ANNOTATED LEADING CASES OF

INTERNATIONAL CRIMINAL TRIBUNALS

VOLUME XXV:

THE INTERNATIONAL CRIMINAL TRIBUNAL FOR RWANDA 2006–2007

André KLIP and Göran SLUITER (eds.)

ANNOTATED LEADING CASES OF

INTERNATIONAL CRIMINAL TRIBUNALS

VOLUME XXV

THE INTERNATIONAL CRIMINAL TRIBUNAL FOR RWANDA 2006–2007

André KLIP and Göran SLUITER (eds.)

intersentia

Antwerp – Oxford – Portland

Distribution for the UK:
Hart Publishing Ltd.
16 C Worcester Place
Oxford OX1 2JW
UK
Tel.: +44 1865 51 75 30
E-mail:mail@hartpub.co.uk

Distribution for the USA and Canada:
International Specialized Book Services
920 NE 58th Ave. Suite 300
Portland, OR 97213
USA
Tel.: +1 800 944 6190 (toll free)
Tel.: +1 503 287 3093
Email: info@isbs.com

Distribution for Austria:
Neuer Wissenschaftlicher Verlag
Argentinierstraße 42/6
1040 Wien
Austria
Tel.: +43 1 535 61 03 24
Email: office@nwv.at

Distribution for other countries:
Intersentia Publishers
Groenstraat 31
2640 Mortsel
Belgium
Tel.: +32 3 680 15 50
Email: mail@intersentia.be

Please cite as: ICTR, Decision on the Prosecutor's Application for Severance and Leave to Amend the Indictment Against Idelphonse Hategekimana, *Prosecutor v. Nizeyimana and Hategekimana*, Case No. ICTR-00-55-I, T. Ch. III, 25 September 2007, Klip/Sluiter, ALC XXV-27.

Annotated Leading Cases of International Criminal Tribunals
André Klip and Göran Sluiter (eds.)
Cover illustration: Eva Sterkens

Antwerp - Oxford - Portland
www.intersentia.com

ISBN 978-90-5095-916-2
D/2010/7849/54
NUR 828

TABLE OF CONTENTS

4. Witness proofing

5. Other evidentiary issues

6. Right to be present

7. Cooperation of States

8. Certification and reconsideration

9. Fair trial (Rule 15*bis* of the ICTR RPE)

PREFACE

This is the twenty-fifth volume in the series 'Annotated Leading Cases of International Criminal Tribunals' and contains the most important decisions of the International Criminal Tribunal for Rwanda (ICTR) from 12 September 2006 up to and including 27 November 2007. It is the ninth volume in the series containing decisions of the ICTR. Further selected volumes on ICTR case law will be volumes 31 and 32, which cover decisions up to 1 January 2009.

The present volume is in its approach and structure similar to previous volumes. Thus, the book contains the full text of all the decisions and judgements, including separate, concurring and dissenting opinions, as well as annexes to the decisions. As with previous volumes, the editors have ensured that the decisions are fully identical to the *written* original text, as issued by the ICTR Press and Information Office and which bears the signatures of the Judges. We are aware that more and more decisions are available on the internet. However, only the written decisions bearing the signatures of the Judges can be considered as authoritative versions. In the course of our editorial work on this and previous volumes, we have occasionally discovered inconsistencies between the written original version of the decision and the internet version, if the latter is available at all. Much of our editorial efforts consist in making the texts in this series identical to the written original version.

We could only include the full text of the decisions in this volume by reducing their original format. Still, we wanted the reader to be able to identify the page number of the original text, which is throughout the text put in brackets [ ]. We are again very happy that a number of scholars in the field of international criminal law were prepared to write interesting and stimulating commentaries regarding the decisions.

A few words regarding the selection of decisions may give the user an insight into our working method. In principle, we select all final judgements. In addition, we publish decisions taken at any stage of the procedure that are important for other reasons: because they deal with a specific legal question, because they are representative of a specific type of decision, or because they enter new legal waters. Of course, we cannot publish all decisions. As a result, we may not publish decisions in which issues have been decided in a way similar or identical to a decision that has already been selected.

The decisions are presented in different parts and under different headings.

Part 1, 'Preliminary Matters', relates to two decisions concerning the indictment and the severance of proceedings.

Part 2 deals with procedural matters. Whereas some decisions concern the way the proceedings are conducted in view of the requirements of a fair trial, others relate to the rights and obligations of witnesses, or to disclosure and the cooperation of states.

Part 3, 'Judgement and Sentencing', contains seven judgements and covers by far the largest part of this volume. As mentioned above, judgements are by definition included in this series, because of their importance, both from a factual and legal perspective.

Part 4, 'Post Conviction or Acquittal Issues', deals with various issues arising after the proceedings have come to an end.

We owe acknowledgements to many persons without whom we could not have completed this twenty-fifth volume. These include Registrar Adama Dieng of the ICTR and his staff, who offered generous assistance in obtaining all the hard copies of decisions. Our publisher Intersentia, in particular Hans Kluwer, Tom Scheirs and Isabelle van Dongen, facilitated our work. We also acknowledge the work of our student assistants, Mariam Pathan (Maastricht), who took over in 2009 from Thom Dieben, and Robert-Jan Winters (Amsterdam), who both assisted with the corrections of the text and without whom we would not be able to publish this series. We are most grateful to Thom for the excellent work he has done for all the volumes since volume 9 on the Special Court for Sierra Leone, which appeared in 2006. The Netherlands School of Human Rights Research stimulated our work. Professor Steven Freeland from the University of Western Sydney,

Australia, offered tremendous help by correcting our English. Last but not least, we wish to thank the distinguished authors for their commentaries on the decisions.

We hope that this volume will contribute to the further dissemination of the important work of the ICTR and that it will provide access to its decisions to practitioners, academics and students.

André Klip and Göran Sluiter

Maastricht/ Amsterdam, April 2010

Tribunal Pénal International pour le Rwanda
International Criminal Tribunal for Rwanda

IN THE APPEALS CHAMBER

Before:	**Judge Fausto Pocar, Presiding** **Judge Mohamed Shahabuddeen** **Judge Mehmet Güney** **Judge Liu Daqun** **Judge Theodor Meron**
Registrar:	**Mr. Adama Dieng**
Decision of:	**18 September 2006**

THE PROSECUTOR

v.

Théoneste BAGOSORA
Gratien KABILIGI
Aloys NTABAKUZE
Anatole NSENGIYUMVA

Case No. ICTR-98-41-AR73

DECISION ON ALOYS NTABAKUZE'S INTERLOCUTORY APPEAL ON QUESTIONS OF LAW RAISED BY THE 29 JUNE 2006 TRIAL CHAMBER I DECISION ON MOTION FOR EXCLUSION OF EVIDENCE

Office of the Prosecutor:

Ms. Barbara Mulvaney
Mr. James K. Stewart
Mr. Neville Weston
Mr. Rashid Rashid
Mr. Abdoulaye Seye

Counsel for the Defence:

Mr. Raphaël Constant
Ms. Allison Turner
Mr. Paul Skolnik
Mr. Frédéric Hivon
Mr. Kennedy Ogetto
Mr. Gershom Otachi Bw'Omanwa

Counsel for Ntabakuze:

Mr. Peter Erlinder
Mr. André Tremblay

[page 1]1. The Appeals Chamber of the International Criminal Tribunal for the Prosecution of Persons Responsible for Genocide and Other Serious Violations of International Humanitarian Law Committed in the Territory of Rwanda and Rwandan Citizens Responsible for Genocide and Other Such Violations Committed in the Territory of Neighbouring States Between 1 January and 31 December 1994 ("Appeals Chamber" and "Tribunal", respectively), is seized of the "Ntabakuze Interlocutory Appeal on Questions of Law Raised by the 29 June 2006 Trial Chamber I 'Decision on Ntabakuze Motion for Exclusion of Evidence'", filed by Aloys Ntabakuze on 20 July 2006 ("Interlocutory Appeal" and "Appellant", respectively).

I. PROCEDURAL HISTORY

2. On 28 March 2006, the Appellant filed a "Motion for the Exclusion of Evidence of Allegations falling outside the Scope of the Indictment" ("Motion"),[1] requesting that Trial Chamber I exclude from its consideration seventeen categories of evidence as irrelevant to the Indictment. On 29 June 2006, the Trial Chamber granted the Motion in part, partially excluding three of the challenged categories of evidence, but denying the request for exclusion in respect of the remaining fourteen categories.[2]

3. On 6 July 2006, the Appellant requested leave to file an interlocutory appeal from the Impugned Decision.[3] On 14 July 2006, the Trial Chamber granted in part the Motion for Certification.[4]

4. The Appellant filed his Interlocutory Appeal on 20 July 2006. The Prosecution responded on 31 July 2006,[5] and the Appellant replied on 4 August 2006.[6] **[page 2]**

II. SCOPE OF THE APPEAL

5. The Interlocutory Appeal is limited by the Certification Decision to questions relating to "the propositions of law articulated in paragraphs 7 and 10" of the Impugned Decision.[7] These paragraphs read as follows:

> 7. Objections play an important role in ensuring that the trial is conducted on the basis of evidence which is relevant to the charges against the accused. The failure to voice a contemporaneous objection does not waive the Accused's rights, but results in a shifting of the burden of proof:
>
>> In the case of objections based on lack of notice, the Defence must challenge the admissibility of evidence of material facts not pleaded in the indictment by interposing a specific objection at the time the evidence is introduced. The Defence may also file a timely motion to strike the evidence or to seek an adjournment to conduct further investigations in order to respond to the unpleaded allegation.
>>
>> ...
>>
>> [A]n accused person who fails to object at trial has the burden of proving on appeal that his appeal [sic] that his ability to prepare his case was materially impaired. Where, however, the accused person objected at trial, the burden is on the Prosecution to prove on appeal that the accused's ability to prepare his defence was not materially impaired.

---

1 An addendum to the Motion was filed on 7 April 2006.

2 "Decision on Ntabakuze Motion for Exclusion of Evidence", 29 June 2006 ("Impugned Decision"), Disposition. The Trial Chamber also observed that the Prosecution conceded the partial exclusion of a fourth category. *Id.*, para. 25.

3 "Ntabakuze Motion for Certification of the 'Decision on Ntabakuze Motion for Exclusion of Evidence' of 29 June 2006, pursuant to Rule 73(B)", 6 July 2006 ("Motion for Certification").

4 "Decision on Request for Certification of Decision on Exclusion of Evidence", 14 July 2006 ("Certification Decision"), p. 5.

5 Prosecutor's Response to "Ntabakuze Interlocutory Appeal on Questions of Law Raised by the 29 June 2006 Trial Chamber I 'Decision on Ntabakuze Motion for Exclusion of Evidence'", 31 July 2006 ("Response").

6 Ntabakuze Reply to "Prosecutor's Response to 'Ntabakuze Interlocutory Appeal on Questions of Law Raised by the 29 June 2006 Trial Chamber I 'Decision on Ntabakuze Motion for Exclusion of Evidence''", 7 August 2006 ("Reply"). The Reply was received by the Tribunal in time on 4 August 2006 but due to a fire in the Tribunal premises, the Reply could not be filed before 7 August 2006. In the circumstances, the Appeals Chamber will consider the Reply as validly filed.

7 Certification Decision, p. 5.

> This standard applies whenever the objection is not raised contemporaneously with the introduction of the evidence.[8]
>
> 10. The Chamber's approach in the sections which follow may be summarized as follows. Where a material fact cannot be reasonably related to the Indictment, then it shall be excluded. Where the material fact is relevant only to a vague or general allegation in the Indictment, then the Chamber will consider whether notice of the material fact was given in the Pre-Trial Brief or the opening statement, so as to cure the vagueness of the Indictment. Material facts which concern the actions of the Accused personally are scrutinized more closely than general allegations of criminal conduct. Other forms of disclosure, such as witness statements or potential exhibits, are generally insufficient to put the Defence on reasonable notice. The Chamber recognizes two exceptions to this principle: first, where the Prosecution filed a motion for the addition of a witness, which was subsequently granted by the Chamber, and which stated the material facts on which the witness would testify (Witness AAA); second, where a lengthy adjournment was ordered by the Chamber for the express purpose of allowing the Defence to meet newly discovered material facts (Witness DBQ).[9]

6. In his Interlocutory Appeal, the Appellant submits that the Trial Chamber erred in its enunciation of the legal principles in both paragraphs. The Appeals Chamber will consider first the principles outlined in paragraph 10 of the Impugned Decision. **[page 3]**

III. CURING DEFECTS IN THE INDICTMENT (PARAGRAPH 10 OF THE IMPUGNED DECISION)

A. Submissions of the Parties

7. The Appellant submits that the Trial Chamber erred in eight respects in paragraph 10 of the Impugned Decision in its description of the standards to apply in determining whether or not to exclude evidence on the basis of lack of notice of the material facts to which the evidence relates:[10]

> -First, the Trial Chamber failed to take into account the exceptional nature of "curing" the indictment, essentially transforming the exception into the rule;[11]
>
> -Second, the Trial Chamber failed to consider that the admission of large amounts of evidence outside the indictment could render the trial unfair since this has the effect of replacing the case in the original indictment with a completely different one, and since the accused never knows precisely the case he has to meet;[12]
>
> -Third, the Trial Chamber failed to define the degree of specificity required in the indictment, in particular with respect to the mode of liability and the locations where the crimes were committed;[13]
>
> -Fourth, the Trial Chamber failed to recognize that evidence of a material fact should be excluded if the latter is not mentioned in the indictment in any form; contrary to what the Trial Chamber found, it is not sufficient that the material fact be "reasonably related to the indictment";[14]
>
> -Fifth, the Trial Chamber "understat[ed] th[e] imperative" that material facts which concern the personal actions of the accused be specifically and clearly pleaded in the indictment;[15]

---

8 Impugned Decision, para. 7, citing *Eliézer Niyitegeka v. The Prosecutor*, Case No. ICTR-96-14-A, Judgement of 9 July 2004 ("*Niyitegeka* Appeal Judgement"), paras 199-200, and referring to *The Prosecutor v. Emmanuel Ndindabahizi*, Case No. ICTR-2001-71-T, Judgement and Sentence of 15 July 2004 ("*Ndindabahizi* Trial Judgement"), para. 29.

9 References omitted. In footnote 22 of the Impugned Decision, the Trial Chamber adds that, in one case, it will also rely on the material supporting the Indictment itself to determine whether notice of the material fact was given so as to cure the vagueness in the Indictment.

10 Interlocutory Appeal, para. 18 (1st para. 18, at p. 7).

11 Interlocutory Appeal, paras 18 (2nd para. 18, at p. 8) and 19.

12 Interlocutory Appeal, paras 20-22. *See also* Reply, paras 7-8, 14.

13 Interlocutory Appeal, paras 23-24.

14 Interlocutory Appeal, paras 25-26.

15 Interlocutory Appeal, paras 27-28.

-Sixth, the Trial Chamber erroneously considered that the Prosecution could include new material facts in the charges against the accused through the filing of a motion for the addition of a witness rather than by seeking to amend the indictment;[16]

-Seventh, the Trial Chamber erred in finding that a lengthy adjournment could be sufficient to allow the Defence to meet newly discovered material facts because, although the adjournment may permit the Defence to better prepare for cross-examination of the witness, "it does not permit the Defence to know whether the Prosecution also intends to add new charges to the indictments [sic]; the Defence is still left in the dark as to the potential use of the newly discovered evidence";[17]

-Eighth, while the Trial Chamber correctly stated that vagueness in the indictment may be cured when additional information is provided in the pre-trial Brief or the opening statement **[page 4]** and that other forms of disclosure such as witness statements and potential exhibits are generally insufficient to put the Defence on reasonable notice, it erred in its application of these principles in the case at hand.[18]

8. The Prosecution responds that most of the arguments made by the Appellant fall outside the scope of the issues for which certification was granted.[19] The Prosecution also contends that the Trial Chamber has discretion in determining which evidence to admit and in deciding on the general conduct of the proceedings, but that the Appellant has not identified any discernable error or abuse in the Trial Chamber's exercise of its discretion.[20] The Prosecution submits that the guiding principles identified by the Trial Chamber at paragraph 10 of the Impugned Decision are consistent with the jurisprudence of the Appeals Chamber and were properly applied.[21]

9. In the Prosecution's view, "[t]he Appellant's erroneous arguments appear to stem from the fact that he equates or mischaracterizes material facts with new charges, claiming that they are allegations outside the scope of the indictment and necessarily cause him material prejudice."[22] The Prosecution recalls that the count or charge is the alleged legal prohibition infringed whereas the materials facts are the acts and omissions of the accused that give rise to that allegation of infringement of a legal prohibition.[23] The Prosecution argues that while communication of timely information cannot cure the omission of a charge in an indictment, it is settled law that it can cure vagueness or imprecision respecting a charge that appears in the indictment.[24] Thus, the failure to plead a material fact in the indictment does not necessarily mean that the Prosecution must seek an amendment to the indictment; the omission of material facts from the indictment can be cured by the provision of timely, clear and consistent information to the Defence.[25] The Prosecution maintains that the Trial Chamber's framework in paragraph 10 of the Impugned Decision follows these principles: when the Trial Chamber required that the material facts be reasonably related to the indictment, it simply required that the material fact be related to a charge in the indictment, as opposed to a charge omitted from it.[26] **[page 5]**

---

16 Interlocutory Appeal, para. 29.
17 Interlocutory Appeal, para. 30.
18 Interlocutory Appeal, para. 31.
19 Response, para. 2.
20 Response, paras 8-9.
21 Response, para. 11.
22 Response, para. 12.
23 Response, para. 12, quoting *The Prosecution v. Tharcisse Muvunyi*, Case No. ICTR-00-55A-AR73, "Decision on Prosecution Interlocutory Appeal Against Trial Chamber II Decision of 23 February 2005", 12 May 2005 ("*Muvunyi* Decision"), para. 19.
24 Response, para. 13, referring to *The Prosecutor v. André Ntagerura et al.*, Case No. ICTR-99-46-A, Judgement of 7 July 2006 ("*Cyangugu* Appeal Judgement"), para. 32.
25 Response, para. 13, referring to *Prosecutor v. Zoran Kupreškić et al.*, Case No. IT-95-16-A, Judgement of 23 October 2001 ("*Kupreškić et al.* Appeal Judgement"), paras 117-121, and *The Prosecutor v. Elizaphan Ntakirutimana and Gérard Ntakirutimana*, Cases Nos. ICTR-96-10-A and ICTR-96-17-A, Judgement of 13 December 2004 ("*Ntakirutimana* Appeal Judgement"), para. 27.
26 Response, para. 13. At paragraph 12 of the Response, the Prosecution also argues that, in the case at hand, the Trial Chamber did not consider that the new material facts (*i.e.*, those not mentioned in the Indictment but found to have been sufficiently disclosed to the Defence) added new charges or changed the nature of the existing charges; rather, the new material facts were reasonably related to existing charges, were relevant, and evidence thereon was admissible.

10. The Prosecution also submits that the Appellant's argument regarding the "exceptional nature of curing" is unconvincing because, even in cases where some of the material facts at issue were known at the time the indictment was filed (and in the present case, this has not been demonstrated), vagueness in the indictment can still be cured by subsequent communications to the Defence.[27] In response to the Appellant's argument that the defects in this case were too numerous to be cured, the Prosecution responds that the essential question is not the number of alleged defects that have been cured, but whether the Defence had clear and unambiguous notice that the material facts would be relied upon as part of the Prosecution's case, and had sufficient opportunity to respond to the charge, so that the fairness of the trial is preserved.[28] Finally, to the Appellant's contention that the Trial Chamber ignored the requirement that material facts which concern the personal actions of the accused be specifically and clearly pleaded in the indictment, the Prosecution responds that the Impugned Decision leaves no doubt that physical perpetration of a criminal act by an accused must be pleaded in the indictment, and that when it was not, the Trial Chamber ruled the evidence inadmissible.[29]

11. The Appellant replies that the question before the Appeals Chamber is not whether the Trial Chamber properly exercised its discretion in admitting or excluding evidence, but rather whether the Trial Chamber correctly formulated the standards to apply in the exercise of that discretion.[30] He adds that if the Appeals Chamber were to find that the Trial Chamber erred in its articulation of these standards, then the Trial Chamber would have to reconsider its previous decision.[31]

12. The Appellant notes the admission of the Prosecution that the Indictment in this case lacked specificity, and submits that in light of this admission, the Prosecution "had an absolute obligation to rectify the lack of 'specificity' regarding the Accused Ntabakuze before the Defence was put to its case," something which it failed to do.[32]

13. The Appellant denies having confused material facts with new charges,[33] and submits that "many of the new *specific events* that emerged in the evidence, which were *never mentioned* in any **[page 6]** form in the Indictment, do, indeed, constitute new 'charges', and are not merely 'material facts' underpinning broad generalities already in the Indictment."[34]

B. Analysis

14. The Appeals Chamber will briefly recall the general principles of admissibility of evidence and sufficiency of the indictment. It will then consider each of the errors alleged to have been committed by the Trial Chamber except the eighth error alleged by the Appellant – that although the Trial Chamber correctly outlined certain relevant principles, it erred in its application of them – as this clearly goes beyond the scope of the certification.

1. Preliminary Question: Standard of Review

15. The Prosecution submits that "[t]he reconsideration envisaged in the Interlocutory Appeal is unwarranted and amounts to an impermissible attempt to overcome the Trial Chamber's discretionary power to admit evidence, during the course of the trial."[35]

16. The Appeals Chamber disagrees. The present appeal does not concern the Trial Chamber's exercise of its discretion in admitting particular categories of evidence, but rather the correctness of the legal principles which it identified as applicable to the exercise of its discretion to admit the disputed evidence. As

27 Response, paras 14-15.
28 Response, para. 15.
29 Response, para. 16.
30 Reply, paras 1-3, 5-6, 9, 15.
31 Reply, para. 6.
32 Reply, para. 7.
33 Reply, paras 10-11.
34 Reply, para. 12 (emphasis in original).
35 Response, para. 9 (references omitted).

the final arbiter of the law, the Appeals Chamber will overturn a Trial Chamber's decision if it is established that the Trial Chamber committed an error of law.[36]

2. Admissibility of Evidence of Material Facts Insufficiently Pleaded in the Indictment

17. It is well established that an accused has a right to be informed in detail of the charges against him or her, and that as a corollary the Prosecution is obliged "to state the material facts underpinning the charges in the indictment, but not the evidence by which material facts are to be proven."[37] No conviction against the accused can be entered on the basis of material facts omitted from the indictment or pleaded with insufficient specificity, unless the Prosecution has cured the **[page 7]** defect in the indictment by provision to the accused of "timely, clear and consistent information detailing the factual basis underpinning the charges against him or her."[38]

18. When the Defence is of the view that the Prosecution introduces evidence of material facts of which it had no notice, it can make an objection to the admission of such evidence for lack of notice.[39] If the Trial Chamber agrees with the Defence that insufficient notice has been given, it should exclude the challenged evidence in relation to the unpleaded material facts,[40] require the Prosecution to amend the indictment, grant an adjournment to allow the Defence adequate time to respond to the additional allegations,[41] or take other measures to preserve the rights of the accused to a fair trial.[42]

3. Alleged Failure to Recognize Relevant Principles

19. The Appellant alleges that the Trial Chamber erred in its articulation of the applicable legal standard at paragraph 10 of the Impugned Decision because it failed to recognize certain relevant principles (first, second and third errors alleged). However, the mere fact that the Trial Chamber did not expressly mention all the applicable principles in paragraph 10 of the Impugned Decision does not necessarily mean that it ignored them. As the first sentence of paragraph 10 explains, the paragraph is merely a summary of the approach the Trial Chamber will take in the rest of its decision. The Trial Chamber was under no obligation to repeat word for word all the statements made by the Appeals Chamber on the subjects of the specificity required in an indictment and the circumstances in which a defective indictment will be deemed cured. Further, the fact that the Trial Chamber was clearly aware of the extent of the jurisprudence established by the Appeals Chamber is demonstrated by its numerous references to the relevant case law in the paragraphs prior to

---

36 *Prosecutor v. Tihomir Blaškić*, Case No. IT-95-14-A, Judgement of 29 July 2004 ("*Blaškić* Appeal Judgement"), para. 15; *Prosecutor v. Miroslav Kvočka et al.*, Case No. IT-98-30/1-A, Judgement of 28 February 2005 ("*Kvočka et al.* Appeal Judgement"), para. 17; *Prosecutor v. Mladen Naletilić, a.k.a. "Tuta" & Vinko Martinović, a.k.a. "Štela"*, Case No. IT-98-34-A, Judgement of 3 May 2006 ("*Naletilić & Martinović* Appeal Judgement"), para. 10. *See also Prosecutor v. Milošević*, Case No. IT-02-54-A-R77.4, Decision on Interlocutory Appeal on Kosta Bulatović's Contempt Proceedings, 29 August 2005, para. 40 & fn. 43.

37 *Kupreškić et al.* Appeal Judgement, para. 88. *See also Niyitegeka* Appeal Judgement, para. 193; *Blaškić* Appeal Judgement, paras 208-209; *Ntakirutimana* Appeal Judgement, para. 25; *Kvočka et al.* Appeal Judgement, para. 27; *Naletilić & Martinović* Appeal Judgement, para. 23; *Cyangugu* Appeal Judgement, para. 21.

38 *Kupreškić et al.* Appeal Judgement, para. 114; *Kvočka et al.* Appeal Judgement, para. 33; *Naletilić & Martinović* Appeal Judgement, para. 26; *Cyangugu* Appeal Judgement, paras 28 & 30.

39 *Prosecutor v. Anto Furundžija*, Case No. IT-95-17/1-A, Judgement of 21 July 2000 ("*Furundžija* Appeal Judgement"), para. 61.

40 In this connection, the Appeals Chamber recalls that a Chamber can find the particular evidence inadmissible to prove a material fact of which the accused was not on notice, but admissible with respect to other allegations sufficiently pleaded: *Arsène Shalom Ntahobali & Pauline Nyiramasuhuko v. The Prosecutor*, Case No. ICTR-97-21-AR73, "Decision of the Appeals by Pauline Nyiramasuhuko and Arsène Shalom Ntahobali on the 'Decision on Defence Urgent Motion to Declare Parts of the Evidence of Witnesses RV and QBZ inadmissible'", 2 July 2004, para. 15; *Pauline Nyiramasuhuko v. The Prosecutor*, Case No. ICTR-98-42-AR73, "Decision on Pauline Nyiramasuhuko's Request for Reconsideration", 27 September 2004, para. 12; *Muvunyi* Decision, para. 55 ("If evidence is relevant to a charge in the current indictment and is probative of that charge, then subject to any other ground for exclusion that may be advanced by the Defence, that evidence should be admissible.").

41 *Kupreškić et al.* Appeal Judgement, para. 92; *Kvočka et al.* Appeal Judgement, para. 31; *Naletilić & Martinović* Appeal Judgement, para. 25.

42 For instance, in certain circumstances, the Trial Chamber could allow the Defence to recall witnesses for cross-examination after the Defence has completed further investigations: *see The Prosecutor v. Édouard Karemera et al.*, Case No. ICTR-98-44-AR73, "Decision on Prosecutor's Interlocutory Appeal Against Trial Chamber III Decision of 8 October 2003 Denying Leave to File an Amended Indictment", 19 December 2003 ("*Karemera* Decision"), para. 28.

[page 8] paragraph 10 in the Impugned Decision.[43] Accordingly, the Appeals Chamber is not persuaded that the Appellant has shown that the Trial Chamber erred simply by failing to comprehensively mention all of the relevant jurisprudence of the Appeals Chamber at paragraph 10 of the Impugned Decision. With this in mind, the Appeals Chamber now considers the specific arguments raised by the Appellant.

(a) First Error Alleged

20. The Appellant submits that the Trial Chamber failed to take into account the exceptional nature of "curing" the indictment, essentially transforming the exception into the rule.

21. The ICTY Appeals Chamber has explained that

> in some instances, a defective indictment can be cured if the Prosecution provides the accused with timely, clear and consistent information detailing the factual basis underpinning the charges against him or her. Nevertheless, in light of the factual and legal complexities normally associated with the crimes within the jurisdiction of this Tribunal, there can only be a limited number of cases that fall within that category.[44]

Thus, "curing" is likely to occur only in a limited number of cases. In this connection, the Appeals Chamber is not convinced by the Trial Chamber's suggestion, at paragraph 4 of the Impugned Decision, that a distinction should be made between cases "where the Prosecution knows of material facts at the time the indictment is filed, but fails to plead them" (in which cases curing would be exceptional) and cases where the material facts "are subsequently discovered" (in which cases curing would not be characterized as exceptional). Indeed, the risk of prejudice to the accused is the same in both types of cases.[45] In both types of cases, the defect in the indictment may be deemed cured only by the provision of timely, clear and consistent information to the accused.

22. This being said, the Appeals Chamber notes that, at paragraphs 2, 3 and 6 of the Impugned Decision, the Trial Chamber referred at length to the jurisprudence of the Appeals Chamber and correctly identified the relevant legal principles in determining whether the defects in the indictment have been cured: the Trial Chamber properly stated that a defect in the indictment can only be deemed cured if the Prosecution has provided timely, clear and consistent information to the accused, which puts him or her in a reasonable position to understand the charges against him or her. Thus, the Appeals Chamber is not persuaded that the error made by the Trial Chamber in paragraph 4 of the Impugned Decision led it to "transform the exception into the rule" or to misapply the relevant legal principles. **[page 9]**

23. The Appeals Chamber also emphasizes that, "if the indictment is found to be defective because it fails to plead material facts or does not plead them with sufficient specificity, the Trial Chamber *must* consider whether the accused was nevertheless accorded a fair trial."[46] Thus, the mere fact that a Trial Chamber considers in a number of instances, as the Trial Chamber did here, whether defects in the indictment have been cured, is not contrary to the principle that there are a limited number of cases wherein a defective indictment will actually be considered to have been cured.

(b) Second Error Alleged

24. The Appellant also contends that the Trial Chamber failed to consider that the admission of large amounts of evidence outside the indictment could render the trial unfair. In the words of the Appellant,

> even if individual defects in the indictment might be said to be "cured" by disclosure, a vast number of such instances in a single trial would render such a "cure" meaningless, because the sheer volume of evidence outside the indictment, which has the effect of replacing one Prosecution case with a completely different case than that set out in the indictment, makes the trial inherently unfair.

---

43 *See* Impugned Decision, paras 2-7 and corresponding footnotes.

44 *Kupreškić et al.* Appeal Judgement, para. 114. *See also Cyangugu* Appeal Judgement, para. 114.

45 The only difference concerns the "level of blame" on the Prosecution: As stated in the *Ntakirutimana* Appeal Judgement (para. 125), "the practice of failing to allege known material facts in an indictment is unacceptable."

46 *Naletilić & Martinović* Appeal Judgement, para. 26 (emphasis added). *See also Kvočka et al.* Appeal Judgement, para. 33, and *Cyangugu* Appeal Judgement, para. 28.

> [...] the Trial Chamber thus erred [in] applying a standard which permits the Prosecution to argue a completely different case than that in the indictment, inasmuch as the allegations falling outside the scope of the indictment significantly outnumber those that are actually mentioned therein. To permit those allegations to stand, without formal amendment of the indictment, by only engaging in an incident by incident analysis without taking into account the totality of new evidence, is to allow the Prosecution to utterly transform the indictment by stealth and stages through the trial, so that the Accused can never really know with any assurance exactly what case he has to meet.[47]

25. In support of this argument, the Appellant refers to paragraph 114 of the *Cyangugu* Appeal Judgement. There, the Appeals Chamber expressed its concern as to the extent of the defects in the indictment that the Prosecution argued had been cured by post-indictment submissions. The Appeals Chamber explained that, even if all defects in the indictment had been deemed cured, it would have had to consider whether the extent of the defects in the indictment, in itself, did not lead to an unfair trial.[48] **[page 10]**

26. The Appeals Chamber agrees that when the indictment suffers from numerous defects, there may still be a risk of prejudice to the accused even if the defects are found to be cured by post-indictment submissions. In particular, the accumulation of a large number of material facts not pled in the indictment reduces the clarity and relevancy of that indictment, which may have an impact on the ability of the accused to know the case he or she has to meet for purposes of preparing an adequate defence. Further, while the addition of a few material facts may not prejudice the Defence in the preparation of its case, the addition of numerous material facts increases the risk of prejudice as the Defence may not have sufficient time and resources to investigate properly all the new material facts. Thus, where a Trial Chamber considers that a defective indictment has been subsequently cured by the Prosecution, it should further consider whether the extent of the defects in the indictment materially prejudice an accused's right to a fair trial by hindering the preparation of a proper defence. The Appeals Chamber finds that the Trial Chamber failed to do so in the Impugned Decision and therefore, instructs the Trial Chamber to reconsider the Impugned Decision on this basis.

(c) Third Error Alleged

27. The Appellant submits that the Trial Chamber erred in failing to define the degree of specificity required in the indictment, in particular with respect to the modes of liability and the locations where the crimes were committed. As explained above, the Appeals Chamber is not convinced that the Appellant has shown that the Trial Chamber erred by failing to define at paragraph 10 of the Impugned Decision the requisite degree of specificity required in the indictment.[49] The Trial Chamber was aware of the jurisprudence of the Appeals Chamber on this question. The Appeals Chamber does not consider that it is necessary here to repeat at length this jurisprudence.[50] Nevertheless, to address some of the specific arguments of the Appellant on this point, the Appeals Chamber would like to emphasize the following:

1-An indictment that fails to "indicate in relation to each individual count precisely and expressly the particular nature of the responsibility alleged" may be ambiguous and could be found defective.[51] In

---

47 Interlocutory Appeal, paras 21-22.

48 *Cyangugu* Appeal Judgement, para. 114:

> La Chambre d'appel doit se montrer préoccupée par la démarche du Procureur dans la présente affaire. Elle ne saurait trop rappeler que l'acte d'accusation, seul instrument de mise en accusation, doit exposer la thèse du Procureur de manière circonstanciée. Si, dans certains cas, un acte d'accusation vicié peut être réputé « purgé », la Chambre d'appel réitère qu'il ne peut exister qu'un nombre limité d'affaires qui entrent dans cette catégorie. Dans le cas d'espèce, la Chambre d'appel est troublée par l'ampleur avec laquelle le Procureur cherche à recourir à cette exception. Même si les arguments du Procureur selon lesquels les Actes d'accusation avaient été purgés de leurs vices s'étaient révélés prospères dans chacun des cas, il aurait malgré tout été du devoir de la Chambre d'appel de considérer si l'ampleur des vices identifiés n'aurait pas rendu le procès inéquitable en soi (no official translation available yet, footnote omitted).

49 *See supra* para. 19.

50 For more on the specificity required in an indictment, *see Kupreškić et al.* Appeal Judgement, paras 89-90; *Prosecutor v. Krnojelac*, Case No. IT-97-25-A, Judgement of 17 September 2003 ("*Krnojelac* Appeal Judgement"), paras 132, 138; *Blaškić* Appeal Judgement, paras 210-219; *Kvočka et al.* Appeal Judgement, paras 28-30, 41-42; *Naletilić & Martinović* Appeal Judgement, para. 24; *Cyangugu* Appeal Judgement, paras 23-26.

51 *Krnojelac* Appeal Judgement, para. 138; *Blaškić* Appeal Judgement, para. 212; *Kvočka et al.* Appeal Judgement, para. 29.

particular, it is essential that the indictment specifies on what legal basis of the Statute an individual is being charged (Article 6(1) and/or 6(3));[52] **[page 11]**

2-The location of the crimes alleged to have been committed should be specified in the indictment. However, the degree of specificity required will depend on the nature of the Prosecution's case.[53] As stated in the *Ntakirutimana* Appeal Judgement, "[t]here may well be situations in which the specific location of criminal activities cannot be listed, such as where the accused is charged as having effective control over several armed groups that committed crimes in numerous locations. In cases concerning physical acts of violence perpetrated by the accused personally, however, location can be very important."[54]

3-Any vagueness or ambiguity in the above respects may be cured in certain cases by the provision of timely, clear and consistent information to the Defence.[55]

4. Alleged Errors in the Statements made in Paragraph 10 of the Impugned Decision

(a) Fourth Error Alleged

28. The Trial Chamber stated that "[w]here a material fact cannot be reasonably related to the Indictment, then it shall be excluded."[56] The Appellant submits that this is an incorrect standard. The Appellant argues that "[a] material fact should be excluded if it is not mentioned in the indictment at all in any concrete form", and that "the failure to mention an accusation *in the indictment* is a defect that can not be remedied."[57]

29. The Appeals Chamber is not convinced by the arguments of the Appellant on this point. The Appeals Chamber first recalls the distinction between counts or charges ("accusations" in French) and "material facts":

> The count or charge is the legal characterisation of the material facts which support that count or charge. In pleading an indictment, the Prosecution is required to specify the alleged legal prohibition infringed (the count or charge) and the acts or omissions of the Accused that give rise to that allegation of infringement of a legal prohibition (material facts).[58]

It is clear that the omission of a count or charge from the indictment cannot be "cured" by the provision of timely, clear, consistent information.[59] Indeed, since the indictment is the only charging instrument,[60] the addition of counts or charges is possible only through amendment, as set out in Rule 50 of the Rules. However, it is also clear that the omission of a material fact **[page 12]** underpinning a charge in the indictment can, in certain cases, be cured by the provision of timely, clear and consistent information.[61]

30. In this connection, the Appeals Chamber stresses that the possibility of curing the omission of material facts from the indictment is not unlimited. Indeed, the "new material facts" should not lead to a "radical transformation" of the Prosecution's case against the accused.[62] The Trial Chamber should always take into account the risk that the expansion of charges by the addition of new material facts may lead to unfairness and prejudice to the accused. Further, if the new material facts are such that they could, on their own, support

52 *Krnojelac* Appeal Judgement, para. 138.

53 *See Kupreškić et al.* Appeal Judgement, para. 89; *Krnojelac* Appeal Judgement, para. 132; *Blaškić* Appeal Judgement, paras. 210, 212-213, 216-218; *Kvočka et al.* Appeal Judgement, para. 28; *Naletilić & Martinović* Appeal Judgement, para. 24; *Cyangugu* Appeal Judgement, paras 23-26.

54 *Ntakirutimana* Appeal Judgement, para. 75.

55 *See supra* footnote 38.

56 Impugned Decision, para. 10.

57 Interlocutory Appeal, para. 25 (emphasis in original), referring to *Cyangugu* Appeal Judgement, para. 32.

58 *Muvunyi* Decision, para. 19.

59 *Cyangugu* Appeal Judgement, para. 32.

60 *Cyangugu* Appeal Judgement, para. 114.

61 *Kupreškić et al.* Appeal Judgement, para. 88; *Kvočka et al.* Appeal Judgement, para. 28; *Naletilić & Martinović* Appeal Judgement, para. 23; *Cyangugu* Appeal Judgement, para. 22.

62 *See Kupreškić et al.* Appeal Judgement, para. 121; *Ntakirutimana* Appeal Judgement, para. 28.

separate charges,[63] the Prosecution should seek leave from the Trial Chamber to amend the indictment and the Trial Chamber should only grant leave if it is satisfied that it would not lead to unfairness or prejudice to the Defence.[64]

31. The Trial Chamber statements in paragraph 10 of the Impugned Decision are in conformity with the principles outlined above. Accordingly, the Appeals Chamber finds that the Appellant has not shown an error on the part of the Trial Chamber.

(b) Fifth Error Alleged

32. The Appellant submits that, by stating that "[m]aterial facts which concern the actions of the Accused personally are scrutinized more closely than general allegations of criminal conduct,"[65] the Trial Chamber "understated the imperative" that material facts which concern the personal actions of the accused must be specifically and clearly pleaded in the indictment.[66]

33. The Appeals Chamber agrees with the Appellant that material facts which concern the personal actions of the accused have to be clearly and specifically pleaded in the indictment.[67] However, the Appeals Chamber does not consider that the Trial Chamber suggested otherwise at paragraph 10 of the Impugned Decision. In addition, the statement at paragraph 10 must be read together with paragraph 5 of the Impugned Decision, where the Trial Chamber stated:

> Allegations of physical perpetration of a criminal act by an accused must appear in an indictment. On the other hand, "less detail may be acceptable if the 'sheer scale of the alleged crimes makes it **[page 13]** impracticable to require a high degree of specificity in such matters as the identity of the victims and the dates for the commission of the crimes'". Many acts attributed to an accused fall on the spectrum between these two extremes. Individual actions of an accused which contribute to crimes will require more specific notice than proof of the crimes themselves, where they are physically committed by others. The specificity of the notice required is proportional to the extent of the Accused's direct involvement.[68]

Accordingly, the Appeals Chamber is not satisfied that the Trial Chamber understated the requirement that personal actions of the accused be clearly and specifically pleaded in the indictment. The above passage from the Impugned Decision clearly shows that the Trial Chamber was aware of the applicable legal principles.

(c) Sixth Error Alleged

34. The Trial Chamber found that notice of a material fact not included in the indictment could be given through a Prosecution motion for the addition of a witness "which was subsequently granted by the Chamber, and which stated the material facts on which the witness would testify."[69] The Appellant contends that this is an error because the addition of a witness cannot "*alter the charges* against the Accused *as already judicially ratified* by the reviewing Judge";[70] if the Prosecution wishes to add new material facts in the charges, it must seek to amend the indictment.[71]

35. The Appeals Chamber reiterates that, while the addition of a charge must necessarily be done through an amendment to the indictment, the omission of material facts from the indictment can in certain circumstances be cured without having to amend the indictment.[72] As to whether notice of a new material

---

63 For examples of new material facts which could support separate charges against an accused, *see Muvunyi* Decision, paras 33 and 35.

64 *Karemera* Decision, para. 28; *Muvunyi* Decision, para. 22. *See also Kvočka et al.* Appeal Judgement, para. 32.

65 Impugned Decision, para. 10.

66 Interlocutory Appeal, paras 27-28.

67 *See Kupreškić et al.* Appeal Judgement, para. 89; *Krnojelac* Appeal Judgement, para. 132; *Niyitegeka* Appeal Judgement, para. 193; *Ntakirutimana* Appeal Judgement, para. 32; *Kvočka et al.* Appeal Judgement, para. 28; *Naletilić & Martinović* Appeal Judgement, para. 24; *Cyangugu* Appeal Judgement, para. 23; *Sylvestre Gacumbitsi v. The Prosecutor*, Case No. ICTR-2001-64-A, Judgement of 7 July 2006 ("*Gacumbitsi* Appeal Judgement"), para. 49.

68 References omitted.

69 Impugned Decision, para. 10.

70 Interlocutory Appeal, para. 29.

71 Interlocutory Appeal, para. 29.

72 *See supra* paras 29-30.

fact could be conveyed through a Prosecution motion to add a witness, the Appeals Chamber recalls that, as a general rule:

> Whether the Prosecution cured a defect in the indictment depends, of course, on the nature of the information that the Prosecution provides to the Defence and on whether the information compensates for the indictment's failure to give notice of the charges asserted against the accused. *Kupreškić* considered that adequate notice of material facts might be communicated to the Defence in the Prosecution's pre-trial brief, during disclosure of evidence, or through proceedings at trial. The timing of such communications, the importance of the information to the ability of the accused to prepare his defence, and the impact of the newly-disclosed material facts on the Prosecution's case are relevant in determining whether subsequent communications make up for the defect in the indictment. As has been previously noted, "mere service of witness statements by the FPğrosecution pursuant to the disclosure requirements" of the Rules does not suffice to inform the Defence of material facts that the Prosecution intends to prove at trial.[73]

In determining whether a defective indictment was cured by timely, clear and consistent information, the Appeals Chamber has looked to the Prosecution pre-trial brief (together with its **[page 14]** annexes and chart of witnesses)[74] or the Prosecution's opening statement.[75] However, the Appeals Chamber never suggested that defects in the indictment could only be cured through the Prosecution pre-trial brief or its opening statement. The Appeals Chamber cannot exclude the possibility that a defect in the indictment could be cured through a Prosecution motion for addition of a witness, provided any possible prejudice to the Defence was alleviated by, for example, an adjournment to allow the Defence time to prepare for cross-examination of the witness. Accordingly, the Appeals Chamber is not convinced that the Trial Chamber erred in stating that although disclosure of witness statements or potential exhibits are generally insufficient to put an accused on reasonable notice, a defect in the indictment could be cured by the information conveyed in a Prosecution motion to add a witness, which clearly states the material facts on which the witness would testify.

(d) Seventh Error Alleged

36. The Trial Chamber found that when a new material fact is discovered at trial, the fairness of the proceedings against the accused may be preserved by granting a lengthy adjournment for the express purpose of allowing the Defence to meet the newly discovered material fact.[76] The Appellant submits that this is in error because simply granting an adjournment does not permit the Defence to know what use will be made of the newly discovered evidence; it is only once the Prosecution seeks an amendment of the indictment that the Defence will have the opportunity to respond and argue the issue.[77]

37. In *Kupreškić*, the Appeals Chamber emphasized that

> the Prosecution is expected to know its case before it goes to trial. It is not acceptable for the Prosecution to omit the material aspects of its main allegations in the indictment with the aim of moulding the case against the accused in the course of the trial depending on how the evidence unfolds. There are, of course, instances in criminal trials where the evidence turns out differently than expected. Such a situation may require the indictment to be amended, an adjournment to be granted, or certain evidence to be excluded as not being within the scope of the indictment.[78]

Thus, when a new material fact is discovered at trial, the Trial Chamber should determine which measure(s) are required in the circumstances of the case to preserve the fairness of the proceedings. If the Trial Chamber decides that an adjournment is warranted, it could also order the Prosecution to **[page 15]** amend the indictment for greater clarity, but this might not be required in every case. Accordingly, the Appeals Chamber

---

73 *Niyitegeka* Appeal Judgement, para. 197 (references omitted).

74 *Kupreškić et al.* Appeal Judgement, para. 117; *Ntakirutimana* Appeal Judgement, paras 46-48; *Kvočka et al.* Appeal Judgement, paras 43-45; *Naletilić & Martinović* Appeal Judgement, paras 27, 45; *Gacumbitsi* Appeal Judgement, paras 57 58.

75 *Kupreškić et al.* Appeal Judgement, para. 118; *Kordić & Čerkez* Appeal Judgement, para. 169; *Kvočka et al.* Appeal Judgement, paras 46-47.

76 Impugned Decision, para. 10.

77 Interlocutory Appeal, para. 30.

78 *Kupreškić et al.* Appeal Judgement, para. 92. *See also Niyitegeka* Appeal Judgement, para. 194; *Blaškić* Appeal Judgement, para. 220; *Ntakirutimana* Appeal Judgement, para. 26; *Kvočka et al.* Appeal Judgement, paras 30-31; *Naletilić & Martinović* Appeal Judgement, para. 25; *Cyangugu* Appeal Judgement, para. 27.

does not find that the Trial Chamber erred in stating at paragraph 10 of the Impugned Decision that the accused was put on reasonable notice of material facts omitted from the indictment where "a lengthy adjournment was ordered by the Chamber for the express purpose of allowing the Defence to meet newly discovered material facts."

IV. TIMELINESS OF OBJECTIONS TO EVIDENCE FOR LACK OF NOTICE (PARAGRAPH 7 OF THE IMPUGNED DECISION)

38. In paragraph 7 of the Impugned Decision, the Trial Chamber held that, when evidence is adduced that purportedly goes beyond the allegations in the indictment, the Defence must raise an objection "contemporaneously with the introduction of the evidence"; if the Defence raises its objection later during trial, it bears the burden of proving that its ability to prepare its case was materially impaired.[79] The Appellant submits that this is erroneous.

39. At the outset, the Appeals Chamber notes that the Parties made several arguments relating not to the statements made in paragraph 7 of the Impugned Decision but rather to their concrete application.[80] This goes beyond the scope of the certification, and these arguments will not be considered.

A. Submissions of the Parties

40. In the Appellant's view, the Trial Chamber considered, erroneously, that "nothing less than a contemporaneous objection, at or very near the time the impugned evidence is offered is a sufficiently timely form of objection."[81] The Appellant submits that the recent jurisprudence of the Appeals Chamber shows that pre-trial objections, objections in Rule 98*bis* proceedings, and even objections in closing arguments, when taken together, are sufficient to maintain the burden of proof on the Prosecutor to show lack of prejudice to the Defence.[82] In fact, argues the Appellant, it may not always be possible to object to the evidence at the time it is adduced since the purpose in **[page 16]** adducing the evidence may become clear only later (for instance, through a motion to amend the indictment or in the Prosecution's closing brief).[83]

41. The Prosecution responds that the statements made in paragraph 7 of the Impugned Decision are consistent with the principles set out in the *Niyitegeka* Appeal Judgement, according to which the Defence must interpose a specific objection at the time the evidence is introduced.[84] The Prosecution submits that blanket objections or generalized claims of lack of notice and prejudice cannot be considered as sufficient and specific.[85] The Prosecution also contends that the determination of whether a timely and appropriate objection has been made is a case-specific exercise, and that the Appellant's reliance on the Appeals Chamber's pronouncements in other cases is thus unhelpful.[86]

B. Analysis

42. In support of its findings at paragraph 7 of the Impugned Decision, the Trial Chamber cited parts of paragraphs 199 and 200 of the *Niyitegeka* Appeal Judgement. It is useful to reproduce the entire discussion in *Niyitegeka:*

> In considering whether a defect in the indictment has been cured by subsequent disclosure, the question arises as to which party has the burden of proof on the matter. Although the Judgement in *Kupreškić* did not address this issue expressly, the Appeals Chamber's discussion indicates that the burden in that case rested with the Prosecution. *Kupreškić* stated that, in the circumstances of that case, a breach of "the substantial safeguards that an indictment is intended to furnish to the accused" raised the presumption "that such a fundamental defect in the ... Indictment

79 Impugned Decision, para. 7.

80 *See, e.g.*, Interlocutory Appeal, para. 35; Response, paras 20-21; Reply, para. 16.

81 Interlocutory Appeal, para. 32.

82 Interlocutory Appeal, paras 33 (1st para. 33 at p. 12), 33 (3rd para. 33 at p. 13), 34, referring to *Naletilić & Martinović* Appeal Judgement, para. 22 and *Gacumbitsi* Appeal Judgement, paras 52-54.

83 Interlocutory Appeal, para. 33 (2nd para. 33 at p. 13).

84 Response, para. 18.

85 Response, para. 19.

86 Response, paras 19-20.

did indeed cause injustice." The defect could only have been deemed harmless through a demonstration "that Fthe Accused'sğ ability to prepare their defence was not materially impaired." *Kupreškić* clearly imposed the duty to make that showing on the Prosecution, since the absence of such a showing led the Appeals Chamber to "uphFoğld the objections" of the accused.

It is noteworthy, however, that *Kupreškić* specifically mentioned the fact that the accused in that case had made a timely objection before the Trial Chamber to the admission of evidence of the material fact in question. In general, "a party should not be permitted to refrain from making an objection to a matter which was apparent during the course of the trial, and to raise it only in the event of an adverse finding against that party." Failure to object in the Trial Chamber will usually result in the Appeals Chamber disregarding the argument on grounds of waiver. In the case of objections based on lack of notice, the Defence must challenge the admissibility of evidence of material facts not pleaded in the indictment by interposing a specific objection at the time the evidence is introduced. The Defence may also choose to file a timely motion to strike the evidence or to seek an adjournment to conduct further investigations in order to respond to the unpleaded allegation.

The importance of the accused's right to be informed of the charges against him under Article 20(4)(a) of the Statute and the possibility of serious prejudice to the accused if material facts crucial to the Prosecution are communicated for the first time at trial suggest that the waiver doctrine should not entirely foreclose an accused from raising an indictment defect for the first time on appeal. Where, in such circumstances, there is a resulting defect in the indictment, an accused person who fails to object at trial has the burden of proving on appeal that his ability to prepare his case was materially impaired. Where, however, the accused person objected at trial, the **[page 17]** burden is on the Prosecution to prove on appeal that the accused's ability to prepare his defence was not materially impaired. All of this is of course subject to the inherent jurisdiction of the Appeals Chamber to do justice in the case.[87]

43. As the above illustrates, the *Niyitegeka* Appeal Judgement outlined a carefully balanced approach taking into account, on the one hand, the principle that "a party should not be permitted to refrain from making an objection to a matter which was apparent during the course of trial, and to raise it only in the event of an adverse finding against that party"[88] and, on the other hand, "the importance of the accused's right to be informed of the charges against him under Article 20(4)(a) of the Statute and the possibility of serious prejudice to the accused if material facts crucial to the Prosecution are communicated for the first time at trial."[89]

44. In *Niyitegeka*, the Appeals Chamber was concerned with the situation of an appellant who had failed to object to the lack of notice at trial, and had raised the issue for the first time on appeal.[90] The present appeal contemplates a different situation: the objection is not raised at the time the evidence is presented, but it is nonetheless raised at the trial stage. This is a crucial difference: the objection is not as late as if it had been raised only on appeal, and there might be more elements militating against a conclusion that the objection was not timely raised. For instance, the objection might not have been raised at the time the evidence was adduced because the purpose for adducing the evidence might have become clear only later.

45. Accordingly, when an objection based on lack of notice is raised at trial (albeit later than at the time the evidence was adduced), the Trial Chamber should determine whether the objection was so untimely as to consider that the burden of proof has shifted from the Prosecution to the Defence in demonstrating whether the accused's ability to defend himself has been materially impaired. In doing so, the Trial Chamber should take into account factors such as whether the Defence has provided a reasonable explanation for its failure to raise its objection at the time the evidence was introduced and whether the Defence has shown that the objection was raised as soon as possible thereafter.

46. In summary, objections based on lack of notice should be specific and timely. The Appeals Chamber agrees with the Prosecution that blanket objections that "the entire indictment is defective" are insufficiently specific.[91] As to timeliness, the objection should be raised at the pre-trial stage (for instance in a motion

87 *Niyitegeka* Appeal Judgement, paras 198-200 (footnotes omitted).

88 *The Prosecutor v. Clément Kayishema and Obed Ruzindana*, Case No. ICTR-95-1-A, Reasons for Judgement of 1 June 2001 ("*Kayishema and Ruzindana* Appeal Judgement"), para. 91.

89 *Niyitegeka* Appeal Judgement, para. 200.

90 *See Niyitegeka* Appeal Judgement, paras 199-200, 205-206, 210, 237.

91 As this falls outside the scope of the appeal, the Appeals Chamber expresses no opinion on the question whether the two motions filed in May and August 2002 by the Ntabakuze Defence constitute sufficiently specific objections.

challenging the indictment) or at the time the evidence of a new **[page 18]** material fact is introduced. However, an objection raised later at trial will not automatically lead to a shift in the burden of proof: the Trial Chamber must consider relevant factors, such as whether the Defence provided a reasonable explanation for its failure to raise the objection earlier in the trial.

47. The Appeals Chamber finds that the statements made by the Trial Chamber at paragraph 7 of the Impugned Decision must be corrected to the extent explained above. As a consequence, the Trial Chamber should reconsider the Impugned Decision on this basis. This reconsideration will be limited to the instances where the Trial Chamber found that the objection had not been raised at the time the evidence was introduced and therefore concluded that the burden of proof had shifted to the Defence.

V. CONCLUSION

48. The Appeals Chamber finds that even if a Trial Chamber finds that the defects in the indictment have been cured by post-indictment submissions, it should consider whether the extent of the defects in the indictment materially prejudices the accused's right to a fair trial by hindering the preparation of a proper defence. The Appeals Chamber instructs the Trial Chamber to reconsider the Impugned Decision on this basis. In all other respects, the Appeals Chamber is of the view that the Trial Chamber did not err in its articulation of the principles at paragraph 10 of the Impugned Decision. As to paragraph 7 of the Impugned Decision, the Appeals Chamber has outlined the approach that should be taken in deciding whether an objection for lack of notice has been timely raised, and, consequently, who bears the burden of proof on this question. The Appeals Chamber instructs the Trial Chamber to reconsider the Impugned Decision to the extent described above.

VI. DISPOSITION

49. For the foregoing reasons, the Interlocutory Appeal is allowed in part.

Done in English and French, the English text being authoritative.

Done this 18th day of September 2006,
At The Hague,
The Netherlands.

Judge Fausto Pocar
Presiding Judge

[Seal of the Tribunal]

International Criminal Tribunal for Rwanda
Tribunal pénal international pour le Rwanda

OR: ENG

TRIAL CHAMBER III

Before Judges: Judge Khalida Rachid Khan, presiding
Judge Lee Gacuiga Muthoga
Judge Emile Francis Short

Registrar: Mr Adama Dieng

Date: 25 September 2007

THE PROSECUTOR

v.

IDELPHONSE NIZEYIMANA
IDELPHONSE HATEGEKIMANA

Case No. ICTR-00-55-I

DECISION ON THE PROSECUTOR'S APPLICATION FOR SEVERANCE AND LEAVE TO AMEND THE INDICTMENT AGAINST IDELPHONSE HATEGEKIMANA

Office of the Prosecutor:
Mr Jonathan Moses
Ms Katya Melluish
Mr Shamus Mangan

Defence Counsel:
Mr Ahlonko Robert Dovi

[page 2] INTRODUCTION

1. The original Indictment against Tharcisse Muvunyi, Idelphonse Nizeyimana, and Ildephonse Hategekimana[1] was confirmed by Judge Yakov Ostrovsky on 2 February 2000 and filed in its current form on 7 November 2000.[2] Tharcisse Muvunyi was arrested on 7 February 2000, Ildephonse Hategekimana was arrested on 16 February 2003, and Idelphonse Nizeyimana remains at large.

2. On 11 December 2003, the Prosecution was granted leave to sever Mr Muvunyi from the original Indictment and ordered to file a separate indictment against him.[3] Mr Muvunyi was subsequently tried and convicted, and his appeal is pending before the Appeals Chamber.[4] Mr Nizeyimana and Mr Hategekimana remain indicted jointly.

3. The Prosecution now seeks to sever the cases of the remaining co-Accused, and if that request is granted, it seeks leave to amend the Indictment against Mr Hategekimana.[5] The Defence for Mr Hategekimana does not oppose the Prosecution's request for severance, but does take issue with some of the requested amendments to the Indictment.[6]

DISCUSSION

The Application for Severance

4. Pursuant to Rule 82(B) of the Rules of Procedure and Evidence (the "Rules"), a Trial Chamber may order that persons accused jointly be tried separately if it is necessary to avoid a conflict of interests that may cause serious prejudice to an accused or to protect the interests of justice. In considering the interests of justice, "the right to be tried fairly and without undue delay, as guaranteed by Article 20 of the Statute, must be taken into account".[7] **[page 3]**

5. The Prosecution submits that severance is in the interests of justice because (i) with their superior, Mr Muvunyi, "having now been tried separately, there is little in the factual allegations connecting the co-accused Mr Nizeyimana and Mr Hategekimana";[8] and (ii) severance is necessary to protect Mr Hategekimana's right to be tried without undue delay, enshrined in Articles 19(1) and 20(4)(c) of the Statute, because Mr Hategekimana has been detained since February 2003 and Mr Nizeyimana remains at large with no indication as to when he might be apprehended, if at all.[9]

6. Two factors favour severance in this case. First, "the issue of delay is especially pertinent in view of the fact that the co-accused has not, to date, been arrested or transferred to the Tribunal's Detention Facilities in Arusha".[10] The Prosecution submits that it is "in the advanced stages of preparing the trial against Mr

---

1 In Annex D of the Prosecution Application, *see infra* footnote 4, the Prosecution indicates that it now believes **Ilde**phonse to be the correct spelling of Mr Hategekimana's first name. In this Decision, the Chamber refers to Mr Hategekimana or the Accused.

2 *Prosecutor v. Muvunyi et al.*, Case No. ICTR-00-55-I, Decision to Confirm the Indictment (TC), 2 February 2000.

3 *Muvunyi et al.*, Case No. ICTR-00-55-I, Decision Regarding the Prosecutor's Motion for Leave to Sever an Indictment and for Directions on the Trial of Tharcisse Muvunyi (TC), 11 December 2003.

4 *Prosecutor v. Muvunyi*, Case No. ICTR-00-55A-T, Judgement and Sentence (TC), dated 12 September 2006.

5 "Application for Severance and Amendment in the Case of the Prosecutor v. Hategekimana and Nizeyimana", filed on 9/10/2006 ("Prosecution Application").

6 "Defence Observations on the Draft Amended Indictment", filed on 20 April 2007.

7 *Prosecutor v. Karemera et al.*, Case No. ICTR-98-44-PT, Decision on Severance of André Rwamakuba and for Leave to File Amended Indictment (TC), 14 February 2005, para. 26 ("Rwamakuba Severance Decision"); *Prosecutor v. Bizimana et al.*, Decision on the Defence Motion in Opposition to Joinder and Motion for Severance and Separate Trials Filed by the Accused Juvénal Kajelijeli (TC), 6 July 2000, par. 30; *Prosecutor v. Nyiramasuhuko et al.*, Case No. ICTR-97-29A-T, Decision on the Defence Motion Seeking a Separate Trial for the Accused Sylvain Nsabimana (TC), 8 September 2000, par. 34; *Prosecutor v. Kamuhanda*, Case No. ICTR-99-54-T, Decision on the Defence Motion for Severance and Separate Trials Filed by the Accused (TC), 7 November 2000, par. 4 ("Kamuhanda Decision"); *Prosecutor v. Muhimana et al.*, Decision on the Prosecutor's Motion for Leave to Sever an Indictment (TC), 14 April 2003.

8 Prosecution Application, paras. 10-13.

9 Prosecution Application, paras. 14-17.

10 *Kamuhanda Decision*, para. 5.

Hategekimana", and therefore severance would allow them to move forward with his trial. Second, the key allegations against Mr Hategekimana are largely distinct from those made against Mr Nizeyimana, so a joint trial is not likely to promote judicial economy. Under these circumstances, the Chamber finds that the requested severance is in the interests of justice as required under Rule 82(B).

The Application for Leave to Amend the Indictment

7. Rule 50(A)(i) of the Rules prescribes that after the initial appearance of the accused, an amendment of an Indictment may only be made by leave granted by a Trial Chamber. In deciding whether to grant leave to amend the indictment, the Chamber shall follow the procedures and apply the standards set out in Sub-Rules 47(E) and (F) in addition to considering any other relevant factors.[11] The Chamber shall therefore examine the proposed amendments to the Indictment, and any supporting materials the Prosecution has provided, to determine whether a *prima facie* case exists against the Accused.[12]

8. Pursuant to the jurisprudence of both *ad hoc* Tribunals, the fundamental issue in relation to granting leave to amend an Indictment is whether doing so will unfairly prejudice the Accused.[13] "Other relevant factors" include the Accused's right to be tried without undue delay, and to be promptly informed and in detail of the nature and cause of **[page 4]** the charges against him or her.[14] In that respect, Chambers have taken into consideration whether the proposed changes more accurately describe the totality of the criminal conduct of the Accused,[15] the ameliorating effect of the changes on the clarity and precision of the case to be met,[16] newly discovered evidence,[17] and the diligence of the Prosecution in bringing the amendment in a timely manner.[18]

9. Consideration of these factors requires an evaluation of the scope of the proposed amendments. The proposed Amended Indictment substantially modifies the current Indictment, with amendments falling into three broad categories. The first category of amendments has the effect of narrowing the case against the Accused by removing extraneous material as well as one count. The second category of amendments improves the Indictment by providing greater detail and adding particulars to various general allegations in the current Indictment; such amendments lend clarity to and may also narrow the case against the Accused. The third category of amendments expands the Indictment by adding new allegations and an additional count.

The First Category of Amendments

10. The first category of amendments includes proposals to remove: (i) general introductory paragraphs concerning historical background, the structure of the government and military, the relationship between political parties and the militias, the existence of an armed conflict, the attack on the presidential plane, and the duties of *préfets*; (ii) paragraphs that deal only with Mr Hategekimana's former co-accused; and (iii) paragraphs that the Prosecution submits were insufficiently pleaded or not supported by the presently

11 Rule 50(A)(ii) of the Rules.

12 Rule 47(E) of the Rules.

13 *Rwamakuba Severance Decision*, para. 35; *Prosecutor v. Zigiranyirazo*, Case No. ICTR-2001-73-I, Decision on Prosecutor's Request for Leave to Amend the Indictment and on Defence Urgent Motion for an Order to Disclose Supporting Material in Respect of the Prosecutor's Motion for Leave to Amend the Indictment (TC), 15 October 2003, par. 19; *Prosecutor v. Simba*, Case No. ICTR-2001-76-I, Decision on Motion to Amend Indictment (TC), 26 January 2004, par. 7; *Prosecutor v. Brdanin and Talic*, Case No. IT-99-36, Decision on Filing Replies (TC), 7 June 2001, par. 3.

14 *Prosecutor v. Bizimungu et al.*, Case No. ICTR-1999-50-I, Decision on the Prosecutor's Request for Leave to File an Amended Indictment (TC), 6 October 2003, para. 28.

15 *Prosecutor v. Nsengiyumva*, Decision on the Prosecutor's Request for Leave to Amend the Indictment (TC), 2 September 1999, para. 4; *Prosecutor v. Barayagwiza*, Decision on the Prosecutor's Request for Leave to File an Amended Indictment (TC), 11 April 2000, para. 4.

16 *Prosecutor v. Muhimana*, Case No. ICTR-1995-1B-I, Decision on Motion to Amend Indictment (TC), 21 January 2004, para. 6.

17 *Prosecutor v. Ndindabahizi*, Case No. ICTR-2001-71-I, Decision on Prosecution Motion for Leave to Amend Indictment, 20 August 2003, para. 4.

18 *Prosecutor v. Ndindiliyimana et al*, Case No. ICTR-2000-56-I, Decision on Prosecutor's Motion under Rule 50 for Leave to Amend the Indictment Issued on 20 January 2000 and Confirmed on 28 January 2000, 26 March 2004, paras. 40-44.

available evidence. The proposed Amended Indictment also drops the count of other inhumane acts as a crime against humanity.

11. The removal of extraneous paragraphs and of the count of other inhumane acts as a crime against humanity makes the indictment clearer and narrows the case against the Accused.

12. The Chamber is not convinced by the Defence submission that the removal of the general introductory paragraphs deprives it of context necessary for the Accused to receive a fair trial. Nor is it convinced by the Defence suggestion that removal of "statements of some of the witnesses" from the Indictment interferes with the rights of **[page 5]** the Defence. These submissions suggest a fundamental misunderstanding of the nature of Indictments and the roles of the Prosecution and Defence at this Tribunal.

13. Article 17 of the Statute empowers the Prosecution to prepare indictments which, pursuant to Rule 47 (C) of the Rules "shall set forth the name and particulars of the suspect, and a concise statement of the facts of the case and of the crime with which the suspect is charged." The Prosecution's obligation to set out concisely the facts of its case must be interpreted in conjunction with Articles 20 (2) and (4)(a) and (b) of the Statute, which "state that in the determination of any charges against him, an accused is entitled to a fair hearing and, more particularly, to be informed of the nature and cause of the charges against him and to have adequate time and facilities for the preparation of his defence."[19]

14. According to the Appeals Chamber, this "translates into an obligation on the part of the Prosecution to state the material facts underpinning the charges in the indictment, but not the evidence by which such material facts are to be proven. Whether certain 'facts' are 'material' depends on the nature of the case."[20] In other words, the degree of specificity required depends on the nature of the Prosecution's case against an accused. Material facts have been defined as those "necessary to determine an issue."[21] For example, the Appeals Chamber has noted, "where the Prosecution alleges that an accused personally committed the criminal acts, the material facts, such as the identity of the victim, the time and place of the events and the means by which the acts were committed, have to be pleaded in detail", though "there may be instances where the sheer scale of the alleged crimes "makes it impracticable to require a high degree of specificity in such matters as the identity of the victims and the dates for the commission of the crimes."[22]

15. The general introductory paragraphs that the Prosecution proposes to remove from the Indictment concern tangential matters including a broad historical background, the structure of the government and military, the relationship between political parties and the militias, the existence of an armed conflict, the attack on President Habyarimana's plane, and the duties of *préfets*. These facts cannot reasonably be described as necessary to determine whether the Accused is responsible for any of the charges against him, and therefore are not "material" to the current or the proposed Amended Indictment. Nor are they necessary to inform the Accused of the nature and cause of the charges against him.

16. Conversely, introductory paragraphs 3 through 5 of the proposed Amended Indictment allege, respectively, the existence of Tutsi minority and Hutu majority ethnic or racial groups in Rwanda, the existence of widespread and/or systematic attacks against Tutsi civilians on the basis of ethnicity or race during the relevant time period, and that **[page 6]** genocide against the Tutsi occurred during the relevant time period. These allegations are material, as they allege that the so-called *chapeau* elements of the crimes charged are met.

17. The Accused is not prejudiced by the removal of these introductory paragraphs; to the extent it can show relevance pursuant to Rule 89 (C) of the Rules, the Accused may adduce evidence of any of the non-material facts the Prosecution seeks to remove from the current Indictment when he presents his case.

---

19 *Prosecutor v. Elizaphan and Gérard Ntakirutimana*, Case Nos. ICTR-96-10 & ICTR-96-17-T, Judgement and Sentence (TC), 24 February 2003, para. 42 (citing *Prosecutor v. Zoran Kupreškić et al.*, Case No. IT-95-16-A, Judgement (AC), 23 October 2001).

20 *Prosecutor v. Elizaphan and Gérard Ntakirutimana*, Case Nos. ICTR-96-10-A & ICTR-96-17-A, Judgement (AC), 13 December 2004, para. 25 (citing *Kupreškić et al.*, Judgement (AC), paras. 88-89).

21 Black's Law Dictionary, p. 977 (6th Ed. West, 1990).

22 *Kupreškić et al.*, Judgement (AC), para. 89.

18. Regarding the Defence submission that witness statements have been removed from the Indictment, the Chamber reiterates that the Prosecution is not obliged to include in the Indictment the evidence by which material facts are to be proven.[23] To the extent the Prosecution is in possession of witness statements or any other evidence pertinent to the Defence, this is generally a matter for disclosure at a later stage pursuant to the Rules.[24]

19. The Chamber concludes that the first category of proposed amendments will streamline and enhance the fairness of the proceedings and will not cause prejudice to the Accused. They are therefore allowed.

The Second Category of Amendments

20. Many of the proposed amendments add specific allegations of fact to the general allegations in the current Indictment, such as dates, places, other additional details regarding events alleged in the current Indictment, and the names of individuals present during and/or involved in the alleged crimes, including individuals with whom the Accused was allegedly involved in a joint criminal enterprise and subordinates of the Accused.[25] The Defence does not specifically oppose any of these proposed amendments.

21. The Prosecution has provided very little information regarding its diligence in investigating the facts underlying the proposed Amended Indictment. With specific regard to the second category of amendments, the Chamber notes that the majority of the supporting materials pre-date the current Indictment. Indeed, the Prosecution disclosed many of the supporting statements to the Accused in March 2003. At the same time, there is nothing to suggest that the Prosecution has sought leave to file the proposed Amended Indictment in order to gain a strategic advantage over the Accused. As such, the Prosecution's failure to show that the Amendments were brought forward in a timely manner must be "measured within the framework of the overall requirement of the fairness of the proceedings."[26] **[page 7]**

22. Although these amendments may cause short term delay in the form of further investigations, consideration of whether any such delay is undue must also be measured within the framework of the overall requirement of the fairness of the proceedings.[27] The Trial Chamber must therefore consider the effect the Amended Indictment will have on the Accused's other rights designed to guarantee a fair trial, for example, his right to be informed in detail of the nature and cause of the charges against him.[28] As explained by the Appeals Chamber:

> [A] Trial Chamber must also examine the effect that the Amended Indictment would have on the overall proceedings Although amending an indictment frequently causes delay in the short term, the Appeals Chamber takes the view that this procedure can also have the overall effect of simplifying proceedings by narrowing the scope of allegations, by improving the Accused's and the Tribunal's understanding of the Prosecution's case, or by averting possible challenges to the indictment or the evidence presented at trial. The Appeals Chamber finds that a clearer and more specific indictment benefits the accused, not only because a streamlined indictment may result in shorter proceedings, but also because the accused can tailor their preparations to an indictment that more accurately reflects the case they will meet, thus resulting in a more effective defence.[29]

23. To the extent that the second category of amendments will require further investigations by the Defence, granting the Prosecution leave to amend may have the result of extending the Accused's period of pre-trial detention. Nonetheless, the Chamber reiterates that the added particulars provide further notice to the Accused of the case against him and will allow the Accused to tailor his investigations and enhance his

---

23 *Prosecutor v. Elizaphan and Gérard Ntakirutimana*, Judgement (AC), para. 42 (citations omitted).

24 *See generally*, Rules 66 and 68 of the Rules of Procedure and Evidence (governing disclosure of exculpatory and other material relevant to the Defence).

25 In particular, see paragraphs 14-16, 18-20, and 26-31 of the proposed Amended Indictment, which describe in detail the general allegations of paragraph 3.46 of the current Indictment.

26 *Prosecutor v. Karemera et al.*, Case No. ICTR-98-44-AR73, Decision on Prosecutor's Interlocutory Appeal against Trial Chamber III Decision of 8 October 2003 Denying Leave to File an Amended Indictment (AC), 19 December 2003, para. 22 (quoting *Prosecutor v. Kovačević* Case No. IT-97-24-AR73, Decision Stating Reasons for Appeals Chamber's Order of 29 May 1998, 2 July 1998).

27 *Id.*, para. 13.

28 Article 20 (4)(a) of the ICTR Statute.

29 *Karemera et al.*, Decision on Prosecutor's Interlocutory Appeal against Trial Chamber III Decision of 8 October 2003 Denying Leave to File an Amended Indictment (AC), para. 15.

ability to prepare his defence. As such, these amendments may result in shortened proceedings overall. Moreover, no date has been set for trial in this matter. Thus, any discussion of the possible extension of the pre-trial detention period is speculative at this time, and, if necessary, the Chamber may grant the Defence more time to investigate without the need to postpone the trial.

24. For the reasons discussed above, the Chamber concludes that the second category of amendments will enhance the fairness of the proceedings and will not cause prejudice to the Accused. They are therefore allowed.

The Third Category of Amendments

25. The third category of amendments consists of new allegations and the addition of a new Count of murder as a crime against humanity. The proposed Amended Indictment contains the following new allegations: (i) throughout the proposed Amended Indictment, the Prosecution now refers to Mr Hategekimana as "Ildephonse Hategekimana alias Bikomago"; (ii) there are several new allegations of material fact supporting existing counts, including, *inter alia*, new rape allegations in support of the existing genocide **[page 8]** count (paragraphs 7, 8 and 17) and new allegations supporting liability pursuant to Article 6(1) of the Statute for the extant count of rape as a crime against humanity (paragraphs 42 through 45), for which the current Indictment charges only command responsibility pursuant to Article 6(3) of the Statute; and (iii) paragraphs 34 through 41 of the proposed Amended Indictment allege a new count of murder as a crime against humanity.

26. As mentioned in footnote 1, the Prosecution alleges that it now believes "Ildephonse", and not "Idelphonse", is the correct spelling of the Accused's first name. Moreover, the proposed Amended Indictment repeatedly refers to the Accused as "Ildephonse Hategekimana alias Bikomago". Statements dating back to 1998 and disclosed to the Defence in 2003 refer to the Accused by the nickname "Bikomago". The Defence argues that references to the Accused as "Bikomago" are intended to associate him with a notorious individual who allegedly committed many crimes and are therefore prejudicial. The Chamber rejects this argument. It is clear from the supporting materials that the proposed Amended Indictment seeks to introduce the use of the nickname "Bikomago" to assist in identifying Mr Hategekimana as well as his alleged crimes, and not to confuse or associate the Accused with any such person named Bikomago who may have committed crimes in Burundi or elsewhere.

27. The proposed Amended Indictment includes new allegations of material fact in support of several of the counts in the current Indictment. In the current Indictment, the count of rape as a crime against humanity is supported by paragraph 3.47 and sub-paragraph 3.47(i), which generally allege that rapes were committed by soldiers under the command of the Accused, and seek to hold the Accused accountable as a superior pursuant to Article 6(3) of the Statute for failing to prevent or punish these acts. The proposed Amended Indictment contains more detailed allegations of the Accused's responsibility for rape and, in addition to seeking Article 6(3) responsibility, seeks to hold him responsible pursuant to Article 6(1) for planning, ordering, instigating, committing or otherwise aiding and abetting in the planning, preparation and or execution of these crimes, as well as for participating in a joint criminal enterprise involving the rape of Tutsi women. Some of these new allegations of material fact are supported by newly obtained evidence. In addition, the proposed Amended Indictment includes the allegations of material fact involving rape as part of the genocide counts. The Defence does not expressly oppose these amendments.

28. The new allegations involving rape contained in paragraphs 7 and 8 of the proposed Amended Indictment under the genocide counts and paragraphs 43 and 44 under the count of rape as a crime against humanity are supported by newly obtained evidence not available to the Prosecution until 2006. Other new allegations, specifically the allegations contained in paragraphs 17 under the genocide counts and paragraphs 45 and 49 under the count of rape as a crime against humanity come from statements previously disclosed to the Accused. While the Prosecution has not offered any explanation regarding its diligence in adding these allegations, there is no suggestion that the Prosecution was trying to obtain unfair advantage by seeking to add them at this time. Moreover, while the additional details are significant, the allegations contained in these paragraphs are consistent with the more general allegations in paragraphs 3.47 and 3.47(i) **[page 9]** of the current Indictment. Like the second category of proposed amendments discussed above, these new

allegations will provide the Accused with better notice of the case against him and will allow the Defence to better focus its investigation and case.

29. The Prosecution also seeks to add a new count of murder as a crime against humanity, which it argues is wholly supported by material facts alleged in support of the existing genocide counts, with the addition of the particulars and specific details the Prosecution seeks to add to the proposed Amended Indictment as a whole. The Defence does not oppose the addition of this count. While the Prosecution offers no explanation for its failure to include this count in the current Indictment, the Chamber finds that, as the new count is not opposed by the Defence and is supported by material facts alleged in the current Indictment, the addition of the new count will not unfairly prejudice the Accused and will not require significant additional investigations or preparation for the Defence.

30. Having considered the proposed new allegations in the context of the overall fairness of the proceedings, the Chamber finds that, as with the second category of amendments, these amendments will not cause undue delay and will not unfairly prejudice the Accused. As there is currently no date set for trial, the Chamber may authorise additional time for the Defence to investigate these allegations, as well as to schedule a further initial appearance as discussed below. The third category of amendments is therefore allowed.

Other Defence Objections

31. In addition to the objections discussed above, the Defence raises other objections related to the specificity of the proposed Amended Indictment. The Chamber notes that, where permission to amend is granted, Rule 50 (C) authorizes a further thirty day period for the Defence to file preliminary motions pursuant to Rule 72, which includes challenges to the form of the Indictment, at least with respect to new charges. The Chamber has nevertheless considered the Defence objections at this stage in the interests of justice and to promote judicial economy. The Chamber recalls its discussion of specificity in paragraphs 13 and 14 above, and considers these Defence objections in light of those principles.

32. The Defence challenges paragraph 6 of the proposed Amended Indictment for failing to add clarity and to simplify the facts and failing to explain the relationship between the Accused and all named co-participants in the alleged joint criminal enterprise. The Chamber notes that paragraph 6 is an introductory paragraph, which alleges that the Accused is responsible for genocide or, alternatively, complicity in genocide pursuant to Article 6 (1) of the Statute. As explained at the end of that paragraph, the particulars relevant to these counts, including the details that the Defence alleges are lacking, follow in paragraphs 7 through 20 of the proposed Amended Indictment. Thus, the Defence's argument is rejected.

33. The Defence submits that in a criminal case, it is necessary to provide exact dates, and objects to the use of any approximate dates in the proposed Amended Indictment. **[page 10]** The Chamber agrees that specificity regarding dates is preferable, but notes that if a precise date cannot be specified, a reasonable range of dates may be provided.[30] Where possible, the Prosecution should provide exact or more specific dates throughout the proposed Amended Indictment, but the Chamber does not find that the dates or date ranges included therein are unreasonable given the nature of the allegations against the Accused.

34. Finally, in addition to the objections based on specificity, the Defence suggests that "it is inadmissible for the Prosecution to take advantage of the amendment procedure to try to rid the Indictment of its inadequacies and contradictions." This argument is unfounded and must be rejected. Neither Rule 50 of the Rules, which governs the amendment process, nor the substantial body of jurisprudence of the *ad hoc* Tribunals regarding amendments, places such a limitation on the Prosecution. On the contrary, amendments that provide better notice to the accused of the nature and cause of the case against him are to be allowed as long as the benefits of better notice are not outweighed by other concerns regarding the rights of, and possible prejudice to, the accused.[31] This is so because, by ridding the Indictment of such inadequacies, amendments

[30] *Prosecutor v. Nchamihigo*, Case No. ICTR-2001-63-I, Decision on Defence Motion on Defects in the Form of the Indictment, 27 September 2006, para. 17 (citing *Prosecutor v. Brdjanin*, Case No. IT-99-36-PT, Decision on Objections to the Form of Amended Indictment (TC), 20 February 2001, at para. 22).

[31] *See e.g.*, *Karemera et al.*, Decision on Prosecutor's Interlocutory Appeal against Trial Chamber III Decision of 8 October 2003 Denying Leave to File an Amended Indictment (AC), para. 15.

that provide better notice to the accused of the nature and cause of the case against him have an overall ameliorative effect on the fairness of the proceedings.

Conclusion

35. The Chamber has considered the materials submitted by the Prosecution in support of its Motion, and finds that a prima facie case has been established with respect to the counts contained in the proposed Amended Indictment against the Accused. The Chamber therefore grants the Prosecution leave to file the proposed Amended Indictment subject to the minor changes detailed in the order, below.

36. The Chamber considers that a further initial appearance is necessary to enable the Accused to enter a plea, pursuant to Rule 50 (B), on the new count of murder as a crime against humanity, the addition of Article 6(1) responsibility for rape as a crime against humanity, and for the new rape allegations in support of the genocide counts.

37. The Chamber notes that second sentence of paragraph 37 of the proposed Amended Indictment repeats the following clause: "After gaining entry to the Maison Généralice". This typographical error should be corrected.

FOR THE ABOVE REASONS, THE CHAMBER [page 11]

I. **GRANTS** the Prosecution leave to sever Mr Ildephonse Hategekimana from the original Indictment, dated 7 November 2000;

II. **DIRECTS** the Registry to designate a new number for the separate Indictment against Mr Hategekimana;

III. **GRANTS** the Prosecution leave to file the Amended Indictment, subject to the above-mentioned directions;

IV. **ORDERS** the Prosecution to file the Amended Indictment with the Registry and the Chamber, within 10 days from the service of this Decision; and

V. **ORDERS** that a further appearance shall be held as soon as practicable, and, accordingly, requests that the Registrar make further arrangements.

Arusha, 25 September 2007

Khalida Rachid Khan
Presiding Judge

Lee Gacuiga Muthoga
Judge

Emile Francis Short
Judge

[Seal of the Tribunal]

Commentary

1. Introduction

The decisions under consideration[1] are directly related to the importance of the indictment as "the primary accusatory instrument"[2] that indicates the formal conclusion of the exclusively investigative phase, establishes the scope of the trial, and permits the material preparation of the defence. The two decisions affirm the intimate connection between the rights of the accused to an effective defence, to be promptly informed of the charges, and to be tried without undue delay.[3] By determining the case of the prosecution, the indictment also sets the scope of the judicial deliberations,[4] considering that evidence introduced before the judges ought to be relevant to demonstrate the guilt or innocence of the accused with respect to the charges contained in the indictment.

2. Confirmation of the indictment and the scope of the trial

In the system of criminal procedure of the ICTR,[5] the prosecution, pursuant to Article 17, paragraph 4 ICTR Statute, "shall prepare an indictment containing a concise statement of the facts with which the accused is charged under the Statute" on the basis of evidence collected during the investigation and upon determining that a *prima facie* case exists. Sub-Rule 47 (B) ICTR RPE seems to articulate a meaning for the expression *prima facie* as employed in the statutory provision, by determining that the prosecution may present an indictment, together with supporting material, for confirmation by a judge "if satisfied in the course of an investigation that there is sufficient evidence to provide reasonable grounds for believing that a suspect has committed a crime within the jurisdiction of the Tribunal". In this sense, the prosecution determines the content and scope of the indictment, the presentation of which, before a Trial Chamber judge, marks the moment when judicial intervention begins to play a considerable role.[6]

Pursuant to Article 18, paragraph 1 ICTR Statute, complemented by Rules 47(E) and (F), while examining the indictment, the judge ought to be satisfied that a "*prima facie* case has been established" with respect to the counts contained in the proposed indictment in order to confirm them. A definition, or a more clear expression of the meaning of *prima facie* case, is not present in the statute or the rules, and it has been argued that there is no need for the reviewing judge to conform to the standard of Rule 47(B),[7] which is drafted to indicate the parameters for the prosecution to present its case.

---

1 ICTR, Decision on Aloys Ntabakuze's Interlocutory Appeal on Questions of Law Raised by the 29 June 2006 Trial Chamber I Decision on Motion for Exclusion of Evidence, *Prosecutor v. Bagosora, Kabiligi, Ntabakuze and Nsengiyumva*, Case No. ICTR-98-41-AR73, A. Ch., 18 September 2006, in this volume, p. 13, (hereinafter "Ntabakuze's Interlocutory Appeal"); and ICTR, Decision on the Prosecutor's Application for Severance and Leave to Amend the Indictment Against Idelphonse Hategekimana, *Prosecutor v. Nizeyimana and Hategekimana,* Case No. ICTR-00-55-I, T. Ch. III, 25 September 2007, in this volume, p. 27, (hereinafter "Hategekimana's Decision").

2 ICTY, Appeal Judgement, *Prosecutor v. Kupreškić, Kupreškić, Kupreškić, Josipović and Šantić*, Case No. IT-95-16-A, A. Ch., 23 October 2001, Klip/ Sluiter, ALC-VIII-429, par. 114. For details on this landmark case, see A. Zahar and G. Sluiter, *infra* note 3, p. 336-340. For a positive view of the tendency of the tribunals to accord growing importance to their own precedents (in particular the Kupreškić appeal judgement), see also Daniel Ntanda Nsereko, Commentary, in Klip/Sluiter ALC-IV-68.

3 See Article 20, paragraph 4 sub a, b and c ICTR Statute. See also Alexander Zahar and Goran Sluiter, International Criminal Law, Oxford, Oxford U.P. 2008, p. 307-309.

4 See Rule 87 ICTR Statute. Robert Cryer *et al.*, An Introduction to International Criminal Procedure, Cambridge, Cambridge U.P. 2007, p. 376-377.

5 The two procedural regimes of the ICTR and the ICTY coincide in the matters under discussion, in spite of the fact that the ICTY RPE are often updated before the ICTR RPE, and that, due to each tribunal's Completion Strategy some peculiarities related to the confirmation of the indictment have been introduced. This commentary refrains from a comparative analysis of ICTR provisions with those of the ICTY and internationalized courts, as well as with the ICC legal framework. Concerning the ICC Statute, it is interesting to note that, at the outcome of the negotiations over the ICC Statute, "application", as a "neutral" term for the document containing the charges, prevailed over "indictment", initially envisaged at the ILC Draft and a source of confusion for many delegations that viewed it as excessively bonded with the common law system (see Fabrizio Guariglia, International Criminal Law Procedures: Investigation and prosecution, in: Roy Lee (ed.), The International Criminal Court: The Making of the Rome Statute, Kluwer, The Hague 1999, p. 235-236).

6 See A. Zahar and G. Sluiter, *supra* note 3, p. 54-59.

7 David Hunt, The Meaning of a "*prima facie*" case for the Purposes of Confirmation, in: Richard May *et al.* (eds.) Essays on ICTY Procedure and Evidence in Honour of Gabrielle Kirk McDonald, Kluwer, The Hague 2001, p. 137-149.

In the procedural law of the *ad hoc* tribunals, the judge is not asked to perform an evidentiary test of reasonableness of grounds for believing that a suspect has committed a crime. A more superficial examination of the indictment would merely require that "the indictment plead facts which, if accepted, are such that a reasonable Trial Chamber *could* be satisfied beyond reasonable doubt of the guilt of the accused".[8]

Judicial intervention at the confirmation of the indictment, while reviewing amendments to the indictment, or at a later stage, while, for example, ruling on the admissibility of evidence of material facts not argued in the indictment, shall be directed at ensuring that the proceedings are fair,[9] and in particular that the defence is fully informed of the charges and of the material facts supporting the charges. Early direct judicial intervention aimed, for example, at restricting the scope of the indictment, may have an overall positive impact on the fairness and the expeditiousness of the trial,[10] and avoid the need to "cure" defects in the indictment, to adjourn the trial to enable the effective preparation of the defence, or to declare parts of the procedure unfair.[11]

Such aspects are present in both decisions, issued at different procedural stages: the Hategekimana decision discusses a case of severance and the admission of different types of amendments to the indictment before the initiation of the trial, while the most interesting part of the Ntabakuze interlocutory appeal deals with the admission of evidence of material facts not pleaded in the indictment at a more advanced stage, considering the duty to give notice to the defence of all material facts supporting the charges.

3. Severance

In the Hategekimana decisions, the Trial Chamber accepted the arguments of the prosecution – unchallenged by the defence – according to which severance of Mr. Hategekimana from the original joint indictment (under Rule 48) would be in the interests of justice, as required by Rule 82(B). The interests of justice would, *in casu*, be characterized by deference to the right of the accused to be tried fairly and without undue delay, and by judicial economy.

There is no doubt that the defence would not have a strong interest in opposing severance, in particular considering the lengthy detention of the accused. Nevertheless, with an eye to the right to be tried without undue delay, it is rather striking that, on 11 December 2003, the prosecution was granted leave to sever Mr. Muvunyi (arrested on 7 February 2000) from the original indictment against the other two co-accused (dated 7 November 2000), although Mr. Hategekimana had already been in detention since 16 February 2003. The arguments for severance of Mr. Hategekimana[12] existed at the time of the severance of Mr. Muvunyi, and could have already been presented by the prosecution. Considering judicial economy, it would have been as true in 2003 that Mr. Hategekimana should be tried separately from the third co-accused, Mr. Nizeyimana, because the allegations against them were of a different nature, regardless of whether their superior, Mr. Muvunyi, would be tried separately. Mr. Hategekimana's trial should have already been envisaged at that time, in order to avoid additional delay, because the third co-accused remained at large.

Based on such facts, already known as at December 2003, the prosecution only requested leave to sever Mr. Hategekimana from the original indictment in October 2006. The reason why the Trial Chamber granted this request only in September 2007 is also revealing of an insufficient standard of expeditiousness. It is noted that such delay would rather be addressed in a request for provisional release than during a decision on the

---

8 *Ibid.*, p. 137-138. The author presents a challenging interpretation of the expression "*prima facie* case", for different stages in the proceedings. Despite the absence of an indication that *prima facie* should have a different meaning in the statutory provisions related to the prosecution's decision to present a case, and to the judicial decision to confirm the counts (*ibid*, p. 146), it would still be possible to argue that the evidence gathered as result of investigations should be more rigorously evaluated by the prosecution than by the judge reviewing the indictment; the latter would be responsible for a superficial assessment of the case, keeping the credibility of the Trial Chamber intact to weigh the evidence as to its admission or exclusion.

9 Article 19, paragraph 1, ICTR Statute.

10 Gillian Higgins, Fair and Expeditious Pre-trial Proceedings, 5 Journal of International Criminal Justice 2007, p. 394-401.

11 See Decision on the Prosecutor's Application for Severance and Leave to Amend the Indictment Against Idelphonse Hategekimana, *Prosecutor v. Nizeyimana and Hategekimana*, T. Ch. III, *supra* note 1, par. 15, 23, 28 and 34; and Decision on Aloys Ntabakuze's Interlocutory Appeal on Questions of Law Raised by the 29 June 2006 Trial Chamber I Decision on Motion for Exclusion of Evidence, *Prosecutor v. Bagosora, Kabiligi, Ntabakuze and Nsengiyumva*, A. Ch., *supra* note 1, par. 26, 27, 30, 35 and 37.

12 Decision on the Prosecutor's Application for Severance and Leave to Amend the Indictment Against Idelphonse Hategekimana, *Prosecutor v. Nizeyimana and Hategekimana*, T. Ch. III, *supra* note 1, par. 5.

severance of a case.[13] However, it is puzzling from a human rights standpoint, notably the right to be tried within a reasonable time,[14] that the factual lengthy detention was not contrasted to the prosecution's arguments, which were all but new. Prosecutorial diligence is, in fact, only marginally mentioned in the Hategekimana decision in connection with a proposed amendment related to new allegations supported by evidence previously available.[15]

4. Effects of amendments to the indictment and of allegations outside the scope of the indictment upon the fairness of the trial

Underscoring the importance of the confirmation of the indictment in the adversarial setting of the *ad hoc* tribunals, Rule 50(A)(i) determines that the prosecution is free to modify the indictment before its confirmation by a Trial Chamber judge. Thereafter, modifications are only possible by leave of a judge; and at or after the initial appearance of the accused, only by leave of the Trial Chamber, following the adversarial procedure set forth at Rule 73. The latter scenario applies to the Hategekimana decision.

In principle, the same threshold relevant for a Trial Chamber judge to confirm an indictment applies to the judicial decision to grant leave to amend the indictment, insofar as it redefines the scope of the indictment. Therefore, pursuant to Rules 47 (E) and (F) and 50 (A)(ii), the proposed amendments to the indictment, and any supporting materials provided by the prosecution, must contribute to meet the requirements of a *prima facie* case against the accused. In addition, the proposed amendments are to be assessed against the fairness of the trial, in particular the right to be informed of the charges, and of the supporting material.[16]

The assessment of the counts in the proposed amended indictment as characterising a *prima facie* case against the accused is done in a very superficial manner in the Hategekimana decision,[17] which focuses on whether different categories of amendments would prejudice the accused's fair trial rights.[18] Similar considerations guide the Appeals Chamber, in the Ntabakuze's interlocutory appeal, in admitting the curing of defects in the indictment by providing details and substantiating vague allegations, or by communication of material facts to the defence in a timely manner.

The first category of amendment discussed in the Hategekimana Decision is related to the removal from the indictment of background information, of general circumstances not directly related to the accused (as non-material facts) and of a count of other inhumane acts as a crime against humanity.[19] This is presented as bringing clarity and narrowing the case against the accused. Since such removal is deemed beneficial to the

---

13 Actually, the procedure related to Mr. Hategekimana is an example of the unfortunate record of the ICTR with regard to the right to be tried within a reasonable time, due to a complex combination of factors. The ICTR Completion Strategy of October 2003 (Security Council resolution 946 of 2003) still displayed a question mark as to Mr. Hategekimana being tried jointly with Mr. Muvunyi (paragraph 14, Table 3). A joint trial would have been a sensible possibility, particularly because no new circumstances whatsoever were presented in the request for severance. The trial of Mr. Hategekimana was further delayed by a request for referral of his case to Rwanda, in late 2007. In pursuance of the Completion Strategy of the tribunal, after the decision on severance of Hategekimana and on amendments to his indictment, the prosecution filed a request for the referral of the Hategekimana case to Rwanda, according to Rule 11*bis*, denied by both Trial and Appeals Chamber on fair trial concerns. The Trial itself only commenced in January 2009. See ICTR, Decision on Prosecutor's request for the referral of the case of Ildephonse Hategekimana to Rwanda, *Prosecutor v. Hategekimana*, ICTR-00-55B-R11bis, Trial Chamber, 19 June 2008; and ICTR, Decision on the Prosecution's Appeal against Decision on Referral under Rule 11*bis*, *Prosecutor v. Hategekimana*, ICTR-00-55B-R11bis, A. Ch., 4 December 2008. For an overview of the United Nations Security Council documents on the ICTR Completion Strategy, see: www.ictr.org/ENGLISH/completionstrat/index.htm (last visit 29 October 2009).

14 Article 9, paragraph 3, ICCPR, and Article 20, paragraph 4, sub c.

15 Decision on the Prosecutor's Application for Severance and Leave to Amend the Indictment Against Idelphonse Hategekimana, *Prosecutor v. Nizeyimana and Hategekimana,* T. Ch. III, *supra* note 1, par. 28.

16 See *inter alia* ICTY, Reasons for Decision on Prosecution's Motion to Use Telephone Interviews, *Prosecutor v. Simić et al.*, Case No. IT-95-9-T, T. Ch. II, 11 March 2003, par. 6.

17 Decision on the Prosecutor's Application for Severance and Leave to Amend the Indictment Against Idelphonse Hategekimana, *Prosecutor v. Nizeyimana and Hategekimana,* T. Ch. III, *supra* note 1, par. 35.

18 *Ibid.*, par. 9-34

19 The difficulty to prosecute someone for such a crime against humanity, formulated as a catchall expression in the Nuremberg Charter, the *ad hoc* tribunals' Statutes and the ICC Statute, is evident. In the system of the ICC, the elements of crime define "other inhumane acts" in a way that could be consistent with the principle of legality. See Machteld Boot and Christopher K. Hall, Article 7, paragraph 1sub k, in Otto Triffterer (ed.), Commentary on the Rome Statute of the International Criminal Court, Munich, C.H. Beck 2008, p. 230-234. It is not clear whether this solution satisfies the basic criminal law requirement that offences be strictly construed.

defendant, the Trial Chamber grants the modification without need for additional measures. The Trial Chamber recognizes that the nature of the case determines the degree of specificity expected of the material facts, which should be those necessary to directly support the charges.[20]

The decision further clarifies that it is not necessary for the indictment to indicate the evidence that will support the allegations of material facts, but evidence should be analysed in the course of the trial considering its probative value within the scope of the indictment.[21] Therefore, as the accused does not suffer substantial prejudice from this category of amendment, no further consequence is envisaged.

The second category of amendments "improves" the indictment by providing greater details of the allegations in the original indictment. However, as several supporting material was known or could have been known by the prosecution at the time of presenting the indictment, the Trial Chamber found it necessary to inquire whether, by communicating them to the defence at a later stage, the prosecution would have gained a strategic advantage over the accused, or whether the fairness of the trial would have been impaired.[22] The Trial Chamber notes that this type of amendment could delay the trial, because of the potential need to adjourn the trial to enable the preparation of the defence after notice of the supporting materials. Although late, the Trial Chamber observes that such amendments have a positive impact on the overall fairness of the proceedings, since they provide further detailed information to the accused of the charges against him, assisting the defence to prepare and streamline its case.[23]

The third category of amendments identified by the Trial Chamber makes use of very similar reasoning to justify admission of new allegations of material facts and the addition of a new count of murder as a crime against humanity, arguably based on material facts alleged in a general manner in the original indictment. The decision takes into account the timeliness of the communication to the defence, allowing it to better prepare its case, and the apparent lack of intention by the prosecution to prejudice the accused.[24]

The Ntabakuze's interlocutory appeal, in line with the precedent of the Kupreškić appeal judgment, noting the risk of prejudice to the accused's fair trial rights, confirms that the possibility to cure a defective indictment is limited. It requires the prosecution to provide the defence with timely, clear and consistent information about material facts supporting the charges against him.[25] However, the scope of the defects in the indictment, such as material facts not pleaded or specified, must also be evaluated. The Appeals Chamber, overruling the Trial Chamber, decided that the addition of a large number of material facts might prejudice the preparation of a proper defence and affect the fair trial rights of the accused: such a large number of defects should not be considered as curable by means of isolated disclosure of relevant information to the defence.

In other words, it is not deemed acceptable that, by informing the defence of new material facts, or by rendering vague allegations present in the indictment more specific, the prosecution builds up a totally different case than the one presented in the indictment. The prosecution should then seek to introduce such modifications and complements to the indictment by means of the amendment procedure, in which the judges decide whether they are satisfied that the accused would not be prejudiced in his right to a fair trial.[26]

---

20 Decision on the Prosecutor's Application for Severance and Leave to Amend the Indictment Against Idelphonse Hategekimana, *Prosecutor v. Nizeyimana and Hategekimana,* T. Ch. III, *supra* note 1, par. 13-15.

21 *Ibid.,* par. 17-18. See also Decision on Aloys Ntabakuze's Interlocutory Appeal on Questions of Law Raised by the 29 June 2006 Trial Chamber I Decision on Motion for Exclusion of Evidence, *Prosecutor v. Bagosora, Kabiligi, Ntabakuze and Nsengiyumva,* A. Ch., *supra* note 1, par. 24-26.

22 Decision on the Prosecutor's Application for Severance and Leave to Amend the Indictment Against Idelphonse Hategekimana, *Prosecutor v. Nizeyimana and Hategekimana,* T. Ch. III, *supra* note 1, par. 21.

23 *Ibid.,* par. 22-23. See Decision on Aloys Ntabakuze's Interlocutory Appeal on Questions of Law Raised by the 29 June 2006 Trial Chamber I Decision on Motion for Exclusion of Evidence, *Prosecutor v. Bagosora, Kabiligi, Ntabakuze and Nsengiyumva,* A. Ch., *supra* note 1, par. 36.

24 Decision on the Prosecutor's Application for Severance and Leave to Amend the Indictment Against Idelphonse Hategekimana, *Prosecutor v. Nizeyimana and Hategekimana,* T. Ch. III, *supra* note 1, par. 26-30.

25 *Ibid.,* par. 20-23.

26 See Decision on Aloys Ntabakuze's Interlocutory Appeal on Questions of Law Raised by the 29 June 2006 Trial Chamber I Decision on Motion for Exclusion of Evidence, *Prosecutor v. Bagosora, Kabiligi, Ntabakuze and Nsengiyumva,* A. Ch., *supra* note 1, par. 29, 30, 35 and 37.

5. Conclusion

The two decisions under consideration reaffirm the findings of the *ad hoc* tribunals' Appeals Chamber in landmark cases, in particular the Kupreškić appeal judgement, and thus apply consistent standards related to the review of indictments. The decisions are not innovative, but they are representative of an effort to streamline the tribunal's procedures, in view of the completion of its mandate, by narrowing the cases or by clarifying the charges, to enable a better preparation of the defence. The reviewed decisions further tackle interesting questions, without fully exploring them, related to the level of control of the proceedings by the judges, in particular the possibility to scrutinise prosecutorial diligence.

This control has direct implications on the exercise of the right to an effective defence. By controlling the content of the indictment, judicial intervention may also influence the scope of international criminal justice, to simply determine individual responsibility, or to set a historical record, or even to lend a voice to the victims of international crimes. The scope of the indictment thus directly bears upon the legacy of international criminal trials.

Celso Eduardo Faria Coracini

Tribunal Pénal International pour le Rwanda
International Criminal Tribunal for Rwanda

IN THE APPEALS CHAMBER

Before:	**Judge Fausto Pocar, Presiding** **Judge Mehmet Güney** **Judge Liu Daqun** **Judge Theodor Meron** **Judge Wolfgang Schomburg**
Registrar:	**Mr. Adama Dieng**
Decision of:	**25 September 2006**

THE PROSECUTOR

v.

Théoneste BAGOSORA
Gratien KABILIGI
Aloys NTABAKUZE
Anatole NSENGIYUMVA

Case No. ICTR-98-41-AR73

Decision on Interlocutory Appeal Relating to Disclosure Under Rule 66(B) of the Tribunal's Rules of Procedure and Evidence

---

Office of the Prosecutor:

Mr. Hassan Bubacar Jallow
Ms. Barbara Mulvaney
Mr. Neville Weston
Mr. Drew White
Ms. Christine Graham
Mr. Rashid Rashid

Counsel for the Defence:

Mr. Raphaël Constant and Ms. Allison Turner for Théoneste Bagosora
Mr. Paul Skolnik and Mr. Frédéric Hivon for Gratien Kabiligi
Mr. Peter Erlinder and Mr. André Tremblay for Aloys Ntabakuze
Mr. Kennedy Ogetto and Mr. Gershom Otachi Bw'Omanwa for Anatole Nsengiyumva

[page 1]1. The Appeals Chamber of the International Criminal Tribunal for the Prosecution of Persons Responsible for Genocide and Other Serious Violations of International Humanitarian Law Committed in the Territory of Rwanda and Rwandan Citizens Responsible for Genocide and Other Serious Violations Committed in the Territory of Neighboring States, between 1 January and 31 December 1994 ("Appeals Chamber" and "Tribunal", respectively) is seized of an interlocutory appeal[1] filed jointly by Anatole Nsengiyumva and Gratien Kabiligi ("Appellants") against a decision of Trial Chamber I,[2] ("Impugned Decision") dismissing Mr. Nsengiyumva's request for the disclosure of documents pursuant to Rule 66(B) of the Tribunal's Rules of Procedure and Evidence ("Rules").

BACKGROUND

2. In April 2005, soon after the defence cases in this case commenced, the Prosecution disclosed that it had documents related to the immigration, refugee, and asylum status of certain defence witnesses that it intended to use during cross-examination for impeachment purposes.[3] On 16 May 2005, one of the Appellants, Mr. Nsengiyumva, requested the disclosure of this material,[4] in part, based on Rule 66(B) of the Rules.[5] On 27 September 2005, the Trial Chamber denied this request and held that the Prosecution would make such documents available at the time of cross-examination in conformity with the normal practice in the case.[6]

3. The Appellants sought certification to appeal the Impugned Decision, which the Trial Chamber granted on 22 May 2006.[7] The Appellants filed their joint appeal brief on 29 May 2006. The Prosecution responded on 8 June 2006,[8] and the Appellants replied on 12 June 2006.[9] **[page 2]**

4. The Appellants argue that in reaching the Impugned Decision the Trial Chamber erred in its interpretation of Rule 66(B) and took account of extraneous considerations, such as the ability of the Appellants to obtain the documents themselves.[10] They submit that the immigration documents are essential in assisting them to assess the potential credibility of their case.[11] Consequently, the Appellants contend that they are being denied the right to make a full answer and defence to the charges against them without the requested disclosure.[12] The Appellants seek an order compelling the Prosecution to disclose the documents in question.[13]

---

1 Kabiligi and Nsengiyumva Joint Appeal under Rule 73(B) of Trial Chamber I's "Decision on Disclosure of Materials Relating to Immigration Statements of Defence Witnesses", 29 May 2006 ("Appeal").

2 *The Prosecutor v. Théoneste Bagosora et al.*, Case No. ICTR-98-41-T, Decision on Disclosure of Materials Relating to Immigration Statements of Defence Witnesses, 27 September 2005 ("Impugned Decision").

3 Impugned Decision, para. 1; Appeal, paras. 4, 5.

4 Based on Nsengiyumva's request, the Trial Chamber described this material as follows: "The Defence motion describes the requested materials as materials, documents, correspondence and any papers in [the Prosecution's] possession, control and/or custody that relate to immigration status and/or records of (i) Witness LIG-2; (ii) Defence Witness LT-1; (iii) any other Defence witnesses on the Nsengiyumva defence list in respect of whom inquiries into immigration, asylum and or refugee status may have been made; and (iv) any potential defence witnesses. According to the motion, such materials include, but are not limited to, any enquiry or correspondence from the Prosecution to any host country; any response from a host country thereto; documents forwarded in such correspondence; and documents relating to immigration, refugee status or record of proceedings relating thereto as disclosed by the host country, UNHCR or any other organization." *See* Impugned Decision, para. 3, footnote 4.

5 Impugned Decision, para. 2. In addition, Mr. Nsengiyumva requested disclosure on the basis of Rule 68, which the Chamber denied. *Id.*, paras. 2, 9, 10. *See also* Appeal, para. 6.

6 Impugned Decision, para. 12.

7 *The Prosecutor v. Théoneste Bagosora et al.*, Case No. ICTR-98-41-T, Decision on Certification of Interlocutory Appeal Concerning Prosecution Disclosure of Defence Witness Statements, 22 May 2006 ("Certification Decision"). The Trial Chamber did not certify the Appellants' appeal on the basis of Rule 68. *Id.*, para. 7.

8 Prosecutor's Response to "Kabiligi and Nsengiyumva Joint Appeal under Rule 73(B) of Trial Chamber I's 'Decision on Disclosure of Materials Relating to Immigration Statements of Defence Witnesses'", 8 June 2006 ("Prosecution Response").

9 Joint Kabiligi and Nsengiyumva Reply to "Prosecutor's Response to Kabiligi and Nsengiyumva Joint Appeal under Rule 73(B) of Trial Chamber I's 'Decision on Disclosure of Materials Relating to Immigration Statements of Defence Witnesses'", 12 June 2006 ("Appellants Reply").

10 Appeal, paras. 14-41.

11 Appeal, paras. 15, 16.

12 Appeal, paras. 34-41. At trial, Mr. Nsengiyumva's fair trial claims also included allegations related to witness intimidation and endangerment. Appeal, para. 6. The Appellants do not address these arguments on appeal and instead focus on their ability to assess the potential credibility of their case.

13 Appeal, para. 42.

5. The Prosecution responds that the Appellants cite no legal authority in support of their reading of Rule 66(B).[14] The Prosecution further refers to domestic legal provisions and national case law in support of the Trial Chamber's approach.[15] The Prosecution disputes that the Trial Chamber relied on any extraneous considerations in interpreting Rule 66(B), such as the ability of the defence to obtain the documents, and notes that this observation referred simply to the lack of prejudice in the present case.[16] In their Reply, the Appellants primarily attempt to distinguish the national case law referred to by the Prosecution.[17]

DISCUSSION

6. In this decision, the Appeals Chamber considers whether the Trial Chamber erred in denying the request for disclosure under Rule 66(B) of the Rules.[18] As the Impugned Decision relates to the general conduct of trial proceedings, this is a matter that falls within the discretion of the Trial Chamber.[19] A Trial Chamber's exercise of discretion will be reversed only if the challenged decision was based on an incorrect interpretation of governing law, was based on a patently **[page 3]** incorrect conclusion of fact, or was so unfair or unreasonable as to constitute an abuse of the Trial Chamber's discretion.[20]

7. Rule 66(B) of the Rules provides for the inspection of certain items which are: (1) "material to the preparation of the defence case", or (2) "intended for use by the Prosecution as evidence at trial".[21] The Trial Chamber ruled that the immigration documents did not fall into either of these categories.[22] It reasoned that the immigration documents were not "material to the preparation of the defence case" because they did not counter the Prosecution's evidence presented during its case-in-chief, but rather concerned the credibility of defence evidence.[23] In addition, for the Trial Chamber, the immigration documents did not constitute material intended for use by the Prosecution at trial because, in its view, this category refers only to evidence for use during the Prosecution's case-in-chief, which is closed.[24]

8. The Appellants contend that, in reaching this conclusion, the Trial Chamber adopted an unduly restrictive interpretation of Rule 66(B) of the Rules contrary to its plain meaning.[25] The Appeals Chamber agrees. The language of Rule 66(B) does not support the Trial Chamber's restrictive approach. The Prosecution refers extensively to domestic legal provisions, in particular United States Federal Rule of Criminal Procedure 16(a)(1)(E),[26] in support of the Trial Chamber's approach.[27] However, the Appeals

---

14 Prosecution Response, para. 6.

15 Prosecution Response, paras. 10-15.

16 Prosecution Response, paras. 22, 23.

17 Appellants Reply, paras. 5-24.

18 Rule 66(B) refers to permitting "inspection". Nonetheless, the provision imposes a disclosure obligation on the Prosecution in the sense of making information available to the Defence. That it is a disclosure obligation in this general sense is reflected in the title of Rule 66, "Disclosure of Materials by the Prosecutor" as well as the language of Rule 66(C) which refers to Prosecution ability to apply to a Trial Chamber in certain circumstances to be relieved from the obligation "to disclose pursuant to Sub-Rules (A) and (B)". The use of the term "inspection" in Sub-Rule (B) simply relieves the Prosecution from providing copies of requested items to the Defence, though a Trial Chamber may nonetheless issue an order this end.

19 *Tharcisse Muvunyi v. The Prosecutor*, Case No. ICTR-00-55A-AR73(C), Decision on Interlocutory Appeal, 29 May 2006, para. 5 ("*Muvunyi* Appeal Decision").

20 *Muvunyi* Appeal Decision, para. 5. *See also The Prosecutor v. Théoneste Bagosora et al.*, Case Nos. ICTR-98-41-AR73, ICTR-98-41-AR73(B), Decision on Interlocutory Appeals of Decisions on Witness Protection Orders, 6 October 2005, para. 3 ("*Bagosora* Appeal Decision").

21 Rule 66(B) states in full: "At the request of the Defence, the Prosecutor shall, subject to Sub-Rule (C), permit the Defence to inspect any books, documents, photographs and tangible objects in his custody or control, which are material to the preparation of the defence, or are intended for use by the Prosecutor as evidence at trial or were obtained from or belonged to the accused."

22 Impugned Decision, para. 6.

23 Impugned Decision, paras. 5, 6.

24 Impugned Decision, paras. 5, 6.

25 Appeal, paras. 14-25.

26 This provision reads: "Upon a defendant's request, the government must permit the defendant to inspect and to copy or photograph books, papers, documents, data, photographs, tangible objects, buildings or places, or copies or portions of any of these items, if the item is within the government's possession, custody, or control and: (i) the item is material to preparing the defense; (ii) the government intends to use the item in its case-in-chief at trial; or (iii) the item was obtained from or belongs to the defendant." This rule was amended in 2002, and what was previously sub-part (C) – which is the reference cited by the Prosecution and the Trial Chamber (Impugned Decision paras. 6, 7; Prosecution Response, para. 12) – was moved with minor amendments to sub-part (E).

27 Prosecution Response, paras. 10-16.

Chamber considers the meaning of Rule 66(B) to be sufficiently clear so as not to require resort to domestic legal provisions in determining its scope.[28] The Appeals Chamber routinely construes the Prosecution's disclosure obligations under the Rules broadly in accord with their plain meaning.[29] Nothing in Rule 66(B) limits an accused's right to inspection **[page 4]** only of material related to the Prosecution's case-in-chief.[30] Rather, this Rule uses much broader language: "material to the preparation of the defence case" and "intended for use ... at trial".

9. The Appellants seek material potentially falling under both categories.[31] In accord with the plain meaning of Rule 66(B) of the Rules, the test for materiality under the first category is the relevance of the documents to the preparation of the defence case. Preparation is a broad concept and does not necessarily require that the material itself counter the Prosecution evidence.[32] Indeed, for the Appellants, the immigration documents are material to the preparation of their defence because these documents may improve their assessment of the potential credibility of their witnesses before making a final selection of whom to call in their defence.[33] The Appeals Chamber cannot exclude that this is an appropriate basis for authorizing the inspection of documents if the requisite showing is made by the defence. There are few tasks more relevant to the preparation of the defence case than selecting witnesses.[34] The Trial Chamber is the appropriate authority to make this case-specific assessment in the first instance under the appropriate standard. Moreover, the use of the phrase "at trial" in the second category of Rule 66(B) signals its applicability throughout the proceedings.[35] As such, at least some of the immigration documents sought are equally subject to inspection to the extent that they are intended as exhibits at trial.

10. The Appeals Chamber observes that this plain reading of Rule 66(B) of the Rules does not create a broad affirmative obligation on the Prosecution to disclose any and all documents which **[page 5]** may be relevant to its cross-examination, as suggested by the Trial Chamber.[36] Rule 66(B) is only triggered by a sufficiently specific request by the defence,[37] which in turn engages reciprocal disclosure obligations on the defence's part under Rule 67(C). In this case, as the Trial Chamber recognized, the defence sought a precise

---

28 This was the same approach taken by the ICTY Appeals Chamber in interpreting the scope of Rule 68. *See The Prosecutor v. Radislav Krstić*, Case No. IT-98-33-A, Judgement, 19 April 2004, para. 179 ("*Krstić* Appeal Judgement").

29 *The Prosecutor v. Edouard Karemera et al.*, Case No. ICTR, 98-44-A73.7, Decision on Interlocutory Appeal Regarding the Role of the Prosecutor's Electronic Disclosure Suite in Discharging Disclosure Obligations, 30 June 2006, paras. 9-13 ("*Karemera* Appeal Decision"). *See also Krstić* Appeal Judgement, para. 180; *The Prosecutor v. Tihomir Blaškić*, Case No. IT-95-14-A, Judgement, 20 July 2004, paras. 265, 266 ("*Blaškić* Appeal Judgement").

30 In contrast, United States Federal Rule of Criminal Procedure 16(a)(1)(E) expressly states that the government's disclosure obligation is limited to items to be used in its "case-in-chief". The United States Supreme Court in turn seized on this language to similarly restrict the category "material to preparing the defense" as well to preparations to counter the government's case-in-chief. *See United States v. Armstrong*, 517 U.S. 456, 462 (1996). It is significant that the Tribunal's Rules omit this reference in favour of a more broad formulation.

31 In addition to prior statements, which could be used for impeachment purposes and possibly tendered as exhibits, the Appellants seek disclosure of a broader category of material, extending to correspondence between the Prosecution and state authorities. *See* Impugned Decision, para. 3, footnote 4 (quoted *supra*).

32 Indeed, even under United States Federal Rule of Criminal Procedure 16, which is limited to disclosure on matters material to the preparation of the defence against the prosecutor's case-in-chief, evidence is material "as long as there is a strong indication that it will play an important role in uncovering admissible evidence, aiding witness preparation, corroborating testimony, or assisting impeachment or rebuttal." *See United States v. Marshall*, 132 F.3d 63, 68 (D.C. Cir. 1998) (emphasis added). Further, it also extends to some extent to information which might dissuade a defendant from pursuing an unmeritorious defence. *Id.*

33 Appeal, para.16.

34 The Prosecution counters that providing possible impeachment material to the defence obviates the purpose of cross-examination and will only result in contrived and perjured testimony. Prosecution Response, para. 9. The Appeals Chamber disagrees. In the present case, the Appellants appear to be seeking disclosure precisely to avoid putting questionable witnesses on the stand. Moreover, the Prosecution still retains the ability to raise questions during cross-examination concerning the witness's preparation in light of the disclosure and make relevant arguments in its final submissions.

35 The Appeals Chamber has held that Rule 66(B) is applicable on appeal as well if the material sought was not available at trial. *See Georges Rutaganda v. The Prosecutor*, Case No. ICTR 96-3-A, Decision on the Prosecution's Urgent Request for Clarification in Relation to the Applicability of Rule 66(B) to Appellate Proceedings and Request for Extension of the Page Limit Applicable to Motions, 28 June 2002, p. 2.

36 *See, e.g.*, Impugned Decision, para. 6 ("Rule 66(B) cannot be interpreted as laying down a blanket obligation for the Prosecutor to disclose documents pertinent to its cross-examination of defence witnesses.").

37 *The Prosecutor v. Tihomir Blaškić*, Case No. IT-95-14-A, Decision on the Appellant's Motions for the Production of Material, Suspension or Extension of the Briefing Schedule, and Additional Filings, 26 September 2000, para. 40.

category of documents, namely immigration-related material, admittedly in the possession of the Prosecution.[38]

11. In addition, the Trial Chamber observed in the Impugned Decision that the defence was aware of the identity and residence of its witnesses and thus was capable of undertaking its own investigations for the material.[39] The Appellants contend that this is an irrelevant consideration and an error of law.[40] The Prosecution responds that the decision was not based on this observation.[41] The Appeals Chamber, for its part, cannot discern whether the Trial Chamber's observation was a basis for denying the motion. Nonetheless, in the Appeals Chamber's view, there is no requirement for the defence to make independent efforts to obtain material prior to receiving requested disclosure under the Rules. A request under Rule 66(B) is one of the methods available to the defence for carrying out investigations.

12. Finally, the Appeals Chamber notes that the Impugned Decision in fact provided for the disclosure of at least some of the requested material, the documents intended as exhibits, at the time of cross-examination.[42] This framework may be appropriate in some circumstances for certain material. The Appeals Chamber affirms that the Trial Chamber is best placed to determine both the modalities for disclosure and also what time is sufficient for an accused to prepare his defence based on the timing of such disclosure.[43] It is evident, however, that disclosure at the time of cross-examination is insufficient to the extent, as in this case, that the requested materials are intended to assist the defence select its witnesses.

CONCLUSION

13. Accordingly, the Appeals Chamber finds that the Trial Chamber erred by narrowly construing the Prosecution's disclosure obligations under Rule 66(B) of the Rules in a manner inconsistent with the plain language of the provision. **[page 6]**

DISPOSITION

14. For the foregoing reasons, the Appeal is **GRANTED**, and the Impugned Decision is **REVERSED**. The Prosecution is **ORDERED** to permit inspection by the defence of all the requested immigration documents that it intends to use as exhibits during cross-examination. Furthermore, with respect to the other immigration documents not intended for use as exhibits, the Appeals Chamber **REMITS** this matter to the Trial Chamber for reconsideration consistent with this decision on whether they are material to the preparation of the defence.

Done in English and French, the English version being authoritative.

Done this 25th day of September 2006,
At The Hague,
The Netherlands.

Judge Fausto Pocar
Presiding

[Seal of the Tribunal]

38 Impugned Decision, para. 3.

39 *See* Impugned Decision, para. 6 ("In relation to the requested immigration documents, the Chamber observes that the Defence is aware of the identify and country of residence of its witnesses and may make inquires as to whether they have been interviewed by immigration authorities. The Defence is therefore in a position to carry out the necessary investigations to prepare its case and, on this basis, select its witnesses."); Prosecution Appeal, para. 8.

40 Appeal, paras. 26-29.

41 Prosecution Response, para. 22.

42 Impugned Decision, para. 12.

43 *The Prosecutor v. Edouard Karemera et al.*, Case No. ICTR, 98-44-A73.6, Decision on Joseph Nzirorera's Interlocutory Appeal, 28 April 2006, paras. 7, 8.

International Criminal Tribunal for Rwanda
Tribunal pénal international pour le Rwanda

OR: ENG

TRIAL CHAMBER III

Before Judges: Dennis C. M. Byron, Presiding
Gberdao Gustave Kam
Vagn Joensen

Registrar: Adama Dieng

Date: 20 September 2007

THE PROSECUTOR

v.

Édouard KAREMERA
Mathieu NGIRUMPATSE
Joseph NZIRORERA

Case No. ICTR-98-44-T

DECISION ON JOSEPH NZIRORERA'S MOTION FOR INSPECTION OF STATEMENT OF PIERRE CELESTIN MBONANKIRA

Rule 66 (B) of the Rules of Procedure and Evidence

Office of the Prosecutor:
Don Webster
Alayne Frankson-Wallace
Iain Morley
Saidou N'Dow
Gerda Visser
Sunkarie Ballah-Conteh
Takeh Sendze

Defence Counsel for Édouard Karemera:
Dior Diagne Mbaye and Félix Sow

Defence Counsel for Mathieu Ngirumpatse:
Chantal Hounkpatin and Frédéric Weyl

Defence Counsel for Joseph Nzirorera:
Peter Robinson and Patrick Nimy Mayidika Ngimbi

[page 2] INTRODUCTION

1. The proceedings in the instant case commenced on 19 September 2005 with the presentation of the Prosecution case. According to Joseph Nzirorera, some Prosecution witnesses in this trial have alleged that Pierre Celestin Mbonankira (also known as "Gafobo") was an *Interahamwe* from Mukingo commune who was present for the training of *Interahamwe*, distribution of weapons, meetings at Mr. Nzirorera's mother house, and attacks against Tutsi.[1]

2. On 31 May 2007, Joseph Nzirorera requested the Prosecutor to allow his defence the inspection of all the statements made by Mr. Mbonankira in the possession of the Prosecutor.[2] The Prosecutor, however, declined the request.[3]

3. Joseph Nzirorera now moves the Chamber, pursuant to Rule 66(B) of the Rules of Procedure and Evidence ("Rules"), to make the necessary order to allow the said inspection.[4] On 18 June 2007, the Prosecutor filed a response not only opposing this application but also, in turn, moving the Chamber to order reciprocal disclosure from Defence under Rule 67.[5] It further requests the Chamber to adopt similar standards in reviewing the Prosecutor's request for reciprocal disclosure, should the Chamber grant Mr. Nzirorera's request for inspection of the statements of Mr. Mbonankira. The Chamber will deal with the Prosecutor's latter request in a separate decision.

DISCUSSION

4. Joseph Nzirorera submits that his defence team is considering including Pierre Celestin Mbonankira on its witness list.[6] Relying on the Appeals Chamber Decision of 25 September 2006 in the *Bagosora et al.* case and on Trial Chambers decisions in the cases of **[page 3]** *Nyiramasuhuko et al., Zigiranyirazo* and *Kamuhanda*,[7] he contends that his request satisfies the requirements for inspection of material under Rule 66 (B) as the documents sought are "material to the preparation of the defence since it will assist his defence to evaluate whether to call the witness at trial".

5. In his response, the Prosecutor submits that this Trial Chamber should deny the Defence's request. Relying on the Declaration of Judges Jorda and Shahabuddeen attached to the Appeals Chamber Decision of 28 June 2002,[8] the Prosecutor submits that the right of inspection under Rule 66 (B) does not apply to witness statements. He contends that both *Bagosora* Appeals Chamber Decision and the Declaration of Judges Jorda and Shahabudeen in the *Rutaganda* case limit Rule 66 (B) inspection to documents that are "real evidence", that is, to "material considered not as an assertion of a state of facts but itself a fact." The Prosecutor further notes that the Appeals Chamber Decision in the *Bagosora* case did not concern inspection of witness statements, but immigration records, and that the Appeals Chamber did not examine the nature of the documents for which inspection was sought.

6. In the Prosecutor's view, requiring him to disclose all of his potential impeachment material, including the statements of prospective Defence witnesses, prior to their examination at trial undermines his ability to confront them effectively.

7. Rule 66 (B) provides that at the request of the Defence, the Prosecutor shall permit the Defence to inspect any books, documents, photographs and tangible objects in his custody or control, which are material

1 Joseph Nzirorera's Motion for Inspection of Statement of Pierre Celestin Mbonankira, filed on 11 June 2007 ("Nzirorera's Motion"), para. 1.

2 See Annex A to Nzirorera's Motion.

3 See Annex B to Nzirorera's Motion.

4 Nzirorera's Motion.

5 Prosecutor Response to Nzirorera Motion for Inspection and Prosecutor's Cross-Motion for Enforcement of Reciprocal Disclosure Pursuant to Rule 67, filed on 18 June 2007, para 22.

6 Nzirorera's Motion, para. 7.

7 *Prosecutor v. Bagosora et al.*, Case No ICTR-98-41-AR73, Decision on Interlocutory Appeal Relating to Disclosure under Rule 66 (B) of the Tribunal's Rules of Procedure and Evidence (AC), 25 September 2006 ("*Bagosora* Appeals Chamber Decision").

8 *Prosecutor v. Georges Rutaganda*, Case No. ICTR-96-3-A, Decision ("Prosecution's Urgent Request for Clarification in Relation to the Applicability of Rule 66(B) to Appellate Proceedings and Request for Extension of the Page Limit Applicable to Motions") (AC), 28 June 2002.

to the preparation of the defence, or are intended for use by the Prosecutor as evidence at trial or were obtained from or belonged to the accused.

8. In cases where the Prosecution refuses such inspection, the Defence may move the Chamber to order such inspection provided that (i) the Defence clearly and sufficiently identifies the material sought; (ii) the material is within the Prosecution's custody or control; and (iii) the Defence makes a *prima facie* showing that the document for which inspection is sought is material to its preparation.[9] **[page 4]**

9. In the present case, it is not disputed that the report sought for inspection is clearly and sufficiently identified, and is in the Prosecution's possession.[10] The issue at stake is whether the statements of Pierre Celestin Mbonankira can be considered as "material to the preparation of the defence."

10. In the *Bagosora et al.* case, Trial Chamber I denied the Defence's requests for inspection of immigration documents of certain defence witnesses that the Prosecution intended to use during cross-examination for impeachment purposes.[11] The Appeals Chamber reversed that decision holding as follows:

> In accord with the plain meaning of Rule 66 (B) of the Rules, the test for materiality under the first category is the relevance of the documents to the preparation of the defence case. *Preparation is a broad concept and does not necessarily require that the material itself counter the Prosecution evidence.* Indeed, for the Appellants, the immigration documents are material to the preparation of their defence because *these documents may improve their assessment of the potential credibility of their witnesses before making a final selection of whom to call in their defence.* The Appeals Chamber cannot exclude that this is an appropriate basis for authorizing the inspection of documents if the requisite showing is made by the defence. There are few tasks more relevant to the preparation of the Defence case than selecting witnesses. The Trial Chamber is the appropriate authority to make this case-specific assessment in the first instance under the appropriate standard. Moreover, the use of the phrase "at trial" in the second category of Rule 66(B) signals its applicability throughout the proceedings. As such, at least some of the immigration documents sought are equally subject to inspection to the extent that they are intended as exhibits at trial."[12]

11. In the Chamber's view, this Appeals Chamber's Decision clearly set out the standards for a Trial Chamber when assessing whether a document is material to the preparation of the Defence, even if the Appeals Chamber did not deal with the nature of the documents as such.

12. According to those principles, the Chamber is of the view that Rule 66(B) may apply to witness statements when these documents may improve the Defence's assessment of the potential credibility of its witnesses before making a final selection of whom to call in their defence. This principle is consistent with the fairness of the proceedings and the rights of the Accused, including his right to be tried without undue delay. Should it indeed be discovered by such inspection that the witness lacks credibility and therefore should not be called as Defence witness, the fairness of the trial will be enhanced by avoiding undue delays. **[page 5]**

13. The Chamber is further not persuaded that the inclusion of witness statements within the purview of Rule 66 (B) will impair the ability of the Prosecutor to effectively cross-examine the Defence witnesses. This plain reading of Rule 66(B) does not create a broad affirmative obligation on the Prosecution to disclose any and all documents which may be relevant to its cross-examination.[13] In each circumstance, the Defence will need to show that the requirements as set forth by Rule 66(B) are indeed met, including the specificity of the material sought.

---

9 *Prosecutor v. Ndayambaje et al.*, Decision on the Defence Motion for Disclosure, (TC) 25 September 2001, para. 10; *Prosecutor v. Bagosora No.ICTR-98-41-AR73,* Decision on Interlocutory Appeal Relating to Disclosure under Rule 66 (B) of the Tribunal's Rules of Procedure and Evidence (AC), 25 September 2006; *Prosecutor v. Delalic et al.*, Case No. IT-96-21-T, Decision on the Motion by the Accused Zejnil Delalic for the Disclosure of Evidence (TC), 26 September 1996. See also *Prosecutor v. Karemera et al*, Case No. ICTR-98-44 T, Decision on Joseph Nzirorera Motion to Compel Inspection and Disclosure (TC), 5 July 2005, para. 9.

10 Annex B to Nzirorera's Motion, which is a letter from Prosecution Counsel in the case.

11 *Bagosora* Appeals Chamber Decision, para. 2.

12 *Bagosora* Appeals Chamber Decision, para 9 (emphasis added and footnotes omitted).

13 *Bagosora* Appeals Chamber Decision, para 10.

14. In light of the Appeals Chamber's standards, the Chamber is satisfied that the witness statements sought are material to the preparation of Joseph Nzirorera's defence in that their inspection may assist his defence in assessing the credibility of Mr. Mbonankira before deciding to list him as a defence witness.

15. The Chamber notes the Prosecutor's contention that since the Defence Counsel for Nzirorera has already interviewed the witness, he is well placed to make an independent assessment of the credibility of the prospective witness and this therefore obviates the need to inspect the statements. As stated by the Appeals Chamber, a request under Rule 66 (B) is one of the methods available to the Defence for carrying out investigations.[14] The fact that the Defence has already conducted some investigations concerning the prospective witness does not prevent the use of inspection to make further or additional investigations.

16. The Prosecutor also adds that in the event that Nzirorera's Motion is granted, the Chamber has the discretionary power to determine the timing of disclosure of the material sought. He stresses out the fact that Appeals Chamber accepted that in some circumstances, it would be appropriate to disclose the material at the commencement of cross-examination.

17. The timing of inspection is indeed within the Trial Chamber's discretion bearing in mind the right of each accused to have adequate time and facilities to prepare his Defence.[15] In the Chamber's view, where the requested materials are intended to assist the Defence in selecting its witnesses, disclosure at the time of cross-examination would not be sufficient to enable the Accused to prepare his defence as suggested by the Prosecutor. **[page 6]**

FOR THESE REASONS, THE CHAMBER

I. **GRANTS** the Defence Motion for inspection of Mr Pierre Celestin Mbonankira's statements; and accordingly

II. **ORDERS** the Prosecutor to permit as soon as practicable the inspection by the Defence for Joseph Nzirorera of the statements of Mr Pierre Celestin Mbonankira in possession of the Prosecutor.

Arusha, 20 September 2007, done in English.

Dennis C. M. Byron Presiding Judge	Gberdao Gustave Kam Judge	Vagn Joensen Judge

[Seal of the Tribunal]

14 *Ibidem.*

15 *Bagosora* Appeals Chamber Decision, para 12.

Commentary

1. Introduction

Although these decisions differ in stature, they merit a comparative analysis because of similar subject matter namely the inspection of prosecution materials by the defence which is a subset of and a means to effect disclosure.[1] The similarity of these two decisions is such that the Appeals decision sets the precedent which is directly applied in the Trial Chamber decision.

2. The Appeals Chamber decision

The Appeals decision concerned a request for disclosure made by the defence to the prosecution. The request was made at a time when the defence had opened its case before the Trial Chamber. The prosecution had documents on certain defence witnesses in particular documents pertaining to refugee, asylum and immigration applications. The prosecution intended to use these documents, which the defence did not have, to cross examine defence witnesses at trial. The defence requested the documents at issue and the Trial Chamber decided that the documents would be made available to it on prosecutorial cross-examination of the relevant defence witnesses.[2] The defence appealed relying on provisions relating to the exercise of judicial discretion.[3]

While making a determination on the exercise of judicial discretion, the Appeals Chamber examined the application of Rule 66 (B).[4] This rule provides for disclosure of prosecution materials to the defence through inspection. The prosecution is obliged, in response to a request from the defence, to allow the defence to inspect any items in its control or custody that are either material to the preparation of the defence case or the prosecution intends to use the items as evidence at trial *inter alia*. The exercise of this rule is subject to Rule 66 sub C which provides for an exception to the prosecutions mandatory obligation to disclose requested information.[5] In particular Rule 66 sub C the prosecution may approach chambers and request that it be released from this duty where disclosure would either prejudice an on going investigation, or where such disclosure would be contrary to public interest or affect the security interests of any state. The prosecution made no such allegation and thus did not rely on this particular set of exceptions. Moreover, the exercise of Rule 66 (B) is additionally subject to Rule 53 and 69. Rule 69 provides an exception for the protection of the identity victims and witnesses. Whilst Rule 53 provides in essence for *in camera* proceedings and thus ensures that certain information is not disclosed to the public as an exception.[6] These exceptions also did not

---

1 ICTR, Decision on Interlocutory Appeal Relating to Disclosure Under Rule 66(B) of the Tribunal's Rules of Procedure and Evidence, *Prosecutor v. Bagosora, Kabiligi, Ntabakuze and Nsengiyumva*, Case No. ICTR-98-41-AR73, A. Ch., 25 September 2006, in this volume, p. 41; ICTR, Decision on Joseph Nzirorera's Motion for Inspection of Statement of Pierre Celestin Mbonankira, *Prosecutor v. Karemera, Ngirumpatse and Nzirorera*, Case No. ICTR-98-44-T, T. Ch. III, 20 September 2007, in this volume, p.47.

2 Decision on Interlocutory Appeal Relating to Disclosure Under Rule 66 (B) of the Tribunal's Rules of Procedure and Evidence, *Prosecutor v Bagosora, Kabiligi, Ntabakuze and Nsengiyumva,* A. Ch., *supra* note 1, par. 2 also see note 4; see also par. 7 for the Trial Chamber's reasoning where it is stated that these documents were excluded because they concerned the credibility of defence witnesses rather than countering the Prosecutions evidence in chief. Secondly, that in the Trial Chambers view these documents were not presented during the Prosecution's evidence in chief which would have been subject to disclosure, effectively limiting disclosure to the Prosecution's case rather than the entire trial.

3 Decision on Interlocutory Appeal Relating to Disclosure Under Rule 66 (B) of the Tribunal's Rules of Procedure and Evidence, *Prosecutor v Bagosora, Kabiligi, Ntabakuze and Nsengiyumva,* A. Ch., *supra* note 1, par. 6 and 9.

4 Decision on Interlocutory Appeal Relating to Disclosure Under Rule 66 (B) of the Tribunal's Rules of Procedure and Evidence, *Prosecutor v Bagosora, Kabiligi, Ntabakuze and Nsengiyumva,* A. Ch., *supra* note 1, par. 7 and in particular 8 wherein the defence argues that the Trial Chamber's approach was unduly restrictive and veered from the plain meaning of Rule 66 sub (B) which permitted a broader interpretation. See also note 18 from paragraph 6 where the Appeals Chamber observes that the obligations in Rule 66 sub B is a disclosure obligation on the prosecution. However, the prosecution is only obliged to make documents available for inspection and there is no obligation on the prosecution to provide the defence with copies. However, copies may be supplied on the request of the defence following such an order from the chamber.

5 International Criminal Tribunal for Rwanda, Rules of Procedure and Evidence, as adopted on 29 June 1995 and amended on 7 June 2005, www.ictr.org/ENGLISH/rules/070605/070605.pdf, accessed 19 August 2009, (ICTR, RPE) Rule 66 B; see also International Tribunal for the Prosecution of Persons Responsible for Serious Violations of International Humanitarian Law Committed in the Territory of the Former Yugoslavia since 1991 Rules of Procedure and Evidence, IT/32/Rev. 34, 22 February 2005, (http://www.icty.org/x/file/Legal%20Library/Rules_procedure_evidence/IT032_rev34_en.pdf), accessed 19 August 2009, (ICTY, RPE), Rule 66 sub B which is similar with the exception that it does not have the built in proviso in respect to Rule 66 sub C.

6 ICTR, RPE, Rule 66 sub B.

apply in the appeals or the trial decision under review. This was because in both instances the witnesses were known to both participants to the proceedings.

In the Appeals decision, Chambers opined that Rule 66 (B) should be interpreted in accordance with the plain meaning or literal interpretation approach. However, the Appeal Chamber found the approach adopted by the Trial Chamber unduly restrictive and favoured instead applying a supposed broader interpretation. The Appeals Chamber took issue with this because such a restrictive interpretation ignored the language in which the rule was couched. In particular with respect to two aspects described here as follows. Firstly and quite aptly the disclosure obligation at issue was relevant to the prosecutions evidence in chief and even extended to the defences evidence in chief. For that matter the Appeal Chamber continued in footnoted *obiter dicta* in certain circumstances this obligation even applied to appeals. Secondly, this disclosure obligation was relevant to any material that was important for the preparation of the defence case and any material that was to be used at trial.[7] Thus the obligation to disclose is operative even after the prosecution has closed its case and the defence has begun to lead its own evidence in chief.

There are important things to bear in mind with regard to the application of this rule. To begin with the Appeals Chamber was very quick to point out that Rule 66 (B) should not be understood as blanket disclosure as contended by the impugned Trial Chamber decision. Rather Rule 66 (B) applies once its triggering mechanism has been activated. That triggering mechanism is a specific request for a specific item or category of items made by the defence to the prosecution. In this case it was a request to inspect immigration, asylum and refugee application documents.[8] This should not be taken lightly. This is in actual fact fairly restrictive or at least has the outcome of limiting in practice the intended broad approach of the Appeal Chamber on this issue.

Moreover, this approach stands in interesting contrast to the rules and procedures of the International Criminal Court (ICC) on inspection and disclosure. In particular Rule 77, which appears to place a blanket obligation on the prosecution to permit the defence to inspect any materials which are in the prosecutors control or possession. This blanket rule applies specifically where these said materials are either material to the preparation of the defence or more crucially, in the context of the decisions under review, intended for use by the prosecution as evidence on trial.[9] Of course it does remain to be seen exactly how the ICC will implement this rule in practical terms. However, contrasting the Appeal Chamber decision and the Rule 77 of the ICC a certain paradox emerges. In particular it is ironic that the Appeal Chamber decision may well have achieved the complete opposite of its intent. The impugned trial decision it sought to remedy produced an outcome inconsistent with the rights of the defence[10] to the extent that it denied the defence an opportunity to inspect requested documents prior to the calling of witnesses. However, the impugned trial decision had in principle adopted an approach consistent with the emerging legislation of the International Criminal Court at least to the extent that it considered Rule 66 (B) as laying down a blanket right to disclosure for the defence.

---

7 Decision on Interlocutory Appeal Relating to Disclosure Under Rule 66 (B) of the Tribunal's Rules of Procedure and Evidence, *Prosecutor v Bagosora, Kabiligi, Ntabakuze and Nsengiyumva,* A. Ch., *supra* note 1, par. 8; see also par. 9 and 10 and its footnote 35 where the Appeals Chamber observes that the obligation for disclosure may also extend to the Appeal where the evidence requested was not available at Trial; see also Rule 77 RPE ICC crucially the last point on the intention of the Prosecutor to use the materials at trial resonates with this Rule from the International Criminal Court.

8 Decision on Interlocutory Appeal Relating to Disclosure Under Rule 66 (B) of the Tribunal's Rules of Procedure and Evidence, *Prosecutor v Bagosora, Kabiligi, Ntabakuze and Nsengiyumva,* A. Ch., *supra* note 1, par. 10; SCSL, Decision on Defence Motion for Disclosure Pursuant to Rules 66 and 68 of the Rules, *Prosecutor v. Sesay, Kallon and Gbao*, Case No. SCSL-2004-15-T, T. Ch., 9 July 2004, Klip/ Sluiter, ALC-IX-499, par. 4 and 25 to 30 ; ICTY, Decision on the Motion by the Accused Zejnil Delalić for the Disclosure of Evidence, *Prosecutor v. Delalić, Mucic, Hazim Delić and Landzo,* Case No. IT-96-21-T, T. Ch. II, 26 September 1996, par. 10. The approach of the Appeal Chamber and Trial Chamber in the decisions under review is consistent with previous jurisprudence on this matter in particular the requirements of specificity when the defence is mounting a challenge on this.

9 International Criminal Court, Rules of Procedure and Evidence, Adopted by the Assembly of State Parties, First Session, 3-10 September 2002, ICC-ASP/1/3 (ICC, RPE), Rule 77, wherein the exercise of this rule is of course subject to certain restrictions relevant to disclosure in Rules 81 and 82. More over the Prosecutor has a reciprocal right to inspect that only extends to items or materials the defence intends to use at Trial in Rule 78.

10 Statute of the International Criminal Tribunal of Rwanda, As adopted on 8 November 1994 and amended on 13 October 2006, www.ictr.org/ENGLISH/basicdocs/statute/2007.pdf), accessed 19 August 2009, (Statute ICTY) Article 20, paragraph 4, in particular the right of the defence to adequate preparation and facilities and the right of the defence to trial with undue delay.

Another important point of convergence which merits discussion in the decisions under review is the point at which the trial had progressed and disclosure for the requested materials had not taken place. As observed earlier, Rule 66 (B) is subject to a number of restrictions. These restrictions provide at least recognised grounds for delayed disclosure in some cases or limited disclosure in other instances. In both the appeal and trial decisions none of these grounds were alleged by the prosecution. This is a pertinent issue because the ICC adopts a different approach, where in all disclosure must take place prior to the commencement of the trial. Moreover disclosure must take place sufficiently in advance ensuring that the defence has adequate time to prepare. In 2008 the Appeal Chamber of the ICC demonstrated just how seriously it regards the failure of the prosecution to disclose materials to the defence prior to trial. While prosecutorial conduct with regard to disclosure was indeed exceptional, the outcome was grave as the Appeals Chamber effectively stayed the intended trial of the accused.[11] Further, the importance of disclosure is emphasised in the rules of Procedure and Evidence wherein disclosure is supposed to take place prior to the commencement of the trial *inter alia.*[12] These protections are linked to the defence rights in the Rome Statute of the International Criminal Court.[13] These rights are translated into obligations of the Trial Chamber which is required to ensure that procedures are in place for the disclosure of information, including that which has not previously been disclosed, in advance of the trials commencement.[14] Thus from the legislation and jurisprudence of the ICC it should not be possible for the prosecution to fail to comply with disclosure at the time that the defence opens its case.

Another interesting point for discussion is the opinion of the Appeals Chamber that this form of disclosure is just one of the methods the defence can use to investigate its case. With this specifically in mind, while the Trial Chambers has the discretion to establish the modalities within the trial disclosure at the time of cross examination in these specific circumstances is inappropriate, given that the documents sought would help the defence decide whether or not to call a certain witness.[15] This is a very important contribution especially considering that the tribunals do not have a specific requirement that all disclosure take place prior to the commencement of the trial.

3. The Trial Chamber decision

Turning now to specific issues emerging from the Trial Chamber decision, it provides an interesting lens with which to assess the impact of the Appeals Chambers decision in this matter. In this trial decision the defence sought to inspect documents in terms of Rule 66 (B). The documents in question were witness statements made by a Mr. Pierre Celestin Mbonankira or Gafobo that were in the possession of the prosecution.[16] Thus invoking the specific triggering mechanism described in the Appeals Chamber decision discussed above. The defence was contemplating adding Mr. Mbonankira to their witness list and relied on the *ratio decidendi* on the Appeals Chamber decision to support their argument, in particular aspects of it that related to items that are material to the defence.[17] The prosecution countered this argument by claiming that Rule 66 (B) did not apply to witness statements, they argued further that the appeals decision only applied to real evidence that is to say, "to material considered not as an assertion of a state of facts but itself a fact".[18] Moreover the prosecution alleged the appeals decision only concerned immigration documents and did not extend to witness statements because the Appeals Chamber had not considered the nature of the documents at issue.[19]

---

11 ICC, Judgement on the Appeal of the Prosecutor Against the Decision of Trial Chamber 1 Entitled, "Decision on the Consequences of Non-Disclosure of Exculpatory Materials Covered by Article 54 (3) (e) Agreements and the Application to Stay the Prosecution of the Accused, Together with Certain Other Issues Raised at the Status Conference on 10 June 2008", *Prosecutor v. Dyilo,* Case No. ICC-01/04-01/06 OA, 13 A. Ch., 21 October 2008. The prosecution of the accused in this matter was stayed because the prosecution had failed to fulfil its disclosure obligations. However, the failure to disclose had taken place on a large scale.

12 RPE ICC, Rule 81 (2), (5) and (6).

13 Rome Statute of the International Criminal Court, Article 67, paragraph 1, sub b and c, read with subsection 2.

14 Rome Statute of the International Criminal Court, Article 64, paragraph 3, sub c.

15 Decision on Interlocutory Appeal Relating to Disclosure Under Rule 66 (B) of the Tribunal's Rules of Procedure and Evidence, *Prosecutor v Bagosora, Kabiligi, Ntabakuze and Nsengiyumva*, A. Ch., *supra* note 1, par. 11 and 12.

16 Decision on Joseph Nzirorera's Motion for Inspection of Statement of Pierre Celestin Mbonankira (Rule 66 (B) of the Rules of Procedure and Evidence), *Prosecutor v. Karemera, Ngirumpatse and Nzirorera*, T. Ch. III, *supra* note 1, par. 2 and 3.

17 *Ibid*, par. 4.

18 *Ibid*, par. 5.

19 *Ibid*, par. 5.

As a point of departure the legal issue that the Trial Chamber was faced with in the decision is whether the requisite witness statements could be regarded as material to the preparation of the defence case.[20] In the Trial Chambers view, the nature of the documents is not important. It is however salient that the Appeals Chamber laid down the standard applicable in terms of Rule 66 (B) applications.[21] Moreover the Trial Chamber in the decision under review stated that if the documents help the defence to decide who to call as a witness then the witness statements are material to the defence case. In addition, the Trial Chamber linked this with right to a fair procedure and the right of the defence to trial without undue delay. It reasoned that access to these documents saves time because then the defence would not waste time by calling a witness with no credibility.[22] It is interesting to note that this linkage to the right of the defence is absent in the Appeal Chamber decision. This is a significant difference in approach which may provide an opportunity in future litigation to link the approach of the tribunals with that of the International Criminal Court.[23]

Moreover, still examining aspects of the trial decision, the prosecution is in a position to question witnesses that are called, linking this with the appeals decision the court added that Rule 66 (B) does not provide for blanket disclosure, instead it has a triggering mechanism. The statements were found to be material to the preparation of the defence case.[24] The trial Chamber also views Rule 66 (B) disclosure as another method through which the defence may legitimately conduct its investigation.[25] Further the Trial Chamber also endorses the Appeal Chambers view that where a matter concerns witness selection then the defence should have advance access to these materials before it makes the decision on who to call.[26] In these decisions both the Trial and Appeals Chamber affirm the importance of adequate access to a document for the defence to prepare we can see the confirmation of a standard in that if the materials sought by the defence impacts on the selection of witnesses it is inappropriate for the prosecution to effect disclosure at the time of cross examination. The defence is entitled to adequate time to see the materials and consider them in the preparation of its defence and crucially prior to its selection of witnesses.

4. Conclusion

The defence in both decisions discussed obtained the outcomes they sought to achieve namely access to specific prosecution documents. However, the appeals decision has set a precedent which may in future come back to haunt aggrieved defence teams should they need to inspect other documents that fall outside the scope of standard set there but are however covered under international human rights law. None the less the fact that the Trial Chamber, unlike the Appeals Chamber, made reference to the rights of the defence may go a long way toward remedying this should it arise. It certainly opened the door for more human rights discourse on this issue in future.

Shamiso Zinzombe

20 *Ibid*, par. 9.

21 *Ibid*, par. 11 and see also 10 which contains a direct quotation of paragraph 9 of the Decision on Interlocutory Appeal Relating to Disclosure Under Rule 66 (B) of the Tribunal's Rules of Procedure and Evidence, *Prosecutor v Bagosora, Kabiligi, Ntabakuze and Nsengiyumva*, A. Ch., *supra* note 1.

22 Decision on Joseph Nzirorera's Motion for Inspection of Statement of Pierre Celestin Mbonankira (Rule 66 (B) of the Rules of Procedure and Evidence), *Prosecutor v. Karemera, Ngirumpatse and Nzirorera*, T. Ch. III, *supra* note 1, par. 12.

23 See above page 3 to 4.

24 Decision on Joseph Nzirorera's Motion for Inspection of Statement of Pierre Celestin Mbonankira (Rule 66 (B) of the Rules of Procedure and Evidence), *Prosecutor v. Karemera, Ngirumpatse and Nzirorera*, T. Ch. III, *supra* note 1, par. 13 and 14.

25 *Ibid.*, par. 15.

26 *Ibid*, par. 17.

International Criminal Tribunal for Rwanda
Tribunal pénal international pour le Rwanda

ORIGINAL: ENGLISH

TRIAL CHAMBER I

Before: Judge Erik Møse, presiding
Judge Jai Ram Reddy
Judge Sergei Alekseevich Egorov

Registrar: Adama Dieng

Date: 6 October 2006

THE PROSECUTOR

v.

Théoneste BAGOSORA

Gratien KABILIGI

Aloys NTABAKUZE

Anatole NSENGIYUMVA

Case No.: ICTR-98-41-T

DECISION ON REQUEST FOR SUBPOENAS OF UNITED NATIONS OFFICIALS

The Prosecution
Barbara Mulvaney
Drew White
Christine Graham
Rashid Rashid
Gregory Townsend

The Defence
Raphaël Constant
Allison Turner
Paul Skolnik
Frédéric Hivon
Peter Erlinder
André Tremblay
Kennedy Ogetto
Gershom Otachi Bw'Omanwa

[page 2] THE INTERNATIONAL CRIMINAL TRIBUNAL FOR RWANDA

SITTING as Trial Chamber I, composed of Judge Erik Møse, presiding, Judge Jai Ram Reddy, and Judge Sergei Alekseevich Egorov;

BEING SEIZED OF the "Request for Subpoenas of Kofi Annan, Iqbal Riza, Shaharyar Khan and Michael Hourigan Pursuant to Rule 54", filed by the Ntabakuze Defence on 25 August 2006;

CONSIDERING the Submissions filed by the Bagosora Defence on 5 September 2006; the Submissions of the United Nations Office of Legal Affairs, dated 7 September 2006; and the Memorandum and Annexes filed by the Ntabakuze Defence on 15 September 2006;

HEREBY DECIDES the motion.

INTRODUCTION

1. The Ntabakuze Defence requests that subpoenas be issued to Kofi Annan and Iqbal Riza, who were officials of the Department of Peacekeeping Operations ("DPKO") in New York in 1994; Shaharyar Khan, who became the Special Representative of the Secretary-General ("SRSG") in Rwanda in the middle of 1994; and Michael Hourigan, a former investigator of the Office of the Prosecutor. The Defence requests that the subpoenas require the latter three to appear before the Chamber to give testimony, whereas the request in respect of Mr. Annan is only that he be compelled to submit to an interview.

2. The Office of Legal Affairs of the United Nations has responded to the motion arguing that the Defence has not yet articulated the legal and factual basis for the appearance of the witnesses, or the need to interview Mr. Annan. The Office of Legal Affairs claims that it has offered extensive cooperation and assistance to the Defence and wishes to continue to do so; its opposition to the requests for subpoenas "does not stem from our unwillingness or refusal to assist [the Defence] but from [its] failure to comply with arrangements that [it] has already repeatedly acknowledged and from which [it] has repeatedly benefited."[1]

DELIBERATIONS

(i) General Principles

3. The applicant for a subpoena requiring a person to give testimony or submit to an interview must show that three conditions are satisfied: (i) reasonable attempts have been made to obtain the voluntary cooperation of the witness; (ii) the prospective witness has information which can materially assist the applicant in respect of clearly identified issues relevant to the trial; and (iii) the witness's testimony must be necessary and appropriate for the conduct and fairness of the trial.[2] It has been said that "subpoenas should not be issued lightly" and that a Chamber must consider "not only the usefulness of the information to the **[page 3]** applicant but … its overall necessity in ensuring that the trial is informed and fair".[3] The Appeals Chamber has elaborated that:

> The applicant seeking a subpoena must make a certain evidentiary showing of the need for the subpoena. In particular, he must demonstrate a reasonable basis for his belief that the prospective witness is likely to give information that will materially assist the applicant with respect to clearly identified issues in the forthcoming trial. To satisfy this requirement, the applicant may need to present information about such factors as the position held by the prospective witness in relation to the events in question, any relation the witness may have had with the accused which is relevant to the charges, any opportunity the witness may have had to observe or learn about those events, and any statements the witness made to the Prosecution or others in relation to them. The Trial Chamber is vested with discretion in determining whether the applicant succeeded in making the required showing, this discretion being necessary to ensure that the compulsive mechanism of the subpoena is not abused. As the Appeals

1 Submissions, p. 6.

2 *Prosecutor v. Krstic*, Case No. IT-98-33-A, Decision on Application for Subpoenas (AC), 1 July 2003, para. 10; *Prosecutor v. Halilovic*, Case No. IT-01-48-AR73, Decision on the Issuance of Subpoenas (AC), 21 June 2004, para. 7 ("*Halilovic* Decision"); *Bagosora et al.*, Decision on Request for a Subpoena (TC), 11 September 2006, para. 5; *Karemera et al.*, Case No. ICTR-98-44-T, Decision on Defence Motion for Issuance of Subpoena to Witness T (TC), 8 February 2006, para. 4.

3 *Halilovic* Decision, para. 7.

> Chamber has emphasized, "Subpoenas should not be issued lightly, for they involve the use of coercive powers and may lead to the imposition of a criminal sanction".[4]

Chambers have considered factors such as the specificity with which the prospective testimony is identified and whether the information can be obtained other than through the prospective witness.[5]

(ii) Application

(a) Kofi Annan and Iqbal Riza

4. The Defence argues that, as the officials who were in charge of the Department of Peacekeeping Operations in 1994, Mr. Annan and Mr. Riza have information relevant to the trial. They are in a position to "explain the circumstances" surrounding the correspondence between UNAMIR officials in Rwanda and DPKO in New York, much of which has been admitted into evidence and on which General Roméo Dallaire and Major Brent Beardsley, among others, have given testimony. The Defence wishes to elicit evidence that the DPKO had no information suggesting that, in the months leading up to April 1994, there was any plan or conspiracy to commit genocide as is alleged in the Indictment. Mr. Annan and Mr. Riza are said to be in a position to testify as to what they were told by General Dallaire and others, on a variety of issues which are specifically enumerated in the motion, and their understanding of events based on that information.[6]

5. The directness of a witness's observation of events is an important criterion in determining whether a subpoena should be issued. Every witness to whom a subpoena has been issued in the present case was an eyewitness to the conduct of the Accused or their **[page 4]** subordinates.[7] Although the Defence attempts to characterize Mr. Annan and Mr. Riza as "eye-witnesses or participants in the events", their prospective testimony concerns information sent to them by UNAMIR officials in Rwanda, and possibly other sources. They are said to be "the only persons who can explain the circumstances described" in the various memos, faxes and code cables exchanged between UNAMIR and the DPKO in New York.[8]

6. The Chamber disagrees that Mr. Annan and Mr. Riza are eyewitnesses. The Defence has not shown that either of them can draw on any personal observation of events for their testimony. Although Mr. Riza did apparently visit Rwanda in May or June 1994, the Defence does not suggest that it wishes to question him about this visit.[9] By contrast, this Chamber has heard from numerous members of UNAMIR who were on the ground in Rwanda: Jacques Roger Booh-Booh, General Dallaire, Major Beardsley, Lt. Colonel Frank Claeys, Colonel Joseph Dewez, Major Donald MacNeil, Colonel Aouilli Tchomi Tchambi, Major Petrus Maggen, Major Robert Van Putten, and Lieutenant Colonel Babacar El Hadj Faye. Indeed, the code cables to United Nations Headquarters in New York City were based on the direct eyewitness observation of these individuals and other UNAMIR officials posted in Rwanda at the time. The impressions of the recipients of those reports in United Nations Headquarters would be of limited weight in comparison to this direct and primary testimony, and does not constitute information which is necessary and appropriate for the conduct and fairness of the trial.

---

4 *Id.*, para. 6.

5 *Bagosora et al.*, Decision on Request for a Subpoena (TC), 11 September 2006, para. 6; *Karemera et al.*, Decision on Nzirorera's *Ex Parte* Motion for Order for Interview of Defence Witnesses NZ1, NZ2 and NZ3 (TC), 12 July 2006, para. 12; *Prosecutor v. Milosevic*, Case No. IT 02 54-T, Decision on Assigned Counsel Application for Interview and Testimony of Tony Blair and Gerhard Schröder (TC), 9 December 2005, paras. 30, 33.

6 Motion, paras. 11-13, 18-20, 24, 26-27.

7 *Bagosora et al.*, Decision on Request for a Subpoena (TC), 11 September 2006 (General Marcel Gatsinzi, former Chief of Staff of Rwandan Army); *Bagosora et al.*, Decision on Request for a Subpoena Compelling Witness DAN to Attend for Defence Cross-Examination (TC), 31 August 2006 (eyewitness of conduct by soldiers allegedly under the command of the Accused); *Bagosora et al.*, Decision on Request for a Subpoena for Major Jacques Biot (TC), 14 July 2006 (military observer present in Gisenyi from 6 to 13 April 1994); *Bagosora et al.*, Decision on Motion Requesting Subpoenas to Compel the Attendance of Defence Witnesses DK 32, DK 39, DK 31, DK 32, DK 311 and DM 24 (TC), 26 April 2005; *Bagosora et al.*, Decision on Defence's Request for a Subpoena Regarding Mamadou Kane (TC), 22 October 2004 (political adviser to the Special Representative of the Secretary-General in Rwanda from December 1993 until May 1994); *Bagosora et al.*, Decision on Prosecutor's Request for a Subpoena Regarding Witness BT (TC), 25 August 2004 (witness allegedly overheard statement made by one of the Accused); *Bagosora et al.*, Decision on Request for Subpoena of Major General Yaache and Cooperation of the Republic of Ghana (TC), 23 June 2004 (subpoena to sector commander of UNAMIR).

8 Motion, para. 11.

9 Motion, Annex 4, p. 9.

7. The perspective of the DPKO, as the central repository of UNAMIR documents, may have a distinct value in one respect. The Defence wishes the DPKO witnesses to confirm that they had no basis to believe that there was a conspiracy or plan to commit genocide leading up to April 1994. To a large extent, however, the documents already disclosed by the DPKO to the Defence, many of which have been entered as exhibits without any dispute as to authenticity, provide a more direct indication as to the information available to the DPKO over time. To the extent that any further confirmation is required from witnesses, the Office of Legal Affairs has offered to continue to cooperate with the Ntabakuze Defence in the preparation of a statement in lieu of oral testimony.[10] In light of this ongoing cooperation, and the nature of the information sought, the Chamber does not consider that the first condition for the issuance of a subpoena – the exhaustion of reasonable attempts to obtain the voluntary cooperation of the witness – is satisfied. Accordingly, there is no need to further consider whether the information is sufficiently important to satisfy the second and third conditions for a subpoena. **[page 5]**

8. Under these circumstances, the Chamber shall not order that a subpoena be issued to either Mr. Annan or Mr. Riza.

(b) Shaharyar Khan

9. The Defence requests a subpoena for Mr. Khan, the SRSG in Kigali from July 1994 until March 1996, in relation to a letter he wrote in 1995 stating that neither the DPKO nor UNAMIR had any warning of an impending genocide prior to April 1994. Furthermore, Mr. Khan purportedly drafted the first list of suspects to be investigated for war crimes in the summer of 1995. The absence of the Accused from that list is said to be an important fact. Finally, Mr. Khan has, according to the Defence, information about a report prepared by the UNHCR concerning alleged massacres of Hutu refugees.[11]

10. The Chamber does not consider that any of the information supposedly in the possession of Mr. Khan justifies the issuance of a subpoena. The state of contemporaneous knowledge of a plan to commit genocide has been addressed in the previous section in relation to the DPKO witnesses, who appear to be in a better position than Mr. Khan to respond to this inquiry. Indeed, the Defence has not indicated that Mr. Khan has any knowledge of this issue other than his retrospective review of the documents which are already in the possession of the Defence. The lack of any mention of the Accused on a list of suspects prepared by Mr. Khan in 1995 constitutes indirect evidence of limited value, and does not justify the issuance of a subpoena. Finally, the relevance of the UNHCR report to the present trial is discussed in a separate decision, rendered today.[12] In light of that decision, Mr. Khan's alleged knowledge of that report does not constitute a valid basis for the issuance of a subpoena.

(c) Michael Hourigan

11. Mr. Hourigan, a former investigator of the Office of the Prosecutor, is said to be able to testify about his investigations into the shooting down of the Presidential airplane on the night of 6 April 1994.[13]

12. The Indictment does not attribute responsibility for the attack on the Presidential airplane to any of the Accused or their alleged co-conspirators. Paragraph 6.2 of the Indictment states neutrally that: "On 6 April 1994 at about 8:30 p.m., the plane carrying, among other passengers, the President of the Republic, Juvénal Habyarimana, was shot down on its approach to Kigali Airport, Rwanda." This event is characterized as the trigger for the massacres which ensued; but, unlike other paragraphs of the Indictment, no involvement of the Accused is alleged. Nor did the Prosecution present evidence during its case-in-chief to prove any responsibility by the Accused in the assassination. The only such suggestion was made during the cross-examination of the Accused Bagosora, when the Prosecution put to Colonel Bagosora that he had been involved in the attack on the Presidential airplane. The Prosecution has made clear, in responding to separate motion by the Bagosora Defence, that this question was posed only for the purpose of challenging the

---

10 Submissions, p. 4.

11 Motion, paras. 14-20.

12 *Bagosora et al.*, Decision on Ntabakuze Motion for Information From the UNHCR and a Meeting With One of Its Officials (TC), 6 October 2006 (denying requests for orders requiring the UNHCR to provide information concerning the report).

13 Motion, paras. 21-24.

witness's credibility, as he had himself discussed responsibility to the attack during his examination-in-chief. The **[page 6]** Prosecution did not suggest, and indeed specifically renounced, that it was seeking to hold the Accused criminally responsibility for the President's assassination.[14]

13. Despite the absence of any charge against the Accused of involvement in the attack on the Presidential airplane, the Defence argues that responsibility for the attack is nevertheless relevant to the trial. The assassination of President Habyarimana is characterized by the Defence as "the initiation of the RPA 'final offensive' to seize power, which knowingly touched off the predicted civilian retaliation killings ... rather than [the result of] any 'plan' or 'conspiracy' by a military that ... lacked the resources to BOTH repel the RPA offensive AND stop the predicted civilian-on-civilian massacres".[15]

14. Legal relevance, as the standard for determining the admission of evidence, is defined in Rule 89 (C): "A Chamber may admit any relevant evidence which it deems to have probative value." This Rule implicates three criteria:

> First, the evidence must be in some way relevant to an element of a crime with which the Accused is charged. Second, the evidence must have some value in proving [or disproving] the elements of the crimes with which an accused is charged. The separate reference to "probative value", and to the requirement that the Chamber must "deem" that the evidence has that quality, suggests that probative value is a different and more complex hurdle than relevance. Third, even where these two criteria are met, Rule 89 (C) does not command, but merely permits, admission of the evidence.
>
> ...
>
> Probative value ... has been described simply as "'evidence that tends to prove an issue'" and is sometimes conceived as overlapping with the concept of relevance: "For one fact to be relevant to another, there must be a connection or a nexus between the two which makes it possible to infer the existence of one from the other. One fact is not relevant to another if it does not have real probative value with respect to the latter."
>
> ...
>
> Relevance, probative value and even prejudice are all relational concepts. The content of the putative facts must be defined and then evaluated in relation to their possible value as proof of the existence of a crime as described in the indictment. The nature of this evaluation explains the discretion conferred on the Trial Chamber by Rule 89 (C).[16]

The putative fact invoked by the Defence is that the RPF is responsible for the attack on the Presidential airplane on the night of 6 April. The question is whether this fact, if true, would tend to disprove any element of any crime with which the Accused has been charged in this case.

15. The conspiracy in which the Accused is alleged to have participated does not include the attack on the Presidential airplane on 6 April 1994. The Chamber summarized the nature of the conspiracy charge against the Accused in its decision on the Defence motions for dismissal following the close of the Prosecution case: **[page 7]**

> The Prosecution asserts that the inter-relationship of the Accused as senior officers within the military sets the stage for what appears to be a series of co-ordinated or even common actions: the promulgation of the definition of the enemy, which may arguably have targeted Tutsi civilians; the dissemination of that definition amongst soldiers in the army by the Accused; the uncanny repetition of that definition by the four Accused on various occasions; support for the *Interahamwe* using the resources of the military; and, finally, the direct evidence of some of the Accused being together on various occasions during one or more acts – speeches, preparing lists, ordering killings – which arguably encouraged the commission of genocide.[17]

Evidence that persons other than the Accused or his alleged co-conspirators were involved in shooting down the Presidential plane does not make any of these allegations any less likely.

16. Nor does responsibility for the assassination of President Habyarimana have any bearing on the offences alleged to have been committed by the Accused and his subordinates after 6 April 1994. Culpability for those crimes would not be reduced because someone other than the Accused created the conditions that led to the commission of those crimes. As this Chamber has previously held in relation to a similar issue:

---

14 Prosecution Response to "Bagosora Defence Urgent Motion for Investigation and Production of (Additional) Evidence...", etc., filed on 19 December 2005.

15 Motion, para. 22.

16 *Bagosora et al.*, Decision on Admissibility of Proposed Testimony of Witness DBY (TC), 18 September 2003, paras. 4, 15, 18 (citations omitted).

17 *Bagosora et al.*, Decision on Motions for Judgement of Acquittal (TC), 2 February 2005, para. 15.

> Descriptions of crimes committed by RPF forces against civilians in geographic areas physically distant from combat between the opposing armed forces in 1994 would not suggest the innocence or mitigate the guilt of the accused. The impact of such events on the criminal conduct with which the accused are charged is too remote and indirect. The Defence submissions have not demonstrated that such information would assist in disproving any element of the offences with which the Accused are charged, or how it could sustain a valid excuse or justification for their alleged conduct.[18]

This said, the Defence is perfectly entitled, of course, to lead evidence concerning the armed conflict with the RPF, the relative strength of forces, and the impact of this context on the crimes for which the Accused is alleged to be responsible.

17. The identity of the killers of President Habyarimana is undoubtedly a matter of contextual significance for the events described in the Indictment against the Accused. On this basis, the Chamber has admitted some evidence concerning this event. On the other hand, the Chamber must exercise its discretion under Rule 89 (C) to ensure that the focus of the present trial is maintained. The admission of detailed evidence on what is, essentially, a matter of collateral and indirect relevance would not assist the Chamber in determining the core issues of this trial.

18. The Defence has failed to establish that the prospective witness has information which can materially assist it in respect of clearly identified issues relevant to the trial, or that his testimony is necessary and appropriate for the conduct and fairness of the trial.[19] Accordingly, no subpoena shall be issued to Mr. Hourigan. **[page 8]**

FOR THE ABOVE REASONS, THE CHAMBER

DENIES the motion.

Arusha, 6 October 2006

Erik Møse Presiding Judge	Jai Ram Reddy Judge	Sergei Alekseevich Egorov Judge

[Seal of the Tribunal]

---

[18] *Bagosora et al.*, Decision on Disclosure of Defence Witness Statements in Possession of the Prosecution Pursuant to Rule 68 (A) (TC), 8 March 2006, para. 7.

[19] This approach is confirmed in numerous decisions in relation to identically or similarly worded indictments: *Kayishema*, Decision (AC), 28 September 2000, p. 3 ("CONSIDERANT qu'au soutien de sa demande le Requérant affirme que le Mémorandum Hourigan donne des indications sur les auteurs présumés de l'attentat contre l'avion du Président rwandais; que le Procureur du Tribunal de l'époque a cru devoir arrêter les enquêtes menées à ce sujet par M. Hourigan; que ces faits, qui n'étaient pas connus lors du process du Requérant, rouvriraient le débat sur la question de la culpabilité de celui ci; CONSIDERANT que le Mémorandum Hourigan n'était bien entendu pas disponible lors du procès en première instance, mais que sa teneur, que le Requérant cite, ne pouvait avoir un rapport avec les questions relatives au genocide sur lesquelles la Chambre de première instance devait se prononcer; qu'il n'est pas dès lors dans l'intérêt de la justice de l'admettre comme moyen de prevue supplémentaire en appel"); *Bizimungu et al.*, Reconsideration of Oral Ruling of 1 June 2005 on Evidence Relating to the Crash of the Plane Carrying President Habyarimana (TC), 23 February 2006, paras. 10-11 ("The potential involvement or responsibility of the RPF or other forces not associated with the government of Rwanda cannot relieve the Accused of responsibility for the crimes they have been charged with. The Chamber is of the opinion that evidence as to who is responsible for the crash of the President's plane would not assist the Chamber in its decision as to the guilt or innocence of the Accused … the jurisprudence of the Tribunal shows that questions relating to the responsibility of the shooting down of the plane may be put to a witness provided that this line of questioning does not go into great detail"); *Karemera et al.*, Décision Relative à la Requête de Joseph Nzirorera aux Fins d'Obtenir la Coopération du Gouvernement Français (TC), 23 February 2005, para. 11 (denying a motion for the Chamber to issue a request to the government of France to disclose to the Defence a report concerning those responsible for shooting down the Presidential plane) *Karemera et al.*, Decision on the Defence Motion for Disclosure of Exculpatory Evidence (TC), 7 October 2003, para. 14 ("The Defence has not shown how such materials, if they exist, could suggest the innocence of the Accused, who is not charged with taking part in the assassination, or how such materials could tend to mitigate the Accused's personal guilt or affect the credibility of the prosecution evidence"); *Kabiligi*, Decision on the Defence motion Seeking Supplementary Investigations (TC), 1 June 2000, para. 19 ("Defence Counsel has failed to establish any causal link between the requested investigation into the responsibility for the plane crash and the acts and omissions which form the basis of the charges against Kabiligi in the Indictment").

Tribunal Pénal International pour le Rwanda
International Criminal Tribunal for Rwanda

BEFORE THE APPEALS CHAMBER

Before: **Judge Fausto Pocar, Presiding**
Judge Mohamed Shahabuddeen
Judge Liu Daqun
Judge Andrésia Vaz
Judge Wolfgang Schomburg

Registrar: **Mr. Adama Dieng**

Decision of: **27 October 2006**

THE PROSECUTOR

v.

Arsène Shalom NTAHOBALI and Pauline NYIRAMASUHUKO

Case No. ICTR-97-21-AR73

DECISION ON "APPEAL OF ACCUSED ARSÈNE SHALOM NTAHOBALI AGAINST THE DECISION ON KANYABASHI'S ORAL MOTION TO CROSS-EXAMINE NTAHOBALI USING NTAHOBALI'S STATEMENTS TO PROSECUTION INVESTIGATORS IN JULY 1997"

Defence Counsel for Mr. Ntahobali
Mr. Normand Marquis, Lead Counsel
Mr. Louis Huot, Co-Counsel

Defence Counsel for Mr. Kanyabashi
Mr. Michel Marchand, Lead Counsel
Ms. Simone Santerre, Co-Counsel

Counsel for the Prosecution
Ms. Silvana Arbia, Senior Trial Attorney
Ms. Adelaide Whest, Trial Attorney
Ms. Holo Makwaia, Trial Attorney
Mr. Gregory Townsend, Trial Attorney
Mr. Althea Alexis-Windsor, Trial Attorney
Mr. Michael Adenuga, Legal Advisor
Ms. Astou Mbow, Case Manager

[page 2]1. The Appeals Chamber of the International Criminal Tribunal for the Prosecution of Persons Responsible for Genocide and Other Serious Violations of International Humanitarian Law Committed in the Territory of Rwanda and Rwandan Citizens Responsible for Genocide and Other Serious Violations Committed in the Territory of Neighbouring States, between 1 January and 31 December 1994 ("Appeals Chamber" and "Tribunal", respectively) is seized of an interlocutory appeal filed by Arsène Shalom Ntahobali on 8 June 2006 ("Interlocutory Appeal").[1] The Defence for Mr. Ntahobali requests that the Appeals Chamber reverse the Trial Chamber's Decision rendered on 15 May 2006 ("Impugned Decision"), which allowed the Defence for the co-accused Mr. Kanyabashi to cross-examine Mr. Ntahobali using previous statements of Mr. Ntahobali made to Prosecution investigators in July 1997 ("Previous Statements").[2] The Defence for Mr. Ntahobali requests that the Appeals Chamber find the Previous Statements inadmissible or alternatively order the Trial Chamber to conduct a *voir dire* procedure to determine whether they were freely and voluntarily provided to the Prosecution investigators.[3] The Prosecution and the Defence for Mr. Kanyabashi filed their responses to the Interlocutory Appeal on 16 and 19 June 2006 respectively.[4] Contrary to the submissions of the Defence for Mr. Ntahobali,[5] both responses were timely filed pursuant to the Practice Direction on Procedure for the Filing of Written Submissions in Appeal Proceedings Before the Tribunal ("Practice Direction").[6] **[page 3]**

1. Background

2. During the cross-examination of Mr. Ntahobali, the Defence for Mr. Kanyabashi sought to challenge the credibility of Mr. Ntahobali using the Previous Statements.[7] The Defence for Mr. Ntahobali objected to the admissibility of the Previous Statements, arguing that they were not freely and voluntarily given[8] and that a *voir dire* procedure should be held in order to assess whether the Previous Statements had been obtained in accordance with the Rules of Procedure and Evidence of the Tribunal ("Rules").[9]

3. In the Impugned Decision, the Trial Chamber found the Previous Statements admissible through a "perusal of the transcripts of [the] interviews as well as through the normal procedure of admissibility of evidence provided under Rule 89(C), and the conditions laid out in Rules 89(D) and 95" on the basis that they fully complied with the requirements of Articles 18 and 20 of the Statute of the Tribunal ("Statute") and Rules 42, 43 and 63 of the Rules.[10] The Trial Chamber limited the admission of the Previous Statements to "cross-examining Ntahobali on issues relating to his credibility" and ruled that the actual admission of each Previous Statement into evidence would be done after the cross-examination of Mr. Ntahobali by each

---

1 *The Prosecutor v. Arsène Shalom Ntahobali and Pauline Nyiramasuhuko*, Case No. ICTR-97-21-AR73 (Joint Case No. ICTR-98-42-T), Appel de l'Accusé Arsène Shalom Ntahobali à l'Encontre de la Décision Intitulée "Decision on Kanyabashi's Oral Motion to Cross-Examine Ntahobali Using Ntahobali's Statements to Prosecution Investigators in July 1997", 8 June 2006 ("Interlocutory Appeal").

2 *The Prosecutor v. Arsène Shalom Ntahobali and Pauline Nyiramasuhuko*, Joint Case No. ICTR-98-42-T, Decision on Kanyabashi's Oral Motion to Cross-Examine Ntahobali Using Ntahobali's Statements to Prosecution Investigators in July 1997, 15 May 2006 ("Impugned Decision").

3 Interlocutory Appeal, pp. 11-12.

4 *The Prosecutor v. Arsène Shalom Ntahobali and Pauline Nyiramasuhuko*, Case No. ICTR-97-21-AR73, Prosecutor's Response to the "Appel de l'Accusé Arsène Shalom Ntahobali à l'Encontre de la Décision Intitulée 'Decision on Kanyabashi's Oral Motion to Cross-Examine Ntahobali Using Ntahobali's Statements to Prosecution Investigators in July 1997'", 16 June 2006, para. 16 ("Prosecutor's Response"); *The Prosecutor v. Arsène Shalom Ntahobali and Pauline Nyiramasuhuko*, Case No. ICTR-97-21-AR73, Réponse de Joseph Kanayabashi á "l'Appeal de l'Accusé Arsène Shalom Ntahobali à l'Encontre de la Décision Intitulée Joseph Kanyabashi's Response to the Appeal by the Accused Arsène Shalom Ntahobali Against the Decision on Kanyabashi's Oral Motion to Cross-Examine Ntahobali Using Ntahobali's Statements to Prosecution Investigator's in July 1997", 19 June 2006, para. 5 ("Kanyabashi's Response").

5 *The Prosecutor v. Arsène Shalom Ntahobali and Pauline Nyiramasuhuko*, Case No. ICTR-97-21-AR73, Réplique de Arsène Shalom Ntahobali à la Réponse du Procureur Intitulée "Appel de de l'Accusé Arsène Shalom Ntahobali à l'Encontre de la Décision Intitulée "Decision on Kanyabashi's Oral Motion to Cross-Examine Ntahobali Using Ntahobali's Statements to Prosecution Investigators in July 1997"", 23 June 2006, paras 4-5 ("Ntahobali's Reply to the Prosecutor"); *The Prosecutor v. Arsène Shalom Ntahobali and Pauline Nyiramasuhuko*, Case No. ICTR-97-21-AR73, Réplique de Arsène Shalom Ntahobali à la Réponse de Joseph Kanayabashi á l'Appeal de l'Accusé Arsène Shalom Ntahobali à l'Encontre de la Décision Intitulée "Decision on Kanyabashi's Oral Motion to Cross-Examine Ntahobali using Ntahobali's Statements to Prosecution Investigators on July 1997", 23 June 2006, paras 2-6 ("Ntahobali's Reply to Kanyabashi ").

6 Practice Direction on Procedure for the Filing of Written Submissions in Appeal Proceedings Before the Tribunal, Section III(8) read together with Section I, permitting ten days from the filing of an interlocutory appeal for the filing of a response.

7 T. 8 May 2006, p. 77; T. 9 May 2006, pp. 3-14. See also Kanyabashi's Response, para. 5; Impugned Decision, paras 1, 65.

8 Impugned Decision, paras 27, 30, 31, 43.

9 Impugned Decision, paras 32-33, 46-56.

10 Impugned Decision, paras 54-55, 64-72, 73-78, 79-82.

party.[11] In addition, the Trial Chamber granted "any other co-Accused's Motion as well as the Prosecution's Motion to cross-examine the Accused Ntahobali using his interviews to challenge his credibility".[12] The Trial Chamber denied the request of the Defence for Mr. Ntahobali to hold a *voir dire* procedure on the basis that it was not the only method by which the Previous Statements could be assessed for their compliance with the Rules and the Statute.[13] The Defence for Mr. Ntahobali sought leave to appeal the Impugned Decision, which the Trial Chamber granted in its Decision on Certification of 1 June 2006.[14]

2. Arguments of the Parties

4. The Defence for Mr. Ntahobali requests the Appeals Chamber to rule that the Trial Chamber erred in finding the Previous Statements admissible.[15] It argues that the Previous Statements, including signed documents by Mr. Ntahobali stating that he understood his rights under Rules 42 and 43 of the Rules, are contrary to his assertions during trial that the Previous **[page 4]** Statements were not free and voluntary.[16] Upon that allegation, the Defence for Mr. Ntahobali submits that the burden was on the Prosecution to prove the free and voluntary nature of the Previous Statements beyond reasonable doubt, and it failed to do so.[17] The Defence for Mr. Ntahobali also argues that the Trial Chamber erred in not considering the alleged inducements or threats to give the Previous Statements on the basis that they occurred "prior to the Accused's 1997 interviews and his arrest".[18] In the alternative, it requests that the Appeals Chamber find the procedure adopted by the Trial Chamber in assessing the admissibility of the Previous Statements erroneous and order the Trial Chamber to conduct a *voir dire* procedure to properly determine admissibility.[19]

5. The Prosecution responds that the Trial Chamber was correct in concluding that it was not obliged to conduct a *voir dire*[20] and exercised its discretion reasonably in assessing the admissibility of the Previous Statements.[21] It submits that there is no evidence of coercion or inducements attributable to the Prosecution investigators[22] and argues that it is not relevant for the Trial Chamber to consider any subjective motivations held by Mr. Ntahobali.[23]

6. The Defence for Mr. Kanyabashi responds that the Trial Chamber correctly applied objective criteria in deciding there was nothing to suggest Mr. Ntahobali provided the Previous Statements as a result of inducements.[24] According to the Defence for Mr. Kanyabashi, Mr. Ntahobali voluntarily surrendered himself to representatives of the Tribunal upon his own assumption that this would secure his father's release from detention by national authorities.[25] The Defence for Mr. Kanyabashi also objects to the argument of Mr. Ntahobali that it was necessary for the Trial Chamber to hold a *voir dire*[26] and argues that the Trial Chamber's "perusal" assessment of the Previous Statements was sufficient.[27]

7. In its reply to the Prosecution, the Defence of Mr. Ntahobali argues that it was not possible for Mr. Ntahobali to give evidence on the veracity of the Previous Statements whilst he was on the stand, as the Previous Statements were only raised during cross-examination and thus it was not open to him to reopen his examination-in-chief to offer evidence on the matter.[28] **[page 5]**

11 Impugned Decision, para. 81

12 Impugned Decision, para. 82

13 Impugned Decision, para. 53.

14 *The Prosecutor v. Arsène Shalom Ntahobali and Pauline Nyiramasuhuko.*, Joint Case No. ICTR-98-42-T, Decision on Kanyabashi's Motion for Certification to Appeal the Chamber's Decision Granting Kanyabashi's Request to Cross-Examine Ntahobali Using 1997 Custodial Interviews, dated 1 June 2006, filed 2 June 2006 ("Decision on Certification").

15 Interlocutory Appeal, paras 14-27, 66.

16 Interlocutory Appeal, para. 17.

17 Interlocutory Appeal, para. 18.

18 Interlocutory Appeal, paras 22-26.

19 Interlocutory Appeal, paras 3-13, 28-66.

20 Prosecutor's Response, paras 9-15.

21 Prosecutor's Response, para. 16.

22 Prosecutor's Response, para. 18.

23 Prosecutor's Response, para. 19.

24 Kanyabashi's Response, paras 20-24.

25 Kanyabashi's Response, para. 22.

26 Kanyabashi's Response, paras 25-40.

27 Kanyabashi's Response, paras 9-16.

28 Ntahobali's Reply to the Prosecutor, paras 15, 19.

8. In its reply to the Defence for Mr. Kanyabashi, the Defence for Mr. Ntahobali further submits that a *voir dire* procedure was necessary to bring forth further evidence on the veracity of the Previous Statements as a perusal of the transcripts of the relevant interviews would not necessarily provide sufficient indication if threats were indeed made.[29]

3. Discussion

9. This Interlocutory Appeal involves two issues: (i) whether the Trial Chamber erred in determining the admissibility of the Previous Statements without holding a *voir dire* procedure; and if the answer to this question is in the negative, (ii) whether the Trial Chamber erred in ruling that the portions of the Previous Statements used in cross-examination to test Mr. Ntahobali's credibility were admissible as evidence. While the Interlocutory Appeal raises these two issues, they will not be addressed separately as they are inextricably linked: the Defence for Mr. Ntahobali argues that a *voir dire* was necessary because there were sufficient indicia to show that the Previous Statements were made by him upon impermissible inducements and threats, which would also render the Previous Statements inadmissible.

10. Decisions relating to the admissibility of evidence and the general conduct of proceedings largely fall within the discretion of the Trial Chamber.[30] An interlocutory appeal challenging the discretion of the Trial Chamber is not a hearing *de novo*.[31] The standard of review on interlocutory appeal for such discretionary matters is therefore not whether the Appeals Chamber agrees with the Trial Chamber's conclusion, but whether the Trial Chamber reasonably exercised its discretion in reaching its decision.[32] The Appeals Chamber affirms that:

> a Trial Chamber's exercise of discretion will be overturned if the challenged decision was (1) based on an incorrect interpretation of governing law; (2) based on a patently incorrect conclusion of fact; or (3) so unfair or unreasonable as to constitute an abuse of the Trial Chamber's discretion. Absent an error of law or a clearly erroneous factual finding, then, the scope of appellate review is quite limited....[33]

11. During cross-examination of Mr. Ntahobali by Defence Counsel for Mr. Kanyabashi, the latter distributed Mr. Ntahobali's Previous Statements to the parties, indicating that he intended to **[page 6]** use them in further cross-examination of Mr. Ntahobali.[34] In response to a query raised by Mr. Ntahobali from the witness box,[35] the Trial Chamber gave the parties the opportunity to present submissions on whether there was sufficient basis to the allegation that the Previous Statements were in violation of the Rules such as to require a *voir dire* procedure.[36]

12. The Defence for Mr. Ntahobali argues that this procedure adopted by the Trial Chamber was impermissibly informal[37] since prior statements of an accused should be subject to an inquiry conducted "in accordance with pre-established rules of law which are known to the parties"[38] and not by merely requiring the parties to indicate their views on whether the Rules were complied with in taking the Previous Statements.[39] The Defence for Mr. Ntahobali has not identified any error in the procedure adopted by the Trial Chamber. The *voir dire* procedure originates from the common law and does not have a strictly defined process in this Tribunal.[40] There are no provisions in the Rules which direct Trial Chambers to adopt a

29 Ntahobali's Reply to Kanyabashi, paras 14-17.

30 *Tharcisse Muvunyi v. The Prosecutor*, Case No. ICTR-00-55A-AR73(C), Decision on Interlocutory Appeal, 29 May 2006, para. 5 ("*Muvunyi* Decision").

31 *The Prosecutor v. Šefer Halilović*, Case No. IT-01-48-AR73.2, Decision on Interlocutory Appeal Concerning Admission of Record of Interview of the Accused from the Bar Table, 19 August 2005, para. 5 ("*Halilović* Decision").

32 *The Prosecutor v. Théoneste Bagosora et al.*, Case Nos. ICTR-98-41-AR73, ICTR-98-41-AR73(B), Decision on Interlocutory Appeals of Decision on Witness Protection Orders, 6 October 2005, para. 3 ("*Bagosora* Appeal").

33 *Prosecutor v. Slobodan Milošević*, Case No. IT-02-54-AR73.7, Decision on Interlocutory Appeal of the Trial Chamber's Decision on the Assignment of Defence Counsel, 1 November 2004, para. 10 ("*Milošević* Decision").

34 T. 8 May 2006, p. 77: the Defence for Mr. Kanyabashi stated "I have distributed the transcripts that we received from the Office of the Prosecutor to the various Defence teams [...]".

35 T. 8 May 2006, pp. 76-77.

36 T. 9 May 2006, p. 3.

37 Interlocutory Appeal, para. 5.

38 Interlocutory Appeal, para. 8.

39 Interlocutory Appeal, para. 6.

40 As an example of the flexibility with which the *voir dire* procedure is utilised at trial, *voir dire* examinations have previously been deferred to the cross-examination stage in determining a Witness's qualification as an Expert Witness: *Prosecutor v. Muvunyi*, Case No. ICTR-2000-55A-T, Decision on the Prosecutor's Motion for Admission of Testimony of Expert Witness Rule 92*bis* of the

formal procedure for determining whether they should conduct a *voir dire*. Instead, Rule 89(B) of the Rules provides that reference may be made to evidentiary rules "which will best favour a fair determination of the matter". This discretion can extend to the conduct of a *voir dire* procedure when it is determined appropriate by the Trial Chamber.[41] The procedure conducted by the Trial Chamber permitted the parties to make submissions as to whether the Prosecution and Co-Accused could use the Previous Statements to impeach Mr. Ntahobali. The Trial Chamber considered the submissions of the parties on whether it was necessary to grant the request for a *voir dire* procedure by the Defence of Mr. Ntahobali, and after finding that it was not necessary, the Trial Chamber determined the admissibility of the Previous Statements on the basis of the submissions made by the parties. At several stages during the hearing[42] the Trial Chamber affirmed that this was the procedure to be followed, in particular when it stated:

> We would like to hear the challenge, the basis of the challenge [to the admissibility of the Previous Statements]. And in the process, certainly, the Trial Chamber will examine the **[page 7]** [admissibility] issue, including whether to determine the issue as presently presented, or whether there would be any need for voir – for trial within a trial, voir dire.[43]

13. Therefore, the parties were informed of the procedure the Trial Chamber was adopting and made submissions pursuant to this procedure.[44] Indeed, the procedure adopted by the Trial Chamber, while characterised as one adopted to determine whether a *voir dire* procedure was necessary, was very similar to a *voir dire*. The Trial Chamber heard the parties on the circumstances surrounding the taking of the Previous Statements, admitting a written affidavit from Mr. Ntahobali into evidence on that issue, and decided that no further evidence was required to determine whether the Previous Statements were in accordance with the Rules. The Appeals Chamber does not see any abuse of the Trial Chamber's discretion in the way that it chose to proceed.

14. The Defence for Mr. Ntahobali further asserts that if it were not for the initiative of the Defence for Mr. Ntahobali, the Trial Chamber "would have proceeded" without his opinion on the matter.[45] This argument is mere speculation. There was no prejudice to Mr. Ntahobali regarding the presentation of his opinion to the Trial Chamber on this matter as he was given an opportunity to present submissions in support of his objection, following which he presented a written affidavit[46] and confirmed in the witness box that he had nothing to add to these submissions.[47]

15. The Defence for Mr. Ntahobali also argues that the Trial Chamber erred in law in finding that the conduct of a *voir dire* is confined to jury trials.[48] The Appeals Chamber does not consider it necessary to address this argument on its merits as the Trial Chamber did not base its decision upon this observation in the Impugned Decision. Rather, it merely acknowledged the common law origins of the procedure in jury trials.[49]

16. The Defence for Mr. Ntahobali further argues that the Trial Chamber erred by distinguishing the Previous Statements (as interviews by the Prosecution investigators) from a confession, in finding that a *voir dire* procedure is inappropriate in this case.[50] The Appeals Chamber notes that a confession does indeed require additional consideration under the Rules as confessions are specially addressed under Rule 92 of the Rules. However, this provision requires the confession to be conducted in strict compliance with Rule 63 of the Rules. Therefore the distinction between confessions and interviews of the accused is not an appropriate basis for deciding when to conduct a **[page 8]** *voir dire* because both forms of statements require the same consideration under Rule 63. However, contrary to submissions of the Defence for Mr. Ntahobali, the Trial Chamber did not merely rely upon such a distinction in deciding not to conduct a *voir dire* procedure as the Trial Chamber additionally found that the "circumstances of the case" did not require further investigation.[51]

Rules, 24 March 2005, para. 27. See also *Halilović* Decision, para. 46 finding that a *voir dire* procedure is not necessarily required for identifying the voluntariness of an interview of an accused, although "there may be certain advantages in doing so."

41 *Halilović* Decision, para. 46.

42 T. 9 May 2006, pp. 3, 16, 42; T. 15 May 2006, p. 16.

43 T. 9 May 2003, p. 16.

44 See the full submissions on T. 8 May 2006 pp. 76-78, T. 9 May 2006, T. 15 May 2006.

45 Interlocutory Appeal, paras 10-11

46 Impugned Decision, para. 73; T. 15 May 2006, p. 4.

47 See T. 15 May 2006, pp. 4-5.

48 Interlocutory Appeal, para. 29.

49 Impugned Decision, paras 47, 50.

50 Interlocutory Appeal, paras 37-39.

51 Impugned Decision, paras 51, 55.

17. Finally, the Defence for Mr. Ntahobali submits that where there is *prima facie* proof of inducements or threats made to an accused during an interview by representatives of the Prosecution, it should be mandatory to conduct a *voir dire*.[52] In support of this argument, the Defence for Mr. Ntahobali refers to Rule 95.[53] Rule 95 provides for the exclusion of evidence which is "obtained by methods which cast *substantial doubt* on its reliability or if its admission is antithetical to, and would *seriously damage*, the integrity of the proceedings" (emphasis added). The Defence for Mr. Ntahobali alleges that he received inducements and threats from representatives of the Prosecution before the 1997 interviews were conducted. These claims, if substantiated, could fall within the terms of Rule 95.[54] The Trial Chamber considered these allegations and heard the parties' submissions. It concluded, however, that there was nothing to suggest that the interviews had been conducted in an improper manner and thus there was no need for further evidence on the matter – Mr. Ntahobali was informed of his rights and the proceedings contained no evidence of oppressive questioning by the Prosecution investigators.[55] The trial record confirms that this was a reasonable conclusion[56] and the submissions in this Interlocutory Appeal have not demonstrated how this aspect of the Impugned Decision was based upon an incorrect interpretation of the governing law or resulted in a patently incorrect conclusion of the factual circumstances of the interview.

18. As the above analysis demonstrates, it has not been shown in this Interlocutory Appeal that the Trial Chamber erred in finding that the Previous Statements were not obtained in a manner violating any provision of the Rules or of the Statute. Given the broad discretion afforded to Trial Chambers in evidentiary matters, the Appeals Chamber finds no error in the procedure employed by the Trial Chamber to determine the admissibility of the Previous Statements and in its decision to **[page 9]** admit portions of the Previous Statements into evidence for the purpose of testing Mr. Ntahobali's credibility during cross-examination.

4. <u>Disposition</u>

19. For the forgoing reasons, the Appeals Chamber **DISMISSES** the Interlocutory Appeal in its entirety.

Done in English and French, the English text being authoritative.

Fausto Pocar
Presiding Judge

Done this 27th day of October 2006,
At The Hague,
The Netherlands.

[Seal of the Tribunal]

52 Interlocutory Appeal, para. 40.

53 Interlocutory Appeal, para. 47.

54 Interlocutory Appeal, para. 59. The Appeals Chamber notes that Mr. Ntahobali made more detailed allegations, which were considered in the Impugned Decision, and the review of the trial record conducted by the Appeals Chamber supports the Trial Chamber's conclusions on these more specific points.

55 Impugned Decision, paras 71-72.

56 English translation of the transcripts from Mr. Ntahobali's interviews with representatives of the Prosecution, 24 July 1997, pp. 2-10; 26 July 1997. For example, the Defence for Mr. Ntahobali alleged before the Trial Chamber that Mr. Ntahobali was handcuffed whilst sleeping (Impugned Decision, para. 43) whereas the Previous Statements reveal that this was discussed in the initial interviews, and it was explained that this was the national procedure in Kenya which the Tribunal representatives had no authority over (K0153-3798, Tape 1, Side A). The Trial Chamber concluded that this was not a violation of the rights of the Accused by the Prosecutor, *see Prosecutor v. Delalić et al.*, Case No. IT-96-21-T, Decision on Mucić's Motion for the Exclusion of Evidence, 2 September 1997, para. 40.

International Criminal Tribunal for Rwanda
Tribunal pénal international pour le Rwanda

OR: ENG

TRIAL CHAMBER III

Before Judges: Inés Mónica Weinberg de Roca, Presiding
Khalida Rachid Khan
Lee Gacuiga Muthoga

Registrar: Mr Adama Dieng

Date: 16 November 2006

THE PROSECUTOR

v.

Protais ZIGIRANYIRAZO

Case No. ICTR-2001-73-T

DECISION ON THE PROSECUTION JOINT MOTION FOR RE-OPENING ITS CASE AND FOR RECONSIDERATION OF THE 31 JANUARY 2006 DECISION ON THE HEARING OF WITNESS MICHEL BAGARAGAZA VIA VIDEO-LINK

Rules 54, 73, 73 Bis(E), and 85 of the Rules of Procedure and Evidence

---

For the Office of the Prosecutor:
Mr Wallace Kapaya
Ms Charity Kagwi-Ndungu
Mr Sylver Ntukamazina
Ms Gina Butler
Mr Iskandar Ismail
Ms Jane Mukangira

Defence Counsel:
Mr John Philpot
Mr Peter Zaduk

[page 2] THE INTERNATIONAL CRIMINAL TRIBUNAL FOR RWANDA ("Tribunal"),

SITTING as Trial Chamber III, composed of Judges Inés Mónica Weinberg de Roca, Presiding, Khalida Rachid Khan, and Lee Gacuiga Muthoga ("Chamber");

BEING SEIZED of the "Prosecutor's Joint Motion for Re-opening of the Prosecution Case (made under Rules 54, 73 and 85 of the Rules of Procedure and Evidence and Appeals Chamber Decision dated 30 October 2006) and Requests for Reconsideration of the Trial Chamber Decision dated 31 January 2006 on the Hearing of Witness Michel Bagaragaza via Video Conference (made pursuant to Rule 73 *bis*(E) of the Rules of Procedure and Evidence)", filed on 6 November 2006 ("Motions", or "Motion for the Re-opening of the Prosecution Case" and "Motion for Reconsideration of the Decision of 31 January 2006", respectively);

CONSIDERING the Defence "Response to Prosecutor's Joint Motion for Re-opening of the Prosecution Case (made under Rules 54, 73 and 85 of the Rules of Procedure and Evidence and Appeals Chamber Decision dated 30 October 2006) and Requests for Reconsideration of the Trial Chamber Decision dated 31 January 2006 on the Hearing of Witness Michel Bagaragaza via Video Conference (made pursuant to Rule 73 *bis*(E) of the Rules of Procedure and Evidence) and Motion to Continue Trial", filed on 7 November 2006 (the "Response");

RECALLING the events leading to the present applications and the Chamber's previous Decisions in respect of Mr. Bagaragaza:

1. Decision on Defence and Prosecution Motions Related to Witness ADE, 31 January 2006 ("Decision of 31 January 2006");
2. Extremely Confidential Decision on Defence Motion Concerning the Hearing of Witness ADE, 5 June 2006 ("Decision of 5 June 2006");
3. Oral Decision on Protais Zigiranyirazo's Application for Certification to Appeal the Extremely Confidential Decision on Defence Motion Concerning the Hearing of Witness ADE ("Oral Decision on Application for Certification to Appeal");[1]

CONSIDERING the Decision on Interlocutory Appeal of the Appeals Chamber, 30 October 2006 ("Appeals Chamber Decision");

CONSIDERING Article 20(4)(d) of the Statute of the Tribunal (the "Statute") and Rules 54, 73, 73 *bis*(E) and 85 of the Rules of Procedure and Evidence (the "Rules");

NOW DECIDES the matter based solely on the briefs of the Parties pursuant to Rule 73(A) of the Rules.

BACKGROUND

1. On 30 October 2006 the Appeals Chamber excluded the testimony of Mr. Bagaragaza in its entirety. The Appeals Chamber held that the Statute affords the Accused with the minimum guarantee of the right to be tried in his presence; fulfilment of this right required the "physical presence" of the Accused in proceedings against him.[2] In so stating, the Appeals Chamber held that the Chamber had erred in hearing Mr. **[page 3]** Bagaragaza's testimony in the Netherlands with the Accused and his lead counsel participating from Arusha via video-link. His "attendance" via video-link was insufficient to constitute the presence guaranteed by the Statute. In excluding the testimony of Mr. Bagaragaza, the Appeals Chamber affirmed that the Trial Chamber remains free to have the witness recalled to testify "in a manner consistent with the Appellant's fair trial rights."[3]

---

1 T. 13 June 2006 pp. 53-54.

2 *See generally* Appeals Chamber Decision.

3 The Chamber notes that the present application by the Prosecutor stems from the Appeals Chamber's holding that the exclusion of witness Michel Bagaragaza's testimony pursuant to Rule 95 "does not prevent the Trial Chamber from exercising its discretion and allowing [the witness] to testify again in a manner consistent with the Appellant's fair trial rights." Appeals Chamber Decision, para. 24. In its footnote to this statement, the Appeal Chamber notes that the Defence acknowledged "that the Prosecution could seek to re-open its case in the interests of justice pursuant to Rule 85 or alternatively that the Trial Chamber could call the witness *proprio motu* under Rule 98." Appeals Chamber Decision, para. 24, fn 65.

2. The Prosecution closed its case on 28 June 2006 and the Defence commenced the presentation of its case on 30 October 2006. On 31 October 2006, in the course of hearing the second defence witness, the parties, having seen the ruling of the Appeals Chamber moved for an adjournment in order that they may have time to consider the import of the Appeals Chamber Decision on their respective cases and to consider the appropriate action in consequence of it.

SUBMISSIONS

The Prosecution Motions

3. The Prosecution submits that, in light of the importance of the testimony of Mr. Bagaragaza, serious prejudice will be caused if the Prosecution is not allowed to re-open its case to receive the testimony. The Prosecution therefore prays that the Chamber allow the re-opening of its case so that Mr. Bagaragaza can be called to testify.

4. Should the Chamber be inclined to grant the Motion for the Re-opening of the Prosecution Case the Prosecution moves, secondly, for the Chamber to reconsider its Decision of 31 January 2006 and allow the Mr. Bagaragaza to be heard via video-link.

5. The Prosecution contends that the criteria for reconsideration are met in the instant situation.[4] The Prosecution argues that the Appeals Chamber's finding of error on the part of the Chamber, and the resultant exclusion of Mr. Bagaragaza's testimony, meet the "high criteria set for the Trial Chamber to reconsider their decision."

6. The Prosecution urges the Chamber to reconsider its reservations on hearing Mr. Bagaragaza via video-link, and raises many of the arguments in favour of video-link that it raised in its original motion. Specifically, the Prosecution argues that (i) Mr. Bagaragaza is important to the Prosecution case and severe prejudice will result if the Chamber does not re-hear his testimony; (ii) his security concerns remain unchanged, and (iii) the Accused will suffer no prejudice as a result of hearing **[page 4]** Mr. Bagaragaza's testimony via video-link. The Prosecution also argues that whereas the use of video-link testimony was previously considered to be less weighty than in-court testimony, technological developments have improved the quality of video-link testimony, allowing judges to assess credibility without impairment. Moreover, video-link testimony is a permissible exception under Rule 75, and it has been utilized and considered adequate in the jurisprudence of both the *ad hoc* Tribunals, even for important and sensitive witnesses.[5]

7. Finally, the Prosecution adds that the "security and legal impediments and concerns of the witness and his counsel are currently being reviewed" and it undertakes to inform the Chamber of any new developments which may entail a change in the modalities surrounding Mr. Bagaragaza's anticipated testimony in this case.

The Defence Response

8. The Defence opposes the reopening of the Prosecution's case and the request for the taking of the testimony of Mr. Bagaragaza by video-link. The Defence argues that the relevant test to determine if a case should be re-opened depends upon the availability of the material sought to be introduced. If the material, through due diligence, could have been obtained, then the case should not be re-opened. If the evidence could not have been obtained through due diligence, then the Chamber must consider: (i) the stage of the trial at the time the application is made; (ii) the delay likely to be caused

[4] Motions, para. 17. According to the Prosecution, a Trial Chamber may reconsider its own prior decision (i) when a fact has been discovered that was not previously known to the Chamber; (ii) where new circumstances have arisen since the filing of the impugned decision that affect the premise of the impugned decision; or, (iii) where a party shows an error of law or the Chamber abused its discretion, and an injustice has been occasioned.

[5] Motions, paras. 22, 26.

by re-opening the case; (iii) the probative value of the evidence must be such that it outweighs prejudice to the Accused; and (iv) the effect of re-opening on any co-accused.[6]

9. According to the Defence, the requirements for the Chamber to reconsider a decision have not been met.[7]

10. The Defence submits that the Prosecution has not met the four-part test for authorizing video-link testimony. Although the Defence agrees that the testimony of Mr. Bagaragaza is sufficiently important, it does not agree that taking the evidence by video-link is in the interests of justice; that Mr. Bagaragaza has given sufficient justification for his inability to come to the Tribunal; or that the rights of the Accused will not be prejudiced.

11. The Defence argues that the rights of the Accused will be severely prejudiced by the re-opening of the Prosecution case and the taking of Mr. Bagaragaza's testimony by video-link. The Defence has already (i) presented the testimony of two witnesses, one of whom commented on Mr. Bagaragaza's original evidence; and (ii) filed its pre-trial brief, witness list, and numerous witness statements. Allowing the Prosecution to lead a key witness after the Defence has revealed so much of its case is unfair and prejudicial to the Accused. Moreover, the Prosecution Motions should be denied due to the potentially lengthy delay it may cause in the case.[8] **[page 5]**

DELIBERATIONS

Motion for the Re-opening of the Prosecution Case

12. The Chamber notes that neither the Statute nor the Rules of this Tribunal or of the International Criminal Tribunal for the former Yugoslavia ("ICTY") provide for the re-opening of a case by either party. Rule 85, which governs the order of presentation of evidence in trial proceedings does not envisage the re-opening of a case by either party to the proceedings and is therefore silent as to a relevant procedure.[9]

13. While an application for the re-opening of the Prosecution's case has never been brought before a Trial Chamber at this Tribunal, under the jurisprudence of the ICTY a Trial Chamber may grant leave to the Prosecution to re-open its case "in order to present new evidence not previously available to it".[10] This view has recently been adopted by a Trial Chamber of the Special Court for Sierra Leone (SCSL).[11]

---

6 Response, paras. 6-9.

7 Response, para. 17.

8 Response, paras. 40-43.

9 Rule 85 on the Presentation of Evidence reads as follows:

(A) Each party is entitled to call witnesses and present evidence. Unless otherwise directed by the Trial Chamber in the interests of justice, evidence at the trial shall be presented in the following sequence:

(i) Evidence for the prosecution;

(ii) Evidence for the defence;

(iii) Prosecution evidence in rebuttal;

(iv) Defence evidence in rejoinder;

(v) Evidence ordered by the Trial Chamber pursuant to Rule 98.

(vi) Any relevant information that may assist the Trial Chamber in determining an appropriate sentence, if the accused is found guilty on one or more of the charges in the indictment.

(B) Examination-in-chief, cross-examination and re-examination shall be allowed in each case. It shall be for the party calling a witness to examine him in chief, but a Judge may at any stage put any question to the witness.

(C) The accused may, if he so desires, appear as a witness in his own defence.

10 *Prosecutor v. Delalić et al.*, Case No. IT-96-21-T, Decision on the Prosecution's Alternative Request to Reopen the Prosecution's Case, 19 August 1998, para. 26 ("*Celebici* Trial Decision"); *see also Prosecutor v. Delalić et al.*, Case No. IT-96-21-A, Judgement (AC), 20 February 2001, para. 279 ("*Celebici* Appeal Judgement"); *Prosecutor v. Blagojević and Jokić*, Case No. IT-02-60-T, Decision on Prosecution's Motion to Admit Evidence in Rebuttal and Incorporated Motion to Admit Evidence Under Rule 92 *bis* in its Case on Rebuttal and to Re-Open its Case for a Limited Purpose, 13 September 2004, para. 7 ("*Blagojević and Jokić* Trial Decision").

11 *Prosecutor v. Alex Tamba Brima, Brima Bazzy Kamara and Santigie Borbor Kanu*, Case No. SCSL-04-16-T, Decision on Confidential Prosecution Motion to Reopen the Prosecution Case to Present an Additional Prosecution Witness, 28 September 2006, at para. 17.

14. In their submissions, the Defence and the Prosecution implicitly accept that in a proper case a Trial Chamber would have jurisdiction to permit a party to re-open its case in the interests of justice.

15. The jurisprudence of both the ICTY and the SCSL require the Prosecution to meet a high threshold should it seek to present new evidence after its case is closed. In the *Milošević* case, the Trial Chamber held that:

> Trial Chambers retain a general discretion under Rule 89(D) to deny re-opening if the probative value of the proposed evidence is substantially outweighed by the need to ensure a fair trial. With respect to this weighing exercise, the Tribunal's jurisprudence clearly establishes that "it is only in exceptional circumstances where the justice of the case so demands" that a Trial Chamber should exercise its discretion to allow the **[page 6]** Prosecution to adduce 'fresh' evidence after the parties to a criminal trial have closed their case. [*Footnotes Omitted*][12]

16. Guided by the *Celebici* Trial Decision and *Celebici* Appeal Judgement, three factors have been identified as being "highly relevant to the fairness to the accused of admission of fresh evidence":[13]

> (1) the stage of the trial at which the evidence is sought to be adduced;
>
> (2) the potential delay in the trial that admission of the evidence could cause, including the appropriateness of a possible adjournment in the overall context of the trial; and
>
> (3) the effect of bringing new evidence against one accused in a multi-defendant case.

17. The Chamber notes that in this case, only the first two factors apply. With regard to the first factor, the tendency has been that "the later in the trial that the application is made the less likely the Trial Chamber is to accede to the request".[14]

18. Having reviewed the relevant jurisprudence, the Chamber finds the instant situation distinguishable on the facts. Whereas the jurisprudence refers to "new evidence not previously available" to the calling party, the Chamber is here confronted with a situation of evidence previously available, but excluded to avoid any "damage [to the] integrity of the proceedings".[15] Protecting the integrity of the proceedings means ensuring fairness in the conduct of the case as far as *both* Parties are concerned. While the Chamber must be diligent in ensuring that the Accused is not deprived of his rights, the Prosecution must also not be unduly hampered in the presentation of its case.

19. The Chamber acknowledges that the discretion to re-open a case is to be exercised only in the interest of justice. Re-opening must never be used as an opportunity for one party to take an unfair advantage over its opponent. Where re-opening is permitted, a Trial Chamber should conduct the proceedings in a manner that ensures that the opposing party is not unfairly prejudiced. In the instant case the Chamber notes that the Defence has already served its Pre-Defence Brief, and a number of defence witness statements and that two witnesses have already testified; thus providing the Prosecution with information it ought not to have before it closes its case. The Chamber will be mindful of this during the taking of the evidence of Mr. Bagaragaza, and in its assessment of his testimony at the conclusion of the case. Given the putative importance of Mr. Bagaragaza's evidence to the Prosecution's case, the circumstances in which his testimony was excluded and the Chamber's ability to ensure that the Accused is not unduly prejudiced, the Chamber finds that **[page 7]** this application is in the interests of justice and therefore grants the Motion for the Re opening of the Prosecution Case.

---

12 *Prosecutor v. Milosević*, Case No. IT-02-54-T, Decision on Application for a Limited Re-Opening of the Bosnia and Kosovo Components of the Prosecution Case with Confidential Annex, 13 December 2005, para. 12.

13 *See Celebici* Trial Decision, para. 27; *Celebici* Appeal Judgement, para. 290, *Blagojević and Jokić* Trial Decision, paras. 10–11.

14 *See Celebici* Trial Decision, para. 27; quoted in *Celebici* Appeal Judgement, para. 280; *Blagojević and Jokić* Trial Decision, para. 10; *Prosecutor v. Hadžihasanović and Kubura*, Case No. IT-01-47-T, Decision on the Prosecution's Application to Re-Open Its Case, 1 June 2005, para. 45.

15 Appeals Chamber Decision, at para. 24.

Motion for Reconsideration of the Decision of 31 January 2006

20. Having granted the Prosecution's application to re-open its case, the Chamber must now consider the Prosecution's request that the Chamber *reconsider* its Decision of 31 January 2006, which denied the Prosecution's original motion to hear Mr. Bagaragaza's testimony by video-link.

21. According to the jurisprudence of the Tribunal, a Chamber can reconsider its own Decision (i) when a new fact has been discovered that was not previously known to the Chamber; (ii) where new circumstances have arisen since the filing of the impugned decision that affect the premise of the impugned decision; or (iii) where a party has successfully shown an error of law or that the Chamber has abused its discretion, and this led to an injustice.[16]

22. In its Decision of 31 January 2006, the Chamber stated that it wished to hear Mr. Bagaragaza "uninterrupted and in person." The Chamber expressed concern as to its ability to effectively and accurately assess the testimony and demeanour of a witness via video-link.

23. The Prosecution suggests that the Appeals Chamber Decision is either a new fact or a new circumstance authorizing reconsideration. The Chamber disagrees. Even if the Appeals Chamber Decision excluding Mr. Bagaragaza's testimony could be considered a new fact or circumstance for the purpose of reconsideration, nothing in the Prosecution's submissions has persuaded the Chamber to re-examine its position. Moreover, the Appeals Chamber Decision does not question the Chamber's exercise of discretion denying the original motion to hear Mr. Bagaragaza via video-link. To the contrary, the following excerpts from the Appeals Chamber Decision acknowledge the legitimacy of the Chamber's concerns:

> 17. The Appeals Chamber agrees that the objectives advanced by the Trial Chamber are of general importance: witness protection, the proper assessment of an important prosecution witness, and the need to ensure a reasonably expeditious trial...
>
> 19. Secondly, the Appeals Chamber also accepts that the Trial Chamber's general concern over its ability to assess the credibility of a key witness is an important interest.[17]

24. Mindful of the general preference that witnesses testify before the Tribunal in Arusha,[18] the Trial Chamber requested the Registrar to submit on whether additional **[page 8]** security measures might allow Mr. Bagaragaza to testify in Arusha.[19] Having reviewed the security threat to Mr. Bagaragaza, the Registrar has submitted that it will be possible to provide a sufficiently high level of security to ensure his safety in Arusha.[20] Based on the Registrar's Confidential and *Ex Parte* Submissions, the Chamber is satisfied that Mr. Bagaragaza's presence in Arusha could be adequately secured so that it is feasible to bring him to Arusha to testify.

FOR THE FOREGOING REASONS, THE CHAMBER HEREBY

GRANTS the Prosecution Motion for the Re-opening of the Prosecution case for the re-call of Mr. Bagaragaza;

DENIES the Motion for Reconsideration of the Decision of 31 January 2006 for Mr. Bagaragaza to be heard by video-link and **DIRECTS** that the witness be heard in Arusha;

---

16 *See, e.g.*, Decision on the Prosecutor's Motion for Reconsideration of the Oral Decision Excluding Evidence on the Meeting of 22 November 1992, or for Certification to Appeal the Same, 31 January 2006, para. 5; *Prosecutor v. Karemera et al.*, Decision on Joseph Nzirorera's Motion for Reconsideration or Certification to Appeal Decision on Motion for Order Allowing Meeting with Defence Witness, 11 October 2005, para. 8; *Prosecutor v. Karemera et al.*, Decision on the Defence Motions for Reconsideration of Protective Measures for Prosecution Witnesses, 29 August 2005, para. 8.

17 Appeals Chamber Decision, paras. 17, 19.

18 *See, e.g., Prosecutor v. Nahimana et al.*, Decision on the Prosecutor's Application to Add Witness X to its List of Witnesses and for Protective Measures, 14 September 2001, para. 36.

19 Request for Submissions Pursuant to Rule 33(B), 9 November 2006.

20 "The Registrar's [Confidential and *Ex Parte*] Submissions in Respect of Trial Chamber III's 'Request for Submissions Pursuant to Rule 33(B)'", filed 14 November 2006 ("Registrar's Confidential and *Ex Parte* Submissions").

ORDERS the transfer of Mr. Bagaragaza from the Detention Centre in The Hague to the Detention Facility in Arusha for hearings at the Tribunal the week beginning 27 November 2006;

REQUESTS the Governments of The Netherlands and of the United-Republic of Tanzania, to cooperate with the Prosecutor and the Registrar and the Witnesses and Victims Support Section of the Tribunal, to take the necessary measures to implement the present decision.

ADJOURNS the proceedings until 27 November 2006.

Arusha, 16 November 2006, done in English.

Inés Mónica Weinberg de Roca	Khalida Rachid Khan	Lee Gacuiga Muthoga
Presiding Judge	Judge	Judge

[Seal of the Tribunal]

International Criminal Tribunal for Rwanda
Tribunal pénal international pour le Rwanda

OR: ENG

TRIAL CHAMBER III

Before Judges: Dennis C. M. Byron, Presiding
Emile Francis Short
Gberdao Gustave Kam

Registrar: Adama Dieng

Date: 11 December 2006

THE PROSECUTOR

v.

Édouard KAREMERA
Mathieu NGIRUMPATSE
Joseph NZIRORERA

Case No. ICTR-98-44-T

DECISION ON PROSECUTION MOTION FOR ADMISSION OF EVIDENCE OF RAPE AND SEXUAL ASSAULT PURSUANT TO RULE 92 *BIS* OF THE RULES; AND ORDER FOR REDUCTION OF PROSECUTION WITNESS LIST

Rules 92*bis* and 73*bis* (D) of the Rules of Procedure and Evidence

Office of the Prosecutor:
Don Webster
Alayne Frankson-Wallace
Iain Morley
Saidou N'Dow
Sunkarie Ballah-Conteh
Takeh Sendze

Defence Counsel for Édouard Karemera
Dior Diagne Mbaye and Félix Sow

Defence Counsel for Mathieu Ngirumpatse
Chantal Hounkpatin and Frédéric Weyl

Defence Counsel for Joseph Nzirorera
Peter Robinson and Patrick Nimy Mayidika Ngimbi

[page 2] INTRODUCTION

1. The trial in this case commenced on 19 September 2005, with the Prosecution calling its first witnesses. Pursuant to Count Five of the Indictment, the Accused are charged with the commission of the crime of rape as a crime against humanity.[1] It is not alleged that the Accused personally physically perpetrated the alleged rapes, but rather that they are responsible for the crime of rape by virtue of their superior responsibility[2] for those who physically perpetrated the rapes or, alternatively, by virtue of an extended form joint criminal enterprise theory.[3]

2. On 4 July 2005, the Prosecution disclosed the statements of 143 witnesses who, it was proposed, would testify on the issue of rape and sexual assault, as pled in Count Five of the Indictment. On 13 December 2005, the Chamber granted the Prosecution's request to remove fifty of those witnesses from its List, and ordered the Prosecution to file any motion seeking the admission of evidence in written form in lieu of oral testimony, as provided for by Rule 92*bis* of the Rules of Procedure and Evidence, by 10 January 2006.[4] That deadline was subsequently extended to 20 February 2006.[5]

3. On that date, the Prosecution filed a Motion[6] seeking the following relief:

- The admission into evidence of the written statements of 63 purported rape witnesses, in lieu of them testifying orally, pursuant to Rule 92*bis* (A) of the Rules.
- The admission into evidence of the transcripts of evidence of eight purported rape witnesses[7] in previous proceedings before this Tribunal, in lieu of them testifying orally, pursuant to Rule 92*bis* (D) of the Rules. **[page 3]**

4. The Prosecution submits that, in the event that the Chamber requires the witnesses in relation to whom it is seeking the admission of their evidence in written form to appear in person for the purposes of cross-examination, the Prosecution prefers to call each witness to give his or her evidence orally, in its entirety. In addition to the aforementioned evidence which it is seeking to have admitted in written form, the Prosecution intends to call 21 witnesses to give evidence on Count Five, orally.

5. The Motion is opposed by the Defence for Joseph Nzirorera,[8] as well as by the Defence for Mathieu Ngirumpatse, which adopts the submissions of the Nzirorera Defence.[9] In addition to opposing the Motion on its merits, the Defence seeks two further forms of relief: firstly, for the Chamber to grant the Defence an extension of time to respond fully to the merits of the Motion, in order for it to be able to investigate the

---

1 *Prosecutor v. Édouard Karemera, Mathieu Ngirumpatse and Joseph Nzirorera ("Karemera et al."),* Case No. 98-44-I, Amended Indictment, 24 August 2005.

2 Paragraph 70 of the Indictment alleges that the rapes were so widespread and systematic that the Accused knew or had reason to know that the *Interahamwe* and other militiamen were about to commit them or that they had committed them; that they had the material capacity to halt or prevent the rapes, or punish or sanction the perpetrators; but that they failed to do so.

3 Paragraph 69 (and 7) of the Indictment alleges that the rapes were the natural and foreseeable consequence of the object of the joint criminal enterprise to destroy the Tutsi as a group, and that the Accused were aware that rape was the natural and foreseeable consequence of the joint criminal enterprise in which they knowingly and wilfully participated. See also paragraphs 4, 5, 6, 7, 8, 14, 15 and 16 of the Indictment which also outline the general allegations of the joint criminal enterprise and relate to Count Five.

4 *Prosecutor v. Karemera et al.,* Case No. 98-44-T, Decision on Variance of the Prosecution Witness List, 13 December 2005.

5 *Prosecutor v. Karemera et al.,* Case No. 98-44-T, Decision on Prosecution Motion Seeking Extension of Time to File Applications Under Rule 92bis, 10 February 2006.

6 See "Prosecution Motion for Proof of Facts Other Than by Oral Evidence Pursuant to Rule 92bis – Admission of 63 witness statements and 9 previous trial testimonies concerning rape and sexual assaults", dated 20 February 2006. See also, "Prosecutor's Reply: Motion for Proof of Facts Other than by Oral Evidence Pursuant to Rule 92*bis* and Prosecutor's Response to Motion for Extension of Time", dated 2 March 2006.

7 Note that the Prosecution originally sought the admission of the previous trial testimony of nine witnesses, pursuant to Rule 92*bis*. However, by Corrigendum dated 3 October 2006, the Prosecution withdrew its application for the admission of the evidence of one of those nine witnesses – Witness FAF (a.k.a. 'TM' and 'RJ') – so that its final application pursuant to Rule 92*bis* (D) relates to the previous trial testimony of eight witnesses only.

8 "Response to Prosecution Motion for Proof of Facts Other than by Oral Evidence Pursuant to Rule 92*bis* and Motion for Extension of Time", filed by the Defence for Joseph Nzirorera, on 27 February 2006.

9 "Mémoire de M. Ngirumpatse sur la Prosecution Motion for Proof of Facts Other Than By Oral Evidence Pursuant to Rule 92 bis et Requête aux Fins D'extension de Délai de Réponse (Confidentiel)", filed on 28 February 2006.

material sought to be admitted with a view to establishing its unreliability; and, secondly, for the Chamber to exclude the evidence of all 72 witnesses and to make an order for the reduction of the Prosecution Witness List, accordingly, on the ground that an excessive number of witnesses is being proposed in relation to Count Five of the Indictment.

DISCUSSION

Applicable Law

General Requirements

6. Rule 92*bis* of the Rules, entitled "Proof of Facts Other Than by Oral Evidence", bestows a discretionary power upon a Trial Chamber to admit, in whole or in part, the evidence of a witness in the form of a written statement (Sub-Rule (A)), or, where the witness has previously given evidence in proceedings before this Tribunal, in the form of a transcript of that evidence (Sub-Rule (D)), in lieu of oral testimony, on the condition that it goes to proof of a matter other than the acts and conduct of the accused as charged in the indictment.

7. In relation to written statements only, a further threshold requirement is provided for by Rule 92*bis* (B), which outlines the formal requirements for the admission of written statements under the Rule. Furthermore, and with respect only to written statements, the Chamber is guided in the exercise of its discretion by the criteria for and against admission, set out in Rule 92 *bis* (A)(i) and (ii), respectively, which are non-exhaustive lists. The factors enumerated include "any other factors which make it appropriate for the witness to attend for cross-examination", which is a factor against the admission of evidence in written form.[10]

8. In relation to the admission of written statements, or transcripts of prior trial testimony under Rule 92*bis*, the general requirements of relevance and probative value, **[page 4]** applicable to all types of evidence under Rule 89 (C), must also be satisfied.[11] Finally, after making a determination that a written statement or transcript of previous trial testimony is admissible in written form, Sub-Rule 92*bis* (E) bestows a further discretionary power upon the Chamber to admit the witness' evidence in whole or in part, and/or to require the witness to appear for cross-examination. The exercise of the Chamber's discretion under Rule 92*bis*, must be governed by the right of the Accused to a fair trial, as provided for in Articles 19 and 20 of the Statute.

The meaning of the phrase "acts and conduct of the accused"

9. The meaning of the term "acts and conduct of the accused as charged in the indictment" has been defined by the Appeals Chamber of the International Criminal Tribunal for the former Yugoslavia ("ICTY"), particularly in relation to cases such as the one before the Chamber, in which the accused are charged with criminal responsibility for the physical acts of subordinates and/or co-perpetrators.

10. The jurisprudence states that the term is a plain expression and should be given its ordinary meaning: deeds and behaviour of the accused himself and not the acts and conduct of his co-perpetrators and/or subordinates.[12] The Appeals Chamber Decision in *Galić* is the leading Appeals Chamber authority on the interpretation of Rule 92*bis*.[13] That Decision held that Rule 92*bis* excludes the acts and conduct of the

10 Sub-Rule 92*bis* (A)(ii)(c).

11 *Prosecutor v. Bagosora et al.*, Case No. ICTR-98-41-T, Decision on Prosecutor's Motion for the Admission of Written Witness Statements Under Rule 92 *bis* (TC), 9 March 2004, para. 12.

12 *Prosecutor v. Milošević*, Case No. IT-02-54-T, Decision on Prosecution's Request to have Written Statements Admitted Under Rule 92 bis (TC), 21 March 2002, para. 22, cited in *Prosecutor v. Galić*, Case No. IT-98-29-AR73.2, Decision on Interlocutory Appeal Concerning Rule 92 bis (C) (AC), 7 June 2002, fn. 28, in support of the Appeals Chamber's statement of principle, at paragraph 10 of its Decision, that the term "acts and conduct of the accused as charged in the indictment" does not refer to the acts and conduct of others for which the accused is charged in the indictment with responsibility.

13 *Prosecutor v. Galić*, Case No. IT-98-29-AR73.2, Decision on Interlocutory Appeal Concerning Rule 92 bis (C) (AC), 7 June 2002. In fact the authority of the *Galić* Decision in relation to the meaning of the term "acts and conduct of the accused" was recently

Accused as charged in the Indictment *which establish his responsibility* for the acts and conduct of others, but does not exclude the acts and conduct of *others* for which the Accused is alleged to be responsible, for example, the acts and conduct of his co-perpetrators or subordinates.[14]

11. According to the jurisprudence, Rule 92*bis* (A) (and by analogy Rule 92*bis* (D)) excludes any written statement (or transcript) which goes to the proof of any act or conduct of the accused upon which the prosecution relies to establish: (1) that the accused personally physically perpetrated any of the crimes charged himself or herself; or (2) that he planned, instigated or ordered the crimes charged; or (3) that he otherwise aided and abetted those who actually did commit the crimes in their planning, preparation or execution of those crimes; or (4) that he was a superior to those who actually did commit the crimes; or (5) that he knew or had reason to know that those crimes were about to be or had been committed by his **[page 5]** subordinates; or (6) that he failed to take reasonable steps to prevent such acts or to punish those who carried out those acts.[15]

12. The proximity to the accused of the acts and conduct which are described in the written statement or transcript is relevant to the exercise of the Trial Chamber's discretion in deciding whether the evidence should be admitted in written form at all.[16] In cases alleging command responsibility and where the crimes charged involve widespread criminal conduct by the alleged subordinates of the accused, there is often but a short step from a finding that the acts constituting the crimes charged were committed by such subordinates to a finding that the accused knew or had reason to know that those crimes were about to be or had been committed by them.[17] In such cases, it may well be that the alleged subordinates of the accused are so proximate to the accused that "the evidence of their acts and conduct which the prosecution seeks to prove by a Rule 92*bis* statement becomes sufficiently pivotal to the prosecution case that it would not be fair to the accused to permit the evidence to be given in written form".[18]

13. Where the Prosecution case is that an accused participated in a joint criminal enterprise, and is therefore liable for the acts of others in that joint criminal enterprise, Rule 92 *bis* also excludes any written statement or transcript which goes to proof of any act or conduct of the accused upon which the prosecution relies to establish that he had participated in that joint criminal enterprise, or that he shared with the person who actually did commit the crimes charged the requisite intent for those crimes.[19] Again, the proximity to the accused of the acts and conduct which are described in the written statement is relevant to the exercise of the Trial Chamber's discretion in deciding whether the evidence should be admitted in written form at all. Where the individual, whose acts and conduct are described in the statement or transcript is proximate to the accused and where the evidence is pivotal to the Prosecution case, the Trial Chamber may decide not to admit the statement or transcript at all.[20] **[page 6]**

---

recalled by the Appeals Chamber in its Decision in this case concerning judicial notice. See *Prosecutor v. Karemera et al.*, Case No. ICTR-98-44-AR73(C), Decision on Prosecutor's Interlocutory Appeal of Decision on Judicial Notice, 16 June 2006, para. 52.

14 See *Prosecutor v. Galić*, Case No. IT-98-29-AR73.2, Decision on Interlocutory Appeal Concerning Rule 92 bis (C) (AC), 7 June 2002, paras. 9-14.

15 *Prosecutor v. Galić*, Case No. IT-98-29-AR73.2, Decision on Interlocutory Appeal Concerning Rule 92 bis (C) (AC), 7 June 2002, para. 10.

16 *Prosecutor v Brđanin & Talić*, IT-99-36-T, *(Confidential)* Decision on the Admission of Rule 92*bis* Statements, 1 May 2002, par 14 [A public version of this Decision was filed on 23 May 2002.]

17 *Prosecutor v. Galić*, Case No. IT-98-29-AR73.2, Decision on Interlocutory Appeal Concerning Rule 92 bis (C) (AC), 7 June 2002, para. 14.

18 *Prosecutor v. Galić*, Case No. IT-98-29-AR73.2, Decision on Interlocutory Appeal Concerning Rule 92 bis (C) (AC), 7 June 2002, para. 15; *Prosecutor v. Blagojević et al.*, Case No. IT-02-60-T, First Decision on Prosecution's Motion for Admission of Witness Statements and Prior Testimony Pursuant To Rule 92 bis (TC), 12 June 2003, para. 12.

19 *Prosecutor v. Galić*, Case No. IT-98-29-AR73.2, Decision on Interlocutory Appeal Concerning Rule 92 bis (C) (AC), 7 June 2002, para. 10; *Prosecutor v. Milošević*, Case No. IT-02-54-T, Decision on Prosecution Motion for the Admission of Transcripts in Lieu of Viva Voce Testimony Pursuant to 92 bis (D) – Foča Transcripts (TC), 30 June 2003, para. 12; *Prosecutor v. Blagojević et al.*, Case No. IT-02-60-T, First Decision on Prosecution's Motion for Admission of Witness Statements and Prior Testimony Pursuant To Rule 92 bis (TC), 12 June 2003, para. 11; *Prosecutor v. Tadić*, Case No. IT-94-1-A, Judgment (AC), 15 July 1999, para. 220.

20 *Prosecutor v. Galić*, Case No. IT-98-29-AR73.2, Decision on Interlocutory Appeal Concerning Rule 92 bis (C) (AC), 7 June 2002, paras. 13-15; *Prosecutor v. Blagojević et al.*, Case No. IT-02-60-T, First Decision on Prosecution's Motion for Admission of Witness Statements and Prior Testimony Pursuant To Rule 92 bis (TC), 12 June 2003, para. 12.

Cross-examination of the Witness

14. According to Rule 92*bis* (A)(ii)(c), a factor against admitting evidence in the form of a written statement is whether there are any other factors which make it appropriate for the witness to attend for cross-examination. In the *Galić* case, the Appeals Chamber considered that in some instances, "the absence of the opportunity to cross-examine the maker of the statement would in fairness preclude the use of the statement in any event".[21]

15. In addition to considering the issue of cross-examination as relevant for the admission of a statement under Rule 92*bis* (A), the Chamber has a discretionary power to decide whether to require the witness to appear for cross-examination, under Rule 92*bis* (E). As the *Galić* Appeals Chamber said,

> … the fact that [a] written statement goes to proof of the acts and conduct of a subordinate of the accused or of some other person for whose acts and conduct the accused is charged with responsibility does, however, remain relevant to the Trial Chamber's decision under Rule 92*bis*. That is because such a decision also involves a further determination as to whether the maker of the statement should appear for cross-examination [under Rule 92*bis* (E)].

In that regard, the proximity to the accused of the acts and conduct which are described in the written statement sought to be admitted is also relevant to the exercise of the Trial Chamber's discretion in deciding whether to require the witness to appear for cross-examination.

16. The principal consideration for determining whether a witness should appear for cross-examination is the overriding obligation of a Chamber to ensure a fair trial under Articles 19 and 20 of the Statute. In that regard, among the matters for consideration are whether the statement or transcript goes to proof of a critical element of the Prosecution's case against the accused.[22] Cross-examination shall be granted if the statement touches upon a critical element of the Prosecution's case, or goes to a live and important issue between the parties, as opposed to peripheral or marginally relevant issue.[23]

Application of Rule 92*bis* to the Material Before the Trial Chamber

17. The Chamber will now consider the substance of the materials sought to be admitted in the light of Rule 92 *bis,* the relevant jurisprudence, and the Parties' submissions.

18. As a preliminary matter, the Chamber finds that the formal requirements of Rule 92*bis* (B) have been met with respect to all 63 statements sought to be admitted under Rule 92*bis* (A). This finding is supported by the submissions of both Parties. **[page 7]**

19. Having reviewed all of the material sought to be admitted, the Chamber notes that none of the rapes and/or sexual assaults alleged are alleged to have been physically perpetrated by any of the Accused in this case. Rather, all of the rapes and/or sexual assaults are alleged to have been physically perpetrated by *Interahamwe* and militiamen, and not by any of the Accused in this case.

20. However, according to the forms of liability pleaded in the Indictment (as outlined in paragraph one of this Decision, and the footnotes thereto) the evidence is to be relied upon to prove that rapes were committed on a widespread and systematic basis by the Accused's subordinates and/or co-perpetrators. These allegations are so pivotal to the Prosecution's case that it would be unfair to the Accused to permit the evidence to be given in written form without an opportunity to cross-examine the witnesses.

21. The Prosecution Motion falls to be rejected. There is therefore no need for the Chamber to rule upon the Defence's application for extension of time in order to be able to conduct investigations with a view to making a factual demonstration of the unreliability of the material sought to be admitted.

---

21 *Prosecutor v. Galić,* Case No. IT-98-29-AR73.2, Decision on Interlocutory Appeal Concerning Rule 92 bis (C) (AC), 7 June 2002, para. 15.

22 *Prosecutor v. Milošević,* Case No. IT-02-54-T, Decision on Prosecution's Request to have Written Statements Admitted Under Rule 92 bis (TC), 21 March 2002, para. 7.

23 *Prosecutor v. Milošević,* Case No. IT-02-54-T, Decision on Prosecution's Request to have Written Statements Admitted Under Rule 92 bis (TC), 21 March 2002, para. 24.

Defence Motion for Order Reducing Prosecution Witness List Pursuant to Rule 73*bis* (D)

22. The Defence submits that the Trial Chamber should exclude the evidence sought to be admitted under Rule 92*bis* of the Rules, in its entirety, by means of an order pursuant to Rule 73*bis*(D) of the Rules.[24] The Prosecutor opposes this application. It finds difficult to conclude that the testimony of 93 witnesses is excessive given the massive scale of the rapes alleged in the Indictment. It submits that, since the Indictment alleges the rape of Tutsi women and girls over the course of three months in five different *préfectures*, the proposed number of 93 witnesses amounts to an average of approximately six witnesses to testify to the rapes, per month, per *préfecture*[25] – a number which the Prosecutor contends is not excessive.

23. According to Rule 73*bis* (D) of the Rules, the Trial Chamber or the designated Judge may order the Prosecutor to reduce the number of witnesses, if it considers that an excessive number of witnesses are being called to prove the same facts.[26]

24. In this case, the Trial Chamber has thus far declined the Defence's request for an order that the Prosecution reduce its Witness List.[27] In its Decision of 13 December 2005, the Chamber noted the Prosecution's intention to file a request seeking admission of written statements for 86 witnesses in lieu of their oral testimony, and therefore found that it was **[page 8]** "premature for the Chamber to order the Prosecution to reduce the number of witnesses it intends to call."[28]

25. Now, as a result of the Chamber's finding in the present Decision rejecting the Prosecution's application for admission of written statements, the Prosecution Witness List will include 93 witnesses to be called to testify on the rape allegations. Considering the particular circumstances of the case, the Chamber is of the view that this number should be drastically reduced.

26. In order to justify the number of witnesses to be called to prove Count Five, the Prosecution offers a mode of calculation based on average of approximately six witnesses to testify to the rapes, per month, per *préfecture*.[29] Should this formula be strictly applied to the allegations as set forth in the Indictment, the Chamber notes that, contrary to the Prosecution's assertion, no more than some 36 witnesses only should be called to testify. The Indictment alleges the commission of rapes in each *préfecture* for a substantially reduced period than the Prosecutor claims: rapes were allegedly committed in Ruhengeri and Butare *préfectures* over a period of two weeks (respectively, from early to mid April; and from mid to late April); in Kigali-*ville* for one month (April); in Kibuye for two months (May and June) and in Gitarama for two months (April and May), and not over the course of three months in each *préfecture* as the Prosecution submits to justify a number of 93 witnesses.

27. The Chamber recalls that in its Decision of 13 December 2005, it denied the Defence's submission to reduce the witness list because, at that time, it received information from the Prosecution that only *seven* witnesses were supposed to be called to give oral evidence on Count Five of the Indictment, related to the rape allegations.[30] Then, the Prosecution indicated its intention to call 21 witnesses to give oral testimony on this Count and sought the admission of written statements of 72 witnesses on the premise that their evidence would be of a cumulative nature. The Chamber also recalls that the Prosecution has acknowledged on prior occasions that its list is too long and has expressed its intention to reduce the number of witnesses as the trial progresses. In that respect, the Prosecution's Motion for judicial notice was sought to reduce the evidence to

---

24 Rule 73*bis* (D) provides: "The Trial Chamber or the designated Judge may order the Prosecutor to reduce the number of witnesses, if it considers that an excessive number of witnesses are being called to prove the same facts".

25 So that the calculation is six witnesses, multiplied by five *préfectures*, multiplied by three months (6 x 5 x 3), which equals a total of ninety witnesses. The Prosecution Witness List currently lists 93 witnesses on the Count of Rape as a Crime Against Humanity – 21 to be called to testify orally, and 72 in respect of whom this application is brought.

26 See *Bagosora et al.*, Case No. ICTR-98-41-T, Order for Reduction of Prosecutor's Witness List (TC), 8 April 2003: the Trial Chamber I ordered *proprio motu* the Prosecution to reduce its witness list from 235 to 100 witnesses.

27 *Prosecutor v. Karemera et al.*, Case No. 98-44-T, Decision on Variance of the Prosecution Witness List, 13 December 2005, para. 20.

28 *Ibidem*.

29 So that the calculation is six witnesses, multiplied by five *préfectures*, multiplied by three months (6 x 5 x 3), which equals a total of ninety witnesses. The Prosecution Witness List currently lists 93 witnesses on the Count of Rape as a Crime Against Humanity.

30 *Karemera et al.*, Case No. 98-44-T, Decision on Variance of the Prosecution Witness List, 13 December 2005, para. 20.

be orally heard during this trial and, in its Decision of even date, the Chamber has taken judicial notice of adjudicated facts concerning rapes committed in Gitarama, Kibuye, Kigali-rural, Ruhengeri and Kigali-ville *prefectures*.

28. In view of the particular circumstances of the case, the Chamber finds that the Prosecution Witness List is excessive and should be drastically reduced with respect to the number of witnesses proposed to give evidence on Count Five of the Indictment. In reaching this conclusion, the Chamber has had regard to: (i) the number of witnesses currently proposed to be called on this Count; (ii) the factual elements that the Prosecution has to establish; (iii) the application of the Prosecution's own formula in submitting to the Chamber that the current number of witnesses is not excessive; (iv) that the use of excessive witnesses wastes judicial resources and time and compromises the administration of justice and the **[page 9]** rights of the accused, and (v) that by Decision of even date, the Chamber has taken judicial notice of a number of adjudicated facts concerning rape and sexual assault.

FOR THOSE REASONS

THE CHAMBER

DENIES the Prosecution's Motion in its entirety; and hereby

ORDERS the Prosecution, pursuant to Rule 73*bis* (D) of the Rules, to drastically reduce the number of witnesses being called to give evidence of rape and sexual assault in relation to Count Five of the Indictment and to file, as soon as possible, with the Chamber, and disclose to the Defence of each of the Accused, a revised Witness List.

Arusha, 11 December 2006, done in English.

Dennis C. M. Byron Presiding	Emile Francis Short Judge	Gberdao Gustave Kam Judge

[Seal of the Tribunal]

International Criminal Tribunal for Rwanda
Tribunal pénal international pour le Rwanda

OR: ENG

TRIAL CHAMBER III

Before Judges:	Dennis C. M. Byron, Presiding Gberdao Gustave Kam Vagn Joensen
Registrar:	Adama Dieng
Date:	25 October 2007

THE PROSECUTOR

v.

Édouard KAREMERA
Mathieu NGIRUMPATSE
Joseph NZIRORERA

Case No. ICTR-98-44-T

DECISION ON PROSECUTION PROSPECTIVE EXPERTS WITNESSES ALISON DES FORGES, ANDRE GUICHAOUA AND BINAIFER NOWROJEE

Rules 89 and 94*bis *of the Rules of Procedure and Evidence

Office of the Prosecutor:
Don Webster
Alayne Frankson-Wallace
Iain Morley
Saidou N'Dow
Gerda Visser
Sunkarie Ballah Conteh
Takeh Sendze
Deo Mbuto

Defence Counsel for Édouard Karemera:
Dior Diagne Mbaye and Félix Sow

Defence Counsel for Mathieu Ngirumpatse:
Chantal Hounkpatin and Frédéric Weyl

Defence Counsel for Joseph Nzirorera:
Peter Robinson and Patrick Nimy Mayidika Ngimbi

[page 2] INTRODUCTION

1. The Prosecution enlisted four prospective expert witnesses, Alison Des Forges, André Guichaoua, Binaifer Nowrojee and Charles Ntampaka, whose reports were filed under Rule 94 *bis* of the Rules of Procedure and Evidence ("Rules") following numerous Trial Chamber decisions.[1]

2. On 21 August 2007, the Chamber granted Joseph Nzirorera's Motion to limit the scope of the evidence of André Guichaoua and Alison Des Forges.[2] On 26 September 2007, addressing another application of Joseph Nzirorera, the Chamber found that Charles Ntampaka was not qualified to provide an expert opinion on issues addressed in the report filed.[3] In this later Decision, the Chamber recalled the applicable law and jurisprudence on the admission of expert evidence.[4] In the 21 August 2007 Decision, the Chamber only dealt with the legal arguments raised by the Parties concerning Guichaoua and Des Forges. However, as the Chamber noted that the Accused had filed a notice that they do not accept the qualification of the prospective experts, it further found it necessary to hear the Parties on that issue.[5]

3. The Accused and the Prosecution filed their submissions accordingly on 8 October 2007. The Accused dispute the qualifications and admissibility of the expert evidence.[6] The **[page 3]** Prosecution submits that the three witnesses are qualified as experts and moves the Chamber to admit in evidence the reports of each of the three proposed expert witnesses, to assign appropriate exhibit numbers to them and to schedule their testimony in this trial.[7]

DISCUSSIONS

4. Rule 94*bis* of the Rules of Procedure and Evidence reads as follows:

> (A) Notwithstanding the provisions of Rule 66(A)(ii), Rule 73*bis*(B)(iv)(b) and Rule 73*ter*(B)(iii)(b) of the present Rules, the full statement of any expert witness called by a party shall be disclosed to the opposing party as early as possible and shall be filed with the Trial Chamber not less than twenty-one days prior to the date on which the expert is expected to testify.
>
> (B) Within fourteen days of filing of the statement of the expert witness, the opposing party shall file a notice to the Trial Chamber indicating whether:
>
> (i) It accepts or does not accept the witness's qualification as an expert;
>
> (ii) It accepts the expert witness statement; or
>
> (iii) It wishes to cross-examine the expert witness.

---

[1] *Prosecutor v. Edouard Karemera, Mathieu Ngirumpatse, Joseph Nzirorera*, Case No. ICTR-98-44-T ("*Karemera et al.*"), Decision on Joseph Nzirorera's Motion For Deadline For Filing of Reports of Experts (TC), 16 May 2005; Decision on Prosecutor's Notice of Delay in Filing Expert Reports and Request for Additional Time to Comply with the Chamber Decision of 16 May 2005 (TC), 9 September 2005; Decision on Motion to Set Deadlines For Filing Expert Reports of Norwojee and Reyntjens (TC), 20 September 2005; Oral Decision on Exclusion of Testimony of Alison Des Forges and Granting Extension of Time for Disclosure of the Expert Report (TC), 3 October 2005; Decision Granting Extension of Time to File Prosecution Expert Report (TC), 8 November 2005; Decision on Prosecution Request for Additional Time to file Expert Report and Joseph Nzirorera's Motion to Exclude Testimony of Charles Ntampaka (TC), 12 December 2005; Order On Filing of Expert Report of Charles Ntampaka (TC). 31 January 2006; Decision on Prosecutor's Notice of Delay In Filing Expert Report Of Professor André Guichaoua; Defence Motion To Exclude The Witness' Testimony; And Trial Chamber's Order To Show Cause (TC), 1 February 2006; Decision on Delay in Filing of Expert Report of Charles Ntampaka (TC), 13 February 2006. The report of Alison Des Forges was filed on 1 November 2005; the report of André Guichaoua was filed on 7 March 2006; the report of Binaifer Nowrojee was filed on 30 September 2005 and the report of Charles Ntampaka was filed on 21 March 2006.

[2] *Karemera et al.*, Decision on Joseph Nzirorera's Motion to Limit the Scope of Testimony of Expert Witnesses Alison des Forges and André Guichaoua (TC), 21 August 2007.

[3] *Karemera et al.*, Decision on Joseph Nzirorera's Motion to Preclude Testimony by Charles Ntampaka (TC), 26 September 2007.

[4] *Ibid.*, paras. 7-8.

[5] *Karemera et al.*, Order for Submissions on the Prosecution Prospective Experts Witnesses (TC), 1 October 2007.

[6] Soumission de Edouard Karemera suite a la "Order for Submissions on the Prosecution Prospective Experts Witnesses" du 01 Octobre 2007 ("Karemera's Submissions"); Observations pour M. Ngirumpatse suite à l' "Order for Submissions on the Prosecution Prospective Experts Witnesses" du 01/10/07 ("Ngirumpaste's Submissions"); Joseph Nzirorera's Submission on the Qualifications of Expert Witnesses ("Nzirorera's Submissions").

[7] Prosecutor's Submissions: Qualifications of Prosecution Expert Witnesses ("Prosecutor's Submissions"), para. 4.

(C) If the opposing party accepts the statement of the expert witness, the statement may be admitted into evidence by the Trial Chamber without calling the witness to testify in person.

Preliminary Matters

Admissibility of the observations of Edouard Karemera and Mathieu Ngirumpatse concerning the admission of Binaifer Nowrojee's evidence

5. The Prosecution notes that only Joseph Nzirorera has filed a notice in accordance with Rule 94*bis* objecting to the qualification of Binaifer Nowrojee as expert witness and to the admission of her report.[8]

6. As held by the Appeals Chamber, nothing in Rule 94 *bis* of the Rules implies that, absent a timely motion from the party opposing an expert, a Trial Chamber is obligated to **[page 4]** admit expert testimony or to accept a witness's qualification as an expert.[9] Failure to file a notice under Rule 94 *bis* cannot be construed as a waiver of the rights of the Accused. The Chamber will therefore consider Edouard Karemera and Mathieu Ngirumpatse's submissions concerning Binaifer Nowrojee.

Scope of the Decision

7. In his submissions, Edouard Karemera suggests that the Chamber's Order of 21 August 2007 was determinative on the question being addressed in the present Decision.[10]

8. In the 21 August 2007 Decision, the Chamber considered the application of Joseph Nzirorera as to whether expert witnesses Alison Des Forges and André Guichaoua should be precluded from offering opinions adverting to the acts, conduct, mental state or criminal responsibility of the Accused on the basis that they go to the ultimate issues in the trial or, alternatively, on the basis that it would be unfair to admit them.[11] The Chamber concluded that such opinions, although not unfair to the Accused, should be excluded on the basis that they usurp the function of the Chamber as they go to the ultimate questions of guilt or innocence of the Accused.[12]

9. The issue here is whether the testimony should be admitted as expert testimony. This is irrespective of the fact that portions of it could not be admitted on the basis that those portions would be determinative of the guilt or innocence of the Accused. Although the testimony, if given, would not be unfair to the Accused it is still within the competence of the Chamber to consider whether it should be admitted as expert testimony in accordance with settled jurisprudence.

Voir Dire

10. The Prosecution submits that, whilst resolving the issue of qualifications by written motion in advance of scheduled testimony may be a welcome departure from the lengthy *voir dire* procedures that have absorbed countless hours in previous trials before the Tribunal, should this Chamber query the qualifications of the proposed experts, or the scope and definition of their expertise, genuine dispute on such matters may be more appropriately addressed by extending the inquiry by additional oral examination of the expert witnesses in a **[page 5]** *voir dire* hearing.[13] In its submissions, the Prosecution recognises that this is a *voir dire* procedure and argues that this could be appropriate. However, it seems to suggest that a non-oral *voir dire* procedure is only appropriate when the Chamber does not have queries, and that any queries should be resolved by an oral hearing

8 Prosecutor's Submissions, para. 1.

9 *Prosecutor v. Sylvestre Gacumbitsi*, Case No: ICTR-2001-64-A, Judgement (AC), 7 July 2006, para. 31 ("*Gacumbitsi* Appeals Chamber Judgement").

10 Karemera's Submissions, para. 3.

11 *Karemera et al.*, Decision on Joseph Nzirorera's Motion to Limit the Scope of Testimony of Expert Witnesses Alison des Forges and André Guichaoua (TC), 21 August 2007.

12 *Ibid.*, para. 3.

13 Prosecutor's Submissions, paras. 5-6.

11. As the Appeals Chamber pointed out, "whereas the Rules lay down a specific procedure for admitting an expert witness's report without hearing the witness, subject to its acceptance by the opposing party, they do not require a "*voir dire*" examination of the person called as an expert."[14] Pursuant to Rule 89(A) of the Rules, the Chamber is not bound by national rules of evidence.

12. Even assuming that there is merit in the argument that certain types of decision-making could be better informed by additional evidence or oral hearing, it would be for the Chamber to conclude that it requires additional material on which to reach its decision. However, in this case the information filed is comprehensive; there are no factual issues that have been raised on the evidence. The argumentation is all about the legal conclusions that should be drawn from the facts that are before the Chamber. The Parties have advanced the legal arguments on which they rely, and oral recitation should not add weight or persuasiveness. In these circumstances, the Chamber is sufficiently informed to draw conclusions and decide without any further hearings of the Parties.

On the Merits

13. Rule 94 *bis* only sets forth a procedure by which an expert's report can be accepted into evidence without that expert testifying.[15] In other respects, the admission of expert testimony is governed only by the general provision of Rule 89, which entrusts the Trial Chamber with broad discretion to employ rules of evidence that "best favour a fair determination of the matter before it and are consonant with the spirit of the Statute and the general principles of law."[16] **[page 6]**

14. An expert's testimony is testimony intended to enlighten the Judges on specific issues of a technical nature, requiring special knowledge in a specific field.[17]

15. This Chamber has already reminded the Parties of settled jurisprudence that expert evidence must meet the following additional requirements in order to be admitted: (i) the Chamber discretionarily deems it necessary to hear an expert on a determined issue; (ii) the prospective witness is an expert on that determined issue; (iii) the statement or report is reliable; (iv) the statement or report is relevant and of probative value; and (v) the substance of the statement or report falls within the expertise of the witness.[18]

16. The Prosecution acknowledges that the qualification of a person as an expert is dependent on two additional factors.[19] Firstly, the witness called as an expert must "possess a relevant specialized knowledge acquired through education, expertise or training in his proposed field of expertise". Secondly, the Chamber must be convinced that the expert evidence could assist it in understanding the evidence presented or in determining a fact in issue.[20] The fact that a person may have been recognized as an expert in other trials does not automatically qualify him or her as an expert witness.[21] As held by the Appeals Chamber, "a witness's qualification as an expert turns on the contribution he or she can make to a Trial Chamber's analysis of a particular case."[22]

---

[14] *Prosecutor v. Georges Anderson Rutaganda,* Case No. ICTR-96-3-A, Judgement (AC), 26 May 2003, para.164; *Prosecutor v. Niyaramasuhuko et al.,* Case No. ICTR-97-21-AR73, Decision on "Appeal Of Accused Arsène Shalom Ntahobali Against the Decision on Kanyabashi's Oral Motion to Cross-Examine Ntahobali Using Ntahobali's Statements to Prosecution Investigators In July 1997" (AC), 27 October 2006, paras. 12-13.

[15] *Gacumbitsi* Appeals Chamber Judgement, para. 31.

[16] *Ibidem.*

[17] *Prosecutor v. Laurent Semanza,* Case No. ICTR-97-20-A, Judgement (AC), 20 May 2005 ("*Semanza* Appeals Chamber Judgement), paras. 303-304.

[18] *Prosecutor v. Jean-Paul Akayesu,* Case No. ICTR-96-4-T, Decision on Defence Motion for Appearance of an Accused as an Expert Witness (TC), 9 March 1998 ("[T]he Tribunal is of the view that there is a fundamental difference between, on the one hand, a witness called to testify about the crimes with which the accused is directly charged and, on the other hand, an expert witness, whose testimony is intended to enlighten the Judges on specific issues of a technical nature, requiring special knowledge in a specific field"). In another more recent case, the Appeals Chamber has confirmed that there was no error in a Trial Chamber's denial to hear an expert witness on international criminal law. See: *Prosecutor v. Milomir Stakic,* Case No.: IT-97-24-A, Judgement (AC), 22 March 2006, par. 164.

[19] Prosecutor's Submissions, para. 14.

[20] *Semanza* Appeals Chamber Judgement, paras. 302-303; *Gacumbitsi* Appeals Chamber Judgement, para. 32.

[21] *Gacumbitsi* Appeals Chamber Judgement, para. 32.

[22] *Gacumbitsi* Appeals Chamber Judgement, para. 32.

17. It is the Prosecution's submission that all three expert witnesses have the requisite specialised experience, knowledge, and skills to be qualified as experts under the criteria established by the jurisprudence of this Tribunal.

Alison des Forges

18. The Prosecution submits that Alison Des Forges is an internationally recognised scholar and human rights advocate with extensive publications in her primary field of **[page 7]** expertise: African history, particularly focused on state structures in the region of the African Great Lakes, including the recent history of human rights abuses, ethnic violence, political instability and genocide in Rwanda. It stresses that she has drawn upon such expertise in offering expert opinion evidence before numerous courts, tribunals and administrative hearings in Europe, North America and in international agencies. Alison Des Forges has already been qualified as an expert in 10 trials before this Tribunal.

19. None of the Accused disputes, as such, the general qualifications of Alison Des Forges as expert in African history and in particular, the Great Lake Region and Rwanda.[23] The Chamber agrees that her expert status to that scope is beyond reasonable dispute and has been recognised in many instances over the years. However, the question still remains whether the Chamber will be assisted by her testimony.

20. In the Pre-Trial Brief, as recalled in its submissions, the Prosecution provided substantial notice of the scope of the evidence of Alison des Forges as related to (i) "[t]he notion of race and ethnicity in Rwandan history and culture and the manner and circumstances under which debates over ethnicity were resurrected by the elites during periods of social strife; the notion of the 'Revolution of 1959'; [the] regionalism as a factor in the perception and manipulation of ethnicity; the treatment of sexual violence in Rwandan culture and society, etc."; (ii) "[t]he mechanisms of social control and mobilization, as manipulated by the state and the elites in Rwandan society, particularly the role of the MRND political party and the territorial administration, but also discussing the role of the church and the legacies of colonialism"; (iii) "[a]n explanation of the social and historical character of Butare and Gitarama in relation to the rest of the country; the character of Kibuye and the northern prefectures of Gisenyi and Ruhengeri, including a discussion of the ethnic composition of Rwandan society in relation to regional patterns of ethnic distribution"; (iv) "[t]he notion of parallel and *de facto* systems of authority and control in Rwandan society"; and (v) the historical context of certain key events "with expanded discussion of their significance, including a review of the history of human rights abuses and ethnic tensions in Rwanda from 1959 onwards".[24]

21. It is the Prosecution's theory that the 1994 genocide was organised by high level government, military and political party authorities, while the Defence's theory is that the **[page 8]** violence was not mobilised and the massive killings were a spontaneous outburst of an enraged population that the Accused were powerless to control.[25] According to the Prosecution, Des Forges's testimony will be of assistance in placing the artifacts of the period 1990-1994 in their social and historical context and to delineate patterns in history and social organisation in Rwanda that will assist the Chamber in its appreciation of the evidence.[26]

22. In the Chamber's view, the factual questions to be decided in the case do not require expert assistance. Review of the proposed testimony of Alison Des Forges indicates that her opinions address issues on which the Chamber has taken judicial notice or heard testimony.

23. The discussions on race and ethnicity are no longer issues on which expert testimony is required. Insofar as they are relevant to the proof of elements of the crimes charged in the Indictment, they are matters of common knowledge. The Chamber recalls its Decisions of 9 November 2005, where it took judicial notice of "the fact that Hutu, Tutsi and Twa were protected groups falling with [sic] the scope of the Genocide

23 Karemera's Submissions, paras. 4-7; Ngirumpaste's Submissions, para. 2; Nzirorera's Submissions, para. 3.

24 Annex B to the Prosecution's Submissions; see: Prosecution Pre-Trial Brief, paras. 20 to 56; and summary of the anticipated testimony attached to the Pre-Trial Brief.

25 Prosecutor's Submissions, para.41.

26 *Ibidem.*

Convention of 1948", and 11 December 2006, following the Appeals Chamber's directives,[27] where it took judicial notice of the commission of a genocide against the Tutsi between 6 April and 17 July 1994.[28] In addition the Chamber has taken judicial notice of numerous adjudicated facts in which issues of ethnicity were addressed.[29] The Chamber therefore considers that it is not necessary to hear expert evidence on the issues of race and ethnicity.

24. The role of the MRND political party and the territorial administration has been the subject of evidence in the trial. Evidence has been heard from officials in the government and the territorial administration, from leaders of the *Interahamwe* and from members of the public. There has been testimony from persons who were actively involved in the events between the period of 1990-1994. The Chamber does not need expert testimony to assist in its evaluation of those testimonies. Whether the Prosecution has proven the elements of the crimes charged will depend on the Chamber's assessment of the credibility of the testimonies that have been adduced; the assistance of expert testimony is not required. **[page 9]**

25. In those circumstances, although the historical dissertations are interesting and informative, the Chamber does not require assistance of the expertise to understand the evidence adduced and come to its conclusions on the guilt or innocence of the Accused.

André Guichaoua

26. According to the Prosecution, André Guichaoua is a highly esteemed scholar with a well-establish career as an academic in the fiercely competitive French university system: he has completed studies in Development Economics and in Sociology to postgraduate level, including a doctoral degree from the University of Paris in the area of Social Sciences, by which he became specialised particularly in the Great Lakes region of Africa. The Prosecution submits that Guichaoua has relevant practical experience in these areas as well, including "socio-political research in Rwanda", and that he was on mission in Rwanda from 4 to 11 April 1994, and is, therefore, an eye-witness to events that occurred during that time. He has several relevant publications to his name, which are listed in his *curriculum vitae*. The Prosecution also recalls that Guichaoua has testified before the Tribunal in the capacity of an expert witness in six previous trials.

27. Based on André Guichaoua's qualifications, practical experience and relevant publications, the Prosecution asserts that he is qualified to offer the expert opinion in the field of socio-political science, as noted in the Prosecution's summary annexed to the Pre-Trial Brief.[30] The Prosecution submits that Guichaoua will assist the Chamber to appreciate the evidence in relation to the MRND's power to mobilise the territorial administration and militias.[31] It stresses that this contribution is even more important given the Chamber's preclusion of the evidence of Ntampaka.[32]

28. Although the Chamber acknowledges the fact that André Guichaoua has earned his reputation as an expert in sociology, it is the Chamber's view that the opinions of an expert, **[page 10]** which are to a large extent based on material similar to that led in evidence in the trial, are not necessary for it to appreciate and evaluate the factual issues in the trial.

---

27 *Karemera et al.*, Case No. ICTR-98-44-AR73(C), Decision on Prosecutor's Interlocutory Appeal of Decision on Judicial Notice (AC), 16 June 2006.

28 *Karemera et al.*, Decision on Prosecution Motion for Judicial Notice (TC), 9 November 2005; Decision on Appeals Chamber Remand of Judicial Notice (TC), 11 December 2006.

29 *Ibidem.*

30 According to the Prosecution's Submissions (Annex B) and the Prosecution Pre-Trial Brief, the expert opinion of André Guichaoua will cover: (i) "[t]he biographies of Karemera, Ngirumpatse and Nzirorera, their family backgrounds, regional affiliations, history of political appointments and allegiances, etc." and the way in which after the dismantling of the MRND as a party-state, the accused maintained their power and influence through the so-called Hutu Power; (ii) "[t]he struggles within the MRND prior to 1994; how regionalism and patronage impacted upon rivalries within the MRND; the forces that led to multipartyism and how the MRND renovated itself to deal with multipartyism"; (iii) the control of the regional territorial administration by the MRND before 1992; (iv) the "mobiliz[ation] [of] the territorial administration, the military, the militias, etc." by the MRND; and (v) "the role of the accused [...] in formulating [the] policies [of the Interim Government] and perpetrating the genocide."

31 Prosecutor's Submissions, para. 42.

32 *Ibidem.*

29. A lot of evidence related to the Accused, their alleged power and influence upon the Hutu Power, their control of MRND and the Interim Government has already been adduced in evidence.[33] The MRND is not on trial. The Chamber will have to assess the individual criminal responsibility of the Accused. The Chamber has been hearing and evaluating the testimony and is satisfied that it can reach its decision without the assistance of an expert.

30. Furthermore, according to the introduction to André Guichaoua's report, his aim is to show the role played by the Accused in the political system and leading up to the 1994 events, notably through the Interim Government, while addressing the professional and political career of each Accused.[34] Many of the opinions he has expressed are determinative of the guilt of the Accused and could therefore not be admitted by the Chamber.

Binaifer Nowrojee

31. The Prosecution describes Binafeir Nowrojee as "a human rights lawyer and scholar with expertise on gender-related crimes in situations of armed conflict". According to her *curriculum vitae*, she has several publications to her name, including a thesis on "Joining Forces: United Nations and Regional Peacekeeping Lessons for Liberia" and has been a lecturer at Harvard University since 1992 where she co–teaches Human Rights Advocacy and supervises students engaged in human rights clinical projects. The Prosecution asserts that she has practical experience in investigating human rights violations, notably gender issues: she conducted human right research and investigative missions on women's rights violations in Kenya, South Africa and Rwanda from 1993 until 1996. She also has testified before the Tribunal in the capacity of an expert witness in two previous cases.

32. According to the Prosecution, Binaifer Nowrojee will offer expert opinion evidence on the foreseeability of gender-based crimes in situations of armed conflict and the gendered **[page 11]** nature of genocide, crimes against humanity, and war crimes.[35] This matter is connected to the Prosecution's allegations that the Accused are responsible for rapes as such crimes were the natural and foreseeable consequence of the object of the joint criminal to kill the Tutsi.[36]

33. Even though Mrs Nowrojee seems to be qualified in relation with sexual violence, as with the previous experts, the subject-area of her report has been addressed by testimony in the trial, which the Chamber is quite capable of evaluating without the assistance of experts. The issue of whether the Accused foresaw rapes as the natural consequence of killing the Tutsi is a question of fact. This has been the subject of testimony of witnesses as well as admitted written statements of rape witnesses and victims, and judicial notice.[37] The assessment of factual evidence in connection with the crimes alleged in the Indictment is not a class of subject on which the Chamber requires any assistance from an expert.

34. Furthermore, the Chamber notes that the material on which the expert's opinion is based is much the same as the material on which the Chamber is being asked to make its findings of fact. The fact that the expert may have accessed a larger material base is not a reason for preferring that opinion to the findings made on the evidence adduced in the trial.

33

34 See for instance at page 7: "An analysis of the role of MRND leaders during that period presupposes understanding of the entire power system that had still been under the stringent control of President Juvénal Habyarimana. [...] it would be proper for me to regularly mention the effective decision-making bodies, their linkage and hierarchy, and especially proceed to the historical relationship between the civilians and soldiers. [...] I have so far base my analysis on a similar approach to the legal one that relies on the victims and the established crimes and then works backwards to the accused and then specifying their possible relationship or responsibility in the instigation or commission of those crimes. I believe that this deductive approach is material to understanding the behavior of subordinates, whose functions, areas of jurisdiction and intervention can be very clearly determined and delimited." See also the conclusions of the author at pages 203-208.

35 Prosecutor's Submissions, para. 43.

36 Count Five of the Indictment. See also paragraphs 4, 5, 6, 7, 8, 14, 15 and 16 of the Indictment which outline the general allegations of the joint criminal enterprise and relate to Count Five.

37 *Karemera et al.*, Decision on Appeals Chamber Remand of Judicial Notice (TC), 11 December 2006; Decision on Reconsideration of Admission of Written Statements and Admission of the Testimony of Witness GAY (TC), 28 September 2007.

35. In view of the circumstances of the case, bearing in mind the evidence adduced thus far and considering the Prosecution's submissions as to the anticipated scope of the proposed expert witnesses, the Chamber is not satisfied that expert evidence is required to analyse and understand the evidence before it.

36. In its submissions, the Prosecution reminds the Chamber that "on several occasions when the prosecution sought to explore certain lines of inquiry with factual witnesses, the defense objected that such questions should be reserved for expert witnesses that were expected to testify in the trial."[38] It recalls that documents from the period 1990 to 1994 have entered the trial record as defense exhibits, often over objection from the Prosecution, "with the understanding that expert witnesses would later be requested to comment on the exhibit to provide context and to explain its significance."[39] The Prosecution also submits that given **[page 12]** the Chamber's inability to fully anticipate the defence case and its arguments, it is highly advisable that the expert opinion evidence from these witnesses be heard and fully considered. It further suggests that the expert reports be admitted in evidence, the witnesses be examined orally before the Chamber, and the reliance to be placed on their opinion evidence be decided subsequently, in light of all of the evidence in the case.

37. The Chamber is not persuaded by the Prosecution's arguments on the necessity of admitting the expert evidence at this stage. As Joseph Nzirorera has submitted, it will be open to the Chamber to call upon expert testimony if at any future time issues arise which require such assistance.[40] However at this point such a need is not foreseen by the Chamber. The argument that the evidence that the Defence may adduce may require expert analysis is also a matter that can be addressed if the need arises, including by calling for the testimony of experts if in the Chamber's opinion it is required.

FOR THESE REASONS, THE CHAMBER

I. **FINDS** that the evidence of Mrs Alison des Forges, André Guichaoua and Binaifer Nowrojee cannot be admitted as expert evidence under Rule 94 *bis* of the Rules and therefore preclude their testimony as expert witnesses.

Arusha, 25 October 2007, done in English.

Dennis C. M. Byron Presiding Judge	Gberdao Gustave Kam Judge	Vagn Joensen Judge

[Seal of the Tribunal]

38 Prosecutor's Submissions, par. 24 at footnote 32.

39 *Ibidem.*

40 Rules of Procedure and Evidence, Rule 98: "A Trial Chamber may *proprio motu* order either party to produce additional evidence. It may itself summon witnesses and order their attendance."

International Criminal Tribunal for Rwanda
Tribunal pénal international pour le Rwanda

OR: ENG

TRIAL CHAMBER III

Before Judges: Dennis C. M. Byron, Presiding
Gberdao Gustave Kam
Vagn Joensen

Registrar: Adama Dieng

Date: 2 November 2007

THE PROSECUTOR

v.

Édouard KAREMERA
Mathieu NGIRUMPATSE
Joseph NZIRORERA

Case No. ICTR-98-44-T

DECISION ON THE PROSECUTION MOTION FOR ADMISSION INTO EVIDENCE OF POST-ARREST INTERVIEWS WITH JOSEPH NZIRORERA AND MATHIEU NGIRUMPATSE

Rules 89 (C) and 95 of the Rules of Procedure and Evidence

Office of the Prosecutor:
Don Webster
Alayne Frankson-Wallace
Iain Morley
Saidou N'Dow
Gerda Visser
Sunkarie Ballah-Conteh
Takeh Sendze
Deo Mbuto

Defence Counsel for Édouard Karemera
Dior Diagne Mbaye and Félix Sow

Defence Counsel for Mathieu Ngirumpatse
Chantal Hounkpatin and Frédéric Weyl

Defence Counsel for Joseph Nzirorera
Peter Robinson and Patrick Nimy Mayidika Ngimbi

[page 2] INTRODUCTION

1. On 27 April 2007, the Prosecution filed a Motion seeking the admission into evidence of fifty UNAMIR documents (Annex A), 10 exhibits admitted in other trials (Annex B) and transcripts[1] of post-arrest interviews with Mathieu Ngirumpatse and Joseph Nzirorera that investigators from the Office of The Prosecutor ("OTP") conducted with the former on 15, 16 and 17 June 1998 and with the latter on 12 and 13 June 1998 (Annex C).[2]

2. The Chamber will consider each Annex separately and rules in the present Decision on the admission into evidence of Annex C to the Prosecutor's Motion. The Defence for each accused opposes the Motion.[3]

DELIBERATION

Applicable law

1. Rule 89 (C) of the Rules of Procedure and Evidence ("the Rules"), provides that a Chamber "may admit any relevant evidence it deems to have probative value". According to the Appeals Chamber, the first step in the determination of whether a document is admissible is to ascertain whether sufficient indicia of reliability have been established.[4] While a Chamber always retains the competence under Rule 89(D) to request verification of the authenticity of evidence obtained out of court, "to require absolute proof of a document's **[page 3]** authenticity before it could be admitted would be to require a far more stringent test than the standard envisioned by Sub-rule 89 (C)."[5]

2. In accordance with jurisprudence, it is to the moving Party to prove that the document has *prima facie* relevance and that it has probative value.[6] In order to establish that evidence is relevant, the applicant must show that a connection exists between the evidence sought to be admitted and the proof of an allegation sufficiently pleaded in the indictment.[7] In order to establish that evidence has probative value, the applicant must show that the evidence tends to prove or disprove an issue.[8]

---

1 The Chamber notes that although only the transcripts are sought to be admitted into evidence, both the audio-tapes and the transcripts of the interviews were made available to the Parties.

2 Prosecutor's Motion for Admission of Certain Materials under Rule 89(c) of the Rules of Procedure and Evidence, filed on 27 April 2007 ("Prosecutor's Motion").

3 Joseph Nzirorera's Response to Prosecution Motion to Admit Exhibits from the Bar Table, filed on 9 May 2007 ("Nzirorera's Response"), para. 99; Mémoire pour M. Ngirumpatse sur la Prosecutor's Motion for admission of certain materials under the rule 89 C of the Rules of Procedure and Evidence, filed on 22 May 2007 ("Ngirumpatse's Response"), paras. 5. 1°/ d) and 6; Soumission de Edouard Karemera suite à la requête du Procureur en admission de certaines pièces sur le fondement de l'Article 89 (C) du Règlement de Preuve et de Procédure, filed on 3 October 2007 ("Karemera's Response"), p. 12. See *Karemera et al.*, Case No ICTR-98-44-T, Décision en prorogation de délai supplémentaire (TC), 17 May 2007; *Karemera et a.,l* Décision accordant une prorogation de délai supplémentaire (TC), 24 May 2007.

4 See *Prosecutor v. Nyiramasuhuko*, Case No. ICTR-98-42-AR73.2, Decision on Pauline Nyiramasuhuko's Appeal on the Admissibility of Evidence (AC), 4 October 2004, para. 7; *Prosecutor v. Georges Anderson Rutaganda*, Case No. ICTR-96-3-A, Judgement (AC), para. 33; *Prosecutor v. Delalic and Delic*, Decision on Application of Defendant Zejnil Delalic for Leave to Appeal Against the Decision of the Trial Chamber of 19 January 1998 for the Admissibility of Evidence (AC), 4 March 1998.

5 *Prosecutor v. Delalic and Delic*, Case No. IT-96-21, Decision on Application of Defendant Zejnil Delalic for Leave to Appeal Against the Decision of the Trial Chamber of 19 January 1998 for the Admissibility of Evidence (AC), 4 March 1998 ("*Delalic* Appeals Decision on the Admissibility of Evidence").

6 *See Prosecutor v. Nyiramasuhuko*, Case No. ICTR-98-42-AR73.2, Decision on Pauline Nyiramasuhuko's Appeal on the Admissibility of Evidence (AC), 4 October 2004, para. 7; *Prosecutor v. Georges Anderson Rutaganda*, Case No. ICTR-96-3-A, Judgement (AC), para. 33; *Prosecutor v. Delalic and Delic*, Decision on Application of Defendant Zejnil Delalic for Leave to Appeal Against the Decision of the Trial Chamber of 19 January 1998 for the Admissibility of Evidence (AC), 4 March 1998.

7 *Prosecution v. Pauline Nyiramasuhuko and Arsène Shalom Ntahobali*, Case No. ICTR-97-21-AR73, Decision on the Appeals by Pauline Nyiramasuhuko and Arsène Shalom Ntahobali on the "Decision on Defence Urgent Motion to Declare Parts of the Evidence of Witnesses RV and ABZ Inadmissible" (AC), 2 July 2004, para. 15; *Prosecution v. Pauline Nyiramasuhuko*, Case No. ICTR-98-42-AR73, Decision on Pauline Nyiramasuhuko's Request for Reconsideration (AC), 27 September 2004, para. 12; *Prosecutor v. Thenoeste Bagosora, Gratien Kabiligi, Aloys Ntabakuze and Anatole Nsengiyumva.*, Case No. ICTR-98-41-T ("*Bagosora et al.*") Decision on Aloys Ntabakuze's Interlocutory Appeal on Questions of Law Raised by the 29 June 2006 Trial Chamber I Decision on Motion for Exclusion of Evidence (AC), 18 September 2006, fn. 40.

8 *Prosecutor v. Blagojevic and Jokic*, Case No. IT-02-60-T, Decision on the Admission into Evidence of Intercept-Related Materials (TC), 18 December 2003, para. 17.

3. Moreover, when deciding on the admissibility of evidence, Trial Chambers must also guarantee the protection of the rights of the accused as prescribed by Articles 19 and 20 of the Statute. The Chamber therefore has the inherent power to exclude evidence if its probative value is substantially outweighed by its prejudicial effect or otherwise by the need to ensure a fair trial.[9]

4. Furthermore, Rule 95 of the Rules provides for the mandatory exclusion of evidence "if obtained by methods which cast substantial doubt on its reliability or if its admission is antithetical to, and would seriously damage, the integrity of the proceedings."[10] According to the ICTY Trial Chamber in *Brdjanin*, when deciding on the exclusion of evidence, "the correct balance must be maintained between the fundamental rights of the accused and the **[page 4]** essential interests of the international community in the prosecution of persons charged with serious violations of international humanitarian law."[11]

Joseph Nzirorera's interview

5. The Defence for Nzirorera, while admitting that the interview otherwise would be of relevance and probative value and need not be authenticated by a witness, submits that the Motion be denied[12] because Joseph Nzirorera's rights were violated in relation to (i) his arrest without a warrant, (ii) the failure to inform him of the reasons for his arrest, (iii) the failure to promptly bring him before a Judge, (iv) the failure to promptly inventory and return his seized property, (v) the failure to record the complete interview with him, and (vi) the failure to respect his rights to silence and to legal assistance.[13]

i) *The Arrest*

6. The Chamber recalls that Trial Chamber II has previously found that the arrest of Joseph Nzirorera had been made on the basis of a case of urgency pursuant to Rule 40 and that the Appeals Chamber confirmed that decision.[14]

7. However, the Defence for Nzirorera disputes that the condition of urgency for his arrest was met.[15] It argues, moreover, that Trial Chamber II's findings have implicitly been overruled by the Appeals Chamber when addressing a similar issue in the *Kalijejeli* Appeals judgement.[16]

8. The Chamber is not satisfied that the Defence for Nzirorera has shown that the exceptional remedy of reconsideration is appropriate in the circumstance and will therefore not revisit the issue. **[page 5]**

(ii) The right to be informed of the reasons for the arrest

9. The Statute prescribes in Article 19(2) that "[a] person against whom an indictment has been confirmed shall ..... be taken into custody, [and be] immediately informed of the charges against him" and in Article 20(4)(a) that the Accused shall be entitled "[t]o be informed promptly and in detail ... of the charge against him or her."

---

9 *See Karemera et al.*, Case No. ICTR-98-44-T, Decision on Defence Oral Motions for Exclusion of XBM's Testimony, for Sanctions Against the Prosecution and for Exclusion of Evidence Outside the Scope of the Indictment (TC), 19 October 2006, para. 29.

10 *See Bagosora et al.*, Decision on the Prosecutor's Motion for the Admission of Certain Materials Under Rule 89 (C) (TC), 14 October 2004, para 21 ("*Bagosora* Decision on the Admission of Certain Materials"); *Prosecutor v. Zigiranyirazo*, Case No. ICTR-2001-73-T, Decision on the Voir Dire Hearing of the Accused's Curriculum Vitae (TC), 29 November 2006, para. 13.

11 *Prosecutor v. Brdjanin*, Case No. IT-99-36-T, Decision on the Defence "Objection to Intercept Evidence" (TC), 3 October 2003, para 62.

12 Rule 95 reads as follows: "No evidence shall be admissible if obtained by methods which cast substantial doubt upon its reliability or if its admission is antithetical to, and would seriously damage, the integrity of the proceedings."

13 Nzirorera's Response, para. 89.

14 *Prosecutor v. Mathieu Ngirumpatse*, Case No. ICTR-97-44-I, Decision on the Defense Motion Challenging the Lawfulness of the Arrest and Detention and Seeking Return or Inspection of Seized Items (TC), 10 December 1999; *Prosecutor v. Joseph Nzirorera*, Case No. ICTR-98-44-T, Decision on the Defence Motion Challenging the Legality of the Arrest and Detention of the Accused and Requesting the Return of Personal Items Seized (TC), 11 September 2000, para. 25-26 ("*Nzirorera* Trial Chamber Arrest Decision"); *Prosecutor v. Joseph Nzirorera*, Case No. ICTR-98-44-A, Arrêt (Relatif à l'appel interlocutoire de la décision de la Chambre de première instance II du 11 septembre 2000) (AC), 4 May 2001, paras. 12-14 ("*Nzirorera* Appeals Chamber Arrest Decision").

15 Nzirorera's Response, para. 46.

16 Nzirorera's Response, para. 49; *Prosecutor v. Kajelijeli*, Case No. ICTR-98-44A-A, Judgement, 23 May 2005; *Nzirorera* Trial Chamber Arrest Decision, para. 27.

10. In his Motion, the Prosecutor asserts that the OTP investigators complied with the "Rules", in particular Rules 42 and 43, but does not comment on the provisions of the Statute.[17] Nor in his Consolidated Reply does he comment on the contention by the Defence for Nzirorera that the requirement of Article 19(2) has not been met.

11. The Chamber notes that Joseph Nzirorera was arrested by the Benin authorities on 5 June 1998 and was interrogated by the OTP investigators on 12 and 13 June 1998. In its decision, Trial Chamber II did not address whether the accused had been promptly informed of the charges against him and limited itself to finding that "the current detention of the Accused did not violate the provisions of the Statute and the Rules."[18]

12. The Chamber further notes that the interview transcript indicates that, at the time of his interview, Joseph Nzirorera did not know of the charges against him, and that the investigators did not provide him with information as to why he was considered a suspect and as to any provisional charges against him.[19] The Chamber notes also that Joseph Nzirorera seemed to indicate in his interview that he was uncertain as to whether he was being charged at all.[20]

13. Therefore, the Chamber is of the view that the Prosecutor has not established that Joseph Nzirorera was informed about the charges or provisional charges against him or the nature and the cause thereof, be it promptly in connection with his arrest or at least before or during the interview sought to be admitted into evidence. **[page 6]**

(iii) The right to be promptly brought before a Judge

14. The Appeals Chamber in the *Kajelijeli* Appeals Judgement discussed the right of a suspect to be promptly brought before a Judge following his or her arrest. It stated as follows:

> (...) Article 9 of the ICCPR provides that upon arrest and provisional detention, everyone has the right to be brought promptly before a Judge or official authorized to exercise judicial power.[21] The Human Rights Committee has interpreted Article 9 to mean that any delay in being brought before a Judge should not exceed a few days.[22] The Human Rights Committee has decided that under this article, four-days' delay is too long,[23] let alone lapses of 11 days, 22 days, or ten weeks.[24] Article 5(3) of the ECHR also requires that the suspect be brought promptly before a Judge or officer able to exercise judicial power upon arrest. The European Court of Human Rights has specified that two days' delay under this article is permissible;[25] however, four days and six hours constitute a violation even in complex cases, let alone one week or longer.[26]

---

17 Prosecutor's Motion, para. 22.

18 *Nzirorera* Trial Chamber Arrest Decision, para. 28.

19 In the following exchange, Joseph Nzirorera asked the OTP interrogator of the charges against him and the OTP interrogated simply responded that there was no official indictment:

> J. (...) For as I told you, this interview, I would like to know the charges against me.
>
> R. We...to also explain to you that there have not been any official indictments. You are being reminded of Article 40, that is, the arrest warrant, that there is no official indictment.

Transcript of Interview with Joseph Nzirorera, part 4, p. 27.

20 See in the following passage:

> J. (...) I was saying that it is against this background that I would like to tell you that...if charges are being brought against me, or will be brought against me regarding the massacres which took place in Rwanda, regarding the misfortune, the misfortune which befell our country, that I personally, my position, had nothing to do with it.

Transcript of Interview with Joseph Nzirorera, part 4, p. 29-30.

21 Article 9(3) of the ICCPR states that "[a]nyone arrested or detained on a criminal charge shall be brought promptly before a judge or other officer authorized by law to exercise judicial power and shall be entitled to trial within a reasonable time or to release...." *See also* ACHR, art. 7(5).

22 *See* U.N. Human Rights Committee, General Comment No. 8, para. 2.

23 *Michael Freemantle v. Jamaica*, CCPR/C/68/D/625/1995, 28 April 2000, para. 7.4.

24 *Dennis Lobban v. Jamaica*, CCPR/C/80/D/797/1998, 13 May 2004, para. 8.3; *Ricardo Ernesto Gomez Casafranca v. Peru*, CCPR/C/78/D/981/2001, 19 September 2003para. 7.2; *Jones v. Jamaica*, para. 9.3.

25 *Arminas Graužinis v. Lithuania*, 37975/97, 10 October 2000, para. 25.

26 *Terence Brogan and Others v. The United Kingdom, 10/1987/133/184-187,* 29 November 1988, paras. 6 and 62; *Talat Tepe v. Turkey,* 31247/96, 21 December 2004, paras. 64-70; *Abdullah Öcalan v. Turkey*, 46221/99, 12 March 2003, para. 106.

15. It further held that.

> The request to the authorities of the cooperating State has to include a notification to the judiciary, or at least, by way of the Tribunal's primacy, a clause reminding the national authorities to promptly bring the suspect before a domestic Judge in order to ensure that the apprehended person's rights are safeguarded by a Judge of the requested State as outlined above. In addition, the Prosecution must notify the Tribunal in order to enable a Judge to furnish the cooperating State with a provisional arrest warrant and transfer order.[27]

16. The Defence for Nzirorera asserts that Joseph Nzirorera's right to be promptly brought before a Judge was not respected.[28] It moreover submits that had it been the case, he or his family may well have contacted a lawyer to advise him on the necessity and wisdom of consenting to an interview with OTP.[29]

17. The Chamber notes that Joseph Nzirorera was not brought before a judge before being transferred from Benin and thus not before the OTP interview. However, the Chamber is not satisfied that this fact in itself – had all his other due process rights been respected – would make the interview inadmissible pursuant to Rule 95. **[page 7]**

(iv) The Inventory and Return of Seized Property

18. Counsel for Nzirorera submits that the Prosecutor did not comply with Rule 41(B) which provides that "[t]he Prosecutor shall draw up an inventory of all materials seized from the accused, ..." and that "[m] aterials that are of no evidentiary value shall be returned without delay to the accused."

19. The Chamber finds that this issue is not sufficiently related to the evidence sought to be admitted so as it makes this evidence inadmissible pursuant to Rule 95.

(v) The full recording of the interview

20. Rule 43 provides that whenever the Prosecutor questions a suspect, the questioning shall be audio recorded or video recorded according to a certain procedure.

21. The Defence for Nzirorera submits that the requirement to audio-record or video record the questioning, contained in Rule 43, was not fully respected during the interview on 12 June 1998.[30] He refers to a number of references in the transcripts of the interview which would demonstrate that the OTP investigators had had a substantive discussion with Joseph Nzirorera concerning his rights and the charges brought against him before the recording began.[31] Accordingly, the Defence requests that, *before admitting the statement into evidence*, the Chamber holds an evidentiary hearing on the contents of the discussions between the OTP and Joseph Nzirorera which took place before the recording began and on their effect on Joseph Nzirorera's decision to participate in the interview.[32]

22. The Chamber notes that the transcripts do seem to indicate that some discussions between the OTP investigators and Joseph Nzirorera took place before the audio recording of his interview began. As to whether what was said during the discussions would make the interview inadmissible pursuant to Rule 95, the Chamber finds that this would require an evidentiary hearing as requested by the Defence. However, since the Chamber will find the interview inadmissible on other grounds, it does not find necessary to conduct an evidentiary hearing and will therefore not address the issue here. **[page 8]**

(vi) The rights to silence and assistance of counsel

23. Article 17(3) of the Statute and Rules 42(A)(i), 42(A)(ii) and 42(B)[33] entitle a suspect with the right to legal assistance and translation during questioning and provide in particular that questioning shall not

27 *Ibid.*, para. 222.
28 Nzirorera's Response, para. 58.
29 Nzirorera's Response, para. 63.
30 Nzirorera's Response, para. 67.
31 *Ibid.*, paras. 67-70 (referring to Transcript of interview tape # 1, p. 1, 3, 6 and 12; Transcript of interview tape # 4, p. 27).
32 Nzirorera's Response, paras. 71-72.
33 Article 17(3) reads as follows: "If questioned, the suspect shall be entitled to be assisted by Counsel of his or her own choice, including the right to have legal assistance assigned to the suspect without payment by him or her in any such case if he or she does

proceed without the presence of counsel, unless the suspect has voluntarily waived his right to counsel. Rule 42(a)(iii) entitles a suspect with the right to silence and to be cautioned that any statement may be used as evidence against him or her.[34]

24. The Trial Chamber in *Bagosora* discussed the right to legal assistance at length:

> 16. Article 17 of the Statute and Rule 42 of the Rules state in unconditional terms that a detainee has a right to the immediate assistance of counsel; and, further, that questioning of the suspect "shall not proceed without the presence of counsel unless the suspect has voluntarily waived his right to counsel". Not all legal systems confer this right on a detainee, but it is deeply and eloquently inscribed in the annals of many national and international legal systems. Along with the right to silence, this right is rooted in the concern that an individual, when detained by officials for interrogation, is often fearful, ignorant and vulnerable; that fear and ignorance can lead to false confessions by the innocent; and that vulnerability can lead to abuse of the innocent and guilty alike, particularly when a suspect is held incommunicado and in isolation.
>
> 17. The importance of the right to counsel, and the precariousness of its exercise by a suspect in detention, is reflected in the stringent requirement in Rule 42 (B) that a suspect has "voluntarily waived his right to counsel" before a custodial interrogation can take place. (...) National courts in which the right to counsel is recognized have elaborated that a waiver cannot be voluntary unless a detainee knows of the right to which he is entitled. To be so informed, the suspect must be informed that the right includes the right to the prompt assistance of counsel, prior to and during any questioning. Any implication that the right is conditional, or that the presence of counsel may be delayed until after the questioning, renders any waiver defective. These rights, and the practical mechanisms for their exercise, must be communicated in a manner that is reasonably understandable to the detainee, and not "simply by some incantation which a detainee may not understand". Generally, a suspect may be taken to comprehend what a reasonable person would understand; but where there are indications that a witness is confused, steps must be taken to ensure that the suspect does actually understand the nature of his or her rights.
>
> 18. Once the detainee has been fully apprised of his right to the assistance of counsel, he or she is in a position to voluntarily waive the right. The waiver must be shown "convincingly **[page 9]** and beyond reasonable doubt". It must be express and unequivocal, and must clearly relate to the interview in which the statement in question is taken.[35]

25. The Chamber recalls that,as stated by the ICTY Chamber in *Delalic*, it is difficult to imagine a statement taken in violation of the fundamental right to the assistance of counsel which would not require its exclusion under Rule 95 as being "antithetical to, and would seriously damage, the integrity of the proceedings".[36]

26. The Prosecutor asserts, in the present case, that Joseph Nzirorera waived his rights in an "express and unequivocal" manner during the interview[37] and in response to questions put to him by the Trial Chamber when he was asked about the voluntary nature of his statements during a court hearing on 16 July 1998.[38] At that time, Nzirorera indicated that, when he was arrested and detained, his rights had been read to him, and that he understood them.[39]

---

not have sufficient means to pay for it, as well as necessary translation into and from a language he or she speaks and understands." Rules 42(A)(i) and (ii)read as follows: "(A) A suspect who is to be questioned by the Prosecutor shall have the following rights, of which he shall be informed by the Prosecutor prior to questioning, in a language he speaks and understands: (i) The right to be assisted by counsel of his choice or to have legal assistance assigned to him without payment if he does not have sufficient means to pay for it; (ii) The right to have the free assistance of an interpreter if he cannot understand or speak the language to be used for questioning". Rule 42(B) reads as follows: "(A) Questioning of a suspect shall not proceed without the presence of counsel unless the suspect has voluntarily waived his right to counsel. In case of waiver, if the suspect subsequently expresses a desire to have counsel, questioning shall thereupon cease, and shall only resume when the suspect has obtained or has been assigned counsel."

34 Rule 42(A)(iii) reads as follows: "(A) A suspect who is to be questioned by the Prosecutor shall have the following rights, of which he shall be informed by the Prosecutor prior to questioning, in a language he speaks and understands: (...) (iii) The right to remain silent, and to be cautioned that any statement he makes shall be recorded and may be used in evidence."

35 *Bagosora et al.*, Case No. ICTR-98-41-T, Decision on the Prosecutor's Motion for the Admission of Certain Materials Under Rule 89 (C) (TC), 14 October 2004, paras. 16-18.

36 *Prosecutor v. Delalic et al.*, Decision on Zdravko Mucic's Motion For the Exclusion of Evidence (TC), 2 September 1997, para. 43; Prosecutor v. Bagosora et al., Case No. ICTR-98-41-T, Decision on the Prosecutor's Motion for the Admission of certain Materials Under Rule 89 (C) (TC), 14 October 2004, para. 21.

37 *See* Waiver dated 12 June 1998-06, Avis des droits-Nzirorera-K0054180 and waiver dated on 13 June 1998 K0054179; Transcription 12 June 1998 p. 1-11; *see also Prosecutor v. Bagosora*, Transcript of 12 June 2006, p.31 (cross examination witness Nzirorera); Prosecutor Consolidated Reply, para. 23.

38 Transcript of 16 July 1998 before Judge Kama, p. 4.

39 *Ibid.*

27. The Chamber notes that the beginning of the interview indicates that Joseph Nzirorera was somewhat confused as to the conditions for the exercise of his rights to counsel and to silence, although he did ultimately state that he understood the content and scope of these rights.[40] The Chamber notes that, at the beginning of the interview, he specifically stated that he would like to conduct the interview in the presence of counsel, and that the OTP investigator, instead of putting an end to the interview at this point as mandated by Rule 42(B), sought instead Joseph Nzirorera's agreement to waive his rights to counsel and silence in respect of non-"tendentious" or "delicate" questions.[41] **[page 10]**

28. The Chamber further notes that on two other instances, Joseph Nzirorera refused to answer specific questions in the absence of counsel.[42] Contrary to their arrangement and to what is required by Rule 42(B), the investigator again proceeded to question Nzirorera in relation these specific issues.[43]

29. The Chamber also finds that, towards the end of the interview, Joseph Nzirorera expressed again his desire to meet with counsel. The OTP investigator sought clarification as to whether this affected Nzirorera's previous waiver of counsel.[44]

30. Moreover, the Chamber finds that the existing doubt as to whether Joseph Nzirorera had any knowledge of the charges or provisional charges against him or any related information as to why he was considered a suspect by the OTP, also entails substantial doubt as to whether he was in an informed position to waive his right to counsel or to answer questions put to him during this interview.[45] **[page 11]**

---

40 Transcript of Interview with Joseph Nzirorera, part 1, p. 1-5, 6, 7, 10 and 13.

41 See below the passage of the interview:

> J. In fact, you have to understand what I mean. I would like to go into the subject with full details, in the presence of my counsel as I mentioned. There are things that you told me yourself might be repeated in two years...
> R. Yeah
> J. ....in three years time. Thus I am telling you that this is a delicate matter. I would have liked to speak in detail about this subject in the presence of counsel.
> R. Okay
> J. These are things that you told me that...if we say certain things, we have to be in a position to repeat them in in two, three years.
> R. Yeah
> J. Thus if I tell you this is a delicate matter, I would prefer to go into all the details with a lawyer.
> R. Okay. That is why...
> J. I do not want to venture alone
> L. Okay
> J. ...into an arena where I do not know the dangers.
> R. Okay. I understand. That is why we have told you that if you feel that one of the questions that I have asked you deals with a tendentious subject or a delicate matter, as you have said, you don't have to answer. You simply state: "I would rather wait to have counsel present to answer that question." Okay? That's it.
> J. That's clear

Transcript of Interview with Joseph Nzirorera, part 1, p. 14.

42 First of all, when questioned on the massacre of the Bagogwe, Transcript of Interview with Joseph Nzirorera, part 2, p. 19. Second of all, when questioned on the murder of members of the government on the night of 6 April 1994, Transcript of Interview with Joseph Nzirorera, part 4, p. 27.

43 Transcript of Interview with Joseph Nzirorera, part 4, p. 27-28.

44 *See* passage below:

> J. (...) I am available at any time to answer any question. Also, as I told you, from...at some point, I had asked you to help me get a lawyer. As I told you, the sensitive nature of the matter is such that as we are not lawyers, I would need the services of a lawyer...to follow-up and assist me and if you get one, you shall bear the cost....of his defending me. Um...
> R. Okay. In order to clarity one point, we shall agree (inaudible) for the questions, for example which we asked today or yesterday, are there questions you would not want to answer without your lawyer?
> J. Um...
> R. ...it is (inaudible) no about what we have just done here. You could have done that, you know I, you have the right to a lawyer, but you decided...
> J. Not....I am aware of that and I signed, I agree with you.
> R. Perfect. Okay, we agree on that?
> J. Ok...

Transcript of Interview with Joseph Nzirorera, part 4, p. 29.

45 In particular, there are certain types of matters which Joseph Nzirorera might not have discussed had he been informed of the provisional charges against him or the information tending to show that he was guilty of a crime within the Tribunal's jurisdiction.

31. Therefore, the Chamber finds that the Prosecutor has not established beyond reasonable doubt that Joseph Nzirorera waived his right to be silent and to be assisted by counsel in an express and unequivocal manner.

Conclusion

32. Based on the foregoing, the Chamber concludes that there is substantial doubt as to the reliability of the interview and that its admission into evidence would be antithetical to and seriously damage the integrity of proceeding, wherefore pursuant to Rule 95, the interview is not admissible.

Mathieu Ngirumpatse's interview

33. The Defence for Ngirumpatse opposes the admission of his interview, submitting (i) that the recordings and hence the transcripts are not reliable, because it appears from the transcripts that the recordings are of extremely poor quality, and because the recordings might have been tampered with, having been in the possession of the Prosecutor for 10 years before the Defence got access to them, (ii) that the Prosecutor has not established the relevance and probative value of the interview, as no foundation has been laid through the testimony of a witness, and as the previous statement of a person who is not a witness before this Chamber is without relevance and purpose, (iii) that Mathieu Ngirumpatse was not informed about the charges against him and was misled into believing that an indictment was in existence, which was not the case, and (iv) that he was ill, in a state of stress as a result of his detention and subject to pressure by investigators, which amounts to threats or coercions and makes the interview inadmissible.[46]

34. The Defence for Nzirorera, joined by the Defence for Karemera and the Defence for Ngirumpatse, further submits, (v) that since parts of Mathieu Ngirumpatse's interview concern the acts of the co-accused, its admission would violate their right pursuant to Article 20(4)(e) of the Statute to cross-examine Mathieu Ngirumpatse, should he decide not to testify in his defence.[47] **[page 12]**

(i) Reliability

35. The Defence for Ngirumpatse requests the Chamber to compare the audio recordings with the transcripts thereof in the determination of the reliability of the transcripts.[48]

36. The Chamber, however, opines that it is for the Defence to substantiate and specify his objections to the transcripts. The Chamber will therefore rely on the transcripts and notes that the recordings seem to be of a poor quality and that a number of passages seem to be incomprehensible.[49] However, this does not in itself render the entire recordings and the transcripts thereof unreliable, but rather constitute an important factor in the assessment of the weight to be given to this evidence.

37. As to the authenticity of the recordings, the Defence's allegation that the recordings might have been tampered with is only substantiated by a reference to other recordings, not originating from OTP,[50] although

---

This is certainly the case in relation to the extended forms of criminal responsibility with which he is charged. During the interview, Nzirorera most notably discussed his meetings and contact with Robert Kajuga (the national president of the Interahamwe and an alleged member of the joint criminal enterprise) and the civil defence programme, military training and weapons distribution, Transcript of Interview with Joseph Nzirorera, part 3, p. 11-12 and 20-22. Nzirorera's lack of awareness of the type of responsibility with which he might be charged comes through most clearly in the following passage, which discusses links between the MRND and the Interahamwe and where the OTP investigator tried to reassure Nzirorera that the information discussed was innocuous:

> R. So there were contacts between the MRND officials and those of the Interahamwe?
> J. Even among the other parties, there were contacts.
> R. Yes. There was absolutely nothing wrong with that.
> J. It's only logical.

Transcript of Interview with Joseph Nzirorera, part 2, p. 46.

46 Ngirumpatse's Reponse, para. 5.

47 Nzirorera's Response, para. 95-96; Karemera's Response, p. 9; Ngirumpatse's Response, para. 5.

48 Ngirumpatse's Response, para. 5 e)b-c-d.

49 As detailed in Ngirumpatse's Response, para. 5. g).

50 Ngirumpatse's Response, para.5 e).

Mathieu Ngirumpatse, as the one having been interviewed, should be in a position to provide the Defence with specifications to substantiate the allegation. Moreover, the Chamber notes that the recordings were made by OTP investigators and have been in the possession of OTP since they were made. It further notes that the Defence does not dispute that it is indeed Mathieu Ngirumpatse's voice which can be heard on the recordings, neither does it dispute the Prosecutor's contention that the audio-tapes of the interview were sealed in Mathieu Ngirumpatse's presence and that he signed a receipt to that effect.

38. The Chamber is therefore satisfied that the Prosecutor has made a *prima facie* showing of the reliability and authenticity of the recordings.

(ii) Relevance and probative value

38. The Chamber recalls that, according to the jurisprudence of the *ad hoc* tribunals, evidence need not be tendered through a witness in order to establish its relevance and probative value and that there are no impediments *per se* to admit previous statements of an accused into evidence.[51] **[page 13]**

39. The Chamber further notes that the interview provides information on the general background of, and to some extent directly on, facts pleaded in the Indictment. The Chamber is therefore satisfied that the Prosecutor has made a *prima facie* showing of relevance and probative value.

(iii) The right to be promptly informed about the charges

40. In his Motion, the Prosecutor asserts that the OTP investigators complied with the "Rules", in particular Rules 42 and 43, but does not comment on Articles 19 and 20 of the Statute. Nor in his Consolidated Reply does he comment on the contention by Counsel that Mathieu Ngirumpatse was not informed about the charges against him.

41. The Chamber notes that the transcripts of Mathieu Ngirumpatse show that, at the begining of the interview, he had been informed by the OTP investigator of his right to be assisted by counsel, to free assistance of an interpreter, and to remain silent. He was also informed that the interview was being recorded and might be used as evidence, and that he could stop the interview at any time and request the service of counsel. The transcript further shows that Mathieu Ngirumpatse explicitly waived his rights, agreeing to be interviewed for the time being without the assistance of counsel, stating that he would engage counsel when he would be transfered to Arusha. The transcripts also shows that in several instances he declined to answer questions or to elaborate on an answer on the ground that he wanted to discuss the matter with his counsel before answering further. The Chamber finds no indication that he was informed about the charges against him or the nature and cause thereof.

42. The Chamber therefore finds that there is a substantive doubt as to whether Mathieu Ngirumpatse's was informed in detail of the nature and cause of the charges against him, according to Article 20(4)(a) of the Statute, be it promptly, before or during the interview. Moreover, the Chamber opines that this fact may likely have influenced Mathieu Ngirumpatse's decision on whether to consent to be interviewed at all or on which questions to answer without the assistance of counsel. Noting that Mathieu Ngirumpatse could not have known or foreseen that he, at a later stage, would be held liable under the extended form of being a participant in a joint criminal enterprise, the Chamber further holds that this fact, although it cannot be attributed to the Prosecution as a failure at the time to respect his due process rights, is a factor to take into consideration when deciding whether the admission of the interview would be consistent with the right of the accused to a fair trial. **[page 14]**

---

[51] *Prosecutor v. Bagosora et al.*, Case No. ICTR-98-41-T, Decision on Request to Admit United Nations Documents into Evidence under Rule 89(C) (TC), 25 May 2006, para. 4; *Prosecutor v. Tihomir Blaskic*, Case No. IT-95-14-T, Judgement (TC), 3 March 2000, para. 35; *Prosecutor v. Kvočka et al.*, Decision on Zoran Zigic's Motion For Rescinding Confidentiality of Schedules Attached to the Indictment Decision On Exhibits (TC), 19 July 2001; *Prosecutor v. Prlic et al.*, IT-04-74-PT, Revised Version of the Decision Adopting Guidelines on Conduct of Trial Proceedings (TC), 28 April 2006; *Prosecutor v. Prlic et al.*, IT-04-74-T, Decision on Admission of Evidence (TC), 13 July 2006.

(iv) Threats or coercion

43. The Chamber notes that the Defence did not attempt to substantiate the allegation that the interview took place under circumstances that would amount to threats or coercion and that the transcripts show no sign thereof. The submission is therefore rejected.

(v) The rights of the co-accused to cross-examination

44. The Prosecutor submits that the admission of the transcripts will not infringe the rights of the co-accused.[52] To support its assertion, it argues that the accused have not articulated inconsistent defenses since, as defense witnesses in other ICTR cases, they have repeated bits and pieces of the same information they provided in the interviews sought to be admitted. Moreover, it submits that this Chamber has already admitted statements from the accused in the form of trial transcripts in other cases.[53] The Prosecutor alleges that the admission of transcripts from OTP interviews would be no different. It argues further that, to the extent that any of the accused can establish that they were unable to confront any one among them during the defense phase of the trial, the current objection can be renewed at the conclusion of the trial and this Chamber can take appropriate steps to afford a remedy.[54]

45. The Chamber notes that the transcripts indeed show that Mathieu Ngirumpatse gave information about the co-accused, in particular about the power struggle between Joseph Nzirorera and himself and that it seems unlikely that Joseph Nzirorera would fully agree on his version of events.

46. The Chamber therefore holds that it would be antithetical to the integrity of the proceedings to admit into evidence those parts of the interview with Mathieu Ngirumpatse that concerns the co-accused before Mathieu Ngirumpatse has indicated a decision to testify in his own defence.

Conclusion

47. Based on the reasons stated under (iii) the Chamber, pursuant to Rule 95, finds that it will be antithetical to the integrity of the proceedings and the right of the accused to a fair trial to admit into evidence any part of the audio recordings and the transcripts thereof of the interview with Mathieu Ngirumpatse. **[page 15]**

FOR THOSE REASONS, THE CHAMBER

DENIES the Prosecutor's Motion for Admission of Certain Materials under Rule 89 (C) as to Annex C.

Arusha, 2 November 2007, done in English.

Dennis C. M. Byron Presiding Judge	Gberdao Gustave Kam Judge	Vagn Joensen Judge

[Seal of the Tribunal]

---

52 Prosecutor's Consolidated Reply, para. 27.

53 Prosecutor's Consolidated Reply, para. 27, citing the following exhibits: P-051; P-061; P-62; P-069; P-070, which are trial transcripts from each of the accused from the testimonies that they have offered as defense witnesses in other cases.

54 *Ibid*, para. 27.

International Criminal Tribunal for Rwanda
Tribunal pénal international pour le Rwanda

OR: ENG

TRIAL CHAMBER III

Before Judges: Dennis C. M. Byron, Presiding
Gberdao Gustave Kam
Vagn Joensen

Registrar: Adama Dieng

Date: 16 November 2007

THE PROSECUTOR

v.

Édouard KAREMERA
Mathieu NGIRUMPATSE
Joseph Nzirorera

Case No. ICTR-98-44-T

DECISION ON PROSECUTION MOTION FOR RECONSIDERATION OF THE DECISION ON PROSPECTIVE EXPERTS GUICHAOUA, NOWROJEE AND DES FORGES, OR FOR CERTIFICATION

Rule 73(B)*bis *of the Rules of Procedure and Evidence

Office of the Prosecutor:
Don Webster
Alayne Frankson-Wallace
Iain Morley
Saidou N'Dow
Gerda Visser
Sunkarie Ballah-Conteh
Takeh Sendze
Deo Mbuto

Defence Counsel for Édouard Karemera
Dior Diagne Mbaye and Félix Sow

Defence Counsel for Mathieu Ngirumpatse
Chantal Hounkpatin and Frédéric Weyl

Defence Counsel for Joseph Nzirorera
Peter Robinson and Patrick Nimy Mayidika Ngimbi

[page 2] INTRODUCTION

1. On 25 October 2007, the Chamber decided that whilst Alison Des Forges, André Guichaoua and Binaifer Nowrojee may be in possession of relevant specialised knowledge in a particular field, their assistance was not necessary for the Chamber to appreciate and evaluate the factual issues on the trial record.[1] Consequently, the Chamber precluded the admission of their evidence as expert witnesses.

2. On 1 November 2007, the Prosecution moved the Chamber to reconsider or, alternatively, grant certification for interlocutory appeal of the Decision of 25 October 2007 ("Impugned Decision").[2] In his response, Joseph Nzirorera opposes the Prosecution's application for reconsideration, but supports the certification to appeal.[3] The Chamber notes that Édouard Karemera and Mathieu Ngirumpatse have not filed any response.

DISCUSSIONS

On the Prosecutor's application for Reconsideration

3. According to the established jurisprudence of the Tribunal, a Chamber has the inherent power to reconsider its decisions. In order for a motion for reconsideration to succeed, the moving party must demonstrate that (i) a new fact has been discovered that was not known to the Chamber at the time it made its original Decision; (ii) there has been a material change in circumstances since it made its original Decision; or (iii) there is reason to believe that its original Decision was erroneous or constituted an abuse of power on the part of the Chamber, resulting in an injustice thereby warranting the exceptional remedy of reconsideration.[4] **[page 3]**

4. The Prosecution proposes that the Chamber maintain the Impugned Decision to exclude the written reports of the proposed experts, given the excessive breadth of their scope, but that the Chamber exercise its discretion to permit Alison Des Forges to testify orally on a limited number of issues during this sixth trial session.[5] The Prosecution further requests that the Chamber reconsiders the possibility of scheduling additional hearings so that André Guichaoua could also testify orally.[6]

---

1 *Karemera et al.*, Decision on Prosecution Prospective Experts Witnesses Alison Des Forges, Andre Guichaoua and Binaifer Nowrojee – Rules 89 and 94bis of the Rules of Procedure and Evidence, filed on 25 October 2007 ("Impugned Decision")

2 Prosecutor's Motion for Reconsideration of Trial Chamber III Decision of 25 October 2007 to Exclude Expert Witnesses, *or alternatively,* Motion for Certification for Interlocutory Appeal, filed on 1 November 2007

3 Joseph Nzirorera's Response to Prosecutor's Motion for Reconsideration of Trial Chamber III Decision of 25 October 2007 to Exclude Expert Witnesses, *or alternatively,* Motion for Certification for Interlocutory Appeal, filed on 6 November 2007; *see also* Prosecutor's Reply to Joseph Nzirorera's Response to Prosecution Motion for Reconsideration or Certification of Decision Excluding Testimony of Expert Witnesses, filed on 8 November 2007.

4 *Karemera et al*, Decision on the Defence Motion for Reconsideration of Sanctions Imposed in Decision on the Defence Request for Leave to Interview Potential Prosecution Witnesses Jean Kambanda, Georges Ruggiu, and Omar Serushago (TC), 10 October 2003 ("6. The Chamber considers that none of the reasons submitted in support of the Motion constitute special circumstances warranting a reconsideration of Order II of the Decision of 29 September 2003. The Chamber particularly emphasizes that the issue raised at paragraph 5(ii) above should have been brought to the Chamber's attention at the time of filing of the Motion dismissed in the Decision of 29 September 2003, as this was an issue that Counsel was aware of at the time."); *Karemera et al*, Decision on the Defence Motions for Reconsideration of Protective Measures for Prosecution Witnesses (TC), 29 August 2005 ("8. The Chamber notes its 'inherent power' to reconsider its own decision [...] [and] reminds itself that reconsideration is an exceptional measure available only in particular circumstances such as (i) when a new fact has been discovered that was not previously known to the Chamber, (ii) where new circumstances have arisen since the filing of the impugned decision that affect the premise of the impugned decision, or (iii) where a party shows an error of law or the Chamber abused its discretion, and an injustice has been occasioned."); *Karemera et al*, Decision on Joseph Nzirorera's Motion for Reconsideration or Certification to Appeal Decision on Motion for Order Allowing Meeting with Defence Witness (TC), 11 October 2005, par. 8; Decision on Reconsideration of Protective Measures for Prosecution Witnesses (TC), 30 October 2006, par. 2; Decision on Reconsideration of Admission of Written Statements in Lieu of Oral Testimony and Admission of the Testimony of Prosecution Witness GAY (TC), 28 September 2007, par. 10; Decision on Joseph Nzirorera's Motion for Reconsideration of Sanctions (TC), 3 October 2007, par. 5. The Appeals Chamber has also rendered decisions on reconsideration in this case: *The Prosecutor v. Edouard Karemera, Mathieu Ngirumpatse, Joseph Nzirorera*, Case No. ICTR-98-44-AR73(c), Decision on Motions for Reconsideration (AC), 1 December 2006 ("6. The Appeals Chamber may reconsider a previous interlocutory decision under its inherent discretionary power if a clear error of reasoning has been demonstrated or if it is necessary to prevent an injustice."); Case No. ICTR-98-44-AR11*bis*, Decision on Motion for Reconsideration of Decision on Joseph Nzirorera's Appeal from Denial of a Request for Designation of a Trial Chamber to Consider Referral to a National Jurisdiction (AC), 21 August 2007, p. 3; Case No. ICTR-98-44-AR73.10, Decision on Ngirumpatse's Motion for Reconsideration (AC), 5 October 2007, p. 3.

5 Prosecutor's Motion, para. 1.

6 *Ibidem.*

5. In support of its application, the Prosecution alleges that the Impugned Decision to preclude the testimony of André Guichaoua and Alison Des Forges was an abuse of discretionary power. It also contends and that there are new circumstances that render it necessary to reconsider the issue of admission of the evidence of these two expert witnesses. The Prosecution clearly accepts the exclusion of Nowrojee by not arguing for her testimony to be admitted or heard.

6. With regard to Alison Des Forges, the Prosecution asserts that her testimony will provide explanations that will enable the informed assessment of documents, speeches and the civil defence and pacification programmes which are the subject of competing characterisations. It concedes to the exclusion of her expert report and asks, instead, that the Chamber allow her oral testimony on a limited number of issues of grave importance, namely "social and historical context", "layered meaning of documents", and "analysis of the pattern, history and socially layered meanings of the 'civil self-defence' and 'pacification / restoring **[page 4]** security' campaigns". It argues that her expert analysis is necessary to enable judicial evaluation of the testimony of factual witnesses that were admitted on the record. It lists the evidence on which it wishes her to opine[7] and states that her analysis would evoke the contradictory nature of documentary evidence, yet reveal the probative elements that make them useful for establishing the allegations of the Indictment.[8]

7. With regard to André Guichaoua, the Prosecution submits that his oral testimony on specified issues should be allowed to introduce into evidence contemporaneously generated documents that he made available as annexes to his report. The Prosecution asserts that Guichaoua's analysis and cross-referencing of diaries and agenda of the Accused and other alleged co-conspirators and his analysis of documentation concerning the use of funds and resources from para-statal enterprises to finance the *Interahamwe* in Butare and other prefectures may assist in the Chamber in its assessment of evidence. The Prosecution further contends that various documents annexed to Guichaoua's report[9] are the *only* prosecution evidence that may be adduced to prove several specified paragraphs of the Indictment and that various paragraphs in the Pre-Trial Brief rely *substantially* on documentation to be presented and analysed by Guichaoua.[10]

8. The Prosecution further submits that Des Forges and Guichaoua's evidence is necessary in view of its compliance with the Chamber's insistence on reducing the number of factual witnesses while admitting defence exhibits during cross-examinations of Prosecution witnesses. The Prosecution contends that it was expected that the expert witnesses would have commented on those documents. **[page 5]**

9. The Prosecution also argues that its new request to adduce their oral testimony on limited relevant issues instead of introducing their full expert reports is a new circumstance which could justify reconsideration.

10. In relation to the interests of justice, the Prosecution contends that the Completion Strategy may have influenced the Chamber's Order, and suggests that Alison des Forges could be heard during the current session of the trial and Andre Guichaoua in the early part of 2008, thereby not causing undue delay.

11. The Chamber is of the view that the Prosecution fails to show any new fact or circumstance or error in law warranting reconsideration of the Impugned Decision.

---

7 The Prosecution requested that Alison Des Forces be allowed to testify as an expert so that she can opine on: 1) The ENI document (a memorandum on the definition of the enemy; disclosed in Tab 004 of the Prosecution Exhibit Bundle) that will be used to prove paragraph 25 of the indictment; 2) The memorandum on civil defense recovered from Prime Minister Jean Kambanda (disclosed in Tab 002 of the Prosecution Exhibit Bundle) that will be used to prove paragraph 26 of the indictment; 3) All documents listed in paragraph 28.3 of the indictment and "civil defense" documents generally; 4) Minutes of the 3 May 1994 "pacification" meeting in Kibuye and transcripts of speeches by authorities at that meeting in relation to paragraphs 33.1 and 52 of the indictment; 5) Speeches by the Accused during a MRND rally in Kigali on 16 January 1994, in relation to paragraph 31.1 of the indictment; 6) President Sindikubwabo's speech in Butare on 19 April 1994, in relation to paragraph 48 of the indictment; 7) Prime Minister Kambanda's Instructions on Restoring Security of 27 April 1994, in relation to paragraph 51 of the indictment; and, 8) Minister of Interior Edouard Karemera's memorandum on implementing the Prime Minister's Directives on Civil Defense of 25 May 1994, in relation to paragraph 57 of the indictment.

8 The Prosecution mentions paragraphs 25, 25.3, 26, 28, 28.1, 28.3, 32.4, 33.1, 33.2, 36, 43, 44, 45, 48, 50, 51, 53, 55, 56, 57, 60, 61, and 64.3 of the Indictment.

9 *See*, in particular, Annexes 16 – 28 concerning notes and memoranda of the Comité de crise prior to the formation of the Interim Government of 8 April 1994; Annex 42 concerning the MRND and its financing of the Interahawme in Butare by the para-statal enterprise SORWAL; and Annex 44, concerning the para-statal enterprise CIMERWA.

10 *See* Prosecutor's Motion, paras. 17 (b) that mentions paragraphs 28, 28.1, 32.4, 43, 45, 46, 50, 56, 60 and 61 of the Indictment; and, paragraphs 53, 54, 105, 115, 120, and 121 from the Pre-trial Brief.

12. When adjudicating on the Prosecutor's submissions for the admission of the evidence of Guichaoua and Des Forges as expert witnesses, the Chamber had considered the evidence adduced in the case thus far, including the exhibits, for which the Prosecution submitted the assistance of these experts was necessary for the Chamber in its analysis of the case. The Chamber also considered the documents annexed to Guichaoua's report. It did not find, however, that the assistance of the witnesses was necessary for the Chamber to analyse those documents.

13. The Chamber acknowledges that André Guichaoua and Alison Des Forges have likely been of value and assistance to the Prosecution in the development of its theories and the selection of evidentiary material to prove them. However, the fact that this assistance was provided to the Prosecution does not mean that the testimony of these experts is necessary for the Chamber in its analysis of this case.

14. The Chamber considers that an expert's testimony is intended to enlighten the Judges on specific issues of a technical nature, requiring special knowledge in a specific field;[11] however, the matters at stake in the present case are not those on which the Chamber requires expert assistance. As explained in details in the Impugned Decision, the Chamber considered that it was able to make its judgment without such assistance.

15. The Chamber considers that the Prosecution statement that the documentation annexed to André Guichaoua's report constitutes the only proof for some paragraphs of the Indictment is contrary to principle and inaccurate. **[page 6]**

16. The Chamber recalls the evidence already adduced to support allegations in the paragraphs of the Indictment for which the Prosecutor claims not to have evidence other than that of the prospective expert witnesses. Prosecution witnesses have testified to various events in the period 6 to 12 April 1994, including activities of the Accused and meetings in which they participated. This testimony addressed the allegations made in Paragraphs 28 and 28.1 of the Indictment. There was also testimony from Prosecution witnesses concerning activities of the Interim Government at Murambi in Gitarama as alleged in paragraphs in Paragraphs 43, 45, 46, 56 and 61 of the Indictment. Prosecution witnesses have testified about the fundraising meetings convened by Kabuga.[12] There has been evidence about meetings in Ruhengeri and the massacres in Bisesero.[13] Some of the documents to which reference was made are already in evidence and others are included in the documents the Prosecutor intends to produce through investigator Baghel.

17. Furthermore, the Prosecution's contention that the admission of Guichaoua's report or his oral testimony is necessary for the introduction of documentary evidence is flawed.

18. Under Rule 89 of the Rules of Procedure and Evidence ("Rules"), the Chamber is not bound by national rules of evidence and may, in cases not otherwise provided for in the Rules, apply rules of evidence which will best favour a fair determination of the matter before it and are consonant with the spirit of the Statute and the general principles of law. Trial Chambers of both *ad hoc* Tribunals have held that documents need not be recognised by a witness in order to have probative value.[14]

19. On prior decisions, the Chamber has applied those principles and admitted without any witness being heard.[15] In that Decision the Chamber applied Rule 89(C) of the Rules, which allows a Chamber to admit documents that are relevant and have probative value once sufficient indicia of reliability have been established. The Chamber remains satisfied that if any of these documents are admitted, it will be able to

11 Prosecutor v. Norman et al., Decision on Prosecution Request for Leave to call Additional Witnesses and for Orders for Protective Measures, Case No. SCSL-04-14-T, T.Ch. I, 21 June 2005, p. 4; Prosecutor v. Akayesu, Decision by a Defence Motion for the Appearance of an Accused as an Expert Witness, Case No. ICTR-96-04-T, Trial Chamber I, 9 March 1998, p. 2.

12 Indictment, para. 50

13 Indictment, para. 32.4

14 *Karemera et al.*,, Decision on the Prosecution Motion for Admission into Evidence of UNAMIR Documents (TC), 30 October 2007.

15 *Karemera et al.*,, Decision on the Prosecution Motion for Admission into Evidence of UNAMIR Documents (TC), 30 October 2007. *Prosecutor v. Bagosora et al.*, Case No. ICTR-98-41-T, Decision on Request to Admit United Nations Documents into Evidence under Rule 89(C) (TC), 25 May 2006, para. 4; *Prosecutor v. Tihomir Blaskic*, Case No. IT-95-14-T, Judgement (TC), 3 March 2000, para. 35; *Prosecutor v. Kvočka et al.*, Decision on Zoran Zigic's Motion For Rescinding Confidentiality of Schedules Attached to the Indictment Decision On Exhibits (TC), 19 July 2001; *Prosecutor v. Prlic et al.*, IT-04-74-PT, Revised Version of the Decision Adopting Guidelines on Conduct of Trial Proceedings (TC), 28 April 2006; *Prosecutor v. Prlic et al.*, IT-04-74-T, Decision on Admission of Evidence (TC), 13 July 2006.

comprehend them and their import **[page 7]** without the assistance of expert testimony. However, should there be any other documents which have no indicia of reliability that is independent from Guichaoua, then the Chamber could consider calling him for that limited purpose.

20. In its submissions, the Prosecution further suggests that the evidence of Alison De Forges is necessary to the extent that the testimony of factual witnesses heard thus far may require expert historical analysis to make a conceptual link to a Conspiracy to Commit Genocide that took form in mid-1992.[16]

21. The Chamber, however, recalls that the established jurisprudence of this Tribunal proscribes expert evidence from usurping the function of the Trial Chamber by offering opinions that are determinative of the guilt or innocence of the Accused or by adverting to the acts, conduct and mental state of the Accused.[17] Admitting the evidence of Des Forges, as suggested by the Prosecution, would be amount to usurping the functions of the Chamber in determining the guilt or not of the Accused.

22. While the Chamber has encouraged the Prosecution to streamline its case and call only witnesses necessary to prove its case, it was the Prosecution that exercised the discretion determining by itself who to call and why, in order to provide sufficient evidence to substantiate its claims. That the expert evidence was not necessary in the Chamber's view has been clearly explained, and the Prosecution has failed to persuade the Chamber that such view was abusive.

23. Contrary to the Prosecution's assertion, the Completion Strategy has not guided it in excluding the evidence of the proposed experts. This trial has come to a point where the Chamber has already heard the majority of the Prosecution evidence. The Chamber is therefore in the position to assess whether the prospective expert evidence could assist it in understanding the issues at stake.

24. In those circumstances, the Chamber is of view that the Prosecution has failed to establish that the Impugned Decision was erroneous and caused any injustice or prejudice to the Prosecution case. **[page 8]**

25. For the same reasons, the Chamber is not persuaded by Prosecution's argument that its change in its strategy – to limiting the scope of testimony of Alison Des Forges and André Guichaoua – amounts to a new fact or circumstance that would justify reconsideration of the Impugned Decision.

26. Reconsideration of the Impugned Decision is not warranted. The Chamber however recalls its prior Decision where it stated that "it will be open to the Chamber to call upon expert testimony if at any future time issues arise which require such assistance."[18]

27. The Chamber will consequently address the alternative Prosecution's request, for certification to appeal.

On the Prosecutor's Alternative Request for Certification to Appeal

28. Under Rule 73(B) of the Rules, a Trial Chamber may certify a decision on a motion for interlocutory appeal if, in its view, the decision (i) "involves an issue that would significantly affect the fair and expeditious conduct of the proceedings or the outcome of the trial" such that (ii) "immediate resolution by the Appeals Chamber may materially advance the proceedings". The Appeals Chamber has recognised that, as a corollary of its discretion concerning whether to certify an interlocutory appeal in the first place, a Trial Chamber also has the discretion to limit the scope of the interlocutory appeal to particular issues. The Trial Chamber's Certification therefore dictates the possible scope of the Appeals Chamber's Decision.[19]

---

16 Prosecution's Motio, para. 17 (h) at p. 6.

17 *Karemera et al.*, Decision on Joseph Nzirorera's Motion to Limit the Scope of the Testimony of Expert Witnesses Alison Des Forges and Andre Guichaoua, 21 August 2007, para. 3. *See also Karemera et al.*, Decision on Prosecution Prospective Experts Witnesses Alison Des Forges, Andre Guichaoua and Dinaifer Nowrojee Rules 89 and 94bis of the Rules of Procedure and Evidence, 25 October 2007. *See also Prosecutor* v. *Hadžihasanović and Kubura, Decision on Report of Prosecution Expert Klaus Reinhardt*, Case No. IT-01-47-T, T. Ch. II, 11 February 2004, p. 4.

18 Rules of Procedure and Evidence, Rule 98: "A Trial Chamber may *proprio motu* order either party to produce additional evidence. It may itself summon witnesses and order their attendance."

19 *See Karemera et al.,* Decision on Prosecutor's Interlocutory Appeal of Decision on Judicial Notice, 16 June 2006, para. 13. *See also Nyiramasuhuko v. Prosecutor*, Case No. ICTR-98-42-AR73, Decision on Pauline Nyiramasuhuko's Request for Reconsideration, 27 September 2004, para. 7.

29. The Prosecution submits that its request for certification to appeal the Chamber's Decision meets both criteria of Rule 73 (B). Regarding the first prong, it asserts that the Impugned Decision significantly affects the fair and expeditious conduct of the proceedings and may affect the outcome of the trial, since it significantly trimmed its original witness list, narrowed the scope of its examinations and consented to the admission of a significant number of Defence exhibits on the understanding that expert opinion evidence that would be offered towards the end of the Prosecution case would provide an opportunity to clarify matters on the trial record. It restates that the expert opinion evidence from all three witnesses is "particularly important" for making its case against the Accused for the crimes of **[page 9]** Conspiracy to Commit Genocide; Direct and Public Incitement to Genocide; and, Rape as a Crime Against Humanity.

30. With respect to the second prong, the Prosecution asserts that a decision from the Appeal Chamber may materially advance the proceedings by ensuring that any subsequent judgment on those three counts by this Trial Chamber will not be assailed on appeal.

31. Joseph Nzirorera does not oppose the Prosecution's alternative request for certification to appeal.[20]

32. The Chamber agrees that the Impugned Decision involves two important issues that may affect the fair and expeditious conduct of the proceedings or the outcome of the trial: (i) the right of a party to adduce what it considers as important evidence in a trial; and (ii) the Trial Chamber's power to control its own proceedings by limiting the appearances of witnesses before it. As such, this second issue is concerned with the very core of any judicial exercise, namely, the issue of judicial independence. Accordingly, the first prong of Rule 73 (B) is satisfied.

33. The Chamber is also satisfied that the second prong of Rule 73 (B) is met. In the Chamber's view, an immediate resolution by the Appeals Chamber on whether the Trial Chamber abused its discretionary power in denying the admission of the evidence of Des Forges and Guichaoua as experts may materially advance the proceedings. The Chamber notes the Appeals Chamber's jurisprudence according to which certification of an appeal has to be the absolute exception when deciding on the admissibility of the evidence, and that it is first and foremost the responsibility of the Trial Chamber, as *trier* of fact, to determine which evidence to admit during the course of the trial.[21] However, in view of the broad scope of the issues concerned by the Impugned Decision and considering the advanced stage of the proceedings, leaving this matter to be resolved in later appeal creates the risk of unnecessarily complicating and delaying the proceedings, all of which could be avoided by having the matter resolved at this stage.[22]

34. In view of these circumstances, the Chamber considers it appropriate to grant certification to appeal to the Decision of 25 October 2007 limiting it only to the matters **[page 10]** related to the exclusion of André Guichaoua and Alison des Forges in the terms referenced on the request for reconsideration.

FOR THESE REASONS, THE CHAMBER

I. DENIES the request for reconsideration;

II. GRANTS the Prosecution's motion for certification to the extent stated in paragraph 34.

Arusha, 16 November 2007, done in English.

Dennis C. M. Byron	Gberdao Gustave Kam	Vagn Joensen
Presiding Judge	Judge	Judge

[Seal of the Tribunal]

20 Nzirorera's Response, at paras. 11 – 13

21 *Nyiramasuhuko et al.*, Decision on Pauline Nyiramasuhuko's Request for Reconsideration (AC), 27 September 2004, para. 10 ("certification of an appeal has to be the absolute exception when deciding on the admissibility of the evidence").

22 Prosecutor v. Milutinović et al., Decision on prosecution request for certification of interlocutory appeal of second decision on addition of Wesley Clark to rule 65 ter list, 14 March 2007, para. 15

Commentary

1. Introduction

It is trite law that to be admissible, evidence must be relevant and have probative value. This basic principle is embodied in Rule 89(D) of the ICTR Rules of Procedure. However, while easily stated, the application of this general principle has long given rise to a plethora of challenges, exercising judicial minds and filling the pages of volumes of academic treatises. The decisions under consideration here all deal with aspects of the admissibility of evidence and the challenges inherent in balancing the interests of the prosecution, the defence and the orderly conduct of proceedings with the interests of fairness and justice.[1]

The first series of four decisions relate to proceedings in Prosecutor v. Karemera, Ngirumpatse and Nzirorera in which the three defendants were charged with rape as a crime against humanity. Responsibility was alleged, not on the basis of actual commission of the acts, but rather on the basis of superior responsibility or, alternatively, by virtue of an extended form of joint criminal enterprise theory. In addition to the findings on the evidentiary questions, this series of decisions demonstrates some of the difficulties inherent in conducting complex, multi-defendant trials.

2. The admissibility of written evidence in *lieu* of oral testimony

The principle issue in the Karemera decision of 11 December 2006[2] relates to the admissibility of written evidence in *lieu* of oral testimony. Article 92*bis* of the Rules of Procedure and Evidence (RPE) of the ICTR sets out the circumstances in which proof of facts may be accomplished by means other than through the taking of oral testimony. Rule 92*bis* sub (A) allows the admission of evidence of a witness in the form of a written statement in lieu of oral testimony while Rule 92*bis* sub (D) allows the submission of evidence in the form of a transcript of evidence given in prior proceedings before the tribunal where, in either case, such evidence goes to the proof of a matter other than the acts and conduct of the accused as charged in the indictment. With respect to written statements, Rule 92*bis* sub (A) sets out a non-exhaustive list of criteria to be considered for and against admission of written statements, including, as a consideration against inclusion, 'any other factors which make it appropriate for the witness to attend for cross-examination'. Rule 92*bis* sub (B) further sets out the procedural requirements that need to be met before such evidence can be admitted.

These rules on admission of written evidence in lieu of oral testimony are intended to assist with the expeditious disposal of trials.[3] However, the general requirements of relevance and probative value must still be met.[4] Moreover, in exercising the discretion to admit such evidence the tribunal must weigh the interests

1 ICTR, Decision on Request for Subpoenas of United Nations Officials, *Prosecutor v. Bagosora, Kabiligi, Ntabakuze and Nsengiyumva,* Case No. ICTR-98-41-T, T. Ch. I, 6 October 2006, in this volume p. 55; ICTR, Decision on "Appeal of Accused Arsène Shalom Ntahobali Against the Decisions on Kanyabashi's Oral Motion to Cross-Examine Ntahobali Using Ntahobali's Statements to Prosecution Investigators in July 1997", *Prosecutor v. Ntahobali and Nyiramasuhuko*, Case No. ICTR-97-21-AR73, A. Ch., 27 October 2006, in this volume p. 61; ICTR, Decision on the Prosecution Joint Motion for Re-Opening its Case and for Reconsideration of the 31 January 2006 Decision on the Hearing of Witness Michel Bagaragaza via Video-Link, *Prosecutor v. Zigiranyirazo*, Case No. ICTR-2001-73-T, T. Ch. III, 16 November 2006 in this volume p. 67; ICTR, Decision on Prosecution Motion for Admission of Evidence of Rape and Sexual Assault Pursuant to Rule 92*bis* of the Rules, and Order for Reduction of Prosecution Witness List, *Prosecutor v. Karemera, Ngirumpatse and Nzirorera*, Case No. ICTR-98-44-T, T. Ch. III, 11 December 2006, in this volume p. 75; ICTR, Decision on Prosecution Prospective Experts Witnesses Alison Des Forges, André Guichaoua and Binaifer Nowrojee, *Prosecutor v. Karemera, Ngirumpatse and Nzirorera*, Case No. ICTR-98-44-T, T. Ch. III, 25 October 2007 in this volume p. 83; ICTR, Decision on the Prosecution Motion for Admission Into Evidence of Post-Arrest Interviews With Joseph Nzirorera and Mathieu Ngirumpatse, *Prosecutor v. Karemera, Ngirumpatse and Nzirorera*, Case No. ICTR-98-44-T, T. Ch. III, 2 November 2007, in this volume p. 91; ICTR, Decision on Prosecution Motion for Reconsideration of the decision on Prospective Experts Witnesses Guichaoua, Nowrojee and Des Forges, or for Certification , *Prosecutor v. Karemera, Ngirumpatse and Nzirorera*, Case No. ICTR-98-44-T, T. Ch. III, 16 November 2007, in this volume p. 101.

2 Decision on Prosecution Motion for Admission of Evidence of Rape and Sexual Assault Pursuant to Rule 92*bis* of the Rules; and Order for Reduction of Prosecution Witness List, *Prosecutor v. Karemera et al.*, T. Ch. III, *supra* note 1.

3 ICTY, Third Decision on the Admission of Written Statements Pursuant to Rule 92*bis*, *Prosecutor v. Brđanin and Talić*, Case No. IT-99-36-T, T. Ch. II, 3 September 2002, Klip/ Sluiter, ALC-XI-349, par. 5.

4 ICTY, Decision on Interlocutory Appeal on the Admissibility of Evidence-In-Chief in the Form of Written Statements, *Prosecutor v. Milošević*, Case No. IT-02-54-AR73.4, A. Ch., 30 September 2003, Klip/ Sluiter, ALC-XIV-437, par. 9.

of expedition against the accused's right to a fair trial as guaranteed by Articles 19 and 20 of the Statute of the ICTR.[5]

In the Karemera case, the prosecution sought to admit, in lieu of oral testimony, the written statements of 63 purported rape witnesses and the written transcripts of eight others, in order to reduce the number of witnesses testifying orally from the proposed total of 93. In declining to grant the motion the Trial Chamber not only declined to accept the written statements and transcripts in evidence but also granted a defence motion, ordering a drastic reduction of the witness list.

The rationale behind requiring oral testimony rested on the interpretation of the phrase 'acts and conduct of the accused'. In this respect the Trial Chamber followed the established jurisprudence of the ICTY in the Galić[6] case which provides for exclusion of any written statement or transcript which goes to the proof of any act or conduct of the accused upon which the prosecution relies to establish: (1) that the accused personally physically perpetrated any of the crimes charged him or herself; or (2) that he planned, instigated or ordered the crimes charged; or (3) that he otherwise aided and abetted those who actually did commit the crimes in their planning, preparation or execution of those crimes; or (4) that he was a superior to those who actually did commit the crimes; or (5) that he knew or had reason to know that those crimes were about to be or had been committed by his subordinates; or (6) that he failed to take reasonable steps to prevent such acts or to punish those who carried out those acts. In addition, in cases of alleged command responsibility and where the crimes charged involve widespread criminal conduct by alleged subordinates, the relationship between a finding that the acts were committed by subordinates and a finding that the accused knew or had reason to know those crimes were about to be or had been committed is a close one. Thus, where evidence of the acts of subordinates is so proximate to the accused that the evidence of those acts becomes pivotal to the prosecution's case, Galić tells us that it would be unfair to the accused to admit that evidence in written form only.[7] Similarly, where the prosecution case rests on allegations of joint criminal enterprise it would be unfair to allow written evidence which goes to prove that the accused participated in a joint criminal enterprise, or shared with the person who actually did commit the crimes charged the requisite intent for those crimes.[8]

Central to any decision on whether to admit written evidence in lieu of oral testimony is the concern to ensure a fair trial through ensuring the availability of cross-examination. In Milosević[9] it was held that where the statement touches upon a critical element of the prosecution's case, or goes to a live and important issue between the parties, as opposed to a peripheral or marginally relevant issue, it would be necessary to ensure the accused's right to cross-examination. In Karemera the Trial Chamber noted that the evidence was to be relied on to prove that rapes had been committed on a widespread and systematic basis by the accused's subordinates and/or co-perpetrators. This evidence was clearly pivotal to the prosecution case such that its admission without the ability to cross-examine would violate the fair trial guarantees.

3. Reducing the witness list

Having decided that cross-examination would be necessary the Trial Chamber then had to address the defence motion for an order reducing the witness list. Rule 73*bis*(D) allows the Trial Chamber to order the prosecution to reduce the number of witnesses being called to prove the same facts if it considers the number to be excessive. The prosecution, for its part, engaged in some interesting mathematical calculations to show that calling 93 witnesses to testify to the massive scale of rapes that had occurred over three months in five prefectures was not excessive. Applying allegedly the same mathematical reasoning, however, the Trial Chamber concluded that the maximum number of witness needed would be 36.

---

5 ICTR, Decision on Prosecution Motion for Admission of Evidence of Rape and Sexual Assault Pursuant to Rule 92*bis* of the Rules, and Order for Reduction of Prosecution Witness List, *Prosecutor v. Karemera, Ngirumpatse and Nzirorea*, T. Ch. III, *supra* note 1, par. 8.

6 ICTY, Decision on Interlocutory Appeal Concerning Rule 92*bis*(C), *Prosecutor v. Galić*, Case No. IT-98-29-AR73.2, A. Ch., 7 June 2002, Klip/ Sluiter, ALC-VIII-281, par. 9-14.

7 *Ibid*., par. 14-15.

8 *Ibid*., par. 10.

9 ICTY, Decision on Prosecution's Request to Have Written Statements Admitted under Rule 92*bis*, *Prosecutor v. Milošević*, Case No. IT-02-54-T, T. Ch. III, 21 March 2002, Klip/ Sluiter, ALC-VIII-269, par. 7 and 24.

While anecdotally, at least, it is well known that a strong correlation exists between mathematical and legal reasoning, the application of a raw 'numbers game' to the fundamentally important issue of the presentation of evidence in a complex multi-defendant, multi-indictment trial seems hardly consistent with the requirements of fairness and justice. Had that been the only rationale expressed by the Trial Chamber serious concerns might arise. However, in reaching its decision the Trial Chamber had regard to a number of factors including: (1) the number of witnesses currently proposed to be called; (2) the factual elements to be established by the prosecution; (3) the application of the prosecution's mathematical formula; and (4) the waste of judicial time and resources and the compromises to the administration of justice and the rights of the accused cause by the use of excessive witnesses. In addition, of critical importance, the Trial Chamber noted that it had already, on the prosecution's own motion, taken judicial notice of a number of adjudicated facts concerning rape and sexual assaults committed in the relevant prefectures.[10] This approach to the use of judicial notice as a means of expediting trials has been the subject of some criticism.[11] Nevertheless, it did allow the Trial Chamber to order to the prosecution to 'drastically' reduce its witness list while appearing confident that this would not prejudice the prosecution's case.

4. Expert Evidence

The Trial Chamber's apparent strictures on the admission of prosecution evidence continued in its decisions of 25 October 2007[12] and 16 November 2007[13] on the admission of expert reports and oral testimony. Rule 94*bis* of the RPE sets out the procedural criteria for the admission of expert evidence. However, admission of such evidence is, as always, subject to the Rule 89 considerations of probity and relevance and to the Trial Chamber's broad discretion to employ rules of evidence that 'best favour a fair determination of the matter before it and are consonant with the spirit of the Statute and the general principles of law'. As previously held in the Semanza[14] and Akayesu[15] cases expert evidence must meet the following criteria to be admitted: (1) the chamber discretionarily deems it necessary to hear an expert on a determined issue; (2) the prospective witness is an expert on that determined issue; (3) the statement or report is reliable; (4) the statement or report is relevant and of probative value; and (5) the substance of the statement or report falls within the expertise of the witness. As for the experts themselves, in order to be so characterised an expert must possess a relevant specialised knowledge acquired through education, expertise or training in his or her proposed field of expertise and the chamber must be convinced that the expert evidence could assist it in understanding the evidence presented or determining a fact in issue.[16]

In the Karemera decision of 25 October 2007 the Trial Chamber did not doubt that each of the persons could be qualified as experts. Rather, the Trial Chamber's determination was based on its assessment of whether it felt their evidence would be of any assistance to it. In the case of the witness Des Forges, the Trial Chamber considered that her proposed testimony consisted only of opinions related to issues on which the Trial Chamber had already taken judicial notice or heard testimony, to wit, the social and historical context of the 1994 genocide. In the case of the witness Guichaoua, the Trial Chamber considered that the opinions were largely based on material similar to material already led in evidence and as such they were not necessary for the Trial Chamber to appreciate and evaluate the factual issues in the trial. Indeed, the Trial Chamber felt that many of the opinions expressed were, in fact, determinative of the guilt of the accused and could therefore not be admitted. Similarly, the evidence and opinions to be introduced by the witness Nowrojee had already been addressed by testimony which the Trial Chamber did not need the assistance of the experts to evaluate. Here, too, it appeared to the Trial Chamber that the experts were simply being put forward to

---

10 ICTY, Decision on defence motion for a ruling that his Honour Judge Canivell is unable to continue sitting in this case, *Prosecutor v. Krajišnik*, Case No. IT-00-39, T. Ch. I, 16 June 2006, to be published in volume XXIX.

11 Ralph Mamiya, Taking Judicial Notice of Genocide? The Problematic Law and Policy of the *Karemera* Decision, 25 Wisconsin International Law Journal 2007-2008.

12 Decision on Prosecution Prospective Experts Witnesses Alison Des Forges, André Guichaoua and Binaifer Nowrojee, *Prosecutor v. Karemera, Ngirumpatse and Nzirorera*, T. Ch. III, *supra* note 1.

13 Decision on Prosecution Motion for Reconsideration of the decision on Prospective Experts Witnesses Guichaoua, Nowrojee and Des Forges, or for, *Prosecutor v. Karemera, Ngirumpatse and Nzirorera*, T. Ch. III, *supra* note1.

14 ICTR, Appeals Chamber Judgement, *Prosecutor v. Semanza*, Case No. ICTR-97-20-A, A. Ch., 20 May 2005, par. 302-304.

15 ICTR, Decision on Defence Motion for Appearance of an Accused as an Expert Witness, *Prosecutor v. Akayesu*, Case No. ICTR-96-4-T, T. Ch. I, 9 March 1998.

16 Appeals Chamber Judgement, *Prosecutor v. Semanza*, A. Ch., *supra* note 14, par. 302-303; ICTR, Judgement, *Gacumbitsi v. Prosecutor*, Case No. ICT R-2001-64-A, A. Ch., 7 July 2006, Klip/ Sluiter, ALC-XXIV-495, par. 31.

make findings of fact, thereby effectively usurping the very function of the Trial Chamber. The Trial Chamber was not satisfied that any expert evidence was needed to assist it to analyse and understand the evidence before it and it therefore precluded the admission of all their evidence as expert witnesses. The Trial Chamber did, however, leave open the possibility that, if at any time in the future issues should arise which did require such assistance, it would be open to the Trial Chamber to call upon such expert testimony.

5. The remedy of reconsideration

The issue was revisited in very quick progression in the decision of 16 November 2007 in which the prosecution asked the Trial Chamber to reconsider its decision of 25 October or, in the alternative, to grant certification for an interlocutory appeal. The prosecution argued that the Trial Chamber had abused its discretionary power in excluding the expert evidence and that the circumstances rendered admission of some of the evidence of at least two of these experts of critical importance.

The test to be met in an application for the exercise of the inherent power of reconsideration is that: (1) a new fact had been discovered that was not known to the chamber at the time it made its original decision; (2) there has been a material change of circumstances since it made its original decision; or (3) there is reason to believe that the original decision was erroneous or constitutes and abuse of power of the part of the chamber, resulting in an injustice thereby warranting the exceptional remedy of reconsideration.[17] It is clear that the exceptional remedy of reconsideration will require exceptional circumstances. It is also clear that no tribunal likes to be told it 'got it wrong' or to be accused of abusing its powers. On this occasion, the Trial Chamber was adamantly of the opinion that no such exceptional circumstances existed, maintaining its opposition to the admission of the expert evidence on the basis that it would simply usurp the function of the Trial Chamber by offering opinions that were determinative of the guilt or innocence of the accused or by adverting to the acts, conduct and mental state of the accused. Moreover, it would waste judicial time and resources by simply repeating evidence that had already been presented through other witnesses or documents.

Nevertheless, undoubtedly mindful of the admonition that justice must not only be done but must be seen to be done, the Trial Chamber did agree to certify a decision on a motion for interlocutory appeal. The test for certification is set out in Rule 73(B) of the RPE. Certification may be granted where the decision (1) involves an issue that would significantly affect the fair and expeditions conduct of the proceedings or the outcome of the trial and (2) is one in which an immediate resolution by the Appeals Chamber may materially advance the proceedings. While it could see no reason to reconsider its decision, the Trial Chamber did agree with the prosecution that the impugned decision involved two important issues that might affect the fair and expeditious conduct of the proceedings or the outcome of the trial, to wit, the right of a party to adduce what it considers as important evidence at trial, and the Trial Chamber's own power to control its own proceedings by limiting appearances of witnesses before it. Indeed, this second aspect goes to the core of the judicial function, namely the issue of judicial independence. Recognising that it was first and foremost the responsibility of the Trial Chamber, as trier of fact, to determine which evidence to admit during the course of the trial, the Trial Chamber accepted that an immediate resolution by the Appeals Chamber on whether the Trial Chamber had abused this discretion could materially advance the proceedings. As the Trial Chamber itself notes, this was undoubtedly a safer course to follow than leaving the matter to be resolved in a later appeal, a delay which could result in prejudice to all.

6. Rights of the accused

The concept of prejudice was also relevant in the final decision in the Karemera proceedings to be considered here, the decision of 2 November 2007,[18] which deals with the issue of the admission into evidence of post-arrest interviews of two of the defendants. Rule 89 of the RPE provides that any relevant, probative evidence may be admitted as long as sufficient indicia of reliability can be established and the rights of the accused to a fair trial are not prejudiced. According to the settled jurisprudence of the ICTY and ICTR, where probative value is substantially outweighed by prejudicial effect or otherwise by the need to ensure a fair trial then the

[17] Decision on Prosecution Motion for Reconsideration of the Decision on Prospective Experts Witnesses Guichaoua, Nowrojee and Des Forges, or for Certification, *Prosecutor v. Karemera, Ngirumpatse and Nzirorera*, T. Ch. III, *supra* note 1, par. 3.

[18] Decision on the Prosecution Motion for Admission Into Evidence of Post-Arrest Interviews With Joseph Nzirorera and Mathieu Ngirumpatse, *Prosecutor v. Karemera, Ngirumpatse and Nzirorera*, T. Ch. III, *supra* note 1.

evidence should be excluded. Indeed, Rule 95 provides for the mandatory exclusion of evidence where it has been obtained by methods which cast substantial doubt on its reliability or if its admission is antithetical to, and would seriously damage, the integrity of the proceedings. In determining whether to exclude evidence it has been noted that 'the correct balance must be maintained between the fundamental rights of the accused and the essential interests of the international community in the prosecution of persons charged with serious violations of international humanitarian law'.[19]

In the Karemera decision of 2 November 2007 two of the accused objected to the admission of their post-arrest interview statements on the grounds that they had been obtained as a result of various violations of their rights. With respect to Joseph Nzirorera's interview, the defence argued that that it should be excluded because: (1) he had been arrested without a warrant; (2) he had not been informed of the reasons for his arrest; (3) he had not been brought promptly before a judge; (4) his property had not been promptly inventoried and returned to him; (5) the complete interview had not been recorded; and (6) his rights to silence and to legal counsel had not been respected. The Trial Chamber rejected the first argument, noting that the Appeals Chamber had already confirmed its decision upholding the validity of his arrest in Benin as having been made as a matter of urgency pursuant to Rule 40 of the RPE.[20] It also rejected the fourth argument on the basis that the issue was not sufficiently related to the evidence sought to be admitted so as to make that evidence inadmissible. In considering the third argument, the Trial Chamber referred to the discussion on point in the Appeals Chamber decision in the Kajelijeli case,[21] in particular noting that the national authorities of Benin should have been reminded to 'promptly bring the suspect before a domestic judge in order to ensure that the apprehended person's rights are safeguarded by a judge of the requested State'. Nevertheless, even though the accused had not been brought before a judge before his transfer from Benin the Trial Chamber was not satisfied that this was enough to render the interview inadmissible.

The Trial Chamber was, however, satisfied that his other rights had been violated. Rule 19 (2) requires a person to be informed of the charges against him or her immediately upon being taken into custody. Rule 20 (4) (a) further requires that an accused be informed promptly and in detail of the charges against him or her. A review of the transcript of the interview made it clear that at the time the interview was conducted the accused did not know of the charges against him and the investigators did not provide him with any information as to why he was considered a suspect or as to any provisional charges against him. Moreover, the transcript indicated that the requirements of Rule 43 had not been met. Rule 43 stipulates that whenever the prosecutor questions a suspect the questioning shall be audio or video recorded according to a certain procedure. Here, the transcripts revealed that discussions had taken place between the accused and the investigators before the interview began. As a general rule, a determination as to whether the content of these discussions would render the subsequent interview inadmissible would require an evidentiary hearing. However, the Trial Chamber did not consider it necessary to conduct such a hearing as it considered the interview inadmissible on other grounds, in particular on the basis that the accused's rights to silence and assistance of counsel had been violated.

The right to counsel is enshrined in Article 17, paragraph 3, of the ICTR Statute and in Rule 42 which provides, in particular, that questioning shall not proceed without the assistance of counsel, unless the suspect has voluntarily waived his or her right to counsel. The right to legal counsel was discussed at length by the Trial Chamber in the Bagosora case,[22] which makes it clear that in order to be voluntary a waiver must be based on clearly communicated and fully understood knowledge of the rights to which the suspect is entitled, including the right to prompt assistance of counsel prior to and during questioning. 'To be effective a waiver must be shown "convincingly and beyond reasonable doubt". It must be express and unequivocal,

---

19 ICTY, Decision on the Defence "Objection to Intercept Evidence", *Prosecutor v. Brđanin*, Case No. IT-99-36-T, T. Ch. II, 3 October 2003, Klip/ Sluiter, ALC-XIV-463, par. 62.

20 ICTR, Decision on the Defense Motion Challenging the Legality of the Arrest and Detention of the Accused and Requesting the Return of Personal Items Seized, *Prosecutor v. Nzirorera*, Case No. ICTR-98-44-1, T. Ch. II, 11 September 2000 and ICTR, Arrêt (Relatif à l'appel interlocutoire de la décision de la Chambre de première instance du 11 septembre 2000), *Prosecutor v. Nzirorera*, Case No. ICTR-98-44-A, A. Ch., 4 May 2001, par. 12-14.

21 ICTR, Judgement, *Kajelijeli v. Prosecutor*, Case No. ICTR-98-44A-A, A. Ch., 23 May 2005, Klip/ Sluiter, ALC-XXII-625, par. 222.

22 ICTR, Decision on the Proescutor's Motion for the Admission of Certian Materials Under Rule 89(C), *Prosecutor v. Bagosora et al.*, Case No. ICTR-98-41-T, T. Ch. I, 14 October 2004, par.16-18.

and must clearly relate to the interview in which the statement in question is taken.'[23] Here the investigator had persisted with the interview in spite of the accused's repeated statements that he would like to have counsel present. Moreover, given that the accused appeared not have had any knowledge of the charges or provisional charges against him or any related information as to why he was considered a suspect, he could not be taken to have waived his rights to counsel or to silence. In the circumstances, admission of the transcript of his interview would be antithetical to and seriously damage the integrity of the proceedings.

A similar result was reached in respect of the interview of Mathieu Ngirumpatse who objected to its introduction on the basis that (1) the recordings and transcripts were unreliable and had possibly been tampered with; (2) their relevance and probative value had not been established by the evidence of any witness; (3) the accused had not been informed of the charges against him and (4) the accused had been subject to threats or coercion. The Trial Chamber found no evidence to support the allegations that the recordings or transcripts were unreliable or of threats or coercion and it was satisfied that the evidence had been shown to be both relevant and probative. However, although the accused had clearly been informed of his rights and had clearly waived his right to counsel for the purposes of the interview, there was no evidence that he had ever been informed of the detail of the nature and cause of the charges against him, be it either promptly, or before, or during the interview. His interview was therefore also inadmissible.

7. Cross-examining a co-accused

An interesting aspect of the decision relates to the difficulty of introducing evidence in multi-defendant trials. Even assuming the transcript of Mathieu Ngirumpatse's interview had been held to be admissible, not all of it would necessarily have been admissible. During his interview he had given information about his co-accused, Joseph Nzirorera. As the Trial Chamber notes, it is likely that the latter would not have agreed with the version of events as given by the former and that Nzirorera would want to cross-examine Ngirumpatse on the statements made. The ability to do so would, however be contingent on Ngirumpatse deciding to testify, something he was not obliged to do. The Trial Chamber therefore considered it would be antithetical to the integrity of the proceedings to admit into evidence those parts of the interview with Mathieu Ngirumpatse that concerned his co-accused before he had indicated a decision to testify in his own defence.

The challenges of allowing one defendant to cross-examine a co-accused on previous statements are illustrated in the Ntahobali decision of 27 October 2006,[24] an interlocutory appeal challenging a decision by the Trial Chamber which allowed the defence for the co-accused Kanyabashi to cross-examine Ntahobli on issues relating to his credibility using previous statements made by Ntahobali to prosecution investigators. Defence for Ntahobli argued that the statements should have been inadmissible as they had not been freely and voluntarily given or, alternately, that at the very least a *voir dire* should have been held to determine whether they had been obtained in accordance with the RPE.

An interlocutory appeal is not a hearing *de novo*. Thus, the standard of review is whether the Trial Chamber reasonably exercised its discretion in reaching its decision.[25] As articulated in the Milosević case, 'a Trial Chamber's exercise of discretion will be overturned if the challenged decision was (1) based on an incorrect interpretation of the governing law; (2) based on a patently incorrect conclusion of fact; or (3) so unfair or unreasonable as to constitute an abuse of the Trial Chamber's discretion. Absent an error of law or a clearly erroneous factual finding, then, the scope of appellate review is quite limited[...]'.[26]

In the Ntahobali decision the Appeals Chamber was unable to find any such error. While the Trial Chamber had not held a dedicated *voir dire*, it had heard the submissions of the parties on the circumstances surrounding the taking of the previous statements and had even admitted a written affidavit from the accused into

---

23 Ibid., par. 18.

24 ICTR, Decision on "Appeal of Accused Arsène Shalom Ntahobali Against the Decisions on Kanyabashi's Oral Motion to Cross-Examine Ntahobali Using Ntahobali's Statements to Prosecution Investigators in July 1997", *Prosecutor v. Ntahobali and Nyiramasuhuko*, Case No. ICTR-97-21-AR73, A. Ch., 27 October 2006, in this volume p. 61.

25 ICTR, Decision on Interlocutory Appeals of Decision on Witness Protection Orders, *Prosecutor v. Bagosora, Kabiligi, Ntabakuze and Nsengiyumva*, Case No. ICTR-98-41-AR73 & ICTR-98-41-AR73(B), A. Ch., 6 October 2005, Klip/ Sluiter, ALC-XXII-189, par. 3.

26 ICTY, Decision on Interlocutory Appeal of the Trial Chamber's Decision on the Assignment of Defense Counsel, *Prosecutor v. Milošević*, Case No. IT-02-54-AR73.7, A. Ch., 1 November 2004, Klip/ Sluiter, ALC-XX-189, par. 10.

evidence on that issue. Based on these submissions the Trial Chamber had decided that no further evidence was required to determine whether the statements were in accordance with the RPE. No abuse of discretion was revealed in this procedure. Moreover, there was nothing to indicate that the Trial Chamber had erred in concluding that there was no need for any further evidence on the matter. There was nothing in the record to suggest that the interviews had been conducted in an improper manner. There was thus neither an incorrect interpretation of the governing law not a patently incorrect conclusion of the factual circumstances of the interview.

8. The *voir dire* procedure

In the course of its reasons the Appeals Chamber makes some interesting observations on the origins of the *voir dire* procedure, noting that it originates from the common law and does not have a strictly defined process in the ICTR. Indeed, Rule 89 (B) specifically provides that reference may be made to evidentiary rules 'which will best favour a fair determination of the matter'. Obviously, defence counsel for Ntahobali was of the opinion that a full *voir dire* procedure would best favour such a fair determination. However, while a Trial Chamber may, in its discretion, decide to hold a *voir dire*, nothing in the RPE compels such a procedure. Indeed, there is force to the suggestion that a full *voir dire* may, as a general rule, be unnecessary in proceedings not involving a jury. Given that the essence of the procedure is to allow the parties to make submissions to the judge on legal issues that arise during the conduct of a trial, it is difficult to argue that an alternative procedure which allows for the hearing of submissions from the parties on the relevant issue is insufficient.

The centrality of the right to cross-examine witnesses was also at issue in the Zigiranyirazo decision of 16 November 2006[27] which deals with the issue of the admissibility of evidence given by video-link. The use of video-link to enable witnesses to give evidence from a location other than the court room is a relatively recent phenomenon. In its early days the physical and technological limitations of the process made it difficult for judges to assess the credibility of witnesses and there was therefore a tendency to place less weight on evidence given by video-link than on in-court testimony. However, as the technology has improved so, too, has the ability to assess credibility without impairment and the procedure is now used in a number of national court systems. Video-link testimony has also been utilised in both the ICTR and the ICTY on a number of occasions, including for receiving the evidence of important and sensitive witnesses where their physical presence in the court room cannot be obtained due to security or other legal impediments.

In Zigiranyirazo a key prosecution witness had given his evidence by video-link from the Netherlands and the prosecution had closed its case. However, shortly after the defence commenced the presentation of its case, the Appeals Chamber excluded the testimony of the witness in its entirety on the basis that the presence of the witness by video-link was not sufficient to constitute fulfilment of the right of the accused to be present in the proceedings against him.[28] The prosecution moved for a re-opening of its case to allow the witness to testify again and for a re-consideration of the Trial Chamber's earlier decision denying the prosecution's original motion to hear the testimony via video-link.

This appears to have been the first time an application for the re-opening of the prosecution's case had been made to the ICTR. The case law of the ICTY[29] and the Trial Chamber of the Special Court for Sierra Leone[30]

---

27 ICTR, Decision on the Prosecution Joint Motion for Re-Opening its Case and for Reconsideration of the 31 January 2006 Decision on the Hearing of Witness Michel Bagaragaza via Video-Link, *Prosecutor v. Zigiranyirazo*, Case No. ICTR-2001-73-T, T. Ch. III, 16 November 2006, in this volume, p. 67.

28 ICTR, Decision on Interlocutory Appeal, *Zigiranyirazo v. Prosecutor*, Case No. ICTR-73-AR73, A. Ch., 30 October 2006, in this volume, p. 303.

29 See, e.g., ICTY, Decision on the Prosecution's Alternative Request to Reopen the Prosecution's Case, *Prosecutor v. Delalić, Mucić, Delić and Landžo*, Case No. IT-96-21-T, T. Ch. II*quater*, 19 August 1998, Klip/ Sluiter, ALC-III-287, par. 26-27; ICTY, Judgement, *Prosecutor v. Delalić, Mucić, Delić and Landžo*, Case No. IT-96-21-A, A. Ch., 20 February 2001, Klip/ Sluiter, ALC-V-369, par. 279-290; ICTY, Decision on Prosecution's Motion to Admit Evidence in Rebuttal and Incorporated Motion to Admit Evidence Under Rule 92bis in its Case on Rebuttal and to re-open is Case for a limited Purpose, *Prosecutor v. Blagojević and Dragan Jokić*, Case No. IT-02-60-T, T. Ch. I, 13 September 2004, par. 7-11; and ICTY, Decision on Application for a Limited Re-Opening of the Bosnia and Kosovo Components of the Prosecution Case With Confidential Annex, *Prosecutor v. Milošević,* Case No. IT-02-54, T. Ch. III, 13 December 2005, to be published in volume XXVIII, par. 12.

30 SCSL, Decision on Confidential Prosecution Motion to Reopen the Prosecution Case to Present an Additional Prosecution Witness, *Prosecutor v. Brima, Kamara and Kanu*, Case No. SCSL-04-16-T, T. Ch. II, 28 September 2006, par. 17.

establishes that, in exceptional circumstances, where the justice of the case requires it, leave may be granted to the prosecution to reopen its case in order to present new evidence not previously available to it. Three factors have been identified as being relevant to the consideration of the fairness to the accused of admission of fresh evidence: (1) the stage of the trial at which the evidence is sought to be adduced; (2) the potential delay in the trial that admission of the evidence could cause; and (3) the effect of bringing new evidence against one accused in a multi-defendant trial. However, the Zigiranyirazo case did not involve the presentation of new evidence not previously available, but rather the re-presentation of evidence previously available but now excluded. The Trial Chamber was therefore in somewhat uncharted territory.

Central to the decision of the Trial Chamber in Zigiranyirazo was the rationale of the Appeals Chamber in excluding the evidence for the purposes of avoiding any damage to the integrity of the proceedings. As the Trial Chamber put it: ' [p]rotecting the integrity of the proceedings means ensuring fairness in the conduct of the case as far as both Parties are concerned. While the Chamber must be diligent in ensuring that the Accused is not deprived of his rights, the Prosecution must not be unduly hampered in the presentation of its case'.[31] It would, of course, be necessary for the Trial Chamber to conduct the re-opened proceedings in such a way as to ensure no unfair prejudice to the defence. However, given the importance of the witness's evidence to the prosecution's case, the circumstances in which it had been excluded, and the Trial Chamber's inherent ability to ensure that the accused was not unduly prejudiced, it agreed that the interests of justice required it to allow the prosecution to re-open its case.

The interests of justice did not, however, require the Trial Chamber to agree to re-hear the evidence by video-link. Indeed, it is difficult to understand the prosecution's motion on this point. The Trial Chamber had previously stated that it wished to hear the testimony 'uninterrupted and in person' and had expressed concern as to its ability to effectively and accurately assess the testimony and the demeanour of a witness via video-link.[32] The Appeals Chamber had now excluded the evidence given by video-link. The logic of an argument that an appeal decision excluding video-link evidence could be considered a new fact or new circumstance requiring reconsideration of the original decision not to admit video-link evidence escapes this commentator, as it did the Trial Chamber. While the prosecution could re-open its case, the witness would have to attend in court in Arusha to give his evidence. This is not to suggest that the Trial Chamber was unsympathetic to the security concerns raised by the prosecution. On the contrary, the Trial Chamber had requested submissions from the registrar, pursuant to Rule 33 regarding what additional security measures might be necessary to enable the witness to testify in Arusha and was satisfied that this could be achieved.

9. The request of a subpoena

The final decision under consideration here deals with a request by the defence to subpoena various United Nations officials either to testify or to submit to an interview. According to established jurisprudence three conditions must be met by the applicant seeking such a subpoena: (1) reasonable attempts must have been made to obtain the voluntary cooperation of the witness; (2) the prospective witness must have information which can materially assist the applicant in respect of clearly identified issues relevant to the trial; and (3) the witness's testimony must be necessary and appropriate for the conduct and fairness of the trial.[33] In addition, in deciding whether to issue a subpoena a chamber must consider 'not only the usefulness of the information to the applicant [...] but its overall necessity in ensuring that the trial is informed and fair'.[34] As was noted in the Halilovic case, a subpoena is not something that is issued lightly since 'they involve the use of coercive powers and may lead to the imposition of a criminal sanction'.[35]

---

31 Decision on the Prosecution Joint Motion for Re-Opening its Case and for Reconsideration of the 31 January 2006 Decision on the Hearing of Witness Michel Bagaragaza via Video-Link, *Prosecutor v. Zigiranyirazo*, T. Ch. III, *supra* note 27, par. 18.

32 ICTR, Decision on Defence and Prosecution Motions Related to Witness ADE, *Prosecutor v. Zigiranyirazo,* Case No. ICTR-2001-73-T, T. Ch. III, 31 January 2006.

33 See, eg., ICTY, Decision on Application for Subpoenas, *Prosecutor v. Krstić*, Case No. IT-98-33-A, A. Ch., 1 July 2003, Klip/ Sluiter, ALC-XIV-521, par. 10; ICTY, Decision on the Issuance of Subpoenas, *Prosecutor v. Halilovic*, Case No. IT-01-48-AR73, A. Ch., 21 June 2004, par. 7; ICTR, Decision on Request for a Subpoena, *Prosecutor v. Bagosora, Kabiligi, Ntabakuze and Nsengiyumva*, Case No. ICTR-98-41-T, T. Ch. I, 11 September 2006, Klip/ Sluiter, ALC-XXIV-315.

34 Decision on the Issuance of Subpoenas, *Prosecutor v. Halilovic*, A. Ch., *supra* note 33, par. 7.

35 Ibid, par. 6.

In the Bagosora decision of 6 October 2006[36] the defence for one of the co-accused, Aloys Ntabakuze, sought to subpoena Kofi Annan and Iqbal Riza who had been officials of the Department of Peacekeeping Operations (DPKO) in 1994 in order to have them explain the circumstances surrounding the correspondence between UNAMIR officials in Rwanda and DPKO in New York to show that DPKO had no information suggesting that the genocide was being planned. The Trial Chamber's refusal to grant the subpoena rested on two rationales. First, it was not possible to consider these men as eye witnesses to the events and their personal impressions as recipients of reports would be of very limited weight in comparison to the direct and primary evidence of real eye witnesses who had been on the ground in Rwanda. Second, the Office of Legal Affairs had clearly indicated its willingness to continue to cooperate with the defendant on the preparation of a statement in lieu of oral testimony. In the circumstances the Trial Chamber found that the first part of the test was not satisfied so there was no need to further consider the other elements of the test.

The request for a subpoena for Shaharyar Khan, Special Representative of the Secretary-General in Rwanda from 1994 to 1996 was similarly dismissed on the basis that any knowledge he could have had of any conspiracy or plan to commit genocide could only have been gained through a retrospective review of documents that were already in the possession of the defence. His testimony could therefore not add anything to the trial. Moreover, the fact that Mr Khan had not entered the accused's name on a list of suspects drawn up in 1995 was, at best, only indirect evidence of extremely limited value on the question of whether the defendant had been involved in any conspiracy. As such it did not justify the issuance of a subpoena.

The final request to subpoena Michael Horrigan, a former investigator in the Office of the Prosecutor, was also refused. Mr. Horrigan's testimony was being sought in relation to his investigations into the shooting down of the Presidential airplane on the night of 6 April 1994, the event which has been characterised as the trigger for the ensuing massacres. However, as the Trial Chamber notes, at no time had any involvement by the accused in the assassination of the President ever been alleged. In any event, responsibility for the assassination was irrelevant to whether the accused and his subordinates had committed the crimes with which they were charged, all of which occurred subsequent to the assassination. In the words of the Trial Chamber: 'culpability for those crimes would not be reduced because someone other than the accused created the conditions that led to the commission of those crimes'.[37] In the circumstances, the Trial Chamber considered that the admission of detailed evidence on what was a matter of collateral and indirect relevance would not assist it in determining the core issues of the trial and the testimony of the witness was therefore neither necessary not appropriate of the conduct and fairness of the trial.

A tribunal will always be wary of issuing a subpoena where it thinks the request amounts to a 'fishing expedition', or where there is a risk of undermining the trial process by focusing on extraneous considerations relating to the knowledge or actions of persons or on other matters of collateral and indirect relevance. In this respect the Trial Chamber's decision to refuse the subpoenas requested on the basis of the need to maintain the focus and integrity of the trial appears to be consistent with both principle and common sense.

10. Conclusion

In conclusion, as these case show, questions relating to the admission of evidence are often vexed and controversial and arise in a myriad of forms. Their resolution requires a complex balancing act of the various interests involved. In balancing those interests there is a preference for evidence to be given in person and in court, so long as the evidence is, in fact, relevant and probative and its admission would not otherwise throw the administration of justice into disrepute.

Rosemary Rayfuse

36 Decision on Request for Subpoenas of United Nations Officials, *Prosecutor v. Bagosora, Kabiligi, Ntabakuze and Nsengiyumva*, T. Ch. I, *supra* note 1.

37 Ibid., par. 16.

International Criminal Tribunal for Rwanda
Tribunal pénal international pour le Rwanda

OR: ENG

TRIAL CHAMBER III

Before Judges:	Dennis C. M. Byron, Presiding Emile Francis Short Gberdao Gustave Kam
Registrar:	Adama Dieng
Date:	15 December 2006

THE PROSECUTOR

v.

Édouard KAREMERA
Mathieu NGIRUMPATSE
Joseph NZIRORERA

Case No. ICTR-98-44-T

DECISION ON DEFENCE MOTIONS TO PROHIBIT WITNESS PROOFING

Rule 73 of the Rules of Procedure and Evidence

Office of the Prosecutor:
Don Webster
Alayne Frankson-Wallace
Iain Morley
Saidou N'Dow
Sunkarie Ballah-Conteh
Takeh Sendze

Defence Counsel for Édouard Karemera
Dior Diagne Mbaye and Félix Sow

Defence Counsel for Mathieu Ngirumpatse
Chantal Hounkpatin and Frédéric Weyl

Defence Counsel for Joseph Nzirorera
Peter Robinson and Patrick Nimy Mayidika Ngimbi

[page 2] Introduction

1. The proceedings in the instant case commenced on 19 September 2005. While the fourth trial session of the Prosecution's case was ongoing, the Defence for Nzirorera moved the Chamber to prohibit, with immediate effect, the Prosecution from "proofing" its witnesses before they testify.[1] To support its application, it relied upon a Decision rendered by Pre-Trial Chamber I of the International Criminal Court ("ICC") in the *Dyilo* case and requested the Chamber to apply the same standards.[2] The Defence for Ngirumpatse joins the application and the Prosecution opposes the Motion.[3]

Deliberations

2. In order to address the Defence Motions, the Chamber will first provide an analysis of the ICC Decision (1), then it will address the practice at the *ad hoc* Tribunals (2) and finally the practice of the Prosecution in this case (3).

1. Comments on the *Dyilo* Decision

3. On 8 November 2006, the Pre-Trial Chamber of the ICC ruled upon whether the practice of proofing witnesses as described by the Prosecution in the *Dyilo* case was admissible in proceedings before the ICC. In reaching its finding, the Pre-Trial Chamber applied the standards of applicable law as set out in Article 21 of its Statute.[4] **[page 3]**

4. The Pre-Trial Chamber divided the notion of "witness proofing" as described by the ICC Prosecution in that case into two components of goals and measures. The Pre-Trial Chamber defined the first component, labelled "witness familiarization" by the Pre-Trial Chamber, as "a series of arrangements to familiarise the witnesses with the layout of the Court, the sequence of events that is likely to take place when the witness is giving testimony, and the different responsibilities of the various participants at the hearing".[5] The Pre-Trial Chamber found that this first component, "witness familiarization", was not only admissible but also mandatory under the ICC Statute.[6] Furthermore, in the Pre-Trial Chamber's view, "the [Witnesses and

---

1 Joseph Nzirorera's Motion to Prohibit Witness Proofing, filed on 13 November 2006.

2 ICC, *Prosecutor v. Thomas Lubanga Dyilo*, Case No. ICC-01/04-01/06, Decision on the Practices of Witness Familiarisation and Witness Proofing (Pre-Trial Chamber), 8 November 2006 ("*Dyilo* Decision").

3 See Ngirumpatse's Motion filed on 17 November 2006; Prosecution Responses filed on 16 and 20 November; Nzirorera's Reply filed on 20 November 2006 and Ngirumpatse's Reply filed on 24 November 2006. The Defence for Nzirorera also orally requested the Chamber to take interim measures prohibiting witness proofing until such a time it will have delivered its decision. The Chamber denied this application for interim measures but reduced the time-limits for the Prosecution to file its response (see T. 14 November 2006).

4 *Dyilo* Decision, paras. 7-9. ICC Statute, Article 21 (Applicable law):

1. The Court shall apply:

(a) In the first place, this Statute, Elements of Crimes and its Rules of Procedure and Evidence;

(b) In the second place, where appropriate, applicable treaties and the principles and rules of international law, including the established principles of the international law of armed conflict;

(c) Failing that, general principles of law derived by the Court from national laws of legal systems of the world including, as appropriate, the national laws of States that would normally exercise jurisdiction over the crime, provided that those principles are not inconsistent with this Statute and with international law and internationally recognized norms and standards.

2. The Court may apply principles and rules of law as interpreted in its previous decisions.

3. The application and interpretation of law pursuant to this article must be consistent with internationally recognized human rights, and be without any adverse distinction founded on grounds such as gender as defined in article 7, paragraph 3, age, race, colour, language, religion or belief, political or other opinion, national, ethnic or social origin, wealth, birth or other status.

5 *Dyilo* Decision, para. 15.

6 *Dyilo* Decision, paras. 14 and 15. These goals and measures encompass:

Assisting the witness testifying with the full comprehension of the Court proceedings, its participants and their respective roles, freely and without fear, through the following measures:

i. To provide the witness with an opportunity to acquaint him/herself with the Prosecution's Trial Lawyer and other whom may examine the witness in Court;

ii. To familiarise the witness with the Courtroom, the Participants to the Court proceedings and the Court proceedings;

iii. To reassure the witness about his/her role in the Court proceedings;

Victims Unit], in consultation with the party that proposes the relevant witness, is the organ of the Court competent to carry out the practice of witness familiarisation from the moment the witness arrives at the seat of the Court to give oral testimony".[7]

5. The Pre-Trial Chamber described the second component of the notion of witness proofing advanced by the ICC Prosecution as measures to review the witness' evidence "by *inter alia* (i) allowing the witness to read his or her statement, (ii) refreshing his or her memory in respect of evidence that he or she will give at the confirmation hearing, and (iii) putting to the witness the very same questions and in the very same orders as they will be asked during the testimony of the witness".[8] The Pre-Trial Chamber found that this second component was not covered by any provision of the Statute, the Rules or the Regulations.[9] It also considered that the ICC Prosecution failed to prove that the goals and measures described under the second component of witness proofing were widely accepted as practice in international criminal law.[10] It observed that the Prosecution did not put forward any jurisprudence from the ICTR authorising the practice of witness proofing as defined by the **[page 4]** Prosecution, and it considered that the sole ICTY Decision rendered in the *Limaj* case did not regulate in detail the content of the practice of witness proofing.[11] The Pre-Trial Chamber also considered that the Prosecution's submission that the practice of witness proofing as defined in the Prosecution Information is a special feature of proceedings carried out before international adjudicatory bodies due to the particular character of the crimes over which such bodies have jurisdiction is also unsupported.[12]

6. In accordance with Article 21 of its Statute, the Pre-Trial Chamber then sought to determine whether the second component of the definition could be embraced by "general principles of law derived by the Court from national laws of legal systems of the world including, as appropriate, the national laws of States that would normally exercise jurisdiction over the crime, provided that those principles are not inconsistent with this Statute and with international law and internationally recognized norms and standards".[13]

7. The Pre-Trial Chamber observed that this second component would be either unethical or unlawful in jurisdictions as different as Brazil, Spain, France, Belgium, Germany, Scotland, Ghana, England and Wales and Australia, whereas in other national jurisdictions, particularly in the United States of America, the practice of witness proofing along the lines advanced by the Prosecution is well accepted, and at times even considered professional good practice.[14] The Pre-Trial Chamber particularly emphasised that the second component of the practice as described by the ICC Prosecution would be in direct breach of the professional standards of the Code of Conduct of the Bar Council of England and Wales that the ICC Prosecution had expressly undertaken to comply with.[15] In light of these circumstances, the Pre-Trial Chamber concluded that

> the second component of the definition of the practice of witness proofing advanced by the Prosecution is *not embraced by any general principle of law* that can be derived from the national laws of the legal systems of the world.[16] On the contrary, if any general principle of law were to be derived from the national laws of the legal systems of the world on this particular matter, it would be the duty of the Prosecution to refrain from undertaking the [above-mentioned] practice of witness proofing".[17] **[page 5]**

---

iv. To discuss matters that are related to the security and safety of the witness, in order to determine the necessity of applications for protective measures before the Court;
v. To reinforce to the witness that he/she is under a strict legal obligation to tell the truth when testifying;
vi. To explain the process of examination-in-chief, cross-examination and reexamination.

7 *Dyilo* Decision, para. 24.

8 *Dyilo* Decision, para. 40, see also paras. 16 and 17.

9 *Dyilo* Decision, para. 28.

10 *Dyilo* Decision, para. 33.

11 *Dyilo* Decision, paras. 31 and 32. *Prosecutor v. Limaj et al.*, Case No. IT 03-66-T, Decision on Defence Motion on Prosecution Practice of "Proofing" Witnesses (TC), 10 December 2004 ("*Limaj* Decision").

12 *Dyilo* Decision, para. 34.

13 ICC Statute, Article 21. See *Dyilo* Decision, paras. 35 and seq.

14 *Dyilo* Decision, para. 37.

15 *Dyilo* Decision, paras. 38-41.

16 *Dyilo* Decision, para. 42 (emphasis added).

17 *Dyilo* Decision, para. 42.

8. In this Chamber's view, the process by which the *Dyilo* Chamber came to its decision is not based on a comprehensive knowledge of the established practice of the *ad hoc* Tribunals, which is justified by the particularities of these proceedings that differentiate them from national criminal proceedings, as explained hereinafter. This was also recently reiterated in the *Milutinovic et al.* case, where the Trial Chamber of the International Criminal Tribunal for Former Yugoslavia ("ICTY") denied a Defence application seeking the Chamber to apply the exact same standards set out in the *Dyilo* Decision.[18]

2. Practice of the *Ad Hoc* Tribunals and the Rights of the Accused

9. Both this Tribunal and the ICTY have consistently allowed the practice of pre-testimony interviews of witnesses for the better administration of justice, in the particular context of their proceedings, and to reduce any element of surprise to the Defence. This practice is in accordance with the Appeals Chamber's finding that each party has the right to interview a potential witness.[19]

10. The practice of witness familiarization not only poses no undue prejudice, but is also a useful and permissible practice.[20] As the *Milutinovic* Trial Chamber recently recalled, there is no reason for limiting witness familiarization to the Witnesses and Victims Support Section of the Tribunal.[21]

11. Although it has not been the subject of specific case-law at the ICTR, witness preparation has been recognized in the jurisprudence in relation to how the content of an interview with a witness is to be disclosed. The Prosecution has developed a practice of disclosing "will-say" or "reconfirmation statements" prior to the testimony of a witness. Contrary to Mathieu Ngirumpatse' assertions, this practice has been sanctioned by the Tribunal's jurisprudence.[22] In the *Simba* case, Trial Chamber I defined a will-say statement as "a communication from one party to the other party and the Chamber anticipating that a witness will testify about matters that were not mentioned in previously disclosed witness **[page 6]** statements."[23] Trial Chambers have considered that will-say statements are in conformity with the Prosecution's obligations under Rule 67(D) of the Rules of the Rules of Procedure and Evidence which require each party to promptly notify the opposing party and the Chamber of the discovery and existence of additional evidence, information and materials that should have been produced earlier pursuant to the Rules.[24] The will-say statement generally supplements or elaborates on information previously disclosed to the Defence, but it may also bring new elements of which the Defence was not put on notice. Although it is not acceptable for the Prosecution to mould its case against the Accused in the course of the trial, it must be admitted that a witness may recall and add details to his or her prior statements. As explained by Trial Chamber I in the *Bagosora et al.* case

> [...] witness statements from witnesses who saw and experienced events over many months which may be of interest to this Tribunal, may not be complete. Some witnesses only answered questions put to them by investigators whose focus may have been on persons other than the accused rather than volunteering all the information of which they are aware.[25]

12. While this practice cannot be considered as permission to train, coach or tamper a witness before he or she gives evidence, the content of these statements under Rule 67(D) encompasses much of the elements described in the second component of witness proofing in the *Dyilo* Decision.

---

18 *Prosecutor v. Milan Milutinovic et al.*, Case No. IT-05-87-T, Decision on Ojdanic Motion to Prohibit Witness Proofing (TC), 12 December 2006 ("*Milutinovic* Decision").

19 *Prosecutor v. Mile Mrksic*, Case No. IT-95-13/1-AR73, Decision on Defence Interlocutory Appeal on Communication with Potential Witnesses of the Opposite Party (AC), 30 July 2003; see also, *Prosecutor v. Sefer Halilovic*, Case No. IT-01-48-AR73, Decision on the Issuance of Subpoenas (AC), 21 June 2004, para. 12 to 15.

20 *Milutinovic* Decision, para. 10.

21 *Ibidem.*

22 See for e,g., *Prosecutor v. Bagosora et al.*, Case No. ICTR-98-41-T, Decision on Admissibility of Witness DBQ (TC), 18 November 2003; *Prosecutor v. Simba*, Case No. ICTR-01-76-T, Decision on the Admissibility of Evidence of Witness KDD (TC), 1 November 2004, par. 9; *Prosecutor v. André Rwamakuba*, Case No. ICTR-98-44C-T, Decision on the Defence Motion Regarding Will-Say Statements (TC), 14 July 2005, para. 4.

23 *Prosecutor v. Simba*, Case No. ICTR-01-76-T, Decision on the Admissibility of Evidence of Witness KDD (TC), 1 November 2004, par. 9; see also *Prosecutor v. André Rwamakuba*, Case No. ICTR-98-44C-T, Decision on the Defence Motion Regarding Will-Say Statements (TC), 14 July 2005, para. 4.

24 *Ibidem.*

25 *Bagosora et al.*, Decision on Admissibility of Witness DBQ (TC), 18 November 2003, para. 29.

13. The ICTY has also developed a consistent practice of "witness proofing". An overview of recent proceedings before the ICTY shows that preparing witnesses, including the practice of putting questions to the witness concerning contradictions between prior statements, is an entire part of the proceedings.[26] In the *Limaj et al.* case, the Trial Chamber **[page 7]** denied a Defence Motion seeking that the Prosecution cease "proofing" witnesses with immediate effect.[27] The Trial Chamber noted that the practice of proofing witnesses, by both parties, has been in place and accepted since the inception of the Tribunal. It also noted that "[i]t is a widespread practice in jurisdictions where there is an adversary procedure". The *Limaj* Chamber considered that this practice has a number of advantages for the due functioning of the judicial process.

14. Recently, in the *Milutinovic et al.* case, the Trial Chamber reaffirmed that "discussions between a party and a potential witness regarding his or her evidence can, in fact, enhance the fairness and expeditiousness of the trial, provided that these discussions are a genuine attempt to clarify a witness' evidence".[28] It considered that "the process by which the *Dyilo* Chamber came to its decisions [was] not applicable to [its] determination of the issue".[29] Considering the situation at the ICTY, which in view of the *Milutinovic* Chamber is radically different than the *Dyilo* case,[30] the *Milutinovic* Chamber found that "reviewing a witness' evidence prior to testimony is a permissible practice under the law of the Tribunal and, moreover, does not *per se* prejudice the rights of the Accused".[31]

15. Under these circumstances, this Chamber is satisfied that a practice of preparing witnesses before they testify has developed and has been sanctioned by both *ad hoc* Tribunals. Provided that it does not amount to the manipulation of a witness' evidence, this practice may encompass preparing and familiarizing a witness with the proceedings before the Tribunal, comparing prior statements made by a witness, detecting differences and inconsistencies in recollection of the witness, allowing a witness to refresh his or her memory in respect of the evidence he or she will give, and inquiring and disclosing to the Defence additional information and/or evidence of incriminatory or exculpatory nature in sufficient time prior to the witness' testimony. It is also admitted that "the practice of witness familiarization not only poses no undue prejudice, but is also a useful and permissible practice".[32]

16. In that respect, the Chamber notes that there are clear standards of professional conduct and ethics which apply to Prosecuting Counsel when conducting interviews. According to the Prosecutor's Regulations No. 2, the members of the Office of the **[page 8]** Prosecutor can be regarded as permanent officers of the court who are "to serve and protect the public interest, including the interests of the international community, victims and witnesses, and to respect the fundamental rights of the suspects and accused" and are "not knowingly to make an incorrect statement of material fact to the Tribunal or offer evidence which Prosecution Counsel knows to be incorrect of false".[33]

---

26 See for e.g., *Prosecutor v. Mile Mrksic*, Case No. IT-95-13/1, T. 26 January 2006; *Prosecutor v. Naser Oric*, Case No. IT-03-68, T. 6 April 2006; *Prosecutor v. Prlic et al.*, Case No. IT-04-74, T. 10 July 2006; see also *Prosecutor v. Vidoje Blagojevic Dragan Jokic*, Case No. IT-02-60-T, Decision on Prosecution's Unopposed Motion For Two Day Continuance For The Testimony of Momir Nikolic (TC), 16 September 2003:

> **FINDING** that there was more than sufficient time for the Prosecution to complete all interviews and final proofing sessions with Mr. Nikolić and to inform the Defence of any new information arising out of such proofing sessions in advance of him being called to testify,
>
> **CONSIDERING** that the Prosecution has only disclosed the final notes from its last proofing sessions to the Defence on 16 September 2003, one day before Mr. Nikolic is to testify, and that this information needs to be translated into B/C/S for Defence review, [...]
>
> **REMINDING** the Prosecution that all such proofing sessions of witnesses – particularly witnesses whom it expects to testify at length – should be completed in sufficient time to allow the Defence to consider any new information gathered through such sessions, [...]

See also *Prosecutor v. Momcilo Krajisnik*, Case No. IT-0039-T, Order for Transfer of Detained Witness Pursuant to Rule90 *bis* (TC), 13 March 2006.

27 *Limaj* Decision.

28 *Milutinovic* Decision, para. 16.

29 *Milutinovic* Decision, para. 13.

30 *Milutinovic* Decision, para. 15.

31 *Milutinovic* Decision, para. 22.

32 *Milutinovic*, para. 10. and *Limaj* Decision.

33 Prosecutor's Regulations No. 2 (1999), Standard of Professional Conduct Prosecution Counsel.

17. The practice of reviewing a witness' evidence prior to testimony is consistent with the specificities of the proceedings before the *ad hoc* Tribunals and may contribute to a proper administration of justice in different circumstances: crimes charged in the indictment occurred many years ago and, in many cases, witness interviews took place a long time ago; matters that were relevant during the course of the investigations may need to be reviewed in light of the case the Prosecution intends to present; there might be differences of perception between the Prosecution investigator and Counsel who is going to lead the witness' evidence in court; the duration of the proceedings and the time elapsed between prior testimonies may require further interviews with a witness before he or she testifies and reduce the effect of surprise to the Defence in cases where the witness recollects elements that were not previously disclosed.[34]

18. This positive effect of meeting a witness before he or she testifies was even acknowledged by the Defence in the present case. The Defence for Nzirorera has requested several times to meet with Prosecution witnesses in order to better prepare its cross-examination and expedite the proceedings.[35] A recent example is that it met with Prosecution Witness GK a few weeks before his anticipated testimony, after the witness had arrived at the Tribunal to testify, and questioned the witness about some discrepancies with testimony in another case and a prior statement.[36] The witness was given an opportunity to explain these discrepancies.

19. In its Motion, the Defence contends that the Prosecution's practice of witness proofing in this case has created many problems of late disclosure and admission of evidence outside the scope of the Indictment.

20. The Chamber is not persuaded that reviewing a witness' evidence prior to testimony necessarily contributes to adduce evidence on matters outside the scope of the Indictment. In any event, should a witness recall and add details to his or her prior statements during the **[page 9]** review of his or her evidence, several remedies are possible such as providing additional time to the Defence for its preparation or, where appropriate, the exclusion of the evidence.[37] Each time, the Chamber will apply the appropriate remedy on a case-by-case basis in conformity with the rights of the Accused, including the right to be tried without undue delay. The Chamber, however, considers that the Prosecution should give notice at the earliest possible date of any additional information the witness is likely to provide during testimony.[38]

3. "Witness Proofing" in the Present Case

21. The Defence for Ngirumpatse claims that, in the present case, the witnesses are actually prepared to recite their testimonies in court that they learnt from the Prosecution. In its view, witness proofing amounts to tampering with the witness and moulding the evidence against the Accused. The Prosecution explicitly "rebuts any suggestion or implication that the pre-trial interview is used to train, coach, and tamper with or in any manner whatsoever, to mould its case against the Accused".

22. While the Defence may query and challenge how the Prosecution prepares its witnesses before he or she testifies, the allegations of tampering with witnesses made by the Defence of Ngirumpatse are serious allegations and making them without any evidence to support or justify them is discourteous at the very least. On the contrary, the Chamber notes that several witnesses have been cross-examined on the conduct of the pre-trial interview and there has been no evidential basis to support such allegations. There is, however, no need to expunge Ngirumpatse's submissions from the Tribunal's record as requested by the Prosecution.[39]

---

34 See *Limaj* Decision.and *Milutinovic* Decision, para. 20

35 See Joseph Nzirorera's Motion for Reconsideration of Witness Protection Order, filed on 25 September 2006.

36 See Will-say Statement of Witness GK, dated 10 November 2006, filed 17 November 2006.

37 *Prosecutor v. Bagosora et al.*, Case No. ICTR-98-41-T, Decision on Admissibility of Evidence of Witness DP (TC), 18 November 2003; *Prosecutor v. Bagosora et al.*, Case No. ICTR-98-41-T, Decision on Admissibility of Evidence of Witness DBQ (TC), 18 November 2003.

38 *Prosecutor v. André Rwamakuba*, Case No. ICTR-98-44C-T, Decision on the Defence Motion Regarding Will-Say Statements (TC), 14 July 2005, para. 7; *Milutinovic* Decision, paras. 22 and 23

39 See Prosecutor's Response.

23. As the Pre-Trial Chamber of the ICC stated, the expression "witness proofing" may encompass various practices which are not necessarily unlawful.[40] Neither the Defence nor the Prosecution provide detailed information as to how the Prosecution prepares its witnesses in this case before calling them to testify. According to disclosures of will-say statements and notices under Rule 67(D) in this case, the Chamber finds that there is a consistent practice by the Prosecution which consists of comparing statements made by a witness, detecting differences and inconsistencies in recollection of the witness, allowing a witness to refresh **[page 10]** his or her memory in respect of the evidence he or she will give, inquiring and disclosing to the Defence additional information and/or evidence of incriminatory or exculpatory nature in sufficient time prior to the witness' testimony.[41] It is not shown by the Defence, nor does it transpire from the said disclosures that the Prosecution puts to the witness the exact questions to be asked during his or her testimony.

24. The Prosecution is presumed to act in good faith[42] and in accordance with standards of professional conduct and ethics. Failure by the Defence to show the contrary, the Chamber is not satisfied that any meeting held prior to the testimony of the witnesses were not in conformity with the established practice.

FOR THE ABOVE REASONS, THE CHAMBER DENIES the Defence Motions.

Arusha, 15 December 2006, done in English.

Dennis C. M. Byron Presiding Judge	Emile Francis Short Judge	Gberdao Gustave Kam Judge

[Seal of the Tribunal]

40 *Dyilo* Decision, para. 12.

41 See for e.g., Prosecutor's Notice for GBU, filed 28 November 2006; Will-say Statement of Witness GK, filed on 17 November 2006.

42 *Karemera et al.*, Decision on Joseph Nzirorera's Interlocutory Appeal (AC), 28 April 2006, para. 17; *Prosecutor v. Dario Kordic and Mario Cerkez*, Case No. IT-95-14/2-A, Judgement (AC), para. 183.

Tribunal Pénal International pour le Rwanda
International Criminal Tribunal for Rwanda

IN THE APPEALS CHAMBER

Before:	**Judge Fausto Pocar, Presiding** **Judge Mohamed Shahabuddeen** **Judge Liu Daqun** **Judge Theodor Meron** **Judge Wolfgang Schomburg**
Registrar:	**Mr. Adama Dieng**
Decision of:	**11 May 2007**

THE PROSECUTOR

v.

Édouard KAREMERA
Mathieu NGIRUMPATSE
Joseph NZIRORERA

Case No. ICTR-98-44-AR73.8

Decision on Interlocutory Appeal Regarding Witness Proofing

Office of the Prosecutor:

Mr. Hassan Bubacar Jallow
Mr. James Stewart
Mr. Don Webster
Ms. Alayne Frankson-Wallace

Counsel for the Defence:

Ms. Dior Diagne Mbaye and Mr. Félix Sow for Mr. Édouard Karemera
Ms. Chantal Hounkpatin and Mr. Frédéric Weyl for Mr. Mathieu Ngirumpatse
Mr. Peter Robinson and Mr. Patrick Nimy Mayidika Ngimbi for Mr. Joseph Nzirorera

[Page 1] 1. The Appeals Chamber of the International Criminal Tribunal for the Prosecution of Persons Responsible for Genocide and Other Serious Violations of International Humanitarian Law Committed in the Territory of Rwanda and Rwandan Citizens Responsible for Genocide and Other Such Violations Committed in the Territory of Neighbouring States, between 1 January and 31 December 1994 ("Appeals Chamber" and "Tribunal", respectively) is seized with an interlocutory appeal filed by Mr. Joseph Nzirorera[1] against a decision taken by Trial Chamber III concerning the practice of "witness proofing".[2] The Prosecution responded on 29 March 2007,[3] and Mr. Nzirorera replied on 2 April 2007.[4]

BACKGROUND

2. On 13 November 2006, Mr. Nzirorera asked the Trial Chamber to prohibit the Prosecution from preparing its witnesses prior to their testimony ("witness proofing"), pointing principally to a decision limiting this practice rendered by Pre-Trial Chamber I of the International Criminal Court ("ICC") in the *Dyilo* case.[5] The Trial Chamber distinguished the *Dyilo* Pre-Trial Decision and denied Mr. Nzirorera's request, ultimately concluding that "the practice of reviewing a witness'[s] evidence prior to testimony is consistent with the specificities of the proceedings before the *ad hoc* Tribunals and may contribute to a proper administration of justice in different circumstances".[6] On 14 March 2007, the Trial Chamber granted Mr. Nzirorera's request for certification to appeal the decision.[7]

DISCUSSION

3. This appeal raises the principal question of whether the practice of witness proofing, as defined by the Trial Chamber in the Impugned Decision, is compatible with the Tribunal's Statute and Rules of Procedure and Evidence ("Rules"). As this matter relates to the general conduct of trial proceedings, it falls within the discretion of the Trial Chamber.[8] The Trial Chamber's exercise of **[page 2]** discretion to permit the continued practice of witness proofing in this case will be reversed only if Mr. Nzirorera can demonstrate that the Trial Chamber made a discernible error in the Impugned Decision because it was based on an incorrect interpretation of governing law, was based on a patently incorrect conclusion of fact, or was so unfair or unreasonable as to constitute an abuse of the Trial Chamber's discretion.[9]

4. The Trial Chamber described the scope of acceptable witness proofing in the Impugned Decision as follows:

> Provided that it does not amount to the manipulation of a witness'[s] evidence, this practice may encompass preparing and familiarizing a witness with the proceedings before the Tribunal, comparing prior statements made

---

1 Joseph Nzirorera's Interlocutory Appeal on "Witness Proofing", 19 March 2007 ("Nzirorera Appeal").

2 *The Prosecutor v. Édouard Karemera et al.*, Case No. ICTR-98-44-T, Decision on Defence Motions to Prohibit Witness Proofing, 15 December 2006 ("Impugned Decision").

3 Prosecutor's Reply to Joseph Nzirorera's Interlocutory Appeal on Witness Proofing, 29 March 2007 ("Prosecution Response").

4 Reply Brief: Joseph Nzirorera's Interlocutory Appeal on "Witness Proofing", 2 April 2007 ("Nzirorera Reply").

5 Impugned Decision, para. 1, referring to *The Prosecutor v. Thomas Lubanga Dyilo*, Case No. ICC-01/04-01/06, Decision on Practices of Witness Familiarisation and Witness Proofing, 8 November 2006 ("*Dyilo* Pre-Trial Decision").

6 Impugned Decision, para. 17.

7 *The Prosecutor v. Édouard Karemera et al.*, Case No. ICTR-98-44-T, Decision on Defence Motion for Certification to Appeal Decision on Witness Proofing, 14 March 2007.

8 *See Protais Zigiranyirazo v. The Prosecutor,* Case No. ICTR-2001-73-AR73, Decision on Interlocutory Appeal, 30 October 2006, para. 9 ("*Zigiranyirazo* Appeal Decision"); *The Prosecutor v. Théoneste Bagosora et al.*, Case No. ICTR 98-41-AR73, Decision on Interlocutory Appeal Relating to Disclosure Under Rule 66(B) of the Tribunal's Rules of Procedure and Evidence, 25 September 2006, para. 6 ("*Bagosora et al.* Appeal Decision (25 September 2006)"); *Tharcisse Muvunyi v. The Prosecutor*, Case No. ICTR-00-55A-AR73(C), Decision on Interlocutory Appeal, 29 May 2006, para. 5 ("*Muvunyi* Appeal Decision"). *See also Prosecutor v. Milan Milutinović et al.*, Case No. IT-05-87-AR73.1, Decision on Interlocutory Appeal against Second Decision Precluding the Prosecution from Adding General Wesley Clark to its 65*ter* Witness List, 20 April 2007, para. 8 ("*Milutinović et al.* Appeal Decision").

9 *Zigiranyirazo* Appeal Decision, para. 9; *Bagosora et al.* Appeal Decision (25 September 2006), para. 6; *Muvunyi* Appeal Decision, para. 5. *See also The Prosecutor v. Théoneste Bagosora et al.*, Case Nos. ICTR-98-41-AR73, ICTR-98-41-AR73(B), Decision on Interlocutory Appeals of Decisions on Witness Protection Orders, 6 October 2005, para. 3 ("*Bagosora et al.* Appeal Decision (6 October 2005)"; *Milutinović et al.* Appeal Decision, para. 10.

by a witness, detecting differences and inconsistencies in recollection of the witness, allowing a witness to refresh his or her memory in respect of the evidence he or she will give, and inquiring and disclosing to the Defence additional information and/or evidence of incriminatory or exculpatory nature in sufficient time prior to the witness'[s] testimony.[10]

5. Relying primarily on the ICC's *Dyilo* Pre-Trial Decision, Mr. Nzirorera challenges the Impugned Decision on three principal grounds. First, Mr. Nzirorera contends that the Trial Chamber erred in finding that the practice of witness proofing is a sanctioned practice at the Tribunal.[11] In this respect, he points to the *Dyilo* Pre-Trial Decision,[12] which held that the Prosecution in the ICC had failed to prove that the practice of witness proofing "is widely accepted practice in international criminal law".[13] Second, he argues that the Trial Chamber erred in distinguishing national prohibitions and in finding that the nature of the cases prosecuted at the international tribunals justified a departure from domestic rules prohibiting the practice.[14] In this respect, he emphasizes that national jurisdictions prosecute similar crimes, notably following Rule 11*bis* transfers.[15] Third, he disputes the Trial Chamber's characterization of witness proofing as a useful practice which does not cause undue prejudice to the accused, highlighting the number of times that the Prosecution has given notice that witnesses will change their testimony after proofing sessions.[16] He requests the **[page 3]** Appeals Chamber to take the same approach to witness proofing as taken in the ICC's *Dyilo* Pre-Trial Decision, and to prohibit it.[17]

6. The crux of Mr. Nzirorera's submissions is the supposition, predicated on his reading of the *Dyilo* Pre-Trial Decision, that witness proofing is considered unethical and unlawful in the ICC and in most major legal systems in the world.[18] Accordingly, he asserts that the Trial Chamber erred in distinguishing the *Dyilo* Pre-Trial Decision, and makes limited or no reference in support of his argument to any provision of the Tribunal's Statute or Rules or to its jurisprudence.[19] The Appeals Chamber finds Mr. Nzirorera's submissions unpersuasive.

7. There is no doctrine of precedence in international law which requires a Trial Chamber to follow practices or decisions adopted by another international court. Accordingly, while a Trial Chamber may find the rulings of another international jurisdiction persuasive, it is not bound to apply them to its own proceedings. Indeed, the Appeals Chamber has previously held that a Trial Chamber is not obligated to follow or to distinguish the decisions of other Trial Chambers of the Tribunal.[20] It is only decisions of the Appeals Chamber that are binding on Trial Chambers of this Tribunal.[21] Therefore, there is no discernible error in the manner in which the Trial Chamber distinguished the *Dylio* Pre-Trial decision, a decision of another international court which cannot bind this Tribunal. The present interlocutory appeal must necessarily turn on an assessment of the Trial Chamber's application of the Tribunal's Statute, Rules, and jurisprudence in the Impugned Decision.

8. The Tribunal's Statute and Rules do not directly address the issue of witness proofing. In the absence of express provisions, Rule 89(B) of the Rules generally confers discretion on the Trial Chamber to apply "rules of evidence which will best favour a fair determination of the matter before it and are consonant with the spirit of the Statute and the general principles of law." It is evident from the jurisprudence of the *ad hoc* Tribunals that, as Trial Chambers have exercised this discretion, a practice of witness proofing has developed and has been accepted in various cases.

---

10 Impugned Decision, para. 15.
11 Nzirorera Appeal, paras. 23, 29-34.
12 Nzirorera Appeal, para. 31, citing *Dyilo* Pre-Trial Decision, para. 33.
13 *Dyilo* Pre-Trial Decision, para. 33.
14 Nzirorera Appeal, paras. 24, 35-40.
15 Nzirorera Appeal, paras. 24, 35-40.
16 Nzirorera Appeal, paras. 25, 41-49.
17 Nzirorera Appeal, para. 50.
18 Nzirorera Appeal, paras. 23-25, 27-29, 35, 50.
19 Nzirorera Appeal, paras. 27-28.
20 *See Bagosora et al.* Appeal Decision (6 October 2005), para. 33 ("Trial Chamber III's Decision in the *Karemera* case is not binding authority on Trial Chamber I, and Trial Chamber I need not have distinguished its Impugned Decision from the *Karemera* Decision."). *See also Prosecutor v. Zlatko Aleksovski*, Case No. IT-95-14/1-A, Judgement, 24 March 2000, para. 114 ("*Aleksovski* Appeal Judgement").
21 *See Aleksovski* Appeal Judgement, para. 113.

9. For example, in the *Gacumbitsi* Appeal Judgement, the Appeals Chamber considered a challenge to a Trial Chamber's decision to credit a particular witness's testimony based, *inter alia*, **[page 4]** on assertions that the witness had been "coached" by the Prosecution.[22] In rejecting this argument, the Appeals Chamber stated that "the passage of Witness TBH's testimony concerning the alleged prosecutorial coaching demonstrates no impropriety."[23] The Appeals Chamber added that it "[saw] no reason to doubt the Prosecution's statement that 'the witness was involved in normal preparation to give evidence, and nothing more'".[24] Significantly, the Appeals Chamber then concluded that "[i]t is not inappropriate *per se* for the parties to discuss the content of testimony and witness statements with their witnesses, unless they attempt to influence that content in ways that shade or distort the truth."[25] The Trial Chamber's definition of acceptable witness proofing in the instant case is consistent with the approach sanctioned by the Appeals Chamber in the *Gacumbitsi* Appeal Judgement.

10. In addition, the decisions referred to in the Impugned Decision further establish the practice of witness proofing. With respect to this Tribunal, the Impugned Decision refers to jurisprudence from the *Simba, Bagosora et al.,* and *Rwamakuba* cases related to the Prosecution's practice of disclosing "will-say" or "reconfirmation statements", a product of proofing sessions, which implicitly condones the practice of witness preparation.[26] The Impugned Decision also refers to ICTY Trial Chamber decisions in the *Milutinović et al., Limaj et al.,* and *Blagojević and Jokić* cases explicitly condoning witness proofing.[27] The Appeals Chamber also recalls that in the *Krstić* case, the ICTY Appeals Chamber acknowledged, in deciding whether it would be appropriate to issue a subpoena to allow a party to meet with prospective witnesses before presenting their testimony as additional evidence on appeal, that it would be contrary to the duty owed by counsel to their client **[page 5]** to act skillfully and with loyalty to force a witness to give evidence "cold" without first knowing what he will say.[28] Mr. Nzirorera does not address this jurisprudence.

11. Furthermore, the submission that a number of national jurisdictions prohibit the practice of witness proofing to varying degrees does not, in the view of the Appeals Chamber, make such practice incompatible with the Tribunal's Statute and Rules or with general principles of law. Indeed, Rule 89(A) of the Rules expressly provides that "[t]he Chambers shall not be bound by national rules of evidence." The Appeals Chamber also notes that, as the *Dylio* Pre-Trial Decision acknowledges, the approach of different national jurisdictions to witness proofing "varies widely",[29] and while it is prohibited in some jurisdictions,[30] others, such as the United States, accept it and consider it good professional practice.[31]

12. Mr. Nzirorera's assertion that the practice of witness proofing is inherently prejudicial focuses primarily on the number of times that the Prosecution has conveyed notices of new material pursuant to Rule

---

22 *Sylvestre Gacumbitsi v. The Prosecutor*, Case No. ICTR-2001-64-A, Judgement, 7 July 2006, para. 73 ("*Gacumbitsi* Appeal Judgement").

23 *Gacumbitsi* Appeal Judgement, para. 74.

24 *Gacumbitsi* Appeal Judgement, para. 74, fn. 176.

25 *Gacumbitsi* Appeal Judgement, para. 74. Mr. Nzirorera attempts to distinguish this holding as a "passing reference". *See* Nzirorera Appeal, fn. 26. However, it is clear from the relevant passages of the *Gacumbitsi* Appeal Judgement that this holding was essential to disposing of the argument advanced on appeal.

26 Impugned Decision, para. 11, citing *The Prosecutor v. Aloys Simba*, Case No. ICTR-01-76-T, Decision on the Admissibility of Evidence of Witness KDD, 1 November 2004, para. 9; *The Prosecutor v. Théoneste Bagosora et al.*, Case No. 98-41-T, Decision on Admissibility of Witness DBQ, 18 November 2003; *The Prosecutor v. André Rwamakuba*, Case No. ICTR-98-44C-T, Decision on the Defence Motion Regarding Will-Say Statements, 14 July 2005.

27 Impugned Decision, paras. 13, 14, citing *Prosecutor v. Fatmir Limaj et al.*, Case No. IT-03-66-T, Decision on Defence Motion on Prosecution Practice of "Proofing" Witnesses, 10 December 2004 ("*Limaj et al.* Decision"); *Prosecutor v. Milan Milutinović et al.*, Case No. IT-05-87-T, Decision on Ojdanić Motion to Prohibit Witness Proofing, 12 December 2006 ("*Milutinović* Decision"); *Prosecutor v. Vidoje Blagojević and Dragan Jokić*, Case No. IT-02-06-T, Decision on Prosecution's Unopposed Motion for Two Day Continuance for the Testimony of Momir Nikolić, 16 September 2003. In the *Milutinović et al.* case, after distinguishing the *Dylio* Pre-Trial Decision and considering the *Limaj et al.* Decision, the Trial Chamber stated: "the Chamber is satisfied that reviewing a witness' evidence prior to testimony is a permissible practice under the law of the Tribunal and, moreover, does not *per se* prejudice the rights of the accused." *Milutinović* Decision, para. 22.

28 *Prosecutor v. Radislav Krstić*, Case No. IT-98-33-A, Decision on Application for Subpoenas, 1 July 2003, para. 8 ("*Krstić* Appeal Decision"). The Dissenting Opinion of Judge Shahabuddeen in that decision expressly refers to witness proofing. *See Krstić* Appeal Decision (Dissenting Opinion of Judge Shahabuddeen), paras. 33-35.

29 *Dylio* Pre-Trial Decision, paras. 36.

30 *Dylio* Pre-Trial Decision, para. 37.

31 *Dylio* Pre-Trial Decision, para. 37.

67(D) of the Rules containing "material which brings the witness'[s] testimony in line with other prosecution evidence in the case".[32] However, the Appeals Chamber observes that the Prosecution's act of disclosing new material to the Defence as a result of a proofing session does not mean that the Trial Chamber will allow the evidence to be led or that it will ultimately credit the testimony in its final assessment of the case.[33] Moreover, in the Impugned Decision, the Trial Chamber expressly prohibited witness preparation to the extent that it involves "manipulation of a witness'[s] evidence".[34] In addition, the Trial Chamber explained that issues of witness preparation have been explored on cross-examination with a number of witnesses, and that it had no basis to conclude that any proofing sessions to date had been improper.[35] Mr. Nzirorera does not dispute this conclusion.

13. The Appeals Chamber observes that there are several ways for parties to address the possibility that witness preparation might have improperly influenced testimony. For example, **[page 6]** through careful cross-examination, a party can explore the impact of preparation on the witness's testimony and use this to call into question the witness's credibility. In addition, intentionally seeking to interfere with a witness's testimony is prohibited, and if evidence of this comes to light, a Trial Chamber can take appropriate action by initiating contempt proceedings under Rule 77 of the Rules and by excluding the evidence pursuant to Rule 95 of the Rules.

14. Accordingly, the Appeals Chamber finds that Mr. Nzirorera has not demonstrated that the Trial Chamber committed a discernible error by permitting the Prosecution to proof its witnesses as described above.

DISPOSITION

15. For the foregoing reasons, the Appeals Chamber **DISMISSES** the Nzirorera Appeal in all respects.

Done in English and French, the English version being authoritative.

Done this 11th day of May 2007,
At The Hague,
The Netherlands.

Judge Fausto Pocar
Presiding

[Seal of the Tribunal]

32 Nzirorera Appeal, para. 47 (citing seven notices of additional evidence filed in the case).

33 For example, in the *Simba* case, the Trial Chamber admitted testimony based on a "will-say" statement, after according the Defence what it deemed sufficient time to prepare for the evidence, but ultimately disregarded the incriminating aspects of this testimony based on credibility concerns. *See, e.g., The Prosecutor v. Aloys Simba*, Case No. ICTR-01-76-T, Judgement and Sentence, 13 December 2005, paras. 40, 259, 268, 278. In particular, the Trial Chamber noted, "[t]he emergence of these incriminating allegations for the first time in a will-say statement disclosed only at the commencement of trial raises too many questions."

34 Impugned Decision, paras. 12, 15.

35 Impugned Decision, paras. 21-24.

Commentary

1. Introduction

These two decisions deal with the admissibility of witness proofing.[1] In line with the jurisprudence of the ICTY[2] and the SCSL,[3] the ICTR Trial Chamber denied Nzirorera's motion to prohibit witness proofing. This decision was confirmed by the Appeals Chamber.

2. Notion of Witness Proofing

The Trial Chamber defines witness proofing in general terms as "pre-testimony interviews of witnesses".[4] A more sophisticated view was presented by the ICTY in Haradinaj *et al.* and later adopted by the ICC prosecutor.[5] According to the ICTY Trial Chamber, "the term 'proofing' refers to a meeting held between a party to the proceedings and a witness, usually shortly before the witness is to testify in court, the purpose of which is to prepare and familiarize the witness with courtroom procedures and to review the witness evidence".[6] A detailed overview on the various components of witness proofing is given by Wydick. According to his experience and knowledge, an American lawyer preparing a witness typically discusses the witness's perception, recollection, and possible testimony about the events in question; reviews documents and other tangible items to refresh the witness's memory or to point out conflicts and inconsistencies with the witness's story; reveals other tangible or testimonial evidence to the witness to find out how it affects the witness's story; explains how the law applies to the events in question; reviews the factual context into which the witness's testimony will fit; discusses the role of the witness and effective courtroom demeanor; discusses probable lines of cross examination that the witness should be prepared to meet; rehearses the witness's testimony, by role playing or other means.[7]

As the ICC Pre-Trial Chamber has pointed out in the Lubanga case, the exact meaning of witness proofing and "the delimitation of what is lawful (or at least what is required as professional good practice), what is contrary to the professional code of ethics, and what could even constitute a criminal offence, greatly differs from jurisdiction to jurisdiction."[8] For the purpose of this commentary, it is, however, sufficient to note that witness proofing includes at least some form of substantive preparation of witnesses with regard to the content of their testimony at trial.

3. The Legal Basis of Witness Proofing

The procedural law of the ICTR does not directly address the admissibility of witness proofing[9]. In such cases, however, Rule 89 (B) of the Rules of Procedure and Evidence[10] directs the chambers to apply 'rules of evidence which will best favour a fair determination of the matter before it and are consonant with the spirit

---

1 ICTR, Decision on Defence Motions to Prohibit Witness Proofing (Rule 73 of the Rules of Procedure and Evidence), *Prosecutor v. Karemera, Ngirumpatse and Nzirorera*, Case No. ICTR9844T, T. Ch. III, 15 December 2006, in this volume p. 117; ICTR, Decision on Interlocutory Appeal Regarding Witness Proofing, *Prosecutor v. Karemera, Ngirumpatse and Nzirorera*, Case No. ICTR9844AR73.8, A. Ch., 11 May 2007, in this volume p. 125.

2 ICTY, Decision on Defence Motion on Prosecution Practice, *Prosecutor v. Limaj et al.*, Case No. IT0366T, T. Ch. II, 10 December 2004; ICTY, Decision on Ojdanić Motion to Prohibit Witness Proofing, *Prosecutor v. Milutinović et al.*, Case No. IT0887, T. Ch. III, 12 December 2006.

3 SCSL, Decision on the Gbao and Sesay Joint Application for the Exclusion of the Testimony of Witness TF1-141, *Prosecutor v. Sesay, Kallon and Gbao*, Case No. SCSL-04-15-T, T. Ch. I, 26 October 2005, Klip/ Sluiter, ALC-XXI-363, par. 33.

4 Decision on Defence Motions to Prohibit Witness Proofing, *Prosecutor v. Karemera, Ngirumpatse and Nzirorera*, T. Ch. III, *supra* note 1, par. 9.

5 ICC, Prosecution submissions regarding the subjects that require early determination: procedures to be adopted for instructing expert witness, witness familiarization and witness proofing, *Prosecutor v. Lubanga,* ICC 01/0401/06952, P-T.Ch. I, 12 September 2007, par. 14.

6 ICTY, Decision on Defence request for audio recording of prosecution witness proofing sessions, *Prosecutor v. Harandinaj et al.*, Case No. IT0484T, T. Ch. I, 23 May 2007, par. 8.

7 Richard C. Wydick, The Ethics of Witness Proofing, 17 Cardozo Law Review 1995, p. 5.

8 ICC, Decision on the Practice of Witness Familiarisation and Witness Proofing, *Prosecutor v. Lubanga,* Case No. ICC01/0401/06, P-T. Ch. I, 8 November 2008, par. 12.

9 Decision on Interlocutory Appeal Regarding Witness Proofing, *Prosecutor v. Karemera, Ngirumpatse and Nzirorera*, A. Ch., *supra* note 1, par. 8.

10 Rules of Procedure and Evidence for the ICTR, adopted on 19 June 1995 as most recently amended on 14 March 2008.

of the statute and the general principles of law'. Thus, it is left to the chambers whether to allow or prohibit witness proofing.

4. Interrelation between the ICTR and the ICC

Nzirorera's motion to challenge a well established practice of the ICTR[11] was clearly inspired by the prohibition of witness proofing in the proceedings before the ICC.[12] Accordingly, the Trial Chamber started its legal analysis with a discussion of the relevant pretrial decision in the Lubanga case.[13] Having summarized the main legal arguments, the Trial Chamber argued that this "decision is not based on a comprehensive knowledge of the established practice of the *ad hoc* tribunals".[14]

The ICC Pre Trial Chamber indeed dealt only briefly with the jurisprudence and practice of ICTY, ICTR, and SCSL.[15] However, a more thorough analysis of the international case law was unnecessary. The Pre-Trial Chamber only had to decide if the *legal framework of the ICC* allows for witness proofing.[16] Pursuant to Article 21 of the Statute of the International Criminal Court (ICC Statute),[17] the chamber has to apply, in the first place, the Statute and its Rules of Procedure and Evidence (ICC RPE)[18], in the second place, where appropriate, applicable treaties and the principles and rules of international law, and then in the third place, general principles of law. Neither the ICC Statute nor the relevant Rules of Procedure and Evidence expressly deal with the admissibility of witness proofing.[19] Even if one argues that the established practice of international tribunals has become a (customary)[20] rule of international law,[21] the ICC enjoys discretion regarding the application of such a rule.[22] In particular, one has to take into account the fact that the legal framework of the ICC establishes a procedural code *sui generis* that differs in parts markedly from those of the *ad hoc* tribunals.[23] The integration of an established practice of the ICTY and ICTR into the proceedings before the ICC may therefore be inappropriate. As the ICC Trial Chamber has clearly demonstrated, witness proofing does not easily fit in the court's general framework.[24] Accordingly, the ICC Pre Trial Chamber has

---

11 See Decision on Defence Motions to Prohibit Witness Proofing, *Prosecutor v. Karemera, Ngirumpatse and Nzirorera*, T. Ch. III, *supra* note 1, par. 9 *et seq.*; Decision on Interlocutory Appeal Regarding Witness Proofing, *Prosecutor v. Karemera, Ngirumpatse and Nzirorera*, A. Ch., *supra* note 1, par. 9 *et seq.;* See also Ruben Karemaker/ B. Don Taylor III/ Thomas Wayde Pittman, Witness Proofing in International Criminal Tribunals: A Critical Analysis of Widening Procedural Divergence, 21 Leiden Journal of International Law 2008, p. 685 *et seq.*

12 Decision on the Practice of Witness Familiarisation and Witness Proofing, *Prosecutor v. Lubanga,* P-T. Ch. I, *supra* note 8. See also the subsequent Trial Chamber's decision in the same case, ICC, Decision Regarding the Practices Used to Prepare and Familiarise for Giving Testimony at Trial, *Prosecutor v. Lubanga*, Case No. ICC01/0401/06, T. Ch. I, 30 November 2007.

13 See Decision on Defence Motions to Prohibit Witness Proofing, *Prosecutor v. Karemera, Ngirumpatse and Nzirorera*, T. Ch. III, *supra* note 1, par. 37.

14 *Ibid.*, par. 8.

15 See Decision on the Practice of Witness Familiarisation and Witness Proofing, *Prosecutor v. Lubanga,* P-T. Ch. I, *supra* note 8, par. 29–35.

16 The differences regarding the applicable law are also stressed in the Decision on Ojdanić Motion to Prohibit Witness Proofing, *Prosecutor v. Milutinović et al.*, T. Ch. III., *supra* note 2, par. 12.

17 Rome Statute of the International Criminal Court of 17 July 1998, entered into force on 1 July 2002, A/CONF. 183/9.

18 Rules of Procedure and Evidence, adopted by the Assembly of State Parties, New York, 310 September 2002, Official Records ICCASP/1/3.

19 See Decision on the Practice of Witness Familiarisation and Witness Proofing, *Prosecutor v. Lubanga,* P-T. Ch. I, *supra* note 8, par. 28; Decision Regarding the Practices Used to Prepare and Familiarise for Giving Testimony at Trial, *Prosecutor v. Lubanga*, T. Ch. I, *supra* note 12, par. 36. See for more detail: Kai Ambos, "Witness proofing" before the ICC: Neither legally admissible nor necessary, in Carsten Stahn/ Göran Sluiter (eds.), The Emerging Practice of the International Criminal Court, Martinus Nijhoff Publishers, Leiden, The Netherlands, p. 602–603; Sergey Vasiliev, Proofing the Ban on 'Witness Proofing': Did the ICC Get it Right?, 20 Criminal Law Forum 2009, p. 208 *et seq.*

20 See Margaret McAuliffe deGuzman, Article 21, paragraph 13, in Otto Triffterer (ed.), Commentary on the Rome Statute of the International Criminal Court, 2nd ed., Beck et al., München 2008.

21 This was indicated by the ICC Prosecution in the Lubanga case: see Decision on the Practice of Witness Familiarisation and Witness Proofing, *Prosecutor v. Lubanga,* P-T. Ch. I, *supra* note 8, par. 29.

22 Margaret McAuliffe deGuzman, *supra* note 20, par. 9.

23 See Claus Kress, The Procedural Law of the International Criminal Court in Outline: Anatomy of a Unique Compromise, 1 Journal of International Criminal Law 2003, p. 603 *et seq.*; Kai Ambos, The Structure of International Procedure: 'Adversarial', 'Inquisitorial' or 'Mixed', in Michael Bohlander (ed.), International Criminal Justice: A Critical Analysis of Institutions and Procedures, Cameron May, London 2007, p. 429 *et seq.* This was also stressed by the T. Ch. in Decision Regarding the Practices Used to Prepare and Familiarise for Giving Testimony at Trial, *Prosecutor v. Lubanga*, T. Ch. I, *supra* note 12, par. 45.

24 This is particularly due to the more civil law orientated division of powers between judges and parties in proceedings before the ICC: Decision Regarding the Practices Used to Prepare and Familiarise for Giving Testimony at Trial, *Prosecutor v. Lubanga*, T.

rightly focused on the question of whether a general principle of law regarding the admissibility of witness proofing exists.[25] These principles have to be derived from *national laws* of legal systems of the world (Article 21 paragraph 1 lit. c) ICC Statute). Even though the practice of the international tribunals may contribute to such a principle,[26] here again one has to respect differences in the procedural law. Thus, as pointed out rightly by the ICC Trial Chamber, the jurisprudence and practice of the *ad hoc* tribunals are not binding on ICC.[27]

Since this is the first case of conflicting jurisprudence between the ICC and the *ad hoc* tribunals, the ICTR Trial Chamber should have dealt with the question of whether the prohibition of witness proofing in proceedings before the ICC limits its discretionary powers regarding the application of additional rules of evidence not expressly provided for in the legal framework of the ICTR. However, as the Appeals Chamber correctly observed, "[t]here is no doctrine of precedence in international law which requires a Trial Chamber to follow practices or decisions adopted by another international court".[28] The ICTR and ICC are, in organization, form and content, independent from each other. Although the ICC has a broader – potential universal – jurisdiction and is constructed as a permanent institution, it is by no means superior to the ICTR. Therefore, the Trial Chamber was not legally obliged to subscribe to the ICC's view on the admissibility of witness proofing.[29]

5. The Impact of National Law and Practice

The ICC Pre Trial Chamber, as well as the ICC Trial Chamber, made an effort to evaluate the national law and practice regarding witness proofing.[30] By contrast, the Nzirorera Trial Chamber did not deal with national examples at all; the Appeals Chamber merely held that "the submission that a number of national jurisdictions prohibit the practice of witness proofing to varying degrees does not [...] make such practice incompatible with the Tribunal's Statute and Rules".[31] As the law of the ICTR does not contain a provision similar to Article 21 paragraph 1 lit. c) ICC Statute, asking for recourse to the legal systems of the world, national precedents traditionally play only a minor role in the jurisprudence of the Tribunal. The ICTR may consider national law, but is not bound by it.[32] Thus, the ICTR Chambers were free to focus on the question of whether or not witness proofing contributes to the fairness of the proceedings.

6. Advantages and Risks of Witness Proofing

In the Trial Chamber's view, witness proofing is "a useful and permissible practice".[33] The Chamber points out that the crimes charged before the ICTY have been committed long ago and that even between the first witness interview in the investigations stage and his or her final testimony at trial, a lot of time, sometimes even years, has gone by. Therefore, pretrial sessions are said to assist the witness in refreshing his or her memory and the parties in the preparation of the trial and thus, "to contribute to a proper administration of

---

Ch. I, *supra* note 12, par. 45. See also Kai Ambos, "Witness proofing" before the ICC: Neither legally admissible nor necessary, *supra* note 19, p. 605. Critically War Crimes Research Office, Witness Proofing at the International Criminal Court, July 2009, p. 27 *et seq.*

25 Decision on the Practice of Witness Familiarisation and Witness Proofing, *Prosecutor v. Lubanga,* P-T. Ch. I, *supra* note 8, par. 35 *et seq.*

26 Kai Ambos, "Witness proofing" before the ICC: Neither legally admissible nor necessary, *supra* note 19, p. 603.

27 Decision Regarding the Practices Used to Prepare and Familiarise for Giving Testimony at Trial, *Prosecutor v. Lubanga*, T. Ch. I, *supra* note 12, par. 44.

28 Decision on Interlocutory Appeal Regarding Witness Proofing, *Prosecutor v. Karemera, Ngirumpatse and Nzirorera*, A. Ch., *supra* note 1, par. 7.

29 *Ibid.* par. 7, see also, Decision on Ojdanić Motion to Prohibit Witness Proofing, *Prosecutor v. Milutinović et al.*, T. Ch. III, *supra* note 2, par. 13.

30 Decision on the Practice of Witness Familiarisation and Witness Proofing, *Prosecutor v. Lubanga,* P-T. Ch. I, *supra* note 8, par. 35; Decision Regarding the Practices Used to Prepare and Familiarise for Giving Testimony at Trial, *Prosecutor v. Lubanga*, T. Ch. I, *supra* note 12, par. 39. See also the comparative overview by Kai Ambos, "Witness proofing" before the ICC: Neither legally admissible nor necessary, *supra* note 19, p. 605 *et seq.*

31 Decision on Interlocutory Appeal Regarding Witness Proofing, *Prosecutor v. Karemera, Ngirumpatse and Nzirorera*, A. Ch., *supra* note 1, par. 11.

32 As to the ICTY: Decision on Ojdanić Motion to Prohibit Witness Proofing *Prosecutor v. Milutinović et al., supra* note 2, par. 13. See also Kai Ambos, *supra* note 19, p. 604.

33 Decision on Defence Motions to Prohibit Witness Proofing, *Prosecutor v. Karemera, Ngirumpatse and Nzirorera*, T. Ch. III, *supra* note 1, par. 10.

justice".[34] Moreover, the chamber believes that pretrial interviews may "reduce the effect of surprise to the Defence in cases where the witness recollects elements that were not previously disclosed".[35] This fits in with the general argumentation of the proponents of witness proofing, which is believed to assist the court in its truth finding function.[36] The alleged advantages of proofing session were summarized concisely by the ICC prosecution as follows:

(i) Providing a detailed review of relevant and irrelevant facts in light of the precise charges to be tried;
(ii) Refreshing the witness's memory of past events through a review of previous statements;
(iii) Ensuring the witness is aware of any issues on which he/she is not permitted to testify about (for instance, due to a previous ruling by the Chamber on inadmissibility of evidence);
(iv) Enabling a more accurate, complete, orderly and efficient presentation of the evidence of a witness in the trial;
(v) Identifying and putting the Defence on notice of any differences in recollection, thereby preventing undue surprise."[37]

Moreover, it should be added that victim-witnesses may benefit from preparation sessions. To testify at an international tribunal with a procedure unknown and unfamiliar to the victims is often a highly stressful event,[38] leading as the case may be to secondary traumatisation.[39] Explaining to them in advance what will happen during their testimony gives them the opportunity to adequately respond to and cope with the situation.[40] This is particular relevant with regard to the preparation of cross-examination, which often has a significant emotional impact on victims.[41]

However, the assumption that witness proofing will contribute to ascertaining the truth is not at all persuasive.[42] As was indicated by Nzirorera's defence,[43] preparation sessions carry the inherent danger of becoming a "rehearsal of in court testimony"[44] conducted in private sessions, which conflicts with the right of the accused to a public trial.[45] The Trial and the Appeals Chamber saw this risk, but decided to take it. The Trial Chamber points out that the manipulation of witness statements is inadmissible,[46] for example, that the prosecution is not allowed to "train, coach, or tamper a witness before he or she gives evidence".[47] Since the defence may challenge in individual cases the manner in which the prosecution has prepared a particular witness, the chamber is convinced that witness proofing is not inherently prejudicial.[48]

---

34 *Ibid.*, par. 17.

35 *Ibid.*

36 Prosecution submissions regarding the subjects that require early determination: procedures to be adopted for instructing expert witness, witness familiarization and witness proofing, *Prosecutor v. Lubanga*, T. Ch. I, *supra* note 5, par. 9; Ruben Karemaker/ B. Don Taylor III/ Thomas Wayde Pittman, *supra* note 11, p. 694.

37 *Ibid.*, par. 16. See also Sergey Vasiliev, Proofing the Ban on 'Witness Proofing': Did the ICC Get it Right?, *supra* note 19, p. 243.

38 This is also stressed by Decision Regarding the Practices Used to Prepare and Familiarise for Giving Testimony at Trial, *Prosecutor v. Lubanga*, T. Ch. I, *supra* note 12, par. 31 *et seq.*

39 See for more detail Herman, Judith Lewis, Complex PTSD: A Syndrome in Survivors of Prolonged and Repeated Trauma, Journal of Traumatic Stress 5, 1992, 377–391.

40 See thereto War Crimes Research Office, Witness Proofing at the International Criminal Court, *supra* note 24, p. 31 *et seq.*

41 Alex C. Lakatos, Evaluating the Rules of Procedure and Evidence for the International Criminal Tribunal in the Former Yugoslawia: Balancing Witnesses' Needs Against Defendants' Rights. 46 Hastings Law Journal 1995, p. 919; Mikaela Heikkilä, International Criminal Tribunals and Victims of Crime, Institute for Human Righs, Saarijärvi 2004, p. 79.

42 In the same vein, see Kai Ambos, *supra* note 19, p. 613.

43 Decision on Defence Motions to Prohibit Witness Proofing, *Prosecutor v. Karemera, Ngirumpatse and Nzirorera*, T. Ch. III, *supra* note 1, par. 21.

44 This expression was used in Decision Regarding the Practices Used to Prepare and Familiarise for Giving Testimony at Trial, *Prosecutor v. Lubanga*, T. Ch. I, *supra* note 12, par. 51. For a criticism of this, see Ruben Karemaker/ B. Don Taylor III/ Thomas Wayde Pittman, Witness Proofing in International Criminal Tribunals: A Critical Analysis of Widening Procedural Divergence, *supra* note 11, p. 693–94.

45 Kai Ambos, "Witness proofing" before the ICC: Neither legally admissible nor necessary, *supra* note 19, p. 614

46 Decision on Defence Motions to Prohibit Witness Proofing, *Prosecutor v. Karemera, Ngirumpatse and Nzirorera*, T. Ch. III, *supra* note 1, par. 15.

47 *Ibid.*, par. 13.

48 *Ibid.*, par. 22. Cf. also War Crimes Research Office, Witness Proofing at the International Criminal Court, *supra* note 24, p. 38 *et seq.*

The Appeals Chamber complemented this argumentation by holding that, "through careful cross examination, a party can explore the impact of preparation on the witness's testimony".[49] In addition, the Appeals Chamber refers to the competence of the Trial Chamber to initiate contempt proceedings and to exclude evidence if appropriate.[50]

In seems, however, highly questionable as to whether these safeguards are sufficient.[51] The main danger does not arise from intentional manipulation of witnesses, which is obviously inconsistent with good professional practice. Rather, chances are that the prosecutor, even if acting in good faith, subconsciously influences the witness by the manner of questioning or his demeanour and actions.[52] In addition, as the ICC Trial Chamber has correctly observed in the Lubanga case, witness preparation may diminish the "helpful spontaneity" of the testimony, which provides the chamber with a useful tool for the assessment of the witness' credibility and for ascertaining the truth.[53]

Moreover, witness preparation may affect the rights of the defence if the witness adds new details to his or her prior statements made in the investigation stage. Late disclosure of incriminatory evidence limits the ability of the defence for trial preparation.[54] The Trial Chamber counters this argument with reference to its powers to take the appropriate measures on a case by case basis.[55] This approach, however, does not adequately guarantee legal certainty.

7. Witness Familiarisation as Solution?

The ICC distinguishes between impermissible witness proofing and admissible witness familiarisation. The latter comprises:

a. Assisting the witness to understand fully the Court proceedings, its participants and their respective roles;
b. Reassuring the witness about her role in proceedings before the Court;
c. Ensuring that the witness clearly understands she is under a strict legal obligation to tell the truth when testifying;
d. Explaining to the witness the process of examination first by the Prosecution and subsequently by the Defence;
e. Discussing matters that are related to the security and safety of the witness in order to determine the necessity of applications for protective measures before the Court; and
f. Making arrangements with the Prosecution in order to provide the witness with an opportunity to acquaint herself with the Prosecution's Trial Lawyer and others who may examine the witness in Court.[56]

---

49 Decision on Interlocutory Appeal Regarding Witness Proofing, *Prosecutor v. Karemera, Ngirumpatse and Nzirorera*, A. Ch., *supra* note 1, par. 13.

50 In a similar vein, see Ruben Karemaker/ B. Don Taylor III/ Thomas Wayde Pittman, Witness Proofing in International Criminal Tribunals: A Critical Analysis of Widening Procedural Divergence, *supra* note 11, p. 695 *et seq.*

51 See also Kai Ambos, 'Witness Proofing' before the International Criminal Court: A Reply to Karemaker, Taylor, and Pittman, 21 Leiden Journal of International Law 2008, p. 915 *et seq.*

52 See for more detail Bender, Der Strafverteidiger 1984, p. 128; Eisenberg, JuristenZeitung 1984, p. 917. In a similar vein, Decision Regarding the Practices Used to Prepare and Familiarise for Giving Testimony at Trial, *Prosecutor v. Lubanga*, T. Ch. I, *supra* note 12, par. 51. As to practical experiences with witness proofing in the USA, see Kai Ambos, *supra* note 50, p. 914 *et seq.* For a different view, see Ruben Karemaker/ B. Don Taylor III/ Thomas Wayde Pittman, Witness Proofing in International Criminal Tribunals: A Critical Analysis of Widening Procedural Divergence, *supra* note 11, p. 695.

53 Decision Regarding the Practices Used to Prepare and Familiarise for Giving Testimony at Trial, *Prosecutor v. Lubanga*, T. Ch. I, *supra* note 12, par. 52. For a different view, see Ruben Karemaker/ B. Don Taylor III/ Thomas Wayde Pittman, Witness Proofing in International Criminal Tribunals: Response to Ambos, 21 Leiden Journal of International Law 2008, p. 920-921; War Crimes Research Office, Witness Proofing at the International Criminal Court, *supra* note 24, p. 30.

54 Kai Ambos, "Witness proofing" before the ICC: Neither legally admissible nor necessary, *supra* note 19, p. 614.

55 Decision on Defence Motions to Prohibit Witness Proofing, *Prosecutor v. Karemera, Ngirumpatse and Nzirorera*, T. Ch. III, *supra* note 1, par. 20. Cf. also Sergey Vasiliev, Proofing the Ban on 'Witness Proofing': Did the ICC Get it Right?, *supra* note 19, p. 243 *et seq.*

56 Decision Regarding the Practices Used to Prepare and Familiarise for Giving Testimony at Trial, *Prosecutor v. Lubanga*, T. Ch. I, *supra* note 12, par. 29.

Witness familiarization, which is carried out by the neutral Victims and Witnesses Unit,[57] ensures that witnesses are sufficiently prepared to testify in an effective manner. Vulnerable witnesses receive the support they need in order to cope with the stressful situation. At the same time, the risk of conscious or subconscious witness manipulation is minimized. Thus, the ICC approach best favours the fairness and efficiency of the proceedings.[58] The ICTR should have taken the chance to adopt this jurisprudence.

Stefanie Bock

[57] Decision Regarding the Practices Used to Prepare and Familiarise for Giving Testimony at Trial, *Prosecutor v. Lubanga*, T. Ch. I, *supra* note 12, par. 27.

[58] In the same vein, see Kai Ambos, "Witness proofing" before the ICC: Neither legally admissible nor necessary, *supra* note 19, p. 612 *et seq.*

Tribunal Pénal International pour le Rwanda
International Criminal Tribunal for Rwanda

APPEALS CHAMBER

Case No. ICTR-99-52-A

ENGLISH
Original: FRENCH

Before: Judge Fausto Pocar, presiding
Judge Mohamed Shahabuddeen
Judge Mehmet Güney
Judge Andrésia Vaz
Judge Theodor Meron

Registrar: Adama Dieng

Date: 20 November 2006

FERDINAND NAHIMANA
JEAN-BOSCO BARAYAGWIZA
HASSAN NGEZE

v.

THE PROSECUTOR

DECISION ON FERDINAND NAHIMANA'S MOTION FOR THE TRANSLATION OF RTLM TAPES IN EXHIBIT C7

Counsel for Ferdinand Nahimana
Jean-Marie Biju-Duval
Diana Ellis

Counsel for Jean-Bosco Barayagwiza
Donald Herbert
Tanoo Mylvaganam

Counsel for Hassan Ngeze
Bharat B. Chadha

Office of the Prosecutor
James Stewart
Neville Weston
George Mugwanya
Linda Bianchi

[page 2] 1. The Appeals Chamber of the International Criminal Tribunal for the Prosecution of Persons Responsible for Genocide and Other Serious Violations of International Humanitarian Law Committed in the Territory of Rwanda and Rwandan Citizens Responsible for Genocide and Other Such Violations Committed in the Territory of Neighbouring States Between 1 January and 31 December 1994 (hereinafter the "Appeals Chamber" and the "Tribunal") is seized by the Appellant Ferdinand Nahimana (hereinafter the "Appellant") of the "Motion to Translate the RTLM Transcripts in Exhibit C7" filed confidentially on 7 April 2006 (hereinafter the "Motion") in which he prays the Chamber to designate a translator to identify, transcribe and translate into the working languages of the Tribunal the excerpts from broadcasts in Exhibit C7 referred to by the Appellant in his Motion.[1] The Appeals Chamber is not persuaded that there is enough justification to classify the Motion as confidential, since the Motion does not deal with protected witnesses and the Appellant does not provide any justification for such classification. Therefore, the Motion and the present Decision must be made public.

2. On 18 April 2006, the Prosecution filed its Response.[2] The Appeals Chamber notes that the Response exceeds the maximum of 10 pages.[3] The Prosecution prays the Appeals Chamber to grant the excess pages, referring to the number of transcripts involved.[4] The Appeals Chamber notes that, in the circumstance, the excess pages are justified and holds that the Response is validly filed.

3. The Appellant has filed no Reply.

I. PROCEDURAL BACKGROUND

4. In July 2000, a series of disclosures about transcripts from "*Radio Télévision Libre des Mille Collines*" (hereinafter "RTLM") was initiated.[5] On 10 January 2001, the Office of the Prosecutor disclosed 21 documents and one box containing 59 RTLM tapes obtained from Witness GO to the Registrar for onward disclosure to the Defence.[6] They were disclosed to the Defence on 15 January 2001.[7] On 20 December 2001, the Prosecution confidentially disclosed a list of 273 RTLM transcripts from October 1993 to July 1994, indicating that they were included in the 345 RTLM transcripts previously disclosed to Counsel for the Appellant (hereinafter the "Defence") under Index Numbers 1-345.[8] The list referred to a translation of 92 transcripts into **[page 3]** at least one of the Tribunal's working languages. The Prosecution undertook to disclose further translations as they became available.[9] In his Motion, the Appellant refers more specifically to the 135 recordings of broadcasts transmitted between October 1993 and 6 April 1994.[10]

5. On 9 January 2002, the Prosecution disclosed to the Defence and to Trial Chamber I (hereinafter the "Trial Chamber") a CD-Rom containing 273 filenames of transcripts of RTLM broadcasts in 1993 and 1994. The purpose of the disclosure was to facilitate access to the content of the broadcasts[11] and the interview of Expert Witness, Mr. Ruzindana,[12] since the Prosecution had stated that those documents had been previously

---

1 Motion, p. 12; *see* also para. 11.

2 Prosecutor's Response to Appellant Nahimana's Motion for Translations of the RTLM Transcripts in Exhibit C7, 18 April 2006 (hereinafter "Response").

3 Practice Direction on the Length of Briefs and Motions on Appeal, 16 September 2002, para. 3.

4 Response, para. 2.

5 *See, e.g., Disclosure of Media Material*, Memorandum of 18 July 2000, from Mr. Elvis Bazawule, disclosing to the Registry and the Accused nine binders containing, *inter alia*, audio tape transcripts; Document Disclosure Binders 54-57, 18 July 2000, containing a total of 48 RTLM transcripts in Kinyarwanda, some with passages in English and French.

6 See Memorandum from Simone Monasebian, Assistant Trial Attorney regarding transmission of material in the Media Case, filed confidentially on 10 January 2001.

7 Dispatch of the Disclosures in the Media Case ICTR-99-52-T, 15 January 2001.

8 Disclosure of Updated List of RTLM Tape Transcriptions and Translations, 20 December 2001 ("Disclosure of 20 December 2001").

9 Disclosure of 20 December 2001, para. 6; as an example of such disclosure, see Memorandum from Stephen Rapp, Senior Trial Attorney, regarding Translation of Radio Broadcasts and the Testimony of Expert-Witness Jean-Pierre Chrétien, 19 June 2002.

10 Motion, para. 2. The Appeals Chamber notes that according to the Prosecution's list, 31 of them had been translated into one of the working languages of the Tribunal; see also Motion, para. 3.

11 Disclosure of 20 December 2001, para. 6.

12 T.14 March 2002, pp. 223-227.

disclosed to the Defence.[13] On 8 March 2002, during the testimony of Expert Witness Rizvi, the Trial Chamber admitted into evidence Exhibits P102 and P103 comprising respectively a list of RTLM transcripts and 210 RTLM tapes.[14]

6. At the close of proceedings on 29 October 2003, the presiding Judge of the Trial Chamber directed the Registry to enter the CD-Rom disclosed by the Prosecution on 9 January 2002 as Exhibit C7 and to inform the parties of the filing thereof.[15]

7. On 3 December 2003, the Trial Chamber rendered its Judgement in the instant case.[16] The Appellant appealed the Judgement and filed his Notice of Appeal on 4 May 2004 and his Appeal Brief on 27 September 2004.[17] The Appeals Chamber notes that in his Notice of Appeal - but not in his Appeal Brief - the Appellant contends that the Trial Chamber erred in law by wrongly defining the ingredients of direct and public incitement to commit genocide, "in particular, by finding that the broadcasts were criminal based on partial, incorrect and unfinished translations thereof".[18] Moreover, the Appeals Chamber notes that the entire submissions on the merits of the appeal contain other allegations about the translation and/or interpretation of the **[page 4]** recordings of RTLM broadcasts.[19] This Decision does not prejudice the Appeals Chamber's ultimate assessment of the grounds of appeal on the merits.

8. At the Status Conference on 9 March 2005, the Appellant requested the translation of a short excerpt of an RTLM broadcast from Exhibit C7 referred to in paragraph 358 of the Judgement. The Pre-Appeal Judge granted the request[20] and the English and French translations were disclosed to the parties on 8 April 2005.[21]

II. DISCUSSION

Submissions by the parties

9. Noting the incompleteness of the translations of the transcripts in Exhibit C7, the Appellant argues that several excerpts of the transcripts selected by the Prosecution were taken into account in the Judgement even though the excerpts were either mistranslated or so truncated as to distort their meaning.[22] Moreover, he asserts that there exists a significant number of transcripts that have not been translated but were nevertheless admitted into evidence as part of Exhibit C7 and which, he contends, confirm that prior to 6 April 1994, RTLM made "[broadcasts aimed at avoiding all forms of ethnic confrontation]".[23] Lastly, he argues that "[the dating of certain excerpts taken into account by the Judges is wrong]".[24]

---

13 *Ibid.*, pp. 226, 229 and 232. The Appeals Chamber notes that the Defence did not contest that these documents had been previously disclosed to it but nonetheless mentioned the potential difficulty in conducting a cross-examination on the basis of documents in Kinyarwanda and requested to be notified about passages that would be used by the Prosecution at trial (*Ibid.*, pp. 240-241).

14 Tapes numbered 0001 to 0344; see T.8 March 2002, p. 27 (P102) and p. 85 (P103).

15 *See* Inter-Office Memorandum from Judge Navanethem Pillay, presiding Judge of the Trial Chamber, 29 October 2003, reproduced in Annex 7 of Appellant Nahimana's Brief in Response, 21 April 2006. Moreover, the memorandum stated that (i) the CD-Rom in question had been mentioned during Alison Des Forges' testimony on 23 May 2002 and in her expert report admitted as Exhibit P158A and (ii) a list of audio tapes including broadcasts contained in the CD-Rom had been tendered as Exhibit P102 during Mr. Kaiser Rizvi's testimony.

16 *The Prosecutor v. Ferdinand Nahimana and Others,* Case No. ICTR-99-52-T, Judgement and Sentence, 3 December 2003 ("Judgement").

17 "Notice of Appeal", 4 May 2004 ("Notice of Appeal"; "Appeal Brief (revised)", 27 September 2004 (confidential version) and 1 October 2004 (public version) ("Appeal Brief").

18 Notice of Appeal, p. 13.

19 *See*, in particular, Appeal Brief, paras. 194, 203, 237-241, 567-569; Defence Response, 21 April 2006 ("Brief in Response"), paras. 61-62, 64-70 and Annex 8 "The language of the transcripts of RTLM broadcasts up until 6 April 1994 (Chambers Exh. C7)".

20 T.9 March 2005, pp. 10-11.

21 Court Management Section's communication of 8 April 2005, pp. 2107/A and 2106/A.

22 Motion, para. 7.

23 *Idem.*

24 *Idem.*

10. The Appellant submits that he only became aware of the transcripts in Exhibit C7 through "[a laborious and time-consuming effort]"[25] and that "[unlike the Judges of the Trial Chamber, who were able to make their determination only on the basis of a tiny selection made by the Office of the Prosecutor, the Appellant has today, for the first time, a representative view of the broadcasts]".[26] Therefore, he requests the designation of an expert to rectify the contested translations and to translate the "[transcripts identified by the Appellant which were admitted into evidence and the content of which could not be reviewed by the Judges]", as well as the correction of the dating of certain broadcasts.[27]

11. In its Response, the Prosecution submits that the Motion must be denied, as it constitutes an abuse of process and an unacceptable attempt to make up for the Appellant's failings at trial.[28] It contends that since the transcripts had been disclosed to the Appellant as early as 2000,[29] **[page 5]** before and during his trial, he could and should have made his request at the first instance stage or in the context of his appeal on the merits.[30] Moreover, such a Motion can only be filed by showing the importance or impact, if any, of the alleged translation errors on the verdict under appeal.[31]

12. In any event, the Prosecution argues that the appeal procedure is not designed to allow an accused to make arguments pertaining to evidence that was before the Trial Chamber or to the Chamber's assessment of that evidence.[32] It argues further that since the Appellant does not raise mere errors of translation or recording, but rather issues of interpretation or assessment of evidence by the Trial Chamber, these issues must be raised in an appeal on the merits rather than in a pre-appeal motion.[33]

Analysis

13. In order to justify, at the appeal stage, a request to revise the translation of exhibits filed in first instance, the Appellant must show that there are legitimate doubts as to the accuracy of the translation and that it is in the interest of justice to clarify such issue at this stage of the proceedings.[34] In view of the advanced stage of the appeal proceedings in the instant case, the Appeals Chamber will grant such a request only if it considers, in the light of the translations referred to by the Appellant, that excluding those documents would lead to a denial of justice. With regard to the request to translate recordings and passages of broadcasts not translated during the trial, the Appeals Chamber will grant the request only if the Appellant can show that he was unable to obtain the translation despite exercising diligence and that the lack of translation of those documents would lead to a miscarriage of justice.[35] Lastly, contesting the Trial Chamber's interpretation of a translated document and alleging that the Trial Chamber failed to consider documents which the Appellant considers to be relevant, including non-translated documents, are matters for the appeal on the merits and will therefore not be considered in the present Decision.

---

25 *Ibid.*, para. 5.

26 *Ibid.*, para. 6.

27 *Ibid.*, para. 8.

28 Response, paras. 1, 3-11.

29 *Ibid.*, para. 6, which refers, with no further details, to a disclosure in July 2000.

30 *Ibid.*, paras. 1, 5-6, 14, 19.

31 *Ibid.*, para. 3.

32 *Ibid.*, para. 13.

33 *Ibid.*, paras. 1, 13.

34 *See*, by analogy, *The Prosecutor v. Elizaphan Ntakirutimana and Gérard Ntakirutimana,* Cases Nos. ICTR-96-10-A and ICTR-96-17-A, Decision on Defence Motion to Strike Annex B from the Prosecution Response Brief and for Re-Certification of the Record, 24 June 2004, p. 3.

35 *See,* further, the Status Conference of 9 March 2005 in which the Pre-Appeal Judge noted, in response to one of the Appellant's questions regarding the translation of briefs before a Trial Chamber, that "I would have thought that we were past the stage of when one's brief's appeal is filed, instead of going back onto the request of translation of documents at trial" (T.9 March 2005, p. 9).

a. Alleged mistranslations [page 6]

14. The Appellant contends that the excerpts of the broadcasts on 30 November 1993,[36] 6 January 1994[37] and 31 March to 1 April 1994[38] taken into consideration by the Trial Chamber were manifestly mistranslated. The Prosecution argues that the Appellant has been in possession of the Kinyarwanda transcripts of the said broadcasts and their contested translations for many years, and that he could thus have made those submissions during his trial or in his Appeal Brief.[39] It further argues that the Appellant did not raise any genuine mistranslation requiring correction[40] and that even if the translation and interpretation suggested by the Appellant were to be accepted, they would not in any way change the Trial Chamber's findings. More specifically, with regard to the 30 November 1993 broadcast, the Prosecution contends that the punishments were targeted at the Tutsi, and that there is no justification for the translation and interpretation suggested by the Appellant.[41] As regards the 6 January 1994 broadcast, the Prosecution points out that the source of the translation of this recording was the International Monitor Institute, which produced summaries of the radio broadcasts rather than exact translations of their verbatim transcripts.[42] Lastly, as regards the broadcast of 31 March to 1 April 1994, the Prosecution notes that the Appellant alleges an interpretation error rather than a translation error.[43]

15. With regard to the 30 November 1993 broadcast,[44] the Appeals Chamber notes that the corrected and completed translation disclosed by the Registrar on 8 April 2005[45] forms part of the appeal file and will be duly taken into account by the Appeals Chamber in its review of the **[page 7]** appeal on the merits.[46] With regard to the corrected version, the Appeals Chamber is of the opinion that the interpretation suggested by the Appellant does not raise any legitimate doubt as to the accuracy of the translation and does not show that a clarification of the translation at this stage of the proceedings is necessary in the interests of justice.

16. As regards the broadcast transmitted on 5 and 6 January 1994, the Appeals Chamber notes that neither Exhibit C7 nor Exhibit P103/45,[47] is explicitly mentioned in paragraphs 352 to 356 of the Judgement. The Trial Chamber's finding in respect of the opinion expressed by Kantano Habimana stems in reality from its analysis of Exhibit 1D9 filed by the Defence and admitted into evidence on 1 November 2000,[48] rather than

---

36 Motion, para. 12, with reference to para. 358 of the Judgement. The Appellant contests the accuracy of the translation admitted into evidence by the Trial Chamber and the translation disclosed by the Registry on 8 April 2005. He submits that the punishments were targeted at the "bad ones", i.e. the *Inkotanyi* fighters rather than the "Tutsis", as shown in the Judgement, or "those who support the bad ones" (a phrase that appeared in the translation of 8 April 2005).

37 Motion, para. 13 with reference to paras. 352-356 of the Judgement. According to the Appellant, this excerpt was mistranslated from Kinyarwanda to English, for the sentence accepted by the Trial Chamber – "You can really feel that they want also to get to power" does not appear in the original text.

38 Motion, para. 14, with reference to paras. 381-383 of the Judgement. The Appellant submits that the Trial Chamber's finding that Hitimana's speeches incited people to take retaliatory action against Dr. André Ngirabanyiginya and his family stems from a translation error.

39 Response, paras. 14, 19, 21and 23.

40 *Ibid.*, para. 12.

41 *Ibid.*, para. 16. The Prosecution submits, *inter alia*, that in any case, the words "the latter" in the uncontested part of the translation clearly refers to the words "the Tutsis" in the previous sentence. Therefore, the meaning of the passage does not change as the sentence "they will be discovered and [...] will receive an appropriate punishment" refers to the Tutsi who allegedly supported the *Inkotanyi*. The Prosecution further argues that this broadcast was analysed by the Trial Chamber as evidence in respect of the period before 6 April 1994, i. e. at a time when the entire Tutsi population was associated or even assimilated to the terms *"Inyenzi"* and *"Inkotanyi"*.

42 *Ibid.*, para. 21. The Prosecution also submits that the Appellant was in possession of the recording and of the original transcript in Kinyarwanda and the French translation and that, in any event, the interpretation suggested by the Appellant would change nothing in the Trial Chamber's findings (Response, paras. 21-22).

43 *Ibid*, para. 24.

44 Admitted as Exhibit P36/5A (Kinyarwanda version) on 20 March 2002 (T.20 March 2002, pp. 133-136 and 169-170) and as Exhibit P36/5B and C (English and French versions) on 5 July 2002 (T.5 July 2002, pp. 89-90).

45 *See* para. 8 above.

46 In this regard, the Appeals Chamber notes that the Appellant contests the relevant Trial Chamber's findings in respect of the RTLM broadcasts as part of his appeal on merits (Appeal Brief, paras. 194 and 203).

47 Exhibit P103/45A (Kinyarwanda version), containing the recording in question, was admitted into evidence on 20 March 2002 (T.20 March 2002, pp. 136-137).

48 Judgement, paras. 351-355. Exhibit 1D9 (English and French versions) was admitted into evidence on 1 November 2000 (T.1 November 2001[*sic*], pp. 72-73). Exhibits 1D9 and C7-044E (pp. K198097 *et seq.*) came from the same text in Kinyarwanda, and contain an excerpt from the broadcast of 5 and 6 January 1994. They contain the same English translation/summary, but the French

Exhibit C7 as the Appellant claims. In this regard, the Appeals Chamber holds that the French and English translations of the transcripts in question appearing in Exhibit 1D9 contain the sentence "*On sent vraiment qu'ils veulent également accéder au pouvoir*" or "You can really feel that they want also to get to power".[49] The Exhibit also contains a "translator's certificate" signed by Ms. Gaudence Mukakigeli, a duly qualified translator accredited by the Tribunal "to translate and interpret from the Kinyarwanda and English/French languages into the English/French and Kinyarwanda languages".[50] In view of the foregoing, the Appeals Chamber finds that the Appellant's Motion to review the translation of a document forming part of Exhibit C7 lacks merit.

17. Lastly, with regard to the broadcast transmitted from 31 March to 1 April 1994, the Appeals Chamber notes that the paragraph in the Judgement contested by the Appellant reads as follows:

> "The Chamber notes the request that if rumours of Dr. Ngirabanyigina's support for the *Inkotanyi* were true, 'let his neighbours telephone us again and tell us that the doctor and his family are no longer in the house', a request, in the Chamber's view, that action be taken against the doctor and his family."[51]

The Appeals Chamber notes that this passage in the Judgement deals with an analysis of Exhibit P103/189C admitted on 23 May 2002[52] and cited in paragraph 381 of the Judgement, not with **[page 8]** Exhibit C7. The Appellant's submission that an error stems from the fact that the sentence in question was taken out of context is therefore unfounded, since Exhibit P103/189C contains the full text of the relevant passage. Moreover, the Appeals Chamber notes that the Appellant does not specifically identify how the translation he is proposing would differ from the one in Exhibit P103/189C, or the impact any correction by him would have on the Trial Chamber's finding. In any event, the Appeals Chamber agrees with the Prosecutor that a submission on an alleged error of interpretation, not of translation, must be raised during the appeal on the merits and is not a matter that can be ruled on during the pre-appeal hearing.[53]

b. Excerpts not translated in full

18. The Appellant submits that "[significant passages]" were omitted in the translation of the excerpts of the broadcasts of 25 and 26 October 2003[54] and 14 March 1994[55] referred to in paragraphs 363 and 377 to 379

---

translation in Exhibit C7-044F is different from the translation in Exhibit 1D9: the sentence "You can really feel that they want also to get to power" appears in the French text in Exhibit 1D9, but not in the translation in Exhibit C7-044F. In the French version of the Judgement, the Trial Chamber cites the French translation in Exhibit 1D9. In their submissions, the Appellant cites the French translation in Exhibit C7-044F, p. K0169341, while the Prosecution refers more generally to Exhibit C7-044K.
The Appeals Chamber also notes a discrepancy in the referencing: CD 44 (recorded as 44-K, 044-E and 044-F for the Kinyarwanda, English and French versions) in Exhibit C7 carries the identification "RTLM 0045 of 05/06/94, Radio Rwanda"; Exhibit P103/45A carries the references "RTLM 0045 of 05/06/94, Radio RTLM"; Exhibit 1D9 is referenced as "RTLM 05-06/01/94".

49 Exhibit 1D9, p. 6 (French version) and p. 3352*bis* (English version).

50 *Ibid.*, pp. 3345*bis* – 3344*bis*.

51 Judgement, para. 383. The Appeals Chamber notes that, in his Motion, the Appellant refers to the French translation of the Judgement, dated 5 April 2004, replaced with the "official version" on 2 March 2006.

52 P. K0162236-38, the disputed passage in this document reads as follows: "Let us now talk about the death of Katumba which sparked off a lot of concern ... It is being reported that yesterday, Kigali town came to a standstill because of his death ... Apart from misleading public opinion, was it only KATUMBA who died in this town, Kigali? Or wasn't it, on the other hand, because of the death of a Tutsi called Maurice? Surely, was it the death of Katumba, a Hutu, which caused the stoppage of all activities in Kigali? Can't such a situation be brought about by the death of a Tutsi? Let them not deceive anybody. Are Katumba's assassins not the same people who killed Maurice to cause confusion, that is to say, in order to give the impression that a Tutsi and a Hutu lost their lives in the same circumstances? We are not stupid. Let them not spread confusion, because from the rumours I have just received, Doctor André NYIRABANYIGINYA, a radiologist at King Fayçal Hospital, the most modern hospital in the country, ... he also works at the CHK on part-time basis, ... huh ... people are saying: "From what we know about him, ha!, he has never stopped saying ... even when he was still in Brussels, that he would support the *Inkotanyi*. Let us assume that those are rumours, but if it is true, let his neighbours telephone us again and tell us that the doctor and his family are no longer in his house".

53 Moreover, the Appeals Chamber notes that in paragraphs 569 of his Appeal Brief, the Appellant already takes issue in general terms, with the Trial Chamber's finding on the existence of a "causal link" between the killing of Tutsi civilians and the message of ethnic targeting for death that was disseminated through RTLM.

54 Motion, para. 16. The Appellant submits that a full translation of this text would enable to ascertain that the person who made the remarks cited in the Judgement was not the RTLM journalist, but a third party.

55 *Ibid*, para. 17. According to the Appellant, the incomplete nature of the translation of this broadcast led the Trial Chamber to make the erroneous finding that "[the Journalist Gahigi listed in an RTLM broadcast 'the names of all the family members' of an *Inkotanyi* called Manzi Sudi]", whereas the "[cut off]" according to him, clarifies the rest of the remarks and "[emphasizes that all

of the Judgement, respectively. He submits that these omissions distort the meaning of the recordings in question, which would explain the Trial Chamber's erroneous analysis.

19. The Prosecution argues that the Appellant's submissions with regard to the deliberate cutting off of excerpts are unfounded and vexatious.[56] Regarding the broadcast of 25 October 1993, the Prosecution notes that the Appellant refers to the official French translation tendered in evidence by the Defence as Exhibit 1D49 and submits that the use of the ellipsis in the **[page 9]** Judgement signals an omission by the Trial Chamber, not by the translator.[57] Moreover, the Prosecution notes that French and English translations of the 14 March 1994 broadcast were admitted in July 2002 and June 2003[58] and that the Appellant then had the opportunity to raise any problems relating to them. It submits further that, in any case, the translation proposed by the Appellant could not in any way change the Trial Chamber's finding.[59]

20. The Trial Chamber cited the RTLM broadcast of 25 October 1993, among others, to illustrate the fact that "[t]he RTLM broadcasts engaged in ethnic stereotyping in economic terms as well as political terms",[60] and found that those broadcasts "show a complex interplay between ethnic and political dynamics".[61] The Appeals Chamber notes that the transcription of that same broadcast appears in Exhibit 1D49C tendered in evidence by the Defence on 24 May 2001. The disputed passage of this broadcast is translated in its entirety, including the sentences identified by the Appellant as being "deliberately omitted by the translator". Consequently, even though it is true that the Trial Chamber in the Judgement refers to Exhibit C7, not Exhibit 1D49C, it is apparent that the Trial Chamber was in possession of the whole translation. The Appeals Chamber considers, moreover, that the Trial Chamber's use of the ellipsis in the disputed passage[62] shows that it was the Chamber, and not the translator, that deliberately omitted to cite the passages referred to by the Appellant, and that the Trial Chamber therefore made its findings with full knowledge of the facts. Lastly, the Appeals Chamber notes that the Appellant takes issue with the Trial Chamber's relevant findings in his appeal on the merits.[63]

21. Regarding the broadcast of 14 March 1994, the Appeals Chamber notes at the outset that the Trial Chamber refers to Exhibit P36/54C admitted on 1 July 2002, not Exhibit C7. The Appeals Chamber notes that this Exhibit comprised only the French translation of the two paragraphs referred to by the Appellant.[64] However, on 3 June 2003, the Trial Chamber admitted Exhibit P36/54E which contained the full French translation of the recording in question.[65] Since the Appellant did not take issue with the accuracy of this translation, the Appeals Chamber considers that his request is therefore unfounded.[66]

22. In the light of the foregoing, the Appellant's request to have the purportedly untranslated excerpts translated by an expert designated by the Appeals Chamber is dismissed.

c. Untranslated broadcasts

23. The Appellant submits that "[a significant number of the untranslated transcripts admitted in evidence confirm that radio RTLM, prior to 6 April 1994, aired broadcasts to avoid any ethnic **[page 10]** confrontation]",[67] and requests their translation. The Prosecutor submits that the Appellant's request

---

the people mentioned were full members of the same RPF clandestine brigade in Biryogo area, without having any family ties with Manzi Sudi Fadil".

56 Response, paras. 28-35 with reference to the Motion, paras. 15-17.

57 *Ibid.*, paras. 29-30.

58 *Ibid.*, para. 33, referring to Exhibits P36/54A, B, C and E.

59 *Ibid.*, para. 33.

60 Judgement, para. 363. The Trial Chamber specified in this respect that during this broadcast "Noël Hitimana discussed the disproportionate Tutsi ownership of taxis".

61 *Ibid.*, para. 468.

62 *Ibid.*, para. 363.

63 *See, e. g.,* Appeal Brief, paras. 194, 203.

64 The whole text of the recording in Kinyarwanda is contained in Exhibit P36/54A admitted on 20 March 2002.

65 *The Prosecutor v. Ferdinand Nahimana et al.*, Decision on the Prosecution's Application to Admit Translations of RTLM Broadcasts and Kangura Articles, 3 June 2003, admitting the French translation of Exhibit P36/54E (*see especially* p. K0249617).

66 Moreover, the Appeals Chamber notes that the Appellant challenges the Trial Chamber's findings on the broadcast of 14 March 1994 in his appeal on the merits, Appeal Brief, paras. 237-241, 567-569.

67 Motion, para. 7.

regarding the untranslated broadcasts is as an abuse of process, in that it constitutes an attempt by the Appellant to make use, at the appeal stage, of evidence that was available to him or had been filed during the first instance proceedings, and which he had knowingly chosen not to use.[68] The Prosecution notes that some of the broadcasts referred to by the Appellant had already been translated into one of the working languages of the Tribunal.[69] In any event, it emphasizes that even if the untranslated broadcasts had been considered at trial, they would not have had the effect of conclusively changing the Trial Chamber's findings.[70]

24. First of all, the Appellant refers to an excerpt from the broadcasts of 29 and 30 November and of 1 December 1993 comprising the remarks made by Gaspard Gahigi, Editor-in-Chief of RTLM, on the occasion of murders committed in Mutura *commune* at the end of November 1993.[71] The Appeals Chamber notes that the passage cited by the Appellant and which he alleges to be untranslated, matches *verbatim* with the passage contained in Exhibit C7,[72] as well as Exhibit P36/5C admitted on 5 July 2002.[73] The Appellant then refers to an excerpt from a broadcast of 17 and 18 March 1994, containing an exchange between two RTLM journalists, Rucogoza and Mbilizi.[74] The Appeals Chamber notes that the excerpt referred to by the Appellant matches word for word the passages in French contained in Exhibit C7,[75] as well as in Exhibit P103/170C admitted on 3 June 2003.[76] Consequently, the Appellant's request regarding the translation of these transcripts is totally without merit.

25. Next, the Appellant proposes translation of the excerpts from untranslated broadcasts of which the transcripts in Kinyarwanda are contained in Exhibit C7. The Appeals Chamber notes however, that all these recordings were disclosed to the Appellant during the trial and were admitted as exhibits well before its conclusion. That was the case for the excerpts from the broadcasts aired: **[page 11]**

- On 2 and 4 December 1993, in which Gaspard Gahigi *inter alia* urged listeners to "[denounce any ethnic provocation]";[77]
- On 3, 6 and 7 December 1993, in which Gaspard Gahigi talks about the role of the Church;[78]
- On 18 and 19 March 1994 in which the speaker asserts, according to the Appellant, that "[Rwandans should develop the spirit of tolerance, live in peace]";[79]
- On 14 and 15 December 1994 in which, according to the Appellant, Journalist Kantano "[denounces people who were instigating others or who were trying to cause violence even at football matches]" and "[calls for the avoidance of violence]";[80]
- On 21 and 22 December 1993, in which Kantano Habimana asserts, according to the Appellant, "[that good coexistence between the *Inkotanyi* and other Rwandans is necessary]";[81]
- On 22, 23 and 24 December 1993, in which, according to the Appellant, Kantano Habimana contradicts those who were accusing radio RTLM of having been against the implementation of the Arusha Accord;[82]

---

68 Response, paras. 1, 36-37.

69 *Ibid.*, paras. 41-42.

70 *Ibid.*, paras. 38-52 referring to the Motion, paras. 18-27.

71 Motion, para. 18 referring to Exhibit C7, 104F, K0159516.

72 File 104F, p. K0159516.

73 K0159516; Exhibit P36/5A (Kinyarwanda version) was admitted on 20 March 2002 (T. 20 March 2002, pp. 169-170) while its translations into English (P36/5B) and into French (P36/5C) were admitted on 5 July 2002 (T.5 July 2002, p. 90).

74 Motion, para. 21.

75 File 131K, pp. K0216692 to K0216698.

76 Exhibit P103/170C, pp. K0249880 *et seq.*; *See The Prosecutor v. Ferdinand Nahimana et al.*, Case No. ICTR-99-52-T, Decision on the Prosecution's Application to Admit Translations of RTLM Broadcasts and Kangura Articles, 3 June 2003.

77 Motion, para. 19, referring to Exhibit C7, 218K, pp. K0224385-K0224386.

78 *Ibid.*, para. 20, referring to Exhibit C7, 219K, p. K0224367.

79 *Ibid.*, para. 22, referring to C7, Files 80, 85, 133. The Appeals Chamber notes that the Appellant does not specifically identify the missing parts of the translations and notes that File 85F is entirely in French and that parts of File 80K and File 133K are also in French.

80 *Ibid.*, para. 23, referring to Exhibit C7, 240K, p. K0139154.

81 *Ibid.*, para. 24, referring to Exhibit C7, 243K, pp. K0164349-K0164351.

82 *Ibid.*, para. 25, referring to Exhibit C7, 244K, K0139293. The Appellant submits that "the part in square brackets [in his translation] had not been transcribed; the Appellant spotted it in the audio part". Immediately, the Appeals Chamber finds that the

- On 5 March 1994 in which, according to the Appellant, Noël Hitimana warned the leaders of RPF against war within Rwanda;[83]
- On 7 and 8 March 1994, in which Kantano urged the listeners to "[continuously cultivate [unity among Tutsi, Hutu and Twa] and to reject ideas which divide Rwandans]".[84]

These excerpts match the recordings in Kinyarwanda contained in Exhibits P103/287A, P103/288A, P36/68A, P36/12A, P36/15A, P103/316A, P103/335A and P36/50A, respectively, admitted in evidence on 20 March 2002.[85]

26. With respect to the evidence tendered well before the conclusion of the trial (unlike Exhibit C7), the Appeals Chamber holds that the Appellant should have requested translation **[page 12]** before the conclusion of the trial. In this connection, the Appeals Chamber notes that the Appellant made this request more than two years after the Judgement was delivered and, what is more, after filing his Appeal Brief. Consequently, the Appeals Chamber is not persuaded that the Appellant exercised due diligence.

27. Consequently, the Chamber will grant such a request only if it finds, in the light of the translations proposed by the Appellant, that excluding these documents would lead to a manifest miscarriage of justice.[86] In general, the Appeals Chamber notes that the Appellant confines himself to submitting passages of which the translation is allegedly missing from the documents contained in Exhibit C7, without referring to the findings of the Trial Chamber to which they supposedly relate.[87] Furthermore, it is for the Appellant to show, in the context of his appeal on the merits, whether some excerpts in Exhibit C7 permit the conclusion that the Trial Chamber committed an error of fact.[88] There is no reason at this stage to order the requested translation, since the Appellant, who has a good command of the Kinyarwanda and French languages, is in possession of all the material needed to prepare his defence; in particular, he can propose his versions of the translations while making his submissions on appeal. If, when ruling on these submissions, the Appeals Chamber finds that there was an error which led to a miscarriage of justice,[89] it will *proprio motu* order, if need be, that the relevant paragraphs shall be translated.

d. Contested dating

28. The Appellant submits that the error in the dating of a broadcast cited in the Judgement[90] "[confirms the need to re-examine the excerpts taken into account by the Judges, without separating them from their context and carefully verify the translation and interpretation given to them]",[91] The Prosecutor submits that the alleged error as to the date of a broadcast by RTLM does not change the Trial Chamber's findings, which were based on an accurate transcript of the recording.[92] **[page 13]**

29. The Appeals Chamber notes that the transcript cited by the Trial Chamber is indeed dated 12 April 1994, not 4 December 1993 as stated in the Judgement.[93] However, given the fact that the transcript in question is available in the working languages of the Tribunal, the Appellant's allegation bears no relation,

---

Appellant's request goes further than a request for translation, since he includes material which was not part of the file before the Trial Chamber. This request will therefore not be considered.

83 *Ibid.*, para. 26, referring to Exhibit C7, 263K, K0168798.

84 *Ibid.*, para. 27, referring to Exhibit C7, 264K, K0169029.

85 T.20 March 2002, pp. 136-137, 169-170.

86 *See supra*, para. 13.

87 Motion, paras. 18-27 under the common heading "Untranslated broadcasts showing the concern of the Editor-in-Chief of RTLM and his journalists to avoid any ethnic confrontation".

88 The Appeals Chamber notes that these submissions are already included in the Appellant's documents on the merits of his appeal – see *inter alia*, Defence Reply, paras. 64-70 and Annex 8, "[Language of the transcripts of the programmes of radio RTLM up to 6 April 1994] (Chambers Exh. C7)".

89 *See* Article 24(1)(b) of the Statute.

90 Motion, para. 28. The Appellant submits that the Trial Chamber, in paragraph 360 of the Judgement, "[gives 4 December 1993 as the date of a programme actually broadcast on 12 April 1994, that is to say, after the beginning of the massacres, at a time when the Appellant no longer had any connections with the radio station and precisely the day when, being evacuated by plane to Bujumbura, he could not pick up any programme]".

91 *Ibid.*, para 30.

92 Response, paras. 53-54.

93 Exhibit C7, file 0004F, p. K0161629 and file 004E, p. K0163179-80.

since it was tendered in evidence, to a request regarding the authenticity of the translation and is clearly a matter for the appeal on the merits.[94] The Appeals Chamber also finds that his general request to "re-examine the excerpts taken into account" based on the example of this error is without merit: at the appeal stage, it is for the Appellant to identify the errors of fact which occasioned a miscarriage of justice and include the submissions relating to them in his Notice of Appeal and his Appeal Brief.

III. DISPOSITION

30. For these reasons, the Appeals Chamber **DISMISSES** the Motion.

Done in French and English, the French text being authoritative.

Done on 20 November 2006, at the Hague, the Netherlands.

Fausto Pocar
Presiding Judge of the Chamber

[Seal of the Tribunal]

94 The Appeals Chamber notes in this regard that one of the Appellant's submissions on the merits of the appeal is precisely the assertion that "[the historical and political context precludes considering the broadcasts made prior to 6 April 1994 as calls for the extermination of the Tutsi population]". (Appeal Brief, p. 27) *See* also Defence Reply, paras. 61-62 and 67).

Tribunal Pénal International pour le Rwanda
International Criminal Tribunal for Rwanda

IN THE APPEALS CHAMBER

Before: Judge Fausto Pocar, Presiding
Judge Mohamed Shahabuddeen
Judge Mehmet Güney
Judge Andrésia Vaz
Judge Theodor Meron

Registrar: Mr. Adama Dieng

Decision of: 27 November 2006

Ferdinand NAHIMANA
Jean-Bosco BARAYAGWIZA
Hassan NGEZE
(Appellants)

v.

THE PROSECUTOR
(Respondent)

Case No. ICTR-99-52-A

PUBLIC REDACTED VERSION

DECISION ON MOTIONS RELATING TO THE APPELLANT HASSAN NGEZE'S AND THE PROSECUTION'S REQUESTS FOR LEAVE TO PRESENT ADDITIONAL EVIDENCE OF WITNESSES ABC1 AND EB

Counsel for Hassan Ngeze
Mr. Bharat B. Chadha
Mr. Behram N. Shroff

Counsel for Ferdinand Nahimana
Mr. Jean-Marie Biju-Duval
Ms. Diana Ellis

Counsel for Jean-Bosco Barayagwiza
Mr. D. Peter Herbert
Ms. Tanoo Mylvaganam

Office of the Prosecutor
Mr. James Stewart
Mr. Neville Weston
Ms. Linda Bianchi
Mr. Abdoulaye Seye
Mr. Alfred Orono Orono

[page 2] 1. The Appeals Chamber of the International Criminal Tribunal for the Prosecution of Persons Responsible for Genocide and Other Serious Violations of International Humanitarian Law Committed in the Territory of Rwanda and Rwandan Citizens Responsible for Genocide and Other Such Violations Committed in the Territory of Neighbouring States, Between 1 January 1994 and 31 December 1994 ("Appeals Chamber" and "Tribunal", respectively) is seized of:

- "Appellant Hassan Ngeze's Motion to Order The Prosecutor to Disclose Material and/or Statement/s of Witness EB Which Might Have Come in his Possession Subsequent to the Presentation of Forensic Expert's Report on Witness EB's Recanted Statement [*sic*]", filed confidentially by Hassan Ngeze ("Appellant") on 19 June 2006 ("Motion of 19 June 2006"), in which the Appellant requests the Appeals Chamber to order the Prosecutor to disclose material connected with the investigations conducted by the Special Counsel to the Prosecutor in relation with the alleged perjury committed by Witness EB;[1]

- "Appellant Hassan Ngeze's Urgent Motion for Leave to Present Additional Evidence (Rule 115) of Witness ABC1 as per Prosecutor's Disclosure of Transcript of Defence Witness ABC1's Testimony in *The Prosecutor v. Bagosora et al.* Filed on 22nd June 2006 Pursuant to Rule 75(F)(ii) and Rule 68 of the Rules of Procedure and Evidence", filed confidentially by the Appellant on 4 July 2006 ("Motion of 4 July 2006"), in which he requests the Appeals Chamber to admit into evidence the testimony of Defense Witness ABC1 given before the Tribunal on 13 June 2006 in *The Prosecutor v. Bagosora et al.,* Case No. ICTR-98-41-T ("*Bagosora et al.* case") and to call [the witness] to testify in the present case;[2]

- "Appellant Hassan Ngeze's in Person Urgent Motion for Leave to Present Additional Evidence (Rule 115) of Witness EB as per Prosecutor's Disclosure Filed on 20th June 2006 of the Relevant Pages of the Gacaca Records Book Given Before the Gacaca on [REDACTED]", filed confidentially by the Appellant on 14 July 2006 ("Motion of 14 July 2006"),[3] in which he seeks admission into evidence of the testimony of Witness EB given before the Gacaca on [REDACTED]; **[page 3]**

- "Appellant Hassan Ngeze's Urgent Motion for Leave to Present *Further* Additional Evidence (Rule 115) of Witness EB", filed confidentially by the Appellant on 28 August 2006 ("Motion of 28 August

---

1 *See also* Prosecutor's Response to "Appellant Hassan Ngeze's Motion to Order The Prosecutor to Disclose Material and/or Statement/s of Witness EB Which Might Have Come in his Possession Subsequent to the Presentation of Forensic Expert's Report on Witness EB's Recanted Statement", 26 June 2006 ("Response to the Motion of 19 June 2006") and Appellant Hassan Ngeze's Reply to the Prosecutor's Response to "Appellant Hassan Ngeze's Motion to Order The Prosecutor to Disclose Material and/or Statements of Witness EB Which Might Have Come in his Possession Subsequent to the Presentation of Forensic Expert's Report on Witness EB's Recanted Statement", 30 June 2006 ("Reply to the Response to the Motion of 19 June 2006").

2 *See also* Prosecutor's Response to "Appellant Hassan Ngeze's Urgent Motion for Leave to Present Additional Evidence (Rule 115) of Witness ABC1 as per Prosecutor's Disclosure of Transcript of Defence Witness ABC1's Testimony in *The Prosecutor v. Bagosora et al.* Filed on 22nd June 2006 Pursuant to Rule 75(F)(ii) and Rule 68 of the Rules of Procedure and Evidence", filed confidentially on 13 July 2006 ("Response to the Motion of 4 July 2006") and Reply to the Prosecutor's Response to "the Appellant Hassan Ngeze's Urgent Motion for Leave to Present Additional Evidence (Rule 115) of Witness ABC1 as per Prosecutor's Disclosure of Transcript of Defence Witness ABC1's Testimony in *The Prosecutor v. Bagosora et al.* Filed on 22nd June 2006 Pursuant to Rule 75(F)(ii) and Rule 68 of the Rules of Procedure and Evidence", filed confidentially on 20 July 2006 ("Reply to the Response to the Motion of 4 July 2006"). The Appeals Chamber notes that the Response to the Motion of 4 July 2006 was served on the Appellant's Counsel by hand-delivery on 17 July 2006. Therefore, the Appeals Chamber considers the Reply to the Response to the Motion of 4 July 2006 to be filed timely.

3 This Motion had initially been filed by the Appellant in person on 3 July 2006 but was returned to him as deficiently filed in light of the Order Concerning Filings by Hassan Ngeze dated 24 May 2004 and Order to the Registrar dated 26 November 2004. On 14 July 2006, the said Motion was forwarded to the Appeals Chamber by the Appellant's Counsel. On 21 September 2006, following the Appeals Chamber's Decision on Hassan Ngeze's Motions Concerning Restrictive Measures of Detention of 20 September 2006, the Appellant's Counsel requested the Registrar (with copy to the Presiding Judge in the present case) to "treat all filings of Hassan Ngeze's Motion in person and forwarded by [Counsel] as having been withdrawn". On 25 September 2006, the Registrar requested the Appellant's Counsel to address to the Registrar and the Appeals Chamber a precise list of motions that he wishes to withdraw. Up to date, no communication in this regard has been received from the Appellant's Counsel. In these circumstances and in light of the Practice Direction on Withdrawal of Pleadings, the Appeals Chamber considers the Motion of 14 July 2006 withdrawn. (*See Prosecutor v. Edouard Karemera et al.*, Case No. ICTR-98-44-AR72.7, Decision on Prosecution Motion to Withdraw Appeal Regarding the Pleading of Joint Criminal Enterprise in a Count of Complicity in Genocide, 25 August 2006, para. 4, and *Prosecutor v. Aloys Simba,* Case No. ICTR-01-76-A, Notice on Prosecutor's Motion Withdrawing Motion Regarding Confidential Filings, 17 May 2006, p. 2).

2006"), in which he requests the Appeals Chamber to admit into evidence "the additional exculpatory statement of witness EB [...] affirming his recanted statement of 5th April 2005";[4]

- "Prosecutor's Motion Pursuant to Rule 115 to Admit the Envelopes in Which Copies of the Letter Purporting to Be a Statement From Witness EB Were Received", filed confidentially by the Prosecutor on 7 September 2006 ("Motion of 7 September 2006"), in which the Prosecution seeks admission of the envelopes in which copies of the alleged recantation statement of Witness EB were received by the Office of the Prosecutor as additional evidence.

I. PROCEDURAL BACKGROUND

2. Trial Chamber I of the Tribunal ("Trial Chamber") rendered its Judgement in this case on 3 December 2003.[5] The Appellant filed his Notice of Appeal on 9 February 2004,[6] amended on 9 May 2005,[7] and the Appellant's Brief on 2 May 2005.[8] The Prosecution filed its Respondent's Brief on 22 November 2005.[9] The Appellant replied on 15 December 2005.[10]

3. By its Decision of 23 February 2006,[11] the Appeals Chamber admitted as additional evidence on appeal handwritten and typed copies of Witness EB's purported recantation statement dated April 2005 ("Recantation Statement")[12] and the Forensic Report of Mr. Antipas Nyanjwa, an expert in handwriting, who assessed the authenticity of Witness EB's statement,[13] pursuant to Rule **[page 4]** 115 of the Rules of Procedure and Evidence of the Tribunal ("Rules"), and ordered that Witness EB be heard by the Appeals Chamber, pursuant to Rules 98 and 107 of the Rules.[14]

4. On 14 June 2006, the Appeals Chamber dismissed the Prosecution's request for an order to the Appellant to produce the original handwritten and typed versions of Witness EB's purported Recantation Statement, and ordered Witness EB to appear, as a witness of the Appeals Chamber, at an evidentiary hearing, pursuant to Rule 115 of the Rules.[15] By the same decision, the Appeals Chamber modified the protective measures applicable to Witness EB and prohibited the parties, their agents or any person acting on their behalf from contacting Witness EB, unless expressly authorized by the Appeals Chamber.[16]

5. On 20 June 2006, the Prosecution disclosed extracts from the [REDACTED] Gacaca Record Book, dated [REDACTED], which it asserts to be relevant to Witness EB's testimony.[17] The Appeals Chamber recalls that this material cannot currently be considered as tendered into evidence and will therefore not address its contents at the present stage.[18] On 22 June 2006, pursuant to Rules 75 (F)(ii) and 68 of the Rules,

4 *See* Prosecutor's Response to "Appellant Hassan Ngeze's Urgent Motion for Leave to Present *Further* Additional Evidence (Rule 115) of Witness EB", filed confidentially on 7 September 2006 ("Response to the Motion of 28 August 2006"). The Appellant has not filed a reply to the Response to the Motion of 28 August 2006.

5 *The Prosecutor v. Ferdinand Nahimana et al.*, Case No. ICTR-99-52-T, Judgement and Sentence, 3 December 2003 ("Trial Judgement").

6 Defence Notice of Appeal (Pursuant to 108 of the Rules of Procedure and Evidence), 9 February 2004.

7 *Confidential* Amended Notice of Appeal, 9 May 2005.

8 *Confidential* Appellant's Brief (Pursuant to Rule 111 of the Rules of Procedure and Evidence), 2 May 2005.

9 Consolidated Respondent's Brief, 22 November 2005.

10 Appellant Hassan Ngeze's Reply Brief (Article 113 of the Rules of Procedures and Evidence), 15 December 2005.

11 *Confidential* Decision on Appellant Ngeze's Six Motions for Admission of Additional Evidence on Appeal and/or Further Investigation at the Appeal Stage, 23 February 2006 ("*Ngeze* Decision on Additional Evidence").

12 *Ngeze* Decision on Additional Evidence, para. 29; *Confidential* Decision on the Prosecutor's Motion for an Order and Directives in Relation to Evidentiary Hearing on Appeal Pursuant to Rule 115, 14 June 2006 ("Decision of 14 June 2006"), p. 3.

13 Report of the Forensic Document Examiner, Inspector Antipas Nyanjwa, dated 20 June 2005, Annex 4 to the "Prosecutor's Additional Submissions In Response to 'Appellant Hassan Ngeze's Urgent Motion for Leave to Present Additional Evidence (Rule 115) of Witness EB'", filed confidentially on 7 July 2005 ("Forensic Report"). *See Ngeze* Decision on Additional Evidence, para. 41.

14 *Ngeze* Decision on Additional Evidence, para. 81.

15 Decision of 14 June 2006, p. 5.

16 *Ibid.*, p. 6.

17 [REDACTED].

18 *See supra*, at footnote 3.

the Prosecution disclosed the transcript of Witness ABC1's testimony in the *Bagosora et al.* case dated 13 June 2006.[19]

6. On 3 August 2006, the Prosecution informed the Appellant and the Appeals Chamber that it received, on 6 July 2006, a copy of the statement purportedly written by Witness EB dated 15 or 16 December [year illegible] "affirming his earlier recanted statement" ("Additional Statement").[20] The copy of the said document (in Kinyarwanda with a translation into French) was transmitted by the Prosecution to the Appellant on 17 August 2006.[21] The English translation was transmitted to the Appellant on 22 August 2006.[22]

7. On 13 September 2006, the Appellant requested the Prosecution to transmit to him the transcript of Witness WFP10 [DW20] testimony in *The Prosecutor v. Casimir Bizimungu et al.*, Case No. ICTR-99-50-T ("*Bizimungu et al.* case") dated 1 through 4 September 2006, partly given in closed session, which, in the Appellant's belief, "contains exculpatory evidence and is relevant to **[page 5]** the evidentiary hearing of the witness EB before the Appeals Chamber".[23] On 4 October 2006, the Prosecution responded that it was not in a position to accommodate this request because it is too general.[24] The Prosecution also affirmed that, upon review of both the closed and open session transcripts of Witness WFP10's testimony in the *Bizimungu et al.* case, it "has not found any exculpatory material within the meaning of Rule 68(A) of the Rules", specifying that the only mention of Witness EB was made in open session and is thus available to the Appellant.[25]

II. MOTION OF 19 JUNE 2006

8. The Appellant requests the Appeals Chamber to order the Prosecution to disclose material related to investigations into the alleged perjury committed by Witness EB which may have come into its possession after the filing of the Forensic Report.[26] The Appellant submits that such material is necessary for the preparation of his defence and cross-examination of Witness EB during the evidentiary hearing.[27] He suggests that the Appeals Chamber can order the production of additional evidence from either party under Rule 98 of the Rules.[28]

9. The Prosecution responds that the Motion of 19 June 2006 should be dismissed. First, the Prosecution contends that it is well aware of its ongoing obligations under Rule 68 of the Rules and has acted in full compliance with them, notably by making its Disclosures of 20 and 22 June 2006, and will continue to do so.[29] Second, it maintains that since the Motion of 19 June 2006 does not refer to any specific document, it amounts to a "fishing expedition".[30] Third, the Prosecution submits that any material uncovered by the Special Counsel during her investigation is privileged and protected by the provisions of Rule 70 (A) of the Rules and thus, will not be disclosed, except if it falls within the scope of Rule 68.[31]

10. The Appellant replies that he is not asking for any material relating to the Special Counsel's report, but for "the material or statement related to the witness EB only",[32] and notes that "it is not clear from the

---

19 Disclosure of Transcript of Defence Witness ABC1's Testimony in the *Prosecutor v. Bagosora et al.* Pursuant to Rule 75(F) (ii) and Rule 68 of the Rules of Procedure and Evidence, filed confidentially on 22 June 2006 ("Disclosure of 22 June 2006").

20 Request for a Further Extension of the *Urgent Restrictive Measures in the Case Prosecutor v. Hassan Ngeze, pursuant to Rule 64* [of the] *Rules Covering the Detention of Persons Awaiting Trial or Appeal Before the Tribunal or Otherwise Detained on the Authority of the Tribunal*, filed confidentially on 3 August 2006.

21 *Id.*

22 Follow up to Prosecutor's Response to [...] Correspondence Dated 15 August 2006 Regarding "Request for Supply of Copy of the Statement of Witness EB Dated 15th December 2005", filed confidentially on 22 August 2006.

23 Request for the Supply of the Court Testimony of Witness Testifying under the Pseudo Name WFP10 [DW20] in Government 1 Case No. ICTR-99-50-T, Bizimungu et al. Given during 1st September to 4th September 2006, as provided under Rule 68 (A) and (E) of the Rules of Procedure and Evidence, filed confidentially on 13 September 2006.

24 Response to [...] "Request for the Supply of the Court Testimony of Witness Testifying under the Pseudo Name WFP10 [DW20] in Government 1 Case No. ICTR-99-50-T, Bizimungu et al. Given during 1st September to 4th September 2006, as provided under Rule 68 (A) and (E) of the Rules of Procedure and Evidence", 4 October 2006, para. 2.

25 *Ibid.*, para. 4.

26 Motion of 19 June 2006, paras 1, 3.

27 *Ibid.*, para. 4.

28 *Ibid.*, para. 6.

29 Response to the Motion of 19 June 2006, para. 3.

30 *Ibid.*, paras 2, 4.

31 *Ibid.*, para. 6.

32 Reply to the Response to the Motion of 19 June 2006, paras 1-2.

Prosecutor's response as to whether the Prosecutor has got any further **[page 6]** statement from the witness EB or not".[33] He assumes that investigators, who were in contact with Witness EB after the filing of the Forensic Report and before the Appeals Chamber's prohibition of contact, might have received further material from Witness EB.[34] Finally, he affirms that, given the circumstances, he is unable to give further description of the materiel required.[35]

11. The Appeals Chamber recalls that the Prosecution has a positive and continuous obligation[36] under Rule 68 of the Rules to, "as soon as practicable, disclose to the Defence any material which in [its] actual knowledge [...] may suggest the innocence or mitigate the guilt of the accused or affect the credibility of Prosecution evidence". Determining what material is subject to disclosure under Rule 68 falls within the Prosecution's discretion and its initial assessment of such exculpatory material must be done in good faith.[37] However, Rule 68(a) does not impose an obligation on the Prosecution to search for material which it does not have knowledge of, nor does it entitle the Defence to embark on a "fishing expedition".[38] Indeed, when an accused requests a Chamber to order the production of material, the accused's request "has to be sufficiently specific as to the nature of the evidence sought and its being in the possession of the addressee of the request".[39] At the same time, such request is not required to be "as specific as to precisely identify which **[page 7]** documents should be disclosed".[40] Finally, if an accused wishes to show that the Prosecution is in breach of these obligations, he/she must identify the material sought, present a *prima facie* showing as to its probable exculpatory nature, and prove the Prosecution's custody or control thereof.[41] Even when the Defence satisfies the Chamber that the Prosecution has failed to comply with its Rule 68 obligations, the Chamber will examine whether the Defence has actually been prejudiced by such failure before considering whether a remedy is appropriate.[42]

---

33 *Ibid.*, para. 5.

34 *Ibid.*, para. 3

35 *Ibid.*, para. 6.

36 Decision on Appellant Jean-Bosco Barayagwiza's Motion Requesting That the Prosecution Disclosure of the Interview of Michel Bagaragaza Be Expunged from the Record, 30 October 2006 ("*Barayagwiza* Decision on Prosecution Disclosure"), para. 6; *The Prosecutor v. Miroslav Bralo*, Case No. IT-95-17-A, Decision on Motions for Access to *Ex Parte* Portions of the Record on Appeal and for Disclosure of Mitigating Material, 30 August 2006 ("*Bralo* 30 August 2006 Decision"), para. 29; *Prosecutor v. Edouard Karemera et al.,* Case No. ICTR-98-44-AR73.7, Decision on Interlocutory Appeal Regarding the Role of the Prosecutor's Electronic Disclosure Suite in Discharging Disclosure Obligations, 30 June 2006 ("*Karemera* 30 June 2006 Decision"), para. 9; *Prosecutor v. Théoneste Bagosora et al.,* Case Nos. ICTR-98-41-AR73 & ICTR-98-41-AR73(B), Decision on Interlocutory Appeals of Decision on Witness Protection Orders, 6 October 2005 ("*Bagosora et al.* 6 October 2005 Decision"), para. 44; *Prosecutor v. Tihomir Blaškić,* Case No. IT-95-14-A, *Confidential* Decision on Prosecution's Application to Seek Guidance from the Appeals Chamber regarding Redaction of the Statement of "Witness Two" for the Purposes of Disclosure to Paško Ljubičić under Rule 68, 30 March 2004 ("*Blaškić* 30 March 2004 Decision"), para. 32; *Prosecutor v. Tihomir Blaškić,* Case No. IT-95-14-A, Decision on the Appellant's Motions for the Production of Material, Suspension or Extension of the Briefing Schedule, and Additional Filings, 26 September 2000 ("*Blaškić* 26 September 2000 Decision"), paras 29-32.

37 Barayagwiza Decision on Prosecution Disclosure, para. 6; *Bralo* 30 August 2006 Decision, para. 30; *Prosecutor v. Juvénal Kajelijeli,* Case No. ICTR-98-44A-A, Judgement, 23 May 2005 ("*Kajelijeli* Appeal Judgement"), para. 262; *Prosecutor v. Dario Kordić and Mario Čerkez*, Case No. IT-95-14/2-A, Appeal Judgement, 17 December 2004 ("*Kordić* Appeal Judgement"), para. 183; *Prosecutor v. Radoslav Brđanin,* Case No. IT-99-36-A, Decision on Appellant's Motion for Disclosure Pursuant to Rule 68 and Motion for an Order to the Registrar to Disclose Certain Materials, 7 December 2004 ("*Brđanin* 7 December 2004 Decision"), p. 3; *Prosecutor v. Tihomir Blaškić,* Case No. IT-95-14-A, Appeal Judgement, 29 July 2004, para. 264; *Prosecutor v. Radislac Krstić*, Case No IT-98-33-A, Judgement, 19 April 2004 ("*Krstić* Appeal Judgement"), para. 190; *Blaškić* 4 March 2004 Decision, para. 44; *Blaškić* 30 March 2004 Decision, paras 31-32; *Blaškić* 26 September 2000 Decision, para. 45.

38 *Bralo* 30 August 2006 Decision, para. 30; *Kajelijeli* Appeal Judgement, paras 262-263, *Blaškić* Appeal Judgement, para. 268; *Prosecutor v. Enver Hadžihasanović et al.,* Case No. IT-01-47-AR73, Decision on Appeal from Refusal to Grant Access to Confidential Material in Another Case, 23 April 2002 ("*Hadžihasanović* 23 April 2002 Decision"), p. 3. *See also Prosecutor v. Casimir Bizimungu et al.,* Case No. ICTR-99-50-T, Decision on Bicamumpaka's Motion for Disclosure of Exculpatory Evidence (MDR Files), 17 November 2004, paras 11-14; *Prosecutor v. Casimir Bizimungu et al.,* Case No. ICTR-99-50-T, Decision on Prosper Mugiraneza's Motion Pursuant to Rule 68 for Exculpatory Evidence Related to Witness GKI (TC), 14 September 2004, paras 8-12.

39 *Bralo* 30 August 2006 Decision, para. 30; *Blaškić* 26 September 2000 Decision, para. 40; *Blaškić* 29 October 1997 Decision, para. 32.

40 *Bralo* 30 August 2006 Decision, para. 30; *Blaškić* 26 September 2000 Decision, para. 40.

41 *Bralo* 30 August 2006 Decision, para. 31; *Kajelijeli* Appeal Judgement, para. 262; *Brđanin* 7 December 2004 Decision, p. 3.

42 *Bralo* 30 August 2006 Decision, para. 31; *Kajelijeli* Appeal Judgement, para. 262; *Krstić* Appeal Judgement, para. 153; *see also Prosecutor v. Edouard Karemera et al.,* Case No. ICTR-98-44-T, Oral Decision on Stay of Proceedings, 16 February 2006, pp 4 and 8-9

12. Under Rule 70(A) of the Rules, "reports, memoranda, or other internal documents prepared by a party, its assistants or representatives in connection with the investigation or preparation of the case, are not subject to disclosure or notification" under Rules 66 and 67. Pursuant to Rule 70(B), with respect to information provided to the Prosecution on a confidential basis and used "solely for the purpose of generating new evidence", the Prosecution shall not disclose it to the Defence unless it obtains the consent of the person or entity providing such information and, in any event, cannot tender it into evidence without prior disclosure to the Defence.

13. The Appeals Chamber recalls that on 7 July 2005, the Prosecution confidentially filed the "Prosecutor's Additional Submissions in Response to 'Appellant Hassan Ngeze's Urgent Motion for Leave to Present Additional Evidence (Rule 115) of Witness EB'", in which it disclosed certain results of the investigations with respect to Witness EB.[43] These submissions were taken into account by the Appeals Chamber when assessing the *prima facie* credibility of Witness EB's additional evidence.[44] On 7 April 2006, the Prosecution specified that, although it was not in the position to provide a date for conclusion of the investigations, it was taking the necessary measures in order to ensure the communication of the results as soon as possible.[45] The Appeals Chamber notes that the Prosecution continually refers to issues related to Witness EB in its submissions concerning the restrictive measures applicable to the Appellant, notably "in the context of the ongoing investigations, led by the Special Counsel to the Prosecutor".[46] It notes, *inter alia*, that such measures are still necessary, "including in light of the recent letter, purportedly written by witness EB, with multiple copies mailed, from both Rwanda and Tanzania, to three Prosecution's **[page 8]** Investigators".[47] Further, on 4 September 2006, the Prosecution claimed that the Additional Statement "can only be construed as further evidence that the restrictive measures are appropriate and should even be strengthened, particularly in light of the upcoming Rule 115 evidentiary hearing".[48] In a Memorandum dated 11 September 2006, the Prosecution reasserted that there was a continuing campaign, involving the Appellant, to interfere with Witness EB.[49]

14. With respect to the Special Counsel's investigations, the Appeals Chamber has already stated that (i) the material produced in the course of these investigations is likely to fall under the scope of Rule 70(A) of the Rules, and (ii) no existing orders or decisions obliged the Prosecution to communicate to the Appellant a report that could be prepared by the Special Counsel following her investigations.[50] At the same time, the Appeals Chamber specifically recalls its jurisprudence on distinctions to be made between witness statements and internal documents falling under Rule 70(A).[51] In any event, neither Rule 70 nor the Decision on Special

---

43 [REDACTED].

44 *Ngeze* Decision on Additional Evidence, para. 20

45 Status Conference, T. 7 April 2006, pp 19-20.

46 [REDACTED].

47 [REDACTED].

48 [REDACTED].

49 [REDACTED]. In its last Memorandum dated 16 November 2006, the Prosecution makes a request for strengthening the restrictive measures in light of the upcoming appeals hearing "in order to safeguard, as much as possible, the integrity and fair outcome of the whole proceedings, as well as the rights to privacy and security of protected witnesses, including Witness EB" [REDACTED].

50 *Décision relative à la Requête de l'Appelant Hassan Ngeze concernant la communication du rapport de l'Avocat général chargé de l'enquête sur les allégations d'entrave au cours de la justice, 23 février 2006* ("Decision on Special Counsel's Report"), paras 15-16 and 19.

51 *Eliézer Niyitegeka v. Prosecutor*, Case No. ICTR-96-14-A, Judgement, 9 July 2004 ("*Niyitegeka* Appeals Judgement"), paras 30-36. The Appeals Chamber specified the following:

> "34. Questions that were put to a witness – thus being part of the witness statement – have to be distinguished from "internal documents prepared by a party", which are not subject to disclosure under Rule 70(A) of the Rules, as an exception to the general disclosure obligation pursuant to Rule 66(A)(ii) of the Rules. A question once put to a witness is not an internal note any more; it does not fall within the ambit and thereby under the protection of Rule 70(A) of the Rules. If, however, counsel or another staff member of the Prosecution notes down a question prior to the interrogation, without putting this question to the witness, such a question is not subject to disclosure. Similarly, any note made by counsel or another staff member of the Prosecution in relation to the questioning of the witness is not subject to disclosure, unless it has been put to the witness.
>
> 35. [...] The Prosecution is obliged to make the witness statement available to the Defence in the form in which it has been recorded. However, something which is not in the possession of or accessible to the Prosecution cannot be subject to disclosure: *nemo tenetur ad impossibile* (no one is bound to an impossibility)." [footnotes omitted].

Counsel should in any way be interpreted as lessening the scope of the Prosecution's Rule 68 obligations described above.[52]

15. The Appeals Chamber takes note of the Prosecution's statement that it is "is well aware of its ongoing disclosure obligations, particularly through Rule 68" and "will continue [...] to honour its disclosure obligations."[53] It also notes that, according to the Prosecution, the Disclosures of 20 and 22 June 2006 were not made in response to the Motion of 19 June 2006, but rather as part of its **[page 9]** obligations to disclose exculpatory or other relevant material.[54] Finally, the Prosecution has specified that it did not provide copies of the Additional Statement to the Appellant prior to his request of 15 August 2006, since the document was at the same time addressed to the Appellant and his Counsel.[55] In these circumstances, although the Appeals Chamber accepts the Appellant's argument that in the present circumstances he cannot identify with more precision the nature of the material to which he seeks access, it finds that the Appellant has provided no indication of any failure of the Prosecution to comply with its disclosure obligation. Therefore, for lack of evidence to the contrary, the Appeals Chamber considers that the Prosecution is acting in good faith.[56] In light of the above, there is no need for the Appeals Chamber to order the Prosecution to comply with its Rule 68 obligations, since "[o]nly where the Defence can satisfy a Chamber that the Prosecution has failed to discharge its obligations should an order of the type sought [...] to be contemplated".[57]

16. In addition, while the parties do not refer to Rule 66(B) of the Rules, the Appeals Chamber notes that the Appellant's request appears to fall under this provision since he is seeking access to documents that would be material to the preparation of his defence with respect to the cross-examination of Witness EB at the evidentiary hearing or might be intended for use by the Prosecution as evidence on that occasion. It has already been clarified that Rule 66(B) applies to appellate proceedings and that, consequently, the Prosecution, on request of the Defence, "has to permit the inspection of any material which is capable of being admitted on appeal or which may lead to the discovery of material which is capable of being admitted on appeal".[58] In this respect, the Appeals Chamber recalls that "purely inculpatory material is not necessarily immaterial for the preparation of the Defence" and that the Prosecution should instead consider "(a) whether the issues to which the material relates are subject of a ground of appeal" or "(b) whether the material could reasonably lead to further investigation by the Defence and the discovery of additional evidence admissible under Rule 115 of the Rules".[59] Therefore, the Appeals Chamber *proprio motu* directs the Prosecution to apply the above-mentioned criteria in order to determine whether it is in possession of any documents that are material to the preparation of the Defence, with the exception of Rule 70 material as discussed above, and then return, if necessary, to the Appeals Chamber for permission to withhold any information provided by these sources under Rule 66(C) of the Rules. **[page 10]**

17. Finally, the Appeals Chamber reiterates that, in compliance with its Decision of 14 June 2006, not only the parties, but also their agents or any other persons on their behalf, are prohibited from contacting or interfering with Witness EB.

See also Prosecutor v. Vidoje Blagojević and Dragan Jokić, Case No. IT-02-60-T, Decision on Vidoje Blagojević's Expedited Motion to Compel the Prosecution to Disclose its Notes from Plea Discussions with the Accused Nikolić & Request for an Expedited Open Session Hearing, 13 June 2003, p. 6: "Rule 70 (A) aims to protect work product from disclosure, as it is in the public interest that information related to the internal preparation of a case, including legal theories, strategies and investigations, shall be privileged and not subject to disclosure to the opposing party".

52 *See supra,* at para. 11. *See also Niyitegeka* Appeals Judgement, para. 30 and footnote 2.

53 Response to the Motion of 19 June 2006, para. 3.

54 Disclosure of 20 June 2006, para. 4 (the Appeals Chamber notes that the Prosecution did not specify whether this disclosure was made under Rule 68 of the Rules); Disclosure of 22 June 2006. para. 2 (it is mentioned in para. 1 that the disclosure is made pursuant to Rules 68 and 73(F)(ii)).

55 Motion of 7 September 2006, para. 13.

56 *Barayagwiza* Decision on Prosecution Disclosure, para. 6; *Bralo* 30 August 2006 Decision, para. 34; *Brđanin* 7 December 2004 Decision, p. 3; *Blaškić* 26 September 2000 Decision, para. 45.

57 *Bralo* 30 August 2006 Decision, para. 31; *Blaškić* 26 September 2000 Decision, para. 45.

58 *Prosecutor v. Radislav Krstić,* Case No. IT-98-33-A, *Confidential* Decision on the Prosecution's Motion to Be Relieved of Obligation to Disclose Sensitive Information Pursuant to Rule 66(C), 27 March 2003, p. 4.

59 *Id.*

III. ADDITIONAL EVIDENCE

A. Applicable Law

18. The Appeals Chamber recalls that according to the jurisprudence of the Tribunal and that of the International Criminal Tribunal for the Former Yugoslavia ("ICTY"), an appeal pursuant to Article 24 of the Statute of the Tribunal (Article 25 of the Statute of the ICTY) is not a trial *de novo* and is not an opportunity to remedy any "failures or oversights" by a party during the pre-trial and trial phases.[60]

19. Rule 115 of the Rules provides for a corrective measure on appeal, and its purpose is to deal "with the situation where a party is in possession of material that was not before the court of first instance and which is additional evidence of a fact or issue litigated at trial".[61] According to this provision, for additional evidence to be admissible on appeal, the following requirements must be met. First, the motion to present additional evidence should be filed "not later than thirty days from the date for filing of the brief in reply, unless good cause or, after the appeal hearing, cogent reasons are shown for further delay".[62] Second, the Appeals Chamber must find "that the additional evidence was not available at trial and is relevant and credible." When determining the availability at trial, the Appeals Chamber is mindful of the following principles:

> [T]he party in question must show that it sought to make "appropriate use of all mechanisms of protection and compulsion available under the Statute and the Rules of the International Tribunal to bring evidence [...] before the Trial Chamber." In this connection, Counsel is expected to apprise the Trial Chamber of all the difficulties he or she encounters in obtaining the evidence in question, including any problems of intimidation, and his or her inability to locate certain witnesses. The obligation to apprise the Trial Chamber constitutes not only a first step in exercising due diligence but also a means of self-protection in that non-cooperation of the prospective witness is recorded contemporaneously.[63] **[page 11]**

With regards to relevance, the Appeals Chamber will consider whether the proposed evidence sought to be admitted relates to a material issue. As to credibility, the Appeals Chamber will only refuse to admit evidence at this stage if "it is devoid of *any* probative value in relation to a decision pursuant to Rule 115"[64], without prejudice to a determination of the weight to be afforded.[65]

20. Once it has been determined that the additional evidence meets these conditions, the Appeals Chamber will determine whether the evidence "could have been a decisive factor in reaching the decision at trial."[66]

---

60 *Prosecutor v. Jean-Paul Akayesu,* Case No. ICTR-96-4-A, Judgement, 1 June 2001, para. 177; Decision on Appellant Hassan Ngeze's Motion for the Approval of the Investigation at the Appeal Stage, Case No. ICTR-99-52-A, 3 May 2005 ("Decision on Investigation"), p. 3; Decision on Jean-Bosco Barayagwiza's Extremely Urgent Motion for Leave to Appoint an Investigator, Case No. ICTR-99-52-A, 4 October 2005 ("Barayagwiza Decision of 4 October 2005"), p. 3; *Ngeze* Decision on Additional Evidence, para. 5; Decision on Appellant Hassan Ngeze's Motion for Approval of Further Investigations on Specific Information Relating to the Additional Evidence of Potential Witnesses, Case No. ICTR-99-52-A, 20 June 2006 ("*Ngeze* Decision on Further Investigations"), para. 4.

61 *Prosecutor v. Zoran Kupreškić et al.*, Case No. IT-95-16-A, Decision on the Motions of Drago Josipović, Zoran Kupreškić and Vlatko Kupreškić to Admit Additional Evidence Pursuant to Rule 115 and for Judicial Notice to be Taken Pursuant to Rule 94 (B), 8 May 2001 ("*Kupreškić et al.* Decision of 8 May 2001"), para. 5; Barayagwiza Decision of 4 October 2005, p. 4; *Ngeze* Decision on Additional Evidence, para. 6.

62 Rule 115 (A) of the Rules as amended on 10 November 2006.

63 *Prosecutor v. André Ntagerura, et al.*, ICTR-99-46-A, Decision on Prosecution Motion for Admission of Additional Evidence, 10 December 2004 ("*Ntagerura et al.* Decision of 10 December 2004"), para. 9. [internal references omitted].

64 *Prosecutor v. Stanislav Galić*, Case No. IT-98-29-A, Decision on the First and Third Rule 115 Motions to Present Additional Evidence Before the Appeals Chamber, 30 June 2005 ("*Galić* 30 June 2005 Decision"), para. 95; *Emmanuel Ndindabahizi v. The Prosecutor*, Case No. ICTR-01-71-A, Decision on the Admission of Additional Evidence, 14 April 2005, p. 6; *See also Prosecutor v. Mladen Naletilić & Vinko Martinović*, Case No. IT-98-34-A, Judgement, 3 May 2006, para. 402; *The Prosecutor v. André Ntagerura et al.*, Case No. ICTR-99-46-A, Decision on Prosecution Motion for Admission of Additional Evidence, 10 December 2004, para. 22; *Georges Anderson Nderubumwe Rutaganda v. The Prosecutor,* Case No. ICTR-96-3-A, Judgement, 23 May 2003, para. 266.

65 *Prosecutor v. Zoran Kupreškić et al.*, Case No. IT-95-16-A, Decision on Motions for the Admission of Additional Evidence filed by the Appellants Vlatko Kupreškić, Drago Josipović, Zoran Kupreškić and Mirjan Kupreškić, 26 February 2001, para. 28; *Kupreškić* Appeal Judgement, para. 63; *Prosecutor v. Blaškić*, Case No. IT-95-14-A, Decision on Evidence, 31 October 2003 ("*Blaškić* Decision of 31 October 2003"), p. 3; *Ngeze* Decision on Additional Evidence, para. 7; *Ngeze* Decision on Further Investigations, para. 5.

66 Rule 115 (B) of the Rules.

To satisfy this, the evidence must be such that it *could* have had an impact on the verdict, *i.e.* it *could* have shown that a conviction was unsafe.[67] Accordingly, the additional evidence must be directed at a specific finding of fact related to a conviction or to the sentence.

21. Although Rule 115 of the Rules does not explicitly provide for this, the Appeals Chamber has considered that, where the evidence is relevant and credible, but was available at trial, or could have been discovered through the exercise of due diligence, the additional evidence may still be admitted if the moving party establishes that the exclusion of the additional evidence *would* amount to a miscarriage of justice inasmuch as, had it been adduced at trial, it *would* have had an impact on the verdict.[68]

22. Finally, the Appeals Chamber recalls that, whether the evidence was available at trial or not, the additional evidence must always be assessed in the context of the evidence presented at trial, and not in isolation.[69] **[page 12]**

B. <u>Motion of 4 July 2006</u>

<u>Submissions of the Parties</u>

23. In his Motion of 4 July 2006, the Appellant seeks the admission of evidence from Witness ABC1 which, he contends, shows that (i) testimony provided by other Prosecution Witnesses was false;[70] and (ii) the Appellant was not a party to the killings which occurred on 7 April 1994 in Gisenyi.[71] The proffered evidence consists of transcripts of Witness ABC1's testimony on 13 June 2006 in the *Bagosora et al.* case, including testimony given in closed session.[72] The Appellant also prays the Appeals Chamber to call the witness to testify in the present case.[73]

24. The Appellant submits that this evidence became available to him only after the Disclosure of 22 June 2006,[74] despite the exercise of due diligence.[75] He submits that it is relevant to the issue relating to his innocence,[76] since it does not implicate him in the killings of 7 April 1994 in Gisenyi, which is in "complete contradiction" with Witness EB's testimony of 15-17 May 2001.[77] In consequence, according to the Appellant, if accepted, this new evidence will "belie the prosecution's story narrated by PWs [*sic*] AGX, Serushago, and AHI" and overturn the Trial Chamber's factual findings at paragraphs 812, 836 and 837 of the Trial Judgement,[78] thus affecting the verdict.[79] Stressing that the finding of credibility of Witness EB was "based upon false evidence", the Appellant avers that the non-admission of Witness ABC1's testimony will result in a miscarriage of justice.[80]

---

67 *Kupreškić* Appeal Judgement, para. 68; *Prosecutor v. Radislav Krstić*, Case No. IT-98-33-A, Decision on Application for Admission of Additional Evidence on Appeal, 5 August 2003 ("*Krstić* Decision of 5 August 2003"), p. 3; *Blaškić* Decision of 31 October 2003, p. 3; *Ngeze* Decision on Additional Evidence, para. 8; *Ngeze* Decision on Further Investigations, para. 6.

68 *Kajelijeli v. Prosecutor*, Case No. ICTR-98-44A-A, Decision on Defence Motion for the Admission of Additional Evidence Pursuant to Rule 115 of the Rules of Procedure and Evidence, 28 October 2004 ("*Kajelijeli* Decision of 28 October 2004"), para. 11; *Ntagerura et al.* Decision of 10 December 2004, para 11; *Ngeze* Decision on Additional Evidence, para. 9; *Ngeze* Decision on Further Investigations, para. 7.

69 *Juvénal Kajelijeli* Decision of 28 October 2004, para. 12; *Ntagerura et al.* Decision of 10 December 2004, para. 12; *Ngeze* Decision on Additional Evidence, para. 10; *Ngeze* Decision on Further Investigations, para. *See* also *Blaškić* Decision of 31 October 2003, p. 3; *Momir Nikolić v. Prosecutor*, Case No. IT-02-60/1-A, Decision on Motion to Admit Additional Evidence, 9 December 2004, para. 25.

70 Motion of 4 July 2006, para. 5a.

71 *Ibid.*, paras 2, 4. [REDACTED]

72 Motion of 4 July 2006, preliminary para. a.

73 *Ibid.*, preambulary para. c.

74 *Ibid.*, paras 1, 3.

75 *Ibid.*, para. 10.

76 *Ibid.*, paras 10-11.

77 *Ibid.*, paras 2, 4, footnote 1, with reference to the *Bagosora et al. case*, T. 13 June 2006, pp 9-14, 16.

78 *Ibid.*, para. 5.

79 *Ibid.*, para. 10.

80 *Ibid.*, para. 6.

25. The Prosecution opposes the Motion of 4 July 2006 and submits that it does not meet the threshold criteria for admission of additional evidence pursuant to Rule 115 of the Rules.[81] First, the Prosecution argues that the Appellant has not shown that the material was unavailable at trial. It contends that Witness ABC1 and the Appellant knew each other and the Appellant thus could have sought to contact [this person] as a potentially useful witness in support of his alibi defence.[82] Second, the Prosecution maintains that the evidence is not relevant to a material issue, since Witness ABC1 only testified [as to not having seen] the Appellant at [Barnabé Samvura's] house on the morning of 7 April 1994, and not about the Appellant's activities outside that house on that day, **[page 13]** in and around Gisenyi.[83] The Prosecution adds that "whether or not a meeting actually took place is not materially relevant to the facts underpinning the Appellant's conviction",[84] the material issue, as presented by Witness EB, being the fact that the Appellant spoke through a loudspeaker, in the street, inciting *Interahamwe* to kill Tutsis.[85] Third, the Prosecution contests the credibility of Witness ABC1 and submits that there is evidence in the *Bagosora et al.* case that contradicts [the] testimony [provided by this witness].[86] Finally, the Prosecution submits that, in any event, the Appellant does not demonstrate that the evidence would or even could have affected the verdict at trial.[87] It points out that the Appellant does not explain why the Trial Chamber would have preferred Witness ABC1's evidence to that of Witness EB[88] or to that of other witnesses concerning his participation in the genocide.[89]

26. In his Reply to the Response to the Motion of 4 July 2006, the Appellant underlines that the Prosecution's contention that the proffered evidence is irrelevant contradicts the fact that it was disclosed to him under Rule 68 as exculpatory and relevant.[90] He maintains that there is no reason to doubt Witness ABC1's credibility, who is an eyewitness and the "most natural witness to describe the true facts which occurred on 7th April, 1994, at [Samvura's] house".[91] He adds that any reference to the evidence of Witness EB is not appropriate at this stage in light of the upcoming evidentiary hearing.[92] Finally, the Appellant concludes that even if another eyewitness' (Witness EB) testimony gave a different version of the incidents of 7 April 1994, Witness ABC1's evidence "is relevant as in that situation according to the principle of evidence neither of the version[s] could be accepted as true".[93]

Discussion

27. As a preliminary matter, the Appeals Chamber considers that there is good cause for the late filing of the Motion of 4 July 2006. Witness ABC1's testimony in the *Bagosora et al.* case, dated 13 June 2006, was made, in the relevant parts, in closed session. The Prosecution disclosed the corresponding transcript on 22 June 2006 and the Motion of 4 July 2006 was filed soon thereafter. The Appeals Chamber therefore recognizes the Motion of 4 July 2006 as timely. **[page 14]**

28. However, with respect to the availability of the proffered evidence at trial, the Appeals Chamber agrees with the Prosecution that the Appellant failed to exercise the due diligence required for the evidence to be admissible on appeal. The Appeals Chamber recalls that "the mere fact that [a witness] gave evidence in another case and that the Appellant was not aware that [the witness was] in possession of this information until then does not in itself suffice to demonstrate unavailability of the evidence at trial."[94] The Appellant

81 Response to the Motion of 4 July 2006, paras 2-3.

82 *Ibid.*, paras 4-6.

83 *Ibid.*, paras 7-8. According to the Prosecution, the Appellant's interpretation of the scope of Witness ABC1's testimony is grossly exaggerated and can only stand for the proposition that she did not see the Appellant at [Samvura's] house that morning, a fact that has no relevance to the Appellant's conviction.

84 Response to the Motion of 4 July 2006, para. 9.

85 *Ibid.*, para. 10.

86 *Ibid.*, paras 8 and 11. [REDACTED]

87 Response to the Motion of 4 July 2006, para. 12.

88 *Ibid.*, para. 13.

89 *Ibid.*, paras 14-15.

90 Reply to the Response to the Motion of 4 July 2006, paras 1 and 3.

91 *Ibid.*, paras 4-5.

92 Reply to the Response to the Motion of 4 July 2006, para. 6.

93 *Ibid.*, para. 7.

94 *Galić* 30 June 2005 Decision, para. 115; *Krstić* Decision of 5 August 2003, p. 3; *Prosecutor v. Radislav Krstić*, Case No. IT-98-33-A, Decision on Application for Subpoenas, 1 July 2003, paras 4-5: "The defence often seeks to satisfy this requirement by

must demonstrate that the "proffered evidence was not available to him at trial in any form" and that he had made use of all mechanisms of protection and compulsion available under the Statute and the Rules to bring the evidence before the Trial Chamber.[95] In the present case, the Appellant has not shown why he could not call [Witness ABC1] [REDACTED] as a Defence witness at trial in order to refute the evidence provided by Witness EB stating that, on the morning of 7 April 1994, he saw the Appellant go into the compound of Samvura's house together with many Interahamwe. Therefore, the Appeals Chamber is not satisfied that this evidence was unavailable at trial.

29. As to the relevance and credibility of the proffered evidence, the Appeals Chamber is satisfied that the *prima facie* requirements have been met. The testimony of Witness ABC1 in the *Bagosora et al.* case is, on its face, in contradiction with the testimony on the same events given by some of the Prosecution witnesses in the present case, and that of Witness EB in particular. The evidence in question thus appears to have some relevance to the Trial Chamber's findings on the credibility of these witnesses as well as to its factual findings with respect to the Appellant's participation in the killings that took place in Gisenyi on the morning of 7 April 1994.[96] Without prejudice to the Trial Chamber's findings in the *Bagosora et al.* case as to the credibility of Witness ABC1 and considering the fact that the testimony was given under solemn oath, the Appeals Chamber is satisfied that the proffered evidence is *prima facie* reasonably capable of belief or reliance.[97] **[page 15]**

30. Having found that the evidence of Witness ABC1 was available at trial and could have been discovered at trial through the exercise of due diligence, the Appeals Chamber must determine whether the non-admission of the additional evidence would amount to a miscarriage of justice.

31. The Appellant claims that Witness ABC1's testimony in the *Bagosora et al.* case would have affected the Trial Chamber's findings as to the credibility of Prosecution Witnesses AHI, EB, AGX and Omar Serushago,[98] hence calling into question the findings of fact made by the Trial Chamber concerning the events in Gisenyi on the basis of the evidence given by those witnesses. The Appeals Chamber notes that, in the *Bagosora et al.* case, Witness ABC1 expressly affirmed that, on the morning of 7 April 1994, there was no meeting held at Samvura's place and that the Appellant was not present in [that] house.[99]

32. The relevant factual findings of the Trial Chamber in the present case appear to be made on the basis of evidence provided by Witness Serushago that the Appellant was transporting weapons on the morning of 7 April 1994[100] corroborated by the evidence of Witness EB that he saw the Appellant "on the morning of 7 April in a red taxi with a loudspeaker".[101] The Trial Chamber also took into account that Witness AHI saw the Appellant early in the morning that day "in military gear, carrying a gun" and that Witness AGX saw him at around 2:30 p.m. "passing by on the road in a vehicle with *Interahamwe* and *Impuzamugambi*, armed with different kinds of weapons and speaking through a megaphone, calling on the public to flush out the enemy and enemy accomplices".[102] Finally, the Trial Chamber noted, on the basis of evidence provided by Witness EB, that "[w]eapons were distributed from a central location, Samvura's house, where Witness EB saw the *Interahamwe* picking them up".[103] On these grounds, the Trial Chamber concluded that

---

asserting that an attempt had been made before or during the trial to ascertain from such prospective witnesses what evidence they could give, but that the prospective witnesses had either failed or declined to co-operate. However, before additional evidence will be admitted pursuant to Rule 115, the defence is obliged to demonstrate not only that the evidence was not available at trial but also that the evidence could not have been discovered through the exercise of due diligence [...]. This obligation of due diligence is therefore directly relevant to the procedures of the Tribunal (in particular, Rule 54) both before and during trial, as well as on appeal." *See also* para. 19 *supra*.

95 *Galić* 30 June 2005 Decision, para. 115; *Krstić* Decision of 5 August 2003, p. 3; *Prosecutor v. Radislav Krstić*, Case No. IT-98-33-A, Decision on Application for Subpoenas, 1 July 2003, paras 4-5.

96 Trial Judgement, paras 825 and 836. The Appeals Chamber finds that the proffered evidence is irrelevant to the Trial Chamber's conclusions at paras 831 and 837 of the Trial Judgement.

97 *See The Prosecutor v. Jean-Paul Akayesu*, Case No. ICTR-96-4-A, Judgement, 1 June 2001, paras 286-287.

98 Motion of 4 July 2006, para. 5, referring to Trial Judgement, paras 812, 813, 824, 775.

99 *Bagosora et al. case*, T. 13 June 2006, p. 10, l. 24-32 [closed session – REDACTED].

100 Trial Judgement, para. 825.

101 *Ibid.*, para. 825.

102 *Id.*

103 *Id.*

> Hassan Ngeze ordered the *Iterahamwe* in Gisenyi on the morning of 7 April 1994 to kill Tutsi civilians and prepare for their burial at the *Commune Rouge*. Many were killed in the subsequent attacks that happened immediately thereafter and later on the same day. [...] The attack that resulted in these and other killings was planned systematically, with weapons distributed in advance, and arrangements made for the transport and burial of those to be killed.[104]

The Appeals Chamber notes that the Trial Chamber considered that Omar Serushago's testimony was not consistently reliable and accepted it "with caution, relying on it only to the extent that it **[page 16]** [was] corroborated".[105] The testimony of Witnesses AHI, AGX and EB was, however, found to be credible.[106]

33. Witnesses AHI and AGX did not specifically testify to the fact that there had been a meeting in Samvura's house on the morning of 7 April 1994, or that the Appellant attended that meeting or participated in the distribution of arms that day.[107] Therefore, their testimony and/or credibility would not be affected by the evidence provided by Witness ABC1 in the *Bagosora et al.* case.[108] However, the Appeals Chamber agrees that the account given by Witness ABC1 can be interpreted as contradicting the testimony of Witness EB in the present case, in particular, when he stated that, on 7 April 1994, at around 07:00 a.m., he saw the Appellant going towards the house of Barnabé Samvura.[109] The same morning, he also saw other people go into the compound of Samvura's house and, thirty minutes later, he heard the Appellant speak through his loudspeaker, telling the *Interahamwe* to kill the Tutsi and that some of them should go to the *Commune Rouge* to dig pits. According to Witness EB, when coming out of Samvura's house, the *Interahamwe* carried nail-studded clubs, rifles and grenades, and the attacks started around 01:00 p.m.[110]

34. The fact that there had been a meeting held at Samvura's house on the morning of 7 April 1994 involving the Appellant and distribution of arms is not in itself decisive for the Trial Chamber's conclusion as to the Appellant's responsibility for killings of the Tutsi civilians in Gisenyi. In fact, the Trial Chamber concluded that there was no evidence that the Appellant was present during the killings of 7 April 1994[111] and that, on that morning, the Appellant ordered the *Interahamwe* to kill the Tutsi and to prepare graves in *Commune Rouge*.[112] Consequently, the principal issue is whether, should the Trial Chamber have had the benefit of hearing the testimony of Witness ABC1, it *would* have disbelieved Witness EB with respect to the events that took place **[page 17]** on the morning of 7 April 1994. In the presence of contradictory accounts of the two witnesses, the Trial Chamber would have had to determine which of the accounts was reliable and, in light of evidence provided by Witness ABC1 in the *Bagosora et al.* case and the fact that [REDACTED], the Appeals Chamber is not satisfied that a reasonable trier of fact *would* have found this witness credible to the detriment of the account provided by Witness EB. Moreover, Witness ABC1 in the *Bagosora et al.* case only testified to the fact that the Appellant was not at [Samvura's] house that morning and that there was no meeting there. The mere fact that [Witness ABC1] did not witness or hear him ordering the killings does not mean that this could

---

104 *Ibid.*, para. 836. *See also* paras 955 and 977A concluding that the Appellant was guilty of genocide, pursuant to Article 6(1) of the Statute of the Tribunal.

105 *Ibid.*, para. 824. *See also Ngeze* Decision on Additional Evidence, paras 26-27.

106 *Ibid.*, paras 775, 813 and 812, respectively.

107 Witness AHI testified that he saw the Appellant on the morning of 7 April in a military outfit accompanied by his bodyguards (T. 4 September 2001, p. 51 l. 13-17 and p. 69 l. 17-25; T. 10 September 2001, p. 17 l. 18-20 and p. 92 l. 17-22). Witness AHI referred to distribution of arms by Colonel Anatole Nsenigyumva on 7 April 1994, but specified that the Appellant was present at a meeting held on 8 April 1994 (T. 4 September 2001, p. 58 l. 7-9 and p. 60 l. 11-19).
Witness AGX saw the Appellant in the afternoon of 7 April 1994 "passing by on the road in a vehicle aboard which were *Interahamwe* as well as *Impuzamugambi* of the CDR" (T. 11 June 2001, p. 39; T. 13 June 2001, p. 39; T. 14 June 2001, pp 40-42).

108 The Appeals Chamber notes that Witness ABC1 also testified that there was no meeting with Anatole Nsengiyumva held in Samvura's house on 7 April 1994 and no distribution of weapons took place there (*Bagosora et al.* case, T. 13 June 2006 (closed session), p. 11 l. 34-35, p. 12 l. 29-31, p. 27 l. 16-18 and 26-31). Witness AHI referred to a meeting of MRND and CDR officials held on 8 April 1994 followed by distribution of weapons (T. 4 September 2001, pp 55-62) and Witness AGX testified that Colonel Nsengiyumva spoke in Gisenyi on 7 April 1994 around 10:00 a.m. saying that the President had been killed by enemies, adding that there were about two hundred people there (T. 11 June 2001, pp 34-39). Consequently, the Appeals Chamber concludes that the three witnesses were referring to different events and no flagrant contradiction affecting their credibility could reasonably be drawn from these accounts.

109 T. 16 May 2001, pp 2-3.

110 *Ibid.*, pp 5-8, 46; T. 17 June 2001, pp 108, 129-134.

111 Trial Judgement, para. 825.

112 *Id.*

not have occurred.[113] The Appeals Chamber notes to this extent that Witness EB testified that the Appellant ordered the killing through a loudspeaker from his vehicle and not *during* the meeting at Samvura's house.[114] Consequently, and in light of the findings above concerning Witnesses AHI and AGX, the Appeals Chamber is not satisfied that the exclusion of the proffered additional evidence would amount to a miscarriage of justice inasmuch as, had it been adduced at trial, it would not have had an impact on the verdict.

C. Motion of 28 August 2006

Submissions of the Parties

35. In his Motion of 28 August 2006, the Appellant prays the Appeals Chamber to admit the Additional Statement of Witness EB purportedly affirming his Recantation Statement of April 2005.[115] The Appellant contends that this evidence is credible and relevant to the evidentiary hearing insofar as, if accepted, it "will clear the doubts of the Prosecution regarding the truthfulness of witness 'EB' [*sic*] first recanted statement".[116] He notes that this evidence, not available at trial, could not have been discovered through the exercise of due diligence, and its exclusion would amount to a miscarriage of justice.[117]

36. The Prosecution does not object to the Motion of 28 August 2006, acknowledging the relevance of the Additional Statement in light of the evidentiary hearing of Witness EB.[118] Nevertheless, it points out that the "agreement on the admissibility of this statement relates *only* to the actual admissibility of the statement, and not to the merits, that is, the reliability or credibility, **[page 18]** of the contents of the document."[119] Furthermore, the Prosecution specifies that the admission of copies of the envelopes in which copies of this letter were received by the Office of the Prosecutor would be necessary.[120]

Discussion

37. The Appeals Chamber notes that in the Additional Statement, Witness EB purportedly states that the reason for this new statement is that after having sent his Recantation Statement, he "learned that officials from the Office of the Prosecutor who had come to see [him] at [his] home had submitted [his] statement to the [Tribunal]" and that "[t]hese employees of the Tribunal, who would usually meet [him] at the *Ubumwe* Hotel threatened [him], asking [him] why [he] had written to the Tribunal to announce [his] recantation". Since he was "annoyed by their threats, and in order to get rid of them, [he] told them the document containing [his] recantation did not come from [him], even though [he] was indeed the one who had written it". According to the Additional Statement, Witness EB met the "employees of the Tribunal" once more when they came back to confirm that he was the author of the Recantation Statement but had not heard from them ever since. Therefore, he decided to write the Additional Statement to confirm that both Recantation Statements of 5 and 27 April 2005 were written and signed by him. In addition to the information contained in Witness EB's purported original Recantation Statement, the Additional Statement specifies that, contrary to his testimony adduced at trial, he never saw the Appellant on 6-9 April 1994 in Gisenyi [REDACTED]. According to the Additional Statement, it was well known to the inhabitants of Gisenyi that the Appellant was arrested following President Habyarimana's death and remained in detention until 9 April 1994; besides, they also knew that the vehicle equipped with megaphones belonged to Hassan Gitoki from *Commune Rouge*

---

113 *See Jean de Dieu Kamuhanda v. The Prosecutor,* Case No. ICTR-99-54A-A, Judgement, 19 September 2005, para. 158.

114 At the same time, the Appeals Chamber recalls that the credibility of Witness EB, the only witness to have testified to the ordering of the killings by the Appellant (the only relevant part of Omar Serushago's testimony that was considered corroborated by the Trial Chamber, and thus reliable, referred to the fact that the Appellant "was transporting arms in a red Hilux vehicle on the morning of 7 April 1994" but not the fact that he ordered that attack), is yet to be re-assessed on the basis of his testimony at the appeals hearing to the subject of his purported Recantation Statement.

115 Motion of 28 August 2006, preambulary para. *See also* para. 6 *supra*.

116 *Ibid., paras* 4, 6.

117 *Ibid.,* paras 5, 7.

118 Response to the Motion of 28 August 2006, para. 2.

119 *Ibid.,* para. 2.

120 *Ibid.,* para. 3.

and not to the Appellant. Finally, in the Additional Statement, Witness EB refers to the Prosecution Witness AFX who allegedly also falsely testified against the Appellant.

38. The Appeals Chamber considers that there is good cause for the late filing of the Motion of 28 August 2006, since, as explained above, the Appellant only received a copy the Additional Statement in August 2006.[121] For the reasons explained in the Ngeze Decision on Additional Evidence,[122] the Appeals Chamber finds that the proffered evidence was unavailable at trial and could not be obtained through the exercise of due diligence. The Appeals Chamber is equally satisfied that the tendered Additional Statement is *prima facie* credible and relevant.[123] Finally, the Appeals Chamber finds that the Additional Statement could have been a decisive factor in **[page 19]** concluding upon the Appellant's responsibility for the events that took place in Gisenyi on 7-9 April 1994.[124] The Appeals Chamber emphasizes that the above findings pertain strictly to the admissibility and not to the merits of the proffered additional evidence.[125]

39. For the foregoing reasons, the Appeals Chamber finds that the Additional Statement is admissible as additional evidence on appeal.

D. Motion of 7 September 2006

40. In its Motion of 7 September 2006, the Prosecution seeks admission of the envelopes containing copies of the Additional Statement as additional evidence on appeal for the purposes of the evidentiary hearing of Witness EB.[126] The Prosecution claims that the information on the envelopes is relevant to the issue of determining the authenticity of the Additional Statement, "which in turn is relevant to the issues [of] the oral hearing, whether EB is recanting his trial testimony or whether the recantation statement is a product of the Appellant['s] efforts to interfere with and suborn the testimony of witnesses".[127] It contends that "[t]he circumstances surrounding the receipt and timing of the letter [...] are suspicious and lead to the inference that someone associated with the Appellant, or at least someone other than EB, has manufactured the letter".[128] The Prosecution, being in the process of obtaining the originals of the envelopes, also seeks direction from the Appeals Chamber as to whether it ought to retain the originals until the evidentiary hearing or whether they should be filed immediately upon their receipt.[129] The Appellant did not respond to the Motion of 7 September 2006.

41. The Appeals Chamber recalls that, pursuant to Rule 115 of the Rules, motions for additional evidence on appeal must be directed towards the *contested* specific finding of fact made by the Trial Chamber. The Appeals Chamber recalls that, while the Rule itself does not expressly prohibit a party from seeking the admission of additional evidence to bolster challenged factual findings, in **[page 20]** the practice of this Tribunal, as well as that of the ICTY, "motions for additional evidence are directed towards supporting an argument of factual error, and if additional evidence is sought to be admitted in support of a factual finding, it is admitted as rebuttal material to that additional evidence admitted in support of a factual error".[130] The Prosecution has not appealed

121 *See* para. 6 *supra*.

122 *Ngeze* Decision on Additional Evidence, para. 23

123 *See ibid.*, paras 19-22.

124 Trial Judgement, paras 836-837. *See also Ngeze* Decision on Additional Evidence, paras 24-29.

125 *See Ngeze* Decision on Additional Evidence, para. 28.

126 Motion of 7 September 2006, para. 1.

127 *Ibid.*, para. 5.

128 *Ibid.*, para. 6. According to the Prosecution, several copies of the Additional Statement – and not the original – were sent to the offices of the ICTR in Arusha and Kigali, to two investigators and an interpreter from OTP, in June 2006, from Tanzania and Rwanda (paras 7-8). According to the Prosecution, "it would seem highly improbable that the date of the Appellant's Motion [of 19 June 2006], seeking admission of an additional statement received from Witness EB, is purely coincidental with the mailing of this letter" (paras 9-11, with reference to para. 3 of the Motion of 19 June 2006, in which the Appellant affirms that "the Prosecutor might have collected or *received* some material and/or statements from witness EB[...]") The Prosecution maintains that the fact that the Additional Statement was allegedly written in December 2005 but only posted in June 2006 militates for a conclusion that Witness EB may have written it under some duress or that the letters were manufactured by someone else (para. 11). It adds that it "is suspicious that a letter purporting to come from Witness EB, an indigent person living in Rwanda, was mailed from Tanzania and Rwanda", the only plausible explanation being that someone other than Witness EB posted several copies to several persons from several places in order to ensure that the letter was received by the Tribunal (para. 12).

129 Motion of 7 September 2006, para. 2.

130 *Prosecutor v. Jovica Stanišić and Franko Simatović*, Case No. IT-03-69-AR65.1, Decision on Stanišić's Application under Rule 115 to Present Additional Evidence in his Response to the Prosecution's Appeal, 3 December 2004, para. 14.

the Trial Judgement and is not, in the circumstances of the instant case, in a position to seek admission of additional evidence. Rather, it should have applied for admission of rebuttal material.

42. The Appeals Chamber finds that it is in the interests of justice to examine *proprio motu* whether the material tendered by the Prosecution in its Motion of 7 September 2006 can be admitted as rebuttal evidence on appeal. It has been well established by the jurisprudence that rebuttal material is admissible if it directly affects the substance of the additional evidence admitted by the Appeals Chamber[131] and, as such, has a different test of admissibility from additional evidence under Rule 115 of the Rules.[132] In light of its findings above with respect to the admissibility of the Additional Statement, the Appeals Chamber finds that copies of envelopes in which the copies of the Additional Statement were purportedly sent to various addressees within the Office of the Prosecutor are directly relevant to the issue of the authenticity of the Additional Statement and *a fortiori* that of the Recantation Statement. Therefore, the Appeals Chamber is satisfied that the proffered material affects the substance of the admitted additional evidence and is thus admissible as rebuttal evidence on appeal.

43. The Appeals Chamber emphasizes that it is highly desirable to have the originals of the said rebuttal evidence, as well as of the Recantation Statement and the Additional Statement, filed and available at the evidentiary hearing.

IV. DISPOSITION

44. For the forgoing reasons, the Appeals Chamber **DISMISSES** the Motion of 19 June 2006; **CONSIDERS** the Motion of 14 July 2006 to be **WITHDRAWN** by the Appellant's Counsel; **DISMISSES** the Motion of 4 July 2006; **GRANTS** the Motion of 28 August 2006 and **ADMITS** the Additional Statement as additional evidence on appeal; **DISMISSES** the Motion of 7 **[page 21]** September 2006. The Appeals Chamber *proprio motu* **ADMITS** as rebuttal evidence on appeal the copies of envelopes annexed to the Motion of 7 September 2006.

45. The Appeals Chamber **INSTRUCTS** the Registrar to provide the following material so far admitted into evidence on appeal with corresponding exhibit numbers:

- copy of the typed statement purportedly signed by Witness EB, index numbers 2223A-2220-A;
- Forensic Report, including the copy of the purported handwritten Recantation Statement, index numbers 3442/A-3413/A;
- copy of the Additional Statement in Kinyarwanda, as well as its translations into English and French, index numbers 8121A-8112/A
- copies of envelopes, index numbers 8183/A-8175/A.

Done in English and French, the English text being authoritative.

Dated this 27th day of November 2006,
At The Hague, The Netherlands.

Fausto Pocar
Presiding Judge

[Seal of the Tribunal]

131 *Prosecutor v. Ramush Haradinaj et al.*, Case No. IT-04-84-AR65.2, Decision on Lahi Brahimaj's Request to Present Additional Evidence under Rule 115, 3 March 2006 ("*Haradinaj* Decision"), para. 44; *Prosecutor v. Miroslav Kvočka et al.*, Case No. IT-98-30/1-A, Decision on Prosecution's Motion to Adduce Rebuttal material, 12 March 2004 ("*Kvočka* Decision"), p. 3; *The Prosecutor v. Tihomir Blaškić*, Case No. IT-95-14-A, Decision on Evidence, 31 October 2003, p. 5.

132 *Haradinaj* Decision, para. 44; *Kvočka* Decision, p. 3.

International Criminal Tribunal for Rwanda
Tribunal pénal international pour le Rwanda

OR: ENG

TRIAL CHAMBER III

Before Judges: Inés Mónica Weinberg de Roca, Presiding
Khalida Rachid Khan
Lee Gacuiga Muthoga

Registrar: Adama Dieng

Date: 29 November 2006

THE PROSECUTOR

v.

Protais ZIGIRANYIRAZO

Case No. ICTR-2001-73-T

DECISION ON THE *VOIR DIRE* HEARING OF THE ACCUSED'S *CURRICULUM VITAE*

Rules 2, 42 and 95 of the Rules of Procedure and Evidence

Office of the Prosecutor:
Wallace Kapaya
Charity Kagwi Ndungu
Sylver Ntukamazina
Gina Butler
Iskandar Ismail
Jane Mukangira

Defence Counsel:
John Philpot
Peter Zaduk

[page 2] Introduction

1. On 27 and 28 June 2006, the Chamber held a *voir dire* hearing on the admissibility of a hand-written document entitled *Curriculum Vitae* ("CV") prepared by the Accused.[1] This document was included in a group of records that was tendered by the Prosecution on 3 October 2005 as Exhibit P2.[2] The CV was subsequently referred to during the Prosecution case. On 2 March 2006, the Defence formally raised an objection to the admissibility of the CV when it was referred to by witness Alison des Forges. According to the Defence, the CV, being a statement by the Accused, is not admissible into evidence because certain procedural safeguards have not been met.[3] The Defence does not contest that the Accused is the author of the document, but contend that it was improperly obtained.[4] The Prosecution contends that this document is already in evidence as Exhibit P2, and may therefore be referred to by Prosecution witnesses. Following these oral submissions, the Chamber decided to provisionally admit the document as part of Exhibit P42 and allow reference to it pending a determination of its final status. The Chamber held that a determination as to the admissibility of this document would be made following a *voir dire* hearing.[5]

Deliberations

Evidence from the Voir Dire Hearing

2. In January of 1998, investigators from the Prosecution received a call from a source, Mr. Pheneas Ruhumuliza, second vice-president of the national committee of the *Interahamwe*, informing them that the Accused had contacted him with a view to arranging a meeting because he wished to collaborate and shed light on the events surrounding the genocide in Rwanda.[6]

3. The investigators met with the Accused for the first time on the 6 or 7 of February 1998. At that initial meeting, the Accused stated he wanted to clear his name with the ICTR.[7] The Accused further claimed that he was wanted by the Rwandan Government. The investigators asked the Accused to prepare a document of what he knew and what he had done before, during and after the genocide.[8]

4. The investigators next met with the Accused around 12 February 1998, where he turned over the first 14 hand-written pages of the document requested by the investigators, now known as the CV. The Accused presented the completed CV, totaling 36 pages, at a third meeting in March 1998.[9]

5. At the last meeting, which occurred on 26 or 27 March 1998, the Accused requested money to repair his "matatu" bus. The investigators then informed the Accused that the **[page 3]** Office of the Prosecutor had analysed the CV and had decided that they were not interested in working with the Accused as there were several contradictions and matters that remained unclear in the CV. The Prosecution was therefore not in a position to assist the Accused.[10]

---

1 The Prosecution does not have the original CV, just a photocopy. T. 27 February 2006, p. 19.

2 T. 3 October 2005 p. 26.

3 T. 2 March 2006 pp. 37-38.

4 T. 27 June 2006, p. 20.

5 T. 2 March 2006 p. 45.

6 T. 27 June 2006, pp. 5-6; T. 28 June 2006, p. 3 (they consulted others at the ICTR before proceeding with the meeting).

7 T. 28 June 2006, p. 3.

8 T. 27 June 2006, pp. 6-7; T. 28 June 2006, p. 4.

9 T. 27 June 2006, pp. 9-11.; T. 28 June 2006, pp. 4-5.

10 T. 27 June 2006, pp. 13-14; T. 28 June 2006, p. 5. The witness testified that the Accused's statements were discredited by statements made by Kambanda after his arrest during Operation NAKI in July 1997, which was a statement given prior to the investigators first meeting with the Accused. T. 28 June 2006, p. 24. In return for the CV and the meetings, the Prosecution maintains that no offers, threats or inducements were made to the Accused, but the Accused did indicate that he wanted the Prosecution "to shed light on the genocide that took place in Rwanda in 1994, to clarify the conditions under which it arose. And he wanted [the Prosecution] to intervene with the Canadian authorities with regard to the document which led to his expulsion when he was in university -- when he was in Canada trying to complete his university studies." T. 27 June 2006, pp. 11-13; T. 28 June 2006, pp. 6, 19-20. One investigator stated that the Accused did not ask for the investigator's assistance with the Canadian government, but that he only informed them that he had been deported from Canada. T. 28 June 2006, p. 23. The investigator's 7 February 1998 report states, as read into the transcript, "[i]n this regard, we inform Mr. Z that it is premature to envisage protection for himself, as well as

6. The Prosecution maintains that at the time of the first meeting the Accused was not a suspect or a target. As far as the investigators were concerned, he was the brother of Agathe Kanziga who was the wife of the late President Habyarimana.[11] The investigators testified that the Accused was not on the list of individuals against whom the Prosecution had issued arrest warrants for Operation NAKI (Nairobi-Kigali) which was carried out in Nairobi and in the various regions.[12]

7. The Prosecution was investigating the RTLM, however, and was in possession of information that the Accused contributed to its establishment.[13] A Prosecution report of 19 January 1998 described the Accused as "allegedly a member of the Death Squad" and a founder of the RTLM, and reported his exile in April of 1994 with members of the Habyarimana family.[14] Moreover, the name of the Accused appears on a 7 March 1997 tracking list,[15] and on the list of the first category of genocide suspects put out by the Rwandan Government, dated 30 August 1996.[16] Further, Witness SFH, who was interviewed by the Prosecution on 11-12 February 1998, stated that the Accused was involved in the killing of "Stanislaus Libakiwe".[17] He was also allegedly implicated in the murder of "Diana (sic) Fossey" and the growing of cannabis in the Nyurgwe (phonetic) region."[18] After each of the meetings with the Accused, the investigators prepared a report.[19] In the investigators report of 17 February 1998, the Accused is referred to as a "suspect".[20] **[page 4]**

The Rights of Suspects

8. Rule 42 of the Rules of Procedure and Evidence (the "Rules"), entitled "Rights of Suspects During Investigation", stipulates that:

> (A) A suspect who is to be questioned by the Prosecutor shall have the following rights, of which he shall be informed by the Prosecutor prior to questioning, in a language he speaks and understands:
>
> (i) The right to be assisted by counsel of his choice or to have legal assistance assigned to him without payment if he does not have sufficient means to pay for it;
>
> (ii) The right to have the free assistance of an interpreter if he cannot understand or speak the language to be used for questioning; and
>
> (iii) The right to remain silent, and to be cautioned that any statement he makes shall be recorded and may be used in evidence.[21]

Rule 42 (B) governs the questioning of a suspect in the absence of counsel, and provides for the possibility of a waiver of the right by the suspect:

> (B) Questioning of a suspect shall not proceed without the presence of counsel unless the suspect has voluntarily waived his right to counsel. In case of waiver, if the suspect subsequently expresses a desire to have counsel, questioning shall thereupon cease, and shall only resume when the suspect has obtained or has been assigned counsel.

---

for members of his family, before the disclosed information is the subject of a -- an exhaustive analysis by the authorities of the Tribunal. It is at that moment that we shall be able to envisage various scenarios concerning his implication, his security, and his possible relocation, contingent upon an official, signed deposition made by himself." T. 28 June 2006, p. 22.

11 T. 27 June 2006, pp. 5-6; T. 28 June 2006, pp. 3, 8.

12 T. 27 June 2006, p. 21; T. 28 June 2006, p. 9.

13 T. 27 June 2006, pp. 27, 34 35.

14 T. 28 June 2006, pp. 13-15.

15 T. 27 June 2006, pp. 39-40.

16 T. 27 June 2006, pp. 40-43 (on the list as number 381).

17 T. 27 June 2006, pp. 45-47. The Indictment charges the Accused with the murder of Stanislas Sinibagiwe, also known as Stanislas Simbizi. *See* Amended Indictment, 8 March 2005, para. 46. It is not clear if Witness SFH was referring to the same person.

18 T. 28 June 2006, pp. 12-14.

19 T. 28 June 2006, p. 6.

20 T. 27 June 2006, p. 20.

21 In addition, Article 17 (3) of the Statute, "Investigation and Preparation of the Indictment", provides: "[i]f questioned, the suspect shall be entitled to be assisted by Counsel of his or her own choice". Article 20 (4)(g) confers on any Accused the right "[n]ot to be compelled to testify against himself or herself or to confess guilt".

9. In order to qualify for the procedural safeguards guaranteed under Rule 42 of the Rules of Procedure and Evidence (the "Rules"), the Accused would have to have been a "suspect" at the time of his meetings with the Prosecution investigators. Rule 2 of the Rules defines a suspect as "[a] person concerning whom the Prosecutor possesses reliable information which tends to show that he may have committed a crime over which the Tribunal has jurisdiction". While the evidence presented during the *voir dire* is not conclusive, there is evidence that the Prosecution possessed information that the Accused had committed crimes over which the Tribunal has jurisdiction. Given this uncertainty and mindful of the rights of the Accused, the Chamber finds that the Accused should have been treated as a suspect during the meetings with Prosecution investigators.

10. The Chamber will now determine whether the Rule 42 procedural safeguards have been met. The Prosecution did not advise the Accused of his rights as enumerated in Rule 42 (A) during any of the meetings. Nor do the circumstances suggest that the Accused's behaviour amounted to a knowing and voluntary waiver of these rights as contemplated in Rule 42 (B).

11. The Chamber is of the view that the procedural safeguards of Rule 42 have not been met. Relying on the principles enumerated above, the Chamber is also of the view that the Prosecution has not discharged its burden of showing that the Accused voluntarily waived his **[page 5]** right to the assistance of counsel, as required by Rule 42 (B). The Chamber will now decide on the appropriate remedy.

12. Rule 95 requires the exclusion of evidence "if obtained by methods which cast substantial doubt on its reliability or if its admission is antithetical to, and would seriously damage, the integrity of the proceedings".

13. The Chamber notes that Rule 95 does not require automatic exclusion of all unlawfully obtained evidence.[22] Rather, "in applying the provisions of Rule 95, this Tribunal considers all the relevant circumstances and will only exclude evidence if the integrity of the proceedings would indeed otherwise be seriously damaged".[23] As stated by the ICTY Chamber in *Delalić et al.*, it is difficult to imagine a statement taken in violation of the fundamental right to the assistance of counsel which would not require its exclusion under Rule 95 as being "antithetical to, and would seriously damage, the integrity of the proceedings".[24]

14. The Chamber finds that keeping the CV of the Accused on the record would seriously damage the integrity of the proceedings.

FOR THE ABOVE REASONS, THE CHAMBER EXPUNGES the CV of the Accused.

Arusha, 29 November 2006, done in English.

Inés Mónica Weinberg de Roca	Khalida Rachid Khan	Lee Gacuiga Muthoga
Presiding Judge	Judge	Judge

[Seal of the Tribunal]

22 *Prosecutor v. Bizimungu et al.*, Decision on Casimir Bizimungu, Justin Mugenzi and Jerome Bicamumpaka's Written Submissions Concerning the Issues Raised at the Hearing of 31 March 2006 in Relation to the Cross Examination of Witness Augustin Kayinamura (Formerly INGA) (TC), 1 November 2006, para. 12 ("*Bizimungu* Decision"); *Prosecutor v. Brdjanin*, Case No. IT-99-36-T, Decision on the Defence "Objection to Intercept Evidence" (TC), 3 October 2003, para. 54 ("*Brdjanin* Decision").

23 *Bizimungu* Decision, para. 12; *Prosecutor v. Bizimungu et al.*, Decision on Prosper Mugirnaeza's Renewed Motion to Exclude His Custodial Statements from Evidence (TC), 4 December 2003, para. 29; *Brdjanin* Decision, para. 61.

24 *Prosecutor v. Delalić et al.*, Case No. IT-96-21-T, Decision on Zdravko Mucić's Motion For the Exclusion of Evidence (TC), 2 September 1997, para. 43; *see also Bagosora* Decision, para. 21.

Tribunal pénal international pour le Rwanda
International Criminal Tribunal for Rwanda

IN THE APPEALS CHAMBER

Before: Judge Fausto Pocar, Presiding
Judge Mohamed Shahabuddeen
Judge Mehmet Güney
Judge Andrésia Vaz
Judge Theodor Meron

Registrar: Mr. Adama Dieng

Decision of: 8 December 2006

Ferdinand NAHIMANA
Jean-Bosco BARAYAGWIZA
Hassan NGEZE
(Appellants)

v.

THE PROSECUTOR
(Respondent)

Case No. ICTR-99-52-A

DECISION ON APPELLANT JEAN-BOSCO BARAYAGWIZA'S MOTIONS FOR LEAVE TO PRESENT ADDITIONAL EVIDENCE PURSUANT TO RULE 115 OF THE RULES OF PROCEDURE AND EVIDENCE

Counsel for Jean-Bosco Barayagwiza
Mr. D. Peter Herbert
Ms. Tanoo Mylvaganam

Counsel for Ferdinand Nahimana
Mr. Jean-Marie Biju-Duval
Ms. Diana Ellis

Counsel for Hassan Ngeze
Mr. Bharat B. Chadha
Mr. Behram N. Shroff

Office of the Prosecutor
Mr. James Stewart
Mr. Neville Weston
Mr. Abdoulaye Seye
Ms. Linda Bianchi

[page 1] 1. The Appeals Chamber of the International Criminal Tribunal for the Prosecution of Persons Responsible for Genocide and Other Serious Violations of International Humanitarian Law Committed in the Territory of Rwanda and Rwandan Citizens Responsible for Genocide and Other Such Violations Committed in the Territory of Neighbouring States Between 1 January and 31 December 1994 ("Appeals Chamber" and "Tribunal", respectively) is seized of five motions by the Appellant Jean-Bosco Barayagwiza ("Appellant"):

- "The Appellant Jean-Bosco Barayagwiza's Motion Giving Notice of the Further Delay in the Filing of the Motion for Additional Evidence Relating to Alison Des Forges, Pursuant to the Decision of 26 May 2006" filed on 26 June 2006 ("Motion Giving Notice of Delay");[1]
- "The Appellant Jean-Bosco Barayagwiza's Motion for Leave to Present Additional Evidence (Rule 115)" filed on 7 July 2006 ("First Rule 115 Motion");[2]
- "The Appellant Jean-Bosco Barayagwiza's Corrigendum Motion Relating to the Appellant's Reply to the Prosecutor's Response to the Appellant's Motion for Leave to Present Additional Evidence (Rule 115) Dated 20th July 2006" filed on 31 July 2006 ("Corrigendum Motion");[3]
- "The Appellant Jean-Bosco Barayagwiza's Motion for Leave to Present Additional Evidence (Rule 115)" filed on 13 September 2006 ("Second Rule 115 Motion");[4]
- "The Appellant Jean-Bosco Barayagwiza's Motion for Leave to Present Additional Evidence (Rule 115)" filed on 14 November 2006 ("Third Rule 115 Motion").[5]

2. In the First Rule 115 Motion, the Appellant requests the Appeals Chamber to admit twelve pieces of additional evidence on appeal to support his allegation that Alison Des Forges, who testified as an expert witness at trial, was biased against the Appellant. The Motion Giving Notice of Delay and the Corrigendum Motion are ancillary to the First Rule 115 Motion. In the Second Rule 115 Motion, the Appellant seeks admission of three documents related to his role within the "*Coalition pour la Défense de la République*" ("CDR") as additional evidence on appeal. In the **[page 2]** Third Rule 115 Motion, the Appellant requests the Appeals Chamber to admit two documents which, in his view, show that the testimony of Witness AGK, who testified at trial, was unreliable.

3. Trial Chamber I rendered its Judgement in this case on 3 December 2003.[6] Pursuant to the decisions of 17 May 2005[7] and 6 September 2005,[8] the Appellant filed both his Notice of Appeal and his Appellant's Brief on 12 October 2005 ("Notice of Appeal" and "Appellant's Brief", respectively). The briefing with respect to the Appellant's appeal was completed on 12 December 2005.[9]

---

1 The Prosecution did not file a response to the Motion Giving Notice of Delay.

2 The Prosecution filed the "Prosecutor's Response to 'The Appellant Jean-Bosco Barayagwiza's Motion for Leave to Present Additional Evidence (Rule 115)'" on 17 July 2006 ("Response to the First Rule 115 Motion"). The Appellant filed "The Appellant Jean-Bosco Barayagwiza's Reply to the Prosecutor's Response to 'The Appellant Jean-Bosco Barayagwiza's Motion for Leave to Present Additional Evidence (Rule 115)'" on 21 July 2006 ("Reply to the First Rule 115 Motion").

3 The Prosecution did not file a reponse to the Corrigendum.

4 The Prosecution filed the "Prosecutor's Response to 'The Appellant Jean-Bosco Barayagwiza's Motion for Leave to Present Additional Evidence (Rule 115)'" on 22 September 2006 ("Response to the Second Rule 115 Motion"), and the Appellant filed "The Appellant Jean-Bosco Barayagwiza's Reply to the Prosecutor's Response to the 'Motion for Leave to Present Additional Evidence (Rule 115)'" on 28 September 2006 ("Reply to the Second Rule 115 Motion").

5 The Prosecution filed the "Prosecutor's Response to 'The Appellant Jean-Bosco Barayagwiza's Motion for Leave to Present Additional Evidence (Rule 115)'" on 22 November 2006 ("Response to the Third Rule 115 Motion") and the Appellant filed confidentially "The Appellant Jean-Bosco Barayagwiza's Reply to the Prosecutor's Response to 'The Appellant Jean-Bosco Barayagwiza's Motion for Leave to Present Additional Evidence (Rule 115)'" ("Reply to the Third Rule 155 Motion") on 30 November 2006. The Appeals Chamber notes that the Appellant gives no reason as to why the Reply to the Third Rule 115 Motion or the present decision need to be confidential and finds that there is no apparent reason for the confidential classification of the Reply to the Third Rule 115 Motion. Consequently, both the Reply to the Third Rule 115 Motion and the present decision should be public.

6 *The Prosecutor v. Ferdinand Nahimana et al.*, Case No. ICTR-99-52-T, Judgement and Sentence, 3 December 2003 ("Trial Judgement").

7 Decision on "Appellant Jean-Bosco Barayagwiza's Urgent Motion for Leave to Have Further Time to File the Appeals Brief and the Appeal Notice", 17 May 2005 ("Decision of 17 May 2005").

8 Decision on Clarification of Time Limits and on Appellant Barayagwiza's Extremely Urgent Motion for Extension of Time to File his Notice of Appeal and his Appellant's Brief, 6 September 2005 ("Decision of 6 September 2005").

9 The Appellant Jean-Bosco Barayagwiza's Reply to the Consolidated Respondent's Brief, 12 December 2005 ("Reply Brief"). For a more detailed procedural background, the Appeals Chamber refers to its earlier decisions in the present case (Decision

APPLICABLE LAW

4. The Appeals Chamber recalls that under the jurisprudence of the Tribunal and that of the International Criminal Tribunal for the Former Yugoslavia ("ICTY"), an appeal pursuant to Article 24 of the Statute of the Tribunal (Article 25 of the Statute of the ICTY) is not a trial *de novo*[10] and is not an opportunity for a party to remedy any "failures or oversights" made during the pre-trial and trial phases.[11] Rule 115 of the Rules of Procedure and Evidence of the Tribunal ("Rules") provides for a mechanism to address "the situation where a party is in possession of material that was not before the court of first instance and which is additional evidence of a fact or issue litigated at trial".[12]

5. According to Rule 115, for additional evidence to be admissible on appeal, the following requirements must be met: first, the motion to present additional evidence should be filed "not later than thirty days from the date for filing of the brief in reply, unless good cause or, after the appeal **[page 3]** hearing, cogent reasons, are shown for a delay.[13] Second, the Appeals Chamber must find "that the additional evidence was not available at trial and is relevant and credible".[14] When determining the availability at trial, the Appeals Chamber will consider whether the party tendering the evidence has shown that it sought to make "appropriate use of all mechanisms of protection and compulsion available under the Statute and the Rules of the International Tribunal to bring evidence [...] before the Trial Chamber."[15] In this respect, the Appeals Chamber has held that

> Counsel is expected to apprise the Trial Chamber of all the difficulties he or she encounters in obtaining the evidence in question, including any problems of intimidation, and his or her inability to locate certain witnesses" and that "[t]he obligation to apprise the Trial Chamber constitutes not only a first step in exercising due diligence but also a means of self-protection in that non-cooperation of the prospective witness is recorded contemporaneously.[16]

With regards to relevance, the Appeals Chamber will consider whether the proposed evidence sought to be admitted relates to a material issue. As to credibility, the Appeals Chamber will only refuse to admit evidence at this stage if it does not appear to be reasonably capable of belief or reliance, without prejudice to a determination of the weight to be afforded.[17]

6. Once it has been determined that the additional evidence meets these conditions, the Appeals Chamber will determine whether the evidence "could have been a decisive factor in reaching the decision at trial."[18] To satisfy this requirement, the evidence must be such that it *could* have had an impact on the verdict, *i.e.* it

---

on Appellant Jean-Bosco Barayagwiza's Motion for Leave to Present Additional Evidence Pursuant to Rule 115, 5 May 2006 ("Decision of 5 May 2006"), paras. 3-5; Decision on Appellant Jean-Bosco Barayagwiza's Motions for Leave to Submit Additional Grounds of Appeal, to Amend the Notice of Appeal and to Correct His Appellant's Brief, 17 August 2006, paras. 5-8).

10 *Confidential* Decision on Appellant Hassan Ngeze's Six Motions for Admission of Additional Evidence on Appeal and/or Further Investigation at the Appeal Stage, 23 February 2006 ("Decision of 23 February 2006"), para. 5; Decision on Jean-Bosco Barayagwiza's Extremely Urgent Motion for Leave to Appoint an Investigator, 4 October 2005 ("Decision of 4 October 2005"), p. 3; *Prosecutor v. Jean-Paul Akayesu,* Case No. ICTR-96-4-A, Judgement, 1 June 2001, para. 177.

11 Decision on Appellant Hassan Ngeze's Motion for the Approval of the Investigation at the Appeal Stage, 3 May 2005, p. 3; *Prosecutor v. Drazen Erdemović*, Case No. IT-96-22-A, Judgement, 7 October 1997, para. 15.

12 Decision of 23 February 2006, para. 6; Decision of 4 October 2005, p. 4; *Prosecutor v. Zoran Kupreškić et al.*, Case No. IT-95-16-A, Decision on the Motions of Drago Josipović, Zoran Kupreškić and Vlatko Kupreškić to Admit Additional Evidence Pursuant to Rule 115 and for Judicial Notice to be Taken Pursuant to Rule 94 (B), 8 May 2001 ("*Kupreškić et al.* Decision of 8 May 2001"), para. 5.

13 Rule 115(A) of the Rules as amended on 10 November 2006.

14 Rule 115(B).

15 *The Prosecutor v. André Ntagerura et al.*, Case No. ICTR-99-46-A, Decision on Prosecution Motion for Admission of Additional Evidence, 10 December 2004 ("*Ntagerura et al.* Decision of 10 December 2004"), para. 9 [internal references omitted].

16 *Id.*

17 Decision of 23 February 2006, para. 7; *Prosecutor v. Zoran Kupreškić et al.*, Case No. IT-95-16-A, Decision on Motions for the Admission of Additional Evidence Filed by the Appellants Vlatko Kupreškić, Drago Josipović, Zoran Kupreškić and Mirjan Kupreškić, 26 February 2001, para. 28; *Prosecutor v. Zoran Kupreškić et al.*, Case No. IT-95-16-A, Appeal Judgement, 23 October 2001 ("*Kupreškić* Appeal Judgement"), para. 63; *Prosecutor v. Tihomir Blaškić*, Case No. IT-95-14-A, Decision on Evidence, 31 October 2003 ("*Blaškić* Decision of 31 October 2003"), p. 3; *Prosecutor v. Mladen Naletilić and Vinko Martinović*, Case No. IT-98-34-A, Decision on Naletilić's Amended Second Rule 115 Motion and Third Rule 115 Motion to Present Additional Evidence, 7 July 2005, para. 12.

18 Rule 115 (B) of the Rules.

could have shown that a conviction was unsafe.[19] Accordingly, the additional evidence must be directed at a specific finding of fact related to a conviction or to the sentence.[20] Although Rule 115 of the Rules does not explicitly provide for this, where the evidence is relevant and credible, but was available at trial, or could have been discovered through the exercise of due diligence, the Appeals Chamber may still allow it to be admitted on appeal provided the moving party can establish that the exclusion of it *would* amount to a miscarriage of justice. **[page 4]** That is, it must be demonstrated that had the additional evidence been adduced at trial, it *would* have had an impact on the verdict.[21]

7. The Appeals Chamber recalls that, whether the additional evidence was or was not available at trial, the additional evidence must always be assessed in the context of the evidence presented at trial, and not in isolation.[22]

THE MOTION GIVING NOTICE OF DELAY

8. As a preliminary matter, the Appeals Chamber turns to the Motion Giving Notice of Delay. The Appellant states that he wishes to notify the Pre-Appeal Judge of the necessity of delaying his motion for additional evidence relating to Alison Des Forges and the reasons for this delay.[23] He thereby requests that, in considering the admissibility of his future Motion for Additional Evidence, the Appeals Chamber recognizes the efforts he made to obtain the additional evidence.[24]

9. As recalled above, the time-limit for the filing of a motion to admit additional evidence is thirty days from the date for filing of the brief in reply, unless good cause is shown for delay.[25] The Appeals Chamber understands that through the Motion Giving Notice of Delay, the Appellant seeks to show good cause for the delayed filing of his First Rule 115 Motion. The Appeals Chamber notes that where arguments are made demonstrating good cause for a late filing after the filing deadline has passed, as a matter of practice, that showing is normally made as part of the Rule 115 motion itself with a request that the motion be recognized as validly filed. Thus, the Appeals Chamber will consider the arguments contained in the Motion Giving Notice of Delay when disposing of the Appellant's submissions concerning good cause for the late filing of his First Rule 115 Motion as follows. **[page 5]**

THE FIRST RULE 115 MOTION

A. Submissions of the Parties

10. In the First Rule 115 Motion, the Appellant requests the admission of twelve documents as additional evidence on appeal,[26] which, he claims, show that Alison Des Forges, by instigating a civil suit in the New

[19] *Zoran Kupreškić* Appeal Judgement, para. 68; *Prosecutor v. Radislav Krstić*, Case No. IT-98-33-A, Decision on Application for Admission of Additional Evidence on Appeal, 5 August 2003 ("*Krstić* Decision of 5 August 2003"), p. 3; *Blaškić* Decision of 31 October 2003, p. 3.

[20] Decision of 23 February 2006, para. 8.

[21] *Juvénal Kajelijeli v. The Prosecutor*, Case No. ICTR-98-44A-A, Decision on Defence Motion for the Admission of Additional Evidence Pursuant to Rule 115 of the Rules of Procedure and Evidence, 28 October 2004 ("*Kajelijeli* Decision of 28 October 2004"), para. 11; *Ntagerura et al.* Decision of 10 December 2004, para. 11. *See* also *Prosecution v. Rasim Delić*, Case No. IT-96-21-R-R119, Decision on Motion for Review, 25 April 2002, para. 18; *Prosecution v. Radislav Krstić*, Case No. IT-98-33-A, Decision on Application for Subpoenas, 1 July 2003, para. 16; *Krstić* Decision of 5 August 2003, p. 4; *Blaškić* Decision of 31 October 2003, p. 3.

[22] *Kajelijeli* Decision of 28 October 2004, para. 12; *Ntagerura et al.* Decision of 10 December 2004, para. 12. *See* also *Blaškić* Decision of 31 October 2003, p. 3; *Momir Nikolić v. Prosecutor*, Case No. IT-02-60/1-A, *Confidential* Decision on Motion to Admit Additional Evidence, 9 December 2004, para. 25.

[23] Motion Giving Notice of Delay, para. 2.

[24] *Ibid.*, para. 9.

[25] The Appeals Chamber notes that, under the provision applicable at the time of the filing of the Motion Giving Notice of Delay, the deadline was set to seventy-five days after the trial judgement.

[26] Statement of Alison Des Forges relating to the Civil Suit against the Appellant lodged in the New York District Court, and the Appellant's letter to the Judge Ceda Baum [presiding over the case] (Annex 1); Extract of the Prosecution's closing arguments on Civil Suits against the Appellant (Annex 2); Extract of the transcript of the cross-examination of Alison Des Forges on 14 June 2004 in the case *Prosecutor v. Casimir Bizimungu et al.* Case No. ICTR-99-50-T (Annex 3); Extract of the transcript of the cross-examination of Alison Des Forges on 1 March 2006 in the case *Prosecutor v. Protais Zigiranyirazo*, Case No. ICTR-01-73-T (Annex

York District Court, "actively pursued the Appellant [...] to neutralize him and undermine the efforts of the Rwandan Interim Government to get support from the United Nations".[27] In addition, the Appellant argues, Alison Des Forges did not disclose her role in the civil suit until her cross-examination in the *Zigiranyirazo* case in March 2006, and the Prosecution, although aware of these facts, did not disclose them to the Appellant.[28] Moreover, documents in Annexes 7 through 11, the Appellant contends, "refute the propaganda disseminated by Alison Desforges [*sic*]"[29] about the intentions of the Interim Government and show that her statement given to the New York District Court was false.[30]

11. The Appellant submits that the evidence only became available to him in June 2006, because the Prosecution did not disclose the information about Alison Des Forges' involvement in the New York civil suit.[31] The Appellant argues that he was not aware of this suit. He admits that he had received a document from the court in 1994, but was not sure whether it was genuine, because it was not served on him by officials.[32]

12. The Prosecution responds that the documents proffered by the Appellant as new evidence do not satisfy the criteria of admissibility under Rule 115 of the Rules.[33] The Prosecution argues that the Appellant was aware of the New York lawsuit, that he sent a letter to the judge who decided the matter, and that he referred to the lawsuit in his book "*Rwanda, le Sang Hutu est-il rouge?*". He was **[page 6]** therefore in the position to look for the documents from this lawsuit and use them at his trial.[34] In addition, the Prosecution argues that Counsel for the Appellant was aware of Alison Des Forges' involvement in the civil suit and cross-examined her about it at trial.[35] Furthermore, the Prosecution submits that Alison Des Forges is neither biased against the Appellant, nor gave any inconsistent or misleading information about her involvement in the civil suit.[36] Regarding the documents related to the policy of the Interim Government in 1994, the Prosecution submits that they are neither new, nor could they have influenced the trial.[37]

13. In reply, the Appellant submits that the Response to the First Rule 115 Motion should be expunged from the record because it exceeds the page limit of ten pages.[38] Regarding the Prosecution's arguments, he submits that he only became aware of the importance of the documents after Alison Des Forges' testimony in the *Zigiranyirazo* case, and that they were therefore not available at trial.[39]

B. <u>Discussion</u>

<u>Preliminary Issues</u>

14. At the outset, the Appeals Chamber notes that the Appellant filed the separate Corrigendum Motion to correct a clerical error in his Reply to the First Rule 115 Motion.[40] The Appeals Chamber recalls that "a party may, *without requesting leave* from the Appeals Chamber, file a corrigendum to their previously filed brief or motion whenever a minor or clerical error in said brief or motion is subsequently discovered and

4); Prosecution's Response to the Appellant's request for disclosure of the case file of the Civil Suit in the New York District Court, dated 22 March 2006 (Annex 5); Letter from the Appellant to the US Ambassador in Cameroon dated 12 April 1996 (Annex 6); five documents related to the activities of the Rwandan Interim Government with regard to the United Nations, taken from a publication "The United Nations and Rwanda 1993 to 1996" (Annexes 7 through 11); and a number of transcripts of interviews with the foreign minister of the Interim Government, Jerome Bicamumpaka in 1994 taken from the BBC summary of world broadcasts (Annex 12)

27 First Rule 115 Motion, para. 16.

28 *Id.*

29 *Ibid.*, para. 17.

30 *Ibid.*, paras 32-43.

31 *Ibid.*, para. 19; Motion Giving Notice of Delay, paras 5-8.

32 First Rule 115 Motion, para. 23.

33 Response to the First Rule 115 Motion, para. 5.

34 *Ibid.*, paras. 7-8.

35 *Ibid.*, para. 9.

36 *Ibid.*, paras. 13-20.

37 *Ibid.*, paras. 21-25.

38 Reply to the First Rule 115 Motion, paras. 2-3.

39 *Ibid.*, para. 7.

40 Corrigendum Motion, para. 1.

where correction of the error is necessary in order to provide clarification".[41] Although it was unnecessary for the Appellant to file a motion to this extent, the Appeals Chamber finds that the submitted amendment indeed corrects an obvious clerical error and does not amount to any substantial change of the Appellant's Reply to the First Rule 115 Motion. Therefore, the Appeals Chamber finds that the Appellant's Reply to the First Rule 115 Motion should be read in accordance with the amendments proposed by the Corrigendum Motion and allowed by the present decision. **[page 7]**

15. Second, the Appellant takes issue with the length of the Prosecution's submission, which, in his view, "deliberately and manifestly" disregards a decision by the Pre-Appeal Judge denying a request for an extension of the page limits for the Prosecution's response to the Appellant's First Rule 115 Motion.[42] The Appeals Chamber notes that, in response to the Appellant's request for an extension of page limits for its First Rule 115 Motion, the Prosecution requested a reciprocal extension for its response. The Pre-Appeal Judge denied the Prosecution's request because she considered the request for an extension of the page limit for a potential response to a motion that had not yet been filed to be unsubstantiated and premature.[43] This decision did not prevent the Prosecution from requesting an extension once the actual motion had been filed, which it did in its Response to the First Rule 115 Motion.[44] Considering the length of the First Rule 115 Motion and the number and size of the documents proffered as additional evidence, the Appeals Chamber finds that the Prosecution has shown good cause for the filing exceeding the regular page limit, and accepts the Response to the First Rule 115 Motion as validly filed.

Late Filing of the First Rule 115 Motion

16. With respect to the Appellant's First Rule 115 Motion, the deadline for the filing of motions under Rule 115 of the Rules expired on 11 January 2006. Any Rule 115 motions filed by the Appellant at the present stage of the proceedings are therefore admissible only if the Appellant shows good cause for the late filing.[45] The Appeals Chamber recalls that "the good cause requirement obliges the moving party to demonstrate that it was not able to comply with the time limit set out in the Rule, and that it submitted the motion in question as soon as possible after it became aware of the existence of the evidence sought to be admitted".[46]

17. The Appeals Chamber notes that most of the documents proffered by the Appellant as additional evidence are more than one year old, the majority of them even dating back to the 1990s. The only argument advanced by the Appellant as explanation for the late filing of these documents is that he became aware of Alison Des Forges' involvement in the New York civil suit only in March 2006.[47] **[page 8]**

18. However, the Appeals Chamber finds that the Appellant knew as soon as 1994 that a civil action had been brought against him in New York. In his letter to Judge Ceda Baum of the New York District Court, he wrote that he had received a document containing a complaint against him, and asked the Judge to dismiss the claim stating "I am persecuted by a so-called human rights organisation which is in fact, an organisation committed to RPF criminal ambitions".[48] This shows that the Appellant was not only aware of the lawsuit but also attributed it to a political campaign against him orchestrated by a human rights organization.[49]

41 Decision on the Appellant Jean-Bosco Barayagwiza's Corrigendum Motions of 5 July 2006, 30 October 2006, p. 2, quoting *Prosecutor v. Željko Mejakić et al.*, Case No. IT-02-65-AR11*bis*.1, Decision on Joint Defense Motion for Enlargement of Time to File Appellants' Brief, 30 August 2005, p. 3.

42 Reply to the First Rule 115 Motion, para. 3.

43 Decision of 26 May 2006, p. 4.

44 Response to the First Rule 115 Motion, paras. 3, 32.

45 Rule 115(A) of the Rules.

46 *Prosecutor v. Dario Kordić and Mario Čerkez*, Case No. IT-95-14/2-A, Decision on Prosecution's Motion to Admit Additional Evidence in Relation to Dario Kordić and Mario Čerkez, 17 December 2004, p. 2; *Prosecutor v. Mladen Naletilić and Vinko Martinović*, Case No. IT-98-34-A, Decision on Naletilić's Motion for Leave to File His Second Rule 115 Motion to Present Additional Evidence Pursuant to Rule 115, 27 January 2005, p. 3.

47 First Rule 115 Motion, para. 21; Motion Giving Notice of Delay, paras 5-8.

48 First Rule 115 Motion, Annex 1, "Appellant's Letter to Judge Ceda Baum".

49 In addition, the documents submitted by the Appellant show that the complaint was served a second time upon the Appellant in Zaire in January 1995: Motion Giving Notice of Further Delay, Annex "U.S. District Court Southern District of New York (Foley Square), Civil Docket for Case#: 1-94-cv-03627-JSM", p. 2.

During trial, Counsel for the Appellant cross-examined Alison Des Forges about her involvement in the lawsuit:

> Q. You did not meet Barayagwiza, but that did not stop you from testifying against him in the United States?
>
> A. I did not testify in any trial against Mr. Barayagwiza. I contributed documentation and witness testimonies to a civil proceeding which was heard without contest, and because there was no contest there was no trial.[50]

Even assuming *arguendo* that the Appellant was not aware of the extent of Alison Des Forges' involvement in this lawsuit, he had sufficient information to show that she was involved in one way or the other in the lawsuit, which he had already in 1994 characterized as a political campaign against him. Given that the relevant documents were all readily accessible, nothing prevented the Appellant from presenting them within the time limit of Rule 115 of the Rules.

19. The extract of the transcript of the *Zigiranyirazo* case dated 1 March 2006 is the only document proffered as additional evidence in the First Rule 115 Motion, which recently became available to the Appellant. However, the Appeals Chamber observes that the Appellant did not submit the relevant parts of this transcript with his First Rule 115 Motion.[51] Furthermore, the Appeals Chamber finds that this document does not reveal any information about the role of Alison Des Forges which would have been new to the Appellant. During her cross-examination in the *Zigiranyirazo* case, with respect to the New York civil suit, she explained that she had "played part in initiating this suit and bringing it to court" by "providing contextual information for the lawyers who prepared the suit in conjunction for the Rwandan plaintiffs"[52]. This is consistent with her testimony in the present case that she contributed documentation to a civil proceeding against the **[page 9]** Appellant.[53] In this context, the Appeals Chamber observes that nothing in the documents proffered by the Appellant supports his assertion that Alison Des Forges was the "driving force"[54] behind the civil suit. Considering that the other documents were earlier available to the Appellant and that the extract of Alison Des Forges' testimony in the *Zigiranyirazo* case presented no new information to the Appellant, the Appeals Chamber finds that it does not justify the late filing of the First Rule 115 Motion. In any case, the extract itself became available to the Appellant soon after the hearing in March 2006, because it was this transcript which occasioned his letter to the Prosecution of 12 March 2006,[55] and the Appellant has not shown good cause for seeking admission of this document as additional evidence more than four months after it became available to him.

20. In light of the above, the Appeals Chamber concludes that the Appellant has not shown good cause for the late filing of any of the documents proffered as additional evidence. The Appeals Chamber thus finds no need to consider the merits of the First Rule 115 Motion[56] and dismisses it in its entirety.

THE SECOND RULE 115 MOTION

A. Submissions of the Parties

21. In the Second Rule 115 Motion, the Appellant submits three documents which show, in his view, that the Trial Chamber erred in finding that he was President of the CDR at the national level.[57] The three documents are two messages by David Rawson, U.S. Ambassador to Rwanda in 1994,[58] and a letter from the CDR, signed by Théoneste Nahimana, the then first Vice-President of the CDR.[59] In the two messages from Ambassador Rawson, the Appellant is referred to as "CDR counselor" or "CDR deputy-designate",

---

50 T. 29 May 2002, p. 217.

51 According to the list of documents attached to the motion, the extract should comprise pages 30-68 of the trial transcript. The actual extract submitted to the Appeals Chamber (Annex 4) comprises only pages 50-54.

52 *Prosecutor v. Protais Zigiranyirazo*, Case No. ICTR-01-73-T, T. 1 March 2006, p. 38.

53 T. 29 May 2002, p. 217.

54 Reply to the First Rule 115 Motion, para. 17

55 Motion Giving Notice of Further Delay, para. 2.

56 *Cf.* Decision of 5 May 2006, para. 27.

57 Second Rule 115 Motion, paras 2-3.

58 *Ibid.*, paras 8-11 and 15.

59 *Ibid.*, paras 12-14.

respectively. This shows, the Appellant argues, that someone as well-informed as the U.S. Ambassador did not consider the Appellant to be the CDR President.[60] Regarding the letter signed by Théoneste Nahimana, the Appellant argues that its content was so important that it would have been signed by the President of the CDR. The fact that **[page 10]** it was not signed by the Appellant therefore shows, in the Appellant's view, that he did not occupy this position.[61]

22. The Prosecution responds that the Appellant overstates the importance of the Trial Chamber's finding about his position in the CDR.[62] Regarding the documents proffered by the Appellant, the Prosecution argues that the Appellant has not demonstrated that the evidence was unavailable at trial in any form and could not have been discovered through the exercise of due diligence.[63] In fact, the Prosecution submits, the Appellant abuses the procedure provided by Rule 115 of the Rules to remedy the consequences of his tactics at trial and failings in this appeal.[64] The Prosecution argues that all the documents were available much earlier than July 2006 and that the Appellant accordingly has not shown good cause for the late filing of the motion. In addition, the Prosecution maintains that none of the documents *could* or *would* have been a decisive factor at trial.[65]

23. The Appellant replies that Defence Counsel imposed on him at trial was incompetent and grossly negligent and, as a result, he was not adequately represented. Therefore, he argues, even evidence which was available at trial, but was not properly used by his Counsel, should be considered as "new".[66]

B. Discussion

24. As with the First Rule 115 Motion, the Second Rule 115 Motion was filed eight months after the expiry of the time period stipulated under Rule 115(A) of the Rules. The Appellant submits that the documents proffered as additional evidence were obtained by him during the month of July 2006, when he received an electronic file called "Alchemy" from the "National Archive", a non-governmental research institute based in the United States which "collects and publishes declassified documents obtained through the Freedom of Information Act".[67] The Appeals Chamber is therefore satisfied that there is good cause justifying the late filing of the Second Rule 115 Motion.

25. With respect to availability of the proffered evidence at trial, the Appeals Chamber is not satisfied that the Appellant was unable to obtain it in spite of the exercise of due diligence. As, the Prosecution points out, the declassifying process of U.S. documents started in 1998 and many **[page 11]** unclassified documents were accessible on the National Security Archive webpage in 2001.[68] The Appeals Chamber finds that the Appellant's reply to this argument, that the Prosecution failed to prove that the documents were declassified before his trial,[69] is misguided; it is for the Appellant to show that the documents were available to him only recently. On the contrary, the Appellant's own arguments seem to suggest that the documents were accessible earlier than 2003: the compilation of documents which the Appellant received is the result of research carried out between 1994 and 2003.[70]

26. In addition, the Appeals Chamber notes that both messages in their relevant parts refer to conversations between the Appellant and Ambassador Rawson.[71] The Appellant was therefore aware that these

60 *Ibid.*, para. 11.
61 *Ibid.*, para. 13.
62 Response to the Second Rule 115 Motion, para. 3.
63 *Ibid.*, para. 7.
64 *Ibid.*, paras. 4-6.
65 *Ibid.*, paras 18-23.
66 Reply to the Second Rule 115 Motion, para. 7.
67 Second Rule 115 Motion, para. 8.
68 Response to the Second Rule 115 Motion, para. 10.
69 Reply to the Second Rule 115 Motion, para. 6.
70 Second Rule 115 Motion, para. 8, fn. 7, referring to a statement by the "National Archive".
71 *Ibid.*, Annex 1: "Message of the US Ambassador Rawson dated 31 March 1994", para. 2: "CDR Counselor, Jean Bosco Barayagwiza, telephoned ambassador about 10:30 PM [illegible word] of 3/30…"; Second Rule 115 Motion, Annex 3: "Message of the US Ambassador Rawson dated 28 March 1994", para. 14: "CDR Deputy-designate Jean-Bosco Barayagwiza called Ambassador morning 3/27…"

conversations had taken place. The point the Appellant wishes to make by proffering the messages is that the U.S. Ambassador "who was monitoring closely the political events in Rwanda, would have been among the first diplomats to be informed" about the Appellant's eventual appointment as CDR President and would have referred to him as such in his messages.[72] The Appellant's role in the CDR was clearly an issue at trial.[73] Given the Appellant's contacts with Ambassador Rawson, the Appellant could have attempted to contact Ambassador Rawson, either to learn about his reports to the U.S. government in 1994 as a reliable and independent source of political information on Rwanda, or with the objective to adduce his live testimony about the Appellant's role in the CDR at trial.

27. Regarding the letter signed by Théoneste Nahimana, the Appellant's submissions show that he was aware of the existence of this letter at trial. The Appeals Chamber also notes that the report by Ambassador Rawson dated 28 March 1994 suggests that the Appellant was at least involved in the drafting of the letter signed by Théoneste Nahimana, as he was informed about his content before it was signed and took suggestions from Ambassador Rawson as to its content.[74] Furthermore, it was the Appellant himself who gave a copy of this letter to Ambassador Rawson in 1994.[75] The Appeals Chamber notes that a number of CDR documents were adduced at trial on behalf of the Appellant.[76] **[page 12]** The Appellant has thus not shown that the letter was unavailable to him at trial or that he had made efforts to obtain a copy thereof in the exercise of due diligence.

28. In light of the above, while the Appeals Chamber finds that the proffered evidence is *prima facie* relevant and credible, it will admit it as additional evidence on appeal only if it concludes that its exclusion would result in a miscarriage of justice, *i.e.* it *would* have had an impact on the verdict if it had been adduced at trial. The Appeals Chamber notes that the Appellant only suggests the proffered evidence *could* have been a decisive factor for the Trial Chamber's finding with respect to the Appellant's position in the CDR.[77]

29. Concerning the letter from the CDR Party to the Prime Minister, the Appellant argues that the letter was of such importance for the CDR that only the President could have signed it; thus, the Appellant claims, the fact that it was signed not by himself, but by Théoneste Nahimana, shows that he was not acting as the president.[78] However, the Appellant does not advance any support for his argument demonstrating why this letter should have been necessarily signed by the president. The Appeals Chamber recalls that Théoneste Nahimana was the first Vice-President of the CDR.[79] The Statute of the CDR, to which the Appellant refers, shows that the first Vice-President was the "first supplementary legal representative" ("*le premier Représentant Légal Suppléant*") of the CDR and was thus able to represent the party.[80] Considering the Trial Chamber's finding that the Appellant was seen as "working to some extent behind the scenes", the fact that the letter was signed by Théoneste Nahimana is not inconsistent with the Trial Chamber's conclusions. Therefore, the Appeals Chamber finds that this piece of evidence, had it been adduced at trial, would not have changed the verdict with regard to the Appellant's position.

30. As regards the messages sent by the U.S. Ambassador, Mr. David Rawson, the Appellant argues that these documents prove that he was not the CDR National President.[81] In light of the evidence adduced at trial, the Appeals Chamber is not satisfied that the Trial Chamber would have arrived at a different conclusion upon examination of the two messages in question. The Appellant has not shown that the Trial Chamber would necessarily opt for the evidence that he now proffers instead of the totality of the evidence that it chose to rely on to conclude that Barayagwiza held the **[page 13]** position of a superior in the CDR including that,

72 Second Rule 115 Motion, para. 11.

73 *Cf.* Trial Judgement, paras 258-277.

74 Second Rule 115 Motion, Annex 3: "Message of the US Ambassador Rawson dated 28 March 1994", para. 15.

75 *Ibid.*, para. 15.

76 Response to the Second Rule 115 Motion, para. 16, referring to Exhibits 2D12 to 2D34.

77 Second Rule 115 Motion, paras 19, 23; *see also* para. 25: "The newly discovered evidence enhances the exculpatory value of the existing material and renders all the more obvious that the finding and the conviction against the Appellant, based on the fact that he succeeded Bucyana as the National President of CDR, are baseless and should be quashed."

78 *Ibid.*, para. 13.

79 *Ibid.*, para. 15.

80 Article 19 of the CDR Statute, Second Rule 115 Motion, Annex 4(1), "CDR Statute (Exhibit 2D9)", p. 29.

81 Second Rule 115 Motion, paras 11 and 15.

after the assassination of Bucyana in February 1994, Barayagwiza succeeded him as President of the CDR at the national level.[82]

31. The Appeals Chamber also rejects the Appellant's argument in relation to the incompetence of his counsel at trial.[83] While it is true that, where the failure resulted solely from counsel negligence or inadvertence, the Appeals Chamber can permit admission of additional evidence to remedy for such negligence or inadvertence, this would only be allowed if the proffered evidence is of such substantial importance to the success of the appeal such as its exclusion would lead to a miscarriage of justice.[84] In these exceptional cases, the Appeals Chamber has reasoned, the interests of justice require that an appellant not be held responsible for the failures of counsel.[85] However, in light of the findings above, the Appeals Chamber is not satisfied that non-admission of the proffered evidence would amount to a miscarriage of justice.

32. Finally, with respect to the Appellant's arguments concerning the "already existing exculpatory material erroneously not taken into account by the [T]rial Chamber",[86] the Appeals Chamber notes that these arguments relate to specific grounds of appeal raised by the Appellant against the Trial Judgement and that they will be appropriately addressed by the Appeals Chamber in rendering its appeals judgement on the Appellant's main appeal.[87] Therefore, the Appeals Chamber will not dispose of them in the present decision.

33. In addition to his request for admission of additional evidence, the Appellant argues that the Prosecution failed to disclose the letter signed by Théoneste Nahimana to him under its obligations pursuant to Rule 68(A) of the Rules and that this failure "should be considered as an abuse of **[page 14]** process and a serious obstruction to a fair trial which deserves a sanction".[88] The Appeals Chamber first observes "that the Prosecution may be relieved of its Rule 68 obligation if the existence of the relevant exculpatory material is known to the Defence and if it is reasonably accessible through the exercise of due diligence".[89] As noted above, the document was known to the Appellant, and he has not demonstrated that the document was not reasonably accessible to him.

34. Second, the Appeals Chamber recalls that "material will fall within the ambit of Rule 68 if it tends to suggest the innocence or mitigate the guilt of the accused, or affects the credibility of Prosecution evidence".[90] The determination of what material meets Rule 68 disclosure requirements is primarily a fact-based judgement made by and under the responsibility of the Prosecution.[91] Therefore, as noted previously,

---

[82] *See, inter alia* Trial Judgement, para. 258 referring to Exhibit 2D9; para. 260 referring to Alison Des Forges' testimony and Exhibit P141; para. 261 referring to the testimony of Alison Des Forges, Omar Serushago, Fançois-Xavier Nsanzuwera and Exhibits P142, P107/37; para. 263 referring to Witness B3; para. 264 referring to the testimony of Thomas Kamilindi, Alison Des Forges, Jean-Pierre Chrétien, Witness AHI, Witness EB, Witness AFX, Witness Omar Serushago; para. 266 referring to the testimony of Witness ABC, Witness LAG, Omar Serushago, Kamilindi, Kabanda and Alison Des Forges and that of Hassan Ngeze; para. 267 referring to Exhibit 2D35 (the book written by the Appellant "*Le Sang Hutu est-il rouge?*"; and paras 273, 276, 977.

[83] Second Rule 115 Motion, para. 16.

[84] *See, by analogy,* Decision on Appellant Jean-Bosco Barayagwiza's Motions for Leave to Submit Additional Grounds of Appeal, to Amend the Notice of Appeal and to Correct his Appellant's Brief, 17 August 2006, para. 12; *Prosecutor v. Vidoje Blagojević and Dragan Jokić*, Case No. IT-02-60-A, Decision on Motion of Dragan Jokić for Leave to File Third Amended Notice of Appeal and Amended Appellate Brief, 26 June 2006, para. 9; *Prosecutor v. Vidoje Blagojević and Dragan Jokić*, Case No. IT-02-60-A, Decision on Motions Related to the Pleadings in Dragan Jokić's Appeal, 24 November 2005, para. 8; *Blagojević* Decision of 14 October 2005, para. 8; *Prosecutor v. Dario Kordić and Mario Čerkez,* Case No. IT-95-14/2-A, Decision Granting Leave to Dario Kordić to Amend His Grounds of Appeal, 9 May 2002, para. 5.

[85] Decision on Appellant Jean-Bosco Barayagwiza's Motions for Leave to Submit Additional Grounds of Appeal, to Amend the Notice of Appeal and to Correct his Appellant's Brief, 17 August 2006, para. 12.

[86] Second Rule 115 Motion, para. 24 referring to Exhibits 2D9, 2D12, P203, P140 and P103/190C.

[87] Appeals Brief, paras 181-193 (Grounds 18-21).

[88] Second Rule 115 Motion, para. 14.

[89] *Prosecutor v. Edouard Karemera et al.*, Case No. ICTR-98-44-AR73.7, Decision on Interlocutory Appeal Regarding the Role of the Prosecutor's Electronic Disclosure Suite in Discharging Disclosure Obligations, 30 June 2006, para. 15; *Prosecutor v. Tihomir Blaškic*, Case No. IT-95-14-A, Appeal Judgement, 29 July 2004 ("*Blaškić* Appeals Judgement"), para. 296.

[90] *Prosecutor v. Krstić*, Case No. IT-98-33-A, Appeal Judgement, 19 April 2004, para. 178.

[91] Decision on Appellant Jean-Bosco Barayagwiza's Motion Requesting that the Prosecution Disclosure of the Interview of Michel Bagaragaza Be Expunged from the Record, 30 October 2006, ("*Barayagwiza* Decision on Disclosure") para. 6; *Prosecutor v. Edouard Karemera et al.*, Case No. ICTR-98-44-AR73.6, Decision on Joseph Nzirorera's Interlocutory Appeal, 28 April 2006, para. 16; *Prosecutor v. Radoslav Brđanin,* Case No. IT-99-36-A, Decision on Appellant's Motion for Disclosure Pursuant to Rule 68

the Appeals Chamber will not intervene in the exercise of the Prosecution's discretion, unless it is shown that the Prosecution abused it and, where there is no evidence to the contrary, will assume that the Prosecution is acting in good faith.[92] In this respect, the Appeals Chamber notes that, if an appellant wishes to show that the Prosecution is in breach of these obligations, he/she must identify specifically the materials sought, present a *prima facie* showing of its probable exculpatory nature, and prove the Prosecutor's custody or control of the materials requested.[93] Finally, even when the Defence satisfies the Chamber that the Prosecution has failed to comply with its Rule 68 obligations, the Chamber will still examine whether the **[page 15]** Defence has actually been prejudiced by such failure before considering whether a remedy is appropriate.[94] The Appeals Chamber is neither satisfied that the document is of *prima facie* exculpatory nature, nor that the alleged Prosecution's failure to communicate it to the Appellant would have caused him any prejudice.[95]

35. For these reasons, the Appeals Chamber finds that the Appellant's argument that the Prosecution did not fulfil its obligations under Rule 68(A) of the Rules by not disclosing the letter, is unfounded.

THE THIRD RULE 115 MOTION

A. Submissions of the Parties

36. In the Third Rule 115 Motion, the Appellant submits another two messages from U.S. Ambassador Rawson, which he obtained from the same source as the two messages submitted in the Second Rule 115 Motion.[96] Both messages are dated 22 February 1994 and relate to a demonstration by CDR members outside the Ministry of Foreign Affairs in Kigali. The Appellant argues that both messages show that the testimony of Witness AGK at trial about the CDR demonstration is false and that, accordingly, the Trial Chamber's findings based on this evidence are unsafe.[97]

37. The Prosecution responds that the Appellant impermissibly tries to use the procedure of Rule 115 to remedy his failings at his trial and on appeal.[98] The Prosecution argues that the evidence proffered by the Appellant is not new and that he does not advance any argument that could constitute good cause for the late filing of the motion.[99] Finally, the Prosecution argues that the new evidence neither could nor would have been a decisive factor at trial.[100]

---

and Motion for an Order to the Registrar to Disclose Certain Materials, 7 December 2004 ("*Brđanin* 7 December 2004 Decision"), p. 3; *Blaškić* Appeals Judgement, para. 264; *Prosecutor v. Tihomir Blaškić,* Case No IT-95-14-A, Decision on Prosecution's Application to Seek Guidance from the Appeals Chamber regarding Redaction of the Statement of "Witness Two" for the purposes of Disclosure to Dario Kordić under Rule 68, 4 March 2004, ("*Blaškić* 4 March 2004 Decision"), para. 44; *Prosecutor v. Tihomir Blaškić,* Case No IT-95-14-A, [confidential] Decision on Prosecution's Application to Seek Guidance from the Appeals Chamber regarding Redaction of the Statement of "Witness Two" for the purposes of Disclosure to Paško Ljubičić under Rule 68, 30 March 2004 ("*Blaškić* 30 March 2004 Decision"), paras 31-32; *Prosecutor v. Tihomir Blaškić,* Case No. IT-95-14-A, Decision on the Appellant's Motions for the Production of Material, Suspension or Extension of the Briefing Schedule, and Additional Filings, 26 September 2000 ("*Blaškić* 26 September 2000 Decision"), paras 38, 45.

92 *Barayagwiza* Decision on Disclosure, para. 6; *Prosecutor v. Miroslav Bralo*, Case No. IT-95-17-A, Decision on Motions for Access to *Ex Parte* Portions of the Record on Appeal and for Disclosure of Mitigating Material, 30 August 2006 ("*Bralo* Decision"), para. 31; *Brđanin* 7 December 2004 Decision, p. 3; *Prosecutor v. Miroslav Kvočka et al.*, Case No. IT 98 30/1-A, Decision, 22 March 2004, p. 3; *Georges Rutaganda v. Prosecutor*, Case No. ICTR-96-3-A, Decision on Urgent Defence Motion for Disclosure and Admission of Additional Evidence and Scheduling Order, 12 December 2002, pp 4-5; *Alfred Musema v. Prosecutor, Case No. ICTR-96-13-A, Decision on the Appellant's Motions for the Production of Material, Suspension of Extension of the Briefing Schedule, and Additional Filings, 18 May 2001, p. 4; Blaškić* 26 September 2000 Decision, para. 39.

93 *Bralo* Decision, para. 31; *Kajelijeli* Appeal Judgement, para. 262; *Brđanin* 7 December 2004 Decision, p. 3.

94 *Bralo* Decision, para. 31; *Kajelijeli* Appeal Judgement, para. 262; *Krstić* Appeal Judgement, para. 153.

95 *See also supra* at para. 29.

96 Third Rule 115 Motion, para. 1.

97 *Ibid.*, paras 6-16.

98 Response to the Third Rule 115 Motion, paras. 4-7.

99 *Ibid.*, paras. 8-10.

100 *Ibid.*, paras. 19-22.

B. Discussion

38. As a preliminary matter, the Appeals Chamber observes that the Reply to the Third Rule 115 Motion was filed after the time-limit for its filing had expired. The Appeals Chamber notes the **[page 16]** Appellant's explanation that he received the Prosecution's Response to the Third Rule 115 Motion only on 27 November 2006, and thus accepts it as validly filed.

39. The Appeals Chamber notes that the Appellant claims to have obtained the two documents attached to the Third Rule 115 Motion from the same compilation of documents, the "National Archive", as the two messages from Ambassador Rawson submitted in the Second Rule 115 Motion.[101] Considering that the Appellant received the material in August 2006 only, the Appeals Chamber is satisfied that the Appellant has shown good cause for the late filing of the Third Rule 115 Motion.

40. The Appeals Chamber is also satisfied that the proffered evidence is *prima facie* relevant and credible. However, the Appeals Chamber finds that the Appellant has failed to show that the evidence was not available to him at his trial or could not be obtained through exercise of due diligence. The Appeals Chamber recalls that the party adducing additional evidence must establish that the said evidence was not available at trial *in any form whatsoever*.[102] As in the Second Rule 115 Motion, the Appellant again merely asserts that the documents "have been declassified only recently" without giving any further details about the declassification process or any earlier attempts to access the material.[103] As the Prosecution points out, unclassified U.S. documents were available during the Appellant's trial, and the possibility to access classified documents through a Freedom of Information Act application also existed.[104] Further, the Appellant has not shown that he tried to contact Ambassador Rawson to adduce his live testimony at trial. Finally, the Appeals Chamber notes that the Appellant acknowledges that other evidence concerning the date of the demonstration, the most important point of the documents proffered as additional evidence, was available to him.[105]

41. Accordingly, the two documents proffered would be admissible as additional evidence only if they *would* have affected the verdict. According to the Appellant, the two messages from Ambassador Rawson show that Witness AGK's testimony at trial about a CDR demonstration was unreliable, because there are significant contradictions between Witness AGK's testimony and the two messages. The main discrepancies noted by the Appellant are the date of the demonstration and the **[page 17]** presence of UNAMIR soldiers.[106]

42. As a preliminary matter, the Appeals Chamber notes that the documents proffered as additional evidence are immaterial to a number of arguments raised by the Appellant, for example, the Trial Chamber's reference to the term "*tubatsembatsembe*" or internal inconsistencies of Witness AGK's testimony.[107] With regard to the date of the demonstration and the presence of UNAMIR soldiers, the Appeals Chamber finds that the Appellant does not show that Witness AGK's testimony and the two messages from Ambassador Rawson relate to the same event. Although the Appellant asserts that there is no evidence that there was more than one demonstration,[108] the very discrepancies noted by the Appellant would suggest that Witness AGK and Ambassador Rawson refer to two different events.

43. Further, the Appeals Chamber notes that the Trial Chamber was aware of the alleged discrepancies in Witness AGK's testimony. The witness was cross-examined about the date he gave for the demonstration (May 1993). Counsel in particular asked the witness whether the demonstration took place before or after the signing of the Arusha accords[109] and explained that the witness referred to the presence of UNAMIR soldiers,

---

101 Third Rule 115 Motion, para. 1. *See supra,* para. 24.

102 *Prosecutor v. Sylvestre Gacumbitsi*, Case No. ICTR-2001-64-A, Decision on "Requête en extrème urgence aux fins d'admission de moyen de preuve supplementaire en appel", 9 February 2006, para. 6.

103 Third Rule 115 Motion, para. 17. *See supra,* para 25.

104 Response to the Third Rule 115 Motion, para. 10, referring to T. 8 July 2002, p. 42 and T. 9 July 2002, pp. 42-44, 69, 75.

105 Reply to the Third Rule 115 Motion, para. 18, referring to Response to the Third Rule 115 Motion, para. 12. The evidence in question includes transcripts from Radio Rwanda broadcasts of 21 February 1994.

106 Third Rule 115 Motion, para. 14.

107 *Id.*

108 Reply to the Third Rule 115 Motion, para. 20.

109 T. 25 June 2001, pp. 28-29.

which would have been impossible in May 1993 because UNAMIR was deployed only after the signing of the Arusha accords.[110] Nevertheless, the Trial Chamber was satisfied that "May 1993 was [Witness AGK's] recollection of the date" and accepted his testimony.[111] Finally, the Appeals Chamber notes that Witness AGK's evidence about the demonstration was only one of several bases for the Trial Chamber's findings regarding the Appellant's role in the CDR.[112]

44. In light of the above, the Appeals Chamber finds that the documents proffered as additional evidence with the Third Rule 115 Motion would not have been a decisive factor in the Trial Chamber's decision. Accordingly, the Appeals Chamber dismisses the Third Rule 115 Motion it in its entirety. **[page 18]**

DISPOSITION

45. For the foregoing reasons, the Appeals Chamber **GRANTS** the Corrigendum Motion; **DISMISSES** the Motion Giving Notice of Delay; and **DISMISSES** the First Rule 115 Motion, the Second Rule 115 Motion and the Third Rule 115 Motion in their entirety.

Done in English and French, the English text being authoritative.

Dated this 8th day of December 2006.
At The Hague, The Netherlands

Fausto Pocar
Presiding Judge

[Seal of the Tribunal]

110 *Ibid.*, p. 30.
111 Trial Judgement, para. 710.
112 *Ibid.*, paras 714-719.

International Criminal Tribunal for Rwanda
Tribunal pénal international pour le Rwanda

OR: ENG

TRIAL CHAMBER III

Before Judges: Dennis C. M. Byron, Presiding
Emile Francis Short
Gberdao Gustave Kam

Registrar: Adama Dieng

Date: 11 December 2006

THE PROSECUTOR

v.

Édouard KAREMERA
Mathieu NGIRUMPATSE
Joseph NZIRORERA

Case No. ICTR-98-44-T

DECISION ON APPEALS CHAMBER REMAND OF JUDICAL NOTICE

Rules 94 of the Rules of Procedure and Evidence

Office of the Prosecutor:
Don Webster
Alayne Frankson-Wallace
Iain Morley
Saidou N'Dou
Sunkaric Ballah-Conteh
Takeh Sendze

Defence Counsel for Édouard Karemera
Dior Diagne Mbaye and Félix Sow

Defence Counsel for Mathieu Ngirumpatse
Chantal Hounkpatin and Frédéric Weyl

Defence Counsel for Joseph Nzirorera
Peter Robinson and
Patrick Nimy Mayidika Ngimbi

[page 2] INTRODUCTION

1. On 9 November 2005, this Chamber ruled upon the Prosecution's request for judicial notice to be taken of six purported facts of common knowledge and 153 purported adjudicated facts.[1] It took judicial notice of three facts of common knowledge, pursuant to Rule 94(A) of the Rules of Procedure and Evidence, and denied the remainder of the request.[2]

2. On 16 June 2006, the Appeals Chamber upheld, in part, the Prosecution's interlocutory appeal of that Decision, directing the Chamber to take judicial notice of certain facts of common knowledge, and to review its findings in the impugned Decision concerning certain purported adjudicated facts.[3]

3. At the Parties' request, the Chamber then issued a Scheduling Order, permitting them to file any further submissions they may have concerning the Trial Chamber's pending review of its findings on judicial notice of adjudicated facts.[4] The Parties duly complied.[5]

4. According to the Defence for Nzirorera, the Defence for each of the Accused agreed to divide their Responses so as each Accused would make submissions with respect to certain Facts only.[6] However, whereas the Defence for Nzirorera adhered to this delineation, the Defence for Ngirumpatse made submissions on almost each and every fact, and the Defence for Karemera made submissions on only some of the facts allocated to it under this division.

5. The Prosecution filed one single Response to all of the Defence submissions. It indicated that it abandoned its application with respect to 10 of the purported adjudicated facts,[7] so that only 137 purported adjudicated **[page 3]** facts remain to be considered by the Trial Chamber.[8]

6. While the Chamber had completed its deliberations pertaining to the Appeals Chamber's remand and was in the final drafting process of its decision, the anticipated testimony of two Prosecution witnesses rendered necessary the delivery of two oral rulings indicating the Chamber's findings concerning certain facts. The Chamber specified that its written Decision on this matter would provide reasons for its ruling, and would be the authoritative statement of the Chamber's findings and reasoning concerning this issue. These rulings allowed the Prosecution to drastically shorten its examination-in-chief.

---

1 The 153 purported adjudicated facts were taken from the *Nahimana et al., Kajelijeli, Kayishema and Ruzindana, Musema, Ntakirutimana, Niyitegeka, Akayesu, Rutaganda* and *Semanza* Judgements.

2 *Prosecutor v. Édouard Karemera, Mathieu Ngirumpatse and Joseph Nzirorera ("Karemera et al.")*, Case No. ICTR-98-44-T, Decision on Prosecution Motion for Judicial Notice (TC), 9 November 2005 ("Impugned Decision"). The facts in relation to which judicial notice was taken were Facts 3 and 4, as proposed by the Prosecution, as well as a slightly modified version of Fact 1. The substance of the denial was the denial of Facts 2, 5 and 6 as facts of common knowledge; and denial of the 153 purported adjudicated facts. Of the adjudicated facts, Fact 153 – that genocide was committed in Rwanda in 1994 against the Tutsi as a group – was pleaded alternatively as a fact of common knowledge and as an adjudicated fact. The Trial Chamber declined to take judicial notice of the fact on either basis.

3 Respectively, Facts two, five and six; and .Facts 1-30, 33-74, and 79-152 listed under Annex B of the Prosecution's Interlocutory Appeal. *Karemera et al*, Case No. ICTR-98-44-AR73(C), Decision on Prosecutor's Interlocutory Appeal of Decision on Judicial Notice (AC), 16 June 2005 ("Appeals Chamber Decision").

4 *Karemera et al*, Case No. ICTR-98-44-T, Scheduling Order, 17 July 2006.

5 Joseph Nzirorera's "Supplemental Submission on Judicial Notice of Adjudicated Facts", filed by on 8 August 2006; "Requête d' Édouard Karemera relative à la demande de la Chambre d'appel pour la reconsidération de la requête du Procureur à propos du constat judiciaire de faits admis", filed on 25 August 2006; "Mémoire complémentaire pour M. Ngirumpatse sur la requête en constat judiciaire et en admission de faits et demande à la Chambre d'entendre les observations orales des parties au soutien de leurs écritures", filed on 28 August 2006; "Prosecutor's Consolidated Response to Defence Submissions on the Motion for Judicial Notice of Adjudicated Facts", filed on 11 September 2006; Joseph Nzirorera's "Reply Brief on Judicial Notice of Adjudicated Facts", filed on 14 September 2006; "Mémoire en réplique pour M. Ngirumpatse sur la *Prosecutor's Motion for Judicial Notice of Adjudicated Facts*", filed on 25 September 2006. On 27 September 2006, the Chamber granted the Defence an extension of time to reply to 2 October 2006 (see *Karemera et al*, Case No. ICTR-98-44-T, Décision Accordant une Prorogation de Délai de Réponse à Deux Requêtes du Procureur (TC), 27 September 2006). Édouard Karemera filed a Reply to the Prosecution Motion was filed on 1 October 2006.

6 See Nzirorera's Supplemental Submission, para. 10. According to this submission, the Defence for Joseph Nzirorera was to address the facts taken from the *Nahimana et al.* and *Kajelijeli* Judgements; the Defence for Mathieu Ngirumpatse was to address the facts taken from the *Akayesu, Rutaganda,* and *Semanza* Judgements, and the Defence for Édouard Karemera was to address the facts taken from the *Kayishema, Musema, Ntakirutimana,* and *Niyitegeka* Judgements.

7 Facts 14, 79-83, and 138-141 – see Prosecutor's Consolidated Response, para. 7.

8 One of which – Fact 153 – is pleaded alternatively as a fact of common knowledge.

DELIBERATIONS

Preliminary Matter

7. The Defence of each of the Accused in this case requested the Appeals Chamber to reconsider, or alternatively, to clarify, its Decision. Pending the Decision of the Appeals Chamber on reconsideration, the Defence for Ngirumpatse asked the Chamber to defer its review of the judicial notice issues, submitting that such a deferral would be in the interests of justice and judicial economy.

8. This request for deferral has been rendered moot since, on 1 December 2006, the Appeals Chamber dismissed the motions for reconsideration in their entirety.[9]

9. The Trial Chamber will therefore begin by considering that part of the Appeals Chamber Decision which directed the Chamber to take judicial notice of certain facts of common knowledge. It will then go on to consider the adjudicated facts aspect of the Appeals Chamber Decision.

I. Facts of Common Knowledge – Rule 94(A)

10. Rule 94 (A) of the Rules states: "A Trial Chamber shall not require proof of facts of common knowledge but shall take judicial notice thereof." This part of the rule is not discretionary;[10] rather Rule 94(A) "commands the taking of judicial notice of material that is 'notorious'".[11] The term "common knowledge" "encompasses facts that are not reasonably subject to dispute: in other words, commonly accepted or universally known facts, such as general facts of history or geography, or the laws of nature.

11. The Appeals Chamber Decision found that this Chamber had erred in failing to take judicial notice of the following facts, which the Appeals Chamber said are facts of common knowledge:[12] **[page 4]**

(i) ***Fact 2*** – "The following state of affairs existed in Rwanda between 6 April 1994 to 17 July 1994: There were throughout Rwanda, widespread or systematic attacks against a civilian population based on Tutsi ethnic identification. During the attacks, some Rwandan citizens killed or caused serious bodily or mental harm to person[s] perceived to be Tutsi. As a result of the attacks, there were a large number of deaths of persons of Tutsi ethnic identity."

(ii) ***Fact 5*** – "Between 1 January 1994 and 17 July 1994 in Rwanda there was an armed conflict not of an international character."

(iii) ***Fact 6*** – "Between 6 April 1994 and 17 July 1994, there was a genocide in Rwanda against the Tutsi ethnic group."

12. Whilst this Chamber only sought further submissions from the Parties on the question of judicial notice of adjudicated facts, the Defence for Ngirumpatse makes submissions concerning whether or not the Trial Chamber is bound to follow the Appeals Chamber's directive. It submits that there is no requirement in the Rules that the Trial Chamber is bound to follow the Appeals Chamber and that instead of carrying out the Appeals Chamber's directive, it should revisit the impugned Decision on the basis of the Appeals Chamber's findings.

13. This contention is, however, contrary to the established jurisprudence, and particularly the recent Appeals Chamber's Decisions. When a fact is considered as a fact of common knowledge, a Trial Chamber has no discretion and must take judicial notice thereof.[13] In the present case, the Appeals Chamber has

[9] *Prosecutor v. Karemera et al.*, Case No. ICTR-98-44-AR73(C), Decision on Motions for Reconsideration (AC), 1 December 2006, para. 28 and "Disposition".

[10] Appeals Chamber Decision, para. 22, *Prosecutor v. Karemera et al.*, Case No. ICTR-98-44-AR73(C), Decision on Motions for Reconsideration (AC), 1 December 2006, para. 24.

[11] Appeals Chamber Decision, para. 22, citing *Prosecutor v. Semanza*, Case No. ICTR-97-20-A, Judgement, 20 May 2005, para. 194 ("*Semanza* Appeals Judgement").

[12] As to Facts 2 and 5, see Appeals Chamber Decision, paras. 26 to 32, particularly, para. 32. As to Fact 6, see Appeals Chamber Decision, paras. 33 to 38, particularly para. 38.

[13] Appeals Chamber Decision, para. 22; *Prosecutor v. Karemera et al.*, Case No. ICTR-98-44-AR73(C), Decision on Motions for Reconsideration (AC), 1 December 2006, para. 24.

determined that Facts 2, 5 and 6 are of common knowledge and accordingly, directed the Trial Chamber to take judicial notice thereof.[14]

14. In the case of *Bizimungu et al.,* Trial Chamber II also considered that "a determination by the Appeals Chamber that any given fact is one of common knowledge and of which judicial notice should be taken under Rule 94(A) is binding upon all Trial Chambers".[15]

15. The Chamber therefore takes judicial notice of Facts 2, 5 and 5 as facts of common knowledge, pursuant to Rule 94(A) of the Rules.

II. Adjudicated Facts – Rule 94(B)

16. Rule 94(B) of the Rules provides:

> At the request of a party or *proprio motu,* a Trial Chamber, after hearing the Parties, may decide to take judicial notice of adjudicated facts or documentary evidence from other proceedings of the Tribunal relating to the matter at issue in the current proceedings.

17. In its Decision of 16 June 2006, the Appeals Chamber remanded the judicial notice matter to the Trial Chamber for further consideration of the majority of the purported adjudicated facts on the basis of two findings. **[page 5]**

18. The Appeals Chamber firstly found that "the Trial Chamber erred to the extent that it found that, under Rule 94(B), it is categorically impermissible to take judicial notice of facts relating directly or indirectly to the defendant's guilt, including facts related to the existence and activity of a joint criminal enterprise."[16] In so doing, the Appeals Chamber also recognised the need for caution in allowing judicial notice of adjudicated facts which were central to the criminal responsibility of the accused. It stated that the Trial Chamber should assess the particular facts of which judicial notice is sought to determine, firstly, whether they are related to the acts, conduct, or mental state of the accused; and, secondly, if not, whether under the circumstances of the case admitting them will advance the objective of expediency without compromising the rights of the accused.[17]

19. The Appeals Chamber secondly considered that a Trial Chamber "can and indeed must decline to take judicial notice of facts if it considers that the way they are formulated – abstracted from the context in the judgement from which they came – is misleading, or inconsistent with the facts actually adjudicated in the cases in question".[18] However, in the present case, the Appeals Chamber was not persuaded that Facts 86 through 110 were actually taken out of context, or improperly combined, in a way which made them inconsistent with the judgements from which they were drawn, as decided by this Chamber. Accordingly, the Appeals Chamber directed the Chamber to reconsider the matter and provide an explanation for its conclusions.[19]

II.1. Applicable Law

20. Under Rule 94(B) judicial notice of adjudicated facts is *discretionary.* Moreover, in order to invoke an exercise of its discretion, the Chamber must be satisfied that the fact in question relates to a matter at issue in the current proceedings.[20]

21. According to the Appeals Chamber, "[t]aking judicial notice of adjudicated facts under Rule 94(B) is a method of achieving judicial economy and harmonising judgements of the Tribunal while ensuring the right of

---

14 Appeals Chamber Decision, para. 57.

15 *Prosecutor v. Casimir Bizimungu et al.,* Case No. ICTR-99-50-T, Decision on Prosecutor's Motion for Judicial Notice (TC), 22 September 2006, para. 7.

16 Appeals Chamber Decision, para. 53.

17 Appeals Chamber Decision, para. 53, emphasis added.

18 Appeals Chamber Decision, para. 55.

19 Appeals Chamber Decision, paras. 56 and 57.

20 *Prosecutor v. Popović et al.,* Case No. IT-05-88-T, Decision on Prosecution Motion for Judicial Notice of Adjudicated Facts with Annex (TC), 26 September 2006, para. 5 ("*Popović* Decision"). The Trial Chamber said, "the fact must have some relevance to an issue in the current proceedings."

the Accused to a fair, public and expeditious trial".[21] The Appeals Chamber also noted the consistency between taking judicial notice of adjudicated facts and the admission of written statements in lieu of oral testimony under Rule 92*bis* of the Rules – both procedural mechanisms adopted "largely for the same purpose".[22]

22. The Appeals Chamber describes adjudicated facts judicially noticed under Rule 94(B) as "merely presumptions that may be rebutted by the defence with evidence at trial."[23] The **[page 6]** Appeals Chamber has clarified how this qualification can be reconciled with the presumption of innocence as follows:

> Judicial notice does not shift the ultimate burden of persuasion, which remains with the Prosecution. In the case of judicial notice under Rule 94(B), the effect is only to relieve the Prosecution of its initial burden to produce [credible and reliable] evidence on the point; the defence may then put the point into question by introducing reliable and credible evidence to the contrary.[24]
>
> Analogously, in the context of alibi evidence, for instance, the accused bears the burden of production with respect to a matter centrally related to the guilt of the accused; yet this shift does not violate the presumption of innocence because, as the Appeals Chamber has repeatedly recognized, the prosecution retains the burden of proof of guilt beyond a reasonable doubt.[25]

23. Trial Chambers of both this Tribunal and the International Criminal Tribunal for the former Yugoslavia ("ICTY") have laid down some guiding principles when deciding whether or not to take judicial notice of purported adjudicated facts. They are consistent with the recent directives given by the Appeals Chamber's in its Decision of 16 June 2006. These principles, which are not exhaustive, can be summarized as follows:

- When ruling on the matter, the Chamber must examine the purported fact in the context of the original judgement.[26]
- With regard to the meaning of the term "adjudicated facts", the jurisprudence outlines a number of requirements before a fact can be considered to be truly adjudicated:
  - A fact sought to be judicially noticed must be distinct, concrete and identifiable.[27]
  - A fact in relation to which judicial notice is sought must be in the same or a substantially similar form to how it was expressed by the original Chamber.[28] Facts altered in a substantial way by the moving party cannot be considered to have been truly adjudicated.[29] However, as the Trial Chamber recently noted in the *Popović* Decision, a minor inaccuracy or ambiguity can be cured *proprio motu* by the Trial Chamber. This is discretionary, and should introduce no

21 Appeals Chamber Decision, para. 39. See also *Prosecutor v. Laurent Semanza,* Case No ICTR-97-20-I, Decision on the Prosecutor's Motion for Judicial Notice and Presumptions of Facts Pursuant to Rules 94 and 54, 3 November 2000 (TC), para. 20; *Prosecutor v. Casimir Bizimungu et al.*, Case No. ICTR-99-50-I, Decision on Prosper Mugiraneza's First Motion for Judicial Notice Pursuant to Rule 94(B) (TC), 10 December 2004, paras. 10, 12; *Prosecutor v. Kajelijeli,* Decision on the Prosecutor's Motion for Judicial Notice pursuant to Rule 94 of the Rules (TC), 16 April 2002, para. 18.

22 Appeals Chamber Decision, para. 51.

23 Appeals Chamber Decision, para. 42, referring to *Prosecutor v. Slobodan Milosevic,* Case No. IT-02-54-AR73.5, Decision on the Prosecution's Interlocutory Appeal Against the Trial Chamber's 10 April 2003 Decision on Prosecution Motion for Judicial Notice of Adjudicated Facts (AC), 28 October 2003, pp. 3-4; *Prosecutor v. Momir Nikolić,* Case No. IT-02-60/1-A, Decision on Appellant's Motion for Judicial Notice (AC), 1 April 2005, paras. 10-11; *Prosecutor v. Momčilo Krajišnik,* Case No. IT-00-39-PT, Decision on Prosecutor's Motion for Judicial Notice and Adjudicated Facts and Admission of Written Statements of Witnesses pursuant to Rule 92*bis* (TC), 28 February 2003, para. 16.

24 Appeals Chamber Decision, paras. 42 and 49.

25 Appeals Chamber Decision, para. 49.

26 *Popović* Decision, para.6, citing *Prosecutor v. Prlić et al.,* Case No. IT-04-74-PT, Decision on Motion for Judicial Notice of Adjudicated Facts Pursuant to Rule 94(B), 14 March 2006, para. 12; *Prosecutor v. Hadžihasanović and Kubura,* Case No. IT-01-47-T, Decision on Judicial Notice of Adjudicated Facts Following the Motion Submitted by Counsel for the Accused Hadžihasanović and Kubura on 10 January 2005 (TC), 14 April 2005, p. 5; *Prosecutor v. Krajišnik,* Case No. IT-00-39-T, Decision on Third and Fourth Prosecution Motions for Judicial Notice of Adjudicated Facts (TC), 24 March 2005, para. 14; *Prosecutor v. Krajišnik,* Case No. IT-00-39-T, Decision on Prosecution Motions for Judicial Notice of Adjudicated Facts and for Admission of Written Statements of Witnesses Pursuant to Rule 92*bis,* 28 February 2003, para. 15; *Prosecutor v. Blagojević and Jokić,* Case No. IT-02-60-T, Decision on Prosecution's Motion for Judicial Notice of Adjudicated Facts and Documentary Evidence, 19 December 2003 ("*Blagojevic* Decision"), para. 16.

27 *Prosecutor v. Krajisnik,* Decision on the Prosecution Motion for Judicial Notice of Adjudicated Facts and for Admission of Written Statements of Witnesses Pursuant to Rule 92*bis,* 10 March 2003; *Blagojevic* Decision.

28 *Blagojevic* Decision.

29 *Popović* Decision, para. 7.

substantive change to the proposed fact. "[T]he purpose of such correction should be to render the formulation consistent with the meaning intended by the original Chamber."[30] **[page 7]**

- Facts proposed for judicial notice must constitute factual findings and must not include legal characterisations.[31]
- A fact cannot be considered as adjudicated in circumstances where those facts *are* or *might be* subject to pending appeal.[32]

- Judicial notice under Rule 94(B) cannot be taken of facts which attest to criminal responsibility of the accused.[33] According to the Appeals Chamber, judicial notice should therefore not be taken of facts relating to the acts, conducts and mental state of the accused.[34] This exclusion does not apply to acts and conduct of other persons for which the accused is alleged to be responsible.[35] Such persons may include, for instance, alleged subordinates whose criminal conduct the accused is charged with failing to prevent or punish, persons said to have participated with the accused in a joint criminal enterprise, and persons the accused is alleged to have aided and abetted.[36]
- Once the Chamber is satisfied that the facts sought for admission are truly adjudicated facts and do not relate to the acts, conduct and mental state of the Accused, it is called upon to invoke an exercise of its discretion for the purpose of expediting the proceedings, only in circumstances where admitting such facts will not compromise the rights of the Accused, including his or her right to a fair and expeditious trial, to hear and confront the witnesses against him or her.[37] In that respect, Trial Chambers of this Tribunal and of the ICTY have considered, in the particular context of their case, that **[page 8]** facts which are core issues should not be judicially noticed.[38] Where a certain fact concerns a core issue in the case, the taking of judicial notice of that fact may place such a significant burden on the Accused to produce rebuttal evidence that it would jeopardise the Accused's right to fair trial.[39] Considering the interests of justice and the particular circumstances of the case at hand, Trial Chambers have also declined to take judicial notice of adjudicated facts

---

30 *Popović* Decision, para. 7.

31 *Prosecutor v. Krajisnik,* Decision on the Prosecution Motion for Judicial Notice of Adjudicated Facts and for Admission of Written Statements of Witnesses Pursuant to Rule 92*bis,* 10 March 2003; *Blagojevic* Decision, para. 16; *Bizimungu et al.*, Decision on the Prosecutor's Motion and Notice of Adjudicated Facts, 10 December 2004, para. 16, citing *Nyiramasuhuko et al.,* Decision on the Prosecutor's Motion for Judicial Notice and Admission of Evidence, 15 May 2002, para. 127, which followed the decision in *Ntakirutimana,* Decision on the Prosecutor's Motion for Judicial Notice of Adjudicated Facts, 22 November 2001, para. 35 and 36.

32 See *Popović* Decision, para. 14, and fn. 50, "[a] Trial Chamber may only judicially notice a purported adjudicated fact if that fact *itself* is clearly not subject to pending appeal or review proceedings." (Emphasis added)

33 *Prosecutor v. Krajisnik,* Decision on the Prosecution Motion for Judicial Notice of Adjudicated Facts and for Admission of Written Statements of Witnesses Pursuant to Rule 92*bis,* 10 March 2003.

34 *Karemera* Appeals Chamber Decision, para. 50

35 Appeals Chamber Decision, para. 52; see also *Popović* Decision para. 13.

36 Appeals Chamber Decision, para. 48; *Popović* Decision, para. 13. Note that the *Karemera* Appeals Chamber referred to the Decision of the Appeals Chamber in the case of *Galić* concerning the application of Rule 92*bis* (*Prosecutor v. Galić,* Case No. IT-98-29-AR73.2, Decision on Interlocutory Appeal Concerning Rule 92*bis* (C) (AC), 7 June 2002, paras. 10-11. In the extract of the Decision quoted, the Appeals Chamber considered whether the exclusion from admission under Rule 92*bis* of any written statement which "goes to proof of the acts and conduct of the accused as charged in the indictment" also mandated the exclusion of any written statement going to proof of the acts and conduct of other persons for whose conduct the accused was alleged to be liable by reason of a joint criminal enterprise theory, or accomplice liability. The Appeals Chamber considered that such an interpretation would denude Rule 92*bis* of any real utility, and that it would be inconsistent with the purpose and terms of the Rule. The *Karemera* Appeals Chamber considered that this analysis was equally applicable to Rule 94 (B).

37 See Articles 19 and 20 of the Statute of the Tribunal. See Appeals Chamber Decision, para. 50. See *Prosecutor v. Semanza,* Case No. ICTR-97-20-I, Decision on the Prosecutor's Further Motion for Judicial Notice Pursuant to Rules 94 and 54, 15 March 2001, para. 10; *Prosecutor v. Ntakirutimana,* Case Nos. ICTR-96-10-T and ICTR-96-17-T, Decision on Prosecutor's Motion for Judicial Notice of Adjudicated Facts, 22 November 2001, para. 28; *Prosecutor v. Simic et al.*, Decision of 25 March 1999 on the Pre-trial motion by the Prosecution requesting the Trial Chamber to take judicial notice of the international character of the conflict in Bosnia-Herzegovina. *Prosecutor v. Krajisnik,* Decision on the Prosecution Motion for Judicial Notice of Adjudicated Facts and for Admission of Written Statements of Witnesses Pursuant to Rule 92*bis,* 10 March 2003; *Blagojevic* Decision, para. 18.

38 *Prosecutor v. Krajisnik,* Decision on the Prosecution Motion for Judicial Notice of Adjudicated Facts and for Admission of Written Statements of Witnesses Pursuant to Rule 92*bis,* 10 March 2003; *Bizimungu et al.*, Decision on the Prosecutor's Motion and Notice of Adjudicated Facts, 10 December 2004; *Popović* Decision, para. 19.

39 *Popović* Decision, para. 16.

in circumstances where evidence has already been heard on the subject matter of the fact sought to be judicially noticed.[40]

II.2. Facts sought for Judicial Notice

24. Generally the Defence for the Accused dispute the accuracy of the facts sought for admission or their character as adjudicated facts. They also contend that some of the facts relate to the acts, conduct and mental of the Accused or of other persons for which the Accused are alleged to be responsible. In their views, the admission of the purported adjudicated facts will seriously impair the rights of the Accused in various ways and will not contribute to the objective of expediency.

25. The Chamber will now consider whether judicial notice should be taken of the 136 purported adjudicated facts in the light of above-mentioned principles and each party's submissions. In order to facilitate the reading of this Decision, it must be noted that the Chamber will not systematically recall each argument submitted by the Parties with respect to each fact, when it has already been addressed.

1. Facts 1 to 9 (*Akayesu* Judgement)

26. The Prosecution requests the Chamber to take judicial notice of nine facts taken from the *Akayesu* Judgement.[41]

27. These facts are relevant to matters at issue in the current proceedings and do not relate to the acts, conduct and mental state of the Accused persons in this case. After reviewing Facts 1 to 9 in the context of the Judgement, the Chamber is also satisfied that they are truly adjudicated facts. Specifically and contrary to Ngirumpatse's assertions, Facts 1 and 8 are similar to how they were expressed in the original Judgement, and Fact 3 does not contain a characterisation of an essentially legal nature.

28. Furthermore, the Defence for Ngirumpatse and the Defence for Karemera request the Chamber not to take judicial notice where the original Trial Chamber has made the particular finding on the basis of the testimony of only one witness.[42] They contend that this deprives the Accused of the same right which has been afforded to the accused person in the case from which the fact has been taken and an opportunity to raise reasonable doubt in the Prosecution's case. **[page 9]**

29. Under Rule 89 of the Rules and according to the established jurisprudence of this Tribunal, corroboration of evidence is not required: a Chamber may rely on a single witness' testimony as proof of a material fact.[43] A Chamber also has a broad discretion to admit hearsay evidence, even when it cannot be examined at its source and when it is not corroborated by direct evidence.[44] The Chamber will therefore not exclude the admission of an adjudicated fact solely because the original Chamber made its finding on the basis of the evidence of only one witness.

30. In view of the particular circumstances of the case, the Chamber is satisfied that taking judicial notice of Facts 1 to 9 will contribute to the objective of expediency while not compromising the rights of the Accused. The Chamber, however, deems it necessary to cure certain minor inaccuracies concerning Fact 9.

2. Facts 15, 65 to 68, 144 and 145 (*Semanza* Judgement)

31. The Prosecution seeks judicial notice of facts taken from the *Semanza* Judgement (Facts 15, 65 to 68, 144 and 145).[45]

---

40 See *Prosecutor v. Bizimungu et al.*, Case No. ICTR-50-T, Decision on the Prosecutor's Motion and Notice of Adjudicated Facts, 10 December 2004, para. 22; *Blagojevic* Decision, paras. 22 and 23.

41 Facts 1 to 9. *Prosecutor v. Jean-Paul Akayesu*, Case No. ICTR-96-4-T, Judgement (TC), 2 September 1998, *ICTR Report 1998*, pp. 44 and seq.

42 The Defence for Karemera also raises this point. Facts 1, 2, 3, 7, 10-24, 36, 41-51, 60, 67, 68, 79, 82, 84, 85, 110, 116-123, 125, 126, 132, 134-141, 144, 145, 148 and 150.

43 See for e.g.: *Prosecutor v. Laurent Semanza*, Case No. ICTR-97-20-A, Judgement (AC), 20 May 2005, para. 153; *Prosecutor v. Sylvestre Gacumbitsi*, Case No. ICTR-2001-64-A, Judgement (AC), 7 July 2006, para. 72.

44 See for e.g.: *Prosecutor v. Jean-Paul Akayesu*, Case No. ICTR-96-4-A, Judgement (AC), 1 June 2001; *Gacumbitsi* Appeal Judgement.

45 *Prosecutor v. Laurent Semanza*, Case No. ICTR-97-20-T, Judgement and Sentence (TC), 15 May 2003.

32. These facts are relevant to matters at issue in the current proceedings and do not relate to the acts, conduct and mental state of the Accused persons in this case. Contrary to Ngirumpatse's assertion, the Chamber is also satisfied that these facts are truly adjudicated facts and are in a substantially similar form to how they were expressed by the original Chamber.

33. The Defence for Ngirumpatse also submits that the Chamber should decline to take judicial notice of Facts 15, 67, 144 and 145 in relation to which the original Chamber did not specify the evidence upon the basis of which the factual finding was made. In its view, where there is lack of transparency, the Accused in this case are unable to bring evidence to rebut those findings.

34. The Chamber has reviewed these facts in the context of the Judgement and does not share the Defence's contention. The *Semanza* Chamber explicitly describes how it assessed and took into consideration the evidence adduced in that trial, including the alibi evidence.

35. Considering the circumstances of the case, the Chamber is of the view that taking judicial notice of Facts 15, 65 to 68 and 144 to 145 will contribute to the objective of expediency without compromising the rights of the Accused.

3. Facts 16 to 24 and 31 to 64 (*Kajelijeli* Judgement)

36. Under Facts 16 to 24 and 31 to 64, the Prosecution moves the Chamber to take judicial notice of facts extracted from the *Kajelijeli* Judgement.[46]

37. Whereas the Defence for Nzirorera concede that none of these facts relates to the acts, conduct and mental state of the Accused, the Defence for Ngirumpatse submits that certain facts must be excluded from admission because they comprise the acts and conduct of the Accused,[47] notably because some of these facts concern the actions of the *Interahamwe* **[page 10]** which, according to the Indictment, are imputed to the Accused.[48] Furthermore, it submits that the Chamber should decline to take judicial notice of facts concerning the synonymous use of the words 'Tutsi' "enemy", "accomplices of the enemy", "infiltrators", "accomplices of the RPF", "*inyenzi*", "*inkotanyi*" for similar reasons.[49]

38. The Chamber is of the view that the facts sought for admission are relevant to matters at issue in the current proceedings. Furthermore, none of them can be said to relate to the acts, conduct and mental state of the Accused in this case.

39. However, some of them directly describe the acts and conducts of Kajelijeli,[50] who according to the Indictment in the present case, is alleged to having directly acted under the instructions of Nzirorera. Paragraph 62 of the Indictment alleges that on 6 or 7 April 1994, or both, Joseph Nzirorera participated in certain decisions taken at a meeting at the residence of Nzirorera's mother in Busogo *secteur* with Juvenal Kajelijeli, amongst others, and ordering the attack and killing of Tutsi population in Mukingo and Nkuli *communes*. It is further alleged that Kajelijeli executed the decisions taken by Joseph Nzirorera.[51]

40. While judicial notice can be taken of acts and conducts of persons for which an accused is alleged to be responsible, the Chamber finds that Facts 19, 40, 50-53, 55-56, 60, 62 and 63 sought for admission are so proximate and central to the criminal responsibility of Joseph Nzirorera following the allegations pleaded in the Indictment that it would compromise the rights of the Accused if judicial notice was taken of these facts.

41. The Chamber finds that Facts 34, which states that killings of the Tutsi in Mukingo *commune* "were not spontaneous reaction of the Hutu populace to the death of the President", touches upon a core issue in the instant case. It has been the consistent Prosecution's theory that the Accused in this case had pre-planned the genocide throughout Rwanda, and the Defence has repeatedly given notice of its intention to rely on the defence that the killings were a spontaneous reaction of the Hutu population. According to the Appeals

46 *Prosecutor v. Juvénal Kajelijeli*, Case No. ICTR-98-44A-T, Judgement and Sentence (TC), 1 December 2003.
47 Facts 33-48, 52-54, 58-60.
48 Facts 16-24, 35, 36, 38-40, 46, 52, 53, 56, 57, 59-63.
49 Facts 19, 34, 35, 42, 43, 49, 52, 54, 55, 57, 58, 61, 64.
50 Facts 19, 36-38, 40, 50-53, 55-56, 60, 62 and 63.
51 Amended Indictment dated 24 August 2005, paras. 62.8 to 62.10.

Chamber, "if the existence of a plan to commit genocide is vital to the Prosecution's case, this must be proved by evidence".[52] Under these circumstances, the Chamber is of the view that it is in the interests of justice to hear oral evidence on this particular issue.

42. With respect to Fact 18,[53] the Prosecution submits that the question of whether there were "widespread attacks" is a question of fact, which having been found proved, can lead to a legal finding. It also submits that, since the Appeals Chamber has found as a fact of common knowledge that there were "throughout Rwanda widespread or systematic attacks against a civilian population based on Tutsi ethnic identification" and rape is one such method of attacking a population, it is proper for the Trial Chamber to take judicial notice of this fact. In the Chamber's view, that rapes and sexual assaults were committed *in the course of* a widespread attack upon the Tutsi civilian population may be considered as a characterisation of an essentially legal nature, which should be left to the ultimate determination of the Trial Chamber. The Chamber therefore declines to take judicial notice of Fact 18. **[page 11]**

43. Considering the context of the *Kajelijeli* Judgement, the Chamber is not satisfied that Facts 36 to 38 reflect the factual findings of the Trial Chamber in the *Kajelijeli* Judgement.[54] They therefore cannot be considered as adjudicated facts and it is therefore appropriate to decline to take judicial notice of them.

44. The Chamber agrees with the Defence that Facts 35, 47 and 48 are vague and not distinct, concrete and identifiable to be judicially noticed. The Chamber is also of the view that Fact 64 may be ambiguous and does

---

52 *Prosecutor v. Karemera et al.*, Case No. ICTR-98-44-AR73(C), Decision on Motions for Reconsideration (AC), 1 December 2006, para. 21.

53 Fact 18 sought for admission reads as follows: "These rapes and sexual assaults were committed in the course of a widespread attack upon the Tutsi civilian population".

54 Fact 36 is extracted from para. 404 of *Kajelijeli* Judgement, which reads as follows:

> The Chamber notes in particular the detailed and reliable account of Prosecution Witness GBH, who stated that the Accused "was the one who gave instructions to the young people who had to do anything. He supervised them and gave them orders… The young people in question were the *Interahamwe*." Witness GBH also testified that "a man of his position as a *bourgmestre* could [have] had the power to stop or lock the young people wearing uniform, engaged in training, singing and dancing." This testimony was further corroborated by Prosecution Witness GBE, who provided testimony that the Accused never bothered the *Interahamwe* even when they were "molesting or harassing" people, though as *bourgmestre* he was both able and obliged to do so. The Chamber finds that these testimonies present a clear picture of the Accused's close association with, and control over, the *Interahamwe*. The Chamber consequently finds that the Accused was a leader of *Interahamwe* with control over the *Interahamwe* in Mukingo *commune*, and that he also had influence over the *Interahamwe* of Nkuli *commune* from 1 January 1994 to July 1994.

Fact 37 is extracted from para. 426 of *Kajelijeli* Judgement, which reads as follows:

> Notwithstanding the fact that the Chamber in its previous findings [Part III, Section H] stated that the Accused was a leader of the *Interahamwe*, the youth wing of the MRND, the Chamber finds, on the basis of the evidence, that there is inconclusive evidence to establish that the Accused was either (a) a registered member of the new MRND, established by the July 1991 Statute; (b) a member of the prefectural committee or a member of the prefectural congress of this party. The aforesaid notwithstanding, the Chamber finds that the Accused was closely associated with the new MRND and its leadership and that, especially from January 1994 to mid-July 1994, he was actively involved in many activities of this party in Mukingo *commune* and the neighbouring areas. He may as well have been a member of the MRND party.

Fact 38 is extracted from Para. 400 of *Kajelijeli* Judgement, which reads as follows:

> The Chamber finds that by 6 April 1994 the Accused was actively involved in the training of the *Interahamwe*. This is evidenced in the eye witness testimony of Prosecution Witness GBH, who stated that the Accused was "seen in the company of the young people while they trained on a football field using the guns, wooden guns." Corroborating evidence is found in the testimonies of Prosecution Witnesses GDD and GAO, both of whom gave similar and largely consistent testimonies of the Accused's involvement in the training of the *Interahamwe*. Witness GDD, a former member of the *Interahamwe*, testified that the Accused and other politicians solicited him to train young *Interahamwe* recruits. Witness GAO, another former member of the *Interahamwe*, also confirmed that when the Accused was *bourgmestre* he [the Accused], together with others, gave *Interahamwe* military training. Witness GAO also testified that the Accused would come to the training grounds every morning, and that the Accused told *Interahamwe* to complete their training quickly so that he [the Accused] could send them to the volcanoes to fight against the "Inkotanyi, the Inyenzi." The Chamber notes in particular, the testimony of Prosecution Witness GAP who stated that the Accused was the leading instructor "responsible for political ideology". Although there are minor ambiguities among them regarding the timing of various training activities of the militia in Mukingo *commune* and the neighbouring areas, the Chamber finds their testimonies consistent and establish beyond reasonable doubt that the Accused did actively participate in the training of *Interahamwe* in Mukingo *commune*. The Chamber finds, however, that there is insufficient evidence that the Accused organized these trainings.

not fairly translate how this finding was expressed by the original Chamber.[55] For this reason, it will not be judicially noticed. **[page 12]**

45. Conversely, Facts 16, 17, 20 to 24, 33, 41 to 46, 49, 54, 57, 58, 59, and 61 are truly adjudicated facts. In particular and contrary to the assertions made by the Defence for Nzirorera and the Defence for Ngirumpatse, Facts 17, 33, 43, 59 are distinct, concrete and identifiable, and Fact 44 does not include a legal characterisation.

46. As already mentioned, the Chamber is also satisfied that Facts 16, 17, 20 to 24, 33, 41 to 46, 49, 54, 57, 58, 59, and 61 do not relate to the acts, conduct and mental state of the Accused persons in this case. In that respect, the Chamber notes that Facts 41 to 46 concern a different meeting to the one which the Indictment alleges that Nzirorera attended and do not contain any allegation that Nzirorera was present at that meeting. This was a meeting held by Kajelijeli on the evening of 6 April 1994 at the Canteen next to the Nkuli *bureau communal*. The Chamber is satisfied that these facts are not too proximate to the Accused.

47. The Defence for Nzirorera, however, objects to their admission submitting that in different ways, it will compromise the rights of the accused and that it will not advance the objective of expediency.

48. According to the Defence, Witnesses ANP and GBU, upon the basis of whose testimony certain factual findings were made by the *Kajelijeli* Trial Chamber, have been found to have committed perjury, and therefore taking judicial notice of facts which are based on the testimony of those witnesses would compromise the Accused's rights.

49. The Chamber notes that Witnesses ANP and GBU were two of several witnesses upon whom the Trial Chamber relied in making the findings from which the adjudicated facts are proposed. The Defence's argument in that respect therefore falls to be rejected.

50. The Defence for Nzirorera contends that the testimony already heard by this Chamber of Witness BTH is a bar to the taking judicial notice of certain facts.

51. As previously mentioned, considering the interests of justice and the particular circumstances of the case, some Trial Chambers have declined to take judicial notice of adjudicated facts in circumstances where evidence has already been heard on the subject matter of the fact sought to be judicially noticed.[56] The fact of a Trial Chamber having heard testimony on a particular fact is, however, not an absolute bar to the taking of judicial notice of that fact. The Chamber must determine whether, having already heard testimony on a particular fact, taking judicial notice of that fact will advance the objective of expediency without compromising the rights of the Accused. Relevant considerations to this determination may include, for example, how much evidence has been heard on a particular fact, how much evidence is still to be heard with respect to the particular fact, how directly a witness has testified on a particular fact, and whether the relevant witness testimony corroborates or contradicts the fact proposed for judicial notice.

52. In the present case, the Chamber has considered the facts allegedly precluded from judicial notice by virtue of Witness BTH's testimony, and is of the view that only Fact 39 should be excluded on this basis in the interests of justice. There might be indeed some divergence with the testimony of Witness BTH on the same fact. Contrary to Nzirorera's assertion, the fact that Witness BTH testified that Kajelijeli was acting at the direction of Nzirorera, does not affect the conclusion that Facts 16, 17, 20 to 24, 33, 41 to 46, 49, 54, 57, 58, 59, and 61 do not relate to the acts, conduct and mental state of the Accused.

53. The Defence for Nzirorera also submits, since the Trial Chamber in *Kajelijeli* found that the Prosecution had failed to prove its allegation that Kajelijeli conspired with Nzirorera **[page 13]** and others,[57] it would be

---

[55] See *Kajelijeli* Judgement, par. 625:

> After careful consideration of all the evidence regarding the massacre at the Ruhengeri Court of Appeal on or around 14 April 1994, the Chamber finds that the Accused played a vital role as an organizer and facilitator of the *Interahamwe* and other attackers. He did this by procuring weapons, rounding up the *Interahamwe* and facilitating their transportation to the Ruhengeri Court of Appeal by supplying them with petrol. The *Interahamwe* were to assist in killing the Tutsis who had been taken from Busengo sub-*prefecture* in Ndusu *Commune* and left at the Ruhengeri Court of Appeal, and who had until that point been successfully resisting attacks by the local militia.

[56] See *Prosecutor v. Bizimungu et al.*, Case No. ICTR-50-T, Decision on the Prosecutor's Motion and Notice of Adjudicated Facts, 10 December 2004, para. 22; *Blagojevic* Decision, paras. 22 and 23.

[57] *Kajelijeli* Judgement, paras. 794-98.

unfair to take judicial notice of selective findings of the Trial Chamber which help the Prosecution.[58] The Chamber is of the view that this argument, on the contrary, favours the admission of Facts 16, 17, 20 to 24, 33, 41 to 46, 49, 54, 57, 58, 59, and 61 since the *Kajelijeli* Trial Chamber did not find that Nzirorera and Kajeljeli were co-conspirators.

54. The Defence for Nzirorera also makes several individual submissions on why taking judicial notice of certain facts will not advance the objective of expediency. Firstly, he submits, Facts 23 and 24 involve events in Kinigi *commune* which are not included in the Amended Indictment, and are not the subject of testimony from any proposed witness on the Prosecution's Witness List. The Defence for Nzirorera submits that, since it will be required to adduce evidence to refute events in Kinigi and Nkuli *communes*, the purpose of expediency will not be advanced. Secondly, with respect to Facts 41 to 50, the Defence submits that these facts are based on findings from the testimony of Witness GDD, who has since died, and that no other witness on the Prosecution's Witness List will testify to these events. It claims that in these circumstances, to take judicial notice of these facts will deprive Nzirorera of his right to cross-examination on matters which are strongly disputed, and will not promote expediency since there are no witnesses whose testimony would not otherwise be needed or whose testimony would be shortened by the taking of judicial notice. The Prosecution acknowledges that Witness GDD has died since his testimony in the *Kajelijeli* case, but says that the Defence will still be able to rebut the facts by calling other witnesses and that there will be other witnesses who will testify about the events in these *communes* whose evidence can be challenged.

55. The Chamber is satisfied that both the Indictment and the Pre-trial Brief make specific mention of massacres in Ruhengeri *prefecture,* within which Kinigi *commune* is located. Furthermore, in the Pre-trial Brief, specific mention is made of Mukingo *commune* and other *communes* which neighbour Kinigi and Nkuli. Having considered the circumstances of the present case, the Chamber is of the view that taking judicial notice of Facts 16, 17, 20 to 24, 33, 41 to 46, 49, 54, 57, 58, 59, and 61 will advance the objective of expediency without compromising the rights of the Accused. Concerning Facts 33 and 54, the Chamber deems it necessary to cure minor inaccuracies (see Annexure to the present Decision)

56. Finally, Facts 31 and 32 have not been appealed, and therefore were not remanded to the Chamber for further consideration. The findings of the Chamber on those facts in the Decision of 9 November 2005 still stand.

*4. Facts 25 to 30 and 146 to 152 (***Rutaganda** *Judgement)*

57. Under Facts 25 to 30 and 146 to 152, the Prosecution seeks judicial notice of facts taken from the *Rutaganda* Judgement.[59]

58. The Defence for Ngirumpatse submits that Facts 27 to 30, 147, 151 and 152 must be excluded from admission because they comprise the acts and conduct of the Accused, or the acts of the *Interahamwe* that can be imputed to the Accused in this case. Furthermore, it contends that the Chamber should decline to take judicial notice of facts concerning the synonymous use of the words 'Tutsi' "enemy", "accomplices of the enemy", "infiltrators", "accomplices of the RPF", "*inyenzi*", "*inkotanyi*" for similar reasons.[60] **[page 14]**

59. The Chamber is satisfied that the purported facts taken from the *Rutaganda* Judgement concern a matter at issue in the current proceedings and none of them relates to the acts, conduct and mental state of the Accused persons in this case. However, Facts 151 and 152 are so central to the allegations against the Accused in this case, that it is preferable to hear *viva voce* evidence on these matters. The Chamber therefore declines to take judicial notice of them.

60. The Chamber also declines to take judicial notice of Fact 150 on the ground of vagueness, and of Facts 148 and 149 because the Chamber is not persuaded that their admission will promote the objective of expediency.

61. Considering the context of the Judgement, Facts 25 to 30 and 146 and 147 are truly adjudicated facts and are in a substantially similar form to how they were expressed in the original Judgement. Considering

58 See paras. 47-49 of Nzirorera's first submissions on this (13 July 2005).

59 *Prosecutor v. Georges Rutaganda*, Case No. ICTR-96-3-T, Judgement and Sentence (TC), 6 December 1999.

60 See Facts 151-152.

the rights of the Accused and the interests of justice, their admission will contribute to expediting the proceedings. The Chamber, however, has cured certain minor inaccuracies *proprio motu,* so as to enable the taking of judicial notice of those facts in a form which does not contain any ambiguity (see Annexure to this Decision; Facts 25 and 28).

*5. Facts 10 to 12, 88 to 90, 92, 99 to 103, 105 to 107, 124, 127 to 131, 133, 134 to 137 (*Niyitegeka *Judgement); Facts 13, 86, 87, 91, 93, 94, 104, 111, 112, 113 (*Musema *Judgement); Facts 69, 71, 74, 84, 85, 95 to 98, 109, 110, 114, 115 (*Kayishema *Judgement); and Facts 70, 72, 73, 108, 116 to 123, 125, 126, 132 (*Ntakirutimana *Judgement)*

62. The Prosecution moves the Chamber to take judicial notice of a series of facts extracted from the *Niyitegeka, Musema*, *Kayishema* and *Ntakirutimana* Judgements,[61] which, among other things concerns attacks on Muyira Hill, in the Bisesero area, on 13 and 14 May 1994.

63. The Defence for Ngirumpatse and the Defence for Karemera submit that these Facts extracted from the *Niyitegeka* Judgement must be excluded because they comprise the acts, conduct and mental state of the Accused persons or concern the acts of the *Interahamwe* that could be imputed to the Accused in this case. They also claim that some of them are vague or taken out of context of the original Judgement.

64. The Chamber declines to take judicial notice of Fact 84 on the basis that, absent the meaning provided by the context of Facts 79 to 83, in respect of which the Prosecution abandoned its application, the fact is devoid of meaning.

65. After reviewing the remaining facts in the context of their original Judgement, the Chamber considers that they are accurate reproductions of the original Chamber's findings from which they were extracted and are truly adjudicated facts which are relevant to matters at issue in the current proceedings. Contrary to the Defence's assertions, the Chamber is also satisfied that none of them concerns the acts, conduct or mental state of the Accused in this case.

66. The Defence for Ngirumpatse and the Defence for Karemera request the exclusion of facts where the original Trial Chamber has made the particular finding on the basis of the **[page 15]** testimony of only one witness. Furthermore, the Defence for Karemera submits that judicial notice of Facts 86 to110 should be denied on the basis that those facts are the subject of reasonable dispute. In its view, since Appeals Judge Lennart Aspergen did not find certain facts pertaining to this incident proven beyond reasonable doubt in his Separate Opinion to the *Musema* Judgement, these facts are the subject of reasonable dispute. The Defence for Karemera also contends that, since Witness HR's testimony, upon whose testimony factual findings were made in the *Musema* Judgement, was disregarded by another Trial Chamber, judicial notice should not be taken of Facts 86 to 107.

67. The Chamber has already indicated that according to the established jurisprudence, a Chamber may rely on a single witness' testimony as proof of a material fact.

68. The *Niyitegeka* Trial Chamber explicitly stated that Witness HR was a credible witness, and accepted his testimony.[62] The Appeals Chamber found the Trial Chamber's assessment of Witness HR to be "detailed and careful", and found no error in the Trial Chamber having relied on his testimony.[63] Furthermore, in the *Musema* trial, Witness HR was one of the witnesses upon whom the Trial Chamber relied in making the findings underpinning other facts.[64] The Trial Chamber expressly stated that it found the cross-examination of the witness in no way impaired his credibility, and that his evidence was reliable. The Appeals Chamber did not question the evaluation of this witness by the Trial Chamber.[65]

---

61 *Prosecutor v. Eliezer Niyitegeka*, Case No. ICTR-96-14-T, Judgement and Sentence (TC), 16 May 2003; *Prosecutor v. Alfred Musema*, Case No. ICTR-96-13-T, Judgement and Sentence (TC), 27 January 2000; *Prosecutor v. Clément Kayishema and Obed Ruzindana*, Case No. ICTR-95-1-T, Judgement (TC), 21 May 1999; *Prosecutor v. Elizaphan and Gérard Ntakirutimana*, Case No. ICTR-96-10 and ICTR-96-17-T, Judgement and Sentence (TC), 21 February 2003.

62 *Niyitegeka* Judgement, para. 108.

63 *Prosecutor v. Niyitegeka,* Case No. ICTR-96-14-A, Judgement (AC), 9 July 2004, para. 138.

64 Facts 86, 87, 91, 93, 94, 104, 111-112.

65 *Musema* Appeals Chamber Judgement, paras. 77-100.

69. While the Chamber considers that issues of witness credibility in an original judgement *may* mitigate against judicial notice of an adjudicated fact, the Chamber is of the view that this depends upon the particular fact in question and the totality of the circumstances surrounding that finding. The question for the Chamber is whether the taking of judicial notice of the fact will compromise the rights of the Accused. The Chamber notes that a witness may be found to be credible by one finder of fact, and not by another. The Chamber also notes that a witness may be found to be telling the truth in a case against one accused, and not in another. The Chamber is not satisfied, with respect to the particular facts proposed for adjudication and said to be tarnished by issues of witness credibility that the rights of the Accused would be compromised. In addition in the present situation, the facts the admission of which is disputed by the Defence were adjudicated by four different Trial Chambers which also heard various witnesses.

70. In these circumstances, the Chamber is satisfied that taking judicial notice of Facts 10 to 12, 88 to 90, 92, 99 to 103, 105 to 107, 124, 127 to 131, 133, 134 to 137, 13, 86, 87, 91, 93, 94, 104, 111, 112, 113, 69, 71, 74, 85, 95 to 98, 109, 110, 114, 115, 70, 72, 73, 108, 116 to 123, 125, 126, 132 is the interests of justice and will promote expediency in this case, without compromising the rights of the Accused.

*6. Facts 142 and 143 (***Nahimana** *Judgement)*

71. The Prosecution seeks judicial notice of two facts taken from the *Nahimana* Judgement (Facts 142 and 143).[66] It claims that while the case is pending appeal, these two facts are not the subject to the appeal and may be judicially noticed. Relying upon the **[page 16]** Separate Opinion of His Honour Judge Shahabuddeen, it submits that judicial notice can be taken of adjudicated facts in cases pending appeal, provided that the particular facts in question do not form part of the appeal.[67]

72. The Chamber notes that one of the Appellants in the *Nahimana* case, Jean-Bosco Barayagwiza, is requesting the annulment of the Judgement on the basis that the proceedings were conducted in his absence. Furthermore, he is alleging a lack of independency of the Tribunal and lack of impartiality of the Judges.[68]

73. In light of these grounds of appeal, the Chamber considers that the Appeals Chamber Judgement has the potential to impact all factual findings of the Trial Chamber Judgement, including the facts sought for judicial notice. Under these circumstances, Facts 142 and 143 cannot be considered to have been finally adjudicated and cannot therefore be judicially noticed.

General Assessment of the Rights of Accused and Expediency of the Proceedings

74. The Defence for each Accused generally submits that taking judicial notice of the facts proposed for notice by the Prosecution compromises the rights of the Accused, including their rights to examine and have examined the witnesses against him. They also claim that the Rule's purpose of expediency will not be advanced, as required by the Appeals Chamber's ruling, since the Accused in this case will be obligated to call evidence to rebut each fact.

75. The Chamber wholly rejects this argument, for if it were to adopt the position, a Chamber could never find that taking judicial notice of any fact would promote expediency.

76. Considering the interests of justice and the entire circumstances of the case, the Chamber is satisfied that taking judicial notice of certain adjudicated facts, as detailed above, will promote expediency without compromising the rights of the Accused. Particularly, the Chamber is of the view that this Decision will not place such a significant burden on the Accused to produce rebuttal evidence that it would jeopardise their right to fair trial.[69] In terms of expediency of the proceedings, the Chamber expects the Prosecution to

---

66 *Prosecutor v. Ferdinand Nahimana, Jean-Bosco Barayagwiza and Hassan Ngeze*, ICTR-99-52-T, Judgement (TC), 3 December 2003.

67 *Prosecutor v. Milošević*, Case No. IT-02-54-AR73.5, Separate Opinion of Judge Shahabuddeen Appended to the Appeal's Chamber's Decision on the Prosecution's Interlocutory Appeal Against the Trial Chamber's 10 April 2003 Decision on Prosecution Motion for Judicial Notice of Adjudicated Facts, 28 October 2003.

68 See Notice of Request for Annulment of Judgement rendered on 3 December 2003 in *The Prosecutor v. Ferdinand Nahimana, Jean-Bosco Barayagwiza and Hassan Ngeze*, ICTR-99-52-T, filed on 3 February 2004.

69 *Popović* Decision, para. 16.

comply with its stated intention to streamline the presentation of its evidence and to reduce the number of witnesses it intends to call as a result of admission of adjudicated facts.

77. However, it is necessary to state that judicial notice is neither taken of the specific order in which these facts have been placed by the Prosecution in its Motion, nor of the headings under which those facts have been placed by the Prosecution. The Chamber takes judicial notice of the facts individually, as extracted from the original Judgements in which the findings were made (for details see Annexure A to this Decision).

FOR THOSE REASONS, THE CHAMBER

I. GRANTS the Prosecution Motion in part, and hereby **[page 17]**

II. TAKES JUDICIAL NOTICE of the following **facts of common knowledge**, pursuant to Rule 94(A) of the Rules:

> (i) The following state of affairs existed in Rwanda between 6 April 1994 to 17 July 1994: There were throughout Rwanda, widespread or systematic attacks against a civilian population based on Tutsi ethnic identification. During the attacks, some Rwandan citizens killed or caused serious bodily or mental harm to person[s] perceived to be Tutsi. As a result of the attacks, there were a large number of deaths of persons of Tutsi ethnic identity.
>
> (ii) Between 1 January 1994 and 17 July 1994 in Rwanda there was an armed conflict not of an international character.
>
> (iii) Between 6 April 1994 and 17 July 1994, there was a genocide in Rwanda against the Tutsi ethnic group.

III. TAKES JUDICIAL NOTICE of the following **adjudicated facts**, pursuant to Rule 94(B) of the Rules, which content is detailed in Annexure A to this Decision:

> Facts 1 to 8, 10 to 13, 15, 16, 17, 20 to 24, 26, 27, 29, 30, 41 to 46, 49, 57 to 59, 61, 65 to 74, 85 to 137, 144 to 147.

III. TAKES judicial notice of the following **adjudicated facts**, pursuant to Rule 94(B) of the Rules, subject to minor corrections deemed necessary and appropriate by the Chamber, appearing in Annexure A to this Decision: Facts 9, 33, 54, 25 and 28.

III. DENIES the remainder of the Prosecution's request and therefore **DECLINES** to take judicial of the following facts, which content is detailed in Annexure B to this Decision:

> Facts 18, 19, 34 to 40, 47, 48, 50-53, 55-56, 60, 62, 63, 64, 84, 142, 143, 148 to 152.

Arusha, 11 December 2006, done in English.

Dennis C. M. Byron	Emile Francis Short	Gberdao Gustave Kam
Presiding	Judge	Judge

[Seal of the Tribunal] **[page 18]**

Annexure A - Adjudicated Facts Judicial Noticed

As explained in this Decision, in some instances the Chamber took judicial notice of adjudicated facts subject to amendments deemed necessary to cure minor inaccuracies or ambiguities. These amendments are highlighted in bold hereinafter when appropriate.

1	During the events of 1994, Tutsi girls and women were subjected to sexual violence, beaten and killed on or near the *bureau communal* premises, as well as elsewhere in the commune of Taba. Hundreds of Tutsi, mostly women and children, sought refuge at the *bureau communal* during this period and many rapes took place on or near the premises of the *bureau communal.*	Akayesu, par. 449.
2	A woman was taken by Interahamwe from the refuge site near the *bureau communal* to a nearby forest area and raped there. She was also raped repeatedly on two separate occasions in the cultural center on the premises of the *bureau communal*, once in a group of fifteen girls and women and once in a group of ten girls and women.	Akayesu, par. 449.
3	Women and girls were selected and taken by the Interahamwe to the cultural center to be raped. Two Interahamwes took a woman and raped her between the *bureau communal* and the cultural center.	Akayesu, par. 449.
4	A woman was taken from the *bureau communal* and raped in a nearby field. Three women were raped at Kinihira, the killing site near the *bureau communal*, and another woman found her younger sister, dying, after she had been raped at the *bureau communal.*	Akayesu, par. 449.
5	Many other instances of rape in Taba took place outside the *bureau communal* - in fields, on the road, and in or just outside houses.	Akayesu, par. 449.
6	Other acts of sexual violence took place on or near the premises of the *bureau communal* - the forced undressing and public humiliation of girls and women.	Akayesu, par. 449.
7	Much of the sexual violence took place in front of large numbers of people, and all of it was directed against Tutsi women.	Akayesu, par. 449.
8	With regard to all rape and sexual violence which took place on or near the premises of the Taba *bureau communal*, the perpetrators were all Interahamwe.	Akayesu, par. 450.
9	Interahamwe are also **identified as** the perpetrators of many rapes which took place outside the *bureau communal.*	Akayesu, par. 450.
10	On 28 June 1994, near the Technical Training College, on a public road **between Charroi Naval and Kibuye,** Niyitegeka ordered Interahamwe to undress the body of a woman who had just been shot dead, to fetch and sharpen a piece of wood, which he then instructed them to insert into her genitalia.	Niyitegeka, paras. 316 and 273.
11	This act was then carried out by the Interahamwe, in accordance with his instructions.	Niyitegeka, par. 316.
12	The body of the woman, with the piece of wood protruding from it, was left on the roadside for some three days thereafter. Niyitegeka referred to the woman as "Inyenzi" by which he meant to refer to Tutsi.	Niyitegeka, par. 316.

13	**Within the area of Gisovu Tea Factory, Twumba Cellule, Gisovu Commune,** Musema ordered the rape of Annunciata Mujawayezu, a Tutsi woman, and the cutting off of her breast to be fed to her son. She was in fact killed.	Musema, paras. 805 and 828.
15	On 13 April 1994 at approximately 10:00 a.m. Semanza directed a group of people to rape Tutsi women before killing them. Victim A was raped by one of the men in the group and that her cousin, Victim B, was taken outside and killed by two other men from the group.	Semanza, par. 261.
16	Ntenzireyerimye and Uyamuremye, members of the Interahamwe, mutilated a Tutsi girl named Nyiramburanga by cutting off her breast and then licking it, on the morning of 7 April 1994 in Rwankeri cellule.	Kajelijeli, par. 678. **[page 19]**
17	Members of the Interahamwe, including Interahamwe from Mukingo commune and neighbouring areas committed rapes and sexual assaults in the Ruhengeri Prefecture between 7 and 10 April 1994.	Kajelijeli, par. 683.
20	The Interahamwe pierced Joyce's side and sexual organs with a spear, and then covered her dead body with her skirt.	Kajelijeli, par. 677.
21	A Tutsi woman was raped by members of the Interahamwe in Busogo Parish and in Kabyaza cellule on 7 April 1994, after having been stopped at a roadblock.	Kajelijeli, par. 679, 918.
22	The handicapped daughter of a Tutsi woman was raped and killed by members of the Interahamwe in Rukoma Cellule, Shiringo Secteur on 7 April 1994.	Kajelijeli, par. 680, 919.
23	A Tutsi woman was raped and sexually mutilated by members of the Interahamwe in Susa secteur, Kinigi commune on 7 April 1994.	Kajelijeli, par. 681, 920.
24	A Tutsi woman was raped by members of the Interahamwe in Susa secteur, Kinigi Commune on 10 April 1994.	Kajelijeli, par. 682, 921.
25	Many of the refugees who escaped or survived the attack at ETO **(*École Technique Officielle*, in Kicukiro sector, Kicukiro *Commune*)** headed in groups towards the Amahoro Stadium.	Rutaganda, **paras. 262 and 300.**
26	Some women were taken forcibly from the group and subsequently raped.	Rutaganda, **par. 300.**
27	Flanked on both sides by *Interahamwe*, approximately 4,000 refugees were then forcibly marched to Nyanza.	Rutaganda, **par. 300.**
28	**At Nyanza, a**n attack took place on 11 April, in the late afternoon and into the evening. Many were killed in this attack.	Rutaganda, **par. 301.**
29	The *Interahamwe* then began killing people with clubs and other weapons.	Rutaganda, **par. 301.**
30	Some girls were selected, put aside, and raped before they were killed. Clothing had been removed from many of the women who were killed.	Rutaganda, **par. 301.**
33	On 7 April 1994 many Tutsi men, women and children were attacked and massacred at a place of shelter within the Mukingo commune, **in this case the place known as Munyemvano's compound in Rwankeri cellule.**	Kajelijeli, par. 597.
41	There was a meeting on the evening of 6 April 1994 following the death of the President, at the Canteen next to the Nkuli bureau communal.	Kajelijeli, par. 469.

42	Kajelijeli seized the leading role in the meeting, and addressed those persons present—who were all of Hutu ethnic origin. And he said to them "[Y]ou very well know that it was the Tutsi that killed—that brought down the Presidential plane. What are you waiting for to eliminate the enemy?"	Kajelijeli, par. 469.
43	By "the enemy", a witness present understood Kajelijeli to mean the Tutsi ethnic group.	Kajelijeli, par. 469.
44	After receiving information from Sendugu Shadrack that there were no weapons available to attack the population, Kajelijeli left the meeting with Deputy Brigadier Boniface Ntabareshya.	Kajelijeli, par. 469.
45	When he returned he informed those present that Major Bizabarumana had agreed to provide them with "equipment" at the commune the following morning.	Kajelijeli, par. 469.
46	Kajelijeli also promised to bring Interahamwe reinforcements from Mukingo commune for the attack on Kinyababa cellule.	Kajelijeli, par. 469.
49	Augustin Habiyambere and Sendugu Shadrack led an attack on the morning of the 7 April 1994, following the delivery of weapons from Mukamira camp in which approximately 100 young militants, including youth from Nkuli commune; recruits from Mukingo led by the CDR President from the Gitwa secteur, Iyakaremye; a group from the Rukoma Mountains; forces from Mukamira; and soldiers in civilian attire from IGA, attacked and killed approximately 12 families of Tutsis, numbering approximately 80 people, residing in Kinyababa cellule in Nkuli commune.	Kajelijeli, par. 487.
54	The attack at Busogo Hill, **Rwankeri *cellule,*** **Mukingo *commune,*** claimed the lives of many Tutsis.	Kajelijeli, **paras. 544 and 549.**
57	The Interahamwe attackers involved in the attack at Munyemvano's compound used traditional weapons, guns and grenades to slaughter their Tutsi victims.	Kajelijeli, par. 597. **[page 20]**
58	There was a killing of a large number of Tutsis at the Convent at Busogo Parish on the morning of 7 April 1994. The number of bodies buried the following day is an indicator that approximately 300 people died in the attack.	Kajelijeli, par. 604.
59	Members of the Interahamwe were involved in the attack.	Kajelijeli, par. 604.
61	At the Ruhengeri Court of Appeal, Interahamwe, who were all Hutus, killed about three hundred Tutsis.	Kajelijeli, par. 622.
65	Tutsi civilians were killed at Musha church by soldiers, gendarmes, and Interahamwe militiamen on 13 April 1994. Semanza participated in this attack by gathering Interahamwe to take part in the attack and by directing the assailants to kill Tutsi refugees.	Semanza, par. 206.
66	In April 1994 there were attacks on mostly Tutsi, civilian refugees on Mwulire Hill.	Semanza, par. 224.
67	Semanza participated in the killings of Tutsi refugees on Mwulire Hill on 18 April 1994	Semanza, par. 228.
68	Semanza was armed and present on 12 April 1994 during the attack on Mabare mosque and that the attack resulted in the death of around 300 Tutsi refugees.	Semanza, par. 244.

69	From about 9 April until 30 June 1994, Tutsis sought refuge in Bisesero from Hutu attacks that had occurred in other parts of Rwanda and, in particularly, other areas of Kibuye Prefecture.	Kayishema, par. 409.
71	Attacks occurred at approximately twelve sites in the Bisesero area.	Kayishema, par. 411.
74	Ruzindana and Kayishema personally attacked Tutsis seeking refuge during the assaults described in Bisesero.	Kayishema, par. 467.
70	Regular attacks occurred in the Bisesero region from 9 April 1994 until about 30 June 1994, and thousands of Tutsi were killed, injured and maimed there.	Ntakirutimana, **paras. 446, 447 and 448.**
72	The attackers consisted of Interahamwe, gendarmes, soldiers, and civilians.	Ntakirutimana, par. 447.
73	The Interahamwe, gendarmes, and soldiers were usually armed with guns and wore uniforms. The civilians were usually armed with clubs, machetes, bows, arrows, spears, hoes, knives, sharpened bamboo sticks, and other traditional weapons.	Ntakirutimana, par. 447.
85	The most severe attacks occurred in the Bisesero area on 13 and 14 May 1994, after an apparent two-week lull in the attacks.	Kayishema, par. 406.
95	Kayishema and Ruzindana were present at the massacres in Muyira Hill and its vicinity beginning on about 13 May 1994.	Kayishema, par. 430.
110	Attacks in the vicinity of Muyira Hill continued into June 1994.	Kayishema, par. 452.
96	Kayishema and Ruzindana arrived at the head of the convoy of vehicles which transported soldiers, members of the Interahamwe, communal police and armed civilians.	Kayishema, par. 565.
97	Kayishema signalled the start of the attacks by firing a shot into the air, directed the assaults by dividing the assailants into groups, and headed one group of them as it advanced up the Hill and verbally encouraged the attackers through a megaphone.	Kayishema, par. 565.
98	Ruzindana also played a leadership role, distributing traditional weapons, leading a group of attackers up the Hill and shooting at the refugees.	Kayishema, par. 565.
109	Ruzindana orchestrated the massacre at the Hole near Muyira Hill, and the assault commenced upon his instruction.	Kayishema, par. 565.
86	On 13 May 1994, a large scale attack occurred on Muyira Hill against up to 40000 Tutsi refugees.	Musema, par. 747.
87	The attack started in the morning.	Musema, par. 747.
91	The attackers were armed with firearms, grenades, rocket launchers and traditional weapons, and sang anti-Tutsi slogans.	Musema, par. 747.
93	Musema was one of the leaders of the attackers coming from Gisovu and drove his red Pajero to the attack. Musema was armed with a rifle. He used the weapon during the attack.	Musema, par. 748.
94	Thousands of unarmed Tutsi men, women and children were killed during the attack at the hands of the assailants and that many were forced to flee for their survival.	Musema, par. 748. **[page 21]**
104	A large scale attack occurred on Muyira Hill 14 May 1994 against Tutsi civilians, and the attackers, numbering as many as 15000, were armed with traditional weapons, firearms and grenades, and sang slogans.	Musema, par. 750.

88	The attackers comprised thousands of Interahamwe, soldiers, policemen and Hutu civilians.	Niyitegeka, par. 178.
89	They were transported in ONATRACOM buses, lorries belonging to COLAS, MINITRAP vehicles, buses, pick-ups, vehicles from the Gisovu Tea Factory and vehicles commandeered from Tutsi.	Niyitegeka, par. 178.
90	These vehicles parked at Kucyapa. The attackers were chanting "Tuba Tsemba Tsembe", which means "Let's exterminate them", a reference to the Tutsi.	Niyitegeka, par. 178.
92	The attackers were armed with guns, machetes, spears, sharpened bamboo sticks and clubs.	Niyitegeka, par. 178.
99	On 13 May, sometime between 7.00 a.m. and 10.00 a.m., Niyitegeka was one of the leaders in a large-scale attack by armed attackers against Tutsi refugees at Muyira Hill.	Niyitegeka, par. 178.
100	Niyitegeka was armed with a gun and was shooting at the Tutsi refugees at the hill. In addition, Niyitegeka instructed the attackers during the attack, showing the attackers where to go and how to attack the refugees.	Niyitegeka, par. 178.
101	Niyitegeka was in the front row leading attackers, together with other leaders.	Niyitegeka, par. 178.
106	The attackers comprised civilians, soldiers, Interahamwe, gendarmes and communal policemen.	Niyitegeka, par. 205.
107	They were carrying guns, spears, clubs, machetes and sharpened objects, and launched a large-scale attack against the Tutsi refugees at Muyira Hill. Niyitegeka was armed with a gun and shot at Tutsi refugees at Muyira Hill.	Niyitegeka, par. 205.
105	On the morning of 14 May, Niyitegeka and others, together with attackers, arrived at Muyira Hill and parked their vehicles at Kucyapa.	Niyitegeka, par. 205.
102	In the evening of 13 May 1994, Niyitegeka held a meeting at Kucyapa after the 13 May attack against Tutsi refugees at Muyira Hill, for the purpose of deciding on the programme of killings for the next day and to organize these killings against the Tutsi in Bisesero, who numbered approximately 60,000. The meeting was attended by about 5,000 people.	Niyitegeka, par. 257.
103	Using a loudspeaker, Niyitegeka thanked attackers for their participation in attacks and commended them for "a good work", which refers to the killing of Tutsi civilians. Niyitegeka told them to share the people's property and cattle, and eat meat so that they would be strong to return the next day to continue the work, that is, the killing.	Niyitegeka, par. 257.
108	Sometime in mid-May 1994 in Muyira Hill, Gérard Ntakirutimana led armed attackers in an attack on Tutsi refugees, as a result of which many Tutsi were killed.	Ntakirutimana, par. 635.
111	Musema participated in an attack on Mumataba hill in mid-May 1994. The assailants, numbering between 120 and 150, included tea factory employees, armed with traditional weapons, and communal policemen.	Musema, par. 755.
112	In the presence and with the knowledge of Musema, tea factory vehicles transported attackers to the location. The attack was launched on the blowing of whistles, and the target of the attack were 2000 to 3000 Tutsis who had sought refuge in and around a certain Sakufe's house.	Musema, par. 756.

113	Musema participated in the attack on Nyakavumu cave at the end of May 1994. Musema was present at the attack during which assailants closed off the entrance to the cave with wood and leaves, and set fire thereto. Over 300 Tutsi civilians who had sought refuge in the cave died as a result of the fire.	Musema, par. 780.
114	At the cave, Kayishema was directing the siege generally and Ruzindana was commanding the attackers from Ruhengeri; both were giving instructions to the attackers and orchestrating the attack.	Kayishema, par. 566.
115	Gendarmes, members of the Interahamwe and various local officials were present and participated.	Kayishema, par. 438. **[page 22]**
116	Elizaphan Ntakirutimana brought armed attackers in the rear hold of his vehicle to Nyarutovu Hill one day in the middle of May 1994, and the group was searching for Tutsi refugees and chasing them. Elizaphan Ntakirutimana pointed out the fleeing refugees to the attackers who then chased these refugees singing "Exterminate them; look for them everywhere; kill them; and get it over with, in all the forests."	Ntakirutimana, par. 594.
117	Elizaphan Ntakirutimana participated in a convoy of vehicles carrying armed attackers to Kabatwa Hill at the end of May 1994, and, later on that day, at neighbouring Gitwa Hill, he pointed out the whereabouts of Tutsi refugees to attackers who attacked the refugees.	Ntakirutimana, par. 607.
118	Three meetings convened in Kibuye town in June 1994.	Ntakirutimana, **paras. 711 and 720.**
119	The first took place around 10 June in the conference room of the prefectural office. The meeting started between 10.00 and 11.00 a.m.	Ntakirutimana, **paras. 711 and 720.**
120	It was attended by Interahamwe and various officials, including Prefect Kayishema, Ruzindana, Musema, Eliézer Niyitegeka, Gérard Ntakirutimana, and the bourgmestres of the communes surrounding Bisesero, seated in the front row.	Ntakirutimana, **paras. 711 and 720.**
121	Ruzindana took the floor and explained to the participants that the meeting was aimed at evaluating their progress in killing Tutsi in the Bisesero area and to decide what still needed to be done to finish that task.	Ntakirutimana, **paras. 711 and 720.**
122	Gérard Ntakirutimana also took the floor, saying that the problem they faced in completing the work was that they had insufficient guns and ammunition. Like other speakers at the meeting, Gérard Ntakirutimana spoke through a microphone connected to loudspeakers.	Ntakirutimana, **paras. 711 and 720.**
123	At those meetings Gérard Ntakirutimana also participated in the distribution of weapons, discussed the planning of attacks at Bisesero, was assigned a role in such an attack, and reported back on its success.	Ntakirutimana, par. 720.
125	There was a second meeting that took place about a week later at the same venue. It also started between 10.00 and 11.00 a.m. and lasted about four hours.	Ntakirutimana, **paras. 712 and 720.**
126	The same officials who attended the first meeting also attended the second. Many other persons, including Interahamwe, were present, inside and outside the room.	Ntakirutimana, **paras. 712 and 720.**
132	Gérard Ntakirutimana was named as a member of the "Ngoma group", which included Enos Kagaba and Mathias Ngirinshuti and was to attack Murambi.	Ntakirutimana, par. 712.

124	Niyitegeka promised to provide weapons for the killing of the Tutsi in Bisesero.	Niyitegeka, par. 225
127	The meeting was held to permit Niyitegeka to answer questions posed at the previous meeting, including in relation to the promise of weapons made at the previous meeting.	Niyitegeka, par. 225.
128	At that meeting, Niyitegeka distributed the weapons to group representatives for use in killings in Bisesero.	Niyitegeka, par. 225.
129	Niyitegeka stated that the attack would take place the next day in Bisesero.	Niyitegeka, par. 225.
130	Niyitegeka presented the attack plan on a blackboard: a circle with "Bisesero" written in the circle. Around this circle were written the names of the designated leaders of each group of attackers and the points of departure for the five groups of attackers, which were Karongi, Rushishi, Kiziba, Gisiza and Murambi.	Niyitegeka, par. 225.
131	Niyitegeka encouraged people to participate in the attack, and was himself a leader for the Kiziba group.	Niyitegeka, par. 225.
133	This plan was carried out in the attack at Kiziba the next day against Tutsi in Bisesero, which attack was led by Niyitegeka and resulted in many victims amongst the Tutsi refugees.	Niyitegeka, par. 225.
134	On or about 18 June, Niyitegeka attended a meeting in the canteen of Kibuye Prefectural Office where he promised to supply gendarmes for the next day's attack and urged bourgmestres and others to do all they could to ensure participation in the attacks so that all the Tutsi in Bisesero could be killed. Another attack took place the next day as planned.	Niyitegeka, par. 229. **[page 23]**
135	Sometime in June, at approximately 5.00 p.m., Niyitegeka spoke at a meeting at Kibuye Prefectural Office, which was attended by Kayishema, Ruzindana, many Interahamwe, and others.	Niyitegeka, par. 232.
136	The Interahamwe were chanting: "Exterminate them, flush them out of the forest", meaning the Tutsi.	Niyitegeka, par. 232.
137	Niyitegeka told the audience that he had come so they could pool their efforts in overcoming the enemy, that is, the Tutsi, and promised they would get his contribution in due course. He promised that not less than a hundred Interahamwe would assist in the attacks against the Tutsi.	Niyitegeka, par. 232.
144	On 8 April 1994 in the morning, Semanza met Rugambarara and a group of Interahamwe in front of a certain house in Bicumbi commune. Semanza told the Interahamwe that a certain Tutsi family had not yet been killed, that no Tutsi should survive, and that the Tutsis should be sought out and killed.	Semanza, par. 271.
145	Later the same day, the Interahamwe searched a field near the house of the family mentioned by Semanza, found four members of that family, and killed them.	Semanza, par. 271.
146	As from an unspecified date in mid-April, a roadblock was erected by *Interahamwe* on the Avenue de la Justice near a traffic light not far from the entrance to the Amgar Garage at the Cyahafi Sector boundary, in Nyarugenge *Commune* of the Kigali-*ville Préfecture*.	Rutaganda, **par. 225.**

147	At the said roadblock, the *Interahamwe* checked the identity cards of those who crossed it and detained those who carried identity cards bearing the "Tutsi" ethnic reference or were otherwise considered as "Tutsi" because they had stated that they were not in possession of an identity card. **[page 24]**	Rutaganda, **par. 225.**

Annexure B - Facts in relation to which judicial notice is denied

18	These rapes and sexual assaults were committed in the course of a widespread attack upon the Tutsi civilian population.	Kajelijeli, par. 922.
19	Pursuant to an order of Kajelijeli given at Byangabo Market on 7 April 1994 to "exterminate the Tutsis" the Interahamwe went to Rwankeri cellule, where a Tutsi woman named Joyce was raped and killed by Interahamwe.	Kajelijeli, par. 917.
34	In Mukingo commune and neighbouring areas in April 1994, the killings of the Tutsi were not a spontaneous reaction of the Hutu populace to the death of the President.	Kajelijeli, par. 161.
35	The killers were, amongst others, Interahamwe who were directed to kill all the Tutsis and received assistance and were supplied with weapons to do so.	Kajelijeli, par. 161.
36	Kajelijeli was a leader of Interahamwe with control over the Interahamwe in Mukingo commune, and he also had influence over the Interahamwe of Nkuli commune from 1 January 1994 to July 1994.	Kajelijeli, par. 404.
37	Kajelijeli was closely associated with the new MRND and its leadership and especially from January 1994 to mid-July 1994, he was actively involved in many activities of this party in Mukingo commune and the neighbouring areas. He may as well have been a member of the MRND party.	Kajelijeli, par. 426.
38	Kajelijeli held and maintained effective control over Interahamwe from Mukingo and Nkuli communes from 6 April until at least 14 April 1994.	Kajelijeli, par. 626.
39	By 6 April 1994, Kajelijeli was actively involved in the training of the Interahamwe in Mukingo commune.	Kajelijeli, par. 400.
40	Interahamwe in Mukingo commune used distinctive uniforms and Kajelijeli participated in the distribution of these uniforms to the Interahamwe in Byangabo Market around 1993	Kajelijeli, par. 402.
47	At the Nkuli bureau communal between 5:00am and 6:00am on the morning of 7 April 1994, a Land Rover arrived from Mukamira military camp.	Kajelijeli, par. 474.
48	The Land Rover had brought Kalashnikovs, grenades and boxes of cartridges.	Kajelijeli, par. 474.
50	The weapons procured by Kajelijeli, which arrived early that morning at the Nkuli bureau communal, were used in the attack.	Kajelijeli, par. 488.
51	Augustin Habiyambere, amongst others, reported back to Kajelijeli at the end of the day on what had been achieved, and assured Kajelijeli that they had "eliminated everything."	Kajelijeli, par. 488.

52	Kajelijeli assembled members of the Interahamwe at Byangabo Market on the morning of 7 April 1994, and instructed them to "[k]ill and exterminate all those people in Rwankeri" and to "exterminate the Tutsis". He also ordered them to dress up and "start to work."	Kajelijeli, par. 531.
53	Kajelijeli participated in this attack by directing the Interahamwe from Byangabo Market towards Rwankeri cellule, to join that attack, and by acting as a liaison with Mukamira camp for military and weapons assistance.	Kajelijeli, par. 549.
55	Tutsis were attacked and killed at the home of Rudatinya. Kajelijeli ordered and supervised this attack and participated in it.	Kajelijeli, par. 555.
56	Kajelijeli was present during the attack on Munyemvano's compound in Rwankeri cellule and, in his position of authority over the Interahamwe attackers, commanded and supervised the attack.	Kajelijeli, par. 597.
60	A feast was held at Kajelijeli's bar on the evening of 7 April 1994 where the Interahamwe feasted together and sang songs after the day's killings. Kajelijeli was present during this event.	Kajelijeli, par. 708.
62	Kajelijeli played a vital role as an organizer and facilitator of the Interahamwe and other attackers in the massacre at the Ruhengeri Court of Appeal on or around 14 April 1994.	Kajelijeli, par. 625.
63	He did this by procuring weapons, rounding up the Interahamwe and facilitating their transportation to the Ruhengeri Court of Appeal by supplying them with petrol.	Kajelijeli, par. 625. **[page 25]**
64	The Tutsis at the Ruhengeri Court of Appeal had been taken from Busengo sub-prefecture in Ndusu Commune.	Kajelijeli, par. 625.
84	Soon after in mid May, the assailants again pursued those seeking refuge from place to place.	Kayishema, par. 406.
142	Radio was the medium of mass communication with the broadest reach in Rwanda. Many people owned radios and listened to RTLM – at home, in bars, on the streets, and at the roadblocks.	Nahimana, par. 488.
143	The Interahamwe and other militia listened to RTLM and acted on the information that was broadcast by RTLM.	Nahimana, par. 488.
148	Rutaganda ordered men under his control to take fourteen detainees, including at least four Tutsis, to a deep hole located near Amgar garage and on his orders and in his presence, his men killed ten of the said detainees with machetes. The bodies of the victims were thrown into the hole.	Rutaganda, par. 261.
149	The attack on the Tutsi population occurred in various parts of Rwanda, such as in Nyanza, Nyarugenge *Commune*, Kiemesakara Sector in the Kigali Prefecture, Nyamirambo, Cyahafi, Kicukiro, Masango.	Rutaganda, par. 372.
150	Rutaganda was present at the mass grave site near the hole behind the École Technique de Muhazi and ordered the burial of bodies. Rutaganda ordered the burial of bodies in order to conceal the dead from foreigners.	Rutaganda, paras. 346, 353, 356.
151	There were meetings held to organise and encourage the targeting and killings of the Tutsi civilian population as such and not as "RPF Infiltrators."	Rutaganda, par. 371.

152	This organisation and encouragement took the form of radio broadcasts calling for the apprehension of Tutsi, the use of mobile announcement units to spread propaganda messages about the *Inkontanyi,* the distribution of weapons to the *Interahamwe* militia, the erection of roadblocks manned by soldiers and members of the *Interahamwe* to facilitate the identification, separation and subsequent killing of Tutsi civilians, and the house to house searches conducted to apprehend Tutsis.	Rutaganda, par. 371.

International Criminal Tribunal for Rwanda
Tribunal pénal international pour le Rwanda

OR: ENG

TRIAL CHAMBER III

Before Judges: Dennis C. M. Byron, Presiding
Gberdao Gustave Kam
Robert Fremr

Registrar: Adama Dieng

Date: 5 February 2007

THE PROSECUTOR

v.

Simion NCHAMIHIGO

Case No. ICTR-2001-63-T

DECISION ON THE PROSECUTOR'S APPLICATION TO ADMIT INTO EVIDENCE THE TRANSCRIPT OF THE ACCUSED'S INTERVIEW AS A SUSPECT AND THE DEFENSE'S REQUEST TO HOLD A *VOIR DIRE*

Article 17 of the Statute; Rules 42,43 and 95 of the Rules of Procedure and Evidence

---

Office of the Prosecutor:
Alphonse Van
Lloyd Strickland
Madeleine Schwarz
Adama Niane

Defence Counsel:
Denis Turcotte
Benoît Henry

[page 2] INTRODUCTION

1. The trial in this case began on 25 September 2006. The first trial session was from 25 September 2006 to 20 October 2006. The second trial session started on 9 January 2007 and concluded on 29 January 2007. During the first trial session, the Prosecutor applied to tender in evidence the transcript of an extra-judicial statement ("Statement") taken by ICTR investigators Mamadou Koné and Moussa Sanogo on 25 and 26 May 2001, from the Accused Nchamihigo.

2. On 20 May 2001, the Prosecutor filed a request under Rule 40 *bis* of the Rules for an Order for the immediate transfer to the premises of the Detention Facilities of the Tribunal (UNDF) in Arusha and for an Order for provisional detention of Simeon Nchamihigo. On 21 May 2001, Judge Mehmet Güney made the Order for Siméon Nchamihigo's transfer as requested.[1] At the time the interview was taken, Nchamihigo had the status of a suspect. The application to admit the Statement was made during the testimony of Prosecution Investigator Jeannette Ebouea, on 26 September 2006, who had not been present during the interview process. The Chamber denied the application on the ground that no evidence had been adduced to indicate whether the procedure governing the rights of suspects during questioning had been observed.

3. On the Prosecutor's application, leave was subsequently granted for investigator Mamadou Koné to be added to the witness list to adduce evidence on the manner on which Nchamihigo's Statement was taken.

4. Investigator Mamadou Koné gave evidence in chief on 9 January 2007 and was crossexamined on 12 and 15 January 2007. During his testimony, the Defence submitted that a *voir dire* should be held. The Chamber directed that submissions be made in writing.[2] Both the Defence and the Prosecutor filed submissions accordingly.

5. The Defence argued that the Chamber should formally determine whether it would conduct a *voir dire* procedure to verify the respect of the rights of the Accused during his questioning, specifically on the matter relating to the waiver of his right to legal assistance of a counsel pursuant to Rule 42 and the procedure for the recording of the Statement pursuant to Rule 43 of the Rules and submitted that the Statement taken by ICTR investigators from the Accused be ruled inadmissible.[3]

6. In its Response[4], the Prosecutor submitted that although the *voir dire* procedure may be conducted by a Trial Chamber of the Tribunal, it is unnecessary in this case. He contended that all the relevant rules were observed, that Nchamihigo was informed of all his rights and waived his right to legal assistance and made the statement voluntarily. **[page 3]**

DISCUSSION

The *Voir* Dire Hearing

7. Decisions relating to the admissibility of evidence and the general conduct of proceedings largely fall within the discretion of the Trial chamber.[5] The *voir dire* procedure originates from common law and does not have any defined process in this Tribunal.[6] There are no provisions in the Rules which direct Trial Chambers to adopt a formal procedure for determining whether they should conduct a *voir dire*. Instead,

---

1 *The Prosecutor* v. *Siméon Nshamihigo,* Order for Transfer and Provisional Detention under Rule 40 *bis* of the Rules of Procedure and Evidence (TC), 21 May 2001.

2 T. 9 January 2007, p. 4.

3 Plaidoirie sur la tenue d'un *voir dire,* filed on 11 January 2007.

4 Réponse du Procureur à la note de pladoirie de la defense de Simeon Nchamihigo sur la tenue d'un voir dire pour violation des articles 42 et 43 du Règlement de procedure et de preuve, filed on 18 January 2007. A Corrigendum was filed on 19 January 2007.

5 *Tharcisse Muvunyi v. The Prosecutor,* Case No. ICTR-200-55A-T, Decision on Interlocutory Appeal (AC), 29 May 2006, para. 5.

6 As an example of the flexibility with which the *voir dire* procedure is utilised at trial, *voir dire* examinations have previously been deferred to the cross-examination stage in determining a Witness's qualification as an Expert Witness: *Prosecufor v. Muvunyi,* Case No. ICTR-200-55A-T, Decision on the Prosecutor's Motion for Admission of Testimony of Expert Witness Rule 92bis of the Rules (TC), 24 March 2005, para. 27. See also *The Prosecutor v. Sefer Halilovic,* Case IT-01-48-T, Decision on Interlocutory Appeal Concerning Admission of Record of Interview of the Accused from the Bar Table (TC), 19 August 2005, para. 46 finding that a *voir dire* procedure is not necessarily required for identifying the voluntariness of an interview of an accused, although "there may be certain advantages in doing so."

Rule 89(B) of the Rules provides that reference may be made to evidentiary rules "which will best favour a fair determination of the matter". This discretion can extend to the conduct of a *voir dire* procedure when it is determined appropriate to do so by the Trial Chamber.[7] The Chamber notes that Black's Law Dictionary describes *voir dire* as "a preliminary examination to test the competence of a witness or evidence".

8. In this case, Defence Counsel did not describe what process he envisaged by his reference to the *voir dire* procedure. In particular, the Defence did not evince an intention or desire to adduce any evidence on the admissibility of the statement. Although the concept or the terminology of *voir dire* was not clarified, the Chamber had indicated that its determination of the admissibility of the proffered Statement would be based on evidence to be adduced on the process by which the Statement was obtained.[8] The Prosecutor applied to add Mr. Koni to the witness list to address this issue and stated that he did not intend to call any other witnesses on the admissibility of the statement.[9] The Defence had clear notice of this. When testimony was given by Mr. Koni, he was subject to cross-examination that was aimed at testing the extent to which there was compliance with the rules governing. admissibility of the Statement.

9. The Chamber has heard all of the available evidence and received oral and written legal submissions and arguments from both the Prosecution and the Defence. The procedure adopted, although not described as such, is either a form of *voir dire* or is similar to it. The Chamber allowed thorough preliminary testing of the competence of the evidence sought to be introduced. The Chamber has sufficient information to rule on the admissibility of the statements and denies the application to make any formal ruling on holding a *voir dire*.

10. The Chamber will now analyse the testimony of Mr. Koné and then apply the legal principles to determine the admissibility of the statement.

The Admissibility of the Statement

11. Mamadou Koné was the only witness called to testify on how the questioning of Nchamihigo was conducted. As a preliminary issue, the Chamber indicates that it relies on his credibility and reliability. There were some instances of inaccuracies in certain aspects of **[page 4]** his testimony, but these were brought to the Chamber's attention by Mr. Koné himself after he had conducted some research. There were some instances where his power of recall was not perfect. However, having considered the entirety of his testimony and his demeanour, the Chamber considers that he is a credible and reliable witness. The Chamber now expresses its findings from his testimony.

12. On Saturday, 19 May 2001, Nchamihigo was arrested by Mr. Paul Schwartzman, duty officer of the ICTR, in the premises of the ICTR.[10] On 25 May 2001, in the morning, Nchamihigo was handed over to ICTR authorities by the Tanzanian authorities[11] in the presence of Mr. Koné.[12]

13. In the afternoon of 25 May 2001, Mr. Koné conducted Nchamihigo's interview in a place which he said was the UNDF Annex.[13] Mr. Koné confessed inability to describe the place where the interview was conducted. He could not say whether it was a prison, but he did see security guards.[14] He could not give its location although he knew it was not in or near the UNDF compound.[15] He could not say how far away it was.[16] He explained the inability to describe the location of the interview to his poor knowledge of Arusha as he hasnever been a resident in the town.[17]

---

7 *The Prosecutor v. Sefer Halilović*, Case IT-01 -48-T, Decision on Interlocutory Appeal Concerning Admission of Record of Interview of the Accused from the Bar Table (TC), 19 August 2005, para. 46.

8 T. 1st February 2007, pp. 7-8 (French).

9 *The Prosecutor* v. *Simdon Nchamihigo,* Case No. ICTR-2001-63-T, Prosecutor's Extremely Urgent Motion foy Leave to Amend its Witness List, 6 October 2006, paras. 6-8.

10 T. 15 January 2007, p. 13; T. 12 January 2007, p. 23.

11 T. 15 January2007, p. 25.

12 T. 15 January2007, p. 14.

13 T. 12 January 2007, p. 26.

14 T. 15 January 2007, p. 36.

15 T. 15 January 2007, p. 35.

16 T. 15 January 2007: p. 37.

17 T. 12 January 2007, p. 26.

14. Mr. Koné could not recall the exact time that Nchamihigo arrived at the place of the interview.[18] He insisted that the only communication before the commencement of the interview were exchanges of pleasantries. The only persons present at the interview were Mr. Koné, Mr. Sanogo and Nchamihigo. He confirmed that no legal counsel was present.[19] The interview was conducted by Mr. Koni in the French language with which Nchamihigo was familiar.

15. Mr. Koné described the process by which the questioning was recorded. He explained that there were two decks on the same recording machine, one deck recording the original and another making the copy.[20]

16. During his cross-examination, Mr. Koné admitted that it was only on some occasions that he recorded the fact and time of breaks in the recording of the interview. After the interview, Mr. Koné delivered the copies of the recording to his superiors and following that, was not involved in their control. Subsequently, he received copies of the transcripts. It was admitted that only 5 of the *6* copies of the recording were sent to the accused.[21]

17. After he was shown extracts from the transcript of the interview, Mr. Koné admitted that it started at 15: 17 pm.[22] He said that he immediately handed Nchamihigo a form, written in French, entitled "Notice of Suspect's Rights" and Nchamihigo read it.[23] This form set out the rights of the suspect that are regulated by Rule 42 of the Rules. Mr. Koné read a part of it to Nchamihigo but omitted to read the section of the form dealing with the right of a suspect **[page 5]** not to be questioned without the presence of counsel unless he voluntarily waived that right.[24] Nchamihigo told Mr. Koné that two attorneys had assisted him that morning when he had appeared before a Tanzanian Court and he wondered whether they could come to assist him at the interview.[25] Mr. Koné indicated that they could not come to assist him unless he had the means to pay them.[26] Nchamihigo said that he did not have the means to pay. Mr. Koné said that if Nchamihigo did not have the means to pay, the Tribunal could assign counsel for him.[27] Whereupon Nchamhigo responded "Agreed. I do not have such means."[28] Mr. Koné said that it was now 3.22 and he was going to turn off the recorder so that Nchamihigo could sign the Notice of Rights. Sirneon Nchamihigo signed the declaration.[29] The questioning continued in the absence of counsel.

18. Mr. Koné, said that at the time the interview was conducted, he did not know that the Tribunal had a practice of appointing duty counsel to assist suspects before their official counsel was appointed.[30] It did not occur to him to defer the questioning to enable Nchamihigo to avail himself of the services of duty counsel, and consequently he did not give Nchamihigo any information or advice about his rights to such assistance. Mr. Koné admitted that since then, he became aware that on the 25 May 2001 the Registrar had appointed Mr. Kirita as duty counsel for Nchamihigo.[31] Nchamihigo was never informed of this during the entire two-day period that he underwent questioning.[32]

19. Mr. Koné also admitted that the appointment of the duty counsel was not mentioned in the "Notice of Suspect's rights";[33] that after reading part of the "Notice of Suspect's Rights", he did not give any further information or explanation about it;[34] that he did not explicitly tell Nchamihigo that he could make use of the services of a lawyer at the time he spoke to him;[35] and that he did not explain that if he did not have the

18 T. 15 January2007, p. 25.
19 T. 15 January 2007, p. 27.
20 T. 12 January 2007, p. 22.
21 Réponse du Procureur à la note de pladoirie de la défense de Siméon Nchamihigo sur la tenue d'un voir dire pour violation des articles 42 et 43 du Règlement de procédure et de preuve », filed on 18 January 2007. A Corrigendum was filed on 19 January 2007, para. 36.
22 T. 15 January 2007, p. 25.
23 T. 15 January2007, p. 40.
24 T. 15 January 2007, pp. 28-29.
25 T. 15 January 2007, p. 38.
26 T. 15 January 2007, p. 38.
27 T. 15 January 2007, p. 39.
28 T. 15 January 2007, p. 39.
29 T. 15 January 2007, p. 40.
30 T. 15 January 2007, p. 33.
31 T. 15 January 2007, p. 33.
32 T. 15 January2007, pp. 33-34.
33 T. 15 Janualy2007, p. 35.
34 T. 15 January 2007, p. 30.
35 T. 15 January 2007, p. 39.

means, the interview could be suspended to allow Nchamihigo to access a lawyer assigned by the Tribunal.[36] He admitted that in the remainder of the interview, at no time did the investigators advise the Accused that he had an immediate right to the assistance of counsel during questioning.[37]

20. Mr. Koné explained that at the commencement of the questioning on the second day, 26 May 2001, at 10:23 am, the investigators re-read the five paragraphs in the "Notice of Suspect's Rights" in the same way it was read to Nchamihigo the first time on 25 May 2001, and no additional explanation was given.[38] The cross-examination contain the following extract:

> "Q. You will, therefore, agree with me, Mr. Koné, that there is no evidence that Mr. Nchamihigo became aware of the waiver of rights; is that correct?
>
> A. Yes.
>
> Q. And this is clear because nowhere is it indicated that the recording was **[page 6]** stopped for him to familiarise him with that waiver between 15:17 and 15:22; is that correct?
>
> A. Yes, that is correct."[39]

21. It is well settled that a statement taken from a suspect would not be admitted into evidence at his trial if his rights during the investigation were not respected. According to Article 17 of the Statute, if questioned, a suspect shall be entitled to be assisted by counsel of his or her own choice, including the right to have legal assistance assigned to the suspect without payment by him or her in any such case if he or she does not have sufficient means to pay for it. Rule 42 of the Rules, prescribes that a suspect who is to be questioned by the Prosecutor must be informed by the Prosecutor prior to questioning, in a language he speaks and understands of the right: (i) to be assisted by counsel of his choice or to have legal assistance assigned to him without payment if he does not have sufficient means to pay for it, (ii) to have the free assistance of an interpreter if he cannot understand or speak the language to be used for questioning; and (iii) to remain silent, and to be cautioned that any statement he makes shall be recorded and may be used in evidence. Rule 42 (B) of the Rules specifically mandates that questioning of a suspect shall not proceed without the presence of counsel unless the suspect has voluntarily waived his right to counsel. In case of waiver, if the suspect subsequently expresses a desire to have counsel, questioning shall thereupon cease, and shall only resume when the suspect has obtained or has been assigned counsel. These rules are supported by the provisions of Rule 44 *bis* requiring the Registrar to summon duty counsel to represent a suspect who is unrepresented at any time after being transferred to the Tribunal as soon as practicable.

22. The Chamber finds that Ncharnihigo's questioning was conducted without the assistance of counsel contrary to Article 17 of the Statute. The Prosecution contended however, that by signing the "Notice of Suspect's Rights" he waived the right to the presence of counsel. The Chamber finds that the testimony of Mr. Koné is inconsistent with that contention. The Prosecutor had argued that Nchamihigo, because of the work he had done in Rwanda as a Deputy Prosecutor, and at the ICTR as an investigator, should have known his rights. In this case that argument does not address Mr. Kone's admission that the Registrar, acting in accordance with Rule 44 *bis,* had appointed Mr. Kirrita to be duty counsel for the suspect on the very day that the questioning commenced, and the investigators never informed him of this fact. The inference from the evidence of Nchamihigo's reference to the lawyers, who had assisted him that morning, was that he expressed a desire to have legal assistance for which he could not pay. The Chamber is of the view that it was the duty of the investigator to stop the questioning at that time to give effect to the rights conferred by Article 17 of the Statute.

23. The Chamber also finds, that at that time of the interview, the Registrar had given effect to Article 17 of the Statute by assigning legal assistance to Nchamihigo, for which he would not have had to pay. Mr. Koné confessed lack of knowledge; not only of the appointment of Mr. Kirita, but also that the system of appointing duty counsel existed. It is difficult for the Chamber to understand this ignorance at the commencement and

[36] T. 15 January 2007, p. 39.

[37] *The Prosecutor v. Théoneste Bagosora ee al,* Case No. ICTR-98-41-T, Decision on the Prosecutor's Motion for the Admission of Certain Materials under Rule 89 (C) (TC), 14 October 2004, para. 19

[38] T. 15 January 2007, p. 40.

[39] T. 15 January 2007, p. 32.

during the two days of the interview process. Even if it is true that the official team representing the Prosecutor at the interview process was ignorant of this, the Chamber must reject the argument that such knowledge should be imputed to the Accused because of the nature of his previous employment.

24. The Chamber considers that no waiver of the right to counsel could be voluntary **[page 7]** unless the suspect knew of the right to which he is entitled.[40] The Chamber is satisfied that Nchaimhigo was not informed by Mr. Koné that a duty counsel was appointed to represent him and was available to him during the questioning. In those circumstances, the Chamber finds that the Prosecutor has not shown that Nchamihigo voluntarily waived his right to counsel and that Mr. Koné should not have proceeded with his questioning. This constitutes a violation of Rule 42 of the Rules.

25. The Chamber also notes that certain provisions of Rule 43 were not carefully implemented. However, the Chamber considers that the violation of Nchamihigo's right to be assisted by counsel during his questioning as a suspect is a sufficient basis for the exercise of its discretion not to allow the Statement of the Accused following that questioning into evidence and does not propose to examine the Rule 43 issues in any further detail.[41]

FOR THOSE REASONS, THE CHAMBER

I. REJECTS the Defence Motion to decide whether to conduct a *voir dire* hearing;

II. REJECTS the Prosecutor's Motion to admit into evidence the transcript of the Accused's interview recorded on 25 and 26 May 2001.

Arusha, 5 February 2007, done in English.

Dennis C. M. Byron Presiding Judge	Gberdao Gustave Kam Judge	Vagn Joensen Judge

[Seal of the Tribunal]

40 *Miranda* p. 475 (right to counsel must be "knowingly and intelligently waived); *R. v. Cullen* 1992 NZLR LEXIS 689 (CA) (*"Cullen"*) p. 10 ("[t]he purpose of making the suspect aware of his rights is so that he may make a decision whether to exercise them and plainly he cannot do that if he does not understand what those rights are"); *R v. Evans* [19911 1 SCR 869 (*"Evans"*), p. 891 ("[A] person who does not understand his or her right cannot be expected to assert it").

41 *Cullen* p. 10 ("[t]the fundamental rights conferred or confirmed by the New Zealand Bill of Rights Act 1990 are not to be regarded as satisfied simply by some incantation which a detainee may not understand. The purpose of making the suspect aware of his rights is so that he make a decision whether to exercise them and plainly he cannot do that if he does not understand what those rights are"); *S v. Melani and others* 1995 SACLR LEXIS 290 pp. 47-48 (Sup. Ct., Eastern Cape) ("[i]n order to give effect to an accused's right in terms of section 25 (l)(c) he or she must be informed of his or her right to consult in manner that it can reasonably he supposed that he or she has understood the content of that right").

Commentary

1. Rights of the suspect during questioning and the rules on recording interrogations

Some of the decisions of the ICTR deal with the fundamental issue of the rights of suspects when interrogated by the inquiring authorities (police and prosecutor). In particular, there are three issues examined by ICTR Trial Chambers. The first concerns the moment from when a person must be considered and treated as suspect[1]. The second deals with the notices that a suspect is entitled to receive, before the beginning of police or prosecutor interrogation.

The third relates to the form in which police and prosecutor must report the operations conducted during the questioning or interrogation. Must they be reported in a written formal way (the French call this a "*procès verbal*", an official police or prosecutor record), or are other forms allowed (for example, the testimony of the police officer who conducted, or attended to the questioning)? Assuming that the preference is given to the written report, what is the consequence when an official record is lacking: must the statements gathered during the questioning be declared inadmissible, or can they be admitted nonetheless, where there are sufficient indicia of their reliability?

If we look at the heart of the matter, all the issues presented in these introductory comments focus on the level at which safeguards for a suspect must be recognised and protected during the investigation phase. The question concerning the moment from when a person must be treated as a suspect represents a traditional critical feature in any criminal investigation. In theory, there are two methods applicable to solve the issue; one of a formal nature and the other of a substantial one. In the first option, a person is considered a suspect only when some investigating or judicial authority – the police, the prosecutor of the investigating judge – formally attributes to him such a status.

With the second method, every person must be treated as a suspect from the first moment in which he is considered as such by the inquiring authorities, regardless whether he was formally defined as such in the official investigation. The positive aspect of the formal solution consists in its certainty, because it is clear when a person becomes a suspect and is entitled to rights as such. However, the negative aspects of this option appear overwhelming. There are risks of mistakes, due to the negligence or the malice of the inquiring authorities. In other words, it could be possible for the police or the prosecutor to perform some act without formally attributing to the person concerned the status of a suspect, in so doing denying his fundamental right and safeguards (for example, the right to be informed of being a suspect, or to consult or be assisted by a counsel). In practice, this happens when the police or the prosecutor question a person making him believe he is a witness, while he is in fact already considered a suspect by them.

Another area in which this issue is relevant is represented by the undercover operations,[2] and by the admissibility of evidence gathered by the police during such operations (such as conversations recording made by undercover agents, or the possibility for police officers to testify as to conversations in which they took part in disguise).

These concerns – involving the risk of some inacceptable abuse being committed by the police or the prosecutor – make the second option preferable. According to this approach, a person is entitled to the rights and safeguards of the suspect, from the first moment in which some indication of criminal responsibility emerges in the course of the investigation against him. In critical cases, judicial authorities – such as pre-trial judges, or trial and appeal chambers – must verify, whether a person had already to be considered as being involved in the facts under investigation, when a certain act was performed. In case of positive answer, if that

---

1 Related issues pertaining to a suspect are dealt with by ICTR, Decision on the Prosecutor's Application to Admit into Evidence the Transcript of the Accused's Interview as a Suspect and the Defense's Request to hold a *Voir Dire, Prosecutor v. Nchamihigo*, Case No. ICTR-2001-63-T, T. Ch. III, 5 February 2007, in this volume, p. 205; ICTR, Decision on the *Voir Dire* Hearing of the Accused's *Curriculum Vitae, Prosecutor v. Zigiranyirazo*, Case No. ICTR-2001-73-T, T. Ch. III, 29 November 2006, in this volume, p. 163.

2 See, on this issue, two interesting articles by Jaqueline E. Ross: Impediments to Transnational Cooperation in Undercover Policing: A Comparative Study of the United States and Italy, 52 American Journal of Comparative Law 2005, p. 303-358; Undercover Policing and the Shifting Terms of Scholarly Debate: The United States and Europe in Counterpoint, 4 Annual Review of Law and Social Science 2008, p. 239–273.

person was treated as a potential witness – in other words, if he was not considered and treated as a suspect – the evidence obtained must be struck out and cannot be used in any way.

The negative aspects of this method follow from its uncertainty. It may be difficult to establish if the police or prosecutor, in executing a certain act, should have treated a person as a suspect, and therefore unjustly denied him the rights and safeguards he was entitled to. However, the high goals associated with the second (substantial) method, oriented as they are to protect the rights and safeguards of the accused throughout the entire criminal proceedings, make it far preferable to the first (formal) one. A practical consequence of the substantial approach, therefore, is that judges will be called in many cases to verify if the police and prosecutor were diligent (and, *a fortiori*, correct) during the investigation phase.

In general, the *ad hoc* international tribunals have traditionally preferred the option endorsed in this commentary, because it is more consistent with the "full respect for the rights of the accused" prescribed by Article 20, paragraph 1, of ICTY Statute and Article 19, paragraph 1, of ICTR Statute respectively. For example, in the Celebici Case, an ICTY Trial Chamber excluded a statement obtained by the Austrian authorities from one of the suspects, Zdravko Mucić, because he had not been interrogated in a way that respected all of the safeguards provided for by the ICTY Statute.[3] At the moment of the interrogation conducted by Austrian police, Mucić could not formally be considered a suspect entitled to the relevant ICTY rights (even though he had been arrested under an order issued by ICTY judicial authorities): in fact, the interrogation had been conducted by Austrian police on their own initiative, and not pursuant to a request by the ICTY Office of the Prosecutor. [4]

Despite this consideration, the Trial Chamber preferred to declare the statements given by him to the Austrian police as inadmissible, because of the disregard of certain safeguards to which Mucić would have been entitled if he had been interrogated by the ICTY inquiring authorities (in particular, the right to have counsel present during the interrogation). In other words, the admission of the "Austrian statements" would have endangered the fairness of the proceedings as a whole and for this reason, they had to be excluded, as provided for by Rule 95 ICTY.

The same approach is applied in the Zigiranyirazo Decision dated 29 November 2006, in which Zigiranyirazo had been invited to provide his *curriculum vitae* to the Office of the Prosecutor of the ICTR, at a time where he would have been considered as a suspect, had the OTP representatives been diligent. For the reasons expressed above, the decision appears not only consistent with the substantial approach, but also fair considering the merits of the case. The Zigiranyirazo decision in fact shows how, if the police or prosecutor do not pay due attention to applying a suspect's safeguards from the first moment in which indications of criminal responsibility emerge against him, the suspect's right to silence may be violated. In other words, there is a danger that the suspect will be induced to render self-incriminating declarations, being unaware of his right to remain silent.

Another issue considered in these decisions[5] concerns the forms to be followed by the police and the prosecutor, during interrogation of suspects. This issue is somewhat twofold. First, it deals with the way of recording the suspect's questioning and interrogation; secondly, it concerns the conditions under which the suspect's waiver of the right to counsel can be accepted as valid under the *ad hoc* tribunal standards.

---

[3] See ICTY, Decision on Zdravko Mucić's Motion for the Exclusion of Evidence, *Prosecutor v. Mucić*, Case No. IT-96-21 -T, T. Ch. II*quater*, 2 September 1997, Klip/ Sluiter, ALC-I-227. The issue was, moreover, dealt with in a trial judgment: see ICTY, Judgement, *Prosecutor v. Delalić, Mucić, Delić and Landžo*, Case No. IT-96-21-T, T. Ch. II*quater*, 16 November 1998, Klip/ Sluiter, ALC-III-363, par. 63. The suspect had been interrogated by Austrian Police, once arrested, as a consequence of an arrest warrant by the ICTY, on 18 March 1996. In the following days (19, 29 and 21 March 1996), he had been questioned by Office of the Prosecutor representatives. On the decisions adopted in the mentioned case, see P. Viseur Sellers, Rule 89 (C) and (D): At Odds or Overlapping with Rule 96 and Rule 95?, in R. May et al. (eds.), Essays on ICTY Procedure and Evidence in Honour of Gabrielle Kirk McDonald, Kluwer Law International, 2001, p. 288-290.

[4] This assertion is confirmed considering that, after his arrest, Mucić was questioned firstly by Austrian authorities, and in the immediately following days, by the Prosecutor of the ICTY. The second interrogation would have not taken place, at least not so soon, if the Austrian authorities had acted with the sole purpose of complying with the ICTY Prosecutor's request.

[5] See Decision on the Prosecutor's Application to Admit into Evidence the Transcript of the Accused's Interview as a Suspect and the Defense's Request to hold a *Voir Dire, Prosecutor v. Nchamihigo*, T. Ch. III, *supra* note 1.

The question of the forms is more important than appears at first glance. One could, in fact, be tempted to observe that the relevant matters are not the forms followed by the enforcement agencies in reporting the operations conducted during interrogations; but rather to ascertain if the person involved was questioned in a manner respecting his rights provided for by law. With this in mind, it could seem excessive to prescribe that only the respect of the specific technicalities relating to the reporting of statements gathered during interrogations by the police and the prosecutor would be sufficient to verify how the suspect was treated. It could therefore appear the same to prove the issue via official record (the French "*procès verbal*"), or via the testimony of the officer who took the statement.

At a deeper analysis, however, things may appear differently. If we look at the reasons underpinning the duty for the police and the prosecutor to write an official record, it emerges that these forms make it more difficult to disregard the rights and safeguards of the persons involved in the interrogation. The record must report the warning given by enforcement authorities to the suspect; it must mention the questions asked and the answers obtained; it must outline the date and time of the operation's commencement, as well as its ending. Finally, it must be signed by the persons who took part in the interrogations.

Sometimes, in national provisions, the official written record must be followed by a video or audio recording, when the operation conducted regards the interrogation of the suspect (or accused). Moreover, the only way to produce the suspect/accused statements collected during investigation by the police and the prosecutor (or by the investigating magistrate) at trial is through the admission as evidence of the written record as such. In other words, in those systems that are, in general, entrenched in the civil law continental family, police testimony on statements given by the accused during investigation is prohibited, because, as already pointed out, a suspect's statements can be used at trial only through the official record in which they are reported. In a nutshell, the official record solution constitutes a sort of *preuve légal* concerning statements given by the suspect or the accused before trial.

These considerations show why the adoption of the official record method is preferable to the free assessment of evidence approach. In spite of the right to cross examination, which undoubtedly constitutes a most useful tool to discover the truth,[6] if it was permitted for those who took part in the suspect interrogation simply to testify on the declarations obtained, it might be too much of a risk that bad practices were inadvertently ignored and would therefore remain unpunished.

Moreover, a reason to opt for the adoption of rigorous forms to record and report statements given by the suspect is because the ICTR legal texts provide for strict prescriptions on the matter. Rule 43 ICTR RPE, specifies certain specific forms to follow during and after questioning: among them, it is worthy to recall the duty of the police and the prosecutor to audio or video record the interrogation (and to make the suspect aware of this), the duty to mention any interruption of the questioning in case of a break, the duty to transcribe the contents of the recording promptly after the conclusion of questioning, and to supply a copy of the transcript to the suspect; finally, the obligation to seal the original recorded tape in the presence of the suspect with the signature of the prosecutor and the suspect.

Even if it is not specified that a violation of the forms specified in Rule 43 must lead to the exclusion of the evidence obtained, due to the large discretion left to the judges by Rule 95 ICTR RPE, it may be asserted that disregard of these requirements gives rise at least to a presumption of the inadmissibility of the statements gathered. It is therefore up to the prosecutor presenting as evidence such statements to prove that, notwithstanding the absence of the formal requirements provided for by Rule 43, all the warnings and safeguards were fully respected in the course of the interrogation.

The approach of Trial Chamber in the Nchamihigo decision seems consistent with this interpretation of the issue. In fact, notwithstanding that the interview of the suspect was not duly recorded according to Rule 43, the omission did not automatically lead to the exclusion of evidence. However, the prosecutor had to prove that all the rights of the person involved in the questioning were completely respected. The inability to prove

---

6 Citing the most famous consideration of John Henry Wigmore: "Cross-examination is the greatest legal engine ever invented for the discovery of truth. You can do anything with a bayonet except sit on it. A lawyer can do anything with cross-examination if he is skillful enough not the impale his own cause upon it.": J. H. Wigmore, Evidence in Trials at Common Law, 3d ed., Boston: Little, Brown, 1940, § 1367. The assertion was reported successively in California v. Green, 399 U.S. 149, 158 (1970).

this with regard to the right to have counsel without charge, lead to the evidence being struck out at the trial.

What could be suggested, as a result of this decision, is that the recording prescribed by Rule 43 starts slightly before the proper questioning, beginning at the moment at which the suspect receives the warning provided for by Rule 42 ICTR RPE.[7] Otherwise, the obligation to record the interview would risk losing its effectiveness, having the aim to ensure that the police and the prosecutor made the suspect plainly aware of his rights and safeguards before the start of the interrogation. Specifically, the audio or video recording of the warnings provided for by Rule 42 should take place when the suspect is not formally summoned in writing, and before he is interrogated.

2. Exculpatory evidence

The Nahimana decision[8] deals, among other issues, with the exculpatory evidence disclosure by the prosecutor. It appears to be consistent with the precedents of ICTY and ICTR on the matter. As previously stressed by the *ad hoc* tribunals, the disclosure of exculpatory evidence is divided in two phases. In the first, the decision is on one party – the prosecutor – who decides autonomously what can be considered exculpatory and, as such, is to be communicated to the accused. The prosecutor is presumed to fulfil its duties correctly.

In the second phase, the defence seems authorised to apply for an additional disclosure. In such a case, when a motion for additional disclosure is raised by the defence, the burden of proof is on the applicant, who must prove a "legitimate forensic purpose"[9] (or a *prima facie* case, as defined in other decisions, such as the current one). This choice has been criticised by some scholars.

With this standard – legitimate forensic purpose or *prima facie* case – ICTY and ICTR judges seek to point out that the applicant must demonstrate that the evidence in the hands of the counterpart is relevant for the preparation of the case, or at least that is likely to be; moreover, the applicant should specify with some precision the evidence requested for additional disclosure, it not being sufficient to make a mere assertion that the other party did not comply with its disclosure duties. Such a demonstration is quite problematic for the defence and in most cases impossible, since the material gathered by the prosecutor is secret, and not

---

7 Rule 42: "Rights of Suspects during Investigation. (A) A suspect who is to be questioned by the Prosecutor shall have the following rights, of which he shall be informed by the Prosecutor prior to questioning, in a language he speaks and understands: (i) The right to be assisted by counsel of his choice or to have legal assistance assigned to him without payment if he does not have sufficient means to pay for it; (ii) The right to have the free assistance of an interpreter if he cannot understand or speak the language to be used for questioning; and (iii) The right to remain silent, and to be cautioned that any statement he makes shall be recorded and may be used in evidence. (B) Questioning of a suspect shall not proceed without the presence of counsel unless the suspect has voluntarily waived his right to counsel. In case of waiver, if the suspect subsequently expresses a desire to have counsel, questioning shall thereupon cease, and shall only resume when the suspect has obtained or has been assigned counsel". See on this issue ICTY, Decision on Bajrush Morina's request for a declaration of inadmissibility and exclusion of evidence, *Prosecutor v. Haraqija and Morina*, Case No. IT-04-84-R77.4, T. Ch. I, 28 August 2008; ICTY, Decision on Lukić request for reconsideration of the trial chamber's admission into evidence of his interview with the Prosecution (Exhibit P948), *Prosecutor v. Milutinović et al.*, Case No. IT-05-87-T, T. Ch. III, 22 May 2008. See also ICTR, Decision on Kanyabashi's Oral Motion to Cross-Examine Ntahobali Using Ntahobali's Statements to Prosecution Investigators in July 1997, *Prosecutor v. Ndayambaje* (Case No. ICTR-96-8-T), *Prosecutor v. Kanyabashi* (Case No. ICTR-96-15-T), *Prosecutor v. Nyiramasuhuko and Ntahobali* (Case No. ICTR-97-21-T) and *Prosecutor v. Nsabimana and Nteziryayo* (Case No. ICTR-97-29-T), Joint Case No. ICTR-98-42-T, T. Ch. II, 15 May 2006, Klip/ Sluiter, ALC-XXIV-95.

8 Decision on Appellant Jean-Bosco Barayagwiza's Motions for Leave to Present Additional Evidence Pursuant to Rule 115 of the Rules of Procedure and Evidence, *Prosecutor v. Nahimana, Barayagwiza and Ngeze*, Case No. ICTR-99-52-A, A. Ch., 8 December 2006, in this volume, p. 167.

9 See on this issue ICTY, Decision on Kolundzija Defence Request to Compel Disclosure of Exculpatory Evidence, *Prosecutor v. Sikirica, Dosen and Kolundzija*, Case No. IT-95-8.T, T.Ch. III, 31 August 2001, par. 2: "[the] defence applied to obtain from the Trial Chamber an order for the Prosecutor to disclose exculpatory evidence, in addition to the elements already communicated. The Prosecutor objected that the Trial Chamber could have granted such a motion only if the defence had proved the occurrence of a *legitimate forensic purpose*. The Trial Chamber agreed with the objection of the Prosecutor and denied the motion of the defence. In the opinion of the judges, if a motion of the defence for additional disclosure was granted under a standard less severe than that adopted in the mentioned case – for example, when the exculpatory nature of an evidence would appear merely possible, the discretion recognised by the system to the Prosecutor in the disclosure phase would have been unreasonably overcome." For a criticism of these arguments, see G. McIntyre, Equality of Arms – Defining Human Rights in the Jurisprudence of the International Criminal Tribunal for the Former Yugoslavia, Leiden Journal of International Law 2003, p. 297. See also R. May – M. Wierda, International Criminal Evidence, Transnational Publishers, New York, p. 77.

accessible to the defence. In addition, it must be noted that the Office of the Prosecutor has at its disposal a huge amount of information concerning a general situation, from which the specific charges against the accused were subsequently selected: this means that some elements are probably set apart by the prosecutor, even though they could be favourable to the accused, if examined from a different perspective.

In practice, the effect of the "*prima facie* case" standard gives rise to the risk that the prosecutorial discretion on the issue of disclosure of exculpatory evidence can be very rarely challenged. This may represent a *vulnus* for the equality of arms principle, which should primarily attribute to the litigants the same chances to prove their case successfully at trial.[10]

Moreover, the system does not appear to adequately sanction the failure of the prosecutor to disclose exculpatory evidence; in general, the judges prefer to opt for a mere postponement of the case, so as to give to the defence sufficient time to prepare its case. In other words, exclusion of evidence or discontinuance of the prosecution are very rarely ordered, in circumstances where there has been a violation of disclosure provisions.[11]

3. Additional Evidence Pursuant to Rule 115 of the Rules of Procedure and Evidence

Two decisions deal with the issue of the admission of additional evidence at the appeal stage.[12] We may conclude that, at the present time, the jurisprudence on this matter has long been constant. [13] The framework

---

[10] "Equality of arms" represents a principle defined in many different, and sometimes incompatible, ways. For a general overview on the various definitions of the principle, see S. Negri, The Principle of "Equality of Arms" and the Evolving Law of International Criminal Procedure, 5 International Criminal Law Review 2005, p. 513–571; G. J. A. Knoops, The Dichotomy between Judicial Economy and Equality of Arms within International and Internationalized Criminal Trials: A Defense Perspective, 28 Fordham International Law Journal 2005, p. 1567-1570. For a reconstruction of the equality of arms principle before international criminal tribunals, see S. Zappalà, The Rights of the Accused, in A. Cassese, P. Gaeta, and J.R.W.D. Jones (eds), The Rome Statute, cit., note 1, vol. II, p. 1328-1333. See also G. McIntyre, *supra* note 9.

[11] In February 2009, a Trial Chamber of ICTR affirmed that "Exclusion of evidence is a remedy which is at the extreme end of a scale of measures available to the Chamber in addressing the prejudice caused to an accused. An accused must demonstrate that he has suffered a degree of prejudice that would justify the extreme remedy of excluding the witnesses' testimony. According to the Appeals Chamber in this case, there can be no conviction of an accused on the basis of facts not charged in the indictment but only introduced by testimonies. Nevertheless, although an allegation may not have been specifically pleaded, this does not in itself render such evidence inadmissible because it may be relevant to the proof of any other allegation pleaded in the indictment" (ICTR, Decision on Alphonse Nteziryayo's motion for exclusion of evidence, *Prosecutor v. Nteziryayo*, Case No. ICTR-97-29-T – *Joint Case No. ICTR 98 42-T*, T. Ch. II, 25 February 2009, par. 26-27). From these words, it is easy to draw the conclusion that the application of procedural sanctions for violation of disclosure provisions is considered highly discretionary. Sometimes, sanctions are at least threatened, even if not applied. See ICTR, Oral decision relating to the late disclosure regarding witness T, *Prosecutor v. Karemera, Ngirumpatse, Nzirorera*, Case No. ICTR-98-44-T, T. Ch. III, 24 May 2006, in which Trial Chamber warned the Prosecutor: "The Defence has asked for disclosure concerning Witness T on several occasions. The request was renewed during this trial session. The Prosecution reiterated that the disclosure was complete. Now, in the middle of the examination-in-chief of Witness T by video link, in a strict time schedule, the Prosecution states that, upon further investigation, it realised that disclosure was not, in fact, complete. The Prosecution should have been diligent in each of the prior requests to ensure that its obligation to disclose as mandated by the rules was properly discharged. This behavior, in the context of this case where the Chamber noted on several occasions the Prosecution's lack of diligence in disclosure matters, is completely unacceptable. This obstructs the proceedings and is contrary to the interests of justice. Accordingly, the Chamber now imposes a warning pursuant to Rule 46(A) so that, if this behavior continues, the Chamber will have the option to impose sanctions". The tendency to merely postpone the trial – refusing to exclude evidence or to order the discontinuance of the case – appears to be followed by the ICC in its early decisions (even of this assertion may be considered arguable under some aspects). See ICC Trial Chamber I, Decision on the Consequences of Non-Disclosure of Exculpatory Materials Covered by Article 54(3)(e) Agreements and the application to stay the prosecution of the accused, together with certain other issues raised at the Status Conference on 10 June 2008, *Prosecutor v. Dyilo*, ICC-01/04-01/06-1401-13-06-2008; ICC Trial Chamber I, Decision on the Release of Mr. Thomas Lubanga Dyilo, *Prosecutor v. Dyilo*, ICC-01/04-01/06-1418-02-07-2008.

[12] ICTR, Decision on Appellant Jean-Bosco Barayagwiza's Motions for Leave to Present Additional Evidence Pursuant to Rule 115 of the Rules of Procedure and Evidence, *Prosecutor v. Nahimana, Barayagwiza and Ngeze*, A. Ch., *supra* note 8; Décision sur la Requête de Ferdinand Nahimana aux fins de Traduction d'enregistrements d'émissions RTLM contenus dans la pièce à conviction C7, *Nahimana, Barayagwiza, Ngeze c. Procureur,* Aff. No. ICTR-99-52-A, A. Ch., 20 Novembre 2006.

[13] See, for example, the case law referred to in Y. M. O. Featherstone, Additional Evidence in the Appeals Proceedings and Review of Final Judgment, in R. May (ed.), Essays on ICTY Procedure and Evidence in Honour of Gabriella Kirk McDonald, Kluwer International, 2001, p. 501. See also ICTY, Decision on the Motions of Drago Josipović, Zoran Kupreškić and Vlatko Kupreškić to Admit Additional Evidence Pursuant to Rule 115 and for Judicial Notice to be Taken Pursuant to Rule 94(B), *Prosecutor v. Kupreškić, Kupreškić, Kupreškić, Josipović and Šantić* Case No. IT-95-16-A, A. Ch., 8 May 2001, Klip/ Sluiter, ALC-VII-135, par. 7 and 10. In this decision, the Appeal Court stressed that the defendant "must put forward its best case in the first instance". It follows that the defendant cannot produce for the first time at the appeal stage evidence he should have presented at trial, if he had been diligent. See the considerations raised by M. Kleijn Hesselink, Commentary, in Klip/ Sluiter, ALC-VII-190. Finally, on the same line of reasoning,

emerging from the decisions involving new evidence in an appeal illustrates a system in which an appeal is not an instrument to remedy to negligent conduct of the parties at trial. Consistent with the adversarial style adopted at trial, and to the orality principle preferred by the system, the parties have one chance to state their case: this is at the trial.

An appeal is essentially a stage to remedy to procedural errors – if these undermine the fairness of the proceedings as a whole – or substantial errors, if without them, the outcome of the proceedings could have been different. An appeal is meant to avoid miscarriages of justice and to control the fairness of the proceeding in its entirety. This is why evidentiary requests at the appeal stage are generally declared inadmissible.

Moreover, it must be noted that, according to Rule 72 ICTR RPE, trial decisions concerning the admission of evidence may be subject to interlocutory appeal, on condition of leave of the Trial Chamber. A party contesting a ruling on evidence made by the Trial Chamber must therefore diligently ask for leave to appeal asserting that the interlocutory appeal "would significantly affect the fair and expeditious conduct of the proceedings or the outcome of the trial", or that "an immediate resolution by the Appeals Chamber may materially advance the proceedings".

As a consequence, a party failing to make use of all the remedies ordinarily consented by the system to protect its rights cannot complain, when it has been shown not to be adequately diligent in presenting its case at the trial. Under a different perspective, if evidence is not admitted at trial, notwithstanding the requesting party having already sought an interlocutory appeal, it is extremely difficult that it would be admitted at the appeal stage, according to Rule 155 ICTR RPE. Such admission, in fact, could be perceived as a sort of *bis in idem*, having the Appeal Chamber already pronounced on the matter. In conclusion, orality and adversariality imply that the parties typically have one opportunity, and they have to use it well, to achieve their goals. There are exceptions, but only to avoid miscarriages of justice, or when the fairness of the proceedings as a whole could be endangered by denying the admission of new evidence at the appeal stage.

4. Judicial notice

The Karemera decision on judicial notice represents a sort of *summa* on the matter. Like for the admission of additional evidence at the appeal stage, with regard to judicial notice, the case law also appears to have been consolidated for years.[14] Rule 94 ICTR RPE is conceived primarily to enhance judicial economy. In particular, judicial notice should help judges and the parties to prove the contextual features of the indictment, which could otherwise require an intolerably long period, if they had to be proved through witness evidence at the trial.

Rule 94 ICTR RPE contains two different provisions. According to subparagraph (A), "A Trial Chamber shall not require proof of facts of common knowledge but shall take judicial notice thereof". This could perhaps be considered superfluous, since in any procedural system, resources must not be spent *inutiliter*. The main problem, however, is that, at least at the earlier work of the *ad hoc* tribunals, it was difficult to apply Rule 94 (A), due to the lack of familiarity of the judges with the contextual features of the people and the land on which they were called to apply the law.

In other words, international judges have more problems than national judges to attain a comprehensive understanding of the historical, social, cultural background that is necessary to fix the facts in their proper dimension. To remedy to this lack of a common shared knowledge among the judges and the parties, Rule 94 (B) was introduced in 1998 in the ICTY, and November 2000 in the ICTR, according to which "At the request

see ICTY, Judgement, *Prosecutor v. Delalić, Mucić, Delić and Landžo*, Case No. IT-96-21-A, A. Ch., 20 February 2001, Klip/ Sluiter, ALC-V-369, (*"Celebici" Appeal Judgment*), par. 283.

[14] See ICTY, Decision on Prosecution Motions for Judicial Notice of Adjudicated Facts and for the Admission of Written Statements of Witnesses Pursuant to Rule 92*bis*, *Prosecutor v. Krajišnik*, Case No. IT-00-39, T. Ch. I, 28 February 2003, par. 15. On the same line of interpretation, see Decision on Prosecution's Motion for Judicial Notice of Adjudicated Facts and Documentary Evidence, *Prosecutor v. Blagojevic*, Case No. IT-02-60, T. Ch. I-A, 19 December 2003, par. 15-18; ICTY, Decision on Judicial Notice of Adjudicated Facts Following the Motion Submitted by Counsel for the Accused Hadzihasanovic and Kubura on 20 January 2005, *Prosecutor v. Hadžihasanović and Kubura*, Case No. IT-01-47-T, T. Ch. II, 14 April 2005; ICTY, Decision on Prosecution Motion for Judicial Notice of Adjudicated Facts, *Prosecutor v. Popović*, Case No. IT-05-88-T, T. Ch. II, 26 September 2006, to be published in volume XXX, par. 5-21. See my commentary in Klip/ Sluiter, ALC-XVIII-177.

of a party or *proprio motu*, a Trial Chamber, after hearing the parties, may decide to take judicial notice of adjudicated facts or documentary evidence from other proceedings of the Tribunal relating to matters at issue in the current proceedings".

Despite some interpretative problems, undoubtedly the provision has given efficacy to the system, permitting the parties to prove more easily the contextual framework of their case in a shorter time they would have required if Rule 94 (B) had not been introduced. However, judicial notice, in the *ad hoc* tribunals' jurisprudence, could not be used to prove the core of the indictment, which is constituted by acts and conduct of the accused.

As for Rule 92 *bis*, documentary evidence can be admitted, in spite of other oral evidence, only if relating to contextual aspect of the case. When the specific behaviour of the defendant is at stake, hearsay exceptions are not admitted (or, at any rate, the defendant must have the opportunity to cross examine crucial witnesses regarding his case).[15] The critical point is represented by acts and conduct of persons close to the defendant involved in the same event. For example, if the defendant is charged with a Joint Criminal Enterprise (JCE),[16] can the acts and conduct of other participants to the JCE be proven via judicial notice, or must they be proven orally at trial?

In theory, whenever the evidence seems crucial for the decision on guilt or innocence, cross examination should be allowed. However, the concept of "crucial evidence" is sometimes quite uncertain, and left to the discretion of the judges. From Rule 94 emerge traditional problems related to the administration of international criminal justice: to achieve a fair outcome within a reasonable time. If the adoption of an oral method, without exceptions, could be considered in theory the optimum, this does not represent a suitable solution.[17] The adoption of the "crucial evidence doctrine" – and the correlative distinction between acts and

---

15 With regard to the concept of "crucial evidence", see ICTY, Decision on defendant ante Gotovina's Motion for admission of evidence of one witness pursuant to Rule 92 bis, *Prosecutor v. Gotovina, Čermak and Markač,* Case No. IT-06-90-T, T. Ch. I, 16 September 2009; ICTY, Decision on Prosecution's motion for admission of evidence of witness Milan Daković pursuant to Rule 92 ter, *Prosecutor v. Dordević,* Case No. IT-05-87/1-T, T. Ch. II, 13 August 2009; ICTY, Decision on Prosecution's Rule 92 bis motion, *Prosecutor v. Milutinović and others*, Case No. IT-05-87-PT, T. Ch. III, 4 July 2006. See also ICTY, Decision on Prosecution motion for admission of testimony of witness KDZ198 and associated exhibits pursuant to Rule 92 *quater*, *Prosecutor v. Karadžić*, Case No. IT-95-5/18-PT, T. Ch. III, 20 August, 2009. In this case, the evidence requested by the prosecutor was admitted since the witness had been already cross examined, in a separate proceeding, by another defendant in a position similar to the Karadžić's one.

16 The JCE represents an essential feature of *ad hoc* international tribunals jurisprudence. On this concept, see C. Del Ponte, Investigation and Prosecution of Large-scale Crimes at the International Level, cit., p. 549-551; G. P. Fletcher – J. D. Ohlin, Reclaiming Fundamental Principles of Criminal Law in the Darfur Case, Journal of International Criminal Justice 2005, p. 548-550. These Authors observed that "Joint criminal enterprise represents a broad theory of complicity. It permits the prosecution of one individual for the crime of a second individual, even if the first did not have the intention of aiding the second and even if the first is unaware of the second's existence [...] The doctrine of joint criminal enterprise is the law of conspiracy dressed up in the jargon of modern economic activity. Joint enterprises were thought to be the Communist path to economic collaboration with the West. Now the West has appropriated the term and its prestige to impose a dubious form of criminal liability" (p. 548). With regard to an application of Rule 92 bis in a case of Joint Criminal Enterprise, see ICTY, Decision on Prosecution's Motion for the Admission of Written Evidence Pursuant to Rule 92 bis of the Rules, *Prosecutor v. Martic*, Case No. IT-95-11-T, T.Ch. I, 16 January 2006, par. 6-9: "proximity *to the accused of the acts and conduct described in the written evidence is relevant to the exercise of the Trial Chamber's discretion in deciding whether the evidence should be admitted in written form at all*" (italics in the text). In 2007, the Journal of International Criminal Justice (vol. 5. no. 1) dedicated an entire issue to JCE. See, among the most relevant contributions, A. Cassese, The Proper Limits of Individual Responsibility under the Doctrine of Joint Criminal Enterprise, p. 109; J. D. Ohlin, Three Conceptual Problems with the Doctrine of Joint Criminal Enterprise, p. 69; K. Gustafson, The Requirement of an "Express Agreement" for Joint Criminal Enterprise Liability, p. 135; E. van Sliedregt, Joint Criminal Enterprise as a Pathway to Convicting Individuals for Genocide, p. 135; K. Ambos, Joint Criminal Enterprise and Command Responsibility, p. 159.

17 See, on this issue, the so-called "Expert's Report", namely "Report of the Expert Group to Conduct a Review of the Effective Operation and Functioning of the International Criminal Tribunal for the Former Yugoslavia and the International Criminal Tribunal for Rwanda", UN Doc. A/54/634 (1999). See also D. A. Mundis, Improving the Operation and Functioning of the International Criminal Tribunals, 94 American Journal of International Law 2000, p. 759. On the amendments to ICTY and ICTR RPE introduced after the Report of Expert Group, see G. Boas, Creating Laws of Evidence for the International Criminal Law: the ICTY and the Principle of Flexibility, 12 Criminal Law Forum 2001, p. 74; G. Boas, Developments in the Law of Procedure and Evidence at the International Criminal Tribunal for the Former Yugoslavia and the International Criminal Court, 12 Criminal Law Forum 2001, p. 174-176; P. L. Robinson, Ensuring Fair and Expeditious Trials at the International Criminal Tribunal for the Former Yugoslavia, 11 European Journal of International Law 2000, p. 575-582; S. Kay, The Move from Oral Evidence to Written Evidence, 2 International Criminal Justice 2004, p. 495.; K. R. Gray, Evidence before the International Criminal Court, in D. McGoldrick, P. Rowe, E. Donnelly, The Permanent International Criminal Court. Legal and Policy Issues, Hart Publishing 2004, p. 289.

conduct of the accused, on one hand, and the contextual feature, on the other - permitted a fair balance of the need to protect the accused's safeguards with the aim of reaching an end of the trial in a reasonable time.

In fact, if regarding the proof of contextual features, the prosecutor could introduce evidence unilaterally formed before trial, which pertains to acts and conduct of the accused, or at any rate when crucial evidence was at stake, the two counterparts can be considered almost entirely on the same level, at least as far as equality seems achievable at the international criminal level. For this reason, judicial notice, as well as the theoretical division between the core of the indictment (the defendants acts and conduct) and contextual features, in spite of some criticisms, can still be considered positively, representing a solution in which the accused is put in the less unequal position, compared to that of the prosecutor. In other words, it seems the only possible way to assure equality of arms in international criminal trials.

Michele Caianiello

Tribunal Pénal International pour le Rwanda
International Criminal Tribunal for Rwanda

IN THE APPEALS CHAMBER

Before:	**Judge Fausto Pocar, Presiding** **Judge Mohamed Shahabuddeen** **Judge Mehmet Güney** **Judge Liu Daqun** **Judge Theodor Meron**
Registrar:	**Mr. Adama Dieng**
Decision of:	**30 October 2006**

Protais ZIGIRANYIRAZO

v.

The Prosecutor

Case No. ICTR-2001-73-AR73

Decision on Interlocutory Appeal

Office of the Prosecutor:

Mr. Hassan Bubacar Jallow
Mr. Wallace Kapaya
Mr. Neville Weston
Ms. Charity Kagwi-Ndungu
Mr. Abdoulaye Seye

Counsel for the Defence:

Mr. John Philpot
Mr. Peter Zaduk

[page 1] 1. The Appeals Chamber of the International Criminal Tribunal for the Prosecution of Persons Responsible for Genocide and Other Serious Violations of International Humanitarian Law Committed in the Territory of Rwanda and Rwandan Citizens Responsible for Genocide and Other Serious Violations Committed in the Territory of Neighboring States, between 1 January and 31 December 1994 ("Appeals Chamber" and "Tribunal", respectively) is seized of an interlocutory appeal,[1] filed by Protais Zigiranyirazo ("Appellant"), against a decision of Trial Chamber III.[2]

BACKGROUND

2. The Appellant submits that the Trial Chamber violated his fundamental right to be tried in his presence, as guaranteed by Article 20(4)(d) of the Statute of the Tribunal. The Appellant argues that this violation resulted from the decision of the Trial Chamber to hear Michel Bagaragaza[3] testify in person in The Netherlands[4] with the Appellant participating in the proceedings only by video-link from Arusha.[5] He contends that the right to be present at trial cannot be satisfied by video-link and instead requires physical presence.[6] The Appellant requests the Appeals Chamber to quash the Trial Chamber's decision of 5 June 2006, which permitted his participation by video-link, and to strike from the record Mr. Bagaragaza's testimony of 13 through 15 June 2006.[7]

3. The present dispute has its origin in the Prosecution's request to have Mr. Bagaragaza testify in this case by video-link from The Netherlands.[8] Both the Trial Chamber and the Prosecution have described him as a key witness.[9] The Appellant opposed the Prosecution's request to hear Mr. **[page 2]** Bagaragaza's testimony by video-link because he wished to confront this witness in person.[10] In addition, the Appellant challenged Mr. Bagaragaza's inability to travel to Arusha, in particular, by disputing the basis of his security concerns and by noting that his agreement with the Prosecution to be heard only by video-link usurped the role of the Trial Chamber in making such decisions.[11]

4. On 31 January 2006, the Trial Chamber denied the Prosecution's request to hear Mr. Bagaragaza's testimony by video-link.[12] In its decision, the Trial Chamber stated that the Appellant had a right to confront this witness in person.[13] In addition, the Trial Chamber expressed concern about its ability "to effectively and accurately assess the testimony and demeanour" of Mr. Bagaragaza if he testified by video-link.[14] The

---

1 Protais Zigiranyirazo Appeal from the Extremely Confidential Decision on Defense Motion Concerning the Hearing of Witness ADE, 19 June 2006 ("Zigiranyirazo Appeal"). The Prosecution responded in "Prosecutor's Response to Appeal from the Extremely Confidential Decision on Defence Motion Concerning the Hearing of Witness ADE", 29 June 2006 ("Prosecution Response"). Mr. Zigiranyirazo replied in "Reply Brief: Appeal from the Extremely Confidential Decision on Defense Motion Concerning the Hearing of Witness ADE", 6 July 2006 ("Zigiranyirazo Reply").

2 *The Prosecutor v. Protais Zigiranyirazo,* Case No. ICTR-2001-73-T, Extremely Confidential Decision on Defence Motion Concerning the Hearing of Witness ADE, 5 June 2006 ("Impugned Decision"). The Appeals Chamber notes that Mr. Bagaragaza is Witness ADE. Mr. Bagaragaza waived the use of a pseudonym at the outset of his testimony. *See The Prosecutor v. Protais Zigiranyirazo,* Case No. ICTR-2001-73-T, T. 13 June 2006 pp. 4-5.

3 Mr. Bagaragaza is an accused person before this Tribunal who is detained exceptionally in the detention facility for the International Tribunal for the Former Yugoslavia ("ICTY") in The Netherlands. Impugned Decision, para. 13. *See also The Prosecutor v. Michel Bagaragaza,* Case No. ICTR-05-86-I, Order for Special Detention Measures, 13 August 2005 (ICTR President); *The Prosecutor v. Michel Bagaragaza,* Case No. ICTR-05-86-I, Order for the Continued Detention of Michel Bagaragaza at the ICTY Detention Unit in The Hague, The Netherlands, 17 February 2006 (ICTR President); *The Prosecutor v. Michel Bagaragaza,* Case No. ICTR-05-86-I, Order for the Continued Detention of Michel Bagaragaza at the ICTY Detention Unit in The Hague, The Netherlands, 17 August 2006 (ICTR President).

4 Zigiranyirazo Appeal, paras. 3, 20-26.

5 Zigiranyirazo Appeal, paras. 3, 9, 16, 20.

6 Zigiranyirazo Appeal, paras. 21-31.

7 Zigiranyirazo Appeal, para. 56.

8 Impugned Decision, para. 13. *See also The Prosecutor v. Protais Zigiranyirazo,* Case No. ICTR-2001-73-T, Decision on Defence and Prosecution Motions Related to Witness ADE, 31 January 2006, paras. 25-34 ("Decision on Prosecution's Request for Video-Link").

9 Impugned Decision, paras. 6, 16; Decision on Prosecution's Request for Video-Link, paras. 26, 32.

10 Decision on Prosecution's Request for Video-Link, para. 32.

11 Decision on Prosecution's Request for Video-Link, para. 28.

12 Decision on Prosecution's Request for Video-Link, p. 10.

13 Decision on Prosecution's Request for Video-Link, para. 32.

14 Decision on Prosecution's Request for Video-Link, para. 32.

Trial Chamber recognized the potential importance of Mr. Bagaragaza's testimony.[15] In addition, the Trial Chamber accepted the Prosecution's submissions that Mr. Bagaragaza faced increased risk to his security if he travelled to Arusha.[16] Consequently, the Trial Chamber decided to hear Mr. Bagaragaza's testimony in person in The Netherlands in the presence of the parties.[17]

5. However, shortly before the anticipated trial session, the Trial Chamber was informed that the Appellant would not be permitted to enter The Netherlands in the foreseeable future.[18] The Trial Chamber does not explain the reason for this, citing only "external variables", though the Registry's submissions point to the absence of a "treaty basis" for the temporary transfer.[19] Consequently, the Trial Chamber modified its arrangements for the hearing of Mr. Bagaragaza's testimony in a Scheduling Order of 26 May 2006.[20] In that Order, the Trial Chamber decided to proceed to hear Mr. Bagaragaza's testimony in person in The Netherlands, beginning 12 June 2006, in the physical absence of the Appellant, who would participate by video-link from Arusha.[21] The Appellant challenged this decision on the grounds that it violated his right to be present at trial and to personally confront the witness.[22] **[page 3]**

6. On 5 June 2006, the Trial Chamber addressed this matter and, after considering various factors, decided that it was in the interests of a fair and expeditious trial to maintain the arrangement for hearing Mr. Bagaragaza's testimony as set forth in the Scheduling Order of 26 May 2006.[23] The Trial Chamber reiterated that its decision to hear Mr. Bagaragaza in person was based primarily on its concern as to its ability to effectively and accurately assess his testimony and demeanour through a video-link.[24] The Trial Chamber decided that the Appellant, however, would be able to follow the proceedings by video-link along with one of his counsel in Arusha.[25] The Trial Chamber's decision also envisioned both parties being represented by counsel in court in The Netherlands.[26] To maintain "procedural equality of arms" between the parties, the Trial Chamber decided that the examination and cross-examination of Mr. Bagaragaza by both parties would be primarily conducted from Arusha via video-link.[27] However, it noted that counsel for both the Prosecution and the Appellant, present in The Netherlands, would also be able to intervene in the proceedings.[28]

7. Following the issuance of the Impugned Decision, the Appellant sought certification to appeal, which the Trial Chamber granted immediately prior to hearing Mr. Bagaragaza's testimony.[29] The Trial Chamber, however, declined to stay the proceedings pending the outcome of the appeal.[30] Accordingly, Mr. Bagaragaza testified from 13 through 15 June 2006. The Prosecution's case closed on 28 June 2006, and the Defence case is set to begin on 30 October 2006.

DISCUSSION

8. Article 20(4)(d) of the Statute provides that an accused has a right "to be tried in his or her presence." This right has been equated with other "indispensable cornerstone[s] of justice", such as the right to counsel,

15 Decision on Prosecution's Request for Video-Link, para. 32.

16 Decision on Prosecution's Request for Video-Link, para. 32. These submissions, as recounted by the Trial Chamber, included Mr. Bagaragaza's fears for his safety stemming from his position as an "insider" witness, the publishing of one of his statements on the internet, the probable murder of Juvénal Uwilingiyimana, and threats to his family, which all contributed to his "sense of vulnerability". *Id.*, para. 26.

17 Decision on Prosecution's Request for Video-Link, para. 33.

18 Impugned Decision, paras. 2, 8, 14.

19 Impugned decision, paras. 8, 14.

20 *The Prosecutor v. Protais Zigiranyirazo*, Case No. ICTR-2001-73-T, Scheduling Order, 26 May 2006 ("Scheduling Order").

21 Scheduling Order, pp. 2-3. *See also* Impugned Decision, para. 2.

22 Impugned Decision, para. 3.

23 Impugned Decision, para. 15.

24 Impugned Decision, paras. 16, 19.

25 Impugned Decision, paras. 15, 18.

26 Impugned Decision, paras. 17, 18.

27 Impugned Decision, para. 18.

28 Impugned Decision, para. 18.

29 *The Prosecutor v. Protais Zigiranyirazo*, Case No. ICTR-2001-73-T, Oral Decision, T. 13 June 2006 pp. 53-54 ("Certification Decision").

30 Certification Decision, pp. 53-54.

the right to remain silent, the right to confront witnesses against them, and the right to a speedy trial.[31] The Trial Chamber concluded that, in the circumstances of this case, the Appellant's presence at his own trial, even during the hearing of a key witness, could be facilitated **[page 4]** through the use of video-link technology.[32] In the present decision, the Appeals Chamber considers whether the Trial Chamber erred in adopting the procedure for hearing the testimony of Mr. Bagaragaza in person in The Netherlands while the accused, Mr. Zigiranyirazo, participated via video-link from Arusha. In the course of this analysis, the Appeals Chamber confronts three principal questions: (1) whether "presence" within the meaning of Article 20(4)(d) refers to physical presence in court before the Trial Judges; (2) if so, whether the right to be physically present in court is categorically inviolable; and (3) if the right may be limited in certain situations, whether the Trial Chamber's restrictions were justified under the present circumstances.

A. Standard of Review

9. Decisions relating to the general conduct of trial proceedings are matters within the discretion of the Trial Chamber.[33] A Trial Chamber's exercise of discretion will be reversed only if the challenged decision was based on an incorrect interpretation of governing law, was based on a patently incorrect conclusion of fact, or was so unfair or unreasonable as to constitute an abuse of the Trial Chamber's discretion.[34]

B. Article 20(4)(d) Provides for Physical Presence at Trial

10. In the Impugned Decision, the Trial Chamber did not directly consider the issue as to what was meant by the term "presence" within the meaning of Article 20(4)(d). On Appeal, the parties dispute whether the term "presence" refers to physical presence in court. The Appellant argues that this language provides him with the right to be physically present at his trial, before the court and the witnesses testifying against him.[35] The Prosecution counters that Article 20(4)(d) does not impose such a "stringent" requirement as physical presence.[36] The Prosecution urges a broader reading of the provision, suggesting that it is simply a "compendious subsection" preventing trial **[page 5]** only where an accused is unaware that the proceedings are being conducted against him and is therefore unable to mount a defence.[37]

11. The Appeals Chamber considers that the physical presence of an accused before the court, as a general rule, is one of the most basic and common precepts of a fair criminal trial. The language and practical import of Article 20(4)(d) of the Statute are clear. First, as a matter of ordinary English, the term "presence" implies physical proximity.[38] A review of the French version of the Statute leads to the same conclusion, in particular

---

31 *Slobodan Milošević v. The Prosecutor*, Case No. IT-02-54-AR73.7, Decision on Interlocutory Appeal of the Trial Chamber's Decision on the Assignment of Defense Counsel, 1 November 2004, paras. 11, 13 ("*Milošević* Appeal Decision").

32 Impugned Decision, para. 15 ("The Chamber considers that the presence and the involvement of the Accused in the testimony of [Mr. Bagaragaza] can be facilitated via video-link, which provides an audio and visual image of the witness and the proceedings.").

33 *The Prosecutor v. Théoneste Bagosora et al.*, Decision on Interlocutory Appeal Relating to Disclosure Under Rule 66(B) of the Tribunal's Rules of Procedure and Evidence, Case No. 98-41-AR73, 25 September 2006, para. 6 ("*Bagosora* Appeal Decision"); *Tharcisse Muvunyi v. The Prosecutor*, Case No. ICTR-00-55A-AR73(C), Decision on Interlocutory Appeal, 29 May 2006, para. 5 ("*Muvunyi* Appeal Decision").

34 *Bagosora* Appeal Decision, para 6; *Muvunyi* Appeal Decision, para. 5. *See also The Prosecutor v. Théoneste Bagosora et al.*, Case Nos. ICTR-98-41-AR73, ICTR-98-41-AR73(B), Decision on Interlocutory Appeals of Decision on Witness Protection Orders, 6 October 2005, para. 3.

35 Zigiranyirazo Appeal, para. 42.

36 Prosecution Response, paras. 2, 5-10.

37 Prosecution Response, paras. 2, 5-10.

38 *See, e.g.*, The Oxford English Dictionary, Second Edition, Volume XII, p. 393 (for the definition of "presence": "The fact or condition of being present; the state of being before, in front of, or in the same place with a person or thing; being there; attendance, company, society, association. Usually with *of* or possessive indicating the person or thing that is present."), p. 395 (for the definition of "present": "An adjective of relation; expressing a local or temporal relation to a person or thing which is the point of reference [...] Being before, beside, with, or in the same place as the person to whom the word has relation; being in the place considered or mentioned; that is here (or there) [...]"); Black's Law Dictionary, Eighth Edition, (for the relevant definition of "presence": "The state or fact of being in a particular place and time [...]. Close physical proximity coupled with awareness [...]"). *See also United States v. Navarro*, 169 F.3d 228, 234-239 (5th Cir. 1999) (interpreting the plain meaning of "presence" as requiring the physical presence of a defendant in court).

in the context of the phrase "*être présente au procès*",[39] conveying unambiguously that Article 20(4)(d) refers to physical presence *at the trial*.[40]

12. Both the Tribunal's legal framework and practice as well as that of the International Criminal Tribunal for the Former Yugoslavia ("ICTY") further reflect that Article 20(4)(d) provides for the physical presence of an accused at trial, as opposed to his facilitated presence via video-link. Initially, the Appeals Chamber observes that such a procedure, over an accused's objection, is unprecedented before the Tribunal and before the ICTY.[41] It is not surprising, therefore, that there are no express provisions in the Statute and Rules of this Tribunal or of the ICTY for the participation of an accused by video-link in his or her own trial.[42] Indeed, Rule 65*bis* of the ICTY **[page 6]** Rules of Procedure and Evidence illustrates very clearly that participation via video-link is not considered presence.[43] The same distinction between actual presence and constructive presence via video-link, which is evident in Rule 65*bis* of the ICTY Rules, also appears in the Statute of the International Criminal Court[44] and the Rules of Procedure and Evidence of the Special Court for Sierra Leone.[45] The Appeals Chamber further observes that other international,[46] regional,[47] and

---

39 Emphasis added.

40 Le Nouveau Petit Robert, p. 1768 (for the definition of "*présente*" : "*Qui est dans le lieu, le groupe se trouve la personne qui parle ou de laquelle on parle*"); Gerard Cornu, Vocabulaire Juridique, p. 664 ("*Qui se trouve ou se trouvait à un moment donné en un lieu déterminé. [...] Qui concourt en personne l'accomplissement d'un acte ou au déroulement de la procédure. [...]*").

41 In the case of Milan Simić before the ICTY, the accused participated in his sentencing hearing towards the end of the trial process via video link because of his health condition. The Trial Chamber expressly noted, however, that during this period Mr. Simic filed a total of twenty-five waivers of his right to be present in court. *See The Prosecutor v. Milan Simić*, Sentencing Judgement, Case No. IT 95-9/2-S, 17 October 2002, para. 8.

42 The Tribunal's Rules and jurisprudence only contemplate the use of video-link technology in order to transmit the testimony of a witness to the court, if justified in narrow circumstances for witness protection concerns, or otherwise in the interests of justice. Rule 75 provides in pertinent part (emphasis added): "(A) A Judge or a Chamber may [...] order appropriate measures to safeguard the privacy and security of victims and witness, provided that the measures are <u>consistent with the rights of the accused</u>. (B) A Chamber may hold an *in camera* proceeding to determine whether to order notably: (i) [...] (c) <u>giving of testimony</u> through [...] closed circuit television [...] (iii) Appropriate measures <u>to facilitate the testimony</u> of vulnerable victims and witnesses, such as one-way closed circuit television." In addition to specific witness protection concerns, the Tribunal's jurisprudence also allows the hearing of a witness by video-link if it is otherwise in the interests of justice. *See, e.g., The Prosecutor v. Théoneste Bagosora et al.*, Case No. ICTR-98-41-T, Decision on Testimony by Video-Conference, 20 December 2004, para. 4 ("Video-conference testimony should be ordered where it is in the interests of justice, as that standard has been elaborated in ICTR and ICTY jurisprudence."). The Rules of Procedure and Evidence of the ICTY authorize this explicitly in Rule 71*bis* ("At the request of either party, a Trial Chamber may, in the interests of justice, order that testimony be received via video-conference link.").

43 Rule 65*bis*(C) of the ICTY Rules provides in pertinent part: "With the written consent of the accused, given after receiving advice from his counsel, a status conference under this Rule may be conducted: (i) in his presence, but with his counsel participating either via tele-conference or video-conference; or (ii) in Chambers in his absence, but with his participation via tele-conference if he so wishes and/or participation of his counsel via tele-conference or video-conference."

44 *See* Statute of the International Criminal Court, Article 63 ("(1) The accused shall be present during the trial. (2) If the accused, being present before the Court, continues to disrupt the trial, the Trial Chamber may remove the accused and shall make provision for him or her to observe the trial and instruct counsel from outside the courtroom, through the use of communications technology, if required. Such measures shall be taken only in exceptional circumstances after other reasonable alternatives have proved inadequate, and only for such duration as is strictly required.").

45 The Appeals Chamber notes that Article 17(4)(d) of the Statute of the Special Court for Sierra Leone is identical to Article 20(4)(d) of the Tribunal's Statute. Notably, similar to the International Criminal Court, Rule 80(B) of the Rules of Procedure and Evidence for the Special Court in Sierra Leone envisions an accused's participation in his or her trial by video-link only after he or she has been removed for persistently disruptive conduct. This Rule provides in pertinent part: "In the event of removal, where possible, provision should be made for the accused to follow the proceeding by video-link."

46 *See supra* notes 44, 45 (discussing the International Criminal Court and the Special Court for Sierra Leone). The Appeals Chamber further observes that the language of Article 20(4)(d) of the Statute tracks Article 14 of the International Covenant on Civil and Political Rights. Under this provision, the Human Rights Committee has referred to an accused's personal attendance at the proceedings as a component of a fair trial. *See Views of the Human Rights Committee under Article 5, Paragraph 4, of the Optional Protocol to the International Covenant on Civil and Political Rights*, Communication No. 289/1988: Panama 8 April 1992, CCPR/C/44/289/1988 (Jurisprudence), para. 6.6 ("The Committee recalls that the concept of a 'fair trial' within the meaning of article 14, paragraph I, must be interpreted as requiring a number of conditions, such as equality of arms and respect for the principle of adversary proceedings. These requirements are not respected where, as in the present case, the accused is denied the opportunity *to personally attend the proceedings*, or where he is unable to properly instruct his legal representative.") (Emphasis added).

47 The European Convention on the Protection of Human Rights and Fundamental Freedoms refers in Article 6(3)(c) to an accused's right "to defend himself in person [...] ". For the European Court of Human Rights, this implies the personal attendance of a defendant at trial as well as in certain procedures on appeal requiring the court to have personal impression of the defendant. *See, e.g., Case of Stoichkov v. Bulgaria, Application no. 9808/02*, Judgment, 24 March 2005, para. 56 ("It may thus be considered that the duty to guarantee the right of a criminal defendant to be present in the courtroom – either during the original proceedings or in a

national[48] systems also share the view that the right to be present at trial implies physical presence. **[page 7]**

13. The Appeals Chamber, therefore, confirms that an accused's right to be tried in his or her presence implies a right to be physically present at trial. Applying the foregoing to the present case leads the Appeals Chamber to conclude that by proceeding as it did, the Trial Chamber restricted the Appellant's right to be present at his trial. However, this does not end the necessary inquiry.

C. The Right To Be Physically Present at Trial Is Not Absolute

14. The parties acknowledge that an accused's right to be tried in his or her presence is not absolute.[49] The ICTY Appeals Chamber has observed as much,[50] and this Appeals Chamber agrees. An accused person can waive or forfeit the right to be present at trial. For example, Rule 80(B) of the Rules allows a Trial Chamber to remove a persistently disruptive accused. Referring to the equivalent provision in the ICTY Rules, the ICTY Appeals Chamber observed that an accused's right to be present for his or her trial can be restricted "on the basis of substantial trial disruptions".[51] In assessing a particular limitation on a statutory guarantee, the Appeals Chamber bears in mind the proportionality principle, pursuant to which any restriction on a

---

retrial after he or she emerges – ranks as one of the essential requirements of Article 6 and is deeply entrenched in that provision."); *Case of Sejdovic v. Italy*, Application no. 56581/00, Judgment, 1 March 2006, para. 84; *Case of Michael Edward Cooke v. Austria*, Application no. 25878/94, Judgement, 8 February 2000, paras. 35, 42, 43. ("The Court recalls that a person charged with a criminal offence should, as a general principle based on the notion of a fair trial, be entitled to be present at the first-instance hearing. However, the personal attendance of the defendant does not necessarily take on the same significance for an appeal hearing."); *Case of Colozza v. Italy*, Application No. 9024/80, Judgment, 12 February 1985, para. 27 ("Although this is not expressly mentioned in paragraph 1 of Article 6 (art. 6-1), the object and purpose of the Article taken as a whole show that a person 'charged with a criminal offence' is entitled to take part in the hearing. Moreover, sub-paragraphs (c), (d) and (e) of paragraph 3 (art. 6-3-c, art. 6-3-d, art. 6-3-e) guarantee to 'everyone charged with a criminal offence' the right 'to defend himself in person', 'to examine or have examined witnesses' and 'to have the free assistance of an interpreter if he cannot understand or speak the language used in court', and it is difficult to see how he could exercise these rights without being present."). *See also* Stefan Trechsel, Human Rights in Criminal Proceedings, pp. 252-253 (2006).

48 Presence is also equated with physical presence in criminal trials in the United States. *See, e.g.*, Federal Rule of Criminal Procedure 43(a). Federal Rules of Criminal Procedure 5 and 10 envision video-conferencing only, with the defendant's consent, at the initial appearance and arraignment. *See also Illinois v. Allen,* 397 U.S. 337, 338 (1970) ("One of the most basic of the rights guaranteed by the Confrontation Clause is the accused's right to be present in the courtroom at every stage of his trial"); *United States v. Navarro,* 169 F.3d 228, 234-239 (5th Cir. 1999) (holding that an accused's participation in his sentencing hearing by video-conference violated his right to be present at trial); *United States v. Reynolds*, 44 M.J. 726, 729 (United States Army Court of Criminal Appeals 1996)("Consequently, the statutory and [Rules for Court Martial] provisions cited above appear to require that the military judge, accused, and counsel all to be at one location for the purpose of a court-martial. This interpretation not only comports with custom and tradition, but also is the one that best guarantees justice. For these reasons, we are satisfied that the telephonic procedures utilized in this case, when based on the meager justification of saving time and travel funds between two installations approximately 150 miles apart, did not comport with any reasonable concept of 'presence' anticipated by the [Uniform Code of Military Justice] and [Rules for Court Martial].")(internal citations omitted); *Riggins v. Nevada*, 504 U.S. 127, 142 (1992)(Kennedy, J., concurring)("It is a fundamental assumption of the adversary system that the trier of fact observes the accused throughout the trial, while the accused is either on the stand or sitting at the defense table. This assumption derives from the right to be present at trial, which in turn derives from the right to testify and rights under the Confrontation Clause. [...] At all stages of the proceedings, the defendant's behavior, manner, facial expressions, and emotional responses, or their absence, combine to make an overall impression on the trier of fact, an impression that can have a powerful influence on the outcome of the trial. If the defendant takes the stand, as Riggins did, his demeanor can have a great bearing on his credibility and persuasiveness, and on the degree to which he evokes sympathy. The defendant's demeanor may also be relevant to his confrontation rights [...]") (internal citations omitted).

In addition, in England and Wales, the right of an accused to be present in court at his or her trial is a matter of common law. *See R. v. Lee Kun* (1916) 1 Kings Bench Reports 337, at 341 ("There must be very exceptional circumstances to justify proceeding with the trial in the absence of the accused. The reason why the accused should be present at the trial is that he may hear the case made against him and have the opportunity [...] of answering it. The presence of the accused means not only that he must be physically in attendance, but also that he must be capable of understanding the nature of the proceedings.").

In Canada, an accused also has the right to be present in court during the trial. The Canadian Criminal Code envisions the possibility of an accused participating in his or her trial by video-link, but not for the hearing of evidence, unless he or she consents. *See* Canadian Criminal Code, Title XX, Section 650.

49 Zigiranyirazo Appeal, para. 44; Prosecution Response, para. 11.

50 *Milošević* Appeal Decision, para. 13 ("If a defendant's right to be present for his trial – which, to reiterate, is listed in the same string of rights and indeed in the same *clause* as the right to self-representation – may thus be restricted on the basis of substantial trial disruption, the Appeals Chamber sees no reason to treat the right to self -representation any differently.").

51 *Milošević* Appeal Decision, para. 13.

fundamental right must be in service of a sufficiently important objective and must impair the right no more than is **[page 8]** necessary to accomplish the objective.[52] The explicit exception provided by Rule 80(B) and the ICTY Appeals Chamber's reference to "substantial trial disruptions" provide a useful measure by which to assess other restrictions on the right to be present at trial.

D. The Present Circumstances Do Not Warrant any Restriction on the Appellant's Right

15. The primary question for the Appeals Chamber is whether the Trial Chamber properly exercised its discretion in its restriction of the Appellant's right to be present at his trial. Because both parties acknowledge that this right is not absolute, the Appeals Chamber does not consider that the Trial Chamber's failure to examine the accused's right to be tried in his presence is of significant consequence. Instead, the primary question for the Appeals Chamber is whether the Trial Chamber properly exercised its discretion in its restriction of the Appellant's right to be present at his trial. The Appeals Chamber recalls that the Trial Chamber's decision was predicated on Mr. Bagaragaza's security concerns, the impact of video-link on the assessment of the witness, and logistical concerns preventing the Appellant from traveling to The Netherlands to attend the proceedings.

16. The Appellant contends that the Trial Chamber failed to apply properly the proportionality principle.[53] He disputes that security concerns in fact prevented Mr. Bagaragaza from testifying in Arusha or that the administrative concerns preventing him from traveling to The Netherlands were insurmountable.[54] The Appellant further takes issue with the procedure for hearing Mr. Bagaragaza's testimony, pointing to the inherent difficulties in following the evidence and visually interacting with the Judges.[55] As a result of these arrangements, the Appellant claims that his participation by video-link meant that neither he nor his lead counsel, who remained with him in Arusha, could observe or hear either the judges or the witness unless the camera was pointed on them.[56] In the Appellant's view, this denied them normal visual interaction with the proceedings.[57] **[page 9]** The Prosecution submits that the procedure adopted by the Trial Chamber was consistent with a fair trial and that Mr. Zigiranyirazo has not demonstrated any prejudice.[58]

17. The Appeals Chamber agrees that the objectives advanced by the Trial Chamber are of general importance: witness protection, the proper assessment of an important prosecution witness, and the need to ensure a reasonably expeditious trial. Nonetheless, the Appeals Chamber is not satisfied that, in the present circumstances, the Trial Chamber properly exercised its discretion in deciding to impose limitations on the Appellant's right to be present at his trial.

18. First, the Appeals Chamber accepts that, by agreeing to cooperate with the Prosecution, Mr. Bagaragaza could be exposed to an increased risk to his security. However, the record does not reflect that the security concern, alluded to by the Trial Chamber,[59] is in fact related to the location of his testimony, or

---

52 *Milošević* Appeal Decision, para. 17. The Appeals Chamber further notes that the situation envisioned under Rule 15*bis*, allowing *inter alia* proceedings to continue for a limited period in the absence of one of the judges, does not inform the present dispute which concerns the absence of the accused.

53 Zigiranyirazo Appeal, para. 47.

54 Zigiranyirazo Appeal, paras. 48, 49.

55 *See generally* Zigiranyirazo Appeal, para. 50; Zigiranyirazo Reply, para. 25.

56 Zigiranyirazo Appeal, para. 50; Zigiranyirazo Reply, para. 25.

57 Zigiranyirazo Reply, para. 25. The Appellant notes that he "'saw' the proceedings through the selective eyes of a camera operated by a third party." He adds: "The experience was dizzying and could have been conducted properly if he and his lead counsel had been able to see his judges. He and his attorney could not speak directly to the judges, gauge their reactions, and adjust the arguments and tenor of pleadings as if they were in open court with the members of the bench." Further, the Appellant claims that the arrangements placed his lead counsel, who conducted the cross-examination, in the difficult position of having to choose to either remain in Arusha and receive direct instruction, or travel to the Netherlands and participate in person, but where communication with the accused would be limited to breaks during the proceedings.

58 Prosecution Response, paras. 2, 13-23. The Prosecution agrees that there was no visual interaction between the bench and the accused unless the camera was pointed at them, but notes that Mr. Zigiranyirazo confirmed each day that he could follow the proceedings. Prosecution Response, paras. 19, 20. Mr. Zigiranyirazo notes, however, that he complained at the beginning of the proceedings and vowed to do his best out of respect for the court. Zigiranyirazo Reply, para. 25.

59 The Appeals Chamber notes that security concerns presented by the Prosecution to the Trial Chamber involved the witness's general feelings of insecurity due to agreeing to cooperate with the Prosecution. The Prosecution also pointed to threats made to Mr.

that injury could only be avoided by having Mr. Bagaragaza testify in The Netherlands.[60] In addition, the record does not show that the Trial Chamber examined the possibility that additional security measures might allay any security threat were Mr. Bagaragaza brought to Arusha to testify.

19. Second, the Appeals Chamber also accepts that the Trial Chamber's general concern over its ability to assess the credibility of a key witness is an important interest. However, the Appeals Chamber considers that if the Trial Chamber had misgivings about its ability to adequately follow the testimony of a key witness through the use of video-link then these same misgivings, if valid, **[page 10]** must apply with equal force to the ability of the accused and his counsel to follow the evidence and proceedings.

20. Third, the Appeals Chamber further observes that none of the "external variables,"[61] alluded to by the Trial Chamber, preventing the Appellant's personal attendance at his own trial, resulted from any action on his part. In addition, there is no indication that the Trial Chamber explored an alternative venue for hearing the testimony, other than The Netherlands. A careful consideration of the feasibility of moving the trial to The Netherlands at the earliest opportunity might have identified the logistical barriers that prevented the Appellant from attending his trial in The Netherlands and allowed the Trial Chamber either to overcome the obstacles or to explore alternative venues or solutions, avoiding the present situation.[62]

21. The Appeals Chamber notes that the Trial Chamber endeavored to ensure that the Appellant had legal representation physically present during the proceedings in The Netherlands. In addition, in an effort to give effect to the principle of equality of arms, the Trial Chamber ordered that the Prosecution also to examine the witness from Arusha. However, the Trial Chamber's attempts to give full respect to both the right to counsel and the principle of equality of arms do not compensate for the failure to accord the accused what is a separate and distinct minimum guarantee: the right to be present at his own trial. Although one of the Appellant's counsel was in the courtroom with the Judges and the witness, the Appellant himself was thousands of kilometres away, connected to the proceedings only by means of audio-visual equipment. The Appellant's sense of being wronged in such circumstances is well-understandable. As the Prosecution and Trial Chamber noted, Mr. Bagaragaza's testimony does not cover simply background information or a matter other than the acts and conduct of the accused. According to the Prosecution's own statement and the Trial Chamber's consideration, Mr. Bagaragaza was a key Prosecution witness against the Appellant.[63]

22. Based on the foregoing, the Trial Chamber's restrictions on the Appellant's fair trial rights were unwarranted and excessive in the circumstances and thus fail the test of proportionality. Accordingly, the Trial Chamber committed a discernible error. **[page 11]**

E. Conclusion

23. After a careful consideration of the circumstances under consideration in this appeal and giving due regard to the accused's right to be present at his or her trial, the Appeals Chamber finds that the Trial

---

Bagaragaza's family and the death of another individual, not in the custody of the Tribunal, who was contemplating cooperating with the Prosecution. The Prosecution explained that this led Mr. Bagaragaza to agree to cooperate if he were not brought to Arusha. *See generally* Impugned Decision, para. 13; Decision on Prosecution's Request for Video-Link, paras. 26, 30, 32. *See also The Prosecutor v. Protais Zigiranyirazo,* Case No. ICTR-2001-73-T, Prosecution's Confidential Request to Allow Witness ADE to Give Testimony Via Video-Link, 21 December 2005. The Appeals Chamber observes that the agreement between Mr. Bagaragaza and the Prosecution that he not be brought to Arusha is not binding on the Trial Chamber.

60 The Appeals Chamber considers that the Trial Chamber is best placed to make the assessment concerning the security of witnesses appearing before it. However, in making a determination that impacts a fundamental right of an accused, a Trial Chamber must do more than simply accept the averments of Prosecution counsel. Rather it must, in accord with Rule 75, undertake an independent inquiry, at a minimum for example by conferring with the relevant sections of the Registry concerned with security and protection of witnesses. The Trial Chamber does not appear to have done this. Moreover, the Appeals Chamber notes that reliance on the President's decision to extraordinarily detain Mr. Bagaragaza in The Hague also does not satisfy this duty. Indeed, there is a significant difference in protecting Mr. Bagaragaza, as an accused, during a lengthy period of pre-trial detention and in ensuring his security when he appears as a witness during three days of testimony before the Tribunal.

61 Impugned Decision, paras. 8, 14.

62 The Appeals Chamber observes that other accused persons have previously attended Tribunal proceedings in The Netherlands in connection with appellate proceedings. *See, e.g., Jean De Dieu Kamuhanda v. The Prosecutor*, Case No. 99-54A-A, Variation of a Scheduling Order, 19 August 2005, p. 2.

63 Impugned Decision, paras. 6, 16; Decision on Prosecution's Request for Video-Link, paras. 26, 32.

Chamber erred in law in holding that the Appellant's right to be present at his trial during the testimony of an apparently key witness against him could be met by video-link. The Appeals Chamber observes that, after certifying its decision for appeal, the Trial Chamber decided not to stay the proceedings and instead proceeded to hear Mr. Bagaragaza's testimony.[64]

24. The precise consequences of the Trial Chamber's error cannot be determined at this stage. However, it cannot be held that the violation of the Appellant's right to be present constitutes harmless error given the length and purported significance of the testimony to the charges against him. Prejudice therefore can only be presumed, as any attempt to prove or disprove actual prejudice from the record in an ongoing trial before any factual findings have been made would be purely speculative. In the view of the Appeals Chamber, allowing the testimony of Mr. Bagaragaza to remain on the record would seriously damage the integrity of the proceedings. In such circumstances, Rule 95 of the Rules plainly requires the exclusion of such testimony. This, however, does not prevent the Trial Chamber from exercising its discretion and allowing Mr. Bagaragaza to testify again in a manner consistent with the Appellant's fair trial rights.[65]

DISPOSITION

25. For the foregoing reasons, the Trial Chamber's decision to hear Mr. Bagaragaza's testimony in person in The Netherlands while Mr. Zigiranyirazo participated by video-link from Arusha is **REVERSED** and the testimony of Mr. Bagaragaza given in such a manner is **EXCLUDED**.

Done in English and French, the English version being authoritative.

Done this 30th day of October 2006,
At The Hague,
The Netherlands.

Judge Fausto Pocar,
Presiding

[Seal of the Tribunal]

64 Certification Decision, pp. 53-54.

65 The Appellant acknowledges that the Prosecution could seek to reopen its case in the interests of justice pursuant to Rule 85 or alternatively that the Trial Chamber could call the witness *proprio motu* under Rule 98. *See Zigiranyirazo* Reply, paras. 26-27.

International Criminal Tribunal for Rwanda
Tribunal pénal international pour le Rwanda

ORIGINAL: ENGLISH

TRIAL CHAMBER I

Before: Judge Erik Møse, presiding
Judge Jai Ram Reddy
Judge Sergei Alekseevich Egorov

Registrar: Adama Dieng

Date: 17 November 2006

THE PROSECUTOR

v.

Théoneste BAGOSORA

Gratien KABILIGI

Aloys NTABAKUZE

Anatole NSENGIYUMVA

Case No.: ICTR-98-41-T

DECISION ON NSENGIYUMVA MOTION FOR ADJOURMENT DUE TO ILLNESS OF THE ACCUSED

The Prosecution
Barbara Mulvaney
Drew White
Christine Graham
Rashid Rashid
Gregory Townsend

The Defence
Raphaël Constant
Allison Turner
Paul Skolnik
Frédéric Hivon
Peter Erlinder
André Tremblay
Kennedy Ogetto
Gershom Otachi Bw'Omanwa

[page 2] THE INTERNATIONAL CRIMINAL TRIBUNAL FOR RWANDA

SITTING as Trial Chamber I, composed of Judge Erik Møse, presiding, Judge Jai Ram Reddy, and Judge Sergei Alekseevich Egorov;

BEING SEIZED OF the "Motion Requesting Suspension of Trial on Medical Grounds", filed by the Nsengiyumva Defence on 8 November 2006;

CONSIDERING the Registrar's Submissions, filed on 13 November 2006;

HEREBY DECIDES the motion.

INTRODUCTION

1. Presentation of evidence by the Nsengiyumva, Bagosora, and Ntabakuze Defence teams closed on 13 October 2006.[1] With the exception of four Bagosora witnesses and one Ntabakuze witness, the present and final session of the trial is devoted exclusively to hearing witnesses on behalf of Kabiligi.[2]

2. On 8 November 2006, Lead Counsel for Nsengiyumva announced that his client was ill and unable to attend proceedings. He indicated that the Accused had no intention of waiving his right to be present, and requested a suspension of the trial until his client was able to return to court.[3] A written motion, filed simultaneously, argued that "most of the witnesses about to take the stand, e.g. ALL 42 and Kambanda are particularly important witnesses whose testimony he absolutely must follow".[4] After an adjournment to allow the Defence time to more fully consult with their client, the Chamber received a medical report from the Registry indicating that "one week rest is recommended for his condition to improve".[5]

3. The Chamber asked whether there were any witnesses of less importance to the Nsengiyumva Defence whom the Accused would consent to be heard in his absence. Lead Counsel responded:

> Now, as I said in the morning, the other witnesses may have nothing obvious, on the face of it, that will have an impact on the defence of the Accused person. But, we do not know what is likely to come out of the cross-examination of those witnesses by the Prosecution, and that is where our difficulty is. So that out of abundant caution, it will be safe that the Accused person is in court to give instructions when issues that are likely to be prejudicial arise during cross-examination either by the Prosecution or by the other Defence teams.[6]

In respect of Witnesses Kambanda and ALL-42, Lead Counsel explained that the situation

> is slightly different. It's both the prejudicial testimony and also the possibility of getting exculpatory testimony from those two witnesses. We will lose that if the **[page 3]** Accused is not in court, because we believe that they have important – particularly, the first one, ALL-42, he has important information that we could elicit from him....[7]

4. After hearing the parties, the Chamber ruled orally that it would proceed with the examination-in-chief of Witness ALL-42, but would reserve its position as to the timing of any possible Nsengiyumva and Prosecution cross-examination of the witness.[8] Upon completion of the witness's examination-in-chief and cross-examination by the two other Defence teams, the Nsengiyumva Defence re-affirmed that it was not in a position to decide whether to cross-examine the witness. The Chamber decided to postpone the remainder of the witness's testimony.[9]

---

1 T. 13 October 2006 p. 1 (Status Conference).

2 *Bagosora et al.*, Decision on Bagosora Motion to Present Additional Witnesses and Vary Its Witness List (TC), 17 November 2006; T. 13 October 2006 p. 6 (Status Conference).

3 T. 8 November 2006 pp. 1-2; T. 14 November 2006 p. 24 (draft).

4 Motion, para. 6.

5 Registrar's Submissions, filed on 13 November 2006; Exhibit DNS-229A.

6 T. 8 November 2006 p. 8.

7 T. 8 November 2006 p. 9.

8 *Id.* pp. 9-11.

9 T. 9 November 2006 p. 30.

5. The Kabiligi Defence then called Witness YC-03. At the end of the examination-in-chief and the Prosecution cross-examination the following day, 9 November 2006, the Nsengiyumva Defence indicated that it was not able to take a position in respect of any additional cross-examination of the witness. The Chamber decided that the witness would remain in Arusha, subject to possible recall by the Nsengiyumva Defence, which should consult with its client on the basis of the transcripts in order to determine whether to cross-examine the witness.[10] After the completion of the examination-in-chief of the next Kabiligi witness, Witness LAX-2, the Nsengiyumva Defence again reserved its right to conduct a cross-examination.[11] On 13 November 2006, the Nsengiyumva Defence repeated its objection to hearing evidence in the absence of the Accused. The Chamber nevertheless heard Kabiligi Witness FB-25, who had previously appeared in the trial as Ntabakuze Witness DM-190.

6. On 13 November 2006, the Chamber received a second medical report from the Registry stating that the Accused would be able to attend trial hearings effective 14 November 2006, subject to being able to take a ten-minute break every two hours, and to elevate his leg.[12] The next day, the Accused was present in court, but complained that he was in significant pain that made it difficult for him to consult meaningfully with his counsel.[13]

DELIBERATIONS

7. Article 20 (4)(d) of the Statute recognizes the right of an accused "to be tried in his or her presence". This right, however, is not absolute; it is subject to "the proportionality principle, pursuant to which any restriction on a fundamental right must be in service of a sufficiently important objective and must impair the right no more than is necessary to accomplish the objective".[14] Furthermore, implied waiver of this right may arise where an accused is given the opportunity to attend trial, but declines to do so without establishing good cause for the absence.[15] No implied waiver will arise where an accused shows good cause, such as the existence of a medical condition that makes attending trial impossible.[16] **[page 4]**

8. Failure to attend proceedings because of illness must be substantiated by a professional medical assessment.[17] The Chamber accepts, on the basis of the first medical report submitted by the Registry, that the Accused was unable to attend trial proceedings on 8, 9, 10 and 13 November 2006. On 14 November 2006, the Accused came to court and addressed the Chamber, saying that he was in pain which prevented him from following the proceedings or engaging in meaningful consultations with his lawyers.[18] Although the Chamber is sympathetic to this claim, it must be guided by the medical report prepared by the attending physician. That report says that the Accused was sufficiently recovered to attend the trial on 14 November 2006. As of that date, the Accused's absence from court has not been substantiated by a professional medical opinion. The Chamber must infer in such circumstances that the Accused's absence is not justified by good cause.[19] Having said this, the Chamber remains open to any further medical reports that may suggest the contrary, and is anxious to ensure that the Accused is closely monitored to ensure that he receives the highest possible standard of health care.[20]

9. The Chamber does not consider that any unjustifiable restriction has been placed on the Accused's right to be present at his trial. First and foremost, the case for the Accused has already closed. None of the witnesses now being called by the other Defence teams appear to be adverse to the Accused. Nsengiyumva argues, nonetheless, that prejudicial testimony might be elicited by the Prosecution from those witnesses, in

10 *Id.* p. 75.

11 T. 10 November 2006 p. 5. The other Defence teams declined to cross-examine the witness.

12 Registrar's Submissions, filed on 13 November 2006; Exhibit DNS-229B.

13 T. 14 November 2006 p. 2 (draft).

14 *Zigiranyirazo*, Decision on Interlocutory Appeal (AC), 30 October 2006, para. 14.

15 *Barayagwiza*, Decision on Defence Counsel Motion to Withdraw (TC), 2 November 2000, paras. 6-7.

16 *Kajelijeli*, T. 2 October 2001 p. 33; *Krstic*, Case No. IT-98-33-T, Decision Adjourning the Trial (TC), 15 January 2001, para. 27.

17 *See e.g. Naletilic and Martinovic*, T. 31 May 2002 pp. 12117-12118, *Kajelijeli*, T. 2 October 2001 p. 33; *Krstic*, Case No. IT 98-33-T, Decision Adjourning the Trial (TC), 15 January 2001, para. 27. In these cases, the Chambers found that there was an implied waiver of the Accused's right to be present.

18 T. 14 November 2006 p. 2.

19 *Naletilic and Martinovic*, T. 31 May 2002 p. 12117-12118; *Kajelijeli*, T. 2 October 2001 p. 33.

20 T. 14 November 2006 pp. 1-3.

particular of Witness ALL-42 and Kambanda, and that the Defence might be able to obtain exculpatory testimony from these and other Kabiligi witnesses.

10. The Chamber has taken measures to address the concerns raised by the Nsengiyumva Defence, to the extent that they are justified. The Prosecution cross-examination of Witness ALL-42 was deferred until 16 November 2006. The testimony of other witnesses has been heard, but the Chamber has indicated its openness to specific submissions to allow the recall of these witnesses for additional questioning and, in one case, directed that a witness remain in Arusha to provide the Nsengiyumva Defence, in consultation with the Accused, an opportunity to decide whether to do so.[21] Transcripts and video-recordings of the testimony are available to the Accused so that he can meaningfully and knowledgeably consult with his Defence team about the need to cross-examine the witness or, at least, to offer more specific submissions concerning the relevance of the their testimony to the Accused.

11. The Nsengiyumva Defence has been unable to show the relevance to the Accused of any testimony heard in his absence. The only specific area of potential interest identified by the Nsengiyumva Defence during the testimony so far concerns a few questions posed to Witness LAX-2 concerning his knowledge of a Prosecution witness.[22] Witness LAX-2 made no reference to Nsengiyumva in his testimony, and the context in which he mentions the Prosecution witness is unrelated to any testimony by that witness against the Accused.[23] The Chamber considers the connection between this testimony and Nsengiyumva to be, at its **[page 5]** highest, marginal. No undue restriction is placed on the Accused's right to be present at his trial by permitting this testimony to be heard under the conditions described above.

12. The Defence has invoked the recent Appeals Chamber decision in *Zigiranyirazo* to reverse a Trial Chamber decision to hear a witness in The Netherlands while the Accused observed proceedings by video-link in Arusha, accompanied by his counsel. A series of factors show that precedent to be inapposite. The witness being heard in that case was considered a "key Prosecution witness" against the accused, whereas the witnesses here are appearing on behalf of another co-Accused and no showing has been made that these witnesses have any particular relevance to Nsengiyumva.[24] A further consideration was the Appeals Chamber's opinion that other options could have been explored to ensure that the Accused was present during the hearing of the witness. The Appeals Chamber did not accept as determinative or as sufficiently established the claims that the witness's security would be at risk by travelling to Arusha, and that the Accused was barred from entering The Netherlands for the hearing.[25] No such considerations are relevant in the present case. Finally, Mr. Zigiranyirazo was being tried alone. Here, the Chamber must consider the potential impact of an adjournment on, in particular, the rights of the Accused Kabiligi. Significant, long-term efforts are often required to ensure the appearance of witnesses before this Tribunal. The risk of losing witnesses poses a much greater threat of prejudice to the Accused Kabiligi than the speculative and remote prejudice to the Accused Nsengiyumva.

FOR THE ABOVE REASONS, THE CHAMBER

DENIES the motion.

Arusha, 17 November 2006

Erik Møse Presiding Judge	Jai Ram Reddy Judge	Sergei Alekseevich Egorov Judge

[Seal of the Tribunal]

21 T. 9 November 2006 p. 76.

22 *Id.* pp. 83-84; T. 10 November 2006 pp. 1-2.

23 T. 9 November 2006 pp. 87-88; T. 10 November 2006 p. 5.

24 *Zigiranyirazo*, Decision on Interlocutory Appeal (AC), 30 October 2006, para. 21.

25 *Id.*, paras. 18, 20.

International Criminal Tribunal for Rwanda
Tribunal pénal international pour le Rwanda

OR: ENG

TRIAL CHAMBER III

Before Judges: Dennis C. M. Byron, Presiding
Gberdao Gustave Kam
Vagn Joensen

Registrar: Adama Dieng

Date: 11 July 2007

THE PROSECUTOR

v.

Édouard KAREMERA
Mathieu NGIRUMPATSE
Joseph NZIRORERA

Case No. ICTR-98-44-T

DECISION ON JOSEPH NZIRORERA'S MOTION FOR STAY OF PROCEEDINGS WHILE HE IS UNFIT TO ATTEND TRIAL OR CERTIFICATION TO APPEAL

Article 20 of the Statute, Rule 73(B) of the Rules of Procedure and Evidence

---

Office of the Prosecutor:
Don Webster
Alayne Frankson-Wallace
Iain Morley
Saidou N'Dow
Gerda Visser
Sunkarie Ballah-Conteh
Takeh Sendze

Defence Counsel for Édouard Karemera
Dior Diagne Mbaye and Félix Sow

Defence Counsel for Mathieu Ngirumpatse
Chantal Hounkpatin and Frédéric Weyl

Defence Counsel for Joseph Nzirorera
Peter Robinson and Patrick Nimy Mayidika Ngimbi

[page 2] INTRODUCTION

1. On 27 June 2007 when Defence Counsel for Mathieu Ngirumpatse was scheduled to continue his cross-examination of Prosecution Witness Jean Bosco Twahirwa, the Chamber received a note from UN Medical Officer Epée Hernandez certifying that Joseph Nzirorera was unfit to attend trial for three days.[1] Defence Counsel for Nzirorera then requested that the cross-examination of the witness be stayed until Nzirorera was fit to attend trial.[2]

2. The Chamber, in an Oral Decision, denied the request and decided to hear the evidence of the witness in the absence of Joseph Nzirorera.[3] When Defence Counsel for Nzirorera indicated that the health situation of his client was likely to recurrently make him unfit to attend trial, the Chamber decided to hold an *in camera* conference with the Parties on how to proceed when an accused is unfit to attend.[4]

3. At the resumption of proceedings on 28 June 2007, Defence Counsel for Joseph Nzirorera made an Oral Motion requesting the Chamber to reconsider its Oral Decision to continue the proceedings in the absence of Nzirorera, or to grant certification to appeal a Chamber's Decision to continue the proceedings in the absence of the Accused.[5]

4. The Chamber granted, in part, the request for reconsideration and modified its previous Oral Decision by allowing the cross-examination by Defence Counsel for Joseph Nzirorera to be postponed until Nzirorera was fit to attend trial again. The Chamber maintained that cross-examination by Defence Counsel for Mathieu Ngirumpatse and Edouard Karemera should continue in the absence of Nzirorera.[6] The Chamber further considered that certification was appropriate in this case. It indicated that it would give its **[page 3]** reasons for granting certification in writing, as well as include guidelines for how to proceed in the future when an accused is unfit to attend trial.[7]

5. The present written Decision must be considered as the authoritative statement of the Chamber's findings and reasoning concerning the above-mentioned oral rulings. The Chamber will first set out relevant guidelines for deciding how to proceed in the absence of an accused person. The Chamber will then will address the issue of certification to appeal its Oral Decision denying Mr. Nzirorera's request to stay the proceedings in the absence of the Accused.

On the Continuation of Proceedings in the Absence of an Accused

6. In support of his motion that proceedings be stayed, the Defence Counsel for Joseph Nzirorera argued that his client wanted to attend the cross-examination and did not consent to it proceeding in his absence. He submitted that since the UN Medical Officer had certified that the Accused was unfit to attend his trial, Rule 82 *bis* of the Rules of Procedure and Evidence ("Rules") providing for the power of the Chamber to continue the proceedings in the absence of an accused person while the later refuses to attend was not applicable. He recalled that the right of an accused to attend his own trial is fundamental. The Defence Counsel acknowledged that this right is not absolute, but submitted that according to the Appeals Chamber's Decision in the *Zigiranyirazo* case ("*Zigiranyirazo* Decision"), these situations are limited to instances where the accused refuses to attend or disrupts the proceedings.[8] Furthermore, in the Defence's view, the Trial Chamber Decision of 19 April 2007 in the *Bagosora et al.* case, in which the Chamber decided to continue in the absence of the Accused Anatole Nsengiyumva,[9] could not be applied under the present circumstances as in that case, the concerned Accused had already closed his case.

[1] T. 27 June 2007, p. 1.
[2] *Ibid*, pp. 1-2.
[3] T. 27 June 2007, p. 11.
[4] *Ibidem.*
[5] T. 28 June 2007, p. 1.
[6] T. 28 June 2007, p. 7
[7] *Ibidem.*
[8] The Defence made a reference to *Prosecutor v. Protais Zigiranyirazo*, Case No. ICTR-2001-73-AR73, Decision on Interlocutory Appeal (AC), 30 October 2006 ("*Zigiranyirazo* Appeals Chamber Decision").
[9] *Prosecutor v. Bagasora et al.*, Case No. ICTR-98-41-T, Decision on Nsengiyumva Motions to Call Doctors and to Recall Eight Witnesses (TC), 19 April 2007, para.1.

7. Defence Counsel for Karemera supported the motion and further argued that it is not sufficient for an accused who is unfit to attend trial to read the transcripts because his illness is also an impediment to reading the transcripts. He further submitted that it is not possible to observe the demeanour of a witness by reading the transcripts.[10] **[page 4]**

8. Defence Counsel for Ngirumpatse also supported the motion and argued further that the Rules only allow for the proceedings to be continued in the absence of an accused when the later refuses to attend; as such, there is no legal basis to order that the proceedings be continued without the consent of the Accused when he wants to attend the proceedings but is unfit to do so.[11]

9. The Prosecution, while conceding that the right of the Accused to be present at his trial is fundamental, argued that the Chamber properly applied the proportionality principle set out in the *Zigiranyirazo* Decision when it decided to continue the proceedings in the absence of Joseph Nzirorera as this Accused had followed the Prosecution witness' examination-in-chief.[12] It furthermore submitted that no information was elicited from the witness concerning any acts of Nzirorera and asserted that by reading the transcripts with the assistance of his Defence Counsel, Nzirorera could follow the witness' testimony during his absence and might – upon showing good cause – request that the witness be recalled for further cross-examination, It submitted that the Chamber's Decision was in line with the Trial Chamber Decision of 19 April 2007 in the *Bagosora et al.* case.

10. The Prosecution further stated that the rights of Witness Jean Bosco Twahirwa should also be taken into account. It recalled that the witness had already been called to Arusha to testify in this trial during the previous session, had been compelled to come again during the present session, and had already waited two weeks before testifying.[13]

11. According to Article 20(4)(d) of the Statute of the Tribunal, an accused has a right to be tried in his or her presence. The Chamber acknowledges that the physical presence of an accused before the Chamber, as a general rule, is one of the most basic and common principles of a fair criminal trial.[14]

12. However, the Chamber notes that the right of an accused to be present at his or her trial is not absolute, as stated by the Appeals Chamber in the *Zigiranyaro* case.[15] In the *Zigiranyirazo* Decision, the Appeals Chamber held:

> In assessing a particular limitation on a statutory guarantee on a fundamental right, the Appeals Chamber bears in mind the proportionality principle, pursuant to which any restriction on a fundamental right must be in service of a sufficiently important objective and must impair the right no more than is necessary to accomplish the objective, The explicit exception provided by Rule 80(B) and the ICTY Appeals Chamber's reference to "substantial **[page 5]** trial disruptions" provide a useful measure by which to assess other restrictions on the right to be present at trial.[16]

13. The issue in the *Zigiranyirazo* case was whether the Trial Chamber had exceeded its discretion by deciding without the consent of the accused to hear a key witness by video link. The Appeals Chamber agreed "that the objectives advanced by the Trial Chamber [were] of general importance: witness protection, the proper assessment of an important prosecution witness and the need to ensure a reasonably expeditious trial", but was not satisfied that the Trial Chamber, in the circumstances of the case, had properly exercised its discretion in deciding to impose limitations on Zigiranyirazo's right to be present at his trial.[17]

14. In the present case, the objective at stake is the need to ensure a reasonably expeditiously trial which, as acknowledged by the Appeals Chamber, is of general importance. The issue at stake is whether there are limitations which can be placed on the access of an accused to the examination of a witness, without

[10] T. 28 June 2007, p. 3.
[11] T.28 June 2007, p. 4.
[12] T. 28 June 2007, p. 5.
[13] T. 28 June 2007, p. 6.
[14] See *Zigiranyirazo* Appeals Chamber Decision, para. 11.
[15] *Zigiranyirazo* Appeals Chamber Decision, para. 14.
[16] *Ibidem* (footnote omitted).
[17] *Zigiranyirazo* Appeals Chamber Decision, para. 17.

materially and disproportionably impairing his rights pursuant to Article 20(4)(d) of the Statute to be tried in his presence.

15. The Chamber recalls that a Trial Chamber may admit witness evidence, not obtained in the presence of an accused, which goes to proof of a matter other than the acts and conduct of the accused as charged in the indictment, either in the form of a written statement pursuant to Rule 92 *bis* or by taking judicial notice of adjudicated facts on the basis of, for instance, witness evidence in other proceedings before the Tribunal pursuant to Rule 94.[18]

16. In a Decision of 16 June 2006, the Appeals Chamber addressed the issue of admitting evidence pursuant to Rule 92 *bis* and Rule 94 in relation to the Accused being charged as members of a joint criminal enterprise, as follows:

> As to all other adjudicated facts relating to the criminal responsibility of the accused, it is for the Trial Chambers, in the careful exercise of their discretion, to assess each particular fact in order to determine whether taking judicial notice of it—and thus shifting the burden of producing evidence rebutting it to the accused—is consistent with the accused's rights under the circumstances of the case. This includes facts related to the existence of a joint criminal **[page 6]** enterprise and the conduct of its members other than the accused—and, more generally, facts related to the conduct of physical perpetrators of a crime for which the accused is being held criminally responsible through some other mode of liability. Contrary to the contentions of Mr. Nzirorera and Mr. Ngirumpatse, there is a distinction between such facts and those related to the acts and conduct of the accused themselves. In the *Galić* case, in the context of Rule 92 *bis*, the ICTY Appeals Chamber considered and rejected an argument similar to that raised by the Accused here:
>
>> The appellant emphasises that Rule 92 *bis* excludes from the procedure laid down any written statement which goes to proof of the acts and conduct of the accused as charged in the indictment. He says that, as the indictment charges the appellant with individual criminal responsibility -
>> (i) as having aided and abetted others to commit the crimes charged, and
>> (ii) as the superior of his subordinates who committed those crimes,
>> the acts and conduct of those others and of his subordinates "represent his own acts". The appellant describes those "others" as "co-perpetrators", and he says that the "acts and conduct of the accused as charged in the indictment" encompasses the acts and conduct of the accused's co-perpetrators and/or subordinates. This argument was rejected by the Trial Chamber.
>> The appellant's interpretation of Rule 92 *bis* would effectively denude it of any real utility. That interpretation is inconsistent with both the purpose and the terms of the Rule. It confuses the present clear distinction drawn in the jurisprudence of the Tribunal between (a) the acts and conduct of those others who commit the crimes for which the indictment alleges that the accused is individually responsible, and (b) the acts and conduct of the accused as charged in the indictment which establish his responsibility for the acts and conduct of those others. It is only a written statement which goes to proof of the latter acts and conduct which Rule 92 *bis* (A) excludes from the procedure laid down in that Rule.89 The Appeals Chamber considers this analysis equally applicable in the Rule 94(B) context."[19]

17. In the Chamber's view, hearing witness evidence which goes to proof of a matter other that the acts and conduct of an accused who is unfit to attend his trial is less intrusive on the accused's right to be present at his trial than admitting witness evidence pursuant to Rule 92 *bis* and Rule 94, bearing in mind that the Defence Counsel of the accused will be present and that the accused – upon showing good cause – may request that witnesses be recalled for further cross-examination.

---

18 Rules 92 *bis* of the Rules of Procedure and Evidence provides:

> A Trial Chamber may admit, in whole or in part, the evidence of a witness in the form of a written statement in lieu of oral testimony which goes to proof of a matter other than the acts and conduct of the accused as charged in the indictment.

Rule 94(B) of the Rules provides:

> At the request of a party or *proprio motu*, a Trial Chamber, after hearing the parties, may decide to take judicial notice of adjudicated facts or documentary evidence from other proceedings of the Tribunal relating to the matter at issue in the current proceedings.

19 *Prosecutor v. Edouard Karemera, Mathieu Ngirumpatse, Joseph Nzirorera* ("*Karemera et al.*"), Case No. ICTR-98-44-AR73(C), Decision on Prosecutor's Interlocutory Appeal of Decision on Judicial Notice (AC), 16 June 2006, para. 52, citing *Prosecutor v. Galić*, Case No. IT-98-29-AR73.2, Decision on Interlocutory Appeal Concerning Rule 92 *bis* (C), 7 June 2002.

18. A similar position was also expressed in the *Bagosora et al.* case. In that trial where four accused are jointly prosecuted in a joint criminal enterprise case, the Trial Chamber held that the examination-in chief by an accused in the absence of a co-accused who was unfit to attend trial did not unfairly impair the right of the co-accused to be tried in his presence as the evidence that was likely to be elicited from the witness would not be directed against him.[20] **[page 7]**

19. Based on these considerations the Chamber finds that hearing the testimony of a witness which goes to proof of matters other than the acts and conduct as charged in the indictment against the said accused, such as the alleged acts and conduct of the co-accused, in the absence of an accused who is unfit to attend his trial, does not materially and disproportionably impair his rights to be present at his trial.

20. In view of this principle, the Chamber is of the view that since the evidence that was likely to be elicited from Witness Jean Bosco Twahirwa only concerned the alleged acts and conduct of the accused Mathieu Ngirumpatse, cross-examination of the witness could continue although Joseph Nzirorera was unfit to attend the trial.

21. However, as the cross-examination by Defence Counsel for Joseph Nzirorera was scheduled to be done on a Friday when the Chamber only sits in the morning, and as Nzirorera, according to the UN Medical Officer, would be fit to attend trial again the following Monday, the Chamber, upon reconsideration of its Decision,[21] found that the need to ensure a reasonably expeditious trial was not seriously affected by allowing the cross-examination by Defence Counsel for Nzirorera to be postponed until the following Monday.

On the Certification to Appeal the Chamber's Decision

22. In support of his motion for certification to appeal the Chamber's Decision, Defence Counsel for Joseph Nzirorera submitted that the Decision to hear evidence in the absence of Nzirorera touches upon a fundamental right of the Accused to be tried in his presence. He further submitted that the issue has not been addressed before by the Appeals Chamber and is likely to occur recurrently due to Nzirorera's health situation and will seriously affect the length of the trial.

23. The Defence Counsels for Edouard Karemera and Mathieu Ngirumpatse and the Prosecutor supported the request for certification. **[page 8]**

24. Rule 73(B) of the Rules provides that Decisions on a party's motion are without interlocutory appeal. However, the Rule confers a discretion on the Chamber to grant certification to appeal when certain clearly delimited conditions are fulfilled: the applicant must satisfy the two prong test and show (i) how the impugned Decision involves an issue that would significantly affect a fair and expeditious conduct of the proceedings or the outcome of the trial, and (ii) that an "immediate resolution by the Appeals Chamber may materially advance the proceedings". Even then, certification to appeal must remain exceptional.[22] Certification is not determined on the merits of the appeal against the impugned decision.[23]

---

20 *Bagosora et al.*, Decision on Nsengiyumva Motions to Call Doctors and to Recall Eight Witnesses (TC), 19 April 2007, para. 1.

21 According to the established jurisprudence, a Chamber has the inherent power to reconsider its decisions when (i) a new fact has been discovered that was not known to the Chamber at the time it made its original Decision, (ii) there has been a material change in circumstances since it made its original Decision, or (ii) there is reason to believe that its original Decision was erroneous or constituted an abuse of power on the part of the Chamber, resulting in injustice thereby warranting the exceptional remedy of reconsideration. See: *Karemera et al.*, Case No. ICTR-98-44-PT, Decision on the Defence Motions for Reconsideration of Protective Measures for Prosecution Witnesses, 29 August 2005, para. 8; *Karemera et al.*, Case No. ICTR-98-44-T, Decision on Defence Motion for Modification of Protective Order: Timing of Disclosure, 31 October 2005, para. 3; *Karemera et al.*, Case No. ICTR-98-44-T, Decision on Motion for Reconsideration or Certification to Appeal Decision on Motion for Order Allowing Meeting with Defence Witness, 11 October 2005, para. 8 (note also the authorities cited in footnotes contained within that paragraph).

22 *Prosecutor v. Arsène Shalom Ntahobali and Pauline Nyiramasuhuko*, Case No. ICTR-97-21-T, Decision on Ntahobali's and Nyiramasuhuko's Motions for Certification to Appeal the 'Decision on Defence Urgent Motion to Declare Parts of the Evidence of Witnesses RV and QBZ Inadmissible' (TC), 18 March 2004, para. 15; *Prosecutor v. Nyiramasuhuko et al.*, Case No ICTR-98-42-AR73, Decision on Pauline Nyiramasuhuko's Request for Reconsideration (AC), 27 September 2004, para. 10.

23 *Karemera et al.*, Decision on Defence Motion for Certification to Appeal Decision Granting Special Protective Measures for Witness ADE (TC), 7 June 2006, para. 5.

25. In the present instance, the Chamber is satisfied that the health of Joseph Nzirorera may make him unfit to attend trial recurrently. Therefore, should all proceedings be stayed during periods when the Accused is unfit to attend trial, the completion of the trial could be further seriously delayed. The Chamber also notes that the Appeals Chamber has not before been seized to address the issue whether evidence can be heard in the absence of an accused who is unfit to attend trial, and this issue touches upon a fundamental right of an accused as previously stated by the Appeals Chamber. Furthermore, should the Chamber's Decision to continue proceedings in the absence of an accused in accordance with the above-mentioned guidelines be overturned upon an appeal of the judgement, it might affect the outcome of the appeal judgment.

26. Accordingly, the Chamber is satisfied that the requirements for granting certification to appeal as articulated in Rule 73(B) are met in the present case.

FOR THE ABOVE MENTIONED REASONS, THE CHAMBER

I. **REJECTS** the Defence Request to stay proceedings in the absence of Joseph Nzirorera;

II. **GRANTS** in part the Defence Request to reconsider its Decision so that the cross-examination by Defence Counsel for Joseph Nzirorera of Witness Jean Bosco Twahirwa be postponed; **[page 9]**

III. **GRANTS** the Defence Motion for certification to appeal the present Decision in all aspects, including the standards set out by this Chamber to continue hearing evidence in the absence of an accused.

Arusha. 11 July 2007, done in English.

Dennis C. M. Byron	Gberdao Gustave Kam	Vagn Joensen
Presiding Judge	Judge	Judge

[Seal of the Tribunal]

Tribunal Pénal International pour le Rwanda
International Criminal Tribunal for Rwanda

IN THE APPEALS CHAMBER

Before:	Judge Fausto Pocar, Presiding Judge Mohamed Shahabuddeen Judge Liu Daqun Judge Theodor Meron Judge Wolfgang Schomburg
Registrar:	Mr. Adama Dieng
Decision of:	5 October 2007

THE PROSECUTOR

v.

Édouard KAREMERA
Mathieu NGIRUMPATSE
Joseph NZIRORERA

Case No. ICTR-98-44-AR73.10

DECISION ON NZIRORERA'S INTERLOCUTORY APPEAL CONCERNING HIS RIGHT TO BE PRESENT AT TRIAL

Office of the Prosecutor:

Mr. James Stewart
Mr. Don Webster
Mr. George W. Mugwanya
Ms. Inneke Onsea

Counsel for the Defence:

Ms. Dior Diagne Mbaye and Mr. Félix Sow for Mr. Édouard Karemera
Ms. Chantal Hounkpatin and Mr. Frédéric Weyl for Mr. Mathieu Ngirumpatse
Mr. Peter Robinson and Mr. Patrick Nimy Mayidika Ngimbi for Mr. Joseph Nzirorera

[page 2] 1. The Appeals Chamber of the International Criminal Tribunal for the Prosecution of Persons Responsible for Genocide and Other Serious Violations of International Humanitarian Law Committed in the Territory of Rwanda and Rwandan Citizens Responsible for Genocide and Other Such Violations Committed in the Territory of Neighbouring States, between 1 January and 31 December 1994 ("Appeals Chamber" and "Tribunal", respectively) is seized of an interlocutory appeal filed by Joseph Nzirorera ("Appellant") on 16 July 2007[1] against a decision rendered by Trial Chamber III on 11 July 2007, concerning the right of an accused to be present at trial.[2] The Prosecution responded on 27 August 2007,[3] and the Appellant replied on 28 August 2007.[4]

A. Background

2. On 27 June 2007, counsel for the Appellant informed the Trial Chamber that the Appellant was ill and that a medical doctor had pronounced him unfit to attend trial for three days.[5] Counsel requested the Trial Chamber to adjourn the proceedings until the Appellant would be medically fit to attend his trial.[6] The Trial Chamber denied the request by oral decision and held that it would proceed with the cross-examination of Prosecution Witness Twahirwa in the absence of the Appellant.[7] The Trial Chamber also requested the assistance of the Registry in ensuring "that the relevant transcripts as well as the minutes of the proceedings" would be provided to the Appellant as soon as available.[8] The Trial Chamber then held an *in camera* conference with the parties and adjourned the proceedings until the following day.[9] **[page 3]**

3. On 28 June 2007, the Appellant requested reconsideration of the Trial Chamber's oral decision to proceed with the cross-examination of Witness Twahirwa in his absence or certification to appeal.[10] The Trial Chamber reconsidered its decision in part and orally ruled that Witness Twahirwa's cross-examination by the Appellant should be stayed until his return to court but that this witness's cross-examination by the Appellant's co-accused should proceed in the Appellant's absence.[11] The Trial Chamber stated that it would set out the reasons for its decision in writing.[12]

4. The Appellant's co-accused continued with their cross-examination of Witness Twahirwa on Thursday, 28 June 2007, in the Appellant's absence, but in the presence of the Appellant's counsel. One of the Appellant's co-accused was unable to conclude his cross-examination on that day, and the Trial Chamber

---

1 Joseph Nzirorera's Appeal from Decision to Proceed in the Absence of the Accused, 16 July 2007 ("Nzirorera's Appeal").

2 *The Prosecutor v. Édouard Karemera et al.*, Case No. ICTR-98-44-T, Decision on Joseph Nzirorera's Motion for Stay of Proceedings while Unfit to Attend Trial or Certification to Appeal – Article 20 of the Statute, Rule 73(B) of the Rules of Procedure and Evidence, 11 July 2007 ("Impugned Decision").

3 Mr. Ngirumpatse and Mr. Karemera also filed appeals against the Impugned Decision on 14 August 2007 and on 21 August 2007, respectively (*Mémoire d'appel pour M. Ngirumpatse contre la Décision* 'on Joseph Nzirorera's Motion for Stay of Proceedings While He Is Unfit to Attend Trial or Certification to Appeal', 14 August 2007; *Mémoire d'appel relatif à la décision rendue le 11 juillet 2007 par la Chambre III. Sur* [sic] *la suspension de la procédure lorsque l'accusé n'est pas en mesure d'assister au procès*, 21 August 2007). On 27 August 2007, the Prosecution filed a consolidated Response to Nzirorera, Ngirumpatse and Karemera's Appeal from Decision to Proceed in the Absence of the Accused ("Response"). In its Decision on Requests for Extension of Time, issued on 29 August 2007, the Appeals Chamber found that Mr. Karemera and Mr. Ngirumpatse had not been granted certification to appeal and it *inter alia* rejected their appeal briefs, *see* Decision on Requests for Extension of Time, 29 August 2007, para. 7. On 30 August 2007, Mr. Ngirumpatse filed a "*Mémoire en intervention pour M. Ngirumpatse au soutien de l'appel de Nzirorera contre la décision* 'on Joseph Nzirorera's Motion for Stay of Proceedings while He Is Unfit to Attend Trial or Certification to Appeal'", which has been rejected by the Appeals Chamber, *see* Decision on Ngirumpatse's Motion for Reconsideration, 5 October 2007. The Appeals Chamber also recognized the Response as validly filed, *see* Decision on Nzirorera's Motion to Reject Prosecution Response, 5 October 2007, p. 4.

4 Reply Brief: Joseph Nzirorera's Appeal from Decision to Proceed in the Absence of the Accused, 28 August 2007 ("Reply").

5 *See* T. 27 June 2007, p. 11.

6 *See* T. 27 June 2007, p. 9.

7 *Id.*, p. 11.

8 *Id.*

9 *See* T. 27 June 2007, p. 23.

10 *See* T. 28 June 2007, p. 1.

11 *See* T. 28 June 2007, p. 7.

12 *Id.*

adjourned the proceedings until Monday, 2 July 2007.[13] On that day, Witness Twahirwa's cross-examination and re-examination were completed in the presence of the Appellant and his counsel.[14]

5. On 11 July 2007, the Trial Chamber issued the Impugned Decision setting out its written reasons for denying the Appellant's request to stay the proceedings in his absence and granting the Appellant certification to appeal.[15]

6. The Appellant submits that in proceeding with the cross-examination of Witness Twahirwa by his co-accused in his absence, the Trial Chamber violated his fundamental right to be tried in his presence, as guaranteed by Article 20(4)(d) of the Statute of the Tribunal ("Statute").[16] The Appellant stresses that he wanted to attend his trial but was unfit to do so for medical reasons.[17] Accordingly, the Appellant seeks exclusion of Witness Twahirwa's testimony taken in his absence.[18] **[page 4]**

B. Standard of Review

7. Decisions relating to the general conduct of trial proceedings are matters within the discretion of the Trial Chamber.[19] The Impugned Decision, which ruled on the right of the accused to be present at trial, was such a discretionary decision to which the Appeals Chamber must accord deference. Such deference is based on the recognition by the Appeals Chamber of "the Trial Chamber's organic familiarity with the day-to-day conduct of the parties and practical demands of the case."[20] A Trial Chamber's exercise of discretion will thus be reversed only if the Appellant demonstrates that the Trial Chamber made a discernible error in the Impugned Decision because it was based on an incorrect interpretation of governing law, was based on a patently incorrect conclusion of fact, or was so unfair or unreasonable as to constitute an abuse of the Trial Chamber's discretion.[21]

C. Alleged violation of the right to be present at trial

8. In the Impugned Decision, the Trial Chamber concluded that the cross-examination of Witness Twahirwa by the Appellant's co-accused could proceed in his absence, despite his request for an adjournment, which was based on medical reasons and prevented his presence in court.

9. The Appellant submits that while the right to be present at one's trial is not absolute,[22] the only permissible exceptions are where an accused waives his right to be present or where his obstructionist conduct in the courtroom warrants a restriction of that right by the Chamber.[23] In identifying those circumstances as the only conditions which justify a court proceeding in his absence, the Appellant draws upon the *Zigiranyirazo* Decision, which held that the right to be present at one's trial can only be limited "where an accused disrupts the trial or in other similar circumstances".[24] The Appellant adds that any further limitations to those envisioned in Rules 82*bis* **[page 5]** and 80(B) of the Rules of Procedure and Evidence of

---

13 *See* T. 28 June 2007, pp. 74-76.

14 *See* T. 2 July 2007, pp. 1, 3.

15 *See* Impugned Decision, paras. 5, 22-26.

16 *See* Nzirorera's Appeal, paras. 5, 8; Nzirorera's Reply, para. 20.

17 *See* Nzirorera's Appeal, paras. 18, 25.

18 *See* Nzirorera's Reply, para. 20.

19 *See The Prosecutor v. Élie Ndayambaje et al.*, Case No. ICTR-98-42-AR73, Decision on Joseph Kanyabashi's Appeals against the Decision of Trial Chamber II of 21 March 2007 concerning the Dismissal of Motions to Vary his Witness List, 21 August 2007 ("*Kanyabashi* Decision"); *The Prosecutor v. Édouard Karemera et al.*, Case No. ICTR-98-44-AR73.8, Decision on Interlocutory Appeal Regarding Witness Proofing, 11 May 2007, para. 3; *Protais Zigiranyirazo v. The Prosecutor*, Case No. ICTR-2001-73-AR73, Decision on Interlocutory Appeal, 30 October 2006 ("*Zigiranyirazo* Decision"), para. 9.

20 *Prosecutor v. Zdravko Tolimir et al.*, Case No. IT-04-80-AR73.1, Decision on Radivoje Miletić's Interlocutory Appeal Against the Trial Chamber's Decision on Joinder of Accused, 27 January 2006, para. 4; *Prosecutor v. Slobodan Milošević*, Case No. IT-02-54-AR73.7, Decision on Interlocutory Appeal of the Trial Chamber's Decision on the Assignment of Defence Counsel, 1 November 2004, para. 9.

21 *See Kanyabashi* Decision, para. 10; *Zigiranyirazo* Decision, para. 9.

22 *See* Nzirorera's Appeal, para. 14; Nzirorera's Reply, para. 2.

23 *See* Nzirorera's Appeal, paras. 15-21.

24 *See* Nzirorera's Appeal, paras. 23-25.

the Tribunal ("Rules") must come from amendments to the Rules, not *ad hoc* decisions of Trial Chambers.[25]

10. The Prosecution responds that a Trial Chamber can validly continue a trial where an accused is absent for reasons other than misconduct or voluntary absence.[26] In this regard, it disputes the relevance of the precedent mentioned by the Appellant, stressing that this jurisprudence does not involve the present circumstance of an accused's absence from trial due to illness.[27]

11. Article 20(a)(d) of the Statute provides that an accused has a right "to be tried in his or her presence". The Appeals Chamber has interpreted the scope of this right as meaning that an accused has a right to be *physically* present at his trial.[28] However, the Appeals Chambers of both this Tribunal and of the International Criminal Tribunal for the former Yugoslavia ("ICTY") have also held that the right to be present at trial is not absolute.[29] In the *Zigiranyirazo* Decision, this Appeals Chamber held that an accused person can waive or forfeit the right to be present at trial.[30] The Appeals Chamber noted that Rule 80(B) of the Rules allows a Trial Chamber to remove an accused for persistent disruption of the proceedings. It further held that in determining to restrict any statutory right of an accused, the Appeals Chamber must take into account "the proportionality principle, pursuant to which any restriction on a fundamental right must be in service of a sufficiently important objective and must impair the right no more than is necessary to accomplish the objective."[31]

12. In the present case, the Trial Chamber cast the proportionality analysis in the following terms:

> [T]he objective at stake is the need to ensure a reasonably expeditious trial which, as acknowledged by the Appeals Chamber, is of general importance. The issue at stake is whether there are limitations which can be placed on the access of an accused to the examination of a witness, without materially and disproportionably impairing his rights pursuant to Article 20(A)(d) of the Statute to be tried in his presence.[32]

The Trial Chamber also took account of the fact that Witness Twahirwa's testimony only concerned the alleged acts and conduct of one of the Appellant's co-accused.[33] **[page 6]**

13. The Appellant contends that the Trial Chamber misapplied the proportionality principle set forth in the *Zigiranyirazo* Decision and used it as "an opportunity to proceed in the absence of the accused if it balanced the prejudice to him against the benefits of an expeditious trial."[34] The Appellant also argues that, in proceeding with Witness Twahirwa's testimony on the premise that it only went to the acts and conduct of his co-accused, the Trial Chamber violated the principle set forth in the Rules that in a joint trial, each accused is to be accorded the same rights as if he were being tried separately.[35] He adds that, "under the Prosecution's joint criminal enterprise and conspiracy theories, Mr. Nzirorera can be convicted for the acts of Mr. Ngirumpatse".[36] The Appellant also disputes the Trial Chamber's reliance in the Impugned Decision on Rules 92*bis* and 94(B) of the Rules.[37]

14. The Prosecution responds that the Trial Chamber reasonably applied the proportionality principle, striking an appropriate balance between the reasonably expeditious resolution of the case and the need to

---

25 *See* Nzirorera's Appeal, paras. 35-36, 38.

26 *See* Response, para. 4.

27 *See* Response, paras. 8-9, 11-12.

28 *See Zigiranyirazo* Decision, paras. 11-13.

29 *See Zigiranyirazo* Decision, para. 14; *Slobodan Milošević v. The Prosecutor*, Case No. IT-02-54-AR73.7, Decision on Interlocutory Appeal of the Trial Chamber's Decision on the Assignment of Defense Counsel, 1 November 2004 ("*Milošević* Decision"), para. 13.

30 *See Zigiranyirazo* Decision, para. 14.

31 *Id.* (footnotes omitted).

32 *See* Impugned Decision, para. 14.

33 *See* Impugned Decision, para. 20.

34 Nzirorera's Appeal, paras. 26, 34. In this connection, the Appellant also submits that, had the Trial Chamber been concerned with the expeditiousness of the trial, it should have considered other alternatives, such as the severance of Nzirorera's trial from his co-accused pursuant to Rule 81(B) of the Rules, *see* Nzirorera's Appeal, paras. 30-33.

35 *See* Nzirorera's Appeal, paras. 30-32. Although the Appellant mentions Rule 81, the Appeals Chamber understands that he is in fact referring to Rule 82 of the Rules.

36 Nzirorera's Appeal, para. 47.

37 *See* Nzirorera's Appeal, paras. 39-51.

protect the fair trial rights of the Appellant.[38] It adds that the reference to Rule 92*bis* of the Rules in the Impugned Decision is correct "merely as a measure by which to assess the fairness of continuing the trial in the absence of the accused."[39]

15. The Appeals Chamber agrees that the right to an expeditious trial as a right guaranteed to all accused by the Statute of the Tribunal was a relevant consideration for the Trial Chamber in balancing whether or not to proceed in the absence of the Appellant. However, in the circumstances of this complex and lengthy case, the Appeals Chamber is not satisfied that the three day delay to the trial was sufficient to outweigh the statutory right of the Appellant to be present at his own trial when the absence of the Appellant was due to no fault of his own. Furthermore, the Appeals Chamber holds that the Trial Chamber's comparison between the limitations placed on the Appellant's "access [...] to the examination of a witness"[40] and the restrictions permitted under Rules 92*bis* and 94(B) of the Rules is misguided. Rules 92*bis* and 94(B) address the proof of facts of a matter other than the acts of the accused. In the present case, the issue was quite different, namely, whether the presence of an accused is required during the cross-examination of a witness by a co-accused or his counsel. In the circumstances of a joint trial, it is irrelevant for the purpose of that determination whether or not the witness's testimony was likely to concern the alleged acts and **[page 7]** conduct of a co-accused only. The Appeals Chamber is therefore not satisfied that in the present circumstances, the Trial Chamber properly exercised its discretion. The Trial Chamber's restrictions on the Appellant's fair trial rights were unwarranted and excessive and thus fail the proportionality test. Accordingly, the Trial Chamber committed a discernible error.

16. In light of the fact that the parties dispute the relevance of the testimony of Witness Twahirwa,[41] the Appeals Chamber will leave the question of whether the portion of Witness Twahirwa's testimony taken in the Appellant's absence should be excluded and whether that witness should be recalled for cross-examination in the presence of the Appellant,[42] to the discretion of the Trial Chamber, which is best placed to assess the significance of Witness Twahirwa's testimony in relation with the charges against the Appellant. The Trial Chamber may order the remedy, if any, that it deems appropriate to cure any prejudice.

D. Disposition

17. On the basis of the foregoing, the Appeals Chamber **GRANTS** Nzirorera's Appeal, **REVERSES** the Impugned Decision, and **REMANDS** to the Trial Chamber the consideration of the prejudice, if any, accrued to the Appellant by proceeding, in his absence, with the cross-examination of Witness Twahirwa by the other co-accused in a manner consistent with this Decision.

Done in English and French, the English version being authoritative.

Dated this 5th day of October 2007,
at The Hague, The Netherlands.

Fausto Pocar
Presiding Judge

[Seal of the Tribunal]

38 *See* Response, paras. 15-17.

39 Response, para. 20.

40 Impugned Decision, para. 14.

41 *See* Nzirorera's Appeal, paras. 45-47; Response, para. 16.

42 Nzirorera's Reply, para. 20 footnote 13; s*ee also* Response, para. 5.

Commentary

1. Introduction

From the time of the first *ad hoc* tribunal's inception, critics have questioned the legitimacy of *ad hoc* tribunals and the way in which the judges have repetitively made laws inapposite to the commonly recognised general principles of law observed by civilised national legal systems. The amalgamation of common law and civil law legal systems in the international criminal proceedings has meant that judges from all corners of the globe have had to find a balance between the two systems. The trial of an accused in *absentia* would definitely raise eyebrows among common law jurists. By contrast, in some civil law legal systems, such a trial would largely go unnoticed. This distinction is a reflection of how trials in *absentia* are perceived in both legal systems but this is very deceptive. In civil law legal systems, restrictions on trials in *absentia* such as, effective service of summons to the accused such that it is clear he has wilfully evaded trial and the accused's right to oppose a judgment in *absentia*, negate the value of such trials. On the other hand, common law legal systems provide for exceptions to the right of a person to be present at trial and these include: where an accused consents to trial in *absentia*; where he is summoned but absconds jurisdiction; where his conduct during trial justifies trial in *absentia*, to mention but a few.[1]

In light of the exceptions under common law legal systems and of the limited value of the convictions under civil law legal systems, some scholars have described the distinction between common law legal systems and civil law legal systems with respect to trials in *absentia,* as being artificial.[2] It can be concluded that both legal systems adhere to the right of an accused to be present at his or her trial; each legal system gives life to this principle in its own way, grounded in its traditions. A bird's eye view through the legislations of countries, where trials in *absentia* are common, points to the fact that such trials largely emanate from the unwillingness of the accused to appear at his trial.[3] The reverse is true for the decisions at hand;[4] in all these decisions, the parties objecting to trials in *absentia* are willing to attend their trials but for reasons beyond their control, they are unable to do so.

The central issue is whether the right to be present at one's trial requires physical presence or whether there are limitations to this right, if so, what criteria are applied in assessing such limitations. At the end of each decision, a reader is confronted with different sub issues. In Zigiranyirazo, the issue arises as to whether the right to be present at one's trial can be satisfied by video link. In Bagosora, the question is whether the Trial Chamber exceeded its discretion when it decided, without the consent of the accused, to continue the trial proceedings in his absence. Finally, in Karemera, the issue at stake is whether in a joint trial, the need to ensure a reasonably expeditious trial and the fact that a witness's testimony is likely to concern the co-accused's alleged acts and conduct, could be justifications for an accused's trial in *absentia*. This commentary reflects on these issues by analysing the substantive and procedural aspects of the decisions above.

2. Whether the right to be present at one's trial can be satisfied by video link?

The decision on interlocutory appeal in the case of Zigiranyirazo emanated from the Trial Chamber's decision to hear the testimony of a key witness for the prosecution in person in the Netherlands while the

[1] Secretariat Memorandum Prepared by the Directorate of Legal affairs, Judgments *in Absentia*, European Committee on Crime Problems, Strasbourg, 3 March 1998, p. 2.

[2] *Ibid.*

[3] Countries where trials *in absentia* are common include, Italy, Germany, Spain, Netherlands, Greece, France, among others.

[4] ICTR, Decision on Interlocutory Appeal, *Zigiranyirazo v. Prosecutor*, Case No. ICTR-73-AR73, A. Ch., 30 October 2006, in this volume p. 219; ICTR, Decision on Nsengiyumva Motion for Adjourment due to Illness of the Accused, *Prosecutor v. Bagosora, Kabiligi, Ntabakuze and Nsengiyumva,* Case No. ICTR-98-41-T, T. Ch. I, 17 November 2006, in this volume, p. 229; ICTR, Decision on Joseph Nzirorera's Motion for Stay of Proceedings While he is Unfit to Attend Trial or Certification to Appeal (Article 20 of the Statute, Rule 73 (B) of the Rules of Procedure and Evidence), *Prosecutor v. Karemera, Ngirumpatse and Nzirorera*, Case No. ICTR-98-44-T, T. Ch. III, 11 July 2007, in this volume, p. 233; ICTR, Decision on Nzirorera's Interlocutory Appeal Concerning his Right to be Present at Trial, *Prosecutor v. Karemera, Ngirumpatse and Nzirorera*, Case No. ICTR-98-44-AR73.10, A. Ch., 5 October 2007, in this volume, p. 239.

accused, Mr. Zigiranyirazo, participated via video-link from Arusha.[5] Below is an analysis of the issue at hand, followed by the highlights of the decision.

2.1 Participation of an accused via video link

The right to be present at one's trial is one of the most fundamental safeguards of the rule of law. The primary interest secured by this right is the ability of the accused to confront his witnesses. In so doing, the witness's reliability and credibility can be verified through reading his or her facial expressions or body language for traces of deception. The rationale behind this is to enable the accused to exercise his right to defence effectively; only after hearing evidence against him can the accused effectively and efficiently rebut such evidence.

In Zigiranyirazo, the appellant claimed that he "'saw' the proceedings through the selective eyes of a camera operated by a third party."[6] He and his attorney could not speak directly to the judges, gauge their reactions, and adjust the arguments and tenor of pleadings as if they were in open court with the members of the bench."[7]

It is highly probable that a video link testimony will portray a partial view of the witness, making it difficult for an accused to fully visualize the witness's body language. In so doing, the video link testimony can undermine the ability of an accused to effectively defend himself or herself. This problem cannot be resolved by the mere presence of the accused's counsel at the trial; it is the accused, not his counsel, who knows how best to confront any witness or evidence against him. In Zigiranyirazo, the presence of the accused during the testimony of the prosecution's key witness was very important for two main reasons: i) with the existence of plea bargaining and lenient sentencing in case of cooperation with the court, information gained from a key witness who at the same time is an accused before the tribunal is the most suspect and the most potentially unreliable type of evidence,[8] ii) assessing reliability of a witness through facial expressions or body language is not a skill that all judges possess and in international criminal proceedings, the situation is made worse by the use of interpreters.

In general, witnesses have testified before international criminal tribunals and the International Criminal Court through interpretations meaning the judges cannot hear the witness, but only the interpreter. Often, there have been misunderstandings caused by interpreters of difficult languages, resulting in both parties to the trial contesting the outcome. Depending on the interpreter's background and the judges' background, there is a likelihood that the body language of a witness from a different background will be misread, for example, behaviours that in western culture are considered evidence of unreliability, such as gaze aversions when talking to someone, are in certain cultures considered a sign of respect. In such cases, if the accused and the witness share the same language and cultural background, the accused is better placed to detect a lie than the judges.

Based on the foregoing, the Appeals Chamber's finding that the Trial Chamber erred in adopting the procedure for hearing the testimony of Mr. Bagaragaza in person in the Netherlands while the accused, participated via video-link from Arusha, is fair and rhymes with the commonly recognised principle of the right to be present at one's trial, observed by international, regional and national legal systems.

2.2 Definition of the term presence and the proportionality principle

The decision is of vast importance in the international arena not only because it defines the scope of the term 'presence' within the meaning of Article 20, paragraph 4 sub d, ICTR Statute, but also because it sets the criteria for assessing limitations to the right to be tried in one's presence. In this regard, the chamber emphasizes the importance of the right to be tried in one's presence and notes that as a matter of ordinary English, the term 'presence' within the meaning of Article 20, paragraph 4 sub d, ICTR Statute implies

5 ICTR, Scheduling Order, *Prosecutor v. Zigiranyirazo*, Case No. ICTR-2001-73-T, T. Ch. III, 26 May 2006, p. 2-3; ICTR, Extremely Confidential Decision on Defence Motion Concerning the Hearing of Witness ADE, *Prosecutor v. Zigiranyirazo*, Case No. ICTR-2001-73-T, 5 June 2006, T. Ch. III, par. 2.

6 ICTR, Protais Zigiranyirazo Appeal from the Extremely Confidential Decision on Defense Motion Concerning the Hearing of Witness ADE, *Prosecutor v. Zigiranyirazo*, Case No. ICTR-2001-73-AR73, A. Ch., 19 June 2006, par. 25.

7 *Ibid.*

8 See, Decision on Interlocutory Appeal, *Zigiranyirazo v. Prosecutor*, A. Ch, *supra* note 4, footnote 3 of the decision, referring to the dual status of Mr. Bagaragaza before the tribunal.

physical proximity.[9] The chamber also states that the right to be physically present at trial is not absolute; a person could waive or forfeit the right to be present at trial.[10] Above all, the chamber notes that in assessing limitations to this right, the proportionality principle must be born in mind; pursuant to this principle, any restriction on a fundamental right must be in service of a sufficiently important objective and must impair the right no more than is necessary to accomplish the objective.[11]

2.3 Balancing the interests of the accused and the obligation of the tribunal to protect witnesses

The decision is a reminder to the Trial Chamber that the balance between the interests of the accused and the obligation of the tribunal in protecting witnesses should be kept as evenly as possible. This balance is very important, especially in light of the code of conduct of judges which encompasses their impartiality and independence. Keeping up with this spirit, the chamber finds that based on the proportionality principle, the circumstances in the case did not warrant any restriction on the appellant's right. On the same point, the chamber notes that the objectives advanced by the Trial Chamber were of general importance, that is to say, i) The record did not reflect that the security concern, alluded to by the Trial Chamber, was related to the location of the witness's testimony;[12] ii) The record did not show that the Trial Chamber examined the possibility that additional security measures would allay any security threat if the witness were to be brought to Arusha to testify;[13] iii) None of the "external variables," alluded to by the Trial Chamber, preventing the appellant's personal attendance at his own trial, resulted from any action on his part;[14] iv) There was no indication that the Trial Chamber explored an alternative venue for hearing the testimony, other than The Netherlands.[15]

2.4 Balance between the rights of an accused and the public interests of judicial efficiency

The decision underscores the importance of striking a balance between the rights of an accused and the public interests of judicial efficiency. This is highlighted in the chamber's reasoning that the Trial Chamber's misgivings about its ability to adequately follow the testimony of a key witness through the use of video-link, if valid, had to apply with equal force to the ability of the accused and his counsel to follow the evidence and proceedings.[16]

3. Whether the Trial Chamber exceeded its discretion when it decided, without the consent of the accused, to continue the trial proceedings in his absence?

In Bagosora, the accused persons were indicted for conspiracy to commit genocide, war crimes and crimes against humanity.[17] The Trial Chamber was tasked with a motion for adjournment due to the illness of Nsengiyumva, one of the accused persons.[18] Relying on the chamber's findings in Zigiranyirazo, the Trial Chamber noted that the right to be tried in one's presence is not absolute and that it is subject to the proportionality principle.[19] The Trial Chamber also considered that implied waiver of this right may arise where an accused is given the opportunity to attend trial, but declines to do so without establishing good cause for the absence.[20]

---

9 Decision on Interlocutory Appeal, *Zigiranyirazo v. Prosecutor*, A. Ch., *supra* note 4, par. 11-13.

10 *Id.*, par. 14.

11 Decision on Interlocutory Appeal, *Zigiranyirazo v. Prosecutor*, A. Ch., *supra* note 4, par. 14; ICTY, Decision on Interlocutory Appeal of the Trial Chamber's Decision on the Assignment of Defense Counsel, *Prosecutor v. Milošević*, Case No. IT-02-54-AR73.7, A. Ch., 1 November 2004, Klip/ Sluiter, ALC-XX-189, par. 13.

12 Decision on Interlocutory Appeal, *Zigiranyirazo v. Prosecutor*, A. Ch., *supra* note 4, par. 18.

13 *Ibid.*

14 *Id.*, par. 20.

15 *Ibid.*

16 Decision on Interlocutory Appeal, *Zigiranyirazo v. Prosecutor*, A. Ch., *supra* note 4, par. 19.

17 ICTR, Judgement and Sentence, *Prosecutor v. Bagosora, Kabiligi, Ntabakuze, Nsengiyumva*, Case No. ICTR-98-41-T, T. Ch. I, 18 December 2008, to be published in volume XXXII, par. 2.

18 ICTR, Motion Requesting Suspension of Trial on Medical Grounds, *Prosecutor v. Bagosora, Kabiligi, Ntabakuze, Nsengiyumva.*, Case No. ICTR-98-41-T, T. Ch. I, 8 November 2006.

19 Decision on Nsengiyumva Motion for Adjourment due to Illness of the Accused, *Prosecutor v. Bagosora, Kabiligi, Ntabakuze and Nsengiyumva*, T. Ch. I, *supra* note 4, par. 7; Decision on Interlocutory Appeal, *Zigiranyirazo v. Prosecutor*, A. Ch., *supra* note 4, par. 14.

20 Decision on Nsengiyumva Motion for Adjourment due to Illness of the Accused, *Prosecutor v. Bagosora, Kabiligi, Ntabakuze and Nsengiyumva*, T. Ch. I, *supra* note 4, par. 7; ICTR, Decision on Defence Counsel Motion to Withdraw, *Prosecutor v. Barayagwiza*, Case No. ICTR-97-19-T, T. Ch. I, 2 November 2000, Klip/ Sluiter, ALC-VI-279, par. 6-7.

Although the Trial Chamber cited the correct law applicable in motions relating to adjournment due to illness, it erred in law and abused its discretion, when it decided to proceed with the trial despite objections from the accused, based on the grounds set out in the decision. In evaluating the Trial Chamber's errors, three main issues arise from its decision, namely: 1) whether an accused's failure to submit a third medical report to substantiate his illness allegations amounts to implied waiver of the right to be tried in his or her presence; 2) whether the closure of the accused's case is a justification for hearing witness testimony of a co-accused, in the absence of the accused; 3) whether the defence's inability to show the relevance to the accused of any witness testimony presented by his co-accused, could be a justification for the accused's trial in *absentia*?

Below is a critical analysis of the different grounds relied on by the Trial Chamber in deciding to deny the Nsengiyumva motion.

3.1 Defence's failure to submit a third medical report to substantiate the accused's illness allegations

With all due respect, the Trial Chamber erred in fact and abused its discretion when it acted in disregard of the registry's first medical report which recommended a week's rest for the accused. By holding that failure to attend proceedings because of illness must be substantiated by a professional medical assessment, the Trial Chamber implies that submission of a medical report is good cause for requesting for adjournment of the trial proceedings.[21] The Trial Chamber admitted that the accused was unable to attend the trial during the week that the registry had recommended for his rest. However, the Trial Chamber did not consider the question whether, in accordance with the proportionality principle, a week's delay of the trial based on the first medical report, was insufficient to outweigh the accused's right to be present. Instead, the Trial Chamber took issue with the accused's two days absence from court without submission of the third medical report and concluded that his absence was not justified by good cause. Although the Trial Chamber noted that it was open to any further medical reports that would suggest the contrary, this could not compensate for the trial of the accused in *absentia* during the registry's recommended week for resting.[22]

It is important to note that the Trial Chamber made the decision after the accused's failure to attend court for two days only, that is, from the time stipulated in the second medical report. Considering that the second medical report had recommended a ten-minute break for the accused every two hours, and elevation of his leg, a reasonable Trial Chamber should have requested the registry for further medical examination of the accused to find out whether his allegations were correct.[23] The recommendation set out in the second medical report was indicative of the fact that the accused had not completely recovered. The possibility of a recurring illness should have been taken into consideration by the Trial Chamber.

3.2 Closure of the accused's defence case and the fact that none of the witnesses called by the other defence teams appeared to be adverse to him

Bearing in mind that the accused persons were indicted for participating in a joint criminal enterprise (JCE), there was an oversight on the part of the Trial Chamber when it denied the defence's motion based on the ground that the case for the accused had already closed and that none of the witnesses being called by the other defence teams appeared to be adverse to the accused. The four accused were charged with conspiracy to commit genocide, genocide, crimes against humanity and serious violations of Article 3 common to the Geneva Conventions and Additional Protocol II (violence to life and outrages upon personal dignity).[24]

---

21 Decision on Nsengiyumva Motion for Adjourment due to Illness of the Accused, *Prosecutor v. Bagosora, Kabiligi, Ntabakuze and Nsengiyumva*, T. Ch. I, *supra* note 4, par. 8; See *e.g.* ICTY, Transcript, *Prosecutor v. Naletilic and Martinovic*, Case No. IT-98-34-A, T. Ch. I, 31 May 2002, p. 12117-12118; ICTR, Transcript, *Prosecutor v. Kajelijeli*, ICTR-98-44A-T, T. Ch. II, 2 October 2001 p. 33; ICTY, *Prosecutor v. Krstic*, Decision Adjourning the Trial, Case No. IT-98-33-T, T. Ch. I, 15 January 2001, par. 27. In these cases, the chambers found that there was an implied waiver of the Accused's right to be present.

22 Decision on Nsengiyumva Motion for Adjourment due to Illness of the Accused, *Prosecutor v. Bagosora, Kabiligi, Ntabakuze and Nsengiyumva*, T. Ch. I, *supra* note 4, par. 8; ICTR, Transcript, *Prosecutor v. Bagosora, Kabiligi, Ntabakuze and Nsengiyumva*, Case No: ICTR-98-41-T, T. Ch. I, 14 November 2006, p. 1-3.

23 ICTR, Registrar's Submissions, *Prosecutor v. Bagosora, Kabiligi, Ntabakuze and Nsengiyumva*, Case No: ICTR-98-41-T, T. Ch. I, filed on 13 November 2006; Exhibit DNS-229B; Decision on Nsengiyumva Motion for Adjourment due to Illness of the Accused, *Prosecutor v. Bagosora, Kabiligi, Ntabakuze and Nsengiyumva*, T. Ch. I, *supra* note 4, par. 6.

24 Judgement and Sentence, *Prosecutor v. Bagosora, Kabiligi, Ntabakuze, Nsengiyumva*, T. Ch. I, *supra* note 17, par. 2.

Nsengiyumva was also accused of direct and public incitement to commit genocide.[25] The prosecution relied on direct or superior responsibility.[26]

In cases involving JCE, the accused persons are considered to be conspirators; an accused can be convicted for crimes committed by co-accused persons in furtherance of a common plan or purpose. The accused can also be convicted for crimes which did not happen as a result of the JCE but were a natural consequence of the JCE or were foreseeable. In effect, the Trial Chamber erred in law when it found that the accused's presence was not important since his case had closed and none of the witnesses being called by the other defence teams appeared to be adverse to him.

3.3 The postponement of witness ALL-42's cross-examination by the prosecution and the Trial Chamber's openness to hearing specific submissions for recalling the witnesses

The Trial Chamber erred in law when it justified the accused's trial in *absentia* based on the fact that the prosecution's cross-examination of witness ALL-42 had been postponed until the return of the accused to court. It is important to note that counsel for the accused had informed the Trial Chamber that witnesses ALL-42 and Kambanda were of great importance to the accused, because of the prejudicial testimony and also the possibility of getting exculpatory testimony from them.[27] Effective cross-examination requires that the defence is well equipped with the testimony that the witness has given during the examination in chief. As noted above, reliance on the witness's testimony depends on the verbal, facial and body expressions. Denying an accused the right to be present during the examination in chief of a witness while postponing the witness's cross examination by the prosecution until the accused is able to attend trial, is unjust as it leads to severance of the witness's testimony. This defect in trial proceedings could lead to a miscarriage of justice.

The Trial Chamber also erred in law and wrongly exercised its discretion when it held that it was open to hearing specific submissions for recalling witnesses heard in the accused's *absentia*. In Zigiranyirazo's decision, the chamber held that a person could waive or forfeit the right to be present at trial; by way of example, the chamber cited Rule 80 (B) of its Rules of Procedure and Evidence, which allows a Trial Chamber to remove a persistently disruptive accused. In the same decision, the chamber noted that none of the "external variables," alluded to by the Trial Chamber, preventing the appellant's personal attendance at his own trial, resulted from any action on his part. It is clear that in Bagosora, the accused's absence during trial resulted from reasons beyond his control, therefore, the Trial Chamber erred in law when it decided that the burden of proof lay on the accused to show that it was necessary to recall the witnesses; the right to be present at one's trial is a fundamental guarantee and the accused need not give justifications for such a right. Naturally, all men have certain inherent rights among which include, enjoying and defending their lives and liberties; such rights are regarded as unalienable. Derogation from such rights requires justifications set out above. The Trial Chamber's decision does not confirm to the exceptions above.

3.4 Availability of transcripts and video-recordings of the testimony to the accused so that he could meaningfully and knowledgeably consult with his defence team about the need to cross-examine the witnesses

As noted above, the primary interest secured by the right to be present at one's trial is the ability of the accused to confront his witnesses. In so doing, the witness's reliability and credibility can be verified through reading his or her facial expressions or body language for traces of deception. It's obvious that such observations can not be fully obtained through reading transcripts. The disadvantages of video-recordings are similar to the disadvantages of video link testimony which are referred to the Zigiranyirazo commentary above. Zigiranyirazo case highlights the importance of physical evidence as opposed to presence by video link; clearly the Trial Chamber in Bagosora misses the main issue in Zigiranyirazo Appeal Decision. As noted by the Nsengiyumva defence, the Trial Chamber should also have taken into consideration the fact that the accused's illness was an impediment to his ability to review transcripts and to watch the videos.[28] By

---

25 *Ibid.*

26 *Ibid.*

27 Decision on Nsengiyumva Motion for Adjourment due to Illness of the Accused, *Prosecutor v. Bagosora, Kabiligi, Ntabakuze and Nsengiyumva*, T. Ch. I, *supra* note 4, par. 2-3.

28 Decision on Nsengiyumva Motion for Adjourment due to Illness of the Accused, *Prosecutor v. Bagosora, Kabiligi, Ntabakuze and Nsengiyumva*, T. Ch. I, *supra* note 4, par. 8; Transcript, *Prosecutor v. Bagosora, Kabiligi, Ntabakuze and Nsengiyumva,* T. Ch. I, *supra* note 22, p. 2.

finding that the transcripts and video recordings of the testimony were available to the accused so that he could consult with his defence team about the need to cross examine the witnesses, the Trial Chamber acts in complete disregard of the registry's medical report which had recommended a week's rest for the accused.

3.5 The Nsengiyumva defence had been unable to show the relevance to the accused of any testimony heard in his absence.

Considering the complexity and length of the JCE trials, relevancy of the witnesses' testimony to the accused is a good factor to take into consideration when evaluating a motion for adjournment. However, if the accused insists that the witnesses are relevant to him, especially, if he indicates that they could provide prejudicial or exculpatory evidence, it is not for defence counsel to show the relevancy of the testimony to the accused. Defence counsel receives instructions from the accused. On several occasions, the defence declined from cross examining witnesses and repetitively insisted that the accused had to be present to provide them with instructions. In this respect, the Trial Chamber erred in law when it relied on the defence's failure to show the relevance to the accused of any testimony, as a justification for his trial in *absentia*. Further, the accused persons in this case were considered conspirators in a JCE; as noted above an accused could be convicted for the crimes of other co-accused persons. In effect, all defence witnesses are either directly or indirectly relevant to each of the accused.

3.6 Distinction between Bagosora and Zigiranyirazo

The Trial Chamber highlighted the difference between the case at hand and Zigiranyirazo. Firstly, the Trial Chamber noted that the witness being heard in that case was considered a "key Prosecution witness" against the accused, whereas the witnesses in Bagosora were appearing on behalf of another co-accused and no showing had been made that these witnesses had any particular relevance to Nsengiyumva.[29]

Secondly, the Trial Chamber pointed out that in Zigiranyirazo, Mr. Zigiranyirazo was being tried alone, however in Bagosora, the potential impact of an adjournment on the rights of the co-accused Kabiligi had to be taken into consideration. In this regard, the Trial Chamber noted that significant long-term efforts are often required to ensure the appearance of witnesses before the tribunal. It concluded that the risk of losing witnesses posed a much greater threat of prejudice to the accused Kabiligi than the speculative and remote prejudice to the accused Nsengiyumva.

In my opinion the two distinctions do not hold water. Whether or not a witness is a key witness does not make a difference since conviction of an accused is based on evaluation of all evidence adduced in relation to the crimes charged. Further, the potential impact of an adjournment on a co-accused and the risks of losing witnesses are issues of general importance pertaining to all trials; the Trial Chamber does not explain how these two issues are related to the case at hand. In the Zigiranyirazo decision, the chamber reversed the Trial Chamber's decision reasoning that the objectives advanced by the Trial Chamber to justify the trial via video link were of general importance.

In Bagosora, the Trial Chamber relies on the potential impact of such adjournment on the rights of the Kabiligi, however, the Trial Chamber does not evaluate the specific impact of such adjournment on Kabiligi. Neither does it ask for Kabiligi's views on the matter. The Trial Chamber also relies on the long-term efforts 'often' required to secure witnesses' presence, however, it does not explore the relevancy of Kabiligi's witnesses to those efforts. In a nutshell, the Trial Chamber erred in law and in fact when it relied on the distinctions above to justify the accused's trial in *absentia*.

4. **Whether in a joint trial, the need to ensure a reasonably expeditious trial and the fact that a witness's testimony concerned the co-accused's alleged acts and conduct, could be a justification for trial of an accused in *absentia*?**

In Karemera, the Trial Chamber was informed by the medical doctor that the accused was unfit to attend trial for three days. The accused requested for an adjournment of the proceedings until he was fit to attend trial.[30] The Trial Chamber reiterated the proportionality principle as set out in Zigiranyirazo. It highlighted the objective at stake which was the need to ensure a reasonably expeditious trial. Further, the Trial Chamber

[29] Decision on Interlocutory Appeal, *Zigiranyirazo v. Prosecutor*, A. Ch, *supra* note 4, par. 21.

[30] ICTR, Decision on Joseph Nzirorera's Motion for Stay of Proceedings While he is Unfit to Attend Trial or Certification To Appeal, *Prosecutor v. Karemera et al.*, Case No. ICTR-98-44-T, T. Ch. III, 11 July 2007, par. 1-2.

drew a comparison between the limitations placed on the appellant's access to the examination of a witness and the restrictions permitted under Rule 92 *bis* and 94 (B) of the Rules, and concluded that the fact that the witness testimony only concerned the alleged acts and conduct of one of the co-accused was a justification for the accused's trial in *absentia*.[31]

Similar to Bagosora, the Trial Chamber misapplies the proportionality principle by relying on general objectives to deny the accused's request for adjournment. The Trial Chamber is correct to take into consideration the right to expeditious trial when evaluating the accused's request, however, the Trial Chamber falls short of evaluating the impact of a three days delay on this right. Neither does it consider the effect of the co-accused's evidence on the accused's conviction.

Not surprising, the chamber reverses the Trial Chamber's decision and holds that a three days delay in such a complex and lengthy case would be insufficient to outweigh the statutory right of the appellant to be present at his own trial, when the absence of the appellant was due to no fault of his own.[32]

The chamber also finds that the Trial Chamber's comparison between the limitations placed on the appellant's access to the examination of a witness and the restrictions permitted under Rules 92 *bis* and 94 (B) of the Rules was misguided.[33] Whereas Rules 92 *bis* and 94 (B) address the proof of facts of a matter other than acts of the accused, Karemera addressed the presence of an accused during the cross-examination of a witness by a co-accused or his counsel.[34] Further, the chamber holds that in a joint trial, whether or not the witness's testimony is likely to concern the alleged acts and conduct of a co-accused is irrelevant in determining the motion above.[35]

Evidently, the Trial Chamber misapplied Rules 92 *bis* and 94 (B) and the chamber's finding in this regard is good law. It is not clear why, having explicitly defined the scope of Rules 92 *bis* and 94 (B), the Trial Chamber goes on to draw a comparison between the Rules and the limitations to the accused's right to be present during trial.[36] *Prima facie,* the examples cited by the Trial Chamber as falling within Rules 92 *bis* and 94 (B), that is, written statements and adjudicated facts do not correspond to the oral evidence that the accused seeks to obtain. Moreover, the Trial Chamber relies on the Bagosora trial decision to justify its finding and as illustrated above, this precedent left a lot to be desired.[37]

5. Conclusion

One way or another, the cases above are similar. In all cases, the accused persons do not consent to being tried in their physical absence; neither do they abscond from jurisdiction. Further, none of the accused persons conducts himself in a manner that justifies his trial in *absentia.* Therefore, all cases do not fall within the ambit of the limitations to the right to be tried in one's presence, recognised by civilised legal systems worldwide.

In cases like the ones above, divergence from commonly recognised principles of law has become inevitable. Depending on the number of accused persons, length of the trial, and complexity of the case, the margin of divergence can be smaller or bigger. International criminal law judges have often sought guidance from judicial interpretations and precedents, principles of natural justice and procedural fairness, among others. The end product is a set of modified principles applicable to similar or different facts. The cases above provide a clear demonstration of how these principles are shaped, applied and checked by the International Criminal Tribunal for Rwanda.

Goreth Kyakuwa

[31] Decision on Joseph Nzirorera's Motion for Stay of Proceedings While he is Unfit to Attend Trial or Certification To Appeal, *Prosecutor v. Karemera et al.*, T. Ch. III, *supra* note 30, par. 12, 14 and 19.

[32] ICTR, Decision on Nzirorera's Interlocutory Appeal Concerning his Right to be Present at Trial, *Prosecutor v. Karemera et al.*, Case No. ICTR-98-44-AR73.10, A. Ch., 5 October 2007, p. 15.

[33] *Ibid.*

[34] *Ibid.*

[35] *Ibid.*

[36] *Id.*, par. 15-17.

[37] Decision on Joseph Nzirorera's Motion for Stay of Proceedings While he is Unfit to Attend Trial or Certification To Appeal, *Prosecutor v. Karemera et al.*, T. Ch. III, *supra* note 30, par. 18.

International Criminal Tribunal for Rwanda
Tribunal pénal international pour le Rwanda

ORIGINAL: ENGLISH

TRIAL CHAMBER I

Before: Judge Erik Møse, presiding
Judge Jai Ram Reddy
Judge Sergei Alekseevich Egorov

Registrar: Adama Dieng

Date: 20 September 2006

THE PROSECUTOR

v.

Théoneste BAGOSORA
Gratien KABILIGI
Aloys NTABAKUZE
Anatole NSENGIYUMVA

Case No.: ICTR-98-41-T

MODALITIES FOR PRESENTATION OF A WITNESS

The Prosecution
Barbara Mulvaney
Drew White
Christine Graham
Rashid Rashid

The Defence
Raphaël Constant
Allison Turner
Paul Skolnik
Frédéric Hivon
Peter Erlinder
André Tremblay
Kennedy Ogetto
Gershom Otachi Bw'Omanwa

[page 2] THE INTERNATIONAL CRIMINAL TRIBUNAL FOR RWANDA

SITTING as Trial Chamber I, composed of Judge Erik Møse, presiding, Judge Jai Ram Reddy, and Judge Sergei Alekseevich Egorov;

BEING SEIZED OF the "Ntabakuze Motion Requesting an Order for a Subpoena", filed on 14 September 2006;

CONSIDERING the Prosecution Response and the Defence "Submissions", both filed on 18 September 2006;

HEREBY DECIDES the motion.

INTRODUCTION

1. The Ntabakuze Defence requests a subpoena for the appearance of a serving colonel in the French military to give testimony before this Chamber. This request follows the receipt of a letter from the Government of France indicating that the colonel is available to testify, but only under certain conditions. After being advised that the procedure proposed by the French Government had been substantially followed during the testimony of a French officer before the International Criminal Tribunal for Yugoslavia, the Defence declared that it was "prepared to accept any measures that the Chamber may deem in its discretion, to be reasonable and warranted, under the circumstances".[1]

2. Aside from insisting that the witness's appearance cannot be used to postpone the deadline for the end of the Defence case, the Prosecution took "no other position on the merits of the Motion".[2]

DELIBERATIONS

3. The French Government proposes five conditions for the appearance of the colonel: (i) that the testimony be heard in closed session; (ii) non-disclosure of the witness's identity; (iii) limiting the scope of examination to matters already covered during a previous interview of the witness, and the same limitation on cross-examination; (iv) the presence of a representative of the Government of France in the proceedings who is authorized to assert a national security privilege; and (v) non-disclosure of the witness's testimony to any party to another proceeding.[3] The letter from the Government of France invokes national security as the basis for these requests.

4. No party to these proceedings has opposed the requests. The Defence has pointed out certain factual differences between the present case and the precedent before the ICTY, but accepts that the general statements of law are applicable to the present case. It has also emphasized that any limitation on cross-examination should not adversely affect the Chamber's ability to assess the witness's credibility. Ultimately, however, the Defence:

> wishes to emphasize that it is prepared to accept any measures that the Chamber may deem, in its discretion, to be reasonable and warranted, under the circumstances. Our **[page 3]** main concern is to have the witness testify in a timely manner to the contents of the questionnaire which he has already answered in the presence of the French authorities, in accordance with the usual French procedure, with which the Ntabakuze Defence has scrupulously complied.[4]

5. In the absence of any objection, the Chamber considers the proposed requests to be acceptable in the circumstances, and finds them permissible under the Rules of Procedure and Evidence. Both parties have, in effect, declared that they have no objection to the limitations on the scope of the examination and cross-examination proposed by the French Government. Furthermore, as this is a Defence witness, such limitations do not impair the rights of the Accused. On the contrary, strict insistence on the usual procedures for disclosure and the scope of cross-examination could lead to the testimony not being heard by the close of the

1 Submissions, para. 5.
2 Response, para. 5.
3 Motion, Annex 1.
4 Submissions, para. 5.

Defence case, which would serve the interests of neither the Accused, nor justice. The Chamber has the power to order non-disclosure of the witness's testimony under Rules 53, 54, 75 and 79. Indeed, the very conditions proposed here were previously accepted by a Trial Chamber of the ICTY in *Blaskić*.[5] This Chamber has itself previously permitted the presence of representatives from a national government to assist a witness under similar circumstances.[6] However, as in the *Blaskić* case, it must be the Chamber which resolves any disputes as to the proper scope of questioning which may arise during the testimony.

6. The measures granted in the present instance must be understood as exceptional. The Government of France has invoked national security and appears to have a credible basis for making that claim. **[page 4]**

FOR THE ABOVE REASONS, THE CHAMBER

DENIES the request for subpoena, in light of the willingness of the Government of France to make the witness available to testify;

DECLARES that (i) the testimony be heard in closed session; (ii) the witness's identity will not be disclosed; (iii) examination and cross-examination shall be limited to matters already covered during previous interviews of the witness; (iv) a representative of the Government of France may be present during proceedings and may request that the witness be relieved from answering questions on the grounds of national security; and (v) the witness's testimony shall not be subject to disclosure to any party in another proceeding.

Arusha, 20 September 2006

Erik Møse Presiding Judge	Jai Ram Reddy Judge	Sergei Alekseevich Egorov Judge

[Seal of the Tribunal]

---

5 *The Prosecutor v. Blaskić*, Decision of Trial Chamber I on Protective Measures for General Philippe Morillon, Witness of the Trial Chamber (TC), 12 May 1999.

6 T. 19 January 2004 p. 2 (representative of Government of Canada permitted to be present to assist with the testimony of General Romeo Dallaire).

International Criminal Tribunal for Rwanda
Tribunal pénal international pour le Rwanda

ORIGINAL: ENGLISH

TRIAL CHAMBER I

Before: Judge Erik Møse, presiding
Judge Jai Ram Reddy
Judge Sergei Alekseevich Egorov

Registrar: Adama Dieng

Date: 19 October 2006

THE PROSECUTOR

v.

Théoneste BAGOSORA
Gratien KABILIGI
Aloys NTABAKUZE
Anatole NSENGIYUMVA

Case No.: ICTR-98-41-T

DECISION ON REQUEST FOR SUBPOENA OF AMI R. MPUNGWE

The Prosecution
Barbara Mulvaney
Drew White
Christine Graham
Rashid Rashid
Gregory Townsend

The Defence
Raphaël Constant
Allison Turner
Paul Skolnik
Frédéric Hivon
Peter Erlinder
André Tremblay
Kennedy Ogetto
Gershom Otachi Bw'Omanwa

[page 2] THE INTERNATIONAL CRIMINAL TRIBUNAL FOR RWANDA

SITTING as Trial Chamber I, composed of Judge Erik Møse, presiding, Judge Jai Ram Reddy, and Judge Sergei Alekseevich Egorov;

BEING SEIZED OF the "Request for Trial Chamber to Order the Government of Tanzania to Cooperate and For Subpoena for Ambassador Mpungwe", filed by the Bagosora Defence on 29 September 2006;

CONSIDERING the "Submissions in Support", filed by the Bagosora Defence on 12 October 2006;

HEREBY DECIDES the motion.

1. The Bagosora Defence requests that a subpoena be issued to Ami R. Mpungwe, requiring his appearance before this Chamber to give testimony. Mr. Mpungwe, a former official of the Government of Tanzania, acted as a facilitator during the negotiation of the Arusha Accords in 1992 and 1993.

2. The applicant for a subpoena compelling the appearance of a person as a witness must show that three conditions are satisfied: (i) reasonable attempts have been made to obtain the voluntary cooperation of the witness; (ii) the prospective witness has information which can materially assist the applicant in respect of clearly identified issues relevant to the trial; and (iii) the witness's testimony must be necessary and appropriate for the conduct and fairness of the trial.[1]

3. This Chamber previously considered a request, filed on 7 July 2006, for a subpoena requiring Mr. Mpungwe to meet with the Defence, and for the assistance of the Government of Tanzania in facilitating such a meeting. In a decision of 29 August 2006, the Chamber held that the second and third conditions for the issuance of a subpoena were satisfied:

> A sufficient basis has been established to suggest that Mr. Mpungwe may have information concerning the conduct of Colonel Bagosora during the Arusha negotiations, on which this Chamber has heard direct and potentially incriminating evidence. Further, the evidence relates to a specific allegation in paragraph 5.10 of the Indictment that the Accused "openly manifested his opposition to the concessions made by the Government representative … to the point of leaving the negotiation table. Colonel Théoneste Bagosora left Arusha saying that he was returning to Rwanda to 'prepare the apocalypse'". The Defence has a reasonable basis to believe that Ambassador Mpungwe may have information which could be material to these allegations.[2] **[page 3]**

4. The request for a subpoena was, nonetheless, denied on the basis that reasonable efforts to obtain the witness's cooperation had not yet been exhausted. Although the Defence, in conjunction with the Registry, had been trying to arrange a meeting with Mr. Mpungwe since 28 April 2006,[3] the impasse appeared attributable to the witness's good faith belief that official authorization was required before he could meet with the Defence:

> It appears that [Mr. Mpungwe] is willing to attend a meeting voluntarily, provided that he is given authorization to do so by the Tanzanian government. The Chamber observes, however, that the meeting must be held expeditiously. The trial is in its closing stages, and the Defence must be given a reasonable opportunity to ascertain the nature of the witness's knowledge and, if necessary, to call him as a witness.[4]

5. Despite the Chamber's instruction that the "meeting must be held expeditiously" and "as soon as possible", five more weeks elapsed before a meeting was finally held on 5 October 2006.[5] On 11 October 2006, after a Defence request for answers to additional written questions, Mr. Mpungwe's lawyer advised the Defence that no further responses would be forthcoming. The following day, the Defence requested,

---

1 *Prosecutor v. Krstic*, Case No. IT-98-33-A, Decision on Application for Subpoenas (AC), 1 July 2003, para. 10; *Prosecutor v. Halilovic*, Case No. IT-01-48-AR73, Decision on the Issuance of Subpoenas (AC), 21 June 2004, para. 7; *Bagosora et al.*, Decision on Request for Subpoenas of United Nations Officials (TC), 6 October 2006, para. 3; *Bagosora et al.*, Decision on Request for a Subpoena (TC), 11 September 2006, para. 5; *Karemera et al.*, Decision on Defence Motion for Issuance of Subpoena to Witness T (TC), 8 February 2006, para. 4.

2 *Bagosora et al.*, Decision on the Bagosora Defence Request for Subpoena of Ambassador Mpungwe and Cooperation of the United Republic of Tanzania (TC), 29 August 2006, para. 3.

3 *Bagosora et al.*, Decision on the Bagosora Defence Request for Subpoena of Ambassador Mpungwe and Cooperation of the United Republic of Tanzania (TC), 29 August 2006, para.1.

4 *Id.* para. 4.

5 *Id.* p. 3.

through Mr. Mpungwe's lawyer, the witness's immediate appearance before the Chamber, and filed the present motion.[6] According to the trial schedule, the deadline for the close of the Bagosora Defence case was 13 October 2006, and the close of the trial is scheduled for 13 December 2006.

6. The Chamber considers that the Defence has made reasonable efforts to obtain the witness's voluntary cooperation, and that a subpoena is now required to ensure his timely appearance. The lengthy delays cannot be attributed to the Defence, which appears to have acted in a diligent manner to secure the witness's testimony before the scheduled close of its case. In light of the imminent completion of the present trial, and the history of delays described above, a subpoena is now required to ensure that Mr. Mpungwe appears during the next trial session. **[page 4]**

FOR THE ABOVE REASONS, THE CHAMBER

GRANTS the motion;

ORDERS the Registrar to prepare a subpoena in accordance with this decision, addressed to Ami R. Mpungwe, requiring his appearance before this Chamber to give testimony in the present case;

DIRECTS the Registry to communicate the subpoena to Mr. Mpungwe through appropriate diplomatic channels, accompanied by a copy of this Decision.

Arusha, 19 October 2006

Erik Møse	Jai Ram Reddy	Sergei Alekseevich Egorov
Presiding Judge	Judge	Judge

[Seal of the Tribunal]

6 Submissions, paras. 6-7.

International Criminal Tribunal for Rwanda
Tribunal pénal international pour le Rwanda

OR: ENG

TRIAL CHAMBER II

Before: Judge William H. Sekule, Presiding
Judge Arlette Ramaroson
Judge Solomy Balungi Bossa

Registrar: Mr Adama Dieng

Date: 1 November 2006

The PROSECUTOR v. Élie NDAYAMBAJE
(Case No. ICTR-96-8-T)
The PROSECUTOR v. Joseph KANYABASHI
(Case No. ICTR-96-15-T)
The PROSECUTOR v. Pauline NYIRAMASUHUKO & Arsène Shalom NTAHOBALI
(Case No. ICTR-97-21-T)
The PROSECUTOR v. Sylvain NSABIMANA & Alphonse NTEZIRYAYO
(Case No. ICTR-97-29-T)

Joint Case No. ICTR-98-42-T

DECISION ON PROSECUTION'S MOTION TO UNSEAL THE TRANSCRIPTS OF WITNESS WDUSA

Office of the Prosecutor
Mr Richard Perras
Ms Silvana Arbia
Ms Adelaide Whest
Mr Gregory Townsend
Ms Holo Makwaia
Ms Althea Alexis Windsor
Mr Cheikh T. Mara
Ms Astou Mbow, Case Manager

Defence Counsel for Ndayambaje
Mr Pierre Boulé
Defence Counsel for Kanyabashi
Mr Michel Marchand
Ms Simone Santerre
Defence Counsel for Nyiramasuhuko
Ms Nicole Bergevin
Mr Guy Poupart
Defence Counsel for Ntahobali
Mr Normand Marquis
Mr Louis Huot
Defence Counsel for Nsabimana
Ms Josette Kadji
Defence Counsel for Nteziryayo
Mr Titinga Frédéric Pacere
Mr Richard Perras

[page 2] THE INTERNATIONAL CRIMINAL TRIBUNAL FOR RWANDA (the "Tribunal"),

SITTING as Trial Chamber II composed of Judge William H. Sekule, Presiding, Judge Arlette Ramaroson and Judge Solomy B. Bossa (the "Chamber");

BEING SEIZED of the "Prosecutor's Motion to Unseal the Transcripts of Witness WDUSA (the "Motion"); filed on 9 October 2006.

HAVING RECEIVED the "*Réponse de Arsène Shalom Ntahobali à la requête du Procureur intitulée* 'Prosecutor's motion to unseal the transcripts of Witness WDUSA (Ntahobali's Response") filed on 12 October 2006;

CONSIDERING the "Prosecutor's Reply to Ntahobali's Response to the Prosecutor's Motion to Unseal Transcripts of Witness WDUSA" ("Prosecution's Reply") filed on 16 October 2006;

NOW DECIDES the Motion, pursuant to Rule 73 (A) of the Rules of Procedure and Evidence (the"Rules"), on the basis of the written submissions of the Parties.

INTRODUCTION

1. Witness WDUSA is a Defence protected witness. The protection he enjoys was ordered pursuant to the Chamber's decision of 15 February 2000 regarding Ntahobali's witnesses. It entails among others, that his identity be concealed from the press and the public. Witness WDUSA testified on 3 and 4 April 2006. Part of his evidence was given in closed session to avoid the disclosure of his identity.

2. On 26 September 2006, the Prosecution filed an *ex-parte* Motion seeking leave from the Chamber to disclose to the Danish authorities the transcripts and other relevant documents pertaining to the testimony of Witness WDUSA in open and closed session.[1] On 9 October 2006, the Chamber instructed the Prosecution to refile the Motion *inter partes,* should it wish to pursue this matter.[2] The same day, the Prosecution refiled the Motion *inter partes.*[3]

SUBMISSIONS OF THE PARTIES

The Prosecution

3. The Prosecution seeks a variance order of the witness protection Decision of 21 April 2001 regarding Ntahobali's witnesses, to be authorised to disclose the open and closed session transcripts of Witness WDUSA's testimony of 3 and 4 April 2006[4] and exhibit D-392, containing the witness's identifying information, to the Danish Special International Crimes Office (*Statsadvokaten Forsverlige Internationale Straffesager*).[5] **[page 3]**

4. The Prosecution submits that under Rules 54, 73, 75 and 66 (C), the Chamber has the authority to vary its own witness protection order and issue the order sought for disclosure. The Prosecution further argues that the sharing of information between the Tribunal and national authorities is consistent with Articles 15 and 28 of the Statute and Security Council Resolution 1503.[6]

5. The Prosecution also submits that Witness WDUSA's written consent annexed to the Motion demonstrates that the disclosure of the witness's own testimony can have no negative repercussions for his protection.[7]

---

1 Prosecutor's Motion to Unseal the Transcripts of Witness WDUSA, filed on 26 September 2006.
2 Facsimile transmission dated 9 October 2006
3 Prosecutor's Motion to Unseal the Transcripts of Witness WDUSA, filed on 9 October 2006.
4 Motion, para 6.
5 Motion, para 10.
6 Motion, para 9
7 Motion, para 8.

6. Further, the Prosecution submits that the disclosure of the transcripts to the Danish Special International Crimes Office will not prejudice Witness WDUSA or any other witnesses, given the guarantees that exist under Danish law and the assurances of the Danish Prosecutor regarding a previous request that: "[I]f the witness statement (transcript) needs to be produced in court the prosecution will request (under Section 729a) a closed session and the court may... order non-disclosure to the public of any records identifying a witness."[8]

Ntahobali's Response

7. The Defence opposes the Motion, arguing that the consent form allegedly signed by Witness WDUSA is the only element supporting the disclosure, and it is not sufficient, and that, in the present case, it is hazardous to disclose the transcripts of WDUSA's testimony to the Danish authorities, as neither the Statute nor the Rules prescribe the possibility of disclosing testimonies heard in closed session before the Tribunal to parties outside the Tribunal.[9]

8. The Defence requests that the witness' consent *a posteriori* and while in detention, be subjected to further verification. Moreover, the Defence argues that there is no reference in the Motion to the fundamental rights of a suspect or an accused in Denmark.

9. The Defence also questions the manner in which the Danish authorities would be bound by the protective orders issued by the Chamber.

Prosecution's Reply

10. The Prosecution submits that its Motion also relied on Rules 54 and 73, which the Defence failed to acknowledge, and which both provide a sufficient basis for granting the Motion.[10] The Prosecution further submits that the sharing of information between the Tribunal and national authorities is consistent with the completion strategy envisaged in Security Council Resolutions 1503 and 1534 and, most recently, in the President's report to the General Assembly on 9 October 2006.[11] **[page 4]**

11. The Prosecution also submits that the signature on the signed consent form of Witness WDUSA is identical to that of exhibit D-392 signed by the witness. In the absence of any evidence, the Defence assertion that the witness may have been subjected to threats, promises or violations of his rights, is mere speculation.[12]

DELIBERATIONS

12. The Chamber recalls that pursuant to Rule 78, "all proceedings before a Trial Chamber, other than deliberations of the Chamber, shall be held in public, unless otherwise provided" and that as such, the transcripts of the testimony of Witness WDUSA heard in open session are accessible to the public without further order by the Chamber.

13. The Chamber also recalls that the Defence had asked for protective measures for Witness WDUSA to safeguard his privacy and safety, and which included the protection of identifying materials from the public's knowledge. Further, parts of the testimony of Witness WDUSA were heard in closed session under Rule 79.A (ii) for reasons of safety, security or non-disclosure of identity of a protected witness, pursuant to Rule 75.[13]

14. However, the Chamber notes that the Danish authorities are aware of the identity of Witness WDUSA and of the fact that he has testified before the Tribunal. Moreover, the Chamber notes and accepts that

8 Motion, para 9.

9 Reference is made to R. 75 (F) which allows disclosure to other Chambers of the Tribunal.

10 Prosecution reply, p.1.

11 Prosecution reply, p.1.

12 Prosecution reply, p.2.

13 *'Décision relative à la requête de la Défense aux fins d'obtenir des mesures de protection pour les témoins de la Défense'*(Chamber's witness protection decision of 15 February 2000.)

Witness WDUSA has given his written consent for his prior statements to be disclosed to the Danish Special International Crimes Office. In the absence of any cogent element indicating the contrary, the Chamber finds the Defence request for the Chamber to inquire further into the consent of the witness to be speculative.

15. The Chamber recognises the uniqueness of the Motion, as disclosure of the transcripts of the testimony of a witness is requested for by Danish authorities; who are not party to any proceedings before the Tribunal. The Chamber considers that the guiding principles of state cooperation under Article 28 (1) of the Statute also apply to requests for cooperation or judicial assistance from States to the Tribunal, in their investigation or prosecution of persons accused of committing serious violations of international humanitarian law. Moreover, the Chamber notes that the Danish authorities' investigation of Witness WDUSA for crimes committed in Rwanda in 1994 is in line with the principles of state cooperation envisaged by the completion strategy in Security Council Resolutions 1503 and 1534.

16. Accordingly, having considered that there is no prejudice to the witness, the Chamber is of the view that it is in the overall interest of justice to vary its order for protective measures for Witness WDUSA, pursuant to Rule 75(A). The Chamber directs the Registry to provide copies of the closed session transcripts of the witness and of exhibit D-392 for the purpose of the proceedings before the Danish Special International Crimes Office. The Chamber further orders that the protective measures granted to Witness WDUSA shall continue to have effect *mutatis mutandis* in any proceedings before the Danish authorities unless and until they are rescinded, varied, or augmented in accordance with the procedure set out in Rule 75. **[page 5]**

FOR THE ABOVE REASONS, THE TRIBUNAL

DIRECTS the Registry to provide the Prosecution with the closed session transcripts of Witness WDUSA's testimony of 3 and 4 April 2006, together with exhibit D-392, for the purpose of disclosure of the same to the Danish Special International Crimes Office. *(Statsadvokaten forsverlige Internationale straffesager).*

With regard to the testimony of Witness WDUSA heard in open session, the Chamber observes that this is accessible to the public without further order of the Chamber.

ORDERS that the protective measures granted to Witness WDUSA shall continue to have effect *mutatis mutandis* in any proceedings before the Danish authorities.

Arusha, 1 November 2006

William H. Sekulee	Arlette Ramaroson	Solomy Balungi Bossa
Presiding Judge	Judge	

International Criminal Tribunal for Rwanda
Tribunal pénal international pour le Rwanda

OR: ENG

TRIAL CHAMBER III

Before Judges: Khalida Rachid Khan, Presiding
Sergei Alekseevich Egorov
Inés M. Weinberg de Roca

Registrar: Adama Dieng

Date: 6 March 2007

THE PROSECUTOR

v.

Michel BAGARAGAZA

Case No. ICTR-2005-86-11bis

SECOND ORDER FOR FURTHER SUBMISSIONS CONCERNING THE REQUEST FOR REFERRAL OF THE INDICTMENT TO THE KINGDOM OF THE NETHERLANDS

Office of the Prosecutor:
Hassan Bubacar Jallow
James Stewart
Wallace Kapaya
Inneke Onsea

Defence Counsel:
Geert-Jan Alexander Knoops

[page 2] 1. On 12 December 2006, the Prosecution submitted a request for referral of the Indictment in this case to the Kingdom of the Netherlands (the "Netherlands").[1] Pursuant to Rule 11 *bis* (A) of the Rules of Procedure and Evidence, the President of the Tribunal designated this Chamber to decide the Motion.[2] On 18 December 2006, the Defence responded to the Prosecution Request.[3] The Prosecution replied on 21 December 2006.[4]

2. On 31 January 2007 the Chamber invited the parties and the Netherlands to provide it with further submissions regarding certain specified issues.[5] On 14 February 2007, the Prosecution filed a submission informing the Chamber that it was relying on the submissions contained in its original request for referral.[6] On 15 February 2007, the Netherlands filed its submissions in response to the Chamber's request.[7] On 21 February 2007, the Prosecution[8] and the Defence[9] filed submissions in response to the Netherlands. Finally, on 2 March 2007, the Netherlands filed an Application to provide additional information as *amicus curiae* pursuant to Rule 74.[10]

3. Rule 74 empowers the Chamber to invite, or grant leave to, any State, organization, or person to make submissions on any specified issue. The Chamber considers the additional information provided by the Netherlands in its "Proposed *Amicus Curiae* brief" to be responsive to the 31 January 2007 Order, and therefore grants the application of the Netherlands to appear as *amicus curiae*.

4. The submissions of the Defence and of the Netherlands in response to the 31 January 2007 Order raised certain issues regarding the jurisdiction of the Netherlands to prosecute genocide allegedly committed by a non-national outside the territory of the Netherlands in 1994. The Chamber requires additional submissions in order to fully assess the legal basis for the Netherlands to exercise criminal jurisdiction over the Accused for the crimes of Conspiracy to Commit Genocide,[11] Genocide,[12] and Complicity in Genocide,[13] and determine **[page 3]** on the basis of this assessment whether there are sufficient legal grounds for referring the case to the authorities of the Netherlands.

FOR THE FOREGOING REASONS, THE CHAMBER

I. INVITES the Netherlands to file, within 14 days from the date of the present Order, copies, in English or French if possible:

(i) of all documents referred to in the "Submission by the Kingdom of the Netherlands pursuant to the Order of the Trial Chamber for Further Submissions Concerning the Request for Referral of the Indictment to the Kingdom of the Netherlands of 31 January 2007", including, but not limited to:

(a) The Genocide Convention Implementation Act of 1964;

---

1 "Prosecutor's Request for Referral of the Indictment to Another Court (the "Request")", 12 December 2006.

2 Designation of Trial Chamber under Rule 11 *bis* (President), 13 December 2006.

3 "Defence Response to 'Prosecutor's Request for Referral of the Indictment to Another Court'", 18 December 2006.

4 "Prosecutor's Reply to the Defence Response to the Prosecutor's Request for Referral of the Indictment to Another Court", 21 December 2006.

5 Order for Further Submissions Concerning the Request for Referral of the Indictment to the Kingdom of the Netherlands (the "31 January 2007 Order"), 31 January 2007.

6 "Prosecutor's Further Submissions in Response to Trial Chamber's Order for Further Submissions concerning the Request for Referral of the Indictment to the Kingdom of the Netherlands", 14 February 2007.

7 "Submission by the Kingdom of the Netherlands pursuant to the Order of the Trial Chamber for Further Submissions Concerning the Request for Referral of the Indictment to the Kingdom of the Netherlands on 31 January 2007", 15 February 2007.

8 "Prosecutor's Responsive Submissions Pursuant to Trial Chamber's Order for Further Submissions concerning the Request for Referral of the Indictment to the Kingdom of the Netherlands", 21 February 2007.

9 "Defence Response to Submission by the Kingdom of the Netherlands Pursuant to the Order of the Trial Chamber for Further Submissions Concerning the Request for Referral of the Indictment to the Kingdom of the Netherlands of 31 January 2007", 21 February 2007.

10 "Application to File an *Amicus Curiae* Brief According to Rule 74 of the Rules of Procedure and Evidence on behalf of the Kingdom of the Netherlands and proposed *Amicus Curiae* brief", 2 March 2007.

11 Count I of the Amended Indictment, dated 1 December 2006.

12 Count II of the Amended Indictment.

13 Count III of the Amended Indictment (alternative to Count II).

(b) Article 4a of the Dutch Criminal Code;

(c) the Decisions of the Dutch District Court of the Hague recognising the special status of ICTR requests in the national and international legal order, dated 16 October 2001 and 14 February 2002 respectively, and referred to in paragraph 4.10 and footnote 6 of the submission of the Netherlands.

(d) the Dutch ICTR implementation law and its Explanatory Memorandum;

(ii) of all public documents relevant to the pending case before a Dutch court in which the Dutch Public Prosecutor is relying on "provisions of law similar to those on which criminal proceedings against the accused would be based", referred to in paragraph 2 of the "Proposed *Amicus Curiae* brief" filed on 2 March 2007;

(iii) of all non-public documents, redacted as necessary, relevant to the pending case before a Dutch court in which the Dutch Public Prosecutor is relying on "provisions of law similar to those on which criminal proceedings against the accused would be based", referred to in paragraph 2 of the "Proposed *Amicus Curiae* brief" filed on 2 March 2007. **[page 4]**

II. INVITES the Netherlands to file, within 14 days from the date of the present Order, further submissions:

(i) in support of the proposition that the ICTR is a "foreign state" for the purposes of Article 4a of the Dutch Criminal Code;

(ii) on the provisions of law the Dutch Public Prosecutor is relying on in the case pending before a Dutch court referred to in paragraph 2 of the "Proposed *Amicus Curiae* brief" filed on 2 March 2007;

(iii) any other issues relevant to the jurisdiction of the Netherlands over the genocide charges against the Accused.

Arusha, 6 March 2007, done in English.

Khalida Rachid Khan Presiding Judge	Sergei Alekseevich Egorov Judge	Inés M. Weinberg de Roca Judge

[Seal of the Tribunal]

International Criminal Tribunal for Rwanda
Tribunal pénal international pour le Rwanda

OR: ENG

TRIAL CHAMBER III

Before Judges: Khalida Rachid Khan, Presiding
Sergei Alekseevich Egorov
Inés M. Weinberg de Roca

Registrar: Adama Dieng

Date: 13 April 2007

THE PROSECUTOR

v.

Michel BAGARAGAZA

Case No. ICTR-2005-86-11bis

DECISION ON PROSECUTOR'S REQUEST FOR REFERRAL OF THE INDICTMENT TO THE KINGDOM OF THE NETHERLANDS

Rule 11* bis *of the Rules of Procedure and Evidence

Office of the Prosecutor:
Hassan Bubacar Jallow
James Stewart
Wallace Kapaya
Inneke Onsea

Defence Counsel:
Geert-Jan Alexander Knoops

[page 2] INTRODUCTION

1. The original Indictment against Michel Bagaragaza was confirmed by Judge Sergei Alekseevich Egorov on 28 July 2005 and charged Mr. Bagaragaza with conspiracy to commit genocide, genocide, and alternatively, complicity in genocide ("genocide counts").[1] Mr. Bagaragaza made an initial appearance before the Tribunal on 16 August 2005, where he pleaded not guilty to all counts.

2. On 15 February 2006, the Prosecution requested referral of the original Indictment against Mr. Bagaragaza to the Kingdom of Norway pursuant to Rule 11 *bis* of the Rules of Procedure and Evidence. Trial Chamber III, composed of Judges Dennis C. M. Byron, presiding, Jai Ram Reddy and Joseph Asoka Nihal de Silva, denied the request on the ground that Norway did not have jurisdiction over the crimes alleged in the original Indictment against the Accused.[2] The Appeals Chamber upheld this decision.[3]

3. On 1 November 2006, the Prosecution sought leave to amend the Indictment, principally by adding a fourth count against Mr. Bagaragaza pursuant to Article 4 of the Tribunal's Statute for killing and causing violence to health and physical or mental well-being as a serious violation of Article 3 common to the Geneva Conventions of 1949 and Additional Protocol II of 1977 ("war crimes"). The Defence did not object to the addition of the charge, as long as the war crimes count was charged only in the alternative to the genocide counts. The Prosecution amended its request accordingly. Trial Chamber III, composed of Judges Khalida Rachid Khan, presiding, Inés M. Weinberg de Roca and Dennis C. M. Byron, granted the Prosecution request on 30 November 2006.[4] Mr. Bagaragaza made a further appearance on 1 December 2006, where he pleaded not guilty to the added war crimes count.

4. The Amended Indictment alleges, *inter alia*, that: Mr. Bagaragaza planned with others the extermination of all members of the Tutsi population because of their association with the RPF; he provided financial assistance to the *Interahamwe*, agreed to raise funds for the *Interahamwe*, and supported the idea of them receiving paramilitary training; he ordered the employees of the Rubaya tea factory to provide fuel to the *Interahamwe* and the Presidential Guard as they were on their way to attack and kill hundreds of Tutsi at Kesho Hill; he ordered one of his drivers from Nyabihu tea factory to transport the *Interahamwe* to Rubaya for another attack; one of his subordinates recruited military reservists as employees, and provided military training, arms and ammunition to other employees of the Rubaya tea factory.

5. On 12 December 2006, the Prosecution submitted a Request for referral of the Amended Indictment to the Kingdom of the Netherlands.[5] Pursuant to Rule 11 *bis* (A) of the Rules of Procedure and Evidence, the President of the Tribunal designated Trial Chamber III **[page 3]** composed of Judges Khalida Rachid Khan, presiding, Sergei Alekseevich Egorov and Inés M. Weinberg de Roca, to decide the Prosecution Request.[6] On 18 December 2006, the Defence responded to the Prosecution Request.[7] The Prosecution replied on 21 December 2006.[8]

6. On 31 January 2007 the Chamber invited the parties and the Kingdom of the Netherlands to provide it with further submissions regarding certain specified issues.[9] On 14 February 2007, the Prosecution filed a submission informing the Chamber that it was relying on the submissions contained in its original request for referral.[10] On 15 February 2007, the Netherlands filed its submissions in response to the Chamber's

---

1 Indictment, filed 28 July 2005; "Decision on Confirmation of an Indictment against Michel Bagaragaza", 28 July 2005.

2 Decision on the Prosecution Motion for Referral to the Kingdom of Norway (TC), 19 May 2006.

3 Decision on Rule 11 *bis* Appeal (AC), 30 August 2006.

4 Decision on the Prosecutor's Application for Leave to Amend the Indictment, 30 November 2006.

5 "Prosecutor's Request for Referral of the Indictment to Another Court", 12 December 2006 (the "Prosecution Request").

6 Designation of Trial Chamber under Rule 11 *bis* (President), 13 December 2006.

7 "Defence Response to 'Prosecutor's Request for Referral of the Indictment to Another Court'", 18 December 2006.

8 "Prosecutor's Reply to the Defence Response to the Prosecutor's Request for Referral of the Indictment to Another Court", 21 December 2006.

9 Order for Further Submissions Concerning the Request for Referral of the Indictment to the Kingdom of the Netherlands, 31 January 2007 (the "31 January 2007 Order").

10 "Prosecutor's Further Submissions in Response to Trial Chamber's Order for Further Submissions concerning the Request for Referral of the Indictment to the Kingdom of the Netherlands", 14 February 2007.

request.[11] On 21 February 2007, the Prosecution[12] and the Defence[13] filed submissions in response to the Netherlands. On 2 March 2007, the Netherlands filed an Application to provide additional information as *Amicus Curiae* pursuant to Rule 74.[14]

7. The submissions of the Defence and of the Netherlands in response to the 31 January 2007 Order raised certain issues regarding the jurisdiction of the Netherlands to prosecute genocide allegedly committed by a non-national outside the territory of the Netherlands in 1994. The Chamber issued a Second Order for further submissions on 6 March 2007, in which it also granted the Netherlands' Application to provide additional information as *Amicus Curiae*.[15] The Netherlands filed further submissions and documents in response to the Second Order on 21 March 2007.[16] The Defence filed responsive submissions to the Netherlands on 26 March 2007.[17] **[page 4]**

DISCUSSION

8. Pursuant to Rule 11 *bis*, there are three requirements that must be met before a Chamber can order referral: (i) the referral State must have jurisdiction, and be willing and adequately prepared to accept the case; (ii) the Chamber must be satisfied that the Accused will receive a fair trial in the courts of the referral State; and (iii) the Chamber must be satisfied that the death penalty will not be imposed or carried out. The parties have raised other issues in their submissions.[18]

A. Jurisdiction, Willingness and Preparedness of the Netherlands

9. A confirmed indictment may be referred to a State (i) in whose territory the crime was committed, or (ii) in which the accused was arrested, or (iii) which has jurisdiction and is willing and adequately prepared to accept the referral.[19] Mr. Bagaragaza's alleged crimes were not committed in the Netherlands, and he was not arrested in the Netherlands, so Mr. Bagaragaza's case may only be referred if the Netherlands has jurisdiction and is willing and adequately prepared to accept the case.

10. The *Note Verbale* of the Netherlands, dated 11 December 2006, which is annexed to the Prosecutor's original Request for referral, clearly expresses the willingness of the Netherlands to accept referral and prosecute Mr. Bagaragaza.[20]

---

11 "Submission by the Kingdom of the Netherlands pursuant to the Order of the Trial Chamber for Further Submissions Concerning the Request for Referral of the Indictment to the Kingdom of the Netherlands on 31 January 2007", 15 February 2007 (the "Submissions of the Kingdom of the Netherlands of 15 February 2007").

12 "Prosecutor's Responsive Submissions Pursuant to Trial Chamber's Order for Further Submissions concerning the Request for Referral of the Indictment to the Kingdom of the Netherlands", 21 February 2007.

13 "Defence Response to Submission by the Kingdom of the Netherlands Pursuant to the Order of the Trial Chamber for Further Submissions Concerning the Request for Referral of the Indictment to the Kingdom of the Netherlands of 31 January 2007", 21 February 2007.

14 "Application to File an *Amicus Curiae* Brief According to Rule 74 of the Rules of Procedure and Evidence on behalf of the Kingdom of the Netherlands and proposed *Amicus Curiae* brief", 2 March 2007 (the "Netherlands' Application").

15 Second Order for Further Submissions Concerning the Request for Referral of the Indictment to the Kingdom of the Netherlands, 6 March 2007 (the "Second Order").

16 "Submission by the Kingdom of the Netherlands pursuant to the Second Order of the Trial Chamber for Further Submissions Concerning the Request for Referral of the Indictment to the Kingdom of the Netherlands of 6 March 2007", 21 March 2007 (the "Submissions of the Kingdom of the Netherlands Pursuant to the Second Order").

17 "Defence Response to Submission by the Kingdom of the Netherlands Pursuant to the Second Order of the Trial Chamber for Further Submissions Concerning the Request for Referrral of the Indictment to the Kingdom of the Netherlands of 6 March 2007", 26 March 2007. In its Second Order for Further Submissions dated 6 March 2007, the Trial Chamber did not invite the parties to respond to the Netherlands' submissions. Nonetheless, the Chamber will consider the Defence submissions in the interests of justice.

18 If referral is granted the Defence requests that the Chamber implement a condition that the Accused be safely and permanently relocated outside the African continent after the completion of his trial, and, if convicted, his sentence. As the Prosecution properly notes, this is not a matter which can be dealt with in the context of an order entered under Rule 11 *bis*. The Prosecution has also raised the issue of witness protection. This issues will be dealt with below.

19 Rule 11 *bis* (A) of the Rules of Procedure and Evidence.

20 Letter from the Embassy of the Kingdom of the Netherlands, 11 December 2006 (attached as Exhibit 3 to the Prosecution Request).

11. According to the Appeals Chamber, "[i]n assessing whether a State is competent within the meaning of Rule 11 *bis* to accept one of the Tribunal's cases, a designated Trial Chamber must consider whether it has a legal framework which criminalizes the alleged conduct of the accused and provides an adequate penalty structure".[21] The Tribunal only has authority to refer cases where the State "will charge and convict [or acquit] only for those international crimes listed in its Statute" as opposed to "ordinary crimes" such as homicide.[22]

12. The Netherlands submits that it has jurisdiction to try Mr. Bagaragaza on the charges in the Amended Indictment. The relevant Dutch legislation includes the War Crimes Act of 1952 and the Genocide Convention Implementation Act of 1964.[23] **[page 5]**

(i) War Crimes

13. The Dutch War Crimes Act of 1952 codifies into Dutch criminal law serious violations of Article 3 Common to the Geneva Conventions and Additional Protocol II of 1977. The Netherlands explains that it has "(secondary) universal jurisdiction" to try individuals for war crimes committed outside the Netherlands in 1994 when the accused is either (i) a Dutch national; or (ii) is present on Dutch territory. Mr. Bagaragaza is presently detained in the Netherlands as the result of an agreement between the ICTR and the government of the Netherlands. In this agreement, the Netherlands waives its right to exercise criminal jurisdiction over Mr. Bagaragaza. If Mr. Bagaragaza's case is referred to Dutch authorities then this waiver will be voided, and the Netherlands will have jurisdiction to prosecute Mr. Bagaragaza's alleged criminal conduct as a result of his presence in the Netherlands. According to their submissions, the Netherlands have previously prosecuted, convicted, and sentenced three non-nationals for war crimes and torture on the basis of their presence on Dutch territory.[24]

14. Under Dutch criminal law, the penalties for conviction for war crimes range from a fine to life imprisonment depending on the severity of the crimes. Where the criminal act, *inter alia*, results in death or serious bodily harm, involves violence with "combined forces", or is "the expression of a policy of systematical (sic) terror or unlawful action against the entire population or against a specific group of that population", then a "term of life imprisonment or a term of twenty years or a fine of the fifth category shall be imposed".[25]

15. On the basis of these submissions, the Chamber finds that the Netherlands has an adequate legal framework criminalizing the alleged war crimes of Mr. Bagaragaza and providing for an adequate penalty structure.

(ii) Genocide

16. The Dutch Genocide Convention Implementation Act of 1964 incorporates the 1948 Genocide Convention into Dutch criminal law. The Netherlands submits that under the Genocide Implementation Act and the Dutch Criminal Code, the Netherlands has jurisdiction to try individuals for violations committed outside the Netherlands in 1994 if (i) the accused is a Dutch national; or (ii) the case is transferred to the Netherlands from another jurisdiction in conformity with Article 4a of the Dutch Criminal Code.

17. Mr. Bagaragaza is not a national of the Netherlands, so jurisdiction over the genocide allegations will depend on the application of Article 4a of the Dutch Criminal Code to the referral. Article 4a states that "the Dutch criminal law is applicable to anyone against whom **[page 6]** prosecution has been transferred from a foreign State to the Netherlands on the basis of a treaty from which the power of the Netherlands to prosecute follows".

---

21 *Prosecutor v. Bagaragaza*, Case No. ICTR-05-86-AR11*bis*, Decision on Rule 11 *bis* Appeal (AC), 30 August 2006, para. 9.

22 *Id.*, para. 16.

23 In 2003, the Netherlands adopted the International Crimes Act, which supersedes both the Genocide Convention Implementation Act of 1964 and the War Crimes Act of 1952. Nonetheless, the Netherlands submits that the International Crimes Act of 2003 cannot be applied retroactively to provide jurisdiction over the acts of the Accused.

24 Submissions of the Kingdom of the Netherlands of 15 February 2007, para. 4.4 (citing Rechtbank Rotterdam (District Court Rotterdam), 7 April 1994 (number 10/000050-03); Gerechtsof's Gravenhage (Court of Appeal of The Hague), 29 January 2007 (Rolnummer: 22-006131-05); Gerechtshof's Gravenhage (Court of Appeals of The Hague), 29 January 2007 (Rolnummer 22-006132-05)).

25 *See id.*, para. 4.1.

(a) Transfer from a Foreign State

18. The Netherlands submits that a United Nations international criminal tribunal with primary jurisdiction such as this Tribunal qualifies as a "foreign state" for the purposes of Article 4a of the Dutch Criminal Code. The Defence questions whether the ICTR could be considered a "foreign state" for the purposes of Article 4a, submitting that the legislative history of Article 4a does not support such a view.

19. The Netherlands acknowledges that the issue of accepting transfer of criminal cases from international tribunals is a recent phenomenon and is therefore unsettled in its law. Nonetheless, it emphasizes the importance placed on cooperation with the ICTR and ICTY under Dutch law, and argues that "an interpretation which would exclude the ICTR from the definition of foreign state would run contrary to past and current views on the importance of cooperation with the ICTR".[26] As support for its position, it points to Article 2, paragraph 2 of the ICTR Implementation Law which incorporates by reference Articles 3 to 18 of the ICTY Implementation Law.[27] Article 9 of the ICTY Implementation Law states, "Requests by the Tribunal for any form whatsoever of legal assistance addressed to the police or any judicial body, named or otherwise, are to be complied with wherever possible".[28] The Netherlands submits that it "believes it important to help to extend international case law on grave breaches of the most fundamental norms of international humanitarian law, such as genocide, crimes against humanity and war crimes".[29]

20. The Defence responds that under Dutch criminal law the Criminal Code is to be interpreted strictly, especially where a more expansive interpretation would be prejudicial to the accused. The Defence also argues that the European Court of Human Rights, interpreting Article 7 of the European Convention (which provides for the principle of legality) has ruled that "the criminal law must not be extensively construed to an accused's detriment, for instance by analogy".[30] The Defence acknowledges that "there will always be a need for adaptation to changing circumstances" and that "Article 7 cannot be read as outlawing the gradual clarification of the rules of criminal liability through judicial interpretation from case to case, provided that the resultant development is consistent with the essence of the offence **[page 7]** and could reasonably be foreseen",[31] but argues that interpreting Article 4a of the Dutch Criminal Code to include the ICTR as a "foreign state" could not reasonably be foreseen by the accused. Thus, the Defence suggests that the phrase "transferred from a foreign State" in Article 4a must be applied only to States, and not international tribunals.

21. Moreover, the Defence suggests that the ICTR and ICTY Implementation Laws relied upon by the Netherlands have to do with cooperation and the provision of legal assistance to the ICTR, and are not relevant to the issue of jurisdiction.

22. Although the issue remains unsettled in Dutch Law and is ultimately an issue for a competent court of the Netherlands, the Chamber is satisfied that the Tribunal will be considered a "foreign state" for the purposes of Article 4a of the Dutch Criminal Code. In addition to the reasons offered by the Netherlands, the Chamber notes that it is an established principle of international law that both the United Nations and States are "subjects of international law and capable of possessing international rights and duties".[32]

---

26 Submissions of the Kingdom of the Netherlands Pursuant to the Second Order, para. 15.

27 Act of 18 December 1997 Containing Provisions Relating to the Establishment of the International Tribunal for the Prosecution of Persons Responsible for Genocide and Other Serious Violations of International Humanitarian Law Committed in the Territory of Rwanda and Rwandan citizens Responsible for Genocide and Other Such Violations Committed in the Territory of Neighbouring States, between 1 January 1994 and 31 December 1994.

28 Act of 21 April 1994 Containing Provisions Relating to the Establishment of the International Tribunal for the Prosecution of Persons Responsible for Serious Violations of International Humanitarian Law Committed in the Territory of the Former Yugoslavia Since 1991.

29 Memorandum from the Minister of Justice and the Minister of Foreign Affairs in response to the report of the house of Representatives' Permanent Committee on Justice concerning the Act of 18 December 1997 ("Nota naar aanleiding van het verslag")

30 *C.R. v. United Kingdom*, ECHR, 22 November 1995, NJ 1997, 1.

31 *Id.*

32 *Reparation for Injuries Suffered in the Service of the United Nations*, Advisory Opinion of 11 April 1949, (1949) ICJ Rep. 174 at 179; *see also Interpretation of the Agreement of 25 March 1951 between the WHO and Egypt*, Advisory Opinion of 20 December 1980, (1980) ICJ Rep. 73 at 89-90; *Cf., Prosecutor v. Rwamakuba*, Case No. ICTR-98-44C-T, Decision on Appropriate Remedy, 31 January 2007, para. 48 (finding the ICTR to be a special subsidiary organ of the United Nations Security Council possessing the international duty to respect generally accepted international human rights norms).

(b) Treaty from which the Power to Prosecute Follows

23. The Netherlands submits that the 1948 Genocide Convention is a treaty from which the power of the Netherlands to prosecute follows for the purposes of Article 4a of the Dutch Criminal Code. Despite the plain language of Article VI of the Genocide Convention limiting trials to a "competent tribunal of the State in the territory of which the act was committed, or by such international penal tribunal as may have jurisdiction with respect to those Contracting Parties which shall have accepted its jurisdiction", the Netherlands suggests that the 1948 Genocide Convention must be read as interpreted by the International Court of Justice ("ICJ") in 1996, in which it ruled that the "rights and obligations enshrined by the [Genocide] Convention are rights and obligations *erga omnes*" and "that the obligation each State thus has to prevent and to punish the crime of genocide is not territorially limited by the Convention".[33]

24. Alternatively, the Netherlands notes (i) the ICTR was established by the Security Council acting pursuant to Chapter VII of the Charter of the United Nations, (ii) the Netherlands is a party to the United Nations Charter, and (iii) that other legal instruments, specifically Security Council Resolution 955 (1994) and Article 28 of the ICTR Statute oblige State parties to the United Nations Charter to cooperate with the Tribunal, and submits that this combination of factors renders the United Nations Charter a treaty from which the power to prosecute follows as required by Article 4a of the Dutch Criminal Code. **[page 8]**

25. Annexed to the Netherlands' 21 March 2007 submissions is the decision of a Dutch investigative judge at the District Court of The Hague declining to institute a preliminary judicial investigation into genocide allegations against a Rwandan asylum-seeker because the investigative judge determined that the Netherlands did not have jurisdiction over genocide. In reaching this conclusion, the investigative judge, applying Article 4a of the Dutch Criminal Code, rejected the Public Prosecutor's assertion that the Genocide Convention of 1948 was a treaty from which the power of the Netherlands to prosecute follows because Article VI of the Genocide Convention limited prosecution to competent tribunals of the State in the territory in which the act was committed, or by an international tribunal.[34] The investigative judge did not refer to the 11 July 1996 ICJ Judgement rejecting any territorial limitation on every States' *erga omnes* obligation to prevent and punish genocide; it is not clear whether the Public Prosecutor raised this argument to the investigative judge.

26. The investigative judge did, however, accept the Public Prosecutor's argument that the United Nations Charter, when read in conjunction with the Statute of the ICTR, and Security Council Resolution 1503 (2003), was a treaty from which the power of the Netherlands to prosecute followed for the purposes of Article 4a of the Dutch Criminal Code. The Public Prosecutor reasoned that Resolution 1503 (2003) authorized transfers, and, read in conjunction with the legal cooperation provisions of the ICTR Statute as applicable to all State Parties to the United Nations Charter, provided the power to prosecute. Although the investigative judge accepted this reasoning, she declined to order a preliminary judicial investigation of genocide because the individual accused in question was not explicitly mentioned in the most recent Completion Strategy of the ICTR, and, as such, she concluded that the transfer of his case was not part of the Completion Strategy. The Prosecution Service has appealed the investigative judge's decision.

27. The Netherlands submits that because Mr. Bagaragaza's case *was* included in the most recent Completion Strategy, the reasoning of the Public Prosecutor's submissions and the investigative judge's decision described above provides another basis for considering the United Nations Charter, when read in conjunction with other legal instruments, specifically the ICTR Statute and Security Council Resolution 1503 (2003), a treaty from which the power of the Netherlands to prosecute genocide follows for the purposes of Article 4a of the Dutch Criminal Code.

28. The Chamber is not the competent authority to make a binding determination as to which treaty referred to above is a treaty from which the power to prosecute genocide follows for the purposes of Article 4a of the Dutch Criminal Code. That is a matter for a court of the Netherlands. The Chamber must, however,

---

[33] *Case concerning application of the Convention on the Prevention and Punishment of the Crime of Genocide (Bosnia-Herzegovina v. Yugoslavia)*, Preliminary Objections, Judgement, 11 July 1996, para. 31 ("11 July 1996 Judgement").

[34] Decision of the Investigative Judge in Criminal Matters of the District Court of The Hague on the Order of the Public Prosecutor of 5 January 2007 to Institute a Preliminary Judicial Investigation Against the Suspect, 11 January 2007.

be satisfied that such a treaty exists. The Chamber is satisfied that the Genocide Convention of 1948, as interpreted by the ICJ in its 11 July 1996 Judgement referenced above, and the United Nations Charter read in conjunction with the ICTR Statute and relevant Security Council Resolutions are treaties from which the power to prosecute genocide follows for the purposes of Article 4a of the Dutch Criminal Code. **[page 9]**

29. Turning to punishment, Article 1 of the Genocide Convention Implementation Act states that "these crimes ... shall be punished with a term of life imprisonment or a term of twenty years or a fine of the fifth category".

30. The Chamber is satisfied that an adequate legal framework criminalizing the alleged conduct of the Accused and providing for punishment exists. Moreover, the Chamber notes that Rules 11 *bis* (D)(iv) and 11 *bis* (F) serve as a potential remedy in the event that a competent court of the Netherlands determines that it does not have jurisdiction to prosecute Mr. Bagaragaza for genocide.[35] Rule 11 *bis* (D)(iv) provides for monitoring of referred proceedings, and Rule 11 *bis* (F) empowers the Chamber to revoke referral at the request of the Prosecutor.

B. Non-Imposition of the Death Penalty

31. According to Rule 11 *bis* (C), the Chamber must satisfy itself that "the death penalty will not be imposed or carried out". The Constitution of the Netherlands prohibits the death penalty. Moreover, the Netherlands has ratified the 13th Protocol to the European Convention on Human Rights on the abolishment of the death penalty in all circumstances. The Chamber is therefore satisfied that the death penalty will not be imposed or carried out if the case is referred to the Netherlands.

C. Fair Trial

32. Rule 11 *bis* (C) also obligates the Chamber to satisfy itself that "the accused will receive a fair trial in the courts of the State concerned". The Netherlands submits that international treaties are an important source of Dutch law on criminal procedures. Article 6 of the European Convention on Human Rights and Fundamental Freedoms (ECHR)[36] and **[page 10]** Article 14 of the International Covenant on Civil and Political Rights (ICCPR)[37] are the guiding principles for Dutch criminal procedure concerning the rights of

---

35 *C.f.*, *Prosecutor v. Stankovic*, Case No. IT-96-23/2-PT, Decision on Referral of Case under Rule 11 *bis* (TC), 17 May 2005, para. 93.

36 Article 6 of the ECHR, entitled Right to a Fair Trial, states:

1. In the determination of his civil rights and obligations or of any criminal charge against him, everyone is entitled to a fair and public hearing within a reasonable time by an independent and impartial tribunal established by law. Judgment shall be pronounced publicly but the press and public may be excluded from all or part of the trial in the interests of morals, public order or national security in a democratic society, where the interests of juveniles or the protection of the private life of the parties so require, or to the extent strictly necessary in the opinion of the court in special circumstances where publicity would prejudice the interests of justice.
2. Everyone charged with a criminal offence shall be presumed innocent until proved guilty according to law.
3. Everyone charged with a criminal offence has the following minimum rights:
   a. to be informed promptly, in a language which he understands and in detail, of the nature and cause of the accusation against him;
   b. to have adequate time and facilities for the preparation of his defence;
   c. to defend himself in person or through legal assistance of his own choosing or, if he has not sufficient means to pay for legal assistance, to be given it free when the interests of justice so require;
   d. to examine or have examined witnesses against him and to obtain the attendance and examination of witnesses on his behalf under the same conditions as witnesses against him;
   e. to have the free assistance of an interpreter if he cannot understand or speak the language used in court.

37 Article 14 of the ICCPR states:

1. All persons shall be equal before the courts and tribunals. In the determination of any criminal charge against him, or of his rights and obligations in a suit at law, everyone shall be entitled to a fair and public hearing by a competent, independent and impartial tribunal established by law. The press and the public may be excluded from all or part of a trial for reasons of morals, public order (ordre public) or national security in a democratic society, or when the interest of the private lives of the parties so requires, or to the extent strictly necessary in the opinion of the court in special circumstances where publicity would prejudice the interests of justice; but any judgement rendered in a criminal case or in a suit at law shall be made public except where the interest of juvenile persons otherwise requires or the proceedings concern matrimonial disputes or the guardianship of children.

the accused. The relevant provisions in the ECHR and the ICCPR are substantially similar to the rights enshrined in Article 20 of the ICTR Statute.[38] **[page 11]**

33. In its original submission, the Prosecution noted that "the taking of witness testimony in Dutch trials is done in a non-public hearing before an examining magistrate in the presence of counsel for both parties. The public trial, therefore, does not involve live witness testimony, but rather the presentation of the evidence taken by the examining magistrate and oral submissions on the facts and law by the parties".[39] The Defence expressed concern that witness statements might be admitted without the effective cross-examination of the witness by the Defence, and requested that the Chamber stipulate to the Netherlands that witness statements should not be admitted in evidence without the right to cross-examination.

34. The Netherlands submits that, under Dutch criminal law, the accused has the right to be present during the trial and the right to investigate the evidence put forward by the Public Prosecution Service and

---

2. Everyone charged with a criminal offence shall have the right to be presumed innocent until proved guilty according to law.
3. In the determination of any criminal charge against him, everyone shall be entitled to the following minimum guarantees, in full equality:
   (a) To be informed promptly and in detail in a language which he understands of the nature and cause of the charge against him;
   (b) To have adequate time and facilities for the preparation of his defence and to communicate with counsel of his own choosing;
   (c) To be tried without undue delay;
   (d) To be tried in his presence, and to defend himself in person or through legal assistance of his own choosing; to be informed, if he does not have legal assistance, of this right; and to have legal assistance assigned to him, in any case where the interests of justice so require, and without payment by him in any such case if he does not have sufficient means to pay for it;
   (e) To examine, or have examined, the witnesses against him and to obtain the attendance and examination of witnesses on his behalf under the same conditions as witnesses against him;
   (f) To have the free assistance of an interpreter if he cannot understand or speak the language used in court;
   (g) Not to be compelled to testify against himself or to confess guilt.
4. In the case of juvenile persons, the procedure shall be such as will take account of their age and the desirability of promoting their rehabilitation.
5. Everyone convicted of a crime shall have the right to his conviction and sentence being reviewed by a higher tribunal according to law.
6. When a person has by a final decision been convicted of a criminal offence and when subsequently his conviction has been reversed or he has been pardoned on the ground that a new or newly discovered fact shows conclusively that there has been a miscarriage of justice, the person who has suffered punishment as a result of such conviction shall be compensated according to law, unless it is proved that the non-disclosure of the unknown fact in time is wholly or partly attributable to him.
7. No one shall be liable to be tried or punished again for an offence for which he has already been finally convicted or acquitted in accordance with the law and penal procedure of each country.

[38] Article 20 of the ICTR Statute, entitled Rights of the Accused, states:
1. All persons shall be equal before the International Tribunal for Rwanda.
2. In the determination of charges against him or her, the accused shall be entitled to a fair and public hearing, subject to Article 21 of the Statute.
3. The accused shall be presumed innocent until proven guilty according to the provisions of the present Statute.
4. In the determination of any charge against the accused pursuant to the present Statute, the accused shall be entitled to the following minimum guarantees, in full equality:
   a. To be informed promptly and in detail in a language which he or she understands of the nature and cause of the charge against him or her;
   b. To have adequate time and facilities for the preparation of his or her defence and to communicate with counsel of his or her own choosing;
   c. To be tried without undue delay;
   d. To be tried in his or her presence, and to defend himself or herself in person or through legal assistance of his or her own choosing; to be informed, if he or she does not have legal assistance, of this right; and to have legal assistance assigned to him or her, in any case where the interests of justice so require, and without payment by him or her in any such case if he or she does not have sufficient means to pay for it;
   e. To examine, or have examined, the witnesses against him or her and to obtain the attendance and examination of witnesses on his or her behalf under the same conditions as witnesses against him or her;
   f. To have the free assistance of an interpreter if he or she cannot understand or speak the language used in the International Tribunal for Rwanda;
   g. Not to be compelled to testify against himself or herself or to confess guilt.

[39] Prosecutor's Request, para. 26.

hand over evidence on his own behalf. The Netherlands also submits that, in line with Article 6 of the ECHR, the accused and the prosecution have the right to cross-examine witnesses.

35. The Chamber is satisfied that the Netherlands will honour Mr. Bagaragaza's right to cross-examine witnesses, and that he will receive a fair trial in a competent court of the Netherlands.

D. Witness Protection

36. Currently the only protective measures in place arise from the decision confirming the original indictment on 28 July 2005, which provided that the witness statements included in the supporting materials could be provided to the Defence in redacted form pending further orders from the Chamber. The Prosecution indicates that it does not foresee the need for further protective measures given its knowledge of the evidence in this case.

37. The Netherlands submits that, generally, witnesses' identities are disclosed in furtherance of the fair trial rights of the accused, but that there are provisions in Dutch law allowing for non-disclosure of the identity of a victim or witness, as well as other protections, in exceptional circumstances. When necessary, these protections may be ordered by the investigating judge. **[page 12]**

38. The Chamber is satisfied that, should they be deemed necessary, adequate witness protection measures can be provided by Dutch courts, and concludes that no matters of witness protection have been identified which preclude referral of this case.

E. Monitoring of the Proceedings

39. Pursuant to Rule 11 *bis* (D)(iv), "the Prosecutor may send observers to monitor the proceedings in the courts of the State concerned". The Appeals Chamber construed the identical ICTY provision as authorizing an ICTY Referral Bench to order the Prosecution to send observers if the Referral Bench finds that this is necessary to safeguard the fair trial rights of the accused.[40] In its submissions, the Prosecution has indicated that it is involved in negotiations with the International Commission of Jurists to provide an independent monitor. The Netherlands notes that its trials are generally public, but requests that if observers are sent, the Dutch authorities be informed in advance so that the president of the relevant court could be informed. **[page 13]**

FOR THE ABOVE REASONS, THE CHAMBER

ORDERS the case of *Prosecutor v. Michel Bagaragaza* to be referred to the authorities of the Kingdom of the Netherlands, so that those authorities should forthwith refer the case to the appropriate court for trial within the Kingdom of the Netherlands;

ORDERS the Registrar to transfer custody of Mr. Bagaragaza, within 30 days of the date of this Decision, to the Kingdom of the Netherlands in accordance with the procedures applicable to transfer of convicted persons to States for service of sentence;

ORDERS the Prosecutor to hand over to the Prosecutor of the Kingdom of the Netherlands, as soon as possible and no later than 30 days from the date of this Decision, the material supporting the Indictment against Mr. Bagaragaza, and all other appropriate evidentiary material;

ORDERS the Prosecutor to inform the authorities of the Kingdom of the Netherlands in advance of sending a monitor from its own office or the International Commission of Jurists or any other organization for the purpose of monitoring and reporting on the proceedings of this case before a court of the Kingdom of the Netherlands;

ORDERS the Prosecutor to file an initial report to the Chamber on the progress made by the Prosecutor of the Kingdom of the Netherlands in the prosecution of Mr. Bagaragaza six weeks after transfer of the

---

40 *Stankovic*, Decision on Rule 11 *Bis* Referral (AC), paras. 50-55.

evidentiary material and, thereafter, every three months, including information on the issue of jurisdiction over the genocide counts and the course of the proceedings of a court of the Kingdom of the Netherlands after commencement of trial, such reports to comprise or include the reports of the International Commission of Jurists or any other organization monitoring or reporting on the proceedings.

Arusha, 13 April 2007, done in English.

Khalida Rachid Khan Presiding Judge	Sergei Alekseevich Egorov Judge	Inés M. Weinberg de Roca Judge

[Seal of the Tribunal]

International Criminal Tribunal for Rwanda
Tribunal pénal international pour le Rwanda

OR: ENG

TRIAL CHAMBER DESIGNATED UNDER RULE 11 *BIS*

Before Judges:	Dennis Byron, presiding Erik Møse Lee Gacuiga Muthoga
Registrar:	Adama Dieng
Date:	17 August 2007

THE PROSECUTOR

v.

Michel BAGARAGAZA

Case No. ICTR-2005-86-11bis

DECISION ON PROSECUTOR'S EXTREMELY URGENT MOTION FOR REVOCATION OF THE REFERRAL TO THE KINGDOM OF THE NETHERLANDS PURSUANT TO RULE 11 *BIS* (F) & (G)

Office of the Prosecutor:
Hassan Bubacar Jallow
Bongani Majola
Silvania Arbia
Richard Karegyesa
Inneke Onsea

Defence Counsel:
Geert-Jan Alexander Knoops

[page 2] INTRODUCTION

1. On 13 April 2007, Trial Chamber III, composed of Judges Khalida Rachid Khan, presiding, Sergei Alekseevich Egorov and Inés M. Weinberg de Roca granted the Prosecution's request to refer the Indictment of Michel Bagaragaza to the authorities of the Kingdom of the Netherlands pursuant to Rule 11 *bis* of the Rules of Procedure and Evidence.[1] In connection with the referral, the Trial Chamber ordered the Prosecution to file an initial report to the Chamber on the progress made by the Dutch Prosecutor in the prosecution of Mr. Bagaragaza six weeks after transfer of the evidentiary material, and, thereafter, every three months. The Chamber specifically requested that the reports include information on the issue of jurisdiction over the genocide counts in Mr. Bagaragaza's Indictment.

2. On 7 May 2007, Mr. Bagaragaza was transferred from the custody of the United Nations Detention Unit ("UNDU") in The Hague to the custody of the Dutch authorities. The Prosecution completed the transfer of Mr. Bagaragaza's case file on 11 May 2007.

3. The Prosecution filed its initial report on the progress made by the Netherlands in prosecuting Mr. Bagaragaza on 22 June 2007,[2] and a confidential supplementary report on 2 August 2007.[3] In the Supplementary Report, the Prosecution informed the Chamber of a decision of the District Court of The Hague in the case of Joseph Mpambara, dated 24 July 2007 (the "*Mpambara* Decision"), in which the court found, *inter alia*, that it did not have jurisdiction to try Mr. Mpambara for genocide. The Dutch Prosecutor had intended to assert the same jurisdictional bases to try Mr. Bagaragaza for genocide as it had for Mr. Mpambara. As a result of this decision, the Dutch Prosecutor suspended proceedings against Mr. Bagaragaza.

4. After consultation with the Dutch authorities, the Prosecution filed an extremely urgent motion requesting that the Trial Chamber revoke the order of referral to the Netherlands pursuant to Rule 11 *bis*.[4] In separate letters annexed to the Motion, representatives of the Dutch Ministry of Justice and National Public Prosecutor's Office noted that Mr. Bagaragaza's period of provisional detention will end on 20 August 2007, after which the Dutch authorities would be forced to free him or attempt to prosecute him despite the lack of jurisdiction.[5] The Defence filed a Response on 13 August 2007,[6] and **[page 3]** the Prosecution replied to that Response on 14 August 2007.[7] Pursuant to Rule 33 (B), the Registrar filed two separate submissions on 16 August 2007.[8]

5. Given the extremely urgent nature of this Motion and noting that the Judges who issued the Referral Decision were away from the seat of the Tribunal in Arusha, Judge Dennis Byron, the President of the Tribunal, composed a bench to hear the Motion. This bench is comprised of Judges Dennis Byron, presiding, Erik Møse, and Lee Gacuiga Muthoga.[9]

---

1 Decision on Prosecutor's Request for Referral of the Indictment to the Kingdom of the Netherlands, 13 April 2007 (the "Referral Decision"). The Chamber will hereinafter refer to the Kingdom of the Netherlands as the "Netherlands" and the authorities thereof as the "Dutch authorities".

2 "The Prosecutor's Initial Report on the Progress Made by the Kingdom of the Netherlands in the Prosecution of Mr. Bagaragaza", filed 22 June 2007 (the "Initial Report").

3 "Prosecutor's Supplementary Report on the Progress Made by the Kingdom of the Netherlands in the Prosecution of Mr. Bagaragaza", filed 2 August 2007 (the "Supplementary Report").

4 "Prosecutor's Extremely Urgent Motion for Revocation of the Referral Order Pursuant to Rule 11 *Bis* (F) & (G)", filed 8 August 2007 (the "Motion").

5 Motion, Annex 1: Letter of Dutch Minister of Justice, p. 2, dated 8 August 2007; Annex 2: Letter of Dutch Prosecutor, Gert Oldekamp, p. 4, dated 8 August 2007

6 "Public Defence Response to Prosecutor's Extremely Urgent Motion for Revocation of the Referral Order Pursuant to Rule 11 *bis* (F) & (G)", filed 13 August 2007 (the "Defence Response").

7 "Prosecutor's Reply to 'Public Defence Response to Prosecutor's Extremely Urgent Motion for Revocation of the Referral Order Pursuant to Rule 11 *bis* (F) & (G)'", filed 14 August 2007 (the "Prosecution Reply").

8 "Registrars Submissions Under Rule 33 (B) of the Rules on Prosecutor's Extremely Urgent Motion and Public Defence Response for Revocation of the Referral Order Pursuant to Rule 11 *Bis* (F) and (G)", filed 16 August 2007 (the "Registrar's First Submissions"); "Registrar's Further Submissions Under Rule 33 (B) of the Rules on Prosecutor's Extremely Urgent Motion and Public Defence Response for Revocation of the Referral Order Pursuant to Rule 11 *Bis* (F) and (G) (Security Issues)", filed 16 August 2007 (the "Registrar's Security Submissions").

9 Designation of Trial Chamber under Rule 11 *bis* (President), filed 14 August 2007.

DISCUSSION

6. The Prosecution requests that the Chamber revoke the order referring the case of Mr. Bagaragaza to the Netherlands pursuant to Rule 11 *bis* (F), which reads:

> At any time after an order has been issued pursuant to this Rule, and before the accused is found guilty or acquitted by a court in the State concerned, the Trial Chamber may, at the request of the Prosecutor and upon having given to the authorities of the State concerned the opportunity to be heard, revoke the order and make a formal request for deferral within the terms of Rule 10.[10]

7. Rule 11 *bis* (F) obliges the Chamber to give "the authorities of the State concerned the opportunity to be heard." In its Motion, the Prosecution notes that the Dutch Minister of Justice does not wish to be heard.[11] This follows from the letter from the Ministry annexed to the Motion.[12] Moreover, both the letter from the Dutch Ministry of Justice and from the National Public Prosecutor's Office explain that, as a result of the *Mpambara* Decision, the Netherlands cannot prosecute Mr. Bagaragaza for genocide and that their jurisdiction to prosecute him for war crimes is also uncertain. As a result, the Dutch authorities support the Prosecution's request that the referral order be revoked. The Chamber is satisfied that the letters annexed to the Motion, are sufficient in relation to Rule 11 *bis* (F).

8. Rule 11 *bis* (F) does not provide the Accused with the right to be heard on the issue of revocation of a referral order. This is in contrast to Rule 11 *bis* (B), which requires that "where the accused is in the custody of the Tribunal", he must be given the **[page 4]** opportunity to be heard on the issue of referral to the authorities of a State. The Chamber nevertheless has considered the Defence submissions in the interests of justice.

9. The Defence argues that Mr. Bagaragaza cannot receive a fair trial if the referral order is revoked because the ICTR cannot possibly allocate time, space and resources for his trial in Arusha. Therefore, the Defence suggests that his case will likely be transferred to Rwanda. The Chamber considers this argument as premature and speculative. If the Prosecution ultimately seeks to refer Mr. Bagaragaza's case to the Rwandan authorities or to the authorities of any other State, he will have a full opportunity to be heard at that time.

10. The Defence submissions refer to an agreement between Mr. Bagaragaza and the Prosecution which provides, *inter alia*, that (i) he will not be prosecuted before the Tribunal; and (ii) a promise to renegotiate where no national court outside the African continent is prepared to prosecute him.[13] The Defence alleges that, in seeking revocation of the referral order and the transfer of Mr. Bagaragaza to Arusha, the Prosecution has violated these provisions of the Agreement. The Chamber finds that the Defence Submissions regarding the alleged violation of his agreement with the Prosecution are unavailing. As the Prosecution acknowledges, this agreement does not bind the Trial Chamber.[14]

11. The Referral Decision was predicated on that Trial Chamber's belief, based on the submissions of the Prosecutor and the Dutch authorities, that the Dutch courts were competent to prosecute Mr. Bagaragaza on the genocide and war crimes charges contained in the Indictment.[15] The *Mpambara* Decision and the submissions from the Dutch Ministry of Justice and the National Public Prosecutor's Office suggest that Dutch courts do not have jurisdiction to prosecute Mr. Bagaragaza for genocide and that jurisdiction over the war crimes counts in the Indictment is uncertain. Jurisdiction to prosecute the acts of an accused as international crimes is a minimum requirement for the referral of a case pursuant to Rule 13 *bis*.[16] The Netherlands no longer appears to have such jurisdiction.

---

[10] Rule 11 *bis* (F) of the Rules of Procedure and Evidence.

[11] Motion, para. 6.

[12] Motion, Annex 1: Letter of Dutch Minister of Justice, p. 3, in which the Ministry official states, "Pursuant to Rule 11 bis (F) of the Rules of Procedure and Evidence, I hereby declare that the authorities of the Netherlands have no wish to make use of the opportunity to be heard in this matter."

[13] Defence Response, paras. 21-30

[14] Prosecution Reply, para. 10. The Chamber notes that it appears premature to form a view on the alleged violations of the agreement.

[15] Referral Decision, paras. 15, 30

[16] *Prosecutor v. Bagaragaza*, Case No. ICTR-05-86-AR11 *bis*, Decision on Rule 11 *bis* Appeal (AC), 30 August 2006, paras. 9, 16-17.

12. For these reasons, the Chamber grants the Prosecution's request for revocation of the referral order of 13 April 2007, and makes a formal request for deferral pursuant to Rule 11 *bis* (F).

13. The Prosecution requests, pursuant to Rule 11 *bis* (G), that, if the Chamber grants its request to revoke the referral order of 13 April 2007, the Chamber (i) issue a warrant for the arrest of Mr. Bagaragaza to the Dutch authorities; and (ii) formally request that the Dutch authorities transfer him into Tribunal custody in Arusha, Tanzania. **[page 5]**

14. The Defence submits that, given the statements Mr. Bagaragaza has made to Prosecution investigators, the security situation in Africa is too dangerous for him to be prosecuted or even detained by the Tribunal. The Defence therefore argues that, if it revokes the referral order, the Chamber should make arrangements for Mr. Bagaragaza's detention and trial outside the African continent. The Defence suggests the possibility that the Trial Chamber order that arrangements be made with the Dutch authorities to detain him at the UNDU in The Hague and for the Tribunal to prosecute him there.[17]

15. The Registry submits that it is aware of the specific circumstances of Mr. Bagaragaza, and that it is prepared to address his security concerns if the Chamber revokes the referral order and orders that he be transferred to the seat of the Tribunal in Arusha. Specifically, the Registry submits (i) that the Commander of the United Nations Detention Facilities ("UNDF") will detain Mr. Bagaragaza without any contact with the other accused; (ii) that the Security and Safety Section of the Tribunal ("SSS"), in conjunction with the Tanzanian Authorities, the UNDF Commander, and the relevant departments of the Tribunal, is making arrangements to ensure his security; and (iii) that the Registrar has instructed the SSS to provide a comprehensive report detailing the security threats faced by Mr. Bagaragaza and the specific security measures that will be but in place to address them.[18]

16. Given the assurances provided by the Registry that the relevant bodies of the Tribunal and the UNDF will be able to adequately provide for the security of Mr. Bagaragaza, the Chamber grants the Prosecution request that it (i) issue a warrant for the arrest of the Accused, and (ii) formally request the transfer of Mr. Bagaragaza to the custody of the Tribunal.[19] Consequently, the Chamber need not consider the Defence suggestion that it order that the Accused be prosecuted by the Tribunal on Dutch soil.

FOR THE ABOVE REASONS, THE CHAMBER

GRANTS the Motion;

REVOKES the Order of 13 April 2007 referring the case of *Prosecutor v. Michel Bagaragaza* to the authorities of the Kingdom of the Netherlands;

REQUESTS that the authorities of the Kingdom of the Netherlands defer to the competence of the Tribunal regarding the case of *Prosecutor v. Michel Bagaragaza* in accordance with Article 28 of the Statute and Rule 10 of the Rules of Procedure and Evidence; **[page 6]**

REQUESTS that the authorities of the Kingdom of the Netherlands comply with the Warrant of Arrest and Order for Transfer and Detention issued by the Tribunal on 17 August 2007.

Arusha, 17 August 2007.

Dennis Byron	Erik Møse	Lee Gacuiga Muthoga
Presiding Judge	Judge	Judge

[Seal of the Tribunal]

17 Defence Response, paras. 33-35, 37. *See also*, Rule 4 of the Rules, which provides that "[a] Chamber or a Judge may exercise their functions away from the Seat of the Tribunal, if so authorized by the President in the interests of justice."

18 Registrar's Security Submissions, paras. 3-4.

19 Warrant of Arrest and Order for Transfer and Detention, filed 17 August 2007.

International Criminal Tribunal for Rwanda
Tribunal pénal international pour le Rwanda

OR: ENG

TRIAL CHAMBER III

Before Judges: Inés M. Weinberg de Roca, Presiding
Lee Gacuiga Muthoga
Robert Fremr

Registrar: Adama Dieng

Date: 8 November 2007

THE PROSECUTOR

v.

Fulgence KAYISHEMA

Case No. ICTR-2001-67-I

DECISION ON THE REQUEST BY HUMAN RIGHTS WATCH FOR LEAVE TO APPEAR AS AMICUS CURIAE IN THE PROCEEDINGS FOR REFERRAL OF THE INDICTMENT AGAINST FULGENCE KAYISHEMA TO RWANDA

Rules 11 bis and 74 of the Rules of Procedure and Evidence

Office of the Prosecutor:
Hassan Bubacar Jallow
Bongani Majola
Silvana Arbia
Alex Obote-Odora
Richard Karegyesa
George Mugwanya
Inneke Onsea
François Nsanzuwera
Florida Kabasinga

Defence Counsel:
Jwani Timothy Mwaikusa
Eliane Nyampinga

* Editor's note: the editors have incorporated in this decision the corrigendum of 1 July 2008 (Corrigendum to the decision on the request by Human Rights Watch for leave to appear as amicus curiae in the proceedings for referral of the indictment against Fulgence Hayishema to Rwanda), Prosecutor v. Kayishema, Case No. ICTR-2001-67-I.

[page 2] INTRODUCTION

1. On 10 June 2001, the Prosecutor of the International Criminal for Rwanda ("the Tribunal") filed an Indictment ("the Indictment") against Fulgence Kayishema ("the Accused"). According to the Indictment, the Accused is charged with genocide, complicity in genocide, conspiracy to commit genocide, crimes against humanity, and serious violations of article 3 Common to the Geneva Convention and Additional Protocol II.[1] The Indictment was confirmed on 4 July 2001 by Judge Lloyd G. Williams.[2]

2. On 11 June 2007, the Prosecutor filed a request for the referral of the Indictment against the Accused to the Republic of Rwanda ("the Referral Request").[3] Pursuant to Rule 11 *bis* of the Rules of Procedure and Evidence ("the Rules"), the President of the Tribunal, on 25 June 2007, designated the present Chamber to decide the motion.[4] The Chamber notes that the Accused is at large and is not represented in the proceedings.

3. On 25 October 2007, Human Rights Watch (hereinafter identified as "HRW") filed a request for leave to appear as a*micus curiae* ("the *amicus* Application")[5] in the instant case. In support of its application, HRW refers to Rule 74 of the Rules and submits that it has valuable information on the current status of the Rwandan judicial system that will assist the Chamber in making a proper determination of the case.[6]

4. HRW presents itself as a non-profit, non-governmental organization headquartered in New York and dedicated to investigating and exposing human rights violations around the world.[7] HRW contends that it is not affiliated with any party to this case.[8] It also asserts that it releases between 60 and 85 reports per year[9] and that its extensive research on human rights violations around the world is often called upon to assist International Tribunals in prosecution of war crimes, crimes against humanity and genocide.[10] In this regard, HRW **[page 3]** explains that its researchers have testified at the *ad hoc* tribunals and have provided assistance to the International Criminal Court.[11]

5. HRW also submits that its work on human rights and justice issues in Rwanda is internationally acknowledged, as evidenced by the number of testimonies given before both the Tribunal and national jurisdictions by Alison Des Forges, senior advisor to its Africa Division, and other HRW researchers.[12] HRW further argues that it has published 15 reports on Rwanda, as of 1991 and has also established an office in Rwanda in since 1995, which is tasked with documenting violations of international humanitarian law in 1994 and with monitoring current human rights and justice issues.[13] HRW contends that its researchers have monitored the judicial system in Rwanda since 2005, following the wide-reaching reforms in the years 2002 through 2004.[14] It explains that its monitoring system, which covers both conventional and *gacaca* trials, conducts interviews of persons working in the field of justice, such as judges, prosecutors, lawyers and staff of Rwandan and international non-governmental organizations.[15]

6. HRW further submits that, although Rwanda has made notable progress in improving its judicial system, there remain serious obstacles to fair and credible prosecutions in Rwanda, especially for persons

---

1 Indictment, 10 June 2001.

2 Decision on Confirmation of the Indictment, 4 July 2001.

3 The Prosecutor's Request for Referral of the Case of Fulgence Kayishema to Rwanda pursuant to Rule 11 *bis* of the Tribunal's Rules of Procedure and Evidence,11 June 2007.

4 Designation of the Trial Chamber for the Referral of the Case Fulgence Kayishema to Rwanda, 25 June 2007.

5 Request for Leave to Appear as *amicus curiae* pursuant to Rule 74 of the ICTR Rules of Procedure and Evidence, 25 October 2007.

6 *Amicus* Application, p. 1.

7 *Amicus* Application, p. 1. .

8 *Amicus* Application, p. 1.

9 *Amicus* Application, p. 1.

10 *Amicus* Application, p. 1.

11 *Amicus* Application, p. 1.

12 *Amicus* Application, p. 1

13 *Amicus* Application, p. 1

14 *Amicus* Application, p. 1

15 *Amicus* Application, pp.1 – 2.

accused of genocide and other crimes relating to the events of 1994.[16] Among issues of concern, HRW alludes to the presumption of an accused person's innocence, the right of an accused to call witnesses in his or her defence and the right to be tried by a competent, independent and impartial court.[17]

7. Finally, HRW requests the Chamber to grant a period of three weeks from the date of this Decision to submit its supporting brief.[18]

8. The Prosecutor filed its Response ("the Prosecutor's Response") on 31 October 2007.[19] The Prosecutor submits that it does not oppose the HRW Application to appear as *amicus curiae in the* instant case.[20] However, the Prosecutor argues that, should the application be granted, HRW should file its *amicus* brief within seven days of the issuance of **[page 4]** the present Decision to avoid undue delay in the proceedings.[21] In support of this request, the Prosecutor contends that HRW has had ample time to submit an Application, insofar as the Referral Request was filed on 11 June 2007.[22] The Prosecutor also submits that HRW has already articulated its position with respect to the issues to be addressed.[23] The Prosecutor further requests leave to file submissions in response to the *amicus curiae* brief, should the Application for *amicus* be granted.[24]

DISCUSSION

9. According to Rule 11 *bis* (A) of the Rules, the Chamber, shall determine whether the State concerned is adequately prepared to accept the reference of an ICTR Indictment. In the instant case, the requirement of adequate preparedness should be addressed with respect to the Judiciary of the Republic of Rwanda, the State concerned by the Referral Request.

10. The Chamber is of the view that a concerned State, such as the Republic of Rwanda in the present case, may be considered as adequately prepared to accept a referral case only if that State can guarantee that the accused will receive a fair trial and that the death penalty will not be imposed or carried out, as indicated in Rule 11 *bis* (C) of the Rules.

11. The Chamber notes that HRW bases its application for *amicus curiae* on several issues related to the ability of the Rwandan Judiciary to guarantee a fair trial to Mr. Kayishema. In this regard the Chamber emphasizes that the issue whether the Accused will receive a fair trial in Rwanda is vital for a proper determination of the case.

12. In determining whether a fair trial is possible, the Chamber needs to consider, amongst other matters, the rights of the Accused as enshrined in Article 20 of the Statute of the Tribunal: specifically the right to a fair and public hearing; the accused's presumption of innocence; the right to have adequate time and facilities for the preparation of a defence; the right to communicate with counsel of the accused's own choosing; the right to be tried without undue delay; the right to be present during all trial proceedings; the right to defend himself or herself in person or through legal assistance and without payment in such case if the accused does not have sufficient means; the right to examine, or have examined, the witnesses against him or her; the right to obtain the attendance and examination of witnesses on the accused's behalf under the same conditions as witnesses testifying against him or her; **[page 5]** the right to free assistance of an interpreter if the accused cannot understand or speak the language used in Court; and the right not to be compelled to testify against himself or herself or to confess guilt.

---

16 *Amicus* Application, pp.1- 2.
17 *Amicus* Application, pp.1 – 2.
18 *Amicus* Application, pp.1 – 2.
19 Prosecutor's Response to "Request for Leave to Appear as Amicus Curiae pursuant to Rule 74 of the ICTR Rules of Procedure and Evidence", filed by Human Rights Watch 25 October 2007
20 Prosecutor's Response, Para.2.
21 Prosecutor's Response Para. 3.
22 Prosecutor's Response Para. 3.
23 Prosecutor's Response Para. 3.
24 Prosecutor's Response, Para. 4.

13. In light of HRW'submission, the Chamber is satisfied that HRW is amply qualified to undertake the role of *amicus* in the present case, pursuant to Rule 74 of the Rules.[25]

14. The Chamber also notes that Rule 74 of the Rules does not impose a specific deadline for an *amicus* to fulfill its mandate. The Chamber may therefore exercise its discretionary power to set a reasonable deadline for submission of the work of the *amicus*. The Chamber is not convinced that a seven day deadline for submission of the *amicus* brief, as suggested by the Prosecutor, would in any case accelerate the trial of the Accused insofar as no trial could commence until the Accused, who is at large, is arrested. In light of the issues to be addressed by the *amicus*, the Chamber is satisfied that a period of 21 days is a reasonable deadline for submission of the *amicus* brief. Upon submission of the *amicus* brief, the Prosecutor, Defence and the Republic of Rwanda may file a Response within 15 days of receipt of the same.

FOR THE FOREGOING REASONS, THE CHAMBER:

I. **GRANTS** leave to HRW to appear as *amicus curiae* in the present case;

II. **REQUESTS** HRW to address, in the form of an *amicus* brief, submissions on the following points:

(i) Whether the Rwandan legal system is able in practice to provide the Accused with assistance in:

a) Securing adequate legal representation;

b) Providing appropriate financial support to an indigent accused;

c) Facilitating travel and investigations for Defence teams;

d) Ensuring security for Defence teams.

(ii) What kind of impediments the Defence of the Accused may face in the discharge of its function? **[page 6]**

(iii) What facilities and procedures exist for ensuring that witnesses and victims can be securely and safely accommodated and transported to the place of trial?

(iv) What procedures exist for ensuring protection of witnesses before, during and after testifying in Court; specifically, whether Rwanda operates a witness protection programme? If so, what are the main features of the witness protection programme?

(v) What kind of threats Prosecution witnesses and/or Defence witnesses may potentially face before, during and after giving testimony in Rwanda?

(vi) What procedures exist for the procurement and the facilitation of safe and secure travel for witnesses, particularly for Rwandan witnesses who reside abroad? Will such witnesses be able to benefit from a safe passage to and from Rwanda?

(vii) Whether Rwanda regulations governing the arrest and detention of an accused will afford to the Accused Fulgence Kayishema the same protection as the protection applied by the Tribunal?

(viii) Whether the detention facilities for accused persons in Rwanda comply with internationally recognized standards.

(ix) Any other relevant issues.

III. **DECIDES** that the *amicus* brief should be filed with the Registry of the Tribunal within 21 days from the date of the present Decision;

---

[25] Rule 74 of the Rules reads as follows: A Chamber may, if it considers it desirable for the proper determination of the case, invite or grant leave to any State, Organization or person to appear before it and make submissions on any issue specified by the Chamber.

IV. **REQUESTS** the Registrar of the ICTR to provide HRW with all the documents related to the present case for a proper discharge of its *amicus* mandate;

V. **REQUESTS** the Registrar to notify, without delay, the present Decision to HRW.

VI. **REQUESTS the Registrar to serve a copy of the *amicus* brief of HRW Association on the Republic of Rwanda upon receipt of same.**

Arusha, 8 November 2007, in English.

Inés M. Weinberg de Roca Presiding Judge	Lee Gacuiga Muthoga Judge	Robert Fremr Judge

[Seal of the Tribunal]

Commentary

1. Introduction

This commentary deals with two groups of decisions. One relates to situations in which states cooperate with the ICTR for the purpose of proceedings before the ICTR itself. The other deals with decisions related to the transfer of proceedings from the ICTR to a state, by means of referral.

2. Cooperation for proceedings at the ICTR

In the Bagasora case, the French authorities made their assistance to the proceedings at the ICTR conditional on no less than five conditions,[1] allegedly all based on national security reasons. The conditions were intended to result in the appearance of a serving colonel in a closed session, without revealing his identity, in the presence of a representative of France whose task it is to assert national security, to respond to questions limited to matters already covered during a previous interview. Additionally, the French stipulated non-disclosure of the testimony to any party in any other proceeding.

Neither of the parties objected to the conditions and the Trial Chamber held that "as this is a Defence witness", the limitations do not impair the rights of the accused. This justification for the acceptance of the conditions is difficult to understand. The Trial Chamber referred to earlier decisions of the ICTY, which allowed for similar arrangements based on national security.[2] However, in the 1999 Blaškić decision, the ICTY required that the state prove to a judge or a Trial Chamber that testifying would put its national security at risk.

There is nothing of that in the current decision. Over time, some 12 years after the relevant facts, it becomes difficult to understand the applicability of national security as an impediment to full cooperation. To what extent is the national security of France in 2006 endangered, when facts of 1993 and 1994 are revealed? In addition, this factual ground for refusal is formulated by the state invoking it, and judged by that state itself as to its applicability.

The second decision in the Bagasora case is an example of a practice, developed by states, not to cooperate with the defence, unless the ICTR orders the subpoena of such a witness.[3] Although formally it is the witness who makes his appearance conditional upon the permission of the state for whom he served as an ambassador, in reality civil servants and military officials do not give evidence as such without consulting their authorities. This practice makes the work of the defence to gather its own evidence difficult and dependant on the Trial Chamber. There is a large number of relevant decisions, starting in 1997 with the Blaškić subpoena judgement,[4] and continuing up to and including more recently commented decisions in Volume 24 of this series.[5]

The third decision relates to an entirely different issue.[6] The Danish authorities wanted to make use of the transcripts of the protected witness WDUSA for a national criminal proceeding. The prosecutor therefore filed a motion to unseal the transcripts and to have them disclosed. The Trial Chamber finds that the protection offered to the protected witness is also guaranteed by the Danish authorities. The identity of the witness will not be disclosed and the testimony read out in a closed session. The Trial Chamber is thus convinced that the protective measures will be respected.

---

1 Modalities for Presentation of a Witness, *Prosecutor v. Bagasora, Kabiligi, Ntabakuze and Nsengiyumva*, Case No. ICTR-98-41-T, T. Ch. I, 20 September 2006, in this volume, p. 251.

2 Decision of Trial Chamber I on Protective Measures for General Philippe Morillon, Witness of the Trial Chamber, *Prosecutor v. Blaškić,* Case No. IT-95-14-T, T. Ch. I, 12 May 1999.

3 Decision on Request for Subpoena of Ami R. Mpungwe, *Prosecutor v. Bagasora, Kabiligi, Ntabakuze and Nsengiyumva*, Case No. ICTR-98-41-T, T.Ch. I, 19 October 2006, in this volume, p. 255.

4 ICTY, Judgement on the Request of the Republic of Croatia for Review of the Decision of Trial Chamber II of 18 July 1997, *Prosecutor v. Blaškić,* Case No. IT-95-14-AR108*bis*, A. Ch., 29 October 1997, Klip/ Sluiter, ALC-I-245.

5 See commentary by Micaela Frulli, Klip/ Sluiter, ALC-XXIV-319.

6 Decision on Prosecution's Motion to Unseal the transcripts of Witness WDUSA, *Prosecutor v. Ndayambaje* (Case No. ICTR-96-8-T), *Prosecutor v. Kanyabashi* (Case No. ICTR-96-15-T), *Prosecutor v. Nyiramasuhuko and Ntahobali* (Case No. ICTR-97-21-T), *Prosecutor v. Nsabimana and Nteziryayo* (Case No. ICTR-97-29-T), Joint Case No. ICTR-98-42-T, T. Ch. II, 1 November 2006, in this volume, p. 259.

The most interesting point of the decision is the mutual recognition of the obligation of states under Article 28 ICTR Statute to cooperate with the ICTR. Article 28 ICTR Statute is also applicable for the ICTR itself in its cooperation with states: the guiding principles of state cooperation under Article 28, paragraph 1, also apply to requests from states to the tribunal. The chamber notes that the Danish authorities are conducting a prosecution for crimes committed in Rwanda in 1994, which is fully in line with the Completion Strategy under Security Council Resolutions 1503 and 1534. In doing so, the Tribunal departs from the purely vertical cooperation model that was established in the early days of the *ad hoc* tribunals.[7] By applying the guiding principles of state cooperation also in the reverse situation, the cooperation has become more equal between states and the ICTR. One may ask whether, in practice, the vertical system has not lost much of its rhetoric over the years. The *ad hoc* tribunals have accepted all kinds of excuses, delays and refusals to cooperate.

3. The failed referral to the Netherlands

The main part of this commentary deals with the referral of the Bagaragaza case to the Netherlands. Already before the final decision was taken, questions arose about the legal possibility under Dutch criminal law to accept a referral by the ICTR.[8] The defence disputed whether the Netherlands had jurisdiction over genocide.

A referral may take place under Rule 11 *bis* ICTR RPE for the purpose of trying the crime before a national court.[9] As is widely known, this rule was introduced as part of the Completion Strategy. Rule 11 *bis* stipulates three requirements for a referral: 1) the referral state must have jurisdiction and be willing and adequately prepared to accept the case; 2) the accused will receive a fair trial in the courts of the referral state; 3) the death penalty will not be imposed or carried out. The discussion in the Bagaragaza case is fully focused on the first requirement. The second and third do not cause much trouble, as the Netherlands is bound by a number of human rights conventions guaranteeing the right to a fair trial and has a constitutional prohibition of the death penalty.[10]

The defence argued that the Netherlands may not have jurisdiction over non-nationals committing genocide outside the territory of the Netherlands. It was undisputed that there is no primary jurisdiction over foreigners committing genocide outside the Netherlands under the 1964 Act implementing the Genocide Convention. It was also argued that the Netherlands could not obtain jurisdiction in a subsidiary manner. The main argument of the defence was that the literal wording of Article 4a Dutch Penal Code, on the basis of which transfer of proceedings may take place, is limited to transfers by foreign states on the basis of a treaty.[11] However, the Trial Chamber followed the assurances of the government of the Netherlands that it will obtain the necessary jurisdiction through the referral.[12] The government argued that the requirement in the national act of "foreign state" is fulfilled by the international tribunal and follows from its obligations under the ICTR Statute.

In its argumentation, the defence partially relied on the principle of legality. This is rather strange. The discussion was not whether genocide was a crime under Dutch criminal law at the time the accused allegedly committed the crime. The 1964 Act to implement the Genocide Convention undisputedly provides for the criminalisation of genocide. The discussion was whether, in the absence of primary jurisdiction over the accused, Dutch law would allow the ICTR's jurisdiction to be conferred on it.[13]

---

7 See further G. Sluiter, International Criminal Adjudication and the Collection of Evidence: Obligations of States, Diss. Utrecht 2002, p. 82-83.

8 See the questions raised in the Second Order for further Submissions Concerning the Request for Referral of the Indictment to the Kingdom of the Netherlands, *Prosecutor v. Bagaragaza*, Case No. ICTR-2005-86-11bis, T. Ch. III, 6 March 2007, in this volume, p. 263.

9 See, on the ICTY case law on referrals, J. Dieckmann and Christina Kerll, UN Ad Hoc Tribunals Under Time Pressure – Completion Strategy and Referral Practice of the ICTY and ICTR from the Perspective of the Defence, 8 International Criminal Law Review 2008, p. 87-108.

10 Decision on the Prosecution Motion for Referral to the Kingdom of Norway, *Prosecutor v. Bagaragaza*, Case No. ICTR-2005-86-11bis, T. Ch. III, 19 May 2006, Klip/ Sluiter, ALC-XXIV-13; Decision on Rule 11*bis* Appeal, *Prosecutor v. Bagaragaza*, Case No. ICTR-05-86-AR11*bis*, A. Ch., 30 August 2006, Klip/ Sluiter, ALC-XXIV-19, with a commentary of Blanco Cordero.

11 "The criminal law of the Netherlands is applicable to anyone against whom proceedings have been transferred to the Netherlands from a foreign state pursuant to a treaty conferring jurisdiction to prosecute on the Netherlands": translation from Bert Swart and André Klip, International criminal law in the Netherlands, Freiburg im Breisgau 1997, p. 252.

12 Decision on Prosecutor's Request for Referral of the Indictment to the Kingdom of the Netherlands, *Prosecutor v. Bagaragaza*, Case No. ICTR-2005-86-11bis, T. Ch. III, 13 April 2007, in this volume, p. 267.

13 It seems ages ago that deferrals were requested. See, for instance, an early commentary by Vander Beken, Klip/ Sluiter, ALC-II-99.

The fears of the defence, which had been probably fueled by an earlier failed referral to Norway in 2006,[14] proved to be justified.[15] The Appeals Chamber in the Norwegian referral did not accept the prosecution's view that "a case" and not "a crime" should be transferred. In hindsight, it might have been more appropriate to follow the prosecutor's view. After the referral in Bagaragaza, the Netherlands courts took decisions in criminal proceedings against Mpambara, a Rwandan who had sought asylum in the Netherlands. They decided that the Netherlands did not have jurisdiction over genocide, and that this jurisdiction could not be obtained by a request of the ICTR prosecutor to deal with the ICTR Statute crimes as well. As a consequence of a decision of the Hague District Court in the Mpambara case,[16] the prosecution filed an urgent motion to revoke the referral of the Bagaragaza case to the Netherlands.[17] The Chamber followed the prosecution in its request and revoked the decision of 13 April on the basis of Rule 11 *bis* (F) RPE.

The decision of the Hague District Court was followed by a decision of the Hague Court of Appeal,[18] which was later confirmed by the Supreme Court of the Netherlands.[19] The Advocate-General at the Supreme Court of the Netherlands suggested that the Bagaragaza case could have had a different outcome from the Mpambara case. Mpambara was arrested in the Netherlands on the initiative of the Netherlands authorities themselves, without a request for referral by the ICTR. Such a formal request on the basis of Rule 11 *bis* could have made the difference.[20]

The Supreme Court could have taken an entirely different decision. With regard to the constitutional requirement applicable in extradition cases, requiring that extradition from the Netherlands may only take place on the basis of a treaty, the government had held in the past that United Nations Security Council Resolutions could be regarded as a sufficient basis to comply with the treaty requirement. That could have been the reasoning in this case, but was not used.

Back in 1996, when the implementing legislation to the ICTR Statute was pending before Dutch Parliament, this author discussed with a Member of Parliament the lacunae in the Dutch legislation on deferral and referral and drafted a new provision for the Penal Code to comply with the obligations under the ICTR Statute.[21] One Member of Parliament raised the matter in the debate in Parliament. However, the Minister of Justice replied that the existing legislation would be sufficient to comply with the obligations.[22]

On 6 October 2009, Minister of Justice Hirsch Ballin published a draft proposal to amend the relevant Dutch legislation.[23] It both extends the jurisdiction of genocide universally, as well as amending Article 4a Penal Code to allow for transfer of proceedings to and from an international criminal tribunal. This will end the incompatibility of Dutch law with requests for referral and deferral.

The question must be raised whether the Trial Chamber could have done anything else than believe that the government would interpret its national law appropriately. The blame is on the Dutch government, which took the risk that a disputed interpretation would not be followed by its courts. One wonders whether the interpretation of Dutch criminal law was provided by the Ministry of Foreign Affairs or the Ministry of

---

14 Decision on the Prosecution Motion for Referral to the Kingdom of Norway, *Prosecutor v. Bagaragaza*, Case No. ICTR-2005-86-11bis, T. Ch. III, 19 May 2006, Klip/ Sluiter, ALC-XXIV-13; Decision on Rule 11*bis* Appeal, *Prosecutor v. Bagaragaza*, Case No. ICTR-05-86-AR11*bis*, A. Ch., 30 August 2006, Klip/ Sluiter, ALC-XXIV-19, with a commentary of Blanco Cordero.

15 In addition, the prosecutor had amended the indictment with an additional war crimes count, for the purpose of encouraging a state to accept a possible transfer: see Decision on the Prosecutor's Application for Leave to Amend the Indictment, *Prosecutor v. Bagaragaza*, Case No. ICTR-05-86-I, T. Ch. III, 30 November 2006, par. 6.

16 The Hague District Court, 24 July 2007, see rechtspraak.nl, BB8462 for the English translation and BB0494 for the Dutch original.

17 This led to the Decision on Prosecutor's Extremely Urgent Motion for Revocation of the Referral to the Kingdom of the Netherlands Pursuant to Rule 11*bis* (F) & (G), *Prosecutor v. Bagaragaza*, Case No. ICTR-2005-86-11*bis*, T. Ch. designated under Rule 11*bis*, 17 August 2007, in this volume, p. 277.

18 Hague Court of Appeal, 17 December 2007, see rechtspraak.nl for an English translation BC1757 and BC0287 for the Dutch original.

19 Supreme Court of the Netherlands, 21 October 2008, Nederlandse Jurisprudentie 2009, 108. I have not been able to trace a translation into English.

20 Opinion of Advocate General Machielse, Nederlandse Jurisprudentie 2009, 108, par. 7.17.

21 Correspondance of 1996 and 1997, on file with the author.

22 Parliamentary Documents 1996-1997, 24818, nr. 5, p. 6 and 7.

23 Draft legislation: Wet ter verruiming van de mogelijkheden tot opsporing en vervolging van internationale misdrijven (Act to extend competences regarding investigation and prosecution of international crimes).

Justice. The arguments given are of an internationalist nature and do not demonstrate any knowledge of the history of the said provision of Dutch law.

4. What happened subsequently to Bagaragaza?

On 20 May 2008, the accused was transferred by the Dutch authorities back to the United Nations Detention Facility in Arusha pending trial. On 17 August 2009, immediately before the trial was scheduled to begin, the parties filed a joint motion for consideration of a guilty plea agreement between the prosecutor and the accused, which included a statement of admitted facts signed by the accused and a guilty plea agreement signed by the prosecutor and the accused. On 17 September 2009, during the hearing on the guilty plea before the chamber, Michel Bagaragaza pleaded guilty to complicity in genocide and not guilty to the three other counts of the amended indictment. The chamber also granted the prosecution's motion for leave to amend the indictment.

That same day, the prosecution filed the operative indictment, charging the accused with individual criminal responsibility pursuant to Article 6, paragraph 1, of the ICTR Statute with one count of complicity in genocide. Bagaragaza was sentenced to 8 years imprisonment on 5 November 2009. With a decision of 1 April 2010, the Trial Chamber deducted the time spent in custody in the Netherlands from that sentence.[24]

5. A fair trial in Rwanda

The prosecution applied in a number of cases for a referral to Rwanda. However, ICTR Trial Chambers have been extremely reluctant to do that. In particular, the human rights situation in Rwanda is increasingly a matter of concern. One decision in the period covered by this volume of the series is evidence of that.[25] Human Rights Watch expressed doubts as to whether the Rwandan judicial system would meet the necessary requirements and sought leave to appear as *amicus curiae*. This was not only granted by the Trial Chamber, but also accompanied by a fair number of general and specific questions as to the status of the Rwandan judicial system. The pertinent questions of the Trial Chamber were a foreboding of the quite critical attitude and reluctance of Trial Chambers to refer cases to Rwanda. In the end, it led to a consistent practice of refusing the request for referral to Rwanda.[26] These decisions will be the subject of a commentary in a later volume of this series.

André Klip

[24] Order regarding the Computation of Time Spent in Custody to be Deducted in Michel Bagaragaza's Sentence, *Prosecutor v. Bagaragaza*, Case No. ICTR-05-86-S, T. Ch. III, 1 April 2010.

[25] Decision on the Request by Human Rights Watch for leave to Appear as Amicus Curiae in the Proceedings for Referral of the Indictment against Fulgence Kayishema to Rwanda, Prosecutor v. Kayishema, Case No. ICTR-2001-67-I, T. Ch. III, 8 November 2007, in this volume, p. 281.

[26] Decision on the Prosecutor's Request for Referral of Case to the Republic of Rwanda, *Prosecutor v. Munyakazi,* Case No. ICTR-97-36-Rll *bis*, T. Ch. III, 28 May 2008; Decision on Prosecutor's Request for Referral to the Republic of Rwanda, *Prosecutor v. Kanyarukiga,* Case No. ICTR-2002- 78-Rll *bis*, T. Ch. 11 *bis*, 6 June 2008; Decision on Prosecutor's Request for the Referral of the Case of Ildephonse Hategekimana to Rwanda, *Prosecutor v. Hategekimana,* Case No. ICTR-00-55B-Rll*bis*, T. Ch. 11 *bis*, 19 June 2008; Decision on Prosecution's Appeal against Decision on Referral Under Rule 11 *bis*, *Prosecutor v. Munyakazi*, Case No. ICTR-97-36-R11*bis*, A. Ch., 8 October 2008; Decision on Defence Judicial and Administrative Application for Deferral in Favour of the ICTR, *Prosecutor v. Nshogoza,* Case No. ICTR-2007-91-PT, T. Ch. III, 5 November 2008; Decision on the Prosecutor's request for referral of case to the Republic of Rwanda, *Prosecutor v. Kayishema*, Case No. ICTR 01 67 R11*bis*, T. Ch. III, 16 December 2008, all to be published in volume XXXI. Additionally, the following decisions were taken on appeal: Decision on the prosecution's appeal against decision on referral under Rule 11*bis*, *Prosecutor v. Kanyarukigal,* Case No.: ICTR-2002-78-R11*bis*, A. Ch., 30 October 2008; Decision on prosecutor's request for referral to the Republic of Rwanda, *Prosecutor v. Gatete*, Case No. ICTR-2 000-61-R 11*bis*, T. Ch. 11 *bis*, 17 November 2008; Decision on the prosecution's appeal against decision on referral under Rule 11 *bis, Prosecutor v. Hategekimana,* Case No. ICTR-00-55B-R11*bis*, A. Ch., 4 December 2008, all to be published in volume XXXI.

Tribunal Pénal International pour le Rwanda
International Criminal Tribunal for Rwanda

IN THE APPEALS CHAMBER

Before:	**Judge Fausto Pocar, Presiding** **Judge Mohamed Shahabuddeen** **Judge Liu Daqun** **Judge Theodor Meron** **Judge Wolfgang Schomburg**
Registrar:	**Mr. Adama Dieng**
Decision of:	**27 September 2006**

ELIÉZER NIYITEGEKA
(Applicant)

v.

THE PROSECUTOR
(Respondent)

Case No. ICTR-96-14-R

DECISION ON REQUEST FOR RECONSIDERATION OF THE DECISION ON REQUEST FOR REVIEW

Counsel for the Prosecution
Mr. Hassan Bubacar Jallow
Mr. James Stewart
Mr. George Mugwanya
Ms. Inneke Onsea

Counsel for Eliézer Niyitegeka
Mrs. Sylvia Geraghty

[page 2] THE APPEALS CHAMBER of the International Criminal Tribunal for the Prosecution of Persons Responsible for Genocide and Other Serious Violations of International Humanitarian Law Committed in the Territory of Rwanda and Rwandan Citizens Responsible for Genocide and Other Such Violations Committed in the Territory of Neighbouring States between 1 January 1994 and 31 December 1994 ("International Tribunal"),

RECALLING that the Appeals Chamber rendered its Judgement in this case on 9 July 2004 ("Appeal Judgement"), in which it sentenced Eliézer Niyitegeka ("Niyitegeka") to life-imprisonment;[1]

RECALLING the "Decision on Request for Review" rendered on 30 June 2006 ("Impugned Decision"), in which the Appeals Chamber dismissed all requests submitted by Niyitegeka on 27 October 2004, 7 February 2005, 17 August 2005, and 10 October 2005 for review of the Appeals Judgement pursuant to Article 25 of the Statute and Rules 120 and 121 of the Rules of Procedure and Evidence of the International Tribunal;[2]

BEING SEIZED OF the "Requête en reconsidération de la 'Decision on Request for Review' du 30 juin 2006" filed by Niyitegeka on 1 August 2006 ("Request for Reconsideration"), in which he: (1) seeks reconsideration of the Impugned Decision on grounds that he is a victim of a miscarriage of justice due to the existence of clear errors in the Appeals Chamber's reasoning in the Impugned Decision that have caused him grave material prejudice;[3] and (2) requests that, prior to the Appeals Chamber's full consideration of his Request for Reconsideration, it extend his Counsel's mandate to assist him in obtaining an Affidavit from Mr. Kambanda and in filing additional submissions that would provide further evidence of the persuasiveness of his alibi;[4]

NOTING the "Prosecutor's Response to Niyitegeka's 'Requête en reconsidération de la Decision on Request for Review du 30 juin 2006'" filed on 10 August 2006;

NOTING the "Réplique de l'Appelant à la Réponse du Procureur à la 'Requête en reconsidération de la Decision on Request for Review du 30 juin 2006'" filed by Niyitegeka on 17 August 2006;

CONSIDERING that the Appeals Chamber recently held that: although it has inherent discretionary power to reconsider its own decisions in exceptional circumstances, "there is no power to reconsider a final judgement" because it is inconsistent with the Statute of the International Tribunal, "which provides for a right of appeal and the right of review but not for a second right of appeal by the avenue of reconsideration of a final judgement"; existing proceedings for appeal and review established under the Statute provide sufficient safeguards for due process **[page 3]** and the right to a fair trial; and it is in the interests of justice for both victims and convicted persons who are entitled to "certainty and finality of legal judgements";[5]

CONSIDERING further that a final judgement is a decision which terminates the proceedings in a case;[6]

FINDING, by majority, that because the Impugned Decision rejected Niyitegeka's requests for review of the Appeal Judgement, it is a final decision closing the proceedings in this case;

HEREBY DISMISSES the Appellant's Request for Reconsideration; and

DECLARES the request therein for extension of Counsel's mandate as moot.

---

1 *Niyitegeka v. The Prosecutor*, Case. No. ICTR-96-14-A, Judgement, 9 July 2004, paras 1, 270.

2 Decision on Request for Review, 30 June 2006, para. 76.

3 Request for Reconsideration, paras. 49, 55, 66, 69.

4 *Id.*, paras 74-75.

5 *Prosecutor v. Žigić*, Case No. IT-98-30/1-A, Decision on Zoran Žigić's "Motion for Reconsideration of Appeals Chamber Judgement IT-98-30/1-A Delivered on 28 February 2005", 26 June 2006, para. 9.

6 *Barayagwiza v. The Prosecutor*, Case No. ICTR-97-19-AR72, Decision (Prosecutor's Request for Review or Reconsideration), 31 March 2000, para. 49.

Done in English and French, the English text being authoritative.

Judge Fausto Pocar
Presiding Judge

Done this 27th day of September 2006,
At The Hague,
The Netherlands.

[Seal of the International Tribunal] [page 4]

DECLARATION OF JUDGE SHAHABUDDEEN

1. On the merits, I agree with the dismissal of the request for reconsideration of the decision denying the appellant's request for review. However, I am not persuaded by the holding of the Appeals Chamber that it has no power to reconsider a decision on a request for review.

2. In *Žigić*, the Appeals Chamber, disagreeing with the rule established by it in *Čelebići*, held that "there is no power to reconsider a final judgement."[1] I disagree with the conclusion of the majority in this case that the Appeals Chamber's "Decision on Request for Review" of 30 June 2006 ("impugned decision") likewise is not subject to the Appeals Chamber's inherent discretionary power to reconsider its own decisions.

3. The impugned decision of the Appeals Chamber did not address, on the merits, the original findings in this case. The Appeals Chamber found that the test for review in Rules 120 and 121 had not been met by the applicant in that he had not presented a new fact that, if proven, could have been a decisive factor in reaching the appeal judgement. No other Chamber previously considered the question whether there was a new fact. This question was raised for the first time in the applicant's Request for Review and decided for the first time in the impugned decision.

4. In *Žigić*, the Appeals Chamber emphasized that the Statute of the Tribunal "provides for a right of appeal and a right of review but not for a second right of appeal by the avenue of reconsideration of a final judgement."[2] The rationale for the rule barring reconsideration of a final judgement is that an appellant, having had the opportunity to contest the original findings against him through appeal and review proceedings, is not entitled to a further bite at the cherry by way of a request for reconsideration. In this case, by contrast, the Appeals Chamber's decision marked the first time that any Chamber considered the applicant's arguments concerning the existence of new facts and their possible impact on the judgement. In my view, the Appeals Chamber has jurisdiction to reconsider such a decision, which is not subject to any further appeal or review proceedings, in order to correct a clear miscarriage of justice. This power should be exercised only in exceptional circumstances. However, consistent with the reasoning in *Žigić* and in the interests of justice, the exercise of this power should not be precluded altogether. **[page 5]**

5. Nonetheless, the applicant has not demonstrated either a clear error of reasoning in the impugned decision or an injustice that warrants the exercise of the Appeals Chamber's inherent jurisdiction to reconsider the impugned decision. For this reason, I support the outcome of the case.

Done in English and in French, the English text being authoritative.

27 September 2006
The Hague
The Netherlands.

Mohamed Shahabuddeen

[Seal of the Tribunal] [page 6]

1 *Prosecutor v. Žigić*, Case No. IT-98-30/1-A, Decision on Zoran Žigić's "Motion for Reconsideration of Appeals Chamber Judgement IT-98-30/1-A Delivered on 28 February 2005," 26 June 2006, para. 9.
2 *Id.*

SEPARATE OPINION OF JUDGE MERON

1. I agree with my learned colleagues that the Appeals Chamber must dismiss the Request for Reconsideration. I write separately, however, because I base my position solely on the fact that Niyitegeka has neither demonstrated a clear error of reasoning in the Impugned Decision nor shown that reconsideration is necessary in order to prevent injustice.[1]

2. In the *Čelebići* Judgement on Sentence Appeal,[2] the Appeals Chamber concluded that it "has an inherent power to reconsider any decision, including a judgment where it is necessary to do so in order to prevent an injustice."[3] Yet in a separate opinion, one colleague and I explained that to decide the matter then before the Appeals Chamber, there was no need to determine whether it has inherent power to reconsider its judgements.[4] We therefore reserved our position on whether the Appeals Chamber has such an inherent power.[5] Recently, the Appeals Chamber overturned the rule it established in the *Čelebići* Judgement on Sentence Appeal, holding instead that "there is no power to reconsider a final judgement."[6] I was not on the bench of the Appeals Chamber that departed from the holding of the *Čelebići* Judgement on Sentence Appeal. In the case where the Appeals Chamber so departed – *Prosecutor v. Žigić* – as in *Čelebići,* I therefore had no occasion to consider whether the Appeals Chamber has the power to reconsider a final judgement that it renders.

3. I continue to reserve my position on this question, as Niyitegeka's Request for Reconsideration must be dismissed regardless of whether the Appeals Chamber may reconsider one of its final judgements. A motion for reconsideration cannot succeed without "demonstrat[ing] the existence of a clear error of reasoning in the [impugned decision], or of circumstances justifying its reconsideration in order to avoid injustice".[7] The Request for Reconsideration raises one frivolous challenge to the manner in which, in one part of the Impugned Decision, the Appeals Chamber applied the requirement that a review request be based on a new fact.[8] Aside from this, the Request **[page 7]** for Reconsideration never attempts to show error in the Appeals Chamber's conclusion that arguments raised in the Request for Review did not pertain to new facts,[9] and that these arguments therefore could not satisfy the four requirements – laid out in paragraph 6

---

[1] *See Prosecutor v. Blagojević and Jokić*, Case No. IT-02-60-A, Decision on Dragan Jokić's Supplemental Motion for Extension of Time to File Appeal Brief, 31 August 2005 ("*Blagojević and Jokić* Decision"), para. 7 (noting that "in order to succeed in a motion for reconsideration, [a party] would have to demonstrate the existence of a clear error of reasoning in the [impugned decision], or of circumstances justifying its reconsideration in order to avoid injustice"); *Prosecutor v. Naletelić and Martinović*, Case No. IT-98-34-A, Decision on Naletelić's Amended Second Rule 115 Motion and Third Rule 115 Motion to Present Additional Evidence, 7 July 2005, para. 20 (making the same point).

[2] *Prosecutor v. Mucić, Delić and Land'o*, Case No. IT-96-21-A*bis*, Judgment on Sentence Appeal, 8 April 2003 ("*Čelebići* Judgement on Sentence Appeal").

[3] *Ibid.*, para. 49.

[4] *Čelebići* Judgement on Sentence Appeal, Separate Opinion of Judges Meron and Pocar, para. 1.

[5] *Ibid.*

[6] *Prosecutor v. Žigić*, Case No. IT-98-30/1-A, Decision on Zoran Žigić's "Motion for Reconsideration of Appeals Chamber Judgement IT-98-30/1-A Delivered on 28 February 2005", 26 June 2006, para. 9.

[7] *Blagojević and Jokić* Decision, para. 7.

Request for Reconsideration, paras 24-25. Niyitegeka points to a paragraph of the Trial Judgement stating that his counsel tried to prove he "was at a government council meeting in Kigali the entire day on 10 April" 1994. Request for Reconsideration, para. 24 (quoting *Prosecutor v. Niyitegeka,* Case No. ICTR-96-14-T, Judgement, 16 May 2003 ("Trial Judgement"), para. 67). He then quotes the Trial Judgement's assertion that he adduced no evidence of this meeting, Request for Reconsideration, para. 24 (quoting Trial Judgement, para. 67), and contends that as "he is being compelled to prove the veracity of his alibi … the factual evidence of the meeting of 10 April 1994" that he sought to introduce in the review proceeding "does constitute a 'new fact'." Request for Reconsideration, para. 25. As the Impugned Decision explained, however, a new fact is "new information of an evidentiary nature of a fact that was not in issue during the trial or appeal proceedings". Impugned Decision, para. 6 (quoting *Prosecutor v. Tadić,* Case No. IT-94-1-R, Decision on Motion for Review, 30 July 2002, para. 25). The new evidence that Niyitegeka offers to show that the 10 April 1994 meeting occurred therefore does not constitute a new fact.

[9] The Request for Reconsideration encourages the Appeals Chamber to "endorse" the views on the "new fact" requirement expressed by Judge Shahabuddeen in a separate opinion in *Prosecutor v. Barayagwiza*. Request for Reconsideration, paras 14-15 (referring to *Prosecutor v. Barayagwiza*, Case No. ICTR-97-19-AR72, Decision (Prosecutor's Request for Review or Reconsideration), 31 March 2000, Separate Opinion of Judge Shahabuddeen, para. 47). The Request for Reconsideration, however, never explains how doing so might prompt the Appeals Chamber, when considering whether arguments raised in the Request for Review pertain to new facts, to reach results different from those reached in the Impugned Decision. In fact, in the cited paragraph, Judge Shahabuddeen explains the "new fact" requirement in a manner consistent with the way it was applied in the "Impugned Decision".

of the Impugned Decision – for obtaining review of a judgement. Though Niyitegeka challenges the Impugned Decision's conclusions that different pieces of alleged "new evidence" could not – if they had been presented in time – have been a decisive factor in the original decision on an issue, the Request for Reconsideration fails to show that the Appeals Chamber clearly erred in reaching these conclusions,[10] or that failure to revisit them would lead to a miscarriage of justice. The Request for Reconsideration likewise fails to show any clear error in the rejection of Niyitegeka's Rule 68 arguments, or that failure to revisit them would lead to a miscarriage of justice.[11] Further, while making clear that Niyitegeka remains concerned about a Prosecution attorney in this case who was subjected to professional discipline in her home jurisdiction,[12] the Request for Reconsideration fails to suggest that in the Impugned Decision, the Appeals Chamber erred: a) in considering only whether newly discovered communications would have led it to handle the issue differently in the Appeals Judgement, and b) in determining that the newly discovered communications would not **[page 8]** have had such an effect, as they relate to an issue the Appeals Chamber did not consider crucial when it addressed the import of the professional discipline to which the attorney was subjected.[13]

4. In sum, the arguments Niyitegeka now raises do not meet the requirements for obtaining reconsideration. I therefore concur in the outcome without joining in the majority's explanation for it.

Done in both English and French, the English text being authoritative.

Done on the 27th day of September 2006
at The Hague, The Netherlands.

Theodor Meron
Judge

[Seal of the International Tribunal]

---

10 Niyitegeka errs when he suggests that the Impugned Decision assumed an accused who raises the defence of alibi has the burden of proving the alibi. *See* Motion for Reconsideration, para. 15 (arguing that the Impugned Decision makes this assumption). Paragraphs of the Impugned Decision cited by Niyitegeka in making this argument do not suggest that an accused has the burden of proof when asserting an alibi defence. *See* Impugned Decision, paras 14, 19, 22, 23, 28, 32, 40.

11 The Request for Reconsideration asserts that, contrary to what the Impugned Decision held, Niyitegeka was prejudiced by the Prosecution's improper failure to disclose transcripts of cassettes AV906, AV 907, and AV 908. Niyitegeka, however, does not explain how the Appeals Chamber might have erred in concluding, at paragraph 57 of the Impugned Decision, that the finding Niyitegeka sought to contest with these transcripts is not "critical to his conviction for any crime". *See* Motion for Reconsideration, paras 21-23. The Request for Reconsideration also challenges the conclusion that Niyitegeka was not prejudiced by the fact that the Prosecution improperly disclosed only 11 of the 29 pages of the transcript of cassette AV/917. Though Niyitegeka asserts that the remaining 18 pages would have helped him to better establish his whereabouts on 16 April 1994, he offers no coherent explanation for why it was clearly erroneous to conclude, on the basis of his submissions during the review proceeding, that these 18 pages would have provided no such assistance. Moreover, he does not explain why failure to reconsider the extent of his prejudice would lead to a miscarriage of justice. *See* Motion for Reconsideration, paras 30-31.

12 *See* Motion for Reconsideration, paras 67-69.

13 *See* Impugned Decision, paras 72-75.

Tribunal Pénal International pour le Rwanda
International Criminal Tribunal for Rwanda

IN THE APPEALS CHAMBER

Before: Judge Mohamed Shahabuddeen, Presiding
Judge Mehmet Güney
Judge Liu Daqun
Judge Theodor Meron
Judge Wolfgang Schomburg

Registrar: Mr. Adama Dieng

Decision of: 4 October 2006

ALOYS NTABAKUZE

("Applicant")

v.

THE PROSECUTOR

Case No.: ICTR-98-41-AR73

DECISION ON MOTION FOR RECONSIDERATION

Counsel for the Applicant
Mr. Peter Erlinder
Mr. André Tremblay

Counsel for the Prosecution
Mr. James Stewart
Ms. Barbara Mulvaney

[page 2] 1. **THE APPEALS CHAMBER** of the International Criminal Tribunal for the Prosecution of Persons Responsible for Genocide and Other Serious Violations of International Humanitarian Law Committed in the Territory of Rwanda and Rwandan Citizens Responsible for Genocide and Other Such Violations Committed in the Territory of Neighbouring States between 1 January 1994 and 31 December 1994 ("Appeals Chamber" and "Tribunal", respectively) is seized of the "Alloys Ntabakuze Motion for Reconsideration of an Appeals Chamber Decision (or to Intervene in Such a Motion) and Ancillary Alternative Motion for Clarification of the Decision" filed on 14 July 2006 ("Motion") in which the Applicant requests

(i) A reconsideration of a decision on interlocutory appeal concerning judicial notice rendered in another case ("Impugned Decision");[1] or, in the alternative,

(ii) Leave to intervene in motions for reconsideration of the Impugned Decision filed by the accused in that case; and

(iii) Clarification of the Impugned Decision.

2. The Prosecution filed a Response opposing the Motion and the Applicant subsequently filed his Reply thereto.[2]

3. **HEREBY RENDERS ITS DECISION** as follows:

I. BACKGROUND

4. On 16 June 2006, the Appeals Chamber issued the Impugned Decision, in which it directed the Trial Chamber in the *Karemera et al.* case to take judicial notice of facts 2, 5 and 6 listed in Annex A of the Prosecution's Interlocutory Appeal.[3] These facts are **[page 3]**

> (i) The following state of affairs existed in Rwanda between 6 April 1994 to 17 July 1994: There were throughout Rwanda widespread or systematic attacks against a civilian population based on Tutsi ethnic identification. During the attacks, some Rwandan citizens killed or caused serious bodily or mental harm to persons perceived to be of a Tutsi ethnic identity;
>
> (ii) Between 1 January 1994 and 17 July 1994 in Rwanda there was an armed conflict not of an international character;
>
> (iii) Between 6 April 1994 and 17 July 1994, there was a genocide in Rwanda against the Tutsi ethnic group.[4]

5. In support of the Motion, the Applicant submits that he has the requisite standing to independently bring this matter before the Appeals Chamber. However, should it be held that he does not have standing, he requests leave to intervene in motions for reconsideration filed by the appellants in the *Karemera et al.* case.[5]

---

1 *The Prosecutor v. Edouard Karemera, Mathieu Ngirumpatse and Joseph Nzirorera*, Case No. ICTR-98-44-AR73(C), Decision on Prosecutor's Interlocutory Appeal of Decision on Judicial Notice, 16 June 2006 ("Impugned Decision").

2 "Prosecutor's Response to 'Aloys Ntabakuze Motion for Reconsideration of an Appeals Chamber Decision (or to Intervene in Such a Motion) and Ancillary Alternative Motion for Clarification of the Decision'", 21 July 2006 ("Response"); "Ntabakuze Reply to 'Prosecutor's Response to Alloys Ntabakuze Motion for Reconsideration of an Appeals Chamber Decision (or to Intervene in Such Motion) and Ancillary Alternative Motion for Clarification of the Decision'", 25 July 2006 ("Reply"). "Appendix to Aloys Ntabakuze Motion for Reconsideration of an Appeals Chamber Decision (or to Intervene in Such a Motion) and Ancillary Alternative Motion for Clarification of the Decision", 20 September 2006, was not considered due to its late filing. Consequently, "The Prosecutor's Motion to Object to the Filing of 'Appendix to Aloys Ntabakuze Motion for Reconsideration of an Appeals Chamber Decision (or to Intervene in Such a Motion) and Ancillary Alternative Motion for Clarification of the Decision' " of 25 September 2006, is moot. The Appeals Chamber will accordingly not consider it or the Applicant's Response of 26 September 2006, entitled "Ntabakuze Response to 'The Prosecutor's Motion to Object to the Filing of Appendix to Aloys Ntabakuze Motion for Reconsideration of an Appeals Chamber Decision (or to Intervene in Such a Motion) and Ancillary Alternative Motion for Clarification of the Decision'".

3 Impugned Decision, para. 57, referring to *The Prosecutor v. Edouard Karemera, Mathieu Ngirumpatse and Joseph Nzirorera*, Case No. ICTR-98-44-AR73(C) ("*Karemera et al.* case").

4 *The Prosecutor v. Edouard Karemera, Mathieu Ngirumpatse and Joseph Nzirorera*, Case No. ICTR-98-44-AR73(C), The Prosecutor's Interlocutory Appeal of Decision on Judicial Notice (Rule 73 (c)). 9 December 2005, Annex A.

5 Motion, para. (i).

6. The Applicant avers that the findings in the Impugned Decision affect all pending cases before the Tribunal and his case in particular.[6] He argues that he has "an immediate, compelling interest" in this matter which he distinguishes from other accused, including the appellants in the *Karemera et al.* case.[7] According to the Applicant, his defence is based on advancing an alternative to the "genocide hypothesis", and his Defence team already introduced evidence in this regard.[8] However, the Impugned Decision has the impact of cutting off the presentation of evidence and eliminating defences which are still the subject of active litigation in his case and while evidence in his defence is still being presented.[9] The Applicant, in his view, is therefore immediately and severely prejudiced based on principles of fair trial.[10]

7. The Applicant submits that the Appeals Chamber has the inherent power to reconsider its decisions in instances where there are new circumstances or where such decisions were erroneous and caused prejudice.[11]

8. The Applicant also, as an alternative remedy, seeks clarification of the Impugned Decision. He submits that the precise parameters of the Impugned Decision must be clearly delineated to avoid any error as to any permissible inferences that may be drawn from it.[12] This will enable him **[page 4]** to determine the evidence that may or may not be presented in concluding his case and the treatment that will be accorded to the evidence already on record.[13]

9. The Prosecution responds that the Applicant has no standing to bring the Motion.[14] In its view, only Rules 74 and 107 of the Rules of Procedure and Evidence of the Tribunal ("Rules") could allow the Appeals Chamber to grant the Applicant standing in this case, but the Applicant has failed to satisfy the criteria set forth therein. Furthermore, the Applicant's request for reconsideration constitutes an exceptional discretionary remedy, and would only be justified where a clear error in reasoning, or injustice was demonstrated.[15] The Motion fails to satisfy this test.[16]

10. In addition, the Prosecution argues that the Applicant did not seek standing to intervene in motions for reconsideration filed in the *Karemera et al.* case in a timely manner.[17] He failed to intervene when the matter relating to the judicial notice of facts was being considered by the Trial Chamber and Appeals Chamber in the *Karemera et al.* case.[18] The Prosecution further argues that the Applicant's request for clarification of the Impugned Decision is baseless. The Prosecution avers that the Impugned Decision is sufficiently clear, and that it is up to the Trial Chamber in the Applicant's case to determine the scope of its application.[19] Accordingly, the Prosecution submits that the Motion should be dismissed in its entirety.

11. The Applicant replies that there is no predetermined regulatory regime that deals with the question of standing in this instance.[20] Rule 74 of the Rules is not applicable in his case as it is apparent that an *Amicus Curiae* is intended to assist a Chamber by being a "friend of the court" where someone else's interests are at stake.[21] In the present case, it is the Applicant's own interests that are at stake.[22] The Applicant argues that reconsideration procedure is based on the inherent jurisdiction and discretion of the Appeals Chamber to act in the interests of justice.[23] The exceptional remedy of reconsideration was created because there is no higher

[6] Motion, para. 1.
[7] Motion, para. 2.
[8] Motion, para. 2.
[9] Motion, para. 3
[10] Motion, para. 3.
[11] Motion, para. 13.
[12] Motion, para. 40.
[13] Motion, paras. 38-41.
[14] Motion, para.6.
[15] Response, para. 8
[16] Response, paras. 8.
[17] Response, para. 9.
[18] Response para. 9.
[19] Response, para. 22
[20] Reply, para. 12.
[21] Reply, para. 11.
[22] Reply, para. 11.
[23] Reply, para. 12.

court to litigate matters that have been decided by the Appeals Chamber. It should therefore not be foreclosed to any one seeking redress on an issue that is causing him or her grave prejudice.[24]

12. The Applicant also submits in reply that there is no explicit Rule that limits standing to the original parties in the dispute. Any party that has been prejudiced by an Appeals Chamber decision **[page 5]** may have standing to seek reconsideration in order to redress the prejudice suffered by that party.[25] The Applicant consequently maintains that he has standing to submit the Motion.

13. According to the Applicant, the Prosecution's submission that he failed to intervene before either the Trial Chamber or Appeals Chamber in the *Karemera et al.* case, has no merit.[26] Unlike the Office of the Prosecutor, which functions as one unit, Defence teams are barred from sharing information as they are bound by witness protection orders and counsel-client confidentiality.[27] The Applicant avers that in his case, the issue of judicial notice has already been decided and the Trial Chamber did not take judicial notice of genocide, or of the ethnic character of the widespread or systematic violence.[28] Consequently, prejudice only became a live issue with the rendering of the Impugned Decision.[29]

II. DISCUSSION

14. The Appeals Chamber notes that the Applicant seeks reconsideration of a decision on interlocutory appeal in a case to which he is not a party. He acknowledges that neither the Statute of the Tribunal ("Statute") nor the Rules prescribe who has standing to seek reconsideration and argues that any party that is prejudiced by a decision may have standing to seek its reconsideration in order to redress the prejudice suffered by that party.[30] The Appeals Chamber confirms that neither the Statute nor the Rules expressly settle the question of standing to seek reconsideration of a decision. However, the Appeals Chamber rejects the assertion that any person who alleges some form of prejudice as a consequence of a particular decision has the requisite standing to seek its reconsideration.

15. As a general principle, only a party to a decision of the Appeals Chamber may ask the Chamber to reconsider that decision. To hold otherwise would open the Appeals Chamber's reconsideration procedures to any non-party who is affected by a decision of the Chamber. In this case, the Applicant is a stranger to the *Karemera et al.* case. Accordingly he has no standing to seek reconsideration of the Appeals Chamber's decision. Also, the Appeals Chamber does not propose to entertain the Applicant's request for intervention at this stage. Moreover, his request for clarification in another case to which he is not a party has no merit.

16. The Appeals Chamber observes that the Applicant is in no way prejudiced. If the Trial Chamber in his own case takes judicial notice of the same or similar facts, he may challenge the **[page 6]** matter there in accordance with his right to be heard. Finally, if the Applicant wants to seek further clarification [see above paragraph 1 (iii)] he may also do so in his own case.

III. DISPOSITION

17. For the aforementioned reasons, the Appeals Chamber **DISMISSES** the Applicant's Motion in its entirety.

---

24 Reply, para. 12.
25 Reply, para. 13.
26 Reply, para. 14.
27 Reply, para. 14.
28 Reply, para. 15.
29 Reply, para. 15.
30 Motion, para. 15.

Done in English and French, the English text being authoritative.

Mohamed Shahabuddeen
Presiding Judge

Done this 4 October 2006,
At The Hague,
The Netherlands.

[Seal of the Tribunal]

International Criminal Tribunal for Rwanda
Tribunal pénal international pour le Rwanda

OR: ENG

TRIAL CHAMBER III

Before Judges: Dennis C. M. Byron, Presiding
Emile Francis Short
Gberdao Gustave Kam

Registrar: Adama Dieng

Date: 30 October 2006

THE PROSECUTOR

v.

Édouard KAREMERA
Mathieu NGIRUMPATSE
Joseph NZIRORERA

Case No. ICTR-98-44-T

DECISION ON DEFENCE MOTION FOR CERTIFICATION TO APPEAL THE CHAMBER'S DECISION ON NZIRORERA'S *EX PARTE* MOTION FOR ORDER FOR INTERVIEW OF DEFENCE WITNESSES NZ1, NZ2 and NZ3

Rule 73(B) of the Rules of Procedure and Evidence

Office of the Prosecutor:
Don Webster
Alayne Frankson-Wallace
Iain Morley
Saidou N'Dow
Sunkarie Ballah-Conteh
Takeh Sendze

Defence Counsel for Édouard Karemera
Dior Diagne Mbaye and Félix Sow

Defence Counsel for Mathieu Ngirumpatse
Chantal Hounkpatin and Frédéric Weyl

Defence Counsel for Joseph Nzirorera
Peter Robinson and Patrick Nimy Mayidika Ngimbi

[page 2] INTRODUCTION

1. The trial in this case started on 19 September 2005. On 12 July 2006, the Chamber denied the Defence request for subpoenas to meet with potential Defence Witnesses DN1, DN2, and DNZ3 ("Impugned Decision").[1] The Defence for Nzirorera now applies to the Chamber for certification to appeal that decision. The Prosecution opposes the Motion.

DISCUSSION

2. The Defence submits that, according to the Appeals Chamber Judgement in the *Tadic* case, "[a Trial] Chamber shall provide every practicable facility it is capable of granting under the Rules and Statute when faced with a request by a party for assistance in presenting its case."[2] It claims that by denying the Defence's motions to issue subpoenas for DNZ1, DNZ2 and DNZ3, the Chamber failed in its duty to provide those facilities, thereby jeopardizing his right to obtain the attendance and examination of witnesses who may be able to rebut the testimony of prosecution witnesses pursuant to Article 20(4)(e) of the Tribunal's Statute.

3. The Chamber notes that the Appeals Chamber has held that "[t]he Chambers are empowered to issue such orders, summonses, subpoenas, warrants and transfer orders as may be necessary for the purposes of an investigation or for the preparation or conduct of the trial."[3] This, however, does not mean that a Chamber must grant all requested facilities by a party because it alleges that it needs assistance. The Chamber must exercise its discretionary power in accordance with the Rules and the Statute. As stated in the Impugned Decision, the Appeals Chamber has determined specific criteria following the outline in the Statute and the Rules, for a Chamber to issue a subpoena and to require a prospective witness to attend at a nominated place and time in order to be interviewed.[4] When an Accused is seeking this particular facility, the Chamber must determine whether it can be granted in accordance with the Statute and the Rules.

4. The Defence argues that the requirements set out for granting certification are met in the instant situation. It also submits that when deciding to grant certification, the Chamber should consider the merits of the appeal against the Impugned Decision as recognized by the Trial Chamber in the *Bagosora* case.[5]

5. Rule 73(B) of the Rules of Procedure and Evidence provides that a decision rendered on Rule 73 motions are without interlocutory appeal except on the Chamber's discretion for the very limited circumstances stipulated in Rule 73 (B). The Trial Chamber has discretion to grant certification when:

1) the decision involves an issue that would significantly affect the fair and expeditious conduct of the proceedings or the outcome of the trial; and **[page 3]**

2) an immediate resolution by the Appeals Chamber may materially advance the proceedings.

6. The moving party must demonstrate that both requirements of Rule 73(B) are satisfied, and even then, certification to appeal must remain exceptional.[6]

---

1 *Prosecutor v. Édouard Karemera, Mathieu Ngirumpatse and Joseph Nzirorera*, Case No. ICTR-98-44-T ("*Karemera et. al*"), Decision on Nzirorera's *Ex Parte* Motion for Order for Interview of Defence Witnesses NZ1, NZ2, and NZ3 (TC), 12 July 2006.

2 *Prosecutor v. Tadic*, Case No. IT-94-1-A, Judgement (AC), 15 July 1999, para. 52.

3 *Prosecutor v. Tadic*, Case No. IT-94-1-A, Judgement (AC), 15 July 1999, para. 52 (emphasis added).

4 *Prosecutor v. Krstic*, Case No. IT-98-33-A, Decision on Application for Subpoenas (AC), 1 July 2003, para. 10; *Prosecutor v. Halilovic*, Case No. IT-01-48-AR73, Decision on the Issuance of a Subpoena (AC), 21 June 2004.

5 The Defence relies upon *Bagosora et. al.*, Decision on Kabiligi Application for Certification Concerning Defence Cross-Examination After Prosecution Cross-Examination (TC), 2 December 2005.

6 *Prosecutor v. Arsène Shalom Ntahobali and Pauline Nyiramasuhuko*, Case No. ICTR-97-21-T, Decision on Ntahobali's and Nyiramasuhuko's Motions for Certification to Appeal the 'Decision on Defence Urgent Motion to Declare Parts of the Evidence of Witnesses RV and QBZ Inadmissible' (TC), 18 March 2004, para. 15; *Prosecutor v. Nyiramasuhuko et al.*, Case No ICTR-98-42-AR73, Decision on Pauline Nyiramasuhuko's Request for Reconsideration (AC), 27 September 2004, para. 10.

7. This Chamber has already decided that the merits should not be considered when addressing an application to certification.[7] Other Trial Chambers have taken the same position.[8] The Chamber is also of the view that the Defence has improperly relied on the *Bagosora* Chamber's view on this issue. In a recent decision not cited by the Defence, the Trial Chamber, I I the Chamber in the *Bagosora* case has also clarified its position on the question whether a Trial Chamber is barred from considering the merits of an appeal in deciding whether leave for that appeal should be granted. It considered that:

> The correctness of a decision is a matter for the Appeals Chamber, should certification be granted. In this sense, it is certainly true that a Trial Chamber is not concerned with the correctness of its own decision when determining whether to grant leave to appeal. On the other hand, Trial Chambers do have a responsibility to screen out requests for certification with no prospect of success and which, accordingly, would not "materially advance the proceedings.[9]

8. In the light of these principles, the Chamber will now determine whether the Defence has shown that both requirements under Rule 73(B) are met.

9. The Defence submits that the Impugned Decision involves an issue that would significantly affect the fair and expeditious conduct of the proceedings because the right of the Accused to a fair trial, and in particular his right to obtain the attendance and examination of witnesses pursuant to Article 20(4)(e) of the Statute, is greatly jeopardized by the Chamber's denial of access to potential witnesses who may be able to rebut the testimony of prosecution witnesses. To support its application, the Defence relies upon prior Decisions rendered by this Tribunal in the *Bagosora et al.* and *Nyiramasuhuko* cases, as well as a Decision from the Special Court in Sierra Leone.[10] It asserts that the issue at hand is similar **[page 4]** to the issues faced in those cases. The Defence also cites other cases that have certified issues concerning the admission and exclusion of evidence, also asserted to be much like the issue at hand, and which have the effect of excluding important potential Defence evidence at the trial.

10. The Defence believes that the resolution of the issue of the Defence obtaining access to potential witnesses by the Appeals Chamber will materially advance the proceedings because this issue is likely to recur as the Defence will request access to more potential Defence witnesses and it will obtain certainty on this issue early in the Prosecution's presentation of evidence and before the Defence begins presenting its case. Should certification be denied and the Trial Chamber be found incorrect in an appeal from a final judgement, the Defence asserts that a new trial would be required to hear the Defence witnesses who had not been originally compelled to testify, thereby significantly delaying the proceedings. The Defence also argues that the potential testimonies are so clearly relevant that since the Chamber did not exercise its power to order a subpoena in this case it is unlikely that it will ever exercise it. Therefore review of the decision will materially advance proceedings.

11. In the Impugned Decision, there has been no general denial of the right of the Accused to examine a witness. Neither has there been a blanket refusal to order subpoenas for all potential witnesses who may

---

7 *Karemera et al.*, Decision on Defence Motion for Certification to Appeal Decision Granting Special Protective Measures for Witness ADE (TC), 7 June 2006, para. 5.

8 See for example, *The Prosecutor v. Casimir Bizimungu et al.*, Case No. ICTR-99-50-T, Decision on Bicamumpaka's Request Pursuant to Rule 73 for Certification to Appeal the 1 December 2004 "Decision on the Motion of Bicamumpaka and Mugenzi for Disclosure of Relevant Material (TC)", 4 February 2005, para. 28. "The *Bizimungu* Chamber agreed that whether there was an error of law or abuse of discretion is not an issue to be considered by the Trial Chamber in its determination of a certification to appeal. It emphasized, however, that the word "significant" in the first prong of the Rule, intends the exclusion of minor or trivial issues that arise in the course of the trial; *Prosecutor v. Nyiramasuhuko et al.*, Case No ICTR-98-42-T, Decision on Prosecutor's Motion for Certification to Appeal the Decision of the Trial Chamber Dated 30 November 2004 on the Prosecution Motion for Disclosure of Evidence of the Defence (TC), 4 February 2005, para. 11; *Prosecutor v. Miloševic*, Case No. IT-02-54-T, Decision on Prosecution Motion for Certification of Trial Chamber Decision on Prosecution Motion for *Voir Dire* Proceeding (TC), 20 June 2005, para. 4.

9 *Bagosora et al.*, Decision on the Motion for Reconsideration Concerning Standards for Granting Certification of Interlocutory Appeal (TC), 16 February 2006, para. 4.

10 *Bagasora et al.*, Certification of Appeal Concerning Prosecution Investigation of Protected Defence Witnesses (TC), 21 July 2005; *Bagasora et al.*, Decision on Certification of Interlocutory Appeal Concerning Prosecution Disclosure of Defence Witness Statements (TC), 22 May 2006; *Prosecutor v. Arsène Shalom Ntahobali and Pauline Nyiramasuhuko,* Case No. ICTR-97-21-T, Decision on Ntabohali's Motion for Certification to Appeal the Chamber's Decision Granting Kanyabashi's Request to Cross-Examine Ntabohali Using 1997 Custodial Interviews (TC), 1 June 2006; *Prosecution v Norman et. al.*, Special Court for Sierra Leone, Case No. SCSL-04-14-T, 28 June 2006.

rebut the testimony of Prosecution witnesses. The Chamber recalls that the Impugned Decision was not concerned with the attendance of witnesses at the trial. It related only to a request to compel attendance at out-of-court interviews. The Chamber was seized of specific requests concerning three potential witnesses and made its ruling on the basis of the information provided by the Defence with respect to these witnesses. No general conclusion can be drawn from the Impugned Decision as to how the Chamber will decide a future motion for subpoena. The Accused is free to submit further requests for subpoenas for out-of-court interviews or to compel their attendance in court when the need arises in this case, which the Chamber will evaluate on a case-by-case basis.

12. The Chamber also finds that the Defence misplaces reliance on several decisions, which it analogizes to the present case and uses to support the claim that the issue in question affects the Accused's right to a fair trial. What distinguishes those cases to the present case is that they all concern issues with a broad scope and a general statement of law which affect a large category of documents or witnesses. The Impugned Decision cannot affect a large category of witnesses, nor does it involve a general statement of law because the evaluation of each request for subpoena was done on a case-by-case basis, and included an exercise of the Chamber's discretion.

13. The Chamber rejects Nzirorera's reliance on the decision from the Special Court for Sierra Leone, which certified a decision from the Trial Chamber after it denied the request to issue a subpoena to call the President of Sierra Leone to testify. In that case, the Trial Chamber was divided in its opinion, the very first considering the issue of pre-testimony interview subpoenas at the Special Court which it claimed would likely arise again, with the majority decision, a concurring opinion, and a dissenting opinion. It was for these reasons that the Trial Chamber certified its decision.[11] This Tribunal has issued other decisions on subpoenas for pre-testimony interviews and the jurisprudence has enunciated that ultimately, the decision to order a subpoena remains discretionary, but also promulgated criteria when **[page 5]** the issuance of a subpoena would be appropriate which the unanimous Chamber in this case took into consideration in the Impugned Decision.

14. Consequently, the Defence failed to show that the Impugned Decision involved an issue that would significantly affect the fair and expeditious conduct of the proceedings or the outcome of the trial. Without satisfying the first requirement needed to grant certification to appeal, the Chamber need not continue its analysis and denies the Defence Motion on that basis.

FOR THE ABOVE REASONS, THE CHAMBER

DENIES the Defence Motion in its entirety.

Arusha, 30 October 2006, done in English.

Dennis C. M. Byron	Emile Francis Short	Gberdao Gustave Kam
Presiding Judge	Judge	Judge

[Seal of the Tribunal]

11 *Prosecution v. Norman et. al.*, at para. 12.

Tribunal Pénal International pour le Rwanda
International Criminal Tribunal for Rwanda

IN THE APPEALS CHAMBER

Before:	**Judge Fausto Pocar, Presiding** **Judge Mohamed Shahabuddeen** **Judge Liu Daqun** **Judge Theodor Meron** **Judge Wolfgang Schomburg**
Registrar:	**Mr. Adama Dieng**
Decision of:	**6 March 2007**

Eliézer NIYITEGEKA

v.

THE PROSECUTOR

Case No. ICTR-96-14-R

Decision on Request for Review

Office of the Prosecutor:

Mr. Hassan Bubacar Jallow
Mr. James Stewart
Ms. Inneke Onsea

The Applicant:

Mr. Eliézer Niyitegeka, *pro se*

[page 2] 1. The Appeals Chamber of the International Criminal Tribunal for the Prosecution of Persons Responsible for Genocide and Other Serious Violations of International Humanitarian Law Committed in the Territory of Rwanda and Rwandan Citizens Responsible for Genocide and Other Such Violations Committed in the Territory of Neighbouring States, between 1 January and 31 December 1994 ("Appeals Chamber" and "Tribunal", respectively), is seized with a request for review, filed on 8 December 2006, by Mr. Eliézer Niyitegeka ("Applicant").[1] The Prosecution responded on 16 January 2007,[2] and the Applicant filed his reply on 1 February 2007.[3]

I. BACKGROUND

2. On 16 May 2003, Trial Chamber I convicted the Applicant, the former Minister of Information in the Rwandan Interim Government in 1994, of genocide, conspiracy to commit genocide, direct and public incitement to commit genocide, and murder, extermination, and other inhumane acts as crimes against humanity, and sentenced him to imprisonment for the remainder of his life.[4] In its Judgement of 9 July 2004, the Appeals Chamber dismissed the Applicant's appeal against his convictions and affirmed his sentence.[5] On 27 October 2004, the Applicant filed his First Request for Review, which was supplemented with additional briefing, including written submissions from assigned counsel.[6] In a decision of 30 June 2006, the Appeals Chamber dismissed the Applicant's First Request for Review.[7]

3. In the Second Request for Review, the Applicant submits several alleged "new facts" principally concerning his alibi. He claims that these "new facts" arise from the **[page 3]** *Rwamakuba* Trial Judgement and an affidavit and agenda provided by Mr. Jean Kambanda, the former Prime Minister of the Rwandan Interim Government in 1994.[8] In addition, the Applicant complains that the Prosecution failed to disclose the agenda of Mr. Kambanda to him as exculpatory material in breach of its obligation to do so under Rule 68 of the Tribunal's Rules of Procedure and Evidence ("Rules").[9] Finally, he seeks the assignment of Tribunal appointed counsel to assist him with his Second Request for Review.[10]

II. DISCUSSION

4. Review proceedings are governed by Article 25 of the Statute of the Tribunal and Rules 120 and 121 of the Rules. Review of a final judgement may be granted only when the moving party satisfies the following cumulative criteria: (1) there is a new fact; (2) the new fact was not known to the moving party at the time of the original proceedings; (3) the lack of discovery of that new fact was not the result of lack of due diligence by the moving party; and (4) the new fact *could* have been a decisive factor in reaching the original decision.[11]

---

1 *Requête en révision de l'Arrêt rendu par la Chambre d'appel le 9 juillet 2004 et, subséquemment, de la décision de la Chambre d'appel du 30 juin 2006*, 8 December 2006 ("Second Request for Review").

2 Prosecutor's Response to Niyitegeka's "*Requête en révision de l'Arrêt rendu par la Chambre d'appel le 9 juillet 2004 et, subséquemment, de la décision de la Chambre d'appel du 30 juin 2006*", 16 January 2007.

3 *Réplique de l'Appelant Niyitegeka à la «Prosecutor's Response to 'Requête en révision de l'arrêt rendu par la Chambre d'appel le 09 juillet 2004 et, subséquemment de la décision de la Chambre d'appel du 30 juin 2006'»*, 1 February 2007.

4 *The Prosecutor v. Eliézer Niyitegeka*, Case No ICTR-96-14-T, Judgement and Sentence, 16 May 2003, paras. 420, 429, 437, 447, 454, 467, 480, 502 ("Trial Judgement").

5 *Eliézer Niyitegeka v. The Prosecutor*, Case No. ICTR-96-14-A, Judgement, 9 July 2004, para. 270 ("Appeal Judgement").

6 In particular, additional briefing was filed on 7 February 2005, 17 August 2005, and 10 October 2005. The Appeals Chamber will refer to these submissions collectively as "First Request for Review". *See Eliézer Niyitegeka v. The Prosecutor*, Case No. ICTR-96-14-R, Decision on Request for Review, 30 June 2006, para. 1, Annex A ("*Niyitegeka* First Review Decision").

7 *See Niyitegeka* First Review Decision, para. 76. On 27 September 2006, the Appeals Chamber denied the Applicant's request for reconsideration of this decision. *See The Prosecutor v. Eliézer Niyitegeka*, Case No. ICTR-96-14-R, Decision on Request for Reconsideration of the Decision on Request for Review, 27 September 2006 ("*Niyitegeka* Reconsideration Decision").

8 Second Request for Review, paras. 30, 33, 45. In addition, the Applicant again raises issues related to the integrity of one of the Prosecution counsel involved in the conduct of the trial. *See* Second Request for Review, paras. 161-167. The Appeals Chamber declines to address this issue as it was exhaustively considered in the Appeal Judgement. *See* Appeal Judgement, paras. 12-23.

9 *See* Second Request for Review, para. 99.

10 *See* Second Request for Review, paras. 23, 168(ii).

11 *Georges Rutaganda v. The Prosecutor*, Case No. ICTR-96-03-R, Decision on Requests for Reconsideration, Review, Assignment of Counsel, Disclosure, and Clarification, 8 December 2006, para. 8 ("*Rutaganda* Review Decision"). *See also The Prosecutor v. Aloys Simba*, Case No. ICTR-01-76-A, Decision on Aloys Simba's Request for Suspension of Appeals Proceedings and Review, 9 January 2007, para. 8 ("*Simba* Review Decision"); *Niyitegeka* First Review Decision, paras. 5-7. *See also The Prosecutor*

In wholly exceptional circumstances, where the second or third criteria are not satisfied, the Appeals Chamber may nevertheless grant review if ignoring the new fact *would* result in a miscarriage of justice.[12]

5. The Appeals Chamber recalls that a "new fact" for the purposes of review refers to new information of an evidentiary nature of a fact that was not in issue during the trial or appeal proceedings.[13] The Appeals Chamber has held that the phrase "not in issue" **[page 4]** means that "it must not have been among the factors that the deciding body could have taken into account in reaching its verdict."[14]

A. <u>Alleged New Facts Arising from the Rwamakuba Case</u>

6. The Applicant submits that, in the *Rwamakuba* Trial Judgement, Trial Chamber III assessed and accepted an alibi similar to the one advanced and rejected in his case related to attendance at a Cabinet Meeting in Kigali on 10 April 1994 and the consequent difficulty of traveling to points outside Kigali at that time.[15] He requests the Appeals Chamber to apply the same reasoning as in the *Rwamakuba* Trial Judgement to his case, not only to events occurring on 10 April 1994, but also to all other instances where he claims that he attended official meetings.[16]

7. The Appeals Chamber is not satisfied that the *reasoning* applied in the *Rwamakuba* Trial Judgement constitutes new information of an *evidentiary nature* of a fact that was not in issue during the trial or appeal proceedings in the Applicant's case. The Applicant concedes that at trial he presented similar arguments to the Trial Chamber concerning attendance at official meetings and the general difficulty of travel at the time.[17] Accordingly, this argument was clearly among the factors that the deciding body took into account in reaching its verdict. Moreover, the fact that the Trial Chamber in the *Rwamakuba* case reached a different conclusion when assessing the weight of alibi evidence with respect to a different accused in a separate trial involving a different factual matrix does not provide a basis for reviewing the assessment of the alibi evidence presented in the Applicant's case.[18] **[page 5]**

B. <u>Alleged New Facts Arising From Mr. Kambanda's Affidavit and Agenda</u>

8. The Applicant next submits an agenda and affidavit supplied by former Prime Minister Kambanda.[19] He argues that these documents confirm the dates of several official meetings and his attendance at those meetings, thereby calling into question his participation in crimes occurring on the same day.[20] In the affidavit relied upon by the Applicant, Mr. Kambanda attests to the Applicant's presence at several Cabinet Meetings on 10 April 1994 in Kigali; on 16 April 1994 and 13 May 1994 in Gitarama; and on 10, 17, and

---

v. Tihomir Blaškić, Case No. IT-95-14-R, Decision on Prosecutor's Request for Review or Reconsideration, 23 November 2006, para. 7 ("*Blaškić* Review Decision").

12 *Simba* Review Decision, para. 8; *Rutaganda* Review Decision, para. 8; *Niyitegeka* First Review Decision, para. 7; *Blaškić* Review Decision, para. 8; *The Prosecutor v. Duško Tadić*, Case No. IT-94-1-R, Decision on Request for Review, 30 July 2002, paras. 26, 27 ("*Tadić* Review Decision").

13 *Rutaganda* Review Decision, para. 9; *Niyitegeka* First Review Decision, para. 6. *See also Blaškić* Review Decision, paras. 14, 15; *Tadić* Review Decision, para. 25.

14 *Rutaganda* Review Decision, para. 9; *Niyitegeka* First Review Decision, para. 6. *See also Blaškić* Review Decision, paras. 14, 15; *Tadić* Review Decision, para. 25.

15 Second Request for Review, paras. 28-33, citing *The Prosecutor v. André Rwamakuba*, Case No. ICTR-98-44C-T, Judgement, 20 September 2006, paras. 91, 98, 117, 156, 214, 215 ("*Rwamakuba* Trial Judgement"). Mr. Rwamakuba, like the Applicant, was also a minister in the Rwandan Interim Government in 1994. *See Rwamakuba* Trial Judgement, para. 3.

16 Second Request for Review, paras. 28, 30, 33.

17 Second Request for Review, para. 30 (noting that he made the same arguments as those advanced in *Rwamakuba* in his case). The Trial Chamber considered these aspects of the Applicant's alibi at, *inter alia*, paras. 67, 79-82, 177, 222, 223, 228, 232, 294-300, 359-362 of the Trial Judgement.

18 *Rutaganda* Review Decision, para. 20. *See also The Prosecutor v. Clément Kayishema and Obed Ruzindana*, Case No. ICTR-95-1-A, Judgement, 1 June 2001, para. 143 ("two judges, both acting reasonably, can come to different conclusions on the basis of the same evidence"). In particular, the Appeals Chamber further observes that the Trial Chamber in the *Rwamakuba* case considered the Prosecution evidence "generally unreliable", a conclusion which the alibi only strengthened. *See Rwamakuba* Trial Judgement, paras. 91, 94-97.

19 The agenda and affidavit are attached as exhibits to the Second Request for Review.

20 Second Request for Review, paras. 34-106, 122-160, Exhibits 1-3.

22 June 1994 in Gisenyi.[21] In his affidavit, Mr. Kambanda also refers to his agenda, which was seized from him at the time of his arrest, to confirm his recollection of the dates and of the approximate duration of each meeting, which he states lasted from 9 a.m. until the afternoon.[22] The Applicant attaches three excerpts from Mr. Kambanda's agenda to his Second Request for Review corresponding to 13 May 1994 and 10 and 17 June 1994.[23]

9. In the following discussion, the Appeals Chamber considers whether the information, arising from Mr. Kambanda's affidavit and his agenda constitutes a new fact in connection with the Applicant's convictions based on the events of 10 and 16 April 1994, 13 May 1994, and 10, 17, and 22 June 1994.[24]

1. 10 April 1994

10. The Trial Chamber found that, on 10 April 1994, the Applicant transported guns in Gisovu commune along with three soldiers.[25] This event, along with a number of others, formed part of the Applicant's conviction for genocide.[26] During the cross-examination of Prosecution Witness GGH, the Applicant, through his counsel, referred to his presence at a Cabinet Meeting in Kigali at the time of this event.[27] However, in considering this exchange, the Trial Chamber noted that the **[page 6]** Applicant did not "adduce any evidence of this meeting" and therefore considered that no alibi had in fact been raised in respect of the event.[28] In his First Request for Review, the Applicant presented evidence of this meeting in the form of a radio broadcast he gave that same day, concerning what occurred at the meeting.[29]

11. In assessing whether the transcripts of the radio broadcast constituted a "new fact" or would have been a decisive factor in reaching the original decision, the Appeals Chamber reasoned as follows in the First Review Decision:

> The Applicant seeks to introduce the transcripts of cassettes in order to prove a fact that he already asserted, albeit without evidence, at trial: that he was in Kigali on 10 April 1994, attending a Cabinet Meeting. [...] The transcripts of the cassettes are information of an evidentiary nature concerning the Applicant's participation in the Cabinet Meeting of 10 April 1994. However, the transcripts relate to the alibi of the Applicant's participation in the Cabinet Meeting of 10 April 1994 in relationship with the credibility of Prosecution Witness GGH, both being matters that were already considered at trial. Accordingly, the transcripts cannot amount to a "new fact" for the purposes of a review application, and the Appeals Chamber is not obliged to examine them further. [...] Furthermore, the particular factual finding of the Applicant transporting arms on 10 April 1994 was not critical to his conviction for any crime. [...] The other evidence relating to the genocide count is overwhelming, such that the conviction on that count would stand even if the transcripts were credited and the factual finding on transport of arms on 10 April 1994 were quashed.[30]

12. In his Second Request for Review, the Applicant relies on the evidence of the radio broadcasts as well as Mr. Kambanda's affidavit attesting to his presence at the Cabinet Meeting.[31] However, for the same reasons quoted above, the Applicant's attempt to bolster his alibi considered at trial does not constitute a new fact for the purposes of review.

---

21 Second Request for Review, Exhibit 1, paras. 4-6.

22 Second Request for Review, Exhibit 1, para. 4.

23 Second Request for Review, Exhibits 2, 3.

24 The Appellant also submits argument concerning his alibi for an event on 20 May 1994. *See* Second Request for Review, paras. 107-121. In his First Request for Review, the Appellant submitted an additional affidavit in support of his alibi for this date, but the Appeals Chamber was not satisfied that it met the threshold for granting review. *Niyitegeka* First Review Decision, paras. 24-28. In his Second Request for Review, the Appellant seeks to relitigate this decision, without submitting any additional new information of an evidentiary nature. The Appeals Chamber, however, will not reconsider its previous decision on this issue and need not address these submissions in detail. *See Niyitegeka* Reconsideration Decision.

25 Trial Judgement, para. 68. The Applicant submits that Gisovu commune is approximately 185 Kilometres from Kigali. Second Request for Review, para. 65.

26 Trial Judgement, para. 411.

27 Trial Judgement, para. 67.

28 Trial Judgement, para. 67.

29 *Niyitegeka* First Review Decision, para. 11.

30 *Niyitegeka* First Review Decision, paras. 12, 13 (internal citations omitted).

31 Second Request for Review, para. 43, 48-71; Exhibit 1, para. 4.

2. 16 April 1994

13. The Trial Chamber found that, "approximately ten days after 6 April 1994", the Applicant procured gendarmes for an attack on Mubuga Church in Kibuye Prefecture.[32] The evidence relied on by the Trial Chamber suggests that this incident occurred "sometime before noon that day".[33] The Trial Chamber, however, declined to rely on **[page 7]** evidence of the actual attack on Mubuga Church as it was uncorroborated hearsay.[34] At trial, the Applicant presented an alibi that, from 14 April until 20 or 30 May 1994, he was in Murambi Centre in Gitarama Town, more than 100 kilometers away with the Interim Government. To establish his alibi, the Applicant relied on the testimony of two witnesses who claimed they saw him there.[35] However, the Trial Chamber rejected the evidence of the two witnesses finding that their testimony was not credible and could not raise a reasonable doubt about the Applicant's role in procuring gendarmes for the attack on Mubuga Church.[36]

14. In his First Request for Review, the Applicant adduced evidence of his attendance at a Cabinet Meeting in Gitarama on 16 April 1994 in the form of a transcript of his radio broadcast, given that same day, concerning what occurred at the meeting.[37] In assessing whether the transcripts of the radio broadcast constituted a "new fact" or would have been decisive in reaching the original decision, the Appeals Chamber reasoned as follows in the First Review Decision:

> The Appeals Chamber is of the opinion that the transcripts of cassette AV/917 constitute information of an evidentiary nature, relating to the Applicant's alibi of participation in the Cabinet Meeting of 16 April 1994 and the credibility of Prosecution Witness KJ. Nonetheless, the alibi and the implications it may have for the credibility of Prosecution Witness KJ, are not new facts, having already been pleaded during the proceedings. Accordingly, the transcripts of cassette AV/917 relating to the said meeting do not amount to a "new fact" for the purposes of a review application and the Appeals Chamber is not obliged to examine them further. Nonetheless, the Appeals Chamber will consider whether, assuming the radio broadcast of the *compte rendu* of the Cabinet Meeting of 16 April 1994 could be characterized as a "new fact", they could have been a decisive factor in reaching the original decision. [...] The Applicant's contends that, before the meeting in the morning of 16 April 1994, he gave an interview which, according to him, was transcribed into a 10-page document. However, he indicates neither the starting nor finishing time or the duration of the interview, making it impossible to determine when he was at the Cabinet Meeting. In the Appeals Chamber's view, the Applicant has failed to demonstrate that the transcripts of the radio broadcast of the *compte rendu* of the Cabinet Meeting of 16 April 1994 could have been a decisive factor in reaching the original decision.[38]

15. In his Second Request for Review, the Applicant refers to the Appeals Chamber's language that "he indicates neither the starting nor finishing time or the duration of the interview, making it impossible to determine when he was at the Cabinet Meeting."[39] Addressing this reasoning, the Applicant points to Mr. Kambanda's affidavit as **[page 8]** confirmation of his presence at this meeting held in Gitarama, from around 9 a.m. until sometime in the afternoon.[40]

16. From the above-quoted text, it clearly follows that the Applicant's alibi for 16 April 1994 is not a new fact and, therefore, his further attempt to bolster this alibi with Mr. Kambanda's affidavit likewise does not present a new fact for purposes of review. While the Applicant may have interpreted this passage from the First Review Decision as suggesting that additional evidence of his attendance at this meeting might have assisted in establishing his alibi, this is not the case. In finding that the Applicant participated in this crime, the Trial Chamber relied on an eye-witness account, which it considered credible. In particular, the Appeals Chamber notes that the Trial Chamber did not fix the date on which the Applicant procured gendarmes for the attack on Mubuga Church as 16 April 1994. Rather, it referred to this timeframe based on the underlying witness's testimony in a more open manner as "approximately ten days after 6 April 1994". Therefore, even

32 Trial Judgement, para. 83.
33 Trial Judgement, para. 70.
34 Trial Judgement, para. 83.
35 Trial Judgement, paras. 79-82.
36 Trial Judgement, paras. 81, 82.
37 *Niyitegeka* First Review Decision, para. 15.
38 *Niyitegeka* First Review Decision, paras. 16, 18, 19 (internal citations omitted).
39 Second Request for Review, para. 74, citing *Niyitegeka* First Review Decision, para. 18.
40 Second Request for Review, paras. 43, 72-88.

accepting as true that the Applicant attended a Cabinet Meeting on 16 April 1994 and that this could constitute a new fact, the Appeals Chamber is still not satisfied that it could have been a decisive factor in reaching the original decision.

3. 13 May 1994

17. The Trial Chamber found that, on the morning of 13 May 1994, the Applicant, among others, led a large-scale attack on Tutsi refugees at Muyira Hill in Kibuye prefecture, resulting in the death of thousands.[41] This event formed part of his conviction for genocide, direct and public incitement to commit genocide, and extermination as a crime against humanity.[42] At trial, as in the case of the events of 16 April 1994, the Applicant advanced an alibi that he was in Gitarama town, which the Trial Chamber rejected for the same reasons mentioned in the preceding sub-section.[43]

18. In his First Request for Review, the Applicant presented video footage from the BBC to confirm that he was at the Cabinet Meeting and at a subsequent press conference in Gitarama.[44] In assessing whether this footage constituted a new fact or would have **[page 9]** been a decisive factor in reaching the original decision, the Appeals Chamber reasoned as follows in the First Review Decision:

> [T]he Applicant's attendance at the Cabinet Meeting/Press Conference of 13 May 1994, which the Applicant aims to prove with the video footage, cannot be considered a "new fact" as the issue was discussed at trial [...]. Even if the Cabinet Meeting/Press Conference were held on 13 May 1994, as testified to by Defence Witness TEN-10, it does not imply that the Applicant could not have participated in the attack in Muyira and the meeting in Kucyapa on that day. Indeed the attack is supposed to have taken place on 13 May 1994 between 7:00 and 10:00 a.m., whereas according to Defence Witness TEN-10 the Cabinet Meetings were held usually from 8:00 a.m. to 2:00 p.m. or beyond. The Applicant has failed to show that he participated in the said Cabinet Meeting/Press Conference from the beginning and that he could not have participated in the attack in Muyira and in the meeting in Kucyapa, and join the Cabinet Meeting/Press Conference at a later stage.[45]

19. In his Second Request for Review, the Applicant refers to the Appeals Chamber's language that "the Applicant has failed to show that he participated in the said Cabinet Meeting/Press Conference from the beginning".[46] In response, the Applicant points to Mr. Kambanda's affidavit and his agenda as confirmation of his presence at this meeting, held in Gitarama, from around 9 a.m. until sometime in the afternoon.[47]

20. The Appeals Chamber's First Review Decision establishes that the Applicant's alibi for 13 May 1994 is not a new fact and, therefore, his further attempt to bolster this alibi with Mr. Kambanda's affidavit likewise does not present a new fact for purposes of review.

4. 10 and 17 June 1994

21. The Trial Chamber found that the Applicant participated with local leaders in two meetings in Kibuye prefecture, respectively, on the mornings of 10 and 17 June 1994 to plan and distribute weapons for an attack on Tutsis in Bisesero.[48] Based on these events, the Trial Chamber convicted the Applicant of conspiracy to commit genocide and direct and public incitement to commit genocide.[49] At trial, the Applicant advanced an alibi, based on the testimony of Defence Witness TEN-10, that he was attending Cabinet Meetings on these dates in Gisenyi prefecture some 200 kilometres away.[50] The Trial Chamber rejected this alibi because it did not find Witness TEN-10 credible, in particular **[page 10]** noting his lack of firsthand or detailed knowledge about who attended and what transpired at the meetings.[51]

41 Trial Judgement, para. 178.
42 Trial Judgement, paras. 413, 433, 451.
43 Trial Judgement, paras. 79-82, 109-114, 177.
44 *Niyitegeka* First Review Decision, para. 20.
45 *Niyitegeka* First Review Decision, paras. 21-22 (internal citations omitted).
46 Second Request for Review, para. 97, citing *Niyitegeka* First Review Decision, para. 22.
47 Second Request for Review, paras. 43, 89-106; Exhibit 1, para. 4; Exhibit 2.
48 Trial Judgement, para. 225.
49 Trial Judgement, paras. 424, 429, 434, 437.
50 Trial Judgement, paras. 214, 224.
51 Trial Judgement, paras. 214, 224.

22. In his First Request for Review, the Applicant presented transcripts of radio broadcasts of his accounts of these meetings given on 11 and 18 June 1994, respectively.[52] In assessing whether this footage constituted a new fact or would have been a decisive factor, the Appeals Chamber reasoned as follows in the First Review Decision:

> [H]aving been raised as such during the proceedings, the Applicant's alibi based on his attendance at the Cabinet Meetings of 10 and 17 June 1994, in support of which the transcripts are introduced, is not a "new fact" within the meaning of Rule 120. [...] [E]ven assuming that Cabinet Meetings were held on 10 and 17 June 1994 in Muramba, and that the Applicant gave an account thereof on the radio, the transcripts do not prove that the Applicant physically participated in the cabinet meetings or that if he was a participant, that he was present throughout the day. [...] The Appeals Chamber finds that the Applicant has failed to establish that the contents of the transcripts of the radio broadcast of the *compte rendu* of the Cabinet Meetings held on 10 and 17 June 1994 could have been a decisive factor in reaching the original decision.[53]

23. In his Second Request for Review, the Applicant refers to the Appeals Chamber's language that "the transcripts do not prove that the Applicant physically participated in the cabinet meetings or that if he was a participant, that he was present throughout the day."[54] In response, the Applicant points to Mr. Kambanda's affidavit and agenda as confirmation of his presence at these meetings, held in Gisenyi prefecture, as well as their duration from around 9 a.m. until sometime in the afternoon.[55]

24. The Appeals Chamber's First Review Decision establishes that the Applicant's alibi for 10 and 17 June 1994 is not a new fact, and, therefore, his further attempt to bolster this **[page 11]** alibi with Mr. Kambanda's affidavit likewise does not present a new fact for purposes of review.[56]

5. <u>22 June 1994</u>

25. The Trial Chamber found that, around 3 p.m. on 22 June 1994, the Applicant was present and rejoiced in the brutal killing and dismemberment of Assiel Kabanda.[57] The Trial Chamber relied on this event, along with other extensive evidence, to infer the Applicant's genocidal intent.[58] As with the events of 10 and 17 June 1994 discussed in the preceding subsection, the Applicant presented evidence through Defence Witness TEN-10 that he attended a Cabinet Meeting in Gisenyi prefecture, which the Trial Chamber rejected for the same reasons.[59]

26. In his First Request for Review, the Applicant presented evidence that a Cabinet Meeting occurred on 22 June 1994 in order to support his alibi.[60] In assessing whether this agenda constituted a new fact or would have been a decisive factor, the Appeals Chamber reasoned as follows in the First Review Decision:

> [T]he Applicant's attendance at the Cabinet Meeting of 22 June 1994, which the agenda seeks to establish, is not a "new fact", since it had been raised during the original proceedings. [...] Regarding the Applicant's attendance at the Cabinet Meeting of 22 June 1994, the entry "MININFOR" at point 4 of the agenda of the said meeting, which according to the Applicant, refers to the "Minister of Information" is not unequivocal. The said entry in the agenda does not rule out the possibility that the Minister of Information may have sent a representative, or that the schedule of the meeting may have been subsequently amended to enable him to address the meeting earlier so that he could leave or that he did not attend the meeting at all. Even if considered to be of impeccable provenance, the agenda is

52 *Niyitegeka* First Review Decision, para. 29.

53 *Niyitegeka* First Review Decision, paras. 30-32 (internal citations omitted).

54 Second Request for Review, para. 126, citing *Niyitegeka* First Review Decision, para. 31.

55 Second Request for Review, paras. 43, 122-142; Exhibit 1, para. 4; Exhibit 3. The Trial Chamber also found that "around 18 June [1994]", the Applicant participated in an attack in Kiziba as well as a subsequent meeting that evening in the Kibuye Prefectural office. *See* Trial Judgement, paras. 215, 229. These findings are based on the same witness, namely Prosecution Witness GGV, whose evidence underlies the Applicant's convictions for the meetings on 10 and 17 June 1994. The Applicant does not make specific arguments about the events of 18 June 1994 in the present submissions. However, the Appeals Chamber understands his submissions to suggest that, if his alibi were accepted for 10 and 17 June 1994, then it would have implications for the credibility of Witness GGV, thereby undermining his convictions based on the events of 18 June 1994 as well.

56 *Niyitegeka* First Review Decision, para. 30.

57 Trial Judgement, para. 312.

58 Trial Judgement, paras. 417, 419.

59 Trial Judgement, paras. 214, 224, 311.

60 *Niyitegeka* First Review Decision, para. 33.

not proof of anything other than the fact that a meeting was scheduled, but not that it actually took place with all anticipated participants present at all or throughout the meeting.[61]

27. In his Second Request for Review, the Applicant refers to the Appeals Chamber's language that "The [entry "MININFOR" at point 4 of the agenda] does not rule out the possibility that the Minister of Information may have sent a representative, or that the schedule of the meeting may have been subsequently amended to enable him to address the meeting earlier so that he could leave or that he did not attend the meeting at all."[62] In response, the Applicant points to Mr. Kambanda's affidavit and agenda as confirming his **[page 12]** presence at this meeting, held in Gisenyi prefecture, as well as the duration from around 9 a.m. until sometime in the afternoon.[63]

28. The Appeals Chamber's First Review Decision indicates that the Applicant's alibi for 22 June 1994 is not a new fact and, therefore, his further attempt to bolster this alibi with Mr. Kambanda's affidavit likewise does not present a new fact for purposes of review.

C. Alleged Disclosure Violation

29. The Applicant also complains in his Second Request for Review that the Prosecution breached its obligation to disclose Mr. Kambanda's agenda to him as exculpatory material pursuant to Rule 68 of the Rules.[64] The Appeals Chamber notes that Mr. Kambanda's agenda does not mention the Applicant by name and simply refers to dates of meetings. However, the agenda's reference to dates of meeting is potential proof that meetings occurred on those dates, and this is consistent with the alibi advanced at trial by the Applicant. As such, the Prosecution did have an obligation to disclose this material to the Applicant pursuant to Rule 68 of the Rules. The Appeals Chamber notes that the failure of the Prosecution to immediately disclose this material may be explained by the fact that, as the Trial Judgement reflects, the Applicant did not give clear advance notice of his intent to rely on an alibi.[65] Nonetheless, a review of the Trial Judgement reveals that having evidence of the existence and exact dates of these meetings was a consideration for the Trial Chamber in evaluating the strength of the alibi that was ultimately advanced.[66] As such, when the importance of these meetings became apparent during the proceedings, the Prosecution had a clear obligation to disclose Mr. Kambanda's agenda, and its failure to do so constitutes a breach of that obligation. However, for the reasons mentioned above, the Appeals Chamber does not consider that this violation prejudiced the Applicant and thus declines to accord any remedy.

D. Assignment of Counsel

30. Though counsel may be assigned in connection with a request for review at the preliminary examination stage for a limited duration if it is necessary to ensure the fairness **[page 13]** of the proceedings,[67] the Appeals Chamber is not satisfied that additional briefing would be of assistance in the present inquiry. In such circumstances, the Applicant's Second Request for Review does not warrant the assignment of counsel under the auspices of the Tribunal's legal aid system.

III. Disposition

31. For the foregoing reasons, the Applicant's Second Request for Review is **DENIED** in all respects.

Judge Shahabuddeen appends a separate declaration.

Judge Meron appends a separate opinion.

---

61 *Niyitegeka* First Review Decision, paras. 34, 37 (internal citations omitted).
62 Second Request for Review, para. 146, citing *Niyitegeka* First Review Decision, para. 37.
63 Second Request for Review, paras. 43, 143-160; Exhibit 1, para. 4; Exhibit 3.
64 *See* Second Request for Review, para. 99.
65 *See, e.g.,* Trial Judgement, paras. 81, 82.
66 *See, e.g.,* Trial Judgement, paras. 67, 214.
67 *Rutaganda* Review Decision, para. 41.

Done in English and French, the English version being authoritative.

Done this 6th day of March 2007,
At The Hague,
The Netherlands.

Judge Fausto Pocar,
Presiding

[Seal of the Tribunal] [page 14]

DECLARATION OF JUDGE SHAHABUDDEEN

1. I am not satisfied on the evidence in this case that the Appeals Chamber's refusal to consider it will lead to a miscarriage of justice. However, I would like to keep the door open to the Appeals Chamber being able to reconsider a case on that exceptional basis should it arise. I understand the existing decisions of the Appeals Chamber to exclude that possibility.[1] I continue to see merit in the idea that the Appeals Chamber should, in a possible case, have the option to consider new evidence proffered by an appellant that does not amount to a new fact, if its exclusion would lead to a miscarriage of justice.[2] In establishing the Tribunal as a judicial body, the Security Council should be seen as having entrusted it with basic judicial functions to administer justice, and consequently with the competence to correct extreme cases of injustice even absent express authority in the Statute to do so.[3] In this respect, I am in agreement with the opinion expressed by Judge Meron.

Done in English and French, the English text being authoritative.

Done this 6th day of March 2007,
At The Hague, The Netherlands.

Mohammed Shahabuddeen
Judge

[Seal of the Tribunal] [page 15]

1 *See Prosecutor v. Zoran Žigić*, Case No. IT-98-30/1-A, Decision on Zoran Žigić's "Motion for Reconsideration of Appeals Chamber Judgement IT-98-30/1-A Delivered on 28 February 2005," 26 June 2006 (*Žigić* Reconsideration Decision"); *The Prosecutor v. Eliézier Niyitegeka*, Case No. ICTR-96-14-R, Decision on Request for Review, 30 June 2006 (*"Niyitegeka* First Review Decision").

2 *See Niyitegeka* First Review Decision, Declaration of Judge Shahabuddeen.

3 *See Žigić* Reconsideration Decision, Declaration of Judge Shahabuddeen, para. 2.

SEPARATE OPINION OF JUDGE MERON

1. In our decision on Niyitegeka's earlier motions for review, Judge Shahabuddeen wrote separately to express his view that the Tribunal has the inherent jurisdiction to reconsider final judgements even where the requirements of Article 25 are not met.[1] This is an issue on which the Appeals Chamber has issued varying decisions,[2] and on which I have twice reserved my position.[3]

2. In the decision at hand, the Appeals Chamber rejects Niyitegeka's motion for review on the grounds that his new evidence does not constitute a "new fact" – as our jurisprudence has interpreted this term – for purposes of Article 25 and Rules 120-121. Unlike in the earlier decision, the Appeals Chamber here mainly declines to address whether in any event this new evidence could have affected the verdict. In light of this choice, I deem it useful to say a few words here about my views on our inherent power to reconsider final judgements.

3. A situation might someday arise in which new evidence that does not amount to a "new fact" under our jurisprudence would nonetheless demonstrate the presence of a serious miscarriage of justice. To pose a hypothetical, suppose that an accused is convicted of murdering a victim. Suppose further that a fact at issue at trial was whether the victim was in fact dead – the Prosecution presented several eye-witnesses who testified to seeing the victim's dead body, whereas the Defence responded with an eye-witness who claimed to have later seen the victim alive. If the victim should turn up alive after the issuance of all final judgements in the case, a clear miscarriage of justice would result from letting the murder conviction stand. This would be true even though under the distinction created by our precedent, this new evidence of the victim's state of being would likely be "additional evidence" that bolsters the Defence's claim at trial that the victim was alive and not a "new fact". **[page 16]**

4. Such situations are unlikely. Like Judge Shahabuddeen, however, I do not think the door should be closed on the exceptional case in which proof of innocence is convincingly demonstrated even though the technical requirements of Article 25 are not satisfied.[4] Should a situation arise where we are presented with convincing evidence of innocence that does not amount to a "new fact" under our jurisprudence, I would likely deem it in the interests of justice to depart from our holding in *Žigić* – a holding that in turn departed from our holding in *Čelebići* – and find that we have inherent jurisdiction to reconsider final judgements when necessary to avoid a clear miscarriage of justice. I have become increasingly concerned that, in departing from *Čelebići*, *Žigić* removed an important safety net for ensuring that justice is done – a departure that is especially problematic in light of our increasingly strict interpretation of the term "new facts". In that respect, I note that allowing for review only of "new facts" as we interpret the term means that we take a stricter approach than that of prominent civil and common law jurisdictions.[5] This Tribunal aims to be a model of due process protections. By refusing to allow convicted persons with an avenue for pursuing claims that do not meet the strict requirements of Article 25 and yet which may be meritorious, we disserve this aim and indeed risk substantive unfairness.

---

1 *The Prosecutor v. Eliézer Niyitegeka*, Case No. ICTR-96-14-R, Decision on Request for Review, Declaration of Judge Shahabuddeen, 30 June 2006.

2 *Compare Prosecutor v. Zdravko Mucić, Hazim Delić, and Esad Landžo*, Case No. IT-96-21-A*bis*, Judgement on Sentencing Appeal, 8 April 2003 ("*Čelebići* Decision"), paras 49-53, *with Prosecutor v. Zoran Žigić*, Case No. IT-98-30/1-A, Decision on Zoran Žigić's "Motion for Reconsideration of Appeals Chamber Judgement IT-98-30/1-A Delivered on 28 February 2005", 26 June 2006 ("*Žigić* Decision"), para. 9.

3 *See Čelebići* Decision, Separate Opinion of Judges Meron and Pocar; *The Prosecutor v. Eliézer Niyitegeka*, Case No. ICTR-96-14-R, Decision on Request for Reconsideration of the Decision on Request for Review ("*Niyitegeka* Reconsideration Decision"), Separate Opinion of Judge Meron, 27 September 2006.

4 *See Žigić* Decision, Declaration of Judge Shahabuddeen, para. 8.

5 *See, e.g.*, Code De Procedure Penal, Art. 622 ("Après une condamnation, vient à se produire ou à se révéler un fait nouveau *ou un élément* inconnu de la jurisdiction au jour due procès, de nature à faire naître un doute sur la culpabilité du condamné") (emphasis added) (France); 28 U.S.C. § 2255 (providing for a review process and further providing for a second review process given "newly discovered *evidence* that, if proven and viewed in light of the evidence as a whole, would be sufficient to establish by clear and convincing evidence that no reasonable fact finder would have found the movant guilty of the offense") (emphasis added) (United States).

5. I recognize that the holding in *Žigić* has been followed in subsequent cases.[6] I will continue to abide by it unless and until the circumstances of a particular case demonstrate that a clear miscarriage of justice will result from doing so. In the case at hand, I do not think that the agenda and affidavit of a convicted war criminal constitutes the sort of convincing and credible evidence needed to show such a miscarriage of justice. Accordingly, I agree with today's outcome.

Done in both English and French, the English text being authoritative.

Done on the 6th day of March 2007 **[page 17]**
At The Hague, The Netherlands.

Theodor Meron
Judge

[Seal of the International Tribunal]

6 *Niyitegeka* Reconsideration Decision, pp. 1-2; *Georges Anderson Nderubumwe Rutaganda v. The Prosecutor*, Decision on Requests for Reconsideration, Review, Assignment of Counsel, Disclosure, and Clarification, 8 December 2006, para. 6.

Tribunal Pénal International pour le Rwanda
International Criminal Tribunal for Rwanda

BEFORE THE APPEALS CHAMBER

Before:	**Judge Mohamed Shahabuddeen, Presiding** **Judge Mehmet Güney** **Judge Liu Daqun** **Judge Theodor Meron** **Judge Wolfgang Schomburg**
Registrar:	**Mr. Adama Dieng**
Order of:	**22 March 2007**

THE PROSECUTOR

v.

Athanase SEROMBA

Case No. ICTR-2001-66-A

ORDER CONCERNING THE FILING OF THE NOTICE OF APPEAL

Counsel for the Prosecution

Mr. Hassan Bubacar Jallow
Mr. James Stewart
Ms. Amanda Reichman

Counsel for the Appellant

Mr. Patrice Monthé
Ms. Sarah N. Bihegué

[page 2] THE APPEALS CHAMBER of the International Criminal Tribunal for the Prosecution of Persons Responsible for Genocide and Other Serious Violations of International Humanitarian Law Committed in the Territory of Rwanda and Rwandan Citizens Responsible for Genocide and Other Such Violations Committed in the Territory of Neighbouring States, between 1 January and 31 December 1994 ("Appeals Chamber" and "Tribunal", respectively);

NOTING that Trial Chamber III pronounced its Judgement ("Trial Judgement") in the present case on 13 December 2006, and issued a reasoned opinion in writing on 19 December 2006;

NOTING the "*Acte d'Appel d'Athanase Seromba*" ("Notice of Appeal"), filed by the Appellant on 19 January 2007;

BEING SEIZED OF the "*Mémoire Complémentaire de la Défense à l'Acte d'Appel du Père Athanase Seromba sur le Fondement de l'Article 7 ter du Règlement de Procédure et de Preuve et du Paragraphe 11 de la Directive Pratique Relative aux Conditions Formelles Applicables au recours en Appel contre un Jugement*" ("Supplementary Brief"), filed by the Appellant on 15 February 2007;

NOTING that, in the Supplementary Brief, the Appellant asserts that his Notice of Appeal was timely filed because the 30-day time limit for the filing of a Notice of Appeal begins to run on the date upon which a party receives notice of the Trial Judgement, which in his case was 19 December 2007;[1]

NOTING that the Appellant "prays the Appeals Chamber to [...] [d]eclare and rule that Father Athanase Seromba's Notice of Appeal was filed in a manner and within the time limit prescribed by the Rules of Procedure and Evidence and the Practice Direction on Formal Requirements for Appeals from Judgement" and that the Notice of Appeal therefore "has been duly filed";[2]

NOTING that the Prosecution has not responded to the Supplementary Brief;[3]

CONSIDERING that Rule 108 of the Rules of Procedure and Evidence of the Tribunal ("Rules") provides that a party seeking to appeal a judgement or sentence must file a notice of appeal "not more than thirty days from the date on which the judgement or sentence was pronounced"; **[page 3]**

CONSIDERING that, contrary to the Appellant's submissions, the time limit for filing his Notice of Appeal began to run from 13 December 2006, the date on which the Trial Judgement was pronounced,[4] and that the Notice of Appeal was due on 12 January 2007;

CONSIDERING that the Notice of Appeal was therefore filed out of time;

CONSIDERING that Rule 116(A) of the Rules provides that the Appeals Chamber may grant a motion to extend a time limit upon a showing of good cause;

CONSIDERING that such a motion should be filed prior to expiry of the relevant time limit;[5]

CONSIDERING that the Appellant failed to file a motion for an extension of the time limit for filing his Notice of Appeal prior to or on 12 January 2007;

CONSIDERING, however, that the Appeals Chamber may "recognize, as validly done any act done after the expiration of a time limit";[6]

---

1 Supplementary Brief, English Translation filed on 8 March 2007, paras. 8-10.

2 *Ibid.*, pp. 1, 3.

3 The time limit for filing a response to the Appellant's Motion expired on 26 February 2007. *See* Practice Direction on Procedure for the Filing of Written Submissions in Appeal Proceedings Before the Tribunal, 8 December 2006, paras. 13, 16.

4 *See The Prosecutor v. Tharcisse Muvunyi*, Case No. ICTR-00-55-A-A, Decision on the Prosecution Motion for Extension of Time for Filing the Notice of Appeal, 22 November 2006 ("*Muvunyi* Decision"), p. 2.

5 *Muvunyi* Decision, p. 2; *Prosecutor v. Jean de Dieu Kamuhanda*, Case No. ICTR-99-54A-A, Decision on Jean de Dieu Kamuhanda's Motion for an Extension of Time, 19 April 2005, pp. 2-3 & n.3.

6 *See* Practice Direction on Formal Requirements for Appeals from Judgement, 4 July 2005, paras. 1, 12. *See also Mikaeli Muhimana v. The Prosecutor*, Case No. ICTR-95-1B-A, Order Concerning the Filing of the Notice of Appeal, 22 February 2006, p. 3.

CONSIDERING that the delayed filing of a Judgement may constitute good cause for the delayed filing of a Notice of Appeal by a period corresponding to the delay in filing the Judgement;[7]

CONSIDERING the importance of the issues involved in this case;

FINDS that the Appellant has established "good cause" within the meaning of Rule 116 of the Rules for the late filing;

HEREBY ORDERS that the filing of the Notice of Appeal be recognized as validly done; and

REMINDS the Appellant that, in accordance with Rule 111 of the Rules, his Appellant's Brief shall be filed no later than 4 April 2007. **[page 4]**

Done in English and French, the English text being authoritative.

Dated this 22 day of March 2007,
At The Hague,
The Netherlands.

Mohamed Shahabuddeen
Presiding Judge

Judge Schomburg appends a declaration to the present decision.

[Seal of the Tribunal] [page 5]

7 *Muvunyi* Decision, p. 3; *Prosecutor v. Blagojević & Jokić*, Case No. IT-02-60-A, Decision on Prosecution Motion for Extension of Time in Which to File the Prosecution Notice of Appeal, 15 February 2005, p. 3.

DECLARATION OF JUDGE SCHOMBURG

It is without consequence whether the time limit for the filing of the Appellant's Notice of Appeal, pursuant to Rule 108 of the Rules, began to run as of 13 December 2006 – the day when the Judgement was pronounced – or as of 19 December 2006 – the day when the Judgement was filed with the Registrar. In both cases, the deadline for the filing of the Notice of Appeal expired on 18 January 2007.[8] However, the Notice of Appeal was filed on 19 January 2007, *i.e.* in any event one day late. The decision does not explain away this one day. While I believe that the Appeals Chamber should not be exceedingly formalistic, it is true that the time limits in the Rules exist for good reason and have to be observed in the interest of justice. The precise observation of forms, including deadlines, is an unalienable part of criminal proceedings. It is also true that the Practice Directions provide that the Appeals Chamber "may recognize as validly done any act done after the expiration of a time limit." However, in light of the higher-ranking Rule 116(A) it is clear that good cause must be shown for a delay. The Appellant has failed to give any reasons why the Notice of Appeal was filed late. To grant only one day without good cause having been shown may set a precedent binding the Appeals Chamber and could open Pandora's Box resulting in an extended non-compliance with time limits. *Obsta principiis!*

Done in English and French, the English text being authoritative.

Done this 22nd day of March 2007,
At The Hague, The Netherlands.

Wolfgang Schomburg
Judge

[8] If assumed that the time limit began to run as of 13 December 2006, it would have expired after thirty days on 12 January 2007. However, the delayed filing of the Judgement (by one week) constituted good cause for an extension of the time limit until 18 January 2007. Assumed that the limit began to normally run as of 19 December 2006 with the filing of the Judgement, the time limit would have likewise expired thirty days later on 18 January 2007.

International Criminal Tribunal for Rwanda
Tribunal pénal international pour le Rwanda

TRIAL CHAMBER I

Before: Judge Erik Møse, presiding
Judge Jai Ram Reddy
Judge Sergei Alekseevich Egorov

Registrar: Adama Dieng

Date: 23 April 2007

THE PROSECUTOR

v.

Théoneste BAGOSORA
Gratien KABILIGI
Aloys NTABAKUZE
Anatole NSENGIYUMVA

Case No. ICTR-98-41-T

DECISION RECONSIDERING EXCLUSION OF EVIDENCE RELATED TO ACCUSED KABILIGI

The Prosecution
Barbara Mulvaney
Drew White
Christine Graham
Rashid Rashid
Kartik Murukutla

The Defence
Raphaël Constant
Allison Turner
Paul Skolnik
Frédéric Hivon
Peter Erlinder
Marc Nerenberg
Kennedy Ogetto
Gershom Otachi Bw'Omanwa

[page 2] THE INTERNATIONAL CRIMINAL TRIBUNAL FOR RWANDA

SITTING as Trial Chamber I, composed of Judge Erik Møse, presiding, Judge Jai Ram Reddy, and Judge Sergei Alekseevich Egorov;

BEING SEIZED OF the "Kabiligi Motion for Reconsideration" etc. of the Trial Chamber's Decision of 18 September 2006, filed on 26 October 2006; the Prosecution response, filed on 30 October 2006; and the Defence reply, filed on 7 November 2006;

NOTING the Appeals Chamber "Decision on Aloys Ntabakuze's Interlocutory Appeal on Questions of Law Raised by the 29 June 2006 Trial Chamber I Decision on Motion for Exclusion of Evidence", rendered on 18 September 2006;

HEREBY RECONSIDERS its earlier decision.

INTRODUCTION

1. On 19 October 2004, the Kabiligi Defence filed a motion to exclude portions of the testimonies of eight Prosecution witnesses, claiming that they testified about allegations which are not mentioned in the Indictment.[1] On 27 September 2005, the Chamber excluded portions of the testimonies given by two witnesses.[2] The Defence filed a second exclusion motion, on 5 April 2006, essentially asking the Chamber to reconsider its previous decision. On 4 September 2006, the Chamber decided to exclude a portion of one witness's testimony.[3] In light of a decision rendered by the Appeals Chamber on 18 September 2006 ("Appeals Chamber Decision"), the present motion asks the Chamber to reconsider its decision of 4 September 2006.[4]

2. In its decision, which relates to exclusion of evidence, the Appeals Chamber found that the Trial Chamber had failed to consider whether the defects in the Indictment which had been cured by the Prosecution nonetheless prejudiced the right of the Accused Ntabakuze to a fair trial by hindering the preparation of a proper defence.[5] Second, the Appeals Chamber instructed the Trial Chamber to reconsider whether the burden of proof had been appropriately placed on the Defence in instances where the Defence had not made a contemporaneous objection concerning lack of notice to the evidence at the time it was introduced.[6] **[page 3]**

DELIBERATIONS

(i) General Remarks

3. Reconsideration is an exceptional measure, available only in particular circumstances.[7] The Appeals Chamber's ruling with regard to the cumulative effect of cured defects in the Indictment constitutes a new circumstance which has arisen since the Trial Chamber's decision of 4 September 2006, and which may affect it. The Chamber therefore finds that reconsideration is justified. The Defence request for reconsideration is made on the basis of the curing issue, but the Chamber will also consider the Defence burden of proof in the light of the Appeals Chamber's decision.

4. Some of the evidence which is contested by the Defence in its present motion was not challenged in its exclusion motions of 19 October 2004 and 5 April 2006 ("Defence exclusion motions"), and hence not

---

1 Kabiligi Defence's «Requête en extrême urgence aux fins de rejet des témoignages sur des faits qui ne figurent pas dans l'acte d'accusation», filed on 19 October 2004 (challenging evidence by Witnesses XAI, ZF, XXY, XXH, LAI, XXQ, DCH, and AAA).

2 *Bagosora et al.*, Decision on Exclusion of Testimony outside the Scope of the Indictment (TC), 27 September 2005, paras. 10, 16 (excluding portions of Witnesses XAI and DCH) ("27 September 2005 Decision").

3 *Bagosora et al.*, Decision on Kabiligi Motion for Exclusion of Evidence (TC), 4 September 2006, para. 18 (excluding a portion of Witness XXH's testimony) ("4 September 2006 Decision").

4 Kabiligi Motion for Reconsideration of the Trial Chamber's 'Decision on Kabiligi Motion for Exclusion of Evidence' in light of the Appeals Chamber Decision of 18 September 2006, filed on 26 October 2006.

5 *Bagosora et al.*, Decision on Aloys Ntabakuze's Interlocutory Appeal on Questions of Law Raised by the 29 June 2006 Trial Chamber I Decision on Motion for Exclusion of Evidence (AC), 18 September 2006, para. 26.

6 Appeals Chamber Decision, paras. 45-47.

7 *See e.g. Bagosora et al.*, Decision on Prosecutor's second motion for reconsideration of the Trial Chamber's "Decision on Prosecutor's motion for leave to vary the witness list pursuant to Rule 73 *Bis* (E)" (TC), 14 July 2004, para. 7.

addressed in the Chamber's decision of 4 September 2006. A motion for reconsideration should normally address issues considered in the challenged decision. However, the Appeals Chamber's subsequent decision warrants the Chamber's consideration of the totality of the Defence submissions in the present motion.

5. The Defence argues that 29 allegations have been made against the Accused and that 21 of them fall outside the scope of the Indictment and Bill of Particulars and have required "curing" by the Prosecution. Without necessarily agreeing with this assertion, the Chamber recalls that, in its exclusion decisions of 27 September 2005 and 4 September 2006, it has already been seized with 14 of these allegations, whereas seven were not raised in the Defence exclusion motions leading to these two decisions.[8]

6. Of the 14 allegations, one was excluded.[9] In respect of four, the burden was placed on the Defence to show prejudice. The Chamber found that the burden was not met.[10] In relation to nine allegations, the Chamber found that the Defence had sufficient notice.

(ii) Burden of Proof

7. In relation to the four of the 14 allegations where the Chamber found that the Defence did not meet its burden of proof, the Chamber declined to exclude the evidence. In light of the Appeals Chamber Decision, the Trial Chamber must reassess its findings concerning these four allegations.

8. The Appeals Chamber summarized the legal situation as follows:

> 45. Accordingly, when an objection based on lack of notice is raised at trial (albeit later than at the time the evidence was adduced), the Trial Chamber should determine **[page 4]** whether the objection was so untimely as to consider that the burden of proof has shifted from the Prosecution to the Defence in demonstrating whether the accused's ability to defend himself has been materially impaired. In doing so, the Trial Chamber should take into account factors such as whether the Defence has provided a reasonable explanation for its failure to raise its objection at the time the evidence was introduced and whether the Defence has shown that the objection was raised as soon as possible thereafter.
>
> 46. In summary, objections based on lack of notice should be specific and timely. The Appeals Chamber agrees with the Prosecution that blanket objections that "the entire indictment is defective" are insufficiently specific. As to timeliness, the objection should be raised at the pre-trial stage (for instance in a motion challenging the indictment) or at the time the evidence of a new material fact is introduced. However, an objection raised later at trial will not automatically lead to a shift in the burden of proof: the Trial Chamber must consider relevant factors, such as whether the Defence provided a reasonable explanation for its failure to raise the objection earlier in the trial.
>
> 47. The Appeals Chamber finds that the statements made by the Trial Chamber at paragraph 7 of the Impugned Decision must be corrected to the extent explained above. As a consequence, the Trial Chamber should reconsider the Impugned Decision on this basis. This reconsideration will be limited to the instances where the Trial Chamber found that the objection had not been raised at the time the evidence was introduced and therefore concluded that the burden of proof had shifted to the Defence.

(a) The Accused's Statement at Gisenyi Hospital about Tutsis

9. Witness XAI testified that the Accused met Colonel Anatole Nsengiyumva in the Gisenyi Hospital on or around 4 July 1994 and said to the sick soldiers that there were still Tutsis in the Kibuye and Bisesero regions who should be prevented from receiving fresh supplies.[11] This allegation was not contemporaneously objected to during the trial. It was first challenged by the Defence in its exclusion motion of 5 April 2006, but the Chamber's decision of 4 September 2006 did not specifically address the allegation.[12]

---

[8] Some of these seven allegations have been challenged through other motions, which were decided by the Trial Chamber before the Appeals Chamber Decision.

[9] 4 September 2006 Decision, excluding the allegation by Witness XXH's that Kabiligi shot a person at the Rusizi 1 roadblock in Cyangugu, in May 1994 (para. 18).

[10] There was a fifth allegation in respect of which the Chamber placed the burden on the Defence but nonetheless examined the issue of notice and concluded that it was provided. This was the allegation by Witness ZF that the Accused was a member of the "zero network" and the Dragons.

[11] T. 9 September 2003 pp. 13-15.

[12] That motion was regarded as a request to reconsider the Chamber's 27 September 2005 Decision, and since in the motion leading to the 27 September 2005 Decision the allegation in question was not challenged, the Chamber's 4 September 2006 Decision

10. At the commencement of Witness XAI's testimony, the Defence objected generally to the late notice it received to some of the facts about which the witness was about to testify.[13] During the examination-in-chief, the Defence raised several objections based on the novelty of the information presented by the witness.[14] However, there was no contemporaneous objection by the Defence when the witness testified about Kabiligi's alleged statements at Gisenyi Hospital. Counsel for Kabiligi crossed-examined the witness that day on this issue.[15] He later reserved the right to conduct further cross-examination in relation to newly discovered information.[16] No further challenge of this allegation was raised until the Defence exclusion motion of 5 April 2006.

11. In light of the very late stage of the trial in which this objection was raised, the Chamber maintains its position that the burden has shifted to the Defence to establish that it **[page 5]** suffered prejudice from the lack of notice. This burden has not been met.

(b) The Accused's Arrival in Bugarama to Distribute Weapons

12. Witness LAI testified that on 28 January 1994, the Accused arrived by helicopter in Bugarama Commune, Cyangugu prefecture, to distribute weapons to *Interahamwe*, and told them that "the enemy was the Tutsi".[17] This allegation was challenged by the Defence in its exclusion motions of 19 October 2004 and of 5 April 2006. In its decision of 27 September 2005, the Chamber found no record of a contemporaneous objection to the allegation. It concluded that therefore the burden of proof lied with the Defence and found that the Defence had not met the burden.[18] The Chamber's decision of 4 September 2006 did not specifically address this allegation.[19]

13. At the beginning of Witness LAI's testimony, the Defence indicated that it had objections to some of the evidence to be presented by the witness, but not to the event in Bugarama.[20] During the examination-in-chief (but not immediately after the witness addressed this event), the Defence indicated that some information proffered by the witness did not appear in his prior statements without specifically referring to this incident. In fact, the Defence explicitly stated that its general statement was not an objection to the testimony.[21] The Defence cross-examined the witness on the allegation in question.[22] Its first challenge to the Bugarama allegation was in its exclusion motion of 19 October 2004, five months after the testimony.

14. In light of the Defence lack of contemporaneous objection and late subsequent challenge of the evidence, the Chamber considers that the burden has shifted to the Defence to establish that it suffered prejudice from the lack of notice. This burden has not been met.

(c) Reprimand of Soldier in Cyangugu for not Killing Tutsi;
(d) Order to Soldiers to Prevent Supplies to Tutsi refugees

15. Witness XXY testified that the Accused reprimanded a soldier in Cyangugu who did not assist the Interahamwe in attacking and killing Tutsi refugees in two refugee camps in August 1994.[23] He also stated that the Accused ordered soldiers to prevent trucks of Operation Turquoise from providing supplies to the

---

did not specifically address the allegation. It is noted that in its exclusion motion of 19 October 2004, the Defence challenged several portions of Witness XAI's testimony, but not the portion containing the allegation in question.

13 T. 8 September 2003 p. 1.

14 *See e.g.* 9 September 2003 pp. 9, 12.

15 T. 9 September 2003 pp. 46-47; T. 10 September 2003 pp. 3-4.

16 T. 10 September 2003 pp. 9-10.

17 T. 31 May 2004 p. 15.

18 27 September 2005 Decision, para. 19.

19 4 September 2006 Decision, para. 22 ("No other grounds have been raised to suggest that the Chamber erred in law or failed to appreciate the relevant facts in the Kabiligi Exclusion Decision. Accordingly, there is no basis to reconsider any other legal or factual finding made therein.")

20 T. 31 May 2004 p. 8.

21 *Id.*, p. 25.

22 *Id.*, p. 48.

23 T. 11 June 2004 pp. 4-6.

Tutsi refugees in Bisesero on 4 July 1994.[24] These allegations were challenged by the Defence in its exclusion motion of 19 October 2004, and later articulated more clearly in its exclusion motion of 5 April 2006. In its decision of 27 September 2005, the Chamber found no record of contemporaneous objections to the allegations, and concluded that the Defence had the burden to establish that it had been prejudiced. It found that the Defence had not met the burden.[25] In its decision of 4 September **[page 6]** 2006, the Chamber did not specifically address these allegations.[26]

16. The Chamber observes that the relevant testimony was given on 11 June 2004, and the challenges were submitted four months later, in the motion of 19 October 2004. There is no indication as to the reason for the lack of contemporaneous objection. The Chamber maintains its findings that the Defence had, and did not meet, the burden of proof.

(iii) Seven Allegations Not Raised in the Two Exclusion Motions

(e) Membership in AMASASU

17. Witness XXQ testified that the Accused was a member of the Amasasu group, which comprised "the senior officers who were living in Kigali"[27] and those who "planned the genocide".[28] During the testimony, the Kabiligi Defence objected generally to new information provided by the witness but not specifically to the Amasasu allegation.[29] Other Defence team objected to that allegation, which concerned their clients as well.[30] The Chamber ruled that there was notice of this material fact in the Prosecution Pre-trial Brief, which was filed on 21 January 2002.[31] Such notice is found in the list of Prosecution exhibits, which contains a reference to death squads and the AMASASU.[32] The Pre-trial Brief also stated that another witness (Witness XAQ) was anticipated to testify about the participation of soldiers in "death squads" in Kigali.[33] The Supporting Material accompanying the original Indictment, filed on 3 August 1998, cites an expert witness saying that "one notes in particular [within the armed forces] the creation of the AMASASU in January 1993 which demanded the establishment of a cleansed army and the elimination of all RPF allies".[34]

18. Paragraphs 1.13 to 1.16 of the Indictment refer to Hutu extremist groups, composed of prominent civilian and military leaders that worked on a strategy to eliminate the Tutsi and political opponents. Although the Accused is not expressly identified as a member of any group preparing such a strategy, the fact that the Accused is the indictee would reasonably suggest that he had some connection to an organization mentioned in his Indictment.

19. Consequently, on the basis of paragraphs 1.13 to 1.16 of the Indictment, the Supporting Material to the original Indictment, and the Prosecution Pre-trial Brief, the Chamber finds that the Accused was reasonably informed that this fact was part of the case against him and does not exclude the allegation by Witnesses XXQ.

20. A similar conclusion was made by the Chamber in a decision addressing challenges **[page 7]** made by Accused Ntabakuze, who is charged with Kabiligi under the same Indictment.[35] It is also recalled that the

---

24 *Id.*, pp. 2-3.

25 27 September 2005 Decision, para. 19.

26 The Chamber only made the general comment in para. 22 of the 4 September 2006 Decision (quoted in footnote 19).

27 T. 11 October 2004 p. 28.

28 *Id.*, p. 31.

29 *Id.*, pp. 6-8, 11, 40.

30 *Id.*, pp. 28-29.

31 *Id.*, p. 40.

32 Prosecution Pre-trial Brief, Annex A, Registry Pagination No. 6461 (document entitled "A.M.A.S.A.S.U. Alliance des Militaires Agacés par les Séculaires Actes Sournois des Unaristes: Naissance et raisons d'être des AMASASU).

33 Prosecution Pre-trial Brief, Annex A, p. 143.

34 Supporting Material, p. 13 (summarizing expert report of André Guichaoua). In addition, the summary for Expert Reyntjens, listed in support of paragraph 5.32 of the Indictment, makes reference to "death squads". Supporting Material, pp. 70-72.

35 *Bagosora et al.*, Decision Reconsidering Exclusion of Evidence Following Appeals Chamber Decision (TC), 17 April 2007, para. 10 (the Defence had sufficient notice of allegations by Witnesses DCH, XAQ, and ZF concerning Ntabakuze's involvement in death squads and the AMASASU).

Chamber has previously denied a Kabiligi request to exclude evidence by Witness ZF concerning related issues (membership of the Accused in "zero network" or "dragon" group).[36]

(f) and (g) Firing of Artillery from Mount Kigali in May and July 1994

21. Witness AAA testified that the Accused fired three mortar rounds from Mount Kigali in direction of Mount Rebero, in presence of the Huye Battalion, on a day between 25 and 30 May 1994. Again, on 3 July 1994, the Accused fired three mortar rounds from Mount Kigali towards Mount Rebero, in presence of Major Ntilikina and Huye Battalion soldiers. He told the soldiers they were good, but were victims of the accomplices.[37]

22. The Defence did not contemporaneously object to this testimony and did not challenge it until the filing of the present motion. This is noteworthy as other portions of Witness AAA's testimony were challenged in the two Defence exclusion motions.[38]

23. Paragraph 4.4 of the Indictment refers to the military authority of the Accused over "units of the sectors of Byumba, Ruhengeri, Mutara and Kigali, as well as the elite units such as the Presidential Guard and the Para-Commando Battalion and the Reconnaissance Battalion". Paragraph 6.30 stipulate that the Accused from "about 10 April to about 31 May 1994 ... encouraged and supported the militiamen who were murdering Tutsi civilians ...".

24. In a motion filed on 24 March 2004, the Prosecution asked to add Witness AAA to its list. The motion summarized the witness's anticipated testimony, and noted that his statements had been disclosed to the Defence on 29 July 2003. The firing of artillery from Mount Kigali was mentioned in the disclosed statements. The motion did not reiterate the facts, but emphasized that the witness's statements include "detailed information about incriminating oral statements made by the accused". It further indicated that the evidence of the witness went directly to the responsibility of the Accused under Article 6 (1) of the Statute.[39] In allowing the Prosecution to add Witness AAA to its list, the Chamber noted that "the evidence appears to have probative value with respect to the charges against ... Kabiligi."[40] The witness testified on 15 June 2004, more than two months later.

25. On the basis of paragraphs 4.4 and 6.30 of the Indictment, the disclosure of the witness's statements in July 2003, and the Prosecution motion of 24 March 2004, the Chamber finds that the Accused was reasonably informed that the above allegations were part **[page 8]** of the case against him, and does not exclude the testimony of Witness AAA.

(h) and (i) Presence and Orders at Saint André College

26. Witness DBQ testified that the Accused was present in the area of Saint André College in Kigali where civilians were killed by *Interahamwe* and soldiers.[41] Witness XXJ testified that the Accused gave orders to soldiers in the same area which resulted in the death of orphans.[42] The Defence filed a motion on 22 September 2003, a day before the witness was anticipated to take the stand, requesting generally to exclude new elements mentioned in belatedly disclosed statements by the witness.[43] The Chamber considers this as a contemporaneous objection.

36 4 September 2006 Decision, paras. 15-16.

37 T. 15 June 2004 pp. 4-6.

38 The Defence exclusion motion of 19 October 2004 challenged two portions of the testimony of Witness AAA: (1) In April 1994, Kabiligi met at the prefecture of Kigali, with persons in charge of local administration, with the aim, among others, to distribute weapons to civilians; (2) in early May 1994, Kabiligi instructed *conseillers* in three sectors to search for accomplices of the *Inkotanyi* and to eliminate them. The second allegation was also challenged in the Defence exclusion motion of 5 April 2006.

39 Prosecutor's Motion for Leave to Vary the Witness List pursuant to Rule 73 *bis* (E), 24 March 2004, paras. 8-9.

40 *Bagosora et al.*, Decision on Prosecutor's Motion for Leave to Vary the Witness List pursuant to Rule 73 *bis* (E) (TC), 21 May 2004, para. 16.

41 T. 23 September 2003 p. 70.

42 T. 14 April 2004 pp. 49-50.

43 Kabiligi Defence's Requête en extrême urgence de la Defence aux fins de rejet de nouvelles déclarations, etc., filed on 22 September 2003. The motion also alleged that the new information was unethically obtained by the Prosecution, in an attempt to pressure the Accused to enter in a plea agreement.

27. Paragraph 6.38 of the Indictment pleads that soldiers under the orders of the Accused massacred Tutsi who sought refuge in a house across from Saint André school, in Kigali, and that these soldiers had been checking the identities and listing the names of the Tutsi refugees, as of May 1994. The Accused was charged with direct responsibility under 6 (1) on the basis of this material fact. Witnesses providing evidence in support of this, even if they testify that the Accused was present or gave orders at the scene of the crime, cannot be regarded as introducing new allegations outside the Indictment.

28. As mentioned above, Witness DBQ's evidence about Kabiligi's presence at Saint André College was challenged by the Defence in a motion filed on 22 September 2003, the day before the testimony. The Chamber found that:

> ... the new elements of testimony were substantially disclosed in the Indictments ... Sufficient notice ... that Kabiligi arrived at the scene after killings occurred, is given by the allegation that he ordered the killing of people at that specific location. The specific actions described are actually less prejudicial than, and may be taken as subsumed within, the accusation in the Indictments that the soldiers at that location were acting under his orders. When combined with the will-say disclosure in accordance with Rule 67(D), the Chamber considers this to be a detail which has been substantially disclosed.[44]

29. In the Supporting Materials accompanying the original Indictment, filed on 3 August 1998, an excerpt of a statement by a potential Prosecution Witness BU was included. It states:

> I would like to repeat here that I personally saw Gratien Kabiligi at Saint André school in Nyamirambo in May-June 1994... He was leading the ex-FAR soldiers, who had taken up position at the school. These were the same soldiers who had killed the civilians at Saint-André. Everything pointed to the fact that they had acted on Kabiligi's orders. In any case, Kabiligi did nothing to prevent the massacres. He even sent soldiers to search **[page 9]** for and kill me.[45]

30. The same witness's anticipated testimony was later summarized in the Prosecution Pre-trial Brief, which was filed on 21 January 2002. The summary indicated that the witness saw the Accused at the Saint André College, and its environs during May and June 1994, and spoke to him. It mentioned that the Accused "was leading the ex-FAR soldiers who'd taken up position at the school and killed civilians there".[46]

31. On the basis of paragraph 6.38 of the Indictment, the Supporting Material accompanying the original Indictment, and the Prosecution Pre-trial Brief, the Chamber finds that the Accused was reasonably informed that the above allegations were part of the case against him. The evidence of Witnesses DBQ and XXJ is not excluded.

(j) Order to Kill at Roadblock in Musambira

32. Witness DY testified that the Accused was present at a roadblock in Musambira and ordered a well-known *Interahamwe* to kill 10 persons there.[47] Four days before the testimony, the Defence submitted a notification in writing that it would object to portions of the evidence based on the witness's statement labelled DY-4, which it received late in the proceedings.[48] During the examination-in-chief, when the Prosecution indicated that it was about to ask the witness questions related to statement DY-4, the Defence objected to the introduction of new information deriving from that statement, including with respect to the event at the roadblock in Musambira.[49] The Chamber considers this as a contemporaneous objection. During the proceedings, the Chamber ruled:

---

44 *Bagosora et al.*, Decision on Admissibility of Evidence of Witness DBQ (TC), 18 November 2003, para. 17. *See also Bagosora et al.*, Decision on Exclusion of Evidence under Rule 95 (TC), 27 January 2004, para. 5 ("the only new element of Witness DBQ's testimony in the will-say statements is that the Accused arrived at a place where Tutsis had previously been killed. It is inconceivable that the Prosecution would hazard the serious misconduct alleged in order to present evidence of such limited significance.")

45 Supporting Material, pp. 129-130.

46 Prosecution Pre-trial Brief, Annex A, p. 21.

47 T. 16 February 2004 pp. 53-56.

48 Defence for Kabiligi's notification to object to the testimony of Witness DY on the basis of witness declaration DY-04, 12 February 2004.

49 T. 16 February 2004 pp. 48-49.

> The Chamber has analysed the two statements previously given by the witness. We note that the information in DY-4 deviates from what is in DY-1 and DY-2, but the core of the event remains the same, namely, that General Kabiligi is passing by a certain location where an incident is taking place, where persons are being arrested, and the end result is that the "Inyenzi" are killed. The new element is the time at which the killing took place. In the Chamber's view, we cannot exclude this evidence. There is clearly a discrepancy between the version in DY-1 or 2, at least on the face of it, compared to DY-4, and it will be a matter for the Chamber, on the merits, to go into this, in particular, after having listened carefully to the cross-examination of this witness. It is also noted that this new issue was given in a will-say statement by the witness on the 14th of January and disclosed to the Defence on the 19th of January, five days later, so that the Defence has had three, four weeks in order to prepare for this change. We will then allow the Prosecution to proceed with this last element in your examination-in-chief.

33. Paragraph 5.1 of the Indictment stipulates that the Accused's plan to exterminate the Tutsi "consisted of, among other things, recourse to hatred and ethnic violence", and that in executing the plan, the Accused "organized, ordered and participated in the massacres perpetrated against the Tutsi population". Paragraph 6.31 refers to the authority of the Accused over military officer and militiamen, who committed massacres throughout Rwanda, **[page 10]** with the Accused's knowledge. This authority was allegedly exercised, among other ways, through giving orders. Accordingly, the Chamber finds that the facts as presented by Witness DY elaborate on the material facts in the Indictment. In the Supporting Materials which accompanied the original Indictment, filed on 3 August 1998, an excerpt of a statement by Witness DY contained a description of the event.[50]

34. The Chamber considers that sufficient notice was given to the Defence through paragraphs 5.1 and 6.31 in the Indictment, the Supporting Materials which accompanied the original Indictment, and Prosecution disclosures. It finds that the Accused was reasonably informed that the above allegation was part of the case against him, and that the evidence of Witness DY shall not be excluded.

(k) Distribution of Arms to Militia or Civilians

35. On 16 February 2004, Witness DY testified that the Accused distributed arms to militia or civilians, including to 150 *Interahamwe* from Gitarama prefecture.[51] There was no contemporaneous objection by the Defence to the evidence. The following day, Counsel for Kabiligi crossed-examined the witness on this issue.[52]

36. This evidence was first contested in the present motion. There is no explanation justifying the lateness of the challenge. The Chamber considers that the Defence has the burden of proof to establish that it had been prejudiced, and that it has not met this burden.

(iv) Nine Allegations Analysed in Previous Decisions

37. Nine allegations have been considered by the Chamber twice, in its decisions of 27 September 2005 and 4 September 2006.[53] The Chamber found that the Defence had sufficient notice through the Indictment,

---

50 Supporting Material, p. 120: "On the road that leads to the Musambira commune office, we found ten or so people who had been stopped by a group of militiamen led by a man named ABDULHAMANI, who was an Interahamwe with a reputation nation-wide. KABILIGI had the armoured vehicle stop at the spot and they told him "Here are the inyenzi that we have arrested and we are still looking for more." KABILIGI told them to remain vigilant so that the Inyenzi would not infiltrate their ranks. We continued on the road to the Musambira market, where we turned back ... On our return, we saw that the people had been killed by the Interahamwe and their bodies were still at the roadblock. KABILIGI did not comment and we returned to Kigali."

51 T. 16 February 2004 p. 43.

52 T. 17 February 2004 p. 27.

53 In respect of eight of them, the burden of proof was placed on the Prosecution. These allegations are that the Accused: (1) presided over a meeting in Ruhengeri on 15 February 1994, where it was decided or announced that the genocide would begin on 23 February 1994; Rwanda and Burundi plotted to prepare and commit the genocide (Witness XXQ); (2) told the conseillers of Nyamirambo, Nyakabanda and Biryogo sectors to eliminate accomplices of the Inkotanyi in their sectors, in early May 1994 (Witness AAA); (3) was present at the scene of the murder of a military deserter at a roadblock in Cyangugu (Witness XXH); (4) killed or had killed 100 persons at the Rusizi 1 roadblock in Cyangugu, which was established by him or his subordinates (Witness XXH); (5) gave a speech encouraging massacres at a meeting on 23 April 1994 with President Sindikubwabo at the MRND building in Cyangugu (Witness XXH); (6) presided over a meeting at the *Cercle Sportif* in Cyangugu, where he collected funds to purchase weapons to distribute to civilians in order to kill Tutsis (Witness XXH); (7) distributed gasoline vouchers to Yussuf Munyakazi (Witness XXH); (8) presided over a meeting in the Byumba military camp in 1992 where he allegedly told the soldiers "that they had

Pre-Trial Brief, and other post-Indictment disclosures. The Appeals Chamber Decision does not provide a basis to re-examine the Trial Chamber's **[page 11]** findings. Accordingly, the Chamber reiterates its findings with relation to these nine allegations, and finds no basis to exclude them.

(v) Cumulative Effect of Cured Defects in the Indictment

38. The Chamber will now look at the totality of cured defects in the Indictment to determine their cumulative effect on the ability of the Accused to prepare his defence.[54] The Appeals Chamber found:

> 26. The Appeals Chamber agrees that when the indictment suffers from numerous defects, there may still be a risk of prejudice to the accused even if the defects are found to be cured by post-indictment submissions. In particular, the accumulation of a large number of material facts not pled in the indictment reduces the clarity and relevancy of that indictment, which may have an impact on the ability of the accused to know the case he or she has to meet for purposes of preparing an adequate defence. Further, while the addition of a few material facts may not prejudice the Defence in the preparation of its case, the addition of numerous material facts increases the risk of prejudice as the Defence may not have sufficient time and resources to investigate properly all the new material facts. Thus, where a Trial Chamber considers that a defective indictment has been subsequently cured by the Prosecution, it should further consider whether the extent of the defects in the indictment materially prejudice an accused's right to a fair trial by hindering the preparation of a proper defence. The Appeals Chamber finds that the Trial Chamber failed to do so in the Impugned Decision and therefore, instructs the Trial Chamber to reconsider the Impugned Decision on this basis.

39. As stated by the Appeals Chamber, fairness is crucial in determining whether the Defence has been materially prejudiced in preparing its case. The question is whether the Accused was in a position to know and understand the allegations against him such that he could prepare a proper defence. The Chamber must determine, in particular, whether a large number of material facts were not pled in the Indictment and whether these defects, even if subsequently cured, prejudiced the right of the Accused to a fair trial.[55]

40. The Defence asserts that because over 70% of the current allegations against the Accused fall outside the Indictment, a substantial change occurred in the Prosecution case from the allegations in the Indictments compared to the strategy pursued at trial. Consequently, the Defence was left guessing at the evidence it had to meet until the close of the Prosecution case.[56] As it is too late to remedy the prejudice by granting the Defence additional time to properly prepare its case, the only available relief is excluding the allegations outside the Indictment.

41. The Chamber disagrees with the Defence that over 70% of the allegations against the Accused are outside the scope of the Indictment. The Defence lists 21 such allegations. Several of these 21 allegations are not material facts but evidence of material facts. Some examples have been considered above (paragraphs 18 and 27). Moreover, it is not correct, as **[page 12]** argued by the Defence, that only eight material facts are included in the Indictment.[57] There are additional material facts in the Indictment, on which responsibility under Article 6 (1) is attributed to the Accused.[58] Furthermore, the Indictment attributed responsibility to the Accused under Article 6 (3) on the basis of facts which were not listed by the Defence in its motion.[59]

---

to be vigilant and capture RPF infiltrators" (Witness XAI). In relation to one allegation, the burden was placed on the Defence but the Chamber nonetheless examined the notice issue: (9) the Accused was a member of the "zero network" and the Dragons (Witness ZF).

54 Subsequent to the Trial Chamber Decision, the Appeals Chamber rendered judgment in the *Ntagerura et al.* case and held that the Chamber has an <u>obligation</u> to determine whether a vague provision in the Indictment has been cured by timely, clear, and consistent information from the Prosecution. *Ntagerura et al.*, Judgment (AC), 7 July 2006, para. 65. The Chamber implicitly did so in making its findings on the impugned evidence, wherein it held that defects had not been cured by proper notice in three instances. Trial Chamber Decision, paras. 31, 54-55, 60.

55 Appeals Chamber Decision, paras. 26, 30 (referencing *Kupreškić et al.* Appeals Chamber Judgement).

56 Motion, paras. 14-21.

57 Motion, para. 12.

58 For example, the Defence listed as a material fact in the Indictment, the allegation that the Accused conspired with others to work out a plan with the intent to exterminate the civilian Tutsi population and eliminate political opponents. It failed to mention that paragraph 5.1 of the Indictment also elaborates on the components of the plan. Additional examples include the material facts alleged in paragraphs 6.29, 6.31, and 6.38 of the Indictment.

59 According to the Indictment, the facts in paragraphs 5.35, 5.36, 6.8, 6.15, 6.16, 6.18, 6.19, 6.25, 6.32 to 6.39, 6.41 to 6.45, 6.47, 6.51 therein provide bases for charges against the Accused under Article 6 (3) of the Statute.

42. As discussed above, in the case of most of the allegations which the Defence claims are outside the Indictment, notice was provided through the Indictment, the Supporting Material, and the Prosecution Pre-trial Brief. The Chamber finds that any curing of defects in the Indictment through notice of new material facts which occurred prior to or at the commencement of trial was sufficient to inform the Accused of the allegations against him such that he could prepare a proper defence. This occurred four years before the Defence would even begin presentation of its case.

43. The Prosecution filed the Supporting Material on 3 August 1998, the Amended Indictment on 13 August 1999, and the Prosecution Pre-trial Brief on 21 January 2002. Trial proceedings began on 2 April 2002 and were then suspended until September 2002. Although thirty-two trial days were held during 2002, the trial did not build real momentum until proceedings resumed before this Trial Chamber in June 2003. The Prosecution closed its case on 14 October 2004. The Kabiligi Defence commenced its case on 6 September 2006.

44. Consequently, the Chamber finds that the number of alleged deficiencies in the Indictment and the timing and means by which they were cured – most often well in advance of trial and years before the Defence began the presentation of its case – did not render the trial unfair and did not materially prejudice the Accused. The Chamber reiterates that the admission of evidence is not to be confused with the ultimate weight to be accorded to the evidence.[60]

45. The Defence also claims that it suffered prejudice because of the demise of potential Defence witnesses who died between the date on which the Indictment was confirmed and when the Prosecution case "finally stopped changing".[61] These individuals could have assisted the Defence in rebutting the additional allegations. In its decision of 4 September 2006, the Chamber dismissed this argument. In light of the additional Defence arguments in the present motion, the Chamber has reconsidered the issue but reiterates its position.[62] **[page 13]**

FOR THE ABOVE REASONS, THE CHAMBER

AFFIRMS its decision of 4 September 2006.

Arusha, 23 April 2007

Erik Møse Presiding Judge	Jai Ram Reddy Judge	Sergei Alekseevich Egorov Judge

[Seal of the Tribunal]

---

[60] *Nyiramasuhuko,* Decision on Pauline Nyiramasuhoko's Appeal on the Admissibility of Evidence (AC), 4 October 2004, paras. 6-7. *See also Bagosora et al.*, Decision on Ntabakuze Motions to Admit Documents Under Rule 92 bis (TC), 12 April 2007, para. 9; *Bagosora et al.*, Decision on Bagosora Motion to Exclude Photocopies of Agenda (TC), 11 April 2007, para. 6.

[61] Motion, para. 22.

[62] 4 September 2006 Decision, para. 12.

International Criminal Tribunal for Rwanda
Tribunal pénal international pour le Rwanda

OR: ENG

TRIAL CHAMBER II

Before: Judge Asoka de Silva, Presiding
Judge Taghrid Hikmet
Judge Seon Ki Park

Registrar: Mr Adama Dieng

Date: 24 April 2007

The PROSECUTOR

v.

Augustin NDINDILIYIMANA
Augustin BIZIMUNGU
François-Xavier NZUWONEMEYE
Innocent SAGAHUTU

Case No. ICTR-00-56-T

DECISION ON DEFENCE REQUEST FOR CERTIFICATION TO APPEAL THE CHAMBER'S DECISION PURSUANT TO RULE 98*BIS*

Office of the Prosecutor:
Mr Ciré Aly Bâ
Mr Moussa Sefon
Mr Segun Jegede
Mr. Lloyd Strickland
Mr Abubacarr Tambadou
Ms Felistas Mushi
Ms Faria Rekkas
Ms Anne Pauline Bodley

Counsel for the Defence:
Mr Gilles St-Laurent and Mr Ronnie MacDonald **for Augustin Bizimungu**
Mr Christopher Black and Mr Patrick De Wolf **for Augustin Ndindiliyimana**
Mr Charles Taku and Ms Beth Lyons **for François-Xavier Nzuwonemeye**
Mr Fabien Segatwa and Mr Seydou Doumbia **for Innocent Sagahutu**

[page 2] INTRODUCTION

1. The trial against the four Accused in this case commenced on 24 September 2004. After presenting 72 witnesses, the Prosecution closed its case on 7 December 2006.

2. On 20 March 2007, the Chamber rendered its Decision on the Defence Motions for Acquittal pursuant to Rule 98*bis* of the Rules of Procedure and Evidence (the "Rules"), denying Nzuwonemeye's request for acquittal on Count 1 (Conspiracy to commit Genocide), Count 4 (Murder as a Crime against Humanity) with respect to paragraph 108 of the Amended Indictment, Count 6 (Rape as a Crime against Humanity) and Count 8 (Rape, Humiliating and Degrading Treatment as War Crimes under Article 3 common to the Geneva Conventions and Additional Protocol II). On 23 March 2007, the Accused Nzuwonemeye filed a Motion requesting the Chamber to grant certification to appeal its Decision of 20 March 2007 (the "Impugned Decision") pursuant to Rule 73(B).[1] The Prosecution did not file a response.

DELIBERATIONS

i) Is a "Judgement of Acquittal" a "decision" under Rule 73?

3. The Defence submits that a decision on a motion for acquittal under Rule 98*bis* could be appealed upon certification granted pursuant to Rule 73(B). The Chamber notes that judicial opinion on this issue still remains divided.[2]

4. Rule 73(B) states that decisions on motions filed after the initial appearance of the accused are without interlocutory appeal except upon certification granted by the Trial Chamber. Rule 98*bis* of the Rules does not expressly provide for a right of appeal. However, this Chamber considers that Rule 73(B) must be interpreted to include the situation where the outcome of a motion under Rule 98*bis* is that the Chamber denies the Defence request for acquittal on one or more counts.[3] Such an interpretation would be consistent with the fact that motions for acquittal fall within the genre of applications brought by the parties 'after the initial appearance of the accused', as required by Rule 73. If the Chamber were to read Rule 98*bis* completely in isolation from Rule 73(B), an accused person who is aggrieved by the Chambers's denial of a motion for acquittal would be left without an immediate remedy. For these reasons, the Chamber finds that the Defence request for certification to appeal was properly brought under Rule 73(B). **[page 3]**

ii) Criteria for certification

5. This Chamber has, on a number of occasions, discussed the criteria for certification under Rule 73(B).[4] In particular, the Chamber stresses the principle that decisions under Rule 73 are "without

---

1 "Motion for Certification of the Decision on Defence Motions pursuant to Rule 98*bis* – Rule 73(B) of the Rules of Procedure and Evidence".

2 In *The Prosecutor v. P. Zigiranyirazo*, Trial Chamber III expressed the view that it was "not convinced that its decision not to enter a judgement of acquittal in favour of the Accused is the proper subject of an interlocutory appeal under Rule ...73(B)." It added that unlike Rule 73, Rule 98*bis* does not provide the right to seek certification to appeal a Trial Chamber's refusal to enter a judgement of acquittal. See "Oral Decision on Defence Motion for Acquittal pursuant to Rule 98*bis* of the Rules of Procedure and Evidence", T. 19 March 2007, p. 69). In *The Prosecutor v. C. Bizimungu et al*, Trial Chamber II, differently constituted, expressed reservations about whether a decision on a motion for judgement of acquittal "is the proper subject of an interlocutory appeal under Rule 73(B)." The Chamber, however, entertained the motion because both parties in that case implicitly agreed that a "Judgement of Acquittal" pursuant to Rule 98*bis* is a 'decision' which can be subject of an interlocutory appeal. See "Decision on Justin Mugenzi's Application for Certification to Appeal the Trial Chamber's Decision on Defence Motions pursuant to Rule 98*bis*", 20 March 2006.

3 See also *The Prosecutor v. Enver Hadzihasanovic and Amir Kubura*, "Decision on the Request for certification to appeal the Decision rendered pursuant Rule 98*bis* of the Rules" (TC), 26 October 2004, p. 2.

4 *The Prosecutor v. Augustin Bizimungu, Augustin Ndindiliyimana, François-Xavier Nzuwonemeye, Innocent Sagahutu*, ICTR-00-56-T, Decision on Sagahutu's Request for Certification to Appeal, 9 June 2005, para. 16; Decision on Bizimungu's Request for Certification to Appeal the Oral Decision Dated 8 June 2005, 30 June 2005, para. 17; Decision on Ndindiliyimana's Request for Certification to Appeal the Chamber's Decision Dated 21 September 2005, 26 October 2005, para. 7; Decision on Bizimungu's Motion for Certification to Appeal the Chamber's Oral Decision of 2 February 2006 Admitting Part of Witness GFA's Confessional Statement into Evidence, 27 February 2006, para. 11; Decision on Ndindiliyimana's Motion for Certification to Appeal the Chamber's Decision Dated 15 June 2006, 14 July 2006, para. 7; Decision on the Defence Requests for Certification to Appeal the Chamber's Decision of 20 October 2006, 7 November 2006, para 7.

interlocutory appeal" and that certification to appeal is an exception that the Chamber may grant, if the two criteria under Rule 73(B) are satisfied. The moving party must show that "the decision involves an issue that would significantly affect the fair and expeditious conduct of the proceedings or the outcome of the trial" and that "in the opinion of the Trial Chamber, an immediate resolution by the Appeals Chamber may materially advance the proceedings."

6. The Defence submits that although the Chamber stated the appropriate legal standard in the Impugned Decision, it did not apply it in its evaluation of the evidence. The Defence claims that the Chamber relied on weak evidence from single witnesses who are incapable of belief, drew incorrect inferences from alleged facts and cited transcripts which did not support these inferences. The Defence argues that the issue affects the fair and expeditious conduct of the proceedings because answering a case that does not exist would waste judicial resources in light of the Completion Strategy and because a reasonable trier of fact could not have concluded that the Accused bears any responsibility for the alleged crimes. Furthermore, the Defence submits that a decision by the Appeals Chamber may materially advance the proceedings because the Trial Chamber has erred in both fact and law and, therefore, to have to present its case on the basis of such an "incorrect and unfair legal footing", would be a waste of judicial resources.

7. The Defence essentially asks the Chamber to evaluate whether or not the Impugned Decision would succeed on appeal. This would be an improper course of action because the correctness of a Trial Chamber decision is a matter for the Appeals Chamber.[5] However, in deciding whether to grant certification to appeal, Trial Chambers "do have a responsibility to screen out requests for certification with no prospect of success and which, accordingly, would not 'materially advance the proceedings'."[6] This is a preliminary assessment aimed at determining whether the requirements of Rule 73(B) are met, rather than a pronouncement on the possible outcome of an appeal if one were certified. In all circumstances therefore, the moving party must still satisfy the cumulative conditions set out in Rule 73(B) of the Rules.[7]

8. The Chamber is not convinced that the first criterion under Rule 73(B) is met. The Impugned Decision did not render a final verdict on the guilt of the Accused. The consequence of that Decision is simply to require the Accused to answer the case he was **[page 4]** confronted with from the start of his trial. That in itself does not affect the fair or expeditious conduct of the proceedings. Furthermore, while the Chamber is aware of the Tribunal's limited resources and time, this cannot be the sole basis for granting certification of appeal. Similarly, the Chamber is not persuaded that the Impugned Decision affects the outcome of the trial. Accepting that the Prosecution evidence is sufficient for the purpose of denying a motion for acquittal, does not preclude the Chamber from ultimately finding that the Prosecution evidence fails to establish the Accused's guilt beyond a reasonable doubt at the close of the case. Indeed, such a finding could be reached even if no defence evidence is adduced.[8] It is a fairly elemental proposition that while at the stage of considering a motion for acquittal the Chamber looks for evidence which, if believed, *could* ground a conviction beyond reasonable doubt, at the stage of final judgement, the Chamber's obligation is to enter a conviction *only* when the evidence in fact establishes the guilt of the accused beyond all reasonable doubt. These two standards must not be confounded.

9. Since the first requirement for certification has not been met, the Chamber does not need to address the second criterion under Rule 73(B).

---

5 *The Prosecutor v. Théoneste Bagosora, Gratien Kabiligi, Aloys Ntabakuze, and Anatole Nsengiyumva,* Case No. ICTR-98-41-T, Decision on the Motion for Reconsideration Concerning Standards for Granting Certification of Interlocutory Appeal (TC), 16 February 2006, para. 4.

6 *Ibid.*

7 *Prosecutor v. Arsène Shalom Ntahobali and Pauline Nyiramasuhuko,* Case No. ICTR-97-21-T, Decision on Ntahobali's and Nyiramasuhuko's Motions for Certification to Appeal the 'Decision on Defence Urgent Motion to Declare Parts of the Evidence of Witnesses RV and QBZ Inadmissible' (TC), 18 March 2004, para. 15.

8 *Prosecutor v. Goran Jelisic,* Case No. IT-95-10-A, Appeals Chamber Judgement, 5 July 2001, para. 37; See also *Prosecutor v. Protais Zigiranyirazo,* Case No. ICTR-01-73-T, Oral Decision on Certification to Appeal the Decision on the Defence Motion Pursuant to Rule 98*bis*, T. 19 March 2007, p. 69.

FOR THE ABOVE REASONS, THE CHAMBER

DENIES the Defence's request for certification to appeal the Impugned Decision.

Arusha, 24 April 2007

Asoka de Silva Presiding Judge	Taghrid Hikmet Judge	Seon Ki Park Judge

[Seal of the Tribunal]

Commentary

1. Introduction

The selected decisions[1] raise the controversial and perplexing question of whether, and under what conditions, the chambers of the International Criminal Tribunal for Rwanda (ICTR) may reconsider or otherwise review their previous decisions and judgments. This encompasses both the procedural issue of the authority of the tribunal to revisit its earlier rulings and, more fundamentally, the philosophical question of the core role of the tribunal itself. In particular, is the ultimate purpose of the tribunal to avoid miscarriages of justice or, on the other hand, to ensure finality and certainty in its judgments? How does the tribunal balance these competing interests? Are there substantive differences between interlocutory decisions and final judgments that should inform this debate? What must an applicant demonstrate in order to obtain relief in this regard? Does the Appeals Chamber possess inherent authority to reconsider its judgments? Are there gaps in the present statutory scheme that necessitate judicial intervention to remedy the defects? These are just some of the intriguing questions this commentary will attempt to answer.

The present commentary will first address the underlying judicial debate over the proper role of the tribunal in matters of reconsideration of final judgments, as reflected in the opposing Appeals Chamber rulings from the International Criminal Tribunal for the former Yugoslavia (ICTY) in Čelebići[2] and Žigić.[3] The article will next provide a detailed treatment of formal "review proceedings," which are a necessary prerequisite to understanding the debate over reconsideration. Following this discussion, the author will focus on issues relating to reconsideration itself and the treatment of the subject as represented in the selected decisions. In addition, the commentary will give an overview of the requirements for certification. Finally, the author will conclude with his thoughts on the importance of providing an avenue for reconsideration from final judgments, even after the passage of years, based upon his personal litigation experience.

2. Justice v. Finality

The debate over whether the Appeals Chamber can reconsider its final judgments is, at the heart, a dispute over the nature of the tribunal itself, i.e., whether the tribunal is to protect against miscarriages of justice or whether it is to promote finality and certainty of its pronouncements, so as to bring closure to the victims and their families, as well as to the sanctity of the tribunal's rulings. This ideological controversy is epitomized in the divergent holdings of the ICTY Appeals eChambers in Čelebići and Žigić.

In Čelebići, the Appeals Chamber held that it "has an inherent power to reconsider any decision, including a judgment[,] where it is necessary to do so in order to prevent an injustice."[4] The Appeals Chamber noted that the decision to reconsider is discretionary in nature.[5] The Appeals Chamber further remarked that, although previous decisions addressing the right to reconsider were concerned "only with interlocutory decisions," as opposed to judgments, it was convinced that it possesses the power to reconsider final judgments where the following grounds are present:

---

1 Decision on Request for Reconsideration of the Decision on Request for Review, *Niyitegeka v. Prosecutor*, Case No. ICTR-96-14-R, A. Ch., 27 September 2006, in this volume, p. 291; Decision on Motion for Reconsideration, *Ntabakuze v. Prosecutor*, Case No. ICTR 98-41-AR73, A. Ch., 4 October 2006, in this volume, p. 297; Decision on Defence Motion for Certification to Appeal the Chamber's Decision on Nzirorera's *Ex Parte* Motion for Order for Interview of Defence witnesses NZ1, NZ2 and NZ3 (Rule 73(B) of the Rules of Procedure and Evidence), *Prosecutor v. Karemera, Ngirumpatse and Nzirorera*, T. Ch. III, Case No. ICTR-98-44-T, 30 October 2006, in this volume, p. 303; Decision on Request for Review, *Niyitegeka v. Prosecutor*, Case No. ICTR-96-14-R, A. Ch., 6 March 2007, in this volume, p. 307; Order Concerning the Filing of the Notice of Appeal, *Prosecutor v. Seromba*, Case No. ICTR-2001-66-A, A. Ch., 22 March 2007, in this volume, p. 319; Decision Reconsidering Exclusion of Evidence Related to Accused Kabiligi, *Prosecutor v. Bagosora, Kabiligi, Ntabakuze and Nsengiyumva,* Case No. ICTR-98-41-T, T. Ch. I, 23 April 2007, in this volume, p. 323; Decision on Defence Request for Certification to Appeal the Chamber's Decision Pursuant to Rule 98*bis*, *Prosecutor v. Ndindiliyimana, Augustin Bizimungu, Nzuwonemeye and Sagahutu*, Case No. ICTR-00-56-T, T. Ch. II, 24 April 2007, in this volume, p. 333.

2 ICTY, Judgment on Sentence Appeal, *Prosecutor v. Mucić, Delić and Landžo*, Case No. IT-96-21-A*bis*, A. Ch., 8 April 2003, Klip/ Sluiter, ALC-XIV-847.

3 ICTY, Decision on Zoran Žigić's "Motion for Reconsideration of Appeals Chamber Judgement IT-98-30/1-A Delivered on 28 February 2005," *Prosecutor v. Žigić*, Case No. IT-98-30/1-A, A. Ch., 26 June 2006.

4 Judgment on Sentence Appeal, *Prosecutor v. Mucić, Delić and Landžo*, A. Ch., *supra* note 2, par. 49.

5 *Ibid.*

"(a) (i) that a clear error of reasoning in the previous judgment has been demonstrated by, for example, a subsequent decision of the Appeals Chamber itself, the International Court of Justice, the European Court of Human Rights or a senior appellate court within a domestic jurisdiction, or
(ii) that the previous judgment was given per *incuriam*; and
(b) that the judgment of the Appeals Chamber sought to be reconsidered has led to an injustice."[6]

According to the Appeals Chamber, the right to reconsider judgments stems from the tribunal's inherent jurisdiction, which derives from "its judicial function," the purpose of which is "to ensure that its exercise of the jurisdiction which is expressly given to it by that statute is not frustrated and that its basic judicial functions are safeguarded."[7] In short, "[t]he principal purpose of the tribunal's existence is to administer justice, and to ensure that its proceedings do not lead to injustice."[8]

Moreover, the Appeals Chamber in Čelebići pointed out that there is only one level of appeal in the tribunal, which is limited in scope and is not *de novo*.[9] Additionally, the right of review, as provided for by statute, is quite narrow and does not adequately fill the gap in terms of preventing potential injustice.[10] Furthermore, absence of a reference to the power to reconsider in either the ICTY's statute or the tribunal's Rules of Procedure and Evidence is no bar to the exercise of such power, as it is not inconsistent with either source.[11] According to the Appeals Chamber, "Justice cannot be denied merely because it may be inconvenient to administer it."[12]

Finally, the Appeals Chamber clarified that its test for reconsideration of judgments "is not satisfied where the Appeals Chamber is satisfied 'just' that its previous decision is wrong; it must also be satisfied that its previous decision has led to an injustice."[13] Although, on its face, this pronouncement seems inherently inconsistent – after all, is there not automatic injustice if the previous decision is wrong? – the tribunal may instead be referring to situations in which the previous decision, though poorly reasoned or otherwise erroneous, could be affirmed on other grounds or where the subject of the previous decision, although wrong, amounted to only harmless error.

On the other hand, in Žigić, the Appeals Chamber expressly disagreed with the conclusion in Čelebići with respect to the right of a reviewing court to reconsider a final judgment.[14] After condemning the practice of appellants simply repeating in their motions to reconsider the same arguments previously advanced on appeal,[15] the Appeals Chamber set forth the philosophical basis for its conclusion that "there is no power to reconsider a final judgment": "To allow a person whose conviction has been confirmed on appeal the right to further contest the original findings against them on the basis of mere assertions of errors of fact or law is not in the interests of justice to the victims of the crimes or the convicted persons, who are both entitled to certainty and finality of legal judgements."[16] The Appeals Chamber further reasoned that because the tribunal's Statute already provides for a right of appeal and for review proceedings, it is inconsistent with the governing Statute to permit "a second right of appeal by the avenue of reconsideration of a final judgement."[17] The Appeals Chamber also opined that appellants are provided with sufficient due process guarantees under the existing statutory procedures.[18] Finally, restricting the scope of its holding to final judgments alone, the Appeals Chamber explained that its disagreement with Čelebići "does not affect the power of the tribunal to reconsider its decisions, which cannot be subject to review proceedings."[19] Judge Shahabuddeen, however,

6 *Ibid.*
7 *Ibid.* par. 50.
8 *Ibid.*
9 *Ibid.* par. 51.
10 *Ibid.*
11 *Ibid.* par. 52 and 53.
12 *Ibid.* par. 53.
13 *Ibid.* par. 52.
14 Decision on Zoran Žigić's "Motion for Reconsideration of Appeals Chamber Judgement IT-98-30/1-A Delivered on 28 February 2005," *Prosecutor v. Žigić*, A. Ch., *supra* note 3, par. 9.
15 *Ibid.* par. 8.
16 *Ibid.* par. 9.
17 *Ibid.*
18 *Ibid.*
19 *Ibid.*

disagreed with the majority's conclusion that the tribunal lacked the legal authority to reconsider a final judgment.[20]

3. Review proceedings

Review proceedings are provided for by Article 25 of the Statute of the International Criminal Tribunal for Rwanda (ICTR Statute), which states: "Where a new fact has been discovered which was not known at the time of the proceedings before the Trial Chambers or the Appeals Chamber and which could have been a decisive factor in reaching the decision, the convicted person or the prosecutor may submit to the International Tribunal for Rwanda an application for review of the judgement." Rules 120 and 121 of the ICTR Rules of Procedure and Evidence (ICTR RPE) further clarify the procedures relative to a request for review. Rule 120(A), ICTR RPE, provides:

> "Where a new fact has been discovered which was not known to the moving party at the time of the proceedings before a Trial Chamber or the Appeals Chamber and could not have been discovered through the exercise of due diligence, the Defence or, within one year after the final judgement has been pronounced, the prosecutor, may make a motion to that chamber for review of the judgement. If, at the time of the request for review, any of the Judges who constituted the original chamber are no longer Judges of the Tribunal, the President shall appoint a Judge or Judges in their place."

Rule 121, ICTR RPE, states, "If the Chamber constituted pursuant to Rule 120 agrees that the new fact, if it had been proven, could have been a decisive factor in reaching a decision, the Chamber shall review the judgement, and pronounce a further judgement after hearing the parties."

Initially, it is important to point out that review proceedings under the aforementioned provisions are applicable only to final judgments, not to interlocutory decisions.[21] Four criteria must be satisfied before review of a final judgment may be granted.[22] First, there must be a new fact,[23] which has been defined as "new information of an evidentiary nature of a fact that was not in issue during the trial or appeal proceedings."[24] Moreover, the phrase "not in issue" means that "it must not have been among the factors that the deciding body could have taken into account in reaching its verdict."[25] Secondly, the moving party must not have been aware of the new fact at the time of the original proceedings.[26] Yet, "it is irrelevant whether the new fact already existed before the original proceedings or during such proceedings. What is relevant is whether the deciding body and the moving party knew about the fact or not."[27] Thirdly, the failure to discover the new fact must not have been the result of a lack of due diligence on the part of the movant.[28] In this context, diligence means that the party must have sought to utilize all available means of compulsion afforded by the ICTR Statute and Rules.[29] Fourthly, it must be demonstrated that the new fact, if proven, "could have been a decisive factor in reaching the original decision."[30]

In addition, it should be noted that there is a marked distinction between review proceedings under Rule 120, ICTR RPE, and an application for the admission of additional evidence under Rule 115, ICTR RPE.[31] The former is related to review proceedings pursuant to Article 25 of the ICTR Statute and the latter, by contrast, is related to Article 24 of the ICTR Statute, which addresses normal appellate proceedings.[32] By way of comparison, requests for review under Article 25 and Rule 120 require a "new fact," while, under Rule 115,

---

20 ICTY, Declaration of Judge Shahabuddeen, on Zoran Žigić's "Motion for Reconsideration of Appeals Chamber Judgement IT-98-30/1-A Delivered on 28 February 2005," *Prosecutor v. Žigić*, Case No. IT-98-30/1-A, A. Ch., 26 June 2006, par. 1-8.

21 ICTR, Decision on Request for Review, *Niyitegeka v. Prosecutor*, Case No. ICTR-96-14-R, A. Ch., 30 June 2006, Klip/ Sluiter, ALC XXIV 957, par. 8

22 *Ibid.* par. 6.

23 *Ibid.*

24 ICTY, Decision on Motion for Review, *Prosecutor v. Tadić*, Case No. IT-94-1-R, A. Ch., 30 July 2002, Klip/ Sluiter, ALC-VIII-1095, par. 25.

25 *Ibid.*

26 Decision on Request for Review, *Niyitegeka v. Prosecutor*, A. Ch., *supra* note 20, par. 6.

27 Decision on Motion for Review, *Prosecutor v. Tadić*, *supra* note 23, par. 25

28 Decision on Request for Review, *Niyitegeka v. Prosecutor*, A. Ch., *supra* note 20, par. 6.

29 *Ibid.*

30 *Ibid.* (emphasis removed).

31 *Ibid.* par. 47.

32 *Ibid.*

the tribunal may accept "any relevant and credible evidence of an issue which has already been considered at trial."[33] A party may not bypass the strictures of Article 25 and Rule 120 by invoking Rule 115.[34]

In Niyitegeka v. Prosecutor, the Appeals Chamber rejected a request for review on several different grounds.[35] First, the applicant submitted the Rwamakuba Trial Judgment, in which Trial Chamber III accepted an alibi defense similar to the one rejected by the Trial Chamber in the applicant's case, namely, that because the defendant was allegedly attending a cabinet meeting he could not have been at another location where the crimes at issue were committed.[36] The Appeals Chamber, however, rejected that this qualified as new information of an evidentiary nature of a fact that was not in issue during the applicant's case.[37] In fact, this very alibi defense was raised at his trial.[38] Furthermore, because the trial of the other accused involved different facts, the Appeals Chamber found that it did not provide a basis to reassess the alibi claim in the applicant's case.[39]

Secondly, the applicant submitted an agenda and an affidavit from the former prime minister in an effort to demonstrate his attendance at a number of official government meetings, thereby bolstering his alibi claim and raising doubt as to his ability to have participated in the crimes alleged against him.[40] Yet, because these alibi claims were previously raised at trial, the Appeals Chamber ruled that they could not constitute "new facts" entitling the applicant to formal review proceedings.[41] In addition, the Appeals Chamber noted that even if these submissions were accepted as new facts, based upon the overwhelming evidence of guilt, they would not have altered the outcome of the original decision.[42]

The Appeals Chamber's decision in this case generated two dissenting commentaries, one from Judge Shahabuddeen, and a second from Judge Meron. Judge Shahabuddeen had previously issued a declaration in the same litigation almost a year before in response to the majority's pronouncement that, despite the strict requirements of Article 25 of the ICTY statute and Rule 120, ICTR RPE, "in 'wholly exceptional circumstances,' where the impact of a 'new fact' on the decision would be such that to ignore it would lead to a miscarriage of justice, review might be possible even though the 'new fact' was known to the moving party, or was discoverable by it through the exercise of due diligence."[43] Therein, Judge Shahabuddeen noted that, in cases that do not fall within the parameters of Article 25, rather than correcting its errors by "artificially and awkwardly disguising what it is doing as an Article 25 review," the Appeals Chamber should recognize its inherent jurisdiction to prevent miscarriages of justice.[44] In the present appeal, he again reiterated that the Appeals Chamber should be able to reconsider a case, even where the evidence submitted by the appellant does not qualify as a "new fact," where its exclusion would lead to an injustice.[45] Furthermore, he remarked that, "[i]n establishing the Tribunal as a judicial body, the Security Council should be seen as having entrusted it with basic judicial functions to administer justice, and consequently with the competence to correct extreme cases of injustice even absent express authority in the Statute to do so."[46]

In Judge Meron's separate opinion, he agreed with Judge Shahabuddeen that the doors of the Appeals Chamber should remain open in a case in which innocence is shown despite the requirements of Article 25 not being met.[47] In his opinion, Judge Meron provided an illustrative hypothetical of a situation where new

---

33 *Ibid.*
34 *Ibid.* par. 48.
35 Decision on Request for Review, *Niyitegeka v. Prosecutor*, A. Ch., *supra* note 1, par. 6-28.
36 *Ibid.* par. 6.
37 *Ibid.* par. 7.
38 *Ibid.*
39 *Ibid.*
40 *Ibid.* par. 8.
41 *Ibid.* par. 10-28.
42 *Ibid.* par. 11, 12, and 16.
43 Decision on Request for Review, *Niyitegeka v. Prosecutor*, A. Ch., *supra* note 21, par. 7.
44 ICTR, Declaration of Judge Shahabuddeen, *Niyitegeka v. Prosecutor*, Case No. ICTR-96-14-R, A. Ch., 30 June 2006, Klip/Sluiter, ALC-XXIV-976, par. 2-3.
45 Declaration of Judge Shahabuddeen, *Niyitegeka v. Prosecutor*, A. Ch., Case No. ICTR-96-14-R, A. Ch., 27 September 2006, in this volume, p. 294, par. 1.
46 *Ibid.*
47 Separate Opinion of Judge Meron, *Niyitegeka v. Prosecutor*, A. Ch., Case No. ICTR-96-14-R, A. Ch., 27 September 2006, in this volume, p. 295, par. 4.

evidence would not qualify under Article 25 as a 'new fact' but would demonstrate a clear miscarriage of justice:

> "[S]uppose that an accused is convicted of murdering a victim. Suppose further that a fact at issue at trial was whether the victim was in fact dead – the Prosecution presented several eye-witnesses who testified to seeing the victim's dead body, whereas the Defence responded with an eye-witness who claimed to have later seen the victim alive. If the victim should turn up alive after the issuance of all final judgements in the case, a clear miscarriage of justice would result from letting the murder conviction stand. This would be true even though under the distinction created by our precedent, this new evidence of the victim's state of being would likely be 'additional evidence' that bolsters the Defence's claim at trial that the victim was alive and not a 'new fact.'"[48]

Judge Meron also remarked that, as a result of the Appeals Chamber's narrow treatment of "new facts," the tribunal was taking a more restrictive approach than major civil and common law national jurisdictions, which, if the Appeals Chamber refused to reconsider final judgments where necessary in order to avoid a manifest miscarriage of justice, would disserve the aim of the tribunal to be "a model of due process protections."[49] Thus, because of the gap in formal review proceedings, both these judges expressed their willingness to embrace the inherent jurisdiction of the Appeals Chamber to remedy gross miscarriages of justice, despite lack of technical compliance with present procedural mechanisms.

4. Reconsideration

Reconsideration is "an exceptional measure, available only in particular circumstances."[50] In order to prevail on a motion for reconsideration, the movant must demonstrate either (1) the existence of a clear error of reasoning or (2) that reconsideration is necessary to avoid injustice.[51] Generally, a request for reconsideration should address only issues considered in the impugned decision.[52]

In Niyitegeka v. Prosecutor, the Appeals Chamber addressed the question of whether the applicant could seek reconsideration of the denial of a request for review proceedings.[53] On 30 June 2006, the Appeals Chamber denied the applicant's request for review pursuant to Article 25 of the statute and Rules 120 and 121, ICTR RPE.[54] Thereafter, on 1 August 2006, the applicant sought reconsideration on the grounds that the impugned decision was based upon erroneous reasoning that was highly prejudicial to him; additionally, he sought leave to extend his counsel's mandate to enable his attorney to collect supplemental material to support his alibi defense.[55] The majority of the Appeals Chamber, however, followed Žigić and, after concluding that its decision denying the request for review was a final judgment – in that it terminated the proceedings – held that it lacked the authority to reconsider a final judgment and thus dismissed the applicant's request for reconsideration.[56] Judges Shahabuddeen and Meron both agreed with the majority that reconsideration was not warranted under the circumstances of the case.[57] Judge Shahabuddeen, however, continued to question the wisdom of Žigić.[58] Judge Meron, for his part, continued to reserve judgment on the issue of the power of the Appeals Chamber to reconsider a final judgment until the appropriate case presented itself.[59]

In Prosecutor v. Bagosora et al., the Trial Chamber considered whether the issuance of an Appeals Chamber decision in a related case constituted a sufficient intervening circumstance to merit reconsideration of a

---

48 *Ibid.* par. 3.

49 *Ibid.* par. 4

50 Decision Reconsidering Exclusion of Evidence Related to Accused Kabiligi, *Prosecutor v. Bagosora, Kabiligi, Ntabakuze and Nsengiyumva*, T. Ch. I, *supra* note 1, par. 3.

51 ICTY, Decision on Dragan Jokić's Supplemental Motion for Extension of Time to File Appeal Brief, *Prosecutor v. Blagojević and Dragan Jokić*, Case No. IT-02-60-A, A. Ch., 31 August 2005, par. 7.

52 Decision Reconsidering Exclusion of Evidence Related to Accused Kabiligi, *Prosecutor v. Bagosora, Kabiligi, Ntabakuze and Nsengiyumva.*, *supra* note 49, par. 4.

53 Decision on Request for Reconsideration of the Decision on Request for Review, *Niyitegeka v. Prosecutor*, A. Ch., supra note 1.

54 *Ibid.*, par. 2.

55 *Ibid.*

56 *Ibid.* par. 2-3.

57 Declaration of Judge Shahabuddeen, *Niyitegeka v. Prosecutor*, A. Ch., *supra* note 44, par. 1 and 5; ICTR, Separate Opinion of Judge Meron, *Niyitegeka v. Prosecutor*, A. Ch., *supra* note 46, par. 1-4.

58 Declaration of Judge Shahabuddeen, *Niyitegeka v. Prosecutor*, *supra* note 44, par. 2-4.

59 Separate Opinion of Judge Meron, *Niyitegeka v. Prosecutor*, *supra* note 46, par. 1-3.

previous Trial Chamber decision.[60] A brief procedural history is necessary for an understanding of the chamber's ruling. On 19 October 2004, defendant Kabiligi filed a motion to exclude various testimony of eight prosecution witnesses on the grounds that they gave testimony about allegations not included in the indictment.[61] On 27 September 2005, the Trial Chamber granted the motion with respect to portions of testimony of two of the challenged witnesses.[62] On 5 April 2006, Kabiligi filed a second exclusion motion, which the chamber construed as a reconsideration motion.[63] On 4 September 2006, the chamber granted this motion as to a portion of one prosecution witness' testimony.[64]

Two weeks later, on 18 September 2006, the Appeals Chamber issued a decision in co-defendant Ntabakuze's interlocutory appeal in the which Appeals Chamber remanded the case to the Trial Chamber for the chamber to consider whether defects in the indictment, despite the prosecution's curative efforts, materially prejudiced Ntabakuze's ability to prepare a defense, as well as to reconsider the placement of the burden of proof in relation to the timeliness of the objection to lack of notice.[65] Based upon this appellate decision in his co-defendant's case, defendant Kabiligi sought reconsideration of the Trial Chamber's 4 September 2006 decision in his case.[66] Here, the Trial Chamber held that the Appeals Chamber's decision on a related legal issue "constitutes a new circumstance which has arisen since the Trial Chamber's decision of 4 September 2006, and which may affect it."[67] Accordingly, the chamber ruled that reconsideration was justified.[68]

In Ntabakuze v. Prosecutor, the Appeals Chamber addressed the question of who has standing to bring a motion for reconsideration.[69] Therein, the movant, Aloys Ntabakuze, who was not a party to the Karemera et al. case, sought reconsideration (or, alternatively, leave to intervene for reconsideration) of an Appeals Chamber decision in the Karemera et al. litigation in which the Appeals Chamber directed the Trial Chamber in Karemera et al. to take judicial notice of certain facts, most prominently, that "[b]etween 6 April 1994 and 17 July 1994, there was a genocide in Rwanda against the Tutsi ethnic group."[70] The applicant argued that he had a compelling interest in the matter, thereby justifying his intervention, because he was advancing, and had already introduced evidence during his trial of, an alternative to the "genocide hypothesis."[71] Further, he alleged that the application of the Appeals Chamber's decision in Karemera et al. would bar his theory of defense and deprive him of a fair trial.[72]

The Appeals Chamber agreed with the applicant's assertion that neither the Statute nor the Rules delineate who has standing to seek reconsideration of a decision.[73] It concluded, however, that "only a party to a decision of the Appeals Chamber may ask the chamber to reconsider that decision."[74] Otherwise, it would open up the chamber's reconsideration procedures to abuse.[75] Moreover, the Appeals Chamber ruled that the applicant was not prejudiced because, in the event that the Trial Chamber in his matter took judicial notice of the same facts, he could challenge the issue in that forum.[76]

---

60 Decision Reconsidering Exclusion of Evidence Related to Accused Kabiligi, *Prosecutor v. Bagosora, Kabiligi, Ntabakuze and Nsengiyumva*, T. Ch. I, *supra* note 49.

61 *Ibid.* par. 1.

62 *Ibid.*

63 *Ibid.*

64 *Ibid.*

65 ICTR, Decision on Aloys Ntabakuze's Interlocutory Appeal on Questions of Law Raised by the 29 June 2006 Trial Chamber I Decision on Motion for Exclusion of Evidence, *Prosecutor v. Bagosora, Kabiligi, Ntabakuze and Nsengiyumva*, Case No. ICTR-98-41-AR73, A. Ch., 18 September 2006, in this volume, p. 13, par. 48.

66 Decision Reconsidering Exclusion of Evidence Related to Accused Kabiligi, *Prosecutor v. Bagosora, Kabiligi, Ntabakuze and Nsengiyumva*, T. Ch. I, *supra* note 49, par. 1.

67 *Ibid.* par. 3.

68 *Ibid.*

69 Decision on Motion for Reconsideration, *Ntabakuze v. Prosecutor*, A. Ch., *supra* note 1.

70 *Ibid.* par. 1, 4, and 5.

71 *Ibid.* par. 6.

72 *Ibid.*

73 *Ibid.* par. 12 and 14.

74 *Ibid.* par. 15.

75 *Ibid.*

76 *Ibid.* par. 16.

Lastly, in Prosecutor v. Seromba, the Appeals Chamber considered whether it could entertain an appeal where the appellant filed a notice of appeal one day beyond the 30-day limit for filing such notices.[77] There, the Appeals Chamber graciously invoked Rule 116(A), ICTR RPE, which provides that "[t]he Appeals Chamber may grant a motion to extend a time limit upon showing of good cause," and found that the appellant had established "good cause."[78] As Judge Schomburg correctly pointed out in his declaration, however, no good cause was demonstrated by the appellant.[79] In fact, the appellant failed to even file a motion for extension of time.[80] Yet, in light of the grave consequences of depriving the defendant of an appeal based upon *de minimus* tardiness, the Appeals Chamber erred on the side of equity and permitted the appeal to proceed.[81] Nevertheless, Judge Schomburg warned, "To grant only one day without good cause having been shown may set a precedent binding the Appeals Chamber and could open Pandora's Box resulting in an extended non-compliance with time limits. *Obsta principiis*!"[82]

5. Certification

Certification procedures are covered under Rule 73(B), ICTR RPE, which provides:

> "Decisions rendered on such motions [i.e., motions filed after the initial appearance of the accused] are without interlocutory appeal save with certification by the Trial Chamber, which may grant such certification if the decision involves an issue that would significantly affect the fair and expeditious conduct of the proceedings or the outcome of the trial, and for which, in the opinion of the Trial Chamber, an immediate resolution by the Appeals Chamber may materially advance the proceedings."

As reflected in the conjunctive language of the rule, a defendant must demonstrate that both of the aforementioned requirements for certification are satisfied.[83] Whether certification is granted is entrusted to the discretion of the Trial Chamber.[84] Moreover, certification is viewed as being exceptional in nature.[85]

In Prosecutor v. Karemera et al., the Trial Chamber addressed the question of whether it should consider the merits of an appeal when deciding on the issue of certification. Therein, the chamber had denied a defense request to subpoena three potential defense witnesses. The defense then sought certification, arguing that the ruling significantly affected the fair and expeditious conduct of the proceedings because the right to a fair trial encompasses the right to compel the attendance of witnesses and, secondly, contending that resolution by the reviewing chamber would materially advance the proceedings because the issue was likely to reoccur and, if not remedied, would require a new trial.[86]

The defense also argued that the Trial Chamber should consider the merits of the appeal in making its certification decision.[87] The chamber, however, rejected this position, holding that "merits should not be considered when addressing an application to certification."[88] In this regard, the chamber pointed out that the correctness of the Trial Chamber's decision is a matter for the Appeals Chamber; however, the Trial Chamber noted that it still has the obligation to screen out nonmeritorious requests for certification as part of its analysis of whether certification would "materially advance the proceedings."[89] In the case at bar, the Trial Chamber rejected the request for certification, finding that the decision to deny subpoenas did not significantly affect the fair and expeditious conduct of the proceedings or the trial's outcome because the request concerned

77 Order Concerning the Filing of the Notice of Appeal, *Prosecutor v. Seromba*, A. Ch., 22 March 2007, *supra* note 1.

78 *Ibid.* p. 3.

79 Declaration of Judge Schomburg, *Prosecutor v. Seromba*, A. Ch., Case No. ICTR-2001-66-A, A. Ch., 22 March 2007, in this volume, p. 322, p. 5.

80 Order Concerning the Filing of the Notice of Appeal, *Prosecutor v. Seromba*, A. Ch., *supra* note 1, p. 3.

81 *Ibid.*

82 Declaration of Judge Schomburg, *Prosecutor v. Seromba*, A.Ch., *supra* note 78, p. 5.

83 Decision on Defence Motion for Certification to Appeal the Chamber's Decision on Nzirorera's *Ex Parte* Motion for Order for Interview of Defence Witnesses NZ1, NZ2, and NZ3 (Rule 73(B) of the Rules of Procedure and Evidence), *Prosecutor v. Karemera, Ngirumpatse and Nzirorera*, T. Ch. III, *supra* note 1, par. 6.

84 *Ibid.* par. 5.

85 *Ibid.* par. 6.

86 *Ibid.* par. 9 and 10.

87 *Ibid.* par. 4.

88 *Ibid.* par. 7.

89 *Ibid.*

compelling attendance for out-of-court interviews, did not involve witnesses at trial, and the denial was not made pursuant to a blanket policy of rejecting subpoenas for all rebuttal witnesses.[90]

Additionally, the question of whether a decision denying a motion for acquittal is subject to certification under Rule 73(B), ICTR RPE, was the subject of discussion in Prosecutor v. Ndindiliyimana et al.[91] After defendant Nzuwonemeye's motion for acquittal was denied, he moved for certification pursuant to Rule 73(B), ICTR RPE.[92] Rule 98*bis*, which addresses motions for judgment of acquittal, provides as follows:

> "If after the close of the case for the prosecution, the Trial Chamber finds that the evidence is insufficient to sustain a conviction on one or more counts charged in the indictment, the Trial Chamber, on motion of an accused filed within seven days after the close of the prosecutor's case-in-chief, unless the Chamber orders otherwise, or *proprio motu*, shall order the entry of judgement of acquittal in respect of those counts."

The Trial Chamber first observed that Rule 98*bis* does not, on its face, provide for a right of appeal.[93] Yet, although noting a division in the Trial Chambers on this issue, Trial Chamber II concluded that certification under Rule 73(B) must be interpreted as including denials of motions for acquittal under Rule 98*bis*.[94] Otherwise, the Chamber reasoned, a defendant aggrieved by an erroneous denial of a motion for judgment of acquittal would be left without any timely remedy.[95] In the case before it, however, the chamber ruled that the first criterion under Rule 73(B) was not satisfied, noting that the denial of a motion for acquittal does not preclude the trier of fact from subsequently concluding that the prosecution failed to prove the defendant guilty beyond a reasonable doubt, because the two legal standards are different.[96]

6. Conclusion

The debate over the role of the tribunal in preventing miscarriages of justice versus guaranteeing the finality of judgments is certainly one of consequence. Yet, in the author's opinion, which is informed by his criminal litigation experience, the latter must yield to the former.

For example, in People v. Dean Cage, the defendant was charged in 1994 with aggravated criminal sexual assault (rape).[97] At trial, Mr. Cage denied that he was in any way involved in the crime and produced an alibi witness, who testified that she was with the defendant at home at the time the rape occurred. The only evidence against Mr. Cage was a single eyewitness identification made almost a week after the offense; however, there was no physical evidence linking Mr. Cage to the crime. Despite these facts, the trial judge, in a bench trial, convicted Mr. Cage and sentenced him to 40 years in prison. On direct appeal, his conviction was affirmed.

Subsequently, in 2002, Mr. Cage filed a *pro se* motion for forensic DNA testing under a statute permitting such applications under Illinois law. The motion was denied by the trial judge. The author was assigned as Mr. Cage's counsel on appeal from the denial of his DNA motion. In reading the record on appeal, counsel discovered that there were several items of the victim's clothing that had never been tested for DNA and that he believed could contain testable genetic material, which could lead to Mr. Cage's exoneration. Despite counsel's pleas to the reviewing court to order the requested testing, the appellate court, based on the arguments of the State, which opposed the appeal, held that Mr. Cage was not entitled to relief based on the technicality that he failed in his *pro se* motion to specifically allege the requested DNA testing methods and that they were unavailable at the time of trial.[98]

Mr. Cage continued to assert his innocence and sought the assistance of the Innocence Project, an organization dedicated to exonerating individuals wrongly convicted of crimes. After several years, the State agreed to allow testing of the clothing items appellate counsel had identified and, lo and behold, the clothing not only

---

90 *Ibid.* par. 11.

91 Decision on Defence Request for Certification to Appeal the Chamber's Decision Pursuant to Rule 98*bis*, *Prosecutor v. Ndindiliyimana, Augustin Bizimungu, Nzuwonemeye and Sagahutu*, T. Ch. II, *supra* note 1.

92 *Ibid.* par. 2.

93 *Ibid.* par. 4.

94 *Ibid.*

95 *Ibid.*

96 *Ibid.* par. 8.

97 Circuit Court of Cook County, Illinois, *People v. Cage*, No. 94 CR 29467.

98 Illinois Appellate Court, Order Pursuant to Rule 23, *People v. Cage*, Case No. 1-02-2898, 26 March 2004, p. 5-6.

contained testable genetic material, but the results conclusively proved that Mr. Cage could not have been the rapist.[99] Shortly thereafter, Mr. Cage was released from the state penitentiary after serving almost 14 years in prison for a crime he did not commit.[100]

Under Žigić, the results of the DNA testing that eventually exonerated Mr. Cage, just as in Judge Meron's hypothetical example of an alleged murder victim later found alive,[101] would not qualify as a "new fact" under Article 25 of the ICTR Statute for the purposes of initiating formal review proceedings because the issue of DNA was already considered during the appeal of the denial of Cage's motion for forensic DNA testing and, thus, the judgment would be considered final and unassailable.

Cases involving wrongful convictions of innocent persons, such as Dean Cage, cry out for a remedy, even if the information exonerating a defendant surfaces many years later. The passage of time cannot erase the stain of an erroneous conviction nor bring certainty to a court's pronouncement of guilt. Admittedly, finality for the victims and their families is important, but can there really be any true closure when the wrong person is confined to a jail cell and the real perpetrator is still at large? Final judgments do not always equate with justice; instead, finality should be measured by the assurance that justice has ultimately been achieved. This goal can only be attained by ensuring that the doors of the tribunal will never be shut to the innocent.

Steven W. Becker

99 M. Possley, DNA Exonerates Inmate on Rape Conviction After 14 Years, Chicago Tribune, 27 May 2008, http://www.chicagotribune.com/news/local/chi-dna-exonerates-prisoner-webmay28,0,5734277.story.

100 *Ibid.*

101 Separate Opinion of Judge Meron, *Niyitegeka v. Prosecutor*, *supra* note 46, par. 3.

International Criminal Tribunal for Rwanda
Tribunal pénal international pour le Rwanda

ORIGINAL: ENGLISH AND FRENCH

TRIAL CHAMBER III

Before Judges: Dennis C. M. Byron, Presiding
Gberdao Gustave Kam
*sitting pursuant to Rule 15*bis *of the Rules of Procedure and Evidence*

Registrar: Adama Dieng

Date: 6 March 2007

THE PROSECUTOR

v.

Édouard KAREMERA
Mathieu NGIRUMPATSE
Joseph NZIRORERA

Case No. ICTR-98-44-T

DECISION ON CONTINUATION OF THE PROCEEDINGS

Rule 15*bis *of the Rules of Procedure and Evidence

Office of the Prosecutor:
Don Webster
Alayne Frankson-Wallace
Iain Morley
Saïdou N'Dow
Sunkarie Ballah-Conteh
Takeh Sendze

Defence Counsel for Édouard Karemera
Dior Diagne Mbaye and Félix Sow

Defence Counsel for Mathieu Ngirumpatse
Chantal Hounkpatin and Frédéric Weyl

Defence Counsel for Joseph Nzirorera
Peter Robinson and Patrick Nimy Mayidika Ngimbi

[page 2] INTRODUCTION

1. The trial in this case started on 19 September 2005 with the presentation of the Prosecution case over four trial sessions. Thirteen Prosecution Witnesses have been heard so far by Trial Chamber III composed of Judge Dennis C. M. Byron, presiding, Emile Francis Short and Gberdao Gustave Kam.

2. On 19 January 2007, Judge Short informed in writing the Presiding Judge that he had decided to withdraw from the case due to recent health challenges he had been undergoing.[1] On the same day, in accordance with Rule 15 *bis* (C) of the Rules of Procedure and Evidence, Judge Byron notified the President of the Tribunal of Judge Short's inability to continue sitting in the instant case.[2]

3. As a result, in accordance with the Rules,[3] the President requested the Defence Counsel to indicate, by 29 January 2007, whether the Accused persons consent to the continuation of the proceedings after the assignment of a new Judge to replace Judge Short, and if not, to state the reasons thereto.[4] In order to minimize any delay in the trial of the co-Accused, the remaining Judges also issued a scheduling order whereby the Parties were instructed to file any submission on the rehearing or continuation of the proceedings by 31 January 2007.[5]

4. In their submissions to the President, Joseph Nzirorera and Mathieu Ngirumpatse indicate that they withhold their consent to the continuation, while Edouard Karemera agrees to a continuation of the proceedings with a substitute Judge provided that the latter ensures his or her perfect knowledge of the case.[6] Under these circumstances, and since the Prosecutor had already started the presentation of his evidence, the President referred **[page 3]** the matter to the remaining Judges in the instant case to decide whether to continue the proceedings with a substitute Judge in accordance with Rule 15 *bis* (D).[7]

5. On 30 and 31 January 2007, the Prosecutor and Joseph Nzirorera respectively filed, with the remaining Judges, their submissions on the continuation of the proceedings.[8] Mathieu Ngirumpatse and Edouard Karemera filed their submissions late,[9] although they were also sent by email and fax to the Court Management Section on 31 January 2007. In the interests of justice and considering the right of the Accused to be heard, the remaining Judges find appropriate to take into consideration these submissions. For the same reasons, the additional submissions filed by Nzirorera as a result of the President's Memorandum referring the matter to the remaining Judges will also be taken into consideration.[10]

DELIBERATIONS

Preliminary Matter

6. Joseph Nzirorera submits that in the Memorandum referring the matter to the remaining Judges, the President has not clearly stated the reasons for his decision, and particularly whether he considered that he

---

1 Letter from Judge Short to Judge Byron dated 19 January 2007, filed confidentially on 25 January 2007.

2 Letter from Judge Byron to the President dated 19 January 2007, filed confidentially on 25 January 2007.

3 Rules of Procedure and Evidence, Rule 15*bis* (C): "If by reason of death, illness, resignation from the Tribunal, non-reelection, non extension of term of office or for any other reason, a Judge is unable to continue sitting in a part-heard case for a period which is likely to be longer than a short duration, the Presiding Judge shall report to the President who may assign another Judge to the case and order either a rehearing or continuation of the proceedings from that point. However, after the opening statements provided for in Rule 84, or the beginning of the presentation of evidence pursuant to Rule 85, the continuation of the proceedings can only be ordered with the consent of the accused, except as provided for in paragraph (D)".

4 Letter from the President filed on 24 January 2007.

5 *Prosecutor v. Edouard Karemera, Mathieu Ngirumpatse and Joseph Nzirorera*, Case No. ICTR-98-44-T ("*Karemera et al.*"), Scheduling Order for the Filing of Submissions (TC), 24 January 2007.

6 Letter from Mr. Robinson to the President, filed on 23 January 2007; Letter from Mrs. Hounkpatin to the President, filed on 29 January 2007; Memorandum from Mrs. Dior Diagne Mbaye and Mr. Moussa Felix Sow to the President, filed on 29 January 2007.

7 Interoffice Memorandum from the President to Judge Byron, filed on 6 February 2007.

8 Prosecutor's Submissions Pursuant to Rule 15 *bis* (D), filed on 30 January 2007; Joseph Nzirorera's Submission to Remaining Judges in Support of a New Trial, filed on 31 January 2007.

9 Soumission pour M. Ngirumpatse sur la Scheduling Order for Filing the Submissions Rules 15 bis D, filed on 1 February 2007 ; Réponse de Edouard Karemera à la « Scheduling Order for the Filing of Submissions Rule 15 bis RPP", filed on 5 February 2007.

10 Joseph Nzirorera's Further Submission to Remaining Judges, filed on 8 February 2007.

had the discretion under Rule 15 *bis* (C) of the Rules to order a rehearing, or, if he believed that he had such discretion, what factors he took into consideration in exercising that discretion not to order a rehearing.[11] According to Nzirorera, should the remaining Judges decide to continue the trial, it will be impossible for the Appeals Chamber to determine how the President exercised his discretion.[12] He also contends that the remaining Judges themselves would benefit from a reasoned opinion from the President as well, since many of the same issues raised before the President will be before the remaining Judges.[13] The Accused therefore requests that before making a decision, the remaining Judges refer the matter back to the President for a reasoned opinion on the issue of whether a rehearing of the trial should be ordered. **[page 4]**

7. The remaining Judges are not an appellate body for the President's decisions and they are therefore not competent to make a finding as to whether he properly exercised his discretionary power under Rule 15 *bis* (C). According to the powers enshrined in the Rules, since the matter has been referred by the President, the remaining Judges have now to determine, in light of all the circumstances of the case and on the basis of the Parties' submissions, whether a rehearing or a continuation of the proceedings would better serve the interests of justice.

8. Furthermore, as emphasized by the Appeals Chamber, there are various safeguards against arbitrariness when the Judges decide upon the continuation or rehearing of the proceedings under Rule 15 *bis* (D): "the decision by the two remaining judges is a judicial one; it is taken after hearing both sides; the two remaining judges know the case as it has so far developed; their decision must be unanimous; an appointment can only be made once".[14] Furthermore, in the present case, the same 66-page submission was filed with both the President and the remaining Judges.[15] Consequently, the submissions made by Joseph Nzirorera before the President will be heard by a judicial organ whose decision is subject to appeal directly to a full bench of the Appeals Chamber.[16] The rights of the Accused are therefore fully guaranteed despite the alleged impossibility for the Appeals Chamber to review the President's Decision.

9. Joseph Nzirorera's request to refer the matter back to the President therefore falls to be rejected.

On the Merits

10. Rule 15 *bis* (D) of the Rules provides that if, after the beginning of the presentation of the evidence, "the accused withholds his consent [for the continuation of the proceedings with a substitute Judge], the remaining Judges may nonetheless decide to continue the proceedings before a Trial Chamber with a substitute Judge if, taking all the circumstances into account, they determine unanimously that doing so would serve the interests of justice". **[page 5]**

11. In the present case, Joseph Nzirorera and Mathieu Ngirumpatse withhold their consent to the continuation of the proceedings with a substitute Judge.[17] Edouard Karemera consents to the continuation provided that some of his concerns are duly taken into consideration.[18] The Prosecutor presents submissions also in favour of a continuation of the proceedings.[19]

12. According to the ordinary meaning of Rule 15 *bis* (D) and as the Appeals Chamber previously emphasized, the remaining Judges must determine that it is in the interests of justice to continue the

---

11 *Ibid.*, para. 7.

12 *Ibid.*, paras. 11 and 12.

13 *Ibid.*, para. 13.

14 *Prosecutor v. Pauline Nyiramasuhuko et al.*, Case No. ICTR-98-42-A15bis, Decision in the Matter of Proceedings Under Rule 15bis (D) (AC), 24 September 2003, para. 18 ("*Nyiramasuhuko* Appeals Chamber Decision on Continuation").

15 Except for a few portions, the content of the submission filed by the Defence for Nzirorera before the President is identical to the one filed with the remaining Judges.

16 See: Rule 15 *bis* (D); *Nyiramasuhuko* Appeals Chamber Decision on Continuation, para. 18.

17 See submissions filed respectively on 31 January 2007 and 1 February 2007.

18 Réponse de Edouard Karemera à la « Scheduling Order for the Filing of Submissions Rule 15 bis RPP", filed on 5 February 2007.

19 Submissions filed on 30 January 2007.

proceedings.[20] Therefore, even if the Judges finds Accused's arguments in favour of a rehearing of the case not persuasive, they still must make the finding that a continuation would best serve the interests of justice.

13. Under the sections hereinafter, the remaining Judges will deal first with the equal right of each co-Accused to be heard on whether or not to continue the proceedings; second, the issue of the fairness of the trial; third, what would best serve the interests of justice in light of all the circumstances of this case, including in light of the parties' submissions.

1. Equal Rights of the Co-Accused to Be Heard on the Continuation, or not, of the Proceedings

14. Joseph Nzirorera, joined by Mathieu Ngirumpatse,[21] submits that while the remaining Judges are able to order the continuation of the trial over the objection of the accused, the lack of consent must be given great weight in the decision whether or not to proceed.[22] To support his assertion, the Accused relies upon the Appeals Chamber decision on continuation in the *Nyiramasuhuko et al.* case.[23]

15. The remaining Judges note that in the *Nyiramasuhuko et al.* case, the Appeals Chamber "takes the view that, though apparently absolute, the right to consent to continuation of the trial was not proprietorial but functional".[24] The Appeals Chamber explained that "[t]he right to consent gave protection against possible arbitrariness in the exercise of the power of the Tribunal to continue the hearing with a substitute judge; consent **[page 6]** was only a safeguard".[25] It found that Rule 15 *bis* as amended in 2003 contains various safeguards which offer an equivalent protection against arbitrariness as offered by the prior Rule when limiting any continuation to the consent of the accused.[26]

16. Contrary to Joseph Nzirorera's assertion, it cannot be concluded from these findings that the Appeals Chamber held the view that the lack of consent is the determining factor in the decision whether or not to proceed. As set forth in Rule 82 of the Rules, "in a joint trial each of the accused shall be accorded the same rights as if he were being tried separately".[27] When deciding upon the continuation of proceedings, the remaining Judges must take into consideration all the circumstances of the case, including the reasons given by the accused for consenting or not to the continuation and the issues raised by the parties. The fact that one of the Accused in the present case has consented to the continuation of the trial is as relevant to the interests of justice as the opposition of two other co-Accused.

2. Fairness of the Trial

17. Joseph Nzirorera, joined by Mathieu Ngirumpatse, submits that the interests of justice would not be served by continuing the trial because this will perpetuate an unfair trial and the proceedings are likely not to be sustained on appeal due to errors of law made during the portion of the trial already completed. He contends that the trial has been rendered unfair due to seven causes: (1) the continuous violation by the Prosecutor of his disclosure obligations under Rules 66(A)(ii), 66(B) and 68 of the Rules; (2) the wholesale admission of material facts not charged in the Indictment; (3) an unjustified use of anonymous witnesses; (4)

---

[20] *Karemera et al.*, Case No. ICTR-98-44-T, Reasons For Decision on Interlocutory Appeals Regarding the Continuation of Proceedings with a Substitute Judge and on Nzirorera's Motion for Leave to Consider New Material (AC), 22 October 2004, para. 49 ("*Karemera* Appeals Chamber Decision on Continuation").

[21] In addition to presenting his own arguments, Mathieu Ngirumpatse joins the arguments developed by Joseph Nzirorera (Ngirumpatse's submissions, para. 5).

[22] Nzirorera's submissions, para. 12.

[23] *Nyiramasuhuko* Appeals Chamber Decision on Continuation.

[24] *Nyiramasuhuko* Appeals Chamber Decision on Continuation, para. 17.

[25] *Ibidem.*

[26] The Appeals Chamber found that "[t]he new Rule 15*bis* contains various safeguards: the decision by the two remaining judges is a judicial one; it is taken after hearing both sides; the two remaining judges know the case as it has so far developed; their decision must be unanimous; an appointment can only be made once. Further, there is an unqualified right of appeal by either party from the decision taken by the two remaining judges direct to a full bench of the Appeals Chamber. Finally, in cases where the Appeals Chamber affirms the Trial Chamber's decision or if no appeal is lodged, the newly assigned judge must certify that he has familiarised himself with the record of the proceedings; if he cannot give the required certificate of familiarisation, he cannot eventually be substituted" (*Nyiramasuhuko* Appeals Chamber Decision on Continuation, para. 18).

[27] See *also Prosecutor v. Nyiramasuhuko et al.*, Joint Case No. ICTR-98-42-A15bis, Dissenting Opinion of Judge David Hunt (AC), 24 September 2003, para. 23.

the presentation by the Prosecutor of perjured testimonies; (5) the failure of the Rwandan authorities to produce statements of Prosecution witnesses; (6) the taking of important testimonies by video-link, and (7) the Prosecutor's interference with the Defence's right to meet witnesses. For each instance, Nzirorera provides details as to the factual circumstances surrounding the issues at stake and the decisions thereto. **[page 7]**

18. Under the subsequent sections, the remaining Judges will consider each issue raised by Joseph Nzirorera to support his assertion that the trial has been rendered unfair.

1. Disclosure Issues

19. Joseph Nzirorera, supported by Mathieu Ngirumpatse, contends that the consistent violation by the Prosecutor of his disclosure's obligations has impeded the cross-examination of virtually every Prosecution witness called so far in the trial and has disrupted the investigation and preparation of the defence.[28]

20. To support its application, Joseph Nzirorera claims the existence of various Prosecutor's failures to disclose documents during the first trial against Edouard Karemera, Mathieu Ngirumpatse, Joseph Nzirorera and André Rwamakuba that started in November 2003.[29] Such violations, if established, are however not relevant to the fairness of the current trial which started afresh on 19 September 2005.[30]

21. Joseph Nzirorera then describes disclosure problems prior to the commencement of this trial as well as during each trial session.[31] He submits that the systematic and cumulative failure to provide timely disclosure amounts to denying his right to fair trial, and particularly his right to cross-examine witnesses. In his view, this cannot be cured by recalling all of these witnesses and confronting them with the results of its post-testimony investigation and disclosures.

22. The remaining Judges note that the disclosure issues raised by Joseph Nzirorera have already been adjudicated upon. Over a period of two years, more than 50 decisions were **[page 8]** delivered on disclosure issues only, including reconsideration of prior decisions and certification to appeal.[32] **[page 9]**

---

28 Nzirorera's submissions, paras. 23-109.

29 *Ibid.*, paras. 26-27.

30 The trial against Edouard Karemera, Mathieu Ngirumpatse, Joseph Nzirorera and André Rwamakuba commenced on 27 November 2003 before Trial Chamber III composed of Judges Vaz, presiding, Arrey and Lattanzi. On 14 May 2004, Judge Vaz withdrew from the case. On 16 July 2004, the remaining Judges decided that it would be in the interests of justice to continue the trial with a substitute Judge. The Appeals Chamber quashed this Decision (*Karemera et al.*, Decision on Interlocutory Appeals Regarding the Continuation of Proceedings with a Substitute Judge and on Nzirorera's Motion for Leave to Consider New Material (AC), 28 September 2004; Reasons For Decision on Interlocutory Appeals Regarding the Continuation of Proceedings with a Substitute Judge and on Nzirorera's Motion for Leave to Consider New Material (AC), 22 October 2004). As a result a rehearing of the case was necessary. Judges Byron, presiding, Short and Kam were then assigned to this trial. At the Prosecution's request, the Chamber granted the severance of André Rwamakuba and ordered that he be tried separately (*Prosecutor v. Edouard Karemera, Mathieu Ngirumpatse, Joseph Nzirorera and André Rwamakuba*, Case No. ICTR-98-44-PT, Decision on Severance of André Rwamakuba and for Leave to File an Amended Indictment (TC), 14 February 2005).

31 Nzirorera's submissions, paras. 28-103.

32 See: Decision on Disclosure of Witness Reconfirmation Statements (TC), 23 February 2005; Scheduling Order (TC), 24 March 2005; *Décision relative à la requête du Procureur en prolongation de délai* (TC), 15 April 2005 ; Decision on Motion To Unseal *Ex Parte* Submissions and To Strike Paragraphs 32.4 and 49 from the Amended Indictment (TC), 3 May 2005; Order For Filing Documents (TC), 5 May 2005; Order For Filing Documents (TC), 11 May 2005; Order Granting Time To Reply To Additional Prosecution's Submission (TC), 16 May 2005; Decision on Joseph Nzirorera's Motion For Deadline For Filing of Reports of Experts (TC), 16 May 2005; Decision on Joseph Nzirorera's Motion to Compel Inspection and Disclosure (TC), 5 July 2005; Decision on Defence Motion for Full Disclosure of Payments to Witnesses and to Exclude Testimony from Paid Witnesses (TC), 23 August 2005; Decision on Prosecutor's Notice of Delay in Filing Expert Reports and Request for Additional Time to Comply with the Chamber Decision of 16 May 2005 (TC), 9 September 2005; Decision on Motions to Compel Inspection and Disclosure and to Direct Witnesses to Bring Judicial and Immigration Records (TC), 14 September 2005; Decision on Continuance of Trial (TC), 14 September 2005; Oral Decision on Ngirumpatse Motion to exclude the 143 Prosecution witness statements filed on 4 July 2005, T. 14 September 2005, p. 1; Decision on Motion to Set Deadlines For Filing Expert Reports of Norwojee and Reyntjens (TC), 20 September 2005; Oral Decision on Joseph Nzirorera's Motion to Exclude the Testimony of Witness GFJ, T. 20 September 2005, p. 2, Oral Decision Joseph Nzirorera's Motion seeking certification to appeal Decision on Motion to Exclude the Testimony of Witness GFJ, T. 20 September 2005, p. 47; Oral Decision on Exclusion of Testimony of Alison Des Forges and Granting Extension of Time for Disclosure of the Expert Report, T. 3 October 2005, p. 26; Decision on Defence Motion for Disclosure of Prosecution *Ex Parte* Motion under Rule 66(C) and Request for Cooperation of a Certain State (TC), 14 October 2005; Decision Granting Extension of Time to File Prosecution Expert Report (TC), 8 November 2005; Decision on Prosecution Request for Additional Time to file Expert Report and Joseph

23. It is not relevant for the remaining Judges to reiterate the prior reasoning and findings which are disputed in the current Joseph Nzirorera's submissions. It is, however, necessary to emphasize that in each relevant instance, the rights of the Accused persons were duly taken into consideration. As a result, the Trial Chamber found that either there was no prejudice caused to the Accused persons[33] or, if there was any, it ordered an appropriate remedy considering the circumstances of the case.[34] In that respect, Nzirorera particularly contends that the recall of a witness is an insufficient remedy to the prejudice resulting from a late disclosure. He further submits that a new cross-examination of Prosecution Witness BTH cannot mitigate the prejudice concerning this witness since he would be now a fugitive and have fled Rwanda.[35] As the Appeals Chamber already noted,[36] the adequacy of this remedy in this instance has not been tested given that Nzirorera has not yet sought to recall any witness, including Witness BTH. In addition, the application

---

Nzirorera's Motion to Exclude Testimony of Charles Ntampaka (TC), 12 December 2005; Scheduling Order (TC), 13 December 2005; Order on Filing of Expert Report of Andre Guichaoua (TC), 15 December 2005; Order On Filing of Expert Report of Charles Ntampaka (TC), 31 January 2006; Decision on Prosecutor's Notice of Delay in Filing Expert Report of Professor André Guichaoua; Defence Motion to Exclude the Witness' Testimony; and Trial Chamber's Order to Show Cause (TC), 1 February 2006; Decision on Delay in Filing Expert Report of Charles Ntampaka (TC), 13 February 2006; Decision on Defence Motion to Report Government of a Certain State to United Nations Security Council and on Prosecution Motions under Rule 66(C) of the Rules (TC), 15 February 2006; Oral Decision on Stay of Proceedings, T. 16 February 2006, pp. 2 and seq.; Oral Decision on Request for Certification of Compliance with Rule 68, T. 22 February 2006, pp. 8 to 10; Oral Decision To Exclude or Postpone the Testimony of Witness UB, T. 22 February 2006, pp. 7 and 8; *Décision relative à la requête aux fins d'inspecter certains documents* (TC), 24 February 2006; Oral Decision on Certification of the Oral Decision of 16 February 2006 For Stay of Proceedings, T. 28 February 2006, p. 41; Oral Decision on the Motion for Inspection of Non-Rule 68 Material, T. 9 March 2006, pp. 16-19; Décision sur la requête d'Edouard Karemera aux fins de certification d'appel (TC), 10 March 2006; Decision on Requests for Certification to Appeal Decision on Defence Motion to Report Government of a Certain State to United Nations Security Council and Prosecution Motions under Rule 66(C) (TC), 14 March 2006; *Décision relative aux requêtes de Mathieu Ngirumpatse aux fins d'exclusion des notices du Procureur ou d'ajournement de l'audition des témoins ALG et AWB* (TC), 15 March 2006; Decision on Requests For Disclosure of Witness T's Immigration Records (TC), 17 March 2006; Decision on Defence Motions To Exclude Testimony of Professor Andre Guichaoua (TC), 20 April 2006; Decision on Defence Motion For Disclosure or Inspection of Hand-Written Notes From OTP Investigator (TC), 26 April 2006; Decision on Defence Motions for Disclosure of Information Obtained From Juvénal Uwilingiyimana (TC), 27 April 2006; Oral Decision on Nzirorera Motion for disclosure of payments and benefits for G and T, T. 23 May 2006, pp. 1 and 2; Oral Decision on late disclosure of Witness T's Statement and Imposing a Warning pursuant to Rule 46(A) to the Prosecution, T. 24 May 2006, pp. 35-36; Oral Decision on disclosure of material from Joseph Serugendo, T. 30 May 2006, pp. 62-64; Oral Decision on Motion for Reconsideration of the Chamber's Decision of 15 February 2006, T. 30 May 2006; Decision On Prosecution's Motion To Permit Limited Disclosure Of Information Regarding Payments And Benefits Provided To Witness ADE And His Family (TC), 21 June 2006; Oral Decision on Five Defence Motions, T. 6 June 2006, pp. 17-18; Decision on Joseph Nzirorera's Notice of Violation of Rule 68 and Motion For Remedial Measures (TC), 4 July 2006; Oral Decision on Late Disclosure regarding Witness XBM, T. 6 July 2006; Oral Decision on the Postponement of the Testimony of Witness G, T. 10 October 2005, p. 18; Decision on Motions to Disclose a Prosecution Witness Statement and to Unseal Confidential Documents (TC), 25 October 2006; Decision on Defence Motion for Disclosure of RPF Material for Sanctions Against the Prosecution (TC), 19 October 2006 (in that Decision, the Chamber also imposed a sanction against the Prosecution pursuant to Rule 46(A) of the Rules and accordingly requested the Registry to serve its Decision on the Prosecutor in person); Decision on Defence Motion to Report Government of Rwanda to United Nations Security Council (TC), 2 October 2006; Decision on Defence Motion to Compel Best Efforts to Obtain and Disclose Statements and Testimony of Witness UB (TC), 10 October 2006; Decision on Motion for Disclosure of Closed Session Transcripts and Exhibits (TC), 12 October 2006; Oral Decision on Disclosure regarding Witness HH, 17 November 2006.

33 See for e.g.: Decision on Prosecutor's Notice of Delay in Filing Expert Reports and Request for Additional Time to Comply with the Chamber Decision of 16 May 2005 (TC), 9 September 2005; Decision on Continuance of Trial (TC), 14 September 2005; Oral Decision on Exclusion of Testimony of Alison Des Forges and Granting Extension of Time for Disclosure of the Expert Report (TC), T. 3 October 2005, p. 26; Decision Granting Extension of Time to File Prosecution Expert Report (TC), 8 November 2005; Decision on Prosecution Request for Additional Time to file Expert Report and Joseph Nzirorera's Motion to Exclude Testimony of Charles Ntampaka (TC), 12 December 2005; Decision on Prosecutor's Notice of Delay in Filing Expert Report of Professor André Guichaoua; Defence Motion to Exclude the Witness' Testimony; and Trial Chamber's Order to Show Cause (TC), 1 February 2006; Decision on Delay in Filing Expert Report of Charles Ntampaka (TC), 13 February 2006; Decision on Defence Motion to Report Government of a Certain State to United Nations Security Council and on Prosecution Motions under Rule 66(C) of the Rules (TC), 15 February 2006; Oral Decision To Exclude or Postpone the Testimony of Witness UB (TC), T. 22 February 2006, pp. 7 and 8; Decision on Defence Motions To Exclude Testimony of Professor Andre Guichaoua (TC), 20 April 2006; Oral Decision on Five Defence Motions (TC), T. 6 June 2006, pp. 17-18; Decision on Joseph Nzirorera's Notice of Violation of Rule 68 and Motion For Remedial Measures (TC), 4 July 2006; Decision on Motions to Disclose a Prosecution Witness Statement and to Unseal Confidential Documents (TC), 25 October 2006.

34 See for e.g.: Oral Decision on late disclosure of Witness T's Statement and Imposing a Warning pursuant to Rule 46(A) to the Prosecution, T. 24 May 2006, pp. 35-36; Oral Decision on disclosure of material from Joseph Serugendo, T. 30 May 2006, pp. 62-64; Oral Decision on Late Disclosure regarding Witness XBM, T. 6 July 2006.

35 Nzirorera's Submissions, para. 76.

36 *Karemera et al.*, Decision on Joseph Nzirorera's Interlocutory Appeal (AC), 28 April 2006, para. 10.

to have the witness recalled is only warranted if the Chamber is satisfied that the seeking party shows a good cause, namely and principally in the present situation that new material produces matters which could be **[page 10]** exculpatory or affect the witness's credibility, which has not been alleged so far by Nzirorera either.[37]

24. It must also be noted that in other circumstances where no prejudice to the rights of the Accused was found, the Trial Chamber, nonetheless, made further arrangements to ensure that the fairness of the trial be preserved.[38]

25. Two of the Trial Chamber's decisions, however, merit particular attention since they addressed a wide range of disclosure issues raised by Joseph Nzirorera, and therefore the issue of the fairness of the trial as a whole.[39] In July 2005, before the commencement of the presentation of the Prosecution evidence, Nzirorera, joined by Mathieu Ngirumpatse, filed a motion seeking a stay of proceedings on the basis, among other things, that disclosures of **[page 11]** Prosecution witness statements and exculpatory material under Rules 66(A)(ii) and 68 of the Rules remained incomplete.[40] The Chamber denied the motion, as follows:

> The Chamber notes that most of the contentious disclosure issues have been addressed by the recent Chamber Decisions. The Expert Reports are scheduled to be disclosed within the next two months, and will not prejudice the rights of the Accused since none of these experts are scheduled to be heard before next year and the Defence has an overall knowledge of prior reports from the same experts. With respect to Rule 68 material, the Chamber recalls that the Prosecution has an ongoing duty to make disclosure as the need arises. There is no evidence before the Chamber to show that the Prosecution has failed to comply with this Rule. In its prior Decisions, the Chamber did not find that the Prosecution breached its obligations under Rules 66(A)(ii) of the Rules, but that in the interests of justice, it should assist the Defence in obtaining specific documents. In addition, the Chamber does not consider

---

[37] In the *Bagosora et al.* case, the Trial Chamber recently recalled the standards for recalling a witness (*Prosecutor v. Bagosora et al.*, Case No. ICTR-98-41-T, Decision on Bagosora Defence Motion to Recall Witness Frank Claeys for Additional Cross-Examination (TC), 19 February 2007, para. 3):

> A party seeking to recall a witness must demonstrate good cause, which previous jurisprudence has defined as a substantial reason amounting in law to a legal excuse for failing to perform a required act. In assessing good cause, the Chamber must carefully consider the purpose of the proposed testimony as well as the party's justification for not offering such evidence when the witness originally testified. The right to be tried with undue delay as well as concerns of judicial economy demand that recall should be granted only in the most compelling of circumstances where the evidence is of significant probative value and not of a cumulative nature.

[38] See for e.g.: Oral Decision on Joseph Nzirorera's Motion to Exclude the Testimony of Witness GFJ, T. 20 September 2005, p. 2:

> The Chamber is of the view that the documents disclosed to the Defence on 8 September 2005, pertaining to Witness GFJ, does not fall within the ambit of Rule 66(A)(ii) of the Rules but merely under the practice which has developed, subject to considerations of the interest of justice, of requiring the intervention of the Prosecution to obtain and disclose certain records, specifically including Rwandan judicial records of Prosecution witnesses. The Prosecution, therefore, did not fail to comply with its disclosure obligations under Rule 66(A)(ii).
>
> In addition, the Chamber notes that the documents were disclosed in Kinyarwanda, a language that the Accused understands. The Chamber, however, accepts the Defence concerns with respect to the fairness of the trial and the preparation of the Defence and is of the view that time and facilities should be granted to the Defence.

See also: Decision on Joseph Nzirorera's Notice of Violation of Rule 68 and Motion For Remedial Measures (TC), 4 July 2006; Oral Ruling on the Extension of Time to Cross-Examine of Witness GFJ, T. 27 October 2005, p. 60; Oral Ruling on Application to Have Witness Ahmed Napoléon Mbonyunkiza Recalled, T. 28 October 2005, pp. 10 and 11.

See also other decisions where the Chamber explicitly recalled that it has the ability to manage the trial to ensure that a delay in disclosure will not manifest in unfairness to the Accused, and that if, when a witness is called to testify, the Chamber is of the view that the Accused has still not had enough time to prepare or investigate and that this has resulted in unfairness to the Accused, it will then be open to the Chamber to consider exclusion of the witness' evidence or other appropriate remedy: Decision on Prosecutor's Notice of Delay in Filing Expert Report of Professor André Guichaoua; Defence Motion to Exclude the Witness' Testimony; and Trial Chamber's Order to Show Cause (TC), 1 February 2006, para. 11; Decision on Delay in Filing Expert Report of Charles Ntampaka (TC), 13 February 2006, para. 7; Decision on Defence Motion to Report Government of a Certain State to United Nations Security Council and on Prosecution Motions under Rule 66(C) of the Rules (TC), 15 February 2006, para. 26; Oral Decision on the Postponement of the Testimony of Witness G (TC), T. 10 October 2005, p. 18.

[39] *Karemera et al.*, Decision on the Continuance of Trial (TC), 14 September 2005; Oral Decision on Stay of Proceedings, T. 16 February 2006.

[40] Motion for Continuance of Trial, filed by the Defence for Nzirorera on 14 July 2005, and Mathieu Ngirumpatse's Joinder, filed on 8 August 2005.

> that the sole remedy for a violation of the Prosecution's disclosure obligation is the postponement of the trial, taking into account the right of the Accused to be tried without undue delay.[41]

26. On 16 February 2006, at the outset of the second trial session, the Trial Chamber had to rule again on a motion for a stay of proceedings until 60 days after all the material identified in the motion was disclosed.[42] The Trial Chamber noted that a number of disclosure issues had effectively been resolved by previous decisions, and that in each case, the Chamber took into consideration the rights of each Accused to a fair trial, including their rights to cross-examine a witness, to have adequate time and facilities to prepare their defence, and to be tried without undue delay.[43] As to the remaining disclosure issues, the Trial Chamber recalled that

> Breach of the Prosecution's obligations do not always create prejudice to the Accused, partly in cases where, as the appeals Chamber stated in the *Niyitegeka* case, the existence of the relevant exculpatory evidence is known and accessible to the Defence.
> When the disclosure of material which could assist the Accused to impeach the testimony of a Prosecution witness is made so late that it has an impact on the fairness of the trial, different lines of remedies have been utilized by Trial Chambers. The evidence could be excluded, the trial or the testimony could be postponed, the cross-examination of the witness could be deferred, or the witness could be re-called. In addition to these remedies, sanctions can be imposed against counsel when there is conduct which wilfully interferes with the administration of justice, obstructs the proceedings, or is contrary to the interests of justice.[44]

In the light of the specific circumstances of the case, the Trial Chamber concluded that the lack of diligence on the part of the Prosecutor in disclosing some statements as well as his failure to comply with his obligations to disclose exculpatory material had not substantially **[page 12]** handicapped the preparation of the defence, nor had it hampered the effective cross-examination of the Prosecution witnesses.[45]

27. It must be noted that the Appeals Chamber dismissed Joseph Nzirorera's appeal against the Chamber's oral Decision of 16 February 2006 in all respects.[46] Particularly, the Appeals Chamber found no error on the part of the Trial Chamber in declining to stay the proceedings and considered that "in long and complicated cases, it is necessary for a Trial Chamber to exercise its discretion to control the progress of the proceedings as appropriate, provided that it does not encroach on fair trial rights".[47] The Appeals Chamber also rejected Nzirorera's assertion that, in reaching its decision, the Trial Chamber had failed to adequately consider the history of disclosure violations by the Prosecution in this case.[48]

28. In light of these circumstances, the remaining Judges are satisfied that the rights of the Accused to a fair trial, including their rights to cross-examine the witnesses against them and to have adequate time and facilities to prepare their defence, were duly guaranteed despite disclosure issues. Where necessary, appropriate remedies and actions have been taken by the Trial Chamber to ensure a fair trial. The Judges do not find any circumstance or fact newly adduced by Joseph Nzirorera in the current submissions that could support another conclusion.

2. Admission of Evidence

29. Joseph Nzirorera, joined by Mathieu Ngirumpatse, contends that the Trial Chamber has, on 35 occasions, allowed the Prosecutor to submit evidence of material facts not included in the Indictment.[49] In his view, the admission of large swaths of evidence outside the Indictment has rendered the trial unfair by effectively replacing the case in the original indictment with a completely different one.[50]

---

41 *Karemera et al.*, Decision on the Continuance of Trial (TC), 14 September 2005, para. 8.

42 Joseph Nzirorera's Motion for Stay of Proceedings, filed on 6 February 2006, and Mathieu Ngirumpatse's Joinder, filed on 9 February 2006. The Defence for Karemera supported only some of the submissions made by the Co-Accused (T. 16 February 2006, p. 5).

43 T. 16 February 2006, pp. 2 and 3.

44 *Ibid.*, p. 4.

45 *Ibid.*, pp. 3 and seq.

46 *Karemera et al.*, Decision on Joseph Nzirorera's Interlocutory Appeal (AC), 28 April 2006.

47 *Ibid.*, para. 8.

48 *Ibid.*, para. 18.

49 Nzirorera's submissions, paras. 110-123.

50 *Ibid.*, para. 111.

30. According to the relevant provisions of the Statute and Rules of Procedure and Evidence, as well as the established jurisprudence of the Appeals Chamber, the Prosecutor has the obligation to state the material facts underpinning the charges in the indictment, but **[page 13]** not the evidence by which such material facts are to be proven.[51] Whether particular facts are "material" depends upon the nature of the Prosecution case. Failure to set forth the specific material facts of a crime constitutes a defect in the indictment. In these circumstances, a Chamber must consider whether a fair trial requires an amendment of the indictment, an adjournment, or the exclusion of evidence outside the scope of the indictment.[52] In addition, according to the established jurisprudence of this Tribunal, a defect in the indictment may be cured where the accused has received timely, clear, and consistent information from the Prosecutor which resolves the ambiguity or clears up the vagueness.[53] When deciding whether a defective indictment has been cured, the essential question is whether, depending on the specific circumstances of each case, the accused was in a reasonable position to understand the charges against him or her and to confront the Prosecution case.[54] Where a Chamber considers that a defective indictment has been subsequently cured by the Prosecutor, it should further consider whether the extent of the defects in the indictment materially prejudices an accused's right to a fair trial by hindering the preparation of a proper defence.[55]

31. The Appeals Chamber has also held that when a material fact has not been sufficiently pleaded in the indictment, this alone does not render the evidence inadmissible.[56] The evidence can be admitted to the extent that it may be relevant to the proof of any allegation **[page 14]** sufficiently pleaded in the indictment.[57] When deciding on the admissibility of evidence, a Chamber must also guarantee the protection of the rights of the Accused.[58]

32. These principles have been applied by the Trial Chamber in this case when adjudicating on the admission of evidence in the course of this trial. Contrary to Joseph Nzirorera's assertions, the Trial Chamber has not systematically admitted material facts which should have been pleaded in the Indictment.

33. In some instances, Defence Counsel for Joseph Nzirorera objected to the presentation of some evidence not on the basis of a defect in the form of the Indictment but on the ground of a lack of adequate notice that these facts pleaded in the Indictment would be included in the examination of the witness called to testify or on the basis that the evidence was not relevant to the charges in the Indictment.[59] On other

---

[51] Statute, Articles 17(4), 19, 20(2), 20(4)(a) and 20(4)(b); Rules of Procedure and Evidence, Rule 47(C); *Prosecutor v. Elizaphan Ntakirutimana and Gérard Ntakirutimana*, Case No. ICTR-96-10-A and ICTR-96-17-A, Judgement (AC), 13 December 2004, paras. 25 and 470 ("*Ntakirutimana* Appeal Judgement"); *Prosecutor v. Georges Anderson Nderubumwe Rutaganda*, Case No. ICTR-96-3-A, Judgement (AC), 26 May 2003, paras. 301-303 ("*Rutaganda* Appeal Judgement"); *Prosecutor v. André Ntagerura, Emmanuel Bagambiki and Samuel Imanishimwe*, Case No. ICTR-99-46-A, Judgement (AC), 7 July 2006, para. 21 ("*Ntagerura* Appeal Judgement"); *Prosecutor v. Mladen Naletilic and Vinko Martinovic*, Case No. IT-98-34-A, Judgement (ICTY AC), 3 May 2006, para. 26 ("*Naletilic* Appeal Judgement").

[52] *Prosecutor v. Bagosora et al.*, Decision on Aloys Ntabakuze's Interlocutory Appeal on Questions of Law Raised by the 29 June 2006 Trial Chamber I Decision on Motion for Exclusion of Evidence (AC), 18 September 2006, para. 18.

[53] *Prosecutor v. Eliézer Niyitegeka*, Case No. ICTR-96-14-A, Judgement (AC), 9 July 2004, para. 195 ("*Niyitegeka* Appeal Judgement"); *Ntagerura* Appeal Judgement, paras. 30; *Prosecutor v. Sylvestre Gacumbitsi*, Case No. ICTR-2001-64-A, Judgement (AC), 7 July 2006, para. 49 ("*Gacumbitsi* Appeal Judgement"); *Naletilic* Appeal Judgement, para. 25.

[54] *Rutaganda* Appeal Judgement, para. 303; see also: *Ntakirutimana* Appeal Judgement, paras. 27 and 469-472; *Ntagerura* Appeal Judgement, paras. 30 and 67; *Gacumbitsi* Appeal Judgement, para. 49.

[55] *Prosecutor v. Bagosora et al.*, Decision on Aloys Ntabakuze's Interlocutory Appeal on Questions of Law Raised by the 29 June 2006 Trial Chamber I Decision on Motion for Exclusion of Evidence (AC), 18 September 2006, para. 26.

[56] *Prosecution v. Nyiramasuhuko et al.*, Case No. ICTR-97-21-AR73, Decision on the Appeals by Pauline Nyiramasuhuko and Arsène Shalom Ntahobali on the "Decision on Defence Urgent Motion to Declare Parts of the Evidence of Witnesses RV and ABZ Inadmissible" (AC), 2 July 2004, para. 15; *Prosecution v. Nyiramasuhuko et al.*, Case No. ICTR-98-42-AR73, Decision on Pauline Nyiramasuhuko's Request for Reconsideration (AC), 27 September 2004, para. 12.

[57] *Ibidem*. See also: *Prosecutor v. Bagosora et al.*, Decision on Aloys Ntabakuze's Interlocutory Appeal on Questions of Law Raised by the 29 June 2006 Trial Chamber I Decision on Motion for Exclusion of Evidence (AC), 18 September 2006, footonote 40.

[58] See *Karemera et al.*, Oral decision, T. 27 February 2006, pp. 7-9, *Karemera et al.*, Decision on Defence Oral Motions for Exclusion of Witness XBM's Testimony, for Sanctions against the Prosecution and for Exclusion of Evidence outside the Scope of the Indictment (TC), 19 October 2006, para. 20. See also International Criminal Tribunal for Former Yugoslavia, Rules of Procedure and Evidence, Rule 89(D).

[59] See for e.g.: Speeches of President Sindikubabwo and Prime Minister Kambanda in Butare on 19 April 1994: T. 23 September 2005, pp. 2 and 4; Mugesera speech and meeting with Mathieu Ngirumpatse following the Mugesera's speech (T. 23 February 2006, pp. 26 and 28; the Defence withdrew its application); CDR party rally at MRND Palace in Gisenyi in March 1994 and Speech of Jean-Bosco Barayagwiza at that rally (T. 21 June 2006, pp. 27-35).

occasions, some evidence was considered as admissible because it was not a material fact that needed to be pleaded in the Indictment.[60] The Trial Chamber also admitted evidence to the extent that it might be relevant to the proof of any allegation sufficiently pleaded in the indictment.[61] In other circumstances, **[page 15]** the Trial Chamber found admissible evidence on some material facts which were not explicitly set forth in the Indictment but of which the Accused had received timely, clear and consistent notice that it would be part of the Prosecution case against them.[62]

34. All along the proceedings, the Trial Chamber bore in mind the rights of the Accused, and found that it was satisfied that their rights to be informed of the charges against them and to have adequate time and facilities for the preparation of their defence were not infringed by the admission of evidence in question.[63] There is no reason for the remaining Judges to depart from the Trial Chamber's prior findings on each individual admission.

---

60 See for e.g.: MRND meeting at Cyasimakamba in Kibungo in 1992 (T. 21 September 2005, pp. 12 and 16 and T. 22 September 2005, p. 19: The Chamber decided that it would not strike the witness' answer merely because he added more information than might have been necessary for the exact answer. The Presiding Judge explained that this evidence was probative, and did not fall within the category of evidence which should be excluded for the reasons of prejudice); Meeting on 7 April 1994 at the Hotel Diplomat between Ngirumpatse, Nzirorera and Interahamwe leaders concerning roadblocks and letter containing instructions (The Chamber noted that paragraphs 36, 37, 38 and 39 of the Indictment unambiguously put on notice the allegation that Mathieu Ngirumpatse participated in the setting of roadblocks and their control and that was part of the Prosecution's case. The Chamber therefore found that ALG's testimony fell within the framework of the allegations that were set out in the Indictment itself. In addition, the Chamber noted that some of the witness' testimony, particularly with regard to the letter and the specific instructions to set up a roadblock resulted from his response to the enquiry about how he knew that the MRND members, including Ngirumpatse, had authorized the roadblocks, T. 30 October 2006, p. 47).

61 See for e.g.: Swearing-in ceremony of President Habyarimana on 5 January 1994 and violence that followed (admitted as historical background, T. 11 October 2005, p. 46); arrests and murders of Tutsis in Kigali in October 1990 (admitted as historical background; the Presiding Judge specified as follows: "we think that you are entitled to lead background information, we don't think that you should go so far as to lead evidence of crimes that were not referred to in the Indictment", T. 23 February 2006, pp. 25-26); Speeches of Mathieu Ngirumpatse at MRND rally in Kibungo in 1993 and in Murambi in 1993 (the Chamber specified: "no convictions can be based on anything that occurred at that meeting", and [...] "what we are permitting this evidence about is purely for the purpose of context and background information; "it has nothing to do with the specific charges in the indictment and cannot be used for that purpose"; T. 27 February 2006, pp. 7-11); Evidence on a network called *réseau zero* (admitted to the extent that it is related to the existence of the *Akazu*; but inadmissible to prove the material fact that the Accused participated in this network, Decision on Defence Oral Motions for Exclusion of Witness XBM's Testimony, For Sanctions Against the Prosecution and for Exclusion of Evidence Outside the Scope of the Indictment (TC), 19 October 2006, para. 28); RTLM Ceremony at Mt. Muhe in September 1993, distribution of weapons in Kabari trading center in September 1993, meeting and distribution of weapons at Mutura commune office in January 1994, meeting of military leaders and population at Meridien Hotel in Gisenyi in May 1994 and massacre of Tutsis at Nyundo parish in Gisenyi (admitted for the sole purpose of showing the collaboration between civilians and military officials, Decision on Defence Oral Motions for Exclusion of Witness XBM's Testimony, For Sanctions Against the Prosecution and for Exclusion of Evidence Outside the Scope of the Indictment (TC), 19 October 2006, para. 42); Killings of Tutsi in Byahi secteur of Gisenyi in 1992 (admitted as a purely "background circumstance", T. 16 May 2006, p. 53); Killings of Tutsi at Mudende University in April 1994 and the participation of Colonel Anatole Nsengiyumva in that killings (admitted for the sole purpose of showing the cooperation between civilians and the military authorities, T. 21 June 2006, p.1: "The massacre itself cannot be a material fact that will be used against the Accused"; see also pp. 11-13); Interahamwe assaults against opposition party members in 1992 (admitted as historical background, "these are matters on which a conviction cannot be based", T. 8 June 2006, p. 25); Meetings between Interahamwe leaders and the accused in Murambi after 12 April 1994 (T. 9 November 2006, p. 26; Nzirorera telephone call to gendarmes to arrange release of Interahamwe who had attacked the Ruhengeri Court of Appeals (T. 4 December 2006, p. 35).

62 See for e.g.: Admission of the speech of Leon Mugesera on 22 November 1992 (T. 10 October 2005, p. 50); the Chamber also allowed the Prosecution to question the witness as to the general reaction to Mugesera's speech. But it did not allow the question which sought to elicit the identity of specific individuals who were killed and the circumstances of their death because this introduced issues which were not pleaded in the Indictment and which adequate notice was not given (T. 10 October 2005, pp. 58-59); Meetings in Gisenyi in 1992 to 1993 and Nzirorera's presence at distribution of weapons in Gisenyi after 6 April 1994 at a ceremony at the 47th Battalion (Decision on Defence Oral Motions for Exclusion of Witness XBM's Testimony, For Sanctions Against the Prosecution and for Exclusion of Evidence Outside the Scope of the Indictment (TC), 19 October 2006, paras. 29-37); Meeting on 10 or 11 April 1994 at the Hotel Diplomat between MRND leaders and Interahamwe and the distribution of weapons after this meeting (T. 27 October 2006, p. 5); Presence of Karemera at 23 October 1993 "Hutu Power" rally and Speech of Karemera at 16 January 1994 MRND rally at Nyamirambo Stadium (T. 27 October 2006, p. 21).

63 See particularly *Karemera et al.*, Decision on Defence Oral Motions for Exclusion of Witness XBM's Testimony, for Sanctions against the Prosecution and for Exclusion of Evidence outside the Scope of the Indictment (TC), 19 October 2006, paras. 11-20; also see references hereinafter.

35. The Trial Chamber also emphasized that curing a defect in the Indictment must be the exception, and that when the indictment suffers from numerous defects, there still may be a risk of prejudice to the Accused, even if the defects are found to be cured:

> In particular, the accumulation of a large number of material facts not plead in the indictment reduces the clarity and relevancy of that indictment, which may have an impact on the ability of the Accused to know the case he or she has to meet for purposes of preparing an adequate **[page 16]** defence.
> Further, while the addition of a few material facts may not prejudice the Defence in the preparation of its case, the addition of numerous material facts increases the risk of prejudice, as the Defence may not have sufficient time and resources to investigate properly all the new material facts.
> Thus, where a Trial Chamber considers that a defective indictment has been subsequently cured by the Prosecution, it should further consider whether the extent of the defects in the indictment materially prejudice an accused's right to a fair trial, by hindering the preparation of a proper defence.[64]

The Trial Chamber clearly held that the admission of evidence by curing an Indictment requires continuous evaluation of their impact on the rights of the Accused. Accordingly, even if at a certain stage some evidence of material fact not pleaded in the Indictment is admitted, this does not prejudice subsequent consideration of the concept of the accumulation of curing.[65]

36. Having therefore also considered, as a whole, Joseph Nzirorera's objections to the admission of some evidence, the remaining Judges are satisfied that the trial has been fair and that the Accused are in a position to understand the charges against them and have benefited from adequate time and facilities to mount their defence.

3. Testimony of Prosecution Witnesses under Pseudonym

37. According to Joseph Nzirorera and Mathieu Ngirumpatse, the Trial Chamber has erred in law and denied their rights to a fair and public trial by granting a blanket authorization for each Prosecution witness to testify under a pseudonym and refusing to reconsider this protective order.[66]

38. This issue has already been adjudicated on several occasions, having due regard for the rights of the Accused. When deciding that the identifying information of protected Prosecution witnesses would not be disclosed to the public, the Trial Chamber explicitly balanced the need to protect witnesses with the rights of the Accused, in accordance with Rules 69 and 75 of the Rules and the established jurisprudence of the Tribunal.[67] The Trial Chamber ruled again later on the matter, when Joseph Nzirorera requested reconsideration of **[page 17]** the protective orders.[68] At that time, the Trial Chamber considered that it was "still satisfied that the protective measures contained in its Order of 10 December 2004 will not prejudice the Defence".[69] In addition to these Decisions, for each Prosecution witness, the Trial Chamber has systematically heard Defence Counsel for Nzirorera on the same issue. In each case, his requests to reconsider the protective orders were dismissed on the ground that he had not shown the existence of any new fact or circumstance to support its application, or that if a new fact or circumstance had been shown to exist, it did not justify reconsideration of the protective orders.[70]

---

64 T. 27 October 2006, pp. 20-21.

65 See for e.g.: *Karemera et al.*, Decision on Defence Oral Motions for Exclusion of Witness XBM's Testimony, for Sanctions against the Prosecution and for Exclusion of Evidence Outside the Scope of the Indictment (TC), 19 October 2006; T. 27 October 2006, pp. 20-21.

66 Joseph Nzirorera's submissions, paras. 124-146.

67 *Prosecutor v. Edouard Karemera, Mathieu Ngirumpatse, Joseph Nzirorera and André Rwamakuba*, Case No. ICTR-98-44-R75, Order on Protective Measures for Prosecution Witnesses (TC), 10 December 2004.

68 *Karemera et al.*, Decision on the Defence Motions for Reconsideration of Protective Measures for Prosecution Witnesses (TC), 29 August 2005, para. 11.

69 *Ibid.*, para. 12.

70 The Defence Counsel submitted his application routinely for each Prosecution witness (see T. 16 February 2006, p. 27; T. 15 May 2006, p. 7; T. 22 May 2006, p. 19; T. 26 October 2006, p. 11; T. 8 November 2006, p. 3; T. 1 December 2006, p. 16; T. 8 December 2006, p. 4). During the trial session held in June 2006, while the Defence Counsel for Nzirorera made his routine application to withdraw the pseudonym (with respect to Witnesses BTH and XBM), he acknowledged that the Chamber had already ruled on that matter, but "wanted to make [his] record". The Chamber referred to its prior findings on the same matter, since this was a routine motion and it did not find a new circumstances justifying reconsideration (T. 8 June 2006, p. 9; T. 20 June 2006, p. 48).

39. To support its assertion that the use of pseudonyms was not warranted in the present case, Joseph Nzirorera alleges, for the first time, that some Prosecution witnesses expressed no security concerns in their reconfirmation statements.[71] After reviewing these statements, the remaining Judges are not persuaded by this argument. The witnesses only state that they do not have any security concern "for the moment", namely at the time when the statement was taken in 2003 or 2004. This elliptic mention must be put in the particular context of the reconfirmation statements which are concise notes of one page drafted by an investigator with a view to reconfirming the content of a witness' anticipated testimony. In the Judge's view, these statements do not contain sufficient and clear information showing a new fact or circumstance justifying a different conclusion that the protective orders were warranted for these witnesses as well.

40. In any event, all along the proceedings, the Trial Chamber has sought to limit as much as possible the protective measures to what was strictly necessary, taking into account the rights of the Accused. Each time a witness has declared that he or she no longer has any security concerns and is ready to testify under his or her real name, the protective orders were **[page 18]** accordingly amended.[72] The Trial Chamber has also always aimed to enhance the fairness and publicity of the proceedings by ensuring that any closed session be reduced to the minimum required, and where it was found that a closed session was ultimately not warranted, it was ordered that the transcripts be considered and reclassified as open sessions.[73] Contrary to Joseph Nzirorera's assertion,[74] the remaining Judges are satisfied that the open session of the testimony of each witness was sufficiently extensive to allow public observation.

41. In light of these circumstances, the remaining Judges holds the view that no unfairness has resulted for the Accused from the use of pseudonyms by Prosecution witnesses.

4. Alleged Presentation by the Prosecutor of Perjured Testimony

42. Joseph Nzirorera, joined by Mathieu Ngirumpatse, contends that the Prosecutor has called witnesses who he knew or should have known would offer false testimony and, by doing so, has violated their right to a fair trial.[75] According to Nzirorera, Prosecution Witnesses Ahmed Mbonyunkiza, UB, ZF, BTH, AWB, ALG, HH and GBU provided evidence containing contradictions with their prior statements and testimonies, or with evidence from other Prosecution witnesses. He also points out that some of these witnesses have acknowledged or been found to have given false testimony in other instances.

43. Again the Accused submissions only reiterate their prior arguments and address Trial Chamber's prior findings thereto.[76] Concerning Witness UB, the Trial Chamber found that **[page 19]** there was an

---

71 Nzirorera's submissions, para. 141. The Defence refers to the reconfirmation statements of Prosecution Witnesses ALZ, taken on 20 January 2004; AMC, taken on 20 January 2004; ANP, taken on 22 October 2003; AJY, taken on 14 January 2004; Witness GBU, taken on 21 October 2003; GBV, taken on 21 October 2003; KGV, taken on 22 January 2004; GOB, taken on 4 June 2003.

72 See Prosecution Witnesses Ahmed Mbonyunkiza (T. 20 September 2005, p. 22). Prosecution Witness Frank Claeys also testified under his name (T. 21 November 2006, p. 39). The Chamber waived the protective measures with regard to Prosecution Witness GBY, as requested by the Prosecutor Counsel who indicated that the witness wished to testify under his real name, subject to reviewing this waiver whereupon questions will have been put to the witness on this issue during his testimony before the Tribunal (T. 8 December 2006, p. 22).

73 See, e.g., T. 20 September 2005, p. 12; T. 19 October 2005, p. 52-54; T. 20 October 2005, p.1-13; T. 20 October 2005, p.18; T. 13 February 2006, p. 9; T. 28 February 2006, p. 46; T. 22 May 2006, p. 1-2; T. 7 November 2006, p. 47; T. 10 November 2006, p. 34; T. 9 November 2006, p. 39 (the Chamber ordered that a portion of the closed session transcript of 8 November 2006 be placed in open session); T. 10 October 2005, p. 18 (the Chamber reconsidered the special protective measures for Witness T and accordingly granted the Defence motion to hear the witness in open session).

74 Nzirorera's submissions, particularly at para. 145.

75 Nzirorera's submissions, paras. 147-203. Prosecution Witnesses Ahmed Mbonyunkiza, UB, ZF, BTH, AWB, ALG, HH, GBU, as well as Prosecution witnesses who were initially called in the first trial to testify against André Rwamakuba while he was still indicted in the joint trial.

76 See T. 14 October 2005, p. 19-21 (The Defence moved the Chamber to order an investigation for false testimony of Prosecution Witness Mbonyunkiza on the grounds that his testimony was in contradiction with the testimony of Prosecution Witness G. The Chamber denied the Motion stating that it was premature and that it could not initiate an investigation every time there was a contradiction of testimony); T. 20 October 2005, p. 54-56 (The Defence invited the Prosecution to withdraw the testimony of Prosecution Witness Mbonyunkiza); T. 1 March 2006, p. 36-37 (The Defence reiterated an application for an investigation for false testimony of Witness Mbonyunkiza during Witness UB's cross-examination). See also references hereinafter. So far, the Chamber has not been seized as such by any Defence Motion for an investigation for false testimony for Prosecution Witnesses ZF, ALG, HH,

insufficient factual basis for initiating an investigation for false testimony.[77] The Trial Chamber also denied the motion filed by Joseph Nzirorera, supported by Mathieu Ngirumpatse, for investigation for false testimony of Witness Mbonyunkiza.[78] On that occasion, the applicable principles for a Chamber to order an investigation for false testimony according to Rule 91(B) of the Rules and the established jurisprudence of this Tribunal were recalled in detail. Specifically, it was emphasized that contradictory evidence between witnesses' testimony is an insufficient basis to demonstrate that a witness intended to mislead a Chamber and to cause harm, and therefore to order an investigation for false testimony.[79]

44. Each time there is an alleged contradiction in the testimony of a witness, it cannot be concluded that the witness has committed perjury. Should the remaining Judges admit the Joseph Nzirorera's interpretation of perjury, there would be no more room for an assessment of the credibility and reliability of the witnesses at the end of the case, while this assessment must be done considering the evidence as a whole.[80] Furthermore, Nzirorera will have an opportunity to rebut or challenge the Prosecution evidence in the presentation of its case. No unfairness can therefore result from the admission of alleged contradictory evidence at this stage. The existence of contradictions is a factor to be used when determining the probative value of the evidence presented by the parties during trial.[81]

45. Furthermore, the remaining Judges cannot see how Joseph Nzirorera and Mathieu Ngirumpatse can be prejudiced by the testimony of witnesses who did not give any evidence in this trial. According to Nzirorera, the Prosecutor had information in his possession from which he should have known that Witness AWB was prepared to give false testimony. This witness, however, refused to testify explaining specifically that he did not want to give false testimony against the Accused persons.[82] Nzirorera also submits that most of the witnesses scheduled to testify against André Rwamakuba during the first trial while the latter was still jointly indicted with Edouard Karemera, Mathieu Ngirumpaste and Joseph Nzirorera, were found to be unreliable. In his view, the Prosecutor also knew that these witnesses had **[page 20]** provided conflicting statements to its own investigators and Rwandan authorities. Nzirorera's reference to witnesses in *Rwamakuba* case is, however, not relevant to the alleged unfairness of this trial since these witnesses were not called in this trial, as a result of the severance of Rwamakuba from this case.[83]

5. Failure of the Rwandan Government to Produce Statements of Prosecution Witnesses

46. Joseph Nzirorera, supported by Mathieu Ngirumpatse, claims that during the trial, the Accused have been required to cross-examine Prosecution witnesses in the absence of prior statements made to Rwandan authorities or on the basis of such statements disclosed at the last minute.[84] Nzirorera submits that his own efforts, the Prosecutor's efforts, and the requests made by the Trial Chamber, have not resulted in the timely production of the prior Rwandan statements of Prosecution witnesses needed for cross-examination.[85] In his view, the Trial Chamber has refused to enforce any of its requests and as a result, he has been denied his right to effectively cross-examine the Prosecution witnesses and therefore his right to a fair trial.[86]

47. Again, Joseph Nzirorera only reiterates arguments upon which the Trial Chamber in the instant case has already adjudicated. Numerous motions have been filed by the Accused on this ongoing issue and, as a

BTH and GBU. In its Decision of 29 December 2006, the Chamber stated the applicable law and necessary requirements for an order to investigate for false testimony

77 T. 28 February 2006, p. 2.

78 *Karemera et al.*, Decision on Defence Motion for Investigation of Prosecution Witness Ahmed Mbonyunkiza for False Testimony (TC), 29 December 2006.

79 *Ibid.*, para. 7.

80 *Prosecutor v. André Rwamakuba*, Case No. ICTR-98-44C-T, Judgement (TC), 20 September 2006, paras. 62-69.

81 *Karemera et al.*, Decision on Defence Motion for Investigation of Prosecution Witness Ahmed Mbonyunkiza for False Testimony (TC), 29 December 2006, para. 7.

82 T. 6 July 2006, pp. 28-29.

83 *Prosecutor v. Edouard Karemera, Mathieu Ngirumpatse, Joseph Nzirorera and André Rwamakuba*, Case No. ICTR-98-44, PT, Decision on Severance of André Rwamakuba and For Leave to File Amended Indictment (TC), 14 February 2005.

84 Nzirorera's submissions, paras. 204-219.

85 Nzirorera's submissions, paras. 218.

86 Nzirorera's submissions, paras. 218 and 219.

result, several decisions have been delivered.[87] The Trial Chamber has provided every practicable facility under the Statue and the Rules in order to assist the Accused in presenting their case, in accordance with the established case-law of the Tribunal. The Prosecutor has also displayed continuous efforts, both past and present, in **[page 21]** seeking to provide the Accused with as many judicial records as possible from Rwandan authorities.[88] Furthermore, it appears that, in some instances, Nzirorera did not use the facilities at his disposal to obtain the documents sought or he failed to adduce any evidence or give any information of the existence of these records or their content or show how these documents may be relevant for the preparation of his defence.[89]

48. Moreover, where appropriate, the Trial Chamber also explicitly considered whether the rights of the Accused, including their rights to have adequate time and facilities for the preparation of their defence and to cross-examine a witness, were impaired by a late disclosure – or the absence of any disclosure – of Rwandan statements.[90] Depending on each circumstance, the Trial Chamber found that there was no prejudice caused to the rights of the Accused or that witnesses could be recalled where necessary. So far there has been no request made by the Accused to recall any witness. A review of the proceedings also shows that the Accused have extensively cross-examined the Prosecution witnesses.[91]

49. In light of all these circumstances, it cannot be concluded that the trial has been rendered unfair by alleged late disclosure, or alleged non-disclosure, of some Rwandan statements. **[page 22]**

6. Taking Testimony of Witnesses G and T by Video-Link

50. Joseph Nzirorera, supported by Mathieu Ngirumpatse, contends that the testimony of two of the most important Prosecution witnesses, Witnesses G and T, by video-link violated their right to confront their

---

87 See: Decision on Motions for Order for Production of Documents by the Government of Rwanda and for Consequential Orders (TC), 13 February 2006; Decision on Defence Requests for Certification to Appeal Decision on Motions for Order for Production of Documents by the Government of Rwanda and for Consequential Orders (TC), 17 March 2006; Decision on Defence Motion to Report Government of Rwanda to United Nations Security Council (TC), 2 October 2006; Decision on Defence Motion to Compel Best Efforts to Obtain and Disclose Statements and Testimony of Witness UB (TC), 10 October 2006; Decision on Defence Motion for Further Order to Obtain Documents in Possession of Government of Rwanda (TC), 27 November 2006; Decision on Defence Motion for Exclusion of Witness GK's Testimony or for Request for Cooperation from Government of Rwanda (TC), 27 November 2006; Decision on Defence Motion to Obtain Documents Pertaining to Witness HH in Possession of Government of Rwanda (TC), 27 November 2006; Decision on Defence Motion for Request for Cooperation to Government of Rwanda: MRND Videotape (TC), 14 December 2006; see also Decision on Motions to Compel Inspection and Disclosure and to Direct Witnesses to bring Judicial and Immigration Records (TC), 14 September 2005, where the Chamber required, pursuant to Rule 98 of the Rules of Procedure and Evidence, the Prosecution to use its best efforts to obtain statements made to Rwandan authorities and records pertaining to the criminal prosecution of the Witnesses AWB, BDW, BGD, HH and KGV, as well as any other witness for whom such materials have not been fully disclosed.

88 See: Decision on Defence Motion for Exclusion of Witness GK's Testimony or for Request for Cooperation from Government of Rwanda (TC), 27 November 2006, para. 11; Decision on Defence Motion for Further Order to Obtain Documents in Possession of Government of Rwanda (TC), 27 November 2006, para. 12 (referring to: Prosecutor's Response to the Motion; see also Prosecutor's Submission Concerning Best Efforts to Obtain Rwanda Judicial Records of Witness HH, filed on 17 November 2006, following the Chamber's Order made orally on 16 November 2006. Further effort has been put in place by the Prosecution. In a recent will-say statement of Witness GK given on 7 November 2006, the witness provides details as to his judicial records, statements and testimonies he gave before Rwandan authorities. As a result, three documents were disclosed to the Defence.)

89 See: Decision on Defence Motion for Further Order to Obtain Documents in Possession of Government of Rwanda (TC), 27 November 2006, paras. 14-15; Decision on Defence Motion for Exclusion of Witness GK's Testimony or for Request for Cooperation from Government of Rwanda (TC), 27 November 2006, paras. 10 and 14.

90 See: Decision on Motions for Order for Production of Documents by the Government of Rwanda and for Consequential Orders (TC), 13 February 2006; Witness HH: T. 17 November 2006, p. 2; Decision on Defence Motion to Obtain Documents Pertaining to Witness HH in Possession of Government of Rwanda (TC), 27 November 2006; Witness GK: Decision on Defence Motion for Exclusion of Witness GK's Testimony or for Request for Cooperation from Government of Rwanda (TC), 27 November 2006, para. 12.

91 The Prosecution Witnesses were cross-examined as follows: Ahmed Napoléon Mbonyunkiza, about six days; ALG, about six days; BTH, about four days; Frank Claeys, about two and a half days; G, about seven days; GK, about two days; GBU, about one and a half days; HH, about five and one quarter days; T, about five and one quarter days; UB, about nine and a half days; XBM, about four and one quarter days; ZF, about three and a half days. See also: Decision on Defence Motion to Obtain Documents Pertaining to Witness HH in Possession of Government of Rwanda (TC), 27 November 2006, para. 10: "The Chamber notes that the Defence has extensively cross-examined Witness HH where he openly admitted in court that he had lied on several occasions in his prior statements. Having heard Witness HH's testimony, the Chamber is of the view that the relevant credibility issues have been explored in a manner which would enable fair evaluation of the witness' credibility."

accusers.[92] While Nzirorera recognizes that this right is not absolute, he contends that there was no necessity for the testimony of these witnesses to be taken by video-link. Relying on the Appeals Chamber Decision in the *Zigiranyirazo* case,[93] he submits that the Trial Chamber in this case erred when ordering the video-link testimony of Witnesses G and T. According to Nzirorera, there is a serious risk that the Appeals Chamber will reverse the Trial Chamber's decisions and exclude the testimony of Witnesses G and T. Accordingly, in his view, the remaining Judges should determine that it would not serve the interests of justice to continue a trial in which the hearing of the two most important prosecution witnesses by video-link constituted a denial of a fair trial to the Accused and will be called into question by a subsequent Appeals Chamber decision.[94]

51. Again, there is no need for the remaining Judges to fully reiterate the articulated reasoning in the Trial Chamber's prior findings on this issue.[95] It must be however emphasized that in its Decision, the Trial Chamber sought a fair and equitable balance between the need to afford full respect to the rights of the Accused and considerations relating to the protection of witnesses. It relied upon the relevant provisions of the Statute and the Rules as well as the established jurisprudence of the Tribunal, and found that granting an order to permit Witnesses G and T to testify by video-link did not infringe the Accused's rights, particularly their right to confront the witness, neither the Accused's ability to observe the demeanour of the witnesses.[96] At the Accused's request, the Trial Chamber also permitted each Defence team and the Prosecutor to send one representative each to the location from **[page 23]** which Witnesses G and T would testify, in order to preserve the integrity of the proceedings.[97]

52. Furthermore, the Trial Chamber has already ruled upon Joseph Nzirorera's requests for disclosure of confidential documents filed by the Prosecutor in support of his motion for special protective measures for Witnesses G and T.[98] In each instance, the rights of the Accused, including their rights to fair and public proceedings and to cross-examine the Prosecution witnesses, were cautiously balanced with the need to protect the witnesses. Where appropriate, the Trial Chamber even ordered that an Annex filed confidentially by the Prosecutor concerning the special protective measures for Witnesses T be disclosed to the Defence in redacted form.[99]

53. Furthermore, a review of the testimony of Witnesses G and T shows that the Accused effectively and extensively exercised their rights to confront and cross-examine the witnesses. It is noteworthy that during the proceedings, Defence Counsel for Joseph Nzirorera described Witness T's testimony as "very truthful" and as "the most accurate testimony" heard during this trial.[100] In his current submissions, Nzirorera contends that some Prosecution witnesses made false testimony by comparing their evidence with the testimony of Witnesses G and T.[101] Such assertions make sense only if Nzirorera acknowledges, to a certain

---

92 Nzirorera's submissions, paras. 220-260.

93 *Prosecutor v. Protais Zigiranyirazo*, Case No. ICTR-2001-73-AR73, Decision on Interlocutory Appeal (AC), 30 October 2006.

94 Nzirorera's submissions, para. 260.

95 In the present case, four decisions were delivered on the same issue as a result of four motions submitted by the Defence for Nzirorera: Decision on the Prosecutor's Motion for Special Protective Measures for Witnesses G and T (TC), 14 September 2005; Decision on the Defence Motion to Unseal and for Application for Certification to Appeal Decision on the Prosecutor's Motion for Special Protective Measures for Witnesses G and T (TC), 7 October 2005; Decision on Defence Motion for Reconsideration of Special Protective Measures for Witness "T" (TC), 9 March 2006; Oral Order, T. 3 October 2005, p. 50.

96 Decision on the Prosecutor's Motion for Special Protective Measures for Witnesses G and T (TC), 14 September 2005, paras 13, 16 and 17. In its Decision of 7 October 2005, the Chamber reiterated that "[t]he special protective Measures ordered by the Chamber in the impugned Decision do not curtail the rights of the Accused, nor does the impugned Decision adversely affect the fairness of the trial." (Decision on the Defence Motion to Unseal and for Application for Certification to Appeal Decision on the Prosecutor's Motion for Special Protective Measures for Witnesses G and T, para. 11).

97 T. 3 October 2005, p. 50; Decision on Defence Motion for Reconsideration of Special Protective Measures for Witness "T" (TC), 9 March 2006.

98 Decision on Joseph Nzirorera's Motion to Compel Inspection and Disclosure (TC), 5 July 2005, paras. 4-6; Decision on Defence Motion for Disclosure of the Affidavit of Richard Renaud Related to Witnesses G & T (TC), 8 August 2005; Decision on Joseph Nzirorera's Motion For Disclosure of a Confidential Annex (TC), 12 September 2005.

99 Decision on Joseph Nzirorera's Motion for Disclosure of a Confidential Annex (TC), 12 September2005.

100 Mr. Robinson stated as follows: "Witness T, I want to, first of all, thank you for your testimony that you've given over the past few days. I think that this has probably been the most accurate testimony that we've heard during this trial. And while we have some differences of recollection and perhaps some differences of opinion, we find your testimony to be very truthful, and I want to thank you for that." (T. 26 May 2006, p. 29).

101 Nzirorera's submissions, paras. 165, 183 and 194.

extent, that the evidence given by Witnesses G and T was truthful. The presence of representatives of each Accused at the location of the testimony of these witnesses also offered additional guarantees as to the fairness of the proceedings.[102]

54. The question is now whether in light of the recent Appeals Chamber decision in the *Zigiranyirazo* case,[103] the Trial Chamber's Decision to authorize the testimony of Witnesses G and T by video-link was erroneous and resulted in an injustice thereby rendering the trial unfair. **[page 24]**

55. In the *Zigiranyirazo* case, the Trial Chamber decided to hear the testimony of Mr. Bagaragaza in person in The Netherlands while the accused, Mr. Zigiranyirazo, participated via video-link from Arusha.[104] The question before the Appeals Chamber was therefore whether the accused's right to be tried in his or her "presence", enshrined in Article 20(4)(d) of the Statute, referred to the physical presence of the accused in court before the Trial Judges.[105] The Appeals Chamber found that "[b]oth the Tribunal's legal framework and practice as well as that of the International Criminal Tribunal for the Former Yugoslavia ("ICTY") further reflect that Article 20(4)(d) provides for the physical presence of an accused at trial, as opposed to his facilitated presence via video-link".[106] As a result and under the specific circumstances of that case, the Appeals Chamber found that it was not satisfied that the Trial Chamber had properly exercised its discretion in deciding to impose limitations on Zigiranyirazo's s right to be present at his trial.[107]

56. The remaining Judges therefore do not agree with Joseph Nzirorera that the circumstances surrounding the testimony by video-link of Witnesses G and T are analogous to the facts in *Zigiranyirazo* case.

57. Furthermore, should the remaining Judges find that a continuation of the proceedings is in the interests of justice and should the Appeals Chamber subsequently find that the rights of the Accused were unwarrantedly and excessively restricted by taking the testimony of Witnesses G and T by video-link and that the Trial Chamber committed a discernible error, then the major risk would be for the Prosecutor to have the evidence of Witnesses G and T excluded.[108] In any event, a rehearing of the case would not be an appropriate remedy.

58. In view of these circumstances, the remaining Judges are satisfied that taking the testimony of Witnesses G and T by video-link did not render the trial unfair. No different conclusion is warranted following the Appeals Chamber's decision delivered in *Zigiranyirazo* case.

7. Interferences with the Right of the Defence to meet with Witnesses

59. Joseph Nzirorera, supported by Mathieu Ngirumpaste, submits that during the trial, the Prosecutor has interfered with the right of the Accused to interview Prosecution witnesses before their testimony.[109] He also claims that the Prosecution had attempted to interfere with **[page 25]** the interview between his Defence Counsel and Georges Rutaganda, who was not a Prosecution witness in this cas, but simply a detainee. In Nzirorera's view, his right to a fair trial was consequently infringed.

60. The remaining Judges note that each of these situations has already been adjudicated. Concerning the interview with Georges Rutaganda, the Trial Chamber in this case ruled twice on this matter, and granted Joseph Nzirorera's request to have his Defence Counsel meet with him without the presence of a representative of the Office of the Prosecutor.[110]

---

102 Witness G: T. 10 October 2005, p.1-2; Witness T: T. 22 May 2006, p. 8.

103 *Prosecutor v. Protais Zigiranyirazo*, Case No. ICTR-2001-73-AR73, Decision on Interlocutory Appeal (AC), 30 October 2006.

104 *Ibid.*, para. 5.

105 *Ibid.*, para. 8.

106 *Ibid.*, para. 12.

107 *Ibid.*, para. 17.

108 *Ibid.*, para. 24.

109 Nzirorera's submissions, paras. 261-279.

110 The Defence for Nzirorera filed a first motion on 24 March 2005 ("Joseph Nzirorera's Motion for Order Allowing Meeting with Defence Witness"); the Chamber granted in part the motion and order that the Defence Counsel meets Georges Rutaganda without the presence of a representative of the Prosecution, but in the presence of a representative of the Registrar (Decision on Joseph Nzirorera's Motion for Order Allowing Meeting with Defence Witness (TC), 13 July 2005). On 11 October 2005, at the

61. The other events raised in Joseph Nzirorera's submissions concern situations where his Defence Counsel requested to meet with Prosecution witnesses just before or during his or her testimony in court in order to show the witness any documents intended to be used during cross-examination and allegedly to save time in court.[111] The Trial Chamber has already dismissed the applications for meeting with Witnesses ZF and XBM considering that they were not warranted in light of the circumstances of the case.[112] It also granted in part Nzirorera's motion to reconsider protective orders as a result of incidents where the Prosecution Counsel had intervened during meetings between Defence Counsel and Prosecution witnesses.[113] On that occasion, the Trial Chamber explicitly referred to the jurisprudence of the Appeals Chamber that although each party has the right to contact and **[page 26]** interview a witness, this is not without limitation; this should not interfere with the course of justice, notably by generating for the witness a feeling of coercion or intimidation.[114] The Trial Chamber also questioned the repetitive requests made by Defence Counsel for Nzirorera to meet with Prosecution witnesses at the outset of their testimony in court without showing a legitimate need which went beyond the need to prepare a more effective cross-examination.[115]

62. It must be noted that there has been no allegation of any difficulty during meetings when the witness was not about to give evidence in court.[116] In the current submissions, Joseph Nzirorera even acknowledges that his Defence Counsel has had no difficulty meeting with witnesses in Rwanda.[117] His Counsel has also had the opportunity to meet with three Prosecution witnesses while they were already present in Arusha for the purpose of testifying before the Chamber.[118] In addition, the Trial Chamber also facilitated the meeting between the Defence Counsel for Nzirorera and 13 potential Prosecution witnesses, who could only be contacted and interviewed in accordance with the protective measures applicable to each of them.[119]

63. In view of these circumstances, the remaining Judges do not consider that the right of the Accused to meet with a witness has been unfairly impaired, or even impaired at all, and that any unfairness of the trial has resulted.

Defence's request (Joseph Nzirorera's Motion for Reconsideration or Certification to Appeal Decision on Motion for Order Allowing Meeting with Defence Witness, filed on 13 July 2005), the Chamber reconsidered its prior decision: it held that the Defence Counsel and Georges Rutaganda could meet without the presence of any third party, and ordered that the latter should not have any documents in his possession during the said meeting (Decision on Joseph Nzirorera's Motion for Reconsideration or Certification to Appeal Decision on Motion for Order Allowing Meeting with Defence Witness (TC), 11 October 2005).

[111] See Joseph Nzirorera's Motion for Reconsideration of Witness Protection Order, filed on 25 September 2006. See also Witness ALG:T. 23 May 2006, p. 26; Witness T: T. 26 October 2006, p. 52; Witness HH: T. 8 November 2006, p. 2; Witness GBU: T. 5 December 2006, p. 19.

[112] The Chamber denied the Defence motion to meet Witness ZF on the ground that he was in the middle of his testimony and that it was therefore not appropriate for the Defence Counsel to meet him (T. 23 May 2006, p. 26). Concerning Witness XBM, the Chamber noted that the witness did agree on conditions that the meeting did take place and during the meeting a problem developed. As previously indicated, the Chamber did not find appropriate to make an order to compel a Prosecution witness to speak with Defence counsel, as requested by the Defence. The Chamber also denied the Defence Motion to exclude the testimony of Witness XBM, considering that it was completely without merit in relation to the factual basis which was apparently being laid (T. 14 June 2006, p. 37).

[113] Decision on Reconsideration of Protective Measures for Prosecution Witnesses (TC), 30 October 2006, para. 4. In its motion filed on 25 September 2006, the Defence submitted that the Prosecution had repeatedly interfered with the right of the Accused to interview Prosecution witnesses who consent to meet with Counsel for the Accused before they give testimony. The Prosecution did not dispute that it intervened during those meetings but submitted that it had no choice in order to avoid any misrepresentation to, or coercion of the witness to obtain the witness' co-operation (see Prosecutor's Response filed on 29 September 2006).

[114] *Ibid.*, paras. 8 and 10; the Chamber relied upon *Prosecutor v. Mile Mrksic*, Case No. IT-95-13/1-AR73, Decision on Defence Interlocutory Appeal on Communication with Potential Witnesses of the Opposite Party (AC), 30 July 2003.

[115] *Ibid.*, para. 10. As a result, the Chamber ordered that "[e]xcept under exceptional circumstances, such meeting should not take place at the outset of the witness' testimony in court".

[116] See *Karemera et al.*, Decision on Reconsideration of Protective Measures for Prosecution Witnesses (TC), 30 October 2006, para. 9.

[117] Nzirorera's submissions, para. 275.

[118] *Ibidem.*

[119] Decision on Defence Written Request to Interview Prosecution Witnesses (TC), 20 September 2005. The Defence requested permission to contact 13 persons who were potential Prosecution witnesses and could have information concerning Witness T. The Chamber granted the Motion, allowing the Defence to meet with Witnesses GMT, COB and CBO without the presence of any representative of the Prosecution; and referred the matter to Trial Chamber I in *Bagosora* case with respect to Witnesses ADD, AHP, APA, APB, APC, APD, APE, DCY, FBU, and Trial Chamber II in *Ndindiliyimana* for Witness HAF, since these Chambers were the competent organs to rule upon the protective measures applying to each of these persons.

64. In conclusion, the remaining Judges note that Joseph Nzirorera's submissions, supported by Mathieu Ngirumpatse, are mainly a repetition of arguments already submitted to the Trial Chamber in this case and upon which it has already ruled. Each issue raised by these co-Accused in their submissions have already been carefully considered, adjudicated and monitored in a manner consistent with the applicable law, including the Statute, the Rules **[page 27]** of Procedure and Evidence and prevailing jurisprudence. Particularly, the Trial Chamber has constantly sought to guarantee a fair trial to each co-Accused and duly taken into account their rights. As a result, depending on each circumstance, the Trial Chamber has either found that the rights of the Accused were not infringed; or ordered the appropriate remedy where necessary. Additional measures have also been decided by the Chamber to continuously enhance the fairness of the proceedings. The remaining Judges do not find in the submissions filed by Joseph Nzirorera and Mathieu Ngirumpatse any factual circumstance or error in law that would justify a different conclusion as to the fairness of the trial.

65. The mere fact that the Trial Chamber has delivered decisions dismissing, in whole or in part, some Accused's requests cannot be considered as rendering the trial unfair. In this case, the Trial Chamber paid, conversely, constant attention to the issues raised by the Accused. Over a period of two years, more than 80 decisions were delivered on Defence motions, which in some circumstances were repetitive applications. This judicial process could furthermore be subject to Appeal Chamber's review at a later stage.

66. Moreover, if Joseph Nzirorera concedes that the appellate process will remedy defects at the trial level then the trial process cannot be said to be unfair, since the appeal is part of this process. It is illogical to say that the possibility of an appellate reversal is an indication that the trial is unfair because appellate review is one of the fair trial guarantees.

67. In view of the circumstances, the remaining Judges consider that there have been no irregularities in the course of the trial which cast doubt on its fairness. The Judges must now determine unanimously what would best serve the interests of justice – a continuation or a rehearing of the proceedings – taking into account all circumstances of the case.

3. Continuation of the Proceedings in the Interests of Justice

68. Joseph Nzirorera, joined by Mathieu Ngirumpatse, contends that the interests of justice would not be served by continuing the trial for various other reasons than the fairness of the trial. In his view, it will take the substitute Judge many months before he or she is in a position to certify sufficient familiarity with the case to join it. Relying upon hours spent in courtroom, the number of exhibits admitted as well as the oral and written motions made, Nzirorera estimates 479 hours of videotapes of trial sessions (for 110 trial days over a 15 month period).[120] In Mathieu Ngirumpatse's view, it is not in the interests of justice to continue the proceedings with a substitute Judge because he or she will have an imperfect **[page 28]** knowledge of the case. Particularly, he contends that the substitute Judge will only have a limited access to many oral decisions delivered by the Trial Chamber in this case.[121] Ngirumpatse also stresses the fact that many decisions related to the evidence were issued by the Trial Chamber during the proceedings – decisions in which the substitute Judge did not participate. Nzirorera further observes that the Trial Chamber sat in absence of Judge Kam for four days during the cross-examination of Prosecution Witness Mbonyunkiza. He therefore contends that the replacement of Judge Short will mean that only one of the three Judges on the Trial Chamber will have observed the demeanour of this witness on cross-examination. As to Edouard Karemera, he consents to the continuation of the proceedings provided that the substitute Judge enjoys enough time to review the videotapes of all the records in the instant proceedings and therefore be familiar with the case.[122]

69. The preference for live testimony to be heard by each and every judge in the adjudicative process is enshrined in the Rules.[123] But this does not form an unbending requirement.[124] The Rules and the case-law

120 Nzirorera's submissions, para. 16.

121 Ngirumpatse' s submissions, para. 8.

122 Karemera's submissions, p. 3.

123 See Rules of Procedure and Evidence, Rule 90 (A). *Nyiramasuhuko* Appeals Chamber Decision on Continuation, para. 25; *Karemera* Appeals Chamber Decision on Continuation, para. 60.

124 *Nyiramasuhuko* Appeals Chamber Decision on Continuation, para. 25.

show that exceptions can be made to live testimony. For example, under Rule 15 *bis* (A) of the Rules, a witness can be heard by two judges over a short period of time.[125] In these circumstances, the absent Judge will review the records of the proceedings, including the transcripts, audio and video-records, to observe the demeanor of the witness. Rule 90 (A), prescribing the general principle of oral testimony, explicitly provides for an exception to hear a witness by means of a deposition.[126] In application of Rules 54 and 75 of the Rules, Trial Chambers have also permitted the hearing of witnesses by video-link where necessary.[127]

70. The Appeals Chamber has also stressed, in case of continuation of proceedings under Rule 15 *bis*, the need to have the substitute Judge "familiarise" himself or herself with "the **[page 29]** record" of the proceedings, whatever that record may contain. This familiarization can be done through the transcripts, audio and video-records of the testimonies.[128]

71. In the present case, 13 witnesses have been heard so far over a list of more than a hundred Prosecution witnesses.[129] Thanks to video-recording of each witness, accurate transcripts, extensive reliance on printed exhibits, significant reliance on filmed and taped evidence, the fidelity and accessibility of the trial record in this case is so high that the gap in mastery of the case between the substitute Judge and the sitting Judges is likely to be of little practical significance. In the opinion of the remaining Judges, a substitute Judge should have little difficulty mastering and being familiar with the case within a reasonable amount of time. The fact that the substitute Judge did not participate in the decision making process of prior decisions of the Trial Chamber will also have little practical significance on the proceedings. First, he or she will review all of them. Second, the existence of these prior decisions will not preclude him or her from expressing his or her view on any issue at any stage of the proceedings.

72. Furthermore, although Judge Kam was indeed absent for four days during the cross-examination of Prosecution Witness Mbonyunkiza,[130] each of the remaining Judges of the Trial Chamber was able to observe, at first-hand, the witness' demeanour for approximately 11 day period, including for the major part of his cross-examination.[131] It must be also stressed that in addition to seeing the witness for those days, Judge Kam reviewed the transcripts, audio and video-records of Witness Mbonyunkiza's testimony for the four days during which he was not present. He is in as good a position as he would have been had he been present throughout the testimony.

73. In view of these circumstances, the remaining Judges are satisfied that the substitute Judge will be in a position to familiarize himself or herself with the records of the proceedings. **[page 30]**

74. As described above, the remaining Judges have already concluded to the overall fairness of the proceedings, despite the contrary contention of Joseph Nzirorera and Mathieu Ngirumpatse.[132]

---

125 Rules of Procedure and Evidence, Rule 15 *bis* (A): "If (i) a Judge is, for illness or other urgent personal reasons, or for reasons of authorised Tribunal business, unable to continue sitting in a part-heard case for a period which is likely to be of short duration, and (ii) the remaining Judges of the Chamber are satisfied that it is in the interests of justice to do so, those remaining Judges of the Chamber may order that the hearing of the case continue in the absence of that Judge for a period of not more than five working days".

126 Rules of Procedure and Evidence, Rule 90 (A): "Witnesses shall, in principle, be heard directly by the Chambers unless a Chamber has ordered that the witness be heard by means of a deposition as provided for in Rule 71". Rule 71 (A) reads as follows: "At the request of either party, a Trial Chamber may, in exceptional circumstances and in the interests of justice, order that a deposition be taken for use at trial, and appoint, for that purpose, a Presiding Officer."

127 *Nyiramasuhuko* Appeals Chamber Decision on Continuation, para. 33; *Karemera* Appeals Chamber Decision on Continuation, para. 58.

128 *Karemera* Appeals Chamber Decision on Continuation, paras. 37-38.

129 On 4 October 2006, the Prosecutor filed an amended witness list. On 11 December 2006, the Chamber ordered him to drastically reduce the number of witnesses being called to give evidence of rape and sexual assault in relation to Count Five of the Indictment (Decision on Prosecution Motion for Admission of Evidence of Rape and Sexual Assault Pursuant to Rule 92*bis* of the Rules; and Order for Reduction of Prosecution Witness List (TC), 11 December 2006, paras. 22-28).

130 See T. 26, 27, 28 and 29 October 2005.

131 The witness started his testimony on 20 September 2005; he was examined in chief for full four days (T. 20, 21 and 22 September 2005; on 23 September 2005, the Chamber adjourned at 11.04 am); he was then cross-examined by Defence Counsel for Ngirumpatse (T. 26 and 27 September 2005, full days), the Defence Counsel for Karemera (T. 27 and 28 September 2006, full days) and the Defence Counsel for Nzirorera (T. 28 September 2006, full day; on 29 September 2006, the Chamber adjourned at 3.40 pm; T. 3 October 2006, full day; T. 24 October 2005, full day; on 21, 25, 27 and 28 October, he testified in alternative with Prosecution Witness G).

132 See above.

75. In that respect, it must be particularly emphasized that the admission of some evidence by the Trial Chamber in this case does not preclude the future Trial Chamber from considering, at a later stage and particularly at the time of the Judgement, whether accumulations of curing the Indictment have resulted in an unfair trial and decide the appropriate remedy, including exclusion of evidence.

76. The remaining Judges are no more persuaded by Joseph Nzirorera's argument that the admission of the evidence in question will expand the scope and therefore the duration of the trial and consequently result in unfairness to the Accused. The Defence does not have the same burden of proof as the Prosecutor and does not have to adduce rebuttal evidence to the Prosecution case. The Defence's evidence must only raise a reasonable doubt within the Prosecution case.[133]

77. A fair trial also encompasses the right of each Accused to be tried without undue delay.[134] This element, as well as the fact that the Accused are currently detained while the proceedings are ongoing, must also be taken into account by the remaining Judges when determining whether a continuation of the proceedings would serve, or not, the interests of justice.

78. Contrary to Mathieu Ngirumpatse's contention, the remaining Judges do not consider that the right of the Accused to be tried without undue delay can no longer be guaranteed. The reasonableness of the length of the current proceedings must be assessed in light of several factors, including the complexity of the case, the complexity of the investigations, the joinder of Accused, the number of motions filed by the parties.[135] **[page 31]**

79. It is the remaining Judges view that the time it would take for familiarization by the substitute Judge is much less than the time required for a rehearing. This is because the review time could be continuous whereas the rehearing process necessitates holding hearings that will be necessarily interrupted and divided in several sessions.

80. Furthermore, the remaining Judges consider that the experience gained during the 15 months of the trial will inform the Trial Chamber's decision-making on the efficient and effective management of the trial process and to the completion of the trial without undue delay, including scheduling for improved and faster presentation of the evidence in the trial and diminishing or eliminating the regurgitation of issues already adjudicated upon.

81. In view of all the circumstances of the case, the remaining Judges finds that a continuation of the proceedings will facilitate the fundamental right of the Accused to be tried without undue delay. This will also contribute to limiting the length of the provisional detention of the Accused.

82. Additionally, the fact that one of the Accused consents to the continuation of the proceedings requires consideration of his rights to a trial without undue delay. An alternative to a continuation would be a bifurcated trial with the additional expenditure of judicial resources. The remaining Judges also consider that a burden would be placed on witnesses who have already testified and are called again. There is a risk of evidence becoming unavailable. Other associated risks would include a change in the current composition or strategy of the Defence teams. These factors are accorded some weight by the Judges in the balancing exercise involved in the present Decision.

---

[133] *Prosecutor v. Clément Kayishema and Obed Ruzindana*, Case No. ICTR-95-1-A, Judgement (Reasons) (AC), 1 June 2001, para. 113; *Prosecutor v. Alfred Musema*, Case No. ICTR-96-13-A, Judgement (AC), 16 November 2001, paras. 205-206; *Niyitegeka* Appeal Judgement, paras. 60-61.

[134] *Nyiramasuhuko* Appeals Chamber Decision on Continuation, para. 24: "a trial is inequitable if it is too long drawn out. Speed, in the sense of expeditiousness, is an element of an equitable trial."

[135] According to the jurisprudence of this Tribunal, which reflects the jurisprudence of international bodies on human rights, the reasonableness of the length of the proceedings must be assessed on a case by case basis, in light of several factors, including: the gravity of the charges against the Accused; the complexity of the case; the complexity of the proceedings, including the complexity of the investigations, the joinder of Accused; the conduct of the Accused; the number of motions filed by the parties; and the conduct of the organs of the Tribunal, including the Prosecution and the Registry. See *Prosecutor v. André Rwamakuba*, Case No. ICTR-98-44C-T, Decision on Defence Motion for Stay of Proceedings (TC), 3 June 2005, para. 19, and the references quoted therein.

83. Joseph Nzirorera also notes that a continuation of the proceedings with a substitute Judge can only be done once according to Rule 15 *bis* (D) of the Rules.[136] Therefore, in his view, any loss of a Judge will require that the trial automatically be restarted, and at a much more advanced stage.

84. In the opinion of the remaining Judges, this argument is purely speculative. It is appropriate here to take in consideration all the circumstances of the case, and not possible unforeseen circumstances that could arise.

85. Joseph Nzirorera, joined by Mathieu Ngirumpatse, also submits that the interests of justice would not be served by continuing the trial because the proceedings, if continued, are unlikely to be completed within the mandate of the Tribunal.[137] He submits that according to **[page 32]** United Nations Security Council resolutions and statements made by the President of the Tribunal, this mandate should be completed by the end of 2008, while in the instant case, the Prosecutor has indicated that he would not be in a position to complete his case until December 2007. The Defence teams have also represented that they will not be able to complete their case by end of 2008. In light of these circumstances, Nzirorera and Ngirumpatse request the remaining Judges to order a rehearing of the case, without any time limit, or even to consider alternatives to continuing the trial, including referring the case to a national jurisdiction other than Rwanda.[138]

86. Although the Co-Accused Edouard Karemera consents to the continuation of the proceedings with a substitute Judge, he also expresses concerns as to the completion strategy of the Tribunal by end of 2008.[139] He queries as to the necessary steps to be taken in order to extend the Tribunal's mandate for the *Karemera et al.* case and also queries whether it would be more appropriate to transfer the case to a national jurisdiction.

87. In the view of the remaining Judges, the completion strategy by 31 December 2008 is not equivalent to the mandate of this Tribunal and is more of a target date. There is nothing to suggest that unfair decisions and actions will be taken with regard to cases that are pending on 31 December 2008. Cases are managed by Trial Chambers taking into account the rights of each and every accused, including the right to a fair trial. In that respect, the remaining Judges do not share the pessimistic view of the Accused that the trial could not be completed within the next two years using appropriate methods in the management of the proceedings while guaranteeing the rights of the Accused. The remaining Judges consider, therefore, that the trial could be completed by 31 December 2008 but that if it is not, reasonable decisions will be taken in the interests of justice and taking into account the rights of each co-Accused.

88. Both Edouard Karemera and Mathieu Ngirumpatse outline the fact that the Prosecutor had many years to present his case.[140] They request to have sufficient time for the preparation and presentation of their defence. Particularly, Karemera requests the remaining Judges to clarify what time will be allotted to the Defence to present its case.

89. Each Accused has a right to adequate time and facilities to prepare his defence. Throughout the trial process, this right has influenced the Trial Chamber's decisions. The recomposed Trial Chamber will continue to guarantee those rights. The actual time to be **[page 33]** allotted to the defence of each Accused will be determined in accordance with particular circumstances and in relation to their rights.

90. Concerning a referral of the Indictment to a national jurisdiction, the remaining Judges note that they have no power to order such a referral because the President has not designated them as a referral Chamber in accordance with Rule 11 *bis* (A) of the Rules.[141]

---

136 Nzirorera's submissions, para. 18.

137 Nzirorera's submissions, paras. 14-20; Ngirumpatse's submissions, para. 8.

138 *Ibidem.*

139 Karemera's submissions, p. 4.

140 Mathieu Ngirumpatse considers that the Prosecution had eight years to prepare its case (from 1998 to 2005); Edouard Karemera estimates that the Prosecution had three years to present its case since 2004.

141 Rules of Procedure and Evidence, Rule 11 *bis* (A) (emphasis added):

If an indictment has been confirmed, whether or not the accused is in the custody of the Tribunal, the *President may designate a Trial Chamber* which shall determine whether the case should be referred to the authorities of a State:

(i) in whose territory the crime was committed; or

(ii) in which the accused was arrested; or

(iii) having jurisdiction and being willing and adequately prepared to accept such a case,

so that those authorities should forthwith refer the case to the appropriate court for trial within that State.

91. In conclusion, considering all the circumstances of the case, and in particular the fairness of the trial, the rights of each Accused to be tried without undue delay and the length of their provisional detention, the remaining Judges find unanimously that a continuation of the proceedings would best serve the interests of justice.

ACCORDINGLY, THE REMAINING JUDGES DECIDE to continue the proceedings with a substitute Judge.

Arusha, 6 March 2007, done in both English and French.

Dennis C. M. Byron
Presiding Judge

With the consent and on behalf of
Gberdao Gustave Kam
Judge
(absent at the time of the signature)

[Seal of the Tribunal]

International Criminal Tribunal for Rwanda
Tribunal Pénal International pour le Rwanda

IN THE APPEALS CHAMBER

Before:	Judge Fausto Pocar, Presiding Judge Mohamed Shahabuddeen Judge Liu Daqun Judge Theodor Meron Judge Wolfgang Schomburg
Registrar:	Mr. Adama Dieng
Decision of:	20 April 2007

THE PROSECUTOR

v.

Édouard KAREMERA
Mathieu NGIRUMPATSE
Joseph NZIRORERA

Case No. ICTR- 98-44-AR15bis.3

DECISION ON APPEALS PURSUANT TO RULE 15*bis* (D)

Counsel for the Defence:

Dior Diagne Mbaye and Félix Sow for Édouard Karemera
Chantal Hounkpatin and Frédéric Weyl for Mathieu Ngirumpatse
Peter Robinson and Patrick Nimy Mayidika Ngimbi for Joseph Nzirorera

Office of the Prosecutor:

James Stewart
Don Webster
Alayne Frankson-Wallace

[page 1] 1. **THE APPEALS CHAMBER** of the International Criminal Tribunal for the Prosecution of Persons Responsible for Genocide and Other Serious Violations of International Humanitarian Law Committed in the Territory of Rwanda and Rwandan Citizens Responsible for Genocide and Other Such Violations Committed in the Territory of Neighbouring States between 1 January 1994 and 31 December 1994 ("Appeals Chamber" and "Tribunal", respectively) is seized of "Ngirumpatse's Motion to Appeal Decision on Continuation of Proceedings" filed by Mathieu Ngirumpatse on 13 March 2007 ("Ngirumpatse Motion") and "Joseph Nzirorera's Appeal from Decision on Continuation of the Proceedings" filed on 13 March 2007 ("Nzirorera Motion") ("Motions" and "Applicants", collectively).

2. On 22 March 2007, the Prosecution filed a consolidated response to the Motions,[1] and Joseph Nzirorera and Matthieu Ngipumpatse filed their replies on 26 March 2007 and 29 March 2007, respectively.[2]

A. Background

3. The trial of the Applicants, who are being tried jointly with Édouard Karemera, commenced on 19 September 2005 before Trial Chamber III composed of Judges Dennis C. M. Byron, Emile Francis Short and Gberdao Gustave Kam.[3] On 19 January 2007, Judge Short withdrew from the trial for health reasons. Judge Byron, who is the Presiding Judge, immediately informed the President of the Tribunal, Judge Erik Møse, of Judge Short's withdrawal.[4] President Møse then requested the Applicants and their Co-Accused to indicate whether they would consent to the continuation of the proceedings with a substitute Judge. The Applicants withheld their consent,[5] and President Møse then referred the matter to Judges Byron and Kam ("remaining Judges") for their determination on whether to continue the proceedings in this case with a substitute Judge.[6] On 6 March 2007, Judges Byron and Kam issued their "Decision on Continuation of the Proceedings" ("Impugned Decision") in which they held that:

> [i]n conclusion, considering all the circumstances of the case, and in particular the fairness of the trial, the rights of each Accused to be tried without undue delay and the length of their provisional **[page 2]** detention, the remaining Judges find unanimously that a continuation of the proceedings would best serve the interests of justice.[7]

The remaining Judges further held that "they have no power to order" the referral of this case to a national jurisdiction for trial because they have not been designated as a referral Chamber by the President.[8]

B. Submissions

1. Ngirumpatse

4. In his Motion, Mr. Ngirumpatse argues that his appeal can only be considered by "a full bench of the Appeals Chamber", which includes Judge Andrésia Vaz. However, Judge Vaz cannot be involved in this appeal due to her previous involvement in his case.[9] On this basis, he argues that the Appeals Chamber will not be in a position to form a "full bench" and, as it cannot consider his appeal in the absence of one of its

---

1 "The Prosecutor's Consolidated Response to Joseph Nzirorera's Appeal from Decision on Continuation of the Proceedings and to the « Mémoire pour M. Ngirumpatse sur l'appel contre la Décision relative à la continuation de la procédure et ensuite de la decision du 14 mars 2007 constituant une formation de jugement de 5 Juges»", 22March 2007 ("Prosecution Response").

2 "Reply Brief: Joseph Nzirorera's Appeal from Decision on Continuation of the Proceedings", 26 March 2007 ("Nzirorera Reply"); "MEMOIRE EN REPLIQUE pour M. NGIRUMPATSE SUR L'APPEL contre la Décision relative à la continuation de la procédure- articlel 5bis du Règlement ensuite de la décision du 14 mars 2007 constituant une formation de jugement de 5 Juges" 29 March 2007 (date of filing) ("Ngirumpatse Reply").

3 Impugned Decision, para. 1.

4 Impugned Decision, para. 2.

5 Impugned Decision, para. 4. Édouard Karemera consented to the continuation of the trial with a substitute Judge provided the said Judge "has perfect knowledge of the case."

6 Impugned Decision, para. 4.

7 Impugned Decision, para. 91.

8 Impugned Decision, para. 90.

9 Ngirumpatse Motion, paras. 5, 6.

members, he requests the Appeals Chamber to stay the consideration of his appeal pending the designation of a substitute Judge.[10]

5. With respect to the Impugned Decision, Mr. Ngirumpatse argues that the remaining Judges erred in determining that his submissions were filed out of time and requests the Appeals Chamber to reverse this determination.[11]

6. Mr. Ngirumpatse states that he will continue to defy the continuation of the proceedings in his case with a substitute Judge even if it means sacrificing his right to "a fair trial without undue delay."[12] He asserts that asking him to consent to the continuation of the proceedings in his case with a substitute Judge "amounts to asking him to pre-endorse the violation of his rights since his arrest".[13]

7. Mr. Ngirumpatse contends that the remaining Judges erred in asserting in the Impugned Decision that 31 December 2008 for the completion of all trials is only a target date.[14] He submits that the reasoning of the remaining Judges in this regard is "simply speculation" and deepens his concern that the proceedings in his case will be predicated on the Tribunal's Completion Strategy. **[page 3]** He suggests that this will lead to a situation where the time allowed for the presentation of his case would be a fraction of the time given to the Prosecution.[15]

8. Further, Mr. Ngirumpatse contends that the remaining Judges erred in rejecting his request to refer his case to a national jurisdiction for trial based solely on Rule 11*bis* (A) of the Rules of Procedure and Evidence of the Tribunal ("Rules").[16] He argues that the remaining Judges erred in their reasoning in that they failed to consider their discretion under Rule 11*bis* (B) of the Rules to order such referral.[17]

9. Finally, Mr. Ngirumpatse submits that the remaining Judges either misunderstood or misinterpreted his submissions on the defects in the proceedings in his case, as he has never requested the remaining Judges to review the decisions rendered by the full Bench.[18]

2. Nzirorera

10. Mr. Nzirorera raises four principal contentions in his appeal of the Impugned Decision. First, he argues that the remaining Judges erred in deciding to continue the proceedings with a substitute Judge when his request to the President to exercise his discretion and order a rehearing of the proceedings[19] was still pending.[20]

11. Second, Mr. Nzirorera contends that the remaining Judges erred in deciding to continue the proceedings in his case in the absence of a decision by the President on his request to designate a Chamber to consider the referral of his case to a national jurisdiction for trial.[21]

12. Third, Mr. Nzirorera contends that the remaining Judges erred in concluding that the completion of his trial by the end of 2008 was not mandatory, and that the trial could be completed without violating the rights of the accused.[22] Finally, Mr. Nzirorera contends that the remaining Judges erred in concluding that the proceedings in his case should continue, despite circumstances which have thus far rendered the trial unfair.[23]

---

10 Ngirumpatse Motion, paras. 6, 7.
11 Ngirumpatse Motion, para. 9.
12 Ngirumpatse Motion, para. 10.
13 Ngirumpatse Motion, para 11.
14 Ngirumpatse Motion, para. 19.
15 Ngirumpatse Motion, paras. 14 – 21.
16 Ngirumpatse Motion, para. 21.
17 Ngirumpatse Motion, para. 22.
18 Ngirumpatse Motion, paras. 23 – 26.
19 Nzirorera Motion, para. 5, referring to "Joseph Nzirorera's Submission in Support of a Rehearing", 29 January 2007.
20 Nzirorera Motion, paras. 13 – 31.
21 Nzirorera Motion, paras. 6, 32 – 51, referring to "Joseph Nzirorera's Request for Designation of a Trial Chamber to Consider Referral to National Jurisdiction", 29 January 2007.
22 Nzirorera Motion, paras. 52 – 60.
23 Nzirorera Motion, paras. 61-133.

13. In light of these contentions, Mr. Nzirorera requests the Appeals Chamber to reverse the Impugned Decision and to order a new trial in his case or alternatively, to refer the matter back to **[page 4]** the President for the exercise of his discretion and a decision pursuant to Rule 15*bis* (C) of the Rules, as well as for his decision on the designation of a Trial Chamber to consider the transfer of his case to a national jurisdiction.[24]

3. Prosecution

14. According to the Prosecution, both appeals are inadmissible and are without merit.[25] In response to Mr. Ngirumpatse's objection relating to the composition of the Appeals Chamber, the Prosecution avers that the Tribunal's Statute states that a full bench of the Appeals Chamber comprises five Judges and not seven.[26] The Prosecution has not responded to the other specific grounds of appeal raised by Mr. Ngirumpatse.

15. In response to Mr. Nzirorera's appeal, the Prosecution contends first that Mr. Nzirorera is proceeding on a misapprehension of the proper interpretation of the discretionary powers provided under Rule 15*bis* (C) and (D) of the Rules.[27] It disputes the premise upon which Mr. Nzirorera bases his contention that the remaining Judges erred in deciding to continue the trial in the absence of an exercise of discretion by the President, and argues that Mr. Nzirorera's interpretation of Rule 15*bis* of the Rules is incorrect.[28]

16. Second, the Prosecution contends that Mr. Nzirorera is in error as to the relevance, scope and application of Rule 11*bis* of the Rules.[29] It argues that the remaining Judges were exercising jurisdiction under Rule 15*bis* and they were never legally enjoined to make any decisions or rulings under Rule 11*bis* of the Rules.[30]

17. Third, the Prosecution contends that the remaining Judges were correct in their determination that it was in the interests of justice to continue the trial with a substitute Judge.[31] According to the Prosecution, both Applicants have failed to identify any discernable error on the part of the remaining Judges.[32] It avers that they have failed to show that the Impugned Decision is based on an incorrect interpretation of the governing law; that it is based on a patently incorrect conclusion of fact; or that it is so unfair or unreasonable so as to amount to an abuse of discretion.[33] **[page 5]**

C. Discussion

18. The Appeals Chamber notes that the Impugned Decision was made pursuant to Rule 15*bis* (D) of the Rules, which provides that if, after the commencement of the presentation of evidence in his case, "the accused withholds his consent [for the continuation of the proceedings with a substitute Judge], the remaining Judges may nonetheless decide to continue the proceedings before a Trial Chamber with a substitute Judge if, taking all the circumstances into account, they determine unanimously that doing so would serve the interests of justice." This rule also allows for an appeal of the Impugned Decision by either party, which the Applicants relied upon in filing their respective appeals. Some of the contentions raised by the Applicants are in common. Where this is the case, the submissions of both Applicants will be considered together.

1. Standard of Review

19. Rules 15*bis* (D) of the Rules confers on the remaining Judges the discretion to determine whether to continue the trial proceedings with a substitute Judge. In exercising this discretion, the remaining Judges

24 Nzirorera Motion, para. 135.
25 Prosecution Response, para. 2.
26 Prosecution Response, paras. 92, 93.
27 Prosecution Response, paras. 18 – 34.
28 Prosecution Response, para. 18.
29 Prosecution Response, paras. 35 – 54.
30 Prosecution Response, para. 35.
31 Prosecution Response, paras. 55 – 91.
32 Prosecution Response, para. 96.
33 Prosecution Response, para. 96.

have "the right to establish the precise point within a margin of appreciation at which a continuation [of the proceedings] should be ordered".[34] The Appeals Chamber has previously stated that it can only intervene in this decision-making process in limited circumstances, as, for example, where it is of the view that there was a failure to exercise the discretion, or that the remaining Judges failed to take into account a material consideration or took into account an immaterial one and that the substance of its decision has in consequence been affected.[35] It is not enough to show that the Appeals Chamber would have exercised the discretion differently.[36]

2. The Composition of the Bench

20. Mr. Ngirumpatse submits that his appeal must be considered by a "full bench" of the Appeals Chamber, which includes Judge Andrésia Vaz.[37] He refers to Rule 15(A) of the Rules and argues that Judge Vaz cannot consider his appeal in light of her prior involvement in his case and therefore, the Appeals Chamber can neither sit as a full bench nor conduct matters in the absence of **[page 6]** one of its members.[38] Mr. Ngirumpatse accordingly requests that the Appeals Chamber stay the consideration of his appeal pending the appointment of a substitute Judge in place of Judge Vaz.[39]

21. The Appeals Chamber notes that a decision by the remaining Judges pursuant to Rule 15*bis* (D) of the Rules may be appealed "directly to a full bench of the Appeals Chamber". This provision must be interpreted in conjunction with Article 11(3) of the Tribunal's Statute, which provides that seven permanent Judges shall be members of the Appeals Chamber but the "Appeals Chamber shall, for each appeal, be composed of five of its members". Therefore a "full bench" of the Appeals Chamber for the purposes of considering this appeal only comprises five Judges. Furthermore, it is noted that Judge Vaz has not been designated as a member of the Bench constituted to consider Mr. Ngirumpatse's appeal.[40] Consequently, the Appeals Chamber finds Mr. Ngirumpatse's contention to be without merit and frivolous.

3. The Alleged Error that Mr. Ngirumpatse's Submission was Filed Out of Time

22. Mr. Ngirumpatse submits that the Impugned Decision is erroneous in that it asserts that his submission before the remaining Judges was filed out of time, and he requests the Appeals Chamber to remedy this error.[41] The Appeals Chamber notes that the remaining Judges did find that Mr. Ngirumpatse's submission was filed out of time even though it may have been faxed on 31 January 2007, however the submission was considered in the "interests of justice" and in light of the "right of the Accused to be heard".[42] If the remaining Judges did err in finding that Mr. Ngirumpatse's submission had been filed out of time, the Appeals Chamber cannot see how this finding could invalidate the Impugned Decision given that Mr. Ngirumpatse has suffered no prejudice as a result of this finding. The Appeals Chamber accordingly finds this contention to be frivolous.

4. The Alleged Error that the Completion of the Trial by the End of 2008 was not Mandatory

23. Mr. Nzirorera submits that when deciding to continue his trial with a substitute Judge, the remaining Judges erred in concluding that the completion of his trial by the end of 2008 was not mandatory,[43] and points to an error in their assessment of Security Council resolution 1503 (2003)[44] and Security Council

34 *The Prosecutor v. Pauline Nyiramasuhuko, Arsène Shalom Ntahobali, Sylvain Nsabimana, Alphonse Nteziryayo, Joseph Kanyabashi and Elie Ndayambaje*, Case No. ICTR-98-42-A15bis, Decision in the Matter of Proceedings Under Rule 15*bis* (D), 24September 2003 ("Butare Decision"), para. 23.

35 Butare Decision, para. 23.

36 Butare Decision, para. 23.

37 Ngirumpatse Motion, paras. 5 -7.

38 Ngirumpatse Motion, para. 6.

39 Ngirumpatse Motion, para. 7.

40 See "Order Assigning Judges to a Case Before the Appeals Chamber", 14 March 2007, p.2 .

41 Ngirumpatse Motion, para. 9.

42 Impugned Decision, para. 5.

43 Nzirorera Motion, paras. 52 – 60.

44 S/RES/1503 (2003) ("Resolution 1503").

resolution 1534 (2004).[45] He argues that the Impugned Decision treats these **[page 7]** resolutions as guidelines rather than deadlines.[46] The Appeals Chamber understands Mr. Nzirorera's contention to be that 31 December 2008 is mandatory for the completion of all trials and that, as such, continuing the proceedings in his case would not serve the interests of justice as his trial could not be "fairly" completed by that date.[47] He therefore asserts that the remaining Judges erred in concluding that his trial could be completed by the end of 2008 without violating his rights.[48] Mr. Ngirumpatse raises a similar contention.[49] Mr. Nzirorera further contends that if his trial is not completed by 31 December 2008, either he will be held hostage to a request to the Security Council for an extension of time to complete his trial or his trial will need to restart in a national jurisdiction.[50]

24. The Appeals Chamber notes that the remaining Judges expressed the view that the completion of all trials by 31 December 2008 is "more of a target date"[51] and that there was "nothing to suggest that unfair decisions and actions will be taken with regard to cases that are pending on 31 December 2008."[52] The Appeals Chamber also notes that resolution 1503 urges the Tribunal to formalise a strategy to enable the Tribunal "to achieve its objective" of completing all trials by the end of 2008[53] and calls on the Tribunal "to take all possible measures" in this regard.[54] The Appeals Chamber is of the view that when assessing the implications of resolution 1503 and resolution 1534 to on-going trials, the overriding consideration must be the strict adherence to the minimum guarantees afforded to accused persons pursuant to Article 20 of the Tribunal's Statute. The Appeals Chamber considers that the remaining Judges properly addressed this overriding consideration and sees no error in their interpretation of their obligations in the context of resolution 1503 and resolution 1534. The remaining Judges considered that the trial in the Applicants' case could be completed fairly and expeditiously by 31 December 2008, by using appropriate trial management methods within their discretion and taking reasonable decisions.[55] In the event of the trial not being completed by the end of 2008, the remaining Judges stated that "reasonable decisions will be taken in the interests of justice [and] taking into account the rights of each co-Accused."[56] The Appeals Chamber finds no error in this approach. **[page 8]**

5. The Alleged Error relating to the Allocation of Time for the Defence Case

25. Mr. Nzirorera argues that the continuation of his trial will not serve the interests of justice because "the trial could not be fairly completed" by 31 December 2008, as the time allocated to the Defence for the presentation of its respective cases must be proportional to that taken by the Prosecution.[57]

26. Mr. Nzirorera avers that the Prosecution is expected to complete the presentation of its case in December 2007, by which time the presentation of the Prosecution case would have taken twenty-six months.[58] He argues that this would leave the three accused with twelve months, which computes to four months each, for the presentation of their respective cases, if the trial is to be concluded by the end of 2008.[59] He asserts that this ratio cannot be justified.[60] Mr. Ngirumpatse raises a similar argument.[61]

45 S/RES/1534 (2004) ("Resolution 1534").
46 Nzirorera Motion, paras. 54 – 57.
47 Nzirorera Motion, para. 53.
48 Nzirorera Motion, paras. 54 – 57.
49 Ngirumpatse Motion, paras. 18 – 21.
50 Nzirorera's Motion, para. 58.
51 Impugned Decision, para. 87.
52 Impugned Decision, para. 87.
53 Resolution 1503, p.2 .
54 Resolution 1503, p.3 at para. 7; Resolution 1534, p.2 at para. 3.
55 Impugned Decision, para. 87.
56 Impugned Decision, para. 87.
57 Nzirorera Motion, para. 53.
58 Nzirorera Motion, para. 52.
59 Nzirorera Motion, paras. 52, 53.
60 Nzirorera Motion, para. 53.
61 Ngirumpatse Motion, 15 – 17.

27. The Appeals Chamber notes that in the Orić case,[62] the ICTY Appeals Chamber stated that:

> [t]he Appeals Chamber has long recognised that "the principle of equality of arms between the prosecutor and accused in a criminal trial goes to the heart of the fair trial guarantee." At a minimum, "equality of arms obliges a judicial body to ensure that neither party is put at a disadvantage when presenting its case," certainly in terms of procedural equity. This is not to say, however, that an [a]ccused is necessarily entitled to precisely the same amount of time or the same number of witnesses as the Prosecution. The Prosecution has the burden of telling an entire story, of putting together a coherent narrative and proving every necessary element of the crimes charged beyond a reasonable doubt. Defence strategy, by contrast, often focuses on poking specifically targeted holes in the Prosecution's case, an endeavour which may require less time and fewer witnesses. This is sufficient reason to explain why a principle of basic proportionality, rather than a strict principle of mathematical equality, generally governs the relationship between the time and witnesses allocated to the two sides.[63]

28. The ICTY Appeals Chamber further held in the Orić Decision that the Trial Chamber has the authority to limit the length of time allocated to the Defence,[64] but that such limitations are always subject to the full respect for the rights of an accused as guaranteed in the Tribunal's Statute.[65] Thus, in addition to whether the time given to an accused is relatively proportional to the time given to the Prosecution, the Trial Chamber must also consider whether the amount of time is **[page 9]** objectively adequate to enable the accused to present his defence in a manner consistent with his rights.[66]

29. The Appeals Chamber has already noted above that the remaining Judges considered the possibility of the trial not being completed by the end of 2008 and indicated that reasonable decisions will nonetheless be taken in the interests of justice and taking into account the rights of each Accused in this case.[67] The remaining Judges also recognised that "[e]ach Accused has a right to adequate time and facilities to prepare his defence"[68] and that "[t]he actual time to be allotted to the defence of each Accused will be determined in accordance with particular circumstances and in relation to their rights".[69] The Appeals Chamber sees no error in this approach and is not satisfied that the Applicants have demonstrated that the remaining Judges failed to consider that full respect for their rights to present their defence must be ensured in accordance with the precedent set in the Orić Decision.

6. The Alleged Error Relating to the Absence of the Exercise of Discretion and a Decision by the President

30. Mr Nzirorera contends that the remaining Judges erred in deciding to continue the trial because the President had not exercised his discretion and had not issued a "reasoned decision" in accordance with Rule 15*bis* (C) of the Rules.[70] He argues that the President had the discretion to order a rehearing of his trial but instead referred the matter to the remaining Judges.[71] He also argues that since he "specifically requested the President to exercise his discretion and order a rehearing",[72] the referral of his case to the remaining Judges "violated his statutory right to a reasoned decision".[73] The Appeals Chamber will consider these two arguments in turn.

31. First, Mr. Nzirorera argues that Rule 15*bis* (C) of the Rules gives the President the "discretion to order a rehearing of the trial."[74] He then raises the issue of whether the President retains the option of ordering a rehearing where the trial has already commenced and where the accused did not consent to the continuation

62 Prosecutor v. Naser Orić, Case No. IT-03-68-AR73.2, Interlocutory Decision on Length of Defence Case, 20July 2005, ("Orić Decision").
63 Orić Decision, para. 7.
64 Orić Decision, para. 8.
65 Orić Decision, para. 8.
66 Orić Decision, para. 8.
67 See para. 25 above.
68 Impugned Decision, para. 89.
69 Impugned Decision, para. 89.
70 Nzirorera Motion, para. 31.
71 Nzirorera Motion, para. 18.
72 Nzirorera Motion, para. 19.
73 Nzirorera Motion, para. 21.
74 Nzirorera Motion, para. 15.

of the trial, instead of referring the matter to the remaining Judges,[75] and argues that if the President does not retain this option, it could lead to an "anomalous situation that the President could order a rehearing where an accused doesn't want one, **[page 10]** but cannot order a rehearing where an accused wants one."[76] He argues that this is contrary to the purpose of the Rule, which is to provide safeguards to an accused who does not consent to the continuation of his trial.[77]

32. The Appeals Chamber is of the view that Rule 15*bis* (C) of the Rules confers on the President the function of assigning a Judge to a part–heard case where one of the Judges in the Trial Chamber is no longer in a position to continue. This function must be understood in the context of the President's overall responsibility of assigning Judges to the Trial Chambers[78] and the coordination of the work of the Chambers.[79] Pursuant to these responsibilities and within the ambit of Rule 15*bis* (C) of the Rules, the President may order "a rehearing or continuation of the proceedings". However, where the opening statement is completed or the presentation of evidence has commenced, the President must seek the consent of the accused before ordering the continuation of the proceedings. The Appeals Chamber agrees with Mr. Nzirorera that where such consent is withheld, the President may either order a rehearing or refer the matter to the remaining Judges for a decision on whether to continue the proceedings with a substitute Judge. However, in the present case, the President did not exercise his discretion to order a rehearing upon establishing that the Applicants withheld their respective consent to the continuation of the proceedings. Rather, in light of the commencement of the presentation of evidence in the Applicants' case, he referred the matter to the remaining Judges for a determination on whether to continue the proceedings with a substitute Judge, which was in his discretion to do pursuant to Rule 15*bis* (D) of the Rules.

33. Second, Mr. Nzirorera submits that the failure of the President to rule on his request for a rehearing of his trial violated his right to a reasoned decision.[80] He argues that he is entitled to have "two chances" to oppose the continuation of his trial, first, by trying to persuade the President and if unsuccessful, by trying to persuade the remaining Judges. He now only has one opportunity due to the President's failure to exercise his discretion and deliver a reasoned decision. The Appeals Chamber notes that the President's consideration of the matter pursuant to Rule 15*bis* (C) of the Rules is triggered by the Presiding Judge reporting to him that one of the Judges is unable to continue with the case. This rule makes no provision for an accused to make a direct request to the President to order a rehearing in his case. In the present case, Mr. Nzirorera has no standing to file a detailed submission to the President requesting a rehearing of the proceedings, and he is not entitled to a reasoned decision from the President in respect of this submission. Therefore, the Appeals **[page 11]** Chamber finds no merit in Mr. Nzirorera's submission that the remaining Judges erroneously rejected his request to refer the matter back to the President.[81] The Appeals Chamber is satisfied that the remaining Judges did not err in reaching the Impugned Decision in the absence of any such reasoned decision from the President.

34. This said, the Appeals Chamber observes that Mr. Nzirorera does have "two chances" to oppose the continuation of his trial, one before the remaining Judges and the other before the Appeals Chamber. He has taken advantage of both these opportunities and has not suffered any prejudice or been denied an opportunity to raise this matter.

7. Alleged Errors Relating to Rule 11*bis*

35. Mr. Ngirumpatse submits that the remaining Judges erred in rejecting the alternative request to refer the case to a national jurisdiction for trial, based solely on Rule 11*bis* (A) of the Rules.[82] He argues that the

---

75 Nzirorera Motion, para. 17.
76 Nzirorera Motion, para. 18.
77 Nzirorera Motion, para. 18.
78 Articlesl 3 (3) and (5) of the Tribunal's Statute.
79 Rule 19 (A) of the Rules.
80 Nzirorera Motion, paras 19, 21.
81 Nzirorera Motion, para. 26.
82 Ngirumpatse Motion, para. 22.

remaining Judges did not take into consideration their discretion to do so under Rule 11*bis* (B) of the Rules.[83]

36. The Appeals Chamber notes in this regard that the remaining Judges stated that:

> [c]oncerning a referral of the Indictment to a national jurisdiction, the remaining Judges note that they have no power to order such a referral because the President has not designated them as a referral Chamber in accordance with Rule 11 *bis* (A) of the Rules.[84]

The Appeals Chamber is satisfied that a "Trial Chamber" may only act in accordance with the provisions of Rule 11*bis* (B) where it has been designated by the President pursuant to Rule 11*bis* (A) of the Rules. The Appeals Chamber therefore finds no merit in Mr. Ngirumpatse's argument.

37. Mr. Nzirorera submits that the remaining Judges erred in deciding to continue the trial in the absence of the President's decision to appoint a Trial Chamber to proprio motu consider the transfer of his case to a national jurisdiction for trial.[85] Mr. Nzirorera argues that he had presented the President with a viable alternative of transferring his case to a national jurisdiction for trial,[86] because his trial could not reasonably be completed by the end of 2008, an issue which directly bears on the Tribunal's Completion Strategy and management of its remaining resources, and was therefore uniquely suited for consideration by the President, instead of the remaining Judges.[87] The **[page 12]** remaining Judges recognised in the Impugned Decision that they were without authority to consider this alternative.[88] Only the President could trigger the consideration of this alternative by designating a Chamber for this purpose.[89]

38. The Appeals Chamber notes that Mr. Nzirorera's appeal is filed pursuant to Rule 15*bis* (D) of the Rules. Hence, the scope of his appeal should relate solely to the exercise of discretion by the remaining Judges in determining whether to continue the proceedings in his case with a substitute Judge. The allegation by Mr. Nzirorera that the remaining Judges "erred in deciding to continue the trial without Mr. Nzirorera having an opportunity to have a decision by an appropriate organ on whether his case could be transferred to a national jurisdiction"[90] falls outside the scope of his appeal under Rule 15*bis* (D) and is irrelevant to the question of whether or not to continue his trial with a substitute Judge. Furthermore, the Appeals Chamber notes that Rule 11*bis* of the Rules makes no provision for an accused to request the transfer of his case to a national jurisdiction for trial. Consequently, the remaining Judges were not obliged to take into consideration Mr. Nzirorera's request to the President pursuant to Rule 11*bis* of the Rules.

8. The Alleged Unfairness of the Trial

39. Mr. Nzirorera contends that the remaining Judges erred in concluding that the trial should be continued despite circumstances which rendered the trial unfair.[91] He states that he declined to consent to the continuation of his trial because he believed the proceedings to this point had been unfair[92] due to the Prosecution's violation of its disclosure obligations; the admission of material facts not charged in the indictment; the unjustified use of anonymous witnesses; the Prosecution's presentation of perjured testimony; the failure of the Rwandan Government to produce statements of Prosecution witnesses; the taking of testimony of important witnesses by video-link; and the Prosecution's interference with the right of the Defence to meet witnesses.[93] Mr. Nzirorera avers that the remaining Judges "held that, in their view, the trial had been fair, and that any prejudice to the rights of the accused could be cured by subsequent

83 Ngirumpatse Motion, para. 22.
84 Impugned Decision, para. 90 (internal citations omitted).
85 Nzirorera Motion, para. 6.
86 Nzirorera Motion, para. 30.
87 Nzirorera Motion, para. 29.
88 Nzirorera Motion, para. 30.
89 Nzirorera Motion, para. 30.
90 Nzirorera Motion, para. 36.
91 Nzirorera Motion, paras. 61-63.
92 Nzirorera Motion, para. 61.
93 Nzirorera Motion, para. 61 – 133.

decisions".[94] He argues that the trial is "too broken to fix" and that only a rehearing will guarantee him a fair trial.[95] **[page 13]**

40. The Appeals Chamber notes that the remaining Judges considered these issues in the Impugned Decision and rejected Mr. Nzirorera's arguments that the trial to date had been unfair. The Appeals Chamber finds, however, that it need not review the remaining Judges' reasoning with regard to these issues. The Appeals Chamber considers the arguments with respect to alleged past violations of fair trial rights in the proceedings to be irrelevant at this stage to the sole question being considered by the remaining Judges of whether to continue the trial with a substitute Judge under Rule 15*bis* (D) of the Rules.

41. Mr. Ngirumpatse additionally submits that his rights are being sacrificed as they are being weighed against each other.[96] He argues that if he withholds his consent to the continuation of the proceedings in his case with a substitute Judge, he would be sacrificing his right to a fair trial without undue delay.[97] If he consents to the continuation of the proceedings, he would be actually consenting to having a substitute Judge who would not have "heard the testimonies of 14 witnesses in the course of 100 days" and also consenting to proceedings that will be "hasty".[98] He also argues that asking him to consent to the continuation of his proceedings is actually asking him to "pre-endorse the violation of his rights since his arrest."[99]

42. The Appeals Chamber considers that the continuation of the proceedings with a substitute Judge in a case where witnesses have already been heard does not necessarily infringe on fair trial rights. As the Appeals Chamber previously stated:

> [t]here is a preference for live testimony to be heard by each and every judge. But that does not represent an unbending requirement. The Rules and the cases show that exceptions can be made. The exceptions may relate even to evidence involving an assessment of demeanour, various ways being available to assist a new judge to overcome any disadvantages.[100]

43. The Appeals Chamber also considers that, pursuant to Rule 15*bis* (D) of the Rules, a substitute Judge may only join the bench "after he or she has certified that he or she has familiarised himself or herself with the record of the proceedings." These safeguards ensure that fair trials rights are not compromised. In the present case, the remaining Judges took into consideration that the substitute Judge will need to review the "records of the proceedings, including the transcripts, audio and video-recordings, to observe the demeanour of the witness" in determining that it would be in the interests of justice to continue the proceedings with a substitute Judge.[101] **[page 14]**

44. On the issue of whether the proceedings in Mr. Ngirumpatse's case will be "hasty" if continued, the Appeals Chamber has already discussed above the remaining Judges' recognition of the right of the Applicants and their Co-Accused to have adequate time and facilities to prepare their respective defences.[102] Based on the approach adopted by the remaining Judges, there is no reason to believe that Mr. Ngirumpatse's rights to a fair trial will be infringed. Furthermore, as mentioned above,[103]any consideration of Mr. Ngirumpatse's argument relating to the alleged violation of rights since his arrest exceeds the scope of appeal envisaged in Article 15*bis* (D) of the Rules and will therefore not be considered.

45. In sum, the Appeals Chamber finds no merit in the arguments raised by the Applicants with respect to alleged errors by the remaining Judges in concluding that the continuation of their trial would not result in a failure to uphold the Applicant's fair trial rights. Furthermore, the Appeals Chamber considers the arguments with respect to alleged past violations of fair trial rights in the proceedings to be irrelevant at this stage to the

94 Nzirorera Motion, para. 63.
95 Nzirorera Motion, para. 63.
96 Ngirumpatse Motion, paras. 10 -12.
97 Ngirumpatse Motion, para. 10.
98 Ngirumpatse Motion, para. 10.
99 Ngirumpatse Motion, para. 11.
100 Butare Decision, para. 25.
101 Impugned Decision, para. 69.
102 See supra para. 28 – 30.
103 See supra para. 40.

sole question being considered by the remaining Judges of whether to continue the trial with a substitute Judge under Rule 15*bis* (D) of the Rules.

9. Conclusion

46. Having considered the submissions made by the Parties, the Appeals Chamber finds that the continuation of the Applicants' trial would not result in a failure to uphold their fair trial rights. The Impugned Decision therefore stands.

D. Disposition

47. For the aforementioned reasons, the Appeals Chamber:

DISMISSES the appeals filed by Mathieu Ngirumpatse and Joseph Nzirorera;

Done in English and French, the English text being authoritative.

Dated this the 20 day of April 2007,
at The Hague,
The Netherlands.

Judge Fausto Pocar,
Presiding

[Seal of the Tribunal]

International Criminal Tribunal for Rwanda
Tribunal pénal international pour le Rwanda

OR: ENG

TRIAL CHAMBER III

Before Judges: Dennis C. M. Byron, Presiding
Gberdao Gustave Kam
*sitting pursuant to Rule 15*bis *of the Rules of Procedure and Evidence*

Registrar: Adama Dieng

Date: 2 May 2007

THE PROSECUTOR

v.

Édouard KAREMERA
Mathieu NGIRUMPATSE
Joseph NZIRORERA

Case No. ICTR-98-44-T

SCHEDULING ORDER FOR THE RESUMPTION OF THE TRIAL

Rules 15* bis *(F) and 54 of the Rules of Procedure and Evidence

---

Office of the Prosecutor:
Don Webster
Alayne Frankson-Wallace
Iain Morley
Saidou N'Dow
Gerda Visser
Sunkarie Ballah-Conteh
Takeh Sendze

Defence Counsel for Édouard Karemera
Dior Diagne Mbaye and Félix Sow

Defence Counsel for Mathieu Ngirumpatse
Chantal Hounkpatin and Frédéric Weyl

Defence Counsel for Joseph Nzirorera
Peter Robinson and Patrick Nimy Mayidika Ngimbi

[page 2] 1. The trial in this case started on 19 September 2005 before Trial Chamber III composed of Judges Dennis C. M. Byron, presiding, Emile Francis Short and Gberdao Gustave Kam. Thus far, four trial sessions have been held for the presentation of the Prosecution case, during which 13 witnesses have been heard.

2. On 19 January 2007, Judge Short decided to withdraw from the case. Although the remaining Judges decided on the continuation of the proceedings with a substitute judge,[1] the trial could not resume as a result of the appeals filed against that decision by Mathieu Ngirumpatse and Joseph Nzirorera.[2] On 20 April 2007, the Appeals Chamber dismissed their applications and affirmed the Trial Chamber's decision to continue the proceedings with a substitute judge.[3]

3. According to the letter of appointment of the United Nations Secretary General and at the request of the President of the Tribunal, Judge Vagn Joensen is assigned to the present case as substitute judge. However, according to Rule 15 *bis* (D) of the Rules of Procedure and Evidence, he can join the bench only after he has certified that he has familiarised himself with the record of the proceedings. While this familiarization process is currently ongoing, there is an urgent need to schedule the resumption of the trial in order to minimize any delay in the trial of the co-Accused persons and ensure the proper administration of justice. Since the President authorized the Trial Chamber, composed of Judges Byron and Kam, to conduct routine matters, such as the delivery of decisions, in the absence of the substitute judge, the scheduling of the trial may be decided at this stage.[4]

4. The parties have been consulted concerning the suitable time-frame for resuming the trial. Each of them expressed a strong view that sufficient time should be given to the substitute judge to familiarize himself with the record of the proceedings and ensure that the **[page 3]** resumption of the trial be not decided hastily, thereby impairing the rights of the Accused to prepare their defence. The Chamber fully shares these views.

5. As previously stated and as affirmed by the Appeals Chamber,[5] the familiarization process is one of the criteria to be taken into account when deciding on the continuation of the proceedings. There is, however, no mathematical or standard rule as how this familiarisation process should take place. Rather, there are different methods and means through which it can be done relying upon transcripts, audio and video-records of the testimonies, documents entered into exhibits and decisions.[6] The length of the familiarization process will also depend on the particularities of each case.

6. In the *Nyiramasuhuko et al.* case, Judge Solomy Balungi Bossa certified that she had familiarized herself with the record of the proceedings less than two months after her assignment to the Tribunal and while 23 witnesses had already been heard by Trial Chamber II over 107 trial days.[7] Judge Emile Francis Short certified that he had familiarized himself with the record of the proceedings in the *Bizimungu et al.*

---

[1] *Prosecutor v. Edouard Karemera, Mathieu Ngirumpatse, Joseph Nzirorera ("Karemera et al.")*, Case No. ICTR-98-44-T, Decision on Continuation of the Proceedings (TC), 6 Mach 2007.

[2] See Rules of Procedure and Evidence, Rule 15 *bis* (D): "If, in the circumstances mentioned in the last sentence of paragraph (C), the accused withholds his consent, the remaining Judges may nonetheless decide to continue the proceedings before a Trial Chamber with a substitute Judge if, taking all the circumstances into account, they determine unanimously that doing so would serve the interests of justice. This decision is subject to appeal directly to a full bench of the Appeals Chamber by either party. If no appeal is taken or the Appeals Chamber affirms the decision of the Trial Chamber, the President shall assign to the existing bench a Judge, who, however, can join the bench only after he or she has certified that he or she has familiarised himself or herself with the record of the proceedings. Only one substitution under this paragraph may be made."

[3] *Karemera et al*, Case No. ICTR-98-44-AR15bis.3, Decision on Appeals Pursuant to Rule 15*bis* (D) (AC), 20 April 2007.

[4] See Rules of Procedure and Evidence, Rule 15 *bis* (F); and Interoffice Memorandum from the President to Judge Byron, filed on 13 March 2007.

[5] *Karemera et al.*, Case No. ICTR-98-44-AR15bis.2, Reasons For Decision on Interlocutory Appeals Regarding the Continuation of Proceedings with a Substitute Judge and on Nzirorera's Motion for Leave to Consider New Material (AC), 22 October 2004, paras. 57-58; *Karemera et al*, Case No. ICTR-98-44-AR15bis.3, Decision on Appeals pursuant to Rule 15*bis* (D) (AC), 20 April 2007, para. 43.

[6] *Karemera et al.*, Case No. ICTR-98-44-AR15bis.2, Reasons For Decision on Interlocutory Appeals Regarding the Continuation of Proceedings with a Substitute Judge and on Nzirorera's Motion for Leave to Consider New Material (AC), 22 October 2004, paras. 57-58.

[7] *Prosecutor v. Nyiramasuhuko et al.*, Joint Case No. ICTR-98-42-T, Certification in the Matter of Proceedings under Rule 15 *bis* (D), 5 December 2003. Judge Bossa was assigned to Trial Chamber II by the President on 20 October 2003.

case, less than 15 days after his assignment to the Tribunal and while 28 witnesses had been heard by Trial Chamber II over 112 trial days.[8]

7. In the present case, the Chamber is of the view that the substitute judge should have little difficulty mastering and becoming familiar with the record of the proceedings by the end of May. In any event, it belongs to the substitute judge, who is appointed on the basis of his high moral character, impartiality and integrity and professional experience at the highest judicial offices, to certify whether he is familiar with the case. Should he consider that he is not familiar within the above mentioned time-estimate, this will be a new circumstance requiring the Chamber to reconsider its scheduling order and postpone the resumption of the trial. **[page 4]**

8. Such an approach will also guarantee that the rights of the Accused are fully protected. The Chamber must ensure that the Accused will benefit from a fair trial, including their right to be tried without undue delay.[9] This element, as well as the fact that the Accused are currently detained while the proceedings are ongoing, must be taken into account when deciding the resumption of the trial and what period of time would be reasonable for the substitute judge to familiarise himself with the proceedings.

9. Concerning the preparation of the Defence, the Chamber notes that as a result of Judge Short's withdrawal, the Defence has enjoyed a break of more than four months since the last trial session. It is not conceivable that the Defence has not optimized this opportunity in order to keep conducting investigations and prepare its case, including the cross-examination of the forthcoming Prosecution witnesses. In addition, the Defence will now have an additional month to prepare the cross-examination of the forthcoming Prosecution witnesses.

FOR THESE REASONS, the **CHAMBER**

I. ORDERS that the Prosecution case resume on 11 June 2007 until 3 August 2007;

I. ORDERS that the Prosecution file a list of the witnesses it intends to call during the aforementioned period, including the expected order of appearance, by 7 May 2007.

Arusha, 2 May 2007, done in English.

Dennis C. M. Byron Presiding Judge	Gberdao Gustave Kam Judge

[Seal of the Tribunal]

[8] *Prosecutor v. Bizimungu et al.*, Case No. ICTR-99-50-T, Certification in the Matter of Proceedings under Rule 15 *bis* (D), 3 June 2004. Judge Short was assigned to Trial Chamber II by the President on 18 May 2004.

[9] *Prosecutor v. Pauline Nyiramasuhuko et al.*, Case No. ICTR-98-42-A15bis, Decision in the Matter of Proceedings Under Rule 15bis (D) (AC), 24 September 2003, para. 24: "a trial is inequitable if it is too long drawn out. Speed, in the sense of expeditiousness, is an element of an equitable trial."

International Criminal Tribunal for Rwanda
Tribunal pénal international pour le Rwanda

THE BUREAU

Before: Judge Arlette Ramaroson
Judge William H. Sekule
Judge Khalida Rachid Khan

Registrar: Adama Dieng

Date: 28 May 2007

THE PROSECUTOR

v.

Théoneste BAGOSORA

Gratien KABILIGI

Aloys NTABAKUZE

Anatole NSENGIYUMVA

Case No. ICTR-98-41-T

DECISION ON MOTION FOR DISQUALIFICATION OF JUDGES

The Office of the Prosecutor

Barbara Mulvaney
Drew White
Christine Graham
Rashid Rashid
Kartik Murukutla

Counsel for Bagosora

Raphaël Constant
Allison Turner

[page 2] THE INTERNATIONAL CRIMINAL TRIBUNAL FOR RWANDA,

SITTING as the Bureau, composed of Judge Arlette Ramaroson, Vice-President of the Tribunal, Judge William H. Sekule, Presiding Judge of Trial Chamber II and Judge Khalida Rachid Khan, Presiding Judge of Trial Chamber III, in accordance with Rule 23 (A) of the Rules of Procedure and Evidence (the "Rules");

NOTING the President's Memorandum ICTR/PRES/037/07 dated 23 May 2007 referring the Bagosora Defence Motion of 17 May 2007 for Disqualification of the Judges to the Bureau in accordance with Rule 15 of the Rules;

BEING SEIZED of "Bagosora Defence Motion to Disqualify Trial Chamber I", filed on 17 May 2007 (the "Motion");

CONSIDERING the "Prosecutor's Response to Bagosora Defence Motion filed 17 May 2007 Requesting Disqualification of Trial Chamber I", filed on 22 May 2007;

CONSIDERING the "Bagosora Defence Reply to Prosecution Response", filed on 24 May 2007;

HEREBY DECIDES the Motion.

INTRODUCTION

1. Théoneste Bagosora requests the disqualification of all three judges hearing his trial, Judge Erik Møse, presiding, Judge Jai Ram Reddy, and Judge Sergei Alekseevich Egorov on the basis of actual bias, or, alternatively, a reasonable apprehension of bias pursuant to Rule 15 of the Rules.

2. Pursuant to Rule 23 (A), the Bureau is composed of the President, the Vice-President and the Presiding Judges of the Trial Chambers. Judge Erik Møse, normally a member of the Bureau in his capacity as President of the Tribunal and Presiding Judge of Trial Chamber I, has recused himself from consideration of the current Motion. The Bureau is therefore presently composed of Judges Arlette Ramaroson, Vice-President of the Tribunal, William H. Sekule, Presiding Judge of Trial Chamber II, and Khalida Rachid Khan, Presiding Judge of Trial Chamber III.

SUBMISSIONS

3. The Accused submits that decisions issued within the past six months consistently and uniquely favour the Prosecution, refuse to consider his submissions, fail to provide a legal basis for their conclusions, and are timed to prejudice the Accused such that they show actual bias or give rise to a reasonable apprehension of bias on the part of the Chamber, which ought to result in disqualification.

4. In addition, the Accused submits that certain decisions expose the Trial Chamber's pre-disposition regarding the guilt of the Accused such that the only course of action to avoid mistrial is dismissal of the Bench.

5. The Prosecution opposes the Motion on the basis that the Accused's failure to persuade the Court is no evidence of bias. The Prosecution submits that the Accused has not demonstrated any actual or reasonably apprehended bias on the part of the Trial Chamber and has not pointed to any decision which was reached by anything other than a proper **[page 3]** process of legal reasoning. The Accused is simply dissatisfied with various rulings and asserts that the Trial Chamber's failure to rule in his favour amounts to judicial bias. Such an argument falls a long way short of displacing the presumption of judicial impartiality.

DELIBERATIONS

6. Rule 15 (A) provides that a Judge may not "sit in any case in which he has a personal interest or concerning which he has or has had any association which might affect his impartiality". This provision has been interpreted broadly to permit any ground of impartiality to be raised before the Bureau as a basis for disqualification.[1] The requirement of impartiality is violated not only where the decision-maker is actually

---

[1] *Prosecutor v. Ntahobali*, Case No. ICTR-97-21-T, Decision on Motion for Disqualification of Judges (Bureau), 7 March 2006, para. 8 (citing *Prosecutor v. Blagojević et al.*, Case No. IT-02-60, Decision on Blagojević's Application Pursuant to Rule 15

biased, but also where there is an appearance of bias.[7] An appearance of bias is established if (a) a Judge is a party to the case, or has a financial or proprietary interest in the outcome of the case, or if the Judge's decision will lead to the promotion of a cause in which he or she is involved; or (b) the circumstances would lead a reasonable observer, properly informed, to reasonably apprehend bias.[3]

7. The apprehension of bias test reflects the maxim that "justice should not only be done, but should manifestly and undoubtedly be seen to be done."[4] Although the standpoint of the Accused is a relevant consideration, the decisive question is whether a perception of lack of impartiality is objectively justified.[5] A mere feeling or suspicion of bias by the accused is insufficient; what is required is an objectively justified apprehension of bias, based on knowledge of all the relevant circumstances.[6] **[page 4]**

8. The Bureau recalls that Judges of this Tribunal enjoy a presumption of impartiality, based on their oath of office and the qualifications for their selection in Article 12 of the Statute, and that the moving party bears the burden of displacing this presumption.[7]

9. The Bureau notes that the Motion does not allege that any interest or association of the Judges gives rise to an apprehension of bias. Rather, it is argued that erroneous legal rulings rendered by the Chamber over the past six months reveal a pattern of bias, actual or reasonably apprehended, against the Accused.

10. With respect to the issue of bias as evidenced through Chamber's decisions, the Bureau held in *Blagojević* that although it "would not rule out entirely the possibility that decisions rendered by a Judge or Chamber by themselves could suffice to establish actual bias, it would be a truly extraordinary case in which they would."[8] Where such allegations are made, the Bureau has a duty to examine the content of the judicial decisions cited as evidence of bias. The purpose of that review is not to detect error, but rather to determine whether such errors, if any, demonstrate that the judge or judges are actually biased, or that there is an appearance of bias based on the objective test described above. Error, if any, on a point of law is insufficient; what must be shown is that the rulings are, or would reasonably be perceived as, attributable to a pre-

---

(B) (Bureau), 19 March 2003, para. 10; *Prosecutor v. Bagosora et al.*, Case No. ICTR-98-41-I, Determination of the Bureau Pursuant to Rule 15 (B) (Bureau), 20 February 2002, paras. 9-11; & *Prosecutor v. Nahimana et al.*, T. 19 September 2000 p. 6).

2 *Prosecutor v. Furundžija*, Case No. IT-95-17/1-A, Judgment (AC), 21 July 2000, paras. 181-88. *See also Prosecutor v. Brđanin and Talić*, Decision on Application by Momir Talic for the Disqualification and Withdrawal of a Judge (TC), 18 May 2000, paras. 9-14.

3 *Furundžija*, Judgment (AC), 21 July 2000, para. 189.

4 *Furundžija*, Judgment (AC), 21 July 2000, para. 195 (*quoting R. v. Sussex Justices* (1923), [1924] 1 K.B. 256, 259 (Lord Hewart)); *Brđanin and Talić*, Decision on Application by Momir Talić for the Disqualification and Withdrawal of a Judge (TC), 18 May 2000, para. 9; *Prosecutor v. Sesay*, Decision on Defence Motion Seeking the Disqualification of Justice Robertson from the Appeals Chamber (Sierra Leone AC), 13 March 2004, para. 16; *Ntahobali*, Decision on Motion for Disqualification of Judges (Bureau), 7 March 2006, para. 9.

5 *Ntahobali*, Decision on Motion for Disqualification of Judges (Bureau), 7 March 2006, para. 9 (*citing Furundžija*, Judgment (AC), 21 July 2000, para. 185). *See also Incal v. Turkey*, (2000) 29 E.H.R.R. 449 (E Ct HR), para. 71: "In deciding whether there is a legitimate reason to fear that a particular court lacks independence or impartiality, the standpoint of the accused is important without being decisive. What is decisive is whether his doubts can be held to be objectively justified".

6 This "objective test" has, in substance, been adopted in a number of decisions before this Tribunal: *Prosecutor v. Seromba*, Case No. ICTR-2001-66-T, Decision on Motion for Disqualification of Judges (Bureau), 25 April 2006, para. 9; *Ntahobali*, Decision on Motion for Disqualification of Judges (Bureau), 7 March 2006, para. 9; *Prosecutor v. Karemera et al.*, Case No. ICTR-98-44-T, Decision on Motion by Karemera for Disqualification of Judges (Bureau), 17 May 2004, para. 9; *Prosecutor v. Nzirorera et al.*, Re. Application for the Disqualification of Judge Mehmet Güney (Bureau), 26 September 2000, paras. 8-9; *Prosecutor v. Nahimana et al.*, Oral Decision (TC), T. 19 September 2000, p. 10; *Nyiramasuhuko and Ntahobali*, Determination of the Bureau in Terms of Rule 15 (B) (Bureau), 7 June 2000, p. 5; *Prosecutor v. Kabiligi*, Decision on the Defence's Extremely Urgent Motion for Disqualification and Objection Based on Lack of Jurisdiction (TC), 4 November 1999, para. 8.

7 *Ntahobali*, Decision on Motion for Disqualification of Judges (Bureau), 7 March 2006, para. 9 (quoting *Prosecutor v. Delalić*, Judgment (AC), para. 707). The reason for this threshold is that while any real appearance of bias on the part of a judge undermines confidence in the administration of justice, it would be equally a threat to the interests of the impartial and fair administration of justice were judges to be disqualified on the basis of unfounded and unsupported allegations of apparent bias. *See id.*: "It needs to be said loudly and clearly that the ground of disqualification is a reasonable apprehension that the judicial officer will not decide the case impartially and without prejudice, rather than that he will decide the case adversely to one party [...] Although it is important that justice must be seen to be done, it is equally important that judicial officers discharge their duty to sit and do not, by acceding too readily to suggestions of apparent bias, encourage parties to believe that, by seeking the disqualification of a judge, they will have their case tried by someone thought to be more likely to decide the case in their favour."

8 *Blagojević et al.*, Decision on Blagojević's Application Pursuant to Rule 15(B) (Bureau), 19 March 2003, para. 14.

disposition against the applicant, and not genuinely related to the application of law, on which there may be more than one possible interpretation, or to the assessment of the relevant facts.[9]

11. The Bureau notes that the submissions of the Accused are, in large part, aimed at the merits of the challenged decisions. To the extent that the Accused appears to be seeking appellate review or reconsideration of the challenged decisions on the basis of alleged errors of law or abuse of discretion, the Bureau reiterates that this is inappropriate pursuant to the jurisprudence discussed above. The Bureau will now examine the challenged decisions in turn.

a) Requests for Disclosure and Investigations Concerning the Assassination of President Habyarimana pursuant to Rule 68

12. The Accused submits that the Trial Chamber's refusal to order the production of this evidence hindered his capacity to present his defence, and is evidence of the Trial Chamber's actual or "latent" bias against the Accused. The use of the term "latent" bias throughout the Motion suggests some confusion on behalf of the Accused. The Bureau stresses that the **[page 5]** objective test does not purport to detect any subjective "latent" bias, but rather to determine whether a reasonable person, properly informed, would reasonably apprehend bias.[10]

13. The Accused alleges that three recent decisions addressing disclosure and investigations concerning the assassination of President Habyarimana show bias or suggest a reasonable apprehension of bias.[11] The Accused argues that the assassination of President Habyarimana is the acknowledged trigger of the massacres and therefore essential to the Prosecution's conspiracy charge and, more generally, informs and underscores its entire case. Therefore, the Accused submits, evidence of the identity of the persons involved in shooting down the President's plane is potentially exculpatory pursuant to Rule 68 of the Rules and of direct relevance to his defence. The Accused argues that, in each of the decisions, the Trial Chamber failed to consider its submissions on the centrality of this event to the case.

14. The Bureau has reviewed the decisions and finds that the Trial Chamber addressed the Accused's submissions regarding the relevance of the identity of the President's assassins to the case. The Trial Chamber has consistently found that: (i) none of the Accused is charged with the assassination of President Habyarimana; (ii) the Prosecution led no direct evidence on this issue; (iii) the issue is collateral; and (iv) evidence of the identity of the President's assassins does not tend to make any of the allegations against the Accused more or less likely.[12] Indeed, the Trial Chamber also addressed these arguments in four decisions issued prior to those challenged here.[13] To the extent that the Accused submits that the sheer number of decisions rendered against his position on this issue somehow suggests bias, the Bureau notes that where a single issue has been the subject of multiple decisions, the consistency of the Trial Chamber's position cannot be the basis for a finding of bias or the appearance thereof.

---

[9] *See e.g., Seromba*, Decision on Motion for Disqualification of Judges (Bureau), 25 April 2006, para. 12 (noting that a showing of an error of law is not sufficient to show bias; "what must be shown is that the rulings are, or would reasonably be perceived as, attributable to a pre-disposition against the applicant"); *Ntahobali*, Decision on Motion for Disqualification of Judges (Bureau), 7 March 2006, para. 12; *Karemera et al.*, Decision on Motion by Karemera for Disqualification of Judges (Bureau), 17 May 2004, para. 13.

[10] *Furundžija*, Judgment (AC), 21 July 2000, para. 189.

[11] The three decisions are: *Bagosora et al.*, Decision on Requests for Disclosure and Investigations Concerning the Assassination of President Habyarimana (TC), 17 October 2006; *Bagosora et al.*, Decision on Request for Certification of Appeal on Disclosure and Investigations Concerning the Assassination of President Habyarimana, 12 December 2006; *Bagosora et al.*, Decision on Ntabakuze Petition for a Writ of Mandamus and Related Defence Requests, 18 April 2007.

[12] *Bagosora et al.*, Decision on Requests for Disclosure and Investigations Concerning the Assassination of President Habyarimana (TC), 17 October 2006, para. 2 (referring to four prior decisions addressing the issue of the relevance of evidence concerning the assassination of President Habyarimana to this trial, and quoting its extensive discussion of this issue from its earlier "Decision on Request for Subpoenas of United Nations Officials (TC)", 6 October 2006, paras. 12-18, which lays out Trial Chamber I's consistent reasoning on this matter); *Bagosora et al.*, Decision on Ntabakuze Petition for a Writ of Mandamus and Related Defence Requests (TC), 18 April 2007, para. 19.

[13] *Bagosora et al.*, Decision on Request for Subpoenas of United Nations Officials (TC), 6 October 2006, paras. 12-18; *Bagosora et al.*, Decision on Ntabakuze Motion for Disclosure of Prosecution Files (TC), 6 October 2006, para. 5; *Bagosora et al.*, Decision on Request for Cooperation of the Government of France (TC), 6 October 2006, paras. 3-6; *Bagosora et al.*, Decision on Disclosure of Defence Witness Statements in Possession of the Prosecution Pursuant to Rule 68 (A) (TC), 8 March 2006, paras. 6-7.

15. The Accused submits that the timing of the 17 October 2006 "Decision on Requests for Disclosure and Investigations Concerning the Assassination of President Habyarimana" demonstrates actual bias against the Accused, or supports finding a reasonable apprehension of bias because it was not issued until almost one year after the Motion was filed. The Accused suggests that this shows bias because if the Trial Chamber had decided to grant his request, then the Prosecution would have had very little time to investigate and search for relevant documents before the end of the trial, which was coming to a close. The Bureau is not persuaded by this wholly speculative argument. The Accused suggests, but does not show, prejudice. Even a showing of actual prejudice, without more, would be insufficient to **[page 6]** show bias.[14] The Bureau recalls that "many factors affect the timing of decisions" and, in the instant case, finds no evidence that the timing of the Decision demonstrates partiality on the part of the Trial Chamber.[15]

16. Finally, the Accused submits that the 12 December 2006 "Decision on Request for Certification of Appeal on Disclosure and Investigations Concerning the Assassination of President Habyarimana" contains evidence of actual bias by the use of language which suggests that a conviction and appeal are foregone conclusions. In denying the Accused's request for certification, Trial Chamber I stated:

> Certification of an interlocutory appeal on these matters would not materially advance the proceedings; on the contrary, it would draw the Appeals Chamber into an unwarranted and premature review of the evidence, which is best reserved for the appeal from the final judgment.[16]

17. The Bureau recognises that, taken in isolation, the phrasing of the final clause of the selected quotation is vague and open to misinterpretation, but does not accept that this proves or even suggests that the Trial Chamber is pre-disposed to believe that the Accused will be convicted. Despite the suggestion that there is more than one extract from these decisions showing evidence of actual bias, the above-quoted passage is the only extract the Accused brought to the Bureau's attention. This isolated remark found in a single decision does not show actual bias or give rise to a reasonable apprehension of bias. Moreover, the Bureau notes that the denial of the request for certification was based on application of the relevant law and assessment of the relevant facts and, thus, does not show bias or give rise to a reasonable apprehension of bias.

b) Request for Exclusion of Bagosora Agenda

18. The Accused submits that three recent decisions related to the admission of a set of photocopied pages alleged to contain his handwriting, known as the "Bagosora agenda", show actual bias or would lead a reasonable observer to apprehend bias.[17] The Accused recalls that he objected to the admission of the "Bagosora agenda" on the basis that the original, complete agenda has never been disclosed, and that the photocopies admitted into evidence contain marks of tampering and falsification. He submits that the Trial Chamber's refusal to both order the production of the original agenda and exclude the photocopied extracts shows bias or gives rise to a reasonable apprehension of bias.

19. Regarding the 11 April 2007 "Decision on Bagosora Motion for Disclosure of Agenda", the Accused submits that the Trial Chamber's deference to the Prosecution's claim that it is not in possession of the entire Agenda demonstrates actual bias against the Accused. Alternatively, it gives rise to a reasonable apprehension of bias by creating a belief that the Chamber will accept the bald assertions of the Prosecution, notwithstanding contrary evidence. The Bureau notes that, in reaching its conclusion, the Trial Chamber considered the submissions of the parties and the relevant evidence concerning the issue, including a **[page 7]** clarification the Chamber requested from the Prosecution.[18] The Bureau finds nothing in the Decision that demonstrates actual bias or would give rise to a reasonable apprehension of bias.

---

14 *Cf.*, *Serumba*, Decision on Motion for Disqualification of Judges (Bureau), 25 April 2006, para. 12 (noting that a showing of an error of law is not sufficient to show bias; "what must be shown is that the rulings are, or would reasonably be perceived as, attributable to a pre-disposition against the applicant").

15 *Karemera et al.*, Decision on Motion by Nzirorera for Disqualification of Trial Judges, 17 May 2004, para. 27.

16 *Bagosora et al.*, Decision on request for certification of appeal on disclosure and investigations concerning the assassination of President Habyarimana (TC), 12 December 2006, para 4.

17 These decisions are: *Bagosora et al.*, Decision on Bagosora Motion for Disclosure of Agenda (TC), 11 April 2007; *Bagosora et al.*, Decision on Bagosora Motion to Exclude Photocopies of Agenda (TC), 11 April 2007; *Bagosora et al.*, Decision on Request for Certification or Reconsideration Concerning the "Bagosora Agenda" (TC), 8 May 2007.

18 *Bagosora et al.*, Decision on Bagosora Motion for Disclosure of Agenda (TC), 11 April 2007, paras. 5 -8.

20. Turning to the 11 April 2007 "Decision on Bagosora Motion to Exclude Photocopies of Agenda", the Accused alleges that the failure of the Trial Chamber to address his concerns regarding the admission of evidence bearing marks of falsification gives rise to a reasonable apprehension of bias. The Bureau does not accept the contention that the Trial Chamber failed to address the Accused's submissions regarding falsification. Noting the distinction between the admissibility of evidence and the weight ultimately attached to it, the Trial Chamber found that the Accused's allegations were relevant to the weight to be attached to the photocopies of the Agenda and would be considered when the Chamber evaluates the evidence as a whole. However, his submissions did not impact admissibility, which was based on the testimony of a handwriting expert.[19] The Bureau considers that this Decision does not give rise to a reasonable apprehension of bias.

21. The Accused submits that the Trial Chamber's refusal to reconsider the merits of his arguments regarding the Agenda in connection with his request to reconsider or certify its decisions regarding the Agenda displays bias or gives rise to a reasonable apprehension thereof. The Accused further submits that the timing of the decision itself displays bias. As the Bureau noted above, the Trial Chamber's consistency on an issue that is the subject of repetitive motions cannot give rise to a reasonable apprehension of bias. With respect to the alleged inconvenient timing of this Decision, the Bureau finds no evidence that it demonstrates partiality on the part of the Judges.[20]

c) Request to Exclude Testimony Adduced in Relation to Immigration Documents

22. The Accused submits that the 30 April 2007 "Decision on Bagosora Motion to Exclude Testimony Relating to Immigration Documents" reinforces the reasonable apprehension of bias by continuing the trend of decisions which ignore the Accused's submissions and consequently favour the Prosecution. The Bureau notes that the Accused does not specify which, if any, of his arguments were ignored, but rather seek to reargue the merits. As noted above, the Bureau's role is not to review or reconsider the Trial Chamber's decisions for possible error, but rather to determine if the decision demonstrates actual bias or gives rise to a reasonable apprehension of bias. The Bureau concludes that the Trial Chamber considered the submissions of the parties, and the Decision was rendered on the basis of applicable law and assessment of relevant facts; it does not suggest actual bias against the Accused or give rise to a reasonable apprehension thereof.

d) Request to Admit Evidence from Witness B-06

23. The Accused submits that the Trial Chamber's Decision, which refused to admit into evidence the written statement of Witness B-06, continued the trend of negative outcomes for the Accused, and increased the likelihood of a reasonable apprehension of bias as perceived by an informed observer.[21] In addition to re-arguing the merits of the Motion, the Accused submits that the Trial Chamber refused to consider his explanations as to why he had not sought admission of Witness B-06's statement at an earlier stage of the proceedings. **[page 8]** According to the Accused, these explanations were submitted in his Reply to the Prosecution Response. The Accused fails to mention that the Reply was filed on 31 March 2007, nearly three weeks after it was due. The Bureau notes that the Trial Chamber provided a reasoned opinion in support of its conclusion based on assessment of the relevant facts and concludes that it does not show bias or give rise to a reasonable apprehension of bias. With regard to the alleged trend of negative outcomes, it is worth noting that on the same day that the Trial Chamber denied the request to admit the statement of Witness B-06, it granted the Accused's request to admit the statement of Witness G-10, noting the importance of G-10's statement to the Defence case.[22]

24. The Accused submits that the Trial Chamber again failed to consider his explanations for the timing of his request to admit the statement of Witness B-06 when it denied his request for certification or reconsideration, and that the Trial Chamber's excessive concern for adherence to the judicial timetable in preference to preservation of the right of the Accused to a fair trial is a further example of the Trial Chamber's actual bias against the Accused. Alternatively, it gives rise to a reasonable apprehension of bias. The Bureau has reviewed the Decision and notes that the Trial Chamber denied the requests based on its finding that the Accused had not met the standard for certification to appeal or the standard for reconsideration.

---

19 *Bagosora et al.*, Decision on Bagosora Motion to Exclude Photocopies of Agenda (TC), 11 April 2007, paras. 5-6.

20 *Cf.*, *Karemera et al.*, Decision on Motion by Nzirorera for Disqualification of Trial Judges, 17 May 2004, para. 27.

21 *Bagosora et al.*, Decision on Bagosora Motion to Tender Statement of Witness B-06, 3 April 2007.

22 *Bagosora et al.*, Decision on Bagosora Motion to Tender Statement of Witness G-10 (TC), 3 April 2007, paras. 4-5.

25. Thus, the Bureau considers that these decisions do not show actual bias. Neither do they give rise to a reasonable apprehension of bias.

e) Request for Suspension of Proceedings and Exclusion of Evidence Falling Outside the Indictment

26. The Accused's submissions related to this section and the following section principally arise from the Trial Chamber's 2 May 2007 "Decision on Bagosora Motion for Additional Time for Closing Brief and On Related Matters". The Accused takes no issue with the first part of the Decision, which grants its second request for an extension of time to file its closing brief. Rather the Accused submits that the Trial Chamber's statements regarding other related matters suggest bias. The first of these statements concerns the Accused's pending request for suspension of proceedings. The Trial Chamber noted that its 13 March 2007 Decision granting the Accused's first request for an extension of time to file his closing brief[23] "made it unnecessary to rule on a Bagosora request to suspend proceedings pending decisions on certain motions".[24]

27. The Accused submits that the Trial Chamber's conclusion that it need not rule on Bagosora's request to suspend proceedings because it had granted the Accused an extension of time to file its closing brief denied the Accused his right to a reasoned opinion. The Accused also submits that not all of the pending motions that were the basis of its request to suspend proceedings had been decided as of 2 May 2007 when the Trial Chamber stated that it considered a ruling on the suspension motion unnecessary. Thus, the Accused submits that this ruling contributes to a reasonable apprehension of bias by creating a perception that not only will the Trial Chamber refuse to consider the submissions of the Accused, in some cases it will refuse to rule at all. The Bureau finds unconvincing the Accused's suggestion that, having twice granted him additional time to file his closing brief, the Trial Chamber **[page 9]** displayed actual or reasonably perceived bias against him by refusing to rule on the motion to suspend proceedings.

28. One of the pending motions that provided the basis for the Accused's request for suspension was a request for exclusion of evidence. The Decision on this motion was rendered on 11 May 2007.[25] The Accused submits that the timing of this Decision - which was rendered nearly one year after the underlying motion was filed and three days before the due date for filing of his closing brief - made any meaningful consideration of its contents impossible before the filing of his closing brief. It is submitted that this gives rise to a reasonable apprehension of bias against the Accused. The Bureau reiterates that many factors affect the timing of decisions and finds no evidence that the timing of the Decision demonstrates any partiality on the part of the Trial Chamber.[26] Moreover, a showing of possible prejudice to the Accused is not sufficient, of itself, to show bias, actual or reasonably apprehended.[27]

f) Request to Hear Testimony of Witness Gatsinzi and for Enforcement of Outstanding Subpoena

29. The 2 May 2007 "Decision on Bagosora Motion for Additional Time for Closing Brief and On Related Matters" also addressed the issue of a pending subpoena against General Marcel Gatsinzi, explaining in brief the history of this issue and noting that General Gatsinzi was unwilling to testify as a witness for the Accused in Arusha and that the Chamber could "do nothing more at this time."[28] The Accused submits that the Trial Chamber's refusal to come to a decision on his outstanding motion for enforcement of the subpoena against General Gatsinzi represents total avoidance of its fundamental duties and notes that the 2 May 2007

---

23 Bagosora et al., Decision on Bagosora Motion Concerning Scheduling of its Closing Brief (TC), 13 March 2007.

24 *Bagosora et al.*, Decision on Bagosora Motion for Additional Time for Closing Brief and on Related Matters (TC), 2 May 2007, para. 4.

25 *Bagosora et al.*, Decision on Bagosora Motion for the Exclusion of Evidence Outside the Scope of the Indictment (TC), 11 May 2007.

26 *Cf.*, *Karemera et al.*, Decision on Motion by Nzirorera for Disqualification of Trial Judges (Bureau), 17 May 2004, para. 27.

27 *Cf.*, *Seromba*, Decision on Motion for Disqualification of Judges (Bureau), 25 April 2006, para. 12 (noting that a showing of an error of law is not sufficient to show bias; "what must be shown is that the rulings are, or would reasonably be perceived as, attributable to a pre-disposition against the applicant").

28 *Bagosora et al.*, Decision on Bagosora Motion for Additional Time for Closing Brief and on Related Matters (TC), 2 May 2007, paras. 5, 7.

Decision is unsupported by any legal authority.[29] The Bureau notes that the Accused disagrees with the Trial Chamber's Decision but reiterates that an error of law, if any, is not sufficient to show actual bias or give rise to a reasonable apprehension of bias.[30] The Bureau finds nothing in the Decision that could lead an independent observer to conclude that the Trial Chamber is pre-disposed against the Accused.

g) Request for Admission into Evidence of Rwandan School Archives

30. The Accused alleges that the Trial Chamber's refusal to admit into evidence Rwandan school archives relating to Prosecution Witness ABQ,[31] and its refusal to **[page 10]** reconsider or certify this Decision for appeal,[32] demonstrate actual bias against the Accused. Alternatively, they create a reasonable apprehension of bias by giving rise to the perception that the Trial Chamber will refuse to consider unavoidable delays in cooperation from sovereign states as sufficient justification for alleged 'late' filings. The Accused further submits that the Trial Chamber's refusal to alter judicial deadlines, even where they may impact the fairness of the proceedings, creates a reasonable apprehension of bias. The Bureau has reviewed the relevant decisions and notes that, in reaching its conclusion, the Trial Chamber considered the submissions of the Accused regarding timeliness, but noted that: (i) Witness ABQ's credibility had been at issue since 2004, (ii) the Accused did not seek the documents until November 2006, and (iii) the Accused did not establish that he had sought to obtain them from Rwandan authorities prior to that time. The Bureau considers that nothing in this Decision demonstrates any actual bias or gives rise to a reasonable apprehension of bias.

CONCLUSION

31. Decisions are rendered on a case by case basis and form part of the inherent discretion and duty of Trial Chambers to control the proceedings in order to ensure a fair and expeditious trial.[33] The Accused has failed to demonstrate that, in rendering the decisions challenged herein, the Judges were animated by any concern other than the relevant legal issues. Neither have the submissions established any trend suggesting a pre-disposition against the Accused. Accordingly, the Bureau finds no evidence of actual bias against the Accused and finds that an objective observer, fully apprised of the relevant circumstances, would not apprehend bias in the instant case.

FOR THE ABOVE REASONS, THE BUREAU

DENIES the Motion.

Arusha, 28 May 2007

Arlette Ramaroson Vice-President	William H. Sekule Presiding Judge, Trial Chamber II	Khalida Rachid Khan Presiding Judge, Trial Chamber III

[Seal of the Tribunal]

---

[29] *Bagosora et al.*, Decision on Bagosora Motion for Additional Time for Closing Brief and on Related Matters (TC), 2 May 2007.

[30] *See e.g., Seromba*, Decision on Motion for Disqualification of Judges (Bureau), 25 April 2006, para. 12 (noting that a showing of an error of law is not sufficient to show bias; "what must be shown is that the rulings are, or would reasonably be perceived as, attributable to a pre-disposition against the applicant"); *Ntahobali*, Decision on Motion for Disqualification of Judges (Bureau), 7 March 2006, para. 12; *Karemera et al.*, Decision on Motion by Karemera for Disqualification of Judges (Bureau), 17 May 2004, para. 13.

[31] *Bagosora et al.*, Decision on Bagosora Defence Request for Admission of Documents (TC), 21 March 2007.

[32] *Bagosora et al.*, Decision on Bagosora Request for certification or reconsideration concerning admission of school documents (TC), 9 May 2007.

[33] *Karemera et al.*, Decision on Motion by Nzirorera for Disqualification of Trial Judges (Bureau), paras. 5, 16, 24, 27 (finding, in response to allegations of unequal treatment, that apparently different outcomes reflect the Chamber's view on the merits of the matters before it).

International Criminal Tribunal for Rwanda
Tribunal Pénal International pour le Rwanda

IN THE APPEALS CHAMBER

Before:	Judge Fausto Pocar, Presiding Judge Mohamed Shahabuddeen Judge Liu Daqun Judge Theodor Meron Judge Wolfgang Schomburg
Registrar:	Mr. Adama Dieng
Decision of:	31 May 2007

THE PROSECUTOR

v.

Édouard KAREMERA
Mathieu NGIRUMPATSE
Joseph NZIRORERA

Case No. ICTR-98-44-AR73.9

DECISION ON "JOSEPH NZIRORERA'S INTERLOCUTORY APPEAL OF DECISION ON OBTAINING PRIOR STATEMENTS OF PROSECUTION WITNESSES AFTER THEY HAVE TESTIFIED"

Counsel for the Defence:

Ms. Dior Diagne Mbaye and Mr. Félix Sow for Édouard Karemera
Ms. Chantal Hounkpatin and Mr. Frédéric Weyl for Mathieu Ngirumpatse
Mr. Peter Robinson and Mr. Patrick Nimy Mayidika Ngimbi for Joseph Nzirorera

Counsel for the Prosecution:

Mr. Hassan Bubacar Jallow
Mr. James Stewart
Mr. Neville Weston Mr. Don Webster

[page 2] 1. **THE APPEALS CHAMBER** of the International Criminal Tribunal for the Prosecution of Persons Responsible for Genocide and Other Serious Violations of International Humanitarian Law Committed in the Territory of Rwanda and Rwandan Citizens Responsible for Genocide and Other Such Violations Committed in the Territory of Neighbouring States between 1 January 1994 and 31 December 1994 ("Appeals Chamber" and "Tribunal", respectively) is seized of "Joseph Nzirorera's Interlocutory Appeal of Decision on Obtaining Prior Statements of Prosecution Witnesses After They Have Testified" filed on 11 April 2007 ("Motion" and "Applicant", collectively).

2. On 23 April 2007, the Prosecution filed its Response, opposing the Motion,[1] and the Applicant filed his Reply on 25 April 2007.[2]

A. Background

3. This is an appeal against the "Decision on Defence Motion for Cooperation of Rwanda to Obtain Statements of Prosecution Witnesses ALG, GK and UB" of 22 March 2007 ("Impugned Decision"), which was rendered by Judges Dennis C. M. Byron and Gberdao Gustave Kam. The Impugned Decision was issued following a motion[3] by the Applicant, which was filed before a full bench of Trial Chamber III composed of Judges Dennis C. M. Byron, Emile Francis Short and Gberdao Gustave Kam.[4] On 19 January 2007, Judge Short withdrew from the bench. According to the Applicant, the Presiding Judge, Judge Byron, requested the President to authorise him and Judge Kam to "conduct routine matters" in his case, pursuant to Rule 15*bis* (F) of the Tribunal's Rules of Procedure and Evidence ("Rules").[5] On receipt of this authorisation, Judges Byron and Kam ("remaining Judges") deliberated on the Motion filed before the Trial Chamber and rendered the Impugned Decision even though, according to the Applicant, he objected to such decision being taken in the absence of a full bench.[6]

4. On 4 April 2007, the remaining Judges granted the Applicant's request for certification to appeal two issues arising from the Impugned Decision namely, whether the remaining Judges had the authority to deliberate and render the Impugned Decision pursuant to Rule 15*bis* (F) of the **[page 3]** Rules; and whether the remaining Judges erred in requiring a "heightened showing of relevance" to obtain undisclosed prior statements of a Prosecution witness after that witness has testified.[7]

B. Submissions

5. The Applicant contends that the remaining Judges exceeded their authority under Rule 15*bis* (F) of the Rules when they deliberated on his Motion, which had been filed before the full bench of the Trial Chamber, and rendered the Impugned Decision.[8] He argues that Rule 15*bis* (F) of the Rules allows for the conduct of routine matters by a Chamber in the absence of one or more of its members, and that his Motion filed before the Trial Chamber was not a routine matter.[9] He requests the Appeals Chamber to vacate the Impugned Decision.[10]

6. The Applicant's second contention is that the remaining Judges erred when they held that "because a greater threshold was required to recall a witness, Mr. Nzirorera was now required to show that the statements sought 'could reveal inconsistencies between the witness' testimony and his prior statements'".[11] In support

---

1 "Prosecution Response to 'Joseph Nzirorera's Interlocutory Appeal of Decision on Obtaining Prior Statements of Prosecution Witnesses After They Have Testified'", 23 April 2007 ("Response").

2 "Reply Brief: Joseph Nzirorera's Interlocutory Appeal of Decision Obtaining Prior Statements of Prosecution Witnesses After They Have Testified", 25 April 2007 ("Reply").

3 "Motion for the Request for Cooperation of [the] Government of Rwanda: Statements of Witnesses ALG, GK, and UB", 2 January 2007 ("Motion filed before the Trial Chamber").

4 Motion, para. 16.

5 Motion, para. 19.

6 Motion, para. 23.

7 Decision on Defence Application for Certification to Appeal Denial of Motion to Obtain Statements of Witnesses ALG and GK, Case No. ICTR-98-44-T, 4 April 2007 ("Decision on Certification"), para. 6 – 10.

8 Motion, para. 38.

9 Motion, para. 32.

10 Motion, para. 38.

11 Motion, paras. 39 – 43.

of this contention, the Applicant submits first that the Prosecution has a continuing duty to disclose prior statements of its witnesses, regardless of the content of those statements;[12] second that prior statements may be relevant and material to the trial even if they are not inconsistent with witness trial testimonies, and therefore the remaining Judges erred in requiring the Applicant to demonstrate that a prior statement was inconsistent with witness trial testimony before requesting it from the Rwandan Government;[13] and finally, the remaining Judges erred in failing to apply the "Legitimate Forensic Purpose Test", which requires a requesting party to show that access to prior testimony could be of material assistance to its case,[14] and claims that the prior statements of Witnesses ALG and GK meet the requirements of this test.[15]

7. In response, the Prosecution calls for a dismissal of the present Motion. It argues that the remaining Judges acted within their jurisdiction in ruling on the Motion filed before the Trial Chamber, as this was a procedural matter which could be properly considered pursuant to Rule 15*bis* (F) of the Rules.[16] It further argues that this rule has the purpose of allowing the remaining Judges to carry out such "administrative and procedural matters as are necessary in order to **[page 4]** continue the trial proceedings".[17] As regards the second issue raised by the Applicant, the Prosecution submits that the remaining Judges correctly exercised their discretion in partially denying the Motion filed before the Trial Chamber.[18]

C. <u>Discussion</u>

8. The Appeals Chamber first considers the Applicant's contention that the Motion filed before the Trial Chamber was not a routine matter within the meaning of Rule 15*bis* (F) of the Rules[19] and that, therefore, the remaining Judges exceeded the authority conferred on them by the President, pursuant to Rule 15*bis* (F) of the Rules, when they rendered the Impugned Decision.[20] In this regard, the Applicant argues that the "delivery of decisions" in the context of this rule, refers to an "act of revealing a decision which has already been made, rather than the making of a decision itself".[21] He further argues that had the remaining Judges "simply published a decision" which had already been deliberated upon and made by the Trial Chamber prior to Judge Short's resignation, they would have been in compliance with Rule 15*bis* (F) of the Rules, but by deliberating on the Motion filed before the Trial Chamber and reaching a decision solely between themselves, they exceeded "the act of delivery of a decision" and therefore the scope of their authority, under Rule 15*bis* (F) of the Rules.[22]

9. The Appeals Chamber notes that, as a general rule, a section of a Trial Chamber shall be composed of three Judges, pursuant to Article 11 of the Statute. However, there are instances provided for in the Rules where a single Judge may act in a case[23] Also, where a Judge is unable to continue sitting in a "part-heard case" for a short duration, the other two Judges of that Trial Chamber may order a continuation of the proceedings in the absence of that Judge, if they are satisfied that it is in the interests of justice to do so.[24] Where a Judge is permanently unavailable, the two remaining Judges of the Trial Chamber may decide whether to continue the proceedings with a substitute Judge[25] which is what has happened in the present case.[26] Furthermore, pursuant

---

12 Motion, paras. 44 – 51.
13 Motion, paras. 52 – 59.
14 Motion, paras. 60 – 68.
15 Motion, paras. 69 – 76.
16 Response, paras. 7 – 14.
17 Response, para. 4.
18 Response, paras. 15 – 22.
19 Motion, paras. 31, 32.
20 Motion, paras. 30 – 38.
21 Motion, para. 33.
22 Motion, para. 33.
23 See Rules 53, 54, 73, 73*bis*, 73ter and 75 of the Rules, which provide for orders and decisions to be issued by a single Judge, and Rule 62 of the Rules, which provides for initial appearance proceedings to be conducted by a single Judge.
24 Rule 15*bis* (A) of the Rules.
25 Rule 15*bis* (D) of the Rules.
26 See Decision on Continuation of the Proceedings, 6 March 2007, where the remaining Judges decided to continue the trial in the Applicant's case with a substitute Judge.

to Rule 15*bis* (F) of the Rules, "the President may, if satisfied that it is in the interest of justice to do so, authorise a Chamber to conduct routine matters, such as the delivery of decisions, in the absence of **[page 5]** one or more of its members". In the present case, the President authorised the Trial Chamber composed of Judges Byron and Kam, to conduct routine matters[27] pending the assignment of a substitute Judge to complete the composition of that Trial Chamber. On receipt of this authorization, the remaining Judges treated the Motion filed before the Trial Chamber as a routine matter and subsequently rendered the Impugned Decision.

10. It has been held at the International Criminal Tribunal for the Former Yugoslavia ("ICTY"), that an initial appearance constitutes a routine matter[28] and a hearing during which issues of sentencing were argued before that Tribunal's Appeals Chamber was also held to have been a routine matter.[29] Furthermore, the ICTY Appeals Chamber has held that "the making of a decision to proceed by way of deposition with regard to the examination of witnesses giving evidence on facts relating to the specific charges made against an accused, thereby having a direct bearing on the determination of the guilt or innocence of the accused, does not [. . .] constitute 'routine matters'".[30] The Appeals Chamber considers that routine matters, within the meaning of Rule 15*bis* (F) of the Rules, are generally matters of a regular and standardised nature, such as the convening of a status conference to organise exchanges between the parties, pursuant to Rule 65*bis* of the Rules. Other matters, both of a substantive and procedural nature, are generally non-routine, for the purposes of Rule 15*bis* (F) of the Rules.

11. In the present case, the Motion filed before the Trial Chamber pertained to a Defence request to the Trial Chamber "to issue a request for cooperation to the Government of Rwanda for it to produce copies of [...] documents" which related to Prosecution Witnesses ALG, GK and UB.[31] It is evident from the Applicant's submissions that the issue of obtaining documents from Rwanda can be traced as far back as 14 September 2005, when the Trial Chamber ordered the Prosecution to use its best efforts to obtain and disclose to the Defence statements made by Prosecution witnesses to the Rwandan Authorities,[32] following a motion by the Applicant. Additionally, on 13 February 2006, the Trial Chamber requested the cooperation of the Government of Rwanda to provide **[page 6]** statements in respect of thirty-seven witnesses, including Witnesses ALG and GK.[33] Witnesses ALG and GK have since testified and their statements have still not been received.[34] Furthermore, the Appeals Chamber notes the Applicant's submission that he has filed five written motions, and that there had been a number of other efforts, including letters to and from the Rwandan Authorities, which eventually culminated in the Motion filed before the Trial Chamber.[35] The Applicant also refers to five previous decisions rendered in his case on issues relating to disclosure of Prosecution witness statements that had been made to the Rwandan Authorities.[36] The Appeals Chamber is of the view that the history of this matter, including the extensive litigation related to it, is indicative of its non-routine nature.

---

27 Impugned Decision, para. 5.

28 *The Prosecutor v. Momir Talić,* Case No. IT-99-36/1, Order of the President for the Conduct of Routine Matters (Initial Appearance), 30 August 1999; *The Prosecutor v. Damir Došen and Dragan Kolundžija,* Order of the President for the Conduct of Routine Matters (Initial Appearance), 26 October 1999.

29 *The Prosecutor v. Duško Tadić,* Case No. IT-94-1, Order of the President Authorising the Appeals Chamber to Conduct a Matter in the Absence of One of its Members, 30 August 1999; See transcript of appeals hearing of 30 August 1999 in *The Prosecutor v. Duško Tadić,* Case No. IT-94-1, pp. 660 - 691.

30 *The Prosecutor v. Zoran Kupreškić et al.,* Case No. IT-95-16-AR73.3, Decision on Appeal by Dragan Papić Against Ruling to Proceed by Deposition, 15 July 1999, para. 14.

31 Impugned Decision, para. 4.

32 Motion, para. 3, referring to Decision on Motions to Compel Inspection and Disclosure and to Direct Witnesses to Bring Judicial and Immigration Records, 14 September 2005, p. 5.

33 See Impugned Decision para. 2 referring to Decision on Motions for Order for Production of Documents by the Government of Rwanda and for Consequential Orders, 13 February 2006.

34 See Impugned Decision, para. 6.

35 Motion, paras. 3 -16.

36 Motion, paras. 3 -14, referring to Decision on Motions to Compel Inspection and Disclosure and to Direct Witnesses to Bring Judicial and Immigration Records, 14 September 2005; Decision on Motions for Order for Production of Documents by the Government of Rwanda and for Consequential Orders, 13 February 2006; Decision on Defence Motion to Report Government of Rwanda to United Nations Security

12. In addition, the remaining Judges took into consideration Article 28 of the Tribunal's Statute, as well as the jurisprudence of both the Tribunal and the ICTY and acknowledged that Witnesses ALG, UN and GK were part of the thirty-seven Prosecution witnesses for whom the Trial Chamber, on 13 February 2006, requested the cooperation of the Rwandan Authorities in furnishing their statements.[37] They reasoned that, at that stage, the Applicant had satisfied the requirements for requesting the cooperation of the Rwandan Authorities to disclose these documents,[38] but the circumstances have since changed,[39] as the Motion filed before the Trial Chamber concerned Prosecution witnesses who have already testified in the Applicant's trial.[40] The Appeals Chamber is of the view that this judicial exercise further reflects the non-routine nature of the issues ruled upon in the Impugned Decision.

13. In sum, the Appeals Chamber considers that in the present case, the issues raised in the Motion filed before the Trial Chamber and ruled upon in the Impugned Decision cannot be considered routine matters within the meaning of Rule 15*bis* (F) of the Rules, by virtue of their complex history and legal nature. **[page 7]**

D. Conclusion

14. On the basis of the foregoing, the Appeals Chamber finds that the remaining Judges exceeded the authority conferred on them by the President, pursuant to Rule 15*bis* (F) of the Rules, in rendering the Impugned Decision. In light of this determination, the Appeals Chamber will not consider the Appellant's contention that the remaining Judges erred by applying an incorrect standard in relation to his request for prior Prosecution witness statements.

E. Disposition

15. For the aforementioned reasons, the Appeals Chamber:

GRANTS the appeal filed by Joseph Nzirorera in part; and

VACATES the Impugned Decision.

Done in English and French, the English text being authoritative.

Dated this the 31 day of May 2007,
at The Hague,
The Netherlands.

Judge Fausto Pocar,
Presiding

[Seal of the Tribunal]

Council, 2 October 2006; Decision on Defence Motion for Further Order to Obtain Documents in Possession of Government of Rwanda, 27 November 2006; Decision on Defence Motion for Exclusion of Witness GK's Testimony or for Request for Cooperation from Government of Rwanda, 27 November 2006.

37 Impugned Decision, paras. 2, 9, 10, referring to Decision on Motions for Order for Production of Documents by the Government of Rwanda and for Consequential Orders, 13 February 2006.

38 Impugned Decision, para. 9.

39 Impugned Decision, paras. 6, 10.

40 Impugned Decision, para. 10.

International Criminal Tribunal for Rwanda
Tribunal pénal international pour le Rwanda

OR: ENG

TRIAL CHAMBER III

Before Judges: Dennis C. M. Byron, Presiding
Gberdao Gustave Kam
Vagn Joensen

Registrar: Adama Dieng

Date: 8 June 2007

THE PROSECUTOR

v.

Édouard KAREMERA
Mathieu NGIRUMPATSE
Joseph NZIRORERA

Case No. ICTR-98-44-T

DECISION ON JOSEPH NZIRORERA'S SUBMISSION TO SUBSTITUTE JUDGE

Office of the Prosecutor:
Don Webster
Alayne Frankson-Wallace
Iain Morley
Saidou N'Dow
Gerda Visser
Sunkarie Ballah-Conteh
Takeh Sendze

Defence Counsel for Édouard Karemera
Dior Diagne Mbaye and Félix Sow

Defence Counsel for Mathieu Ngirumpatse
Chantal Hounkpatin and Frédéric Weyl

Defence Counsel for Joseph Nzirorera
Peter Robinson and Patrick Nimy Mayidika Ngimbi

[page 2] INTRODUCTION

1. The trial in this case started on 19 September 2005 before a bench of the Trial Chamber composed of Judges Dennis C. M. Byron, presiding, Emile Francis Short and Gberdao Gustave Kam. On 19 January 2007, Judge Short decided to withdraw from the case.

2. Under Rule 15 *bis* (D) of the Rules of Procedure and Evidence ("Rules"), the remaining Judges decided on the continuation of the proceedings with a substitute Judge.[1] On 20 April 2007, the Appeals Chamber affirmed that Decision.[2]

3. Judge Vagn Joensen was then appointed by the Secretary-General as an *ad litem* Judge to form part of the bench in the present case.[3] This appointment was subject to his familiarisation with the record of the proceedings in accordance with Rule 15 *bis* (D) of the Rules. On 8 June 2007, Judge Joensen certified that he has familiarised himself with the record of the proceedings.[4] He therefore joined the bench in the current matter.

4. Meanwhile, on 24 April 2007, the Defence for Nzirorera filed a submission to be transmitted to the substitute Judge requesting him (i) to review some specific material in view of the familiarisation process and (ii) to detail the specific steps taken to familiarise himself with the proceedings.[5] Not only did the Prosecution request that the Chamber deny the Motion in its entirety but also that costs be disallowed in respect of this filing.[6]

DISCUSSION

5. In the present motion, the Defence for Nzirorera requests that the substitute Judge carefully review the video-tapes of the testimony of each of the 13 prosecution witnesses on direct and cross examination. It also requests that when viewing the video tapes of the testimony, the substitute Judge consult the exhibits in the same way in which he would have been consulting them had he been hearing the testimony in real time. The substitute Judge is further invited to consult a Procedural History compiled by the Defence. Furthermore, the Defence requests that when making the certification, the substitute Judge detail the specific steps taken to familiarize himself with the proceedings "so that there are no questions or **[page 3]** lingering doubts that the substitute Judge has viewed the video recordings of all of the testimony and otherwise properly carried out the expectations of the remaining Judges, Appeals Chamber, and the parties".

6. Rule 15 *bis* (D) of the Rules of Procedure and Evidence prescribes as follows:

> If, in the circumstances mentioned in the last sentence of paragraph (C), the accused withholds his consent, the remaining Judges may nonetheless decide to continue the proceedings before a Trial Chamber with a substitute Judge if, taking all the circumstances into account, they determine unanimously that doing so would serve the interests of justice. This decision is subject to appeal directly to a full bench of the Appeals Chamber by either party. If no appeal is taken or the Appeals Chamber affirms the decision of the Trial Chamber, the President shall assign to the existing bench a Judge, *who, however, can join the bench only after he or she has certified that he or she has familiarised himself or herself with the record of the proceedings.* Only one substitution under this paragraph may be made."[7]

7. There is no discussion, as previously stated, that the fact that the substitute Judge will be able to familiarise himself with the record of the proceedings is a core element when determining that it would be

---

1 *Prosecutor v. Edouard Karemera, Mathieu Ngirumpatse, Joseph Nzirorera ("Karemera et al.")*, Case No. ICTR-98-44-T, Decision on Continuation of the Proceedings (TC), 6 March 2007 ("Decision on Continuation").

2 *Karemera et al.*, Decision on Appeals Pursuant to Rule 15 *bis* (D) (AC), 20 April 2007 ("Rule 15 *bis* Appeals Chamber Decision").

3 Judge Joensen was sworn in on 2 May 2007.

4 Certification under Rule 15 *bis* (D) of the Rules of Procedure and Evidence, filed on 8 June 2007.

5 Joseph Nzirorera's Submission to Substitute Judge, filed on 24 April 2007 ("Defence Motion").

6 Prosecutor's Response to Joseph Nzirorera's Submission to Substitute Judge, filed on 25 April 2007.

7 Emphasis added.

in the interests of justice to continue the proceedings.[8] This is one of the safeguards to ensure that fair trials rights are not compromised.[9]

8. The Rules, however, neither describe how a substitute Judge is expected to familiarise himself with the record of the proceedings nor require that the substitute Judge provides details as to how he familiarised himself with the record. According to the jurisprudence of the Tribunal, this familiarisation process can be done through different methods and means such as relying upon transcripts, audio and video-records of the testimonies, exhibits and decisions.[10] The length of the familiarisation process will depend on the particularities of each case and on each Judge who is expected to familiarise himself or herself with the record.[11] There is no mathematical or Standard rule as how this familiarisation process should **[page 4]** take place. The Appeals Chamber has never considered that there is only one method or Standard rule for such a process.[12]

9. Contrary to what the Defence seems to suggest,[13] the familiarisation process should not be confused with the assessment of the credibility and reliability of a witness. The Chamber agrees with the Defence that the assessment of the credibility of a witness, including through the observation of his or her demeanour in court, is a major issue.[14] However, the probative value to be attached to testimony, including the credibility and reliability of the witness, is to be determined at a later stage, when considering the evidence adduced by each party as a whole.[15]

10. The Chamber takes note of the suggestions made by the Defence for Nzirorera in view of assisting the substitute Judge in his familiarisation with the record of the proceedings. The Chamber, however, does not find appropriate that the substitute Judge provides detail as to the specific steps taken to familiarise himself with the record of the proceedings.

11. The judges are appointed to the Tribunal on the basis of their high moral character, impartiality and integrity and professional experience at the highest judicial offices.[16] It should be expected that each Judge, as a professional Judge, has his own method when seeking to familiarise himself with the proceedings. Requesting a Judge to detail how he prepares for and masters a case would not only be offensive and challenge

---

8 Decision on Continuation, para. 70. *Karemera et al.*, Case No. ICTR-98-44-AR15bis.2, Reasons For Decision on Interlocutory Appeals Regarding the Continuation of Proceedings with a Substitute Judge and on Nzirorera's Motion for Leave to Consider New Material (AC), 22 October 2004, paras. 57-58; *Karemera et al*, Case No. ICTR-98-44-AR15bis.3, Decision on Appeals pursuant to Rule 15*bis* (D) (AC), 20 April 2007, para. 43.

9 Rule 15 *bis* Appeals Chamber Decision, para. 43.

10 *Karemera et al.*, Case No. ICTR-98-44-AR15bis.2, Reasons For Decision on Interlocutory Appeals Regarding the Continuation of Proceedings with a Substitute Judge and on Nzirorera's Motion for Leave to Consider New Material (AC), 22 October 2004, paras. 57-58.

11 In the *Nyiramasuhuko et al.* case, Judge Solomy Balungi Bossa was assigned to Trial Chamber II by the President on 20 October 2003. Judge Bossa certified that she had familiarized herself with the record of the proceedings less than two months after her assignment to the Tribunal and while 23 witnesses had already been heard by Trial Chamber II over 107 trial days (*Prosecutor v. Nyiramasuhuko et al.*, Joint Case No. ICTR-98-42-T, Certification in the Matter of Proceedings under Rule 15 *bis* (D), 5 December 2003). In the *Bizimungu et al.* case, Judge Emile Francis Short was assigned to Trial Chamber II by the President on 18 May 2004. Judge Short certified that he had familiarized himself with the record of the proceedings less than 15 days after his assignment to the Tribunal and while 28 witnesses had been heard by Trial Chamber II over 112 trial days *(Prosecutor v. Bizimungu et al.*, Case No. ICTR-99-50-T, Certification in the Matter of Proceedings under Rule 15 *bis* (D), 3 June 2004).

12 The Appeals Chamber explicitly made reference to the Decision on Continuation of the Proceedings noting: "In the present case, the remaining Judges took into consideration that the substitute Judge will need to review the "records of the proceedings, including the transcripts, audio and video-recordings, to observe the demeanour of the witness" in determining that it would be in the interests of justice to continue the proceedings with a substitute Judge". (para. 43)

13 Defence Motion, para. 5.

14 *Ibidem.*

15 *Prosecuiion v. Nyiramasuhuko et al.*, Case No. ICTR-97-21-AR73, Decision on the Appeals by Pauline Nyiramasuhuko and Arsène Shalom Ntahobali on the "Decision on Defence Urgent Motion to Declare Parts of the Evidence of Witnesses RV and ABZ Inadmissible" (AC), 2 July 2004, para. 15; *Prosecutor v. Georges Anderson Rutaganda*, Case No. ICTR-96-3-A, Judgement (AC), para. 33; *Prosecutor v. Detalic and Delic*, Decision on Application of Defendant Zejnil Delalic for Leave to Appeal Against the Decision of the Trial Chamber of 19 January 1998 for the Admissibility of Evidence (AC), 4 March 1998.

16 Statute, Art. 12: "The permanent and *ad litem* Judges shall be persons of high moral character, impartiality and integrity who possess the qualifications required in their respective countries for appointment to the highest judicial offices. In the overall composition of the Chambers and sections of the Trial Chambers, due account shall be taken of the experience of the Judges in criminal law, international law, including international humanitarian law and human rights law."

his capacities as a Judge, but also intrudes upon his judicial function. The Defence request therefore falls to be rejected. **[page 5]**

12. Although the Defence indeed should refrain from filing frivolous motions,[17] the Chamber does not find that sanctions against the Defence Counsel are warranted, as per requested by the Prosecution.

FOR THOSE REASONS, THE CHAMBER

I. DENIES the Defence Motion in its entirety;

II. DENIES the Prosecution request that the costs of the Motion be disallowed.

Arusha, 8 June 2007, done in English.

Dennis C. M. Byron	Gberdao Gustave Kam	Vagn Joensen
Presiding Judge	Judge	Judge

[Seal of the Tribunal]

[17] See Rule 73 (F) of the Rules: "In addition to the sanctions envisaged by Rule 46, a Chamber may impose sanctions against Counsel if Counsel brings a motion, including a preliminary motion, that, in the opinion of the Chamber, is frivolous or is an abuse of process. Such sanctions may include non-payment, in whole or in part, of fees associated with the motion and/or costs thereof".

International Criminal Tribunal for Rwanda
Tribunal pénal international pour le Rwanda

OR: ENG

TRIAL CHAMBER III

Before Judges: Dennis C. M. Byron, Presiding
Gberdao Gustave Kam
Vagn Joensen

Registrar: Adama Dieng

Date: 17 July 2007

THE PROSECUTOR

v.

Édouard KAREMERA
Mathieu NGIRUMPATSE
Joseph NZIRORERA

Case No. ICTR-98-44-T

DECISION ON MOTIONS TO VACATE DECISIONS

Rules 15* bis *(F) and 73 of the Rules of Evidence and Procedure

Office of the Prosecutor:
Don Webster
Alayne Frankson-Wallace
Iain Morley
Saidou N'Dow
Gerda Visser
Sunkarie Ballah-Conteh
Takeh Sendze

Defence Counsel for Édouard Karemera
Dior Diagne Mbaye and Félix Sow

Defence Counsel for Mathieu Ngirumpatse
Chantal Hounkpatin and Frédéric Weyl

Defence Counsel for Joseph Nzirorera
Peter Robinson and Patrick Nimy Mayidika Ngimbi

[page 2] INTRODUCTION

1. The trial in this case started on 19 September 2005 before Trial Chamber III composed of Judges Dennis C. M. Byron, presiding, Emile Francis Short and Gberdao Gustave Kam. On 19 January 2007, Judge Short withdrew from the case.

2. Under Rule 15 *bis* (D) of the Rules of Procedure and Evidence ("Rules"), the remaining Judges decided on the continuation of the proceedings with a substitute judge.[1] That Decision was affirmed by the Appeals Chamber in April 2007.[2]

3. Although Judge Vagn Joensen was appointed on 2 May 2007 as substitute judge in the present case, he first had to certify that he had familiarised himself with the record of the proceedings before joining the Bench.[3]

4. Meanwhile, according to the authorization given by the President of the Tribunal to the Trial Chamber composed of Judges Dennis Byron and Gberdao Gustave Kam, to conduct routine matters under Rule 15 *bis* (F) of the Rules,[4] the remaining Judges delivered decisions in the absence of the substitute judge.

5. Between 14 March 2007 and 10 May 2007, 11 decisions were delivered accordingly by this Chamber composed of Judges Dennis Byron and Gberdao Gustave Kam. However, the Defence for Nzirorera lodged an appeal against one of these decisions, arguing, among other things, that the remaining Judges exceeded their authority under Rule 15 *bis* (F) of the Rules because the Motion on which they deliberated was not a routine matter.[5] In its Decision of 31 May 2007, the Appeals Chamber granted this appeal and vacated the **[page 3]** Impugned Decision.[6] It also laid down standards and principles defining what should be considered a routine matter under Rule 15 *bis* (F) of the Rules.

6. On 4 June 2007, as a result of the Appeals Chamber's Decision, the Defence for Nzirorera moved that five decisions delivered by the Chamber composed of Judges Dennis Byron and Gberdao Gustave Kam be vacated.[7] It also requested that these Judges disqualify themselves from all further deliberations on the concerned decisions, including the Impugned Decision that was vacated by the Appeals Chamber on 31 May 2007.[8]

---

1 *Prosecutor v. Edouard Karemera, Mathieu Ngirumpatse, Joseph Nzirorera ("Karemera et al.")*, Case No. ICTR-98-44-T, Decision on Continuation of the Proceedings (TC), 6 March 2007.

2 *Karemera et al.*, Decision on Appeals Pursuant to Rule 15 *bis* (D) (AC), 20 April 2007.

3 See Rules of Procedure and Evidence, Rule 15*bis* (D): "If, in the circumstances mentioned in the last sentence of paragraph (C), the accused withholds his consent, the remaining Judges may nonetheless decide to continue the proceedings before a Trial Chamber with a substitute Judge if, taking all the circumstances into account, they determine unanimously that doing so would serve the interests of justice. This decision is subject to appeal directly to a full bench of the Appeals Chamber by either party. If no appeal is taken or the Appeals Chamber affirms the decision of the Trial Chamber, the President shall assign to the existing bench a Judge, who, however, can join the bench only after he or she has certified that he or she has familiarised himself or herself with the record of the proceedings. Only one substitution under this paragraph may be made."

4 See: Interoffice Memorandum from the President to Judge Byron, filed on 13 March 2007; Rules of Procedure and Evidence, Rule 15 *bis* (F): "In case of illness or an unfilled vacancy or in any other similar circumstances, the President may, if satisfied that it is in the interests of justice to do so, authorise a Chamber to conduct routine matters, such as the delivery of decisions, in the absence of one or more of its members."
See: Interoffice Memorandum from the President to Judge Byron, filed on 13 March 2007.

5 See: Joseph Nzirorera's Interlocutory Appeal of Decision on Obtaining Prior Statements of Prosecution Witnesses After They Have Testified", filed on 11 April 2007; also Decision on Defence Motion for Certification to Appeal Denial of Motion to Obtain Statements of Witnesses ALG and GK (TC), 4 April 2007.

6 *Karemera et al.*, Case No. ICTR-98-44AR73.9, Decision on "Joseph Nzirorera's Interlocutory Appeal of Decision on Obtaining prior Statements of Prosecution Witnesses after they have testified" (AC), 31 May 2007.

7 Joseph Nzirorera's Motion to Vacate Decisions and For Disqualification of Judges Byron and Kam, filed on 4 June 2007 ("Nzirorera's Motion"), see also the Reply filed on 11 June 2007. In addition to the Decision on Defence Motion for Cooperation of Rwanda to Obtain Statements of Witnesses ALG, GK and UB which was vacated by the Appeals Chamber, the Defence seeks that the following Decisions be vacated: Decision on Defence Motion for Certification to Appeal Decision on Appeals Chamber Remand of Judicial Notice (TC), 22 March 2007; Decision on Prosecutor's Motion for an Order to File Notice of Alibi (TC), 22 March 2007; Decision on Defence Motion for Certification to Appeal Decision on False Testimony (TC), 23 March 2007; Scheduling Order for the Resumption of the Trial (TC), 2 May 2007; Decision on Defence Motion for Subpoenas to Prosecution Witnesses (TC), 10 May 2007.

8 Nzirorera's Motion and Reply.

7. The issue of the disqualification was referred to the Bureau in accordance with Rule 15 (B) of the Rules.[9] On 14 June 2007, the Bureau composed of the Vice-President of the Tribunal and the Presiding Judges of each Trial Chamber denied Nzirorera's application for disqualification of Judges Dennis Byron and Gberdao Gustave Kam of any further deliberations on the prior decisions he seeks to be vacated.[10] It held that

> The possibility that, having previously decided the relevant issues on the merits, Judges Byron and Kam are pre-disposed to apply the law and assess the facts in the same manner is insufficient as a matter of law to displace the presumption of impartiality and show bias, either actual or reasonably apprehended.[11]

8. In addition to Nzirorera's Motion for vacating some of the prior Decisions delivered under Rule 15 *bis* (F), it must be noted that in the Decision of 10 May 2007, the Chamber composed of Judges Dennis Byron and Gberdao Gustave Kam also noted the appeal lodged by the Defence for Nzirorera against a prior decision delivered under Rule 15 *bis* (F). While considering that the application at stake was a routine matter falling within the ambit of its authority, the said Chamber indicated that **[page 4]**

> Should the Appeals Chamber lay out standards and principles in the interpretation of the phrase "to conduct routine matters", the Chamber will then determine whether reconsideration of the decisions rendered pursuant to its Rule 15 *bis* (F), including this Decision, is warranted in light of these standards and principles.[12]

9. In view of those circumstances, the Chamber, now fully composed, is ready to rule on Nzirorera's Motion to vacate prior decisions as well as review other decisions delivered under Rule 15 *bis* (F) for which the Defence for Nzirorera does not seek vacation, considering the Appeals Chamber's principles set out in the Decision of 31 May 2007.

10. It must be noted that the Defence for Ngirumpatse joins in part the application made by the Defence for Nzirorera to vacate some prior decisions.[13] The Prosecution does not object to the Chamber vacating three of the prior Decisions as requested by the Defence for Nzirorera.[14]

DISCUSSION

11. In its Decision of 31 May 2007, the Appeals Chamber considered that

> routine matters, within the meaning of Rule 15*bis* (F) of the Rules, are generally matters of a regular and standardised nature, such as the convening of a status conference to organise exchanges between the parties, pursuant to Rule 65*bis* of the Rules. Other matters, both of a substantive and procedural nature, are generally non-routine, for the purpose of Rule 15*bis* (F) of the Rules.[15]

---

9 Interoffice Memorandum from Judge Dennis Byron, Presiding Judge in the case and President of the Tribunal to Judge Khalida Rachid Khan, Vice-President dated 11 June 2007.

10 As noted in the Bureau's Decision, Judge Byron, who is also the President of the Tribunal, had "recused himself from consideration of Joseph Nzirorera's Motion for disqualification since the decision at issue involved him" (see *Karemera et al.*, Decision on Motion to Vacate Decisions and For Disqualification of Judges Byron and Kam (Bureau), 14 June 2007, para. 1).

11 *Karemera et al.*, Decision on Motion to Vacate Decisions and For Disqualification of Judges Byron and Kam (Bureau), 14 June 2007, para. 15.

12 Decision on Defence Motion for Subpoenas to Prosecution Witnesses (TC), 10 May 2007, para. 9.

13 *Mémoire pour M. Ngirumpatse sur la Joseph Nzirorera's Motion to Vacate Decision*, filed on 11 June 2007. The Defence for Ngirumpatse moves the Chamber to vacate: Decision on Defence Motion for Certification to Appeal Decision on Appeals Chamber Remand of Judicial Notice; Decision on Defence Motion for Certification to Appeal Decision on False Testimony; Scheduling Order for the Resumption of the Trial. It objects to the Chamber vacating the Decision on Prosecutor's Motion for an Order to File Notice of Alibi.

14 Prosecutor's Response to Joseph Nzirorera's Motion to Vacate Decisions and for Disqualification of Judges Byron and Kam, para. 2. The Prosecution does not object to the Chamber vacating its orders with regard to Decision on Defence Motion for Certification to Appeal Decision on Appeals Chamber Remand of Judicial Notice; Decision on Defence Motion for Certification to Appeal Decision on False Testimony; Decision on Defence Motion for Subpoenas to Prosecution Witnesses.

15 *Karemera et al.*, Case No. ICTR-98-44AR73.9, Decision on "Joseph Nzirorera's Interlocutory Appeal of Decision on Obtaining prior Statements of Prosecution Witnesses after they have testified" (AC), 31 May 2007, para. 10.

The Appeals Chamber also took into account the fact that a matter was subject to extensive litigation and judicial exercise as indicative of its non-routine nature.[16] **[page 5]**

12. The Chamber notes that, concerning two prior decisions, the issue of whether routine matters were concerned – and whether these decisions should therefore be vacated – is now moot.[17] The Appeals Chamber has already ruled on the issues in connection with the Decision on Defence Motion for Certification to Appeal Decision on Witness Proofing and the Chamber, acting under Rule 15 *bis* (F).[18] The Chamber is also of the view that the matter in connection with the Decision granting disclosure of closed session transcripts to the Canadian Authorities is now moot as those documents were disclosed.[19] In that respect, it must be recalled that the Defence for Nzirorera did not object to such disclosure.[20] The Chamber further notes that the Defence for Nzirorera does not seek vacation of any of the above-mentioned two decisions.

13. In view of the Appeals Chamber's standards, the Chamber considers that the prior Orders for the transfer of Prosecution Witnesses from Rwanda as well as the prior Decisions granting an extension of time to respond to a Prosecution Motion must be considered as dealing with routine matters within the meaning of Rule 15 *bis* (F) of the Rules.[21] The Chamber further notes that the Defence for Nzirorera does not seek the vacation of these decisions and that the Defence for Karemera and Ngirumpatse had submitted that extension of time for filing submissions is a routine matter.[22] There is therefore no need to vacate those decisions.

14. The Chamber also recalls its oral Decision of 12 June 2007, where it found that in view of the Appeals Chamber standards, a scheduling order is a routine matter for the purposes of Rule 15 *bis* (F) of the Rules.[23] In reaching this conclusion, the Chamber held that **[page 6]**

> The commencement of a trial is based on other factors than the scheduling order itself. The goal of the scheduling order is to provide the parties, and also the Registrar, and other organs of the Tribunal concerned, by judicial organisation, an advance notice as to when the trial session will take place. In these circumstances, the trial session could have resumed today, even if a scheduling order had not been made.[24]

The Scheduling Order of 2 May 2007 is therefore maintained.[25]

15. Conversely, in view of the standards set out by the Appeals Chamber and in particular the fact that the issues at stake were subject to extensive litigation, the Chamber finds that the Defence Motion for Certification

---

16 See *Karemera et al.*, Case No. ICTR-98-44AR73.9, Decision on "Joseph Nzirorera's Interlocutory Appeal of Decision on Obtaining prior Statements of Prosecution Witnesses after they have testified" (AC), 31 May 2007, at para. 11: "The Appeals Chamber is of the view that the history of this matter, including the extensive litigation related to is, is indicative of its non-routine nature."

See at paragraph 12 (footnotes omitted):

> In addition, the remaining Judges took into consideration Article 28 of the Tribunal's Statute, as well as the jurisprudence of both the Tribunal and the ICTY and acknowledged that Witnesses ALG, UN and GK were part of the thirty-seven Prosecution witnesses for whom the Trial Chamber, on 13 February 2006, requested the cooperation of the Rwandan Authorities in furnishing their statements. They reasoned that, at that stage, the Applicant had satisfied the requirements for requesting the cooperation of the Rwandan Authorities to disclose these documents, but the circumstances have since changed, as the Motion filed before the Trial Chamber concerned Prosecution witnesses who have already testified in the Applicant's trial. The Appeals Chamber is of the view that this judicial exercise further reflects the non-routine nature of the issues ruled upon in the Impugned Decision.

17 Decision on Defence Motion for Certification to Appeal Decision on Witness Proofing (TC), 14 March 2007; Decision on Defence Motion for Certification to Appeal Denial of Motion to Obtain Statements of Witnesses ALG and GK (TC), 4 April 2007.

18 *Karemera et al.*, Case No. ICTR-98-44AR73.8, Decision on Interlocutory Appeal Regarding Witness Proofing (AC), 11 May 2007.

19 Decision on Prosecution's Motion to Unseal and Disclose to the Canadian Authorities the Transcripts of Witness CEA (TC), 22 March 2007.

20 *Ibid.*, para. 4.

21 Order for the Transfer of Prosecution Witnesses from Rwanda (TC), 26 April 2007; Decision Supplementing the Chamber's Prior Order For The Transfer Of Prosecution Witnesses From Rwanda (TC), 8 May 2007; *Décision accordant une prorogation de délai de réponse a une requête du Procureur* (TC), 10 May 2007.

22 See: *Décision accordant une prorogation de délai de réponse a une requête du Procureur* (TC), 10 May 2007, para. 6.

23 T. 12 June 2007, pp. 17-18.

24 T. 12 June 2007, p. 18.

25 Scheduling Order for the Resumption of the Trial (TC), 2 May 2007.

to Appeal Decision on Appeals Chamber Remand of Judicial Notice and the Defence Motion for Certification to Appeal Decision on False Testimony could not be considered as routine matters upon which Judges Byron and Kam could rule in the absence of the third Judge. Consequently, the prior Decisions on these motions are to be vacated, as requested by the Defence for Nzirorera and the Defence for Ngirumpatse.[26]

16. As already indicated for similar reasons, the Chamber also finds that the prior Decision on Defence Motion for Subpoenas to Prosecution Witnesses needs to be vacated.[27]

17. The Defence for Ngirumpatse opposes that the Decision on Prosecutor's Motion for an Order to File Notice of Alibi be vacated.[28] It submits that Nzirorera has no interest in claiming that this Decision be vacated, and that if the Prosecutor was not satisfied with this Decision, he could have applied for a certification to appeal the Decision.

18. The Chamber does not agree with this submission. In view of the Appeals Chamber standards in the Decision of 31 May 2007, the issue of filing a notice of alibi cannot be considered as a routine matter. It does not have a regular and standardised nature and it certainly raises extensive litigation between the parties. Therefore, having found that the Chamber composed of Judges Byron and Kam acting under Rule 15 *bis* (F) of the Rules committed an error of law, this Chamber has the inherent power to reconsider prior decisions **[page 7]** in light of the Appeals Chamber's principles.[29] The Chamber further notes that since then, the Prosecution filed another motion for enforcement of a notice of alibi by the Defence with a broader scope than the initial motion which was decided on 22 March 2007 by the two remaining Judges.[30] In view of these circumstances, the Chamber finds that the Decision on Prosecutor's Motion for an Order to File Notice of Alibi must also be vacated.

FOR THOSE REASONS, THE CHAMBER

I. **GRANTS** in part the Motions of Joseph Nzirorera and Mathieu Ngirumpatse;

II. **AND DECIDES** to vacate the following:

1) Decision on Defence Motion for Certification to Appeal Decision on Appeals Chamber Remand of Judicial Notice, 22 March 2007;

2) Decision on Defence Motion for Cooperation of Rwanda to Obtain Statements of Witnesses ALG, GK and UB, 22 March 2007;

3) Decision on Prosecutor's Motion for an Order to File Notice of Alibi, 22 March 2007;

4) Decision on Defence Motion for Certification to Appeal Decision on False Testimony, 22 March 2007; and

5) Decision on Defence Motion for Subpoenas to Prosecution Witnesses, 10 May 2007.

---

26 Decision on Defence Motion for Certification to Appeal Decision on Appeals Chamber Remand of Judicial Notice (TC), 22 March 2007; Decision on Defence Motion for Certification to Appeal Decision on False Testimony (TC), 23 March 2007. See Nzirorera's Motion, para. 1; Ngirumpatse's Motion, para.7; the Prosecution does not oppose this request (See Prosecutor's Response, para. 1).

27 Decision on Defence Motion for Subpoenas to Prosecution Witnesses (TC), 10 May 2007; See: T. 13 June 2007, pp. 5-6 and Decisions on Joseph Nzirorera's Motions to Vacate the Decision on Defence Motion for Subpoenas to Prosecution Witnesses, to Exclude the Testimony of Witnesses AMB, ANU, AWD, AWE, FH, and KGV, and to postpone the testimony of Witness ANU (TC), 14 June 2007.

28 Decision on Prosecutor's Motion for an Order to File Notice of Alibi (TC), 22 March 2007; Ngirumpatse's Motion, paras. 3-5.

29 According to the established jurisprudence, a Chamber has the inherent power to reconsider its decisions when (?) a new fact has been discovered that was not known to the Chamber at the time it made its original Decision, (ii) there has been a material change in circumstances since it made its original Decision, or (ii) there is reason to believe that its original Decision was erroneous or constituted an abuse of power on the part of the Chamber, resulting in injustice thereby warranting the exceptional remedy of reconsideration. See: *Karemera et al.*, Case No. ICTR-98-44-PT, Decision on the Defence Motions for Reconsideration of Protective Measures for Prosecution Witnesses, 29 August 2005, para. 8; *Karemera et al.*, Case No. ICTR-98-44-T, Decision on Defence Motion for Modification of Protective Order: Timing of Disclosure, 31 October 2005, para. 3; *Karemera et al.*, Case No. ICTR-98-44-T, Decision on Motion for Reconsideration or Certification to Appeal Decision on Motion for Order Allowing Meeting with Defence Witness, 11 October 2005, para. 8 (note also the authorities cited in footnotes contained within that paragraph).

30 Prosecutor's Cross-Motion for Enforcement of Reciprocal Disclosure Pursuant to Rule 67, filed on 18 June 2007.

III. DENIES the remainder of Joseph Nzirorera's and Mathieu Ngirumpatse's Motions.

Arusha, 17 July 2007, done in English.

Dennis C. M. Byron	Gberdao Gustave Kam	Vagn Joensen
Presiding Judge	Judge	Judge

[Seal of the Tribunal]

Commentary

1. Introduction

The inability of a judge to continue sitting in a part-heard case has proved to be a rather thorny issue for the *ad hoc* criminal tribunals.[1] Even after a pertinent amendment was introduced in the Rules of Procedure and Evidence to address the problem, Trial Chambers have not always been able to put together a coherent set of criteria to respond to the dilemma of whether to reinstitute the trial *de novo,* or continue with a substitute judge. Each solution comes with its own advantages and disadvantages: restarting the trial does seem to preserve the credibility of the procedure, as well as guaranteeing fair trial rights; at the same time, however, it entails unavoidable delay, and also brings about probative drawbacks, as there are no assurances that the evidence formerly produced will be available in the new trial.[2]

On the other hand, continuing the trial with a substitute judge avoids these problems; however, it endangers a fair trial, which is why it has to be carried out only in the presence of adequate safeguards. During the last few years, it has not gone unnoticed that an additional factor has had its bearing on this whole debate, the so-called "completion strategy" of the two *ad hoc* criminal tribunals,[3] necessitating speediness in concluding trials.

In the Karemera case, both the Trial[4] and the Appeals Chamber[5] of the International Criminal Tribunal for Rwanda (ICTR) dealt with the question of whether to restart the trial afresh, or continue with a substitute judge, eventually opting for the latter solution.[6] In arriving at this conclusion, the pertinent decisions addressed a number of questions entailing interpretation of Rule 15*bis* that indeed merit some attention. Accordingly, this commentary begins by placing the provisions of that Rule in a broader context (2), as well as addressing the interplay between the competence of the president and the remaining judges under Rule 15*bis*(C), a matter raised by one of the defendants in the case at hand. Subsequently, part 3 discusses the safeguards necessarily accompanying a decision to continue the trial, as outlined in the rules of Procedure and Evidence and applied by the tribunal. Lastly, an effort is made (4) to approach the keystone of the provision in question, namely whether continuation is "in the best interests of justice", by itemizing its elements.

2. The history and application of Rule 15*bis*

The Rules of Procedure and Evidence distinguish between the inability of a judge to sit in a part-heard case for a period that is likely to be of (1) short or (2) long duration. The former situation is regulated under Rules 15*bis*(A) and (B), and does not appear to cause particular problems in practice. Specifically, the rules

---

1 ICTR, Decision on Continuation of the Proceedings, *Prosecutor v. Karemera, Ngirumpatse and Nzirorera*, Case No. ICTR-98-44-T, T. Ch. III, 6 March 2007, in this volume, p. 347; ICTR, Decision on Appeals Pursuant to Rule 15*bis* (D), *Prosecutor v. Karemera, Ngirumpats and Nzirorera*, Case No. ICTR-98-44-AR15*bis*.3, A. Ch., 20 April 2007, in this volume p. 369; ICTR, Scheduling Order for the Resumption of the Trial (Rules 15*bis* (F) and 54 of the Rules of Procedure and Evidence), *Prosecutor v. Karemera, Ngirumpatse and Nzirorera*, Case No. ICTR-98-44-T, T.Ch. III, 2 May 2007, in this volume, p. 381; ICTR, Decision on Motion for Disqualification of Judges, *Prosecutor v. Bagosora, Kabiligi, Ntabakuze and Nsengiyumva,* Case No. ICTR-98-41-T, The Bureau, 28 May 2007, in this volume, p. 385; ICTR, Decision on "Joseph Nzirorera's Interlocutory Appeal of Decision on Obtaining Prior Statements of Prosecution Witnesses After They Have Testified", *Prosecutor v. Karemera, Ngirumpatse and Nzirorera*, Case No. ICTR-98-44-AR73.9, A. Ch., 31 May 2007, in this volume, p. 393; ICTR, Decision on Joseph Nzirorera's Submission to Substitute Judge, *Prosecutor v. Karemera, Ngirumpatse and Nzirorera*, Case No. ICTR-98-44-T, T. Ch. III, 8 June 2007, in this volume, p. 399; ICTR, Decision on Motions to Vacate Decisions, *Prosecutor v. Karemera, Ngirumpatse and Nzirorera,* Case No. ICTR-98-44-T, T. Ch. III, 17 July 2007, in this volume p. 403.

2 This is primarily a concern as regards witnesses, who may not be in a position to testify anew, for a variety of reasons.

3 On the completion strategy of the *ad hoc* criminal tribunals, see generally R. Cryer *et al*., An Introduction to International Criminal Law and Procedure, Cambridge University Press, Cambridge 2007, p. 109 *et seq.*; W. Schabas, The UN International Criminal Tribunals: The former Yugoslavia, Rwanda and Sierra Leone, Cambridge University Press, Cambridge 2006, p. 40 *et seq.*; M. Bohlander, Last Exit Bosnia. Transferring War Crimes Prosecution from the International Tribunal to Domestic Courts, Criminal Law Forum 2003, p. 59; D. Raab, Evaluating the ICTY and its Completion Strategy, Journal of International Criminal Justice 2005, p. 82.

4 Decision on Continuation of the Proceedings, *Prosecutor v. Karemera, Ngirumpatse, Nzirorera*, T. Ch. III, *supra* note 1.

5 Decision on Appeals pursuant to Rule 15*bis* (D), *Prosecutor v. Karemera, Ngirumpatse, Nzirorera*, A. Ch., *supra* note 1.

6 See Decision on Continuation of the Proceedings, *Prosecutor v. Karemera, Ngirumpatse, Nzirorera*, T. Ch. III, *supra* note 1, par. 91; Decision on Appeals pursuant to Rule 15bis (D), *Prosecutor v. Karemera, Ngirumpatse, Nzirorera*, A. Ch., *supra* note 1, par. 45-47.

authorize the remaining judges of the chamber to order that the hearing of the case continue in the absence of a judge, if they are satisfied that it is in the interests of justice to do so, and for a period of no more than five working days.[7] In such an event, the remaining judges are not prevented from conducting those matters in relation to which they are satisfied it is in the interests of justice to dispose of, but the presiding judge is also entitled to adjourn the proceedings. Although the use of the phrase "in the interests of justice" both as a criterion for deciding whether to order continuation and as the only defining attribute of matters entrusted with the remaining judges appears somewhat vague, the short duration of the absence (hence of the continuation) tends to mitigate the hazards for the defence.[8]

When it comes to the inability of a judge to continue sitting in a part-heard case for a long duration, however (which in practice has resulted in withdrawal of a judge from the case), things tend to become more complicated. Initially, the Rules of Procedure and Evidence (for both the ICTY and the ICTR) provided for continuation of the trial with a substitute judge, on the condition that the defendant(s) consented thereto. This was the case, for instance, in Prosecutor v. Blaškić, where Rule 15*bis* was applied repeatedly.[9] In the event of non-consent, restarting the trial *de novo* appeared to be the only available path.[10] This set of rules was soon deemed to be impracticable, particularly in view of the fact that the defence was thus offered a chance to stall the procedure. This is why the Rules of Procedure and Evidence were amended in 2003,[11] so as to allow for continuation of the trial with a substitute judge, even in the face of the defendant's objections.

The new rule was applied by the ICTR in the Butare case. The problem was spawned when Judge Maqutu's term of office was extended by the Security Council, so that he could finish two cases that were nearing completion, but not a third one, which was the case in question. Although the trial was already in progress at the time of the amendment,[12] and despite the fact that only one of the six defendants consented to continuation, the Trial Chamber decided to continue the trial with a substitute judge,[13] considering that such continuation would not prejudice fair trial rights.[14]

Interestingly, the Trial Chamber weighed fair trial concerns not only against the need for speedy conclusion of the trial already in progress, but also against the need to precipitate other trials pending before the tribunal, whose commencement would be delayed in the event of restarting the trial.[15] In the opinion of the remaining judges, lack of consent on the defendants' part had been effectively compensated for[16] by safeguards of an equivalent value.[17] The ICTR Appeals Chamber upheld this decision.[18]

---

7 See Rule 15(A).

8 For instance, the Appeals Chamber of the ICTR has applied this rule so as to allow for delivery of the Appeal Judgment in the absence of a judge who was present throughout the proceedings: see ICTR, Scheduling Order, *Gacumbitsi v. The Prosecutor*, Case No. ICTR-2001-64-A, A. Ch., 26 May 2006.

9 For a brief summary of how the composition of the bench was finalized in that particular case, see ICTY, Judgement, *Prosecutor v. Blaškić*, Case No. IT-95-14-T, T. Ch. I, 3 March 2000, Klip/ Sluiter, ALC-IV-477, par. 20-21.

10 Only routine matters could be dealt with in the meanwhile, based on (former) Rule 15 *bis* (D), which later became Rule 15*bis* (F).

11 Specifically, such amendment took place on May 27, 2003, and was modeled after an identical amendment of the ICTY RPE that had taken place in late 2002.

12 Under Rule 6(C), "[a]n amendment shall enter into force immediately, but shall not operate to prejudice the rights of the accused in any pending case".

13 ICTR, Decision on the Matter of Proceedings Under Rule 15bis (D*), Prosecutor v. Nyiramasuhuko and Ntahobali* (Case No. ICTR-97-21-T), *Nsabimana and Nteziryayo* (Case No. ICTR-97-29A&B-T), *Kanyabashi* (Case No. ICTR-96-15-T), *and Ndayambaje* (Case No. ICTR-96-8-T), Joint Case No. ICTR-98-42-T, T. Ch. II, 15 July 2003, Klip/ Sluiter, ALC-XII-105, (Butare case).

14 *Id.*, par. 15 *et seq.*

15 *Id.*, par. 33(g). Also see W. Schabas, The UN International Criminal Tribunals: The former Yugoslavia, Rwanda and Sierra Leone, *supra* note 3, p. 413-414. Other concerns previously put forward by the ICTR include the argument that restarting the trial afresh would amount ignore the hundreds of thousands of dollars, representing the cost of the procedure that has already taken place: see ICTR, Decision on Continuation or Commencement *de novo* of Trial, *Prosecutor v. Bagosora, Kabiligi, Ntabakuze and Nsengiyumva*, Case No. ICTR-98-41-T, T. Ch. I, 11 June 2003, Klip/ Sluiter, ALC-XII-99, at footnote 6 in the decision.

16 Decision on the Matter of Proceedings Under Rule 15bis (D*), Prosecutor v. Nyiramasuhuko and Ntahobali, Nsabimana and Nteziryayo, Kanyabashi and Ndayambaje, supra* note 13, par. 26 *et seq*. Providing consent was not deemed to constitute a "substantive right", and therefore could be revoked even while the trial was in progress.

17 See P. Robinson, Fair but Expeditious Trials, in H. Abtahi / G. Boas / R. May (eds.), The Dynamics of International Criminal Justice: Essays in Honour of Sir Richard May, Martinus Nijhoff Publishers, Leiden 2005, p. 176 *et seq.*

18 ICTR, Decision in the Matter of Proceedings under Rule 15bis (D), *Prosecutor v. Nyiramasuhuko and Ntahobali* (Case No. ICTR-97-21-T), *Nsabimana and Nteziryayo* (Case No. ICTR-97-29A&B-T), *Kanyabashi* (Case No. ICTR-96-15-T), *and Ndayambaje* (Case No. ICTR-96-8-T), Joint Case No. ICTR-98-42-A15bis, A. Ch., 24 September 2003, Klip/ Sluiter, ALC-XII-121.

The ICTY has also made use of the new provision. When President May was forced to resign due to health problems while sitting in the Milošević case, the defendant neither refused continuation nor expressly consented thereto.[19] Nonetheless, it was decided that continuation of the trial with a substitute judge would best serve the interests of justice.[20] Again, the decision was made by the remaining judges of the Trial Chamber.

However, the competence to make such determination is not always discharged by the Trial Chamber itself. One of the issues raised in the Karemera case related to the distribution of competence between the president on the one hand and the remaining judges of the bench on the other. According to Rule 15*bis* (C), the primary responsibility for addressing the inability of a judge to continue sitting in a part-heard case lies with the president, who "may assign another judge to the case and order either a rehearing or continuation of the proceedings". The provision further stipulates a point in the procedure up until which such competence of the president is exclusive, namely the opening statements (of the trial)[21] or the beginning of the presentation of evidence.[22] After that point, continuation of the proceedings can only be ordered either with the consent of the accused or by unanimous decision of the remaining judges, subject to an appeal before a full bench of the Appeals Chamber.[23]

Based on the Rules, it is evident that the president shall at all times retain the right to order a rehearing. What is temporally limited is his exclusive prerogative to order continuation, which only exists until the actual commencement of the trial. Such distribution of competence makes sense: indeed, before the commencement of the trial under Rules 84 and 85, ordering a continuation only poses minor hazards – if any - to fair trial rights, and it is only reasonable to allow such discretion in the president, in the context of his general authority over the function of the chambers.

Thereafter, the progress of the case brings two factors into play: *first*, the interests of the defendant himself, and, *secondly*, the proximity to the case of the judges sitting at the bench. Therefore, the president shall only be competent to order continuation after obtaining the defendant's consent; otherwise, he will have to yield such competence to the remaining judges.

Competence to order a rehearing or continuation of the trial

	Prior to opening statements or beginning of presentation of evidence	**After opening statements or beginning of presentation of evidence**
Rehearing	President	President
Continuation	President	President with defendant's consent *Or* Trial Chamber (remaining judges) subject to appeal

According to one of the defendants, upon referral of the question of continuation to the remaining judges under Rule 15*bis*(D), the president must provide a reasoned opinion justifying his decision. In the defendant's opinion, this would be necessary to allow him "two chances" to rebut continuation. The Appeals Chamber rightly determined that there was no such obligation incumbent on the president under the rules.[24] Indeed, Rule 15 *bis* (D) specifies that the remaining judges shall be the ones responsible to assess whether continuation

[19] See L. N. Sadat, W. Schabas, S. Trechsel, C. Van den Wyngaert, D. Sloss, The Influence of International Law and International Tribunals on Harmonized or Hybrid Systems of Criminal Procedure, Transcriptions of the Centennial Universal Congress of Lawyers Conference, Washington University Global Studies Law Review 2005, p. 658-659.

[20] ICTY, Order pursuant to Rule 15*bis* (D), *Prosecutor v. Milošević*, Case No. IT-02-54-T, T. Ch. III, 29 March 2004.

[21] See Rule 84.

[22] See Rule 85.

[23] Based on a combination of Rules 15*bis*(C) *in fine* and (D).

[24] See Decision on Appeals pursuant to Rule 15bis (D), *Prosecutor v. Karemera, Ngirumpatse, Nzirorera*, A. Ch., *supra* note 1, par. 32-33.

serves the interests of justice, such assessment being subject to an appeal before the Appeals Chamber. The rules do not require any reasoned opinion of the president at this stage,[25] only that he refer the matter to the remaining judges.

3. The safeguards accompanying continuation of the trial

A decision to continue the trial with a substitute judge must invariably be accompanied by a number of safeguards, which are to be fulfilled *cumulatively*. The combined effect of these safeguards has been considered to effectively counterbalance the defendant's lack of consent. Both the Trial and Appeals Chamber decisions under scrutiny made some interesting findings related thereto. Specifically:

3.1 Every defendant has the right to be heard prior to a decision for continuation: this right derives from Rule 15*bis*(C) *in fine,* in conjunction with (D). Although consent is no longer recognized as an absolute prerequisite to continuation, "hearing both sides" has steadily been regarded as a necessary safeguard.[26] Under the rules as they currently stand, the process to substitute a judge necessarily begins by obtaining the defence's views on the matter. Only after the defence withholds its consent are the remaining judges seized of the matter. The term "withhold consent" in section (D) can only mean that the defence is entitled to fully rebut continuation within a reasonable period of time. This was acknowledged both by the Trial Chamber[27] and the Appeals Chamber[28] in the Karemera Case. In fact, before the remaining judges of the Trial Chamber issued their decision for continuation, the defendants were all given the right to file their submissions on the matter both before the president[29] and the remaining judges.[30]

3.2 The decision for continuation by the remaining judges has to be "unanimous": although the use of the term "unanimous" to describe a decision adopted by *two* judges appears somewhat unusual, this requirement has not caused particular problems in practice. The practical effect of the provision is that dissent by one of the remaining judges is enough to lead to a mandatory rehearing of the case. In sum, after the trial has begun, continuation with a substitute judge requires: *first*, that the president did not opt for a rehearing, thus referring the matter to the two remaining judges; and *secondly*, that neither of the two remaining judges opted for a rehearing either.

3.3 The decision for continuation shall be subject to appeal before a full bench of the Appeals Chamber: the Appeals Chamber in the Karemera case was faced with two issues relating to the right to an appeal against a decision ordering continuation. The first issue related to what constitutes a "full bench" within the meaning of Rule 15*bis* (D). This was a particularly charged question, as one of the defendants (Mathieu Ngirumpatse) argued that a "full bench" would have to comprise *all* members appointed to the Appeals Chamber, one of which had to be excluded due to her prior involvement in this case.[31] The Appeals Chamber was correct in countering that a "full bench" would be constituted according to Article 11, paragraph 3, of the ICTR Statute, dictating that the "Appeals Chamber shall, for each appeal, be composed of five of its members".[32] Given that the judge previously involved in the case had not been designated to sit as a member of the bench considering the appeal, no violation of the rules had occurred.

A more important issue arises with respect to the "standard of review" adopted by the Appeals Chamber in hearing the appeal. Specifically, the Appeals Chamber acknowledged that discretion as to whether

25 That being noted, it is quite doubtful as to whether the Appeals Chamber actually recognized two chances at disputing the Trial Chamber's assessment of what the "interests of justice" dictate, unlike its declaration to the contrary. On this matter, see *infra*, see point 3.3.

26 See, for example, Decision in the Matter of Proceedings under Rule 15bis (D), *Prosecutor v. Nyiramasuhuko and Ntahobali, Nsabimana and Nteziryayo, Kanyabashi and Ndayambaje,* A. Ch., *supra* note 18, par. 18.

27 Decision on Continuation of the Proceedings, *Prosecutor v. Karemera, Ngirumpatse, Nzirorera*, T. Ch. III, *supra* note 1, par. 8.

28 Decision on Appeals pursuant to Rule 15bis (D), *Prosecutor v. Karemera, Ngirumpatse, Nzirorera*, A. Ch., *supra* note 1, par. 22.

29 It has already been noted, however, that this right did not extend to require a reasoned opinion by the president.

30 The Trial Chamber did note that one of the defendants dissenting to continuation (namely Joseph Nzirorera) had chosen to file essentially the same brief both to the president and the remaining Judges: Decision on Continuation of the Proceedings, *Prosecutor v. Karemera, Ngirumpatse, Nzirorera*, T. Ch. III, *supra* note 1, par. 8.

31 This was Judge Andrésia Vaz: see Motion filed by Mathieu Ngirumpatse, par. 5-7.

32 Decision on Appeals pursuant to Rule 15bis (D), *Prosecutor v. Karemera, Ngirumpatse, Nzirorera*, A. Ch., *supra* note 1, par. 21.

continuation with a substitute judge is in order, is essentially vested in the remaining judges of the Trial Chamber.[33] Subsequently, it noted that its own appellate jurisdiction was confined to limited circumstances, such as the failure of the remaining judges to exercise their discretion.[34] It concluded by stating that it would not be enough for the defendant to show that the Appeals Chamber would have exercised its discretion differently.[35]

These observations merit clarification, lest they reduce the object of the appeal under section (D) to something less than the rules envisioned. To begin with, it is quite obvious that the Appeals Chamber is competent to discuss any "technical" violation of Rule 15*bis* leading to continuation, despite the lack of consent by the defence: such a violation could, for instance, be the denial of the defence's right to be heard. In reality, however, the core issue that will normally be at stake in similar situations is whether continuation serves the interests of justice, and it would be erroneous to completely exclude that question from the subject of the appeal.[36]

Just like the remaining judges of the Trial Chamber, the Appeals Chamber is called to render a "judicial decision",[37] which will review – if necessary - the exercise of discretion as expressed in the impugned decision. This conclusion is further supported by the decision in the Butare case, which was relied upon by the Appeals Chamber. There it was aptly stated that:

[...] even if a trial court has not otherwise erred, the appellate court must, if necessary, examine anew the relevant facts and circumstances to exercise a discretion by way of review if it thinks that the judge's ruling may have resulted in injustice to the appellants.[38]

As has already been accepted, fair trial concerns lie at the heart of the "interests of justice". By definition, then, an error in judgment regarding this matter will result in injustice, and therefore ought to be reviewable by the Appeals Chamber. Besides, if the Appeals Chamber were confined to mere technicalities, then the right to an appeal would be reduced to a mere mechanism for overseeing the safeguards provided for in section (D), as opposed to a safeguard *in and of itself.* That does not appear to emanate from the structure or language of the rule in question.

3.4 The substitute judge can join the bench only after he has certified that he has familiarized himself with the record of the proceedings: this requirement, aimed at preserving the integrity of the procedure, is expressly provided for in section (D). In the case at hand, the Trial Chamber fittingly described this requirement as a "safeguard to ensure that fair trial rights are not compromised", as well as "a core element in determining that it would be in the interests of justice to continue the proceedings".[39]

In view of the silence of the rules as to the modalities of such familiarization, case law appears to be flexible as to the method and time limits of this process.[40] For example, when Judge Short was assigned as a substitute judge in the Bizimungu case, it took only two weeks before he was prepared to certify that he had familiarized himself with almost four months of trial material.[41]

The means by which the substitute judge is supposed to familiarize himself with the procedure consist of transcripts, exhibits, previous decisions issued during the trial and, most notably, audio and video records of

---

33 *Id.*, par. 19.

34 *Ibid.*

35 *Ibid.*

36 If that were indeed the case, and given that the president does not render a reasoned opinion in referring the matter to the remaining Judges, this would mean that there is just one opportunity for the defence to put forward its own views as regards the interests of justice, i.e. before the remaining Judges of the Trial Chamber.

37 See Decision in the Matter of Proceedings under Rule 15bis (D), *Prosecutor v. Nyiramasuhuko and Ntahobali, Nsabimana and Nteziryayo, Kanyabashi and Ndayambaje,* A. Ch., *supra* note 18, par. 18.

38 *Id.*, par. 23.

39 Decision on Joseph Nzirorera's Submission to Substitute Judge, *Prosecutor v. Karemera, Ngirumpatse and Nzirorera*, T. Ch. III, *supra* note 1, par. 7.

40 It has been pointed out, that "there is no mathematical or standard rule as to how this process is to take place": *id.*, par. 8.

41 See ICTR, Certification in the Matter of Proceedings under Rule 15 *bis* (D), *Prosecutor v. Bizimungu et al.*, Case No. ICTR-99-50-T, T. Ch. II, 3 June 2004.

previous testimonies.[42] It has been correctly noted that, if for some reason no such records are available, rehearing the case should take prevalence over continuation, as adequate familiarization with the case by the substitute judge would become virtually impossible.[43] The Trial Chamber was correct in disassociating the familiarization process under Rule 15*bis* (D) from questions pertaining to the credibility and reliability of witnesses, which are to be examined at a later stage of the proceedings.[44]

It is noteworthy, however, that the Trial Chamber emphasized the experience and integrity of the substitute judge as factors allowing him to determine *how* and *when* familiarization is to take place. Since the requirement of Rule 15*bis*(D) is met if the substitute judge himself certifies his familiarization with the case, and given the reticence of Trial Chambers to review such certification, the actual value of this safeguard may lie in determining the "interests of justice", as delineated below.[45]

3.5 Only one substitution is permitted per trial: this requirement –introduced in Rule 15*bis*(D) *in fine* - did not cause particular problems in the Karemera case. Generally speaking, the rationale behind it is simple: given the fact that Trial Chambers are comprised of three judges, it was deemed appropriate to ensure that at least the majority will have sat at the trial from its beginning.

3.6 Lastly, an additional "safeguard" – albeit one introduced in a different fashion than the previous ones – relates to the competence entrusted with the Chamber during the absence of a judge. Under Rule 15*bis*(F), such competence only extends to conducting routine matters, such as the delivery of decisions, upon authorization by the president. In the Karemera Case, the authorization by the president was in fact exceeded by the Trial Chamber, which engaged in an effort to obtain documents from the Rwandan Government.

The Appeals Chamber noted that routine matters within the meaning of Rule 15*bis* (F) are those of a "regular and standardized nature", as would be, for example, the convening of a status conference to organize exchanges between the parties.[46] On the other hand, it has been held that non-routine matters would include any decision that might have a bearing on the guilt or innocence of the accused, including decisions regarding the procurement of evidence.[47]

For the purposes of our present discussion, one would have to consider that the latter category (that of non-routine matters) would also encompass any question affecting rights of the accused. Addressing such questions would require legal determinations, as opposed to mere application of procedural provisions. The actions of the Trial Chamber in this case entailed non-routine matters, and were therefore rightly held to be inconsistent with Rule 15*bis* (F).

4. Identifying the "interests of justice" under Rule 15 *bis* (D)

Having examined the safeguards introduced under Rule 15*bis* as applied in the *Karemera* Case, it is now time to discuss what might form part of the substantive content of "the interests of justice", the core element of a decision ordering continuation of a trial. As a general remark, the interests of justice will have to be delimited around two independent poles: the rights of the accused on the one hand, and the proper function of the tribunal on the other.[48] Still, the concept has to be interpreted so as to encompass something more than

---

42 ICTR, Reasons for Decision on Interlocutory Appeals Regarding the Continuation of Proceedings With a Substitute Judge and on Nzirorera's Motion for Leave to Consider New Material, *Karemera, Ngirumpatse, Nzirorera and Rwamakuba v. Prosecutor*, Case No. ICTR-98-44-AR15*bis*.2, A. Ch., 22 October 2004, Klip/ Sluiter, ALC-XVIII-213, par. 57-58.

43 See dissenting opinion of Judge David Hunt in the Decision in the Matter of Proceedings under Rule 15bis (D), *Prosecutor v. Nyiramasuhuko and Ntahobali, Nsabimana and Nteziryayo, Kanyabashi and Ndayambaje*, A. Ch., *supra* note 18, par. 26-27.

44 Decision on Joseph Nzirorera's Submission to Substitute Judge, *Prosecutor v. Karemera, Ngirumpatse and Nzirorera*, T. Ch. III, *supra* note 1, par. 9.

45 See part 4 of this commentary.

46 See Rule 65*bis*.

47 Decision on "Joseph Nzirorera's Interlocutory Appeal of Decision on Obtaining Prior Statements of Prosecution Witnesses After They Have Testified", *Prosecutor v. Karemera, Ngirumpatse and Nzirorera*, A. Ch., *supra* note 1, par. 10, citing further examples derived from previous case law.

48 According to the ICTY, Decision on Prosecution's Motion for Order Appointing Counsel to Assist Vojislav Šešelj with his Defence, *Prosecutor v. Šešelj*, Case No. IT-03-67-PT, T. Ch. II, 9 May 2003, Klip/ Sluiter, ALC-XIV-217, par. 21: The phrase 'in the interests of justice' potentially has a broad scope [and] includes the right to a fair trial, which is not only a fundamental right of the Accused, but also a fundamental interest of the Tribunal related to its own legitimacy. In the context of the right to a fair trial, the length of the case, its size and complexity need to be taken into account.

the safeguards that are already provided for. Thus, one might distinguish between five elements that have to be jointly evaluated by the remaining judges in deciding whether to continue hearing the case with a substitute judge:

4.1 Fairness of the trial: This would appear to be the primary consideration in deciding whether or not to continue the trial. The ICTY has accepted that the "interests of justice" will have to be interpreted based on the fair trial standards under Article 21 of the tribunal's statute.[49] However, in the Karemera Case there was a lack of common ground as to what makes up such "fairness". In the opinion of one of the defendants, continuation would result in unfairness, due to repeated violations of fair trial rights that had already taken place before the issue of substitution was even brought up.[50] Such violations included disclosure issues, admission of evidence, as well as alleged errors in the use of witness testimonies by the prosecution. The defendant summarized his argument by arguing that only a rehearing could guarantee a fair trial, as the trial in progress was "too broken to fix".[51]

As regards these allegations, the Trial Chamber engaged in a copious effort to address them one by one, attempting to establish that no fair trial rights had actually been violated.[52] In doing so, the remaining judges of the Trial Chamber put themselves in the awkward position of evaluating the legality of their own actions. The approach taken by the Appeals Chamber was much simpler, its reasoning being that any alleged violations that had taken place (in the presence of all three judges in the Trial Chamber) were completely irrelevant as such vis - à - vis the matter of continuation with a substitute judge. As a result, the Appeals Chamber decided that it need not (and in fact did not) enter into a discussion as to whether these alleged violation had taken place.[53]

This latter approach seems to be correct: it is indeed one thing to assess fairness in evaluating the "interests" of justice, and a totally different task to discuss whether the trial as a whole has been a fair one at the time of a discussion on continuation. In other words, the real question posed under Rule 15 *bis* (D) is whether continuation *per se* will result in unfairness.

That being said, the Appeals Chamber could have noted that the way in which a trial is conducted until the question of substitution is raised might have a bearing on the fairness of the subsequent procedure, and is thus a factor to be evaluated. For instance, this correlation was pointed out by Judge David Hunt in his dissenting opinion in the Appeals Chamber Decision in the Butare case.[54] According to Judge Hunt, a key factor underlining the fairness of the trial is that each judge be given the opportunity to independently observe and assess for himself the demeanor of each witness.[55] The fact that certain witnesses had testified on the condition of anonymity, however, meant that no video records were available, hence rendering such first hand assessment impossible. It thus follows that certain practices – albeit not irregular *per se* - might become an affront to a fair trial in view of the question of continuation with a substitute judge. This leads to the second factor to be evaluated in determining the "interests of justice" under Rule 15*bis* (D).

4.2 Familiarization of the substitute judge with the record of the case: As noted above, the Trial Chamber correctly characterized this familiarization process as a core element of whether continuation would be in the interests of justice.[56] Admittedly, a crucial parameter of the fairness of the procedure is whether the substitute judge can reasonably be expected to be *au fait* with the record of the case. Thus, familiarization plays a dual role in the broader context of Rule 15*bis* (D). On the one hand, the fact that the trial may not resume until the substitute judge has certified that he has familiarized himself with the case is a safeguard in the sense described above.[57]

---

49 See, for example, ICTY, Decision pursuant to Rule 15*bis* (D), *Prosecutor v. Momcilo Krajišnik*, Case No. IT-00-39-T, 16 December 2004, par. 10.

50 Motion filed by Joseph Nzirorera, par. 61 *et seq.*

51 *Id.*, par. 63.

52 Decision on Continuation of the Proceedings, *Prosecutor v. Karemera, Ngirumpatse, Nzirorera*, T. Ch. III, *supra* note 1, par. 18 *et seq.*

53 Decision on Appeals pursuant to Rule 15bis (D), *Prosecutor v. Karemera, Ngirumpatse, Nzirorera*, A. Ch., *supra* note 1, par. 40 and 45.

54 *Op. cit.*, par. 15 *et seq.*

55 *Id.*, par. 25 and 33.

56 See *supra* note 38.

57 See part 3 of this commentary.

On the other, what forms part of the decision on continuation is whether the substitute judge can be expected to adequately prepare for trial within a reasonable period of time, so as to form an opinion on the trial's progress thus far. This is a projection that has to be done by the Trial Chamber, based on what has *already* taken place in trial.[58] It has been pointed out that case law so far does not appear to discern a hard and fast relationship between the number of witnesses that have already testified and the decision on whether to continue the trial or order a rehearing.[59]

Admittedly, however, the general rule should be that the more lengthy and complex a trial has been, the more difficult it would be for the substitute judge to achieve such level of familiarization. Thus, continuation would emerge as a less viable option if the evidentiary phase of the trial is approximating completion. In any event, the remaining judges must be absolutely certain that the substitute judge can familiarize himself with the case before issuing their decision on continuation. This would make up one aspect of the "familiarization requirement", the one to be assessed by the remaining judges when deciding for continuation. One cannot ignore, however, the role to be played by the substitute judge himself, who (as stated above) can effectively force a rehearing by failing to certify familiarization with the case *within a reasonable period of time*.

From the substitute judge's point of view, the notion of "familiarization" cannot be confined merely to having enough time to skim through the record of the case. It should be interpreted so as to also denote: (a) that the substitute judge has familiarized himself with the substance of what each witness had to offer to the bench. For instance, if the substitute judge considers that certain witnesses were never asked important questions that would have shed light on the case,[60] familiarization will not be achieved even if the substitute judge has thoroughly gone through the pertinent testimonies;[61] (b) additionally, possible irregularities that had occurred during the trial (prior to substitution) can have a bearing on the substitute judge's stance *vis-à-vis* the trial in progress. If, for instance, the substitute judge considers that what has taken place so far is inconsistent with the concept of a fair trial, he cannot be said to have familiarized himself with the outcome of the evidentiary phase.

Certifying familiarization under certain circumstances would indeed mean that the substitute judge adopts practices that he himself would never have subscribed to had he been a member of the bench from the beginning. It follows that substitution does not merely require familiarization with the case record in the strict sense, but also connotes that the substitute judge *identify himself* with what has taken place so far in the trial.

4.3 Undue delay: The unavoidable delay that would accompany a decision ordering rehearing has been invoked both as a hazard to the defendant's rights and as a factor encroaching on the proper function of the tribunal.[62] In assessing undue delay, the Trial Chamber compared the time it would take the substitute judge to familiarize himself with the case with the amount of time that would be required in the event of a *de novo* trial.[63] It also considered that a rehearing of the case would unduly prolong the provisional detention of the defendants.[64] This would in particular constitute an aggravating circumstance for a defendant who has consented to continuation,[65] which brings us to the next factor.

---

58 See Decision on Continuation of the Proceedings, *Prosecutor v. Karemera, Ngirumpatse, Nzirorera*, T. Ch. III, *supra* note 1, par. 68-75.

59 W. Schabas, The UN International Criminal Tribunals: The former Yugoslavia, Rwanda and Sierra Leone, *supra* note 3, p. 414-415. Also see Decision in the Matter of Proceedings under Rule 15bis (D), *Prosecutor v. Nyiramasuhuko and Ntahobali, Nsabimana and Nteziryayo, Kanyabashi and Ndayambaje,* A. Ch., *supra* note 18, par. 27. The ICTY has also expressly rejected such a correlation: see Decision pursuant to Rule 15*bis* (D), *Prosecutor v. Momcilo Krajišnik*, *supra* note 49, par. 13.

60 Note the important observation of Judge Hunt in his dissenting opinion in the Decision in the Matter of Proceedings under Rule 15*bis* (D), *Prosecutor v. Nyiramasuhuko and Ntahobali, Nsabimana and Nteziryayo, Kanyabashi and Ndayambaje,* A. Ch., *supra* note 18, par. 25 *et seq.* regarding the issue of examining witnesses.

61 On the reasons why ordering a recall of certain witnesses does not necessarily address this concern, see dissenting opinion of Judge Hunt, *id.*, par. 35-37. One might add that the recall of witnesses would, in any event, tend to introduce certain risks of rehearing into continuation of the trial under Rule 15*bis* (D). For example, certain witnesses may no longer be available to testify.

62 See Decision on Continuation of the Proceedings, *Prosecutor v. Karemera, Ngirumpatse, Nzirorera*, T. Ch. III, *supra* note 1, par. 77 *et seq.*

63 *Id.*, par. 79.

64 *Id.*, par. 77 and 81.

65 *Id.*, par. 82.

4.4 In the event of multiple defendants (a very frequent occurrence before the two *ad hoc* criminal tribunals), consent for continuation of the trial with a substitute judge under Rule 15*bis* (C) would have to be obtained from *each* defendant. Even if one of the defendants withholds consent,[66] the president will have to refer the matter to the remaining judges, in which case continuation can only take place under the requirements listed in section (D). However, the fact that one or more of the defendants consented to continuation – albeit not determinative *per se* - is relevant in deciding what is in the interests of justice. In the words of the Trial Chamber, "the fact that one of the Accused in the present case has consented to the continuation of the trial is as relevant to the interests of justice as the opposition of two other co-Accused".[67]

Indeed, the defendants are often in a better position to measure their rights up against the possibility of continuation. Thus, the more defendants who consent to continuation, the easier it becomes for the remaining judges to decide upon continuation, as opposed to rehearing (provided, of course, the fairness of the trial is preserved).

4.5 Risks of rehearing: Aside from the inevitable delay it brings about, ordering that a *de novo* trial take place also entails other unavoidable risks. For instance, there is no guarantee that the witnesses who had testified will be available again, and there is always the chance that the new trial will take a wholly different course than the initial one. In the Karemera Case, the defence attempted to reverse such reasoning by putting forward two risks that were supposedly inherent in a decision to continue. Specifically, the defendant argued that there was always the risk of "losing another judge".[68] If continuation were to take place, and given that only one substitution is permitted per trial under Rule 15 *bis* (F), such occurrence would effectively lead to an order for rehearing at a much later stage of the proceedings.

The Trial Chamber rejected this assertion as purely speculative, refusing to regard it as a parameter encroaching on the interests of justice.[69] One might add that accepting such a "risk" as a factor blocking continuation would in effect render Rule 15 *bis* (D) moot, as the risk of losing a second judge can never really be dispensed with until the trial is over.

The second assertion put forward by the defence was that there would be no realistic prospect of the trial being concluded by the end of 2008,[70] which was the target date for the tribunal's "completion strategy".[71] The Trial Chamber responded by labeling the end of 2008 as an indicative date, which could not be invoked as a ground for non-continuation.[72] In reality, one can only assume that the remaining judges of the Trial Chamber had two things in mind: first, the probability of extension of the tribunal's mandate, which indeed took place; secondly, that a potential decision ordering a rehearing of the case would *a fortiori* leave the tribunal with less than enough time to complete the case within its mandate.

Hence, the real problem emerges, that the completion strategy of the tribunal tends to tip the balance in favor of continuation of trials with a substitute judge.[73] Although the Trial Chamber was right in that the completion strategy cannot function *per se* as grounds for rehearing the case or referring it to a national jurisdiction without more, it should also not become a pretext for relaxing the safeguards of continuation.[74]

66 For the right to be heard as a safeguard for the accused, see above, in part 3 of this commentary. *Cf.* Rule 82, according to which, "in a joint trial each of the accused shall be accorded the same rights as if he were being tried separately".

67 Decision on Continuation of the Proceedings, *Prosecutor v. Karemera, Ngirumpatse, Nzirorera,* T. Ch. III, *supra* note 1, par. 16.

68 Submissions filed by Joseph Nzirorera, par. 18.

69 Decision on Continuation of the Proceedings, *Prosecutor v. Karemera, Ngirumpatse, Nzirorera*, T. Ch. III, *supra* note 1, par. 83-84

70 Submissions filed by Joseph Nzirorera, par. 14 *et seq. Cf.* submissions filed by Mathieu Ngirumpatse, par. 8.

71 Therefore, the defendants suggested that the matter be referred to a national jurisdiction under Rule 11*bis*. The Trial Chamber rejected such claim on the grounds of lack of competence on its part under the Rules: see Decision on Continuation of the Proceedings, *Prosecutor v. Karemera, Ngirumpatse, Nzirorera*, T. Ch. III, *supra* note 1, par. 90. The Appeals Chamber affirmed such finding: see Decision on Appeals pursuant to Rule 15bis (D), The *Prosecutor v. Karemera, Ngirumpatse, Nzirorera*, A. Ch., *supra* note 1, par. 35-38.

72 Decision on Continuation of the Proceedings, *Prosecutor v. Karemera, Ngirumpatse, Nzirorera*, T. Ch. III, *supra* note 1, par. 87.

73 See the concerns expressed by Judge David Hunt in his dissenting opinion in the Decision in the Matter of Proceedings under Rule 15bis (D), *Prosecutor v. Nyiramasuhuko and Ntahobali, Nsabimana and Nteziryayo, Kanyabashi and Ndayambaje,* A. Ch., *supra* note 18, par. 17.

74 For a discussion on the correlation between the completion strategy of the tribunal and the right to a fair trial see Decision on Appeals pursuant to Rule 15bis (D), *Prosecutor v. Karemera, Ngirumpatse, Nzirorera*, A. Ch., *supra* note 1, par. 25-29, 44.

In conclusion, ordering a rehearing of the case is by definition accompanied by certain "risks". Such risks, however, cannot *per se* render a rehearing as a non-viable option. Again, the real question posed is whether continuation appears to contradict a fair trial in each specific situation, in which case rehearing becomes the *only* available option, its risks necessarily being assumed by the Trial Chamber.

5. Conclusion

Summing up, the "interests of justice" indeed comprise more than concerns related to the administration of justice (such as judicial economy), encompassing the defence's interests as well. In addition, one cannot fail to notice that all the parameters delimiting the "interests of justice" seem to be intertwined. Continuation with a substitute judge by definition poses fair trial concerns, the form and extent of which may vary depending on the particularities of each trial. Rehearing the case has certain drawbacks on its part, mainly the delay it brings about.

The degree of familiarization likely to be achieved by the substitute judge, as well as the safeguards introduced by the rules, serve as a measure for the balancing of rights and interests that is required. Overall, this is not just about weighing the defendant's rights against each other, although this is necessarily part of the process.

Following on from the above analysis, certain general conclusions can be drawn regarding the "permissibility" of continuation:

- Continuation of the trial is deprived of its object if the evidentiary phase has virtually been concluded, in which case all that is pending is the judgment itself.
- Continuation should not be opted for if the trial has reached the point where the volume of the evidence already examined does not *safely* allow the conclusion that the substitute judge can *adequately familiarize himself*[75] with the record of the case *within a reasonable period of time.*
- Continuation should not be opted for in as much as special measures have been applied (for instance, the use of anonymous witnesses whose testimonies have not been recorded), which – albeit not irregular as such - pose an obstacle to the process of familiarization of the substitute judge with the record of the case, and are thus incompatible with Rule 15 *bis* (D).
- Continuation should not be opted for when a fair trial cannot be guaranteed, no matter whether the completion strategy of the tribunal (or some other factor) points towards speediness.
- The possible risks of rehearing cannot *per se* block the rehearing of the case, and the need to avoid them should certainly not take prevalence over the preservation of a fair trial.
- It is up to the remaining judges to establish with absolute certainty that continuation best serves the interests of justice.[76] The defence does not carry the burden to establish that rehearing the case would be a more suitable solution.

Overall, the question of whether to order a rehearing or continuation of the trial is to be dealt with consecutively by the president of the tribunal, the remaining judges of the chamber, and the Appeals Chamber (in exercising its appellate jurisdiction). Each one of these organs may, in fact, force a rehearing of the case. In addition, the substitute judge himself could bar continuation by failing to certify his familiarization with the case. A decision for continuation will thus have to pass through all these various "filters" in order to take effect.

Maria Kaiafa-Gbandi
Yannis Naziris

---

[75] In the sense described above, in part 4.2 of this commentary, i.e. taking into account the fairness of the trial as a vital component of the familiarization process.

[76] Decision on Continuation of the Proceedings, *Prosecutor v. Karemera, Ngirumpatse, Nzirorera*, T. Ch. III, *supra* note 1, par. 12.

International Criminal Tribunal for Rwanda
Tribunal pénal international pour le Rwanda

OR: ENG

TRIAL CHAMBER II

Before Judges: Khalida Rachid Khan, presiding
Lee Gacuiga Muthoga
Emile Francis Short

Registrar: Mr. Adama Dieng

Date: 29 May 2007

THE PROSECUTOR

v.

CASIMIR BIZIMUNGU
JUSTIN MUGENZI
JÉRÔME-CLÉMENT BICAMUMPAKA
PROSPER MUGIRANEZA

Case No. ICTR-99-50-T

DECISION ON PROSPER MUGIRANEZA'S SECOND MOTION TO DISMISS FOR DEPRIVATION OF HIS RIGHT TO TRIAL WITHOUT UNDUE DELAY

Articles 19 and 20(4)(c) of the Statute of the Tribunal

Office of the Prosecutor:
Mr. Paul Ng'arua
Mr. Ibukunolu Babajide
Mr. Justus Bwonwonga
Mr. Elvis Bazawule
Mr. George William Mugwanya
Mr. Shyamlal Rajapaksa

Counsel for the Defence:
Ms. Michelyne C. St. Laurent and Ms. Alexandra Marcil for **Casimir Bizimungu**
Mr. Ben Gumpert and Mr. Jonathan Kirk for **Justin Mugenzi**
Mr. Pierre Gaudreau and Mr. Michel Croteau for **Jérôme-Clément Bicamumpaka**
Mr. Tom Moran and Ms. Marie-Pierre Poulain for **Prosper Mugiraneza**

[page 2] INTRODUCTION

1. By Motion dated 11 December 2006,[1] the Defence for Prosper Mugiraneza moves the Chamber to order a permanent stay of proceedings – to dismiss the Indictment in this case with prejudice – as a remedy to the alleged violation of his right to be tried without undue delay, recognised as a minimum guarantee by Article 20(4)(c) of the Statute of the Tribunal. The Defence complains of pre-trial and intra-trial delay, as well as the expected time for any appeal from final judgement.

2. This is the second motion of such nature to be filed by Prosper Mugiraneza during his case,[2] the primary substantive difference being that his First Motion complained solely of a violation of the Accused's right to a trial without undue delay on the basis of pre-trial delay. The Trial Chamber denied Prosper Mugiraneza's First Motion, finding that there had been no violation of the Accused's right guaranteed by Article 20(4)(c) of the Statute.[3]

3. The Prosecution opposes the Defence Motion in light of the previous litigation on this issue in Prosper Mugiraneza's case. The Prosecution submits that the issues raised in the Defence Motion are barred from re-litigation by virtue of the doctrine of *res judicata.* Further, it submits, the Defence's submissions are speculative and an abuse of court process.[4]

DELIBERATIONS

I. Preliminary matter – *res judicata*

4. The Prosecution opposes the Defence Motion on the ground of *res judicata* – that since this issue has already been litigated before the Trial Chamber, it is barred from re-litigation by virtue of the doctrine of *res judicata*. Further, the Prosecution submits, the arguments raised by the Defence in support of its application are identical to those which were raised – and rejected by the Chamber – in its First Motion. The Chamber must therefore determine, as a preliminary matter, whether the issue before it is procedurally barred from **[page 3]** consideration. If so, the Chamber will not consider the merits of the Defence Motion. If not, the Chamber will go on to consider the substantive arguments raised by the Parties in determining whether or not there has been undue delay in this case, and, if so, how the Accused should be compensated.

5. In its Reply,[5] the Defence raises three arguments as to why the doctrine of *res judicata* should not apply to its Motion. Firstly, the Defence submits, the doctrine of *res judicata* applies only to cases in which there has been a final judgement; since there has been no final judgement in this case, the Prosecutor's arguments are without merit.[6]

---

1 *Prosecutor v. Casimir Bizimungu et al.*, Case No. ICTR-99-50-T, "Prosper Mugiraneza's Second Motion to Dismiss for Deprivation of his Right to Trial Without Undue Delay" ("Defence Motion" or "Second Motion"), dated 11 December 2006, filed on 12 December 2006.

2 See *Prosecutor v. Prosper Mugiraneza et al.*, Case No. ICTR-99-50-T, "Prosper Mugiraneza's Motion to Dismiss the Indictment for Violation of Article 20(4)(C) of the Statute, Demand for Speedy Trial and for Appropriate Relief" ("First Motion"), filed on 17 July 2003.

3 See *Prosecutor v. Prosper Mugiraneza et al.*, Case No. ICTR-99-50-T, Decision on Prosper Mugiraneza's Application for a Hearing or other Relief on his Motion for Dismissal for Violation of his Right to Trial without Undue Delay (TC), 3 November 2004, generally, and particularly the findings at para. 34. See also *Prosecutor v. Prosper Mugiraneza et al.*, Case No. ICTR-99-50-T, Decision on Prosper Mugiraneza's Motion to Dismiss the Indictment for Violation of Article 20(4)(C) of the Statute, Demand for Speedy Trial and for Appropriate Relief (TC), 2 October 2003. Note that certification to appeal the Trial Chamber's Decision of 2 October 2003 was granted, the Appeals Chamber subsequently vacating the Trial Chamber's Decision and remanding the matter back to the Trial Chamber for reconsideration of its decision (*Prosecutor v. Casimir Bizimungu et al.*, Case No. ICTR-99-50-A73, Decision on Prosper Mugiraneza's Interlocutory Appeal from Trial Chamber II Decision of 2 October 2003 Denying the Motion to Dismiss the Indictment, Demand Speedy Trial and for Appropriate Relief (AC), 27 February 2004). The Trial Chamber's subsequent reconsideration of its Decision of 2 October 2003 led to its Decision of 3 November 2004.

4 *Prosecutor v. Casimir Bizimungu et al.*, Case No. ICTR-99-50-T, "Prosecutor's Response to Prosper Mugiraneza's Second Motion to Dismiss for Deprivation of his Right to Trial Without Undue Delay", dated 18 December 2006.

5 *Mugiraneza et al,* Prosper Mugiraneza's Reply to the Prosecutor's Response to Prosper Mugiraneza's Second Motion to Dismiss for Deprivation of his Right to Trial Without Undue Delay, 26 December 2006.

6 Defence Reply, para. 15.

6. The Chamber does not accept the Defence's argument. The Prosecution uses the term *res judicata* synonymously with what is known in some national jurisdictions as *issue estoppel*. As the jurisprudence of this Tribunal demonstrates, the Trial Chambers have often considered and applied arguments concerning the doctrine of *res judicata* (or *issue estoppel*) in relation to interlocutory matters in cases which have not yet reached the stage of final judgement.[7] In fact this Trial Chamber recently addressed – and rejected - an argument of *res judicata* raised by Prosper Mugiraneza's co-Accused, when considering the merits of the Prosecution's Motion for Judicial Notice.[8] The Chamber therefore considers that the Prosecution is not prevented from making an argument of *res judicata* (more accurately *issue estoppel*) in relation to this application despite the case not having yet reached final judgement.

7. A further argument of the Defence as regards the issue of *res judicata* is that the Prosecution should be estopped from asserting *res judicata* in circumstances where it has itself sought reconsideration of other issues previously determined by the Chamber.

8. The Chamber considers this Defence position to be confused and erroneous. The doctrine of *res judicata* is not to be confused with the Trial Chamber's inherent power to reconsider its own decisions, which is well established before this Tribunal. The Prosecution's position is not that the Trial Chamber cannot reconsider its own decisions but rather that the Trial Chamber should not consider the Defence's application because it has already ruled on an identical application previously brought by the Accused; that, by virtue of the doctrine of *res judicata,* the issue has already been ruled upon by the Chamber. The Chamber considers that the Prosecution is in no way "estopped" from arguing that the Defence's application should be rejected on the grounds of the doctrine of *res judicata.* **[page 4]**

9. Finally, as regards the issue of *res judicata,* the Defence argues that the doctrine does not apply in these circumstances because the First Motion only complained of pre-trial delay, whereas its Second Motion complains of pre-trial delay, intra-trial delay, and future delay in the determination of the case by the Appeals Chamber.

10. The Chamber is persuaded by this Defence argument and is of the view that it may consider the merits of the Defence Motion on the basis that it is a fresh application due to the time which has lapsed since its previous determination of a similar issue in November 2004. The Chamber therefore rejects the Prosecution argument that the Chamber is barred from considering the issue before it by virtue of the doctrine of *res judicata.*

II. Substance of the Defence Motion

11. Having found that there is no procedural bar to its consideration of the merits of the Defence Motion, the Chamber will now address the substance of the application. Essentially, the Chamber must address two issues: firstly, has the Accused's right to trial without undue delay been violated? Secondly, if yes, is a permanent stay of proceedings – a dismissal of the Indictment in this case with prejudice - the appropriate remedy?

12. The Defence Motion is brought pursuant to Article 20(4)(c) of the Statute of this Tribunal which provides:

> In the determination of any charge against the accused pursuant to the present Statute, the accused shall be entitled to the following minimum guarantees, in full equality:
>
> [...]
>
> (c) To be tried without undue delay

---

[7] See, for example, *Prosecutor v. Tharcisse Muvunyi,* Case No. ICTR-2000-55A-T, Decision on Muvunyi's Motion to Include all Testimony of Witness AOG/D/X/006 in the Appellate Record (TC), 5 June 2006, para. 7; *Prosecutor v. Tharcisse Muvunyi,* Case No. ICTR-2000-55A-T, Decision on Muvunyi's Motion for Judgement of Acquittal Pursuant to Rule 98*bis* (TC), 13 October 2005, para. 21; *Prosecutor v. Pauline Nyiramasuhuko,* Case No. ICTR-97-21-T, Decision on Defence Motion for Certification to Appeal the "Decision on Defence Motion for a Stay of Proceedings and Abuse of Process" (TC), 19 March 2004, para. 28; *Prosecutor v. Simon Bikindi,* ICTR-2001-72-PT, Decision on the Amended Indictment and the Taking of a Plea Based on the Said Indictment (TC), 11 May 2005, para. 3; *Prosecutor v. Pauline Nyiramasuhuko,* Case No. ICTR-97-21-T, Decision on Nyiramasuhuko's Oral Motion Regarding Prosecution's Use of Material Under Seal (TC), 27 April 2004, para. 29; *Prosecutor v. Edouard Karemera et al.,* Case No. ICTR-98-44-PT, Decision on Motion to Vacate Sanctions (TC), 23 February 2005, para. 10.

[8] See *Prosecutor v. Casimir Bizimungu et al.,* Case No. ICTR-99-50-T, Decision on Prosecutor's Motion for Judicial Notice (TC), 22 September 2006, para. 8.

13. Article 19 of the Statute further requires the Trial Chamber to ensure that the trial is fair and expeditious, and that proceedings are conducted in accordance with the Rules of Procedure and Evidence, with full respect for the rights of the accused and due regard for the protection of victims and witnesses.

14. The Appeals Chamber jurisprudence of this Tribunal – arising from previous litigation in this case - states that a determination of whether an Accused person's right to be tried without undue delay has been violated must necessarily include a consideration of, *inter alia*, the following factors:[9]

(1) The length of the delay;
(2) The complexity of the proceedings, such as the number of charges, the number of accused, the number of witnesses, the volume of evidence, the complexity of facts and law;
(3) The conduct of the parties;
(4) The conduct of the relevant authorities; and
(5) The prejudice to the accused, if any. **[page 5]**

15. As previously outlined by this Chamber, the Appeals Chamber's jurisprudence indicates that there cannot be a determination of whether the right to trial without undue delay was violated without considering the totality of the above-mentioned five criteria.[10] Furthermore, a finding of undue delay will depend on the circumstances of the case.[11]

16. Before going on to assess the merits of the Defence Motion in light of the Appeals Chamber criteria, however, the Chamber must address two arguments raised by the Defence in its Motion – the issue of burden of persuasion, as well as the issue of binding authority on the Trial Chamber.

<u>Burden of Persuasion</u>

17. The Defence contends that, by virtue of the fact that the Prosecution did not respond to the merits of the Defence's Motion – arguing only a procedural bar to the Chamber's consideration of the Motion - the Prosecution has given up its right to provide an explanation for the undue delay alleged in this case.

18. The Chamber considers that, as a matter of law, the onus is on the Defence as the moving party to make out the circumstances which it says amount to undue delay on the basis of those matters, *inter alia,* outlined by the Appeals Chamber Decision.[12] The question for the Chamber is not whether the Prosecution has satisfied a reverse onus, but rather, whether the Defence has made out the undue delay alleged, on the basis of those matters, *inter alia,* outlined by the Appeals Chamber Decision. The Prosecution's failure to respond to the merits of the Defence's claims is a matter which the Chamber will take into consideration in determining whether or not the Defence has succeeded in showing that there has been undue delay in this case. However, the Prosecution's failure to respond to the substance of the Defence's allegations does not automatically lead to a finding in favour of the Defence.

---

[9] *Prosecutor v. Prosper Mugiraneza et al.,* Case No. ICTR-99-50-A73, Decision on Prosper Mugiraneza's Interlocutory Appeal from Trial Chamber II Decision of 2 October 2003 Denying the Motion to Dismiss the Indictment, Demand Speedy Trial and for Appropriate Relief (AC), 27 February 2004, p. 2.

[10] Note that this position is consistent with this Trial Chamber's previous decisions on this issue; see *Prosecutor v. Prosper Mugiraneza et al.,* Case No. ICTR-99-50-T, Decision on Prosper Mugiraneza's Application for a Hearing or other Relief on his Motion for Dismissal for Violation of his Right to Trial without Undue Delay (TC), 3 November 2004, para. 28.

[11] *Prosecutor v. Joseph Kanyabashi,* Case No. ICTR-96-15-I, Decision on the Extremely Urgent Motion on Habeas Corpus and for Stoppage of Proceedings (TC), 23 May 2000.
"The Chamber notes that the issue of reasonable length of proceeding has been addressed by the U.N. Human Rights Committee, the European Court of Human Rights and the Inter-American Commission on Human Rights. "The reasonableness of the period cannot be translated into a fixed number of days, months or years, since it is dependent on other elements which the judge must consider". In the opinion of the European Court of Human Rights, "the reasonableness of the length of proceedings coming within the scope of Article 6(1) must be assessed in each case according to the particular circumstances. The Court has to have regard, *inter alia*, to the complexity of the factual or legal issues raised by the case, to the conduct of the applicants and the competent authorities and to what was at stake for the former, in addition to complying with the "reasonable time" requirement. [four factors]". [Footnotes omitted]

[12] This view is consistent with this Chamber's approach in *Prosecutor v. Prosper Mugiraneza et al.,* Case No. ICTR-99-50-T, Decision on Prosper Mugiraneza's Application for a Hearing or other Relief on his Motion for Dismissal for Violation of his Right to Trial without Undue Delay (TC), 3 November 2004, para. 33 – "The burden for proving prejudice does indeed lie with the Defence."

Status of ECHR and HRC Authority on the Trial Chamber

19. In support of its Motion, the Defence relies upon a number of case authorities from the European Court of Human Rights ("ECHR") and the Human Rights Committee ("HRC") (established pursuant to Part IV and Optional Protocol I to the International Covenant on **[page 6]** Civil and Political Rights). In addition, the Defence refers extensively to the recent decision of Trial Chamber III in the case of *Prosecutor v. André Rwamakuba,*[13] in which the Trial Chamber relied upon decisions of the HRC and noted the binding nature of "generally accepted norms of human rights" on the Tribunal.

20. Firstly, the Chamber fully accepts the binding nature of "generally accepted norms of human rights" on the Tribunal. Secondly, however, whilst the jurisprudence of the ECHR and HRC may be persuasive in nature to the Tribunal, the Chamber considers that it should only have recourse to such authorities to the extent that the Tribunal's statutory instruments and jurisprudence are deficient. In this respect, the Chamber notes that the fundamental guarantees afforded to the Accused are derived firstly from the Tribunal's statutory instruments – in particular Articles 19 and 20 of the Statute. The Chamber further notes the binding nature of the above-mentioned Appeals Chamber criteria which gives some guidance in the application of the Tribunal's Statute. With respect to the *Rwamakuba* case, the Chamber notes that the Decision had recourse to HRC jurisprudence because there was a deficit in binding Tribunal jurisprudence on the issue under consideration[14] (in that case, since the Chamber had found a violation of Rwamakuba's rights, the question concerned appropriate remedy for that violation); it was therefore necessary in that case to seek guidance from persuasive authorities.

21. For the aforementioned reasons, therefore, the Chamber's Decision will focus on the jurisprudence which is binding upon it in making a determination as to whether the delay in this case – if any - is undue.

Application of the Appeals Chamber criteria to the facts

(1) *The length of the delay*

22. The Defence argues that the undue delay in this case is constituted by:

- the length of time between Mugiraneza's arrest at the request of the Prosecutor in April 1999 to the start of his trial in November 2003;
- the length of the trial, including the estimate of the remaining time given by the President of the Tribunal to the Security Council on 1 June 2006;
- the anticipated length of any post judgement appeals.

23. The Defence submits that Prosper Mugiraneza has been incarcerated since April 1999, and that, therefore, at the time of filing the Motion he had been incarcerated for more than seven years. The Defence speculates that judgement in this case will not be rendered prior to 2008, and that if there is an appeal from final judgement, the Accused will have been incarcerated for 11 years without final determination of the case. It is the Defence's submission that a delay in excess of 10 years constitutes undue delay for the purposes of the Statute no matter what the circumstances. **[page 7]**

24. Relying upon General Comment 13 to the International Covenant on Civil and Political Rights,[15] as well as upon jurisprudence of the Human Rights Committee[16] and the European Court of Human Rights,[17]

[13] *Prosecutor v. André Rwamakuba*, Case No. ICTR-98-44C-T, Decision on Appropriate Remedy (TC) ("*Rwamakuba* Decision"), 31 January 2007.

[14] *Rwamakuba* Decision, 31 January 2007, paras. 21-22.

[15] Office of the High Commissioner for Human Rights, General Comment No. 13 (1984), para. 10. http://www.unhchr.ch/tbs/doc.nsf/0/bb722416a295f264c12563ed0049dfbd? Open document (visited 5 December 2006), cited at footnote 17 of the Defence Motion.

[16] UN Doc. CCPR/C/60/D/533/1993, *Elahie v. Trinadad and Tobago,* para. 8.2 (1996), cited at footnote 37 of the Defence Motion.

[17] See, for example, *Bunkate v. The Netherlands,* No. 26/1992/371/445 (ECHR 1993), cited at footnote 18 of the Defence Motion.

the Defence submits that the right to trial without undue delay "includes not only the pre-trial phase but the trial itself and the following appellate process."[18]

25. It should firstly be noted that an assessment of whether the Accused's right to trial without undue delay has been violated will be made only as at today's date. This means that the Chamber, at the date of signature of this Decision, is making a determination as to whether or not the Accused's right to trial without undue delay has been violated - *to date*. The Chamber will not enter into any speculation about whether – at date of judgement, or at date of appeal from final judgement, if any – the Accused's right to trial without undue delay will have been violated. This Trial Chamber is only empowered to determine whether there has been any violation of the Accused's rights as at the present date.

26. The Chamber notes the authorities relied upon by the Defence in support of its submission that the right to trial without undue delay includes not only the pre-trial phase but the trial itself and the following appellate process. The Chamber's position is not inconsistent with this line of authority because the authorities in question only require the judicial body to consider the totality of the proceedings *which have already transpired* at the time it is making its assessment.[19] For example, if the proceedings are in pre-trial phase, the judicial body must determine whether there has been undue delay up until that point; if, on the other hand, the proceedings are in the phase of appeal from final judgement, the judicial body must determine whether there has been undue delay in the pre-trial, trial, and appeal phases.

27. The Chamber also rejects the Defence's submission that a delay in excess of 10 years constitutes undue delay *per se* for the purposes of the Statute no matter what the circumstances. In this respect, the Chamber notes that the jurisprudence of this Tribunal is clear on this issue - the reasonableness of the period of delay cannot be translated into a fixed number of days, months or years, since it is dependent on other elements which the judge must consider,[20] notably the totality of those matters outlined by the Appeals Chamber. As **[page 8]** this Chamber previously noted, "the Strasbourg organs have deemed trials that lasted longer than 10 years to be compatible with Article 6(1) of the ECHR, on the other hand holding that undue delay has occurred in others which lasted less than one year."[21]

28. The Chamber notes that it has been some eight years from the date of the Accused's arrest. However, as outlined by the Appeals Chamber, the duration of the proceedings alone will not necessarily give rise to a violation of the Accused's right to trial without undue delay. Rather, the question is whether the duration of the proceedings, in the context of other matters to be considered by the Chamber, gives rise to a violation of the Accused's right.

(2) *The complexity of the proceedings*

29. It is the Defence's submission that this case is *not* a complex case. The Defence submits that this is essentially "an eyewitness case no different than a bank robbery case other than the fact that a large number

---

18 Defence Motion, paras. 6-7.

19 See paragraph 10 of the Office of the High Commissioner for Human Rights, General Comment No. 13 (1984), para. 10. http://www.unhchr.ch/tbs/doc.nsf/0/bb722416a295f264c12563ed0049dfbd? Open document (visited 5 December 2006), cited at footnote 17 of the Defence Motion, which reads: "Subparagraph 3(c) provides that the accused shall be tried without undue delay. This guarantee relates not only to the time by which a trial should commence, but also the time by which it should end and judgement be rendered; all stages must take place "without undue delay". To make this right effective, a procedure must be available in order to ensure that the trial will proceed "without undue delay", both in first instance and on appeal." See also UN Doc. CCPR/C/60/D/533/1993, *Elahie v. Trinadad and Tobago,* para. 8.2 (1996), cited at footnote 37 of the Defence Motion. In that case, the Committee considers only the history of the "author's" (ie. complainant's) detention. The case of *Bunkate v. The Netherlands,* No. 26/1992/371/445 (ECHR 1993), cited at footnote 18 of the Defence Motion, is also consistent with the Chamber's view.

20 *Prosecutor v. Kanyabashi*, Case No. ICTR-96-15-I, Decision on the Defense Extremely Urgent Motion on Habeas Corpus and For Stoppage of Proceedings (TC), 23 May 2000, par. 68; *Prosecutor v. Joseph Kanyabashi*, Case No. ICTR-96-15-T, Decision on the Defense Motion for the Provisional Release of the Accused (TC), 21 February 2001 par. 11; *Prosecutor v. André Rwamakuba,* Case No. ICTR-98-44C-PT, Decision of Defence Motion for Stay of Proceedings (TC), 3 June 2005, para. 29; *Prosecutor v. Mugiraneza et al.*, Case No.ICTR-99-50-T, Decision on Prosper Mugiraneza's Application for a Hearing or Other Relief on His Motion for Dismissal for Violation of His Right to a Trial without Undue Delay (TC), 3 November 2004, para. 31.

21 *Prosecutor v. Mugenzi et al.*, Case No. ICTR-99-50-I, Decision on Justin Mugenzi's Motion for Stay of Proceedings or in the Alternative Provisional Release (Rule 65) and in Addition Severance (Rule 82(B) (TC), 8 November 2002, para. 33, citing *Prosecutor v. Kanyabashi*, Case No. ICTR-96-15-I, Decision on the Defence Extremely Urgent Motion on Habeas Corpus and For Stoppage of Proceedings (TC), 23 May 2000, para. 68.

of witnesses were called by the Prosecutor because it was presenting evidence of numerous events."[22] Further, the Defence submits, even though a large number of exhibits have been introduced in the case, many are of little relevance and few require complex analysis.[23]

30. The Chamber disagrees with the Defence's view as regards the complexity of these proceedings. The Chamber considers - in light of some of the factors highlighted by the Appeals Chamber as relevant to a determination of the complexity of the proceedings (ie. number of charges, the number of accused, the number of witnesses, the volume of evidence, the complexity of facts and law) - that the instant case is a complex one. There are four accused persons in this case, each of whom is answering to an Indictment containing up to eight counts.[24] To date, the Chamber has heard some 57 witnesses for the Prosecution, and more than 40 witnesses for the Defence of two Accused persons. Those witnesses have been a mixture of factual and expert witnesses. The Trial Chamber has rendered more than 200 written decisions in this case. Furthermore, in excess of 25 volumes of documentary exhibits have been tendered into evidence in this trial. The evidence in this case – in terms of both oral testimony and documentary exhibits – is therefore voluminous. The Chamber is of the view that this case is complex both factually and legally, particularly having regard to the Prosecution's case being based on an allegation of conspiracy, and the modes of responsibility attaching to the counts remaining in the Indictment against the Accused.

31. As regards the Defence's submissions concerning the "little relevancy" of many of the exhibits in this case, the Chamber notes, firstly, that in order for any exhibit to be tendered into evidence before this Tribunal, it must satisfy a threshold relevancy requirement pursuant to Rule 89(C) of the Rules. All documents which have become exhibits in this case are therefore "relevant" for the purposes of these proceedings. Secondly, the Chamber will not comment to any degree upon the weight to be afforded to any exhibits nor the level of analysis to be engaged in with respect to those exhibits for the purposes of this application. Such matters are to be deliberated upon in the final stages of these proceedings.

(3) *The conduct of the parties*

32. The Defence alleges a lack of sense of urgency in these proceedings on the part of the Prosecution, mainly prior to the commencement of the trial, and in bringing the case to trial, but also in relation to the filing of the motion seeking to amend the Indictment.[25] The Defence further alleges delays in disclosure on the part of the Prosecution. The Defence submits that of the delay occasioned thus far, only two days are attributable to Mugiraneza.

33. The Chamber notes that none of the issues raised by the Defence – except the issue of the Prosecution's late filing of his motion seeking to amend the Indictment – concerns the conduct of the Prosecution *since* the Chamber rendered its Decision of 3 November 2004 concerning undue delay. Addressing similar arguments raised by the Defence in its Decision of 3 November 2004, the Chamber found that "the delay in this case, if any, is not attributable to the OTP."[26]

34. The Chamber has considered the Defence argument concerning the late filing of the Prosecution's Motion to amend the Indictment (filed in August 2006). The Chamber rejects the argument that the Prosecution in someway contributed to undue delay in this case by the late filing of the said motion. The Chamber recalls that it denied the Prosecution motion on the very basis that granting it may cause delay in the trial. Therefore, to the contrary, the Chamber's denial of the Prosecution's motion to amend the Indictment in this case contributed towards an objective of preventing delay in this case.

---

22 Defence Motion, para. 57.

23 Defence Motion, para. 58.

24 Pursuant to the Indictment in this case, each of the Accused was charged with 10 counts. However, following the acquittal of certain of the Accused in respect of certain counts in the Indictment and/or modes of responsibility, the Accused Justin Mugenzi is now answering eight counts, the Accused Casimir Bizimungu is now answering eight counts, the Accused Jerôme Bicamumpaka is now answering seven counts, and the Accused Prosper Mugiraneza is now answering seven counts. See *Prosecutor v. Casimir Bizimungu et al.*, Case No. ICTR-99-50-T, Decision on Defence Motions Pursuant to Rule 98*bis* (TC), 22 November 2005, p. 32.

25 Defence Motion, paras. 59-60.

26 *Prosecutor v. Mugiraneza et al.*, Case No.ICTR-99-50-T, Decision on Prosper Mugiraneza's Application for a Hearing or Other Relief on His Motion for Dismissal for Violation of His Right to a Trial without Undue Delay (TC), 3 November 2004, para. 32.

(4) *The conduct of the relevant authorities*

35. The Defence submits that the remainder of the delay in this case has been "due to lack of resources such as courtrooms, judges and prosecutors; bureaucratic infighting between the Office of the Prosecutor and the Registry; lack of prompt action by the Security Council and the General Assembly in providing needed resources; and the considered decisions by the Office of the Prosecutor in indicting more persons than could be tried without undue delay and to join accused in multi-defendant trial which take more time than individual trials."[27] The Defence further alleges that the trial has "come to a screeching halt due to lack of witnesses" and says that the Trial Chamber should take "judicial notice" of this allegation.[28]

36. The Chamber notes that, despite strong allegations, the Defence has failed to give details concerning how the conduct of the relevant authorities has resulted in or contributed to undue delay in this case. For example, as regards the Defence allegation concerning lack of witnesses in this case, the Defence provides the Chamber with only one example of a loss of two days of trial time as the result of witness-related issues. As regards the other far-reaching allegations – such as "bureaucratic infighting", lack of prompt action by the Security Council and the General Assembly, etc. – the Defence fails to show how such issues have translated into delay in this case. The Chamber therefore cannot find that the conduct of the relevant authorities has contributed to delay – if any – in this case.

(5) *The prejudice to the accused, if any*

37. The Defence submits that the prejudice to the Accused is his incarceration since April 1999 while presumptively innocent.[29] The Defence further submits that the delay in this case has impacted upon his ability to present his Defence – "witnesses have died, become unavailable or have disappeared… [and] over time, memories fade."[30]

38. The Chamber has already noted that the Accused has been in custody for some eight years; however, this matter must be considered in light of the totality of the criteria laid down by the Appeals Chamber. As regards the impact of the delay in these proceedings on the Accused's ability to present his Defence, again the Defence has failed to give substantive details concerning its allegation, but the Chamber has taken note of this submission. Furthermore, in its Decision of 3 November 2004 the Chamber found that "the Defence ha[d] failed to show how the delay of four years, six months and 28 days ha[d] prejudiced the Accused such as to prevent a fair trial and necessitate a dismissal of the Indictment against him."[31] Since the date of this Decision, the trial in this case has advanced with the Prosecution closing its case in June 2005 and the completion of the hearing of the defence of one of the accused. The defence of a second accused is now almost nearing completion. Therefore, considering the Chamber's finding of 3 November 2004, as well as the matters put forward by the Accused in his Motion, the Chamber is of the view that the Defence has failed to show that the delay occasioned up to this time in this case has caused prejudice to the Accused.

Conclusion

39. Having considered the submissions of the Parties in the light of the totality of the criteria laid down by the Appeals Chamber (the length of the delay; the complexity of the proceedings, such as the number of charges, the number of accused, the number of witnesses, the volume of evidence, the complexity of facts and law; the conduct of the parties; the conduct of the relevant authorities; and the prejudice to the accused, if any), and taking into account the stage which the trial has now reached, the Chamber is of the view that the Defence has failed to show a violation of the Accused's right to be tried without undue delay, **[page 11]** guaranteed by Article 20(4)(c) of the Statute, having regard to the complexity of the case and the absence of any wrongdoing on the part of the Prosecution or the relevant authorities.

27 Defence Motion, para. 10.
28 Defence Motion, para. 67.
29 Defence Motion, para. 76.
30 Defence Motion, para. 78.
31 *Prosecutor v. Mugiraneza et al.*, Case No.ICTR-99-50-T, Decision on Prosper Mugiraneza's Application for a Hearing or Other Relief on His Motion for Dismissal for Violation of His Right to a Trial without Undue Delay (TC), 3 November 2004, para. 33.

40. Having found that the Defence has failed to show that Prosper Mugiraneza's right to trial without undue delay has been violated, the Chamber need not consider the arguments of the Defence concerning appropriate remedy for any violation thereof.

FOR THE FOREGOING REASONS, THE CHAMBER

DENIES the Defence Motion in its entirety.

Arusha, 29 May 2007

Khalida Rachid Khan	Lee Gacuiga Muthoga	Emile Francis Short
Presiding Judge	Judge	Judge

[Seal of the Tribunal]

International Criminal Tribunal for Rwanda
Tribunal pénal international pour le Rwanda

OR: ENG

TRIAL CHAMBER II

Before Judges:	Khalida Rachid Khan, presiding Lee Gacuiga Muthoga Emile Francis Short
Registrar:	Mr. Adama Dieng
Date:	14 June 2007

THE PROSECUTOR

v.

CASIMIR BIZIMUNGU
JUSTIN MUGENZI
JÉRÔME-CLÉMENT BICAMUMPAKA
PROSPER MUGIRANEZA

Case No. ICTR-99-50-T

DECISION ON JUSTIN MUGENZI'S MOTION ALLEGING UNDUE DELAY AND SEEKING SEVERANCE

Office of the Prosecutor:
Mr. Paul Ng'arua
Mr. Ibukunolu Babajide
Mr. Justus Bwonwonga
Mr. Elvis Bazawule
Mr. Shyamlal Rajapaksa
Mr. Olivier De Schutter
Mr. William Mubiru

Counsel for the Defence:
Ms. Michelyne C. St. Laurent and Ms. Alexandra Marcil for **Casimir Bizimungu**
Mr. Ben Gumpert and Mr. Jonathan Kirk for **Justin Mugenzi**
Mr. Pierre Gaudreau and Mr. Michel Croteau for **Jérôme-Clément Bicamumpaka**
Mr. Tom Moran and Ms. Marie-Pierre Poulain for **Prosper Mugiraneza**

[page 2] INTRODUCTION

1. The Defence for Justin Mugenzi alleges a violation of Mr. Mugenzi's right to trial without undue delay, guaranteed by Article 20(4)(c) of the ICTR Statute.[1] In support of its argument, the Defence relies upon the legal arguments presented in Prosper Mugiraneza's Second Motion to Dismiss for Deprivation of His Right to Trial Without Undue Delay (the "Mugiraneza Motion").[2]

2. As a remedy for the alleged violation of his right to a trial without undue delay, Mr. Mugenzi urges the Chamber to sever his case under Rule 82 of the Rules of Procedure and Evidence.[3] Mr. Mugenzi has previously requested severance, but the Chamber denied the request, stating its intention to remain "alive to the matter."[4]

3. Prosper Mugiraneza supports Mr. Mugenzi's allegation of undue delay and his request for severance, so long as severance of Mr. Mugenzi does not violate Mr. Mugiraneza's right to a trial without undue delay and does not prejudice him in any way.[5]

4. The Prosecution opposes the Motion, submitting: (i) that the issue is *res judicata*, and therefore barred; (ii) that it is time-barred under Rule 72(A); and (iii) that Mr. Mugenzi has not suffered any prejudice. In addition, the Prosecution argues that the Defence concerns about the health of one of the judges and the end date of the trial are speculative and unsupported by evidence.[6]

5. Mr. Mugiraneza submits that the Prosecution's argument based on the doctrine of *res judicata* is misplaced since no final judgment has been entered in the instant case.[7]

DISCUSSION

Preliminary Matters – Time-bar and Res judicata

6. The Prosecution submits that the present motion is barred by virtue of the doctrine of *res judicata* based on the 8 November 2002 Decision.[8] The Chamber is not persuaded **[page 3]** by this argument. The doctrine of *res judicata* – or more accurately under the circumstances, issue estoppel – does not bar the Chamber from considering the merits of a second motion alleging undue delay where the second motion alleges a new basis for undue delay.[9] Mr. Mugenzi's previous motion was based on an allegation of undue delay during the pre-trial proceedings and the present motion alleges undue delay during the trial. Therefore, for the same reasons articulated by this Chamber in the Mugiraneza Decision,[10] the Chamber determines that this issue is not barred as *res judicata*.

7. In addition, the Prosecution argues that the present motion is time-barred pursuant to Rule 72(A)(iii) of the Rules, which provides that a motion seeking a separate trial under Rule 82(B) must be "brought not later than thirty days after" disclosure by the Prosecution under Rule 66(A)(i). Rule 72(F) states that "[f] ailure to comply with the time limits prescribed in this Rule shall constitute a waiver of the rights. The Trial Chamber may, however, grant relief from the waiver upon showing of good cause."[11]

1 "Justin Mugenzi's Motion for Severance Under Rule 82", filed 28 March 2007, paras 2, 18 (The "Mugenzi Motion").

2 "Prosper Mugiraneza's Second Motion to Dismiss for Deprivation of His Right to Trial Without Undue Delay", filed 11 December 2006, (the "Mugiraneza Motion").

3 Mugenzi Motion, paras 1-2, 20-25.

4 *See Prosecutor v. Bizimungu et al.*, Case No. ICTR-99-50-I, Decision on Justin Mugenzi's motion for stay of proceedings or in the alternative provisional release (Rule 65) and in addition severance (Rule 82(b)), 8 November 2002, para 43 (the "8 November 2002 Decision").

5 "Prosper Mugiraneza's response to Justin Mugenzi's Motion for Severance under Rule 82", filed 30 March 2007, para 4.

6 "Prosecutor's Response to Justin Mugenzi's Motion for Severance Under Rule 82", filed 3 April 2007 (the "Prosecution's Response").

7 "Prosper Mugiraneza's Reply to the Prosecutor's Response to Justin Mugenzi's Motion for Severance under Rule 82", filed 4 April 2007.

8 Prosecutor's Response, para 11.

9 Mugiraneza Decision, paras 9-10.

10 Mugiraneza Decision, para 10.

11 Prosecutor's Response, paras 4-8.

8. The Chamber notes that the focus of Mr. Mugenzi's Motion is the alleged violation of his right to trial without undue delay. Severance is merely the requested remedy. Therefore, the Motion shall be considered as having been brought under Rule 73, which allows for motions at any time after the initial appearance of the accused.

Undue Delay

9. The Defence submits that Mr. Mugenzi has been denied his right to a trial without undue delay guaranteed by Article 20(4)(c) of the Statute, which provides, "In the determination of any charge against the accused pursuant to the present Statute, the accused shall be entitled to the following minimum guarantees, in full equality: [...] to be tried without undue delay". In addition to the Statute, the Defence for Mr. Mugenzi incorporates the arguments set forth in the Mugiraneza Motion,[12] which relied, *inter alia*, on the jurisprudence of the *ad hoc* Tribunals, as well as Article 14(3) of the International Covenant on Civil and Political Rights (ICCPR), comments issued by the Human Rights Committee interpreting the ICCPR,[13] and jurisprudence of the European Court of Human Rights.[14]

10. In the Mugiraneza Decision, the Chamber acknowledged the binding nature of generally accepted human rights norms on the Tribunal, stating, "while the jurisprudence of the ECHR and HRC may be persuasive to the Tribunal, the Chamber considers that it should only have recourse to such authorities to the extent that the Tribunal's statutory instruments and jurisprudence are deficient."[15] **[page 4]**

11. The Appeals Chamber has previously held that a determination of whether an Accused person's right to be tried without undue delay has been violated must necessarily include a consideration of, *inter alia*, the following factors:[18]

1. The length of the delay;
2. The complexity of the proceedings, such as the number of charges, the number of accused, the number of witnesses, the volume of evidence, the complexity of facts and law;
3. The conduct of the parties;
4. The conduct of the relevant authorities; and
5. The prejudice to the accused, if any.

(1) *The length of the delay*

12. The Defence notes that Mr. Mugenzi has been incarcerated since 6 April 1999 and was charged on 2 September 2002. His trial began on 6 November 2003 and the Prosecution finished presenting his evidence on 23 June 2005, after 178 days of trial.

13. The Defence estimates that the remaining Co-Accused will not complete presentation of their evidence until 2009.[19] The Defence further speculates that one of the judges might choose to withdraw from this case and, if so, that this might have an effect on Mr. Mugenzi's right to a trial without undue delay.[20]

---

12 Mugenzi Motion, para 18 (citing the Mugiraneza Motion, paras 5 to 7).

13 *Id.*, paras 5-6, 12-14, 25-32, 35.

14 Mugiraneza Motion, para 7 (citing *Bunkate v. Netherlands*, No. 26/1992/371/445 (ECHR 1993)).

15 Mugiraneza Decision, para 20.

18 *Prosecutor v. Bizimungu et al.*, Case no. ICTR-99-50-AR73, Decision on Prosper Mugiraneza's Interlocutory Appeal from Trial Chamber II Decision of 2 October 2003 Denying the Motion to Dismiss the Indictment, Demand Speedy Trial and for Appropriate Relief (AC), 27 February 2004, p. 3.

19 Mugenzi Motion, paras 7-11.

20 *Id.*, paras 14-17.

14. When making a determination as to whether there has been undue delay, the Chamber will only consider any delay up to the present. The Chamber will not speculate on whether the Accused's right to trial without undue delay might be violated at a future date.[21]

15. The Chamber notes that Mr. Mugenzi is in his ninth year of incarceration. When analyzing undue delay, however, this Chamber has made clear that the reasonableness of a period of delay cannot be translated into a fixed length of time and is dependant on consideration of the other factors articulated by the Appeals Chamber.[22] **[page 5]**

(2) *The complexity of the proceedings*

16. The Defence for Mr. Mugenzi offers no additional submissions regarding the complexity of the proceedings, relying instead on the Mugiraneza Motion, which alleges that these proceedings are not complex.[23] This Chamber has already had the opportunity to consider the complexity of the proceedings in the Mugiraneza Decision, and has found that they are complex.[24]

(3) *The conduct of the parties*

17. The Defence presents no additional evidence of delay caused by the Prosecution, but refers to and relies upon the relevant allegations in the Mugiraneza Motion. The Mugiraneza Motion alleged a lack of a "sense of urgency" on behalf of the Prosecution, delays in disclosure,[25] delays due to leadership vacancies,[26] and delays related to the request to amend the Indictment.[27]

18. In the Mugiraneza Decision the Chamber rejected these arguments and found no delay attributable to the Prosecution.[28] For the same reasons these arguments are rejected here.

(4) *The conduct of the relevant authorities*

19. The Mugenzi Motion refers to a "chronic lack of court space"[29] and the Mugiraneza Motion describes shortages of *ad litem* judges and translation facilities,[30] delays due to the Security Council, the General Assembly, disagreements between the Prosecution and the Registry, and the amount of time allocated to the trial by the Tribunal President.[31]

20. The Chamber has already rejected these arguments, including the allegations of a lack of court space, in the Mugiraneza Decision.[32] The Defence for Mr. Mugenzi has not adduced any more details and relies entirely on the Mugiraneza Motion. The Chamber therefore finds that Mugenzi has not raised any new arguments showing how the delay is attributable to the listed authorities. Accordingly, the arguments are rejected here as well. **[page 6]**

---

21 *See* Mugiraneza Decision, para 25.

22 *See, e.g., The Prosecutor v. Kanyabashi*, Case No. ICTR-96-15-I, Decision on the Defence Extremely Urgent Motion on Habeas Corpus and for Stoppage of Proceedings (TC), 23 May 2000, para 68; *The Prosecutor v. Kanyabashi*, Case No. ICTR-96-15-T, Decision on the Defence Motion for the Provisional Release of the Accused (TC), 21 February 2001, para 11; *Prosecutor v. Bizimungu et al.*, Case No. ICTR-99-50-T, Decision on Prosper Mugiraneza's Second Motion to Dismiss for Deprivation of His Right to Trial Without Undue Delay, 29 May 2007, para 27.

23 Mugiraneza Motion, paras 56-58.

24 Mugiraneza Decision, paras 30-31.

25 Mugiraneza Motion, paras 59-61.

26 Mugiraneza Motion, paras 40-43.

27 Mugiraneza Motion, para 60.

28 , para 34.

29 Mugenzi Motion, paras 13, 18.

30 *Id.* paras 44-48.

31 Mugiraneza Motion, paras 10, 40-51, 64-65, 71.

32 Mugiraneza Decision, para 36.

(5) *The prejudice to the accused, if any*

21. The Defence presents no arguments that Mr. Mugenzi has been prejudiced. The Mugiraneza Motion argued prejudice due to witnesses dying or their memories fading.[33] Mr. Mugiraneza's arguments regarding prejudice are specific to his own case and are not relevant to Mr. Mugenzi. Mr. Mugenzi fails to allege how he has been prejudiced.

Conclusion

22. The Defence has proposed severance of Mr. Mugenzi's case as a remedy for the alleged undue delay suffered by the Accused. The Chamber finds that Mr. Mugenzi has not been denied his right to a trial without undue delay. It is therefore unnecessary for the Chamber to consider whether severance is an appropriate remedy.

FOR THESE REASONS, the Chamber

DENIES the Defence Motion

Arusha, 14 June 2007

Khalida Rachid Khan Presiding Judge	Lee Gacuiga Muthoga Judge	Emile Francis Short Judge

[Seal of the Tribunal]

33 Mugiraneza Motion, paras 78.

Commentary

1. Introduction

Both decisions[1] come from the same case and both co-accused complained to the Trial Chamber about the violation of their right to be tried without undue delay. Their complaints are exclusively concerned with this right, as an element of the right to a fair trial, and not the right not to be detained on remand for an unreasonable period of time. Having regard to the facts of the case, as well as the facts in certain other ICTR cases, the right, as enshrined in, for example, Article 5, paragraph 3, of the ECHR, to 'be entitled to trial within a reasonable time or to release pending trial' may very well be applicable. However, this right is, contrary to the right to be tried without undue delay, not part of the ICTR Statute, although that should not prevent it from being respected.

A more cogent reason for defence counsel to refrain from invoking the right to a reasonable period of pre-trial detention seems that it is not capable of producing the remedy of dismissal of the case – or a permanent stay of proceedings. Only when a fair trial can no longer be conducted, which could be the case when undue delay occurs, can it be argued that a stay of proceedings must be put in place.[2] The logical remedy in case of a breach of the right to reasonable pre-trial detention period is provisional release, which a) may not be the remedy the defence is after, and b) is as good as impossible to obtain at the ICTR.[3]

Overall, the manner in which the Trial Chamber has handled the matter of undue delay is disappointing and indicative of a lack of a proper understanding of international human rights law. I will concentrate on the first decision, the motion brought by Mugiraneza. The second decision, triggered by the motion brought by co-accused Mugenzi, follows fully the analysis and result of the first decision, and thus needs no separate discussion.

2. The Trial Chamber's approach to international human rights law

The Trial Chamber in its approach to the defence motion gave some puzzling statements on the status of the major international supervisory mechanisms on human rights law, the European Court of Human Rights and the Human Rights Committee. It states that recourse to the case law of international human rights courts and bodies should only be had when the 'Tribunal's statutory instruments and jurisprudence are deficient.'[4] It is then noted by the chamber that both the statutory guarantees – Articles 19 and 20 – and case law from the ICTR Appeals Chamber on undue delay, make it unnecessary to seek guidance from international human rights law.[5]

This line of reasoning is indicative of the uneasy relationship between international criminal tribunals and human rights law. On several occasions, Chambers of the ICTY and ICTR have sought to restrict the relevance and/ or applicability of international human rights norms to international criminal proceedings.[6] At no time has there been any serious discussion on the nature of human rights as minimum standards, inherent in human dignity, which should apply to all criminal proceedings.[7] Instead, there is a strong preference, as in this case, for self-referential rhetoric.

---

1 ICTR, Decision on Prosper Mugiraneza's second motion to dismiss for deprivation of his Right to Trial without Undue Delay, *Prosecutor v. Bizimungu, Mugenzi, Bicamumpaka, Mugiraneza*, Case No. ICTR-99-50-T, T. Ch. II, 29 May 2007, in this volume, p. 419; ICTR, Decision on Justin Mugenzi's Motion Alleging Undue Delay and Seeking Severance, *Prosecutor v. Bizimungu, Mugenzi, Bicamumpaka, Mugiraneza*, Case No. ICTR-99-50-T, T. Ch. II, 14 June 2007, in this volume, p. 429.

2 In this respect, it is worth citing the ICC Trial Chamber in the Lubanga case: 'If, at the outset, it is clear that the essential preconditions of a fair trial are missing and there is no sufficient indication that this will be resolved during the trial process, it is necessary – indeed, inevitable – that the proceedings should be stayed,': ICC, Decision on the consequences of non-disclosure of exculpatory materials covered by Article 54(3)(e) agreements and the application to stay the prosecution of the accused, together with certain other issues raised at the Status Conference on 10 June 2008, *Prosecutor v. Lubanga Dyilo*, Case No. ICC-01/04-01/06-1401, T. Ch. I, 13 June 2008, par. 91.

3 I refer to the many commentaries in this series dealing with the matter of provisional release.

4 Decision on Prosper Mugiraneza's second motion to dismiss for deprivation of his Right to Trial without Undue Delay, *Prosecutor v. Bizimungu, Mugenzi, Bicamumpaka, Mugiraneza*, T. Ch. II, *supra* note 1, par. 20.

5 *Ibid.*

6 See M. Fedorova and G. Sluiter, Human Rights as Minimum Standards in International Criminal Proceedings, 3 Human Rights and International Legal Discourse 2009, p. 9 – 56.

7 *Ibid.*

It is illusory, as the Trial Chamber did in the present case, to think that the tribunal can come to an autonomous and isolated interpretation of the right to be tried without undue delay. The standard set out in the ICTR statute is not an invention, but rather an exact copy of the same right protected in Article 14 ICCPR and Article 6 ECHR. For a proper interpretation of that right, recourse to the origins and interpretations given by human rights courts is inevitable. The case law of the ICTR cannot itself substitute interpretations provided for by international bodies and courts that have been entrusted with the task of supervising respect for these norms; that would be presumptuous.

The Trial Chamber also suffers from selective memory. There is case law from the ICTR Appeals Chamber supporting the binding effect and direct applicability of human rights law for the ICTR. This does not impose as a condition that 'the Tribunal's statutory instruments and jurisprudence are deficient':

> The Report of the U.N. Secretary-General establishes the sources of law for the Tribunal. The International Covenant on Civil and Political Rights is part of general international law and is applied on that basis. Regional human rights treaties, such as the European Convention on Human Rights and the American Convention on Human Rights, and the jurisprudence developed thereunder, are persuasive authority which may be of assistance in applying and interpreting the Tribunal's applicable law. Thus, they are not binding of their own accord on the Tribunal. They are, however, authoritative as evidence of international custom.[8]

The reason why the Trial Chamber created this condition of 'deficiency of statutory instruments and jurisprudence' can be easily understood. It is an excuse for not having to consider and carefully examine human rights law itself. Indeed, from a human rights perspective, there is much to criticize in the decision. Such criticism could have been avoided – or at least mitigated – if the chamber would have done a better job in its reasoning.

3. Undue delay at the ICTR

Getting to the substance of the case - why was undue delay not established - the Trial Chamber's approach is, overall, very defensive and in no way makes it transparent to the reader when undue delay *can* be established at the ICTR. With the emphasis on factors that explain delay, and using these as valid justifications, any delay – even undue delay – can be defended. The result of this decision, as well as the recent Trial Chamber judgement in Military I case,[9] is that the protection against undue delay in the ICTR Statute is very much a dead letter.

The first point to be examined is the determination of the period. What do we mean by the right to be tried without undue delay? The decision does not inform us much on this point. The case law of the ECtHR offers important guidance as to the start of the period, as well as the different parts constituting the period (trial at first instance, appellate proceedings and proceedings at the supreme court), and the desired length per part and for the total period.[10] National courts have even transformed ECtHR case law in very concrete terms to their lower courts.[11] In such case law, there exist norms of aspiration – two years for finalization of the case at first instance after the arrest of the individual concerned[12] – concerning undue delay. Clearly, with similar norms lacking at the ICTR, although perhaps sometimes for good reasons, any delay seems permissive.

The good thing about norms of aspiration is that infringement thereof triggers a reversal of the burden of proof. It would be for the state to offer evidence justifying delay beyond these norms. At the ICTR, however, the lack of norms of aspiration means that the burden of proof, even in the most extreme cases, lies with the defendant.

3.1 Criteria determining undue delay

The Trial Chamber blindly follows the Appeals Chamber's criteria for assessing the existence of undue delay. The Appeals Chamber, in its earlier decision in this same case in 2004, listed the following criteria:

---

8 ICTR, Decision, *Barayagwiza v. Prosecutor*, Case No. ICTR-97-19-AR72, A. Ch., 3 November 1999, Klip/ Sluiter, ALC II-129, par. 40.

9 ICTR, Judgement and Sentence, *Prosecutor v. Bagosora et al.*, Case No. ICTR-98-41-T, T. Ch. I, 18 December 2008. In par 73 – 84, the Trial Chamber in Bagosora *et al* 'accepted' a period of 11 years until the judgement at first instance.

10 For an overview and discussion of relevant ECtHR case law on this matter, see S. Trechsel, Human Rights in Criminal Proceedings, Oxford University Press, Oxford 2005, p. 137 – 141.

11 See the Dutch Supreme Court, in its Judgement of 3 October 2000, NJ 2000, 721.

12 Or any other official act that leads to the reasonable belief that one will be prosecuted.

1. length of the delay;
2. complexity of the proceedings;
3. conduct of the parties;
4. conduct of relevant authorities;
5. prejudice to the accused, if any.

These criteria in and of themselves are already subject to criticism. As will be demonstrated below, their application to the facts also leaves much to be desired. First of all, it is my view that two factors in this list should play no role. The length of delay, to start with, only makes sense when we have a norm of aspiration, or starting point, such as is the case in the case law of ECtHR. Even then, it is not a factor of assessment, but we are in a position to determine the degree to which the norm of aspiration has been transgressed. Is this a matter of days, months or even years? Depending on the degree of transgression, we can then make a meaningful evaluation of factors that could - or could not - justify this transgression. Clearly, the longer the transgression, the more demanding one must be in respect of factors accounting for it. However, the length of delay as a factor in determining undue delay makes no sense, without at least some starting point as to what constitutes a reasonable period.

Secondly, it is astonishing that prejudice to the accused has been invented by the Appeals Chamber as a criterion, a factor for assessing undue delay. This is as absurd as requiring a person unlawfully detained or not enjoying legal representation to demonstrate prejudice. The prejudice consists and follows directly from the violation of fair trial rights. Any (implicit) requirement of additionally proving this means that these rights are not taken seriously and brings with it the significant risk that violations are not established, even where they should be. This factor is absent in human rights case law.[13]

The risks in imposing this factor are easily demonstrated by its application to the facts in ICTR case law. In the decision under review, for example, prejudice was measured by the accused's ability to present his defence, and it was concluded that no such prejudice was suffered. However, nowhere was it explained why prejudice had to be related to the accused's ability to prepare his defence; the latter is a separate and autonomous right that has been falsely taken into this equation. One must be equally critical of the view, as expressed in Military I, that no prejudice was suffered because the accused was eventually convicted to a sentence of life imprisonment.[14] If this is the prevailing approach, many human rights violations can be justified.

It bears stressing that the prejudice suffered in a case of undue delay is direct: it is the fact that there has been uncertainty for too long a period of time as to what would eventually happen with the accused. This prolonged uncertainty is the prejudice, because it prevents individuals from moving on with their lives (in case of acquittal) or adjusting to and making preparations for radically changed circumstances (in case of conviction). It demonstrates a fundamental lack of understanding of human rights law if the view is adopted that a showing of additional prejudice would be required. The remaining three factors as developed by the ICTR Appeals Chamber are relevant and are: a) the complexity of the proceedings; b) the conduct of the parties; and c) the conduct of the relevant authorities. When compared to human rights case law, there is a seemingly innocent mix-up between factors b and c. However, this can have serious implications and is at the heart of the difficulties in applying human rights law in international criminal proceedings.

3.2 The relevant authorities

The ECtHR does not distinguish between parties and authorities, because they can be identical. The prosecutor is a party, but also an authority, in the sense that its conduct is generally attributable to the state. Thus, the ECtHR makes a distinction between the conduct of the defence/ accused and the conduct of the authorities. This is of great importance, because of the obligations incumbent upon the state to ensure protection of rights attributed to individuals. In the relationship the individual and the state, it is only self-evident that conduct of the individual accounting for delay may weigh against establishing undue delay,

13 See, S. Trechsel, Human Rights in Criminal Proceedings, *supra* note 10, p. 142 – 148.

14 The Trial Chamber in that case said: 'the Chamber cannot identify any [prejudice], in particular since both have received life sentences in view of the gravity of their crimes' (Judgement and Sentence, *Prosecutor v. Bagosora et al.*, T. Ch. I, *supra* note 9, par.83).

whereas conduct of authorities causing delay will weigh in support of determining undue delay. 'Authorities' must be understood in a broad sense, including all organs the conduct of which can be attributed to the state. As a result, it is not restricted to the prosecuting authorities, but also includes the judges, as well as state organs responsible for organizing the criminal justice system effectively.

The deviation in ICTR criteria from established human rights case law is therefore unfortunate. It fails to take into account that, if the international community sets up criminal justice mechanisms, it carries the responsibility to ensure expeditious justice. That responsibility starts with the UN Security Council and includes the judges and prosecutor. From a human rights perspective, all these organs would qualify as 'authorities'. Otherwise, an imperfect, under-staffed system, could always serve as justification for violations of the right to a trial without undue delay. It needs to be borne in mind that the excuses that the ICTR could seek to advance are by no means original. The justification of excessive case load has often been brought to the ECtHR and has always been rejected, on the basis of arguments that are directly applicable to the ICTR as well; the ECtHR has regularly stated that the ECHR places the contracting states under a duty to organize their legal systems so as to enable the courts to comply with the requirements of Article 6, paragraph 1, including that of trial within a "reasonable time".[15]

There is no reason why this should be different for the ICTR, and it also means that the assessment of conduct of authorities should encompass a broad range of organs, including the UN Security Council. Within the category of 'relevant authorities' - a notion that remains undefined in the decision under review - all UN organs involved in setting up, organizing and financing the ICTR should thus be included, as well as organs within the ICTR itself.

3.3 The conduct of the relevant authorities

It transpires from human rights case law that the conduct of relevant authorities is by far the most important factor in determining undue delay. Trechsel refers to this as the only decisive element, far more important than the complexity of the case:

> Whether the case is complex or not is in essence entirely irrelevant – a violation will only be found when there have been periods during the proceedings where no action was taken, although something could and should have been done.[16]

Clearly, the respective ICTR chambers have not applied the criteria to the facts at all in this way. They do not give decisive weight to the conduct of authorities; rather it seems, also in this decision, that the complexity of the case is emphasized and taken as the major justification for serious delay. There is no separate attention to the (long) periods of inaction in the case and the role of the authorities during that period.

In the decision under review, the Trial Chamber takes an unfair and incorrect view of the criterion 'conduct of relevant authorities'. As was already mentioned, it failed to indicate the scope of 'relevant authorities', which should include the UN Security Council and the judges themselves. More important is the standard of proof imposed upon the defendant. In fact, the chamber reproaches the defence that it 'has failed to give details concerning how the conduct of the relevant authorities has resulted in or contributed to undue delay in this case.'[17] This seems to impose an absurd standard. The problem with delay is that it generally is the result of inaction. When the chamber asks for 'details' of 'conduct', it seems to assume the existence of deliberate activities. Details of inaction are difficult, if not impossible, to provide.

Instead of imposing this impossible burden on the defence, human rights law takes a radically different approach. It is only for the individual suffering from delay to prove that the authorities contributed to it, when the latter have remained fully active in the investigation and prosecution. Conversely, the burden is on the authorities, certainly not the defence, to prove that inaction has not caused delay or can be justified under the circumstances. It is thus not for the defence to prove, as the Trial Chamber said, how mismanagement and

---

15 S. Trechsel, Human Rights in Criminal Proceedings, *supra* note 10, p. 147.

16 *Ibid.*, p. 145.

17 Decision on Prosper Mugiraneza's second motion to dismiss for deprivation of his Right to Trial without Undue Delay, *Prosecutor v. Bizimungu, Mugenzi, Bicamumpaka, Mugiraneza*, T. Ch. II, *supra* note 1, par. 36.

other such issues have translated into delay in a concrete case.[18] The burden is on the authorities to offer a plausible and reasonable explanation for delay caused.

4. Recommendations on the right to be tried without undue delay

I will make a short attempt to sketch what in my view should be the basic contours of the right to be tried without undue delay in international criminal proceedings. As a starting point, there should be a norm of aspiration. It is reasonable, given the entirely different nature and complexity of cases, when compared to ordinary domestic criminal proceedings, to set this norm at four years (instead of the two years at the ECHR). This would concern the period from arrest until judgement at first instance. This is based on an average case complexity at the ICTR or ICTY, and means that longer durations may be justified by increased complexity in individual cases. Conversely, less complex cases should be finalized in less than four years.

I also propose that a stricter attitude is taken towards delays resulting from inaction, ineffective and under-staffed institutions, mismanagement, bureaucracy etc. The case law of the ECtHR should be considered and shows us that most of these excuses are not accepted. However, it can be argued that, in the early years of existence of international criminal tribunals, problems related to setting up an effective organisation and management might serve as justification for some delay. However, this must remain exceptional and could no longer serve as an excuse in the decision under review.

It is my view that a proper determination in the decisions under review, if human rights law and case law would be properly appreciated and duly taken into account, should result in the decision that the accused's right to be tried without undue delay has been violated. I think this should be the determination in a number of other ICTR cases as well, such as the Military I case.[19]

However, this determination thus does not necessarily mean that, as a remedy, the proceedings should be stayed or the case dismissed. There is flexibility in the choice of remedies, and one of them could very well be a reduction in the sentence, in case of conviction, proportionate to the violation. This remedy is not unusual, and has been applied at the ICTR in a number of cases.[20]

5. Conclusion

In conclusion, the ICTR case law on undue delay leaves much to be desired. It is unworthy of the role model that the ICTR should be in criminal proceedings. It is, furthermore, proof of the lack of proper understanding of human rights law in international criminal proceedings. Finally, although it exceeds the scope of this commentary, this poor case law adds important fuel to the idea of having a human rights supervisory mechanism ensuring proper respect for human rights law at the ICTR. Apparently, the institution is incapable of doing this itself.

Göran Sluiter

---

[18] *Ibid.*

[19] See S. Trechsel, Human Rights in Criminal Proceedings, *supra* note 10.

[20] See, for example, ICTR, Judgement, *Kajelijeli v. Prosecutor*, Case No. ICTR-98-44A-A, A. Ch., 23 May 2005, Klip/ Sluiter, ALC-XXII-625, par. 320; ICTR, Decision, Semanza v. Prosecutor, Case No. ICTR-97-23-A, A. Ch., 31 May 2000, Klip/ Sluiter, ALC-VI-167; ICTR, Decision (Prosecutor's Request for Review or Reconsideration), Barayagwiza v. Prosecutor, Case No. ICTR-97-19-AR72, A. Ch., 31 March 2000, Klip/ Sluiter, ALC-VI-223.

International Criminal Tribunal for Rwanda
Tribunal pénal international pour le Rwanda

OR: ENG

TRIAL CHAMBER III

Before Judge: Dennis C. M. Byron, Presiding
Karin Hökborg
Gberdao Gustave Kam

Registrar: Adama Dieng

Date: 20 September 2006

THE PROSECUTOR

v.

André RWAMAKUBA
Case No. ICTR-98-44C-T

JUDGEMENT

Office of the Prosecutor:
Dior Fall
Iain Morley
Adama Niane
Tamara Cummings-John

Defence Counsel
David Hooper and Andreas O'Shea

TABLE OF CONTENTS

[page 3] INTRODUCTION

1. This Tribunal has the authority to prosecute persons responsible for serious violations of international humanitarian law, including genocide and crimes against humanity, committed in the territory of Rwanda and Rwandan citizens responsible for such crimes committed in the territory of neighbouring States, between 1 January 1994 and 31 December 1994.[1] Under Article 2 of the Statute, genocide is an act committed with the intent to destroy, in whole or in part, a national, ethnical, racial or religious group, as such.[2] The crime against humanity is defined as a crime committed as part of a widespread or systematic attack against any civilian population on national, political, ethnic, racial or religious grounds.[3]

2. The Appeals Chamber has held that genocide against Tutsi and widespread or systematic attacks against a civilian population based on Tutsi ethnic identification occurred in Rwanda between April and July 1994 are facts of common knowledge not subject to reasonable dispute.[4] As the Appeals Chamber recalled, this ruling does not lessen the Prosecution's burden of proof: it must still demonstrate that the specific events alleged in an Indictment constituted genocide or a crime against humanity and that the conduct and mental state of an Accused establishes his culpability for such crimes.

3. The Accused, André Rwamakuba, was born in 1950 in Nduba, Gikomero *commune*, Kigali rural *préfecture*. He is qualified as a doctor having studied at Butare University, **[page 4]** Rwanda, in Zaïre (now the Democratic Republic of Congo) and in Belgium.[5] He was a public health specialist and in 1992 was appointed Director of the Kigali Health Region. In 1994, after the death of Rwandan President Juvénal Habyarimana, he was appointed Minister of Primary and Secondary Education in the Interim Government, and took oath on 9 April 1994. He was a member of the *Mouvement démocratique du Rwanda* (MDR) party.[6]

4. André Rwamakuba was first arrested on 2 August 1995 upon what appears to have been an independent initiative of the Namibian authorities. Once contacted, the Prosecution indicated that it had instructed its office in Kigali to take urgent steps to ascertain whether it was interested in the prosecution of Rwamakuba on charges within the Tribunal's jurisdiction.[7] A month later, the Prosecution notified the Namibian

---

1 Statute, Articles 1 to 4.

2 Statute, Article 2(2): Genocide means any of the following acts committed with the intent to destroy, in whole or in part, a national, ethnical, racial or religious group, as such:
- (a) Killing members of the group;
- (b) Causing serious bodily or mental harm to members of the group;
- (c) Deliberately inflicting on the group conditions of life calculated to bring about its physical destruction in whole or in part;
- (d) Imposing measures intended to prevent births within the group;
- (e) Forcibly transferring children of the group to another group.

3 Statute, Article 3: The International Tribunal for Rwanda shall have the power to prosecute persons responsible for the following crimes when committed as part of a widespread or systematic attack against any civilian population on national, political, ethnic, racial or religious grounds:
- (a) Murder;
- (b) Extermination;
- (c) Enslavement;
- (d) Deportation;
- (e) Imprisonment;
- (f) Torture;
- (g) Rape;
- (h) Persecutions on political, racial and religious grounds;
- (i) Other inhumane acts.

4 *Karemera et al.*, Decision on Prosecutor's Interlocutory Appeal of Decision on Judicial Notice (AC), paras. 29 and 35; see also: *Semanza* Appeal Judgement, para. 192.

5 Curriculum vitae of André Rwamakuba (Exh. D. 184); Prosecution Closing Brief, para. 6 and footnote 3; Defence Closing Brief, pp. 2-5.

6 Indictment, para. 1; Prosecution Pre-Trial Brief, para. 11; Prosecution Closing Brief, paras. 7-10; Defence Closing Brief.

7 See Prosecution's letter of 22 December 1995, attached to the Defence "Additional Evidence in Support of Motion for Stay of Proceedings on Grounds of Undue Delay of 13 May 2005", filed on 1 June 2005; *Rwamakuba*, Decision on André Rwamakuba's Motion for Severance (TC), paras. 30 and 32.

authorities that it did not possess evidence which would entitle it to request his detention.[8] Rwamakuba was subsequently released on 8 February 1996.

5. Three years after that initial arrest, the Prosecution did file an indictment against André Rwamakuba and seven other co-Accused.[9] Rwamakuba was arrested by the Namibian authorities on 21 October 1998, in compliance with a Tribunal warrant of arrest and Order for transfer and detention,[10] and transferred to the United Nations Detention Facilities ("UNDF") in Arusha the following day. Rwamakuba pleaded not guilty to all the charges against him.[11]

6. After four of his co-Accused were severed from the 1998 Indictment,[12] the trial against André Rwamakuba and the three remaining co-Accused, namely Edouard Karemera, Mathieu Ngirumpaste and Joseph Nzirorera, commenced on 27 November 2003. Thirteen Prosecution witnesses were heard before the trial was interrupted in May 2004 as a result of the Presiding Judge's withdrawal from the case. A rehearing of the case with a different bench was then **[page 5]** necessary.[13] The new Chamber subsequently granted the Prosecution's request for severance of Rwamakuba from the joined Indictment and ordered a separate trial pursuant to an Amended Indictment.[14] This Indictment filed 10 days later charges André Rwamakuba with genocide, or in the alternative complicity in genocide, and crimes against humanity.[15] At a further initial appearance held on 21 March 2005, the Chamber entered a plea of not guilty to all counts in the absence of the Accused.[16] The Defence for André Rwamakuba did not dispute that genocide occurred in Rwanda in 1994, but contested the Accused's participation in any of the crimes alleged in the Indictment.[17] Following the Chamber's rulings on the defects in the form of the Indictment, the Prosecution filed its final version on 10 June 2005.[18]

7. The trial in the instant case commenced on 9 June 2005. Eighteen Prosecution witnesses were heard, including one investigator and one expert witness, over 39 trial days.[19] Two Prosecution witnesses refused to testify. The Chamber was not requested to issue a subpoena order for these witnesses to appear before the Tribunal. Rather, the Prosecution moved for an adjournment of the proceedings until some unspecified time in October 2005.[20] After several opportunities were given to the Prosecution to clarify if and when these witnesses would testify, the Chamber denied the Prosecution's application considering the interests of justice and the right of the Accused to be tried without undue delay.[21] In its ruling, it found that the Prosecution demonstrated a lack of diligence and had failed to persuade the Chamber that these two witnesses were critical to the case against the Accused.[22] **[page 6]**

8 See Prosecution's letter of 18 January 1996, attached to the Defence "Additional Evidence in Support of Motion for Stay of Proceedings on Grounds of Undue Delay of 13 May 2005", filed on 1 June 2005.

9 *Bizimana et al.*, Confirmation and Non-Disclosure of the Indictment, 29 August 1998.

10 *Rwamakuba*, Warrant of Arrest and Order for Transfer and Detention (TC).

11 See: Initial Appearance, T. 7 April 1999.

12 See *Bizimana et al.* Case, Decision on the Defence Motion in Opposition to Joinder and Motion for Severance and Separate Trial Filed by the Accused Juvénal Kajelijeli (TC); *Bizimana et al.*, Decision on the Prosecutor's Motion for severance of Félicien Kabuga's Trial and for Leave to the Accused's Indictment (TC); *Bizimana et al.*, Decision on the Prosecutor's Motion for Separate Trials and for Leave to File an Amended Indictment (TC).

13 *Karemera et al.*, Decision on Interlocutory Appeals Regarding the Continuation of Proceedings with a Substitute Judge and on Nzirorera's Motion for Leave to Consider New Material (AC); *Karemera et al.*, Reasons for Decision on Interlocutory Appeals Regarding the Continuation of Proceedings with a Substitute Judge and on Nzirorera's Motion for Leave to Consider New Material (AC).

14 *Karemera et al.*, Decision on severance of André Rwamakuba and for Leave to File Amended Indictment (TC).

15 Amended Indictment filed on 10 June 2005, counts 1 to 4.

16 André Rwamakuba did not appear before the Chamber. His Counsel asserted that Rwamakuba had been provided with the Indictment and had been apprised of its content (T. 21 March 2005). The Amended Indictment was filed on 23 February 2005 and re-filed on 9 March 2005, due to typographical errors and in accordance with the Chamber's Order to Re-File the Amended Indictment (TC).

17 See for e.g.: T. 21 April 1994, p. 35.

18 *Rwamakuba*, Decision on Defects in the Form of the Indictment (TC). See also: T. 6 June 2005; T. 9 June 2005.

19 The Prosecution conducted its case during two trial sessions: from 9 June to 15 July 2005 and from 22 August to 13 September 2005. The expert witness was heard in part via teleconference; both parties agreed on it (T. 22, 23 and 24 August 2005).

20 T. 13 September 2005, p. 3. See *Rwamakuba*, Decision on Prosecution Motion for Reconsideration or, in the Alternative, Certification to Appeal Chamber's Decision Denying Request for Adjournment (TC).

21 T. 13 September 2005, pp. 13-14.

22 *Rwamakuba*, Decision on Prosecution Motion for Reconsideration or, in the Alternative, Certification to Appeal Chamber's Decision Denying Request for Adjournment (TC).

8. The Defence case commenced on 7 November 2005 and 31 witnesses were called over 39 days.[23] The Chamber undertook a site visit in Rwanda with the parties in January 2006.[24] Key locations relevant to the charges against André Rwamakuba were viewed in Kigali, Gikomero and Butare areas.[25] The closing arguments of both parties were heard on 21 April 2006, approximately 10 weeks after the close of the Defence case.[26]

9. From the outset André Rwamakuba refused to attend court proceedings. According to his Counsel, this was due to the Accused's belief that the evidence against him was being manipulated.[27] The Chamber nevertheless regularly invited him to attend the proceedings, through the Registrar and his Counsel.[28] The trial proceeded in the absence of the Accused in accordance with Rule 82*bis* of the Rules.[29]

10. The charges against the Accused are discussed in **Chapter I**. The Chamber then reviews the evidence adduced during the trial and will reach its findings in **Chapter II**. **Chapter III** pertains to the rights of the Accused and **Chapter IV** contains the verdict.

CHAPTER I – CHARGES AGAINST THE ACCUSED

11. In its Closing Brief, the Prosecution contends that by his acts and omissions, André Rwamakuba is criminally responsible under Article 6(1) of the Statute for having planned, ordered, instigated and committed the crimes of genocide, or complicity in genocide, murder and extermination as crimes against humanity in Gikomero *commune* and at Butare University Hospital during April 1994.[30] It also submits that as Minister of Primary and Secondary Education, Rwamakuba "did nothing, either to denounce the crimes committed against the Tutsi, [o]r to dissociate himself from the [Interim Government]". It submits that by **[page 7]** these omissions, Rwamakuba directly failed to discharge the duties entrusted to him, which he had sworn to fulfil, and that he encouraged the genocidal activities.[31]

12. The Prosecution further contends that "a Trial Chamber may find an accused guilty when it is satisfied that the accused participated in a crime by committing any one of the acts covered by the Statute, *even if the Chamber does not endorse the Prosecution's case*".[32] It adds that "[a]s a Tribunal of fact and law, the Chamber may accept any argument that it finds relevant to the facts of the case, on condition that the said argument is consistent with the provisions of Article 6(1) of the Statute".[33] In the Prosecution's view, the question of notifying the Accused of the charges against him in that respect does not arise, since he was informed of the forms of responsibility under Article 6(1) of the Statute for which he was being prosecuted and which have been established by the Prosecution.[34]

13. Article 17(4) of the Statute and Rule 47(C) of the Rules require the Prosecution to set forth in the Indictment a concise statement of the facts of the case and of the crime(s) with which the suspect is charged. This obligation must be interpreted in light of the rights of the accused to a fair trial, to be informed of the charges against him, and to have adequate time and facilities for the preparation of his defence.[35] According to the jurisprudence of both *ad hoc* Tribunals, this translates into an obligation on the part of the Prosecution

23 The Defence case was conducted during two trial sessions: from 7 November to 16 December 2005 and from 17 January to 9 February 2006. At the Defence's request, four witnesses testified via video-link. The Prosecution did not oppose. See: *Rwamakuba*, Decision on Confidential Motion for the Testimony of Defence Witness 1/15 (TC); T. 18 January 2006, p. 37; T. 19 January 2006, p.3.

24 *Rwamakuba*, Decision on Defence Motion for A View Locus In Quo (TC).

25 Minutes for the Site Visit to Rwanda in the *Rwamakuba* case, 13-16 January 2005.

26 T. 21 April 2006.

27 See: T. 6 June 2005, pp. 2-3.

28 See for e.g.: T. 6 June 2005, p. 4; T. 27 June 2005, p. 2; T. 4 July 2005, pp. 1-2; T. 11 July 2005, pp. 1-2; T. 22 August 2005, pp. 1-2; T. 29 August 2005, p. 1; T. 1 November 2005, p. 1; T. 7 November 2005, p. 1; T. 14 November 2005, p. 1; T . 17 January 2006, p. 3.

29 A chronology of the case is annexed to this Judgement (Annex II).

30 Prosecution Closing Brief, paras. 19, 208, 216-217, 239, 243-244, 248, 268 and 269.

31 Prosecution Closing Brief, para. 265.

32 Prosecution Closing Brief, para. 266 (emphasis added).

33 *Ibidem*.

34 Prosecution Closing Brief, para. 266.

35 Statute, Articles 19, 20(2), 20(4)(a) and 20(4)(b).

to state the material facts underpinning the charges in the Indictment, but not the evidence by which such material facts are to be proven.[36]

14. The Indictment, therefore, has to fulfil the fundamental purpose to inform the Accused of the charges against him with sufficient particularity to enable him to mount his defence.[37] Failure to set forth the specific material facts of a crime constitutes a material defect in the Indictment. This defect may nonetheless be cured, and a conviction entered, where the accused has received timely, clear, and consistent information from the Prosecution which resolves the ambiguity or clears up the vagueness.[38] In assessing whether a defective **[page 8]** indictment was cured, the Chamber must determine whether the accused was in a reasonable position to understand the charges against him or her and to confront the Prosecution's case.[39]

15. In the present case, after a brief description of the Accused, his authority and legal duties,[40] the four counts of the Indictment charge André Rwamakuba pursuant to Articles 2, 3 and 6(1) of the Statute, with genocide, or in the alternative, complicity in genocide, and extermination and murder as crimes against humanity regarding events that took place on or between 6 and 30 April 1994 in Gikomero *commune* and at Butare University Hospital.[41] These four counts set out the crimes for which the Accused is charged. The respective succeeding paragraphs set out the concise statement of facts on which the allegations are based.[42]

16. Paragraph 11 of the Indictment details how between 10 and 20 April 1994, in Gikomero *commune*, the Accused allegedly delivered machetes that were subsequently used in killing or attempting to kill Tutsi. Paragraphs 12, 13, 23 and 26 of the Indictment describe how during the same period and in the same *commune*, the Accused allegedly ordered and participated in the killing of three persons identified as Tutsi and in the massacre of Tutsi refugees at the Kayanga Health Centre. The alleged participation of the Accused in massacres at Butare University Hospital between 18 and 25 April 1994 is set forth at paragraphs 15 to 16, 23 and 26 of the Indictment.

17. The Indictment also describes André Rwamakuba's alleged political status and related political activities. It sets out how he conducted sensitization campaigns against Tutsi in Gikomero *commune* between 26 July 1993 and June 1994.[43] It alleges that as a Minister of Primary and Secondary Education of the Interim Government of 8 April 1994, he took part in the conception and the implementation of the Government's policies to exterminate the Tutsi throughout Rwanda.[44] The Accused is also defined as a member of the extremist wing of the *Mouvement Démocratique du Rwanda*, MDR "Hutu Power", which was allegedly created on or about 26 July 1993 and had a specific ideology of exterminating the Tutsi.[45] **[page 9]**

18. The Indictment does not allege the Accused's criminal responsibility as superior for crimes committed by subordinates.[46] In addition to alleging complicity in genocide,[47] the Indictment includes only a general reference to Article 6(1) of the Statute in relation to each of the four counts. In accordance with the settled jurisprudence, such general reference implies that the Accused is prosecuted for all forms of individual participation set out by Article 6(1) of the Statute, namely planning, instigating, ordering, committing and

36 *Ntakirutimana* Appeal Judgement, paras. 25 and 470 ; *Rutaganda* Appeal Judgement, paras. 301-303; *Ntagerura* Appeal Judgement, para. 21; *Naletilic* Appeal Judgement, para. 26.

37 *Ntakirutimana* Appeal Judgement, paras. 25 and 470; *Ntagerura* Appeal Judgement, para. 22.

38 *Niyitegeka* Appeal Judgement, para. 195; *Ntagerura* Appeal Judgement, paras. 30; *Gacumbitsi* Appeal Judgement, para. 49.

39 *Rutaganda* Appeal Judgement, para. 303; see also: *Ntakirutimana* Appeal Judgement, paras. 27 and 469-472; *Ntagerura* Appeal Judgement, paras. 30 and 67; *Gacumbitsi* Appeal Judgement, para. 49.

40 See Indictment, paras. 1 and 2.

41 The Amended Indictment was filed on 10 June 2005, and is attached to the present Judgement (see Annex 1).

42 See the use of the words "as follows" at the end of each Introductory paragraph of each Count.

43 Indictment, paras. 3 to 5.

44 Indictment, paras. 1, 7, 9, 14 and 19

45 Indictment, para. 3.

46 Statute, Article 6(3): The fact that any of the acts referred to in Articles 2 to 4 of the present Statute was committed by a subordinate does not relieve his or her superior criminal responsibility if he or she knew or had reasons to know that the subordinate was about to commit such acts or had done so and the superior failed to take the necessary and reasonable measures to prevent such acts or to punish the perpetrators thereof.

47 According to the jurisprudence, complicity in genocide is a form of liability. See: *Ntakirutimana* Appeal Judgement, para. 500; *Semanza* Appeal Judgement, para. 316; *Krstić* Appeal Judgement, para. 139.

aiding and abetting in the planning, preparation or execution of a crime.[48] The Appeals Chamber and some Trial Chambers have stated that this provision is interpreted "[to cover] first and foremost the physical perpetration of a crime by the offender himself, or the culpable omission of an act that was mandated by a rule of criminal law."[49] In the present case, there is no allegation of any legal duty under which the Accused was mandated to act and which failure to do so would constitute a criminal act.

19. Reading the Indictment as whole, the Chamber concludes that the allegations describing the political activities of the Accused provide the context or background from which inferences could be drawn either concerning his intent, his disposition or other elements of his individual participation in specific crimes in Gikomero *commune* and at Butare University Hospital between 6 and 30 April 1994. This conclusion is in accordance with the clear and consistent notice given by the Prosecution throughout its representations of the case, its Pre-Trial Brief and Opening Statement, and its evidence adduced during the trial, as described hereinafter.

20. When André Rwamakuba was jointly indicted with three co-Accused, all were charged with conspiracy to commit genocide, direct and public incitement to genocide, genocide, or alternatively complicity in genocide, rape and extermination as crimes against humanity, and serious violations of Article 3 Common to the Geneva Conventions.[50] That **[page 10]** Indictment pleaded not only the direct criminal responsibility of the four Accused as perpetrators or accomplices but also as superiors for the crimes committed by their subordinates. The Prosecutor's theory alleged a "huge government conspiracy of State-sponsored genocide".[51]

21. In 2004, before the rehearing of the trial began, the Prosecution requested the severance of André Rwamakuba from the joint Indictment. It contented that "it [was] not necessary to support a joint trial to prosecute Rwamakuba effectively" and that it intended to focus the case entirely on Rwamakuba's "direct participation in crimes", thereby removing any allegation of conspiracy to commit genocide or joint criminal enterprise responsibility.[52]

22. The Prosecution reiterated this affirmation several times.[53] It stated in open court that the entire case was to be based on André Rwamakuba's own acts and omissions and that it was not going to "attempt to bring in proof of Rwamakuba's meeting and conspiring with other interim government ministers and other MRND leaders to commit genocide".[54] The Prosecution also indicated that any pleading of 'common purpose' implicating Rwamakuba as a co-perpetrator of crimes committed throughout Rwanda in furtherance of a government conspiracy to commit genocide had been removed from the Indictment.[55]

---

48 *Ntakirutimana* Appeal Judgement, para. 473.

49 See: *Tadić* Appeal Judgement, para. 188; *Kayishema* Appeal Judgement, para. 187; *Musema* Judgement, para. 123; *Bagilishema* Judgement, para. 29 and footnote 19; *Kamuhanda* Judgement, para. 595; *Kajelijeli* Judgement, para. 764; *Ntagerura* Judgement, para. 659.

50 In 1998, the Prosecution filed an Indictment against Augustin Bizimana, Félicien Kabuga, Juvénal Kajelijeli, Edouard Karemera, Mathieu Ngirumpaste, Callixte Nzabomimana, Joseph Nzirorera and André Rwamakuba. As a result of the severance of four of these co-Accused, the Prosecution charged André Rwamakuba jointly with Edouard Karemera, Mathieu Ngirumpatse and Joseph Nzirorera (see: Amended Indictment filed on 18 February 2004).

51 See Prosecutor's Consolidated Motion to Sever Rwamakuba from the Joint Indictment and to Try Him Separately, For Leave to File a Separate Amended Indictment against Rwamakuba, and For Leave to File a Separate Amended Indictment against Karemera, Ngirumpatse and Nzirorera, filed on 20 December 2004, para. 11; see also Prosecutor's Motion for Leave to File an Amended Separate Indictment against Karemera, Ngirumpatse and Nzirorera, filed on 19 November 2004, para. 14.

52 Prosecutor's Motion of 19 November 2004, paras. 14 and 21.

53 See T. 25 November 2004, p. 13; Prosecutor's Consolidated Motion.

54 T. 25 November 2004, p. 13.

55 Prosecutor's Consolidated Motion of 20 December 2004, para. 15.

23. At first, André Rwamakuba opposed the Prosecution's application for severance.[56] Subsequently, his Defence altered its position on the premise of the Prosecution's stated new theory against the Accused.[57] It stressed the significance of that understanding in determining **[page 11]** its advice to the Accused and to his subsequent consent not to oppose severance.[58] The Prosecution replied that "it [was] evident that the Prosecutor [intended] to establish Rwamakuba's criminal responsibility under the Statute for commission of crimes in Gikomero and Butare and [would] *not rely upon the doctrine of joint criminal enterprise or seek to establish his criminal responsibility for acts and omissions of the Interim Government throughout Rwanda*".[59] The Prosecution further submitted that the question of what evidence it may adduce to establish his responsibility was different and that it intended to offer evidence of his ministerial appointment, "*to prove elements of the Prosecution case such as* mens rea *for genocide*".[60] The Chamber granted the severance of André Rwamakuba on the basis of the Prosecution's assertions and its stated revised theory against the Accused.[61]

24. Later, when replying to the Defence Motion on Defects in the Form of the Indictment, the Prosecution reiterated the same position.[62] In the light of these submissions, the Chamber ruled that one particular paragraph which could have raised ambiguities concerning the exact nature of the responsibility alleged against the Accused was to be struck from the Indictment.[63]

25. The Prosecution's Pre-Trial Brief also presents the factual allegations against the Accused divided between events in Gikomero *Commune* and at Butare University Hospital, and alleges his criminal responsibility under Article 6(1) of the Statute for crimes committed in those specific locations.[64] The Prosecution Opening Statement was consistent with this theory.[65]

26. Until the submission made at the latest stage by the Prosecution in its Closing Brief, there was therefore no indication in the Indictment, the Pre-Trial Brief or the Opening Statement that the charges against the Accused included a responsibility, as a Minister of the **[page 12]** Interim Government, for not having denounced the crimes committed against the Tutsi or for not dissociating himself from the Government, and for a failure to discharge the duties entrusted to him as a member of the Government. On the contrary, from the outset, the Prosecution gave clear and consistent information both to the Accused and to the Chamber that its case was limited to Rwamakuba's direct participation in criminal activities in two specific locations[66] within a specific time-frame.[67] Before and during the presentation of the evidence at trial, the Prosecution never claimed to revise this stated position.

---

[56] At that stage, the Defence considered that a joint trial would assist the Chamber in placing in context the nature of Rwamakuba's activities as a Minister and would assist to controvert the prosecution's theory of a concerted government plan to which all Ministers were party. The Defence further expressed its concern that the proposed Separate Indictment at that time did not reflect the stated intent of the Prosecution in its severance motion. It contended that the proposed Separate Indictment did not in fact reduce the substance of the Prosecution case against the Accused. The Defence was therefore of the view that the Accused's interests were best served within a joint trial, rather than dealt with in a less coherent manner to support indirect responsibility by virtue of his alleged influence and effective control as a Minister and so called "high ranking member of Hutu power" (Response on Behalf of Dr Rwamakuba to the Prosecutor's Motions for Separate Trials, filed on 24 November 2004, paras. 36-38).

[57] Rwamakuba's Response to the Prosecution's Motion to Sever and File a Separate Amended Indictment, filed on 10 January 2005, p. 2.

[58] *Ibid.*, pp. 2 and 4: [The Defence] have altered [its] position and provided advice to the Accused in the light of the increased clarity of the Prosecution position expressed in the renewed motion, and on the premise that the Prosecution will adhere to their expressed position. [...] It is therefore [the Defence] understanding that the position is that, on severance, the Prosecution seeks to prove culpability solely through evidence of events in Gikomero and Butare that concern Rwamakuba [...] [and] does not intend to rely on the doctrine of joint criminal enterprise.

[59] Prosecutor's Reply to the Defence Submissions on the Consolidated Motion to Sever Rwamakuba from the Joint Indictment and for Leave to Amend the Indictment, filed on 10 February 2005, para.2 (emphasis added).

[60] Prosecutor's Reply, filed on 10 February 2005, para. 3 (emphasis added).

[61] *Karemera et al.*, Decision on Severance of André Rwamakuba and For Leave to File Amended Indictment (TC).

[62] *Réponse du Procureur à la requête de la Défense en date du 27 avril 2005, intitulée* "Preliminary Motion on Behalf of the Accused on Defects in the Form of the Indictment of 23 February 2005", filed on 4 May 2005.

[63] *Rwamakuba*, Decision on Defects in the Form of the Indictment (TC), para. 18.

[64] Prosecution Pre-Trial Brief, paras. 15 to 29, 30 to 40 and 74.

[65] T. 9 June 2005.

[66] Gikomero *Commune* and Butare University Hospital.

[67] Between 6 and 30 April 1994.

27. The Chamber notes that in its closing arguments the Defence reiterated its understanding of the Prosecution's case against the Accused. It emphasised that it had conducted the Defence of André Rwamakuba on the plain understanding that "command responsibility, joint criminal enterprise, were out and that the relevance of his being a minister was confined to disposition and ideology".[68]

28. It would therefore be contrary to the fundamental right of the Accused to a fair trial, including his right to defend himself and to know the charges against him, if the Chamber were to accede to a Prosecution request to find the Accused criminally responsible for omissions which were neither set forth in the Indictment nor subsequently notified by timely, clear, and consistent information from the Prosecution.[69] The Prosecution is expected to know its case before it goes to trial rather than seek to mould its case at the end of the trial depending on how the evidence unfolded.

29. The Chamber therefore considers that in the present case, the Prosecution charges André Rwamakuba, pursuant to Article 6(1) of the Statute,[70] with genocide, or alternatively, complicity in genocide, and crimes against humanity for acts allegedly committed between 6 and 30 April 1994 in Gikomero *commune* and at Butare University Hospital, as pleaded in Counts 1 to 4 of the Indictment. Any factual allegation related to André Rwamakuba's political activities or role as a member of the MDR party or as Minister of the Interim **[page 13]** Government must be considered as context or background from which inferences could be drawn concerning, for instance, his intent, disposition or other elements of the crimes.[71]

CHAPTER II - FINDINGS

30. Before addressing its factual findings **(II)**, the Chamber briefly discusses two applicable rules on evidentiary matters **(I)**.

I. RULES ON EVIDENTIARY MATTERS

31. In the Chamber's view, there are two principles especially significant in the assessment of the evidence: first, the presumption of innocence of each accused person **(I.1.)**; and second, the Chamber's discretionary power concerning the assessment of the evidence in view of a fair determination of the matter **(I.2.)**.

I.1. Presumption of Innocence

32. Each accused is presumed innocent.[72] Accordingly, the Prosecution bears the onus of establishing the accused's guilt beyond reasonable doubt.[73] The Defence does not have to adduce rebuttal evidence to the Prosecution's case. The Prosecution will fail to discharge its persuasive burden of proof if the Defence's evidence raises a reasonable doubt within the Prosecution's case.[74] This principle also applies when the accused denies commission of the crimes with which he is charged because he was not at the scene of the crime at the time of its commission: "the Prosecution's burden is to prove the accused's guilt as to the alleged crimes beyond reasonable doubt in spite of the proffered alibi".[75] According to the settled jurisprudence, if the defence is reasonably possibly true, it must be successful.[76] **[page 14]**

---

68 T. 21 April 2006, pp. 37 and 39.

69 Compare with *Ntagerura* Judgement, para. 34, in which the Trial Chamber did not consider the Prosecutor's argument, *which were advanced for the first time during the presentation of closing arguments*, to hold the accused criminally responsible based on the theory of joint criminal enterprise. The Appeals Chamber confirmed this finding (*Natgerura* Appeal Judgement, paras. 33-46).

70 For planning, instigating, ordering, committing or otherwise aiding and abetting in the planning, preparation or execution of these crimes.

71 See: Indictment, paras. 3 to 9, 14 and 17-19.

72 Statute, Article 20(3).

73 See also Rule 87(A):

32. [...] A finding of guilt may be reached only when a majority of the Trial Chamber is satisfied that guilt has been proved beyond reasonable doubt.

74 *Kayishema* Judgement, para. 117; *Musema* Judgement, para. 213; *Niyitegeka* Judgement, paras. 60-61.

75 *Kajelijeli* Judgement, para. 43.

76 *Niyitegeka* Judgement, paras. 60-61.

I.2. Chamber's Discretionary power in the Assessment of the Evidence

33. The Rules of Procedure and Evidence govern the proceedings. The Chamber is not bound by national rules of evidence and may, in cases not otherwise provided for in the Rules, apply rules of evidence which will best favour a fair determination of the matter before it and are consonant with the spirit of the Statute and the general principles of law.[77] A Chamber may also admit any relevant evidence which it deems to have probative value.[78]

34. Considering these principles, corroboration of evidence is not necessarily required: a Chamber may rely on a single witness' testimony as proof of a material fact.[79] A Chamber also has a broad discretion to admit hearsay evidence, even when it cannot be examined at its source and when it is not corroborated by direct evidence.[80]

35. The probative value to be attached to testimony is determined according to its credibility and reliability. When a witness is found to be credible, a Chamber must also determine whether his or her evidence is reliable. When applying these criteria, a Chamber must consider the evidence as a whole, including other witnesses' testimonies and the exhibits admitted.[81]

II. FACTUAL FINDINGS

36. In the present case, the Prosecution's evidence consisted mainly of hearsay evidence concerning both the content of the allegations and also the identification of André Rwamakuba. Five of the 18 Prosecution witnesses claimed to have direct knowledge of Rwamakuba.[82] Two witnesses also gave uncorroborated evidence to support specific allegations in the Indictment.[83] The Prosecution did not specify why this was the case and it must be presumed that this was the best evidence available. The Defence called witnesses who had both direct and indirect knowledge of Rwamakuba and many of them claimed to have been eyewitnesses to events alleged in the Indictment. **[page 15]**

37. The Chamber will assess the evidence in order to determine whether the Prosecution has proved beyond reasonable doubt that any of the criminal acts pleaded in the Indictment[84] were planned, instigated, ordered, committed or aided and abetted by the Accused, or with respect to the genocide that he was complicit in these acts, in Gikomero *commune* and at Butare University Hospital in April 1994. If established, the Chamber will determine whether these criminal acts were committed with the specific intent to destroy, in whole or in part, the Tutsi group, and whether these acts were committed as a part of a widespread or systematic attack against the Tutsi civilian population on political, ethnic, or racial grounds. Pursuant to the established jurisprudence, the criminal intent of an accused may be proved through inferences from the facts and circumstances of a case.[85] This approach does not relieve the Prosecution of its burden of proving each element of its case, including genocidal intent, beyond reasonable doubt.[86]

38. The case against the Accused revolves around two sets of events allegedly committed in Gikomero *commune* and at Butare University Hospital. They are reviewed in Sections II.1. and II.2. respectively.

---

77 Rules 89(A) and (B).

78 Rules 89(C).

79 See for e.g.: *Semanza* Appeal Judgement, para. 153; *Gacumbitsi* Appeal Judgement, para. 72.

80 See for e.g.: *Akayesu* Appeal Judgement, para. 286; *Kajelijeli* Judgement, para. 45; *Gacumbitsi* Appeal Judgement.

81 *Ntagerura* Appeal Judgement, paras. 172-174.

82 See: Prosecution Witnesses GLM and GIT claimed that they personally knew André Rwamakuba's family; Prosecution Witnesses GIN and ALA claimed that they were personally introduced to Rwamakuba; Prosecution Witness XV testified that he used to see Rwamakuba when the latter was a student.

83 See Prosecution Witness GAC with respect to the delivery of machetes at Kamanzi's house, and Prosecution Witness GIN regarding the killing of three people at the Gikomero *secteur* office.

84 According to the Indictment: killings, or causing serious bodily or mental harm to the Tutsi population, or deliberately inflicting conditions of life upon the Tutsi population that were calculated t bring about its physical destruction in whole or in part, as genocide, and murder or extermination as crimes against humanity.

85 *Gacumbitsi* Appeal Judgement, paras. 39-41; *Rutaganda* Appeal Judgement, para. 525; see also: *Akayesu* Judgement, paras. 523-524; *Bagilishema* Judgement, para. 63; *Gacumbitsi* Judgement, para. 252.

86 *Gacumbitsi* Appeal Judgement, para. 41.

39. For each allegation, the Chamber will bear in mind that the Indictment is the main accusatory instrument. As discussed in Chapter I, the Pre-Trial Brief and the Opening Statement may, in some circumstances, resolve any ambiguities in the Indictment, provided that the Accused was in a reasonable position to understand the charges against him and confront the Prosecution case.

40. The evidence will be assessed as a whole, although the different elements of the assessment of the evidence are divided into sub-sections in the interests of clarity. For each allegation, the Chamber discusses the identification of the Accused, and the credibility and reliability of the Prosecution and Defence witnesses, including the alibi evidence. The Chamber will use various criteria in its assessment of the evidence, such as internal discrepancies in the witness' testimony, inconsistencies with other witnesses' testimony, inconsistencies with the witness' prior statements, relationship between the witness and the Accused and other witnesses, the criminal record of the witness, the impact of trauma on a **[page 16]** witness' memory, discrepancies in translation, social and cultural factors, and the demeanour of the witness. References to admitted exhibits will also be made where appropriate.

41. Most Prosecution and Defence witnesses were granted protective measures in order to prevent public disclosure of their identities.[87] The Chamber seeks to set forth the basis of its reasoning as clearly as possible, whilst avoiding disclosure of any information that may reveal the identity of protected witnesses.

II.1. Alleged Criminal Acts Committed by André Rwamakuba in Gikomero *Commune*

42. The *commune* of Gikomero, presently named Gasabo District, lies approximately 25 kilometres north of Kigali town.[88] In 1994, it was within the *préfecture* of Kigali Rural and was divided into ten *secteurs*, including the Bumbogo, Gasabo, Gicaca, Gikomero, Gishaka, Kayanga, Nduba, Rutunga, Sha and Shango *secteurs*.[89] Each *secteur* was divided into *cellules*. Gikomero *commune* was surrounded by the *communes* of Giti, Gikoro, Rubungo, Rutongo and Mugambazi.[90] The Chamber and the parties went to Gikomero *commune* in January 2006 and viewed specific locations relevant to the case including the Trading Centre, the *secteur* Office, the Protestant School site, Kayanga School, Kayanga Health Centre and the Ndatemwa Trading Centre.[91]

43. The Indictment alleges that from 26 July 1993 until June 1994, André Rwamakuba travelled around various *secteurs* of the Gikomero *commune* organizing and participating in meetings which called upon the Hutu majority to exterminate the Tutsi, recruiting members for "MDR-Hutu Power" and supporting the "Hutu Power" **(II.1.1.)**. It further alleges that between 10 and 11 April 1994, after these sensitization campaigns, Rwamakuba delivered weapons that were to be used to kill the Tutsi to the homes of André Muhire, near Ndatemwa Trading Centre in Gasabo *secteur*, and Etienne Kamanzi, located in the Kayanga *secteur* **(II.1.2)**. He is also alleged to have instigated the killing of three unknown men, but identified **[page 17]** as Tutsi, at the Gikomero *secteur* office **(II.1.3.)**.[92] Finally, between 13 and 15 April 1994, Rwamakuba allegedly went to the Kayanga Health Centre where he signalled the beginning of the massacres against Tutsi refugees and witnessed their killing committed by soldiers and *Interahamwe* **(II.1.4.)**.

44. The Chamber will address each of these allegations in turn, and assess the related evidence. Neither the Indictment nor the Prosecution Pre-Trial Brief and Opening Statement are very explicit, but they seem to suggest, as does the evidence adduced, that for each event alleged, the Accused commuted between Kigali town and the various locations in Gikomero *commune*.[93]

---

87 *Karemera et al.*, Order on Protective Measures for Prosecution Witnesses (TC); *Rwamakuba*, Decision on Defence Motion for Protective Measures (TC), and Decision on Prosecution Motion For Variation, or in Alternative Reconsideration of the Decision on Protective Measures for Defence Witnesses (TC).

88 Distance between Kigali town and Gikomero *secteur* Office, Exh. P. 2. The Defence acknowledges that the routes to Gikomero *commune* are reasonably reviewed in that document (Defence Closing Brief, p. 22).

89 See: Testimony of Prosecution investigator Upendra Baghel, T. 13 June 2005, pp. 8-9; Defence Closing Brief, para. 23.

90 See Exh. P. 2.

91 Minutes for the Site Visit to Rwanda in the *Rwamakuba* case, 13-16 January 2005 (Annex A).

92 Exh. P. 2.

93 See also the Prosecution Pre-Trial Brief, Opening Statement and Prosecution Closing Brief.

45. The Prosecution and Defence witnesses agree that in April 1994, attacks and massacres were committed in Gikomero *commune* against the Tutsi population, and specifically at the Ndatemwa Trading Centre, Gikomero Protestant School, Gishaka Parish and the Kayanga Health Centre.[94] Prosecution and Defence witnesses also described an *Interahamwe* named Ephrem Nyirigera, the communal *brigadier* named Michel Nyarwaya and the communal accountant named Mathias Rubanguka as three of the main leaders of the attacks and massacres against Tutsi throughout Gikomero *commune* during the 1994 genocide.[95] The Defence denies that André Rwamakuba was involved in any of those attacks and massacres.

II.1.1. Alleged Public Instigation in Gikomero from July 1993 through June 1994

46. The Prosecution alleges at paragraphs 3 to 5 of the Indictment that

> 3. [...] After the establishment of MDR "Power" on 26 July 1993 or thereabouts, **André RWAMAKUBA,** practically every weekend, up to and including January 1994, and often accompanied by local authorities and officials of MDR "Power", traveled about his home *commune* in Gikomero, Kigali-rural *préfecture.* He organized meetings and participated in rallies in Kayanga, Gikomero, Rutunga, Gasabo and Gicaca *secteurs.* During the rallies, **André RWAMAKUBA** distributed songs of the Parmehutu party. The ***Accused's*** objective at the time was to recruit members for MDR "Power" party and to support "Hutu Power". The *Accused* called upon the Hutu majority to oppose the Arusha Peace Accords and to exterminate the Tutsi.
>
> 4. During those "sensitization" campaigns in Gikomero *commune*, particularly in January 1994, **André RWAMAKUBA** occasionally went about in a vehicle equipped with a public address system exhorting Hutu to unite in order to get rid of Tutsi. His announcements, the objective of which was to exhort Hutu to unite in order to get rid of Tutsi, included repeated statements that "the time has come for you, Hutu, to get rid of the enemy". **[page 18]**
>
> 5. During the period from January through June 1994, **André RWAMAKUBA** made statements at various meetings and public gatherings in Gikomero *commune*, or publicly associated himself with statements or acts by other persons at such gatherings. Thus, from January 1994 and during the entire period preceding the events of April 1994 in Sha, Nduba, Shango, Kayanga and Gikomero *secteurs,* and in the *communes* adjoining Gikomero, namely Rutungo, Rubungo and Kanombe, he publicly instigated participants to combat "the enemy", all the Tutsi being characterized as "the enemy", "accomplices of the enemy" or "accomplices of RPF". After these gatherings, during which the Accused called for the extermination of Tutsi, the participants became excited, aggressive and disposed to physically attack and destroy the Tutsi as a group. Such speeches by the **Accused** signaled the start of killings in the *commune.* Furthermore, after the killings began in early April 1994, **André RWAMAKUBA** often praised and congratulated militiamen publicly for and on having killed Tutsi, thereby instigating other militias and armed civilians to participate in further attacks and massacres against the Tutsi population.

(1) Evidence Adduced

47. Six Prosecution Witnesses testified that between 1992 and March 1994, André Rwamakuba came to Gikomero *commune* several times.[96] Some of them attested that during that period, he participated in MDR party meetings at Kayanga Primary School **(1.1)**, and in political rallies in four *secteurs* **(1.2.)**. It was also said that Rwamakuba was present at gatherings in bars, and used a vehicle equipped with a loudspeaker in order to call for the extermination of the Tutsi **(1.3.)** and to recruit members for the MDR extremist wing, "Hutu Power" **(1.4.)**.

48. The Prosecution contends that the sensitization campaigns allegedly conducted by the Accused between 23 July 1993 and April 1994 were principally aimed at laying the groundwork for the struggle against the Tutsi in which André Rwamakuba personally involved himself.[97] This Tribunal is only competent to prosecute individuals for crimes committed between 1 January and 31 December 1994.[98] Evidence of events prior to 1994 that can establish a "pattern, design or systematic course of conduct by the accused" or

---

94 These events are discussed below.

95 See Prosecution Witnesses GAB, GAC and GIN; Defence Witnesses 3/1, 4/16, 6/10, 7/18 and 9/20.

96 See Prosecution Witnesses ALA, GAB, GAC, GIQ, GIT and GLM.

97 Prosecution Closing Brief, para. 49.

98 Statute, Article 1.

provide a context or background to crimes falling within the temporal jurisdiction of the Tribunal is however admissible.[99] Moreover, in the light of the discussion under Chapter I regarding the charges against the Accused, the Chamber will consider the evidence on the alleged public instigation in Gikomero *commune* discussed hereinafter as circumstantial evidence that could be relevant concerning the alleged crimes committed by the Accused in the Gikomero *commune* in April 1994. **[page 19]**

(1.1.) MDR Party Meetings at Kayanga Primary School

49. Prosecution Witnesses GIQ, GAC and GAB did not personally know André Rwamakuba, but testified that they saw him at an MDR party meeting or several such party meetings held at Kayanga Primary School. None of them could recollect the exact date of the meeting or meetings. Witness GIQ placed a meeting at the school in 1992 "before the split of the MDR party", GAC could not specify the year of the event,[100] and GAB testified that a meeting took place in 1993 at Kayanga Primary School.

50. Prosecution Witness GIQ testified that in 1992, he saw André Rwamakuba with MDR leaders Anastase Gasana, Faustin Twagiramungu and Aloys Munyangazu recruiting members for their party in the courtyard of Kayanga Primary School. The witness recognized Anastase Gasana and Aloys Munyangazu because he knew them prior to that event.[101] He also recognized Twagiramungu because he used to hear him on the radio and was able to recognize his voice.[102] Along with the other party dignitaries, Rwamakuba was introduced to the crowd by Gasana,[103] as a native of Gikomero. They were told that those dignitaries were united and that they all belonged to the MDR party. Rwamakuba did not make any public statement on that day.

51. Prosecution Witness GAC also testified about an MDR rally organized by Faustin Twagiramungu at an unspecified date in the courtyard of Kayanga Primary School, which MRND party members also attended out of curiosity.[104] According to the witness, Twagiramungu, the then Prime Minister Agathe Uwilingiyimana, Jean De Dieu Kamuhanda and André Rwamakuba were introduced at the rally by the person conducting the ceremony. The witness heard approximately five people giving speeches, including Twagiramungu, who made a long speech about the MDR in his capacity as chairman of the party.[105] He also heard Rwamakuba addressing the population using language which, in the witness' view, amounted to calling on the audience to attack and kill Tutsi.[106] GAC also attested that the objective of the Kayanga Primary School rally was to call on the people to accept the coalition between **[page 20]** the MDR-Power, the MDR-PARMEHUTU and the MRND-Power. He further testified that "Twagiramungu taught the Hutu to kill the Tutsi", and that the participants, including Twagiramungu, implemented the killing of Tutsis.[107]

52. Prosecution Witness GAB also testified to an MDR Power party meeting held in the courtyard of Kayanga Primary School in 1993, where he saw André Rwamakuba and other authorities attending that meeting.[108] The witness asserted that Twagiramungu and Gasana were not present.[109] According to GAB, the main objective of the rally was to sensitize members of the MDR, Hutus in general, to the fact that their enemy was the Tutsi "who had attacked Rwanda".[110] The witness heard the MDR Power representative say

---

99 *Simba*, Decision on Interlocutory Appeal Regarding Temporal Jurisdiction (AC); *Nahimana* Judgement, para. 101.

100 T. 4 July 2005, p. 50; T. 5 July 2006, p. 43. Although the English transcript mentions the year "1992", the witness was testifying to a 1993 meeting (see: French version of the transcript at p. 43).

101 T. 15 June 2005, p. 53.

102 T. 15 June 2005, p. 53.

103 T. 15 June 2005, p. 55.

104 T. 4 July 2005, p. 46.

105 T. 4 July 2005, p. 46.

106 According to the witness, André Rwamakuba said: "According to you, who are those who are many more than the others: is it people who have tinned roofs or those who have thatched roof?" Rwamakuba added: "if you were asked to burn down the house of people, which houses are with thatched roofs would it take much time?" GAC explained that he understood it as "If I were to order today that Tutsis be killed from now, would you think – did you think that there would be survivors?" (T. 4 July 2005, pp. 6 and 45).

107 T. 4 July 2005, p. 44.

108 T. 5 July 2005, p. 19.

109 T. 5 July 2005, p. 45.

110 T. 5 July 2005, p. 19.

that the enemy of the MDR and of the Hutu in general was "the Tutsi who collaborate with the *Inkotanyi*." As soon as the witness heard this statement, he left the meeting. He did not know whether Rwamakuba took the floor to make a speech on that day.[111] The witness testified that after this meeting, there was a conflict between the Hutu and the Tutsi in Kayanga.[112]

(1.2.) Political Rallies in Sha, Nduba, Shango and Kayanga secteurs

53. Prosecution Witnesses GLM and GIT claimed to know André Rwamakuba personally,[113] and testified to various rallies that took place between 1993 and March 1994 in Sha, Nduba, Shango and Kayanga *secteurs* where Rwamakuba was said to have been present. None of them attended any of those rallies, but rather learned of them from other persons present.[114] These witnesses further testified that prior to each rally they heard or saw a vehicle equipped with a loudspeaker which was used to invite the population to attend the rallies.

54. Around October 1993, on a Sunday "about two months after the Hutu Power wing of the MDR had been created", Witness GLM saw André Rwamakuba pass where the witness lived on his way to and from Nduba *secteur*. He saw him in a car equipped with a megaphone calling out to people to attend a rally.[115] The witness was not present at the rally in Nduba, but **[page 21]** a man[116] later told him that Rwamakuba had been there.[117] According to that man, Rwamakuba spoke to the public at the rally and explained the political situation in the country, and specifically that "the Hutu needed to unite their forces so that they can exterminate the Tutsi." He is also alleged to have said that "all the evils that the country was faced with were due to the Tutsi; the Tutsi were at the origin of all these evils, so they needed to be exterminated so that the country could be governed properly after having gotten rid of that problem."[118]

55. The witness testified that a similar event occurred at the end of November 1993, also on a Sunday.[119] Witness GLM was standing close to his house and saw a passing vehicle equipped with loudspeakers calling on the people to attend an MDR Power meeting to learn about the ideals and program of the party.[120] He saw André Rwamakuba driving the vehicle while the person next to him was speaking into the loudspeaker. On the following day, a man[121] who had attended the meeting met the witness at his workplace[122] and told him that Rwamakuba had publicly addressed a meeting held in Shango *secteur*. According to this informant, the meeting was related to the extermination of the Tutsi. It was allegedly said that since the Tutsis were behaving like traitors to the country, they had to be exterminated. Party members were told that the MDR Power was the party which contained the word «power,» representing the force or the strength of Hutu to be counted on to exterminate the Tutsi. Witness GLM asserted that it was Rwamakuba who addressed the population about the MDR Power and the party's program.[123]

56. In January 1994, GLM again heard a vehicle equipped with a loudspeaker pass on the hill opposite his house. The message from the loudspeaker called upon the people to attend a rally at Kayanga *secteur*. Slogans of MDR Power were diffused asking the Hutu to unite. GLM was not able to see the person driving the

---

111 T. 5 July 2005, p. 20.

112 T. 5 July 2005, p. 20.

113 GLM and GIT are brothers. They both stated that their family and Rwamakuba's family were well acquainted since they were neighbours. GIT knew Rwamakuba when he was a secondary school pupil. He would have visited Rwamakuba's parents several times and met the Accused on these occasions. GLM was also used to see André Rwamakuba on visits to Gikomero. In particular, he met him at a parents' meeting of the free secondary school in Nduba, the *École Technique Libre* (ETL), which had been created by Rwamakuba and in which GLM had registered one of his elder brother's children. (See: T. 21 June 2005, pp. 65-66; T. 16 June 2005, p. 4).

114 T. 16 June 2005, p. 10.

115 T. 16 June 2005, p. 11.

116 The name of the man was provided by Witness GLM, Exh. P. 32 (under seal).

117 T. 16 June 2005, p. 11. The name of the man has been written down by Witness GLM, Exh. P. 32 (under seal).

118 T. 16 June 2005, p. 12.

119 T. 16 June 2005, p. 13.

120 T. 16 June 2005, pp. 12-13

121 The name of the man was provided by Witness GLM, Exh. P. 32 (under seal).

122 T. 16 June 2005, p. 13 and Exh. P. 32 (under seal).

123 T. 16 June 2005, p. 14.

vehicle, because it passed too far away from him.[124] The witness did not attend the Kayanga rally, but again, a man[125] who had attended told him that André Rwamakuba and other people who had come from Kigali were introduced **[page 22]** to the audience. During the rally, the ideals of the MDR Power – the extermination of the Tutsi in particular – were "taught". It was said that the Hutu should not scatter into several parties but should instead unite into one party in order to exterminate the Tutsi.[126]

57. Prosecution Witness GIT was told about rallies or meetings organized in the centre of Sha *secteur*, in the square near the Kayanga School of Kayanga *secteur* and on the football field of Nduba *secteur* between August 1993 and March 1994. He did not attend these meetings but he did see André Rwamakuba going to the rallies on five separate occasions, driving a red pick-up truck, the last occasion being in March 1994.[127] Witness GIT would see Rwamakuba passing because he lived at a distance of 15 meters from the road coming from Kigali and going in the direction of the rallies.[128] He saw other people in the vehicle with Rwamakuba but did not know their names. According to the witness, they were singing in praise of their party and wearing caps and small flags bearing the MDR Power emblem.[129] Two people informed the witness about the content of the meetings and Rwamakuba's participation at the various rallies.[130] The latter had allegedly taken the floor and said that the time had come to eliminate the enemy Tutsi who were causing problems throughout the country.[131]

(1.3.) Calls for the Extermination of the Tutsi

58. Prosecution Witnesses GLM and ALA testified that they once heard André Rwamakuba personally call for the extermination of the Tutsi. Witness ALA saw him during the third week of January 1994 in his cellule on a Sunday, around one o'clock in the afternoon.[132] The witness was in his house, which is near the commercial centre. He heard a voice coming from a megaphone and went to see what was happening. He saw a khaki coloured Peugeot model 505 equipped with a megaphone, which was idling near the commercial centre with three people on board.[133] As ALA was approaching the vehicle, he was called by one of its passengers, Anastase Gasana who knew the witness, and asked to **[page 23]** repair the vehicle.[134] Gasana then introduced the witness to the other two people in the vehicle, Aloys Munyangazu and André Rwamakuba.[135] As the witness was attempting to repair the car, Rwamakuba took the megaphone and called out to the people saying several times that "it was time for the Hutus to get rid of the enemy". The witness asserted that a reasonable person would have understood that Rwamakuba was referring to the Tutsi when speaking about the enemy.[136] Witness GLM testified that in February 1994,[137] he saw Rwamakuba in Froduard Birasa's bar in Nduba Centre[138] and heard him say that the Tutsis were a big problem and it was time to get rid them.[139] Rwamakuba is alleged not to have gone into greater depth on the matter because of GLM's presence. The witness stated that this was the only time he heard Rwamakuba speak such words.[140] In GLM's view, the people present at the bar planned to exterminate the Tutsi and later implemented this extermination plan.[141]

---

124 T. 16 June 2005, pp. 14-15.
125 T. 16 June 2005, p. 15. The name of the man was provided by Witness GLM, Exh. P. 32 (under seal).
126 T. 16 June 2005, p. 17.
127 T. 22 June 2005, p. 5.
128 T. 21 June 2005, p. 69.
129 T. 21 June 2005, p. 71. According to the witness, the caps and flags were red and black – the colour of their party. Some others wore the *Interahamwe* uniform of the MRND.
130 T. 21 June 2005, p. 73.
131 T. 22 June 2005, p. 2.
132 T. 14 June 2005, pp. 47 and 75.
133 T. 14 June 2005, p. 46.
134 The witness explained that he knew Anastase GASANA from when he was still a Professor at Nyakinama University. The witness was a friend of GASANA's borther and therefore used to visit them (T. 14 June 2005, p. 46).
135 T. 14 June 2005, p. 46.
136 T. 14 June 2005, p. 75.
137 T. 16 June 2005, p. 31.
138 T. 16 June 2005, p. 17.
139 T. 16 June 2005, pp. 9-10 and 30-31.
140 T. 20 June 2005, p. 55.
141 T. 16 June 2005, p. 19.

(1.4.) Recruitment of Members for the MDR "Hutu Power"

59. Prosecution Witnesses GIQ and ALA testified that they saw or heard André Rwamakuba recruiting members for the MDR party. In January 1994, Witness GIQ saw him in Emmanuel Rubagumya's bar. Rwamakuba had bought people drinks and was telling them that they should join the MDR party, recruit other members and that they should kill anyone who refused to join the party.[142] GIQ also testified that he saw Rwamakuba in 1992 or in 1993 in a white vehicle which was equipped with loudspeakers playing songs glorifying the MDR-Power Hutu.[143] The songs were asking the Hutu to unite, and claiming that due to this unity, they would overcome. Rwamakuba was accompanied by the then Minister of Information, Pascal Ndengejeho. The vehicle was going slowly, ensuring that people could hear what was being said including GIQ who was standing close to where the vehicle passed.[144] Witness ALA testified that he saw Rwamakuba in the third week of October 1993, on or about 22 **[page 24]** October 1993, in a vehicle passing by in Kayanga.[145] He was speaking to Mathias Rubanguka and Gérard Gakuba from his car.[146] Later, Rubanguka informed the witness that Rwamakuba was recruiting members for the "MDR power", and was looking for people whom he could trust to assist him with additional recruitment.

(2) Assessment of the Evidence

60. In the Chamber's view, the Prosecution witnesses' testimonies on the alleged sensitization campaigns led by the Accused in Gikomero are not consistent with certain allegations in the Indictment **(2.1.)**. Furthermore, the Prosecution evidence is tainted by internal contradictions **(2.2.)** and directly contradicted by the defence alibi evidence **(2.3.)**.

(2.1.) Lack of Consistency between the Indictment and the Prosecution Evidence

61. Testimony was given on eleven instances between 1992 and March 1994 during which André Rwamakuba allegedly came to Gikomero *commune*. It has not been shown that towards the end of 1993 and in early January 1994, the Accused went to Gikomero *commune* "practically every week-end", as alleged in paragraph 3 of the Indictment. None of the witnesses testified about meetings held in Gikomero, Rutunga, Gasabo and Gicaca *secteurs*, or in the adjoining *communes* of Rutungo, Rubungo and Kanombe, although one Prosecution witness testified that he saw Rwamakuba passing by in a vehicle in Rutunga and Gasabo *secteurs* at the beginning of 1994.[147] The Prosecution, therefore, failed to prove that during meetings in these *secteurs* and *communes*, the Accused instigated participants to "combat" and exterminate the Tutsi, as alleged in paragraph 5 of the Indictment.

(2.2.) Reliability Issues

62. The identification of the Accused raises a number of concerns. Witnesses GIT and GLM, who are brothers, are the sole witnesses claiming to know André Rwamakuba personally. They said they were neighbours of Rwamakuba's parents, and have known him for a long time. Neither of them, however, could give a satisfactory description of **[page 25]** Rwamakuba nor much detail concerning how they came to know

142 T. 15 June 2005, pp. 30-32. According to the witness, the following persons were also in the bar: Callixte Kabarira, Sebahinzi, Joseph Ayirwanda and his son Frédéric Turatsinze. Emmanuel Rubagumya, Callixte Kabarira, and Sebahinzi are in prison in Remera. Ayirwanda and Frederic Turatsinze are both dead.

143 T. 15 June 2005, pp. 30-31.

144 T. 15 June 2005, pp. 31 and 59.

145 T. 14 June 2005, pp. 48 and 70.

146 T. 14 June 2005, p. 71.

147 Witness GIQ did not hear or see André Rwamakuba say anything and did not see him do anything (T. 15 June 2005, p. 32).

him.[148] It is interesting to note that Witness GIT claimed not to know whether his brother was testifying in this case, although they live near one another and both testified in this case within a short space of time.[149]

63. Both GAB and GAC testified that they saw André Rwamakuba for the first time at the stone-laying ceremony of a primary school in Rutunga, in the company of the then Minister of Primary and Secondary School, Faustin Munyanzesa.[150] GAB could not specify the exact date of this ceremony, except that it was before 1994, but GAC placed the event in 1992. Neither witness had any prior knowledge of Rwamakuba. The latter was pointed out to GAC by a young man who used to live in Rutunga.[151] He was also told that Rwamakuba was working in the Ministry of Health. GAB stated that the Accused was introduced to the assembly as "the doctor André Rwamakuba, a native of Gikomero *commune.*"[152] It is noteworthy that GAB was only fifteen years old at that time and was not able to provide any details about the event. In contrast to Witness GAB's testimony, GAC did not specify that Rwamakuba was introduced during the alleged rally held in 1993 at Kayanga Primary School.

64. The lack of consistency between the Indictment and the testimonies adduced on this aspect of the case was compounded by witnesses who gave different and irreconcilable versions of the facts. Witnesses GAC, GAB, GIQ, GLM and GIT testified about various rallies held in Gikomero *commune*. The Prosecution seemed to present these as separate rallies held on different occasions.[153] It is however uncertain as to whether the witnesses testified to the same rallies or to different ones. Different dates were given for a meeting at Kayanga Primary School, which the same authorities were alleged to have attended and at which similar speeches were given. In his testimony, Witness GAC could not specify the year of the Kayanga School meeting, but in a previous signed statement, had attested that it took **[page 26]** place at the end of 1993.[154] Witness GAB testified to the presence of Rwamakuba at a Kayanga meeting in 1993, and although Witness GIQ acknowledged the existence of a meeting in 1993 in Kayanga he specified that Rwamakuba was not in attendance.[155]

65. The Chamber recalls that the evidence of GIT and GLM is indirect and mostly hearsay in many respects. The source of Witness GIT's information casts doubt upon the reliability of his testimony. According to this witness, his informer was respectable and honest, but Witness GLM asserted that a man with the same name as GIT's informer was partial, biased and disrespectful towards others.[156]

66. Some major aspects of GLM's testimony are also vague and inconsistent. When the Prosecution asked who GLM thought had called for the extermination of Tutsi, the witness replied that the person usually there to speak about MDR Power was André Rwamakuba.[157] He also recalled the Nduba *secteur* rally as having been held on a Sunday, whereas later, he stated that he *was told* that it was on a Sunday.[158] Similarly, he first said that he saw André Rwamakuba holding the megaphone and calling on people to come and attend the Nduba rally,[159] but during cross-examination, stated instead that Rwamakuba was driving the car and that

---

148 Prosecution Witness GIT described André Rwamakuba as follows: "Someone who was of average size. Now, as for his complexion, his skin was between light complexion and dark complexion, the light complexion being the more dominant. He was not a fat man, nor was he thin; between the two. [...] He was someone who was solid in build, and he was neither too big nor too thin." (T. 23 June 2005, p. 53).

62. Prosecution Witness GLM described Rwamakuba as follows: "a man of average size, his complexion was neither dark nor light, medium. He seemed to have a tendency to have chubby cheeks and very little hair." "He was a well built man and I would say that he wasn't thin." "His voice was deep and somewhat rough." (T. 20 June 2005, p. 4).

149 T. 22 June 2005, p. 20; T. 24 June 2005, pp. 12 and16.

150 T. 4 July 2005, p. 35.

151 T. 4 July 2005, p. 37.

152 T. 5 July 2005, p. 43.

153 Prosecution Closing Arguments, paras. 33-48.

154 Exh. D. 34 A and B (under seal). In the same statement, he declared that the meeting took place at the Kayanga *secteur* office and that he could no longer remember what André Rwamakuba said on that occasion. On the contrary, the witness testified in court that the meeting took place in the courtyard of the Kayanga School. He further stated the alleged speech made by Rwamakuba on that occasion.

155 T. 15 June 2005, p. 58.

156 T. 20 June 2005, p. 2 and Exh. P. 32.

157 T. 16 June 2005, p. 14.

158 T. 20 June 2005, p. 57.

159 T. 16 June 2005, p. 11.

the person sitting beside him was speaking through the megaphone.[160] The witness placed the event at Birasa's bar in February 1994,[161] then at the end of the year in 1993, only to later reaffirm that it was in February 1994.[162] This important event at Birasa's bar, where Witness GLM allegedly heard Rwamakuba calling for the extermination of Tutsi, was mentioned for the first time in court. Also mentioned for the first time in court was Rwamakuba's alleged discussion about the split in MDR-Hutu Power. GLM claimed that he had already mentioned these details to the Prosecution, but that the first investigators recorded only a summary and the subsequent team of investigators made many mistakes in the document and did not return to him to enable the necessary corrections to be made.[163] The Chamber however notes that on 11 February 1998, GLM signed a statement describing Rwamakuba's political and anti-Tusti **[page 27]** activities which mentioned Birasa as one of the extremists with whom Rwamakuba used to work.[164]

67. The testimony of these witnesses is also contradicted by other Prosecution witnesses' testimonies. Witness ALA described an incident where André Rwamakuba travelled with Anastase Gasana and called for the extermination of the Tutsi in Gasana's presence. GAC alleged that at the Kayanga Primary School meeting, Faustin Twagiramungu "taught to kill the Tutsi". Witnesses GIT, GIQ and Prosecution Expert Witness Alison Des Forges, however, testified that Anastase Gasana and Faustin Twagiramungu were all moderate MDR politicians.[165] Witness GIQ stated that he would have been surprised to see Rwamakuba and Gasana together.[166] GAC's placing of Jean de Dieu Kamuhanda at the MDR meeting in Kayanga was also contradicted by evidence that Kamuhanda was an MRND politician.[167]

68. GLM's testimony concerning a meeting in Nduba *secteur* around October 1993, "about two months after" the creation of the MDR-Power wing[168] is also inconsistent with the Prosecution expert witness' evidence. She described the process of division within the MDR as starting from February 1993 (when the Rwandan Patriotic Front ("RPF") violated the ceasefire and launched a massive military advance across the northern part of Rwanda causing the displacement of hundreds of thousands of people) until 23 July 1993 when Twagiramungu was expelled from the MDR party because he wished, *inter alia*, to maintain the party's collaboration with the RPF.[169] Twagiramungu's expulsion was confirmed by Defence Witness Jean-Marie Nkezebera, a former member of the MDR's political bureau and vice-president of the party in the Kigali area. Therefore, GLM's assertion that Twagiramungu attended an MDR-Power meeting around October 1993 appears inherently unlikely. In addition, the expert witness stated that, after the October 1993 assassination of the Burundian President – the first freely and fairly elected Hutu President – by Tutsi soldiers, Froduald Karamira introduced the concept of Hutu Power at a massive political rally at the Amohoro stadium in Kigali.[170] Although the expert witness was told that there was a meeting in Gitarama in September 1993 where the term "Hutu power" was used, she agreed that the term originated at the rally in October 1993. This testimony conflicts with GAC's testimony, who instead **[page 28]** testified to the use of the term or slogan "power" at rallies in 1992 and in the earlier parts of 1993.

69. These inconsistencies cannot be justified by the time elapsed, translation discrepancies, or the manner in which the statements were taken. They become still more significant when viewed against the alibi evidence adduced by the Defence.

---

160 T. 20 June 2005, p. 57.
161 T. 16 June 2005, p. 31.
162 T. 16 June 2005, pp. 17, 22, 30 and 31; T. 20 June 2005, pp. 53-55; T. 21 June 2005, p. 2.
163 T. 20 June 2005, pp. 55-56; T. 21 June 2005, pp. 2-3.
164 Exh. D. 19 A and B (under seal).
165 GIT testified that when the MDR party came into conflict, Gasana joined the moderate wing (T. 21 June 2005, p. 67); T. 15 June 2005, pp. 54-55.
166 T. 15 June 2005, p. 56.
167 See Defence Witness 1/5, T. 13 December 2005, p. 28. This was not disputed by the Prosecution.
168 T. 16 June 2005, p. 11.
169 T. 14 July 2005, pp. 15-16.
170 T. 14 July 2005, p. 17.

(2.3.) Alibi

70. The Defence alleges that André Rwamakuba could not have participated in the alleged public instigations in Gikomero between September 1993 and March 1994 because he was not in Rwanda for most of that time.[171] Evidence was adduced that between 23 September 1993 and 10 March 1994, the Accused was studying at the Prince Leopold Institute in Antwerp, Belgium, and that between 17 and 29 March 1994, he attended a World Health Organization (WHO) Conference in Aswan, Egypt. The Defence put the Prosecution on notice of the Belgian alibi at a preliminary hearing held in 2000.[172] In addition, the Defence served notice of the alibi to the Prosecution at the outset of trial and disclosed the names and addresses of witnesses and other evidence which it intended to rely upon in the presentation of this defence.[173]

71. To support the alibi, the Defence called six witnesses who mostly relied on their own diaries or personal documents to recollect the exact dates when they met André Rwamakuba during the time in question.[174] The Prosecution did not dispute and the Chamber accepts that the Accused was trained as a medical doctor, studying medicine in Belgium between 1970 and 1974 and then at Butare University between 1975 and 1978,[175] and had a career as a public health specialist, being appointed Director of the Kigali Health Region in 1992.[176]

72. Defence Witnesses Henri Van Balen and Pierre Mercenier are co-founders of the Prince Leopold Institute (Institute of Tropical Medicine) in Antwerp, Belgium.[177] Both of them have had long medical careers working with both Belgian authorities and international **[page 29]** organizations such as the World Health Organization.[178] In 1993-1994, they were both professors of public health at the Antwerp Institute of Tropical Medicine. Relying on various documents,[179] both testified that André Rwamakuba participated in a training course at the Institute in Belgium between 27 September 1993 and March 1994. According to Professor Mercenier's attestation, the training course ended on 9 March 1994.[180] The report drafted by Rwamakuba and the attestation signed by Professor Van Balen, however, mentioned the end date of the course as 27 March 1994.[181] The explanation given for the discrepancy in this date was that since the training report submitted by Rwamakuba was made to the Belgian Technical Cooperation for scholarship purposes and had to cover a six months period, it did not correspond with the exact end date of the course.[182] Professor Van Balen explained further that in May 1995, Rwamakuba, who was in Namibia at the time, wrote him a letter requesting certification of his training in Antwerp. In his letter, Rwamakuba explained that he was looking for work in Namibia and had had to leave Rwanda where he abandoned all of his documents. Since Professor Mercenier was already retired when Henri Van Balen received the letter, the latter drafted the certificate on the basis of Rwamakuba's training report. The witness stated that as he had personal knowledge that Rwamakuba had completed the six-month scholarship, he therefore did not pay attention to the exact dates.

171 Defence Closing Brief, p. 230 and seq.

172 *Prosecutor v. André Rwamakuba*, Case No. ICTR-98-44-I, T. 7 November 2000.

173 See Confidential Alibi Notice, filed on 8 June 2005, Corrigendum to Confidential Alibi Notice, filed on 14 June 2005 and Further Alibi Details, filed on 21 June 2005.

174 Defence Witness Edith Van Wynsberghe, Pierre Mercenier, Henri Van Balen, François Monet, 1/1 and 3/A. Due to the particularly close relationship between the Accused and Witness 3/A and the age of the witness at the time of the event, the Chamber is of the view that it will be more appropriate to set aside this evidence.

175 Curriculum vitae of André Rwamakuba (Exh. D. 184) and Prosecution Closing Brief at para. 6, footnote 3: "The Prosecutor does not dispute the periods and the studies undertaken by the Accused."

176 Exh. D. 184; Prosecution Closing Brief, para. 6 and Defence Closing Brief, pp. 2-5.

177 T. 14 December 2005, p. 2.

178 *Ibidem*,

179 Both witnesses relied upon their own diaries. Professor Van Balen produced the following documents: Training report drafted by André Rwamakuba, attestation signed by Professor Van Balen in May 1995, letter drafted by the Secretary of the Institute dated 28 January 1993, attestation by Professor Mercenier, letter drafted by the Secretary of the Institute dated 25 February 1994 (Exh. D. 186).

180 Exh. D. 186(B).

181 Exh. D. 186 (A and D); T. 6 December 2005, pp. 34-35 and 42-43.

182 T. 6 December 2005, p. 43; T. 14 December 2005, pp. 8, 15 and 17.

73. Professors Van Balen and Pierre Mercenier could not categorically attest to André Rwamakuba's presence every day in Belgium during the period of his training,[183] but they specified that it was a full-time course and that he would have had to stay in Belgium for its duration. Professor Mercenier testified that initially he would have seen Rwamakuba about once per week and later on, about once a fortnight. Both Professors also saw him from time to time in passing in the corridors of the Institute.[184] They further testified to specific dates when meetings had been arranged with him, as recorded in their diaries. Henri Van Balen noted that his diary mentions a meeting with Rwamakuba on 13 October 1993 to discuss a colloquium,[185] and Pierre Mercenier stated that he met Rwamakuba on 21 February 1994 in **[page 30]** Belgium to discuss the end of the training and his prospective mission to Rwanda in April 1994.[186]

74. Doctor Francis Monet is a doctor specialized in tropical medicine who was working for the Belgian Technical Cooperation in Rwanda from 1990 to 1994.[187] He came to know André Rwamakuba when the latter was appointed as the Director of the Kigali Health Region in 1992. They used to meet on a daily basis when they were both in Rwanda.[188] Doctor Monet confirmed that he was present at the airport when Rwamakuba left Rwanda on 23 September 1993, between 6.30 and 7 a.m., for Belgium. The witness relied on his diary,[189] but could also recall that event because, on that occasion, he had been somewhat upset that Rwamakuba had arrived very late to the airport for his flight. He also testified that he was at the airport for Rwamakuba's return to Rwanda on the morning of 10 March 1994. According to the witness, Rwamakuba did not return to Rwanda between 23 September 1993 and 10 March 1994. While the witness did not recall receiving any news from the Accused during that period, he submitted that it was practically impossible for Rwamakuba to return to Rwanda without him knowing about it. Even if Rwamakuba had not contacted him directly, he was still certain that others would have told him of his return.[190]

75. Defence witness Edith Van Wynsberghe met Andre Rwamakuba during his medical studies in Belgium in 1973. She stated that she saw him approximately ten times while he was attending the training course at the Tropical Institute of Antwerp in Belgium, between September 1993 and March 1994. Relying on various receipts,[191] the witness was able to recollect specific dates when she met Rwamakuba during that period. She saw him sometime between the end of November 1993 and the beginning of December 1993, when she went to Antwerp to order a sewing machine.[192] She later visited him for his birthday on 27 December 1993, at his house in Antwerp.[193] She could not confirm where Rwamakuba was between about 1 December 1993 and 27 December 1993.[194] Around 6 January 1994, the witness and **[page 31]** her daughter accompanied Rwamakuba to look for a used car in another town in Belgium.[195] On 2 March 1994, she took Rwamakuba to a pharmacy in Antwerp to buy medical supplies.[196] She also accompanied the Accused to the airport on 9 March 1994 when he left Belgium for Rwanda.[197]

76. Defence Witness 1/1, who is a close relative of André Rwamakuba, testified that he left Rwanda to pursue a program of study in Belgium between late September 1993 and March 1994.[198] Witness 1/1

183 T. 6 December 2005, pp. 35, 42 and 44; T. 14 December 2005, p.15.

184 T. 14 December 2005, pp. 4 -12 (Witness Van Balen) and T. 6 December 2005, p. 43 (Witness Mercenier).

185 T. 14 December 2005, p. 4.

186 T. 6 December 2005, pp. 36 and 45.

187 T. 14 December 2005, p. 23.

188 Witness Monet came to know André Rwamakuba in particular as a result of the latter's appointment in 1992 as Director of the Kigali Health Region. The witness stated that he met Rwamakuba on a daily basis (T. 14 December 2005, p. 24).

189 Exh. D. 187. Only one page of his diary was entered into evidence, the entire diary was offered for inspection by the Chamber.

190 T. 14 December 2005, pp. 26-27, 38-39, 48-49.

191 Exh. D. 182.

192 The receipt is dated 8 December 1993; the witness came to Antwerp a week or so before the delivery date.

193 T. 1 December 2005, p. 57.

194 T. 2 December 2005, p.3.

195 T. 1 December 2005, p. 57.

196 T. 1 December 2005, pp.57-58; Exh. D. 182.

197 The witness recollected this meeting by producing the customs documents concerning the medical supplies bought which were stamped and dated by the Belgian customs authorities; T. 1 December 2005, pp.60-61 and Exh. D. 182.

198 Witness 1/1 placed the return day of André Rwamakuba in Rwanda on 14 March 1994. Confronted with Rwamakuba's passport, the witness conceded that the date was given according to the witness' recollection; T. 14 December 2005, p. 58; T. 15 December, pp. 25, 32-35.

confirmed that Rwamakuba never came back to Rwanda during that period. The witness further provided some correspondence received by Rwamakuba at an address in Belgium where Edith Vanwynsberghe testified having visited him for his birthday and Rwamakuba's diary from 1993 diary with references to his stay in Belgium.[199]

77. The Defence also adduced evidence concerning André Rwamakuba's presence in Egypt between 17 and 29 March 1994. Edith Van Wynsberghe saw Rwamakuba again on 18 March 1994, while he was in transit at the airport in Brussels.[200] Doctor Francis Monet testified that he met him in Kigali on the evening of his return from Egypt at the Regional Health Centre offices on 29 March 1994.[201] Professor Henri Van Balen testified that Rwamakuba was to attend an international conference organized by the WHO in Egypt upon completion of the course in Belgium. The secretary of the Institute told Professor Van Balen that she had made reservations for Rwamakuba to attend this conference, but that these were not final tickets. Finally, Witness 1/1 also testified that André Rwamakuba left Rwanda on 17 March 1994 and returned on 29 March 1994 from a seminar in Egypt.

78. Defence Witness Monet testified that between André Rwamakuba's return from Belgium and departure to Egypt, he saw him every day at the Regional Health Centre since they were working together. On 11 March 1994, they went together with a delegation of Belgian members of Parliament to Rutungo Hospital.[202] Witness 1/1 testified that during the **[page 32]** same period, Rwamakuba visited his parents once in Gikomero to console them over the death of a relative who died in February.[203]

79. The Defence tendered into evidence the Rwandan passport of André Rwamakuba, which was in the custody of the UNDF and provided to the parties for inspection.[204] This passport was issued in Kigali in August 1993, with a visa for studies (as intern) issued by the Belgian Embassy on 2 September 1993, an entry stamp dated 23 September 1993 for Belgium and an exit stamp dated 9 March 1994 from Belgium, a single-entry visa for Egypt issued on 17 March 1994, entry and exit stamps for Egypt, a transit stamp for Kenya dated 28 March 1994, and an exit stamp from Kenya dated 29 March 1994.[205]

80. The Chamber finds these Defence witnesses individually credible and reliable. Henri Van Balen, Pierre Mercenier and François Monet were professors and colleagues of André Rwamakuba and nothing has emerged to indicate that they would have any particular interest in protecting him by providing false testimony. Their evidence is supported by various documents admitted into exhibit. Edith Van Wynsberghe, although closer to the Accused, also gave a fair and probable account of the facts, which was based on her analysis of the specific documents she had in her possession and which were tendered into exhibit. None of these documents admitted into evidence were rebutted by the Prosecution. The Chamber took particular care with the evidence of Defence Witness 1/1, as a close relative of the Accused; it is nonetheless satisfied that she was also reliable.

81. The Chamber accepts the explanation given by Professors Van Balen and Mercenier concerning the inconsistency between the dates of André Rwamakuba's attendance at the training program in Belgium on the certificates and in the report. It is noteworthy that the Accused requested Van Balen's confirmation of his attendance at the training program before his arrest by the Namibian authorities in 1995.[206]

82. The Chamber also notes that the Prosecution failed to rebut the alibi evidence. It acknowledged that the Accused was in Belgium between September 1993 and March 1994, but submitted that he must have come back to Rwanda at the times the witnesses testified to having seen him. The Prosecution was aware of the defence alibi a long time before the beginning of the trial and was therefore in a position to conduct a

199 Exh. D. 190 and D. 193.

200 T. 1 December 2005, pp.60-61. The witness assisted André Rwamakuba in buying a mobile phone and a fax. She relied on a receipt dated 18 March 1994 (Exh. D. 182).

201 T. 14 December 2005, pp. 28-29. The witness referred to his diary which also had an entry on 17 March 1994 stating the day André Rwamakuba left for Egypt.

202 T. 14 December 2005, p. 27

203 T. 15 December 2005, pp. 3, 24-25.

204 T. 22 August 2005, pp. 12-13; T. 24 August 2005, p. 68; T. 7 September 2005, pp. 4-5.

205 Exh. D. 151.

206 The Accused was arrested on 2 August 1995.

proper investigation,[207] it **[page 33]** did, however, not adduce any evidence to support its theory, nor did it explain the fact that there were no records of these alleged trips in Rwamakuba's passport which was in the UNDF's possession.[208] The Prosecution did rely upon a copy of a page from another Rwandan passport belonging to Rwamakuba, containing a picture of the Accused and a description of his identity,[209] but it was not able to tender other pages failing to possess the entire document and was not able to provide any other information concerning its source.[210]

83. In the Chamber's view, the proffered alibi concerning André Rwamakuba's absence from Rwanda between 23 September 1993 and 29 March 2004 is sufficient to cast reasonable doubt upon the allegations regarding the Accused's participation in public meetings and gatherings during that period in Gikomero *commune*. The Chamber notes that paragraph 5 of the Indictment could be interpreted as alleging the participation of the Accused in sensitization meetings beyond 29 March 2004, extending through June 1994. This possible contention was not clarified, nor supported by the Prosecution evidence. Witnesses ALA, GAB, GAC, GIQ, GIT and GLM testified to meetings held only until March 1994, and not beyond. Other Prosecution witnesses testified to the Accused's participation in specific attacks against Tutsi in April 1994 during which he congratulated militiamen,[211] but their testimonies did not include any statements made by the Accused at various meetings or that he participated in any specific gatherings. This lack of clarity of the charges in the Indictment and the Prosecution's evidence cannot, for reasons of fairness, be interpreted to the disadvantage of the Accused.

84. In light of the earlier conclusions regarding inconsistencies in the Prosecution evidence and the unreliability of the Prosecution witnesses and considering the proffered alibi, the Chamber finds that the Prosecution has failed to prove, beyond reasonable doubt, the allegations set forth in paragraphs 3 to 5 of the Indictment. **[page 34]**

II.1.2. Alleged Delivery of Machetes by André Rwamakuba in Gikomero Commune in April 1994

85. The Prosecution alleges at paragraph 11 of the Indictment that

> Between 10 and 20 April 1994, **André RWAMAKUBA** delivered bags of machetes to the home of André Muhire, near Ndatemwa trading center in Gasabo *secteur,* in his home *commune* of Gikomero, Kigali-rural *préfecture*. On that occasion, between 10 and 11 April, **André RWAMAKUBA** held a meeting with several influential local members of MDR "Hutu Power" political party, including the persons known as Joas Habimana, Chairman of MDR "Power" in Rutunga *secteur*, Ndamage and André Muhire. Several days later, about 13 April, André Muhire distributed the machetes to local residents, who then used them to attack and massacre the Tutsi population. Following such attacks, many Tutsi were killed, including residents of Ndatemwa Centre, namely the wife of a man called Gakumba and her son, Kambanda, and the persons known as Kanuma, Rwihimba, Kankidi, Rutembya, Rutembesa, and many unidentified refugees from Rutongo, Nkuzuzu and Rutanga *secteurs*. Again, between 10 and 11 April 2004, **André RWAMAKUBA** delivered bags of machetes to the home of Etienne Kamanzi, the director of the Kayanga Health Center. The Accused knew, or had reasons to know, that the machetes would be used in attacks against the Tutsi in those areas, thereby aiding and abetting the killing campaign against the Tutsi population.

86. The Chamber will address first the delivery of machetes to André Muhire's home **(II.1.2.1.)** and then the one to Etienne Kamanzi's home **(II.1.2.2.)**.

II.1.2.1. Alleged Delivery of Machetes to André Muhire and Subsequent Massacres of Tutsi at Ndatemwa Trading Centre

87. Despite the large time-frame pleaded at the beginning of paragraph 11 of the Indictment, "between 10 and 20 April 1994", the subsequent sentence of this paragraph specifies that the Accused delivered bags of

---

207 *Prosecutor v. Andre Rwamakuba*, Case No. ICTR-98-44-I, T. 7 November 2000.

208 Exh. D. 151.

209 Exh. P. 3.

210 Exh. P. 3.

211 See below: evidence on the alleged murder of three Tutsi near the Gikomero office *secteur* and on the massacre at the Kayanga Health Centre.

machetes to the home of André Muhire "*between 10 and 11 April*"[212] and that the machetes were distributed "*several days later, about 13 April*". As confirmed in the Prosecution Pre-Trial Brief, Opening Statement and Closing Arguments, there is no doubt that it was the Prosecution's case that this event took place "between10 and 11 April 1994".[213] The Chamber will therefore take into consideration this more specific time-frame when dealing with the assessment of the evidence.

(1) Evidence Adduced

88. Ndatemwa Trading Centre is located in the Gasabo *secteur* of the Gikomero *commune*, approximately 36 kilometres from Kigali town,[214] where André Rwamakuba was living at the **[page 35]** time of the allegations in the Indictment. Both Prosecution and Defence witnesses testified that between 9 and 11 April 1994, two Tutsi named Rutembya and Rutembesa, were beaten up at that Centre and then taken to Kayanga Health Centre where they were subsequently killed.[215] These witnesses also testified that an attack was led against the Tutsi population at Ndatemwa Trading Centre on 13 April 1994.[216] The detailed recollection of this event differs between Prosecution and Defence witnesses.

89. Prosecution Witness GII stated that, between 10 and 11 April 1994 in the afternoon, while he was standing on the road a few meters from Muhire's house in Ndatemwa Trading Centre, he saw five bags unloaded from the boot of a white car and taken into Muhire's house. André Rwamakuba had already come out of the car. Prosecution Witnesses AVD and AVC affirmed that they saw a car with a similar description arriving at Ndatemwa Centre,[217] although they placed this event on a different date than Witness GII: AVD asserted that this event occurred on 12 April 1994 in the afternoon;[218] AVC stated first that he saw the car between 10 and 13 April 1994, and during cross-examination he said that it could have been on 12 April 1994.[219] Witness AVD saw three bags being unloaded from the boot of the car and taken into Muhire's house. AVC testified that the vehicle stayed at Muhire's home for less than an hour,[220] but GII and AVD indicated that Rwamakuba remained at Muhire's house for approximately one to two hours in the company of other persons.[221] According to Witness GII, Joas Habimana, Ndamage and other people were also in Muhire's house; and Witness AVD placed Ndoli and Murangira at the house. Witness AVC was also told that Rwamakuba went to Muhire's house on that occasion with an *Interahamwe* named Ephrem.[222] The Prosecution Witnesses asserted that machetes were distributed by Muhire to young people from Rutungo and Gasabo *secteurs*[223] during the night of 12 April or the morning of 13 April **[page 36]** 1994.[224] Witness AVD further stated that Muhire was assisted by Ndoli and Murangira on that occasion. The Prosecution witnesses testified that after that distribution, houses of Tutsi were attacked and destroyed. According to Witness GII, Tutsi from the commune but also Tutsi refugees from Rubungo and Kanombe were killed.

---

212 Emphasis added.

213 Prosecution Pre-Trial Brief, para. 19; Opening Statement, T. 9 June 2005, p. 8; Prosecution Closing Brief, paras. 50-52.

214 See Exh. P. 2: distance between Kigali/Remera and Gikomero *secteur* office is 25 kilometres; the distance between this office and Ndatemwa Centre is 11 kilometres.

215 Prosecution Witness AVC testified that Rutembya and Rutembesa were beaten up on 9 or 11 April 1994 (T. 27 June 2005, pp. 33-35); Prosecution Witness AVD said that this event took place during the same week of Habyarimana's death but before André Rwamakuba's arrival at the Ndatemwa Trading Centre (T. 28 June 2005, pp. 5-6); Prosecution Witness GII testified that this event took place on or about 11 April 1994 (T. 23 June 2005, pp. 43-44). According to Defence Witnesses 9/20, Rutembya and Rutembesa were beaten up on 11 April 1994 (T. 7 November 2005, p. 22); and Defence Witness 4/16 said that it happened between 11 and 12 April 1994 (T. 19 January 2006, p. 57).

216 Defence Closing Brief, p. 83.

217 T. 28 June 2005, pp. 19 and 39; T. 27 June 2006, p. 12.

218 Witness AVD testified that the event took place "four or five days after Habyarimana's death". Responding to the Defence Counsel, the witness said that Rwamakuba arrived on 12 April 1994 in the afternoon (T. 28 June 2006, pp. 7 and 31).

219 T. 27 June 2006, pp. 12 and 35.

220 The witness stated that the vehicle stayed for approximately 10 to 15 minutes (T. 27 June 2005, p. 54).

221 T. 28 June 2005, p. 9.

222 T. 27 June 2005, pp. 12-13 and 54.

223 AVD specified that they were young *Interahamwe*, Hutus.

224 AVC testified that the machetes were distributed after Rwamakuba's departure, in the night of 12 April 1994; GII stated that the machetes were distributed on 13 April 1994, around 9.40 am; AVD situated the distribution on the "morning of the third day" after the beating up of two people at the Centre (T. 28 June 2006, p. 30).

90. Defence Witnesses 9/20 and 4/16 gave very different accounts of the events at Ndatemwa Trading Centre. They stated that the events took place on13 April 1994 and, on that day, Ephrem Nyirigera, accompanied by three communal policemen, about fifteen *Interahamwe* from Ruhengeri as well as refugees from Gitega and members of the local population, looted houses belonging to Tutsi and threatened the people with machetes and clubs.[225] That attack was stopped by the intervention of the *Conseiller* from Gasabo *secteur*, named Ntamuhanga, who was assisted by soldiers. The Defence witnesses asserted that no killings occurred in Ndatemwa[226] or Gasabo *secteur*,[227] except for the two brothers, named Rutembesa and Rutembya, who were beaten on or about 11 April 1994 and then subsequently killed at Kayanga Health Centre.[228] They also asserted that André Rwamakuba never came to Ndatemwa during that period.

(2) Assessment of the Evidence

91. The Chamber notes that the testimonies of the Prosecution witnesses are not consistent with the allegations against the Accused **(3.1.)**. In addition, they are generally unreliable, especially when considering the evidence adduced to support the Accused's alibi **(3.2.)**.

(2.1.) Lack of Consistency between the Indictment and the Prosecution Evidence

92. Witnesses AVC's and AVD's testimonies that Rwamakuba delivered machetes to Muhire's home on 12 April 1994 are inconsistent with the allegation that this event took place between 10 and 11 April 1994.[229] **[page 37]**

93. Witnesses GII, AVC and AVD also testified that two Tutsi named Rutembya and Rutembesa were *beaten up* on 9 or 11 April 1994 at the Ndatemwa Centre, *before* the alleged delivery of machetes at Muhire's house, and were killed later at the Kayanga Health Centre. This evidence, corroborated by testimony from Defence witnesses,[230] is inconsistent with the allegation that Rutembya and Rutembesa were killed as a result of attacks against some Tutsi after the delivery of machetes by Rwamakuba at Ndatemwa Trading Centre.

(2.2.) Reliability Issues

94. The identification of André Rwamakuba at the time of the alleged machetes delivery to Muhire's home is unreliable. AVC and AVD had no prior knowledge of him when he allegedly arrived at Ndatemwa Trading Centre. Their identification of the Accused is based on untested hearsay evidence. Witness AVC who was hiding in a clump of bushes and could not see the people in the car, was told by two men that the person who had arrived in the car was Rwamakuba.[231] AVD testified that he could not see the people in the car due to the crowd surrounding it. In court, AVC and AVD were not able to offer any physical description of the person they claim to be Rwamakuba.

95. GII is the sole Prosecution witness who claimed to have prior knowledge of André Rwamakuba. GII allegedly saw Rwamakuba when the latter came to attend a meeting at Muhire's house, on 4 or 5 April 1994, with the President of MDR-Power in Rutunga *secteur*, Joas Habimana, and the MDR-Power representative at Gasabo, Ndamage. On that occasion, people told GII that it was Rwamakuba who had come to attend this meeting. GII claimed that a few days later, when Rwamakuba came to deliver machetes at Muhire's place, he recognized him as the man who was identified to him on 4 or 5 April 1994.

---

225 T. 7 November 2005, pp. 24-25 (Witness 9/20); T. 19 January 2006, pp. 57-58 (Witness 4/16).

226 Witness 9/20.

227 Witness 4/16.

228 T. 7 November 2005, pp. 22-24 (Witness 9/20); T. 19 January 2006, pp. 57-58 (Witness 4/16).

229 Indictment, para. 11; Prosecution Pre-Trial Brief, para. 19, Opening Statement, T. 9 June 2005, p. 8; Prosecution Closing Brief, paras. 50-52.

230 See: Witness 9/20 and 4/16.

231 T. 27 June 2005, pp. 44, 50 and 54. According to AVC, one of these men had also just met André Rwamakuba. He is dead now and the second man who identified him as Rwamakuba to AVC is in exile but the witness does not know whether he is still alive.

96. The Chamber notes that GII identified André Rwamakuba from information given to him by unknown and unidentified people. The witness described him in very general terms[232] and was only able to specify that he wore spectacles. The Defence, however, challenged that Rwamakuba wore spectacles at that time and tendered into evidence a letter from the UNDF Commanding Officer stating that the Accused had "no spectacle in his possession upon his **[page 38]** transfer to the UNDF".[233] In addition, Defence witnesses who had personal knowledge of Rwamakuba, testified that he never wore glasses.[234]

97. Alibi evidence from the Defence strengthens the doubt on GII's reliability to identify André Rwamakuba. According to Defence Witness François Monet, Rwamakuba spent the day of 5 April 1994 from 7.30 a.m. to 5.30 p.m. with himself and Pierre Mercenier.[235] Not only did he rely on his diary entries to confirm this date,[236] but the witness also asserted that he remembered very well Rwamakuba's presence on that day since the latter had been leading the delegation when they met with the Director General of Health. Although Pierre Mercenier could not actually remember whether the Accused was present on 5 April 1994, he claimed that he would have been surprised if he had not met him on that day. The other possible date given by Witness GII as having met Rwamakuba was 4 April 1994. That day was Easter Monday, and testimony was given that Rwamakuba spent the day with his family in Kigali.[237] Considering GII's untested indirect evidence on Rwamakuba's identification and the reliability of the Defence witness' testimony, the Chamber finds that there is some reasonable doubt that GII would have seen Rwamakuba on 4 or 5 April 1994 when the Accused allegedly came to attend a meeting at Muhire's place. This doubt is supported by the Defence evidence on the road access to Gikomero in April 1994.

(2.3.) Road Access to Gikomero

98. The Defence disputed that the Accused could have been present in Gikomero *commune* at the time of the alleged event. The parties agreed and the Chamber accepts that André Rwamakuba was sworn in as a Minister of the Interim Government on 9 April 1994, attended a governmental meeting held in Kigali at the *Hotel des Diplomates* on 11 April 1994,[238] and was living in Kigali until 12 April 1994 when he went to Gitarama with the convoy of the Interim Government.[239] The admission of these facts has a major impact on the Prosecution's theory since at the onset of this trial, the Defence challenged the accessibility from and to Gikomero *commune* due to geographical and military obstacles to road travel in **[page 39]** April 1994. In its Closing Brief, the Prosecution submitted that the Defence did not show that it was impossible to move to Gikomero at that time.[240] It further contended that as a Minister, Rwamakuba could move more easily around the country than an ordinary citizen.[241] No evidence, however, was adduced in support of that submission. The Chamber recalls that, contrary to the Prosecution's assertion, the Accused is presumed innocent and does not have to prove anything. If the evidence adduced by the Defence raises reasonable doubt, the Prosecution has failed to establish the guilt of the Accused.

99. In the present case, the Prosecution decided not to call any witness to rebut the Defence allegation "but preferred to focus on the credibility and limited knowledge of Defence witnesses on this point".[242] It only called investigator Upendra Baghel who testified to a study he conducted in 2003, and who spoke of several routes between Kigali and Gikomero *commune*. According to his report, the average distance between

---

232 The witness said: "His skin is not too dark. He's not very big, but he's quite robust, quite solid, average size, average height, neither too tall nor too short; he was wearing a jacket and also spectacles."

233 Exh. D. 215.

234 See: Edith Van Wynsberghe (T. 1 December 2005, p. 61); Witness 1/1 (T. 14 December 2005, p. 65); Witness 1/15 (T. 18 January 2006, p. 14) and Witness 9/1 (T. 29 November 2005, pp. 37 and 63-65).

235 They first met in the morning at the Kigali Regional Health headquarters. Then, the three of them also spent the afternoon together, including at meeting with the director general of public health in the Ministry, during which they discussed the project and the work they were planning to do in Rwanda.

236 Exh. D. 187.

237 Witness 1/1, T. 15 December 2005, pp. 35-36. The Prosecution Counsel did not dispute that the 4th April 1994 was Easter Monday.

238 These are facts not disputed by the parties. See Prosecution Closing Brief, para. 68; Defence Closing Brief.

239 *Ibidem.*

240 Prosecution Closing Brief, paras. 190-192.

241 Prosecution Closing Brief, para. 192.

242 Prosecution Closing Brief, para. 178.

Kigali and Ndatemwa Trading Centre is approximately 36 kilometres which would have taken one and a half hours to travel.[243] The Defence acknowledged that the routes and timing of journeys to Gikomero *commune* were reasonably reviewed in that document, "with the caveat that [the timings] were based on a journey in a good, four wheel drive vehicle, in the dry season, and in peace time".[244] The Prosecution investigator admitted that the routes were hilly and difficult, and that he had no knowledge of the conditions for travel in that area in 1994.[245] He also denied having knowledge of the positions occupied by the military between 8 and 30 April 1994. The weight of his evidence is therefore less than that of a witness who was present in the relevant area in 1994.

100. Defence witnesses, who were present in Gikomero or tried to get there in April 1994, testified that shortly after 7 April 1994, four main routes between Kigali and Gikomero *commune* were all effectively severed by military positions of the RPF.[246] According to Witness 9/20, it was impossible that André Rwamakuba came to Ndatemwa between 10 and 13 April 1994, because the people who lived there could not move about and were ordered to stay home.[247] The witness explained that the road from Kigali to Ndatemwa was impassable **[page 40]** and that vehicles could only travel from Rutunga to Ndatemwa and could go no further.[248] The witness asserted that no Minister came to Gikomero in the days in leading up to 13 April 1994.[249] Defence Witness 6/10 stated that from 9 April 1994, roads, especially those from Rutongo, were not practicable because the RPF had already taken control of that area. He could not see how a vehicle would have left Kigali and come to the east.[250] Defence Witness 7/3 confirmed this evidence and stated that between President Habyarimana's death and 14 April 1994, it was not easy to travel from Gikomero to Kigali because the RPF had overrun strategic positions, especially on Gikomero hills.[251] According to Defence Witnesses 1/5, 3/13 and 3/4, several roads from Kigali leading up to Gikomero could not be used after 8 or 9 April 1994 because of the RPF's presence and ongoing fighting.[252] Defence Witness 3/22 also testified that it was not possible to get to and from Kigali after 12 April 1994 because there were soldiers on the roads.[253] He acknowledged that there were other secondary roads that might have been used to Gikomero, but those small roads were connected to the main road coming from Kigali, which was blocked.[254] His testimony was corroborated by Defence Witness 4/12 who lived close to the road. This witness asserted that, after 12 April 1994, he did not see any other vehicle apart from the four vehicles carrying soldiers who were going to fight the *Inkotanyi*.[255] He claimed that the road was not safe and Rwamakuba would not have risked his life to get from Kigali to Gikomero at that time.[256] Defence witness 2/18 stated that after 13 April 1994, no one could leave Kigali to get to Gikomero because Kigali and Remera were already captured.[257]

101. It was also a major part of the Defence case that André Rwamakuba's name was not mentioned during the *Gacaca* proceedings in relation to the events that took place in Gikomero *commune* in April 1994. This was supported by the evidence given by several **[page 41]** Defence witnesses who lived in the area in 1994, or were participating in *Gacaca* proceedings in the *commune*. Defence Witnesses 3/1, 3/22, 3/11 and 4/16 asserted that they never saw or heard of a Minister coming to Gikomero in the days leading up to 13 April

243 Exh. P. 2.
244 Defence Closing Brief, p. 22.
245 T. 13 June 2005, pp. 39-40.
246 See references below.
247 T. 7 November 2005, p. 27.
248 T. 9 November 2005, p. 6.
249 T. 9 November 2005, p. 6.
250 T. 24 November 2005, p. 8.
251 T. 19 January 2006, pp. 14-15.
252 The RPF was occupying Remera (road near the Kigali Stadium and Hotel Amahoro) and the "CND" (Parliament – road from German Radio Station *Deutsche Welle*) and the road that goes out towards Kanombe. See: Defence Witnesses 3/4 (T. 17 January 2006, p. 6-12); 3/13 (T. 24 January 2006, pp. 15, 30 and 32); 1/5 (T. 13 December 2005, pp. 24 and 38). Moreover, Defence Witness 2/18 said that after 13 April 1994, no one could leave Kigali to get to Gikomero because Kigali and Remera were captured at that time (T. 23 January 2006, p. 28), and Defence Witness 3/22 testified that Defence Witness 3/22 further testified that after 12 April 1994, it was no longer possible to get to and from Kigali because there were soldiers on the roads (T. 30 November 2005, p.16).
253 T. 30 November 2005, p.16.
254 T. 30 November 2005, pp.29-31.
255 T. 22 November 2005, pp. 22-23.
256 T. 22 November 2005, pp. 22-23.
257 T. 23 January 2006, p. 28.

1994.[258] Defence Witnesses 7/18 and 9/31 said that Rwamakuba never came to Gikomero after 6 April 1994.[259] Witnesses 1/5, 4/12, 6/10 and 7/18 asserted that they never heard that Rwamakuba played any role in the genocide.[260] Particularly, several Defence Witnesses also contended that they did not hear any mention of the Accused's name in the *Gacaca* hearings concerning the 1994 massacres in Gikomero.[261] Defence Witness 3/10, however, testified that, in September or October 2005 after the beginning of the present trial, two of the Prosecution Witnesses mentioned André Rwamakuba's name in the *Gacaca* hearings in the witness' cellule.[262]

102. The Chamber finds that these Defence witnesses generally gave a consistent and objective account of the facts sufficient to levy a reasonable doubt on the Prosecution's case. Witnesses 9/20 and 3/1 had no personal relationship with the Accused: they do not know him personally and admit that they would not recognize him.[263] They are both Tusti, whose family members were killed during the genocide in 1994.[264] One of them is a coordinator of a local *Gacaca* court in Rwanda. Witness 1/5 did not know André Rwamakuba very well.[265] It was not shown that these witnesses would have any particular interest to defend him. For instance, the Prosecution did not attempt to question Witness 3/4 concerning his knowledge of Rwamakuba or the existence of any relationship with him.[266] The Chamber notes that Defence Witnesses 3/10, 6/10 and 7/18 knew Rwamakuba's family very well and that Witnesses 4/16 and 7/3 have criminal records. Due to these individual circumstances, the Chamber has taken particular care in assessing their testimonies.[267] The evidence adduced from these witnesses **[page 42]** does corroborate the testimony of the other Defence witnesses. The Prosecution's cross-examination of Defence Witnesses 3/10, 6/10, 7/18, 4/16 and 7/3 did not raise any convincing element to show that they were unbelievable or unreliable, nor did the Prosecution adduce any evidence to rebut their testimonies on the above issues.

103. Furthermore, the evidence given on the content of the alleged bags delivered and the subsequent massacres of Tutsi people was merely hearsay evidence. None of the Prosecution witnesses actually saw the content of the bags. They were told later that machetes were brought and the inhabitants were requested to start killing the Tutsi.[268] They also did not see the alleged massacres of Tutsi since they fled the area on 13 April 1994 and only learned about it when they returned to the Centre months later and when human skeletal remains were found. These witnesses did not mention the name of any particular victims of the 13 April 1994 attack at Ndatemwa Trading Centre. Their evidence was challenged by the Defence. There was direct testimony that André Muhire never distributed any machetes. Evidence was also adduced regarding the criminal charges against Muhire in Rwanda. It was specified that he was never prosecuted for distributing machetes and that André Rwamakuba's name was never mentioned in his Rwandan judicial records. Witness 9/20 furthermore stated that no new machetes were distributed at that time in Ndatemwa because individuals used their own weapons which they took from their own houses.[269]

---

258 T. 10 November 2005, p. 8 (Witness 3/1); T. 30 November 2005, p.17 (Witness 3/22); Witness 1/5 never heard of André Rwamakuba coming to Gikomero *commune* between 8 and 17 April 1994 (T. 12 December 2005, p. 26).

259 T. 1 December 2005, p. 33 (Witness 7/18). Defence Witness 9/31 stated that he never saw André Rwamakuba in Gikomero *secteur* during April 1994 (T. 1 February 2006, p. 8).

260 T. 12 December 2005, p. 26 (Witness 1/5); T. 24 November 2005, p. 7 (Witness 4/12); T. 24 November 2005, p. 24 (Witness 6/10). Witness 7/18 added that she had not heard people at Gikomero or in the Rutare camp for displaced persons discussing Rwamakuba in connection with the massacres (T. 1 December 2005, p. 9).

261 See: Defence Witnesses 3/1 (T. 10 November 2005, p. 9); 3/22 (T. 30 November 2005, p. 34); 4/12 (T. 24 November 2005, p. 7); 4/16 (T. 19 January 2006, p. 55); 5/16 (T. 2 February 2006, p. 34); 9/31 (T. 1 February 2006, p. 9); 6/10 (T. 24 November 2005, p. 25).

262 T. 15 November 2005, pp. 19-20.

263 T. 7 November 2005, p. 26; T. 10 November 2005, p. 25.

264 T. 7 November 2005, pp. 19, 31 and 32; T. 10 November 2005, p. 3.

265 T. 12 December 2005, p. 26 (Witness 1/5).

266 T. 17 January 2005.

267 Defence Witness 3/10 knew Rwamakuba's family very well; 4/16 is charged in his country with killings of four people but claims his innocence. Defence Witnesses 6/10 and 7/18 were very closed to the Accused's family; they are moreover relatives. Defence Witness 7/14 was Prosecution Witness GIN's relative and Defence Witness 7/3 has a criminal record related to the 1994 genocide.

268 See: Witnesses AVC, AVD and GII.

269 The witness added that, during the *Gacaca* sessions, she never heard about the distribution of new machetes at Ndatemwa Trading Centre (T. 7 November 2005, p. 27).

104. The absence of any reliable identification of the Accused at the time and place of the alleged event, his undisputed presence to certain locations during the considered period, the evidence on the potential hazards of travel to and from Gikomero, the absence of any reliable evidence on the exact context of the alleged event, all cumulatively contribute to cast a reasonable doubt that the Accused delivered machetes to André Muhire at Ndatemwa Trading Centre as alleged in paragraph 11 of the Indictment.

II.1.2.2. Alleged Delivery of Machetes to Etienne Kamanzi Used in Attacks against Tutsi

105. The Prosecution alleges that, between 10 and 11 April 1994, the Accused delivered bags of machetes to the home of Etienne Kamanzi, director of the Kayanga Health Centre, **[page 43]** and that he knew, or had reasons to know, that the machetes would be used in attacks against the Tutsi in the areas.[270] Kamanzi's home was located in Kayanga *secteur*, Gikomero *commune*, which is approximately six kilometres from the Ndatemwa Trading Centre and 30 kilometres northeast of Kigali town where André Rwamakuba resided until 12 April 1994. On that date, he moved to Gitarama which is 53 kilometres southwest of Kigali.[271]

(1) Evidence Adduced

106. Prosecution Witness GAC, who claimed to be an eyewitness of this event, was the sole witness called to testify on this allegation. He also claimed that he knew André Rwamakuba since he had already seen him on three occasions before that event.[272]

107. The witness testified that "on the day following the death of [President] Habyarimana"[273] or a few days after the President's death, between 10 and 13 April 1994,[274] he saw André Rwamakuba unloading bags containing machetes from a white car and giving them to Etienne Kamanzi.[275] The witness heard Rwamakuba blaming Kamanzi for continuing to provide medical treatment to Tutsi at the Kayanga Health Centre.[276] He saw Rwamakuba give machetes to Kamanzi indicating that it was the "medicine to treat them", namely to kill the Tutsi.[277] Witness GAC then saw a woman named Anatalie Mukarulinda telling Rwamakuba and Kamanzi that she had six "Abakigas"[278] who could work and she requested machetes for them. Kamanzi then gave, in the presence of Rwamakuba, six machetes to Mukarulinda.[279] GAC saw Mukarulinda distributing the machetes to the six Abakigas.[280] The witness did not see machetes being distributed to other persons, but he attested that when the killing began, everyone was provided with a new and recently sharpened machete.[281] **[page 44]**

108. Witness GAC claimed to be "aware"[282] that the Abakigas used the machetes to kill Tutsi. The witness learnt from a *conseiller* that a policeman named Nyarwaya had taken part in a meeting in Nduba the day before the attacks, with *Interahamwe*, policemen and *conseillers*, where instructions were issued.[283] According to the witness, on or about 13 April 1994, the six Abakigas went toward Rutunga Trading Centre.[284] Then, Nyarwaya, who was standing at the Rutunga marketplace, shot his gun in the air and told

---

270 Indictment, para. 11.
271 Exh. P. 2.
272 See above: Alleged Public Instigation in Gikomero from July 1993 through June 1994.
273 T. 4 July 2005, p. 7
274 T. 4 July 2005, pp. 50-53.
275 T. 4 July 2005, pp. 8 and 58
276 According to Witness GAC, André Rwamakuba asked Kamanzi: "You mean you are continuing to give treatment to the Tutsis?" (T. 4 July 2005, pp. 8-9 and 18).
277 T. 4 July 2005, pp. 6, 7, 9, 11 and 18.
278 Witness GAC explained that the Abakigas were Rwandan natives of Adukiga, located in Byumba and Ruhengeri, who had come from their own region, to flee the war that was being waged by the *Inkotanyi* (T. 4 July 2005, p. 12).
279 T. 4 July 2005, pp. 11 and 58.
280 T. 4 July 2005, pp. 18 and 58.
281 T. 4 July 2005, p. 18.
282 T. 4 July 2005, p. 12.
283 T. 4 July 2005, pp. 15-16.
284 T. 4 July 2005, p. 12.

the Abakigas to "begin".[285] The witness was not present at the market at that time.[286] After the gunshot, the Abakigas began burning down houses, looting and assaulting neighbouring persons, beginning with Mukarulinda's neighbours.[287] According to Witness GAC, the victims of the attacks were Tutsi and the perpetrators were Hutu. These attacks by the Abakigas marked the beginning of the massacres in Kayanga. The witness stated that the first person who was killed was an inhabitant;[288] then Tutsi patients of the Kayanga Health Centre were killed after 13 April 1994 and until the end of the week by *Interahamwe* from Gasabo.[289]

(2) Assessment of the Evidence

109. The Chamber notes that Witness GAC was a Prosecution witness in the *Kamuhanda* case. The Defence submits that his evidence should not be admitted since the Trial Chamber in the *Kamuhanda* case found him not credible.[290] It contends that once a Trial Chamber finds a witness not credible, in respect of significant and substantial testimony, it is only appropriate in the most exceptional circumstances for the Prosecution to tender him as a witness of truth in another trial. In the Defence's view, failure to follow such good practice is likely to bring the administration of justice into disrepute and the Chamber should refuse the admission of such evidence as an abuse of process.[291]

110. The Chamber has discretionary power to assess the evidence brought before it and cannot be bound by the assessment of Witness GAC's credibility made in the *Kamuhanda* case. The Chamber, however, already found his testimony unreliable concerning the political **[page 45]** meetings in Kayanga.[292] Moreover, Witness GAC's testimony on the alleged delivery of machetes to Kamanzi also appears to be tainted with major internal inconsistencies which seriously challenge his credibility **(2.1.)**. This challenge is reinforced by the Defence evidence on the road access to Gikomero at the time of the event **(2.2.)**.

(2.1.) Credibility Issues

111. Witness GAC's testimony is not consistent concerning the date when the alleged event took place. The witness first testified that the delivery of machetes by the Accused to Kamanzi took place "the day *following the death of Habyarimana*". Later in his testimony, he asserted that the event had taken place *a few days* after the President was killed, around 10 and 13 April 1994.[293] Similarly, the witness stated that a *conseiller*, who was his neighbour, informed him about the meeting in which Nyarwaya participated the day before the attacks in Nduba. Later in his testimony, he denied that this *conseiller* was a neighbour and added that he is no longer alive.[294]

112. The witness' account of the event is also subject to concerns. After Witness GAC saw the alleged distribution of machetes, he did not directly inform his family but continued on his way and went off for a drink in a bar.[295] Such behaviour is odd when considering the particular insecure context of threats against the Tutsi people as described by the witness himself. The witness' testimony as to his presence when the massacres started at the Rutunga Trading Centre on 13 April 1994 also seemed unlikely: he both affirmed that he was present on the spot when massacres started and that he fled Kayanga on the same day.[296]

113. In addition to these internal inconsistencies and unlikely behaviours and actions, Witness GAC's testimony substantially differed from his statement to the Prosecution on 8 November 2004.[297] In that

285 T. 4 July 2005, p. 12.
286 T. 5 July 2005, p. 3.
287 T. 4 July 2005, pp. 12 and 15.
288 T. 4 July 2005, pp. 18 and 60
289 T. 4 July 2005, pp. 18-19
290 *Kamuhanda* Judgement, para. 287; Defence Closing Brief, pp. 191-193.
291 Defence Closing Brief, pp. 192-193.
292 See: Alleged Public Instigation in Gikomero from July 1993 through June 1994.
293 T. 4 July 2005, pp. 50-53.
294 T. 5 July 2005, p. 2.
295 T. 4 July 2005, p. 62.
296 T. 4 July 2005, pp.29-30.
297 Exh. D. 34 A and B (under seal).

statement, the witness declared that Kamanzi opened the bag of machetes which had been unloaded *on Rwamakuba's order*, but in the courtroom, he testified that it was Rwamakuba who had opened his car and was giving machetes to Kamanzi himself.[298] In the same statement, the witness specified that he clearly heard Rwamakuba *ask* Kamanzi to give Mukarulinda the machetes, while in his testimony the machetes were given **[page 46]** to her *at her request*. In 2004, he also gave the name of three companions, including Alexis Karekezi, who were present when he saw Rwamakuba giving the machetes. According to his statement, these three persons were then killed at the Kayanga Health Centre. In court, the witness testified that *only* Alexis Karakezi was with him on that occasion and that there were *Interahamawe* who were not far away.[299] The witness' statement does not contain any information concerning the alleged attacks of the six Abakigas against Tutsi at the Rutunga Trading Centre, the meeting held the day before the attacks where instructions to kill Tutsi were issued, and the incident with Nyarwaya firing his gun in the air and telling the Abakigas to begin the attacks, all of which he testified extensively about in court. The witness also qualified Etienne Kamanzi as the Head of the Kayanga Health Centre in his 2004 statement,[300] but in court he referred to him as a nurse at the Kayanga Health Centre.[301]

114. These discrepancies cannot be justified by the time elapsed since the event or translation discrepancies. They are significant in the assessment of the credibility of this witness who omitted any reference to André Rwamakuba in his early statements to the Prosecution investigators. Witness GAC gave a statement in 1999 to the Prosecution and testified in the *Kamuhanda* case in 2002 about the activities of Kamuhanda and Kamanzi in the distribution of weapons in Kayanga between 8 and 12 April 1994. He testified on the occasions where he saw Kamanzi prior to the massacres. It was not until he gave his statement in 2004 that he mentioned Rwamakuba for the first time. He explained the prior omission by the fact that he was not questioned about Rwamakuba at the time. Even if that were the case, the Chamber does not find this to be a satisfactory explanation, as the absence of certain questions would not preclude a witness, who wanted to give a credible picture of an event, from volunteering information.[302]

115. Witness GAC's demeanour in court supports the Chamber's conclusion that the witness cannot be found credible. Although the Chamber acknowledges that a witness' behaviour may be influenced by the fact that he or she is responding to the opposite party, in the present case, the witness was particularly reluctant or unwilling to respond to the **[page 47]** Defence's questions in cross-examination.[303] He was also extremely disinclined to speak about or comment on his previous testimony in the *Kamuhanda* case.[304]

116. The defence evidence on the potential hazards of travel between Kigali and Gikomero *commune* at the time of the event reinforces the Chamber's doubts on GAC's credibility.

(2.2.) Road Access to Gikomero

117. Neither the Indictment nor the Prosecution's evidence seems to suggest that the delivery of machetes to Kamanzi's house took place on the same day as the alleged delivery of machetes at Muhire's place in Ndatemwa Trading Centre.[305] The Prosecution did not provide any chronology of the alleged four occasions when the Accused came to Gikomero over a period of five days. According to Witness GAC, André Rwamakuba met Kamanzi and decided to give him machetes by chance. There is no other explanation or account of that event. However, in the Chamber's view, the chronology of the facts was particularly relevant to the Prosecution case. As previously discussed, it was admitted that the Accused attended other activities

298 T. 4 July 2005, pp. 9 and 58.
299 T. 4 July 2005, pp. 59-60.
300 Exh. D. 34.
301 T. 4 July 2005, p. 7.
302 It is interesting to note that GAC gave his first statement as a result of a visit to the United Nations office in Kigali. As he was requesting free medical assistance, an investigator asked him whether he had information about the crimes committed by a man named André Rwamakuba in Gikomero in April 1994 (T. 4 July 2005, pp. 32-33).
303 See for e.g.: T. 4 July 2005, pp. 11, 27, 39-42 and 51.
304 T. 4 July 2005, pp. 45-48.
305 See above the testimonies of Prosecution Witnesses AVC, AVD and GII on the alleged delivery of machetes to Muhire's house.

in Kigali on 11 April 1994.[306] The Prosecution did not attempt to explain how the Accused moved from that town to deliver machetes in a location 30 kilometres apart or how he came over a period of two days to two different locations six kilometres apart,[307] whereas the Defence adduced evidence that it was hazardous to travel to and from Gikomero after 7 April 1994, that Rwamakuba never came to Gikomero *commune* in the days leading up to 13 April 1994 and that his name was never mentioned in relation to the massacres in the *commune* in April 1994.[308] The Chamber already found the Defence evidence consistent and objective enough to levy a reasonable doubt on the Prosecution's case.[309]

118. The lack of credibility of Witness GAC, the admitted presence of André Rwamakuba in other activities, the evidence on the potential hazards to travel, cumulatively contribute to reasonable doubt on the alleged presence of the Accused in Kayanga *secteur,* Gikomero *commune* between 10 and 13 April 1994. Since Witness GAC was the sole witness called and **[page 48]** no additional evidence was adduced that between 10 and 11 April 1994, the Accused delivered bags of machetes to the home of Etienne Kamanzi, the Prosecution failed to prove this allegation.

II.1.3. Alleged Murder of Three Tutsi near Gikomero Secteur Office

119. At paragraph 12 of the Indictment, the Prosecution alleges that

> Between 10 and 20 April 1994, **André RWAMAKUBA** went to Gikomero *commune* where, during a rally near the *secteur* office, accompanied by RUTAGANIRA, *bourgmestre* of the *commune*, Brigadier NYARWAYA, Mathias KABANGUKA, accountant of the *commune*, and two men unknown but who were identified as policemen, he asked persons in the crowd why the massacres had not started. He then seized documents belonging to two unknown youths, but who were identified as Tutsi, tore the documents and ordered the crowd to seize the youths and kill them. Persons present in the crowd armed with firearms, machetes and clubs, including NGIRUWOSANGA, a *secteur* inhabitant, NGARAMBE and KAYIBANDA, and two communal policemen, immediately seized the two young men that **André RWAMAKUBA** had designated, led them away to a wooded area and killed them as the ***Accused***, who was not far, looked on. Thereafter, this same crowd stopped an unidentified man on a motorcycle claiming to flee the massacres in Rutongo *commune*. **André RWAMAKUBA,** while speaking to the crowd, stated that the motorcyclist could not be a Hutu since only Tutsi were fleeing, and decided that the youth should be killed. At the instigation of and following orders from **André RWAMAKUBA**, the same armed crowd led him away to a wooded area to kill him. The ***Accused*** then told the crowd that it had just started the killings and that it was a good start. The same day, in the afternoon, Interahamwe militiamen, elements of the Presidential Guard, with the assistance of members of the population, following such orders and instigations, began to massacre Tutsi refugees, in Gikomero *commune*, notably at Kayanga Health Center, Gikomero Protestant School and Gicaca. Thousands were massacred, including refugees from Remera, in Kigali town centre, refugees from the neighbouring *commune* of Gikoro and Kabuga *secteur*, Rubungo *commune*.

(1) Evidence Adduced

120. The Gikomero *secteur* office is approximately 25 kilometres northeast of Kigali town, where André Rwamakuba was living until 12 April 1994; 11 kilometres from Ndatemwa Trading Centre and five kilometres from Kayanga *secteur.* From Kigali town it is 53 kilometres southwest to Gitarama where Rwamakuba moved to on 12 April 1994.[310]

121. To support the allegation at paragraph 12 of the Indictment, the Prosecution only called Witness GIN, who claimed to have been present at this event. This witness also asserted that she was introduced to André Rwamakuba for the first time in 1992 at a wedding in the family of a man named Karuyonga who, according

---

306 On 11 April 1994, André Rwamakuba participated in a governmental meeting held in Kigali at the *Hotel des Diplomates*. See: Statement of Admissions by the Parties and Other Matters not in Dispute, filed on 3 June 2005; Prosecution Witness GLM and Prosecution Expert Witness Des Forges.

307 When he allegedly came to Ndatemwa Trading Centre to deliver machetes to Muhire's house (see above) and when he allegedly came to Kayanga to deliver machetes to Kamanzi's house.

308 See paras 100-101.

309 See para. 102.

310 Exh. P. 2.

to the witness, seemed to be Rwamakuba's friend.[311] She saw the Accused again at Nyamirambo, Kigali *ville*, in 1992 **[page 49]** when he came to visit her family.[312] The witness testified that she saw Rwamakuba a third time in Gikomero *commune* between 10 and 14 of April 1994, between 10.00 a.m. and 11.00 a.m. He was in the company of *Bourgmestre* Rutaganira, the accountant Mathias Rubanguka, the brigadier Nyarwaya, two *commune* policemen, Ngarambe and Kayibanda, and other members of the population such as François-Xavier Kamanzi, Ngiruwosanga and Mivumbi.[313]

122. According to Witness GIN, when André Rwamakuba got to the centre, the inhabitants had stopped two young people and were asking them to show their identity cards. As these young people showed their certificates instead of their identity cards, Rwamakuba tore them up[314] and said that these young people were Tutsi because they had refused to show their identity cards.[315] He then ordered that they be arrested and killed. The two young men were taken off to a wooded area by the same group, which included Rwamakuba, Ngiruwosanga, Murekezi, Runyota, Ngarambe, Kayibanda, Rubanguka and Rutaganira.[316] They were armed with machetes, clubs, and some carried guns.[317] There was a distance of 70 to 100 meters between the entrance to the yard of GIN's house where she was standing and the place in the woods where the two men were taken. They stayed in the woods for about one and a half hours.[318] GIN heard the two young persons screaming as they were beaten up and she concluded that they were killed because the people who took them away returned alone.[319] GIN cannot confirm whether Rwamakuba went right to the spot where the people were killed, but she asserted that he was there and he saw what was happening.[320]

123. After the two young people were killed, André Rwamakuba allegedly encouraged and gave instructions to members of the population to continue the killings. He is also alleged to have thanked them for starting the killings in the *commune*.[321]

124. Then, still according to GIN, while André Rwamakuba was still there, a young man showed up on a motorcycle. He was stopped and was required to show his identification documents. GIN heard Rwamakuba say that only Tutsis were fleeing and he then gave orders for the motorcyclist to be killed.[322] The witness saw that the same armed group took the **[page 50]** motorcyclist into the same woods as the two young people. This time, Rwamakuba allegedly remained with the *bourgmestre* in an open area,[323] as the motorcyclist was killed. GIN testified that he left shortly thereafter.[324]

(2) Assessment of the Evidence

125. In the Chamber's view, GIN's evidence is not consistent with the Prosecution's allegation set forth in the Indictment **(2.1.)**. It is also highly improbable that the alleged killing of three people at the Gikomero *secteur* office between 10 and 14 April 1994 would have occurred as described by Witness GIN **(2.2.)**.

(2.1.) Lack of Consistency between the Dates in the Indictment and the Evidence

126. In addition to GIN's testimony, evidence has also been adduced by both parties that in April 1994, Tutsi refugees from Mbandazi and from Rubungo *communes* were attacked and killed by *Interahamwe* at Gikomero Protestant School. GIN was not present at the location but was informed that this massacre took

311 T. 29 June 2005, p. 9. The Chamber notes an interpretation discrepancy between the French ("Karuyonga") and English transcript ("Kayiranga").
312 T. 29 June 2005, p. 10; T. 30 June 2005, pp. 27-29 and 32-33.
313 T. 29 June 2005, p. 10.
314 T. 29 June 2005, pp. 11-12.
315 T. 29 June 2005, p. 12.
316 T. 29 June 2005, p. 13.
317 T. 29 June 2005, p. 14.
318 T. 29 June 2005, p. 14.
319 T. 29 June 2005, pp. 13, 16 and 28.
321 T. 29 June 2005, pp. 14-15.
322 T. 29 June 2005, p. 15.
323 T. 29 June 2005, p. 16.
324 T. 29 June 2005, p. 16.

place between 8 and 12 April 1994. She asserted that André Rwamakuba was not involved in that massacre.[325] Defence Witnesses 2/18, 3/1,[326] 3/11, 9/31 who were present at the time and location of the event, were more specific and all affirmed that the Tutsi refugees were killed on 12 April 1994, between 1.00 p.m. and 2.00 p.m. This date was confirmed by Defence Witnesses 3/22, 4/12 and 7/3 following information they received from others.[327] Prosecution Witnesses GAB and GII also testified that on 12 April 1994, Tutsi refugees were killed at the Gishaka parish in Gikomero *commune.*[328] Both parties accepted that this massacre took place at that time.[329]

127. Consequently, the suggestion made by GIN that the killings at the Gikomero *secteur* office could have taken place after 12 April 1994, on 13 or 14 April 1994, is inconsistent with the Prosecution's allegation that the day of the killings of three people at the Gikomero *secteur* office, *after* Rwamakuba's departure, in the afternoon, *Interahamwe* militiamen, **[page 51]** elements of the Presidential Guard, with the assistance from members of the population, began to kill Tutsi refugees, notably at the Gikomero Protestant School.

(2.2.) Credibility Issues

128. GIN's evidence includes major discrepancies between her prior statements and testimony, and is also seriously challenged by facts admitted by both parties and the evidence adduced by the Defence.

129. A comparison between her testimony regarding the identification of André Rwamakuba, and her prior statements and testimony in the *Kamuhanda* case reveals important discrepancies. In her first statement of 3 February 1998,[330] she stated that her husband told her that it was Rwamakuba who came to Gikomero in April 1994, and that she recognized him as well because she used to see him driving his car in Gikomero *commune*. GIN confirmed this information in the investigator's report dated 13 February 2004,[331] but two months later, she stated that she met Rwamakuba for the first time at a wedding between 1991 and 1992.[332] She then specified that the wedding took place at Karuyonga's house who was her mother's neighbour in Gicaca, and not Rwamakuba's friend, as she declared in court.[333] In the *Kamuhanda* case, in 2001, prior to her amended statement, the witness gave a different account of her knowledge of Rwamakuba: she testified that she saw him for the first time in front of her house in 1994.[334]

130. Witness GIN's physical description of André Rwamakuba was also extremely vague[335] and contradictory. In her earlier statements, she described him wearing clothes with the colours and emblem of the MRND party.[336] Despite giving several other statements,[337] it was not until April 2004 that she changed her statement and specified that Rwamakuba was not wearing the MRND colours.[338] During her testimony, when confronted with the obvious discrepancy because of Rwamakuba's membership in the opposing MDR party, the witness **[page 52]** explained that the investigator made a mistake when taking notes of her description of Rwamakuba's attire. She maintained, however, that he was wearing a cap with the MRND colours and emblem.[339] This explanation and comment are not satisfactory and raises further doubts on her credibility.

---

325 T. 29 June 2005, p. 27.

326 The witness stated that the victims at the Gikomero Protestant School included members of her family that came from Mbandazi (T. 10 November 2005, p. 7).

327 T. 30 November 2005 (Witness 3/22); T. 22 November 2005, pp. 12-14 (Witness 4/12); T. 19 January 2006, p. 11 (Witness 7/3).

328 T. 23 June 2005, pp. 44-45 (Witness GII); T. 6 July 2005, p. 22 (Witness GAB).

329 T. 5 July 2005, p. 52.

330 Exh. D. 35 A and B (under seal).

331 Exh. D. 38 (under seal).

332 See: Notice of Additional Evidence Pursuant to Rule 67(D), Exh. D. 39 (under seal).

333 *Ibidem.*

334 *Prosecutor v. Jean de Dieu Kamuhanda*, Case No. ICTR-98-54A-T, T. 17 April 2001, p. 68 (Exh. D. 43).

335 T. 30 June 2005, pp. 30-32. According to Witness GIN, André Rwamakuba was "not very tall, he was fat but not very fat. He was not obese. As for his colour, he was somewhere between dark and light; fair skinned." The witness further added that he "was a well built man. He was stout".

336 Statement of 3 February 1998, Exh. D 35 (under seal).

337 Witness GIN made a statement to Prosecution on 3 February 1998 (Exh. D. 35); and interview reports were taken on 27 March 2002 (Exh. D. 36); 27 May 2003 (Exh. D. 37) and 13 February 2004 (Exh. D. 38).

338 See: Notice of Additional Evidence Pursuant to Rule 67(D), Exh. D 39 (under seal), p. 2.

339 T. 30 June 2005, pp. 32-33.

131. The witness' account of the event is also radically different from her prior statements made with the Prosecution and her testimony in the *Kamuhanda* case. In court, she testified that André Rwamakuba arrived at the Gikomero *secteur* office between 10 and 14 April 1994 and that three Tutsi people were killed on that occasion. She also testified that massacres took place at the Gikomero Protestant School between 8 and 12 April 1994. In 1998, however, the witness explicitly affirmed that the killing of the three people at Gikomero *secteur* office took place on 12 April 1994, a date on which according to the witness' statement, the killings had not yet started in the *commune*. In the same statement, she stated that Rwamakuba came to launch the beginning of the massacre in the *commune* and that as soon as he left, in the afternoon, Tutsi refugees were killed at the Gikomero Protestant School. In that statement, she asserted that she did not see him again after that massacre. In 2001 in the *Kamuhanda* case, the witness testified that the killings at the Protestant School were the first killings in the *secteur*. Later, in 2003, the witness stated that she did not see Rwamakuba exactly on 12 April 1994 but between 12 and 20 April 1994.[340] This declaration was amended again a year later when she stated that she saw him, after the killings at the Gikomero Protestant School between 6 and 20 April 1994.[341] In this case, GIN testified that Rwamakuba came with the crowd to the wooden area where the two young people were killed, but in 2003 she requested the investigator to amend her prior statement and indicated that the Accused did not follow the crowd to the wooded area but stayed by his car in front of the *secteur* office, from where he was able to see the killings. The witness also gave an inconsistent account of her whereabouts in April 1994. She admitted that she had gone to Kibobo with her sister in law to seek refuge, but she was uncertain on the dates.[342] This is a major matter of concern considering that Defence witnesses testified that GIN was not in Gikomero at the time of the alleged murders.[343] The Defence challenged GIN on her prior statements and testimonies. The Chamber found her answers to be inconsistent and unconvincing. **[page 53]**

132. These major inconsistencies between GIN's testimony and her prior statements cannot be explained by the time elapsed, translation discrepancies, the manner in which the statements were taken or the impact of trauma inflicted upon the witness. Neither can they be considered additional details provided to the witness' prior statements.

133. Several Defence witnesses also gave testimony to Witness GIN's personality. The Chamber has considered and weighed this information with great caution due to the personal relationship between GIN and some of the Defence witnesses. During the genocide, the witness lost her mother and one of her siblings.[344] According to Defence Witness 3/22 who has known GIN since she was very young, and Defence Witness 5/15, who also has a close relationship to GIN, she has been greatly affected by her experience in 1994 and had changed since then. Witness 3/22 described GIN as someone who is highly emotional, dishonest,[345] and not trustworthy.[346] Witness 7/14 submitted that GIN was plotting with other people to fabricate evidence against key figures of Gikomero.[347] Witness GIN's criminal record indicating a conviction in Rwanda for the murder of a colleague, was also raised by the Defence to undermine her credibility.[348]

134. Her credibility is further challenged by the admitted fact that on 11 April 1994 the Accused was in Kigali,[349] and the day after was moving from there to Gitarama.[350] The Indictment and the Prosecution evidence did not provide a chronological account of the Accused's alleged activities in Gikomero in April 1994. GIN's testimony seemed to require that the Accused made a separate or third trip to the area in addition to the alleged delivery of machetes to Muhire and Kamanzi.[351] The evidence adduced by the Defence

340 Interview Report of 27 May 2003 (Exh. D. 37).
341 Interview Report of 13 February 2004 (Exh. D. 38).
342 T. 1 July 2005, pp. 14-15.
343 See: Defence Witnesses 7/14 and 3/31 who personally knew GIN (T. 25 January 2006, p.22; T. 11 November 2005, p. 10).
344 T. 29 June 2005, p. 42.
345 T. 30 November 2005, p. 20.
346 See: Defence Witness 3/1 (T. 10 November 2005, pp. 9 and 29).
347 T. 25 January 2006, pp. 16-19; T. 03 February 2006, pp. 12-14 and 43.
348 Exh. D. 213 (under seal)
349 See: Prosecution Witness GLM; Prosecution Witness Des Forges; Prosecution Closing Brief, footnote 5; Defence Closing Brief.
350 Statement of Admissions by the Parties and Other Matters not in Dispute, filed on 3 June 2005; see also: Prosecution Witness GLM and Prosecution Expert Witness Des Forges.
351 See above, para. 85 and seq.

that travel between Kigali and Gikomero was difficult and hazardous at that time due to the presence of RPF troops reinforces the doubt on GIN's credibility.[352]

135. In view of the major inconsistencies in the witness' evidence, her particular personality and judicial record, the admitted presence of the Accused on other locations at the **[page 54]** time of the alleged event, the potential hazards of access to the commune at the time of the event, Witness GIN cannot be found credible. Since no other evidence has been adduced to establish the allegation in the Indictment, the Chamber finds that the Prosecution failed to prove beyond reasonable doubt André Rwamakuba's involvement in the killings of three Tutsi people in Gikomero *commune* between 10 and 20 April 1994.

II.1.4. Alleged Participation of André Rwamakuba to the Massacre at Kayanga Health Centre

136. The Prosecution alleges at paragraph 13 of the Indictment that

> Between 13 and 15 April 1994, in the morning, **André RWAMAKUBA,** accompanied by local authorities, including Mathias RUBANGUKA, accountant of the *commune*, Callixte KABARERA, Inspector of Schools, Brigadier NYARWAYA, RUTAGANIRA, *bourgmestre* of Gikomero *commune*, Thomas MABANGO, *conseiller* of Kanyanga [sic],[353] and soldiers and *Interahamwe* militiamen, arrived at the Kayanga Health Center in Kayanga *secteur*, where many Tutsi fleeing the massacres that had started in their *secteurs* had sought refuge. At a man unknown but identified as the deputy director's request, they assembled in the courtyard of the Health Centre [sic][354]. Upon his arrival, **André RWAMAKUBA** stated that the killings had started everywhere else and that he realized that nothing had been done at the Health Centre. The ***Accused***, stating that he was showing the example, then brandished a firearm, signaling the start of the massacres to soldiers and *Interahamwe* who began, in his presence, to attack and kill the Tutsi with firearms, machetes and clubs. Shortly after the beginning of the killings, while it was raining, **André RWAMAKUBA**, referring to the bodies of Tutsi, demanded that such filth be cleared. The ***Accused*** witnessed the killings until he left the Health Centre, while the soldiers and *Interahamwe* continued the killings for several hours. No one survived the massacre in which about a hundred people are alleged to have died. The bodies of the victims were thrown into a mass grave. These victims were mostly in-patients and Tutsi refugees fleeing the killings in the neighbouring *secteurs*, notably the killings in the Parishes of Gikomero and Gicaca.

(1) Evidence Adduced

137. Kayanga Health Centre is located in Kayanga *secteur*,Gikomero *commune*, which is approximately 80 kilometres from Gitarama where André Rwamakuba resided at the time of the event.[355]

138. There is no dispute in the present case that there were killings at Kayanga Health Centre in April 1994 and that the victims were murdered solely because they were Tutsi.[356] **[page 55]** Both parties adduced evidence on this event. The alleged participation of the Accused, however, is disputed.

139. Five Prosecution witnesses gave evidence on this massacre,[357] including Witness GAB who said that he was the sole survivor and eyewitness of the event.[358] On 13 April 1994, after the massacres had started in his *secteur*, Prosecution Witness GAB began to flee.[359] He testified that he arrived at Kayanga Health Centre between 13 and 15 April 1994.[360] He spent the night in the courtyard between the rooms, the open space at the Centre.[361] The morning after his arrival, around 8.00 a.m., the Deputy Director of the Centre, Etienne Kamanzi, arrived with *Interahamwe*. The witness and the people who were in the wards as well as refugees

352 See above, paras.100 and 102.

353 The French version of the Indictment, which is the original language, reads as follows: "Kayanga".

354 The French version of the Indictment reads as follows: "Ils étaient, à la demande d'un homme inconnu, mais identifié comme étant le Directeur-adjoint, rassemblés dans la cour du Centre."

355 See: Exh. P. 2: the distance between Kigali and Kayanga is approximately 30 kilometres; and Gitarama is 53 kilometres southwest from Kigali.

356 Defence Closing Brief, p. 167, para. 6; See: Prosecution Witnesses ALA, AVC, GAC, GIN and GAB; Defence Witnesses 3/1, 7/14, 6/10, 7/18.

357 Witnesses ALA, AVC, GAB, GAC and GIN.

358 T. 5 July 2005, p. 35; see also: Prosecution Closing Brief, para. 62.

359 T. 5 July 2005, p. 22.

360 T. 6 July 2006, p. 8.

361 T. 6 July 2006, p. 7.

were taken out with the Tutsis and collected in the big courtyard in front of the Centre.[362] They were told to sit down and not to move. Around 10.00 a.m., four vehicles arrived, including a military truck. The witness saw the Accused, *Bourgmestre* Rutaganira, the *brigadier* Nyarwaya, the accountant and the school inspector.[363] When he saw them, the witness hid in a nearby sorghum field near the Centre.[364] From that place, he heard Rwamakuba say "[e]verywhere I have been, they have began to work - and "work" meant to kill – so what are you waiting for?"[365] The *brigadier* Nyarwaya replied that they did not start to kill because they did not have enough materials for the task.[366] The witness then saw Rwamakuba take out a pistol, wave it in the air, and say "Here is the pistol; the Interahamwe are present. The material is available; I don't see why you continue to raise that question while everything is ready."[367] After that, many people, mostly Tutsi, were shot or attacked with machetes, clubs and bludgeons.[368] The witness also heard the Accused stating that the Tutsis should be killed "so that in [the] future, a Hutu who is born asks what a Tutsi look[ed] like".[369] Rwamakuba allegedly left with the other vehicles in the direction of Gikomero, around midday when people had already been killed.[370] After his departure, the *Interahamwe* **[page 56]** and the soldiers went on killing, until everybody was killed.[371] According to GAB, around one hundred persons died in this massacre.[372]

140. Prosecution Witness GIN testified that "about four or five days" after the killing of the three young people in Gikomero centre between 10 and 14 April 1994,[373] she saw André Rwamakuba arrive at the trading centre in a white station wagon.[374] He stopped for a few minutes and spoke to some inhabitants from his vehicle. Some of the people who were present at that time included one person named Callixte, Twagirayezu, Drocella Mukayiranga, Ngiruwosanga, Mirumbi, a policeman by the name of Ngarambe, Gihanga and Gatinseyi.[375] Then, Rwamakuba allegedly went on his way towards Kayanga.[376] Later, two vehicles, with Mathias Rubanguka,[377] Nzaramba, and the *brigadier* Nyarwaya aboard, came to collect *Interahamwe* as well as *communal* policemen. They were carrying firearms, guns and grenades.[378] One of the vehicles stopped in front of GIN's house and the other stopped in front of Karekezi's house.[379] GIN's husband, *Interahamwe* and other people got into the vehicles and went off together to Kayanga. When GIN's husband came back from Kayanga, he told her that he had found Rwamakuba in the company of the person in charge of the Kayanga Health Centre, Kamanzi. He also told GIN that Rwamakuba ordered the massacre of the Tutsi people, that the massacre actually began and then Rwamakuba left Kayanga Health Centre.[380]

141. Prosecution Witnesses ALA and AVC were told that attacks against Tutsi people took place at Kayanga Health Centre.[381] ALA specified that the attack claimed about a hundred victims.[382] AVC said that this happened some time between May and June 1994.[383] He was told that people were killed there, including four of his brothers and other people who had sought refuge at Kayanga Health Centre.[384] Witness GAC testified that Tutsi patients of Kayanga Health Centre were killed after 13 April 1994 and until the end of the week by

362 T. 6 July 2005, p. 7.
363 T. 5 July 2005, p. 24.
364 T. 5 July 2005, p. 24.
365 T. 5 July 2005, p. 25.
366 T. 5 July 2005, p. 26.
367 T. 5 July 2005, p. 26.
368 T. 5 July 2005, p. 26.
369 T. 5 July 2005, p. 26.
370 T. 5 July 2005, p. 27.
371 T. 5 July 2005, p. 27.
372 T. 5 July 2005, p. 28.
373 See above
374 T. 29 June 2005, p. 21.
375 T. 29 June 2005, p. 21.
376 T. 29 June 2005, p. 22.
377 T. 29 June 2005, p. 22. The Chamber notes an interpretation discrepancy between the French ("Rubanguka") and English transcript ("Rubaruka").
378 T. 29 June 2005, p. 23.
379 T. 29 June 2005, p. 23.
380 T. 29 June 2005, p. 25.
381 T. 14 June 2005, p. 53 (Witness ALA); T. 27 June 2005, p.67 (Witness AVC).
382 T. 14 June 2005, p. 53.
383 T. 27 June 2005, p 19.
384 T. 27 June 2005, p 18.

the **[page 57]** *Interhamwe* from Gasabo.[385] He did not specify whether he was present at the time of the event.

142. Defence Witnesses 6/10, 7/18 and 7/3 testified that they were survivors of the Kayanga Health Centre massacre that, according to them, took place on 15 April 1994 and was led by the *brigadier* Nyarwaya.[386]

(2) Assessment of the Evidence

143. In the Chamber's view, the Prosecution's evidence is inconsistent with the allegation set forth in the Indictment **(2.1.)** and suffers major challenges as far as the witness' credibility is concerned **(2.2.)**.

(2.1.) Lack of Consistency between the Indictment and the Prosecution Evidence

144. Witnesses ALA, AVC and GAC did not provide any evidence on the presence of the Accused at the Kayanga Health Centre massacre in April 1994. ALA and AVC gave hearsay evidence, and AVC's testimony that the massacre took place between May and June 1994 contradicts the other evidence adduced by both parties and does not support the charges against the Accused which place this event between 13 and 15 April 1994.

(2.2.) Credibility Issues

145. The Chamber has already found that Witness GIN was not a credible witness as far as her evidence concerned the alleged participation of the Accused in the murder of three Tutsi near the Gikomero *secteur* office.[387] For the present event, she provided hearsay evidence from her deceased husband. It is noteworthy that she mentioned the Kayanga Health Centre massacre of April 1994 and André Rwamakuba's participation in the massacre for the first time in April 2004,[388] in her fifth meeting with the Prosecution.[389] In particular, in her first statement dated 3 February 1998,[390] she asserted that she had not seen Rwamakuba after the **[page 58]** killing of the three people at the Gikomero *secteur* office.[391] Such a major inconsistency seriously undermines GIN's credibility regarding her evidence of Rwamakuba's participation to the Kayanga Health Centre massacre.

146. Witness GAB is the only one who claims to be an eyewitness of the event. As already noted,[392] this Chamber is not bound by the prior finding made by the Trial Chamber in the *Kamuhanda* case where the witness was found not credible. However, after reviewing and assessing the evidence as a whole, this Chamber finds that there are serious doubts as to GAB's credibility in the present case.

147. The Chamber has already found that the identification of the Accused by the witness raises serious concerns.[393] In addition, his testimony contains several irreconcilable inconsistencies between his prior statement to the Prosecution, his testimony in the *Kamuhanda* case,[394] and also within his own testimony given in court.

148. GAB first testified that he arrived at Kayanga Health Centre in the night of 13 April 1994.[395] During cross-examination, however, he claimed that he did not give the exact date of his arrival at the Centre, but

385 T. 4 July 2005, pp. 18-19.

386 T. 19 January 2006, p. 14. Defence Witness 9/20 also learnt that people were killed at the Kayanga Health Centre on 15 April 1994.

387 See above.

388 Notice of Additional Evidence pursuant to Rule 67(D), filed on 23 April 2004, Exh. D. 39.

389 Witness GIN made statements to Prosecution on 3 February 1998 (Exh. D. 35); and interview reports were taken on 27 March 2002 (Exh. D. 36); 27 May 2003 (Exh. D. 37) and 13 February 2004 (Exh. D. 38).

390 Exh. D 35.

391 Exh. D. 35 to 38.

392 See above: Alleged Public Instigation in Gikomero from July 1993 through June 1994.

393 See above: Alleged Public Instigation in Gikomero from July 1993 through June 1994.

394 Exh. D. 33 A and B.

395 T. 6 July 2005, p.23.

that he arrived between 13 and 15 April 1994.[396] In his statement of 4 November 2004, which was read into the record by the Defence Counsel, the witness provided a more specific date: he stated that he started fleeing on the night of 13 April 1994 towards Kayanga Health Centre, where he arrived in the morning.[397] A mere comparison of the witness' testimony and his prior statements shows other inconsistencies. In his 2004 statement, it is said that after 8.00 a.m., he, along with the other people at the Centre, was instructed to stay in the Centre's courtyard, and that prior to Rwamakuba's arrival, he lagged behind the rest of the people by creeping and was able to reach the rear of the building where he hid in an adjoining sorghum farm. In court, however, GAB testified that he hid *after* Rwamakuba's arrival at the Centre around 10.00 a.m. In his statement of 1999, which was read into the record by the Defence Counsel, the witness stated that a week after 13 April 1994, the RPF soldiers "*arrived and assembled and took [them]* to Rutare".[398] The witness gave a different account of this fact in court: he testified that he *went* to Rutare the night he left the Centre after hiding in the sorghum field, since Rutare was a secure place occupied by **[page 59]** RPF.[399] This account also differs from GAB's evidence in the *Kamuhanda* case, where he said that he was moving from one hiding place to another, and around 15 April 1994, he surrendered to the attackers.[400]

149. Such inconsistencies in the chronology of facts cannot be explained by the time elapsed, translation discrepancies or considered as additional information provided by the witness. On the contrary, they directly challenge the truthfulness of his account. This challenge is reinforced by the disturbing similarities between GAB's testimony in this case and in the *Kamuhanda* case. In this trial, the witness described André Rwamakuba's behaviour and the account of the events in the same way as he described Kamuhanda's criminal acts when testifying as Prosecution witness in that case; he also attributed much of the same words to Kamuhanda and Rwamakuba.[401] GAB explained in court that he was not able to recall the contents or the purport of his evidence in the *Kamuhanda* trial,[402] and further submitted that Kamuhanda and Rwamakuba used almost the same words because these were statements that held the same logic.[403]

150. This explanation is not persuasive, especially since the witness only mentioned André Rwamakuba's name for the first time in November 2004 after making a statement to the Prosecution in 1999 and testifying in the *Kamuhanda* case in 2001. He explained his failure to mention Rwamakuba's name at an earlier time by stating he was not previously questioned about the Accused. Although this is a fairly common explanation provided by both Prosecution and Defence Witnesses, this is not a satisfactory explanation considering the fact that the Kayanga Health Centre massacre is the only one that Witness GAB allegedly witnessed. The witness' obvious reluctance to answer questions from the Defence,[404] **[page 60]** particularly in relation to his testimony in the *Kamuhanda* case, further contributes to challenge his overall credibility.[405]

151. The Defence's evidence reinforces the Chamber's doubt on the Prosecution's case. The Prosecution did not provide a chronology of Rwamakuba's movement to and from Gikomero area over the five days-

396 T. 5 July 2005, p. 52; T. 6 July 2005, p. 5.

397 T. 6 July 2005, p. 3.

398 Statement of 24 June 1999, p. 4.

399 T. 5 July 2005, p. 27.

400 T. 6 July 2005, p.17.

401 In the *Kamuhanda* case, Witness GAB said that when Jean de Dieu Kamuhanda arrived on 12 April, he said: "Everywhere I went, even in Kigali, the *Interahamwe* and CDR have been killing people. What are you doing?" Nyarwaya and Rubanguka who were present, then said: "What we are doing at this time is detailing them and when we get the necessary instruments to accomplish our task, we shall accomplish our task." (see Extract read by the Defence, T. 6 July 2005, p. 13).

149. In the present trial, Witness GAB testified that André Rwamakuba said: "Everywhere I have been, they have began to work – and "work" meant to kill – so what are you waiting for?" Then, the Brigadier Nyarwaya took the floor and replied that they did not start to kill because they had not material enough for the task. Then the witness saw Rwamakuba taking out a pistol, waving it in the air, and saying that "Here is the pistol; the *Interahamwe* are present. The material is available; I don't see why you continue to raise that question while everything is ready." (T. 5 July 2005, pp. 25-26).

402 T. 6 July 2005, p. 13.

403 T. 6 July 2005, p. 23.

404 See for e.g.: about the distances between his house and the field, between his place and the Kayanga Health Centre (T. 5 July 2005, pp. 3-4); between the sorghum field and the Centre when he was hiding (T. 6 July 2005, p. 12); whether the date 13 April has been chosen for the reburial ceremony in 2004 because it was the date of the massacres (T. 6 July 2005, p. 14-15); about the exact date when the witness reached the RPF secured zones (T. 6 July 2005, p.15); about the details of the stone laying ceremony at the Rutunga School (T. 5 July 2005, pp. 41-42).

405 See for e.g.: T. 5 July 2005, pp. 47-50.

period, during which it is alleged that he delivered machetes at two different locations, ordered the killing of three Tutsi people and went to Kayanga Health Centre. The parties agreed that after 12 April 1994, the Accused moved to Gitarama with his family, along with the Interim Government.[406] The present allegation would therefore have required that the Accused made a fourth trip there. Such theory was seriously challenged by the Defence evidence on the hazardousness and difficulties to move from and to Gikomero *commune* after 7 April 1994.[407] There were also testimonies that the Accused never went to Kayanga Health Centre during the massacre. Defence Witnesses 6/10 and 7/18 testified that they were present at Kayanga Health Centre on 15 April 1994 when the massacres against the Tutsi took place. While they were hiding in a room in the maternity ward of the Centre,[408] they saw refugees dragged out, beaten up, taken out of the Centre and finished off by the *brigadier* Nyarwaya, who was with Mathias Rubanguka, the *communal* policeman Kayibanda, and other *Interahamwe*.[409] Both witnesses knew Rwamakuba very well. Witness 6/10 denied any Rwamakuba's involvement in the 1994 killings in Gikomero *commune* and Witness 7/18 stated that the Accused never came to Gikomero during the genocide.[410] Defence Witness 7/3 who admitted to having played a direct role in the killings which took place at Kayanga Health Centre on 15 April 1994 and claimed to know Rwamakuba very well,[411] also testified that the attack was led by the *brigadier* Nyarwaya in the company of policemen. He asserted that Rwamakuba was not involved in these killings.[412] Defence Witness 3/1 was told that patients were killed at Kayanga Health Centre and that the *brigadier communal* and communal officers were the ones responsible. She asserted that no one ever **[page 61]** mentioned Rwamakuba as playing a part in the killings at Kayanga Health Centre[413] Defence Witness 7/14, who knew Witness GIN very well, stated that GIN's husband stayed in Gikomero and never went to Kayanga Health Centre.[414] Due to their individual circumstances, the evidence of Defence Witnesses 6/10, 7/18, 7/3 and 7/14 was assessed with great caution.[415] The Chamber, however, found their accounts consistent and objective enough to challenge the Prosecution's evidence.

152. In the Chamber's view, the major inconsistencies in Prosecution Witnesses GAB and GIN testimonies cast serious doubt on their credibility. This doubt is supported by the Defence evidence on the improbable presence of the Accused at the scene of the crimes. In addition to testimonies on the potential hazards of road access to Gikomero *commune* in April 1994, there was detailed and consistent evidence from other witnesses which identified the *brigadier communal* Nyarwaya and other communal officers as the leaders of this massacre. They denied Rwamakuba's involvement. The other Prosecution witnesses who mentioned Kayanga Health Centre massacre in their testimonies never spoke of Rwamakuba as playing a role in it. Considering the evidence as a whole, the Chamber finds that the allegations of the Accused's participation in the massacre at Kayanga Health Centre in April 1994 have not been proved beyond reasonable doubt.

Conclusion on the Alleged Criminal Acts Committed by André Rwamakuba in Gikomero Commune

153. The Chamber first notes that there was no evidence adduced on certain allegations concerning the events in Gikomero *commune* and that some of the Prosecution witnesses' testimonies were inconsistent with the Indictment. Specifically, no evidence was given about the alleged meetings or public instigations in which André Rwamakuba allegedly participated in Gikomero, Rutunga, Gasabo and Gicaca *secteurs* or in Rutungo, Rubungo and Kanombe *communes*. There was also no evidence on the various statements made by Rwamakuba at various meetings and gatherings in Gikomero *commune* between March and June 1994. **[page 62]**

406 Prosecution Closing Brief, para. 68; Defence Closing Brief.

407 See paras. 100 and 102.

408 T. 24 November 2005, p. 2.

409 T. 24 November 2005, pp. 3 and 35; T. 30 November 2005, pp. 55 and 57. According to Witness 7/18, one of the victims was called Rutembesa.

410 T. 24 November 2005, p. 7; T. 1 December 2005, p. 33.

411 T. 19 January 2006, p. 33. Defence Witness 7/3 claimed that he knew Rwamakuba very well as he hailed from their *commune* and was an intellectual present at *communal* meetings.

412 T. 19 January 2006, pp. 8-10 and 18-19.

413 T. 10 November 2005, p. 9.

414 T. 25 January 2006, p. 16.

415 Defence Witnesses 6/10 and 7/18 seemed close to André Rwamakuba's family; they are moreover relatives. Defence Witness 7/14 was Prosecution Witness GIN's relative and Defence Witness 7/3 has a criminal record related to the 1994 genocide.

154. Then, the Prosecution evidence on the sensitization campaigns allegedly conducted by the Accused in Gikomero *commune* between 1992 and March 1994 was unreliable in many instances, including the Prosecution witnesses' identification of Rwamakuba at the time and place of the events. This conclusion is supported by the Defence evidence indicating that the Accused participated in two events in his capacity as a doctor during the time in question. A reasonable probability has been shown that between 23 September 1993 and 10 March 1994, Rwamakuba attended a training course at the Institute of Tropical Medicine in Antwerp, Belgium, and that between 17 and 29 March 1994, he attended an international colloquium organized by the WHO in Egypt. The Chamber therefore finds that the Prosecution failed to prove beyond reasonable doubt the allegations set forth in paragraphs 3 to 5 of the Indictment.

155. Both parties adduced evidence that attacks and massacres took place against Tutsi in Gikomero *commune* in April 1994, including in Ndatemwa Trading Centre, at Gikomero Protestant School, Gishaka Parish and Kayanga Health Centre. The Prosecution called six witnesses to support its allegations that during a period of five days between 10 and 15 April 1994, André Rwamakuba went to four different locations in Gikomero *commune* to deliver machetes that were to be used in killings against the Tutsi, to encourage and give instructions to kill Tutsi, and to launch the beginning of the attacks against Tutsi in the *commune*.

156. The Prosecution witnesses' testimonies were tainted of major deficiencies which could not be justified by the time elapsed, translation discrepancies, the manner in which the prior statements were taken or the impact of trauma inflicted upon the witnesses. In the Chamber's view, these inconsistencies undermined the witnesses' credibility or reliability. Furthermore, the Defence disputed that the Accused could have been present in Gikomero *commune* at the time of the alleged event. The parties agreed and the Chamber accepted that André Rwamakuba was sworn in as a Minister of the Interim Government on 9 April 1994, attended a governmental meeting held in Kigali at the *Hotel des Diplomates* on 11 April 1994,[416] and was living in Kigali until 12 April 1994 when he went to Gitarama with the convoy of the Interim Government.[417] The admission of these facts had a major impact on the Prosecution's case since the Defence challenged the accessibilities from and to Gikomero *commune* in April 1994. The Prosecution did not provide a chronological account of the Accused's alleged activities in Gikomero in April 1994, and seemed to suggest that on each event alleged, the Accused commuted between Kigali or Gitarama and the various locations in Gikomero **[page 63]** *commune*.[418] There was, however, reliable evidence on the potential hazards to travel to and from Gikomero *commune* after 7 April 1994. Reliable testimonies were also given that Rwamakuba's name was not mentioned before Rwandan local courts in relation to the crimes committed in Gikomero *commune* in April 1994 and that he was not present at the scene of the crimes. This evidence, however, was not satisfactorily rebutted by the Prosecution.

157. The absence of any reliable identification of André Rwamakuba at the time and location of the alleged events, the lack of credibility or reliability of the Prosecution witnesses, the admitted facts that the Accused participated in other activities during the period alleged in the Indictment, the potential hazards of travel to the locations of the alleged crimes, cumulatively contribute to raise a reasonable doubt on the Prosecution's case.

158. The Chamber therefore finds that the Prosecution failed to prove at all or beyond reasonable doubt the charges against the Accused in Gikomero *commune* as pleaded at paragraphs 3 to 5, 10 to 13, 23 and 26 of the Indictment. The Chamber will now address André Rwamakuba's alleged participation in the killings at Butare University Hospital in April 1994.

II.2. Alleged Participation of André Rwamakuba to killings at Butare University Hospital in April 1994

159. Butare University Hospital is located in Butare town, Butare *préfecture*, approximately 136 kilometres from Kigali in south west Rwanda.[419] The Hospital has barely changed since the events of April 1994.[420] The

416 These are facts not disputed by the parties. See Prosecution Closing Brief, para. 68; Defence Closing Brief.

417 *Ibidem*.

418 See the Indictment, the Prosecution Pre-Trial Brief, the Opening Statement and the Prosecution Closing Brief.

419 See: Exh. P. 2.

420 See: Exh. P. 2; Defence Closing Brief, p. 282.

site is not very large and is composed of six main buildings.[421] During the trial, various pictures and sketches of the Hospital were admitted into evidence and the Chamber visited the building premises with the parties on 15 January 2005.[422]

160. At paragraphs 15 and 16 of the Indictment, the Prosecution alleges that

> 15. Between 18 and 25 April 1994, at Butare University Hospital, **André RWAMAKUBA**, along with Dr. Geoffroy Gatera, soldiers, militiamen and armed civilians, ordered, instigated, committed, or otherwise aided and abetted killings of Tutsi patients and displaced persons seeking refuge at Butare University Hospital with intent to destroy, in whole or in part, the **[page 64]** Tutsi ethnic group. Thus, during an official delegation's visit to the Hospital, he asked a woman unknown but identified as the head of Doctors Without Borders not to treat Tutsi casualties, to get rid of them and not to admit any others. During the above-mentioned period, **André RWAMAKUBA,** armed with a small axe hung on his belt, and often accompanied by Dr. Gatera, armed soldiers, *Interahamwe* militiamen and civilians armed with machetes, axes and clubs, went around the hospital wards checking identity cards and identifying Tutsi refugees and patients, selecting them and putting them on board a vehicle manned by *Interahamwe* armed with clubs and machetes. The persons taken away were never seen again. During this period, in the morning or afternoon, during his rounds, **André RWAMAKUBA** regularly removed drips from patients, in particular, in a ward where sick women were admitted.
>
> 16. Concurrently with the events related above, **André RWAMAKUBA** directly caused the death of several persons identified as Tutsi. Thus, during his ward rounds, he caused the death of an unknown Tutsi patient by wounding him in the head with an axe. The militiamen subsequently took away the body of that person. Five of the patients referred to above as having been in the in-patients ward, and who were identified as Tutsi, died from axe wounds inflicted by **André RWAMAKUBA.** The ***Accused*** wounded Tutsi found in the corridors of the Hospital by striking them on the head with an axe. Some of them, including the persons called Rukara and Mutabazi, who suffered serious bodily harm caused by **André RWAMAKUBA**, were subsequently finished off by *Interahamwe*. As a result of such orders and instigation by the ***Accused***, many Tutsi refugees and patients were massacred in Butare University Hospital. The victims included the persons known as Déogène, Placide and the parents of several survivors of the killings. The bodies of hundreds of victims of the massacres organized by **André RWAMAKUBA** at Butare University Hospital were gathered and buried in mass graves located behind the Hospital.

161. The Chamber will first provide a brief and general description of the evidence adduced on the Butare University Hospital massacre in April 1994 and the alleged involvement of the Accused **(II.2.1.)**. The content of the evidence will then be more detailed in the second section when discussing the credibility and reliability of the witnesses **(II.2.2)**.

II.2.1. Evidence Adduced

162. The existence of a massacre against Tutsi at Butare University Hospital in April 1994 was not a contentious matter and both parties adduced evidence on that event. The Defence, however, disputed any involvement of the Accused therein.

163. The Prosecution called six witnesses who asserted their presence at Butare University Hospital at the same time as André Rwamakuba allegedly committed the crimes outlined in the Indictment. Prosecution Witnesses ALV, ALW, GIO, HF and RJ placed the events on different dates between 21 and 25 April 1994, and Prosecution Witness XV, the only one who claimed to know Rwamakuba personally, testified that they took place in May 1994. The Prosecution witnesses generally stated that Rwamakuba came to Butare University Hospital at various times, during which he conducted the identification and injured some of the Tutsi **[page 65]** patients with an axe, removed drips from Tutsi patients, which killed some of them, and gave orders to *Interahamwe* and soldiers to kill or take away to kill Tutsi patients in a pick-up truck. The witnesses specified that during those events, Rwamakuba was often in the company of Doctors Gatera, Twagirayezu and Jotham. In addition, Prosecution Witness XV testified that Rwamakuba took part in a government meeting at the Hospital on 15 May 1994, which was to assess whether the killings were being satisfactorily conducted in Butare. Prosecution expert witness Alison Des Forges also testified to reports of a massacre of

---

421 Archives building, Clinic and ORL/ENT, Surgery, Paediatrics, Hospitalization and Maternity wards; see: Exh. P. 2 and D. 48.

422 See: Exh. P. 2, P. 33, D. 48, D. 53, D. 78, D. 105, D. 106, D. 112 and D. 124; and Minutes for the Site Visit to Rwanda in the *Rwamakuba* case, 13-16 January 2005 (Annex B).

about 170 patients and staff members at Butare University Hospital on 24 April 1994.[423] She did not give evidence on the presence of the Accused at the Hospital during the massacre, but commented on an extract from a Radio Rwanda news broadcast which said that "Doctor Rwamakuba refuse[d] the information that was being broadcast by a foreign radio station, talking about the massacres of 200 people by members of the national army who might have found the victims in the Butare Hospital".[424]

164. The Defence called six witnesses to testify on the same event. They confirmed that there were attacks on patients and meetings at Butare University Hospital,[425] and that criminal acts took place under the supervision of military and armed civilians or militiamen. They denied André Rwamakuba's presence or involvement in those acts.

II.2.2. Assessment of the Evidence

165. After reviewing the evidence adduced as a whole, the Chamber is of the view that the Prosecution evidence is inconsistent with some of the allegations against the Accused **(1)**. The identification of André Rwamakuba at the time and place of the alleged event also raises serious doubt **(2)** and the internal discrepancies in the Prosecution witnesses' testimonies, notably when considering their prior statements and testimonies in Rwandan proceedings, cast doubt on their credibility and reliability **(3)**. The Defence evidence supports this conclusion since it tends to show that Rwamakuba was not present at the scene of the crimes **(4)**.

(1) Lack of Consistency between the Indictment and the Prosecution Evidence

166. None of the Prosecution witnesses testified, as alleged at paragraph 15 of the Indictment, that "during an official delegation's visit to the Hospital, [Rwamakuba] asked a **[page 66]** woman unknown but identified as the head of Doctors Without Borders not to treat Tutsi casualties, to get rid of them and not to admit others". No evidence either was adduced on the allegation at paragraph 16 of the Indictment that persons known as Rukara, Déogène, Placide were massacred in the Butare University Hospital.

167. Since Witness XV asserted that André Rwamakuba committed crimes at Butare University Hospital in May 1994, his testimony cannot support the allegation in the Indictment that these offences took place between 18 and 25 April 1994.[426]

168. This witness also testified that André Rwamakuba attended a government meeting at the Hospital on 15 May 1994.[427] While paragraph 18 of the Indictment does plead a meeting held by the Prime Minister Kambanda at the Faculty of Medicine of the Hospital on that day, it does not allege the presence of the Accused.[428]

(2) Identification of André Rwamakuba

169. **Witness XV** was the only witness to the Butare University Hospital events who claimed prior knowledge of André Rwamakuba. In the Chamber's view, the witness gave an unsatisfactory account of when he actually met him. The witness allegedly knew Rwamakuba when the latter attended the Faculty of Medicine at Butare "from 1974 until he went to do his internship that concluded his studies".[429] He said that doctors studied for six years and then the seventh year was devoted to an internship. When Rwamakuba began his internship, Witness XV had not yet began to work at the Hospital but was at the University. He declared that he lived near the Hospital and used to go to the students' residence to do their washing or to sell

423 T. 14 July 2005, pp.70-71.

424 T. 14 July 2005, pp. 72-73.

425 See: Witnesses 5/7, 5/13, 5/15, 5/16, 9/17 and 9/29.

426 Indictment, para. 15-16; Prosecution Pre-Trial Brief, paras. 30-38; Opening Statement, T. 9 June 2005, p. 10.

427 T. 30 August 2005, pp. 52-54

428 Indictment, para. 18: "Massacres of Tutsi at Butare University Hospital continued and intensified through late May 1994, particularly after a meeting, held at the Faculty of Medicine on or about 15 May 1994, where Prime Minister Jean Kambanda addressed university authorities, encouraging them to "continue the fight until ultimate victory".

429 T. 30 August 2005, p. 25. In his will-say statement dated 6 August 2005, XV also stated that he remembered André Rwamakuba from a strike at the University in around 1974 (Exh. D. 121 A and B, under seal).

cigarettes.[430] He allegedly saw Rwamakuba more than ten times over a period of one or two years, but never actually spoke to him. The witness said that Rwamakuba was already doing his internship when he, himself, started to work at the Hospital in 1981. Witness XV also testified that around 1973 or 1974, he saw Rwamakuba at the University, actively participating in unrest where Tutsi were chased away from the University.[431] The witness saw **[page 67]** Rwamakuba on two additional occasions before April 1994: towards the end of 1993 in a dancing bar in Butare, and in January 1994 during a rally organized at the Huye stadium.[432]

170. Witness XV testified to two occasions when he saw André Rwamakuba during the genocide. The first time was at a meeting of Government Ministers at the Faculty of Medicine at Butare University Hospital, and the second was at the maternity ward when Rwamakuba was giving instructions to some *Interahamwe* to get Tutsi people into the pick-up truck in order for them to be killed.[433] He claimed that, on that occasion, he was also put into the pick-up truck but was able to escape and went into hiding at the Hospital until he left on 6 June.[434] The witness asserted, on one hand, that he arrived at Butare University Hospital between 21 and 22 April 1994[435] and that the incident with the pick-up truck occurred two weeks after his arrival at the Hospital;[436] on the other hand, he testified that the meeting of Government Ministers was on 15 May 1994.[437] The witness' chronological account of the facts is mistaken and therefore unreliable because two weeks after 21 or 22 April – the alleged second occasion he saw Rwamakuba – would fall before 15 May 1994 – the alleged first occasion he saw the Accused.

171. Witness XV' identification of André Rwamakuba is contradicted by admitted facts and reliable Defence evidence. The parties agreed and the Chamber accepts that the Accused studied in Belgium between 1970 and 1974 and in Butare between 1975 and 1978.[438] Contrary to XV's assertion, Rwamakuba was not a student at the Faculty of Medicine of Butare University either before 1975 or after 1979. Further, the Chamber has already found that the Defence's evidence raised serious doubt that the Accused was in Rwanda between 23 September 1993 and 10 March 1994.[439] XV, therefore, could not have reasonably seen him chasing Tutsi students in 1973 or 1974, nor doing his internship after 1980, in a bar at the end of 1993 or at a meeting in Rwanda in the beginning of January 1994.

172. Witness XV's testimony in court was furthermore inconsistent with testimonies in other cases and prior statements. The witness testified in three cases in Rwanda between 1997 and 1999 where he never mentioned Rwamakuba's name. He was also interviewed by the **[page 68]** Prosecution nine times between 1997 and 2005.[440] In his first statement in November 1997, XV gave a detailed statement about the events he witnessed at Butare University Hospital in 1994. In that statement, he referred to a man named Rwamakuba who was an *Interahamwe* leader, a native of Huye *commune* and who had also been a second lieutenant during the Kayibanda regime.[441] The description of that man was inconsistent with the Accused André

---

430 T. 30 August 2005, pp. 25-26. The Witness however did not do washing for Rwamakuba.

431 T. 30 August 2005, p. 28.

432 T. 30 August 2005, pp. 28, 30, 35 and 36.

433 T. 30 August 2005, p. 36.

434 T. 30 August 2005, pp. 36 and 64.

435 T. 31 August 2005, p. 6.

436 T. 30 August 2005, p. 39.

437 T. 30 August 2005, p. 52.

438 Curriculum vitae of André Rwamakuba (Exh. D. 184) and Prosecution Closing Brief at para. 6, footnote 3: "The Prosecutor does not dispute the periods and the studies undertaken by the Accused."

439 See above at para. 70 and seq.

440 See: Statement of 25 November 1997, Exh. D. 113 A and B (under seal); 7 December 2000, Exh. D. 114 A and B (under seal); 22 February 2001, Exh. D. 115 A and B (under seal); 19 April 2001, Exh. D. 116 A and B (under seal); 5 June 2001, Exh. D. 117 A and B (under seal); 28 June 2001, Exh. D. 118 A and B (under seal); 5 December 2001, Exh. D. 119 A and B (under seal). All these statements were signed by the witness. See also: "Witness Confirmation", 8 July 2003, Exh. D. 120 A and B (under seal); Will-Say Statement, 26 August 2005, Exh. D. 121 A and B (under seal). These documents were not signed by the witness but, following the usual practice, drafted by Prosecution's representative.

441 In his statement dated 25 November 1997 (Ex. D. 113), XV stated: "I also recall a man named *Rwamakuba* coming to the university hospital from Sovu hospital in an ambulance which he had requisitioned to transport *Interahamwe*. I no longer recall the date. He was dressed in civilian clothing and the *Interahamwe* accompanying him were armed with hoes and clubs. I recognized him because he was a native of Huye *commune*. He was a second lieutenant during the Kayibanda regime and a driver for a DGB project until the war broke out. He was a member of MDR Power and was very active in the meetings. He had even become the *Interahamwe* leader when the war started." (para. 9, emphasis added).

Rwamakuba. In 2003, after six more signed statements which have no mention of Rwamakuba, in an interview to confirm his statements before his testimony in the first trial in this case, the witness specified that the mention of man named Rwamakuba in his 1997 statement was a mistake and that the right person was a man named Nkiramakuba. He then referred to meeting Rwamakuba as a student at Butare University in 1982, and to the meeting of Government Ministers of 15 May 1994, but he did not refer to the incident with the red pick-up truck nor did he specify that he had been a victim of Rwamakuba's actions. There was no mention of the attempted abduction which was meant to lead to his death, as he testified in court. This traumatic event was mentioned to the Prosecution for the first time, less than one week before XV gave evidence in this trial.[442] In court, the witness corrected himself again and stated that the man mentioned in his 1997 statement was actually Emmanuel Rekeraho.[443] He asserted that he only knew one man named Rwamakuba, but realized that the person he used to call Rwamakuba was in fact Rekeraho.[444]

173. Witness XV explained that the absence of any reference to the Accused in seven of his prior statements was due to the fact that "[he] could only think of [Rwamakuba] when it was the time of his trial".[445] The Chamber notes that in 2003, XV was on the Prosecution's witness list for the first trial against André Rwamakuba, and his reconfirmation statement was **[page 69]** made in Arusha in preparation for his testimony in that trial. This reconfirmation statement, however, did not mention major elements of the evidence that he gave in this trial.

174. Witness XV did not appear to know what André Rwamakuba looked like. First, as acknowledged by the witness, he confused Rwamakuba with one Rekeraho. Then, when shown a picture in court, he confused Rwamakuba with a priest.[446] He also testified that Rwamakuba wore glasses. This assertion was seriously challenged by the Defence which provided a letter from UNDF Commanding Officer, who stated that the Accused had "no spectacle in his possession upon his transfer to the UNDF",[447] and called witnesses who had personal knowledge of the Accused and denied that he wore glasses at that time.[448] In view of these circumstances and the major inconsistencies in Witness XV's testimony, the Chamber is of the view that his evidence is subject to serious doubt and cannot be relied upon.

175. Except for Witness XV, none of the other Prosecution witnesses had prior knowledge of André Rwamakuba. Their identification of Rwamakuba is based on untested hearsay evidence or on XV's evidence which has already been found unreliable.

176. Witnesses **ALV** and **ALW** said that André Rwamakuba was identified him to them by refugees and students when they were at Butare University Hospital.[449] These people, however, are now dead.[450] Witness **RJ** was made aware of who Rwamakuba was by two persons: first by a Hutu lady who helped the witness at the Hospital and then, by XV while the witness was in the corridor of the surgery unit.[451] It is important to note that RJ was not able to recognize in court a picture of the priest who helped her during the genocide and took her to the Hospital in April 1994.[452] Witness **GIO** testified that Rwamakuba was first identified her by Witness RJ and then some students told her that his first name was André.[453] It is noteworthy that during her evidence, Witness GIO identified, on the basis of a picture showed by the Defence, the man named Rekeraho as probably being André Rwamakuba. **[page 70]** Witness **HF** testified that while in the presence of Witness

---

442 Will-Say Statement, 26 August 2005, Exh. D. 121.

443 T. 31 August 2005, pp. 55-59; T. 1 September 1994, pp. 9-10.

444 T. 31 August 2005, pp. 56-59.

445 T. 30 August 2005, p. 63.

446 T. 1 September 2005, pp. 21-22.

447 Exh. D. 215.

448 See: Edith Van Wynsberghe (T. 1 December 2005, p. 61); Witness 1/1 (T. 14 December 2005, p. 65); Witness 1/15 (T. 18 January 2006, p. 14) and Witness 9/1 (T. 29 November 2005, pp. 37 and 63-65).

449 Witness ALV stated that other refugees who knew Rwamakuba because some of them worked in the Hospital or knew him from when he was a student and intern identified him to her (T. 6 July 2005, pp. 28 and 46). Witness ALW said that she learned the identity of André Rwamakuba by other refugees and students (T. 25 August 2005, pp. 13-14, 26; T. 26 August 2005, p. 15).

450 T. 6 July 2005, p. 50. Witness ALW gave the name of the student who informed her but said that he was dead (T. 25 August 2005, p. 26; T. 30 August 2005, p. 16).

451 T. 2 September 2005, pp. 24- 26; T. 5 September, pp. 2-3; Exh. P. 71 (under seal).

452 See Exh. D. 143. Witness RJ even stated that she "[did] not know the person on the photograph." (T. 5 September 2005, p. 9).

453 T. 24 August 2005, p. 9.

RJ, Witness XV pointed out Rwamakuba to them.[454] The Chamber also notes that the description of the Accused provided by Witnesses ALV, HF and RJ was particularly vague.[455]

177. In view of these circumstances, the identity of the person who the Prosecution's witnesses claim to have seen committing the alleged crimes raises serious doubt. Other elements, as discussed below, also contribute to the Chamber's doubt on Rwamakuba's involvement in the massacres at Butare University Hospital as alleged in the Indictment.

(3) Internal Discrepancies

178. Apart from Prosecution Witness XV, Prosecution Witnesses ALV, ALW, GIO, HF and RJ testified that they saw André Rwamakuba committing crimes at Butare University Hospital at different times and places between 21 and 25 April 1994. As a preliminary matter, the Chamber can accept that if found reliable, these testimonies are not necessarily contradictory since it is reasonably acceptable that the Prosecution witnesses saw Rwamakuba on different times and rooms while at the Hospital.

179. The Chamber will discuss the evidence for each of the Prosecution witnesses. For a clearer assessment, the discussion will be preceded by a brief summary of the relevant part of their testimony.

180. **Witness ALV** was 16 years old in 1994. Fleeing from Ngoma with her father, she arrived at Butare University Hospital on 20 April 1994.[456] She saw André Rwamakuba on two occasions at the Hospital. She first saw him on the evening of 21 April 1994 when he was pulling out drips from some of the Tutsi patients in the intensive care unit while in the company of Doctor Gatera, Colonel Muvunyi, Sister Theopiste, and Doctor Jotham.[457] She next saw him on 22 April 1994, about 11 a.m. when he was with the same people, including **[page 71]** some soldiers, and he took away her father from his hiding place in the kitchen.[458] She testified that, as she followed the group to see where her father was being taken, Rwamakuba hit her on the back.[459] Witness ALV's account of this fact was particularly confused. She first testified that she did not see who struck the blow, but was told later that it was Rwamakuba.[460] Then, she explained that she lost consciousness after the hit, but not really,[461] and after a few moments, she turned and saw that it was Rwamakuba who had hit her.[462] ALV then testified that the refugees were forced to leave the Hospital and go the *préfecture*, where she met her two sisters. They stayed for two days and then went to her grandmother's house where they stayed for about one hour before they had to flee from assailants. They then returned to the *préfecture* from where they were taken to a centre at Rango where they stayed for a month and a half.

181. Witness ALV evidence substantially differs from her prior statements to the Prosecution investigators which she verified and signed.[463] Her first statement contains a detailed account of the events she suffered in 1994, particularly at Butare University Hospital, without any mention of André Rwamakuba.[464] In that statement, she described the abduction of her father from the Hospital storeroom by Sister Theopiste and soldiers without any mention of the Accused, Doctor Gatera, Colonel Muvunyi, or Doctor Jotham being present or participating. She gave a detailed account of her stay at the Hospital for a week after that incident, and described how Doctor Jotham ordered the refugees to be removed from the *préfecture* as filth. In her

454 T. 11 July 2005, pp. 11, 13, 14; T. 12 July 2005, p. 11.

455 Witness ALV described Rwamakuba as follows: "a medium-sized man, neither too big nor too short; colour of skin somewhere between light and dark, thick lips and a strong jaw; sort of nose which Hutus generally have." (T. 6 July 2005, p. 57). Witness HF said: "This is a man of average height, who has a nose like the nose of the Hutus. He has broad lips, with big cheeks." (T. 11 July 2005, p. 29). Witness RJ stated that Rwamakuba was "dark skinned with a large nose, of medium height, and he was somewhat quite corpulent, but not too fat (T. 2 September 2005, p. 25).

456 T. 6 July 2005, p. 27.

457 T. 6 July 2005, pp. 27-29 and 45.

458 T. 6 July 2005, pp. 31-32, 50 and 63.

459 T. 6 July 2005, p. 54.

460 T. 6 July 2005, p.33.

461 Witness ALV specified that she did not really lost consciousness, but that she was tremendously scared, and, however, maintained consciousness all the time. T. 6 July 2005, pp. 33 and 34.

462 T. 6 July 2005, pp. 33 and 55.

463 Witness ALV stated that she signed these statements as she was satisfied that everything contained therein reflected what she had said (T. 6 July 2005, pp. 26 and 43).

464 Statement of 29 November 2000 (Exh. D. 49 A and B, under seal).

second statement of 13 November 2003, she said she was forced to leave on the same day, under orders from Doctor Gatera and the soldiers just as in her testimony in court.[465] In her second statement, she also described with significant detail how she followed Rwamakuba and saw the atrocities he committed in the intensive care ward. She specified that he took away her father, and even hit her on the shoulder.[466] The statement described that she saw Rwamakuba and his entourage leave the ward where she stayed for another 20 minutes, in contradiction with her testimony in court when she claimed that she **[page 72]** was in the unit for about 20 minutes and left *before* Rwamakuba.[467] Witness ALV's prior statements also present a different and irreconcilable account of the facts she presented of what happened after she had left Butare University Hospital. Specifically, in her first statement, the witness stated that after leaving the Hospital, she spent two weeks at the Butare *préfecture* office, giving details about her activities during that period, which included witnessing the murder of her brother by *Interahamwe*, but in her second statement and in her testimony, she said that she stayed there for only two days.[468] In the first statement she said that she was taken to Rango after two weeks at the *préfecture*. In the second statement, she stated that she left the *préfecture* and took refuge first in her grandmother's house, then with her aunt at Cyarwa, and asserted that they are both alive today and reside in Butare. There is no mention of going to Rango.

182. In view of these omissions and inconsistencies which cannot be explained by the passage of time, translation discrepancies or the way the statements were taken, the Chamber cannot find Witness ALV's evidence reliable, mainly when considering the witness' affirmation that "[André Rwamakuba's] image remained engraved in [her] memory" because he hit her at the Hospital.[469] The witness explained in court that she omitted his name from her first statement because she was suffering from "anterograde" amnesia. The Chamber is not satisfied by this explanation that is not supported by any medical or other report and that is inconsistent with a prior explanation she gave in her 2003 statement. In that statement, she stated that she did not mention Rwamakuba "because the investigators did not ask [her] any question about him".[470] In addition, were the witness' amnesia established, this would strengthen the Chamber's doubt on her reliability. ALV's testimony cannot support a conviction against the Accused in the present case.

183. **Witness ALW** arrived with her wounded aunt at Butare University Hospital on 21 April 1994.[471] About three days after her arrival, she saw André Rwamakuba for the first time when he was with Doctor Gatera; he was removing the drips from five Tutsi patients in the surgical ward and then striking them on the head with a small axe.[472] They were immediately removed and put on a red pick-up truck. On or around 27 April 1994, the witness also saw **[page 73]** Rwamakuba strike two men named Mutabazi and Kazasumaho with the same axe.[473] He said that "there was no hiding place for snakes". The two men fell down from the blows and were immediately taken away by *Interahamwe* and put in a red pick-up tuck. During cross-examination, the witness confirmed that Rwamakuba in fact killed the seven people she saw him hit with an axe.[474]

184. Witness ALW's account of the event suffered from internal discrepancies,[475] and was mainly inconsistent with her evidence given in the *Gatera* case in Rwanda.[476] In that case, ALW testified about the killing of Mutabazi and Kazasumaho. She said that Doctor Gatera, who was with soldiers, stabbed them with

465 Exh. D. 50 A and B (under seal).
466 Statement of 13 November 2003 (Exh. D. 50 A and B, under seal).
467 T. 6 July 2005, p. 49.
468 T. 6 July 2005, pp.35 and 60.
469 T. 6 July 2005, p. 34.
470 Statement of 13 November 2003 (Exh. D. 50 A and B, under seal).
471 T. 25 August 2005, p. 25.
472 T. 29 August 2005, p. 12; T. 25 August 2005, p. 28.
473 T. 25 August 2005, pp. 28-29 and 35; T. 29 August 2005, pp. 22-23; T. 30 August 2005, p. 18.
474 T. 26 August 2005, p. 3.
475 For instance, Witness ALW evidence was inconsistent on whether the five Tutsi patients hit by André Rwamakuba were actually killed by him, whether she saw that he killed them or blood on Rwamakuba's axe (T. 29 August 2005, p.17; T. 30 August 2005, p. 7). Likewise, ALW's account of the attack of two men by Rwamakuba contains contrary information. For instance, the witness said that she knew the two men very well but was not able to give their first name; she also placed the pick-up once opposite to the maternity, and then behind; she said first that she met the two men in the corridor, but also said that at that moment, she was standing close to the tents where the other refugees were.
476 Exh. D. 108 and D. 109.

bayonets and beat them with a small club saying that their time had come. The soldiers then took them beside the medicine intern block in order to kill them. Rwamakuba is not mentioned as being present or participating. Before this Chamber, the witness explained that she did not mention Rwamakuba during the *Gatera* trial because she did not know where he was and because she was only asked about Gatera's participation.[477] She further asserted that her account was consistent because Rwamakuba was with Gatera and that they acted together.[478] In the present case, the witness did not mention Gatera's presence when Rwamakuba allegedly attacked Mutabazi and Kazasumaho, although she specifically testified that Gatera was with Rwamakuba when the latter was removing drips from Tutsi patients. Witness ALW's explanation of these contradictory accounts of the same event is not convincing. Evidence about the abduction of these two men, their female relative and a fourth man was given by Defence Witnesses 9/17 and 9/29, who are also Tutsi survivors and were present at Butare University Hospital in April 1994. Witness 9/17 explicitly denied any involvement of Rwamakuba in the attacks of Mutabazi and Kazasumaho,[479] and Witness 9/29 provided a complete description of the event with no mention of Rwamakuba's involvement at all.[480] The Chamber also notes that Witness ALW's **[page 74]** evidence in this trial on when and how she left the Hospital differs from her testimony in the *Gatera* trial.[481] In the Chamber's view, the internal discrepancies in ALW's testimony and inconsistencies with her prior statements and testimonies cannot be explained by the time elapsed or translation discrepancies, and seriously undermine her credibility. ALW's evidence cannot support a conviction against the Accused in the present case.

185. On or about 22 or 23 April 1994, **Witness GIO** went to Butare University Hospital with her brother who was wounded.[482] The witness testified that two days after her arrival, André Rwamakuba, along with a group of five or six doctors and *Interahamwe*, was checking identity cards of the patients in the surgical ward, and identified that GIO's brother was Tutsi. Doctor Gatera then killed him by a blow on his head with an axe.[483] According to the witness, another patient was similarly attacked. Then, Rwamakuba, Doctor Gatera and some *Interahamwe* allegedly put those people they had killed in a pick-up truck that was parked near the maternity ward.[484]

186. Witness GIO gave substantially different accounts of the events at the Hospital both in her prior statements[485] and testimonies before both this Tribunal and Rwandan courts.[486] The core element of her evidence is the attack of her brother which description in court is the opposite of what she said previously. In a statement signed by the witness in 1997, she stated that her brother had been taken away in a pick-up truck and that she never saw him again.[487] There was no mention of an attack with an axe or her brother being killed in her presence. During her testimony in December 2003 in the prior joint case involving André Rwamakuba and three other Accused, she added that Doctor Gatera put her brother in a pick-up truck. She testified that she never saw her brother being killed by an axe and that she never said that **[page 75]** Doctor

477 T. 30 August 2005, p. 6.

478 T. 30 August 2005, p. 8.

479 T. 12 December 2005, p. 13.

480 T. 27 January 2006, pp. 12-13 and 6 February 2006, pp. 11-13: Witness 9/29 stated that stated that Mutabazi and Kazasumaho were taken away in a wooded area. She never saw them again.

481 In court, the witness testified that the refugee's tents at the Hospital were removed towards the end of April, beginning of May, before she left the Hospital. On the contrary, in the *Gatera* trial, she testified that the tents had already been dismantled upon her arrival at the Hospital. The witness explained that she returned to the Hospital between May and June to find out whether her aunt was still alive and that at that time, she realized that the tents were dismantled. The witness also stated that her aunt was still alive when she left the Hospital, while in the *Gatera* trial she said that she left the Hospital *after her aunt was killed*, at the end of May. (See T. 29 August 2005, p. 30 and T. 30 August 2005, p. 19).

482 T. 22 August 2005, p. 24.

483 T. 22 August 2005, pp. 26-27.

484 T. 22 August 2005, pp. 29-30 and 38.

485 Statement of 5 May 1998 (Exh. D. 71 A, B and C, under seal); 19 May 1998 (Exh. D. 72, under seal); 7 May 1999 (Exh. D. 73 A, B and C, under seal); 7 February 2000 (Exh. D. 74, under seal); Transcripts of December 2003 (Exh. D. 76, under seal); 17 September 1997 (Exh. D. 75). On 7 July and 22 November 2003, she confirmed the content of her statement (Exh. D. 80, under seal).

486 The Witness testified before Rwandan courts: *Gatera* case (Exh. D. 71 and D. 72), *Twagirayezu* case (Exh. D. 73) and *Mukabandora* case (Exh. D. 74) and in the prior joint trial in the case *Prosecutor v. Édouard Karemera, Mathieu Ngirumpatse, Joseph Nzirorera, André Rwamakuba*, Case No. ICTR-98-44.

487 Statement of 17 September 1997 (Exh. D XX).

Gatera killed her brother.[488] In a statement taken in 1998, by Rwandan authorities, prior to her first testimony before this Tribunal,[489] Witness GIO gave a third different account of this event: Rwamakuba was not present, and Doctor Gatera, who was inspecting the wounded patients, immediately struck her brother on the head with a small axe saying that he was an *Inkotanyi*.[490] This version of the facts is again modified a year later in a statement given by the witness in another case in Rwanda: GIO stated that Doctor Gatera ordered a man named "Athanas" to kill her brother, which he did; she fails to mention Rwamakuba's name.[491] These major inconsistencies cannot be explained by the time elapsed or translation discrepancies. It must be noted that, in her will-say statement, GIO directly addressed these inconsistencies.[492] She stated that she could not remember a meeting with the Prosecution's investigators in 1997 or whether the document was read to her, even if she signed it. She even denied her signature on some other documents. In light of the above-mentioned inconsistencies, these explanations are not convincing and, conversely, support the conclusion that Witness GIO lacks credibility as far as her evidence in this case is concerned.

187. **Witness HF** arrived at Butare University Hospital on 18 April 1994 because her sister had gone there to give birth, and left on 29 April 1994 for the Butare *préfecture*.[493] After three days, she allegedly saw André Rwamakuba with Doctor Gatera in the maternity ward ordering Tutsi patients to get up and then delivered them to the *Interahamwe* who took them away in a pick-up truck.[494] She then saw Rwamakuba on the same day in the afternoon, in the surgical ward with Doctors Gatera and Twagirayezu and some *Interahamwe*. On that occasion, Rwamakuba allegedly hit the head of a Tutsi patient with an axe, woke up another patient and stepped on his neck, and then proceeded to give them to the *Interahamwe*, who subsequently put them in a pick-up truck.[495] Witness HF saw Rwamakuba for the third time, on the next day, in front of the paediatrics ward while he was selecting people to be taken away in a pick-up truck. The witness however also said that on this third occasion, she saw Rwamakuba in the maternity ward, when he took away the witness' sister. This account was **[page 76]** not consistent. HF identified her elder sister, her brother and a nurse as victims of the massacres at the Hospital.

188. During her testimony, Witness HF denied important factual elements that she consistently mentioned in her three prior statements.[496] The different accounts of the events the witness gave in her three successive interviews with the Prosecution and in court are also critical in the assessment of her credibility.[497] In a statement taken in 1997, Witness HF affirmed that she went to the Hospital to "seek refuge"; there is no mention of her sister or brother and she then stated that she did not recall the names of any victim.[498] She stated that she saw André Rwamakuba dressed in banana leaves. In 2001, she declared that she went to the Hospital "to take care of [her] sister [...] who was sick"; she also specified that this sister and her brother who had come to seek medication were killed and taken away in a pick-up truck.[499] She again said she saw Rwamakuba dressed in banana leaves and when he passed by, people whispered that he was an *Interahamwe* leader. In her testimony, she denied all this, along with other matters recorded in those statements. In 2003, she stated that she was at the Hospital helping her "sister who had given birth to a premature baby"; this

---

488 *The Prosecutor v. Édouard Karemera, Mathieu Ngirumpatse, Joseph Nzirorera, André Rwamakuba*, Case No. ICTR-98-44-T, T. 12 December 2003, 51-52. The witness said: "Yes. I'm saying that we are testifying because we saw Mr. Rwamakuba and Gatera, but I never said Gatera used an axe to kill my brother. I say that he put them into a vehicle, but I never said that Gatera used an axe to kill my brother. [...] I never saw my brother being killed by an axe. I don't know where you're getting this information from."

489 Statement of 5 May 1998 (Exh. D. 71).

490 Exh. D. 71 A, B and C (under seal).

491 Exh. D. 73 A, B and C (under seal).

492 Exh. D. 79. The will-say statement is the results of two meetings between the witness and the Prosecution Counsel.

493 T. 11 July 2005, p. 9.

494 T. 11 July 2005, pp. 10 and 17; T. 12 July 2005, p. 38.

495 T. 11 July 2005, pp. 10 and 17; T. 12 July 2005, pp. 38 and 47.

496 Contrary to what she stated in 2001 and 2003 (see Exh, D. 55 and 54), in court she denied that she left the Butare University Hospital on 25 April 1994. As opposed to what she stated in 1997, 2001 and 2003 (see Exh. D. 56, 55 and 54) in court she denied that André Rwamakuba wore banana leaves and that he disembowelled a pregnant women.

497 Witness HF gave a statement respectively on 11 September 1997, Exh. D. 56 A and B (under seal), on 6 and 8 February 2001, Exh. D. 55 A and B (under seal); and on 12 March 2003, Exh. D. 54 A and B (under seal). The witness also testified during the joint trial in the case the *Prosecutor v. Edouard Karemera, Mathieu Ngirumpatse, Joseph Nzirorera and André Rwamakuba* (Case No. ICTR-98-44) before the severance of André Rwamakuba in December 2003.

498 Statement of 11 September 1997, Exh. D. 56 A and B (under seal).

499 Statement of 6 and 8 February 2001, Exh. D. 55 A and B (under seal).

sister, her baby and her brother were then killed while lying "in their hospital beds".[500] During her testimony, Witness HF provided a fourth account of the same event, saying that, on two different dates, her wounded brother and her sister with her baby were both taken away by the *Interahamwe* while lying in their beds respectively in the surgical and maternity wards of the Hospital.[501]

189. The Chamber notes that Witness HF's account of facts also differs from her evidence in Rwandan proceedings. In the *Gatera* case, the witness stated that she went to the Hospital to take care of her sister who was pregnant, but she gave a different name from the one provided in her statements and testimony in this case.[502] Doctor Gatera came into the ward selected the victims, including her sister and brother, and put them in a pick-up truck. There is no mention of André Rwamakuba being present. In another Rwandan case held in 1997, the **[page 77]** witness testified that her sister was shot by a man named Rurangirwa in a specific *secteur* in Butare *préfecture*. The name of this sister was exactly the same Christian name as the one of her sister allegedly killed at Butare University Hospital.[503] In this trial, when confronted with the judgement in that case, the witness explained that she had twin sisters with the same Christian name. The Chamber is not convinced by this explanation. In that respect, it is noteworthy that the Rwandan court in the above-mentioned case denied the witness' claim against Rurangirwa for payment of pain and suffering because she could not provide any communal death certificate for the sister and brother who she said were abducted by Rwamakuba.[504] In December 2003, in the first trial in this case, the witness testified that she had never claimed that Rugangirwa had killed her sister and that she had never lodged any compensation claim nor was even aware of any claim being made in relation to her brother and sister.[505]

190. The Chamber is of the view that the above-mentioned inconsistencies in Witness HF's evidence cannot be explained by the time elapsed, translation discrepancies or mistakes in the way the statements were taken by Prosecution investigators. In addition to these major inconsistencies, the Chamber notes that Witness HF's evidence is contradicted by other Prosecution evidence. For example, the witness testified that after she left Butare University Hospital on 29 April 1994, she witnessed a massacre in the Kabakobwa. This evidence is in conflict with the testimony of Prosecution Expert Witness Alison des Forges, who placed the Kabakobwa massacre on 22 April 1994,[506] and also with the Prosecution's allegations in the Indictment against Joseph Kanyabashi, which plead that the Kabakobwa massacre took place on 21 or 22 April 1994.[507] If this massacre took place on 21 or 22 April 1994 and HF was there at that moment, she could not have been at Butare University Hospital to witness the events about which she testified. The Chamber also finds that the demeanour of Witness HF in court is relevant. She was extremely reluctant to answer questions on her prior statements and testimonies. The witness was disinclined to admit having given a statement in the *Gatera* case and denied that what was read in court was that statement. She even alleged that the **[page 78]** document which had been received from the Rwandan authorities was false.[508] There were similar denials in relation to information in the statements taken by Prosecution investigators. In view of these circumstances, the Chamber finds that Witness HF is not credible and her evidence cannot support a conviction against the Accused in the present case.

191. On 21 April 1994, **Witness RJ** arrived at Butare University Hospital where she was taken by a priest to receive medical assistance.[509] She testified that she saw André Rwamakuba three times at the Hospital in April 1994: at the tents, when a delegation of doctors, including Rwamakuba and some military inspected

500 Statement of 12 March 2003, Exh. D. 54 A and B (under seal).
501 T. 12 July 2005, p. 39.
502 This statement was read to the witness in open court, see T. 12 July 2005, pp. 54-55.
503 See: *Procès-Verbal* of the Public Hearing dated 17 November 1997 (Exh. D. 61 A, B and C); Judgement in the *Sahera* case, dated 23 March 1998 (Exh. D. 59 and D. 60 A and B). HF admitted that she was a witness in that case and accepted the Judgement exhibited (T. 13 July 2005, pp. 3 and 8; T. 12 July 2005, p. 66); she however denied her signature on the *Procès-Verbal* of the Public Hearing dated 17 November 1997 (T. 13 July 2005, p. 15).
504 Judgement in the *Sahera* case, dated 23 March 1998 (Exh. D. 59 and D. 60 A and B).
505 *Prosecutor v. Édouard Karemera, Mathieu Ngirumpatse, Joseph Nzirorera and André Rwamakuba*, Case No. ICTR-98-44-T, T. 11 December 2003, pp. 13-14 (see: Exh. D. 76).
506 Expert Report by Alison Des Forges prepared for the *Butare* case ICTR-98-42-T, 1 June 2001, Exh. D. 101.
507 *Prosecutor v. Joseph Kanyabashi*, Case No. ICTR-96-15-I, Indictment, filed on 11 June 2001, Exh. D. 51.
508 T. 12 July 2005, pp. 49-53.
509 T. 2 Sept. 2005, pp. 11-12.

identification cards from the patients;[510] when Rwamakuba and Doctor Gatera came to the maternity ward; and when she saw Rwamakuba removing drips from patients in the surgical ward and ordering them to get onto a red pick-up truck. She allegedly saw him assault a man in plaster. She testified that her child was beaten by Doctor Gatera in the presence of Rwamakuba, but she could not remember whether this happened at the first, the second or the third instance when she saw him.[511] She fled from the Hospital and went to the *préfecture* office, and while she was there, she saw Rwamakuba and heard him say to the *préfet* that the Tutsi had to be killed.

192. Witness RJ's prior accounts of the events to which she testified were substantially different from her in-court testimony. In a statement taken by the Rwandan authorities in the *Gatera* case before her statement to the Prosecution in this case, she stated that Doctor Gatera was the person who ordered the soldiers to beat her and other Tutsi;[512] she did not mention André Rwamakuba.[513] Similarly, in a statement taken in June 1998 by the Rwandan authorities in the *Kageruka* case, Witness RJ failed to mention Rwamakuba in her recollection of the events that took place at the Hospital, and Doctors Gatera and Kageruka are described as the main perpetrators of the attacks. Particularly, she stated that Doctor Kageruka took identity cards of Tutsi patients and tore them up and together with Doctor Gatera, put the Tutsi patients in a vehicle and told them to "look at the world for the last time".[514] In a statement taken a year later in another Rwandan proceeding, Witness RJ presented Doctor Twagirayezu as the main perpetrator of the killings. She declared that Doctor Gatera was also present, but she did not mention Doctor Kageruka and described Rwamakuba as committing **[page 79]** the same acts and saying the same words as were previously attributed to Doctor Kageruka in her *Kageruka* statement of 1998.[515] Witness RJ also made a statement in the *Misago* case in 1999 where she stated that she did not stay at Butare University Hospital at all because they refused to keep her there; she went then to Butare *préfecture*.[516] The same year, she also gave an interview published in a report by *African Rights*, where she described soldiers from the *Ecole des Sous-Officiers* (ESO) at the centre of the crimes committed at Butare University Hospital; she did not mention Rwamakuba; and she stated that the soldiers *threw them out of the Hospital* and *told them* to go to the office of the *préfecture*.[517]

193. These various inconsistencies regarding the same events are not reconcilable and cannot be reasonably explained by the time elapsed or translations discrepancies. The Chamber notes that the witness was particularly reluctant to discuss her prior statements. She eventually denied the content of each of the Rwandan statements and of the *African Rights* Report, and she claimed that her words were distorted.[518] She even alleged that her signature must have been forged.[519] In view of these circumstances, the Chamber finds that Witness RJ lacks credibility.

194. The Chamber finds that the Prosecution witnesses on the alleged crimes committed by the Accused at Butare University Hospital lack credibility and reliability. This conclusion is supported by the alibi evidence.

---

510 T. 2 September 2005, pp. 12-16.

511 T. 5 September 2005, p. 5.

512 Statement in *Gatera* case, 30 April 1997 (Exh. D. 137 A, B and C, under seal). In that statement, Witness RJ did not state that Dr. Gatera also had beaten her child.

513 Exh. D. 137 A, B and C (under seal).

514 Exh. D. 139 A, B and C (under seal).

515 Statement in *Twagirayezu* case, 6 May 1999, Exh. D. 138 A, B and C (under seal). André Rwamakuba is described as arriving aboard a vehicle, where Tutsi patients were then put on and taken away. The witness stated that he told them "to look at the world for the last time". In the *Kageruka* statement, RJ said that her elder sister who had given birth to a *boy* at the Hospital was put on the vehicle by Dr. Gatera and Kageruka; but in 1999, she stated that her elder sister and her *two twins whom she had just given birth*, were taken away by Dr. Gatera and Twagirayezu.

516 Statement in *Misago* case, 21 April 1994, Exh. D. 145 A, B and C (under seal). Witness RJ stated that when she arrived at Butare University Hospital, they refused to keep her there. She then went to the Butare *préfecture*.

517 See Exh. D. 140 (under seal). In court, Witness RJ testified that she fled to a nearby sorghum field and then made her way to the *préfecture* office; in the *African Rights* Report, she stated: "the soldiers *threw us out of the hospital* and *told us* to go to the office of the prefecture" (emphasis added).

518 See for e.g.: T. 5 September 2005, p. 28.

519 T. 5 September 2005, pp. 31 and 35; T. 6 September 2005, pp. 2 and 11.

(4) Alibi

195. It was also the Defence case that the Accused would not have been able to spend time in Butare to the extent suggested by the Prosecution witnesses because between 18 and 25 April 1994, the period during which André Rwamakuba is alleged to have committed crimes **[page 80]** at Butare University Hospital, he was first staying in Gitarama and then, after 20 April 1994, in Gisenyi.[520]

196. The parties agreed and the Chamber accepted that on 12 April 1994, the Accused moved to Gitarama with the convoy of the Interim Government.[521] Prosecution investigator Upendra Baghel also gave evidence that the distance between Gitarama and Butare is approximately 83 kilometres and between Gisenyi and Butare 247 kilometres.[522] The Defence accepted these figures[523] and provided evidence that the Accused was not present at the scene of the crimes.

197. According to Defence Witnesses 1/1, André Rwamakuba was in Gitarama from 12 to 20 April 1994. During that period, the witness saw him each morning, at lunch, and again each evening starting from around 5.00 p.m. Defence Witnesses 1/1 and 9/1 testified to Rwamakuba's presence in Gisenyi from 20 April to 2 May 1994. They each gave an account of his daily activities including attempts to get air tickets for his family to leave Rwanda. Specifically, from 20 to 24 April 1994, they stated that Rwamakuba spent his days and nights at home with his wife and his family. Witness 1/15 also testified that he met with Rwamakuba in Gisenyi between 20 and 22 April 1994 as he assisted the witness to get a new passport and a visa to Zaïre.[524] Copies of that document were tendered into evidence by the Defence.[525]

198. The testimonies of Witnesses 1/1 and 9/1 are corroborated to a certain extent by Witnesses 5/16, 5/7, 9/17, 5/13, 5/15 and 9/29 who testified that they never saw André Rwamakuba at Butare University Hospital during the genocide in April and May 1994. Witnesses 5/16, 5/7, and 5/15 who were employees of Butare University Hospital in April and May 1994, said that they never saw Rwamakuba there and that they never heard any such allegation against him. They testified that they would come to work at the Hospital in the morning and find that people had been abducted and were told that the killings were done by soldiers during the night. Witness 5/13 was at Butare University Hospital in the surgical ward with his relative throughout the time Rwamakuba was alleged to have been there and confirmed that he did not see him. The witness stated that he was familiar with all of the doctors at the Hospital because they greeted each other as neighbours. He also never heard **[page 81]** that a Minister was at the Hospital taking part in the genocide, except a woman named Nyiramasuhuko.

199. The Prosecution did not call any direct witness to rebut these testimonies. Only the Expert witness testified that on 19 April 1994, several members of the Government, including André Rwamakuba, went to Butare to publicly remove the Tutsi *préfet* who had attempted to stop the killings against the Tutsi.[526] A transcript of Prime Minister Kambanda's speech made on that date mentioning the presence of the Minister of Primary and Secondary Education was also admitted into evidence.[527] The Prosecution did not attempt to present a comprehensive chronology of the Accused's presence in Butare, particularly concerning his attendance at the government meeting of 19 April 1994 and then between 21 and 25 April 1994, as asserted by the Prosecution witnesses.

200. The Chamber assessed with particular caution the evidence given by Defence Witnesses 1/1 and 9/1 due to their close relationship with André Rwamakuba, but it should be acknowledged that these witnesses testified with great detail and answered questions on cross-examination in a steady demeanour. In addition, none of Witnesses 5/16, 5/7, 9/17, 5/13, 5/15 and 9/29 knew Rwamakuba personally. They did not appear to

---

520 See Defence Witnesses 1/1, 9/1 and 1/15. Defence Witness 3/A gave a similar evidence. However, due to the particularly close relationship between the Accused and this witness, and the age of the witness at the time of the event, the Chamber will set aside this evidence.

521 *Ibidem.*

522 Exh. P. 2.

523 Defence Closing Brief, p. 283.

524 T. 18 January 2006, pp. 10-13 and 16-17.

525 Exh. D. 198.

526 T. 14 July 2005, p. 40.

527 Exh. P. 64.

have any special interest in defending the Accused and their cross-examination by the Prosecution did not raise any convincing element to show that they were unbelievable or unreliable. In the Chamber's view, their testimonies were consistent and objective enough to levy an additional doubt on the Prosecution's case.

Conclusion on the Alleged Participation of André Rwamakuba to Crimes at Butare University Hospital

201. As discussed above, first, the Prosecution did not adduce evidence on some allegations at Butare University Hospital and adduced evidence inconsistent with some of the allegations in the Indictment.

202. Then, the identity of the person who the Prosecution witnesses saw committing the alleged crimes at Butare University Hospital in April 1994 raised doubt. Apart from Witness XV who claimed to have personally known André Rwamakuba, the identification of the Accused was either based on untested hearsay evidence or on Witness XV's identification. **[page 82]** Specifically, Witness XV pointed out Rwamakuba to Witnesses HF and RJ, who in turn identified him to Witness GIO. In that respect, it is remarkable that Witness XV was confusing Rwamakuba with a man named Rekeraho. This confusion was also entertained by Witness GIO. As developed in detail above, Witness XV's evidence contained many inconsistencies that cannot be reasonably explained or reconciled. His personal knowledge and identification of Rwamakuba is therefore unreliable.

203. In addition to these identification issues, the credibility and reliability of the Prosecution witnesses also raised serious concerns. In the Chamber's view, the major inconsistencies between the witnesses' testimonies and their prior statements and testimonies in other cases cannot be explained by the time elapsed, translation discrepancies, the manner in which the prior statements were taken or the impact of trauma inflicted upon the witnesses. They undermine the credibility and reliability of the Prosecution witnesses. In addition, the Prosecution did not satisfactorily rebut the Defence evidence that Rwamakuba did not participate in the killings at Butare University Hospital or that, during the considered period, he was staying in Gitarama and Gisenyi, and could not have been in Butare to the extent suggested by the Prosecution witnesses.

204. The absence of any reliable identification of André Rwamakuba at the time and location of the event, the lack of credibility and reliability of the Prosecution witnesses and the Defence alibi evidence, cumulatively contribute to levy reasonable doubt on the Prosecution's case.

205. Consequently, the Chamber finds that the Prosecution failed to prove at all or beyond a reasonable doubt the allegations against the Accused at the Butare University Hospital, as set forth in paragraphs 15 to 16, 23 second and third limbs and 26 second to fourth limbs of the Indictment. The Chamber will now address the other allegations in the Indictment.

II.3. Other Allegations in the Indictment

206. In addition to the charges pertaining to events in Gikomero and Butare events, the Indictment contains allegations regarding André Rwamakuba's political status and related political activities. It alleges that as the Minister of Primary and Secondary Education of the Interim Government of 8 April 1994, he took part in the conception and the implementation **[page 83]** of the Government's policies to exterminate the Tutsi throughout Rwanda.[528] It is said that between 27 and 29 April 1994, he was spokesman for the Interim Government.[529] On 17 May 1994, he was allegedly assigned to the Civil Defence Forces (CDF) program with other ministers.[530] This program would have been used to identify, search out and kill the Tutsi population.[531] The Accused is also described as a member of the MDR extremist wing, MDR "Hutu Power", which would have been created on or about 26 July 1993 and which would have had a specific ideology of exterminating the Tutsi.[532] He is alleged to have mobilized the physical and logistical resources of the MDR "Hutu Power", the other parties allied with the *Mouvement Révolutionnaire National pour le Développement* (MRND) and

[528] Indictment, paras. 7 and 19.

[529] Indictment, paras. 1 and 14.

[530] Indictment, para. 9.

[531] Indictment, para. 8.

[532] Indictment, para. 3. It is specifically said that André Rwamakuba was a member of the Executive Committee of MDR "Power" Political Party and was a member of that party's *comité préfectoral* in Kigali-Rural *préfecture* (see Indictment, para. 2).

"Hutu Power", the Interim Government Ministries controlled by those parties and the military to execute a campaign sought to kill or destroy the Tutsi as a group.[533]

207. It is noted that no evidence was adduced concerning what the Accused could or should have done as Minister or what he failed to do. The Prosecution also did not bring any evidence to prove its contentions regarding the structures of the MDR "Hutu Power", André Rwamakuba's alleged authority over local administrative officials, his alleged mobilization of the physical and logistical resources of the other parties that were allied with MRND and "Hutu Power", the Interim Government ministries controlled by these parties and the military to execute the campaign of destruction of the Tutsi throughout Rwanda. No direct evidence was adduced concerning the responsibilities of Rwamakuba with regard to the program of civilian self defence or how he might have used it to kill Tutsi. There was also no evidence that on or about 28 April 1994 he announced on Radio Rwanda that "security had been restored in Butare because the Inyenzi had been suppressed".

208. As discussed under Chapter I, André Rwamakuba was not alleged to be criminally responsible as a member of the Interim Government for failing to denounce the crimes committed against the Tutsi, for not dissociating himself from the Government or for failing to discharge his duties as Minister. In view of the charges against the Accused set forth in the Indictment and according to the clear and consistent notice given by the Prosecution, the above-mentioned allegations pertaining to Rwamakuba's political role and activities are **[page 84]** considered as context or background from which inferences concerning his intent, disposition or other required elements of the crimes could be drawn.

209. Since the Prosecution failed to prove beyond reasonable doubt the charges against the Accused pertaining to Gikomero *commune* and Butare University Hospital as detailed above, the Chamber need not to discuss the allegations and evidence concerning his criminal intent or disposition in relation to these alleged incidents.

Conclusion

210. That genocide against Tutsi and widespread or systematic attacks against a civilian population based on Tutsi ethnic identification occurred in Rwanda between April and July 1994 are notorious facts not subject to reasonable dispute,[534] and nor were they disputed by the Defence in the present case. This Tribunal was established to contribute to the process of reconciliation and to the restoration of peace and security in Rwanda.[535] The Tribunal's contribution in this area is by conducting impartial criminal proceedings where the burden of proving the guilt of an individual accused is on the Prosecution.

211. In the present case, André Rwamakuba was charged with specific acts committed in Gikomero *commune* and at Butare University Hospital between 6 and 30 April 1994. No charges were brought on the basis of his acts, omissions or duties as Minister of the Interim Government in 1994.

212. The Chamber heard 49 Prosecution and Defence witnesses, 94 Prosecution and 218 Defence exhibits were admitted into evidence over 78 trial days. The Prosecution case was largely circumstantial, and much evidence adduced was of hearsay character. Five of the 18 Prosecution witnesses claimed to have direct knowledge of André Rwamakuba. Two witnesses also gave uncorroborated evidence to support specific allegations in the Indictment. The Defence witnesses were mainly issued from different ranges of the Rwandan society, including victims of the genocide, they had both direct and indirect knowledge of Rwamakuba, and many of them claimed to have been eyewitnesses to events alleged in the Indictment.

213. The parties agreed that that Tutsi people were attacked and massacred in the Gikomero *commune* in April 1994, including at the Ndatewma Trading Centre, the Gikomero Protestant **[page 85]** School, the Gishaka Parish and the Kayanga Health Centre, and at Butare University Hospital. Both the Prosecution and the Defence adduced substantial evidence on these massacres. The Defence, however, denied the Accused's involvement in any of them.

533 Indictment, para. 6.

534 *Karemera et al.*, Decision on Prosecutor's Interlocutory Appeal of Decision on Judicial Notice (AC).

535 UN S.C. Res. 955 (1994), 8 November 1994.

214. After assessing the evidence as a whole, the Chamber found that all of the Prosecution witnesses not to be credible or reliable. Their testimonies were either inconsistent with the Indictment or contained other discrepancies which could not be satisfactorily explained. The absence of any credible or reliable identification of André Rwamakuba at the time and place of the alleged crimes, the lack of credibility or reliability of the Prosecution witnesses, the participation of the Accused in other activities during periods alleged in the Indictment and the Defence alibi evidence, cumulatively raise a reasonable doubt regarding the Prosecution's case.

215. Consequently, in the Chamber's view, the Prosecution has failed to prove beyond reasonable doubt that André Rwamakuba participated in sensitization campaigns in Gikomero *commune* from June 1993 up to and including June 1994; that between 10 and 11 April 1994, Rwamakuba delivered machetes to Muhire's house in Ndatemwa Trading Centre; that around the same period, he delivered machetes to Kamanzi's house in Kayanga Centre; that between 10 and 20 April 1994, at the Gikomero *secteur* office, he ordered the killings of three Tutsi people and encouraged the beginning of the massacres against Tutsi in the commune; and that between 13 and 15 April 1994, he participated in the massacre at Kayanga Health Centre. The Prosecution also failed to prove beyond reasonable doubt that the Accused committed criminal acts against Tutsi people between 18 and 25 April 1994 at Butare University Hospital.

216. Before concluding on the verdict, the Chamber will address a particular issue concerning the violation of the rights of the Accused.

CHAPTER III RIGHTS OF THE ACCUSED

217. In a Decision of 12 December 2000,[536] Trial Chamber II, composed of Judges Laïty Kama, presiding, William H. Sekule and Mehmet Güney, considered that the Tribunal had no jurisdiction over André Rwamakuba's conditions of detention by the Namibian authorities between 2 August 1995 and 7 February 1996 since he had not been arrested at the Tribunal's request. That same Chamber found that there was a violation of Rwamakuba's right to legal **[page 86]** assistance during the first months of his detention at the UNDF, from 22 October 1998 until 10 March 1999, and that the delay in assigning him duty Counsel further caused a delay in his initial appearance.[537]

218. The Appeals Chamber held that "any violation of the accused's rights entails the provision of an effective remedy pursuant to Article 2(3)(a) of the [International Covenant on Civil and Political Rights]."[538] The Appeals Chamber has previously ordered or decided the reduction of an accused's sentence where he was found guilty at trial.[539] In the *Barayagwiza* and *Semanza* cases, it also decided that "if the [accused] [was] not found guilty, he shall receive financial compensation."[540]

219. In the present case, the Appeals Chamber moreover considered that "it [was] open to [Rwamakuba] to invoke the issue of the alleged violation of his fundamental human rights by the Tribunal in order to seek reparation as the case may be, at the appropriate time".[541]

220. Since a violation of the Accused's right to legal assistance during the first months of his detention was found, André Rwamakuba is at liberty to file an application seeking an appropriate remedy after the time-limit to file an appeal against this Judgement has elapsed. The Prosecution and the Registry are also at liberty to file any related submissions.

---

536 *Rwamakuba*, Decision on the Defence Motion concerning the Illegal Arrest and Illegal Detention of the Accused (TC).

537 *Ibidem*.

538 See: *Barayagwiza*, Decision (Prosecutor's Request for Review or Reconsideration) (AC), paras. 74-75; *Kajelijeli* Appeal Judgement, paras. 255 and 322; *Semanza*, Decision of 31 May 2000 (AC), para. 125: "The Appeals Chamber nevertheless finds that any violation, even if it entails only a relative degree of prejudice, requires a proportionate remedy."

539 *Ibidem*.

540 *Barayagwiza*, Decision (Prosecutor's Request for Review or Reconsideration) (AC), para. 75; *Semanza*, Decision of 31 May 2000 (AC), disposition.

541 *Rwamakuba*, Decision (Appeal Against Dismissal of Motion Concerning Illegal Arrest and Detention) (AC).

CHAPTER IV – VERDICT

I. For the foregoing reasons, having considered all the evidence and the arguments of the parties, the Chamber **FINDS** André Rwamakuba, unanimously:

Count 1: Not Guilty of Genocide

Count 2: Not Guilty of Complicity in Genocide

Count 3: Not Guilty of Crimes against Humanity (Extermination)

Count 4: Not Guilty of Crimes against Humanity (Murder)

Accordingly, André Rwamakuba is **ACQUITTED** on all counts in the Indictment. **[page 87]**

II. Pursuant to Rule 99 (A) of the Rules, the Chamber **ORDERS** the immediate release of André Rwamakuba from the Tribunal's Detention Facilities and **REQUESTS** the Registrar to make all necessary arrangements in the implementation of this decision. This order is without prejudice to any further order that may be made by the Chamber pursuant to Rule 99 (B) of the Rules.

III. The Defence is at liberty to file any application seeking appropriate remedy to the violation of his right to legal assistance between 22 October 1998 and 10 March 1999 no later than 23 October 2006; the Prosecution and the Registry to file their respective submissions no later than 30 October 2006; and the Defence to file any reply thereto no later than 6 November 2006. This order is subject to any appeal to be filed within a 30 days time-limit as set out in Rule 108 of the Rules.

Arusha, delivered on 20 September 2006, done in English.

Dennis C. M. Byron Presiding Judge	Karin Hökborg Judge	Gberdao Gustave Kam Judge

[Seal of the Tribunal]

ANNEX I: INDICTMENT

International Criminal Tribunal for Rwanda
Tribunal pénal International pour le Rwanda

Case No. ICTR-98-44C-I

ENGLISH
Original: FRENCH

THE PROSECUTOR

against

ANDRÉ RWAMAKUBA

INDICTMENT
of 9 June 2005

The Prosecutor of the International Criminal Tribunal for Rwanda ("The Prosecutor"), pursuant to the authority stipulated in Article 17 of the Statute of the International Criminal Tribunal for Rwanda (the "Statute of the Tribunal"), charges:

ANDRÉ RWAMAKUBA

Pursuant to Article 2 of the Statute of the Tribunal, with:

(i) **GENOCIDE** ***or, alternatively,***
(ii) **COMPLICITY IN GENOCIDE**

Pursuant to Articles 3 of the Statute of the Tribunal, with:

(iii) **EXTERMINATION,** ***and***
(iv) **MURDER**, *as* **CRIMES AGAINST HUMANITY**

[page 1] The Accused

I. Particulars of the Accused

1. **André RWAMAKUBA** was born in 1950 in Gikomero *commune,* Kigali-rural *préfecture,* Rwanda. **André RWAMAKUBA** was trained as a physician and was Minister of Primary and Secondary Education in the Interim Government of 8 April 1994, taking the oath of office on 9 April 1994 and continuing in that capacity until the Interim Government fled from Rwanda in July 1994. **André RWAMAKUBA** also served as "spokesman" for the Interim Government, and was a member of MDR political party, associated with that party's "Hutu Power" wing.

II. Authority and Legal Duties of the Accused

2. **André RWAMAKUBA** was a member of the Executive Committee of MDR "Power" political party and was a member of that party's *comité préfectoral* in his *préfecture* of origin. As Minister of Primary and Secondary Education in the Interim Government, he had authority and influence over local administrative officials that executed his instruction. The Accused exercised the same authority and control over regional and local leaders of the "civil defense force", particularly over the *Interahamwe* and related militias in Gikomero, his home *commune,* and militiamen that were present in and around the Butare University Hospital.

Charges

Count 1: Genocide

The Prosecutor charges **André RWAMAKUBA** with **Genocide,** pursuant to Articles 2 and 6(1) of the Statute of the Tribunal in that on or between 6 April and 30 April 1994, in Gikomero *commune* and at Butare University Hospital, he was responsible for killing or causing serious bodily or mental harm to members of the Tutsi population, or deliberately inflicting conditions of life upon the Tutsi population that were calculated to bring about its physical destruction, with the intent to destroy, in whole or in part, the Tutsi racial or ethnic group;

Or, alternatively,

Count 2: Complicity in Genocide

The Prosecutor charges **André RWAMAKUBA** with **Complicity in Genocide,** pursuant to Articles 2 and 6(1) of the Statute of the Tribunal in that on or between 6 April and 30 April 1994, in Gikomero *commune* and at Butare University Hospital, he instigated or provided the means to other persons to kill or cause serious bodily or mental harm to members of the Tutsi population, or to deliberately inflict conditions of life upon the Tutsi population that were calculated to bring about its physical destruction, knowing that those other persons intended to destroy, in whole or in part, the Tutsi racial or ethnic group, committed as follows: **[page 2]**

3. Following an extraordinary congress of MDR political party held at Kabusunzu in Kigali on or about 26 July 1993, **André RWAMAKUBA** became associated with the party's extremist "Hutu Power" wing as a member of its executive team, along with Frodouald Karamira, a leader of the party, and Jean Kambanda, a leading politician who would subsequently become Prime Minster of the Interim Government of 8 April 1994. After the establishment of MDR "Power" on 26 July 1993 or thereabouts, **André RWAMAKUBA** practically every weekend, up to and including January 1994, and often accompanied by local authorities and officials of MDR "Power", traveled about his home *commune* in Gikomero, Kigali-rural *préfecture.* He organized meetings and participated in rallies in Kayanga, Gikomero, Rutunga, Gasabo and Gicaca *secteurs.* During the rallies, **André RWAMAKUBA** distributed songs of the Parmehutu party. The ***Accused's*** objective at the time was to recruit members of MDR "Power" party and to support "Hutu Power". The *Accused* called upon the Hutu majority to oppose the Arusha Peace Accords and to exterminate the Tutsi.

4. During those "sensitization" campaigns in Gikomero *commune,* particularly in January 1994, **André RWAMAKUBA** occasionally went about in a vehicle equipped with a public address system exhorting Hutu

to unite in order to get rid of Tutsi. His announcements, the objective of which was to exhort Hutu to unite in order to get rid of Tutsi, included repeated statements that "the time has come for you, Hutu, to get rid of the enemy".

5. During the period from January through June 1994, **André RWAMAKUBA** made statements at various meetings and public gatherings in Gikomero *commune,* or publicly associated himself with statement or acts by other persons at such gatherings. Thus, from January 1994 and during the entire period preceding the events of April 1994 in Sha, Nduba, Shango, Kayanga and Gikomero *secteurs,* and in the *communes* adjoining Gikomero, namely Rutungo, Rubungo and Kanombe, he publicly instigated participants to combat "the enemy", all the Tutsi being characterized as the "the enemy", "accomplices of the enemy" or "accomplices of RPF". After these gatherings, during which the accused called for the extermination of Tutsi, the participants became excited, aggressive and disposed to physically attack and destroy the Tutsi as a group. Such speeches by the **Accused** signaled the start of killings in the *commune.* Furthermore, after the killings began in early April 1994, **André RWAMAKUBA** often praised and congratulated militiamen publicly for and on having killed Tutsi, thereby instigating other militias and armed civilians to participate in further attacks and massacres against the Tutsi population.

6. Between 1 January and 17 July 1994, **André RWAMAKUBA** participated in a killing campaign against Tutsi in Gikomero *commune* and in Butare *prefecture,* instigated or ordered others to participate in this campaign, or otherwise aided and abetted the planning, preparation or execution of the campaign. In so doing, the Accused mobilized the physical and logistical resources of the political party, MDR "Power", the other parties that were allied with MRND and "Hutu Power", the Interim Government ministries controlled by those parties, and the military, to target Rwanda's Tutsi population as "the enemy" or "accomplices of the enemy", and to execute this campaign that sought to attack, kill and destroy the Tutsi as a group.

7. **André RWAMAKUBA** participated in formulating, articulating, publicizing, and legitimizing the policies of the Interim Government of 8 April 1994. Such policies were **[page 3]** elaborated and used to implement a vast campaign of violence against the Tutsi population throughout Rwanda.

8. In this regard, **André RWAMAKUBA** utilized a state-endorsed program of "civilian self defense", whereby officials in the territorial administration [*préfets, bourgmestres* and *conseillers*] and officials in MRND and MDR "Power" political parties recruited civilians, usually local Hutu youth, and consolidated them with political party "youth wing" militias under the authority of retired military officers and reservists. The militias were used to mount and control roadblocks that tracked and killed Tutsi civilians. Furthermore, this "civilian self defense" corps was deployed in armed patrols to identify, search out, and kill the Tutsi population.

9. On or about 17 May 1994, during a meeting of the *Conseil des ministres,* the Interim Government implemented measures to manage the "civil defense force", formally entrusting responsibility for this program to **André RWAMAKUBA** and other ministers.

10. **André RWAMAKUBA** planned, instigated, ordered, committed or otherwise aided and abetted attacks against the Tutsi population in his home *commune* of Gikomero. All those acts were intended to destroy, in whole or in part, the Tutsi as a group.

11. Between 10 and 20 April 1994, **André RWAMAKUBA** delivered bags of machetes to the home of André Muhire, near Ndatemwa trading center in Gasabo *secteur,* in his home *commune* of Gikomero, Kigali-rural *préfecture.* On that occasion, between 10 and 11 April **André RWAMAKUBA** held a meeting with several influential local members of MDR "Hutu Power" political party, including the persons known as Joas Habimana, Chairman of MDR "Power" in Rutunga *secteur,* Ndamage and André Muhire. Several days later, about 13 April, André Muhire distributed the machetes to local residents, who then used them to attack and massacre the Tutsi population. Following such attacks, many Tutsi were killed, including residents of Ndatemwa Centre, namely the wife of a man called Gakumba and her son, Kambanda and the persons known as Kanuma, Rwihimba, Kankidi, Rutembya, Rutembesa, and many unidentified refugees from Rutongo, Nkuzuzu and Rutanga *secteurs.* Again, between 10 and 11 April 2004, **André RWAMAKUBA** delivered bags of machetes to the home of Etienne Kamanzi, the director of the Kayanga Health Center. The Accused knew, or had reasons to know, that the machetes would be used in attacks against the Tutsi in those areas, thereby aiding and abetting the killing campaign against the Tutsi population.

12. Between 10 and 20 April 1994, **André RWAMAKUBA** went to Gikomero *commune* where, during a rally near the *secteur* office, accompanied by RUTAGANIRA, *bourgmestre* of the *commune,* Brigadier NYARWAYA, Mathias KABANGUKA, accountant of the *commune,* and two men unknown but who were identified as policemen, he asked persons in the crowd why the massacres had not started. He then seized documents belonging to two unknown youths, but who were identified as Tutsi, tore the documents and ordered the crowd to seize the youths and kill them. Persons present in the crowd armed with firearms, machetes and clubs, including NGIRUWOSANGA, a *secteur* inhabitant, NGARAMBE and KAYIBANDA, and two communal policemen, immediately seized the two young men that **André RWAMAKUBA** had designated, led them away to a wooded area and killed them as the ***Accused,*** who was not far, looked on. Thereafter, this same crowd stopped an unidentified man on a motorcycle claiming to flee the massacres in Rutongo *commune.* **André RWAMAKUBA,** while speaking to the crowd, stated that the motorcyclist could not be a Hutu since only Tutsi were fleeing, and decided that the youth should be killed. At the **[page 4]** instigation of and following orders from **André RWAMAKUBA**, the same armed crowd led the youth away to a wooded area to kill him. The ***Accused*** then told the crowd that it had just started the killings and that it was a good start. The same day, in the afternoon, *Interahamwe* militiamen, elements of the Presidential Guard, with the assistance of members of the population, following such orders and instigations, began to massacre Tutsi refugees, in Gikomero *commune,* notably at Kayanga Health Center, Gikomero Protestant School, and Gicaca. Thousands were massacred, including refugees from Remera, in Kigali town centre, refugees from the neighbouring *commune* of Gikoro, and Kabuga *secteur,* Rubungo *Commune.*

13. Between 13 and 15 April 1994, in the morning, **André RWAMAKUBA,** accompanied by local authorities, including Mathias RUBANGUKA, accountant of the *commune,* Callixte KABARERA, Inspector of Schools, Brigadier NYARWAYA, RUTAGANIRA, *bourgmestre* of Gikomero *commune,* Thomas MABANGO, *conseiller* of KANYANGA, and soldiers and *Interahamwe* militiamen, arrived at the Kayanga Health Center in Kayanga *secteur,* where many Tutsi fleeing the massacres that had started in their *secteurs* had sought refuge. At a man unknown but identified as the deputy director's request, they assembled in the courtyard of the Health Centre. Upon his arrival, **André RWAMAKUBA** stated that the killings had started everywhere else and that he realized that nothing had been done at the Health Centre. The ***Accused,*** stating that he was showing the example, then brandished a firearm, signaling the start of the massacres to soldiers and *Interahamwe* who began, in his presence, to attack and kill the Tutsi with firearms, machetes and clubs. Shortly after the beginning of the killings, while it was raining, **André RWAMAKUBA,** referring to the bodies to Tutsi, demanded that such filth be cleared. The ***Accused*** witnessed the killings until he left the Health Centre, while the soldiers and *Interahamwe* continued the killings for several hours. No one survived the massacre in which about a hundred people are alleged to have died. The bodies of the victims were thrown into a mass grave. These victims were mostly in-patients and Tutsi refugees fleeing the killings in the neighbouring *secteurs,* notably the killings in the Parishes of Gikomero and Gicaca.

14. Between 27 and 29 April, the thereabouts, **André RWAMAKUBA** was spokesman for the Interim Government and, in that capacity, delivered radio addresses and communiqués on Radio Rwanda and RTLM encouraging the *Interahamwe* and the listening audience to continue the hunt for Tutsi, Moreover, from May to June 1994, **André RWAMAKUBA** made several radio broadcasts in which he urged *Interahamwe* militiamen and the listening audience to continue to hunt down the Tutsi wherever they were hiding and to exterminate them.

15. Between 18 and 25 April 1994, at Butare University Hospital, **André RWAMAKUBA,** often accompanied by Dr. Geoffroy Gatera, soldiers, militiamen and armed civilians, ordered, instigated, committed, or otherwise aided and abetted killings to Tutsi patients and displaced persons seeking refuge at Butare University Hospital with intent to destroy, in whole or in part, the Tutsi ethnic group. Thus, during an official delegation's visit to the Hospital, he asked a woman unknown but identified as the head of Doctors without Borders not to treat Tutsi casualties, to get rid of them and not to admit any others. During the above-mentioned period, **André RWAMAKUBA,** armed with a small axe hung on his belt, and often accompanied by Dr. Gatera, armed soldiers, *Interahamwe* militiamen and civilians armed with machetes, axes and clubs, went around the hospital wards checking identity cards and identifying Tutsi refugees and patients, selecting them and putting them on board a vehicle manned by *Interahamwe* armed with clubs and machetes. The persons taken away **[page 5]** were never seen again. During this period, in the morning or afternoon, during

his rounds, **André RWAMAKUBA** regularly removed drips from patients, in particular, in a ward where unidentified sick Tutsi women were admitted.

16. Concurrently with the events related above, **André RWAMAKUBA** directly caused the death of several persons identified as Tutsi. Thus, during his ward rounds, he caused the death of an unknown Tutsi patient by wounding him in the head with an axe. The militiamen subsequently took away the body of that person. five of the patients referred to above as having been in the in-patients ward, and who were identified as Tutsi, died from axe wounds inflicted by **André RWAMAKUBA.** The ***Accused*** wounded Tutsi found in the corridors of the hospital by striking them on the head with an axe. Some of them, including the persons called Rukara and Mutabazi, who suffered serious bodily harm caused by **André RWAMAKUBA**, were subsequently finished off by *Interahamwe.* As a result of such orders and instigation by the ***Accused,*** many Tutsi refugees and patients were massacred in Butare University Hospital. The victims included the persons known as Déogène, Placide and the parents of several survivors of the killings. The bodies of hundreds of victims of the massacres organized by **André RWAMAKUBA** at Butare University Hospital were gathered and buried in mass graves located behind the Hospital.

17. On or about 28 April 1994, **André RWAMAKUBA** announced on Radio Rwanda that "security had been restored in Butare because the *Inyenzi* had been suppressed", referring to massacres of Tutsi residents that had taken place after the sensitization campaign of 25 April 1994 of thereabouts conducted by an Interim Government delegation in which he had participated.

18. Massacres of Tutsi at Butare University Hospital continued and intensified through late May 1994, particularly after a meeting, held at the Faculty of Medicine on or about 15 May 1994, where Prime Minister Jean Kambanda addressed university authorities, encouraging them to "continue the fight until ultimate victory".

19. By the time the Interim Government fled Rwanda in mid-July 1994, hundreds of thousands of unarmed men, women and children had been killed as a direct result of policies formulated and authorized by MRND and affiliated "Hutu Power" political parties, and executed through the instrumentalities of the State. **André RWAMAKUBA** contributed to formulating and implementing those policies and is directly responsible for the killing of hundreds of Tutsi in Gikomero *commune* and Butare University Hospital, and intended those killings to destroy the Tutsi as a group.

Count 3: Extermination as a Crime Against Humanity

The Prosecutor charges **André RWAMAKUBA** with **Extermination as a Crime against Humanity,** pursuant to Articles 3 and 6(1) of the Statute of the Tribunal in that on or between 6 April and 30 April 1994, in Gikomero *commune* and at Butare University Hospital, he was responsible for killing persons, or causing persons to be killed, as part of a widespread or systematic attack against a civilian population on political, ethnic, or racial grounds. **[page 6]**

20. The allegations contained in paragraphs 1 through 19, above, are reiterated and incorporated herein by reference as a concise statement of facts to support the charges under this specific count of the indictment.

21. Between 6 April 1994 and 17 July 1994, throughout Rwanda there were widespread or systematic attacks against a civilian population based on Tutsi ethnic or racial identification, or political opposition to MRND and "Hutu Power" political parties. **André RWAMAKUBA** planned, instigated, ordered, committed or otherwise aided and abetted the planning and execution of killings of persons perceived to be Tutsi or deemed to be political opponents to "Hutu Power", as set forth above.

22. **André RWAMAKUBA** is responsible, by act or by omission for killing numerous persons in Gikomero *commune,* Kigali-rural *préfecture,* and at the Butare University Hospital in that he planned, instigated, ordered, committed or otherwise aided and abetted the planning, preparation and execution of the crimes detailed above.

23. As recounted in paragraphs 11, 12, 13 and 15, between 10 and 25 April 1994, **André RWAMAKUBA** instigated attacks against Tutsi in Gikomero *commune* and at Butare University Hospital that claimed hundreds of victims.

The victims of the said attacks included:

- Many persons identified as Tutsi residing or seeking refuge in Gikomero *commune,* precisely at Ndatemwa Health Centre, and those seeking refuge at Kayanga Health centre where there were no survivors;
- Many Tutsi refugees and patients foreibly taken out of Butare University Hospital in mid-April by armed militiamen and killed upon the instructions of **André RWAMAKUBA;**
- Many persons killed by armed militiamen in the premises of Butare University Hospital, during the second half of April 1994, upon the orders or instigation of **André RWAMAKUBA,** or in his presence;

Count 4: Murder as a Crime Against Humanity

The Prosecutor charges **André RWAMAKUBA** with **Murder as a Crime against Humanity,** pursuant to Articles 3 and 6(1) of the Statute of the Tribunal in that on or between 6 April and 30 April 1994, in Gikomero *commune* and at Butare University Hospital, he was responsible for killing persons, or causing persons to be killed, as part of a widespread or systematic attack against a civilian population on political, ethnic, or racial grounds.

24. The allegations contained in paragraphs 1 through 23 above are reiterated and incorporated herein by reference as a concise statement of facts to support the charges under this specific count of the Indictment.

25. **André RWAMAKUBA** is responsible, by act or by omission, for killing numerous persons in Gikomero *commune,* Kigali-Rural *préfecture,* and at the Butare University **[page 7]** Hospital in that he planned, instigated, ordered, committed or otherwise aided and abetted the planning, preparation and execution of the crimes detailed above.

26. As recounted in paragraphs 12 and 16, between 10 and 25 April, during the systematic and widespread attacks carried out at Butare University Hospital against Tutsi refugees and patients, **André RWAMAKUBA** was personally responsible for the death of:

- Three unkown youths, but who were identified as Tutsi in a crowd that had gathered near the Gikomero *secteur* office;
- A man who was a patient at Butare University Hospital, unknown but identified as a Tutsi, who was struck on the head with an axe. His body was subsequently taken away by the *Interahamwe;*
- The persons known as Rukura and Mutabazi, two Tutsi encountered in the corridors of Butare University Hospital whom he struck on the head with an axe, seriously wounding them. The said persons were immediately finished off by armed *Interahamwe;*
- Five unknown patients, who were identified as Tutsi, in a Butare University Hospital ward by striking them on the head with an axe, while pulling out their drips.

The acts and omissions of André RWAMAKUBA detailed herein are punishable pursuant to Articles 22 and 23 of the Statute of the Tribunal.

Dated : Arusha, this 9 day of June 2005:

Hassan Bubacar Jallow

Prosecutor

[page i] ANNEX II: CHRONOLOGY OF THE CASE

The main factual elements and decisions pertaining to the case are presented in chronological order under the present section.

1995

2 August 1995: André Rwamakuba is arrested at the initiative of the Namibian authorities

1996

8 February 1996: André Rwamakuba is released by the Namibian authorities following the ICTR Prosecutor's notification that he did not possess evidence to request Rwamakuba's further detention

1998

29 August 1998: Prosecutor files an Indictment against Augustin Bizimana, Félicien Kabuga, Juvénal Kajelijeli, Edouard Karemera, Mathieu Ngirumpaste, Callixte Nzabomimana, Joseph Nzirorera and André Rwamakuba

29 August 1998: Judge Pillay confirms the Indictment and orders non-disclosure of the Indictment

8 October 1998: Judge Pillay issued a warrant of arrest against André Rwamakuba and ordered for his transfer and detention

21 October 1998: André Rwamakuba is arrested by the Namibian authorities in accordance with the Tribunal's warrant of arrest and transferred to the Tribunal

1999

7 April 1999: Initial appearance of André Rwamakuba

27 September 1999: Rescission of the Order for non disclosure of 29 August 1998 **[page ii]**

2000

6 July 2000: Trial Chamber II grants the Defence motion for severance and separate trial of Juvénal Kajelijeli and orders the Prosecutor to file a separate indictment pertaining only to that accused

12 December 2000: Trial Chamber II denies the Defence Motion seeking severance of André Rwamakuba from the Indictment

22 September 2000: Trial Chamber II grants the Prosecutor's Motion for Protective Measures for Witnesses

2001

25 April 2001: Trial Chamber II finds defects in the form of the Indictment and orders its amendment

21 November 2001: Prosecutor files the Amended Indictment against Augustin Bizimana, Félicien Kabuga, Edouard Karemera, Mathieu Ngirumpaste, Callixte Nzabomimana, Joseph Nzirorera and André Rwamakuba

2003

1 September 2003: Trial Chamber III grants the severance of Félicien Kabuga

8 October 2003: Trial Chamber III grants the severance of Augustin Bizimana and Callixte Nzabonimana and grants in part the amendment of the Indictment

27 November 2003: The trial starts before Trial Chamber III composed of Judges Andresia Vaz, presiding, Flavia Lattanzi and Florence Rita Arrey.

11 December 2003: End of the first trial session

2004

13 February 2004: Trial Chamber III grants in part the Prosecution request for leave to amend the Indictment

18 February 2004: Prosecutor files an Amended indictment against Edouard Karemera, Mathieu Ngirumpaste, Joseph Nzirorera and André Rwamakuba **[page iii]**

23 February 2004: Further Initial Appearance of Edouard Karemera, Mathieu Ngirumpaste, Joseph Nzirorera and André Rwamakuba

14 May 2004: Judge Andresia Vaz withdraws from the case

24 May 2004: The remaining Judges order the continuation of the proceedings with a substitute Judge

21 June 2004: Appeals Chamber allows Joseph Nzirorera's appeal on the continuation of the proceedings, and remands the matter to the remaining Judges for reconsideration

16 July 2004: The remaining Judges orders the continuation of the proceedings with a substitute Judge

28 September 2004: Appeals Chamber quashes the Trial Chamber's Decision to continue the proceedings with a substitute Judge

22 October 2004: Reasons for Appeals Chamber Decision of 28 September 2004 and Declaration of Judge Shahabudeen

23 October 2004: Declaration of Judge Schomburg on the Appeals Chamber Decision of 28 September 2004

2005

14 February 2005: Trial Chamber III, composed of Judges Dennis Byron, Presiding, Emile Francis Short and Gberdao Gustave Kam, grants severance of André Rwamakuba and leave to file an Amended Indictment

15 February 2005: Corrigendum to the Decision on Severance

23 February 2005: Prosecutor files the Amended Indictment against André Rwamakuba

3 March 2005: Order directing the Prosecution to provide additional information on its Motion to renew and extend transfer of a Detained Prosecution Witness

8 March 2005: Order to re-file the Amended Indictment

21 March 2005: Further Initial Appearance of André Rwamakuba: a not guilty plea is entered for all charges

24 March 2005: Status Conference and Scheduling Order (commencement of the Prosecution case) **[page iv]**

6 May 2005: *Proprio Motu* Order requesting the Prosecution to file Additional Information for its Motion for Temporary Transfer of Witnesses

23 May 2005: Decision granting the transfer of Witness GIQ

26 May 2005: Decision on Defects in the Form of the Indictment and Decision granting extension of time to file any statement of admitted or contested facts and law

27 May 2005: Judges Dennis C. M. Byron, Presiding, Karin Hökborg and Gberdao Gustave Kam are appointed to compose the Trial Chamber for the trial

1 June 2005: Decision ordering transfer of detained Witness GIN under Rule 90*bis* of the Rules.

Prosecutor files the Amended Indictment in compliance with the Chamber's Decision of 26 May 2005.

3 June 2005: Decision denying Defence Motion for a stay of proceedings

6 June 2005: Pre-Trial Conference

8 June 2005: Prosecutor files a new Amended version of the Indictment in accordance with the Chamber oral Order of 6 June 2005

9 June 2005: (TD1) Prosecution case starts with the Prosecutor's Opening Statements

From 10 June to 15 July 2005: (TD 2 to 23) 14 witnesses testified, including Prosecution Investigator Upendra Baghel and Expert Witness Alison Des Forges

10 June 2005: Prosecutor files a new Amended version of the Indictment in accordance with the Chamber oral Order of 9 June 2005

14 June 2005: Decision on Prosecution Motion for Notice of Alibi and Reciprocal Inspection

14 July 2005: Decision denying Defence Motion seeking directives from the Chamber to get signatures on will-say statements

From 22 August to 6 September 2005: (TD 25 to 36) Continuation of the Prosecution's case: 5 witnesses testified, including continuation of the testimony of Expert Witness Alison Des Forges (teleconference)

7 September 2005: (TD 37) Hearing on the issue of the willingness of two Prosecution witnesses to testify in the case **[page v]**

9 September 2005: (TD 38) Hearing on the issue of the willingness of two Prosecution witnesses to testify in the case

13 September 2005: (TD 39) Hearing on the issue of the willingness of two Prosecution witnesses to testify in the case and the Chamber oral Decision denying the Prosecution's request for adjournment. End of the Prosecution case.

21 September 2005: Decision granting the Defence Motion for Protective Measures

29 September 2005: Decision denying the Prosecution motion for Reconsideration or, in the alternative, Certification to the Appeal Chamber's Decision Denying Request for Adjournment

4 October 2005: Decision granting the Prosecution motion for disclosure of the Defence Witness Statements

7 October 2005: Status Conference

10 October 2005: Scheduling Order (commencement of the Defence Case)

28 October 2005: Decision denying Defence motion for Judgment of acquittal

1 November 2005: Pre-Defence Conference

2 November 2005: Decision granting in part the Prosecution motion to modify the Decision on Protective measures for Defence witnesses

From 7 November to 16 December 2005: (TD 40 to 64) Defence case starts with the Defence Opening Statements: 19 witnesses testified

29 November 2005: (TD 55) Decision granting the Defence motion on protective measures regarding one Defence witness

8 December 2005: Decision granting the Defence motion for the testimony of Defence Witness 1/15 to be taken by video-link

16 December 2005: Decision requesting the Registry to prepare a subpoena addressed to Witnesses 5/16, 5/7, 5/15 and 4/4, ordering their appearance before the Chamber for the next trial scheduled in January 2006; Scheduling Order (Video-Link); Decision granting a site visit to Rwanda **[page vi]**

2006

9 January 2006: Decision ordering the transfer of detained Witnesses 7/3, 4/16 and 9/22 from Rwanda

13-16 January 2006: Site Visit in Rwanda

From 17 January to 9 February 2006: (TD 65-79) Continuation of the Defence's case: 12 witnesses testified

20 January 2006: Decision requesting the Registry to enquire on the availability of Witnesses 9/22 and 4/18 to testify by video-transmission and report back; and dismissing the Defence motion to subpoena Witnesses 9/21 and 4/7

17 February 2006: Scheduling Order (closing briefs and arguments)

5 April (but filed on 10 April) 2006: Decision denying the Defence request to take judicial notice, and ordering the admission into evidence of three documents

21 April 2006: Closing Oral Arguments

[page i] ANNEX III: DEFINED TERMS AND JURISPRUDENCE

1. List of Abbreviations

Abbreviated Form	*Long Form*
Defence Closing Brief	*Prosecutor v. André Rwamakuba, Case No. ICTR-98-44C-I*, Defence Closing Brief (confidential) 18 April 2006
Indictment	*Prosecutor v. André Rwamakuba, Case No. ICTR-98-44C-I*, Amended Indictment, filed 10 June 2005
Prosecution Closing Brief	*Prosecutor v. André Rwamakuba, Case No. ICTR-98-44C-I, Réquisitoire du Procureur*, 18 April 2006
Prosecution Pre-Trial Brief	*Prosecutor v. André Rwamakuba, Case No. ICTR-98-44C-I, Mémoire préalable au procès*, 23 May 2005
Rules	Rules of Procedure and Evidence of the International Criminal Tribunal for Rwanda
Statute	Statute of the International Criminal Tribunal for Rwanda
T.	Transcript. Unless otherwise indicated, all reference to the transcripts are to the official English transcript in the case *Prosecutor v. André Rwamakuba*, Case No. ICTR-98-44C-T

2. Jurisprudence

2.1. Appeals Chamber Judgements

Abbreviated Form	*Long Form*
Akayesu Appeal Judgement	*Prosecutor v. Jean-Paul Akayesu*, Case No. ICTR-96-4-A, Judgement (AC), 1 June 2001
Gacumbitsi Appeal Judgement	*Prosecutor v. Sylvestre Gacumbitsi*, Case No. ICTR-2001-64-A, Judgement (AC), 7 July 2006
Kajelijeli Appeal Judgement	*Prosecutor v. Juvenal Kajelijeli*, Case No. ICTR-98-44A-A, Judgement (AC), 23 May 2005
Kayishema Appeal Judgement	*Prosecutor v. Clément Kayishema and Obed Ruzindana*, Case No. ICTR-95-1-A, Judgement (Reasons) (AC), 1 June 2001 **[page ii]**
Krstić Appeal Judgement	*Prosecutor v. Radislav Krstić,* Case No. IT-98-33-A, Judgement (ICTY AC), 19 April 2004
Naletilic Appeal Judgement	*Prosecutor v. Mladen Naletilic and Vinko Martinovic*, Case No. IT-98-34-A, Judgement (ICTY AC), 3 May 2006
Niyitegeka Appeal Judgement	*Prosecutor v. Eliézer Niyitegeka*, Case No. ICTR-96-14-A, Judgement (AC), 9 July 2004
Ntagerura Appeal Judgement	*Prosecutor v. André Ntagerura, Emmanuel Bagambiki and Samuel Imanishimwe*, Case No. ICTR-99-46-A, Judgement (AC), 7 July 2006
Ntakirutimana Appeal Judgement	*Prosecutor v. Elizaphan Ntakirutimana and Gérard Ntakirutimana,* Case No. ICTR-96-10-A and ICTR-96-17-A, Judgement (AC), 13 December 2004
Rutaganda Appeal Judgement	*Prosecutor v. Georges Anderson Nderubumwe Rutaganda*, Case No. ICTR-96-3-A, Judgement (AC), 26 May 2003
Semanza Appeal Judgement	*Prosecutor v. Laurent Semanza,* Case No. ICTR-97-20-A, Judgement (AC), 20 May 2005
Tadić Appeal Judgement	*Prosecutor v. Duško Tadić,* Case No. IT-94-1-A, Judgement (ICTY AC), 15 July 1999

2.2. Appeals Chamber Decisions

Abbreviated Form	***Long Form***
Barayagwiza, Decision (Prosecutor's RequestforReviewor Reconsideration) (AC)	*Prosecutor v. Jean Bosco-Barayagwiza*, Case No. ICTR-97-19-AR72, Decision (Prosecutor's Request for Review or Reconsideration) (AC), 31 March 2000, *ICTR Report 2000*, pp. 240 and seq.
Karemera et al., Decision on Prosecutor's Interlocutory Appeal of Decision on Judicial Notice (AC)	*Prosecutor v. Edouard Karemera, Mathieu Ngirumpatse and Joseph Nzirorera*, Case No. ICTR-98-44-AR73(C), Decision on Prosecutor's Interlocutory Appeal of Decision on Judicial Notice (AC), 16 June 2006
Rwamakuba, Decision (Appeal Against Dismissal of Motion Concerning Illegal Arrest and Detention) (AC)	*Prosecutor v. André Rwamakuba*, Case No. ICTR-98-44-A, Decision (Appeal Against Dismissal of Motion Concerning Illegal Arrest and Detention) (AC), 11 June 2001
Semanza, Decision of 31 May 2000 (AC)	*Prosecutor v. Laurent Semanza*, Case No. ICTR-97-23-A, Decision (AC), 31 May 2000, *ICTR Report 2000*, pp. 2252 and seq.
Simba, Decision on Interlocutory Appeal Regarding Temporal Jurisdiction (AC)	*Prosecutor v. Aloys Simba*, Case No. ICTR-01-76-AR72.2, Decision on Interlocutory Appeal Regarding Temporal Jurisdiction (AC), 29 July 2004 **[page iii]**

2.3. Trial Chambers Judgements

Abbreviated Form	***Long Form***
Akayesu Judgement	*Prosecutor v. Jean-Paul Akayesu*, Case No. ICTR-96-4-T, Judgement (TC), 2 September 1998, *ICTR Report 1998*, pp. 44 and seq.
Bagilishema Judgement	*Prosecutor v. Ignace Bagilishema*, Case No. ICTR-95-1A-T, Judgement (TC), 7 June 2001
Gacumbitsi Judgement	*Prosecutor v. Sylvestre Gacumbitsi*, Case No. ICTR-2001-64-T, Judgement (TC), 17 June 2004
Kajelijeli Judgement	*Prosecutor v. Juvénal Kajelijeli*, Case No. ICTR-98-44A-T, Judgement and Sentence (TC), 1 December 2003
Kamuhanda Judgement	*Prosecutor v. Jean de Dieu Kamuhanda*, Case No. ICTR-99-54A-T, Judgement and Sentence (TC), 22 January 2003
Musema Judgement	*Prosecutor v. Alfred Musema*, Case No. ICTR-96-13-T, Judgement and Sentence (TC), 27 January 2000
Nahimana Judgement	*Prosecutor v. Ferdinand Nahimana, Jean-Bosco Barayagwiza and Hassan Ngeze*, Case No. ICTR-99-52-T, Judgement and Sentence (TC), 3 December 2003

2.4. Trial Chambers Decisions

Abbreviated Form	***Long Form***
Bizimana et al. Case, Decision on the Defence Motion in Opposition to Joinder and Motion for Severance and Separate Trial Filed by the Accused Juvénal Kajelijeli (TC)	Prosecutor v. Augustin Bizimana, Félicien Kabuga, Juvénal Kajelijeli, Edouard Karemera, Mathieu Ngirumpaste, Callixte Nzabomimana, Joseph Nzirorera and André Rwamakuba, Case No. ICTR-98-44-T, Decision on the Defence Motion in Opposition to Joinder and Motion for Severance and Separate Trial Filed by the Accused Juvénal Kajelijeli (TC), 6 July 2000

Bizimana et al., Decision on the Prosecutor's Motion for severance of Félicien Kabuga's Trial and for Leave to the Accused's Indictment (TC)	*Prosecutor v. Augustin Bizimana, Félicien Kabuga, Edouard Karemera, Mathieu Ngirumpaste, Callixte Nzabomimana, Joseph Nzirorera and André Rwamakuba*, Case No. ICTR-98-44-PT, Decision on the Prosecutor's Motion for severance of Félicien Kabuga's Trial and for Leave to the Accused's Indictment (TC), 1 September 2003 **[page iv]**
Bizimana et al., Decision on the Prosecutor's Motion for Separate Trials and for Leave to File an Amended Indictment (TC)	*Augustin Bizimana, Félicien Kabuga, Edouard Karemera, Mathieu Ngirumpaste, Callixte Nzabomimana, Joseph Nzirorera and André Rwamakuba*, Case No. ICTR-98-44-PT, Decision on the Prosecutor's Motion for Separate Trials and for Leave to File an Amended Indictment (TC), 8 October 2003
Karemera et al., Decision on Interlocutory Appeals Regarding the Continuation of Proceedings with a Substitute Judge and on Nzirorera's Motion for Leave to Consider New Material (AC)	*Prosecutor v. Edouard Karemera, Mathieu Ngirumpatse, Joseph Nzirorera and André Rwamakuba*, Case No. ICTR-98-44-A, Decision on Interlocutory Appeals Regarding the Continuation of Proceedings with a Substitute Judge and on Nzirorera's Motion for Leave to Consider New Material (AC), 28 September 2004
Karemera et al., Reasons for Decision on Interlocutory Appeals Regarding the Continuation of Proceedings with a Substitute Judge and on Nzirorera's Motion for Leave to Consider New Material (AC)	*Prosecutor v. Edouard Karemera, Mathieu Ngirumpatse, Joseph Nzirorera and André Rwamakuba*, Case No. ICTR-98-44-A, Reasons for Decision on Interlocutory Appeals Regarding the Continuation of Proceedings with a Substitute Judge and on Nzirorera's Motion for Leave to Consider New Material (AC), 22 October 2004
Karemera et al., Order on Protective Measures for Prosecution Witnesses (TC)	*Prosecutor v. Edouard Karemera, Mathieu Ngirumpatse, Joseph Nzirorera and André Rwamakuba*, Case No. ICTR-98-44-R75, Order on Protective Measures for Prosecution Witnesses (TC), 10 December 2004
Karemera et al., Decision on severance of André Rwamakuba and for Leave to File Amended Indictment (TC)	*Prosecutor v. Edouard Karemera, Mathieu Ngirumpatse, Joseph Nzirorera and André Rwamakuba*, Case No. ICTR-98-44-PT, Decision on severance of André Rwamakuba and for Leave to File Amended Indictment (TC), 14 February 2005
Rwamakuba, Warrant of Arrest and Order for Transfer and Detention (TC)	*Prosecutor v. André Rwamakuba*, Case ICTR-98-44-I, Warrant of Arrest and Order for Transfer and Detention (TC), 8 October 1998, *ICTR Report* 1998, p. 954.
Rwamakuba, Decision on André Rwamakuba's Motion for Severance (TC)	*Prosecutor v. Rwamakuba*, Case No. ICTR-98-44-T, Decision on André Rwamakuba's Motion for Severance (TC), 12 December 2000, *ICTR Report 2000*, pp. 784 and seq.
Rwamakuba, Decision on the Defence Motion concerning the Illegal Arrest and Illegal Detention of the Accused (TC)	*Prosecutor v. André Rwamakuba*, Case No. ICTR-98-44-T, Decision on the Defence Motion concerning the Illegal Arrest and Illegal Detention of the Accused (TC), 12 December 2000, *ICTR Report 2000*, p. 784.
Rwamakuba, Order to Re-File the Amended Indictment (TC)	*Prosecutor v. André Rwamakuba*, Case No. ICTR-98-44C-PT, Order to Re-File the Amended Indictment (TC), 8 March 2005 **[page v]**
Rwamakuba, Decision on Prosecution Motion for Notice of Alibi and Reciprocal Inspection (TC)	*Prosecutor v. André Rwamakuba*, Case No. ICTR-98-44C-R72, Decision on Prosecution Motion for Notice of Alibi and Reciprocal Inspection (TC), 14 June 2005
Rwamakuba, Decision on Defence Motion for Protective Measures (TC)	*Prosecutor v. André Rwamakuba*, Case No. ICTR-98-44C-T, Decision on Defence Motion for Protective Measures (TC), 21 September 2005

Rwamakuba, Decision on Prosecution Motion for Reconsideration or, in the Alternative, Certification to Appeal Chamber's Decision Denying Request for Adjournment (TC)	*Prosecutor v. André Rwamakuba*, Case No. ICTR-98-44C-T, Decision on Prosecution Motion for Reconsideration or, in the Alternative, Certification to Appeal Chamber's Decision Denying Request for Adjournment (TC), 29 September 2005
Rwamakuba, Decision on Prosecution Motion For Variation, or in Alternative Reconsideration of the Decision on Protective Measures for Defence Witnesses (TC)	*Prosecutor v. André Rwamakuba*, Case No. ICTR-98-44C-T, Decision on Prosecution Motion For Variation, or in Alternative Reconsideration of the Decision on Protective Measures for Defence Witnesses (TC), 2 November 2005
Rwamakuba, Decision on Confidential Motion for the Testimony of Defence Witness 1/15 (TC)	*Prosecutor v. André Rwamakuba*, Case No. ICTR-98-44C-T, Decision on Confidential Motion for the Testimony of Defence Witness 1/15 (TC), 8 December 2005
Rwamakuba, Decision on Defence Motion for A View Locus In Quo (TC)	*Prosecutor v. André Rwamakuba*, Case No. ICTR-98-44C-T, Decision on Defence Motion for A View Locus In Quo (TC), 16 December 2005

Commentary

1. Introduction: The problem of perjury

Academic literature on the ad hoc international tribunals has all but ignored the problem of perjury. Until recently,[1] moreover, commentators had failed to problematize the weak foundations of fact-finding at the tribunals and all that this entails for our faith in the convictions – and occasional acquittals – the tribunal judges hand down.

In this paper I examine the problem of perjury, or false testimony, at the ICTR, with particular reference to the Rwamakuba trial judgement,[2] which did more to reveal the extent of the problem than any tribunal decision before it. The *problem* of perjury may be defined as a reluctance to prosecute the offence where its commission is suspected. The hypothesis explored in this paper is that the problem of perjury at the ICTR has combined with a systemic temptation for Rwandan witnesses to testify falsely, thus encouraging actual perjury. Along with other factors, the above combination contributes to the unreliability of judicial fact-finding at the ICTR and the risk of conviction of innocent persons. The discussion that follows fits within a broader questioning, begun by Combs, of the ability of international criminal tribunals to discover the truth.[3]

2. The prosecution's "unconvincing" witnesses in Rwamakuba

Several features combine to make André Rwamakuba's case unusual: he was arrested by the Namibian authorities (not clear why) in 1995, released upon a request of the ICTR prosecutor in 1996, and arrested again in 1998;[4] more than five years elapsed before his trial could start; soon after it opened, it was abandoned when the presiding judge withdrew (she had co-habited, for a short period of time, with the prosecutor);[5] the indictment was amended and finalized only in June 2005; a new trial commenced in the same month, almost seven years after Rwamakuba's re-arrest;[6] the accused never attended his trial, protesting from his cell the falsehood of the allegations against him.[7] In September 2006 Rwamakuba was acquitted of all charges when the prosecution's evidence was thrown out after the close of the hearings.[8]

Of all the peculiar aspects of the case, I will focus on the last.

Rwamakuba faced four main allegations of genocide: that he supplied machetes which were later used in killings; that he ordered and participated in the killing of three Tutsi persons; that he carried out large-scale killings at a health centre; and that he took part in other killings at a university hospital.[9]

The Trial Chamber judges observed that the case against him "consisted mainly of hearsay evidence concerning both the content of the allegations and also the identification" of the accused, with only five of the eighteen prosecution witnesses claiming to have direct knowledge of him.[10] The key witnesses suffered from remarkably messy memories, giving "irreconcilable versions of the facts",[11] which the judges, unusually for the ICTR, made little effort to smooth over.[12] Accounts of facts supposedly recalled by the witnesses kept

---

1 See Nancy Combs's seminal Factfinding Without Facts: The Uncertain Evidentiary Foundations of International Criminal Convictions, Cambridge University Press, New York 2010.

2 Judgement, *Prosecutor v. Rwamakuba*, Case No. ICTR-98-44C-T, T. Ch. III, 20 September 2006, in this volume, p. 439.

3 See Nancy Combs, Fact-finding Without Facts: The Uncertain Evidentiary Foundations of International Criminal Convictions, *supra* note 1.

4 Judgement, *Prosecutor v. Rwamakuba*, T. Ch. III, *supra* note 2, par. 4-5.

5 *Ibid.*, par. 6.

6 *Ibid.*, par. 6-7.

7 *Ibid.*, par. 9.

8 Up until Rwamakuba's acquittal, the ICTR had convicted 34 persons and acquitted four. Seventeen more convictions have followed. There has been one further acquittal.

9 Judgement, *Prosecutor v. Rwamakuba*, T. Ch. III, *supra* note 2, par. 16.

10 *Ibid.*, par. 36.

11 *Ibid.*, par. 64.

12 On this point, see A. Zahar, Witness Memory and the Manufacture of Evidence at the International Criminal Tribunals, in C. Stahn and L. van den Herik (eds), Future Perspectives in International Criminal Justice, TMC Asser Press/Cambridge University Press, Cambridge 2010, p. 600-610. In Rwamakuba the judges evidently had a hunch that the prosecution's case was unacceptably weak, and worked backwards from their theory to dismiss every incriminating allegation. The ICTR's usual practice is to move backward from a theory of guilt to a reconciled evidentiary basis, using techniques described in the cited paper. Some techniques

shifting over the years;[13] critical facts were dredged up for the first time when a witness spoke in court,[14] or were contradicted by the evidence of other prosecution witnesses;[15] or they simply made no sense.[16]

The evidence concerning the supply of machetes was quickly dismissed as essentially meaningless.[17] A witness dubbed GAC was linked to the machete allegations. GAC already had been condemned as unreliable by another ICTR trial bench.[18] That he was recycled by the prosecution in the Rwamakuba case is a sign of desperation if not want of professionalism. The Rwamakuba judges said of GAC that his evidence was "tainted with major internal inconsistencies which seriously challenge his credibility".[19] They repeated their concerns about him several times.[20]

Witness GIN was called to support the allegation about the killing of the three Tutsi. In her several prior out-of-court statements, her story about Rwamakuba's role and other aspects of the incident kept changing. She did not hold up under cross-examination.[21] The Trial Chamber concluded that "These major inconsistencies between GIN's testimony and her prior statements cannot be explained by the time elapsed, translation discrepancies, the manner in which the statements were taken or the impact of trauma inflicted upon the witness"[22] – marking off some of the techniques commonly used at the ICTR to excuse difficulties in prosecution witness recollection. Moreover, "Neither can they be considered additional details provided to the witness's prior statements."[23]

What, then, *can* they be considered? And if the aforementioned inconsistencies cannot be explained by the factors listed, what *does* explain them? Evidently, to the reader of the judgement, they were lies. A witness who first denies that the accused was present at the scene of a crime and later insists that indeed he was present must at least be *suspected* of lying.[24] But the judges stopped short of calling GIN a liar. Why they stopped short they never explained.[25]

GAB claimed to be an eyewitness to the killings at the health centre. Like GAC, he had been found to be not credible by a prior ICTR case, but he was called anyway.[26] GAB supposedly heard Rwamakuba call out to the assembled fighters that the Tutsi should be killed "so that in [the] future, a Hutu who is born asks what a Tutsi look[ed] like" (brackets in original).[27] We first come across this leitmotif of the 1994 lore in the Akayesu case. There, witnesses testified that one Kubwimana had said during a public meeting chaired by Akayesu that all the Tutsi were to be killed "so that someday Hutu children would not know what a Tutsi looked like".[28] Possibly in elaboration of this theme, Akayesu himself is said to have called out to men committing rape, "Never ask me again what a Tutsi woman tastes like".[29] Anyone with experience of prosecution witness testimony at the ICTR (whether direct experience of the testimony, or indirect from study of the transcripts) will have been struck by certain clichéd renditions of events, hackneyed set pieces of evil-doing, so idealized

---

used by the Rwamakuba judges to discard evidence (for example, Judgement, *Prosecutor v. Rwamakuba*, T. Ch. III, *supra* note 2, par. 114, 150) are just as implausible as those used in other settings to repair it.

13 For example Judgement, *Prosecutor v. Rwamakuba*, T. Ch. III, *supra* note 2, par. 113, 131, 145, 172 and 188.

14 For example, *ibid.*, par. 66 and 173.

15 For example, *ibid.*, par. 68.

16 For example, *ibid.*, par. 112 and 170-1.

17 *Ibid.*, par. 104 and 110.

18 *Ibid.*, par. 109-110.

19 *Ibid.*, par. 110.

20 *Ibid.*, par. 114-16 and 118.

21 *Ibid.*, par. 131.

22 *Ibid.*, par. 132.

23 *Ibid.*, par. 132.

24 *Ibid.*, par. 145.

25 GIN was the source of much of the evidence against Jean de Dieu Kamuhanda, who was convicted more than two years before the *Rwamakuba* case was decided, ICTR, Judgment and Sentence, *Prosecutor v. Kamuhanda*, Case No. ICTR-95-54A-T, T. Ch. II, 22 January 2004, Klip/ Sluiter, ALC-XVII-531. GIN was witness GEK in that case. The different pseudonyms help disguise cross-case identities.

26 Judgement, *Prosecutor v. Rwamakuba*, T. Ch. III, *supra* note 2, par. 146.

27 *Ibid.*, par. 139.

28 ICTR, Judgement, *Prosecutor v. Akayesu*, Case No. ICTR-96-4-T, T. Ch. I, 2 September 1998, Klip/ Sluiter, ALC-II-399, par. 118.

29 *Ibid.*, par. 422.

that witnesses easily transpose them from one case to another, changing few details except the identity of the accused.

A remarkable feature of the Rwamakuba judgement is that this phenomenon, or syndrome, is, for the first time, noticed and remarked upon by a bench of judges. The judges observed that GAB's testimony in the ICTR's Kamuhanda case had been "disturbingly similar" to that in Rwamakuba, for GAB "described André Rwamakuba's behaviour and the account of the events in the same way as he described Kamuhanda's criminal acts [...] he also attributed much of the same words to Kamuhanda and Rwamakuba."[30] This was actually pointed out to the witness, and GAB conceded that he had attributed to the two accused the "same logic".[31] He was a witness of logic, it seems, not fact.

The judges "cast serious doubt" on GAB's credibility, but took no further action.[32] They observed that a second witness, RJ, had testified using what we might henceforth call the logical (or is it analogical?) method,[33] but took no action against her either, except to declare her not credible.[34]

The university hospital allegations portrayed Rwamakuba as Doctor Death.[35] Of the six witnesses summoned for this episode, only XV claimed personal knowledge of the accused.[36] XV clearly had set out to smear Rwamakuba, deciding to backdate the accused's anti-Tutsi sentiments all the way to 1973. It was a reckless gamble, and he was effortlessly exposed.[37] XV had not troubled even to find out what Rwamakuba looked like in 1973 or 1994, as the court was soon to discover.[38] He too eagerly made last-minute adjustments to his stories to fit to Rwamakuba the model (or logic) he was working from:

> Witness XV explained that the absence of any reference to the Accused in seven of his prior statements was due to the fact that "[he] could only think of [Rwamakuba] when it was the time of his trial". The Chamber notes that in 2003, XV was on the Prosecution's witness list for the first trial against André Rwamakuba [in which Rwamakuba was one of four co-accused], and his reconfirmation statement was made in Arusha in preparation for his testimony in that trial. This reconfirmation statement, however, did not mention major elements of the evidence that he gave in this trial.[39]

We can see in this passage strong indicators, even intimations, of deliberate falsification by XV, but the Trial Chamber would not bring itself to say so openly. As XV's evidence evaporated, so the significance of the other hospital witnesses diminished. All of them relied on hearsay to place Rwamakuba at the hospital.[40] I will briefly refer to the court's findings on one of these witnesses, HF. HF claimed to have seen Rwamakuba committing crimes at the hospital while dressed in banana leaves.[41] The leaves are another leitmotif of the Rwandan civil war. According to the lore, fighters resorted to traditional tribal gear when decking out for violence.[42] Projecting the image onto Rwamakuba, HF did not think it odd that a resident doctor would put on banana leaves before setting off on his round of the wards to kill Tutsi patients. In the event, when HF came before the court, "she denied all this", observed the chamber dryly, "along with other matters recorded in [her prior] statements".[43] She did claim, though, that her sister was abducted from the hospital and killed. When it emerged that HF had testified in a Rwandan (state) court that a sister of hers with the same first name as her hospital sister was killed in totally different circumstances, HF "explained that she had twin sisters with the same Christian name". The reaction to these revelations at the ICTR? "The Chamber is not convinced

30 Judgement, *Prosecutor v. Rwamakuba*, T. Ch. III, *supra* note 2, par. 149. Footnote 401 of the judgement illustrates the transposition between the two cases.

31 *Ibid.*, par. 149.

32 *Ibid.*, par. 152.

33 *Ibid.*, par. 192.

34 *Ibid.*, par. 193.

35 See the indictment paragraphs reproduced at *ibid.*, par. 160.

36 *Ibid.*, par. 163.

37 The effort is dismissed in *ibid.*, par. 171.

38 *Ibid.*, par. 174. Rwamakuba's boycott of the proceedings was an advantage to him in this respect.

39 *Ibid.*, par. 173.

40 *Ibid.*, par. 175-7.

41 *Ibid.*, par. 188.

42 Banana leaves come to prominence in ICTR, Judgement and Sentence, *Prosecutor v. Musema*, Case No. ICTR-96-13-T, T. Ch. I, 27 January 2000, Klip/ Sluiter, ALC-VI-469, par. 372, and then much is made of them in ICTR, Judgement, *Prosecutor v. Bagilishema*, Case No. ICTR-95-1A-T, T. Ch. I, 7 June 2001., Klip/ Sluiter, ALC-X-617.

43 Judgement, *Prosecutor v. Rwamakuba*, T. Ch. III, *supra* note 2, par. 188.

by this explanation."[44] Is that it? Just *not convinced*? The comment is typical of a studied, unnatural understatement that mars the judgement.

Having decided that all the key prosecution witnesses had been, in effect, making up evidence against Rwamakuba, the judges, instead of instituting proceedings against them for suspected perjury, acquitted the accused and called the proceedings to a close. By that point, Rwamakuba had been in the tribunal's custody for nearly eight years.[45]

What are the roots of apathy towards falsification in the Rwamakuba judgement? There is no doubt that the Trial Chamber was aware of a serious underlying problem. "The Prosecution witnesses' testimonies were tainted of [sic] *major deficiencies* which could not be justified by the time elapsed, translation discrepancies, the manner in which the prior statements were taken or the impact of trauma inflicted upon the witnesses."[46] But the chamber evidently felt no obligation to get to the bottom of the major deficiencies. It saw no connection, it would appear, between them and the integrity of the proceedings. The chamber had an acknowledged obligation to "ascertain the truth",[47] but it seems to have construed "truth" narrowly. It fully accepted that "This Tribunal was established to contribute to the process of reconciliation and to the restoration of peace and security in Rwanda",[48] but did not ask how the deficient prosecution of Rwamakuba was compatible with that aim.

3. Influence of the Akayesu case on the interpretation of Rule 91 at the ICTR

In a 1999 paper which is probably the earliest academic comment on the power of the ad hoc international tribunals to punish false testimony, Klip wrote:

> Perjury hinders the course of justice and might even lead to miscarriages of justice. Especially in the serious cases pending before the International Criminal Tribunal it is important that the Trial Chamber can rely on those giving evidence. Whenever this trust is abused it deserves a reaction.[49]

It is hard to disagree with this statement of principle. Klip cannot have known at that early date that the perjury power against witnesses would remain remarkably underutilized at the tribunals.[50] At the ICTR, the contribution of the Akayesu Trial Chamber to this effect was critical. The Akayesu case's influence was both jurisprudential and ideological, as I will try to explain.

In the Akayesu case, the defence complained that witness R's testimony was so self-contradictory as to constitute false testimony. The Trial Chamber, in its decision,[51] stated that where a party moves for a Rule 91 investigation, "the onus is on th[e] party *to convince the Chamber* that there exist strong grounds for believing that a witness has knowingly and wilfully given false testimony".[52]

This interpretation of Rule 91 is inaccurate and misleading. The clear meaning of the rule is not that a party must *convince* the chamber of any thing, but that it must show, *to the satisfaction* of the chamber, that there exist strong grounds for believing that a witness has knowingly and wilfully given false testimony. In other words, the moving party need only satisfy the trial judges that there exists a sufficient suspicion of perjury to warrant a formal investigation.

---

44 *Ibid.*, par. 189.

45 *Ibid.*, par. 5 (noting that Rwamakuba was arrested on 21 October 1998 and transferred to the tribunal the following day).

46 *Ibid.*, par. 156, emphasis added.

47 ICTR RPE, Rule 90(F).

48 Judgement, *Prosecutor v. Rwamakuba*, T. Ch. III, *supra* note 2, par. 210.

49 A. Klip, Commentary on Decisions Relating to the False Testimony of Dragan Opacić, Klip/ Sluiter, ALC-I-214. Klip was commenting on *Prosecutor v. Miroslav Tadić*, Order for the Prosecution to Investigate the False Testimony of Dragan Opacić, Trial Chamber, 10 December 1996. The case against Opacić was discontinued: ICTY, Order for the Return of a Detained Witness, *Prosecutor v. Miroslav Tadić*, Case No. IT-94-1-ST, IT-95-7-Misc.1, T. Ch. II, 27 May 1997, Klip/ Sluiter, ALC-I-211.

50 Klip goes on to argue in his paper that the ICTY has no jurisdiction to prosecute persons for false testimony, the power is not inherent, and the tribunal ought to have sought such jurisdiction from the UN Security Council. While I agree with this assessment, and have taken a similar line myself with respect to the contempt power more generally (A. Zahar, International Court and Private Citizen, 12 New Criminal Law Review 2009, p. 569-589), I will assume, for the purposes of the present comment, that the jurisdictional issue does not arise. It certainly is not a *reason* for the paucity of perjury prosecutions at the tribunals.

51 ICTR, Decision on the Defence Motions to Direct the Prosecutor to Investigate the Matter of False Testimony by Witness "R", *Prosecutor v. Akayesu*, Case No. ICTR-96-4-T, T. Ch. I, 9 March 1998.

52 *Ibid.*, emphasis added. Several of these early decisions do not use paragraph numbers.

At the ICTR (as at the ICTY) the early formulation of Rule 91 (entitled "False Testimony under Solemn Declaration") was succeeded after several years by an elaborated version. I reproduce the key provisions of each:

> **Rule 91 (June 1995-May 2003)**
>
> (A) A Chamber, on its own initiative or at the request of a party, may warn a witness of the duty to tell the truth and the consequences that may result from a failure to do so.
>
> (B) If a Chamber has strong grounds for believing that a witness *has*[53] knowingly and wilfully given false testimony, it may direct the Prosecutor to investigate the matter with a view to the preparation and submission of an indictment for false testimony. [...]
>
> **Rule 91 (May 2003-present)**
>
> (A) A Chamber, *proprio motu* or at the request of a party, may warn a witness of the duty to tell the truth and the consequences that may result from a failure to do so.
>
> (B) If a Chamber has strong grounds for believing that a witness has knowingly and wilfully given false testimony, it may:
>
> (i) direct the Prosecutor to investigate the matter with a view to the preparation and submission of an indictment for false testimony; or
>
> (ii) where the Prosecutor, in the view of the Chamber, has a conflict of interest with respect to the relevant conduct, direct the Registrar to appoint an *amicus curiae* to investigate the matter and report back to the Chamber as to whether there are sufficient grounds for instigating proceedings for false testimony.
>
> (C) If the Chamber considers that there are sufficient grounds to proceed against a person for giving false testimony, the Chamber may:
>
> (i) in circumstances described in paragraph (B) (i), direct the Prosecutor to prosecute the matter; or
>
> (ii) in circumstances described in paragraph (B) (ii), issue an order in lieu of an indictment and direct *amicus curiae* to prosecute the matter. [...]
>
> (H) Paragraphs (B) to (G) apply *mutatis mutandis* to a person who knowingly and willingly makes a false statement in a written statement taken in accordance with Rule 92 *bis* ["Proof of Facts Other Than by Oral Evidence"] which the person knows or has reason to know may be used as evidence in proceedings before the Tribunal.

The basic test on the face of the rule is both perspicuous and constant.

To further confuse matters, the Akayesu Trial Chamber stated later in the same decision that "the onus is on the party pleading a case of false testimony to *prove*: the falsehood of the witness['s] statements; that these statements were made with harmful intent, or at least that they were made by a witness who was fully aware that they were false; and the possible bearing of the said statements upon the judge's decision".[54]

Whatever one makes of the last requirement in this passage, which is quite unclear, a glance at either version of Rule 91, above, reveals the incorrectness of contending that the moving party must *prove* both the actus reus and the mens rea of the offence. For if that were the case, the rule's continuation, that the chamber "may direct the Prosecutor to investigate the matter", is rendered senseless. Also senseless becomes the rule's

---

[53] Emphasis added. In several editions of the RPE after 1995 and before 2003 (available from the ICTR's web site), the "has" in this position has mistakenly been changed to "may have", thus radically altering the test. The first (1995) edition of the ICTR RPE correctly shows the "has", which of course was copied verbatim from the ICTY RPE. The post-1995 transcription error in the RPE was transmitted to ICTR decisions. For example, in ICTR, Decision on the Request of the Defence for the Chamber to Direct the Prosecutor to Investigate a Matter with a View to the Preparation and Submission of an Indictment for False Testimony, *Prosecutor v. Bagilishema*, Case No. ICTR-95-1A-T, T.Ch. I, 11 July 2000, par. 3, the Trial Chamber incorporates the incorrect "may have" version of the rule; similarly in ICTR, Decision on Defence Request for an Investigation Into Alleged False Testimony of Witness DO, *Prosecutor v. Bagosora, Kabiligi, Ntabakuze and Nsengiyumva*, Case No. ICTR-98-41-T, T. Ch. I, 3 October 2003, Klip/ Sluiter, ALC-XII-331, par. 8.

[54] Decision on the Defence Motions to Direct the Prosecutor to Investigate the Matter of False Testimony by Witness "R", *Prosecutor v. Akayesu*, T. Ch. I, *supra* note 51, emphasis added.

requirement that a perjury indictment must be decided by a Trial Chamber *other* than the one deciding the Rule 91 motion.[55]

In truth, "proof" in the framework of Rule 91 is something to be pursued not by the party raising the suspicion, but upon an indictment by an amicus investigator/prosecutor before a different bench of judges; it has nothing to do with the original Trial Chamber's determination or the burden of the party initiating the action.

The Akayesu Trial Chamber denied the motion in question on the ground that the defence had not "demonstrated" witness R's mens rea. The defence's arguments were said to be "pertinent only to raising doubts as to the credibility of the statements made by the witness". They were not "sufficient to establish" that R knowingly and wilfully gave false testimony.

The Rutaganda case, on the heels of Akayesu (and with the same judges), gave rise to three decisions. The first concerned defence evidence that prosecution witness E had falsely denied that he had a criminal record. The motion was dismissed using a nearly identical text as the Akayesu decision.[56] In a second motion, the defence claimed that the witness had contradicted himself in relation to incidents he had witnessed. The prosecution responded that the issue went to weight and was a matter for evaluation in the context of all the evidence adduced. The chamber again dismissed the motion using the words of the Akayesu decision.[57]

The Rutaganda decisions went on appeal, presenting the ICTR Appeals Chamber with its first opportunity to comment on the current interpretation of Rule 91.[58] Rutaganda's complaint on appeal was that the Trial Chamber had used an improperly high legal standard. He argued that the test should be set at the level of ICTR Rule 47(A) ("satisfied that there is sufficient evidence to provide reasonable grounds for believing that a suspect has committed a crime"). The Appeals Chamber dismissed the appeal as inadmissible on procedural grounds. However, it inserted the following, remarkable, comment: "an investigation for false testimony is ancillary to the proceedings and does not impact on the accused's right to a fair trial [...] a credibility determination may be based, but does not necessarily depend, on a judicial finding that a witness has given false testimony".[59] We see in this idea a strikingly narrow conception of what impacts an accused's right to a fair trial. The witness who knows that a casual approach to the truth might trigger an investigation for perjury obviously is in a different position from the witness who believes that a fabrication, should it be noticed, will be treated as an inconsistency going to weight. The Appeals Chamber did not consider the broader consequences of its dictum.

In the Bagilishema case,[60] the defence submitted evidence tending to show that witness H's claim that certain people were in the presence of the accused at certain times could not possibly be true. The Trial Chamber adopted the Akayesu test, requiring "proof" of the elements of the offence. It said that while there was evidence of a "contradiction" in H's account, "This does not *suffice to demonstrate* that the witness intended to mislead the Chamber and to cause harm."[61] The chamber added that "contradiction" is common in criminal cases, and deferred its decision on the credibility of H until such time as all evidence in the case was presented.[62]

Already by the time of Bagilishema, then, a patterned judicial response to Rule 91 defence motions is clear.

---

55 Rule 91(D) of the pre-May 2003 ICTR RPE; and Rule 91(F) of the post-May 2003 ICTR RPE.

56 ICTR, Decision on the Defence Motion to Direct the Prosecutor to Investigate the Matter of False Testimony by Witness "E", *Prosecutor v. Rutaganda*, Case No. ICTR-96-3-T, T. Ch. I, 10 March 1998.

57 ICTR, Decision on the Defence Motion to Direct the Prosecutor to Investigate the Matter of False Testimony by Witness "CC", *Prosecutor v. Rutaganda*, Case No. ICTR-96-3-T, T. Ch. I, 10 March 1998.

58 ICTR, Decision on Appeals Against the Decision by Trial Chamber I Rejecting the Defence Motions to Direct the Prosecutor to Investigate the Matter of False Testimony by Witnesses "E" and "CC", *Prosecutor v. Rutaganda*, Case No. ICTR-96-3-A, A. Ch., 8 June 1998, Klip/ Sluiter, ALC-II-233 (text of oral summary of decision).

59 The first part of this quoted statement is later repeated by ICTR, Judgement, *Simba v. Prosecutor*, Case No. ICTR-07-76-A, A. Ch., 27 November 2007, in this volume, p. 817, par. 33.

60 Decision on the Request of the Defence for the Chamber to Direct the Prosecutor to Investigate a Matter with a View to the Preparation and Submission of an Indictment for False Testimony, *Prosecutor v. Bagilishema*, T. Ch. I, *supra* note 53.

61 *Ibid.*, par. 6, emphasis added.

62 *Ibid.*, par. 7.

In the next case, Nahimana, the defence claimed that, under cross-examination, prosecution witness AEN had contradicted his own evidence-in-chief. In the resulting Rule 91 decision,[63] the Trial Chamber proceeded directly to review AEN's answers under questioning, concluding that while there had been a lack of clarity, there had been no obvious contradiction. It then restated the Akayesu test, about the need for "proof", and reaffirmed the position in the Rutaganda decision on witness CC[64] that such matters are best left to the end of a case, when witness credibility determinations can be made in the context of all the evidence.

In Bagosora, one aspect of witness DO's testimony on indictment-related events was highly implausible. The witness, who was serving a life sentence in Rwanda, also made allegations about current threats against him by the family of one of the accused; but when questioned further, he was not able to substantiate them. In its Rule 91 decision,[65] the Trial Chamber affirmed the Akayesu test, noting that while the rule "does not *expressly* require a party to prove false testimony as a prerequisite to the Chamber exercising its power to direct an investigation [...] an onus rests on the requesting party to *prove* that the testimony was given knowingly and willfully".[66] There is a "strong preference", added the chamber, "for considering such matters as part of the evaluation of credibility".[67] The motion was denied on the ground that the highly implausible aspect of the testimony "[did] not concern a matter material to the case",[68] whereas the allegations against the family had been retracted by DO almost as soon as they were made, casting doubt, it was said, on the existence of mens rea.[69] Again, Bagosora contains no explanation of its departure from the plain meaning of the rule. Akayesu is thus unreflectively recycled.

Rule 91 actions came to some prominence in the ICTR's Butare case. In one action,[70] the defence argued that witness QY had given evidence with an intention to falsely incriminate the accused, citing inconsistencies with statements made by her in another tribunal case, as well as her "harebrained" explanations of them.[71] The defence conceptualized litigation under Rule 91 as going beyond the immediate concerns about QY; the procedure, according to the defence, held out the promise of a "public sanction [...] to deter other potential witnesses from following this course of action".[72] The Trial Chamber dismissed the motion with minimal reasoning.[73]

However, some time after the first QY decision, QY and SJ (another witness in the Butare case) appeared as witnesses in a trial in Canada against one Munyaneza. In the light of what transpired at that trial, the two witnesses were recalled to the ICTR for further cross-examination in the Butare case. This resulted in admissions by both witnesses that they had testified falsely in the course of their earlier ICTR appearances.[74] A new Rule 91 motion was filed by the defence. The Trial Chamber cited Akayesu as the authority for the applicable test.[75] But because the witnesses had already admitted to lies and manipulation, the question of "proof" did not require (or attract) any comment by the chamber.[76] The real puzzle in this case is why the judges, who had all the information they needed to initiate Rule 91 proceedings themselves, passively waited for a motion to this effect from the defence. In the event, the chamber ordered the appointment of an amicus investigator with a broad mandate, under both Rules 91 and 77 (contempt of court).[77]

---

63 ICTR, Decision on the Defence Motion to Direct the Prosecutor to Investigate the Matter of False Testimony by Witness "AEN" in Terms of Rule 91(B), *Prosecutor v. Nahimana*, Case No. ICTR-96-11-I, T. Ch. I, 27 February 2001.

64 See above.

65 Decision on Defence Request for an Investigation Into Alleged False Testimony of Witness DO, *Prosecutor v. Bagosora, Kabiligi, Ntabakuze and Nsengiyumva*, T. Ch. I, *supra* note 53.

66 *Ibid.*, par. 9, emphasis added.

67 *Ibid.*

68 *Ibid.*, par. 11.

69 *Ibid.*, par. 13.

70 ICTR, Decision on Arsène Shalom Ntahobali's Motion to Have Perjury Committed by Prosecution Witness QY Investigated, *Prosecutor v. Nyiramasuhuko and Ntahobali*, Case No. ICTR-97-21-T ,T. Ch. II, 23 September 2005.

71 *Ibid.*, par. 5.

72 *Ibid.*, par. 6.

73 *Ibid.*

74 ICTR, Decision on Ntahobali's Motion for an Investigation into False Testimony and Kanyabashi's Motion for an Investigation into Contempt of Court Relative to Prosecution Witnesses QY and SJ, *Prosecutor v. Nyiramasuhuko and Ntahobali,* Case No. ICTR-98-42-T, T. Ch. II, 19 March 2009, par. 13.

75 *Ibid.*, par. 10.

76 *Ibid.*, par. 14.

77 *Ibid.*, par. 17.

One defendant in the Karemera case, Joseph Nzirorera, made three separate motions in the course of the prosecution's case to have the first prosecution witness in that case, M, investigated for false testimony.[78] Nzirorera complained that later prosecution witnesses had been contradicting M.[79] His motion was denied. The Trial Chamber, referring to decisions in Akayesu, Bagilishema, and other ICTR cases, distilled the following principle:

> Contradictory evidence between witnesses' testimony is insufficient evidence to demonstrate that a witness intended to mislead the Chamber and to cause harm. Instead, contradictory evidence is used when determining the probative value of the evidence presented by the parties during trial.[80]

This is an illogical view, both of evidence and of the role of the judge. The Trial Chamber seems to be saying that contradictory evidence merely lessens the probative value of that evidence and nothing more; alternatively, that the role of the judge is limited to weighing up the evidence and making a judgement on probative value in relation to a fact in issue. Both these positions omit to mention the essence of fact-finding, namely that the judge's assessment of testimonial evidence ultimately comes down to the credibility of witnesses. Whether by intuitive means or through analysis of what a witness says over time, a decision is made about his or her credibility. Where the question concerns what to do with a witness who is found not to be credible, and who may have been lying, a judge, contrary to the Karemera Chamber's suggestion in the excerpt above,[81] need not wait until after all the evidence in the case has been presented to make a determination on credibility. The determination can be made, and the possibility of lying investigated, even before the very first witness in the case (as M was) has completed his or her testimony.[82]

In another Karemera decision,[83] the Rule 91 issue arose from the use of forged documents, which renders the Trial Chamber's decision to deny the motion unexpected, to say the least. Prosecution witnesses ALG and HH, both of whom were in detention in Rwanda on criminal charges, claimed to have had contemporaneous knowledge of letters written by one of the accused in April 1994 exhorting the Interahamwe militia to kill Tutsi persons. The letters, which were introduced into evidence by another witness, were later independently determined to be forgeries.[84] Quite apart from the fact that this discovery creates at least a presumption of false testimony on behalf of the two witnesses, it was known to the Trial Chamber that HH had confessed to being part of a "conspiracy to frame" another ICTR accused, François Karera.[85] Despite the Karera incident, the Karemera judges took the following position:

> in the Chamber's view, at this stage, the evidentiary foundation for the allegations of the Defence does not constitute strong grounds for believing in any harmful intent of the witnesses concerned nor that their testimony results from a plan to subvert the trial as submitted. Furthermore, the allegations made by [the accused] concerning a conspiracy to make false accusations against them are part of their challenge to the Prosecution's case and reflect a theory that the Defence has been advocating. The Chamber, however, recalls that *the burden of proof is on the Prosecution and cannot be made to shift to the Defence.* [...] The interests of justice do not require or make it desirable for the Chamber to engage an investigation on a collateral exercise on the basis of the unsupported suspicions expressed by the Defence. This goes outside what is necessary for justice to be done in this case.[86]

If the disinclination to proceed on a "collateral exercise" alludes to the common law's finality rule, this would constitute a misapplication of the rule, in light of the well-established exceptions going to bias, partiality, and prior inconsistency of the witness. And while the Chamber's statement, above, is open to

78 ICTR, Decision on Defence Motion for Investigation of Prosecution Witness Ahmed Mbonyunkiza for False Testimony, *Prosecutor v. Karemera et al.*, Case No. ICTR-98-44-T, T. Ch. III, 29 December 2006, par. 1.

79 *Ibid.*, par. 2.

80 *Ibid.*, par. 7.

81 Later in the decision this is made explicit (*ibid.*, par. 11): "any alleged discrepancy in the testimony of Witness Mbonyunkiza will be addressed by this Chamber at a later stage when assessing the evidence adduced by each party in the present case as a whole. To make a finding now on allegedly contradictory evidence would be pre-judging the issues and is premature."

82 At the time of writing, Nzirorera's case was still in trial and the Trial Chamber's determination, finally, of M's credibility was still unknown.

83 ICTR, Decision on Defence Motions for Appointment of Amicus Curiae, Trial Chamber, *Prosecutor v. Karemera et al*, Case No. ICTR-98-44-T, T. Ch. III, 26 September 2007.

84 *Ibid.*, par. 2 and 9.

85 *Ibid.*, par. 5.

86 *Ibid.*, par. 9-11, emphasis added.

attack on many sides, the italicized portion is perhaps the most surprising. After years of recycling the *Akayesu* test, to the effect that the moving party must "prove" its allegations, here the tribunal descends deeper into misconception about who must prove what in the context of Rule 91. The italicized text makes no sense at all.

In yet another Rule 91 decision in the same case,[87] BTH was a prosecution witness who admitted lying both in the Karemera trial and in other ICTR proceedings. All parties, including the prosecution, wanted him investigated for perjury. In the Trial Chamber's decision, nominal reference was made to the Akayesu decision,[88] but no need arose to reflect on the test at any length, or, in fact, at all, given that BTH had practically confessed. The Chamber gave orders for an amicus investigator to be appointed, with powers to investigate, as well, the extent to which the witness's perjury had been procured by others.

The BTH decision in Karemera is part of a small constellation of decisions late in the life of the ICTR that have ordered Rule 91 investigations. Another is Butare's QY decision, discussed above; chronologically it comes after the BTH order. The case that revitalized the discourse on perjury, however, and began to help the ICTR out of the rut dug by Akayesu, was the GAA case, which began life in 2005. I will consider the GAA case further below.

Witness BTH also testified under the pseudonym GFA in the ICTR's Bizimungu case.[89] Some three years after his testimony in Bizimungu, GFA arranged to meet with representatives of the prosecutor and the defence to confess that he had given false testimony against one of the accused. He said that while he was imprisoned in Rwanda, he and other prisoners had colluded to fabricate stories they would tell the ICTR.[90] He was recalled by both the Karemera and the Bizimungu Trial Chambers for further cross-examination; however, at one point, BTH/GFA "absconded" and has not been heard from since.[91]

The Bizimungu decision restates the Akayesu "proof" requirement.[92] Clearly, however, here too, the chamber's decision to order a Rule 91 investigation of GFA was made on the brute strength of the extraordinary facts. By contrast, the chamber dismissed the motion with respect to witnesses GAP and GKB, even though they had been fellow prisoners of GFA – and, according to GFA, fellow colluders – and had presented inconsistent testimonies, albeit, in the case of GAP at least, of a more conventional fault-profile than that of GFA.[93] The relatively powerful and unusual evidence for a Rule 91 action against GKB did not seem to move the chamber, however.[94]

4. GAA is jailed

At the time of writing (August 2009), GAA is the only person to have been convicted of false testimony at the ICTR and ICTY.[95] GAA was also charged with, and pleaded guilty to, contempt of court.[96] His was thus also the only case where acts amounting to perjury resulted in a conviction for contempt.[97] GAA appeared before the ICTR Appeals Chamber in May 2005 and recanted testimony he had given before the Trial Chamber in the Kamuhanda case. He claimed that, despite what he had said at first instance, he had never witnessed unlawful acts by the accused, Kamuhanda. Later, in August 2007, he recanted his recantation and confessed to have "knowingly and wilfully" testified falsely on this matter (i.e. his bogus recantation) before the Appeals Chamber.[98]

87 ICTR, Decision on Prosecutor's Confidential Motion to Investigate BTH for False Testimony, *Prosecutor v. Karemera et al.*, Case No. ICTR-98-44-T, T. Ch. III, 14 May 2008.
88 *Ibid.*, par. 5.
89 ICTR, Decision on Defence Motion Seeking the Appointment of *Amicus Curiae* to Investigate Possible False Testimony by Witnesses GFA, GAP and GKB, *Prosecutor v. Bizimungu et al.*, Case No. ICTR-99-50-T, T. Ch. II, 23 July 2008.
90 *Ibid.*, par. 10.
91 *Ibid.*, par. 13.
92 *Ibid.*, par. 6.
93 *Ibid.*, par. 18.
94 *Ibid.*, par. 24-28.
95 ICTR, Judgement and Sentence, *Prosecutor v. GAA*, Case No. ICTR-07-90-R77-I, T. Ch. II, 4 December 2007, par. 7.
96 *Ibid.*, par. 3.
97 *Ibid.*, par. 7.
98 *Ibid.*, par. 5.

In determining the sentence to be imposed, the Trial Chamber to which GAA's case had been referred, said of the gravity of the offence of false testimony:

> The Chamber considers false testimony under solemn declaration and contempt of the Tribunal as very grave offences, as they constitute a direct challenge to the integrity of the trial process. Maintaining the integrity of the administration of justice is particularly important in trials involving serious criminal offences. [...] Although all perjury is serious, the Chamber is of the view that the most serious category is where the perjured evidence is being given to lead to the conviction of an innocent person and the second most serious category is where, as in this case, the perjured evidence is given in the hope of procuring the acquittal of a guilty person. The Chamber therefore considers that the gravity of the offence requires that a custodial sentence must be imposed.[99]

GAA was sentenced to nine months' imprisonment. Because this penalty was for perjury of the lesser kind (as distinguished in the text above), it follows from the view expressed by the Trial Chamber that a witness found to have knowingly and wilfully testified falsely to attain "the conviction of an innocent person" (meaning, in fact, any person on trial) could expect a jail term of *at least* nine months, assuming, that is, that he or she were prepared to plead guilty to the charge of perjury. Without a guilty plea, and in the absence of other mitigating circumstances going in the defendant-perjurer's favour, he or she would surely be advised to expect a jail term considerably longer than nine months if convicted.[100]

As seen from the material presented in this paper, almost all instances of apparent false testimony at the ICTR fall into the "most serious category" of false incrimination.

It is perhaps no surprise that GAA was not allowed to escape Rule 91 proceedings after changing his trial testimony and confronting the Appeals Chamber with a new version of events.[101] Clearly, GGA's case did not consist merely of the constantly shifting witness accounts seen, for example, in Rwamakuba; it had an extra dimension.[102] The same is true of the three other instances mentioned above (BTH, GFA, and QY) in which a Trial Chamber ordered a Rule 91 investigation. In all these cases, the perjury had been effectively admitted. Even there, however, none of the decisions taken was pursuant to a Rule 91 process initiated by the Trial Chamber itself. The judges remained apathetic until they were moved to action.

5. Explaining a tradition of apathy in the face of perjury

The above review of Rule 91 decisions at the ICTR does not reflect the full extent of the problem of perjury at the tribunal. As the Rwamakuba trial judgement itself illustrates, most instances of apparent perjury are passed over, by the parties as much as by the judges, without any comment except on the credibility, for evidentiary purposes, of the witness. In the footnotes, I refer to some of the most striking cases of apparent perjury, where the "strong grounds" of the Rule 91 test abound.[103] In some we see the judges acknowledging evidence of the mens rea of the offence, yet never taking any action.[104]

---

99 *Ibid.*, par. 10.

100 GAA's sentence would have been even higher had it not been for evidence that he had been suborned by one Léonidas Nshogoza (*ibid.*, par. 11). Moreover, mitigating factors, in addition to the guilty plea, were taken into account (*ibid.*, par. 12).

101 For an explanation of the Appeals Chamber's finding that GAA testified falsely on appeal, see ICTR, Judgement, *Kamuhanda v. Prosecutor*, Case No. ICTR-99-54A-A, A. Ch., 19 September 2005, Klip/ Sluiter, ALC-XXII-721, par. 216-221.

102 At the same time, it is remarkable that the other witness in GAA's case, known as GEX, who had not testified at the trial but had given a statement to the prosecution implicating the accused, sought to retract her statement and support GAA's story about pressure having been put on the pair to falsify evidence against the accused. GAA and GEX were really in the same boat, as far as the facts revealed (*ibid.*, par. 222-226). GEX's case was no less extra-dimensional. Yet the Appeals Chamber branded *her* testimony at the appellate hearing merely "unreliable" (*ibid.*, par. 226), as opposed to the "not credible" (*ibid.*, par. 221) for GAA, and initiated proceedings only against GAA.

103 ICTR, Judgment and Sentence, *Prosecutor v. Kamuhanda*, Case No. ICTR-95-54A-T, T. Ch. II, 22 January 2004, Klip/ Sluiter, ALC-XVII-531, par. 282; ICTR, Judgement and Sentence, *Prosecutor v. Ntagerura, Bagambiki and Imanishimwe*, Case No. ICTR-99-46-T, T. Ch. III, 25 February 2004, Klip/ Sluiter, ALC-XVIII-267, par. 321 (the allegation that the accused had cut out the hearts of seventeen victims and eaten them is particularly striking); *Prosecutor v. Ndindabahizi*, ICTR, Judgement and Sentence, *Prosecutor v. Ndindabahizi*, Case No. ICTR-2001-71-I, T. Ch. I, 15 July 2004, Klip/ Sluiter, ALC-XVIII-645, par. 197; and ICTR, Judgement, *Prosecutor v. Seromba*, Case No. ICTR-2001-66-T, T. Ch. III, 13 December 2006, in this volume p. 523, par. 254.

104 ICTR, Judgement and Sentence, *Prosecutor v. Rutaganda*, Case No. ICTR-96-3-T, T. Ch. I, 6 December 1999, Klip/ Sluiter, ALC-II-709, par. 298 ("The inference to be drawn is that this defence was an afterthought and that the account of dates was tailored by the Accused and Defense Witness DDD, following the conclusion of the Prosecution's case ICTR, Judgement and Sentence, *Prosecutor v. Niyitegeka*, Case No. ICTR-96-14-T, T. Ch. I, 16 May 2003, Klip/ Sluiter, ALC-XII-731, par. 222 ("As the witness claimed that he had made a false statement, the Chamber finds that Witness TEN-6's evidence is of questionable veracity"); ICTR,

Explanations of the ICTR judges' apathy towards possible perjury might include a misapprehension that it is for the parties to initiate proceedings. Or perhaps the judges consider perjury proceedings to be too trivial or too tangential to the main case. They might view the Rule 91 process as a drain on tribunal resources, or be concerned that heavy-handed tactics could scare away witnesses. They likely pity some of the evidently damaged witnesses. And they have to contend with the authoritarian government of Rwanda, still controlled by the war's victors, on whose pleasure depends the smooth operation on the tribunal (including facilitation of witness travel).[105]

None of these are valid justifications, of course. They trivialize that which is self-evidently serious. We have seen evidence of systemic pressures operating on witnesses resident in Rwanda, which are aimed at, or serve as incentives for them to distort their testimonies when they come before the ICTR.[106] It is difficult to understand how such disturbing evidence can be ignored by the tribunal judges, who must be assumed to have some concern about defending the integrity of their own proceedings.

We have also seen that when the Trial Chamber came to punish GAA, it described perjury as relatively serious on the scale of offences. False testimony in the ICTR's rules became more, not less, serious over the years. The maximum penalty of imprisonment for false testimony initially was set at twelve months.[107] As of 2003 it was increased to five years.[108] It is noteworthy that the ICTR's maximum penalty for false testimony was initially set twice as high as the imprisonment penalty for contempt (Rule 77). The latter was held at a six-month upper limit[109] until 2003, when it too was raised to five years.[110] Only since 2003, then, have the maxima of Rules 77 and 91 been equalized at the ICTR; for eight years, false testimony was regulated as an offence of greater consequence than contempt of court.[111]

Judgement and Sentence, *Prosecutor v. Ntagerura, Bagambiki and Imanishimwe*, Case No. ICTR-99-46-T, T. Ch. III, 25 February 2004, Klip/ Sluiter, ALC-XVIII-267, par. 322 and 438 ("leaves the impression of fabrication [...]leaves the impression that his testimony is for sale [...] Witness LAP admitted to falsifying evidence related to other cases"); Judgement, *Prosecutor v. Seromba*, T. Ch. III, *supra* note 103, par. 92 ("Witness FE36 is not credible, as he admits having lied before the Chamber"); *ibid.*, par. 237 ("The witness provided no convincing explanation for these contradictions, merely claiming that the statements were occasionally false, occasionally incomplete or drafted under duress or with a view to financial compensation"); *ibid.*, par. 249 ("Witness FE32 explained that he made this statement 'in order to please some people who wanted me to implicate Father Seromba'"); and ICTR, Judgement, *Prosecutor v. Nahimana, Barayagwiza, Ngeze*, Case No. ICTR-99-52-A, A. Ch., 28 November 2007, par. 446 ("Witness EB denies before the Chamber being the author of a recantation statement, but an expert retained by the Prosecutor unhesitatingly attributes to him the handwriting and signature on that statement; and [...] several genocide survivors consider him ready to do anything for money").

105 See A. Zahar, Witness Memory and the Manufacture of Evidence at the International Criminal Tribunals, in C. Stahn and L. van den Herik (eds), Future Perspectives in International Criminal Justice, TMC Asser Press/Cambridge University Press, 2010, p. 600-610.

106 There is much compelling evidence that prosecution witnesses often experience pressure by individuals and groups in Rwanda to testify falsely against ICTR defendants. In addition to evidence cited elsewhere in the paper, see, ICTR, Decision on Kanyabashi's and Nsabimana's Motions to Cross-Examine Prosecution Witness QA on Additional Topics, *Prosecutor v. Kanyabashi (*Case No. ICTR-96-15-T), *Prosecutor v. Nsabimana* (Case No. ICTR-97-29-T), Joint Case No. ICTR-98-42-T, T. Ch. II, 28 October 2008. See also ICTR, Judgment and Sentence, *Prosecutor v. Kajelijeli*, Case No. 98-44A-T, T. Ch. II, 1 December 2003, Klip/ Sluiter, ALC-XVII-27, par. 94 (AVEGA representatives ask witness to make false allegations against the accused by saying he raped her in 1994; in return they promise to assist the witness to recover her property and to receive a government pension); and ICTR, Decision on the Defence Preliminary Motion Objecting to the Form of the Amended Indictment (Rule 72 (A) (ii) of the Rules of Procedure and Evidence), *Prosecutor v. Zigiranyirazo*, Case No. ICTR-2001-73-I, T. Ch. III, 15 July 2004, Klip/ Sluiter, ALC-XVIII-41, par. 111 ("Witness DF charges that Witness CGH, while working as a prison guard, boasted that he was going to manufacture evidence against the Accused. Witness DC alleges that Witness CGH took him to see the inspector of judicial police, who was with two white people. They offered to pay him fifty dollars if he testified about crimes committed by the accused. When he refused, Witness CGH implied that he would be deprived of prison privileges because of his failure to cooperate").

107 ICTR RPE, 29 June 1995, Rule 91(E).

108 ICTR RPE, 27 May 2003, Rule 91(G).

109 ICTR RPE, 29 June 1995, Rule 77(A).

110 ICTR RPE, 27 May 2003, Rule 77(G).

111 The ICTY moved to equalization and stiffer penalties for both offences almost five years before the ICTR. It, too, started out with a twelve-month maximum for false testimony and a six-month maximum for contempt (ICTY RPE, 11 February 1994, Rules 91(E) and 77(A), respectively). In 1998, it increased the imprisonment limit for false testimony to seven years (ICTY RPE, 4 December 1998, Rule 91(E)). For contempt, it distinguished between two categories; in effect, lesser and greater contempt. The new rule limited the sentencing maxima for these forms of contempt to twelve months and seven years of imprisonment, respectively (ICTY RPE, 4 December 1998, Rule 77(H)). (This distinction has since been abandoned: ICTY RPE, 12 July 2002, Rule 77(G).) Thus, just over four years after the first ICTY Rules were promulgated in 1994, during which period perjury was regarded as surpassing contempt in seriousness, the ICTY came to regard contempt and false testimony as potentially equally grave offences,

I have argued that the constellation of decisions late in the life of the ICTR ordering perjury investigations against GAA, BTH/GFA, and QY must be categorized as exceptional on the facts. The Rwamakuba judgement's monolithic presence in the ICTR's twilight years can only reasonably be explained as the product of a long tradition which is only partly jurisprudential; a good part of it is cultural or ideological. I have described the jurisprudential tradition in terms of Akayesu's setting of an almost impossibly high test for a party-initiated Rule 91 inquiry.[112] The ideological tradition is also the Akayesu case's making. I give an outline of it below.

The Akayesu trial judgement initiated a tradition at the ICTR of excusing inaccuracies or inconsistencies in witness evidence. Shifting testimonies were to be seen as *natural* to human beings, psychologistic intuitions were to be deployed to explain away gaps and contradictions in evidence led by the prosecution, and judicial ingenuity in smoothing over evidentiary issues was to be prized. The threshold indication of false testimony was thus raised even higher than the artificially high jurisprudential threshold.

Here is a sample of the Akayesu case's ideology, dressed as an empirically grounded psycho-physiology:

> an often levied criticism of testimony is its fallibility. Since testimony is based mainly on memory and sight, two human characteristics which often deceive the individual, this criticism is to be expected. Hence, testimony is rarely exact at to the events experienced. To deduce from any resultant contradictions and inaccuracies that there was false testimony, would be akin to criminalising frailties in human perceptions. [...] Memory over time naturally degenerates, hence it would be wrong and unjust for the Chamber to treat forgetfulness as being synonymous with giving false testimony.[113]

The Akayesu judgement – the ICTR's defining judgement – proceeded to add a moral gloss to its pro-prosecution rhetoric of the senses. If "victims" had to be cared for, so had their testimony:

> The possible traumatism of these witnesses caused by their painful experience of violence during the conflict in Rwanda is a matter of particular concern to the Chamber. The recounting of this traumatic experience is likely to evoke memories of the fear and the pain once inflicted on the witness and thereby affect his or her ability fully or adequately to recount the sequence of events in a judicial context. [...] The Chamber is unable to exclude the possibility that some or all of these witnesses did actually suffer from post traumatic or extreme stress disorders [...] Inconsistencies or imprecisions in the testimonies, accordingly, have been assessed in the light of this assumption, personal background and the atrocities they have experienced or have been subjected to.[114]

In other words, to question evidence is to question victimhood.

The baleful influence of the Akayesu case has combined with an inexorable fact about applied international criminal law, *viz.* that the culturally remote judges at the international criminal tribunals have experienced great difficulty in "reading" witnesses as persons. They much prefer to read them as text.[115] The preference

---

and moreover as significantly graver offences than the ICTR with its lesser maxima has ever done. Another peculiar difference between the two tribunals is that whereas the ICTY increased the monetary fine for both contempt and false testimony from US$10,000 to €100,000 at the same time it raised the limits on incarceration, the ICTR has, from the start, kept the fine for the two offences unchanged at US$10,000 (ICTR RPE, 14 March 2008, Rules 77(G) and 91(G)). As for the International Criminal Court, false testimony is penalized under Article 70 of the ICC Statute. The maximum term of imprisonment for the offence is five years (ICC Statute, Article 70, paragraph 3). The ceiling of the monetary fine is unquantified, although it is limited with reference to the convicted person's assets (ICC RPE, Rule 166(3)). The ICC's other contempt powers are also controlled by Article 70; however, they are much narrower than those claimed by the ad hoc tribunals.

112 The Akayesu case's "proof" test has never been overturned. In addition to the citations already given, *Akayesu*'s test is reiterated with approval in ICTR, Judgement and Sentence, *Prosecutor v. Musema*, Case No. ICTR-96-13-T, T. Ch. I, 27 January 2000, Klip/ Sluiter, ALC-VI-469, par. 99; ICTR, Judgement and Sentence, *Prosecutor v. Niyitegeka*, Case No. ICTR-96-14-T, T. Ch. I, 16 May 2003, Klip/ Sluiter, ALC-XII-731, par. 42; ICTR, Judgement, *Niyitegeka v. Prosecutor*, Case No. ICTR-96-14-A, A. Ch., 9 July 2004, Klip/ Sluiter, ALC-XVIII-563, par. 253; and Judgement, *Simba v. Prosecutor*, A. Ch., *supra* note 59, par. 31 (where the chamber's "conviction" about the elements of the offence is said to be required). Consider also Judgment and Sentence, *Prosecutor v. Kajelijeli*, T. Ch. II, *supra* note 106, par. 683 ("the Chamber finds, in the *absence of corroboration* of Witness ZLA's allegation, insufficient evidence to determine that subornation of perjury or intimidation attempts *did in fact occur*", emphasis added; note that nowhere does the Trial Chamber make any finding to the effect that ZLA is not a credible witness).

113 Judgement, *Prosecutor v. Akayesu*, T. Ch. I , *supra* note 28, par. 140.

114 *Ibid.*, par. 142-143. The Trial Chamber is careful to point out that this is the proper attitude towards both prosecution and defence witnesses.

115 I have discussed this issue in A. Zahar, Witness Memory and the Manufacture of Evidence at the International Criminal Tribunals, in C. Stahn and L. van den Herik (eds), Future Perspectives in International Criminal Justice, TMC Asser Press/Cambridge University Press 2010, p. 600-610.

we have seen expressed time and again in the material cited in this paper for making credibility determinations only once all the evidence has been admitted is a subterfuge for a deep anxiety shared by ICTR judges. Once all the evidence is admitted, they can go into seclusion with the text. They look forward to that moment, because it is easier to take the measure of a typed narrative than a genuine person.

The tribunal judge's in-court alienation from the Rwandan witness, accounts, in my view, for the tendency we have seen in these pages, of Trial Chambers, in effect, postponing the Rule 91 procedure until the conclusion of the evidentiary hearings. The problem, by that stage, however, is that there is no advantage, at least for the defence, in pursuing the matter through Rule 91. A case in point is Rwamakuba. Following his acquittal, instead of expending resources on written motions for Rule 91 prosecutions of witnesses, which of course could not have resulted in any personal benefit to himself, Rwamakuba sought monetary compensation from the tribunal for "grave and manifest injustice occasioned, inter alia, by the manipulation of evidence against him during his case".[116]

In closing arguments and briefs, defence teams continue their attacks on the credibility of prosecution witnesses, but no longer on the basis of Rule 91.[117] For the defence, at that stage, the meaningful moment has passed. Judicial apathy takes care of the rest. With no pursuer left, the matter is forgotten.

6. No justice for Rwamakuba

The Trial Chamber which dealt with Rwamakuba's petition for monetary compensation was the same one which acquitted him. While not affirming that there had been a grave and manifest injustice in his prosecution, it did not *dispute* the claim.[118] It concentrated instead on Rwamakuba's argument that Article 85, paragraph 3, of the ICC Statute (which states that "In exceptional circumstances, where the Court finds conclusive facts showing that there has been a grave and manifest miscarriage of justice, it may in its discretion award compensation [...]") represents customary international law. The judges found that it does not. Rwamakuba appealed.

The Appeals Chamber confirmed the Trial Chamber's finding on the law.[119] But it did not stop there. Perhaps feeling that the Trial Chamber's decision left the impression, as indeed it does, that if only the law were different Rwamakuba might have qualified for compensation, the Appeals Chamber, in dismissing the appeal, took the additional, and strictly unnecessary step of purporting to refute Rwamakuba's claim that there had been a grave and manifest injustice in his case. The Appeals Chamber's argument[120] is not only too brief, it is transparent in its tendentiousness. It asserts that, but does not explain why, Rwamakuba's claim is defeated by the fact that at no point prior to the final trial judgement was the evidence against him found to be unconvincing. An informed reader knows, however, that that fact was a consequence of the Trial Chamber's insistence on making such a determination only once it had all the evidence before it, at the end

---

116 ICTR, Decision on Appropriate Remedy, *Prosecutor v. Rwamakuba*, Case No. ICTR-98-44C-T, T. Ch. III, 31 January 2007, in this volume p. 907, par. 5.

117 The defence tactic in the concluding stages of a case is to evoke conspiracies; see, for example, Judgement, *Prosecutor v. Akayesu*, T. Ch. I , *supra* note 28, par. 44 (collusion in syndicate of informers); ICTR, Judgement and Sentence, *Prosecutor v. Elizaphan Ntakirutimana and Ntakirutimana*, Cases No. ICTR-96-10 and ICTR-96-17-T, T. Ch. I, 21 February 2003, Klip/ Sluiter, ALC-XII-383, par. 751 (organized propaganda effort); ICTR, Judgement and Sentence, *Prosecutor v. Niyitegeka*, Case No. ICTR-96-14-T, T. Ch. I, 16 May 2003, Klip/ Sluiter, ALC-XII-731, par. 42 and 397 (subornation by RPF and IBUKA); Judgment and Sentence, *Prosecutor v. Kajelijeli*, T. Ch. II, *supra* note 106, par. 117 and 683 (fabricated testimonies); ICTR, Judgement and Sentence, *Prosecutor v. Nahimana, Barayagwiza and Ngeze*, Case No. ICTR-99-52-T, T. Ch. I, 3 December 2003, Klip/ Sluiter, ALC-XVII 221, par. 851-74 (subornation by IBUKA); and Judgment and Sentence, *Prosecutor v. Kamuhanda*, T. Ch. II, *supra* note 103, par. 70 (witnesses were out to discredit the accused and cause mischief). Such conspiracy theories are relatively easily – but often too easily – dismissed by the Trial Chambers, which always reduce the problem to whether individual witnesses are credible; for example, Judgement, *Prosecutor v. Akayesu*, T. Ch. I , *supra* note 28, par. 46-7; Judgement and Sentence, *Prosecutor v. Elizaphan Ntakirutimana and Ntakirutimana*, T. Ch. I, see above, par. 751-77; Judgement and Sentence, *Prosecutor v. Niyitegeka*, T. Ch. I, see above, par. 397-401; Judgement and Sentence, *Prosecutor v. Nahimana, Barayagwiza and Ngeze*, T. Ch. I, see above, par. 851-74; and Judgment and Sentence, *Prosecutor v. Kamuhanda*, T. Ch. II, *supra* note 103, par. 71.

118 Decision on Appropriate Remedy, *Prosecutor v. Rwamakuba*, T. Ch. III, *supra* note 116, par. 21-31. In the trial judgement, the judges repeatedly referred to the prosecution's "failure" to make its case (e.g. *Judgement*, par. 158), stopping short, however, of calling it a sham.

119 Decision on Appeal Against Decision on Appropriate Remedy, *Rwamakuba v. Prosecutor*, Case No. ICTR-98-44C-A, A. Ch., 13 September 2007, in this volume, p. 439, par. 10.

120 *Ibid.*, par. 11-12.

of the case. How, then, *could* the Trial Chamber have expressed any intermediate lack of conviction in the evidence when it had postponed such consideration to the final stages of deliberation? But even if the Trial Chamber had not taken that approach, there is no legal basis for the Appeals Chamber's position that the Trial Chamber's uncritical assessment of the evidence along the way, in particular its no-case-to-answer (Rule 98 bis) decision at the end of the prosecution's case, were unreviewable by the Appeals Chamber in the context of a compensation claim.

In the end, Rwamakuba paid a price for the Trial Chamber's reluctance, typical of ICTR judges, to make credibility findings before the close of the hearings. We sense the elements of a vicious circle: Rule 91 does not work for defendants in the course of trial; at the end of trial, it is irrelevant for those who have been acquitted; and if the latter ask for compensation, their claim is undermined by the fact that they had no success in attacking witness credibility midstream in the process. The Appeals Chamber in its decision on the compensation issue also wrongly asserted that Rwamakuba's alibi played a big role in his acquittal.[121] As I outlined earlier, the Trial Chamber found against the prosecution witnesses primarily for reasons unrelated to the alibi. The Appeals Chamber's alibi argument is not just inaccurate, it is irrelevant; the prosecution had been notified of the alibi long before the trial,[122] which makes it even harder to understand why it pressed ahead with such a weak case.

André Rwamakuba was brought to trial on the basis of the testimony of five lying witnesses. A whole trial was conducted at great expense to the international community and untold inconvenience to the accused. Both the prosecution lawyers and the lying witnesses walked away from the disaster unscathed. The judges, captives of a judicial mindset, took no action to correct the injustice. Now there is nothing more to be done.

Alexander Zahar

121 *Ibid.*, par. 12.

122 Judgement, *Prosecutor v. Rwamakuba*, T. Ch. III, *supra* note 2, par. 82.

International Criminal Tribunal for Rwanda
Tribunal pénal international pour le Rwanda

TRIAL CHAMBER

Case No. ICTR-2001-66-I

ENGLISH
Original: FRENCH

Before: Andrésia Vaz, presiding
Karin Hökborg
Gberdao Gustave Kam

Registrar: Adama Dieng

Date: 13 December 2006

THE PROSECUTOR

v.

ATHANASE SEROMBA

JUDGEMENT

Office of the Prosecutor:
Silvana Arbia
Jonathan Moses
Gregory Townsend
Althea Alexis-Windsor
Tolulope Olowoye

Counsel for the Defence:
Patrice Monthé
Barnabé Nekuie
Sarah Ngo Bihegué

TABLE OF CONTENTS

[page 8] CHAPTER I: INTRODUCTION

1. This Judgement is rendered by Trial Chamber III (the "Chamber") of the International Criminal Tribunal for Rwanda (the "Tribunal"), composed of Judge Andrésia Vaz, presiding, Judge Karin Hökborg and Judge Gberdao Gustave Kam, in the case of the *Prosecutor v. Athanase Seromba.*

2. The Tribunal is governed by its Statute (the "Statute")[1] annexed to Security Council Resolution 955, and by its Rules of Procedure and Evidence (the "Rules").[2]

3. The Tribunal has jurisdiction to prosecute persons responsible for serious violations of international humanitarian law committed in the territory of Rwanda and Rwandan citizens responsible for such violations committed in the territory of neighbouring States. Its jurisdiction is limited to acts of genocide, crimes against humanity and serious violations of Article 3 common to the Geneva Conventions and Additional Protocol II,[3] committed between 1 January 1994 and 31 December 1994.[4]

4. The Chamber recalls that in the present case, it has already taken judicial notice of the fact that widespread killings occurred in Rwanda in 1994,[5] and that this fact is no longer subject to reasonable dispute. The Chamber further recalls that it has also taken judicial notice of the fact that during the events referred to in this Indictment, Tutsi, Hutu and Twa were identified as ethnic or racial groups.[6]

5. In addition, it notes that the Appeal Chamber recently stated in *Karemera* that the genocide perpetrated in Rwanda is a fact of common knowledge.[7] The Trial Chamber nevertheless emphasizes that taking judicial notice of facts of common knowledge does not relieve the Prosecution of its burden to prove that the Accused was criminally responsible for the specific events alleged in the Indictment.[8]

6. The Accused, Athanase Seromba, was born in 1963 in Rutziro *commune*, Kibuye *préfecture*, Rwanda. Trained at the Nyakibanda major seminary,[9] he was ordained a priest in July 1993.[10] In April 1994, he was a priest in Nyange parish, Kivumu *commune*. **[page 9]**

7. In the Indictment dated 8 June 2001 (the "Indictment"), registered with the Tribunal Registry on 5 July 2001,[11] the Prosecutor preferred four charges against Athanase Seromba:

8. Count 1: Genocide:[12] The Prosecutor of the International Criminal Tribunal for Rwanda charges Athanase Seromba with genocide, a crime stipulated in Article 2(3)(a) of the Statute, in that on or between 6 April 1994 and 20 April 1994, in Kivumu *commune*, Kibuye *préfecture*, Rwanda, Seromba was responsible for killing or causing serious bodily or mental harm to members of the Tutsi population, with intent to destroy, in whole or in part, a racial or ethnic group; and pursuant to Article 6(1) of the Statute: by virtue of his affirmative acts, in planning, instigating, ordering, committing, or otherwise aiding and abetting the planning, preparation or execution of the crime charged.

9. Count 2: Complicity in genocide:[13] The Prosecutor of the International Criminal Tribunal for Rwanda charges Athanase Seromba of complicity in genocide, a crime stipulated in Article 2(3)(e) of the Statute, in that on or between the dates of 6 April 1994 and 20 April 1994, in Kivumu *commune*, Kibuye *préfecture*, Rwanda, Athanase Seromba was an accomplice to the killing or causing serious bodily or mental harm to

---

[1] United Nations Document S/RES/955 (1994), 8 November 1994.

[2] The Rules were adopted on 5 July 1995 by the Judges of the Tribunal and amended most recently on 7 June 2005. The Statute and the Rules are available on the Tribunal site: www.ictr.org.

[3] Articles 2, 3 and 4 of the Statute.

[4] Article 1 of the Statute.

[5] Decision on Prosecutor's Motion for Judicial Notice, 14 July 2005, p. 7.

[6] *Idem.*

[7] *The Prosecutor v. Édouard Karemera et al.*, ICTR-98-44-T, Decision on Prosecutor's Interlocutory Appeal on Judicial Notice (Appeal Chamber), 16 June 2006, para. 35.

[8] *Ibid.*, para. 37.

[9] Transcript, 20 April 2006, p. 6 (closed session).

[10] Letter of the Accused to the Archbishop of Florence (Exhibit P-8).

[11] The French version of the Indictment was filed with the Registry of the Tribunal on 9 July 2001.

[12] Indictment, p. 2.

[13] Indictment, p. 3.

members of the Tutsi population, committed with intent to destroy, in whole or in part, a racial or ethnic group; and pursuant to Article 6(1) of the Statute: by virtue of his affirmative acts, in planning, instigating, ordering, committing, or otherwise aiding and abetting the planning, preparation or execution of the crime charged.

10. Count 3: Conspiracy to commit genocide:[14] The Prosecutor of the International Criminal Tribunal for Rwanda charges Athanase Seromba of conspiracy to commit genocide, a crime stipulated in Article 2(3)(b) of the Statute, in that on or between 6 April 1994 and 20 April 1994, in Kivumu *commune*, Kibuye *préfecture*, Rwanda, Athanase Seromba, a priest responsible for Nyange Parish, did agree with Grégoire Ndahimana, *bourgmestre* of Kivumu *commune*, Fulgence Kayishema, a police inspector of Kivumu *commune*, Télesphore Ndungutse, Gaspard Kanyikuriga and other persons not known to the Prosecution, to kill or cause serious bodily or mental harm to members of the Tutsi population, with intent to destroy, in whole or in part, a racial or ethnic group; and pursuant to Article 6(1) of the Statute: by virtue of his affirmative acts, in planning, instigating, ordering, committing, or otherwise aiding and abetting the planning, preparation or execution of the crime charged.

11. Count 4: Crimes against humanity (extermination):[15] The Prosecutor of the International Criminal Tribunal for Rwanda charges Athanase Seromba with extermination as crime against humanity as stipulated in Article 3(b) of the Statute, in that on or between 7 April 1994 and 20 April 1994, in Kibuye *préfecture*, Rwanda, Athanase Seromba was responsible for killing **[page 10]** persons, or causing persons to be killed, during mass killing events as part of a widespread or systematic attack against a civilian population on political, ethnic or racial grounds; and pursuant to Article 6(1) of the Statute: by virtue of his affirmative acts, in planning, instigating, ordering, committing, or otherwise aiding and abetting the planning, preparation or execution of the crime charged.

12. The full text of the Indictment is attached to this Judgement.[16]

13. The Accused, Athanase Seromba, who went into exile in Florence, Italy, surrendered to the authorities of the Tribunal on 6 February 2002 without the warrant of arrest[17] issued by the Tribunal against him being executed by the Italian authorities who had received notification thereof on 10 July 2001.[18] The Accused made his initial appearance before Justice Navanethem Pillay on 8 February 2002 and entered a plea of not guilty.[19] His trial started on 20 September 2004 and was ended on 27 June 2006.[20] **[page 11]**

CHAPTER II: FACTUAL FINDINGS

1. PRELIMINARY MATTERS

1.1 Defects in the Indictment

1.1.1 The Law applicable to motions on defects in the form of the Indictment

14. The Chamber notes that under Article 72 of the Rules of Procedure and Evidence, defects in the form of the Indictment must, in principle be raised during the pre-trial phase of the proceedings,[21] unless leave is granted by the Chamber to a party to do so at a later stage in the proceedings.

15. In the present case, the Chamber finds that the Defence failed to comply with the aforementioned procedural requirement by alleging defects in the Indictment in its final trial brief, i.e. after the close of hearing, rather than during the pre-trial phase. The Chamber further notes that until the close of hearing, the

14 Indictment, p. 11.
15 Indictment, p. 15.
16 See Annex III: Indictment.
17 *Seromba*, Decision on the Prosecutor's Ex Parte Request for Search, Seizure, Arrest and Transfer, 3 July 2001; *Seromba*, Warrant of Arrest and Order for Transfer, 4 July 2001.
18 See letter of the Italian Justice Ministry dated 11 July 2001 addressed to the Registrar of the International Criminal Tribunal for Rwanda.
19 Transcript, 8 February 2002, p. 16 (open session).
20 See Annex I: History of proceedings.
21 *Simba*, Trial Judgement, 13 December 2005, para. 15.

Defence neither sought nor obtained leave from the Trial Chamber to file an application alleging defects in the form of the Indictment.

16. The Chamber recalls that, as to whether a trial chamber may, after the close of hearing, rule that an indictment was defective, the Appeals Chamber stated in *Ntagerura* that it could not do so without first giving the parties the opportunity to be heard, which entails reopening the hearing.[22]

17. In view of the foregoing, the Chamber is of the opinion that an amendment of a defective indictment may be allowed even at the stage of deliberations of the Trial Chamber only if the Trial Chamber has first ordered a reopening of the hearing. Consequently, the Chamber considers that the issue here is to determine whether the Defence arguments submitted in support of its allegations of defects in the Indictment are such as would justify an amendment of the Indictment for the sake of fairness of the trial. In such a case, the Chamber would have to reopen the hearing. **[page 12]**

18. In addressing this issue, the Chamber will examine in turn the arguments advanced by the Defence in its final trial brief,[23] even if that may appear redundant.

1.1.2 Examination of Defence arguments

The Defence allegations with respect to paragraph 5 of the Indictment

19. The Chamber notes the Defence submission that the Prosecutor merely states that Athanase Seromba, "a priest responsible for Nyange parish [...] and others not unknown to the Prosecution", prepared and executed a plan of extermination of the Tutsi population, without specifying the nature of the said plan, the date and location of its conception, the persons who allegedly conceived it, the methods used to execute it, or the exact role allegedly played by the Accused in its conception, elaboration and execution.

20. The Chamber also notes the Defence allegation that, by merely stating that after the death of the Rwandan President on 6 April 1994 attacks were perpetrated against the Tutsi in Kivumu *commune*, causing the death of several of them, the Prosecutor does not provide sufficient information as to identify the perpetrators of the attacks, the planners of the attacks, the location where such attacks occurred, the manner in which they were executed or even as to whether Athanase Seromba participated in them.

21. The Chamber considers the aforementioned Defence allegations irrelevant, as the issues raised have been pleaded with sufficient particularity. The Court consequently finds that these allegations fail to prove the existence of defects in the Indictment.

The other Defence allegations

22. The Defence also alleged a lack of precision in paragraphs 7, 8, 11, 14, 15, 16 and 17 of the Indictment which alleged respectively that: the Accused drew up a list of refugees; several meetings were held, and the Accused attended them; the Accused expelled Tutsi employees from the parish; the doors of the church were closed; and a meeting was held on 14 April 1994. On these different points, the Chamber considers that the Defence allegations are unfounded, insofar as the material facts are set forth both in the Indictment and in the Prosecutor's pre-trial brief which was disclosed to the Defence in a timely manner, to enable the Defence to prepare for trial.

---

22 *Ntagerura*, Appeal Judgement, 7 July 2006, para. 55: "In the present matter, the Appeals Chamber considers that, once the Trial Chamber decided to reconsider its pre-trial decisions relating to the specificity of the Indictments at the stage of deliberations, it should have interrupted the deliberation process and reopened the hearings. At such an advance stage of the proceedings, after all the evidence had been heard and the parties had made their final submissions, the Prosecution could not move to amend the Indictment. On the other hand, reopening the hearings would have allowed the Prosecution to try to convince the Trial Chamber of the correctness of its initial pre-trial decisions on the form of the Indictment, or to argue that any defects had since been remedied. The Appeals Chamber finds that the Trial Chamber erred in remaining silent on its decision to find the abovementionned parts of the Indictments defective until the rendering of the Trial Judgement. "

23 Defence Closing Argument, pp. 40-42.

1.1.3 Findings of the Chamber

23. In view of the foregoing, the Chamber considers that the arguments raised by the Defence do not permit the conclusion that the Indictment contains defects that might have warranted an **[page 13]** amendment. The Chamber therefore dismisses the Defence allegations that the Indictment is defective and accordingly, finds that there are no grounds for reopening the hearing.

1.2 Evidence of the good character of the Accused

24. In its final trial brief, the Defence submitted that evidence of the good character of an accused may be relevant in determining whether the accused could have committed the crimes with which he is charged.[24] The Prosecution did not contest this point.

25. It is the Chamber's opinion that the evidence to be considered during deliberations, for determining probative value, is, in principle, the evidence which the parties presented at the hearing, in accordance with the provisions of Rules 89 to 98 *bis*.

26. The Chamber notes that evidence of the good character of the accused prior to the events for which he is indicted is, generally, of limited probative value in international criminal law.[25]Rather, evidence of prior good character is taken into consideration at the time of sentencing.[26]The Chamber, however, observes that such evidence may be relevant if it is shown to be particularly probative in relation to the charges against the accused.[27]

27. In the present case, the Chamber finds that the Defence only adduced evidence of the Accused's good character after the hearing had been declared closed, thus making ot impossible for the Prosecution to present arguments on this point. Furthermore, the Chamber finds that by merely submitting that the Accused's conduct had "[...] had never been viewed with disfavour by the faithful of Nyange parish prior to the events of 6 April 1994 [...]",[28] the Defence has failed to show that evidence of the Accused's good character is particularly probative to the charges against him.

28. In view of the foregoing, the Chamber will not accept evidence of the Accused's good character at this stage, but will possibly take it into consideration at the time of sentencing.

1.3 General allegations in the Indictment

29. The Chamber finds that judicial notice has already been taken of the facts alleged in paragraph 1 of the Indictment, namely, that the population of Rwanda was divided into three ethnic groups: Tutsi, Hutu and Twa.[29] The Chamber therefore, considers it to be a general allegation. **[page 14]**

30. The Chamber finds that paragraph 24 of the Indictment only provides a general description of the attacks against refugees and the intentions of the attackers, without charging Accused Athanase Seromba with any specific act or event. Consequently, the Chamber considers this allegation to be general.

31. The Chamber finds that the arrival of a bus, alleged in paragraph 18 of the Indictment, is of no relevance to the crimes charged against Accused Athanase Seromba. Consequently, the Chamber considers it to be a general allegation.

32. The Chamber finds that the allegations made in paragraphs 5, 33, 34, 35 and 45 of the Indictment allude to a plan of extermination involving the Accused, even though he is not charged with any specific act. Consequently, the Chamber considers them as general allegations.

---

24 Defence Final Trial Brief, p. 6.

25 *Kupreškic*, Decision on evidence of the good character of the accused and the Defence of *tu quoque* (Ch.), 17 February 1999, para. (i).

26 *Kambanda*, Trial Judgement, 4 September 1998, para. 34.

27 *Bagilishema*, Trial Judgement, 7 June 2001, para. 116.

28 Defence Final Trial Brief, p. 7.

29 Decision on the Prosecutor's Motion for Judicial Notice, 14 July 2005, p. 7.

33. The Chamber finds that the allegation in paragraph 32 of the Indictment that the Accused embezzled all the assets of the parish is not supported by evidence. Consequently, the Chamber considers it to be a general allegation.

34. The Chamber finds that the allegation contained in paragraph 50 of the Indictment falls within the general context of the events which occurred in Nyange in April 1994. Consequently, the Chamber considers it to be a general allegation.

35. In view of the foregoing, the Chamber does not deem it necessary to consider such allegations in its factual findings.

2. KIVUMU *COMMUNE*, NYANGE PARISH AND THE DUTIES EXERCISED BY THE ACCUSED

36. Kivumu *commune* is located in Kibuye *préfecture*, Republic of Rwanda.[30] In 1994, this *commune* had a population of about 53,000 inhabitants, including approximately 6,000 Tutsi.[31]

37. Nyange parish is located in Nyange *secteur*, Kivumu *commune*. The Nyange church measured 55 metres x 19 metres (55m x 19m).[32] The church had a seating capacity of at least 1,500.[33] **[page 15]**

38. The Chamber notes that at the time of events referred to in the Indictment, Athanase Seromba was a priest in Nyange parish, where he had been assigned as a vicar.[34] Several witnesses testified that the parish priest of Nyange, Father Straton, had already left this parish at the time of the events which occurred during April 1994.[35] These same witnesses also testified that Seromba had assumed the daily management of the parish, while waiting to take up his duties in the parish of Crête Zaïre Nil, where he had been posted since 17 March 1994.[36] The Chamber further notes, in light of those testimonies and the factual findings made above, that Seromba acted in a number of ways which show that he was responsible for the daily management of Nyange parish during the April 1994 events.[37] Accordlingly, the Chamber is of the view that Accused Seromba was acting as Nyange parish priest during the April 1994 events.

3. EVENTS FROM 6 TO 10 APRIL 1994 IN KIVUMU COMMUNE

3.1 The Indictment

39. The Indictment alleges as follows:

> "6. After the death of the Rwandan President, on 6 April 1994, attacks against the Tutsi began at KIVUMU *commune*, causing the deaths of some Tutsi civilians, including Grégoire NDAKUBANA, Martin KARAKEZI and Thomas MWENDEZI.

---

30 Transcript, 27 September 2004, ppF-6 (open session), *Preliminary report on identification of sites of the genocide and massacres that took place in Rwanda from April-July 1994* (P-4), pp. 138 and 165, Kibuye map (P-1) and annotated Kibuye map (P-1B).

31 Witness FE56 testified that the population of Kivumu *commune* stood at 53,000 (Transcript, 4 April 2006, p. 28 (closed session)). Witness FE27 testified that during the 1993 census, 55,000 persons were resident in Kivumu, including approximately 6,000 Tutsi (Statement of Witness FE27 before Tribunal investigators on 14 September 2000 (P.-41), p. 3).

32 *Preliminary report on identification of sites of the genocide and massacres that took place in Rwanda from April-July 1994* (P-4), p. 166.

33 The estimates of witnesses are: CBK: 3,000 (Transcript of 19 October 2004, p. 8 (closed session)); CNJ: 1,400 (Transcript, 25 January 2005, p. 31 (open session)); CBT: 2,000 (Transcript, 7 October 2004, p. 3 (closed session)); CF23: between 1,200 and 2,000 (Transcript, 3 April 2006, pp. 1- 2 (open session)); FE32: between 1,500 and 2,000 persons (Transcript, 6 April 2006, p. 16 (open session)); FE27: 1,500 (Transcript, 23 March 2006, p. 64 (closed session)).

34 See Letter of 17 March 1994 from the Bishop of Nyundo to Father Athanase Seromba (Exhibit D-5).

35 See YAT: Transcript, 30 September 2004, pp. 19 and 21 (open session); CBI: Transcript, 4 October 2004, pp. 23 (open session); BZ4: Transcript, 1 November 2005, p. 56 (open session); CF23: Transcript, 3 April 2006, pp. 5 (open session); PA1: Transcript, 20 April 2006, p. 7 (closed session).

36 See Exhibit D-5.

37 See CDL: Transcript, 19 January 2005, pp. 8, 14 and 19 (open session); CBK: Transcript, 20 October 2004, p. 7 (closed session); CF23: Transcript, 31 March 2006, pp. 36-37 (closed session), Transcript, 3 April 2006, pp. 5-6 (open session); BZ4: Transcript, 1 November 2005, pp. 57 (open session). See findings of the Chamber in Section 4.3.2.

7. To escape the attacks directed against them, Tutsis from the different sectors of KIVUMU commune fled their homes to seek refuge in public buildings and churches, including the Nyange church. The *Bourgmestre* and communal police gathered and transported the refugees from the different sectors of KIVUMU *commune* to Nyange parish.

8. Athanase SEROMBA questioned the refugees transferred to the Parish about those not yet present, then noted the names of the remaining refugees on a list he gave to the *Bourgmestre* Grégoire NDAHIMANA for the purpose of looking for and bringing them to the Parish. **[page 16]**

9. A Tutsi named Alexis KARAKE, his wife and his children (more than six) were brought from Gakoma cellule to Nyange church through that list.

[...]

39. On or about 12 April 1994, the *Bourgmestre* Grégoire NDAHIMANA ordered members of the communal police to search for Tutsi civilians from the list prepared by Athanase SEROMBA, as described above, and bring them to the church."

3.2 The allegation that attacks were perpetrated against the Tutsi in Kivumu *commune,* resulting in the death of certain Tutsi civilians, including Grégoire Ndakubana, Martin Karekezi and Thomas Mwendezi

3.2.1 The evidence

Prosecution witnesses

40. Witness CDL, a Hutu,[38] testified that in the night of 7 to 8 April 1994, an attack led by Ndungutse was launched against the Ndakubana Tutsi family.[39] CDL further testified that in the night of 9 to 10 April 1994 at Nyange centre, a trader and an agricultural monitor named Martin were killed.[40] Lastly the witness testified that communal authorities, namely the *Bourgmestre*, the IPJ (judicial police inspector) and other communal officials violated the very law that they were supposed to enforce.[41]

41. Witness CBJ, a Tutsi,[42] stated that the massacres which occurred in Murambi *cellule* where he resided, commenced on 7 April 1994. He also explained that in the night of 7 April 1994, members of the Rudakubana family were killed by a teacher named Télesphore Ndungutse. He further testified that between 7 and 9 April 1994, Martin, a Tutsi who hailed from Ngobagoba *secteur*, Gasake *commune* was killed during an attack launched by a businessman, Gaspard Kanyarukiga.[43]

42. Witness CBN, a Tutsi,[44] testified that a certain Thomas was killed during the attacks against the Tutsi shortly after the death of the President.[45]

Defence witnesses **[page 17]**

43. Witnesses FE31, FE13, FE56 and CF14 testified that Hutu assailants attacked the Ndakubana Tutsi family.[46] FE13 and CF14 stated *inter alia* that following this incident, insecurity increased throughout the *commune* in the night of 7 to 8 April 1994.[47] They further explained that during the same night, family members of Thomas Mwendezi, a Tutsi, were killed during an attack in Kigali *secteur*.[48]

---

38 Witness information sheet (P-19).

39 Transcript, 19 January 2005, pp. 7-8 and 40 (open session).

40 Transcript, 19 January 2005, p. 7 (open session).

41 Transcript, 19 January 2005, pp. 45-47 (open session).

42 Witness information sheet (P-15).

43 Transcript, 13 October 2004, p. 8 (open session).

44 Witness information sheet (P-16).

45 Transcript, 15 October 2004, p. 51 (open session).

46 FE31: Transcript, 29 March 2006, p. 11 (closed session); FE13: Transcript, 7 April 2006, p. 17 (closed session); FE56: Transcript, 4 April 2006, p. 43 (open session); CF14: Transcript, 16 November 2005, p. 27 (close session).

47 Transcript, 7 April 2006, p. 17 (closed session); Transcript, 16 November 2005, p. 27 (closed session).

48 Transcript, 7 April 2006, p. 17 (closed session); Transcript, 16 November 2005, p. 27 (closed session).

3.2.2 Findings of the Chamber

44. The Chamber finds the testimonies of Witnesses CDL, CBJ and CBN to be credible with regard to the murder of Ndakubana. Not only are they consistent, they are also corroborated by the evidence of Defence witnesses. Consequently, the Chamber finds that it has been proven beyond a reasonable doubt that attacks were perpetrated against the Tutsi in Kivumu *commune*, resulting in the death of some of them, including Grégoire Ndakubana, Martin Karakezi and Thomas Mwendezi.

3.3 The allegation that Tutsi sought refuge in public buildings and churches, including the Nyange church.

3.3.1 The evidence

Prosecution witnesses

45. Witnesses YAU, a Tutsi woman,[49] and CBS, a Tutsi man,[50] testified that upon arriving at the church on 12 April 1994, they found other refugees there, the majority of whom were Tutsi.[51]

46. Witness CBI, a Tutsi,[52] testified that several persons arrived at the parish on board vehicles, including a white Toyota driven by a certain Yohana or Jean, also called Jigoma.[53] The witness also testified that some officials were involved in transporting refugees to the parish. Some of the officials he cited were Grégoire Ndahimana, Clément Kayishema, Gaspard Kanyarukiga and Télesphore Ndungutse.[54] **[page 18]**

47. Witness CBN, a Tutsi,[55] stated that he sought refuge in Nyange church as from 12 April 1994.[56] He added that several persons arrived at the parish on board a vehicle belonging to a certain Rwamasirabo.[57]

48. Witness CBJ[58] testified that he found Tutsi refugees at Nyange parish upon his arrival there on 10 April 1994. He further testified that in the evening of 10 April 1994, Athanase Seromba asked a night watchman named Canisius Habiyambere and the major seminarian, Apollinaire Hakizimana, to count the refugees who were going to spend the night there. Lastly, Witness CBJ testified that these were 48 of them.[59]

49. Witness CBK, a Hutu,[60] explained that Tutsi who were attacked by the Hutu sought refuge in Nyange parish, which they considered to be a "safe haven". He further stated that the first refugees arrived in the parish on or about 8 April 1994.[61]

50. Witness CDL, a Hutu,[62] testified that the Tutsi willingly sought refuge at the Nyange parish or at the communal office.[63]

Defence witnesses

51. Witness BZ3, a Hutu,[64] testified that he met refugees in Nyange church when she attended the morning mass on 11 April 1994.[65] The witness also stated that the refugees also attended the mass,[66] adding that they

49 Witness information sheet (p-9).
50 Witness information sheet (p-12).
51 Transcript, 29 September 2004, p. 12 (open session); Transcript, 5 October 2004, pp. 8-9 (open session).
52 Witness information sheet (p-11).
53 Transcript, 4 October 2004, p. 28 (open session).
54 Transcript, 1 October 2004, pp. 41-42 (open session)
55 Witness information sheet (P-16).
56 Transcript, 15 October 2004, p. 40 (open session).
57 Transcript, 15 October 2004, p. 58 (open session).
58 See Section 3.2.1.
59 Transcript, 13 October 2004, p. 10 (open session).
60 Transcript, 19 October 2004, p. 6 (closed session); Witness information sheet (P-17).
61 Transcript, 19 October 2004, p. 73 (open session).
62 See Section 3.2.1.
63 Transcript, 19 January 2005, p. 47 (open session).
64 Transcript, 8 November 2005, p. 29 (open session).
65 Transcript, 31 October 2005, p. 44 (open session).
66 Transcript, 8 November 2005, p. 27 (open session).

were not many.[67] According to the witness, the Tutsi sought refuge in the church because the Hutu were burning down their houses.[68] Witness BZ3 also testified that she saw refugees heading towards the communal office while returning home after mass.[69] She added that when they arrived there, they were directed towards the church.[70] Lastly the witness testified that she saw several persons being led to the communal office on board a vehicle belonging to Aloys Rwamasirabo and driven by Jigoma.[71] **[page 19]**

52. Witness CF14, a Hutu,[72] testified that he saw no refugees at the communal office on 12 April 1994, but however did learn that the *bourgmestre* had "transported" other persons very early that morning to the parish.[73]

53. Witness FE32, a Hutu,[74] explained that Tutsi fled to the church as soon as they noticed that they were being persecuted.[75] He further explained that Tutsi sought refuge in Nyange church because they believed that this location could secure them protection against attacks as in the past. Lastly, the witness testified that the Tutsi went to the church on their own volition[76].

3.3.2 Findings of the Chamber

54. The Chamber finds that all the statements of both Prosecution and Defence witnesses are consistent with respect to the fact that Tutsi who lived in Kivumu *commune* voluntarily sought refuge in public buildings, such as the communal office, or in churches, including the Nyange parish church. The Chamber therefore considers that this fact has been established beyond all reasonable doubt.

3.4 The allegation that Athanase Seromba provided the *Bourgmestre* of the *commune* with a list of Tutsi for the purpose of looking for and bringing them to Nyange church

3.4.1 The evidence

Prosecution witness

55. Witness CBI[77] stated that he gave to Athanase Seromba, at his request, the names of several persons of the Tutsi ethnic group who lived in Nyange and who were not present at the parish. He also testified that the Accused prepared a list which he subsequently handed to Grégoire Ndahimana, the *bourgmestre* of the *commune*.[78] Some of the names Witness CBI testified to having disclosed to Seromba are Antoine Karake, Aloys Rwemera and those of his family members: Épimaque Kuratsire and Vénust Ryanyundo.[79] The witness further testified that on 13 April 1994, Antoine Karake arrived at Nyange church on board a vehicle that had been confiscated.[80] **[page 20]**

56. During cross-examination, Witness CBI testified that he arrived at Nyange church on Tuesday, 12 April 1994 in the evening,[81] adding that he found approximately 1,000 persons there who had come to seek refuge. He also stated that he met Athanase Seromba the day following his arrival and that Athanase Seromba asked him if there were still persons remaining in certain *secteurs* of the *commune*. The witness stated that he answered in the affirmative, disclosing the names of certain persons.[82] Asked by Defence

67 Transcript, 31 October 2005, p. 45 (open session).
68 Transcript, 31 October 2005, p. 45 (open session).
69 Transcript, 31 October 2005, p. 45 (open session).
70 Transcript, 31 October 2005, p. 45 (open session).
71 Transcript, 8 November 2005, p. 22 (open session).
72 See Section 3.2.1.
73 Transcript, 16 November 2005, pp. 40 and 42 (closed session).
74 See Section 3.2.1.
75 Transcript, 29 March 2006, p. 8 (open session); Transcript, 29 March 2006, p. 163 (closed session).
76 Transcript, 29 March 2006, p. 17 (closed session).
77 See Section 3.3.1.
78 Transcript, 4 October 2004, p. 7 (open session).
79 Transcript, 4 October 2004, p. 7 (open session).
80 Transcript, 1 October 2004, p. 46 (open session).
81 Transcript, 4 October 2004, p. 27 (open session).
82 Transcript, 4 October 2004, p. 30 (open session).

Counsel how the witness have determined that these persons were not in a crowd that he had himself estimated at around 1,000 persons, the witness responded that there was a difference between "counting people and recognising them", adding subsequently that he had noticed that these persons were absent simply because he knew them.[83]

Defence witnesses

57. Witness PA1, a Hutu,[84] testified that he arrived in Nyange parish on Sunday, 10 April 1994.[85] He stated that he had never heard about a list of persons of Tutsi origin.[86]

58. Witness FE32 is a Hutu who testified openly as Anastase Nkinamubanzi. He stated that during the events of April 1994, he was working for the Astaldi company, which was responsible for the construction of the Rubengera-Gisenyi road.[87] He also stated that the driver of the bulldozer which demolished Nyange church.[88] He testified that he was a Rwandan court sentenced him to life imprisonment for this act.[89] Finally, the witness testified that a Tutsi list never existed.[90]

59. Witness FE27, a Hutu,[91] testified that he was not aware of the existence of any list of persons prepared by Athanase Seromba, adding that if such a list existed he would have been informed of it.[92]

3.4.2 Findings of the Chamber

60. The Chamber notes that Witness CBI is the only Prosecution witness who testified that Athanase Seromba prepared a list of Tutsi which he allegedly handed to the *bourgmestre,* so that the Tutsi could be sought out and brought to Nyange parish. The Chamber finds implausible **[page 21]** Witness CBI's testimony that upon arrival in Nyange parish on 12 April 1994, he could immediately determine the absence of 10 people from a crowd of 1,000 persons. In fact, the witness merely stated that he noticed the absence of these persons simply because he knew them, even however specifying the observations or reasons that must have led him to such a conclusion. The Chamber therefore finds that Witness CBI is not credible. Accordingly, the Chamber finds that the Prosecution has not established beyond a reasonable doubt that Athanase Seromba prepared a list which he handed to the *bourgmestre* in order to seek out the persons on the list and bring them to Nyange parish.

4. THE EVENTS OF 10 TO 11 APRIL 1994

4.1 The Indictment

61. The Indictment alleges as follows:

> "10. On or about 10 April 1994, several important meetings were held at the Parish of Nyange and the communal office. Athanase SEROMBA, Fulgence KAYISHEMA, Gaspard KANYARUKIGA and others not known to the Prosecutor attended these meetings.
>
> 11. During these said meetings, it was decided to request Kibuye prefecture for gendarmes, to gather all Tutsi civilians of KIVUMU commune at Nyange church to exterminate them
>
> [...]
>
> 36. On or about 10 April 1994, several important meetings were held at the Parish of Nyange and the communal office. Athanase SEROMBA, Fulgence KAYISHEMA, Gaspard KANYARUKIGA and others not known to the Prosecution attended these meetings.

83 Transcript, 4 October 2004, pp. 30-31 (open session).
84 Transcript, 20 April 2006, p. 38 (closed session).
85 Transcript, 20 April 2006, p. 7 (closed session).
86 Transcript, 20 April 2006, p. 26 (closed session).
87 Transcript, 28 March 2006, p. 25 (open session).
88 Transcript, 28 March 2006, p. 35 (open session).
89 Transcript, 5 April 2006, p. 30 (open session).
90 Transcript, 28 March 2006, p. 55 (open session).
91 Transcript, 23 March 2006, pp. 38 and 54 (closed session).
92 Transcript, 23 March 2006, p. 27 (open session).

37. During these said meetings, they decided to request Kibuye prefecture for gendarmes, to gather all Tutsi civilians of Kivumu commune at Nyange church to exterminate them."

4.2 The 10 April 1994 Meeting

4.2.1 The evidence

Prosecution witness

62. Witness YAT, a Tutsi,[93] testified that a parish council meeting was held at the presbytery on or about 10 April 1994,[94] which was attended by Athanase Seromba, Kabwana, *Bourgmestre* **[page 22]** Ndahimana, Criminal Investigation Police Inspector, Fulgence Kayishema, Inspector Aloys Uwoyiremye and other members of the parish council.[95] He explained that it was an extraordinary meeting held to address the state of insecurity that prevailed in the *commune* following the death of President Habyarimana and the attacks being perpetrated against the Tutsi.[96] Witness YAT also testified that during the meeting Seromba stated his opinion that President Habyarimana had been killed by the *Inkotanyi* and that the issue of persons killed was a political problem which did not fall within the jurisdiction of the parish council as such.[97] The witness also stated that that parish council meeting was the last he attended.[98]

63. Witness YAT further stated that Fulgence Kayishema informed him on 11 April 1994 that a meeting was held on 10 April 1994 in Nyange parish during which the decision to kill Tutsi was taken. He added that Kanyarukiga, Athanase Seromba, *Bourgmestre* Ndahimana and Kayishema were present at the meeting.[99]

Defence witness

64. Witness FE27 testified that during the meeting of 11 April 1994, *Bourgmestre* Grégoire Ndahimana stated that he met with Athanase Seromba the day before this meeting and that Seromba had spoken to him of Tutsi who had sought refuge in Nyange church.[100]

4.2.2 Findings of the Chamber

65. The Chamber notes that the Defence has not adduced any evidence to contradict Witness YAT's testimony that a parish council meeting was held in Nyange church on 10 April 1994. In fact, Defence Witness FE27 in no way contradicted Witness YAT when he testified to having heard the *bourgmestre* inform participants in the 11 April 1994 meeting that he had met with Athanase Seromba the previous day, i.e. 10 April 1994. The Chamber is of the view that such a meeting could been part of the 10 April 1994 parish council meeting referred to by Witness YAT, who testified that he was a member of the council, a point which was not challenged by the Defence. The Chambe also finds that details provided by Witness YAT about the meeting are consistent. The Chamber therefore considers his testimony that a parish council meeting was held on 10 April 1994 to be credible. However, Witness YAT's testimony that a second meeting was held on 10 April 1994 in Nyange parish cannot be deemed credible, as the information which was disclosed to him is not supported by any other evidence. Finally, as regards Witness FE27, who did not testify specifically about the parish council meeting of 10 April 1994, the Chamber nevertheless finds his testimony that a meeting was held at the parish on 10 April 1994 to be credible, as it is corroborated by that of Witness YAT. **[page 23]**

93 Witness information sheet (P-10).
94 Transcript, 29 September 2004, p. 49 (open session).
95 Transcript, 29 September 2004, p. 49 (open session).
96 Transcript, 29 September 2004, p. 49 (open session).
97 Transcript, 29 September 2004, pp. 48-49 (open session); Transcript, 30 September 2004, p. 22 (open session).
98 Transcript, 30 September 2004, p. 22 (open session).
99 Transcript, 29 September 2004, p. 49 (open session).
100 Transcript, 23 March 2006, p. 22 (closed session).

66. In view of the foregoing, the Chamber finds that the Prosecution has established beyond a reasonable doubt that a parish council meeting was held on 10 April 1994 in Nyange parish in which Witness YAT, Athanase Seromba and other persons participated.

4.3 The 11 April 1994 Meeting at the Communal Office

4.3.1 The evidence

Prosecution witnesses

67. Witness CNJ, a Hutu,[101] testified that his uncle informed him that a meeting was held at the communal office on 11 April 1994, during which decisions were taken, including the decision to assemble the Tutsi at the Nyange church.[102] He also testified that since he did not attend the meetings, he was not in a position to state precisely when the decision to destroy the church had been taken.[103]

68. Witness CDL, a Hutu,[104] explained that security committee meetings were held in the communal office or at the parish, adding that the meetings were held regularly at the instance of the *bourgmestre.*[105] He also stated that department heads and religious authorities were invited to participate in the meetings.[106] The witness finally stated that Athanase Seromba participated in the 11 April 1994 meeting of the security committee.[107]

Defence witnesses

69. Witness FE13 stated that the 11 April 1994 meeting was chaired by *Bourgmestre* Grégoire Ndahimana,[108] who informed those in attendance that the meeting would be dealing with security issues and the fate of Tutsi refugees.[109] He added that only an exceptional situation could justify the holding of any such meeting.[110] The witness further explained that, in general, meetings dealing with security issues were also attended by *conseillers de secteur*, who were to convey recommendations to the authorities,[111] the *IPJ* (Criminal Investigations Officer) in charge of security in the *commune* and the president of the *canton tribunal.*[112] He also mentioned that **[page 24]** many Tutsi, including Charles Mugenzi, head of the Nyange health centre, Boniface Gatare, a youth counsellor in the *commune* and Lambert Gatare, a political party official, also attended the meeting.[113] Finally, Witness FE13 stated that decisions taken at the meeting include the decision to assemble Tutsi refugees at Nyange parish[114] and to make a request for military reinforcements from Kibuye *prefecture.*[115]

70. Witness FE27, a Hutu,[116] testified that he attended the meeting of 11 April 1994, held in the communal office. He indicated that this meeting, which usually dealt with problems related to the economic development of the *commune*, was transformed into a security committee meeting on the initiative of the *bourgmestre.*[117] The witness added that Athanase Seromba did not participate in this meeting.[118] He further stated that during the meeting *Bourgmestre* Ndahimana read out a letter sent to him by Seromba, in which the latter informed him that he would not attend, but would adhere to the decisions the meeting would take.

101 Transcript, 24 January 2005, p. 31 (open session); Witness information sheet témoin (P-24).
102 Transcript, 24 January 2005, p. 27 (closed session).
103 Transcript, 25 January 2005, p. 18 (open session).
104 See Section 3.2.1.
105 Transcript, 19 January 2005, p. 19 (closed session).
106 Transcript, 19 January 2005, pp. 8-9 (closed session).
107 Transcript, 19 January 2005, p. 51 (open session).
108 Transcript, 12 April 2006, cross-examination, p. 19 (open session).
109 Transcript, 7 April 2006, p. 21 (open session).
110 Transcript, 7 April 2006, p. 18 (closed session).
111 *Idem.*
112 *Idem.*
113 Transcript, 7 April 2006, pp. 19-20 (closed session).
114 *Idem.*
115 Transcript, 7 April 2006, p. 21 (open session).
116 See Section 3.2.1.
117 Transcript, 7 April 2006, p. 19 (closed session).
118 Transcript, 7 April 2006, p. 22 (open session).

71. Witness CF23, a Hutu,[119] testified that the 11 April 1994 meeting was convened by the *bourgmestre* of the *commune*, Ndahimana. He added that the purpose of this meeting was to review the situation, to take all the necessary measures to stop the killings and lastly to discuss the organisation of receiving refugees into Nyange parish.[120] He indicated that Tutsi, including Charles Mugenzi and Boniface Gatare, actively participated in this meeting.[121] The witness emphasised that participants in this meeting were opposed to the killings. He also stated that Athanase Seromba did not attend the meeting, but had written a letter to the *bourgmestre* which was read out at the meeting.[122] In that letter, the witness continued, Seromba asked the *commune* authorities to ensure the protection of refugees, as well as their food supply, suggesting to the authorities that they solicit the assistance of the Caritas. Finally, Witness CF23 explained that at the end of the meeting, the *bourgmestre* requested gendarme reinforcement from Kibuye *préfecture* as had been recommended to him by those in attendance.[123]

4.3.2 Findings of the Chamber

72. The Chamber finds that the testimonies of CNJ and CDL are not reliable. It notes that CNJ's testimony is hearsay. As to CDL, the Chamber observes that nothing in his testimony shows that he personally attended the meeting of 11 April 1994. In fact, when Counsel for the Defence put a question to him with respect to the 13 April 1994 meeting, the witness stated as **[page 25]** follows: "I think that I have already said in my testimony there are certain events which I heard and saw myself, [...] and other events that were reported to me; in particular, this meeting".[124]Furthermore, the witness was unable to state convincingly why he failed to mention the presence of the clergy in his prior statements, whereas he does so in his testimony before the Chamber. In fact, when asked by Counsel for the Defence why he did not mention, before the Rwandan courts, the names of the clergy when he was giving the names of participants in security meetings, the witness stated that when he began to testify in 1999, he was unable to "say everything in one go because at the time it was not easy to understand the reasons and to say the whole truth".[125]

73. Witnesses FE27 and CF23 cannot be considered credible on this point, as their testimonies are inconsistent with their prior statements. With respect to FE27, the Chamber notes that in his 25 January 2002 statement, he stated: "Father Seromba also attended the meeting for the issue of gathering of the refugees at the church to ensure their security was considered".[126]The witness confirmed that he signed the prior statement and made the statements therein.[127] On the other hand, he admitted that he lied to members of the "truth" committee "because they were telling me that if I were to say that Father Seromba was at the meeting I was going to be released".[128] As for CF23, the Chamber notes that in his 14 August 2002 pre-trial statement, this witness stated as follows: "[...] several persons attended that meeting, I remember recognising [...] Reverend Father Seromba [...]".[129] The witness testified that he had only signed the last page of his 14 August 2002 statement, even though his signature appears on each of the pages of the statement.[130] The witness also challenged the validity of the statement, pointing out that the excerpts which were read out to him did not reflect what he had said and that he gave credence only to the documents he wrote himself, such as his confessional statements.[131] Finally, the witness stated at trial that he had referred to Seromba's letter in his statement to the investigators of the Tribunal. The Chamber notes, however, that such reference is not contained in the statements.[132]

119 Transcript, 30 March 2006, pp. 9-10 (closed session); Witness information sheet (D-74).
120 Transcript, 31 March 2006, (closed session), p. 3.
121 *Idem.*
122 Transcript, 31 March 2006, p. 5 (closed session).
123 Transcript, 31 March 2006, p. 10 (open session).
124 Transcript, 19 January 2005, p. 54 (open session).
125 Transcript, 19 January 2005, pp. 53-54 (open session).
126 Statement of Witness FE27 to the "truth" committee on 25 January 2002 (P-42), p. 2.
127 Transcript, 24 March 2006, p. 17 (closed session).
128 Transcript, 24 March 2006, p. 18 (closed session).
129 Statement of Witness CF23 to investigators of the Tribunal on 14 August 2002 (P-49), p. 3.
130 Transcript, 3 April 2006, p. 27 (closed session).
131 Transcript, 3 April 2006, pp. 30-31 (closed session).
132 Transcript, 3 April 2006, p. 12 (closed session).

74. The Chamber finds Witness FE13 credible because of the duties he performed at the *commune,*[133] his presence at the meeting and the account he gave of the meeting. Moreover, FE13's testimony concerning the reading of the letter from Athanase Seromba during the meeting has been corroborated by the testimonies of Witnesses FE27 and CF23. **[page 26]**

75. In view of the foregoing, the Chamber finds that it has been proven beyond a reasonable doubt that a meeting known as "security meeting", was held in the communal office on 11 April 1994. It finds, however that it has not been established beyond a reasonable doubt that Athanase Seromba attended this meeting.

4.4 Arrival at Nyange church of gendarmes coming from Kibuye *préfecture*

4.4.1 The evidence

Prosecution witness

76. Witness CDL, a Hutu,[134] testified that he saw gendarmes on 10 or 11 April 1994. He stated that he was unaware of the circumstances surrounding the arrival of the gendarmes, who according to him, came together with the *bourgmestre*. The witness also testified that he did not know whether the gendarmes had come at the request of Athanase Seromba. He did, however, remark that a gendarme was constantly at Seromba's side during the April 1994 events.[135]

Defence witnesses

77. Witness FE55, a Hutu,[136] testified that during the 11 April 1994 meeting, the decision was taken to seek gendarme reinforcements from Kibuye *préfecture* to ensure the security of refugees in Nyange parish.[137]

78. Witness BZ1, a Hutu,[138] testified that there were about four armed gendarmes stationed at the parish. He further testified that the gendarmes arrived there on or about 13 April 1994, shortly before the situation worsened.[139]

79. Witness PA1[140] testified that four gendarmes arrived in Nyange parish on Tuesday, 12 April 1994.[141]

4.4.2 Findings of the Chamber

80. The Chamber notes that the statements of Prosecution Witness CDL and Defence Witnesses FE55, BZ1 and PA1 are consistent with respect to the presence of gendarmes in Nyange parish at the time of the April 1994 events, although they differ slightly as to the date of arrival on the location. The Chamber further notes that Witness FE55 also stated that the arrival **[page 27]** of the gendarmes was the result of a decision taken at the 11 April 1994 meeting, referred to as a "security meeting". This contention is corroborated by Witness FE13 and CF23 in their respective testimonies.[142]

81. In view of the foregoing, the Trial Chamber finds that CDL, FE55 and BZ1 are credible witnesses. Consequently, the Chamber considers that it has been established beyond a reasonable doubt that on 11 April 1994 gendarmes from Kibuye *préfecture* arrived at Nyange church.

133 Transcript, 7 April 2006, p. 11 (closed session), p. 23 (open session), p. 35 (closed session); Witness information sheet (D-86).
134 See Section 3.2.1.
135 Transcript, 19 January 2005, p. 71 (open session).
136 Statement of Witness FE55 to Tribunal investigators on 13 March 2003 (P-61), p. 1.
137 Transcript, 12 April 2006, p. 42 (open session).
138 Transcript, 10 November 2005, p. 30 (open session).
139 Transcript, 2 November 2005, pp. 66-67 (open session).
140 See Section 3.4.1.
141 Transcript, 20 April 2006, p. 16 (closed session).
142 See Section 4.3.1.

5. EVENTS OF 12 TO 14 APRIL 1994 AT NYANGE PARISH

5.1 The Indictment

82. The Indictment alleges as follows:

> 12. From about 12 April 1994, refugees were confined by the gendarmes and surrounded by the militiamen and *Interahamwe* armed with traditional and conventional weapons. Father Athanase SEROMBA did prevent the refugees from taking food and instructed the gendarmes to shoot any "*Inyenzi*" (reference to Tutsi) who tried to take some food from the Presbytere or the parish banana groves. He refused to celebrate mass for them and stressed that he didn't want to do that for the *Inyenzi*.
>
> 13. On or about 12 April 1994, Father Athanase SEROMBA expelled from the Parish four Tutsi employees (Alex, Félécien, Gasore and Patrice). He forced them to leave the parish, while *Interahamwe* and militiamen were beginning the attacks against refugees of the parish.
>
> 14. Father Athanase SEROMBA knew that removing the employees would cause their death. In fact, only one of them (Patrice) was able to return to the parish, seriously wounded, which did not prevent Athanase SEROMBA from preventing his access to the church. He was killed by the *Interahamwe* and the militiamen
>
> [...]
>
> 38. On or about 12 April 1994, Father SEROMBA chaired a meeting in his parish office, with, among others, Grégoire NDAHIMANA and Fulgence KAYISHEMA. Immediately after this meeting, Fulgence KAYISHEMA said that KAYIRANGA (a prosperous Tutsi businessman) must be found and brought to the church.
>
> 40. The second step of the plan consisted of keeping the refugees inside the church, surrounding the Church with *Interahamwe* and militiamen and inflicting on the refugees conditions of life calculated to weaken them physically. The plan also included regular attacks by *Interahamwe* and militiamen of the refugees to defeat their endurance. **[page 28]**
>
> 41. To this end, from about 12 April 1994, gendarmes confined the refugees at the Nyange church, which was surrounded by *Interahamwe* and the militiamen.
>
> 42. Athanase SEROMBA prevented the refugees from having access to sanitary places in the parish or from taking food, ordering gendarmes to shoot any *Inyenzi* who tried to take food from the Presbytere or the banana groves of the parish.
>
> 43. On or about 12 April 1994, in the afternoon, Father Athanase SEROMBA chaired a meeting with Grégoire NDAHIMANA and Fulgence KAYISHEMA. Soon after, the *bourgmestre* NDAHIMANA declared, "*We choose the richest to be killed, the others can go back to their houses*"

5.2 Encirclement of refugees by militia and *Interahamwe* armed with traditional and conventional weapons

5.2.1 The evidence

Prosecution witnesses

83. Witness CBS[143] testified that the church was surrounded by gendarmes.[144] Witness CBK[145] testified that the church was encircled by attackers.[146]

Defence witnesses

84. Witness PA1[147] testified that the evening of 11 April 1994, "a lot of people" surrounded the church where the refugees were.[148] Witness FE56, a Hutu,[149] testified that Kayishema had Nyange church surrounded

---

143 See Section 3.3.1.
144 Transcript, 5 October 2004, p. 9 (open session).
145 See Section 3.3.1.
146 Transcript of19 October 2004, pp. 19-20 (closed session)
147 See Section 3.4.1.
148 Transcript, 20 April 2006, p. 14 (closed session).
149 See Section 3.2.1.

by "people".[150] He further testified added that soldiers were positioned near the doors of the presbytery, in order to block the entrance.[151]

5.2.2 Findings of the Chamber

85. The Trial Chamber notes that, with the exception of Witness CBS who testified that only gendarmes surrounded the church, the fact that from 12 April 1994, militiamen and other *Interahamwe* surrounded Nyange church where the refugees were confined is corroborated both by Prosecution Witness CKB and Defence Witnesses PA1 and FE56. Consequently, the Chamber considers this fact established beyond a reasonable doubt. **[page 29]**

5.3 Athanase Seromba's order prohibiting the refugees from seeking food in the banana plantation of the parish and his alleged order to gendarmes to shoot any *"Inyenzi"* who attempted to pick any bananas

5.3.1 The evidence

Prosecution witnesses

86. Witness CBS[152] stated on three occasions that Athanase Seromba prevented the refugees from getting food from the parish banana plantation.[153] He explained, *inter alia,* that on Wednesday, 13 April 1994, some teachers, who were among the Tutsi refugees, asked for food from Seromba, but Seromba refused to give it to them. Following this refusal, certain refugees went on their own initiative into the banana plantation of the parish to harvest bananas, which they roasted in the parish courtyard.[154] The witness further explained that upon seeing the refugees, Seromba prohibited them from returning to the banana plantation and also gave orders to the gendarmes to shoot at any refugee who ventured there, treating the refugees as *"Inyenzi"*. Finally the witness stated that he was near Seromba when the latter made these remarks.[155]

87. Witness CBJ[156] also testified that the refugees had asked Athanase Seromba for food and that Seromba refused to give it to them. He also explained that he, together with other refugees, went to harvest bananas in the parish banana plantation. When Seromba saw the bananas, he became angry and scolded them for not showing him respect by going into the banana plantation. Seromba then addressed the gendarmes in these terms: "Whoever goes back to the banana plantation to cut the bananas, you should shoot at the persons."[157]

88. Witness CBN, a Tutsi,[158] stated on two occasions that Athanase Seromba prohibited refugees from getting food from the banana plantation on 14 April 1994, adding that Seromba ordered the gendarmes to shoot at any refugee who returned there.[159]

Defence witness

89. Witness CF23[160] stated twice during his testimony that Athanase Seromba never prohibited refugees from entering the banana plantation and that he saw refugees in the banana **[page 30]** plantation when he personally went there on 13 April 1994.[161] He also testified that, on the same date, he spotted refugees

150 Transcript, 3 April 2006, p. 54 (closed session).
151 Transcript, 3 April 2006, p. 54 (closed session).
152 See Section 3.3.1.
153 Transcript, 5 October 2004, pp. 10 and 18-19 (open session); Transcript of 6 October 2004, pp. 29-30 (open session).
154 Transcript, 6 October 2004, p. 30 (open session).
155 Transcript, 5 October 2004, p. 19 (open session).
156 See Section 3.3.1.
157 Transcript, 11 October 2004, p. 54 (open session).
158 See Section 3.3.1.
159 Transcript, 15 October 2004, p. 43 (open session); Transcript, 18 October 2004, p. 3 (open session).
160 See Section 4.3.1.
161 Transcript, 31 March 2006, p. 24 (open session).

moving about freely in the churchyard and even going to cut bananas.[162] The witness finally stated that he was not present on the location on 14 April 1994.[163]

5.3.2 Findings of the Trial Chamber

90. The Trial Chamber considers Witness CBS' description of the location and the banana plantations to be reliable.[164] Furthermore, his testimony at cross-examination is consistent with his testimony-in-chief. Moreover, there are not any major inconsistencies between his prior statements and his testimony before the Trial Chamber.[165] In this regard, the Trial Chamber considers that the failure to mention the events in issue in his 14 February 1999 statement[166]cannot be perceived as an inconsistency, insofar as no question on the said events was put to him at the time he made the statement. Furthermore, the Trial Chamber notes that the witness was at the location at the time the events occurred. From the foregoing, the Chamber finds Witness CBS reliable both with respect to the prohibition and the order that Seromba allegedly gave to the gendarmes.

91. The Chamber finds that Witness CBJ is also reliable on these two points. In fact, it finds no contradiction between the prior statements of the witness and his testimony before the Chamber. In this regard, that the events in issue are not mentioned in the statements the witness made on 23 March 1997[167] and 24 June 1997[168] can be explained by the fact that no question in relation thereto was put to him at the time he made the statements. The Chamber observes that only minor inconsistencies relating to the number of Hutu attackers,[169] the number of Tutsi refugees in the church[170] and the number of Tutsi in Kivumu *commune*[171] were noted, and are not such as would impugn the credibility of witness CBJ. **[page 31]**

92. The Trial Chamber also considers that the contradictory testimony given by Witness FE36[172] does not impugn the credibility of Witness CBJ. No question was put to Witness CBJ on FE36's account of the events. The Chamber also notes that Witness FE36 is not credible, as he admits having lied before the Chamber.[173] In this connection, the Chamber notes, in particular, that Witness FE36 testified that CBJ stated that his entire family had been killed, whereas CBJ had, in fact, only stated that certain members of his family were dead.[174]

93. The Trial Chamber considers that the testimony of CBN is not reliable on this point. What the witness said during his examination contradicts a statement made on 17 August 2000.[175] In the statement, the witness on the contrary claimed that the prohibition against entering the banana plantation was made by a gendarme in the presence of Athanase Seromba. Furthermore, the discussion between Seromba and the gendarmes allegedly did not take place in front of the church but in the banana plantation. The witness testified that the true account was that given before the Trial Chamber, and that the earlier account is the result of a

162 Transcript, 3 April 2006, p. 15 (closed session)

163 Transcript, 3 April 2006, p. 15 (closed session).

164 Transcript, 6 October 2004, p. 31 (open session).

165 There is a minor inconsistency between the witness's testimony and his 17 August 2000 statement (Statement of witness CBS to Tribunal investigators on 17 August 2000 (Statement not tendered as Prosecution exhibit)), p. 3; read out to the witness: Transcript, 6 October 2004 p. 28 (open session). In his statement, the witness states that refugees had delegated a group of teachers to go and ask for food from Athanase Seromba, whereas in his testimony, the witness testified that it was the teachers who took the initiative to meet Seromba. During cross-examination, Counsel for the Defence asked the witness to explain this inconsistency, referring erroneously to the statement of 15 November 1995. The witness then explained that there was a transcription error, adding that the refugees had never sent a delegation and that the teachers themselves took the initiative to meet the priest (Transcript, 6 October 2004, pp. 27-29 (open session)).

166 Statement of Witness CBS to the Rwandan judicial authorities on 14 October 1999 (D-19).

167 Statement of Witness CBJ to Tribunal investigators on 23 March 1997 (D-26).

168 Statement of Witness CBJ to Tribunal investigators on 24 June 1997 (D-25).

169 Transcript, 13 October 2004, pp. 31-32 (open session).

170 Transcript, 13 October 2004, pp. 10, 12 and 15 (open session).

171 Transcript, 13 October 2004, pp. 14-15 (open session).

172 Transcript, 21 November 2005, pp. 17-19 (closed session).

173 Transcript, 28 November 2005, pp. 4 and 6 (closed session). *Seromba*, Decision on Defence Motion for an Investigation into the Circumstances and Actual Causes Underlying Retracting by Witness FE36, 20 April 2006.

174 FE36: Transcript, 28 November 2005, p. 7 (closed session); CBJ: Transcript, 15 October 2004, p. 48 (open session).

175 Statement of Witness CBN to Tribunal investigators on 17 August 2000 (statement not submitted as Prosecution exhibit), p. 3; read out to the witness: Transcript, 18 October 2004, p. 3 (open session).

misunderstanding, as it was Seromba who gave the order not to go into the banana plantation, which order was subsequently repeated by the gendarme.[176]

94. With respect to Defence Witness CF23, the Chamber notes that he acknowledged not having been present at the location on 14 April 1994. Moreover, the Chamber finds the witness's testimony that the refugees could move freely between the churchyard and the banana plantation to be hardly consistent with reality, especially as on 13 April 1994, the day he alleges to have witnessed this event, the church was already surrounded by numerous militiamen and other *Interahamwe,* whose violent attacks on the previous days justified the choice of the church as a sanctuary for refugees. In the light of the foregoing observations, the Chamber finds that Witness CF23 is not credible.

95. In view of the foregoing, the Trial Chamber finds that it has been proven beyond a reasonable doubt that between 13 and 14 April 1994, Athanase Seromba prohibited refugees from going into the Parish banana plantation to get food, and that he also ordered gendarmes to shoot at any refugees who ventured there.

96. The Chamber finds on the other hand that the Prosecutor did not adduce evidence in support of the allegation that Seromba prohibited Tutsi refugees from getting food at the presbytery. The Chamber therefore finds that this fact was not proved beyond a reasonable doubt. **[page 32]**

5.4 Refusal of Athanase Seromba to celebrate mass for "*Inyenzi*"

5.4.1 The evidence

Prosecution witnesses

97. Witness CBN[177] testified that on 14 April 1994 Athanase Seromba was approached by several Tutsi refugees, including some teachers, namely Bonera, Ruteghesa and Rwakayiro, who asked him to celebrate a mass for them.[178] The witness further testified that Athanase Seromba refused to celebrate the mass, arguing that he couldn't "waste his time".[179] The witness also explained that such refusal went against the wishes of the refugees who wanted the mass to be said.[180] He further explained that a Tutsi refugee then announced to other refugees that they should pray together, as Seromba had refused to say a mass for them.[181] Finally, the witness stated that Seromba was in front of the church when he expressed his refusal.[182]

98. Witness CBI[183] testified that, on or about 13 April 1994, Athanase Seromba entered the church to remove chalices, which he took to the presbytery, "on the first floor of his residential quarters".[184]

99. Furthermore, Witness CBJ[185] testified that there was no mass celebrated in Nyange parish on Sunday, 10 April 1994, explaining that it was not possible to celebrate mass because the "situation was rather critical".[186] The witness also testified that on 14 April 1994, Athanase Seromba removed priests' cassocks and chalices filled with communion from the church. Finally, the witness stated that he learned subsequently that Seromba had taken the objects with him to the presbytery.[187]

100. Witness CBK[188] testified that masses were celebrated in the old meeting hall during the events which occurred in Nyange parish in April 1994.[189] **[page 33]**

---

176 Transcript, 18 October 2004, pp. 3-4 (open session).
177 See Section 3.3.1.
178 Transcript, 15 October 2004, pp. 60-61 (open session).
179 Transcript, 15 October 2004, p. 41 (open session).
180 Transcript, 18 October 2004, p. 1 (open session).
181 Transcript, 18 October 2004, p. 49 (closed session).
182 Transcript, 15 October 2004, p. 60 (open session).
183 See Section 3.3.1.
184 Transcript, 1 October 2004, p. 42 (open session).
185 See Section 3.2.1.
186 Transcript, 13 October 2004, p. 15 (open session)
187 Transcript, 12 October 2004, p. 3 (open session).
188 See Section 3.3.1.
189 Transcript, 20 October 2004, p. 45 (closed session).

Defence witness

101. Witness PA1[190] testified that as of 11 April 1994, the decision was taken to no longer celebrate mass in Nyange church because of the huge number of refugees and the presence of animals there, adding that masses were celebrated in the oratory, located in the presbytery.[191]

102. When Counsel for the Defence asked if the removal by Athanase Seromba of Communion hosts and sacerdotal ornaments had met with resistance on the part of the refugees, Witness PA1 answered: "There were no problems whatsoever. We believe that the sacrament is something that is highly respected by Catholics, and the sacred vases could not have stayed there because of the respect due to such ornaments. So there was no opposition. We believed it was our mission to have all our sacraments respected and put them in a safe place."[192]

5.4.2 Findings of the Chamber

103. The Chamber finds Witness CBN credible. There are only minor inconsistencies between his trial testimony and prior statements as to the exact location where Athanase Seromba expressed his refusal to celebrate the mass[193] and what he said on this occasion.[194] The Trial Chamber does not consider such inconsistencies to be crucial, given the lapse of time since the occurrence of the events, on the one hand, and the numerous references by witnesses to Seromba's refusal to celebrate mass for Tutsi refugees.[195]

104. Moreover, the Chamber notes that Witnesses CBI, CBJ and CBK testified that Athanase Seromba removed objects that are useful for celebrating mass between 10 and 13 April 1994.

105. The Chamber considers that the testimony of PA1, member of a religious order, clearly shows that from 11 April 1994, no mass was celebrated in Nyange church. On this point, Witness PA1 is corroborated by Witness CBI, as the Trial Chamber considers it in significance that CBI, unlike PA1, gave the date of the decision to no longer celebrate mass in church as being rather 10 April 1994. The Chamber considers, therefore, that these two witnesses are credible on this point. The Chamber is also of the view that Witness PA1 is credible with respect to the fact that sacred objects (Communion hosts and sacerdotal ornaments) were removed from the church.

106. That the refugees did not put up any resistance, as asserted by Witness PA1, to the removal by Seromba of sacred objects does not, in the opinion of the Chamber, exclude in any way the possibility that the refugees requested that a mass be said for them. In this regard, the **[page 34]** Chamber is aware of the fact that Tutsi refugees in Nyange church knew that they were in constant danger of death during the events of April 1994, given that members of their ethnic group were being persecuted throughout the Rwandan territory. Under these circumstances, the Chamber considers it highly probable that the most fervent among them could have requested that Seromba celebrate a mass for them. The Chamber further considers that Seromba's removal of sacred objects could be interpreted as a denial of the refugees' request, particularly in view of the fact that he continued to celebrate mass in the oratory as from 11 April 1994. Consequently, the Chamber finds Witness CBN credible as to his testimony that refugees presented a mass request to Seromba which he turned down.

107. In view of the foregoing, the Trial Chamber finds that it has been established beyond a reasonable doubt that Athanase Seromba refused to celebrate mass for Tutsi refugees in Nyange church.

190 Transcript, 20 April 2006, p. 38 (closed session).
191 Transcript, 20 April 2006, p.11 (closed session).
192 Transcript, 20 April 2006, p.11 (closed session).
193 Transcript, 20 April 2006, p. 60 (open session).
194 Transcript, 15 October 2004, pp. 61-62 (open session).
195 Transcript, 18 October 2004, p. 3 (open session).

5.5 Dismissal of four Tutsi employees (Alex, Félécien, Gasore and Patrice) from the parish by Athanase Seromba and the death of Patrice who was refused access to the presbytery by Seromba

5.5.1 The evidence

Prosecution witness

108. Witness CBK[196] testified that after the death of the Rwandan President, Alex, Félécien, Gasore and Patrice, all of whom were Tutsi and employees in Nyange parish, told him that they had been suspended from work by Athanase Seromba, whereupon they left the parish.[197]

109. Witness CBK explained that these employees returned to the parish on 13 April 1994, but were turned back by Athanase Seromba, who informed them that there was no refuge for them there.[198] The witness also observed that the security situation had worsened considerably, such that any Tutsi who went outside ran the risk of being killed.[199] He further testified that he saw Patrice in the rear courtyard of the presbytery, wounded in both the arms and the legs, adding that he approached Seromba and asked him to help Patrice. According to the witness, Seromba refused; rather, he asked Patrice to leave the premises. Noticing that Patrice delayed complying with his order, Seromba asked the gendarmes to forcefully expel him. Finally, the witness testified that he subsequently saw the lifeless body of Patrice in the rear courtyard of the presbytery.[200] **[page 35]**

Defence witness

110. Witness NA1, born of Hutu and Tutsi parents,[201] testified that he arrived at Nyange church on 15 April 1994.[202] He also indicated that he had previously worked in Nyange parish between 1992 and 1993.[203] The witness explained that when he returned to this parish in April 1994, he observed that none of the employees of the parish had been dismissed. He added that he met Alexis on site, who even greeted him.[204]

111. During cross-examination, Witness NA1 explained, *inter alia*, that he had no idea which employees were to be found among the refugees. He also stated that he was not there to take a census of the parish,[205] nor was he in any position to know who was an employee of the parish and who was not.[206]

5.5.2 Findings of the Trial Chamber

112. The Trial Chamber finds Witness CBK credible. No contradiction exists between his testimony and his prior statements. The Chamber also considers witness CBK's account of how athanase Seromba turned back Tutsi employees to be consistent and plausible, particularly in view of the circumstances which prevailed in Nyange parish in April 1994.

113. Furthermore, the Chamber is of the view that NA1's is not reliable on this point. The Chamber notes that Witness NA1 only arrived in Nyange parish on 15 April 1994 and, therefore, could not properly testify on events he did not witness. Furthermore, it observes that the witness spoke in general terms, as his testimony focussed simply on staff changes which were made between the time he left Nyange in 1993 and when he returned in April 1994. Finally, as the witness himself admits, he was in no position to identify employees present at the time he arrived at the church, due to the very large number of refugees and attackers that were on the premises.[207]

196 See Section 3.3.1.
197 Transcript, 19 October 2004, pp. 7, 14 and 15 (closed session).
198 Transcript, 19 October 2004, p. 15 (closed session).
199 Transcript, 19 October 2004, p. 15 (closed session).
200 Transcript, 19 October 2004, pp. 15-16 (closed session).
201 Transcript, 7 December 2005, p. 75 (closed session).
202 Transcript, 7 December 2005, pp. 15-16 (closed session).
203 Transcript, 7 December 2005, pp. 10-12 (closed session).
204 Transcript, 7 December 2005, p. 19 (closed session).
205 Transcript, 7 December 2005, p. 19 (closed session).
206 Transcript, 7 December 2005, p. 10 (closed session).
207 Transcript, 7 December 2005, p. 21 (closed session); Transcript, 8 December 2005, p. 13 (closed session).

114. In view of the foregoing, the Trial Chamber finds that it has been proved beyond a reasonable doubt that on 13 April 1994, art the time when the security situation in Kivumu *commune* had become precarious, Athanase Seromba dismissed four Tutsi employees from the parish, including a certain Patrice, who, upon returning the following day, was killed by attackers after having been turned back from the presbytery by Seromba. **[page 36]**

5.6 The meeting in the parish office on 12 April 1994

5.6.1 The evidence

Prosecution witness

115. Witness CBJ[208] testified that on 12 April 1994, he saw Athanase Seromba engaged in discussion on the balcony of the "second floor" of the presbytery with Grégoire Ndahimana, Gaspard Kanyarukiga, Fulgence Kayishema and Télesphore Ndungutse.[209] He added that the discussion lasted between 15 and 20 minutes.[210] He finally stated that these persons did not go into any room or hall to hold discussions.[211]

5.6.2 Findings of the Chamber

116. The Chamber finds that CBJ's testimony is insufficient to prove that a meeting presided over by Seromba took place in the parish office on 12 April 1994. Accordingly, the Chamber finds that the Prosecution has not proved this fact beyond a reasonable doubt.

6. EVENTS OF 14 TO 15 APRIL 1994 IN NYANGE PARISH

6.1 The Indictment

117. The Indictment alleges as follows:

> "15. On or about 13 April 1994, the *Interahamwe* and militiamen surrounding the parish, launched an attack against the refugees in the church. The refugees defended themselves by pushing the attackers out of the church, to a place named "*la statue de la Sainte Vierge*". The attackers in turn, threw a grenade causing many deaths between the refugees. The survivors quickly tried to return to the Church, but Father Athanase SEROMBA ordered that all doors be closed, leaving many refugees (about 30) outside to be killed
>
> 16. On or about 14 April 1994, in the afternoon, Father SEROMBA met Fulgence KAYISHEMA and Gaspard KANYARUKIGA in his Parish office. Soon afterwards, Fulgence KAYISHEMA went to bring some fuel, using one of the KIVUMU commune official vehicles. That fuel was used by the *Interahamwe* and militiamen to burn down the church, while the gendarmes and members of the communal police threw grenades.
>
> 17. On that same day, Athanase SEROMBA chaired a meeting in his Parish Office with Fulgence KAYISHEMA, Grégoire NDAHIMANA, Gaspard KANYARUKIRA and **[page 37]** others unknown to the Prosecution. Immediately after this meeting, following a request by refugees for protection, *bourgmestre* Grégoire NDAHIMANA replied that this war was caused by the *Inyenzi* who killed the President.
>
> 18. On or about 15 April, a bus transporting armed *Interahamwe* and a priest named KAYIRANGWA, arrived in Nyange parish, from KIBUYE prefecture. Soon thereafter, Father SEROMBA held a meeting with priest KAYIRANGWA, Fulgence KAYISHEMA, KANYARUKIGA and others unknown to the Prosecution.
>
> 19. After this meeting, Father Athanase SEROMBA ordered the *Interahamwe* and militiamen to launch attacks to kill the Tutsi, beginning with the intellectuals. Following his orders, an attack was launched against the refugees by the *Interahamwe*, militiamen, gendarmes and communal police officers, equipped with traditional weapons and firearms, causing the deaths of numerous refugees.
>
> 20. On or about 15 April, in the afternoon, the attacks intensified against the refugees of the Church. The *Interahamwe* and militiamen attacked with traditional arms, and poured fuel through the roof of the church, while gendarmes and communal police officers launched grenades and killed the refugees.

208 See Section 3.2.1.
209 Transcript, 11 October 2004, p. 51 (open session).
210 Transcript, 11 October 2004, p. 53 (open session).
211 Transcript, 11 October 2004, p. 52 (open session).

21. During these attacks, Father SEROMBA handed over to the gendarmes a Tutsi teacher named GATARE who was killed immediately. This act encouraged and motivated the attackers.

22. Again during these attacks, some refugees left the church for the Presbytere. Father SEROMBA found them and informed gendarmes about their hiding place. Immediately thereafter, they were attacked and killed. Among the victims were two Tutsi women (Alexia and Meriam).

[...]

25. During the attacks described above, Athanase SEROMBA, Grégoire NDAHIMANA, Fulgence KAYISHEMA, Télesphore NDUNGUTSE, Judge Joseph HABIYAMBERE, assistant *bourgmestre* Védaste MUPENDE, and other authorities not known to the Prosecution, were supervising the massacres.

[...]

44. On or about 13 April 1994, the *Interahamwe* and militiamen surrounding the parish launched an attack against the refugees in the church, killing about 30 refugees.

[...]

46. The massive attack against the Tutsi refugees was conducted on or about 15 April 1994 under the supervision of Father SEROMBA, Fulgence KAYISHEMA, Grégoire NDAHIMANA, Télesphore NDUNGUTSE, Gaspard KANYIRUKIGA and others unknown to the Prosecution. **[page 38]**

[...]

48. On or about 13 April, the *Interahamwe* and militiamen surrounding the parish launched an attack against the refugees in the church. The attackers having been pushed away and out of the church, to a placed named "la statue de la Sainte Vièrge". The attackers threw a grenade causing many deaths among the refugees. The survivors quickly tried to return to the church, but Father Athanase SEROMBA ordered that all doors be closed, leaving many refugees outside (about 30) to be killed.

6.2 The attack against Nyange church followed by resistance from the refugees countered by the throwing of grenades by the attackers

6.2.1 The evidence

Prosecution witnesses

118. Witnesses CNJ,[212] CBR,[213] CBJ,[214] CDK,[215] CBS[216] and CDL[217] stated that a confrontation took place between the attackers and Tutsi refugees in the morning of 15 April 1994, near the Caritas restaurant. They, *inter alia,* explained that the assailants attacked the refugees with stones and traditional weapons, and that the refugees managed to push them back right up to the Codecoki. The attackers only regained control when a reservist named Théophile Rukara climbed on the roof of a house and began throwing grenades, wounding and killing many Tutsi refugees. The refugees then retreated towards Nyange church in order to avoid fighting the attackers.[218] Witness CBR, in particular, added that communal officials, including Ndahimana, Fulgence Kayishema, Habiyambere, Védaste Muraginabugabo and Gaspard Kanyarukiga[219] were present at the scene of fighting and encouraged the attackers to attack the refugees.[220]

[212] See Section 3.3.1.
[213] Transcript, 20 January 2005, p. 45 (open session); Witness information sheet (P-23).
[214] See Section 3.2.1.
[215] Witness information sheet (P-14); Transcript, 7 October 2004, pp. 77-78 (closed session).
[216] See Section 3.3.1.
[217] See Section 3.2.1.
[218] CNJ: Transcript, 24 January 2005, p. 16 (open session); CBR: Transcript, 20 January 2005, p. 37 (open session); CBJ: Transcript, 12 October 2004, pp. 5-6 (open session); CDK: Transcript, 7 October 2004, pp. 60-61 (open session) and Transcript, 11 October 2004, p. 15 (open session); CBS: Transcript, 5 October 2004, p. 20 (open session); CDL: Transcript, 19 January 2005, p. 48 (open session).
[219] Transcript, 20 January 2005, p. 37 (open session).
[220] Transcript, 20 January 2005, p. 37 (open session).

Defence witnesses

119. Witnesses FE31,[221] BZ14,[222] BZ1[223] and BZ4[224] stated that grenades were thrown at Tutsi refugees during the attack which occurred in the morning of 15 April 1994. They also mentioned **[page 39]** that following the grenade attack, which left some of them dead, the refugees fell back and barricaded themselves inside the church to better protect themselves.[225]

6.2.2 Findings of the Chamber

120. The Trial Chamber notes that Prosecution and Defence witnesses alike confirmed that in the morning of 15 April 1994, an attack was launched against Tutsi refugees which met with stiff resistance, and that the attackers subsequently used grenades, causing the death of several refugees. The Chamber therefore finds that these facts have been proven beyond a reasonable doubt.

6.3 The order given by Athanase Seromba to shut the doors of the church, leaving about 30 refugees outside to be killed

6.3.1 The evidence

Prosecution witnesses

121. Witness CBJ[226] testified that in the evening of 14 April 1994, Athanase Seromba, accompanied by gendarmes, asked Tutsi refugees to go inside the church, and then locked them inside.[227] He also testified that the following morning, Seromba, still accompanied by gendarmes, returned to open the doors of the church.[228] Witness CBJ also explained that during the attacks of 15 April 1994, the Tutsi refugees themselves took the decision to barricade themselves inside, abandoning outside the church some people "who did not succeed to do so", and so they were killed.[229]

122. Witnesses CBK,[230] CDL[231] and CNJ testified that during the attack of 15 April 1994, the refugees barricaded themselves inside the church for protection.[232] **[page 40]**

Defence witnesses

123. Witnesses BZ4,[233] FE56,[234] BZ14[235] and FE34[236] testified that following the attacks of 15 April 1994, the refugees retreated towards the church and barricaded themselves inside.[237]

---

221 See Section 3.2.1.
222 Transcript, 1 November 2005, p. 42 (open session).
223 See Section 4.4.1.
224 Transcript, 1 November 2005, pp. 52-54 (open session).
225 FE31: Transcript, 29 March 2006, pp. 18-19 and 23 (closed session); Transcript, 29 March 2006, p. 48 (open session); BZ1: Transcript, 2 November 2005, pp. 57 58 (open session); BZ14: Transcript, 1 November 2005, p. 22 (open session) and Transcript, 1 November 2005, p. 28 (open session); BZ4: Transcript, 1 November 2005, pp. 5860 (open session).
226 See Section 3.2.1.
227 Transcript, 12 October 2004, pp. 2-4 (open session); Transcript, 13 October 2004, pp. 36-37 (open session).
228 Transcript, 12 October 2004, p. 10 (open session); Transcript, 13 October 2004, p. 41 (open session).
229 Transcript, 13 October 2004, p. 42 (open session).
230 See Section 3.3.1.
231 See Section 3.2.1.
232 CBK: Transcript, 19 October 2004, p. 24 (closed session); CDL: Transcript, 19 January 2005, p. 23 (open session); CNJ: Transcript, 24 January 2000, p. 41 (open session).
233 See Section 6.2.1.
234 See Section 3.2.1.
235 See Section 6.2.1.
236 Transcript, 30 March 2006, p. 7 (closed session).
237 BZ4: Transcript, 1 November 2005, pp. 58-60 (open session); FE56: Transcript, 3 April 2006, p. 56 (closed session); BZ14: Transcript, 1 November 2005, pp. 22, 26 and 28 (open session); FE34: Transcript, 30 March 2006, p. 51 (open session).

6.3.2 Findings of the Chamber

124. The Chamber notes that both the Indictment and the Prosecutor's pre-trial brief contain the allegation that Athanase Seromba ordered that the church doors be locked, leaving about 30 refugees outside, who were then killed. The Chamber notes, however, that these two pleadings are inconsistent as to the date of the events. While the Indictment alleges that the events occurred on or about 13 April 1994, the pre-trial brief refers to 14 April 1994.

125. The Chamber, moreover, considers that although Witness CBJ alleges that Athanase Seromba locked the doors of the church in the evening of 14 April 1994 and opened them again in the morning of 15 April 1994, he does not blame Seromba for the death of the Tutsi refugees who were killed on account of the fact that they could not gain access to the inside of the closed church. The Chamber also notes that the same witness testified that on 15 April 1994, refugees who were already inside the church took the decision to barricade themselves, abandoning some of their own who were left outside at the mercy of the attackers. The Chamber finally notes that Prosecution and Defence witnesses alike confirm the fact that it was the refugees themselves who took the decision to barricade the doors of the church on 15 April 1994.

126. In the light of the foregoing, the Trial Chamber is of the view that the available evidence is consistent with respect to the dates of the events and the sequence thereof. The Chamber therefore finds that the Prosecution has not proved beyond a reasonable doubt that Athanase Seromba locked the doors of the church, leaving outside approximately 30 refugees who were subsequently killed.

6.4 That Athanase Seromba held meetings with communal authorities and other persons unknown to the Prosecutor

6.4.1 The evidence **[page 41]**

Prosecution witnesses

127. Witness CBI[238] testified that several communal authorities, including Fulgence Kayishema, regularly came to the church while he was still there, adding that the authorities visited Athanase Seromba[239] to seek information on what was happening in the rear courtyard of the presbytery.[240] During cross-examination, Witness CBI stated that the meetings which planned the "killing" of Tutsi were also being held at Seromba's home.[241] Questioned by Defence Counsel as to what he meant by "meeting", the witness responded in these terms: "And you can conclude that it was a meeting when people are together."[242]

128. Witness CBJ[243] testified that the gendarmes, after discussing with Athanase Seromba, travelled to the Codecoki, in the centre of Nyange. He added that when Athanase Seromba returned to the presbytery after the Codecoki meeting, the *Interahamwe*, armed with spears, machetes, swords and bamboo pickets, began killing refugees.[244] He further testified that a meeting was held on 14 April 1994 in Nyange parish which was attended by Seromba, *Bourgmestre* Grégoire Ndahimana, Criminal Investigations Officer Fulgence Kayishema, Télesphore Ndungutse, the businessman Gaspard Kanyarukiga, Brigadier Christophe Mbakirirehe and other persons whom the witness stated he was unable to identify.[245] The witness explained that he observed the holding of this meeting from the church tower where he was with members of the charismatic group.[246] During cross-examination, Witness CBJ reiterated that participants in this meeting planned the killing of Tutsi.

238 See Section 3.3.1.
239 Transcript, 4 October 2004, p. 14.
240 Transcript, 4 October 2004, p. 16.
241 Transcript, 4 October 2004, p. 65.
242 Transcript, 4 October 2004, p. 65 (open session).
243 See Section 3.2.1.
244 Transcript, 12 October 2004, pp. 5-6 (open session).
245 Transcript, 12 October 2004, p. 4 (open session).
246 Transcript, 12 October 2004, p. 32 (closed session).

129. Witness CDK[247] testified that he spotted Athanase Seromba in the vicinity of the church, in the company of Fulgence Kayishema, Grégoire Ndahimana, Gaspard Kanyarukiga and Télesphore Ndungutse.[248] The witness also stated that he saw them emerge at approximately 11 a.m. from the office of the Codecoki where they had just held a meeting. The witness testified that he did not participate in the meeting, adding that he was in front of Gaspard Kanyarukiga's pharmacy at the time of this event.[249] He finally stated that after the meeting, Athanase Seromba returned in the direction of the church, accompanied by Grégoire Ndahimana, Fulgence Kayishema and Télesphore Ndungutse, while Gaspard Kanyarukiga rejoined the population gathered near the statue where they were waiting for him.[250] **[page 42]**

130. Witness CBK[251] testified that between 13 and 16 April 1994, Athanase Seromba organised several meetings in Nyange parish attended by Gaspard Kanyarukiga, Fulgence Kayishema, Grégoire Ndahimana, Ndungutse and Rushema. The witness also testified that the meetings were often held in a room located "on the upper floor of the presbytery building".[252]

131. Witness CBN[253] stated that he saw Athanase Seromba welcome several authorities including *Bourgmestre* Ndahimana, Kanyarukiga and Criminal Investigations Officer Kayishema.[254] Witness CBN also testified that he was informed that communal *conseillers* held meetings.[255]

132. Witness CBS[256] alleged that the authorities had come to Nyange parish to meet Athanase Seromba. Among them, the witness cited *Bourgmestre* Ndahimana, Criminal Investigations Officer Kayishema, Brigadier Mbakirirehe, a teacher, Télesphore Ndungutse, and a businessman, Kanyarukiga.[257]

Defence witnesses

133. Witness PA1[258] testified that no meeting was held at the presbytery by Athanase Seromba and the communal authorities for the purpose of exterminating the refugees.[259] He pointed out he, together with other religious persons, had asked Seromba to contact the *bourgmestre* so as to be apprised of the situation which prevailed in Nyange parish on Friday, 15 April 1994. On his return from this mission, Seromba explained to them that he could not meet the *bourgmestre,* as he was absent attending a burial.[260] Witness PA1 further testified that Grégoire Ndahimana and Fulgence Kayishema came to the parish in the evening. The witness stated that the clergymen asked the authorities to tell them what to do with the corpes strewn in the churchyard.[261] The *bourgmestre* then promised to send bulldozers the following day to bury the bodies.[262] The witness finally testified that it was not possible that Seromba could organise these meetings without him knowing about it, since they were always together.[263] **[page 43]**

134. Witness BZ3[264] stated that there was no "relationship" between Athanase Seromba and the authorities.[265] He furthermore stated that he had never heard of any meetings between Seromba, Fulgence Kayishema, Grégoire Ndahimana and Télesphore Ndungutse prior to 16 April 1994.[266]

247 See Section 6.2.1.
248 Transcript, 11 October 2004, p. 11 (open session).
249 Transcript, 11 October 2004, pp. 12-13 (open session).
250 Transcript, 7 October 2004, pp. 60-61 (open session).
251 See Section 3.3.1.
252 Transcript, 19 October 2004, pp. 16-17 (closed session).
253 See Section 3.3.1.
254 Transcript, 15 October 2004, pp. 44-45(open session).
255 Transcript, 15 October 2004, p. 55 (open session).
256 See Section 3.3.1.
257 Transcript, 5 October 2004, p. 19 (open session).
258 See Section 3.4.1.
259 Transcript, 20 April 2006, p. 18 (closed session).
260 Transcript, 20 April 2006, p. 23 (closed session).
261 Transcript, 20 April 2006, p. 24 (closed session).
262 Transcript, 20 April 2006, p. 24 (closed session).
263 Transcript, 20 April 2006, p. 31 (closed session).
264 Transcript, 8 November 2005, p. 29 (open session).
265 Transcript, 31 October 2005, p. 49 (open session).
266 Transcript, 8 November 2005, p. 23 (open session).

135. Witness CF23[267] testified that meetings of Nyange *commune* were always held at the communal office[268] and that he was always kept informed of them. He also added that no meeting of the communal authorities took place in Nyange parish. He furthermore indicated that no official meeting of the communal authorities had on its agenda the extermination of the Tutsi.[269]

6.4.2 Findings of the Chamber

136. The Chamber finds that the statements of Prosecution Witnesses CBI, CBJ, CBK, CDK and CBS are consistent with respect to the fact that Athanase Seromba held meetings or discussions with the communal authorities. In this regard, it notes that the testimony of Defence Witness PA1 corroborates the testimony of these witnesses when he states, *inter alia,* that Seromba had been asked to contact the *bourgmestre* to find a solution concerning the corpes that were strew all over the church courtyard. The Chamber, however, considers that the testimonies of CBI, CBJ, CBK, CDK and CBS do not lead to the conclusion that any meeting attended by Seromba or any discussion he may have had with the communal authorities was for the purpose of planning the extermination of the Tutsi. In fact, none of these witnesses participated in such meetings or discussions. Therefore, the Chamber considers that reference by some of them to an extermination plan is nothing more than a reflection of their own opinions.

137. The Chamber notes that Witness PA1 was heard on 8 October 2003 within the framework of a Letter Rogatory. At the hearing, the witness admitted that he was not always with Athanase Seromba at the presbytery, adding that it was highly probable that certain persons came to the presbytery without him being informed.[270] The Chamber finds this statement inconsistent with PA1's testimony that he was always alongside Seromba. The Chamber therefore concludes that this witness is not credible.

138. The Chamber is also of the view that the testimonies of BZ3 and CBN are not reliable, as they are hearsay. **[page 44]**

139. The Chamber also considers that the evidence given by Witness CF23 is not probative, as he recounts that meetings were held by the communal authorities in the *commune* office, without any reference to the presence of Athanase Seromba at the meetings.

140. In view of the foregoing, the Trial Chamber finds that the Prosecution has established beyond a reasonable doubt that meetings or discussions were held between Athanase Seromba and *commune* authorities. On the other hand, the Chamber finds that it has not been established beyond a reasonable doubt that the purpose of the meetings or discussions was to plan the extermination of the Tutsi.

6.5 That Athanase Seromba ordered the *Interahamwe* and militia to attack refugees

6.5.1 The evidence

Prosecution witnesses

141. Witness CDK[271] testified that he saw Gaspard Kanyarukiga, Télesphore Ndungutse and Fulgence Kayishema give orders and instructions to the attackers on 15 April 1994.[272]

142. Witness CBR[273] testified that Athanase Seromba was not the one leading the attackers on 15 April 1994. However, he added that before the attackers received any instructions from the authorities, the latter first held discussions with Seromba. He stated however that he was not privy to the discussions.[274] The

267 See Section 4.3.1.
268 Transcript, 31 March 2006, p. 20 (open session).
269 Transcript, 31 March 2006, p. 10 (open session).
270 Statement, WItness PA1 as part of the Letter Rogatory on 8 October 2003 (D-90), p. 4.
271 See Section 6.2.1.
272 Transcript, 11 October 2004, p. 3 (open session).
273 See Section 6.2.1.
274 Transcript, 24 January 2005, p. 4 (open session).

witness also testified that Fulgence Kayishema stated that it was necessary to attack the *Inyenzi* who were located in Nyange church.[275]

143. Witness CNJ[276] testified that when he arrived in Nyange parish with his group, Fulgence Kayishema and Grégoire Ndahimana welcomed them. They told them to cover themselves with banana leaves to distinguish themselves from the Tutsi. The witness further testified that Fulgence Kayishema directed them to a location where they were to assist others in fighting the Tutsi.[277] Witness CNJ admitted that they were pushed back as far as the pharmacy belonging to Kanyarukiga. Kayishema then told them to go back up and throw stones at the Tutsi.[278]

144. Witness YAU[279] testified that when the *Interahamwe* arrived in the courtyard of the church, Athanase Seromba told them not to attack the refugees immediately, as there were few of **[page 45]** them.[280] Seromba allegedly told them to stop the fighting because, in his words, "you are in inadequate numbers".[281] The witness further testified that Seromba ordered the *Interahamwe* to start by killing the intellectuals.[282] Furthermore, he claimed that during the same day, Seromba addressed an *Interahamwe* woman, saying to her: "find all these people who are hiding in here and take them out and kill them!".[283]

Defence witnesses

145. Witness NA1[284] testified that during the 15 April 1994 attack, Athanase Seromba was always with him and other persons in the presbytery. He also stated that while they were in the living room of the presbytery, Kayiranga came to inform them about the massacre of refugees who remained outside the buildings.[285]

146. Witness BZ1[286] testified that, on 15 April 1994, the attackers were led by communal authorities, including the *bourgmestre*, the Criminal Investigations Officer and an MRND official, who worked in close collaboration with these authorities. He stated that he at no time saw Athanase Seromba or other clergymen on 15 April 1994.[287]

147. Witness FE31[288] testified that he arrived at Nyange church in the morning of 15 April 1994, between 10 a.m. and 10.30 a.m.[289] The witness stated that he saw Fulgence Kayishema, a communal police officer, a businessman, Anastase Rushema, Léonard Abayisenga, Théophile Rukura, Boniface Kabalisa, Ephrem Nzabigerageza and other persons holding a meeting, but did not hear what they discussed.[290] He, furthermore, indicated that these persons were leading the attack.[291] Witness FE31 also stated that Athanase Seromba was not present at this meeting,[292] as he did not see him at the location that day.[293] The witness stated, *inter alia,* as follows: "We were [*sic*] attacked because we were incited to do so by the authorities ... [Seromba] could not be attacked and be leading the attack, whereas he was targeted by the assailants."[294] **[page 46]**

275 Transcript, 20 January 2005, pp. 36-37 (open session).
276 See Section 3.3.1.
277 Transcript, 24 January 2005, p. 15 (open session).
278 Transcript, 24 January 2005, p. 16 (open session).
279 See Section 3.3.1.
280 Transcript, 30 September 2004, p. 77 (closed session).
281 Transcript, 29 September 2004, p. 17 (open session).
282 Transcript, 1 October 2004, p. 2 (open session).
283 Transcript, 29 September 2004, p. 21 (open session).
284 See Section 5.5.1.
285 Transcript, 7 December 2005, p. 22 (closed session).
286 See Section 4.4.1.
287 Transcript, 2 November 2005, p. 59 (open session).
288 See Section 3.2.1.
289 Transcript, 29 March 2006, p. 19 (closed session).
290 Transcript, 29 March 2006, p. 48 (open session).
291 Transcript, 29 March 2006, p. 23 (closed session).
292 Transcript, 29 March 2006, p. 22 (closed session).
293 Transcript, 29 March 2006, pp. 25 and 28 (open session).
294 Transcript, 29 March 2006, p. 28 (open session).

148. Witness FE36[295] testified that Télesphore Ndungutse was behind the killings perpetrated in Nyange parish.[296]

149. Witness FE55[297] testified that on 15 April 1994, Gaspard Kanyarukiga solicited the recruitment of persons from Kibilira "to attack the church". He also allegedly stated that everything had to be done to kill the Tutsi, including destroying the church, if necessary.[298] The witness finally testified that on the same day he saw Fulgence Kayishema distributing whistles from his vehicle, inciting the Hutu to kill Tutsi refugees in Nyange parish.[299]

150. Witness FE56[300] explained that on 15 April 1994, Fulgence Kayishema wanted to expel the refugees from the church. The witness also stated that Télesphore Ndungutse gave him a watering can containing fuel and ordered him to spray it on the windows of the church.[301]According to the witness, the objective was to frighten the refugees, so that they would be forced to come out of the church, which was surrounded on the orders of Fulgence Kayishema.[302] The witness testified that Télesphore Ndungutse and Fulgence Kayishema supervised the attacks.[303]He explained that these persons went to negotiate with Astaldi company to obtain trucks for the transport of attackers from Kibilira to Nyange parish.[304] Witness FE56 finally testified that he did not see Athanase Seromba in Nyange parish on 15 April 1994.[305]

6.5.2 Findings of the Chamber

151. The Chamber notes that Witness YAU is the sole Prosecution witness who stated that Seromba ordered *Interahamwe* to start by killing Tutsi intellectuals on 15 April 1995. The Chamber observes, however, that the circumstances under which this witness may have heard Athanase Seromba give such an order do not clearly emerge from his testimony. Consequently, the Chamber finds that Witness YAU is not reliable.

152. The Chamber notes that the testimonies of CDK, CBR, CNJ, NA1, BZ1, FE31, FE36, FE55 and FE56 are consistent with respect to the fact that it was the communal authorities who led the attackers, made up of *Interahamwe* and militiamen, and gave them orders to attack the refugees. **[page 47]**

153. In view of the foregoing, the Chamber finds that the Prosecution has not proved beyond a reasonable doubt that Athanase Seromba ordered the *Interahamwe* and militiamen to attack the refugees.

6.6 That the *Interahamwe* and militia, assisted by gendarmes and communal police officers, launched attacks against the refugees and attempted to burn down the Nyange church

6.6.1 The evidence

Prosecution witnesses

154. Witness CBI[306] testified that on 15 April 1994, most of the assailants were carrying traditional weapons, while their leaders were carrying guns.[307] He also testified that this attack caused numerous deaths among the refugees, leaving the church courtyard strewn with their dead bodies.[308]

---

295 Transcript, 21 November 2005, p. 6 (closed session).
296 Transcript, 21 November 2005, p. 21 (closed session).
297 See Section 4.4.1.
298 Transcript, 12 April 2006, pp. 41-43 (open session).
299 Transcript, 12 April 2006, p. 50 (open session).
300 See Section 3.2.1.
301 Transcript, 3 April 2006, p. 54 (closed session).
302 Transcript, 3 April 2006, p. 54 (closed session).
303 Transcript, 3 April 2006, p. 55 (closed session); Transcript, 3 April 2006, p. 58 (closed session); Transcript, 4 April 2006, p. 6 (open session).
304 Transcript, 3 April 2006, p. 57 (closed session).
305 Transcript, 3 April 2006, p. 58 (closed session).
306 See Section 3.3.1.
307 Transcript, 4 October 2004, p. 11 (open session).
308 Transcript, 4 October 2004, p. 12 (open session).

155. Witness CBR[309] testified that the attacks continued in the afternoon of 15 April 1994,[310]adding that the attackers attempted to burn down the church by spraying it with petrol and using banana leaves and "sticks of dynamite".[311]

156. Witness CDK[312] stated that another attack occurred during the afternoon of 15 April 1994, while the church was still surrounded by the attackers. He testified that communal police officers and gendarmes opened fire in the direction of the church and attempted to burn it down using gasoline and dynamite.[313] Finally, the witness estimated that more than 100 persons were killed in that attack.[314]

157. Witness CBK[315] testified that on 15 April 1994 there was a "large scale" attack against refugees in Nyange church. The witness stated that the attackers had increased in number and were armed with spears, machetes, small hoes and sharpened and wooden sticks. He added that the refugees defended themselves using stones and were forced to barricade themselves inside the church to protect themselves. The witness also testified that Fulgence Kayishema, Télesphore **[page 48]** Ndungutse and Grégoire Ndahimana attempted to burn down the church by spraying petrol on it and throwing grenades against the doors.[316]

158. Witness CBT[317] testified that during the 15 April 1994 attack, Faustin sprayed petrol on the church, adding that the attackers climbed on the roof of the church from where a grenade was thrown.[318]

159. Witness CDL[319] testified that during the 15 April 1994 attack, the objective of the attackers was to enter the church. He explained, *inter alia,* that they initially attempted to break down the doors of the church using dynamite and that when they failed, they unsuccessfully tried to burn it down using gasoline.[320]

6.6.2 Findings of the Chamber

160. The Chamber finds that all the testimonies of Prosecution witnesses are consistent with respect to the fact that the attackers launched an attack against the refugees in Nyange church on 15 April 1994 and that they also attempted to burn down the church on the same day.

161. The Chamber notes that the Defence adduced no evidence to refute this allegation.

162. In view of the foregoing, the Trial Chamber finds that the Prosecutor has proved beyond a reasonable doubt that on 15 April 1994, the *Interahamwe* and militiamen, assisted by gendarmes and communal police officers, launched attacks against Tutsi refugees and attempted to burn down Nyange church.

6.7 Supervision of the attacks by Athanase Seromba

6.7.1 The evidence

Prosecution witnesses

163. Witness CDL[321] testified that Athanase Seromba was present at the 15 April 1994 attack and that he was standing in front of the parish secretariat.[322] The witness further testified added that he saw Seromba again later in the day when Seromba was standing in front of the priest's residence.[323] The witness also stated that Seromba advised the attackers to attack Tutsi who were **[page 49]** inside the church rather than those

309 See Section 6.2.1.
310 Transcript, 20 January 2005, p. 38 (open session).
311 Transcript, 20 January 2005, pp. 40-41 (open session).
312 See Section 6.2.1.
313 Transcript, 7 October 2004, pp. 62-63 (open session).
314 Transcript, 7 October 2004, p. 63 (open session).
315 See Section 3.3.1.
316 Transcript, 19 October 2004, pp. 20-21 (closed session).
317 Witness information sheet (P-13).
318 Transcript, 6 October 2004, pp. 61-62 (open session).
319 See Section 3.2.1.
320 Transcript, 19 January 2005, pp. 23-24 (open session).
321 See Section 3.2.1.
322 Transcript, 19 January 2005, pp. 18-19 (closed session).
323 Transcript, 19 January 2005, p. 19 (closed session).

who were inside the presbytery.[324] The witness furthermore stated that the *bourgmestre* and Ndungutse informed him that they had discussed with Seromba, who wanted them to bury the numerous bodies strewn all over the church courtyard. In fact, Witness CDL stated, *inter alia*, as follows: "So Father Seromba deemed it necessary to first bury the bodies and then to resume the killings afterwards."[325] The witness explained that Seromba did nothing to protect the refugees.[326]

164. Witness CBR[327] explained that during the 15 April 1994 attack, when there were no longer any refugees outside the church, the attackers wanted to attack the refugees hidden in the presbytery courtyard. He testified that Kayishema and Ndungutse led these attacks. He stated that Seromba and the gendarmes prevented the attackers from entering the presbytery courtyard. He explained that Kayishema and Ndungutse held a discussion with Seromba and subsequently told the attackers that Seromba had asked them to stop the killings and to "first" remove the bodies and debris lying on the ground. The witness alleged that Seromba made the following remarks: "Listen, look around, first of all, clear this filth." He also stated that Kayishema and Ndungutse uttered the following remarks: "Seromba did not even allow us to enter the courtyard of the presbytery before we removed the filth." The witness furthermore indicated that he was standing 10 metres away from Kayishema, Ndungutse and Seromba when they were discussing. He also stated that the numerous bodies were removed in less than an hour, using a bulldozer belonging to Astaldi company. He alleged that Seromba did nothing to protect the refugees or to oppose the attack.[328] During cross-examination, Witness CBR confirmed that he had personally heard Seromba refer to the bodies as filth.[329] The witness further testified that the attacks resumed after the bodies had been removed.[330] Finally, he testified that he never saw Seromba lead the attackers on 15 April 1994 or 16 April 1994, while indicating that "before the authorities gave us any instructions, whatsoever, they had to discuss with the pastor".[331]

165. Witness CNJ[332] stated that during the 15 April 1994 attack, the attackers pursued the refugees who were trying to hide in the presbytery and that Athanase Seromba prevented them, saying "first of all, remove the dead bodies that were in front of the secretariat". The witness stated that he personally heard Seromba utter these words,[333] and that the attacks resumed after the bodies had been removed. Witness CNJ stated as follows: "We removed the dead bodies, and afterwards we went into the back courtyard, the place where he was stopping us from entering before we removed the dead bodies."[334] **[page 50]**

166. Witness CBJ[335] explained that following the 15 April 1994 attacks, Athanase Seromba congratulated some of the assailants by throwing down bottles of beer to them from the "second floor" of the presbytery. The witness testified that he saw Seromba later in the evening at the secretariat, holding a discussion with the *Interahamwe* and the gendarmes. Seromba allegedly asked them to bring a mechanical digger to remove the bodies strewn on the ground in front of the church.[336] Witness CBJ furthermore testified that when the killings began on 15 April 1994, he saw Seromba on the "second floor" of the presbytery, in the company of Édouard Nturiye, Emmanuel Kayiranga and the *grand séminariste* Apollinaire Hakizimana watching the massacres that were taking place.[337]

167. Witness CDK[338] testified that he saw Athanase Seromba in company with Kanyarukiga and Kayishema in Nyange parish towards 2 p.m. The witness explained that the three of them were standing in front of the office of the Parish secretariat and that he was at a short distance from them at that time.[339]

---

324 Transcript, 19 January 2005, p. 65 (open session).
325 Transcript, 19 January 2005, p. 65 (open session).
326 Transcript, 19 January 2005, p. 19 (closed session).
327 See Section 6.2.1.
328 Transcript, 20 January 2005, pp. 38-39 and 52-54 (open session).
329 Transcript, 24 January 2005, p. 3 (open session).
330 Transcript, 20 January 2005, p. 40 (open session).
331 Transcript, 24 January 2005, p. 4 (open session).
332 See Section 3.3.1.
333 Transcript, 24 January 2005, p. 17 (open session).
334 Transcript, 24 January 2005, p. 18 (open session).
335 See Section 3.2.1.
336 Transcript, 12 October 2004, p. 6 (open session).
337 Transcript, 13 October 2004, p. 45 (open session).
338 See Section 6.2.1.
339 Transcript, 7 October 2004, p. 62 (open session).

Defence witnesses

168. Witness BZ1[340] testified that he never saw Athanase Seromba at the time the attacks were perpetrated in the church up until the collapse of the bell tower.[341] He claimed to have seen Seromba for the last time during a mass celebration which took place on 11 April 1994.[342]

169. Witness BZ4[343] stated that he never saw Athanase Seromba in the company of the attackers.[344] The witness also testified that he did not see Seromba on 15 and 16 April 1994.[345]

170. Witness FE31[346] testified that he did not see Athanase Seromba at the locus of the 15 April 1994 attack[347]. The witness stated that the assailants attacked Seromba and that Seromba could not have led an attack, whereas he was himself being targeted by the assailants[348]. **[page 51]**

171. Witness FE35[349] testified that he did not see the priest during the 15 April 1994 attack. He stated that he only saw employees of the *commune* and members of the general public.[350]

172. Witness PA1[351] stated that he did not come out of the presbytery following the attacks which occurred upon the arrival of the bus on 15 April 1994. The witness testified that Seromba came out outraged by the fact that "people" were being killed. He added that he did not remember the time during which Seromba remained outside the presbytery.[352] He explained that he witnessed a meeting between Seromba, Kariramba, Kayiranga, Nturiye, the *bourgmestre* and Kayishema during which the question of numerous bodies which were strewn on the ground in the parish courtyard was being addressed. The witness stated, *inter alia*, that the priest requested the *bourgmestre* "to do something" with a view to burying the bodies. The *bourgmestre* then told them that he would contact the person in charge of the site in order to obtain a bulldozer for that purpose.[353]

173. Witness YA1, a Hutu,[354] testified that he saw no clergymen on 15 April 1994.[355]

174. Witness NA1[356] explained that on 15 April 1994, at approximately 6 p.m., the priests met in the presbytery and asked Athanase Seromba to contact the *bourgmestre* of the *commune* and inform him of the progress of events. The witness stated that when Seromba returned to the presbytery, he explained that he was unable to meet the *bourgmestre*, as the latter had gone to attend a burial.[357] Witness NA1 furthermore stated that he learned later in the evening that the *bourgmestre* had come to the parish that same evening and that he had told the priest that on the following day he would take necessary measures to bury the bodies. The witness finally stated that he did not attend this meeting, and therefore, did not see the *bourgmestre* in the parish during the evening of 15 April 1994.[358]

---

340 Transcript, 10 November 2005, p. 30 (open session).
341 Transcript, 2 November 2005, p. 64 (open session).
342 Transcript, 2 November 2005, p. 64 (open session).
343 See Section 6.2.1.
344 Transcript, 1 November 2005, pp. 59 and 60 (open session).
345 Transcript, 10 November 2005, p. 8 (open session).
346 See Section 3.2.1.
347 Transcript, 29 March 2006, pp. 25, 28 and 55 (open session).
348 Transcript, 29 March 2006, pp. 28 and 31-32 (open session).
349 Transcript, 22 November 2005, p. 29 (closed session).
350 Transcript, 22 November 2005, p. 18 (closed session).
351 Transcript, 20 April 2006, p. 38 (closed session).
352 Transcript, 21 April 2006, p. 13 (closed session).
353 Transcript, 21 April 2006, p. 15 (closed session).
354 See Section 6.2.1.
355 Transcript, 14 November 2005, p. 37 (open session).
356 See Section 5.5.1.
357 Transcript, 7 December 2005, pp. 28-29 (closed session).
358 Transcript, 7 December 2005, pp. 28-29 (closed session).

6.7.2 Findings of the Chamber

175. The Chamber notes that the testimony of Witness CDL is hearsay. Consequently, his allegations that Athanase Seromba ordered assailants to attack the refugees inside the church and to remove the bodies prior to resuming the killings are not credible.

176. In view of the foregoing, the Chamber finds that the Prosecution has not proved beyond a reasonable doubt that Athanase Seromba supervised the 15 April 1994 attacks in Nyange parish. **[page 52]**

177. The Chamber notes, furthermore, that three Prosecution witness, Witnesses CDL, CBR and CNJ stated in similar testimonies that, during the 15 April 1994 attack, Athanase Seromba prevented attackers from entering the courtyard of the presbytery where refugees were hiding. Witness CDL explained, *inter alia*, that Seromba held discussions with the *bourgmestre* and Ndungutse, while Witness CBR referred rather to a meeting between Seromba, Kayishema and Ndungutse. Witness CNJ claimed that Seromba personally addressed the attackers.

178. The Chamber notes that Witness CDL's evidence on the content of the meeting is hearsay, whereas Witnesses CBR and CNJ stated that they personally heard the remarks made by Athanase Seromba. Contrary to the first two witnesses, CNJ did not state that Seromba referred to the bodies as filth. Furthermore, Witnesses CBR and CNJ alleged that the massacres resumed after the bodies had been removed.

179. The Chamber considers Witness CBR to be credible. In fact, during cross-examination, Witness CBR confirmed what he had said in the examination-in-chief.[359] Counsel for the Defence challenged Witness CBR on his assertions that he heard Kayishema and Ndungutse say that Athanase Seromba had asked for the bodies to be removed and that he had personally heard Seromba say these words.[360] Witness CBR explained that there was no discrepancy between the two assertions. He stated that he heard the priest utter those words and that the authorities conveyed to the attackers what the priest had told them.[361]

180. Witness CNJ gave a consistent account of the events which occurred on 15 April 1994, except with respect to the time of his arrival at the location[362]. The Chamber finds that no evidence casts doubt on the credibility of his factual evidence.

181. Witness CBJ also stated that Athanase Seromba requested that the bodies be removed, although he estimated this event as having occurred in the evening of 15 April 1994. No other evidence supports his own evidence that Seromba congratulated the assailants. The Chamber therefore declines to admit CBJ's evidence on this point.

182. The Chamber finds that the evidence given by CBR, CBJ, CBI and CDK is consistent with respect to the presence of Athanase Seromba on the site during the 15 April 1994 attacks.

183. The Chamber finds that BZ1's evidence on this point is not reliable. In fact, after first declaring in the examination-in-chief that he had not seen Athanase Seromba on 15 April 1994, the witness subsequently admitted during cross-examination the following: "At any rate, I am telling you that these people were speaking to him. I can't say that I certainly saw him, but when **[page 53]** they were speaking to him, I could hear what they were saying. In fact, I could say I had a glance of him…"[363]

184. The Trial Chamber finds the testimony of BZ4 unreliable, as he testified that he did not stay in Nyange parish for a long time on 15 April 1994.[364]

185. The Chamber holds that Witness FE31 is not credible on this point. In fact, after first declaring that Athanase Seromba was not present during the 15 April 1994 attack, he subsequently stated that the assailants attacked Seromba. However no other witness stated that Seromba was attacked on 15 April 1994.

---

359 Transcript, 24 January 2005, p. 2 (open session).
360 Transcript, 24 January 2005, p. 2 (open session).
361 Transcript, 24 January 2005, p. 3 (open session).
362 Transcript, 24 January 2005, pp. 55-56 (open session).
363 Transcript, 10 November 2005, p. 20 (open session).
364 Transcript, 9 November 2005, pp. 48-49 (open session).

186. Furthermore, the Chamber notes that Witness F31 stated that he arrived at the church at approximately 10.30 a.m.,[365] went to the statue of the Virgin Mary, and then returned to the church courtyard, where he remained only for 10 minutes, without going inside the presbytery.[366]The Chamber points out that the witness claimed in his previous statements that he was not present in Nyange parish on 15 April 1994. In fact, during cross-examination, the Prosecutor read out Question 6, appearing on the statement made by the witness to the Rwandan authorities on 14 January 2000 as follows: "You are accused of having participated in the bloody attack on the church. That was in broad daylight, and many people saw you. What is your response?" The Chamber notes that the witness answered as follows: "It is a pure lie. I never went there."[367] The Prosecutor also read out the answer which the witness gave to Question 7 as follows: "I never went to the church. If I had gone there, people would have seen me."[368] The Prosecutor finally read out to Witness FE31 an excerpt from his statement to the Rwandan authorities on 19 November 1999: "What are your grounds of defence in respect of the acts for which you are accused by the legal officer?; Answer: I did not commit these offences. I stayed in the house. I did not go anywhere. I did not go to the church."[369] In view of the foregoing, the Chamber finds that Witness FE31's statements are inconsistent.[370]

187. The Chamber also finds Witness FE35 unreliable, having stated that he did not see Athanase Seromba during the attacks. Incidentally, the Chamber notes that his evidence that he left the church sometime between 1 and 4 p.m. is vague.[371] **[page 54]**

188. The Chamber considers PA1's evidence inconclusive. In fact, he testified on what Athanase Seromba did or said when he left the presbytery, even though he did not follow Seromba to personally ascertain his conduct. The Chamber therefore finds PA1's evidence unreliable.

189. The Chamber also considers NA1's evidence to be inconclusive, as he did not attend the meeting during which the *bourgmestre* allegedly promised the priests, in the evening of 15 April 1994, that he would bring in some bulldozers to remove the bodies.

190. The Chamber considers that Witness YA1 is not credible. In fact, his testimony is full of contradictions: at times he claims to have been present at the 15 April 1994 events, standing near the statue of the Virgin Mary. On other occasions, he states that he did not go to the parish on 15 April 1994.[372]

191. In view of the foregoing, the Trial Chamber finds that it has been proven beyond a reasonable doubt that on 15 April 1994, Athanase Seromba asked the assailants, who were preparing to attack the Tutsi in the presbytery courtyard, to stop the killings and to first remove the bodies. The Chamber also finds that the attacks against Tutsi refugees resumed after the bodies had been removed.

6.8 That numerous Tutsi refugees, including the teacher called Gatare, and two Tutsi female refugees, Alexia and Meriam, were killed.

6.8.1 The evidence

Prosecution witnesses

192. Witness CBT[373] testified that around noon, on 15 April 1994, he saw Athanase Seromba on the staircase, in front of the secretariat, in the company of a teacher called Anicet Gatare.[374]The witness stated

365 Transcript, 29 March 2006, p. 47 (open session).
366 Transcript, 29 March 2006, pp. 52-53 (open session).
367 Statement of Witness FE31 to the Rwandan judicial authorities on 14 January 2000 (P-45), p. 1, read out to the witness: Transcript, 29 March 2006, p. 63 (open session).
368 Statement of Witness FE31 to the Rwandan judicial authorities on 14 January 2000 (P-45), p. 2, read out to the witness: Transcript, 29 March 2006, p. 66 (open session).
369 Statement of Witness FE31 to the Rwandan judicial authorities on 19 November 1999 (P-46), p. 1, read out to the witness: Transcript, 29 March 2006, p. 68 (open session).
370 Transcript, 29 March 2006, pp. 65-68 (open session).
371 Transcript, 23 November 2005, p. 28 (closed session).
372 Transcript, 14 November 2005, p. 28 (open session).
373 See Section 6.3.1.
374 Transcript, 7 October 2004, p. 31 (open session).

that Seromba accompanied Anicet Gatare up to the door of the secretariat where he handed him over to three gendarmes who were on duty. He further stated that the gendarmes took away Anicet Gatare and killed him with one bullet.[375] He explained that during this incident, Seromba was on the veranda of the parish secretariat.[376] He also testified that after handing over Anicet Gatare to the gendarmes, Seromba returned to the "inner courtyard".[377] **[page 55]**

193. Witness CBJ[378] testified that he knew Meriam during his sojourn at Nyange church from 10 to 16 April 1994. He added that Meriam was among a group of privileged Tutsi to whom Athanase Seromba had provided accommodation inside the presbytery until 14 April 1994. The witness also pointed out that following the 14 April 1994 meeting, the purpose of which, in his view, was to plan the killing of Tutsi, all the persons to whom accommodation had been provided in the presbytery were sent away by Seromba.[379] He also testified that the refugees came out after the doors of the church were opened on the morning of 15 April 1994. Among other things, he recounted how Meriam returned to the presbytery to avoid the *Interahamwe* who had started attacking the refugees. Witness CBJ furthermore explained that these attacks occurred between 1 p.m. and 3 p.m., and that Seromba, once again, sent away all the persons of Tutsi origin, including Meriam, who were in the rear courtyard of the presbytery. He further recounted how Meriam was "beaten up" in front of the secretariat and dragged on the ground up to the front of the church by Muringanyi while Fulgence Kayishema held her by the head and was banging it against the ground in the courtyard.[380] The witness stated that he personally saw the naked, mortal remains of Meriam.[381] He also stated that on the same day, at approximately 7 p.m., he heard Seromba call his night watchman, Canisius Habiyambere, and order him to search the rear courtyard of the presbytery to see whether any Tutsi were hidden there.[382] Finally, Witness CBJ testified that he saw a gendarme in front of the corridor near the ground floor shoot Anicet Gatare at point-blank range who, struck by a bullet in the chest, died thereafter.[383]

194. Witness CBK[384] testified that he saw numerous victims among whom he was able to identify Adrienne, a religious novice from Nyinawajambo *commune*, Anicet Gatare, a teacher, Boniface Gatare, a youth counsellor in Kivumu *commune* and Kanamugire, a *MINITRAP* employee.[385] The witness stated that Anicet Gatare was killed by gendarmes on 13 April 1994. He recounted how he learned from gendarmes that Anicet Gatare had offered them money so as to be killed by shooting, as he did not want to be killed with a machete.[386] Witness CBK also stated that Fulgence Kayishema killed Meriam by banging her head against bricks,[387] while Seromba, who was present on site, did nothing to prevent the killing.[388] **[page 56]**

Defence witnesses

195. Witness BZ1[389] testified that when Anicet Gatare saw the attackers arriving, he asked a gendarme to kill him in order to avoid an atrocious death. He testified that the attackers accused Athanase Seromba of complicity with the *Inkotanyi* because he did not want to hand over persons found in the parish to the attackers.[390]

---

375 Transcript, 6 October 2004, pp. 58-59 (open session).

376 Transcript, 6 October 2004, p. 59 (open session). Witness CBT identified Prosecution Exhibit P3-1 as being a photograph of the office in question.

377 Transcript, 7 October 2004, p. 41 (open session).

378 See Section 3.2.1.

379 Transcript, 12 October 2004, pp. 9-10 (open session).

380 Transcript, 12 October 2004, pp. 10-11 (open session).

381 Transcript 12 October 2004, p. 10 (open session).

382 Transcript, 12 October 2004, p. 12 (open session); Transcript, 13 October 2004, p. 46 (open session).

383 Transcript, 12 October 2004, pp. 10-11 (open session).

384 See Section 3.3.1.

385 Transcript, 19 October 2004, p. 32 (closed session).

386 Transcript, 19 October 2004, p. 33 (closed session).

387 Transcript, 19 October 2004, p. 35 (closed session).

388 Transcript, 19 October 2004, p. 35 (closed session).

389 See Section 4.4.1.

390 Transcript, 2 November 2005, p. 65 (open session).

196. Witness BZ2[391] testified that he learned that many persons, including his friend, Meriam and a teacher named Anicet Gatare had died in Nyange parish.[392]

197. Witness FE31[393] testified that he was told that Anicet Gatare asked the gendarmes to shoot him, to avoid death by machete. The witness also stated that he was unaware that he had been handed over to the gendarmes, adding that the attackers found Anicet Gatare on site and killed him by striking him with a machete.[394]

198. Witness FE55[395] testified that Meriam and Anicet Gatare were killed on Friday, 15 April 1994.[396]

6.8.2 Findings of the Chamber

199. The Chamber notes that Witnesses CBT, CBJ, CBK, BZ2 and FE55 confirmed the death of Tutsi refugees Anicet Gatare and Meriam. The Chamber further notes that Witnesses BZ1 and FE31 only referred to the death of Anicet Gatare. The Trial Chamber finally observes that no witness in the present matter made reference to the death of Alexia. Consequently, the Chamber is of the view that the murders of Meriam and Anicet Gatare have been proved beyond a reasonable doubt.

200. With respect to the murder of Anicet Gatare, the Chamber notes that the statements of Witnesses CBT and CBJ are not consistent as to the circumstances of his death. The Trial Chamber, however, accepts the evidence of Witnesses CBK, BZ1 and FE31 that Anicet Gatare was killed by a gendarme who agreed to shoot him in exchange for a sum of money, so as to avoid being killed with a machete.

201. With respect to the murder of Meriam, the Chamber accepts CBJ's testimony that Athanase Seromba turned back several refugees from the presbytery, including Meriam, and that Meriam was subsequently killed by the attackers. The Chamber finds CBJ's testimony credible. **[page 57]** The Chamber further observes that Witness CBK gave a consistent account of the circumstances surrounding the death of Meriam. The Chamber finds this witness credible.

202. In the light of the foregoing, the Trial Chamber finds that the Prosecution has not proven beyond a reasonable doubt that Athanase Seromba handed over Anicet Gatare to the gendarmes. The Trial Chamber is, however, of the view that it has been proved beyond a reasonable doubt that Seromba turned back several refugees, including Meriam, from the presbytery.

7. EVENTS OF 16 APRIL 1994 IN NYANGE PARISH

7.1 The Indictment

203. The Indictment alleges as follows:

> "23. Many refugees were killed during these attacks. A bulldozer was used by three employees of Astaldi company (Mitima, Maurice and Flanbeau) to remove the numerous corpses of the victims from the Church. Two additional drivers were requested from Fulgence KAYISHEMA to complete the removal. One of them, Evarist RWAMASIRABO, who had refused to participate, was killed immediately.
>
> [...]
>
> 26. When the corpses of victims were removed from the church, Védaste MUPENDE ordered the driver (Athanase alias 2000) to demolish the Church. The latter refused since the church was the house of God.
>
> 27. Immediately thereafter, Védaste MUPENDE, Fulgence KAYISHEMA and Grégoire NDAHIMANA requested the intervention of Athanase SEROMBA, who came and ordered Athanase alias 2000 to destroy the church, telling him that Hutu people were numerous and could build another one.
>
> 28. Athanase bulldozed the church and its roof collapsed, killing more than 2,000 Tutsi refugees gathered inside. The few survivors were attacked by the *Interahamwe*, anxious to finish them off.

391 Transcript, 2 November 2005, pp. 79 and 81 (open session).
392 Transcript, 7 November 2005, p. 7 (open session).
393 See Section 3.2.1.
394 Transcript, 12 April 2006, p. 43 (open session).
395 See Section 4.4.1.
396 Transcript, 29 March 2006, p. 26 (open session).

29. On or about 16 April 1994, after the destruction of the church, the authorities held a meeting in the Parish. Soon after, Father SEROMBA ordered the *Interahamwe* to clean the "rubbish". The bodies of victims were placed into common graves.

30. The transfer of corpses into common graves took about two days, under the supervision of Athanase SEROMBA, Fulgence KAYISHEMA, Grégoire NDAHIMANA and others unknown to the Prosecution.

[...] **[page 58]**

47. After the complete destruction of the church, Father Athanase SEROMBA met with Fulgence KAYISHEMA, Grégoire NDAHIMANA, Gaspard KANYIRUKIGA and the drivers of the caterpillar bulldozer and sat drinking beer together.

[...]

49. On or about 15 April 1994, Father Athanase SEROMBA ordered or planned, abetted and encouraged the destruction of the church with more than 2,000 Tutsi trapped inside, causing their deaths.

7.2 The presence of a bulldozer in the church courtyard

7.2.1 The evidence

Prosecution witnesses

204. Witnesses CBK,[397] CDK[398] and CBT[399] mentioned the presence of a bulldozer in Nyange parish.[400] Witnesses CBJ,[401] CBR[402] and CDL,[403] for their part, testified to the presence of two bulldozers.[404]

Defence witnesses

205. Witnesses BZ1,[405] BZ3,[406] BZ4,[407] BZ14,[408] CF14,[409] CF23,[410] FE27,[411] FE32,[412] PA1[413] and YA1[414] testified to the presence of a bulldozer at Nyange church.[415] Witnesses FE35,[416] FE34,[417] FE56[418] and NA1[419] rather testified that there were two bulldozers there.[420] **[page 59]**

397 See Section 3.3.1.
398 See Section 6.2.1.
399 See Section 6.6.1.
400 CBK: Transcript, 19 October 2004, p. 30 (closed session); CDK: Transcript, 7 October 2004, p. 63 (open session); CB: Transcript, 6 October 2004, p. 64 (open session).
401 See Section 3.2.1.
402 See Section 6.2.1.
403 See Section 3.2.1.
404 CBJ: Transcript, 12 October 2004, p. 11 (open session); CBR: Transcript, 20 January 2005, pp. 38-39 (open session); CDL: Transcript, 19 January 2005, p. 22 (closed session).
405 See Section 4.4.1.
406 See Section 4.4.1.
407 See Section 6.2.1.
408 See Section 6.2.1.
409 See Section 3.2.1.
410 See Section 4.3.1.
411 See Section 3.4.1.
412 See Section 3.4.1.
413 See Section 3.4.1.
414 See Section 6.2.1.
415 BZ1: Transcript, 2 November 2005, p. 60 (open session); BZ3: Transcript, 31 October 2005, p. 55 (open session); BZ4: Transcript, 2 November 2005, pp. 4-5 (open session); BZ14: Transcript, 1 November 2005, pp. 31-32 (open session); CF14: Transcript, 17 November 2005, pp. 16-17 (closed session); CF23: Transcript, 31 March 2006, p. 24 (open session); FE27: Transcript, 23 March 2006, p. 28 (open session); FE32: Transcript, 5 April 2006, p. 15 (open session); PA1: Transcript, 21 April 2006, p. 16 (closed session); YA1: Transcript, 14 November 2005, p. 8 (closed session).
416 See Section 6.7.1.
417 See Section 6.3.1.
418 See Section 3.2.1.
419 See Section 5.5.1.
420 FE35: Transcript, 22 November 2005, pp. 19, 20 and 24 (closed session); FE34: Transcript, 30 March 2006, p. 19 (open session); FE56: Transcript, 4 April 2006, p. 13 (open session); NA1: Transcript, 7 December 2005, p. 38 (closed session).

7.2.2 Findings of the Chamber

206. The Chamber notes that 13 witnesses testified to having seen a bulldozer at Nyange church, while 7 others mentioned the presence of two bulldozers. It is the Chamber's opinion that the discrepancy between the witness accounts is due to the difficulty they had in identifying the type of vehicles present at Nyange church. The Chamber therefore finds that the Prosecution has proved beyond a reasonable doubt that there was at least one bulldozer at Nyange church on 16 April 1994.

7.3 Murder of Driver Evarist Rwamasirabo

7.3.1 The evidence

Defence witnesses

207. Witness FE32, one of the drivers of the bulldozer that demolished Nyange church,[421]testified that on 16 April 1994, towards 9.30 a.m., Fulgence Kayishema visited him at his home.[422] He explained that Fulgence Kayishema was looking for drivers of Astaldi company and asked them why they were so reluctant to "help the others". The witness further recounted how they answered to him that they had not come to kill "people". He stated that Fulgence Kayishema harassed them and that they were forcefully led to the church by gendarmes.[423] The witness testified that Kayishema told them that they had to help the "others" to bury the bodies. The witness explained that following a quarrel, a gendarme shot Evariste Ntahomvukiye in the head, causing his death.[424] The witness explained that this murder occurred on the Gitarama main road leading up to the church, between the statue of the Virgin Mary and[425] the *Caritas* main office.[426] **[page 60]**

7.3.2 Findings of the Chamber

208. The Chamber considers that Witness FE32 is not credible on this point. In fact, the Chamber notes that he is the only witness who made mention of this murder, whereas it occurred in a public place. Furthermore, the Chamber observes that the witness showed an inclination to use the alleged death of Evariste Ntahomvukiye to support the argument that he only demolished the church under duress.

209. In view of the foregoing, the Chamber considers that the Prosecution has not established the murder of Evarist Rwamasirabo.

7.4 The order given by Athanase Seromba to demolish the church

7.4.1 The evidence

Prosecution witnesses

210. Witness CBJ[427] testified that a meeting was held at the Codekoki on 16 April 1994, attended by Athanase Seromba, Businessman Gaspard Kanyarukiga, Criminal Investigations Officer Fulgence Kayishema, a teacher, Télesphore Ndungutse, Judge Habyambere, Businessman François Gashugi and many others who worked with these persons. He explained that the attackers who stood close by the Codekoki building were waiting for the signal to launch attacks,[428]adding that he observed this meeting while he was in the church bell tower[429]. Witness CBJ stated that he saw Seromba in front of the office of the priest's secretariat at the time when the bulldozers started to move on 16 April 1994. He also testified that he saw *Interahamwe* and the bulldozer driver, Anastase, penetrate into the courtyard of the presbytery and re-

421 See Section 3.4.1.
422 Transcript, 28 March 2006, p. 28 (open session).
423 Transcript, 28 March 2006, p. 29 (open session).
424 Transcript, 28 March 2006, p. 31 (open session).
425 Transcript, 6 April 2006, p. 1 (open session).
426 Transcript, 6 April 2006, p. 2 (open session).
427 See Section 3.2.1.
428 Transcript, 12 October 2004, p. 14 (closed session).
429 Transcript, 12 October 2004, p. 31 (closed session).

emerge. He stated that he was witness to discussions between Anastase and Seromba, an account of which he gives as follows:

> "[...] he spoke to him saying, 'Really, father, do you accept that I should destroy this church?' I saw Father Athanase Seromba nod. The driver spoke to him again, to Father Seromba. And then for a third time, 'Father, do you accept that I should destroy this church', and Father Seromba answered in these words, 'Unless you, yourselves, are *Inyensi*, destroy it. All we want is to get rid of the *Inyenzi*. As for the rest of it, we the Hutus are many. If we get rid of the *Inyenzi*, we will build another church. We will build a new church'."[430] **[page 61]**

211. Witness CBJ explained that following this meeting, he saw Athanase Seromba pull out an object from his pocket and hand it to the bulldozer driver. The driver then started demolishing the church.[431]

212. Witness CBK[432] testified that he saw Athanase Seromba, Kayishema, Ndahimana, Kanyarukiga and other persons holding a meeting at the secretariat in the morning of 16 April 1994. He testified that he heard Kayishema say that the church tower had to be destroyed because there were Tutsi intellectuals hiding there. He mentioned that he was at least three metres away from the place where the meeting was being held. He explained that after this conversation, Seromba and those persons climbed to the "upper floor of the building".[433]

213. Furthermore, Witness CBK stated that the bulldozer driver was called Anastase, and that Athanase Seromba was present when he arrived with the bulldozer. On four occasions, he related the following conversation between the driver and Seromba:

> "[...] he asked Father Seromba thrice: 'Should we destroy this church?' And then Father Seromba answered, 'Destroy the church. We, the Hutu, are many in number and, furthermore, in the house of God. Demons have gotten in there ... that we, the Hutus, were many in number and that we were going to build another'".[434]
>
> "Anastase asked Seromba: 'Do you want me to destroy this church?' And he put the question to him three times. And he told him, 'Destroy it.' [...] Furthermore, he stated that: 'We, the Hutus, are many and we can build another church'."[435]
>
> "[...] the driver who came to destroy the church asked him on three occasions, three times, if he should destroy the church. Now, he said, 'Destroy it!'".[436]
>
> "It was Anastase who asked Father Seromba whether the church would be destroyed. and Seromba told him: 'you can destroy it. There are many of us. We can rebuild it. When there are demons in the church, it should be destroyed'."[437]

214. According to witness CBK, the ex-*bourgmestre* of Gisovu *commune*, the Criminal Investigations Officer of the *commune*, the deputies of the *bourgmestre* and the communal police officers of Kivumu *commune* were present during this conversation. The driver then began demolishing the church. The witness further stated that Athanase Seromba did nothing to prevent the demolition of the church. At the time when the church was being destroyed, the witness was with Seromba in front of the church secretariat. He testified that he told Seromba that he was **[page 62]** afraid, and that Seromba reassured him by saying that only the Tutsi were targets of these killings.[438]

215. Furthermore, Witness CBK testified that it was Kayishema who gave the order to bring in the bulldozer.[439] The witness alleges that Athanase Seromba was responsible for the destruction of the church, considering the comments that0 he made to the bulldozer driver.[440] He stated that he saw Seromba watching the killings that continued after the collapse of the church tower.[441]

---

430 Transcript, 12 October 2004, p. 18 (open session).
431 Transcript, 12 October 2004, p. 18 (open session).
432 See Section 3.3.1.
433 Transcript, 19 October 2004, pp. 17-18 (closed session).
434 Transcript, 19 October 2004, pp. 28-29 (closed session).
435 Transcript, 20 October 2004, p. 17 (closed session).
436 Transcript, 19 October 2004, p. 45 (closed session).
437 Transcript, 20 October 2004, p. 19 (closed session).
438 Transcript, 19 October 2004, pp. 28-29 (closed session).
439 Transcript, 20 October 2004, p. 18 (closed session).
440 Transcript, 19 October 2004, p. 45 (closed session).
441 Transcript, 19 October 2004, p. 29 (closed session).

216. Witness CNJ[442] testified that Athanase Seromba collaborated with the attackers, although he did not give the order to destroy the church.[443] He also referred to the comments that the authorities made in relation to Seromba and the destruction of the church: "Seromba was coming, that was to decide as to whether the church was going to be totally destroyed or whether he had another solution, to enable people to get into the church".[444] He explained that after this conversation, Kayishema went to the rear of the church, close to the presbytery, and returned five minutes later accompanied by Seromba. According to the witness, Seromba approached the bulldozer and greeted the authorities who were standing close to it. The witness explained that Kayishema gave the bulldozer driver the order in the presence of Seromba, to start destroying the church. The witness specified that he was approximately two metres away from the scene. Seromba then said to the driver: "Watch out, make sure the wall doesn't fall on you." He stated that he was standing approximately four metres away from Seromba when Seromba said those words. He testified that these events occurred between 9 a.m. and 10 a.m.[445] The witness finally stated that on 16 April 1994, Seromba moved forward with the authorities to follow the movements of the bulldozers as they were destroying the church.[446]

217. Witness CDL[447] testified that he was witness to a discussion between the *bourgmestre* and Athanase Seromba in the morning of 16 April 1994, towards 7.30 a.m. He explained that after the discussion, the *bourgmestre* held conversations with other *commune* authorities, including Ndungutse, Habiyambere, Kayishema and police officers and reservists. He further explained that various authorities took the decision to use bulldozers to destroy the church, and that, subsequently, these authorities went to see Seromba who was standing in front of the secretariat and told him that they no longer had any means, other than the bulldozers, to destroy the church, so as to reach the refugees. Seromba then said to them: "If you have no other means, bring the bulldozers then, and destroy the church." The witness stated that he was not far from **[page 63]** the place where Seromba said those words.[448] He explained that the decision to destroy the church had been taken by these authorities and that Seromba accepted the decision.[449]

218. Witness CDL further testified that Athanase Seromba advised bulldozer drivers to start demolishing the church from the side of the sacristy.[450] The witness also reported the following: "As I have already said, he was showing the fragile or weak part that one needed to start in order to kill the Tutsis, and he was talking – they were talking with the father. Nothing was done without his consent. At least, he did not show any desire to come to the assistance of the refugees in question".[451]

219. Witness CBR[452] testified that on 16 April 1994 he saw Ndahimana, Kayishema, Kanyarukiga, Ndungutse, Habiyambere and Murangwabugabo, enter the courtyard of the presbytery and emerge from there several moments later in the company of Athanase Seromba.[453] The witness stated that Athanase Seromba was not the one leading the attackers on 16 April 1994, adding that: "[b]efore the authorities gave us any instructions, whatsoever, they had to discuss with the pastor. I couldn't tell you what they were saying because they were on one side. So our authorities, the leaders, before they gave us any instructions, they had to speak with the father, be it on the 15th or the 16th. Before we did anything whatsoever, the authorities had to speak with the father."[454]

---

442 See Section 3.3.1.
443 Transcript, 24 January 2005, pp. 21-23 and 49-51 (open session).
444 Transcript, 24 January 2005, p. 44 (open session).
445 Transcript, 24 January 2005, pp. 21-23 (open session).
446 Transcript, 24 January 2005, pp. 21-23 and 49-51 (open session).
447 See Section 3.2.1.
448 Transcript, 19 January 2005, pp. 25-27 (open session).
449 Transcript, 19 January 2005, p. 28 (open session).
450 Transcript, 19 January 2005, p. 28 (open session).
451 Transcript, 19 January 2005, p. 29 (open session).
452 See Section 6.2.1.
453 Transcript, 20 January 2005, p. 42 (open session).
454 Transcript, 24 January 2005, p. 4 (open session).

Defence witnesses

220. Witness FE32, the bulldozer driver who demolished the Nyange church,[455] testified that Védaste Murangwabugabo and Anastase Rushema led the operations on 16 April 1994. He stated that it was Kayishema, and not Athanase Seromba, who forced him to demolish the church. He explained that he reiterated to Rushema on three occasions that it was forbidden to destroy a church. The witness explained that went ahead to demolish the church after having been threatened with death. He testified that when he had started destroying the church, Seromba actually ran up to complain to Rushema, saying: "I forbad you yesterday to kill people here and you have just demolished the church." The witness stated that he did not see Seromba again during the destruction of the church. According to him, Seromba was powerless in the face of such a situation.[456] The witness also mentioned that he was not informed of any meeting during which the decision to bring the bulldozers was taken, adding, finally, that he was a "mere driver", and could not be aware of the holding of any such meeting.[457] **[page 64]**

221. Witness BZ1, a Hutu,[458] stated that he never saw Athanase Seromba from the moment when the attacks were perpetrated at the church up until the collapse of the bell tower.[459] He stated that he saw Seromba for the last time when Seromba said mass on 11 April 1994, and that he no longer saw him thereafter.[460]

222. Furthermore, Witness BZ1 stated that he arrived at the scene when the bulldozer was destroying the bell tower. According to him, the bulldozer had been brought to bury the bodies that were lying there. Subsequently, the objective of bringing the bulldozers was changed; it was, now, to demolish the church.[461] The witness claimed that it was the communal authorities, namely Kayishema, Ndungutse and Ndahimana who sent for a bulldozer on day the church was destroyed.[462] The witness testified to having heard the following: "the people said, '[t]here were people inside the church. We can get to them [*sic*]. So a decision was made to demolish the church. The order was given to the bulldozer driver to demolish the church'."[463]

223. Furthermore Witness BZ1 denies having joined the group of attackers during the attacks against the Tutsi and the destruction of the church. He testified that he went to the location to attend the tragic events which were occurring there.[464] He stated that he did not see Athanase Seromba on 15 and 16 April 1994.[465]

224. Witness BZ4[466] stated that he arrived at Nyange parish on the morning of 16 April 1994, more specifically at the Nyange commercial centre.[467] He testified that he heard that people held a discussion and thought that the bulldozer could be used for the destruction of the church. The witness further testified that Fulgence Kayishema was cited as the person who had asked the driver, Nteziryayo, to use the bulldozer to destroy the church where the refugees were hiding.[468]

225. Witness BZ4 stated that he saw neither Athanase Seromba nor any other cleric at the scene when the church was being destroyed, and that he never heard that it was Seromba who had ordered the destruction of the church.[469] He added that he left the location after the destruction of the church.[470] He also mentioned that he did not see Seromba on 15 and 16 April 1994.[471] **[page 65]**

455 See Section 3.4.1.
456 Transcript, 28 March 2006, pp. 34-35 (open session).
457 Transcript, 28 March 2006, p. 49 (open session).
458 Transcript, 10 November 2005, p. 30 (open session).
459 Transcript, 2 November 2005, p. 64 (open session).
460 Transcript, 2 November 2005, p. 64 (open session).
461 Transcript, 10 November 2005, p. 30 (open session).
462 Transcript, 10 November 2005, p. 29 (open session).
463 Transcript, 10 November 2005, p. 30 (open session).
464 Transcript, 10 November 2005, p. 30 (open session).
465 Transcript, 10 November 2005, p. 30 (open session).
466 See Section 6.2.1.
467 Transcript, 2 November 2005, pp. 4-5 (open session).
468 Transcript, 2 November 2005, p. 6 (open session).
469 Transcript, 2 November 2005, p. 6 (open session).
470 Transcript, 2 November 2005, p. 6 (open session).
471 Transcript, 10 November 2005, p. 8 (open session).

226. The witness further stated that he arrived at the scene during the morning, but could not give the exact time of his arrival, or that of the bulldozer at the church. The witness, however, added that he was present at the location when the bulldozer arrived.[472] He testified that he travelled to Nyange on the day the church was demolished in order to see how the situation was unfolding, adding that he did not participate in the attacks.[473]

227. Witness CF23[474] stated that the bulldozer was driven by Anastase Nkinamubanzi and other *Zaïrois* drivers.[475] He stated that Anastase Rushema and Ndungutse were co-ordinating the demolition activities.[476] The witness testified that by the time he arrived at the church its destruction was already underway, adding that he remained there for only a few minutes, before deciding to return home.[477]

228. Witness FE35, a Hutu,[478] testified that he had never heard that Athanase Seromba had met with communal authorities to plan the demolition of the church.[479] The witness further testified that the bulldozer drivers had been requisitioned by Anastase Kayishema, Télesphore Ndungutse and the police officers and that they were working under orders from them.[480] The witness pointed out that the "leaders" of the attackers did not act in concert with Athanase Seromba.[481] In the opinion of Witness FE35, Seromba did not order the destruction of the church and never supported the attackers who destroyed the church. The witness emphasized that Seromba did not play any role in the massacres perpetrated in Nyange[482] and that he never saw him at the church when it was being destroyed.[483]

229. Furthermore, Witness FE35 explained that Kayishema, Anastase Rushema and Ndahimana escorted the bulldozers and were at he scene supervising the destruction of the church.[484]

230. Witness PA1[485] explained that at the time destruction of the church had commenced, the priests, including Athanase Seromba were in the presbytery. He testified that the heard "a very loud noise" and subsequently realized that the church was being destroyed. He further explained **[page 66]** that Seromba immediately came out of the presbytery, furious.[486] Witness PA1 finally stated that he did not see Seromba issue any order to destroy the church.[487]

231. Witness NA1[488] testified that on 16 April 1994, towards 8 a.m., he went to the refectory and noticed that there were attackers who had surrounded the church and a tractor that was removing the bodies. The witness also stated that later on, he heard a noise and saw dust rising. At that moment, curious to know what was going on, the priests went up to the upper floor. The witness added that the priests observed the destruction of the church without making any comments.[489]

232. Furthermore, Witness NA1 testified that the clergymen subsequently approached the gendarmes to ask them to salvage the situation. The gendarmes responded that they were not in sufficient numbers to confront the attackers and that they had no orders to shoot at people.[490]

472 Transcript, 10 November 2005, p. 3 (open session).
473 Transcript, 10 November 2005, pp. 3-4 (open session).
474 See Section 4.3.1.
475 Transcript, 31 March 2006, p. 24 (open session).
476 Transcript, 31 March 2006, p. 25 (open session).
477 Transcript, 31 March 2006, p. 24 (open session); Transcript, 3 April 2006, p. 24 (closed session).
478 Transcript, 22 November 2005, p. 29 (closed session).
479 Transcript, 22 November 2005, p. 20 (closed session).
480 Transcript, 22 November 2005, p. 20 (closed session).
481 Transcript, 22 November 2005, p. 21 (closed session).
482 Transcript, 22 November 2005, p. 23 (closed session).
483 Transcript, 22 November 2005, p. 23 (closed session).
484 Transcript, 23 November 2005, p. 32 (closed session).
485 See Section 3.4.1.
486 Transcript, 20 April 2006, pp. 25-26 and 28 (closed session).
487 Transcript, 20 April 2006, p. 29 (closed session).
488 See Section 5.5.1.
489 Transcript, 7 December 2005, pp. 26, 28 and 31 (closed session).
490 Transcript, 7 December 2005, pp. 31-32 (closed session).

7.4.2 Findings of the Chamber

233. The Trial Chamber considers Witness CBJ credible[491] on the point under discussion. In fact, there is no contradiction between his testimony and his prior statement. Furthermore, in his statement made before the Rwandan judicial authorities on 24 June 1997, the witness accused Anastase Rushema, but made no allusion either to Athanase Seromba or to the destruction of the church in an in-depth manner, merely stating that Seromba collaborated with Rushema in the attacks of 15 and 16 April 1994.[492] In another statement made before the Rwandan judicial authorities on 25 March 1997, Witness CBJ, in response to the question as to who perpetrated the killings and destroyed the church, stated that "Abbot Seromba ... also played a role".[493]

234. The Chamber considers that Witness CBJ is also credible as to two alleged events namely that Seromba and other persons held a meeting on 16 April 1994 and that Seromba handed an object to the bulldozer driver. The Chamber, however, considers his testimony on the remarks Seromba made to the bulldozer driver not to be reliable, because of his location at the time the remarks were made. In fact, the Chamber finds that from the church tower, it was physically impossible to hear the conversation between Seromba and the bulldozer driver at the parish secretariat, given the distance separating the two locations.[494] **[page 67]**

235. The Chamber finds Witness CBK credible, notwithstanding a discrepancy between his 15 August 2000 statement and his in-court testimony on the identity of the bulldozer driver. In fact, Witness CBK testified that the bulldozer was driven by Anastase.[495] However, when challenged by Counsel for the Defence on his 15 August 2000 statement wherein he alleged that Flambeau, a Zaïrois, was the "bulldozer driver",[496] the witness responded that he actually meant to say that "Flambeau oversaw the road construction", and that "it was Anastase who drove the bulldozer".[497] In the Chamber's view, the discrepancy concerning the identity of the victims does not discredit the evidence of the witness, particularly in the light of the testimonies of Witnesses FE32 and CF23 who referred to the presence of several Zaïrois drivers[498] and, more specifically, the testimony of Witness FE32 that he was replaced by another driver during the destruction of the church.[499] Finally, with respect to the allegations by the witness concerning Athanase Seromba, the witness consistently referred to Anastase as being the bulldozer driver.

236. The Chamber also considers Witness CBK to be credible as regards a meeting allegedly held on the morning of 16 April 1994 and attended by Athanase Seromba and other persons. During that meeting, Kayishema allegedly said that it was necessary to destroy the church tower in order to kill Tutsi intellectuals hiding inside. The Chamber also finds the witness credible with respect to the conversation between the bulldozer driver and Seromba in the course of which the driver asked Seromba three times whether he should destroy the church. Seromba allegedly responded in the affirmative. The testimony of the witness is plausible, given that he was very close to the persons in question when these events occurred.

237. The Trial Chamber considers that Witness CNJ is not credible. In fact, during cross-examination, Counsel for the Defence pointed out that in four different prior statements Witness CNJ declared that he arrived after the demolition of the church had begun. The witness provided no convincing explanation for

---

491 For a discussion on the general credibility of Witness CBJ, see Section 5.3.2.

492 Statement of Witness CBJ to Rwandan authorities on 24 June 1997 (D-25), pp. 1-2.

493 Statement of Witness CBJ to Rwandan authorities on 25 March 1997 (D-26), p. 2.

494 Investigator Rémy Sahiri stated that the distance separating the presbytery from the principal entrance to the Nyange church was 48 metres (Transcript, 27 September 2004, p. 12, open session). Although Witness Rémy Sahiri did not specify the distance between the secretariat and the church, the Trial Chamber is of the view, on the basis of Prosecution Exhibit P-02, representing a layout of the premises, that the distance separating the secretariat from the church is approximately the same as that extending from the presbytery to the entrance to the parish.

495 Transcript, 20 October 2004, p. 18 (closed session).

496 Statement of Witness CBK to Tribunal investigators on 15 August 2000 (statement not filed as exhibit), p. 5, read to the witness: Transcript, 20 October 2004, p. 18 (closed session).

497 Transcript, 20 October 2004, p. 19 (closed session).

498 FE32: Transcript, 28 March 2006, pp. 30-31 (open session); CF23: Transcript, 31 March 2006, p. 24 (open session).

499 Transcript, 28 March 2006, p. 38 (open session).

these contradictions, merely claiming that the statements were occasionally false, occasionally incomplete or drafted under duress or with a view to financial compensation.[500] **[page 68]**

238. The Chamber considers Witness CDL to be credible. In fact, it notes that there are no inconsistencies in his testimony. Furthermore, the Chamber has no doubt about the witness's presence at the discussions that he referred to in his testimony. The Chamber further notes that Counsel for the Defence raised only one omission – a trivial discrepancy between CDL's testimony and the letter he wrote to the Rwandan authorities on 16 April 1999.[501] Thus, Counsel for the Defence pointed out to the witness that in that letter, the witness made no mention of the fact that the *bourgmestre* had met with Athanase Seromba before giving the signal of the attacks. The witness responded that he did not provide all particulars in his prior statements, as he did not deem it necessary at the time.[502] In this same statement (letter), the witness however stated the following: "At about ten o'clock, the *bourgmestre*, the IPJ and the gendarmes agreed with Seromba to demolish the church".[503]

239. The Chamber considers that Witness CDL is also credible as to two other alleged events: first, the meeting held by Athanase Seromba, Kayishema, Ndahimana, Kanyarukiga, Habarugira and other persons, during which Seromba approved the decision to destroy the church, saying: "If you have no other means of doing it, bring these bulldozers and destroy the church", and secondly, the advice that Seromba gave to the drivers concerning the fragile side of the church.

240. The Chamber finds that Witness CBR is credible. Defence Counsel raised two points during cross-examination which are insufficient to impugn the credibility of the witness because of the explanations that he subsequently provided. More particularly, Defence Counsel challenged Witness CBR on the statement he made on 29 August 2000 in which he declared as follows: "After noticing that the attacks launched by the *bourgmestre* were not sufficiently efficient, the group with the *bourgmestre* went towards the presbytery to meet with Father Seromba: Ndahimana, Muraginabugabo, Kayishema, Ndungutse, Habarigira, Kanyarukiga, Habyambere."[504] Defence Counsel then put to the witness that he had previously stated that he saw Seromba only once on 16 April 1994. The witness explained that on 16 April 1994, the persons whose names he mentioned went to the presbytery and upon their return from there, they started shooting at the church.[505]

241. Counsel for the Defence then read out another part of Witness CBR's statement of 29 August 2000 wherein he stated as follows: "After the entire church had collapsed the authorities held a meeting with Father Seromba, after which I heard him ordering the removal of the rubbish in front of his house -- by "rubbish", he meant the bodies of the refugees."[506] **[page 69]** Defence Counsel then asked Witness CBR whether this statement did not mean that he saw Seromba after the church had been destroyed. The witness answered in the negative.[507] He stated that he saw Seromba on the morning of 16 April 1994 and did not see him thereafter. The witness recalled having returned home after the collapse of the church. He averred that Seromba uttered these remarks on "getting rid of the rubbish" on 15 April 1994 and that the meeting was held on 15 April 1994 and not 16 April 1994. Witness CBR claimed that there was a confusion of dates in the transcription of his statement made in Kinyarwanda.[508]

500 Information supplement to the file concerning confession and guilty plea of 28 December 1998 (D-39), read back to the witness: Transcript, 24 January 2005, p. 58 (open session); Confession of guilt of the witness on 21 August 2000 (D-40B), read back to the witness: Transcript, 24 January 2005, pp. 2 and 62 (open session); 27 May 2001 witness statement (D-41), read back to the witness: Transcript, 25 January 2005, p. 15 (open session).

501 Letter of Witness CDL to Rwandan authorities dated 16 April 1999 (statement not filed as exhibit), p. 3; read back to the witness: Transcript, 20 January 2005, p. 4 (open session).

502 Transcript, 20 January 2005, p. 5 (open session).

503 Letter of Witness CDL to Rwandan authorities dated 16 April 1999 (statement not filed as exhibit), p. 3; read back to the witness: Transcript, 20 January 2005, p. 4 (open session)

504 Statement of Witness CBR to Tribunal investigators on 29 August 2000, (statement not filed as exhibit), p. 4; read back to the witness: Transcript, 20 January 2005, p. 59 (open session).

505 Transcript, 20 January 2005, p. 61 (open session).

506 Statement of Witness CBR to Tribunal investigators on 29 August 2000, (statement not filed as exhibit), p. 4; read back to the witness: Transcript, 20 January 2005, p. 61 (open session).

507 Transcript, 20 January 2005, p. 61 (open session).

508 Transcript, 20 January 2005, pp. 62-63 (open session).

242. In view of the foregoing, the Chamber considers that Witness CBR is also credible with respect to another event: the discussions and meetings between Athanase Seromba and the authorities on 16 April 1994.

243. The Chamber finds that Defence Witness FE32 is not credible as to the events of 16 April 1994, due to the numerous contradictions in his testimony and prior statements on the one hand, as well as between his testimony and his prior statements on the other hand. Here, the Chamber will mention only the most serious contradictions.

244. In the African Rights Information Bulletin No. 2, Witness FE32 stated:

> "Father Seromba who was in favour of that solution said the following: 'They should be destroyed so that we can get rid of the enemy. When the enemy was no longer there we can build another'.
> Anastase refused to bulldoze the church but he said Seromba made him afraid. Father Seromba said the following: 'There are many Christians abroad. That church -- this church will be rebuilt in three days'."[509]

245. Witness FE32 asserted that these statements were untrue, insisting that the Rwandan authorities refuse to admit that he was forced to bulldoze the church.[510]

246. In a statement to Rwandan authorities on 27 August 1996, Witness FE32 stated as follows:

> "They ordered me to destroy this church, and let me add that the priest of this parish, by the name Seromba, was there, and he said nothing with regard to the demolition of the church. I carried out the orders in order to save my life. Apart from those soldiers, IPJ Kayishema, as well as the priest of the said parish, Seromba – no one else was on the **[page 70]** spot. I performed that duty over a three day period and he was watching over me so as to prevent me from escaping – they were watching so as to prevent me from escaping".[511]

247. Witness FE32 specified that he made this statement under duress to "save my skin".[512]

248. In a statement to Rwandan authorities on 19 April 1995, Witness FE32 identified "Seromba the parish priest of Nyange parish" as one of his collaborators. He stated that Athanase Seromba was present when Kayishema, the *bourgmestre*, and the presiding judge of the canton tribunal ordered him to bring in the bulldozer.[513] The witness did not contest the validity of this document and the information contained therein, except the entries related to Seromba. He explained that he made this statement under duress.[514]

249. In a statement to Rwandan authorities on 22 July 1997, Witness FE32 stated as follows: "When I asked Kayishema what was going to happen now that people had been killed in that church, that he went to rear courtyard of the presbyterian with Father Seromba: The priest asked me to destroy the church and added that they were going to build another one. I put the following question to him, 'Are we going to destroy the house of God?' And he replied, 'Destroy it. We will build another one'."[515] Witness FE32 explained that he made this statement "in order to please some people who wanted me to implicate Father Seromba".[516]

250. In a statement made to Tribunal investigators on 27 July 2000, Witness FE32 stated that he initially refused to demolish the church, that the authorities then went to the presbytery and returned accompanied by Athanase Seromba, who directly addressed him in the following terms: "'It has been decided that indeed has to be destroyed. We shall build another one."[517]Commenting on this excerpt, Witness FE32 explained that the Tribunal investigators had their own objectives in relying solely on statements made to the Rwandan

---

509 *Information bulletin No. 2 of African Rights* (P-5), p. 15; read back to the witness: Transcript, 5 April 2006, p. 20 (open session).

510 Transcript, 5 April 2006, p. 21 (open session).

511 Statement of Witness FE32 to the Rwandan judicial authorities on 27 August 1996 (D-77), p. 2, read back to the witness: Transcript, 5 April 2006, p. 37 (open session).

512 Transcript, 5 April 2006, p. 38 (open session).

513 Statement of Witness FE32 to the Rwandan judicial authorities on 19 April 1995 (P-54), p. 1; read back to the witness: Transcript, 6 April 2006, p. 14 (open session).

514 Transcript, 6 April 2006, p. 14 (open session).

515 Statement of Witness FE32 to the Rwandan judicial authorities on 22 July 1997 (D-82), p. 5; read back to the witness: Transcript, 6 April 2006, p. 15 (open session).

516 Transcript, 6 April 2006, p. 16 (open session).

517 Statement of Witness FE32 to Tribunal investigators on 27 July 2000 (P-55), p. 5, read back to the witness: Transcript, 6 April 2006, p. 29 (open session).

authorities which, he claimed, were obtained under duress.[518] Another excerpt from this statement was read to the witness, wherein the witness stated that after having demolished the right wall near the bell tower, Seromba approached him and said: "Destroy all those walls. Nothing must be left standing."[519] **[page 71]**

251. Witness FE32 admitted to having signed the statement, but stated that Tribunal investigators did not first read it back to him and made that the interpreters were not trustworthy.[520] The statement the witness made to Tribunal investigators on 4 April 2002, which included his 27 July 2000 statement, was shown to him. The 4 April 2002 statement indicated that the 27 July 2000 statement of the witness was read back to him and that he made no changes to it.[521] The witness explained that Tribunal investigators had forced him to sign the statement and refused to allow him to make the slightest change.[522] A confirmation of his 4 April 2002 statement dated 11 February 2003,[523] which indicated that the investigators had read back to him his 4 April 2002 statement, to which he made a change which was recorded in the final version, was shown to him. This is acknowledged by the witness.[524] The Chamber notes that this negates the witness' allegations that Tribunal investigators refused to make any amendments to his statements.

252. In his letter to the Supreme Court of Rwanda, written on 7 November 2001,[525] Witness FE32 stated as follows:

> "The truth admitted before the court in which I still stand by up to today, is that I demolished the church with a bulldozer in execution of the order issued by the *commune* and church leaders at the time."[526]
>
> "On the 15th April 1994, they had me and my friend Everiste Ntahokiriye – Kigali, Byumba brought in order to destroy the church but we refused. Immediately they killed him, my friend, on the spot. Having witnessed that, I felt weak and carried out their orders. They just had Father Seromba brought in, and later informed us that that was the decision that had been taken."[527]
>
> "The Court did not pay any attention to the statements made by the Prosecution witness who testified that he saw IPJ, Kayishema, when he brought me and forced me to demolish the church. I refused to comply until the arrival of Father Seromba. After that the church was destroyed."[528] **[page 72]**

253. The witness refused to comment on this letter, merely insisting that his request had been rejected by the Supreme Court of Rwanda.[529] He then stated that he wrote this letter with the assistance of another person, but that an error had slipped into it.[530]

254. Witness FE32 was unable to provide explanations as to the numerous contradictions between his testimony before the Chamber and the remarks he made before African Rights, on the one hand, and Rwandan authorities and Tribunal investigators on the other, over a period of 10 years. Nor could he provide any explanation for the contradictions which are still to be found in his letter to the Supreme Court of Rwanda.

255. With respect to Defence claims that the witness acted under duress, the Chamber recalls that it is up to the Defence to adduce evidence of duress.[531] In the present case, the Chamber considers that the Defence

518 Transcript, 6 April 2006, pp. 29-30 (open session).

519 Statement of Witness FE32 to Tribunal investigators on 27 July 2000 (P-55), p. 5, read back to the witness: Transcript, 6 April 2006, pp. 30-31 (open session).

520 Transcript, 6 April 2006, pp. 21-24 (open session).

521 Statement of Witness FE32 to Tribunal investigators on 4 April 2002 (D-80), p.3, read back to the witness: Transcript, 6 April 2006, p. 21 (open session).

522 6 April 2006 Transcripts, p. 24 (open session).

523 Confirmation of Witness FE32 of his 4 April 2002 statement on 11 February 2003 (P-56); read back to the witness: Transcript, 6 April 2006, p. 25 (open session).

524 Transcript, 6 April 2006, p. 26 (open session).

525 A signed version of this letter was filed with the Trial Chamber as Exhibit C-1.

526 Letter from Witness FE32 to the Supreme Court of Rwanda dated 7 November 2001 (P-57), p. 2, read back to the witness: Transcript, 6 April 2006, p. 35 (open session).

527 Letter from Witness FE32 to the Supreme Court of Rwanda dated 7 November 2001 (P-57), p. 2, read back to the witness: Transcript, 6 April 2006, p. 38 (open session).

528 Letter from Witness FE32 to the Supreme Court of Rwanda dated 7 November 2001 (P-57), pp. 3-4, read back to the witness: Transcript, 6 April 2006, p. 40 (open session).

529 Transcript, 6 April 2006, pp. 35-36 (open session).

530 Transcript, 6 April 2006, p. 38 (open session).

531 *Bagosora,* Decision on Motion Concerning Alleged Witness Intimidation (TC), 28 December 2004, paras. 8-10.

has not adduced any evidence to show that the prior statements of Witness FE32 were obtained under duress. The Chamber notes that the witness was inconsistent in his explanations on the occasions when he did not refuse to provide one. Furthermore, the Chamber notes that the witness had never previously stated that he had been tortured or that he gave any statements under duress, either before Tribunal investigators or those of the Defence. Finally, the Chamber notes that in the course of his testimony, in response to a question from the Prosecution concerning the letter he sent to the Supreme Court of Rwanda, the witness stated: "Why does the Prosecutor continue to rely on this document? In my opinion – in my opinion this document has no value. You are coercing me – you are bringing pressure to bear on me. Just like when you appear before Rwandan courts, I believe there is also the form of coercion."[532] In view of the numerous contradictions in this witness' statements, the Trial Chamber holds that the excerpt is insufficient to establish that he may have suffered any form of duress.

256. The Chamber also notes that Witness FE32 appears to be a witness seeking to exculpate Athanase Seromba. Thus, to justify his decision to testify as a Defence witness and not as a Prosecution witness, as previously envisaged, Witness FE32 stated: "[...] Life is short on earth. And I didn't want to be on bad terms with my God."[533]

257. In view of the foregoing, the Chamber finds that the testimony of Witness FE32 concerning the events which occurred on 16 April 1994 is not credible.

258. The Chamber finds that Witness BZ1's evidence is not conclusive. He expressed himself in general terms, and his claim that he did not see Athanase Seromba on 15 and 16 April 1994 is insufficient to establish that Seromba was not present at the scenes of the events. Indeed, it is even possible that the witness did not see Seromba in the huge crowd at the church. Incidentally, the witness only arrived on site after the demolition of the church had begun. Finally, Witness **[page 73]** BZ1's testimony about the persons who brought the bulldozer constitutes hearsay and, as such, is of little probative value.

259. The Chamber finds that the testimony of Witness BZ4 is not conclusive. In fact, the witness expressed himself in general terms, and his testimony lacks precision with respect to the sequence of the events. For instance, he was unable to give the exact time of his arrival or the arrival of the bulldozer at the church on 16 April 1994.[534] The assertion that he did not see Athanase Seromba on 15 or 16 April 1994 is insufficient to establish that Seromba was not present at the scene of the events. Indeed, it is even well possible that the witness did not spot Seromba in the huge crowd which had gathered at the church.[535] Finally, Witness BZ4's assertions about the persons who brought the bulldozer constitute hearsay and, as such, have little probative value.

260. The Chamber considers that Witness CF23 is not credible. The Chamber notes that when this witness arrived in the vicinity of the church, the destruction of the church was already underway. Consequently, the Chamber attaches no weight to his testimony concerning the events which occurred on 16 April 1994 at Nyange church.

261. The Chamber finds that the testimony of Witness FE35 is not credible. The Chamber notes that the witness expressed himself in general terms, and that there were many inconsistencies between his testimony and prior statements.[536]

262. The Trial Chamber finds that Witness PA1 is not credible. The Chamber notes that his testimony and prior statements as to the events of 16 April 1994 contain many contradictions. For example, in his statement to the Defence on 27 January 2005,[537] the witness did not mention the fact that Athanase Seromba was furious when he left the presbytery, whereas he made this assertion in his testimony.[538] The Prosecution read out to the witness an excerpt from his 27 January 2005 statement where the witness stated that the priests did

---

532 Transcript, 6 April 2006, p. 39 (open session).
533 Transcript, 5 April 2006, p. 58 (open session).
534 Transcript, 10 November 2005, p. 3 (open session).
535 Transcript, 2 November 2005, p. 6 (open session).
536 Transcript, 23 November 2005, pp. 12, 15-24 and 32-34 (closed session).
537 Statement of Witness PA1 to Defence Counsel on 27 January 2005 (P-62).
538 Transcript, 21 April 2006, p. 16 (closed session).

not dare to approach the attackers.[539] The Prosecutor pointed out that this contradicted the testimony of the witness, who nevertheless asserted that Seromba went outside. To justify this omission, the witness merely stated that it was nothing more than an involuntary memory lapse,[540] adding that in the phrase "we did not dare approach", there is no reference to any particular moment, but was merely trying to describe the situation that prevailed. The witness, once again, referred to the powerlessness of the priests in the face of such a situation. He reiterated that Seromba emerged from the presbytery expressing his anger and incomprehension.[541] **[page 74]**

263. Witness PA1 was also examined as to the content of his 8 October 2003 statement. Counsel for the Prosecution read out the following excerpt to the witness: "Question: 'What did the attackers do?' Answer: 'They entered the house of the priest and they asked Seromba why he kept me by his side. For they considered me to be a Tutsi because of my appearance but Seromba replied to them that I was a Hutu.'"[542] The witness confirmed that the content of the excerpt corresponded to what he had said before the Chamber.[543] Counsel for the Prosecution read out a second excerpt to the witness: "Each time the authorities came to the presbytery to find out the attitude to adopt in the face of these problems."[544] The witness stated that that statement was false.[545] Counsel read out a third excerpt to the witness: "Question: 'Are you in a position to confirm that those people never came to the presbytery without your knowledge?' Answer: 'It is possible that they came without my knowledge since I was hiding and I was not always outside the room to see what was happening.'"...[546] The witness stated that this was a summary of what he said and that his intention was to explain to the investigators that "It is as if we were linked by some umbrical cord. I wasn't really with him all times".[547] Counsel for the Prosecution read out a fourth excerpt to the witness: "Question: 'Was the *bourgmestre* physically present during the trench digging?' Answer: 'I do not know, since I did not see the machine. As far as I am concerned, I remained shut up in my room.'"[548] The witness declared the statement to be false.[549] The Trial Chamber considers all of the witness' explanations to be implausible.

264. Finally, the Chamber notes that Witness PA1 admitted that he did not go out with Athanase Seromba and was not in direct contact with him at that time. Therefore, he could not have heard the remarks that Seromba made outside the presbytery at the time the church was being destroyed.[550]

265. The Chamber finds that Witness NA1 is not credible. His account of the events of 16 April 1994 contains many contradictions. For instance, in his 9 December 1996 statement, the witness stated: "It is Seromba who played a role in the killings. However, I do not accuse him of any particular offence, but I saw him moving about with the authorities."[551] Commenting on this portion of his statement, Witness NA1 merely stated that his answers were being oriented towards a particular goal and that, in any event, the Rwandan authorities wrote down whatever **[page 75]** they wanted. He added that at the time he made this statement, he wanted to save his skin and that it was important not to forget the context in Rwanda in 1996.[552]

266. The Chamber notes contradictions in Witness NA1's testimony as to the order to bring in the bulldozer. In the course of his in-court testimony, the witness testified that Athanase Seromba never asked "people" to collect the bodies. The witness claimed to have learned that the bulldozer was there, and that the *bourgmestre*

539 Statement of Witness PA1 to Defence Counsel on 27 January 2005 (P-62), p. 4: read back to the witness: Transcript, 21 April 2006, p. 17 (closed session).

540 Transcript, 21 April 2006, p. 17 (closed session).

541 Transcript, 21 April 2006, pp. 17-19 (closed session).

542 Statement of Witness PA1 to the Rogatory Commission on 8 October 2003 (D-90), p. 3.

543 Transcript, 21 April 2006, p. 26 (closed session).

544 Statement of Witness PA1 to the Rogatory Commission on 8 October 2003 (D-90), p. 5.

545 Transcript, 21 April 2006, p. 27 (closed session).

546 Statement of Witness PA1 to the Rogatory Commission on 8 October 2003 (D-90), p. 5.

547 Transcript, 21 April 2006, p. 27 (closed session).

548 Statement of Witness PA1 to the Rogatory Commission on 8 October 2003 (D-90), p. 5.

549 Transcript, 21 April 2006, p. 30 (closed session).

550 Transcript, 21 April 2006, p. 19 (closed session).

551 Statement of Witness NA1 to the Rwandan judicial authorities on 9 December 1996 (P-37), p.1, read back to the witness: Transcript, 7 December 2005, p. 83 (closed session).

552 Transcript, 7 December 2005, pp. 83-85 (closed session).

had said that he was going to send in a bulldozer to remove the bodies.[553] The Prosecutor challenged the witness on his 9 December 1996 statement in which he mentioned that the following day, Seromba asked people to collect the bodies, but that they refused, and that it was at that time that *bourgmestre* Ndahimana and Seromba ordered that a bulldozer be brought in to remove the bodies.[554] The witness responded that this statement should be understood in the context within which his trial was conducted. He furthermore stated that the document was poorly punctuated and that this shows that the person who examined him did so with a specific aim in mind.[555] The witness stated: "[...] Father Seromba asked the people to collect the bodies, but they refused. *Bourgmestre* Grégoire decided to bring in the bulldozer to evacuate the bodies. When I speak of Grégoire, they always insert Seromba because they wanted me to accuse Seromba".[556] The witness explained that he had actually stated that they asked Seromba to go and see the *bourgmestre*, but that he was not personally present when the decision to remove the bodies was being taken.[557]

267. In view of the foregoing, the Chamber finds that the Prosecution has not proved beyond a reasonable doubt that Athanase Seromba personally gave the order to destroy the church.

268. The Chamber, however, finds that the Prosecution has proved beyond a reasonable doubt that Athanase Seromba was informed by the authorities of their decision to destroy the church and that he accepted the decision.

269. The Chamber also finds that the Prosecution has established beyond a reasonable doubt that Athanase Seromba said such words to bulldozer driver FE32 as would encourage him to destroy the church. The Chamber notes that when bulldozer driver FE32 received the order from the authorities to destroy the church, he asked Seromba whether he should destroy the church. Seromba answered in the affirmative, assuring to the witness that Hutu would be able to build it again. Furthermore, the Trial Chamber finds that Seromba gave advice to the bulldozer drivers concerning the fragile side of the church. **[page 76]**

7.5 Destruction of Nyange church using the bulldozer thus causing the death of at least 1,500 persons

7.5.1 The evidence

Prosecution witnesses

270. Witness CBR[558] testified that the destruction of Nyange church began at about 10 a.m. on 16 April 1994. He explained that the walls were demolished first, and that the tower eventually collapsed at about 5 p.m.[559]

271. Witness CBJ[560] testified that he was in the church tower on 16 April 1994. The witness also claimed that demolition of the church began at about 3 p.m. and lasted three hours.[561] He estimated the number of persons who perished in the demolition at more than 1,500.[562]

272. Witness CBK[563] testified that he was in front of the secretariat when the church was being destroyed. He claimed that its destruction began at about 10 a.m. and that the tower was the last part of the building to collapse.[564]

---

553 Transcript, 8 December 2005, p. 14 (closed session).

554 Statement of Witness NA1 to the Rwandan authorities on 11 November 1996 (P-38), pp. 3-4, read back to the witness: Transcript, 8 December 2005, p. 16 (closed session).

555 Transcript, 8 December 2005, p. 17 (closed session).

556 Transcript, 8 December 2005, p. 17 (closed session).

557 Transcript, 8 December 2005, pp. 17-18 (closed session).

558 See Section 6.2.1.

559 Transcript, 20 January 2005, p. 42 (open session).

560 See Section 3.2.1.

561 Transcript, 14 October 2004, pp. 26-27 (closed session).

562 Transcript, 12 October 2004, p. 19 (open session).

563 See Section 3.3.1.

564 Transcript, 19 October 2004, pp. 28-29 (closed session).

273. Witness CDL[565] testified that he was on the site when the church was being destroyed. He claimed that he saw two bulldozers destroy the church and the tower at about 10 a.m. He also alleged that on 15 April 1994, there were between 1,500 and 2,000 refugees gathered in the parish[566] and estimated that approximately 1,500 persons were killed in the destruction of Nyange church.[567]

274. Witness CBI[568] estimated that approximately 2,000 refugees were at the church when he arrived there, adding that this number rose to 5,000 persons.[569]

275. Witness CBS[570] testified that when he arrived at Nyange church on 12 April 1994, there were approximately 2,000 persons on the site.[571] **[page 77]**

276. Witness CNJ[572] estimated the number of persons killed at approximately 2,000.[573] He explained that between 15[574] and 16[575]April 1994 nearly 2,000 Tutsi were killed.[576]

277. Witness CBN[577] estimated the number of Tutsi refugees gathered at the church on 15 April 1994 to be 2,000.[578]

Defence witnesses

278. Witness FE32[579] testified that the destruction of the church began at about 10.30 a.m. on 16 April 1994 and ended at about 3 p.m. or 4 p.m.[580] He explained that there were no refugee survivors of the destruction of the church,[581] and that there were "fewer than" 2,000 persons inside the church at the time of its destruction.[582]

279. Witness BZ1[583] testified to having seen the bulldozer demolish the church and the bell tower. The witness added that the destruction of the church lasted between three and five hours and that the bell tower collapsed at about 3 p.m.[584] He also claimed that following the collapse of the bell tower, he left the site, adding that he did not see "any other refugees on the site".[585]

280. Witness BZ8[586] testified that in April 1994, he was living in Kivumu *commune*.[587] The witness claimed that he watched the destruction of the church from a distance. He explained that the machine arrived and began to destroy the rear walls of the church.[588] He further explained that the entire church building did not collapse immediately and that the bell tower was only destroyed the following day.[589] Finally, he stated that he was not sure about the dates.[590]

565 See Section 3.2.1.
566 Transcript, 19 January 2005, p. 11 (open session).
567 Transcript, 19 January 2005, p. 28 (open session).
568 See Section 3.3.1.
569 Transcript, 4 October 2004, p. 8 (open session).
570 See Section 3.3.1.
571 Transcript, 5 October 2004, p. 9 (open session).
572 See Section 3.3.1.
573 Transcript, 24 January 2005, p. 16 (open session).
574 Transcript, 24 January 2005, p. 16 (open session).
575 Transcript, 24 January 2005, p. 25 (open session).
576 Transcript, 24 January 2005, p. 25 (open session).
577 See Section 3.3.1.
578 Transcript, 15 October 2004, p. 46 (open session).
579 See Section 3.4.1.
580 Transcript, 28 March 2006, pp. 37-38 (open session).
581 Transcript, 28 March 2006, p. 40 (open session).
582 Transcript, 28 March 2006, pp. 40-41 (open session).
583 Transcript, 10 November 2005, p. 30 (open session).
584 Transcript, 2 November 2005, pp. 62-64 (open session).
585 Transcript, 2 November 2005, p. 67 (open session).
586 Transcript, 15 November 2005, p. 43 (open session).
587 Transcript, 15 November 2005, p. 28 (open session).
588 Transcript, 15 November 2005, p. 37 (open session).
589 Transcript, 15 November 2005, p. 39 (open session).
590 Transcript, 16 November 2005, p. 2 (open session)

281. Witness FE35[591] testified that part of the wall of the church building was destroyed first, followed by the other part. He added that the bell tower collapsed at about noon.[592] **[page 78]**

7.5.2 Findings of the Chamber

282. The Chamber notes that Witness Rémy Sahiri, an investigator with the Office of the Prosecutor,[593] prepared a report titled *Rapport préliminaire d'identification des sites du génocide et des massacres d'avril-juillet 1994 au Rwanda* [Preliminary report identifying the sites of Genocide and Massacres in April-July 1994 in Rwanda]. In the report, he stated that Nyange church was destroyed.[594] He also submitted to the Chamber an album of photographs showing the location of Nyange parish and the ruins of the former church.[595]

283. The Chamber finds both Prosecution and Defence witnesses to be credible. In fact, all of them gave consistent evidence with respect to the fact that Nyange church was destroyed on 16 April 1994, using a bulldozer.

284. In view of the foregoing, the Chamber finds that the Prosecution has proved beyond a reasonable doubt that Nyange church was destroyed on 16 April 1994, using a bulldozer.

285. The Chamber further notes that the body of evidence points to the fact that the destruction of the church resulted in the death of many Tutsi refugees who had sought refuge there, with some witnesses estimating the number of victims to be 1,500, while others put it at 2,000. In this regard, the Chamber recalls its findings that Nyange church had a holding capacity of at least 1,500 persons.[596] This leads to the conclusion that on 16 April 1994, the destruction of Nyange church resulted in the death of at least 1,500 refugees who had sought refuge there to flee from the attacks of the assailants.

7.6 The order given by Athanase Seromba to bury the bodies

7.6.1 The evidence

Defence witnesses

286. Witness FE35[597] testified that after the demolition of the church, Athanase Seromba did not hold any meeting in the parish with the communal authorities. He averred that after the destruction of Nyange church, trucks from ASTALDI company buried the bodies of the victims in a mass grave which had been dug in the banana plantation owned by the priests.[598] The **[page 79]** witness stated that it was not Seromba who gave the order to bury the bodies. He explained that Kayishema, in the company of Ndahimana, gave the order to the *Interahamwe*.[599]

287. Witness FE32[600] testified that he buried in a mass grave the bodies of persons killed when the church was destroyed.[601]

288. Witness FE34[602] testified that the graves were dug using a bulldozer which had been brought there for the purpose of burying the bodies of persons killed as a result of the destruction of Nyange church.[603] He

591 See Section 6.7.1.
592 Transcript, 22 November 2005, pp. 20-21 (closed session).
593 Transcript, 27 September 2004, p. 5 (open session).
594 Preliminary report identifying the sites of genocide and massacres in April-July 1994 in Rwanda (P-4), p. 166.
595 Exhibit P2-7.
596 See Section 2.
597 See Section 6.7.1.
598 Transcript, 22 November 2005, p. 24 (closed session).
599 Transcript, 22 November 2005, p. 24 (closed session).
600 See Section 2.
601 Transcript, 6 April 2006, pp. 10-12 (open session).
602 See Section 6.3.1.
603 Transcript, 30 March 2006, p. 17 (open session).

asserted that it was the *bourgmestre* who gave the order to bury the bodies, although he admitted that he did not hear him give the order.[604]

289. Witness FE13[605] testified that a bulldozer that was on the site on 16 April 1994 was used to dig a grave in which the bodies of victims of the destruction of the church were buried.[606]

7.6.2 Findings of the Chamber

290. The Chamber notes that the Prosecution has not produced any evidence in support of the above allegation. The Chamber further notes that no Defence witness gave evidence to the effect that Athanase Seromba gave the order to bury the bodies after the destruction of the church.[607] In fact, the witnesses aver that this order came from the authorities. In the light of the foregoing, the Chamber considers that the Prosecution has not proved this fact beyond a reasonable doubt.

7.7 The meeting between Athanase Seromba and the authorities after the demolition of the church

7.7.1 The evidence

Prosecution witness

291. Witness CBK[608] stated that after the 16 April 1994 massacres, Athanase Seromba, Fulgence Kayishema, Colonel Nzapfakumunsi, Gaspard Kanyarukiga, Grégoire Ndahimana, **[page 80]** Anastase Rushema and Télésphore Ndungutse met upstairs in the presbytery building to drink banana beer and wine.[609] The witness added that Seromba was standing on the "upper floor" of the presbytery building and was distributing beer to the attackers who were in the rear courtyard of the presbytery. He testified that there was a party atmosphere on this occasion and that all the persons there were satisfied with the massacre that had just been perpetrated.[610]

Defence witnesses

292. Witness FE32[611] testified that he neither saw Athanase Seromba drink nor rejoice at the destruction of the church, adding that he did not receive any beer from Seromba.[612]

293. Witness PA1[613] testified that it was impossible that Athanase Seromba rewarded those who demolished the church by giving them beer.[614] The witness stated that he did not see anyone come to thank Seromba for the destruction of the church, and considered it as inconceivable: "And the state in which he was, his frame of mind, I don't think anybody could dare approach him [...]."[615] He finally stated that the person who demolished the church did not receive any remuneration.[616]

604 Transcript, 30 March 2006, p. 50 (open session)

605 See Section 3.2.1.

606 Transcript, 7 April 2006, p. 29 (open session).

607 CBR is the only Prosecution witness who claims to have heard Athanase Seromba order that the "rubbish" be removed from the church courtyard during a meeting held on 16 April 1994. However, during cross-examination, he stated that this meeting was held in the parish on 15 April and not on 16 April 1994 (Transcript, 20 January 2005, pp. 62-63 (open session)).

608 See Section 3.3.1.

609 Transcript, 19 October 2004, pp. 41-42 (closed session).

610 Transcript, 19 October 2004, pp. 31-32 (closed session).

611 See Section 3.1.1.

612 Transcript, 28 March 2006, p. 48 (open session).

613 See Section 3.4.1.

614 Transcript, 20 April 2006, pp. 28-29 (closed session).

615 Transcript, 20 April 2006, p. 29 (closed session).

616 Transcript, 20 April 2006, p 30 (closed session).

7.7.2 Findings of the Chamber

294. The Chamber is of the view that the testimony of CBK is not reliable on this point. In fact, he is the only witness who claims that Athanase Seromba rejoiced at the destruction of the church. The Chamber considers that there subsists a reasonable doubt as to the veracity of the account given by Witness CBK.

295. The Chamber finds that Witnesses FE32 and PA1 are not credible. In fact, their testimonies are nothing but a reflection of their personal opinions.

296. In view of the foregoing, the Chamber finds that the Prosecution has not proved beyond a reasonable doubt that Athanase Seromba celebrated the destruction of the church in the company of other persons. **[page 81]**

CHAPTER III: LEGAL FINDINGS OF THE TRIAL CHAMBER

297. In setting out its legal findings, the Chamber will rely on the factual findings set forth in Chapter II above.

298. The Indictment contains four counts: genocide, complicity in genocide, conspiracy to commit genocide and crimes against humanity (extermination).

299. The first two counts of the Indictment, that is genocide and complicity in genocide, are alternative counts, whereas Counts 1, 3 and 4 are cumulative. Consequently, the Chamber will consider whether the Prosecution has adduced evidence of the Accused's liability under each of the counts.

1. Mode of participation in the crimes

1.1 The Indictment

300. The Indictment charges the Accused with criminal liability under Article 6(1) of the Statute which provides as follows: "A person who planned, instigated, ordered, committed or otherwise aided and abetted in the planning, preparation or execution of a crime referred to in Articles 2 to 4 of the present Statute, shall be individually responsible for the crime."

1.2 Applicable law

301. The different modes of participation set forth in Article 6(1) include a number of acts for which the Accused incurs individual criminal responsibility under the counts charged against him. The different modes of participation in an offence referred to in Article 6(1) of the Statute are briefly set out below:

302. Participation by "committing" means the direct physical or personal participation of the accused in the perpetration of a crime or the culpable omission of an act that was mandated by a rule of criminal law.[617]

303. Participation by "planning" presupposes that one or several persons contemplate designing the commission of a crime at both the preparatory and execution phases.[618] With respect to this mode of participation, the Prosecution must demonstrate that the level of participation of the accused was substantial[619] and that the planning was a material element in the commission of the crime.[620] **[page 82]**

304. Participation by "instigating" implies urging or encouraging another person to commit a crime.[621] Proof of this mode of participation requires the Prosecution to establish that the instigation was a factor

617 *Krstić*, Judgement (TC), 2 August 2001, para. 601; *Kayishema*, Judgement (AC), 1 June 2001, para. 187.

618 *Akayesu*, Judgement (TC), 2 September 1998, para. 480.

619 *Bagilishema*, Judgement (TC), 7 June 2001, para. 30: "The level of participation must be substantial, such as formulating a criminal plan or endorsing a plan proposed by another."

620 *Krstić*, Case No. IT-98-33, Judgement (TC), 2 August 2001, para. 601.

621 *Bagilishema*, Judgement (TC), 7 June 2001, para. 30; *Krstić*, Case No. IT-98-33, Judgement (TC), 2 August 2001, para. 601.

element substantially contributing to the conduct of another person committing the crime. It is, however, not mandatory to prove that the crime would not have been committed without the intervention of the accused.[622]

305. Participation by "ordering" presupposes that a person in a position of authority orders another person to commit an offence. This mode of participation implies the existence of a superior-subordinate relationship between the person who gives the order and the one who executes it.[623] A formal superior-subordinate relationship is, however, not required.[624] A superior-subordinate relationship is established by showing a formal or informal hierarchical relationship involving an accused's effective control over the direct perpetrators.[625]

306. The requisite *mens rea* for the four modes of responsibility referred to above is the direct intent of the perpetrator in relation to his own planning, instigating, or ordering.[626]

307. Participation by "aiding and abetting" refers to any act of assistance or support in the commission of the crime.[627] Such mode of participation may take the form of tangible assistance, or verbal statements. It may also consist in the mere presence of the accused at the scene of the crime, conceptualized in the theory of the "approving spectator".[628] Aiding and abetting must have a substantial effect on the commission of the crime, but does not necessarily constitute an indispensable element, i.e. a *conditio sine qua non,* of the crime.[629] Except in the case of the "approving spectator", assistance may be provided prior to or during the commission of the crime, and it is not necessary for the person providing assistance to be present during the commission of the crime.[630] **[page 83]**

308. In the case of the "approving spectator", the mere presence of the accused at the scene of the crime is insufficient in itself to establish that he has aided and abetted the commission of the crime, unless it is shown to have a significant legitimizing or encouraging effect on the actions of the principal offender.[631] The criminal responsibility of the "approving spectator" is incurred only where he is actually present at the scene of the crime or, at the very least, in the immediate vicinity of the scene of the crime, such that his presence is interpreted by the principal perpetrator of the crime as an approval of his conduct.[632] The authority of the accused constitutes an important factor in assessing of the impact of the accused's presence.[633]

309. The *mens rea* of aiding and abetting requires that the accused be aware that his conduct would contribute substantially to the commission of the *actus reus* of the offence or that the perpetration of the crime would be the possible and foreseeable result of his conduct.[634] The accused must be aware of the essential elements of the crime, including the *mens rea* of the principal offender. It is not necessary, however, that the accused share the *mens rea* of the principal offender.[635]

---

622 *Bagilishema*, Judgement (TC), 7 June 2001, para. 30: "By urging or encouraging another person to commit a crime, the instigator may contribute substantially to the commission of the crime. Proof is required of a causal connection between the instigation and the *actus reus* of the crime." *Akayesu*, Judgement (TC), 2 September 1998, paras. 478-482.

623 *Bagilishema*, Judgement (TC), 7 June 2001, para. 30; *Akayesu*, Judgement (TC), 2 September 1998, para. 483; *Rutaganda*, Judgement (TC), 6 December 1999, para. 39.

624 *Kordić* Judgement (AC), 17 December 2004, para. 28.

625 *Semanza* Judgement, para. 415.

626 *Kordić* Judgement (AC), 17 December 2004, paras. 26-29.

627 *Bagilishema* Judgement (TC), 7 June 2001, para. 33; *Akayesu* Judgement (TC), 2 September 1998, para. 484; *Kayishema* Judgement (AC), 1 June 2001, para. 186; *Kayishema* Judgement (TC), 21 May 1999, paras. 200-202.

628 *Kayishema* Judgement (AC), 1 June 2001, paras. 201-202, *Kayishema*, Judgement (TC), 21 May 1999, para. 198;

629 *Bagilishema*, Judgement (TC), 7 June 2001, para. 33; *Furundñija*, Case No. IT-95-17/1-T, Judgement (TC), 10 December 1998, paras. 209-226.

630 *Bagilishema*, Judgement (TC), 7 June 2001, para. 33; *Rutaganda*, Judgement (TC), 6 December 1999, para. 43; *Kayishema*, Judgement (TC), 21 May 1999, para. 200; *Akayesu*, Judgement (TC), 2 September 1998, para. 484.

631 *Krnojelac*, Judgement (TC), 15 March 2002, para. 89; *Bagilishema*, Judgement (TC), 7 June 2001, para. 36.

632 *Aleksovski*, Case No. IT-95-14/1, Judgement (TC), 25 June 1999, paras. 64 and 65.

633 *Aleksovski*, Case No. IT-95-14/1, Judgement (TC), 25 June 1999, para. 65. See also the following cases: *Aleksovski*, Case No. IT-95-14/1, Judgement (TC), 25 June 1999, paras. 64-65; *Tadić*, Case No. IT-94-1, Judgement (TC), 7 May 1997, para. 690; *Akayesu*, Judgement (TC), 2 September 1998, para. 693 and *Furundñija*, Case No. IT-95-17/1-T, Judgement (TC), 10 December 1998, para. 274.

634 *Bagilishema*, Judgement (TC), 7 June 2001, para. 32; *Furundñija*, Case No. IT-95-17/1-T, Judgement (TC), 10 December 1998, para. 246.

635 *Krnojelac*, Judgement (TC), 15 March 2002, para. 90; *Krnojelac*, Judgement (AC.), 17 September 2003, para. 52; *Ntakirutimana*, Case No. ICTR-96-10, Judgement (AC.), 13 December 2004, paras. 500-502; *Krstić*, Case No. IT-98-33, Judgement

310. The requisite *mens rea* in the more specific case of the "approving spectator" is for the accused to know that his presence would be seen by the perpetrator of the crime as encouragement or support.[636] The *mens rea* of the approving spectator may be deduced from the circumstances, and may include prior concomitant behaviour, for instance allowing crimes to go unpunished or providing verbal encouragement to commit such crimes.[637]

1.3 Findings of the Chamber as to the mode of participation of the Accused in the offences charged against him

The mode of participation of the Accused in the offences charged against him

311. On the basis of its factual findings, the Trial Chamber considers that Accused Athanase Seromba can incur criminal responsibility only for his participation by aiding and abetting in the offences for which he may be convicted. **[page 84]**

312. The Chamber finds that the Prosecution has not proved beyond reasonable doubt that Seromba planned or committed the massacres of Tutsi refugees.[638] With respect to participation by instigating or by ordering, the Prosecution has not proved that Athanase Seromba had the specific genocidal intent or *dolus specialisis* to incur liability under these two modes of participation. More specifically, in relation to ordering, the Chamber finds that the Prosecution has not established that Accused Athanase Seromba exercised effective control over the principal perpetrators of the crimes.

Exclusion of the theory of the approving spectator in the present case

313. The Chamber notes in the instant case that, in its Final Trial Brief, the Defence advanced arguments on the theory of the *approving spectator*.[639] The Chamber, however, notes that neither the Indictment nor the Prosecutor's Pre-Trial Brief refers to the theory of the *approving spectator*. It therefore deduces that the Prosecutor had no intention of arguing this form of participation in relation to the charges against Accused Athanase Seromba. Consequently, the Chamber will not consider the theory of the *approving spectator* in its findings.

2. Count 1 – Genocide

2.1 The Indictment

314. In the Indictment, the Prosecutor of the International Criminal Tribunal for Rwanda charges Athanase Seromba with genocide, pursuant to Article 2(3)(a) of the Statute, in that on or between 6 April 1994 and 20 April 1994, in Kivumu *commune*, Kibuye *préfecture*, Rwanda, Athanase Seromba was responsible for killing or causing serious bodily or mental harm to members of the Tutsi population, committed with intent to destroy, in whole or in part, a racial or ethnic group.

2.2 Applicable law

315. Article 2(2) of the Statute[640] provides that:

> Genocide means any of the following acts committed with intent to destroy, in whole or in part, a national, ethnical, racial or religious group, as such:
>
> (a) killing members of the group;
> (b) causing bodily or mental harm to members of the group; **[page 85]**

(AC.), 19 April 2004, paras. 134-140.

636 *Bagilishema*, Judgement (TC), 7 June 2001, para. 36.

637 *Bagilishema*, Judgement (TC), 7 June 2001, para. 36.

638 See Chapter II, Sections 3.4, 4.2, 4.3, 5.6, 6.3, 6.4, 6.5, 6.7 and 7.4. See also Chapter III, Section 4.2.

639 Defence Final Brief, pp. 25-28.

640 The definition of genocide, as given in Article 2 of the Statute of the Tribunal, is culled from Articles 2 and 3 of the Convention for the Prevention and Punishment of the Crime of Genocide. Rwanda signed this Convention but declared it was not bound by Article 9 of the Convention (on this point see the Legislative Decree of 12 February 1975, *Journal Officiel de la République Rwandaise*, 1975, p. 230).

(c) deliberately inflicting on the group conditions of life calculated to bring about its physical destruction in whole or in part;
(d) imposing measures intended to prevent births within the group;
(e) forcibly transferring children of the group to another group.

316. The constituent elements of the crime of genocide are: first, that one of the acts listed under Article 2(2) of the Statute was committed; secondly, that this act was committed against a specifically targeted national, ethnic, racial or religious group, as such, and thirdly, that the act was committed with intent to destroy, in whole or in part, the targeted group.

317. In the Indictment, the Prosecutor charges the Accused, *inter alia*, with acts of killing and causing serious bodily or mental harm to members of the group. In its analysis in relation to each of these acts, the Chamber will rely on the definition to be found in the relevant jurisprudence. Thus, in *Musema*, the Trial Chamber defined "killing" as "homicide committed with intent to cause death".[641] With respect to "causing serious bodily or mental harm", the Trial Chamber, in *Kayishema*, held that the phrase could be construed to include "harm that seriously injures the health, causes disfigurement or causes any serious injury to the external, internal organs or senses".[642] "Serious mental harm" entails more than minor or temporary impairment to mental faculties.[643] It includes, but is not limited to, acts of bodily or mental torture, inhumane or degrading treatment, rape, sexual violence, and persecution.[644] It need not, however, entail permanent or irremediable harm.[645]

318. As for the notion of "members of the group" which represents belonging to a group, case-law considers this from a subjective standpoint, holding that the victim is perceived by the perpetrator of the crime as belonging to the group targeted for destruction.[646] The determination of the targeted group is to be made on a case-by-case basis.[647]

319. Genocide is distinct from other crimes because it requires a special intent: an accused may not be convicted for the crime of genocide unless it is established that he committed one of the acts listed in Article 2(2) of the Statute with specific intent to destroy, in whole or in part, a particular protected group. The notion "destruction of the group" means "the material destruction of a group either by physical or by biological means, not the destruction of the national, linguistic, religious, cultural or other identity of a particular group".[648] There is no numeric **[page 86]** threshold of victims necessary to establish genocide.[649] To establish specific genocidal intent, it is not necessary to prove that the perpetrator intended to achieve the complete annihilation of a group throughout the world,[650] but, at least, to destroy a substantial part thereof.[651]

320. In the light of the Tribunal's jurisprudence, the specific intent of genocide may be inferred from certain facts or indicia, including but not limited to (a) the general context of the perpetration of other culpable acts systematically directed against that same group, whether these acts were committed by the same offender or by others, (b) the scale of atrocities committed, (c) their general nature, (d) their execution in a region or a country, (e) the fact that the victims were deliberately and systematically chosen on account of their membership of a particular group, (f) the exclusion, in this regard, of members of other groups, (g) the political doctrine which gave rise to the acts referred to, (h) the repetition of destructive and discriminatory

---

641 *Musema*, Judgement (TC), 27 January 2000, para. 155.
642 *Kayishema*, Judgement (TC), 21 May 1999, para. 109.
643 *Kayishema*, Judgement (TC), 21 May 1999, para. 110.
644 *Musema*, Judgement (TC), 27 January 2000, para. 156.
645 *Musema*, Judgement (TC), 27 January 2000, para. 156.
646 *Rutaganda*, Judgement (TC), 6 December 1999, para. 56; *Musema*, Judgement (TC), 27 January 2000, para. 155; *Semanza*, Judgement (TC), 15 May 2003, para. 317.
647 *Semanza*, Judgement (TC), 15 May 2003, para. 317.
648 Report of the International Law Commission on the Work of its Forty-Eighth Session, 6 May-26 July 1996, Official documents of the UN General Assembly, suppl. No 10, p. 90, (A/51/10) (1996). See *Semanza*, Judgement (TC.), 15 May 2003, para. 315.
649 *Semanza*, Judgement (TC), 15 May 2003, para. 316.
650 *Kayishema*, Judgement (TC), 21 May 1999, para. 95.
651 *Semanza*, Judgement (TC), 15 May 2003, para. 316.

acts and (i) the perpetration of acts which violate the very foundation of the group or considered as such by their perpetrators.[652]

2.3 Findings of the Chamber

321. Paragraphs 1 to 32 of the Indictment concisely set out the allegations relating to the charge of genocide. The Chamber has already discussed these allegations in Chapter II, Sections 3, 4, 5, 6 and 7 under its factual findings.

322. In the light of its factual findings, the Chamber considers that the Prosecution has not proved beyond a reasonable doubt that Athanase Seromba planned, instigated, ordered or committed massacres against Tutsi refugees in Nyange.[653] The Chamber, however, finds that Athanase Seromba, by his words and actions on 12, 14, 15 and 16 April 1994, aided and abetted in the commission of murders and causing serious bodily or mental harm to the Tutsi who had sought refuge in Nyange church during the events covered in the Indictment.

2.3.1 Causing serious bodily or mental harm to members of the Tutsi ethnic group.

The actus reus *in relation to causing serious bodily or mental harm to the refugees in Nyange church*

323. With respect to paragraph 12 of the Indictment, the Chamber finds that Athanase Seromba prohibited the refugees from getting food from the banana plantation belonging to the **[page 87]** parish and that he ordered gendarmes to shoot at any refugees found there.[654] The Chamber further finds that Seromba refused to celebrate mass for the Tutsi in Nyange church.[655]

324. With respect to paragraphs 13 and 14 of the Indictment, the Chamber finds that on 13 April 1994, at a time when the security situation in Kivumu *commune* had become precarious, Athanase Seromba turned four Tutsi employees out of the parish, including a certain Patrice, who returned the next day and was killed by attackers after, once again, being turned back from the presbytery.[656]

325. With respect to paragraph 22 of the Indictment, the Chamber finds that Seromba turned out several refugees from the presbytery, including Meriam, who was subsequently killed by the attackers.[657]

326. It is the Chamber's opinion that Seromba's order prohibiting refugees from getting food from the banana plantation, his refusal to celebrate mass in Nyange church, and his decision to expel employees and Tutsi refugees from the parish and the presbytery facilitated the perpetration of acts causing serious mental harm to the Tutsi refugees in Nyange church. Indeed, the Chamber considers that when the Tutsi sought refuge in Nyange church, they were very vulnerable, having previously been the target of numerous attacks.[658] Furthermore, Nyange church, where the refugees had sought refuge and thought they could be protected from the attacks, had been surrounded by militiamen and *Interahamwe* since 12 April 1994.[659] It would therefore appear that the refugees in Nyange church lived in a constant state of anxiety, inasmuch as they knew that their lives, and those of relatives were under constant threat. The Chamber is convinced that by adopting such a line of conduct, Seromba contributed substantially to the commission of acts causing serious mental harm to Tutsi refugees in Nyange church.

327. The Chamber also finds that the order by Athanase Seromba prohibiting refugees from getting food from the banana plantation facilitated the perpetration of acts causing serious bodily harm to the refugees. Indeed, on 14 April 1994, the refugees lacked food and had very limited access to basic foodstuffs from the

652 *Akayesu*, Judgement (TC), 2 September 1998, paras. 523-524; *Kayishema*, Judgement (TC), 21 May 1999, paras. 93-94; *Musema*, Judgement (TC), 27 January 2000, para. 166; *Rutaganda*, Judgement (TC), 6 December 1999, paras. 60-62; *Bagilishema*, Judgement (TC), 7 June 2001, paras. 62-63.

653 See Chapter II, Sections 3.4, 4.2, 4.3, 5.6, 6.3, 6.4, 6.5, 6.7 and 7.4; see also Chapter III, Section 4.2.

654 See Chapter II, Section 5.3.

655 See Chapter II, Section 5.5.

656 See Chapter II, Section 5.5.

657 See Chapter II, Section 6.8.

658 See Chapter II, Section 3.2.

659 See Chapter II, Section 5.2.

outside, due to the encirclement of the church. Under such circumstances, Seromba's refusal to allow the refugees to get food from the banana plantation substantially contributed to their physical weakening, as they were deprived of food. The Chamber is satisfied that by his conduct, Seromba substantially contributed towards the commission of acts causing serious bodily harm to the Tutsi refugees in Nyange church. **[page 88]**

328. In the light of the foregoing, the Chamber finds that the *actus reus* of the assistance provided by the Accused in the commission of acts causing serious bodily or mental harm to refugees in Nyange church has been proved beyond a reasonable doubt.

The mens rea *of Accused Athanase Seromba in relation to causing serious bodily or mental harm to refugees in Nyange church*

329. The Chamber is convinced that Athanase Seromba could not have been unaware that his prohibition of refugees from getting food from the banana plantation, his refusal to celebrate mass for them and the expulsion of employees and Tutsi refugees would certainly have a negative impact on the morale of the refugees who were faced with an extremely difficult situation related to the persecutions which they had been suffering during the events of April 1994.

330. The Chamber is also satisfied that Athanase Seromba knew that the refugees lacked food.[660] The Chamber therefore considers that he was fully aware that his refusal to allow the refugees to get food from the banana plantation would substantially contribute towards weakening them physically.

331. In view of the foregoing, the Chamber is satisfied that the Prosecution has proved beyond a reasonable doubt the *mens rea* of the Accused's assistance in the commission of acts causing serious bodily or mental harm to the refugees in Nyange church.

2.3.2 Killing members of the Tutsi group

The actus reus *in relation to the killing of Tutsi refugees in Nyange church*

332. With respect to paragraphs 13, 14 and 22 of the Indictment, discussed earlier, the Chamber found that Athanase Seromba turned employees and Tutsi refugees out of Nyange parish.[661] It is the Chamber's opinion that, by so acting, Seromba assisted in the killing of several Tutsi refugees, including Patrice and Meriam.

333. With respect to paragraphs 24 and 25 of the Indictment, the Chamber finds that on 15 April 1994, Athanase Seromba requested assailants, who were getting ready to attack the Tutsi refugees gathered in the presbytery courtyard, to stop the killings and collect the bodies that were strewn throughout the church yard. The Chamber also finds that the attacks against Tutsi refugees resumed after the bodies had been removed.[662] However, the Chamber finds that it has not been proved beyond reasonable doubt that this request constitutes aiding or abetting in the killing of Tutsi refugees. **[page 89]**

334. With respect to paragraphs 26 and 27 of the Indictment, the Chamber finds that Athanase Seromba held discussions with the communal authorities and accepted their decision to destroy the church. The Chamber also concludes that Seromba spoke with the bulldozer driver and said certain words to him which encouraged him to destroy the church. Lastly, the Chamber finds that Seromba even gave advice to the bulldozer driver as to the fragile side of the church building.[663]The Chamber is satisfied that by adopting such a line of conduct, Seromba substantially contributed to the destruction of the Nyange church, causing the death of more than 1,500 Tutsi refugees.

335. In view of the foregoing, the Chamber is satisfied beyond a reasonable doubt that the Accused had committed the *actus reus* of aiding and abetting killing of refugees in Nyange church.

660 See Chapter II, Section 5.3.
661 See Chapter II, Sections 5.5 and 6.8.
662 See Chapter II, Section 6.7.
663 See Chapter II, Section 7.4.

The mens rea *of Accused Athanase Seromba in relation to the killing of Tutsi refugees in Nyange church*

336. The Chamber is satisfied that, given the security situation which prevailed in Nyange parish, Athanase Seromba could not have been unaware that by turning refugees out of the presbytery, he was substantially contributing to their being killed by the attackers.

337. Furthermore, the Chamber is of the view that Athanase Seromba could not have been unaware of the legitimising effect that his words would have on the actions of the communal authorities and the bulldozer driver. The Chamber is also of the view that Seromba knew perfectly well that his approval of the decision by the authorities to destroy Nyange church and his words of encouragement to the bulldozer driver would contribute substantially towards the destruction of the church and the death of the numerous refugees trapped inside.

338. In view of the foregoing, the Chamber is satisfied that the *mens rea* of the Accused in aiding and abetting the killing of refugees in Nyange church has been proved beyond reasonable doubt.

2.3.3 The constituent elements of genocide

339. The Chamber considers as established that the Tutsi constituted an ethnic group in Kivumu *commune* at the time of the events referred to in the Indictment[664] and that they were therefore a protected group within the meaning of Article 2(2).

340. The Chamber also considers that it is beyond dispute that during the events of April 1994 in Nyange church, the attackers and other *Interahamwe* militiamen committed murders of Tutsi refugees in Nyange church and caused serious bodily or mental harm to them on ethnic grounds, with the intent to destroy them, in whole or in part, as an ethnic group. **[page 90]**

341. The Chamber finds that, in his capacity as the priest in charge of Nyange parish during the events of April 1994, and given the situation which prevailed throughout Rwanda, the attacks he personally witnessed[665] and the words he heard or uttered,[666] Accused Athanase Seromba could not have been unaware of the intention of the attackers and other *Interahamwe* militiamen to commit acts of genocide against Tutsi refugees in Nyange parish.

342. Consequently, the Chamber finds it established that Accused Athanase Seromba aided and abetted the crime of genocide as alleged in Count 1 of the Indictment.

3. Count 2 – Complicity in genocide

343. Count 2 is alternative to Count 1 of the Indictment.[667] Hence, having already found the Accused guilty of genocide under Count 1 of the Indictment, the Chamber will not consider the count of complicity in genocide and therefore dismisses it.

4. Count 3 – Conspiracy to commit genocide

4.1 The Indictment

344. The Prosecutor of the International Criminal Tribunal for Rwanda charges Athanase Seromba with conspiracy to commit genocide pursuant to Article 2(3)(b) of the Statute, in that on or between 6 and 20 April 1994, in Kivumu *préfecture*, Rwanda, Seromba did agree with Grégoire Ndahimana, *bourgmestre* of Kivumu *commune*, Fulgence Kayishema, police inspector of Kivumu *commune*, Télesphore Ndungutse, Gaspard Kanyarukiga and other persons not known to the Prosecutor, to kill or to cause serious bodily or

664 Decision on Prosecution Motion for Judicial Notice, 14 July 2005.

665 See Chapter II, Sections 6.7-6.8.

666 See Chapter II, Section 7.4.

667 *Akayesu*, Judgement (TC), 2 September 1998, para. 532.

mental harm to members of the Tutsi population with the intent to destroy, in whole or in part, a racial or ethnic group.

4.2 Applicable law

345. The Chamber relies on the Tribunal's jurisprudence which defines conspiracy to commit genocide as "an agreement between two or more persons to commit the crime of genocide".[668]Thus, the essential element of the crime of conspiracy to commit genocide is "the act of conspiracy itself, in other words, the process ("*procédé*") of conspiracy [...] and not its result".[669]

346. The Chamber also notes that in *Nahimana*, the Appeals Chamber held that conspiracy to commit genocide can be inferred from coordinated actions of individuals who have a common **[page 91]** purpose and are acting within a unified framework.[670] Also in *Niyitegeka*, the Chamber inferred the existence of conspiracy to commit genocide from the participation by the Accused in meetings held for the purpose of planning the massacre of Tutsi, his words and the leadership he exercised during those meetings, his involvement in the planning of attacks against the Tutsi and his role in the distribution of weapons to the attackers.[671]

347. The *mens rea* of the crime of conspiracy to commit genocide is the same as the intent required for the crime of genocide, and rests on the specific intent to commit genocide.[672]

4.3 Findings of the Chamber

348. Paragraphs 33 to 47 of the Indictment set forth concise allegations relating to the count of conspiracy to commit genocide. The Chamber discussed the allegations mainly in sections 3, 4, 5, 6 and 7 of Chapter II dealing with its factual findings. This part of the Indictment describes the three-phase plan, drawn up for the extermination of the Tutsi in Kivumu *commune*. This part also alleges that Athanase Seromba prepared a list of Tutsi to be sought, that he prohibited the refugees from getting food from the presbytery or banana plantation, refused to celebrate mass and that he supervised the massacre of refugees.

349. The Trial Chamber held in its factual findings that the Prosecution has not established beyond a reasonable doubt that Athanase Seromba participated in meetings with the communal authorities on 11[673] and 12 April 1994.[674] The Chamber also found that it has not been established beyond a reasonable doubt that Accused Seromba held meetings with the communal authorities on 10,[675] 15[676] and 16[677]April 1994 for the purpose of planning the extermination of Tutsi refugees in Nyange parish.

350. Furthermore, the Chamber finds that the Prosecution has not established beyond a reasonable doubt that Athanase Seromba prepared a list of Tutsi sought after,[678]or that he ordered or supervised the attack against the refugees on 15 April 1994[679] or that he ordered the destruction of Nyange church on 16 April 1994.[680] As regards the facts established against Seromba, such as prohibiting the refugees from getting food from the banana plantation, or refusing to celebrate mass, the Chamber is of the view that these facts, in and of themselves, are not sufficient to establish the existence of a conspiracy to commit genocide. **[page 92]**

668 *Musema*, Judgement (TC), 27 January 2000, para. 191.
669 *Musema*, Judgement (TC), 27 January 2000, para. 193.
670 *Nahimana*, Judgement (TC), 3 December 2003, para. 1047
671 *Niyitegeka*, Judgement (TC), 16 May 2003, paras. 427-248.
672 *Musema*, Judgement (TC), 27 January 2000, para. 192.
673 See Chapter II, Section 4.3.
674 See Chapter II, Section 5.6.
675 See Chapter II, Section 4.2.
676 See Chapter II, Section 6.4.
677 See Chapter II, Section 7.4.
678 See Chapter II, Section 3.4.
679 See Chapter II, Sections 6.5 and 6.7
680 See Chapter II, Section 7.4.

351. Consequently, the Chamber finds that the Prosecution thus has not proved beyond a reasonable doubt that Athanase Seromba conspired with other persons to commit genocide as alleged in Count 3 of the Indictment.

5. Count 4 – Crime against humanity (extermination)

5.1 The Indictment

352. The Prosecutor of the International Criminal Tribunal for Rwanda charges Athanase Seromba with Extermination as a crime against humanity, as stipulated in Article 3(b) of the Statute, in that on or between the dates of 7 April 1994 and 20 April 1994, in Kibuye *préfecture*, Rwanda, Athanase Seromba was responsible for killing persons or causing persons to be killed during mass killing events as part of a widespread or systematic attack against the civilian population on political, ethnic or racial grounds.

5.2 Applicable law

353. Article 3 of the Statute provides that:

> The International Tribunal for Rwanda shall have the power to prosecute persons responsible for the following crimes when committed as part of a widespread or systematic attack against any civilian population on national, political, ethnic, racial or religious grounds:
>
> (a) Murder;
> (b) Extermination;
> (c) Enslavement;
> (d) Deportation;
> (e) Imprisonment;
> (f) Torture;
> (g) Rape;
> (h) Persecutions on political, racial and religious grounds;
> (i) Other inhumane acts.

354. Article 3 of the Statute, which deals with crimes against humanity, contains a general element that is applicable to all the acts listed therein: perpetration of any of those acts by an accused will constitute a crime against humanity only if it was committed as part of a widespread or systematic attack against any civilian population on national, political, ethnic, racial or religious grounds. **[page 93]**

355. The concept of attack, within the meaning of Article 3, refers to any unlawful act, or event or series of events, of the kind listed in Article 3 of the Statute.[681]

356. This attack must be widespread or systematic.[682] In practice, these two criteria tend to overlap.[683] "Widespread" may be defined as massive, frequent, large scale action, carried out collectively with considerable seriousness and directed against a multiplicity of victims.[684]"Systematic" may be defined as thoroughly organised and following a regular pattern on the basis of a common policy involving substantial public or private resources.[685] The existence of a policy or plan may be evidentially relevant, in that it may be useful in establishing that the attack in question was widespread or systematic, but it should not be considered as a separate element of the crime.[686]

357. It is in not a requirement that the criminal act must, in and of itself, be widespread or systematic. A single murder may constitute a crime against humanity if it is perpetrated within the context of a widespread or systematic attack.[687]

---

681 *Semanza*, Judgement (TC), 15 May 2003, para. 327; *Musema*, Judgement (TC), 27 January 2000, para. 205; *Rutaganda*, Judgement (TC), 6 December 1999, para. 70; *Akayesu*, Judgement (TC), 2 September 1998, para. 581.

682 *Akayesu*, Judgement (TC), 2 September 1998, para. 579.

683 *Bagilishema*, Judgement (TC), 7 June 2001, para. 77.

684 *Akayesu*, Judgement (TC), 2 September 1998, para. 580.

685 *Akayesu*, Judgement (TC), 2 September 1998, para. 580.

686 *Semanza*, Judgement (TC), 15 May 2003, para. 329.

687 *Akayesu*, Judgement (TC), 2 September 1998, para. 580; *Tadić*, Case No. IT-94-1, Judgement (TC), 7 May 1997, para. 649.

358. The attack must be directed against a civilian population, i.e. "people who are not taking any active part in the hostilities, including members of the armed forces who laid down their arms and those persons placed *hors de combat* by sickness, wounds, detention or any other cause".[688] The presence of certain non-civilians in this group does not change its civilian character.[689]

359. The attack against a civilian population must have been committed with discriminatory intent. That is, it must have been committed against a population "on national, political, ethnic, racial or religious grounds". This qualifier characterises only the nature of the attack in general and not the criminal intent of the accused.[690]

360. There must be a nexus between the criminal act and the attack.[691] The accused must have acted with knowledge of the broader context of the attack and knowledge that his acts formed part of a widespread or systematic attack against a civilian population.[692] **[page 94]**

361. In the Indictment, the Prosecutor charges the Accused with a crime listed under Article 3, namely "extermination". By its legal description, the crime of extermination requires proof that the accused participated in a widespread or systematic massacre, or in subjecting a widespread number of people to conditions of living that would inevitably lead to death.[693] Extermination differs from murder or killing in that it requires an element of mass destruction of life,[694]without, however, any suggestion of a numerical minimum.[695] The *mens rea* for extermination is intent to commit or participate in a mass killing.[696]

5.3 Findings of the Chamber

362. Paragraphs 48 to 50 of the Indictment set forth concise allegations relating to the count of crime against humanity. The Chamber has already discussed these allegations in Sections 5, 6 and 7 of Chapter II dealing with its factual findings.

363. With respect to paragraph 48 of the Indictment, the Chamber finds that the Prosecutor has failed to establish that Athanase Seromba ordered the closure of the church doors so as to expose the Tutsi refugees inside Nyange church to death.[697] Consequently, the Chamber finds that Seromba incurs no responsibility for that act.

Actus reus *in relation to the destruction of Nyange church*

364. With respect to paragraph 49 of the Indictment, the Trial Chamber finds that Athanase Seromba held discussions with the authorities and accepted their decision to destroy the church. The Chamber further found that Seromba also discussed with the bulldozer driver and said words which encouraged him to destroy the church. The Chamber finally found that Seromba even gave advice to the bulldozer driver concerning the fragile side of the church.[698] The Chamber is satisfied that by his conduct, Seromba substantially contributed to the destruction of Nyange church.

365. The Chamber is of the view that the destruction of the church, which resulted in the death of 1,500 Tutsi refugees,[699] constitutes the crime of extermination within the meaning of Article 3 of the Statute. **[page 95]**

---

688 *Akayesu*, Judgement (TC), 2 September 1998, para. 582.

689 *Bagilishema*, Judgement (TC), 7 June 2001, para. 79; *Tadić*, Case No. IT-94-1, Judgement (TC), 7 May 1997, para. 638.

690 *Bagilishema*, Judgement (TC), 7 June 2001, para. 81; *Akayesu*, Judgement (TC), 2 September 1998, para. 469; *Kayishema*, Judgement (TC), 21 May 1999, paras. 133-134.

691 *Tadić*, Case No. IT-94-1, Judgement (AC), 15 July 1999, para. 271.

692 *Semanza*, Judgement (TC), 15 May 2003, para. 332.

693 *Ntakirutimana*, Judgement (AC), 13 December 2004, para. 522; *Ndindabahizi*, Judgement (TC), 15 July 2004, para. 480.

694 *Ntakirutimana*, Judgement (AC), 13 December 2004, para. 516; *Ndindabahizi*, Judgement (TC), 15 July 2004, para. 479; *Semanza*, Judgement (TC), 15 May 2003, para. 340.

695 *Ntakirutimana*, Judgement (AC), 13 December 2004, para. 516.

696 *Ntagerura*, Judgement (TC), 25 February 2004, para. 701; *Ntakirutimana*, Judgement (AC), 13 December 2004, para. 522.

697 See Chapter II, Section 6.3.

698 See Chapter II, Section 7.4.

699 See Chapter II, Section 7.5.

366. In view of the foregoing, the Chamber is satisfied beyond reasonable doubt that the Accused aided and abetted the crime of extermination of the Tutsi refugees at Nyange church.

Mens rea *of Athanase Seromba in relation to the destruction of Nyange church*

367. The Chamber further finds that Athanase Seromba could not have been unaware of the legitimising effect his words would have on the actions of the communal authorities and the bulldozer driver. Furthermore, the Chamber finds that Seromba knew perfectly well that his approval of the authorities' decision to destroy Nyange church and his encouraging words to the bulldozer driver, would substantially contribute to the destruction of the church and the death of the numerous refugees inside.

368. In view of the foregoing, the Chamber finds that the Accused's *mens rea* in aiding and abetting the crime of extermination of Tutsi refugees at Nyange church has been proven beyond reasonable doubt.

The constituent elements of crime against humanity

369. The Chamber finds that the conditions required for the commission of crime against humanity have been satisfied in this case. Indeed, the Chamber is satisfied that there were attacks against the Tutsi in Kivumu *commune* in April 1994.[700] The attack which culminated in the destruction of Nyange church on 16 April 1994 was "widespread" in the sense that it was massive, carried out collectively and directed against a multiplicity of victims. The attack was also "systematic" inasmuch as the factual findings tend to show that it was thoroughly organized and followed a regular pattern, starting with the surrounding of the church on 12 April 1994 up to its destruction on 16 April 1994, coupled with the intensification of the attacks against the refugees on 14 and 15 April 1994. Lastly, the Chamber finds that the attack was directed against the Tutsi civilian population that had sought refuge in Nyange church on discriminatory grounds.

370. Furthermore, the Chamber finds that Accused Athanase Seromba had knowledge of the widespread and systematic nature of the attack and the underlying discriminatory grounds. The Chamber is satisfied that Seromba also knew that the crime of extermination committed against the Tutsi refugees was part of that attack.

371. Accordingly, the Chamber considers that it has been proved beyond reasonable doubt that Accused Athanase Seromba committed a crime against humanity (extermination), as alleged in Count 4 of the Indictment. **[page 96]**

CHAPTER IV: VERDICT

372. For the reasons set out in this Judgement, the Chamber unanimously finds as follows:

Count 1: Genocide	**GUILTY**
Count 2: Complicity in genocide	**DISMISSED**
Count 3: Conspiracy to commit genocide	**NOT GUILTY**
Count 4: Crimes against humanity (extermination)	**GUILTY [page 97]**

CHAPTER V: SENTENCE

1. INTRODUCTION

373. Having found Accused Athanase Seromba guilty of genocide and crime against humanity (extermination) by aiding and abetting, the Chamber now considers the appropriate sentence.

374. In its Final Trial Brief, the Prosecution requested the Chamber to sentence Athanase Seromba to concurrent life sentences for each of the counts of the Indictment where the Chamber found him guilty.[701]

700 See Chapter II, Section 3.2.
701 Prosecutor's Final Trial Brief, para. 692.

The Prosecution highlighted the gravity of the crimes and the aggravating circumstances that the Chamber should take into account in determining sentence.

375. In its final brief, the Defence made no submission with respect to sentence. It stated that the Accused had a good reputation and was respected by Hutu and Tutsi parishioners of Nyange prior to the events of 6 April 1994.[702]

2. APPLICABLE LAW

376. The Chamber has unfettered discretion in sentencing persons found guilty of crimes falling within its jurisdiction.[703] The Chamber recalls that the aims of sentencing are retribution, deterrence, reprobation, rehabilitation, national reconciliation, protection of society and restoration of peace.

377. In the determination of sentence the Chamber is governed by the following legal provisions: Article 23 of the Statute and Rule 101 of the Rules.

378. Under Article 23 of the Statute, the Chamber, in imposing sentence, shall have recourse to the general practice regarding prison sentences in the courts of Rwanda (Article 23(1)) and take into account the gravity of the offence and the individual circumstances of the convicted person (Article 23(2)). Pursuant to Rule 101(B) of the Rules, the Chamber must also take into account the following factors:

(i) Any aggravating circumstances;
(ii) Any mitigating circumstances, including the substantial co-operation with the Prosecutor by the convicted person before or after conviction;
(iii) The general practice regarding prison sentences in the courts of Rwanda;
(iv) The extent to which any penalty imposed by a court of any state on a convicted person for the same act has already been served (...) **[page 98]**

379. The Chamber considers that in imposing sentence, it may also take into account any other factor which fully reflects the circumstances of the case.[704]

3. FINDINGS OF THE CHAMBER

3.1 Gravity of the offences

380. The Chamber notes that in its Final Trial Brief, the Prosecution argued that the crimes committed by Accused Athanase Seromba are serious.[705] In support of this argument, the Prosecution asserts that Athanas Seromba acted with premeditation,[706] and without constraint.[707]

381. The Chamber recalls that an evaluation of the gravity of offences is based on the crimes charged against the accused, that is, the individual circumstances under which the offences were committed, and not on a hierarchy of crimes.[708]

382. The Chamber notes that in this case the Prosecutor did not prove beyond a reasonable doubt that Accused Athanase Seromba either planned or ordered, as a principal, the commission of the offences for which he has been found guilty. Nor does the Trial Chamber accept the argument of premeditation advanced by the Prosecutor. Lastly, the Trial Chamber considers that the Accused did not act under duress when he approved that the church be destroyed using the bulldozer. Accordingly, the Trial Chamber concludes that the offences of genocide and crimes against humanity by aiding and abetting for which Accused Athanase Seromba has been found guilty are of the most extreme gravity.

702 *Conclusions finales de la Défense*, p. 7.
703 See *Ruggiu*, Judgement (TC), 1 June 2000, para. 52; *Kambanda*, ICTR-97-23-S, Judgement (TC), 4 September 1998, para. 11.
704 See *Rutaganda*, Judgement (TC), 6 December 1999, para. 454.
705 Prosecutor's Final Trial Brief, para. 651.
706 Prosecutor's Final Trial Brief, paras. 672 (p. 138).
707 Prosecutor's Final Trial Brief, para. 652.
708 *Mucić*, Judgement (TC), 16 November 1996, para. 1226; *Kayishema*, Judgement (AC), 1 June 2001, para. 367.

3.2 Individual circumstances of the Accused

383. The Chamber recalls that the individual circumstances of the accused are perceived in the jurisprudence of the *ad hoc* tribunals as a factor for individualizing the penalty.[709] The Chamber further considers that individual circumstances should be understood to be any personal circumstance of the accused which may either aggravate or mitigate sentence.

384. The Chamber further notes that the Prosecution submitted in its Final Trial Brief that nothing in the individual circumstances of Athanase Seromba mitigates the gravity of the crimes charged against him. **[page 99]**

385. The Chamber notes that Accused Athanase Seromba was ordained priest on 18 July 1993.[710] It is the Chamber's opinion that his training as a priest and his experience within the church should have enabled him to understand the reprehensible nature of his conduct during the events.

386. The Chamber notes, moreover, that Accused Athanase Seromba was present at Nyange church only at the end of the summer or early autumn 1993.[711] The Chamber further notes that Athanas Seromba was only a curate in Nyange parish during the April 1994 events, and was put in charge of the parish because there was no parish priest there.[712]

3.3 Aggravating circumstances

387. In its Final Trial Brief, the Prosecution cited several aggravating circumstances. The Prosecution cited the fact that Athanase Seromba was known in Nyange community,[713] that he was directly involved in the massacre of Tutsi.[714] The Prosecution also averred that the Accused betrayed the trust of his parishioners.[715] The Prosecution pointed out that the crimes committed during the events of April 1994 in Nyange parish were accompanied by excessive violence and the victims went through humiliation[716] and a lot of suffering before dying.[717]

388. The Chamber recalls that aggravating circumstances must be proved beyond a reasonable doubt.[718] A particular circumstance shall not be retained as aggravating if it is included as an element of the crime in question.[719]

389. The Chamber will, in this case, examine as aggravating circumstances the status of the Accused and betrayal of the trust placed in him by the Tutsi refugees,[720] as well as the flight of the Accused after the destruction of the church.

Status of the Accused and betrayal of trust

390. The Chamber recalls that Athanase Seromba, a Catholic priest, was in charge of Nyange parish at the time of the events referred to in the Indictment.[721] The Accused was known and **[page 100]** respected in the

---

709 For a list of factors to take into account in the individualisation of the sentence, see: *Kambanda*, Judgement (TC), 4 September 1998, para. 29; *Erdemović*, Judgement (TC), 29 November 1996, para. 44.

710 See letter dated 18 May 1993 from the Bishop of Nyundo to Athanase Seromba (D-10).

711 See, *inter alia*, Witness CBK: Transcript, 19 October 2004, p. 8 (closed session); Witness CBJ: Transcript, 12 October 2004, pp. 26-27 (open session); Witness FE27: Transcript, 23 March 2006, p. 11 (closed session).

712 See Section 2.

713 Prosecutor's Final Trial Brief, para. 658.

714 Prosecutor's Final Trial Brief, paras. 665-666.

715 Prosecutor's Final Trial Brief, paras. 657-671.

716 Prosecutor's Final Trial Brief, para 675.

717 Prosecutor's Final Trial Brief, para. 676.

718 Judgement (TC), para. 693; *Ndindabahazi*, Judgement (TC), 15 July 2004, para. 502.

719 *Blagojević & Jokić*, Judgement (TC), 17 January 2005, para. 849; *Ndindabahazi*, Judgement (TC), 15 July 2004, para. 502; *Ntakirutimana*, Judgement (TC), 21 February 2003, para. 893.

720 *Ndindabahazi*, Judgement (TC), 15 July 2004, para. 508; *Ntakirutimana*, Judgement (TC), 21 February 2003, paras. 899-902; *Nahimana*, Judgement (TC), 3 December 2003, para. 1099.

721 See Chapter II, Section 2.

Catholic community of Nyange. The Chamber recalls that it has been established that many Tutsi from Kivumu *commune* sought refuge in Nyange church in order to escape attack.[722] The Chamber considers as an aggravating circumstance the fact that the Accused took no concrete action whatsoever to earn the trust of those persons who believed they were safe by seeking refuge at Nyange parish. Consequently, the Chamber finds that the status of the Accused and betrayal of trust constitute aggravating circumstances.

Flight of the Accused after destruction of church

391. The Chamber notes that it is not in contention that the Accused used an identity other than his own to go into exile in Italy, as attested to by the passport issued to him by the then Zaïrian authorities.[723] The Chamber notes, however, that other priests who were with the Accused at Nyange church during the events of April 1994 did not adopt this stratagem. Furthermore, these priests who remained in Rwanda were even prosecuted, but all of them were acquitted.[724] Therefore, the Chamber finds that the flight of Athanase Seromba represents an aggravating circumstance.

3.4 Mitigating circumstances

392. In its Final Trial Brief, the Prosecution submitted that Athanase Seromba should not benefit from any mitigating circumstance, as his surrender was not "voluntary", and as he did not cooperate with the Prosecutor, but rather obstructed the proceedings throughout the trial. The Prosecution added that the Accused has shown no remorse for the role he played in the commission of the crimes charged. Finally, the Prosecutor stressed that no evidence of the Accused's good conduct before and after the crimes charged against him has been adduced.[725]

393. In its Final Trial Brief, the Defence submitted that the Accused had a good reputation and was respected by both Hutu and Tutsi parishioners of Nyange prior to the events of April 1994.[726]

394. The Chamber recalls that mitigating circumstances have to be proved on a balance of probabilities.[727] The weight to be attached to mitigating circumstances is a matter of discretion for the Trial Chamber.[728] In the instant case, the Chamber will discuss the following points: the **[page 101]** good reputation of the Accused prior to the events, voluntary surrender of the Accused and the age of the Accused.

Athanase Seromba's good reputation prior to the events of April 1994 in Nyange parish

395. Evidence of Athanase Seromba's good reputation was provided by several Prosecution and Defence witnesses. Such witnesses include CBJ,[729] CBK,[730] BR1,[731] BZ1[732] and BZ4[733] who testified that, as a priest, Athanase Seromba was respected by the public. Accordingly, the Chamber finds that this fact constitutes a mitigating circumstance in determining the sentence to be imposed on the Accused.

Surrender of the Accused

396. The Prosecutor argues that Athanase Seromba's surrender cannot be considered as a mitigating circumstance, as it was not voluntary.[734] The Prosecutor contends that the Accused surrendered only once

722 See Chapter II, Section 3.3.

723 See the following exhibits: Italian immigration document of Athanase Sumba Bura (P-6) and Zaïrian passport of Athanase Sumba Bura (P-7).

724 See Rwandan court files disclosed by the Prosecutor.

725 Prosecutor's Final Trial Brief, paras. 682-685.

726 *Conclusions finales de la Défense*, p. 7.

727 See, e.g., *Niyitegeka*, Judgement (TC), 16 May 2003, para. 488; *Ntakirutimana*, Judgement (TC), 21 February 2003, para. 893.

728 *Kambanda*, Judgement (AC), 19 October 2000, para. 124.

729 Transcript, 12 October 2004, p. 23 (closed session).

730 Transcript, 19 October 2004, p. 46 (closed session).

731 Transcript, 25 November 2005, p. 36 (open session).

732 Transcript, 2 November 2005, p. 71 (open session).

733 Transcript, 2 November 2005, p. 7 (open session).

734 Prosecutor's Final Trial Brief, paras. 677-683; Transcript, 28 June 2006, p. 42 (open session).

his arrest by the Italian authorities became imminent.[735] The Prosecutor further submits that if indeed the Accused surrendered, his surrender does not constitute a mitigating circumstance, because it does not meet the criteria set forth in the *Babić* Judgement.[736]

397. The Chamber notes that voluntary surrender of an accused may constitute a mitigating circumstance.[737] The Chamber considers that the circumstances and time frames surrounding the surrender of the accused must be assessed on a case by case basis. Thus, for example, in *Blaškić*, the fact that the accused surrendered only after having prepared his defence,[738] and in *Simić*, the fact that the accused surrendered three years after the surrender of other individuals in the same circumstances, limited the mitigating effect of those surrenders.[739] The Chamber notes, on the contrary, that in *Babić*, the voluntary surrender of the accused was considered as a mitigating circumstance because it happened "soon after the confirmation of an indictment against him",[740]while in *Plavšić*, the voluntary surrender of the accused to the Tribunal's authorities 20 days after having learned about the Indictment, was considered as a mitigating circumstance.[741] **[page 102]**

398. In this case, the Chamber notes that Accused Athanase Seromba surrendered to the authorities of the Tribunal on 6 February 2002, without the arrest warrant issued against him being executed by the Italian authorities.[742] The Chamber finds this to be a voluntary surrender and, therefore, considers the voluntary surrender of the Accused as a mitigating circumstance in determining the sentence.

The young age of the Accused

399. The Chamber notes the relatively young age of Accused Athanase Seromba, who was 31 years old at the time of the events,[743] and the possibility of his rehabilitation.

3.5 Sentence

The general practice regarding prison sentences in Rwanda

400. The Chamber notes that the Rwandan law of 26 January 2001[744] classifies persons prosecuted for aiding and abetting the genocide and crime against humanity in category 1(b): "(b) Persons who acted in positions of authority at the national, provincial or district level, in political parties, the army, religious organizations or the militiamen, and who committed or encouraged others to commit such crimes".

401. The Chamber also notes that Rwanda, like other countries that have incorporated genocide or crimes against humanity in their domestic law, has provided very severe penalties for these crimes.[745]

---

735 Prosecutor's Final Trial Brief, paras. 682-683.

736 *Babić*, Judgement (TC), 29 June 2004, paras. 85-86.

737 *Serushago*, Judgement (TC), 6 April 2000, para. 24.

738 *Blaškić*, Judgement (TC), 3 March 2000, para. 776.

739 *Simić*, Judgement (TC), 17 October 2003, para. 1086.

740 *Babić*, Judgement (TC), 29 June 2004, para. 86.

741 *Plavšić*, Judgement (TC), 27 February 2003, paras. 82 to 84.

742 *Seromba*, Decision on the Prosecutor's Ex-Parte Request for Search, Seizure, Arrest and Transfer, 3 July 2001; *Seromba*, Warrant of Arrest and Order for Transfer, 4 July 2001; see letter dated 11 July 2001 from the Italian Justice Ministry to the Registrar of the International Criminal Tribunal for Rwanda.

743 See the following exhibits: Italian immigration document for Athanase Sumba Bura (P-6) and Zaïrian passport for Athanase Sumba Bura (P-7) which certify that the Accused was born in 1963.

744 Article 51 of Organic Law No. 40/2000 of 26/01/2001 Setting up Gacaca Jurisdictions and Organizing Prosecutions for Offences Constituting Genocide or Crimes Against Humanity Committed between l October 1990 and 31 December 1994.

745 Defendants coming within the first category who did not want to have recourse to the confession and guilt plea procedure within conditions set in Article 56 of this organic law or whose confession and guilt plea have been rejected, incur a death penalty or life imprisonment. Defendants who have made recourse to the confession and guild plea procedure within conditions provided for in Article 56 of this organic law are sentenced to imprisonment ranging from 25 years to life imprisonment". Article 68 of Organic Law No. 40/2000 of 26/01/2001 setting up Gacaca Jurisdictions and Organizing Prosecutions for Offences Constituting the Crime of Genocide or Crimes Against Humanity Committed between October 1, 1990 and December 31, 1994.

402. The Trial Chamber recalls, however, that Rwandan law and sentences passed by the Rwandan courts are to be used only as a reference,[746] since such reference is but one of the factors that must be taken into account in determining sentence.[747] In fact, the Tribunal can only **[page 103]** impose on the Accused a sentence of imprisonment for the remainder of his life and not the death sentence, which is applied in Rwanda.[748]

403. Furthermore, the Chamber notes that direct participation of an accused in crimes committed generally attracts a higher sentence than criminal participation by way of aiding and abetting the commission of the crimes.[749] Thus, a sentence of life imprisonment is generally imposed upon persons who directly planned or ordered the criminal acts, particularly those who clearly had authority and influence at the time the crimes were committed, as well as those who participated in those crimes with particular zeal or sadism.[750]

Multiple sentences

404. Under Rule 101(C) of the Rules, the Chamber has discretion to determine whether the sentences it has passed are to be served consecutively or concurrently.[751] In this regard, the Chamber recalls that the Appeals Chamber held that "nothing in the Statute or Rules expressly states that a Chamber must impose a separate sentence for each count on which an accused is convicted".[752] The Chamber further notes that in *Blaškić*, the Appeals Chamber held *inter alia* as follows: "The crimes ascribed to the accused have been characterised in several distinct ways but form part of a single set of crimes committed in a given geographic region during a relatively extended time-span ... In light of this overall consistency, the Trial Chamber finds that there is reason to impose a single sentence for all the crimes of which the accused has been found guilty".[753]

Credit for time served

405. Accused Athanase Seromba surrendered to the Tribunal's authorities on 6 February 2002. Consequently, the Chamber will grant him credit for the period spent in custody from the date of his arrest to the date of this Judgement, pursuant to Article 101(D) of the Rules of Procedure and Evidence. **[page 104]**

CHAPTER VI: DISPOSITION

FOR THE FOREGOING REASONS, the Trial Chamber, delivering this judgement in public, inter parties and in the first instance, pursuant to the Statute and the Rules of Procedure and Evidence;

HAVING CONSIDERED all of the evidence and arguments of the parties;

HAVING FOUND Athanase Seromba **GUILTY** of the crime of genocide and crime against humanity (extermination);

SENTENCES Athanase Seromba to a single sentence of fifteen (15) years imprisonment;

RULES that this sentence shall be enforced immediately;

RULES that pursuant to Rule 101(D) of the Rules, the time that Athanase Seromba spent in custody, calculated from the date of his surrender on 6 February 2002, and any additional period spent in custody, pending a decision to appeal, shall be deducted from this sentence;

746 Article 23(1) of the Statute and Article 101(B)(iii) of the Rules.

747 *Kambanda*, Judgement (TC), 4 September 1998, para. 23.

748 The Chamber notes in this regard that Rwanda is currently considering abolishing the death penalty.

749 See *Semanza*, Judgement (AC), 20 May 2005, para. 388.

750 *Muhimana*, Judgement (TC), 28 April 2005, paras. 604-616; *Musema*, Judgement (AC), 16 November 2001, para. 383.

751 *Kambanda*, Judgement (AC), 19 October 2000, para. 102.

752 *Kambanda*, Judgement (AC), 19 October 2000, para. 102.

753 Ibid., paras. 109-10.

RULES that pursuant to Rule 103 of the Rules, Athanase Seromba shall remain in the custody of the Tribunal until the necessary arrangements have been made for his transfer to the State where he shall serve his sentence.

Done at Arusha, this Wednesday, 13 December 2006.

[Signed]	[Signed]	[Signed]
Andrésia Vaz Presiding Judge	Karin Hökborg Judge	Gustave G. Kam Judge **[page 105]**

ANNEX I: PROCEDURAL BACKGROUND

1. Pre-trial phase

1. The Indictment against Athanase Seromba was filed by the Prosecutor on 8 June 2001 and confirmed on 3 July 2001 by Judge Lloyd Williams, subject to the correction of grammatical and typographical errors.[754] Following a request by the Prosecutor, the Presiding Judge also ordered the non-disclosure to the public, the media or to the suspect of the names of the witnesses and suspects identified in the supporting materials that accompagnied the Indictment or any other information that might permit their identification.

2. On 4 July 2001, Judge Lloyd Williams issued a warrant of arrest against the Accused.[755]On 10 July 2001, in execution of the order for transfer issued by the said Judge, the Registrar of the Tribunal transmitted the warrant of arrest and the Indictment to the Italian Minister of Justice.

3. On 6 February 2002, the Accused surrendered to the authorities of the Tribunal and was placed in detention. The Accused made his initial appearance before Judge Navanethem Pillay on 8 February 2002 and entered a plea of not guilty to each of the counts in the Indictment.[756] On 12 February 2002, the Prosecutor served a first request for interview on the Accused.

4. On 14 May 2002, the Prosecutor filed a motion for protective measures for witnesses.

5. In a motion filed on 3 June 2002, the Prosecutor requested the President of the Tribunal to authorize the Trial Chamber to exercise its functions away from the seat of the Tribunal and to hold the trial of the Accused in Rwanda.[757] On 20 June 2002, Judge Navanethem Pillay postponed making a decision on the matter until the Registrar assigned a Defence Counsel for the Accused.[758]

6. On 10 September 2002, the Prosecutor filed an addendum to his motion for witness protection measures.

7. On 3 March 2003, the Registrar assigned Mr. Alfred Pognon as Lead Counsel for the Defence.

8. On 17 April 2003, the Prosecutor wrote a letter to the Defence inviting the Accused to review the evidence. **[page 106]**

9. On 2 May 2003, the Defence filed a motion to annul or withdraw the Indictment, on the grounds that the Prosecutor's failure to question the suspect before issuing an indictment against him amounted to a procedural defect invalidating the Indictment.

10. On 30 June 2003, Judge Erik Møse granted the Prosecutor's motion for protective measures for victims and witnesses, ordering the Prosecution to disclose any unredacted witness statements 21 days prior to resumption of the trial.[759]

11. On 8 January 2004, the Prosecutor withdrew his motion for trial in Rwanda.[760]

12. On 13 January 2004, the Trial Chamber, sitting in the person of Judge Erik Møse, dismissed the Defence motion to annul or withdraw the Indictment,[761] and ruled that neither the Statute nor the Rules required the Prosecution to interview a suspect prior to indicting.

754 *Seromba*, "Decision on the Prosecutor's Ex Parte Request for Search, Seizure, Arrest and Transfer", 4 July 2001 (Judge Lloyd G. Williams asked the Prosecutor to correct paragraphs 2, 5, 8, 11, 17, 19, 25, 28, 32, 33, 35, 38, 39, 40, 43, 48 and Count 4 of the Indictment).

755 *Seromba*, Warrant of Arrest and Order for Transfer, 4 July 2001.

756 Transcript, 8 February 2002, p. 16 (open session).

757 *Seromba*, Office of the Prosecutor, "Prosecutor's Motion for Trial in Rwanda", 3 June 2002.

758 *Seromba*, Interoffice Memorandum from Judge Navanethem Pillay to Prosecutor Carla Del Ponte, 20 June 2002.

759 *Seromba*, "Decision on the Prosecutor's Motion for Protective Measures for Victims and Witnesses", 30 June 2003.

760 *Seromba*, Office of the Prosecutor, "Request by the Prosecutor to Withdraw Motion for Trial in Rwanda", 8 January 2004.

761 *Seromba*, "Decision on the Defence Motions to Annul or Withdraw the Indictment", 13 January 2004.

13. A status conference to assess progress of the preparation for commencement of the trial was also held on 13 January 2004. The Chamber invited the Prosecutionr to file its Pre-Trial Brief.[762] The Defence submitted that it would be ready only in September 2004.[763]

14. On 14 January 2004, Judge Erik Møse granted the Prosecutor's request to withdraw its motion for trial in Rwanda.[764]

15. On 20 January 2004, the Prosecutor filed the initial version of his Pre-Trial Brief.

16. On 20 August 2004, the Prosecution disclosed its list of exhibits to the Defence.

17. On 27 August 2004, the Prosecutor filed the final version of the Pre-Trial Brief. Exhibits were filed on 30 August 2004. A corrigendum to the Pre-Trial Brief was filed on 7 September 2004. On 15 September 2004, other exhibits were filed, as well as the order of appearance of Prosecution witnesses.

18. A pre-trial conference was held on 20 September 2004. The Chamber noted the absence of the Accused at that conference.[765] The Prosecution stated that it had fully discharged its pretrial obligations, in particular with respect to disclosure of materials to the Defence.[766] The **[page 107]** Defence requested that the Prosecution disclose to it the witness statements referred to in decisions of the Rwandan courts and filed by the Prosecution.[767]

2. Trial phase

19. The trial of the Accused commenced on 20 September 2004. The Accused participated in a strike ation called by some accused persons of the Tribunal and so did not attend the first three days of the trial. Defence Counsel, Messrs. Pognon and Monthé, explained that their client had asked them not to represent him during the strike.[768] The Chamber ruled that the Accused's instructions did not amount to a termination of the Defence Counsel's assignment to represent the Accused and ordered them to continue to represent the Accused for as long as he refused to appear before the Chamber.[769] After stating that they could not represent the Accused without his authorization, the Defence Counsel left the court room, thus compelling the Chamber to adjourn the trial until 27 September, that date on which they returned.

20. In letters dated 24 September 2004 and 27 September 2004 respectively, Defence Counsel and the Accused, as well as the *Association des avocats de la défense* (*ADAD*), in an application to appear as *amicus curiae*, requested the Chamber to reconsider its Oral Decision of 21 September 2004. The Chamber dismissed this first motion, having concluded that the warning of 21 September 2004 did not constitute a sanction,[770] and that the decision to warn Counsel was well-founded in law, falling within its inherent powers to direct and control the proceedings and, therefore, is not open to any challenge, even in the face of special circumstances.[771] With respect to the *ADAD* application, the Chamber refused to authorize the association to appear as *amicus curiae*, having found that the Brief submitted by *ADAD* raised no such relevant issues as would enlighten the Chamber.[772]

21. The Chamber heard 15 Prosecution witnesses: 12 witnesses from 27 September to 22 October 2004 and 3 witnesses from 19 January to 25 January 2005, the date the Prosecution closed its case.

22. On 20 January 2005, the Defence filed a motion for protective measures for witnesses.

---

762 Transcript, 13 January 2004, p. 21 (closed session).

763 *Ibid.*, p. 26 (closed session).

764 *Seromba*, Decision on the "Prosecution Request to Withdraw its Motion for Trial in Rwanda", 14 January 2004.

765 Transcript, 20 September 2004, Pre-Trial Conference, p. 2 (open session).

766 *Ibid.*, pp. 3-4 (open session).

767 *Ibid.*, p. 8 (open session).

768 Transcript, 20 September 2004, Trial, p. 2 (open session); *Seromba*, Transcript, 21 September 2004, p. 1 (open session).

769 Transcript, 21 September 2004, p. 3 (open session).

770 *Seromba*, *Décision sur les requêtes en annulation de sanction et en intervention en qualité* d'amicus curiae, 22 October 2004, para. 14.

771 *Ibid.*, para. 18.

772 *Ibid.*, para. 21.

23. A status conference was held on 25 January 2005. The Chamber requested the Defence to file its list of witnesses as quickly as possible and ordered that the trial resume on 1 March 2005.[773] **[page 108]**

24. On 31 January 2005, the Chamber rendered a decision authorizing protective measures for the Defence witnesses and ordered the Defence to disclose unredacted statements of its witnesses 21 days prior to the resumption of trial.[774]

25. On 9 February 2005, the Defence filed a motion for extension of the time-limit for disclosing the unredacted statements of its witnesses, and another motion for the same purpose on 17 February 2005. On 1 March 2005, the Chamber ordered the Defence to file, no later than 14 March 2005, its Pre-Defence Brief, the complete and precise list of witnesses which it intended to call to testify, a summary of facts and the estimated length of the testimony of each witness.[775] The Chamber adjourned the trial to 4 April 2005 for the commencement of the Defence case.[776]

26. On 11 March 2005, the Defence filed a new motion for further extensions. During a status conference held on 5 April 2005, the Trial Chamber postponed resumption of the trial to 10 May 2005 and ordered the Defence to file its Pre-Defence Brief, the summaries and the statements of its witnesses within the prescribed time-limit, so that the trial could resume on 10 May 2005.[777]

27. On 9 April 2005, the Accused sent a letter to his Lead Counsel, Mr. Pognon, stating that he no longer wanted to be represented by him because he had lost confidence in him.

28. On 13 April 2005, the Chamber ordered the Defence to disclose to the Prosecution the unredacted statements of its witnesses no later than 21 days prior to resumption of trial.[778]

29. On 15 April 2005, the Accused wrote to the Registrar requesting the withdrawal of the assignment of his Lead Counsel, Mr. Pognon. On 18 April 2005, Mr. Pognon agreed to step down and to withdraw immediately.

30. On 19 April 2005, the Defence filed a Pre-Defence Brief, but did not comply with the orders for disclosure of unredacted Defence witness statements.

31. On 10 May 2005, given the withdrawal of Mr. Pognon and the absence of Mr. Monthé, the Chamber decided to adjourn the trial *sine die*.[779] **[page 109]**

32. On 19 May 2005, the Chamber directed the Registrar to respond, no later than 27 May 2005, to the Accused's Motion of 15 April 2005 concerning the assignment of a new counsel.[780] On 20 May 2005, the Registrar withdrew the assignment of the Lead Counsel,[781] and on 8 June 2005, assigned Mr. Monthé in his place.

33. On 23 June 2005, the Defence filed a motion to withdraw the Pre-Defence Brief filed by the previous Lead Counsel.

34. During the status conference held on 24 June 2005, the Chamber granted the Defence's request for adjournment and set the date of 31 October 2005 for resumption of trial.[782]

35. In a 7 July 2005 Decision,[783] the Chamber authorized the Defence to file a new Pre-Defence Brief and ruled that the Defence motion for withdrawal of the 19 April 2005 Preliminary Brief was without merit. The

773 Transcript, 25 January 2004, Status Conference, p. 13 (open session).

774 *Seromba, Décision relative à la requête aux fins de prescription de mesures de protection des témoins de la Défense*, 31 January 2005.

775 *Seromba, Décision relative à la requête de la Défense aux fins de délai*, 1 March 2005, para. 21.

776 *Ibid.*, para. 20.

777 Transcript, 5 April 2005, Pre-Trial Conference, p. 19.

778 *Seromba, Décision relative à la requête du Procureur aux fins de communication des déclarations des témoins de la Défense*, 13 April 2005.

779 Transcript, 10 May 2005, p. 22 (open session).

780 *Seromba*, Order, 19 May 2005, p. 19.

781 *Seromba*, Registrar, Decision to withdraw the assignment of Mr. Alfred Pognon as Counsel for Athanase Seromba, 20 May 2005.

782 Transcript, 24 June 2005, Status Conference, p. 8.

783 *Seromba, Décision relative à la fixation d'une date de reprise du procès*, 7 July 2005.

Chamber also authorized the Prosecution to inspect the exhibits that the Defence intended to rely on, at least 21 days prior to the commencement of the Defence case. The Chamber ordered the Defence to disclose its new Preliminary Brief and the unredacted statements of its witnesses to the Prosecution at least 21 days prior to the resumption of trial, as well as the redacted and unredacted statements of Defence witnesses at least 60 days and 21 days respectively prior to the resumption of the trial.

36. On 10 October 2005, the Defence filed a new Pre-Defence Brief, which was subsequently amended on 19 October 2005. On 25 and 27 October 2005, the Defence filed the statements of its witnesses without disclosing their identity. On 28 October 2005, the Defence filed the order of appearance of the Defence witnesses, without disclosing their identity.

37. On 31 October 2005, the Defence opened its case.

38. On 16 December 2005, the Chamber rendered five decisions: a decision setting 13 February 2006 as the date of resumption of the trial;[784] a decision ordering the transfer of detained witnesses to Arusha;[785] a decision ordering the opening of an investigation into the retraction of testimony by Witness FE36;[786] a decision ordering the opening of an investigation into the request for long-term protection measures for Witnesses FE36, FE35 and CF14;[787] and a **[page 110]** decision ordering the Prosecution to disclose to the Defence, through the Witnesses and Victims Support Section, the identity and addresses of certain witnesses whom it no longer intended to call and authorising the Defence to enter into contact with some of those witnesses.[788]

39. In a memorandum dated 7 February 2006, the President of the Tribunal postponed the date of resumption of the trial to 23 March 2006.

40. On 7 March 2006, the Defence filed a motion to add Witnesses PS1 and PS2 to its witness list and to drop witnesses CF3 and FE25.

41. The Defence resumed presentation of its evidence on 23 March 2006.

42. On 24 March 2006, the Chamber granted the motion to add Witnesses PS1 and PS2 to the list of Defence witnesses.[789]

43. On 29 March 2006, the Chamber granted the Prosecution's motion for sites visit in Rwanda.[790] From 8 to 11 April 2006, the Chamber, the Defence, the Prosecutor and the Registrar visited sites in Kivumu, Rwanda.

44. On 12 April 2006, the Defence dropped Witnesses CF4 and CF13 from its list of witnesses and modified the order of appearance of Witnesses PA1, PS1, PS2 and the Accused. The Chamber adjourned the trial to 18 April 2006.[791]

45. On 18 April 2006, the Defence dropped PS1 from its witness list and informed the Chamber that Witness PS2 could not testify in Arusha before May 2006.[792]

46. On 20 April 2006, the Chamber granted the Defence motion for the deposition of witness PS2 to be taken by means of a video-conference.[793]

---

784 *Seromba, Décision portant fixation de la date de reprise du procès au 13 février 2006*, 16 December 2005.

785 *Seromba, Ordonnance relative à la requête de la Défense aux fins du transfert des témoins détenus*, 16 December 2005.

786 *Seromba, Décision relative à la requête de la Défense aux fins de voir ordonner l'ouverture d'une enquête sur les circonstances et les causes réelles de rétraction du témoin portant le pseudonyme FE36*, 16 December 2005.

787 *Seromba, Décision relative à la requête de la Défense aux fins de voir ordonner des mesures de protection à long terme à l'égard des témoins de la Défense portant les pseudonyme CF14, FE35 et FE36*, 16 December 2005.

788 *Seromba, Décision relative à la Requête aux fins d'obtenir la divulgation de l'identité et de l'adresse des témoins de l'accusation CAN, CNY, CBW, CNV, CBX, CNP, CNE, CNI, CNO, [...] non retenus sur la liste finale du Procureur et l'autorisation de prendre contact avec ces derniers*, 16 December 2005.

789 Transcript, 24 March 2006, p. 39 (open session).

790 *Seromba*, Decision on the "Prosecutor's Motion for Site Visits in Rwanda", 29 March 2006.

791 Transcript, 12 April 2006, pp. 55-57 (open session).

792 Transcript, 18 April 2006, p. 1 (open session).

793 *Seromba*, Decision on the "Defence Motion for the Deposition of Witness PS2 to be Taken by Video-Conference", 20 April 2006.

47. On 21 April 2006, the Chamber ordered the Accused to testify on 24 April 2006[794] and authorized the parties to send representatives to South Africa for the deposition of Witness PS2 by video-link.[795] **[page 111]**

48. On 21 April 2006, the Defence argued that the Accused could not testify before Witness PS2's deposition is given and requested the Chamber to reconsider its Oral Decision of 21 April 2006.[796] The Chamber dismissed the Defence request, given that its 21 April 2006 Decision violated neither Article 20 of the Statute nor Rule 85 of the Rules, and that it had not forced the Accused to testify against his will, but had simply reversed the order of appearance of Witness PS2 and the Accused in order to meet the deadline for the close of the Defence case.[797]The Chamber also dismissed the Defence's request for certification for appeal of that Decision.[798]

49. The Defence, subsequently, filed a motion with the Bureau of the Tribunal for disqualification of the Judges of the Trial Chamber. On 25 April 2006, the Bureau dismissed the Defence motion.[799]

50. The trial resumed on 26 April 2006. The Defence disclosed that it was appealing the decision of the Bureau and asked that the trial be adjourned pending a decision by the Appeal Chamber.[800] The Chamber dismissed the Defence motion to adjourn the proceedings.[801] With the Defence having refused to examine Witness PS2, the Chamber held that it had waived its right to examine the witness.[802] The Chamber adjourned the proceedings to the following day to enable the Accused to be present at the hearing.[803]

51. On 27 April 2006, the Defence declared that the Accused had decided not to attend the proceedings until the Appeal Chamber ruled on the Defence appeal against the Bureau's decision on the disqualification motion.[804] The Trial Chamber concluded that the Defence had waived its right to examine the Accused and, therefore there was no other witness to be heard, and that the Defence had closed its case. The Chamber ordered that the Prosecutor's Final Brief be filed no later than 26 May 2006, that of the Defence no later than 16 June 2006, and that the parties should present their closing arguments on 27 June 2006.[805]

52. On 22 May 2006, the Appeal Chamber dismissed the Defence appeal against the decision of the Bureau of the Tribunal on the motion for disqualification.[806]

53. On 5 June 2006, the Defence filed a motion for extention of the time-limit for the filing of its Closing Brief on 22 June 2006. The Chamber granted that motion on 8 June 2006.[807] **[page 112]**

54. The Prosecutionr filed its Closing Brief on 26 May 2006, while the Defence filed its own Brief on 22 June 2006. The Defence also filed a corrigendum to its Closing Brief on 26 June 2006.

55. The parties presented their closing arguments on 27 and 28 June 2006.

56. On 28 June 2006, the Chamber granted the Prosecutor's motion to exclude as out of time the corrigendum to the Defence Final Trial Brief and ordered its exclusion from the proceedings.[808] **[page 113]**

---

794 Transcript, 21 April 2006, p. 1 (closed session).
795 *Ibid.*, p. 42 (closed session).
796 Transcript, 24 April 2006, pp. 1-2 (open session).
797 *Ibid.*, pp. 6-7 (open session).
798 *Ibid.*, p. 7 (open session).
799 *Seromba*, Decision on Motion for Disqualification of Judges, 25 April 2006.
800 Transcript, 26 April 2006, p. 4 (open session).
801 *Ibid.*, p. 7 (open session).
802 *Ibid.*, p. 8 (open session).
803 *Ibid.*, p. 20 (open session).
804 Transcript, 27 April 2006, p. 3 (open session).
805 *Ibid.*, p. 5 (open session).
806 *Seromba*, Decision on Interlocutory Appeal of a Bureau Decision, 22 May 2006.
807 *Seromba*, Decision on "Defence Motion for an Extension [of Time] to file the Final Trial Brief", 8 June 2006.
808 *Seromba*, Decision on "Prosecutor's Extremely Urgent Motion to Exclude as Out of Time the Corrigendum to the Defence Final Trial Brief (Reasons for the Oral Decision of 27 June 2006)", 28 June 2006.

ANNEX II: LIST OF SOURCES CITED AND ABBREVIATIONS

A. List of Judgements

Long form	*Short form*
The Prosecutor v. Akayesu, Case No. ICTR-96-4, Judgement (TC), 2 September 1998.	*Akayesu*, Judgement (TC), 2 September 1998.
Prosecutor v. Babić, Case No. IT-03-72-S, Judgement (TC), 29 June 2004.	*Babić*, Judgement (TC), 29 June 2004.
The Prosecutor v. Bagilishema, Case No. ICTR-95-1, Judgement (TC), 7 June 2001.	*Bagilishema*, Judgement (TC), 7 June 2001.
Prosecutor v. Blagojević & Jokić, Case No. IT-02-60 T, Judgement (TC), 17 January 2005.	*Blagojevic & Jokić*, Judgement (TC), 17 January 2005.
Prosecutor v. Blaškić, Case No. IT-95-14, Judgement (TC), 3 March 2000.	*Blaškić*, Judgement (TC), 3 March 2000.
Prosecutor v. Erdemović, Case No. IT-96-22, Judgement (TC), 29 November 1996.	*Erdemović*, Judgement (TC), 29 November 1996.
The Prosecutor v. Kambanda, Case No. ICTR-97-23 S, Judgement (TC), 4 September 1998.	*Kambanda*, Judgement (TC), 4 September 1998.
The Prosecutor v. Kambanda, Case No. ICTR-97-23 S, Judgement (AC), 19 October 2000.	*Kambanda*, Judgement (AC), 19 October 2000.
The Prosecutor v. Kayishema, Case No. ICTR-95-1, Judgement (TC), 21 May 1999.	*The Prosecutor v. Kayishema*, Case No. ICTR-95-1, Judgement (TC), 21 May 1999.
The Prosecutor v. Kayishema, Case No. ICTR-95-1 A, Judgement (AC), 1 June 2001.	*Kayishema*, Judgement (AC), 1 June 2001.
Prosecutor v. Kordić, Case No. IT-95-14/2, Judgement (AC), 17 December 2004.	*Kordić*, Case No. IT-95-14/2, Judgement (AC), 17 December 2004.
Prosecutor v. Krnojelać, Case No. IT-97-25, Judgement (TC), 15 March 2002.	*Krnojelać*, Judgement (TC), 15 March 2002.
Prosecutor v. Krnojelać, Case No. IT-97-25, Judgement (AC), 17 September 2003.	*Krnojelać*, Judgement (AC), 17 September 2003.
Prosecutor v. Krstić, Case No. IT-98-33, Judgement (TC), 2 August 2001.	*Krstić*, Judgement (TC), 2 August 2001. **[page 114]**
The Prosecutor v. Mucić, Case No. no IT-96-21, Judgement (TC), 16 November 1996.	*Mucić*, Judgement (TC), 16 November 1996.
The Prosecutor v. Muhimana, Case No. ICTR-95-1, Judgement (TC), 28 April 2005.	*Muhimana*, Judgement (TC), 28 April 2005.
The Prosecutor v. Musema, Case No. ICTR-96-13, Judgement (TC), 27 January 2000.	*Musema*, Judgement (TC), 27 January 2000.

The Prosecutor v. Musema, Case No. ICTR-96-13-T, Judgement (AC), 16 November 2001.	*Musema*, Judgement (AC), 16 November 2001.
The Prosecutor v. Nahimana, Case No. ICTR-99-52 T, Judgement (TC), 3 December 2003.	*Nahimana*, Judgement (TC), 3 December 2003.
The Prosecutor v. Ndindabahizi, Case No. ICTR-2001-71-T, Judgement (TC), 15 July 2004.	*Ndindabahizi*, Judgement (TC), 15 July 2004.
The Prosecutor v. Niyitegeka, Case No. ICTR-96-14, Judgement (TC), 16 May 2003.	*Niyitegeka*, Judgement (TC), 16 May 2003.
The Prosecutor v. Ntagerura, Case No. ICTR-99-46-T, Judgement (TC), 25 February 2004.	*Ntagerura*, Judgement (TC), 25 February 2004.
The Prosecutor v. Ntagerura, Case No. ICTR-99-46 T, Judgement (AC), 7 July 2006.	*Ntagerura*, Judgement (AC), 7 July 2006.
Prosecutor v. Plavšić, Case No. IT-00-39, Judgement (TC), 27 February 2003	*Plavšić*, Judgement (TC), 27 February 2003.
The Prosecutor v. Ruggiu, Case No. ICTR-97-32-I, Judgement (TC), 1 June 2000.	*Ruggiu*, Judgement (TC), 1 June 2000.
The Prosecutor v. Rutaganda, Case No. ICTR-96-3, Judgement (TC), 6 December 1999.	*Rutaganda*, Judgement (TC), 6 December 1999.
The Prosecutor v. Semanza, Case No. ICTR-97-20-T, Judgement (TC), 15 May 2003.	*Semanza*, Judgement (TC), 15 May 2003.
The Prosecutor v. Semanza, Case No. ICTR-97-20-T, Judgement (AC), 20 May 2005.	*Semanza*, Judgement (AC), 20 May 2005.
The Prosecutor v. Serushago, Case No. ICTR-98-39 A, Judgement (TC), 6 April 2000.	*Serushago*, Judgement (TC), 6 April 2000.
The Prosecutor v. Simba, Case No. ICTR-01-76, **[page 115]** Judgement (TC), 13 December 2005. **[page 116]**	*Simba*, Judgement (TC), 13 December 2005.
Prosecutor v. Simić, Case No. IT-95-9/2-S, Judgement (TC), 17 October 2002.	*Simić*, Judgement (TC), 17 October 2002.
Prosecutor v. Tadić, Case No. IT-94-1, Judgement (AC), 15 July 1999.	*Tadić*, Judgement (AC), 15 July 1999.

D. List of decisions and orders

Long form	*Short form*
The Prosecutor v. *Bagosora et al.*, Decision on Motion Concerning Alleged Witness Intimidation (TC), 28 December 2004.	*Bagosora,* Decision on Motion Concerning Alleged Witness Intimidation (TC), 28 December 2004.
The Prosecutor v. Karemera et al., Case No. ICTR-98-44-AR73(C), Decision on Interlocutory Appeal of the Prosecutor's Decision on Judicial Notice (AC), 16 June 2006.	*Karemera,* Decision on Interlocutory Appeal of the Prosecutor's Decision on Judicial Notice (AC), 16 June 2006.

Prosecutor v. Kupreškić, Case No. IT-95-16, Decision on Evidence of the Good Character of the Accused and the Defence of *Tu Quoque* (TC), 17 February 1999.	*Kupreškić*, Decision on Evidence of the Good Character of the Accused and the Defence of *Tu Quoque* (TC), 17 February 1999.
The Prosecutor v. Seromba, Case No. ICTR2001-66-I, Decision on the Prosecutor's *Ex Parte* Request for Search, Seizure, Arrest and Transfer, 3 July 2001.	*Seromba*, Decision on the Prosecutor's *Ex Parte* Request for Search, Seizure, Arrest and Transfer, 3 July 2001.
The Prosecutor v. Seromba, Case No. ICTR2001-66-I, Warrant of Arrest and Order for Transfer, 4 July 2001.	*Seromba*, Warrant of Arrest and Order for Transfer, 4 July 2001.
The Prosecutor v. Seromba, Case No. ICTR2001-66-I, *Décision relative à la requête de la Défense aux fins de voir ordonner l'ouverture d'une enquête sur les circonstances et les courses réelles de retraction du témoins portent le pseudonyme FE36,* 20 April 2006.	*eromba, Décision relative à la requête de la Défense aux pris de voir ordonner l'ouverture dune enquête sur les circonstances et les causes réelles de retraction du témoin portent le pseudonyme FE36,* 20 April 2006.

C. List of Rwandan laws

- *S-Décret-loi du 12 février 1975, Journal Officiel de la République Rwandaise*, 1975.

[page 117]

- Organic Law No. 40/2000 of 26 January 2001 Setting up "Gacaca Jurisdictions" and Organizing Prosecutions for Offences Constituting the Crime of Genocide or Crimes against Humanity committed between October 1, 1990 and December 31, 1994.

D. Other document

- United Nations Report of the International Law Commission on the Work of its Forty-Eighth Session, 6 May to 26 July 1996, General Assembly Official Record, Fifty-First Session, Supplement No. 10, p. 90, (A/51/10) (1996).

E. List of abbreviations

Long form	*Short form*
Association des avocats de la Défense	*ADAD*
Trial Chamber III	Chamber
United Nations Security Council	Security Council
United Nations	UN
Rules of Procedure and Evidence of the International Criminal Tribunal for Rwanda	Rules
Statute of the International Criminal Tribunal for Rwanda	Statute
International Criminal Tribunal for Rwanda	Tribunal
Trial Chamber	TC
Appeals Chamber	AC

[page 118]

ANNEX III: THE INDICTMENT

[page 1] INTERNATIONAL CRIMINAL TRIBUNAL FOR RWANDA

Case No. ICTR-2001-66-1

THE PROSECUTOR

AGAINST

Athanase SEROMBA

INDICTMENT

I. The Prosecutor of the International Criminal Tribunal for Rwanda, pursuant to the authority stipulated in Article 17 of the Statute of the International Criminal Tribunal for Rwanda (the "Statute of the Tribunal") charges.

Athanase SEROMBA

with **GENOCIDE;** or in the alternative **COMPLICITY IN GENOCIDE; CONSPIRACY TO COMMIT GENOCIDE;** and **CRIMES AGAINST HUMANITY** for **EXTERMINATION;** offenses stipulated in Articles 2 and 3 of the Statute of the Tribunal, as set forth below.

II. THE ACCUSED:

Father **Athanase SEROMBA** was born at Rutziro commune, KIBUYE préfectue, Rwanda. He was a catholic priest at the parish of Nyange, located in sector Nyange, KIVUMU commune, KIBUYE préfecture.

III. CHARGES, *including a* CONCISE STATEMENT OF FACTS:

Count 1: GENOCIDE:

The Prosecutor of the International Criminal Tribunal for Rwanda charges **Athanase SEROMBA** with ***GENOCIDE,*** *a crime stipulated in Article 2(3)(a) of the Statute,* in that on or between the dates of 6 April 1994 and 20 April 1994, in KIVUMU commune, KIBUYE *préfecture,* Rwanda Athanase SEROMBA was responsible for killing or causing serious bodily or mental harm to members of the Tutsi population with intent to destroy, in whole or in part, a racial or ethnic group; **[page 2]** *Pursuant to Article 6(1) of the Statue:* by virtue of his affirmative acts in planning, instigating, ordering, committing, or otherwise aiding and abetting the planning, preparation or execution of the crime charged.

Or alternatively
ount 2: COMPLICITY IN GENOCIDE:

The Prosecutor of the International Criminal Tribunal for Rwanda charges Athanase SEROMBA with ***COMPLICITY IN GENOCIDE,*** *a crime stipulated in Article 2(3)(e) of the Statute,* in that on or between the dates of 6 April 1994 and 20 April 1994 in KIVUMU commune, KIBUYE *prefecture,* Rwanda, Athanase SEROMBA was an accomplice to the killing or causing serious bodily or mental harm to members of the Tutsi population with intent to destroy, in whole or in part, a racial or ethnic group.

Pursuant to Article 6(1) of the Statute: by virtue of his affirmative acts in planning, instigating, ordering, committing, or otherwise aiding and abetting the planning, preparation or execution of the crime charged.

Concise statements of facts for Count 1 and Count 2

1. During the events referred to in this indictment, Tutsi, Hutu, and Twa were identified as ethnic or racial groups.
2. KIVUMU is one of the communes of KIBUYE préfecture, Republic of Rwanda. During the events described in this indictment it was a commune with a large concentration of Hutu resident, nearly 50,000 Hutu and only 6000 Tutsi.
3. The Nyange Parish was located in Nyange sector, KIVUMU commune, KIBUYE préfecture. Its Church (Nyange Church) had a seating capacity for 1500 persons.
4. During the events referred to in this indictment, Father Athanase SEROMBA was the parish priest, in charge of the Parish of Nyange.
5. During the events referred to in this indictment, Athanase SEROMBA, a priest responsible for Nyange Parish, Grégoire NDAHIMANA, the *bourgmestre* of KIVUMU commune; Fulgence KAYISHEMA, a police inspector of KIVUMU commune and others not known to the Prosecution, prepared and executed a plan of extermination of the Tutsi population.
6. After the death of the Rwandan President, on 6 April 1994, attacks against the Tutsi began at KIVUMU commune, causing the deaths of some Tutsi civilians, including, Grégoire NDAKUBANA, Martin KARAKEZI and Thomas MWENDEZI.
7. To escape the attacks directed against them, Tutsis from the different sectors of KIVUMU commune, fled their homes to seek refuge in public buildings **[page 3]** and Churches, including the Nyange Church. The *bourgmestre* and communal police gathered and transported the refugees from the different sectors of KIVUMU commune to Nyange Parish.
8. Athanase SEROMBA questioned the refugees transferred to the Parish about those not yet present, then noted the names of the remaining refugees on a list he gave to the bourgmestre Grégoire NDAHIMANA for the purpose of looking for and bringing them to the Parish.
9. A Tutsi named Alexis KARAKE, his wife and his children (more than six) were brought from Gakoma cellule to Nyange Church through that list.
10. On or about 10 April 1994, several important meetings were held at the Parish of Nyange and the communal office. Athanase SEROMBA, Fulgence KAYISHEMA, Gaspard KANYARUKIGA and others not known to the Prosecutor attended these meetings.
11. During the said meetings it was decided to request Kibuye prefecture for gendarmes, to gather all Tutsi civilians of KIVUMU commune at Nyange Church in order to exterminate them.
12. From about 12 April 1994, refugees were confined by the gendarmes and surrounded by the militia and Interahamwe armed with traditional and conventional weapons. Father Athanase SEROMBA did prevent the refugees from taking food and instructed the gendarmes to shoot any "Inyenzi" (reference to Tutsi) who tried to take some food from the *Presbytere* or the Parish banana groves. He refused to celebrate mass for them and stressed that he didn't want to do that for the Inyenzi.
13. On or about 12 April 1994, Father Athanase SEROMBA expelled from the Parish four Tutsi employees (Alex, Félécien, Gasore, and Patrice). He forced them to leave the Parish, while Interahamwe and militia were beginning the attacks against refugees of the Parish.

14. Father Athanase SEROMBA knew that removing the employees would cause their death. In fact, only one (Patrice) of these people was able to return to the Parish, having been gravely wounded, but Athanase SEROMBA prevented him from entering the Church. He was killed by the Interahamwe and the milita.

15. On or about 13 April 1994, the Interahamwe and the militia surrounding the Parish, launched an attack against the refugees in the Church. The refugees defended themselves by pushing the attackers out of the Church, to a place named *"la statue de la Sainte Viérge"*. The attackers in turn, threw a grenade causing many deaths among the refugees. The survivors quickly tried to return to the Church, but Father Athanase SEROMBA ordered that all doors be closed, leaving many refugees (about 30) outside to be killed.

16. On or about 14 April 1994, in the afternoon, Father SEROMBA met Fulgence KAYISHEMA and Gaspard KANYARUKIGA in his Parish Office. Soon afterwards, Fulgence KAYISHEMA went to bring some fuel, using one **[page 4]** of the KIVUMU commune officila vehicles. That fuel was used by the Interahamwe and the militia to burn down the Church, while the gendarmes and members of the communal police launched grenades.

17. On that same day, Athanase SEROMBA chaired a meeting in his Parish Office with Fulgence KAYISHEMA, Grégoire NDAHIMANA, Gaspard KANYARUKIRA and others unknown to the Prosecution. Immediately after this meeting, following a request from the refugees for protection, the *bourgmestre* Grégoire NDAHIMANA replied that this war was caused by the Inyenzi who killed the President.

18. On or about 15 April 1994, a bus transporting armed Interahamwe and a priest named KAYIRANGWA arrived at Nyange Parish, from KIBUYE préfecture. Soon thereafter, father SEROMBA held a meeting with priest KAYIRANGWA, Fulgence KAYISHEMA, KANYARUKIGA and others unknown to the Prosecution.

19. After this meeting, Father Athanase SEROMBA ordered the Interahamwe and the militia to launch attacks to kill the Tutsi, beginning with the intellectuals. Following his orders, an attack was launched against the refugees by the Interahamwe, militia, gendarmes and communal police, armed with traditional weapons and firearms, causing the deaths of numerous refugees.

20. On or about 15 April 1994, in the afternoon, the attacks intensified against the refugees of the Church. The Interahamwe and the militias attacked with traditional arms and poured fuel through the roof of the Church, while gendarmes and communal police launched grenades and killed the refugees.

21. During these attacks, Father SEROMBA handed over to the gendarmes a refugee, a Tutsi teacher named GATARE who was killed immediately. This event encouraged and motived the attackers.

22. Again during these attacks, some refugees left the Church for the *Presbytere*. Father SEROMBA found them and informed gendarmes about their hiding place. Immediately thereafter, they were attacked and killed. Among the victims were two Tutsi women (Alexia and Meriam).

23. Many refugees were killed during these attacks. A bulldozer was used by three employees of Astaldi company (Mitima, Maurice and Flanbeau,) to remove the numerous corpses of the victims from the Church. Two additional drivers were requested from Fulgence KAYISHEMA to complete the removal. One of them, Evarist RWAMASIRABO, who had refused to participate was killed immediately.

24. In the meantime Interahamwe, militias, gendarmes and communal police, continued their attacks but were unable to kill all the refugees in the Church.

25. During the attacks described above, Athanase SEROMBA, Grégoire NDAHIMANA, Fulgence KAYISHEMA, Télesphore NDUNGUTSE, Judge **[page 5]** Joseph HABIYAMBERE, assistant *bourgmestre* Védaste MUPENDE and other authorities not known to the Prosecution, were supervising the massacres.

26. When the corpses of victims were removed from the Church, Védaste MUPENDE ordered the driver (Athanase alias 2000) to demolish the Church. The latter refused since the Church was the house of God.

27. Immediately thereafter, Védaste MUPENDE, Fulgence KAYISHEMA and Grégoire NDAHIMANA requested the intervention of Athanase SEROMBA, who came and ordered Athanase alias 2000 to destroy the Church, telling him that Hutu people were numerous and could build another one.

28. Athanase bulldozed the Church and its roof crashed killing more than 2000 Tutsi refugees gathered inside. The few survivors were attacked by the Interahamwe, anxious to finish them off.

29. On or about 16 April 1994, after the destruction of the Church, the authorities held a meeting in the Parish. Soon after, Father SEROMBA ordered the Interahamwe to clean the "rubbish". The corpses of victims were placed into common graves.

30. The transfer of corpses into common graves took about two days, under the supervision of Athanase SEROMBA, Fulgence KAYISHEMA, Grègoire NDAHIMMANA and others unknown to the Prosecution.

31. After the destruction of the Church, almost all the Tutsi population of KIVUMU was killed, and in July 1994, there was no Tutsi known in KIVUMU commune.

32. Before leaving Rwanda, Athanase SEROMBA embezzled all assets of the Parish, including a car.

Count 3: CONSPIRACY TO COMMIT GENOCIDE:

The Prosecutor of the International Criminal Tribunal for Rwanda charges Athanase SEROMBA with ***CONSPIRACY TO COMMIT GENOCIDE,*** *a crime stipulated in Article 2(3)(b) of the Statute,* in that on or between the dates of 6 April 1994 and 20 April 1994, in KIVUMU *prefecture,* Rwanda, Athanase SEROMBA a priest responsible for Nyange Parish, did agree with Grégoire NDAHIMANA, *bourgmestre* of Kivumu commune, Fulgence KAYISHEMA, a police inspector of Kivumu commune, Télesphore NDUNGUTSE, Gaspard KANYIKURIGA and other persons not known to the Prosecution, to kill or cause serious bodily or mental harm to members of the Tutsi population with the intent to destroy, in whole or in part, a racial or ethnic group;

Pursuant to Article 6(1) of the Statute: by virtue of his affirmative acts in planning, instigating, ordering, committing, or otherwise aiding and abetting the planning, preparation or execution of the crime charged. **[page 6]**

33. Father Athanase SEROMBA, Grégoire NDAHIMANA, Fulgence KAYISHEMA, Télesphore NDUNGUTSE, and Gaspard KANYIKURIGA did agree to kill the Tutsi ethnic group, and established a plan or a common scheme to execute the extermination of Tutsi in KIVUMU commune.

34. They held regular meetings at Nyange Parish and the communal office, between the dates of 6 April 1994 and 20 April 1994. During these meetings, they did agree on a common strategy to kill and exterminate all Tutsi in the KIVUMU commune.

35. This plan was carried out following three main actions. First to force Tutsi civilians of KIVUMU commune to leave their homes and take refuge in Nyange Church. For this purpose between 7 and 10 April 1994 local authorities and members of communal police launched attacks against Tutsi in their houses, resulting in the killing of some civilians, and forcing the survivors to take refuge in Nyange Church.

36. On or about 10 April 1994, several important meetings were held at the Parish of Nyange and the communal office. Athanase SEROMBA, Fulgence KAYISHEMA, Gaspard KANYARUKIGA and other not known to the Prosecution attended these meetings.

37. During these said meetings they decided to request Kibuye prefecture for gendarmes, to gather all Tutsi civilians of Kivumu commune at Nyange Church to exterminate them.

38. On or about 12 April 1994, Father SEROMBA chaired a meeting in his Parish Office with, among others, Grégoire NDAHIMANA, and Fulgence KAYISHEMA. Immediately after this meeting, Fulgence KAYISHEMA said that KAYIRANGA (a prosperous Tutsi businessman) must be found and brougth to the Church.

39. On or about 12 April 1994, the bourgmestre Grégoire NDAHIMANA ordered members of the communal police to search for Tutsi civilians, from the list prepared by Athanase SEROMBA, as described above, and bring them to the Church.

40. The second step of the plan consisted of keeping the refugees inside the Church, surrounding the Church with Interahamwe and militias and inflicting on the refugees conditions of life calculated to weaken them physically. The plan also included regular attacks by Interahamwe and militias against the refugees to defeat their endurance.

41. To this end from about 12 April 1994, the gendarmes confined the refugees at the Nyange Church, which was surrounded by the Interahamwe and the militias.

42. Athanase SEROMBA prevented the refugees from having access to sanitary places in the Parish and from taking food, ordering the gendarmes to shoot any **[page 7]** "Inyenzi" who tried to take food from the *Presbytere* or the banana groves of the Parish.

43. On or about 12 April 1994, in the afternoon, Father Athanase SEROMBA chaired a meeting with Grégoire NDAHIMANA and Fulgence KAYISHEMA. Soon after the *bourgmestre* NDAHIMANA said, *"We choose the richest to be killed, the others can go back to their houses"*.

44. On or about 13 April 1994, Interahamwe and militias surrounding the Parish, launched an attack against the refugees in the Church, killing about 30 refugees.

45. The third and final step of the plan consited in assembling a consistent number of killers, including Hutu civilians, to kill all the refugees. That was done with the demolition of the Church, using a caterpillar Bulldozer with more than 2000 Tutsi civilians trapped inside the Church as described above.

46. The massive attack against the Tutsi refugees was conducted on or about 15 April 1994, under the supervision of Father SEROMBA, Fulgence KAYISHEMA, Grégoire NDAHIMANA, Télesphore NDUNGUTSE, Gaspard KANYIRUKIGA and others unknown to the Prosecution.

47. After the complete destruction of the Church, Father Athanase SEROMBA, met with Fulgence KAYISHEMA, Grégoire NDAHIMANA, Gaspard KANYIRUKIGA and the drivers of the caterpillar bulldozer and sat drinking beer togeter.

Count 4: EXTERMINATION as a CRIME AGAINST HUMANITY.

The Prosecutor of the International Criminal Tribunal for Rwanda charges Athanase SEROMBA with ***EXTERMINATION as a CRIME AGAINST HUMANITY,*** *as stipulated in Article 3(b) of the Statute,* in that on or between the dates of 7 April 1944,and 20 April 1994, in KIBUYE *préfecture,* Rwanda, Athanase SEROMBA was responsible for killing persons, or causing persons to be killed, during mass killing events as part of a widespread or *systematic* attack against a civilian population on political, ethnic or racial grounds, as follows:

Pursuant to Article 6(1) of the Statute: by virtue of his affirmative acts in planning, instigating, ordering, committing or otherwise aiding and abetting the planning, preparation or execution of the crime charged.

48. On or about 13 April 1994, the Interahamwe and the militia surrounding the Parish, launched an attack against the refugees in the Church. The attackers having been pushed away and out of the Church, to a place named *"la statue de la Sainte Vièrge"*. The attackers threw a grenade causing many deaths among the refugees. The survivors quickly tried to return to the Church, but Father

Athanase SEROMBA ordered that all doors be closed, leaving many refugees outside (about 30) to be killed. **[page 8]**

49. On or about 15 April 1994, Father Athanase SEROMBA ordered or planned abetted and encouraged the destruction of the Church with more than 2000 Tutsi trapped inside causing their deaths.

50. After the destruction of the Church, most of the Tutsi from KIVUMU commune were killed, and in July 1994, there was no Tutsi Known in KIVUMU commune.

The acts and omissions of Athanase SEROMBA detailed herein are punishable in reference to Articles 22 and 23 of the Statute of the Tribunal.

Dated in Arusha: this day of 2001

____

Carla Del Ponte
Prosecutor

Commentary

1. Introduction

On 8 June 2001, Athanase Seromba was indicted by the international criminal tribunal for Rwanda (ICTR) under four charges: genocide, complicity in genocide, conspiracy to commit genocide and extermination as a crime against humanity. On 13 December 2006, Trial Chamber III rendered its judgment, finding the accused guilty of aiding and abetting genocide and of extermination as a crime against humanity and sentencing him to fifteen years imprisonment.[1] Although subsequently overruled by the Appeals Chamber, which re-qualified the individual criminal responsibility of the defendant as that of a principal perpetrator rather than as that of an aider and abettor thereby substituting this sentence with life imprisonment,[2] the Trial Chamber's judgment remains noteworthy on a number of points.

Perhaps surprisingly, the first preliminary remarks the Seromba decision calls for go beyond the strict ambit of the law. Rather than constituting yet another decision on the international criminal law front, the case at issue reveals an intriguing storyline, which has as much to do with the sequence of events than with the ambiguous personality of the defendant. The judicial saga which followed the indictment of Athanase Seromba, a priest in Nyange parish in Rwanda, is indeed worth recalling here.

Seromba was indicted by the ICTR prosecutor on 8 June 2001. He surrendered from Italy eight months later, on 6 February 2002. This lapse of time notwithstanding, the Trial Chamber still found that the defendant had voluntarily surrendered to the authorities of the tribunal insofar as 'the arrest warrant issued against him [had not been] executed by the Italian authorities'[3] and thus considered his surrender as a circumstance mitigating punishment,[4] a finding subsequently upheld by the Appeals Chamber.[5] Analyses as to the circumstances and qualification of Seromba's surrender differ and, while Zorzi Giustiniani concurs with the judicial findings, noting that 'Italy refused to hand over the accused to the Tribunal, claiming a lack of a legal basis in Italian legislation to execute the arrest warrant, but on 6 February 2002 Seromba spontaneously turned himself in',[6] Townsend observes that 'Seromba surrendered only when Italian national legislation that would permit his extradition was pending approval. Italy adopted such legislation on 2 August 2002',[7] thus pointing to the fact that his surrender might have been a calculated move rather than a spontaneous effort to cooperate with the ICTR.

This assertion seems to be further corroborated by the events that ensued, which revealed clear signs of obstruction to justice on the part of the defendant. As noted by Venturini, Seromba refused to testify and 'continuously obstructed the proceedings, first suspending his counsel's authorization to represent him, then requesting the disqualification of the judges hearing the trial (request rejected on 25 April 2006) and submitting documents after the designated deadlines'.[8]

The ambiguous personality of the defendant notwithstanding, it must also be recognized – and simultaneously regretted – that the judicial saga did not stop at the issuing of the Trial Chamber's judgment. And indeed, disturbingly, and as noted by several commentators,[9] the decision remained unjustifiably unavailable for over a year, a truly unprecedented situation. Without embarking on irrelevant extrapolations which would

1 ICTR, Judgement, *Procureur v. Seromba*, Case No. ICTR-2001-66-T, T. Ch. III, 13 December 2006, in this volume p. 523.

2 See ICTR, Judgement, *Prosecutor v. Seromba*, Case No. ICTR-2001-66-A, A. Ch., 12 March 2008, to be published in volume XXXI.

3 Judgement, *Prosecutor v. Seromba*, T. Ch. III, *supra* note 1, par. 398.

4 *Ibid.*

5 Judgement, *Prosecutor v. Seromba*, A. Ch., *supra* note 2, par. 236. See G. Townsend, Committing Genocide by Integral-Part Participation: The ICTR Appeals Chamber judgement in Prosecutor v. Seromba, 3 Hague Justice Journal 2008, p. 42-43.

6 F. Zorzi Giustiniani, Stretching the Boundaries of Commission Liability – The ICTR Appeal Judgment in *Seromba*, 6 Journal of International Criminal Justice 2008, p. 784.

7 Here referring to the enactment of Law No. 181 (O.J. No. 190 of 14 August 2002) on judicial assistance and cooperation with the ICTR. G. Townsend, Committing Genocide by Integral Part Participation: The ICTR Appeals Chamber judgement in Prosecutor v. Seromba, *supra* note 5, p. 42-43.

8 G. Venturini, Rwanda's Unanswered Screams: Still seeking justice after the Seromba trial, 28 February 2007, available on The Hague Justice Portal at: http://www.haguejusticeportal.net/eCache/DEF/7/123.html, footnote omitted.

9 See e.g. W. A. Schabas, Seromba Overturned on Appeal, but Where is the Trial Chamber Judgment?, weblog 19 March 2008, available at: http://humanrightsdoctorate.blogspot.com/2008/03 /seromba-overturned-on-appeal-but-where.html

amount to pure speculation, the fact is that the Seromba judgment remained nowhere to be seen for a very long period of time, thereby inspiring both unease and distrust towards international criminal justice. Suffice here to recall Townsend's analysis to easily measure the degree of suspicion that might have been generated by this unexplained absence:

> Gabriella Venturini noted that in 1999, when the London-based non-governmental organisation African Rights publicised the allegations that Seromba committed genocide in Nyange, Rwanda in April 1994 and identified that he was living under a false name in Florence, Italy, the Roman-Catholic Church "immediately [...] reassigned [Seromba] to a different parish." The Church secured residence permits for Seromba under his false name.[10]

Although a resolved matter, the unavailability of the Seromba trial judgment was highly detrimental to the credibility of international criminal justice as it could still be seen as a clear indicator of the powerful links between politics and international criminal justice, a very worrisome observation to say the least. Moving beyond this extra-legal anticipation, these concerns should nonetheless remain at their right place and certainly not be the focus of the present commentary. Yet, an analysis of the judgment reveals that the Trial Chamber might have been rather cursory in reaching its decision, arguably to the benefit of the defendant. And indeed, in its application of international criminal law, it seems that the Trial Chamber might have dealt rather swiftly with the definitions of the crimes for which the defendant stood trial, both in terms of their *actus reus* and of their *mens rea,* and might have ultimately erred in its judicial findings.

This assertion seems to be supported by the subsequent Appeals judgment, which overruled the Trial Chamber's judgment, re-qualified his individual criminal responsibility as that of a principal perpetrator and substituted the initial sentence of fifteen years imprisonment with life imprisonment. The obvious difference in the appreciation of the facts and of the individual criminal responsibility of the defendant as well as in the degree of severity of the punishment unavoidably raises questions as to the application of the law and the coherence of the judicial findings. While it would probably be both misplaced and incorrect to assert that the Trial Chamber here showed complacency for the defendant, the fact still remains that, through the velocity in its consideration of the crimes, the Trial Chamber allowed for a certain degree of vagueness to infiltrate its findings, arguably paving the way for a questionable qualification of the acts committed and a rather lenient form of sentence.

2. An elliptic understanding of the crime of genocide

The authoritative definition of the crime of genocide as encapsulated in Article II of the Genocide Convention,[11] and as reproduced *verbatim* in Article 2 of the ICTR Statute, defines genocide as a series of specific acts, perpetrated against specific groups with the specific intent to bring about the destruction of the given group. And indeed, as explained by the different Chambers of the international criminal tribunals, '[t]he *actus reus* of genocide is found in each of the five acts enumerated in Article 2 paragraph 2 of the Statute'[12] and

> [t]hus, for a crime of genocide to have been committed, it is necessary that one of the acts listed under Article 2(2) of the Statute be committed, that the particular act be committed against a specifically targeted group, it being a national, ethnical, racial or religious group. Consequently, in order to clarify the constitutive elements of the crime of genocide, the Chamber will first state its findings on the acts provided for under

10 G. Townsend, Committing Genocide by Integral-Part Participation: The ICTR Appeals Chamber judgement in Prosecutor v. Seromba, *supra* note 5, p. 42, footnote omitted.

11 Convention for the Prevention and Punishment of the Crime of Genocide, United Nations, 1948. Approved and proposed for signature, ratification or accession by the General Assembly of the United Nations, Resolution 260 A (III) of 9 December 1948 (Entry into force: 12 January 1951).

12 ICTR, Judgement, *Prosecutor v. Gacumbitsi*, Case No. ICTR-2001-64-T, T. Ch. III, 17 June 2004, Klip/ Sluiter, ALC-XVIII-481, par. 251. See also ICTR, Judgement, *Prosecutor v. Kayishema and Ruzindana*, Case No. ICTR-95-1-T, T. Ch. II, 21 May 1999, Klip/ Sluiter, ALC-II-555, par. 100; ICTR, Judgement and Sentence, *Prosecutor v. Semanza*, Case No. ICTR-97-20-T, T. Ch. III, 15 May 2003, Klip/ Sluiter, ALC-XII-599, par. 318; ICTR, Judgment and Sentence, *Prosecutor v. Kajelijeli*, Case No. 98-44A-T, T. Ch. II, 1 December 2003, Klip/ Sluiter, ALC-XVII-27, Judgment and Sentence, par. 812; ICTR, Judgment and Sentence, *Prosecutor v. Kamuhanda*, Case No. ICTR-95-54A-T, T. Ch. II, 22 January 2004, Klip/ Sluiter, ALC-XVII-531, par. 631.

> Article 2(2)(a) through Article 2(2)(e) of the Statute, the groups protected by the Genocide Convention, and the special intent or *dolus specialis* necessary for genocide to take place.[13]

In other words, so as to find the accused guilty of genocide, the Trial Chamber had to establish that both the *actus reus* and the *mens rea* of the crime of genocide were met and ultimately found the defendant guilty of having aided and abetted the commission of two different genocidal acts namely, the act of causing serious bodily or mental harm to members of the Tutsi ethnic group as well as the act of killing members of the Tutsi group.

2.1. A laconic approach to the genocidal *actus reus*

2.1.1. Causing serious bodily or mental harm to members of the group

The act of 'causing serious bodily or mental harm to members of the group', as listed in the exhaustive enumeration of prohibited acts in Article 2 of the ICTR Statute,[14] has been subject to jurisprudential elaboration, if only because the Statute – just like the Genocide Convention itself – fails to provide for a definition of this act. Several cases – which, interestingly, the Trial Chamber fails to mention here – have accordingly addressed the issue and have tried to draw a definition of this admittedly vague category of acts, which seems to cover a whole series of non fatal acts.[15] It was notably specified that:

> The serious bodily or mental harm [...] can be informed by the Tribunal's interpretation of the offence of wilfully causing great suffering or serious injury to body or health under Article 2 of the Statute. The latter offence was defined in the *Celebici* Judgement as "an act or omission that is intentional, being an act which, judged objectively, is deliberate and not accidental, which causes serious mental or physical suffering or injury".[16]

And that:

> serious harm need not cause permanent and irremediable harm, but it must involve harm that goes beyond temporary unhappiness, embarrassment or humiliation. It must be harm that results in a grave and long-term disadvantage to a person's ability to lead a normal and constructive life. In subscribing to the above case-law, the Chamber holds that inhuman treatment, torture, rape, sexual abuse and deportation are among the acts which may cause serious bodily or mental injury.[17]

Rather interestingly, the ICTR and its Yugoslav counterpart have both used the vagueness of this notion to interpret and define it in such a way that it now undoubtedly encompasses acts which were initially not covered by the conventional scope of application. And indeed, based on the double predicament that both 'serious bodily harm' and 'serious mental harm' are 'not defined in the Statute'[18] and that the act of '[c]ausing serious bodily or mental harm to members of the group does not necessarily mean that the harm is permanent and irremediable',[19] it has been recognized that it includes acts of bodily or mental torture,[20] inhumane or

---

13 ICTR, Judgement, *Prosecutor v. Akayesu*, Case No. ICTR-96-4-T, T. Ch. I, 2 September 1998, Klip/ Sluiter, ALC-II-399, par. 499.

14 Here reproducing verbatim Article 2 of the Genocide Convention.

15 See e.g. ICTR, Judgement and Sentence, *Prosecutor v. Semanza*, Case No. ICTR-97-20-T, T. Ch. III, 15 May 2003, Klip/ Sluiter, ALC-XII-599, par. 320; ICTR, Judgement and Sentence, *Prosecutor v. Ntagerura, Bagambiki and Imanishimwe*, Case No. ICTR-99-46-T, T. Ch. III, 25 February 2004, Klip/ Sluiter, ALC-XVIII-267, par. 664.

16 ICTY, Judgement, *Prosecutor v. Krstić*, Case No. IT-98-33-T, T. Ch. I, 2 August 2001, Klip/ Sluiter, ALC-VII-575, par. 484, footnote omitted.

17 *Ibid.*, at par. 486, footnote omitted.

18 Judgement and Sentence, *Prosecutor v. Semanza*, T. Ch. III, *supra* note 15, par. 320-321. In this respect, the ICTR Appeals Chamber expressly referred to the '*quintessential examples* of serious bodily harm are torture, rape, and non-fatal physical violence that causes disfigurement or serious injury to the external or internal organs. Judgement, *Prosecutor v. Seromba*, A. Ch., *supra* note 2, par. 46. Emphasis added.

19 Judgement, *Prosecutor v. Akayesu*, T. Ch. I, *supra* note 13, par. 502; Judgement, *Prosecutor v. Kayishema and Ruzindana*, T. Ch. II, *supra* note 12, par. 110; ICTR, Judgement and Sentence, *Prosecutor v. Rutaganda*, Case No. ICTR-96-3-T, T. Ch. I, 6 December 1999, Klip/ Sluiter, ALC-II-709, par. 51; ICTR, Judgement and Sentence, *Prosecutor v. Musema*, Case No. ICTR-96-13-T, T. Ch. I, 27 January 2000, Klip/ Sluiter, ALC-VI-469, par. 156, ICTR, Judgement, *Prosecutor v. Bagilishema*, Case No. ICTR-95-1A-T, T. Ch. I, 7 June 2001, Klip/ Sluiter, ALC-X-617, par. 59; Judgement and Sentence, *Prosecutor v. Semanza*, T. Ch. III, *supra* note 15, par. 320-322; ICTY, Judgement, *Prosecutor v. Stakić*, Case No. IT-97-24-T, T. Ch. II, 31 July 2003, Klip/ Sluiter, ALC-XIV-545, par. 516; Judgment and Sentence, *Prosecutor v. Kajelijeli*, T. Ch. II, *supra* note 12, par. 815.

20 ICTR, Judgement and Sentence, *Prosecutor v. Muhimana*, Case No. ICTR-95-1B-T, T. Ch. III, 28 April 2005, Klip/ Sluiter, ALC-XXII-413, par. 502.

degrading treatment, cruel treatment,[21] persecution,[22] deportation,[23] rape[24] and sexual violence,[25] mutilations and interrogations combined with beatings, and/or threats of death.[26] As a matter of fact, in the Seromba case, the Appeals Chamber further noted that 'nearly all convictions for the causing of serious bodily or mental harm involve rapes or killings'.[27] Not only do such acts fall outside the express enumeration provided by the Genocide Convention – and the Statutes of the international criminal tribunals – but the international criminal tribunals have also specified that the conventional list remains purely illustrative.[28]

With respect to 'causing serious bodily harm' more specifically, the ICTR seems to have been satisfied with the preconceived idea that this act was, to a large extent, 'self-explanatory. This phrase could be construed to mean harm that seriously injures the health, causes disfigurement or causes any serious injury to the external, internal organs or senses'.[29] Encouraged by this rather wide understanding of this genocidal act, constant case law now considers that '[t]he phrase serious bodily harm should be determined on a case-by-case basis, using a common sense approach'.[30]

Adopting a similar case-by-case approach in its determination of the act of 'causing serious mental harm', the ICTR was able to move beyond the initial understanding of the act, which originally only covered harm caused by the use of narcotics. As explained by Robinson, 'a study, tracing the history and giving a lucid interpretation of the Convention and its various articles, [...] would have made absolutely clear that 'mental harm', within the meaning of the Convention, can be caused only by the use of narcotics'.[31] According to Bryant, mental harm includes 'anything from racial or ethnic slurs by individuals directed at members of a group, to an overt pattern of governmental discrimination or harassment of a group, to deliberate debilitation and demoralization of a group through the use of addictive narcotic drugs'.[32] Although the ICTR expressly recognized that '[r]eference to serious mental harm, in the context of the Genocide Convention, appears to have been restricted originally to the injection of pharmacological substances occasioning the serious impairment of mental faculties',[33] it nonetheless opted for a case-by-case determination of serious mental harm[34] and remained rather vague in its delimitation of the notion, finding that 'serious mental harm can be construed as some type of impairment of mental faculties, or harm that causes serious injury to the mental state of the victim.'[35] Here also giving an illustrative list of acts, the ICTR found that 'serious mental harm' included such acts as the infliction of strong fear or terror, intimidation or threat.[36]

---

21 ICTY, Review of the Indictments Pursuant to Rule 61 of the Rules of Procedure and Evidence, *Prosecutor v. Karadžić and Mladić*, Case Nos. T-95-5-R61, IT-95-18-R61, T. Ch. I, 11 July 1996, Klip/ Sluiter, ALC-I-679, par. 93.

22 Judgement, *Prosecutor v. Akayesu*, T. Ch. I, *supra* note 13, par. 504. See also Judgement and Sentence, *Prosecutor v. Rutaganda*, T. Ch. I, *supra* note 19, par. 51.

23 Review of the Indictments Pursuant to Rule 61 of the Rules of Procedure and Evidence, *Prosecutor v. Karadžić and Mladić*, T. Ch. I, *supra* note 21, par. 93.

24 *Ibid.*

25 Judgement and Sentence, *Prosecutor v. Muhimana*, T. Ch. III, *supra* note 20, par. 502.

26 See notably Judgement, *Prosecutor v. Akayesu*, T. Ch. I, *supra* note 13, par. 706-707 and 711-712. See also Judgement, *Prosecutor v. Kayishema and Ruzindana*, T. Ch. II, *supra* note 12, par. 108; Judgement, *Prosecutor v. Stakić*, T. Ch. II, *supra* note 19, par. 516; Judgment and Sentence, *Prosecutor v. Kajelijeli*, T. Ch. II, *supra* note 12, par. 815.

27 Judgement, *Prosecutor v. Seromba*, A. Ch., *supra* note 2, par. 46.

28 Judgement, *Prosecutor v. Akayesu*, T. Ch. I, *supra* note 13, par. 502; Judgement, *Prosecutor v. Kayishema and Ruzindana*, T. Ch. II, *supra* note 12, par. 110; Judgement and Sentence, *Prosecutor v. Rutaganda*, T. Ch. I, *supra* note 19, par. 51; Judgement and Sentence, *Prosecutor v. Musema*, T. Ch. I, *supra* note 19, par. 156; Judgement and Sentence, *Prosecutor v. Semanza*, T. Ch. III, *supra* note 15, par. 320-321; Judgement, *Prosecutor v. Seromba*, T. Ch. III, *supra* note 1, par. 317.

29 Judgement, *Prosecutor v. Kayishema and Ruzindana*, T. Ch. II, *supra* note 12, par. 109. See also Judgement and Sentence, *Prosecutor v. Semanza*, T. Ch. III, *supra* note 15, par. 320. Judgement and Sentence, *Prosecutor v. Ntagerura, Bagambiki and Imanishimwe*, T. Ch. III, *supra* note 15, par. 664; Judgement, *Prosecutor v. Seromba*, T. Ch. III, *supra* note 1, par. 317.

30 See e.g. Judgement, *Prosecutor v. Kayishema and Ruzindana*, T. Ch. II, *supra* note 13, par. 108; Judgment and Sentence, *Prosecutor v. Kajelijeli*, T. Ch. II, *supra* note 12, par. 815.

31 N. Robinson, The Genocide Convention – A Commentary, New York: Institute of Jewish Affairs, 1960, p. ix.

32 B. Bryant, Substantive Scope of the Convention, 16 Harvard International Law Journal 1975, p. 693.

33 Judgement, *Prosecutor v. Akayesu*, T. Ch. I, *supra* note 15, par. 502.

34 Judgement, *Prosecutor v. Kayishema and Ruzindana*, T. Ch. II, *supra* note 12, par. 110 and 113.

35 Judgement, *Prosecutor v. Gacumbitsi*, Case No. ICTR-2001-64-T, T. Ch. III, *supra* note 12, par. 291, footnote omitted. See also Judgement and Sentence, *Prosecutor v. Muhimana*, T. Ch. III, *supra* note 20, par. 502.

36 Judgement, *Prosecutor v. Kayishema and Ruzindana*, T. Ch. II, *supra* note 12, par. 110; Judgement and Sentence, *Prosecutor v. Semanza*, T. Ch. III, *supra* note 15, par. 321; Judgement, *Prosecutor v. Seromba*, A. Ch., *supra* note 2, par. 46.

Although arguably keeping in line with these findings in its Seromba decision, the Trial Chamber interestingly made hardly any mention of these valid precedents and generally refrained from referring to earlier case law, merely asserting that

> It is the Chamber's opinion that Seromba's order prohibiting refugees from getting food from the banana plantation, his refusal to celebrate mass in Nyange church, and his decision to expel employees and Tutsi refugees from the parish and the presbytery facilitated the perpetration of acts causing serious mental harm to the Tutsi refugees in Nyange church. Indeed, the Chamber considers that when the Tutsi sought refuge in Nyange church, they were very vulnerable, having previously been the target of numerous attacks. Furthermore, Nyange church, where the refugees had sought refuge and thought they could be protected from the attacks, had been surrounded by militiamen and *Interahamwe* since 12 April 1994. It would therefore appear that the refugees in Nyange church lived in a constant state of anxiety, inasmuch as they knew that their lives, and those of relatives were under constant threat. The Chamber is convinced that by adopting such a line of conduct, Seromba contributed substantially to the commission of acts causing serious mental harm to Tutsi refugees in Nyange church.[37]
>
> The Chamber also finds that the order by Athanase Seromba prohibiting refugees from getting food from the banana plantation facilitated the perpetration of acts causing serious bodily harm to the refugees. Indeed, on 14 April 1994, the refugees lacked food and had very limited access to basic foodstuffs from the outside, due to the encirclement of the church. Under such circumstances, Seromba's refusal to allow the refugees to get food from the banana plantation substantially contributed to their physical weakening, as they were deprived of food. The Chamber is satisfied that by his conduct, Seromba substantially contributed towards the commission of acts causing serious bodily harm to the Tutsi refugees in Nyange church.[38]

Based on this purely factual reasoning, the Trial Chamber succinctly concluded that:

> In the light of the foregoing, the Chamber finds that the *actus reus* of the assistance provided by the Accused in the commission of acts causing serious bodily or mental harm to refugees in Nyange church has been proved beyond a reasonable doubt.[39]

This lack of jurisprudential support in the Seromba judgment is all the more questionable in light of the fact that, as mentioned earlier, neither the Genocide Convention nor the ICTR Statute provide for a clear definition of what is covered by the act of 'causing serious bodily or mental harm', thus prompting the international criminal tribunals – including the ICTR Trial Chamber in the present case - to themselves define the notion and to arguably include within the definitional scope of the crime of genocide acts which had not been contemplated by the drafters of the Genocide Convention. While it is not the purpose here to discuss the validity of such jurisprudential construction, potentially problematic from a legality perspective, the observation may still be made that, in engaging with such activism, the Seromba Trial Chamber should have cautiously supported its findings, notably by reference to earlier case law. This is all the more surprising considering that the international criminal tribunals generally motivate their decisions by express reference to supporting judicial precedents. While the above mentioned findings do indicate that, faced with conventional and statutory silence, the international criminal tribunals have read the act of 'causing serious bodily or mental harm' in an extensive fashion, they simultaneously reveal that, in doing so, the tribunals have proved reasonable and realistic and have clearly refrained from unduly stretching and trivializing the crime's definitional scope. In other words, what remains truly questionable in the Seromba trial judgment is not so much the qualification of the acts as 'causing serious bodily or mental harm' than the absence of legal reasoning and motivation.

This lack of judicial rigour shown by the Seromba Trial Chamber was severely addressed by the Appeals Chamber which unequivocally noted 'that the Trial Chamber did not clearly differentiate the *actus reus* of the underlying crime and the *actus reus* for aiding and abetting that crime'[40] and expressly qualified the Trial Chamber's statements as 'vague'.[41] It further observed that:

> The Trial Chamber failed to define the underlying crime to which Athanase Seromba's actions supposedly contributed. It also had a duty to marshal evidence regarding the existence of the underlying crime that

37 Judgement, *Prosecutor v. Seromba*, T. Ch. III, *supra* note 1, par. 326, footnote omitted.
38 *Ibid.*, par. 327.
39 *Ibid.*, par. 328.
40 Judgement, *Prosecutor v. Seromba*, A. Ch., *supra* note 2, par. 47.
41 *Ibid.*

> caused serious bodily or mental harm, and its *parsimonious statements* fail to do so. In the absence of such evidence, the Appeals Chamber cannot equate *nebulous invocations* of "weakening" and "anxiety" with the heinous crimes that obviously constitute serious bodily or mental harm, such as rape and torture.[42]

As a result, the Appeals Chamber found that 'the Trial Chamber failed to establish with sufficient precision the crime of "causing serious bodily or mental harm"; therefore, Athanase Seromba's conviction for aiding and abetting such a crime cannot stand.'[43] It accordingly unanimously quashed 'the Trial Chamber's finding that Athanase Seromba aided and abetted genocide by substantially contributing to the causing of serious bodily or mental harm by prohibiting the Tutsi refugees from getting food from the Nyange Parish's banana plantation and by refusing to celebrate mass for them'[44] and held, by majority, that 'Athanase Seromba committed genocide as well as extermination as a crime against humanity, by virtue of his role in the destruction of the church in Nyange Parish'.[45]

2.1.2. Killing members of the group

The other genocidal act Athanase Seromba was found guilty of aiding and abetting by the Trial Chamber is the act of 'killing members of the group'. Although seemingly clear and straightforward, the inclusion of the act of 'killing' within the restrictive list of genocidal acts did raise some definitional and interpretative questions. And indeed, as explained by Quigley, '[t]he term "killing" reads oddly in this context. "Killing" is not a term ordinarily used to define crime in English-speaking countries, since it implies no culpability. A killing can be accidental, or in self-defense.'[46] This 'oddity' was further reinforced by the fact that the French version of the Genocide Convention refers to '*meurtre*', a penal qualification requiring culpability, which does not apply to non-culpable homicide. In its groundbreaking Akayesu decision, Trial Chamber I of the ICTR addressed the matter by concurring with the French version of the text:

> With regard to Article 2(2)(a) of the Statute, like in the Genocide Convention, the Chamber notes that the said paragraph states *"meurtre"* in the French version while the English version states "killing". The Trial Chamber is of the opinion that the term "killing" used in the English version is too general, since it could very well include both intentional and unintentional homicides, whereas the term *"meurtre"*, used in the French version, is more precise. It is accepted that there is murder when death has been caused with the intention to do so, as provided for, incidentally, in the Penal Code of Rwanda which stipulates in its Article 311 that "Homicide committed with intent to cause death shall be treated as murder".[47]

This jurisprudential choice in favour of the French terminology was subsequently confirmed by the Kayishema and Ruzindana Trial Chamber, which, after noting that the 'French language version refers to *meurtre,* a term that requires the additional mental element of intent',[48] observed that

> the *Akayesu* Judgement does not fully define the term "killing." It is the opinion of the Trial Chamber that there is virtually no difference between the term "killing" in the English version and *"meurtre"* in the French version of Article 2 (2)(a) of the Statute within the context of genocidal intent. Hence "killing" or "meurtre" should be considered along with the specific intent of genocide, that is, the intent to destroy in whole or in part, a national, ethnical, racial or religious group as such.[49]

This judicial interpretation of the genocidal act of 'killing' since became constant jurisprudence[50] and, although it does overcome the linguistic obstacle by bringing a welcomed harmonization between the two versions of the Genocide Convention, it does however fail to ensure a clear and precise definition of the proscribed act. In the Musema case, Trial Chamber I of the ICTR succinctly defined 'killing' as 'homicide

---

42 *Ibid.*, par. 48. Emphasis added.

43 *Ibid.*, par. 49.

44 *Ibid.*, par. 240. See also par. 66.

45 *Ibid.*

46 J. Quigley, The Genocide Convention: An International Law Analysis, Ashgate Publishing, Aldershot 2007, p. 94.

47 Judgement, *Prosecutor v. Akayesu*, T. Ch. I, *supra* note 13, par. 500. See also Judgement and Sentence, *Prosecutor v. Rutaganda*, T. Ch. I, *supra* note 19, par. 50; Judgement and Sentence, *Prosecutor v. Musema*, T. Ch. I, *supra* note 19, par. 155; Judgement, *Prosecutor v. Bagilishema*, T. Ch. I, *supra* note 19, par. 57.

48 Judgement, *Prosecutor v. Kayishema and Ruzindana*, T. Ch. II, *supra* note 12, par. 101.

49 *Ibid.*, par. 104, footnote omitted.

50 See e.g. Judgement, *Prosecutor v. Bagilishema*, T. Ch. I, *supra* note 19, par. 58.

committed with intent to cause death'[51] while, on several occasions, Trial Chambers II and III of the ICTR, supported by Trial Chamber III of the ICTY, were merely satisfied with the presupposition that '"Killing" in sub a needs no further explanation. As regards the underlying acts, the word "killing" is understood to refer to intentional but not necessarily premeditated acts.'[52] In other words,

> In order to be held criminally liable for genocide by killing members of a group, in addition to showing that an accused possessed an intent to destroy the group as such, in whole or in part, the Prosecutor must show the following elements: (1) the perpetrator intentionally killed one or more members of the group, without the necessity of premeditation; and (2) such victim or victims belonged to the targeted ethnical, racial, national, or religious group.[53]

The conventional lack of definition notwithstanding, the international criminal tribunals have, here also, refrained from any abusive interpretation and have very much remained within the spirit of the conventional text. As the above judicial findings highlight, they have proceeded to a strict but reasonable reading of the act of 'killing members of the group' and have clearly explained their reasoning... a far cry from the Seromba Trial Chamber, which, although arguably not departing from earlier case law, simply asserted that 'the Accused had committed the *actus reus* of aiding and abetting killing of refugees in Nyange church',[54] and failed to fully review previous supporting case law. In spite of the fact that this lack of judicial motivation was not commented upon on appeals, it is still to be regretted here as the Trial Chamber probably missed an opportunity to clarify both its reasoning and the act of 'killing members of the group' itself.

2.2. A negative approach to the genocidal *mens rea*

As specified earlier, the conventionally prohibited acts will only be characterized as genocidal if, and only if, perpetrated with the 'intent to destroy, in whole or in part, a national, ethnical, racial or religious group, as such'.[55] In strictly all their consideration of the crime of genocide, the international criminal tribunals have consistently put the emphasis on this specific genocidal intent, without which the criminal act will simply not be considered as constitutive of genocide.[56]

According to constant case law however, genocidal intent needs to be proven only when individual criminal responsibility is incurred for having committed or instigated the crime of genocide: with respect to aiding and abetting, the criminal *mens rea* lies in the knowledge of the principal perpetrator's genocidal intent. As expressed by the ICTY Appeals Chamber in the Blaškić case, 'knowledge on the part of the aider and abettor that his acts assist in the commission of the principal perpetrator's crime suffices for the *mens rea* requirement of this mode of participation'.[57]

As the Trial Chamber here based its decision on the presupposition that 'Accused Athanase Seromba [could] incur criminal responsibility only for his participation by aiding and abetting in the offences for which he may be convicted',[58] there was admittedly no need for it to assess the existence of the genocidal intent. Yet, it may still be regretted that, once again, the Trial Chamber failed to support its findings by reference to relevant judicial precedents. This may have indirectly contributed to the requalification of Seromba's criminal responsibility on appeal, when the presupposition of the Trial Chamber was quashed as the Appeals Chamber found that the role of the defendant in the destruction of the church in Nyange parish was that of a principal perpetrator:

> The Appeals Chamber observes, Judge Liu dissenting, that Athanase Seromba's conduct was not limited to giving practical assistance, encouragement or moral support to the principal perpetrators of the crime,

[51] Judgement and Sentence, *Prosecutor v. Musema*, T. Ch. I, *supra* note 19, par. 155. See Judgement, *Prosecutor v. Seromba*, T. Ch. III, *supra* note 1, par. 317.

[52] See Judgement, *Prosecutor v. Stakić*, T. Ch. II, *supra* note 19, par. 515. See also Judgment and Sentence, *Prosecutor v. Kamuhanda*, T. Ch. II, *supra* note 12, par. 632; Judgement and Sentence, *Prosecutor v. Ntagerura, Bagambiki and Imanishimwe*, T. Ch. III, *supra* note 15, par. 664.

[53] Judgement and Sentence, *Prosecutor v. Semanza*, T. Ch. III, *supra* note 15, par. 319. Footnotes omitted. See also Judgment and Sentence, *Prosecutor v. Kajelijeli*, T. Ch. II, *supra* note 12, par. 813.

[54] Judgement, *Prosecutor v. Seromba*, T. Ch. III, *supra* note 1, par. 335.

[55] Article 2 of the Genocide Convention.

[56] See e.g. Judgement, *Prosecutor v. Akayesu*, T. Ch. I, *supra* note 13, par. 499.

[57] ICTR, Judgement, *Prosecutor v. Blaškić*, Case No. IT-95-14-A, A. Ch., 29 July 2004, Klip/ Sluiter, ALC-XX-295, par. 49.

[58] Judgement, *Prosecutor v. Seromba*, T. Ch. III, *supra* note 1, par. 311.

> which would merely constitute the *actus reus* of aiding and abetting. Quite the contrary, the findings of the Trial Chamber allow for only one conclusion, namely, that Athanase Seromba was a principal perpetrator in the killing of the refugees in Nyange church. The Appeals Chamber therefore finds that Athanase Seromba's conduct can only be characterized as "committing" these crimes.[59]

While an analysis of the Appeals Judgment falls beyond the scope of the present commentary, it may still be observed that this rather unexpected reevaluation of the facts of the case and of the evidence presented – arguably prompted by the vagueness of the Trial Chamber – raises some serious questions as to the role of the Appeals Chamber. As pointed out by Zorzi Giustiniani,

> The Appeals Chamber's approach to reviewing the evidence in Seromba is also unconvincing. In applying the correct legal standard to the facts of the case, the Appeals Chamber supplemented the Trial Chamber's findings with the testimony of witnesses on the sole basis that the Trial Chamber considered them credible. The Appeals Chamber had previously decided, in Blaškić, that after having established an error of law it will apply the correct legal standard to the case at hand. Yet, the application of this approach to the present case shows the dangers inherent when the Appeals Chamber assumes the role of a trier of fact.
>
> [...]
>
> This way of proceeding also raises the question of how far the Appeals Chamber can go in revaluating the evidence without applying the standard of review applicable to errors of fact. The applicability of such a standard to the present case was implicitly supported by the dissenting Judge Liu, who, referring to the jurisprudence on errors of fact, affirmed that the Appeals Chamber may substitute its own finding for that of the Trial Chamber only where the evidence relied upon by the latter could not have been accepted by any reasonable tribunal of fact or where the evaluation of the evidence is 'wholly erroneous'.[60]

The role played by the Appeals Chamber in this case and the reasons behind it put aside, what is perhaps more noteworthy here is the fact that the Trial Chamber unexpectedly resorted to a negative formula, thus contenting itself with the finding that the defendant 'could not have been unaware' of the consequences of his acts. With respect to the act of 'causing serious bodily or mental harm', the Trial Chamber indeed held that

> The Chamber is convinced that Athanase Seromba could not have been unaware that his prohibition of refugees from getting food from the banana plantation, his refusal to celebrate mass for them and the expulsion of employees and Tutsi refugees would certainly have a negative impact on the morale of the refugees who were faced with an extremely difficult situation related to the persecutions which they had been suffering during the events of April 1994.[61]

Similarly, for the act of 'killing members of the group', it found that:

> Furthermore, the Chamber is of the view that Athanase Seromba could not have been unaware of the legitimising effect that his words would have on the actions of the communal authorities and the bulldozer driver. The Chamber is also of the view that Seromba knew perfectly well that his approval of the decision by the authorities to destroy Nyange church and his words of encouragement to the bulldozer driver would contribute substantially towards the destruction of the church and the death of the numerous refugees trapped inside.[62]

As explained by Venturini, an

> element that may raise some doubts is the qualification of the *mens rea* by the Chamber. While the judgment repeatedly explains that the accused was perfectly aware that his behavior would substantially contribute to the commission of homicides and extermination, his knowledge of the principal perpetrators' specific genocidal intent is merely deduced by a negative statement ("he could not have ignored"). A positive assessment would have been more persuasive.[63]

59 Judgement, *Prosecutor v. Seromba*, A. Ch., *supra* note 2, par.172, Footnote omitted.

60 F. Zorzi Giustiniani, Stretching the Boundaries of Commission Liability – The ICTR Appeal Judgment in *Seromba*, 6 Journal of International Criminal Justice 2008, p. 796, footnotes omitted.

61 Judgement, *Prosecutor v. Seromba*, T. Ch. III, *supra* note 1, par. 329.

62 *Ibid.*, par. 337.

63 G. Venturini, Rwanda's Unanswered Screams: Still seeking justice after the Seromba trial, 28 February 2007, available on The Hague Justice Portal at: http://www.haguejusticeportal.net/eCache/DEF/7/123.html

And indeed, while it is admitted here that the *mens rea* of an aider and abettor differs from that of a principal perpetrator, it still seems that the mere assertion that the defendant could not have been unaware of the situation stands in too sharp a contrast with the specific intent required to qualify a crime as genocide. The lack of motivation and judicial reasoning on the part of the Seromba Trial Chamber, coupled with the nebulous negative statement as to the *mens rea,* not only seems at odds with constant case law, it also holds the risk of ultimately trivializing the crime of genocide. It could indeed set up an extremely dangerous precedent according to which aiding and abetting the commission of one of the most serious international crimes, labeled the 'crime of crimes' by the ICTR itself,[64] could become a more ordinary offence, constituted when individuals 'could not have been unaware' of the fact that their acts assisted in the commission of genocide.

3. The enigmatic distinction between genocide and extermination as a crime against humanity

Athanase Seromba also stood accused of having aided and abetted extermination as a crime against humanity and it seems fair to assert that the Seromba Trial Chamber's reasoning is here far less enigmatic. The Trial Chamber indeed referred to earlier relevant case law so as to qualify the facts and establish the responsibility of the defendant. It clearly assessed the existence of the constitutive elements of crimes against humanity, reviewing the characteristics of the attack as either widespread or systematic[65] and as directed against a civilian population.[66]

Yet, it seems equally fair to assert that the Seromba Trial Chamber failed to enter into great detail and, although it did motivate its findings, its reasoning would have benefited from further development. As noted by Singh,

> In the *Seromba* Trial Chamber judgment, the court cites *Akayesu's* definition of civilian population and does not cite any ICTY authority. Seemingly, the Court continues the unbroken chain created by the *Akayesu* Trial Chamber, while not acknowledging the *Bisengimana* Trial Chamber's attempt to extend the definition of civilian population even further than the *Akayesu* Trial Chamber and its progeny.[67]

The fact that the Seromba Trial Chamber kept in line with the Akayesu judgment is not in itself questionable. What might be more problematic here is the lack of discussion and of engagement with previous case law. The swift judicial elaboration on extermination as a crime against humanity is to be regretted as the Trial Chamber arguably here missed an opportunity to clarify the law on one of the gravest international crimes. This regret becomes even more acute in light of the decision reached by the Trial Chamber which, after having qualified the destruction of the Nyange church as genocide,[68] subsequently characterized it as extermination as a crime against humanity.

It may indeed legitimately be questioned why the Trial Chamber qualified the exact same facts as constitutive of both genocide and extermination as a crime against humanity, a double characterization which becomes close to absurd when one compares the following finding of the Trial Chamber:

> With respect to paragraphs 26 and 27 of the Indictment, the Chamber finds that Athanase Seromba held discussions with the communal authorities and accepted their decision to destroy the church. The Chamber also concludes that Seromba spoke with the bulldozer driver and said certain words to him which encouraged him to destroy the church. Lastly, the Chamber finds that Seromba even gave advice to the bulldozer driver as to the fragile side of the church building. The Chamber is satisfied that by adopting such a line of conduct, Seromba substantially contributed to the destruction of the Nyange church, causing the death of more than 1,500 Tutsi refugees.[69]

---

64 ICTR, Judgement and Sentence, *Prosecutor v. Kambanda*, Case No. ICTR-97-23-5, T. Ch. I, 4 September 1998, Klip/ Sluiter, ALC-II-793, par. 16; ICTR, Sentence, *Prosecutor v. Serushago*, Case No. ICTR-98-39-5, T. Ch. I, 5 February 1999, Klip/ Sluiter, ALC-II-823, par. 15.

65 Judgement, *Prosecutor v. Seromba*, T. Ch. III, *supra* note 1, par. 356

66 *Ibid.*, par. 358.

67 H. Singh, Critique of the Mrkšić Trial Chamber (ICTY) Judgment: A re-evaluation on Whether Soldiers *Hors de Combat* Are Entitled to Recognition as Victims of Crimes Against Humanity, 8 The Law and Practice of International Courts and Tribunals 2009, p. 271, footnote omitted.

68 Judgement, *Prosecutor v. Seromba*, T. Ch. III, *supra* note 1, par. 340.

69 *Ibid.*, par. 334, footnote omitted.

> In view of the foregoing, the Chamber is satisfied beyond a reasonable doubt that the Accused had committed the *actus reus* of aiding and abetting killing of refugees in Nyange church.[70]

With this subsequent finding:

> With respect to paragraph 49 of the Indictment, the Trial Chamber finds that Athanase Seromba held discussions with the authorities and accepted their decision to destroy the church. The Chamber further found that Seromba also discussed with the bulldozer driver and said words which encouraged him to destroy the church. The Chamber finally found that Seromba even gave advice to the bulldozer driver concerning the fragile side of the church. The Chamber is satisfied that by his conduct, Seromba substantially contributed to the destruction of Nyange church.[71]
>
> The Chamber is of the view that the destruction of the church, which resulted in the death of 1,500 Tutsi refugees, constitutes the crime of extermination within the meaning of Article 3 of the Statute.[72]

This confusion is all the more to be regretted as it somehow spoils the other parts of the decision and notably the findings of the Trial Chamber on the defendant's responsibility for having aided and abetted extermination as a crime against humanity, findings which were however clear and firmly grounded in both fact and law:

> The Chamber finds that the conditions required for the commission of crime against humanity have been satisfied in this case. Indeed, the Chamber is satisfied that there were attacks against the Tutsi in Kivumu *commune* in April 1994. The attack which culminated in the destruction of Nyange church on 16 April 1994 was "widespread" in the sense that it was massive, carried out collectively and directed against a multiplicity of victims. The attack was also "systematic" inasmuch as the factual findings tend to show that it was thoroughly organized and followed a regular pattern, starting with the surrounding of the church on 12 April 1994 up to its destruction on 16 April 1994, coupled with the intensification of the attacks against the refugees on 14 and 15 April 1994. Lastly, the Chamber finds that the attack was directed against the Tutsi civilian population that had sought refuge in Nyange church on discriminatory grounds.[73]
>
> Furthermore, the Chamber finds that Accused Athanase Seromba had knowledge of the widespread and systematic nature of the attack and the underlying discriminatory grounds. The Chamber is satisfied that Seromba also knew that the crime of extermination committed against the Tutsi refugees was part of that attack.[74]

There is little doubt that genocide and extermination do share some striking similarities and it can hardly be debated that genocide finds its origins in the Nuremberg creation of 'crimes against humanity'[75] and that the 'crime of genocide is a type of crime against humanity'.[76] Yet, the crime of genocide and crimes against humanity, thus including extermination, have been recognized as distinct by international criminal law and their constitutive elements and definitional requirements indeed remain inherently different. Notwithstanding the fact that the 'definition of the crime of genocide was based upon that of crimes against humanity, that is, a combination of "extermination and persecutions on political, racial or religious grounds"',[77] the international criminal tribunals have consistently insisted – and rightly so – on the fact that '[g]enocide, however, is different from other crimes against humanity'.[78]

It is therefore crucial that judicial findings remain within this line of reasoning and clearly delineate the contours of each notion, resisting any form of equalization and avoiding a confusion which would be detrimental to both the definition of genocide and that of crimes against humanity. In the Seromba judgment, the absence of legal reasoning with respect to the crime of genocide, coupled with the lack of legal discussion on extermination as a crime against humanity, has led to a problematic consequence: it has indeed allowed for the same criminal acts to fall under two distinct criminal qualifications. In this respect, the Seromba Trial Chamber here not only missed an opportunity to clarify the law on genocide and on extermination – an admittedly arduous task –, it has also reinforced the confusion and amalgams between the two crimes.

---

70 *Ibid.*, par. 335.
71 *Ibid.*, par. 364, footnote omitted.
72 *Ibid.*, par. 365, footnote omitted
73 *Ibid.*, par. 369, footnote omitted.
74 *Ibid.*, par. 370.
75 See Article 6 (c) of the Nuremberg Charter.
76 Judgement, *Prosecutor v. Kayishema and Ruzindana*, T. Ch. II, *supra* note 12, par. 89.
77 *Ibid.*
78 *Ibid.*

3. The contentious appreciation of the individual circumstances of the defendant

Sentencing in international criminal trials is arguably a perilous exercise for any Trial Chamber. Considering the enormity of the crimes perpetrated, no sentence could ever be seen as appropriate and adequate. In considering the personal circumstances of Athanase Seromba, the Trial Chamber recalled 'that the individual circumstances of the accused are perceived in the jurisprudence of the *ad hoc* tribunals as a factor for individualizing the penalty. The Chamber further consider[ed] that individual circumstances should be understood to be any personal circumstance of the accused which may either aggravate or mitigate sentence.'[79]

It accordingly reviewed such circumstances and interestingly held that the defendant's 'training as a priest and his experience within the church should have enabled him to understand the reprehensible nature of his conduct during the events'[80] before considering 'as an aggravating circumstance the fact that the Accused took no concrete action whatsoever to earn the trust of those persons who believed they were safe by seeking refuge at Nyange parish' and finding 'that the status of the Accused and *betrayal of trust* constitute aggravating circumstances.'[81] Yet, it also – surprisingly – found that Athanase Seromba's good reputation 'constitute[d] a mitigating circumstance in determining the sentence to be imposed'.[82] In light of the crimes for which the defendant stood accused and for which he was convicted, such consideration appears rather dubious, to say the least.

Intriguingly, this finding in Seromba is not the first of this sort and a parallel can here be drawn with the Ntakirutimana judgment when, also assessing the individual circumstances of an accused with religious ranking and affiliation, the Trial Chamber had, rather astonishingly, held that:

> the Accused was a highly respected personality within the Seventh Day Adventist Church of the West-Rwanda Field and beyond, in the Kibuye prefecture. It heard and reviewed moving testimony from colleagues and supervisors of the Accused within the Seventh-Day Adventist Church. This evidence consistently described the Pastor's exemplary life as a church leader, a highly religious and tolerant person, who did not show ethnic bias, even in times of unrest and ethnic tension, for over half a century. Significantly, one such colleague praised "a faithful and honest worker who manifested courage in confronting irregularities with workers of either tribal affiliation" while an other described Pastor Ntakirutimana as "a kind Christian gentleman", an outstanding worker whom he found to be fair and trustworthy, whom he never saw lose his temper, who "worked well with the Hutus and the Tutsis" and whom he never saw making any distinction in their respect. As already stated, the Chamber accepts this evidence and finds that Elizaphan Ntakirutimana was essentially a person of good moral character until the events of April to July 1994 during which he was swept along with many Rwandans into criminal conduct.[83]

Such finding did not remain unnoticed and, as Sloane rightly pointed out,

> the idea that Ntakirutimana's prior good character should be a mitigating circumstance is quite dubious. Unlike the thousands of poor, uneducated, rank and file *génocidaires* who were 'swept along... into criminal conduct', Ntakirutimana, by virtue of his status, education, and religious and moral leadership, could have and should have resisted the tide; his prior 'character' and 'exemplary life', that is, would seem to render him more, not less, culpable.[84]

Clearly, the same remark could be made with respect to Athanase Seromba whose religious faith and leadership 'would seem to render him more, not less, culpable'. The consideration by the Trial Chamber of questionable mitigating circumstances added to the vagueness of the legal findings and the unavailability of the judgment for over a year may have shed a shadow of doubt on the credibility of the judgment, perhaps even prompting erroneous accusations of leniency. And if the intention of the Trial Chamber ever was to show some complacency towards a representative of the Catholic Church, it can safely be asserted that this

79 Judgement, *Prosecutor v. Seromba*, T. Ch. III, *supra* note 1, par. 383, footnote omitted.
80 *Ibid.*, par. 385, footnote omitted.
81 *Ibid.*, par. 390, emphasis added.
82 *Ibid.*, par. 395.
83 ICTR, Judgement and Sentence, *Prosecutor v. Elizaphan Ntakirutimana and Ntakirutimana*, Cases No. ICTR-96-10 and ICTR-96-17-T, T. Ch. I, 21 February 2003, Klip/ Sluiter, ALC-XII-383, par. 895, footnote omitted.
84 R. D. Sloane, Sentencing for the 'Crime of Crimes' The Evolving 'Common Law' of Sentencing of the International Criminal Tribunal for Rwanda, 5 Journal of International Criminal Justice 2007, p. 731.

totally backfired as, on appeals, the Appeal Chamber proved extremely severe. As noted by Zorzi Giustiniani,

> The *Seromba* Appeal Judgment is one of the few cases in which the ICTR Appeals Chamber has not only reversed the Trial Chamber's decisions, but also increased the sentence.[85] This was a direct consequence of the application of a broad conception of commission as a form of responsibility.[86]

She further specified that:

> In substance, a careful reading of the Appeal Judgment leaves the impression that the Appeals Chamber was primarily inspired by the need to impose an exemplary punishment on Father Seromba. This is also apparent from Appeals Chamber's remainder-of-life sentence which, unlike a life sentence, implies that Seromba may not be eligible for any form of clemency under the domestic laws of the state in which he will serve his sentence.[87]

Could it be that the Appeals Chamber here aimed at issuing an exemplary decision? It is possible that it reacted to the opacity of the Trial Chamber's judgment, which arguably generated misconceptions as to both the qualification of the acts committed and the individual responsibility of the accused, thus paving the way for a loose appreciation of the individual circumstances and a rather lenient sentencing. An analysis of the Appeal judgment could indeed reveal the willingness of the Appeals Chamber to preserve the reputation of impartiality and independence of international criminal justice and to unequivocally dismiss any suggestion of bias and tolerance towards genocidal behaviour, even when committed by religious leaders.

Caroline Fournet

---

85 The other ICTR cases where the sentence was increased on appeal were ICTR, Judgement, *Semanza v. Prosecutor*, Case No. ICTR-97-20-A, A. Ch., 20 May 2005, Klip/ Sluiter, ALC-XXII-525, par. 389 and ICTR, Judgement, *Gacumbitsi v. Prosecutor*, Case No. Case No. ICTR-2001-64-A, A. Ch., 7 July 2006, Klip/ Sluiter, ALC-XXIV-495, par. 205. At the ICTY, the Appeals Chamber raised the sentence in *Aleksovski* ICTY, Judgement, *Prosecutor v. Aleksovski*, Case No. IT-95-14/1-A, A. Ch., 24 March 2000, Klip/ Sluiter, ALC-IV-361, par. 191, ICTY, Judgement, *Prosecutor v. Galić*, Case No. IT-98-29-A, A. Ch., 30 November 2006, par. 456, ICTY, Judgement, *Prosecutor v. Krnojelac*, Case No. IT-97-25-A, A. Ch., 17 September 2003, Klip/ Sluiter, ALC-XIV-753, par. 264 and ICTY, Judgement, *Prosecutor v. Delalić, Mucić, Hazim, Delić and Landžo*, Case No. IT-96-21-A, A. Ch., 20 February 2001, Klip/ Sluiter, ALC-V-369, par. 853.

86 F. Zorzi Giustiniani, Stretching the Boundaries of Commission Liability – The ICTR Appeal Judgment in *Seromba*, 6 Journal of International Criminal Justice 2008, p. 783-784.

87 *Ibid.*, par. 798, footnote omitted.

Tribunal pénal international pour le Rwanda
International Criminal Tribunal for Rwanda

IN THE APPEALS CHAMBER

Before: **Judge Wolfgang Schomburg, Presiding**
Judge Mohamed Shahabuddeen
Judge Mehmet Güney
Judge Liu Daqun
Judge Theodor Meron

Registrar: **Mr. Adama Dieng**

Judgement of: **16 January 2007**

EMMANUEL NDINDABAHIZI
(Appellant)

v.

THE PROSECUTOR
(Respondent)

Case No. ICTR-01-71-A

JUDGEMENT

Counsel for the Appellant:

Mr. Michel Konitz
Ms. Magali Pirard

The Office of the Prosecutor:

Mr. Hassan Bubacar Jallow
Mr. James K. Stewart
Mr. George Mugwanya
Ms. Inge Onsea
Mr. Abdoulaye Seye
Mr. Alfred Orono Orono

CONTENTS

[page 1] 1. The Appeals Chamber of the International Criminal Tribunal for the Prosecution of Persons Responsible for Genocide and Other Serious Violations of International Humanitarian Law Committed in the Territory of Rwanda and Rwandan Citizens Responsible for Genocide and Other Such Violations Committed in the Territory of Neighbouring States between 1 January 1994 and 31 December 1994 ("Tribunal") is seized of an appeal by Emmanuel Ndindabahizi against the Judgement rendered by Trial Chamber I on 15 July 2004 in the case of *The Prosecutor v. Emmanuel Ndindabahizi* ("Trial Judgement").[1]

I. INTRODUCTION

A. The Appellant

2. The Appellant, Emmanuel Ndindabahizi, was born in 1950[2] in Gashuru, Gitesi Commune, Kibuye Prefecture, Rwanda. Between September 1992 and 6 April 1994, he was *Directeur de Cabinet* in the Ministry of Finance, second in authority, reporting to the Minister only. In 1993 he was elected Executive Secretary of the *Social Democratic Party* (PSD) in Kibuye. He was sworn in as Minister of Finance of the Interim Government on 9 April 1994. The Appellant left Rwanda for Goma in the Democratic Republic of Congo (formerly Zaire) on 13 or 14 July 1994.[3]

B. The Amended Indictment

3. The amended indictment ("Indictment") of 1 September 2003 charges the Appellant with three counts, pursuant to Articles 2 and 3 of the Statute: genocide; extermination, a crime against humanity; and murder, a crime against humanity. The Indictment charges the Appellant with individual criminal responsibility under all modes of liability pursuant to Article 6(1) of the Statute for these crimes. Charges of direct and public incitement to commit genocide pursuant to Article 2(3)(c) of the Statute and of rape as well as all allegations of superior responsibility under Article 6(3) of the Statute had been withdrawn from the Indictment at the request of the Prosecution.[4] **[page 2]**

C. The Judgement

4. The Trial Chamber primarily found that, on 23 through 24 April 1994, the Appellant transported attackers to Gitwa Hill, distributed weapons there and expressly urged the attackers to kill Tutsi people.[5] For these acts, resulting in the death of thousands of Tutsi, the Trial Chamber convicted the Appellant pursuant to Article 6(1) of the Statute for instigating and aiding and abetting genocide (Count 1).[6] The Trial Chamber also convicted him for committing or, alternatively, instigating and aiding and abetting extermination as a crime against humanity at Gitwa Hill (Count 2).[7]

5. The Trial Chamber further found that in late May 1994 the Appellant encouraged those manning a roadblock at a place called Gaseke to stop and kill Tutsi, and that he distributed machetes and money to these men, who soon after the Appellant's departure apprehended and killed one person named Mr. Nors.[8] The Trial Chamber convicted the Appellant for these acts pursuant to Article 6(1) of the Statute for instigating

---

1 Two annexes are appended to this Judgement: Annex A – Procedural Background and Annex B – Cited Materials/Defined Terms.

2 The Appellant stated at trial that no further particulars as to the day or month are given in his documents, T. 24 November 2003, p. 1.

3 Trial Judgement, para. 6.

4 Decision on Prosecution Request to Amend Indictment, 30 June 2003, granting leave to the Prosecution "to amend its indictment so as to withdraw the charge of incitement to commit genocide, and related factual allegations" (p. 2). *See also* Decision on Prosecution Motion for Leave to Amend Indictment, 20 August 2003, and the oral Decision of the Trial Chamber on the first day of trial, T. 1 September 2003, pp. 1-2. Also, the Prosecution stated in closing arguments that it would not offer evidence in relation to paras 6, 7, 14, 17, 18, 22, 23, 24 and 26 of the Indictment, T. 1 March 2003, pp. 52-53; T. 2 March 2003, p. 54.

5 Trial Judgement, paras 179-80.

6 Trial Judgement, para. 464.

7 Trial Judgement, para. 485.

8 Trial Judgement, paras 230-31.

and aiding and abetting genocide (Count 1),[9] and for instigating and aiding and abetting murder as a crime against humanity (Count 3).[10]

6. The Trial Chamber handed out a single sentence of imprisonment for the remainder of the Appellant's life.

D. The Appeal

7. The Appellant is appealing against all convictions and the sentence,[11] dividing his remaining ten grounds of appeal[12] into two categories, namely errors of law and errors of fact. The Appeals Chamber points out that several aspects of the grounds of appeal are inextricably intertwined. Therefore, related grounds of appeal have been grouped together as follows:

- Alleged vagueness of the Indictment (Ground of Appeal 1)
- Alleged error in finding that the Appellant was in Gitwa (Grounds of Appeal 9 and 10)
- Judgement allegedly rendered beyond the scope of the Indictment (Ground of Appeal 2) **[page 3]**
- Alleged non-disclosure of exculpatory evidence (Ground of Appeal 4)
- Alleged errors in the assessment of Defence evidence (Grounds of Appeal 5 and 3)
- Alleged error in finding that the Appellant was at the Gaseke roadblock (Ground of Appeal 11)
- Alleged error in finding a legal basis for the genocide conviction (Ground of Appeal 7)
- Appeal against the sentence (Ground of Appeal 13)

E. The Standard for Appellate Review

8. The settled standards of appellate review pursuant to Article 24 of the Statute are set out in the jurisprudence of the Tribunal.[13] The Appeals Chamber reviews only errors of law invalidating the decision of the Trial Chamber and errors of fact which have occasioned a miscarriage of justice.

9. As regards errors of law, the Appeals Chamber has repeatedly stated:

> Where a party alleges that there is an error of law, that party must advance arguments in support of the submission and explain how the error invalidates the decision. However, if the appellant's arguments do not support the contention, that party does not automatically lose its point since the Appeals Chamber may step in and, for other reasons, find in favour of the contention that there is an error of law.[14]

10. As regards errors of fact, it is settled jurisprudence that

> [w]here the Defence alleges an erroneous finding of fact, the Appeals Chamber must give deference to the Trial Chamber that received the evidence at trial, and it will only interfere in those findings where no reasonable trier of fact could have reached the same finding or where the finding is wholly erroneous. Furthermore, the erroneous finding will be revoked or revised only if the error occasioned a miscarriage of justice.[15]

11. A party cannot merely repeat on appeal arguments that did not succeed at trial, unless it can demonstrate that the Trial Chamber's rejection of those arguments constituted an error warranting the intervention of the Appeals Chamber.[16] Arguments which do not have the potential to cause the impugned decision to be reversed or revised need not be considered on the merits.[17]

---

9 Trial Judgement, paras 472-73.

10 Trial Judgement, para. 490.

11 Appellant's Brief, para. 319.

12 Of the original thirteen grounds of appeal, the Appellant has abandoned grounds of appeal 6, 8 and 12. Ground of appeal 3 was merged with ground of appeal 5 and ground of appeal 9 with ground of appeal 10: *see* Appellant's Brief, pp. 2 and 3.

13 *Gacumbitsi* Appeal Judgement, paras 6-10; *Ntagerura et al.* Appeal Judgement, paras 11-14.

14 *Gacumbitsi* Appeal Judgement, para. 7 (with further references).

15 *Ibid.*, para. 8 (with further references).

16 *Ibid.*, para. 9 (with further references).

17 *Ibid.*, (with further references).

12. In order for the Appeals Chamber to assess the appealing party's arguments, the appealing party must provide precise references to relevant transcript pages or paragraphs in the decision or judgement to which the challenge is being made, and "the Appeals Chamber cannot be expected to **[page 4]** consider a party's submissions in detail if they are obscure, contradictory, vague or suffer from other formal and obvious insufficiencies."[18] Also, the Appeals Chamber has inherent discretion in selecting which submissions merit a detailed reasoned opinion in writing and will dismiss arguments which are evidently unfounded without providing detailed reasoning.[19]

13. Finally, "there are situations where the Appeals Chamber may raise questions *proprio motu* or agree to examine alleged errors which will not affect the verdict but which do, however, raise an issue of general importance for the case-law or functioning of the Tribunal."[20] As the final arbiter of the law applied by the Tribunal, the Appeals Chamber must give the Trial Chambers guidance for their interpretation of the law.[21]

II. ALLEGED VAGUENESS OF THE INDICTMENT (SUB-GROUND OF APPEAL 1 – GITWA HILL)

A. Submissions of the Parties

14. The Appellant submits that the Trial Chamber committed an error of law in rendering a judgement on the basis of the vague and defective paragraphs 15 and 20 of the Indictment, which alleged that the attacks at Gitwa Hill took place on unknown days between 13 and 26 April 1994.[22]

15. The Prosecution submits that the Trial Chamber read paragraph 15 together with paragraph 16 of the Indictment and gave a holistic reading to paragraph 20,[23] thus finding that "[t]he dates in the Indictment gave the defence a good idea of when the alleged events in question occurred".[24] The Prosecution submits that no prejudice was caused and that the Appellant did not raise any objection to the pertinent evidence during trial.[25] **[page 5]**

B. Discussion

1. Alleged Defect in the Indictment – Applicable Law

16. The form of an indictment is primarily governed by Article 17(4) of the Statute requiring the Prosecution to set out, *inter alia*, a concise statement of the facts and the crime(s) charged, and Article 20(4) of the Statute enshrining, *inter alia*, an accused's right to be informed promptly and in detail of the nature and cause of the charge against him or her.[26] An indictment is defective if it does not state the material facts underpinning the charges with enough detail to enable an accused to prepare his or her defence.[27] Whether a fact is material depends on the nature of the Prosecution case.[28] The Appeals Chambers of both the ICTR and the ICTY have specified several factors that can determine the materiality of facts: for example, if the personal physical commission of criminal acts is charged, the indictment should set forth the victim's identity, the place and time of the events and the means by which the acts were committed.[29] The Appeals

18 *Ibid.*, para. 10 (with further references).
19 *Ibid.*, para. 10 (with further references).
20 *Kordić and Čerkez* Appeal Judgement, para. 1031 (with further reference).
21 *Ibid.*
22 Appellant's Brief, paras 14, 17-20, 28-29.
23 Respondent's Brief, paras 22, 25-27. Paragraphs 28 and 35 refer to jurisprudence supporting this point, citing *Rutaganda* Appeal Judgement, paras 297, 304.
24 Respondent's Brief, para. 20, referring to Trial Judgement, para. 34.
25 Respondent's Brief, paras 25, 44 and 51-55, pointing out that the Appellant did not raise any objection to the testimony of Witness CGC describing the killing of Mr. Nors. According to the Respondent, the doctrine of waiver applies on appeal because the Appellant does not explain how he was prejudiced.
26 *See also* Rule 47 of the Rules.
27 *See Kamuhanda* Appeal Judgement, para. 17, and *Kupreškić et al.* Appeal Judgement, para. 88.
28 *Kamuhanda* Appeal Judgement, para. 17, referring to *Kupreškić et al.* Appeal Judgement, para. 89.
29 *Ntakirutimana* Appeal Judgement, para. 25.

Chamber recalls, however, that "such detail need not be pleaded if the 'sheer scale of the alleged crimes makes it impracticable to require a high degree of specificity in such matters'."[30]

2. Findings of the Trial Chamber

17. The Trial Chamber referred to paragraphs 15 and 16 (genocide, Count 1) and paragraph 20 (extermination, Count 2)[31] when convicting the Appellant for the massacre at Gitwa Hill.

18. The Trial Chamber addressed the objections placed before it with respect to the date range of 13 days for the massacre at Gitwa Hill pleaded in paragraph 15 (genocide) and paragraph 20 (extermination) of the Indictment. It recalled that the Defence did not object during trial to the admission of evidence relating to Gitwa Hill on the basis of lack of notice in the Indictment, that the Defence bore the burden of showing that it was materially prejudiced in the preparation of its case, and that no such showing was made.[32] The Trial Chamber noted that the testimony of the three Prosecution witnesses testifying to the events at Gitwa Hill provided dates that fell within the date **[page 6]** range set out in the Indictment.[33] Furthermore, the Trial Chamber made the following statements when finding that the Indictment was not defective:

> The dates in the Indictment gave the Defence a good idea of when the alleged events in question occurred, and a reasonable opportunity to investigate them and discover exculpatory information. The Indictment does not give the impression that the Accused participated in an attack on a single date throughout the period, but rather than [*sic*] he participated over the course of several days. The date range was not unreasonable in light of the nature of the events. [...] Given the continuity and notoriety of the attacks at Gitwa, it was not unreasonable for the Prosecution to have used the duration of the attacks to define the possible dates of the Accused's involvement. The Defence was reasonably able to meet the Prosecution case as presented in the Indictment.[34]

3. Analysis

19. The Indictment pleaded the time period for the events at Gitwa Hill with sufficient specificity. A date may be considered to be a material fact if it is necessary in order to inform a defendant clearly of the charges so that he may prepare his defence.[35] If a date is found to constitute a material fact, it must be pleaded with sufficient specificity, as stated by the ICTY Appeals Chamber:

> An indictment may also be defective when the material facts are pleaded without sufficient specificity, such as, unless there are special circumstances, when the times refer to broad date ranges [...].[36]

20. The precision with which dates have to be charged varies from case to case.[37] It has also been acknowledged by the ICTY Appeals Chamber that "[...] an accused may be charged with having participated [...] in an extensive number of attacks on civilians that took place over a prolonged period of time and resulted in large numbers of killings [...]."[38] Also, the ICTY Appeals Chamber held that "there may be instances where the sheer scale of the alleged crimes 'makes it impracticable to require a high degree of specificity in such matters as the identity of the victims and the dates for the commission of the crimes'."[39] In cases where timing is of material importance to the charges, more specific information should be provided.[40] However, in particular in light of the events that occurred in Rwanda in 1994, the Appeals Chamber is mindful of the fact that it is not always possible to be precise as to the specific date on which the

30 *Ntakirutimana* Appeal Judgement, para. 25, referring to *Kupreškić et al.* Appeal Judgement, para. 89.

31 Trial Judgement, paras 458-64; 481-85. The remaining paragraphs under the extermination count referring to dates were withdrawn, *see supra* note 4. The allegation of throwing an explosive grenade in paragraph 16 of the Indictment has not been found to be proven.

32 Trial Judgement, para. 35.

33 Trial Judgement, paras 33-34.

34 Trial Judgement, para. 34 (references omitted).

35 *Tadić* Trial Judgement, para. 534, referring to Halsbury's Laws of England (London, Butterworths, 1990), Volume 11(2), para. 926; *see also Kupreškić et al.* Appeal Judgement, para. 88; *Ntakirutimana* Appeal Judgement, para. 25.

36 *Kvo~ka et al.* Appeal Judgement, para. 31.

37 *See supra* para. 16.

38 *Kupreškić et al.* Appeal Judgement, para. 90.

39 *Kupreškić et al.* Appeal Judgement, para. 89 (citing other ICTY Decisions).

40 *See Kayishema and Ruzindana* Trial Judgement, para. 86.

crimes charged were committed. Nevertheless, these considerations have to be balanced with the accused's right to be **[page 7]** informed in detail about the nature and cause of the charge against him in order to allow a comprehensive defence to be raised.

21. The Indictment alleges that over the course of 13 days a continued attack was sustained against Tutsi refugees taking shelter at Gitwa Hill.[41] Thus, the Prosecution case was premised upon a series of attacks which took place over the course of several days. The Defence itself also characterised the Prosecution case in this manner during closing arguments when it stated that the Appellant was accused in paragraphs 15 and 20 of the Indictment of "being in charge of a series of attacks".[42]

22. Given the nature of the Prosecution case, the date range of 13 days sufficiently specified the date range for the crimes alleged. It provided the Appellant with enough information to know the nature of the charges against him and to prepare his defence.[43] His participation was found to have occurred at various specific dates within the time period pleaded in the Indictment.[44]

23. Consequently, the first sub-ground of appeal in relation to the events at Gitwa Hill is rejected.

III. ALLEGED ERROR IN FINDING THAT THE APPELLANT WAS IN GITWA (GROUNDS OF APPEAL 9 AND 10)

A. Submissions of the Parties

24. The Appellant submits that the Trial Chamber erred in fact in relying on the testimonies of Witnesses CGY and CGN to find that he went to Gitwa Hill on 23 and 24 April 1994.[45] The Appellant does not present arguments about his alleged activities at Gitwa Hill, but denies that the trial record supports the finding that he was present.

25. The Prosecution responds that the Appellant merely repeats arguments that did not succeed at trial and fails to show how and why the Trial Chamber's findings are so unreasonable that they **[page 8]** warrant appellate intervention.[46] The Prosecution submits that the Trial Chamber was entitled to make findings based solely on the uncorroborated evidence of Witnesses CGY and CGN.[47]

B. Discussion

1. Dates of Events at Gitwa Hill

26. The Appellant submits that, on the basis of Witness CGN's testimony alone, the Trial Chamber erroneously dated acts imputed to the Appellant at Gitwa Hill on 24 April 1994, while the Prosecution dated these acts on 20 April 1994.[48]

27. During closing arguments, the Prosecution stated that

> [t]he second event [at Gitwa] is on the 20th of April, and that's Witness CGN. He says he saw the Accused arriving at Gitwa hill on the 20th of April [...].[49]

---

41 Indictment, paras 15 and 20.

42 T. 2 March 2004, p. 10.

43 The Appeals Chamber also notes that a date range of 13 days was accepted in the *Semanza* Trial Judgement in para. 48 (this finding was not appealed), and that a period of six days was not found to be too vague in the *Ntakirutimana* Appeal Judgement at para. 47.

44 Trial Judgement, paras 179-81: namely 23 and 24 April 1994.

45 Appellant's Brief, paras 187-243. The Appeals Chamber notes that the date of the final attack on 26 April 1994 is not disputed by the Parties.

46 Respondent's Brief, paras 193-96.

47 Respondent's Brief, paras 197-200. In reply, the Appellant submits that he "is prepared to admit that the testimony of a single witness may suffice to prove a material fact, but only where such testimony is free of any contradictions or inaccuracies; but such is certainly not the case with Witnesses CGY and CGN" (Appellant's Reply, para. 51).

48 Appellant's Brief, paras 200-06, 236; Appellant's Reply, para. 57.

49 T. 1 March 2004, p. 31.

Later in closing arguments, however, the Prosecution argued:

> Witness CGN's statement says it was around [...] 20th to 25th of April [...].[50]

Furthermore, the Prosecution stated in its Pre-Trial Brief that Witness CGN saw the Appellant "between 20 and 25 April",[51] and the Prosecution Closing Brief referred to the testimony of Witness CGN when stating that he saw the Appellant at Gitwa "[a]round the 20th of April".[52] It is evident from the Trial Judgement records that the alleged discrepancies in the dates were not put to Witness CGN during cross examination.[53]

28. The Trial Chamber found that Witness CGN saw the Appellant in Gitwa on 24 April 1994, deducing this date from Witness CGN's statements that he saw the Appellant between 20 and 24 April, two days before the large attack dispersing the refugees from Gitwa Hill which was found to have occurred on 26 April 1994.[54] **[page 9]**

29. The question before the Appeals Chamber is whether this finding amounts to an error of fact occasioning a miscarriage of justice. The Appellant takes issue with the Trial Chamber assessing the evidence in its totality to "infer"[55] the date, when Witness CGN was only able to provide references that were non-date specific, *i.e.* the timing of an event in relation to another major event, namely the large attack and massacre which dispersed the refugees from Gitwa Hill. The Appeals Chamber notes that it was open for the Trial Chamber to make factual findings on the date of the events by examining the evidence as a whole[56] and, indeed, this may be particularly necessary when determining dates, as often witnesses may not recall an exact date but describe the timing of the event in relation to other variables.[57] The Appeals Chamber finds that the Trial Chamber reasonably concluded that Witness CGN was referring to events taking place on 24 April 1994.

30. Further, the Appellant complains that the submissions of the Prosecution caused the Defence to "focus" on 20 April 1994 in structuring their rebuttal case.[58] The Appeals Chamber notes that the trial transcripts show that the Defence stated during cross-examination: "[w]hen you [Witness CGN] saw Mr. Ndindabahizi between the 20th and 24th of April [...]",[59] which suggests that the Defence was aware of Witness CGN's time frame for the events in Gitwa. The Appeals Chamber finds that the Defence had notice of a reasonable timeframe relevant for Witness CGN's evidence, that is around 20 to 25 April 1994, and that the Prosecution did not narrow the allegations to 20 April 1994, as discussed above in this section.

31. For the reasons set out above, the Appellant has not demonstrated that the relevant findings of the Trial Chamber were unreasonable.

2. Inconsistencies in Witness CGY's Testimony

32. According to the Appellant, Witness CGY claimed that he travelled between Gitwa Hill and Karongi FM Hill every day between 15 and 26 April 1994,[60] apparently contradicting Witness CGN who allegedly demonstrated that it was not possible to travel between Gitwa Hill and Karongi FM Hill at that time.[61] The Trial Chamber expressly considered whether Witness CGN's testimony made it implausible that Witness

---

50 T. 1 March 2004, p. 50.

51 Prosecution Pre-Trial Brief, Appendix A, p. 8.

52 Prosecution Closing Brief, para. 40. *See also* Prosecution Closing Brief, note 134, referencing T. 8 September 2003, p. 5, which is the Prosecution's summary of the statement of Witness CGN made at T. 8 September 2003, p. 4.

53 Trial Judgement, para. 154.

54 Trial Judgement, para. 149, note 175. Trial Judgement, para. 181, referring to the testimony of Witnesses CGY, CGN, and DC. *See also* written statement of Witness CGN, 27 April 2001, p. 3. This was affirmed by Witness CGN during trial, T. 8 September 2003, p. 4.

55 Trial Judgement, para. 149, note 175.

56 *Rutaganda* Appeal Judgement, para. 304, referring to holistic reading of the Indictment.

57 *See, e.g., Kajelijeli* Appeal Judgement, para. 115.

58 Appellant's Brief, para. 205.

59 T. 8 September 2003, p. 19.

60 Appellant's Brief, paras 207-20; Appellant's Reply, paras 59-64.

61 Appellant's Brief, paras 208-210: the Appellant refers to Witness CGN's testimony on the number of attacks and attackers, and the difficulty of escape.

CGY could have made daily trips between Gitwa Hill and Karongi FM Hill.[62] The Appellant submits that the Trial Chamber incorrectly reconciled the **[page 10]** testimonies of Witness CGN and Witness CGY by referring to Witness CGN's lack of specificity as to the time when Gitwa Hill was surrounded, while Witness CGN in fact stated that from 14 through 20 April "attackers surrounded the hill and made escape impossible."[63]

33. The Appellant does not cite the full reasoning employed by the Trial Chamber in assessing the testimony of Witness CGY. The question of when Gitwa Hill was surrounded was not the sole basis for the Trial Chamber's finding that Witness CGY shuttled between Gitwa Hill and Karongi FM Hill. The Trial Chamber also found that Witness CGY explained that he moved at night and had a particular imperative to travel and care for his family hiding in different places in the locality, and the Trial Chamber noted that it did not have precise information on the positioning of the attackers.[64] Also, while travelling between two locations can be regarded as impossible by one witness, it can be reasonably assessed as possible by another witness. In this regard, it is notable that Witness CGY's testimony centred on his need to move between his different family members, whereas Witness CGN does not discuss such an imperative. Thus, the Appellant has failed to show a factual error in the Trial Chamber's finding.

34. The Appeals Chamber notes the findings of the Trial Chamber that Witness CGY "moved at night, which obviously reduced the risk of being discovered".[65] This finding could be inconsistent with the Trial Chamber's finding that Witness CGY was credible when he testified that he saw the Appellant at Gitwa Hill on 23 April 1994 at about 11.00 a.m.[66] It is noted, however, that Witness CGY also stated that he was involved in reconnaissance missions, including ascertaining "whether attacks were coming."[67] The Appeals Chamber also notes that the Trial Chamber extensively considered Witness CGY's testimony as to these missions.[68] While being hidden in a bush and conducting reconnaissance missions may appear contradictory, it must be recalled that a trier of fact often has to reconcile conflicting evidence of a witness, and that the Trial Chamber was **[page 11]** best placed to assess Witness CGY's evidence in its entirety together with his demeanour. In light of these considerations, it was reasonable for the Trial Chamber to conclude that Witness CGY was seeking to observe activities of the attackers,[69] whereas during the night he was providing for his family which was hiding in various locations.[70] It is notable in this context that, contrary to the Appellant's assertion,[71] the trial record shows that the two hills were located on the same side of the road, and the vantage point from which Witness CGY observed the Appellant was on the same side of this road,[72] therefore limiting the risk that Witness CGY would encounter roadblocks during the daytime, as alleged by the Appellant. Consequently, it has not been shown how the Trial Chamber was unreasonable in its findings.

---

62 Trial Judgement, paras 134-36.

63 Appellant's Brief, para. 210, referring to the Trial Judgement, para. 151.

64 Trial Judgement, para. 136.

65 Trial Judgement, para. 136.

66 Trial Judgement, paras 134-36, 142; Appellant's Brief, paras 215-16. *See also* T. 8 September 2003, p. 53.

67 *See* written statement for Witness CGY, 10 May 2001, p. 4, cited at Trial Judgement, para. 135.

68 T. 8 September 2003, pp. 55-56, referred to in Trial Judgement, para. 135, notes 160, 166:

> Q. [...] What was the object of those missions for information gathering, as it were?
> A. I will answer you. It was an important mission because this enabled us – we became [sic] to know where the attackers were coming from as well as the people, the inhabitants who were not supporting these attacks, and we were thus able to know the places where the attackers were coming from.
> Q. During these fact-finding missions did you have to go away from Gitwa hill, to go towards the attackers so that you could get better information regarding their numbers, for instance?
> A. This information could not be collected or gathered by one single individual. There were people who needed to go and look for the information, and since Gitwa was surrounded by more than three secteurs -- Gitwa is located in Rubanzo, next door there's Gitesi, Gitarama secteur, and Bishura and Kangabiro as well as the Rubanzo secteur -- so, you will realise that there must have been many people who needed to go and try and find information from all corners, and it was not to me alone that that task was assigned.

69 *See* written statement for Witness CGY, 10 May 2001, p. 4 cited at Trial Judgement, para. 135 and T. 8 September 2003, p. 41.

70 T. 8 September 2003, p. 53.

71 Appellant's Brief, para. 216.

72 Exh. P2, page L0019869.

35. The Appellant further submits that Witness CGY contradicted himself during his oral testimony by stating that he did not travel to Karongi FM Hill after 21 April 1994.[73] Already in his Closing Brief, the Appellant argued that Witness CGY initially stated that he was shuttling between Karongi FM Hill and Gitwa Hill between 15 and 26 April 1994,[74] whereas later he asserted that he did not go back to Karongi FM Hill after 21 April 1994. Nonetheless, Witness CGY stated that he saw the Appellant at a roadblock on 23 April 1994 about 600 metres from Karongi FM Hill.[75] The Trial Chamber addressed the issue in finding that "Witness CGY testified that he moved regularly between Gitwa Hill and the two places on Karongi Hill where his family was hidden, *at least until* 20 April."[76] The footnote to this text reads as follows:

> [...] At first, the witness testified that he moved back and forth between the two hills every day between 15 and 26 April, but then he later corrected himself to say that these journeys ceased on 20 April when his wife and children joined him on Gitwa Hill [...].[77]

From the trial transcripts, it is apparent that the confusion over the relevant dates arose during cross-examination when Defence counsel asked Witness CGY the following questions:

> MR. BESNIER (Defence): Did you do the shuttling between Karongi and Gitwa hill between the 15th of April and 26th of April regularly, everyday?
>
> WITNESS CGY: Yes. **[page 12]**
>
> MR. BESNIER: So each day you moved from the Gitwa hill to see your family at Karongi, and when you were reassured on the assault, you came back to the Gitwa hill; is that correct?
>
> WITNESS CGY: Yes, and that was the only way to cater for the food needs of my family, because we left some food items with some family friends who were taking care of them for us.
>
> MR. BESNIER: Why simply not remain with your family on the Karongi hill?
>
> WITNESS CGY: I told you and I repeat, just in case you did not understand. It was as if there were two distinct families. My family was living outside the refugee camp in the village, and another part of my family living within the camp.[78]

Witness CGY clarified soon after that:

> "[...] I was shuttling between the camp and these two places [Gitwa Hill and Karongi FM Hill]. It was as if I was living in these – all these places." [...]
>
> MR. BESNIER: My question is as follows: did you stay on Karongi FM hill between 15th April 1994 and 21 April 1994 without moving? [...]
>
> WITNESS CGY: [...] Well, I would be coming, going. I would go there and I would go back to where I came from. I would spend nights at Karongi. During the night I needed to move, to go to Gitwa and provide food, because I am the one who prepared meals for those people."[79]

Later during cross-examination, as identified by the Trial Chamber, Witness CGY clarified the date range, although it was through answering a "yes or no" question from Defence counsel:

> MR. BESNIER: Witness, to summarise some of the statements that we went through yesterday, will it be correct to say that you left Karongi on 20th April 1994, and that you hid yourself in a bush between the 20th and the 26th of April with your wife and your children?
>
> WITNESS CGY: Yes, that is correct.[80]

36. As stated above, Witness CGY made contradictory statements as to whether he went back to Karongi FM Hill after 21 April 1994. However, the Trial Chamber's finding that Witness CGY "moved regularly

---

73 Appellant's Brief, para. 207.

74 Defence Closing Brief, pp. 129-30, Appellant's Brief, paras 213-18.

75 Appellant's Brief, paras 212-15. This distance has been inferred by the Defence from Exh. P2, *see* Appellant's Brief, notes 156-58.

76 Trial Judgement, para. 129, citations omitted (emphasis added).

77 Trial Judgement, para. 129, note 143.

78 T. 8 September 2003, p. 50.

79 T. 8 September 2003, pp. 52-53.

80 T. 9 September 2003, p. 1.

between Gitwa Hill and the two places on Karongi FM Hill where his family was hidden, at least until 20 April" is consistent with Witness CGY's statement that he saw the Appellant at a roadblock about 600 metres away from Karongi FM Hill on 23 April 1994.

37. Also, Witness CGY's testimony that he was hiding in a bush with his family between 20 and 26 April 1994 is not inconsistent with the finding that he saw the Appellant on 23 April 1994 about 600 metres from Karongi FM Hill. Witness CGY testified to constantly moving in the region of Karongi FM Hill and Gitwa Hill to care for his family which was located in different positions, and he stated that he conducted reconnaissance missions.[81] As stated above, while being hidden in a bush and conducting reconnaissance missions may appear contradictory, it must be recalled that a **[page 13]** trier of fact often has to reconcile conflicting evidence of a witness, and that the Trial Chamber was best placed to assess Witness CGY's evidence in its entirety together with his demeanour. The Appeals Chamber finds that the Appellant has failed to show that the finding of the Trial Chamber is unreasonable.

38. The Appellant further submits that there is a corroboration requirement given that the Defence argues that Witness CGY was contradicted by Witness CGN. The Appellant relies upon the *Bagilishema* Trial Judgement which states that the Prosecution must be "especially careful to rub out grey areas" of the testimony of witnesses who "while purportedly in hiding and in fear of their lives, nonetheless are able to move around from one crime scene to the next, gathering intelligence along the way."[82] However, the Appellant fails to cite the remainder of this passage in which the Trial Chamber points out that the Prosecution "hurried Witness O through her evidence", and another Prosecution witness gave evidence that was not consistent with Witness O.[83] Neither of these allegations can be made against the current case in point. It has already been demonstrated that the Appellant's concerns regarding Witness CGN's contradiction of Witness CGY on the possibility of movement around Gitwa Hill are unfounded, and thus there was no Prosecution witness contradicting Witness CGY. Furthermore, the Prosecution carefully led Witness CGY through his evidence and the Defence had an adequate opportunity to cross-examine.[84] Also, it is recalled that there is no requirement for corroboration.[85] Thus, the Appellant has failed to demonstrate how the findings of the Trial Chamber were unreasonable with respect to Witness CGY.

39. Finally, the Appellant argues that trial testimony of Witness CGY in the present case is contradicted by the following exchange from the *Musema* case:

> MR. PHILLIPS (PROSECUTOR): Whilst you were in the bush did you witness another attack?
>
> WITNESS CGY: There were no other attacks.
>
> MR. PHILLIPS (PROSECUTOR): On the 26 of April 1994 did you witness an attack?
>
> WITNESS CGY: Yes, there were many attacks from several places at the same time.[86]

40. Defence counsel put this alleged discrepancy to Witness CGY during trial. Witness CGY asserted that his testimony had been improperly recorded and the Prosecution suggested that the witness had not mentioned the attacks on 24 and 25 April 1994 as they were of minor significance **[page 14]** compared to the large scale attack on 26 April 1994. The Trial Chamber accepted the explanation from the Prosecution, and also added that

> "[w]hether there were any attacks between 18 and 26 April does not appear to have been a matter of significance in the prior testimony and, accordingly, the witness may have omitted mention of relatively small-scale attacks. The Chamber notes that according to his prior statement of 10 May 2001, quoted by the Defence, the witness said that there were attacks on Gitwa Hill almost every day, but that they were small. The statement also refers to a small attack on 25 April."[87]

81 T. 8 September 2003, pp. 55-56.
82 *Bagilishema* Trial Judgement, para. 860.
83 *Bagilishema* Trial Judgement, para. 860.
84 T. 8 September 2003, pp. 30-61; T. 9 September 2003, pp. 1-20.
85 In the Appellant's Brief, para. 54. *See also Kamuhanda* Appeal Judgement, para. 239.
86 Exh. D7, *Musema* T. 30 April 1999, pp. 44-45. *See* Appellant's Brief, paras 221-28; Appellant's Reply, paras 65-67.
87 Trial Judgement, para. 140.

41. The Appellant has not demonstrated how this finding of the Trial Chamber is unreasonable. The Appellant does not address the full discussion in the Trial Judgement which also refers to the prior written statement of Witness CGY of 10 May 2001; in this statement, Witness CGY had said that there were attacks on Gitwa Hill almost every day. Furthermore, the different context of his testimony in *Musema* has to be considered. It is also noted that the citation from the *Musema* case provided by the Appellant omits the following passage:

> The Chamber notes that in such cases, witnesses may have provided conflicting evidence under solemn declaration. The Chamber will, in accordance with the general principles of the assessment of evidence [...], assess such evidence on a case-by-case basis. It will address the admissibility of such evidence, and, in evaluating the probative value of the evidence, will address the explanations given by the witness for the discrepancies between his or her testimonies, and the materiality of such apparent discrepancies.[88]

42. The Appeals Chamber notes with approval the need to assess prior contradicting testimony on a case-by-case basis. In the present case, the Trial Chamber discussed Witness CGY's prior testimony. The Trial Chamber stated that the attacks prior to 26 April 1994 did not appear to be of significance in *Musema*,[89] and it is noted that the transcripts show that the testimony in *Musema* focused on the attacks where the accused in that case was present.[90] The Trial Chamber in the present case further referred to Witness CGY's written statement that attacks occurred "almost every day"[91] as supported by his testimony at trial.[92] The Appeals Chamber is mindful of the fact that the Trial Chamber did not accept Witness CGY's testimony that his testimony in *Musema* had been improperly recorded. In so doing, the Trial Chamber addressed the explanations given by the witness for the discrepancies in his testimonies. The materiality of such discrepancies was addressed by the Trial Chamber when it rejected Witness CGY's explanation and accepted that of the Prosecution. Again, it is recalled that the Appeals Chamber will not lightly overturn findings of **[page 15]** a trier of fact which is able to directly assess the demeanour of a witness giving live testimony.[93] For these reasons, the Appeals Chamber finds that the Appellant has not shown that the Trial Chamber's conclusion is one which no reasonable trier of fact could have made.

3. Identification of the Accused by Witness CGN

43. The Appellant argues that the Trial Chamber erroneously found that Witness CGN had sufficient prior knowledge from his alleged work at Trafipro in Kibuye to identify him in Gitwa on 24 April 1994, as the Appellant was working exclusively in Kigali at that time.[94]

44. The Appellant misrepresents the findings of the Trial Chamber. The Appellant states that, on the basis of Witness CGV's testimony,[95] the Trial Chamber found that the Appellant was a manager of the Trafipro shop in Kibuye.[96] However, the testimony of Witness CGV was only accepted in part by the Trial Chamber: While he was found not to be credible in claiming that the Appellant participated in an attack on Gitwa Hill on or about 17 April 1994[97] and in stating that he was the manager of the Trafipro shop in Kibuye,[98] this finding did not extend to Witness CGV's testimony as to the Appellant's presence at Trafipro in Kibuye.[99] Instead, the Trial Chamber stated that the "Accused's *occasional* presence at the Kibuye Trafipro is

---

88 *Musema* Trial Judgement, para. 88.

89 Trial Judgement, para. 140.

90 Exh. D7, *Musema* T. 30 April 1999, p. 45, *cf.* p. 24. Witness CGY confirmed both these attacks on 18 April 1994 and 26 April 1994 where Musema was present on examination by the President, T. 9 September 2003, p. 3.

91 Trial Judgement, para. 140.

92 T. 8 September 2003, pp. 41, 55 (stating "It wasn't every day that there would be an attack but there were four attacks" line 8); T. 9 September 2003, pp. 5, 11.

93 *Kajelijeli* Appeal Judgement, para. 50; *Kamuhanda* Appeal Judgement, para. 7; *Ntakirutimana* Appeal Judgement, para. 12; *Niyitegeka* Appeal Judgement, para. 8.

94 Appellant's Brief, paras 229-34. "Trafipro" was a consumer cooperative with headquarters in Kigali.

95 The Appeals Chamber notes that the Appellant erroneously referred to "Witness CGC" in para. 232 of his Appellant's Brief In the Corrigendum to the Appellant's Brief, p. 3, he stated that he meant Witness CGV.

96 Appellant's Brief, para. 232.

97 Trial Judgement, para. 128.

98 Trial Judgement, paras 125, 128.

99 Trial Judgement, paras 117, 124, 125, 158.

corroborated by Witness [...] CGV" in supporting the testimony of Witness CGN.[100] Thus, the Trial Chamber's finding that Witness CGV "made conflicting remarks about his basis for identifying the Accused"[101] was limited to remarks referring to the Appellant's status as a manager of the Trafipro shop in Kibuye, not to remarks on his occasional visits there.[102] It is recalled that it is permissible for a Trial Chamber to accept some elements of a witness's testimony while rejecting other elements.[103] Thus, the Trial Chamber was entitled to find that Witness CGV supported the conclusion that the Appellant's occasional presence at Trafipro in Kibuye provided a sufficient basis for Witness CGN's identification of the Appellant at Gitwa Hill.

45. As to Witness CGX, the Appellant correctly states that the Trial Chamber erroneously referred to him as one of the sources of the assertion that the Appellant was seen at the Trafipro **[page 16]** shop in Kibuye.[104] However, it is obvious that this mistake is merely a typographical error and that the Trial Chamber intended to refer to Witness CGM and not to Witness CGX. The Trial Chamber considered at length Witness CGM's testimony relating to Trafipro in Kibuye both before and after the relevant finding and accepted his account on the sighting of the Appellant there.[105]

46. The Appellant also states that the Trial Chamber accepted the testimony of Prosecution witnesses stating that they saw him at the Kibuye Trafipro between 1980 and 1985, although he was working for Elektrogaz in Kigali between 1981 and 1985.[106] The Trial Chamber found that the Appellant's work for Trafipro in Kigali from 1976 to 1981 "is not inconsistent with his occasional visits to the branch store in Kibuye during that period."[107] The Trial Chamber repeated this finding later, stating that Witness CGN "did not insist that the Accused has formal employment there."[108] The Trial Chamber was, thus, asserting that regardless of the location of the Appellant's work, it was still reasonable for him to have been present at the Kibuye Trafipro and seen by Prosecution witnesses to the extent needed as a foundation for prior identification. Thus, the findings of the Trial Chamber are reasonable.

47. Finally, the Trial Chamber accepted Witness CGN's testimony as to the vehicle which the Appellant "customarily used" when Witness CGN testified to seeing the Appellant on several occasions prior to 1994.[109] The question of the car used by the Appellant on 24 April 1994 appears to be only peripheral and does not affect the ability of Witness CGN to identify the Appellant. The Appellant has not demonstrated how the resolution of which car the Appellant normally used could have rendered unreasonable the Trial Chamber's assessment of Witness CGN's testimony concerning the events on 24 April 1994.

48. Consequently, the ninth and tenth grounds of appeal are rejected. **[page 17]**

IV. JUDGEMENT ALLEGEDLY RENDERED BEYOND THE SCOPE OF THE INDICTMENT (GROUND OF APPEAL 2)

A. Submissions of the Parties

49. The Appellant submits that the Trial Chamber erred in law in making factual findings on three elements not contained in the Indictment, and requests the Appeals Chamber to set them aside:[110] first, his position as Minister of Finance in the Interim Government of Rwanda in April-June 1994; second, his

100 Trial Judgement, para. 158 (emphasis added).
101 Trial Judgement, para. 128.
102 Trial Judgement, paras 128, 158.
103 *Kupreškić et al.* Appeal Judgement, paras 332-33; *Kajelijeli* Appeal Judgement, para. 167; *Ntakirutimana* Appeal Judgement para. 280; *Kamuhanda* Appeal Judgement para. 248.
104 Appellant's Brief, para. 230, referring to Trial Judgement, para. 158.
105 Trial Judgement, paras 125, 252, 254-255, 258.
106 Appellant's Brief, para. 230.
107 Trial Judgement, para. 125.
108 Trial Judgement, para. 158, note 192.
109 Appellant's Brief, para. 233; Trial Judgement, paras 149, 153.
110 Appellant's Brief, para. 65. *See also* Appellant's Reply, paras 1-4, where the Appellant asks the Appeals Chamber to disregard as irrelevant the evidence of the Appellant's role in the demission of Witness GKH and in the events at Nyabahanga Bridge.

participation in discussions at a meeting in Kibuye on 3 May 1994;[111] and third, his role in the resignation of Witness GHK as a Member of Parliament in June 1994.[112]

50. The Prosecution responds that the Trial Chamber did not rely on any of the elements challenged by the Appellant to find intent in convicting him.[113] The Prosecution submits that the Trial Chamber rightly explained that the evidence on these matters was only relevant as background or contextual information.[114]

B. Discussion

1. Appellant's Position in the Interim Government

51. The Appeals Chamber notes that the Appellant's position in the Interim Government was expressly mentioned twice in the Indictment.[115] Accordingly, this contention of the Appellant need not be discussed any further.

52. The Appellant also contends that the Trial Chamber improperly relied on his position in the Interim Government to find that he had the requisite criminal intent to commit the crimes charged. However, the Trial Chamber expressly stated that it was not persuaded that the Appellant's position was relevant to his *mens rea*, adding that "[t]he direct evidence of the Accused's conduct, if believed, provides ample indication of the state of mind of the Accused in respect of the specific **[page 18]** acts with which he is charged."[116] The Trial Chamber then found that the Appellant had the requisite *mens rea* in relation to the crimes for which he was convicted, based on evidence of his conduct in the particular events.[117]

53. Similarly, the Appellant contends that the fact that he was a minister in the Interim Government was misused by the Trial Chamber to establish his motive to commit the crimes charged in the Indictment. This argument presupposes that the Prosecution was under an obligation to establish the Appellant's motive to secure a conviction. However, pursuant to settled jurisprudence, it is the intent (*mens rea*) that is decisive for liability purposes, not the motive (which can only be relevant to sentencing, if at all).[118] The Appellant did not show that the Trial Chamber erred in this regard. Indeed, while the Trial Chamber noted that his position in the Interim Government could be relevant to a possible motive,[119] it immediately cautiously added that this had little probative value to establish the charges and might be prejudicial to the Appellant.[120]

54. The Appellant further contends that the reference to his position in the Interim Government was an impermissible attempt to reintroduce a charge of superior responsibility.[121] However, he did not demonstrate that, by presenting evidence on his position in the Interim Government, the Prosecution intended to reintroduce such a charge. Also, the Trial Chamber did not understand the reference to the Appellant's position in the Interim Government as a charge of superior responsibility, and he was convicted for his own acts, not for those committed by his subordinates.

---

111 Appellant's Brief, paras 47-48, 51-54 ("The Defence still believes that the Prosecution cunningly raised the issue of the Accused's participation in the meeting of 3 May 1994 in order to circumvent the issue of formally adding new charges, which would require using the procedure for amending an indictment."); Appellant's Reply, para. 19. Also, the Appellant denies having exhorted the PSD youth to serve in the civilian defence, or even having made reference to any RPF accomplices in the past in the PSD (Appellant's Brief, para. 52).

112 Appellant's Brief, paras 30-33, 34-35, 60-63; Appellant's Reply, paras 16, 20-22.

113 Respondent's Brief, paras 62-67.

114 Respondent's Brief, paras 65, 68-71.

115 *See* Indictment, Section I. The Accused, and Section II. Charges, para. 1.

116 Trial Judgement, para. 51.

117 *See* Trial Judgement, paras 462 (finding that the Appellant had the requisite intent to be convicted of genocide in relation to the events at Gitwa Hill) and 483 (finding that he had the requisite intent to be convicted of extermination for the same events). While the Trial Chamber did not expressly find that the Appellant had the requisite intent for genocide and murder in relation to the events at the Gaseke roadblock, this is implicit in paras 472-73 and 490.

118 *See, e.g.*, *Niyitegeka* Appeal Judgement, paras 52-53; *Kayishema and Ruzindana* Appeal Judgement, para. 161; *Tadić* Appeal Judgement, paras 269, 272.

119 Trial Judgement, para. 50.

120 Trial Judgement, para. 50.

121 A charge previously withdrawn from the Indictment, *see* Decision on Prosecution Request to Amend Indictment, 30 June 2003.

55. For the above reasons, the Appeals Chamber finds that the Appellant has not shown that the Trial Chamber improperly relied on his position in the Interim Government to convict him. Further, the Trial Chamber correctly recognized that the evidence of the Appellant's participation in the Interim Government could be relevant only for certain limited purposes, for instance as a matter of background information and in relation to his ability to incite and lead others to commit crimes.[122] **[page 19]**

2. Participation in the Meeting of 3 May 1994 and Alleged Role in the Resignation of Witness GKH

56. It is undisputed that the Indictment did not plead the Appellant's participation in the meeting of 3 May 1994 and his alleged role in the resignation of Witness GKH. The Appellant objected at trial to the admission of evidence on these elements[123] and maintained his objection on appeal; thus, there was no waiver. Accordingly, the Appeals Chamber will first consider whether the Trial Chamber convicted the Appellant on the basis of his participation in the meeting of 3 May 1994 or his alleged role in the resignation of Witness GKH. Even if this is not the case, the Appeals Chamber will consider whether the proceedings against the Appellant were rendered unfair because of the Trial Chamber's discussion of the evidence on these elements.

(a) Whether the Appellant's Convictions were Based on Material Facts not pleaded in the Indictment

57. As explained above,[124] a Trial Chamber cannot convict an accused on the basis of material facts not pleaded in the indictment (unless the defect has been cured subsequently by the provision of timely, clear and consistent information). Thus, irrespective of whether the Appellant's participation in the meeting of 3 May 1994 and his alleged role in the resignation of Witness GKH were material facts that had to be pleaded in the Indictment,[125] the crucial question is whether the Trial Chamber relied on these elements to convict the Appellant. The Trial Chamber explicitly refused to consider the evidence related to the Appellant's participation in the meeting of 3 May 1994 and to his alleged role in the resignation of Witness GKH as evidence of his *mens rea*;[126] instead, as already discussed, it relied on other evidence to conclude that he had the requisite intent.[127] The Trial Chamber did not otherwise rely on the Appellant's participation in the 3 May meeting or his alleged role in the resignation of Witness GKH to convict the Appellant. Therefore, the Appeals Chamber finds that the Trial Chamber did not convict the Appellant on the basis of material facts which were not pleaded in the Indictment. **[page 20]**

(b) Whether the Appellant was Otherwise Prejudiced by the Trial Chamber's Consideration of these Elements

58. The Trial Chamber stated that the evidence of the Appellant's participation in the meeting of 3 May 1994 "could be probative of an alleged motivation to actively pursue a government policy of genocide against Tutsi,"[128] and later referred to this as an aggravating circumstance.[129] As discussed below, this conclusion was open to the Trial Chamber.[130]

---

122 *See* Trial Judgement, paras 48, 68 and 483.

123 *See* Trial Judgement, para. 47.

124 *See supra* para. 16.

125 In this context, the Appeals Chamber recalls that while the Prosecution must plead the material facts underpinning the charges in the indictment, it need not plead the evidence that will be used to prove those material facts. *See Stakić* Appeal Judgement, para. 116; *Ntakirutimana* Appeal Judgement, para. 25; *Kupreškić et al.* Appeal Judgement, para. 88; *Furundžija* Appeal Judgement, para. 147.

126 Trial Judgement, paras 51 and 69.

127 *See supra* para. 52.

128 Trial Judgement, para. 69.

129 Trial Judgement, para. 508 (ii) ("The Chamber considers it particularly aggravating that instead of promoting peace and reconciliation in his capacity as Minister, he supported and advocated a policy of genocide").

130 *See infra*, para. 134. Further, since no effect on the verdict or the sentence has been shown, it is unnecessary to consider the Appellant's challenges to the use of the evidence on this event by the Trial Chamber.

59. As to the alleged role of the Appellant in the resignation of Witness GKH, it is unclear why the Trial Chamber made a finding on this.[131] Indeed, the Trial Chamber did not expressly refer to this finding later in the Trial Judgement. However, as no effect on the judgement has been shown, the Appeals Chamber considers that the proceedings against the Appellant were not rendered unfair by the Trial Chamber's discussion of this evidence.[132]

60. Accordingly, the second ground of appeal is rejected.

V. ALLEGED NON-DISCLOSURE OF EXCULPATORY EVIDENCE (GROUND OF APPEAL 4)

A. Submissions of the Parties

61. The Appellant submits that the Prosecutor failed to disclose[133] four documents which were in the possession of the Prosecution since 20 June 2001,[134] the first being a letter dated 20 June 2001 from the Governor of the National Bank of Rwanda ("Governor") forwarding the following three documents, which were allegedly drafted and signed by the Appellant in Kigali,[135] to the Prosecutor: two separate letters dated 13 and 23 April 1994 from the Appellant to the Governor, and an agreement signed by the Appellant relating to a grant by the Bank of a special advance to the State of Rwanda dated 23 April 1994. The Appellant argues that the documents show that he was in **[page 21]** Kigali and not in Gitwa on 13 and 23 April 1994 (the latter a Saturday).[136] The Appellant also submits that if the Trial Chamber had these documents, it is highly probable that it would not have assessed the testimony from Witnesses CGN and CGY as reliable evidence.[137]

62. The Prosecution acknowledges that the documents ought to have been disclosed under Rule 68,[138] but argues that the admission of this additional evidence on appeal provided a sufficient remedy.[139] The Prosecution submits that the non-disclosure did not cause material prejudice because the Appellant was able to adduce other evidence on the substance of what the documents record.[140] Additionally, according to the Prosecution, the consequences of non-disclosure only touch upon the Appellant's alibi for 23 April 1994 and do not affect the findings concerning 24 April 1994 and the events at the Gaseke roadblock; therefore, the non-disclosure does not affect the convictions for genocide, and extermination and murder as crimes against humanity.[141]

63. The Prosecution questions why the Appellant did not attempt to secure the three documents which had his signature and argue a "Kigali alibi" at trial.[142] The Prosecution also argues that the potential "Kigali alibi" contained in the new documents is inconsistent with the "Gitarama alibi" which he argued earlier at trial,[143] and that under Rule 67(A) a new alibi cannot be argued on appeal.[144] Furthermore, it argues that it

---

131 The Trial Chamber found that "in early or mid-June 1994 the Accused pressured Witness GKH to relinquish his post as an elected Member of Parliament for Kibuye Prefecture because he had a Tutsi wife" (Trial Judgement, para. 109).

132 Again, since no effect on the verdict or the sentence has been shown, it is unnecessary to consider the Appellant's challenges to the use of the evidence on this event by the Trial Chamber. As to the allegation that the Trial Chamber exhibited bias in assessing the evidence of Witness DN, this has not been established: *see infra* para. 80.

133 Appellant's Brief, paras 70-74.

134 Appellant's Brief, para. 70.

135 Appellant's Brief, paras 69 and 75, also referring to the admitted documents under Rule 115 in the Appeals Chamber's Decision on the Admission of Additional Evidence, 14 April 2004.

136 Appellant's Brief, paras 66-67, 72-79.

137 Appellant's Brief, paras 75-81

138 Respondent's Brief, paras 134, 139.

139 Respondent's Brief, paras 134 and 141; Decision on the Admission of Additional Evidence, 14 April 2005.

140 Respondent's Brief, paras 135, 141-42.

141 Respondent's Brief, paras 137, 167, 171.

142 Respondent's Brief, paras 148-50.

143 Respondent's Brief, para. 154.

144 Respondent's Brief, paras 136, 155. The Respondent submits the rule is designed to enable the Prosecutor to investigate both places and witnesses relating to an alibi. The presence of the Appellant in Kigali after 12 April was not raised at trial. The lack of opportunity to investigate is allegedly not due to non-disclosure, because if the Appellant genuinely had a Kigali alibi then he should have raised it at trial.

was routine for official documents to bear the Kigali letterhead even after the seat of the Interim Government was moved from Kigali to Gitarama.[145]

B. Discussion

64. With the additional evidence, the Appellant seeks to support an alibi different to the one raised at trial where he relied on Witness DP as an alibi witness. Witness DP testified that he saw the Appellant once or twice a day, excluding weekends, from 15 April to about 28 May 1994, at various times of day, either at the Appellant's office in the government compound or at one of the two commercial banks where Witness DP worked in Gitarama, as well as at occasional social meetings.[146] Thus, the alibi at trial placed the Appellant in Gitarama.[147] The Trial Chamber found **[page 22]** that this testimony carried "very little weight" as the alibi could not account for the time outside of the meetings between Witness DP and the Appellant.[148]

65. The Appellant now seeks to rely on the documents admitted on appeal under Rule 115 to argue that he was in Kigali on the dates the documents were signed:[149] two of them are dated 23 April 1994 and one is dated 13 April 1994.[150] As to the former date, the Appellant argues that, as the document is purported to have been signed in Kigali, he could not have been in Gitwa on 23 April 1994, a date on which the Trial Chamber found that he had participated in attacks.[151]

66. The first issue is whether an Appellant is permitted to raise a new alibi on appeal. Pursuant to Rule 67(A)(ii)(a), the Prosecution has to be provided with notice of an alibi argument as early as practicable and prior to the commencement of trial. While Rule 67(B) states that failure to provide such notice "shall not limit the right of the accused" to rely on an alibi defence, the jurisprudence permits a Trial Chamber to consider the failure to provide the requisite notice in its assessment of the alibi.[152] The same legal principle applies in a situation where an alibi is raised for the first time on appeal. Rule 67 provides that the Defence can still raise an alibi even if no prior notice is provided; however, if for example the Appellant could have been reasonably expected to raise the new alibi during trial, the Appeals Chamber can take particular note of the failure to provide timely notice to the Prosecution in its assessment of the alibi. This does not contradict the finding of the ICTY Appeals Chamber that an "accused, generally, cannot raise a defence for the first time on appeal".[153] The Appeals Chamber recalls

> that an alibi 'does not constitute a defence in its proper sense'. In general, a defence comprises grounds excluding criminal responsibility although the accused has fulfilled the legal elements of a criminal offence. An alibi, however, is nothing more than the denial of the accused's presence during the commission of a criminal act.[154]

67. The second issue is that the alibi raised on appeal is different from the Gitarama Alibi raised at trial where Witness DP supported the Appellant's contention that he could not have committed the alleged crimes as he was working in Gitarama. The Appellant now argues that the additional evidence shows that he was in Kigali on the dates reflected therein. **[page 23]**

68. In assessing alibi evidence a Chamber must consider whether the Defence raised a reasonable doubt about the Prosecution's allegations.[155] On appeal, the Appeals Chamber then has to consider whether the

---

145 Respondent's Brief, paras 158-63. Note 214 refers to the Appellant's passport Exh. D.63 which was purportedly issued in Kigali but Witness DP testified the Appellant remained in Gitarama in May and June.

146 Trial Judgement, para. 171.

147 Trial Judgement, paras 170-81.

148 Trial Judgement, paras 177-78 and 265.

149 Appellant's Brief, paras 67, 75-81.

150 The evidence in relation to this date is not relevant for the purposes of the conviction for crimes committed at Gitwa Hill.

151 Trial Judgement, para. 179.

152 *Kajelijeli* Trial Judgement, paras 164-67; *Kamuhanda* Trial Judgement, para. 82; *Kayishema and Ruzindana* Trial Judgement, paras 233-39; *Kayishema and Ruzindana* Appeal Judgement, paras 106, 110-11; *Musema* Trial Judgement para. 107; *Niyitegeka* Trial Judgement, para. 50; *Semanza* Trial Judgement, para. 82.

153 *Aleksovski* Appeal Judgement, para. 51.

154 *Kamuhanda* Appeal Judgement, para. 167.

155 *Kamuhanda* Appeal Judgement, para. 167: "An alibi, in contrast to a defence, is intended to raise *reasonable doubt* about the presence of the accused at the crime site, this being an element of the prosecution's case, thus the burden of proof is on the prosecution" (emphasis added); *Kajelijeli* Appeal Judgement, para. 42; *Ntakirutimana* Appeal Judgement, paras 170-71.

Trial Chamber's method of assessing the alibi evidence was erroneous.[156] If additional evidence has been admitted, the Appeals Chamber will first determine, on the basis of the trial record alone, whether a reasonable trier of fact could have reached the conclusion of guilt beyond reasonable doubt. Only if this is the case, will it determine whether, on the basis of the trial record and additional evidence admitted on appeal, it is itself convinced beyond reasonable doubt.[157]

69. The Trial Chamber considered the Gitarama Alibi pertaining to 23 April 1994 to be inadequate.[158] The Appeals Chamber sees no error in the finding. Thus, the Appeals Chamber now turns to the question whether the documents admitted as additional evidence on appeal show that the Appellant was in Kigali on 23 April 1994.

70. The Appeals Chamber finds that the documents admitted as additional evidence do not establish the veracity of the Kigali alibi nor do the documents render the finding of the Trial Chamber on the Gitarama alibi unreasonable[159] or, read together, cast any doubt on the Trial Chamber's finding on the Appellant's presence at the crime site on 23 April 1994. The Appellant merely asserts that the letterheads of the documents bearing his signature show that he was in Kigali at the time of the indicated dates. If he was indeed in Kigali at these times working on the documents, his delay in raising the alibi affects the probative value of the documents: he would have been able to recall his own actions independently from the admission of the new documents, and he does not provide a reasonable explanation for the delay in raising the Kigali alibi. Also, the Appellant did not show that the documents admitted as additional evidence are different from a class of documents which could have been just routinely marked as being created in Kigali, the established seat of government, although they were signed at some other location.

71. The Appeals Chamber recalls that in the Rule 115 Decision of April 2005 it held that the question whether or not the Prosecution was under an obligation to disclose the four documents pursuant to Rule 68 of the Rules to the Appellant has to be dealt with only in the appeal judgement, **[page 24]** as it refers to the Appellant's fourth ground of appeal.[160] No doubt the Prosecution should have disclosed these documents to the Appellant.[161]

72. However, in light of the above findings, it is neither necessary to consider the Appellant's submissions concerning the impact of the new alibi on the testimony of Witnesses CGY and CGN,[162] nor to further consider the Prosecution's alleged breach of its obligations under Rule 68.[163] The Appeals Chamber reiterates, however, that the onus on the Prosecution to comply with Rule 68 to the best of its ability is not a secondary obligation, and is as important as the obligation to prosecute.[164]

73. Consequently, the fourth ground of appeal is rejected.

VI. ALLEGED ERRORS IN THE ASSESSMENT OF DEFENCE EVIDENCE (GROUNDS OF APPEAL 5 AND 3)

74. The Appellant submits that the Trial Chamber violated his right to fair proceedings by ignoring some of the evidence he presented, by examining it in a manner that was systematically unfavourable to him, and by omitting to address fundamental points raised by the Defence.[165] The Prosecution responds that the Trial Chamber adhered to the relevant principles relating to the assessment of evidence.[166]

156 *Kamuhanda* Appeal Judgement, para. 210.
157 *See Blaškić* Appeal Judgement, para. 24(c).
158 Trial Judgement, paras 170-81.
159 *See Blaškić* Appeal Judgement, para. 24(c).
160 Decision on the Admission of Additional Evidence, 14 April 2005, p. 8.
161 This has also been admitted by the Prosecution, Respondent's Brief, paras 134, 139.
162 Appellant's Brief, paras 75-81.
163 Appellant's Brief, paras 70-74.
164 *See Kordić and Čerkez* Appeal Judgement, para. 242.
165 Appellant's Brief, paras 84-146.
166 Respondent's Brief, paras 80, 83-92, 132-33.

75. Each of the instances raised by the Appellant will now be briefly discussed; the Appeals Chamber will then consider whether the Appellant has shown that his right to fair proceedings was infringed. At the outset, the Appeals Chamber recalls that:

> [T]he Trial Chamber is not under the obligation to justify its findings in relation to every submission made during the trial [...]. [I]t is in the discretion of the Trial Chamber as to which legal arguments to address. With regard to the factual findings, the Trial Chamber is required only to make findings of those facts which are essential to the determination of guilt on a particular count. It is not necessary to refer to the testimony of every witness or every piece of evidence on the trial record. It is to be presumed that the Trial Chamber evaluated all the evidence presented to it, as long as there is no indication that the Trial Chamber completely disregarded any particular piece of evidence [...]. If the Trial Chamber did not refer to the evidence given by a witness, even if it is in contradiction to the Trial Chamber's finding, it is to be presumed that the Trial Chamber assessed and weighed the evidence, but found that the evidence did not prevent it from arriving at its actual findings.[167] **[page 25]**

A. Witness DQ

1. Submissions of the Parties

76. The Appellant avers that the Trial Chamber ignored crucial elements of the testimony of Witness DQ, in particular his evidence that the Appellant was absent from the scenes of genocide in Kibuye Prefecture and his statements as to the morality of the Appellant before the start of the massacres.[168]

77. The Prosecution responds that the features of Witness DQ's testimony which the Appellant claims the Trial Chamber ignored were not so centrally important that the Trial Chamber was required to assess them in detail.[169]

2. Discussion

78. It has not been shown that the Trial Chamber ignored parts of Witness DQ's evidence or that its assessment thereof was unreasonable. The Trial Chamber did refer to Witness DQ's evidence in the Trial Judgement[170] and, even though it did not refer expressly to the parts of Witness DQ's evidence mentioned by the Appellant, the Appellant has not shown that no reasonable trier of fact could have reached the findings reached by the Trial Chamber:

1) Witness DQ's testimony that the Appellant was never identified as one of the persons responsible for the massacres constituted hearsay evidence of unverifiable reliability; it would have been reasonable for a Trial Chamber to prefer the direct evidence of Prosecution witnesses incriminating the Appellant;

2) As to Witness DQ's evidence of the Appellant's morality before the start of the massacres, a reasonable trier of fact could have found that this was insufficient to cast doubt on the evidence of his involvement in the massacres.

B. Witness DN

1. Submissions of the Parties

79. In the Appellant's view, while the Trial Chamber admitted parts of Witness DN's testimony, it unfairly rejected or ignored other important parts of his testimony,[171] *inter alia*, portions of his evidence pertaining to a meeting on 3 May 1994,[172] his evidence that the Appellant did not force **[page 26]** Witness GKH to

[167] *Kvočka et al.* Appeal Judgement, para. 23 (references omitted).

[168] Appellant's Brief, paras 85-91; Appellant's Reply, para. 27.

[169] Respondent's Brief, paras 94-97.

[170] *See* Trial Judgement, para. 106.

[171] Appellant's Brief, paras 92-101. At paragraphs 126-128, the Appellant contends that Exh. D.41 (a written statement of Witness DN to the State Prosecutor of Kibuye, dated 26 March 2001) buttresses the credibility of his testimony.

[172] Appellant's Brief, para. 93.

resign from his post of deputy,[173] and his evidence absolving the Appellant from the massacres.[174] The Prosecution responds that the Trial Chamber reasonably rejected part of Witness DN's evidence.[175]

2. Discussion

80. The Appellant has failed to show that the Trial Chamber unfairly rejected or ignored parts of Witness DN's evidence.

81. The argument of the Appellant with respect to the Trial Chamber's assessment of Witness DN's evidence on the meeting of 3 May 1994 is unclear.[176] The Appellant seems to suggest that the Trial Chamber erred in accepting Witness DN's testimony as to the statements made by the Appellant during the meeting while at the same time rejecting Witness DN's suggestion that the Appellant had been obliged to make those statements at the meeting because of his vulnerability as a member of the PSD.[177] However, it has not been shown that the Trial Chamber was unreasonable in accepting his testimony as to the statements made by the Appellant and in rejecting his suggestion as to why the Appellant made the statements. In particular, as the Trial Chamber noted, this suggestion was speculative and based on vague remarks about the position of PSD members at the time.[178]

82. With respect to the resignation of Witness GKH, the Trial Chamber reasonably preferred the testimony of Witness GKH to that of Witness DN:

1) The Trial Chamber rightly considered that Witness DN was not completely dispassionate on this issue.[179] The Appellant's argument that the Trial Chamber should not have invoked "confidential reasons" to rule on the credibility of this witness[180] is unconvincing: the "confidential reasons" were known to the Parties and it is only to protect the identity of Witness DN that the Trial Chamber spoke of "confidential reasons" in the Trial Judgement. Also, the Trial Chamber found that "Witness DN's testimony on this question appeared evasive and **[page 27]** uncertain."[181] The Appellant does not argue that this assessment was unreasonable.

2) Witness DN's testimony did not undermine Witness GKH's evidence on his resignation. As explained by the Trial Chamber, "Witness DN had no direct knowledge of the conversation between Witness GKH and the Accused; his testimony was only that Witness GKH had not mentioned that the Accused had threatened him in order to induce his resignation."[182] The Trial Chamber was reasonable in concluding that it was unlikely that Witness GKH would have mentioned the threats of the Appellant to Witness DN.[183] It was reasonable for the Trial Chamber to find that "Witness DN's testimony concerning the reasons for the resignation of Witness GKH is not credible and deserves little weight."[184]

83. Finally, the Appellant argues that the Trial Chamber ignored Witness DN's evidence absolving the Appellant from any responsibility for the massacres in Kibuye Prefecture. In this connection, the Appellant points to the following three grounds: First, in Exh. D.41 (a letter written by Witness DN to the Rwandan

---

173 Appellant's Brief, paras 93, 100.

174 Appellant's Brief, paras 95-99, 126-27. The Appellant recalls that Witness DN stated (Exh. D.41) that he had nothing to say about the activities of the Appellant during the period of the massacres. The Appellant argues that Witness DN testified that the Appellant was never mentioned as a person responsible of the massacres in meetings held during the war to convince the local population to cease the killings or in the *Gacaca* organized by detainees of Kibuye prison.

175 Respondent's Brief, paras 100-05, 123-27.

176 *See* Appellant's Brief, para. 93 ("Furthermore, Trial Chamber I found Witness DN to be credible as to the speech Emmanuel Ndindabahizi allegedly made during this meeting, and isolated this part of the testimony from its context so as to present it in an unfavourable light for the Defence.")

177 *See* Trial Judgement, paras 87-88.

178 *See* Trial Judgement, para. 88 and T. 4 November 2003, pp. 33-34 (Witness DN alleges that the PSD was perceived as too supportive of the RPF and that the Appellant could not have spoken openly against the killings).

179 *See* Trial Judgement, paras 102-03.

180 *See* Appellant's Brief, para. 94.

181 Trial Judgement, paras 103; *see also* para. 105.

182 Trial Judgement, para. 104. *See also* para. 100.

183 *See* Trial Judgement, para. 104.

184 Trial Judgement, para. 105.

Prosecutor), Witness DN "said nothing about the activities of the Appellant during the period of the massacres";[185] second, Witness DN testified that, at the end of April 1994, he organized meetings with the local population in an attempt to stop the killings; nobody identified the Appellant as one of the persons responsible for the violence;[186] third, none of Witness DN's co-detainees in a national prison in Rwanda ever incriminated the Appellant in relation to the massacres in Kibuye Prefecture.[187] However, the Appellant has not shown that, presented with this evidence, no reasonable trier of fact could have found as the Trial Chamber did. It was reasonable for the Trial Chamber to prefer the direct evidence of Prosecution witnesses implicating the Appellant in the crimes to Witness DN's hearsay evidence.

C. Witness DU

1. Submissions of the Parties

84. The Appellant submits that the Trial Chamber ignored Witness DU's evidence, which contradicted Witness CGM's testimony and exculpated the Appellant from any responsibility for the killing of Tutsi women married to Hutu men.[188] The Prosecution responds that the Trial Chamber correctly held that Witness DU's evidence had limited significance.[189] **[page 28]**

2. Discussion

85. The Trial Chamber found, on the basis of Witness CGM's testimony, that the Appellant encouraged those at Nyabahanga Bridge roadblock to kill Tutsi women married to Hutu men.[190] However, the Appellant did not incur any liability in this relation because the Trial Chamber found that the evidence of Witness CGM was insufficient to establish that the conduct of the Appellant directly and substantially contributed to killings.[191] Thus, even if the Appeals Chamber were to prefer the evidence of Witness DU on this, the verdict would not be affected.

86. The Appeals Chamber notes that, although the Trial Chamber did not refer to the evidence of Witness DU in relation to the distribution of weapons and incitement at Nyabahanga Bridge at the end of May 1994, it did refer to it elsewhere in its Judgement.[192] As explained above,[193] the Trial Chamber is presumed to have taken into account the evidence before it, and the Appellant will be successful only if he can show that no reasonable trier of fact would have decided as the Trial Chamber did. In the present case, the Trial Chamber was presented with two competing accounts: First, the testimony of Witness CGM that Tutsi women married to Hutu men only started being killed after the Appellant incited these killings at the end of May 1994;[194] and second, the testimony of Witness DU that Tutsi women married to Hutu men were killed from the beginning of the war, and that these killings ceased after the Appellant called for an end to them when he came to the region in June 1994.[195] The Appellant argues that the Trial Chamber erred in accepting the account of Witness CGM, but his arguments are limited to asserting that the testimony of Witness DU contradicted that of Witness CGM, and he does not show that a reasonable trier of fact presented with the testimony of Witness DU would necessarily have rejected the testimony of Witness CGM.

---

185 Appellant's Brief, para. 95.
186 Appellant's Brief, para. 98, referring to T. 3 November 2003, pp. 33-34.
187 Appellant's Brief, paras 96, 99, referring to T. 3 November 2003, p. 35.
188 Appellant's Brief, paras 102-04.
189 Respondent's Brief, para. 107, referring to Trial Judgement, paras 363 and 365.
190 Trial Judgement, para. 264.
191 Trial Judgement, para. 474.
192 *See* Trial Judgement, paras 362-65.
193 *See supra*, para. 75.
194 T. 15 September 2003, pp. 7-9.
195 T. 28 October 2003, p. 48.

D. Expert Witness Bernard Lugan

1. Submissions of the Parties

87. The Appellant asserts that the Trial Chamber erred in rejecting the evidence of Defence Expert Witness Bernard Lugan that the Appellant's accession to the Interim Government and his participation in the meeting of 3 May 1994 in Kibuye were part of a survival strategy.[196] **[page 29]**

2. Discussion

88. The Appellant merely repeats arguments that did not succeed at trial, without showing that the Trial Chamber's assessment of the evidence of Defence Expert Lugan was unreasonable and led to a miscarriage of justice.

E. Witness DX

1. Submissions of the Parties

89. The Appellant submits that the Trial Chamber unfairly denied his motion for the admission of Witness DX's written statement.[197] The Appellant argues that first, the Trial Chamber should not have considered the arguments of the Prosecution in response to the motion because the deadline to file a response had lapsed;[198] and second, that in dismissing the motion, the Trial Chamber did not understand the importance of Witness DX's statement for the Defence, particularly in that it showed that the Appellant was manipulated by the investigators of the ICTR and that the Indictment against him was fraudulent.[199]

90. In response, the Prosecution argues that the Appellant merely repeats arguments that were unsuccessful at trial without demonstrating how the Trial Chamber erred.[200] First, in rejecting the motion, the Trial Chamber did not have to decide whether the Prosecution's response to the motion was timely, nor did it give the Prosecution's arguments great weight;[201] and second, the Trial Chamber provided a detailed, clear and reasoned decision, specifying that parts of the written statement did not go to "proof of a matter other than the acts and conduct of the accused" (as required by Rule 92*bis* of the Rules) and that the other parts were so intertwined with the rest of the statement that it was difficult to split the statement into parts that could be admitted.[202]

2. Discussion

91. In its Decision on Rule 92*bis* Motion, the Trial Chamber found first that sections of the statement proffered (to wit, the sections stating that the Appellant could not have committed the crimes for which he was indicted because that would have been contrary to his character) were not admissible under Rule 92*bis* of the Rules because they went to the acts and conduct of the **[page 30]** Appellant.[203] The Trial Chamber also refused to admit other parts of the statement because cross-examination on these parts would not be possible in light of the unwillingness of Witness DX to appear before the Trial Chamber.[204] Finally, the Trial Chamber

---

196 Appellant's Brief, paras 105-11. At paragraphs 107-08, the Appellant contends that, contrary to what the Prosecution asserted at trial, Dr. Lugan cannot be said to be postulating a racist, negativist and revisionist history of Rwanda.

197 Appellant's Brief, paras 112-19. At paragraph 113, the Appellant submits that his motion met the formal requirements of Rule 92*bis* of the Rules. This is irrelevant as the Trial Chamber did not find that the motion failed to meet the formal requirements of Rule 92*bis* of the Rules: *see* T. 28 November 2003, pp. 24-26 ("Decision on Rule 92*bis* Motion").

198 Appellant's Brief, paras 114-15.

199 Appellant's Brief, paras 117-19, 142.

200 Respondent's Brief, para. 112.

201 Respondent's Brief, para. 114.

202 Respondent's Brief, paras 112, 116-17.

203 Decision on Rule 92*bis* Motion, pp. 24-25.

204 Decision on Rule 92*bis* Motion, p. 25 ("[...] we have noted in this document several matters which calls [*sic*] for cross-examination, such as page 7, when it is a matter of how the witness left Rwanda; at page 18 and 20, about Mr. Ndindabahizi's relationships to colleagues in various governments and also the parts concerning the legitimacy of the investigation by ICTR employees and the assertion that the Accused was subjected to some kind of blackmail.")

considered whether the remaining parts of the statement could still be admitted pursuant to Rule 92*bis* of the Rules but refused to do this because it found that "everything is intertwined."[205] Thus, the Trial Chamber held that the statement proffered could not be admitted pursuant to Rule 92*bis* of the Rules.

92. The Appeals Chamber must consider whether the Appellant has shown that the Trial Chamber erred in its Decision on Rule 92*bis* Motion. A preliminary question is whether, as argued by the Appellant, the Trial Chamber improperly considered the Prosecution's arguments in response to the motion.

(a) Whether the Trial Chamber Improperly Considered the Prosecution's Arguments

93. The Appellant filed his motion on 27 October 2003.[206] The Prosecution filed a response on 27 November 2003.[207] At the hearing on 28 November 2003, the Trial Chamber invited the parties to make further oral submissions on the Rule 92*bis* Motion (and on the question whether the Prosecution had filed a timely response[208]). The Trial Chamber then rejected the Rule 92*bis* Motion, stating at the end that, "[w]ith this conclusion, the question doesn't arise whether the Prosecution's response is timely under Rule 92 *bis* (E), and we do not have to decide that matter."[209]

94. The Appellant argues that the Trial Chamber should not have considered the written response filed by the Prosecution nor should the Prosecution have been given a further chance to make oral submissions.[210] But the Appellant does not go as far as to argue that if the Prosecution's arguments were time-barred then the Trial Chamber was bound to admit the statement of **[page 31]** Witness DX. This is correct because, irrespective of the arguments made by the parties, the Trial Chamber must itself be convinced that the statement proffered meets the requirements of Rule 92*bis* of the Rules.[211] In particular, the Trial Chamber must be satisfied that the written statement "goes to proof of a matter other than the acts and the conduct of the accused as charged in the indictment."[212] Further, even if this requirement is met, the decision of the Trial Chamber is not an automatic one: the Trial Chamber must weigh "[f]actors in favour of admitting evidence in the form of a written statement" and "[f]actors against admitting evidence in the form of a written statement."[213] In this connection, the submissions of the parties may be useful to the Trial Chamber, but they are by no means indispensable.

95. The Appeals Chamber need not decide whether the Trial Chamber erred in not ruling on the admissibility of the Response to Rule 92*bis* Motion or in allowing the Prosecution to make oral representations on the Rule 92*bis* Motion because no prejudice to the Appellant has been shown.

(b) Whether the Trial Chamber Erred in Dismissing the Rule 92bis Motion

96. The Trial Chamber found that Witness DX's assertions that the Appellant was incapable of committing the crimes with which he was charged because of his character went to the matter of his acts and conduct.[214]

---

205 Decision on Rule 92*bis* Motion, p. 25.

206 "Requête aux fins d'admission d'un témoignage écrit (Article 92 bis du Règlement de procédure et de preuve)", filed confidentially on 27 October 2003 ("Rule 92*bis* Motion").

207 "Prosecutor's Response to the Defence Motion for Admission of a Written [Statement of] Witness DX into Evidence under Rule 92 *bis* of the Rules of Procedure and Evidence", filed 27 November 2003 ("Response to Rule 92*bis* Motion").

208 On this last point, *see* T. 28 November 2003, p. 18.

209 Decision on Rule 92*bis* Motion, p. 26. Rule 92*bis* (E) of the Rules reads:

> Subject to any order of the Trial Chamber to the contrary, a party seeking to adduce a written statement or transcript shall give fourteen days notice to the opposing party, who may within seven days object. The Trial Chamber shall decide, after hearing the parties, whether to admit the statement or transcript in whole or in part and whether to require the witness to appear for cross-examination.

210 Appellant's Brief, paras 114-15.

211 *See Stakić* Appeal Judgement, para. 196, stating that even if the Prosecution does not object, the plain language of Rule 92*bis* gives the Trial Chamber discretion to decide whether to admit such statements.

212 Rule 92*bis* (A) of the Rules.

213 Rule 92*bis* (A)(i) and (ii) of the Rules. *See* also Rule 92*bis* (E) of the Rules ("The Trial Chamber shall decide, after hearing the parties, whether to admit the statement or transcript in whole or in part and whether to require the witness to appear for cross-examination.")

214 Decision on Rule 92*bis* Motion, pp. 24-25.

Therefore, it held that these parts of the statement were inadmissible pursuant to Rule 92*bis* of the Rules.[215] The Appellant offers no argument to challenge this. Accordingly, it has not been shown that the Trial Chamber erred in this regard.

97. The Appellant takes issue with the Trial Chamber's decision not to admit Witness DX's assertions relating to the contacts between the Appellant and the investigators of the Office of the Prosecution starting in 1996 up to the moment the Appellant was indicted and arrested in 2001. The Appellant submits that this evidence was of considerable importance to prove that he had been manipulated by the ICTR investigators, and that he had been indicted only as a result of the failure of the discussions between him and the ICTR investigators.[216]

98. As recalled above, the decision on whether to admit written statements (or parts thereof) is a discretionary one. In the case at hand, the Trial Chamber refused to admit the relevant parts of **[page 32]** Witness DX's statement because of the impossibility of cross-examining the witness.[217] The Appellant has not demonstrated that the Trial Chamber abused its discretion or rendered his trial unfair in deciding as it did. First, Rule 92*bis* of the Rules itself provides that the existence of "factors which make it appropriate for the witness to attend for cross-examination" weighs against admitting evidence in the form of a written statement.[218] The Appellant offers no argument that the Trial Chamber erred in finding that cross-examination was needed with regard to a series of elements of Witness DX's written statement[219] or that other factors in favour of admitting this evidence should have prevailed. Second, as to the Appellant's contention that Witness DX's statement would have shown that he was manipulated by the investigators of the ICTR or that the indictment against him was "fraudulent", the Appeals Chamber considers that in principle, the exercise of the discretion of who to indict is vested in the Prosecution. The role of the Confirming Judge is in principle limited to deciding whether a *prima facie* case has been established, and the role of the Trial Chamber is similarly limited to deciding whether the Prosecution has proved its case beyond reasonable doubt.[220] This is what the Trial Chamber did.

99. As to the remainder of Witness DX's statement, the Appellant provides no argument that the Trial Chamber erred in finding that it could not be admitted pursuant to Rule 92*bis* of the Rules because everything was "intertwined."[221] Thus, it has not been shown that the Trial Chamber erred in rejecting the remaining parts of Witness DX's written statement.

F. Exhibit D.34

100. The Appellant contends that, while the Trial Chamber accepted that Exh. D.34 was authentic, it failed to give proper weight to this exhibit when making its findings.[222] This argument has been considered under Ground 11, as it relates to the Trial Chamber's factual findings with respect to the events at the Gaseke roadblock. **[page 33]**

---

215 Decision on Rule 92*bis* Motion, p. 25.

216 Appellant's Brief, paras 117-119.

217 Decision on Rule 92*bis* Motion, p. 25. In his motion, the Appellant had stated that "au debut du mois de septembre 2003, le témoin DX a fait état de difficultés tenant tout á la fois á son état de santé, á sa sécurité et á ses obligations professionnelles, et a finalement refusé d'effectuer le déplacement á Arusha pour y comparaître devant la Chambre de Première Instance I"(Rule 92*bis* Motion, para. 2).

218 Rule 92*bis* (A)(ii)(c) of the Rules.

219 The Trial Chamber referred to the issues of "how the witness left Rwanda[,] Mr. Ndindabahizi's relationships to colleagues in various governments and also the parts concerning the legitimacy of the investigation by ICTR employees and the assertion that the Accused was subjected to some kind of blackmail" (Decision on Rule 92*bis* Motion, p. 25).

220 The Prosecution has discretion to decide who to indict (Articles 15, 17 of the Statute). While the indictment must be confirmed by a judge (Article 18 of the Statute and Rule 47 of the Rules), the role of the judge is limited to determining that a *prima facie* case has been established against the individual (Article 18 of the Statute). In the case at hand, the Appellant does not challenge the Confirming Judge's determination that a *prima facie* case had been made against him. The Appeals Chamber notes that ICTY Rule 73*bis* of the Rules does not form part of the ICTR Rules and in any event only permits the Trial Chamber to direct the Prosecution to limit the counts on which it proceeds.

221 Decision on Rule 92*bis* Motion, p. 25.

222 Appellant's Brief, paras 120-25.

G. Exhibit D.52

1. Submissions of the Parties

101. The Appellant submits that the Trial Chamber unfairly failed to attach any weight to the fact that the *Preliminary Report on Identification of Sites of the Genocide and Massacres that took place in Rwanda from April to July 1994*[223] does not mention him even though it purports to identify the perpetrators of the massacres at the sites of the genocide. The Appellant also argues that the report was presented by the Prosecution in other cases and that it is unfair not to accord it any probative value when used in support of the Defence's case.[224]

102. The Prosecution argues that it was within the Trial Chamber's discretion not to accord any weight to Exh. D.52, especially as the Chamber was unable to assess its reliability and found that it did not contradict Prosecution evidence.[225]

2. Discussion

103. The Trial Chamber explicitly considered this issue:

> The Defence has also at various points asserted that the absence of incriminatory statement regarding the Accused in certain documents should be considered by the Chamber as exculpatory evidence. Reference has been made, for example, to a preliminary report of a commission which had purportedly conducted extensive investigations into killings in Rwanda in 1994. The Defence tendered this lengthy report as an exhibit in connection with testimony by its expert witness, Dr. Bernard Lugan, who testified that there was no mention of the Accused in the report. The Chamber notes that the report, dated February 1996, is entitled "Preliminary". According to its preface, the document does not claim to be authoritative or exhaustive in its coverage. None of the authors of the report were called before the Chamber; there was no discussion of its methodology, particularly in reference to the specific events alleged in the Indictment; and there was no testimony on whether the preliminary report had been superseded by a final report. In these circumstances, the Chamber is unable to assess its reliability, and does not consider its contents to contradict Prosecution evidence.[226]

104. The Appellant merely reiterates the arguments he raised at trial, without demonstrating that the Trial Chamber erred in its assessment of this evidence. The Appeals Chamber finds no error in the Trial Chamber's analysis. As to the argument that the report was considered in support of the Prosecution's case in other cases, this does not show that the Appellant was treated unfairly. A Trial Chamber has discretion in the appreciation of evidence presented by the parties in the case before it, and there is no unfairness simply because another Trial Chamber decided otherwise in another case in respect of a particular piece of evidence. The Appellant has not shown in what way the jurisprudence mentioned by the Appellant is helpful to his case. **[page 34]**

H. Conclusion

105. As discussed above, the Trial Chamber's assessment of the evidence presented by the Defence was reasonable. Thus, the Appellant has failed to establish that the Trial Chamber abused its discretion or exhibited bias in assessing the evidence. The fifth and the third grounds of appeal are rejected.[227]

---

223 Exh. D.52.

224 Appellant's Brief, paras 129-35, 145. *See also* Appellant's Reply, para. 28.

225 Respondent's Brief, paras 128-31.

226 Trial Judgement, para. 52 (reference omitted).

227 As explained above, the Appellant's contentions relating to Exh. D.34 will be considered together with his arguments under Ground 11 of the appeal.

VII. GROUNDS OF APPEAL 6 AND 8 – WITHDRAWN

VIII. ALLEGED ERROR IN FINDING THAT THE APPELLANT WAS AT THE GASEKE ROADBLOCK (GROUND OF APPEAL 11)

A. Submissions of the Parties

106. The Appellant argues that the Trial Chamber based its finding on his alleged visit to the Gaseke roadblock at the end of May 1994 solely upon the basis of the uncorroborated testimony of Witness CGC which was inconsistent with other evidence[228] and incorrect as to dates.[229]

107. The Prosecution states that reliance on uncorroborated evidence in a holistic way is permissible[230] and that the Trial Chamber did not err in accepting Witness CGC's evidence.[231]

B. Discussion

1. Alleged Contradiction Between the Testimonies of Witness CGC and Other Witnesses

108. The Appellant submits that the Trial Chamber's findings on contradictions between Witness CGC's testimony and the testimonies of Witness DC and Witness DB occasioned a miscarriage of justice. **[page 35]**

(a) Witness DC

109. The Appellant argues that while the Trial Chamber found that Witness DC was not present at the roadblock prior to and during the killing of Mr. Nors,[232] it later referred to Witness DC's presence at the roadblock.[233] A careful review of the two findings reveals that they are reconcilable. It was reasonable for the Trial Chamber to accept Witness DC's testimony that he was *asked* to stay at the roadblock to assist in killing Mr. Nors, and to find also that Witness DC was in fact not present prior to or during the killing of Mr. Nors. The scenario envisaged in the Trial Judgement is as follows: Witness DB was found to have accompanied Mr. Nors through the Gaseke roadblock.[234] Witness DC then arrived at the roadblock and was asked to stay to assist in killing Mr. Nors on his return.[235] Witness DC states that he waited for three hours.[236] However, the evidence accepted by the Trial Chamber shows that Witness DB and Mr. Nors stayed for at least a day in Kibuye.[237] Therefore, the remainder of Witness DC's testimony was not found to be credible, namely his assertion that he waited at the roadblock for three hours and then assisted in the killing of Mr. Nors, without having seen the Appellant.[238] Witness CGC, however, was accepted to have been at the roadblock during the return journey of Witness DB and Mr. Nors, and to have seen the Appellant before their arrival.[239] The Appellant has advanced no further arguments on this issue. The Appeals Chamber finds that he did not show

228 Appellant's Brief, paras 252, 255 referring to Trial Judgement, paras 227, 229. Appellant's Reply, paras 87-88.

229 Appellant's Brief, paras 244-50, 289-91. The Appellant reiterates his submissions with respect to the alleged lies of Witness CGC concerning Mr. Nors, the contradictions in Witness CGC's testimony and the identification of the Appellant, Appellant's Reply, paras 77-78, 79-86.

230 Respondent's Brief, paras 226, 241-42, 244, citing case law from Australia, England, and Canada.

231 Respondent's Brief, paras 227-28, 231-32, 234-39. The Appeals Chamber notes that the Prosecution submits in para. 246 that any finding other than that the Appellant was at the roadblock on or around 20 May 1994, as described by Witness CGC, "would be perverse". The Appeals Chamber is aware that the use of this term is appropriate in some legal systems. However, in other jurisdictions this term may have very different connotations. In German law, for instance, a reference to "perverted justice" could be equated with the last phase of the jurisprudence of the *Reichsgericht* during the Nazi-regime. In order to avoid any ambiguity, the Appeals Chamber calls upon the Prosecution to avoid employing this language in future proceedings.

232 Appellant's Brief, para. 252, referring to Trial Judgement, para. 229.

233 Appellant's Brief, paras 253-55, referring to Trial Judgement, para. 470. *See* in this context *Semanza* Appeal Judgement, para. 155.

234 Trial Judgement, para. 207.

235 Trial Judgement, paras 213, 470.

236 Trial Judgement, para. 214.

237 Trial Judgement, para. 229.

238 Trial Judgement, paras 227, 229.

239 Trial Judgement, paras 217-18.

that the Trial Chamber's findings with respect to the alleged inconsistencies between Witness DC's and Witness CGC's testimony were unreasonable.

(b) Witness DB

110. The Appellant submits that the Trial Chamber erroneously accepted, first, the evidence of Witness CGC that the Appellant came to Gaseke on 20 May 1994 and that Mr. Nors was murdered shortly thereafter, and second, the logbook of Witness DB (Exh. D.34), which places the murder of Mr. Nors on 26 May 1994.[240] **[page 36]**

111. The Prosecution responds that the Appellant does not show that the Trial Chamber erred in its assessment of Exh. D.34 or that its findings on the killing of Mr. Nors were unreasonable.[241]

112. In his examination-in-chief, Witness CGC could only approximate the date he saw the Appellant at the Gaseke roadblock;[242] in cross-examination, however, he was adamant that it happened on 20 May 1994 "though he could cite no reason for remembering the date as such."[243] He admitted that, contrary to what he asserted in his prior statement, he had not witnessed the killing of Mr. Nors at the roadblock, but had heard about the killing later.[244] Witness DB testified that his passenger Mr. Nors was killed on 26 May 1994, based on an entry in his logbook.[245]

113. The Trial Chamber found that Witness CGC's change in his testimony concerning his recollection of the date was "slightly surprising", as he did not offer any convincing explanation for this change.[246] Nevertheless, it accepted that the events to which Witness CGC testified took place "on or about 20 May 1994."[247] The Trial Chamber also found Witness DB to be credible and found that "the anomalies in the logbook are minor and it appears to be a routinely updated document."[248] The Trial Chamber then concluded that "in late May, 1994 the Accused encouraged those manning a roadblock at Gaseke to stop and kill Tutsi, and distributed machetes and money to them [...]. [O]n the same day, shortly after the Accused's departure, a man named Nors, also known by the name Nturusu, was apprehended there and killed at the Gaseke roadblock."[249]

114. The Trial Chamber did not expressly resolve the apparent contradiction between the dates given by Witnesses CGC and DB (and his logbook), but simply found that the events in question occurred in late May 1994. Since it accepted the testimony of Mr. Nors's driver – Witness DB –that the killing occurred on 26 May 1994, the Trial Chamber was under an obligation to discuss more thoroughly whether both witnesses were indeed testifying as to the same day. In this context, it is recalled that the Trial Chamber accepted Witness CGC's testimony that he "heard that a person named Nturusu [...] was killed at the roadblock about five minutes after his own release."[250] This is the only evidence placing the murder of Mr. Nors shortly after the visit of the Appellant at the **[page 37]** roadblock.[251] However, Witness CGC did not provide any explanation as to why he could be sure that the killing happened shortly after the Appellant's visit. This is what Witness CGC stated during his examination-in-chief:

> Q. Nturusu, was this person killed before or after Mr. Ndindabahizi's visit? Can you recall?
>
> A. **If my memory serves me right, that person was killed after Ndindabahizi's departure.**

---

240 Appellant's Brief, paras 120-25, 284-93.
241 Prosecution Response, paras 118-22.
242 T. 29 September 2003, pp. 23, 25.
243 Trial Judgement, para. 215; T. 29 September 2003, pp. 45-46, 48, 52.
244 T. 29 September 2003, pp. 33-34, 48, 51. Witness CGC referred to the victim as "Nturusu" or "Nturuso" (T. 29 September 2003, pp. 33, 48-49).
245 Exh. D.34; T. 28 October 2003, pp. 82-83, 88, 92.
246 Trial Judgement, para. 215.
247 Trial Judgement, para. 215.
248 Trial Judgement, para. 224. These anomalies referred to "dates in the date column [that] appeared to be out of sequence, and some of them, including the entry of the date of 26 May, appeared to be in a different handwriting than the rest", *ibid.*, para. 223.
249 Trial Judgement, paras 230-31.
250 Trial Judgement, para. 205.
251 T. 29 September 2003, pp. 33-34, 48, 51.

Q. But would I be correct in saying that that person was not killed in your presence? You didn't see this, did you?

A. **That person, yes, you're quite right. When this person was killed I was not present.**

Q. Do you know if anything else happened at the roadblock whilst you were there, before your uncle rescued you, apart from Mr. Ndindabahizi's drive through there?

A. People were being killed at that roadblock. Nothing else.

Q. Were these people killed at the roadblock in your presence or before or after you had left? Can you help me with that?

A. Before I arrived, people were being killed there, and even after I left the roadblock. I'm saying this because those who were manning the roadblock there only were to kill people. [...]

Q. Do you recall making a statement to investigators, Mr. Witness, on the 10th of November 2000?

A. I don't recall the date, because after that I experienced a problem and I fell ill. So I cannot remember those dates.

Q. Okay. In that statement you referred to a Rwandan half-caste being killed after Mr. Ndindabahizi's departure. Do you recall saying that in the statement?

A. I did not quite understand the term that you used. Yes, I made that statement.

Q. Now, was this person killed in your presence or was this something you were told, Mr. Witness?

A. **I have explained to you that that person was killed after my departure**, but I do not know how the investigators took down my statement. I think I explained to you that this person was killed after my departure.

Q. So any reference in that statement to the fact that you were present at the roadblock when that incident happened is wrong, is it not, Mr. Witness?

A. Do you mean the incident in which that person was killed?

Q. Yes, Mr. Witness. You were not present, were you?

A. **I have explained to you that that person was killed after my departure and that I do not know how the investigators took down my statement in that manner, because I had already left when that person was killed.**[252] **[page 38]**

When cross-examined, Witness CGC responded to questions on this issue as follows:

Q. The half-caste who was killed subsequently at the roadblock, and the person called Nturuso, is it the same -- is the one and the same person?

A. It is that person called Nturuso, he was the half-caste.

Q. But you admit today that you did not witness that killing, whereas you said the contrary in your statement to the investigators of the ICTR?

A. Counsel, I expressed reservation and I did say that the investigators might have got it wrong or maybe the interpreter got it wrong, or for some other reason.

Q. I understand, Witness. I just want to know, based on what you were told, if the killing of the half-caste had anything to do with the visit of Emmanuel Ndindabahizi to the roadblock?

A. I have already said that regarding Ndindabahizi and the killing of that person, the killing of this person occurred subsequent to Ndindabahizi's departure. I don't know if you understand me, Counsel.

Q. Very well. But this killing occurred after, but was it after, in the course of the same day, in the course of the week? Do you have any further information on this?

A. Well, Counsel, I don't know if you understand what I'm saying. There wasn't a long lapse of time. I don't know if you need someone else to explain what I'm telling you, but I believe it's clear.

MR. PRESIDENT: What did you say now, Mr. Witness, can you repeat your answer?

252 T. 29 September 2003, pp. 33-34 (emphases added).

> THE WITNESS: I said that it was not after a long time -- it was not a long time thereafter. I cannot even say hours, let alone days. It was soon after the departure of Ndindabahizi.[253]

And in response to questions asked by Judge Bossa:

> JUDGE BOSSA: You mentioned that you were taken to the roadblock at around 11 o'clock in the morning; is that correct?
>
> THE WITNESS: I cannot tell you that that is the absolute truth. It was not during the evening, but neither was it very early in the morning. I gave a period of time which was approximate.
>
> JUDGE BOSSA: In the morning; okay. How long after that did the Accused arrive?
>
> THE WITNESS: Just a little after my arrival at that place.
>
> JUDGE BOSSA: Okay. And how long after that was the half-caste killed? Because you said he was killed in the morning as well.
>
> THE WITNESS: Briefly, that happened about five minutes after I left the roadblock.[254]

115. Thus, Witness CGC never explained (nor was he asked to[255]) how he learned that Mr. Nors was killed at the roadblock about five minutes after he (Witness CGC) had left.[256] Thus, the Trial **[page 39]** Chamber did not know how the person – or persons – who told Witness CGC about the killing knew about it; also, the Trial Chamber did not know on which basis the person – or persons –came to the conclusion that the killing happened some minutes after his departure. The finding that Mr. Nors was killed shortly after the Appellant's visit was thus based only on vague and unverifiable hearsay. While hearsay evidence is not *per se* inadmissible, it is well established that a Trial Chamber must be cautious in considering such evidence.[257] Hence, the Appeals Chamber finds, by majority, Judge Shahabuddeen dissenting, that the Trial Chamber failed to adhere to this principle and that no reasonable trier of fact could have reached the conclusion beyond reasonable doubt that Mr. Nors was killed shortly after the Appellant's visit on or about 20 May 1994.

116. In relation to the question whether the Appellant's actions on 20 May 1994 substantially contributed to the killing of Mr. Nors on 26 May 1994 – if Witness DB and Exh. D.34 were to be believed – the Appeals Chamber notes that Witness CGC testified that people were killed at the roadblock even before the Appellant's visit, that is, without his contribution.[258] Also, it is not established whether the persons who were instigated by the Appellant on 20 May 1994 were those who killed Mr. Nors on 26 May 1994. Thus, it is unclear whether the Appellant's acts substantially contributed to Mr. Nors's killing had it occurred six days after these acts or even later.

117. Also, the Trial Chamber did not make a finding on any criminal act of the Appellant during mid-April 1994 (*see* paragraph 25 of the Indictment) that could have substantially contributed to the murder of Mr. Nors in late May 1994 (*see* paragraph 11 of the Indictment). Thus, the Prosecution failed to establish a link between the murder of Mr. Nors at the Gaseke roadblock and a substantial contribution of the Appellant. Without that

---

253 T. 29 September 2003, p. 48.

254 T. 29 September 2003, p. 51.

255 The fact that Defence counsel did not question Witness CGC as to how he could be sure that Nturusu had been killed five minutes after the witness had left the roadblock should not be held against the Appellant as it was the onus of the Prosecution to prove that the hearsay evidence was reliable and credible.

256 Witness CGC testified that many people were killed at that roadblock both before and after the Appellant's visit. But Witness CGC did not explain why he recalled specifically that the murder of Nturusu (which murder he did not witness) happened shortly after the Appellant's visit. In fact, Witness CGC himself at first was not entirely certain that the murder of Nturusu occurred after the Appellant's departure: *see* T. 29 September 2003, p. 33 ("If my memory serves me right, that person was killed after Ndindabahizi's departure").

257 *Rutaganda* Appeal Judgement, para. 34; *Akayesu* Appeal Judgement, paras 286-92; *Niyitegeka* Trial Judgement, para. 43; *Ntakirutimana* Trial Judgement, para. 33; *Bagilishema* Trial Judgement, para. 25; *Musema* Trial Judgement, para. 51. *See also Naletilić and Martinović* Appeal Judgement, para. 516; *Kordić and Čerkez* Appeal Judgement, para. 281. This principle was recognized by the Trial Chamber in this case: *see* Trial Judgement, para. 23. In this context, the Appeals Chamber notes that the Trial Chamber held in para. 216 of the Trial Judgement that "Rwandans do not always express clearly the difference between what they have seen with their own eyes and what they have heard". The Appeals Chamber does not accept this characterization as being specific to Rwandans. Rather, it interprets the Trial Chamber's finding as a general reference to inaccuracies which often occur in the testimony of witnesses, regardless of their nationality.

258 T. 29 September 2003, p. 33.

crime being committed, the Appellant cannot be held liable for instigating and aiding and abetting genocide for the murder of Mr. Nors **[page 40]** pursuant to Article 6 of the Statute.[259] Instigating means prompting another person to commit an offence, thus requiring a subsequent criminal action.[260] Similarly, a conviction for aiding and abetting presupposes that the support of the aider and abetter has a substantial effect upon the perpetrated crime.[261] No reasonable trier of fact could have concluded beyond reasonable doubt that the killing of Mr. Nors was a result attributable to the Appellant's acts. In this context, the Appeals Chamber recalls that the Prosecution had withdrawn the charge of direct and public incitement to commit genocide.[262] Hence, the Trial Chamber erroneously convicted the Appellant for instigating and aiding and abetting the murder of Mr. Nors as a crime against humanity.

118. In this context, the Appeals Chamber notes that the pleadings of the parties have to be clear and unambiguous. On the basis of ambiguous submissions made by the Prosecution during closing arguments, the Appeals Chamber might have come to the conclusion that the Prosecution had abandoned its case in relation to the killing of Mr. Nors.

2. Conclusion

In light of the above, the Appellant's eleventh ground of appeal is granted.

IX. ALLEGED VAGUENESS OF THE INDICTMENT (SUB-GROUND OF APPEAL 1 - GASEKE ROADBLOCK)

119. As the eleventh ground of appeal is granted on the basis of the reasoning set out above, it is not necessary for the Appeals Chamber to consider under the first sub-ground of appeal relating to the Gaseke roadblock whether the case concerning Mr. Nors was withdrawn by the Prosecution.[263] By the same token, it is not necessary to consider allegations of the vagueness of the Indictment relating to Mr. Nors[264] as both issues are rendered moot. **[page 41]**

X. ALLEGED ERROR IN FINDING A LEGAL BASIS FOR THE GENOCIDE CONVICTION (GROUND OF APPEAL 7)

120. In addition, for the reasons set out above under the eleventh ground of appeal, it is not necessary for the Appeals Chamber to consider whether the Appellant was erroneously convicted of instigating and aiding and abetting genocide at the Gaseke roadblock on the basis of the killing of Mr. Nors. Consequently, the seventh ground of appeal has become moot.

XI. GROUND OF APPEAL 12 – WITHDRAWN

XII. ALTERNATIVE CONVICTIONS

121. The Appeals Chamber *proprio motu* raises the issue of alternative convictions arising from paragraph 485 of the Trial Judgement:[265]

---

259 The modes of liability as regulated under Article 6(1) of the Statute are also applicable to the crime of genocide pursuant to Article 2 of the Statute, *Ntakirutimana* Appeal Judgement, para. 500. *See also Krstić* Appeal Judgement, para. 138.

260 *Kordić and Čerkez* Appeal Judgement, para. 27.

261 *Blaškić* Appeal Judgement, para. 48.

262 *See supra* note 4. As the offence of direct and public incitement to commit genocide is an inchoate offence, the legal assessment of such a charge may have been different.

263 Appellant's Brief, paras 22, 172-77, referring to closing arguments, T. 1 March 2004, pp. 14-15, Appellant's Reply, paras 41-42.

264 Appellant's Brief, paras 21-29. This argument was also raised during the appeal hearing: the Defence argued that ambiguity must be resolved in favour of the Appellant, at T. 6 July 2006, p. 18, *see also* T. 6 July 2006, pp. 26-27, 34, 64. The Prosecution argued that the act of instigation was not limited to Mr. Nors, T. 6 July 2006, p. 52.

265 Upon invitation of the Appeals Chamber, this issue was discussed at the Appeals Hearing: T. 6 July 2006, pp. 53, 54, 58: the Prosecution argued that although conviction in the alternative is incorrect, it is not sufficient grounds to overturn the Trial Judgement, and suggested the term "additionally" would have been more appropriate. The Defence replied that it is not permissible to substitute language for the Trial Chamber, T. 6 July 2006, p. 67.

> [T]he Chamber finds that the Accused himself committed the crime of extermination. He participated in creating, and contributed to, the conditions for the mass killing of Tutsi on Gitwa Hill on 26 April 1994, by distributing weapons, transporting attackers, and speaking words of encouragement that would have reasonably appeared to give official approval for an attack. **Alternatively**, the Chamber finds that by these words and deeds, the Accused directly and substantially contributed to the crime of extermination committed by the attackers at Gitwa Hill, and is thereby guilty of both instigating, and of aiding and abetting, that crime. (emphasis added).

122. While an accused can be convicted for a single crime on the basis of several modes of liability, alternative convictions for several modes of liability are, in general, incompatible with the principle that a judgement has to express unambiguously the scope of the convicted person's criminal responsibility. This principle requires, *inter alia*, that the sentence corresponds to the totality of guilt incurred by the convicted person. This totality of guilt is determined by the *actus reus* and the *mens rea* of the convicted person. The modes of liability may either augment (*e.g.*, commission of the crime with direct intent) or lessen (*e.g.*, aiding and abetting a crime with awareness that a crime will probably be committed[266]) the gravity of the crime.[267] Thus, the criminal liability of a convicted person has to be established unequivocally.

123. However, the Appeals Chamber finds, by majority, Judge Güney dissenting, that the Trial Chamber did not convict the Appellant in the alternative. Rather, the Trial Chamber was seeking to **[page 42]** provide a further characterisation of the Appellant's criminal conduct. The Trial Chamber was convinced beyond a reasonable doubt that the Appellant committed acts constituting extermination,[268] namely by distributing weapons, transporting attackers and speaking words of encouragement. Furthermore, the Trial Chamber also found that by such encouragement, the Appellant instigated and aided and abetted the crime of extermination. Therefore, the Trial Chamber wanted to emphasize that a full characterisation of the Appellant's conduct had to cumulatively refer to various modes of liability. The Appeals Chamber notes, however, that it is for a Trial Chamber to identify unambiguously the mode(s) of liability for which an accused is convicted and the relation between them. It has to be stated already here that the underlying acts and the crime itself remain the same, and no reduction or increase of the sentence is merited.

XIII. APPEAL AGAINST the SENTENCE (GROUND OF APPEAL 13)

A. Submissions of the Parties

124. The Appellant submits that the Trial Chamber erred in fact and in law in concluding that the aggravating circumstances outweighed the mitigating circumstances in his case.[269]

125. With respect to the aggravating circumstances, the Appellant contends first that the fact that he was well-known and influential in the region where the crimes were committed and the fact that he held an official position in the Interim Government do not constitute two separate aggravating circumstances but express the same idea, since his position in the Interim Government explains why he had become a more well-known figure than the other workers of the public administration in Kibuye Prefecture. Further, argues the Appellant, his position in the Interim Government cannot, by itself, constitute an aggravating circumstance, because the Prosecution still has to establish the causal link between this position and the influence he used in his official capacity to facilitate the commission of genocide and crimes against humanity.[270] **[page 43]**

---

[266] *See Blaškić* Appeal Judgement, para. 50.

[267] In this context, the Appeals Chamber recalls that in *Krstić*, the ICTY Appeals Chamber stated that it had taken into account the sentencing practice of the courts of the former Yugoslavia applicable in that case, in particular the practice that "the sentence of a person who aided a principal perpetrator to commit a crime can be reduced to a sentence less than the one given to the principal perpetrator", *Krstić* Appeal Judgement, para. 270 (note omitted).

[268] The Trial Chamber stated that "[e]xtermination may be committed less directly than murder, as by participation in measures intended to bring about the deaths of a large number of individuals, but without actually committing a killing of any person" (Trial Judgement, para. 479). The words "without actually committing a killing" could mean, in the ordinary sense of the word, "without causing death". The Appeals Chamber finds, however, that the word "actually" in this context rather describes what other judgements have referred to as "indirectly" causing death, in particular as these judgements are referred to in para. 479 of the Trial Judgement: *Krstić* Trial Judgement, para. 498; *Vasiljević* Trial Judgement, para. 227; *Kayishema and Ruzindana* Trial Judgement, paras 143, 146.

[269] Appellant's Brief, paras 301-19.

[270] Appellant's Brief, paras 305, 311-13. Appellant's Reply, paras 90-91.

126. The Appellant also argues that the Trial Chamber erred in concluding that he supported a policy of genocide in his capacity as minister in the Interim Government, which was considered an aggravating factor by the Trial Chamber at sentencing. In his view, it has not been established that he committed any act of government relating to genocide.[271]

127. The Appellant further argues that the Trial Chamber erred in considering as an aggravating circumstance a summary of the substantive grounds that the Prosecutor charged in paragraph 21 of the Indictment.[272] The Appellant submits that the Trial Chamber should not look to the Indictment to find aggravating or mitigating circumstances.[273]

128. The Appellant also submits that the Trial Chamber erred in considering as an aggravating circumstance that he influenced and encouraged others to commit crimes because this influence and encouragement already constituted elements of the crimes for which he was convicted.[274] The Appellant further argues that the Trial Chamber contradicted itself in finding first that it had not been established that he instigated or aided and abetted the killing of Tutsi women married to Hutu men, and second that his statements encouraging the killing of Tutsi women who were married to Hutus constituted an aggravating circumstance.[275]

129. As to mitigating circumstances, the Appellant submits that he recently became aware of an allegedly new mitigating circumstance, specifically that "Fidèle Uwiyeze, one of the unprotected Prosecution witnesses in *Bizimungu et al.* [...] thanked [the Appellant] for saving his children's lives."[276]

130. The Prosecution responds that the Trial Chamber did not err in sentencing and, in particular, was free to consider the Appellant's ministerial position as an aggravating factor in sentencing: First, it was not an integral element of the crimes; and second, the jurisprudence of the Tribunal recognizes the abuse of a position of influence and authority in society as an aggravating factor.[277]

131. The Prosecution responds that the first two aggravating circumstances identified by the Trial Chamber are distinct: the Trial Chamber referred first to the abuse by the Appellant of the influence he had on the local population and second to the fact that the Appellant also had influence at the **[page 44]** national level, which he should have used to promote peace and reconciliation instead of supporting and advocating a policy of genocide.[278] As to the third aggravating circumstance, the Prosecution submits that the Trial Chamber rightly considered that the Appellant actively influenced others to commit crimes by distributing machetes and money and that he publicly encouraged the killing of Tutsi women who were married to Hutu men.[279]

B. Discussion

132. The Appeals Chamber recalls the applicable standard of review for sentencing:

> The Appeals Chamber's review of an appeal of the sentencing portion of a judgement is not *de novo*. Trial Chambers are vested with broad discretion to tailor the penalties to fit the individual circumstances of the accused and the gravity of the crime. As a general rule, the Appeals Chamber will not revise a sentence unless the Trial Chamber has committed a "discernible error" in exercising its discretion. It is for the Appellant to demonstrate how the Trial Chamber ventured outside its discretionary framework in imposing the sentence. A Trial Chamber's sentencing decision may therefore only be disturbed on appeal if the Appellant shows that the Trial Chamber erred in the

271 Appellant's Brief, para. 44.

272 Appellant's Brief, para. 315.

273 Appellant's Brief, para. 314.

274 Appellant's Brief, para. 305. *See also ibid.*, paras 314-15, where the Appellant submits that the third aggravating circumstance is a reproduction of "the material elements that the Indictment put forward to support the charge of genocide and crimes against humanity (extermination and murder)" and that "the Indictment should not serve the Chamber in its search for aggravating or mitigating circumstances."

275 Appellant's Brief, para. 316, referring to Trial Judgement, paras 474 and 508(iii).

276 Appellant's Brief, paras 310, 318. Appellant's Reply, para. 92.

277 Respondent's Brief, paras 72-73; 254-56, 258-59.

278 Respondent's Brief, paras 248-50.

279 Respondent's Brief, paras 251-52. The Prosecution contends that there was no contradiction in the reasoning of the Trial Chamber in this respect and it refers to paragraphs 508 and 264 of the Trial Judgement.

weighing process either by taking into account what it ought not to have considered or by failing to take into account what it ought to have considered.[280]

133. The Trial Chamber identified the following as aggravating circumstances:

> (i) The Accused was a well-known and influential figure in his native prefecture of Kibuye, where his crimes were committed. As such, the Accused abused the trust placed in him by the population.
>
> (ii) At the time of the events, the Accused held an official position at the national level, as a member of the Interim Government. The Chamber considers it particularly aggravating that instead of promoting peace and reconciliation in his capacity as Minister, he supported and advocated a policy of genocide. He also participated in the commission of the massacres in Gitwa Hill, during which thousands of persons were killed.
>
> (iii) The Accused actively influenced others to commit crimes, by distributing machetes and money. He publicly encouraged the killing of Tutsi women who were married to Hutu.[281]

134. The Appellant has not demonstrated that the first two aggravating circumstances identified by the Trial Chamber are in fact the same aggravating circumstance. While it is arguable that the influence of the Appellant at the local level also derived to some extent from his position in the Interim Government, the important element in the first aggravating circumstance is the abuse of **[page 45]** trust. This differs from the second aggravating circumstance, in which the Trial Chamber considered, first, the fact that, instead of promoting peace and reconciliation as would be the duty of a Minister, the Appellant supported and advocated a policy of genocide;[282] and second, the large number of victims at Gitwa Hill.[283] There is thus no double-counting of the same aggravating circumstance.

135. Also, the Trial Chamber did not err in considering the large number of victims at Gitwa Hill as an aggravating circumstance relevant to the sentence. As to the conviction for genocide, there need not be a large number of victims to enter a genocide conviction. As for extermination, the *actus reus* requires "killing on a large scale".[284] While this does not "suggest a numerical minimum",[285] a particularly large number of victims can be an aggravating circumstance in relation to the sentence for this crime if the extent of the killings exceeds that required for extermination. In the present case, there is no indication that, in considering aggravating circumstances, the Trial Chamber looked at only those killings required for extermination when it specifically cited the fact that "thousands" of people were killed.[286]

136. The Appellant also argues that his position in the Interim Government does not *per se* constitute an aggravating circumstance. The Appeals Chamber agrees, recalling that:

> [a] high rank in the military or political field does not, in itself, merit a harsher sentence. But a person who abuses or wrongly exercises power deserves a harsher sentence. Consequently, what matters is not the position of authority taken alone, but that position coupled with the manner in which the authority is exercised.[287]

Thus, the Trial Chamber was entitled to refer to the Appellant's position as a Minister in the Interim Government in sentencing, in accordance with the case law of the Tribunal which recognizes that the abuse of a position of influence and authority in society can be taken into account as an aggravating factor.[288] The

---

280 *Semanza* Appeal Judgement, para. 312 (references omitted); *see also* as to ICTY jurisprudence: *Naletilić and Martinović* Appeal Judgement, para. 593:

> With regard to sentencing, Trial Chambers are vested with broad discretion in determining the appropriate sentence due to their obligation to individualise the penalties to fit the circumstances of the accused and the gravity of the crime. As a general rule, the Appeals Chamber will not substitute its own sentence for that of a Trial Chamber unless it can be shown that the Trial Chamber committed a discernible error in exercising its discretion or failed to follow the applicable law (internal references omitted).

281 Trial Judgement, para. 508.

282 *See also* the Trial Chamber's earlier findings concerning the meeting of 3 May 1994, *supra* para. 58.

283 *See infra* para. 142.

284 *Ntakirutimana* Appeal Judgement, para. 516.

285 *Ntakirutimana* Appeal Judgement, para. 516.

286 Trial Judgement, para. 508(ii).

287 *Babić* Judgement on Sentencing Appeal, para. 80, referring to *Krstić* Trial Judgement, para. 709 and *Kayishema and Ruzindana* Appeal Judgement, paras 358-59.

288 *See, e.g., Akayesu* Appeal Judgement, paras 414-15; *Ntakirutimana* Appeal Judgement, para. 563; *Kamuhanda* Appeal Judgement, paras 347-348; *Stakić* Appeal Judgement, para. 411.

Trial Chamber did not find that the Appellant's position in the Interim Government in itself called for a harsher sentence. Instead, it found that it was the wrongful exercise of his powers that constituted the aggravating circumstance. The Appeals Chamber finds no error in this. **[page 46]**

137. As to the third challenged circumstance, the Appeals Chamber recalls that "where an aggravating factor for the purposes of sentencing is at the same time an element of the offence, it cannot also constitute an aggravating factor for the purposes of sentencing."[289] In the present case, the Trial Chamber convicted the Appellant for instigating and aiding and abetting genocide at Gitwa Hill,[290] as well as for committing, instigating and aiding and abetting extermination at Gitwa Hill.[291] These convictions were based on the factual finding that the Appellant transported assailants at Gitwa Hill, distributed weapons there and encouraged the killing of Tutsi.[292] The Trial Chamber could not also refer to these same factual findings as aggravating circumstances. Accordingly, the Trial Chamber erred in finding that the fact that the Appellant "actively influenced others to commit crimes, by distributing machetes and money"[293] constituted an aggravating circumstance.

138. However, the Trial Chamber correctly recalled that the sentence had to be first and foremost commensurate to the gravity of the offence,[294] and that the Appellant had been convicted of the most serious crimes.[295] The Trial Chamber then considered the mitigating and aggravating circumstances, finding that "the aggravating circumstances outweigh the mitigating circumstances".[296] There is only one genocide that was committed in Rwanda between 6 April 1994 and 17 July 1994 and that resulted in the killings of hundreds of thousands of Tutsi. In sentencing, acts in furtherance of this one genocide and attributable to the accused can be taken into account.

139. The Appeals Chamber notes that while the genocide in Rwanda cost the lives of hundreds of thousands of people, the Appellant's individual criminal responsibility has to be measured according to his own contributions and the killings resulting therefrom, taking into account his own position. The Appeals Chamber finds that the acquittal for the killing of Mr. Nors at the Gaseke roadblock does not materially diminish the gravity of the crimes for which the Appellant has been found guilty. The Appeals Chamber therefore finds no error in the Trial Chamber's assessment of the gravity of the Appellant's acts when determining the appropriate sentence.

140. The Trial Chamber also found that the Appellant "encouraged those at the roadblock [near Nyabahanga Bridge] to kill Tutsi women married to Hutu men"[297] without convicting the Appellant on this basis because it found that there was "insufficient evidence to establish that the **[page 47]** [Appellant's] conduct at the roadblocks [*sic*] directly and substantially contributed to the killing of Tutsi women married to Hutu men, or their children."[298] However, the Trial Chamber considered that the Appellant's encouragement of the killing of Tutsi women who were married to Hutu could be considered as an aggravating factor.[299]

141. There was no contradiction in the Trial Chamber's findings in this respect. The Trial Chamber did not impose liability because it found that there was insufficient evidence that the Appellant's words directly and substantially contributed to killings of Tutsi women married to Hutu men, but it did find that the Appellant effectively made statements encouraging such killings. This behaviour could therefore be considered as an aggravating factor.

142. The life sentence already stands on the basis of the Appellant's participation in genocide and extermination at Gitwa Hill, which resulted in the death toll of thousands of human beings. Having affirmed the sentence of life imprisonment, the acquittal for the crimes related to the killing of Mr. Nors at the Gaseke

289 *Blaškić* Appeal Judgement, para. 693. *See also Vasiljević* Appeal Judgement, paras 172-73.
290 Trial Judgement, paras 462-64.
291 Trial Judgement, para. 485.
292 Trial Judgement, paras 179-80.
293 Trial Judgement, para. 508(iii).
294 Trial Judgement, para. 510.
295 *See* Trial Judgement, para. 499.
296 Trial Judgement, para. 509.
297 Trial Judgement, para. 264.
298 Trial Judgement, para. 474.
299 *See* Trial Judgement, para. 508(iii).

roadblock does not merit a reduction in sentence. By the same token, the question of further aggravation of sentence as found by the Trial Chamber for the Appellant's acts in encouraging the killing of Tutsi women who were married to Hutu need not be addressed.

143. A motion of the Appellant for the admission of allegedly mitigating evidence pursuant to Rule 115 of the Rules was rejected,[300] as was the request for reconsideration of this decision.[301]

144. The Appeals Chamber notes that the Appellant was arrested at Verviers, Belgium, on 12 July 2001 and was transferred to the United Nations Detention Facility in Arusha, Tanzania, on 25 September 2001. **[page 48]**

XIV. DISPOSITION

For the foregoing reasons, **THE APPEALS CHAMBER**,

PURSUANT to Article 24 of the Statute and Rule 118 of the Rules;

NOTING the written submissions of the parties and their oral arguments presented at the hearing on 6 July 2006;

SITTING in open session;

VACATES the Appellant's conviction for genocide under Count 1 in relation to the events at Gaseke roadblock;

VACATES the Appellant's conviction for murder under Count 3;

AFFIRMS the Appellant's convictions for genocide and extermination as a crime against humanity under Counts 1 and 2 in relation to the events at Gitwa Hill, pursuant to Article 6(1) of the Statute;

DISMISSES the appeal in all other respects;

AFFIRMS unanimously the sentence imposed by the Trial Chamber, subject to credit being given under Rule 101(D) and Rule 107 of the Rules for the period in which Emmanuel Ndindabahizi was deprived of his liberty for the purposes of this case, that is from 12 July 2001;

RULES that this Judgement shall be enforced immediately pursuant to Rule 119 of the Rules; and

ORDERS, in accordance with Rules 103(B) and 107 of the Rules, that Emmanuel Ndindabahizi is to remain in the custody of the Tribunal pending his transfer to the State in which his sentence will be served. **[page 49]**

Done in English and French, the English text being authoritative.

Wolfgang Schomburg
Presiding Judge

Mohamed Shahabuddeen
Judge

Mehmet Güney
Judge

Liu Daqun
Judge

Theodor Meron
Judge

Judge Shahabuddeen appends a separate opinion.

300 Decision on the Admission of Additional Evidence, 4 April 2006.

301 Decision on Defence "Requête de l'appelant en reconsidération de le décision du 4 avril 2006 en raison d'une erreur matérielle", 14 June 2006.

Judge Güney appends a partially dissenting opinion.

Signed on the tenth day of January 2007 in The Hague,

Issued on the sixteenth day of January 2007 in Arusha

[SEAL OF THE TRIBUNAL] [page 50]

XV. SEPARATE OPINION OF JUDGE SHAHABUDDEEN

1. I support the judgement rendered by the Appeals Chamber today, but regret that I do not have the good fortune to agree with the reasoning of my colleagues on one point. The point concerns the Trial Chamber's finding that Mr Nors was killed shortly after the visit by the appellant to the Gaseke roadblock. The Appeals Chamber considers that the finding was erroneous; I am of the opposite view.

A. Preliminary

2. In 1994, there was genocide in Rwanda[302]; Tutsis were being killed[303]; a roadblock was set up at Gaseke.[304] The Trial Chamber found that the appellant, who was the Minister of Finance and a Hutu, visited the roadblock. He distributed machetes and money to the persons who were manning the roadblock and asked them why Tutsis were being allowed to go through the roadblock without being killed;[305] he then left.[306] The Trial Chamber also found that a Mr Nors was killed by those manning the roadblock shortly after the appellant's visit[307]; he was killed because he was perceived to be a Tutsi.[308] Among the issues raised in the oral arguments on appeal is the question of the interval between the visit and the killing. The question concerns the causal relationship between the two events.

B. In his written arguments the appellant contended that he did not visit the roadblock at all

3. The question of the interval between the visit and the killing was not raised in the written arguments on appeal. It was raised orally at the appeal hearing, possibly in reaction to questions asked by the Appeals Chamber.[309] The written arguments on appeal raised only the question whether the appellant did in fact visit the roadblock, not the question, if he did make the visit, what was the interval between the visit and the killing. For example, the eleventh ground of appeal states as follows:

> La Chambre de Première Instance I a commis une erreur de fait qui a entraîné un déni de justice en concluant que l'appelant s'est rendu sur un barrage routier à Gaseke fin mai 1994. **[page 51]**
>
> La Chamber a fondé sa conviction sur les seules déclarations du témoin CGC qui s'avèrent erronées quant aux dates et aux éléments factuels, contradictoires et incompatibles avec les déclarations d'autres témoins. Les preuves retenues par la Chambre à cet effet ne sont pas conformes aux standards de la preuve en matière de justice pénale internationale.[310]

4. Given the appellant's contention that he did not visit the roadblock at all, it is legitimate to assume that he judged that it would have been contradictory for him, in his written arguments on appeal, to take the position that the visit did occur but that it occurred too long before the killing to support a causal link between the two events. The date of the two events was indeed in discussion, but only from the point of view advanced by the appellant that he did not make the visit at all. The Appeals Chamber having allowed him to raise additional matters, he is free to argue the question. But his original stand has to be taken into account for the purpose of evaluating his new position.

C. Whether the appellant visited the roadblock at all

302 *Karemera*, ICTR -98-44-AR73(c), Decision on Prosecutor's Interlocutory Appeal of Decision on Judicial Notice, 16 June 2006, para. 57 and Annex A.

303 *Ibid.*

304 Trial Judgement, para. 230.

305 *Ibid.*, para. 204, and Trial Chamber's Transcript, 29 September 2003, pp. 29, 31, Witness CGC.

306 Trial Judgement, para. 204.

307 *Ibid.*, paras. 230-231.

308 *Ibid.*, paras 231, 469.

309 *See* Scheduling Order, ICTR-01-71-A, 11 May 2006, and a letter from the Presiding Judge to the parties dated 26 June 2006 asking questions.

310 Acte d'appel, onzième moyen d'appel. *See also* Appellant's Brief, paras. 244ff; Respondent's Brief of the Prosecutor, paras. 222 ff; and Response to Respondent's Brief, paras. 76 ff.

5. Because of the importance of the issue, it is proposed to consider first the appellant's original stand, namely, that he made no visit to the roadblock at all. The Trial Chamber found that he had. The appellant seeks to controvert this finding by appealing to a certain discrepancy. The Trial Chamber referred to the testimony of Witness CGC, whom it regarded as credible, that he saw the appellant visit the roadblock.[311] By contrast, the evidence of Witness DB, whom the Trial Chamber also regarded as credible and who it found was also at the roadblock, was that he did not see or hear of any visit by the appellant to the roadblock. So, if the witnesses had in mind the same time, here was a possible discrepancy as to whether the appellant visited the roadblock at all. How could it be resolved?

6. The Trial Chamber explained itself by saying the following in paragraph 221 of its judgement (footnote omitted):

> The Chamber now turns to Witness DB, who was of the view that the Accused played no role in the killing of Nors, based on his investigations into the circumstances of the Gaseke roadblock conducted after 1994. Aside from being hearsay evidence, the witness did not indicate the source of his information. Under these circumstances, the Chamber considers the evidence of what he subsequently discovered to have little weight against the eyewitness testimony of Witness CGC.

In paragraph 225 of its judgement, the Trial Chamber added:

> Witness DB's account of the killing of Nors is not inconsistent with Witness CGC's. Witness CGC testified that the Accused departed before the killing of Nors. The only basis for contradicting Witness CGC's evidence of the Accused's presence at the roadblock before the arrival of Nors, is Witness DB's unreliable hearsay evidence. Accordingly, the Chamber finds that Witness DB's testimony does not weaken or detract from Witness CGC's credibility. **[page 52]**

7. Thus, although the Trial Chamber found in favour of the credibility of Witness DB, that finding was not unqualified: the Trial Chamber made it clear that it did not accept his evidence on all points. On the specific question of the appellant's visit, it preferred the evidence of Witness CGC. And, as seen, it gave its reasons. On the assumption (which I later argue is correct) that the witnesses were speaking of the same time, there was indeed a conflict in evidence as to whether the appellant visited the roadblock. The Trial Chamber resolved the conflict by electing to believe one witness and not the other. That was the right of the Trial Chamber.

D. The appellant did not contend that his visit took place before the killing of Mr Nors

8. The Appeals Chamber does not have a roving magisterial jurisdiction to ensure, of its own motion, that the Trial Chamber was acting correctly in every detail; it may do that to avoid a miscarriage of justice, but not otherwise, and I do not think that that exceptional authority is attracted in this case. Criminal courts nowadays have a pre-trial procedure under which parties state what are the issues dividing them; and it is usual for an appellate court to say that there is no dispute on a point where there is none. An appeal is not an opportunity for shadow-boxing; it is concerned with real issues. It is therefore appropriate to have regard to what were the issues in contention before the Appeals Chamber.

9. Various theoretical questions could be asked of the stage at which the visit was made by the appellant in relation to the killing of Mr Nors. The possibility that the killing took place before the visit was rightly excluded by Mr Konitz, counsel for the appellant, when he said that the appellant "stopped at the roadblock several days before the crime, and there is absolutely no proof of any causal link".[312] A little earlier he explained this; he said, "[W]hat I'm asking is whether there was any investigation to find out that those who were manning the roadblock were the same, or whether they were replaced by others".[313] In other words, if the visit was long before the killing, the effect of any instructions given by the appellant during the visit might abate with time, especially if there was meanwhile a change of personnel: causality would be in question.

311 Trial Judgement, paras. 215, 219, 225, 230-231.

312 Transcript of the oral arguments in the Appeals Chamber, 6 July 2006, p. 20; emphasis added.

313 *Ibid.*, p. 19.

10. That is the nub of the problem raised by Mr Konitz: the sole issue was as to how long after the visit was the killing done. The appeal raises no issue as to the killing taking place before the visit. No such issue has in fact been raised, but it is important to set correctly the parameters of the question to be answered. **[page 53]**

E. How long after the visit was made did the killing occur?

11. Now to be considered is the question raised in the oral arguments of Mr Konitz as to how long after the visit was made did the killing occur. The answer is made difficult by evidential discrepancies, particularly as to dates. Evidential discrepancies often occur in trials. When they do, it is the responsibility of the Trial Chamber to resolve them. The Appeals Chamber accepts the Trial Chamber's solution, absent clear error. The Trial Chamber cannot of course draw inferences from non-existent facts, but one has to be on solid ground before criticising it for doing so. I do not think that the Trial Chamber did so.

12. The matter is complicated because, as part of its reasoning on the question whether the Trial Chamber erred in holding that the killing took place shortly after the visit, the Appeals Chamber considers that Witness CGC gave no admissible evidence of the killing itself. This was because Witness CGC said that he learnt of the killing, without disclosing the source of his information or any other material relevant to the issue of reliability.[314] I respectfully agree with the Appeals Chamber that, although hearsay evidence is admissible, in the absence of disclosure of the bases of reliability, the evidence is not admissible. It seems to me, however, that there was other evidence of the killing, and that the failure of Witness CGC to give admissible evidence on it is not by itself germane to the question whether the killing took place shortly after the visit.

13. The Trial Chamber found in favour of the credibility of Witness CGC and, for the purposes at hand, of Witness DB also. Witness DB's evidence showed that Witness DB drove a car to the roadblock, with Mr Nors as a passenger.[315] As for Witness CGC, the Trial Chamber said, "Witness CGC testified that Witness DB was indeed the driver of the car carrying Nors when it was stopped at the roadblock".[316] It may be questioned whether in this passage the Trial Chamber meant to say that it found that Witness CGC was himself present when the car arrived at the roadblock. I consider that the natural sense of the Trial Chamber's language and of the proven events is that Witness CGC was indeed present.

14. Witness CGC's recorded evidence, given under cross-examination, was this:

> Q. Did you know him yourself?
>
> A. No, it was only at that location that I learnt of his existence and people spoke about him saying that he was called Nturuso.
>
> Q. Do you know any other name that he might have had or a nickname? **[page 54]**
>
> A. How would you want me to know that, Counsel?
>
> Q. In your written statement you mentioned the fact that this half-caste was in his vehicle and that his driver was driving. Did you also come by this information through other persons?
>
> A. You are referring to the driver? No, no, I knew the driver before. That is not something which was reported to me. I knew the driver.
>
> Q. And the driver did indeed answer to the name which you mentioned in your written statement? I don't want to mention the name out loud, but you stated that he was driving his vehicle and you mentioned the name. Do you remember the name that you mentioned? Don't say it out loud.
>
> A. Yes, of course, I know that name. I do remember his name but of course I won't say it out loud.[317]

There then followed a procedure in the Trial Chamber whereby Witness CGC disclosed the protected name of Witness DB; so the driver was indeed Witness DB. I should add that there is no dispute that "Nors" was the same as "Nturuso".

---

314 Appeal Judgement, para. 115.

315 Trial Judgement, paras. 209, 224-225.

316 *Ibid.*, para. 224. *See also* Trial Chamber's Transcript, 29 September 2003, pp. 49, 50.

317 Trial Chamber's Transcript, 29 September 2003, p. 49.

15. Whatever was the precise legal status of Witness CGC's written statement, the appellant had succeeded in placing on the record of the Trial Chamber what in my opinion amounted to an averment that Witness CGC was in a position to see both the half-caste and the driver. It also appears that the appellant did not separate himself from that averment. Accordingly, there was no debate suggesting that Witness CGC was not present when the car arrived with two people. The assumption of the appellant, put forward to the Trial Chamber in the above excerpt of the cross-examination of Witness CGC, was that Witness CGC was present when a car with two people arrived at the roadblock.

16. The real concern of the appellant was not with whether Witness CGC was present when the car arrived, but with whether Witness CGC personally knew enough of the two persons in the car to have been able to identify them. The appellant denied that the driver was Witness DB and that the passenger was Mr Nors. But if, as the appellant contended, Witness CGC was incapable of identifying Nors, he was not incapable of identifying Witness DB; as has been seen, Witness CGC's testimony was that he "knew the driver [Witness DB] before. That is not something which was reported to me. I knew the driver".[318] So Witness CGC knew Witness DB. And Witness DB plainly knew his passenger Mr Nors; Witness DB, an ambulance driver, knew Mr Nors as a medical assistant at the local hospital, and Mr Nors had asked Witness DB to give him a ride.[319] Also, **[page 55]** Witness DB gave clear and graphic testimony from which it could be reasonably inferred that Mr Nors was killed at the roadblock later that day.[320]

17. Since Witness CGC was present during the appellant's visit to the roadblock, since, in my view, he was also present when Witness DB and Mr Nors arrived there later that day, and since, according to Witness DB Mr Nors was killed shortly after leaving the roadblock, it follows from the above circumstances that Mr Nors was killed the same day on which the appellant visited the roadblock.[321]

18. A straight nexus is thus established between the appellant's visit to the roadblock and the killing of Mr Nors, the latter occurring after the former but both taking place on the same day. The killing may not have occurred five minutes after the visit, but the Trial Chamber would have been right to find that it took place "shortly after".[322] Further, proof of the nexus does not depend on hearsay evidence: it does not require proof of the killing by the unreliable hearsay evidence of Witness CGC.

19. Various dates for the killing of Mr Nors were suggested. Dates from about 20 May 1994 to 26 May 1994 were mentioned. The Trial Chamber found that the killing occurred "in late May, 1994",[323] which included that period. The difficulty of estimating time and of recalling precise dates on which events occurred many years before in circumstances of extreme trauma has to be taken into account in resolving conflicts of evidence as to exact dates. A solution is to be found by focusing on the factual events, as sought to be done above.

20. When the evidence is thus approached, there is no basis on which the Appeals Chamber can find that no reasonable trier of fact could have reached the conclusion, beyond reasonable doubt, "that in late May, 1994"[324] Mr Nors was killed and that the killing took place "shortly after the Accused's departure" from the Gaseke roadblock.[325] Other triers of fact might have reached a different conclusion, but that is not sufficient to show that "no reasonable trier of fact could have reached" the conclusion reached by the Trial Chamber.

21. Finally, it has to be remembered that the particular point as to the interval between the visit and the killing was not raised in the written arguments on appeal. As mentioned before, the point **[page 56]** was raised only orally, in possible reaction to questions asked by the Appeals Chamber preparatory to the hearings.

F. Conclusion

318 *Ibid.*
319 Trial Judgement, para. 207. *See also* Trial Chamber's Transcript, 28 October 2003, p. 81, Witness DB.
320 Trial Judgement, para. 209. *See also* Trial Chamber's Transcript, 28 October 2003, pp. 83-84, Witness DB.
321 Trial Chamber's Transcript, 29 September 2003, p. 48, Witness CGC.
322 Trial Judgement, para. 231.
323 *Ibid.*, paras. 230-231.
324 *Ibid.*
325 *Ibid.*, para. 231.

22. For these reasons, I regret that I am not able to support the reasoning of the majority of the Appeals Chamber. The different reason why I agree with the Appeals Chamber to acquit the appellant in respect of the killing of Mr Nors is that, towards the end of the trial, the prosecution created an ambiguity as to whether in fact the charge was withdrawn, with the result that the accused would have to be given the benefit of the doubt on the question of fact as to whether there was a withdrawal. The Appeals Chamber can choose the ground of its decision, but it is worth noting that the question whether there was a withdrawal is logically prior to the merits of the arguments relating to the charge that was allegedly withdrawn. Normally the question of withdrawal should be treated first. But there is no point in elaborating.

Done in English and in French, the English text being authoritative.

Mohamed Shahabuddeen
Judge

Signed 10 January 2007
At The Hague
The Netherlands

And delivered
16 January 2007
At Arusha
Republic of Tanzania

[Seal of the Tribunal] [page 57]

XVI. PARTIALLY DISSENTING OPINION OF JUDGE GÜNEY

1. I agree with the Appeals Chamber's resolution of Emmanuel Ndindabahizi's appeal and with most of the reasons provided in today's Judgement. However, with respect, I am unable to accept the Appeals Chamber's affirmation *proprio motu* of the Trial Chamber's finding that Emmanuel Ndindabahizi himself committed the crime of extermination.[326] I therefore regret that I cannot support the findings of the Appeals Chamber with respect to paragraph 123.

2. In its Judgement, the Appeals Chamber finds *proprio motu* that "alternative convictions for several modes of liability are, in general, incompatible with the principle that a judgement has to express unambiguously the scope of the convicted person's criminal responsibility",[327] a statement with which I agree. In paragraph 123 of its Judgement, the Appeals Chamber also holds that "a full characterisation of the Appellant's conduct had to cumulatively refer to various modes of liability", *i.e.*, committing, instigating and aiding and abetting the crime of extermination.[328] The Appeal Judgement does not assess the characterisation by the Trial Chamber of the Appellant's criminal conduct; it simply upholds the Trial Judgement's finding, without considering its correctness. I have difficulty with the approach taken by the majority in this regard. More importantly, I disagree with the Trial Chamber's finding, upheld by the majority, that based on the circumstances of this case, the Appellant's conduct constitutes the "commission" of extermination. My reasons are as follows.

3. The Trial Chamber found that "[e]xtermination may be committed less directly than murder, as by participation in measures intended to bring about the deaths of a large number of individuals, but without actually committing a killing of any person."[329] In defining the *actus reus* for extermination, the Trial Chamber went beyond the findings of this Appeals Chamber in the *Ntakirutimana* Appeal Judgement and those of the ICTY Appeals Chamber in the *Stakić* Appeal Judgement. The Appeals Chambers in these cases defined the *actus reus* of extermination as "the act of killing on a large scale"[330] or the "systematical[] subject[ion of] a number of people to conditions of living that would inevitably lead to death."[331] If these precedents had been followed in this case, the acts of the Appellant could not have been characterised as "committing extermination".[332] Indeed, the Trial Chamber found that the evidence did not establish that the **[page 58]** Appellant himself killed any person by his acts at Gitwa Hill.[333] The Trial Chamber found that the Appellant committed the crime of extermination by distributing weapons, transporting attackers and encouraging them.[334] This cannot be considered as "systematically subjecting a number of people to conditions of living that would inevitably lead to death".[335] Moreover, it cannot be maintained that the killing of the refugees at Gitwa Hill would have occurred without the actions of the attackers themselves.

4. The Appeal Judgement does not provide reasons for upholding the Trial Chamber's characterisation of the Appellant's conduct as "committing" extermination. However, in a footnote, the majority suggests that "indirectly" causing death could also constitute committing extermination.[336] This seems to follow the approach in the *Gacumbitsi* case, in which the majority held that committing means not only "physically perpetrating the *actus reus* of the crime [or] participating in a joint criminal enterprise", but also "other acts of participation."[337] In my Partially Dissenting Opinion in *Gacumbitsi*,[338] I explained that this finding departs from prior decisions of both the ICTR and the ICTY Appeals Chambers without providing cogent reasons. I also explained that it blurs the essential distinction between "committing" a crime and other forms of liability

326 Appeal Judgement, paras 121 and 123.
327 *Ibid.*, para. 122.
328 *See* Trial Judgement, para. 485.
329 Trial Judgement, para. 479.
330 *Ntakirutimana* Appeal Judgement, para. 516; *Stakić* Appeal Judgement, para. 259.
331 *Ntakirutimana* Appeal Judgement, para. 522; *Stakić* Appeal Judgement, para. 259.
332 Except perhaps in the sense of participation in a joint criminal enterprise, but such mode of liability was not pleaded in this case.
333 Trial Judgement, para. 481.
334 *Ibid.*, para. 485.
335 *Ntakirutimana* Appeal Judgement, para. 522; *Stakiœ* Appeal Judgement, para. 259 (emphasis added).
336 Appeal Judgement, footnote 269.
337 *Gacumbitsi* Appeal Judgement, paras 60-61.
338 *Gacumbitsi* Appeal Judgement, Partially Dissenting Opinion of Judge Güney, paras 2-9.

recognised by the Statute and the jurisprudence. If any act of participation in a crime amounts to committing the crime, then all modes of liability are subsumed in the expression "committed" in Article 6(1) of the Statute and become redundant. This, at the very least, runs contrary to the principle *ut res magis valeat quam pereat*, according to which all provisions in the Statute should be given effect.

5. In my view, the criminal conduct of the Appellant can only be characterised as instigating and aiding and abetting the crime of extermination; it does not constitute "committing" that crime. In the circumstances of this case, the attackers at Gitwa Hill committed the crime. Their actions directly resulted in the deaths of the refugees and there were no other agents intervening between their acts and the death of the victims. The Appellant assisted, encouraged and lent moral support to these attackers, and his acts had a substantial effect upon the perpetration of the crime.

6. I conclude that the Trial Chamber erred in finding that Mr. Ndindabahizi "himself committed the crime of extermination".[339] I regret that the Appeal Judgement upholds this erroneous finding without considering the matter further. For the reasons stated above, I depart **[page 59]** from the majority and disagree with paragraph 123 of the Appeal Judgement.

Done in English and French, the English text being authoritative.

Mehmet Güney
Judge

Signed on the tenth day of January 2007,
in The Hague, The Netherlands,

Issued on the sixteenth day of January 2007,
in Arusha, Tanzania.

[Seal of the Tribunal] [page 60]

339 Trial Judgement, para. 485.

XVII. ANNEX A – PROCEDURAL BACKGROUND

A. Notice of Appeal and Briefs

1. The Trial Judgement was delivered in the original English version on 15 July 2004. On 13 August 2004, the Appellant filed his Notice of Appeal, including 13 grounds of appeal. On 24 August 2004, the Appellant filed a motion seeking an extension of time for filing his Appellant's Brief on the basis that the French translation of the Trial Judgement was not yet available.[340] The request was granted on 26 August 2004, and the Appellant was ordered to file the Appellant's Brief within seventy-five days of receipt of the French translation of the Trial Judgement.[341] On 29 December 2004, the Appellant filed a motion seeking a suspension of the deadline for filing his Appellant's Brief on the basis that his lead counsel was quitting the profession of attorney.[342] The request was granted on 6 January 2005, and the Appellant was ordered to file the Appellant's Brief within seventy-five days after the assignment of new lead counsel by the Registrar.[343] On 1 April 2005, the Appellant again sought to extend the deadline for the Appellant's Brief on the grounds that his co-counsel and lead counsel required more time to acquaint themselves with the case.[344] This request was denied on 5 April 2005.[345]

2. The Appellant filed his Appellant's Brief in which grounds of appeal 6, 8 and 12 were withdrawn[346] on 9 May 2005.[347] On 14 June 2005, he filed a Corrigendum to his Appellant's Brief.[348] The Prosecution filed its Respondent's Brief on 17 June 2005[349] and a Corrigendum on 5 June 2006.[350] The Appellant requested an extension of the deadline for filing his Brief in Reply[351] which was granted until 15 days after receipt of the French translation of the Respondent's Brief.[352] The Appellant submitted a further request for delay in filing his Brief in Reply on the basis that he had not received the full translation of the Respondent's Brief until 31 October 2005.[353] This **[page 61]** request was granted by the Appeals Chamber who ordered that the Brief in Reply, if any, be filed no later than 14 November 2005.[354] The Appellant submitted his Brief in Reply on that day.[355] On 9 November 2006, the Appellant filed a public version of the Appellant's Brief.[356]

B. Assignment of Judges

3. On 24 August 2004, the following Judges were assigned to hear the appeal: Judge Theodor Meron, Presiding; Judge Florence Mumba; Judge Mehmet Güney; Judge Wolfgang Schomburg; and Judge Inés Weinberg de Roca. Judge Schomburg was designated as Pre-Appeal Judge on 24 August 2004[357] and as

---

340 Requête aux fins de prorogation de délai pour le dépôt du mémoire en appel – articles 111 et 116 du règlement de procédure et de preuve, 24 August 2004.
341 Decision on Emmanuel Ndindabahizi's Motion for an Extension of Time, 26 August 2004.
342 Requête urgente aux fins de suspension des délais, 29 December 2004. This latter submission replaced the earlier submission, Requête urgente aux fins de prorogation de délai pour le dépôt du mémoire en appel, 14 December 2004.
343 Decision on Emmanuel Ndindabahizi's Motion for an Extension of Time, 6 January 2005.
344 Requête urgente aux fins de prorogation de délai pour le dépôt du mémoire en appel, 1 April 2005.
345 Decision on 'Requête urgente aux fins de prorogation de délai pour le dépôt du mémoire en appel', 5 April 2005.
346 Appellant's Brief, para. 11.
347 Mémoire d'Appel, 9 May 2005.
348 Corrigendum au Mémoire d'Appel, 14 June 2005.
349 Respondent's Brief, 17 June 2005.
350 Corrigendum to the Respondent's Brief of the Prosecutor, 5 June 2006.
351 Requête urgente aux fins de prorogation de délai pour le dépôt de la réplique de l'appelant, 22 June 2005.
352 Decision on Requête urgente aux fins de prorogation de délai pour le dépôt de la réplique de l'appelant, 28 June 2005.
353 Requête urgente en extension de délai pour le dépôt de la réplique au procureur, 28 October 2005, and Requête en clarification de la date de réception du Mémoire de l'Intimé, 7 November 2005. The Prosecutor only replied to the former in: Prosecutor's Response to Appellant Emmanuel Ndindabahizi's Requête urgente en extension de délai pour le dépôt de la réplique au procureur, 1 November 2005.
354 Order on Appellant's Requête urgente en extension de délai pour le dépôt de la Réplique au procureur and Requête en clarification de la date de réception du mémoire de l'intimé, 9 November 2005.
355 Reply Brief, 14 November 2005.
356 Mémoire d'Appel Version publique, 20 October 2006, filed on 9 November 2006.
357 Order of the Presiding Judge Assigning Judges and Designating the Pre-Appeal Judge, 24 August 2004.

Presiding Judge on 21 November 2005. Subsequently, Judge Shahabuddeen was assigned to replace Judge Inés Weinberg de Roca,[358] and Judge Liu Daqun was assigned to replace Judge Florence Mumba.[359]

C. Additional Evidence and Further Motions

4. On 27 September 2004, the Appellant filed a motion seeking leave to present additional evidence in the form of four documents relating to his alleged alibi.[360] The Appeals Chamber granted the motion and gave leave to present the four documents as additional evidence pursuant to Rule 115 of the Rules.[361] On 28 February 2006, the Appellant filed a second motion seeking leave to present additional evidence relating to mitigating circumstances[362] which was dismissed by the **[page 62]** Appeals Chamber on 4 April 2006.[363] On 24 April 2006, the Appellant filed a request for reconsideration of this decision of the Appeals Chamber,[364] which was rejected on 14 June 2006.[365]

5. Status conferences were held on 8 March 2005, 19 September 2005 and 8 February 2006. In the status conference on 8 February 2006, both parties were invited to make submissions on the definition of the crime against humanity of extermination.[366] Both parties made submissions,[367] and on 2 March 2006 the Presiding Judge invited the parties to respond to each other's submissions,[368] which both parties did.[369]

D. Hearing of the Appeal

6. Pursuant to a Scheduling Order of 11 May 2006,[370] the Appeals Chamber heard the parties' submissions on the appeal on 6 July 2006 in Arusha, Tanzania. **[page 63]**

---

358 Order Replacing a Judge, 15 July 2005.

359 Order Replacing a Judge, 18 November 2005.

360 Requête de la défense en présentation de moyens de preuve supplémentaires – Art 115 du Règlement, 27 September 2004; Prosecutor's Response to Requête de la défense en présentation de moyens de preuve supplémentaires – Art 115 du règlement, 7 October 2004; Réplique de l'appelant (requête en présentation de moyens de preuve supplémentaires – Art 115 du règlement), 12 October 2004; Corrigendum to Prosecutor's Response to Requête de La Défense En Présentation de Moyens de Preuve Supplémentaires-Art. 115 du Règlement, 8 March 2005; Prosecutor's Additional Submission in Response to the 'Requête de La Défense En Présentation de Moyens de Preuve Supplémentaires-Art. 115 du Règlement (Pre-Appeal Judge's Directive of 8 March 2005), 22 March 2005; Observations de la Défense sur les Documents Communiqués par le Bureau du Procureur, 22 March 2005.

361 Decision on the Admission of Additional Evidence, 14 April 2005.

362 The Appellant's Second Motion to Present Additional Evidence (R.115), 28 February 2006; Prosecutor's Response to the Appellant's Second Motion to Present Additional Evidence (R.115), 10 March 2006; Réponse aux observations de l'intimé sur la deuxième requête de l'appelant en présentation de moyens de preuve supplémentaires, 20 March 2006.

363 Decision on the Admission of Additional Evidence, 4 April 2006.

364 Requête de l'appelant en reconsidération de la décision du 4 avril 2006 en raison d'une erreur matérielle, 24 April 2006; Prosecutor's Response to Requête de l'appelant en reconsidération de la décision du 4 avril 2006 en raison d'une erreur matérielle, 26 April 2006.

365 Décision on Defence Requête de l'appelant en reconsidération de la décision du 4 avril 2006 en raison d'une erreur matérielle, 14 June 2006.

366 Scheduling Order, 6 January 2006.

367 Mémoire supplémentaire de l'appelant sur l'élément matériel et moral de l'extermination, 28 February 2006; Prosecutor's Submissions on Elements of Extermination as a Crime against Humanity, 1 March 2006.

368 Letter to the Parties: Invitation to Respond to Submissions on Extermination, 2 March 2006.

369 Prosecutor's Response to Ndindabahizi's Mémoire supplémentaire de l'appelant sur l'élément matériel et moral de l'extermination, 15 March 2006; Réponse de l'appelant aux observations du procureur sur les éléments de l'extermination en tant que crime contre l'humanité, 15 March 2006.

370 Scheduling Order, 11 May 2006.

XVIII. ANNEX B – CITED MATERIALS/DEFINED TERMS

A. List of Cited Tribunal Decisions

ICTR

AKAYESU
Prosecutor v. Jean-Paul Akayesu, Case No. ICTR-96-4-A, Judgement, 1 June 2001 ("*Akayesu* Appeal Judgement")

BAGILISHEMA
Prosecutor v. Ignace Bagilishema, Case No. ICTR-95-1A-T, Judgement, 7 June 2001 ("*Bagilishema* Trial Judgement")

GACUMBITSI
Prosecutor v. Sylvestre Gacumbitsi, Case No. ICTR-01-64-A, Judgment, 7 July 2006 ("*Gacumbitsi* Appeal Judgement")

KAJELIJELI
Prosecutor v. Juvénal Kajelijeli, Case No. ICTR-98-44A-T, Judgement and Sentence, 1 December 2003 ("*Kajelijeli* Trial Judgement")

Prosecutor v. Juvénal Kajelijeli, Case No. ICTR-98-44A-A, Judgement, 23 May 2005 ("*Kajelijeli* Appeal Judgement")

KAMUHANDA
Prosecutor v. Jean de Dieu Kamuhanda, Case No. ICTR-99-54A-T, Judgement and Sentence 22 January 2003 ("*Kamuhanda* Trial Judgement")

Prosecutor v. Jean de Dieu Kamuhanda, Case No. ICTR-95-1-A, Judgement, 19 September 2005 ("*Kamuhanda* Appeal Judgement")

KAYISHEMA AND RUZINDANA
Prosecutor v. Clément Kayishema and Obed Ruzindana, Case No. ICTR-95-1-T, Judgement,21 May 1999 ("*Kayishema and Ruzindana* Trial Judgement")

Prosecutor v. Clément Kayishema and Obed Ruzindana, Case No. ICTR-95-1-A, Judgement (Reasons), 1 June 2001 ("*Kayishema and Ruzindana* Appeal Judgement ")

MUSEMA
Prosecutor v. Alfred Musema, Case No. ICTR-96-13-T, Judgement, 27 January 2000 ("*Musema* Trial Judgement")

NIYITEGEKA
Prosecutor v. Eliézer Niyitegeka, Case No. ICTR-96-14-T, Judgement and Sentence, 16 May 2003 ("*Niyitegeka* Trial Judgement and Sentence")

Prosecutor v. Eliézer Niyitegeka, Case No. ICTR-96-14-T, Appeal Judgement, 9 July 2004 ("*Niyitegeka* Appeal Judgement") **[page 64]**

NTAKIRUTIMANA
Prosecutor v. Elizaphan and Gérard Ntakirutimana, Case No. ICTR-96-10 & ICTR-96-17-T, Judgement and Sentence, 21 February 2003 ("*Ntakirutimana* Trial Judgement and Sentence")

Prosecutor v. Elizaphan and Gérard Ntakirutimana, Case No. ICTR-96-10 & ICTR-96-17-A, Appeal Judgement, 9 December 2004 ("*Ntakirutimana* Appeal Judgement")

NTAGERURA *ET AL.*
Prosecutor v. André Ntagerura, Emmanuel Bagambiki and Samuel Imanishimwe, Case No. ICTR-99-46-A, Judgement and Sentence, 7 July 2006 ("*Ntagerura et al* Appeal Judgement and Sentence")

RUTAGANDA

Prosecutor v. Georges Anderson Nderubunwe Rutaganda, Case No. ICTR-96-3-A, Judgement, 26 May 2003 ("*Rutaganda* Appeal Judgement")

SEMANZA

Prosecutor v. Laurent Semanza, Case No. ICTR-97-20-T, Judgement and Sentence, 15 May 2003 ("*Semanza* Trial Judgement and Sentence")

Prosecutor v. Laurent Semanza, Case No. ICTR-97-20-A, Judgement, 20 May 2003 ("*Semanza* Appeal Judgement")

ICTY

ALEKSOVSKI

Prosecutor v. Zlatko Aleksovski, Case No. IT-95-14/1-A, Judgement, 24 March 2000 ("*Aleksovski* Appeal Judgement")

BLAŠKIĆ

Prosecutor v. Tihomir Blaškić, Case No. IT-95-14-A, Judgement, 29 July 2004 ("*Blaškić* Appeal Judgement")

FURUNDŽIJA

Prosecutor v. Anto Furundžija, Case No. IT-95-17/1-A, Judgement, 21 July 2000 ("*Furundžija* Appeal Judgement")

KRSTIĆ

Prosecutor v. Radislav Krstić, Case No. IT-98-33-T, Judgement, 2 August 2001 ("*Krstić* Trial Judgement")

Prosecutor v. Radislav Krstić, Case No. IT-98-33-A, Judgement, 19 April 2004 ("*Krstić* Appeal Judgement")

Z. KUPREŠKIĆ, M. KUPREŠKIĆ, V. KUPREŠKIĆ, JOSIPOVIĆ, (PAPIĆ) AND SANTIĆ

Prosecutor v. Zoran Kupreškić, Mirjan Kupreškić, Vlatko Kupreškić, Drago Josipović and Vladimir Santić, Case No. IT-95-16-A, Appeal Judgement, 23 October 2001 ("*Kupreškić et al.* Appeal Judgement")

NALETILIĆ AND MARTINOVIĆ

Prosecutor v. Mladen Naletilić and Vinko Martinović, Case No. IT-98-34-A, Appeal Judgement, 3 May 2006 ("*Naletilić and Martinović* Appeal Judgement") **[page 65]**

STAKIĆ

Prosecutor v. Milomir Stakić, Case No. IT-97-24-A, Appeal Judgement, 22 March 2006 ("*Stakić* Appeal Judgement")

D. TADIĆ

Prosecutor v. Duško Tadić a/k/a "Dule", Case No. IT-94-1-T, Judgement, 7 May 1997 ("*Tadić* Trial Judgement")

Prosecutor v. Duško Tadić, Case No. IT-94-1-A, Judgement, 15 July 1999 ("*Tadić* Appeal Judgement")

VASILJEVIĆ

Prosecutor v. Mitar Vasiljević, Case No. IT-98-32-T, Judgement, 29 November 2002 ("*Vasiljević* Trial Judgement")

Prosecutor v. Mitar Vasiljević, Case No. IT-98-32-A, Judgement, 25 February 2004 ("*Vasiljević* Appeal Judgement")

B. List of Abbreviations

According to Rule 2 (B), of the Rules of Procedure and Evidence, the masculine shall include the feminine and the singular the plural, and vice versa.

Accused	Emmanuel Ndindabahizi
AT	Transcript page from hearings on appeal in the present case. All transcript page numbers referred to are from the unofficial, uncorrected version of the transcript, unless specified otherwise.
cf.	[Latin: *confer*] (Compare)
Defence	The Accused, and/or the Accused's counsel
Exh(s).	Exhibit(s)
ICTR	International Criminal Tribunal for the Prosecution of Persons Responsible for Genocide and Other Serious Violations of International Humanitarian Law Committed in the Territory of Rwanda and Rwandan Citizens responsible for genocide and other such violations committed in the territory of neighbouring States, between 1 January 1994 and 31 December 1994
ICTY	International Tribunal for the Prosecution of Persons Responsible for Serious Violations of International Humanitarian Law Committed in the Territory of the Former Yugoslavia since 1991
Indictment	*Prosecutor v. Emmanuel Ndindabahizi*, Case No. ICTR-01-71-I, Amended Indictment (Pursuant to Trial Chamber I's Decision of 1 September 2003), dated 1 September 2003
Ndindabahizi Appeal Brief	*Prosecutor v. Emmanuel Ndindabahizi*, Case No. ICTR-01-71-A, Appellant's Brief, filed 9 May 2005
Ndindabahizi Closing Brief	*Prosecutor v. Emmanuel Ndindabahizi*, Case No. ICTR-01-71-T, Defence Closing Brief, filed on 6 February 2003 **[page 66]**
Ndindabahizi Reply Brief	*Prosecutor v. Emmanuel Ndindabahizi*, Case No. ICTR-01-71-A, Response to Respondent's Brief, filed 14 November 2005
Notice of Appeal	*Prosecutor v. Emmanuel Ndindabahizi*, Case No. ICTR-01-71-T, Acte d'Appel, filed on 13 August 2004
Prosecution	Office of the Prosecutor
Prosecution Response	*Prosecutor v. Emmanuel Ndindabahizi*, Case No. ICTR-01-71-A, Respondent's Brief of the Prosecutor, filed on 17 June 2005
Prosecution Pre-trial Brief	*Prosecutor v. Emmanuel Ndindabahizi*, Case No. ICTR-01-71-I, Prosecutor's Pre-Trial Brief, filed 1 August 2003
Prosecution Closing Brief	*Prosecutor v. Emmanuel Ndindabahizi*, Case No. ICTR-01-71-T, Prosecutor's Closing Brief, filed on 20 January 2004
Rules	Rules of Procedure and Evidence of the ICTR
Statute	Statute of the International Tribunal for Rwanda established by Security Council Resolution 955 (1994)

T.	Transcript page from hearings at trial in *Prosecutor v. Emmanuel Ndindabahizi*, Case No. ICTR-2001-71-I. All transcript page numbers referred to are from the unofficial, uncorrected version of the transcript, unless specified otherwise.
UN	United Nations
UNDF	United Nations Detention Facilities for persons awaiting trial or appeal before the ICTR **[page 67]**

Commentary

1. Introduction

This judgement[1] by the Appeals Chamber of the International Criminal Tribunal for Rwanda (ICTR) deals with yet another conviction by a Trial Chamber of the ICTR of a senior government official for serious crimes committed during the carnage that took place in Rwanda between April-June 1994.[2] In the case of Emmanuel Ndindabahizi, this also included a conviction for the 'crime of crimes',[3] the crime of genocide, as defined in Article 2 of the ICTR Statute. This followed previous convictions for genocide of former government officials, including Jean Kambanda, the former prime minister of Rwanda (who had pleaded guilty), Jean-Paul Akayesu, the former *bourgmestre* of Taba and Sylvestre Gacumbitsi, the former *bourgmestre* in the commune of Rusomo.

2. The appellant

Between September 1992 and 6 April 1994, Emmanuel Ndindabahizi had been the second highest official working in the Rwandan ministry of finance. He subsequently became minister of finance in the interim government on 9 April 1994, following the death of president Juvenal Habyarimana on 6 April, and held that position at the time of the events that lead to his conviction.

Following the fall of the interim government in Rwanda in July 1994, the appellant fled to the Democratic Republic of the Congo and eventually found his way to Belgium in early 2001, where he took up residence pending an (ultimately unsuccessful) request for asylum. He was arrested in Verviers, Belgium on 12 July 2001, and was transferred to the seat of the ICTR on 25 September of that year, making his initial appearance before the tribunal on 19 October 2001.

The original indictment regarding the appellant was confirmed on 5 July 2001. A modified indictment was filed, with leave, by the prosecution on 5 October 2001, and included a separate charge of crimes against humanity (rape), and allegations of superior responsibility under Article 6, paragraph 3 of the ICTR Statute in respect of the charges of genocide and crimes against humanity (murder, extermination and rape). The prosecution requested further amendments to the indictment by a motion filed 9 May 2003, which included withdrawal of the counts concerning direct and public incitement to commit genocide, crimes against humanity (rape), and the charge of superior responsibility. An amended indictment (the indictment) was filed on 1 September 2003.

Emmanuel Ndindabahizi was found guilty by Trial Chamber I of the ICTR on 15 July 2004, pursuant to Article 6, paragraph 1 of the ICTR Statute, of the crimes of genocide, crimes against humanity (extermination) and crimes against humanity (murder). These convictions related to the actions of the appellant in support of the attackers at Gitwa Hill during April 2004 – where "thousands of Tutsi" had sought refuge only to be subsequently killed – and at a roadblock at Gaseke in May 2004, including in relation to the death of a half-caste called Mr Nors (also known as Nturuso).

Following his conviction, he was sentenced by the Trial Chamber to a single sentence of life imprisonment.

The appellant appealed against all of these convictions and also against the sentence handed down by the Trial Chamber. This commentary deals with the judgement of the Appeals Chamber in relation those appeals.

3. The appeal

The appellant raised a total of ten grounds of appeal, alleging both errors of fact and errors of law in the judgment handed down by Trial Chamber 1. These grounds were grouped in various ways by the Appeals Chamber and dealt with one by one (see below). In undertaking this task, the Appeals Chamber took note of

1 ICTR, Judgement, *Ndindabahizi v. Prosecutor*, Case No. ICTR-01-71-A, A. Ch., 16 January 2007, in this volume, p. 620.

2 ICTR, Judgement and Sentence, *Prosecutor v. Ndindabahizi*, Case No. ICTR-2001-71-I, T. Ch. I, 15 July 2004, Klip/ Sluiter, ALC-XVIII-645.

3 ICTR, Judgement, *Prosecutor v. Akayesu*, Case No. ICTR-96-4-T, T. Ch. I, 2 September 1998, Klip/ Sluiter, ALC-II-399, par. 16.

the "settled standards of appellate review" in relation to proceedings under Article 24 of the ICTR Statute. It is worthwhile repeating these here. In relation to alleged errors of law, the Appeals Chamber noted:

> "[w]here a party alleges that there is an error of law, that party must advance arguments in support of the submission and explain how the error invalidates the decision. However, if the appellant's arguments do not support the contention, that party does not automatically lose its point since the Appeals Chamber may step in and, for other reasons, find in favour of the contention that there is an error of law."[4]

As regards alleged errors of fact, it was reiterated that:

> "[w]here the Defence alleges an erroneous finding of fact, the Appeals Chamber must give deference to the Trial Chamber that received the evidence at trial, and it will only interfere in those findings where no reasonable trier of fact could have reached the same finding or where the finding is wholly erroneous. Furthermore, the erroneous finding will be revoked or revised only if the error occasioned a miscarriage of justice."[5]

After considering the various grounds of appeal, the Appeals Chamber:

a) affirmed the conviction of the appellant for the crimes of genocide (but only in relation to the events at Gitwa Hill) and crimes against humanity (extermination) (Judge Güney dissenting);

b) unanimously vacated the appellant's conviction for crimes against humanity (murder), although the reasoning of the majority on this point differs from that of Judge Shahabuddeen. The Appeals Chamber having reached this conclusion, it followed that the conviction for genocide in relation to the events at the Gaseke roadblock were also vacated; and

c) unanimously affirmed the sentence of life imprisonment imposed on the appellant by the Trial Chamber, despite the Appeals Chamber vacating a number of the convictions.

4. Discussion of the Appeals Chamber decision

The discussion below deals in turn with each of the grounds of appeal considered by the Appeals Chamber.

4.1 Alleged vagueness of the indictment (Gitwa Hill)

The appellant referred to various discrepancies in relation to the dates specified in the indictment on which the massacre at Gitwa Hill took place. The indictment referred to a period – from 13 to 26 April – during which the events occurred, without specifying the precise date(s) on which the appellant was alleged to have been involved. The appellant argued that this constituted an error of law, while the prosecution submitted that no prejudice on the appellant had arisen and that, in any event, he had not raised any objection in relation to this point before the Trial Chamber.

The Appeals Chamber concluded that the time period had been stated in the indictment "with sufficient specificity".[6] It noted that a "continued attack" took place at Gitwa Hill during the 13 day period specified in the indictment, and accepted that, in the words of the Trial Chamber, these attacks had "notoriety".[7] Beyond this, however, the Appeals Chamber provided very little by way of analysis or explanation as to why the time range was sufficiently clear in the circumstances. In this regard, the Appeals Chamber simply assumed that the reference to this time period did, in fact, satisfy the appellant's right to be informed in detail about the nature and cause of the charge against him, which is one of the 'minimum guarantees' to be afforded to all accused before the tribunal.[8] Accordingly, the Appeals Chamber rejected this ground of appeal.

Whilst this was, in the circumstances, most likely a correct conclusion, it would have been preferable had the Appeals Chamber perhaps provided a clearer (and thus more transparent) explanation as to why the wording of the indictment was acceptable in the circumstances of this case. It could, for example, be argued that the notoriety of the events on its own did not constitute a sufficient justification for accepting that the time range

---

4 Judgement, *Ndindabahizi v. Prosecutor*, *supra* note 1, par. 9.
5 *Ibid.*, par. 10.
6 *Ibid.*, par. 19.
7 *Ibid.*, par. 21.
8 See ICTR Statute, Article 20, paragraph 4, sub a.

was sufficient to satisfy such an important right of the appellant, and it therefore would have been helpful for the elimination of any doubt if the Appeals Chamber had provided additional reasons.

4.2 Alleged error in finding that the appellant was in Gitwa

The appellant argued that the Trial Chamber committed an error of fact by accepting the testimonies of various witnesses – in this instance, witnesses CGY and CGN – in relation to his alleged actions at Gitwa Hill. The prosecution, whilst acknowledging that the evidence presented by these witnesses was uncorroborated, submitted that the Trial Chamber was nonetheless entitled to rely on it. It also argued that, in relation to this ground of appeal, the appellant was merely repeating arguments that had been rejected at the trial by Trial Chamber I.

In relation to the claims by the appellant, it must be remembered, as noted above, that for such a ground to succeed, the appellant must demonstrate that the relevant findings of fact by the Trial Chamber (based on the witness testimonies) were *unreasonable*. As is illustrated in the discussion of the Appeals Chamber, this is a difficult burden for an appellant to overcome, particularly given the fact that, as was noted by the Appeals Chamber itself: "the Appeals Chamber will not lightly overturn findings of a trier of fact which is able to directly assess the demeanour of a witness giving live testimony."[9]

In essence, herein lay the problem for the appellant. In dealing with this ground of appeal, the Appeals Chamber did agree that there were a number of inconsistencies in the evidence of the relevant witnesses. Yet, at the same time, it noted that it was often the case that a trier of fact had to consider and deal with conflicting evidence, even by the same witness (witness CGY), but that, within the structure of the *ad hoc* tribunals, the Trial Chamber is typically "best placed" to assess the evidence of a witness "in its entirety".[10] Thus, it is permissible, and indeed quite common, for a Trial Chamber "to accept some elements of a witness's testimony while rejecting other elements" of the same witness testimony.[11]

The end result of this thought process seems to be that, in the absence of what would clearly be wholly unreasonable conclusions on the part of the Trial Chamber, an Appeals Chamber is unlikely to overturn findings of fact. Naturally, this is a pragmatic and perhaps logical general approach – the nature of the appeals process at the *ad hoc* tribunals is generally that witness testimony is not 'reheard', since this would make the entire process unwieldy and (even more) time-consuming. Moreover, given the time pressures imposed by the relevant 'completion strategy' of each of the *ad hoc* tribunals,[12] they simply cannot afford the luxury of allowing for witness testimony – even where it is contradictory and may (thus) go to the heart of the appeal itself – to be re-presented before the Appeals Chamber.

Similarly, and in all likelihood related to the same time-related reasons, one might also sense a general reluctance on the part of the Appeals Chamber to make a statement/ finding as to the effect of the inconsistencies it has found and, on that basis, then send matters back to a Trial Chamber for retrial, even though the Appeals Chamber has the power to do precisely that.[13]

Yet, this pragmatism may sometimes leave an observer with a slightly uneasy feeling. It is, of course, perfectly understandable that, in the complex, traumatic and confused circumstances in which catastrophes such as the genocide in Rwanda took place, witnesses may have difficulty remembering precise details of events that transpired perhaps many years previously, thus giving rise to sometimes conflicting testimony. However, one must always remember that these trials are also about the guilt and innocence of accused persons and that inconsistency in testimony of those persons upon whom any conviction is to be based must be thoroughly considered.

---

9 Judgement, *Ndindabahizi v. Prosecutor*, *supra* note 1, par. 42.

10 *Ibid.*, par. 34.

11 *Ibid.*, par. 44.

12 See United Nations Security Council Resolution 1503 (2003), 28 August 2003, U.N. Doc. S/Res/1503, which refers in preambular paragraph 8 to the 'ICTR Completion Strategy' involving the completion of investigations by the end of 2004, of all trial activities at first instance the end of 2008 and of all of the work of the Tribunal in 2010. Paragraph 3 of United Nations Security Council Resolution 1534 (2004), 26 March 2004, U.N. Doc. S/Res/1534, (emphasizes the "importance" of each of the *ad hoc* tribunals implementing their respective completion strategies and called upon the tribunals to "plan and act accordingly".

13 See Rule 118, paragraph C of the ICTR Rules of Evidence and Procedure (RPE), which provides that "[i]n appropriate circumstances the Appeals Chamber may order that the accused be retried before the Trial Chamber."

In this sense – and there is probably no other practical way in the context of these trials – it is left to the (trial) judges to 'pick and choose' what evidence they will and will not accept, even from the same witness. Given that the judges in these trials are both adjudicators of the (relevant) law and finders of fact, much depends upon their skills, professionalism and ability to decipher what, in the circumstances, is the 'truth' and what is not. Once this has been done, it will often be difficult for an Appeals Chamber to question those findings. I plan to briefly return to this issue in the concluding comments to this commentary.

4.3 Judgement allegedly rendered beyond the scope of the indictment

The appellant argued that the Trial Chamber had erred in law in relation to certain factual findings not contained in the indictment as follows: a) his position as minister of finance in the interim government; b) his participation at a meeting on 3 May 1994; and c) his role in the resignation of witness GHK as a member of parliament in June 1994.

Regarding his position as minister of finance, the Appeals Chamber, having dispensed with the claim by the appellant that this was not included in the indictment (in fact, his position was referred to twice in the indictment), concluded that the Trial Chamber did not improperly rely on his position in order to convict him. The Appeals Chamber noted that the Trial Chamber had concluded that the appellant's position was not relevant to his *mens rea*, which was instead evidenced by his actual conduct.

Nor, in the opinion of the Appeals Chamber, did the Trial Chamber use his position to substantiate a motive to commit the crimes charged. Indeed, as confirmed by the Appeals Chamber on the basis of settled jurisprudence,[14] the motive of an accused is of relevance *only* with respect to sentencing if at all, and certainly not for "liability purposes". This does rather beg the question as to why the Trial Chamber raised the question of a possible motive at all. As explained by the Appeals Chamber, the Trial Chamber seems that to have raised the issue of motive in the context of the appellant's position, only to have then dismissed it as having "little probative value". This approach does not sit entirely squarely with the way in which the Appeals Chamber explains the question of motive, a conclusion that is reiterated by the Appeals Chamber's affirmation that his position in the interim government "could be relevant only for certain limited purposes".[15]

With respect to the two other factual issues raised by the appellant, the Appeals Chamber agrees that neither was referred to in the indictment. In this regard, the question that must therefore be determined is whether the Trial Chamber relied on these facts to convict the appellant. On this point, the Appeals Chamber accepts the express statement of the Trial Chamber that it did not rely on of these 'facts' either to conclude that the appellant had the requisite *mens rea*, or in any other way. Yet, as noted by the Appeals Chamber, the Trial Chamber did subsequently make reference to the appellant's attendance at the meeting as perhaps "probative of an alleged motivation" and also as an aggravating circumstance.[16]

Despite this apparent error by the Trial Chamber, the Appeals Chamber, which was unable to determine why the Trial Chamber made such a finding, concluded (again without any analysis or explanation) that "no effect on the judgement has been shown" such that the proceedings were rendered unfair.[17] Once again, this indicates the difficulties that the appellant had in seeking to overturn the findings of the Trial Chamber.

4.4 Alleged non-disclosure of exculpatory evidence

The appellant argued that the prosecution, which was under a duty to disclose exculpatory evidence pursuant to Rule 68 of the ICTR Rules of Procedure and Evidence (RPE), failed to disclose to the appellant four documents that had been in its possession for over three years prior to the date of the trial judgement. On the basis of these documents, the appellant sought to raise a 'new' *alibi* – one that was different from an *alibi* he had unsuccessfully presented before the Trial Chamber.

The prosecution acknowledged that the four documents "ought to have been disclosed". This was confirmed by the Appeals Chamber.[18] The failure to do so constituted a clear breach by the prosecution of its obligations

---

14 Judgement, *Ndindabahizi v. Prosecutor*, *supra* note 1, par. 53.
15 *Ibid.*, par. 55.
16 *Ibid.*, par. 58.
17 *Ibid.*, par. 59.
18 *Ibid.*, par. 71.

under Rule 68 – although the Appeals Chamber, whilst stating that this was an important obligation, also added that this obligation extended only "to the best of its [the prosecution's] ability", even though those qualifying words do not appear in the rule itself.[19] This gloss is also surprising given the fact that the prosecutor is not only a party to the proceedings, but is also an organ of the tribunal, and is therefore also responsible for the proper conduct of international criminal 'justice' in the *ad hoc* tribunals.

Perhaps this was indicative of the way in which the Appeals Chamber viewed the submissions by the appellant on this issue. The fact that the appellant was now seeking to rely on an *alibi* that was different from that which he had alleged during the trial obviously went to the credibility (or lack thereof) of the claim. Rather than focusing on the breach of the prosecution's obligations, the main thrust of the discussion by the Appeals Chamber was whether the appellant could, in fact, raise this (new) *alibi* and what the effect of the documents (and the new *alibi*) were in relation to the reasonableness of the Trial Chamber's decision to convict the appellant.

The Appeals Chamber confirmed that the appellant could, pursuant to Rule 67, paragraph A, sub ii, sub a of the ICTR RPE, raise a new *alibi*, after having given notice to the prosecution "[a]s early as reasonably practicable and in any event prior to the commencement of the Trial".[20] Whilst the "[f]ailure [...] to provide such notice [...] shall not limit the right of the accused to rely" on the *alibi*,[21] the Appeals Chamber noted that the Trial Chamber was entitled to consider such failure in its overall assessment of the alibi. This of course makes perfect sense, and the general circumstances of this case are a perfect illustration of why this is so.

However, one should bear in mind that, due to the breach by the prosecution of its disclosure obligations, the appellant did *not*, prior to and during the trial, have access to the documents upon which he claimed to base this *alibi*. Despite this, the Appeals Chamber notes that "his delay in raising the alibi affects the probative value of the documents".[22] Whilst the conclusion by the Appeals Chamber that this new *alibi* does not raise a reasonable doubt about the finding of guilt appears to be correct, it is perhaps unsatisfactory that the Appeals Chamber seems to gloss over the slight illogicality of its own argument.

Interestingly, one might note in this regard the importance of the obligations to provide an accused with exculpatory evidence in the case of the first accused in the custody of the International Criminal Court (ICC), Thomas Lubanga Dyilo. Following the failure of the ICC prosecution to properly comply with its obligations to disclose exculpatory material to the accused,[23] the ICC Trial Chamber ordered that he be immediately released.[24] In the end this did not actually happen – that order was suspended pending an appeal by the prosecution and, as at the time of writing this commentary, that trial is currently underway.

However, and acknowledging that the circumstances in Lubanga were completely different from the case in hand, this illustrates all too clearly how respect for rules regarding exculpatory evidence are a vital element in the implementation of a transparent and credible process of international criminal justice. The obligation on the prosecution under Rule 68 represents an important element in the 'truth seeking' character of the tribunal.

4.5 Alleged errors in the assessment of defence evidence

The appellant alleged that the Trial Chamber had erred in its assessment of various aspects of the evidence that he had presented, thus resulting in a violation of his right to a fair trial. The Appeals Chamber considered each aspect of this evidence, whilst noting that the Trial Chamber had discretion as to what evidence to

[19] *Ibid.* Rule 68 paragraph a of the Rules of Procedure and Evidence of the International Criminal Tribunal for Rwanda (ICTR RPE) provides as follows: "The Prosecutor shall, as soon as practicable, disclose to the Defence any material, which in the actual knowledge of the Prosecutor may suggest the innocence or mitigate the guilt of the accused or affect the credibility of Prosecution evidence."

[20] Rule 67, paragraph A, sub ii, sub a of the ICTR RPE.

[21] Rule 67, paragraph B of the ICTR RPE.

[22] Judgement, *Ndindabahizi v. Prosecutor, supra* note 1, par. 70.

[23] See, ICC, Decision on the Consequences of Non-Disclosure of Exculpatory Materials Covered by Article 54(3)(e) Agreements and the Application to Stay the Prosecution of the Accused, Together With Certain Other Issues Raised at the Status Conference on 10 June 2008, *Prosecutor v. Dyilo,* Case No. ICC-01/04-01/06, T. Ch. I, 13 June 2008.

[24] ICC, Decision on the Release of Thomas Lubanga Dyilo, *Prosecutor v. Dyilo,* Case No. ICC-01/04-01/06, T. Ch. I, 2 July 2008.

accept, which legal arguments to address and what evidence it wished to refer to in handing down its judgement. Having done so, the Appeals Chamber concluded that the assessment of this evidence by the Trial Chamber was reasonable, thus rejecting each of the claims by the appellant.

Much of the discussion by the Appeals Chamber relates to the details of the particular evidence and does not merit any specific comment here. However, there are a few points to note in the conclusions of the Appeals Chamber. First, the Appeals Chamber accepts that it was reasonable of the Trial Chamber to prefer direct evidence in relation to several factual issues, rather than the hearsay evidence relied upon by the appellant. Unlike traditional common law criminal trials, hearsay evidence is not *per se* inadmissible before the *ad hoc* tribunals, with the trial judges being solely responsible for weighing the probative value of such evidence.

However, as the Appeals Chamber itself notes later (in relation to the issue of whether the appellant was at the Gaseke roadblock), "it is well established that a Trial Chamber must be cautious in considering such [hearsay] evidence".[25] The tribunal's largely unrestricted discretion regarding such evidence must always be considered in the light of ensuring the fairness of the proceedings. Indeed, by majority (Judge Shahabuddeen dissenting), the Appeals Chamber rejects the conclusion reached by the Trial Chamber, which was based on such evidence, regarding the events at the Gaseke roadblock.

Secondly, the Appeals Chamber confirmed that the discretion of a Trial Chamber in relation to its assessment of evidence presented to it at a trial is to be determined on a case-by-case basis. This is, of course, to be expected, given that each trial relates to separate accused, separate charges, specific circumstances *etc.* However, in the case at hand, this does lead to the somewhat surprising conclusion that it was reasonable for the Trial Chamber *not* to consider the contents of a preliminary report prepared by a commission and presented by the appellant, even though another Trial Chamber at the ICTR *had* considered that same report when it was presented by the prosecution in other cases before the tribunal.

At first glance, this may appear to be unfair (as is claimed by the appellant) and, once again, it would have been preferable for the purposes of transparency for the Appeals Chamber to explain why this was not so in these circumstances. As it was, the Appeal Chamber merely stated that "there is no unfairness" arising from an apparent inconsistency in approach between various Trial Chambers of the ICTR.[26]

4.6 Alleged error in finding that the appellant was at the Gaseke roadblock

As noted earlier, the Appeals Chamber (by majority) did not accept the conclusion of the Trial Chamber that had linked the murder of Mr Nors at the Gaseke roadblock with "a substantial contribution of the appellant".[27] Applying the relevant standard of review that it had outlined earlier, the majority held that no reasonable trier of fact could have concluded beyond reasonable doubt that this murder was attributable to the appellant's actions. It based its conclusion on its determination that the hearsay evidence of witness CGC was "vague and unverifiable",[28] since the prosecution had not satisfied its *onus* to prove that it was otherwise.

It is worthwhile noting that the Appeals Chamber pointed out – without making a comment – that the witness was never asked to explain how he learned that Mr Nors had been killed at the Gaseke roadblock about five minutes after he (witness CGC) had left the scene. It seems that the Trial Chamber judges themselves did not see it as appropriate to ask the pertinent question (given that neither the prosecution nor defence counsel had done so), even when it seemed that such a question might have been a necessary step towards establishing the 'truth' of what occurred at the roadblock. Nor did the Appeals Chamber judges find it necessary to remark on this apparent oversight.

By contrast, in his separate opinion, Judge Shahabuddeen took the view that, in fact, "[a]straight nexus" was established by the evidence between the appellant's visit to the roadblock and the murder of Mr Nors (par. 18).[29] Interestingly, despite his vehemence on this point, he concedes that "[o]ther triers of fact might have

25 Judgement, *Ndindabahizi v. Prosecutor, supra* note 1, par. 115.
26 *Ibid.*, par. 104.
27 *Ibid.*, par. 117.
28 *Ibid.*, par. 115.
29 ICTR, Separate Opinion of Judge Shahabuddeen, *Ndindabahizi v. Prosecutor*, Case No. ICTR-01-71-A, A. Ch., 16 January 2007, in this volume, p. 620, par. 18.

reached a different conclusion".[30] Yet, in his opinion, this is not sufficient to justify the application of the 'no reasonable trier of fact' standard, thus once again indicating how difficult this standard might be to apply in practice. Somewhat paradoxically, it seems from what Judge Shahabuddeen is saying that either conclusion by a Trial Chamber would be acceptable; or perhaps more accurately, would not be sufficiently unreasonable as to be rejected by an Appeals Chamber.

Despite his conclusion as to the responsibility of the appellant for the death of Mr Nors, Judge Shahabuddeen agreed with the conclusion of the majority to acquit the appellant on this charge, giving the appellant the benefit of the doubt as to whether the charge had, in fact, been withdrawn by the prosecution.

It should also be noted that the Appeals Chamber takes the rather unusual step of advising the prosecution not to use language such as 'perverse' in future proceedings. By contrast, the Appeals Chamber is far more tolerant of the equally unfortunate remarks made by the Trial Chamber in relation to certain characteristics of 'Rwandans'.[31]

4.7 Alleged vagueness of the indictment; and alleged error in finding a legal basis for the genocide convection

In view of the conclusions of the Appeals Chamber regarding the murder of Mr Nors, it was not necessary for it to deal with either of these grounds of appeal.

4.8 Alternate convictions

The Appeals Chamber *proprio motu* raised the possibility that, by its wording in par. 485 of the Trial judgment (reproduced at par. 121), the Trial Chamber might have entered alternate convictions against the appellant. The Appeals Chamber affirmed that alternate convictions may not be compatible with the principles requiring certainty as to the actual criminal responsibility of a convicted person.

By majority, the Appeals Chamber concluded that the Trial Chamber was not purporting to convict the appellant in relation to the charge of crimes against humanity (extermination) in the alternative, despite the fact that the word 'alternatively' is expressly used by Trial Chamber I. The argumentation of the majority is not particularly convincing on this point and, it is submitted, Judge Güney provides what appears to be a more logical conclusion in relation to this charge.

4.9 Appeal against the sentence

The appellant submitted that the Trial Chamber, in determining the (life imprisonment) sentence, erred in both law and fact, specifically with regard to its consideration of what were argued to be the mitigating and aggravating circumstances in his case.

The Appeals Chamber repeated the applicable standard of review for sentencing from previous jurisprudence of both of the *ad hoc* Tribunals. It highlighted the "broad discretion" of a Trial Chamber in determining a sentence – an exercise that involves a "weighing process" of any applicable mitigating and aggravating circumstances.[32] This is, of course, an exercise that has been repeatedly undertaken by the *ad hoc* tribunals. In the end, the Appeals Chamber, whilst determining that the Trial Chamber had erred in certain respects – specifically by considering a factual element leading to a conviction as also being an aggravating circumstance – decided that, in all the circumstances, the life sentence should be affirmed.[33] This was also notwithstanding the fact that it had acquitted the appellant of any criminal involvement in the murder of Mr Nors.

The predominant determining factor was the gravity of the offence, and the appellant had been convicted of the most serious of crimes. Although it tinkered at the edges in relation to the surrounding circumstances, the Appeals Chamber found no error in the overall assessment by the Trial Chamber of the gravity of the offence in the light of the applicable mitigating and aggravating circumstances. In this regard, it should be

30 *Ibid.*, par. 20.

31 Judgement, *Ndindabahizi v. Prosecutor, supra* note 1, footnote 257.

32 *Ibid.*, par. 132, citing ICTR, Judgement, *Semanza v. Prosecutor*, Case No. ICTR-97-20-A, A. Ch., 20 May 2005, Klip/ Sluiter, ALC-XXII-525, par. 312.

33 *Ibid.*, par. 137.

noted that the Appeals Chamber did not expressly consider in its reasons every argument raised by the appellant, although it seems that this would not have made any difference to its ultimate conclusion.

5. Concluding comments

The ICTR has been charged by the international community with the important task of bringing to justice the perpetrators of some of the most serious crimes committed in living memory. The factual circumstances underlying these criminal proceedings are often highly complex, traumatic and difficult. Emotions may run high for those affected, even many years after the event, and first-hand witness and victim recollections of what (might have) happened may often be confused, contradictory and unverifiable. The judges of the tribunal have to wade through this sometimes opaque compilation of claim and counter claim, allegation and rebuttal, and ultimately reach a conclusion based on their impression of the witnesses and the evidence presented. While this is, of course, also the role of a judge in most national criminal law systems, the complexity of the circumstances, the wide reaching effects of the alleged crimes and the broad goals of these mechanisms of international justice make this task all the more difficult for international criminal law judges.

Furthermore, unlike the typical common law national criminal trial, there are no lay juries, so that these international criminal law judges must at the same time adjudicate according to the relevant legal principles – some of which may be unique and previously untested - and also be the 'finders' of fact. The experience and abilities of these judges is therefore constantly being out to the test. Increasingly, all of this is to be done under time constraints that may put some additional pressure on the entire process. It is perhaps no coincidence that the judges of the *ad hoc* tribunals have sometimes taken to referring to themselves as 'professional' judges.

In this context, it is to be expected that the Appeals Chamber will not lightly disturb a Trial Chamber's factual findings, which have been based on a careful assessment of the veracity of the witness under both examination and cross-examination and within the confines of the trial itself. In the vast majority of cases, the Appeals Chamber will not be able to have the benefit of such direct experience of the presentation of evidence, and thus will generally find it difficult to differ widely from the factual conclusions reached by the Trial Chamber.

Of course, it does happen – indeed it did so in the case at hand in relation to the appellant's alleged involvement in the murder of Mr Nors – but that was, for the majority of the Appeals Chamber, relatively easy given that they considered the Trial Chamber's conclusion was principally based on unsubstantiated hearsay evidence. Apart from this, however, this case does illustrate again the difficulties that a convicted appellant may have in seeking to overturn important factual findings made during the trial proceedings.

Steven Freeland

International Criminal Tribunal for Rwanda
Tribunal pénal international pour le Rwanda

OR: English

TRIAL CHAMBER II

Before: Judge Arlette Ramaroson, Presiding
Judge William Hussein Sekule
Judge Solomy Balungi Bossa

Registrar: Mr Adama Dieng

Date: 23 February 2007

The PROSECUTOR

v.

Joseph NZABIRINDA
Case No. ICTR-2001-77-T

SENTENCING JUDGEMENT

The Prosecution
Mr William Egbe
Ms Veronic Wright
Mr Patrick Gabaake
Mr Suleyman Khan
Ms Amina Ibrahim

The Defence
Mr François Roux
Mr Jean Haguma
Mr Célestin Buhuru
Ms Charlotte Moreau

TABLE OF CONTENTS

[page 4] 1. The Judgement in the case of *Prosecutor v. Joseph Nzabirinda* is rendered by Trial Chamber II of the International Criminal Tribunal for Rwanda (the "Tribunal"), composed of Judge Arlette Ramaroson, presiding, Judge William H. Sekule, and Judge Solomy B. Bossa.

I. Introduction

2. Joseph Nzabirinda (the "Accused") was born in 1957 in Sahera *secteur*, Ngoma *commune,* Butare *préfecture.*[1] He was a youth *encadreur* (organizer) in Butare *préfecture* from 1976 to 1992 and became Managing Director of SECOBE in Kigali. He was also a founding member of the *Parti Social Démocrate* ("PSD") in 1990.

3. On 21 December 2001, Joseph Nzabirinda was arrested in Brussels by the Belgian authorities based on an arrest warrant issued by Judge Navanethem Pillay,[2] which was annexed to an indictment dated 6 December 2001 confirmed by the same Judge on 13 December 2001.[3] The indictment contained four counts.[4] On 20 March 2002, the Accused was transferred to the United Nations Detention Facility in Arusha (the "UNDF"). On 27 March 2002, the Accused made his initial appearance and pleaded not guilty to all four counts.[5]

4. On 20 November 2006, the Prosecutor filed a motion to amend the indictment of 13 December 2001.[6] On 8 December 2006, the Chamber granted the motion and accepted the withdrawal of the previous indictment and the filing of a new indictment with one count of murder, as a crime against humanity.[7] Under the Amended Indictment, dated 9 December 2006 and filed on 11 December 2006 (the "Indictment"), Joseph Nzabirinda is only charged with aiding and abetting murder, a crime against humanity, under Articles 3 (a) and 6 (1) of the Statute of the Tribunal (the "Statute"), as an accomplice by omission in the preparation of the commission of the crime.

5. The Indictment alleges that after 19 April 1994 the Accused attended several "pacification meetings" in Sahera *secteur* where only the Hutu and killers of his *secteur* were present.[8] Following the meetings, systematic attacks were launched against Tutsi families living on the Accused's hill. During one of these attacks, the *Interahamwe* killed Pierre Murara near the **[page 5]** location of the "pacification meetings" where Joseph Nzabirinda was present as an "approving spectator".[9]

6. Joseph Nzabirinda is also charged with the murder of Joseph Mazimpaka killed near the Kabuga roadblock which he manned on two occasions after 19 April 1994, at the request of the authorities. The Indictment alleges that in appearing beside the killers at the roadblock as an "approving spectator," the Accused encouraged the murder.[10]

---

1 T. 14 December 2006 p. 6.

2 Warrant of Arrest and Order for Transfer and Detention, 13 December 2001.

3 Decision on the Confirmation of the Indictment, 13 December 2001.

4 The four counts are: genocide, complicity in genocide in the alternative, extermination as a crime against humanity and rape as a crime against humanity.

5 T. 27 March 2002 p. 9.

6 Prosecutor's Request for Leave to Amend an Indictment Pursuant to Rules 72, 73, 50 and 51 of the Rules of Procedure and Evidence, filed on 20 November 2006. The same day, the Prosecution and the Defence filed a joint motion for consideration of a guilty plea agreement between Joseph Nzabirinda and the Office of the Prosecutor. On 27 November 2006, the Chamber issued a confidential Scheduling Order instructing the Prosecution to provide material in support of the new count of murder as a crime against humanity and to clarify certain aspects of the proposed amended indictment dated 20 November 2006, within three days. On 29 November 2006, the Prosecution requested an extension of time to provide the aforementioned supporting material. The Chamber granted an extension until 4 December 2006. On that date, the Prosecution filed the supporting material and a new proposed amended Indictment.

7 Decision on the Prosecution's Under Seal and Confidential Motion For Leave to Amend the Indictment, 8 December 2006.

8 Indictment, para. 14.

9 Indictment, para. 15.

10 Indictment, paras. 18, 19.

II. The Guilty Plea

A. Background

7. On 12 December 2006, the Parties filed a joint motion for consideration of a guilty plea and a plea agreement between Joseph Nzabirinda and the Office of the Prosecutor. The Motion sets forth the facts and the legal characterization for the Accused's guilty plea.

8. The Chamber notes that the provisions governing guilty pleas and plea agreements are Rule 62 (B) and Rule 62 *bis* of the Rules of Procedure and Evidence (the "Rules").[11]

9. On 14 December 2006, on his further appearance, Joseph Nzabirinda pleaded guilty to aiding and abetting murder, a crime against humanity, as accomplice by omission in the preparation of the commission of the crime.[12] The Chamber proceeded to verify the validity of the plea.[13]

10. The Chamber informed the Accused of the consequences of his plea. The Chamber stated that when an accused pleads not guilty, he is presumed innocent unless guilt is established beyond reasonable doubt. An accused who pleads not guilty therefore has a right to a fair trial, including, the right to cross-examine Prosecution witnesses, to call Defence witnesses, and to **[page 6]** testify in his defence. The Chamber asked the Accused whether he understood that in entering a plea, he would renounce these rights. The Accused responded in the affirmative.[14]

11. Pursuant to Rule 62 (B)(i), (ii), and (iii) of the Rules, the Chamber first asked if the guilty plea was made freely and voluntarily that is, if the Accused was entering his plea knowingly and without threats or promises. The Accused responded that he had done so without threats or promises.[15]

12. Secondly, the Chamber asked the Accused if the plea was informed: that is if the Accused clearly understood the nature of the charges brought against him. The Accused responded in the affirmative.[16]

13. Thirdly, the Chamber asked whether the plea was unequivocal: that is whether the Accused understood that he could not challenge any facts alleged in the indictment. The Accused responded that his plea was unequivocal.[17]

14. In its oral ruling of 14 December 2006, the Chamber was satisfied that there was no material disagreement between the Accused and the Prosecution on the acknowledged facts forming the basis of the

---

11 Rule 62: Initial Appearance of Accused and Plea
(B) If an accused pleads guilty in accordance with Rule 62 (A)(v), or requests to change his plea to guilty, the Trial Chamber shall satisfy itself that the guilty plea:
(i) is made freely and voluntarily;
(ii) is an informed plea;
(iii) is unequivocal; and
(iv) is based on sufficient facts for the crime and accused's participation in it, either on the basis of objective indicia or of lack of any material disagreement between the parties about the facts of the case.
Thereafter the Trial Chamber may enter a finding of guilt and instruct the Registrar to set a date for the sentencing hearing.
Rule 62 *bis*: Plea Agreement Procedure
(A) The Prosecutor and the Defence may agree that, upon the accused entering a plea of guilty to the indictment or to one or more counts of the indictment, the Prosecutor shall do one or more of the following before the Trial Chamber:
(i) apply to amend the indictment accordingly;
(ii) submit that a specific sentence or sentencing range is appropriate;
(iii) not oppose a request by the accused for a particular sentence or sentencing range.
(B) The Trial Chamber shall not be bound by any agreement specified in paragraph (A)
(C) If a plea agreement has been reached by the parties, the Trial Chamber shall require the disclosure of the agreement in open session or, on a showing of good cause, in closed session, at the time the accused pleads guilty in accordance with Rule 62 (A) (v), or requests to change his or her plea to guilty.

12 T. 14 December 2006 p. 6.

13 T. 14 December 2006 p. 6.

14 T. 14 December 2006 p. 7.

15 T. 14 December 2006 p. 7.

16 T. 14 December 2006 p. 7.

17 T. 14 December 2006 p. 7.

plea agreement, which facts were sufficient to establish the crimes and the Accused's participation in the crimes.

B. Applicable Law

1. Individual Criminal Responsibility for Aiding and Abetting

15. Article 6 (1) reflects the principle that criminal responsibility for any crime in the Statute is incurred not only by individuals who physically commit the crime, but also by individuals who participate in and contribute to the commission of the crime in other ways, such as aiding and abetting.[18]

16. Aiding and abetting is a form of accessory liability. The *actus reus* of the crime is not performed by the accused but by another person.[19] The accused's participation may take place at the planning, preparation or execution stage of the crime and may take the form of a positive act or an omission, occurring before or after the act of the principal offender.[20]

17. With respect to criminal responsibility incurred through omission, a person's mere presence at the crime scene may constitute aiding and abetting where it is demonstrated that his **[page 7]** presence had a significant encouraging effect on the principal offender, particularly if the individual standing by was the superior of the principal offender or was otherwise in a position of authority.[21] In such circumstances, an omission to act may constitute the *actus reus* of aiding and abetting, provided that the failure to act had a decisive effect on the commission of the crime.[22] This form of criminal responsibility "is derived not from the omission alone, but from the omission combined with the choice to be present."[23]

18. Unlike other forms of aiding and abetting, "criminal responsibility as an 'approving spectator' does require actual presence during the commission of the crime or at least presence in the immediate vicinity of the scene of the crime, which is perceived by the actual perpetrator as approval of his conduct."[24]

19. The *mens rea* of an aider and abettor is demonstrated by proof of his knowledge that his act is assisting the commission of the crime by the principal offender.[25] The aider and abettor must have known the intent of the principal offender, and although he need not know the precise offence being committed by the principal offender, he must be aware of the essential elements of the crime.[26]

2. Murder as a Crime Against Humanity

a. General Elements of a Crime Against Humanity

20. For an enumerated act under Article 3 of the Statute to qualify as a crime against humanity, it must be proved that the crime was committed as part of a widespread or systematic attack against any civilian population on national, political, ethnic, racial or religious grounds.

---

[18] "Aiding" means assisting another to commit a crime. "Abetting" means facilitating, encouraging, advising or instigating the commission of a crime. The two terms are so often used conjunctively that they are treated as a single broad legal concept. (*Kajelijeli*, Judgement (TC), para. 765; *Semanza*, Judgement (TC), para. 384, referring to Mewett & Manning, *Criminal Law* (3rd ed. 1994) p. 272 (noting that aiding and abetting are "almost universally used conjunctively")).

[19] *Kunarać et al.*, Judgement (TC), paras. 391-392.

[20] *Kajelijeli*, Judgement (TC), para.766; *Semanza*, Judgement (TC), para. 385; *Rutaganira*, Judgement (TC) para. 64; The Prosecution is required to demonstrate that the accused carried out an act of substantial practical assistance, encouragement, or moral support to the principal offender, culminating in the latter's actual commission of the crime (*Kayishema and Ruzindana*, Judgement (AC), para. 186; *Kamuhanda*, Judgement (TC), para. 597; *Akayesu*, Judgement (TC), paras. 473-475; *Rutaganda*, Judgement (TC), para. 43. While the assistance need not be indispensable to the crime, it must have a substantial effect on the commission of the crime (*Bagilishema*, Judgement (TC), para. 33)

[21] *Kajelijeli*, Judgement (TC), para. 769; *Furundžija*, Judgement (TC), paras. 34-35 ; *Mpambara*, Judgement (TC), para. 22.

[22] *Blaškic*, Judgement (TC), para. 284; *Tadić*, Judgement (TC), para. 686; *Akayesu*, Judgement (TC), para. 705.

[23] *Mpambara*, Judgement, (TC), para. 22.

[24] *Kayishema and Ruzindana*, Judgement (TC), para. 201; *Semanza* (TC), para. 386; *Bagilishema* (TC), paras. 34, 36 ; *Mpambara*, Judgement (TC), para. 23.

[25] *Blaškic*, Judgement (AC), para. 49; *Kayishema and Ruzindana*, Judgement (AC), para. 186.

[26] *Kajelijeli*, Judgement (TC), para. 768; *Semanza*, Judgement (TC), para. 388; *Bagilishema*, Judgement (TC), para. 32; *Kayishema and Ruzindana*, Judgement (TC), para. 201; *Kayishema and Ruzindana*, Judgement (AC), para. 186.

21. First, the Chamber recalls that 'attack' has been defined as "an unlawful act, event, or series of events of the kind listed in Article 3 (a) through (i) of the Statute."[27] The Chamber adopts the *Kajelijeli* Judgement's definition of "widespread" which is "large scale, involving many victims"[28] and of "systematic" which describes the organised nature of the attack.[29]

22. Second, the attack must be directed against a civilian population.[30] As stated in the *Semanza* Judgement, "a civilian population remains civilian in nature even if there are individuals within it who are not civilians."[31] **[page 8]**

23. Third, the attack must be committed on discriminatory grounds. The Chamber recalls the *Akayesu* Judgement, where the "discriminatory grounds" element was considered to be jurisdictional in nature, limiting the jurisdiction of the Tribunal to crimes committed on "national, political, ethnic, racial or religious grounds."[32] Nonetheless, in the *Kajelijeli* Judgement the Chamber noted that:

> such acts committed against persons outside the discriminatory categories need not necessarily fall out with the jurisdiction of the Tribunal, if the perpetrator's intention in committing these acts is to support or further the attack on the group discriminated against on one of the enumerated grounds.[33]

24. Finally, with respect to the mental element of crimes against humanity, the Chamber agrees with the reasoning in the *Kajelijeli* Judgement that "the accused must have acted with knowledge of the broader context of the attack and knowledge that his act formed part of the attack on the civilian population."[34]

b. Murder

25. Murder is the intentional killing of a person by an act or an omission,[35] or the intentional infliction of grievous bodily harm, committed by the offender with knowledge that such harm is likely to cause the victim's death or with reckless disregard as to whether or not death will result, with no lawful justification or excuse.[36] The commission of a positive act is not an absolute requirement of criminal responsibility.[37] Murder is punishable as a crime against humanity when it has been committed as part of a widespread or systematic attack against a civilian population on discriminatory grounds.

26. The *mens rea* as an aider or abettor of murder, as a crime against humanity, is that the accused knew of the criminal intent of the principal perpetrator and knew that his actions or omissions assisted the principal to commit the crime.[38]

---

27 *Kajelijeli*, Judgement (TC), para. 867; *Semanza*, Judgement (TC), para. 327.

28 *Kajelijeli*, Judgement (TC), para. 871.

29 *Kajelijeli*, Judgement (TC), para. 872.

30 As noted in the *Blaškic* Judgement, "the specific situation of the victim at the moment the crimes were committed, rather than his status, must be taken into account in determining his standing as a civilian."(*Blaškic,* Judgement (TC), para. 214, cited in *Bagilishema*, Judgement (TC), para. 79 and *Kajelijeli*, Judgement (TC), para. 874.) Moreover, the term "population" does not require that crimes against humanity be directed against the entire population of a geographical territory or area (*Kajelijeli*, Judgement (TC), para. 875; *Bagilishema*, Judgement (TC), para. 80; *Tadić*, Judgement (TC), para. 644). The Trial Chamber in the *Semanza* Judgement further clarified that: "The victim(s) of the enumerated act need not necessarily share geographic or other defining features with the civilian population that forms the primary target of the underlying attack, but such characteristics may be used to demonstrate that the enumerated act forms part of the attack." (*Semanza*, Judgement (TC), para. 330, cited in *Kajelijeli,* Judgement (TC), para. 875).

31 *Semanza*, Judgement (TC), para. 330.

32 *Akayesu*, Judgement (AC), paras. 464-465, also cited in *Kajelijeli*, Judgement (TC), para. 877.

33 *Kajelijeli*, Judgement (TC), para. 878; *Rutaganda*, Judgement (TC), para. 74; *Musema*, Judgement (TC), para. 209; *Semanza*, Judgement (TC), para. 331.

34 *Kajelijeli*, Judgement (TC), para. 880, *Semanza*, Judgement (TC), para. 332; *Musema*, Judgement (TC), para. 206; *Ntakirutimana et al.*, Judgement (TC), para. 803; *Bagilishema*, Judgement (TC), para. 94; *Kayishema and Ruzindana*, Judgement (TC), para. 134; *Kunarać et al.*, Judgement (AC), para. 102.

35 *Kvočka et al.*, Judgement (AC), para. 261 ; *Galić*, Judgement (AC), para. 149.

36 *Akayesu* Judgement (TC), para. 586 ; *Ndindabahizi* Judgement, (TC), para. 487.

37 *Galić,* Judgement (AC), para. 149.

38 *Blaškic*, Judgement (AC), para. 49; *Semanza*, Judgement (TC), para. 388.

C. Findings

27. The Chamber noted that the facts contained in the Plea Agreement – from paragraphs 31 to 49- conformed to the facts contained in the Indictment in support of the count of murder- namely from paragraphs 1 to 20.

28. The Chamber stated that the requirements of Rule 62 (B) were met and it therefore declared the Accused guilty for having aided and abetted the crime of murder as a crime against **[page 9]** humanity of Pierre Murara and Joseph Mazimpaka pursuant to Articles 3 (a) and 6 (1) of the Statute.[39]

29. The Chamber found the Accused guilty of aiding and abetting the crime of murder as a crime against humanity based on the following reasoning.

30. The Accused admitted that following the meeting held by President Sindikubwabo in Butare *préfecture* on 19 April 1994, widespread killings of Tutsi and opponents of the regime began in the *préfecture* and in particular, in Sahera *secteur*.[40]

31. The Accused admitted that he attended several meetings at the Sahera *secteur* office where only Hutu and killers that the Accused knew as his neighbours were present. He admitted that he was present at such meetings as an "approving spectator."[41] He also admitted that, following the meetings, systematic attacks were launched on Tutsi families living on his hill. He further admitted that during one attack, Pierre Murara was murdered at a location close to the meeting place, where the Accused was present as an "approving spectator.[42]

32. Although he knew that systematic killings had occurred after the meetings, the Accused never stopped attending them, knowing that the purpose of the meetings was in reality to prepare and encourage the hunting down and killing of Tutsi. At the meetings, the Accused did not at any time or in no manner openly object to these killings.[43]

33. The Accused admitted that as a former youth *encadreur*, political personality, intellectual and a relatively affluent businessman, he did exert obvious moral authority over the population of his *secteur*, especially its youth, and over the country people living on his hill. The Accused also admitted that his presence at the meetings had a decisive influence on the criminal elements in their midst as he was a person held in high esteem by his fellow citizens, and with the circumstances prevailing in his *secteur*, conveyed the impression of his being an "approving spectator." He also knew that his silence would be considered by the assailants as tacit approval of the preparations for the killings.[44]

34. The Accused also admitted that after 19 April 1994, roadblocks were erected in his *secteur* and that he knew that they were used for identity checks and were one of the means employed in the campaign of killings in the *secteur*;[45] that, at the request of the authorities, he had manned the Kabuga roadblock on two occasions, along with some *Interahamwe* of Sahera *secteur*;[46] that he had encouraged the murder of Joseph Mazimpaka by Mugenzi near the Kabuga roadblock where the Accused was present as an "approving spectator."[47]

35. The Accused admitted that the murders of Joseph Mazimpaka and Pierre Murara were committed in his *secteur*, at a location close to those of the meetings and roadblocks respectively where he was present as an "approving spectator."[48] **[page 10]**

---

39 T. 14 December 2006 p. 17.
40 Plea Agreement, paras. 40, 41.
41 Plea Agreement, paras. 43, 44.
42 Plea Agreement, para. 44.
43 Plea Agreement, para. 45.
44 Plea Agreement, paras. 39, 46.
45 Plea Agreement, para. 47.
46 Plea Agreement, para. 48.
47 Plea Agreement, para. 48.
48 Plea Agreement, para. 49.

36. On the basis of the facts admitted by the Accused, the Chamber was convinced that widespread and systematic attacks had been carried out against a civilian population on discriminatory grounds in Sahera *secteur* in April 1994. The Chamber was also satisfied that the only logical conclusion to be drawn from the facts admitted by the Accused was that both Pierre Murara and Joseph Mazimpaka were murdered as a result of these attacks and because of their Tutsi ethnicity.

37. The Chamber was convinced that Joseph Nzabirinda knew that the *secteur* meetings, which he repeatedly attended, and the Kabuga roadblock, which he manned on two occasions were some of the means employed in the campaign of killings; that the murders of Pierre Murara and Joseph Mazimpaka were part of the widespread and systematic attacks against Tutsis civilians on ethnic ground; that the Accused knew the criminal intent of the perpetrators of the murders; that because of the moral authority he exercised, he knew that his presence at the Sahera *secteur* meetings and at the Kabuga roadblock would be crucial in encouraging the preparation and the commission of the murders.

38. On the basis of the facts acknowledged by the Accused with respect to the murders of Pierre Murara and Joseph Mazimpaka, the Chamber found the Accused criminally responsible not only for the attendance and encouragement that he provided as an "approving spectator" at the preparatory meetings but also for his presence as an "approving spectator" close to the locations where Pierre Murara and Joseph Mazimpaka were murdered.

39. The Chamber held that the Accused was criminally responsible, pursuant to Article 6 (1) of the Statute, for aiding and abetting the murders of Pierre Murara and Joseph Mazimpaka in Sahera *secteur* in April 1994.

III. Applicability of the *Non Bis in Idem* Principle to the Counts Withdrawn

40. On 14 December 2006, the Chamber indicated that it would address the question of the application of the *non bis in idem* principle to the counts that had been withdrawn in its sentencing judgement.[49]

A. Background

41. On 20 November 2006, the Prosecution requested the withdrawal of the counts of genocide, complicity in genocide, crimes against humanity (rape and extermination), with prejudice. It submitted that such withdrawal should trigger the application of the doctrine of *non bis in idem*.[50]

42. On 8 December 2006, the Chamber granted the withdrawal of the counts but determined that the prayer to declare that the withdrawal of counts attracted the application of the *non bis in idem* principle was premature at that stage of the proceedings.[51]

43. In the Plea Agreement, the Prosecution submitted that if the Chamber accepted Nzabirinda's plea, it would not refer the case to any other jurisdiction.[52] **[page 11]**

44. On 14 December 2006, the Prosecution recalled that the Chamber, in its Decision of 8 December 2006, had granted the withdrawal of the counts of genocide, complicity in genocide, and crimes against humanity (rape and extermination). The Prosecution further submitted that, pursuant to Article 9 of the Statute, the Chamber should rule that the *non bis in idem* principle applies to counts withdrawn even though no trial on the merits had been held thereon.[53] The Prosecution submitted that, after five years of investigations, it would not succeed in proving the counts that had been withdrawn "because the evidence is not there."[54] The Defence supported the Prosecution application.[55]

---

49 T. 14 December 2006 p. 17.

50 Prosecutor's Request to Amend an Indictment, para. 4.

51 Decision on the Prosecutor's Under Seal and Confidential Motion for Leave to Amend the Indictment, 8 December 2006, para. 13.

52 Plea Agreement, para. 58.

53 T. 14 December 2006 p. 11.

54 T. 14 December 2006 p.12.

55 T. 14 December 2006 p.14.

B. Findings

45. The Chamber recalls that Article 9 (1) of the Statute prohibits against a second trial of an accused for the same serious violation of international humanitarian law. The *non bis in idem* principle applies to persons who have been tried by the ICTR (Article 9(1)), or to persons who have been tried before a national court (Article 9(2)) for acts constituting serious violations of international humanitarian law.[56]

46. As the Appeals Chamber observed, "the term 'tried' implies that proceedings in the national court constituted a trial for the acts covered by the indictment brought against the Accused by the Tribunal and at the end of which trial a final judgement is rendered."[57] Accordingly, in the particular circumstances of this case where counts have been withdrawn without a final judgement, the principle of *non bis in idem* does not apply and cannot be invoked to bar potential subsequent trials of the accused before any jurisdiction.

47. In the instant case, the Chamber recalls that the charges were withdrawn when the Prosecution sought to amend the indictment under Rule 50 of the Rules and that a trial on the merits was yet to commence. The Chamber therefore denies the Prosecution's Motion.

IV. Issues Relating to the Sentence

48. On 17 January 2007, the Chamber held a Pre-Sentencing Hearing. The Chamber heard five character witnesses and admitted two witness statements under Rule 92 *bis* (A).[58] **[page 12]**

A. Applicable Texts and Principles

49. The Tribunal was established to prosecute and punish the perpetrators of the atrocities in Rwanda in 1994 so as to end impunity.[59] It was also created to contribute to the process of national reconciliation, the restoration and maintenance of peace and to ensure that the violations of international humanitarian law in Rwanda are halted and effectively redressed.[60] The Chamber considers that a fair trial and, in the event of a conviction, a just sentence, contribute towards these goals. Deterrence, retribution and rehabilitation are fundamental principles considered by the Chamber when imposing a sentence.[61]

50. The Chamber will sentence Joseph Nzabirinda pursuant to the provisions of Articles 22 and 23 of the Statute and Rules 100 and 101 of the Rules. The Tribunal can only impose a prison term. Under Rule 101 (A) of the Rules, such a term shall not exceed life imprisonment. The Statute and the Rules do not provide for specific penalties for any of the crimes within the jurisdiction of the Tribunal.

51. Consequently, the determination of the sentence is left to the discretion of the Chamber. In exercising that discretion, the Chamber shall, however, pursuant to Article 23 (2) of the Statute and Rule 101 (B) of the

---

56 A person tried by a national jurisdiction under those circumstances may be tried by the ICTR only under certain conditions described in Article 9 (2)(a) and (b) of the Statute.

57 *Semanza v. Prosecutor*, Decision (AC), 31 May 2000, para. 74 (footnotes omitted).

58 On 11 December 2006, the Defence filed a motion for protective measures for its character witnesses, Witnesses LZI, LBH, LBG, CAN and LDK. The Chamber granted some of the measures sought in its Decision on the Nzabirinda's Under Seal-Extremely Urgent Motion for Protective Measures for Character Witnesses dated 13 December 2006. On 9 January 2007, the Defence and the Prosecution filed a joint Pre-Sentencing Brief in French. On 12 January 2007, the Defence filed a complementary Pre-Sentencing Brief. On 12 January 2007, the Defence filed a motion for protective measures for another character witness, Witness LZB2, which was partially granted by the Chamber in its Decision on the Defence's Extremely Urgent Confidential Motion for Protective Measures for Witness LBZ2 dated 16 January 2007. On 16 January 2007, the Defence filed a motion for the admission of Witness LBZ2's and Mr. Saidou Guindo's written statements in lieu of oral testimony under Rule 92 *bis* (A) and (B). In its oral decision of 17 January 2007, the Chamber granted the motion and admitted the written testimony of Witness LBZ2 and the attestation of good conduct of the Accused issued by Mr Saidou Guindo, Commander of the UNDF. On 17 January 2007, Witness Jean-Baptiste Nkuliyingoma (formerly known as LBH), Witnesses CAN, LZI, LDK and LBG testified. During the same hearing, the Defence orally moved the Chamber to vary its witness list so that the Witness bearing the pseudonym LDK, referred to in the Decision of 13 December 2006 be substituted by another witness who would bear the same pseudonym, i.e. LDK and requested protective measures for that witness. The Chamber granted the motions.

59 *Serugendo*, Judgement (TC), para. 31 citing *Rutaganda*, Judgement (TC), para. 455.

60 Security Council Resolution 955, 8 November 1994.

61 *Serugendo*, Judgement (TC), para. 33; *Aleksovski*, Judgement (AC), para. 185; *Mucić et al*, Judgement (AC), para. 806.

Rules, consider a number of factors, including the gravity of the offence, any aggravating or mitigating circumstances, the personal circumstances of the convicted person and the general practice regarding prison sentences in the courts of Rwanda.

52. The Chamber understands its obligation to ensure that the sentence is commensurate with the individual circumstances of the offender.[62]

53. The Chamber recalls that aggravating circumstances must be proved beyond reasonable doubt, while mitigating circumstances must be proved on a balance of probabilities.[63]

B. Gravity of the Offence

1. Submissions

54. The Prosecution submitted that the gravity of the offence is the first element to consider in determining an appropriate sentence. The determination of the gravity of the crime requires a consideration of the particular circumstances of the case, as well as the form and degree of the participation of the accused person in the crime.[64] According to the Prosecution, the serious nature of the crime, and its impact on the victims, ought to be taken into consideration.[65]

2. Findings

55. The seriousness of the crimes and the extent of the involvement of Joseph Nzabirinda in their commission are factors to be considered in sentencing. **[page 13]**

56. Genocide and crimes against humanity are inherently very serious offences because they are heinous in nature and shock the collective conscience of mankind.[66]

57. The Chamber finds that Joseph Nzabirinda's participation in aiding and abetting murder, as a crime against humanity, constitutes a very serious offence and a gross violation of international humanitarian law.

C. Aggravating Circumstances

1. Submissions

58. The Prosecution has indicated that it would not plead any aggravating circumstances other than those already accepted by the Parties in the Plea Agreement.[67] It argued that the presence of the Accused in the vicinity of the two murders as an "approving spectator" knowing that widespread and systematic attacks were under way, make the murder charge extremely serious.

59. Joseph Nzabirinda acknowledged the relevance of Paragraph 120 of the *Bisengimana* Judgement to his case, in the sense that he is an educated person who could appreciate the dignity and value of human life, and is aware of the need for and value of peaceful co-existence between communities.[68]

2. Findings

60. The Chamber is mindful that "where an aggravating factor for the purposes of sentencing is at the same time an element of the offence, it cannot also constitute an aggravating factor for the purposes of sentencing."[69]

---

62 *Mucić et al.*, Judgement (AC), para. 717; *Muhimana*, Judgement (TC), para. 594.

63 *Kajelijeli,* Judgement (AC), para. 294.

64 T.17 January 2007 p. 46.

65 T. 17 January 2007 p. 46.

66 *Ruggiu*, Judgement (TC), para. 48.

67 Plea Agreement, para. 59.

68 T. 17 January 2007 p. 51.

69 *Blaškić*, Judgement (AC), para. 693 cited in *Ndindabahizi*, Judgement (AC), para. 137.

61. It is well established in the Jurisprudence of the ICTR and ICTY that, while a position of authority by itself does not amount to an aggravating factor, the manner in which the accused exercised his command or the abuse of an accused's personal position in the community may be considered as aggravating factors.[70]

62. The Chamber considers that Joseph Nzabirinda - a youth organizer, an intellectual and a successful businessman held in high esteem in the community – had abused the obvious moral authority he exerted on the youth of his *commune* and the population of his *secteur*. The Chamber is of the view that Joseph Nzabirinda's abuse of position of influence constitutes an aggravating factor.

63. As the Defence has acknowledged, Joseph Nzabirinda "was an educated person who could appreciate the dignity and value of human life and was aware of the need for a peaceful co-existence between communities."[71] The Chamber considers this factor to be aggravating. **[page 14]**

D. Mitigating Circumstances

1. Applicable Law

64. Mitigating circumstances may not be directly related to the offence.[72]

65. According to the jurisprudence of this Tribunal and that of the ICTY, a guilty plea may have a mitigating effect on the sentence, by: the showing of remorse,[73] repentance,[74] the contribution to reconciliation,[75] the establishment of the truth,[76] the encouragement of other perpetrators to come forward,[77] the sparing of a lengthy investigation and a trial and thus time, effort and resources,[78] and the fact that witnesses are relieved from giving evidence in court.[79] The timing of the guilty plea is also a factor to be considered in sentencing.[80]

2. The Guilty Plea and Public Expression of Remorse

a. Submissions

66. The Parties have argued that, in principle, a guilty plea should entail a reduction of the sentence; that a guilty plea is important to establish the truth; that, because the Accused has pleaded guilty before his trial, judicial time and resources have been saved; and that the plea contributes to the prevention of revisionism and contributes to the process of reconciliation.[81]

67. On 14 December 2006, in his further appearance before the Chamber, the Accused indicated his decision to change his initial plea of "not guilty," after long reflection in detention. He requested forgiveness from the families of the two victims, Pierre Murara and Joseph Mazimpaka, and from the people of Rwanda for the crimes for which he is responsible by his omission to act for which he suffers deep remorse. The Accused also expressed the hope that his guilty plea will assist and encourage others to commit themselves to the path of truth.[82] These elements were also stated in the Plea Agreement, in the Joint Sentencing Brief and during the Pre-Sentencing Hearing.[83]

---

[70] *Akayesu*, Judgement (AC), paras. 414-415, *Kambanda*, Judgement (TC), paras. 61, 62 quoted with approval in *Kambanda*, Judgement (AC) para. 119 ; *Aleksosvki*, Judgement (AC), para. 183 ; *Kayishema and Ruzindana*, Judgement (AC), paras. 357, 358 ; *Ntakirutimana et al.*, Judgement (AC), para. 563 ; *Kamuhanda*, Judgement (AC), paras. 347-348; *Bisengimana*, Judgement (TC), para. 120 ; *Serugendo*, Judgement (TC), para. 48 ; *Ndindabahizi*, Judgement (AC), para. 136 .

[71] *Bisengimana*, Judgement, para. 120.

[72] *Nikolić*, Judgement (TC), para. 145; *Deronjić*, Judgement (TC), para. 155.

[73] *Plavšić*, Judgement (TC), para. 73.

[74] *Ruggiu*, Judgement (TC), para. 55.

[75] *Plavšić*, Judgement, (TC), paras. 80-81.

[76] *Erdemović*, Judgement, (TC) (1998), para. 21; *Nikolic*, Judgement (TC), para. 248; *Serugendo*, Judgement (TC), para. 55.

[77] *Erdemović*, Judgement, (TC) (1998), para. 16; *Ruggiu*, Judgement (TC), para. 55.

[78] *Ruggiu*, Judgement (TC), para. 53.

[79] *Kambanda*, Judgement (TC), para. 54; *Serugendo*, Judgement (TC), paras. 52, 57.

[80] *Kambanda*, Judgement (TC), paras. 52,53; *Sikirica et al.*, Judgement (TC), para.150 ; *Serugendo*, Judgement (TC), para. 54.

[81] *Mémoire conjoint*, paras. 21-23.

[82] T. 14 December 2006 p. 8.

[83] Plea Agreement, paras. 2-22 ; *Mémoire conjoint*, para. 33 ; T. 17 January 2007, p. 60.

b. Findings

68. The Chamber recalls that an acknowledgement of guilt may constitute proof of the perpetrator's honesty, that some form of consideration should be afforded to those who have confessed their crimes, in order to encourage others to come forward, and that a guilty plea may contribute to the process of national reconciliation in Rwanda.[84] **[page 15]**

69. For remorse to be considered mitigating, the Chamber must be satisfied that the remorse is sincere.[85]

70. After considering Joseph Nzabirinda's public expression of regrets and remorse for the crimes he committed, the Chamber is satisfied that Joseph Nzabirinda's expression of remorse is sincere.

71. The Chamber finds that Joseph Nzabirinda's change of plea to one of guilty together with public regrets and remorse constitutes recognition of his responsibility, has saved judicial time and resources, and may contribute to the process of national reconciliation in Rwanda. Therefore, the Chamber finds that Joseph Nzabirinda's guilty plea is a factor to be considered in mitigation of the sentence.

3. Cooperation with the Prosecution

a. Submissions

72. Joseph Nzabirinda has offered to cooperate with the Prosecution. Both Parties argued that this offer indicates his desire to participate in the effective search for truth and might encourage others to also confess their crimes.[86]

b. Findings

73. It is for the Trial Chamber to weigh the circumstances relating to any cooperation,[87] and "the evaluation of the accused's co-operation depends both on the quantity and quality of the information he provides."[88]

74. There is no dispute regarding Joseph Nzabirinda's offer to cooperate with the Prosecution in the future. However, at this stage of the proceedings, the Chamber considers that this offer cannot be considered as a mitigating circumstance in and of itself, insofar as there has been no demonstration of any substantial cooperation, within the meaning of Rule 101 (B)(ii), apart from the Guilty Plea which the Chamber has already taken into account.

4. Assistance Provided to Certain Individuals

a. Submissions

75. The Defence submitted that the Accused personally saved the lives of individuals[89] which the Prosecution does not dispute.[90]

76. The Defence called Witnesses CAN,[91] LZI[92] and LDK[93] to testify about Nzabirinda's role in assisting Tutsi refugees during the 1994 events. The statement of Witness LBZ-2, admitted under Rule 92 *bis*, corroborates the evidence of the above witnesses.[94] **[page 16]**

---

84 *Bisengimana*, Judgement (TC), para. 139.
85 *Banović*, Judgement (TC), para. 72 (footnotes omitted).
86 Plea Agreement, para. 55 ; *Mémoire conjoint*, paras 24, 25.
87 *Jelisić*, Judgement (AC), para. 124.
88 *Blaškić* Judgement (TC), para. 774
89 Plea Agreement, para. 50 ; *Mémoire conjoint*, paras. 26, 27.
90 Plea agreement, para. 60.
91 T. 17 January 2007 pp. 14-16.
92 T. 17 January 2007 pp. 20, 21.
93 T.17 January 2007 pp. 30-32.
94 Defence Exhibit D.5.

b. Findings

77. After considering the testimonies of witnesses and a witness statement admitted under Rule 92 *bis*(A), the Chamber is of the view that there is sufficient evidence that Joseph Nzabirinda personally assisted Tutsi refugees by way of moral, financial and material support in Sahera *secteur* during the 1994 events and that he assisted in organising the departure of certain refugees to Burundi. According to the evidence submitted, Joseph Nzabirinda's acts contributed to saving the lives of some of the Tutsi refugees. Therefore, the Chamber finds that Joseph Nzabirinda's assistance to certain victims constitutes a mitigating factor.

5. Personal and Family Situation

a. Submissions

78. Both Parties argued that the jurisprudence of the Tribunal has taken into consideration, as mitigating factor, personal circumstances, such as the Accused's family situation as proof of his capacity for reintegration into society.[95]

79. The Defence called Witness LBG who testified favourably about Nzabirinda's personal and family situation.[96]

b. Findings

80. The Chamber notes that the fact that an accused is married and has children may, under certain circumstances, be considered mitigating.[97]

81. In the instant case, the personal and family situation of the Accused, a married man with children, leads the Chamber to believe in his chances of rehabilitation after his release. The Chamber therefore finds this personal situation to be a mitigating circumstance.

6. Lack of Personal Participation in the Crimes

a. Submissions

82. Both Parties argued that the Accused's omission is not a mitigating circumstance, but a mode of participation in the acknowledged crimes. However, referring to the *Bisengimana* Judgement, both Parties submitted that the particular circumstances of the case should be taken into account, including the mode and degree of the Accused's participation in the murders. They further submit that Nzabirinda did not commit any violent act during the massacres and did not personally participate in committing the two murders to which he has pleaded guilty, but in their preparation. Although the murders were committed close to the respective sites of the meetings and the roadblock, where the Accused was present, he did not "watch" the murders.[98]

83. The Accused admitted that he was present not at the crime scene, but at the preparatory meeting for that crime:[99] He was, therefore, not physically present at the venue of the murder, but at the meeting and at the roadblocks where those crimes were prepared.[100] **[page 17]**

---

95 *Mémoire conjoint*, paras. 28-31.
96 T. 17 January 2007 pp. 35-40.
97 *Kunarać et al.*, Judgement (AC), para. 362; *Vasiljević*, Judgement (TC), para. 300; *Serushago*, Judgement (TC), para. 39; *Rutaganira*, *Jugement* (TC), paras. 120-121.
98 *Mémoire conjoint*, paras. 34-36.
99 T. 17 January 2007 p. 49.
100 T. 17 January 2007 p. 50.

b. Findings

84. The Chamber is mindful of the need to take into account the particular circumstances of the case, including the form and the degree of the Accused's participation in the crime.[101]

85. The Chamber recalls that Joseph Nzabirinda did not personally commit the two murders or any violent act related to the murders. However, the Chamber finds that Joseph Nzabirinda who aided and abetted the preparation of the murders at meetings, and the commission of the crimes while being in the vicinity, had full knowledge that the *secteur* meetings and the Kabuga roadblock were used in the campaign of killings raging in Sahera *secteur* at the time. The Chamber is mindful that Joseph Nzabirinda participated in the *secteur* meetings and manned the Kabuga roadblock, knowing that his presence would lend obvious moral authority to the killers, signal approval of the killings and provide encouragement to the assailants. The Chamber also considers that Joseph Nzabirinda did not disassociate himself from those who organised the attacks during the *secteur* meetings, which he attended nor from the assailants who murdered Joseph Mazimpaka near the roadblock that he manned. The Chamber further recalls that Joseph Nzabirinda did not stop attending the so-called "pacification meetings" while he knew that they prepared the systematic hunting down and killing of Tutsi.

86. In accordance with the jurisprudence of the Tribunal, the "approving spectator" doctrine requires "actual presence during the commission of the crime or at least presence in the immediate vicinity of the scene of the crime."[102] In that respect, the Chamber recalls that Joseph Nzabirinda admitted that Pierre Murara was killed by the *Interahamwe* near the location where the meetings were held and where he was present as an "approving spectator"[103] and that, in appearing beside the killers at the roadblock, he encouraged the murder by Mugenzi of Joseph Mazimpaka near the roadblock that he was manning and while he was present.[104] Based on these admitted facts, the Chamber considers that Joseph Nzabirinda's presence as an "approving spectator" in the vicinity of the crime scenes, encouraged the preparation and the commission of the murders of Pierre Murara and Joseph Mazimpaka. Accordingly, the Chamber rejects the Defence arguments that the fact that Joseph Nzabirinda was not physically present at the venue of the murder is a mitigating factor as it is established that he was in the immediate vicinity of the crime scenes and knew that he would encourage the commission of the crimes.

87. Therefore, the Chamber does not consider that this form of participation warrants consideration as a mitigating factor in sentencing.

7. Character of the Accused, Attitude Towards Tutsi Before and During Events, Lack of Prior Criminal Convictions and Good Conduct in Detention

a. Submissions

88. Both Parties submitted that Nzabirinda was a person of good character with no history of extremism prior to the events of 1994.[105] The Parties further submitted that prior to the 1994 **[page 18]** events, the Accused was considered by the persons with whom he was close to be a good, open and generous man, popular both on a professional and a personal level.

89. The Parties submitted that the Accused was indifferent to ethnicity, never discriminated on that basis and had excellent relationships and friendships with Hutu and Tutsi alike. Further, the Accused's wife is Tutsi and the relations he had with his family-in-law went further than simple cordiality.

---

101 *Mucić et al.*, Judgement (AC), para. 731 quoting *Kupreskić*, Judgement (AC) para. 442 ; *Aleksovski*, Judgement (TC), para. 243.

102 *Kayishema and Ruzindana*, Judgement (TC), para. 201; *Semanza*, Judgement (TC), para. 386; *Bagilishema*, Judgement (TC), paras. 34, 36 ; *Mpambara*, Judgement (TC), para. 23.

103 Plea Agreement, para. 44. See also Indictment, para. 15.

104 Plea Agreement, para. 48. See also Indictment, para. 19.

105 Plea Agreement, para. 56.

90. While it has been impossible to obtain the Accused's criminal record, the Defence submitted that the Accused has a clean record and has never been convicted. Further, as attested by Saidou Guindo, the UNDF Commanding Officer, the Accused was well-behaved during his five year detention.[106]

91. Defence Witnesses Jean-Baptise Nkuliyingoma,[107] LZI[108] and LBG[109] testified favourably about Nzabirinda's good character.

b. Findings

92. On the basis of the witnesses' testimonies, the Chamber is satisfied that Joseph Nzabirinda was a person of good character before his involvement in the crimes committed in Sahera *secteur* in April 1994, with no history of ethnic discrimination. The Chamber is also satisfied, on balance, that Joseph Nzabirinda had no previous criminal record. Finally, the Chamber considers that the statement of the UNDF Commanding Officer demonstrates Joseph Nzabirinda's good conduct while in detention. The Chamber finds that these factors constitute mitigating circumstances.

8. Circumstances of Necessity

a. Submissions

93. The Parties submit that, if the Accused had directly opposed the events in Sahera *secteur* there would have been a real risk that he or a member of his close family would have been killed. Indeed, as a PSD party member he was personally threatened, and a target for the *Interahamwe* and the soldiers who were responsible for the massacres in Butare. Further, the lives of the Accused's wife, a Tutsi, and their children were also threatened. Therefore the Parties submitted that the prevailing circumstances faced by the Accused and his family should be considered as a factor in mitigation of the sentence.

94. Witness LZI testified that Nzabirinda was threatened during the events.[110] Joseph Nzabirinda also submitted in court that he was under psychological pressure, which forced him to take part in meetings and to go to the roadblocks in order not to confirm the suspicion that being a member of the PSD party was equivalent to being an accomplice of the enemies.[111]

b. Findings

95. The Chamber considers that this submission in respect of prevailing circumstances of necessity contradicts the facts in the Plea Agreement in which Joseph Nzabirinda acknowledged **[page 19]** that he attended several meetings at the Sahera *secteur*; that he never stopped attending those meetings even though he knew that systematic killings resulted from the first meeting; at no time or in any manner did he openly object to the killings at such meetings; and he knew that his silence would be regarded by the killers as tacit approval of the preparations for the killings.[112] Moreover, Joseph Nzabirinda admitted that he manned the Kabuga roadblock twice, at the request of the authorities, whereas he knew that roadblocks were one of the means employed in the campaign of killings in the *secteur.*

96. The Chamber notes that the Plea Agreement does not assert that Joseph Nzabirinda was compelled, under duress, to a criminal conduct. The Chamber is not convinced by the testimony of Witness LZI that Joseph Nzabirinda had no option but to attend the meetings and to man the Kabuga roadblock. The Chamber therefore rejects this purported mitigating circumstance.

---

106 Defence Exhibit D. 6 admitted under Rule 92 *bis*; T. 17 January 2007, pp. 42, 43.
107 T. 17 January 2007 pp. 3-7.
108 T. 17 January 2007 pp. 17-22.
109 T. 17 January 2007 pp. 35-40.
110 T. 17 January 2007 pp. 18, 19.
111 T. 17 January 2007 p. 60.
112 Plea Agreement, paras. 45-46.

E. Sentencing Recommendations by the Parties

97. Both Parties recommend a term of imprisonment ranging from five to eight years' imprisonment, with credit given for time already served and that he serve his sentence in a European country, preferably in France, as it is close to Belgium, where the Accused's wife and children reside. The Parties are aware that this is entirely within the Chamber's discretion.[113] Both acknowledge that the Chamber is not bound by their sentencing recommendations.[114]

98. The Prosecution submitted that the Chamber should consider the objectives of retribution, deterrence and rehabilitation in sentencing.[115] The Prosecution added that the agreement of the Parties regarding the recommended sentencing range is reasonable and consistent with the practice of both this Tribunal and the ICTY. In *Furundzija*, the Trial Chamber sentenced the Accused, who was a person of authority, to eight years' imprisonment for encouraging, by his presence, outrages upon personal dignity and rape. In *Rutaganira*, the Accused was found guilty and sentenced to a term of six years' imprisonment for having encouraged, by his presence and by omission, the perpetration of extermination as a crime against humanity.

99. The Defence submitted that the Accused has no blood on his hands, exercised no *de jure* authority and is charged with the murders of only two persons and not with extermination, as in the *Bisengimana* case.[116]

100. Citing a judgement from the Cyangugu High Court in Rwanda dated 29 April 2005, the Defence further submitted that the Chamber should apply the lower scale of the sentencing range.[117] In that case, Athanase Murwanashyaka who was charged with very serious offenses, including murder, extermination, and rape, was found guilty of genocide. Following a guilty plea, Athanase Murwanashyaka was sentenced to seven year's imprisonment, with credit for three and-a-half years already spent in detention. The Defence emphasized that the facts related to the crimes for which Athanase Murwanashyaka was charged are not commensurate with the case at bar. **[page 20]**

101. The Defence submitted that Articles 82 and 83 of the Rwandan Penal Code provide that, where mitigating circumstances are accepted or admissible, the death penalty shall be replaced by a sentence of no less than five years' imprisonment; a sentence of life imprisonment shall be replaced by a sentence of no less than two years' imprisonment; and a sentence of up to 25 years' imprisonment shall be reduced to a sentence of no more than one year's imprisonment.[118]

F. Findings

1. The General Sentencing Practice in the Courts of Rwanda

102. The Chamber recalls Article 23 of the Statute and Rule 101 of the Rules, which obliges the Tribunal to take into account the general practice regarding prison sentences in the courts of Rwanda.

103. Under the Rwandan Penal Code, serious offences, such as murder, carry a maximum sentence of death or life imprisonment, depending on the nature of the accused's participation.[119] Article 89 of the Code specifically provides that accomplices may be subject to the same sentence as the principal perpetrator.

104 The Chamber considers that the Rwandan Organic Law setting up "*Gacaca* Jurisdictions"[120] may be relevant for the sake of comparison in the instant case because it addresses the procedure for persons pleading

---

113 Plea Agreement, para. 60 ; *Mémoire conjoint*, paras. 48-53 and p. 12.
114 Plea Agreement, para. 64; *Mémoire conjoint*, para. 13.
115 T. 17 January 2007 p. 45.
116 T. 17 January 2007 p. 50.
117 T. 17 January 2007 p. 49.
118 T. 17 January 2007 p. 59.
119 *Code Pénal Rwandais, Décret-Loi* n° 21/77, 18 August 1977, modified by *Décret-Loi* n° 23/81, 13 October 1981, Articles 311-317.
120 Organic Law N°16/2004 of 19/6/2004 Establishing the Organisation, Competence and Functioning of Gacaca Courts Charged with Prosecuting and Trying the Perpetrators of the Crime of Genocide and Other Crimes Against Humanity, Committed Between October 1, 1990 and December 31, 1994. (Organic Law of 19 June 2004)

guilty to crimes against humanity. A person who aided to commit an offence,[121] may, after pleading guilty and under certain conditions,[122] be sentenced to a prison sentence of seven to twelve year's imprisonment.[123]

2. Conclusion

105. The Chamber is mindful that sentences of like individuals in like cases should be consistent. However, it is also mindful that the Appeals Chamber in the *Kupreškic* Judgement held that a Chamber is "under no obligation to expressly compare the case of one accused to that of another,"[124] and notes that "any given case contains a multitude of variables, ranging from the number and type of crimes committed to the personal circumstances of the individual."[125] The Chamber also understands its obligation to ensure that the sentence is commensurate with the individual circumstances of the offender.[126]

106. The Chamber recalls that it has found Joseph Nzabirinda's participation in aiding and abetting murder, as crimes against humanity, constitutes a very serious offence and is a gross violation of international humanitarian law.

107. The Chamber also found that Joseph Nzabirinda's moral authority in the community and the fact that Joseph Nzabirinda is an educated person are aggravating factors. However, the **[page 21]** Chamber further found the following circumstances to be mitigating: Joseph Nzabirinda's guilty plea accompanied by a public expression of remorse, his personal and family situation, his good character prior to the 1994 events, his lack of prior criminal convictions, his good conduct in detention, and the assistance he provided to certain victims.

108. Nonetheless, while Joseph Nzabirinda's personal circumstances (personal and family situation, good character, lack of prior criminal conviction and good conduct in detention) are relevant in the mitigation of the sentence, the Chamber is of the view that such factors cannot play a significant role in mitigating international crimes and the weight to be accorded to them is limited.[127]

109. The Chamber is mindful of the reasoning in the *Semanza* Judgement that a higher sentence is likely to be imposed on "one who orders rather than merely aids and abets exterminations."[128] The Chamber further recalls that "the modes of liability may either augment (*e.g.*, commission of the crime with direct intent) or lessen (*e.g.*, aiding and abetting a crime with awareness that a crime will probably be committed) the gravity of the crime."[129]

110. On examination of the sentencing practice of this Tribunal and that of the ICTY, the Chamber notes that principal perpetrators convicted of crimes against humanity, such as murder, have received sentences ranging from ten years' to life imprisonment.[130] Persons convicted of secondary forms of participation have generally received lower sentences.[131] The Chamber is mindful that the sentence should reflect the totality of the criminal conduct of the accused.[132]

---

121 Article 51 of Organic Law of 19 June 2004.

122 Article 56 of the Organic Law of 19 June 2004.

123 Article 73 of the Organic Law of 19 June 2004.

124 *Kupreškic*, Judgement (AC), para. 443.

125 *Kvočka*, Judgement (AC), para. 681.

126 *Mucić et al.*, Judgement (AC), paras. 717-719; *Muhimana,* Judgement (TC), para. 594.

127 *Banović,* Judgement, (TC), para. 76 (footnotes omitted); *Ntakirutimana*, Judgement (TC), para. 898; *Bisengimana*, Judgement (TC), para. 175.

128 *Semanza,* Judgement (AC), para. 388.

129 *Ndindabahizi*, Judgement (AC), para. 122 (fooотnote omitted).

130 *Muhimana*, Judgement (TC), para. 618; *Ntakirutimana et al.*, Judgement (TC), paras. 922, 924.

131 Laurent Semanza was sentenced to eight years' imprisonment for instigating the murder of six persons as a crime against humanity *(Semanza,* Judgement (TC), para. 588); Vincent Rutaganira was sentenced to six years' imprisonment after having pleaded guilty to complicity by omission in extermination as a crime against humanity (*Rutaganira*, *Jugement* (TC), *Dispositif*); Elizaphan Ntakirutimana was sentenced to ten years' imprisonment for aiding and abetting genocide (*Ntakirutimana et al.,* Judgement (TC), paras. 790, 921), and this sentence has been upheld by the Appeals Chamber (*Ntakirutimana et al.,* Judgement (AC), para. 570.); Paul Bisengimana was sentenced to 15 years' imprisonment after having pleaded guilty to aiding and abetting extermination as a crime against humanity (*Bisengimana*, Judgement (TC), para. 203); Joseph Serugendo was sentenced to six years' imprisonment after having pleaded guilty to direct and public incitement to commit genocide and persecution as a crime against humanity (*Serugendo*, Judgement (TC), Section VI).

132 *Mucić et al.,* Judgement (AC), para. 772.

111. However, the Chamber recalls that, it did not accept, in the instant case, Joseph Nzabirinda's form of participation as a mitigating circumstance. The Chamber considers that Joseph Nzabirinda's presence amounts to a very serious form of participation that relates to a cognizant, a positive choice. The Chamber also considers that Joseph Nzabirinda did not disassociate himself from those who organised the attacks during the *secteur* meetings, which he attended nor from the assailants who murdered Joseph Mazimpaka near the roadblock that he manned. Moreover, the Chamber finds that Joseph Nzabirinda knew that his presence and moral authority would encourage the killers to execute their crimes. **[page 22]**

3. Credit for Time Served in Custody

112. Pursuant to Rule 101 (D) of the Rules, "credit shall be given to the convicted person for the period, if any, during which the convicted person was detained in custody pending his surrender to the Tribunal or pending trial or appeal."

113. The Chamber considers 21 December 2001 as the beginning of Joseph Nzabirinda's detention, this being the date on which he was arrested and detained. The Chamber recognizes that Joseph Nzabirinda is entitled to credit for the time in detention since this date, including any additional time that he may serve pending an appeal.

V. Verdict

114. Recalling the guilty verdict of 14 December 2006;

115. Having considered the Statute and the Rules, the general practice regarding prison sentences in Rwanda, the Parties' pre-sentencing submissions and the evidence;

116. Having weighed the gravity of the offence, the aggravating and mitigating circumstances, the Chamber convicts and sentences Joseph Nzabirinda for the single count of murder, as a crime against humanity, pursuant to Article 3 (a) of the Statute, to a sentence of Seven years' imprisonment

117. The Chamber finds that Joseph Nzabirinda is entitled to credit for the time spent in detention from 21 December 2001 to the date of this judgement.

118. In accordance with Rule 102 (A) of the Rules, the sentence shall run as of the date of this judgement.

119. Pursuant to Rule 103 of the Rules, Joseph Nzabirinda shall remain in the custody of the Tribunal, pending a decision on where his sentence will be served, pursuant to Article 26 of the Statute and Rule 103 (A). The Chamber has noted the Parties' submissions, with respect to the recommended State in which the sentence will be served, but recalls that the President of the Tribunal, in consultation with the Chamber, will designate the State. The Government of Rwanda and the designated State shall be so notified by the Registrar.

120. Pursuant to Rule 102 (A) of the Rules, if notice of appeal is given, the enforcement of this judgement shall be stayed until the decision on appeal has been delivered, while the convicted person remains in detention.

Done in English

Arusha, 23 February 2007

Arlette Ramaroson	William H. Sekule	Solomy B. Bossa
Presiding Judge	Judge	Judge

[Seal of the Tribunal] **[page 23]**

Annexes

A. Jurisprudence and Defined Terms

1. ICTR

Prosecutor v. Akayesu, Case No.ICTR-96-4-T, Judgement (TC), 2 September 1998.

Prosecutor v. Akayesu, Case No.ICTR-96-4-A, Judgement (AC), 1 June 2001.

Prosecutor v. Bagilishema, Case No. CTR-95-1A-T, Judgement (TC), 7 June 2001.

Prosecutor v. Bisengimana, Case No.ICTR-00-60-S, Judgement and Sentence (TC), 13 April 2006.

Prosecutor v. Kajelijeli, Case No. ICTR-99-44-T, Judgement (TC), 1 December 2003.

Prosecutor v. Kajelijeli, Case No. ICTR-99-44-A, Judgement (AC), 23 May 2005.

Prosecutor v. Kambanda, Case No. ICTR- 97-23-S, Judgement (TC), 4 September 1998.

Prosecutor v. Kambanda, Case No. ICTR-97-23-A, Judgement (AC), 19 October 2000.

Prosecutor v. Kamuhanda, Case No. ICTR-95-54-T, Judgement (TC), 22 January 2004.

Prosecutor v. Kamuhanda, Case No. ICTR-95-54-A, Judgement (AC), 19 September 2005.

Prosecutor v. Kayishema and Ruzindana, Case No. ICTR-95-1-T, Judgement (TC), 21 May 1999.

Prosecutor v. Kayishema and Ruzindana, Case No. ICTR-95-1-A, Judgement (AC), 1 June 2001.

Prosecutor v. Mpambara, Case No. ICTR-01-65-T, Judgement (TC), 11 September 2006.

Prosecutor v. Muhimana, Case No. ICTR-95-1B-T, Judgement (TC), 28 April 2005.

Prosecutor v. Musema, Case No. ICTR-96-13-T, Judgement (TC), 27 January 2000.

Prosecutor v. Ndindabahizi, Case No. ICTR-2001-71-I, Judgement (TC), 15 July 2004.

Prosecutor v. Ndindabahizi, Case No. ICTR-2001-71-A, Judgement (AC), 16 January 2007.

Prosecutor v. Ntagerura et al., Case No. ICTR-99-46-T, Judgement (TC), 25 February 2004.

Prosecutor v. Ntakirutimana et al., Cases No. ICTR-96-10-T and ICTR-96-17-T, Judgement (TC), 21 February 2003.

Prosecutor v. Ntakirutimana et al., Cases No. ICTR-96-10-A and ICTR-96-17-A, Judgement (AC), 13 December 2004.

Prosecutor v. Ruggiu, Case No. ICTR-97-32-T, Judgement (TC), 1 June 2000.

Prosecutor v. Rutaganda, Case No. ICTR-96-3-T, Judgement (TC), 6 December 1999. **[page 24]**

Prosecutor v. Rutaganira, Case No. ICTR-95-1C-T, *Jugement* (TC), 14 *mars* 2005.

Prosecutor v. Semanza, Case No. ICTR-97-20-T, Judgement (TC), 15 May 2003.

Prosecutor v. Semanza, Case No. ICTR-97-20-A, Judgement (AC), 20 May 2005.

Prosecutor v. Serugendo, Case No. ICTR-2005-84-I, Judgement and Sentence (TC), 12 June 2006.

Prosecutor v. Serushago, Case No. ICTR-98-39-T, Judgement (TC), 5 February 1999.

2. ICTY

Prosecutor v. Aleksovski, Case No. IT-95-14/1-T, Judgement (TC), 25 June 1999.

Prosecutor v. Aleksovski, Case No. IT-95-14/1-A, Judgement (AC), 24 March 2000.

Prosecutor v. Banović, Case No. IT-02-65/1S, Judgement (TC), 28 October 2003.

Prosecutor v. Blaškić, Case No. IT-94-14-S, Judgement (TC), 3 March 2000.

Prosecutor v. Blaškić, Case No. IT-94-14-A, Judgement (AC), 29 July 2004.

Prosecutor v. Deronjić, Case No. IT-02-61-S, Judgement (TC), 30 March 2004.

Prosecutor v. Erdemović, Case No. IT-96-22-Tbis, Judgement (TC), 5 March 1998.

Prosecutor v. Furundžija, Case No. IT-95-17/1-T, Judgement (TC), 10 December 1998.

Prosecutor v. Galić, Case No. IT-98-29-A, Judgement (AC), 30 November 2006.

Prosecutor v. Jelisić, Case No. IT-95-10-A, Judgement (AC), 5 July 2001.

Prosecutor v. Kunarać et al., Case No. IT-96-23-T & 96-23/1-T, Judgement (TC), 22 February 2001.

Prosecutor v. Kunarać et al., Case No. IT-96-23-A & 96-23/1-A, Judgement (AC), 12 June 2002.

Prosecutor v. Kupreškić et al., Case No. IT-95-16-A, Judgement (AC), 23 October 2001.

Prosecutor v. Kvočka, Case No. IT-98-30-A, Judgement (AC), 28 February 2005.

Prosecutor v. Mucić et al. ("Čelebići"), Case No. IT-96-21-T, Judgement (TC), 16 October 1998.

Prosecutor v. Mucić et al. ("Čelebići"), Case No. IT-96-21-A, Judgement (AC), 20 February 2001. **[page 25]**

Prosecutor v. Dragan Nikolić, Case No. IT-02-60/1-S, Judgement (TC), 18 December 2003.

Prosecutor v. Plavšić, Case No. IT 00 39 & 40/1-S, Judgement (TC), 27 February 2003.

Prosecutor v. Sikirica et al., Case No. IT-95-8-T, Judgement (TC), 13 November 2001.

Prosecutor v.Dusko Tadić, Case No. IT-94-1, Judgement (TC), 7 May 1997.

Prosecutor v. Vasiljević, Case No. IT-98-32-S, Judgement (TC), 29 November 2002.

3. Defined Terms

Chamber
Trial Chamber II

Indictment
Prosecutor v. Nzabirinda, Case No. ICTR-2001-77-I, Amended Indictment, filed on 11 December 2006 in English and French.

Plea Agreement
Prosecutor v. Nzabirinda, Case No. ICTR-2001-77-I, Plea agreement between Joseph Nzabirinda and the Office of the Prosecutor, filed on 12 December 2006.

Prosecutor's Request for Leave to Amend an Indictment
Prosecutor v. Nzabirinda, Case No. ICTR-2001-77-I, Prosecutor's Request for Leave to Amend an Indictment Pursuant to Rules 72, 73, 50 and 51 of the Rules of Procedure and Evidence, filed on 20 November 2006.

Joint Sentencing Brief -*Mémoire conjoint*
Prosecutor v. Nzabirinda, Case No. ICTR-2001-77-T, *Mémoire conjoint entre Joseph Nzabirinda et le Bureau du Procureur préalable au prononcé de la sentence* filed on 9 January 2007.

Judgement
Prosecutor v. Nzabirinda, Case No. ICTR-2001-77-T, Sentencing Judgement, XX 2007.

T.
Official transcripts of the proceedings in English unless otherwise indicated.

B. Indictment

[page 1] THE PROSECUTOR

v.

JOSEPH NZABIRINDA

AMENDED INDICTMENT
Pursuant to Decision of 8 December 2006
UNDER SEAL

1. The Prosecutor of the International Criminal Tribunal for Rwanda pursuant to the authority stipulated in Article 17 of the Statute of the International Criminal Tribunal for Rwanda (the "Statute of the Tribunal") charges:

JOSEPH NZABIRINDA

with MURDER as a CRIME AGAINST HUMANITY under Articles 3(a) and 61 of the Statute of the Tribunal, as set forth below:

II. THE ACCUSED

1. Joseph NZABIRINDA, aka BIROTO, was born on 1 July 1957 in Rwanda, Sahera *Secteur* (Ngoma *Commune,* Butare *Préfecture*). After secondary education and training at the Youth Training Centre, he became *Encadreur* [Organizer] of Youth and Sports in Ngoma Urban *Commune,* Butare, in 1976 and was promoted to the post of *Encadreur* of Youth and Cooperatives, Butare *Préfecture,* in 1984; later, he became Managing Director of the firm SECOBE in Kigali, where he settled in 1992.

2. As the *Commune Encadreur,* Joseph NZABIRINDA, aka BIROTO, was officially responsible for the youth of his *commune,* and in particular for their training in craft skills and literacy and their initiation into "socio-economic groupings", but also for civic education, sports, recreational and cultural activities; at the *Préfecture,* he supervised *Commune Encadreurs.*

3. In 1990, Joseph NZABIRINDA aka BIROTO was one of the founding members of the PSD, which led him to return frequently to his home region to organize political meetings and to raise awareness among the population regarding his Party's policies.

4. In 1994, as Managing Director of SECOBE, Joseph NZABIRINDA aka BIROTO owned property in Rwanda and was considered to be rich and well-to-do.

5. when he returned to Sahera on 12 April 1994, Joseph NZABIRINDA aka BIROTO was regarded by the population not only as Youth *Encadreur,* but also as one of those who opposed the regime in power, symbolized in the *Secteur* by *Conseiller* Pascal Habyarimana, his acknowledged political adversary. **[page 2]**

6. Joseph NZABIRINDA aka BIROTO, as both former Youth *Encadreur* and a political personality, had moral authority in the eyes of the population in his *Secteur,* and in particular of the young people of whom he had been *Encadreur.* As a successful businessman and intellectual, Joseph NZABIRINDA aka BIROTO enjoyed a certain authority over the people living on his hill.

III. THE CHARGE

MURDER as a CRIME AGAINST HUMANITY under Articles 3(a) and 6.1 of the Statute

The Prosecutor of the International Criminal Tribunal for Rwanda charges Joseph NZABIRINDA aka BIROTO with having aided and abetted MURDER as a crime against humanity under Articles 3(a) and 6.1 of the Statute of the Tribunal, as accomplice by omission in the preparation of the commission of the crime.

7. During the period of the crime referred to in this Indictment, Tutsi, Hutu and Twa were identified as ethnic or racial groups.

8. After the death of the President of Rwanda, Juvénal Habyarimana, on 6 April 1994, there were in Rwanda in 1994 widespread or systematic attacks against a section of the civilian population, notably Tutsi and moderate Hutu, on political or ethnic grounds, resulting in the deaths of thousands of people, mostly civilians, throughout Rwanda.

9. Between 7 April and mid-July 1994, the massacre of the civilian population was for the most part aimed at the Tutsi in Rwanda. This is evidenced by the indiscriminate nature of the killings, which targeted unarmed women, children, young persons and the aged alike, who were massacred at roadblocks or places where they sought refuge, such as in the *préfecture* and *commune* offices, schools, churches and stadia in Butare *Préfecture.*

10. On 12 April 1994, Joseph NZABIRINDA aka BIROTO, together with his children, fled Kigali, where widespread massacres were taking place, and arrived in Sahera *Secteur,* Ngoma *Commune,* Butare *Préfecture.* A certain Antoine Mbarushimana Antoine, aka Bernier, and a soldier called Eugène, had also left Kigali for Sahera *Secteur.*

11. On 19 April 1994, the interim President Theodore Sindikubwabo held a meeting at Butare *Préfecture* with local authorities, including Prefect Sylvain Nsabimana and the *Bourgmestre* of Ngoma *Commune,* Joseph Kanyabashi. On that occasion, the local authorities assured the President that his wishes would be complied with.

12. Following that meeting, widespread killings of Tutsi and opponents of the regime began in Butare *Préfecture,* which had hitherto been peaceful, and in particular in Sahera *Secteur,* where Joseph NZABIRINDA then was. **[page 3]**

13. Starting form 6 April 1994, *Secteur Conseiller* Pascal Habyarimana held a number of "pacification meetings".

14. After 19 April, Joseph NZABIRINDA aka BIROTO attended meetings where only the Hutu of his *secteur* and those who participated in the Sahera killings were present. Joseph NZABIRINDA knew the killers because they were his neighbours, including Yacinthe Rurangirwa, Jean Baptiste Ntawangaheza, Joseph Ufiteyezu, Eugène and others.

15. After these meetings, systematic attacks were launched on the Tutsi families living on the Accused's hill, and these attacks *inter alia* led to the death of Pierre MURARA, who was killed by *Interahamwe* near the location where the meetings were held and where Joseph NZABIRINDA aka BIROTO was present as an approving spectator.

16. The Accused, Joseph NZABIRINDA aka BIROTO, attended several meetings organized at the Sahera *Secteur* office by the *secteur conseiller.* He never stopped attending those meetings, even though he knew that systematic killings had resulted from the first meetings he had attended. That clearly showed that the pacification activities organized in the course of those meetings, in reality, prepared and encouraged the hunting down and killing of Tutsis. At no time or in any manner, did the Accused openly object to those killings at such meetings.

17. Joseph NZABIRINDA aka BIROTO enjoyed such moral authority that, as a person held in high esteem by his fellow-citizens, his attendance was liable to have a decisive influence on the criminals attending the meetings, in light of the particular circumstances prevailing in his *secteur;* Joseph NZABIRINDA aka BIROTO thus gave the appearance of an "approving spectator" and knew that his silence would be regarded by the killers as tacit approval of the preparations for killings.

18. On 19 April 1994, the local authorities erected roadblocks throughout Sahera *Secteur,* and in particular at Kabuga; the roadblocks were used for identity checks, and were one of the means employed in the campaign of killings raging in the *secteur,* a fact of which Joseph NZABIRINDA was aware.

19. At the request of the authorities, during this same period Joseph NZABIRINDA aka BIROTO went twice to the roadblock at Kabuga to take his turn at manning it; on two occasions he was on duty at the roadblock along with some *Interahamwe* of Sahera *Secteur.* In thus appearing beside the killers, and as an approving spectator at the roadblock, the Accused encouraged the murder of Joseph Mazimpaka, killed by Mugenzi near the roadblock where Joseph NZABIRINDA aka BIROTO was.

20. Furthermore, the murders of Joseph Mazimpaka and Pierre Murara were committed in his *secteur,* at a location close to those of the meetings and roadblocks where the Accused, Joseph NZABIRINDA aka BIROTO, was present as an "approving spectator".

The crimes alleged against Joseph NZABIRINDA aka BIROTO in the present Amended Indictment are punishable under Articles 22 and 23 of the Statute of the Tribunal. **[page 4]**

Done in Arusha, this 9th December 2006

Hassan Bubacar Jallow
Prosecutor

Commentary

1. Introduction

On 23 February 2007, ICTR Trial Chamber II sentenced Nzabarinda to seven years imprisonment.[1] The accused had been arrested in Brussels on 21 December 2001. Since, pursuant to Rule 101(D) of the RPE, an accused is entitled to credit for the time spent in detention, pending both surrender to the tribunal and trial/ appeal, Nzabarinda was released in December 2008 after completing his sentence.[2]

The accused had pleaded guilty to aiding and abetting murder, as a crime against humanity, as an accomplice by omission in the preparation of the commission of the crime. He had attended so-called pacification meetings, which were organized for the purpose of preparing attacks on Tutsi and moderate Hutus. Apart from that, he had manned a roadblock, in the vicinity of which a victim called Joseph Mazimpaka had been murdered. By his presence at the 'preparation meetings' and his appearance at the roadblock, the accused had assumed the role of an "approving spectator" and had thereby encouraged the murders. The Trial Chamber accepted that, because of the moral authority he exercised as a former youth organizer, political personality, intellectual and businessman, Nzabarinda 'knew that his presence at the Sahera *secteur* meetings and at the Kabuga roadblock would be crucial in encouraging the preparation and the commission of the murders'.[3]

In arriving at the sentence, the Trial Chamber first considered the gravity of the offence, which comprised the usual statement that '[g]enocide and crimes against humanity are inherently very serious offences because they are heinous in nature and shock the collective conscience of mankind'.[4] It accepted as aggravating circumstances the fact that Nzabarinda has abused his position of influence,[5] and that he, as an educated person, 'could appreciate the dignity and value of human life and was aware of the need for peaceful co-existence between communities'.[6] His guilty plea – in combination with his public statements of regret and remorse – his personal assistance (in the form of 'moral, financial and material support') to Tutsi refugees, which had contributed to the saving of lives, his personal situation as a married man with children, his good character prior to the 1994 events, his lack of a criminal record and his good behaviour while in UN detention were all accepted as mitigating circumstances.

The Chamber subsequently stressed the importance of ensuring that the 'sentences of like individuals in like cases' are consistent, while, at the same time, respecting the principle of individualized sentencing.[7] Therefore, before imposing the seven year sentence, it considered the Rwandan Organic law that established the *Gacaca* jurisdictions, and then applied the specific circumstances relating to the case and the accused, also taking into account ICTR and ICTY sentencing case law.

As well as the Nzabarinda Sentencing Judgement, this commentary will examine in general terms the *ad hoc* tribunals' sentencing practices and discuss the main sentencing factors accepted therein. Such an exercise will serve the purpose of the final part of this commentary, where consideration will be given to the question as to whether and how the sentencing factors are guided by the principles that are supposed to direct international sentencing. In examining the tribunals' case law in a search for these rationales or principles, this author refers to his other commentary listed in this same volume of the Annotated Leading Cases series.

---

1 ICTR, Sentencing Judgement, *Prosecutor v. Nzabirinda*, Case No. ICTR-2001-77-T, T. Ch. II, 23 February 2007, in this volume, p. 679.

2 Unlike at the ICTY, no person convicted by the ICTR has ever been granted early release.

3 Sentencing Judgement, *Prosecutor v. Nzabirinda*, T. Ch. II, *supra* note 1, par. 37.

4 *Ibid.*, par. 56. See, in a similar vein, ICTR, Judgement and Sentence, *Prosecutor v. Muhimana*, Case No. ICTR-95-1B-T, T. Ch. III, 28 April 2005, Klip/ Sluiter, ALC-XXII-413, par. 603 and ICTR, Judgement and Sentence, *Prosecutor v. Ruggiu*, Case No. ICTR-97-32-I, T. Ch. I, 1 June 2000, Klip/ Sluiter, ALC-VI-637, par. 48.

5 Sentencing Judgement, *Prosecutor v. Nzabirinda*, T. Ch. II, *supra* note 1, par. 62.

6 *Ibid.*, par. 63, referring to ICTR, Judgement and Sentence, *Prosecutor v. Bisengimana*, Case No. ICTR-00-60-T, T. Ch. II, 13 April 2006, Klip/ Sluiter, ALC-XXIV-429, par. 120.

7 Sentencing Judgement, *Prosecutor v. Nzabirinda*, T. Ch. II, *supra* note 1, par. 105.

2. The ad hoc tribunals' sentencing practices

2.1 General remarks

From Article 23 of the ICTR statute and Rule 101 of the ICTR RPE, it follows that, in imposing a sentence, a Trial Chamber must take into account the following sentencing factors:[8] (i) the gravity of the offence;[9] (ii) the general practice regarding prison sentences in the courts of Rwanda;[10] (iii) the individual circumstances of the accused, including aggravating and mitigating circumstances;[11] (iv) credit to be given for any time spent in detention pending surrender to the international tribunal, trial or appeal;[12] and (v) the extent to which any penalty imposed by a court of any State on the convicted person for the same act has already been served.[13]

Discretion is an important factor in identifying, weighing and interpreting the different sentencing factors. As an apparently automatic response to requests by either the prosecution or defence for more structure and clarity in sentencing, the Appeals Chamber has referred to the Trial Chamber's discretionary powers.[14] While discretion does, of course, not necessarily result in arbitrary decision making, and may be indispensable in order to avoid a too rigid equality in sentencing,[15] it might obscure judicial decision making, particularly if the principle of reasoned decision making is disregarded, which, in turn, may negatively affect the expressive function of the sentencing.[16]

Thus, although the sentencing regime outlined below may appear quite balanced and rational, one should not overlook the fact that sentencing is not a mathematical exercise. Non-sentencers cannot look into the judges' minds at the time of sentencing. In other words, if a sentencing chamber fails to provide insights as to how the different factors relate to each other in a concrete case, and how much weight is given to each of those factors, it is impossible to exactly follow, let alone control, the judges' endeavours.

2.2 Gravity of the crime

The two *ad hoc* tribunals have repeatedly stressed that the gravity of the offence is by far the most important consideration in sentencing, being regarded as the 'litmus test' for determining the appropriate

[8] ICTR, Judgment, *Prosecutor v. Akayesu*, Case No. ICTR-96-4-A, A. Ch., 1 June 2001, Klip/ Sluiter, ALC-X-335, par. 410; ICTR, Judgement, *Kajelijeli v. Prosecutor*, Case No. ICTR-98-44A-A, A. Ch., 23 May 2005, Klip/ Sluiter, ALC-XXII-625, par. 290; Judgement and Sentence, *Prosecutor v. Bisengimana*, T. Ch. II, *supra* note 6, par. 109; ICTY, Judgement, *Prosecutor v. Blaškić*, Case No. IT-95-14-A, A. Ch., 29 July 2004, Klip/ Sluiter, ALC-XX-295, par. 679.

[9] Article 23, paragraph 2, ICTR Statute. See also Judgement, *Kajelijeli v. Prosecutor*, A. Ch., *supra* note 8, par. 290; ICTY, Judgement, *Prosecutor v. Delalić, Mucić, Delić and Landžo (also referred to as Čelebići),* Case No. IT-96-21-A, A. Ch., 20 February 2001, Klip/ Sluiter, ALC-V-369, par. 429.

[10] Article 23, paragraph 1, ICTR Statute; Rule 101 (B) (iii). See, further, ICTY, Judgment in Sentencing Appeals, *Prosecutor v. Tadić*, Case No. IT-94-1-A and IT-94-1-A*bis*, A. Ch., 26 January 2000, Klip/ Sluiter, ALC-IV-439, par. 21, 70;ICTY, Judgement, *Prosecutor v. Aleksovski*, Case No. IT-95-14/1-A, A. Ch., 24 March 2000, Klip/ Sluiter, ALC-IV-361, par. 188. See also ICTR, Judgement, *Kajelijeli v. Prosecutor*, Case No. ICTR-98-44-A-A, A. Ch., 23 May 2005, Klip/ Sluiter, ALC-XXII-625, par. 290.

[11] Article 23, paragraph 2, ICTR Statute; Rule 101(B)(i) and (ii). See, further, ICTR, Judgement, *Kajelijeli v. Prosecutor*, Case No. ICTR-98-44-A-A, A. Ch., 23 May 2005, Klip/ Sluiter, ALC-XXII-625, par. 290.

[12] Rule 101(C); Judgment in Sentencing Appeals, *Prosecutor v. Tadić*, A. Ch., *supra* note 10, par. 38, 75. See also ICTR, Judgement, *Kajelijeli v. Prosecutor*, Case No. ICTR-98-44-A-A, A. Ch., 23 May 2005, Klip/ Sluiter, ALC-XXII-625, par. 290.

[13] Rule 101(B)(iv) referring to Article 9, paragraph 3, ICTR Statute. See also Judgement, *Kajelijeli v. Prosecutor*, A. Ch., *supra* note 8, par. 290.

[14] See, for example, Judgement, *Prosecutor v. Delalić, Mucić, Delić and Landžo,* A. Ch., *supra* note 9, par. 776 and 777, where it is held that '[a]s a matter of law, a Trial Chamber is obliged to take account of mitigating circumstances in imposing sentence. However, the weight to be attached is a matter within its discretion.' See also ICTY, Judgment, *Prosecutor v. Jelisić*, Case No. IT-95-10-A, A. Ch., 5 July 2001, Klip/ Sluiter, ALC-VII-513, par. 103; ICTY, Judgement on sentencing appeal, *Prosecutor v. Dragan Nikolić*, Case No. IT-94-2-A, A. Ch., 4 February 2005, to be published in volume XXVI, par. 74; ICTY, Judgement, *Prosecutor v. Stakić*, Case No. IT-97-24-A, A. Ch., 22 March 2006, to be published in volume XXIX, par. 375; ICTY, Judgement, *Prosecutor v. Furundžija*, Case No. IT-95-17/1-A, A. Ch., 21 July 2000, Klip/ Sluiter, ALC-V-291, par. 250; ICTY,Judgement, *Prosecutor v. Krstić*, Case No. IT-98-33-A, A. Ch., 19 April 2004 , Klip/ Sluiter, ALC-XIX-539, par. 248; ICTR, Judgement and Sentence, *Prosecutor v. Semanza*, Case No. ICTR-97-20-T, T. Ch. III, 15 May 2003, Klip/ Sluiter, ALC-XII-599, par. 562-564; ICTR, Judgement, *Kambanda v. Prosecutor*, Case No. ICTR-97-23-A, A. Ch., 19 October 2000, Klip/ Sluiter, ALC-VI-659, par. 101; ICTR, Judgement and Sentence, *Prosecutor v. Niyitegeka*, Case No. ICTR-96-14-T, T. Ch. I, 16 May 2003, Klip/ Sluiter, ALC-XII-731, par. 483; ICTY, Judgement, *Prosecutor v. Blaškić*, Case No. IT-95-14-T, T. Ch. I, 3 March 2000, Klip/ Sluiter, ALC-IV-477, par. 807.

[15] J. de Hullu, Materieel Strafrecht, Over algemene leerstukken van strafrechtelijke aansprakelijkheid naar Nederlands recht, Kluwer, Deventer 2006, p. 27.

[16] See, further, this author's commentary, in this volume, p. 807.

sentence.[17] Determining the gravity of the crime does not take place in abstract,[18] but requires a consideration of the particular circumstances of the case, as well as the form and degree of the participation of the accused in the crime.[19] A Trial Chamber must consider the totality of the accused's culpability,[20] which includes the impact of the crime upon the victim(s), the effects on relatives of the immediate victims[21] and, more generally, the consequences of the criminal conduct.[22] Other variables that have been taken into account when determining the gravity of the crime include the discriminatory nature of the crimes (where this is not considered an element of the crime),[23] and the vulnerability of the victims.[24]

Some of these variables have, occasionally, also been accepted by the tribunals as aggravating circumstances.[25] Particularly in their earlier sentencing judgements, ICTR Trial Chambers appeared confused over the distinction between, and the functions of, these two sentencing factors when they, for example, discussed gravity elements under the heading of aggravating circumstances.[26]

The practice of not clearly distinguishing between the variables to be considered when determining the gravity of the offence and those belonging to the category of aggravating circumstances, apart from not contributing to transparency, also hinders the development of a consistent and logical sentencing regime. Coupled with the absence of an obligation on Trial Chambers to expressly mention all sentencing variables that have been taken into account in a concrete case,[27] effective control by the Appeals Chamber is impossible.

---

17 ICTY, Judgement, *Prosecutor v. Delalić, Mucić, Delić and Landžo*, Case No. IT-96-21-T, T. Ch. II*quater*, 16 November 1998, Klip/ Sluiter, ALC-III-363, par. 1225; Judgement, *Prosecutor v. Delalić, Mucić, Delić and Landžo*, A. Ch., *supra* note 9, par. 731; ICTY, Appeal Judgement, *Prosecutor v. Kupreškić, Kupreškić, Kupreškić, Josipović and Šantić* , Case No. IT-95-16-A, A. Ch., 23 October 2001, Klip/ Sluiter, ALC-VIII-429, par. 442; Judgement, *Prosecutor v. Blaškić*, A. Ch., *supra* note 8, par. 683; Judgement, *Prosecutor v. Aleksovski*, A. Ch., *supra* note 10, par. 182; ICTR, Judgement and Sentence, *Prosecutor v. Rutaganira*, Case No. ICTR-95-1C-T, T. Ch. III, 14 March 2005, Klip/ Sluiter, ALC-XXII-373, par. 117; Judgement and Sentence, *Prosecutor v. Serugendo*, T. Ch. I, *supra* note 17, par. 39.

18 Judgement and Sentence, *Prosecutor v. Semanza*, T. Ch. III, 15 May 2003, *supra* note 14, par. 555.

19 ICTY, Judgement, *Prosecutor v. Kupreškić, Kupreškić, Kupreškić, Josipović, Papić and Šantić* , Case No. IT-95-16-T, T.Ch. II, 14 January 2000, Klip/ Sluiter, ALC-IV-703, par. 852, cited in Judgement, *Prosecutor v. Aleksovski*, A. Ch., *supra* note 10, par. 182. See also Judgement, *Prosecutor v. Delalić, Mucić, Delić and Landžo*, A. Ch., *supra* note 9, par. 731; Judgement, *Prosecutor v. Blaškić*, A. Ch., *supra* note 8, par. 683; ICTY, Judgement, *Prosecutor v. Galić*, Case No. IT-98-29-A, A. Ch., 30 November 2006, par. 409; Judgement and Sentence, *Prosecutor v. Serugendo*, T. Ch. I, *supra* note 17, par. 39.

20 Appeal Judgement, *Prosecutor v. Kupreškić, Kupreškić, Kupreškić, Josipović and Šantić* , A. Ch., *supra* note 17, par. 451; ICTR, Judgement and Sentence, *Prosecutor v. Ndindabahizi*, Case No. ICTR-2001-71-I, T. Ch. I, 15 July 2004, Klip/ Sluiter, ALC-XVIII-645, par. 502.

21 Judgement, *Prosecutor v. Blaškić*, A. Ch., *supra* note 8, par. 683. In Krnojelac, the Appeals Chamber considered that 'even where no blood relationships have been established, a trier of fact would be right to presume that the accused knew that his victim did not live cut off from the world but had established bonds with others'; see Judgement, *Prosecutor v. Krnojelac*, A. Ch., *supra* note 21, par. 270.

22 Appeal Judgement, *Prosecutor v. Kupreškić, Kupreškić, Kupreškić, Josipović and Šantić* , A. Ch., *supra* note 17, par. 442.

23 Judgement, *Prosecutor v. Blaškić*, A. Ch., *supra* note 8, par. 683, referring to ICTY, Judgement, *Prosecutor v. Kvočka, Kos, Radić, Žigić and Prcać*, Case No. IT-98-30/1-T, T. Ch. I, 2 November 2001, Klip/ Sluiter, ALC-VIII-581, par. 702.

24 Judgement, *Prosecutor v. Blaškić*, A. Ch., *supra* note 8, par. 683, referring to ICTY, Judgement, *Prosecutor v. Kunarac et al.*, Case No. IT-96-23&IT-96-23/1-A, A. Ch., 12 June 2002, Klip/ Sluiter, ALC-VIII-911, par. 352.

25 In Vasiljević, the Appeals Chamber found that the method and circumstances surrounding a killing are factors that normally would be taken into account in a Trial Chamber's consideration of the 'inherent gravity' of the offence. The Vasiljević Trial Chamber had considered it an aggravating factor. The Appeals Chamber held that the Trial Chamber did not err in doing so: ICTY, Judgement, *Prosecutor v. Vasiljević*, Case No. IT-98-32-A, A. Ch., 25 February 2004, Klip/ Sluiter, ALC-XIX-465, par. 157. See further par. 167, where the long term effect of the trauma on the victims was taken into account as an aggravating factor. See, in a similar vein, Judgement, *Prosecutor v. Blaškić*, A. Ch., *supra* note 8, par. 686. In ICTY, Judgment on Sentencing Appeal, *Prosecutor v. Momir Nikolić*, Case No. IT-02-60/1-A, A. Ch., 8 March 2006, to be published in volume XXVIII, par. 66, the impact of the crime on survivors was considered an aspect of the gravity of the offence. See also Judgement, *Prosecutor v. Kunarac et al.*, A. Ch., *supra* note 24, par. 357. In Judgement, *Prosecutor v. Krnojelac*, A. Ch., *supra* note 21, par. 259, the impact on the relatives of the victims was considered an aggravating circumstance.

26 See, for example, ICTR, Judgement and Sentence, *Prosecutor v. Rutaganda*, Case No. ICTR-96-3-T, T. Ch. I, 6 December 1999, Klip/ Sluiter, ALC-II-709, par. 468; Judgement and Sentence, *Prosecutor v. Ruggiu*, T. Ch. I, *supra* note 4, par. 47-48; ICTR, Judgment and Sentence, *Prosecutor v. Kamuhanda*, Case No. ICTR-95-54A-T, T. Ch. II, 22 January 2004, Klip/ Sluiter, ALC-XVII-531, par. 759-764.

27 See, for example, ICTY, Judgement, *Prosecutor v. Kordić and Čerkez*, Case No. IT-95-14/2-A, A. Ch., 17 December 2004, to be published in volume XXVI, par. 1051 and 1054, where the Appeals Chamber held that mitigating factors do not need to be expressly taken into account. See, in a similar vein, ICTR, Judgement and Sentence, *Prosecutor v. Ntagerura, Bagambiki and Imanishimwe*, Case No. ICTR-99-46-T, T. Ch. III, 25 February 2004, Klip/ Sluiter, ALC-XVIII-267, par. 436.

Admittedly, it has been repeatedly stressed in the tribunals' case law that factors that Trial Chambers take into account when determining the gravity of the offence cannot in the same case also be included as aggravating circumstances and *vice versa*.[28] However, in Deronjić, although the Appeals Chamber acknowledged that the Trial Chamber had not addressed the distinction between the gravity of the offence and aggravating circumstances, it accepted that this, by itself, did not yet imply that the Trial Chamber had engaged in impermissible "double counting".[29] It appears to follow that, as long as it is not manifest that "double counting" has occurred, it does not matter whether a particular variable is considered under the heading of gravity or as an aggravating circumstance. However, since, as stated, Trial Chambers are under no clear obligation to expressly mention all the variables they have taken into account, merely sanctioning manifest cases of double counting hardly provides an adequate safety net.

In trying to clarify the distinction between the gravity of the offence and aggravating circumstances, it has been argued that aggravating (and mitigating) circumstances only relate to *personal* circumstances concerning the accused.[30] However, in Deronjić, the Appeals Chamber held that this view, which was expressed by the Kunarac et al. Trial Chamber, 'is not to be taken as a rule'.[31] It explained that this remark should rather be understood as reflecting the 'general principle of individual responsibility that underlies criminal law: a person cannot be held responsible for an act unless something he himself has done or failed to do justifies holding him responsible.'[32]

Some of the factors that have been recognized in the tribunals' case law as contributing to the determination of the gravity of the crime will be discussed here. In relation to the mode of participation, it is generally accepted that aiders and abettors deserve a lower sentence than co-perpetrators.[33] Further, as held by the Muhimana Appeals Chamber, the principle of gradation in sentencing 'suggests that sentences should be graduated, that is, that the most senior levels of the command structure should attract the severest sentences, with less severe sentences for those lower down the structure'.[34] It also follows from Kvočka *et al.*, that participation in a 'multi-perpetrator offence' is not considered a circumstance that increases the gravity of the crime,[35] in contrast to those national jurisdictions where 'multi-perpetrator offences' are often accorded a more severe punishment. The Appeals Chamber thus recognizes the special context of international crimes, in which a multitude of perpetrators is the rule rather than the exception.

A second factor that influences the determination of the gravity of the offence is the 'relative significance' of the role of the accused in the broader conflict,[36] and his level in the command structure,[37] the latter being of

[28] ICTY, Judgement on Sentencing Appeal, *Prosecutor v. Deronjić*, Case No. IT-02-61-A, A. Ch., 20 July 2005, to be published in volume XXVII, par. 106; ICTY, Sentencing Judgement, *Prosecutor v. Plavšić*, Case No. IT-00-39&40/1-S, T. Ch. III, 27 February 2003, Klip/ Sluiter, ALC-XI-933, par. 58; ICTY, Judgment, *Prosecutor v. Krnojelac*, Case No. IT-97-25-T, T. Ch. II, 15 March 2002, Klip/ Sluiter, ALC-VIII-755, par. 517; ICTY, Sentencing Judgement, *Prosecutor v. Perdrag Banović*, Case No. IT-02-65/1-S, T. Ch. III, 28 October 2003, Klip/ Sluiter, ALC-XV-701, par. 53; ICTY, Sentencing Judgement, *Prosecutor v. Obrenović*, Case No. IT-02-60/2-S, T. Ch. I, Section A, 10 December 2003, Klip/ Sluiter, ALC-XIX-639, par. 101; ICTY, Sentencing Judgement, *Prosecutor v. Češić*, Case No. IT-95-10/1-S, T. Ch. I, 11 March 2004, Klip/ Sluiter, ALC-XIX-755, par. 53; Sentencing Judgement, *Prosecutor v. Nzabirinda*, T. Ch. II, *supra* note 1, par. 60.

[29] Judgement on Sentencing Appeal, *Prosecutor v. Deronjić*, A. Ch., *supra* note 28, par. 106. See, in a similar vein, Judgement, *Prosecutor v. Galić*, A. Ch., *supra* note 19, par. 409, footnote 1229.

[30] See ICTY, Judgement, *Prosecutor v. Kunarac, Kovač and Vuković*, Cases No. IT-96-23-T and IT-96-23/1-T, T. Ch. II, 22 February 2001, Klip/ Sluiter, ALC-V-617, par. 850.

[31] Judgement on Sentencing Appeal, *Prosecutor v. Deronjić*, A. Ch., *supra* note 28, par. 124.

[32] *Ibid.*, par. 124.

[33] Judgement, *Prosecutor v. Krstić*, A. Ch., *supra* note 14, par. 237, 240, 251 and 268. Judgement, *Prosecutor v. Mitar Vasiljević*, A. Ch., *supra* note 25, par. 149, 182; ICTR, Judgment and Sentence, *Prosecutor v. Kajelijeli*, Case No. 98-44A-T, T. Ch. II, 1 December 2003, Klip/ Sluiter, ALC-XVII-27, par. 963; Judgement, *Prosecutor v. Krstić*, A. Ch., *supra* note 14, par. 268; ICTR, Judgement and Sentence, *Prosecutor v. Simba*, Case No. ICTR-01-76-T, T. Ch. I, 13 December 2005, Klip/ Sluiter, ALC-XXIV-325, par. 434.

[34] ICTR, Judgement, *Muhimana v. Prosecutor*, Case No. ICTR-95-1B-A, A. Ch., 21 May 2007, in this volume, p. 717, par. 233.

[35] ICTY, Judgement, *Prosecutor v. Kvočka, Radić, Žigić and Prcac*, Case No. IT-98-30/1-A, A. Ch., 28 February 2005, to be published in volume XXVI, par. 703.

[36] Judgment in Sentencing Appeals, *Prosecutor v. Tadić*, A. Ch., *supra* note 10, par. 55; Judgement, *Prosecutor v. Krstić*, A. Ch., *supra* note 14, par. 253, 273.

[37] *Ibid.*, par. 56; Appeal Judgement, *Prosecutor v. Kupreškić, Kupreškić, Kupreškić, Josipović and Šantić*, A. Ch., *supra* note 17, par. 404.

particular importance in combination with him actively participating in the criminal conduct.[38] It has, more generally, been acknowledged that it would be 'wrong to assume that responsibility for criminal conduct as a superior is less grave than for acts committed by a subordinate'.[39] This does not imply that, if an accused's rank in the chain of command was by comparison low, a more lenient sentence should automatically be imposed;[40] a Trial Chamber must take into account all specific circumstances of an individual case.[41]

In Čelebići, it was stipulated that, in connection with the assessment of the gravity of offences committed under Article 7, paragraph 3, ICTY Statute, two aspects need be considered: (i) the gravity of the underlying crime committed by the convicted person's subordinate; and (ii) the gravity of the convicted person's own conduct in failing to prevent or punish the underlying crime.[42] A superior directly engaging in committing crimes adds to the gravity of the superior's failure to prevent or punish those acts and may therefore aggravate the sentence.[43] Also, the duration of the period in which the superior failed to prevent or punish the criminal acts of his subordinates co-determines the overall gravity of the crime.[44]

Another important consideration in this respect is that, where criminal responsibility for an offence is alleged under one count, pursuant to both Article 7, paragraph 1, and Article 7, paragraph 3, of the Statute, and where both forms of responsibility are proved, this must be taken into account in sentencing, although a Trial Chamber is allowed to enter only one conviction.[45] Thus, direct responsibility, under Article 7, paragraph 1, of the Statute, is considered graver if accompanied by a perpetrator's position of authority[46] and *vice versa*. Whereas a position of authority cannot aggravate a conviction under Article 7, paragraph 3, of the ICTY Statute,[47] the *abuse* of such an authoritative position can.[48]

A third factor that influences the gravity of an offence is the principle of proportionality. This author has elsewhere pointed to the unfortunate absence in the tribunals' sentencing practices of a sufficient consideration for Von Hirsch's distinction between 'ordinal' and 'cardinal' proportionality.[49] Ordinal scaling of punishment comes down to the question of how severe crimes should be punished, when compared to each other, whereas cardinal scaling of punishment refers to the 'overall levels of onerousness that should be chosen to anchor

---

38 Judgement, *Prosecutor v. Aleksovski*, A. Ch., *supra* note 10, par. 182; Judgement, *Prosecutor v. Krstić*, A. Ch., *supra* note 14, par. 239; Judgement, *Prosecutor v. Kvočka, Radić, Žigić and Prcac*, A. Ch., *supra* note 35, par. 797.

39 Judgement, *Prosecutor v. Delalić, Mucić, Delić and Landžo*, A. Ch., *supra* note 9, par. 735.

40 *Ibid.*, par. 847. See also Judgement, *Prosecutor v. Kvočka, Radić, Žigić and Prcac*, A. Ch., *supra* note 35, par. 716; ICTY, Judgement on Sentencing Appeal, *Prosecutor v. Jokić*, Case No. IT-01-42/1-A, A. Ch., 30 August 2005, to be published in volume XXVII, par. 28.

41 Judgement, *Prosecutor v. Delalić, Mucić, Delić and Landžo*, A. Ch., *supra* note 9, par. 849. See also Judgement, *Prosecutor v. Krstić*, A. Ch., *supra* note 14, par. 254, where the Appeals Chamber stated that, although 'guilt should be assessed on a personal basis and [...] the comparative guilt of other alleged co-perpetrators, not adjudicated [...], is not a relevant consideration, [...] the Trial Chamber was entitled to consider the conduct of Krstić in the proper context, which includes the conduct of alleged co-perpetrators. A comprehensive understanding of the facts of a particular case not only permits a consideration of the culpability of other actors; indeed, it requires it in order to accurately comprehend the events in question and to impose the appropriate sentence [...]'. See also footnote 418, where it is acknowledged that the Tribunal has recognized the practice of 'gradation of sentence'. See, further, Judgement, *Prosecutor v. Aleksovski*, A. Ch., *supra* note 10, par. 184; Judgement and Sentence, *Prosecutor v. Serugendo*, T. Ch. I, *supra* note 17, par. 39.

42 Judgement, *Prosecutor v. Delalić, Mucić, Delić and Landžo*, A. Ch., *supra* note 9, par. 732.

43 *Ibid.*, par. 736; Judgement, *Prosecutor v. Aleksovski*, A. Ch., *supra* note 10, par. 183.

44 Judgement, *Prosecutor v. Delalić, Mucić, Delić and Landžo*, A. Ch., *supra* note 9, par. 739.

45 *Ibid.*, par. 745, ICTY, Judgement on Sentence Appeal, *Prosecutor v. Mucić, Delić and Landžo*, Case No. IT-96-21-A*bis*, A. Ch., 8 April 2003, Klip/ Sluiter, ALC-XIV-847, par. 35. See also Judgement on Sentencing Appeal, *Prosecutor v. Jokić*, A. Ch., *supra* note 40, par. 27: 'Based on settled jurisprudence [...] only one conviction under each count can be entered against the Appellant pursuant to Article 7(1) of the Statute. Thus, the Appeals Chamber vacates the Appellant's convictions for Counts 1 through 6 insofar as they are based on a finding of the Appellant's superior responsibility under Article 7(3) of the Statute'.

46 Appeal Judgement, *Prosecutor v. Kupreškić, Kupreškić, Kupreškić, Josipović and Šantić* , A. Ch., *supra* note 17, par. 451; Judgement, *Prosecutor v. Kvočka, Radić, Žigić and Prcac*, A. Ch., *supra* note 35, par. 797; Judgement, *Prosecutor v. Naletilić and Martinović*, A. Ch., *supra* note 46, par. 613.

47 *Ibid.*, par. 613.

48 ICTR, Judgement, *Prosecutor v. Ntagerura, Bagambiki and Imanishimwe*, Case No. ICTR-99-46-A, A. Ch., 7 July 2006, Klip/ Sluiter, ALC-XXIV-595, par. 818; Judgement and Sentence, *Prosecutor v. Serugendo*, T. Ch. I, *supra* note 17, par. 48; Sentencing Judgement, *Prosecutor v. Nzabirinda*, T. Ch. II, *supra* note 1, par. 62.

49 See Denis Abels, Commentary, in Klip/ Sluiter, ALC-XIV-875, referring to Andrew von Hirsch and Andrew Ashworth, Proportionate Sentencing, Exploring the Principles, Oxford University Press, Oxford 2005, p. 131.

the system of penalties'.[50] Ordinal proportionality thus requires that persons convicted for criminal acts of comparable gravity should receive punishments that are comparable in severity.

The ICTY Appeals Chamber has made clear that, in its view, proportionality does not see to comparing sentences imposed in distinct cases. As it held in Nikolić, '[t]he principle of proportionality [...] by no means encompasses proportionality between one's sentence and the sentence of other accused'.[51]

Although the ICTY Appeals Chamber has acknowledged that, eventually, as the number of convictions rendered by the tribunal increases, a pattern of sentences will emerge that Trial Chambers would be obliged to consider, it has also stressed that such obligation would merely exist in *considering* previously imposed sentences, not in being bound by them.[52] For the tribunals to develop a fair and consistent sentencing regime, it is, however, a prerequisite to attribute a significant role to ordinal proportionality. As Danner has pointed out, '[o]ne of the fundamental elements in any rational and fair system of criminal justice is consistency in punishment.'[53]

However, things seem to have improved somewhat, at least at the ICTR. The ICTR's sentencing chambers, in more recent years, tend to make comparisons of the circumstances of the case before them with those of previous cases before both *ad hoc* tribunals.[54]

2.3 Sentencing practices of the courts of the former Yugoslavia and Rwanda

Although Trial Chambers must have recourse to the general practices regarding prison sentences in the national courts of the former Yugoslavia and Rwanda, Trial Chambers are not obliged to conform to such practices.[55] In Tadić, it was held that the wording of Sub-Rule 101 paragraph A, which empowers Trial Chambers to impose life sentences, shows that a Trial Chamber's discretion in imposing sentence is not bound by any maximum term of imprisonment applied in a national system.[56] In the same vein, the principle of *lex mitior*[57] is not applicable, because "different criminal laws are relevant and applicable to the law governing the sentencing consideration of the International Tribunal".[58]

---

50 See Denis Abels, Commentary, in Klip/ Sluiter, ALC-XIV-875, referring to Andrew von Hirsch and Andrew Ashworth, Proportionate Sentencing, Exploring the Principles, Oxford University Press, Oxford 2005, p. 138.

51 Judgement on Sentencing Appeal, *Prosecutor v. Dragan Nikolić*, A. Ch., *supra* note 14, par. 21. This should be seen in light of the argument held by the Appeals Chamber in Čelebići, that 'comparison with other cases is often of limited assistance', because 'often the differences are more significant than the similarities, and the mitigating and aggravating factors dictate different results. They are therefore not reliable as the sole basis for sentencing an individual'. See Judgement, *Prosecutor v. Delalić et al.*, A. Ch., *supra* note 8, par. 719 and 821. See also Judgement, *Prosecutor v. Kordić and Čerkez*, A. Ch., *supra* note 27, par. 1064; Judgement, *Prosecutor v. Kvočka, Radić, Žigić and Prcac*, A. Ch., *supra* note 35, par. 681: 'The underlying question is whether the particular offences, the circumstances in which they were committed, and the individuals concerned can truly be considered 'like'. Any given case contains a multitude of variables, ranging from the number and type of crimes committed to the personal circumstances of the individual. Often, too many variables exist to be able to transpose the sentence in one case *mutatis mutandis* to another.' See further Judgment on Sentencing Appeal, *Prosecutor v. Momir Nikolić*, A. Ch., *supra* note 25, par. 38; ICTY, Judgement, *Prosecutor v. Stakić*, A. Ch., *supra* note 14, par. 381; Judgement, *Prosecutor v. Naletilić and Martinović*, A. Ch., *supra* note 46, par. 615; ICTY, Separate and Partially Dissenting Opinion of Judge Meron, *Prosecutor v. Galić*, A. Ch., *supra* note 19, par. 8.

52 Judgement, *Prosecutor v. Furundžija*, A. Ch., *supra* note 14, par. 237; Judgement, *Prosecutor v. Krstić*, A. Ch., *supra* note 14, par. 248.

53 Allison Marston Danner, Constructing a Hierarchy of Crimes in International Law Sentencing, 87 Virginia Law Review Association 2001, p. 441.

54 See, for example, Judgement and Sentence, *Prosecutor v. Serugendo*, T. Ch. I, *supra* note 17, par. 86-87; Judgement and Sentence, *Prosecutor v. Simba*, T. Ch. I, *supra* note 33, par. 437.

55 Judgement, *Prosecutor v. Delalić, Mucić, Delić and Landžo*, A. Ch., *supra* note 9, par. 813, footnote 1390; ICTR, Reasons for Judgment, *Serushago v. Prosecutor*, Case No. ICTR-98-39-A, A. Ch., 6 April 2000, Klip/ Sluiter, ALC-VI-627, par. 30; Judgment in Sentencing Appeals, *Prosecutor v. Tadić*, A. Ch., *supra* note 10, par. 21; Appeal Judgement, *Prosecutor v. Kupreškić, Kupreškić, Kupreškić, Josipović and Šantić* , A. Ch., *supra* note 17, par. 415; Judgement, *Prosecutor v. Jelisić*, A. Ch., *supra* note 14, par. 117; Judgement, *Prosecutor v. Kunarac et al.*, A. Ch., *supra* note 24, par. 347; Judgement, *Prosecutor v. Krstić*, A. Ch., *supra* note 14, par. 262; Judgement, *Prosecutor v. Blaškić*, A. Ch., *supra* note 8, par. 681; Judgement on Sentencing Appeal, *Prosecutor v. Dragan Nikolić*, A. Ch., *supra* note 14, par. 84; ICTY, Judgement, *Prosecutor v. Stakić*, A. Ch., *supra* note 14, par. 398; Judgement, *Prosecutor v. Galić*, A. Ch., *supra* note 19, par. 398; ICTR, Judgement, *Semanza v. Prosecutor*, Case No. ICTR-97-20-A, A. Ch., 20 May 2005, Klip/ Sluiter, ALC-XXII-525, par. 377.

56 Judgment in Sentencing Appeals, *Prosecutor v. Tadić*, A. Ch., *supra* note 10, par. 21, referred to in Judgement, *Prosecutor v. Kunarac et al.*, A. Ch., *supra* note 24, par. 377.

57 See Judgement on Sentencing Appeal, *Prosecutor v. Dragan Nikolić*, A.Ch., *supra* note 14, par. 81.

58 Judgement on Sentencing Appeal, *Prosecutor v. Dragan Nikolić*, A.Ch., *supra* note 14, par. 80, 81: 'It is an inherent element of this principle [of *lex mitior*] that the relevant law must be binding upon the court. [...] The principle of *lex mitior* is thus only

The underlying rationale for such a lack of obligation was given in Kunarac *et al.*, where it was held that expert witness testimony regarding the sentencing practices in the national courts is of little relevance, because such practice 'generally centers upon crimes committed during peacetime'[59] and 'the severity of crimes falling under the jurisdiction of the tribunal is, in general, decidedly greater than that of their national counterpart'.[60] In Krstić, it was concluded that the nature, scope and scale of the offences tried before the international tribunal do not allow for an automatic application of the sentencing practices of the former Yugoslavia.[61]

This explains why ICTR Trial Chambers find somewhat more guidance in the Rwandan Organic Law, which established the *Gacaca* jurisdictions that specifically deal with alleged perpetrators of crimes against humanity.[62] It may also explain why ICTY Trial Chambers merely tend to automatically cite some provisions found in the national criminal code of the former Yugoslavia, only to immediately conclude that such provisions do not bind them. Further, the statute and the rules refer to the practices of the courts of the former Yugoslavia, not to the courts in the entities emerging from the dissolution of the former Yugoslavia,[63] nor to the practices of the courts in each of the constituent republics of the former Yugoslavia.[64] Trial Chambers thus do not need to take such practices into account.

Related to this sentencing factor is the principle of *nulla poena sine lege*. According to Schabas, this sentencing factor was initially included in the tribunals' statutes because of the fear of violating the *nulla poena* principle.[65] However, as outlined by Van Zyl Smit, the attempt to create legal certainty, by inserting this in the statutes of the *ad hoc* tribunals, has proved irrelevant;[66] although Trial Chambers have imposed higher sentences than were possible under the criminal code of the SFRY,[67] violation of the *nulla poena* principle has not been accepted in ICTY case law.

In reply to the criticism that it was not possible for courts in the former Yugoslavia to impose a life sentence – the gravest sentence being the death penalty with the possibility of substituting a fixed term of twenty years imprisonment[68] – it has simply been held that, because a Trial Chamber is bound to apply the law of the tribunal and not that of national jurisdictions, the contention that the *nulla poena* principle would be violated is without merit.[69] It has further been argued that, since the customary penalty for war crimes is the death penalty, any sentence up to and including the remainder of a person's life does not violate the principle of *nulla poena sine lege*.[70]

In Čelebići, the Appeals Chamber referred to ECHR case law, from which it follows that, as long as punishment is foreseeable and accessible, the principle of *nulla poena* is not violated.[71] It that case, it simply found that '[t]here can be no doubt that the accused must have been aware of the fact that the crimes for which

applicable if a law that binds the International Tribunal is subsequently changed to a more favourable law by which the International Tribunal is obliged to abide'. See also Judgement, *Prosecutor v. Blaškić*, A. Ch., *supra* note 8, par. 681, footnote 1433.

59 Judgement, *Prosecutor v. Kunarac et al.*, A. Ch., *supra* note 24, par. 402.

60 Judgement, *Prosecutor v. Kunarac et al.*, A. Ch., *supra* note 24, par. 402. See also Judgement, *Prosecutor v. Kordić and Čerkez,* A. Ch., *supra* note 27, par. 1085; Judgement on Sentencing Appeal, *Prosecutor v. Dragan Nikolić,* A. Ch., *supra* note 14, par. 69. Schabas refers to a study by Janković and Vasiljević, in which they would have concluded that the number of relevant prosecutions before national courts is 'far too small to allow for meaningful inferences regarding sentencing practices.' William A. Schabas, Sentencing by International Tribunals: A Human Rights Approach, 7 Duke Journal of Comparative and International Law 1997, p. 477.

61 Judgement, *Prosecutor v. Krstić*, A. Ch., *supra* note 14, par. 260; Judgement, *Prosecutor v. Blaškić*, A. Ch., *supra* note 8, par. 682.

62 Sentencing Judgement, *Prosecutor v. Nzabirinda*, T. Ch. II, *supra* note 1, par. 104.

63 Judgement, *Prosecutor v. Jelisić,* A. Ch., *supra* note 14, par. 114.

64 *Ibid.*, par. 114, 115; Judgement, *Prosecutor v. Krstić*, A. Ch., *supra* note 14, par. 261; Judgement on Sentencing Appeal, *Prosecutor v. Dragan Nikolić*, A. Ch., *supra* note 14, par. 74.

65 William A. Schabas, Sentencing by International Tribunals: A Human Rights Approach, 7 Duke Journal of Comparative and International Law 1997, p. 468.

66 Dirk van Zyl Smit, Punishment and Human Rights in International Criminal Justice, 2 Human Rights Law Review 2002, p. 7.

67 *Ibid.*, p. 7 and 8.

68 ICTY, Judgement, *Prosecutor v. Stakić*, Case No. IT-97-24-T, T. Ch. II, 31 July 2003, Klip/ Sluiter, ALC-XIV-545, par. 889.

69 ICTY, Judgement, *Prosecutor v. Stakić*, A. Ch., *supra* note 14, par. 398.

70 Allison Marston Danner, Constructing a Hierarchy of Crimes in International Law Sentencing, 87 Virginia Law Review Association 2001, p. 433.

71 Judgement, *Prosecutor v. Delalić, Mucić, Delić and Landžo*, A. Ch., *supra* note 9, par. 817, referring in footnote 1400 to ECHR, *SW v. The United Kingdom* and *CR v. The United Kingdom*, Judgement of 22 November 1995, par. 34-36 and 43.

they were indicted are the most serious violations of international humanitarian law, punishable by the most severe penalties.'[72]

2.4 Aggravating circumstances

The Statute and rules of the *ad hoc* tribunals do not exhaustively list the variables that may be taken into account in mitigation or aggravation of a sentence. Such a determination is left to the Trial Chambers' discretion.[73] If an aggravated circumstance is present and is not also an element of the crime, it may be considered in aggravation of the sentence.[74] Aggravating circumstances must be proved by the prosecution beyond reasonable doubt.[75] Further, the absence of a mitigating factor cannot serve as an aggravating factor.[76] Although it possesses a large margin of discretion in accepting variables under this factor, a Trial Chamber does not have complete freedom; it must provide convincing reasons for its choice of variables.[77]

Aggravating circumstances recognized in the case law of the *ad hoc* tribunals include the following:

(i) The accused's position of leadership, his status, level in the command structure, or role in the broader conflict.[78] In Babić, it was, however, noted that a high rank in the military or political field does not, in itself, merit a harsher sentence. However, a person who *abuses or wrongly exercises power* would deserve a harsher sentence.[79]

(ii) Duration of the period in which the crime was committed.[80]

(iii) Active and direct criminal participation combined with a high level position in the command structure[81] and active participation of a superior in the criminal acts of subordinates.[82]

---

72 Judgement, *Prosecutor v. Delalić, Mucić, Delić and Landžo*, A. Ch., *supra* note 9 par. 817; Appeal Judgement, *Prosecutor v. Kupreškić, Kupreškić, Kupreškić, Josipović and Šantić* , A. Ch., *supra* note 17, par. 423, 424; Judgement, *Prosecutor v. Blaškić*, A. Ch., *supra* note 8, par. 681.

73 Judgement, *Prosecutor v. Delalić, Mucić, Delić and Landžo*, A. Ch., *supra* note 9 par. 780; Judgement, *Prosecutor v. Blaškić*, A. Ch., *supra* note 8, par. 685.

74 Judgement, *Prosecutor v. Blaškić*, A. Ch., *supra* note 8, par. 683; Judgement, *Prosecutor v. Mitar Vasiljević*, A. Ch., *supra* note 25, par. 172-173; ICTY, Sentencing Judgement, *Prosecutor v. Todorović*, Case No. IT-95-9/1-S, T. Ch. I, 31 July 2001, Klip/ Sluiter, ALC-VII-773, par. 57; Judgement on Sentencing Appeal, *Prosecutor v. Dragan Nikolić*, A. Ch., *supra* note 14, par. 27; Judgement, *Prosecutor v. Galić*, A. Ch., *supra* note 19, par. 408; Sentencing Judgement, *Prosecutor v. Nzabirinda*, T. Ch. II, *supra* note 1, par. 60.

75 Judgement, *Prosecutor v. Blaškić*, A. Ch., *supra* note 8, par. 686; Judgement, *Prosecutor v. Delalić, Mucić, Delić and Landžo*, A. Ch., *supra* note 9, par. 763; Sentencing Judgement, *Prosecutor v. Nzabirinda*, T. Ch. II, *supra* note 1, par. 53.

76 Sentencing Judgement, *Prosecutor v. Plavsić*, T. Ch. III, *supra* note 28, par. 64.

77 ICTY, Judgement, *Prosecutor v. Stakić*, A. Ch., *supra* note 14, par. 414.

78 ICTY, Sentencing Judgement, *Prosecutor v. Jokić*, Case No. IT-01-42/1-S, T. Ch. I, 18 March 2004, Klip/ Sluiter, ALC-XIX-779, par. 61-62; Judgment in Sentencing Appeals, *Prosecutor v. Tadić*, A. Ch., *supra* note 10, par. 55-56; Judgement, *Prosecutor v. Kordić and Čerkez*, A. Ch., *supra* note 27, par. 1088; ICTY, Judgement on Sentencing Appeal, *Prosecutor v. Babić*, Case No. IT-03-72-A, A. Ch., 18 July 2005, to be published in volume XXVII, par. 79; ICTY, Judgement, *Prosecutor v. Brđanin*, Case No. IT-99-36-T, T. Ch. II, 1 September 2004, par. 1099; Judgement, *Prosecutor v. Galić*, A. Ch., *supra* note 19, par. 412; ICTR, Judgement, *Prosecutor v. Seromba*, Case No. ICTR-2001-66-T, T. Ch. III, 13 December 2006, in this volume, p. 523, par. 390; ICTR, Judgement and Sentence, *Prosecutor v. Simba*, Case No. ICTR-01-76-T, T. Ch. I, 13 December 2005, Klip/ Sluiter, ALC-XXIV-325, par. 438; Judgement and Sentence, *Prosecutor v. Semanza*, T. Ch. III, *supra* note 14, par. 571.

79 Judgement on Sentencing Appeal, *Prosecutor v. Babić*, A.Ch., *supra* note 78, par. 80; ICTY, Judgement, *Prosecutor v. Krstić*, Case No. IT-98-33-T, T. Ch. I, 2 August 2001, Klip/ Sluiter, ALC-VII-575, par. 709; ICTR, Judgment (Reasons), *Prosecutor v. Kayishema and Ruzindana*, Case No. ICTR-95-1-A, A. Ch., 1 June 2001, Klip/ Sluiter, ALC-X-495, par. 358-359; ICTR, Judgement, *Prosecutor v. Elizaphan Ntakirutimana and Ntakirutimana*, Cases Nos. ICTR-96-10-A and ICTR-96-17-A, A. Ch., 13 December 2004, Klip/ Sluiter, ALC-XVIII-755, par. 563; ICTY, Judgement, *Prosecutor v. Stakić*, A. Ch., *supra* note 14, par. 411; ICTR, Judgement, *Prosecutor v. Ntagerura, Bagambiki and Imanishimwe*, A. Ch., *supra* note 48, par. 818; Judgement and Sentence, *Prosecutor v. Serugendo*, T. Ch. I, *supra* note 17, par. 48; Sentencing Judgement, *Prosecutor v. Nzabirinda*, T. Ch. II, *supra* note 1, par. 62; Judgement and Sentence, *Prosecutor v. Muhimana*, T. Ch. III, *supra* note 4, par. 604; Judgement and Sentence, *Prosecutor v. Ndindabahizi*, T. Ch. I, *supra* note 20, par. 508; ICTR, Judgement and Sentence, *Prosecutor v. Nahimana, Barayagwiza and Ngeze*, Case No. ICTR-99-52-T, T. Ch. I, 3 December 2003, Klip/ Sluiter, ALC-XVII-221, par. 1099; ICTR, Judgement and Sentence, *Prosecutor v. Elizaphan Ntakirutimana and Ntakirutimana*, Cases No. ICTR-96-10 and ICTR-96-17-T, T. Ch. I, 21 February 2003, Klip/ Sluiter, ALC-XII-383, par. 900.

80 Judgement, *Prosecutor v. Kunarac et al.*, A. Ch., *supra* note 24, par. 356 and 382; Sentencing Judgement, *Prosecutor v. Todorović*, *supra* note 74, par. 65; Judgement and Sentence, *Prosecutor v. Niyitegeka*, T. Ch. I, *supra* note 14, par. 499.

81 Judgement, *Prosecutor v. Blaškić*, A. Ch., *supra* note 8, par. 686, citing Judgement, *Prosecutor v. Krstić*, T. Ch. I, A.Ch., *supra* note 79, par. 708.

82 Judgement, *Prosecutor v. Blaškić*, A. Ch., *supra* note 8, par. 686; Judgement, *Prosecutor v. Delalić, Mucić, Delić and Landžo*, A. Ch., *supra* note 9 par. 736-737.

(iv) The zealous, particularly violent or cruel, willing or enthusiastic participation in the crime.[83]
(v) Premeditation and motive.[84]
(vi) The sexual, violent, and humiliating nature of the acts and the vulnerability of the victims.[85]
(vii) The victims' youthful or elderly age, the number of victims and the effect of the crimes on the victims.[86]
(viii) The behaviour of the accused during trial proceedings, as relevant for a Trial Chamber to determine (lack of) remorse and compassion.[87]
(ix) The threatening of witnesses.[88]
(x) The professional background of the accused.[89]

Not considered as aggravating circumstances are the failure on the part of the accused to give testimony,[90] a failure to enter a guilty plea,[91] or the late timing of a guilty plea.[92]

2.5 Mitigating circumstances

Most of the remarks made above in connection with aggravating circumstances also apply to mitigating circumstances. As with aggravating circumstances, discretion is accorded to Trial Chambers in determining what may constitute mitigating circumstances and the weight to be attached to them.[93] The only two mitigating factors expressly mentioned in the legal framework of the *ad hoc* tribunals are 'substantial co-

---

83 Judgement, *Prosecutor v. Blaškić*, A. Ch., *supra* note 8, par. 686, citing Judgement, *Prosecutor v. Jelisić*, A. Ch., *supra* note 14, par. 86; Judgement, *Prosecutor v. Elizaphan Ntakirutimana and Ntakirutimana*, A. Ch., *supra* note 79, par. 351. See also Judgement on Sentencing Appeal, *Prosecutor v. Dragan Nikolić*, A. Ch., *supra* note 14, par. 30; Judgement and Sentence, *Prosecutor v. Muhimana*, T. Ch. III, *supra* note 4, par. 610; ICTR, Judgement and Sentence, *Prosecutor v. Niyitegeka*, T. Ch. I, *supra* note 14, par. 499; ICTR, Judgement, *Prosecutor v. Kayishema and Ruzindana*, Case No. ICTR-95-1-T, T. Ch. II, 21 May 1999, par. 18.

84 Judgement, *Prosecutor v. Blaškić*, A. Ch., *supra* note 8, par. 686, citing Judgement, *Prosecutor v. Krstić*, T. Ch. I, A. Ch., *supra* note 79, par. 711-712; Judgement, *Prosecutor v. Krstić*, A. Ch., *supra* note 14, par. 258. See also Judgment (Reasons), *Prosecutor v. Kayishema and Ruzindana*, A. Ch., *supra* note 79, par. 161, cited in ICTR, Judgment, *Prosecutor v. Niyitegeka*, Case No. ICTR-96-14-A, A. Ch., 9 July 2004, par. 52.

85 Judgement, *Prosecutor v. Blaškić*, A. Ch., *supra* note 8, par. 686, citing Judgement, *Prosecutor v. Kunarac, Kovač and Vuković*, T. Ch. II, *supra* note 30, par. 867; Judgement, *Prosecutor v. Kunarac et al.*, A. Ch., *supra* note 24, par. 353; Judgement and Sentence, *Prosecutor v. Muhimana*, T. Ch. III, *supra* note 4, par. 613.

86 Judgement, *Prosecutor v. Blaškić*, A. Ch., *supra* note 8, par. 686, citing Judgement, *Prosecutor v. Kunarac, Kovač and Vuković*, T. Ch. II, *supra* note 30, par. 864, 866; Judgement, *Prosecutor v. Kunarac et al.*, A. Ch., *supra* note 24, par. 355. See also Judgement, *Prosecutor v. Kordić and Čerkez*, A. Ch., *supra* note 27, par. 1088; Judgment on Sentencing Appeal, *Prosecutor v. Momir Nikolić*, A. Ch., *supra* note 25, par. 66; ICTR, Judgement and Sentence, *Prosecutor v. Simba*, Case No. ICTR-01-76-T, 13 December 2005, par. 440; Judgement and Sentence, *Prosecutor v. Muhimana*, T. Ch. III, *supra* note 4, par. 87; Judgement and Sentence, *Prosecutor v. Ndindabahizi*, T. Ch. I, *supra* note 20, par. 508; Judgement and Sentence, *Prosecutor v. Niyitegeka*, T. Ch. I, *supra* note 14, par. 499; Judgement and Sentence, *Prosecutor v. Semanza*, T. Ch. III, *supra* note 14, par. 571.

87 Judgement, *Prosecutor v. Blaškić*, A. Ch., *supra* note 8, par. 686, citing Judgement, *Prosecutor v. Delalić, Mucić, Delić and Landžo*, A. Ch., *supra* note 9 par 788; Judgement and Sentence, *Prosecutor v. Rutaganira*, T. Ch. III, *supra* note 17, par. 143.

88 Judgement, *Prosecutor v. Delalić, Mucić, Delić and Landžo*, A. Ch., *supra* note 9 par. 789.

89 Judgement, *Prosecutor v. Kvočka, Radić, Žigić and Prcac*, A. Ch., *supra* note 35, par. 678. In Ntakirutimana, the Trial Chamber held that 'the Accused simply abandoned the Tutsi patients. This behaviour is not in conformity with the general picture painted by the Defence of the Accused as a medical doctor who cared for his patients': Judgement and Sentence, *Prosecutor v. Elizaphan Ntakirutimana and Ntakirutimana*, *supra* note 79, par. 153.

90 Judgement, *Prosecutor v. Delalić, Mucić, Delić and Landžo*, A. Ch., *supra* note 9 par. 781, 783; Judgement, *Prosecutor v. Blaškić*, A. Ch., *supra* note 8, par. 687, citing Sentencing Judgement, *Prosecutor v. Plavsić*, T. Ch. III, *supra* note 28, par. 64; Judgment on Sentencing Appeal, *Prosecutor v. Momir Nikolić*, A. Ch., *supra* note 25, par. 126.

91 Judgement, *Prosecutor v. Blaškić*, A. Ch., *supra* note 8, par. 714.

92 Judgment on Sentencing Appeal, *Prosecutor v. Momir Nikolić* A. Ch., *supra* note 25, par. 126; ICTY, Sentencing Judgement, *Prosecutor v. Momir Nikolić*, Case No. IT-02-60/1-S, T. Ch. I, 2 December 2003, par. 234; Sentencing Judgement, *Prosecutor v. Predrag Banović*, T. Ch. III, *supra* note 28, par. 71.

93 Judgement, *Kambanda v. Prosecutor*, A. Ch., *supra* note 14, par. 124, ICTR, Judgement, *Musema v. Prosecutor*, Case No. ICTR-96-13-A, A. Ch., 16 November 2001, Klip/ Sluiter, ALC-X-863, par. 396; Judgement on Sentencing Appeal, *Prosecutor v. Nikolić* A. Ch., *supra* note 14, par. 27; Judgement, *Prosecutor v. Krstić*, A. Ch., *supra* note 14, par. 265; Judgement, *Prosecutor v. Blaškić*, A. Ch., *supra* note 8, par. 696; Judgement, *Prosecutor v. Kordić and Čerkez*, A. Ch., *supra* note 27, par. 1053; Judgement, *Prosecutor v. Jelisić*, A. Ch., *supra* note 14, par. 131; Judgement, *Prosecutor v. Kvočka, Radić, Žigić and Prcac*, A. Ch., *supra* note 35, par. 715; Judgement on Sentencing Appeal, *Prosecutor v. Jokić*, A. Ch., *supra* note 40, par. 57; Judgment on Sentencing Appeal, *Prosecutor v. Momir Nikolić*, A. Ch., *supra* note 25, par. 91; ICTY, Judgement on Sentencing Appeal, *Prosecutor v. Bralo*, Case No. IT-95-17-A, A. Ch., 2 April 2007, par. 83.

operation with the Prosecutor by the convicted person before or after conviction'[94] and the fact that an accused acted pursuant to a superior order.[95] Although Article 24, paragraph 2, of the ICTY statute and Rule 101 paragraph B sub ii oblige Trial Chambers to take into account mitigating circumstances,[96] they are not obliged to search for mitigating circumstances themselves, if the defence fails to adduce these.[97]

Further, whereas the prosecution is required to prove aggravating circumstances beyond reasonable doubt, the defence needs only to prove mitigating circumstances on the balance of probabilities.[98] A Trial Chamber is not required to set out in detail each mitigating factor it relied upon, or to explain exactly under what heading a specific mitigating variable is taken into consideration, even if such specific circumstance is mentioned in one of the Parties' submissions.[99]

Moreover, it is not incumbent upon a Trial Chamber to specify the reduction of the term of imprisonment to be accorded to each mitigating factor.[100] In Niyitegeka, the ICTR Appeals Chamber held that proof of mitigating circumstances does not automatically entitle an accused to a reduction of sentence; instead, it 'simply requires the Trial Chamber to consider such mitigating circumstances in its final determination'.[101] In Musema, it indicated that, even if a cause for mitigation is found, a Trial Chamber can still impose a life sentence, if the gravity of the offence requires the imposition of the maximum sentence.[102] On appeal, any modification of sentence needs to be assessed in light of all the circumstances of the case and 'cannot be limited to a simple mathematical diminuation of the sentence otherwise to be imposed'.[103]

Mitigating circumstances recognized in the case law of the a*d hoc* tribunals include the following:

(i) The accused's co-operation with the prosecution.[104]

---

94 Rule 101(B).

95 Article 7, paragraph 2, ICTY Statute; Article 6, paragraph 2, ICTR Statute.

96 See also Reasons for Judgment, *Serushago v. Prosecutor*, A. Ch., *supra* note 55, par. 22; Judgement, *Prosecutor v. Kordić and Čerkez*, A. Ch., *supra* note 27, par. 1051; Judgement, *Prosecutor v. Musema*, A. Ch., *supra* note 93, par. 395.

97 Judgement, *Prosecutor v. Kvočka, Radić, Žigić and Prcac*, A. Ch., *supra* note 35, par. 674; Appeal Judgement, *Prosecutor v. Kupreškić, Kupreškić, Kupreškić, Josipović and Šantić* , A. Ch., *supra* note 17, par. 414.

98 Judgement, *Prosecutor v. Blaškić*, A. Ch., *supra* note 8, par. 687; Judgement, *Prosecutor v. Kunarac, Kovač and Vuković*, T. Ch. II, *supra* note 30, par. 847; Judgement on Sentencing Appeal, *Prosecutor v. Babić*, A.Ch., *supra* note 78, par. 65; Judgement, *Prosecutor v. Seromba*, T. Ch. III, *supra* note 78, par. 388 and 394.

99 Appeal Judgement, *Prosecutor v. Kupreškić, Kupreškić, Kupreškić, Josipović and Šantić* , A. Ch., *supra* note 17, par. 430. The Trial Chamber did not expressly list each factor it considered in mitigation of Šantić's sentence. According to the Appeals Chamber, this alone did 'not support the contention that the factors pointed out were neither evaluated nor weighed'. It held that '[a] reading of the Trial Judgement as a whole supports a finding that the Trial Chamber considered the circumstances of his case as a whole'. See also Judgement, *Prosecutor v. Kordić and Čerkez*, A. Ch., *supra* note 27, par. 1051; Judgement on Sentencing Appeal, *Prosecutor v. Bralo*, A. Ch., *supra* note 93, par. 29; Judgement, *Prosecutor v. Musema*, A. Ch., *supra* note 93, par. 395; Judgement and Sentence, *Prosecutor v. Ntagerura, Bagambiki and Imanishimwe*, T. Ch. III, *supra* note 27, par. 436.

100 Judgement, *Prosecutor v. Delalić, Mucić, Delić and Landžo,* A. Ch., *supra* note 9 par. 841.

101 Judgment, *Prosecutor v. Niyitegeka*, A. Ch., *supra* note 83, par. 267; Judgement on Sentencing Appeal, *Prosecutor v. Babic*, A. Ch., *supra* note 78, par. 44; Judgement on Sentencing Appeal, *Prosecutor v. Bralo*, A. Ch., *supra* note 93, par. 83.

102 Judgement, *Prosecutor v. Musema*, A. Ch., *supra* note 93, par. 396; Judgement, *Kambanda v. Prosecutor*, A. Ch., *supra* note 14, par. 126. In *Stakić*, the Appeals Chamber found that it could not conclude, solely on the basis of the fact that a life sentence was imposed, that the Trial Chamber failed to consider mitigating factors. See ICTY, Judgement, *Prosecutor v. Stakić*, A. Ch., *supra* note 14, par. 407.

103 Judgement on Sentencing Appeal, *Prosecutor v. Bralo*, A. Ch., *supra* note 93, par. 85.

104 Rule 101(B)(ii). See also Sentencing Judgement, *Prosecutor v. Jokić*, T. Ch. I, *supra* note 78, par. 95-96; Sentencing Judgement, *Prosecutor v. Todorović*, *supra* note 74, par. 88; Judgement, *Prosecutor v. Jelisić*, A. Ch., *supra* note 14, par. 124. According to the Bralo Appeals Chamber, non-substantial co-operation also counts as a mitigating circumstance; Judgement on Sentencing Appeal, *Prosecutor v. Bralo*, A. Ch., *supra* note 93, par. 51. Further, a distinction is made between co-operation before and after conviction; See Appeal Judgement, *Prosecutor v. Kupreškić, Kupreškić, Kupreškić, Josipović and Šantić* , A. Ch., *supra* note 17, par. 463. According to the Appeals Chamber, with respect to co-operation with the Prosecution after conviction, a cautious approach is required, since appellate proceedings are not intended to permit a *de novo* review of sentence. It stated, however, that, in light of Rule 101(B)(ii), 'in appropriate cases, co-operation between conviction and appeal could be a factor that the Appeals Chamber too may consider in order to reduce sentence'; Sentencing Judgement, *Prosecutor v. Jokić*, T. Ch. I, *supra* note 78, par. 95; Judgement on Sentencing Appeal, *Prosecutor v. Jokić*, A. Ch., *supra* note 40, par. 88; Judgement, *Prosecutor v. Krnojelac*, A. Ch., *supra* note 21, par. 261, 262; Judgement on Sentencing Appeal, *Prosecutor v. Dragan Nikolić*, A. Ch., *supra* note 14, par. 62; Judgement on Sentencing Appeal, *Prosecutor v. Babić*, A.Ch., *supra* note 78, par. 70; ICTR, Judgement and Sentence, *Prosecutor v. Serugendo*, Case No. ICTR-2005-84-I, T. Ch. I, 12 June 206, par. 62; Judgement and Sentence, *Prosecutor v. Ruggiu*, T. Ch. I, *supra* note 4, par. 56-58; ICTR, Sentence, *Prosecutor v. Serushago*, Case No. ICTR-98-39-5, T. Ch. I, 5 February 1999, Klip/ Sluiter, ALC-II-823, par. 31-33.

(ii) A guilty plea, or an admission of guilt.[105]
(iii) An expression of remorse.[106]
(iv) Voluntary surrender.[107]
(v) The good character of the convicted person and lack of prior criminal convictions.[108]
(vi) The accused's behaviour while in UN detention.[109]
(vii) The accused's family situation and other personal circumstances.[110]
(viii) The behaviour and character of the accused subsequent to the conflict.[111]
(ix) Duress.[112]
(x) Indirect participation.[113]

---

105 Judgement, *Prosecutor v. Blaškić*, A. Ch., *supra* note 8, par. 696, citing Judgement, *Prosecutor v. Jelisić*, A. Ch., *supra* note 14, par. 122; Sentencing Judgement, *Prosecutor v. Jokić*, T. Ch. I, *supra* note 78, par. 76; Appeal Judgement, *Prosecutor v. Kupreškić, Kupreškić, Kupreškić, Josipović and Šantić* , A. Ch., *supra* note 17, par. 464; Judgement on Sentencing Appeal, *Prosecutor v. Dragan Nikolić*, A. Ch., *supra* note 14, par. 49; Judgement on Sentencing Appeal, *Prosecutor v. Babić*, A. Ch., *supra* note 78, par. 68; Judgment on Sentencing Appeal, *Prosecutor v. Nikolić*, A. Ch., *supra* note 25, par. 83; Judgement and Sentence, *Prosecutor v. Ruggiu*, T. Ch. I, *supra* note 4, par. 53-55; Judgement and Sentence, *Prosecutor v. Serugendo*, T. Ch. I, *supra* note 17, par. 60; Sentence, *Prosecutor v. Serushago*, T. Ch. I, *supra* note 104, par. 35.

106 Judgement, *Prosecutor v. Blaskic*, A. Ch., *supra* note 8, par. 696, citing Sentencing Judgement, *Prosecutor v. Jokić*, T. Ch. I, *supra* note 78, par. 89; ICTY, Sentencing Judgement, *Prosecutor v. Erdemović*, Case No. IT-96-22-T*bis*, T. Ch. II*ter*, 5 March 1998, Klip/ Sluiter, ALC-I-657, par. 16(iii). For remorse to be accepted as a mitigating factor, the Judges must believe it to be sincere; see Judgement, *Prosecutor v. Jelisić*, A. Ch., *supra* note 14, par. 103; Judgement, *Prosecutor v. Mitar Vasiljević*, A. Ch., *supra* note 25, par. 177; Judgement on Sentencing Appeal, *Prosecutor v. Dragan Nikolić*, A. Ch., *supra* note 14, par. 59; *Judgement, Prosecutor v. Kvočka, Radić, Žigić and Prcac*, A. Ch., *supra* note 35, par. 715; Judgement on Sentencing Appeal, *Prosecutor v. Jokić*, A. Ch., *supra* note 40, par. 52; Judgement on Sentencing Appeal, *Prosecutor v. Babić*, A. Ch., *supra* note 78, par. 72; Judgement and Sentence, *Prosecutor v. Ruggiu*, T. Ch. I, *supra* note 4, par. 69-72; Judgement and Sentence, *Prosecutor v. Serugendo*, T. Ch. I, *supra* note 17, par. 106; ICTR, Judgement and Sentence, *Prosecutor v. Musema*, Case No. ICTR-96-13-T, T. Ch. I, 27 January 2000, Klip/ Sluiter, ALC-VI-469, par. 1006-1007; Sentence, *Prosecutor v. Serushago*, T. Ch. I, *supra* note 104, par. 40-41.

107 Judgement, *Prosecutor v. Blaškić*, A. Ch., *supra* note 8, par. 696, citing Sentencing Judgement, *Prosecutor v. Jokić*, T. Ch. I, *supra* note 78, par. 73. See also *Blaškić* Appeal Judgement par. 701; Judgement, *Prosecutor v. Kordić and Čerkez*, A. Ch., *supra* note 27, par. 1090; Judgement, *Prosecutor v. Kordić and Čerkez*, A. Ch., *supra* note 27, par. 75. Although mere facilitation of a transfer process cannot be considered voluntary surrender, such facilitation may be considered in mitigation of sentence. See Judgement, *Prosecutor v. Naletilić and Martinović*, A. Ch., *supra* note 46, par. 600; Judgement, *Prosecutor v. Seromba*, T. Ch. III, *supra* note 78, par. 398; Sentence, *Prosecutor v. Serushago*, T. Ch. I, *supra* note 104, par. 34.

108 Judgement, *Prosecutor v. Blaškić*, A. Ch., *supra* note 8, par. 696, citing Sentencing Judgement, *Prosecutor v. Erdemović*, T. Ch. IIter, *supra* note 106, par. 16(i); Appeal Judgement, *Prosecutor v. Kupreškić, Kupreškić, Kupreškić, Josipović and Šantić* , A. Ch., *supra* note 17, par. 459. See also Judgement, *Prosecutor v. Krnojelac*, A. Ch., *supra* note 21, par. 251; Judgement, *Prosecutor v. Blaškić*, A. Ch., *supra* note 8, par. 706; Judgement, *Prosecutor v. Kordić and Čerkez*, A. Ch., *supra* note 27, par. 1090; Judgement and Sentence, *Prosecutor v. Ruggiu*, T. Ch. I, *supra* note 4, par. 59-60; Judgement and Sentence, *Prosecutor v. Elizaphan Ntakirutimana and Ntakirutimana*, T. Ch. I, *supra* note 79, par. 895.

109 Judgement, *Prosecutor v. Blaškić*, A. Ch., *supra* note 8, par. 696, citing ICTY, Sentencing Judgement, *Prosecutor v. Jokić*, T. Ch. I, *supra* note 78, par. 100; Sentencing Judgement, *Prosecutor v. Nikolić*, T. Ch. I, *supra* note 92, par. 268. See, also, Judgement, *Prosecutor v. Kordić and Čerkez*, A. Ch., *supra* note 27, par. 1090; Judgement and Sentence, *Prosecutor v. Rutaganira*, T. Ch. III, *supra* note 17, par. 131.

110 Judgement, *Prosecutor v. Blaškić*, A. Ch., *supra* note 8, par. 696; Judgement, *Prosecutor v. Kunarac et al.*, A. Ch., *supra* note 24, par. 362, 408. In Erdemović, the circumstance that the accused had a young child was considered a mitigating factor; Sentencing Judgement, *Prosecutor v. Erdemović*, T. Ch. IIter, *supra* note 106, par. 16. In Blaškić, the accused, being a father of two young children, a professional soldier of conviction and a man of duty and professionalism, were all taken into account; Judgement, *Prosecutor v. Blaškić*, A. Ch., *supra* note 8, par. 708. See further Judgement, *Prosecutor v. Kordić and Čerkez*, A. Ch., *supra* note 27, par. 1090; Judgement and Sentence, *Prosecutor v. Elizaphan Ntakirutimana and Ntakirutimana*, T. Ch. I, *supra* note 79, par. 896, Sentence, *Prosecutor v. Serushago*, T. Ch. I, *supra* note 104, par. 39.

111 Judgement, *Prosecutor v. Blaškić*, A. Ch., *supra* note 8, par. 696, citing Sentencing Judgement, *Prosecutor v. Jokić*, T. Ch. I, *supra* note 78, par. 90, 91 and 103. See also Judgement, *Prosecutor v. Krnojelac*, A. Ch., *supra* note 21, par. 251; Judgement on Sentencing Appeal, *Prosecutor v. Babić*, A. Ch., *supra* note 78, par. 55; Judgement on Sentencing Appeal, *Prosecutor v. Jokić*, A. Ch., *supra* note 40, par. 51. The Plavsić Trial Chamber accorded significant weight to Plavsić's post-conflict conduct as a mitigating factor – her contribution to the advancement of the Dayton Agreement and her attempt to remove obstructive officials from office – and concluded that 'she made a considerable contribution to peace in the region'; see Sentencing Judgement, *Prosecutor v. Plavsić*, T. Ch. III, *supra* note 28, par. 85-93. See also Judgement on Sentencing Appeal, *Prosecutor v. Bralo*, A. Ch., *supra* note 93, par. 72.

112 Judgement, *Prosecutor v. Blaškić*, A. Ch., *supra* note 8, par. 696, citing Sentencing Judgement, *Prosecutor v. Erdemović*, T. Ch. IIter, *supra* note 106, par. 17.

113 Judgement, *Prosecutor v. Blaškić*, A. Ch., *supra* note 8, par. 696; Judgement, *Prosecutor v. Krstić*, A. Ch., *supra* note 14, par. 273.

(xi) Diminished mental responsibility.[114]
(xii) Age of the convicted person.[115]
(xiii) Assistance to other victims or refugees.[116]
(xiv) Poor health.[117]
(xv) (Particularly) long detainment of the accused, pending a final outcome in his case.[118]
(xvi) The criminal responsibility of the accused being limited to a relatively short duration.[119]
(xvii) A protected witness status and its impact on the family of the accused.[120]
(xviii) The lack of genocidal intent on behalf of an aider and abettor to genocide.[121]

The absence of serious consequences for the victims,[122] the 'chaotic context' of a conflict,[123] voluntary intoxication,[124] and lack of discriminatory behavior,[125] are not considered in mitigation.

3. Sentencing factors and rationales

As argued by Bagarić and Morss, in order to justify the application of specific variables in sentencing, it is necessary to identify the sentencing aims that are being invoked and to show how the variables serve the aim

[114] Judgement, *Prosecutor v. Blaškić*, A. Ch., *supra* note 8, par. 696, citing Judgement, *Prosecutor v. Delalić, Mucić, Delić and Landžo*, A. Ch., *supra* note 9 par. 590. See also par. 841 where it is stated that '[a]lthough the Trial Chamber accepted evidence that Landžo suffered from a personality disorder, it considered that, despite this, he was able to control his actions, therefore rejecting any "defence" of diminished responsibility. The Chamber nevertheless did take into account Landžo's personality traits'.

[115] Judgement, *Prosecutor v. Blaškić*, A. Ch., *supra* note 8, par. 696, citing Sentencing Judgement, *Prosecutor v. Jokić*, T. Ch. I, *supra* note 78, par. 100. See, also, Judgement, *Prosecutor v. Jelisić*, A. Ch., *supra* note 14, par. 129. See, in connection to 'advanced age', Judgement, *Prosecutor v. Krnojelac*, A. Ch., *supra* note 21, par. 251; Judgement, *Prosecutor v. Kvočka, Radić, Žigić and Prcac*, A. Ch., *supra* note 35, par. 720. See, further, Judgement on Sentencing Appeal, *Prosecutor v. Jokić*, A. Ch., *supra* note 40, par. 49; Judgement and Sentence, *Prosecutor v. Elizaphan Ntakirutimana and Ntakirutimana*, T. Ch. I, *supra* note 79, par. 898; Judgement and Sentence, *Prosecutor v. Rutaganira*, T. Ch. III, *supra* note 17, par. 136; Judgement, *Prosecutor v. Seromba*, T. Ch. III, *supra* note 78, par. 399; ; Sentence, *Prosecutor v. Serushago*, T. Ch. I, *supra* note 104, par. 39.

[116] Judgement, *Prosecutor v. Blaškić*, A. Ch., *supra* note 8, par. 696, citing ICTY, Sentencing Judgement, *Prosecutor v. Sikirica, Došen and Kolundžija*, Case No. IT-95-8-S, T. Ch. III, 13 November 2001, Klip/ Sluiter, ALC-VIII-1033, par. 195, 229. See also Judgement, *Prosecutor v. Delalić, Mucić, Delić and Landžo*, A. Ch., *supra* note 9 par. 775, 776; Judgement, *Prosecutor v. Kvočka, Radić, Žigić and Prcac*, A. Ch., *supra* note 35, par. 693; Judgement and Sentence, *Prosecutor v. Ruggiu*, T. Ch. I, *supra* note 4, par. 73-74; Judgement and Sentence, *Prosecutor v. Elizaphan Ntakirutimana and Ntakirutimana*, T. Ch. I, *supra* note 79, par. 909; Judgement and Sentence, *Prosecutor v. Niyitegeka*, T. Ch. I, *supra* note 14, par. 494; Sentence, *Prosecutor v. Serushago*, T. Ch. I, *supra* note 104, par. 38.

[117] Judgement, *Prosecutor v. Blaškić*, A. Ch., *supra* note 8, par. 696; Judgement, *Prosecutor v. Krstić*, A. Ch., *supra* note 14, par. 271; ICTY, Judgement, *Prosecutor v. Milan Simić et al.*, Case No. IT-95-9-T, T. Ch. II, 17 October 2003, par. 98; Judgement, *Prosecutor v. Kvočka, Radić, Žigić and Prcac*, A. Ch., *supra* note 35, par. 720; Judgement, *Prosecutor v. Galić*, A. Ch., *supra* note 19, par. 436; Judgement and Sentence, *Prosecutor v. Elizaphan Ntakirutimana and Ntakirutimana*, T. Ch. I, *supra* note 79, par. 898; Judgement and Sentence, *Prosecutor v. Serugendo*, T. Ch. I, *supra* note 17, par. 74; Judgement and Sentence, *Prosecutor v. Rutaganira*, T. Ch. III, *supra* note 17, par. 136.

[118] Judgement, *Prosecutor v. Blaškić*, A. Ch., *supra* note 8, par. 728. The Appeals Chamber held that this factor can be of specific importance in the case of voluntary surrender and stated further that 'in this case, the time spent in custody before and during the proceedings is a factor in mitigation of sentence. This is because in this case the International Tribunal has been hampered by the complexity of these proceedings, and the Appeals Chamber has had to deal with the sheer volume of additional material submitted on appeal [...] which was beyond the parties' control'.

[119] Judgement, *Prosecutor v. Kordić and Čerkez*, A. Ch., *supra* note 27, par. 1090.

[120] Judgement on Sentencing Appeal, *Prosecutor v. Babić* , A. Ch., *supra* note 78, par. 45.

[121] Judgement, *Prosecutor v. Krstić*, A. Ch., *supra* note 14, par. 268.

[122] Judgement, *Prosecutor v. Kunarac et al.*, A. Ch., *supra* note 24, par. 361.

[123] The Appeals Chamber stipulated in Blaškić that 'a finding that a 'chaotic' context might be considered as a mitigating factor in circumstances of combat operations risks mitigating the criminal conduct of all personnel in a war zone. Conflict is by its nature chaotic, and it is incumbent on the participants to reduce that chaos and to respect international humanitarian law'. See Judgement, *Prosecutor v. Blaškić*, A. Ch., *supra* note 8, par. 711. See also Judgement, *Prosecutor v. Galić*, A. Ch., *supra* note 19, par. 418: 'The Appeals Chamber considered that Galić's argument that he received his command of the SRK units 'practically in the state of chaos' was not an argument the Trial Chamber was bound to consider in mitigation. As a military commander Galić had the authority and competence to order lawful combat operations, and it was his duty to work towards an effective chain of command'.

[124] Judgement, *Prosecutor v. Kvočka, Radić, Žigić and Prcac*, A. Ch., *supra* note 35, par. 707.

[125] Judgement, *Prosecutor v. Galić*, A. Ch., *supra* note 19, par. 429. The Appeals Chamber noted that '[r]espect towards all people, regardless of their nationality, ethnicity or religion, is the demeanour expected of any individual and does not constitute a factor to be considered in mitigation of sentence'.

relied upon, this in order to develop a rational and defensible system of punishment.[126] In a similar vein, this author has elsewhere argued that the different sentencing factors recognized in the *ad hoc* tribunals' case law must serve the sentencing purposes, in order to arrive at a rational, structured and coherent sentencing regime.[127] Although the question as to whether the main sentencing purposes find optimum expression in the sentencing factors can, of course, not be answered in the context of a modest case note, a brief attempt will nonetheless be undertaken here.

It is outlined by this author elsewhere in this volume of the Annotated Leading Cases that retribution and deterrence have been recognized by the international criminal tribunals as the main sentencing purposes.[128] What these rationales have in common – according to their definitions as adhered to by both *ad hoc* tribunals – is their emphasis on norm strengthening. The declaratory or expressive function of international sentencing is considered, on basis of a perusal of sentencing case law, as its most important. The international community declares the wrongfulness of specific conduct for the purpose of reprobation itself (retribution), and in order to prevent similar atrocities in the future, by socio-educative norm-strengthening (deterrence).[129]

However, as noted, the tribunals do not distinguish clearly between the variables that are to be considered when determining the gravity of the crime and those that may be accepted as aggravating circumstances. This does not contribute to transparency and expressiveness of sentencing and, in combination with the absence of an obligation on Trial Chambers to expressly mention all the variables that they have taken into account, renders effective control impossible. Furthermore, the perceived overall fairness of the sentencing regime is endangered. It is thus clear that the main sentencing purposes suffer from this lack of coherence.

Although the different circumstances present in distinct cases demand attention – which implies that abstract distinctions between crimes may, but should not always, be determinative of the outcome – it is this author's view that international judges who impose sentences should compare as much as possible the circumstances of distinct cases, in order to arrive at a consistent and transparent sentencing regime, in line with and supportive of the expressive function of punishment.

The same argument goes for the sentencing factor of 'referring to the sentencing practice of the national courts of the affected States'. It was stated above that, in particular ICTY Trial Chambers, appear to merely automatically cite some provisions of the relevant national criminal codes, only to conclude that they are not bound by those provisions.

Such empty rhetoric does not enhance the public's trust in the sentencing regime and is, therefore, in clear violation of the tribunal's sentencing purposes. If Trial Chambers are not bound by national sentencing practices, and if such practices are usually not perceived as being of much assistance to judges, it would be better to leave out such repetitive considerations altogether, unless, of course, they would be of demonstrable assistance in a concrete case.

In relation to mitigating circumstances, although it was recognized that, according to the tribunals' statutes and rules, a Trial Chamber must take mitigating circumstances into account, it has been shown that Trial Chambers are under no obligation to set out in detail each factor relied upon, or to explain exactly under what heading a specific circumstance is taken into account. It was also mentioned that it is not incumbent upon a Trial Chamber to indicate the precise reduction of sentences determined in relation to each mitigating factor. However, a transparent and fair sentencing system requires that the public and the accused must be able to understand whether and why specific mitigating circumstances have or have not been accepted in a concrete case, and as to how they have influenced the imposed sentence.

However, quite a number of variables accepted in international sentencing do seem to serve the main sentencing purposes. According to Van Zyl Smit, the tribunals' emphasis on retribution is often 'encapsulated

126 Mirko Bagarić and John Morss, International Sentencing Law: In Search of a Justification and Coherent Framework, 6 International Criminal Law Review 2006, p. 194.

127 Denis Abels, Commentary, this volume, p. 703. See, in a similar vein, Judgement, *Prosecutor v. Kordić and Čerkez*, A. Ch., *supra* note 27, par. 1083.

128 Denis Abels, Commentary, this volume, p. 703.

129 *Ibid.*, p. 703.

in the proposition that the most important sentencing consideration is the gravity of the offence'.[130] Further, international judges, by taking into account the specific role of the accused in the overall conflict, address the criticism that retributive punishment – by emphasizing individual guilt – negates the 'collective' character of systematic criminality. Retribution is reflected in practically all aggravating circumstances. A discriminatory intent, an active participation in the crime, a long period over which the crime was committed, or sexual and particularly violent acts all demand additional reprobation and condemnation.

In attributing weight to the accused's cooperation with the prosecution, the tribunals recognize the difficulties inherent in investigating and prosecuting international crimes. At first blush, this does not serve the rationale of retribution. This being said, if such cooperation eventually leads to more perpetrators being brought before the international criminal fora, this *does* contribute to retribution and deterrence. A similar pragmatism and justification underlies the tribunals' recognition of guilty pleas and voluntary surrender as mitigating circumstances.

Apart from retribution and deterrence, the sentencing rationale of rehabilitation is reflected in some of the mitigating circumstances. In Kordić and Čerkez, for example, the Appeals Chamber pointed to Čerkez's 'extraordinarily good behaviour at UNDU', which would indicate, according to the Appeals Chamber, good rehabilitative prospects.[131] Keller notices that in Erdemović, although the Trial Chamber – in theory – rejected rehabilitation as an important sentencing purpose,[132] the sentencing judges did cite various factors that would demonstrate the likelihood of his successful rehabilitation, such as the accused's personal characteristics, his remorse, admission of guilt, cooperation with the prosecution and the duress under which he committed the crimes.[133]

It is clear that the *ad hoc* tribunals have made some attempts to develop a sentencing regime that is particularly suited to the international context. On the basis of the above, a tentative conclusion must be that, unfortunately, in some respects, their sentencing regimes do not accord with the overarching principles.

Denis Abels

---

130 Dirk van Zyl Smit, Punishment and Human Rights in International Criminal Justice, 2 Human Rights Law Review 2002, p. 10, footnote 35.

131 Judgement, *Prosecutor v. Kordić and Čerkez*, A. Ch., *supra* note 27, par. 1091.

132 ICTY, Sentencing Judgement, *Prosecutor v. Erdemović*, Case No. IT-96-22-T*bis*, T. Ch. I, 29 November 1996, Klip/ Sluiter, ALC-I-503, par. 66. See also William A. Schabas, Sentencing by International Tribunals: A Human Rights Approach, 7 Duke Journal of Comparative and International Law 1997, p. 504.

133 See Andrew N. Keller, Punishment for Violations of International Criminal Law: An Analysis of Sentencing at the ICTY and ICTR, 12 Indiana International and Comparative Law Review 2001, p. 62 and 63, referring to Sentencing Judgement, *Prosecutor v. Erdemović*, Case No. IT-96-22-T, T. Ch. I, *supra* note 132, par. 16. Keller also points to Serushago, where the ICTR Trial Chamber found substantial mitigating circumstances indicating a possibility for rehabilitation; Sentence, *Prosecutor v. Serushago*, T. Ch. I, *supra* note 104.

Tribunal pénal international pour le Rwanda
International Criminal Tribunal for Rwanda

IN THE APPEALS CHAMBER

Before:	**Judge Fausto Pocar, Presiding** **Judge Mohamed Shahabuddeen** **Judge Mehmet Güney** **Judge Liu Daqun** **Judge Wolfgang Schomburg**
Registrar:	**Mr. Adama Dieng**
Judgement of:	**21 May 2007**

MIKAELI MUHIMANA

v.

THE PROSECUTOR

Case No. ICTR-95-1B-A

JUDGEMENT

Counsel for Mikaeli Muhimana:

Prof. Nyabirungu mwene Songa
Mr. Kazadi Kabimba
Mr. Mathias Sahinkuye

The Office of the Prosecutor:

Mr. Hassan Bubacar Jallow
Mr. James Stewart
Ms. Linda Bianchi
Mr. Abdoulaye Seye
Mr. François Xavier Nsanzuwera

CONTENTS

[page 1] 1. The Appeals Chamber of the International Criminal Tribunal for the Prosecution of Persons Responsible for Genocide and Other Serious Violations of International Humanitarian Law Committed in the Territory of Rwanda and Rwandan Citizens Responsible for Genocide and Other Such Violations Committed in the Territory of Neighbouring States between 1 January 1994 and 31 December 1994 ("Appeals Chamber" and "Tribunal", respectively) is seized of an appeal by Mikaeli (also known as Mika) Muhimana ("Appellant") against the Judgement and Sentence rendered by Trial Chamber III of the Tribunal on 28 April 2005 in the case of *The Prosecutor v. Mikaeli Muhimana* ("Trial Judgement").[1]

I. INTRODUCTION

A. The Appellant

2. The Appellant was born on 24 October 1961 in Kagano Cellule, Gishyita Sector, Gishyita Commune, Kibuye Prefecture, Rwanda.[2] The Appellant was the *conseiller* of Gishyita Sector from 1990 through the relevant period covered by his Indictment in 1994.[3]

B. The Judgement and Sentence

3. The Trial Chamber convicted the Appellant pursuant to Article 6(1) of the Statute of the Tribunal ("Statute") for instigating, committing, and abetting crimes between April and June 1994 at various locations in Kibuye Prefecture, including Gishyita Town, Mubuga Church, Mugonero Complex, and the Bisesero area comprising, *inter alia*, Nyarutovu Cellule, Ngendombi Hill, Kanyinya Hill, and Muyira Hill.[4] Specifically, the Trial Chamber determined that the Appellant participated in various attacks by shooting and throwing a grenade at Tutsi refugees and raping numerous Tutsi women or women whom he believed to be Tutsi.[5] Additionally, the Trial Chamber found that the Appellant disembowelled a pregnant woman who died as a result of her injuries.[6] The Trial Chamber also found that the Appellant abetted others who raped women as well as instigated individuals to kill victims in his presence.[7] For these crimes, the Trial Chamber convicted the Appellant of genocide (Count 1), rape as a crime against humanity (Count 3), and murder as a crime **[page 2]** against humanity (Count 4).[8] The Trial Chamber sentenced the Appellant to imprisonment for the remainder of his life on each count.[9]

C. The Appeal

4. The Appellant appeals his convictions and challenges his sentences. He requests the Appeals Chamber to overturn his convictions and to release him.[10] In the alternative, he requests the Appeals Chamber to order a retrial or, as a further alternative, to quash his life sentences and substitute them with an appropriate fixed-term sentence.[11] The Appellant has divided his grounds of appeal into three categories: errors of law and fact relating to general issues, erroneous factual findings related to specific events, and sentencing errors. Within these categories, the Appeals Chamber has identified sixteen grounds of appeal. The Prosecution responds that all grounds of appeal should be dismissed.[12]

---

1 For ease of reference, two annexes are appended to this Judgement: Annex A – Procedural Background; Annex B – Cited Materials and Defined Terms.

2 Trial Judgement, para. 4.

3 Trial Judgement, paras. 4, 132, 604.

4 Trial Judgement, paras. 508-519, 552-563, 570-583.

5 Trial Judgement, paras. 512, 513, 552, 570.

6 Trial Judgement, paras. 557, 570-576.

7 Trial Judgement, paras. 553, 570.

8 Trial Judgement, paras. 519, 562, 563, 582, 583, 585. Having found the Appellant guilty of genocide, the Trial Chamber dismissed the charge of complicity in genocide (Count 2). Trial Judgement, paras. 520, 586.

9 Trial Judgement, paras. 618, 619.

10 Notice of Appeal, Ch. IV.

11 Notice of Appeal, Ch. IV.

12 *See* Respondent's Brief, para. 21.

5. The Appeals Chamber heard oral submissions regarding this appeal on 15 January 2007. Having considered the written and oral submissions of the parties, the Appeals Chamber hereby renders its Judgement. **[page 3]**

II. STANDARDS OF APPELLATE REVIEW

6. The Appeals Chamber recalls some of the applicable standards of appellate review pursuant to Article 24 of the Statute. The Appeals Chamber reviews only errors of law which invalidate the decision of the Trial Chamber and errors of fact which have occasioned a miscarriage of justice.

7. As regards errors of law, the Appeals Chamber has stated:

> Where a party alleges that there is an error of law, that party must advance arguments in support of the submission and explain how the error invalidates the decision. However, if the appellant's arguments do not support the contention, that party does not automatically lose its point since the Appeals Chamber may step in and, for other reasons, find in favour of the contention that there is an error of law.[13]

8. As regards errors of fact, it is well established that the Appeals Chamber will not lightly overturn findings of fact made by the Trial Chamber:

> Where the Defence alleges an erroneous finding of fact, the Appeals Chamber must give deference to the Trial Chamber that received the evidence at trial, and it will only interfere in those findings where no reasonable trier of fact could have reached the same finding or where the finding is wholly erroneous. Furthermore, the erroneous finding will be revoked or revised only if the error occasioned a miscarriage of justice.[14]

9. A party cannot merely repeat on appeal arguments that did not succeed at trial, unless it can demonstrate that the Trial Chamber's rejection of those arguments constituted an error warranting the intervention of the Appeals Chamber.[15] Arguments which do not have the potential to cause the impugned decision to be reversed or revised may be immediately dismissed by the Appeals Chamber and need not be considered on the merits.[16]

10. In order for the Appeals Chamber to assess arguments on appeal, the appealing party must provide precise references to relevant transcript pages or paragraphs in the decision or judgement to which the challenge is made.[17] Further, the Appeals Chamber cannot be expected to consider a party's submissions in detail if they are obscure, contradictory, vague or suffer from other formal **[page 4]** and obvious insufficiencies.[18] Finally, the Appeals Chamber has inherent discretion in selecting which submissions merit a detailed reasoned opinion in writing and will dismiss arguments which are evidently unfounded without providing detailed reasoning.[19] **[page 5]**

III. ALLEGED ERRORS RELATING TO THE DEFINITION OF *INTERAHAMWE*, ITS STRUCTURE, AND THE APPELLANT'S ROLE THEREIN (GROUND OF APPEAL 1)

11. The Appellant submits that the Trial Chamber erred in law and in fact by finding that he had authority over the *Interahamwe* and that he was in a position to order them to commit genocide and crimes against

[13] *See Gacumbitsi* Appeal Judgement, para. 7, quoting *Ntakirutimana* Appeal Judgement, para. 11 (internal citations omitted). *See also Kajelijeli* Appeal Judgement, para. 5; *Stakić* Appeal Judgement, para. 8; *Vasiljević* Appeal Judgement, para. 6.

[14] *Gacumbitsi* Appeal Judgement, para. 8, quoting *Krstić* Appeal Judgement, para. 40 (internal citations omitted). *See also Kajelijeli* Appeal Judgement, para. 5.

[15] *Ndindabahizi* Appeal Judgement, para. 11; *Gacumbitsi* Appeal Judgement, para. 9; *Niyitegeka* Appeal Judgement, para. 9. *See also Stakić* Appeal Judgement, para. 11; *Naletilić and Martinović* Appeal Judgement, para. 13.

[16] *Ndindabahizi* Appeal Judgement, para. 11; *Kajelijeli* Appeal Judgement, para. 6; *Ntakirutimana* Appeal Judgement, para. 13. *See also Stakić* Appeal Judgement, para. 11; *Naletilić and Martinović* Appeal Judgement, para. 13.

[17] Practice Direction on Formal Requirements for Appeals from Judgement, para. 4(b). *See also Ndindabahizi* Appeal Judgement, para. 12; *Gacumbitsi* Appeal Judgement, para. 10; *Kajelijeli* Appeal Judgement, para. 7; *Stakić* Appeal Judgement, para. 12; *Vasiljević* Appeal Judgement, para. 11.

[18] *Vasiljević* Appeal Judgement, para. 12. *See also Ndindabahizi* Appeal Judgement, para. 12; *Naletilić and Martinović* Appeal Judgement, para. 14; *Kajelijeli* Appeal Judgement, para. 7.

[19] *Gacumbitsi* Appeal Judgement, para. 10; *Kajelijeli* Appeal Judgement, para. 8; *Niyitegeka* Appeal Judgement, para. 11. *See also Stakić* Appeal Judgement, para. 13; *Blaškić* Appeal Judgement, para. 13.

humanity, thereby incurring individual criminal responsibility pursuant to Article 6(1) of the Statute.[20] He further submits that the Trial Chamber erred in fact when it "linked" him to the *Interahamwe* without first defining the *Interahamwe* and his position in it.[21]

12. The essence of the Appellant's submission under this ground of appeal is that the Trial Chamber erred in finding that he had authority over the *Interahamwe* and that he was in a position to order them to commit crimes for which he was held responsible. The Appeals Chamber finds no merit in this submission. The Trial Chamber did not find that the Appellant had authority over the *Interahamwe* or that he ordered them to commit crimes for which he was then held responsible. Rather, the Trial Chamber held the Appellant responsible for personally committing genocide,[22] committing and abetting rape as a crime against humanity,[23] and committing and instigating murders as crimes against humanity.[24] None of these holdings is founded upon any finding that the Appellant had authority over the *Interahamwe* or that he ordered the *Interahamwe* to commit these crimes. Consequently, there was no need for the Trial Chamber to define the *Interahamwe*, its structure, or the Appellant's position in it.

13. Accordingly, this ground of appeal is dismissed. **[page 6]**

IV. ALLEGED ERROR RELATING TO THE BURDEN OF PROOF (GROUND OF APPEAL 2)

14. The Appellant submits that the Trial Chamber erred in law by reversing the burden of proof and essentially requiring him to prove the impossibility of his presence at the scene of crimes or that the crimes could not have occurred, rather than simply requiring him to "induce a reasonable doubt as to whether his version might not be true".[25] The Appellant illustrates this alleged legal error under this ground of appeal by pointing to the Trial Chamber's findings on the rapes of Languida Kamukina and Goretti Mukashyaka.[26]

15. Based on the uncorroborated testimony of Prosecution Witness AP,[27] the Trial Chamber inferred that the Appellant raped these two women, reasoning as follows:

> Although Witness AP was not an eyewitness to the rape of Goretti and Languida, the Chamber infers that the Accused raped them on the basis of the following factors: the witness saw the Accused take the girls into his house; she heard the victims scream, mentioning the Accused's name and stating that they "did not expect him to do that" to them; finally the witness saw the Accused lead the victims out of his house, stark naked, and she noticed that they were walking "with their legs apart".[28]

16. In asserting that the Trial Chamber reversed the burden of proof, the Appellant points to the following passage from the Trial Judgement:

> The Chamber finds that the mere fact that several Defence witnesses did not hear of rapes committed by the Accused in his house on 7 April 1994 does not mean that they *could not have occurred*. The witnesses advanced no reason to support the implied assertion that, if the Accused had committed rapes, they would have heard of them. The Chamber does not find this argument persuasive. The Chamber does not accept the contention that under Rwandan culture it is impossible for a man to rape a woman in the matrimonial home. The Chamber accepts that in any society such behaviour would be considered unacceptable. However, this fact *does not preclude the possibility that it could occur*.[29]

17. The Appellant contends that his evidence considered under the proper legal standard at the very least raised doubt as to the commission of the rapes, especially as Witness AP was not an eye-witness to the actual crimes.[30] The Appeals Chamber considers here the Appellant's legal argument concerning the burden of

---

20 Appellant's Brief, para. 23.
21 Notice of Appeal, p. 2, Ch. I, para. 1; Appellant's Brief, paras. 21, 22.
22 Trial Judgement, paras. 513, 519.
23 Trial Judgement, paras. 552, 553, 562.
24 Trial Judgement, paras. 570, 571, 582.
25 Appellant's Brief, para. 27, quoting *Čelebići Case* Trial Judgement, para. 603. *See also* Notice of Appeal, p. 2, Ch. I, para. 2; Appellant's Brief, paras. 25-31.
26 Appellant's Brief, para. 26.
27 Trial Judgement, paras. 17-19, 22.
28 Trial Judgement, para. 32.
29 Appellant's Brief, paras. 26, 28, quoting Trial Judgement, para. 25 (emphasis added).
30 Appellant's Brief, paras. 28-30.

proof, and it addresses the Trial Chamber's reliance on Witness AP in connection with these events in Ground of Appeal 8. **[page 7]**

18. The Appeals Chamber considers that some of the language used in paragraph 25 of the Trial Judgement, highlighted by the Appellant, could be perceived as a shift in the burden of proof to the Appellant, when viewed in isolation. An accused does not need to prove at trial that a crime "could not have occurred" or "preclude the possibility that it could occur". Nonetheless, it is apparent from the Trial Chamber's approach as a whole that it did not place the burden on the Appellant to establish that the rapes could not have occurred.

19. The Trial Chamber's statement that "the mere fact that several Defence witnesses did not hear of [the] rapes [...] does not mean that they could not have occurred" reflects the appreciation that simply not hearing of something does not necessarily rebut the evidence that established that the rapes had been committed. Notably, the Trial Chamber observed that the Defence witnesses "advanced no reason to support the implied assertion that, if the [Appellant] had committed rapes, they would have heard of them."[31] This analysis does not demonstrate a shift of burden of proof to the Appellant. Rather, it reflects the Trial Chamber's assessment of the limited probative value of the evidence presented by the Appellant in the context of the totality of evidence presented by both parties.

20. In addition, the Trial Chamber's statement that: "[t]he Chamber accepts that in any society such behaviour would be considered unacceptable. However, this fact does not *preclude* the possibility that it could occur",[32] when considered in the context of the Trial Judgement, also does not evidence a shift in the burden of proof to the Appellant. The Appeals Chamber considers that the Trial Chamber's assessment of the Appellant's evidence relating to standards of behaviour in a particular society simply reflects the limited probative value of such evidence in raising reasonable doubt when weighed against Prosecution evidence that the rapes did occur, which the Trial Chamber considered to be credible.

21. Accordingly, this ground of appeal is dismissed. **[page 8]**

V. ALLEGED ERRORS RELATING TO THE POWERS OF *CONSEILLER DE SECTEUR* (GROUND OF APPEAL 3)

22. The Appellant submits that the Trial Chamber erred in law and in fact by not defining the scope of his legal authority as a *conseiller* as well as his position, role and subordinates, in accordance with the Rwandan Law of 23 November 1963 on Territorial Administration and the *Bagilishema* Trial Judgement.[33] He argues that, as a result of this alleged error, his conviction for "ordering" has no legal basis.[34]

23. The Appeals Chamber observes that the Trial Chamber did not find the Appellant responsible for ordering any of the crimes of which it convicted him; rather, the Trial Chamber held him responsible for committing, abetting, and instigating.[35] The Appeals Chamber therefore finds that the Appellant has failed to show how the fact that the Trial Chamber did not address the powers of a *conseiller* amounted to an error.

24. Accordingly, this ground of appeal is dismissed. **[page 9]**

VI. ALLEGED ERRORS RELATING TO THE ALIBI (GROUND OF APPEAL 4)

25. The Appellant submits that the Trial Chamber erred in law and in fact by unfairly considering his alibi based on the circumstances surrounding the death of his child on 8 April 1994 and the ensuing mourning period.[36] He argues that the Trial Chamber erred in discrediting his alibi based on the testimony of Defence

---

31 Trial Judgement, para. 25.
32 Emphasis added.
33 Notice of Appeal, p. 2, Ch. I, para. 3; Appellant's Brief, paras. 32-36, citing *Bagilishema* Trial Judgement, para. 198.
34 Appellant's Brief, para. 35.
35 Trial Judgement, paras. 513, 519, 552, 553, 562, 570, 576, 582.
36 Notice of Appeal, p. 2, para. 4; Appellant's Brief, para. 37.

Witness DC, who proved to be a "hostile witness".[37] The Appellant contends that the Trial Chamber could have admitted the alibi that he continuously remained at home at least until 12 April 1994, when Witness DC allegedly saw him at Mubuga Church.[38]

26. The Appellant does not make any reference to any part of the Trial Judgement in support of the present submission, nor does he explain the significance of the claim that Witness DC was a "hostile witness". The Appeals Chamber has reviewed the relevant paragraphs of the Trial Judgement and notes the following:

> At trial, the Accused raised an alibi to establish that he could not have committed the crimes, which occurred outside his home, for which he was indicted. The Accused called a number of witnesses to say that he remained at his home in Gishyita continuously mourning his dead son from 8 to 16 April 1994.[39]

27. The Appeals Chamber also notes that the Trial Chamber followed established jurisprudence when it considered the Appellant's alibi and correctly reasoned as follows:

> The Trial Chamber is satisfied that the evidence of the Defence witnesses does not raise a reasonable doubt as to whether the Accused was present at the various locations where he is alleged to have committed or participated in the commission of crimes. This finding in no way undermines the Accused's presumption of innocence, and the Trial Chamber has made its factual findings bearing in mind that the Prosecution alone bears the burden of proving beyond a reasonable doubt the allegations made against the Accused.[40]

28. A review of the Trial Judgement shows that the Trial Chamber considered the Appellant's alibi in the context of the allegations against him during the period of 8 to 16 April 1994.[41] The Appeals Chamber notes that, in this assessment, Witness DC was only one of many eyewitnesses to have placed the Appellant outside his home during this period.[42] Furthermore, the Trial Chamber **[page 10]** noted that the evidence in support of the alibi was not convincing.[43] There is, therefore, no merit in the Appellant's contention that, even if the Trial Chamber relied on Witness DC, it should have accepted his alibi until 12 April 1994. Moreover, the Appellant's unsubstantiated submission that Witness DC was a "hostile witness" does not demonstrate that no reasonable trier of fact could have relied on his evidence.

29. Accordingly, this ground of appeal is dismissed. **[page 11]**

VII. ALLEGED ERRORS RELATING TO THE INTENT TO COMMIT GENOCIDE (GROUND OF APPEAL 5)

30. The Appellant submits that the Trial Chamber erred in law and in fact by finding that he had the intent to commit genocide when it was established at trial that he had a Tutsi wife whom he protected to the end of the war; that he had saved Tutsi people in Gishyita; that he had saved Witness AQ, a Tutsi woman; and that he had married a Tutsi woman during his flight to Zaire.[44] The Appellant argues that "a person cannot have the intent to commit genocide [...] and at the same time carry out protective and goodwill acts for members of the same group."[45]

31. The Appeals Chamber observes that the Trial Chamber took the following factors into account in determining that the Appellant had intent to commit genocide:

> 515. The Chamber finds that the attacks mentioned [...] above were systematically directed against the *Tutsi* group. Before the attacks on Mubuga Church commenced, *Hutu* refugees, who were intermingled with the *Tutsi*, were instructed to come out of the church. Similarly, both Prosecution and Defence witnesses testified that the refugees who had gathered on Kanyinya and Muyira Hills were predominantly *Tutsi*.

---

37 Appellant's Brief, paras. 37, 38.

38 Appellant's Brief, para. 37.

39 Trial Judgement, para. 12.

40 Trial Judgement, paras. 13-15, citing *Niyitegeka* Appeal Judgement, para. 60, *Musema* Appeal Judgement, para. 108.

41 Trial Judgement, paras. 63, 160, 203. The Appellant has raised specific challenges against these findings in other grounds of his appeal. *See* Grounds of Appeal 10, 11.

42 *See, e.g.,* Trial Judgement, paras. 63, 203.

43 Trial Judgement, paras. 63, 160, 203.

44 Notice of Appeal, p. 2, para. 5; p. 8, para. 6; Appellant's Brief, paras. 39-44.

45 Appellant's Brief, para. 45.

> 516. Factors such as the sheer scale of the massacres, during which a great number of *Tutsi* civilians died or were seriously injured, and the number of assailants who were involved in the attacks against *Tutsi* civilians, lead the Chamber to the irresistible conclusion that the massacres, in which the Accused participated, were intended to destroy the *Tutsi* group in whole or in part.
>
> 517. The Accused targeted *Tutsi* civilians during these attacks by shooting and raping *Tutsi* victims. He also raped a young *Hutu* girl, Witness BJ, whom he believed to be *Tutsi*, but later apologised to her when he was informed that she was *Hutu*. During the course of some of the attacks and rapes, the Accused specifically referred to the *Tutsi* ethnic identity of his victims.
>
> 518. Thus, the Chamber finds that the Accused's participation in the attacks, and his words and deeds demonstrate his intent to destroy, in whole or in part, the *Tutsi* group.[46]

32. The Appeals Chamber notes that the Trial Chamber's finding that the Appellant participated in killing and seriously injuring Tutsi victims with the intention to commit genocide, was based on evidence which the Appellant has failed to successfully impugn. The Appellant attempts to show error in the finding of his intent by pointing to his acts of protecting individual Tutsis, including his wives. This evidence was before the Trial Chamber. The Trial Chamber was free to consider that it did not suffice to impeach the evidence of the Appellant's individual acts of violence against the Tutsis which formed the basis of its finding that he had the requisite intent to commit genocide. In **[page 12]** general, evidence of limited and selective assistance towards a few individuals does not preclude a trier of fact from reasonably finding the requisite intent to commit genocide.[47]

33. Accordingly, this ground of appeal is dismissed. **[page 13]**

VIII. ALLEGED ERRORS RELATING TO THE PLOT BY PASCAL NKUSI AND CERTAIN WITNESSES (GROUND OF APPEAL 6)

34. The Appellant submits that the Trial Chamber erred in law and in fact by failing to consider his arguments advanced at trial in relation to a plot by Pascal Nkusi against him, his family, and his property[48] and by failing to draw all necessary inferences from the contention that Prosecution Witness AP was biased in her testimony against him in light of her relationship with Pascal Nkusi.[49] The Appellant explains that Pascal Nkusi fraudulently obtained his property[50] and that Prosecution Witness AQ is also benefiting from it.[51] He further avers that Pascal Nkusi intimidated Defence Witness DQ.[52] The Appellant contends that Pascal Nkusi recruited witnesses for the Prosecution who were "attached" to him and who were enjoying the Appellant's property to appear before the Tribunal and lie.[53] He further submits that Pascal Nkusi provided the Prosecution with Witnesses AP, AX, AQ, BB, BU, BF, AW, BE, and BC, and that no reasonable trier of fact would have found their testimonies to be credible in light of this plot.[54]

35. The Trial Judgement reflects that the Trial Chamber explicitly considered many of the arguments relating to the alleged plot by Pascal Nkusi and his alleged relationship with certain witnesses. In relation to Witness AP, the Trial Chamber reasoned as follows:

---

46 Trial Judgement, paras. 515-518.

47 *See Rutaganda* Appeal Judgement, para. 537 ("[T]he Appeals Chamber holds the view that a reasonable trier of fact could very well not take account of some of the illustrations [of assisting Tutsi] provided by the Appellant, which appear immaterial within the context of the numerous atrocities systematically and deliberately perpetrated against members of the Tutsi group, owing to their being members of thereof."). *See also Kvočka et al.* Appeal Judgement, paras. 232, 233 (referring to persecution as a crime against humanity, which is also a specific intent crime).

48 Notice of Appeal, p. 2, para. 6; Appellant's Brief, para. 46.

49 Appellant's Brief, paras. 50, 82-86. According to the Appellant this follows from the testimonies of Witnesses DA, DT, and DJ. The Appellant advances these arguments primarily under Ground of Appeal 8 challenging the evidence of Witness AP in connection with the rapes of Languida Kamukina and Goretti Mukasyaka, but the Appeals Chamber finds it appropriate to consider them here in connection with his other arguments concerning Pascal Nkusi.

50 Appellant's Brief, para. 46.

51 Appellant's Brief, paras. 49, 84.

52 Appellant's Brief, para. 48.

53 Appellant's Brief, paras. 46, 48.

54 Appellant's Brief, paras. 46, 47.

> The Chamber has also noted the Defence challenge to Witness AP's credibility that she is related to the current *conseiller* of Gishyita *Secteur*, who replaced the Accused, and that her testimony is therefore biased, and part of a plot against the Accused by the *conseiller* to deprive the Accused of his property. The Chamber notes that the Defence never put this allegation of bias to the witness during cross-examination. Moreover, in assessing the credibility of Witness AP, the Chamber has taken note of this allegation of bias and is satisfied that it does not in any way discredit her testimony.[55]

36. The Appeals Chamber notes that the Trial Chamber assessed the challenges to Witness AP's testimony in the Trial Judgement and found her to be credible.[56] Having reviewed the Trial Chamber's assessment of Witness AP's evidence, the Appeals Chamber finds no error in the Trial Chamber's acceptance of and reliance on her testimony. **[page 14]**

37. In relation to Witness AQ, the Trial Chamber took into consideration the Appellant's arguments concerning her alleged connection to Pascal Nkusi when assessing her testimony. The Trial Chamber reasoned as follows:

> The Chamber is mindful of the Defence submission regarding the partiality of Witness AQ and has, accordingly, considered her testimony with the necessary caution. Nevertheless, the Chamber finds her recollection of the events credible and reliable.[57]

38. The Appellant's argument that Witnesses AX, BB, BU, BF, AW, BE, and BC are biased given their relationship with Pascal Nkusi is not substantiated by any reference to evidence in the record.[58] Therefore, the Appeals Chamber declines to consider it further.

39. The Appeals Chamber concludes that there is no merit in the Appellant's contention that the Trial Chamber did not consider his arguments in relation to the alleged plot and finds that the Appellant has failed to demonstrate any error of law or fact on the part of the Trial Chamber in this regard.

40. Accordingly, this ground of appeal is dismissed. **[page 15]**

IX. ALLEGED ERROR RELATING TO THE ATTACKS AT NYARUTOVU HILL AND THE NEIGHBOURING AREAS OF KIZIBA, NYARUTOVU, AND NGENDOMBI (GROUND OF APPEAL 7)

41. The Appellant submits that the Trial Chamber erred in fact when it found that the attacks at Nyarutovu Hill and the neighbouring areas of Kiziba, Nyarutovu, and Ngendombi between 8 and 11 April 1994 had been established,[59] whereas Prosecution Witnesses AT, BJ, and AV testified that "the poor climate had set in in Ngoma, Mubuga and Gishyita three or four days after the death of the President".[60] Relying on excerpts of evidence given by Witnesses AT and BJ,[61] the Appellant contends that, according to Witness AT, no massacres had taken place in the six days following President Habyarimana's death[62] and that, according to Witness BJ, war had only broken out on 16 April 1994.[63]

42. The Appeals Chamber notes that the Trial Chamber relied on the evidence given by two eyewitnesses, Witnesses AW and W, to find that between 8 and 11 April 1994, the Appellant took part in two attacks at Nyarutovu Hill and neighbouring areas.[64] The Appellant argues that three other Prosecution witnesses,

---

55 Trial Judgement, para. 30.

56 *See, e.g.*, Trial Judgement, paras. 23-31.

57 Trial Judgement, para. 106.

58 Appellant's Brief, paras. 46, 48. The Appellant suggests that all individuals "invoke" Pascal Nkusi's name, but does not cite to a specific exhibit. *See* Appellant's Brief, para. 48 fn. 50. Additionally, the Appellant directs the Appeals Chamber to review paragraph 79 of the Defence Closing Brief, which indicates that these witnesses have "a particular relationship with Pascal Nkusi." *See* Appellant's Brief, para. 46, citing Defence Closing Brief, para. 79. The Appeals Chamber notes that while the Appellant generically references "identification sheets" in the Defence Closing Brief, he does not point to any specific exhibit.

59 Notice of Appeal, p. 2, Ch. II, para. 1; p. 9, para. 8; Appellant's Brief, paras. 51-55, citing Trial Judgement, paras. 64-67. The Appeals Chamber notes that the Appellant also challenges these factual findings under Ground of Appeal 9.

60 Appellant's Brief, para. 56. *See also* Notice of Appeal, p. 9, para. 8.

61 Appellant's Brief, paras. 57, 59, 60.

62 Appellant's Brief, para. 58.

63 Appellant's Brief, para. 61.

64 Trial Judgement, paras. 63-68.

namely Witnesses AT, BJ, and AV, contradicted the Trial Chamber's findings when they testified that on the relevant dates, between 8 and 11 April 1994, the hostilities had not yet started.

43. It is apparent from the Trial Judgement that Witnesses AT and BJ were among the Tutsi refugees at the Mugonero Complex in Ngoma in the days immediately following the assassination of President Juvenal Habyarimana.[65] Both witnesses focussed in their testimonies on the events at Mugonero Complex and, in particular, on the events of 16 April 1994.[66] The Appellant does not show how these testimonies would support the contention that attacks did not take place at other locations, namely Nyarutovu Hill and the neighbouring areas, on other dates. The Appellant cites an excerpt of Witness AT's testimony that "poor climate" set in in his area three to four days after President Habyarimana's death.[67] The Appeals Chamber notes that this excerpt, however, clearly refers to a specific location, namely the place of the witness's residence, which is irrelevant to the **[page 16]** Trial Chamber's findings related to attacks at Nyarutovu Hill and the neighbouring areas.[68] Similarly, the testimony of Witness BJ referred to by the Appellant in this connection does not establish that the Trial Chamber erred in making the findings in question. Finally, the Appellant has not provided any argument or references in relation to Witness AV.[69]

44. For the foregoing reasons, the Appeals Chamber finds that the Appellant has not demonstrated in this ground of appeal that Witnesses AT, BJ, and AV contradicted the Trial Chamber's findings as to the attacks at Nyarutovu Hill and the neighbouring areas between 8 and 11 April 1994.

45. Accordingly, this ground of appeal is dismissed. **[page 17]**

X. ALLEGED ERRORS RELATING TO THE RAPES OF LANGUIDA KAMUKINA AND GORETTI MUKASHYAKA (GROUND OF APPEAL 8)

46. The Trial Chamber found that, on 7 April 1994, the Appellant raped two Tutsi women, Languida Kamukina and Goretti Mukashyaka, in his home and, as a result, convicted him of rape as a crime against humanity.[70] In making this finding, the Trial Chamber relied on the evidence of Prosecution Witness AP, holding as follows:

> Although Witness AP was not an eyewitness to the rape of Goretti and Languida, the Chamber infers that the Accused raped them on the basis of the following factors: the witness saw the Accused take the girls into his house; she heard the victims scream, mentioning the Accused's name and stating that they "did not expect him to do that" to them; finally the witness saw the Accused lead the victims out of his house, stark naked, and she noticed that they were walking "with their legs apart".[71]

47. The Appellant submits that the Trial Chamber erred in law and in fact in relying on Witness AP's uncorroborated circumstantial evidence of the rapes, in assessing Witness AP's credibility, and in assessing Defence evidence.[72] Recalling the elements of rape as defined in the *Kunarac et al.* case at the ICTY,[73] the Appellant alleges that, because Witness AP was not an eyewitness, she was not in a position to establish the *actus reus* of rape.[74]

48. The Prosecution responds that any crime under the jurisdiction of the Tribunal may be established through circumstantial evidence and that there is no rule requiring direct evidence to prove the *actus reus* of

65 Trial Judgement, paras. 227, 247.
66 Trial Judgement, para. 227.
67 Appellant's Brief, para. 57, citing T. 19 April 1994 pp. 4, 5.
68 The Appeals Chamber has reviewed Prosecution Exhibit 17 (under seal) containing Witness AT's particulars, including a reference to his residence in April 1994.
69 *See* Appellant's Brief, para. 56. The Appellant only provided a reference to T. 1 April 2004 p. 5 which, the Appeals Chamber notes, is not a transcript of Witness AV's testimony.
70 Trial Judgement, paras. 32, 552, 563.
71 Trial Judgement, para. 32.
72 Notice of Appeal, pp. 2, 3, Ch. II, paras. 2-7; pp. 9, 10, paras. 8-14; Appellant's Brief, paras. 30, 62-88. In addition, the Appellant also raises other arguments concerning this event in Ground of Appeal 2.
73 Appellant's Brief, para. 65, quoting *Kunarac* Trial Judgement, para. 460, *Kunarac* Appeal Judgement, para. 127.
74 Appellant's Brief, para. 66.

rape.[75] Moreover, the Prosecution submits that Witness AP gave both direct and circumstantial evidence, which was "detailed, credible and 'internally consistent'".[76]

49. The Appeals Chamber recalls that it is permissible to base a conviction on circumstantial evidence[77] and that a Trial Chamber has the discretion to decide in the circumstances of each case whether corroboration of evidence is necessary.[78]

50. The Trial Chamber's finding that the Appellant raped Languida Kamukina and Goretti Mukashyaka is based on the testimony of Witness AP who described their maltreatment.[79] In such **[page 18]** circumstances, the Appeals Chamber can identify no factual error on the part of the Trial Chamber in concluding that these two women were raped in the Appellant's home. The above-quoted text, in particular coupled with the evidence of widespread rape committed in the course of the crimes perpetrated by the Appellant, provides a sufficient basis for this conclusion.

51. However, it is apparent from Witness AP's testimony that the Appellant was not alone with the young women in the house at the relevant time.[80] Witness AP testified that "[a]mongst the voices coming from inside the house, the witness also recognised the voice of *Bourgmestre* Sikubwabo, telling the girls to 'shut up'."[81] Consequently, the Appeals Chamber is not persuaded that the Trial Chamber acted reasonably in determining that it was the Appellant who raped the two women, rather than another person present in the house, such as Sikubwabo.

52. Accordingly, the Appeals Chamber finds, Judge Shahabuddeen and Judge Schomburg dissenting, that the Trial Chamber erred in fact in convicting the Appellant for committing rape based on this event and reverses this factual finding. Even if Witness AP's evidence, as accepted by the Trial Chamber, demonstrated that the Appellant could bear criminal responsibility for the rapes of these women as an aider and abettor, the Prosecution did not charge this form of criminal responsibility in connection with these rapes,[82] and, therefore, it would not be appropriate for the Appeals Chamber to uphold the conviction on this basis.

53. The Trial Chamber's error of fact, however, did not occasion a miscarriage of justice because no conviction on any count of the Indictment rested solely on these rapes. The Appellant's conviction for rape as a crime against humanity, for which he was sentenced to life imprisonment, rests on his commission of or complicity in the rapes of ten other individuals.[83] Accordingly, the Appeals Chamber is not satisfied that its finding of error on the part of the Trial Chamber with **[page 19]** respect to the rape of Languida Kamukina and Goretti Mukashyaka is sufficient to impugn his conviction for rape as a crime against humanity. The Appeals Chamber is also not satisfied that this error affects the Appellant's sentence of imprisonment for the remainder of his life in view of the other crimes and the appropriateness of considering this event in

---

75 Respondent's Brief, paras. 107, 108.

76 Respondent's Brief, paras. 109, 110, quoting Trial Judgement, para. 23.

77 *Gacumbitsi* Appeal Judgement, para. 115.

78 *Kajelijeli* Appeal Judgement, para. 170, citing *Niyitegeka* Appeal Judgement, para. 92 ("The Appeals Chamber has consistently held that a Trial Chamber is in the best position to evaluate the probative value of evidence and that it may, depending on its assessment, rely on a single witness's testimony for the proof of a material fact.").

79 *See* Trial Judgement, para. 32 ("[T]he witness saw the Accused take the girls into his house; she heard the victims scream, mentioning the Accused's name and stating that they "did not expect him to do that" to them; finally the witness saw the Accused lead the victims out of his house, stark naked, and she noticed that they were walking "with their legs apart".).

80 Trial Judgement, para. 14. *See also* T. 30 April 1994 pp. 24, 27 ("I could hear voices of many people, and amongst these voices, I could hear the voice of the *bourgmestre*. [...] Q. Now, can you tell me when Mika arrived at the house with the two girls, was there anybody else present inside that house, at that time, apart from Mika and the girls? A. Listen, I didn't enter the house. I can only say that there were many people. The only person whose voice I recognised was the *bourgmestre*.").

81 Trial Judgement, para. 18.

82 Paragraph 6 of the Indictment alleges that the Appellant "committed rape". More specifically, with respect to this event, paragraph 6(a)(i) of the Indictment reads:

> On or about 7 April 1994 in Gishyita town Gishyita sector, Gishyita commune, Mikaeli Muhimana brought two civilian women Goretti Mukashyaka and Languida Kamukina into his house and raped them. Thereafter he drove them naked out of his house and invited *Interahamwe* and other civilians to come and see how naked Tutsi girls looked like. Mikaeli Muhimana then directed the *Interahamwe* to part the girls' legs to provide the onlookers with a clear view of the girls' vaginas.

83 *See* Trial Judgement, paras. 552, 553.

aggravation. Accordingly, the Appeals Chamber finds no basis for disturbing the Appellant's conviction or sentence due to this error of fact. **[page 20]**

XI. ALLEGED ERRORS RELATING TO THE ATTACKS AGAINST TUTSIS ON NYARUTOVU HILL AND NGENDOMBI HILL AND RELATING TO THE RAPE OF ESPERANCE MUKAGASANA (GROUND OF APPEAL 9)

54. The Trial Chamber found that, between 8 and 11 April 1994, the Appellant participated in two "large scale" attacks against Tutsi refugees at Nyarutovu Hill.[84] In addition, the Trial Chamber found that, between 9 and 11 April 1994, the Appellant participated in an attack on Ngendombi Hill.[85] The Trial Chamber's findings reflect that the second attack on Nyarutovu Hill occurred on the same day as the attack on Ngendombi Hill.[86] The Trial Chamber convicted the Appellant of genocide based in part on his participation in the attacks on these two hills.[87] In another event, which is not related to the attacks on Nyarutovu and Ngendombi Hills, the Trial Chamber found that in mid-April 1994, the Appellant raped Esperance Mukagasana at his residence.[88] The Trial Chamber convicted the Appellant of rape as a crime against humanity based in part on this crime.[89] The Appeals Chamber addresses in turn the Appellant's three sub-grounds of appeal challenging the factual and legal findings on the attacks at Nyarutovu Hill and Ngendombi Hill, as well as the rape of Esperance Mukagasana.

A. Alleged Errors relating to the Attacks on Nyarutovu Hill

55. The Trial Chamber found that, on 8 or 9 April 1994, the Appellant participated in the first attack on Nyarutovu Hill by supplying the assailants with ammunition and by shooting and wounding a Tutsi man named Emmanuel.[90] In making these findings, the Trial Chamber relied on the evidence of Prosecution Witnesses AW and W.[91] The Trial Chamber found that the Appellant participated in a second attack on Nyarutovu Hill, as well as other neighbouring areas, including Ngendombi Hill, between 9 and 11 April 1994.[92] In making findings concerning the second attack **[page 21]** at Nyarutovu Hill, the Trial Chamber relied solely on the evidence of Witness W.[93] Under this ground of appeal, the Appellant submits that the Trial Chamber erred in law and in fact in its assessment of Witnesses AW and W and in its failure to consider other Defence evidence.[94] The Appeals Chamber has already considered the Appellant's other challenges to the findings related to the two attacks on Nyarutovu Hill under Ground of Appeal 7.

84 Trial Judgement, paras. 64-68.

85 Trial Judgement, paras. 67, 76-79.

86 The Trial Judgement refers to the second attack on Nyarutovu Hill as occurring on 11 April 1994 based on the evidence of Witness W. The Trial Chamber further found based on this witness's account that, on the same day as the second attack on Nyarutovu Hill, the Appellant participated in attacks on neighbouring areas including Nyarutovu, Kiziba, and Ngendombi. *See* Trial Judgement, para. 67. However, the Trial Chamber also found that the attack on Ngendombi Hill occurred between 9 and 11 April 1994, relying in part on Prosecution Witness W's account as corroboration for Prosecution Witnesses BB and BC. Trial Judgement, para. 76. As discussed below in connection with the Appellant's sub-ground of appeal related to the attacks at Ngendombi Hill, the Appeals Chamber finds that the Trial Chamber intended the broader date range of 9 to 11 April 1994 to apply equally to the second attack at Nyarutovu Hill.

87 Trial Judgement, paras. 513, 519.

88 Trial Judgement, paras. 103, 108.

89 Trial Judgement, paras. 552, 563.

90 Trial Judgement, paras. 64-66, 513.

91 Trial Judgement, paras. 63-66.

92 Trial Judgement, paras. 67, 76. The Trial Chamber also found that, on the day of the second attack on Nyarutovu Hill, the Appellant also participated in attacks in neighbouring areas such as Nyarutovu, Kiziba, and Ngendombi. The Trial Chamber discussed in detail only the attacks on Nyarutovu Hill and Ngendombi Hill and its findings on genocide are based only on those two locations. Trial Judgement, paras. 63-79, 513. The parties also do not address these other attacks in detail, and the Appeals Chamber therefore sees no need to address them.

93 Trial Judgement, paras. 46-50, 67.

94 Notice of Appeal, p. 3, paras. 8-10, 13; pp. 10-11, paras. 15-21; Appellant's Brief, paras. 89-106, 111-116.

1. Alleged Errors in the Assessment of Witness AW

56. The Appellant submits that the Trial Chamber erred in law and in fact in relying on the testimony of Witness AW in making findings in relation to the attack on Nyarutovu Hill, arguing that his testimony was uncorroborated, inconsistent, and implausible.[95] In this respect, the Appellant raises six principal arguments which are discussed below in turn.

57. The Appellant initially submits that the Trial Chamber erred in fact in relying on the testimony of Witness AW because he contradicted himself by first stating that the Appellant arrived on 8 April 1994 in the Bisesero area in a red minivan and subsequently noting that he arrived during the attack in a white Toyota.[96] In this regard, the Appellant also submits that it was established by other witnesses that the commune did not have a red-coloured van.[97]

58. A review of the transcripts reveals that Witness AW made reference to a red minivan at the beginning of his testimony[98] and, when specifically questioned by the Prosecution about the vehicle, identified it as a white Toyota.[99] In recounting Witness AW's testimony in the Trial Judgement, the Trial Chamber referred only to the Appellant arriving in a "red minivan" and did not explicitly address this contradiction.[100] The Appeals Chamber recalls that, while a Trial Chamber is required to consider inconsistencies and any explanations offered in respect of them when weighing the probative value of evidence,[101] it does not need to individually address them in the Trial Judgement.[102] Furthermore, the presence of inconsistencies within or amongst witnesses' **[page 22]** testimonies does not *per se* require a reasonable Trial Chamber to reject the evidence as being unreasonable.[103] The Appeals Chamber notes that Witness AW's testimony was consistent as to the owner and occupants of the vehicle.[104] The Appeals Chamber is therefore not convinced that no reasonable trier of fact could have relied on his testimony, notwithstanding the discrepancy concerning the colour of the vehicle.

59. The Appellant also submits that the Trial Chamber erred in fact in relying on Witness AW's testimony given his account that from Nyarutovu Hill he could see vehicles parked close to the Appellant's house in Gishyita town.[105] The Appellant submits that this would have been impossible in light of the witness's testimony that it would take approximately thirty minutes to walk from one location to the other, which the Appellant surmised corresponded to a distance of about two-and-a-half kilometres.[106]

60. A review of the relevant transcript shows that the witness found it difficult to estimate the distance between Gishyita town and Nyarutovu Hill, given the "roundabout pathways that lead from one place to the other."[107] Yet, the witness considered that "the distance was not very large" and could be covered in a thirty minute walk.[108] In this context, the witness was also asked to explain the location of a place called Kiziba in relation to Nyarutovu Hill and Gishyita town.[109] The witness stated that Kiziba was located between the two

95 Notice of Appeal, p. 3, paras. 8, 9; pp. 10-11, paras. 15-17, 19; Appellant's Brief, paras. 89-102, 111-114.

96 Appellant's Brief, paras. 90, 91, 96, 97, 111-114. At paragraph 111 of the Appellant's Brief, the Appellant refers to alleged contradictions between the evidence given by Witness AW and Witness W relating to the "means" the Appellant used to arrive at Nyarutovu Hill. The Appellant however goes on to illustrate this with an alleged internal inconsistency in Witness AW's testimony. Appellant's Brief, paras. 112, 113.

97 Notice of Appeal, p. 10, para. 16. The Appeals Chamber notes that this argument was not mentioned in the Appellant's Brief and that the Appellant does not provide citation to evidence on the record.

98 T. 14 April 2004 p. 5.

99 T. 14 April 2004 p. 7.

100 Trial Judgement, para. 39.

101 *Niyitegeka* Appeal Judgement, para. 96.

102 *Niyitegeka* Appeal Judgement, para. 124. *See also Musema* Appeal Judgement, para. 20.

103 *Niyitegeka* Appeal Judgement, para. 95, quoting *Kupreškić et al.* Appeal Judgement, para. 31.

104 T. 14 April 2004 pp. 5, 7, 41.

105 Appellant's Brief, paras. 92, 96, 97.

106 Notice of Appeal, p. 10, para. 15; Appellant's Brief, para. 92. In the Notice of Appeal, the Appellant also submits that the hills Kirunga, Rurebero, and Gitovu were located between the Appellant's house and Nyarutovu Hill and, therefore, obstructed the view from one location to the other. *See* Notice of Appeal, p. 10, para. 15. This argument has not been presented or developed in the Appellant's Brief and, therefore, will not be addressed.

107 T. 14 April 2004 p. 6.

108 T. 14 April 2004 p. 6.

109 T. 14 April 2004 p. 6.

places.[110] He also stated that the distance between Kiziba and Nyarutovu Hill measured between thirty and fifty metres and that, in relation to Nyarutovu Hill, Kiziba was located in the valley below.[111] In challenging Witness AW's testimony on this point, the Appellant advances his own view of the situation based on speculation and selective references to the witness's testimony, which fail to account for the witness's elevated location on a hill. Therefore, the Appeals Chamber is not convinced that the Appellant has demonstrated that no reasonable trier of fact could have relied on this aspect of Witness AW's testimony. **[page 23]**

61. The Appellant further submits that the Trial Chamber erred in fact in relying on Witness AW's testimony because the witness's account of when the attack unfolded is not consistent with his testimony on the timeframe when he was on Nyarutovu Hill.[112] The Appellant submits that Witness AW testified that the attack started at 11 a.m., although he attested to arriving at Nyarutovu Hill at 1 p.m., and, consequently, could not have witnessed the attack.[113] In addition, the Appellant argues that, if the witness arrived after the attack had begun, then this is inconsistent with his evidence that he and the refugees left the hill when the attackers arrived.[114]

62. The record reveals that the witness did not state that he personally witnessed the beginning of the attack, but merely testified that the attack started at 11 a.m. and was already under way when he arrived at 1 p.m.[115] Moreover, although the witness stated that he left Nyarutovu Hill when the attackers arrived,[116] it is evident from his examination that he was not referring to leaving the hill at the exact moment when the attackers arrived. Rather, when viewed in context, the exchange relied on by the Appellant for this point is simply a broad statement of what the refugees did as a result of the attack. During cross-examination, the witness further stated: "I tried to flee. Everybody was just running away [...] if I wanted to die, I would have stayed there, but I didn't want to and I ran away".[117] The Appeals Chamber does not consider the fact that the witness fled at some point after the Appellant's arrival as the attack unfolded as contradicting evidence of what he saw before he left the hill. In particular, the witness's testimony reflects that he observed the Appellant and other assailants arrive and saw the killing of several Tutsis.[118] Therefore, the Appeals Chamber is not convinced that the Appellant has shown that the Trial Chamber erred in its assessment of this evidence.

63. The Appellant submits that the Trial Chamber erred in fact in relying on Witness AW's testimony because the witness was not certain whether he met Kabanda on 7 April 1994 at Kabanda's shop or home.[119] The transcripts reflect that the witness was cross-examined by the Defence and questioned by the Trial Chamber on this particular point and that he explained that, **[page 24]** although Kabanda lived in Bisesero, he owned houses in Gishyita "where he plied his trade".[120] The Appeals Chamber is therefore not convinced that the Appellant has demonstrated the existence of any contradiction in Witness AW's account on this point that would call into question the Trial Chamber's overall credibility assessment.

64. The Appellant also submits that the Trial Chamber erred in fact in relying on Witness AW because of an alleged discrepancy about when he met the Appellant.[121] The Appellant points to a prior witness statement of Witness AW noting that he knew the Appellant "precisely after secondary school" and Witness AW's trial

---

110 T. 14 April 2004 p. 6.

111 T. 14 April 2004 pp. 41, 42. The witness explained that from Kiziba, the attackers had to climb up the hill to pursue the refugees. T. 14 April 2004 pp. 41, 42.

112 Appellant's Brief, paras. 93-97.

113 Appellant's Brief, para. 93.

114 Appellant's Brief, para. 94.

115 T. 14 April 2004 p. 6 ("Q. Now, let's talk about your going to seek refuge on Nyarutovu hill on the 8th of April. What time, do you recall, sir, that you went to that place? A. It is from 11 a.m. that an attack was launched on Nyarutovu, and this attack lasted until 4 p.m. Q. No. What time did you get there? A. As concerns the time at which I reached that locality, it was at about 1 p.m., and people were saying that we needed to fight back at the thieves. We thought they were thieves whereas it had to do with assailants that were attacking the hill.").

116 T. 14 April 2004 p. 8 ("And when they came on the Nyarutovu hill, we continued to Bisesero, with the refugees, that is.").

117 T. 14 April 2004 p. 46.

118 T. 14 April 2004 pp. 5-8.

119 Appellant's Brief, paras. 98, 99.

120 T. 14 April 2004 pp. 32, 35, 36.

121 Appellant's Brief, paras. 100, 101.

testimony indicating that he did not know if the Appellant attended secondary school.[122] The Appellant further notes that the witness then denied saying "secondary school" to the investigators even though he acknowledged his pre-trial statement by signing it.[123]

65. A review of the record reveals that Witness AW testified that he first knew the Appellant "when [the Appellant] finished school, when [the Appellant] just started trading".[124] The witness's testimony reflects that he did not know when the Appellant finished school or whether he went to secondary school.[125] The witness did state, however, that the Appellant went to primary school and began his trade when he was still young.[126] When confronted with his pre-trial statement referring to "secondary school", the witness explained that at the time he referred only to "studies", not to "secondary school".[127] The witness further explained that he did not write the pre-trial statement because he cannot read or write.[128] Given this explanation, the Appeals Chamber is not convinced that no reasonable trier of fact could have relied on Witness AW's evidence despite this alleged discrepancy.

66. Finally, the Appellant submits that the Trial Chamber erred in law in relying on Witness AW's uncorroborated testimony as to the first attack at Nyarutovu Hill in light of the foregoing challenges to his credibility.[129] The Appellant's characterization of Witness AW's testimony as uncorroborated is unfounded. The Trial Chamber determined that the Appellant participated in the first attack on Nyarutovu Hill on 8 or 9 April 1994 based on the corroborated testimonies of **[page 25]** Witnesses AW and W.[130] Moreover, it is clear from the Trial Judgement that, with respect to the details of the Appellant's involvement in the attack, the Trial Chamber relied primarily on the evidence of Witness W.[131]

67. Accordingly, the Appellant's arguments in respect of Witness AW are dismissed.

2. Alleged Errors in the Assessment of Witness W

68. The Appellant submits that the Trial Chamber erred in fact in finding that there were two attacks on Nyarutovu Hill on the basis of Witness W's testimony.[132] The Appellant contends that, according to Witness W, there were no victims and the attackers were either unarmed or fired into the air.[133] The Appellant further submits that Witness W's evidence in the *Kayishema and Ruzindana* case, where the witness testified to having taken refuge on Bisesero Hill on 9 April 1994, is irreconcilable with his testimony about attacks on Ngendombi Hill on 11 April 1994 in the present case.[134]

69. The Appeals Chamber notes that the Appellant misrepresents Witness W's testimony in respect of the victims during the two attacks. Contrary to the Appellant's assertions, the witness testified that firearms were used, that some people were injured, and that he saw the Appellant shoot a young Tutsi man named Emmanuel during the attack on Nyarutovu Hill.[135] Furthermore, the witness testified that the Appellant participated in several attacks on 11 April 1994, during which many people were shot at and killed.[136] In addition, the Appeals Chamber is not persuaded by the Appellant's arguments regarding the alleged discrepancies in Witness W's testimony. The Appellant was confronted with his testimony from the *Kayishema and Ruzindana* trial and explained that he moved among several hills during the period in question.[137] The Appellant has not demonstrated that the Trial Chamber erred in accepting this explanation.

122 Appellant's Brief, para. 100.
123 Appellant's Brief, para. 100.
124 T. 14 April 2004 p. 23.
125 T. 14 April 2004 p. 23.
126 T. 14 April 2004 p. 23.
127 T. 14 April 2004 pp. 23-25.
128 T. 14 April 2004 p. 25.
129 Appellant's Brief, para. 102.
130 Trial Judgement, paras. 64, 65.
131 Trial Judgement, para. 66.
132 Notice of Appeal, p. 3, paras. 10, 13; pp. 10, 11, paras. 17, 18; Appellant's Brief, paras. 103, 105, 110, 115, 135.
133 Appellant's Brief, paras. 103, 105, 110, 115.
134 Appellant's Brief, para. 136.
135 Trial Judgement, paras. 43, 44.
136 Trial Judgement, paras. 46-50.
137 T. 27 April 2004 p. 35; T. 29 April 2004 p. 34.

Therefore, the Appellant has failed to demonstrate that no reasonable trier of fact could have made the Trial Chamber's findings regarding the attacks at Nyarutovu Hill, based in part on Witness W's testimony. **[page 26]**

3. Alleged Inconsistency between the Testimonies of Witnesses AW and W

70. The Appellant submits that the Trial Chamber erred in fact in finding that testimonies of Witnesses AW and W corroborated each other because they provided different dates for the initial attack at Nyarutovu Hill.[138] The Trial Chamber addressed this issue as follows:

> The Chamber notes the discrepancy between the testimonies of Witnesses AW and W in relation to the date of the first attack at Nyarutovu. Whereas Witness AW testified that the attack occurred on 8 April 1994, Witness W recalled the date of the attack as 9 April 1994. The Chamber is of the view that in situations where witnesses are called to testify on events which took place over a decade ago, discrepancies relating to the time and date of the event may occur.[139]

The Appellant has not shown that no reasonable trier of fact could have accepted this explanation for this discrepancy. Accordingly, the Appellant's argument on this point is dismissed.

4. Alleged Error in Failing to Consider the Testimony of Witnesses DI and DT

71. The Appellant submits that the Trial Chamber erred in law in failing to consider the testimony of Defence Witnesses DI and DT with regard to the attacks at Nyarutovu Hill.[140]

72. The Appeals Chamber observes that the Appellant has not explained how the evidence of Witnesses DI and DT would have been relevant to the Trial Chamber's findings on the events at Nyarutovu Hill. Moreover, the Trial Chamber expressly considered the evidence provided by Witness DI in connection with other findings,[141] although it made no reference to the testimony of Witness DT. This, however, does not mean that the Trial Chamber did not consider the testimony of Witness DT. A Trial Chamber is not required to expressly reference and comment upon every piece of evidence admitted onto the record.[142]

73. In view of the foregoing discussion, the Appeals Chamber finds that the Appellant has failed to demonstrate that no reasonable trier of fact could have made the Trial Chamber's findings as to the events at Nyarutovu Hill. This sub-ground of appeal is therefore dismissed.

B. Alleged Errors relating to the Attack on Ngendombi Hill

74. The Trial Chamber found that, between 9 and 11 April 1994, the Appellant participated in the search for and attack on Tutsi civilians at Ngendombi Hill and that many Tutsis died or were **[page 27]** seriously injured in the attack.[143] The Trial Chamber determined that the Appellant was armed with a gun and grenades and that he threw a grenade into a crowd of Tutsi refugees, causing many deaths.[144] In addition, the Trial Chamber found that, after the attack, the Appellant attacked Witness BC with a machete, cutting off her left hand, and that he killed her three children.[145] In finding that the Appellant participated in the attack on Ngendombi Hill, the Trial Chamber relied on the evidence of Prosecution Witnesses BC, BB, and W, which it considered "consistent and corroborative".[146] The Trial Chamber convicted the Appellant of genocide based in part on his role in this attack.[147] On appeal, the Appellant submits that the Trial Chamber erred in

138 Notice of Appeal, p. 11, para. 17; Appellant's Brief, para. 104.
139 Trial Judgement, para. 65.
140 Notice of Appeal, p. 3, para. 14; p. 11, para. 21; Appellant's Brief, para. 116.
141 *See* Trial Judgement, paras. 20, 21, 26, 87, 100, 235, 236, 250, 251, 446, 449, 475.
142 *Musema* Appeal Judgement, para. 20.
143 Trial Judgement, paras. 76, 78, 79.
144 Trial Judgement, para. 76.
145 Trial Judgement, para. 77.
146 Trial Judgement, paras. 69, 74, 76.
147 Trial Judgement, paras. 513, 519.

law and in fact in considering the notice provided by paragraph 5(d)(iv) of the Indictment and in assessing the evidence of Witnesses BC, BB, and W.[148]

1. Alleged Defect in the Form of the Indictment

75. The Appellant submits that the Trial Chamber erred in law in failing to address at trial his arguments pertaining to the vagueness of the Indictment.[149] He argues that paragraph 5(d)(iv) of the Indictment lacks precision and fails to plead any physical act of genocide.[150]

76. The charges against an accused and the material facts supporting those charges must be pleaded with sufficient precision in the Indictment so as to provide notice to the accused.[151] The Appeals Chamber has held that criminal acts that were physically committed by the accused personally must be set forth in the indictment specifically, including where feasible "the identity of the victim, the time and place of the events and the means by which the acts were committed."[152] An indictment lacking this precision is defective; however, the defect may be cured if the Prosecution provides the accused with timely, clear, and consistent information detailing the factual basis underpinning the charge.[153] **[page 28]**

77. Paragraph 5(d)(iv) of the Indictment reads: "In April 1994 Mikaeli Muhimana, along with Clement Kayishema, Obed Ruzindana and *Interahamwe* participated in [the] search for and attacks on Tutsi civilians taking refuge in Mutiti and Ngendombi hills in Bisesero." In connection with this paragraph, the Trial Chamber found that in April 1994, the Appellant participated in the "search for and attack" on Tutsi civilians at Ngendombi Hill.[154] The Trial Chamber found, more specifically, that the Appellant threw a grenade into a crowd of Tutsi refugees, causing many deaths.[155] The Trial Chamber further found that the Appellant killed Witness BC's three children and cut her on her hands, shoulder and head with a machete, cutting off her left hand.[156] The Appeals Chamber notes that, in its legal findings on genocide, the Trial Chamber only highlighted the wounding of Emmanuel with respect to the attacks on Nyarutovu Hill and Ngendombi Hill.[157] However, it appears that the Trial Chamber also convicted the Appellant of the grenade attack and crimes committed against Witness BC and her children since it made specific factual findings as to these events,[158] referred to Witness BC's anticipated evidence as alleging the Appellant's *actus reus* of genocide,[159] and cross-referenced in the legal findings the entire section encompassing these factual findings.[160]

78. The Trial Chamber considered that the allegation in Paragraph 5(d)(iv) of the Indictment that the Appellant "participated in [the] search for and attacks on *Tutsi* civilians" provided adequate notice of his role in the crime.[161] The Appeals Chamber disagrees. In the *Ntakirutimana* Appeal Judgement, the Appeals Chamber determined that the phrase "participated in an attack on [...] Mugonero Complex" did not provide sufficient notice that the accused was being charged with the murder of a specific individual.[162] The Appeals Chamber reached a similar conclusion in the *Gacumbitsi* Appeal Judgement, where the indictment alleged that the accused "killed persons by his own hands" but failed to mention with respect to a massacre at a

148 Notice of Appeal, pp. 11, 12, paras. 21-25; Appellant's Brief, paras. 106-109, 117-147.

149 Notice of Appeal, p. 12, para. 23; Appellant's Brief, paras. 127-133. In addition, the Appellant submits that the Trial Chamber erred in law in making findings on the attack at Ngendombi Hill, as alleged in paragraph 5(d)(iv) of the Indictment, because in the concluding paragraph of its findings on this attack it referred to paragraph 5(d)(ii) of the Indictment, which relates to Nyarutovu Hill. *See* Notice of Appeal, p. 12, para. 25; Appellant's Brief, paras. 141, 146, 147. A review of the Trial Judgement reveals that this is simply a typographical error and occasions no miscarriage of justice.

150 Appellant's Brief, paras. 127-133.

151 *Gacumbitsi* Appeal Judgement, para. 49. *See also Ndindabahizi* Appeal Judgement, para. 16.

152 *Gacumbitsi* Appeal Judgement, para. 49; *Ntakirutimana* Appeal Judgement, para. 32, quoting *Kupreškić et al.* Appeal Judgement, para. 89. *See also Ndindabahizi* Appeal Judgement, para. 16.

153 *Gacumbitsi* Appeal Judgement, para. 49. *See also Ntagerura et al.* Appeal Judgement, paras. 28, 65.

154 Trial Judgement, para. 78.

155 Trial Judgement, para. 76.

156 Trial Judgement, para. 77.

157 Trial Judgement, para. 513.

158 Trial Judgement, paras. 76, 77.

159 Trial Judgement, para. 73.

160 Trial Judgement, para. 513 fn. 473, citing to Chapter II, Section E.

161 Trial Judgement, para. 73.

162 *Ntakirutimana* Appeal Judgement, paras. 30, 33.

church a specific killing or the accused's personal participation in the killings there.[163] The Appeals Chamber considers that the Indictment in this case does not contain any greater specificity than the cited portions of the indictments in the *Ntakirutimana* and *Gacumbitsi* cases. The Appellant could not have known, on the basis of the Indictment alone, that he was being charged as part of this attack with personally killing Tutsis with a grenade, seriously wounding Witness BC, and killing her children. **[page 29]**

79. While in certain circumstances, "the sheer scale of the alleged crimes makes it impracticable to require a high degree of specificity in such matters as the identity of the victims and the dates for the commission of the crimes",[164] this is not the case with respect to these events. The Prosecution should have expressly pleaded the grenade attack, the wounding of Witness BC, as well as the killing of her three children, particularly since it had this information in its possession before the amended Indictment was filed.[165] The Indictment was thus defective in this respect.

80. A review of the trial record, including the evidence of Witnesses BB and BC, reveals that the Appellant did not object to the form of this paragraph of the Indictment before trial or to the evidence led pursuant to it during the relevant testimonies. However, the Trial Chamber considered the Appellant's allegations of vagueness raised in the Defence Closing Brief in the Trial Judgement.[166] The Appeals Chamber has held that, where a Trial Chamber has treated a challenge to an indictment as being adequately raised, the Appeals Chamber should not invoke the waiver doctrine.[167] The Appeals Chamber will therefore treat the Appellant's objection as having been timely raised. It therefore falls to the Prosecution to prove that the Appellant's defence was not materially impaired by this defect.[168]

81. The Prosecution points to the Trial Chamber's finding that paragraph 5(d)(iv) of the Indictment was sufficiently specific, its observation that paragraphs 54 to 58 of the Pre-Trial Brief provided additional details, and the summary of Witness BC's anticipated evidence in an annex to the Pre-Trial Brief in an effort to show that the defect in the Indictment was cured by subsequent timely, clear, and consistent information provided to the Appellant.[169] Paragraphs 54 to 58 of the Pre-Trial Brief speak only generally about Tutsi refugees fleeing to the Bisesero region and provide no greater specificity as to the nature of the Appellant's conduct during the attack on Ngendombi Hill. However, a review of the summary of Witness BC's anticipated testimony in an annex to the Pre-Trial Brief contains an allegation that the Appellant cut off the witness's arm with a machete **[page 30]** and killed her three children on Ngendombi Hill.[170] It further mentions that the Appellant shot at refugees and threw grenades resulting in death.[171]

82. In the *Gacumbitsi* Appeal Judgement, the Appeals Chamber held that a summary of an anticipated testimony in an annex to the Prosecution's pre-trial brief could, in certain circumstances, cure a defect in an indictment.[172] The circumstance at hand is similar to that in the *Gacumbitsi* case in that the summary of the anticipated testimony provides greater detail that is consistent with a general allegation pleaded in the Indictment.[173] The Pre-Trial Brief therefore provided the Appellant with timely, clear, and consistent information sufficient to put him on notice that he was being charged with committing genocide by throwing a grenade at Tutsis, wounding Witness BC, and killing her three children at Ngendombi Hill. Therefore, the

163 *Gacumbitsi* Appeal Judgement, para. 50.

164 *Gacumbitsi* Appeal Judgement, para. 50, citing *Kupreškić et al.* Appeal Judgement, para. 89 (internal citations omitted).

165 Indeed, the Prosecution had the information in its possession since Witness BC provided her statement on 29 November 1999.

166 Trial Judgement, para. 73.

167 *Gacumbitsi* Appeal Judgement, para. 54. *See also Ntakirutimana* Appeal Judgement, para. 23.

168 *Gacumbitsi* Appeal Judgement, para. 51.

169 Respondent's Brief, paras. 148, 149, referring to Trial Judgement, para. 73.

170 Pre-Trial Brief, Annex A, p. 8. The summary further connects this allegation with paragraph 5(d) of the Indictment. The Appeals Chamber further notes that the Prosecution in the body of its Pre-Trial Brief specifically states that Witness BC will testify to the Appellant's acts of genocide in the various attacks in the Bisesero area. Pre-Trial Brief, para. 58.

171 Pre-Trial Brief, Annex A, p. 8.

172 *Gacumbitsi* Appeal Judgement, paras. 57, 58. *See also Ntakirutimana* Appeal Judgement, para. 48 (holding that a witness statement, when taken together with "unambiguous information" contained in a pre-trial brief and its annexes may be sufficient to cure a defect in an indictment). This approach is consistent with ICTY jurisprudence. *See Naletilić and Martinović* Appeal Judgement, para. 45.

173 *Gacumbitsi* Appeal Judgement, para. 58.

Appellant has failed to demonstrate that the Trial Chamber erred in its consideration of his arguments pertaining to the vagueness of paragraph 5(d)(iv) of the Indictment.

2. Alleged Errors in the Assessment of Witness BC

83. The Appellant submits that the Trial Chamber erred in law and in fact in relying on Witness BC in light of inconsistencies in her account as to the death of her children and as to when she was at Ngendombi Hill.[174] The Appellant contends that Witness BC initially testified that her children were killed by a grenade and later testified that they were dismembered with a machete.[175]

84. The Trial Chamber addressed the Appellant's arguments regarding Witness BC's evidence and concluded that there was no "contradiction in the witness' [*sic*] account of how her children were killed".[176] On appeal, the Appellant has failed to show that no reasonable trier of fact could have made this finding. A review of the transcripts reveals that Witness BC did not suggest that her children were killed by a grenade. Rather, the witness stated that people died as a result of a **[page 31]** grenade that the Appellant had placed on the road and that only subsequently, when "[t]hose who did not die were finished off", the Appellant killed her children with a machete.[177]

85. The Appellant also asserts that Witness BC was not in a position to testify about the events at Ngendombi Hill on 10 April 1994 because on 9 April 1994 she had already taken refuge in Kigarama in the Bisesero area, and no evidence was adduced to show that she subsequently returned to Ngendombi Hill.[178]

86. The Appeals Chamber has reviewed the relevant transcripts which show that, according to Witness BC's testimony, she fled on Saturday, 9 April 1994, from Kigarama to the Bisesero region.[179] She specified that the first hill she reached was Kigarama Hill in the Bisesero region.[180] The witness then testified that Kigarama was not safe and that they "spent the day running".[181] She testified that on Sunday she witnessed the Appellant launch an attack at Ngendombi Hill in the Bisesero region.[182] The witness testified that, after the attack, during which she was wounded by the Appellant, her husband took her to Kigarama, a "*secteur* or *colline* of Bisesero,"[183] where she stayed for a few months.[184] The Appellant's submissions therefore fail to demonstrate that no reasonable trier of fact could have accepted Witness BC's testimony concerning the attack on Ngendombi Hill.

3. Alleged Errors in the Assessment of Witness BB

87. The Appellant submits that the Trial Chamber erred in law by failing to address the contradictions within Witness BB's testimony, which the Appellant had raised at trial.[185] To substantiate this submission, the Appellant merely refers to a paragraph of the Defence Closing Brief, without providing further reasoning and without attempting to demonstrate any error on the part of the Trial Chamber. Consequently, the Appeals Chamber will not consider this submission further. **[page 32]**

4. Alleged Errors in Finding that Witnesses BB, BC, and W Corroborate Each Other

88. The Appellant submits that the Trial Chamber erred in fact in finding that the testimonies of Witnesses BB, BC, and W were coherent and corroborative.[186] The Appellant points to discrepancies in the accounts of

174 Notice of Appeal, p. 3, paras. 11, 15; p. 11, paras. 21, 22; Appellant's Brief, paras. 107-109, 120-124, 126, 137, 138, 140.
175 Appellant's Brief, paras. 107-109.
176 Trial Judgement, para. 75.
177 T. 20 April 2004 pp. 40, 41.
178 Appellant's Brief, paras. 120-124, 126, 137, 138.
179 T. 20 April 2004 p. 57.
180 T. 20 April 2004 pp. 40, 57.
181 T. 20 April 2004 p. 40.
182 T. 20 April 2004 pp. 40-42, 57.
183 T. 20 April 2004 p. 43.
184 T. 20 April 2004 pp. 42-44.
185 Appellant's Brief, para. 140.
186 Notice of Appeal, p. 3, para. 17; pp. 11, 12, paras. 21, 22, 24; Appellant's Brief, paras. 106, 117-120, 126, 135, 137-139, 140.

these three witnesses concerning when the attack on Ngendombi Hill unfolded, as well as in the evidence of Witnesses BB and BC with respect to the manner in which the Appellant killed his victims. The Appeals Chamber addresses each argument in turn.

89. The Appellant notes that Witness BB testified that the attack occurred on 9 April 1994, while Witness BC stated that the attack took place on 10 April 1994, and Witness W testified that it occurred on 11 April 1994 and was "categorical that on Sunday 10 April there was no attack."[187]

90. The Appeals Chamber considers that the alleged inconsistencies relating to the dates of the attack do not affect the Trial Chamber's finding that "the attack on Tutsi refugees on Ngendombi Hill took place between 9 and 11 April 1994".[188] As the Trial Chamber stated in reconciling the discrepancy in the dates between the testimonies of Witnesses AW and W in connection with the date of the first attack on Nyarutovu Hill: "The Chamber is of the view that in situations where witnesses are called to testify on events which took place over a decade ago, discrepancies relating to the time and date of the event may occur."[189] It appears that the Trial Chamber applied this same approach to reconciling the different dates provided by Witnesses BB, BC, and W for the attack on Ngendombi Hill and that it focused instead on the consistency of the testimonies regarding specific features of the attack.[190] This is illustrated by the following passage:

> Based on the testimonies of Witnesses BB, BC, and W, the Chamber finds that the attack on Tutsi refugees on Ngendombi Hill took place between 9 and 11 April 1994, and that the Accused, with two *commune* policemen, including Ruzindana, led a group of *Interahamwe* in carrying out the attack. Based on the consistent and corroborative testimonies of all three witnesses, the Chamber finds that the Accused was armed with a gun and grenade and that he threw a grenade into a crowd of *Tutsi* refugees, causing many deaths.[191] **[page 33]**

91. Beyond disputing the discrepancy in dates, the Appellant makes no submissions challenging the other common features of the accounts of these three witnesses, such as the identity of the assailants accompanying him and the grenade attack. In addition, the Appellant has also not advanced any argument suggesting that the passage of time in the circumstances of this case is not a reasonable explanation for justifying the discrepancy as to the precise date of the attack. Therefore, the Appeals Chamber is not convinced that the Trial Chamber erred in considering and in relying on the evidence of Witnesses BB, BC, and W as "consistent and corroborative" in making its findings concerning the events at Ngendombi Hill.

92. The Appellant additionally points to an alleged inconsistency between the testimonies of Witnesses BC and BB concerning how Witness BC's children were killed.[192] The Appellant submits that Witness BC testified that her children were dismembered, while Witness BB testified that the Appellant "didn't have a machete" and that, as a leader, he would "not soak himself in blood".[193]

93. Contrary to the Appellant's submission, there appears to be no contradiction between the testimony of Witness BC and Witness BB on this matter. The fact that Witness BB saw the Appellant armed with a gun and grenades around 1 p.m.[194] does not preclude a reasonable Trial Chamber from relying on Witness BC's testimony that she saw the Appellant close to sundown, killing her children with a machete.[195] This sub-ground of appeal is therefore dismissed.

---

187 Appellant's Brief, paras. 125, 135-137.
188 Trial Judgement, para. 76.
189 Trial Judgement, para. 65.
190 The Appeals Chamber notes that the Trial Chamber referred to the specific date of 11 April 1994 in connection with Witness W and the specific date of 10 April 1994 in connection with Witness BC. *See* Trial Judgement, paras. 67, 77. Given the Trial Chamber's statements in paragraphs 64 and 76 of the Trial Judgement reconciling discrepancies in dates, the Appeals Chamber considers that these specific references simply reflect the estimates given by the witnesses and are not in and of themselves factual findings. Indeed, the Appeals Chamber notes that Witness BC, when questioned on a specific date, noted: "We were like mad people, traumatised people. Don't ask me about the time. I cannot tell you." *See* T. 20 April 2004 p. 57. Indeed, in light of such testimony, it would have been unreasonable to rely on Witness BC alone in order to assign any particular date to the attack.
191 Trial Judgement, para. 76.
192 Appellant's Brief, para. 139.
193 Appellant's Brief, para. 139, quoting T. 16 April 2004 p. 6.
194 Trial Judgement, para. 53.
195 Trial Judgement, paras. 58, 77.

C. Alleged Errors relating to the Rape of Esperance Mukagasana

94. The Trial Chamber found that, "during the first week after the eruption of hostilities", the Appellant raped Esperance Mukagasana in his home on several occasions.[196] In making this finding, the Trial Chamber relied solely on the eyewitness testimony of Prosecution Witness AQ, who lived in the Appellant's house at that time.[197] The Trial Chamber convicted the Appellant of rape as a crime against humanity in part based on this event.[198] The Appellant submits that the Trial Chamber erred in law and in fact in its assessment of Witness AQ.[199] His submission is supported by **[page 34]** arguments related to a credibility finding on Witness AQ in relation to another event, allegations of bias, internal inconsistencies in the witness's account, lack of corroboration, and implausibility in light of Defence evidence.[200] The Appeals Chamber addresses each argument in turn.

1. Alleged Failure to Consider a Previous Finding on Witness AQ

95. The Appellant submits that the Trial Chamber erred in law and in fact in finding Witness AQ credible, even though it dismissed her uncorroborated testimony on the unlawfulness of a meeting held in Gishyita in mid-April 1994.[201]

96. The Appeals Chamber observes that, contrary to the Appellant's contention, the Trial Chamber did not decline to rely upon the evidence given by Witness AQ concerning a meeting held in Gishyita nor did it question the reliability of her testimony. The Trial Chamber considered her evidence that "some time before the meeting, she overheard the Accused state that he was going to hold a meeting to encourage the *Hutu* population to go out and kill *Tutsi*"[202] and found that this evidence was insufficient "to prove the allegations contained in Paragraph 6 (a) of the Indictment and Paragraph 40 of the Pre-Trial Brief that the Accused and others held meetings at which plans to attack *Tutsi* civilians were made."[203] Accordingly, the Appellant's argument on this point is dismissed.

2. Alleged Failure to Consider Bias

97. The Appellant also argues that the Trial Chamber erred in law and in fact because it failed to take into account his allegation of bias in respect of Witness AQ.[204] The Appeals Chamber observes that the Trial Chamber noted that it was "mindful of the Defence submission regarding the partiality of Witness AQ and [that it] has, accordingly, considered her testimony with the necessary caution."[205] Notwithstanding, the Trial Chamber found Witness AQ's "recollection of the events credible and reliable."[206] The Appeals Chamber considers that the Appellant has failed to demonstrate an error in the Trial Chamber's approach or that no reasonable trier of fact could have reached the Trial Chamber's conclusion. **[page 35]**

---

196 Trial Judgement, paras. 103, 108, 552.

197 Trial Judgement, paras. 90-94, 102-108.

198 Trial Judgement, paras. 552, 563.

199 Notice of Appeal, pp. 3, 4, paras. 19-21; Appellant's Brief, paras. 151-174. In addition, the Appellant submits a related error of law and fact arguing that the Trial Chamber relied on, but failed to assess the credibility of Defence Witnesses TQ13, TQ14, DI, NT1, DS, DR, and DI. Notice of Appeal, p. 12, para. 26; Appellant's Brief, paras. 148-150. In this respect, the Appellant points to paragraphs 82 to 87 of the Trial Judgement relating to another event involving Witness AQ. In respect to that other event, the Trial Chamber was not satisfied that the Prosecution had proved the allegations charged in paragraph 6(a) of the Indictment related to this event, namely that "the Accused and others held meetings at which plans to attack *Tutsi* civilians were made". *See* Trial Judgement, para. 88. The Appellant's cursory submissions on this point fail to relate this challenge in any detail to other relevant aspects of this ground of appeal. The Appeals Chamber therefore will not consider this argument further.

200 Notice of Appeal, pp. 3, 4, paras. 19-21; Appellant's Brief, paras. 151-174.

201 Appellant's Brief, paras. 152-156.

202 Trial Judgement, para. 81.

203 Trial Judgement, para. 88.

204 Appellant's Brief, paras. 158, 169-174.

205 Trial Judgement, para. 106.

206 Trial Judgement, para. 106.

3. Alleged Failure to Consider Inconsistencies in Witness AQ's Testimony and Statements

98. The Appellant submits that the Trial Chamber erred in law and in fact in failing to consider a number of inconsistencies in the witness's testimony and prior statements.[207] The Appellant highlights a number of inconsistencies mentioned in the Defence Closing Brief and his closing arguments, which the Trial Chamber allegedly failed to address.[208]

99. The Appeals Chamber observes that a review of the transcripts shows that the witness was cross-examined on the alleged contradictions and that her explanations are on record. The Appellant again highlighted the alleged contradictions in his Defence Closing Brief. The Appeals Chamber reiterates that a Trial Chamber does not need to individually address alleged inconsistencies and contradictions and does not need to set out in detail why it accepted or rejected a particular testimony.[209] The Trial Chamber, when considering Witness AQ's credibility, stated the following:

> The Chamber finds the testimony of Prosecution Witness AQ credible. The Chamber is satisfied that Witness AQ, who lived in the Accused's house, was an eyewitness to the rape of Esperance. She gave a detailed description of how the Accused raped Esperance several times. The Witness did not exaggerate her evidence and was prepared to admit that she was not able to see the alleged rape of Esperance by Gisambo, because he closed the door.[210]

100. In addition, the Trial Chamber explicitly stated that it considered Witness AQ's evidence with caution.[211] The Appeals Chamber is not satisfied that the Appellant has demonstrated that the Trial Chamber erred in its assessment of any alleged inconsistency in Witness AQ's evidence.

4. Alleged Error relating to Lack of Corroboration

101. The Appellant submits that the Trial Chamber erred in law in relying on the evidence of Witness AQ concerning the rape of Esperance Mukagasana, given that her evidence was uncorroborated.[212] The Appeals Chamber recalls that a Trial Chamber has the discretion to rely on uncorroborated, but otherwise credible, witness testimony.[213] The Appellant has not demonstrated an error by the Trial Chamber in this regard.

5. Alleged Error relating to Inconsistencies with other Evidence

102. The Appellant submits that the Trial Chamber erred in fact when it convicted him of the rape of Esperance Mukagasana when the evidence given by Defence Witnesses DQ, TQ1, NT1, **[page 36]** DR, DI, DJ, and Prosecution Witness BF shows that it would have been "not only impossible, but also implausible" that he committed this act.[214]

103. A review of the Trial Judgement demonstrates that the Trial Chamber evaluated the evidence given by Defence witnesses on this point.[215] Additionally, the Trial Chamber explained why it did not to rely on the evidence the Appellant now highlights:

> The Chamber has already found that, even though some Defence witnesses testified that they did not hear of rapes committed by the Accused in his house on 7 April 1994, it does not follow that such rapes did not occur. The Chamber rejects the testimony of Defence witnesses who testified that it was not possible for the Accused to rape women in his own house, where his wife lived. These witnesses did not advance any convincing reason for this assertion.[216]

The Appeals Chamber cannot find any error in the Trial Chamber's finding. The Appellant merely points the Appeals Chamber to evidence that had been considered at trial without, however, demonstrating any error.

---

207 Appellant's Brief, paras. 157-160.
208 Appellant's Brief, paras. 157-159.
209 *Niyitegeka* Appeal Judgement, para. 124. *See also Musema* Appeal Judgement, para. 20.
210 Trial Judgement, para. 102.
211 Trial Judgement, para. 106.
212 Appellant's Brief, para. 151.
213 *Gacumbitsi* Appeal Judgement, para. 72; *Niyitegeka* Appeal Judgement, para. 92.
214 Appellant's Brief, paras. 161-168.
215 Trial Judgement, paras. 95-101, 104.
216 Trial Judgement, para. 104.

Additionally, the Appellant's arguments regarding Witness BF are also unpersuasive. His assertion that the witness "must have been well informed" but had never witnessed the rape or death of Esperance Mukagasana is not supported by a direct reference to the record and fails to demonstrate that no reasonable trier of fact could have made the Trial Chamber's findings. The Appeals Chamber recalls that when faced with competing versions of events, it is the duty of the Trial Chamber which heard the witnesses to determine which evidence it considers more probative.[217] In the case at hand, the Appellant has not shown that the Trial Chamber erred in making this determination.

104. Accordingly, this sub-ground of appeal is dismissed.

D. Conclusion

105. For the foregoing reasons, this ground of appeal is dismissed in its entirety. **[page 37]**

XII. ALLEGED ERRORS RELATING TO THE EVENTS AT MUBUGA CHURCH FROM 11 TO 15 APRIL 1994 (GROUND OF APPEAL 10)

106. The Trial Chamber found that, between 8 and 13 April 1994, many Tutsis sought refuge at Mubuga Church in Gishyita Commune[218] and that, on 14 April 1994, the Appellant was in the church presbytery where "looters" took the refugees' food supplies.[219] The Trial Chamber further found that, on the morning of 15 April 1994, the Appellant, along with others, launched an attack on the Tutsis at the church resulting in the deaths of hundreds of people[220] and concluded that the Appellant threw a grenade into the church, killing a Tutsi man named Kaihura.[221] The Trial Chamber convicted the Appellant of genocide and murder as a crime against humanity based, in part, on his participation in this attack.[222] The Appellant raises three challenges with respect to these findings relating to the assessment of Defence Witness DC, his alibi, and the burden of proof.[223]

A. Alleged Error in the Assessment of Witness DC

107. The Appellant submits that the Trial Chamber erred in fact in finding, based on the evidence of Defence Witness DC, that he was at Mubuga Church on 12 *and* 13 April 1994 during the looting of the food supplies.[224] In this respect, the Appellant submits that Witness DC's testimony referred to the looting taking place only on one day, 12 *or* 13 April 1994.[225]

108. A review of the Trial Judgement reveals that the Trial Chamber did not find, as the Appellant suggests, that the Appellant was present at Mubuga Church during the looting of food supplies on 12 *and* 13 April 1994. Rather, the Trial Chamber found that the Appellant was present at Mubuga Church during the looting of food supplies on 14 April 1994, based primarily on the eyewitness testimony of Prosecution Witness AF.[226] The Appellant's reference to the passage in the Trial Judgement that Witness DC testified that the looting occurred on 12 *and* 13 April 1994 merely highlights a typographical error in the Trial Chamber's description of Witness DC's testimony.[227] Elsewhere in the Trial Judgement, the Trial Chamber correctly referred to the date provided by Witness DC as "12 *or* 13 April" 1994.[228] The Appellant makes no submissions on the possible **[page 38]** impact that this error might have had on the Trial Chamber's assessment of Witness AF's evidence. In addition, he points to no deficiencies in the Trial Chamber's approach in reconciling the

217 *Gacumbitsi* Appeal Judgement, para. 81; *Rutaganda* Appeal Judgement, para. 29.
218 Trial Judgement, para. 127.
219 Trial Judgement, paras. 130-132.
220 Trial Judgement, paras. 164, 167.
221 Trial Judgement, paras. 164-167.
222 Trial Judgement, paras. 513, 519, 570, 583.
223 Notice of Appeal, pp. 13, 14, paras. 32-35; Appellant's Brief, paras. 175-185.
224 Appellant's Brief, para. 175.
225 Appellant's Brief, para. 176.
226 Trial Judgement, paras. 123, 130-132.
227 Trial Judgement, para. 131 ("although [Witness DC] testified that the looting occurred on 12 and 13 April 1994").
228 Trial Judgement, paras. 121, 160 (emphasis added).

accounts of Witness AF and Witness DC, or in its assessment of Witness AF's evidence. The Appellant, therefore, has failed to demonstrate that no reasonable trier of fact could have made the Trial Chamber's finding on his presence at Mubuga Church during the looting of the food supplies. Moreover, the Appellant has not articulated how this error invalidated any part of the Trial Judgement. The Appeals Chamber observes that, although this event was charged in the Indictment, the Trial Chamber did not rely on it to establish the Appellant's responsibility for genocide.[229]

B. Alleged Error relating to the Alibi

109. The Appellant submits that the Trial Chamber erred in fact and in law in finding that he participated in the attack on the Mubuga Church on 15 April 1994.[230] He points to an alleged factual error in the Trial Chamber's assessment of his alibi and disputes that the evidence of Defence Witness TQ28, who saw him at the CCDFP building in Gishyita centre,[231] contradicts that he remained constantly at home.[232] In this respect, the Appellant asserts that CCDFP and his home "are basically in the same location [...] not even 70 metres apart."[233]

110. The Appeals Chamber observes that the Appellant has failed to substantiate his claim about the proximity of the CCDFP building to his home with any reference to the record. Putting this aside, however, the Appeals Chamber notes that this was only one of several factors which the Trial Chamber considered in rejecting the Appellant's alibi for this event. In particular, the Trial Chamber noted that the alibi evidence presented by other Defence witnesses was internally inconsistent and lacked credibility.[234] Moreover, the Trial Chamber pointed to the evidence of Witness DC, who also placed the Appellant at the church, further undermining the Appellant's claim that he remained continuously at home during the period covered by the alibi.[235] The Appellant does not address these other reasons for rejecting his alibi and thus has not demonstrated any error in the Trial Chamber's findings with respect to it. **[page 39]**

C. Alleged Error relating to the Burden of Proof

111. The Appellant argues that the Trial Chamber erred in law in its application of the burden of proof.[236] The Appellant suggests that the Trial Chamber required him to prove that he was not at Mubuga Church rather than cast reasonable doubt on the Prosecution's evidence.[237] Moreover, the Appellant argues that the Trial Chamber applied a standard of proof below beyond reasonable doubt in finding that he participated in the attacks on Mubuga Church.[238] In this respect, the Appellant points to the evidence of Defence Witnesses DZ and DAA, who were patrolling the church, and who testified that they did not see the Appellant during the attack.[239] The Appellant further alleges that the Trial Chamber made a related factual error in discrediting Witness DZ because he was not at the church.[240] According to the Appellant, Witness DZ was only a short distance away, approximately the length of the courtroom.[241]

112. In support of his contention that the Trial Chamber erred in law by requiring him to prove his absence from the church and that his participation in the attack was not proven beyond reasonable doubt, the Appellant points primarily to the following passage from the Trial Judgement pertaining to Witnesses DZ and DAA: "While it is quite possible that these witnesses would have recognized the Accused if they had seen him

229 Trial Judgement, paras. 487, 513.
230 Appellant's Brief, paras. 177-185.
231 The Trial Chamber did not define "CCDFP".
232 Appellant's Brief, para. 177.
233 Appellant's Brief, para. 177.
234 Trial Judgement, para. 160.
235 Trial Judgement, para. 160.
236 Appellant's Brief, paras. 178-184.
237 Appellant's Brief, paras. 178, 180, 183, 184.
238 Appellant's Brief, paras. 178, 180-184.
239 Appellant's Brief, para. 179.
240 Appellant's Brief, para. 185.
241 Appellant's Brief, para. 185.

during the attack, it is also quite possible that they would have missed seeing him."[242] The Appeals Chamber is not persuaded that this language demonstrates that the Trial Chamber shifted the burden of proof onto the Appellant, or that in making its findings, the Trial Chamber did not apply the beyond reasonable doubt standard in assessing the Prosecution's evidence.

113. In discussing its assessment of alibi evidence, the Trial Chamber specifically recalled that "it is incumbent on the Prosecution to establish beyond reasonable doubt that, despite the alibi, the facts alleged are nevertheless true."[243] A review of the Trial Judgement reveals that, in finding that the Appellant participated in the attack on Mubuga Church and that he killed Kaihura, the Trial Chamber relied on the eyewitness accounts of Prosecution Witnesses AF and AV, which it found to be credible.[244] The Appellant does not address this evidence, which underlies the factual findings on his role in the attack. Moreover, the Appeals Chamber finds no deviation from the principles related to the assessment of alibi evidence in the Trial Chamber's assessment of the testimonies of **[page 40]** Witnesses DZ and DAA. In making the impugned statement, the Trial Chamber simply considered the limited probative value that evidence of this nature has in the context of a large scale assault involving hundreds of attackers.[245]

114. In addition, the Appeals Chamber finds no error of fact in the Trial Chamber's statement, in assessing Witness DZ's evidence, that the witness "admitted that he was not stationed at the church itself, but rather on the road close to the church".[246] In the Appellant's view, the Trial Chamber failed to appreciate how close Witness DZ's position was to the church.[247] A review of the Trial Judgement reveals, however, that the Trial Chamber was mindful of the witness's proximity to the events since it expressly noted that he was "on the road close to the church".[248]

D. Conclusion

115. Accordingly, this ground of appeal is dismissed. **[page 41]**

XIII. ALLEGED ERRORS RELATING TO THE RAPE OF AGNES MUKAGATARE AT MUBUGA CEMETERY ON 15 APRIL 1994 (GROUND OF APPEAL 11)

116. The Trial Chamber found that, on 15 April 1994 after the attack on Mubuga Church, the Appellant and a group of *Interahamwe* brought six young Tutsi women to a cemetery near the church where the Appellant raped one of them, Agnes Mukagatare.[249] The Trial Chamber based its findings on the eyewitness account of Prosecution Witness AV.[250] The rape of Agnes Mukagatare forms part of the Appellant's conviction for rape as a crime against humanity.[251]

117. The Appellant submits that the Trial Chamber erred in fact[252] in finding that he raped Agnes Mukagatare on the basis of Witness AV's testimony because her evidence was internally inconsistent, lacked corroboration, and was inconsistent with the testimonies of other Prosecution and Defence witnesses, in

242 Appellant's Brief, para. 181, quoting Trial Judgement, para. 161.

243 Trial Judgement, paras. 13-15, quoting *Niyitegeka* Appeal Judgement, para. 60.

244 Trial Judgement, paras. 156, 165.

245 In this respect, the Trial Chamber was not satisfied that the Prosecution proved that the Appellant played a leadership role. *See* Trial Judgement, para. 157. Moreover, Witnesses DZ and DAA referred to a large number of attackers. *See* Trial Judgement, paras. 147, 151 (Witness DZ spoke of "eight hundred Hutu men" and Witness DAA referred to "about 2,000 gendarmes and about 1,500 civilians").

246 Trial Judgement, para. 161.

247 Appellant's Brief, para. 185.

248 Trial Judgement, para. 161.

249 Trial Judgement, paras. 198, 204.

250 Trial Judgement, paras. 170, 171, 191, 198, 199.

251 Trial Judgement, para. 552.

252 The Appellant initially describes the errors related to the assessment of Witness AV's evidence in the Appellant's Brief as an error of law. *See* Appellant's Brief, para. 186. However, it is clear from the nature of his submissions and the language used elsewhere in this ground of appeal and the Notice of Appeal that he is alleging errors of fact. *See, e.g.*, Appellant's Brief, paras. 192, 195, 198-200; Notice of Appeal, p. 14, paras. 36-38.

particular with respect to when the event occurred.[253] The Appellant further contends that the Trial Chamber erred in fact in rejecting his alibi for this period based on the evidence of Witness DC.[254]

A. Alleged Errors in the Assessment of Witness AV

118. The Appellant points to a number of alleged inconsistencies in the evidence of Witness AV, which he claims undermine her credibility and the possibility of her observing the rape. Witness AV's evidence reflects that, at the time she saw the Appellant, she was walking from the church to the nearby dispensary to find the bodies of her parents after learning of their death from her sister.[255] The Appellant contends that the ability of Witness AV and her sister to walk to and from Mubuga Church is contradicted by her evidence and that of Witness AF about the attack and the fact that *Interahamwe* were posted around the perimeter of the church at the time.[256] A review of the Trial Judgement and the record, however, reveals that these submissions lack merit. The Trial Chamber noted that Witness AV learned of the death of her parents and left the church on 15 April **[page 42]** 1994 after "the attack had subsided".[257] However, the Appellant cites testimony from Witness AF referring to *Interahamwe* surrounding the church preventing people from leaving on 14 April 1994, a day before the witness walked toward the dispensary.[258] The Appellant also claims that Witness AV gave contradictory testimony about whether her sister was at the church or the nearby dispensary where their parents were killed.[259] The Appeals Chamber, however, is not convinced that the portion of Witness AV's evidence referred to by the Appellant reflects a discrepancy in her account about whether her sister was at the church or the dispensary.[260] Therefore, these arguments do not demonstrate any error in the Trial Chamber's findings on Witness AV's credibility and her ability to be in a position to observe the Appellant's crime.

119. The Appellant argues that Witness AV's lack of knowledge concerning Agnes Mukagatare's age, home, and family background undermines the Trial Chamber's findings on her credibility.[261] Although the Trial Chamber did not expressly discuss in the Trial Judgement the basis of Witness AV's identification of the victim, a review of her evidence reflects that the witness knew Agnes Mukagatare as a nurse in the dispensary.[262] The Appellant has not shown this to be an unreasonable basis for identifying the victim.

120. The Appellant contends that Witness AV's evidence of the rape on the afternoon of 15 April 1994 is uncorroborated and conflicts with the evidence of Witness AF and Defence Witnesses DF and DG, who refer to a number of women being taken from the Mubuga Church and killed in the nearby cemetery on the night of 14 April 1994.[263] While Witness AV's testimony was not corroborated, the Appeals Chamber has consistently held that a Trial Chamber has the discretion to rely on uncorroborated, but otherwise credible, witness testimony.[264] The Trial Chamber found **[page 43]** Witness AV's account to be credible and explained

---

253 Notice of Appeal, p. 14, paras. 36-38; Appellant's Brief, paras. 186-199.

254 Notice of Appeal, p. 15, para. 40; Appellant's Brief, paras. 200-203.

255 Trial Judgement, paras. 170, 171.

256 Appellant's Brief, paras. 187-189, 191.

257 Trial Judgement, para. 170.

258 Appellant's Brief, para. 191, quoting T. 28 April 2004 p. 27. The Appellant in his submissions attempts to characterize this passage of Witness AF's testimony as indicating the conditions at the church "*from* 14 April 1994" (emphasis added). However, a review of the transcript reveals that the witness referred only to the conditions *on* 14 April 1994. *See* T. 28 April 2004 p. 27 ("Q. Now, what was the situation inside the Mubuga church *on the 14th* of April? [...] A. *On the 14th* the situation was not a good one for the refugees because they could not get out of the church for one. [...]") (emphasis added).

259 Appellant's Brief, para. 189.

260 It is clear from the exchange that the questions posed during cross-examination were very general and did not specify a time-frame and that Witness AV's sister ultimately came to the church. *See* T. 1 April 2004 pp. 54-55 ("Q. While you were in the church [...] were you there with any other member of your family? A. Yes, I was with some. [...] Q. All your brothers and all your sisters? A. Yes. Q. And how did you learn of your parents' death at the dispensary? A. My younger sister told me so. She was with them at the dispensary. Q. So all your sisters were not at the Catholic Church? A. Yes, that sister was not at the Catholic Church. Q. When did your junior sister join you? A. I do not recall the hour, but it was before midday, around midday.").

261 Appellant's Brief, para. 190.

262 T. 1 April 2004 p. 55 ("Q. Regarding the six girls, you could fully identify one of them and you could only identify the first names of two of them and the three others you can't remember their names. Can you talk to us about Mutagatare, whom you knew the best? A. She was a nurse at the dispensary, and that is why I knew her.").

263 Appellant's Brief, paras. 186, 192-199.

264 *Gacumbitsi* Appeal Judgement, para. 72.

that she "clearly recognized the Appellant" and had a "clear and unobstructed view" of his crime.[265] A review of the Trial Judgement reveals that the Trial Chamber considered the evidence of the killings on the night of 14 April 1994 in making its factual findings based on Witness AV's testimony.[266] The Trial Chamber was not satisfied that Witness AV and Witnesses DF and DG were referring to the same events.[267] The Trial Chamber's rejection of the Appellant's position at trial that the rape described by Witness AV and the crimes referred to by Witnesses DF and DG were the same appears reasonable, particularly given Witness AV's eyewitness account and the marked differences in the time of the events and the names and numbers of the victims.[268]

121. The Trial Chamber did not expressly consider whether Witness AV's account of the rape of Agnes Mukagatare on 15 April 1994 conflicted with Witness AF's evidence of women from the church being raped on the night of 14 April 1994. Nonetheless, it follows from the Trial Judgement that Witness AV's testimony was considered in the context of Witness AF's account.[269] The Appeals Chamber is not convinced that the evidence of Witness AF renders erroneous the Trial Chamber's findings based on Witness AV's testimony in light of the explanation provided by the Trial Chamber in connection with the alleged discrepancy of testimony of Witnesses DF and DG.

B. Alleged Errors related to the Alibi

122. In challenging the rejection of his alibi of remaining continuously at home on 15 April 1994, the Appellant notes that the Trial Chamber misstated the date when Witness DC placed him at Mubuga Church.[270] In particular, he notes that Witness DC testified that the Appellant was at the church on 12 or 13 April 1994, but the Trial Chamber, in rejecting his alibi for 15 April 1994, reflected that the witness saw him at the church on the day of the attack of 15 April 1994.[271] The Appeals Chamber agrees with the Appellant that the Trial Chamber misstated Witness DC's testimony in this portion of the Trial Judgement.[272] Nonetheless, the Appeals Chamber is not **[page 44]** satisfied that the Appellant has demonstrated an error occasioning a miscarriage of justice. Elsewhere in the Trial Judgement, including a section assessing the alibi, the Trial Chamber correctly reflected the date on which Witness DC saw the Appellant as "12 *or* 13 April" 1994.[273] The Appeals Chamber observes that the purpose of the Trial Chamber's inclusion of Witness DC's evidence in the assessment of the alibi was to reflect that the Appellant's proposition that he remained *continuously* at home from 8 to 16 April 1994 was exaggerated, not to demonstrate that the Appellant was at the church on 15 April 1994.[274]

123. Moreover, Witness DC's evidence that he saw the Appellant at the church on 12 or 13 April 1994 was only one of several factors the Trial Chamber took into account in finding that the alibi evidence for 15 April 1994 lacked credibility.[275] In particular, in rejecting the alibi for 15 April 1994, the Trial Chamber relied on the corroborated eyewitness accounts of Witnesses AV and AF who placed the Appellant at the church on 15 April 1994.[276] In addition, the Trial Chamber observed that the alibi evidence lacked credibility.[277] The

---

265 Trial Judgement, para. 197.

266 Trial Judgement, paras. 172, 179-186, 202. The Appeals Chamber notes that Witness AF heard that the women were raped, though Witnesses DF and DG stated that they were killed, but not that they were raped.

267 Trial Judgement, para. 202.

268 *Cf.* Trial Judgement, paras. 170, 171 *with* Trial Judgement, paras. 180-185. The Appeals Chamber also notes the Appellant's submission that the Trial Chamber erred in law and unfairly treated differently the discrepancies with respect to the timing of events when considering Prosecution and Defence evidence. Notice of Appeal, para. 39; Appellant's Brief, para. 197. The Appeals Chamber, in this instance, is not persuaded by this argument. For the Trial Chamber, the discrepancies reflected that Witness AV and Witnesses AF, DF, and DG were referring to different events, not that the Defence evidence lacked credibility. Trial Judgement, para. 202.

269 The Trial Chamber summarized Witness AF's account immediately after the evidence of Witness AV. Trial Judgement, paras. 170, 172.

270 Appellant's Brief, paras. 200-203.

271 Appellant's Brief, paras. 200, 201.

272 *See* Trial Judgement, para. 203.

273 Trial Judgement, paras. 121, 160.

274 Trial Judgement, paras. 12, 15, 160.

275 Trial Judgement, paras. 160, 203.

276 Trial Judgement, paras. 156, 203.

277 Trial Judgement, para. 160.

Appellant's submissions fail to demonstrate the unreasonableness of these other, independent grounds for rejecting his alibi, and thus he has not demonstrated that the Trial Chamber's findings with respect to it are erroneous.

124. Accordingly, this ground of appeal is dismissed. **[page 45]**

XIV. ALLEGED ERRORS RELATING TO THE ATTACK AGAINST TUTSI REFUGEES AT MUGONERO COMPLEX ON 16 APRIL 1994 (GROUND OF APPEAL 12)

125. The Trial Chamber found that the Appellant participated in an attack against Tutsi civilians at Mugonero Complex on 16 April 1994.[278] The Trial Chamber further found that the Appellant was present when the attacks were launched and that he used a gun to kill and inflict injuries on Tutsi civilians targeted by the attackers.[279] Additionally, the Trial Chamber determined that the Appellant committed and abetted rapes during this attack.[280] The Trial Chamber relied, in part, on its findings relating to the attack on the Mugonero Complex in convicting the Appellant of genocide,[281] rape as a crime against humanity,[282] and murder as a crime against humanity.[283] The Appellant raises several challenges to the Trial Chamber's assessment of the evidence and the credibility of Prosecution witnesses which the Trial Chamber relied upon in making findings relating to his participation in this attack. The Appeals Chamber discusses each of these challenges in turn below.

A. Alleged Error relating to Witness DI

126. The Appellant submits that the Trial Chamber erred in fact by attributing statements to Witness DI that he had not made, thereby distorting the witness's evidence to suggest that the Appellant killed with guns and grenades.[284] The Appellant contends that Witness DI's evidence instead establishes that the Appellant was not present during the attack against Tutsi refugees at Mugonero Complex on 16 April 1994.[285]

127. In summarizing Witness DI's testimony, the Trial Chamber stated that "Witness DI testified that the Accused never clubbed anyone to death, as only the assailants without guns or grenades killed victims in this manner."[286] The transcript reflects that the witness had testified that the *witness* himself, rather than the Appellant, had never clubbed anyone to death at the Mugonero Complex, **[page 46]** stating that "guns and grenades" were used in the attack.[287] This error in the summary was made only after the Trial Chamber had correctly recounted Witness DI's testimony, which indicated that "[a]ccording to Witness DI, 'Mika wasn't present' during the attack".[288] In determining whether the Appellant participated in the attacks at Mugonero Complex on 16 April 1994, the Trial Chamber recalled Witness DI's testimony that the Appellant "could not have been present during the attacks,"[289] but concluded, nonetheless, that it did not consider Witness DI's evidence to be credible.[290] Moreover, the Trial Chamber did not rely on Witness DI's testimony to establish that the Appellant "used his gun to kill and inflict injuries on Tutsi civilians targeted by the attackers" at Mugonero Complex.[291] Thus, the Appeals Chamber considers that the Trial Chamber's error in summarizing

278 Trial Judgement, para. 246. Relying on the same witnesses, the Trial Chamber considered the specific crimes committed by the Appellant during the attack in a separate section of the Trial Judgement. *See* Trial Judgement, paras. 261-306. These crimes are discussed under Ground of Appeal 13.

279 Trial Judgement, para. 259.

280 Trial Judgement, paras. 273-275, 302-304, 552, 553.

281 Trial Judgement, paras. 513, 519.

282 Trial Judgement, paras. 552, 553, 562, 563.

283 Trial Judgement, paras. 570, 582, 583.

284 Notice of Appeal, p. 15, para. 41; Appellant's Brief, paras. 204, 205 (emphasis added).

285 Appellant's Brief, para. 204.

286 Trial Judgement, para. 236.

287 T. 1 September 2004 p. 56 ("Q. Now, how many Tutsi refugees did you club to death at the complex? A. No one. We used guns and grenades. Guns and grenades were used. They could not have been hit with clubs, whereas there were guns and grenades that could be used.").

288 *Cf.* Trial Judgement, para. 236 *with* T. 1 September 2004 pp. 40, 57.

289 Trial Judgement, para. 250.

290 Trial Judgement, paras. 250, 251.

291 Trial Judgement, paras. 246, 259.

Witness DI's testimony does not demonstrate that the Trial Chamber's assessment of the evidence was unreasonable or resulted in a miscarriage of justice.

128. Accordingly, this sub-ground of appeal is dismissed.

B. Alleged Errors relating to Witness BG

129. The Appellant submits that the Trial Chamber erred in law and in fact in the assessment of Witness BG's credibility.[292] In this respect, the Appellant argues that portions of her account were scientifically inaccurate and points to inconsistencies between her pre-trial statements and her trial testimony.

1. Alleged Error in Relying on Witness BG's Testimony Given the Scientific Impossibility of Aspects of her Evidence

130. The Appellant submits that the Trial Chamber erred in law and in fact in finding Witness BG to be credible given her testimony "that 'a fire set by assailants at Mugonero Church with petrol was put out because of the blood everywhere'".[293] The Appellant argues that the witness's account is scientifically inaccurate.[294] Consequently, the Appellant suggests that Witness BG's testimony **[page 47]** could "only be a mistake or a lie," and that the Trial Chamber erred in law in disregarding "scientific truth".[295]

131. In assessing Witness BG's evidence, the Trial Chamber highlighted the Appellant's submissions challenging the scientific accuracy of Witness BG's testimony.[296] The Trial Chamber considered that the account, "even if scientifically inaccurate," did not "tarnish" the credibility of the witness.[297] Consequently, the Trial Chamber relied partially on Witness BG's testimony in finding that the Appellant participated in the attack on Mugonero Complex.[298]

132. The Appeals Chamber notes that the Trial Chamber made no findings as to whether blood put out the fire at Mugonero Church. This notwithstanding, a reasonable trier of fact may disregard certain parts of a witness's testimony while relying on other parts of the testimony which it considers credible and reliable.[299] In the present case, the Trial Chamber assessed Witness BG's credibility in light of the same challenge that the Appellant has brought on appeal.[300] Moreover, in finding that the Appellant participated in the 16 April 1994 attack on Mugonero Complex, the Trial Chamber also relied on corroborating evidence provided by several other witnesses.[301] Accordingly, the Appellant has failed to demonstrate that the Trial Chamber erred in relying, in part, on Witness BG's evidence in its findings related to the events at Mugonero Complex.

2. Alleged Failure to Address Discrepancies between Witness BG's Witness Statement and her Subsequent Evidence

133. The Appellant argues that the Trial Chamber erred in law and in fact in failing to address all of his objections relating to discrepancies between Witness BG's pre-trial statement of 14 November 1995 and a subsequent statement of 24 October 1999, as well as her trial testimony.[302] First, the Appellant argues that Witness BG provided inconsistent accounts regarding where she hid after leaving Mugonero Hospital.[303] The Appellant argues that Witness BG's 14 November 1995 statement indicates that she spent a week in

292 Notice of Appeal, p. 15, paras. 42, 43, Appellant's Brief, paras. 206-221.
293 Notice of Appeal, p. 15, para. 42; Appellant's Brief, paras. 206-208.
294 Appellant's Brief, para. 208.
295 Appellant's Brief, paras. 206, 208.
296 Trial Judgement, para. 248.
297 Trial Judgement, para. 248.
298 Trial Judgement, para. 259.
299 *See, e.g.*, *Ntagerura et al.* Appeal Judgement, para. 214; *Semanza* Appeal Judgement, paras. 155, 156; *Kajelijeli* Appeal Judgement, para. 167; *Kamuhanda* Appeal Judgement, para. 248.
300 Trial Judgement, para. 248.
301 Trial Judgement, paras. 246, 259.
302 Notice of Appeal, p. 15, para. 43; Appellant's Brief, para. 209.
303 Appellant's Brief, para. 209.

Gishyita and then stayed in Kibuye town for two weeks before moving to Zaire.[304] The Appellant notes that the witness's 24 October 1999 statement and her trial testimony indicated that upon leaving the hospital she climbed the hills towards Gitwa on **[page 48]** her way to the Bisesero area.[305] The Appellant argues that this discrepancy is relevant to whether the witness observed the events in the Bisesero area and to whether she could have been captured on 22 April 1994 and subsequently raped.[306]

134. Second, the Appellant emphasizes that Witness BG never mentioned rape and sexual violence in her 14 November 1995 statement, even though this statement was taken much closer to the events.[307] The Appellant suggests that Witness BG's explanations concerning this discrepancy at trial were so confusing that a reasonable trier of fact would have rejected her testimony.[308] Third, the Appellant argues that the Trial Chamber acted unreasonably in relying on the witness's later statement without providing any reason for disregarding the earlier statement.[309] Finally, the Appellant contends that the Trial Chamber erred in law in accepting the testimony of Witness BG,[310] as she ought to have been disqualified as a witness due to her incapacity to testify because she had suffered from "mental dementia and trauma".[311]

135. The Appeals Chamber recalls that the primary responsibility for assessing the credibility of witnesses and the probative value of evidence lies with the Trial Chambers.[312] In fulfilling this responsibility, a Trial Chamber has the duty to evaluate inconsistencies that may arise in the evidence.[313] Where a Trial Chamber has based its findings on testimony that is inconsistent with prior out-of-court statements or other evidence, this does not necessarily constitute an error.[314] However, the Trial Chamber is bound to take into account inconsistencies and any explanations offered in respect of them when weighing the probative value of the evidence.[315]

136. The Appeals Chamber notes that Witness BG's statement of 24 October 1999 was not tendered into evidence. Nonetheless, the relevant transcripts indicate that Witness BG was confronted with this statement during her cross-examination.[316] The Trial Judgement reflects that **[page 49]** the Trial Chamber considered the Appellant's arguments related to this document when making its findings.[317] Specifically, the Trial Chamber noted:

> The Defence submits that because of Witness BG's conflicting prior written statements, dated 14 November 1995 and 24 October 1999, as well as inconsistencies in her testimony, the evidence of this witness should be rejected.[318]

The Trial Chamber relied on Witness BG's evidence and that of several other witnesses in finding that the Appellant participated in attacks on Mugonero Complex on 16 April 1994.[319] However, the Trial Judgement does not explicitly address where she went upon leaving Mugonero Hospital or her failure to mention being raped in her 14 November 1995 statement.

---

304 Appellant's Brief, para. 210.

305 Appellant's Brief, paras. 209-211.

306 Appellant's Brief, paras. 212, 216. The Appellant has also been convicted of abetting the rape of Witness BG when on 22 April 1994 he "permitted" an *Interahamwe* named Mugonero to abduct Witness BG knowing that Mugonero wanted to rape her. Trial Judgement, paras. 318, 319, 323, 553, 563. The Appellant challenges this conviction under Ground of Appeal 13.

307 Appellant's Brief, para. 213.

308 Appellant's Brief, para. 214.

309 Appellant's Brief, para. 217.

310 Appellant's Brief, para. 221.

311 Appellant's Brief, para. 221.

312 *See, e.g., Niyitegeka* Appeal Judgement, para. 95; *Rutaganda* Appeal Judgement, para. 188; *Musema* Appeal Judgement, para. 18; *Kayishema and Ruzindana* Appeal Judgement, paras. 319, 323, 324; *Akayesu* Appeal Judgement, para. 132; *Aleksovski* Appeal Judgement, para. 63; *Tadić* Appeal Judgement, para. 64; *Kupreškić et al.* Appeal Judgement, paras. 31, 32, 156; *Čelebići Case* Appeal Judgement, para. 491.

313 *Kupreškić et al.* Appeal Judgement, para. 31 (internal citations omitted).

314 *Niyitegeka* Appeal Judgement, para. 96.

315 *See Kupreškić et al.* Appeal Judgement, para. 31. *See also Niyitegeka* Appeal Judgement, para. 96.

316 *See* T. 6 April 2004 pp. 13, 17, 22, 25-27.

317 *See* Trial Judgement, paras. 248, 249.

318 Trial Judgement, para. 248.

319 Trial Judgement, paras. 246, 247, 259. Additionally, the Trial Chamber relied on Witness BG's evidence alone in finding that the Appellant abetted Mugonero in raping her. *See* Trial Judgement, paras. 318-323, 553. This event is discussed under Ground of Appeal 13.

137. A review of the trial record reveals that Witness BG was cross examined regarding her failure to mention rape in her 14 November 1995 statement:

> A. I wasn't asked questions relating thereto, but I think, given the situation in which I found myself, even if questions were asked [of] me on that subject, I don't think I could have talked about it. For a Rwandan it is difficult to talk about such events. It is subsequently, after having gotten some training, some counsel from a number of people that have talked about it; otherwise I wouldn't have been able to talk about those events at that particular time.
>
> Q. Can we know what kind of training you received?
>
> A. On several occasions we were told that for those who were traumatised we needed to meet doctors and that these doctors told us that we should talk about those various events, which were difficult for us, and they told us that by talking about them it will be better for us to put them in perspective and to be aware of our state of health. And it is under those conditions that we, therefore, that had the courage of talking about them.[320]

The Trial Chamber sought clarification from the witness regarding her 14 November 1995 statement on this point.[321] Moreover, Witness BG was cross-examined on her failure to describe the attacks in Bisesero in her 14 November 1995 statement.[322] Subsequent to these questions and responses, Witness BG was also cross-examined regarding discrepancies in her 14 November 1995 statement concerning where she went after leaving Mugonero Hospital:

> Q. And when you left the basement, madam, where did you go?
>
> A. I went up through the Gitwe hill going towards the Bisesero region.
>
> Q. Since this has to do with the statement of the 14th November 1995 I will simply recall what we read, that is: 'I spent one week at Gishyita and then I was housed there for a week in Kibuye **[page 50]** town and then I moved on to Zaire.' You state, in your statement of 24 October, that you went to Bisesero; is that correct?
>
> A. Yes, that is true. I went to Bisesero.[323]

138. The Appellant has not demonstrated that the witness's explanations concerning the discrepancies among her accounts based on the trauma she suffered after being raped were unreasonable or that no reasonable trier of fact could have relied on Witness BG's evidence in light of the arguments advanced under this ground of appeal. In addition, the Appeals Chamber is satisfied that the Trial Chamber considered the discrepancies arising between Witness BG's 14 November 1995 statement and her subsequent statement and trial testimony. The Appeals Chamber recalls that the Trial Chamber is not obliged in its Judgement to recount and justify its findings in relation to every submission made during trial.[324] A Trial Chamber has the discretion to accept a witness's evidence, notwithstanding inconsistencies between trial testimony and his or her previous statements.[325] Accordingly, the Appeals Chamber is not convinced that the Trial Chamber erred in not explaining why it preferred certain aspects of Witness BG's evidence over others.

139. Finally, the Appellant argues that, as a matter of law, the Trial Chamber should have rejected Witness BG's evidence because she admitted that in 1995 she was "suffering from mental dementia and trauma"[326] and that no subsequent evidence was led to establish that she regained mental health. However, a review of the trial record reveals that at no point did Witness BG suggest that she suffered from "dementia". Moreover, the witness indicated that she had received counselling for the trauma she suffered.[327] Additionally, the Appellant fails to cite any evidence on the record revealing that Witness BG was incapable of understanding her obligations while testifying as a witness before the Tribunal. Therefore, the Appeals Chamber is not convinced that the Trial Chamber erred in relying on her testimony.

140. Accordingly, this sub-ground of appeal is dismissed.

---

320 T. 6 April 2004 pp. 7-8.
321 T. 6 April 2004 pp. 8-9.
322 T. 6 April 2004 p. 8.
323 T. 6 April 2004 p. 13.
324 *Čelebići Case* Appeal Judgement, para. 498.
325 *Kajelijeli* Appeal Judgement, para. 96.
326 Appellant's Brief, para. 221.
327 T. 6 April 2004 pp. 7-8.

C. Alleged Errors relating to Witnesses DS and DK

141. The Appellant submits that the Trial Chamber erred in law in rejecting the testimonies of Defence Witnesses DS and DK, who testified that, in Gishyita Prison and during *gacaca* sessions, his name was not mentioned in relation to the attack at Mugonero Complex.[328] He argues that the **[page 51]** Trial Chamber did not provide any reason for rejecting this exculpatory evidence and that this failure amounts to an error of law, which invalidates the Trial Chamber's decision.[329]

142. The Appeals Chamber notes that, in assessing the evidence of Witnesses DS and DK, the Trial Chamber did not find these witnesses persuasive because they were not eyewitnesses to the crimes committed at Mugonero Complex and their testimonies related to what they had heard years later in Gishyita Prison and during *gacaca* sessions.[330] The Appellant has not shown that the Trial Chamber's assessment of this evidence was unreasonable, particularly in light of the other evidence the Trial Chamber considered in relation to the crimes committed at Mugonero Complex.

143. Accordingly, this sub-ground of appeal is dismissed.

D. Alleged Error relating to Witness AV

144. The Appellant submits that the Trial Chamber erred in law by relying on the testimony of Witness AV as one of the Prosecution witnesses who testified about the attack at Mugonero Complex.[331] He contends that the entire testimony of Witness AV related exclusively to the "Mubuga site" and cannot be relied upon to support the allegations relating to the "Mugonero events".[332]

145. The Appeals Chamber notes that the Trial Chamber mentioned Witness AV once in its findings on the attacks at Mugonero Complex.[333] However, it is clear that this is a mere typographical error as the Trial Chamber did not summarize Witness AV's evidence alongside other Prosecution evidence on this event and because it did not discuss this witness's testimony in its analysis of the relevant evidence. Rather, the Trial Chamber relied on the evidence of Prosecution Witnesses BG, BI, BJ, AT, and AU.[334] Consequently, the Appeals Chamber finds that this error did not cause prejudice to the Appellant and did not invalidate the decision.

146. Accordingly, this sub-ground of appeal is dismissed.

E. Conclusion

147. For the foregoing reasons, this ground of appeal is dismissed in its entirety. **[page 52]**

XV. ALLEGED ERRORS RELATING TO THE RAPES AND MURDERS COMMITTED AT MUGONERO COMPLEX AND THE RAPE OF WITNESS BG (GROUND OF APPEAL 13)

148. The Trial Chamber found that, during the attack on Mugonero Complex on 16 April 1994, the Appellant played a role in the rape and murder of several women in three separate incidents which occurred in the basement of Mugonero Hospital.[335] Based on these findings, the Trial Chamber convicted the Appellant of genocide,[336] rape as a crime against humanity,[337] and murder as a crime against humanity.[338] In another event on 22 April 1994, which is not related to the attack on the complex, the Trial Chamber also found that

---

328 Notice of Appeal, p. 16, para. 44; Appellant's Brief, paras. 222-225.
329 Appellant's Brief, para. 225.
330 Trial Judgement, para. 254.
331 Notice of Appeal, p. 16, para. 45; Appellant's Brief, paras. 226-228.
332 Appellant's Brief, para. 227.
333 Trial Judgement, para. 259.
334 Trial Judgement, para. 247.
335 Trial Judgement, paras. 273, 274, 276, 291, 302, 552, 553, 570.
336 Trial Judgement, paras. 513, 519.
337 Trial Judgement, paras. 552, 553, 563.
338 Trial Judgement, paras. 570, 583.

the Appellant "permitted" an *Interahamwe* named Mugonero to "take away" Prosecution Witness BG with knowledge that Mugonero wanted to rape her.[339] Based on this event, the Trial Chamber convicted the Appellant for rape as a crime against humanity for abetting the rape of Witness BG.[340] The Appeals Chamber addresses in turn the Appellant's four sub-grounds of appeal challenging the factual and legal findings on the three incidents occurring at the Mugonero Hospital, as well as the events surrounding the rape of Witness BG.

A. Alleged Errors relating to the Rape and Murder of Mukasine Kajongi and Amos Karera's Two Daughters

149. The Trial Chamber found that, on 16 April 1994, the Appellant raped Mukasine Kajongi and abetted two other assailants accompanying him to rape the two daughters of Amos Karera in the basement of Mugonero Hospital.[341] The Trial Chamber further found that, after those rapes, the Appellant instigated the two other assailants to murder these three women.[342] The Trial Chamber relied on the evidence of a single witness, Prosecution Witness AT, who observed the events while under a pile of dead bodies.[343] The Trial Chamber convicted the Appellant for these rapes and **[page 53]** murders for genocide,[344] rape as a crime against humanity,[345] and murder as a crime against humanity.[346]

150. The Appellant submits that the Trial Chamber erred in law and in fact in convicting him for these crimes on the basis of the evidence of Witness AT. In particular, the Appellant alleges a number of inconsistencies between Witness AT's evidence and his previous statements, the lack of clarity in his evidence concerning the location of the crime, and the lack of corroboration.[347] In addition, the Appellant submits that the Trial Chamber erred in fact in relying on the evidence of Prosecution Witness AU in convicting him for this event.[348] The Appeals Chamber addresses each of the Appellant's arguments in turn.

1. Alleged Errors relating to Inconsistencies between Witness AT's Testimony and Pre-Trial Statements

151. With respect to alleged discrepancies between Witness AT's testimony and his prior statements, the Appellant submits that the Trial Chamber erred in fact in relying on Witness AT's account based on his written statement of 12 November 1999, instead of his earlier account provided in his statement of 20 June 1996.[349] He argues that the Trial Chamber ought to have relied upon the earlier statement, which makes no reference to rape, as this was taken closer in time to the events.[350] He also argues that a reasonable trier of fact would have found the later statement to be unreliable "in the absence of any plausible explanation" as to why the witness did not mention rape in the earlier statement.[351]

152. The Appeals Chamber considers that the Appellant's present line of argument, suggesting that Witness AT did not see the Appellant's crimes because they were not mentioned in his first pre-trial statement, is not convincing. As the Appeals Chamber has previously held, "to suggest that if something were true a witness would have included it in a statement or a confession letter is obviously speculative and, in general, it cannot

[339] Trial Judgement, paras. 318, 323, 553.
[340] Trial Judgement, paras. 553, 563.
[341] Trial Judgement, paras. 273, 274, 552, 553.
[342] Trial Judgement, paras. 276, 570. The Trial Chamber's factual findings refer to the murder of only one of Amos Karera's daughters while its legal findings refer to the killing of both daughters. Neither party raises this discrepancy on appeal. A review of the transcripts of Witness AT's testimony, in particular the French version, reveals that the witness indicated that both daughters were killed. *See* T. 19 April 2004 p. 16; T. 19 April 2004 p. 17 (French version).
[343] Trial Judgement, para. 272.
[344] Trial Judgement, paras. 513, 519.
[345] Trial Judgement, paras. 552, 553, 563.
[346] Trial Judgement, paras. 570, 583.
[347] Notice of Appeal, pp. 16-18, paras. 46-54, 56-58; Appellant's Brief, paras. 229-248, 250-257.
[348] Notice of Appeal, p. 18, para. 55; Appellant's Brief, para. 249.
[349] Appellant's Brief, paras. 230-234.
[350] Appellant's Brief, para. 230.
[351] Appellant's Brief, para. 233.

substantiate a claim that a Trial Chamber erred in assessing the witness's credibility."[352] Moreover, the Appellant presented these arguments to the Trial Chamber.[353] The Trial Chamber undertook "a careful review of the written statements and the **[page 54]** oral testimony of Witness AT," in particular with respect to the omission of rape in the first statement.[354] The Trial Chamber considered any discrepancies between them to be minor and was not satisfied that the omission of rape in the first statement affected the witness's credibility.[355] The Appellant has failed to show how the Trial Chamber erred in considering his arguments and, accordingly, has failed to show any error of law or fact in the Trial Chamber's assessment of Witness AT's credibility with respect to the alleged inconsistencies in his statements.

2. Alleged Error relating to the Location of the Crime

153. The Appellant submits that the Trial Chamber erred in fact in relying on Witness AT's unreliable and uncorroborated evidence to establish that these crimes were committed and that the basement of Mugonero Hospital was the crime scene.[356] The Appellant points to several discrepancies in Witness AT's testimony and prior statements with respect to the details of this location.[357] He argues that the Trial Chamber minimized these discrepancies in its assessment of his testimony and, therefore, failed to clarify the exact location of the crime.[358] He submits that this alleged error of fact resulted in a further error of law because the location of a crime is a material fact which is necessary to prove the existence of the crime itself.[359]

154. The Trial Chamber concluded that the rape and murder of Mukasine Kajongi and Amos Karera's two daughters occurred in the basement of Mugonero Hospital.[360] In making this finding, the Trial Chamber considered the various alleged inconsistencies in Witness AT's account, in particular related to the location of the crime, and concluded, notwithstanding, that the witness gave credible evidence.[361]

155. Beyond general complaints that the Trial Chamber minimized the specific discrepancies to which he alludes, the Appellant alleges only one specific error in the Trial Chamber's assessment of Witness AT's account of the location of the crime.[362] The Appellant claims that the Trial Chamber misstated Witness AT's testimony in justifying an alleged discrepancy about the number of rooms **[page 55]** in the surgical area.[363] The Trial Chamber stated: "Witness AT did not assert that the surgical theatre consisted of many rooms. Rather, the witness testified only that there were more than two rooms in the surgical area, located in the basement of the hospital."[364] The Appellant contends that the Trial Chamber erred in stating that Witness AT never testified that there were several rooms in the "surgical area".[365]

156. The Appeals Chamber considers that the Appellant has failed to appreciate the Trial Chamber's distinction in this passage between the terms "surgical theatre" and "surgical area" and finds no contradiction between this statement and the witness's testimony. The Appellant has therefore not pointed to any factual error in the Trial Chamber's assessment of the various discrepancies advanced by him at trial. The Trial Chamber reasoned that any inconsistency in Witness AT's account related to "minor details" and, with respect to discrepancies as to the location of the crime, simply resulted from trauma, the passage of time, and the witness's lack of familiarity with the surgical theatre.[366] The Appellant has not demonstrated that, in

---

352 *Kajelijeli* Appeal Judgement, para. 176.
353 Trial Judgement, paras. 269, 270.
354 Trial Judgement, paras. 269, 270.
355 Trial Judgement, paras. 269, 270. The Trial Chamber noted, *inter alia,* that "the witness' explanation, during cross-examination, that the 1996 statement focused on the attack itself, not on particular incidents which occurred during the course of the attack", and that "the witness was consistent in his description of the rape of Mukasine Kajongi." *Id.,* para. 270.
356 Appellant's Brief, paras. 235, 236, 242-245.
357 Appellant's Brief, paras. 237-244.
358 Appellant's Brief, paras. 236, 242.
359 Appellant's Brief, paras. 245, 247.
360 Trial Judgement, paras. 274, 276.
361 Trial Judgement, paras. 269, 271.
362 Appellant's Brief, para. 244.
363 Appellant's Brief, para. 244.
364 Trial Judgement, para. 271.
365 Appellant's Brief, para. 244.
366 Trial Judgement, paras. 269, 271.

these circumstances, this was an unreasonable basis for assessing any discrepancy or vagueness in the witness's evidence related to the location of the crime. A review of Witness AT's testimony reveals that he consistently stated that he sought refuge in a room with around thirty dead bodies in the basement of Mugonero Hospital, where he witnessed the rape and murder of three women.[367]

157. The Appeals Chamber is not satisfied that the Appellant has shown that no reasonable trier of fact could have made the Trial Chamber's findings with respect to the location of the crime. Therefore, the Appellant's further argument that the Trial Chamber erred in law by failing to establish the location of the crime need not be addressed.

3. Alleged Error relating to Lack of Corroboration

158. The Appellant submits that the Trial Chamber erred in law in relying on the uncorroborated evidence of Witness AT.[368] In this respect, in addition to the arguments raised above, he argues that Witness AT engaged in collusion, lied about his relationship with Witness BJ, and was involved in a murder.[369] **[page 56]**

159. It is well established that a Trial Chamber has the discretion to rely on uncorroborated, but otherwise credible, witness testimony.[370] The Trial Chamber assessed Witness AT, an eyewitness to this event, and found him to be credible.[371] As discussed above, the Appeals Chamber is not satisfied that the Appellant has pointed to any factual or legal error in this assessment with respect to the alleged inconsistencies in the witness's account.

160. In asserting that Witness AT colluded with other witnesses, the Appellant points to the following passage from his testimony:

> Q. You told the Prosecution investigator the following: "Regarding rape and other sexually related crimes, which is the purpose of your investigations, I knew about some cases, in particular three cases of rape and one case of sexual mutilation." Can you confirm that statement?
>
> A. I made that statement, but then haven't you heard women who came to testify here? I'm sure you must have listened to their testimonies.[372]

The Appeals Chamber considers that this passage simply reflects Witness AT's awareness that women had been raped and does not evidence collusion with other witnesses.

161. The Appeals Chamber is also not satisfied that the Appellant has demonstrated any error on the part of the Trial Chamber with respect to his allegation that Witness AT lied about his relationship with Witness BJ, who also attested to an incident of rape at the Mugonero Complex.[373] A review of the record reveals that, although Witness AT stated during cross-examination that he did not have a "relationship" with Witness BJ,[374] he provided additional clarification on this matter during his re-examination.[375] Therefore, the Appellant has not demonstrated that the witness misrepresented his relationship with Witness BJ. Moreover, this issue was fully explored during the witness's testimony and raised during closing arguments,[376] and it was thus before the Trial Chamber when assessing the witness's credibility. Finally, beyond referring to allegations advanced during closing arguments, the Appellant has not substantiated his claim that Witness AT was involved in a murder.

162. Accordingly, the Appellant has not demonstrated any error of fact or law on the part of the Trial Chamber in relying on the uncorroborated testimony of Witness AT. **[page 57]**

---

367 T. 19 April 2004 pp. 11-13, 37-38.
368 Appellant's Brief, paras. 246, 254, 257.
369 Appellant's Brief, paras. 251 257.
370 *Gacumbitsi* Appeal Judgement, para. 72, citing *Semanza* Appeal Judgement, para. 153.
371 Trial Judgement, paras. 269, 272, 273.
372 T. 19 April 2004 p. 25.
373 *See* Trial Judgement, paras. 284-286, 288.
374 T. 19 April 2004 pp. 28, 30.
375 T. 20 April 2004 pp. 25-26.
376 T. 19 April 2004 pp. 26-34; T. 20 April 2004 pp. 24-26; T. 20 January 2005 p. 35.

4. Alleged Error relating to Witness AU

163. The Appellant submits that the Trial Chamber erred in fact in relying on Witness AU's testimony to establish the murder of Mukasine Kajongi and Amos Karera's two daughters.[377] He argues that this witness never testified about this event.[378] The Appeals Chamber observes that in its factual findings on these murders, the Trial Chamber referred to Witness AU hearing the assailants' gunfire.[379] However, a review of the Trial Judgement and record reveals that this is simply a typographical error. The evidence misattributed to Witness AU is clearly set out in the summary of the evidence in connection with Witness AT.[380] Therefore, the Appeals Chamber is not satisfied that this typographical error resulted in a miscarriage of justice.

164. Accordingly, this sub-ground of appeal is dismissed.

B. Alleged Errors relating to the Rape of Witness BJ, Mukasine, and Murekatete

165. The Trial Chamber found that, on 16 April 1994 in the basement of Mugonero Hospital at the Mugonero Complex, the Appellant raped Prosecution Witness BJ, a young Hutu woman whom he mistook for a Tutsi.[381] The Trial Chamber further found that at the same time two assailants, who accompanied the Appellant, raped Mukasine and Murekatete, whose ethnicity was not established at trial.[382] The Trial Chamber found that the Appellant abetted these rapes.[383] In part, on the basis of these events, the Trial Chamber convicted the Appellant of rape as a crime against humanity.[384] On appeal, the Appellant raises three principal legal and factual challenges related to an alleged defect in the form of the Indictment, the ethnicity of the victims, and the credibility of Witness BJ.[385]

1. Alleged Defect in the Form of the Indictment

166. The Appellant submits that the Trial Chamber erred in law[386] in convicting him on the basis of the rapes of Witness BJ, Mukasine, and Murekatete because the Indictment failed to provide him with sufficient notice of the place of these crimes.[387] He submits that the Indictment alleges that the **[page 58]** rapes were committed at Mugonero Complex, which is "huge and comprises several buildings, including a hospital, a church, and a school".[388]

167. The charges against an accused and the material facts supporting those charges must be pleaded with sufficient precision in the indictment so as to provide notice to the accused.[389] The Appeals Chamber has held that criminal acts that were physically committed by the accused personally must be set forth in the indictment specifically, including where feasible "the identity of the victim, the time and place of the events and the means by which the acts were committed."[390]

168. Paragraph 6(c)(ii) of the Indictment reads:

> On 16 April 1994, at the Mugonero complex, Mikaeli Muhimana and *Interahamwe* collectively raped civilian *Tutsi* women Mukasine and Murekatete staff maids at Mugonero hospital, and a civilian *Hutu* lady BJ-K. Mikaeli Muhimana subsequently apologised to BJ-K for the 'mistake' of raping her as he initially thought she was *Tutsi*.

---

377 Appellant's Brief, para. 249.
378 Appellant's Brief, para. 249.
379 Trial Judgement, para. 276.
380 *See* Trial Judgement, para. 265.
381 Trial Judgement, paras. 291, 552.
382 Trial Judgement, paras. 291, 553.
383 Trial Judgement, para. 553.
384 Trial Judgement, paras. 552, 553, 563.
385 Notice of Appeal, pp. 18-19, paras. 59-62; Appellant's Brief, paras. 258-267.
386 The Appellant refers to this as an error of fact. However, the Appeals Chamber treats claims of lack of notice as errors of law. *See, e.g., Gacumbitsi* Appeal Judgement, para. 46; *Niyitegeka* Appeal Judgement, para. 191.
387 Notice of Appeal, p. 18, para. 59; Appellant's Brief, paras. 258-262.
388 Appellant's Brief, para. 259.
389 *See supra* para. 76. *See also Gacumbitsi* Appeal Judgement, para. 49; *Ndindabahizi* Appeal Judgement, para. 16.
390 *Gacumbitsi* Appeal Judgement, para. 49, quoting *Ntakirutimana* Appeal Judgement, para. 32, quoting *Kupreškić et al.* Appeal Judgement, para. 89. *See also Ndindabahizi* Appeal Judgement, para. 16.

On the basis of this paragraph, the Trial Chamber concluded, *inter alia*, that the Appellant raped Witness BJ and abetted the rapes of Mukasine and Murekatete in the basement of Mugonero Hospital at the Mugonero Complex.[391] From the Indictment alone, the Appellant would have known that he was being charged in connection with these rapes at Mugonero Complex. The Indictment, however, does not indicate that these crimes specifically occurred in the basement of the Mugonero Hospital.

169. The question remains whether the failure to further specify the location of these crimes within the Mugonero Complex as the basement of the Mugonero Hospital renders this paragraph defective with respect to the location of these crimes. The Appeals Chamber notes that the Prosecution was in a position to provide the exact location of these rapes as early as 15 November 1999.[392] Nonetheless, the Appeals Chamber is not satisfied that the failure to plead the exact location of these crimes within the complex resulted in a defect in the Indictment.

170. In the *Ntakirutimana* Appeal Judgement, the Appeals Chamber concluded that Gérard Ntakirutimana had adequate notice that he murdered Charles Ukobizaba at the Mugonero Hospital during this same attack on Mugonero Complex.[393] In that case, Gérard Ntakirutimana challenged **[page 59]** his indictment, alleging that it did not, *inter alia*, set forth the place of this crime in sufficient detail.[394] The Appeals Chamber notes that, as with the events in this case, the murder occurred at the Mugonero Hospital and the indictment referred to the location of the crime only as "Mugonero Complex".[395] Beyond the assertion that Mugonero Complex is "huge",[396] the Appellant has not advanced any argument indicating why further specificity was required in this particular case.

171. Accordingly, the Appellant has failed to demonstrate that the Indictment was defective with respect to the location of these crimes.

2. Alleged Errors relating to the Ethnic Identity of the Victims

172. In addition, the Appellant submits that the Trial Chamber erred in fact in finding in paragraph 288 of the Trial Judgement that Mukasine and Murekatete were Tutsi when it referred to them as "two *Tutsi* staff maids".[397] He notes that Witness BJ testified that she did not know the ethnicity of Mukasine and Murekatete.[398] Moreover, the Appellant submits that, in failing to establish the ethnic identity of these women, the Trial Chamber erred in law in convicting him for genocide on the basis of this event.[399]

173. Paragraph 288 of the Trial Judgement, which the Appellant challenges, is not a factual finding, but simply a summary of allegations contained in paragraph 6(c)(ii) of the Indictment. Contrary to the Appellant's assertion, the Trial Chamber observed in its factual findings on this incident that the ethnicity of Mukasine and Murekatete was unknown.[400] Moreover, the Appellant's contention that the Trial Chamber erred in law in entering a conviction against him for genocide based on this event is without merit. The Trial Chamber

391 Trial Judgement, paras. 291, 552.

392 *See* Respondent's Brief, para. 209 ("In her statement of 15 November 1999, Witness BJ stated that, 'I did not identify those spearheading the attack because I was scared; my only concern then was to arrive at the hospital as swiftly as possible and hide. At about 9 am, a man named MIKA came into the room with two other men.'").

393 *Ntakirutimana* Appeal Judgement, paras. 30-44.

394 *Ntakirutimana* Appeal Judgement, para. 21.

395 *Ntakirutimana* Appeal Judgement, paras. 30, 33-44. The Appeals Chamber concluded in the *Ntakirutimana* Appeal Judgement that the indictment was defective because it failed to plead the specific murder. The Pre-Trial Brief along with the witness statements, which the Appeals Chamber concluded cured this defect, also did not further specify the location of the crime beyond referring to Mugonero Complex.

396 Appellant's Brief, para. 259.

397 Appellant's Brief, para. 264.

398 Appellant's Brief, para. 263.

399 Appellant's Brief, paras. 263, 264. The Appellant makes reference to the failure to establish that the women belonged to a "protected group" within the meaning of the Genocide Convention and the Statute. Appellant's Brief, para. 263. Thus, the Appeals Chamber understands his submissions as challenging his conviction for genocide.

400 Trial Judgement, para. 291.

stated in its legal findings that the Appellant's conviction for genocide, insofar as it related to acts of rape at Mugonero Complex, encompassed only the rapes of Tutsi women.[401] **[page 60]**

174. Rather, the Appellant was convicted of the rapes of Mukasine and Murekatete as a crime against humanity,[402] and he does not dispute that these crimes were part of the "discriminatory, widespread, and systematic attacks [...] directed against groups of *Tutsi* civilians in Gishyita *Commune* and in the Bisesero area, between April and June 1994."[403] Accordingly, the Appellant has not demonstrated any error related to the Trial Chamber's findings related to the ethnicity of the victims which might result in a miscarriage of justice.

3. Alleged Error in the Assessment of Witness BJ

175. The Appellant submits that the Trial Chamber erred in fact and in law in failing to address all but one of the nineteen arguments raised in the Defence Closing Brief relating to the reliability of Witness BJ's testimony.[404] He argues that this failure deprived him of a fair trial, which includes the right to be guaranteed that the evidence and arguments presented by the Defence have been heard and carefully considered.[405]

176. The Appeals Chamber notes that the fact that the Trial Chamber did not refer to every one of the Appellant's arguments in relation to Witness BJ's testimony in its reasoning, does not mean that those arguments had not been considered. A Trial Chamber is not required to set out in detail why it accepted or rejected a witness's testimony, or justify its evaluation of testimony in cases where there are discrepancies in the evidence.[406] It is also not obliged in its judgement to recount and justify its findings in relation to every submission made at trial.[407] Moreover, the Appeals Chamber declines to consider the Appellant's remaining eighteen arguments allegedly impugning the credibility of Witness BJ in particular as they are incorporated merely by reference from the Defence Closing Brief, without any additional argument justifying their consideration on appeal.

177. Accordingly, this sub-ground of appeal is dismissed.

C. Alleged Errors relating to the Rape of Witness AU

178. The Trial Chamber found that, on 16 April 1994 during the attack on Mugonero Complex, the Appellant raped Witness AU twice in the basement of Mugonero Hospital.[408] The Trial Chamber convicted him, in part, based on this event for genocide[409] and rape as a crime against **[page 61]** humanity.[410] The Appellant submits errors of fact and of law in the notice given to him in the Indictment for this event and in the assessment of Witness AU's testimony.[411]

1. Alleged Defect in the Form of the Indictment

179. The Appellant contends that the Indictment alleges that the rape took place at "Mugonero School of Medicine", which does not exist, and that it therefore does not give notice that the event occurred in the basement of Mugonero Hospital.[412]

---

401 Trial Judgement, para. 513 ("The Chamber finds that, through personal commission, the Accused killed and caused serious bodily or mental harm to members of the *Tutsi* group: [...] (c) By taking part in attacks at Mugonero Complex, where he raped *Tutsi* women and shot at *Tutsi* refugees. Many *Tutsi* refugees died or were injured in the attack.").

402 Trial Judgement, paras. 553, 563.

403 Trial Judgement, para. 533.

404 Appellant's Brief, paras. 265, 266.

405 Appellant's Brief, para. 266.

406 *Musema* Appeal Judgement, para. 20.

407 *Čelebići Case* Appeal Judgement, para. 498.

408 Trial Judgement, paras. 302, 552.

409 Trial Judgement, paras. 513, 519.

410 Trial Judgement, paras. 552, 563.

411 Notice of Appeal, p. 19, para. 63; Appellant's Brief, paras. 268-274. The Appellant also raises an argument in his Notice of Appeal concerning the credibility of her account concerning the number of attackers, which he does not develop in his brief. Notice of Appeal, p. 19, para. 63.

412 Appellant's Brief, paras. 270, 274.

180. Paragraph 6(c)(iv) of the Indictment reads:

> On 16 April 1994, at the Mugonero complex, Mikaeli Muhimana, acting in concert with *Interahamwe* went to one of the operating rooms in the medical school building in the Mugonero complex and collectively raped Tutsi women AU-K, Immaculate Mukabarore, Josephine Mukankwaro. In particular Mikaeli Muhimana raped AU-K.

181. On the basis of the Indictment alone, the Appellant would have known that he was being charged with the rape of Witness AU at the Mugonero Complex. As the Appeals Chamber noted above in this ground of appeal, this is sufficient notice of the location of this crime in the context of these events. In light of the reference to "operating room" and "medical school building", the Appeals Chamber is satisfied that it would have been apparent that this was a reference to the Mugonero Hospital. Accordingly, the Appellant has failed to demonstrate that the Indictment was defective with respect to the location of this crime.

2. Alleged Errors in the Assessment of Witness AU

182. The Appellant submits that the Trial Chamber erred in fact in finding that Witness AU was raped in the basement of Mugonero Hospital because the witness gave conflicting testimony about the location of the crime and could not clearly indicate where it occurred.[413] The Appellant points to passages in the witness's testimony where she refers both to "the church" and "the hospital surgery" and to a contradiction in the witness's testimony and her pre-trial statement concerning whether she was alone in the room before the Appellant raped her.[414] **[page 62]**

183. As the Appellant submits, Witness AU apparently stated that she observed other women "lying down on the ground in the church", referring to the same location where she was raped.[415] The Appeals Chamber notes that immediately after this reference the interpreters asked the witness to move closer to the microphone because they were having difficulty hearing her.[416] The witness then indicated that, when the attackers arrived, she and other refugees were on the ground of the church, and subsequently went to the surgical room.[417] A review of the transcripts reveals that, other than this one instance, Witness AU consistently attested to fleeing the church to the hospital where she was raped in the hospital basement.[418] In addition, her testimony also reflects that at some points she used the term "church" to refer to the entire Mugonero Complex.[419] Therefore, the Appeals Chamber is not convinced that no reasonable trier of fact could have relied on her account despite this discrepancy.

184. A certain degree of ambiguity is apparent in Witness AU's account of whether she was in the room alone or with others when the Appellant raped her.[420] The Trial Chamber, however, was aware of this, as it sought clarification from her on this point during her testimony.[421] The Appeals Chamber considers that the Trial Chamber appears to have exercised an appropriate degree of caution in assessing her testimony as reflected in its rejection of certain portions of her account relating to other rapes she claimed to have witnessed.[422] Accordingly, the Appeals Chamber is not satisfied that these apparent contradictions show that no reasonable trier of fact could have made the Trial Chamber's finding that this crime occurred in the basement of the Mugonero Hospital.

---

413 Appellant's Brief, paras. 268-274.

414 Appellant's Brief, paras. 271-273.

415 T. 7 April 2004 p. 5 ("Q. [...] You said the *Interahamwes* were maltreating these girls and raping them. A. That is correct. Q. It was – and you also indicated this is the same room where Mika Muhimana had sexual intercourse with you. A. Yes, these other people were lying down on the ground in the church. I was able to identify some of these people.").

416 T. 7 April 2004 p. 5.

417 T. 7 April 2004 p. 5 ("Q. Thank you, Madam Witness. We were talking about the *Interahamwes* who were raping the girls, and as a follow-up to that, I want to ask a question whether Mika Muhimana was present when these *Interahamwes* were raping the girls. A. He was present, and when he came in he was accompanied by a large crowd of *Interahamwe*. We were on the floor in the church, and afterwards we went to the surgical room.").

418 T. 7 April 2004 pp. 4-5, 7, 18, 21-23, 29.

419 *See, e.g.,* T. 7 April 2004 p. 3 ("We were at the hospital in Ngoma, in a church [...]. We saw people running away. We went towards the church. When we arrived at the church, the president was dead. We learnt of this when we reached the hospital.").

420 T. 7 April 2004 pp. 25-30.

421 T. 7 April 2004 p. 30.

422 Trial Judgement, para. 303.

D. Alleged Errors relating to the Rape of Witness BG

185. The Trial Chamber found that the Appellant "permitted" an *Interahamwe* called Mugonero to "take away" Witness BG with the knowledge that Mugonero intended to rape her.[423] The Trial Chamber found that, based on this, the Appellant encouraged Mugonero to rape Witness BG and **[page 63]** that this encouragement contributed substantially to the subsequent rape.[424] The Trial Chamber, therefore, found the Appellant responsible for abetting the rape of Witness BG and convicted him for rape as a crime against humanity, in part based on this event.[425]

186. The Appellant alleges that the Trial Chamber erred in law in convicting him of a crime that is not provided for in the Statute.[426] The Appellant argues that he was convicted for "authorising" Mugonero to abduct and rape Witness BG, which is not a mode of participation under Article 6(1) of the Statute.[427] Moreover, the Appellant further argues that, to the extent that "authorising" means "ordering", Mugonero allegedly asked for a "favour" and thus was not compelled to commit the crime.[428]

187. The Trial Chamber convicted the Appellant for abetting the rape of Witness BG.[429] Abetting is one of the modes of participation under Article 6(1) of the Statute. Therefore, the Appellant's argument that he was convicted of a crime or for a mode of participation that is not in the Statute is without merit.

188. In addition, the Appellant argues that the Trial Chamber erred in fact in failing to establish the structure of the *Interahamwe* in Gishyita Commune, his role in the *Interahamwe*, and a superior-subordinate relationship between him and Mugonero.[430] He submits that the Trial Chamber was required to establish his position of authority in order to show that he used his authority to "persuade or force another person to commit a crime."[431]

189. The Appeals Chamber has explained that an aider and abettor carries out acts specifically directed to assist, encourage, or lend moral support to the perpetration of a specific crime, and that this support has a substantial effect on the perpetration of the crime.[432] The requisite mental element of aiding and abetting is knowledge that the acts assist the commission of the specific crime of the **[page 64]** principal perpetrator.[433] For an accused to be convicted of abetting an offence, it is not necessary to prove that he had authority over the principal perpetrator.[434]

190. The Appeals Chamber is not convinced that the Trial Chamber erred in convicting the Appellant for abetting the rape of Witness BG when he gave permission to Mugonero to "take away" Witness BG. The Trial Chamber concluded that the Appellant was a well-known and influential person in his community.[435] The Trial Chamber further found that the Appellant knew that Mugonero wanted to rape the witness.[436] The Appeals Chamber considers that a reasonable trier of fact could find that the Appellant's actions in such circumstances amounted to encouragement which had a substantial affect on Mugonero's subsequent rape of Witness BG. In the *Semanza* Appeal Judgement, the Appeals Chamber reached a similar conclusion in

---

423 Trial Judgement, paras. 318, 323, 553.
424 Trial Judgement, para. 553.
425 Trial Judgement, paras. 553, 563.
426 Notice of Appeal, p. 20, para. 69; Appellant's Brief, paras. 276-284. In addition, in his Notice of Appeal, the Appellant raised a number of challenges to the credibility of Witness BG, but he did not develop them in his Appellant's Brief under this ground. Notice of Appeal, pp. 19-20, paras. 65-68. The Appeals Chamber, however, discusses these issues in connection with the Appellant's challenge to Witness BG's credibility under Ground of Appeal 12.
427 Appellant's Brief, paras. 276-284.
428 Appellant's Brief, paras. 282, 283.
429 Trial Judgement, para. 553.
430 Appellant's Brief, paras. 275, 285-290.
431 Appellant's Brief, paras. 285, 290.
432 *Ntakirutimana* Appeal Judgement, para. 530; *Vasiljević* Appeal Judgement, para. 102.
433 *Ntakirutimana* Appeal Judgement, para. 530; *Vasiljević* Appeal Judgement, para. 102.
434 *Cf. Semanza* Appeal Judgement, para. 257 (referring to instigation).
435 Trial Judgement, para. 604.
436 Trial Judgement, para. 323.

respect of an "influential" accused who encouraged the rape of Tutsi women by giving "permission" to rape them.[437]

191. Accordingly, this sub-ground of appeal is dismissed.

E. Conclusion

192. In view of the foregoing, this ground of appeal is dismissed in its entirety. **[page 65]**

XVI. ALLEGED ERRORS RELATING TO THE ATTACK AT KANYINYA HILL IN MAY 1994 (GROUND OF APPEAL 14)

193. The Trial Chamber found that, "on a morning during May 1994", the Appellant called the Tutsi refugees on Kanyinya Hill together for a meeting and, when one of them stepped forward to speak to him, he told the individual that he would return the next day with "white people who would bring food and medicine".[438] The Trial Chamber concluded that on the next day the Appellant returned to the hill with busloads of armed assailants and unleashed a devastating attack.[439] The Trial Chamber found that the Appellant actively participated in this attack by shooting and wounding a Tutsi man named Nyagihigi.[440] In making these findings, the Trial Chamber relied primarily on the evidence of Prosecution Witness AP, which it found was corroborated by Prosecution Witness AW.[441] The Trial Chamber convicted the Appellant of genocide in part based on his role in this attack.[442] On appeal, the Appellant raises three principal factual and legal challenges with respect to the Trial Chamber's assessment of the notice provided by the Indictment, the Prosecution evidence, and the standard applied in assessing Defence evidence.[443] The Appeals Chamber addresses these arguments in turn.

A. Alleged Defect in the Form of the Indictment

194. The Appellant submits that the Trial Chamber erred in law in failing to address his arguments pertaining to the vagueness of the Indictment.[444] He argues that paragraph 5(d)(v) of the Indictment lacks precision and fails to plead any physical act of genocide.[445]

195. As noted above, the charges against an accused and the material facts supporting those charges must be pleaded with sufficient precision in the Indictment so as to provide notice to the accused.[446] Applying the standard of notice articulated previously in this Judgement, where an accused is alleged to have personally committed a crime, the indictment must specify the criminal acts physically committed by the accused.[447] An indictment lacking this precision is defective; **[page 66]** however, the defect may be cured if the Prosecution provides the accused with timely, clear, and consistent information detailing the factual basis underpinning the charge.[448]

196. Paragraph 5(d)(v) of the Indictment reads: "In May 1994, Mikaeli Muhimana along with Clement Kayishema, Obed Ruzindana, *Interahamwe* and *gendarmes*, searched for and attacked *Tutsi* civilians taking refuge in Kabakobwa, Gitwa, Kanyinya and Ngendombi hills in Bisesero area." In connection with this allegation, the Trial Chamber found that the Appellant participated in an attack on Kanyinya Hill in May

---

437 *Semanza* Appeal Judgement, paras. 256, 257, quoting *Semanza* Trial Judgement, para. 478.
438 Trial Judgement, para. 339.
439 Trial Judgement, para. 340.
440 Trial Judgement, para. 513.
441 Trial Judgement, paras. 338-340.
442 Trial Judgement, para. 513.
443 Notice of Appeal, p. 20, paras. 70-73; Appellant's Brief, paras. 291-314.
444 Notice of Appeal, p. 20, para. 73; Appellant's Brief, para. 314.
445 Appellant's Brief, para. 314.
446 *See supra* paras. 76, 167. *See also Gacumbitsi* Appeal Judgement, para. 49, *Ndindabahizi* Appeal Judgement, para. 16.
447 *Gacumbitsi* Appeal Judgement, para. 49; *Ntakirutimana* Appeal Judgement, para. 32, quoting *Kupreškić et al.* Appeal Judgement, para. 89. *See also Ndindabahizi* Appeal Judgement, para. 16.
448 *Gacumbitsi* Appeal Judgement, para. 49. *See also Ntagerura et al.* Appeal Judgement, paras. 28, 65.

1994 and participated in this massacre of Tutsis, *inter alia*, by shooting and wounding a Tutsi man named Nyagihigi.[449]

197. On the basis of the Indictment alone, the Appellant could not have known that he was being charged with personally shooting and wounding Nyagihigi during this attack. While in certain circumstances, "the sheer scale of the alleged crimes makes it impracticable to require a high degree of specificity in such matters as the identity of the victims and the dates for the commission of the crimes",[450] this is not the case with respect to the shooting of Nyagihigi.[451] The Prosecution should have expressly pleaded this shooting and wounding as it had the information in its possession before the amended Indictment was filed.[452] The Indictment was thus defective in this respect.

198. A review of the trial record, including the evidence of Witness AP, reveals that the Appellant did not object to the form of this paragraph before trial or during the witness's testimony. The Prosecution, however, argues only that the Appellant failed to raise this argument in the Defence Closing Brief.[453] The Appeals Chamber notes that the Appellant did challenge the evidence that he shot and wounded Nyagihigi after the close of the Defence case before closing arguments in a motion to strike Witness AP's testimony, along with other Prosecution evidence, on grounds of lack of notice.[454] In deciding on the Appellant's motion to strike, the Trial Chamber held that it would consider these issues in reaching final judgement and invited the parties to present their submissions on this point in their closing briefs.[455] A review of the Defence Closing Brief also **[page 67]** reveals that the Appellant raised an objection in it based on the inadequacy of the notice provided by paragraph 5(d)(v) of the Indictment.[456]

199. The Appeals Chamber has held that, where a Trial Chamber has treated a challenge to an indictment as being adequately raised, the Appeals Chamber should not invoke the waiver doctrine.[457] In this case, the Trial Chamber did not consider the Appellant's objection based on lack of notice in its motion to strike as untimely, but rather invited the parties to present arguments on this point in their final submissions.[458] In addition, although it did not specifically address the Appellant's claims of lack of notice in respect to this paragraph of the Indictment in the Trial Judgement, the Trial Chamber considered other similar challenges made in the Defence Closing Brief as timely.[459] The Appeals Chamber will therefore treat the Appellant's objection as having been timely raised. It therefore falls to the Prosecution to prove that the Appellant's defence was not materially impaired by this defect.[460]

200. The question remains whether the defect in the Indictment was cured by subsequent timely, clear, and consistent information provided to the Appellant. The Prosecution makes no submissions in this regard, simply referring to the sheer scale of the massacre.[461] Nonetheless, the Appeals Chamber observes that the Appellant conceded in his motion to strike that he received more detailed notice of this incident in the Pre-Trial Brief.[462] A review of the summary of Witness AP's anticipated testimony in an annex to the Pre-Trial

449 Trial Judgement, paras. 340, 513.

450 *Gacumbitsi* Appeal Judgement, para. 50, citing *Kupreškić et al.* Appeal Judgement, para. 89 (internal citations omitted).

451 The Trial Chamber did not refer to the Appellant's initial visit to assess the situation and to call on the refugees to gather together on the date of the massacre as part of his participation in the attack. Trial Judgement, para. 513.

452 Indeed, the Prosecution had this information in its possession since Witness AP provided statements between 1999 and 2000.

453 Respondent's Brief, para. 250.

454 *See The Prosecutor v. Mikaeli Muhimana*, Case No. ICTR-95-1B-T, *Requête en irrecevabilité des témoignages relatifs à des charges ne figurant pas dans l'acte d'accusation modifié ou n'ayant pas été soutenues devant la Chambre ou ayant été rétractées par le Procureur*, 6 September 2004, para. 6 (requesting exclusion of Witness AP's testimony in part on the basis that the shooting of Nyagihigi is not pleaded in the Indictment).

455 *Muhimana*, Order in Relation to Defence Motion on Inadmissibility of Witness Testimony.

456 Defence Closing Brief, paras. 177, 194.

457 *Gacumbitsi* Appeal Judgement, para. 54. *See also Ntakirutimana* Appeal Judgement, para. 23.

458 *Muhimana*, Order in Relation to Defence Motion on Inadmissibility of Witness Testimony.

459 *See, e.g.*, Trial Judgement, paras. 403, 404, 571-575.

460 *Gacumbitsi* Appeal Judgement, para. 51.

461 Respondent's Brief, paras. 249-252.

462 *See The Prosecutor v. Mikaeli Muhimana*, Case No. ICTR-95-1B-T, *Requête en irrecevabilité des témoignages relatifs à des charges ne figurant pas dans l'acte d'accusation modifié ou n'ayant pas été soutenues devant la Chambre ou ayant été rétractées par le Procureur*, 6 September 2004, para. 6.

Brief contains an allegation that the Appellant was among the leaders attacking the refugees at Kanyinya Hill and that sometime in mid-May 1994 she saw the Appellant shoot and kill Nyagihigi.[463]

201. In the *Gacumbitsi* Appeal Judgement, the Appeals Chamber held that a summary of an anticipated testimony in an annex to the Prosecution's pre-trial brief could, in certain circumstances, cure a defect in an indictment.[464] The present circumstance is similar to that in *Gacumbitsi* where the summary of the anticipated testimony provides greater detail in a consistent manner with a **[page 68]** general allegation pleaded in the Indictment.[465] The Pre-Trial Brief therefore provided the Appellant with timely, clear, and consistent information sufficient to put him on notice that he was being charged with committing genocide by shooting Nyagihigi at Kanyinya Hill. Therefore, the Appellant has failed to demonstrate that the Trial Chamber erred in failing to consider his arguments pertaining to the vagueness of paragraph 5(d)(v) of the Indictment.

B. Alleged Errors in the Assessment of Witnesses AP and AW

202. The Appellant submits that the Trial Chamber erred in fact in assessing the evidence of Witnesses AP and AW and in making factual findings on the basis of it.[466]

203. The Appellant submits that Witness AW's evidence reflects that no attack occurred at Kanyinya Hill because, contrary to his direction, the refugees did not assemble in order to receive the promised humanitarian assistance.[467] The Appeals Chamber, however, is not satisfied that the Appellant has demonstrated any contradiction between Witness AW's account on this point and the Trial Chamber's findings that an attack occurred.

204. The Appellant further submits that Witness AW's account of the Appellant's conversation with Witness AW during his initial visit to Kanyinya Hill is implausible and that no reasonable trier of fact could have relied on this evidence to establish the Appellant's role in the attack.[468] The Appellant argues that the conversation could not have taken place because, if, as the Prosecution contended, the Appellant was armed and a "genocide hangman [...] whose job was to exterminate Tutsi", he would have simply killed Witness AW, a Tutsi, at this meeting.[469] The Appeals Chamber is not convinced that this submission, which is mere speculation, calls into question the reasonableness of the Trial Chamber's reliance on Witness AW's testimony. This is especially so because this conversation took place not on the day of the attack, but earlier.[470]

205. Next, the Appellant submits that the Trial Chamber erred in fact in finding that Witness AW corroborated Witness AP's evidence in light of several alleged discrepancies between their accounts related to the timing of the events and what transpired during the Appellant's initial meeting with **[page 69]** the refugees.[471] In particular, the Appellant notes that Witness AW described the Appellant arriving for the initial visit with Obed Ruzindana and two soldiers and stated that the attack occurred two days later.[472] The Appellant submits that, in contrast, Witness AP described the Appellant arriving with communal police and stated that the attack occurred one day later.[473] The Appellant observes that neither witness placed this event

---

463 Pre-Trial Brief, Annex A, p. 2. The summary, however, does not refer the Appellant to paragraph 5(d)(v) of the Indictment.

464 *Gacumbitsi* Appeal Judgement, paras. 57, 58. *See also Ntakirutimana* Appeal Judgement, para. 48 (holding that a witness statement, when taken together with "unambiguous information" contained in a pre-trial brief and its annexes may be sufficient to cure a defect in an indictment). This approach is consistent with ICTY jurisprudence. *See Naletilić and Martinović* Appeal Judgement, para. 45.

465 *Gacumbitsi* Appeal Judgement, para. 58.

466 Notice of Appeal, p. 20, paras. 70, 71; Appellant's Brief, paras. 291-304. The Appellant also points to an apparent contradiction between the evidence of Witnesses AP and AW and Witness BI as to the location where the Appellant told the refugees to assemble after his initial visit. Appellant's Brief, para. 295. However, as the Appellant acknowledges, the Trial Chamber did not rely on Witness BI's testimony in making findings on this event. *See* Trial Judgement, para. 338.

467 Appellant's Brief, paras. 291, 292.

468 Appellant's Brief, paras. 293, 294.

469 Appellant's Brief, para. 294.

470 Trial Judgement, paras. 329, 338.

471 Appellant's Brief, paras. 296-304.

472 Appellant's Brief, paras. 300, 303.

473 Appellant's Brief, paras. 300, 301

in mid-May 1994, noting that Witness AP stated that it occurred at the beginning of May 1994.[474] Finally, the Appellant's submissions suggest that Witness AW's description of a group of refugees interacting with the Appellant is inconsistent with the Trial Chamber's finding that one individual stepped forward to speak with him.[475]

206. The Trial Chamber did not explicitly assess these discrepancies between the accounts of Witnesses AP and AW, which, the Appeals Chamber notes, are for the most part readily apparent in the summary of their evidence presented in the Trial Judgement.[476] Rather, in assessing their evidence, the Trial Chamber focused on the similarities in the accounts of Witnesses AW and AP, noting that both testified that the Appellant arrived in a red vehicle accompanied by others and promised to return with assistance for the refugees.[477] The Appeals Chamber observes that these witnesses provided a broadly consistent description and chronology of the events in question and notes that Witness AP attested to giving estimates with respect to dates and times.[478] The Appeals Chamber also finds no error in the finding that the event occurred in mid-May 1994, a broad time frame, which is not inconsistent with the general description provided by the witnesses.[479]

207. Moreover, a review of the Trial Judgement reveals that the Trial Chamber relied primarily on the evidence of Witness AP in making findings on the details of this event.[480] While not every aspect or detail of Witness AP's account was corroborated by Witness AW, the Appeals Chamber has consistently held that a Trial Chamber has the discretion to rely on uncorroborated, but **[page 70]** otherwise credible, witness testimony.[481] The Trial Chamber determined that Witness AP was credible,[482] and the Appellant has not shown this finding to be erroneous.

208. Accordingly, the Appellant has not demonstrated that no reasonable trier of fact could have considered the testimony of Witness AW as corroborating the testimony of Witness AP and made findings on the basis of their evidence.

C. Alleged Error in the Assessment of Defence Evidence

209. The Appellant submits that the Trial Chamber erred in law by applying a stricter standard in assessing the credibility of Defence witnesses in respect of this event than in assessing the Prosecution evidence and by reversing the burden of proof, leading it to reject the Defence evidence.[483] The Appellant argues that the Trial Chamber accepted a certain degree of vagueness in assessing descriptions of the events provided by Prosecution witnesses, noting that it was understandable given the passage of time.[484] However, the Appellant asserts that, in assessing the credibility of Defence witnesses, the Trial Chamber used similar vagueness in their accounts to reject their evidence.[485] In addition, the Appellant submits that the Trial Chamber's rejection of testimonies of Defence witnesses who stated that they did not see him during the attack essentially required him to prove that he did not participate in the crimes.[486]

474 Appellant's Brief, paras. 298, 299.
475 Appellant's Brief, paras. 291-294.
476 Trial Judgement, paras. 326-329.
477 Trial Judgement, para. 338.
478 Trial Judgement, para. 326 ("Witness AP told the Chamber that she could not recall the specific dates of events that occurred when she was in the Bisesero Hills.").
479 Prosecution Witness AW placed this event between 10 and 14 May 1994. T. 14 April 2004 p. 54 ("This happened in the month of May, I would say between the 10th and the 14th, before the attacks that were launched on Muyira hill."). Prosecution Witness AP estimated that this event occurred sometime after 8 May 1994. Her testimony reflects that she arrived in the Bisesero area on 8 April 1994 and saw the Appellant there about a month after her arrival. *See* Trial Judgement, para. 326; T. 30 March 2004 pp. 32, 33 ("I only got to Bisesero on the 8th [of April] [...]. Well, we could not recall dates. We do not even know the day of the week. Night followed day. We didn't know which day it was. It was in the month of May. We had just spent a month in Bisesero.").
480 Trial Judgement, paras. 326-328, 339, 340.
481 *Gacumbitsi* Appeal Judgement, para. 72.
482 Trial Judgement, para. 338.
483 Notice of Appeal, p. 20, para. 72; Appellant's Brief, paras. 305-313.
484 Appellant's Brief, paras. 306, 308.
485 Appellant's Brief, paras. 307, 309, 310, 313.
486 Appellant's Brief, paras. 312, 313.

210. In assessing the credibility of Defence Witnesses DY, DK, DL, and DF, who admitted to participating in various attacks in the Bisesero area, the Trial Chamber observed that they gave "vague descriptions of the time and place of the attacks in which they participated and sketchy details about their own roles in the killing."[487] However, the vagueness in their accounts was not the principal reason for rejecting their evidence. Rather, as the Trial Chamber noted, "[t]he thrust of the Defence evidence was that these witnesses neither saw the Accused during the attacks nor heard, during *gacaca* sessions held in prison in Rwanda, that the Accused participated in the attacks."[488] The Appellant has thus not established that the Trial Chamber erred by applying a more stringent standard to its assessment of the Defence evidence than in its assessment of the Prosecution evidence. **[page 71]**

211. Moreover, the Appeals Chamber is also not satisfied that the Appellant has shown that, in rejecting this Defence evidence, the Trial Chamber reversed the burden of proof. Noting that "these attacks involved thousands of assailants spread over a large area", the Trial Chamber simply reflected the limited probative value that evidence of this nature has in the context of a large-scale assault.[489] Accordingly, the Appeals Chamber dismisses these arguments.

D. Conclusion

212. In view of the foregoing, this ground of appeal is dismissed in its entirety. **[page 72]**

XVII. ALLEGED ERRORS RELATING TO THE MURDER OF PASCASIE MUKAREMERA (GROUND OF APPEAL 15)

213. The Trial Chamber found that, in mid-May 1994 on Rugona Hill, the Appellant cut a pregnant woman, Pascasie Mukaremera, with a machete and removed her child, who cried before dying.[490] The victim died as a result of the injuries.[491] The Trial Chamber convicted the Appellant of murder as a crime against humanity, in part based on this event.[492]

214. The Trial Chamber found that the relevant paragraph of the Indictment was defective with respect to the timing of this event, its location, and the form of the Appellant's participation in the crime.[493] Paragraph 7(d)(i) of the Indictment reads: "Towards the end of May 1994, at Nyakiyabo hill in the Bisesero area an *Interahamwe* named Gisambo killed Pascasie Mukarema, on instructions of Mikaeli Muhimana." The Trial Chamber observed that the Appellant disputed this allegation based on lack of notice with respect to the time and place of the event, but not as to the nature of his role in the murder.[494] The Trial Chamber considered that a summary of the testimonies of Prosecution Witnesses BI and AW, contained in an annex to the Prosecution's Pre-Trial Brief, as well as the disclosure of Witness AW's written statement cured these defects.[495]

215. On appeal, the Appellant submits that the Trial Chamber erred in law[496] in convicting him of the murder of Pascasie Mukaremera because the Indictment failed to give him proper notice of the time and place of the crime and his role in it.[497] In addition, he disputes the Trial Chamber's conclusion that he failed to contest the variance between the description of him in the Indictment as instructing Gisambo to kill Pascasie Mukaremera and the finding that he personally committed the crime.[498] He argues that this variance

487 Trial Judgement, para. 342.

488 Trial Judgement, para. 342. For the same reasons, the Trial Chamber rejected the evidence of Defence Witness DD who was a refugee on Kanyinya Hill at the time. *See* Trial Judgement, para. 343.

489 Trial Judgement, paras. 342, 343.

490 Trial Judgement, paras. 402, 570, 576.

491 Trial Judgement, para. 576.

492 Trial Judgement, paras. 570, 576, 582, 583.

493 Trial Judgement, paras. 404, 574.

494 Trial Judgement, paras. 403, 404, 575. The Trial Chamber refers only to "the Defence submission" without referring to a particular document. The Trial Chamber appears to be referring to the Defence's Closing Brief.

495 Trial Judgement, paras. 403, 404, 574.

496 The Appellant refers to this as an error of fact. *See* Appellant's Brief, para. 315. However, the Appeals Chamber treats claims of lack of notice as errors of law. *See, e.g., Gacumbitsi* Appeal Judgement, para. 46; *Niyitegeka* Appeal Judgement, para. 191.

497 Notice of Appeal, paras. 74, 75; Appellant's Brief, paras. 315-340.

498 Appellant's Brief, paras. 331-334.

was not simply a defect in the legal qualification of the crime, but instead indicated that the Indictment pleaded a different act.[499]

216. The Prosecution responds that the Appellant had sufficient notice of the time and location of the murder of Pascasie Mukaremera and his role in it through the Pre-Trial Brief and through the **[page 73]** disclosure of the statement of Witness AW.[500] The Prosecution acknowledges that the Indictment was defective as to the legal qualification of the Appellant's role in the crime, but that it was within the Trial Chamber's discretion to reclassify the Appellant's mode of participation and enter a finding of guilt for personal commission, rather than ordering the murder.[501] The Prosecution further adds that the Appellant failed to object to the legal qualification of the crime at trial and has failed to demonstrate prejudice on appeal.[502] In this respect, the Prosecution observes that ordering and personal commission are both direct forms of participation in a crime.[503]

217. Applying the standard of notice articulated previously in this Judgement, where an accused is alleged to have personally committed a crime, the indictment must specify the criminal acts physically committed by the accused.[504] An indictment lacking this precision is defective; however, the defect may be cured if the Prosecution provides the accused with timely, clear, and consistent information detailing the factual basis underpinning the charge.[505]

218. As the Trial Chamber observed, the Indictment is defective because it fails to allege the correct time and location of the murder and that the Appellant physically committed it.[506] The Appellant, therefore, could not have known, on the basis of the Indictment alone, that he was being charged with personally killing Pascasie Mukaremera in mid-May 1994 on Rugona Hill. A review of the transcripts of Prosecution Witness AW, whose uncorroborated testimony supports this conviction, reveals that the Appellant did not make a specific objection at the time the evidence was presented. However, he did raise an objection based on lack of notice in his Defence Closing Brief.[507] Although the Prosecution submits that the Appellant failed to make a contemporaneous objection to the evidence of Witness AW at trial,[508] the Trial Chamber did not describe the Appellant's objection based on lack of notice in its closing brief as untimely. The Appeals Chamber has held that, where a Trial Chamber has treated a challenge to an indictment as being adequately raised, the Appeals Chamber should not invoke the waiver doctrine.[509]

219. The question arises whether the Appellant's objection pertained solely to the time and place of the murder or whether he also objected to the description of his alleged role in the killing. Both **[page 74]** the Trial Chamber in its Judgement, and the Prosecution on appeal, consider that the Appellant failed to dispute the defect in the description in the Indictment of his role in the crime and, in this respect, only challenged evidence related to it on its merits.[510] However, a review of the Defence Closing Brief reveals that the Appellant also challenged the Indictment based on its failure to plead his physical perpetration of this crime.[511] Accordingly, the Appeals Chamber considers that the Appellant raised a timely objection to all defective aspects of this paragraph of the Indictment at trial. It therefore falls to the Prosecution to prove that the Appellant's defence was not materially impaired by these defects.[512]

220. The question remains whether the defect in the Indictment was cured by the disclosure of Witness AW's written statement and the summary of the evidence of Prosecution Witnesses BI and AW in an annex

499 Appellant's Brief, paras. 325-328, 340.
500 Respondent's Brief, paras. 254-264.
501 Respondent's Brief, para. 261.
502 Respondent's Brief, para. 263.
503 Respondent's Brief, para. 264.
504 *See supra* paras. 76, 167, 195. *See also Gacumbitsi* Appeal Judgement, para. 49; *Ntakirutimana* Appeal Judgement, para. 32, quoting *Kupreškić et al.* Appeal Judgement, para. 89, *Ndindabahizi* Appeal Judgement, para. 16.
505 *Gacumbitsi* Appeal Judgement, para. 49. *See also Ntagerura et al.* Appeal Judgement, paras. 28, 65.
506 Trial Judgement, paras. 403, 404, 574.
507 Defence Closing Brief, paras. 318, 321.
508 Respondent's Brief, para. 259.
509 *Gacumbitsi* Appeal Judgement, para. 54. *See also Ntakirutimana* Appeal Judgement, para. 23.
510 Trial Judgement, para. 575; Respondent's Brief, para. 263.
511 Defence Closing Brief, paras. 318, 321.
512 *Gacumbitsi* Appeal Judgement, para. 51. *See also Ntagerura et al.* Appeal Judgement, paras. 31, 138.

to the Prosecution's Pre-Trial Brief. On appeal, the Prosecution does not point to any additional filings or oral submissions beyond those mentioned by the Trial Chamber when considering whether the Indictment defects were cured.[513]

221. The Appeals Chamber observes that the summary of Witness BI's testimony in the annex refers to a different, although strikingly similar event allegedly occurring on Nyakiyabo Hill, rather than to the one presented at trial, occurring on Rugona Hill.[514] The summary provides:

> In Bisesero the witness was hiding in one of the hills, Nyakiyabo [*sic*] saw Muhimana shoot dead a child Mukasine was carrying and proceed to rape Mukasine. After raping the girl, Gisambo raped the same girl before shooting her.

The summary does not indicate that this anticipated testimony goes to Paragraph 7(d)(i) of the Indictment, which is at issue.[515] Moreover, the summary clarifies in a column entitled "Reconfirmations/Notice on New Evidence/Discrepancies" that Gisambo, not Muhimana, killed Mukasine's child, who was seven years old, not an infant.[516]

222. The summary of Witness AW's anticipated testimony in the annex to the Pre-Trial Brief, based on Witness AW's pre-trial statement dated 12 December 1999,[517] states in pertinent part: "[...] Witness fled to Rugona hill. In mid-May 1994, witness saw Muhimana opening the stomach **[page 75]** of a pregnant Tutsi woman called Pascasie Mukaremera."[518] This summary further indicates that this information is relevant to paragraph 7(d)(i) of the Indictment, which is quoted above.[519]

223. In the *Gacumbitsi* Appeal Judgement, the Appeals Chamber held that a summary of an anticipated testimony in an annex to the Prosecution's pre-trial brief could, in certain circumstances, cure a defect in an indictment.[520] In that case, the indictment alleged generally that "Gacumbitsi killed persons by his own hands".[521] The Appeals Chamber found this allegation to be vague, in particular as it referred to the physical commission of murder of a particular person.[522] However, a summary of anticipated testimony contained in an annex to the pre-trial brief referred to a specific killing and connected it to the crime of genocide.[523] The Appeals Chamber also observed that the summary did not conflict with any other information that was provided to the accused and was provided in advance of trial.[524] The information in the annex to the pre-trial brief was thus found to be timely, clear, and consistent and to provide sufficient notice of the allegation of the specific murder mentioned in the summary.[525]

224. The circumstances presented in this instance, however, are different. The summary of Witness AW's anticipated testimony does not simply add greater detail in a consistent manner with a more general allegation already pleaded in the Indictment. Rather, the summary modifies the time, location, and physical perpetrator, matters that were already specifically pleaded in the Indictment, albeit in a materially different manner. In such circumstances, the summary of Witness AW's anticipated testimony in the annex of the Pre-Trial Brief and the disclosure of his witness statement do not provide clear and consistent information sufficient to put the Appellant on notice that he was being charged with physically committing the murder of Pascasie Mukaremera on Rugona Hill in mid-May 1994. The summary of Witness AW's testimony does not supplement or provide greater detail, but materially alters key facets of this paragraph. This discrepancy

513 *See* Respondent's Brief, para. 256.
514 *See* Pre-Trial Brief, Annex A, p. 4.
515 *See* Pre-Trial Brief, Annex A, p. 4. Instead, it refers to Paragraphs 5(c) and 6(c) of the Indictment which relate to the events at the Mugonero Complex. *Id.*
516 *See* Pre-Trial Brief, Annex A, pp. 1, 4.
517 *See* Ex. D 16(f).
518 Pre-Trial Brief, Annex A, p. 6.
519 Pre-Trial Brief, Annex A, p. 6.
520 *Gacumbitsi* Appeal Judgement, paras. 57, 58. *See also Ntakirutimana* Appeal Judgement, para. 48 (holding that witness statements, when taken together with "unambiguous information" contained in a pre-trial brief and its annexes may be sufficient to cure a defect in an indictment). This is consistent with ICTY jurisprudence. *See Naletilić and Martinović* Appeal Judgement, para. 45.
521 *Gacumbitsi* Appeal Judgement, para. 58.
522 *Gacumbitsi* Appeal Judgement, para. 50.
523 *Gacumbitsi* Appeal Judgement, paras. 57, 58.
524 *Gacumbitsi* Appeal Judgement, para. 58.
525 *Gacumbitsi* Appeal Judgement, para. 58.

should have been immediately apparent to the Prosecution as it prepared its Pre-Trial Brief and listed the anticipated testimony of Witness AW in support of a paragraph of the Indictment that materially conflicted with it, in particular given that the Prosecution had shortly prior to that added this allegation to the **[page 76]** Indictment for the purpose of providing specificity to the Accused.[526] The Prosecution however did not seek to clarify this discrepancy with a clear, timely, and consistent communication.

225. In addition, contrary to the observation in the Trial Judgement, the summary of Witness BI's testimony did not provide any notice that the location of the crime for which the Appellant was convicted is Rugona Hill because the summary appears to refer to a different event on Nyakiyabo Hill.[527] Rather, the summary of Witness BI's testimony simply adds greater confusion given its mention of Nyakiyabo Hill, which is in fact the location of the crime pleaded in paragraph 7(d)(i).

226. Moreover, the Appeals Chamber is not persuaded that these defects were not prejudicial, as indicated by the Trial Chamber, because the witness's testimony with respect to the date of the incident was consistent with his statement; because Rugona Hill, like Nyakiyabo Hill, is in the Bisesero area; and because the Indictment is merely defective in its legal qualification of the Appellant's act.[528] First, the question of proper notice is not whether the witness's testimony is consistent with his or her prior statement, but rather whether the notice provided is clear, consistent, and timely.[529] Second, as to the fact that Rugona Hill, like Nyakiyabo Hill, is in the Bisesero area, in the *Niyitegeka* Appeal Judgement, the Appeals Chamber concluded that the Trial Chamber erred in convicting the Appellant based on his participation in a massacre where the Indictment referred only generally to the Bisesero area, which did not give notice of a specific attack at a named location on a specific date.[530] Finally, the defect is not simply a mischaracterization of the legal qualification of the crime, but an error in the description of the material facts of the crime itself.

227. In sum, the failure to properly plead Pascasie Mukaremera's murder in the Indictment was not cured and the Prosecution has failed to rebut the presumption of material impairment of the defence. Accordingly, the Appeals Chamber finds, Judge Schomburg dissenting, that the Trial Chamber erred in law in relying on this evidence in convicting the Appellant for this murder. His conviction for murder as a crime against humanity for this event on this count is therefore **[page 77]** invalidated. As a consequence, the Appeals Chamber need not address the Appellant's remaining arguments under this ground of appeal.[531]

228. This error of law, however, does not invalidate the conviction of the Appellant for murder because this conviction did not rest solely on this murder. In addition, though the Trial Chamber described this particular attack as a "highly aggravating factor",[532] the Appeals Chamber is not satisfied that this error invalidates the Appellant's sentence of imprisonment for the remainder of his life in view of the other crimes[533] as well as the other aggravating factors considered by the Trial Chamber.[534] Accordingly, the Appeals Chamber finds no basis for disturbing the Appellant's conviction for murder as a crime against humanity despite its finding that the Trial Chamber erred in finding this incident established. **[page 78]**

---

526 *Muhimana*, Decision on Motion to Amend Indictment, paras. 7, 9 ("A comparison of the general allegations and facts described in the current Indictment with the detailed account in the proposed Indictment shows that the fairness of the trial will be very substantially enhanced. [...] The new Indictment provides more precise particulars as to the location of killings and other criminal acts. [...] Rather than changing or extending geographical scope, the effect of the proposed Indictment is to specify more precise locations within the broad area defined in the current Indictment. In that sense, the Defence cannot reasonably argue that it has had no notice that events at these locations are part of the Prosecution's case.").

527 *See* Pre-Trial Brief, Annex A, p. 4.

528 Trial Judgement, paras. 403, 404, 571-574.

529 *Gacumbitsi* Appeal Judgement, para. 49. *See also Ntagerura et al.* Appeal Judgement, paras. 28, 65.

530 *Niyitegeka* Appeal Judgement, paras. 229-235.

531 *See* Notice of Appeal, paras. 76-78; Appellant's Brief, paras. 342-346.

532 Trial Judgement, para. 612.

533 In addition to the Appellant's convictions for genocide and rape as a crime against humanity, for which he was sentenced respectively to two concurrent terms of life imprisonment, the conviction and life sentence for murder also rests on the Appellant's commission of or complicity in the killing of five other individuals. *See* Trial Judgement, para. 570.

534 *See generally* Trial Judgement, paras. 604-616 (discussing the Appellant's individual circumstances).

XVIII. ALLEGED ERROR RELATING TO THE SENTENCE (GROUND OF APPEAL 16)

229. The Trial Chamber, having found the Appellant guilty of genocide (Count 1), rape as a crime against humanity (Count 3), and murder as a crime against humanity (Count 4), sentenced him to imprisonment for the remainder of his life on each of the three counts.[535] The Trial Chamber found no mitigating circumstances.[536] In so doing, the Trial Chamber noted that the Appellant did not "extensively address the issue of mitigating circumstances".[537] The Trial Chamber quoted the Appellant's closing arguments, stating that he would rely on the Trial Chamber's "knowledge of the case file" and its "high sense of justice" to impose a "proportionate" sentence that reflected the "precise role that [he] might have played".[538]

230. The Appellant submits that the Trial Chamber erred in law by failing to consider any mitigating circumstances and in imposing on him an excessive and disproportionate sentence.[539] Referring to Article 23 of the Statute, Rule 101 of the Rules, and the jurisprudence of the ICTR and ICTY, the Appellant asserts that the Trial Chamber was obliged to consider mitigating circumstances.[540] He argues that the following factors should have mitigated his sentence. First, he had no prior criminal convictions and had a good reputation in Gishyita Commune.[541] Second, he was only thirty-three years old during the relevant period and is the father of nine young children.[542] Third, during the events in 1994, he protected several Tutsis.[543] Finally, he submits that, given his relatively low position in the Rwandan administrative structure and existing case law, his three life sentences are unreasonable.[544]

231. Pursuant to Rule 101(B)(ii) of the Rules, a Trial Chamber is required to take into account any mitigating circumstances in determining a sentence.[545] The accused, however, bears the burden of establishing mitigating factors by a preponderance of the evidence.[546] The Appeals Chamber notes that the Appellant made no sentencing submissions at trial.[547] In such circumstances, the Trial Chamber's determination that there were no mitigating circumstances was within its discretion and **[page 79]** does not constitute a legal error. If an accused fails to put forward relevant information, the Appeals Chamber considers that, as a general rule, a Trial Chamber is not under an obligation to seek out information that counsel did not see fit to put before it at the appropriate time.[548] Rule 86(C) of the Rules clearly indicates that sentencing submissions shall be addressed during closing arguments, and it was therefore the Appellant's prerogative to identify any mitigating circumstances instead of directing the Trial Chamber's attention to the record in general. The Appellant is simply advancing arguments on appeal that he failed to put forward at the trial stage, and the Appeals Chamber "does not consider itself to be the appropriate forum at which such material should first be raised".[549]

232. In any event, the Appellant's submissions fail to demonstrate that the Trial Chamber's finding of "no mitigating circumstances" is unreasonable.[550] The Appellant cites several cases, which, in his view, suggest that his age, status as a father, lack of prior criminal history, and his assistance to Tutsis should have mitigated the sentence.[551] Notwithstanding the fact that the Appellant's submissions do not identify evidence in the

535 Trial Judgement, paras. 618, 619.
536 Trial Judgement, para. 616.
537 Trial Judgement, para. 602.
538 Trial Judgement, para. 602.
539 Notice of Appeal, pp. 21-22, paras. 79-85; Appellant's Brief, paras. 347-372.
540 Appellant's Brief, paras. 352, 354.
541 Appellant's Brief, paras. 356-359.
542 Appellant's Brief, paras. 360-365.
543 Appellant's Brief, para. 366.
544 Appellant's Brief, para. 367-374.
545 *Kamuhanda* Appeal Judgement, para. 354; *Kajelijeli* Appeal Judgement, para. 294.
546 *Kajelijeli* Appeal Judgement, para. 294.
547 Trial Judgement, para. 602.
548 *Kupreškić et al.* Appeal Judgement, para. 414.
549 *Kamuhanda* Appeal Judgement, para. 354, quoting *Kvočka et al.* Appeal Judgement, para. 674
550 Trial Judgement, para. 616.
551 Appellant's Brief, paras. 356-365, citing *Blaškić* Trial Judgement, paras. 778-780, 782; *Jelisić* Trial Judgement, para. 124; *Jelisić* Appeal Judgement, paras. 128-132; *Furundžija* Trial Judgement, para. 284; *Čelebići Case* Trial Judgement, paras. 1278, 1283; *Erdemović I* Sentencing Judgement, paras. 108, 111; *Erdemović II* Sentencing Judgement, para. 16; *Serushago* Sentencing Judgement, para. 39; *Kayishema and Ruzindana* Sentencing Order, 21 May 1999, para. 12. The Appeals Chamber notes that the Appellant makes

record substantiating his claim regarding his prior criminal record,[552] the Appellant points to no authority suggesting that the circumstances he now identifies require, as a matter of law, the mitigation of his sentence. The Appeals Chamber notes that comparing sentences with other cases that have been subject to final determination is of limited assistance in challenging one's sentence.[553]

233. Additionally, the Appellant's arguments, citing the *Tadić* Sentencing Appeal Judgement discussing the principle of gradation, are equally unpersuasive. The principle suggests that sentences should be graduated, that is, that the most senior levels of the command structure should attract the severest sentences, with less severe sentences for those lower down the structure.[554] While the Trial Judgement makes no explicit reference to the role played by the Appellant in the larger Rwandan political or administrative structure, it did consider the Appellant's position, and, contrary to his assertions, determined that he exercised influence.[555] Moreover, the principle is subject to the proviso that the gravity of the offences committed is the primary consideration when **[page 80]** imposing a sentence.[556] The ICTY Appeals Chamber has held that "[i] n certain circumstances, the gravity of the crime may be so great that even following consideration of any mitigating factors, and despite the fact that the accused was not senior in the so-called command structure, a very severe penalty is nevertheless justified."[557]

234. Finally, the Appeals Chamber considers that the Trial Chamber correctly noted that the sentence should be commensurate with the gravity of the offences and the degree of liability of the convicted person.[558] In addition, the Trial Chamber also noted its obligation to consider the individual circumstances of the Appellant and his role in the crimes, including any mitigating circumstances, but found it appropriate to impose the maximum sentence.[559] In imposing life sentences on all counts, the Trial Chamber recounted the vast impact, as well as the violent and cruel nature of the Appellant's conduct.[560] The Appellant makes no submission suggesting that the crimes for which he was convicted, many of which involved his direct participation, are not grave. The Appeals Chamber recalls that even where mitigating circumstances exist, a Trial Chamber "is not precluded from imposing a sentence of life imprisonment, where the gravity of the offence requires the imposition of the maximum sentence provided for."[561] Mindful of the gravity of the Appellant's crimes, the Appeals Chamber does not find, even if it accepted the Appellant's submissions as to mitigating factors, any discernible error in sentencing that has resulted in a miscarriage of justice.

235. Accordingly, this ground of appeal is dismissed. **[page 81]**

XIX. DISPOSITION

For the foregoing reasons, **THE APPEALS CHAMBER**,

PURSUANT to Article 24 of the Statute and Rule 118 of the Rules;

NOTING the written submissions of the parties and their oral arguments presented at the hearing on 15 January 2007;

---

no specific reference to cases supporting his contention that his assistance to Tutsis warrants mitigation. *See* Appellant's Brief, para. 366.

552 Appellant's Brief, para. 357. The Appeals Chamber notes that elsewhere in the Appellant's Brief, the Appellant cites evidence in the record supporting his contention that he assisted Tutsis. *See* Appellant's Brief, paras. 39-44.

553 *See Babić* Sentencing Appeal Judgement, para. 32; *Čelebići Case* Appeal Judgement, paras. 717, 720, 821.

554 *Musema* Appeal Judgement, paras. 382, 383. *See also Tadić* Sentencing Appeal Judgement, paras. 55, 56; *Čelebići Case* Appeal Judgement, para. 849; *Aleksovski* Appeal Judgement, para. 184.

555 Trial Judgement, para. 604.

556 *Musema* Appeal Judgement, para. 382; *Čelebići Case* Appeal Judgement, paras. 847-849; *Aleksovski* Appeal Judgement, para. 182.

557 *Čelebići Case* Appeal Judgement, para. 847.

558 Trial Judgement, paras. 591, 617.

559 Trial Judgement, paras. 591, 594, 604-617. The Appeals Chamber considered the impact of its decision to reverse the Trial Chamber's findings on the Appellant's role in the rapes of Languida Kamukina and Goretti Mukashyaka under Ground of Appeal 8 as well as in killing Pascasie Mukaremera, which the Trial Chamber considered as a "highly aggravating factor", under Ground of Appeal 15.

560 *See* Trial Judgement, paras. 604-615.

561 *Niyitegeka* Appeal Judgement, para. 267, quoting *Musema* Appeal Judgement, para. 396.

SITTING in open session;

AFFIRMS unanimously the Appellant's conviction for genocide (Count 1); and **AFFIRMS** unanimously his sentence of imprisonment for the remainder of his life entered for that conviction;

ALLOWS, in part, Judge Shahabuddeen and Judge Schomburg dissenting, the Appellant's eighth ground of appeal; **REVERSES**, Judge Shahabuddeen and Judge Schomburg dissenting, the Trial Chamber's finding that he bears criminal responsibility for the rapes of Goretti Mukashyaka and Languida Kamukina; **AFFIRMS** unanimously his conviction for rape as a crime against humanity (Count 3) in all other respects; and **AFFIRMS** unanimously his sentence of imprisonment for the remainder of his life entered for that conviction;

ALLOWS, in part, Judge Schomburg dissenting, the Appellant's fifteenth ground of appeal; **REVERSES**, Judge Schomburg dissenting, the Trial Chamber's finding that he bears criminal responsibility for the murder of Pascasie Mukaremera; **AFFIRMS** unanimously his conviction for murder as a crime against humanity (Count 4) in all other respects; and **AFFIRMS** unanimously his sentence of imprisonment for the remainder of his life entered for that conviction;

DISMISSES unanimously the Appellant's appeal of his convictions and sentences in all other respects;

RULES that this Judgement shall be enforced immediately pursuant to Rule 119 of the Rules;

ORDERS, in accordance with Rule 103(B) and Rule 107 of the Rules, that Mikaeli (also known as Mika) Muhimana is to remain in the custody of the Tribunal pending his transfer to the State in which his sentence will be served. **[page 82]**

Done in English and French, the English text being authoritative.

Fausto Pocar	Mohamed Shahabuddeen	Mehmet Güney
Presiding Judge	Judge	Judge

Liu Daqun	Wolfgang Schomburg
Judge	Judge

Judge Mohamed Shahabuddeen and Judge Wolfgang Schomburg append a Joint Partly Dissenting Opinion.

Judge Wolfgang Schomburg appends a Partly Dissenting Opinion on the Interpretation of the Right to be Informed.

Dated this 21st day of May 2007 at Arusha, Tanzania.

[Seal of the Tribunal] [page 83]

XX. JOINT PARTLY DISSENTING OPINION OF JUDGE SHAHABUDDEEN AND JUDGE SCHOMBURG

1. We are in general agreement with the outcome of the judgement. However, in relation to Ground of Appeal 8 we cannot agree with the finding of the majority. The Trial Chamber found:

> [T]he witness saw the Accused take the girls into his house; she heard the victims scream, mentioning the Accused's name and stating that they "did not expect him to do that" to them; finally the witness saw the Accused lead the victims out of his house, stark naked, and she noticed that they were walking "with their legs apart".[1]

This was based on the evidence of Witness AP. The credibility of Witness AP was not at stake. The appellate exercise was confined to determining the reasonableness of the Trial Chamber's finding that the accused had raped the girls in accordance with the applicable standard of proof.

2. It was open to the Trial Chamber to determine that rape had been committed. Indeed, we do not find that the Appeals Chamber holds otherwise. Its difficulty was whether it was the appellant who raped the girls. On this, we consider that it was open to the Trial Chamber to find that it was the appellant who raped the girls: it was he who led them into his house, who led them out of it, and whose name they called out saying that they "did not expect him to do that" to them. Furthermore, when he led them out of the house they were "stark naked" and were walking "with their legs apart".

3. There might have been other possibilities. But it is common to crime situations that there might have been alternative possibilities. It is the function of the trial court (if it can) to sort out these possibilities. The Trial Chamber found that it could sort out the situation. In our view, it cannot be said that the inference which it drew did not accord with the standard of proof in that no reasonable trier of fact could have come to this conclusion beyond reasonable doubt.

4. We consider that no intervention by the Appeals Chamber is warranted. In consequence, we respectfully dissent. **[page 84]**

Done in English and French, the English text being authoritative.

Mohamed Shahabuddeen	Wolfgang Schomburg
Judge	Judge

Dated this 21st day of May 2007 at Arusha, Tanzania.

[Seal of the Tribunal] [page 85]

1 Trial Judgement, para. 32.

XXI. PARTLY DISSENTING OPINION OF JUDGE SCHOMBURG ON THE INTERPRETATION OF THE RIGHT TO BE INFORMED

1. I am in general agreement with the outcome of the Judgement. However, I am concerned about the finding by the majority of the Appeals Chamber in relation to Ground of Appeal 15 that the Trial Chamber erred in law when relying on the evidence presented by the Prosecution in the attachments of the Pre-Trial Brief in relation to the murder of Pascasie Mukaremera. Therefore, I wish to offer some remarks on the right of the accused to be informed promptly and in detail about the nature and cause of the charge against him.

2. The right of the accused to be informed about the charges is a fundamental guarantee of the fairness of proceedings. Reflecting this - repeating *verbatim* the wording of Art. 14(3)(a) and (b) International Covenant on Civil and Political Rights of 16 December 1966[1], to which *inter alia* Article 7(a) of the African Charter on Human and Peoples Rights' of 26 June 1981[2] makes reference - the Statute of the Tribunal includes the following provisions:

> Article 21: Rights of the accused
>
> [...] 4. In the determination of any charge against the accused pursuant to the present Statute, the accused shall be entitled to the following minimum guarantees, in full equality:
>
> (a) to be informed promptly and in detail in a language which he understands of the nature and cause o the charge against him;
>
> (b) to have adequate time and facilities for the preparation of his defence and to communicate with counsel of his own choosing; [...].

3. This provision also corresponds to the rights guaranteed in many other human rights conventions. For example, Article 6(3) of the European Convention for the Protection of Human Rights and Fundamental Freedoms of 4 November 1950 reads:

> Everyone charged with a criminal offence has the following minimum rights:
>
> (a) to be informed promptly, in a language which he understands and in detail, of the nature and cause of the accusation against him;
>
> b) to have adequate time and facilities for the preparation of his defence; [...]. **[page 86]**

4. In the case at hand the Indictment alleged the accused to have instructed another person to commit murder. It informed the accused of the legal nature of the charge brought against him (committing murder), but did not inform the accused in detail about the underlying factual allegations. It has to be noted, however, that the summary of Witness AW's anticipated testimony, as appended to the Pre-Trial Brief[3], gives sufficiently clear and consistent information to notify the Appellant unequivocally that he was charged with physically committing the murder of Pascasie Mukaremera on Rugona Hill in mid-May 1994. It indicated the time, place and manner in which the crime was committed. The relevant part of the annex reads as follows:

> Witness fled to Rugona hill. In mid-May 1994, witness saw Muhimana opening the stomach of a pregnant Tutsi woman called **Pascasie Mukaremera.**[4]

This summary refers to paragraph 7(d)(i) of the Indictment, thus linking these detailed factual allegations unambiguously to the charge on this unique conduct. The reference to Witness AW's statement makes it abundantly clear that the Appellant was alleged to have committed the murder himself and not to have instructed another person to do it. Moreover, the different alleged crime scenes are in the same region and the difference between the end of May and mid-May is not substantial as there is no doubt about the concrete alleged crime.

---

1 Article 14(3) of which reads: "In the determination of any criminal charge against him, everyone shall be entitled to the following minimum guarantees, in full equality: (a) To be informed promptly and in detail in language which he understands of the nature and cause of the charge against him; (b) To have adequate time and facilities for the preparation of his defence and to communicate with counsel of his choosing; [...]."

2 OAU Doc. CAB/LEG/67/3/Rev.5. The *African Charter of Human and Peoples' Rights* was adopted on 27 June 1981 at the 18th Ordinary Session of the Assembly of Heads of State and Government in Banjul, Gambia. It entered into force on 21 October 1986.

3 Pre-Trial Brief, Appendix A, page 6.

4 *Ibid.*

5. The Indictment is the first guiding instrument for the criminal proceedings. According to the jurisprudence of the Tribunals, however, the Indictment is not to be seen in isolation. Other sources of information have to be taken into consideration as well, such as the Pre-Trial Brief including appended witness statements.

In *Gacumbitsi* the Appeals Chamber held:

> The charges against an accused and the material facts supporting those charges must be pleaded with sufficient precision in the Indictment so as to provide notice to the accused. The Appeals Chamber has held that "criminal acts that were physically committed by the accused personally must be set forth in the indictment specifically, including where feasible 'the identity of the victim, the time and place of the events and the means by which the acts were committed.'"[Footnote 117: *Ntakirutimana* Appeal Judgement, para. 32, quoting *Kupreškić et al.* Appeal Judgement, para. 89] An indictment lacking this precision may, however, be cured if the Prosecution provides the accused with timely, clear and consistent information detailing the factual basis underpinning the charge. [Footnote 118: *Ntakirutimana* Appeal Judgement, para. 27, referring to *Kupreškić et al.* Appeal Judgement, para. 114] When an appellant raises a defect in the indictment for the first time on appeal, then he bears the burden of showing that his ability to prepare his defence was materially impaired. [Footnote 119: *Niyitegeka* Appeal Judgement, para. 200; *Kvočka et al.* Appeal Judgement, para. 35] In cases where an accused has raised the issue of lack of notice before the Trial Chamber, in contrast, the burden rests on the Prosecution to demonstrate that the **[page 87]** accused's ability to prepare a defence was not materially impaired. [Footnote 120: *Niyitegeka* Appeal Judgement, para. 200; *Kvočka et al.* Appeal Judgement, para. 35][5]

In *Naletilić and Martinović* the Appeals Chamber even more precisely held:

> As to whether the defects were cured, the information in the Prosecution Pre-Trial Brief, filed on 11 October 2000, as well as in its Chart of Witnesses and List of Facts, filed on 18 July 2000, was provided to Naletilić and Martinović in a timely manner, as these documents were filed eleven and fourteen months prior to the commencement of trial, respectively. With regard to unlawful labour in locations other than the frontline, the Prosecution Pre-Trial Brief states that "prisoners were forced to work at the premises of Martinović" and that "detainees were forced by Martinović to loot the homes of Bosnian Muslims who had been evicted across the front-line into East Mostar". The Prosecution Chart of Witnesses and List of Facts provides that Martinović forced Muslim detainees to perform "work such as construction, maintenance, repairs on the front line or at other locations either in support of the military effort of the Croatian forces or for their personal gain".[6]

6. The European Court of Human Rights has dealt with the possible violation of Article 6(3)(a) and (b) of the Convention. In this context it held:

> The Court reiterates that in criminal matters the provision of full, detailed information to the defendant concerning the charges against him – and consequently the legal characterisation the court might adopt in the matter – is an essential prerequisite for ensuring that the proceedings are fair. Additionally, as regards the complaints under Article 6 § 3 (b) of the Convention, the Court considers that sub-paragraphs (a) and (b) of Article 6 § 3 are connected and that the right to be informed of the nature and the cause of the accusation must be considered in the light of a defendant's right to prepare his defence.[7]

In another case, the European Court of Human Rights stated:

> The scope of the above provision must in particular be assessed in the light of the more general right to a fair hearing guaranteed by Article 6 § 1 of the Convention. The Court considers that in criminal matters the provision of full, detailed information concerning the charges against a defendant, and consequently the legal characterisation that the court might adopt the matter, is an essential prerequisite for ensuring that the proceedings are fair.
>
> **Article 6 § 3 (a) does not impose any special formal requirement as to the manner in which the accused is to be informed of the nature and cause of the accusation against him.**
>
> Lastly, as regards the complaint under Article 6 § 3 (b) of the Convention, the Court considers that sub-paragraphs (a) and (b) of Article 6 § 3 are connected and that the right to be informed of the nature and the cause of the accusation must be considered in the light of the accused's right to prepare his defence.[8]

7. Consequently, according to the above cited cases, the Indictment is not the only way to inform the appellant about the charges against him. In many cases, the Prosecution will not be in a position to know all the evidence at the early stage of proceedings in which the Indictment is filed. It is unrealistic to believe that

---

5 *Gacumbitsi* Appeal Judgement, para. 49 (original footnotes in square brackets).

6 *Naletilić, a.k.a. "Tuta", and Martinović, a.k.a. "Štela"*, Appeal Judgement, para. 33 (footnotes omitted).

7 ECtHR, Case of *Borisova v. Bulgaria*, Appl. No. 56891/00, Judgment, 21 December 2006, para. 41 (further references omitted).

8 ECtHR, Case of *Pélissier and Sassi v. France*, Appl. No. 25444/94, Judgement 25 March 1999, paras 52-54 (further references omitted, emphasis added).

the Prosecution is not confronted with changing evidence throughout **[page 88]** the whole course of the proceedings. It would be incredible or, at the very least, surprising, if the factual basis of an Indictment remained unchanged after the finalization of investigations. Even in cases where trial proceedings are already ongoing, it has to be and is possible to add fresh information to the case.

8. As it is at the same time still important to keep the accused informed about the charges against him, it is a generally accepted principle in criminal law, both in Anglo-Saxon and Romano-Germanic influenced jurisdictions, that such additional information can also be given by an indication that the factual basis and/ or the legal assessment might be varied.

9. Before continuing, I would like to apologize for restricting my following comments to German law and jurisprudence. Unfortunately, the workload does not allow for in-depth comparative research. However, the quoted regulations and case law may serve as an example for many similar systems. Moreover, up until today nobody has successfully claimed that this approach violates the fundamental rights to be informed and to be heard.

10. The German Code of Criminal Procedure allows explicitly for legal indications by the court. The respective provision reads:

> Section 265. [Change in Legal Reference]
>
> (1) The defendant may not be sentenced on the basis of a penal norm other than the one referred to in the charges admitted by the court without first having his attention specifically drawn to the change in the legal reference and without having been afforded an opportunity to defend himself.
>
> (2) The same procedure shall be followed if special circumstances appear only at the hearing which in accordance with the penal norm increase criminal liability [...].
>
> (3) The main hearing shall be suspended upon the defendant's application if, alleging insufficient preparation for defense, he contests newly discovered circumstances which admit the application of a more severe penal norm against the defendant than the one referred to in the charges admitted by the court, or which forms part of the circumstances indicated in subsection (2).
>
> (4) The court shall, in other cases as well, suspend the main hearing upon an application or proprio motu, if in consequence of the change in circumstances it appears reasonable for adequate preparation of the charges or of the defense.[9]

11. In order to avoid injustice by the barring principle of *ne bis in idem*, a regulation like this is necessary in the well understood interest of justice. It is inherent to any criminal proceedings that the underlying facts might be discovered only during the trial. To hold otherwise would make a public hearing with its inherent dynamics superfluous. In such a hearing, for example, a witness **[page 89]** might testify spontaneously or confronted in cross-examination in a totally different way. As a consequence the bench might reach different conclusions.

12. The above cited provisions show that there are ways to introduce new facts into the proceedings while at the same time safe-guarding the fundamental rights of the accused. In this context, it has to be noted that according to settled German jurisprudence a hearing can even be re-opened in order to hear new evidence when the court is handing down the reasons for the judgement – at a point in German criminal proceedings when the disposition has already been read out.[10] Not to allow a party to continue to bring new facts until the very end of the proceedings and to seek, if necessary, legal requalification would render the proceedings unfair, provided of course that these new facts or the new evidence were not previously known or available. However, the question of untimely disclosure is not at stake in this case.

13. From the outset, according to settled German jurisprudence, any legal indication, which enables the accused and his defence counsel to align the defence strategy accordingly is necessary and at the same time sufficient.[11] Certain inaccuracies in relation to the factual allegations are considered to be inherent to any indictment. A legal indication has to be given as soon as a more accurate description of the underlying facts

---

9 Courtesy translation provided by the German Ministry of Justice. Emphasis added.

10 Lutz Meyer-Goßner, Strafprozessordnung, 50th ed., C.H. Beck (2007), Section 268, marginal number 14 (with further references).

11 German Federal Supreme Court (*Bundesgerichtshof*), Judgement of 16 October 1962, BGHSt 18, 56, guiding principles.

is possible.[12] In cases, where in the course of the trial certain aspects of the factual allegations are simply specified further, however, a legal indication is only considered to be obligatory where the rights of the accused to be heard and to be protected against unexpected decisions so demand.[13]

14. In predominantly party-driven proceedings, like those before this Tribunal, such an indication has to be given by the Prosecution or, to avoid unfairness, by the bench (*iura novit curia*). As it is unrealistic to believe that the facts as described in the Indictment will always be proven in exactly that way at trial, it is important that such an indication can be given at any time during the proceedings. Just as in other criminal proceedings, our main concern should be to strive to find the truth. The possibility to introduce new facts in the course of the proceedings is therefore essential. In particular in light of our specific mandate under Chapter VII of the Charter of the United Nations[14], it is irresponsible to acquit an accused who was informed about the charges **[page 90]** against him and had the possibility (and made indeed use of it) to defend himself against a slightly varied charge, however concrete and known in detail to him. In the case before us, the accused was in no doubt about the alleged concrete criminal conduct against which he had to defend himself. This is all that matters.

15. Ultimately, and in accordance with the rights guaranteed not only in the Statute[15], it is decisive that an accused is informed well in advance before a judgement is rendered. The question of delayed disclosure is irrelevant as long as the accused is able to defend himself against all the allegations. As the right to be informed cannot be viewed in isolation and must be seen in the context of the right to prepare a defence, the decisive factor in determining whether the accused's rights were in fact impaired has to be whether he was able to frame his defence accordingly. In the case at hand, the modification was presented even before the trial started. The Defence was clearly informed about the material facts underlying the alleged crime. Defence Counsel referred to the crime as described by Witness AW in cross-examination, thus showing that the Defence was completely aware of the time, place and manner of the alleged crime[16], and in particular that the Appellant was alleged to have committed the crime himself. Consequently, the defects of the Indictment were cured and the defence was in no way prejudiced.

16. By not taking into consideration at least the allegation as presented by the Prosecution in the Pre-Trial Brief and its appendices, the jurisprudence of the Tribunal ultimately runs the risk of hitting a dead-end, leading at the end of the day to injustice. Therefore, it would have been preferable to use this opportunity to clarify the jurisprudence of this Tribunal in the case before us. It is for these reasons that, with all due respect, I have to dissent in relation to Ground of Appeal 15. **[page 91]**

Done in English and French, the English text being authoritative.

Wolfgang Schomburg

Judge

Dated this 21st day of May 2007 in Arusha, Tanzania.

[Seal of the Tribunal] [page 92]

---

12 German Federal Supreme Court (*Bundesgerichtshof*), Judgement of 29 July 1998, BGHSt 44, 153, guiding principles.

13 German Federal Supreme Court (*Bundesgerichtshof*), Judgement of 20 February 2003, BGHst 44, 153, guiding principles.

14 United Nations Security Council Resolution of 8 November 1994, S/Res/955 (1994) reads: "[...] Determined to put an end to such crimes and to take effective measures to bring to justice the persons who are responsible for them, [...]." In this context, please also note the famous words of former UN Secretary-General *Kofi Annan*: "There is no peace without justice; there is no justice without truth.", referring *inter alia* to *Prophet Mohammed,* Hadith: "If you see a wrong you must right it; with your hand if you can, or, with your words, or, with your stare, or in your heart, and that is the weakest of faith"; *Pope Paul VI*: "If you want peace, work for justice"; *Rabban Simeon Ben Gamaliel*: "The world rests on three pillars: on truth, on justice, and on peace"; a Talmudic commentary adds to this: "The three are really one. If justice is realized, truth is vindicated and peace results."

15 *See supra* paras 2 and 3.

16 T. 14 April 2004 p. 49-51.

XXII. ANNEX A – PROCEDURAL BACKGROUND

1. The main aspects of the appeal proceedings are summarized below.

A. Notice of Appeal

2. The Trial Chamber rendered its judgement at a hearing on 28 April 2005 and issued the written judgement in English on 26 May 2005. On 20 May 2005, the Appellant filed a motion seeking an extension of time for the filing of his Notice of Appeal on the basis that the French and Kinyarwanda texts of the Trial Judgement were not available.[1] On 2 June 2005, the Appeals Chamber ordered the Appellant to file his Notice of Appeal no later than thirty days from the date of the filing of the French translation of the Trial Judgement.[2] The French translation of the Trial Judgement was filed on 19 December 2005.[3]

3. The Appellant filed his Notice of Appeal on 26 January 2006.[4] On 22 February 2006, the Appeals Chamber accepted the Notice of Appeal as validly filed, requested the Registry to designate the Notice of Appeal as a confidential document, and ordered the Appellant to file a public and redacted version within sixty days of the filing of the order.[5] The Appellant filed a public and redacted version of the Notice of Appeal on 24 April 2006.[6]

B. Appellant's Brief

4. The Appellant filed a confidential brief in support of his appeal on 12 April 2006,[7] and a public, redacted version on 30 August 2006.[8] On 22 May 2006, the Prosecution filed its Respondent's Brief, partly in English and partly in French.[9] On 14 June 2006, the Appellant filed a motion requesting that the prescribed time limit for the filing of the Brief in Reply start to run from 10 July 2006, in case the French version of the Respondent's Brief was made available between 14 June 2006 and 10 July 2006.[10] On 21 June 2006, the Pre-Appeal Judge rendered a decision disallowing the Appellant's request for an extension of time and reminded the Appellant to file his **[page 93]** Brief in Reply within fifteen days of service of the French translation of the Respondent's Brief.[11] The French text of the Respondent's Brief was filed on 13 October 2006 and was served on the Appellant on 16 October 2006.[12]

5. On 14 November 2006, the Appeals Chamber noted in its Scheduling Order that the Appellant had not filed a Brief in Reply in accordance with Rule 113 of the Rules and that the time for the filing had lapsed.[13] The Appellant filed his Brief in Reply on 14 November 2006.[14] On 16 November 2006, the Prosecution filed a motion to expunge the Brief in Reply from the record.[15] On 17 November 2006, the Appellant filed a motion

---

[1] *Requête de la Défense aux fins du Report du Délai de Dépôt de l'Acte d'Appel*, 20 May 2005.

[2] Decision on Motion for Extension of Time for Filing of Notice of Appeal, 2 June 2005.

[3] *See* Order Concerning the Filing of the Notice of Appeal, 22 February 2006 (noting the date of filing of the French translation of the Trial Judgement).

[4] *Acte d'Appel*, 26 January 2006.

[5] Order Concerning the Filing of the Notice of Appeal, 22 February 2006.

[6] An English translation of the public and redacted Notice of Appeal was filed on 23 May 2006.

[7] An English translation of the confidential Appellant's Brief was filed on 27 June 2006.

[8] *Mémoire d'Appel public et caviardé*, 30 August 2006.

[9] An English translation of the Respondent's Brief was filed on 4 September 2006.

[10] *Requête de l'Appelant aux fins de réaménagement du calendrier judiciaire*, 14 June 2006. The Prosecution filed a response in French on 16 June 2006 (*Réponse du Procureur à la "Requête de l'Appelant aux fins de réaménagement du calendrier judiciaire"*).

[11] Decision on Appellant's Motion for Extension of Time to File a Brief in Reply and Postponement of a Status Conference, 21 June 2006. On 27 June 2006, the Appellant filed a reply (*Réplique de l'Appelant à la réponse du Procureur à la requête du 16 juin 2006, relative au réaménagement du calendrier judiciaire*).

[12] Registrar's Submission under Rule 33(B) of the Rules on Decision on Appellant's Motion to Note the Failure to File the Respondent's Brief within the Prescribed Time Limit of 11 September 2006, 18 October 2006.

[13] Scheduling Order, 14 November 2006.

[14] *Réplique de l'Appelant au mémoire de l'Intimé,* 14 November 2006.

[15] Prosecutor's Motion to Expunge from the Record the Late and Over-Sized Reply Brief filed by the Appellant on 14 November 2006, 16 November 2006.

requesting the Appeals Chamber to declare his Brief in Reply validly filed.[16] On 11 January 2007, the Appeals Chamber dismissed the Appellant's motion, having found that the Appellant had failed to show good cause for the late filing within the ambit of Rule 116 of the Rules and granted the Prosecution's motion of 16 November 2006.[17] Consequently, the Appeals Chamber did not consider the Appellant's Brief in Reply.

C. Assignment of Judges

6. On 31 May 2005, the following Judges were assigned to hear the appeal: Judge Theodor Meron, Presiding; Judge Mohamed Shahabuddeen; Judge Mehmet Güney; Judge Fausto Pocar; and Judge Wolfgang Schomburg.[18] Judge Fausto Pocar was designated as Pre-Appeal Judge.[19] By Order of 1 February 2006, the following Judges were reassigned to hear the appeal: Judge Fausto Pocar, Presiding; Judge Mohamed Shahabuddeen; Judge Mehmet Güney; Judge Liu Daqun; and Judge Wolfgang Schomburg.[20] Judge Liu Daqun was assigned to replace Judge Fausto Pocar as Pre-Appeal Judge.[21] **[page 94]**

D. Motions related to the Admission of Additional Evidence

7. On 13 March 2006, the Appellant filed a motion for extension of time to file a motion to present additional evidence.[22] The Prosecution filed a response on 17 March 2006 opposing the extension of time,[23] and the Appellant filed a reply on 29 March 2006.[24] On 25 April 2006, the Appellant filed a motion to present additional evidence.[25] On 26 April 2006, the Pre-Appeal Judge denied the Appellant's 13 March 2006 motion for extension of time to file a motion to present additional evidence.[26] On 5 May 2006, the Prosecution filed a response to the Appellant's 25 April 2006 motion to present additional evidence.[27] On 26 September 2006, the Appeals Chamber denied the Appellant's 25 April 2006 motion for admission of additional evidence.[28] On 14 December 2006, the Appellant filed a second motion to admit additional evidence.[29] The Prosecution filed its response opposing this motion on 19 December 2006,[30] and the Appellant replied on 29 December 2006.[31] On 12 January 2007, the Appeals Chamber denied this second motion.[32] Hearing of the Appeal

8. On 15 January 2007, the parties presented their oral arguments at a hearing held in Arusha, Tanzania, in accordance with the Scheduling Order of 14 November 2006.[33] At the close of the hearing, the Appellant addressed the Appeals Chamber. **[page 95]**

---

16 *Requête de l'Appelant aux fins de la recevabilité de la Réplique au mémoire de l'intimé*, 17 November 2006.

17 Decision on the Admissibility of the Appellant's Brief in Reply, 11 January 2007.

18 Order of the Presiding Judge Assigning Judges to an Appeal before the Appeals Chamber, 31 May 2005.

19 Order of the Presiding Judge Assigning Judges to an Appeal before the Appeals Chamber, 31 May 2005.

20 Order Re-Assigning Judges to a Case before the Appeals Chamber and Re-Appointing a Pre-Appeal Judge, 1 February 2006.

21 Order Re-Assigning Judges to a Case before the Appeals Chamber and Re-Appointing a Pre-Appeal Judge, 1 February 2006.

22 *Requête de l'Appelant aux fins de prorogation de délai pour la présentation des moyens de preuve supplémentaires*, 13 March 2006.

23 *Réponse du Procureur à la requête de l'Appelant aux fins de prorogation de délai pour la présentation des moyens de preuve supplémentaires*, 17 March 2006.

24 *Réplique de l'Appelant à la réponse du Procureur à la requête aux fins de prorogation de délai pour la présentation des moyens de preuve*, 29 March 2006.

25 *Requête de l'Appelant aux fins de la présentation des moyens de preuve supplémentaires*, 25 April 2006.

26 Decision on Appellant's Request for Extension of Time to File Additional Evidence Motion, 26 April 2006.

27 Prosecutor's Response to "*Requête de l'Appelant aux fins de la présentation des moyens de preuve supplémentaires*", 5 May 2006.

28 Decision on Appellant's Motion to Present Additional Evidence, 26 September 2006.

29 *Requête de l'Appellant aux fins de présentation d'un moyen de preuve supplémentaire nouveau sur base de l'article 115 du Règlement de preuve et de procédure*, 14 December 2006.

30 *Réponse du Procureur à la "Requête de l'Appelant aux fins de présentation d'un moyen de preuve supplémentaire nouveau sur base de l'article 115 du Règlement de preuve et de procédure"*, 19 December 2006.

31 *Réplique de l'Appellant à la Réponse du Procureur relative à la présentation d'un moyen de preuve supplémentaire nouveau sur bas de l'article 115 du R.P.P.*, 29 December 2006.

32 Decision on the Appellant's Request to Admit Additional Evidence Pursuant to Rule 115 of the Rules of Procedure and Evidence, 12 January 2007.

33 Scheduling Order, 14 November 2006.

XXIII. ANNEX B – CITED MATERIALS AND DEFINED TERMS

A. Jurisprudence

1. ICTR

Akayesu

The Prosecutor v. Jean-Paul Akayesu, Case No. ICTR-96-4-A, Judgement, 1 June 2001 ("*Akayesu* Appeal Judgement")

Bagilishema

The Prosecutor v. Ignace Bagilishema, Case No. ICTR-95-1A-T, Judgement, 7 June 2001 ("*Bagilishema* Trial Judgement")

The Prosecutor v. Ignace Bagilishema, Case No. ICTR-95-1A-A, Judgement (Reasons), 3 July 2002 ("*Bagilishema* Appeal Judgement")

Gacumbitsi

Sylvestre Gacumbitsi v. The Prosecutor, Case No. ICTR-2001-64-A, Judgement, 7 July 2006 ("*Gacumbitsi* Appeal Judgement")

Kajelijeli

Juvénal Kajelijeli v. The Prosecutor, Case No. ICTR-98-44A-A, Judgement, 23 May 2005 ("*Kajelijeli* Appeal Judgement")

Kamuhanda

Jean de Dieu Kamuhanda v. The Prosecutor, Case No. ICTR-95-54A-A, Judgement, 19 September 2005 ("*Kamuhanda* Appeal Judgement")

Kayishema and Ruzindana

The Prosecutor v. Clément Kayishema and Obed Ruzindana, Case No. ICTR-95-1-A, Sentence, 29 May 2001 ("*Kayishema and Ruzindana* Sentencing Order")

The Prosecutor v. Clément Kayishema and Obed Ruzindana, Case No. ICTR-95-1-A, Judgement (Reasons), 1 June 2001 ("*Kayishema and Ruzindana* Appeal Judgement")

Muhimana

The Prosecutor v. Mikaeli Muhimana, Case No. ICTR-95-IB-I, Decision on Motion to Amend Indictment, 21 January 2004 ("*Muhimana*, Decision on Motion to Amend Indictment")

The Prosecutor v. Mika Muhimana, Case No. ICTR-95-IB-T, Order in Relation to Defence Motion on Inadmissibility of Witness Testimony, 13 September 2004 ("*Muhimana*, Order in Relation to Defence Motion on Inadmissibility of Witness Testimony") **[page 96]**

Musema

Alfred Musema v. The Prosecutor, Case No. ICTR-96-13-A, Judgement, 16 November 2001 ("*Musema* Appeal Judgement")

Ndindabahizi

Emmanuel Ndindabahizi v. The Prosecutor, Case No. ICTR-01-71-A, Judgement, 16 January 2007 ("*Ndindabahizi* Appeal Judgement")

Niyitegeka

Eliézer Niyitegeka v. The Prosecutor, Case No. ICTR-96-14-A, Judgement, 9 July 2004 ("*Niyitegeka* Appeal Judgement")

Ntagerura et al.

Le Procureur c/ André Ntagerura, Emmanuel Bagambiki and Samuel Imanishimwe, Affaire n° ICTR-99-46-A, Arrêt, 7 juillet 2006 ("*Ntagerura et al.* Appeal Judgement")

Ntakirutimana

The Prosecutor v. Elizaphan Ntakirutimana and Gérard Ntakirutimana, Cases Nos. ICTR-96-10-A and ICTR-96-17-A, Judgement, 13 December 2004 ("*Ntakirutimana* Appeal Judgement")

Rutaganda

Georges Anderson Nderubumwe Rutaganda v. The Prosecutor, Case No. ICTR-96-3-A, Judgement, 26 May 2003 ("*Rutaganda* Appeal Judgement")

Semanza

The Prosecutor v. Laurent Semanza, Case No. ICTR-97-20-T, Judgement and Sentence, 15 May 2003 ("*Semanza* Trial Judgement")

Laurent Semanza v. The Prosecutor, Case No. ICTR-97-20-A, Judgement, 20 May 2005 ("*Semanza* Appeal Judgement")

Serushago

The Prosecutor v. Omar Serushago, Case No. ICTR-98-39-S, Sentence, 5 February 1999, ("*Serushago* Sentencing Judgement")

2. ICTY

Aleksovski

The Prosecutor v. Zlatko Aleksovski, Case No. IT-95-14/1-A, Judgement, 30 May 2001 ("*Aleksovski* Appeal Judgement")

Babić

The Prosecutor v. Milan Babić, Case No. IT-03-72-A, Judgement on Sentencing Appeal, 18 July 2005 ("*Babić* Sentencing Appeal Judgement") **[page 97]**

Blaškić

The Prosecutor v. Tihomir Blaškić, Case No. IT-95-14-T, Judgement, 3 March 2000 ("*Blaškić* Trial Judgement")

The Prosecutor v. Tihomir Blaškić, Case No. IT-95-14-A, Judgement, 29 July 2004 ("*Blaškić* Appeal Judgement")

Čelebići Case

The Prosecutor v. Zejnil Delalić et al., Case No. IT-96-21-T, Judgement, 16 November 1998 ("*Čelebići Case* Trial Judgement")

The Prosecutor v. Zejnil Delalić et al., Case No. IT-96-21-A, Judgement, 20 February 2001 ("*Čelebići Case* Appeal Judgement")

Erdemović

The Prosecutor v. Drazen Erdemović, Sentencing Judgement, IT-96-22-T, 29 November 1996 ("*Erdemović I* Sentencing Judgement")

The Prosecutor v. Drazen Erdemović, Sentencing Judgement, IT-96-22, 5 March 1998 ("*Erdemović II* Sentencing Judgement")

Furundžija

The Prosecutor v. Anto Furundžija, Case No. IT-95-17/1-T, Judgement, 10 December 1998 ("*Furundžija* Trial Judgement")

Jelisić

The Prosecutor v. Goran Jelisić, Case No. IT-95-10-T, Judgement, 14 December 1999 ("*Jelisić* Trial Judgement")

The Prosecutor v. Goran Jelisić, Case No. IT-95-10-A, Judgement, 5 July 2001 ("*Jelisić* Appeal Judgement")

Krstić

The Prosecutor v. *Radislav Krstić*, Case No. IT-98-33-A, Judgement, 19 April 2004 ("*Krstić* Appeal Judgement")

Kunarac et al.

The Prosecutor v. Dragoljub Kunarac et al., Case Nos. IT-96-23-T & IT-96-23/1-T, Judgement, 22 February 2001 ("*Kunarac et al.* Trial Judgement")

The Prosecutor v. Dragoljub Kunarac et al., Case No. IT-96-23&IT-96-23/1-A, Judgement, 12 June 2002 ("*Kunarac et al.* Appeal Judgement")

Kupreškić et al.

The Prosecutor v. Zoran Kupreškić et al., Case No. IT-95-16-A, Judgement, 23 October 2001 ("*Kupreškić et al.* Appeal Judgement") **[page 98]**

Kvočka et al.

The Prosecutor v. Miroslav Kvočka et al., Case No. IT 98 30/1 A, Judgement, 28 February 2005 ("*Kvočka et al.* Appeal Judgement")

Naletilić and Martinović

The Prosecutor v. Mladen Naletilić and Vinko Martinović, Case No. IT-98-34-A, Judgement, 3 May 2006 ("*Naletilić and Martinović* Appeal Judgement")

Stakić

The Prosecutor v. Milomir Stakić, Case No. IT-97-24-A, Judgement, 22 March 2006 ("*Stakić* Appeal Judgement")

Tadić

The Prosecutor v. Duško Tadić a/k/a "Dule", Case No. IT-94-1-A, Judgement, 15 July 1999 ("*Tadić* Appeal Judgement")

The Prosecutor v. Duško Tadić a/k/a "Dule", Case No. IT-94-1-A and IT-94-1-*Abis*, Judgement in Sentencing Appeals, 26 January 2000 ("*Tadić* Sentencing Appeal Judgement")

Vasiljević

The Prosecutor v. Mitar Vasiljević, Case No. IT-98-32-A, Judgement, 25 February 2004 ("*Vasiljević* Appeal Judgement")

B. Defined Terms and Abbreviations

Appellant

Mikaeli (aka "Mika") Muhimana and the Counsel for the Defence of Mikaeli Muhimana

Appellant's Brief

The Defence of Mikaeli Muhimana Appeal Brief, filed in French (*Mémoire d'Appel*) on 12 April 2006

Defence Closing Brief

The Final Trial Brief of the Defence of Mikaeli Muhimana, English translation filed on 29 November 2004

Ex. D

Defence Exhibit

Ex. P

Prosecution Exhibit **[page 99]**

Genocide Convention

Article II of the Convention on the Prevention and Punishment of Crime of Genocide, 9 December 1948

ICTR

International Criminal Tribunal for the Prosecution of Persons Responsible for Genocide and Other Serious Violations of International Humanitarian Law Committed in the Territory of Rwanda and Rwandan Citizens Responsible for Genocide and Other Such Violations Committed in the Territory of Neighbouring States, between 1 January 1994 and 31 December 1994

ICTY

International Tribunal for the Prosecution of Persons Responsible for Serious Violations of International Humanitarian Law Committed in the Territory of the Former Yugoslavia since 1991

Notice of Appeal

The Defence of Mikaeli Muhimana Notice of Appeal, filed in French (*Acte d'Appel*) on 26 January 2006

p. (pp.)

page (pages)

para. (paras.)

paragraph (paragraphs)

Practice Direction on Formal Requirements for Appeals from Judgement

Practice Direction on Formal Requirements for Appeals from Judgement, 4 July 2005

Pre-Trial Brief

Pre-Trial Brief of the Office of the Prosecutor of the International Criminal Tribunal for Rwanda (Filed Pursuant to Rule 73(B)(i)*bis* of the Rules of Procedure and Evidence), filed in English on 27 February 2004

Respondent

The Office of the Prosecutor of the International Criminal Tribunal for Rwanda

Respondent's Brief

Prosecution Response to Appeal Brief of the Defence of Mikaeli Muhimana, filed partly in French and partly in English (*Mémoire de l'intimé*) on 22 May 2006

Rules

Rules of Procedure and Evidence of the International Criminal Tribunal for Rwanda **[page 100]**

Statute

Statute of the International Criminal Tribunal for Rwanda established by Security Council Resolution 955

T.

Transcript

Trial Judgement

The Prosecutor v. Mikaeli Muhimana, Case No. ICTR-95-1B-T, rendered orally on 28 April 2005, written judgement released in English on 26 May 2005

Commentary

1. The irrelevance of the victims' ethnicity in the context of rape as a crime against humanity

1.1

The Trial Chamber found the defendant guilty of *inter alia* abetting to the rape of two girls of unknown ethnicity (Muraketete and Mukasine).[1] The defendant appealed against the decision, on the grounds that the Trial Chamber, having failed to establish the ethnic identity of the victims, erred in law in convicting him for genocide solely on the basis of this event.[2] However, as the Appeals Chamber rightly observes, the Trial Chamber did not rely on those facts to enter a conviction of genocide, but rather of rape as a crime against humanity. As the appellant did not dispute that such crimes were part of the 'discriminatory, widespread, and systematic attacks [...] directed against groups of Tutsi civilians in Gishyita *Commune* and in the Bisesero area, between April and June 1994', the Appeals Chamber found the appeal without merit.[3]

It is clear that the Tutsi ethnicity of the victims would be crucial for the rape to qualify as genocide. Although the issue was not expressly addressed by the appellant, the question remains whether the same applies to crimes against humanity.

1.2

Customary law describes the context element of crimes against humanity as a 'general context of criminal conduct, consisting of a widespread or systematic practice of unlawful attacks against the population'.[4] Nevertheless, Article 3 of the Statute of the international criminal tribunal for Rwanda (ICTR) narrows this definition,[5] by adding the requirement that the attack be based on certain discriminatory grounds.[6] Thus, it is debatable whether the victims of the enumerated offences must actually pertain to the group of civilians targeted by the discriminatory attack – or, at least, whether the enumerated offences must also be (subjectively) based on the discriminatory grounds that underlie the attack, so as to establish that the offence is part of such attack.

To answer those questions, it is important to understand the precise nature and role of the restriction introduced by the Security Council in Article 3 regarding the relevant attacks.

As to the former question, Trial Chamber I found in Bagilishema that 'the qualifier "on national, political, ethnic, racial or religious grounds", which is peculiar to the ICTR Statute should, as a matter of construction, be read as a characterisation of the nature of the "attack" rather than of the *mens rea* of the perpetrator'.[7] As to the latter question, the Appeals Chamber held in Akayesu that the discriminatory nature of the attack required by Article 3 of the Statute 'introduces no additional element in the legal ingredients of the crime as these are known in customary international law'; instead, it is a pure jurisdictional element that limits the powers of the tribunal.[8]

Both findings are correct. Nevertheless, it should be added that the attack does not have to actually succeed in the intended discrimination: it suffices that it is undertaken on discriminatory grounds. As a consequence, the ICTR has jurisdiction over crimes committed as part of an attack that was meant to be directed against a certain, ethnical group, even if it was actually undertaken, by mistake, against a different group of the population, which was not intended to be so discriminated against and harmed.

---

1 ICTR, Judgement and Sentence, *Prosecutor v. Muhimana*, Case No. ICTR-95-1B-T, T. Ch. III, 28 April 2005, Klip/ Sluiter, ALC-XXII-413, par. 291 and 553.

2 ICTR, Judgement, *Muhimana v. Prosecutor*, Case No. ICTR-95-1B-A, A. Ch., 21 May 2007, in this volume, p. 717.

3 Judgement and Sentence, *Prosecutor v. Muhimana*, T.Ch. III, *supra* note 1, par. 172-174.

4 Antonio Cassese, International Criminal Law, 2 ed., Oxford U. P., New York 2008, p. 109 (emphasis omitted).

5 See Kai Ambos, Internationales Strafrecht. Strafanwendungsrecht. Völkerstrafrecht. Europäisches Strafrecht, 2 ed., Beck, München 2008, p. 237.

6 'The International Tribunal for Rwanda shall have the power to prosecute persons responsible for the following crimes when committed as part of a widespread or systematic attack against any civilian population on national, political, ethnic, racial or religious grounds: [...]'.

7 ICTR, Judgement, *Prosecutor v. Bagilishema*, Case No. ICTR-95-1A-T, T. Ch. I, 7 June 2001, Klip/ Sluiter, ALC-X-617, par. 81. Endorsing this interpretation, see also Kai Ambos, Internationales Strafrecht. Strafanwendungsrecht. Völkerstrafrecht. Europäisches Strafrecht, *supra* note 5, p. 237.

8 ICTR, Judgment, *Prosecutor v. Akayesu*, Case No. ICTR-96-4-A, A. Ch., 1 June 2001, Klip/ Sluiter, ALC-X-335, par. 465.

1.3

Still, the preceding considerations do not answer the question of how the jurisdictional element reflects (if at all) on the scope of the norms punishing crimes against humanity, so as to establish that a given offence was part of an attack with a discriminatory nature. In this respect, the case law of the ICTR on the construction of the enumerated offences in the light of Article 3 of the Statute has followed two divergent approaches. Some decisions assert that the enumerated offences must themselves be discriminatory [*infra*, (i)], whereas other decisions find it sufficient that the offences can further the discriminatory attack, or even that there is no need for discriminatory grounds in the perpetration of the specific offences [*infra*, (ii)].

(i) In Akayesu, Trial Chamber I ruled that 'inhumane acts committed against the civilian population must be committed on "national, political, ethnic, racial or religious grounds" (...)',[9] and considered that 'inhumane acts committed against persons not falling within any one of the categories could constitute crimes against humanity if the perpetrator's intention was to further his attacks on the group discriminated against on one of the grounds mentioned in Article 3 of the Statute. The perpetrator must have the requisite intent for the commission of crimes against humanity'.[10]

In Kayishema and Ruzindana, Trial Chamber II assumed that the enumerated acts must have a discriminatory nature and, on that basis, made a distinction between two scenarios: 'in a scenario where the perpetrator's intention is to exterminate the Tutsi group and, in furtherance of this intent, he kills a Belgium [sic] Priest who is protecting the Tutsi, the Trial Chamber opines that such an act, would be based on discrimination against a Tutsi group. The second relevant scenario is where the perpetrator attacks people on the grounds and in the *belief* that they are members of a group but, in fact, they are not (...). In [this] scenario, the Trial Chamber opines that the prosecution must show that the perpetrator's belief was objectively reasonable – based upon real facts – rather than being mere speculation or perverted deduction'.[11]

In Rutaganda – and despite having pondered the stance taken by the ICTY in the Tadic Appeal, according to which the discriminatory intent is not an element of crimes against humanity in general[12] – Trial Chamber I maintained the reasoning adopted in Akayesu, on the grounds that 'there is a material and substantial difference in the elements of the offence that constitute crimes against humanity. This stems from the fact that Article 3 of the ICTR Statute expressly provides the enumerated discriminatory grounds of "national, political, ethnic, racial or religious", in respect of the offences of Murder; Extermination; Deportation; Imprisonment; Torture; Rape; and; Other Inhumane Acts, whilst the ICTY Statute does not stipulate any discriminatory grounds in respect of these offences'.[13]

A similar approach was taken in Muhimana, where Trial Chamber III found that 'the victim's membership in a national, political, ethnic, racial or religious group is irrelevant, provided that the perpetrator's intention is to support or further an attack against a civilian population on one of the enumerated discriminatory grounds'.[14]

(ii) A different interpretation was followed by the ICTR in several other decisions.

In Akayesu, the Appeals Chamber, having construed the discriminatory nature of the attack as a jurisdictional element, held that 'discrimination is not a requirement for the various crimes against humanity, except where persecution is concerned'. In that light, 'the meaning to be collected from Article 3 of the Statute is that even

---

9 In the same sense, William Schabas, Commentary, in Klip/ Sluiter, ALC-II-550: 'The Statute of the Rwanda Tribunal stipulates that inhumane acts committed against the civilian population must be committed on "national, political, ethnic, racial, or religious grounds" '.

10 ICTR, Judgement, *Prosecutor v. Akayesu*, Case No. ICTR-96-4-T, T. Ch. I, 2 September 1998, Klip/ Sluiter, ALC-II-399, par. 583-584.

11 ICTR, Judgement, *Prosecutor v. Kayishema and Ruzindana*, Case No. ICTR-95-1-T, T. Ch. II, 21 May 1999, Klip/ Sluiter, ALC-II-555, par. 131 and 132.

12 ICTY, Judgement, *Prosecutor v. Tadić*, Case No. IT-94-1-A, A. Ch., 15 July 1999, Klip/ Sluiter, ALC-III-761, par. 288 *et seq.* and 305.

13 ICTR, Judgement and Sentence, *Prosecutor v. Rutaganda*, Case No. ICTR-96-3-T, T. Ch. I, 6 December 1999, Klip/ Sluiter, ALC-II-709, par. 75 and 76; almost *verbatim*, ICTR, Judgement and Sentence, *Prosecutor v. Musema*, Case No. ICTR-96-13-T, T. Ch. I, 27 January 2000, Klip/ Sluiter, ALC-VI-469, par. 210 and 211.

14 ICTR, Judgement and Sentence, *Prosecutor v. Muhimana*, Case No. ICTR-95-1B-T, T. Ch. III, 28 April 2005, Klip/ Sluiter, ALC-XXII-413, par. 529.

if the accused did not have a discriminatory intent when he committed the act charged against a particular victim, he nevertheless knew that his act could further a discriminatory attack against a civilian population; the attack could even be perpetrated by other persons and the accused could even object to it. As a result, where it is shown that the accused had knowledge of such objective nexus, the prosecutor is under no obligation to go forward with a showing that the crime charged was committed against a particular victim with a discriminatory intent'.[15]

In Bagilishema, after having circumscribed the relevance of the discriminatory grounds to the nature of the attack, Trial Chamber I found that '[t]he perpetrator may well have committed an underlying offence on discriminatory grounds identical to those of the broader attack; but neither this, nor for that matter any discriminatory intent whatsoever, are prerequisites of the crime, so long as it was committed as part of the broader attack'.[16]

Finally, in Semanza, Trial Chamber III followed the Appeals Chamber in Akayesu: when describing the relationship between the attack and the enumerated offences, the court ruled that '[a]cts committed against persons outside the discriminatory categories may nevertheless form part of the attack where the act against the outsider supports or furthers or is intended to support or further the attack on the group discriminated against on one of the enumerated grounds' and, in relation to the requisite *mens rea*, held that 'the accused need not necessarily share the purpose or goals behind the broader attack. There is no requirement that the enumerated acts other than persecution be committed with discriminatory intent'.[17]

1.4

At this point, it might be helpful to recall that the purpose underlying the prohibition of crimes against humanity is to protect 'the individual from violations of his most important rights in situations where those rights are facing extreme danger, i.e. in cases of widespread or systematic attacks against civilians'.[18] This means that there must be an objective connection between the enumerated offences and the attack, even if only at a situational level. However, it is not apparent why the offence should be required to further or support (or, even less, intend to further or support) the attack. If, for instance, a Rwandan citizen, irrespective of his or her ethnic identity, had taken advantage of the situation of lawlessness to murder a fellow citizen not included in the discriminated group, but who has become equally vulnerable by virtue of the attack,[19] not only would the ICTR have jurisdiction over the act, but such an act would also constitute a crime against humanity.

This said, it is clear that Article 3 of the Statute does not require a particular form of *mens rea* (the discriminatory intent) for the commission of 'murder-type' crimes against humanity.[20] It is sufficient that the perpetrator knows the existence of a widespread or systematic attack against a civilian population and that his act is part of such attack. In theory, the perpetrator does not even have to be aware of the discriminatory nature of the attack, since *mens rea* is not supposed to cover the elements of jurisdiction.[21]

Therefore, the special feature of Article 3 of the Statute lies (exclusively) in the circumstance that the enumerated offences must be objectively linked to an attack of a discriminatory nature, but they do not have to be (objectively) discriminatory in and of themselves or capable of furthering the attack, nor do they have to be perpetrated with a discriminatory intent.

In the case at hand, the defendant was convicted of rape as a crime against humanity for abetting the rape of two women of unknown ethnicity, in the context of an attack against the civilian population based on ethnic

---

15 Judgment, *Prosecutor v. Akayesu*, A. Ch., *supra* note 8, par. 466 and 467.

16 Judgement, *Prosecutor v. Bagilishema*, T. Ch. I, *supra* note 7, par. 81.

17 ICTR, Judgement and Sentence, *Prosecutor v. Semanza*, Case No. ICTR-97-20-T, T. Ch. III, 15 May 2003, Klip/ Sluiter, ALC-XII-599, par. 331 and 332.

18 Kai Ambos/ Steffen Wirth, Commentary, in Klip/ Sluiter, ALC-II-704.

19 See Kai Ambos/ Steffen Wirth, The current law of crimes against humanity. An analysis of UNTAET Regulation 15/2000, 13 Criminal Law Forum 2002, p. 14 and 36.

20 For the distinction between 'murder-type' and 'persecution-type' crimes against humanity, see Antonio Cassese, International Criminal Law, *supra* note 4, p. 118 *et seq.*

21 Pedro Caeiro, Fundamento, Conteúdo e Limites da Jurisdição Penal do Estado: o Caso Português, doctoral thesis, Coimbra, 2007 (publication forthcoming), p. 236 *et seq.*

grounds that was well known to him. For the reasons set above, the ethnic identity of the victims was immaterial, as well as the beliefs that the perpetrator might have had in this respect.

2. Defects in the substance of the indictment and the right of the defendant to be given proper notice of the charges

2.1

The Trial Chamber convicted the defendant of murder as a crime against the humanity, in part based on the finding that, in mid-May 1994, at Rugona Hill, he had killed a pregnant woman with a machete and removed her child, who cried before dying. However, the relevant paragraph of the indictment read: 'Towards the end of May 1994, at Nyakiyabo hill in the Bisesero area an *Interahamwe* named Gisambo killed Pascasie Mukarema, on instructions of Mikaeli Muhimana'. On appeal, the defendant submitted that the Trial Chamber erred in law in convicting him for the murder of Pascasie Mukaremera, because the indictment failed to give him proper notice of the time and place of the crime and his role in it.

The Appeals Chamber considered that the defendant had raised a timely objection to all the defective aspects of this part of the indictment and that it fell to the prosecution to prove that the defence was not materially impaired by these defects. The question remained whether the defects of the indictment were cured by the disclosure of witness AW's written statement, and the summary of the evidence of witnesses BI and AW in an annex to the prosecution's pre-trial brief.[22]

After having examined the summary of witness BI's testimony, the Appeals Chamber concluded that it referred to a different event that occurred at Nyakiyabo Hill, where Muhimana and Gisambo allegedly raped a different victim (Mukasine), who was killed by Gisambo, together with a seven year old child she was carrying.

The summary of evidence given by witness AW stated that, in mid-May 1994, she saw Muhimana opening the stomach of a pregnant Tutsi woman called Pascasie Mukaremera in Rugona Hill; the summary indicated that the information was relevant to the paragraph of the indictment, where the murder of Pascasie Mukaremera was alleged.

In view of these circumstances, the Appeals Chamber found that the reference to the summary of witness BI's testimony, which seemed to relate to a different set of facts, only 'add[ed] greater confusion'. The majority also found (Judge Schomburg dissenting) that, considering the discrepancy with the indictment, the summary of witness AW's testimony did not 'provide clear and consistent information sufficient to put the appellant on notice that he was being charged with physically committing the murder of Pascasie Mukaremera on Rugona Hill in mid-May 1994'. Furthermore, the majority observed that the defect in the indictment was not 'simply a mischaracterization of the legal qualification of the crime, but an error in the description of the material facts of the crime itself', ruling that 'the Trial Chamber erred in law in relying on this evidence in convicting the Appellant for this murder'.

2.2

Judge Schomburg appended a partly dissenting opinion on the right to be informed, where he held that the indictment informed the defendant 'of the legal nature of the charge brought against him (committing murder), but did not inform the accused in detail about the underlying factual allegations'. However, in Judge Schomburg's view, the summary of witness AW's testimony gave 'sufficiently clear and consistent information to notify the Appellant unequivocally that he was charged with physically committing the murder of Pascasie Mukaremera on Rugona Hill in mid-May 1994'. The Judge then cited some case law of the Appeals Chamber and of the European Court of Human Rights that allows for the conclusion that the indictment is not the only way of informing an accused about the charges brought against him, as well as a Section of the German Code of Criminal Procedure (*StPO*), which that regulates the case where the penal norm to be applied by the court differs from the one set out in the indictment.[23]

Judge Schomburg added that, as the main concern of the tribunal should be 'to strive to find the truth', the 'possibility to introduce new facts in the course of the proceedings is therefore essential'. Thus, it would be

22 See Judgement, *Muhimana v. Prosecutor*, A. Ch., *supra* note 2, par. 220 et seq.

23 Section 265 – Change in Legal Reference (§ 265 *StPO – Hinweispflicht auf die Veränderung des rechtlichen Gesichtspunktes*).

'irresponsible to acquit an accused who was informed about the charges against him and had the possibility (and made indeed use of it) to defend himself against a slightly varied charge'. Finally, as the defence had been shown to be 'completely aware of the time, place and manner of the alleged crime, and in particular that the Appellant was alleged to have committed the crime himself, (...) the defects of the Indictment were cured and the defence was in no way prejudiced'.

2.3

All the judges seemed to agree that the indictment was defective in substance and that the summary of witness BI's testimony was of no relevance to that matter, because it referred to a <u>different</u> set of facts, <u>other than</u> the acts indicted (a <u>different</u> victim, who was not pregnant and who was carrying a seven year old child). However, there was no unanimity as to whether the summary of witness AW's testimony could cure the defects of the indictment.

It is submitted that such a discussion should start by acknowledging that the indictment is not just one of the ways in which the prosecution may present its case, on equal footing with other documents or procedural acts, but rather the fundamental piece of the accusatorial procedure, where the factual and legal elements of the charges must be described in a precise manner. The role of the indictment is to provide the defendant with sufficient knowledge of the charges brought against him, so as he can defend himself, but also to set the object of the case and, consequently, the limits of the court's cognisance.[24] That is the reason why, in certain circumstances, the indictment is said to be defective (because it lacks the information or precision it is supposed to bear), and why the court evaluates whether such defects have somehow been cured. It is also why the Rules allows the prosecution to present amended indictments, which would not be necessary if the relevant information could be provided by any means during the course of the proceedings.

2.4

It is true that domestic and international systems accept that certain details regarding the crimes indicted can be provided by other documents or acts, as long as the defendant has a fair opportunity to defend himself against them.[25] Nevertheless, as the majority of the Appeals Chamber correctly observed in the case at hand, there is an important difference between adding 'greater detail' to the acts pleaded in the indictment and modifying 'key facets' of the acts indicted – at least, this author would add, when such modification causes those acts to be no longer the same. In other words, a defective indictment can be cured if the information provided in subsequent briefs, adequately develops or specifies the acts referred to in the indictment, but the overriding principle according to which the defendant cannot be convicted of acts for which he has not been indicted forbids that such briefs and communications replace the indictment in describing the *actus reus*.

2.5

Arguably, the inconsistencies of the time and place of the crime were not *per se* substantial, and should perhaps not be decisive.[26] However, ordering the murder of a pregnant woman is quite different from opening her abdomen and extracting her living baby, thus killing both of them. The summary of witness AW's testimony did not specify or complement the acts indicted: it changed the material acts that form the *actus reus* themselves. As both sets of allegations refer to the same perpetrator and victim, they should be seen as contradictory, because it is not possible to impute the victim's death to a material act of the defendant and to the material act of a third person acting under the former's orders. Were both allegations present in the same count of the indictment, it would probably be invalid for duplicity, except if they were pleaded in the alternative.[27]

24 See ICTR, Separate Declaration of Pavel Dolenc Regarding Decision on Preliminary Motion, *Prosecutor v. Rukundo*, Case No. ICTR-2001-70-I, T. Ch. III, 4 March 2003, in Klip/ Sluiter, ALC-XII-37, par. 12, and the corresponding Commentary, Pedro Caeiro, Klip/ Sluiter, ALC-XII- 47.

25 See, for instance, ICTR, Judgement, *Gacumbitsi v. Prosecutor*, Case No. Case No. ICTR-2001-64-A, A. Ch., 7 July 2006, Klip/ Sluiter, ALC-XXIV-495, par. 49 *et seq.*, with further references.

26 But see Judgement, *Muhimana v. Prosecutor*, A. Ch., *supra* note 2, par. 226, with further references.

27 For an explanation of the difference between cumulative and alternative charges, see the Separate Declaration of Pavel Dolenc Regarding Decision on Preliminary Motion, *Prosecutor v. Rukundo*, T. Ch. III, *supra* note 24 and Commentary, Pedro Caeiro, *supra* note 24, p. 49 *et seq.*

Moreover, the imputation of the crime as indicted (ordering) would obviously require proof that Gisambo was the material perpetrator of the crime and that the defendant enjoyed a 'position of authority' over him.[28] Theoretically, the defendant might have relied on the circumstance that the prosecution provided no such evidence[29] and that the evidence brought by witness AW did not relate to the acts indicted.

Finally, since the indictment had not been amended before the commencement of the trial – as it should have been, pursuant to Rules 50 or 73 of the Rules of Procedure and Evidence (RPE) (in the version then in force)[30] – and bearing in mind that the two versions of the facts are incompatible, why should the defendant trust that the prosecution would plead the murder of the victim according to the summary of witness AW's testimony, and not in the terms of its own indictment?[31]

2.6

For the reasons set above, the summary of witness AW's testimony should not be seen as simply leading to a different qualification of the same acts: it was a change in the factual basis of the case (due to the prevalence of the summary of witness AW's testimony over the indictment) that led the Trial Chamber to convict the defendant under a different mode of liability.

In this respect, it is doubtful that the *rationale* underlying norms such as those enshrined in Sections 265 and 266 of the German Code of Criminal Procedure[32] (or other similar domestic law)[33] could serve as a source of inspiration for this type of decision.[34] These norms confer upon the court the power to extend its cognisance, subject to certain conditions, to acts that are not described in the indictment, in the context of a procedural system where the court has some investigative powers (derived from the so-called 'inquisitorial model'), which make it unnecessary to provide for amendments of the indictment. However, it is known that international criminal procedure (or, at least, the procedural rules embodied in the Statute of the ICTR) bears a marked influence of the so-called 'adversarial model'[35] and the very existence of RPE 50 and 73 is a strong argument against the admissibility of the court extending its cognisance beyond the material acts indicted. This construction does not necessarily leave the 'new' acts unpunished, since the *non bis in idem* bar only covers the acts that form the 'object' of the case (i. e., the acts that could have been tried by the court); thus, the prosecution may, if it so wishes, plead new charges in fresh proceedings.

2.7

In conclusion, it is this author's view that the Appeals Chamber was correct in invalidating the conviction of Muhimana for murder as a crime against humanity for this event, no matter how difficult the taking of such a decision might have been in view of the atrocious act at hand.

However, it is respectfully submitted that the indictment was not 'defective' in relation to the murder of Pascasie Mukaremera, because it gave clear and sufficient notice of the time and place of the alleged crime

---

28 Judgement, *Gacumbitsi v. Prosecutor,* A. Ch., *supra* note 24, par. 143.; Kai Ambos, Internationales Strafrecht. Strafanwendungsrecht. Völkerstrafrecht. Europäisches Strafrecht, *supra* note 4, p. 153; Antonio Cassese, International Criminal Law, *supra* note 4, p. 230.

29 As a matter of fact, there were other allegations concerning the perpetration of crimes by Gisambo under the instructions of the defendant, but the Judgement of Trial Chamber makes no reference to the position of authority of the latter over the former.

30 As the Appeals Chamber suggests, Judgement, *Muhimana v. Prosecutor*, A. Ch., *supra* note 2, par. 224: '[t]his discrepancy should have been immediately apparent to the Prosecution as it prepared its Pre-Trial Brief and listed the anticipated testimony of Witness AW in support of a paragraph of the Indictment that materially conflicted with it, in particular given that the Prosecution had shortly prior to that added this allegation to the Indictment for the purpose of providing specificity to the Accused. The Prosecution however did not seek to clarify this discrepancy with a clear, timely, and consistent communication'.

31 Let alone the summary of witness BI's testimony, where the Trial Chamber saw an additional cure for the defects of the relevant paragraph of the indictment, even if it referred to a different paragraph: Judgement, *Muhimana v. Prosecutor*, A. Ch., *supra* note 2, par. 220 and 221.

32 Respectively, '*Veränderung des rechtlichen Gesichtspunktes*', ('Change in legal reference'), and '*Erhebung der Nachtragsanklage*' (Supplementary Charges). An English version of these norms, provided by the German Ministry of Justice, is available at <http://www.iuscomp.org/gla/statutes/StPO.htm#266>.

33 For instance, articles 358º and 359º of the Portuguese Code of Criminal Procedure.

34 I wish to thank Prof. Martin Böse for his kind help with the interpretation of German procedural law, namely in what concerns the difference between the substantive and the procedural concepts of "criminal act" (*Tat*). Indeed, the responsibility for any mistakes rests with me.

35 See Antonio Cassese, International Criminal Law, *supra* note 4, p. 369 *et seq.*

and of the defendant's role in it. Rather, the indictment recounted a set of facts that were simply not proven at trial[36] and this should have sufficed to set aside the defendant's responsibility. The testimony of witness AW should have been deemed irrelevant for the purposes of the case, since it referred to the perpetration of a crime that was not included in the indictment.

Lastly, it is indisputable that the approach taken by the Appeals Chamber leads to the impossibility of introducing fresh charges against the defendant for personally committing the murder of the victim, because this act was considered as having been indicted (albeit in a defective manner). That conclusion would probably not apply if the Appeals Chamber would have followed the submitted line of reasoning, for it would have come to the conclusion that the physical perpetration of the murder by the defendant fell outside the boundaries of the court's cognisance and, arguably, the force of *res judicata* would therefore not extend to it.

Pedro Caeiro

[36] 'Towards the end of May 1994, at Nyakiyabo hill in the Bisesero area an *Interahamwe* named Gisambo killed Pascasie Mukarema, on instructions of Mikaeli Muhimana'.

International Criminal Tribunal for Rwanda
Tribunal pénal international pour le Rwanda

OR: ENG

TRIAL CHAMBER II

Before:	Judge Asoka de Silva, Presiding Judge Taghrid Hikmet Judge Seon Ki Park
Registrar:	Mr. Adama Dieng
Date:	16 November 2007

The PROSECUTOR
v.
Juvénal RUGAMBARARA

Case No. ICTR-00-59-T

Sentencing Judgement

Office of the Prosecutor
Mr. Charles Adeogun-Phillips
Mr. Peter Tafah
Ms. Memory Maposa

Counsel for the Defence
Mr. Maroufa Diabira
Mr. Boubou Diabira

[page 2] I. Introduction

1. Juvénal Rugambarara was born in 1959 in Bumba *secteur*, Tare *commune*, Kigali-Rural *préfecture*.[1] He lived most of his adult life in Bicumbi *commune*, where he worked as a medical officer.[2] He was appointed *bourgmestre* of Bicumbi *commune*, Kigali-Rural *préfecture* on 4 August 1993, having succeeded Laurent Semanza.[3] Juvénal Rugambarara served as the *bourgmestre* of Bicumbi *commune* from 16 September 1993 until 20 April 1994.[4]

2. The Indictment against Rugambarara, containing nine counts, was confirmed on 13 July 2000 by Judge Pavel Dolenc.[5] He was charged with genocide, complicity in genocide, conspiracy to commit genocide, direct and public incitement to commit genocide, extermination, torture and rape as crimes against humanity and serious violations of common Article 3 of the Geneva Conventions of 12 August 1949, pursuant to Articles 2, 3, 4 and Articles 6(1) and 6(3) of the Statute of the Tribunal (the "Statute").[6] On 14 July 2000, Judge Pavel Dolenc issued the first warrant of arrest and order for the transfer and detention of Rugambarara.[7] On 11 August 2003, Rugambarara was arrested in Uganda[8] and on 13 August 2003 transferred to the Tribunal. On 15 August 2003, he made his initial appearance and pleaded not guilty to all counts of the Indictment.[9]

3. On 12 June 2007, the Prosecution filed a Motion, requesting the Chamber to amend the Indictment.[10] The Defence supported the Prosecution Motion.[11] On 28 June 2007, the Chamber accepted the withdrawal of the previous indictment and the filing of an Amended Indictment with one count.[12] The Amended Indictment of 2 July 2007 (the "Indictment") charged Juvénal Rugambarara with extermination as a crime against humanity pursuant to Article 3(b) of the Statute, for having failed in his duty to take the necessary and reasonable measures to commission an investigation into the crimes committed by his subordinates between 7 and 20 April 1994, with a view to apprehending and referring the perpetrators thereof to the competent authorities for **[page 3]** appropriate punishment pursuant to Article 6(3) of the Statute.[13] More specifically, the Indictment alleges that, between 7 and 20 April 1994, subordinates under Juvénal Rugambarara's effective control (*conseillers*, communal policemen, local administrators and militiamen) had launched attacks on the Tutsi gathered at Mwulire, Mabare and Nawe *secteurs* in Bicumbi *commune* of Kigali-Rural *préfecture*, resulting in the deaths of thousands of Tutsi civilians.[14] The attacks took place between 13 and 18 April 1994 at the Mwulire camp, on or about 13 April at the Mwulire *secteur* office, between 12 and 18 April 1994 in Mabare *secteur*, between 16 and 18 April 1994 at Mabare Mosque and on 8 April 1994 in Nawe *secteur*.[15]

---

1 Amended Indictment, 2 July 2007 ("Indictment"), para. 2.

2 Indictment, para. 2.

3 Indictment, para. 3.

4 Indictment, para. 3.

5 Confirmation of the Indictment and Order for Non-Disclosure of the Indictment and Protection of Victims and Witnesses (TC).

6 *Ibid.*

7 Warrant of Arrest and Order for Transfer and Detention (TC), 14 July 2000; this was followed by the issuance of 2 further warrants for the arrest of Rugambarara: Warrant of Arrest and Orders for Transfer and Detention and for Search and Seizure (TC), 1 June 2001; and Warrant of Arrest and Orders for Transfer and Detention and for Search and Seizure (TC), 15 February 2002.

8 The Warrant of Arrest and Order for Transfer and Detention of the Accused Juvénal Rugambarara was communicated by the ICTR Registrar to the Ugandan Minister of Justice on 11 August 2003.

9 T. 15 July 2003, pp. 6, 8, 11, 13, 16, 17, 20, 24 and 26.

10 Prosecutor's Request for leave to amend an Indictment pursuant to Rules 73, 50 and 51 of the Rules of Procedure and Evidence.

11 *Réponse de la Défense à la requête du Procureur demandant l'autorisation de modifier un acte d'accusation conformément aux articles 73, 50 et 51 du Règlement de Procédure et de Preuve,* filed on 13 June 2007.

12 Decision on the Prosecution Motion to Amend the Indictment (TC).

13 Indictment, paras. 14-15.

14 Indictment, para. 16.

15 Indictment, paras. 17-33.

II. Background

A. The Guilty Plea

4. On 13 June 2007, the Parties filed a Joint Motion for Consideration of a Guilty Plea Agreement between Rugambarara and the Office of the Prosecutor.[16] The Motion sets forth the factual basis and legal requirements of the Accused's guilty plea, for the Chamber's consideration pursuant to Rules 62(B) and 62*bis* of the Rules of Procedure and Evidence (the "Rules").[17]

5. On 13 July 2007, at his further appearance, Juvénal Rugambarara pleaded guilty for having failed in his duty to take the necessary and reasonable steps to ensure the punishment of his subordinates for the crimes they committed between 7 and 20 April 1994.[18] **[page 4]**

6. The Chamber proceeded to verify the validity of the plea. After questioning the Accused, the Chamber was satisfied that Rugambarara understood that when an accused pleads not guilty, he is presumed innocent until proven guilty beyond reasonable doubt and that in pleading guilty, he was waiving his right to a fair trial, including the right to cross-examine Prosecution witnesses.[19] Rugambarara also understood that his plea, if accepted, would result in a conviction with imprisonment associated thereto. Furthermore, Rugambarara acknowledged the existence of the Plea Agreement. He confirmed that his Counsel had fully explained to him the terms of the Plea Agreement, and that he understood the nature of the charges against him.[20]

7. The Accused indicated that his guilty plea was made out of his own free will and with no guarantees or promises, other than those set out in the Plea Agreement. The Accused confirmed that he was satisfied with the explanations provided in the Indictment and that he could not challenge any of the facts alleged in the Indictment after the plea.[21] Rugambarara further confirmed that his plea was made without any pressure or coercion.[22]

B. Findings on the Guilt of Rugambarara

8. The Chamber was satisfied that the guilty plea by the Accused was made freely, voluntarily, unequivocally and was informed. In its Oral Ruling of 13 July 2007, the Chamber found that there was no disagreement between the Accused and the Prosecution on the acknowledged facts forming the basis of the Plea Agreement and that such facts were sufficient to establish the crimes to which he confessed. The Chamber found the facts set out in the Indictment satisfy the different elements of a crime against humanity:

---

16 Joint Motion for Consideration of a Guilty Plea Agreement between Juvénal Rugambarara and the Office of the Prosecutor ("Joint Motion").

17 Rule 62: Initial Appearance of Accused and Plea

(B) If an accused pleads guilty in accordance with Rule 62(A)(v), or requests to change his plea to guilty, theTrial Chamber shall satisfy itself that the guilty plea:

(i) is made freely and voluntarily;
(ii) is an informed plea;
(iii) is unequivocal; and
(iv) is based on sufficient facts for the crime and accused's participation in it, either on the basis of objective indicia or of lack of any material disagreement between the parties about the facts of the case. Thereafter the Trial Chamber may enter a finding of guilt and instruct the Registrar to set a date for the sentencing hearing.

Rule 62*bis*: Plea Agreement Procedure

(A) The Prosecutor and the Defence may agree that, upon the accused entering a plea of guilty to the indictment or to one or more counts of the indictment, the Prosecutor shall do one or more of the following before the Trial Chamber:

(i) apply to amend the indictment accordingly;
(ii) submit that a specific sentence or sentencing range is appropriate;
(iii) not oppose a request by the accused for a particular sentence or sentencing range.

(B) The Trial Chamber shall not be bound by any agreement specified in paragraph (A).

(C) If a plea agreement has been reached by the parties, the Trial Chamber shall require the disclosure of the agreement in open session or, on a showing of good cause, in closed session, at the time the accused pleads guilty in accordance with Rule 62(A)(v), or requests to change his or her plea to guilty.

18 T. 13 July 2007, p. 8.

19 T. 13 July 2007, pp. 8, 10.

20 T. 13 July 2007, p. 9.

21 T. 13 July 2007, pp. 9-10.

22 T. 13 July 2007, pp. 8-10.

the attacks were widespread and directed against the Tutsi civilian population on ethnic grounds.[23] Furthermore, the scale of the killings undoubtedly amounts to extermination.[24] **[page 5]**

9. Based on the premises above, the Chamber declared the Accused guilty of the crime of extermination as a crime against humanity pursuant to Articles 3(b) and 6(3) of the Statute.[25]

III. Sentencing

10. On 13 July 2007, the Chamber scheduled a sentencing hearing for 17 September 2007.[26] The Parties filed their sentencing briefs on 12 September 2007 and the hearing was held on 17 September 2007. The Defence called five character witnesses and was permitted to adduce one witness statement under Rule 92*bis*.[27]

A. Applicable Law

11. The Tribunal was established to prosecute and punish the perpetrators of the atrocities in Rwanda in 1994 so as to end impunity. It was also created to contribute to the process of national reconciliation, the restoration and maintenance of peace and to ensure that the violations of international humanitarian law in Rwanda are halted and effectively redressed.[28] The Chamber considers that a fair trial and, in the event of a conviction, a just sentence, contribute towards these goals. Furthermore, deterrence, retribution and rehabilitation are relevant principles considered by the Chamber when imposing a sentence.[29]

12. The penalty imposed by the Chamber is limited to imprisonment, as per Article 23 of the Statute and Rule 101 of the Rules. Such a term shall not exceed life imprisonment.[30] The Statute and the Rules do not provide for specific penalties for any of the crimes within the jurisdiction of the Tribunal.

13. Consequently, the determination of the sentence is left to the discretion of the Chamber. In exercising that discretion, the Chamber shall consider a number of factors, including the gravity of the offence, any aggravating or mitigating circumstances, the personal circumstances of the convicted person and the general practice regarding prison sentences in the courts of Rwanda.[31] **[page 6]**

---

23 Article 3 of the Statute: Crimes against Humanity
The International Tribunal for Rwanda shall have the power to prosecute persons responsible for the following crimes when committed as part of a widespread or systematic attack against any civilian population on national, political, ethnic, racial or religious grounds:
(a) Murder;
(b) Extermination;
(c) Enslavement;
(d) Deportation;
(e) Imprisonment;
(f) Torture;
(g) Rape;
(h) Persecutions on political, racial and religious grounds;
(i) Other inhumane acts.

24 *The Prosecutor v. Ndindabahizi*, Case No. ICTR-2001-71-A, Judgement (AC), 16 January 2007, para. 135, citing *The Prosecutor v. Ntakirutimana*, Case No. ICTR-96-10/ICTR-96-17, Judgement (AC), 13 December 2004, para. 516.

25 T. 13 July 2007, p. 14.

26 T. 13 July 2007, p. 16.

27 On 14 September 2007, the Defence for Rugambarara filed a Motion requesting the admission of 4 witness statements under Rule 92*bis* and a Motion requesting the admission of documentary evidence under Rule 100(A). During the sentencing hearing, the Chamber noted that only one of the witness statements met the requirements of Rule 92*bis*. The Chamber also rejected the Defence Motion requesting admission of documentary evidence on the basis that the Defence should have filed the material by 12 September 2007 in accordance with Rule 100(A) and no good reasons had been given for its late filing (T. 17 September 2007, pp. 25-26).

28 Security Council Resolution 955, 8 November 1994.

29 *Prosecutor v. Joseph Serugendo*, Case No. ICTR-2005-84-I, Judgement and Sentence (TC), 12 June 2006, para. 33; *Prosecutor v. Zlatko Aleksovski*, Case No. IT-95-14/1-A, Judgement (AC), 24 March 2000, para. 185; *Prosecutor v. Mucić et al.*, Case No. IT-96-21-A, Judgement (AC), 20 February 2001, para. 806.

30 Rule 101(A).

31 Article 23: Penalties
2. In imposing the sentences, the Trial Chambers should take into account such factors as the gravity of the offence and the individual circumstances of the convicted person.

14. Aggravating circumstances must be proved beyond reasonable doubt, while mitigating circumstances must be proved on a balance of probabilities.[32]

15. The Chamber understands its obligation to ensure that the sentence is commensurate with the individual facts of the case and the individual circumstances of the offender.[33]

16. Recommendations on the range of the sentence as suggested in the Joint Motion for Consideration of the Plea Agreement are not binding on the Chamber.[34]

B. Gravity of the Offence

1. Submissions

17. The Prosecution submits that the gravity of the offence is the first element to consider in determining an appropriate sentence. According to the Prosecution, the crimes for which Rugambarara has been charged with and to which he pleaded guilty are inherently crimes of extreme gravity, the scale of which shock the collective conscience. The Prosecution further submits that the mass killings, as alleged in the Indictment, occurred as part of a wider plan to exterminate the Tutsi civilians throughout Rwanda between April and June 1994. To that end, the factual allegations against Rugambarara should not be considered in isolation, but rather in the overall context of the events that occurred in Rwanda in 1994, and more specifically in Kigali-Rural *préfecture* within the same period.[35]

18. The Defence submits that Rugambarara fully recognizes his responsibility. The Defence submits, however, that Rugambarara did not personally participate in any of the massacres committed in Bicumbi *commune* nor did he order or encourage them.[36]

2. Findings

19. The seriousness of the crime, including the form and the degree of the Accused's participation in the crime,[37] are factors to be considered in sentencing. Crimes against **[page 7]** humanity are very serious offences because they are heinous in nature and shock the collective conscience of mankind.[38]

20. The Chamber finds that Rugambarara's failure to act constitutes a very serious offence and a gross violation of international humanitarian law. The Chamber also recalls that "Trial Chambers, when assessing the gravity of the offence, have no obligation to take into account what the accused did *not* do".[39] Furthermore the Chamber is not required to give the Accused credit for the fact that he did not order, plan or instigate the crimes.[40] The Chamber notes, however, that the Accused is only charged with *post facto* knowledge of the crimes. Saving lives was therefore not at stake, which makes the crime less serious than if it were otherwise.

Rule 101: Penalties
(B) In determining the sentence, the Trial Chamber shall take into account the factors mentioned in Article 23(2) of the Statute, as well as such factors as:
(i) Any aggravating circumstances;
(ii) Any mitigating circumstances including the substantial cooperation with the Prosecutor by the convicted person before or after conviction;
(iii) The general practice regarding prison sentences in the courts of Rwanda;
(iv) the extent to which any penalty imposed by a court of any State on the convicted person for the same act has already been served, as referred to in Article 9(3) of the Statute.

32 *The Prosecutor v. Juvénal Kajelijeli,* Case No. ICTR-98-44A-A, Judgement (AC), 23 May 2005, para. 294.

33 *Mucić et al.,* Judgement (AC), para. 717; *Prosecutor v. Mikaeli Muhimana,* Case No. ICTR-95-1B-T, Judgement and Sentence (TC), 28 April 2005, para. 594; *Prosecutor v. Fatmir Limaj et al.,* Case No. IT-03-66A, Judgement (AC), 27 September 2007, paras. 127, 133, 135.

34 T. 13 July 2007, p. 10.

35 Prosecutor's Sentencing Brief, para. 33.

36 Defence Sentencing Brief, para. 49.

37 *Mucić et al.,* Judgement (AC), para. 731; *Prosecutor v. Zoran Kupreskić,* Case No. IT-95-16-A, Judgement (AC), 23 October 2001, para. 442; *Prosecutor v. Zlatko Aleksovski,* Case No. IT-95-14/1-T, Judgement (TC), 25 June 1999, para. 243.

38 *Prosecutor v. Georges Ruggiu,* Case No. ICTR-97-32-I, Judgement and Sentence (TC), 1 June 2000, para. 48.

39 *Prosecutor v. Momir Nikolic,* Case No. IT-02-60/1-A, Judgement on Sentencing Appeal (AC), 8 March 2006, para. 56.

40 *Ibid.,* para. 56.

C. Aggravating Circumstances

1. Nature of the Crime

a. Submissions

21. The Prosecution submits that the gravity and heinous nature of extermination as a crime against humanity and its absolute prohibition in international law make its commission inherently aggravating. The Prosecution further submits that the magnitude of such a crime involving the killings of several thousands of civilians in Rwanda over a period of 100 days constitutes an aggravating factor.[41]

b. Findings

22. The Chamber is mindful that "where an aggravating factor for the purposes of sentencing is at the same time an element of the offence, it cannot also constitute an aggravating factor for the purposes of sentencing."[42]

23. Although the *actus reus* of the crime of extermination requires "killing on a large scale", this does not suggest a "numerical minimum." A particularly large number of victims, however, can be an aggravating circumstance in relation to the sentence for this crime if the extent of the killings exceeds that required for extermination.[43]

24. The crimes to which Rugambarara confessed involve the deaths of thousands of Tutsi civilians in Mwulire, Mabare and Nawe *secteurs,* Bicumbi *commune.*[44] The Chamber finds this to be a particularly large number of victims and that it therefore constitutes an aggravating factor for the purpose of sentencing. **[page 8]**

2. Position of Juvénal Rugambarara

a. Submissions

25. The Prosecution submits that, as *bourgmestre* of Bicumbi *commune* in Kigali-Rural *préfecture* between 4 August 1993 and 20 April 1994, Juvénal Rugambarara was in the first rank of leadership at the communal level, had administrative authority over the entire commune and represented executive power at the communal level. He was a prominent member of the civilian community in the said *commune.* The Prosecution further submits that a particularly aggravating factor is that Rugambarara was charged with the specific enforcement of laws and regulations, and failed in his duty to take the necessary and reasonable measures within his powers to ensure the punishment of his subordinates. The Prosecution submits that by failing in this duty, Rugambarara failed to create or sustain an environment of discipline and respect for the law amongst the persons under his control and abused the trust placed in him when such authority was entrusted to him. The Prosecution further submits that Rugambarara's position of authority and proximity to the local population placed him under a duty to uphold the principles laid down in the constitution of Rwanda and exhibit a higher than average degree of morality, both of which he failed to do. The Prosecution also submits that Rugambarara is well educated and in a position to know and appreciate the dignity and value of human life. Finally, the Prosecution submits that the involvement of the peasant population in the massacres of Tutsi civilians in Bicumbi *commune* was facilitated by their misplaced belief and confidence in their leadership and an understanding that the encouragement of said authorities guaranteed them immunity to kill the Tutsi and loot their property.[45] The Prosecution requests the Chamber to treat all these factors relating to Rugambarara's position of authority as aggravating.

---

41 Prosecutor's Sentencing Brief, p. 7, para. 36; T. 17 September, p. 27.

42 *Prosecutor v. Tihomir Blaškić*, Case No. IT-95-14A, Judgement (AC), 29 July 2004, para. 693 cited in *Ndindabahizi,* Judgement (AC), para. 137; *Limaj et al.,* Judgement (AC), para. 143.

43 *Ndindabahizi,* Judgement, (AC), para. 135, citing *Ntakirutimana* Judgement (AC), para. 516.

44 A Plea Agreement between Mr. Juvénal Rugambarara and the Office of the Prosecutor ("Plea Agreement"), 13 June 2007, paras. 38, 40, 41, 42, 44, 46-48, 49-50 and 52, annexed to Joint Motion.

45 Prosecutor's Sentencing Brief, para. 47; T. 17 September 2007, pp. 28-29.

b. Findings

26. The Chamber recalls that an element of the offence itself cannot constitute an aggravating factor. As such, Rugambarara's position as a superior is not aggravating since it constitutes an element of the crime under Article 6(3) of the Statute. However, the Chamber notes that although certain modes of liability require a position of authority, a high level of authority is not an element of the mode of liability and may still be considered as an aggravating factor.[46]

27. Furthermore, it is well established in the jurisprudence of the ICTR and ICTY that the manner in which the accused exercised his command or the abuse of an accused's personal position in the community may be considered as aggravating factors.[47] **[page 9]**

28. The Chamber considers that Juvénal Rugambarara did not hold a high level of authority. His position as *bourgmestre* of Bicumbi *commune* made him an immediate superior and can therefore not constitute an aggravating factor.

29. The Chamber also notes that the Prosecution deliberately expands its allegations against Rugambarara beyond the scope of the Indictment by lending a role to him over the behaviour of the peasant population and by further vilifying the manner in which he exercised his authority. The Chamber dismisses these allegations.

D. Mitigating Circumstances

1. Applicable Law

30. Mitigating circumstances may not be directly related to the offence.[48] A guilty plea may have a mitigating effect on the sentence by: the showing of remorse,[49] repentance,[50] the contribution to reconciliation,[51] the establishment of the truth,[52] the encouragement of other perpetrators to come forward,[53] the sparing of a lengthy investigation and a trial and thus time, effort and resources,[54] and the fact that witnesses are relieved from giving evidence in court.[55] The timing of the guilty plea is also a factor to be considered in sentencing.[56]

2. Personal Mitigating Circumstances

a. The Guilty Plea and Public Expression of Remorse

i) Submissions

31. The Parties contend that, in principle, a guilty plea is a mitigating factor. Specifically, they argue that, because Rugambarara pleaded guilty before the start of his trial, judicial time and resources have been

---

46 *The Prosecutor* v. *Galic*, Case No. IT-98-29-A, Judgement (AC), 30 November 2006, para. 412.

47 *Aleksovski,* Judgement (AC), para. 183; *Prosecutor v. Clément Kayishema and Obed Ruzindana,* Case No. ICTR-95-1-A, Judgement (Reasons) (AC), 1 June 2001, paras. 357, 358; *Ntakirutimana*, Judgement (AC), para. 563; *The Prosecutor v. Jean de Dieu Kamuhanda,* Case No. ICTR-99-54A-A, Judgement (AC), 19 September 2005, paras. 347-348; *Prosecutor v. Paul Bisengimana,* Case No. ICTR-00-60-T, Judgement and Sentence (TC), 13 April 2006, para. 120; *Serugendo*, Judgement (TC), para. 48; *Ndindabahizi* Judgement (AC), para. 136.

48 *Prosecutor v. Dragan Nikolic*, Case No. IT-94-2-S, Sentencing Judgement (TC), 18 December 2003, para. 145; *The Prosecutor v. Miroslav Deronjić*, Case No. IT-02-61-S, Sentencing Judgement (TC), 30 March 2004, para. 155.

49 *Prosecutor v. Biljana Plavšić,* Case No. IT-00-39&40/S, Sentencing Judgement (TC), 27 February 2003, para. 73.

50 *Ruggiu,* Judgement (TC), para. 55.

51 *Plavšić*, Judgement (TC), paras. 80-81.

52 *Prosecutor v. Drazen Erdemović,* Case No. IT-96-22, Sentencing Judgement (TC), 5 March 1998, para. 21; *Nikolić,* Judgement (TC), para. 248; *Serugendo*, Judgement (TC), para. 55.

53 *Ruggiu*, Judgement (TC), para. 55.

54 *Ibid.*, para. 53.

55 *Serugendo*, Judgement (TC), paras. 52, 57.

56 *Prosecutor v. Jean Kambanda*, Case No. ICTR-97-23-S, Judgement and Sentence (TC), 4 September 1998, para. 52; *Prosecutor v. Dusko Sikirica et al.*, Case No. IT-95-8, Sentencing Judgement (TC), 13 November 2001, para. 150; *Serugendo*, Judgement (TC), para. 54.

saved; victims of the attacks in Bicumbi *commune* in 1994 have been spared the ordeal of giving testimony before the Chamber; and the plea will assist in the administration of justice as well as in the process of national reconciliation in Rwanda.[57] The Prosecution further submits that the guilty plea is important to establish the truth and that by pleading guilty, Rugambarara should be seen **[page 10]** as setting an example that may encourage others like him to acknowledge their personal involvement in the events in Rwanda in 1994.[58]

32. On 13 July 2007, during his further appearance before the Chamber, Juvénal Rugambarara indicated his decision to change his initial plea of "not guilty" after a period of long reflection during which he became fully aware of both the consequences and scope of the offences he had committed in Rwanda in 1994.[59] He asked the families of the victims in Bicumbi *commune* in particular and the people of Rwanda in general for forgiveness for his failure to punish his subordinates and added that he felt deep remorse.[60]

ii) Findings

33. The Chamber accepts the Prosecution's position that a guilty plea not only saves time but may also encourage others to come forward, thus contributing to the process of national reconciliation in Rwanda.[61] For remorse to be considered mitigating, the Chamber must be satisfied that the expression of remorse is sincere.[62]

34. After considering Rugambarara's public expression of regret and remorse, the Chamber is satisfied that Rugambarara's expression of remorse is sincere.

35. Rugambarara's change of plea has indeed saved judicial time and resources, and may contribute to the process of national reconciliation in Rwanda. The Chamber considers these factors as mitigating.

b. Assistance Provided to Certain Individuals

i) Submissions

36. The Defence submits that Rugambarara assisted Tutsi refugees in the Bicumbi communal office during the events in 1994.[63] The Defence called Witnesses JRR10, JRR11, JRR23 and JRR24 to support this contention.[64]

ii) Findings

37. After considering the testimonies of the above witnesses, the Chamber accepts the evidence that Rugambarara personally assisted Tutsi refugees by way of moral and material support in Bicumbi *commune* during the 1994 events. Rugambarara's acts contributed to saving some of their lives. In the Chamber's view, this constitutes a mitigating factor. **[page 11]**

c. Personal and Family Situation

i) Submissions

38. The Defence argues that the jurisprudence of the Tribunal and the ICTY has taken into consideration, as mitigating factors, personal circumstances such as the accused's family situation. It puts forth the fact that

---

57 Prosecutor's Sentencing Brief, paras. 50, 54; Defence Sentencing Brief, paras. 60-62; T.17 September 2007, p. 29.
58 Prosecutor's Sentencing Brief, para. 55; T.17 September 2007, p. 29.
59 Plea Agreement, para. 8.
60 T. 13 July 2007, pp. 11-13.
61 *Bisengimana,* Judgement (TC), para. 139; *Prosecutor v. Joseph Nzabirinda*, Case No. ICTR-2001-77-T, Sentencing Judgement (TC), 23 February 2007, para. 68.
62 *Prosecutor v. Predrag Banović*, Case No. IT-02-65/1-S, Sentencing Judgement (TC), 28 October 2003, para. 72.
63 Defence Sentencing Brief, paras. 75, 76.
64 T. 17 September 2007, pp. 6, 9, 12-13, 15-16.

Rugambarara is married and has six children as proof of his capacity for reintegration into society.[65] The Defence called Witness JRK01, who is Rugambarara's wife, who testified favourably about the Accused's personal and family situation.[66]

ii) Findings

39. The Chamber notes that the fact that an accused is married and has children may, under certain circumstances, be considered as mitigating.[67] In the instant case, the personal and family situation of the Accused, as a married man with children, leads the Chamber to believe in his chances of rehabilitation after his release. The Chamber therefore finds this personal situation to be a mitigating circumstance.

d. Character of the Accused, Lack of Prior Criminal Record and Good Conduct in Detention

i) Submissions

40. Both Parties submit that Rugambarara was a person of good character with no history of extremism before the events of 1994.[68]

41. The Defence adduced evidence that as a medical assistant, Rugambarara took care of all his patients without discrimination and had excellent relationships with Tutsi, some of whom were close friends of his family.[69] The Defence further submits that as *bourgmestre*, Rugambarara abolished the practice of reinserting the Tutsi ethnicity of ID holders who had changed their ethnicity to Hutu in the 1960s, and that he spearheaded an initiative at the national level to abolish the reference to ethnicity on identification cards.[70]

42. The Defence submits that the Accused has a clean record and has never been convicted of a crime, an assertion which was not challenged by the Prosecution.[71] The Chamber also accepted, pursuant to Rule 92*bis*, a statement from the UNDF **[page 12]** Commanding Officer, stating that the Accused exhibited good behaviour during his four-year detention.[72]

ii) Findings

43. The Chamber accepts that Rugambarara was a person of good character before the events of 1994, with no history of ethnic discrimination. The Chamber also accepts the unchallenged assertion that Rugambarara had no previous criminal record. Finally, the Chamber considers that the statement of the UNDF Commanding Officer demonstrates Rugambarara's good conduct while in detention. The Chamber accepts these as mitigating factors.

3. Prevailing Circumstances in Bicumbi *Commune* in April 1994

a. Absence of Hierarchical Superior in April 1994

i) Submissions

44. The Defence submits that Rugambarara had knowledge of the crimes committed by his subordinates only on or about 18 April 1994. The Defence further submits that Rugambarara fled when the RPF took control of Bicumbi *commune* on 20 April 1994. This left Rugambarara with only 48 hours to report to his hierarchical superiors and to inform them about the crimes committed by his subordinates. The Defence also

65 Defence Sentencing Brief, paras. 65-68; T. 17 September 2007, p. 39.

66 T. 17 September 2007, pp. 18-23.

67 *Prosecutor v. Dragoljub Kunarać et al.*, Case No. IT-96-23&23/1, Judgement (AC), 12 June 2002, para. 362; *Prosecutor v. Mitar Vasiljević*, Case No. IT-98-32-T, Judgement (TC), 29 November 2002, para. 300; *Prosecutor v. Vincent Rutaganira*, Case No. ICTR-95-1C-T, *Jugement et Sentence*, (TC), 14 March 2005, paras. 120-121.

68 Prosecutor's Sentencing Brief, para. 53; Defence Sentencing Brief, paras. 71-74; T. 17 September 2007, p. 29.

69 Defence Sentencing Brief, paras. 71-74; Testimony of JRK01, T. 17 September 2007, pp. 20-22.

70 Defence Sentencing Brief, paras. 77-78.

71 Defence Sentencing Brief, para. 69.

72 T. 17 September 2007, p. 26.

submits that the Public Prosecutor of Kigali at the time, who was Rugambarara's judicial superior and to whom Rugambarara would have had to report, had already fled.[73]

ii) Findings

45. The Chamber finds the Defence submission, concerning the circumstances of Rugambarara's failure to act as pleaded in the Indictment, misplaced. By pleading guilty, the Accused admitted that he had effective control over his subordinates and the material ability to punish the perpetrators or commission an investigation into the said crimes. The suggestion that it was almost materially impossible for him to report to his hierarchical superior is not supported by any evidence and casts a shadow on the unequivocal acknowledgement of responsibility. The Chamber does not consider this a mitigating factor.

b. War Situation in Bicumbi *Commune* in April 1994

i) Submissions

46. The Defence submits that the Chamber should take into consideration the circumstances prevailing in Bicumbi *commune* in April 1994: i) the existence of an armed conflict; ii) the renewed political intolerance and inter-ethnic tensions within the commune; iii) an influx of refugees into the *commune*, people displaced by the war, infiltrators and RPF recruitment in the region; and iv) the insufficient number of communal police.[74] **[page 13]**

ii) Findings

47. Although the Defence did not adduce evidence to sustain these assertions, the Chamber accepts as facts of common knowledge that there was an armed conflict in Rwanda in 1994 and as a result there was renewed political intolerance, interethnic tensions and an influx of refugees into the Bicumbi *commune*. The Chamber accepts that this particular environment could have made it difficult for Rugambarara to exercise his full authority. The Chamber considers this as a mitigating factor. Other facts relied upon by the Defence do not bear the character of indisputability so as to warrant their acceptance without proof. The Chamber rejects, therefore, the Defence contention that there were infiltrators in Bicumbi *commune* in 1994 and that RPF recruitment took place in the region. Furthermore, the Chamber finds the Defence submission that the communal police was understaffed is not necessarily relevant to Rugambarara's failure, which forms the basis of his criminal responsibility.

E. Sentencing Recommendations by the Parties

48. In the Joint Motion for Consideration of a Guilty Plea Agreement between Rugambarara and the Office of the Prosecutor, the Prosecution recommended a term of imprisonment ranging from nine to twelve years imprisonment, with due credit given for time spent in detention.[75] However, in its Sentencing Brief, the Prosecution appears to depart from the sentencing range agreed upon and recommends a term of imprisonment of not less than twelve years.[76] The Prosecution further submits that the Chamber should consider the principal aims of sentencing, namely justice, retribution, deterrence and rehabilitation.[77] The Defence requests the Chamber to take into account in the determination of the sentence, all mitigating factors, including the personal situation of Rugambarara and his desire for reintegration.[78] The Defence submits that the sentence should be fair, should reflect the chances of rehabilitation and reinsertion into society and should foster national reconciliation.[79] Both Parties acknowledge, however, that the Chamber is not bound by their sentencing recommendations.[80]

---

73 Defence Sentencing Brief, paras. 32, 55.
74 Defence Sentencing Brief, paras. 18-22, 29-33, 51, 54, 56-57.
75 Plea Agreement, para. 56.
76 Prosecutor's Sentencing Brief, para. 57; T. 17 September 2007, p. 30.
77 Prosecutor's Sentencing Brief, para. 17.
78 Defence Sentencing Brief, para. 79; T. 17 September 2007, p. 40.
79 Defence Sentencing Brief, paras. 35-37.
80 Plea Agreement, para. 59.

49. The Defence requests the Chamber to order that Rugambarara serve his sentence in Europe, preferably France, a neighbouring country to Belgium, where his family resides.[81] The Prosecution supports that application.[82]

F. Findings

1. The General Sentencing Practice in the Courts of Rwanda

50. Article 23 of the Statute and Rule 101 of the Rules mandate the Tribunal to take into account the general practice regarding prison sentences in the courts of Rwanda. **[page 14]**

51. Under Rwandan Law, serious offences, such as genocide or crimes against humanity, carry a maximum sentence of life imprisonment or life imprisonment with special provisions, depending on the nature of the accused's participation.[83] If the defendant confesses to the crime, pleads guilty, repents and apologizes, the sentence may range from 25 to 30 years of imprisonment.[84]

52. The Chamber, though not bound by the Rwandan law, regards this as one factor supporting the imposition of a heavy penalty upon the convicted person.

2. Conclusion

53. The Chamber is mindful that sentences of individuals in similar cases should be consistent. However, a Chamber is "under no obligation to expressly compare the case of one accused to that of another,"[85] and "any given case contains a multitude of variables, ranging from the number and type of crimes committed to the personal circumstances of the individual."[86]

54. The Chamber recalls that it has found that Rugambarara's superior responsibility for the crime of extermination as a crime against humanity constitutes a very serious offence and is a gross violation of international humanitarian law. The Chamber also recalls that the gravity of his crime is reduced by the fact, as set forth in the Plea Agreement, that the Accused only had *post facto* knowledge of the crimes committed by his subordinates.

55. The Chamber has found as an aggravating circumstance the high number of victims.

56. The Chamber found the following circumstances to be mitigating: the Accused's guilty plea accompanied by a public expression of remorse which the Chamber found to be sincere, his personal and family situation, his good character prior to the 1994 events, his lack of prior criminal convictions, his good conduct in detention, and the assistance he provided to certain individuals.

57. Nonetheless, while Rugambarara's personal circumstances are relevant in the mitigation of the sentence, the Chamber is of the view that such factors cannot play a significant role in mitigating international crimes and therefore the weight to be accorded to them is limited.[87]

58. On examination of the sentencing practice of this Tribunal, the Chamber notes that there is only limited authority on sentencing for superior responsibility in relation to the **[page 15]** crime of extermination.[88]

---

81 Defence Sentencing Brief, para. 80.

82 Plea Agreement, para. 58.

83 Articles 51 and 72 of the Organic Law N. 16/2004 of 19/6/2004 Establishing the Organisation, Competence and Functioning of Gacaca Courts Charged with Prosecuting and Trying the Perpetrators of the Crime of Genocide and Other Crimes against Humanity, Committed between October 1, 1990 and December 31, 1994 and Articles 2, 3, 5, 6(1) and 18(3) of the Law N. 33 bis/2003 of 06/09/2003 Repressing the Crime of Genocide, Crimes against Humanity and War Crimes as amended by Articles 3 and 4 of Organic Law N. 31/2007 of 25 July 2007.

84 Article 72(2) of Organic Law N. 16/2004.

85 *Kupreskić*, Judgement (AC), para. 443.

86 *Prosecutor v. Miroslav Kvočka et al.*, Case No. IT-98-30/1-A, Judgement (AC), 28 February 2005, para. 681.

87 *Banović*, Sentencing Judgement (TC), para. 76; *Nzabirinda*, Sentencing Judgement (TC), para. 108.

88 In a judgement yet to be decided on appeal (which further limits its authority), Jean-Bosco Barayagwiza was convicted of, *inter alia*, genocide pursuant to Articles 2 and 6(3) of the Statute for his active engagement in the management of RTLM prior to 6 April 1994, and his failure to take necessary and reasonable measures to prevent the killing of Tutsi civilians instigated by RTLM (*The Prosecutor v. Jean-Bosco Barayagwiza*, Case No. ICTR 99-52, Judgement (TC), 3 December 2003, para. 973) and extermination

Furthermore, the Chamber notes that the case law on guilty plea sentencing concerning extermination does not follow a consistent pattern.[89] Finally, the Chamber is mindful that the sentence should reflect the totality of the criminal conduct of the accused.[90]

3. Credit for Time Served in Custody

59. Pursuant to Rule 101(D) of the Rules, "credit shall be given to the convicted person for the period, if any, during which the convicted person was detained in custody pending his surrender to the Tribunal or pending trial or appeal."

60. The Chamber considers 11 August 2003[91] as the beginning of Rugambarara's detention, this being the date on which he was arrested and detained. The Chamber recognizes that Rugambarara is entitled to credit for the time spent in detention from this date, including any additional time that he may serve pending an appeal. **[page 16]**

IV. Verdict

61. The Chamber sentences Juvénal Rugambarara to **11 years imprisonment.**

62. The sentence shall run as of the date of this judgement.

63. Juvénal Rugambarara is entitled to credit for the time spent in detention from 11 August 2003 to the date of this sentencing judgement.

64. Juvénal Rugambarara shall remain in the custody of the Tribunal, pending a decision on where his sentence will be served.

65. The request to designate France as the country where Rugambarara will serve his sentence is premature and is therefore denied. The President of the Tribunal, in consultation with the Chamber, will designate the State in due course. The Government of Rwanda and the designated State will be so notified by the Registrar.

Done in English
Arusha, 16 November 2007

Asoka de Silva Presiding Judge	Taghrid Hikmet Judge	Seon Ki Park Judge

[Seal of the Tribunal] **[page 17]**

---

as a crime against humanity under Article 3(b), pursuant to Article 6(3) of the Statute of the Tribunal for RTLM broadcasts in 1994 that caused the killing of Tutsi civilians (*Barayagwiza*, Judgement (TC), para. 1064). The Trial Chamber considered that the appropriate sentence for Barayagwiza, in light of all the counts on which he was convicted, was imprisonment for the remainder of his life (*Barayagwiza*, Judgement (TC), para 1106). However due to the violation of Barayagwiza's rights, the Trial Chamber reduced the sentence to 35 years imprisonment in respect of all the counts on which he was convicted (*Barayagwiza*, Judgement (TC), para 1107). Alfred Musema was sentenced to a single sentence of life imprisonment for the counts of genocide, extermination as a crime against humanity pursuant to Articles 6(1) and 6(3) of the Statute (*Musema*, Judgement (TC), para 951).

[89] Jean Kambanda entered a guilty plea and was sentenced to life imprisonment for, *inter alia*, extermination as a crime against humanity pursuant to both Articles 6(1) and 6(3) of the Statute (*Kambanda*, Judgement (TC), para. 40, Verdict). Paul Bisengimana was sentenced to 15 years imprisonment after having pleaded guilty to aiding and abetting extermination as a crime against humanity (*Bisengimana*, Judgement (TC), para. 203). Omar Serushago was also sentenced to 15 years imprisonment after having pleaded guilty to genocide, murder, extermination and torture as crimes against humanity (*Prosecutor v. Serushago,* ICTR-98-39-S, Sentence (TC), 5 February 1999, Disposition). The Trial Chamber considered many mitigating factors in determining the sentence of Serushago, including his family circumstances and the fact that he helped some Tutsi to avoid capture (*Serushago*, Sentence (TC), paras. 31-35). Vincent Rutaganira was sentenced to six years imprisonment after having pleaded guilty to complicity by omission in extermination as a crime against humanity (*Rutaganira*, Judgement (TC), Disposition).

[90] *Mucić et al.*, Judgement (AC), para. 772; *Gacumbitsi*, Judgement (TC), para. 354; *Semanza*, Judgement (TC), para. 563.

[91] Transmission of Warrant of Arrest and Order for Transfer and Detention of the Accused Juvénal Rugambarara, dated 11 August 2003.

Annexes

A. Jurisprudence and Defined Terms

1. ICTR

Prosecutor v. Akayesu, Case No. ICTR-96-4-T, Judgement (TC), 2 September 1998.

Prosecutor v. Barayagwiza, Case No. ICTR 99-52, Judgement (TC), 3 December 2003.

Prosecutor v. Bisengimana, Case No. ICTR-00-60-T, Judgement and Sentence (TC), 13 April 2006.

Prosecutor v. Gacumbitsi, Case. No. ICTR-01-64, Judgement (TC), 17 June 2004.

Prosecutor v. Gacumbitsi, Case. No. ICTR-01-64, Judgement (AC), 7 July 2006.

Prosecutor v. Kajelijeli, Case No. ICTR-98-44-T, Judgement (TC), 1 December 2003.

Prosecutor v. Kajelijeli, Case No. ICTR-98-44-A, Judgement (AC), 23 May 2005.

Prosecutor v. Kambanda, Case No. ICTR- 97-23-S, Judgement (TC), 4 September 1998.

Prosecutor v. Kamuhanda, Case No. ICTR-99-54-T, Judgement (TC), 22 January 2004.

Prosecutor v. Kamuhanda, Case No. ICTR-99-54-A, Judgement (AC), 19 September 2005.

Prosecutor v. Kayishema and Ruzindana, Case No. ICTR-95-1-A, Judgement (AC), 1 June 2001.

Prosecutor v. Muhimana, Case No. ICTR-95-1B-T, Judgement (TC), 28 April 2005.

Prosecutor v. Musema, Case No. ICTR-96-13-T, Judgement (TC), 27 January 2000.

Prosecutor v. Musema, Case No. ICTR-96-13-T, Judgement (AC), 16 November 2001.

Prosecutor v. Nahimana, Case No. ICTR-99-52, Judgement (TC), 3 December 2003.

Prosecutor v. Ndindabahizi, Case No. ICTR-2001-71-I, Judgement (TC), 15 July 2004.

Prosecutor v. Ndindabahizi, Case No. ICTR-2001-71-A, Judgement (AC), 16 January 2007.

Prosecutor v. Niyitegeka, Case No. ICTR-96-14, Judgement (TC), 16 May 2003.

Prosecutor v. Ngeze, Case No. ICTR-99-52, Judgement (TC), 3 December 2003.

Prosecutor v. Ntakirutimana et al., Cases No. ICTR-96-10-T and ICTR-96-17-T, Judgement (TC), 21 February 2003.

Prosecutor v. Ntakirutimana et al., Cases No. ICTR-96-10-A and ICTR-96-17-A, Judgement (AC), 13 December 2004.

Prosecutor v. Nzabirinda, Case No. ICTR 2001-77-T, Sentencing Judgement, 23 February 2007.

Prosecutor v. Ruggiu, Case No. ICTR-97-32-I, Judgement (TC), 1 June 2000.

Prosecutor v. Rutaganda, Case No. ICTR-96-3-T, Judgement (TC), 6 December 1999.

Prosecutor v. Rutaganda, Case No. ICTR-96-3-T, Judgement (AC), 26 May 2003. **[page 18]**

Prosecutor v. Rutaganira, Case No. ICTR-95-1C-T, *Jugement* (TC), 14 *mars* 2005.

Prosecutor v. Semanza, Case No. ICTR-97-20-T, Judgement (TC), 15 May 2003.

Prosecutor v. Semanza, Case No. ICTR-97-20-A, Judgement (AC), 20 May 2005.

Prosecutor v. Seromba, Case No. ICTR 01 66, Judgement (TC), 13 December 2006

Prosecutor v. Serugendo, Case No. ICTR-2005-84-I, Judgement and Sentence (TC), 12 June 2006.

Prosecutor v. Serushago, Case No. ICTR-98-39-S, Sentence (TC), 5 February 1999.

2. ICTY

Prosecutor v. Aleksovski, Case No. IT-95-14/1-T, Judgement (TC), 25 June 1999.

Prosecutor v. Aleksovski, Case No. IT-95-14/1-A, Judgement (AC), 24 March 2000.

Prosecutor v. Banović, Case No. IT-02-65/1-S, Judgement (TC), 28 October 2003.

Prosecutor v. Blaškić, Case No. IT-95-14-A, Judgement (AC), 29 July 2004.

Prosecutor v. Deronjić, Case No. IT-02-61-S, Judgement (TC), 30 March 2004.

Prosecutor v. Erdemović, Case No. IT-96-22, Judgement (TC), 5 March 1998.

Prosecutor v. Galić, Case No. IT-98-29-A, Judgement (AC), 30 November 2006.

Prosecutor v. Kunarać et al., Case No. IT-96-23 & 23/1, Judgement (AC), 12 June 2002.

Prosecutor v. Kupreškić et al., Case No. IT-95-16-A, Judgement (AC), 23 October 2001.

Prosecutor v. Kvočka, Case No. IT-98-30/1-A, Judgement (AC), 28 February 2005.

Prosecutor v. Limaj, et al., Case No. IT-03-66A, Judgement (AC), 27 September 2007.

Prosecutor v. Mucić et al. ("Čelebići"), Case No. IT-96-21-A, Judgement (AC), 20 February 2001.

Prosecutor v. Dragan Nikolić, Case No. IT-94-2, Judgement (TC), 18 December 2003.

Prosecutor v. Momir Nikolić, Case No. IT-02-60/1-A, Judgement on Sentencing Appeal (AC), 8 March 2006.

Prosecutor v. Plavšić, Case No. IT-00-39 & 40/1-S, Judgement (TC), 27 February 2003.

Prosecutor v. Sikirica et al., Case No. IT-95-8-T, Judgement (TC), 13 November 2001.

Prosecutor v. Vasiljević, Case No. IT-98-32, Judgement (TC), 29 November 2002. **[page 19]**

3. Defined Terms

Chamber
Trial Chamber II

ICTR
International Criminal Tribunal for the Former Yugoslavia

Indictment
Prosecutor v. Rugambarara, Case No. ICTR-2000-59-I, Amended Indictment, filed on 2 July 2007.

Judgement
Prosecutor v. Rugambarara, Case No. ICTR-2000-59-I, Sentencing Judgement, 16 November 2007.

Plea Agreement
Prosecutor v. Rugambarara, Case No. ICTR-2000-59-I, Plea Agreement between Mr. Juvénal Rugambarara and the Office of the Prosecutor, filed on 13 June 2007.

T.
Official transcripts of the proceedings in English.

B. Indictment

[page 1] INTERNATIONAL CRIMINAL TRIBUNAL FOR RWANDA

(CASE No.ICTR-2000-59-I)

THE PROSECUTOR

vs.

JUVENAL RUGAMBARARA

AMENDED INDICTEMENT

The Prosecutor of the International Criminal Tribunal for Rwanda, pursuant to the authority stipulated under Article 17 of the Statute of the International Criminal Tribunal for Rwanda (the "Statute of the Tribunal") charges:

JUVENAL RUGAMBARARA

With EXTERMINATION AS a CRIME AGAINST HUMANITY pursuant to Article 3 (b) of the Statute of the Tribunal.

1. The events set out hereinafter occurred in Mwulire, Mabare and Nawe secteurs in Bicumbi commune, Kigali-Rural prefecture, Republic of Rwanda between 7 and 20 April 1994 unless otherwise stated.

THE ACCUSED

2. Juvenal Rugambarara was born in 1959, in Bumba secteur, Tare commune, Kigali-Rural prefecture, in the Republic of Rwanda. Juvenal Rugambarara lived most of his adult life in Bicumbi commune where he worked as a medical officer.

3. Juvenal Rugambarara was appointed *bourgmestre* of Bicumbi commune, Kigali-Rural on 4 August 1993, succeeded Mr. Laurent Semanza. Juvenal Rugambarara served as the *bourgmestre* of Bicumbi commune from 16 September 1993 until 20 April 1994. **[page 2]**

4. Juvenal Rugambarara was appointed as *bourgmestre* of Bicumbi commune by the President of the Republic of Rwanda upon the recommendations of the Minister of the Interior, who was also his hierarchical superior.

5. As *bourgmestre* of Bicumbi commune Juvenal Rugambarara had administrative authority over Mwulire, Mabare and Nawe secteurs which were all located in Bicumbi commune where the crimes he is charged of were committed by his subordinates over who he had effective control.

6. As *bourgmestre* of Bicumbi commune, Kigali-Rural préfecture between 7 and 20 April 1994, Juvenal Rugambarara was the highest ranking civilian authority in the said commune and in that regard, had both the authority to serve as the chief administrator as well as the chief law enforcement officer of Bicumbi commune.

7. As *bourgmestre* of Bicumbi commune, Juvenal Rugambarara had administrative authority over the entire commune and in that regard was responsible for the enforcement of laws and regulations.

8. Juvenal Rugambarara was also responsible for ensuring peace, public order, safety of people and property and implementing government programme. Juvenal Rugambarara was also responsible for informing the central government of any situation worthy of interest in Bicumbi commune.

9. As *bourgmestre* of Bicumbi commune, Juvenal Rugambarara was the representative of the central government at the communal level and thus the embodiment of communal authority therein. To that end, Juvenal Rugambarara had hierarchical authority over all conseillers, communal policemen, and local government officials.

10. In that regard, a superior-subordinate relationship existed between Juvenal Rugambarara and all the conseillers, communal policemen, local administrators, and armed militiamen located in Mwulire, Mabare and Nawe secteurs in Bicumbi commune between 7 and 20 April 1994.

11. In addition, as *bourgmestre* of Bicumbi commune Juvenal Rugambarara had effective control over these categories of persons who were responsible for perpetrating attacks on Tutsi civilians at various locations in Mwulire, Mabare and Nawe secteurs in Bicumbi commune between 7 and 20 April 1994 as outlined in the indictment.

12. Based on his position as the highest ranking civilian authority in Bicumbi commune, Juvenal Rugambarara subsequently came to know that the categories of persons who had participated in attacks resulting in the death of thousands of Tutsi civilians in various locations in Mwulire, Mabare and Nawe secteurs of Bicumbi commune between 7 and 20 April 1994, were his subordinates over whom he had effective control. **[page 3]**

13. In that regard Juvenal Rugambarara in his position as the highest ranking civilian authority in Bicumbi commune, in addition to his duties to enforce amongst other things, the laws and regulations, had a duty to take necessary and reasonable measures to commission investigations into crimes committed by people who were his subordinated and over whom he had effective control, with a view to apprehending and referring the perpetrators of such crimes to the competent authorities for appropriate punishment, but failed to do so.

THE CHARGE

Count 1: EXTERMINATION, as a CRIME AGAINST HUMANITY *pursuant to Article 3(b) of the Statute of the Tribunal*

14. Between 7 and 20 of April 1994 Juvenal Rugambarara through the criminal acts of his subordinates, was responsible, pursuant to Article 6(3) of the Statute, for killing or causing persons to be killed, during mass killing events in Mwulire, Mabare and Nawe secteurs in Bicumbi commune of Kigali-Rural prefecture, Republic of Rwanda, as part of a widespread and systematic attack against a civilian population on political, ethnic or racial grounds.

15. The Accused, Juvenal Rugambarara is charged with: extermination as a crime against humanity by virtue of the fact that having subsequently known that subordinates under his effective control had committed one or more of the acts referred to in Article 3(b) of the Statute of the Tribunal, Juvenal Rugambarara failed in his duty to take the necessary and reasonable measures to commission an investigation into the said crimes, with a view to apprehending and referring the perpetrators thereof to the competent authorities for appropriate punishment pursuant to Article 6(3) of the Statute.

16. Furthermore, as consequence of Juvenal Rugambarara's acts and omissions thousands of Tutsi civilian men, women and children were killed in Mwulire, Mabare and Nawe secteurs of Bicumbi commune between 7 and 20 April 1994.

Particulars of the offence

Events in Mwulire Secteur, Bicumbi commune.

17. On or about 18 April 1994, Juvenal Rugambarara came to know that, several attacks had been launched on the Tutsi refugees gathered at the Mwulire Camp Mwulire secteur in Bicumbi commune between 13 and 18 April 1994 resulting in the death of hundreds of the Tutsi refugees. **[page 4]**

18. On or about 18 April 1994, Juvenal Rugambarara came to know that, several civil public officers, including *conseillers* and communal policemen employed at Bicumbi communal office acting in concert with armed militiamen from the said commune, had participated in the attacks against Tutsi refugees gathered at Mwulire camp in Mwulire secteur in Bicumbi commune.

19. In particular, on or about 18 April 1994, Juvenal Rugambarara came to know that the attacks on the Tutsi civilians gathered at Mwulire Camp had been organized by Theodore Nsengiyumva, the Assistant Bourgmestre of Bicumbi commune, Francois Fungameza the conseiller of Muyumbu secteur, Deo Nkuriyingoma, the conseiller of Bicumbi secteur, Mathias Karuhie, the conseiller of Mabare secteur, Ngabonziza, conseiller of Rubona secteur, Sekimonyo, conseiller of Mabare secteur, and several policemen from Bicumbi commune among who were: Mathias Gasana, Rwabugabo, Shabayiro and Munyakayanza.

20. In that regard, having subsequently known of the attacks on the Tutsi refugees gathered at Mwulire camp as described above, Juvenal Rugambarara, as bourgmestre of Bicumbi commune, failed to take the necessary and reasonable measures to commission an investigation into the said crimes, with a view to apprehending and referring his subordinates who perpetrated these criminal acts that resulted in the death of hundrerds of Tutsi refugees, to the competent authorities for appropriate *punishment.*

21. On or about the 18 April 1994, Juvenal Rugambarara came to know that, on or about 13 April 1994, the conseiller of Bicumbi secteur, one Nkuliyingoma and a communal policeman from Bicumbi commune named Munyakayanza and militiamen armed with traditional weapons left for Mwulire secteur office following which they launched an attack on the Tutsi refugees gathered at the secteur office resulting in the death of hundreds of Tutsi refugees.

22. In that regard, as bourgmestre of Bicumbi commune, Juvenal Rugambarara, having subsequently known that these crimes had been committed, failed to take the necessary and reasonable measures to commission an investigation into the said crimes, with a view to apprehending and referring his subordinates who were responsible for these criminal acts at Mwulire secteur office which resulted in the death of several Tutsi civilians to the competent authorities for appropriate punishment.

Events in Mabare Secteur

23. On or about 18 April 1994, Juvenal Rugambarara came to know that, between 12 and 18 April 1994, several attacks were launched on Tutsi civilians in Mabare secteur, Bicumbi commune, which resulted in the death of hundreds of Tutsi civilians. **[page 5]**

24. On or about the same date, Juvenal Rugambarara further knew that the said attacks on Tutsi civilians located at Mabare secteur in Bicumbi commune which took place between 12 and 18 April 1994 were led by armed communal policemen and militiamen over who he exercised effective control.

25. Having become aware that his subordinated had committed crimes in Mabare secteur, Juvenal Rugambarara as bourgmestre of Bicumbi commune, failed to take the necessary and reasonable measures to commission an investigation into the said crimes, with a view to apprehending and referring his subordinates responsible for these criminal acts which resulted in the death of hundreds of Tutsi civilians to the competent authorities for appropriate punishment.

Events at the Mabare mosque located in Mabare secteur

26. On or about 18 April 1994, Juvenal Rugambarara came to know that attacks had been launched on several Tutsi civilians gathered at the Mabare mosque located in Mabare secteur Bicumbi commune between 16 and 18 April 1994, resulting in the death of hundreds of Tutsi refugess.

27. On or about 18 April 1994, Juvenal Rugambarara also knew that the Tutsi refugees gathered at the Mabare mosque and who had initially resisted the attacks launched upom them by armed militiamen, were subsequently overpowered and killed with the assistance of armed communal policemen from Bicumbi commune who provided reinforcements to the armed militiamen.

28. On or about 18 April 1994, Juvenal Rugambarara came to know that, the Tutsi refugees gathered at the Mabare mosque were attacked by persons who, in his capacity as bourgmestre of Bicumbi commune, were his subordinates and over who he had effective control.

29. Having known that his subordinated had committed attacks at the Mabare mosque between 16 and 18 of April 1994, Juvenal Rugambarara as bourgmestre of Bicumbi commune, failed in his duty to take the necessary and reasonable measures to commission an investigation into the said crimes, with a view to apprehending and referring his subordinates responsible for these criminal acts which resulted in the death of hundreds of Tutsi refugees, to the competent authorities for appropriate punishment.

Events in Nawe secteur

30. On or about 18 April Juvenal Rugambarara came to know that Jean Baptiste Gatete, a census officer employed at the Bicumbi communal office, had, on or about 8 April 1994, publicly instigated and encouraged members of the civilian Hutu population in Nawe secteur, to exterminate their Tutsi counterparts in order to avenge **[page 6]** the death of the President of Rwanda, following which, Jean Baptiste Gatete himself led attacks against Tutsi in Nawe secteur often in concert with communal policemen and militiamen.

31. In that regard, on or about 18 April 1994, Juvenal Rugambarara also came to know that Jean-Baptiste Getete had led three (3) policemen employed by Bicumbi commune namely: Shabayiro, Rwabugabo and Ntabara and several armed militiamen in attacks on Tutsi civilians located in Nawe Secteur on or about 8 April 1994. The said attacks resulted in the death of hundreds of Tutsi civilians in Nawe secteur, in Bicumbi commune.

32. As *bourgmestre* of Bicumbi commune, Juvenal Rugambarara had effective control over Jean-Baptiste Gatete, the communal policemen and the militiamen who were involved in the said attacks in Nawe secteur.

33. Having known of the criminal acts of his subordinates, Juvenal Rugambarara as bourgmestre of Bicumbi commune, failed in his duty to take the necessary and reasonable measures to commission an investigation into the said crimes, with a view to apprehending and referring his subordinates who were responsible for the massacres of Tutsi civilians in Nawe Secteur Bicumbi commune on or about 8 April 1994, to the competent authorities for appropriate punishment.

34. The acts and omissions of Juvenal Rugambarara herein are punishable under Articles 22 and 23 of the Statute of the Tribunal.

Signed at Arusha this .... day of July 2007.

Hassan Bubacar Jallow
Prosecutor

Commentary

1. Introduction

On 16 November 2007, an ICTR Trial Chamber rendered its Sentencing Judgement in the case against Juvénal Rugambarara.[1] The Trial Chamber had convicted the accused on 13 July 2007, on the basis of a guilty plea, for the crime of extermination as a crime against humanity. The chamber had accepted as fact that Rugambarara's subordinates – he had been *bourgmestre* of Bicumbi *commune* in the period from 16 September 1993 until 20 April 1994 – had launched attacks on Tutsi civilians between 13 and 18 April 1994, which had led to thousands of Tutsi being killed. Rugambarara was found guilty of 'having failed in his duty to take the necessary and reasonable measures to commission an investigation into the crimes committed by his subordinates', 'with a view to apprehending and referring the perpetrators thereof to the competent authorities for appropriate punishment pursuant to Article 6(3) of the Statute'.[2]

The Trial Chamber first summed up the applicable law and, subsequently, discussed the primary factor to be considered in sentencing – the gravity of the crime. It held that Rugambarara's failure to act constituted a 'very serious offence' and stressed that it was 'not required to give the Accused credit for the fact that he did not order, plan or instigate the crimes'.[3] It acknowledged, however, that Rugambarara was only charged with '*post facto* knowledge of the crimes', explaining that '[s]aving lives was therefore not at stake, which makes the crime less serious than if it were otherwise'.[4]

The Trial Chamber accepted the particularly large number of victims as an aggravating circumstance,[5] and noted as mitigating circumstances Rugambarara's guilty plea, his expression of remorse – which it found to be sincere - the assistance Rugambarara had rendered to several Tutsi refugees during the events in 1994, his personal and family situation as a married man with children (which led the chamber 'to believe in his chances of rehabilitation after his release'),[6] his pre-1994 good conduct and good conduct while in detention at the United Nations Detention Facility and, finally, the Rwandan situation of 1994, in which an armed conflict was ongoing as well as 'political intolerance, interethnic tensions and an influx of refugees into the Bicumbi *commune*', which, according to the chamber, 'could have made it difficult for Rugambarara to exercise his full authority'.[7] The Trial Chamber, after noting the sentencing recommendations made by the parties and acknowledging Rugambarara's entitlement to credit for the time he had already spent in detention, sentenced him to eleven years imprisonment.[8]

After this brief outline of the Rugambarara Sentencing Judgement, this commentary will identify the sentencing rationales, by perusing the sentencing case law of the two *ad hoc* tribunals, in order to find out whether these two institutions employ corresponding definitions of these rationales.

2. Sentencing rationales

The Trial Chamber, when outlining the law applicable to sentencing, pointed to the principles of deterrence, retribution and rehabilitation, and held that these must guide the chamber in sentencing. While referring to United Nations Security Council Resolution 955, it recalled that the tribunal was established to end impunity, and 'to contribute to the process of national reconciliation, the restoration and maintenance of peace and to ensure that the violations of international humanitarian law in Rwanda are halted and effectively redressed'.[9] These remarks – which are repeated in all of the tribunal's sentencing decisions – both fail to give a definition of the underlying principles and to explain how they direct a Trial Chamber in sentencing.

1 ICTR, Sentencing Judgement, *Prosecutor v. Rugambarara*, Case No. ICTR-00-59-T, T. Ch. II, 16 November 2007, in this volume, p. 789.
2 *Ibid.*, par. 3 and 5.
3 *Ibid.*, par. 20.
4 *Ibid.*, par. 20.
5 *Ibid.*, par. 23 and 24.
6 *Ibid.*, par. 39.
7 *Ibid.*, par. 47.
8 *Ibid.*, par. 61.
9 *Ibid.*, par. 11.

In light of the guidance that both *ad hoc* tribunals claim to find in each other's sentencing practices,[10] it must be seen whether the two institutions employ corresponding interpretations of the sentencing principles of deterrence, retribution and rehabilitation.[11] If this is not the case, the two institutions are seriously misinformed in looking for guidance in each other's sentencing practices. Notwithstanding a general absence of explanatory remarks on the ICTR's sentencing theory in its sentencing case law, in Rutaganira, the Trial Chamber went to some length to clarify its understanding of the most important sentencing principles.[12]

2.1 Retribution

The Rutaganira Sentencing Chamber, referring to the Aleksovski Appeals Judgement, identified retribution, deterrence and rehabilitation as the main purposes of punishment. It defined retribution as 'the expression of the social disapproval attached to a criminal act and to a perpetrator and demands punishment for the latter for what he has done' and concluded that '[t]he sentences handed down by the International Criminal Tribunal are therefore an expression of humanity's outrage against the serious violations of human rights and international humanitarian law which an accused has been found guilty of committing. Retribution meets the need for justice and may also appease the anger caused by the crime to the victims and within the community as a whole'.[13]

The Appeals Chamber, in Bralo, recognized retribution as probably the most important purpose in international sentencing.[14] Retribution, as defined by the ICTY Appeals Chamber in Blaškić, must be understood as public reprobation and stigmatization by the international community.[15] The ICTY Judges have repeatedly emphasized that punishment expresses the international community's condemnation of the criminal act and the perpetrator.[16] It appears to follow that the ICTY Judges exclude the Old Testament[17] and Kantian[18] maxim of a *jus tallionis*.

In Aleksovski, the Appeals Chamber affirmed this view, when it held that retribution is not to be understood as fulfilling a desire for revenge, but rather as 'duly expressing the outrage of the international community at these crimes' and that sentences rendered by the international tribunal 'should make plain the condemnation of the international community of the behavior in question and show that 'the international community [is] not ready to tolerate serious violations of international humanitarian law and human rights.'[19]

---

10 In Krstić, the Appeals Chamber, reacting to the argument of the prosecution that the imposed sentence was inconsistent with ICTR jurisprudence in comparable genocide cases, expressly stated that it is important that due regard is given to, *inter alia*, the jurisprudence of the ICTY and the ICTR. See ICTY,Judgement, *Prosecutor v. Krstić*, Case No. IT-98-33-A, A. Ch., 19 April 2004 , Klip/ Sluiter, ALC-XIX-539, par. 248. For ICTR Sentencing Chambers making reference to ICTY sentencing practice, see for example ICTR, Judgement and Sentence, *Prosecutor v. Ndindabahizi*, Case No. ICTR-2001-71-I, T. Ch. I, 15 July 2004, Klip/ Sluiter, ALC-XVIII-645, par. 510; ICTR, Judgment and Sentence, *Prosecutor v. Kamuhanda*, Case No. ICTR-95-54A-T, T. Ch. II, 22 January 2004, Klip/ Sluiter, ALC-XVII-531, par. 765.

11 There has been some criticism concerning the disparity in sentencing between the ICTR and the ICTY. See, for example, Stephen M. Sayers, Defence Perspectives on Sentencing Practice in the International Criminal Tribunal for the Former Yugoslavia, 16 Leiden Journal of International Law, 2003, p. 753 and Allison Marston Danner, Constructing a Hierarchy of Crimes in International Law Sentencing, 87 Virginia Law Review Association 2001, p. 441 and 442.

12 ICTR, Judgement and Sentence, *Prosecutor v. Rutaganira*, Case No. ICTR-95-1C-T, T. Ch. III, 14 March 2005, Klip/ Sluiter, ALC-XXII-373, par. 107-114.

13 *Ibid.*, par. 108 footnote omitted.

14 ICTY, Judgement on Sentencing Appeal, *Prosecutor v. Bralo*, Case No. IT-95-17-A, A. Ch., 2 April 2007, par. 81.

15 ICTY, Judgement, *Prosecutor v. Blaškić*, Case No. IT-95-14-A, A. Ch., 29 July 2004, Klip/ Sluiter, ALC-XX-295, par. 678.

16 ICTY, Sentencing Judgement, *Prosecutor v. Jokić*, Case No. IT-01-42/1-S, T. Ch. I, 18 March 2004, Klip/ Sluiter, ALC-XIX-779, par. 31 and 32; Judgement, *Prosecutor v. Blaškić*, A. Ch., *supra* note 15, par. 678; Judgement on Sentencing Appeal, *Prosecutor v. Bralo*, A. Ch., *supra* note 14, par. 81; ICTY, Judgement, *Prosecutor v. Kunarac, Kovač and Vuković*, Case No. IT-96-23&IT-96-23/1-A, A. Ch., 12 June 2002, Klip/ Sluiter, ALC-VIII-911, par. 385.

17 Genesis 9:6; Exodus 21:24. See Danilo Zolo, Peace Through Criminal Law (Editorial Comment), 2 Journal of International Criminal Justice 2004, p. 733, who also points to Catholic medieval theology.

18 D. Hazewinkel-Suringa and J. Remmelink, Inleiding tot de studie van het Nederlandse Strafrecht, Goua Quint, Deventer 1996, p. 883-895. See, further, Immanuel Kant, Fundering voor de metafysica van de zeden, Boom, Amsterdam 1997 and Antoine Mooij, Psychiatrie, recht en de menselijke maat. Over verantwoordelijkheid, Boom, Amsterdam 2004, p. 189.

19 ICTY, Judgement, *Prosecutor v. Aleksovski*, Case No. IT-95-14/1-A, A. Ch., 24 March 2000, Klip/ Sluiter, ALC-IV-361, par. 185. See also ICTY, Judgement, *Prosecutor v. Kordić and Čerkez*, Case No. IT-95-14/2-A, A. Ch., 17 December 2004, to be published in volume XXVI, par. 1075, where it is stated that 'retribution should not be misunderstood as a way of expressing revenge or vengeance'. Similarly, Nuremberg Prosecutor Robert H. Jackson held that '[t]he satisfaction of instincts of revenge and retribution for the sake of retribution are obviously the least sound basis of punishment. If punishment is to lead to progress, it must be carried out in a manner which world opinion will regard as progressive and as consistent with the fundamental morality of the Allied case.'

On a closer look, however, this may be no more than wishful thinking. Communities certainly want to see the perpetrators punished *because* of the heinous acts they have committed. In essence, such sentiments belong to the classical retributive paradigm.[20] As Hannah Arendt argued, '[w]e refuse, and consider as barbaric, the propositions "that a great crime offends nature, so that the very earth cries out for vengeance; that evil violates a natural harmony which only retribution can restore; that a wronged collectivity owes a duty to the moral order to punish the criminal" (Yosal Rogat). And yet I think it is undeniable that it was precisely on the ground of these long-forgotten prepositions that Eichmann was brought to justice to begin with, and that they were, in fact, the supreme justification for the death penalty.'[21]

Some may also argue that, since the death penalty is not considered an acceptable form of punishment in international criminal law, punishment at the international tribunals can never be truly retributive. However, apart from the fact that the death penalty can be considered equally inadequate when dealing with crimes of this magnitude,[22] this argument does not necessarily deny retribution its role as a sentencing purpose. It rather appears that retribution applies up to a certain point, where human rights considerations take the lead and deny the possibility of inflicting corporal punishment or the death penalty upon a convicted person.

Relevant to international criminal tribunals employing a 'more modern' understanding of retribution as a purpose in sentencing - retribution as public reprobation and stigmatization in order to affirm a society's norms and values and to prevent the victims or their relatives from taking the law into their own hands[23] - is the need for the existence of an international community, one that is able to express uniform values, in order for these to be strengthened.[24] One may argue that such a community does not exist and therefore cannot express universal values.[25] Accordingly, it would be inappropriate to apply the above defined understanding of retribution to the international context. This author, however, agrees with Kok and van der Wilt that such an argument, which presumably has its basis in cultural relativism, is misinformed.[26]

International criminal justice generally deals with the most heinous crimes; there should be no doubt that the international community condemns such acts and that we can, accordingly, speak of truly universal norms. Carcano further argues that such skepticism is at odds with the broad range of shared values that constitute

Cited in William A. Schabas, Sentencing by International Tribunals: A Human Rights Approach, 7 Duke Journal of Comparative and International Law 1997, p. 500.

20 See William A. Schabas, Sentencing by International Tribunals: A Human Rights Approach *supra* note 19, p. 501, who warns that '[a]ccompanying the new focus of human rights law upon the battle against impunity, the significance of retribution as an objective in sentencing is heard with disconcerting frequency. Activists whose social vision is normally pervaded by tolerance and forgiveness become, in the name of retribution, militant advocates of severe punishment.'

21 Hannah Arendt, Eichmann in Jerusalem. A Report on the Banality of Evil, New York 1963, p. 277.

22 See *ibid.*, p. 250, where she writes that '[t]he most common argument was that Eichmann's deeds defied the possibility of human punishment, that it was pointless to impose the death penalty for crimes of such magnitude […]'.

23 Hart states that '[i]n its most interesting form modern retributive theory has shifted the emphasis, from the alleged justice or intrinsic goodness of the return of suffering for moral evil done, to the value of the authoritative expression, in the form of punishment, of moral condemnation for the moral wickedness involved in the offence. This theory […] is termed by some of its modern advocates a theory of reprobation rather than retribution.' See H.L.A. Hart, Punishment and Responsibility, Essays in the Philosophy of Law, Oxford 1968, p. 235. See also Joel Feinberg, Doing & Deserving, Essays in the Theory of Responsibility, Princeton 1970, p. 98, where he argues that 'punishment is a conventional device for the expression of attitudes of resentment and indignation, and of judgments of disapproval and reprobation, on the part either of the punishing authority himself or of those "on whose name" the punishment is inflicted. Punishment, in short, has a *symbolic significance* largely missing from other kinds of penalties' (emphasis in the original). The importance of the expressive function of punishment in the international criminal justice context has been acknowledged by various scholars. See William A. Schabas, Sentencing by International Tribunals: A Human Rights Approach, *supra* note 19, p. 516; Ruth Kok en Harmen van der Wilt, Kanttekeningen bij de straftoemeting voor het Joegoslavië Tribunaal, 2 Strafblad 2004, p. 63; Edward M. Wise, The International Criminal Court: A Budget of Paradoxes, 8 Tulane Journal of International and Comparative Law 2000, p. 267; Ralph Henham, Some Issues for Sentencing in the International Criminal Court, 52 International & Comparative Law Quarterly 2003, p. 84, 111; Allison Marston Danner, Constructing a Hierarchy of Crimes in International Law Sentencing, *supra* note 11, p. 419.

24 Edward M. Wise, The International Criminal Court: A Budget of Paradoxes, *supra* note 23, p. 268.

25 Henham, for example, states that '[t]here […] exists cogent evidence to suggest that international agreement on matters of sentencing rationales and principles is problematic. Consequently, not only may globality and locality posit contrary values which lead to conflict, paradox and disharmony are disguised, submerged and ignored in the overwhelming nature of the rhetoric of retribution and vengeance' (footnotes omitted); see Ralph Henham, Some Issues for Sentencing in the International Criminal Court, *supra* note 23 p. 90.

26 Ruth Kok en Harmen van der Wilt, Kanttekeningen bij de straftoemeting voor het Joegoslavië Tribunaal, *supra* note 23, p. 63.

the groundwork for the enormous expansion of human rights law over the past half a century.[27] Henham argues that the educative role ascribed to retribution through reprobation and norm strengthening may have more effect at the international level than at a domestic one, in a postmodern pluralistic Western society, because of the 'symbolism of the international forum as an effective platform for publicizing what are perceived as acceptable moral values [...]'.[28]

Where such skepticism is, in this author's view, based on the correct understanding that a *civitas maxima* does not (yet) fully exist,[29] instead of supporting the argument that the modern concept of retribution cannot be applied to the international context, this buttresses a call for more symbolic affirmation, in order to strengthen the fundamental norms of this infant international community.[30]

Such reasoning takes the norms of the international community as frame of reference; the premise must thus also be that it is the international community that provides the moral framework to which the intensity of the punishment must relate. However, the interests and objectives of international and domestic communities may easily come into conflict, an example of which is found in Rwandan objections against the absence of the death penalty as a possible mode of punishment in the ICTR legal framework.

Henham and Drumbl argue that both the international and the municipal community must be taken into account in international sentencing.[31] In this respect, Henham emphasizes the need to take the 'contextual reality' into consideration.[32] Arguably, however, in light of, on the one hand, the very diverse norms of various municipal communities for which international criminal justice tries to provide justice and, on the other, the necessity for a mature international criminal procedure to have a consistent sentencing practice, it is rather the international community and its norms and values that should be the point of reference in international sentencing.

In the *ad hoc* tribunals' definition of retribution, the international community is the sole point of reference. This focal point is also present in the already noted habit of both tribunals' Sentencing Chambers to look for guidance in each other's sentencing practices. Although their legal frameworks oblige them to have recourse to the general practice regarding prison sentences in Rwanda or the former Yugoslavia,[33] Trial Chambers do not have to conform to such domestic practice.[34] The result has been that Sentencing Chambers tend to

---

27 Andrea Carcano, Sentencing and the Gravity of the Offence in International Criminal Law, 51 International & Comparative Law Quarterly 2002, p. 585.

28 Ralph Henham, The Philosophical Foundations of International Sentencing, 1 Journal of International Criminal Justice 2003, p. 76.

29 Danilo Zolo, Peace Through Criminal Law (Editorial Comment), *supra* note 17, p. 727. Edward M. Wise, The International Criminal Court: A Budget of Paradoxes, *supra* note 23, p. 261 and 264.

30 See, in a similar vein, Edward M. Wise, The International Criminal Court: A Budget of Paradoxes, *supra* note 23, p. 261.

31 Mark A. Drumbl, Collective Violence and Individual Punishment: The Criminality of Mass Atrocity, 99 Northwestern University Law Review 2005, p. 541. On the one hand, he states that '[s]ince these assaults are constructed as being of concern to humanity as a whole, international institutions putatively representative of the global community become appropriate conduits to dispense justice and inflict punishment'; on the other, he holds that '[i]nternational criminal law interventions would do well to engage with those practices that actually reflect the customs, procedures and mores of those individuals affected by violence (as perpetrators and victims)'. See, further, Ralph Henham, Some Issues for Sentencing in the International Criminal Court, *supra* note 23 p. 84.

32 See Ralph Henham, Some Issues for Sentencing in the International Criminal Court, *supra* note 23 p. 84 and 90, and Ralph Henham, The Philosophical Foundations of International Sentencing, *supra* note 28, p. 78. On p. 76, he holds that '[...] where national and international punishment norms fail to coincide, victim communities may well perceive this denunciatory aspect of retributive punishment as remaining unfulfilled, thereby undermining any morally justifiable claim for retributivism to have satisfied public opinion and restored public confidence in the punishment process'.

33 See Article 24, paragraph 1, ICTY Statute, Article 23 ICTR Statute and Rule 101 (B) (iii) of the ICTY RPE. See also ICTY, Judgement, *Prosecutor v. Delalić, Mucić, Delić and Landžo*, Case No. IT-96-21-A, A. Ch., 20 February 2001, Klip/ Sluiter, ALC-V-369, par. 813 and ICTR, Reasons for Judgment, *Serushago v. Prosecutor*, Case No. ICTR-98-39-A, A. Ch., 6 April 2000, par. 30.

34 *Ibid.*, par. 813, footnote 1390, citing ICTR, Reasons for Judgment, *Serushago v. Prosecutor*, Case No. ICTR-98-39-A, A. Ch., 6 April 2000, Klip/ Sluiter, ALC-VI-627, par. 30 and ICTY, Judgment in Sentencing Appeals, *Prosecutor v. Tadić*, Case No. IT-94-1-A and IT-94-1-A*bis*, A. Ch., 26 January 2000, Klip/ Sluiter, ALC-IV-439, par. 21. See also ICTY, Appeal Judgement, *Prosecutor v. Kupreškić, Kupreškić, Kupreškić, Josipović and Šantić*, Case No. IT-95-16-A, A. Ch., 23 October 2001, Klip/ Sluiter, ALC-VIII-429, par. 415. In Jelisić, it was held that '[t]his general practice provides general guidance and does not bind a Trial Chamber to act exactly as a court of the former Yugoslavia would. For example, even if the general practice were otherwise, this would not prohibit the imposition of a sentence of life imprisonment; a fortiori, it would not stand in the way of a sentence of 40 years' imprisonment'. See ICTY, Judgment, *Prosecutor v. Jelisić*, Case No. IT-95-10-A, A. Ch., 5 July 2001, Klip/ Sluiter, ALC-

merely cite some domestic provisions on sentencing, while immediately stressing that they are not bound by domestic legislation. The net result is that such domestic legislation lacks any significant influence on international sentencing.

It was stipulated in Nikolić, however, that the underlying aim in sentencing is to 'come as close as possible to justice for both victims and their relatives and the Accused, justice being of paramount importance for the restoration and maintenance of peace',[35] which idea also found expression in the above quotation from the Rutaganira case. Henham is correct where he argues that the international criminal tribunals' 'general justifying aim'[36] of reconciliation might seriously be impeded, if the victimized community does not regard the punishments imposed by international judges as effectively retributing the crimes committed. It seems to follow from the Appeals Chamber's above quoted remarks in Dragan Nikolić, that it, in fact, shares this viewpoint. However, some sort of 'proxy justice'[37] - in which the international judges act on behalf of the various local communities[38]- would lead to unfavourable results, in light of the above mentioned need for consistency in international sentencing.

In this author's view, as long as the *harm* done to victims and their communities is acknowledged and such acknowledgement finds expression in sentencing, the international community can further be taken as the point of reference in respect of the *norms* that are to be expressed, and in determining the appropriate intensity of the punishment.[39] This author agrees with Sloane that, particularly in the international context of diverging standards, the noted challenges can at best be reduced and not eliminated; in his words, the 'responsiveness of international criminal tribunals to municipal communities will probably never be perfect'.[40]

Thus, it is the affirmation of societal norms through reprobation, condemnation and stigmatization, which constitute the core of both *ad hoc* tribunals' interpretation of the principle of retribution. This corresponds to a large extent with Durkheim's views on the role of punishment in a given society, which he argues 'is not what it is ordinarily perceived to be. It does not serve, or serves only incidentally, to reform the offender or to scare off potential imitators. Its effectiveness in these respects is questionable – at any rate, mediocre. Its real function is to maintain intact the cohesion of society by sustaining in all its vigor communal consciousness'.[41] As formulated by Wise, 'punishment reaffirms and reinforces collective beliefs about what constitutes right and wrong [...] it helps hold the community together.'[42]

VII-513, par. 117. See also, Judgement, *Prosecutor v. Kunarac, Kovač and Vuković.*, A. Ch., *supra* note 16, par. 347; ICTY, Judgement, *Prosecutor v. Krstić*, A. Ch., *supra* note 10, par. 262; Judgement, *Prosecutor v. Blaškić*, A. Ch., *supra* note 15, par. 681; Judgement on sentencing appeal, *Prosecutor v. Nikolić*, Case No. IT-94-2-A, A. Ch., 4 February 2005, to be published in volume XXVI, par. 84; ICTY, Judgement, *Prosecutor v. Stakić*, Case No. IT-97-24-A, A. Ch., 22 March 2006, to be published in volume XXIX, par. 398; ICTY, Judgement, *Prosecutor v. Galić*, Case No. IT-98-29-A, A. Ch., 30 November 2006, par. 398. See, further, this author's other commentary, in this volume, p. 807.

35 ICTY, Sentencing Judgement, *Prosecutor v. Momir Nikolić*, Case No. IT-02-60/1-S, T. Ch. I, Section A, 2 December 2003, Klip/ Sluiter, ALC-XV-731, par. 4. See also Judgement on Sentencing Appeal, *Prosecutor v. Bralo*, A. Ch., *supra* note 14, par. 82.

36 The term 'general justifying aim of punishment' is borrowed from H.L.A. Hart; see H.L.A. Hart, Punishment and Responsibility, *supra* note 23, p. 8-13.

37 This term is borrowed from Robert Sloane; see Robert Sloane, The Expressive Capacity of International Punishment, Columbia Public Law & Legal Theory Working Papers 2006, NELLCO, http://lsr.nellco.org/cgi/viewcontent.cgi?article=1024&context=columbia_pllt

38 *Ibid.*, p. 12.

39 Schabas warns that, although the retributive sentiments of victims and their communities must be taken into account, 'their encouragement may have unwanted and unhappy side effects, particularly where society is concerned with rebuilding and reconciliation. It should not be forgotten that many of the most appalling crimes in both the former Yugoslavia and Rwanda were committed in the name of retribution for past grievances.' William A. Schabas, Sentencing by International Tribunals: A Human Rights Approach, *supra* note 19, p. 502.

40 See Robert Sloane, The Expressive Capacity of International Punishment, *supra* note 37, p. 14 and 15. Sloane states, in relation to the ICC, that it 'may be able to bolster local efforts at national justice and improve its solicitude for the victims, but it neither can nor should radically restructure itself in response to the highly divergent local circumstances and legal, political, and social cultures implicated by each situation referred to it'. At p. 16, he further argues that '[t]he drafters of the Rome Statute did not design the Court with a view to the satisfaction of local penal interests'.

41 Cited in Edward M. Wise, The International Criminal Court: A Budget of Paradoxes, *supra* note 23, p. 266.

42 Edward M. Wise, The International Criminal Court: A Budget of Paradoxes, *supra* note 23, p. 266.

2.2 Deterrence

In Rutaganira, the ICTR Trial Chamber, while referring to the ICTY Todorović Trial Judgement, held that - apart from the retributive objective - 'an attempt is made to deter, that is, to discourage people from committing similar crimes', while '[t]he main result sought is to discourage people from committing a second offence (special deterrence)'.[43] Pointing to the Tadić Trial Judgement, it further stated that 'the penalty should also in discourage other people from carrying out their criminal plans (general deterrence)'.[44] It clarified its use and understanding of these notions when it held that '[w]ith respect to general deterrence, a sentence would contribute to strengthening the legal system which criminalizes the conduct charged and to assuring society that its criminal system is effective' and, further, that '[t]he Chamber shall assess the factors relevant to "special deterrence" in considering circumstances in mitigation'.[45]

In a similar vein, the ICTY Appeals Chamber in Blaškić outlined that '[t]he deterrent effect of punishment consists in discouraging the commission of similar crimes. The main effect sought is to turn the perpetrator away from future wrongdoing (special deterrence), but it is assumed that punishment will also have the effect of discouraging others from committing the same kind of crime under the Statute (general deterrence).'[46] Some Trial Chambers of both the ICTY and the ICTR have ignored special deterrence or even expressly held that its applicability is less fitting in an international context.[47] Special deterrence may, indeed, to some extent,[48] be considered of less significance when dealing with international crimes: systematic criminality takes place in and is dependent on a certain political, social and historical context – a context that surpasses a mere individual's evil inclinations.[49]

Although various scholars have criticized the *ad hoc* tribunals for listing deterrence among the sentencing purposes - the effectiveness of deterrence, in the sense of directly discouraging potential violators of international humanitarian law by punishing others, is argued to be highly dubious[50]- it is notable that the ICTY Appeals Chamber has acknowledged that a general deterrent effect is merely 'assumed', cautiously explaining that 'with regard to general deterrence, imposing a punishment serves to strengthen the legal order in which the type of conduct involved is defined as criminal and to reassure society of the effectiveness of its penal provisions.'[51] Although a direct discouraging effect of punishment on future perpetrators has not been persuasively proven,[52] in accordance with the Appeals Chamber's working definition, it has been

---

43 ICTR, Judgement and Sentence, *Prosecutor v. Rutaganira*, Case No. ICTR-95-1C-T, T. Ch. III, 14 March 2005, Klip/ Sluiter, ALC-XXII-373, par. 110.

44 *Ibid.*, par. 110.

45 *Ibid.*, par. 111 and 112.

46 Judgement, *Prosecutor v. Blaškić*, A. Ch., *supra* note 15, par. 678; ICTY, Sentencing Judgement, *Prosecutor v. Milan Babić*, Case No. IT-03-72-S, T. Ch. I, 29 June 2004, to be published in volume XX, par. 45.

47 ICTR, Judgement and Sentence, *Prosecutor v. Kambanda*, Case No. ICTR-97-23-5, T. Ch. I, 4 September 1998, Klip/ Sluiter, ALC-II-793, par. 28; ICTR, Sentence, *Prosecutor v. Kayishema and Ruzindana*, Case No. ICTR-95-1-T, T. Ch. II, 21 May 1999, Klip/ Sluiter, ALC-II-693, par. 2; ICTR, Judgement and Sentence, *Prosecutor v. Elizaphan Ntakirutimana and Ntakirutimana*, Cases No. ICTR-96-10 and ICTR-96-17-T, T. Ch. I, 21 February 2003, Klip/ Sluiter, ALC-XII-383, par. 882; ICTR, Judgement and Sentence, *Prosecutor v. Niyitegeka*, Case No. ICTR-96-14-T, T. Ch. I, 16 May 2003, Klip/ Sluiter, ALC-XII-731, par. 484; ICTY, Judgment, *Prosecutor v. Vasiljević*, Case No. IT-98-32-T, T. Ch. II, 29 November 2002, Klip/ Sluiter, ALC-XI-609, par. 273. See, for an opposite view, Judgement, *Prosecutor v. Kordić and Čerkez*, A. Ch., *supra* note 19, to be published in volume XXVI, par. 1076; Judgement on Sentencing Appeal, *Prosecutor v. Nikolić* , A. Ch., *supra* note 34, par. 45.

48 The argument adduced here may not apply equally to all individuals accused of international crimes. In particular, it may not apply to heads of state and other highly ranked figures.

49 See William A. Schabas, The UN International Criminal Tribunals, The former Yugoslavia, Rwanda and Sierra Leone, Cambridge 2006, p. 558.

50 Edward M. Wise, The International Criminal Court: A Budget of Paradoxes, *supra* note 23, p. 267; Ralph Henham, Some Issues for Sentencing in the International Criminal Court, *supra* note 23 p. 88; Danilo Zolo, Peace Through Criminal Law (Editorial Comment), *supra* note 17, p. 729-731. The latter author states that 'the many questions about such models raised by Western criminology and philosophy of punishment during the 20th century have been disregarded' and that 'Judges and Prosecutors seem to assume as a self-evident axiom that an exemplary punishment of crimes committed by one or both of the conflicting parties may decisively contribute to peace-making' and, finally, that the ''exemplary' character of criminal penalties retains elements of that ancestral irrationality which confers a victimizing and sacrificial function on punishment.' See, further, Ruth Kok en Harmen van der Wilt, Kanttekeningen bij de straftoemeting voor het Joegoslavië Tribunaal, *supra* note 23, p. 56. See, also, Judgement in Sentencing Appeals, *Prosecutor v. Tadić*, A. Ch., *supra* note 34, par. 43.

51 Judgement, *Prosecutor v. Blaškić*, A. Ch., *supra* note 15, par. 678.

52 See Andrew Ashworth, Sentencing and Criminal Justice, Oxford U. P., London 1992; Andrew Ashworth, Sentencing, in: Mike Maguire, Rod Morgan and Robert Reiner (eds.), The Oxford Handbook of Criminology, Oxford University Press, Oxford 2002; and, Edward M. Wise, The International Criminal Court: A Budget of Paradoxes, *supra* note 23, p. 267.

recognized in a domestic context that punishment, in the long run, may have a deterrent effect, through the gradual strengthening of a society's legal norms.[53] Or, as Wise puts it, '[t]here is reason to believe [deterrence] operates more subtly and indirectly, in part by helping to form and reinforce popular perceptions and social norms about what constitutes right and wrong [...]'.[54]

Apparently, the Blaškić Appeals Chamber subscribed to this latter understanding of deterrence as also being applicable to the context of international criminal justice. A corresponding viewpoint was expressed in Kordić and Čerkez, where the Appeals Chamber held that, in the context of international justice, deterrence 'refers to the attempt to integrate or to reintegrate those persons who believe themselves to be beyond the reach of international criminal law', and '[i]n modern criminal law this approach to general deterrence is more accurately described as deterrence aiming at reintegrating potential perpetrators into the global society.'[55]

Furthermore, although the tribunals have recognized deterrence as one of the main purposes in sentencing, they have, at the same time, cautioned that this rationale must not be accorded undue prominence in the assessment of the appropriate sentence to be imposed in a concrete case.[56] It was held in Delalić *et al.* that, although 'in adopting resolution 827, the Security Council established the international tribunal with the stated purpose of bringing to justice persons responsible for serious violations of international humanitarian law in the former Yugoslavia, thereby *deterring future violations* and contributing to the re-establishment of peace and security in the region',[57] 'the Trial Chamber's duty remains to tailor the penalty to fit the individual circumstances of the accused and the gravity of the crime.'[58] One recognizes the teachings of Hart, where he holds that general justifying aims do influence the distribution of sentences, but that, at the same time, distributive purposes (which may be at variance with the general justifying aims), as well as general principles of criminal justice as, for example, due process rights, require compromises being made.[59]

A further differentiation made by the Appeals Chamber in Blaškić, concerned the applicability of the deterrence rationale to various kinds of perpetrators. It held that deterrence is of particular importance in relation to commanders,[60] whilst acknowledging that different sentencing purposes might need to be applied with respect to other perpetrators. This reasoning appears to be in accordance with the argument that, in the context of international crimes, punishment might not effectively deter the rank and file, who have often been indoctrinated for years or who act under strong socio-psychological pressure, in societies where the universal norms of international humanitarian law have been obscured by a genocidal or otherwise extreme violence, but nonetheless with conventional morality.[61] This is important in light of the notion of deterrence being intrinsically connected to the question as to whether an individual can exercise his free will – whether one may adhere to the portrayal of man as a rational and calculating individual.[62]

The Rutaganira sentencing chamber, in referring to the ICTY's definition of (general) deterrence, appears to embrace these qualifications of the rationale in ICTR case law. Both presumably subscribe to an understanding

---

53 Robert Sloane, The Expressive Capacity of International Punishment, *supra* note 37, p. 44; Ralph Henham, The Philosophical Foundations of International Sentencing, *supra* note 28, p. 78; Edward M. Wise, The International Criminal Court: A Budget of Paradoxes, *supra* note 23, p. 267.

54 Edward M. Wise, The International Criminal Court: A Budget of Paradoxes, *supra* note 23, p. 267.

55 Judgement, *Prosecutor v. Kordić and Čerkez*, A. Ch., *supra* note 19, par. 1078.

56 ICTY, Judgement, *Prosecutor v. Aleksovski*, Case No. IT-95-14/1-A, A. Ch., 24 March 2000, Klip/ Sluiter, ALC-IV-361, par. 185; Judgement, *Prosecutor v. Delalić, Mucić, Delić and Landžo*, *supra* note 33, A. Ch., par. 801-803; Judgement, *Prosecutor v. Kordić and Čerkez*, A. Ch., *supra* note 19, par. 1078; Judgement on Sentencing Appeal, *Prosecutor v. Nikolić*, A. Ch., *supra* note 34, par. 46.

57 Judgement, *Prosecutor v. Delalić, Mucić, Delić and Landžo*, A. Ch., *supra* note 33, par. 800 (emphasis added), citing ICTY, Decision on the Defence Motion for Interlocutory Appeal on Jurisdiction, *Prosecutor v. Tadić*, Case No. IT-94-1-AR72, A. Ch., 2 October 1995, par. 72. It is noted, however, that deterrence is used here as a general justifying aim for the establishment of the ICTY, not as a sentencing rationale to be used for ascertaining the appropriate measure of punishment in a concrete case.

58 Judgement, *Prosecutor v. Delalić, Mucić, Delić and Landžo*, A. Ch., *supra* note 33, par. 717; ICTY, Judgement on Sentencing Appeal, *Prosecutor v. Nikolić*, A. Ch., *supra* note 34, par. 46.

59 See, H.L.A. Hart, Punishment and Responsibility, *supra* note 23, p. 14.

60 Judgement, *Prosecutor v. Blaškić*, A. Ch., *supra* note 15, par. 678.

61 See Robert Sloane, The Expressive Capacity of International Punishment, *supra* note 37, p. 26, 27. See also Harald Welzer, Täter. Wie aus ganz normalen Menschen Massenmörder werden, S. Fischer Verlag, Frankfurth 2005.

62 Andrew Ashworth, Sentencing and Criminal Justice, *supra* note 52, p. 60.

of the concept of deterrence as preventing crimes by punishing perpetrators through socio-educative norm strengthening.

2.3 Rehabilitation

Rehabilitation was defined by the Trial Chamber in Rutaganira – by referring to the Čelebići Appeals Judgement and the Banović Trial Judgement - as 'the need to take into account the ability of the person found guilty to be rehabilitated; such rehabilitation goes hand in hand with his reintegration into society'.[63] Rehabilitation has been defined by the ICTY Judges as 'taking into account in sentencing the circumstances of reintegrating the guilty accused into society'.[64] Accused have at times argued that the Trial Chamber erred by not taking into account rehabilitation as a sentencing purpose in their case.[65] The Appeals Chamber, however, held in Čelebići that rehabilitation usually has a role to play 'when younger, or less educated, members of society are found guilty of offences. It therefore becomes necessary to re-integrate them into society so that they can become useful members of it and enable them to lead normal and productive lives upon their release from imprisonment. The age of the accused, his circumstances, his ability to be rehabilitated and availability of facilities in the confinement facility can, and should, be relevant considerations in this respect'.[66]

The Appeals Chamber pointed to the serious nature of the crimes falling under the jurisdiction of the tribunal, and argued that these cases could not simply be compared to domestic criminal cases. It held that, therefore, rehabilitation cannot 'play a predominant role in the decision-making process of a Trial Chamber of the tribunal' and 'cannot be given undue weight.'[67]

Although rehabilitation, as Schabas argues, appears important in the context of human rights violations, 'because of the need for 'reconstruction and reconciliation' in the affected societies',[68] the Appeals Chamber's position is quite acceptable. The grave nature of the crimes dealt with by the international criminal institutions, the trials of which - particularly at the ICTR - often result in the imposing of life sentences or long fixed terms of imprisonment, necessarily reduces the relevance of the principle of rehabilitation to international sentencing.[69]

The question is, of course, what is meant with 'not giving the principle undue weight'. In this regard, in Furundžija, the Appeals Chamber reiterated that retribution and deterrence must be considered the main purposes in international sentencing,[70] while expressing 'support for rehabilitative programs in which the accused may participate while serving his sentence.'[71] The chamber thus acknowledged rehabilitation's role

---

63 Judgement and Sentence, *Prosecutor v. Rutaganira*, T. Ch. III, *supra* note 43, par. 113.

64 Judgement, *Prosecutor v. Delalić, Mucić, Delić and Landžo*, A. Ch., *supra* note 33, par. 805; Judgement, *Prosecutor v. Kordić and Čerkez*, A. Ch., *supra* note 19, par. 1079.

65 See, for example, Judgement, *Prosecutor v. Delalić, Mucić, Delić and Landžo*, A. Ch., *supra* note 33, par. 804.

66 *Ibid.*, par. 805.

67 *Ibid.*, par. 806; Judgement, *Prosecutor v. Kordić and Čerkez*, A. Ch., *supra* note 19, par. 1079; ICTY, Judgement on Sentencing Appeal, *Prosecutor v. Deronjić*, Case No. IT-02-61-A, 20 July 2005, A. Ch., to be published in volume XXVII, par. 136. See, in this regard, also ICTY, Judgement, *Prosecutor v. Stakić*, A. Ch., *supra* note 34, par. 371, where the Appellant argued that the Trial Chamber erred in refusing to hear the evidence of an expert criminologist or psychiatrist, which would have been relevant to sentencing, as it related to his propensity to commit crimes. The Appellant claimed that such evidence was essential to his case and would have led to a lesser sentence. The Appeals Chamber held that a Trial Chamber has the discretion to determine which experts it wants to hear, depending on the circumstances of the case. It was stated in Blaškić that, in light of the gravity of many of the crimes, the weight of rehabilitative considerations may be limited in some cases; see ICTY, Judgement, *Prosecutor v. Blaškić*, Case No. IT-95-14-T, T. Ch. I, 3 March 2000, Klip/ Sluiter, ALC-IV-477, par. 782.

68 William A. Schabas, Sentencing by International Tribunals: A Human Rights Approach, *supra* note 19, p. 503. He argues that '[i]t may be difficult or impossible for society to reconcile and rebuild without serious rehabilitation efforts undertaken within the context of effective action against impunity.'

69 However, the limited relevance of rehabilitation to *international sentencing* must not be understood as in any way diminishing the full applicability of rehabilitation to the *enforcement* of international sentences, in respect of which the tribunals are under a human rights obligation pursuant to Article 10, paragraph 3, ICCPR.

70 ICTY, Judgement, *Prosecutor v. Furundžija*, Case No. IT-95-17/1-A, A. Ch., 21 July 2000, Klip/ Sluiter, ALC-V-291, par. 291; ICTY, Judgement on Sentencing Appeal, *Prosecutor v. Deronjić*, A. Ch., *supra* note 67, par. 136. See also Judgement, *Prosecutor v. Kordić and Čerkez*, A. Ch., *supra* note 19, par. 1079, in which it was stated that '[i]t would violate the principle of proportionality and endanger the pursuit of other sentencing purposes if rehabilitative considerations were given undue prominence in the sentencing process'.

71 Judgement, *Prosecutor v. Furundžija*, A. Ch., *supra* note 70, par. 291 (emphasis added). See also ICTY, Sentencing Judgement, *Prosecutor v. Erdemović*, Case No. IT-96-22-T*bis*, T. Ch. II*ter*, 5 March 1998, Klip/ Sluiter, ALC-I-65, par. 16 and ICTY, Judgement, *Prosecutor v. Zoran Kupreškić, Mirijan Kupreškić, Vlatko Kupreškić, Josipović, Papić and Šantić*, Case No. IT-95-16-T,

in connection to an enforcement regime, while qualifying the rationale's relevance in connection to sentencing.

In view of the Rutaganira Trial Chamber making reference to the Nikolić Trial Chamber's findings and, further, its expressly linking of rehabilitation to an individual's potential for reintegration into society, it appears that the ICTR sentencing chamber shares the ICTY judges' viewpoint about rehabilitation's limited role in international sentencing.

3. Conclusion

Retribution and deterrence have thus been recognized as the main purposes in international sentencing. What these sentencing rationales have in common - according to their definition as adhered to by the *ad hoc* tribunals - is an emphasis on norm strengthening. The declaratory or expressive function of international sentencing must therefore be considered as its most important. The international community declares the wrongfulness of specific conduct for the purposes of reprobation itself (retribution), and in order to prevent similar atrocities in the future, by socio-educative norm-strengthening (deterrence).[72]

This finds further support in the oft encountered phrase, that the general aim is to influence 'the legal awareness of the accused, the victims, their relatives, the witnesses, and the general public in order to reassure them that the legal system is being implemented and enforced.'[73] The Appeals Chamber has recognized the similarities and the gradual transition between the two rationales' meaning, where it held that reprobation and stigmatization are closely related to affirmative prevention.[74]

The tribunals, as human rights' role models, should provide 'enlightened justice'.[75] By applying the more modern working definitions of retribution and deterrence, supplemented where possible with the rehabilitative ideal, these institutions might just succeed in this task.

However, in light of their emphasis on norm strengthening, it is a prerequisite that international sentencing is sufficiently expressive – expressly mentioning and explaining the factors that have led to the imposed punishment. The applied rationales require express reasoning, in order to 'bring the message across'. The statement by the Nikolić Appeals Chamber, that Trial Chambers in concrete cases neither need to mention each of the applicable sentencing purposes, nor to explain why certain purposes were or were not applicable, does not correspond with the requirement of expressive and explicit reasoning.[76] As is also the case with respect to the Sentencing Judgement under review, the Trial Chamber's repetitively summing up the sentencing rationales - without any explanation as to their content or any indication as to why and how they are applicable to the case at issue – also fails to provide explicit and expressive reasoning.

All in all, the question that prompted the above examination of the tribunals' sentencing practice has been answered. These institutions appear to work with practically identical working definitions of the rationales that are central to their sentencing, which therefore, at least from this perspective, permits them to look for guidance in each other's sentencing practices for the sake of consistency in sentencing.

Denis Abels

T.Ch. II, 14 January 2000, Klip/ Sluiter, ALC-IV-703, par 819. This appears to be in accordance with this author's views expressed, *supra* note 69.

72 See, for the same view as to the most important function of international punishment, *inter alia*, William A. Schabas, Sentencing by International Tribunals: A Human Rights Approach, *supra* note 19, p. 516; Ruth Kok en Harmen van der Wilt, *supra* note 26, p. 63; Edward M. Wise, The International Criminal Court: A Budget of Paradoxes, *supra* note 23, p. 267.

73 Judgement, *Prosecutor v. Blaškić*, A. Ch., *supra* note 15, par. 678.

74 Judgement, *Prosecutor v. Kordić and Čerkez*, A. Ch., *supra* note 19, par. 1081.

75 This term is borrowed from Schabas. William A. Schabas, Sentencing by International Tribunals: A Human Rights Approach, *supra* note 19, p. 516.

76 Judgement on Sentencing Appeal, *Prosecutor v. Nikolić* , A. Ch., *supra* note 34, par. 47. See also, Judgement, *Prosecutor v. Delalić, Mucić, Delić and Landžo*, A. Ch., *supra* note 33, par. 806.

Tribunal pénal international pour le Rwanda
International Criminal Tribunal for Rwanda

IN THE APPEALS CHAMBER

Before:	**Judge Fausto Pocar, Presiding** **Judge Mehmet Güney** **Judge Liu Daqun** **Judge Theodor Meron** **Judge Wolfgang Schomburg**
Registrar:	**Mr. Adama Dieng**
Judgement of:	**27 November 2007**

ALOYS SIMBA

v.

THE PROSECUTOR

Case No. ICTR-01-76-A

JUDGEMENT

Counsel for Aloys Simba:

Mr. Sadikou Ayo Alao
Mr. Wenceslas de Souza
Mr. Jean Kiwallo
Mr. Salim A. Kolawolou

The Office of the Prosecutor:

Mr. Hassan Bubacar Jallow
Mr. James Stewart
Mr. George William Mugwanya
Ms. Inneke Onsea
Ms. Evelyn Kamau

CONTENTS

[page 3] I. INTRODUCTION

1. The Appeals Chamber of the International Criminal Tribunal for the Prosecution of Persons Responsible for Genocide and Other Serious Violations of International Humanitarian Law Committed in the Territory of Rwanda and Rwandan Citizens Responsible for Genocide and Other Such Violations Committed in the Territory of Neighbouring States between 1 January 1994 and 31 December 1994 ("Appeals Chamber" and "Tribunal", respectively) is seized of appeals by Aloys Simba ("Appellant") and the Prosecution against the Judgement and Sentence rendered by Trial Chamber I on 13 December 2005 in the case *The Prosecutor v. Aloys Simba* ("Trial Judgement").[1]

A. Background

2. The Appellant, Aloys Simba, was born in 1938 in Musebeya Commune, Gikongoro Prefecture, Rwanda. The Appellant is a retired lieutenant colonel, a member of the "Comrades of the fifth of July", who participated in the *coup d'état* that brought former President Juvénal Habyarimana to power in 1973, and was a member of parliament from 1989 to 1993.[2]

3. The Appellant was tried on the basis of an amended indictment dated 10 May 2004 ("Indictment"),[3] which charged him with individual criminal responsibility for his alleged participation in five massacres committed against the Tutsi population in the Gikongoro Prefecture and in the Butare Prefecture between 14-29 April 1994.[4] At the close of trial, the Prosecution withdrew the charges of complicity in genocide (Count 2) and of murder as a crime against humanity (Count 4) and declined to pursue a conviction for superior responsibility under Article 6(3) of the Statute of the Tribunal ("Statute").[5] The Trial Chamber found the Appellant guilty of genocide (Count 1) based on his participation in a joint criminal enterprise ("JCE") to kill Tutsi civilians at Murambi Technical School and Kaduha Parish.[6] It also convicted him of extermination as a crime against humanity (Count 3), based on the same facts underlying the count of genocide.[7] It imposed a single sentence of 25 years' imprisonment,[8] with credit being given for time already served since he was arrested in Senegal, on 27 November 2001.[9] **[page 4]**

B. The Appeals

4. The Appellant appeals his convictions and challenges his sentence.[10] He alleges several errors of law relating to his right to a fair trial (Ground 1), the burden of proof (Ground 2) and the assessment of evidence (Ground 3). The Appellant submits that the Trial Chamber erred by making contradictory findings (Ground 4) and failing to give a reasoned opinion on certain elements of evidence (Ground 5). He alleges several errors relating to the Trial Chamber's findings concerning his criminal responsibility as a participant in a JCE (Ground 6), and in particular his responsibility for genocide (Ground 7) and extermination as a crime against humanity (Ground 8). He submits that the Trial Chamber committed errors of fact, in particular regarding his presence at Murambi Technical School and Kaduha Parish on 21 April 1994 (Ground 9) and the Public Meeting in Ntyazo on 22 May 1994 (Ground 10). He further submits that the Trial Chamber erred by distorting facts (Ground 11), in assessing his alibi (Ground 12), and in taking certain interlocutory

---

1 *The Prosecutor v. Aloys Simba*, Case No. ICTR-01-76-T, Judgement and Sentence, 13 December 2005 ("Trial Judgement"). For ease of reference, two annexes are appended to this Judgement: Annex A: Procedural Background; Annex B: Cited Materials/ Defined Terms.

2 Trial Judgement, paras 7, 54, 56.

3 The Trial Judgement erroneously refers to the "Indictment of 6 May 2004" (Trial Judgement, para. 4). The Amended Indictment annexed to the Trial Judgement was filed on 10 May 2004.

4 Trial Judgement, para. 10.

5 Trial Judgement, para. 13.

6 Trial Judgement, paras 419, 427.

7 Trial Judgement, paras 426-427.

8 Trial Judgement, para. 445.

9 Trial Judgement, paras 444, 446.

10 Notice of Appeal, filed in French on 22 June 2006 ("Simba Notice of Appeal"); Appellant's Brief, originally filed in French on 6 September 2006 and refiled in French on 16 October 2006 ("Simba Appeal Brief"); Simba Brief in Reply, filed in French on 2 March 2007 ("Simba Reply").

decisions (Ground 13). Finally, the Appellant presents several challenges to the verdict and the sentence of 25 years' imprisonment imposed upon him (Ground 14).

5. The Prosecution responds that all grounds of appeal raised by the Appellant should be dismissed.[11]

6. The Appeals Chamber points out that several aspects of the Appellant's grounds of appeal are inextricably intertwined. Therefore, for ease of analysis, related grounds of appeal have been grouped together. Further, the Appeals Chamber will address the Appellant's grounds of appeal in an order different from that presented.

7. The Prosecution presents two grounds of appeal.[12] The Prosecution claims that the Trial Chamber erred when not finding the Appellant criminally responsible for his participation in the Cyanika Parish Massacre of 21 April 1994 (Ground 1). It also submits that the Trial Chamber erred **[page 5]** in imposing a single sentence of 25 years' imprisonment on the Appellant (Ground 2). The Appellant objects to the grounds of appeal raised by the Prosecution.[13]

C. Standards of Appellate Review

8. The Appeals Chamber recalls some of the applicable standards of appellate review pursuant to Article 24 of the Statute. Article 24 addresses errors of law which invalidate the decision and errors of fact which occasion a miscarriage of justice. A party alleging an error of law must advance arguments in support of the submission and explain how the error invalidates the decision. However, even if the appellant's arguments do not support the contention, the Appeals Chamber may step in and, for other reasons, find in favour of the contention that there is an error of law.[14]

9. As regards errors of fact, it is well established that the Appeals Chamber will not lightly overturn findings of fact made by a Trial Chamber. Where an erroneous finding of fact is alleged, the Appeals Chamber will give deference to the Trial Chamber that received the evidence at trial, as it is best placed to assess the evidence, including the demeanour of witnesses. The Appeals Chamber will only interfere in those findings where no reasonable trier of fact could have reached the same finding or where the finding is wholly erroneous. Furthermore, an erroneous finding of fact will be quashed or revised only if the error occasioned a miscarriage of justice.[15]

10. A party cannot merely repeat on appeal arguments that did not succeed at trial, unless it can demonstrate that the Trial Chamber's rejection of those arguments constituted an error warranting the intervention of the Appeals Chamber. Arguments which do not have the potential to cause the impugned decision to be reversed or revised may be immediately dismissed by the Appeals Chamber and need not be considered on the merits.[16]

11. In order for the Appeals Chamber to assess arguments on appeal, the appealing party must provide precise references to relevant transcript pages or paragraphs in the decision or judgement to which the challenge is made.[17] Further, the Appeals Chamber cannot be expected to consider a party's submissions in

---

[11] Respondent's Brief, originally filed on 24 November 2006 and refiled on 1 December 2006 following the Order Concerning the Prosecution's Respondent's Brief, 30 November 2006 ("Prosecution Response").

[12] Prosecutor's Notice of Appeal, filed on 12 January 2006 ("Prosecution Notice of Appeal"); Prosecutor's Appellant's Brief, filed on 27 March 2006, as amended by the Corrigendum to Prosecutor's Appellant's Brief, filed on 28 March 2006 ("Prosecution Appeal Brief"); Prosecutor's Brief in Reply, filed on 31 October 2006 ("Prosecution Reply"). On 17 August 2006, the Appeals Chamber dismissed a Prosecution request to add two new grounds of appeal (*see The Prosecutor v. Aloys Simba*, Case No. ICTR 01 76-A, Decision on 'Prosecutor's Motion for Variation of Notice of Appeal Pursuant to Rule 108', 17 August 2006 ("Decision on Motion for Variation of Notice of Appeal of 17 August 2006")). Accordingly, the Appeals Chamber will not consider the arguments made in the Prosecution Appeal Brief which are related to these additional grounds of appeal.

[13] Simba Respondent Brief, filed in French on 18 October 2006 ("Simba Response").

[14] *Muhimana* Appeal Judgement, para. 7, *Ntagerura et al.* Appeal Judgement, para. 11

[15] *Ntagerura et al.* Appeal Judgement, para. 12; *Semanza* Appeal Judgement, para. 8; *Niyitegeka* Appeal Judgement, para. 8.

[16] *Muhimana* Appeal Judgement, para. 9; *Ndindabahizi* Appeal Judgement, para. 11; *Gacumbitsi* Appeal Judgement, para. 9; *Naletilić and Martinović* Appeal Judgement, para. 13; *Blaškić* Appeal Judgement, para. 13; *Kordić and Čerkez* Appeal Judgement, para. 21.

[17] Practice Direction on Formal Requirements for Appeals from Judgement, 4 July 2005 ("Practice Direction on Appeals of 4 July 2005"), para. 4(b). *See also Muhimana* Appeal Judgement, para. 10; *Ndindabahizi* Appeal Judgement, para. 12; *Gacumbitsi* Appeal Judgement, para. 10.

detail if they are obscure, contradictory, vague or suffer from other formal **[page 6]** and obvious insufficiencies.[18] Finally, the Appeals Chamber has inherent discretion in selecting which submissions merit a detailed reasoned opinion in writing and will dismiss arguments which are evidently unfounded without providing detailed reasoning.[19] **[page 7]**

II. THE APPEAL OF ALOYS SIMBA

A. Interlocutory Decisions

12. The Appellant challenges, on various grounds, a series of interlocutory decisions made by the Trial Chamber. The Appeals Chamber notes that none of the errors alleged was pleaded properly in the Appellant's Notice of Appeal, which merely lists the decisions challenged and states with respect to each one that the Trial Chamber "erred" or "erred in law" in denying the defence motions underlying these decisions.[20] The notice thus fails to indicate the substance of the alleged errors and the relief sought as required by Rule 108 of the Tribunal's Rules of Procedure and Evidence ("Rules").[21] However, the Prosecution does not object to this failure, arguing instead that the Appeal Brief itself suffers from similar shortcomings. Where an Appellant fails to properly raise its argument and the Prosecution fails to object, the Appeals Chamber possesses the discretion to consider the Appellant's arguments in order to ensure the fairness of the proceedings. It chooses to do so in the instant case.

1. Decisions on Site Visits (31 January and 4 May 2005)

13. The Appellant alleges that the Trial Chamber erred in law by rejecting two Defence requests for on-site visits in Rwanda.[22] Based on the "discovery of new information" he submits that such an on-site visit would have enabled the Trial Chamber to obtain this information at the time when he made the requests.[23] This would have had presumably cast doubt on the Trial Chamber's findings regarding the Appellant's presence at both Murambi Technical School and Kaduha Parish.[24]

14. The Prosecution responds that the interlocutory decisions were not subject to any application by the Appellant for leave to appeal.[25] It submits that the Trial Chamber's decisions denying the requests are supported by the Tribunal's established jurisprudence and that the Trial Chamber did not commit any error in taking these decisions.[26] **[page 8]**

15. In its Decision of 31 January 2005, the Trial Chamber dismissed the Defence request for on-site visits, noting that "a number of photographs and maps have been tendered into evidence" and that "[a]s the trial proceeds, it is expected that more evidence from Defence witnesses will shed light on the relevant locations and that additional photographs, maps and measurements will be submitted for consideration".[27] It concluded that at that stage of the trial it was not persuaded that the requested visits would "be instrumental in the discovery of the truth and determination of the matter before the Chamber", but left it open to the Defence to renew its request later if required.[28] On 4 May 2005, the Trial Chamber dismissed a renewed Defence

18 *Muhimana* Appeal Judgement, para. 10; *Ndindabahizi* Appeal Judgement, para. 12.

19 *Muhimana* Appeal Judgement, para. 10; *Gacumbitsi* Appeal Judgement, para. 10.

20 Simba Notice of Appeal, III-1 to III-6.

21 *See also* Practice Direction on Appeals of 4 July 2005, para. 1(c)(i), providing that a Notice of Appeal shall contain "the grounds of appeal, clearly specifying in respect of each ground of appeal [...] any alleged error on a question of law invalidating the decision [...]".

22 Simba Notice of Appeal, III-1 and III-2; Simba Appeal Brief, paras 395-397, referring to *The Prosecutor v. Aloys Simba*, Case No. ICTR-01-76-T, Decision on the Defence Request for Site Visits in Rwanda, 31 January 2005 ("Decision on Site Visits of 31 January 2005"); *The Prosecutor v. Aloys Simba*, Case No. ICTR-01-76-T, Decision on Renewed Request for Site Visits in Rwanda, 4 May 2005 ("Decision on Site Visits of 4 May 2005").

23 Simba Appeal Brief, para. 396.

24 Simba Appeal Brief, para. 396. *See also* Simba Reply, paras 136, 138,139, 141.

25 Prosecution Response, para. 191.

26 Prosecution Response, paras 196-198.

27 Decision on Site Visits of 31 January 2005, para. 2.

28 Decision on Site Visits of 31 January 2005, para. 3.

request for site visits, finding that "the evidence on the record is sufficient to allow the Chamber to make a proper assessment of the credibility of the witnesses and the charges against the Accused".[29]

16. The Appeals Chamber notes that "managerial decisions, such as whether to make a site visit, are left to the discretion of the Trial Chamber".[30] In the instant case, the Appellant does not demonstrate that the Trial Chamber abused its discretion in finding that site visits were unnecessary to assess the credibility of the evidence and the charges against the Appellant. The Appellant's challenge to the Trial Chamber's decisions solely rests on purportedly "newly discovered material" which does not form part of the trial record, and which the Appeals Chamber will therefore not consider.[31] No further argument is submitted by the Appellant on this issue. Accordingly, these sub-grounds of appeal are dismissed.

2. Decision on the Admission of Certain Exhibits (7 July 2005)

17. The Appellant challenges the Trial Chamber's Decision on the Admission of Certain Exhibits,[32] in which it denied the Appellant's request to admit several exhibits on the ground that the Appellant had not been questioned on the basis of these documents, despite having identified them during his examination-in-chief. These exhibits include two written statements of a person whom the Appellant intended to call as a witness in his defence but who eventually refused to testify (BJK1), a *pro justitia* statement of Simon Bikindi as well as a copy of his passport, and a letter from Marcel Gatsinzi.[33] The Appellant claims, however, that he had indeed been questioned **[page 9]** during his examination-in-chief about the documents relating to Simon Bikindi[34] and the letter from Marcel Gatsinzi,[35] and submits that he referred to BJK1 during his testimony several times.[36] He affirms that the Trial Chamber violated his right to a fair trial by rejecting these pieces of evidence.[37] The Appellant finally asserts that BJK1 was the only witness able to corroborate the Appellant's entire alibi and since BJK1 refused to testify before the Tribunal, the admission of his statements was crucial to the Appellant's defence.[38]

18. The Prosecution responds that the Appellant's challenge to the Decision on the Admission of Certain Exhibits of 7 July 2005 suffers from deficiencies which render it inadmissible under Article 24 of the Statute.[39] It further submits that, given that the Appellant was not questioned on the basis of these documents, it was well within the Trial Chamber's discretion not to "require their admission to provide additional context for the Accused's examination".[40] The Prosecution submits that the Appellant fails to demonstrate any error in the exercise of the Trial Chamber's discretion which would necessitate appellate intervention.[41]

19. The Appeals Chamber recalls that the decision to admit or exclude evidence pursuant to Rule 89(C) of the Rules is one that falls within the discretion of the Trial Chamber and therefore, warrants appellate intervention only in limited circumstances.[42] It further recalls that in exercising its discretion to admit witness testimony, the Trial Chamber shall be guided by the general principle, enshrined in Rule 90(A) of the Rules, that witnesses be heard directly by the Chambers.

---

29 Decision on Site Visits of 4 May 2005, para. 2.

30 *Galić* Appeal Judgement, para. 50.

31 The Appeals Chamber will consider below under Sections D and E the Appellant's arguments related to the credibility of the Prosecution and Defence witnesses who testified in relation to the massacres at Murambi Technical School and Kaduha Parish.

32 Simba Notice of Appeal, III-3, referring to *The Prosecutor v. Aloys Simba*, Case No. ICTR-2001-76-T, Decision on the Admission of Certain Exhibits (Corrigendum), 7 July 2005 ("Decision on the Admission of Certain Exhibits of 7 July 2005").

33 Simba Appeal Brief, para. 399, referring to Decision on the Admission of Certain Exhibits of 7 July 2005, paras 9-10.

34 Simba Appeal Brief, para. 401.

35 Simba Appeal Brief, para. 402.

36 Simba Appeal Brief, para. 400.

37 Simba Appeal Brief, para. 403.

38 Simba Appeal Brief, para. 400.

39 Prosecution Response, para. 202.

40 Prosecution Response, para. 205, quoting Decision on the Admission of Certain Exhibits of 7 July 2005, para. 10.

41 Prosecution Response, paras 206-207, 209.

42 *Prosecutor v. Théoneste Bagosora et al.*, Case Nos. ICTR-98-41-AR93 & ICTR-98-41-AR93.2, Decision on Prosecutor's Interlocutory Appeals Regarding Exclusion of Evidence, 19 December 2003, para. 11. *See also Naletilić and Martinović* Appeal Judgement, para. 257; *Kordić and Čerkez* Appeal Judgement, para. 236.

20. The Appeals Chamber recognises, however, that there are well established exceptions to the Tribunal's preference for direct, live, in-court testimony[43] and agrees with the Trial Chamber's reasoning that, as a matter of law, statements of non-testifying individuals used during cross-examination may be admitted into evidence, even if they do not conform to the requirements of **[page 10]** Rules 90(A) and 92*bis* of the Rules, provided the statements are necessary to the Trial Chamber's assessment of the witness's credibility and are not used to prove the truth of their contents.[44]

21. The Appeals Chamber notes that the Trial Chamber, after having reviewed the transcript of the examination-in-chief and cross-examination of the Appellant, found that he had not been questioned on the basis of BJK1's statements, the *pro justitia* statement or passport of Simon Bikindi, or the letter from Marcel Gatsinzi and therefore did "not require their admission to provide additional context for the [Appellant's] examination".[45]

22. The Appeals Chamber observes, however, that the Appellant was in fact questioned on the basis of the documents relating to Simon Bikindi[46] and the letter of Marcel Gatsinzi during his examination-in-chief.[47] Despite this, and putting aside the relevance of the distinction, if any, between the Appellant being questioned on the basis of the documents during his examination-in-chief rather than during his cross-examination, the Appeals Chamber considers that the Appellant has failed to demonstrate how the Trial Chamber's decision to exclude these documents affected the verdict.[48] The Appeals Chamber recalls that arguments of a party that do not have the potential to cause the impugned decision to be reversed or revised may be immediately dismissed by the Appeals Chamber and need not be considered on the merits.[49]

23. Turning to the Appellant's claim that the contents of BJK1's statements would have corroborated his alibi, the Appeals Chamber observes that the Appellant does not allege that he was questioned on the basis of these statements but rather claims that they should have been admitted "if only pursuant to Rule 93(C) (*sic*) of the Rules [...], especially as the Appellant referred to [...] BJK1 several times during his testimony".[50]

24. The Appeals Chamber notes that the Trial Chamber could have admitted BJK1's statements solely on the basis that they had been necessary to the assessment of the Appellant's testimony. The Appellant, however, fails to provide any specific reference to BJK1's statements which would have provided the necessary additional context to his testimony. Moreover, it should be recalled that **[page 11]** "[c]orroboration is simply one of many potential factors in the Trial Chamber's assessment of a witness's credibility".[51] It is indeed well established that the trier of fact is far better suited to the task of assessing the credibility of witnesses,[52] and here the Appellant has not demonstrated any error on the part of the Trial Chamber in assessing his credibility.

25. Accordingly, this sub-ground of appeal is dismissed.

---

43 For instance, Rule 90(A) of the Rules provides that a Chamber may order that a witness be heard by means of deposition under Rule 71 of the Rules, and Rule 92 *bis* of the Rules allows for the admission of written witness statements in lieu of oral testimony which do not go to proof of the acts and conduct of the accused as charged in the indictment.

44 Decision on the Admission of Certain Exhibits of 7 July 2005, para. 7. *See also* T. 3 November 2004 pp. 37-38; *Akayesu* Appeal Judgement, para. 134.

45 Decision on the Admission of Certain Exhibits of 7 July 2005, para. 10.

46 Simba Appeal Brief, para. 401.

47 T. 23 March 2005 pp. 23-29 and 43-48.

48 The Appeals Chamber notes that the letter of Marcel Gatsinzi merely establishes that the Appellant and Marcel Gatsinzi only met once, after 5 July 1994, without providing any information which could support the Appellant's case (Simba Appeal Brief, Annex 37); the admission of the documents related to Simon Bikindi was sought in order to challenge Witness KEI's testimony relating to the allegations of paragraphs 67 and 68 of the Indictment under Count 4, Murder as a Crime Against Humanity (T. 23 March 2005 p. 41), for which the Appellant was found not guilty by the Trial Chamber (Trial Judgement, para. 427.)

49 S*ee above* Chapter I, Section C, para. 10.

50 Simba Appeal Brief, para. 400.

51 *Ntakirutimana* Appeal Judgement, para. 132.

52 *Ntakirutimana* Appeal Judgement, para. 177. *See also Musema* Appeal Judgement, para. 18.

3. Decisions on Defence Requests related to Witnesses YH and KXX (23 September and 10 November 2004)

26. The Appellant claims that the Trial Chamber erred when it rejected his oral motions requesting the Prosecution to investigate Prosecution Witness YH, "for crimes and false testimony" in relation to alleged discrepancies between the witness's self-incriminating testimony before the Trial Chamber and his confession given to officials in Rwanda.[53] The same error is alleged in relation to Prosecution Witness KXX, for similar reasons.[54] The Appellant submits that the Trial Chamber further erred when it denied his request for a report on whether prosecutions were underway against Witnesses YH and KXX.[55] The Appellant finally requests that the Appeals Chamber invalidate their testimonies, pursuant to Rule 95 of the Rules, "as well as their effects on the [Trial] Judgement".[56]

27. The Prosecution responds that the Trial Chamber properly exercised its discretion when assessing the evidence provided by Witnesses YH and KXX[57] and that the Appellant fails to show how the Trial Chamber's denial of the Appellant's request for a report on the Prosecution's investigation on these two witnesses constitutes an error capable of invalidating the Trial Chamber's verdict. It further affirms that the Trial Chamber correctly based the challenged decisions on Articles 15(2) and 17 of the Statute, according to which the Prosecution evaluates and decides independently whether to initiate proceedings.[58] **[page 12]**

28. The Appeals Chamber notes that the oral motion brought by the Appellant before the Trial Chamber on 23 September 2004 sought directions by the Trial Chamber to the Prosecution to initiate investigations concerning Witness YH's alleged participation in the genocide and his alleged false testimony.[59] On the same day, in an oral decision, the Trial Chamber rejected both requests. In relation to Witness YH's alleged participation in the genocide, the Trial Chamber stated that the Prosecutor has the discretionary power to initiate investigations with respect to crimes that fall within the Tribunal's mandate. With regard to the allegation of false testimony, the Trial Chamber did not find it expedient to make any order under Rule 91 of the Rules.[60] The next day, the Appellant requested that the Trial Chamber "consider the implementation of Rule 91 of the Rules [...]" in relation to Witness KXX's testimony.[61] The Trial Chamber dismissed the Appellant's request to implement Rule 91 of the Rules in respect of Witness KXX on the same basis that it had rejected the Appellant's request in respect of Witness YH, namely, that it did not find it expedient to make an order under Rule 91, reserving its position on the merits of any alleged discrepancies until after having heard the totality of the evidence.[62]

29. On 25 October 2004, the Appellant filed a request seeking a report, within one month, on the measures and judicial actions the Prosecution had taken against Witnesses YH and KXX.[63] The Trial Chamber dismissed the Defence Motion of 25 October 2004 in its Decision on the Request for Information Related to Witnesses YH and KXX of 10 November 2004 on the basis that the Prosecution had not initiated any proceedings and had no intention of doing so.[64]

---

53 Simba Notice of Appeal, III-4, III-6, referring to *The Prosecutor v. Aloys Simba*, Case No. ICTR-01-76-T, Decision on Defence Request for Information Related to Witnesses YH and KXX, 10 November 2004 ("Decision on the Request for Information Related to Witnesses YH and KXX of 10 November 2004"), and to the oral decision of 23 September 2004 ("Simba Oral Decision of 23 September 2004"). *See also* Simba Appeal Brief, paras 404-405.

54 Simba Appeal Brief, para. 406.

55 Simba Notice of Appeal, III-6; Simba Appeal Brief, paras 407-408, referring to *The Prosecutor v. Aloys Simba*, Case No. ICTR-2001-76-I, *Requête de la défense en vue d'enjoindre au Procureur d'avoir à fournir la preuve que des poursuites judiciaires ont été engagées contre les témoins "KXX" et "YH" lesquels se sont accusés du crime de génocide*, 25 October 2004 ("Simba Defence Motion of 25 October 2004") and Decision on the Request for Information Related to Witnesses YH and KXX of 10 November 2004, paras 4-5.

56 Simba Appeal Brief, paras 409-411.

57 Prosecution Response, paras 214-215, referring to Trial Judgement, paras 164-169.

58 Prosecution Response, para. 216.

59 T. 23 September 2004 p. 28.

60 T. 23 September 2004 p. 29.

61 T. 24 September 2004 p. 60.

62 Decision on the Request for Information Related to Witnesses YH and KXX of 10 November 2004, para. 4.

63 Simba Defence Motion of 25 October 2004, prayer, p. 4.

64 Decision on the Request for Information Related to Witnesses YH and KXX of 10 November 2004, disposition.

30. The Appeals Chamber dismisses the Appellant's contention that the Trial Chamber erred in its Decision on the Request for Information Related to Witnesses YH and KXX of 10 November 2004. With regard to the Appellant's request for a report, the Appeals Chamber considers that given that the Prosecution had not initiated any proceedings against these witnesses and had no intention to do so the Appellant's request for such a report was not yet ripe for adjudication at the time of the decision. With regard to the Appellant's contention that the Trial Chamber "erred in denying [...] the Defence motion to order the Prosecutor to investigate Witness KXX for participation in genocide",[65] the Appeals Chamber notes that at the trial the Appellant limited his argument to the implementation of Rule 91 of the Rules with respect to Witness KXX and thus failed to raise this argument before the Trial Chamber. **[page 13]**

31. Turning to the Appellant's contention in relation to Witness YH,[66] the Appeals Chamber recalls that the Prosecutor has independent authority to initiate investigations on statutory crimes and to assess whether the information forms a sufficient basis to proceed against persons suspected of having committed such crimes.[67] However, Rule 91(B)(i) of the Rules specifically provides that "[i]f a Chamber has strong grounds for believing that a witness has knowingly and wilfully given false testimony, it may direct the Prosecutor to investigate the matter with a view to the preparation and submission of an indictment for false testimony". Such action lies within the discretion of the Trial Chamber and is contingent on its conviction that a witness "has knowingly and wilfully given false testimony".[68] On the other hand, a credibility determination may be based, but does not necessarily depend, on a judicial finding that a witness has given false testimony.[69]

32. The Appeals Chamber stresses that the mere existence of discrepancies between a witness's testimony and his earlier statements does not constitute strong grounds for believing that a witness may have knowingly and wilfully given false testimony.[70] In the instant case, it is apparent from the Trial Chamber's reasoning that it did not believe Witness YH to have wilfully given false testimony. Indeed, the Trial Chamber accepted Witness YH's explanation that he planned to make a full confession before the *Gacaca* courts and considered "that he simply attempted, at earlier stages of his proceeding in Rwanda, to minimize his involvement in the genocide".[71] Therefore, the Appellant does not show that the Trial Chamber erred in not directing the Prosecution to investigate Witness YH for false testimony.

33. In any event, the Appeals Chamber is only required to grant relief for a violation of the Rules where a party has objected in a timely manner and has suffered material prejudice.[72] The Appellant clearly fails to show how the Oral Decision of 23 September 2004 has prejudiced him. The Appeals Chamber recalls that an investigation for false testimony is only ancillary to proceedings and does not necessarily affect the rights of an accused.[73] **[page 14]**

34. For the foregoing reasons, this sub-ground of appeal is dismissed.

---

[65] Simba Notice of Appeal, III-6.

[66] Simba Notice of Appeal, III-3 and III-6.

[67] *See* Articles 15(2) and 17(1) of the Statute.

[68] The Appeals Chamber finds the following statement persuasive: "[F]alse testimony is a deliberate offence which requires wilful intent on the part of the perpetrator to mislead the Judge and thus to cause harm" (*Rutaganda* Trial Judgement, para. 20).

[69] *The Prosecutor v. Georges Anderson Nderumwe Rutaganda*, Case No. ICTR 96-3-A, Decision on Appeals Against the Decisions by Trial Chamber I Rejecting the Defence Motions to Direct the Prosecutor to Investigate the Matter of False Testimony by Witnesses "E" and "CC", 8 June 1998 ("*Rutaganda* Decision Rejecting the Defence Motions to Direct the Prosecutor to Investigate the Matter of False Testimony by Witnesses "E" and "CC" of 8 June 1998"), para. 28.

[70] *Rutaganda* Trial Judgement, para. 20.

[71] Trial Judgement, para. 165.

[72] *Gacumbitsi* Appeal Judgement, para. 11, fn. 24, referring to Rule 5 of the Rules.

[73] *See The Prosecutor v. Georges Anderson Nderumwe Rutaganda*, Case No. ICTR 96-3-A, Decision on Appeals Against the Decisions by Trial Chamber I Rejecting the Defence Motions to Direct the Prosecutor to Investigate the Matter of False Testimony by Witnesses "E" and "CC", 8 June 1998, para. 28.

4. Decision on the Defence Request to Preclude the Testimony of Witness KDD under Oath (28 October 2004)

35. The Appellant submits that the Trial Chamber erred in law by denying the Defence objection to the admission of Prosecution Witness KDD's testimony under oath.[74] The Appellant submits that Witness KDD had been condemned to death by Rwandan courts and, therefore, under Rwandan law, was deprived of his civil rights, including his ability to testify. According to the Appellant, Witness KDD's testimony could thus only be considered as simple information.[75]

36. The Prosecution responds that the Trial Chamber denied the motion by finding that, in accordance with Rule 89(A) of the Rules and Appeals Chamber's jurisprudence, a Trial Chamber is not bound by national rules of evidence.[76] Recalling the margin of discretion accorded to Trial Chambers in the admission, assessment and evaluation of evidence, it submits that the Appellant fails to demonstrate how the Trial Chamber exceeded its discretion.[77] The Prosecution avers that in any event, the Trial Chamber's reliance on the witness's testimony, if any, was limited, and caused the Appellant no prejudice.[78]

37. In its Decision of 28 October 2004, the Trial Chamber denied the Defence motion to preclude the anticipated testimony of Witness KDD. The Trial Chamber noted that

> according to Rule 89 (A) the Tribunal is not bound by national rules of evidence. The witness's legal status in Rwanda in no way impacts his capacity to testify or the manner in which he would give evidence before this Tribunal. The Chamber is also unwilling to pre-judge the credibility and reliability of a witness's anticipated testimony.[79]

38. The Appeals Chamber notes that this sub-ground of appeal is limited to the Trial Chamber's decision to admit Witness KDD's evidence, and is not concerned with the assessment of its reliability or credibility. It is well established that according to Rule 89 of the Rules, a Trial Chamber is not bound by national rules of evidence and has the discretion to admit any relevant evidence it deems to have probative value.[80] The Appellant does not attempt to demonstrate an abuse of the Trial Chamber's discretion. The Appellant's argument that the loss of Witness KDD's **[page 15]** civil rights under Rwandan law warrants *per se* the preclusion of his evidence is evidently unfounded and warrants the dismissal of the sub-ground.

39. In light of the foregoing, this ground of appeal is dismissed in its entirety.

B. Alleged Violation of the Appellant's Right to Call Witnesses in his Defence

40. The Appellant submits that he did not receive a fair trial since he was prevented from calling two individuals to testify in his defence, HBK and BJK1, who, due to interference by Rwandan government officials, refused to appear before the Tribunal. The Appellant claims that these testimonies would have been crucial for his defence,[81] and that the Trial Chamber erred in law by failing to acquit him under those circumstances. Moreover, the Appellant contends that the Trial Chamber committed an error of law in making contradictory findings as to whether Rwandan authorities interfered with HBK and BJK1.[82] The

---

74 Simba Notice of Appeal, III-5, referring to the *The Prosecutor v. Aloys Simba*, Case No. ICTR-2001-76-T, Decision on the Defence Request to Preclude the Testimony of Prosecution Witness KDD under Oath, 28 October 2004 ("Decision of 28 October 2004"); Simba Appeal Brief, paras 412-415; Simba Reply, para. 147.

75 Simba Appeal Brief, para. 412.

76 Prosecution Response, para. 219.

77 Prosecution Response, para. 220.

78 Prosecution Response, para. 221.

79 Decision of 28 October 2004, para. 3 (footnotes omitted).

80 *The Prosecutor v. Édouard Karemera et al.*, Case No. ICTR-98-44-AR73.8, Decision on Interlocutory Appeal Regarding Witness Proofing, 11 May 2007 ("*Karemera* Decision on Interlocutory Appeal Regarding Witness Proofing of 11 May 2007"), para. 11; *Akayesu* Appeal Judgement, fn. 577.

81 On 21 May 2007, the Appeals Chamber issued a confidential decision in which it rejected, *inter alia*, the Appellant's request, brought pursuant to Rule 115 of the Rules, that BJK1 and HBK be subpoenaed to testify before the Appeals Chamber. *See Aloys Simba v. The Prosecutor*, Case No. ICTR-01-76-A, Decision on Appellant Aloys Simba's Request to Present Additional Evidence, 21 May 2007 ("Decision on Rule 115 Evidence of 21 May 2007").

82 Simba Notice of Appeal, I-A-1, I-D-2, I-D-3, II-C-2, II-C-3; Simba Appeal Brief, paras 20-45, 257-258, 365; Simba Reply, paras 49-50.

Prosecution responds that the Appellant's right to a fair trial was not violated and that the Trial Chamber did not err by convicting the Appellant.[83]

41. The Appeals Chamber can conceive of situations where a fair trial is not possible because witnesses crucial to the Defence case refuse to testify due to State interference. In such cases, it is incumbent on the Defence to, first, demonstrate that such interference has in fact taken place and, second, exhaust all available measures to secure the taking of the witness's testimony.[84]

1. BJK1

42. The Appellant submits that BJK1 refused to testify in the instant case due to interference by Rwandan authorities, and that, as a consequence, he was deprived of the only witness who could have corroborated his alibi in its entirety.[85] In support of this argument, the Appellant submits that the Witness and Victims Support Section ("WVSS") confirmed that BJK1 refused to testify because of threats to his security[86] and that, based on a report of that section, the Trial Chamber acknowledged that it was futile to issue a subpoena because its implementation required the **[page 16]** cooperation of Rwandan authorities.[87] In the Appellant's view, the fact that the Trial Chamber subsequently ordered the Registry to subpoena the witness and requested the Rwandan authorities to take all appropriate measures to ensure BJK1's protection, was merely a "last-ditch effort" which the Trial Chamber knew in advance was futile.[88] In this respect, the Appellant points out that following the Trial Chamber's decision, the Rwandan authorities failed to comply with the Trial Chamber's request[89] and BJK1 remained unwilling to testify.[90]

43. The Prosecution responds that the Appellant's submission is misleading.[91] It argues that BJK1 could not have testified to the entire alibi, that his testimony would not have raised a reasonable doubt with respect to the Prosecution's case, and that the Appellant suffered no prejudice since the testimony would not have had any impact on the verdict.[92] The Prosecution further submits that it was always open for the Appellant to seek an adjournment or other forms of redress in order to ensure that BJK1 be heard.[93]

44. The Appeals Chamber observes that, contrary to the Appellant's submissions, WVSS did not at any time confirm the existence of threats against BJK1. It is clear from the communication issued by WVSS on 24 March 2005[94] and the oral submissions made by a representative of this section on 29 March 2005,[95] that WVSS merely informed the Trial Chamber that BJK1 himself cited security concerns as the reason for his refusal to come to Arusha to testify. The fact that, during the status conference held on 29 March 2005, the Trial Chamber initially stated that it would be futile to subpoena BJK1[96] is immaterial since it subsequently reconsidered its position.[97] Moreover, in a written decision issued on 4 May 2005, the Trial Chamber ordered the Registry to issue subpoenas to BJK1 and HBK, and requested the Rwandan authorities to take all

83 Prosecution Response, paras 9-34, 106.

84 *See Tadić* Appeal Judgement, para. 55.

85 Simba Notice of Appeal, I-A-1(a); Simba Appeal Brief, paras 21, 22, 25, 27; AT. 22 May 2007 pp. 10-12, 41-42.

86 Simba Appeal Brief, paras 24, 25; Simba Reply, paras 10, 11.

87 Simba Appeal Brief, para. 24.

88 Simba Reply, para. 17.

89 Simba Appeal Brief, para. 26; Simba Notice of Appeal, II-C-2 (second part).

90 Simba Reply, paras 17-18.

91 Prosecution Response, paras 13-14.

92 Prosecution Response, paras 29-31.

93 Prosecution Response, para. 14; AT. 22 May 2007 pp. 25-26.

94 Simba Appeal Brief, Annex 2 (E-mail of 24 March 2005 by Ms. Sylvie Becky, WVSS, addressed to Mr. Alao, Defence. The relevant section reads: "Le témoin BJK1 a rencontré à plusieurs reprises des représentants de notre Section en vue de son témoignage dans le procès Simba. Il n'est ni disposé à voyager à Arusha aux fins de témoignage, ni prêt à témoigner par vidéo-conférence à Kigali. Au regard des confidences faites par le témoin à nos officiers, celui-ci ne souhaite à aucun prix se rendre à Arusha ni témoigner par vidéo-conférence pour des raisons sécuritaires même s'il faisait l'objet d'une citation à comparaître.").

95 Representation made by WVSS representative Mr. Essombe on 29 March 2005 (T. 29 March 2005 pp. 23, 24, 26).

96 T. 29 March 2005 p. 28.

97 T. 29 March 2005 p. 31. It is noteworthy that the Trial Chamber gave every assistance the Appellant requested to ensure the taking of the witness's testimony. While, on 4 February 2005, it denied a Defence request to subpoena BJK1 along with two other Defence witnesses, it authorised the taking of their testimony via video-link from Kigali in order to allay their reluctance to appear voluntarily, *see The Prosecutor v. Aloys Simba*, Case No. ICTR-01-76-T, Decision Authorizing the Taking of the Evidence of Witnesses IMG, ISG, and BJK1 by Video-Link, 4 February 2005. ("Decision of 4 February 2005").

appropriate measures to ensure their protection and to provide any other assistance requested by the Registry to **[page 17]** facilitate the proposed witnesses' attendance at trial.[98] The Appellant has not advanced any evidence to support his contention that the Rwandan authorities did not comply with the Trial Chamber's Decision, and has failed to demonstrate that any interference with BJK1 occurred.

45. For the foregoing reasons, these sub-grounds of appeal are dismissed.

2. HBK

46. The Appellant further contends that he did not receive a fair trial since he was prevented from calling HBK, who refused to testify due to interference by Rwandan authorities.[99] In support of this contention, the Appellant presents several arguments which the Appeals Chamber will address in turn.

47. The Appellant argues that the Trial Chamber erred in considering that the onus was on him to prove that Rwandan authorities had interfered with HBK.[100] The Appeals Chamber notes however that the Trial Chamber found that interference by Rwandan authorities with HBK had indeed occurred.[101] Accordingly, this matter is not contentious and the Appeals Chamber declines to consider it.

48. The Appellant further submits that the Trial Chamber erred in finding that the Defence failed to request a stay of proceedings until appropriate arrangements could be made for the witness to come to testify.[102] In particular, he argues that it would have been "offensive" and "foolhardy" on his part to make such a request since the Trial Chamber had emphasised that the dates set for the submission of final trial briefs and closing arguments would not be changed, and since it had stated that HBK was unwilling to testify.[103] In this respect, the Appellant refers to paragraph 4 of the Decision on Subpoenas of 4 May 2005,[104] where the Trial Chamber held: **[page 18]**

> The timing for hearing of the evidence of these witnesses [HBK and BJK1] does not alter the deadlines for submission of the final trial briefs on 22 June 2005 or closing arguments on 7-8 July 2005 … [T]he prospective evidence of these witnesses may be fully discussed during oral arguments (emphasis omitted).[105]

49. In response, the Prosecution argues that the Appellant was given every opportunity to call HBK to testify.[106] It submits that the passage of the Decision on Subpoenas of 4 May 2005 referred to by the Appellant shows that the Trial Chamber allowed the hearing of the testimony of HBK and BJK1 after the filing of the closing briefs but before closing arguments, following a procedure similar to that under Rule 115 of the Rules.[107] In this regard, the Prosecution refers to footnote 4 of the Decision on Subpoenas of 4 May 2005, which reads as follows:

> Hearing additional witnesses after the filing of final briefs and prior to argument would be consistent with the practice of the Appeals Chamber when it takes additional evidence on appeal.[108]

---

98 *The Prosecutor v. Aloys Simba*, Case No. ICTR-01-76-T, Decision on Defence Request for Subpoenas, 4 May 2005 ("Decision on Subpoenas of 4 May 2005"), Disposition. On 13 July 2007, the Appeals Chamber ordered the Registrar, pursuant to Rule 33(B) of the Rules, to submit a detailed written submission on the steps taken by the Registry in order to secure the attendance of BJK1 at trial no later than 13 August 2007, *see Aloys Simba v. The Prosecutor*, Case No. ICTR-01-76-A, Order to Registrar Regarding BJK1, 13 July 2007 ("Order to Registrar Regarding BJK1 of 13 July 2007"). On 13 August 2007, the Registry confidentially filed the requested submission (The Registrar's Submission Pursuant to Rule 33(B) of the Rules of Procedure and Evidence Regarding Securing the Attendance at Trial of Defence Witness BJK1, 13 August 2007). In light of the Registrar' s submission, the Appeals Chamber is satisfied that WVSS and the Tribunal undertook all possible steps to secure BJK1's testimony and that BJK1's failure to testify was due to personal reluctance and concerns on the part of the witness, and beyond the control of WVSS and the Tribunal.

99 Simba Notice of Appeal, I-A-1(b) to I-A-1(c), I-D-3, II-C-2 (first part), II-C-3; Simba Appeal Brief, paras 21, 28-45, 258; AT. 22 May 2007 p. 12.

100 Simba Appeal Brief, para. 30.

101 Trial Judgement, paras 49-50.

102 Simba Appeal Brief, paras 28, 31-36.

103 Simba Notice of Appeal, I-A-1(b); Simba Appeal Brief, paras 33-35.

104 Simba Appeal Brief, para. 33.

105 While quoting paragraph 4, the Appellant erroneously points to paragraph 5 of the Decision on Subpoenas of 4 May 2005.

106 Prosecution Response, paras 11, 18-24.

107 Prosecution Response, paras 18, 19.

108 Prosecution Response, para. 18, quoting Decision on Subpoenas of 4 May 2005, fn. 4.

The Prosecution concludes that since the Appellant failed to seek appropriate measures to secure the witness's testimony and instead accepted to close the case, he waived his right to raise the matter on appeal.[109]

50. The Appeals Chamber notes that the Trial Chamber's statement that the hearing of HBK would "not alter the deadlines for submission of the final trial briefs on 22 June 2005 or closing arguments" was made in its Decision on Subpoenas of 4 May 2005, two months ahead of the date scheduled for closing arguments. The Appeals Chamber does not accept that in light of this statement it was reasonable for the Defence to presume that the dates were irrevocably fixed and that the Trial Chamber would not grant a request for postponement of closing arguments.[110] Moreover, at the outset of the hearing of the parties' closing arguments on 7 July 2005, the Presiding Judge noted that HBK had expressed his willingness to testify but that it had been impossible to arrange his transfer to Arusha before closing arguments.[111] He recalled that the parties had been informed of the situation earlier that week and that the Defence had not objected to proceeding and closing the case.[112] The Presiding Judge's statement suggests that the Trial **[page 19]** Chamber would have been ready to duly consider any such request. The Appeals Chamber therefore considers that the Trial Chamber did not err when it found that the Defence failed to request a stay of proceedings until appropriate arrangements could be made for the proffered witness to come to testify.[113]

51. Finally, the Appellant appears to argue that it was apparent from the circumstances that HBK would never agree to testify and that a request for a stay of proceedings would have been futile.[114] The Appeals Chamber cannot agree. As noted above, the Presiding Judge had informed the parties before 7 July 2005, the date of closing arguments, that HBK had expressed his willingness to testify but that it had been impossible to arrange his transfer to Arusha before closing arguments.

52. The Appellant further submits that the Trial Chamber erred in law[115] in finding that in any event HBK's failure to testify did not cause him material prejudice.[116] He emphasises that HBK is being prosecuted in Rwanda for the massacres at Kaduha Parish of 21 April 1994.[117] He also argues that by virtue of his position at the time and his involvement in the events, HBK had information concerning the massacres and was therefore able to testify to whether the Appellant was present at Kaduha Parish on 21 April 1994.[118] In this regard, the Appellant points out that the Trial Chamber had acknowledged that HBK's testimony "may be of interest".[119] He further claims that since Witness KXX's testimony would have supported that of HBK, the Trial Chamber "discounted the testimony of Witness KXX, so as to render moot that of [...] HBK".[120]

53. The Prosecution responds that the Appellant was not convicted for the events at the Kaduha Trading Centre, that the Trial Chamber did not accept the testimony of Witness KXX with respect to the events at the Trading Centre, and that accordingly the testimony of HBK in this regard could not have had an impact on

---

109 Prosecution Response, paras 12, 16, 25.

110 On that basis the Appeals Chamber dismisses the allegation in Ground I-D-3 that paragraph 52 of the Trial Judgement contradicted the Decision on Subpoenas of 4 May 2005 by faulting the Appellant for not requesting a stay of the proceedings until the appearance of HBK (*See* Notice of Appeal, I-D-3 (first part); Simba Appeal Brief, para. 258).

111 T. 7 July 2005 pp. 1-2.

112 T. 7 July 2005, pp. 1-2. Following this statement, the Appellant did not intervene and the Prosecution made its closing arguments (T. 7 July 2005 pp. 2-13). *See also* T. 8 July 2005 p. 10. The Appeals Chamber recalls its Decision on Rule 115 Evidence of 21 May 2007. At paragraph 32 of said decision, the Trial Chamber found that at that stage of the proceedings, at least two avenues were open to the Appellant to secure the hearing of HBK's testimony. In particular, the Appellant could have requested a stay of proceedings until appropriate arrangements were made to move the proposed witness to Arusha, or he could have requested the taking of the witness's testimony via video-link from Kigali.

113 Trial Judgement, para. 52.

114 Simba Notice of Appeal, I-A-1(b) (first part) and I-D-3 (second part). The Appellant highlights that a period of one and a half months to two months had elapsed between the issuance of the Decision on Subpoenas of 4 May 2005 and the date envisaged for the witness's testimony without the witness being released for trial, and that WVSS failed to give any indication as to when HBK could be transferred (Simba Reply, paras 7-8).

115 The Appeals Chamber notes that according to the structure of the Simba Appeal Brief, the Appellant is alleging an error of law. It however appears from the nature of his submission that he is alleging an error of fact.

116 Simba Appeal Brief, paras 37-45.

117 Simba Appeal Brief, para. 39 (a).

118 Simba Appeal Brief, paras 39 (b), 40.

119 Simba Appeal Brief, paras 41-42, 44, quoting Decision on Subpoenas of 4 May 2005, para. 3.

120 Simba Reply, para. 26; Simba Appeal Brief, paras 37, 42.

the verdict.[121] The Prosecution emphasises that the Appellant confirmed that HBK was not an alibi witness.[122] **[page 20]**

54. The Trial Chamber provided the following reasoning in concluding that HBK's failure to testify did not cause material prejudice to the Appellant:

> In any event, [...] HBK's intended testimony dealt primarily with the events surrounding the massacre at Kaduha Parish on 21 April 1994. His proposed testimony about the massacre would have been second-hand and therefore of limited probative value. The Chamber is mindful that Prosecution Witness KXX placed [...] HBK with Simba in the Kaduha Trading Centre in the days before the attack. [...] HBK's testimony would have been relevant and direct in this respect. However, the Chamber did not find Witness KXX to be credible on matters relating to [...] HBK. Therefore, the Chamber can find no material prejudice.[123]

55. The Appellant's argument that due to his position, HBK was aware of the massacres and was therefore able to testify to whether the Appellant was at Kaduha Parish on 21 April 1994 is without merit. It appears from HBK's pre-trial statements[124] that he was not present during the massacres at Kaduha Parish,[125] and that he would have been restricted to giving testimony to the effect that he had never heard anyone else mentioning the Appellant's name in relation to this event.[126] The Trial Chamber's finding that the witness's testimony would have been of limited probative value was therefore reasonable.

56. The Appeals Chamber notes that HBK's testimony would also have concerned the events at Kaduha Trading Centre. It was reasonable for the Trial Chamber to conclude that while HBK's testimony would have been direct in this respect, no conviction was entered on the basis of these events and accordingly the witness's failure to testify was not prejudicial to the Appellant.

57. The Appeals Chamber finally notes that the Appellant fails to submit any argument in support of his contention that the Trial Chamber discounted the testimony of Witness KXX so as to render moot that of HBK. The Appeals Chamber accordingly declines to consider it.

58. The Appellant has not shown any error in the Trial Chamber's finding on this point. Accordingly, these sub-grounds of appeal are dismissed.

3. Alleged Contradiction in the Trial Judgement

59. The Appellant submits that the Trial Chamber contradicted itself when it considered, on the one hand, that the Defence failed to establish that Rwandan authorities had interfered with the **[page 21]** proceedings, while, on the other hand, it recognized that such interference had in fact taken place.[127] The Prosecution responds that the Appellant misrepresents the Trial Chamber's finding.[128]

60. The Appeals Chamber observes that the Appellant's argument clearly rests on a misreading of the Trial Chamber's finding. The Trial Chamber made different findings with respect to the two proffered witnesses. It found that Rwandan government authorities had interfered with HBK,[129] while it found with respect to BJK1 that the Defence had not established such interference on the balance of probabilities.[130] The Appellant's argument on this point is therefore without merit.

61. Accordingly, this sub-ground of appeal is dismissed.

---

121 Prosecution Response, para. 34.
122 Prosecution Response, para. 34, referring to T. 29 March 2005 p. 30.
123 Trial Judgement, para. 53 (footnote omitted).
124 R.P. 3178*bis*, 3177*bis*.
125 HBK's pre-trial statement of 27 July 2004, R.P. 3178*bis*: « Les massacres à la paroisse de Kaduha ont eu lieu dans la nuit du 20 au 21 avril. Pendant ce temps, je suis resté chez moi. »
126 HBK's pre-trial statement of 11 January 2005, R.P. 3177*bis*: « Mais, je n'ai jamais vu SIMBA sur les lieux et je n'ai jamais entendu parler de lui à cette époque. » *See also* Decision on Rule 115 Evidence of 21 May 2007, para. 35.
127 Simba Notice of Appeal, I-D-2; Simba Appeal Brief, para. 257, referring to Trial Judgement, paras 48-50.
128 Prosecution Response, para. 105.
129 Trial Judgement, paras 49-50.
130 Trial Judgement, para. 48.

C. Alleged Defects in the Form of the Indictment

62. The Appellant makes several submissions to the effect that the Indictment failed to clearly plead the theory of JCE as well as the material facts supporting that theory. The Appellant further contends that the Trial Chamber erred in law by making findings on several material facts not pleaded in the Indictment and in finding that, as a matter of law, post-indictment communications may cure defects in the Indictment. The Appellant argues that since he lacked notice of the charges against him, his trial was rendered unfair and, accordingly, his convictions should be reversed.[131] The Prosecution responds that the Appellant was informed in detail of the nature and cause of the charges against him.[132]

63. Charges against an accused and the material facts supporting those charges must be pleaded with sufficient precision in the indictment so as to provide notice to the accused.[133] Whether particular facts are "material" depends on the nature of the Prosecution's case.[134] In cases where the Prosecution intends to rely on a theory of JCE, the Prosecution must plead the purpose of the enterprise, the identity of its participants, the nature of the accused's participation in the enterprise and the period of the enterprise.[135] The Indictment should also clearly indicate which form of JCE is **[page 22]** being alleged.[136] Failure to specifically plead JCE, including the supporting material facts and the category, constitutes a defect in the indictment.[137]

64. If the indictment is found to be defective because it fails to plead material facts or does not plead them with sufficient specificity, the Trial Chamber must consider whether the accused was nevertheless accorded a fair trial.[138] Where the Prosecution provides the accused with timely, clear and consistent information detailing the factual basis underpinning the charges, defects in the indictment may be considered cured.[139] In determining whether a defective indictment was cured, the Appeals Chamber has previously looked at information provided in the Prosecution's pre-trial brief,[140] its opening statement,[141] as well as the witness charts annexed to the Prosecution pre-trial brief.[142] The Appeals Chamber has furthermore held that an accused's submissions at trial, for example the motion for judgement of acquittal, final trial brief or closing arguments, may assist in some instances in determining to what extent the accused was put on notice of the Prosecution's case.[143]

65. As a preliminary matter, in light of the applicable law set out above, the Appellant's argument that the Trial Chamber erred by finding that, as a matter of law, post-indictment communications may cure defects in the Indictment, is readily dismissed.[144]

---

131 Simba Notice of Appeal, I-A-2 to I-A-5, I-D-1, I-F-1 to I-F-5, I-F-11; Simba Appeal Brief, paras 46-79, 256, 273-283, 294-298; Simba Reply, para. 79.

132 Prosecution Response, paras 35-58, 117-138.

133 *Muhimana* Appeal Judgement, paras 76, 167, 195; *Gacumbitsi* Appeal Judgement, para. 49; *Simić et al.* Appeal Judgement, para. 20.

134 *Naletilić and Martinović* Appeal Judgement, para. 24.

135 *Simić et al.* Appeal Judgement, para. 22; *Ntagerura et al.* Appeal Judgement, para. 24.

136 *Simić et al.* Appeal Judgement, para. 22; *Gacumbitsi* Appeal Judgement, para. 162, referring to *Kvočka et al.* Appeal Judgement, paras 28, 42.

137 *Simić et al.* Appeal Judgement, para. 22; *Gacumbitsi* Appeal Judgement, para. 162; *Kvočka et al.* Appeal Judgement, paras 43-54.

138 *Naletilić and Martinović* Appeal Judgement, para. 26, referring to *Kvočka et al.* Appeal Judgement, para. 33.

139 *Muhimana* Appeal Judgement, paras 76, 195, 217; *Simić et al.* Appeal Judgement, para. 23; *Gacumbitsi* Appeal Judgement, para. 49; *Ntagerura et al.* Appeal Judgement, para. 28.

140 *Naletilić and Martinović* Appeal Judgement, para. 27, referring to *Kupreskić et al.* Appeal Judgement, paras 115-117.

141 *Naletilić and Martinović* Appeal Judgement, para. 27, referring to *Kordić and Čerkez* Appeal Judgement, para. 169.

142 *Muhimana* Appeal Judgement, paras 81, 82, 200, 201; *Gacumbitsi* Appeal Judgement, paras 56-58; *Naletilić and Martinović* Appeal Judgement, paras 40-42. Pursuant to Rule 73 *bis*(B)(iv) of the Rules, the Prosecution may be ordered at the Pre-Trial conference, to file a list of witnesses it intends to call including, *inter alia*, a summary of the facts on which each witness is expected to testify.

143 *Simić et al.* Appeal Judgement, para. 24; *Naletilić and Martinović* Appeal Judgement, para. 27, referring to *Kvočka et al.* Appeal Judgement, paras 52-53; *Kordić and Čerkez* Appeal Judgement, para. 148.

144 Simba Notice of Appeal, I-A-4, I-D-1, I-F-2, I-F-3 (in part); Simba Appeal Brief, paras 70-79, 256, 281, 282(c).

1. Alleged Errors Relating to JCE

(a) Theory of JCE

66. The Appellant submits that the Trial Chamber misinterpreted the Indictment, in particular paragraphs 14 and 58, in order to find that he was charged with JCE liability and to enter a conviction on that basis, while the only possible interpretation was that he was charged with **[page 23]** planning, preparing and committing the massacres "as a head or leader, not as an executant".[145] In addition, the Appellant submits that it was not clear from the Indictment that the Prosecution intended to rely on JCE liability since paragraphs 14 and 15 thereof clearly charged him with complicity in genocide, which is incompatible with other forms of participation.[146] The Prosecution responds that the Appellant was put on notice that he was charged with JCE liability.[147]

67. The Appellant's argument on this point is readily dismissed. Under each Count of the Indictment the Appellant is explicitly charged for his participation in a JCE.[148] It is clear from the concise statement of facts that the alleged common criminal purpose comprised the killing of Tutsi at Murambi Technical School, Kaduha Parish, Cyanika Parish, and Kibeho Parish in Gikongoro prefecture, and Gashoba Hill and Rugongwe Trading Centre in Butare prefecture. The fact that the material facts underpinning this theory of responsibility reflect that he was charged with taking a leading position within the JCE is not in any way incompatible with his participation in that enterprise. Moreover, the Appeals Chamber notes that commission and complicity in genocide are two different punishable acts of genocide[149] which may both be pleaded in an Indictment.[150]

68. For the foregoing reasons, the Appeals Chamber is satisfied that the Indictment put the Appellant adequately on notice that he was being charged with participation in a JCE. Accordingly, the Appellant's argument on this point is dismissed. **[page 24]**

(b) Identity of the Participants in the JCE

69. The Appellant challenges the Trial Chamber's finding that the identities of the participants in the JCE were adequately pleaded. He contends that the Prosecution failed to put the Appellant on notice that it intended to allege the participation of the physical perpetrators in the JCE.[151] In this respect, the Appellant submits that the Trial Chamber erred by finding that the Prosecution Pre-Trial Brief and opening statement confirmed that the physical perpetrators were also considered as participants in the JCE since the Prosecution's opening statement merely referred to the persons "named in his Indictment".[152] The Appellant argues that

---

145 Simba Notice of Appeal, 1-A-5, 1-F-1 and 1-F-3 (in part); Simba Appeal Brief, paras 274-280, 282(d). In support of this contention, the Appellant argues that while the Prosecution alleges that he "acted in concert" with the individuals listed at paragraph 14 of the Indictment, including *Interahamwe*, gendarmes, and soldiers, it nonetheless considered him as leader of this group and did not clearly plead a case of JCE (Simba Appeal Brief, para. 275). The Appellant further submits that while paragraph 58 of the Indictment reads: "Aloys Simba intended to commit the acts [...], this intent being shared [...]", the Trial Chamber altered its meaning by considering that it was alleged that "Simba shared the same intent" with the other individuals (Simba Appeal Brief, paras 278-279, 282, quoting Trial Judgement, para. 393 (emphasis in the Simba Appeal Brief)).

146 Simba Appeal Brief, para. 282(b); Simba Reply, para. 80. The Appeals Chamber notes that the alleged error was not pleaded in the Notice of Appeal. However, since the Prosecution does not object to this failure and responds to the Appellant's submission, the Appeals Chamber will exercise its discretion to consider the Appellant's argument.

147 Prosecution Response, paras 123-127.

148 Under each Count, the Indictment states the Appellant's alleged responsibility "in concert with others as part of a joint criminal enterprise" (*See* Indictment, pp. 2, 11, 12). As will be discussed in further detail below, the Appellant was also given notice that the Prosecution intended to rely on JCE liability in the Prosecution Pre-Trial Brief as well as in a series of pre-trial decisions regarding the form of the Indictment (*See* Indictment Decision of 26 January 2004, para. 8; Decision on the Defects in the Form of the Indictment of 6 May 2004, paras 9-12, Disposition; Decision on Amended Indictment of 14 July 2004, paras 5-11).

149 *Semanza* Appeal Judgement, para. 316.

150 The Appeals Chamber has previously held that both cumulative and alternative charging on the basis of the same acts is generally allowed on the basis that "prior to the presentation of all of the evidence, it is not possible to determine to a certainty which of the charges brought against an accused will be proven" (*Naletilić and Martinović* Appeal Judgement, para. 103, quoting *Kupreškić et al.* Appeal Judgement, paras 385-386. *See also Semanza* Appeal Judgement, paras 307-309).

151 Simba Notice of Appeal, I-F-4, I-F-5, I-F-11; Simba Appeal Brief, paras 294-298; AT. 22 May 2007 pp. 7-8.

152 Simba Reply, paras 71, 72. The Appellant refers to footnote 403 of the Trial Judgement which in turn quotes an excerpt of the Prosecution's opening statement.

the fact that the Prosecution included, without explanation, a new list of participants in its Final Trial Brief, adding seven names and removing one name as well as the reference to individuals "unknown to the Prosecution", reveals that the identity of the participants in the JCE had not been adequately pleaded.[153] Finally, the Appellant submits that the Indictment fails to refer to any sort of "organization" among these individuals.[154]

70. The Prosecution responds that it did not amend the list of participants in the JCE in its Final Trial Brief, but that the names listed there already appeared in various paragraphs throughout the Indictment.[155] It submits that the Appellant does not demonstrate how the Trial Chamber erred in finding that, given the nature of the Prosecution's case, the Prosecution had adequately pleaded the identity of the participants in the JCE.[156]

71. A review of the Trial Judgement reveals that the Trial Chamber discussed in detail whether the Appellant had been adequately put on notice of the identity of the participants in the JCE. The Trial Chamber found as follows:

> 392. With respect to the participants in the joint criminal enterprise, paragraph 14 of the Indictment lists eight officials with whom, the Prosecution claims, Simba "planned" and "prepared" the genocide. The paragraph states that these named individuals "acted in concert" with Simba, echoing the language used in the count along with the specific reference to joint criminal enterprise. The Indictment also adequately identifies the participants alleged to have materially committed the crimes forming part of the common criminal purpose. Some are named in various paragraphs throughout the Indictment in connection with planning of the attacks.
>
> 393. In most cases, the participants who physically perpetrated the crimes are identified in each section of the Indictment dealing with a particular massacre site by broad category, such as *Interahamwe* or gendarmes, and then further identified with geographic and temporal details. In the context of this case and given the nature of the attacks, the Chamber is not satisfied that the Prosecution could have provided more specific identification. The Indictment alleges Simba's **[page 25]** interactions with the attackers in such a way as to reflect concerted action. In addition, paragraph 58 of the Indictment affirms that the attackers are participants when it pleads the *mens rea* for the basic form of joint criminal enterprise by stating that Simba shared the same intent to commit the pleaded crimes with "all other individuals involved in the crimes perpetrated". Moreover, the Prosecution Pre-trial Brief and opening statement also confirm that the named individuals as well as the attackers should be considered as participants in the joint criminal enterprise.[157]

72. The Appellant has not advanced any reason why the notice provided through paragraphs 14 and 58 of the Indictment read together with the different sections of the Indictment[158] identifying the physical perpetrators by category for each particular massacre site was insufficient to put him on notice that the Prosecution intended to plead the physical perpetrators as participants in the JCE. Accordingly, the Appeals Chamber cannot find the Indictment defective in this respect. It further observes that the Trial Chamber stated that "the Prosecution Pre-trial Brief and opening statement also confirm that [...] the attackers should be considered as participants in the joint criminal enterprise".[159]

73. With respect to the participants listed in the Prosecution Final Trial Brief,[160] the Appeals Chamber finds the Appellant's argument misconceived. Prosecution final trial briefs are only filed at the end of a trial, after the presentation of all the evidence, and are therefore not relevant for the preparation of an accused's case.

74. Finally, the Appeals Chamber cannot find any merit in the Appellant's argument that the Indictment fails to refer to any sort of "organization" among these individuals. It is well established that a JCE need not

153 Simba Appeal Brief, paras 294, 296-298, quoting Trial Judgement, para. 393; Simba Reply, paras 70, 73.

154 Simba Appeal Brief, para. 295.

155 Prosecution Response, para. 137.

156 Prosecution Response, para. 137.

157 Trial Judgement, paras 392-393 (internal footnotes omitted).

158 The Appeals Chamber recalls that in order to determine whether an accused was adequately put on notice of the nature and cause of the charges against him the indictment must be considered as a whole (*Gacumbitsi* Appeal Judgement, para. 123).

159 Trial Judgement, para. 393.

160 *The Prosecutor v. Aloys Simba*, Case No. ICTR-01-76-T, The Prosecutor's Closing Brief, filed on 22 June 2005 ("Prosecution Final Trial Brief"), para. 35.

be previously arranged or formulated and may materialise extemporaneously.[161] Since "organization" is not an element of JCE, it need not be pleaded in the Indictment.

75. For the foregoing reasons, the Appellant's submission that he was not adequately put on notice of the identity of the participants in the JCE is dismissed.[162] **[page 26]**

(c) Category of JCE

76. The Appellant submits that the Indictment fails to indicate the category of JCE on which the Prosecution intended to rely, and that only the Prosecution Final Trial Brief specified the Prosecution's intention to rely on the basic category.[163] The Appellant further claims that the Prosecution did not give notice of the constituent elements of all three categories of JCE and that this would have also been a "mission impossible" since the categories are mutually incompatible.[164] In addition, he submits that the Trial Chamber erred in finding that paragraph 58 of the Indictment adequately pleaded the *mens rea* for the basic form of JCE.[165] The Prosecution concedes that the Indictment fails to specify the category of JCE it intended to rely on but that it was apparent to the Appellant from the Prosecution Pre-Trial Brief as well as the Decision on Amended Indictment of 14 July 2004 that it intended to rely on all three categories of JCE.[166]

77. The Appeals Chamber recalls that while the JCE categories are mutually incompatible to the extent that a defendant may not be convicted of multiple categories based on the same conduct, an indictment may charge a defendant cumulatively with multiple categories.[167] The Appeals Chamber notes that the Appellant was convicted for his participation in a JCE based on the first category, and therefore restricts its inquiry to whether he was put on notice that the Prosecution intended to rely on that specific category.[168] In this regard, the Appeals Chamber recalls that the three categories of JCE vary only with respect to the *mens rea* element, not with regard to the *actus reus*.[169] Accordingly, an accused will have sufficient notice of the category of JCE with which he is being charged where the indictment pleads the *mens rea* element of the respective category.

78. The Appeals Chamber observes that in the instant case, the Indictment indeed failed to specifically name the category of JCE the Prosecution intended to rely on. However, paragraph 58 of the Indictment states that "Aloys Simba intended to commit the acts above, this intent being shared by all other individuals involved in the crimes perpetrated." Read together with the paragraphs of the Indictment which set out the acts and crimes alleged,[170] the Appeals Chamber is **[page 27]** satisfied that the specific state of mind of the first category of JCE was explicitly pleaded. Consequently, the Appellant had sufficient notice that he was being charged on that basis.

---

161 *Kvočka et al.* Appeal Judgement, para. 117; *Tadić* Appeal Judgement, para. 227 (ii). *See* also *Vasiljević* Appeal Judgement, para. 100.

162 The Appellant also argues that the Trial Chamber erred when it considered paragraph 14 of the Indictment in its factual findings since this paragraph was impermissibly vague (Simba Notice of Appeal, I-A-3; Simba Appeal Brief, paras 60-69; Simba Reply, para. 43). As discussed above, the Trial Chamber did not make any finding on the basis of this paragraph alone. It considered paragraph 14 as "introductory paragraph" providing "a summary list of various individuals that are mentioned elsewhere in the Indictment interacting with Simba in the context of specific events" which needed to be "read in the context of the Indictment as a whole" (Trial Judgement, para. 18). Therefore, the Appellant's contention on this point need not be discussed any further.

163 Simba Appeal Brief, para. 282(c); Simba Reply, para. 90; AT 22 May 2007 pp. 6-7.

164 Simba Reply, paras 87-88.

165 Simba Notice of Appeal, I-F-5; Simba Appeal Brief, para. 279; Simba Reply, para. 83.

166 Prosecution Response, paras 132-134

167 *See, e.g. Delalic et al.* Appeal Judgement, para. 400 ("Cumulative charging is to be allowed in light of the fact that, prior to the presentation of all of the evidence, it is not possible to determine to a certainty which of the charges brought against an accused will be proven. The Trial Chamber is better poised, after the parties' presentation of the evidence, to evaluate which of the charges may be retained, based upon the sufficiency of the evidence. In addition, cumulative charging constitutes the usual practice of both this Tribunal and the ICTR.").

168 The Appellant's arguments concerning the other categories, including the contention that it is a "mission impossible" to prove the elements of all three categories since they are mutually incompatible, need not be addressed as they could not have had any impact on the verdict.

169 *Tadić* Appeal Judgement, paras 227, 228.

170 Indictment, paras 26-57.

79. This conclusion is also reached when viewing the notice provided to the Appellant against the backdrop of a series of pre-trial decisions regarding the form of the Indictment. On 6 May 2004, the Trial Chamber issued a decision in which it ordered the Prosecution, *inter alia*, "to amend the amended Indictment by providing (...) details (...) with respect to the *mens rea* element of joint criminal enterprise."[171] On 10 May 2004, and in response to the Trial Chamber's decision, the Prosecution filed a second amended Indictment which included the above-cited paragraph 58. On 14 July 2004, the Trial Chamber dismissed a Defence motion challenging the Second Amended Indictment and found, *inter alia*, that the Second Amended Indictment pleaded with sufficient precision the *mens rea* element of all three forms of JCE.[172] It is also noteworthy that the Trial Chamber explicitly stated with respect to the material facts pleaded at paragraph 23 of the Indictment that these are "*also* relevant to establishing the general intent to commit the underlying crimes."[173] Moreover, the Prosecution explicitly stated in the Pre-Trial Brief that it intended to rely on all three categories of JCE.[174]

80. For the foregoing reasons, the Appellant's submissions on this point are dismissed.

2. Alleged Errors Relating to Other Material Facts Not Pleaded in the Indictment

(a) The Appellant's Stature as an Aggravating Factor

81. The Appellant submits that the Trial Chamber erred in finding that he was not an "ordinary citizen" and that this constituted an aggravating circumstance. He submits that this fact was not pleaded in the Indictment and should therefore not have been considered by the Trial Chamber in **[page 28]** sentencing.[175] The Prosecution responds that the Appellant's stature in Rwanda was pleaded in detail in the Indictment.[176]

82. The Appeals Chamber recalls that the charges against an accused and the material facts supporting those charges must be pleaded with sufficient precision in the Indictment so as to provide notice to the accused.[177] By the same token, for sentencing purposes, a Trial Chamber may only consider in aggravation circumstances pleaded in the Indictment.[178]

83. A review of the Indictment reveals that it specifies that before 1994, the Appellant had held the positions of Colonel of the Rwandan Armed Forces, *Deputé* in the National Assembly and President of the *Mouvement révolutionnaire national pour la démocratie et le développement* ("MRND") in Gikongoro Prefecture; and that from mid-May 1994, he was designated by the Minister of Defence of the interim government as *Conseiller* of the civil defence for Gikongoro and Butare prefectures.[179] The Indictment describes the Appellant as one of the wealthiest citizens in Gikongoro Prefecture and alleges that he also

---

171 *The Prosecutor v. Aloys Simba*, Case No. ICTR-2001-76-I, Decision on Preliminary Defence Motion Regarding Defects in the Form of the Indictment, 6 May 2004, Disposition. The Appellant's participation in a joint criminal enterprise was not explicitly pleaded in the Initial Indictment. On 26 January 2004, the Trial Chamber granted a Prosecution's motion to amend the Indictment, *see The Prosecutor v. Aloys Simba,* Case No. ICTR-2001-76-I, Decision on Motion to Amend Indictment, 26 January 2004 ("Simba Indictment Decision of 26 January 2004"). The Trial Chamber noted, *inter alia*, that "the specific allegation of a joint and criminal enterprise gives the Accused clear notice that the Prosecution intends to argue this theory of commission of crimes" (Simba Indictment Decision of 26 January 2004, para. 8). On 16 February 2004, the Prosecution filed an amended indictment which specified with respect to each count that it intended to rely on joint criminal enterprise liability.

172 Decision on Amended Indictment of 14 July 2004, paras 8-11.

173 Decision on Amended Indictment of 14 July 2004, fn. 8 (emphasis added).

174 *The Prosecutor v. Aloys Simba*, Case No. ICTR-2001-76-I, The Prosecutor's Pre-Trial Brief Pursuant to Article 73 *bis* (B)(i) of the Rules of Procedure and Evidence, filed on 16 February 2004 ("Prosecution Pre-Trial Brief"), paras 125-136.

175 Simba Notice of Appeal, I-A-2-(a); Simba Appeal Brief, paras 47, 49.

176 Prosecution Response, paras 38-41.

177 *Gacumbitsi* Appeal Judgement, para. 49; *Simić et al.* Appeal Judgement, para. 20.

178 *Delalić et al.* Appeal Judgement, para. 763 ("The Appeals Chamber agrees that only those matters which are proved beyond reasonable doubt against an accused may be the subject of an accused's sentence or taken into account in aggravation of that sentence."); *Kunarac et al.* Trial Judgement, para. 850 ("Only those circumstances directly related to the commission of the offence charged and to the offender himself when he committed the offence, such as the manner in which the offence was committed, may be considered in aggravation. In other words, circumstances not directly related to an offence may not be used in aggravation of an offender's sentence for that offence. To permit otherwise would be to whittle away the purpose and import of an indictment.").

179 Indictment, p. 1.

derived authority from his close association with President Habyarimana.[180] All of these clearly allege that the Appellant was no ordinary citizen. The Appellant's contention is therefore without merit.

(b) The Distribution of Weapons

84. The Appellant challenges the Trial Chamber's findings that he distributed weapons to the physical perpetrators of the crimes at Murambi Technical School and Kaduha Parish, and that he had a cache of weapons for distribution, which certainly would have come from civilian or military authorities.[181] The Appellant submits that neither the fact that he had a cache of weapons nor the source of these weapons appears in the Indictment, the trial record or in any of the Trial Chamber's **[page 29]** findings.[182] The Prosecution responds that the source of the weapons is not a material fact which the Prosecution was required to plead.[183]

85. The Appeals Chamber notes that paragraph 32 of the Indictment states that during the attack at Kaduha Parish, "Aloys SIMBA replenished the ammunition of the attackers on several occasions." By the same token, paragraph 42 of the Indictment states that the Appellant arrived in Murambi "in a truck loaded with machetes which he subsequently distributed to the Interahamwe." The Appellant's argument that the Indictment failed to plead the Appellant's distribution of weapons is therefore without merit. The fact that the weapons distributed by the Appellant originated from "civilian and military authorities" and had been stored by the Appellant in a cache was not a material fact which the Prosecution was required to plead to put the Appellant on notice of the charges against him. Rather, the material fact was the Appellant's distribution of the weapons. Accordingly, the Appellant has failed to demonstrate that the Indictment was defective with respect to the Appellant's distribution of weapons.

86. Accordingly, this sub-ground of appeal is dismissed.

(c) The Appellant's Motive

87. The Appellant argues that his motive with respect to genocide or crimes against humanity was not pleaded in the Indictment.[184] Moreover, he contends that the Trial Chamber's finding relating to his motive is merely an assumption leading to a doubt which must be considered in favour of the Appellant.[185] The Prosecution responds that an accused's motive does not constitute an element of an international crime and therefore need not be pleaded in the Indictment.[186]

88. The Trial Chamber did not consider motive to be an element of the crimes at issue, but considered that a possible motive did not preclude the possession of genocidal intent.[187] This finding is in accordance with established jurisprudence.[188] As a result there was no need for the Prosecution to plead the motive in the Indictment. Accordingly, this sub-ground of appeal is dismissed. **[page 30]**

(d) The Formulation of a Genocidal Plan

89. The Appellant contests the Trial Chamber's finding that it "is also possible that local authorities formulated a plan of attack and then requested Simba to assist in implementing it", on the basis that no such

180 Indictment, p. 3.

181 Trial Judgement, para. 404.

182 Simba Notice of Appeal, I-A-2(b); Simba Appeal Brief, para. 51; Simba Reply, paras 34, 51. The Appeals Chamber will address the Appellant's argument that this finding is without support in the evidence (Simba Notice of Appeal, II-C-14) below under Chapter II, Section F-1.

183 Prosecution Response, para. 44; AT. 22 May 2007 pp. 33-34, 52-53.

184 Simba Notice of Appeal, I-A-2-(c); Simba Appeal Brief, para. 53; Simba Reply, para. 37; AT. 22 May 2007 p. 20.

185 Simba Appeal Brief, paras 54-55.

186 Prosecution Response, paras 46-47.

187 Trial Judgement, para. 417.

188 *Kvočka et al.* Appeal Judgement, para. 106; *Niyitegeka* Appeal Judgement, para. 53; *Jelisić* Appeal Judgement, para. 49; *Kayishema and Ruzindana* Appeal Judgement, para. 161; *Tadić* Appeal Judgement, para. 269.

plan was pleaded in the Indictment.[189] The Prosecution responds that "planning" is not an element of JCE liability and thus need not be pleaded in the Indictment.[190]

90. The Appeals Chamber notes that, contrary to what the Appellant seems to suggest, the Trial Chamber did not enter any conviction on the basis of the contested finding. To the contrary, having considered that it was not the only reasonable inference available from the evidence, it dismissed the allegation that the Appellant participated in the planning of the massacres of 21 April 1994 at Murambi, Cyanika, and Kaduha.[191] Moreover, it is well established that "planning" is not an element of a JCE.[192] The material element of a JCE is the "common purpose", and it is on this basis that the Trial Chamber convicted the Appellant for his participation in a JCE. Accordingly, this sub-ground of appeal is dismissed.

(e) Appellant's Presence and Utterances at Kaduha Parish as a Sign of Approval of the Attackers' Conduct

91. The Appellant submits, without elaboration, that the Trial Chamber erred in law by finding, at paragraph 403 of the Trial Judgement, that the attackers perceived the Appellant's alleged presence at Kaduha Parish and the remarks he made as a sign that he and the government approved of their conduct, since he had not been put on notice of this allegation.[193]

92. As a preliminary matter, the Appeals Chamber finds that the invocation of the government by the Appellant was not a material fact which the Prosecution was required to plead in the Indictment. Rather, the material fact was that the Appellant encouraged the assailants by his presence, acts and utterances. A review of the Indictment shows that it provided detailed information with respect to both the Appellant's presence, acts, and utterances at Kaduha Parish and his position of "power" and "authority" in Rwanda, and in particular in Gikongoro and Butare prefectures.[194] The Appeals Chamber is therefore satisfied that the Appellant was properly given **[page 31]** notice by the Indictment that the Prosecution intended to plead that his presence at Kaduha Parish and his acts and utterances encouraged the assailants.

93. In any event, the Prosecution Pre-Trial Brief repeatedly describes the Appellant's presence at the massacre sites as tacit encouragement and demonstration of his support to the attackers. A whole subsection in the Prosecution Pre-Trial Brief is entitled "Presence at or in the vicinity of Crime Scenes: Tacit Encouragement of the Crimes" and deals with this issue.[195] Similarly, paragraphs 89 and 147 of the Prosecution Pre-Trial Brief read:

> 89. Aloys SIMBA was present at or in the vicinity of various massacre sites/scenes. He knew that widespread and systematic killings targeting Tutsis were taking place throughout Gikongoro and in some communes in Butare prefecture bordering Gikongoro. He did not take any action to prevent or oppose the massacres. As a person in authority, his failure to take action amounts to tacit encouragement of the killings and other acts of violence.[196]
>
> (...)
>
> 147. Although Aloys SIMBA knew that throughout Rwanda, Tutsi civilians were being targeted and systematically and massively killed on ethnic grounds, he did not publicly disavow the killings, thereby demonstrating his support for the massacres.[197]

---

189 Simba Notice of Appeal, I-A-2 (d); Simba Appeal Brief, paras 56-59; Simba Reply, para. 38.

190 Prosecution Response, para. 48.

191 Trial Judgement, para. 405.

192 *Kvočka et al.* Appeal Judgement, para. 117 ("Joint criminal enterprise requires the existence of a common purpose which amounts to or involves the commission of a crime. The common purpose need not be previously arranged or formulated; it may materialize extemporaneously" (footnote omitted)). *See also* Section C-1(b), fn. 167.

193 Simba Notice of Appeal, I-F-8. The Appellant does not develop this claim in his Appeal Brief.

194 Indictment, paras 3, 5, 7-11, 27-34.

195 Prosecution Pre-Trial Brief, paras 169-174.

196 Prosecution Pre-Trial Brief (Section D(i): Prosecutor's Case Theory, General theory), para. 89.

197 Prosecution Pre-Trial Brief (Section D(iv)(a): Prosecutor's Case Theory, Article 6(1) Applied to the Facts of the Case, Participation in a Joint or Common Criminal Enterprise), para. 147.

94. Consequently, the Trial Chamber found at paragraph 403 as follows:

> Simba participated in the joint criminal enterprise through his acts of assistance and encouragement to the physical perpetrators of the crimes at Murambi Technical School and Kaduha Parish. In the Chamber's view, Simba's actions at those two sites had a substantial effect on the killings which followed. Witness KSY noted that the attackers at Murambi continued with renewed enthusiasm after Simba's departure. Moreover, the use of guns and grenades, which Simba distributed at Kaduha Parish, was a decisive factor in the success of these assaults. The Chamber notes that Simba was a respected national figure in Rwandan society and well-known in his native region. Therefore, the assailants at those places would have viewed his presence during the attacks, however brief, as approval of their conduct, particularly after Simba's invocation of the government.[198]

95. The Trial Chamber further found at paragraph 406 of the Trial Judgement that the Appellant "shared the common purpose of killing Tutsi at Murambi Technical School and Kaduha Parish based on his presence and specific actions at the two sites."[199]

96. It is apparent from the language of paragraph 403 of the Trial Judgement quoted above, that the Trial Chamber correctly treated the Appellant's actions in aggregate, finding that taken together, they clearly indicated the Appellant's intent to participate in and to encourage the massacres. In light of the above, the Appeals Chamber is also satisfied that the Appellant was put on notice regarding the nature of the charges for which he was convicted. **[page 32]**

97. The Appellant's argument that he lacked notice regarding the effect of his apparent presence and utterances at Kaduha Parish, including his invocation of the government, is therefore without merit. Accordingly, this sub-ground of appeal is dismissed.

D. <u>Alleged Errors in the Assessment of the Prosecution Evidence</u>

98. The Appellant submits, under various sub-grounds of appeal, that the Trial Chamber committed errors of law and fact in finding that he was present during and participated in the attacks at Murambi Technical School and Kaduha Parish on 21 April 1994.

99. The Appeals Chamber notes that some of the Appellant's submissions are advanced without any supporting argument.[200] The Appeals Chamber declines to address these submissions as they do not meet the minimum criteria for a challenge on appeal. Moreover, the Appeals Chamber will not address alleged errors with respect to the assessment of Prosecution Witness KDD's testimony,[201] given that no factual findings in the Trial Judgement are based on the evidence challenged.

100. The Appeals Chamber will consider in turn the Appellant's allegations of error relating to the respective weight the Trial Chamber accorded to oral evidence and documentary evidence; the Appellant's presence at and participation in the attacks at Murambi Technical School and Kaduha Parish; the impossibility to drive between these two places in the lapse of time compatible with the evidence; and the speech given by the Appellant at a public meeting in Ntyazo Commune on 22 May 1994.

---

198 Footnotes omitted.

199 Trial Judgement, para. 406.

200 These include submissions to the effect that (i) "[i]t is contradictory to acknowledge that Prosecution witnesses had credibility problems and nevertheless to accept certain aspects of their testimonies and to go as far as to explain their inconsistencies and contradictions" (Simba Appeal Brief, paras 165-166, 261 in relation to Simba Notice of Appeal, I-C-6 and I-D-6); (ii) the Trial Chamber erred in finding, in relation to the assessment of the credibility of Witness YH, "that the issue of the RPA attack was not developed further by the Defence" (Simba Notice of Appeal, I-B-5. Neither the Defence nor the Trial Judgement clarifies "RPA". The Trial Judgement at paragraph 167 appears to point to the armed branch of the RPF); (iii) the Trial Chamber applied a standard lower than "beyond a reasonable doubt" to find that he was present at Murambi Technical School and Kaduha Parish on 21 April 1994 and participated in criminal activities (Simba Notice of Appeal, I-B-6); (iv) the Trial Chamber erred in failing to disqualify Witnesses YH, KEI and KXX on the ground that the Prosecution dropped Count 4 (Murder as a crime against humanity) (Simba Notice of Appeal, I-C-8; Simba Appeal Brief, paras 171-173); (v) the Trial Chamber erred in using a different standard for assessing the evidence of Witness KEL, on the one hand, and Witnesses YH and KSY, on the other hand (Simba Notice of Appeal, I-C-9); and (vi) the Trial Chamber erred in failing to apply the "notion of any reasonable doubt must benefit to the Accused"(Simba Notice of Appeal, I-C-13).

201 Simba Notice of Appeal, III-5, I-C-4; Simba Appeal Brief, paras 109-111, 412-415.

1. Alleged Error Relating to the Hierarchy of Evidence

101. The Appellant contends that the Trial Chamber erred in law in giving more weight to the testimony of Prosecution witnesses than to documentary evidence used to confront them during **[page 33]** cross-examination.[202] To this end he asserts that in all legal systems the rule for assessing evidence ranks documentary evidence above oral evidence.[203] He contends that by failing to apply this legal standard to the assessment of the evidence of Prosecution Witnesses KEI,[204] KSY,[205] YH,[206] and KXX,[207] the Trial Chamber erred in giving more weight to their in-court testimony than to their prior statements.[208]

102. The Prosecution responds that contrary to the Appellant's claim it has been set out by the Appeals Chamber that live testimony is primarily accepted as being the most persuasive evidence before a court.[209]

103. The Appeals Chamber limits its analysis at this stage to the assertion that the rule for assessing evidence ranks documentary evidence above oral evidence.[210] The Appeals Chamber recalls that pursuant to Rule 89(C) of the Rules, a chamber may admit any relevant evidence which it deems to have probative value. Contrary to the Appellant's submissions, there is a general,[211] though not absolute,[212] preference for live testimony before this Tribunal. As stated in the *Akayesu* Appeal Judgement,

> the general principle is that Trial Chambers of the Tribunal shall hear live, direct testimony [and] prior statements of witnesses who appear in court are as a rule relevant only insofar as they are necessary to a Trial Chamber in its assessment of the credibility of a witness. It is not the case [...] that they should or could generally in and of themselves constitute evidence that the content thereof is truthful. For this reason, live testimony is primarily accepted as being the most persuasive evidence before a court. [...] [I]t falls to the Trial Chamber to assess and weigh the evidence before it, in the circumstances of each individual case, to determine whether or not the evidence of the witness as a whole is relevant and credible.[213]

This is consistent with Rule 90(A) of the Rules which states in part that witnesses shall, in principle, be heard directly. As the primary trier of fact, it is the Trial Chamber that has the main responsibility to resolve any inconsistencies that may arise within and/or amongst witnesses' testimonies. It is within the discretion of the Trial Chamber to evaluate any inconsistencies, to consider whether the evidence taken as a whole is reliable and credible and to accept or reject the "fundamental features" of the evidence. It may do this by relying on live testimony or documentary **[page 34]** evidence.[214] The Appeals Chamber finds no merit in the Appellant's contention and, accordingly, this sub-ground of appeal is dismissed.

2. Alleged Errors Relating to the Appellant's Presence at and Participation in the Attack at Murambi Technical School on 21 April 1994

104. The Appeals Chamber will now consider the Appellant's arguments relating to the alleged errors made in the assessment of the respective testimonies of Witnesses KSY and KEI.

---

202 Simba Notice of Appeal, I-C-5; Simba Appeal Brief, para. 112. *See also* Simba Reply, para. 47.

203 Simba Appeal Brief, para. 117.

204 Simba Appeal Brief, paras 113-115, 118.

205 Simba Appeal Brief, para. 119.

206 Simba Appeal Brief, paras 120-127.

207 Simba Appeal Brief, para. 133.

208 Simba Notice of Appeal, I-C-6.

209 Prosecution Response, paras 81-82.

210 Other errors alleged in relation to the assessment of the evidence of Prosecution Witnesses KEI, KSY, YH and KXX and Exhibit D 147 will be addressed below under Sections D-2 and D-3.

211 *See The Prosecutor v. Pauline Nyiramasuhuko et al.*, Joint Case No. ICTR-98-42-A15*bis*, Decision In the Matter of Proceedings under Rule 15 *bis*(D), 24 September 2003, para. 25.

212 *See* Rules 71, 89(C), 92 *bis*, 94 *bis*(C) of the Rules.

213 *Akayesu* Appeal Judgement, paras 134-135.

214 *Kupreškić et al.* Appeal Judgement, para. 31.

(a) Witness KSY

105. The Appellant makes several submissions to the effect that the Trial Chamber committed errors of law and fact in its assessment of Prosecution Witness KSY's evidence. The Prosecution submits that the Trial Chamber's assessment of Witness KSY's credibility and reliability, in light of his whole testimony, was correct, careful and detailed.[215] The Appeals Chamber will consider the Appellant's submissions in turn.

(i) Alleged Discrepancies Between Witness KSY's Oral Testimony and Pre-Trial Statement of 16 June 2000

106. The Appellant alleges that Witness KSY's in-court testimony contradicts his statement to Prosecution investigators dated 16 June 2000 ("Statement of 16 June 2000") as to whether he was standing or lying down when he saw the Appellant at Murambi.[216] The Prosecution responds that the Trial Chamber discussed the alleged inconsistencies at length and gave a reasoned and reasonable explanation as to why it accepted his evidence as being credible.[217]

107. The alleged discrepancy was addressed by the Trial Chamber at paragraph 118 of the Trial Judgement which reads:

> The Chamber notes, however, that the witness explained that when the Accused arrived, the attackers shouted: "Here's our Simba". Witness KSY also observed Simba during a lull in the fighting, which lasted around fifteen minutes. The witness was at a slightly elevated area and standing at various times. During cross-examination, the Defence pointed out that the witness indicated in his 16 June 2000 statement to Tribunal investigators, that he was lying down when Simba arrived, not standing up. The witness responded that he was both lying down and standing up when he saw Simba. The Chamber accepts this explanation.

108. The Trial Chamber then considered the totality of the witness's evidence, including his explanations with regard to alleged inconsistencies; the fact that he heard the attackers shouting **[page 35]** "Here's our Simba"; his observation of the Appellant during a lull in the fighting; as well as his prior familiarity with the Appellant and his ability to identify him in court.[218] The Trial Chamber concluded its assessment of Witness KSY's credibility by finding that he "provided a consistent and convincing firsthand narrative of the attacks against the Tutsi refugees at Murambi Technical School" and that "[c]ontrary to Defence suggestions, [his] testimony about [the Appellant] was generally in conformity with his previous statement to Tribunal investigators, dated 16 June 2000."[219]

109. The Appeals Chamber notes that at trial Witness KSY gave a much more detailed account of these events than in his Statement of 16 June 2000, where this sequence of events is summarised in only a few lines.[220] During his examination-in-chief, Witness KSY specified that he was standing in the courtyard of the Murambi Technical School when the Appellant arrived around 7 a.m. and that he saw him from an approximate distance of 70-100 metres. During cross-examination, Witness KSY was questioned extensively on the circumstances of his sighting of the Appellant. Witness KSY explained that, before the arrival of the Appellant at the site, he was lying down "pretending to be dead", but that he stood up in order to assist the refugees who were coming back to the front to resume the fight against the assailants.[221] He later clarified that he stood up after the Appellant's arrival and that he could see him from the slightly elevated area where

---

215 Prosecution Response, para. 186.

216 Simba Notice of Appeal, I-C-6, and II-A-1(c); Simba Appeal Brief, para. 119.

217 Prosecution Response, para. 82.

218 Trial Judgement, para. 118.

219 Trial Judgement, para. 114.

220 In the Statement of 16 June 2000 Witness KSY stated: "On the 21st April, we were attacked (...). [A]t about 6:00 hrs from where I was lying, I saw the Prefet BIKIBARUTA, Capt SEBUHURA and SEMUKWAVU coming to the entrance. SEBUHURA gave more ammunition to the gendarmes and those Interahamwe who had guns. The prefet then directed that some of the Interahamwe should go to reinforce those who were attacking and killing Tutsi refugees at Cyanika. They then left, and after about one hour, Lt Col SIMBA came to the entrance. He was dressed in military uniform and he was being driven in a red pickup which was carrying a lot of pangas (machetes). He then distributed some machetes to the Interahamwe militiamen and left thereafter. I was lying about 100 metres away and I recognised him very well. I knew Simba well – he had on many times campaigned in our area for election to parliament before" (Exh. D 1A, p. 4 (filed strictly confidentially)).

221 T. 30 August 2004 pp. 27-30, 57-62.

he was standing, despite the presence of around 100 refugees at the front.[222] The Appeals Chamber finds that the Trial Chamber's assessment of the credibility of Witness KSY is consistent with the evidence on the record and that it did not exceed its discretionary power when finding that, contrary to the Appellant's contention, Witness KSY's testimony was in general conformity with his Statement of 16 June 2000. **[page 36]**

110. The Appellant has failed to demonstrate that the Trial Chamber erred, in light of the totality of Witness KSY's evidence, when accepting the witness's explanations. Accordingly, this sub-ground of appeal is dismissed.

(ii) The Omission from Prior Statements of the Appellant's Name with Respect to Events at Murambi on 21 April 1994

111. The Appellant contends that the Trial Chamber misrepresented the facts when it accepted Witness KSY's explanation that he had omitted the Appellant's name from a previous statement "because he intended to provide evidence against persons in his neighbourhood".[223] The Appellant submits that according to Witness KSY's testimony the Appellant had not been seen at the site.[224]

112. The Trial Chamber considered this issue at paragraph 115 of the Trial Judgement, which reads:

> The Defence referred to three *pro justitia* statements to Rwandan authorities, where the witness made no mention of Simba. In relation to two of the statements, the witness expressed doubts as to whether they were his statements. Leaving aside the issue of their authenticity, the Chamber observes that the first of these two documents, dated 9 September 1996, was a complaint against Israel Nsengiumva involving several locations. Another statement of 22 November 1996 related to a person who allegedly had killed a relative of the witness and did not concern the Murambi massacre in particular. Consequently, the lack of reference to Simba in these two documents is not significant. However, his *pro justitia* declaration of 22 November 1996 dealt generally with the massacre in Murambi. The Chamber accepts the witness's explanation that he intended to provide evidence against persons in his neighbourhood and, therefore, did not include Simba. The witness also observed that some of his statements to Rwandan authorities appeared forged. The Chamber does not find these explanations convincing.[225]

113. As a preliminary matter, the Appeals Chamber notes that there appears to be an inconsistency in the way certain statements are referred to by the Appellant and the Trial Chamber: where the former refers to the statements of 22 September 1996[226] and 20 November 1996,[227] the Trial Chamber refers to a "*pro justitia* declaration of 22 November 1996".[228] According to the trial record, there is no *pro justitia* declaration of 22 November 1996, which clearly indicates that the Trial Chamber erred in labeling the statement at issue. While proper identification of the statement is not aided by the fact that the Trial Chamber did not specify the exhibit number of the document, the Appeals Chamber has been able to establish, on the basis of the translation of Exhibits D3, D4 **[page 37]** and D5, that the Trial Chamber intended to refer to the statement of 22 May 1996, admitted as Exhibit D4.[229] The subsequent analysis is therefore undertaken on this basis.

---

222 T. 30 August 2004 pp. 57-62. Still during cross-examination, Witness KSY was questioned on the alleged contradiction between his in-court testimony and the Statement of 16 June 2000 with regard to his posture. He explained the following: "I have told you that I did not spend the whole day lying down. I would stand up every now and then, and then I would lie down, and even while lying, I could see what was happening. [...] While I was lying down I saw him, and when I stood up, I still saw him" (T. 31 August 2004 pp. 10-11).

223 Simba Appeal Brief, para. 369.

224 Simba Notice of Appeal, II-C-7; Simba Appeal Brief, paras 369-370.

225 Trial Judgement, para. 115 (footnotes omitted).

226 Simba Appeal Brief, para. 119. The Appeals Chamber notes that the Appellant refers to the statement of 22 September 1996 as "Exhibit D4".

227 Simba Appeal Brief, paras 369-370. The Appeals Chamber notes that the Appellant refers to the statement of 20 November 1996 as "Exhibits D5A, D5B".

228 Trial Judgement, para. 115.

229 The Appeals Chamber notes that at paragraph 115 of the Trial Judgement, the Trial Chamber considered three statements made by Witness KSY to Rwandan authorities and also stated that the "pro justicia declaration of 22 November 1996 dealt generally with the massacre in Murambi" (Trial Judgement, para. 115). Indeed, the statement of 22 May 1996, admitted as Exhibit D4 is the only one of the three statements made by Witness KSY to the Rwandan authorities and admitted as exhibit, that dealt principally with the massacre at Murambi. Exhibits D3 and D5 do not mention this massacre (*See* Regisrar's Submissions under Rule 33(B) of the Rules on Order for Translation, 16 July 2007). *See also* T. 31 August 2004 pp. 36-38.

114. The Appeals Chamber notes that in reaching its conclusion that the omission of the Appellant's name from the statement of 22 May 1996 was not significant, the Trial Chamber relied solely on the explanation by Witness KSY that his intention in the statement was to provide evidence against persons in his neighborhood. During cross-examination, Witness KSY explained that he mentioned the names of the people who were present when he was lodging his complaint and that he did not mention the people who had been absent. He was thinking that as soon as he saw them, he would be able to lodge his complaint against them.[230]

115. As stated by the Trial Chamber, Witness KSY explained that he intended to mention only the names of persons whom he could see at the time of the interviews. He explained that regarding the other people from the other localities, he was thinking that if questions were put to him concerning them, he was going to respond. According to him, in fact, when one gives a statement, one does not remember all the names; "[i]t is only later on that if [one] remember[s] names, if it is necessary, [one] can mention them."[231] It was in this context that the witness specified that he was complaining against the people who were his neighbours. Thus, while Witness KSY's later explanations for the omission may have focused on him only mentioning persons who were "well known" in the area,[232] it does not follow that the Trial Chamber misrepresented Witness KSY's earlier explanation that he intended to provide evidence against persons in his neighbourhood.

116. The Appeals Chamber will not lightly overturn findings of a trier of fact who was able to directly assess the demeanor of a witness giving live testimony.[233] The Appellant has not shown that no reasonable Trial Chamber could have accepted Witness KSY's explanation that "he intended [in this statement] to provide evidence against persons in his neighbourhood and, therefore, did not include [the Appellant]".[234] Accordingly, this sub-ground of appeal is dismissed. **[page 38]**

117. In conclusion, the Appeals Chamber finds that the Appellant has failed to show that the Trial Chamber abused its discretion in finding Witness KSY credible and erred in relying on his testimony with regard to the presence of the Appellant at Murambi Technical School on 21 April 1994.

(b) Witness KEI

118. The Appellant alleges that the Trial Chamber minimised the inconsistencies between Prosecution Witness KEI's testimony and his prior statements made to Prosecution investigators and Rwandan judicial authorities in which he did not implicate the Appellant in the distribution of weapons.[235] The Appellant submits that the Trial Chamber violated his right to a fair trial when it justified "the inconsistencies of Witness KEI in the Respondent's stead".[236]

119. The Appellant further alleges that the Trial Chamber erred by relying on Witness KEI's testimony despite the doubts it expressed about his credibility.[237] The Appellant asserts that Witness KEI "was unable to explain why in a camp where there were gendarmes, some of whom were among the killers in Murambi, the Appellant, Captain Sebuhura and *Préfet* Bucyibaruta preferred his services (though he was not a gendarme) to those of their subordinates", and though he claimed to have been a butcher at the gendarmerie camp, he did not know the camp's cooks, the commander or any gendarme at the camp.[238] In addition, the Appellant contends that the Trial Chamber did not take into account existing contradictions between Witnesses KEI's and KSY's respective testimonies.[239]

120. The Prosecution responds that the Trial Chamber did not minimise the alleged inconsistencies in Witness KEI's testimony and submits that, on the contrary, in view of his questionable credibility, the Trial

230 T. 31 August 2004 pp. 20-21.
231 T. 31 August 2004 p. 21.
232 T. 31 August 2004 pp. 22-24.
233 *Ndindabahizi* Appeal Judgement, para. 42; *Kajelijeli* Appeal Judgement, para. 50; *Kamuhanda* Appeal Judgement, para. 7; *Ntakirutimana* Appeal Judgement, para. 12; *Niyitegeka* Appeal Judgement, para. 8.
234 Trial Judgement, para. 115.
235 Simba Notice of Appeal, I-C-5, I-C-6; Simba Appeal Brief, paras 113-118, 176-177.
236 Simba Appeal Brief, para. 115.
237 Simba Appeal Brief, paras 176-177. *See also* Simba Reply, paras 47-48.
238 Simba Notice of Appeal, I-C-6; Simba Appeal Brief, paras 137-143.
239 Simba Appeal Brief, para. 144.

Chamber declined to accept his testimony without corroboration.[240] The Prosecution further states that the Appellant's submission is misguided "given that the Trial Chamber did not rely on Witness KEI to convict the Appellant".[241]

121. The Appeals Chamber finds that, contrary to the Appellant's assertion, the Trial Chamber did not minimise or justify the contradictions between Witness KEI's testimony and his prior statements. After having acknowledged the existence of contradictions, the Trial Chamber carefully reviewed them and concluded that, in the absence of convincing explanations, they called into **[page 39]** question the credibility of the witness.[242] The Trial Chamber accordingly considered Witness KEI's testimony with caution[243] and concluded that in "view of Witness KEI's questionable credibility, [it] declines to accept his testimony without corroboration".[244] The Appeals Chamber sees no error in this approach particularly as there is no legal requirement for the corroboration of evidence. In the instant case, the Appeals Chamber notes that the Trial Chamber's findings related to these events are primarily based on evidence given by Witness KSY, a witness whose credibility has not been successfully challenged on appeal. In preferring the evidence of Witness KSY where it differed from that of Witness KEI, the Trial Chamber clearly took into account differences in the testimony of the two witnesses. Accordingly, these sub-grounds of appeal are dismissed.

3. Alleged Errors Relating to the Appellant's Presence at and Participation in the Attack at Kaduha Parish on 21 April 1994

122. The Appeals Chamber will in turn consider the Appellant's arguments to the effect that the Trial Chamber erred in assessing the evidence of Witnesses YH, KXX and KSK and that the testimonies of Witnesses YH and KXX are contradictory with respect to the time of arrival of the Appellant at Kaduha Parish.

(a) Witness YH

123. The Appellant alleges that the Trial Chamber erred in finding Witness YH's testimony credible with respect to the Appellant's presence at and participation in the attack at Kaduha Parish on 21 April 1994. In this effect, the Appellant submits that the error is twofold: first, concerning the discrepancies between Witness YH's testimony at trial and his pre-trial statement of 1 October 1997 (regarding the duration of his military service and his purported detention from April to July 1994); and, second, the failure to consider Exhibit D147 authoritative as to the location of the officer whom Witness YH claimed to have accompanied to Gikongoro prefecture in April 1994.[245]

124. The Prosecution responds that the Trial Chamber duly acknowledged problematic aspects and discrepancies in Witness YH's testimony, carefully assessed them and decided that they did not call into question the witness's first-hand account at trial.[246] **[page 40]**

(i) Alleged Discrepancies Between Witness YH's Testimony and His Statement of 1 October 1997

125. The Appellant contends[247] that the Trial Chamber erred "by ruling that Witness YH's testimony in court is credible and reliable as regards the Appellant's participation in the Kaduha massacre, even though

240 Prosecution Response, para. 82.
241 Prosecution Response, para. 109.
242 Trial Judgement, paras 107-112.
243 Trial Judgement, paras 106-107.
244 Trial Judgement, para. 112.
245 Simba Notice of Appeal, I-C-5, I-C-7, II-C-8, II-C-9; Simba Appeal Brief, paras 122-127, 371-376. The Appeals Chamber will not consider the Appellant's contention that the Trial Chamber distorted the evidence of Witness YH in relation to his prosecution in Rwanda in 1995, for "the sole purpose of lending to [him] credibility" (Notice of Appeal, II-C-8; Simba Appeal Brief, paras 371-373). The Appellant does not explain how the purported distortion would in any way affect the credibility of Witness YH.
246 Prosecution Response, paras 82, 186.
247 Simba Notice of Appeal, I-C-5, I-C-18, II-C-9, II-A-2(b) where the Appellant reiterates similar assertions in the context of his allegation that it was impossible for him to be present at both Murambi Technical School and Kaduha Parish on 21 April 1994 between 7 a.m. and 9 a.m.; AT. 22 May 2007 pp. 15-17.

the Trial Chamber had found the witness's testimony doubtful and had particularly noted discrepancies between his testimony and prior statements".[248] In support, the Appellant alleges contradictions between Witness YH's testimony and his prior statements in relation to the period he spent in the army,[249] and between the witness's oral assertion that he participated in the Kaduha attacks and the statement of 1 October 1997 in which he stated that he was in jail between April and July 1994.[250] The Appellant submits that the latter contradiction and the fact that Witness YH never confessed to and was never prosecuted in Rwanda for genocide in Kaduha, demonstrate that the witness admitted his participation in the Kaduha massacre for the sole purpose of implicating the Appellant in that massacre.[251]

126. The Appellant further contends that the Trial Chamber erred in finding, at paragraph 166 of the Trial Judgement, that "the discrepancies between [Witness YH's] testimony and his 1 October 1997 statement to Rwandan authorities simply reflected the witness's attempts to distance himself from the crimes which he later acknowledged".[252]

127. At trial, Witness YH gave evidence that his military service lasted from 1991 until mid-April 1994 and that he participated in events at Kaduha Parish in April 1994. This evidence contrasted with his statement of 1 October 1997 which indicated that he left the army in August 1993 and was in prison from April to July 1994.[253] When cross-examined, the witness explained that he was beaten by Rwandan officials during his interview of 1 October 1997 and that some passages of this statement were given under duress.[254] He stated that the portion of the statement mentioning that he was in the Kigali prison from April to July 1994, when he was transferred to Nyanza, was "invented",[255] and that he never said that he left the army in August 1993.[256] He further asserted that during the period from April to July 1994 there were no prisoners in **[page 41]** Rwanda.[257] The witness could not say why the Rwandan authorities might want to indicate that he left the Rwandan army in August 1993, rather than April 1994.[258]

128. At the outset of its assessment of Witness YH's testimony, the Trial Chamber expressly stated that because the witness was an alleged accomplice of the Appellant, his testimony would be viewed with appropriate caution.[259] With respect to the issue of credibility, the Trial Chamber acknowledged "that there [were] some problematic aspects of Witness YH's testimony", notably his failure to disclose his own role in the Kaduha Parish massacre to Rwandan authorities and the discrepancy between his trial testimony and prior statements concerning his military service,[260] but concluded that "Witness YH provided a convincing, credible and reliable first-hand testimony concerning [the Appellant's] participation in the massacre at Kaduha Parish".[261] The Trial Chamber also noted that Witness YH had prior familiarity with the Appellant and identified him in court. The Trial Chamber concluded "that the problematic aspects of Witness YH's testimony [...] [did] not call into question his first-hand account at trial".[262]

129. Thus, having considered all the existing discrepancies in Witness YH's testimony, the Trial Chamber concluded that his explanations "simply reflect[ed] the witness's attempts to distance himself from the crimes which he [had] later acknowledged".[263] This conclusion is consistent with the explanation given by Witness YH in relation to his failure to disclose his role in the Kaduha Parish massacre to the Rwandan authorities. He said that he was "awaiting the *gacaca* court system to confess that crime".[264] The Trial

248 Simba Appeal Brief, para. 120 (emphasis omitted).
249 Simba Appeal Brief, para. 121.
250 Simba Appeal Brief, paras 122-123.
251 Simba Appeal Brief, paras 123, 125.
252 Simba Appeal Brief, para. 124.
253 Trial Judgement, paras 140, 166; Exh. P 12.
254 T. 22 September 2004 pp. 13-14.
255 T. 22 September 2004 p. 15.
256 T. 22 September 2004 p. 16.
257 T. 23 September 2004 p. 12.
258 T. 22 September 2004 pp. 16-17.
259 Trial Judgement, para. 164.
260 Trial Judgement, paras 165-167.
261 Trial Judgement, para. 168.
262 Trial Judgement, para. 168.
263 Trial Judgement, para. 166.
264 T. 23 September 2004 p. 19.

Chamber accepted this explanation and found that the witness "simply attempted, at earlier stages of his proceeding in Rwanda, to minimize his involvement in the genocide".[265] The Appeals Chamber notes that the witness also acknowledged that his limited confession facilitated his provisional release as a criminal of the "second category".[266] The Appeals Chamber finds that the Appellant has not demonstrated that the Trial Chamber exceeded its discretion when finding that the discrepancies between Witness YH's testimony and his statement of 1 October 1997 could be explained by his attempt to distance himself from the crimes which he later acknowledged.

130. This sub-ground of appeal is dismissed. **[page 42]**

(ii) Exhibit D147

131. The Appellant submits that the Trial Chamber erred in finding that Exhibit D147 did not necessarily reflect the location of all officers in mid-April.[267] He submits that this document "is authentic, since it was produced by the Prosecution in another case of this Tribunal" and contends that "judicial notice should have been taken thereof under Rule 94(B) of the Rules".[268] The Appellant asserts that Exhibit D147 as well as the prior statements of Witness YH prove that this witness did not go to Kaduha on 21 April 1994. The Appellant further contends that the Trial Chamber erred by according lower probative value to these documents than to the in-court evidence of Witness YH, thereby violating Rule 89(B) and (C) of the Rules.[269]

132. The Appeals Chamber recalls that it has already dismissed the argument that as a matter of law documentary evidence should be preferred to oral testimony.[270] Here the Appellant further submits that because the Prosecution presented a document in evidence in another case before the Tribunal, it must be authentic, probative and subject to judicial notice.[271] The Appeals Chamber rejects this argument as a matter of principle: the probative value of a document may be assessed differently in different cases, depending on the circumstances. In the instant case, the Trial Chamber considered Exhibit D147,[272] a document allegedly showing the location of Rwandan Army officers as of 5 March 1994, and found that, in the context of the events which followed the death of the President of Rwanda, the locations of officers in mid-April 1994 could have been different from those mentioned in this document.[273] The Appellant has failed to demonstrate that no reasonable Trial Chamber could have reached the same conclusion. Accordingly, this sub-ground of appeal is dismissed.

(b) Witness KXX

133. The Appellant contends that the Trial Chamber erred by relying on Prosecution Witness KXX's testimony.[274] He submits that in prior statements before the Rwandan authorities, Witness KXX never mentioned his own participation in the massacre at Kaduha Parish,[275] and that in court **[page 43]** he was unable to give a consistent chronology of the attack against Kaduha[276] or to identify the Appellant.[277] The Appellant asserts that the falsity of Witness KXX's testimony was demonstrated when he admitted that at

265 Trial Judgement, para. 165.
266 T. 23 September 2004 p. 19.
267 Simba Notice of Appeal, I-C-7; Simba Appeal Brief, paras 126-127.
268 Simba Appeal Brief, paras 126-127.
269 Simba Appeal Brief, para. 127. *See also* Simba Reply, paras 47-48.
270 *See above* Section D-1, paras 101-103.
271 Simba Appeal Brief, paras 126-127.
272 Exh. D147, admitted on 29 March 2005. The document itself is dated 5 March 1994. It arguably emanates from the "Ministère de la Défense Nationale, Armée Rwandaise, *Etat-Major* G1" and shows the situation of the officers of the Rwandese army as of 1 March 1994.
273 Trial Judgement, para. 167.
274 Simba Notice of Appeal, I-C-6, I-C-18. II-A-2(c) where the Appellant reiterates similar assertions in the context of his allegation that it was impossible for him to be present at both Murambi Technical School and Kaduha Parish on 21 April 1994 between 7 a.m. and 9 a.m. *See also* Simba Reply, paras 47, 132-133; AT. 22 May 2007 p. 17.
275 Simba Appeal Brief, para. 130.
276 Simba Appeal Brief, paras 131, 160.
277 Simba Appeal Brief, paras 131, 157-159.

Kaduha Parish he had stood at a place where he could not see events a hundred metres away.[278] He submits that, in accordance with the case law, in such circumstances Witness KXX should have been disqualified.[279]

134. The Appellant also submits that the Trial Chamber erred in finding at paragraph 169 of the Trial Judgement that there was no evidence of the witness's prior knowledge of the Appellant.[280] He further contends that the Trial Chamber erred in giving more weight to Witness KXX's in-court testimony than to the discrepancies in his prior statements.[281]

135. The Prosecution responds that the Trial Chamber's approach to the assessment and application of Witness KXX's evidence is correct, careful and detailed, and, therefore, reasonable.[282]

136. The Appeals Chamber notes that Witness KXX is one of three witnesses, together with Witnesses YH and KSK, who placed the Appellant at Kaduha Parish during the attack on 21 April 1994. As Witness KXX was an alleged accomplice of the Appellant, the Trial Chamber stated that it viewed his testimony with "appropriate caution".[283] It also identified a number of problems with Witness KXX's testimony,[284] and stated that it would "only accept his testimony, if it [was] adequately corroborated, as where it [was] consistent with Witness YH's account".[285]

137. As the question whether the Trial Chamber erred in relying on Witness KXX's testimony is closely linked to alleged contradictions between the respective testimonies of Witnesses YH and KXX, the Appeals Chamber considers that it would be best addressed below in the context of the **[page 44]** analysis of the possible contradictions.[286] The Appeals Chamber will not consider the Appellant's submission regarding the alleged error in the Trial Chamber's finding that there was no evidence of Witness KXX's prior knowledge of the Appellant, as no conviction was entered on the basis of the Trial Chamber's allegedly erroneous finding and the Appellant's claim does not have the potential to cause the verdict to be reversed or revised.

(c) Witness KSK

138. The Appellant submits that the Trial Chamber erred in relying on the evidence of Witness KSK to conclude that the Appellant was at Kaduha on 21 April 1994 and in finding that Witness KSK was credible and corroborative of Witness KXX's account despite noting inconsistencies and expressing doubt as to their testimonies.[287] He also contends that the Trial Chamber showed more leniency towards Witness KSK than towards alibi witnesses.[288] The Prosecution does not present any specific argument in response.

139. The Appeals Chamber observes that, contrary to the Appellant's assertion, the Trial Chamber did not rely on Witness KSK's testimony to find that the Appellant was at Kaduha Parish on 21 April 1994. While not calling into question Witness KSK's general credibility, the Trial Chamber found that there was insufficient evidence showing "a satisfactory basis of knowledge" which would have allowed the witness to

---

278 Simba Appeal Brief, para. 161.

279 Simba Appeal Brief, para. 132.

280 Simba Appeal Brief, para. 158. The Appellant makes a related submission that the Trial Chamber erred in fact in finding that no evidence was presented to show that Witness KXX had prior knowledge of the Appellant establishing that he was able to accurately identify him during the genocide (Simba Notice of Appeal, II-C-10).

281 Simba Appeal Brief, para. 133.

282 Prosecution Response, paras 82, 186.

283 Trial Judgement, para. 164.

284 Trial Judgement, para 169. The Trial Chamber noted that Witness KXX "had problems providing a clear chronology of the events surrounding the Kaduha Parish massacre"; there was no evidence of his prior knowledge of the Appellant establishing that he was able to accurately identify him during the events; he could not identify the Appellant in court; and in prior statements, he did not specifically mention the Appellant's presence at Kaduha Parish on the morning of 21 April 1994.

285 Trial Judgement para. 169. On this basis, the Trial Chamber declined to accept "Witness KXX's [...] uncorroborated testimony that [the Appellant] addressed a crowd in Kaduha Trading Centre and delivered weapons to the sub-prefecture office in the days before the attack on Kaduha Parish".

286 *See below* Section D-3(d).

287 Simba Notice of Appeal, I-C-6, I-C-12, II-A-2(a), II-A-2(d); Simba Appeal Brief, paras 163-164, 167, 170, 181, 183, 236, 333.

288 Simba Notice of Appeal, I-C-12.

identify the Appellant at the crime site.[289] With respect to her estimate that the attack started around 5:00 a.m., the Trial Chamber found that this was not inconsistent with the accounts of Witnesses YH and KXX. The Appellant has failed to demonstrate that the Trial Chamber erred in so finding. Neither has the Appellant demonstrated how the Trial Chamber might have showed more leniency toward Witness KSK than toward alibi witnesses. Accordingly, these sub-grounds of appeal are dismissed.

(d) Alleged Contradictions between the Testimonies of Witnesses YH and KXX

140. The Appellant submits that the respective testimonies of Witnesses YH and KXX regarding the Appellant's arrival time at Kaduha Parish are inconsistent. He argues that while Witness YH testified that the Appellant arrived at Kaduha Parish at 8.20 a.m., Witness KXX testified that the Appellant only arrived around 9 a.m. The Appellant contends that the testimonies of Witnesses YH **[page 45]** and KXX were not corroborative and therefore could not form the basis of a conviction beyond reasonable doubt.[290]

141. The Prosecution responds that the Appellant fails to demonstrate any error in the Trial Chamber's assessment of the evidence. In particular, it submits that the Trial Chamber applied the correct approach with respect to Witnesses YH and KXX, alleged accomplices of the Appellant, in stating that it "viewed their testimonies with appropriate caution".[291]

142. The Appeals Chamber notes that the witnesses' testimonies do in fact differ as to the time of the Appellant's arrival at Kaduha Parish. While according to Witness KXX, Simba arrived at Kaduha Parish "around 9.00 a.m.", Witness YH testified that the Appellant arrived at around 8.20 a.m.[292] As noted above, the Trial Chamber identified a number of problems in Witness KXX's testimony and therefore decided to only accept it if adequately corroborated by Witness YH.[293] The Trial Chamber, however, ignored its own holding by finding that the Appellant arrived at Kaduha Parish "around 9 a.m.",[294] thereby relying solely on the testimony given by Witness KXX.

143. The Appeals Chamber finds that the Trial Chamber committed an error of law in making this finding. While a trier of fact is not obliged to detail every step of its reasoning, in view of its concerns regarding the credibility of Witness KXX and its decision to accept his testimony only where corroborated,[295] the Trial Chamber was compelled to explain why it relied on the uncorroborated account of Witness KXX instead of Witness YH's testimony with regard to the time of the Appellant's arrival at Kaduha Parish. The Appeals Chamber will consider below whether, and if necessary, to what extent, the Trial Chamber's error affects its findings relating to the Appellant's participation in the attacks at Murambi Technical School and Kaduha Parish on 21 April 1994 within the time frame emerging from the relevant testimonies. **[page 46]**

4. Alleged Errors Relating to the Possibility of the Appellant's Presence at Both Murambi Technical School and Kaduha Parish on 21 April 1994 in the Lapse of Time Accepted by the Trial Chamber

144. The Appellant alleges that the Trial Chamber erred in fact[296] in finding that he took part in the massacres at Murambi Technical School and Kaduha Parish on 21 April 1994, thereby ignoring the Appellant's submissions that it was physically impossible for him to be present at both sites within the time

---

289 Trial Judgement, paras 170-175.

290 Simba Notice of Appeal, I-C-6, II-A-2(a), II-C-5; Simba Appeal Brief, paras 167-170. While the Appellant alleges several inconsistencies between the respective testimonies of Witnesses YH, KXX and KSK, he specifies only one alleged contradiction between the testimonies of Witnesses YH and KXX, to which the Appeals Chamber will limit its consideration. The Appeals Chamber will not consider the Appellant's argument to the effect that the case law requires that when a conviction is based on uncorroborated testimony it must be established beyond reasonable doubt (Simba Appeal Brief, para. 169), since that standard does not vary according to whether the testimony is corroborated or not.

291 Prosecution Response, para. 86 .

292 Trial Judgement, para. 142.

293 *See above* Section D-3(b), para. 136.

294 Trial Judgement, para. 175.

295 Trial Judgement, para. 169.

296 The Appeals Chamber notes that the Appellant alleges an error of fact. However, it appears from the nature of his submission that he alleges both an error of law (failure to provide a reasoned opinion) and an error of fact (findings that the Appellant had been successively at Murambi Technical School and Kaduha Parish on 21 April 1994).

frame which emerges from the relevant testimonies.[297] The Appellant also submits that his presence at both sites was not proven beyond reasonable doubt.[298]

145. The Appellant points out that he was allegedly seen at Murambi Technical School from 7 a.m. (by Witness KSY) to 8.20 or 8.30 a.m. or even 9.20 to 9.30 a.m. at the latest (by Witness KEI), while he allegedly arrived at Kaduha Parish at 8.20 a.m. (according to Witness YH) or around 9 a.m. at the latest (following Witness KXX's account).[299] He submits that in the "most optimistic scenario" it could be inferred that he traveled from Murambi Technical School to Kaduha Parish in less than 40 minutes.[300] He alleges that the distance between the two places is either 72 or 79 kilometers by road; the shortest road takes nearly three hours to travel;[301] and the road conditions, particularly in April during the heavy rainy season, in addition to the restrictions on movements in April 1994, would have rendered this scenario impossible.[302]

146. The Appellant also submits that, when finding that the three massacre sites were located "not far from one other",[303] the Trial Chamber might have been misled by the maps in the Prosecution Investigator's file.[304] He submits that, while one of these maps "indicates an area called **[page 47]** 'Murambi' as being close to Kaduha Parish", the actual site of Murambi Technical School is between 72 and 79 kilometers away from Kaduha.[305]

147. The Prosecution responds that the Appellant has not demonstrated any error committed by the Trial Chamber in assessing the relevant evidence and merely tries to re-litigate matters that were fully explored at trial.[306] According to the Prosecution, the Trial Chamber closely considered factors such as the distance between the two locations, the credibility of Prosecution witnesses, and the Appellant's participation in the crimes at the two locations. In particular, the Prosecution submits that the Trial Chamber "was fully alive to the issue of time-gap between the Appellant's participation in the perpetration of crimes at the two locations".[307]

148. The Prosecution further submits that the Appellant misrepresents the Trial Chamber's findings in relation to the time-frame within which he was found to have participated in the crimes at Murambi Technical School and Kaduha Parish, in particular by representing this as a maximum of 40 minutes[308] and by engaging in "some arithmetic exercise, which attempts to provide rather exact time-frames".[309] In addition, the Prosecution submits that the Appellant's allegations with regard to the time necessary for driving from Murambi Technical School and Kaduha Parish are based on estimations which can vary from one driver to the other, and that his assertion regarding the state of the roads during the rainy season is not sustained by any evidence.[310]

149. In reply, the Appellant contends that the Trial Chamber "failed to display objectivity" when finding that the Appellant was seen at Murambi Technical School at 7:00 a.m. on 21 April 1994 and at Kaduha Parish

297 Simba Notice of Appeal, II-A-3; Simba Appeal Brief, paras 333-355; AT. 22 May 2007 pp. 13, 20-22, 45.

298 Simba Notice of Appeal, II-A-1, II-A-2; Simba Appeal Brief, paras 333, 343-344. Under Grounds II-A-1 and II-A-2, the Appellant also makes submissions which do not point strictly toward the impossibility to be present at both sites in the lapse of time accepted by the Trial Chamber. These sub-grounds were dealt with above under Sections D-1to D-3.

299 Simba Appeal Brief, para. 344.

300 Simba Appeal Brief, para. 345.

301 The Appellant submits that his arguments are supported by the Defence Expert Report which states that it "took at least three hours to travel from Murambi to Kaduha" (Simba Appeal Brief, para. 347, referring to Defence Expert Report of 27 March 2005 (Exh. D 156), p. 49).

302 Simba Appeal Brief, paras 345-346, 349-353.

303 Trial Judgement, para. 401.

304 Simba Appeal Brief, para. 353. The English version of Simba Appeal Brief mentions "Exhibits 7 and 8". However, it seems that the Appellant is referring to maps numbered 7 and 8 annexed to the Investigator's file titled "Documents relating to the Investigator's testimony". This file contains documents prepared by the Prosecution's Investigator, Mr. Karugaba ("Witness Karugaba"), and was disclosed on 11 May 2004 (R.P. 1572 2086). The Appeals Chamber further notes that these maps were not admitted as exhibits. Exhibits P18, P19 and P20 are the only maps, which were admitted before the Trial Chamber.

305 Simba Appeal Brief, para. 353.

306 Prosecution Response, paras 167, 169-170, 181.

307 Prosecution Response, para. 169.

308 Prosecution Response, para. 179.

309 Prosecution Response, para. 174. *See also* para. 179.

310 Prosecution Response, paras 179-180.

at 9:00 a.m. the same day, when it should have considered "all possible time-sequence combinations", including the distance between the places and the time necessary to travel between them.[311] He further submits that the Trial Chamber erred by failing to question the credibility of the Prosecution witnesses given that Witness KEI did not testify that the Appellant went to Kaduha Parish after leaving Murambi Technical School.[312] With respect to the issue of the time necessary to travel from one crime scene to the other, the Appellant submits that there is a clerical mistake in the Defence Expert Report and that it should read that the alleged distance travelled by the Appellant on 21 April 1994 could only be done in 5 "hours" rather than "days".[313] The Appellant seeks the admission of Witness TER's statement as additional evidence and submits **[page 48]** that refusing this new evidence would occasion a miscarriage of justice. In the alternative, he requests that the Appeals Chamber visit the crime sites or assign an independent expert to do so.[314]

150. At the outset, the Appeals Chamber notes that it has already dismissed the Appellant's arguments regarding the credibility of Prosecution witnesses who testified in relation to the massacres at Murambi Technical School and Kaduha Parish, with the exception of the contention that the Trial Chamber erred in relying on Witness KXX with regard to the time of the Appellant's arrival at Kaduha Parish.[315] These arguments will not be revisited here. Moreover, the Appeals Chamber recalls that some of the Appellant's requests related to this issue have previously been considered and rejected in the Decision on Rule 115 Evidence of 21 May 2007. Witness TER's statement was neither found to be part of the trial record nor admitted as additional evidence on appeal. Similarly, the Appellant's requests for the Appeals Chamber to either conduct a site-visit or assign an independent expert to do so were rejected.[316] The Appeals Chamber therefore restricts its consideration here to the issue of the alleged impossibility for the Appellant to be present at both massacres sites in the time-frame emerging from the credible evidence.

151. With regard to the Appellant's argument that the Trial Chamber might have been misled by a map annexed to the Prosecution investigator's file which shows that there is another place named Murambi located closer to Kaduha than the actual Murambi Technical School, where the massacre took place on 21 April 1994, the Appeals Chamber finds this to be mere speculation unsupported by any evidence. Under these circumstances, the Appeals Chamber can only conclude that the Trial Chamber did not take into account this map in its assessment of the geographical aspects of the case.[317]

152. Turning to the issue of distance and driving time, the Appeals Chamber recalls that a Trial Chamber has the obligation to provide a reasoned opinion,[318] but is not required to articulate the reasoning in detail.[319] Although certain evidence may not have been referred to by a Trial Chamber, in the particular circumstances of a given case it may nevertheless be reasonable to assume that the Trial Chamber took it into account.[320] There is no guiding principle on the question to determine **[page 49]** the extent to which a Trial Chamber is obliged to set out its reasons for accepting or rejecting a particular testimony.[321]

153. The Appeals Chamber notes that the material fact at issue during trial was whether the Appellant was present at both Murambi Technical School and Kaduha Parish in the early morning of 21 April 1994. The Trial Chamber found that there was evidence of the Appellant's presence there. The issue to be resolved by the Appeals Chamber is therefore whether the Trial Chamber erred in fact by finding that the evidence presented by the Appellant did not cast any reasonable doubt on the Appellant's presence at the two places. One way for the Appellant to cast reasonable doubt on this evidence was to show that it was impossible to travel between the two places in a lapse of time compatible with the time-frame arising from the testimonies

---

311 Simba Reply, paras 111-115.

312 Simba Reply, paras 115-118.

313 Simba Reply, para. 128.

314 Simba Reply, paras 124 -125, 129.

315 *See above* Sections D-2 and D-3.

316 Decision on Rule 115 Evidence of 21 May 2007, paras 18-19, 61.

317 *See above* fn. 304.

318 Article 22(2) of the Statute and Rule 98(C) of the Rules.

319 *Kamuhanda* Appeal Judgement, para. 32; *Kajelijeli* Appeal Judgement, para. 59; *Semanza* Appeal Judgement, paras 130, 149; *Niyitegeka* Appeal Judgement, para 124; *Rutaganda* Appeal Judgement, para. 536; *Musema* Appeal Judgement, paras 18, 277; *Delalić et al.* .Appeal Judgement, para. 481.

320 *Musema* Appeal Judgement, para. 19.

321 *Musema* Appeal Judgement, para. 18.

of Witnesses KSY and YH.[322] The Trial Chamber's findings that the Appellant was successively at Murambi Technical School and then Kaduha Parish on that morning indicate that it did not view the evidence introduced by the Appellant on this point as being sufficient to cast any reasonable doubt on his presence at either site.[323]

154. The Trial Chamber did not explicitly address the issues of distance and driving times in the Trial Judgement, merely noting that Murambi Technical School, Kaduha Parish and Cyanika Parish were "geographically proximate locations".[324] The Appeals Chamber notes that findings on both the distance between and the time necessary to travel from one site to the other were of importance as they directly affected whether it would have been possible for the Appellant to participate in the massacres at both sites in the relatively short time-frame at issue. The Trial Chamber accepted the time-frame given by the Prosecution witnesses regarding the Appellant's presence at both sites. Relying on Witness KSY, the Trial Chamber concluded that the Appellant was at Murambi around 7:00 a.m. on 21 April 1994.[325] There is no specific finding as to when the Appellant left the area, but the Trial Chamber observed that Witness KSY saw the Appellant for around 15 minutes. On the basis of the testimony of Witness KXX, the Trial Chamber found that the Appellant arrived at Kaduha Parish around 9:00 a.m. the same day, discarding the earlier arrival time (around 8:20 a.m.) suggested by Witness YH.[326] **[page 50]**

155. Having made these findings as to times of arrival at the two massacre sites, the Trial Chamber failed to expressly discuss the Defence evidence to the effect that it was impossible for the Appellant to travel from Murambi Technical School to Kaduha Parish within this time-frame. The issue was clearly controversial and the evidence presented by the parties in this respect was contradictory. The Trial Chamber should have been clearer in finding that the Appellant was at both Murambi Technical School and Kaduha Parish, which the Trial Chamber deemed geographically proximate, thereby rejecting his argument regarding impossibility. However, the failure to be more explicit does not indicate the lack of a reasoned judgement, particularly in light of the approximate nature of the evidence offered by Witnesses KSY, YH and AJT1 as discussed in subsequent paragraphs.

156. Contrary to the Appellant's contention, the Trial Chamber was not compelled to question the credibility of the Prosecution witnesses in light of the fact that Witness KEI did not testify that the Appellant went directly to Kaduha Parish after leaving Murambi Technical School. The Trial Chamber expressly rejected all uncorroborated aspects of Witness KEI's testimony; it is thus consistent that it did not accept the witness's account that the Appellant went to the Gendarmerie camp after the attack against Murambi Technical School.[327]

157. According to Prosecution Witness Karugaba, the shortest non-tarmac road between the two massacre sites was 25-30 km long.[328] Defence Witness AJT1 testified that the distance between the two locations could be covered in one and a half hours.[329] This evaluation is not necessarily contradicted by the Defence Expert Report, which stated that during the rainy season this trip could take three hours, with a solid car.[330] No

---

322 *See Kamuhanda* Appeal Judgement, para. 40.

323 *Kamuhanda* Appeal Judgement, para. 40.

324 Trial Judgement, para. 401. The other paragraphs of the Trial Judgement quoted in the Prosecution Response do not give any relevant information about the Trial Chamber's reasoning in support of its findings that the Appellant was seen successively at Murambi Technical School and Kaduha Parish in the early morning of 21 April 1994. *See* Prosecution Response, para. 169, fn. 250, referring to Trial Judgement, paras 134, 399, 401, 402.

325 Trial Judgement, paras 113, 117.

326 The Appeals Chamber has already concluded that this finding is erroneous since it contradicts the Trial Chamber's previous finding that it would rely on Witness KXX only if corroborated (*see above* Section D(3)(d), para. 143).

327 *See* Trial Judgement, para. 112, read together with paras 100, 107 (on the ground that the credibility of Witness KEI was questionable).

328 Witness Karugaba pointed out the locations on a map which was admitted as Exhibit P19. He estimated the driving distance between Gikongoro town and Kaduha as 50 km via Cyanika and 25-30 km via Murambi, and the driving distance between Gikongoro town and Murambi as 2 km. (T. 8 November 2004 pp. 7-8).

329 T. 11 March 2005 p. 27.

330 According to the Defence Expert Report, it would have taken three hours during the rainy season to travel between them, without taking into account the presence of road-blocks. The Defence Expert Report also asserted that it would have taken five days to travel the distances which the Appellant had, according to the Indictment, travelled on 21 April 1994 (Exh. D 156, Defence Expert Report, p. 47). The Appeals Chamber notes that the Appellant submits that this was in fact a clerical error, and that the expert meant

evidence was brought that showed that the road conditions **[page 51]** were affected by rain at the relevant time; the simple fact that April falls within the rainy season is not sufficient to demonstrate that the roads were actually in bad condition on the day at issue.[331]

158. The Appeals Chamber notes that both Witness KSY and Witness YH gave only approximate times of their respective sightings of the Appellant on the 21 April at Murambi Technical School. Witness KSY testified that he saw the Appellant arriving at Murambi Technical School at "around" 7:00 a.m. on 21 April 1994 and that he observed the Appellant during a period of "about" 15 minutes.[332] A reading of the relevant transcripts clearly shows that Witness KSY only intended to give estimated times.[333] Similarly, Witness YH did not give a precise time for the arrival of the Appellant at Kaduha Parish. Witness YH first indicated during the examination-in-chief that he (Witness YH) arrived at Kaduha Parish "between about 8:00 and 9:00 in the morning [of 21 April 1994]"[334] and that the Appellant arrived 20 minutes after his arrival at Kaduha Parish.[335] The Trial Chamber duly acknowledged the fact that these witnesses intended in general to provide an approximate time-frame for the events they reported in their testimony.

159. Similarly, nothing in Defence Witness AJT1's testimony indicates that she intended to provide an exact calculation of the minimum travel time required to go from Kaduha to Murambi.[336] The Appeals Chamber finds that in light of the troubling context of the events reported by the witnesses and the long period of time that elapsed between the events and the taking of the testimony (a decade in the instant case), the times indicated by the witnesses must be considered as mere approximations, the approach taken by the Trial Chamber. In light of the approximations given by the witnesses, a reasonable trier of fact could have found beyond a reasonable doubt that **[page 52]** the times articulated by them were, in fact, quite flexible and created a window during which Simba could have been present at both Murambi Technical School and Kaduha Parish on the morning of 21 April 1994. The Appeals Chamber finds, therefore, that the Appellant has not demonstrated that the Trial Chamber erred in so finding.

5. The Ntyazo Public Meeting of 22 May 1994

160. The Appellant contends that the Trial Chamber erred by relying on the uncorroborated testimony of Witness YC to find that the Appellant made an inflammatory speech against Tutsi at a public meeting in Ntyazo Commune on 22 May 1994, and by rejecting the Appellant's account of that speech which was

---

"5 hours" rather than five days, without presenting arguments in support of this submission. However, since the issue at stake is limited to the question of the distance between Murambi and Kaduha and the time necessary to cover that distance, and not the time necessary to travel all the distances which the Indictment alleged that the Appellant covered on 21 April 1994, the Appeals Chamber does not deem it necessary to make any findings on this point. *See also Corrigendum à l'annexe Ia des conclusions de la Défense d'Aloys Simba*, 4 July 2005 (strictly confidentially filed); Prosecution closing arguments (T. 7 July 2005 pp. 11-12); Defence closing arguments (T. 7 July 2005 pp. 57-58).

331 The Appeals Chamber notes that the Defence failed to ask the witnesses if it was raining on 21 April 1994. It asked Witness Karugaba (T. 9 November 2004 pp. 8-10) and Witness KSY whether it was the rainy season at that time. However, in contrast with the line of questioning pursued by the Defence, Witness KSY answered that indeed it was normally the rainy season, but on the days before 21 April 1994 it had not rained in the area of Murambi (T. 31 August 2004 p. 13).

332 T. 30 August 204 p. 28; Trial Judgement, para. 92.

333 Trial Judgement, paras 113, 117, 118. T. 30 August 2004 p. 28 ("Q. Now, at around what time of the morning did Aloys Simba arrive at Murambi Technical Institute? A. It was around 7:00 in the morning."). T. 30 August 2004 p. 29 ("Q. And, approximately, how long did this visit by Simba last, Witness? A. He was there for about 15 minutes."). In cross-examination, the Defence asked Witness KSY to confirm the time of arrival of the Appellant at Murambi Technical School. Witness KSY did not respond directly. The Defence did not enquire further on this question (T. 30 August 2004 p. 47).

334 T. 21 September 2004 p. 35 ("Q. And at around what time of the day did you see Aloys Simba at Kaduha parish on the 21st of April 1994? A. It was between about 8:00 and 9:00 in the morning.").

335 T. 21 September 2004 p. 35 ("A. [...] So we got up early, between 7 and 9 a.m., and 20 minutes after my arrival, Colonel Simba also arrived there [Kaduha Parish] and I saw him."). T. 21 September 2004 pp. 36-37 (Later, still in examination-in-chief, "A. We got to Kaduha at around 8:00. Q. And approximately how long after your arrival did Colonel Simba arrive at Kaduha parish? A. He got there some minutes after our arrival."). The Defence did not question Witness YH on the times of the Appellant's arrival and stay at Kaduha Parish (T. 22 September 2004; T. 23 September 2004).

336 T. 11 March 2005 p. 27. During cross-examination, the Prosecution questioned Witness AJT1 on the time it would take to travel between Kaduha Parish and Murambi ("A. [w]ell, Murambi is farther away than Kaduha, and you have to pass through Kaduha to reach Murambi, so you have to add one and an half hour [...]".). The Prosecution did not pursue this line of questioning to Witness AJT1 (T. 11 March 2005 p. 27).

corroborated by Witness GM1.[337] He submits that it is absurd to find that he would have suddenly decided to incite people to kill the Tutsi a moment after he had urged the members of the population to embrace peace and defend their homeland alongside the national army.[338] The Appellant further argues that the fact that Witness YC was better placed than Witness GMI to hear the Appellant's speech does not mean that Witness YC was more credible than the latter.[339] He also contends that the Trial Chamber should have considered Witness YC's testimony with caution since he confessed to having participated in the genocide, and since his cooperation with the Rwandan authorities was clearly an attempt to obtain a reduced sentence.[340] Finally, the Appellant submits that Witness YC's testimony was inaccurate insofar as it described the Appellant as a civil defence advisor in Butare and Gikongoro.[341]

161. The Prosecution responds that the Trial Chamber adopted the correct approach in assessing the testimonies of Witnesses YC and GM1 and that the Appellant has failed to demonstrate any error of fact leading to a miscarriage of justice.[342]

162. The Appeals Chamber notes that the Trial Chamber's finding that the Appellant made an inflammatory speech against Tutsi at a public meeting in Ntyazo Commune on 22 May 1994 does not underlie any conviction, nor does it support any subsequent finding in relation to the sentence. Indeed, the Trial Chamber found that the Prosecution did not prove the allegation that Tutsi were killed as a result of the Appellant's speech. As the Appellant fails to demonstrate that the alleged errors occasioned a miscarriage of justice, this sub-ground of appeal is dismissed. **[page 53]**

E. Alleged Errors in the Assessment of the Defence Evidence

163. The Appellant submits, under various sub-grounds of appeal, that the Trial Chamber committed errors of law and fact in its assessment of Defence evidence.

164. As a preliminary matter, the Appeals Chamber declines to address a number of the Appellant's submissions for lack of arguments. First, the Appellant alleges that the Trial Chamber contradicted itself in finding that the Appellant was in Kigali and Gitarama from 6-13 April 1994 and that "he might have left Gitarama on 12 April when the Interim Government was being installed there".[343] The Appeals Chamber notes that the Trial Chamber accepted the Appellant's alibi with respect to the period of 6-13 April 1994[344] and no convictions rest on the findings pertaining to this period. As a result, the Appeals Chamber's intervention is not warranted since the alleged error could not have occasioned a miscarriage of justice.

165. Similarly, the Appeals Chamber will not consider the Appellant's claim that the Trial Chamber erred by distorting the facts in finding that the Appellant was on his way to Gikongoro when he met Witness MIB and his wife[345] since he has failed to elaborate on this sub-ground of appeal in his Appeal Brief.[346]

166. Further, the Appellant claims that the Trial Chamber erred by declining to accept in its entirety the alibi for the period of 14-24 April 1994, despite the multiple corroborations of alibi witnesses.[347] In this

337 Simba Notice of Appeal, II-B-1 and II-B-2.

338 Simba Appeal Brief, para. 357.

339 Simba Appeal Brief, para. 358.

340 Simba Notice of Appeal, II-B-1.

341 Simba Notice of Appeal, II-B-1. *See also* Simba Reply, para. 131.

342 Prosecution Response, para. 183.

343 Simba Notice of Appeal, I-D-9; Simba Appeal Brief, para. 264, referring to Trial Judgement, paras 343-377. *See* Prosecution Response, paras 112-103, 112; Simba Reply, paras 49-50; AT. 22 May 2007 pp. 18-19.

344 Trial Judgement, paras 341-349

345 Simba Notice of Appeal, II-C-12. *See also* Simba Appeal Brief, para. 379; Simba Reply, para. 133. In his Appeal Brief (para. 379) the Appellant merely refers to another part of the same brief (paras 191-212), but does not elaborate on the specific contention that the Trial Chamber misrepresented Witness MIB's testimony. The Appeals Chamber notes that the Appellant's submissions point erroneously to paragraph 464 of the Trial Judgement, while paragraphs 374 to 376 of the Trial Judgement seem more relevant to the Appellant's apparent argument. However, contrary to the Appellant's contention, these paragraphs show clearly that the Trial Chamber took into account the evidence that the Appellant was travelling to Gikongoro "in order to see if the roads were sufficiently safe to relocate there" and accepted that he turned back to Gitarama town when he was warned by Witness MIB that it was too dangerous to continue his way with Tutsi accompanying him (Trial Judgement, para. 375).

346 Simba Appeal Brief, para. 379, referring to Simba Appeal Brief, paras 191-212.

347 Simba Notice of Appeal, II-D-2; Simba Appeal Brief, para. 384, referring to Simba Appeal Brief, paras 184-252.

respect, the Appellant relies on arguments advanced in the context of other sub-grounds of appeal which are addressed elsewhere in the Trial Judgement. As no separate error on the part of the Trial Chamber is advanced, the Appeals Chamber need not address these arguments here.

167. The Appeals Chamber also declines to address the challenge that the Trial Chamber contradicted itself when it allegedly failed to conclude that "the alibi had raised a reasonable doubt **[page 54]** in the Prosecution case".[348] The Appellant is in fact asserting that the Trial Chamber erred in law in failing to apply the proper legal standard to the alibi evidence. This general contention overlaps with the Appellant's more specific allegations of error relating to the assessment of the alibi evidence which will be considered below, and does not call for a separate analysis by the Appeals Chamber.

168. The Appeals Chamber further declines to address the Appellant's contention that the Trial Chamber erred in failing to consider the Defence Expert Report in relation to the massacres that occurred at Murambi Technical School and Kaduha Parish, since this report makes only limited submissions to the effect that the Indictment exaggerated the number of victims at these places, an issue which is not at stake on appeal.[349]

169. Finally, the Appeals Chamber will not address the following allegations of error since they fall outside the scope of the grounds set out in the Notice of Appeal: in relation to Prosecution Witness YH's testimony placing the Appellant at a meeting at *Centre Intercommunal de perfectionnement du personnel* ("CIPEP") around 16 April 1994, and the link between these statements and Defence Witness SBL1's testimony;[350] in the assessment of the diary of the Appellant;[351] and in the assessment of the Appellant's letters with respect to dates of his departure from Gikongoro.[352]

170. The Appeals Chamber will now address the remaining arguments in turn.

1. Alleged Failure to Consider Report by Defence Expert Witness Dr. Pascal Ndengejeho

171. The Appellant contends that the Trial Judgement failed to consider the Defence Expert Report of Dr. Pascal Ndengejeho in relation to the massacres that occurred at various sites, the physical impossibility of committing the crimes charged because of the distance between Murambi Technical School and Kaduha Parish, the Appellant's alibi, or his motive.[353] According to the Appellant, the Trial Chamber implicitly suggested that the report was irrelevant[354] when it "touched **[page 55]** upon crucial issues" such as the Appellant's alibi.[355] The Appellant claims that this failure occasioned a miscarriage of justice.[356] As a corollary submission, the Appellant contends that the Trial Chamber erred by refusing to admit statements of BJK1, since they were discussed in and annexed to the Defence Expert Report, which was admitted into evidence and not challenged by the Prosecution.[357]

172. The Prosecution responds that the Trial Judgement mentions the evidence of this Defence expert witness and the fact that it was considered and assessed by the Trial Chamber. The Prosecution submits that "[i]n the absence of any substantiated submission of the Appellant supporting an allegation of erroneous assessment of evidence and failure to provide a reasoned opinion, it is reasonable to assume that the Trial

348 Simba Notice of Appeal I-D-8; Simba Appeal Brief, para. 263.

349 Defence Expert Report, pp. 48-49.

350 Simba Appeal Brief, paras 224-227, referring to Trial Judgement, para. 378. The latter paragraph refers to Witness YF. This is evidently a typographical error, as confirmed by reference to paragraph 144 of the Trial Judgement where the same testimony is said to have been given by Witness YH.

351 Simba Appeal Brief, paras 230-232.

352 Simba Appeal Brief, paras 233-236.

353 Simba Notice of Appeal, I-C-1, I-C-3, I-E-4, II-D-6; Simba Appeal Brief, paras 102-107, 271-272, 393-394. The Appeals Chamber need not consider here the Appellant's challenge to the extent it relates to the motive of the Appellant to commit the crimes. This is considered above under Section C2(c), paras 87-88 and below under Section H-3, paras 261-270.

354 Simba Appeal Brief, para. 102.

355 Simba Appeal Brief, para. 103.

356 Simba Notice of Appeal, II-D-6; Simba Appeal Brief, paras 393-394. *See also* Prosecution Response, para. 79; Simba Reply, paras 47, 49-50, 134.

357 Simba Appeal Brief, para. 104.

Chamber has taken the report into account".[358] With respect to the Appellant's submission regarding BJK1's statements, the Prosecution responds that no error on part of the Trial Chamber is demonstrated.[359]

173. The Appeals Chamber recalls that, while required to give a reasoned opinion, the trier of fact is not obliged to articulate every step of its reasoning.[360] In that light, the Appellant clearly fails to demonstrate how the Trial Chamber erred in not considering the Defence Expert Report in explicit terms. The Appeals Chamber further recalls its earlier finding that the evidence provided in the Defence Expert Report did not necessarily contradict the evidence that the Appellant was present at the two massacre sites within the relevant time-frame.[361] Therefore this challenge can be readily dismissed.

174. The Appeals Chamber further notes that the evidence of an expert witness is meant to provide specialised knowledge that may assist the fact finder to understand the evidence presented.[362] It is for the Trial Chamber to decide whether, on the basis of the evidence presented by the parties, the person proposed can be admitted as an expert witness.[363] Just as for any other **[page 56]** evidence presented, it is for the Trial Chamber to assess the reliability and probative value of the expert report and testimony.

175. In the instant case, the Appeals Chamber notes that, contrary to the Appellant's assertion,[364] the Defence Expert Report was admitted subject to express reservations entered by the Prosecution,[365] disputing both the qualifications of the Defence Expert Witness and the contents of the report. However, the Appeals Chamber need not address the question as to whether the Defence Expert Report was validly admitted[366] since the Prosecution is not challenging this point.

176. The Defence Expert Report was mentioned once in the Trial Judgement, in paragraph 12, with the Trial Chamber noting that the Report "focuses primarily on the role of civil defence", a statement consistent with the title of the Defence Expert Report. However, only a limited express reference to the Defence Expert Report does not imply that the Trial Chamber failed to consider it or considered that it was "irrelevant".

177. Regarding the issue of the alibi, the Defence Expert Report was of limited assistance to the Trial Chamber, merely summarising prospective defence evidence and setting out the Appellant's theory that the Appellant was in Gitarama from 13-22 or 23 April 1994 and only arrived in Gikongoro on 23 April 1994.[367] It provided no expert opinion which could have assisted the Trial Chamber in its analysis, but instead ventured beyond the scope of the expertise and provided an opinion on the ultimate issue on the case.

178. The Appeals Chamber further notes that no less than 18 pages of the Trial Judgement address the alibi.[368] On the basis of a careful review of the alibi evidence, the Trial Chamber found it to be convincing with respect to the period 6-13 April 1994,[369] but not for the period 14-24 April 1994. The Trial Chamber

358 Prosecution Response, para. 78.

359 Prosecution Response, para. 79.

360 *Gacumbitsi* Appeal Judgement, para. 65; *Kajelijeli* Appeal Judgement, para. 147..

361 *See above* Section D-4, paras 157-159.

362 *Semanza* Appeal Judgement, para. 303. *See also* The *Prosecutor v. Casimir Bizimungu, Justin Mugenzi, Jérôme-Clément Bicamumpaka, Prosper Mugiraneza,* Case No. ICTR-99-50-T, Decision on Casimir Bizimungu's Urgent Motion for the Exclusion of the Report and Testimony of Déo Sebahire Mbonyinkebe (Rule 89(C)), 2 September 2005, para. 11; *The Prosecutor v. Théoneste Bagosora et al.,* Case No. ICTR-98-41-T, Decision on Motion for Exclusion of Expert Witness Statement of Filip Reyntjens, 28 September 2004, para. 8; *The Prosecutor v. Jean-Paul Akayesu,* Case No. ICTR-96-4-T, Decision on a Defence Motion for the Appearance of an Accused as an Expert Witness, 9 March 1998, p. 2.

363 *The Prosecutor v. Sylvestre Gacumbitsi*, Case No. ICTR-01-64-T, Decision on Expert Witnesses for the Defence, Articles 54, 73, 89 and 94 *bis* of the Rules of Procedure and Evidence, 11 November 2003, para. 8.

364 The Appellant claimed that the Expert Report was accepted by the Trial Chamber and the Prosecutor, who at no time criticised its content or its author's qualifications (Simba Appeal Brief, para. 105).

365 The Prosecution Notice in Respect of the Defence Expert Report of Dr. Pascal Ndengejeho, filed on 29 March 2005, p. 2.

366 It appears that the Trial Chamber admitted the report as evidence without following the procedure prescribed in Rule 94 *bis* of the Rules which envisages cross-examination of the expert where a report's contents are challenged by the other party. It is unclear whether the Trial Chamber considered before admitting the Defence Expert Report whether Dr. Pascal Ndengejeho had specialised knowledge that could assist the Trial Chamber to understand the evidence presented at trial.

367 The Defence Expert Report made only a brief reference to the alibi at pages 41-42 (The Simba Appeal Brief refers to pages 41-50, but only page 42 is directly related to the alibi). It refers in passing to the statements of Witness AJT1 and three persons who did not testify at trial: Witnesses HWH, HJT1, and Alison Des Forges.

368 Trial Judgement, paras 296-384.

369 Trial Judgement, paras 349-384.

considered the evidence given by 10 Defence witnesses (the Appellant, SML2, MIB, FMP1, FKP2, AJT1, AJG7, SIH, GMA3 and GL3).The Appeals Chamber recalls that a trier of fact is not obliged to state in detail, each step of its reasoning. Thus, the absence of **[page 57]** reference to the Defence Expert Report in this respect does not mean that the Trial Chamber did not take it into account in its assessment.

179. With regard to the statements of BJK1, the alleged error concerning the denial of their separate admission has been addressed and dismissed above and will not be revisited here.[370] Concerning their status as annexes to the Defence Expert Report, these statements form part of the trial record only to the extent that they support the Defence Expert's analysis regarding the issues addressed in the Report, which the Appeals Chamber already found to be of limited assistance.

180. The Appellant has not demonstrated that the Trial Chamber erred by failing to consider the Defence Expert Report.

2. Alleged Errors in Relation to the Alibi

181. The Appellant makes several other submissions to the effect that the Trial Chamber erred in relation to the alibi.[371]

(a) Alleged Error Relating to the Burden of Proof

182. The Appellant contends that the Trial Chamber impermissibly reversed the burden of proof with respect to the alibi evidence[372] in particular when it concluded at paragraph 384 of the Trial Judgement as follows:

> However, when considering the evidence of the alibi, together with the Prosecution evidence, the Chamber has no doubt that on 21 April Simba was in Gikongoro prefecture at Murambi Technical School and at Kaduha Parish.

The Appellant submits that the language of this paragraph suggests that the Trial Chamber "compared" the merits of the alibi with the Prosecution evidence, while the correct legal standard required the Trial Chamber to assess whether the alibi evidence cast reasonable doubt on the Prosecution's case.[373] According to the Appellant, the Trial Chamber should have drawn the inference that the alibi had raised a reasonable doubt with respect to the Prosecution case.[374] **[page 58]**

183. The Prosecution responds that the Appellant has not identified any error in the Trial Chamber's approach, and that his allegations should be dismissed.[375]

184. The Trial Chamber correctly set out the legal standard on alibi evidence when stating:

> In assessing the alibi, the Chamber recalls that it is settled jurisprudence before the two *ad hoc* Tribunals that in putting forward an alibi, a defendant need only produce evidence likely to raise a reasonable doubt in the Prosecution case. The alibi does not carry a separate burden. The burden of proving beyond reasonable doubt the facts charged remains squarely on the shoulders of the Prosecution. Indeed, it is incumbent on the Prosecution to establish beyond reasonable doubt that, despite the alibi, the facts alleged are nevertheless true.[376]

185. The Appeals Chamber is further satisfied that the Trial Chamber correctly applied this standard in its subsequent findings on alibi. The Trial Chamber first found that, although the alibi evidence for the period of 6-13 April 1994 "[did] not account for every moment of [the Appellant's time], viewed as a whole and

---

370 *See above* Chapter II, Section A-2, paras 19-25.

371 Simba Notice of Appeal, I-B-4, I-B-7; AT. 22 May 2007 pp. 8-9, 44.

372 Simba Notice of Appeal, I-B-4, I-B-7; Simba Appeal Brief, paras 83, 86, 92, 94. *See also* Prosecution Response, paras 61-63, 111; Simba Reply, paras 49-50. The Appeals Chamber need not consider the unsubstantiated allegation made under Ground I-B-4 that the Trial Chamber erred in its findings at paragraph 378. The Appeals Chamber also declines to consider the Appellant's unsubstantiated contention that the Trial Chamber failed to apply "the principles governing the burden of proof, for [Defence] witnesses [AJT1 and SML2 who] raise a reasonable doubt" as to the Prosecution's allegations (Simba Appeal Brief, para. 219); AT. 22 May 2007 pp. 14-15.

373 Simba Appeal Brief, para. 94.

374 Simba Appeal Brief, para. 263.

375 Prosecution Response, paras 61-63.

376 Trial Judgement, para. 303 (footnote omitted).

when weighed against the Prosecution evidence, it [provided] a reasonable and satisfactory explanation for [the Appellant's] activities [for this period]."[377] The Appeals Chamber notes that this wording reflects that in assessing the alibi evidence for this period the Trial Chamber did not require the Defence to prove its case beyond reasonable doubt. Instead, the Trial Chamber found that the Prosecution had not eliminated the reasonable possibility that the Appellant was in Kigali between 6-13 April 1994, that this reinforced the doubt the Trial Chamber expressed in relation to Prosecution Witness KEL's testimony, and that there was not "sufficient and reliable evidence to establish that [the Appellant] on or about 9 April urged *Interahamwe* to kill Tutsi in Kibeho, as alleged in paragraphs 23(d) and 56 of the Indictment".[378]

186. It is apparent that the Trial Chamber applied the same standard with regard to the second period of the alibi, 14-24 April 1994, but that, this time, it did not find that the alibi had raised doubt with respect to the Prosecution evidence:

> After viewing the evidence of the alibi in its totality, it is understandable that Simba stayed for a brief period of time in Gitarama town after his arrival on 13 April. In the Chamber's view, however, the concerns outlined above, as well as first-hand corroborated Prosecution evidence, eliminate the reasonable possibility that he remained in Gitarama after 16 April. The Chamber accepts that Simba might have continued to travel to various localities outside of Gikongoro after that time. However, when considering the evidence of the alibi, together with the Prosecution evidence, the Chamber has no doubt that on 21 April Simba was in Gikongoro prefecture at Murambi Technical School and at Kaduha Parish.[379]

The Appeals Chamber sees no error of law in this finding. **[page 59]**

187. Similarly, the Appellant fails to show that the Trial Chamber shifted the burden of proof with regard to the allegations in relation to the attacks against Murambi Technical School and Kaduha Parish when it stated that the "numerous inconsistencies in the alibi eliminate the reasonable possibility that [the Appellant] was in Gitarama at the time of the attack[s]".[380] It is clear from paragraph 384 of the Trial Judgement that the Trial Chamber found that the Prosecution had proven the Appellant's presence at Murambi Technical School and Kaduha Parish on 21 April 1994 beyond reasonable doubt. It is equally clear that it found that the alibi relied upon by the Appellant did not cast any doubt on the Prosecution's case. The Appellant's argument on this point is therefore without merit.

188. The Appellant further alleges that at paragraph 121 of the Trial Judgement, the Trial Chamber shifted the burden of proof by finding Prosecution Witness KSY credible based on the sole fact that the alibi contained numerous contradictions.[381]

189. The Appeals Chamber notes that the Appellant's challenge regarding Witness KSY is based on a misreading of paragraph 121 of the Trial Judgement. The Trial Chamber assessed the witness's credibility in detail at paragraphs 114-115 and 117-119 of the Trial Judgement, before it concluded at paragraph 121 that "Witness KSY's reliable testimony and the numerous inconsistencies in the alibi eliminate the reasonable possibility that Simba was in Gitarama at the time of the attack". The conclusion regarding Witness KSY's credibility is based on the detailed analysis of his evidence set out in the Trial Judgement. The reference to inconsistencies in the alibi merely highlights the fact that the alibi failed to raise a reasonable doubt with respect to the Prosecution case.

190. Finally, the Appellant alleges that in paragraph 177 of the Trial Judgement, the Trial Chamber shifted the burden of proof by finding Prosecution Witness YH credible based on the fact that the alibi contained inconsistencies.[382] The Appeals Chamber disagrees. As noted above, the Trial Chamber assessed Witness YH's credibility in detail.[383] The Trial Chamber's conclusion that "Witness YH's reliable and corroborated testimony as well as the numerous inconsistencies in the alibi eliminate the reasonable possibility that Simba

377 Trial Judgement, para. 349.
378 Trial Judgement, para. 85.
379 Trial Judgement, para. 384.
380 Trial Judgement, paras 121, 177.
381 Simba Notice of Appeal, I-B-4; Simba Appeal Brief, para. 83.
382 Simba Notice of Appeal, I-B-4; Simba Appeal Brief, para. 86.
383 Trial Judgement, Chapter II, Section 6-3.

was in Gitarama at the time of the attack" reflects only that the Prosecution proved its case beyond reasonable doubt, and that the alibi failed to raise a reasonable doubt in this regard.

191. Accordingly, these sub-grounds of appeal are dismissed. **[page 60]**

(b) Alleged Errors in the Assessment of the Evidence on Alibi

(i) Alleged Errors Relating to the Assessment of the Evidence of Witnesses AJT1 and SML2

192. The Appellant submits that the Trial Chamber made a number of errors in its assessment of evidence given by Defence witnesses. First, it is submitted that the Trial Chamber distorted the facts in relation to the testimonies of the Appellant and of Defence Witnesses AJT1 and SML2 with regard to the date of his departure for Gikongoro.[384] This claim is not supported by any further argument and is therefore dismissed without further consideration.

193. The Appeals Chamber readily dismisses the contention that the Trial Chamber distorted the evidence of Witness SML2 when it stated at paragraph 377 of the Trial Judgement that "Witness SML2's account of the journey to Gikongoro prefecture also suggests an earlier departure [since she] described *Interahamwe* surrounding Kaduha Parish as the group passed the parish". In his brief the Appellant merely asserts without demonstration that this finding is inconsistent with Witness SML2's testimony.[385]

194. By the same token, the Appeals Chamber readily dismisses the Appellant's submissions that the Trial Chamber erred in both law and fact by failing to consider "the satisfaction expressed by the [Prosecution] regarding [his] alibi" and to draw the proper inferences therefrom, following investigations conducted by the Prosecution in Kigali, Gitarama and Musebeya.[386] The Appellant fails to demonstrate that the Prosecution did indeed accept the alibi evidence of Witness AJT1. The Appellant's submission appears to be based on a misinterpretation of an internal Prosecution e-mail forwarded to the Defence on 16 March 2005 (Defence Exhibit 138). In this message, B. Egbe, Senior Trial Attorney for the Prosecution, declared that photographs taken at a compound shown to him by Witness AJT1 at Gitarama came out blank and that he "was satisfied with the written and signed statement of the witness and therefore saw no need to ask for another mission to repeat the snap shots of the compounds".[387] The satisfaction expressed in this message clearly relates to the description and location of the compound by Witness AJT1 and not to the entire testimony of that witness in relation to the alibi. Contrary to the Appellant's submission, nothing in B. Egbe's statement indicates that the Prosecution accepted the Appellant's alibi. As it is the duration and the continuous nature of the stay of the Appellant at Gitarama between 14 and 24 April 1994 that is at **[page 61]** issue in the present appeal and not the characteristics of the compound where they stayed, Defence Exhibit 138 was not of relevance to the Trial Chamber in its task.

195. The Appellant submits that the Trial Chamber erred in law by failing to rule on the non-disclosure of pictures taken by the Prosecution investigators in Gitarama and of the Prosecution's investigators report.[388] These pictures were subsequently disclosed during the appeal proceedings,[389] following which the Appellant failed to show how the preparation of his case had been materially prejudiced as a result of the Prosecution's failure to disclose the pictures at trial.[390]

---

384 Simba Notice of Appeal, II-C-11. In his Appeal Brief, the Appellant merely refers to other parts of his brief, without articulating any argument in support of his claim (Simba Appeal Brief, para. 378, referring to paras 213-223).

385 Simba Appeal Brief, para 221

386 Simba Notice of Appeal, I-E-2, II-D-5; Simba Appeal Brief, paras 391, 392, 395. *See also* Simba Reply, paras 49-50, 135.

387 Simba Appeal Brief, para. 95.

388 Simba Notice of Appeal, I-E-3. *See also* Prosecution Response, para. 114; Simba Reply, paras 49-50. There is no need to discuss the Appellant's claim related to the non-disclosure of the Prosecution's investigator's report since the Prosecution has informed the Appeals Chamber that such a report does not exist (Prosecution's Memorandum, 18 May 2007, para. 2).

389 Prosecution's Memorandum, 18 May 2007.

390 During the appeal hearing, the Appellant claimed that an earlier disclosure of the pictures would have enabled the Defence "to, at the very least, question the witness on specific points, on specific witnesses, and on the sites, so as to consolidate the conviction of the Trial Chamber" (AT. 22 May 2007 pp. 9-10).

196. The Appellant also submits that the Trial Chamber erred in law in its assessment of the evidence of Witnesses AJT1 and SML2 with regard to the Appellant's stay at Gitarama.[391] He submits that the Trial Chamber failed to take into account the fact that these witnesses gave corroborated accounts as to the Appellant's continuous presence. The Appellant also alleges that the Trial Chamber failed to apply the same "treatment or understanding" in assessing Prosecution and Defence alibi witnesses.[392]

197. With respect to the discrepancy noted by the Trial Chamber "between Witness AJT1's testimony and her statement to Tribunal investigators, which indicates that Simba departed Gitarama around the time the interim government relocated there",[393] the Appellant contends that any mistakes were understandable given the stress associated with the long period of time (nearly 11 years) which had elapsed since the events had occurred, her low level of education and the fact that her concentration might have been impaired by the environment of the Tribunal's courtroom.[394]

198. The Appellant further submits that the Trial Chamber confirmed the difficulties encountered by Witness AJT1 as to the dates[395] but that, contrary to the Trial Chamber's observation, Witness AJT1 never testified that she went to Kabgayi on 1 May 1994.[396] He submits that the Trial Chamber should have concluded that the witness confused the dates, since she could not have been informed **[page 62]** on 16 April by the Kaduha survivors of events that had taken place on 21 April 1994.[397] The Appellant alleges that the Trial Chamber used the witness's confusion against the Appellant "in defiance of the principles of presumption of innocence", and in breach of Articles 19 and 20 of the Statute and Rule 89 (B) and (C) of the Rules.[398]

199. The Appeals Chamber notes that the Appellant does not explain how the Trial Chamber erred in its assessment of the evidence of Witnesses AJT1 and SML2. He is merely requesting that the Appeals Chamber substitute an alternative and more favourable assessment of the evidence, without showing how the Trial Chamber erred in law. The Trial Chamber correctly took into account Witness AJT1's inconsistencies as to the dates of her journey to Kabgayi, inconsistencies which the Appellant acknowledges. These dates were crucial to the weight and probative value to be given to her testimony, and it was accordingly open to the Trial Chamber to conclude that the testimony was not capable of casting doubt on the Appellant's presence at Kaduha Parish and Murambi Technical School on 21 April 1994.

200. This sub-ground of appeal is accordingly dismissed.

(ii) Alleged Error Relating to the Date of Arrival of the Appellant at Gikongoro

201. The Appellant submits that the Trial Chamber erred in law in its assessment of the evidence of several Defence Witnesses in relation to his date of arrival at Gikongoro.[399] He contends that the Trial Chamber erred in not accepting that the Appellant arrived at the Crête-Zaïre-Nil Project towards the end of April 1994, more specifically on 24 April, on the basis of the concurring testimonies of Witnesses GMA3, GL3, SIH, SML2, AJT1, AJG7 and the Appellant, as corroborated by Annex XVIII (Annexes 15 and 16) of the Defence Expert Report. The Appellant further claims that "at the very least, these corroborating testimonies cast on the Prosecution's theory a doubt that must benefit the Appellant" and that the discretion of a judge should be based on concurring evidence, and not on biased and unfair assumptions.[400] **[page 63]**

---

391 Simba Notice of Appeal, I-C-15.

392 Simba Appeal Brief, para. 184.

393 Simba Appeal Brief, para. 213, referring to Trial Judgement, para. 378.

394 Simba Appeal Brief, para. 214.

395 Simba Appeal Brief, para. 215, referring to Trial Judgement, fn. 371.

396 Simba Appeal Brief, para. 216.

397 Simba Appeal Brief, paras 215-218, referring to Trial Judgement, fn. 371, where the Trial Chamber notes in relation to the discrepancies between Witness AJT1's testimony and her prior statements that "[i]n addition, the witness's account of seeing the survivors of the Kaduha Parish massacre at Kabgayi on 16 April suggests that she perhaps instead accompanied Simba there on his visit from Gikongoro prefecture on 1 May".

398 Simba Appeal Brief, para. 219; Simba Reply, para. 47.

399 Simba Notice of Appeal, I-C-16; Simba Appeal Brief, paras 210-235. The Appeals Chamber readily dismisses the Appellant's contention that the Trial Chamber's finding that the Appellant arrived in Gikongoro before 21 April 1994 is contradicted by other findings, since it is manifestly unfounded. None of the alleged contradictions are demonstrated (Simba Notice of Appeal, II-D-4(a) to II-D-4(d); Simba Appeal Brief, paras 386-390).

400 Simba Appeal Brief, paras 239-243. *See also* Simba Reply, para. 134.

202. The Trial Chamber considered the evidence of Witnesses GMA3, AJG7, GL3 and SIH on this point and accorded them "little or no weight, particularly when viewed in the context of the corroborated Prosecution evidence placing [the Appellant] in Gikongoro prefecture during this time".[401]

203. The Appeals Chamber recalls that the Trial Chamber had the discretion to assess the relevance and weight of evidence given by both Prosecution and Defence witnesses when reaching a decision as to the Appellant's date of arrival in Gikongoro. The Appellant has not demonstrated how the Trial Chamber abused its discretion in assessing the totality of the alibi evidence to find that it did not cast any doubt on the fact that the Appellant was at the relevant massacre sites on 21 April 1994.[402] Similarly, the Appellant has not demonstrated that no reasonable trier of fact could have come to the conclusion that the Appellant arrived in Gikongoro on that date. This sub-ground is accordingly dismissed.

(iii) Alleged Error Relating to the Assessment of Witness FKP2's evidence

204. The Appellant claims that the Trial Chamber treated Defence Witness FKP2's testimony unfairly in comparison to Prosecution witnesses, by disallowing the witness's account that he saw the Appellant at a meeting in Gitarama on 20 April on the grounds that, during cross-examination, the witness instead placed that meeting between 13-30[403] April 1994.[404] The Appellant submits that Witness FKP2's testimony raises a doubt that must be of benefit to the Appellant.

205. The Appeals Chamber notes that the Appellant fails to give a full account of the Trial Chamber's relevant findings. The Trial Chamber noted that Witness FKP2, when confronted during cross-examination with his prior statement in which he stated that he had met the Appellant twice in Gitarama between 13-30 April, explained that he had given a broad range of dates because he was not certain of when the second meeting occurred.[405] The Appellant has failed to demonstrate how the Trial Chamber abused its discretion in assessing Witness FKP2's evidence. The Trial Chamber could reasonably conclude that Witness FKP2's evidence with regard to the second meeting with the Appellant was not accurate as to the date and therefore not capable of casting doubt on the **[page 64]** Appellant's presence at Kaduha Parish and Murambi Technical School on 21 April 1994.[406] This sub-ground of appeal is therefore dismissed.

(c) Alleged Error in Failing to Accept the Alibi Evidence in its Entirety and in Taking into Account the Purported Relationship of Witnesses with the Appellant or Members of his Family

206. The Appellant submits that the Trial Chamber erred in law and in fact by holding that certain witnesses were credible with respect to the Appellant's presence in Kigali in April 1994 but not with respect to the Appellant's stay in Gitarama, and also by failing to accept the evidence of the alibi witnesses in their entirety.[407] In addition, the Appellant claims that the Trial Chamber erred in asserting that these alibi witnesses were inclined to testify in a manner favourable to the Appellant because they had a close relationship with him. Similarly, the Appellant submits that the Trial Chamber erred in fact by finding that elements of exaggeration or embellishment in their testimonies could be explained by a desire to assist him.[408]

207. The Appellant submits that purported personal ties between Defence witnesses and the Appellant or members of his family should *a priori* not have any impact on credibility assessments.[409] The Appellant further alleges that it has not been established that all of the alibi witnesses had personal ties to the Appellant

401 Trial Judgement, para. 383.
402 Trial Judgement, para. 384.
403 In the Simba Appeal Brief it is suggested that according to paragraph 382 of the Trial Judgement Witness FKP2 stated in cross-examination that he met the Appellant twice in Gitarama during the period 13 -20 April 1994, when in fact the said paragraph of the Trial Judgement mentions the period 13 -30 April (Simba Appeal Brief, para 238).
404 Simba Notice of Appeal, I-C-12; Simba Appeal Brief, paras 237-238. *See also* Simba Reply, para. 47.
405 Trial Judgement, para. 382.
406 *See* Trial Judgement, paras 382, 384.
407 Simba Notice of Appeal, II-D-1 and II-D-2; Simba Appeal Brief, paras 185-188.
408 Simba Notice of Appeal, II-D-1; Simba Appeal Brief, paras 185-188.
409 Simba Appeal Brief, paras 185-186.

or members of his family.[410] By way of example, he submits that he had no personal relationship with Witnesses SIH, FMP1, GMA3, GL3, and Monique Mujawamariya, and that even though he and Witness FKP2 had been colleagues in Parliament, he could not be considered to be close to him.[411]

208. The Prosecution submits that it "was within [the Trial Chamber's] discretion to take certain factors, like the personal relationship with either the Appellant or a member of his family, into consideration in assessing the evidence of the alibi witnesses, and, based upon discrepancies and inconsistencies, to accord little or no weight to their evidence, when viewed in the context of the corroborated Prosecution evidence placing the Appellant in Gikongoro during this time".[412]

209. The Trial Chamber divided its assessment of the alibi into two phases.[413] The Trial Chamber found the alibi evidence sufficiently credible to cast doubt on the evidence supporting the **[page 65]** Prosecution's allegations in relation to the period 6-13 April 1994,[414] but did not find that a reasonable doubt had been cast on the Prosecution evidence for the period 14-24 April 1994.[415]

210. With regard to the contention that the Trial Chamber erred in law by taking into account the purported links between alibi witnesses and the Appellant or members of his family, the Appeals Chamber notes that, in the course of its assessment of the relevant alibi evidence, the Trial Chamber observed that "most of the Defence witnesses providing evidence in support of the alibi have a close personal relationship with either [the Appellant] or members of his family",[416] and noted that "[w]hile these relationships do not invalidate their testimonies, it does suggest that any lapse in their recollections might be resolved in a manner favorable to [the Appellant]".[417] While these observations suggest that the Trial Chamber viewed with caution the evidence given by Defence witnesses who had close relationships with the Appellant or with members of his family, it does not demonstrate *per se* that the Trial Chamber erred in law in its assessment of this evidence.

211. As for the submission that the Trial Chamber erred in fact by finding elements of exaggeration or embellishment in the witness testimonies with respect to the period 14-24 April 1994, the Appeals Chamber recalls that it is primarily for the Trial Chamber to determine whether a witness is credible and to decide which witness testimony to prefer.[418] The Appeals Chamber points out that the Trial Chamber, in addressing the alibi for this period, did not find that all the relevant alibi witnesses had personal ties with the Appellant or members of his family, but only that most of them did. The Trial Judgement makes no reference to the nature of the Appellant's relationship with Witnesses SIH, FMP1, GMA3, GL3, and Monique Mujawamariya, contrary to what the Appellant appears to infer. With respect to Witness FKP2, the Trial Judgement merely notes that he had prior professional ties to the Appellant, a view supported by that witness's testimony.[419] Furthermore, it is apparent that the Trial Chamber took into account the purported relationships simply as one of a number of factors which were determinant with respect to the credibility of alibi witnesses for the period of 14-24 April 1994. The Appeals Chamber notes that the Trial Chamber took into consideration, *inter alia*: discrepancies between Witness AJT1's testimony and her prior statements;[420] discrepancies between the Appellant's testimony and his prior statement;[421] the fact that the accounts of the Appellant's "time in Gitarama town provided by [the Appellant himself] **[page 66]** and Witnesses AJT1 and SML2 [were] not particularly detailed and convincing";[422] inconsistencies with respect to meeting dates in Witness

410 Simba Appeal Brief, para. 187.
411 Simba Appeal Brief, para. 187.
412 Prosecution Response, para. 94.
413 Trial Judgement, paras 298-299.
414 Trial Judgement, paras 347-349.
415 Trial Judgement, para. 384.
416 Trial Judgement, para. 381.
417 Trial Judgement, para. 381.
418 *Kupreškić et al.* Appeal Judgement, para. 32; quoted in *Kunarac et al.* Appeal Judgement, para. 40.
419 T. 15 December 2004 p. 11.
420 Trial Judgement, para. 377.
421 Trial Judgement, paras 379-380.
422 Trial Judgement, para. 381, noting that these witnesses remained at the compound where the Appellant stayed at Gitarama, engaged in domestic household matters.

FKP2's testimony and his prior statement;[423] the lack of detail in and the second-hand nature of the evidence of Witnesses GMA3 and AJG7 on the Appellant's arrival in Gikongoro towards the end of April 1994; the uncertainty with regard to the date and the generally limited probative value of Witness GL3's testimony regarding a sighting of the Appellant; and the limited significance of Witness SIH's testimony with regard to the date of arrival of the Appellant in Gikongoro.[424] On the basis of all of the evidence considered, the Trial Chamber concluded that the factual finding pertaining to the alibi did not cast doubt on the Prosecution's evidence relating to the second period.[425]

212. With regard to the Appellant's submission that the Trial Chamber erred by not accepting the alibi evidence in its entirety, the Appeals Chamber recalls that a party must, when alleging an error of law, identify the alleged error, present arguments in support of its claim and explain how the error invalidates the judgement.[426] In the present case, the Appellant fails to articulate any argument based on applicable law or jurisprudence to the effect that the Trial Chamber was required to accept or reject the alibi evidence in its entirety. In general, it is not unreasonable for a Trial Chamber to accept certain parts of a witness's testimony and reject others.[427] When challenging factual findings made by the Trial Chamber, an appellant has first to identify the alleged error[428] and prove that the challenged factual finding is one which no reasonable trier of fact could have reached.[429] Here, the Appellant does not clearly identify the alleged error of fact which would demonstrate that no reasonable trier of fact could have found that the alibi evidence cast doubt on the finding regarding the first period and not the second. **[page 67]**

213. The Appellant has not demonstrated that the Trial Chamber erred in law or fact in not accepting the evidence of alibi witnesses in their entirety or in noting personal and family ties. This sub-ground of appeal is accordingly dismissed.

(d) Alleged Error Relating to the Appellant's Purported Influence

214. The Appellant submits that the Trial Chamber erred by "raising the possibility that [he] did not remain in Gitarama for as long as he and his witnesses claimed he did" and in finding that it could "eliminate the possibility that [the Appellant] remained in Gitarama after 16 April" on the basis of, *inter alia,* his purported influence on military and administrative authorities.[430] Specifically, the Appellant appears to allege that the Trial Chamber erred in finding in paragraph 376 of the Trial Judgement that the Appellant's stature in Rwandan society allowed him to obtain the assistance of authorities to facilitate movement[431] and that he admitted that he had little fear of roadblocks in Gikongoro.[432] The Appellant contends that in a situation of widespread chaos, it was not obvious that he would have been respected everywhere, especially since he was

[423] Trial Judgement, para. 382.

[424] Trial Judgement, para. 383.

[425] *See* Trial Judgement, para. 384.

[426] *Limaj et al.* Appeal Judgement, para. 9; *Blagojević and Jokić* Appeal Judgement, para. 7; *Brđanin* Appeal Judgement, para. 9; *Galić* Appeal Judgement, para. 7; *Stakić* Appeal Judgement, para. 8; *Kvočka et al.* Appeal Judgement para. 16, referring to *Krnojelac* Appeal Judgement, para. 10.

[427] *Blagojević and Jokić* Appeal Judgement, para. 82; *Kupreškić et al.* Appeal Judgement, para. 333. *See also Ntagerura et al.* Appeal Judgement, para. 214; *Kamuhanda* Appeal Judgement, para. 248.

[428] *See* for example, *Niyitegeka* Appeal Judgement, para. 172; *Krnojelac* Appeal Judgement, para. 25.

[429] *See Akayesu* Appeal Judgement, para. 178, quoting *Delalić et al.* Appeal Judgement, paras 434-435 ("The test to be applied in relation to the issue as to whether the evidence is *factually* sufficient to sustain a conviction is whether the conclusion of guilt beyond reasonable doubt is one which no reasonable tribunal of fact *could* have reached. If an appellant is not able to establish that the Trial Chamber's conclusion of guilt beyond reasonable doubt was one which no reasonable tribunal of fact could have reached, it follows that there must have been evidence upon which such a tribunal could have been satisfied beyond reasonable doubt of that guilt. Under those circumstances, the latter test of legal sufficiency is therefore redundant, and the appeal must be dismissed. Similarly, if an appellant is able to establish that no reasonable tribunal of fact could have reached a conclusion of guilt upon the evidence before it, the appeal against conviction must be allowed and a Judgment of acquittal entered. In such a situation it is unnecessary for an appellate court to determine whether there was evidence (if accepted) upon which such a tribunal could have reached such a conclusion").

[430] Simba Notice of Appeal, II-D-3, referring to Trial Judgement, paras 376-379, 384.

[431] Simba Appeal Brief, paras 190-201.

[432] Simba Appeal Brief, para. 202, referring implicitly to Trial Judgement, para. 376.

traveling with Tutsi.[433] The Appellant also submits that he was not as well-known and influential in the prefecture of Gikongoro as the Trial Chamber held.[434]

215. The Prosecution does not specifically respond to the Appellant's argument.[435]

216. The Trial Chamber made the impugned findings in the context of its assessment of the evidence given by the Appellant and Witness MIB to the effect that the latter had warned the Appellant in Nyanza, Butare Prefecture, on 16 April 1994, of the danger of traveling "any further with the Tutsi accompanying him", with the consequence that the Appellant returned back to Gitarama where he stayed the next eight days. The relevant passage of the Trial Judgement reads as follows:

> 374. As discussed above, Simba provided a reasonable explanation for his activities from 6 until 13 April 1994 when he relocated to Gitarama town. From 14 to 24 April 1994, Simba claimed that he remained in Gitarama town, taking periodic trips during the day to Kigali or other neighbouring localities. His version of the events is corroborated, to varying degrees by several witnesses. However, the evidence for this part of the alibi contains a number of elements which call into serious question the reasonableness of Simba's account and, in fact, lend support for an earlier arrival date in Gikongoro. **[page 68]**
>
> 375. In particular, Simba acknowledged travelling with three others toward Gikongoro prefecture on 16 April, in order to see if the roads were sufficiently safe to relocate there. Witness MIB confirmed that Simba was travelling toward Gikongoro prefecture at this time when she met him along the road in Nyanza, Butare prefecture. According to the evidence, Simba then turned back to Gitarama town on the advice of Witness MIB who warned that it was too dangerous to travel any further with Tutsi accompanying him. As a result, Simba returned to Gitarama town. According to the Accused's testimony, and that of Witnesses SML2 and AJT1, Simba spent the next eight days playing cards, going to the market, and making short trips to Kigali or other nearby areas.
>
> 376. The Chamber notes that on 16 April, Simba was travelling in southern Rwanda toward his native area. He was a prominent figure in Rwanda based on his prior military and political career. The Chamber is certain that Simba was an imposing figure, particularly when he travelled in uniform. The Accused's own testimony reflects that when confronted at a roadblock between Kigali and Gitarama, he threatened to kill an assailant rather than surrender one of the Tutsi in his care. Though he lacked formal ties to the government and military, the evidence shows that Simba's stature in Rwandan society allowed him to obtain the assistance of authorities to facilitate movement. This point is illustrated by his ability to contact high ranking personnel in Kibungo prefecture to assist Witness SML2 in her return to Kigali. In addition, Simba had no difficulty convincing gendarmes and soldiers to accompany him to rescue various individuals throughout Kigali in the first few days after the death of the president. Simba also acknowledged that he had little fear of roadblocks in Gikongoro prefecture because he was well-known in the area.
>
> 377. In this context, it is not plausible that Witness MIB's warning would have dissuaded Simba if he had wanted to relocate to Gikongoro prefecture at the time. The Chamber also notes that, contrary to Simba's testimony, Witness MIB indicated that he was travelling with a number of people under his care, including Witness SML2. Witness SML2's account of the journey to Gikongoro prefecture also suggests an earlier departure. She described *Interahamwe* surrounding Kaduha Parish as the group passed the parish. The Chamber recalls that in the days before the final assault on 21 April against Murambi Technical School, Cyanika Parish, and Kaduha Parish, *Interahamwe* clashed with Tutsi refugees at those sites. Moreover, the Chamber has noted the discrepancy between Witness AJT1's testimony and her statement to Tribunal investigators, which indicates that Simba departed Gitarama around the time the interim government relocated there.[436]

217. The Appeals Chamber notes that the Trial Chamber's findings with respect to the Appellant's stature and influence rest on multiple observations: the Appellant was able to travel on 16 April 1994, he dared to assert his authority in the face of an assailant at a roadblock between Kigali and Gitarama, and he managed to obtain the assistance of gendarmes and other authorities in order to facilitate his movements and the movements of others. The Trial Chamber took into consideration not only his past military and governmental career but also elements contemporaneous to the events which were demonstrative of his prominence.[437] The

[433] Simba Appeal Brief, para. 200.

[434] Simba Appeal Brief, para. 201. The Appeals Chamber will consider below the correlated arguments relating to the alleged marginalisation of the Appellant (*see below* Section F-2, paras 237-242).

[435] The Prosecution addresses the issue of the Appellant's purported influence in relation to the Appellant's ground of appeal on the sentence (*see below* Sections F(2) paras 237-242 and K para. 283).

[436] Trial Judgement, paras 374-377 (internal footnotes omitted).

[437] Trial Judgement, paras 56-60, 375-376.

Appellant's claim that he was seriously marginalised does not demonstrate that the Trial Chamber erred in finding that he was a prominent and imposing figure.

218. With regard to the Appellant's challenge to the finding that he had acknowledged that he did not fear roadblocks in Gikongoro prefecture because he was well-known in the area, the Appeals Chamber notes that the Trial Judgement does not refer to any specific part of the Appellant's testimony in support. However, the Trial Judgement does refer to the Appellant's statement that on **[page 69]** 24 April 1994 he was able to pass a roadblock at Kaduha because he was well-known.[438] This passage in turn refers to the transcripts of the Appellant's testimony, which in relevant part read as follows:

> At the roadblock set up at the office of the sub-*préfecture*, I stopped -- of course I was followed by the other vehicle. There were civilians. I asked the whereabouts of the *sous-préfet*. I was told that he was not present, that he had gone hitherto. I continued on my way. I arrived at the other roadblock near the market. Since I was fairly well known, they stopped me, and I stopped and I asked them to open the roadblock. They saw my name Simba, so they allowed me to pass.[439]

219. The Appellant has not demonstrated that no reasonable trier of fact could have found on the basis of this evidence that, due to his notoriety, the Appellant had little fear of roadblocks in the Gikongoro area. In the absence of any demonstration that the Trial Chamber erred in linking the Appellant's ability to travel within Gikongoro at the relevant time to his notoriety or influence, this sub-ground is dismissed.

3. Alleged Errors Relating to the Assessment of Defence Witnesses NGJ2 and SBL1

220. The Appellant submits that the Trial Chamber erred in law "in failing to attach more weight to the testimonies of Defence Witnesses SBL1 [and] NGJ2, veritable informed local figures in Gikongoro, who are, moreover, implicated in the crimes perpetrated in that locality".[440] He asserts that the Trial Chamber further erred in law and contradicted itself in disregarding the testimonies of these witnesses while noting that they were implicated in the attack, without any evidentiary basis.[441] In addition, he submits that the Trial Chamber distorted the facts and thus erred in fact when noting that these witnesses were both implicated in the attack against Murambi Technical School, while no evidence in the trial record supports this assertion.[442]

221. The Appellant submits that Witness SBL1 testified that, as far as he knew, the Appellant did not participate in the massacres at Murambi and Kaduha and that in fact he was not there. The Appellant argues that since this witness was "the most senior administrative authority in Gikongoro *préfecture* at the time of the genocide, [he] must have been fully aware of the events that took place in Murambi and Kaduha". The Appellant also refers to the fact that the Indictment charges both Witness SBL1 and the Appellant as participants in a JCE.[443] **[page 70]**

222. The Appellant submits that Witness NGJ2, an administrative official in the Gikongoro prefecture with the Murambi Commune under his authority, also testified that the Appellant did not participate in the massacre at Murambi.[444]

223. The Appellant submits that the Trial Chamber "systematically" dismissed the testimonies of these witnesses with regard to his alleged presence at Murambi and Kaduha during the massacres on the ground that their information is second-hand and of questionable probative value, and preferred to rely on the "suspect testimonies of witnesses imprisoned for perpetrating genocide".[445]

224. The Prosecution responds that the Appellant's submission merely suggests an alternative assessment of the respective testimonies of Witnesses SBL1 and NGJ2, more favourable to him. The Prosecution submits

---

438 Trial Judgement, para. 357.

439 T. 22 March 2005 pp. 71-72.

440 Simba Notice of Appeal, I-C-17, referring to Trial Judgement, paras 120, 137, 163.

441 Simba Notice of Appeal, I-D-7.

442 Simba Notice of Appeal, II-C-6, Simba Appeal Brief, para. 368, referring to Simba Appeal Brief, paras 245-252 and Trial Judgement, para. 120.

443 Simba Appeal Brief, paras 246-248.

444 Simba Appeal Brief, para. 249.

445 Simba Appeal Brief, para. 250. *See also* Prosecution Response, paras 97-98.

that nothing has been shown on appeal to indicate that the Trial Chamber erred in the assessment of these testimonies.[446]

225. The Appeals Chamber is not convinced that the Appellant has demonstrated that the Trial Chamber erred in the exercise of its discretion by failing to attach weight to the assertions of Witnesses NGJ2 and SBL1 that the Appellant was not present at Murambi Technical School and Kaduha Parish during the massacres which took place there on 21 April 1994. The Trial Chamber considered that the evidence of these two witnesses regarding the attacks against Murambi Technical School was "based principally on their assertions that they did not hear about [the Appellant's] involvement".[447] It subsequently found that this evidence was "not a sufficient basis of knowledge for [it] to make any findings concerning [the Appellant's] activities at the relevant time".[448] The Appellant has not demonstrated that the Trial Chamber abused its discretion in making this finding. Similarly, Witness SBL1 gave evidence that he was not present during the attack at Kaduha Parish, limiting his testimony to the fact that he had not heard that the Appellant was involved in the massacre. This being the case, it was within the discretion of the Trial Chamber to conclude that the information given by the witness was second-hand and of questionable probative value.[449]

226. The fact that Witnesses SBL1 and NGJ2 were informed local administrative authorities[450] does not by itself suffice to demonstrate that the Trial Chamber erred in not relying on their second-hand testimonies. Furthermore, and contrary to the Appellant's assertion, the Trial Chamber did not **[page 71]** "systematically" dismiss Witnesses SBL1 and NGJ2 testimonies. In fact, it took these testimonies into account and gave them some credit with respect to other allegations in the Indictment which were dismissed.[451]

227. The Appeals Chamber also dismisses the Appellant's submission that the Trial Chamber contradicted itself in disregarding the testimonies of Witnesses SBL1 and NGJ2 while noting their implication in the attacks at Murambi Technical School and Kaduha Parish. The Trial Chamber's observation that the witnesses were both implicated in attacks[452] in the area is not incompatible with a finding that their testimonies are second-hand regarding the Murambi Technical School and Kaduha Parish massacres, since according to their own testimonies they were not present at these attacks.[453] Accordingly, no legal error has been demonstrated.

228. With regard to the Appellant's related submission that the Trial Chamber erred in fact in finding that Witnesses SBL1 and NGJ2 were implicated in the attacks, the Appeals Chamber first notes that the Trial Chamber did not actually find that they participated in the attacks against Murambi Technical School and Kaduha Parish. It noted only that it had taken into account their implication in the attacks,[454] while assessing the evidence of these witnesses. In any case, both witnesses gave second-hand evidence and neither witness's testimony was of relevance to the issue of the Appellant's participation in the attacks.

229. These sub-grounds of appeal are accordingly dismissed.

4. Alleged Differential Treatment of Prosecution and Defence Witnesses

230. The Appellant submits that the Trial Chamber showed bias in applying different approaches to Prosecution and Defence evidence. He submits that while the Trial Chamber accepted Prosecution witnesses' testimonies even when they "were not credible and on which moreover it expressed serious doubts, the Chamber strove to get the said testimonies to corroborate each other". He contends that the Trial Chamber

446 Prosecution Response, paras 97-98.
447 Trial Judgement, para. 120.
448 Trial Judgement, paras 104-105, 120.
449 Trial Judgement, paras 163, 176.
450 Simba Appeal Brief, paras 245-249.
451 *See* Trial Judgement, paras 208, 210, with respect to the distribution of weapons at Rukondo Commune; Trial Judgement, paras 256, 258, with respect to the distribution of weapons at Kinyamakara commune office.
452 *See* Trial Judgement, paras 120, 276 (the latter in relation to the meeting at CIPEP on 26 April 1994)
453 Witness SBL1 stated that he was not at Kaduha from April to July 1994 and that at the time of the attack against Murambi Technical School, he was at home in Gikongoro, sleeping (T. 23 February 2005 pp. 35-36). Witness NGJ2 stated that when the attack against refugees at Murambi started he heard gunshots from a distance and that he was not a witness to the attack at Murambi (T. 21 March 2005 pp. 15-16). Witness NGJ2 stated that he did not know what happened in Kaduha (T. 21 March 2005 p. 62).
454 *See* Trial Judgement, paras 120, 276 (the latter in relation to the meeting at CIPEP on 26 April 1994).

failed to adopt the same approach regarding Defence witnesses, particularly the alibi witnesses, rejecting Defence witness testimony even when corroborated, while **[page 72]** "using such testimonies in a biased manner when they corroborated Prosecution witnesses' testimonies".[455]

231. Overall, the Appellant submits that the Trial Chamber was more lenient towards Prosecution witnesses than towards Defence alibi witnesses.[456] Specifically, the Appellant submits that the Trial Chamber treated leniently Prosecution Witnesses KEI, KSY, KSK, KXX, YC and YH while Defence alibi witnesses, such as Witness FKP2[457] and the Appellant himself, did not benefit from the same treatment.[458]

232. In response, the Prosecution submits that the Trial Chamber used the same approach in assessing Defence and Prosecution evidence. It stresses that the Trial Chamber rejected certain Prosecution allegations as unproven because it found a number of Prosecution witnesses not to be reliable and credible, while at the same time it accepted the alibi evidence for the period from 6-13 April 1994. It asserts that, in essence, the Appellant disputes the Trial Chamber's findings which are unfavourable to him without demonstrating that they were so unreasonable that they warrant appellate intervention.[459]

233. Under the present sub-grounds of appeal the Appellant alleges Trial Chamber errors relating to the assessment of both Prosecution and Defence evidence. The Appeals Chamber has already addressed these submissions in previous sections of the Appeal Judgement, and has dismissed all but one.[460] While it found that the Trial Chamber erred in relying on Witness KXX with regard to the time of the Appellant's arrival at Kaduha Parish on 21 April 1994,[461] this error does not demonstrate any bias in the Trial Chamber's assessment of the evidence. Accordingly, the Appeals Chamber does not need to revisit the challenges here. The Appellant's submissions with respect to the biased or differential treatment of Prosecution and Defence evidence are dismissed. **[page 73]**

F. Alleged Distortion of Facts

234. The Appellant makes a number of submissions to the effect that the Trial Chamber erred in fact by distorting the facts before it.[462] The Appeals Chamber notes that most of these submissions have been dealt with elsewhere in this Judgement.

1. The Appellant's Possession of a Cache of Weapons

235. The Appellant alleges that the Trial Chamber erred in finding that he had a cache of weapons, and that this finding is unsupported in the evidence.[463] The Prosecution responds that the Appellant's allegations of error are unmeritorious and should be dismissed.[464]

236. The Appeals Chamber notes that the Trial Chamber found at paragraph 404 of the Trial Judgement that the Appellant "had a cache of weapons, including firearms and grenades for distribution, which certainly would have come from civilian or military authorities". No conviction is based on the finding that the

455 Simba Notice of Appeal, I-C-10 and I-C-11.
456 Simba Notice of Appeal, I-C-10 to I-C-12.
457 Simba Appeal Brief, paras 237-238.
458 Simba Appeal Brief, paras 174-244.
459 Prosecution Response, paras 91-96.
460 *See above* Sections D-1 to D-3 and E-1 to E-3.
461 *See above* Section D-3(d), para. 143.
462 Simba Notice of Appeal, II-C-1 to II-C-14. Under the present section, the Appeals Chamber will only consider the allegations of errors under sub-grounds II-C-1 and II-C-14. Sub-grounds II-C-2 to II-C-13 are considered elsewhere in the Appeal Judgement.
463 Simba Notice of Appeal, II-C-14; Simba Appeal Brief, para. 51, 381, referring to Trial Judgement, para. 404; AT. 22 May 2007 pp. 44-45. In his Appeal Brief the Appellant goes beyond his original submission concerning this sub-ground and alleges that the Trial Chamber erred in basing its finding of the Appellant's guilt in the distribution of weapons solely on the finding of his possession of such weapons (Simba Appeal Brief, para. 51). The Appeals Chamber notes that the Appellant's submission is based on a misreading of the Trial Judgement as the Trial Chamber made an independent finding on the Appellant's distribution of weapons, including by relying on Witness KSY's testimony [specifically related to the Appellant's distribution of weapons] (*see* Trial Judgement, paras 113, 117-118, *see also* paras 175, 178). Therefore, the Appellant's submission is clearly unfounded and is readily dismissed.
464 Prosecution Response, paras 42-45.

Appellant had a cache of weapons. Rather, the legal findings related to the Appellant's participation in a JCE encompassing the massacres at Murambi Technical School and Kaduha Parish are grounded on his acts and deeds at these places during the attacks, and in particular, that he distributed weapons at Kaduha Parish. This sub-ground is thus without merit and is accordingly dismissed.

2. The Appellant's Stature

237. The Appellant alleges that the Trial Chamber distorted the facts relating to his stature in Rwandan society and his relationship with governmental and military authorities.[465] In particular, he alleges that the Trial Chamber erred by finding that he was a national hero simply because he fought the *Inkotanyi* in the sixties and had been part of the "Comrades of the fifth July 1973" who led the military *coup d'état* in 1973, whereas he had only fought the *Inyenzi* and those who had participated in the *coup d'état* were considered traitors.[466] To this end, the Appellant points to **[page 74]** setbacks he suffered in his political and military career.[467] The Appellant further submits that the Trial Chamber distorted the facts by considering the Appellant's appointment to the civil defence as a sign of his special prominence, whereas it had been clearly demonstrated at trial that he was not the only retired officer contacted to become a civil defence advisor.[468] The Appellant requests that the Appeals Chamber exclude these "distortions" as well as the related legal findings.[469]

238. The Prosecution responds that the Trial Chamber made reasonable conclusions with respect to the Appellant's stature and his relationship with governmental and military authorities, based on evidence adduced at trial.[470]

239. The Appeals Chamber notes that in finding that the Appellant was a prominent former political and military figure in Rwandan society, the Trial Chamber provided a detailed analysis and took into consideration numerous factors.[471]

240. It is not clear how the Appellant's first contention, that the Trial Chamber distorted the facts when it found that he fought the *Inkotanyi* in the sixties whereas he had only fought the *Inyenzi*, advances the Appellant's case. Regardless, it is evidently based on a misrepresentation of the Trial Chamber's finding and is therefore readily dismissed. At no point did the Trial Chamber make the finding regarding the *Inkotanyi* suggested by the Appellant. Instead, the Trial Chamber found that "between 1963 and 1967, he led several units fighting against the *Inyenzi* and in 1964 fought alongside President Mobutu Sese Seko of Zaire."[472] By the same token, the Appeals Chamber dismisses the Appellant's related contention that those who had

465 Simba Notice of Appeal, II-C-1; Simba Appeal Brief, paras 360-362; Simba Reply, paras 132-133.

466 Simba Notice of Appeal, II-C-1; Simba Appeal Brief, paras 360-362.

467 Simba Appeal Brief, para. 362.

468 Simba Notice of Appeal, II-C-4; Simba Appeal Brief, para. 363.

469 Simba Appeal Brief, para. 364.

470 Prosecution Response, para. 186.

471 In particular, the Trial Chamber took into account:
– the Appellant's military career (namely the fact that he had led several units in the fights against the *Inyenzi* between 1963 and 1967 and had fought alongside President Mobutu Sese Seko of Zaire; his work at Camp Kanombe between 1967 and 1973 where he had earned the military ranks of commander and major; the fact that he had been a member of the "Comrades of the fifth of July", the group which led the military *coup d'état* in 1973; and his position of commander of Camp Kigali between 1980 and 1988) (Trial Judgement, paras 54-56);
– his positions within the national government after the 1973 *coup d'état* (Trial Judgement, para. 55);
– his position as a member of parliament on behalf of Gikongoro prefecture from 1989 to 1993 and as MRND party chairman for Gikongoro prefecture from 1991 to 1993 (Trial Judgement, para. 56);
– his "substantial wealth" (Trial Judgement, para. 59);
– his own testimony that "his military and political career gained him prominence" (Trial Judgement, para. 54).
The Trial Chamber found "that after his resignation [of his post within the MRND, in September 1993], Simba maintained connections with influential officials and continued to garner substantial deference due to his prior professional life". According to the Appellant's testimony, after the 6 April 1994, "he used his connections and stature, for example, to acquire military escorts throughout Kigali, contact military and government authorities to arrange for the evacuation of Witness SML2, and move through roadblocks" (Trial Judgement, paras 57, 58). Finally, the Trial Chamber considered his appointment as Gikongoro's Civil Defense Advisor in May 1994 as one of the factors which underscored "his continued prominence with the Rwandan state at that time" (Trial Judgement, para. 60).

472 Trial Judgement, para. 54.

participated in the *coup d'état* were considered traitors. This does not find any support in the material referred to by the Appellant. The **[page 75]** Appeals Chamber further observes that the Trial Chamber's consideration of the Appellant's appointment as Gikongoro's Civil Defence Advisor in May 1994 as one of the factors which underscored "his continued prominence with the Rwandan state at that time" is not rendered unreasonable by the contention that the Appellant was not the only retired officer who was contacted to become a civil defence advisor.

241. Finally, the Appeals Chamber understands the Appellant to be arguing that the fact that he suffered setbacks in his political and military career contradicts the Trial Chamber's finding on his prominent position in Rwandan society,[473] a submission with which the Appeals Chamber cannot agree. The Appeals Chamber notes that the Trial Chamber accepted that after the 1973 *coup d'état* the Appellant "began to experience professional and personal difficulties", and acknowledged "the possibility that Simba throughout his life and career suffered some professional setbacks".[474] The Trial Chamber, however, concluded that "the evidence on the record in no way reflects that he was ever simply an ordinary Rwandan citizen".[475] It found that "while he might not have achieved the apex of his own career aspirations, he nonetheless held prominent posts in the military, government, and his political party for most of his professional life, which gained him national recognition".[476] In light of the overall evidence before the Trial Chamber, the Appellant has not demonstrated that no reasonable trier of fact could have reached the same finding on this point.

242. Accordingly, these sub-grounds of appeal are dismissed.

G. Alleged Errors in Convicting the Appellant pursuant to JCE for Crimes Committed at Murambi Technical School and Kaduha Parish

243. The Appellant contends that the Trial Chamber erred in convicting him for genocide and extermination as a crime against humanity under the mode of liability of JCE.[477] The Appellant raises a number of arguments in this regard concerning notice, motive and genocide,[478] which are addressed elsewhere in the Trial Judgement and will not be considered here.[479] **[page 76]**

1. Alleged Error in Finding the Appellant Responsible under the Third Category of JCE

244. The Appellant submits that the Trial Chamber erred in finding that the Prosecution had proven beyond reasonable doubt the existence of a JCE and his participation therein.[480] In this respect, he submits that the Trial Chamber erred in finding him responsible under the third category of JCE, when the Prosecution relied on the first category and "various indications in the [Trial] Judgement suggest that what is involved is the first form".[481]

245. In response, the Prosecution submits that the Trial Chamber held the Appellant responsible for crimes pursuant to the first category of JCE, not the third category.[482]

246. The Appeals Chamber is satisfied that, contrary to the Appellant's assertions, the Trial Chamber held the Appellant responsible for genocide and extermination as a crime against humanity pursuant to the first category of JCE, rather than the third category. In its legal findings, the Trial Chamber noted that the Prosecution was primarily pursuing a case based on the first category.[483] It subsequently found the Appellant

---

473 Under sub-ground of appeal I-D-4 the Appellant asserts that the Trial Chamber's assessment of the Appellant's motive for participating in the genocide contradicted its findings that the Appellant had suffered military and political setbacks as well as social marginalisation. The Appeals Chamber will address this sub-ground below under Section H-3.

474 Trial Judgement, para. 57.

475 Trial Judgement, para. 57.

476 Trial Judgement, para. 57.

477 Simba Notice of Appeal, I-F-1 to I-F-11; Simba Appeal Brief, paras 273-314.

478 *See* Simba Notice of Appeal, I-F-1 to I-F-5, I-F-8, I-F-11; Simba Appeal Brief, paras 273-283.

479 *See above* Section C-1 and C-2 and *see below* Section H.

480 Simba Notice of Appeal, I-F-6.

481 Simba Appeal Brief, paras 290, 292, referring to Trial Judgement, para. 386.

482 Prosecution Response, para. 140.

483 Trial Judgement, para. 386.

responsible as a participant in the JCE, for which he "shared the common purpose of killing Tutsi at Murambi Technical School and Kaduha Parish".[484] The Appellant has not indicated how this implies a finding of responsibility pursuant to the third category of JCE. While it is true, as submitted by the Prosecution,[485] that the Trial Chamber at least once used language that is more appropriate to an analysis of the *mens rea* for the third category of JCE, this was with respect to the alleged acts at Cyanika Parish for which the Appellant was not found responsible, and therefore the matter is not contentious on appeal. As all convictions were pursuant to the first category of JCE, the Appeals Chamber will not address the Appellant's further challenges concerning the third category.

2. Alleged Error Relating to Planning

247. The Appellant submits that a conviction for JCE is untenable in law "since the Prosecution failed to adduce evidence of pre-conceived JCE"[486] and the Trial Chamber recognised that the Prosecution did not prove beyond a reasonable doubt the allegations in the Indictment as to prior planning.[487] He specifically challenges as "mere speculation" the finding that it was possible that the local authorities formulated their plan of attack and then requested the Appellant to assist in **[page 77]** implementing it.[488] The Appellant submits that the Trial Chamber erred in assuming that his alleged presence indicated that he would have joined in either the plan of the attackers or that of the government officials.[489]

248. In response, the Prosecution submits that the Appellant's arguments do not demonstrate any error as it is not necessary prior to a conviction as a co-perpetrator in a JCE to establish the existence of an agreement or plan.[490]

249. In this respect, the Trial Chamber held:

> 405. The Prosecution argues that Simba participated in the planning of the three massacres on 21 April. There is no direct evidence of this. Moreover, the Chamber is not satisfied that this is the only reasonable inference available from the evidence. It is also possible that local authorities formulated a plan of attack and then requested Simba to assist in implementing it.[491]
>
> (...)
>
> 435. At the time of the events, Simba had no formal position within the government, military, or political structures of the government. He assumed the post of civil defence adviser on 18 May 1994. However, he is not charged with any criminal conduct based on this position. In addition, the Chamber is not convinced beyond reasonable doubt that Simba was the architect of the massacres at Murambi Technical School and Kaduha Parish or that he played a role in their planning. In addition, the manner in which Simba participated in the joint criminal enterprise did not evidence any particular zeal or sadism on his part. In particular, he did not physically participate in killings and did not remain at the sites of the massacres for more than a brief period.[492]

250. The Appeals Chamber does not find any error on the part of the Trial Chamber. It is well-established that in a JCE, it is not necessary for a participant to have participated in its planning. All that is required is the participation of an accused in the common design involving the perpetration of one of the crimes provided for in the Statute.[493] Further, the Appellant has not demonstrated that the Trial Chamber erred in stating that it was possible that the local authorities formulated their plan of attack and then requested the Appellant's assistance in implementing it. Read in context, the Trial Chamber was merely demonstrating that there was more than one reasonable inference possible from the available evidence. The finding set out above

484 Trial Judgement, para. 406.
485 Prosecution Response Brief, para. 149.
486 Simba Appeal Brief, para. 284.
487 Simba Notice of Appeal, I-F-7.
488 Simba Notice of Appeal, I-D-10 and I-F-9.
489 Simba Appeal Brief, para. 312.
490 Prosecution Response, para. 155.
491 Trial Judgement, para. 405.
492 Trial Judgement, para. 435 (internal footnotes omitted).
493 *Kayshema & Ruzindana* Appeal Judgement, para. 193; *Tadić* Appeal Judgement, para. 227. *See above* Chapter II, Section C-1(b), fn. 161.

demonstrates that this inference was not held against the Appellant. Accordingly, this sub-ground of appeal is dismissed. **[page 78]**

3. Alleged Error in Finding the Appellant Responsible under the First Category of JCE

251. The Appellant submits that his responsibility based on the first category of JCE was not established during trial,[494] and that the Trial Chamber erred in finding that he "shared the common purpose of killing Tutsi" in Murambi and Kaduha merely as a result of his presence and conduct there, and that, in any event the Prosecution did not prove his presence there beyond reasonable doubt.[495] He argues that the Trial Chamber erred in finding that the attackers would have viewed his alleged presence at Kaduha Parish and the remarks he made as a sign that he and the government approved of their conduct.[496]

252. The Prosecution submits that the Trial Chamber did not err in finding that the Appellant bore first category JCE liability for the crimes encompassed by the common purpose. The Prosecution argues, that the Trial Chamber's legal analysis of the requirements for establishing the *actus reus* for JCE and the application of the law to the factual findings do not show any error prejudicial to the Appellant. Regarding the *mens rea*, the Prosecution submits that the Trial Chamber did not err in law in finding that the Appellant, as a participant in the first category of JCE, shared the required specific intent for the crime of genocide.[497]

253. The Appeals Chamber finds the Appellant's contention to be without merit. The Trial Chamber took into account various factors in finding generally that a common criminal purpose existed between a plurality of persons to kill Tutsi at Murambi Technical School, Cyanika Parish and Kaduha Parish.[498] With respect to the Appellant's personal participation in the JCE, which was found to be limited to the attacks at Murambi Technical School and Kaduha Parish, the Trial Chamber found both that he was present at the two massacre sites and that his acts of assistance and encouragement provided substantial assistance to the killings which followed.[499] At Murambi Technical School the Appellant distributed traditional weapons to the attackers and addressed the assailants who then proceeded to attack the refugees with "renewed ardour".[500] At Kaduha Parish, the Appellant distributed guns and grenades, which were a decisive factor in the success of the assaults, and urged the attackers to "get rid of the filth".[501] The Trial Chamber also found that the mere presence of the Appellant at both places would have been seen by the assailants as approval of **[page 79]** their conduct.[502] On this basis, the Trial Chamber found that the Appellant shared the intent to carry out the common purpose of killing Tutsi at Murambi Technical School and Kaduha Parish.

254. The Appellant fails to demonstrate that the Trial Chamber committed any legal error in reaching its conclusion. In addition, the Appeals Chamber has already rejected another challenge to the Trial Chamber's finding of responsibility, based on physical impossibility.[503]

255. These sub-grounds of appeal are accordingly dismissed.

H. Alleged Errors Relating to the Conviction for Genocide

256. The Appellant submits numerous arguments to the effect that the Trial Chamber erred in holding him responsible for genocide with respect to the events at Murambi Technical School and Kaduha Parish when the constitutive elements of the crime, both acts and intent, were not proven beyond reasonable doubt.[504] The

---

494 Simba Appeal Brief, para. 301.
495 Simba Notice of Appeal, I-F-10; Simba Appeal Brief, paras 299, 312-313.
496 Simba Notice of Appeal, I-F-8.
497 Prosecution Response, paras 143-146.
498 Trial Judgement, para. 402.
499 Trial Judgement, paras 403, 433.
500 Trial Judgement, paras 92, 118.
501 Trial Judgement, paras 403, 406.
502 Trial Judgement, paras 398, 400, 403.
503 *See above* Section D-4, paras 144-159.
504 Simba Notice of Appeal, I-G; Simba Appeal Brief, paras 299, 313, 315-327; Simba Reply, para. 108.

Prosecution responds that the Trial Chamber applied the correct legal requirements of the crime of genocide to the facts before it.[505]

257. The Appeals Chamber observes that some of the arguments advanced under this ground of appeal challenge the Trial Chamber's factual findings as well as its findings related to notice.[506] The Appeals Chamber has already discussed these arguments in the respective sections of this Judgement.[507] To the extent that no additional arguments are presented under this ground of appeal, no further discussion is warranted.

1. Alleged Failure to Determine Whether the Killings at Murambi and Kaduha Could Be Legally Characterised as Genocide

258. The Appellant's primary submission is that the Trial Chamber erred by failing to determine whether the large-scale killings at Murambi and Kaduha could be legally characterised as genocide.[508] This contention is evidently unfounded and readily dismissed.[509] The Trial Chamber **[page 80]** carefully made this determination[510] and the Appellant does not advance any argument to demonstrate that the Trial Chamber erred in its application of the law to the facts.

2. Alleged Error Relating to the Existence of a Plan or Policy as Element of the *Actus Reus* of Genocide

259. The Appellant argues that the Trial Chamber failed to require the Prosecution to prove the existence of a plan or policy as a fundamental element of the *actus reus* of this crime.[511] In this regard, the Appellant also emphasises that the Trial Chamber found that his involvement in planning the crime had not been established.[512] The Prosecution responds that the Trial Chamber correctly defined the applicable law and applied it to the facts before it.[513]

260. The Appeals Chamber recalls that according to the jurisprudence of this Tribunal as well as that of the ICTY the existence of an agreement or a plan is not an element required for a conviction for genocide.[514] The Appellant's contention on this point is therefore without merit.

3. Alleged Errors Relating to the Requisite *Mens Rea* of Genocide

261. The Appellant makes numerous submissions to the effect that the Trial Chamber erred in finding that he had the requisite specific intent for genocide.[515] The Prosecution responds that the Appellant's assertions are unsubstantiated and that the Trial Chamber did not commit any error.[516]

262. The Appellant submits that the Trial Chamber erred in finding, without any evidence, that he possessed specific intent to commit genocide at the moment of the events.[517] This contention is without merit. The Trial

---

505 Prosecution Response, para. 151.

506 These include the Appellant's assertions that the Trial Chamber erred in finding that the Appellant gave encouragement and provided arms (Simba Notice of Appeal, I-G-1; Simba Appeal Brief, para. 319), and that the Trial Chamber breached the Appellant's right to be informed of the charges against him when it dropped the allegation of prior coordination and instead relied on a "spontaneous" JCE (Simba Notice of Appeal, I-G-7; Simba Appeal Brief, para. 320).

507 *See above* Sections C and D.

508 Simba Appeal Brief, para. 316. The Appeals Chamber notes that the Appellant does not dispute that large-scale killings occurred at Murambi Technical School and Kaduha Parish (Simba Appeal Brief, para. 317).

509 The Appeals Chamber also notes that the Appellant fails to raise this argument in his Notice of Appeal.

510 *See* Trial Judgement, paras 415-416.

511 Simba Notice of Appeal, I-G-10; Simba Appeal Brief, para. 317.

512 Simba Appeal Brief, para. 318, referring to Trial Judgement, para. 405.

513 Prosecution Response, paras 152, 155.

514 *Semanza* Appeal Judgement, para. 260; *Jelisic* Appeal Judgement, para. 48.

515 Simba Notice of Appeal, I-G-2 to I-G-9; Simba Appeal Brief, paras 320-325. The Appeals Chamber notes that for a few of the Appellant's submissions, the Appellant brings no arguments in support, consequently the Appeals Chamber declines to consider them. Falling into this category is the Appellant's assertion that the Trial Chamber erred in finding that all of the participants in the JCE, including the Appellant, shared the intent to commit genocide by reason of the scale of the massacres and the context within which they were perpetrated (Simba Notice of Appeal, I-G-2).

516 Prosecution Response, paras 153, 156.

517 Simba Notice of Appeal, I-G-8 and I-G-9.

Chamber considered in detail the evidence before it prior to concluding that the Appellant acted with genocidal intent at the moment of the massacres. The relevant passage of the Trial Chamber's analysis reads as follows:

> Simba was physically present at two massacre sites. He provided traditional weapons, guns, and grenades to attackers poised to kill thousands of Tutsi. Simba was aware of the targeting of Tutsi throughout his country, and as a former military commander, he knew what would follow when he **[page 81]** urged armed assailants to "get rid of the filth". The only reasonable conclusion, even accepting his submissions as true, is that at that moment, he acted with genocidal intent.[518]

263. The Appellant next submits, without elaboration, that the Trial Chamber erred in finding that he had the requisite *mens rea* for genocide because it dismissed the allegations of *mens rea* set out in paragraphs 4 and 23 of the Indictment.[519] The Appeals Chamber understands the Appellant to effectively be arguing that, as a result, there was no notice given that could sustain a finding that he possessed the requisite specific intent.

264. The Appeals Chamber finds that the Trial Chamber did dismiss said allegations,[520] as argued by the Appellant. However, it observes that the Appellant has not advanced any argument to show how this dismissal would affect and invalidate the Trial Chamber's assessment of the Appellant's specific intent on the basis of the evidence before it. The Appeals Chamber has previously held that genocidal intent can be proven through inference from the facts and circumstances of a case.[521] Correspondingly, the Appeals Chamber has held that it is sufficient if the evidentiary facts from which the state of mind is to be inferred are pleaded.[522] It is apparent from the above-cited portion of the Trial Judgement that the Trial Chamber inferred the requisite specific intent of the Appellant and the other participants in the JCE from several facts and circumstances that it found established beyond reasonable doubt.

265. The Appellant has not challenged the Trial Chamber's findings from which his genocidal intent is inferred, nor has he challenged the pleading of the material facts forming the basis of these findings. Consequently, the Appeals Chamber can identify no discernible error in the Trial Chamber's decision on that particular point.

266. The Appellant further contests the Trial Chamber's finding that he possessed the requisite *mens rea* for genocide arguing that the Trial Chamber inferred his intent from his alleged presence at the crime sites alongside the assailants whose intent was to kill the Tutsi under a *"spontaneous"* **[page 82]** JCE.[523] In his view, for the crime of genocide to occur, the intent to commit genocide must be formed *prior* to the commission of genocidal acts.[524] The Appeals Chamber finds no merit in this submission. The inquiry is not whether the specific intent was formed prior to the commission of the acts, but whether at the moment of commission the perpetrators possessed the necessary intent. The Trial Chamber correctly considered whether the Appellant and the physical perpetrators possessed genocidal intent at the time of the massacres.[525] The Appellant's argument on this point is therefore without merit.

267. The Appellant argues that the Trial Chamber erred by ignoring credible evidence of Defence Witness Monique Mujawamariya and the Defence Expert Report of Pascal Ndengejeho that demonstrated that he

---

518 Trial Judgement, para. 418.

519 Simba Notice of Appeal, I-G-4; Simba Appeal Brief, para. 324. Paragraph 4 of the Indictment alleges that in January 1993, Simba directed a rally against the Arusha Accords in the town of Gikongoro. Paragraph 23 of the Indictment lists "various rallies and meetings in Gikongoro and Butare prefectures" where the Appellant allegedly "publicly expressed his intent to destroy the Tutsis and incited others to do likewise" "before and during the events of April to July 1994".

520 The Trial Chamber expressly declined to make findings with respect to paragraphs 4 and 23(c) and (f) of the Indictment on the basis of the Prosecution's concession that no evidence had been brought in support of these allegations (Trial Judgement, para. 13). It further found paragraph 23(a) of the Indictment defective and noted that the Prosecution did not seek any conviction on that basis (Trial Judgement, fn. 26). Finally, the Trial Chamber found that the Prosecution did not prove the allegations contained in paragraphs 23(b) (Trial Judgement, para. 225) and 23(d) (Trial Judgement, para. 85). The Appeals Chamber notes that while the Trial Chamber considered the allegation in paragraph 23(g) of the Indictment partly established (it found that "Simba addressed a crowd in Ntyazo commune and delivered an inflammatory speech against Tutsi"), the Trial Chamber did not explicitly rely on this finding in its assessment of the Appellant's intent (Trial Judgement, para. 295).

521 *Gacumbitsi* Appeal Judgement, para. 40; *Rutaganda* Appeal Judgement, para. 525.

522 *Blaskić* Appeal Judgement, para. 219 (internal footnotes omitted).

523 Simba Notice of Appeal, I-G-7; Simba Appeal Brief, para. 320.

524 Simba Appeal Brief, paras 299, 320.

525 Trial Judgement, paras 416, 418.

could not have had the intent to commit genocide.[526] The Appeals Chamber cannot find any merit in the Appellant's argument. It is well established that a Trial Chamber need not articulate in its judgement every factor it considers in reaching a particular finding.[527] In reaching the conclusion that the "genocidal intent was shared by all participants in the JCE, including [the Appellant]",[528] the Trial Chamber explicitly noted that it had "considered the arguments of the Defence that Simba could not have committed genocide, given his close association with Tutsi and his tolerant views, which it suggests resulted in his marginalization and attacks against his family in Gikongoro".[529] A closer review of the Defence arguments in question reveals that these concerned, *inter alia*, the testimony of Monique Mujawamariya as well as the Defence Expert Report of Pascal Ndengejeho.[530]

268. Finally, the Appellant submits that the Trial Chamber erred in affirming, in its attempt to establish his motive, that it could not be excluded that he participated in genocide out of a misguided sense of patriotism or to ensure the protection of himself and those in his care by basing its convictions on these "assumptions".[531] The Appellant contends that the Trial Chamber erred by relying on the *Kvočka* Appeal Judgement in support of this finding.[532] Further, he submits that his alleged presence at the crime scenes was in itself an insufficient motive to commit genocide.[533] **[page 83]**

269. The Appeals Chamber notes that the Appellant's contention clearly rests on a misreading of the Trial Chamber's finding. The Trial Chamber did not find motive to be an element of the crime of genocide. To the contrary, it found, in accordance with established jurisprudence,[534] that a possible personal motive for participating in the JCE did not preclude a finding that he possessed the intent to commit genocide.[535] The Appellant's argument on this issue is therefore evidently unfounded and dismissed. Accordingly, the Appeals Chamber need not address the Appellant's remaining arguments relating to motive.[536]

270. For the foregoing reasons, the Appeals Chamber dismisses the present ground of appeal in its entirety.

I. Alleged Errors Relating to the Conviction for Extermination as a Crime Against Humanity

271. The Appeals Chamber observes that most of the arguments advanced under this ground of appeal concern the Trial Chamber's legal findings on criminal responsibility and genocide as well as its factual findings.[537] These include the Appellant's contentions that the Trial Chamber erred in attributing to him responsibility for his participation in a JCE aimed at killing Tutsi in Kaduha and Murambi, when there was no proof of a JCE or of the Appellant's participation therein, and in presuming his participation based on his presence at the crime sites when such presence was physically impossible.[538] The Appellant further points to

---

526 Simba Notice of Appeal, I-G-5; Simba Appeal Brief, para. 324.

527 *See above* fn. 360. *See also Niyitegeka* Appeal Judgement, para. 115; *Musema* Appeal Judgement, para. 18; *Delalić et al.* Appeal Judgement, para. 48.

528 Trial Judgement, para. 416.

529 Trial Judgement, para. 417.

530 Trial Judgement, fn. 414, referring to Defence Final Trial Brief, paras 1045-1097.

531 Simba Notice of Appeal, I-G-3; Simba Appeal Brief, paras 321-323, 325.

532 Simba Notice of Appeal, I-G-6; Simba Appeal Brief, paras 322-323.

533 Simba Appeal Brief, para. 313.

534 *Kvočka* Appeal Judgement, para. 106; *Niyitegeka* Appeal Judgement, para. 53; *Jelisić* Appeal Judgement, para. 49; *Kayishema and Ruzindana* Appeal Judgement, para. 161; *Tadić* Appeal Judgement, para. 269.

535 Trial Judgement, para. 417.

536 Under sub-grounds of appeal I-D-4 and I-D-5, the Appellant submits that the Trial Chamber erred in law by making contradictory findings in relation to his motive. He alleges that the Trial Chamber contradicted itself when it found on the one hand that the Appellant had suffered military and political setbacks and social marginalisation and that he was tolerant and entertained close relationships with Tutsi, while on the other hand it supposed that he participated in the genocide out of a sense of patriotism or allegiance (Simba Notice of Appeal, I-D-4 and I-D-5, Simba Appeal Brief, paras 259-260). The Appellant also alleges that the Trial Chamber distorted the facts in making the same supposition (Simba Notice of Appeal, II-C-13; Simba Appeal Brief, para. 380, referring to Simba Appeal Brief, paras 53-55). Under sub-ground of appeal I-E-4, the Appellant submits, *inter alia*, that the Trial Chamber in its assessment of the Appellant's motive failed to consider the Report of Defence Expert Witness Dr. Pascal Ndengejeho (Simba Notice of Appeal, I-E-4; Simba Appeal Brief, paras 271-272). To the extent that sub-grounds of appeal I-D-4 and I-D-5 relate to the Trial Chamber's findings on mitigating circumstances, they will be considered below under Section K.

537 Simba Notice of Appeal, I-H; Simba Appeal Brief, paras 328-332; Simba Reply, para. 109.

538 Simba Notice of Appeal, I-H-2; Simba Appeal Brief, para. 329.

his submissions regarding JCE and genocide, which, in his view, invalidate the charges of both genocide and extermination as a crime against humanity.[539] The Appeals Chamber has addressed these arguments in the respective sections elsewhere in this Judgement.[540] No additional arguments are presented in relation to the alleged ground and accordingly no further discussion is warranted. **[page 84]**

272. Moreover, the Appeals Chamber need not address the Appellant's argument that the Trial Chamber erred by holding him responsible for meetings of other local officials, in which, the Trial Chamber itself confirmed, he did not participate,[541] on the basis that no conviction was entered on that ground.

273. The remaining arguments under this ground of appeal pertain to cumulative charges and cumulative convictions for genocide and extermination as a crime against humanity.[542] These submissions will be dealt with in a separate section below.[543]

J. Alleged Errors Relating to Cumulative Charges and Convictions

274. The Appellant submits that the Trial Chamber erred in law in finding that cumulative charges for extermination as a crime against humanity and genocide could be brought and in entering convictions for both crimes, based on the same underlying conduct.[544] The Prosecution responds that it is settled law that genocide and extermination are composed of different legal elements, and that therefore convictions for both crimes are properly cumulative.[545]

275. Under Count 1 of the Indictment and pursuant to Articles 2(3)(a), 2(2)(a) and 2(2)(b) of the Statute, the Appellant was charged with genocide for killing or causing serious bodily harm to members of the Tutsi population, *inter alia* for his participation in the massacres at Murambi Technical School and Kaduha Parish.[546] In addition, the Appellant was charged under Count 3 of the Indictment, *inter alia* on the basis of these same facts, with extermination as a crime against humanity pursuant to Article 3(b) of the Statute.[547] On the ground that the Appellant was criminally responsible for his participation in a JCE to kill Tutsi civilians at Murambi Technical School and Kaduha Parish the Trial Chamber found him guilty of both genocide (Count 1)[548] and extermination as a crime against humanity (Count 3).[549]

276. The Appeals Chamber recalls that it is established jurisprudence that cumulative charging is allowed on the basis that "prior to the presentation of all of the evidence, it is not possible to **[page 85]** determine to a certainty which of the charges brought against an accused will be proven".[550] Under this reasoning, cumulative charging on the basis of the same set of facts is permissible.

277. Furthermore, it is well established that cumulative convictions entered under different statutory provisions but based on the same conduct are permissible if each statutory provision involved has a materially distinct constitutive element not contained in the other.[551] An element is materially distinct from another if it requires proof of a fact not required by the other.[552] Applying this principle, the Appeals Chamber has previously held that

> the crime of genocide under Article 2 of the Statute and the crime of extermination under Article 3 of the Statute each contained a materially distinct element not required by the other. The materially distinct element of genocide is the specific intent to destroy, in whole or in part, a national, ethnical, racial or religious group. The materially

539 Simba Appeal Brief, para. 331, pointing to the Appellant's submissions under Grounds of Appeal, I-F and I-G.

540 *See above* Section D-4, G and H.

541 Simba Notice of Appeal, I-H-3; Simba Appeal Brief, para. 332.

542 Simba Notice of Appeal, I-H-1 and IV-1; Simba Appeal Brief, para. 330.

543 *See below* Section J.

544 Simba Notice of Appeal, I-H-1 and IV-1; Simba Appeal Brief, para. 330.

545 Prosecution Response, para. 160.

546 Indictment Count 1 and Concise Statement of Facts for Counts 1 and 2 (Indictment, paras 3-58).

547 Indictment Count 3 and Concise Statement of Facts for Count 3 (Indictment, paras 59-65, incorporating by reference paragraphs 1 through 58 of the Indictment).

548 Trial Judgement, paras 411, 419, 427. Having noted at paragraph 414 of the Trial Judgement that the Prosecution, in its Final Trial Brief, only pointed to evidence of killing, the Trial Chamber did not consider acts enumerated in Article 2(2)(b) of the Statute.

549 Trial Judgement, paras 420, 426, 427.

550 *Naletilić and Martinović* Appeal Judgement, para. 103, quoting *Kupreskić et al.* Appeal Judgement, paras 385-386.

551 *Ntagerura et al.* Appeal Judgement, para. 425; *Ntakirutimana* Appeal Judgement, para. 542.

552 *Ntagerura et al.* Appeal Judgement, para. 425; *Ntakirutimana* Appeal Judgement, para. 542.

> distinct element of extermination, as a crime against humanity, is the requirement that the crime was committed as part of a widespread or systematic attack against a civilian population.[553]

Accordingly, convictions for genocide and extermination as a crime against humanity, based on the same facts are, as a matter of law, permissible.[554] The Appellant's argument on this point is therefore without merit.

278. For the foregoing reasons, this ground of appeal is dismissed.

K. Alleged Errors Relating to the Sentence

279. The Appellant contends that the Trial Chamber erred in sentencing him to 25 years' imprisonment and raises a number of arguments in support of this claim.[555] The Prosecution opposes all of the Appellant's arguments.[556] The Appeals Chamber will consider the Appellant's arguments in turn.

280. The Appeals Chamber has already considered and dismissed the Appellant's claims that the Trial Chamber erred in convicting him for genocide and extermination as a crime against humanity on the basis of the same set of facts.[557] In his Appeal Brief,[558] the Appellant merely submits that the same alleged error on the conviction occasioned an additional error on the sentence and provides no **[page 86]** further elaboration in support. As the basis for this alleged sentencing error has not been demonstrated, this sub-ground is dismissed without further consideration.

281. The Appellant contends that the Trial Chamber erred in the exercise of its discretion in not according greater weight to mitigating circumstances in determining the sentence.[559] The Prosecution responds that this claim is unsupported and that, as the Appellant acknowledges,[560] the Trial Chamber accepted some mitigating circumstances.[561] The Appeals Chamber finds that the Appellant merely presents factual assertions[562] without showing how the mitigating circumstances were undervalued by the Trial Chamber. Therefore, the Appellant has not demonstrated that the Trial Chamber committed a discernible error in its assessment of the individual mitigating circumstances. This sub-ground of appeal is accordingly dismissed.

282. The Appellant's contention that the Trial Chamber erroneously failed to consider, in assessing mitigating circumstances, the fact that the Appellant had family relationships with Tutsi, some of whom he saved, and the tolerance he always showed in his relations with them,[563] is readily dismissed. Contrary to the Appellant's allegation, the Trial Chamber did consider in mitigation the fact that he provided selective assistance to members of his family[564] and acknowledged the evidence showing that the Appellant had a close relationship and worked harmoniously with Tutsi.[565]

283. The Appellant submits that the Trial Chamber misconceived his stature in Rwandan society when stating that he was a prominent former political and military leader, and erred in considering this as an aggravating circumstance.[566] He argues that the evidence adduced at trial showed that, at the time of the

---

553 *Ntakirutimana* Appeal Judgement, para. 542, referring to *Musema* Appeal Judgement, para. 366.

554 *Ntakirutimana* Appeal Judgement, para. 542, referring to *Musema* Appeal Judgement, para. 366. The Appeals Chamber also notes that the Trial Chamber explicitly referred to the law applicable to cumulative convictions. It noted that "[a] conviction for genocide or complicity in genocide is not impermissibly cumulative with the convictions for crimes against humanity" (Trial Judgement, fn. 424, quoting *Semanza* Appeal Judgement, para. 318).

555 Simba Notice of Appeal, IV-1 to IV-6; Simba Appeal Brief, paras 416-435; AT. 22 May 2007 pp. 22-23.

556 Prosecution Response, paras 226-235.

557 *See above* Section J.

558 Simba Appeal Brief, para. 420. In his Notice of Appeal, the Appellant is only challenging his conviction for both crimes, without challenging specifically the sentence.

559 Simba Notice of Appeal, IV-2; Simba Appeal Brief, paras 424, 434.

560 Simba Appeal Brief, para. 425.

561 Prosecution Response, para. 228.

562 Simba Appeal Brief, paras 426-432 (stating *inter alia* that the Appellant was marginalised and even considered a traitor by Hutus; that he had suffered professional setbacks; that he had no motive for participating in the genocide; and that he was an isolated, ordinary man, without power or influence over the authorities). The Appellant provides no reference to the trial record.

563 Simba Notice of Appeal, I-D-5; Simba Appeal Brief, para. 260. This sub-ground of appeal is presented under the heading "Contradiction in the Judgement" together with a correlated argument in relation to motive which has been considered above under Section H-3, paras 261-269.

564 Trial Judgement, para. 442.

565 Trial Judgement, para. 61.

566 Simba Notice of Appeal, IV-3; Simba Appeal Brief, paras 426-427, 429-430, 433.

events in question, the Appellant had been marginalised and had lost all social and professional standing.[567] The Prosecution responds that the Appellant merely re-argues this point without demonstrating how the Trial Chamber erred.[568] **[page 87]**

284. The Appeals Chamber has already considered and dismissed the Appellant's claim that the Trial Chamber erred in concluding that he was a prominent political and military figure and therefore need not address this challenge again.[569] Turning to the question of whether the Trial Chamber erred in taking his stature into account as an aggravating circumstance, the Appeals Chamber recalls that it is settled in the jurisprudence of the Tribunal and the ICTY that a superior position in itself does not constitute an aggravating factor. Rather, it is the abuse of such position which may be considered as an aggravating factor.[570]

285. A review of the Trial Chamber's findings on this point reveals that it not only took into account the Appellant's stature, but also the influence he derived from his stature[571] and the use he made of his influence by lending encouragement and approval to the participants in the killings.[572] The Appeals Chamber finds that the Trial Chamber thus implicitly found that the Appellant abused his position and influence in order to facilitate the commission of the crimes. Accordingly, the Appeals Chamber finds no discernable error in the Trial Chamber's findings. Therefore this sub-ground of appeal is dismissed.

286. The Appellant further claims that the Trial Chamber erred in considering that his participation in the massacres resulted from misguided notions of patriotism and government allegiance rather than extremism and ethnic hatred.[573] The Prosecution submits that this cannot advance his case for a reduction of the sentence.[574] The Appeals Chamber notes that, contrary to what the Appellant seems to suggest, the Trial Chamber actually mentioned this possible motive in its discussion of mitigating factors.[575] The question of whether it took it into account will be determined below.[576]

287. The Appellant further submits that the sentence imposed is unjustified in view of the Appellant's age and health condition.[577] The Prosecution submits that the Appellant's unelaborated claim concerning his age does not justify appellate intervention as his age fails to meet the threshold set by the Appeals Chamber.[578] It further argues that even if the Appellant's age were to be **[page 88]** considered, it alone, is not decisive.[579] The Appeals Chamber recalls that the age and state of health of an accused person may be relevant factors in sentencing.[580] In the instant case, the Appellant has failed to substantiate his contention concerning his health either in his briefs or at the appeal hearing,[581] and the Appeals Chamber accordingly gives it no further consideration. With regard to his age, the Appellant merely submits that, because he was 65 years old at the time of his conviction, a sentence of 25 years would in effect be equivalent to a sentence to prison for the rest of his life since "life expectancy in sub-Sahara Africa for males is 45 years".[582] This does not demonstrate how the Trial Chamber abused its discretion in determining the sentence. This sub-ground of appeal is therefore dismissed.

---

567 Simba Appeal Brief, para. 426; Simba Reply, paras 150-151.

568 Prosecution Response, para. 231.

569 *See above* Section F-2, paras 237-242.

570 *Stakić* Appeal Judgement, para. 411, quoting *Kayishema and Ruzindana* Appeal Judgement, paras 358–359; *Babić* Sentencing Appeal Judgement, para. 80; *Kamuhanda* Appeal Judgement, para. 347; *Aleksovski* Appeal Judgement, para. 183; *Ntakirutimana* Appeal Judgement, para. 563; *Krstić* Trial Judgement, para. 709.

571 Trial Judgement, para. 439.

572 Trial Judgement, para. 433.

573 Simba Notice of Appeal, IV-4; Simba Appeal Brief, paras 428, 431.

574 Prosecution Response, para. 229.

575 Trial Judgement, para. 441.

576 *See below* Chapter III, Section B-1(c)(ii), paras 327-330.

577 Simba Notice of Appeal, IV-6; Simba Appeal Brief, para. 435.

578 Prosecution Response, para. 234.

579 Prosecution Response, para. 235.

580 *Ntakirutimana* Appeal Judgement, para. 569.

581 At the appeal hearing, the Appellant submitted the following: "We also stated that to our mind the sentence was unfair because of the age of the witness *(sic)*, and also because of the medical files in the possession of the UNDF. It not possible for us to mention the health status of an individual for which information is available in the files of the Tribunal" (AT. 22 May 2007 p. 67).

582 AT. 22 May 2007 pp. 22, 23. The Appeals Chamber notes that this argument is being raised for the first time on appeal as it was not raised during closing arguments nor in the Defence Closing Brief. *See* Defence Closing Brief Against the Amended Indictment of 10 May 2004; T. 7 and 8 July 2005.

288. Finally, the Appellant claims that the Trial Chamber erred in sentencing him to 25 years' imprisonment, when the charges against him were not proven beyond reasonable doubt.[583] In response, the Prosecution submits that the Trial Chamber committed no error as to justify a reduction in sentence.[584] The Appeals Chamber finds that, under this sub-ground of appeal, the Appellant merely reiterates arguments already presented elsewhere in support of his claim that the Trial Chamber erred in the factual and legal findings supporting his conviction for genocide and extermination as a crime against humanity. These arguments were already dismissed and since no distinct argument is advanced demonstrating that the Trial Chamber made a specific error in sentencing, these sub-grounds of appeal are dismissed. **[page 89]**

III. THE APPEAL OF THE PROSECUTION

A. Alleged Errors in Finding that Aloys Simba was not Criminally Responsible for his Participation in the Cyanika Parish Massacre

289. The Prosecution contends that the Trial Chamber erred in fact and in law by failing to find the Appellant criminally responsible for his participation in the Cyanika Parish Massacre on 21 April 1994.[585] Under this ground of appeal, the Prosecution submits, first, that the Trial Chamber erred in fact by requiring proof that the Appellant was physically present at Cyanika Parish before holding him responsible for genocide and extermination as a crime against humanity for the acts that took place there;[586] and, secondly, that it erred in law by requiring a direct and substantial contribution by the Appellant to the massacre at Cyanika Parish as a pre-condition for holding him criminally responsible for that specific massacre.[587]

290. The Appeals Chamber will consider the Prosecution's arguments in turn.

1. Alleged Errors in Requiring Proof that the Appellant was Physically Present at Cyanika Parish

291. The Prosecution submits that the Trial Chamber erred in fact by requiring proof that the Appellant was physically present at Cyanika Parish before it would hold him responsible for the killings there, instead of considering his presence and all of his actions at Murambi Technical School and Kaduha Parish, both on 21 April 1994, as proof of his active role in furthering the common purpose of the JCE that encompassed all three massacre sites.[588] It contends that while physical presence at a massacre site might be an indicator of a co-perpetrator's contribution,[589] it is not necessary in order to incur liability under a JCE theory.[590]

292. The Prosecution submits that although the Trial Chamber correctly set out the applicable law with respect to JCE, it failed to apply it accurately to the factual findings with respect to the nature and extent of the Appellant's criminal responsibility for the Cyanika Parish massacre.[591] On the basis of the Trial Chamber's findings, the Prosecution asserts that the only reasonable conclusion is that a single JCE existed with the common purpose of killing Tutsi at Murambi **[page 90]** Technical School, Cyanika Parish and Kaduha Parish. The Trial Chamber erred in "breaking up" this single enterprise and in finding that the Appellant was not criminally responsible for the killing of Tutsi at the Cyanika Parish.[592]

293. The Appellant submits that the Prosecution's request that the Appellant be found responsible for the Cyanika Parish massacre without any factual basis is unjustified, as the theory of "on-site or spontaneous joint criminal enterprise" in itself has no basis in law.[593] He argues that his participation in the Cyanika

583 Simba Notice of Appeal, IV-5; Simba Appeal Brief, paras 421-423.

584 Prosecution Response, para. 223

585 Prosecution Notice of Appeal, Ground 1, paras 1-5; Prosecution Appeal Brief, para. 26; AT. 22 May 2007 pp. 46-53.

586 Prosecution Appeal Brief, para. 27; AT. 22 May 2007 p. 46.

587 Prosecution Appeal Brief, para. 27. In its Appeal Brief, the Prosecution also contends that the Trial Chamber erred in applying the *mens rea* for the first category of JCE (Prosecution Appeal Brief, paras 67-74). The Appeals Chamber will not consider this alleged error since it was not included in the Prosecution Notice of Appeal, and because it has previously decided to disregard paragraphs 65-74 of the Prosecution Appeal Brief (*see* Decision on 'Prosecutor's Motion for Variation of Notice of Appeal Pursuant to Rule 108' of 17 August 2006).

588 Prosecution Notice of Appeal, Ground 1, para. 2, Prosecution Appeal Brief, paras 27, 40-45.

589 Prosecution Appeal Brief, para. 44.

590 Prosecution Appeal Brief, para. 40.

591 Prosecution Appeal Brief, para. 34.

592 AT. 22 May 2007 p. 49.

593 Simba Response, para. 42.

Parish massacre was not established beyond reasonable doubt at trial,[594] and that the Trial Chamber erred in linking the Cyanika Parish massacre to those of Murambi and Kaduha.[595]

294. The Appeals Chamber notes that the Prosecution originally alleged in its Notice of Appeal that the Trial Chamber erred in fact. Subsequently, in its Appeal Brief, it expanded this to encompass an error of law. It is not entirely clear on what basis the error of fact is alleged. As the alleged error appears to more closely resemble an error of law, the Appeals Chamber will address it as such.

295. The Appeals Chamber agrees that the Trial Chamber concluded that there was a single JCE encompassing all three massacre sites, stating that, "[i]n the Chamber's view, the only reasonable inference from the evidence is that a common criminal purpose existed to kill Tutsi at these three sites."[596] However, the Appeals Chamber notes that, in respect of the Appellant's personal responsibility, this finding is clearly qualified by subsequent Trial Chamber findings. While not expressly stated, it is clear that the Trial Chamber found that there was in effect a separate JCE limited to Murambi Technical School and Kaduha Parish, in which the Appellant was a participant.[597]

296. The Appeals Chamber agrees with the Prosecution that physical presence at the time a crime is committed by the physical perpetrator is not required for liability to be incurred by a participant **[page 91]** in a JCE.[598] However, as conceded by the Prosecution,[599] it may be taken as an indicator of a co-perpetrator's contribution. Here, the Trial Chamber considered that there was "no direct evidence of the presence of Simba" at Cyanika Parish.[600] This appears to have been relevant primarily as a basis for the Trial Chamber's finding that there was no evidence to support the idea that he shared the intent to participate in the common purpose of killing Tutsi there.[601] After finding generally that a common purpose existed to kill Tutsi at the three sites, it found that the Appellant shared the common purpose of killing Tutsi at Murambi Technical School and Kaduha Parish, but expressed its doubt that he equally shared the common purpose of killing Tutsi at Cyanika Parish.[602] As explained by the Trial Chamber, this doubt arose from the fact that there was "no direct evidence linking the Appellant to Cyanika Parish or indicating that he knew and accepted that it would also form part of the operation".[603] It is apparent from this language that the Trial Chamber's consideration of this issue focused on his intent to participate in the common purpose to kill the Tutsi at this site.[604] Therefore the Trial Chamber's inquiry was broader than mere physical presence. The Appeals Chamber sees no error in this approach.

297. Accordingly, this sub-ground of appeal is dismissed.

2. Alleged Error in Requiring a Direct and Substantial Contribution by the Appellant to the Massacre at Cyanika Parish as a Pre-Condition to Holding him Criminally Responsible

298. The Prosecution further claims that the Trial Chamber erred in law in requiring a direct and substantial contribution by the Appellant to the Cyanika Parish massacre as a precondition for holding him criminally

594 Simba Response, para. 41.

595 Simba Response, para. 43.

596 Trial Judgement, para. 402.

597 Trial Judgement, para. 419: "The Trial Chamber finds beyond reasonable doubt that Simba is criminally responsible under Article 6(1) of the Statute based on his participation in a joint criminal enterprise to kill Tutsi civilians at Murambi Technical School and Kaduha Parish." *See also* para. 415: "The Trial Chamber has found that Simba participated in a joint criminal enterprise to kill Tutsi civilians at Murambi Technical School and Kaduha Parish by providing weapons and lending encouragement and approval to the physical perpetrators."; and paragraph 425: "Simba participated in this large-scale killing as a participant in the joint criminal enterprise to kill Tutsi at these two sites by distributing weapons and lending approval and encouragement to the physical perpetrators."; and paragraph 426: "Simba is criminally responsible under Article 6(1) of the Statute based on his participation in a joint criminal enterprise to kill Tutsi civilians at Murambi Technical School and Kaduha Parish."

598 Prosecution Appeal Brief, para. 40; *Kvočka* Appeal Judgement, paras 112-113, 276.

599 Prosecution Appeal Brief, para. 44.

600 Trial Judgement, para. 399. *See also* para. 134.

601 Trial Judgement, para. 407.

602 Trial Judgement, paras 406-407.

603 Trial Judgement, para. 407. The Trial Chamber noted that the "only evidence directly connecting him to the massacre comes from Witness KSU", but noted that this evidence had been excluded (Trial Judgement, para. 134).

604 Trial Judgement, paras 134-136.

responsible for that massacre as a participant in a JCE encompassing all three massacre sites.[605] It submits that a participant in a JCE need only perform actions that "in some way" are directed to the furtherance of the common purpose.[606] The Prosecution adds that, although the Trial Chamber correctly noted that there is no requirement to make a substantial contribution, it erroneously required such contribution.[607]

299. The Prosecution notes that the Trial Chamber found that the three massacres on 21 April 1994 could only be described as a highly coordinated operation involving local militiamen backed **[page 92]** by gendarmes, armed with guns and grenades, and with the organisational and logistical support offered by local authorities and prominent personalities such as the Appellant.[608] The Prosecution submits that the massacre at Cyanika Parish was clearly an essential part of the highly coordinated operation, due to geographic proximity and the participation of the same attackers in the massacres at both Murambi Technical School and Cyanika Parish.[609]

300. The Prosecution submits that the Appellant participated in this JCE by distributing weapons and lending approval and encouragement to the physical perpetrators of the crimes committed at Murambi Technical School and Kaduha Parish.[610] It notes the Trial Chamber's findings regarding the effect that the Appellant had on the enthusiasm of the attackers at Murambi, and the decisive role played in these assaults by the guns and grenades distributed by the Appellant at Kaduha Parish. The Prosecution notes that the Trial Chamber considered that, in light of the fact that the Appellant was a respected national figure in Rwandan society and well known in his native region, the assailants at those places considered the Appellant's presence during the attacks as approval of their conduct, particularly after the Appellant's invocation of the government. Moreover, given the Appellant's stature in Rwandan society as a prominent former political and military figure, the Trial Chamber found that his participation would have had a similar effect on other prominent participants in the JCE such as Prefect Bucyibaruta, Captain Sebuhura, and Bourgmestre Semakwavu.[611]

301. The Appellant responds that the Prosecution was unable to prove beyond reasonable doubt that he had taken part in or in any way contributed to the Cyanika Parish massacre[612] and that the Trial Chamber's findings linking the Cyanika massacre to those of Kaduha and Murambi by assuming a "hypothetical and un-proven plan" are erroneous.[613] Accordingly, he submits that the Prosecution's request that he be found responsible for the killings at Cyanika Parish has no basis.[614]

302. The Appellant also makes a number of submissions regarding whether JCE was established at trial[615] or properly pleaded,[616] the vagueness of the Indictment,[617] the category of JCE applied by **[page 93]** the Trial Chamber,[618] his involvement in planning the three massacres,[619] and motive.[620] These are dealt with in other sections of the Trial Judgement and will not be addressed here.

303. The Appeals Chamber is unable to agree that the Trial Chamber required the Appellant's participation in a JCE at Cyanika Parish to be substantial. The basis for this Prosecution argument appears to be the Trial Chamber's findings that the Appellant provided substantial assistance at the massacres at Murambi Technical School and Kaduha Parish.[621] The Appeals Chamber notes that the Trial Chamber expressly acknowledged

605 Prosecution Notice of Appeal, Ground 1, para. 3; Prosecution Appeal Brief, paras 27, 30, 46, 63; AT. 22 May 2007 p. 47.
606 Prosecution Appeal Brief, paras 47, 52.
607 Prosecution Appeal Brief, paras 48-49, referring to the Trial Judgement, paras 403, 415, 425 and footnote 407.
608 Prosecution Appeal Brief, para. 55.
609 Prosecution Appeal Brief, paras 58-59.
610 Prosecution Appeal Brief, paras 56, 54, 51 (the latter referring to Trial Judgement, paras 403, 415, 419, 425, 426.).
611 Prosecution Appeal Brief, para. 56.
612 Simba Response, para. 41.
613 Simba Response, para. 43.
614 Simba Response, para. 42.
615 Simba Response, paras 19-21.
616 Simba Response, para. 12.
617 Simba Response, para. 11.
618 Simba Response, paras 14-15, 29, referring to Trial Judgement, paras 398-408, 412-426.
619 Simba Response, paras 16, 24.
620 Simba Response, para. 28.
621 *See e.g.* Trial Judgement, para. 403: "Simba participated in the joint criminal enterprise through his acts of assistance and encouragement to the physical perpetrators of the crimes at Murambi Technical School and Kaduha Parish. In the Chamber's view, Simba's actions at those two sites had a *substantial effect* on the killings which followed" (footnote omitted) (emphasis added); Trial

that a showing of substantial contribution is not required as a matter of law.[622] The Trial Chamber correctly interpreted the law on this matter. The Appeals Chamber recalls that although an accused's contribution to a JCE need not be necessary or substantial, it should at least be a significant contribution to the crimes for which the accused is found to be responsible.[623]

304. The fact that the Appellant's actions at Murambi Technical School and Kaduha Parish were found to have provided substantial assistance at those sites does not necessarily imply that this was therefore required for a finding of responsibility for the crimes at Cyanika Parish. The Appellant's actions with respect to Cyanika Parish were clearly addressed by the Trial Chamber, which found that there was "no direct evidence linking him to Cyanika Parish or indicating that he knew and accepted that it would also form part of the operation."[624] In so doing, it considered the Appellant's contribution to the Cyanika Parish massacre only insofar as it could have provided any evidence that would allow for a finding that he possessed the requisite *mens rea* with respect to the JCE at that site. The Prosecution has therefore demonstrated no legal error on the part of the Trial Chamber. As the Prosecution has not properly challenged on appeal the Trial Chamber's findings on the *mens rea* elements for a JCE encompassing the killing of Tutsi at Cyanika Parish,[625] the Appeals Chamber need not consider whether the Trial Chamber erred in its finding in this respect. Accordingly, this ground of appeal is dismissed in its entirety. **[page 94]**

B. Alleged Errors Relating to the Sentence

305. The Prosecution makes several submissions to the effect that the Trial Chamber erred in law by imposing a sentence of 25 years' imprisonment instead of imprisonment for the remainder of the Appellant's life.[626] The Prosecution affirms that the Trial Chamber abused its sentencing discretion and committed three discernible errors of law invalidating its decision: (1) in failing to consider or give proper weight to relevant aggravating factors while erroneously according weight to irrelevant factors in mitigation; (2) in imposing a sentence that is manifestly disproportionate to the gravity of the crimes and the Appellant's role; and (3) in imposing a sentence that is in disparity with the Tribunal's sentencing practice.[627]

306. The Appeals Chamber recalls that the Trial Chamber has considerable discretion in determining an appropriate sentence, which includes the weight given to mitigating and aggravating circumstances.[628] As a general rule, the Appeals Chamber will not revise a sentence unless "it believes that the Trial Chamber has committed an error in exercising its discretion, or has failed to follow applicable law."[629] The Appeals Chamber will only intervene if a Trial Chamber ventures outside its "discretionary framework" in imposing a sentence and commits a "discernable" error.[630] It therefore falls, in the present appeal, on the Prosecution to demonstrate how the Trial Chamber ventured outside its discretionary framework in making the decisions challenged.

1. Alleged Failure to Consider or Give Proper Weight to Relevant Aggravating Factors and Erroneously According Weight to Irrelevant Factors in Mitigation.

307. The Prosecution contends that the Trial Chamber erroneously failed to consider or give adequate weight to aggravating factors, while taking extraneous and irrelevant considerations into account as

Judgement, para. 425: "Simba participated in this large-scale killing as a participant in the joint criminal enterprise to kill Tutsi at these two sites by distributing weapons and lending approval and encouragement to the physical perpetrators. In its findings on criminal responsibility, the Chamber described this assistance as having a *substantial effect* on the killings that followed" (footnotes omitted) (emphasis added); Trial Judgement, para. 433: "The Chamber determined that Simba's acts of assistance and encouragement provided *substantial assistance*." (emphasis added).

622 Trial Judgement, fn. 407.

623 *Brđanin* Appeal Judgement, para. 430.

624 Trial Judgement, para. 407.

625 *See* Decision on Motion for Variation of Notice of Appeal of 17 August 2006.

626 Prosecution Notice of Appeal, Ground 2, paras 6-11; AT. 22 May 2007 pp. 53-61.

627 Prosecution Notice of Appeal, Ground 2, paras 6-11; Prosecution Appeal Brief, para. 76. The Appeals Chamber will not consider the additional arguments presented in paragraphs 108 to 114 of the Prosecution Appeal Brief, since it has already decided to disregard them (*see* Decision on Motion for Variation of Notice of Appeal of 17 August 2006, in which the Appeals Chamber denied a Prosecution request for an amendment of its Notice of Appeal which invited the Appeals Chamber to consider the sentencing practice of Rwanda).

628 *Brđanin* Appeal Judgement, para. 500.

629 *Delalić et al.* Appeal Judgement, para. 725.

630 *Delalić et al.* Appeal Judgement, para. 725.

mitigating circumstances.[631] The Prosecution submits that the Trial Chamber erred by (a) failing to accord full weight to the Appellant's stature in Rwandan society and his authority;[632] (b) giving undue weight in mitigation to the absence of zeal and sadism demonstrated by the Appellant **[page 95]** while committing the crimes;[633] and (c) according undue weight to extraneous and irrelevant considerations in mitigation.[634] The Appeals Chamber will consider these arguments in turn.

(a) Alleged Failure to Accord Full Weight to Aloys Simba's Stature and Authority in Rwanda

308. The Prosecution alleges that although the Trial Chamber noted the Appellant's stature in Rwandan society as a prominent former political and military figure, and stated that the influence derived from this status would have made it likely that others would follow his example, it erred by not according full weight to this aggravating factor. It further contends that the Trial Chamber should have accorded full weight to this factor regardless of whether the Appellant's authority and influence were formal or *de facto*.[635] The Prosecution submits that the Appellant wielded the same authority, albeit *de facto*, when he committed the crimes as when he occupied formal positions within the government, military and political structure. He was able to use that authority to instigate others to commit crimes[636] or to stop them from doing certain acts.[637] It further submits that the Appellant's use of his stature to commit crimes constituted an abuse of public trust.[638]

309. The Appellant opposes the Prosecution's submissions on his stature. He submits that he had been deprived of rank and promotion for a long time and that his relations with the Tutsi earned him criticism within Rwandan society and in the press. He also submits that as the Prosecution abandoned at trial, due to lack of evidence, its allegations that the Appellant had *de facto* authority over Hutu civilians, local administrative authorities, and soldiers and gendarmes, it cannot on appeal make arguments based on an alleged abuse of formal or *de facto* authority or adduce new factual evidence to this effect on appeal without violating his rights.[639]

310. The Trial Chamber found that the influence the Appellant derived from his stature made it likely that others would follow his example, and that this was an aggravating factor.[640] The Appeals Chamber recalls that the Trial Chamber implicitly found that the Appellant abused this influence.[641] This interpretation is supported by the Trial Chamber's findings that the Appellant participated in the attack against Murambi Technical School and Kaduha Parish by lending encouragement and **[page 96]** approval to the attackers and that, since the Appellant was a respected national figure in Rwandan society and well-known in his native region (Gikongoro), the assailants at those places would have viewed his presence during the attacks as approval of their conduct, particularly after his invocation of government support.[642] In so doing, the Trial Chamber did not distinguish between his formal or *de facto* authority and influence, but limited itself to established facts. The Trial Chamber therefore did fully take into account as aggravating factors the Appellant's stature in Rwanda society, as well as the abuse of the influence he derived from it.

311. This sub-ground of appeal is accordingly dismissed.

---

631 Prosecution Notice of Appeal, Ground 2, paras 8-10; Prosecution Appeal Brief, paras 76, 79, 101-107; AT. 22 May 2007 p. 53.

632 Prosecution Notice of Appeal, Ground 2, para. 8; Prosecution Appeal Brief, paras 80-91.

633 Prosecution Notice of Appeal, Ground 2, para. 9. In its Appeal Brief, the Prosecution further affirms that the Trial Chamber should have found that the Appellant acted with sadism and zeal and that this constituted an aggravating factor (Prosecution Appeal Brief, paras 92-100).

634 Prosecution Notice of Appeal, Ground 2, para. 10.

635 Prosecution Appeal Brief, para. 80, referring to Trial Judgement paras 434-435, 439; Prosecution Appeal Brief, paras 84-85, referring to *Semanza* Appeal Judgement, para. 336.

636 Prosecution Appeal Brief, para. 81.

637 Prosecution Appeal Brief, para. 82.

638 Prosecution Appeal Brief, paras 82-83.

639 Simba Response, paras 50-53.

640 Trial Judgement, para. 439, referring to its previous factual findings on the Appellant's stature in Rwandan society (*see* Trial Judgement, paras 54-60).

641 *See* above Chapter II, Section K, para. 285.

642 Trial Judgement, paras 400, 403. The Trial Chamber thus did not regard as an aggravating circumstance the fact that the Appellant encouraged and approved of the attacks, as these were elements of the crime, but rather took into account the fact that he abused his influence by doing so.

(b) Alleged Failure to Give Proper Weight to the Sadism and Zeal of the Appellant

312. The Prosecution submits that the Trial Chamber erred in law by "treating its finding that the [Appellant] did not commit the crimes with sadism and zeal, in effect, as a mitigating factor".[643] The Prosecution further argues that the Trial Chamber took into account erroneous factors to reach this finding[644] and that, contrary to the Trial Chamber's conclusion, the criminal conduct of the Appellant evidences zeal and sadism.[645]

313. The Prosecution submits that the Appellant's own conduct and his targeting of refugees at sites traditionally regarded as safe havens, such as churches and schools, overwhelmingly evidenced zeal and sadism.[646] The Prosecution argues that attacks against such places have traditionally been characterised as evidencing zeal, and as constituting an aggravating factor in sentencing.[647] Further, the Prosecution submits that the Appellant's zeal and sadism is demonstrated by his use of language, describing the victims as "filth" and urging others to "wipe them away".[648] It adds that, in any case, sadism is inherent in mass crimes such as those he committed.[649]

314. The Prosecution also asserts that the impact of the Appellant's criminal conduct was profound, despite the brevity of his visit to the massacre sites.[650] The Prosecution affirms that the fact that the Appellant did not physically participate in killings and that he made only brief visits to the massacre sites is irrelevant in the present case since the Appellant has been found responsible **[page 97]** for "committing" the crimes as a member of a JCE, distributing weapons and giving words of encouragement "set[ting] in motion a process that culminated in the massacres of thousands of victims".[651]

315. The Appellant does not specifically respond to this Prosecution argument.

316. The Trial Chamber held at paragraph 435:

> At the time of the events, Simba had no formal position within the government, military, or political structures of the government. He assumed the post of civil defence adviser on 18 May 1994. However, he is not charged with any criminal conduct based on this position. In addition, the Chamber is not convinced beyond reasonable doubt that Simba was the architect of the massacres at Murambi Technical School and Kaduha Parish or that he played a role in their planning. In addition, the manner in which Simba participated in the joint criminal enterprise did not evidence any particular zeal or sadism on his part. In particular, he did not physically participate in killings and did not remain at the sites of the massacres for more than a brief period.[652]

317. The Appeals Chamber is unable to agree that the finding of a lack of zeal or sadism was considered in mitigation of the Appellant's sentence. The Appeals Chamber observes that paragraph 435 of the Trial Judgement is not included in the section entitled "Individual, Aggravating, and Mitigating Circumstances" but in the section of the sentencing deliberations entitled "Gravity of the Offence". The finding thus appears to have been considered in the context of determining the gravity of the Appellant's crimes, as evidenced by the subsequent paragraph.

318. The Appeals Chamber further notes that the Trial Chamber listed, in the section on "Individual, Aggravating, and Mitigating Circumstances", a number of mitigating factors that it considered in the determination of the Appellant's sentence. The fact that he did not exhibit any particular zeal or sadism was not included in this section. The Appeals Chamber finds, therefore, that the finding regarding a lack of zeal or sadism did not influence the Trial Chamber's decision with respect to factors mitigating the Appellant's sentence.

319. With respect to the Prosecution's arguments to the effect that the Trial Chamber erred in not taking into account the Appellant's sadism and zeal as an aggravating factor, the Appeals Chamber notes that these

---

643 Prosecution Notice of Appeal, Ground 2, para. 9.
644 AT. 22 May 2007 p. 57.
645 Prosecution Appeal Brief, para. 92, referring to Trial Judgement, para. 435.
646 Prosecution Appeal Brief, paras 94, 97; AT. 22 May 2007 p. 61.
647 Prosecution Appeal Brief, para. 97, referring to *Kayishema and Ruzindana* Trial Judgement, para. 16, and *Kayishema and Ruzindana* Appeal Judgement, paras 360-361.
648 Prosecution Appeal Brief, para. 96.
649 Prosecution Appeal Brief, paras 94, 100.
650 Prosecution Appeal Brief, para. 92, referring to Trial Judgement para. 435.
651 Prosecution Appeal Brief, para. 93.
652 Trial Judgement, para. 435 (footnote omitted).

are raised for the first time in the Appeal Brief.[653] The Prosecution Notice of Appeal does not explicitly allege that the Trial Chamber erred by not finding that the Appellant acted with zeal and sadism and by failing to take these factors into account in aggravation. Hence, the Prosecution clearly failed to "indicate the substance of the alleged errors" as required by Rule **[page 98]** 108 of the Rules. Accordingly, the Appeals Chamber declines to consider the Prosecution's arguments at issue.

320. However, the Appeals Chamber holds, *proprio motu*, Judge Liu dissenting, that the Trial Chamber erred when it assessed the gravity of the offence in light of its finding that "the manner in which Simba participated in the joint criminal enterprise did not evidence any particular zeal or sadism."[654] The Appeals Chamber notes that the aforementioned factors are neither elements of the crime of genocide or extermination nor factors indicating the gravity of the crimes as such. The Appeals Chamber raises this issue *proprio motu* in order to clarify that zeal and sadism are factors to be considered, where appropriate, as aggravating factors rather than in the assessment of the gravity of an offence. Nonetheless, given the fact that the Appeals Chamber has already rejected the Prosecution's claim that the Trial Chamber erred in not taking into account the Appellant's sadism and zeal in aggravation on procedural grounds in the preceding paragraph, this error can not have any impact upon the Appellant's sentence.

321. Accordingly, this sub-ground of appeal is dismissed.

(c) Alleged Errors in According Weight to Extraneous and Irrelevant Considerations in Mitigation, or Undue Weight to Mitigating Factors.

322. The Prosecution submits that the Trial Chamber committed a discernible error by according weight to extraneous and irrelevant considerations in mitigating the Appellant's sentence.[655] In particular, the Prosecution contends that the Trial Chamber erred (i) in according weight in mitigation to the selective assistance that the Appellant provided to some people, and (ii) considering in mitigation that the Appellant "might have acted out of patriotism and government allegiance rather than extremism or ethnic hatred".[656]

323. The Appellant does not specifically respond to this argument, submitting that he will not discuss the Trial Chamber's exercise of its discretionary sentencing power for "crimes in respect of which the physical possibility that [he] committed them remains unproven".[657]

324. The Appeals Chamber will consider these arguments in turn.

(i) The Trial Chamber Accorded Weight in Mitigation to the Selective Assistance Provided by the Appellant to Members of his Family **[page 99]**

325. The Prosecution contends that the Trial Chamber erred, at paragraph 442 of the Trial Judgement, in according weight in mitigation to the selective assistance provided by the Appellant to some people. It argues that the Appellant extended assistance only to members of his family and close friends, some of whom happened to be Tutsi, and thus did not provide assistance because they were members of the Tutsi ethnic group. Consequently, his assistance should not have been given any weight in mitigation.[658]

326. The Appeals Chamber notes that this argument was not included in the Prosecution's Notice of Appeal. Consequently the Prosecution is precluded from adducing it on appeal.

(ii) The Trial Chamber Accorded Weight in Mitigation to the Possibility that the Appellant Acted Out of Patriotism and Government Allegiance rather than Extremism or Ethnic Hatred

327. The Prosecution contends that the Trial Chamber erroneously considered in mitigation that the Appellant "might have acted out of patriotism and government allegiance rather than extremism or ethnic hatred." It submits that possible motivation could not amount to a mitigating factor in the circumstances of

---

653 Prosecution Appeal Brief, para. 97.
654 Trial Judgement, para. 435.
655 Prosecution Notice of Appeal, Ground 2, para. 10; Prosecution Appeal Brief, para. 101.
656 Prosecution Appeal Brief, paras 102, 104; Trial Judgement, paras 441-442.
657 Simba Response, para. 49.
658 Prosecution Appeal Brief, para. 104.

this case.[659] The Prosecution adds that it "is incorrect [...] to use as a mitigating factor, only something that may have existed or could possibly have existed".[660]

328. The Appeals Chamber recalls that neither the Statute nor the Rules exhaustively define the factors which may be considered as mitigating factors.[661] Consequently, under the jurisprudence of this Tribunal, "what constitutes a mitigating circumstance is a matter for the Trial Chamber to determine in the exercise of its discretion."[662] The burden of proof which must be met by an accused with regard to mitigating circumstances is not, as with aggravating circumstances, proof beyond reasonable doubt,[663] but proof on the balance of probabilities – the circumstance in question must exist or have existed "more probably than not".[664] Once a Trial Chamber determines that certain evidence constitutes a mitigating circumstance, the decision as to the weight to be accorded to that mitigating circumstance also lies within the wide discretion afforded to the Trial Chamber at sentencing.[665] **[page 100]**

329. In the instant case, the Trial Chamber found that

> [the Appellant] spent much of his life and career before 1994 engaged in professions devoted to the public service of his country. His political views before April 1994 appear to have been relatively moderate. Such evidence can in no way exonerate or excuse [him] for his participation in the killings. However, it provides a somewhat nuanced picture and may imply that his participation in the massacres resulted from misguided notions of patriotism and government allegiance rather than extremism or ethnic hatred. The Chamber also notes that [the Appellant] does not deny the existence of genocide in Rwanda and condemned the massive slaughter that occurred.[666]

330. The Appeals Chamber finds that the Prosecution allegation at issue is based on a misreading of the Trial Judgement. It is clear from paragraph 441 that the Trial Chamber took into account only two mitigating factors, the Appellant's prior moderate political views and his service to his country. In the view of the Trial Chamber, these two mitigating factors demonstrated that the Appellant might have acted with another motive. However, this was merely speculation on the part of the Trial Chamber and did not reflect a finding that this motive was itself a separate mitigating factor. This being the case, the Prosecution has not demonstrated that the Trial Chamber erroneously considered in mitigation that the Appellant "might have acted out of patriotism and government allegiance rather than extremism or ethnic hatred."

2. Alleged Error in Imposing on the Appellant a Sentence that Was Manifestly Disproportionate to the Gravity of his Crimes and his Role in Them

331. The Prosecution submits that the Trial Chamber erred by failing to take sufficient account of either the inherent gravity of the crimes of which the Appellant was convicted or his individual circumstances.[667] The Prosecution submits that the jurisprudence of the international tribunals shows that the gravity of the crimes is the most important consideration in arriving at an appropriate sentence.[668] In the instant case, the Appellant was convicted of genocide and extermination as a crime against humanity, both inherently grave crimes, with the former the "gravest crime known to the international criminal justice system."[669] As a result, the Prosecution argues that the Trial Chamber did not impose the sentence the crimes deserved.[670]

---

659 Prosecution Notice of Appeal, Ground 2, para. 10; Prosecution Appeal Brief, paras 102-103.
660 AT. 22 May 2007 p. 55.
661 *Kajelijeli* Appeal Judgement, para. 294.
662 *Musema* Appeal Judgement, para. 395.
663 *Delalić et al.* Appeal Judgement, para. 763.
664 *Delalić et al.* Appeal Judgement, para. 590.
665 *Niyitegeka* Appeal Judgement, para. 266, referring to *Musema* Appeal Judgement, para. 396 and *Kayishema and Ruzindana* Appeal Judgement, para. 366; *Kajelijeli* Appeal Judgement, para. 294.
666 Trial Judgement, para. 441 (internal footnotes omitted).
667 Prosecution Notice of Appeal, Ground 2, para. 8; Prosecution Appeal Brief, para. 115.
668 Prosecution Appeal Brief, para. 116, referring to *Akayesu* Appeal Judgement para. 413, *Kayishema and Ruzindana* Appeal Judgement para. 593, *Delalić et al.* Appeal Judgement, para. 731; *Kupreškić* Appeal Judgement, para. 442; *Aleksovski* Appeal Judgement, para. 182.
669 Prosecution Appeal Brief, para. 117, quoting *Semanza* Appeal Judgement, Separate Opinion of Judge Shahabuddeen and Judge Güney, para. 2.
670 Prosecution Appeal Brief, para. 117.

332. The Prosecution contends that the Appellant's participation and the impact of such participation were "pre-eminent", and that "the short duration of the [Appellant's] stay at the **[page 101]** massacre site is irrelevant since the *impact* of his actions was profound."[671] The Trial Chamber held that the use of guns and grenades, which the Appellant distributed at Kaduha Parish, was a "decisive" factor in the success of these assaults.[672]

333. The Prosecution adds that the Trial Chamber erred in focusing solely on the fact that the Appellant did not physically perpetrate the crimes himself as opposed to looking at the impact of his actions.[673] The Prosecution submits that the Trial Chamber erred by removing the Appellant from the category of "principle perpetrators", limiting those to persons who planned and ordered atrocities.[674]

334. The Prosecution finally submits that even assuming that there were some mitigating factors, this does not automatically entitle the Appellant to "credit" in the determination of the sentence.[675] It argues that given the gravity of crimes of which the Appellant was convicted, the shocking number of lives lost, the Appellant's pre-eminent role and the totality of the circumstances of this case, the Appellant deserved no credit and the Trial Chamber should not have "moved him away from the category of convicts deserving of a life sentence".[676]

335. The Appellant does not specifically respond to these Prosecution arguments.

336. The Appeals Chamber observes that the Trial Chamber correctly noted that it has "considerable, though not unlimited, discretion on account of its obligation to individualize penalties to fit the individual circumstances of an accused and to reflect the gravity of the crimes for which the accused has been convicted".[677] The Appeals Chamber also endorses the view taken by the Trial Chamber that there are a "multitude of variables, ranging from the number and types of crimes committed to the personal circumstances of the individual"[678] which need to be taken into account in order to individualise sentences. In the instant case, the Trial Chamber expressly recognised the gravity of the crimes for which the Appellant was responsible[679] while at the same time taking into consideration his role in the commission of these crimes.[680] The Prosecution advances a different view of the gravity of the crimes and the Appellant's role therein, apparently arguing against any discretion in sentencing where an accused is a "principal perpetrator" who has committed grave crimes. For the reasons stated above, the Appeals Chamber, Judge Schomburg **[page 102]** dissenting, is unable to agree that the Trial Chamber was so restricted in the exercise of its discretion and reaffirms the requirement to individualise sentences. In the instant case, the Prosecution has not demonstrated how the Trial Chamber may have committed an error in exercising its discretion or departed from the Tribunals' case law by imposing a sentence of 25 years' imprisonment. The Appeals Chamber, Judge Schomburg dissenting, accordingly dismisses this sub-ground of appeal.

3. The Sentence is Allegedly Inconsistent with the Tribunal's Sentencing Practice

337. The Prosecution submits that the Trial Chamber erred by imposing a sentence that is manifestly inconsistent with the Tribunal's sentencing practice in similar cases.[681]

338. This argument goes beyond the scope of the Prosecution Notice of Appeal. It is also noted that a previous attempt by the Prosecution to amend its Notice of Appeal in order to incorporate a similar ground

671 Prosecution Appeal Brief, para. 118.
672 Prosecution Appeal Brief, para. 118.
673 Prosecution Appeal Brief, para. 119.
674 Prosecution Appeal Brief, para. 120.
675 Prosecution Appeal Brief, para. 123, referring to *Niyitegeka* Appeal Judgement, para. 267.
676 Prosecution Appeal Brief, para. 124.
677 Trial Judgement, para. 431.
678 Trial Judgement, para. 432, referring to *Kvočka et al* Appeal Judgement, para. 681.
679 Trial Judgement, para. 436.
680 Trial Judgement, para. 435.
681 Prosecution Appeal Brief, para. 125.

of appeal was rejected by the Appeals Chamber.[682] Accordingly, this sub-ground is dismissed without further consideration. **[page 103]**

IV. DISPOSITION

For the foregoing reasons, **THE APPEALS CHAMBER**,

PURSUANT to Article 24 of the Statute and Rule 118 of the Rules;

NOTING the written submissions of the parties and their oral arguments presented at the hearing on 22 May 2007;

SITTING in open session;

DISMISSES in all respects the grounds of appeal raised by Aloys Simba, and the Prosecution in their respective appeals;

AFFIRMS the Appellant's convictions for genocide and extermination as a crime against humanity under Counts 1 and 3;

AFFIRMS, Judge Schomburg dissenting, the Appellant's sentence of twenty-five (25) years' imprisonment entered for these convictions, subject to credit being given under Rule 101(D) and Rule 107 of the Rules for the period already spent in detention since 27 November 2001;

RULES that this Judgement shall be enforced immediately pursuant to Rule 119 of the Rules; and

ORDERS in accordance with Rules 103(B) and 107 of the Rules, that Aloys Simba is to remain in the custody of the Tribunal pending his transfer to the State in which his sentence will be served. **[page 104]**

Done in English and French, the English text being authoritative.

Fausto Pocar	Mehmet Güney	Liu Daqun
Presiding Judge	Judge	Judge
Theodor Meron	Wolfgang Schomburg	
Judge	Judge	

Judge Schomburg appends a partially dissenting opinion.

Judge Liu appends a partially dissenting opinion.

Signed on the 21st day of November 2007 at The Hague, The Netherlands, and delivered on this 27th day of November 2007 at Arusha, Tanzania.

[Seal of the Tribunal]

682 Simba Prosecutor's Motion for Variation of the Notice of Appeal Pursuant to Rule 108 of 27 March 2006, para. 9.

[page 1] V. PARTIALLY DISSENTING OPINION OF JUDGE LIU DAQUN

1. I support the Appeals Chamber's findings in this case. However, with due respect, I am in disagreement with the Majority that "the Trial Chamber erred when it assessed the gravity of the offence in light of its finding that 'the manner in which Simba participated in the joint criminal enterprise did not evidence any particular zeal or sadism'".[1] I further disagree with the Majority's view that because neither zeal nor sadism are "elements of the crime of genocide or extermination nor factors indicating the gravity of crimes as such [...] zeal and sadism are factors to be considered, where appropriate, as aggravating factors rather than in the assessment of the gravity of an offence."[2]

2. I agree that zeal and sadism are not elements of genocide and extermination, however, they may still be correctly taken into account as "particular circumstances" relevant to the gravity of the offence. It is established in the jurisprudence of the Appeals Chamber of this Tribunal and the ICTY that "[w]hen assessing the gravity of the offence, a Trial Chamber must take into account the inherent gravity of the crime and the criminal conduct of the accused, *the determination of which requires a consideration of the particular circumstances of the case* and the crimes for which the accused was convicted, as well as the form and degree of the participation of the accused in the crime."[3] Thus, by taking zeal and sadism into account in the context of assessing "the manner in which Simba participated"[4] in the JCE, the Trial Chamber acted in conformity with the case law.

3. In the jurisprudence of this Tribunal and that of the ICTY, the consideration of zeal and sadism in sentencing has not been restricted to the determination of "aggravating factors", although they are factors which when relevant have been considered in the framework of enhancing a sentence. In the *Ntakirutimana* case, the Trial Chamber considered zeal and sadism in the context of the principle of gradation of sentences, not as an aggravating circumstance.[5] Although this was **[page 2]** noted by the Appeals Chamber on appeal,[6] the Appeals Chamber did not find an error on the part of the Trial Chamber for not taking it into account as an aggravating circumstance. Similarly, the *Ndindabahizi* Trial Chamber and *Niyitegeka* Trial Chamber did not consider zeal and sadism in the context of aggravating circumstances but in the context of gradation of sentences.[7] Although both the *Ndindabahizi* Appeals Chamber and the *Niyitegeka* Appeals Chamber considered errors in sentencing, neither Appeals Chamber made a *proprio motu* finding of an error on the part of the Trial Chamber, for not taking it into account as an aggravating circumstance.

4. In a very recent ICTY Appeals Chamber Judgement, the Appeals Chamber in *Limaj*, dismissed a ground of appeal by the Prosecution, opining that the absence of a sadistic motive was not considered by the Trial Chamber as a mitigating circumstance but "taken into account as particular circumstances when assessing the gravity of the crimes".[8] This approach is directly on point and consistent with that taken by the Trial Chamber in the present case. However, the Appeals Chamber in *Limaj* did not *proprio motu* find that the Trial Chamber had erred. Similarly, in the *Dragan Nikolić* case, the Trial Chamber held that the manner in which crimes were committed is an important consideration in assessing the gravity of the offence and considered in this context, that he sadistically beat detainees.[9] This was assessed by the Appeals Chamber

1 Appeal Judgement, para. 320.

2 *Ibid.* While I disagree with the Majority that the Trial Chamber erred, I do not support the crediting by the Trial Chamber of the Appellant for something he did not do in its assessment of the gravity of the offence, that is, in considering that his manner of participation in the JCE "*did not evidence* any particular zeal or sadism" (emphasis added). In this regard, I note the Appeals Chamber's holding in the *Momir Nikolić* Appeals Judgement, para. 56, that "Trial Chambers, when assessing the gravity of the offence, have no obligation to take into account what the accused did *not* do." (emphasis in original). Since this aspect of the verdict is not in issue in the present Judgement, I will not address it further.

3 (Emphasis added). *Akayesu* Appeal Judgement, para. 413; *Blaškić* Appeal Judgement, para. 683; *Vasiljević* Appeal Judgement, para. 182; *Furundžija* Appeal Judgement, para. 249; *Aleksovski* Appeal Judgement, para. 182.

4 Trial Judgement, para. 435.

5 *Ntakirutimana* Trial Judgement, para. 884.

6 *Ntakirutimana* Appeal Judgement, para. 550.

7 *Ndindabahizi* Trial Judgement, para. 500; *Niyitegeka* Trial Judgement, para. 486.

8 *Limaj* Appeal Judgement, para. 133.

9 *Dragan Nikolić* Trial Judgement, paras 186, 189.

which found no error *proprio motu* on the part of the Trial Chamber for not taking it into account as an aggravating circumstance.[10]

5. Furthermore, the Appeals Chamber has emphasised in previous Judgements that sentencing is a discretionary decision and that it is inappropriate to set down a definitive list of sentencing guidelines, given the discretionary nature of sentencing.[11] Up until this point, the practice of the Appeals Chamber has been consistent with this principle, generally allowing a Trial Chamber to decide the categorisation of elements as relevant to factors such as gravity on one hand and aggravating on the other. s a result, certain factors have in the jurisprudence been considered both as aggravating factors and under the gravity of the offence (although not in the same case). In my respectful view, the above-mentioned finding of the Majority marks an unfortunate departure from this principle.

6. In sum, the Majority's decision to *proprio motu* find that the Trial Chamber erred in considering zeal and sadism in its assessment of the gravity of the offence is unsupported by the jurisprudence which has broadly defined elements that may be considered under "gravity". It is not **[page 3]** clear why the Majority decided to act *proprio motu* in this case, particularly as the Prosecution ground relating to this issue was summarily dismissed for lack of notice. In my view, this finding marks an encroachment into the discretionary framework of the Trial Chambers, who are best placed to determine the relevant factors in sentencing. It is for the foregoing reasons that I cannot support the Majority's finding of an error by the Trial Chamber in the exercise of its sentencing discretion.

Done in both English and French, the English text being authoritative.

Signed on the 21st day of November 2007 at The Hague, The Netherlands,

Issued on the 27th day of November 2007 in Arusha, Tanzania.

Liu Daqun
Judge

[Seal of the Tribunal]

10 *Dragan Nikolić* Appeal Judgement, para. 30.

11 *Blaškić* Appeal Judgement, para. 680.

[page 1] VI. PARTIALLY DISSENTING OPINION OF JUDGE SCHOMBURG

1. With all due respect, I cannot find any reason to depart from the International Tribunal's established jurisprudence on sentencing and uphold the sentence of 25 years' imprisonment for Aloys Simba. The Trial Chamber simply took this sentence from the wrong shelf.[1] The only adequate sentence in this case is life imprisonment. I cannot identify any factors which would permit a distinction to be made between this judgement and previous cases, in particular *Gacumbitsi v. The Prosecutor.*

2. Furthermore, pursuant to Article 23(1) of the International Tribunal's Statute, we shall have recourse to the general practice regarding prison sentences in the courts of Rwanda. This International Tribunal was established to avoid impunity. It would be contrary to this mandate to mete out punishment which is more lenient than sentences handed down in Rwanda, in particular vis-à-vis subordinates, as opposed to those standing trial as their superiors before the International Tribunal.

3. Finally, I need to point out that in this case, unlike in most of the other cases before the International Tribunal in which those convicted for the crime of genocide have received less than life sentence, there were no significantly distinguishing circumstances.[2] In fact, Aloys Simba was a principal perpetrator with stature in Rwandan society as a prominent former political and military figure who abused his position and influence to encourage the death of thousands, proven not only for one occasion. Like Sylvestre Gacumbitsi, he was a "primary player."[3] **[page 2]**

Done in English and French, the English text being authoritative.

Signed on the 21st day of November 2007 at The Hague, The Netherlands,

Issued on the 27th day of November 2007 in Arusha, Tanzania.

Wolfgang Schomburg

Judge

[Seal of the Tribunal]

1 *See Galić* Appeal Judgement, para. 455; *Gacumbitsi* Appeal Judgement, para. 205.

2 Simba's case is not comparable to those cases in which an individual convicted of genocide or extermination has been sentenced to less than life imprisonment. In the *Serushago* Sentencing Judgement (upheld on appeal) and the *Ruggiu* Sentencing Judgement, a fixed term of imprisonment was imposed in cases where the convicted person had pleaded guilty. In the *Semanza* Appeal Judgement (para. 389 and Disposition) and the *Kajelijeli* Appeal Judgement (paras 324-325), the sentences reflected the fact that the pre-trial rights of the convicted persons had been infringed. In the *Kayishema and Ruzindana* Trial Judgement (Sentence, para. 28), upheld on appeal in the *Kayishema and Ruzindana* Appeal Judgement (para. 372), and *Ntakirutimana* Appeal Judgement (para. 564 and Disposition), the fixed sentences reflected other mitigating factors such as age and level of culpability of the accused.

3 *Gacumbitsi* Appeal Judgement, para. 204.

[page 1] ANNEX A: PROCEDURAL BACKGROUD

A. Notices of Appeal and Briefs

1. The Trial Judgement was delivered in English on 13 December 2005. The Prosecution and the Appellant both submitted Notices of Appeal against the Trial Judgement.

1. Prosecution's Appeal

2. The Prosecution filed its Notice of Appeal on 12 January 2006 and its Appeal Brief on 27 March 2006.[1] On 17 August 2006, the Appeals Chamber dismissed a Prosecution motion for variation of the Notice of Appeal.[2] In its decision, the Appeals Chamber informed the parties that paragraphs 65-74 and 108-114 of the Prosecution Appeal Brief, which were related to the amendment the Prosecution sought to introduce in its Notice of Appeal, would be disregarded.

3. On 18 October 2006, the Appellant filed his response to the Prosecution Appeal Brief.[3] The Prosecution filed its Brief in Reply on 31 October 2006.[4]

2. Appellant's Appeal

4. On 16 December 2005, the Appeals Chamber granted the Appellant's Motion for Extension of Time for Filing his Notice of Appeal.[5] The Appellant was ordered to file his Notice of Appeal no later than thirty days from the date of the filing of the French translation of the Trial Judgement.[6] The French translation of the Trial Judgement was filed on 15 May 2006,[7] and the Appellant filed his Notice of Appeal on 22 June 2006.[8] **[page 2]**

5. The Appellant filed confidentially his Appeal Brief on 6 September 2006.[9] The Prosecution filed two motions, on 8 September and 27 September 2006 respectively, objecting to the Appellant's Appeal Brief.[10] On 29 September 2006, the Pre-Appeal Judge rejected the filings of both the electronic version and the hard copy of the Appellant's Appeal Brief, and ordered the Appellant to re-file, by 6 October 2006, his Appeal Brief in strict compliance with the Practice Direction on the Length of Briefs and Motions on Appeal and directed the Registrar to withhold the payment of fees, if claimed, associated with the rejected filings.[11]

---

[1] Prosecutor's Notice of Appeal, 12 January 2006; Prosecutor's Appellant's Brief, 27 March 2006, as amended by the Corrigendum to Prosecutor's Appellant's Brief, 28 March 2006.

[2] Decision on Motion for Variation of Notice of Appeal of 17 August 2006.

[3] *The Prosecutor v. Aloys Simba*, Case No. ICTR-2001-76-A, Respondent Brief, filed on 17 October 2006. On 13 April 2006, the Pre-Appeal Judge had granted an extension of time to the Appellant to file his response to the Prosecution Appeal Brief for the reason that a French translation of the documents was not available (Decision on Respondent's Motion for Extension of Time, 13 April 2006).

[4] Prosecutor's Brief in Reply, filed on 31 October 2006.

[5] *Requête en extrême urgence de la Défense en vue d'obtenir un report de délai pour le dépôt de son Acte d'appel contre le jugement de la première Chambre du TPIR rendu le 13/12/05 (Article 166B) du RPP)*, 14 December 2005.

[6] Decision on Motion for Extension of Time for Filing of Notice of Appeal, 16 December 2005.

[7] *See also* Decision on Registrar's Request for Extension of Time for Filing an Official Translation of the Trial Judgement, 25 January 2005; *Observations du Greffier relatives à la seconde ordonnance de la décision relative à la requête visant à obtenir un report de délai pour le dépôt de l'acte d'appel rendue par la Chambre d'Appel le 16 décembre 2005*, 21 December 2005.

[8] *Acte d'appel de la Défense (Article 24 du Statut du TPIR),* 22 June 2006. The Appeals Chamber notes that the French translation of the Trial Judgement was only served to the Appellant on 23 May 2006 (*see* Decision on Defence Motion for Extension of Time to Respond to the Prosecutor's Appellant's Brief, 20 June 2006, fn. 6).

[9] *Mémoire d'appel de la Défense,* 6 September 2006. An electronic copy had been transmitted on 5 September 2006. The annexes were filed on 18 September 2006. The original hard copy of the Appellant's Appeal Brief was filed on 21 September 2006. *See* Order Concerning Aloys Simba's Appellant's Brief, 29 September 2006, p. 2.

[10] Prosecutor's Urgent Motion Objecting to "Mémoire d'appel de la Défense", 8 September 2006; Prosecutor's Urgent Motion Objecting to "Mémoire d'appel de la Défense" and Annexes as Filed on 21 September 2006 and 18 September 2006, Respectively", 27 September 2006.

[11] Order Concerning Aloys Simba's Appellant's Brief, 29 September 2006. *See* also *Requête en extrême urgence de la Défense en vue de solliciter le réexamen de l' « Ordonnance relative au Mémoire d'appel de Simba »,* 2 October 2006; Prosecutor's Response to « Requête en extrême urgence de la Défense en vue de solliciter le réexamen de l' «Ordonnance relative au Mémoire d'appel de

6. The Appellant filed his Appeal Brief on 16 October 2006.[12] The Prosecution filed its Response Brief on 1 December 2006.[13] On 2 March 2007, the Appellant filed his Brief in Reply.[14]

B. Assignment of Judges

7. On 16 December 2005, the following Judges were assigned to hear the appeal: Judge Fausto Pocar, Presiding; Judge Mehmet Güney; Judge Liu Daqun; Judge Theodor Meron; and Judge Wolfgang Schomburg.[15] On 24 January 2006, Judge Liu Daqun was designated as Pre-appeal Judge.[16] **[page 3]**

C. Review Motions

8. On 22 July 2006, the Appellant filed a motion before the Trial Chamber requesting a review of the Trial Judgement pursuant to Rule 120 of the Rules.[17] On the same date, the Appellant filed a request before the Appeals Chamber for the suspension of the time limits in the appeal proceedings and the return of the case to the Trial Chamber for the purposes of conducting a review.[18] On 15 August 2006, the Pre-Appeal Judge confirmed the continuation of the pre-appeal proceedings in this case.[19] On 30 August 2006, the Prosecution asked the Trial Chamber to dismiss the request for review and direct the Appellant to file it before the Appeals Chamber.[20] On 11 September 2006, the Appellant filed a motion requesting the Appeals Chamber to send the request for review to the Trial Chamber for the consideration of its merits, or in the alternative to admit the request for review and to find that it has merit.[21] On 9 January 2007, the Appeals Chamber dismissed the Request for Review and the Request for Suspension of Appeal Proceedings.[22] On 17 August 2007, the Trial Chamber rejected the Defence requests for review and the Motion for Clarification and Additional Relief as moot.[23]

Simba (Article 73 du RPP)»», 2 October 2006; Decision on the Appellant's Request for Reconsideration of the Order Concerning Aloys Simba's Appellant's Brief, 8 November 2006.

12 *Mémoire d'appel d'Aloys Simba*, 16 October 2006. On 4 October 2006, in response to the Appellant's motion requesting an extension of the word limit and authorisation to transmit his Appeal Brief via express mail (*Requête en extrême urgence de la Défense en vue de solliciter exceptionnellement l'interprétation du paragraphe C1a) de la Directive Relative à la Longueur des mémoires et des requêtes en appel et l'autorisation de dépasser le nombre des mots limité et de transmettre le mémoire d'appel uniquement par courrier express (article 73 du RPP)*, 3 October 2006) the Pre-Appeal Judge ordered the Appellant, *inter alia*, to file an Appeal Brief not exceeding 30,000 words, allowed the Appellant to submit his Appeal Brief by express mail, and requested him to take the necessary measures to ensure that the brief reached the Registry of the Tribunal in Arusha, no later than 13 October 2006 (Decision on Aloys Simba's Motion to File his Appellant's Brief, 4 October 2006).

13 Prosecutor's Respondent's Brief, 1 December 2006. The Prosecution filed a first respondent's brief on 24 November 2006. On 30 November 2006, the Pre-Appeal Judge ordered the Prosecution to re-file its respondent's brief no later than 7 December 2006 in strict compliance with the Practice Direction on the Length of Briefs and Motions on Appeal (Order Concerning the Prosecution's Respondent's Brief, 30 November 2006).

14 *Mémoire en réplique de l'Appelant*, 2 March 2007.

15 Order of the Presiding Judge Assigning Judges to an Appeal before the Appeals Chamber, 16 December 2005.

16 Order Appointing a Pre-Appeal Judge, 24 January 2006.

17 *Requête en extrême urgence de la Défense en vue de la Révision du Jugement en date du 13 Décembre 2005 pour cause de faits nouveaux*, 22 July 2006.

18 *Requête de la Défense en vue de la suspension de tous les délais de la procédure en appel en cours*, 22 July 2006 ("Request for Suspension of Appeal Proceedings"); Prosecutor's Response to "Requête de la Défense en vue de la suspension de tous les délais de la procédure en appel en cours", 1 August 2006; *Réplique de la Défense à la Réponse du Procureur suite à la requête de la Défense en vue de la suspension de tous les délais de la procédure en appel en cours*, 7 August 2006.

19 Scheduling Order, 15 August 2006.

20 Motion for Clarification and Additional Relief, 30 August 2006.

21 *Requête en extrême urgence de la Défense en vue de la Révision du Jugement en date du 13 Décembre 2005 pour cause des faits nouveaux et/ou de renvoi de la cause devant la 1ère Chambre du TPIR pour en connaître au fond*, 11 September 2006 ("Request for Review"); Prosecutor's Response to « Requête en extrême urgence de la Défense en vue de la Révision du Jugement en date du 13 Décembre 2005 pour cause des faits nouveaux et/ou de renvoi de la cause devant la 1ère Chambre du TPIR pour en connaître au fond», 21 September 2006; *Réplique à la Réponse du Procureur suite à la «Requête en extrême urgence de la Défense en vue de la Révision du Jugement en date du 13 Décembre 2005 pour cause des faits nouveaux et/ou de renvoi de la cause devant la 1ère Chambre du TPIR pour en connaître au fond»*, 25 October 2006.

22 Decision on Aloys Simba's Requests for Suspension of Appeal Proceedings and Review, 9 January 2007.

23 Ruling on Defence Requests for Review of Trial Judgement and on Prosecution Motion, 17 August 2007.

D. Motions Related to the Admission of Additional Evidence

9. On 3 April 2007, the Appellant filed a motion for the admission of additional evidence.[24] On 24 April 2007, and following an Order of the Pre-Appeal Judge,[25] the Appellant submitted several **[page 4]** documents in support of his Rule 115 application.[26] On 21 May 2007, the Appeals Chamber dismissed the Appellant's motion in its entirety.[27]

E. Hearing of the Appeals

10. Pursuant to a Scheduling Order of 3 April 2007, the Appeals Chamber heard the parties' oral arguments on 22 May 2007 in Arusha, Tanzania.[28]

F. Post-Hearing Proceedings

1. Order for Translation

11. On 3 July 2007, the Appeals Chamber issued an order for the translation of Exhibits D3, D4, D5-A and D5-B, which were admitted at trial in Kinyarwanda only.[29] The Appeals Chamber instructed the parties to file those unofficial translations of the exhibits which were in their possession and requested the Registry to provide certified translations of the exhibits into English and French. The Appellant and Prosecution filed confidentially their submissions on 9 and 11 July 2007 respectively.[30] On 16 July 2007, the Registry filed confidentially the official translations.[31]

2. Order to Registrar Regarding BJK1

12. On 13 July 2007, the Appeals Chamber issued an order in which it requested the Registrar to submit a detailed written submission on the steps taken by the Registry in order to secure the attendance at trial of BJK1.[32] On 13 August 2007, the Registrar filed a confidential submission re BJK1.[33] **[page 5]**

---

24 *Requête en extrême urgence de la Défense en vue d'obtenir l'autorisation de présenter des moyens de preuve supplémentaires (Articles 73 et 115 du RPP)*, 3 April 2007; Prosecutor's Response to "*Requête en extrême urgence de la Défense en vue d'obtenir l'autorisation de présenter des moyens de preuve supplémentaires (Article 73 et 115 du RPP)*", 27 April 2007. Corrigendum, filed on 30 April 2007; *Réplique de la Défense suite à la Réponse du Procureur à la "Requête en extrême urgence de la Défense en vue d'obtenir l'autorisation de présenter des moyens de preuve supplémentaires (Article 73 et 115 du RPP)»*, 11 May 2007. The Appellant filed the annexes to the motion on 12 April 2007.

25 Order Concerning Aloys Simba's «Requête en extrême urgence de la Défense en vue d'obtenir l'autorisation de présenter des moyens de preuve supplémentaires», 18 April 2007.

26 *Transmission des pièces suite à l'ordonnance du juge de la mise en état en date du 18 avril 2007*, 24 April 2007.

27 Decision on Appellant Aloys Simba's Request to Present Additional Evidence, 21 May 2007 (confidential filing).

28 Scheduling Order, 3 April 2007.

29 Order for Translation, 3 July 2007.

30 *Transmission par la Défense des traductions non-officielles en Français des pièces D3, D4, D5A, et D5B*, 9 July 2007; Prosecutor's Response to the Appeals Chamber's "Order for Translation" Dated 3 July 2007, 11 July 2007.

31 Registrar's Submissions Under Rule 33(B) of the Rules on Order for Translation, 16 July 2007. On 3 August 2007, the Registry submitted additional information on the origin of Exhibit D4 (Registrar's Submissions Under Rule 33(B) of the Rules on Order for Translation, 3 August 2007).

32 Simba Order to Registrar Regarding BJK1 of 13 July 2007.

33 The Registrar's Submission filed pursuant to Rule 33(B) of the Rules of Procedure and Evidence Regarding Securing the Attendance At Trial of Witness BJK1, 13 August 2007 (confidential filing).

ANNEX B: CITED MATERIALS/DEFINED TERMS

A. List of Court Decisions

1. ICTR

AKAYESU

The Prosecutor v. Jean-Paul Akayesu, Case No. ICTR-96-4-A, Judgement, 1 June 2001 ("*Akayesu* Appeal Judgement")

BAGILISHEMA

The Prosecuter v. Ignace Bagilishema, Case No. ICTR-95-1A-A, Judgement, 3 July 2002, ("*Bagilishema* Appeal Judgement")

BAGOSORA ET AL.

Prosecutor v. Théoneste Bagosora et al., Case Nos. ICTR-98-41-AR93 & ICTR-98-41-AR93.2, Decision on Prosecutor's Interlocutory Appeals Regarding Exclusion of Evidence, 19 December 2003 ("*Bagosora* Decision on Prosecutor's Interlocutory Appeals Regarding Exclusion of Evidence of 19 December 2003")

BIZIMUNGU ET AL.

The Prosecutor v. Bizimungu, Case No. ICTR-99-50-T, Decision on Prosecution's Interlocutory Appeals Against Decisions of the Trial Chamber on Exclusion of Evidence, 25 June 2004

"BUTARE CASE"

The Prosecutor v. Pauline Nyiramasuhuko et al., Joint Case No. ICTR-98-42-A15*bis* Decision In the Matter of Proceedings under Rule 15 *bis*(D), 24 September 2003 ("*Butare Case* Decision In the Matter of Proceedings under Rule 15 *bis*(D) of 24 September 2003")

GACUMBITSI

The Prosecutor v. Sylvestre Gacumbitsi, Case No. ICTR-01-64, Trial Judgment, 17 June 2004 ("*Gacumbitsi* Trial Judgement")

The Prosecutor v. Sylvestre Gacumbitsi, Case No. ICTR-01-64-A, Judgment, 7 July 2006 ("*Gacumbitsi* Appeal Judgement") **[page 6]**

KAJELIJELI

Juvénal Kajelijeli v. The Prosecutor, Case No. ICTR-98-44A-A, Judgement, 23 May 2005 ("*Kajelijeli* Appeal Judgement")

KAMBANDA

Jean Kambanda v. The Prosecutor, Case No. ICTR-97-23-A, Judgement, 19 October 2000 ("*Kambanda* Appeal Judgement")

KAMUHANDA

Jean de Dieu Kamuhanda v. The Prosecutor, Case No. ICTR-99-54A-A, Judgement, 19 September 2005 ("*Kamuhanda* Appeal Judgement")

KAREMERA ET AL.

The Prosecutor v. Édouard Karemera et al., Case No. ICTR-98-44-AR73.8, Decision on Interlocutory Appeal Regarding Witness Proofing, 11 May 2007 ("*Karemera* Decision on Interlocutory Appeal Regarding Witness Proofing of 11 May 2007")

KAYISHEMA AND RUZINDANA

The Prosecutor v. Clément Kayishema and Obed Ruzindana, Case No. ICTR-95-1-T, Judgement, 21 May 1999 ("*Kayishema and Ruzindana* Trial Judgement ")

The Prosecutor v. Clément Kayishema and Obed Ruzindana, Case No. ICTR-95-1-A, Judgement (Reasons), 1 June 2001 ("*Kayishema and Ruzindana* Appeal Judgement ")

MUHIMANA

Mikaeli Muhimana v. The Prosecutor, Case No. ICTR-95-1B-A, Judgement, 25 May 2007 ("*Muhimana* Appeal Judgement")

MUSEMA

Alfred Musema v. The Prosecutor, Case No. ICTR-96-13-A, Judgement, 16 November 2001 ("*Musema* Appeal Judgement") **[page 7]**

MUVUNYI

Prosecutor v. Tharcisse Muvunyi, Case No. ICTR-00-55A-T, Judgement and Sentence, 12 September 2006 ("*Muvunyi* Trial Judgement")

NDINDABAHIZI

The Prosecutor v. Emmanuel Ndindabahizi, Case No. ICTR-01-71-I, Judgement and Sentence, 15 July 2004 ("*Ndindabahizi* Trial Judgement")

Emmanuel Ndindabahizi v. The Prosecutor, Case No. ICTR-01-71-A, Judgement, 16 January 2007 ("*Ndindabahizi* Appeal Judgement")

NIYITEGEKA

The Prosecutor v. Eliézer Niyitegeka, Case No. ICTR-96-14-T, Judgement and Sentence, 16 May 2003 ("*Niyitegeka* Trial Judgement")

Eliézer Niyitegeka v. The Prosecutor, Case No. ICTR-96-14-A, Judgement, 9 July 2004 ("*Niyitegeka* Appeal Judgement")

NTAGERURA ET AL.

The Prosecutor v. André Ntagerura et al., Case No. ICTR-99-46-T, Judgement and Sentence, 25 February 2004 ("*Ntagerura et al.* Trial Judgement")

The Prosecutor v. André Ntagerura et al., Case No. ICTR-99-46-A, Arrêt, 7 July 2005 ("*Ntagerura et al.* Appeal Judgement")

NTAKIRUTIMANA

The Prosecutor v. Elizaphan and Gérard Ntakirutimana, Case Nos. ICTR-96-10 & ICTR-96-17-T, Judgement and Sentence, 21 February 2003 ("*Ntakirutimana* Trial Judgement")

The Prosecutor v. Elizaphan Ntakirutimana and Gérard Ntakirutimana, Case Nos. ICTR-96-10-A & ICTR-96-17-A, Judgement, 13 December 2004 ("*Ntakirutimana* Appeal Judgement")

RUTAGANDA

The Prosecutor v. Georges Anderson Nderumwe Rutaganda, Case No. ICTR 96-3-A, Decision on Appeals Against the Decisions by Trial Chamber I Rejecting the Defence Motions to Direct the Prosecutor to Investigate the Matter of False Testimony by Witnesses "E" and "CC", 8 June 1998 **[page 8]** ("*Rutaganda* Decision Rejecting the Defence Motions to Direct the Prosecutor to Investigate the Matter of False Testimony by Witnesses "E" and "CC" of 8 June 1998")

Georges Anderson Nderubumwe Rutaganda v. The Prosecutor, Case No. ICTR-96-3-T, Judgement, 6 December 1999 ("*Rutaganda* Trial Judgement")

Georges Anderson Nderubumwe Rutaganda v. The Prosecutor, Case No. ICTR-96-3-A, Judgement, 26 May 2003 ("*Rutaganda* Appeal Judgement")

SEMANZA

Laurent Semanza v. The Prosecutor, Case No. ICTR-97-20-A, Judgement, 20 May 2005 ("*Semanza* Appeal Judgement")

SEROMBA

The Prosecutor v. Athanase Seromba, Case No. ICTR-01-66-I, Judgement, 13 December 2006 ("*Seromba* Trial Judgement")

SERUGENDO

The Prosecutor v. Joseph Serugendo, Case No. ICTR-05-84-I, Judgement and Sentence, 12 June 2006 ("*Serugendo* Trial Judgement")

SIMBA

The Prosecutor v. Aloys Simba, Case No. ICTR-01-76-I, Decision on Motion to Amend Indictment, 26 January 2004 ("Indictment Decision of 26 January 2004")

The Prosecutor v. Aloys Simba, Case No. ICTR-01-76-I, Decision on Preliminary Defence Motion Regarding Defects in the Form of the Indictment, 6 May 2004 ("Decision on the Defects in the Form of the Indictment of 6 May 2004")

The Prosecutor v. Aloys Simba, Case No. ICTR-01-76-I, Decision on Defence's Preliminary Motion Challenging the Second Amended Indictment, 14 July 2004 ("Decision on Amended Indictment of 14 July 2004")

Aloys Simba v. The Prosecutor, Case No. ICTR-2001-76-AR72.2, Decision on Interlocutory Appeal Regarding Temporal Jurisdiction, 29 July 2004 ("Appeal Decision on Temporal Jurisdiction of 29 July 2004") **[page 9]**

The Prosecutor v. Aloys Simba, Case No. ICTR-2001-76-T, Decision on the Defence Request to Preclude the Testimony of Prosecution Witness KDD under Oath, 28 October 2004 ("Decision of 28 October 2004")

The Prosecutor v. Aloys Simba, Case No. ICTR-2001-76-T, Decision on Defence Request for Information Related to Witnesses YH and KXX, 10 November 2004 ("Decision on the Request for Information Related to Witnesses YH and KXX of 10 November 2004")

The Prosecutor v. Aloys Simba, Case No. ICTR-2001-76-T, Decision on the Defence Request for Site Visits in Rwanda, 31 January 2005 ("Decision on Site Visits of 31 January 2005")

The Prosecutor v. Aloys Simba, Case No. ICTR-2001-76-T, Decision Authorizing the Taking of the Evidence of Witnesses IMG, ISG, and BJK1 by Video-Link, 4 February 2005 ("Decision on Taking of the Evidence by Video-Link of 4 February 2005")

The Prosecutor v. Aloys Simba, Case No. ICTR-2001-76-T, Decision on Renewed Request for Site Visits in Rwanda, 4 May 2005 ("Decision on Site Visits of 4 May 2005")

The Prosecutor v. Aloys Simba, Case No. ICTR-2001-76-T, Decision on Defence Request for Subpoenas, 4 May 2005 ("Decision on Subpoenas of 4 May 2005")

The Prosecutor v. Aloys Simba, Case No. ICTR-2001-76-T, Decision on the Admission of Certain Exhibits, 23 June 2005 ("Decision on the Admission of Certain Exhibits of 23 June 2005")

The Prosecutor v. Aloys Simba, Case No. ICTR-2001-76-T, Decision on the Admission of Certain Exhibits (Corrigendum), 7 July 2005 ("Decision on the Admission of Certain Exhibits of 7 July 2005")

The Prosecutor v. Aloys Simba, Case No. ICTR-01-76-T, Judgement and Sentence, 13 December 2005 ("Trial Judgement")

Aloys Simba v. The Prosecutor, Case No. ICTR-01-76-A, Decision on Motion for Extension of Time for Filing of Notice of Appeal, 16 December 2005 ("Decision of Extension of Time for Filing of Notice of Appeal of 16 December 2005")

The Prosecutor v. Aloys Simba, Case No. ICTR-01-76-A, Decision on Respondent's Motion for Extension of Time, 13 April 2006 ("Decision of Extension of Time of 13 April 2006") **[page 10]**

Aloys Simba v. The Prosecutor, Case No. ICTR-01-76-A, Decision on Appellant Aloys Simba's Request to Present Additional Evidence, 21 May 2007 ("Decision on Appellant's Request to Present Additional Evidence of 21 May 2007")

Aloys Simba v. The Prosecutor, Case No. ICTR-01-76-A, Order to Registrar Regarding BJK1,13 July 2007 ("Order to Registrar Regarding BJK1 of 13 July 2007")

Aloys Simba v. Prosecutor, Case No. ICTR-01-76-A, Registrar's Submissions under Rule 33(B) of the Rules on Order For Translation, 16 July 2007 ("Registrar's Submissions on Order for Translation of 16 July 2007"), confidential

The Prosecutor v. Aloys Simba, Case No. ICTR-01-76-A, Decision on 'Prosecutor's Motion for Variation of Notice of Appeal Pursuant to Rule 108', 17 August 2006 ("Decision on Motion for Variation of Notice of Appeal of 17 August 2006")

The Prosecutor v. Aloys Simba, Case No. ICTR-01-76-A, Order Concerning the Prosecution's Respondent's Brief, 30 November 2006 ("Order Concerning the Prosecution's Respondent's Brief of 30 November 2006")

Aloys Simba v. The Prosecutor, Case No. ICTR-01-76-A, Decision on Appellant Aloys Simba's Request to Present Additional Evidence, 21 May 2007 ("Decision on Rule 115 Evidence of 21 May 2007")

2. ICTY

ALEKSOVSKI

The Prosecutor v. Zlatko Aleksovski, Case No. IT-95-14/1-A, Judgement, 24 March 2000 ("*Aleksovski* Appeal Judgement")

BABIĆ

The Prosecutor v. Milan Babić, Case No. IT-03-72-A, Judgement on Sentencing Appeal, 18 July 2005 ("*Babić* Sentencing Appeal")

BLAŠKIĆ

The Prosecutor v. Tihomir Blaškić, Case No. IT-95-14-A, Judgement, 29 July 2004 ("*Blaškić* Appeal Judgement") **[page 11]**

BRĐANIN

The Prosecutor v. Radoslav Brđanin, Case No. IT-99-36-A, Judgement, 3 April 2007 ("*Brđanin* Appeal Judgement")

DELALIĆ ET AL.

The Prosecutor v. Zejnil Delalić et al., Case No. IT-96-21-T, Judgement, 16 November 1998 ("*Delalić et al.* Trial Judgement")

The Prosecutor v. Zejnil Delalić et al., Case No. IT-96-21-A, Judgement, 20 February 2001 ("*Delalić et al.* Appeal Judgement")

FURUNDŽIJA

Prosecutor v. Anto Furundžija, Case No. IT-95-17/1-A, Judgement, 21 July 2000 ("*Furundžija* Appeal Judgement")

GALIĆ

The Prosecutor v. Stanislav Galić, Case No. IT-98-29-T, Judgement and Opinion, 5 December 2003 ("*Galić* Trial Judgement")

The Prosecutor v. Stanislav Galić, Case No. IT-98-29-A, Judgement, 30 November 2006 ("*Galić* Appeal Judgement")

JELISIĆ

The Prosecutor v. Goran Jelisić, Case No. IT-95-10-A, Judgement, 5 July 2001 ("*Jelisić* Appeal Judgement")

KORDIĆ AND ČERKEZ

The Prosecutor v. Dario Kordić and Mario Čerkez, Case No. IT-95-14/2-A, Judgement, 17 December 2004 ("*Kordić and Čerkez* Appeal Judgement")

KRNOJELAC

The Prosecutor v. Milorad Krnojelac, Case No. IT-97-25-A, Judgement, 17 September 2003 ("*Krnojelac* Appeal Judgement") **[page 12]**

KRSTIĆ

The Prosecutor v. *Radislav Krstić*, Case No. IT-98-33, Judgement, 2 August 2001 ("*Krstić* Trial Judgement")

The Prosecutor v. *Radislav Krstić*, Case No. IT-98-33-A, Judgement, 19 April 2004 ("*Krstić* Appeal Judgement")

KUNARAC ET AL.

The Prosecutor v. Dragoljub Kunarac et al., Case Nos. IT-96-23-T & IT-96-23/1-T, Judgement, 22 February 2001 ("*Kunarac et al.* Trial Judgement")

The Prosecutor v. Dragoljub Kunarac et al., Case Nos. IT-96-23 & IT-96-23/1-A, Judgement, 12 June 2002 ("*Kunarac et al.*, Appeal Judgement")

KUPREŠKIĆ ET AL.

The Prosecutor v. Zoran Kupreškić et al., Case No. IT-95-16-A, Judgement, 23 October 2001 ("*Kupreškić et al.* Appeal Judgement")

KVOČKA ET AL.

The Prosecutor v. Miroslav Kvočka et al., Case No. IT-98-30/1-A, Judgement, 28 February 2005 ("*Kvočka et al.* Appeal Judgement")

LIMAJ ET AL.

The Prosecutor v. Limaj et al., Case No. IT-03-66-A, Judgement, 27 September 2007 ("*Limaj et al.* Appeal Judgement")

NALETILIĆ AND MARTINOVIĆ

The Prosecutor v. Mladen Naletilić and Vinko Martinović, Case No. IT-98-34-A, Judgement, 3 May 2006 ("*Naletilić and Martinović* Appeal Judgement")

M. NIKOLIĆ

Momir Nikolić v. Prosecutor, Case No. IT-02-60/1-A, Judgement on Sentencing Appeal, 8 March 2006 ("*M. Nikolić Appeal* Judgement") **[page 13]**

SIMIĆ ET AL.

The Prosecutor v. Blagoje Simić et al., Case No. IT-95-9-A, Judgement, 28 November 2006 ("*Simić et al.* Appeal Judgement")

STAKIĆ

The Prosecutor v. Milomir Stakić, Case No. IT-97-24-A, Judgement, 22 March 2006 ("*Stakić* Appeal Judgement")

TADIĆ

The Prosecutor v. Duško Tadić, Case No. IT-94-1-A, Judgement, 15 July 1999 ("*Tadić* Appeal Judgement")

VASILJEVIĆ

The Prosecutor v. Mitar Vasiljević, Case No. IT-98-32-A, Judgement, 25 February 2004 ("*Vasiljević* Appeal Judgement")

B. Defined Terms and Abbreviations

The Appellant	Aloys Simba
cf.	[Latin: *confer*] (Compare)
CIPEP	*Centre intercommunal de perfectionnement du personnel*
Defence	The Appellant, and/or the Appellant's counsel
Exh(s).	Exhibit(s)
fn.	footnote
ICTY	International Tribunal for the Prosecution of Persons Responsible for Serious Violations of International Humanitarian Law Committed in the Territory of the Former Yugoslavia since 1991
Indictment	*The Prosecutor v. Aloys Simba*, Case No. ICTR-01-76-I, Amended Indictment (Pursuant to 6 May 2004 Decision), dated 10 May 2004
Amended Indictment	*The Prosecutor v. Aloys Simba*, Case No. ICTR-01-76-I, Amended Indictment, dated 20 November 2003 and filed on 27 January 2004 (Pursuant to 26 January 2004 Decision) **[page 14]**
Initial Indictment	*The Prosecutor v. Aloys Simba*, Case No. ICTR-01-76-I, Indictment, dated 4 January 2002
JCE	Joint criminal enterprise
MRND	*Mouvement révolutionnaire national pour la démocratie et le développement*
Prosecution	Office of the Prosecutor
para. (paras)	paragraph (paragraphs)
Prosecution Appeal Brief	The Prosecutor v. Aloys Simba, Case No. ICTR-01-76-A, Prosecutor's Appellant's Brief, filed on 27 March 2006
Prosecution Corrigendum to Appeal Brief	The Prosecutor v. Aloys Simba, Case No. ICTR-01-76-A, Corrigendum to Prosecutor's Appellant's Brief, filed on 28 March 2006
Prosecution Final Trial Brief	*The Prosecutor v. Aloys Simba*, Case No. ICTR-2001-76-T, The Prosecutor's Closing Brief, filed on 22 June 2005

Prosecution Pre-Trial Brief	*The Prosecutor v. Aloys Simba*, Case No. ICTR-01-76-I, The Prosecutor's Pre-Trial Brief Pursuant to Article 73 bis (B)(i) of the Rules of Procedure and Evidence, filed on 16 February 2004
Prosecution Notice of Appeal	Prosecutor's Notice of Appeal, filed on 12 January 2006
Prosecution Response	*The Prosecutor v. Aloys Simba*, Case No. ICTR-2001-76-A, Prosecutor's Respondent's Brief, filed on 1 December 2006
Prosecution Reply	*The Prosecutor v. Aloys Simba*, Case No. ICTR-2001-76-A, Prosecutor's Brief in Reply, filed on 31 October 2006
R.P.	Registry Page (reference to page number in case file maintained by the Registry)
Rules	Rules of Procedure and Evidence of the ICTR
Simba Appeal Brief	*The Prosecutor v. Aloys Simba*, Case No. ICTR-2001-76-A, Appellant's Brief, filed in French on 16 October 2006 (Mémoire d'Appel d'Aloys Simba).
Simba Final Trial Brief	*The Prosecutor v. Aloys Simba*, Case No. ICTR-2001-76-T, "Conclusions de la Défense contre l'Acte d'Accusation modifié en date du 10 Mai 2004", filed on 22 June 2005. Note: English *draft* translation available
Simba Notice of Appeal	*The Prosecutor v. Aloys Simba*, Case No. ICTR-2001-76-A, Defence Notice of Appeal, filed in French (Acte d'Appel de la Défense) on 22 June 2006 **[page 15]**
Simba Reply	*The Prosecutor v. Aloys Simba*, Case No. ICTR-2001-76-A, Appellant's Brief in Reply, filed in French (Mémoire en Réplique de l'Appelant) on 2 March 2006
Simba Response	*The Prosecutor v. Aloys Simba*, Case No. ICTR-2001-76-A, Respondent Brief, filed on 17 October 2006
Statute	Statute of the International Tribunal for Rwanda established by Security Council Resolution 955 (1994)
T.	Transcript page from hearings in *Prosecutor v. Aloys Simba*, Case No. ICTR-01-76. All references are to the official English transcript, unless otherwise indicated.
AT.	Transcript page from hearings in *Aloys Simba v. The Prosecutor,* Case No. ICTR-01-76-A. All references are to the official English transcript, unless otherwise indicated.
CRA	French Transcript (Compte rendu d'audience) page from hearings in *Prosecutor v. Aloys Simba*, Case No. ICTR-01-76
Tribunal or ICTR	International Criminal Tribunal for the Prosecution of Persons Responsible for Genocide and Other Serious Violations of International Humanitarian Law Committed in the Territory of Rwanda and Rwandan Citizens responsible for genocide and other such violations committed in the territory of neighbouring States, between 1 January 1994 and 31 December 1994
UN	United Nations
UNDF	United Nations Detention Facilities for persons awaiting trial or appeal before the ICTR
WVSS	Witness and Victims Support Section

C. Other Documents cited

The Prosecutor v. Aloys Simba, Case No. ICTR-01-76-I, Simba Defence's Motion Challenging Jurisdiction and Alleging Substantial Defects in the Form of the Amended Indictment of 10 May 2004 (Rules 72 and 73 of the Rules of Procedure and Evidence), 9 June 2004 ("Motion Challenging Jurisdiction and Defects in the Form of the Amended Indictment of 10 May 2004")

The Prosecutor v. Aloys Simba, Case No. ICTR-01-76-I, Requête de la défense en vue d'enjoindre au procureur d'avoir à fournir la *preuve* que des poursuites judiciaires ont été *engagées* contre les témoins "KXX" et "YH" lesquels se sont accusés du crime de *génocide*, 25 October 2004 ("Motion of 25 October 2004") **[page 16]**

The Prosecutor v. Aloys Simba, Case No. ICTR-2001-76-T, Corrigendum à l'Annexe Ia des Conclusions de la Defense d'Aloys Simba, 4 July 2005 ("Corrigendum Conclusions de la Defense of 4 July 2005")

The Prosecutor v. Aloys Simba, Case No. ICTR-01-76-A, Prosecutor's Motion for Variation of the Notice of Appeal Pursuant to Rule 108, 27 March 2006 ("Prosecutor's Motion for Variation of the Notice of Appeal Pursuant to Rule 108 of 27 March 2006")

Aloys Simba v. The Prosecutor, Case No. ICTR-01-76-A, Corrigendum to Prosecutor's Appellant's Brief, 28 March 2006 ("Corrigendum to Prosecutor's Appellant's Brief of 28 March 2006")

Commentary

1. Introduction

Aloys Simba (hereinafter the appellant) is an ex-lieutenant colonel in the Rwandan armed forces. In 1973, he participated in the *coup d'état* against the then President of Rwanda, Juvénal Habyarimana. Between 1989 and 1993, he was a member of the Rwandan parliament.[1] On 13 December 2005, a Trial Chamber of the ICTR found him guilty of genocide and extermination as a crime against humanity, for his participation in a joint criminal enterprise to murder Tutsi civilians at Murambi Technical School and Kadusha Parish. For these crimes he was given a single sentence of 25 years imprisonment.[2] The appellant appealed against both of the convictions and the sentence; the prosecutor, against the acquittal of one charge of the indictment and the sentence.[3] On 27 November 2007, the ICTR Appeals Chamber rendered the judgement annotated below.

The judgement deals with many factual and legal issues. This annotation focuses on a selected number of issues, namely the standard of appellate review, the assessment of witness statements and cultural factors, the theory of joint criminal enterprise, the material element of the crime of genocide, cumulative convictions, and the determination of the term of imprisonment.

2. The standard of appellate review

Article 24 of the ICTR statute lays down the general principles of appellate proceedings before the tribunal. According to this provision, only errors of law invalidating the decision or errors of fact causing a miscarriage of justice may be the subject of an appeal. The ICTR Appeals Chamber has developed a series of basic standards of review pursuant to this provision, which it usually recalls at the outset of each appeal judgement.[4] Some of these standards are the following: a party alleging an error of law must advance arguments in support of the submission and explain how the error invalidates the decision;[5] errors of fact will be revised or reversed only where no 'reasonable trier of fact' could have arrived at the same finding, or where the finding is totally mistaken, and only if the error caused a miscarriage of justice;[6] arguments rejected by the Trial Chamber will not be considered on appeal, unless the rejection amounted to an error deserving the intervention of the Appeals Chamber;[7] and the Appeals Chamber will not deal in detail with submissions that are unclear, contradictory, or vague.[8] These basic standards are from earlier jurisprudence of the tribunal.[9]

It is worth noting that the first basic standard of review mentioned above does not exclude the *iura novit curia* principle from the applicable law of the ICTR. Thus, in the case of errors of law, the arguments of the parties do not end the discussion, because the Appeals Chamber is allowed, as the final arbiter of the applicable law, to find in favor of an appellant on grounds other than those put forward, in other words, *iura novit curia.* Since its early practice, the Appeals Chamber has recognized that it has the power to apply the *iura novit curia* principle if the circumstances of the case so require.[10]

Against this background, it is worth observing that none of the grounds of appeal submitted by the appellant and the prosecutor were consistent with the basic standards of review. As a result, the Appeals Chamber

1 ICTR, Judgement, *Simba v. Prosecutor*, Case No. ICTR-07-76-A, A. Ch., 27 November 2007, in this volume, p. 789, par. 2.

2 ICTR, Judgement and Sentence, *Prosecutor v. Simba*, Case No. ICTR-01-76-T, T. Ch. I, 13 December 2005, Klip/ Sluiter, ALC-XXIV-325. For a commentary see Klip/ Sluiter, ALC-XXIV-421.

3 Judgement, *Simba v. Prosecutor*, Case No. ICTR-07-76-A, A. Ch., *supra* note 1, par. 2, 5 and 7.

4 See, for example, Judgement, *Simba v. Prosecutor*, Case No. ICTR-07-76-A, A. Ch., *supra* note 1, par. 8-11.

5 *Ibid.*, par. 8.

6 *Ibid.*, par. 9.

7 *Ibid.*, par. 10.

8 *Ibid.*, par. 11.

9 The precedent recalled by the Appeals Chamber is ICTR, Judgement, *Niyitegeka v. Prosecutor*, Case No. ICTR-96-14-A, A. Ch., 9 July 2004, Klip/ Sluiter, ALC-XVIII-563, par. 8.

10 ICTR, Judgement, *Kambanda v. Prosecutor*, Case No. ICTR-97-23-A, A. Ch., 19 October 2000, Klip/ Sluiter, ALC-VI-659, par. 98. For a commentary on this judgement, see ALC-VI-681. On the *iura novit curia* principle, see Fabián Raimondo, General principles of law in the decisions of international criminal courts and tribunals, Martinus Nijhoff Publishers, The Hague 2008, p. 123, 147, 148, 171 and 194.

dismissed all of them, affirmed the appellant's convictions for genocide and extermination as a crime against humanity, and affirmed the sentence of 25 years imprisonment.[11]

3. Witness statements and cultural factors

The impact of cultural issues on international criminal proceedings has, to a large extent, been neglected in the ever-growing literature on international criminal law. Cultural factors, such as language and demeanour, may complicate the assessment of evidence in international trials, because they may impact on the credibility of witnesses statements. For example, in many decisions, the ICTR has pointed out the complexities of receiving and assessing witness statements from persons whose language is different from the tribunal's working languages (English and French). In the *Akayesu* case,[12] the Trial Chamber expressly recognized the difficulties arising from the fact that the large majority of witnesses spoke Kinyarwanda.[13]

In that case, the Trial Chamber realized that some possible contradictions between the statements of a number of witnesses at trial and earlier statements by these witnesses given to ICTR's investigators were due to the fact that the grammar and daily modes of expression in the Kinyarwanda language were extremely difficult to translate into the ICTR's working languages. According to the Trial Chamber, additional cultural factors affecting the assessment of witnesses statements encompassed, for instance, the fact that Rwandans report facts as if they had personally witnessed these (even if they are recounting somebody else's account); the reason for this is that Rwandans live in an oral tradition.[14]

In view of these reasons, it is welcome that the Appeals Chamber made clear from the outset of the judgement that, where an error of fact is alleged, it will pay special respect to the Trial Chamber that received the evidence at trial, as that chamber is best positioned to evaluate the evidence, 'including the demeanour of witnesses'.[15]

4. The theory of joint criminal enterprise

Both the appellant and the prosecutor submitted grounds of appeal relating to the theory of joint criminal enterprise. As is well known, the ICTY usually bases joint responsibility on this theory as a mode of criminal participation.[16] This form of criminal participation is deemed to be part of customary international law.[17] This appeals judgement does not add anything new in respect of the theory of joint criminal enterprise. However, it is a leading decision in the context of the ICTR for the reason that it reaffirms the very first conviction of the tribunal to be based on this theory.[18]

In the appellate proceedings leading to the decision *sub examine*, the appellant affirmed that the Trial Chamber erred in convicting him for genocide and extermination as a crime against humanity pursuant to the theory of joint criminal enterprise.[19] In this regard, he submitted, among other reasons, that the Trial Chamber erred in assuming that his supposed presence at the crime scene indicated that he would have joined in the attackers' or government officials' plans.[20] However, the Appeals Chamber found there to be no mistake in the Trial Chamber's assessment. It held that, in a joint criminal enterprise, it is not essential for a

11 Judgement, *Simba v. Prosecutor*, Case No. ICTR-07-76-A, A. Ch., *supra* note 1, disposition.

12 See ICTR, Judgement, *Prosecutor v. Akayesu*, Case No. ICTR-96-4-T, T. Ch. I, 2 September 1998, Klip/ Sluiter, ALC-II-399.

13 *Ibid.*, par. 145-154.

14 *Ibid.*, par. 155-156. See also Ida Bostian, Cultural relativism in international war crimes prosecutions: The International Criminal Tribunal for Rwanda, 12 ILSA Journal of International and Comparative Law 2005, p. 24.

15 Judgement, *Prosecutor v. Akayesu*, T. Ch. I, *supra* note 12, par. 8.

16 The leading case being ICTY, Judgement, *Prosecutor v. Tadić*, Case No. IT-94-1-A, A. Ch., 15 July 1999, Klip/ Sluiter, ALC-III-761, par. 194 *et seq.*

17 *Ibid.*

18 This does not mean that the ICTR had not discussed issues pertaining to the theory of joint criminal enterprise in previous cases. In these cases, however, the defendants were convicted on the basis of other forms of criminal participation. See, for example, ICTR, Judgment (Reasons), *Prosecutor v. Kayishema and Ruzindana*, Case No. ICTR-95-1-A, A. Ch., 1 June 2001, Klip/ Sluiter, ALC-X-495, par. 193.

19 Judgement, *Simba v. Prosecutor*, Case No. ICTR-07-76-A, A. Ch., *supra* note 1, par. 244.

20 *Ibid.*, par. 247.

participant to have participated in its planning; all that is needed is the accused's participation in the common plan involving the commission of one of the crimes within the subject matter jurisdiction of the ICTR.[21]

To this commentator, the Appeals Chamber's finding is uncontroversial. It conforms with the case law of the ICTR and ICTY, which establish that a common plan can be in existence without apparent forethought.[22] In other words, the common plan need not be formed before the offence is perpetrated.[23]

As far as the prosecutor's ground of appeal is concerned, it was particularly based on the argument that the Trial Chamber erred in law in demanding a direct and substantial contribution by the appellant to the Cyanika Parish killing as a prerequisite for holding him liable for that killing as a participant in a joint criminal enterprise.[24] However, contrary to the prosecutor's submission, the Appeals Chamber found that the Trial Chamber did not actually impose that requirement.[25]

The Trial Chamber, the prosecutor, and the Appeals Chamber were correct in affirming that the contribution that must be made by every participant in the joint criminal enterprise is not subject to particular requirements. The so-called 'basic form' of joint criminal enterprise, the form under which the Trial Chamber found the appellant responsible, covers transactions in which a group of individuals shares the intent to perpetrate an international crime and the crime is executed in light of a common purpose.[26]

Case law and scholars agree that the contribution to a joint criminal enterprise by the offender may consist of any kind of assistence and need not be related to execution.[27] To put it differently, although the contribution by the participant in the joint criminal enterprise must not necessarily be direct and substantial,[28] it should be no less than a significant contribution to the offences for which the accused is found responsible.[29]

5. The material element of the crime of genocide

The appellant challenged the conviction for genocide, *inter alia* because of an alleged error relating to the existence of a plan or policy as an element of the *actus reus* of genocide.[30]

The crime of genocide is different from crimes against humanity, because it does not require the existence of a systematic attack against a civilian population; it does not have a contextual element. The peculiarity of the crime of genocide lies in the necessary subjective element or *mens rea*, - the specific intent to destroy in whole or in part a national, ethnic, racial, or religious group.[31] Hence, at least in theory, a single person having the specific *mens rea* could, without this intent having been supported by any organisation in which other persons participated, be responsible for the crime of genocide.[32]

For these reasons, an official plan or policy to carry out the crime of genocide is not an autonomous material element of the crime, under customary international law.[33] Nevertheless, the existence of such a plan or

21 *Ibid.*, par. 250.

22 Judgment (Reasons), *Prosecutor v. Kayishema and Ruzindana*, A. Ch., *supra* note 18, par. 193; Judgement, *Prosecutor v. Tadić*, A. Ch, *supra* note 18, par. 227.

23 Gerhard Werle, Principles of international criminal law, 2nd edition, Asser Press, The Hague 2009, p. 173.

24 *Ibid*, par. 298.

25 *Ibid*, par. 303.

26 Judgement, *Prosecutor v. Tadić*, A. Ch, *supra* note 18, par. 195.

27 *Ibid*, par. 196 *et seq.* and 227; Albin Eser, in Antonio Cassese *et al.* (eds.), The Rome Statute of the International Criminal Court, Vol. 1, Oxford University Press, New York 1999, p. 791 *et seq.*; Gerhard Werle, Principles of international criminal law, *supra* note 23, p. 174.

28 ICTY, Judgement, *Prosecutor v. Kvočka, Radić, Žigić and Prcac*, Case No. IT-98-30/ 1-A, A. Ch., 28 February 2005, to be published in volume XXVI, par. 97, 104 and 187.

29 ICTY, Judgement, *Prosecutor v. Brđanin*, Case No. IT-99-33-A, A. Ch., 3 April 2007, par. 430.

30 Judgement, *Simba v. Prosecutor*, Case No. ICTR-07-76-A, A. Ch., *supra* note 1, par. 259.

31 See Article II of the 1948 Convention on the Prevention and Punishment of the Crime of Genocide; ICTR, Judgement, *Prosecutor v. Kayishema and Ruzindana*, Case No. ICTR-95-1-T, T. Ch. II, 21 May 1999, Klip/ Sluiter, ALC-II-555, par. 94; ICTY, Judgement, *Prosecutor v. Jelisić*, Case No. IT 95 10 T, T. Ch. I, 14 December 1999, Klip/ Sluiter, ALC IV 669, par. 100; Werle, Gerhard, Principles of international criminal law, *supra* note 23, p. 271.

32 Judgement, *Prosecutor v. Jelisić*, T. Ch. I, *supra* note 31, par. 100.

33 ICTR, Judgement, *Semanza v. Prosecutor*, Case No. ICTR-97-20-A, A. Ch., 20 May 2005, Klip/ Sluiter, ALC-XXII-525, par. 260; ICTY, Judgment, *Prosecutor v. Jelisić*, Case No. IT-95-10-A, A. Ch., 5 July 2001, Klip/ Sluiter, ALC-VII-513, par. 48; Gerhard Werle, Principles of international criminal law, *supra* note 23, p. 271.

policy may evidence the specific *mens rea* of the perpetrator. Against this background, it is clearly not surprising that the Appeals Chamber promptly and correctly dismissed the appellant's argument.[34]

6. Cumulative convictions

The appellant challenged the Trial Chamber's cumulative convictions for extermination as a crime against humanity and genocide;[35] in his view, the Trial Chamber erred in law in convicting him for both crimes, based on one and the same conduct.[36]

The cases before international criminal courts and tribunals show that the conduct of a perpetrator may meet the definitions of different offences. Thus, for example, rape or torture may amount to war crimes and crimes against humanity. The statute of the ICTR (and of the ICTY) does not regulate the issue of *concursus delictorum*; the ICTR and the ICTY have settled this issue by having recourse to customary law and general principles of law.[37]

In this connection, the ICTY has developed jurisprudence to the effect that cumulative charging is permissible, the reason being that, before the presentation of all the evidence, it is impossible to ascertain which of the charges brought against an accused will be proven.[38]

In addition, the ICTR has reaffirmed ICTY's jurisprudence to the effect that cumulative convictions entered under different provisions of the statute, but based on the same conduct, are allowed, provided that each provision at stake has a materially different constitutive element not contained in the other.[39] Against this backdrop, the Appeals Chamber quickly dismissed the appellant's argument.[40]

7. Determination of the term of imprisonment

Both the appellant and the prosecutor put forward grounds of appeal concerning the sentence imposed by the Trial Chamber. Not surprisingly, the appellant submitted that the Trial Chamber erred in sentencing him to 25 years imprisonment (the term of imprisonment being too severe in view of his age, health, and other mitigating factors),[41] whereas the prosecutor argued that the Trial Chamber should have imposed life imprisonment, in light of the seriousness of the offence, the appellant's role, and certain aggraviting circumstances.[42]

To this commentator, the most interesting issue in this regard is the one raised by Judge Schomburg in his partially dissenting opinion. In Judge Schomburg's view, the imposition of sentences by the ICTR on persons with prominent social status in Rwandan society, such as the appellant, which are less severe than sentences imposed in Rwanda on subordinates, would be contrary to the mandate of the tribunal to fight against impunity.[43] Further, in this regard, one cannot fail to observe that a less severe sentence would possibly pay insufficient attention to the needs of Rwandan victims to see justice done in a manner that meets their expectations.

8. Conclusion

This judgment does not deal with fresh legal problems: it does not determine new rules of international (criminal) law and does not offer new interpretations of the law applicable by the ICTR. Of course, this is not

34 Judgement, *Simba v. Prosecutor*, Case No. ICTR-07-76-A, A. Ch., *supra* note 1, par. 260.

35 *Ibid.*, par. 274.

36 *Ibid.*

37 Fabián Raimondo, General principles of law in the decisions of international criminal courts and tribunals, *supra* note 10, p. 119-124.

38 ICTY, Appeal Judgement, *Prosecutor v. Kupreškić, Kupreškić, Kupreškić, Josipović and Šantić*, Case No. IT-95-16-A, A. Ch., 23 October 2001, Klip/ Sluiter, ALC-VIII-429, par. 385-386; Judgement, *Prosecutor v. Naletilic and Martinovic*, Case No. IT-98-34-A, A. Ch., 3 May 2006, to be published in volume XXIX, par. 103.

39 ICTR, Judgement and Sentence, *Prosecutor v. Ntagerura, Bagambiki and Imanishimwe*, Case No. ICTR-99-46-T, T. Ch. III, 25 February 2004, Klip/ Sluiter, ALC-XVIII-267, par. 425; ICTR, Judgement, *Prosecutor v. Elizaphan Ntakirutimana and Ntakirutimana*, Cases Nos. ICTR-96-10-A and ICTR-96-17-A, A. Ch., 13 December 2004, Klip/ Sluiter, ALC-XVIII-755, par. 542.

40 Judgement, *Simba v. Prosecutor*, Case No. ICTR-07-76-A, A. Ch., *supra* note 1, par. 278.

41 *Ibid.*, par. 279-288.

42 *Ibid.*, par. 305-338.

43 ICTR, Judgement, Partially dissenting opinion of Judge Schomburg, *Simba v. Prosecutor*, Case ICTR-01-76-A, A.Ch., 27 November 2007, in this volume, p. 817, par. 2.

a fault, let alone a fault attributable to the Appeals Chamber; it is the result of the preexistence of well established case law elaborated by both the ICTR and the ICTY, which does not offer, at this point it time, serious legal gaps.

To this author, the most important contribution of this judgement to international (criminal) law is the reaffirmation of the jurisprudence of the ICTR and the ICTY in respect of issues such as standards of appellate review, assessment of witness statements, the theory of joint criminal enterprise, the material element of the crime of genocide, and cumulative convictions.

On the other hand, the confirmation of the sentence imposed by the Trial Chamber is the most significant shortcoming of the appeal judgement; a sentence of 25 years imprisonment is at odds with the sentencing practice of the Rwandan courts for similar crimes and certainly it does not meet the expectations of the victims of the crimes perpetrated by the appellant.

Fabián Raimondo

International Criminal Tribunal for Rwanda
Tribunal pénal international pour le Rwanda

OR: ENG

TRIAL CHAMBER III

Before Judges: Dennis C. M. Byron, Presiding
Karin Hökborg
Gberdao Gustave Kam

Registrar: Adama Dieng

Date: 31 January 2007

THE PROSECUTOR

v.

André RWAMAKUBA

Case No. ICTR-98-44C-T

DECISION ON APPROPRIATE REMEDY

Office of the Prosecutor:
Dior Fall
Iain Morley
Adama Niane

Defence Counsel:
David Hooper
Andreas O'Shea

[page 2] INTRODUCTION

1. On 20 September 2006, the Chamber rendered its Judgement in the present case, acquitting André Rwamakuba of all charges and consequently ordering his immediate release.[1]

2. In a decision dated 12 December 2000,[2] Trial Chamber II found that the Registrar had failed to appoint Duty Counsel for André Rwamakuba during the initial months of his detention at the United Nations Detention Facilities ("UNDF"), from 22 October 1998 until 10 March 1999, in breach of Rule 44 *bis* of the Rules of Evidence and Procedure.[3] It further held that this was a violation of Rwamakuba's right to legal assistance and that the delay in assigning him duty Counsel had caused a delay in his initial appearance.[4] Trial Chamber II did not consider that the said delays in providing Rwamakuba with legal representation and in his initial appearance had caused him a serious and irreparable prejudice.[5] Concluding that there was no accumulation of violations of André Rwamakuba's rights, Trial Chamber II dismissed the Defence motion for his immediate and unconditional release.[6]

3. On 11 June 2001, the Appeals Chamber dismissed the appeal filed by André Rwamakuba against Trial Chamber II's Decision. It found that the notice of appeal did not meet the requirements for an interlocutory appeal challenging the Indictment. The Appeals Chamber, however, considered that "it [was] open to [Rwamakuba] to invoke the issue of the alleged violation of his fundamental human rights by the Tribunal in order to seek reparation as the case may be, at the appropriate time."[7]

4. In its Judgement of 20 September 2006, the Chamber held that in light of the previous finding of a violation of André Rwamakuba's right to legal assistance, he was at liberty to file an application seeking an appropriate remedy for the violation of his right to legal assistance between 22 October 1998 and 10 March 1999.[8] The Chamber further invited the Prosecution and the Registrar to file any submission on this issue.

5. On 25 October 2006, the Defence filed an "Application for Appropriate Remedy,"[9] by which it claims an appropriate remedy not only for the violation of André Rwamakuba's right to legal assistance, but also for the alleged grave and manifest injustice occasioned, inter alia, by the manipulation of evidence against him during his case. In its submission, the Defence requests that the Chamber order that the Registrar: (i) provide Rwamakuba with an apology; (ii) seek the good offices of the State where Rwamakuba's family is present to facilitate some temporary status for him in that State; (iii) seek the good offices of that State to ensure the uninterrupted schooling of Rwamakuba's children; and (iv) provide financial compensation **[page 3]** to Rwamakuba.[10] With respect to the violation of Rwamakuba's right to legal assistance, it specifically seeks compensation covering a minimum of 2,000 US dollars (USD) per month for loss of earnings and 10,000 USD for emotional stress.[11]

6. On 2 November 2006, the Registrar filed his response, in accordance with an extension of time granted by the Chamber,[12] in which he opposes the Defence application on various grounds.[13] On 9 November 2006,

---

1 *Prosecutor v. André Rwamakuba*, Case No. ICTR-98-44C-T, Judgement (TC), 20 September 2006.

2 *Rwamakuba*, Decision on the Defence Motion concerning the Illegal Arrest and Illegal Detention of the Accused (TC), 12 December 2000 ("Decision on Illegal Arrest and Detention").

3 Rule 44 *bis* (d) reads: "If an accused, or suspect transferred under Rule 40 *bis*, is unrepresented at any time after being transferred to the Tribunal, the Registrar shall as soon as practicable summon duty counsel to represent the accused or suspect until counsel is engaged by the accused or suspect, or assigned under Rule 45."

4 *Rwamakuba*, Decision on Illegal Arrest and Detention (TC), 12 December 2000, at para. 43.

5 *Ibid.*, at para. 45.

6 *Ibid.*

7 *Rwamakuba*, Decision on Appeal against Dismissal of Motion Concerning Illegal Arrest and Detention (AC), 11 June 2001.

8 *Ibid.*, at paras. 217-220 and Order III.

9 Defence for André Rwamakuba, Application for Appropriate Remedy, 25 October 2006 ("Defence Application").

10 *Ibid.*, pp. 10-11.

11 *Ibid.*, p. 10.

12 See *Rwamakuba*, Decision Granting Extension of Time to File Submissions (TC), 31 October 2006.

13 The Registrar, "The Registrar's Submissions Regarding André Rwamakuba's Request for an Appropriate Remedy," 2 November 2006 ("Registrar's Submissions").

the Defence filed a Reply to the Registrar's Submissions.[14] The Registrar filed additional submissions on 24 November 2006 and 7 December 2006.[15] The Prosecutor did not file any submissions on this issue.

DELIBERATIONS

7. Before ruling on the merits, the Chamber will first address two preliminary matters relating to the timeliness and scope of the submissions filed by the Defence and the Registrar. The Chamber will then determine if any violation of André Rwamakuba's rights entitles him to an appropriate remedy, and what, in the circumstances of the case, constitutes an appropriate remedy.

1. Preliminary Matters

1.1 Timeliness of the Submissions filed by the Defence and the Registrar

8. The Defence Application is dated 23 October 2006, but was filed on 25 October 2006, two days after the deadline for submissions set out in Order III of the Judgement.[16] The Chamber considers however that it is in the interests of justice to accept this late submission.

9. In addition to the submissions filed in accordance with the Chamber's Order, the Registrar filed two additional submissions on 24 November and 7 December 2006, respectively[17] The Defence has not responded to any of these additional submissions.

10. In the filing of 24 November 2006, the Registrar contends that the Defence misunderstands a number of his arguments and therefore requests the right to present some clarifications.[18] In its submissions of 2 November 2006, the Registrar undertook to seek the **[page 4]** legal advice of the Office of Legal Affairs ("OLA") of the UN Secretary-General on the Defence Application. The additional submission filed by the Registrar on 7 December 2006 relays the substance of the OLA's legal advice on the Defence Application.

11. According to Order III of the Chamber's Judgement, the Registrar was supposed to file only one submission. Nevertheless, the Chamber decides to take into consideration the Registrar's Additional Submissions of 24 November 2006 since the arguments developed therein with respect to the powers of the Chamber and the prior positions expressed by the Presidents of the ICTR and ICTY were already contained in his two initial submissions and since the Additional Submissions of 24 November 2006 only amount to providing the Chamber and the parties with documents which were either publicly available or were previously communicated to the Defence. With respect to the Additional Submissions of 7 December 2006, the Chamber also decides to consider the arguments developed in this submission, reproducing the OLA's advice, as they do not in substance constitute new arguments on the issues under consideration and because they were not previously available.

---

[14] Defence for André Rwamakuba, "Reply to the Registrar's Submissions Regarding André Rwamakuba's Request for an Appropriate Remedy," 9 November 2006 ("Defence Reply").

[15] The Registrar, "The Registrar's Additional Submissions in regard to the Defence Application for Remedy," 24 November 2006 ("Registrar's Additional Submissions of 24 November 2006"); The Registrar, "The Registrar's Additional Submissions in regard to the Defence Application for Remedy," 7 December 2006 ("Registrar's Additional Submissions of 7 December 2006").

[16] *Rwamakuba*, Judgement (TC), 20 September 2006, Order III: "The Defence is at liberty to file any application seeking appropriate remedy to the violation of his right to legal assistance between 22 October 1998 and 10 March 1999 no later than 23 October 2006."

[17] These submissions were filed pursuant to Rule 33(B) of the Rules, whereby the Registrar may make a submission to Chambers on any issue arising in the context of a specific case which affects or may affect the discharge of his functions.

[18] The Registrar clarifies that he questions the appropriateness of making a claim for compensation for unwarranted proceedings and prolonged detention before the Chamber. In that respect, the Registrar refers to letters from Presidents of this Tribunal or of the International Criminal Tribunal for Former Yugoslavia ("ICTY") indicating that the Tribunals do not have the mandate, under their respective Statutes, to provide compensation to persons wrongly accused and then acquitted by the Tribunal. The Registrar contends that the United Nations Secretary-General, through his Legal Counsel, might be in a better position to direct the concerned party to the organ or party which could effectuate payment in compensation to André Rwamakuba, should such relief be considered appropriate. The Registrar also attached an Inter-Office Memorandum by the Court Management Section, dated 16 February 2000, concerning the issue of the assignment of Duty Counsel to André Rwamakuba at that time "to assist this Chamber in its deliberations on this issue." (Registrar's Additional Submissions of 24 November 2006, at para. 8).

1.2 Scope of the Defence's Application and Orders of the Judgement

12. The Registrar submits that the Defence Application exceeds Order III of the Judgement in that the Defence also seeks an appropriate remedy for the grave and serious miscarriage of justice due to the time André Rwamakuba spent in the custody of the Tribunal prior to his acquittal and alleged manipulation of evidence.[19]

13. While this Defence request exceeds the Order III of the Judgement, the Chamber finds that it is in the interests of justice to discuss it since it could pertain to the fundamental rights of a former accused of the Tribunal.

2. Violation of the Rights of André Rwamakuba Entitling Him to an Effective Remedy

14. The Defence claims an appropriate remedy for the violation of André Rwamakuba's right to legal assistance as well as for the alleged grave and manifest miscarriage of justice occasioned in his case. The Chamber will separately address these two issues hereinafter.

2.1 Violation of André Rwamakuba's Right to Legal Assistance

15. The Registrar submits that, in its Decision of December 2000, Trial Chamber II did not find that André Rwamakuba suffered serious or irreparable prejudice as a result of the Registrar's failure to appoint a Duty Counsel as soon as practicable. The Registrar also emphasizes the particular circumstances of the case at that time. The Registrar explains first, that the duty to appoint a Duty Counsel had not been enshrined in the Rules until just over four months before Rwamakuba arrived in Arusha; second, the initial appearance would have taken place in a reasonable time had Rwamakuba advised the Registrar in due time of his **[page 5]** wish to have Defence Counsel assigned to him, based on a claim of indigence; third, as the Registrar was taking diligent steps to implement the new practice imposed by the new Rule, there was a limited number of counsel practising in Arusha who qualified as Duty Counsel for the Tribunal; and fourth, a statement of the rights possessed by an accused had already been served on Rwamakuba, who is an intelligent, educated man who has held senior ministerial office in his government.[20] The Registrar further submits that the delay in Rwamakuba's initial appearance was partly attributable to the difficulty in assigning Defence Counsel to the co-accused.[21] To support its submission, the Registrar provides copy of an Inter-Office Memorandum by the Court Management Section, dated 16 February 2000, which was made available to the parties and Trial Chamber II at the time of its deliberations on the Defence Motion concerning the illegal arrest and detention of Rwamakuba.[22]

16. The Chamber is not persuaded by the Registrar's arguments regarding the seriousness of the breach of André Rwamakuba's right to legal assistance as set forth in Rule 44 *bis* of the Rules. Even if the specific circumstances of this case could explain the reason why Rwamakuba's right was violated – as claimed by the Registrar – and even if the prejudice was not as serious and irreparable as to justify his immediate release, Trial Chamber II clearly established the existence of the violation of one of Rwamakuba's fundamental rights while he was an accused before this Tribunal.[23] Moreover, it is a fundamental principle of international human rights law, as recalled by the Appeals Chamber, that any violation of a human right entails the provision of an effective remedy.[24]

17. Furthermore, Rule 44 *bis* gives effect to one of the most important fair trial rights of an accused, the right to legal assistance.[25] While it is true that this rule was included in the Rules on 8 June 1998, just over

19 Registrar's Submissions, at para. 7.

20 Registrar's Submissions, at paras. 11-17.

21 Registrar's Additional Submissions of 24 November, at para. 10.

22 Registrar's Additional Submissions of 24 November, at para. 8.

23 *Rwamakuba*, Decision on Illegal Arrest and Detention (TC), 12 December 2000, at para. 43.

24 See, below, at paras. 40-44.

25 See *Pham Hoang v. France*, Judgement of 25 September 1992, Series A no. 243, p. 23, at para. 39; *Prosecutor v. Slobodan Miloševic,*, Case No. IT-02-54-AR73.7, Decision on Interlocutory Appeal of the Trial Chamber's Decision on the Assignment of Defense Counsel (TC), 1 November 2004, at paras. 11 & 13 (on the fundamental importance of the right to counsel).

four months before the breach started to take place, it is nonetheless clearly established under international human rights law that the right to counsel attaches at the investigative and pre-trial stages.[26] What is more, an infringement of Rule 44 *bis* would generally be considered as a violation of the right to legal assistance as enshrined in international human rights law. Indeed, it is in the interests of justice that legal assistance be provided to the accused in international criminal law from the earliest stages of the proceedings as it involves complex cases, concerns serious offences and entails significant potential sentences.[27] **[page 6]**

18. As decided in its Judgement,[28] this Chamber must therefore address the issue of the effective and appropriate remedy concerning the violation of André Rwamakuba's rights.

2.2 Alleged Grave and Manifest Injustice

19. The Defence also claims a remedy on the basis of a grave and manifest miscarriage of justice.[29] It submits that André Rwamakuba was indicted and prosecuted on false and manipulative evidence. In the Defence's view, this circumstance, combined with the length of his pre-trial and trial detention which amounts to a total of nine years, constitutes a miscarriage of justice.[30]

20. In support of its application, the Defence relies upon Article 85(3) of the Statute of the International Criminal Court ("ICC") which provides for compensation to an acquitted person in circumstances involving a grave and manifest miscarriage of justice.[31] In the Defence's view, irregularities in the detention of an accused, long detention before trial and evidence of foul play in the bringing of a prosecution are factors which might be considered by Judges in determining whether a grave and manifest miscarriage of justice has taken place in a given case.[32]

21. Neither the Statute nor the Rules of Procedure and Evidence of this Tribunal provide for the power to accord compensation to an acquitted person in circumstances involving a grave and manifest miscarriage of justice. Nor is there any decision from this Tribunal applying such a principle. Likewise, the Statute and the Rules of Procedure and Evidence of the International Criminal Tribunal for Former Yugoslavia ("ICTY"), which was established by the United Nations Security Council in similar circumstances as this Tribunal a year before the ICTR, do not include such a provision.

22. The Chamber must therefore determine whether the ground of compensation provided for in Article 85(3) could be applied by this Tribunal as a rule established under customary international law.[33] According to the jurisprudence of the International Court of Justice, the existence of a customary international law

---

26 See Concluding Observations of the Human Rights Committee: Georgia, 1 April 1997 P 27, U.N. Doc. CCPR/C/79/Add.74 (1997); *Kelly v. Jamaica*, Communication No. 253/1987, U.N. Doc. CCPR/C/41/D/253/1987 at 60 (1991) at para. 5.10 ("*Kelly v. Jamaica*"); *S v. Switzerland*, 12629/87; 13965/88 (1991) ECHR 54 (28 November 1991); *Brennan v. the United Kingdom*, 39846/98 (2001) ECHR 596 (16 October 2001); Inter-American Commission on Human Rights, *Report on the Situation of Human Rights in El Salvador*, OEA/Ser.L/V/II.85, rev. February 11, 1994, at 5.

27 Under both the International Covenant on Civil and Political Rights and the European Convention on Human Rights, whether the right to legal assistance has been violated in a given case will depend on the circumstances of that case: whether the accused or suspect lacks sufficient means to pay for legal assistance and whether it is consequently required in the interests of justice to provide him with free legal assistance. The complexity of the case (*Pham Hoang v. France*, 13191/87 (1992) ECHR 61 (25 September 1992) ("*Pham Hoang v. France*")) as well as the seriousness of the offence with which the accused is charged and the potential sentence involved (*Kelly v. Jamaica*, at para. 5.10; *Boner v. UK*, 18711/91 (1994) ECHR 36 (28 October 1994)) are relevant factors in the assessment of whether it is in the interests of justice to provide the right to legal assistance to an accused.

28 *Rwamakuba*, Judgement (TC), 20 September 2006, at para. 220.

29 Defence Application, at para. 7.

30 *Ibid.*, at para. 24.

31 *Ibid.*, at paras. 18-19 & 22 (referring to the Rome Statute of the International Criminal Court, 2187 U.N.T.S. 3, entered into force July 1, 2002, Article 85(3) of which reads as follows: "In exceptional circumstances, where the Court finds conclusive facts showing that there has been a grave and manifest miscarriage of justice, it may in its discretion award compensation, according to the criteria provided in the Rules of Procedure and Evidence, to a person who has been released from detention following a final decision of acquittal or a termination of the proceedings for that reason.")

32 *Ibid.*, at para. 19.

33 The Appeals Chamber has recalled on several occasions that the sources of law of this Tribunal encompass customary international law, see *Prosecutor v. Jean-Bosco Barayagwiza*, Case No. ICTR-97-19-AR72, Decision (AC), 3 November 1999, at para. 40; *Prosecutor v. Kajelijeli*, Case No. ICTR-98-44A, Judgement (AC), 23 May 2005, at, para. 209. See also Report of the Secretary-General pursuant to Paragraph 2 of Security Council Resolution 808, 3 May 1993, U.N. Doc. S/25704, at paras. 33-34 ("Secretary-General's Report on the Establishment of the ICTY"); Report of the Secretary-General pursuant to Paragraph 5 of

requires the demonstration of two elements: (i) an extensive and virtually uniform State practice (material element of custom) and (ii) the **[page 7]** acceptance by States of this practice as law (subjective element of custom).[34] To this end, the Chamber will therefore have regard to the practice and positions of States as expressed in international criminal law and international human rights law.

23. The ICC Statute is the only constitutive instrument of an International Criminal Tribunal to include a provision for compensation for an acquitted person in circumstances involving a grave and manifest miscarriage of justice.[35] In the only other Statute which expressly provides for compensation to an accused person, the Statute of the Special Panel for Serious Crimes in East Timor ("SPSCET"), a provision for this ground of compensation was not included.[36]

24. As well, international human rights law does not provide for this ground of compensation, only providing a right to compensation in circumstances involving either an unlawful arrest or detention[37] or an unjust conviction.[38] Since the adoption of the ICC Statute, these instruments have not been amended to include a ground for compensation to an acquitted person for a miscarriage of justice.

25. As such, other than the ICC Statute, no instrument in international criminal law or international human rights law includes a provision for compensation for an acquitted person in circumstances involving a grave and manifest miscarriage of justice while some of them do provide for compensation under other circumstances. **[page 8]**

26. What is more, the inclusion of Article 85(3) was not without controversy during negotiations of the ICC Statute. The Report of the Working Group on Procedural Matters at the Rome Conference includes the following comment: "There are delegations which believe that there should not be an unfettered right to compensation where a person is acquitted or released prior to the end of the trial. The text of paragraph 3 is intended to limit the right to compensation to cases of grave and manifest miscarriage of justice. Other delegations considered this text to be too restrictive."[39]

Security Councl Resolution 955, presented 13 Febuary 1995, U.N. Doc. S/1995/134, at paras. 11-12 ("Secretary-General's Report on the Establishment of the ICTR").

34 See *North Sea Continental Shelf Cases* (Federal Republic of Germany v. Denmark; Federal Republic of Germany v. The Netherlands), Judgment of 20 Feb. 1969, (1969) ICJ Rep. 3, at para. 74; *Continental Shelf Case* (Lybian Arab Jamahiriya/Malta), Judgement of 3 June 1985, (1985) ICJ Rep. 13 at para. 27; *Legality of the Threat or Use of Nuclear Weapons*, Advisory Opinion of 8 July 1996, (1996) ICJ Rep. 226 at para. 64.

35 The International Criminal Tribunal for Rwanda, the International Criminal Tribunal for the Former Yugoslavia, the Special Court for Sierra Leone, the Special Panel for Serious Crimes in East Timor and the Extraordinary Chambers in the Courts of Cambodia for the Prosecution of the Crimes Committed during the Period of Democratic Kampuchea do not provide for this ground of compensation.

36 Article 52 of the SPSCET provides a right to compensation in regard to unjust convictions and unlawful arrests or detentions (Statute of the SPSCET, Regulation 2000/30, September 25, 2000, as amended by regulation 2001/25, September 14, 2001, s. 52).

37 International Covenant on Civil and Political Rights, G.A. res. 2200A (XXI), 21 U.N. GAOR Supp. (No. 16) at 52, U.N. Doc. A/6316 (1966), 999 U.N.T.S. 171, entered into force Mar. 23, 1976, art. 9(5) ("ICCPR"). Convention for the Protection of Human Rights and Fundamental Freedoms, 213 U.N.T.S. 222, entered into force Sept. 3, 1953, as amended by Protocols No 3, 5, 8, and 11 which entered into force on 21 September 1970, 20 December 1971, 1 January 1990, and 1 November 1998 respectively, art. 5(5) ("ECHR"). An arrest or detention will be considered unlawful if there has been a violation of the provisions relating to the right to liberty and security (articles 9(1) to (4) of the ICCPR, articles 5(1) to 5(4) of the ECHR) or a relevant provision of domestic law.

38 ICCPR, Art. 14(6): "When a person has by a final decision been convicted of a criminal offence and when subsequently his conviction has been reversed or he has been pardoned on the ground that a new or newly discovered fact shows conclusively that there has been a miscarriage of justice, the person who has suffered punishment as a result of such conviction shall be compensated according to law, unless it is proved that the non-disclosure of the unknown fact in time is whole or partly attributable to him."; ECHR, Protocol no 7, art. 3: "When a person has by a final decision been convicted of a criminal offence and when subsequently his conviction has been reversed, or he has been pardoned, on the ground that a new or newly discovered fact shows conclusively that there has been a miscarriage of justice, the person who has suffered punishment as a result of such conviction shall be compensated according to the law or the practice of the State concerned, unless it is proved that the non-disclosure of the unknown fact in time is whole or partly attributable to him."; ACHR, Art. 10: "Every person has the right to be compensated in accordance with the law in the event he has been sentenced by a final judgement through a miscarriage of justice." This right to compensation is therefore limited to cases where an accused person was convicted through a miscarriage of justice, specifically with respect to the ICCPR and ECHR where this miscarriage of justice has been conclusively shown to exist on the basis of a new or newly discovered fact.

39 Report of the Working Group on Procedural Matters at the Rome Conference, Document A/CONF.183/C.1/WGPM/L.2/Add.7 (13 July 1998), art. 85.

27. On the basis of the above, the Chamber considers that there is insufficient evidence of State practice or of the recognition by States of this practice as law to establish that customary international law provides for compensation to an acquitted person in circumstances involving a grave and manifest miscarriage of justice.

28. Moreover, even if Article 85(3) of the ICC Statute had achieved customary status, the Chamber observes that it remains a narrowly drafted provision. It firstly does not as such provide a right to compensation, but rather provides that the Court *may in its discretion* make an award for financial compensation. It secondly provides that such an award will be appropriate in *exceptional circumstances* where *conclusive facts* establish that there has been a grave and manifest miscarriage of justice.[40]

29. This being said, the Chamber finds it, however, necessary to emphasize the importance and the relevance of the principle set forth in Article 85(3) of the ICC Statute in light of the long and complex trials in this Tribunal. The significance of this principle must be understood with reference to the right of any individual to freedom, including the corresponding principle that detention should remain exceptional or, at least, limited to what is reasonable and necessary.[41]

30. In that respect, it is notable that under the Tribunal's Rules, an accused person who is sentenced is given credit for the period during which he was detained in custody pending his or her surrender to the Tribunal or pending trial or appeal.[42] By analogy, the Chamber is of the view that the possibility to grant some sort of remedy or compensation would be fair in circumstances where, although the arrest or detention of an acquitted person was not unlawful, he or she was subject to a lengthy detention during the pre-trial and trial stages. Such an award of compensation would be exercised in light of the circumstances of the case, and could not be applied, for instance, where an accused had intentionally caused his or her arrest or where it would be unreasonable to award compensation. In the Chamber's view, such a provision would offer an acceptable balance between the fundamental right to freedom of any individual and the realities of the investigation and prosecution of international crimes. **[page 9]** The Chamber notes that a number of States provide for the award of compensation in such circumstances subject to a number of conditions or exceptions.[43]

31. For the above reasons, while the Chamber acknowledges the importance of the principle provided for in Article 85(3) of the ICC Statute, it does not find that at present customary international law provides for a right to compensation for an acquitted person in circumstances involving a grave and manifest miscarriage of justice. In the absence of a provision in its Statute and Rules or any other applicable source of law in this regard, the Chamber therefore denies the Defence's claim for compensation on this basis. The Chamber considers that the Security Council would have to amend the Statute of the Tribunal, or take any other action, as the case may be, for such a claim or any other claim for compensation to be admissible in the context discussed.

3. Effective Remedy

32. The Chamber will first determine whether it has the power to provide for an effective remedy in case of violation of the rights of a person while he or she was an accused before this Tribunal. In particular, it will

---

40 See however Salvatore Zappalà, "Compensation to a n Arrested or Convicted Person" in Antonio Cassese, Paola Gaeta and John R.W. Jones, eds., *The Rome Statute of the International Criminal Court: A Commentary* (Oxford: OUP, 2002) 1577 at 1583 (arguing that a grave and manifest injustice should be considered ipso facto as an exceptional circumstance.)

41 ICCPR, Art. 9(1), 9(3) & 9(4); ECHR, Art. 5(1), 5(3) & 5(4); ACHR, 7(2), 7(5) & 7(6).

42 Rule 101(D) reads as follows: "Credit shall be given to the convicted person for the period, if any, during which the convicted person was detained in custody pending his surrender to the Tribunal or pending trial or appeal."

43 See, e.g, Austria: Compensation (Criminal Proceedings) Act 1969, Sect. 2(1)(b) and 6; Iceland: Act No. 36/1999, Section 175; Italy: Code of Criminal Procedure, Article 314; Latvia: Law on Indemnification against Loss Resulting from Unlawful or Unsubstantiated Actions of the Investigation Entity, Prosecution Office or Court; Sweden: SFS 1974:515, as amended by SFS 1998:714; The Netherlands: Dutch Code of Criminal Procedure, Articles 89 and 591a; Norway: Code of Criminal Procedure, Articles 444-446; United Kingdom: The UK has a policy of making ex-gratia payments to acquitted persons for wrongful conviction or charge or in exceptional circumstances (Policy Statement of the Home Secretary Douglas Hurd, 29 November 1985, H.C. Deb., cols 691-692, quoted in *Regina v. Secretary of State for the Home Department (Appellant) ex parte Mullen (Respondent),* [2004] UKHL 18, at para. 28).

determine whether it has the power to order a financial compensation as an effective remedy. Finally, it will address the question of the effective remedy in view of the specific circumstances of the case.

3.1 The Chamber's Power to Provide an Effective Remedy in Case of Violation of the Rights of an Accused Person

33. The Defence submits that the Chamber possesses the power to grant an effective remedy to André Rwamakuba under Rule 5, Rule 54 or an implied power.[44]

34. The Chamber cannot accept the Defence argument regarding Rule 54.[45] This Rule provides that a Chamber may issue any such orders as may be necessary for the preparation or conduct of the trial. The Chamber is of the opinion that an award for compensation in respect of a former accused's rights, following the end of his trial, cannot be considered as being necessary for the preparation or conduct of his trial.

35. Concerning the Defence's argument relying upon Rule 5, the Registrar submits that according to the French version of this provision, a remedy can only be awarded against a party to the case[46] and that the Registrar is not a party to this case within the meaning of the Rule.[47] **[page 10]**

36. Rule 5 of the Rules provides that "[w]here an objection on the ground of non-compliance with the Rules or Regulations is raised by a party at the earliest opportunity, the Trial Chamber shall grant relief, if it finds that the alleged non-compliance is proved and that it has caused material prejudice to that party." The Chamber notes that the French version of this provision differs from the English version in that it seems to limit its scope to non-compliance with the Rules or Regulations by a party only.[48]

37. Under Rule 7, in case of discrepancy between the two versions of a Rule, "the version which is more consonant with the spirit of the Statute and the Rules shall prevail."[49] In this regard, the Chamber finds the Registrar's interpretation of Rule 5 unsustainable as it goes against the ordinary meaning and spirit of the Rule. First of all, neither the English nor French texts specify what kind of relief may be ordered by the Chamber if it finds that the non-compliance has caused material prejudice to the claiming party. In some instances, a Trial Chamber may consider that the provision of relief will require action by a person to whom the non-compliance is not attributable. This could therefore cover situations where the Registrar is ordered to take the necessary measures while not being responsible for the non-compliance. Second of all, the violations for which relief could be ordered under Rule 5 cannot be limited to violations by "parties" to the proceedings as this would defeat the purpose of the Rule which seeks to provide relief for non-compliance with the Tribunal's Rules and Regulations. The Chamber cannot accept that the Tribunal could escape liability for non-compliance with the Rules or Regulations because the non-compliance was by an organ or a person or authority who was not a "party" to the proceedings. Consequently, the Chamber finds that Rule 5 must grant protection against any breach of the rules and regulations and that the party against whom relief may be ordered includes the Tribunal itself.

38. In the present case, it was found that the Registrar failed to act pursuant to Rule 44 *bis* of the Rules so as to appoint a Duty Counsel for André Rwamakuba pending assignment of his Counsel and that this omission resulted, notably, in the absence of legal assistance for Rwamakuba, while he was an accused, over an extended period of time in contradiction with his fundamental right enshrined in Article 20 (4) (c) of the Statute.[50] According to Rule 5 of the Rules, the Chamber must now establish whether the Registrar's non-

---

44 Defence Reply, at para. 5.

45 Rule 54 reads: "At the request of either party or proprio motu, a Judge or a Trial Chamber may issue such orders, summonses, subpoenas and warrants as may be necessary for the purposes of an investigation or for the preparation or conduct of the trial."

46 Rule 2(A) provides that only the Prosecution and the Accused are parties to a given case.

47 Registrar's Submissions, at para. 21.

48 The French version of Rule 5 (A) reads: "Toute exception d'une partie à l'égard d'un acte d'une autre partie, fondée sur une violation du Règlement ou des règlements internes, doit être soulevée dès que possible; la Chambre de première instance accorde réparation si la preuve de la violation présumée est rapportée et si celle-ci a effectivement fait subir un préjudice substantiel à cette partie."

49 See also Vienna Convention on the Law of Treaties, 22 May 1969, 1155 U.N.T.S. 331, art. 33(4) (when a comparison of a text authenticated in two or more languages discloses a difference of meaning, "the meaning which best reconciles the texts, having regard to the object and purpose of the treaty, shall be adopted.")

50 *Rwamakuba*, Decision on Illegal Arrest and Detention (TC), 12 December 2000, at para. 43.

compliance with Rule 44 *bis* caused material prejudice to Rwamakuba. In light of Trial Chamber II's finding that this breach had not caused Rwamakuba a serious and irreparable prejudice,[51] the Chamber finds that he did not suffer a material prejudice within the meaning of Rule 5. As such, the Chamber deems it unnecessary to consider whether the relief contemplated in Rule 5 would confer upon the Chamber the power to make orders for financial compensation.

39. Having determined that Rule 5 is not applicable on the facts to the present case, in the absence of the showing that André Rwamakuba suffered material prejudice, the Chamber will now consider whether the violation of his right to legal assistance may be redressed on the basis of any other applicable law. **[page 11]**

40. The Chamber agrees with the parties that neither the Statute, nor the Rules of this Tribunal provide for a right to an effective remedy for violations of human rights. However, this right undoubtedly forms part of customary international law and is expressly provided for in the following instruments: the Universal Declaration of Human Rights,[52] the ICCPR,[53] the Convention on the Elimination of All Forms of Racial Discrimination,[54] the Convention against Torture and Other Cruel, Inhuman or Degrading Treatment,[55] the Convention Concerning Indigenous and Tribal Peoples in Independent Countries,[56] the UN Declaration of Basic Principles of Justice for Victims of Crime and Abuse of Power,[57] the ECHR,[58] the American Declaration of the Rights and Duties of Man[59] and the American Convention of Human Rights.[60]

41. Relying upon international human rights instruments, and particularly the International Covenant on Civil and Political Rights, the Appeals Chamber of this Tribunal has recognized on several occasions that an Accused has a right to an effective remedy.[61]

42. In the *Kajelijeli* case, the Appeals Chamber relied upon the various sources of law applicable to the Tribunal, including the Statute, the Rules and customary international law as reflected in the ICCPR as well as referred to the provisions of regional human rights treaties as persuasive authority and evidence of international custom.[62] It set out, on the basis of existing standards in international human rights law, that

---

51 *Ibid.*, at para. 45.

52 G.A. Res. 217A (III), U.N. Doc. A/810 (1948) art. 8 (providing that everyone has the right to an effective remedy by the competent national tribunals for acts violating the fundamental rights granted hum by the constitution or law).

53 ICCPR, art. 2(3)(a) (obliging State Parties to ensure that any person whose rights have been violated shall have a effective remedy). See also articles 9(5) and 14(6) which provide that a enforceable right to compensation according to law for unlawful arrests or detentions and unjust convictions.

54 21 December 1965, entered into force 4 January 1969, 660 U.N.T.S. 195, art. 6 (obliging State Parties to assure effective protection and remedies against any acts of racial discrimination as well as the right to seek just and adequate reparation or satisfaction for any damage suffered as a result of such discrimination).

55 10 December 1984, entered into force 26 June 1987, G.A. Res. 39/46, 39 U.N. GAOR, Supp. No. 51, U.N. Doc. A/39\51, 197, art. 14 (obliging State Parties to ensure that a victim of an act of torture obtains redress and has an enforceable right to fair and adequate compensation)

56 I.L.O. No. 169, 27 June 1989, entered into force 5 September 1991, (1989) 28 I.L.M. 1382. The Convention refers to "fair compensation for damages" at Art. 15(2), "compensation in money" at Art. 16(4) and full compensation for "any loss or injury" at Art. 16(5).

57 G.A. Res. 40/34 of 29 November 1985, at para. 4 (stating that victims are entitled to access to the mechanisms of justice and prompt redress for the harm they have suffered) and at para. 8 (providing that where appropriate restitution should be made to victims, their families or dependants by offenders or third parties responsible for their behaviour).

58 ECHR, Art. 13 (stating that victims are entitled to an effective remedy before a national authority). See also article 41 (formerly article 50) which provides, upon a finding of a violation and the absence of total reparation in domestic law, that the European Court of Human Rights shall afford just satisfaction to the injured party.

59 2 May 1948, O.A.S. Res. XXX, adopted by the Ninth International conference of American States (1948), reprinted in Basic Documents Pertaining to Human Rights in the Inter-American System, OEA/ser.L/V/II.92, doc.31 rev. 3 at 17 (1996), Art. XVII (guaranteeing the right to resort to the courts to ensure respect for legal rights and to obtain protection from acts of authority which violate fundamental constitutional rights).

60 O.A.S. Treaty Series No. 36, 1144 U.N.T.S. 123, entered into force July 18, 1978, reprinted in Basic Documents Pertaining to Human Rights in the Inter-American System, OEA/Ser.L.V/II.82 doc.6 rev.1 at 25 (1992), Art. 25 (entitling everyone to effective recourse against acts that violate the fundamental rights recognized by the constitution, laws of the state or the Convention), ("ACHR"). See also Articles 1(1), 8, 10 & 63(1).

61 See *Prosecutor v. Barayagwiza*, Case No. ICTR-97-19, Decision (Prosecutor's Request for Review or Reconsideration) (AC), 31 March 2000, at paras. 74-75; *Kajelijeli*, Judgement (AC), 23 May 2005, at paras. 255 and 322; *Prosecutor v. Semanza,* Case No.ICTR-97-20, Decision (AC), 31 May 2000, at para. 125.

62 *Kajelijeli*, Judgement (AC), 23 May 2005, at para. 209.

"any violation of the accused's **[page 12]** rights entails the provision of an effective remedy pursuant to Article 2(3) (a) of the ICCPR."[63] In that case, the Appeals Chamber ordered a reduction in sentence as the appropriate remedy with respect to the violations of the Appellant's rights.[64]

43. In the *Barayagwiza* case, the Appeals Chamber also affirmed that all violations of rights demand a remedy.[65] In his Separate Declaration, Judge Rafael Nieto-Navia shed further light on the Appeals Chamber decision by stating as follows:

> 28. Human rights treaties provide that when a state violates fundamental human rights, it is obliged to ensure that appropriate domestic remedies are in place to put an end to such violations and in certain circumstances to provide for fair compensation to the injured party.
> 29. Although the Tribunal is not a State, it is following such a precedent to compensate the Appellant for the violation of his human rights. As it is impossible to turn back the clock, I think that the remedy decided by the Appeals Chamber fulfills the international requirements.[66]

44. In the present case, the Appeals Chamber has stated that "it [was] open to [Rwamakuba] to invoke the issue of the alleged violation of his fundamental human rights by the Tribunal in order to seek reparation as the case may be, at the appropriate time."[67]

45. On the basis of the above Appeals Chamber decisions, the Chamber holds the view that its power to provide an accused or former accused with an effective remedy for violations of human rights arises out of the combined effect of the Tribunal's inherent powers and its obligation to respect generally accepted international human rights norms.

46. The doctrine of inherent powers provides that a court should be recognized as having been implicitly conferred the powers which prove necessary to the exercise of its mandate.[68] The Appeals Chamber has previously recognized the existence of certain inherent powers accruing to a Trial Chamber by virtue of its nature as a judicial body. In the *Tadic* case, the Appeals Chamber explained that the Tribunal was not simply a subsidiary organ of the Security Council, but was a judicial body:

> To assume that the jurisdiction of the International Tribunal is absolutely limited to what the Security Council "intended" to entrust it with, is to envisage the International Tribunal exclusively as a "subsidiary organ" of the Security Council (see United Nations Charter, Arts. 7(2) & 29), a "creation" totally fashioned to the smallest detail by its "creator" and remaining totally in its power and at its mercy. But the Security **[page 13]** Council not only decided to establish a subsidiary organ (the only legal means available to it for setting up such a body), it also clearly intended to establish a special kind of "subsidiary organ": a tribunal.[69]

47. In the Chamber's view, the power to give effect to the right to an effective remedy for violations of the rights of an accused or former accused accrues to the Chamber because this power is essential for the carrying out of judicial functions, including the fair and proper administration of justice. This is all the more true in the present case as the right at issue, the right to legal assistance, is one of the core fair trial rights held by an accused in criminal proceedings.[70]

---

63 *Ibid.*, at para. 255. See also at para. 322.

64 *Ibid.*, at para. 324.

65 *Barayagwiza*, Decision (AC), 31 March 2000, at para. 74. In his Separate Opinion, Judge Shahabuddeen did not address the issue of financial compensation as such, arguing on the basis of rule 40 *bis*, that the accused's release was the only possible remedy (*Barayagwiza*, Separate Opinion of Judge Mohamed Shahabuddeen on Prosecutor's Request for Review or Reconsideration (AC), 31 March 2000, at para. 42).

66 *Barayagwiza*, Declaration of Judge Rafael Nieto-Naviam on Prosecutor's Request for Review or Reconsideration (AC), 31 March 2000, at paras. 28 & 29. In his Declaration, Judge Lal Chand Vohrah indicated that he approved of Judge Nieto-Naviam' statement as it related to human rights principles (*Barayagwiza*, Declaration of Judge Lal Chand Vohrah on Prosecutor's Request for Review or Reconsideration (AC), 31 March 2000, at para. 3).

67 *Rwamakuba*, Decision on Illegal Arrest and Detention (AC), 11 June 2001.

68 See, e.g., *Nuclear Tests Case* (Australia. v. France; New Zeland v. France), Judgement of 20 Dec. 1974, (1974) I.C.J. Rep. 253 at 259-260; *Bremer Vulkan Schiffbau und Maschinenfabrik v. S. India Shipping Corp.*, (1981) 1 All E.R. 289, 295 (H.L.).

69 *Prosecutor v. Tadic*, Case No. IT-94-1, Decision on the Defence Motion for Interlocutory Appeal on Jurisdiction (AC), 2 October 1995, at para. 15. See also *Prosecutor v. Blaskic*, Case No. IT-95-14, Judgement on the Request of the Republic of Croatia for Review of the Decision of Trial Chamber II of 18 July 1997 (AC), 29 October 1997, at para. 33; *Tadic*, Judgement (AC), 15 July 1999, at para. 322.

70 See *Prosecutor v. Slobodan Milošević*, Case No. IT-02-54-AR73.7, Decision on Interlocutory Appeal of the Trial Chamber's Decision on the Assignment of Defense Counsel (TC), 1 November 2004, at paras. 11 & 13 (on the fundamental importance of the

48. Moreover, this power accrues to the Chamber because the Tribunal, as a special kind of subsidiary organ of the U.N. Security Council, is bound to respect and ensure respect for generally accepted human rights norms. Indeed, the United Nations, as an international subject, is bound to respect rules of customary international law, including those rules which relate to the protection of fundamental human rights.[71] This result is in keeping with the United Nations' stated purposes as well as its internal practices. According to its constitutional instrument, one of the purposes of the United Nations is to achieve international co-operation in promoting and encouraging respect for human rights and for fundamental freedoms for all.[72] In many instances, the U.N. Security Council has recalled **[page 14]** this purpose by adopting resolutions aiming to promote and protect human rights.[73] The Security Council and the Secretary-General have also recalled that the members of peace-keeping missions as well as transitional authorities for the administration of territory must observe fundamental human rights.[74] In particular, when reporting to the Security Council on the establishment of the ICTY, the U.N. Secretary General underlined that: "It is axiomatic that the International Tribunal must fully respect internationally recognized standards regarding the rights of the accused at all stages of its proceedings."[75] This result is furthermore in keeping with the principle that States cannot evade their obligations under international legal obligations by creating an international organization that would not be bound by the legal limits imposed upon them. As the Member States of the United Nations are bound to respect their international human rights obligations when prosecuting international crimes within their domestic national legal systems, they cannot establish an International Criminal Tribunal which would not be bound to respect the same human rights obligations.[76]

---

right to counsel); *Pham Hoang v. France*, at para. 39 (noting that the "right of a person charged with a criminal offence to free legal assistance is one element, amongst others, of the concept of a fair trial in criminal proceedings").

[71] This is implicit in two of the International Court of Justice's advisory opinions: *Interpretation of the Agreement of 25 March 1951 between the WHO and Egypt*, Advisory Opinion of 20 Dec. 1980, (1980) ICJ Rep. 73 at 89-90 ("International organizations are subjects of international law and, as such, are bound by obligations incumbent upon them under general rules of international law, under their constitutions or under international agreements to which they are parties."); *Reparation for Injuries Suffered in the Service of the United Nations*, Advisory Opinion of 11 April 1949, (1949) ICJ Rep. 174 at 179 (holding that an international organization is "a subject of international law and capable of possessing international rights and duties."). See also CESCR, General Comment 8, The Relationship between Economic Sanctions and Respect for Economic, Social and Cultural Rights, 12/12/97, E/C.12/1997/8 at para. 11 ("The second set of obligations relates to the party or parties responsible for the imposition, maintenance or implementation of the sanctions, whether it be the international community, an international or regional organization, or a State or group of States. In this respect, the Committee considers that there are three conclusions which follow logically from the recognition of economic, social and cultural human rights.) ("General Comment no 8"). At the EU level, see *Nold v. Commission*, Case 4/73, 1974 E.C.R. 491 (holding that fundamental rights were applicable to the EU on the basis of the constitutional traditions common to the member states and from the guidelines supplied by international treaties for the protection of human rights on which the member states have collaborated or of which they are signatories (including the European Convention of Human Rights)).

[72] See *Charter of the United Nations*, 26 June 1945, entered into force 24 Oct. 1945, 1 U.N.T.S. xvi, Art. 1(3). Article 1(3) has most notably been invoked by the General Assembly with respect to the improvement within of the effective enjoyment of human rights (see, e.g., G.A. Res. 34/46, 23 Nov. 1979; 36/133, 14 Dec. 1981; 38/124, 16 Dec. 1983; 339/145, 14 Dec. 1984; 40/124, 13 Dec. 1985). See also the Preamble and Art. 55 (c), the latter of which states that the United Nations shall promote "universal respect for, and observance of, human rights and fundamental freedoms for all without distinction as to race, sex, language or religion." It is notable that according to the *travaux préparatoires*, the inclusion of the term "observance" was considered to strengthen this provision (United Nations Conference on International Organization, at 324). The French version of Article 55(c) even refers to the "respect effectif" (effective observance) of human rights obligations. Article 55(c) thus forms the basis for the activities of the United Nations in respect of human rights. It was for instance invoked, along with Article 56, in the Preamble to the Universal Declaration of Human Rights, UN GA Res. 217 A(III), 10 Dec. 1948, UN Doc. A/810 at 71 (1948).

[73] See, e.g., SC. Res. 1244, 22 U.N. SCOR, 4011th mtg., U.N. Doc. S/RES/1244 (1999) para. 11(j) (specifying that the responsibilities of the international administrations in Kosovo and Timor include "protecting and promoting human rights.").

[74] UNTAET, Reg. No. 1999/1 On the Authority of the Transitional Administration in East Timor, UNTAET/REG/1991/1, 27 Nov. 1999 and UNMIK, Reg. No. 1999/1 On the Authority of the Interim Administration in Kosovo, UNMIK/REG/1999/1, 25 July 1999 (both providing that "[i]n exercising their functions, all persons undertaking public duties or holding public office [in the respective territories] shall observe internationally recognized human rights standards."); UN Secretary-General's Bulletin on the Observance by UN Forces of International Humanitarian Law, 6 August 1999, U.N. Doc. ST/SGB/1999/13 (1999) at para. 1.1.

[75] Secretary-General's Report on the Establishment of the ICTY, at para. 106.

[76] The Committee of the International Law Association on the Accountability of International Organisations has stated as follows: "States cannot evade their obligations under customary law and general principles of law by creating an international organization that would not be bound by the legal limits imposed upon its Member States." (ILA Final Report 2004, at 18). See General Comment no 8 at para. 8 (emphasizing the treaty obligations of the members of the Security Council), *Waite and Kennedy v. Germany*, 26083/94 [1999] ECHR 13 (18 February 1999), at para. 67 and *Matthews v. UK*, 24833/94 [1999] ECHR 12 (18 February 1999), at para. 32 (holding that the responsibilities of Member States under the ECHR continue even after the transfer of competences to international organisations).

49. In light of the above-mentioned principles and as there is no explicit provision of the Statute or the Rules providing for an organ of this Tribunal to grant an effective remedy, the Chamber finds that it has the inherent power to provide an accused or former accused with an effective remedy for violations of his or her human rights while being prosecuted or tried before this Tribunal. Such power necessarily accrues to the Chamber as it is essential both for the carrying out of its judicial functions and for complying with its obligation to respect generally accepted international human rights norms.

3.2 The Chamber's Power to Order Financial Compensation as an Effective Remedy

50. The Chamber will now consider whether its power to give effect to an accused's or former accused's right to an effective remedy includes the power to grant financial compensation as claimed by the Defence.

51. Under international human rights law, the right to an effective remedy endows an individual who has been the victim of a human rights violation with the right to seek a **[page 15]** remedy before a competent tribunal and to obtain financial compensation as a remedy if appropriate. To begin with, the Human Rights Committee has stated the following view on the obligations entailed by the right to an effective remedy under Article 2(3) of the ICCPR:

> Article 2, paragraph 3, requires that States Parties make reparation to individuals whose Covenant rights have been violated. Without reparation to individuals whose Covenant rights have been violated, the obligation to provide an effective remedy, which is central to the efficacy of article 2, paragraph 3, is not discharged. In addition to the explicit reparation required by articles 9, paragraph 5, and 14, paragraph 6, the Committee considers that the Covenant generally entails appropriate compensation. The Committee notes that, where appropriate, reparation can involve restitution, rehabilitation and measures of satisfaction, such as public apologies, public memorials, guarantees of non-repetition and changes in relevant laws and practices, as well as bringing to justice the perpetrators of human rights violations.[77]

52. Moreover, according to the European Court of Human Rights, an effective remedy entails that "where an individual has an arguable claim to be the victim of a violation of the rights set forth in the Convention, he should have a remedy before a national authority in order both to have his claim decided and, if appropriate, to obtain redress."[78] Finally, the Inter-American Commission of Human Rights has interpreted the right to an effective remedy as "the right of every individual to go to a tribunal when any of his rights have been violated [...], to obtain a judicial investigation conducted by a competent, impartial, and independent tribunal that will establish whether or not a violation has taken place and will set, when appropriate, adequate compensation."[79] Under the American Convention of Human Rights, an effective remedy must therefore be both adequate and efficacious:

> The American Convention requires the States to offer effective recourses to human rights violations victims. The formal existence of such recourses is not sufficient to demonstrate their effectiveness; to be effective, a recourse must be adequate and efficacious. Adequate means that the function of the recourse in a State's domestic legal system must be appropriate for protecting the juridical situation affected. A recourse is efficacious when it is capable of producing the result for which it was designed.[80]

53. In the present case, the Registrar disputes the Chamber's power to grant financial compensation to André Rwamakuba for the violation of his right to legal assistance. It submits that orders to financially compensate those whose rights have been violated are only under development within the general principles of law as understood in Article 38 of the ICJ Statute and have not yet been enshrined in UN Charter principles, treaty law, or customary law.[81]

---

77 Human Rights Committee, General Comment No. 31 Nature of the General Legal Obligation Imposed on States Parties to the Covenant, 26 May 2004, U.N. Doc. CCPR/C/21/Rev.1/Add.13, at para. 16.

78 *Silver v. UK*, 5947/72; 6205/73; 7052/75;... [1983] ECHR 11 (24 October 1983), at para. 113.

79 *Raquel Martí de Mejía v. Perú*, Case 10.970, Report No. 5/96, Inter-Am.C.H.R., OEA/Ser.L/V/II.91 Doc. 7 (1996) 157 at 190-191. See also *Carranza v. Argentina*, Case 10.087, Report No. 30/97, Inter-Am.C.H.R., OEA/Ser.L/V/II.98, Doc. 7 rev. (1998) 254 at 266-267.

80 *Raquel Martí de Mejía v. Perú*, at 193. See also *Velásquez Rodríguez Case*, Judgement of July 29, 1988, Inter-Am Ct. H.R. (Ser. C) No. 4 (1988), at paras. 63, 64 & 66.

81 Registrar's Submissions, at para. 18.

54. The Chamber is not persuaded by the Registrar's argument. To begin with, five international human rights instruments expressly refer to a right to compensation or **[page 16]** restitution.[82] In particular, the International Covenant on Civil and Political Rights, which was adopted under the auspices of the United Nations, provides for a right to financial compensation in circumstances involving either an unlawful arrest or detention[83] or an unjust conviction.[84] Other regional instruments on human rights also provide for a right to financial compensation under these circumstances.[85] With respect to violations of the right to life, the *Special Rapporteur*, in a 1994 report to the UN Human Rights Commission, characterized the duty to provide compensation to victims of such violations as an international obligation: "The recognition of the duty to compensate victims of human rights violations, and the actual granting of compensation to them, presupposes the recognition by the Government of its obligation to ensure effective protection against human rights abuses on the basis of the respect for the fundamental rights and freedoms of every person."[86]

55. In addition, the Inter-American Court of Human Rights and the European Court of Human Rights are empowered to make awards for financial compensation to victims of human rights violations.[87] Consequently, financial compensation has been awarded to victims of human rights violations on numerous occasions by the Inter-American Court of Human Rights[88] and the European Court of Human Rights.[89] The former stated as follows in *Velazquez-Rodriguez* in regard to the concept of reparations: "Reparation of harm brought about by the violation of an international obligation consists in full restitution (*restitutio integrum*) which includes the restoration of the prior situation, the reparation of the consequences of the violation, and indemnification and patrimonial and non-patrimonial **[page 17]** damages, including emotional harm."[90] The latter has held that while just satisfaction cannot be claimed as a right under the ECHR, the Court has the discretion to grant just satisfaction the basis of equity, though not of its own motion.[91] Bodies without express provisions allowing for the award of financial compensation have also accepted in principle the need for an award of compensation and have made recommendations to that effect. The African Commission on Human and Peoples' Rights,[92] the UN Human Rights Committee[93] and the Committee on the Elimination of all

---

82 The Convention on the Elimination of All Forms of Racial Discrimination, art. 6; the Convention against Torture and Other Cruel, Inhuman or Degrading Treatment, art. 14; the Convention Concerning Indigenous and Tribal Peoples in Independent Countries, art. 15(2), 16(4) & 16(5); and the UN Declaration of Basic Principles of Justice for Victims of Crime and Abuse of Power, at para. 4.

83 ICCPR, art. 9(5): "Anyone who has been the victim of an unlawful arrest or detention shall have an enforceable right to compensation." ECHR, art. 5(5): "Everyone who has been the victim of arrest or detention in contravention with the provisions of this Article shall have an enforceable right to compensation."

84 ICCPR, art. 14(6): "When a person has by a final decision been convicted of a criminal offence and when subsequently his conviction has been reversed or he has been pardoned on the ground that a new or newly discovered fact shows conclusively that there has been a miscarriage of justice, the person who has suffered punishment as a result of such conviction shall be compensated according to law, unless it is proved that the non-disclosure of the unknown fact in time is whole or partly attributable to him."

85 ECHR, Protocol no 7, art. 3: "When a person has by a final decision been convicted of a criminal offence and when subsequently his conviction has been reversed, or he has been pardoned, on the ground that a new or newly discovered fact shows conclusively that there has been a miscarriage of justice, the person who has suffered punishment as a result of such conviction shall be compensated according to the law or the practice of the State concerned, unless it is proved that the non-disclosure of the unknown fact in time is whole or partly attributable to him."; ACHR, art. 10: "Every person has the right to be compensated in accordance with the law in the event he has been sentenced by a final judgement through a miscarriage of justice."

86 E/CN.4/1993/46, at para. 79(g). See also at para. 11.

87 ECHR, art. 41: "If the Court finds that there has been a violation of the Convention or the Protocols thereto, and if the internal law of the High Contracting Party concerned allows only partial reparation to be made, the Court shall, if necessary, afford just satisfaction to the injured party."; ACHR, art. 63(1): "1. If the Court finds that there has been a violation of a right or freedom protected by this Convention, the Court shall rule that the injured party be ensured the enjoyment of his right or freedom that was violated. It shall also rule, if appropriate, that the consequences of the measure or situation that constituted the breach of such right or freedom be remedied and that fair compensation be paid to the injured party."

88 See, e.g., *Velasquez Rodriguez v. Honduras*, Judgement of 29 July 1988, (1988) Inter-Am.Ct.H.R. (ser. C) no. 4; *Suarez Rosero v. Ecuador (Reparations)*, Judgement of 20 January 1999, (1999) 44 Inter-Am.Ct.H.R. (ser. C); *Aloeboetoe et al. v. Surinam (Reparations)*, Judgement of 10 September 1993, (1994) Inter-Am.Ct.H.R. (Ser. C) No. 15.

89 See below footnote 121.

90 *Velasquez Rodriguez v. Honduras*, Judgement of 29 July 1988, (1988) Inter-Am.Ct.H.R. (ser. C) no. 4, at para. 26.

91 *Sunday Times v. UK (No.1)*, 6538/74 (1980) ECHR 6 (6 November 1980); *Francesco Lombardo v. Italy*, 11519/85 (1992) ECHR 72 (26 November 1992).

92 *Embga Mekongo Louis v. Cameroon*, 8th Annual Report of the ACHPR 1994-1995, ACHPR/8TH/ACT/RPT/XVII, Annex IX.

93 See, e.g, *Irene Bleier Lewenhoff and Rosa Valiño de Bleier v. Uruguay*, Communication No. 30/1978, U.N. Doc. CCPR/C/OP/1 at 109 (1985); *Guillermo Ignacio Dermit Barbato and Hugo Haroldo Dermit Barbato v. Uruguay*, Communication No. 84/1981,

Forms of Racial Discrimination[94] have all recommended paying compensation as an appropriate remedy for a human rights violation. Moreover, two International Criminal Tribunals now include express provisions granting a right to financial compensation for violations of the rights of an accused.[95]

56. As a result, the Chamber holds the view that it cannot be said that orders to financially compensate those whose rights have been violated are only under development in international law.

57. The Registrar further disputes the Chamber's power to grant financial compensation to André Rwamakuba for the violation of his right to legal assistance because there is no provision in the Statute that allows the Tribunal or Chambers to grant financial compensation to individuals it has allegedly wronged.[96] In support of its submission, it relies upon letters written by Judge Claude Jorda, former President of the ICTY, Judge Navanethem Pillay, former President of the ICTR, Judge Theodore Meron, former president of the ICTY and Judge Erik Møse, President of the ICTR, in which they take the position that the Security Council would have to amend the Statutes of the Tribunals for a Chamber to be able to make an order for compensation.[97] The Registrar also points out that the Tribunal does not have budgetary provisions allowing payment to individuals in compensation for the Tribunal's actions and that financial compensation could not be effected from present budget lines without breaching the financial rules of the Tribunal.[98] It argues that a claim for compensation would be more appropriately lodged with the U.N. Secretary-General, through his Legal Counsel,[99] and that pursuant to Section 2 of the Convention on the Privileges and Immunities of the United Nations 1946,[100] the Registrar should be able to request that the Secretary-General of the United Nations waive the immunity of the Tribunal, or to seek **[page 18]** clarification from the Secretary-General that the waiver is unnecessary, before any Chamber's finding on this issue.[101]

58. In light of the above-mentioned instruments on human rights and their applications by human rights bodies, the Chamber concludes that its inherent power to give effect to an accused's or former accused's right to an effective remedy encompasses the power to grant financial compensation where, in the specific circumstances of a case, it constitutes the appropriate remedy to redress a violation of the human right in question. Should the Chamber not have this power, it would lead to the untenable conclusion that it could not give effect to the right to an effective remedy in circumstances where financial compensation formed the only effective for a human rights violation. As such, the fact that this power is not explicitly provided for in the Tribunal's Statute or Rules is immaterial.

59. In the letters written by the former and current Presidents of the ICTR and ICTY to the U.N. Secretary-General, referred by the Registrar in support its submissions, the Presidents did not discuss the possibility that the Chamber possessed an inherent power to grant financial compensation, nor did they comment on the right to an effective remedy as they were not acting as a judicial body as this Chamber is in the present case. They only indicated their interest "in having the International Criminal Tribunal for Rwanda placed in a position to fully respect internationally recognized obligations"[102] – an objective shared by this Chamber. Similarly to the present Decision, the Presidents recalled that acts of the Tribunals, as subsidiary organs of

---

U.N. Doc. Supp. No. 40 (A/38/40) at 124 (1983); *Husband of Maria Fanny Suarez de Guerrero v. Colombia*, Communication No. R.11/45 (5 February 1979), U.N. Doc. Supp. No. 40 (A/37/40) at 137 (1982).

94 *LO. Karim v. the Netherlands*, Communication No. 4/1991, U.N. Doc. CERD/C/42/D/4/1991.

95 Article 52 of the SPSCET; Article 85 of the ICC Statute.

96 Registrar's Submissions, at para. 23.

97 Registrar's Additional Submissions of 24 November 2006, at paras. 4-5; Registrar's Additional Submissions of 7 December 2006, at paras. 6-9.

98 Registrar's Submissions, at para. 29.

99 Registrar's Additional Submissions of 24 November 2006, at para. 6.

100 1 U.N.T.S. 15, 13 February 1946, II, sec. 2: "The United Nations, its property and assets wherever located and by whomsoever held, shall enjoy immunity from every form of legal process except insofar as in any particular case it has expressly waived its immunity. It is, however, understood that no waiver of immunity shall extend to any measure of execution."

101 Registrar's Submissions, at para. 25.

102 Letter dated 26 September 2000 from the President of the International Criminal Tribunal for Rwanda addressed to the Secretary-General annexed to Letter dated 28 September 2000 from the Secretary-General addressed to the President of the Security Council, UN Doc. S/2000/925, at 3 [Letter from the President of the ICTR of 26 September 2000]. See also Letter dated 19 September 2000 from the President of the International Criminal Tribunal for the Former Yugoslavia addressed to the Secretary-General annexed to Letter dated 26 September 2000 from the Secretary-General addressed to the President of the Security Council, UN Doc. S/2000/904, at 3 [Letter from the President of the ICTY of 18 September 2000].

the Security Council, were imputable to the United Nations[103] and further observed that the United Nations, considering itself bound by generally accepted norms of human rights law such as articles 9(5) and 14(6) of the ICCPR relating to unlawful detentions and unjust convictions, would be under an obligation to ensure that compensation was paid to a person whose rights, enshrined in these articles, had been violated.[104] In this regard, the Chamber holds the view that the Security Council cannot have intended that the Tribunal would be in breach of generally accepted international human rights norms and as such must have accorded it the powers necessary to comply with such norms and thus carry out its functions as a judicial body. The lack of an appropriate mechanism to provide redress to an accused or former accused of this Tribunal, including the award of financial compensation when appropriate, when he or she is the victim of a human rights violation in fact justifies the Chamber's decision to entertain Rwamakuba's claim.

60. In the Chamber's view, since Article 16(1) of the Statute provides that the Registrar "shall be responsible for the administration and servicing of the International Criminal Tribunal for Rwanda",[105] the Registrar forms the entity with the necessary powers and **[page 19]** responsibilities to give effect to financial compensation that could be ordered as an effective remedy for the violation by the Tribunal of the rights of an accused person. However, questions relating to the mechanisms for giving effect to an order for compensation, such as budgetary matters or the appropriate body for lodging a claim, constitute extra-legal considerations which cannot constitute bars to the provision of financial compensation when it appears to be the effective remedy for a human rights violation. In addition, the Chamber considers that the internal rules of the United Nations may not be invoked as justification for its failure to comply with an international obligation, in the present case, the obligation to respect André Rwamakuba's right to an effective remedy.[106]

61. Furthermore, the Chamber also finds that the Convention on the Privileges and Immunities of the United Nations cannot apply to an order by the Chamber to the Registrar, both of which are part of a special kind of subsidiary organ of the U.N. Security Council as the immunities recognized to the United Nations are primarily applicable to its relations with States.[107]

62. The Chamber concludes therefore that in accordance with its obligation to give full effect to an accused's or former accused's right to an effective remedy, it must have the inherent power to make an award of financial compensation. Were the provision of financial compensation never available, then an individual's right to an effective remedy would be unjustifiably restricted in cases where such compensation was necessary to adequately and efficaciously address the prior human rights violation.

---

103 Letter from the President of the ICTY of 18 September 2000, at 3; Letter from the President of the ICTR of 18 September 2000, at 3.

104 Letter from the President of the ICTY of 18 September 2000, at 3-5, Letter from the President of the ICTR of 18 September 2000, at 3-4.

105 See also Secretary-General's Report on the Establishment of the ICTR, at para. 20: "Article 30 of the Statute provides that the expenses of the Tribunal shall be the expenses of the Organization in accordance with Article 17 of the Charter. In clearly distinguishing between the competence of the Security Council to establish the International Tribunal and the budgetary authority of the General Assembly to decide on its financing, the Security Council did not pronounce itself on the mode of financing, i.e., regular budget or a special account."

106 See, by analogy, Article 27(2) of the Vienna Convention on the Law of Treaties between States and international organizations or between international organizations, 21 March 1986, not yet in force, Official Records of the United Nations Conference on the Law of Treaties between States and International Organizations or between International Organizations, vol. II (Vienna: United Nations, 1986).: "An international organization party to a treaty may not invoke the rules of the organization as justification for its failure to perform the treaty."

107 According to the Preamble to the UN Convention on Privileges and Immunities, this Convention is primarily meant to apply to the relations between the UN and Member States:

> "Whereas Article 104 of the Charter of the United Nations provides that the Organization shall enjoy in the territory of each of its Members such legal capacity as may be necessary for the exercise of its functions and the fulfillment of its purposes and
> Whereas Article 105 of the Charter of the United Nations provides that the Organization shall enjoy in the territory of each of its Member such privileges and immunities as are necessary for the fulfillment of its purposes and that representatives of the Members of the United Nations and officials of the Organization shall similarly enjoy such privileges and immunities as are necessary for the independent exercise of their functions in connection with the Organization."

63. This finding conforms to the jurisprudence of the Appeals Chamber. In the *Semanza* and *Barayagwiza* cases, the Appeals Chamber found that the accused's rights had been violated, and ordered as a remedy that when judgement was rendered by the Trial Chamber, if the accused was found not guilty, he would be entitled to financial compensation from the Tribunal.[108] However, since in both cases the accused were found guilty, no financial compensation has been ordered so far.[109] **[page 20]**

64. Contrary to the Registrar's assertions,[110] the orders made by the Appeals Chamber in those cases cannot be considered as purely declaratory statements about the remedy to which an accused is in principle entitled. By including an order either for a reduction in sentence or for financial compensation in its disposition, the Appeals Chamber must have intended that its order be complied with depending on the outcome. And indeed, the Trial Chambers complied with the Appeals Chamber's orders when at the conclusion of these two trials, they decided to reduce the sentences against the accused in accordance with the Appeals Chamber decisions.[111]

65. The Registrar also considers that this Chamber cannot rely upon the Appeals Chamber's decision in the *Barayagwiza* case because it did not specify the legal basis for compensation and the Registrar was not invited to address submissions to the Appeals Chamber on this issue. The Registrar moreover asserts that the Appeals Chamber's decision in *Semanza* merely alluded to the Tribunal's mandate to protect international public order and relied on Rule 5, a rule which the Registrar argues does not in fact provide the Chamber with the power to make awards for financial compensation to individuals whose rights it has infringed.[112]

66. The Chamber is of the opinion that the Registrar misreads the Appeals Chamber Decisions. Both Decisions relied upon the principle that all violations of rights of an accused person demand a remedy.[113] In any event, as this Chamber has already explained above, it has the inherent power to grant an appropriate remedy to redress any violation of the rights of an accused. Such a remedy may include, depending on the circumstances of the case, a financial compensation. There is therefore no need to comment further on the Appeals Chamber's prior Decisions and if the Registrar seeks to dispute these Decisions and be heard by the Appeals Chamber, his application lies with the Appeals Chamber.

3.3 The Effective Remedy in this Case

67. The Defence requests for the violation of André Rwamakuba's right to legal assistance during the initial months of his detention at the Tribunal's detention facilities, that the Chamber order that the Registrar: (i) provide Rwamakuba with an apology; (ii) seek the good offices of the State where Rwamakuba's family is present to facilitate some temporary status for him in that State; (iii) seek the good offices of that State to ensure the uninterrupted schooling of Rwamakuba's children; and (iv) provide financial compensation to Rwamakuba.[114] It also seeks compensation covering a minimum of 2,000 USD per month for loss of earnings and 10,000 USD for emotional stress.[115] **[page 21]**

68. According to jurisprudence on human rights, an effective remedy must be granted on a case-by-case basis, taking into account the subject matter as well as the nature of the right allegedly violated.[116]

69. Before international criminal proceedings, the only remedy thus far utilized by a Trial Chamber with respect to the violation of an accused's right to legal assistance has been the exclusion of evidence.[117] Under

---

108 *Barayagwiza*, Decision (AC), 31 March 2000, at para. 75.

109 *Semanza*, Judgement (TC), 15 May 2003, at paras. 579-582; *Media Case*, Judgement (TC), 3 December 2003, at para. 1106.

110 Registrar's Additional Submissions of 7 December 2006, at para. 10.

111 *Semanza*, Judgement (TC), 15 May 2003, at paras. 579-582; *Media Case*, Judgement (TC), 3 December 2003, at para. 1106.

112 Registrar's Submissions, at para. 20.

113 *Barayagwiza*, Decision (AC), 31 March 2000, at para. 74; *Semanza*, Decision (AC), 31 May 2000, at para. 125. With respect to the *Semanza* Decision, the Chamber observes that while the Appeals Chamber only discussed the appropriateness of ordering a remedy under Rule 5 of the Rules; on the facts before it, it dismissed the application of Rule 5 having found that the violation of the accused's right had not caused him a material prejudice (*Semanza*, Decision (AC), 31 May 2000, at para. 124.)

114 Defence Application, pp. 10-11.

115 *Ibid.*, p. 10.

116 ECHR, *Hasan and Chaush v. Bulgaria*, 30985/96 (2000) ECHR 511 (26 October 2000), at para. 99. See also footnotes 77-80.

117 *Prosecutor v. Delalic*, Case No. IT-96-21-I, Decision on Zdravko Mucic's Motion for the Exclusion of Evidence (TC), September 2, 1997. The Trial Chamber excluded a statement made by the accused to Austrian authorities because the accused had not been informed of his right to counsel or permitted counsel.

international human rights law, in *Kelly v. Jamaica*, the Human Rights Committee concluded that as a result of a violation of his right to legal assistance, the petitioner was entitled to a remedy entailing his release.[118] Neither remedy is of course applicable to the present case. There is also significant case-law regarding the appropriate remedy for a violation of the right to legal assistance under the ECHR.[119] The European Court of Human Rights has awarded non-pecuniary damages to applicants in circumstances where the outcome would have been different had the infringement of the right to legal assistance not taken place[120] or where it was satisfied that the applicant had suffered some injury from the infringement itself, such as distress, frustration, confusion or feelings of abandonment and isolation.[121] The Court has yet to award pecuniary damages to an applicant for a violation of his right to legal assistance. Indeed, the Court has concluded that it could not speculate as to the outcome of the proceedings had the applicant been provided with legal assistance and therefore that no causal link between the violation and the alleged pecuniary damage had been established.[122] In cases where it has found neither, the Court has held that a finding of a violation was sufficient satisfaction for the violation.[123]

70. Drawing on the persuasive jurisprudence of the European Court of Human Rights, the Chamber will therefore consider, with respect to both pecuniary and non-pecuniary damages, whether the outcome would have been different had André Rwamakuba's right to legal assistance not been infringed. In addition, the Chamber will also ascertain whether he suffered some injury from the infringement itself. **[page 22]**

71. With respect to the first question, the Chamber considers that the Defence has not established that the length of André Rwamakuba's detention would have been shorter had he been provided with legal assistance upon his arrival in Arusha. While Trial Chamber II established that the violation of Rwamakuba's right to legal assistance caused a delay in his initial appearance,[124] the Defence has not established that this delay lengthened the duration of his time in detention. The Chamber therefore concludes that there is no causal link between the violation found and his alleged loss in earnings, nor between the violation found and any non-pecuniary injury he may have suffered as a result of his detention.

72. With respect to the second question, the Chamber considers that Trial Chamber II's finding that the prejudice caused to André Rwamakuba's defence was not serious or irreparable[125] is not necessarily determinative of whether he suffered some moral injury as a result of this infringement. While this finding makes clear that the violation of Rwamakuba's right to legal assistance did not affect the overall fairness of the trial, it does not as such address the need for reparations arising out of any emotional harm which may have been caused by the infringement itself.

73. The Chamber finds that, in the specific circumstances of this case, André Rwamakuba must have suffered some moral damage as a result of the violation of his right to legal assistance which cannot be adequately compensated by the sole finding of a violation and the provision of an apology by the Registrar. Bearing in mind the complexity of international criminal proceedings, his unfamiliarity with the Tribunal's

---

118 *Kelly v. Jamaica*, at para. 7.

119 The Inter-American Commission of Human Rights and the Inter-American Court of Human Rights have yet to consider communications alleging violations of the right to legal assistance.

120 *Perks v. UK*, 25277/94; 25279/94; 25280/94;... (1999) ECHR 89 (12 October 1999). In respect of one of the applicants, the Court held it was unlikely that the magistrates would have made the order for the applicant's detention had he been represented at the hearing before them. It awarded the applicant GBP 5,500 (at paras. 80 & 81). In respect of all other applicants, the Court concluded that it was impossible for it to speculate as to whether the magistrates would have made the order for the applicants' detention had they been represented at the hearing before them. It held that the finding of a violation was sufficient satisfaction (at para. 82).

121 See *Twalib v. Greece*, 24294/94 (1998) ECHR 54 (9 June 1998), at para. 66 ("*Twalib v. Greece*"); *R.D. v. Poland*, 29692/96;34612/97 (2001) ECHR 868 (18 December 2001), at para. 57; *Artico v. Italy*, 6694/74 (1980) ECHR 4 (13 May 1980), at para. 46; *Quaranta v. Switzerland*, 12744/87 (1991) ECHR 33 (24 May 1991), at para. 43; *Berlinski v. Poland*, 27715/95; 30209/96 (2002) ECHR 303 (20 June 2002), at para. 83; *Bibu v. Greece*, 33170/96 (2000) ECHR 426 (26 September 2000), at para. 35; *Granger v. UK*, 11932/86 (1990) ECHR 6 (28 March 1990), at para. 52.

122 See, e.g., *Twalib v. Greece*,), at para. 62; *Pham Hoang v. France*, at para. 41.

123 See, e.g., *Pakelli v. Germany*, 8398/78 (1983) ECHR 6 (25 April 1983), at para. 46; *Benham v. UK*, 19380/92 (1996) ECHR 22 (10 June 1996), at para. 68; *Pham Hoang v. France*, at para. 45; *Maxwell v. UK*, 18949/91 (1994) ECHR 38 (28 October 1994), at para. 43.

124 *Rwamakuba*, Decision on Illegal Arrest and Detention (TC), 12 December 2000, at para. 43.

125 *Ibid.*, at para. 45.

proceedings, the seriousness of the charges and the potential sentence involved,[126] in all probability, Rwamakuba suffered feelings of confusion, isolation, and distress as a result of the failure to provide him with duty counsel over a four and a half month period.

74. In addition to his claim for financial compensation, André Rwamakuba also moves the Chamber to order that the Registrar seek the good offices of the State where Rwamakuba's family is present to facilitate some temporary status for him in that State and to ensure the uninterrupted schooling of Rwamakuba's children.

75. The Registrar responds that he is unable to determine the success or failure of such efforts and that none of these requests are within the power of the Registry to effect.[127]

76. According to the Statute and Rules, the Registrar has the duty to give effect and implement any Chamber's Decision or Judgement.[128] In its Judgement of 20 September 2006, this Chamber also requested the Registrar to make all necessary arrangements in the implementation of the decision of acquittal of André Rwamakuba.

77. In the present case, contrary to the Registrar's assertions, the Defence only seeks that good efforts are used to facilitate the temporary residence of André Rwamakuba and schooling of his children in a certain State. These are obligations of means and not of result and they derive from the judgment of acquittal itself and form a necessary element of its **[page 23]** implementation. Without interfering with the powers and responsibilities of the Registrar, the Chamber cannot see any obstacle for the Registrar to act as requested by the Defence. In the Chamber's view, these requests should be granted not as a result of Rwamakuba's violation of his right to legal assistance, but as a matter of course.

78. The Chamber further observes that on the basis of Article 28 of the Statute, States have to cooperate with the Tribunal in the "prosecution of persons accused of committing serious violations of international humanitarian law."[129] The term "prosecution" includes compliance not only with orders included in sentencing judgements, but also with orders in judgements of acquittal as either result forms the natural consequence of any prosecution.[130] In that respect, the Chamber holds the view that this meets one of the Tribunal's objectives of contributing to the process of national reconciliation in Rwanda, as decided by the Security Council acting under Chapter VII of the Charter.[131] As such, the Chamber has no doubt that States will cooperate with the Tribunal in facilitating the relocation of Rwamakuba and his family. The Chamber emphasizes that whoever has been found to be not guilty should be treated as such, without consideration as to whether elements of doubt persist.[132]

79. The Chamber notes that the present decision does not fall within the ambit of Rule 73 for the purposes of appeal.

FOR THE ABOVE REASONS, THE CHAMBER

I. DISMISSES the Defence's claim for financial compensation for a grave and manifest miscarriage of justice;

126 The European Court of Human Rights has inferred that applicants must have suffered moral injury arising out of the violation of the right to legal assistance in circumstances involving complex proceedings or serious consequences for the applicant or where the applicant right to legal assistance was violated over a significant period of time. See above footnote 121.

127 Registrar's Submissions, at para. 8.

128 See Article 16 of the Statute and Rule 33 of the Rules.

129 Article 28(2) includes a non-exhaustive list of requests for assistance and orders issued by a Trial Chamber with which States shall comply.

130 The French version of Article 28 is even clearer in this respect, referring to the "jugement" of such persons.

131 UNSC Resolution 955, UN Doc. S/RES/955 (1994), 8 November 1994. Article 39 of the UN Charter reads as follows: "The Security Council shall determine the existence of any threat to the peace, breach of the peace, or act of aggression and shall make recommendations, or decide what measures shall be taken in accordance with Articles 41 and 42, to maintain or restore international peace and security."

132 The European Court of Human Rights has held numerous times that following an acquittal, the voicing of suspicions of guilt constitutes a violation the presumption of innocence set out in Article 6(2) of the ECHR. See, e.g., *Asan Rushiti v. Austria*, 28389/95 [2000] ECHR 106 (21 March 2000), at paras. 24-32 (in the context of proceedings for compensation on acquittal).

II. **HOLDS** that there has been a breach of André Rwamakuba's right to legal assistance, as provided for in Article 20 (4) (d) of the Statute, resulting from the Registrar's failure to appoint Duty Counsel for Rwamakuba during the initial months of his detention at the United Nations Detention Facilities, from 22 October 1998 until 10 March 1999;

III. Accordingly, **ORDERS** that the Registrar provide André Rwamakuba with an apology for the violation of his right to legal assistance;

IV. **ORDERS** that the Registrar provide André Rwamakuba with financial compensation in the amount of 2,000 (two thousand) US dollars for the moral injury sustained as a result of this violation;

V. **ORDERS** that the Registrar use all available means to seek the good offices of the State where André Rwamakuba's family is present to facilitate some temporary status for him **[page 24]** in that State and to seek the good offices of that State to ensure the uninterrupted schooling of his children.

Arusha, 31 January 2007, done in English.

Dennis C. M. Byron	Karin Hökborg	Gberdao Gustave Kam
Presiding Judge	Judge	Judge

[Seal of the Tribunal]

Tribunal Pénal International pour le Rwanda
International Criminal Tribunal for Rwanda

IN THE APPEALS CHAMBER

Before:	**Judge Fausto Pocar, Presiding** **Judge Mohamed Shahabuddeen** **Judge Liu Daqun** **Judge Theodor Meron** **Judge Wolfgang Schomburg**
Registrar:	**Mr. Adama Dieng**
Decision of:	**13 September 2007**

André RWAMAKUBA

v.

THE PROSECUTOR

Case No. ICTR-98-44C-A

Decision on Appeal against Decision on Appropriate Remedy

Counsel for André Rwamakuba:

Mr. David Hooper
Mr. Andreas O'Shea

[page 2] 1. The Appeals Chamber of the International Criminal Tribunal for the Prosecution of Persons Responsible for Genocide and Other Serious Violations of International Humanitarian Law Committed in the Territory of Rwanda and Rwandan Citizens Responsible for Genocide and Other Such Violations Committed in the Territory of Neighbouring States, between 1 January and 31 December 1994 ("Appeals Chamber" and "Tribunal", respectively), is seized of an appeal filed by Mr. André Rwamakuba[1] against a decision taken by Trial Chamber III ("Trial Chamber").[2] In its decision of 18 April 2007, the Appeals Chamber dismissed the Prosecution's appeal against the Impugned Decision,[3] but allowed the Registrar to make submissions pursuant to Rule 33(B) of the Rules of Procedure and Evidence of the Tribunal ("Rules") on all aspects of it.[4] The Registrar and Mr. Rwamakuba filed their initial briefs on 2 May 2007[5] and their response briefs on 14 and 17 May 2007,[6] respectively. No replies have been filed.

I. BACKGROUND

2. In its Judgement of 20 September 2006, the Trial Chamber acquitted Mr. Rwamakuba of all charges against him and ordered his immediate release.[7] At that point, Mr. Rwamakuba had been detained by the Tribunal for nearly eight years.[8] The Trial Judgement also invited submissions from the parties and the Registrar concerning a potential violation of Mr. Rwamakuba's right to legal assistance, which resulted in a delay in his initial appearance, occurring shortly after his arrest and transfer to the Tribunal.[9] Pursuant to the Trial Judgement, Mr. Rwamakuba requested a remedy for this violation.[10] In addition, he sought a separate remedy for the "grave and manifest injustice" he **[page 3]** suffered as a result of his lengthy detention and prosecution on allegedly false and manipulative evidence.[11] The Registrar opposed both applications, and the Prosecution filed no submissions.[12]

3. On 31 January 2007, the Trial Chamber awarded Mr. Rwamakuba two thousand United States dollars upon finding that there had been a violation of his right to legal assistance and, as a further reparation for this violation, ordered the Registrar to provide an apology to Mr. Rwamakuba, and to use his good offices in resettling him with his family and in ensuring his children's continued education.[13] The Trial Chamber, however, denied Mr. Rwamakuba's separate claim for compensation arising from the alleged "grave and manifest injustice" related to his lengthy detention and allegedly tainted prosecution.[14] Mr. Rwamakuba now appeals the dismissal of this latter claim and requests the Appeals Chamber to find that the Trial Chamber

---

1 Defence Notice of Appeal of Decision dated 31 January 2007, 12 February 2007 ("Rwamakuba Notice of Appeal").

2 *The Prosecutor v. André Rwamakuba*, Case No. ICTR-98-44C-T, Decision on Appropriate Remedy, 31 January 2007 ("Impugned Decision").

3 Decision on Prosecution's Notice of Appeal and Scheduling Order, 18 April 2007, paras. 6, 9 ("Scheduling Order").

4 Scheduling Order, paras. 7, 9 ("As for the Registrar's Notice, the Appeals Chamber notes that the Impugned Decision is directed at the Registrar, who participated in the proceedings below on this matter upon invitation from the Trial Chamber to do so. Accordingly, the Appeals Chamber finds it appropriate and within the scope of Rule 33(B) of the Rules in the present circumstances to allow the Registrar to make submissions on all aspects of the Impugned Decision, including the award of compensation for the violation of Mr. Rwamakuba's right to legal counsel.").

5 Registrar's Submissions in Respect of the Trial Chamber III Decision on Appropriate Remedy of 31 January 2007 Pursuant to Rule 33(B) of the Rules of Procedure and Evidence, 2 May 2007 ("Registrar's Submissions"); Defence Brief on Appeal Concerning Appropriate Remedy, 2 May 2007 ("Rwamakuba Appeal Brief").

6 Registrar's Submissions in Response to Defence Brief on Appeal Concerning Appropriate Remedy, Pursuant to Rule 33(B) of the Rules of Procedure and Evidence, 14 May 2007 ("Registrar's Response Brief"); Appellant's Response to Registrar's Submissions on Appeal Concerning Appropriate Remedy, 17 May 2007 ("Rwamakuba Response Brief"). The Appeals Chamber granted Mr. Rwamakuba a brief extension of time to file his response brief. *See* Decision on Request for Extension of Time to File a Response, 10 May 2007, para. 5.

7 *The Prosecutor v. André Rwamakuba*, Case No. ICTR 98-44C-T, 20 September 2006, Chapter IV ("Trial Judgement").

8 Trial Judgement, para. 5 (noting that Mr. Rwamakuba was arrested on 21 October 1998 and transferred to the Tribunal the following day). The Namibian authorities first arrested and detained Mr. Rwamakuba, apparently on their own initiative, from 2 August 1995 until 8 February 1996. During this period, the Prosecution informed the Namibian authorities on 22 December 1995 that it was determining whether it was interested in prosecuting Mr. Rwamakuba. However, on 18 January 1996, the Prosecution informed the Namibian authorities that it had no evidence against him. *See* Trial Judgement, para. 4.

9 Trial Judgement, Chapter IV.

10 Impugned Decision, paras. 5, 14.

11 Impugned Decision, paras. 5, 14, 19.

12 Impugned Decision, para. 6.

13 Impugned Decision, pp. 23-24 (disposition).

14 Impugned Decision, paras. 19-31.

had the authority to award compensation on that claim as well.[15] In his submissions, the Registrar objects to the Trial Chamber's award of financial compensation to Mr. Rwamakuba for the violation of his right to legal assistance.[16]

4. The Appeals Chamber will first address Mr. Rwamakuba's appeal concerning compensation for the lengthy detention and allegedly tainted prosecution. It will then turn to the Registrar's objection to the award of financial compensation to Mr. Rwamakuba for the violation of his right to legal assistance.

II. ALLEGED ERROR RELATING TO THE TRIAL CHAMBER'S DECISION NOT TO PROVIDE COMPENSATION IN VIEW OF THE ACQUITTAL

A. Background

5. In his application before the Trial Chamber, Mr. Rwamakuba claimed that he was indicted and prosecuted on false and manipulative evidence, which, coupled with his lengthy pre-trial and trial detention, resulted in "a grave and manifest miscarriage of justice".[17] As a legal basis for this **[page 4]** claim, Mr. Rwamakuba pointed primarily to Article 85(3) of the Statute of the International Criminal Court ("ICC Statute"), which envisions the possibility of compensation to an acquitted person in such circumstances.[18]

6. The Trial Chamber, however, was not satisfied that it had the power to provide such a remedy.[19] First, it noted that neither the Statute nor the Rules of the Tribunal provides for compensation to an acquitted person.[20] Second, it observed that, in the context of the existing international courts, only the ICC Statute provides for the possibility of compensation in the event of an acquittal[21] and even then, only in exceptional circumstances.[22] Finally, given the lack of uniform practice at national and international levels, the Trial Chamber concluded that a right to compensation for an acquitted person does not exist in customary international law.[23]

B. Submissions

7. Mr. Rwamakuba asserts that the Trial Chamber erred in law in finding that it lacked authority to award compensation in the event of an acquittal involving "a grave and manifest miscarriage of justice".[24] In this respect, he submits that both customary international law and the Trial Chamber's inherent authority provide a basis to award him compensation.[25] In particular, he points to the Trial Chamber's extensive discussion of the right to compensation as a remedy for violations of fair trial rights both in customary international law and in the exercise of its inherent authority.[26] Accordingly, Mr. Rwamakuba presents his claim to the Appeals Chamber as a violation of his fair trial and human rights.[27]

---

15 Rwamakuba Notice of Appeal, paras. 5, 6; Rwamakuba Appeal Brief, paras. 7, 13. In his Notice of Appeal, Mr. Rwamakuba asks the Appeals Chamber to award appropriate compensation and, in the alternative, to remit the matter to the Trial Chamber. However, in his Appeal Brief, Mr. Rwamakuba requests only that his claim be remanded for further consideration.

16 Registrar's Submissions, paras. 22, 23, 36-39, 40-72. In addition, the Registrar's Submissions also address the question of whether compensation is available for an acquittal as well as the Trial Chamber's construction of Rule 5 of the Rules. *See* Registrar's Submissions, paras. 6-21, 24-39. The Appeals Chamber has considered the Registrar's submission on the issue of compensation to an acquitted person in the context of Mr. Rwamakuba's appeal. The Appeals Chamber however does not need to address his submissions on the Trial Chamber's construction of Rule 5 of the Rules, as the Trial Chamber expressly stated that this rule was inapplicable to its findings. *See* Impugned Decision, para. 39.

17 Impugned Decision, para. 19.

18 Impugned Decision, para. 20

19 Impugned Decision, paras. 21, 31.

20 Impugned Decision, para. 21.

21 Impugned Decision, paras. 21-25. The Trial Chamber observed that the Special Panel for Serious Crimes in East Timor provides for a right to compensation for unjust convictions and unlawful arrests and detentions. *See* Trial Judgement, para. 23, fn. 36.

22 Impugned Decision, para. 28.

23 Impugned Decision, paras. 27, 31.

24 Rwamakuba Notice of Appeal, para. 5; Rwamakuba Appeal Brief, paras. 32-53

25 Rwamakuba Appeal Brief, paras. 32-53.

26 Rwamakuba Appeal Brief, para. 32.

27 Rwamakuba Appeal Brief, para. 32 ("The Trial Chamber held that there was not sufficient evidence of State practice and *opinion (sic) juris* to support a customary right to compensation for grave and manifest miscarriage of justice. In our respectful

8. In particular, Mr. Rwamakuba submits that he suffered a "grave and manifest injustice" because he was indicted and prosecuted on evidence that was "false and manipulative", "palpably dishonest", and "inherently unsatisfactory and tainted".[28] Mr. Rwamakuba claims that the **[page 5]** Prosecution failed to take adequate measures against the use and presentation of false evidence.[29] In addition, Mr. Rwamakuba points to his lengthy pre-trial and trial detention, resulting from the alleged failings in the collection and presentation of evidence against him, and argues that he was denied the right to an expeditious trial.[30] In particular, he notes that he made an early unsuccessful request for the severance of his case.[31] Ultimately, Mr. Rwamakuba requests the Appeals Chamber to find that the Trial Chamber has the authority to award financial compensation in such circumstances and to remand his case for further consideration of the merits of his claim.[32]

9. The Registrar opposes Mr. Rwamakuba's appeal.[33] The Registrar argues that the Tribunal has no authority to award compensation in circumstances where an accused has been acquitted after trial or for alleged unfairness in the proceedings.[34] In any event, the Registrar submits that Mr. Rwamakuba has failed to substantiate both factually and legally his claim of a grave and manifest miscarriage of justice.[35] The Registrar concludes by noting that "[w]hen the Tribunal acquits an Accused because the evidence fails to establish the crime beyond reasonable doubt, then the rights of an Accused to be judged fairly upon the evidence are vindicated."[36]

C. Discussion

10. The Appeals Chamber can identify no error on the part of the Trial Chamber in finding that it lacked authority to award compensation to Mr. Rwamakuba for having been prosecuted and acquitted. As the Trial Chamber observed, the Statute and Rules of the Tribunal do not provide a basis for compensation in such circumstances.[37] Nor is any found in the jurisprudence of this Tribunal or of the International Criminal Tribunal for the Former Yugoslavia ("ICTY"). In the past, the Presidents of this Tribunal and the ICTY requested the Security Council to amend the Statutes of the two Tribunals to provide for such authority.[38] These efforts were unsuccessful and underscore the inability of the Tribunal to provide such a remedy in either its express or implied powers.[39] As **[page 6]** the Trial Chamber observed, the practice of providing compensation for an acquittal varies at both national and international levels.[40] In this respect, the International Covenant on Civil and Political Rights ("ICCPR") refers to a right of compensation only where

submission, the Chamber has posed the question in the wrong way. The Trial Chamber accepts that there is a right to an effective remedy under customary international law when addressing the other claim. This, it is suggested, is well established in international law. The real question in our submission is whether the right to an effective remedy under customary law could be applied to the accused in these circumstances.").

28 Rwamakuba Appeal Brief, paras. 12, 20, 22.

29 Rwamakuba Appeal Brief, paras. 22, 43, 46.

30 Rwamakuba Appeal Brief, paras. 17, 18, 23, 46, 47.

31 Rwamakuba Appeal Brief, para. 16.

32 Rwamakuba Appeal Brief, para. 13.

33 Registrar's Response Brief, para. 2.

34 Registrar's Submissions, paras. 18-21; Registrar's Response Brief, paras. 21-26.

35 Registrar's Response Brief, paras. 4-29.

36 Registrar's Response Brief, para. 29.

37 Impugned Decision, para. 21.

38 *See* Letter dated 28 September 2000 from the Secretary General Addressed to the President of the Security Council, U.N. Doc. S/2000/925* (6 October 2000)(annexing letter from President Pillay of the Tribunal)("ICTR Submission"). *See also* Letter dated 26 September 2000 from the Secretary General Addressed to the President of the Security Council, U.N. Doc. S/2000/904 (26 September 2000)(annexing letter from President Jorda of the ICTY)("ICTY Submission"); Letter dated 18 March 2002 from the Secretary General Addressed to the President of the Security Council, U.N. Doc. S/2002/304 (18 March 2002)(annexing letter from President Jorda of the ICTY). These letters specifically annexed a copy of Article 85 of the ICC Statute.

39 *Cf. The Prosecutor v. Radovan Stanković*, Case No. IT-96-23/2-AR11bis.1, Decision on Rule 11*bis* Appeal, 1 September 2005, paras. 14-17 (holding that the Security Council's endorsement of the ICTY's Completion Strategy, which included the referral of cases to national jurisdictions, reflected that the Tribunal was authorized to do so under the Statute)("*Stanković* Appeal Decision").

40 Impugned Decision, paras. 25, 27.

an individual already convicted by a final decision has been exonerated by newly discovered facts.[41] A person in such circumstances who has been convicted and has suffered punishment as a result of the conviction may receive compensation.[42] Mr. Rwamakuba, however, was not convicted and punished; he was acquitted in the first instance.

11. Furthermore, the Appeals Chamber finds no merit in Mr. Rwamakuba's submission that he is entitled to financial compensation for his acquittal on the basis that the proceedings against him violated certain rights resulting in a grave and manifest injustice to him. First, he presents no evidence or convincing argument to substantiate his assertion that the Prosecution presented false or tainted evidence against him in order to arrest and try him. His argument consists primarily of reiterating reasons why the Prosecution witnesses presented at his trial lacked credibility and reliability.[43]

12. In that respect, the Appeals Chamber notes that prior to commencement of trial, the Trial Chamber reviewed the evidence supporting the amended indictment against Mr. Rwamakuba after his case was severed from the *Karemera et al.* case and found that a *prima facie* case was established by the Prosecution.[44] In addition, in dismissing Mr. Rwamakuba's motion for judgment of acquittal at the end of the Prosecution case, the Trial Chamber rejected his principal contention that the Prosecution evidence was inherently unreliable.[45] Mr. Rwamakuba's submission that the Prosecution evidence was palpably false relies principally on the strength of his alibi, of which Mr. **[page 7]** Rwamakuba gave notice only on the eve of his separate trial on 8 June 2005.[46] While the Trial Judgement reflects that the Trial Chamber eventually found that the Prosecution evidence lacked credibility upon a final analysis of all the evidence as a whole, including the alibi,[47] this does not lead to the conclusion that the Prosecution evidence - which was initially considered to be sufficiently credible and reliable by the Trial Chamber to charge Mr. Rwamakuba and to deny his motion for judgement of acquittal - was therefore false or tainted.

13. Second, his assertion on appeal that he was denied the right to an expeditious trial is similarly unsupported and somewhat belied by his failure to develop this argument before the Trial Chamber.[48] He points only to the length of his proceedings and his early unsuccessful request for severance on 11 October

---

41 Article 14(6) of the ICCPR provides: "When a person has by a final decision been convicted of a criminal offence and when subsequently his conviction has been reversed or he has been pardoned on the ground that a new or newly discovered fact shows conclusively that there has been a miscarriage of justice, the person who has suffered punishment as a result of such conviction shall be compensated according to law, unless it is proved that the non-disclosure of the unknown fact in time is wholly or partly attributable to him."

42 *Id.*

43 Rwamakuba Appeal Brief, paras. 25-27.

44 *The Prosecutor v. Édouard Karemera et al.*, Case No. ICTR-98-44-PT, Decision on Severance of André Rwamakuba and For Leave to File Amended Indictment, 14 February 2005, para. 48 ("Considering the evidence presented by the Prosecution in support of its Motion, the Chamber finds that a *prima facie* case has been established with respect to the counts contained in the proposed Amended Indictment against Rwamakuba and grants leave to file it subject to further amendments detailed in the order.") ("*Karemera et al.* Severance Decision"). The Trial Chamber observed that his case changed "substantially" from his initial indictment to his trial, removing allegations of joint criminal enterprise and focusing on his alleged direct role. *See Karemera et al.* Severance Decision, paras. 28, 37.

45 *See The Prosecutor v. André Rwamakuba*, Case No. ICTR-98-44C-T, Decision on Defence Motion for Judgement of Acquittal, 28 October 2005, para. 13 ("The Chamber has very cautiously reviewed all the arguments of both parties as well as the transcripts in the current proceedings. The contradictions raised by the Defence with respect to the witnesses' testimony are not so irreconcilable that the Prosecution case should be considered as having completely broken down.").

46 *The Prosecutor v. André Rwamakuba*, Case No. ICTR. 98-44C-PT, Decision on Prosecution Motion for Notice of Alibi and Reciprocal Inspection, 14 June 2005, para. 5.

47 Trial Judgement, paras. 212, 214 ("The Chamber heard 49 Prosecution and Defence witnesses, [and] 94 Prosecution and 218 Defence exhibits were admitted into evidence over 78 trial days. [...] *After assessing the evidence as a whole*, the Chamber found all of the Prosecution witnesses not to be credible or reliable. Their testimonies were either inconsistent with the Indictment or contained other discrepancies which could not be satisfactorily explained. The absence of any credible or reliable identification of André Rwamakuba at the time and place of the alleged crimes, the lack of credibility or reliability of the Prosecution witnesses, the participation of the Accused in other activities during periods alleged in the Indictment and the Defence alibi evidence, *cumulatively* raise a reasonable doubt regarding the Prosecution's case.")(emphasis added).

48 *The Prosecutor v. André Rwamakuba*, Case No. ICTR-98-44C-T, Application for Appropriate Remedy, 25 October 2006, para. 24 ("We submit it is not necessary to demonstrate a violation of the right to trial without undue delay for this to be weighed into the question of whether there has been a miscarriage of justice.")("*Rwamakuba* Trial Submissions").

2000.[49] In this respect, he does not address the complexity or nature of the proceedings against him when his case formed part of a joint trial alleging a government-wide joint criminal enterprise.[50]

14. Finally, the Appeals Chamber sees no basis for remanding Mr. Rwamakuba's claim to the Trial Chamber in order for him to develop it further. Mr. Rwamakuba already had an opportunity to present these arguments to the Trial Chamber and, indeed, he expressly based his application below in part on the assertion that his rights were violated at one or more stages of the proceedings.[51] However, Mr. Rwamakuba took the position before the Trial Chamber that it was unnecessary for him to demonstrate that he was denied the right to an expeditious trial.[52] In addition, as to the alleged violation based on the nature of the Prosecution evidence presented in his case, Mr. **[page 8]** Rwamakuba raised similar issues at the delivery of his Trial Judgement[53] and cited the Prosecution's use of "false and manipulative" evidence in his submissions at trial.[54] The Trial Chamber expressly considered these submissions in the Impugned Decision, even though they exceeded the scope of its scheduling order.[55] These arguments were therefore before the Trial Chamber and were not accepted as a basis for compensation.

D. Conclusion

15. In sum, Mr. Rwamakuba has not demonstrated that the Trial Chamber erred in law in finding that it lacked authority to award him compensation for his acquittal. Furthermore, Mr. Rwamakuba fails to substantiate his claim that he suffered a grave and manifest injustice from the proceedings brought against him because he was indicted and prosecuted on false and manipulative evidence and because of his lengthy pre-trial detention. Accordingly, his appeal is dismissed.

III. ALLEGED ERROR RELATING TO THE TRIAL CHAMBER'S DECISION TO AWARD COMPENSATION

A. Background

16. The Registrar's submissions concern the Trial Chamber's decision to award Mr. Rwamakuba two thousand United States dollars as compensation for a violation of his right to legal assistance.[56] The history of the proceedings related to the violation of Mr. Rwamakuba's rights to legal assistance and to an initial appearance without delay is set forth in the Trial Judgment and in a number of decisions in this case.[57] It suffices to note here that the Namibian authorities arrested Mr. Rwamakuba on 21 October 1998 and

---

49 Rwamakuba Appeal Brief, para. 16. *See also The Prosecutor v. André Rwamakuba*, Case No. ICTR-98-44C-T, Decision on André Rwamakuba's Motion for Severance, 12 December 2000, para. 44.

50 *See Karemera et al.* Severance Decision, para. 29 ("The proposed Amended Indictment against Rwamakuba incorporates only allegations that are unique and relevant to him. The charge of joint criminal enterprise, which formed the basis of the joinder and was one of the reasons why the Prosecution previously opposed the severance, has been removed. The Prosecution has indicated that the severance of Rwamakuba has allowed it to narrow the allegations of joint criminal enterprise from the large level of the government apparatus to the level of the MRND party, and to focus primarily on the control of *Interahamwe* militias.").

51 *Rwamakuba* Trial Submissions, para. 7.

52 *Rwamakuba* Trial Submissions, para. 24.

53 *See* T. 20 September 2005 pp. 11, 14 ("But for all that, it's our submission that there has been a deliberate attempt -- to use the phrase that's often been used -- to poison the waters of justice and to bring before you, the Judges, false allegations that have essentially resulted in André Rwamakuba being detained for seven years, totally separated from family -- and work, and opportunity and effectively having his life broken on those lies.").

54 Impugned Decision, para. 19; *Rwamakuba* Trial Submissions, para. 24.

55 Impugned Decision, paras. 12, 13.

56 Registrar's Submissions, paras. 19-23, 36-72.

57 Trial Judgement, paras. 217; Impugned Decision, paras. 2-4; *The Prosecutor v. André Rwamakuba et al.*, Case No. ICTR-98-44-T, Decision on the Defence Motion Concerning the Illegal Arrest and Illegal Detention of the Accused, 12 December 2000, p. 2, paras. 35-44 ("*Rwamakuba* Arrest and Detention Decision"); *André Rwamakuba v. The Prosecutor*, Case No. ICTR-98-44-A, Decision (Appeal Against Dismissal of Motion Concerning Illegal Arrest and Detention), 11 June 2001, pp. 2-4 ("*Rwamakuba* Appeal Decision"). The Trial Chamber described the violation of Mr. Rwamakuba's rights as a violation of his "right to legal assistance", noting that it resulted in a delay in his initial appearance. Impugned Decision, paras. 14-18, 71. However, the Appeals Chamber has previously explained in a similar context that the right to legal assistance and the right to an initial appearance without delay are in fact two distinct rights. *Juvénal Kajelijeli v. The Prosecutor,* Case No. ICTR-98-44A-A, Judgement, 23 May 2005, paras. 242-253 ("*Kajelijeli* Appeal Judgement").

transferred him to the Tribunal the following day.[58] The **[page 9]** Tribunal did not assign him counsel under the Tribunal's legal aid system until 24 February 1999.[59] This delay was explained in part by Mr. Rwamakuba's delay in proposing an attorney to represent him.[60] However, during this four month period, the Tribunal did not offer Mr. Rwamakuba the assistance of a duty counsel as required under Rule 44*bis* of the Rules.[61] In addition, the Tribunal did not hold his initial appearance, in part due to his lack of representation, until 7 April 1999.[62]

17. On 18 April 2000, Mr. Rwamakuba requested Trial Chamber II, which was originally seized of this case, to dismiss the charges against him and to immediately release him, alleging violations of his fundamental rights during his arrest and detention.[63] Trial Chamber II determined that the Registrar's failure to assign duty counsel in accordance with Rule 44*bis* "resulted in an absence of any legal assistance for the Accused over an extended period of time in contradiction with, notably, Article 20(4)(c) of the Statute, and, further, in the delay in the Accused's initial appearance."[64] Trial Chamber II, however, concluded that the delay did not cause him "serious and irreparable prejudice" and denied the motion for immediate release.[65] On 11 June 2001, a Bench of the Appeals Chamber dismissed Mr. Rwamakuba's appeal of this decision, on the ground that the issues surrounding Mr. Rwamakuba's arrest and detention did not raise jurisdictional matters.[66] The Bench of the Appeals Chamber added, however, that "it is open to the Appellant to invoke the issue of the alleged violation of his fundamental human rights by the Tribunal in order to seek reparation as the case may be at the appropriate time."[67]

18. Pursuant to the Trial Judgement, Mr. Rwamakuba filed an application for a remedy for the violation of his right to legal assistance.[68] In the Impugned Decision, the Trial Chamber granted this application and ordered the Registrar to issue a formal apology[69] and to pay him two thousand United States dollars in financial compensation for his "moral injury".[70] The Trial Chamber reasoned that it had authority to provide a remedy to Mr. Rwamakuba for this violation based on the **[page 10]** right to a remedy for human rights violations, as reflected in numerous international instruments,[71] as well as the jurisprudence of the Appeals Chamber, notably the *Kajelijeli* Appeal Judgement and the *Barayagwiza* case.[72] More particularly, the Trial Chamber recalled that a Bench of the Appeals Chamber in this case indicated that Mr. Rwamakuba could seek reparation for this violation.[73] In addition, the Trial Chamber relied on its inherent authority.[74]

---

58 Trial Judgement, para. 5; *Rwamakuba* Arrest and Detention Decision, p. 2, para. 35.

59 *Rwamakuba* Arrest and Detention Decision, para. 38. The Appeals Chamber notes that Trial Chamber II mistakenly referred to the year of the assignment of Mr. Rwamakuba's counsel as 2000, rather than the correct year of 1999. *See* Rwamakuba Appeal Brief, Annex A (indicating date of appointment as 24 February 1999).

60 *Rwamakuba* Arrest and Detention Decision, paras. 38-40.

61 *Rwamakuba* Arrest and Detention Decision, paras. 41-43. *See also* Trial Judgement, para. 217.

62 *Rwamakuba* Arrest and Detention Decision, p. 2, paras. 35, 43. *See also* Impugned Decision, para. 2. The Tribunal scheduled his initial appearance for 10 March 1999, but adjourned it at the request of his assigned counsel until 7 April 1999.

63 *Rwamakuba* Arrest and Detention Decision, p. 2, paras. 1-7.

64 *Rwamakuba* Arrest and Detention Decision, para. 43.

65 *Rwamakuba* Arrest and Detention Decision, para. 44.

66 *Rwamakuba* Appeal Decision, p. 4.

67 *Rwamakuba* Appeal Decision, p. 4.

68 Impugned Decision, paras. 5, 14, 19.

69 Impugned Decision, pp. 23-24 (Disposition). In addition, the Trial Chamber ordered the Registrar to use his good offices in resettling him with his family and in ensuring his children's continued education. The Trial Chamber noted that "[t]hese are obligations of means and not of result". Impugned Decision, para. 77. The Registrar does challenge this aspect of the decision.

70 Impugned Decision, pp. 23-24 (Disposition).

71 Impugned Decision, para. 40 (referring to Universal Declaration of Human Rights, the International Covenant on Civil and Political Rights, the International Convention on the Elimination of All Forms of Racial Discrimination, the Convention against Torture and Other Cruel, Inhuman or Degrading Treatment or Punishment, the Convention Concerning Indigenous and Tribal Peoples in Independent Countries, the United Nations Declaration of Basic Principles of Justice for Victims of Crime and Abuse of Power, the European Convention on Human Rights, the American Declaration of the Rights and Duties of Man and the American Convention of Human Rights)(internal citations omitted).

72 Impugned Decision, para. 41-43, citing *Kajelijeli* Appeal Judgement, paras. 255, 322; *Jean-Bosco Barayagwiza v. The Prosecutor*, Case No. ICTR-97-19-AR72, Decision (Prosecutor's Request for Review or Reconsideration), 31 March 2000, para. 74 ("*Barayagwiza* Appeal Decision").

73 Impugned Decision, para. 44, citing *Rwamakuba* Appeal Decision, p. 4.

74 Impugned Decision, paras. 45-49.

19. On the issue of financial compensation for the violation of Mr. Rwamakuba's right to legal assistance, the Trial Chamber acknowledged that no specific provision of the Statute or Rules expressly envisioned such a remedy.[75] However, the Trial Chamber reviewed various international instruments,[76] decisions of human rights bodies,[77] and the decisions of the Appeals Chamber in the *Barayagwiza* and *Semanza* cases,[78] all referring to compensation as part of an effective remedy. From this, the Trial Chamber concluded that it had inherent authority to award financial compensation.[79]

B. Submissions

20. The Registrar submits that the Trial Chamber erred in law in finding that it had the authority to award financial compensation as part of an effective remedy.[80] In this respect, he contends that the Tribunal's Statute and Rules do not provide for compensation as a remedy and submits that the right to compensation for human rights violations is simply an "emerging norm".[81] He describes the Appeals Chamber findings in the *Barayagwiza* and *Semanza* cases, which envisioned an award of financial compensation to the accused in those cases if they were acquitted, as "anticipatory" and **[page 11]** "declaratory".[82] In particular, he notes that the Presidents of this Tribunal and of the ICTY unsuccessfully sought an amendment of the Statute from the Security Council to provide for financial compensation as a remedy for fair trial rights violations in the Statute, shortly after these decisions were taken.[83]

21. Finally, the Registrar takes issue with the merits of the decision. Pointing to the Trial Chamber's finding that the violation did not materially prejudice Mr. Rwamakuba's case, he submits that the award of financial compensation is unwarranted and that other forms of reparation awarded to Mr. Rwamakuba in the Impugned Decision, such as the formal apology, sufficed.[84] He adds that the Trial Chamber's award of damages for the "moral injury" has no basis in fact.[85]

22. Mr. Rwamakuba responds that the Statute was not meant to be an exhaustive document on the authority of the Tribunal but rather a basic jurisdictional framework.[86] He submits that an effective remedy therefore falls within the Tribunal's mandate to do justice and to foster reconciliation.[87] Furthermore, Mr. Rwamakuba contends that the award of moral damages was "a fair and humane demonstration of the Trial Chamber's capacity to understand the real hurt occasioned to an accused by such circumstances."[88]

C. Discussion

23. There is no question that, as the Trial Chamber recognized and held in the Impugned Decision, Mr. Rwamakuba is entitled to an effective remedy for the violation of his right to legal assistance as well as his right to an initial appearance without delay. Trial Chamber II recognized the existence of these violations,[89]

---

[75] Impugned Decision, paras. 40, 58.

[76] Impugned Decision, paras. 54, 55 (referring to the International Covenant on Civil and Political Rights, European Convention on Human Rights, American Convention on Human Rights, and the Statutes of the Inter-American Court of Human Rights as well as the European Court of Human Rights).

[77] Impugned Decision, paras. 51, 52, 55 (discussing decisions or recommendations of the European Court of Human Rights, Inter-American Court of Human Rights, the African Commission on Human and Peoples' Rights, The United Nations Human Rights Committee, Committee on the Elimination of all Forms of Racial Discrimination).

[78] Impugned Decision, para. 63, citing *The Prosecutor v. Laurent Semanza*, Case No. ICTR-97-20-T, Judgement and Sentence, 15 May 2003, paras. 579-582, *Barayagwiza* Appeal Decision, para. 75.

[79] Impugned Decision, para. 62.

[80] Registrar Submissions, paras. 19, 20, 40-61.

[81] Registrar Submissions, paras. 40-56.

[82] Registrar Submissions, para. 41. He also quotes an opinion from the Office of Legal Affairs of the United Nations in support of this proposition. *Id.*, para. 20(iii).

[83] Registrar Submissions, paras. 20, 41.

[84] Registrar Submissions, paras. 36-39, 67-69.

[85] Registrar Submissions, paras. 62-66.

[86] Rwamakuba Response Brief, para. 15.

[87] Rwamakuba Response Brief, paras. 16, 17.

[88] Rwamakuba Response Brief, para. 23.

[89] *Rwamakuba* Arrest and Detention Decision, para. 43.

and the Appeals Chamber indicated that Mr. Rwamakuba could "seek reparation" for them.[90] Moreover, the Appeals Chamber, after considering nearly identical violations in the *Kajelijeli* Appeal Judgement, reached the same conclusion and, accordingly, reduced the sentence imposed in that case.[91] The two principal questions for the Appeals Chamber **[page 12]** are whether the Tribunal is empowered to award financial compensation as an effective remedy for a violation of the fundamental rights of the accused and, if so, whether it was appropriate to award Mr. Rwamakuba financial compensation as an effective remedy in the present case.

24. The Appeals Chamber has previously held that "any violation, even if it entails a relative degree of prejudice, requires a proportionate remedy."[92] It follows very plainly from the Appeals Chamber's decisions in the *Barayagwiza* and *Semanza* cases that a remedy for a violation of the rights of the accused may include an award of financial compensation, as both decisions envisioned financial compensation being fixed at the time of judgement, if the accused were acquitted.[93] In this respect, the Appeals Chamber is not persuaded by the Registrar's submissions that the absence of an explicit provision providing for financial compensation in the Statute for violations of the rights of the accused as well as the Security Council's decision not to amend the Statute to expressly include such a remedy indicate that it is not available.

25. First, while there is no right to compensation for an acquittal *per se*, there is a right in international law to an effective remedy for violations of the rights of the accused, as reflected in Article 2(3)(a) of the ICCPR.[94] In this respect, the ICCPR specifically envisions compensation as an appropriate remedy in certain circumstances, such as the case of unlawful arrest or detention.[95] The Appeals Chamber has previously held that the ICCPR is a persuasive authority in determining the Tribunal's powers under international law.[96] **[page 13]**

26. The authority in the Statute to provide an effective remedy flows from Article 19(1) of the Statute, which obliges the Trial Chambers to ensure a fair trial and full respect for the accused's rights. The existence of fair trial guarantees in the Statute necessarily presumes their proper enforcement.[97] In this respect, the

---

90 *Rwamakuba* Appeal Decision, p. 4.

91 *Kajelijeli* Appeal Judgement, paras. 237, 242-250, 253, 323, 324 (finding violations of the right to counsel, resulting from a failure to provide duty counsel in accord with Rule 44*bis* of the Rules, and the right to an initial appearance without delay). The Appeal Chamber noted that the accused was in the custody of the Tribunal for a total of 211 days prior to any initial appearance during which he was without assigned counsel for 147 days. *Kajelijeli* Appeal Judgement, para. 237. In the present case, Mr. Rwamakuba was detained in the Tribunal's detention facilities for a total of 167 days from the date of his transfer on 22 October 1998 until his initial appearance held on 7 April 1999, of which he spent 125 days without assigned counsel. *See supra* para. 16. It should also be noted, however, that the Appeals Chamber found additional violations in the *Kajelijeli* case. *See Kajelijeli* Appeal Judgement, para. 251, 252 (finding that the rights of the accused were violated based on his arbitrary provisional detention in Benin without charge for 85 days, and detention in Benin without appearance before a Judge for a total of 95 days, which was attributable to the Prosecution).

92 *Laurent Semanza v. The Prosecutor*, Case No. ICTR-97-20-A, Decision, 31 May 2000, para. 125 ("*Semanza* Appeal Decision").

93 *Semanza* Appeal Decision, p. 34 ("[T]hat for the violation of his rights, the Appellant is entitled to a remedy which shall be given *when judgement is rendered by the Trial Chamber*, as follows:(a) If he is found not guilty, the Appellant shall be entitled to financial compensation [...]")(emphasis added); *Barayagwiza* Appeal Decision, para 75(iii)("DECIDES that for the violation of his rights the Appellant is entitled to a remedy, *to be fixed at the time of judgement at first instance*, as follows: a) If the Appellant is found not guilty, he shall receive financial compensation [...]")(emphasis added).

94 Article 2(3) of the ICCPR states: "Each State Party to the present Covenant undertakes: (a) To ensure that any person whose rights or freedoms as herein recognized are violated shall have an effective remedy, notwithstanding that the violation has been committed by persons acting in an official capacity; (b) To ensure that any person claiming such a remedy shall have his right thereto determined by competent judicial, administrative or legislative authorities, or by any other competent authority provided for by the legal system of the State, and to develop the possibilities of judicial remedy; (c) To ensure that the competent authorities shall enforce such remedies when granted." *See also* Basic Principles and Guidelines on the Right to a Remedy and Reparation for Victims of Gross Violations of International Human Rights Law and Serious Violations of International Humanitarian Law, G.A. Res. 60/147 (16 December 2005).

95 *See, e.g.*, ICCPR, Article 9(5)("Anyone who has been the victim of unlawful arrest or detention shall have an enforceable right to compensation.").

96 *See Kajelijeli* Appeal Judgement, para. 209. In addition, the Appeals Chamber has previously recognized that the rights of the accused in Article 20 of the Statute track the rights in the ICCPR. *See, e.g., Protais Zigiranyirazo v. The Prosecutor,* Case No. ICTR-2001-73-AR73, Decision on Interlocutory Appeal, 30 October 2006, para. 12, fn. 46 ("*Zigiranyirazo* Appeal Decision").

97 *Cf. Stanković* Appeal Decision, para. 14 ("It is true, as the Appellant points out, that the Statute of the Tribunal does not contain an explicit legal basis for Rule *11bis*. But the explicit language of the Statute is neither an exclusive nor an exhaustive index

Appeals Chamber observes that the Statute and Rules do not expressly provide for other forms of effective remedy, such as the reduction of sentences, yet such a remedy has been accorded on several occasions.[98] Moreover, the submissions of the Presidents of this Tribunal and of the ICTY seeking an amendment of the Statute from the Security Council to provide for financial compensation do not suggest that an effective remedy in the form of financial compensation cannot be ordered and paid in the absence of an express provision. At the time of making the submissions, the Appeals Chamber had already issued two decisions envisioning possible awards of compensation to remedy fair trial rights violations and the submissions themselves recognized the authority of the Tribunals to order financial compensation as an effective remedy in the form of an "exceptional ruling" or an "*ex gratia* payment".[99] The request for a statutory amendment merely expressed the preference of the Presidents for a specific statutory provision so that it would be beyond dispute that any award of compensation would be paid "according to law".[100] Against this backdrop, the Appeals Chamber will not assume that the Security Council's inaction was intended to interfere with the Tribunal's inherent authority to order compensation in appropriate circumstances. Accordingly, the Appeals Chamber can identify no error of law on the part of the Trial Chamber in finding that it had the authority in general to award an effective remedy for the violations of Mr. Rwamakuba's rights as an accused person, including financial compensation.

27. The question remains, however, whether it was appropriate for the Trial Chamber to award Mr. Rwamakuba financial compensation in the present case, as part of the remedy for the violations **[page 14]** of his right to legal assistance and to an initial appearance without delay. The jurisprudence of the Appeals Chamber reflects that the nature and form of the effective remedy should be proportional to the gravity of harm that is suffered.[101] In practice, the effective remedy accorded by a Chamber for violations of an accused's fair trial rights will almost always take the form of equitable or declaratory relief.[102] In the past, the Appeals Chamber has envisioned financial compensation as a form of effective remedy only in situations where, amongst other violations, an accused was impermissibly detained without being informed of the charges against him.[103] This is in line with Article 9(5) of the ICCPR which provides for an enforceable right to compensation in the event of an unlawful arrest or detention.[104]

28. Bearing this in mind, the Appeals Chamber recalls that Mr. Rwamakuba was detained in the Tribunal's detention facilities for a total of 167 days from the date of his transfer on 22 October 1998 until his initial appearance held on 7 April 1999, of which he spent 125 days without assigned counsel.[105] As the Appeals

---

of the Tribunal's powers. It is axiomatic under Article 9 of the Statute that it was never the intention of those who drafted the Statute that the Tribunal try all those accused of committing war crimes or crimes against humanity in the Region. The Tribunal was granted primary – but explicitly not exclusive – jurisdiction over such crimes. In this regard, it is clear that alternative national jurisdictions have consistently been contemplated for the 'transfer' of accused.")(internal citations omitted).

98 *See generally Semanza* Appeal Decision, p. 34; *Barayagwiza*, Appeal Decision, para. 75; *Kajelijeli* Appeal Judgement, para. 324.

99 ICTR Submission, p. 4 ("Such mechanisms include, inter alia, arbitration, ex gratia payment, resolutions of the General Assembly authorizing limited liability and amendment of the Statute"); ICTY Submission p. 4 ("These mechanisms include, among other things, arbitration, exceptional ruling, General Assembly resolutions recognizing limited responsibility and amendment of the Tribunal's Statute.").

100 ICTR Submission, p. 4 ("In this connection, it is essential to note that the United Nations would not be able to comply with its international obligations simply by paying the individuals concerned an appropriate sum in compensation. The obligations which are codified within article 9, paragraph 5, and article 14, paragraph 6, of the International Covenant on Civil and political Rights are not simply to ensure that persons whose cases fall within the scope of these provisions are compensated *simpliciter*, but rather to guarantee that they are vested with žan enforceable right to compensation" (in the case of article 9(5)) and are compensated "according to the law" (in the case of article 14 (6)"); *See also* ICTY Submission p. 5.

101 *Semanza* Appeal Decision, para. 125.

102 *See, e.g., Zigiranyirazo* Appeal Decision, para. 24 (excluding testimony taken in violation of an accused's right to be present during his trial); *The Prosecutor v. André Ntagerura et al.*, Case No. ICTR-99-46-A, Judgement, 7 July 2006, paras. 164, 165 (setting aside a guilty verdict where accused's right to notice of charges against him was violated); *Kajelijeli* Appeal Judgement, para. 324 (reduction of sentence for period of unlawful arrest and detention in Benin and right to legal assistance and initial appearance at Tribunal); *Georges Rutaganda v. The Prosecutor*, Case No. ICTR-96-03-R, Decision on Requests for Reconsideration, Review, Assignment of Counsel, Disclosure, and Clarification, 8 December 2006, para. 37 (recognition of violation and warning of possible future sanctions for the Prosecution's violation of Rule 68 of the Rules).

103 *Semanza* Appeal Decision, paras. 87, 90; *Barayagwiza* Appeal Decision, paras. 54, 55.

104 ICCPR, article 9(5)("Anyone who has been the victim of unlawful arrest or detention shall have an enforceable right to compensation.").

105 *See supra* paragraph 16.

Chamber in the *Kajelijeli* case already pointed out in relation to the rights of a suspect,[106] a judge is called upon to make an accused familiar with the charges, to verify an accused's identity, to examine any obvious challenges to the case, to inquire into the medical condition of an accused, and to notify a person enjoying the confidence of the detainee[107] and consular officers.[108] The Appeals Chamber further stressed that:

> Rule 62 is unequivocal that an initial appearance is to be scheduled without delay. There are purposes for an initial appearance apart from entering a plea including: reading out the official charges against the accused, ascertaining the identity of the detainee, allowing the Trial Chamber or Judge to ensure that the rights of the accused while in detention are being respected, giving an opportunity for the accused to voice any complaints, and scheduling a trial date or date for a sentencing hearing, in the case of a guilty plea, without delay.[109]

The Appeals Chamber considers the violations of Mr. Rwamakuba's rights attributable to the Tribunal and financial compensation to be an effective remedy. The nature of the violations **[page 15]** suffered by Mr. Rwamakuba is no less significant than in other cases where such compensation was envisioned to be fixed at the time of judgement if the accused were found not guilty (as opposed to a reduction in sentence in case the accused were found guilty).[110] Accordingly, the Appeals Chamber can identify no error on the part of the Trial Chamber in finding that financial compensation is an appropriate form of an effective remedy to address the violations of Mr. Rwamakuba's rights.

29. Moreover, the Appeals Chamber is not persuaded by the Registrar's submission that the award of two thousand United States dollars has no basis in fact. It is not disputed that Mr. Rwamakuba's suffered serious violations of his fundamental rights. In the *Kajelijeli* Appeal Judgement, the Appeals Chamber did not demand or cite additional proof of specific harm in according an appropriate remedy in that case, which involved a significant reduction in sentence.[111] Moreover, as noted above, the Appeals Chamber in the *Barayagwiza* and *Semanza* cases envisioned the award of compensation, in the event of an acquittal, to be fixed at the time of judgement.[112]

30. Finally, the Appeals Chamber also agrees with the Trial Chamber that internal institutional considerations related to the execution of an order, including budgetary matters, are separate considerations from the Tribunal's authority to award an effective remedy in the form of financial compensation in appropriate circumstances and in compliance with its international obligations.[113] Budgetary considerations cannot interfere with the Tribunal's authority to award financial compensation as an effective remedy for a human rights violation; similarly, at the domestic level, a State cannot advance the argument that there are no budgetary resources available to justify a refusal to award compensation. The Appeals Chamber has confirmed the Tribunal's general authority to award compensation in appropriate and limited circumstances. In addition, it has affirmed the reasonableness of the award in the present case.

D. <u>Conclusion</u>

31. Accordingly, the Appeals Chamber concludes that the Trial Chamber did not err in awarding Mr. Rwamakuba two thousand United States dollars as financial compensation as part of an effective remedy for the violations in the present case. **[page 16]**

---

106 *Kajelijeli* Appeal Judgement, para. 221.

107 *See* Standard Minimum Rules for the Treatment of Prisoners, approved by ECOSOC Res. 663(C) (XXIV) of 31 July 1957 and Res. 2076 (LXII) of 13 May 1997 (UN Doc. E/5988 (1977)); *Kajelijeli* Appeal Judgement, fn. 451.

108 Vienna Convention on Consular Relations, Article 36(B).

109 *Kajelijeli* Appeal Judgement, para. 250 (internal citations omitted).

110 *See, e.g., Kajelijeli* Appeal Judgement, para. 323 (considering an accused's detention without being informed of the charges against him and his detention without an initial appearance as equally impermissible).

111 *Kajelijeli* Appeal Judgement, paras. 253, 323, 324. The Appeals Chamber set aside the convicted person's two life-sentences and fifteen years' sentence imposed by the Trial Chamber and converted them into a single sentence consisting of a fixed term of imprisonment of 45 years.

112 *Semanza* Appeal Decision, p. 34; *Barayagwiza* Appeal Decision, para 75(iii).

113 *See* Impugned Decision, para. 60.

IV. DISPOSITION

32. For the foregoing reasons, the Appeals Chamber **DISMISSES** Mr. Rwamakuba's appeal, **AFFIRMS** the Trial Chamber's award of two thousand United States dollars in compensation to him and **ORDERS** the Registry to make appropriate arrangements for the payment of the award.

Done in English and French, the English version being authoritative.

Done this thirteenth day of September 2007,
At The Hague,
The Netherlands.

Judge Fausto Pocar
Presiding

[Seal of the Tribunal] [page 17]

PARTLY DISSENTING OPINION OF JUDGE SHAHABUDDEEN

1. I agree with the Appeals Chamber's dismissal of Mr. Rwamakuba's appeal relating to the Trial Chamber's decision not to provide compensation in view of his acquittal. My hesitation is over paragraph 32 of the decision of the Appeals Chamber, in which the Appeals Chamber "ORDERS the Registry to make appropriate arrangements for the payment of the award" in respect of related matters. As the Registry is headed by the Registrar, the flexibility of this formula does not conceal the fact that it is directed to him and that it assumes that he has the capacity to make payment. That gives me difficulty.

2. I accept that the Tribunal may declare that the appellant's human rights have been violated. It may also award compensation for such a violation, provided that the particular methods of award are within its competence, as has been the case in some instances. But it seems to me that the Tribunal has no competence to order the Registrar to make appropriate arrangements for financial payment. It is not merely a question of the lack of budgetary provision, but also a question of the lack of authority under the Statute.

3. The Appeals Chamber suggests that it is granting 'an effective remedy'. What therefore has to be seen is whether the remedy granted will prove effective. In my view, it will not prove effective, for the reason that the Registrar will lack the means of compliance. As indicated by the Appeals Chamber itself, the Presidents of this Tribunal and of the ICTY sought an appropriate amendment of the Statute from the Security Council to allow for financial compensation to be paid by the Tribunal in such a situation, but their quest was unsuccessful; that was in September 2000.[1] By its long silence, the Security Council may be taken to have affirmed that the Tribunals have no competence to order payment of financial compensation.

4. The practical implications of the Appeals Chamber's order must also be considered. If the order stands and the Registrar (including anyone from the Registry) does not make the payment, his obligation can be enforced, at the instance of Mr. Rwamakuba, by a contempt order. The Registrar's probable defence in contempt proceedings will be that he is unable to make the payment because of the lack of budgetary provision and the impossibility of such provision being made in view of the lack of statutory authority. If the Tribunal accepts this defence, it will merely have postponed the decision that the Trial Chamber lacked authority to order the Registrar to pay financial compensation to Mr. Rwamakuba. If the Registrar's defence is dismissed, the Registrar **[page 18]** may have to go to prison. That prospect looks unlikely. If the Registrar succeeds at that stage, Mr Rwamakuba would have to content himself with an illusion in place of an effective remedy.

5. The international legal system, if it may be called a system, is not perfect. In this respect, it is unlike the national legal systems addressed by the various human rights instruments. The question is not how a function given to the Tribunal is to be exercised by it, but whether the function has in the first place been given to it. In this case, it is not possible to fill the imperfections in the Tribunal's system by recourse to the idea of inherent authority. Both Tribunals have in several cases properly relied on the concept of inherent authority, and I recognize that the competence which the concept gives is not confined to trivial matters. However, it seems to me that it is available only for the better discharge of a function which was given to the Tribunals, at least in essence, by the Statute; it is not available to justify the acquisition of a wholly new function, more particularly one which involves the expenditure of monies provided by United Nations member states.

6. *South West Africa* has been justly criticized. However, the criticisms do not affect the validity of the International Court of Justice's pronouncement that in 'the international field, the existence of obligations that cannot in the last resort be enforced by any legal process, has always been the rule rather than the exception ...'.[2] As Immanuel Kant saw in 1784, 'The greatest problem for the human species is that of

---

1 *See* Letter dated 28 September 2000 from the Secretary General Addressed to the President of the Security Council (U.N. Doc. S/2000/925)(annexing a letter from President Pillay of the ICTR). *See also* Letter dated 26 September 2000 from the Secretary General Addressed to the President of the Security Council, U.N. Doc. S/2000/904 (26 September 2000)(annexing a letter from President Jorda of the ICTY).

2 *I.C.J.Reports 1966*, 6, 46, para. 86.

attaining a civil society which can administer universal justice'.[3] That is true of the administration of international justice to states; it is equally true of the administration of international justice to individuals.

7. The problem in this case is a real one; some of the dicta in past decisions may have led to it. However, it is not possible to supply the deficit in the manner indicated by the Appeals Chamber.

Done in English and French, the English text being authoritative.

Dated 13 September 2007

At The Hague

The Netherlands

Mohamed Shahabuddeen

[Seal of the Tribunal]

3 Cited in J.L. Gaddis, *The Cold War, A New History* (New York, 2005), 158.

Commentary

1. Introduction

For the first time in the history of the international criminal tribunals, a person who has claimed that his human rights have been violated in international criminal proceedings has been granted financial compensation as a means of redress for that alleged violation.[4] That, however, is not the only reason why these decisions on appropriate remedy in the Rwamakuba case merit closer examination. They are equally important because they also make clear that there is no right to redress in several situations that are unjust to the accused. Ultimately, the possibility that an accused can obtain redress depends very much on whether or not the grievance claimed may be qualified as a human rights violation. If so, then the tribunal may award redress. Although this might seem a reasonable system, the case of Rwamakuba proves that it is not necessarily so.

The ICTR acquitted André Rwamakuba – a doctor who was minister of primary and secondary education in the Rwandan Interim Government during the Rwandan genocide – of all charges against him and consequently ordered his immediate release on 20 September 2006.[5] At that point, the applicant had been in detention in the United Nations Detention Facilities (UNDF) for almost eight years, since 22 October 1998. Moreover, in contravention of Rule 44 *bis* section d of the ICTR Rules of Procedure and Evidence, the registrar had failed to appoint duty counsel for Rwamakuba during the initial 125 days of his detention at the UNDF, from 22 October 1998 until 24 February 1999. No redress could be granted for the eight years of detention, but Rwamakuba was offered compensation and satisfaction for the violation of Rule 44 *bis* section d, which was qualified as a human rights violation.

2. A violation of the international human right to legal assistance?

In its Decision on Appropriate Remedy of 31 January 2007, Trial Chamber III ordered the registrar to provide Rwamakuba with financial compensation in the amount of 2,000 US dollars for the moral injury sustained as a result of the violation of his right to legal assistance. This order was confirmed by the Appeals Chamber on 13 September 2007. Ultimately, the substantive basis of the order is the assumption that the violation of Rule 44 *bis* section d of the ICTR Rules of Procedure and Evidence also constitutes a violation of the human right to legal assistance.[6] With a reference to the ICCPR, but without further analyses or explanation, this was first suggested in the Judgment of Trial Chamber III of 20 September 2006 by which Rwamakuba was acquitted.[7] An explanation for the assumption that a human right was violated was, however, offered in the Decision on Appropriate Remedy of 31 January 2007 by Trial Chamber III. This Chamber held that Rule 44 *bis* gives effect to one of the most important fair trial rights of an accused, the right to legal assistance.[8]

In the abstract this is certainly true, but it does not necessarily mean that the right afforded by Rule 44 *bis* and the human right to legal assistance are identical in content and scope. In fact they are not. A fundamental difference between them is that Rule 44 *bis* section d, provides a positive obligation on the authorities to 'as soon as practicable summon duty counsel to represent the accused or suspect', while the human right in the pre-trial phase entails a right to have access to counsel, which right is primarily complemented by a negative obligation on the state not to infringe that right. The crucial question therefore is whether the human right to legal assistance can indeed be regarded as having been violated in this particular case.

---

4 ICTR, Decision on Appropriate Remedy, *Prosecutor v. Rwamakuba*, Case No. ICTR-98-44C-T, T. Ch. III, 31 January 2007, in this volume, p. 907; ICTR, Decision on Appeal Against Decision on Appropriate Remedy, *Rwamakuba v. Prosecutor*, Case No. ICTR-98-44C-A, A. Ch., 13 September 2007, in this volume, p. 927.

5 ICTR, Judgement, *Prosecutor v. Rwamakuba*, Case No. ICTR-98-44C-T, T. Ch. III, 20 September 2006, in this volume p. 439.

6 See, Decision on Appropriate Remedy, *Prosecutor v. Rwamakuba*, T. Ch. III *supra* note 1, section 3.1, especially par. 40-45; Decision on Appeal Against Decision on Appropriate Remedy, *Rwamakuba v. Prosecutor*, A. Ch., *supra* note 1, particularly par. 18-19, 25 and 27.

7 Judgement, *Prosecutor v. Rwamakuba*, T. Ch. III, *supra* note 2, par. 217-220. Cf. ICTR, Decision on the Defence Motion Concerning the Illegal Arrest and Illegal Detention of the Accused, *Prosecutor v. Rwamakuba and others*, Case No. ICTR-98-44-T, T. Ch. II, 12 December 2000, Klip/ Sluiter, ALC-VI-207, par. 43-44, in which the ICTR still only found a violation of Rule 44 *bis* (and thus not of the human right to legal assistance).

8 Decision on Appropriate Remedy, *Prosecutor v. Rwamakuba*, T. Ch. III, *supra* note 1, par. 17.

Rule 44 *bis* was breached because the registrar had failed to appoint duty counsel for Rwamakuba during the initial 125 days of his pre-trial detention, which started on 22 October 1998. This was clearly in violation of section d of this provision, which states that the Registrar shall as soon as practicable summon duty counsel to represent an unrepresented accused or suspect. In order to determine whether this default also infringes the human right to legal assistance, it is vital to establish the moment from which this human right applies. True, as Trial Chamber III held, international human rights law clearly establishes that the right to counsel attaches at the investigative and pre-trial stages.[9] But, as such, this does not at all settle the matter, since it does not take into consideration that the right is much more limited in the pre-trial stage than during the trial, nor does it clarify the exact point at which the right starts to apply.

Meanwhile, international human rights law itself also does not provide an imperative and consistent answer. Only some soft law expressly specifies that untried prisoners are entitled, as soon as they are imprisoned, to choose their legal representation and to receive visits from their legal adviser.[10] Furthermore, the Committee against Torture has recognised that the right for all persons deprived of their liberty to receive prompt, independent legal assistance is an important guarantee against torture and ill-treatment.[11] Nowhere, however, does it state that this right constitutes a human right as such; it merely seems to consider it as a commendable guarantee for the prohibition of torture and ill-treatment.

Therefore, more relevant here and also more compelling (albeit not legally binding, even for state parties to the ICCPR) are the views of the Human Rights Committee (HRC). It is clear that the committee holds the opinion that barring a detainee from access to legal assistance (of his own choosing) will constitute a violation of Article 14, paragraph 3, ICCPR.[12] Attached to this negative obligation on the state is the positive obligation to inform the detainee of his right to legal assistance.[13] So from which moment do these obligations then apply? In the case of Kelly versus Jamaica, the detainee had not been given the opportunity to speak with a lawyer of his choosing until five days after being taken into custody. The committee held that 'in the circumstances', the right to communicate with counsel (Article 14, paragraph 3 sub b, ICCPR) was violated.[14] It therefore seems that the ICCPR entails a right that detainees have access to a lawyer from the beginning of their deprivation of liberty.

This, however, might only be a qualified right, since the committee clearly attaches the finding of the violation to the circumstances of the case. Two such circumstances are expressly referred to: Jamaican law establishes a right to consult with an attorney following arrest, and Kelly had immediately stated that he wanted to speak to his lawyer.[15] With Rule 44 *bis,* the first of these circumstances was also present in the case of Rwamakuba. By contrast, this was not so with regard to the latter of these circumstances: Rwamakuba had apparently not advised the authorities (viz. the registrar) of his wish to have defence counsel assigned to him prior to 17 February 1999 (after which counsel was assigned to him on 24 February 1999).[16] Moreover, the accused had been invited within eight days following his transfer to the tribunal on 22 October 1998 to file a request for assignment of counsel if he would declare himself indigent.[17] Thus, the right to have access to legal assistance in Article 14, paragraph 3, ICCPR does not as such seem to have been violated in the case of Rwamakuba.

---

9 *Ibid.*, par. 17.

10 See, for example, Rule 93 of the Standard Minimum Rules for the Treatment of Prisoners as adopted by the Committee of Ministers of the Council of Europe by Resolution (73) 5 of 19 January 1973; The European Committee for the Prevention of Torture and Inhuman or Degrading Treatment or Punishment (CPT), Report of 24 April 2002 on Turkey (CPT/Inf(2002)8); AfCionHPR, Principles and Guidelines on the Right to a Fair Trial and Legal Assistance in Africa, 2001, under M, section 2 (f).

11 General Comment no. 2, 24 January 2008 (CAT/C/GC/2), par. 13.

12 See, for example, HRC, View of 27 March 1981, *Carballal v. Uruguay*, Comm. 33/1978, par. 9 and 13, and HRC, View of 21 July 1983, *Caldas v. Uruguay*, Comm. 43/1979, par. 13.3 and 14.

13 HRC, View of 3 November 2004, *Rolando v. The Philippines*, Comm. 1110/2002, par. 5.6.

14 HRC, View of 17 July 1996, *Kelly v. Jamaica*, Comm. 537/1993, par. 9.2.

15 See also HRC, View of 20 July 2000, *Gridin v. Russian Federation*, Comm. 770/1997, par. 8.5.

16 Decision on the Defence Motion Concerning the Illegal Arrest and Illegal Detention of the Accused, *Prosecutor v. Rwamakuba and others, supra* note 4, par. 38-39; Decision on Appropriate Remedy, *Prosecutor v. Rwamakuba,* T. Ch. III, *supra* note 1, par. 15. As a matter of fact, these decisions erroneously make mention of 17 February 2000 and 24 February 2000, instead of 1999.

17 Decision on the Defence Motion Concerning the Illegal Arrest and Illegal Detention of the Accused, *Prosecutor v. Rwamakuba and others, supra* note 4, par. 38 and 39. See also Decision on Appropriate Remedy, *Prosecutor v. Rwamakuba,* T. Ch. III, *supra* note 1, par. 15.

However, the committee's view in the case of Kelly – or for that matter in any other case – does not solve the question of whether the mere fact that a detainee is only informed of his right to legal assistance after eight days – as in the case of Rwamakuba – may constitute a violation of Article 14, paragraph 3, ICCPR. Even if an eight-day delay could constitute a violation, this provision would probably still not be regarded as being breached in the case of Rwamakuba. First, Rwamakuba took a rather long time before he actually requested legal assistance after being informed of his right.[18] This at least appears to imply that the eight-day delay is not relevant.[19] Moreover, the consequences of the omission had been duly considered before and during his trial, as a result of which it might not have to be regarded any longer as a violation of the right to legal assistance.[20]

This still leaves unanswered the question of whether the right to access to a lawyer under Article 14, paragraph 3, ICCPR entails a positive obligation on the authorities to provide an indigent detainee with legal assistance almost immediately after arrest. Relevant in this regard is the case of Borisenco v. Hungary, which appears to imply that such an obligation may indeed result from this provision.[21] The committee's view makes clear that the state has to ensure and if necessary provide effective representation during a hearing on detention.[22] The same possibly applies with regard to police interrogations.[23] However, none of the ICTR's decisions and judgments referred to in this annotation indicate that Rwamakuba was without legal assistance during either a hearing on his detention (or on the case) or an interrogation.

What is more, there is nothing to assume that this positive obligation is so far-reaching that it even requires from the authorities that, almost immediately after arrest, they provide legal assistance to a detainee who did not ask for it, even though he had been informed that he could make such request. There seems to be little or no basis to conclude that the violation of Rule 44 *bis* section d of the ICTR Rules of Procedure and Evidence in the Rwamakuba case also constituted a violation of the human right to legal assistance under the ICCPR. This does not seem to be different due to the fact – to which the ICTR rightly points – that proceedings at international criminal tribunals involve complex cases, concern serious offences and potentially entail significant sentences.[24] In fact, in cases in which a capital sentence may be pronounced on the accused, the committee does not even demand that the state shall provide free counsel long before any preliminary hearing relating to the case, any hearing on the detention, or any interrogation by the police (this is a sentence, of course, that the tribunals may not impose anyhow).[25]

A similar conclusion seems to follow when the violation of Rule 44 *bis* section d in the case of Rwamakuba is reviewed against the European Convention on Human Rights (ECHR) and the case law thereon pronounced by the European Court of Human Rights (ECtHR). Indeed, the right to legal assistance under Article 6, paragraph 3 sub c, ECHR may also be relevant in the pre-trial phase, when 'the fairness of the trial is likely to be seriously prejudiced by an initial failure to comply with' it.[26] Particularly in the case of police interrogation, Article 6 will normally require that the accused be allowed to benefit from the assistance of a lawyer.[27] However, the right to have access to legal assistance does not necessarily apply from the moment someone is detained. Matters may be different when a detainee needs access to counsel in order to prevent his being ill-treated or tortured in detention. There have not, however, been any claims by the defence that, because of the violation of Rule 44 *bis* section d, Rwamakuba was ill-treated in the UNDF.

---

18 This even holds true if one follows the Defence's claim that a request for assignment of counsel was already submitted on 8 December 1998 (instead of 17 February 1999), since that would still be more than five weeks after Rwamakuba had been informed of his right to legal assistance; see Decision on the Defence Motion Concerning the Illegal Arrest and Illegal Detention of the Accused, *Prosecutor v. Rwamakuba and others, supra* note 4, par. 39.

19 Cf. HRC, View of 27 July 1998, *Whyte v. Jamaica*, Comm. 732/1997, par. 7.4.

20 Cf. HRC, View of 28 October 2002, *Hendricks v. Guyana*, Comm. 838/1998, par. 3.1 and 6.2.

21 HRC, View of 14 October 2002, *Borisenco v. Hungary*, Comm. 852/1999, par. 7.5.

22 This right may under specific circumstances also flow from the right to freedom from arbitrary detention, more particularly the right to habeas corpus in Article 9, paragraph 4, ICCPR. The violation of Rule 44 *bis* section d of the ICTR Rules of Procedure and Evidence has, however, not been raised by the defendant, nor has it been assessed by the ICTR in this regard; see particularly, Decision on the Defence Motion Concerning the Illegal Arrest and Illegal Detention of the Accused, *Prosecutor v. Rwamakuba and others, supra* note 4.

23 Cf. HRC, View of 7 August 2003, *Aliev v. Ukraine*, Comm. 781/1997, par. 7.2.

24 Decision on Appropriate Remedy, *Prosecutor v. Rwamakuba*, T. Ch. III, supra note 1, par. 17.

25 See, for example, HRC, View of 3 November 1998, *Marshall v. Jamaica*, Comm. 730/1996, par. 6.2 and particularly 6.4.

26 ECtHR, Judgment of 24 November 1993, *Imbrioscia v. Switzerland*, Appl. 13972/88, par. 36.

27 ECtHR, Grand Chamber Judgment of 27 November 2008, *Salduz v. Turkey*, Appl. 36391/02, par. 52.

Furthermore, the European Convention does not contain an absolute right to legal assistance in detention proceedings, nor are the authorities obliged to provide a detainee with free legal aid in that context.[28] Therefore, the fact that Rwamakuba was not provided with counsel during the first approximately four months of his detention does not seem to be in contravention of the law of the European Convention.[29]

The foregoing seems to justify the conclusion that the ICTR (*i.e.* Trial Chamber III[30] and the Appeals Chamber[31]) has incorrectly asserted that the violation of Rule 44 *bis* section d in the Rwamakuba case also constitutes a violation of the internationally recognized human right to legal assistance. At the least, the tribunal has inadequately substantiated its assertion. As a result, the award of 2,000 US dollars is based on a invalid grounds.[32]

3. Redress for human rights violations against acquitted persons

In deciding on the question of redress, the ICTR starts from the justified assertion that it is a fundamental principle of international human rights law that any violation of a human right entails the provision of an effective remedy.[33] This right includes a procedural aspect (the right of access to an impartial body that can offer redress) and a substantive one (the right to receive redress). Given that the ICTR Rules of Procedure and Evidence do not provide for a right to an effective remedy for violations of human rights, at least not in this case, it is international human rights law that is ultimately taken by the tribunal as the substantive basis for its order to grant redress.[34] The ICTR points at many human rights instruments that entail the obligation on states to offer an effective remedy, in case fundamental rights have been violated.[35] Relevant to the case of Rwamakuba are Article 2, paragraph 3, ICCPR, Article 13 ECHR, Article 25 American Convention on Human Rights (ACHR), and Article 7 African Charter on Human and Peoples' Rights (AfChHPR).

Under the ICCPR and the ECHR, the obligation on the authorities to provide an effective remedy applies only to the violation of rights that are guaranteed in these instruments, while the ACHR and the AfChHPR also apply to the violation of fundamental rights contained in, for example, national laws and constitutions. This means – since the violation of Rule 44 *bis* in the case of Rwamakuba does not constitute a violation of international human rights law – that the ICCPR and the ECHR would not require an effective remedy, nor redress, for the fact that Rwamakuba was without legal assistance for the first approximately four months of his detention. All things considered, in my view the same holds true for the ACHR and the AfChHPR. There seems to be little or no ground in both international law and national constitutional law to hold that Rule 44 *bis* entails a fundamental right in those aspects that were violated in the case of Rwamakuba, the moreso since this rule is not part of the ICTR statute, but rather of a much lower hierarchy.

Nevertheless, let us assume here that the human right to legal assistance was violated, as the ICTR asserted. Analogical application of international human rights law to the tribunals' proceedings would then indeed involve an obligation on the ICTR to offer an effective remedy to the defendant. This remedy could have been offered by the Chamber trying the case, but instead it decided that Rwamakuba should file a separate application for remedy after the trial.[36] Although this course of action is not in violation of the human right to an effective remedy, it nevertheless was unnecessary, as will become clear further on.

---

28 See Article 5 ECRH and ECtHR, Judgment of 25 October 2007, *Lebedev v. Russia*, Appl. 4493/04, par. 84.

29 For other regional systems, see Article 8, paragraph 2 sub (d) and (e), ACHR and Article 7, paragraph 1 sub (c), AfChHPR, which provisions and the case law thereon also do not seem to support a claim that the human right to legal assistance was violated against Rwamakuba, either. See, for example, Malcolm Evans & Rachel Murray, The African Charter on Human and Peoples' Rights, Cambridge University Press, Cambridge 2008, p. 203-204.

30 Judgment, *Prosecutor v. Rwamakuba*, *supra* note 2; Decision on Appropriate Remedy, *Prosecutor v. Rwamakuba*, T. Ch. III, *supra* note 1, section 3.1, especially par. 40-45.

31 Decision on Appeal Against Decision on Appropriate Remedy, *Rwamakuba v. Prosecutor,* A. Ch., *supra* note 1, particularly par. 18-19, 25 and 27.

32 Meanwhile, it is far from certain that the compensation order will ever be executed. The registrar has refused to pay the award, choosing instead simply to refer the Trial Chamber's order to the Security Council. For further information on the legal difficulties Rwamakuba met after he was acquitted, see Kevin Jon Heller, What Happens to the Acquitted?, 21 Leiden Journal of International Law 2008, p. 663-680.

33 Decision on Appropriate Remedy, *Prosecutor v. Rwamakuba*, T. Ch. III, *supra* note 1, section 3.1, especially par. 16 and 40-41; Decision on Appeal Against Decision on Appropriate Remedy, *Rwamakuba v. Prosecutor,* A. Ch., *supra* note 1, par. 24-26.

34 Decision on Appropriate Remedy, *Prosecutor v. Rwamakuba*, T. Ch. III, supra note 1, par. 34-39, 45 and 49.

35 *Ibid.*, par. 40.

36 Judgment, *Prosecutor v. Rwamakuba*, *supra* note 2, par. 220.

The question now is: are the tribunal's decisions on redress, particularly the order of financial compensation, supported by international (human rights) law? In this respect, it is important that, when applying international human rights law to the proceedings of the tribunals, these tribunals must be equated to states or national authorities, and not to international human rights courts, commissions and committees. That these international bodies are entitled to order states to provide redress is therefore – although the ICTR suggests differently –without relevance to the question of whether the ICTR is permitted or obligated to make such an order (although it does of course denote that financial compensation is an accepted form of redress for human rights violations).[37]

It is, however, relevant that question that the European Convention only demands that the state, offer redress for human rights violations in so far as national law (here by analogy; ICTR law) allows reparation to be made for the consequences of a breach (Article 41 ECHR).[38] Since the tribunal holds that the ICTR Statute and Rules, and the internal rules of the United Nations, do not offer the possibility to provide for reparation, analogical application of the ECHR to the ICTR's procedures appears to imply that the tribunal – contrary to what it asserts – is not required to provide for it.[39] Such a conclusion would be in line with the point of view of Judge Shahabuddeen in his partly dissenting opinion in the decision of the Appeals Chamber.

However, it seems to me that this conclusion cannot be drawn from Article 41 ECHR. This provision holds that the European Court shall, if necessary, afford just satisfaction (financial compensation) to the injured party, if the internal law of the state concerned allows only partial reparation to be made. This clearly means that states (here by analogy; the ICTR) cannot avoid having to pay financial compensation by arguing that their internal law does not allow for it, because it is exactly such compensation that the ECtHR is allowed to impose on the state in any case. Nor is this all. In contrast to the European system, the Human Rights Committee, as well as the Inter-American Court of Human Rights (I-ACtHR), seem de facto to hold that domestic law (here by analogy; ICTR law) may not (never) be used as an excuse for not providing full reparation.[40]

Thus, supposing that international human rights law does apply to international criminal law procedures – which the ICTR argues very well it does[41] – the tribunal has good reasons to stretch its implied powers in order to be able to make orders on redress.[42] To put it differently: under analogical application of international human rights law (including European human rights law), there does not seem to be room for the point of view that Judge Shahabuddeen defends. The tribunal (Trial Chamber III and the Appeals Chamber) has thus rendered convincing and important case law by its decision that the tribunal is obligated to offer redress, if necessary in the form of financial compensation, when human rights have been violated in its justice system. However, that does not yet mean that the order to pay financial compensation was substantively justified in this concrete situation. What is more; it most probably is not.

It is generally accepted in international (human rights) law that the authorities have two principle obligations of redress when human rights are violated: to cease the violation immediately, if it still continues, and to make full reparation.[43] Only the latter is relevant to the case under consideration. The basic form of reparation is *restitution in integrum,* which has primacy over the other forms of reparation, viz., financial compensation and satisfaction.[44] *Restitution in integrum* is, in principle, understood as re-establishing the situation that existed before the violation took place and, alternatively, as establishing the situation that would have existed if the violation had not materialized. Of course, a situation in which someone was not provided with legal assistance for a period of 125 days is as such irreversible. However, by avoiding or removing the consequences

[37] Decision on Appropriate Remedy, *Prosecutor v. Rwamakuba*, T. Ch. III, *supra* note 1, par. 55.

[38] See ECtHR, Judgment of 23 January 2001, *Brumărescu v. Romania*, Appl. 28342/95, par. 19-20.

[39] Decision on Appropriate Remedy, *Prosecutor v. Rwamakuba*, T. Ch. III, *supra* note 1, par. 57-60; Decision on Appeal Against Decision on Appropriate Remedy, *Rwamakuba v. Prosecutor*, A. Ch., *supra* note 1, par. 30.

[40] HRC, General Comment No. 31, The Nature of the General Legal Obligation Imposed on States Parties to the Covenant, 29 March 2004, par. 16; I-ACtHR, Judgment of 30 October 2008, *Bayarri v. Argentina*, par. 123.

[41] Decision on Appropriate Remedy, *Prosecutor v. Rwamakuba*, T. Ch. III, *supra* note 1, par. 48.

[42] *Ibid.*, par. 58 and 62.

[43] Cf. HRC, General Comment No. 31, The Nature of the General Legal Obligation Imposed on States Parties to the Covenant, 29 March 2004, par. 16 and 19; ECtHR, Judgment of 23 January 2001, *Brumărescu v. Romania*, Appl. 28342/95, par. 19-20, and ECtHR, Judgment of 31 October 1995, *Papamichalopoulos v. Greece*, Appl. 14556/89, par. 34; I-ACtHR, Judgment of 30 October 2008, *Bayarri v. Argentina*, par. 119-121, and I-ACtHR, Judgment of 21 July 1989, *Velásquez Rodríguez v. Honduras*, para. 25-26.

[44] Cf. Articles 30 to 37 of the Articles on the Responsibility of States for Internationally Wrongful Acts.

of the violation that are unfavourable, it is to a great extent possible to place the defendant in a position similar to the one he would have been in if the violation had not occurred.

In fact, it is that position in which Rwamakuba found himself after the criminal case had ended. Already, long before then, Trial Chamber II did 'not consider that the said delay in providing the accused with legal representation and thus, in the accused's initial appearance, has caused him a serious and irreparable prejudice.'[45] Both Trial Chamber III and the Appeals Chamber confirmed this.[46] Moreover, and more importantly, the absence of legal assistance at the beginning of his pre-trial detention had not adversely influenced his case, since he was acquitted. None of the purposes of the human right to legal assistance had been thwarted by the violation. These purposes are: prevention of ill-treatment and torture in detention, effectively guaranteeing the right to remain silent and, more generally, the right to a fair trial. In fact, there was little or nothing that required repair.[47] Even apart from that, however, a large degree of *restitution in integrum* was in any case effected by Rwamakuba's acquittal.

Still, there is one potential aspect of violations that can never be repaired: non-pecuniary damages, such as suffering, anxiety, inconvenience, uncertainty, loss of opportunities. For that, financial compensation is indeed – as the ICTR explains[48] – recognized in international human rights law as an appropriate form of redress. But were there any such damages in this case? The ICTR does believe so, for it grants financial compensation of 2,000 US dollars for the moral injury sustained as a result of the violation of the right to legal assistance. The question now is whether this injury requires financial compensation under international human rights law.

Although it is hard to say what an international human rights expert body would decide in a specific situation, a closer look at human rights law suggests that this form of redress was not required in this case. Crucial to that assessment is the fact that there is little to suggest that Rwamakuba actually suffered from being without a lawyer for approximately four months. On the contrary; for many months he did not request to be provided with counsel, even while he knew he had the right to do so. In view of this, it is hard to comprehend how the ICTR comes to conclude that 'in all probability, Rwamakuba suffered feelings of confusion, isolation, and distress as a result of the failure to provide him with duty counsel'.[49] Nor is there any indication that he lost vital opportunities because of the delay. Again, on the contrary; he was acquitted.

Against this background, it is important that the Human Rights Committee seems to demand financial compensation only in cases in which the suffering is manifest (killings, ill-treatment, arbitrary or 'unlawful' arrest and detention, miscarriages of justice, confiscation of property that cannot be returned, undue delay of proceedings). I have not been able (and neither was the ICTR) to find a single case in which the committee asserted an obligation on the state to award compensation in circumstances where the suffering did not significantly exceed that of Rwamakuba.[50]

In cases in which a violation only caused slight non-pecuniary damage to the (adult) defendant, the European Court usually holds that a finding of the violation in itself constitutes sufficient just satisfaction. That also applies when the right to legal assistance is violated during the pre-trial stages, even when this might have had material consequences for the outcome of the case.[51] It seems that this may also apply in cases of non-pecuniary damage if the national authorities have, either expressly or in substance, acknowledged that the convention has been breached.[52] Moreover, the ECtHR holds that there is no requirement under existing case

---

45 Decision on the Defence Motion Concerning the Illegal Arrest and Illegal Detention of the Accused, *Prosecutor v. Rwamakuba and others, supra* note 4, par. 44.

46 Decision on Appropriate Remedy, *Prosecutor v. Rwamakuba*, T. Ch. III, *supra* note 1, par. 38; Decision on Appeal Against Decision on Appropriate Remedy, *Rwamakuba v. Prosecutor,* A. Ch., *supra* note 1, par. 17.

47 Cf. Decision on Appropriate Remedy, *Prosecutor v. Rwamakuba,* T. Ch. III, *supra* note 1, par. 71-72.

48 *Ibid.*, par. 53-56. The Appeals Chamber also does not offer any convincing or factual reasons for that, see Decision on Appeal Against Decision on Appropriate Remedy, *Rwamakuba v. Prosecutor,* A. Ch., *supra* note 1, par. 28.

49 See Decision on Appropriate Remedy, *Prosecutor v. Rwamakuba*, T. Ch. III, *supra* note 1, par. 73.

50 Cf. Individual Opinion by Mr. Scheinin on HRC, View of 31 March 1998, *McTaggart v. Jamaica*, Comm. 749/1997.

51 See, for example, ECtHR, Judgment of 10 March 2009, *Böke and Kandemir v. Turkey*, Appl. 71912/01, par. 79; ECtHR, Judgment of 19 February 2009, *Shabelnik v. Ukraine*, Appl. 16404/03, par. 64.

52 See, for example, ECtHR, Decision of 16 December 2008, *Lobanovskaya v. Russia*, Appl. 31755/03; ECtHR, Judgment of 6 November 2008, *Ponushkov v. Russia*, Appl. 30209/04, par. 69-71; ECtHR, Decision of 1 April 2008, *Davidchuk v. Russia*, Appl. 37041/03; ECtHR, Decision of 21 June 2005, *I.H v. the United Kingdom*, Appl. 17111/04, par. 2; ECtHR, Decision of 10 May 2005,

law that the domestic authorities (here by analogy; the ICTR) should award the same sum by way of compensation as the court would be likely to award under Article 41 of the Convention.[53]

In other words, if the European Court itself would not afford financial compensation for non-pecuniary damage in a certain situation, then there is even less of a demand that the authorities (here by analogy; the ICTR) should do so of their own accord. The bottom line is that the level of just satisfaction granted by the national authorities (here by analogy; the ICTR) must not be manifestly inadequate in the particular circumstances of the case. The tribunal's decisions do not sufficiently explain that denying financial compensation would indeed be inadequate, and with that it has not been properly argued that there was an obligation to afford financial compensation in the case of Rwamakuba.

Nor does it seem that such arguments can be derived from the case law of the Inter-American Court of Human Rights. Similarly to the ECtHR, the American Court holds the view that international judgments in which human rights violations are found constitute in and of themselves a form of reparation.[54] Nevertheless, in many cases in which the non-pecuniary damage was substantial and obvious, the I-ACtHR has obligated states to pay compensation. But the violations in these cases (including those to which the ICTR refers)[55] are of a fundamentally different order than the alleged human rights violation against Rwamkuba, while the suffering in those other cases was much more substantial and obvious.[56]

Thus, in the case of a human rights violation, the redress afforded needs to be adequate and sufficient. That also applies to non-pecuniary damages. There is no indication in international human rights law that adequate and sufficient redress required financial compensation in the case of Rwamakuba for the non-pecuniary damage that resulted from the violation of Rule 44 *bis* section d. Even assuming that this violation constitutes a breach of the human right to legal assistance (which it actually does not), the express recognition by the ICTR of that breach would have sufficed in and of itself. Nor did the tribunal leave it at that, for it also ordered that the registrar provide Rwamakuba with an apology for the violation of his right to legal assistance, and, furthermore, that the registrar use all available means to seek the good offices of the state where Rwamakuba's family is present to facilitate some temporary status for him in that state and to ensure the uninterrupted schooling of his children.

4. Redress for detention in remand undergone by acquitted defendants?

The real distress caused to Rwamakuba is that he had to undergo nearly eight years of detention at the UNDF before he was acquitted and released.[57] The defence attempted to persuade the tribunal that the indictment and prosecution was based on false and manipulated evidence. They argued that this, in combination with the length of the pre-trial and trial detention, constituted a miscarriage of justice, for which compensation may be granted by analogical application of Article 85, paragraph 3, of the Statute of the International Criminal Court. Both Trial Chamber III and the Appeals Chamber convincingly denied that a 'miscarriage of justice' had occurred, while they furthermore made clear that they would not have had the power to make an award for financial compensation if it had occurred.[58]

Arrigo & Vella v. Malta, Appl. 6569/04, par. 2; ECtHR, Decision of 12 September 2000, *Nikishina v. Russia*, Appl. 45665/99 (it follows from these decisions that, after the national authorities had repaired the violation as such, their acknowledgment of the violation constituted appropriate redress, which implies that no compensation had to be afforded for any non-pecuniary damage). Cf. also ECtHR, Judgment of 30 June 2008, *Gäfgen v. Germany*, Appl. 22978/05, par. 80; ECtHR, Decision of 18 November 2008, *Lukić v. Bosnia and Herzegovina*, Appl. 34379/03.

53 ECtHR, Judgment of 13 November 2008, *Ommer v. Germany (no. 1)*, Appl. 10597/03, par. 69.

54 See, with many references to other case law, for example I-ACtHR, Judgment of 7 June 2003, *Juan Humberto Sánchez v. Honduras*, par. 172; ECtHR, Judgment of 22 November 2005, *Palamara-Iribarne v. Chile*, par. 247.

55 Decision on Appropriate Remedy, *Prosecutor v. Rwamakuba*, T. Ch. III, *supra* note 1, par. 55 (footnote 88).

56 Cf. of many cases, for example, I-ACtHR, Judgment 27 November 2008, *Ticona Estrada et al. v. Bolivia*, par. 130; I-ACtHR, Judgment of 27 November 2003, *Maritza Urrutia v. Guatemala*, par. 166. For a case in which it was found that the I-ACtHR's judgement per se constituted adequate redress for non-pecuniary damage, see for example, I-ACtHR, Judgment of 5 February 2001, *'The Last Temptation of Christ' Case*, par. 99.

57 Rwamakuba also spent time in detention in Namibia (see Judgment, *Prosecutor v. Rwamakuba*, *supra* note 2, par. 4). The tribunal cannot be held responsible for that period; cf., for example, ECtHR, Decision of 3 February 2009, *Hoischen v. Germany*, Appl. 22683/04, par. 1.

58 See respectively Decision on Appropriate Remedy, *Prosecutor v. Rwamakuba*, T. Ch. III, *supra* note 1, par. 21-25, and Decision on Appeal Against Decision on Appropriate Remedy, *Rwamakuba v. Prosecutor*, A. Ch., *supra* note 1, par. 10-15.

The defence did not argue that the length of the detention as such was in violation of human rights, more particularly the human right to a trial within a reasonable time, nor did the tribunal *ex officio* find such a human rights violation. Instead, the tribunal correctly asserts that international human rights law does provide for a right to compensation in circumstances involving either an unlawful arrest or detention, or an unjust conviction, but not after an acquittal.[59] There was, thus, nobody to qualify the eight years of detention as a human rights violation. With that, the power to order redress – which power the tribunal had, after all, advanced with regard to the violation of human rights and for human rights violations only (see above) – could not come into play. Again, the question of whether a human rights violation had occurred was thus crucial to the question of redress.

It seems very arbitrary that no redress can be afforded to someone who has spent nearly eight years in detention before being acquitted for lack of proof beyond a reasonable doubt, while that same person was indeed offered compensation because the authorities failed to provide him with legal assistance (which the defendant nevertheless knew he could request, but failed to do so for a long period, even though this deficiency had no bearing on the case). Therefore, it is no surprise that in many (European) countries, courts have the competence to grant compensation on an equitable basis for defendants who have been held in detention while the trial against them did not result in a conviction.[60]

This case illustrates that international criminal justice may result in the removal of up to at least eight years of an individual's freedom, who had to be regarded as innocent before, during and after the trial (cf. the presumption of innocence). It seems to me that the responsibility of the international community for the injustice caused to an individual entails at least a significant moral obligation to offer compensation to that person. The international community and the international criminal tribunals should therefore make provision for that.

Meanwhile, it remains to be seen whether it was impossible for the tribunal to provide redress or compensation. For that, it is thus crucial to ascertain whether the nearly eight years of detention (which included over five[61] or six and a half[62] years of pre-trial detention, the rest being trial detention) did or did not constitute a human rights violation. Unfortunately, international human rights law does not offer an entirely indisputable answer to that question, for it does not set an absolute time limit on detention nor on the duration of the case from the charge or arrest until the end of the trial. Nevertheless, human rights law points firmly to the conclusion that the human right to trial within a reasonable time was actually violated in the case of Rwamakuba. This right is included in the right against arbitrary detention (see, for example, Article 9, paragraph 3, ICCPR and Article 5, paragraph 3, ECHR)[63] as well as the right to a fair trial (see, for example, Article 14, paragraph 3 sub (c), ICCPR and Article 6, paragraph 1, ECHR). Both are relevant here, but since the requirement to prevent unreasonable terms of detention is the strictest of these, I shall focus on that.

International human rights law holds that pre-trial detention should be the exception and as short as possible.[64] In principle, a period of over approximately 18 months of detention will constitute a violation of the reasonable time requirement in Article 9, paragraph 3, ICCPR, if no explanation is offered for the

---

59 Decision on Appropriate Remedy, *Prosecutor v. Rwamakuba*, T. Ch. III, *supra* note 1, par. 24-25; Decision on Appeal Against Decision on Appropriate Remedy, *Rwamakuba v. Prosecutor*, A. Ch., *supra* note 1, par. 10.

60 See, for example, Belgium (Article 28 Act on the compensation for inefficacious preventive detention/ Wet betreffende de vergoeding voor onwerkzame voorlopige hechtenis), Estonia (Compensation for Damage Caused by State to Person by Unjust Deprivation of Liberty Act/ Riigi poolt isikule alusetult vabaduse võtmisega tekitatud kahju hüvitamise seadus), France (Articles 149-150 CCP/ Code de Procedure Penale), Germany (section 2 Act on Compensation for Measures of Criminal Prosecution/ Gesetz über die Entschädigung für Strafverfolgungsmaßnahmen), Italy (Article 314 CCP/ Codice di Procedura Penale), The Netherlands (Articles 89-93 CCP/ Wetboek van Strafvordering), and Norway (Articles 444-446 CCP/ Straffeprosessloven).

61 Judgment, *Prosecutor v. Rwamakuba*, supra note 2, par. 6 (the initial trial commenced on 27 November 2003).

62 *Idem*, par. 7 (the trial in the instant case commenced on 9 June 2005).

63 See also Article 7, paragraph 5, ACHR. The detainee's right to trial within a reasonable time is, however, not expressly provided in Article 6 AfChHPR, which concerns the right to liberty. The African Commission has, however, been able to read it into the fair trial requirement of Article 7, paragraph 1 sub (d); see AfCionHPR, Decision of 16-30 May 2007, *Article 19 v. The State of Eritrea*, Comm. 275/ 2003 (2007), under Decision on the merits.

64 HRC, General Comment No. 8, Right to liberty and security of persons (Article 9), 30 June 1982, par. 3; ECtHR, Judgment of 24 July 2003, *Smirnova v. Russia*, Appl. 46133/99, par. 58-64.

delay.[65] The Human Rights Committee has nevertheless hinted that even seven years and eight months of detention might be compatible with Article 9, paragraph 3, ICCPR, if special circumstances justify such delay, such as impediments to the investigations attributable to the accused or to his representative.[66] Otherwise, this will be in violation of the provision.

At the same time, however, it is not very easy to convince that such circumstances exist.[67] The longest period of detention accepted by the Human Rights Committee that I have been able to find is 12 months, which may of course not be regarded as the limit of detention.[68] Although international criminal justice is faced with complicated, large-scale cases that require time-consuming investigations that depend greatly on the cooperation of states, it is far from certain that the nearly eight years of detention would be acceptable under the ICCPR.

The same appears to apply from the point of view of the European Convention, more particularly Article 5, paragraph 3, ECHR. As a rule, any detention exceeding two years – from the first day of custody until the day when the charge is determined[69] – is likely to violate this provision.[70] However, in the very exceptional case of Chraidi v. Germany, the ECtHR held that nearly five and a half years of detention (before the defendant was convicted on more than 100 counts) did not constitute a violation.[71] The court makes clear that detention exceeding five years will in principle always constitute a violation, but in this case, very special circumstances applied. The case involved a particularly complex investigation and trial concerning serious offences of international terrorism that were committed by criminal associations acting on a global scale. The offences caused the death of three victims and serious suffering to more than one hundred. The investigation and trial concerned serious charges against the defendant and four co-defendants (who had 15 lawyers), necessitated the hearing of 169 witnesses (on 281 separate hearing days), involved 106 joint plaintiffs (who had 29 lawyers) and resulted in a judgement of 380 pages.[72]

Thus, the Chraidi case bears some resemblance to the Rwamakuba case, as well as to many other cases that are tried by international criminal tribunals. At this moment, however, it is not possible to compare these cases precisely. What can be ascertained, though, is that Rwamabuka's detention of nearly eight years was some two and a half years longer even than that of Chraidi, and this while Ramakuba was acquitted and Chraidi convicted. Nevertheless, the case law of the ECtHR does not yet offer conclusive criteria on the question of whether such a long period of detention is in contravention of Article 5, paragraph 3, although it can very well be argued that it is.

But should any period of detention, no matter how long, always be assessed with regard to whether the particular circumstances of the case justify that period under the relevant criteria? In my opinion, the answer is no. It is argued that nearly eight years of deprivation of freedom to an unconvicted person is so excessive that this must be considered as constituting a human rights violation, if that person is not substantially responsible for the delay. This means that even in the most complicated, large-scale cases, states as well as international criminal tribunals are under the obligation to take all necessary measures to sufficiently speed

---

65 HRC, View of 1 April 2002, *Teesdale v. Trinidad and Tobago*, Comm. 677/1996, par. 9.3 (17 months detention, including 16 months pre-trial detention); HRC, View of 23 October 2008, *Smantser v. Belarus*, Comm. 1178/2003, par. 10.3 (22 month detention from arrest till conviction in appeal trial). Violations regarding the lengths of pre-trial detention (period from arrest to opening of trial) were also found in: HRC, View of 30 July 1998, *Perkins v. Jamaica*, Comm. 733/1997, par. 11.3 (21 months); HRC, View of 17 July 1997, *Lewis v. Jamaica*, Comm. 708/1996, par. 8.1 (23 months); HRC, View of 25 July 1996, *Henry and Douglas v. Jamaica*, Comm. 571/1994, par. 9.3 (2 and a half years); HRC, View of 26 October 1995, *Seerattan v. Trinidad and Tobago*, Comm. 434/1990, par.7.2 (over 3 years).

66 HRC, View of 28 July 1997, *Elahie v. Trinidad v. Tobago*, Comm. 533/1993, par. 8.2. See a similar view, but relating to 4 years and 7 months: HRC, View of 21 October 1994, *Koné v. Senegal*, Comm. 386/1989, par. 8.7.

67 See references in preceding footnotes. See also HRC, View of 19 July 1995, *Barroso v. Panama*, Comm. 473/1991, par. 8.5 (3 and a half years; complex factual situation and protracted investigations could not sufficiently explain the delay).

68 HRC, View of 31 March 1998, *McTaggart v. Jamaica*, Comm. 749/1997, par. 8.2.

69 See recently ECtHR, Judgment of 25 June 2009, *Bakhmutskiy v. Russia*, Appl. 36932/02, par. 131.

70 D.J. Harris, M. O'Boyle, E.P. Bates and C.M. Buckley, Law of the European Convention on Human Rights, Oxford: Oxford University Press 2009, p. 181.

71 ECtHR, Judgement of 26 October 2006, *Chraidi v. Germany*, Appl. 65655/01, par. 33 and 49.

72 *Ibid.*, par. 43.

up criminal proceedings.[73] Therefore, it seems that the wrong caused to Rwamakuba of nearly eight years of detention constitutes the only human rights violation in this case, and a fundamental one at that.

Piet Hein van Kempen

73 Cf. Gillian Higgins, Fair and Expeditious Pre-trial Proceedings. The Future of International Criminal Trials, 5 Journal of International Criminal Justice 2007 p. 394-401.

International Criminal Tribunal for Rwanda
Tribunal pénal international pour le Rwanda

OR: ENG

Before: Dennis Byron, President

Registrar: Adama Dieng

Date: 30 August 2007

THE PROSECUTOR

v.

Samuel IMANISHIMWE

Case No.: ICTR-99-46-S

DECISION ON SAMUEL IMANISHIMWE'S APPLICATION FOR EARLY RELEASE

Counsel for the Accused

Marie Louise Mbida

[page 2] THE PRESIDENT OF THE INTERNATIONAL CRIMINAL TRIBUNAL FOR RWANDA,

BEING SEIZED OF Samuel Imanishimwe's Request for Early Release, filed on 14 June 2007 ("the Application");

RECALLING that, on 25 February 2004, Trial Chamber III convicted Samuel Imanishimwe of genocide and extermination as a crime against humanity with sentences of two terms of 15 years imprisonment to be served consecutively, as well as, murder, imprisonment, and torture as crimes against humanity with sentences of ten, three, and ten years imprisonment respectively and serious violations of Common Article 3 for murder, torture, and cruel treatment with a sentence of twelve years imprisonment;[1]

RECALLING that, on 7 July 2006, the Appeals Chamber rendered its Judgement and Sentence in *The Prosecutor v. Samuel Imanishimwe*, in which it upheld the Trial Chamber's convictions for murder, imprisonment and torture as crimes against humanity and serious violations of Common Article 3 but set aside Samuel Imanishimwe's convictions of genocide and extermination as a crime against humanity resulting in a reduction of sentence to twelve years of imprisonment to run from 11 August 1997;[2]

NOTING that Samuel Imanishimwe has not been transferred to a State for the enforcement of his sentence and remains in the custody of the Tribunal in Arusha, Tanzania;

NOTING that, under Article 27 of the Statute of the Tribunal, there shall only be pardon or commutation of sentence if the President so decides in the interests of justice and following notification by the State in which the convicted person is imprisoned that he or she is eligible for pardon or commutation of sentence pursuant to the applicable law of that State;

COGNISANT that, there is precedent for the instant application, in that a previous request for commutation of sentence was found admissible despite the fact that the individual was serving his sentence at the Tribunal's Detention Facility, while awaiting transfer to a designated State;

CONSIDERING Rule 125 of the Rules of Procedure and Evidence ("Rules") which authorises the President to determine any request for commutation of sentence in consultation with the Bureau and any remaining Permanent Judges of the Sentencing Chamber, following notification to the Republic of Rwanda;

HAVING carried out the consultations prescribed by Rule 125 and **NOTING** that the Government of Rwanda was notified of the Application on 24 August 2007;

CONSIDERING that under Rule 126 of the Rules, the President shall, in determining whether pardon or commutation is appropriate, take into account, *inter alia*, the gravity of the crime or crimes for which the prisoner was convicted, the treatment of similarly-situated prisoners, the prisoner's demonstration of rehabilitation and any substantial cooperation of the prisoner with the Prosecutor; **[page 3]**

NOTING that the crimes for which Imanishimwe was sentenced include those of significant gravity, including murder, imprisonment, and torture as crimes against humanity and serious violations of Common Article 3 for murder, torture, and cruel treatment;

CONSIDERING that to date, no person convicted by this Tribunal has had their sentence commuted or been released early, and that those persons granted early release by the International Criminal Tribunal for the former Yugoslavia have not been convicted for the same combination of crimes as Samuel Imanishimwe;[3]

OBSERVING that the instant application for early release refers, *inter alia*, to Samuel Imanishimwe's lack of prior criminal record, good behaviour in his country of asylum, and his age;

---

[1] *Prosecutor v. André Ntagerura, Emmanuel Bagambiki, and Samuel Imanishimwe*, Case No. ICTR-99-46-T, Judgement and Sentence, 25 February 2004.

[2] *Prosecutor v. André Ntagerura, Emmanuel Bagambiki, and Samuel Imanishimwe*, Case No. ICTR-99-46-T, Judgement (AC), 7 July 2006.

[3] *See* Order of the President on the Early Release of Dragan Kolundzija, Case No. IT-95-8-S, President, ICTY, 5 December 2001; Order of the President for the Early Release of Majolica Kos, Case No. IT-98-30/1-A, President, ICTY, 30 July 2002.

NOTING that the Judgement already considered these factors as mitigating when determining Samuel Imanishimwe's sentence;

HAVING carefully considered Samuel Imanishimwe's submissions that his remorse for victims, good behaviour within detention, family situation, potentially fragile health, and desire to reintegrate and complete his education in order to be of use to Rwanda warrant early release;

FINDING that these factors, at the present stage, do not warrant early release given the gravity of the crimes in question;

FOR THE ABOVE REASONS,

DENIES the Application.

Arusha, 30 August 2007

Dennis Byron
President

[Seal of the Tribunal]

Commentary

1. Introduction

Early release, pardon and commutation of sentence are all instruments that aim to serve justice, although in cases when they are applied too strictly, they may instead be regarded as producing injustice. This not only corresponds to what appears to be a quite common view, it also results from international human rights law, as will become clear below. In order to analyse and explain the decision by the president of the ICTR on Samuel Imanishimwe's application for early release,[1] human rights law will be frequently referred to. I shall take particular note of the relevant findings of the Human Rights Committee (HRC) on the International Covenant on Civil and Political Rights (ICCPR), the European Court of Human Rights (ECtHR) on the basis of the European Convention on Human Rights (ECHR), and the Inter-American Commission and Court of Human Rights (I-ACionHR and I-ACtHR) on the American Convention on Human Rights (ACHR).

It will be useful first to briefly introduce the case. On 7 July 2006, the Appeals Chamber sentenced Imanishimwe, a former lieutenant of the Rwandan army, effectively to 12 years of imprisonment for murder, imprisonment and torture as crimes against humanity and serious violations of common Article 3.[2] Since the sentence runs from 11 August 1997 – the date on which the applicant was arrested and subsequently transferred to the tribunal – the end of the prison term is 11 August 2009. As of 6 December 2008, the applicant was detained in Mali.[3] His request for early release was filed on 14 June 2007. At that point the applicant had not been transferred to a state and was still in the custody in the United Nations Detention Facility (UNDF) in Arusha.

2. An instrument sui generis

Both the ICTR Statute (Article 27) and the ICTR Rules of Procedure and Evidence (Rules 124-126) provide for the possibility of pardon or commutation of sentences.[4] Strictly speaking, however, these provisions do not apply to the applicant's request, first of all because they literally only apply to convicted persons who are imprisoned under the authority of a state, and thus not to those who are detained in UNDFs. Following the Yugoslavia Tribunal on early release,[5] from the first request for early release that was submitted to the Rwanda Tribunal, the ICTR president relied on his inherent powers and applied these provisions analogically to convicted persons detained in the Arusha UNDF.[6] That precedent is adhered to in this decision.

Second, the provisions make no mention of early release – which should be distinguished from pardon and commutation of sentence.[7] Whereas the president of the ICTY implicitly regards early release as a form of pardon, the ICTR president in his decisions seems to equate it primarily with commutation.[8] From a dogmatic point of view, this is incorrect. Commutation of sentences involves an adjustment of the judgment as regards the sentence; early release merely means that the convicted person is (conditionally) entitled to remain free for the remainder of the sentence. The applicant only requests the latter. As a rule, prisoners become eligible (discretionary release system) or entitled (mandatory release system) to release under national legal systems when they have served a fixed period of time or a proportion of the sentence (usually

1 ICTR, Decision on Samuel Imanishimwe's Application for Early Release, *Prosecutor v. Imanishimwe*, Case No. ICTR-99-46-S, Pres., 30 August 2007, in this volume, p. 951.

2 ICTR, ICTR, Judgement, *Prosecutor v. Ntagerura, Bagambiki and Imanishimwe*, Case No. ICTR-99-46-A, A. Ch., 7 July 2006, Klip/ Sluiter, ALC-XXIV-595, par. 444.

3 ICTR, Decision on the Enforcement of Sentence, *Prosecutor v. Imanishimwe*, Case No. ICTR-99-46, Pres., 3 November 2008.

4 On early release of prisoners who are transferred to states, see Mark A. Drumbl, Atrocity, Punishment, and International Law, Cambridge University Press, Cambridge 2007, p. 53-55 and 160.

5 On the relevant case law of the ICTY, see André Klip, Commentary, Klip/Sluiter, ALC-VIII-1091; Denis Abels, Commentary, Klip/Sluiter, ALC-XV-796-800; Inés Mónica Weinberg de Roca and Christopher M. Rassi, Sentencing and Incarceration in the Ad Hoc Tribunals, 44 Stanford Journal of International Law 2008, p. 50-53.

6 For the first application to the Rwanda Tribunal, see ICTR, Decision of the President on the Application for Early Release of Georges Ruggiu, *Prosecutor v. Ruggiu*, Case No. ICTR-97-32-S, Pres., 12 May 2005.

7 See André Klip, Commentary, *supra* note 5.

8 See also ICTR, Decision on the Motion for Reconsideration of the Denial of Early Release, *Prosecutor v. Rutaganira*, Case No. ICTR-1995-1C-R73, Pres., 13 February 2008, par. 4.

half or two-thirds of the full term).[9] Considering that such a legal framework for early release for UNDF prisoners is absent, while the provisions on pardon and commutation of sentence are instead being adopted to assess early release requests, one must in fact conclude that the presidents of the ICTY and ICTR have developed an early release instrument *sui generis*.

As such, this is not necessarily problematic. It seems hardly possible for international criminal justice to function in the same way as national systems, if only because the international structure, much more than a national system, depends on many other systems which, moreover, differ significantly from each other. This also applies to the imprisonment of convicts and their possible early release, for which the international tribunals chiefly depend on the cooperation of states and the nature of their criminal, legal and prison systems. All the same, the international system should also be clear in substance and scope, and its consequences should be foreseeable.

3. International human rights law and the scope and grounds of early release

Some elucidation is possibly offered in the "Practice Direction on the Procedure for the Determination of Applications for Pardon, Commutation of Sentence and Early Release of Persons Convicted by the International Criminal Tribunal for Rwanda" of 10 May 2000. But this direction has not been made public. This leaves us with the decision under consideration here. This decision offers only slight additional clarification to what already follows from Article 27 of the Statute and Rules 124-126 of the ICTR Rules of Procedure and Evidence. I shall therefore discuss the decision more closely in the light of international human rights law, in order to further analyse and explain the mechanism of early release.

The involvement here of human rights is not without basis. The general touchstone for pardon and commutation of sentences that follows from Article 27 of the ICTR Statute is made up of the "interest of justice" and the "general principles of law". This provision is applied analogously to early release, albeit that the president in this decision does not clarify the meaning of these principles in that regard. It nevertheless seems that human rights standards must be considered as being relevant, particularly as part of the "general principles of law". With that, the mechanisms of early release, as well as pardon and commutation, have to meet the requirements of international human rights law. Indeed, the ICTR regards itself as bound by international human rights law.[10]

Meanwhile, the criterion of the 'interest of justice' is also not without relevance for early release. Bearing in mind that the tribunal's mechanism of early release must be regarded as an instrument *sui generis*, this criterion offers, for example, the possibility to take into consideration the aims of punishment as recognized by the tribunals - retribution, deterrence, reprobation, rehabilitation, national reconciliation, protection of society and restoration of peace.[11]

Since early release has to date never been granted by the ICTR, it is not very clear under what conditions and in exactly what circumstances a request for such release will be successful. Some guidelines nevertheless seem to be evident from the ICTR president's case law on early release. Four of these grounds are derived from Rule 126 of the ICTR Rules of Procedure and Evidence; two grounds are not.

Grounds that may particularly support early release are the prisoner's demonstration of rehabilitation and any substantial cooperation by the prisoner with the Prosecutor. The first of these grounds – both of which are stated in Rule 126 – particularly appears to be applied with some latitude. In reviewing the rehabilitation ground, it is not only regarded as potentially relevant that the applicant has no prior criminal record, that he displayed good behaviour in his country of asylum and within detention, that he showed remorse for victims, and that he has a desire to reintegrate and complete his education. It emerges that the president in examining

---

[9] Cf. Principle No. 5 of the Council of Europe Recommendation Rec (2003) on conditional release (parole). Information on the conditional release systems of twenty countries (European and other) is provided in Peter J.P. Tak and Manon Jendly (eds.), Prison Policy and Prisoners' Rights, Wolf Legal Publishers 2008.

[10] See ICTR, Decision on Appropriate Remedy, *Prosecutor v. Rwamakuba*, Case No. ICTR-98-44C-T, T. Ch. III, 31 January 2007, in this volume, p. 907, par. 48, with commentary by Piet Hein van Kempen.

[11] ICTR, Judgement, *Procureur v. Seromba*, Case No. ICTR-2001-66-T, T. Ch. III, 13 December 2006, in this volume, p. 523, par. 376.

this ground also takes in to consideration the applicant's age, family situation, and potentially fragile health.

In a narrow sense, these factors are not "demonstrations" of rehabilitation but rather potential humanitarian reasons for early release. This is indeed important, since under international human rights law, humanitarian circumstances may call for a prisoner's early release. For example, Principle 14 of Recommendation no. R (93) 6 of the Committee of Ministers states that "Prisoners with terminal HIV disease should be granted early release, as far as possible, and given proper treatment outside the prison."[12] So with the acceptance of humanitarian circumstances as a possible ground for early release, the ICTR meets a relevant condition of international human rights law.

A ground mentioned in Rule 126 as well as in the decision, which may work either for or against an application for early release, is the treatment of similarly situated prisoners. Whether this ground, in which the principle of equality is manifested, will support early release or act against it depends on whether or not the applications for early release of other such prisoners have been granted. I shall return to the problem of applying early release in conformity with the principle of non-discrimination (see section 5). Another ground that may work either for or against an applicant is the length of the term of imprisonment served up to the date of the decision. Neither Rule 126 nor this decision refers explicitly to this ground, but it is expressly reviewed in a decision on a request for early release in another case.[13] It seems that the term already served will normally be a factor that is taken into account, either expressly or implicitly, when deciding whether or not a UNDF prisoner shall be released early.

Finally, there appear to be two grounds that as such will never be able to serve as an argument for early release, but might very well be a reason to deny it. First, there is the question of whether the facts and reasons put forward for early release have or have not already been considered in the judgment when determining the sentence. Naturally, this ground can only apply to facts and reasons for early release, that already existed prior to the conviction. This ground did in fact work against the applicant in this case. The same applies to the other ground: the gravity of the crime or crimes for which the prisoner was convicted, which is contained in Rule 126. In another case, an important reason to reject the request for early release was that the crimes for which the applicant was sentenced included the direct and public incitement to commit genocide.[14]

In the case under consideration here, however, the applicant was acquitted of genocide on appeal, and convicted of the only marginally less severe crimes of murder, imprisonment and torture as crimes against humanity and serious violations of common Article 3.[15] The applicant adduced several facts and reasons for early release that had only come into existence after his conviction on appeal. All of these were trumped by the gravity of the crime. Therefore, this ground serves to be most decisive of all. This approach is not contrary to international human rights law. Indeed, the European Court seems to be of the opinion that the severity of the offence should not be the only element taken into consideration when deciding on early release.[16] However, the several grounds offered in Rule 126 of the Rules of Procedure and Evidence, and the fact that these are actually being reviewed by the ICTR, clearly imply conformity with this requirement. Moreover, the European Court (or any other international human rights supervisory body for that matter) does not prohibit making a distinction between different types of offence or the gravity thereof.[17] Such a

---

12 Recommendation no. R (93) 6 of the Committee of Ministers to member states concerning prison and criminological aspects of the control of transmissible diseases including Aids and related health problems in prison. For a similar provision, see Guidelines for State Action annexed to Guideline 4 of the UN International Guidelines on HIV/Aids and Human Rights: "Compassionate early release of prisoners living with AIDS should be considered."

13 See, Decision of the President on the Application for Early Release of Georges Ruggiu, *Prosecutor v. Ruggiu*, Pres., *supra* note 6.

14 Decision of the President on the Application for Early Release of Georges Ruggiu, *Prosecutor v. Ruggiu*, Pres., *supra* note 6.

15 Cf. yet another case in which the request for early release was denied primarily because the conviction of the applicant concerned the grave crime of extermination as a crime against humanity: ICTR, Decision on Request for Early Release, *Prosecutor v. Rutaganira*, Case No. ICTR-95-IC-T, Pres., 2 June 2006, Klip/ Sluiter, ALC-XXIV-947; ICTR, Decision on Appeal of a Decision of the President on Early Release, *Prosecutor v. Rutaganira*, Case No. ICTR-95-IC-AR, A. Ch., 24 August 2006.

16 ECtHR, Decision of 10 February 2009, *Streicher v. Germany*, Appl. 40384/04.

17 See, for example, ECtHR, Grand Chamber Judgment of 8 July 1999, *Gerger v. Turkey*, Appl. 24919/94, par. 69; ECtHR, Decision of 30 August 2005, *Gök and Güler v. Turkey*, Appl. 74307/01.

practice is in itself not a breach of the right to liberty, nor the prohibition of discrimination (see also section 5 below). So the possibility of pardon, commutation of sentences and early release may be excluded for the gravest crimes (albeit not categorically, as is discussed further below).

Certainly, the decision in the case of Imanishimwe is again an important demonstration of the possibility of early release of convicted prisoners in UNDFs – at least in theory, for it has never been granted by the ICTR up to the time of writing. The absence of specific provisions means that these prisoners do not know if and when they might become eligible for early release. Notably, this particular decision also does not state when the applicant may qualify for early release.[18] The president merely submits that it is not warranted "at the present stage".

Interestingly, the applicant had already served just over fourth- fifths of his sentence when this decision was rendered. That is quite a bit more than the above- mentioned requirement of half or two-thirds of the sentence. It is therefore clear that the president does not wish to adopt a similar system for early release as is common in many countries. An important consequence of this is that convicted persons who are imprisoned in the UNDF of Arusha, as the applicant was, will in all probability have to serve a longer sentence than convicts who have been transferred to a state. To these latter persons the early release regime of the country they are sent to will be applied in principle, and that will most likely be a more favourable system. This raises several important issues, a few of which will be discussed below.

4. A human right to early release and a human rights restriction to granting it?

The answer to the important question of whether prisoners do have a human right to pardon, commutation of sentence or early release is, in principle, in the negative. The European Court of Human Rights (ECtHR) holds that the Convention does not confer, in general, a right to amnesty, to release on licence or to have a sentence reconsidered by a national authority, judicial or administrative, with a view to its remission or termination.[19] There is nothing to suggest that a different view is held by the Human Rights Committee on the basis of the ICCPR, or the I-ACionHR and I-ACtHR on the basis of the American Convention. However, if and when early release is granted, the right to liberty (see, for example, Article 9 ICCPR, Article 7 ACHR, and Article 5 ECHR) demands that the prisoner is released without delay the moment his release is provided for by domestic law, according to the European Court.[20]

The absence of a general right to pardon, commutation of sentence or early release does not signify that there is no pressure to arrange for such mechanisms or to apply them. A provision that appears to have close analogous relevance for the practice of international criminal tribunals is Article 6, paragraph 4, of Protocol II to the Geneva Conventions: "At the end of hostilities, the authorities in power shall endeavour to grant the broadest possible amnesty to persons who have participated in the armed conflict, or those deprived of their liberty for reasons related to the armed conflict, whether they are interned or detained." Furthermore, international human rights law gives rise to obligations to offer the possibility of early release, to consider applying it, or to actually apply it when certain specific circumstances arise.

At first such obligation occurs when a sentence of life imprisonment is involved – which was not so in the case of Imanishimwe, but which has been imposed on several others by the ICTR. In its case law, the European Court has consistently ruled that the imposition of a sentence of life imprisonment on an adult offender is not in itself prohibited by or incompatible with the European Convention. Yet, where the life sentence is "irreducible", this may raise an issue under the prohibition of torture and inhuman and degrading treatment and punishment in Article 3 ECHR.[21] The crucial factor here is the fact that there is no chance whatsoever that the sentence or its execution will be reduced.

[18] Cf. Article 8 of the Practice Direction of 8 August 2006 on the Procedure for the Determination of Applications for Pardon, Commutation of Sentence and Early Release of Persons Convicted by the International Tribunal (It/146/Rev.1).

[19] See, for example, ECtHR, Grand Chamber Judgment of 12 February 2008, *Kafkaris v. Cyprus*, Appl. 21906/04, par. 99; ECtHR, Judgement of 6 March 2007, *Gębura v. Poland*, Appl. 63131/00, par. 32; Decision of 30 August 2005, *Gök and Güler v. Turkey*, *supra* note 17; ECtHR, Decision of 16 December 2003, *Jankauskas v. Lithuania*, Appl. 59304/00.

[20] Judgement of 6 March 2007, *Gębura v. Poland*, *supra* note 19, par. 31-37.

[21] See, for example, Grand Chamber Judgment of 12 February 2008, *Kafkaris v. Cyprus*, *supra* note 19, par. 97; ECtHR, Judgment of 19 February 2009, *A. and Others v. the United Kingdom*, Appl. 3455/05, par. 128; Decision of 10 February 2009,

Where national law affords the possibility for commutation, remission or termination of the life sentence or the conditional release of the prisoner, this will be sufficient to satisfy Article 3 ECHR.[22] This does not mean that someone who is sentenced to life imprisonment must necessarily be released sooner or later, it is just that the prisoner may not be deprived of all hope of it. Furthermore, this obligation will only come into play if the continued detention actually causes at least considerable mental or physical suffering. The ICTR's practice seems to be in conformity with this. After all, the possibility of pardon, commutation and early release exists for everyone convicted by the ICTR, while the president, neither for Imanishimwe nor for anybody else, has permanently excluded the possibility thereto.

Interestingly, the case law of the European Court also implies that extradition should be refused when the individual concerned runs the risk of being sentenced to life imprisonment without any possibility of early release. Applied to the practice of the ICTR (or for that matter the ICTY or ICC), this means that the tribunal may not transfer a prisoner to a state in order to serve his or her sentence of life imprisonment if that state does not allow for reduction of that sentence in its execution.[23] From this point of view, Rule 124 of the ICTR Rules of Procedure and Evidence incorrectly appears to leave room for the possibility that a state in which a convicted person is imprisoned does not offer the possibility of pardon, commutation of sentence or early release, as far as the sentence entails life imprisonment.

The Human Rights Committee has not yet decided any of these matters, as far as I have been able to ascertain. It has, however, recommended that states seriously consider early release as a means of redress for violations of, for example, the right to humane treatment of prisoners (Article 10 ICCPR) and the right to a fair trial (Article 14 ICCPR).[24] The Inter-American Commission on Human Rights has formulated similar obligations.[25] From a human rights point of view, the need to offer redress (in the form of non-financial compensation) for human rights violations committed against a prisoner might thus require pardon, commutation of sentence or early release of that prisoner. While neither the Rules of Procedure and Evidence nor the ICTR president have recognized the offer of redress as a ground for early release, Rule 126 of the Rules does provide the possibility for that, since it only offers a non-exhaustive account of grounds. This, however, is probably not of great practical relevance. Considering the position of international criminal tribunals – individuals cannot complain of the procedures and decisions of these tribunals to international human rights bodies – redress of human rights violations by reducing a punishment will usually have to be done immediately when deciding on the sentence. Indeed, the ICTR has been offering redress in this way.[26]

I reiterate that under international human rights law, humanitarian circumstances may sometimes call for a prisoner's early release. Thus, international human rights law does indeed recognize that pardon, commutation of sentence and early release may be important for the course of justice. As I have already mentioned, too simplistic an application of these instruments may instead result in injustice. Human rights therefore also limit the possibilities for pardon, commutation of sentence, early release and similar instruments. I mention only some restrictions.

First, international (human rights) law contains obligations with regard to many crimes entailing the appropriate and effective punishment of the perpetrators of these crimes. See, for example, Article 4 of the UN Convention against Torture and Other Cruel, Inhuman or Degrading Treatment or Punishment (1984). A more precise formulation of such positive obligations is offered in the case law of the European Court of

---

Streicher v. Germany, *supra* note 16. To date, the Human Rights Committee has sidestepped decisions on this matter; see Human Rights Committee, View of 3 April 2003, *Weiss v. Austria*, Comm. 1086/2002, par. 9.4 (see also 4.6 and 6.7-6.8).

22 Cf. Article 6, paragraph 4, ICCPR and Article 4, paragraph 4, ACHR. These provisions signify that every person condemned to death (which is not a sentence that may be imposed by the ICTR) shall have the right to apply for amnesty, pardon, or commutation of sentence, and that these may be granted in all cases. Cf. also Article 75 of the Geneva Convention relative to the Protection of Civilian Persons in Time of War, and Article 6 of the Revised Arab Charter on Human Rights 2004.

23 ECtHR, Decision of 26 May 2005, *Parlanti v. Germany*, Appl. 45097/04, par. 6; ECtHR, Decision of 16 October 2001, *Einhorn v. France*, Appl. 71555/01, par. 27.

24 See, for example, Human Rights Committee, View of 21 September 1997, *Aliev v. Ukraine*, Comm. 781/1997, par. 8 and 9; Human Rights Committee, View of 21 March 2003, *Evans v. Trinidad and Tobago*, Comm. 908/2000, par. 7 and 8.

25 See, for example, I-ACionHR, Report of 15 April 1999, *Briggs v. Trinidad and Tobago*, Report 44/99, par. 68; I-ACionHR, Report of 21 April 1999, *Hilaire v. Trinidad and Tobago*, Report 66/99.

26 See, for example, ICTR, Judgement, *Kajelijeli v. Prosecutor*, Case No. ICTR-98-44A-A, A. Ch., 23 May 2005, Klip/ Sluiter, ALC-XXII-625, par. 325.

Human Rights, which holds that killing and life-endangering offences, as well as torture or serious ill-treatment, including rape and sexual abuse, may not go unpunished.[27] The punishment imposed should be proportional to the gravity of the act. As a result, the application of, for example, pardon or early release may not de facto produce a punishment which is manifestly disproportional.[28]

Secondly, with regard to some offences, pardon, commutation of sentence and early release are banned. The ECtHR asserts that pardon and amnesty should not be permissible in the case of, for example, torture by state agents.[29] This ban, formulated in absolute terms, may conflict with the obligations of states discussed above: that they must offer possibilities for early release, consider applying it, or actually apply it when certain specific circumstances arise. In that case, these obligations must, in my opinion, take priority over the prohibition against pardon, commutation of sentence and early release, primarily because the result of a different approach would be that the negative obligation not to torture or ill-treat a person would be violated. In other words, the positive obligation to punish individuals is limited by the negative obligation not to subject anyone to torture or inhuman treatment and punishment, the prohibition of which is the basis upon which these human rights obligations offer (the possibility) of pardon, commutation or early release.

5. The principle of non-discrimination

Much has been written about the problem of how international criminal tribunals can guarantee equal treatment as between themselves in respect of the punishment of convicted persons.[30] I shall therefore discuss only a few issues. First, it should be mentioned that, although there is no general obligation nor right to provide for an early release mechanism, if a prison pre-release scheme is operated, this must be done in a non-discriminatory manner.[31] Secondly, there is the problem that, as mentioned before, convicted persons who are imprisoned in a UNDF will in all probability have to serve a longer sentence than convicts who have been transferred to a state. Although this practice is highly questionable, it probably does not constitute a human rights violation. This would seem to follow from at least the case law of the European Court. In the case of Csoszánszki v. Sweden, the applicant was transferred from Sweden to Hungary in order to serve the remainder of his ten year prison sentence there. In Hungary, the applicant was eligible for conditional release at the earliest around 13 months later than in Sweden (the applicant now had to serve fourth-fifths instead of two-thirds of his sentence). The ECtHR did not regard this to be in violation of the right to liberty in Article 5 ECHR.[32] As an important reason, the European Court asserted that international cooperation in the administration of justice should not be thwarted by laying down a strict requirement that the sentence served in the administering country should not exceed the sentence that would have to be served in the sentencing country.

This observation also seems to be valid for the international criminal tribunals. Since they are dependent on co-operation with national states, also as regards the execution of sentences, differences in early release mechanisms between the tribunals and national states, as well as between the co-operating countries themselves, have to be accepted. Otherwise international criminal justice will become virtually impossible. Of course, the situation in the Csoszánszki case is different from that of UNDF prisoners: their grievance is not that they are transferred, it is that they are not transferred. But if the international transfer of a prisoner to a less favourable regime does not constitute a human rights violation, then it seems to me that the refusal to transfer him to a regime which is more sympathetic to him does not either.[33]

---

[27] See, of many, ECtHR, Judgment of 20 December 2007, *Nikolova and Velichkova v. Bulgaria*, Appl. 7888/03, par. 57(e); ECtHR, Judgment of 12 April 2007, *Ivan Vasilev v. Bulgaria*, appl. 48130/99, § 75; ECtHR, Grand Chamber Judgment of 30 November 2004, *Oneryildiz v. Turkey*, Appl. 48939/99, par. 96; ECtHR, Judgment of 4 December 2003, *M.C. v. Bulgaria*, Appl. 39272/98, par. 153, 166, and 185.

[28] Cf. Judgment of 20 December 2002, *Nikolova and Velichkova v. Bulgaria*, *supra* noto 27, par. 57, 60 and particularly 62.

[29] ECtHR, Judgment of 2 November 2004, *Abdulsamet Yaman v. Turkey*, Appl. 32446/96, par. 55; ECtHR, Judgment of 17 Oktober 2006, *Okkalı v. Turkey*, Appl. 32067/99, par. 76.

[30] See, for example, Inés Mónica Weinberg de Roca and Christopher M. Rassi, Sentencing and Incarceration in the Ad Hoc Tribunals, 44 Stanford Journal of International Law 2008, p. 48-62; Denis Abels, Commentary, Klip/Sluiter, ALC-XV-796-800.

[31] European Commission of Human Rights, Decision of 4 March 1987, *Webster v. the United Kingdom*, Appl. 12118/86.

[32] ECtHR, Decision of 27 June 2006, *Csoszánszki v. Sweden*, Appl. 22318/02, par. 1.

[33] Cf. ECtHR, Judgment of 18 January 2007, *Estrikh v. Latvia*, Appl. 73819/01, par. 83-84.

However, the European Court does set some limits. First of all, the sentence to be served may not exceed the sentence imposed in the original criminal proceedings. Secondly, a flagrantly longer de facto term of imprisonment in the administering state could still give rise to an issue under the right to liberty. So the longer de facto term of imprisonment in one regime must not be too disproportionate compared to the term of imprisonment that would have to be served in the other regime. It seems to me that this constitutes an important obligation on the international tribunals and the states to which sentenced persons are transferred: they need to seriously monitor and improve the early release mechanisms that apply to those convicted persons, so that the inequality in actual prison terms they serve will be kept to a minimum.

A third issue that merits attention is whether the mechanism of early release is equally applied by the various international criminal tribunals. It is noted in the Imanishimwe decision that those persons granted early release by the ICTY have not been convicted for the same combination of crimes as the applicant in this case. This brief comparison seems to imply that equal application of the instrument is indeed intended. But it remains questionable as to whether the decision actually guarantees such an equal approach. In itself it is, as has already been mentioned, not contrary to human rights law to make a distinction between different types of offence or the gravity thereof, when assessing whether or not early release may be granted (see section 3). It seems that the ICTR in principle (apart from very specific circumstances, such as, probably, urgent humanitarian reasons) does not grant early release in case of convictions for genocide,[34] extermination as a crime against humanity[35], or combinations of offences in which violation of Common Article 3 on crimes against humanity is included, as was the position in the Imanishimwe case. With this, the ICTR appears to proceed in conformity with international human rights law.

However, such an application of the principle of non-discrimination to my eye constitutes a very general approach: an approach that could easily result in a practice by which prisoners are denied early release on the basis of the crime for which they are sentenced, while they are actually responsible for less grave conduct than those who are granted such release. It is not only the nature of the crime for which applicants are convicted that should therefore be taken into consideration in the comparison, but, for example, also the number of their convictions, the actual conduct for which they are convicted, the sentences passed on them, and whether the possibility of early release has been taken into account when calculating the sentence.[36] Only then can genuinely non-discriminatory application of the early release mechanism by the various international criminal tribunals be guaranteed.

Admittedly, in this regard there does not seem to have been any flagrant inequality in the application of the early release mechanism as between the ICTR and the ICTY to date. The cases in which the ICTY granted early release not only involved less serious crimes than the cases in which the ICTR denied this measure; the applicants in those cases were also sentenced to less severe punishments.

6. Conformity with the principle of legality and the right to a fair trial?

Since the ICTR's law on early release is somewhat indefinite, another issue that presents itself is whether it is in conformity with the principle of legality or *nullum crimen, nulla poena sine praevia lege poenali,* as it is recognized in international human rights law. Under this principle, offences and punishments must be clearly formulated in law, which implies qualitative requirements, including those of accessibility and foreseeability. The question is now whether those conditions also apply to early release. In its case law, the European Court has consistently stated that early release is related to questions of enforcement of the sentence, rather than to the penalty and, as such, it falls outside the scope of the legality principle in Article 7 of the European Convention.[37] As a consequence, the principle of legality would not impose requirements on the early release mechanism.

---

34 Decision of the President on the Application for Early Release of Georges Ruggiu, *Prosecutor v. Ruggiu*, Pres., *supra* note 6.

35 Decision on the Motion for Reconsideration of the Denial of Early Release, *Prosecutor v. Rutaganira*, Pres., *supra* note 8, par. 9-10.

36 On taking account of early release, see Daryl A. Mundis and Fergal Gaynor, Current Developments at Ad Hoc International Criminal Tribunals, 3 Journal of International Criminal Justice 2005, p. 1149-1150.

37 Grand Chamber Judgment of 12 February 2008, *Kafkaris v. Cyprus*, *supra* note 19, par. 142; ECtHR, Decision of 29 November 2005, *Uttley v. the United Kingdom*, Appl. 36946/03; ECtHR, Judgement of 10 July 2003, *Grava v. Italy*, Appl. 43522/98, par. 51.

It seems, however, that this has become more of a basic assumption than an absolute rule. In the case of Kafkaris v. Cyprus, the Grand Chamber of the Court all of a sudden made it clear that if the law governing sentences and early release, taken as a whole, is not formulated with sufficient precision to enable one to discern the scope of a penalty and the manner of its execution, this may in specific circumstances be in violation of the Article 7 requirement of the "quality of law".[38] Although this judgment is very problematic, for it is legally and logically impossible to breach this requirement without also violating the principle of "no punishment without law", the fact remains that the lack of quality of the law on early release was decisive for the European Court to find a violation of Article 7 ECHR. With this, the legality principle now thus implies that the law and practice of early release may not lack a sufficient degree of clarity such that one cannot foresee the maximum extent to which a sentence may actually be executed. In the case of Kafkaris there was nothing to suggest at the time the offence was committed that the sentence of life imprisonment could actually result in imprisonment for over 20 years.

Unfortunately, the views of the Human Rights Committee do not offer any additional clarification of the meaning of the principle of legality for early release, since it has never applied the principle to this issue. At the same time, however, nor has it not sought to rule out such an application when it had the opportunity to do so.[39]

Even if the early release framework were to be reviewed against the legality principle, it is far from certain that it would be regarded as insufficiently clear. Indeed, it barely explains when and in what kind of cases a UNDF prisoners may become eligible for conditional release. Nonetheless, the analogous application to early release of Article 27 of the Statute and Rules 124-126 of the ICTR Rules of Procedure and Evidence in the ICTR's case law does offer a legal framework that does not leave UNDF prisoners completely in the dark, because they know that complete execution of their sentences is a real option. If not strictly legally necessary, elucidation of that framework is nevertheless still advisable from the point of view of the principle of legal certainty, which in international law is also recognised as important to the law on early release.[40]

Therefore, it would be at least welcome to make public the Practice Direction on the Procedure for the Determination of Applications for Pardon, Commutation of Sentence and Early Release of Persons Convicted by the International Criminal Tribunal for Rwanda of 10 May 2000. That would meet the requirement of accessibility. Meanwhile, the problem that the early release mechanism is not very clear might increase when the ICTR (and ICTY) cease to exist. The Completion Strategy will also have to come up with a solution for the problem of supervising and taking decisions on pardon, commutation of sentences, and early release.[41]

The principle of legal certainty also implies that the procedure for early release should be as transparent as possible. Yet, this does not mean that this procedure should meet the requirements of the right to a fair trial. At any rate, the European Court of Human Rights holds that Article 6 of the Convention is not applicable here, since procedures for measures such as early release and pardon do not involve the determination of "a criminal charge".[42] The consequence of this is that decisions on early release do not necessarily have to be taken by courts.[43]

---

38 Grand Chamber Judgment of 12 February 2008, *Kafkaris v. Cyprus*, *supra* note 19, par. 149-152. See also, Decision of 10 February 2009, *Streicher v. Germany*, *supra* note 16, in which the Court suddenly applied, as a sub-standard for Article 7 ECHR, a criterion as to whether early release was applied consistently.

39 See particularly Human Rights Committee, View of 7 April 1982, *Van Duzen v. Canada*, Comm. 50/1979, par. 10.1-10.4, and furthermore Human Rights Committee, View of 14 October 1982, *MacIsaac v. Canada*, Comm. 55/1979, par. 10-14. However, mandatory supervision in case of remission of sentence is not considered as equivalent to a penalty, the imposition of which must be compatible with the guarantees laid down in Article 15 of the Covenant; see Human Rights Committee, View of 28 October 1981, *A. R. S. v. Canada*, Comm. 91/1981, par. 5.1-5.3.

40 See Principles 5, 16, 22, 23, and 32 of the Council of Europe Recommendation Rec(2003) on conditional release (parole). See furthermore Judgement of 6 March 2007, *Gębura v. Poland*, *supra* note 19, par. 29.

41 Cf. Erik Møse, The ICTR's Completion Strategy – Challenges and Possible Solutions, 6 Journal of International Criminal Justice 2008, p. 675.

42 ECtHR, Decision of 5 January 2006, *Kuolelis et.al. v. Lithuania*, Appl. 74357/01 *et.al.*; Decision of 27 June 2006, *Csoszánszki v. Sweden*, *supra* note 32, par. 2; Decision of 16 December 2003, *Jankauskas v. Lithuania*, *supra* note 19. See also Stefan Trechsel, Human Rights in Criminal Proceedings, Oxford University Press, Oxford 2006, p. 57-58.

43 ECtHR, Decision of 16 June 2005, *Hajiyev v. Azerbaijan*, Appl. 5548/03, par. 3.

In this respect, the fact that the ICTR's president adjudicates on requests for early release offers a higher standard than that required by human rights law. That procedures on early release are not equated to criminal trials also implies the inapplicability of, for example, the right to an appeal in criminal cases (cf. Article 14, paragraph 5, ICCPR, Article 8, paragraph 2 sub h, ACHR, and Article 2 Protocol No. 7 ECHR). Thus, it is not in violation of human rights law either that such appeal is not offered against the president's decisions on early release.[44] Nevertheless, as long as the detention persists, the prisoner may always make a new request for pardon, commutation of sentence or early release, and the president may then once again deny it, although only within the limits of international human rights law.

Piet Hein van Kempen

---

44 See, Decision on Appeal of a Decision of the President on Early Release, *Prosecutor v. Rutaganira*, A. Ch., *supra* note 15, par. 3.

INDEX

J

K

L

M

N

O

P

R

S

CONTRIBUTORS AND EDITORS

Denis Abels studied criminal law at the University Of Amsterdam. In the past, he has been a lecturer in Dutch criminal procedure at the University of Amsterdam. Currently, he is a PhD candidate in international prison law, at the Amsterdam Center for International Law. In 2007, he was awarded a 'Toptalent' subsidy by the Netherlands Organisation for Scientific Research (NWO Toptalent 2007, 'Prisoners of the International Community'). In the framework of that research, he conducted a field-research at the International Criminal Tribunal for Rwanda (2008) and at the Special Court for Sierra Leone (2009). He wrote several other commentaries for these series.

Steven W. Becker is an Assistant Appellate Defender at the Office of the State Appellate Defender in Chicago, Illinois, USA, where he represents indigent defendants in criminal appeals in the Illinois Appellate and Supreme Courts. He currently serves as a Senior Research Fellow at the DePaul University College of Law's International Human Rights Law Institute and as Co-editor in Chief of the 'Revue Internationale de Droit Pénal,' a comparative criminal law journal published in France. He also recently served as a Fulbright Senior Specialist in Croatia and co-edited a book with Professor Davor Derenčinović entitled 'International Terrorism: The Future Unchained?'

Stefanie Bock studied law at the University of Hamburg. She has worked as a research assistant at the University of Hamburg and as an intern at the International Criminal Court in The Hague. In her Ph.D. thesis, she has dealt with the status of victims in the proceedings before the International Criminal Court. Moreover, she has published several articles on international criminal law and criminal law. At present, she works as a research assistant for Prof. Dr. Kai Ambos at the Institute for Criminal Law and Criminal Justice, University of Göttingen. Besides her research activities, she teaches criminal law.

Pedro Caeiro studied law at the Faculty of Law of the University of Coimbra, where he graduated (1990) and received his LL.M degree in Criminal Law with a thesis on bankruptcy crimes (1995). He received his PhD degree with a thesis on the fundament, contents and limits of the State's jurisdiction in criminal matters (2008). He is Assistant Professor of Criminal Law and Criminal Procedure at the same Faculty, where he teaches general criminal law and international cooperation in criminal matters, and, since 1997, a post-graduate course on European and International Criminal Law. He has published a monograph and several articles, in collective books and magazines, the more recent ones on European and International criminal law. He is a founding member and contact point for Portugal of ECLAN (European Criminal Law Academic Network).

Michele Caianiello, is an Associate Professor in Criminal Procedure, and European and International Criminal Procedure at the University of Bologna, Faculty of Law. He graduated cum laude in 1994, with a thesis on the detention pending proceedings. From 2000, he has been undertaking a PhD in Criminal Procedure, with a thesis on the international criminal tribunals. He also lectures in European Criminal Procedure at the LUISS University of Rome. In his academic career he studied the subject of the decision to charge a suspect with a crime, particularly the powers recognised by the law to the victims and to the private citizens on this issue. He also conducted research in the area of Evidence Law in the International Criminal Justice Systems. He is the author of 2 books: 'Poteri dei privati nell'esercizio dell'azione penale' (Giappichelli, 2003) and 'Ammissione della prova e contraddittorio nelle giurisdizioni penali internazionali' (Giappichelli, 2008). He is a lawyer since 1998, and practiced until 2006, in the field of criminal law.

Celso Eduardo Faria Coracini is an associate expert at the Terrorism Prevention Branch of the United Nations Office on Drugs and Crime. He holds a masters degree in criminal law from the University of São Paulo.

Caroline Fournet (LLM Lund, DEA Strasbourg, PhD Leicester) is a senior lecturer in law at the University of Exeter (United Kingdom). Her research interests are Public International Law, Human Rights Law, International Humanitarian Law and International Criminal Law, with a particular emphasis on the law of genocide. Her publications include two monographs: International Crimes – Theories, Practice and Evolution, with a foreword by Professor Malcolm N. Shaw QC (London: Cameron May, 2006) and The Crime of Destruction and The Law of Genocide: Their Impact on Collective Memory (Ashgate Publishing, 2007).

Steven Freeland is Professor in International Law at the University of Western Sydney, Australia. He is also a Visiting Professor in International Law at the University of Copenhagen, a Visiting Professional (Chambers) at the International Criminal Court and has been a special advisor to the Danish Foreign Ministry in matters related to the International Criminal Court. Among other activities, he is chair of the international law action group of the Lawyers Reform Association, a member of the management committee of the International Law Association (Australian Branch), a member of the Australian and New Zealand Society of International Law and a member of the SUR Human Rights University Network. He also sits on the editorial board of the 'Australian Journal of Human Rights', the 'Australian International Law Journal' and a new series of books entitled 'Studies in Space Law'.

Maria Kaiafa-Gbandi is a Professor of criminal law at Aristotle University of Thessaloniki and the National School of Judges, as well as a member of the Special Supreme Court of Greece. She has lectured and published extensively on issues pertaining to Greek, European and international criminal law. She is co-author of the treatise 'War Crimes' (published in Greek under the auspices of the Defense Analyses Institute), identifying the steps necessary to ensure the effective harmonization of Greek law to international humanitarian law generally, as well as to the Statute of the International Criminal Court in particular.

Piet Hein van Kempen is Professor of Law at Radboud University Nijmegen, The Netherlands, and holds the Chair of Criminal Law and Criminal Procedure (Department of Criminal Law), as well as the Chair of Human Rights Law (Department of International and European Law). He is a part time Judge at the 's-Hertogenbosch Court of Appeal. Van Kempen is furthermore Secretary General of the International Penal and Penitentiary Foundation (IPPF). He is also a member of the editorial board of the book series on criminal law, 'Studiepockets Strafrecht', as well as of the Dutch Journal of Human Rights, 'Nederlands Tijdschrift voor de Mensenrechten', and he is a member of the board of the Dutch Association for Comparative Law. He can be contacted via p.h.vankempen@jur.ru.nl or http://www.ru.nl/law/vankempen/.

André Klip is Professor of criminal law, criminal procedure and international criminal law at Maastricht University and head of the Department of criminal law and criminology. He is a Judge at the 's-Hertogenbosch Court of Appeal (2002). He is president of the Dutch section of the international association of penal law. He is also a member of the standing committee of experts on international immigration, refugee and criminal law, a member of the editorial board of 'Delikt en Delinkwent – Tijdschrift voor Strafrecht', as well as of the 'International Criminal Law Review' and co-editor of the 'Commentary on Dutch Law on International Cooperation in Criminal Matters'.

Goreth Kyakuwa obtained an LLM in Gobalisation & Law from Universiteit Maastricht in the Netherlands, a Bachelor of Laws degree from Makerere University and a Diploma in Legal Practice from Law Development Centre in Uganda. She has worked as a legal assistant for Donge & Co. Advocates in Uganda and as a legal Intern at the International Criminal Court, the International Criminal Tribunal for the Former Yugoslavia and the Coalition for the International Criminal Court in the Netherlands. She is currently working as a Visiting Professional at the International Criminal Court.

Yannis Naziris is an attorney and a doctoral candidate at Aristotle University in the field of international criminal law, currently associated with the University's Criminal Law department. He has lectured and written on criminal law, criminal procedure, and international criminal law. He is co-author of the treatise War Crimes (published in Greek under the auspices of the Defense Analyses Institute), identifying the steps necessary to ensure the effective harmonization of Greek law with international humanitarian law generally, as well as with the ICC Statute in particular.

Fabián Raimondo is Assistant-Professor of Public International Law at Maastricht University. He graduated as Abogado and Magíster en Relaciones Internacionales at the Universidad Nacional de La Plata (Argentina) and he holds a diploma of Doctor from the University of Amsterdam. He is a member of the Colegio de Abogados de La Plata (Argentina) and the List of Counsel of the ICC.

Rosemary Rayfuse is a Professor of International Law at the Faculty of Law, University of New South Wales in Sydney, Australia. She specialises in the law of the sea where she is known internationally for her work in international fisheries law and high seas governance. She also teaches and researches in other areas of international law including international humanitarian law, international criminal law and international environmental law. She is the Founding Editor of the ICSID Reports and the Australian Indigenous Law Reporter and is on the editorial board and advisory boards of a number of international law journals.

Göran Sluiter is Professor of international criminal law at the University of Amsterdam and a judge at the Utrecht district court. In the past, he has worked for the Department of international law, the Netherlands institute of human rights and the Willem Pompe Institute of criminal law and criminology at Utrecht University. His doctoral dissertation is entitled 'International Criminal Adjudication and the Collection of Evidence: Obligations of States' (Intersentia, 2002), for which he received the Max van der Stoel human rights award. He is a member of the editorial committees of the 'Journal of International Criminal Justice' and the 'International Criminal Law Review'.

Alexander Zahar is a lecturer in international law at Griffith University Law School in Australia. Formerly he was a Legal Officer at the ICTR and ICTY. Dr Zahar has published extensively on international criminal law, including a book he wrote in collaboration with G. Sluiter: *International Criminal Law: A Critical Introduction* (Oxford University Press, 2008).

Shamiso Zinzombe, B. Soc. Sci (Cape Town 1996), LLB (Cape Town 2000), LLM cum laude (Utrecht 2005) in International and European Protection of Human Rights. Presently a PhD Researcher in the area of health and human rights at the Institute of Health Policy and Management – Erasmus University Rotterdam. She has worked for the Legal Resources Centre, the International Criminal Court – Victims and Witnesses Unit and Gweru Legal Projects Centre amongst others. She is a specialist in human rights law, with a particular interest in human rights including economic, social and cultural rights in international criminal justice, economic and social justice particularly related to health and the rights of victims and witnesses.